WITCHCRAFT

Catalogue of the Witchcraft Collection in Cornell University Library

Introduction by Rossell Hope Robbins

Edited by Martha J. Crowe

Index by Jane Marsh Dieckmann

kto press

A U.S. Division of Kraus-Thomson Organization Limited

Millwood, New York

1977

PREFACE

The Witchcraft Collection in Cornell University Library is a research collection of historical and scholarly materials pertaining to the phenomenon of witchcraft in Europe and North America. The main topics included are demonic possession, theological and legal disputations, witchcraft trials, and torture. Not included in the collection are materials dealing largely or solely with alchemy, astrology, cabala, magic, the occult, prophecies, and superstition. Nevertheless, many of these topics are listed in the index because brief discussions of them are contained in some of the books in the collection.

The basic collection, growing constantly and consisting mainly of older and rare imprints, is housed in the Department of Rare Books of the John M. Olin Library. These items have "Witchcraft" above the call number. Entries with a different rubric, or none at all above the call number, are located elsewhere within the library system. Added entries for title, editor, translator, etc. are not included for works outside the main collection if those works are also represented in the basic collection. Main entries, added entries, and subject entries referring to persons and their works, and bibliographies, are interfiled in one alphabet. Topical subject references, such as *Demonology* and *Trials*, are to be found in the index. When looking for a personal name, the reader should check both the main section of the catalogue and the index. All manuscripts are listed in a special section at the end of the alphabet, but bound manuscripts are also included in the body of the catalogue.

The filing of entries basically conforms to the *American Library Association Rules for Filing Catalog Cards* (Chicago, 1942). Some selected rules follow:

Items are arranged word by word.
>New England
>New York
>Newark

The letters *ä, ö, ü* are filed as if spelled *ae, oe, ue*.

Latin *i* and *j* are filed as distinct letters, but Gothic type *v* (for *u*) and *vv* (for *w*) are filed as *u* and *w*.

Foreign articles and prepositions with the final vowel elided are filed as separate words.
>d'histoire
>de la révolution

Hyphenated words are filed as separate words.
>book-plate
>bookbinding

Proper names with prefixes are filed as if one word.
>Eldorado
>El Paso
>Le Strange, Guy
>L'Estrange, Roger

Articles in the nominative case are disregarded when they are the initial words of titles, but not otherwise.

When there is more than one edition of the same work, entries are arranged by date, earliest edition first.

Works entered under the author's name are filed in the following order:
- Works by the person.
- Collected works in alphabetical order.
- Individual works in alphabetical order, each title by date.
- Criticism of an individual work follows immediately after the work criticized. (Headings are typed in red on the original cards and indicated in the book catalogue by underlining the last element of the call number.)
- Entries for the same person as editor, illustrator, or translator of works by another author.
- Subject entries for the person. (Headings are typed in red on the original cards and indicated in the book catalogue by underlining the last element of the call number.)

Three cataloguers are to be thanked for their contribution to the cataloguing of the collection: Elizabeth Mayer, Carl Anderson, and Dorothy Grosser. However, the basic organization of the card catalogue and the greater part of the cataloguing we owe to the diligent and erudite efforts of Barbara Kauber. In addition, we are grateful to Jane Woolston and Rebecca Rudman for their clerical assistance in preparing this book catalogue from the card file.

M.J.C.

INTRODUCTION

Rossell Hope Robbins

PREFACE

In the early summer of 1958, after having spent four uninterrupted years studying witchcraft, Mrs. Robbins and I came to Cornell. Our arrival was not a parallel to the Israelites entering their Promised Land, for our exile had prospered in American libraries such as the New York Public, the Pierpont Morgan, Columbia University and Columbia Law School, and Union Theological Seminary; and outside New York in the Lea Library (University of Pennsylvania), Harvard University, and Yale Law School, as well as the Library of Congress and the libraries of Duke University and the University of North Carolina. Each of these libraries, as indeed every other major research library, can supply adequate materials for serious studies on witchcraft.

What made Cornell memorable for us (and still continues to astound us on our annual return each summer) was that here in the Witchcraft Collection we found God's plenty—perhaps "Devil's plenty" would be more appropriate. I recall the thrill when I saw side by side on one shelf no fewer than fourteen editions of the *Malleus maleficarum*, certainly the most notorious of all the works on witchcraft, the rare first edition "before 15 April 1487," followed by editions of 1490, 1494, 1519 (Lyons), 1519 (Nuremberg), 1520, 1580, 1582, 1584, 1588, 1595, 1604, 1620, and 1660. Whereas some other libraries would proudly display their one copy, here at Cornell were fourteen. And we reveled in the incunabula, all seventeen of them; a Girolamo Visconti of 1490, an Alphonsus de Spina of about 1471, with its original wooden boards and metal corners, or a Thomas Murner of 1490; and the early printed books, 204 before 1600, such as Samuel de Cassini (1505), Gianfrancesco Ponzinibio (1563), and the unique copies of Heinrich von Schultheis (1634) or Johann Matthäus Meyfart (1635), which have so radically changed my own approach to the witchcraft delusion.

In 1958 the Witchcraft Collection was housed in the vaults of what is now the Uris Undergraduate Library, adjoining the clock tower. To reach it, one undertook a roundabout navigation over shaky iron bridges, through heavy doors, down narrow steel steps. The vaults actually had windows, for at that point the ground slopes so precipitously that even four or five flights into the bowels of the building got one down merely to the ground level. Here, provided with the umbilical cord of a telephone, we were locked in and left free to explore this array of treasure. For this inestimable privilege we will forever be in debt to the then Curator of Rare Books, George H. Healey, whom we came to respect and love more and more over the passing years until his brave death in the fall of 1971.

The old vaults in Uris now serve different purposes, and the Witchcraft Collection is consolidated in twelve bays each with eight shelves in meticulously air-controlled vaults in the Department of Rare Books of the Olin Library. Having been asked to write the introduction to this Catalogue by the Librarian of the Department of Rare Books, Donald D. Eddy, who has so graciously continued the unique privileges granted by Healey, and by Herbert Finch, Assistant Director of Libraries for Special Collections, good friends both, I feel a very personal sense of involvement and commitment. Until very recently, the catalogue was incomplete, many cards being temporary handwritten entries by George Lincoln Burr. Only now, with the appearance of this Catalogue, is a full use of the Witchcraft Collection in Cornell University Library possible.

The Witchcraft Collection was conceived and laboriously acquired by Cornell's first president, Andrew Dickson White, and by his personal assistant, friend, and librarian, George Lincoln Burr. While the familiar designation "White Collection" is no longer accurate, the whole collection reflects White's aims and interests: the rationalist tradition of the nineteenth-century historians, one in which Lea and Lecky would be thoroughly at home. It is a tradition which I too can share, having been the last student at Cambridge of the great medieval historian, G. G. Coulton. Writing this introduction in 1976 has brought my own scholarly direction full cycle: here I sit at Andrew Dickson White's table in the guest suite of the mansion White built for his wife and himself in 1874. Surrounded by memorabilia of White, pictures that recall his stay in Moscow in 1893, his inlaid armoire, looking out over the "President's Walk," the beeline connecting White's home to the library, I feel a surge of gratitude to humane men with means who planned for the future, who were devoted to the acquisition and dissemination of knowledge, and who were even more dedicated to the proposition that knowledge could and should conquer ignorance and bigotry and superstition: a comprehension of the witchcraft delusion was but one aspect of that crusade. This is the central message of White's original holdings, and an ideal my wife and I in our own limited way have tried to follow.

R.H.R

THE FOUNDING OF THE COLLECTION

Whether or not the Witchcraft Collection at Cornell University is the largest in the world, it is surely the most important. George Lincoln Burr, for so many years the librarian of the White Collection, the core of the present holdings, back in 1894 considered that it lacked very few important books on witchcraft, "except things so rare that it was almost futile to look for them."[1] Roland Bainton, who wrote Burr's biography, claimed it was "the finest collection in the world on the persecution of witches in Christendom."[2] The only other comparable library, in view of the monumental importance of his three-volume *Materials toward a History of Witchcraft*, is that of Henry Charles Lea (since 1925 in the University of Pennsylvania), with whom in 1889 Burr had discussed the building of a witchcraft collection at Cornell.[3] Lea modestly described his own "good many books" as "sufficient for working purposes, but without the slightest pretence of completeness."[4] In 1895 Burr visited the Lea Library and was impressed by its superiority over the White books in such fields as the Spanish Inquisition, torture, Canon Law and Procedure; but of the one other area (witchcraft) in which comparison could be made,[5] he considered the White Library much the richer and "yet larger."[6] For several decades thereafter, Burr continued to recommend additions to the Witchcraft Collection, still further increasing its usefulness. With the recent acquisitions of the Kurt Seligmann Library and of the William P. Wreden collection of 166 items, all earlier than 1800, there is no question now that the Witchcraft Collection at Cornell outranks any other similar collection in the world.[7]

From my own researches on witchcraft over the past twenty-five years, I know that in no other library will be found so many of the classic works, and that in no other library will be found the half dozen or so contemporary exposés of the witchcraft trials without which any comprehensive account is impossible. Much reading and research on witchcraft can be done satisfactorily in any of the great libraries of the western world,[8] but ultimately scholars must make their pilgrimage to the center of learning high above Cayuga's waters. Only now, with the publication of this Catalogue of the Witchcraft Collection, will they find the riches there readily available.

It must be remembered that along with this special Witchcraft Collection housed in the Department of Rare Books of the Olin Library, consisting of the older standard source books (covering four centuries of "uncivilization") and the standard critical works, the Cornell University Libraries have quite an extensive repository of witchcraft literature in the open stacks. At the time of writing this introduction, there are several hundred titles not in the Department of Rare Books.[9] A library has to make provision for its professors and graduate students who may wish to inform themselves—about witchcraft, say—and take out books for home use. Consequently, many of the recent serious studies on witchcraft, sparked by the renewed attention given to the occult, as well as to the folklore, psychology, anthropology, and sociology of witchcraft, are not in this Catalogue

of the Witchcraft Collection, but are nevertheless available in the library. In addition to these scholarly books, the Olin Library, as every major library is compelled to do if it wishes its holdings to be as complete as possible, has its share of the unsubstantiated and often bizarre approaches to witchcraft. The reader of this Catalogue will also note here a few older unusual books (such as those of Eliphas Alphonse Louis Constant Lévi),[10] which by now have acquired the patina of historical curiosa. This support section is naturally of inestimable value to the scholar working with the primary source materials, and there will be times, when a book from the stacks is in use, he would wish every book on witchcraft throughout the whole Cornell University system were kept on reserve. But if this were so, then this Catalogue would never be finished; nor would its significance be much increased, for it already covers most of the writings on heretical witchcraft from the fifteenth to the eighteenth century, upon which all future studies inevitably rest.[11]

The present Witchcraft Collection has sometimes been familiarly called the White Witchcraft Collection, and of course its inception was due to Cornell's first president, Andrew Dickson White. White was possibly more devoted to books than he was to administration or to diplomacy. He recalled starting his own library as early as 1850 at the age of eighteen and enjoying the "little student's library in my college building."[12] He not only collected extensively in history, in which discipline he became a professor, both at Michigan and at Cornell, but in his "pet extravagance," architecture, donating "certainly one of the largest, if not the largest, of the architectural libraries in the United States" to his university.[13] Fortunately, White had the financial resources to purchase the books he wanted, and sometimes Burr had to chide him for paying exaggerated prices. On one occasion, Burr wrote: "*I* do not look on the opportunity as either rare or a bargain. I will concur if you urge it, but my judgment rebels. It is a book that we must some day own, but I wish it were not *now*, and from these funds."[14] On another occasion (March 25, 1887), having bought some books on Salem witchcraft, Burr annotated the acquisitions log: "The prices of this lot of books are thus exorbitant because of my ignorance of the American book-sale custom of rating lots by the piece."[15] When he retired in 1885, White gave to the University his historical and general collection of some 30,000 volumes and some 10,000 pamphlets, "one of the largest and, in its field, one of the best collections of books in the United States."[16]

In various logs and diaries and notebooks kept by Burr (and preserved in the University Archives), one can trace the growth of the witchcraft acquisitions. In the beginning, Burr drew on Graesse's *Bibliotheca magica et pneumatica* (1843) for suggestions to White about what books to buy; Burr's own copy in the Witchcraft Collection is interleaved and hand annotated. Sometimes in the records, books are simply lumped together, as on December 6, 1897: "G. E. Stechert, Books on Witchcraft, $6.75," and again on December 14, 1897: "G. E. Stechert, Books on Witchcraft, French Revolution, MSS., etc., $126.93."[17] At other times come detailed acquisition lists; often a single month would indicate priceless new

Introduction

treasures, like August, 1886, a month that saw the collection grow with a Gramineau (1594), Binsfeld (1623), Müller (1830), Diefenbach (1866), Leitschuh (1883), Binz (1885), and Carnap's facsimile copy of the famous *De vera et falsa magia* by Cornelius Loos (at a cost of $27.32). The following month (September) was equally exciting: Nider's *Formicarius* (1476), Agricola's *Ob Zauberey* (1597), Lercheimer's *Christlich Bedencken von Zauberey* (1598), Binsfeld's *Tractatus* (1591), Godelmann's *Tractatus* (1601), and the *Formulae instrumentorum* (1504) were among the more spectacular acquisitions.

Probably this decade (1881-1890) proved the most fruitful for the expansion of the Witchcraft Collection. In addition to purchases just mentioned, standard source materials acquired in these years included Carpzov, Boulton, Wagstaff, Michaelis, Cotta, Sinclair, Mather, Hallywell, and most important, the Flade manuscript (about 1589) on February 3, 1883, the subject of an extended essay by Burr, all that was left of his ill-fated doctoral dissertation at Leipzig (1885).[18] In 1889 White bought the famous (and still unedited) Maria Renata manuscripts and succeeded in getting the dealer, Joseph Baer, to reduce the price. Books continued to flow in after the turn of the century. Early in 1900 White acquired the "Bamberg Hexenprozesse" (1614-1630) from the same dealer, and on June 1 of that year he bought the 1621 Edict of the Bishop of Bamberg from Ludwig Rosenthal (paying $1.98 for the postage). In 1906 White got manuscripts of witchcraft trials dated 1624-1630 from a dealer in Munich, and brought off a big coup on July 22, 1907, obtaining from Basler Buch the manuscript of the trial of Hermann Löher (at a cost then of $178.95), and in addition the "Hexenprozesse aus dem Steinthal" (Alsace) dated 1606-1675. He obtained in 1910 from Stechert manuscripts of witchcraft trials of 1630-1631, in 1913 from Baer in Frankfurt a manuscript of the Hexenprozesse of Catherine Büchler, and from Goodspeeds' Book Shop the manuscript of William Good's petition of 1710 (the only original Salem manuscript at Cornell). Meanwhile, books on English witchcraft were being picked up, and a collection of English witchcraft tracts was bought for Cornell in 1913 by the celebrated authority, Wallace Notestein, in a pleasant example of scholarly cooperation.[19]

In September and October of 1891 White's entire private collection was moved into a handsome set of galleries—separated from the main library space—in the new Sage Library, and continued under the direction of its own librarian (since 1878), George Lincoln Burr. But in its new home the White Collection was little by little inadvertently dissipated: "White" books in fields other than history were shelved with the university volumes; and on the other hand university holdings in history were merged into the "White Library." The planned separation of university and White books (identified only by their book plates)[20] was further complicated by the fact that White continued to make valuable gifts to both divisions, not always distinguished in the librarian's annual reports, such as the acquisitions after 1900 for witchcraft from the royalties of White's *History of the Warfare of Science with Theology*.[21] Continuing and increasing demands for library space, further dispersal of some White books to the general stacks, and the

later removal of most of the witchcraft books to the vaults of the Department of Rare Books in fact diminished the precision of a "White Collection."

In the more spacious quarters of the Olin Library, opened in 1961, the original witchcraft books from the Sage Library (now redesignated Uris), augmented considerably by major acquisitions, are consolidated into one unified collection kept in one special location. This collection of 2,659 printed works (in 3,181 volumes) and 215 manuscripts is now known as the Witchcraft Collection, and it is this collection that this Catalogue describes.

Quite apart from its numbers, the Witchcraft Collection is significant in a way no other parallel collection can or could be: it was initiated, inspired, collected, and assembled by two historians who agreed—even if their points of view on other matters sometimes varied—that "interference with science in the supposed interest of religion . . . has resulted in the direst evils both to religion and science . . . and untrammeled scientific investigation . . . has invariably resulted in the highest good both of religion and of science." [22] By drawing attention to the stranglehold of dogma on thinking, the two scholars hoped to dispel superstition and ignorance and usher in a more informed and consequently more rational way of living in society. Their library therefore concentrated on historical periods or historical phenomena illustrative of this interference with freedom—of which witchcraft was one.[23] "Witchcraft," wrote Burr on a slip of paper found in his notes, "is the shadow on the dial whose recession marks the upward course of the sun of civilization." [24]

This concern with witchcraft as theology, as a religious heresy, rather than as folklore or anthropology, forms the justification for the presence of most of the books in the original witchcraft collection. White and Burr deliberately excluded works in fringe areas; they spent frugally on related topics such as exorcism, prophecies, diabolism, hell, on literary works about the devil, alchemy, astrology, cabala, folklore, magic, and of course the "magic of the Church" (miracles and hocus-pocus literature).[25] The resultant collection thus took on a quite different shape from that inspired by the distinguished Harvard professor and author of the erudite but limited *Witchcraft in Old and New England*, George Lyman Kittredge.[26] An even greater contrast in principles and objectives is provided by the Mellon Collection of Alchemy and the Occult at Yale University, very few of whose books would have been welcomed by White and Burr.[27] On the other hand, the White-Burr approach to witchcraft was also the justification for the Lea Library, and therefore the *Materials toward a History of Witchcraft*, Lea's notes on the books in his own library, can serve very well as a limited descriptive catalogue to many of the volumes of the Witchcraft Collection at Cornell. Frequent reference will be made to Lea's *Materials* throughout the documentation to this introduction.

The genesis, growth, and aims of what amounted to a crusade for humanistic rationalism have been told by White himself in his *History of the Warfare of Science with Theology* and in his *Autobiography*.[28] Irked by slanderous attacks on Cornell University for its "irreligion," the first president took the offensive in

1875 in a well-publicized lecture at Cooper Union [now Institute] in New York on "The Battle-fields of Science." This lecture, actually presented much earlier in lesser-known arenas such as the University of Michigan on December 7, 1872,[29] grew into two magazine articles, "then into a little book [1876] which was widely circulated at home... expanded into a series of articles in the 'Popular Science Monthly,' and finally (1894) wrought into [the] book on *The Warfare of Science with Theology*," published in two volumes in 1896.[30] White wrote that the ideas had been growing in his mind for about twenty years and that his main reading, even for his different courses of lectures, had more or less connection with it.[31] He was simply trying "to aid in letting the light of historical truth into that decaying mass of outworn thought which attaches the modern world to mediaeval conceptions of Christianity and which still lingers among us—a most serious barrier to religion and morals, and a menace to the whole normal evolution of society."[32] All the books in the White Library, one might say, served as footnotes for White's *Warfare*.

White's books were catalogued by Burr, who became White's personal librarian in 1878. In that year or the next Burr, with a view to publication, made a start at the task, which included cataloguing those books kept in White's house in Syracuse.[33] Only three volumes of the four projected for the catalogue were completed: *The Protestant Reformation and Its Forerunners* in 1889, *The French Revolution* in 1894, and a *Miscellanea* in 1897. Volume Three, reserved for a catalogue of the witchcraft collection, never appeared, although Burr said he had been readying one in 1889.[34] One reason for holding back was that the whole library was growing so rapidly that Burr's catalogues were almost out of date by the time they were printed. For example, a colleague (Morse Stephens) increased the holdings of the French Revolution Collection far beyond the extent of the catalogue,[35] and Burr himself added considerably after his own catalogue of 1889 to the books on the Protestant Reformation. "He resolved in consequence," wrote Bainton, "to keep up card entries for the witchcraft materials, but not to publish until in the course of new studies he had rounded out the bibliography and filled the gaps which would certainly come to light."[36] Burr counseled further delay to White: "With the witchcraft we have nothing to gain and all to lose by haste. Every study in this field which you will first leave me time to publish will add to the prestige as well as to the worth of the catalogue. And what can you use it for in the mean time? The reputation of the collection is already international."[37]

Although the Witchcraft Collection has grown considerably since 1894 (when Burr wrote the above), the basis of the present Catalogue lies in Burr's handwritten cards, which he continued preparing as late as 1915 or even 1921.[38] In addition to bibliographical description, Burr sometimes wrote critical comments on his library cards, on scraps of paper inserted between pages, or even on the flyleaves or covers of the books. These remarks clearly illustrate his point of view as well as his erudition. He found *The Compleat Wizard* (London, 1770) "a shameless plundering of Glanvill's *Saducismus Triumphatus*." He wrote a long and detailed note on the *Instrvctio pro formandis processionibus in causis strigum*,

sortilegiorum, et maleficorum, "perhaps the only printed copy existing of an official paper of very great interest for the history of witchcraft." [39] He commented on a passage in the *History of European Morals* (p. 90) where Lecky states that through believing themselves witches because of the Christian treatment of the insane, "many thousands were burned as witches": "an exaggeration, but well worth research." Andrew Dickson White also "annotated" the books. For example, on the copy of Michelet's *La Sorcière* which he had purchased in March, 1863, White wrote: "An erratic book full of whimsies and the genius of Michelet. . . . It was seized by the French police at its appearance and I had much difficulty in obtaining this copy from the first *unexpurgated* edition." What adds further interest to this note was its proximity on the shelf to a book published the same year, a study of Michelet by Gabriel Séailles translated into English by L. J. Trotter. On the flyleaf of *Die Hexenprozesse* by Carl Haas (Tübingen, 1865), White wrote: "This is a book written from the clerical point of view and as 'good as a play' in its use of the *suppressio veri* and *suggestio falsi.*" White never forgot the human aspect of the books he was collecting; thus, on one copy of Binsfeld's *Tractatus de confessionibus maleficorum et sagarum* ([Trier], 1589)—"This is the book . . . which brought such horrible suffering to Flade, and torture and death to Loos."

Because of the absence of any catalogue save Burr's handwritten cards augmented by the slowly growing entries prepared by professional bibliographers, the Collection was virtually off limits to scholars, who had almost to guess at its treasures from the two brilliant (and neglected) articles by Burr, "The Literature of Witchcraft" (1889) and "A Witchhunter in the Bookshops" (1902).[40] In many ways, these two papers still form the finest introduction to the books of the original collection. The latter essay is especially evocative in capturing the excitement of participating in the building of a truly great collection, and Burr is at his scholarly best describing the joys and occasional sorrows of book hunting. One paragraph in particular might be quoted as a humble memorial to a scholar to whom all subsequent researchers will be forever indebted:

> Aye, and the long vacation tours by rail or foot through all those book-rich lands, now threading the cluttered windings of Paternoster Row, now stooping for a grain of wheat in the waste of chaff which litters the quays of Paris, now locked from morn till eve in the back-street warehouse where a Bologna bookseller keeps his reserves, now haggling with the Neapolitan huckster who knows his volumes only by their shape and begs you to make out yourself the bill already receipted for him by the wayside notary. Oh, the joys of those *Wanderjahre!* And if to the quest for printed book one join the quest for manuscripts, then a wider orbit. What precious scraps may then lurk among the coins and armor of the antiquary's den! What rare old parchment may not be rescued from the rag-dealer before he weighs it out by the ounce to the goldbeaters! Yes, and the private hoards, the rummage of castle-chests and peasant-garrets, the hermit-lairs of the art-misers, the cabinets of canny schoolmasters! [41]

But this great research tool has never been put to work. Two brilliant theses by Burr's students, "Peter Binsfeld and Cornelius Loos" by Mabel Elisabeth Hodder (1911) and "Some Rhenish Foes of Credulity and Cruelty" by Lois Oliphant Gib-

bons (1920),[42] along with an unpublished transcription "in three cases" by Bertha Merritt (Bertha Sutermeister) in 1926 of a mass of witch trials from Alsace-Lorraine, are about all the tangible products. Apart from Burr's articles, the only publicity the Collection received was a piece by Heinrich Schneider, buried in *Hessische Blätter für Volkskunde* in 1950, who observed: "it is neither very well-known, nor has it been used very often."[43] And indeed my own *Encyclopedia of Witchcraft and Demonology* (1959) was the first work to draw on the Cornell holdings extensively. Even since then, it is only an occasional scholar who stops by. With the publication of this Catalogue, almost a century after the inception of the Collection, this ignorance becomes a relic of the past, and Burr's hope that "the collection be not without its use"[44] may now become a reality.

WITCHCRAFT, SORCERY, AND HERESY

Reference has been made to Kittredge, to whom witchcraft was synonymous with sorcery, "the common heritage of humanity."[45] Sorcery, in the words of Henry Guerlac (who wrote an appreciation of Burr) represents the "timeless and widespread belief that certain persons have magical powers or endowments or skills by which they can bring injury to others; and consequently it is not a phenomenon limited by time or geography, but could equally well be studied among the Chaldeans, the Shanti, the Piwtes, or the subjects of James I."[46] Burr in 1911 challenged Kittredge's position in his valuable paper, "New England's Place in the History of Witchcraft."[47] It is notable not only because it shows the rationale of White and Burr in assembling the Witchcraft Collection, but because it is the best extended explanation of the cleavage between two schools of witchcraft studies: one that interprets witchcraft as a historical phenomenon in western European Christendom and another that interprets western European witchcraft as the local manifestation of a universal prevalence of magic.

The latter view, in my opinion unfortunately, has been dominant in witchcraft studies over the past two or three decades, for it is considered intellectually chic to harness documented events in "time and geography" to speculative assumptions in anthropology, psychology, or folklore, whether or not the connection clarifies them. A recent book claiming to use anthropological methodology admits, "although anthropologists have provided some useful analytic distinctions, these do not really help in a number of societies."[48] Another learned, and indeed well-documented, study which acknowledges "the studies made by modern social anthropologists of similar beliefs held in Africa or elsewhere,"[49] observes: "In general, therefore, the anthropological distinction between witchcraft and sorcery is of limited utility when applied to England."[50] And I would add, to western Europe. In 1976 possibly the most prominent historiographer of compara-

tive religion was not merely blurring this distinction but insisting on its elimination:

> As a matter of fact, all the features associated with European witches are—with the exception of Satan and the Sabbath—claimed also by Indo-Tibetan yogis and magicians. They too are supposed to fly through the air, render themselves invisible, kill at a distance, master demons and ghosts, and so on. Moreover, some of these eccentric Indian sectarians boast that they break all the religious taboos and social rules: that they practice human sacrifice, cannibalism, and all manner of orgies, including incestuous intercourse, and that they eat excrement, nauseating animals, and devour human corpses. In other words, they proudly claim all the crimes and horrible ceremonies cited *ad nauseam* in the western European witch trials.[51]

The all-important words, "with the exception of Satan and the Sabbath," are sloughed off as an aside. The Witchcraft Collection at Cornell would give no support to the foregoing hypothesis, and Burr would have countered that the crime of witchcraft was the surrender of one's self to the service of the devil, and was based upon a personal compact between the witch and Satan.[52] When time and geography are handily ignored, and only then, can the new antihistoricism be safely promulgated: "Gradually it becomes evident that witchcraft cannot be satisfactorily understood without the help of other disciplines, such as folklore, ethnology, sociology, psychology, and history of religions."[53] Would that fashionable writers and their trendy publishers had heeded the words of a professional anthropologist, Geoffrey Parrinder, who in his *Witchcraft in Europe and Africa* (1958) emphasized the distinction that the whole Witchcraft Collection upholds: "People have included witchcraft under the same heading as magic. But the two are essentially distinct, and no progress can be made in understanding what witchcraft is about until the consideration of magic in the same category is abandoned."[54]

Burr's essay on New England witchcraft is still a *sine qua non* for the definition of witchcraft, and with his two earlier essays, must be studied and absorbed by any investigator of the whole subject, for these are the keys to the Witchcraft Collection at Cornell.[55] And the big key, the *clavis major*, is Burr's realization—along with Lea, Lecky, and White, with Hansen, with Soldan and Heppe and Bauer, with Baissac, with Cauzons, and with the rest of the great historians of the nineteenth century—that witchcraft is a *Christian* heresy: "Whatever in universal human experience, anthropology or folklore may find akin to it, the witchcraft our fathers feared and fought was never universal, in place or time. It belonged alone to *Christian* thought and modern centuries."[56]

Far too many educated persons, even those historically oriented,[57] still misconceive typical witches as, in the words of Reginald Scot, women "commonly old, lame, bleare-eied, pale, fowle, and full of wrinkles."[58] Archbishop Samuel Harsnett some twenty years after Scot, in 1603, in his *Declaration of Egregious Popish Impostures*, similarly described the then popular view of a witch: "An old weather-beaten crone, having the chin and her knees meeting for age, walking like a bow, leaning on a staff; hollow-eyed, untoothed, furrowed on her face, having her limbs trembling with palsy, going mumbling in the streets."[59]

The witch in her black conical hat, riding a broomstick or communing with her cat, is part of the folklore of magic and sorcery. Unfortunately, this notion obscures the fact that very many persons accused as witches—possibly a majority—were not old women casting spells. A contemporary description of witches is provided in a letter written by the chancellor of the prince-bishop of Würzburg in 1629:

> Ah, the woe and the misery of it—there are still four hundred in the city, high and low, of every rank and sex, nay, even clerics, so strongly accused that they may be arrested at any hour. It is true that, of the people of my gracious Prince here, some out of all offices and faculties must be executed: clerics, electoral councilors and doctors, city officials, court assessors, several of whom Your Grace knows. There are law students to be arrested. The Prince-Bishop has over forty students who are soon to be pastors; among them thirteen or fourteen are said to be witches. A few days ago, a Dean was arrested; two others who were summoned have fled. The notary of our Church consistory, a very learned man, was yesterday arrested and put to the torture. In a word, a third part of the city is surely involved. The richest, most attractive, most prominent, of the clergy are already executed. A week ago a maiden of nineteen was executed, of whom it is everywhere said that she was the fairest in the whole city, and was held by everybody as a girl of singular modesty and purity. She will be followed by seven or eight others of the best and most attractive persons.... And thus many are put to death for renouncing God and being at the witch-dances, against whom nobody has ever else spoken a word. To conclude this wretched matter, there are children of three and four years, to the number of three hundred, who are said to have had intercourse with the Devil. I have seen put to death children of seven, promising students of ten, twelve, fourteen, and fifteen. Of the nobles—but I cannot and must not write more of this misery.[60]

Just what was this crime of witchcraft for which so many people were put to death? At the time when witchcraft dominated men's thinking, living, and dying—1550-1750, with its peak about 1600—every judge, lawyer, theologian, priest, physician, whether living in Germany, France, England, or Scotland, was agreed on a very precise definition of witchcraft. The French jurist Jean Bodin in 1580 defined a witch as "one who knowing God's law tries to bring about some act through an agreement with the Devil."[61] The Spanish-born Martin Del Rio, a Jesuit and at one time attorney general for Brabant, wrote in 1599 that witchcraft is "an art which, by the power of a contract, entred into with the Devill, some wonders are wrought which passe the common understanding of man."[62] Side by side with Del Rio, Sir Robert Filmer quoted the Calvinist divine William Perkins, who used almost identical terms: "Witchcraft is an Art serving for the working of Wonders, by the assistance of the Devill, so far as God shall permit."[63] And Cotton Mather, almost forty years later, in 1689, joined the American colonies to the unanimous European opinion: "Witchcraft is the Doing of Strange (and for the most part Ill) Things by the help of evil Spirits, Covenanting with (and usually Representing of) the woful children of men."[64]

Witchcraft, which was invented, introduced, and imposed by the establishment of church and state, meant one thing only: league with the Christian devil to do evil and so overthrow the Christian God. Alleged acts of sorcery of *maleficia*, such as hexing, fascination, ligature, storm-raising, or poppet-pricking, were but indications (*indicia*) of witchcraft. The more dangerous witch, in fact, tried to

deceive men by living an outwardly virtuous life. As William Perkins put it: "Though the witch were in many respects profitable, and did no hurt but procured much good, yet, because he hath renounced God his king and governor and hath bound himself by other laws to the service of the enemies of God and his church, death is his portion justly assigned him by God: he may not live." [65] And Perkins was followed by Fuller in his *Holy and Profane State*: "The white and black [witch] are both guilty alike in compounding with the devil." [66]

The various laws in western European countries were correspondingly specific about the offense. A convenient example is the statute of James I in 1604, under which most English trials were conducted and which provided the legality for the Salem trials in 1692. It tried to spell out the pact with the devil, making it a felony (entailing the death penalty) to "practise or exercise any Invocation or Conjuration of any evil and wicked Spirit, or [to] consult, covenant with, entertaine, employ, feed, or reward any evil and wicked Spirit to or for any intent or purpose." [67] Even in England, where witch trials were completely different from those on the Continent in that some evidence of evildoing to property, animals, or humans was generally presented, in 1645 seven women were hanged on the sole charge of entertaining evil spirits (which appeared to them in the forms of a white dog, a greyhound, and a polecat).[68]

What all witches had in common was their denial of God, open or secret, and in their minds joining the spiritual forces of what the Church termed evil. Unlike sorcery, witchcraft was not primarily a matter of wicked acts; it was a matter of wicked opinions and wicked ideas. A noted Protestant preacher, George Gifford, spelled out this view: "A witch by the word of God ought to die the death not because she killeth men—for that she cannot, unless it be those witches which kill by poison, which either they receive from the Devil or he teacheth them to make—but because she dealeth with devils." [69]

This constant emphasis on allegiance to the devil and on treason to God not only explains the enormity of the criminal sin of witchcraft in the eyes of those in authority, but removes witchcraft from folklore, anthropology, or sociology and puts it unequivocally in theology. "This fact, that witchcraft was heresy, and that persecution for witchcraft was persecution for heresy," wrote George Lincoln Burr, "we cannot bear too carefully in mind, for it is the essence of the matter." [70] This definition of witchcraft explains the nature of the sources for its study, in the main theological, legal, and historical.

SOURCE MATERIALS

The source materials in the Witchcraft Collection at Cornell University may conveniently be grouped in five major areas: (1) Early Writers on Witchcraft; (2)

Introduction   xxi

The Classic Demonologists; (3) The Penologists; (4) Court Records of Trials; (5) The Opponents. Nearly all modern writers on witchcraft depend heavily on the classic demonologists but are ignorant of or have slighted the third, fourth, and fifth areas, although these (in my opinion) provide the correct understanding of the witchcraft phenomenon. And in the fifth area the Witchcraft Collection is unique.

Some discussion of the contributions these five areas make to the concept of witchcraft points to the research that the Witchcraft Collection may encourage.

EARLY WRITERS ON WITCHCRAFT

Witchcraft was first mooted in the thirteenth and fourteenth centuries, when the Inquisition began equating sorcery with heresy by the simple expedient of declaring that sorcery was possible only with the help of the Christian devil. Sorcerers were transformed into heretics and were therefore subject to the discipline of the Inquisition.[71]

The ascription of guilt to people for what they thought, or imagined—or rather were forced by torture to admit having thought or imagined—was the achievement of the Inquisition. The function of the Inquisition was thought control: to change the opinion of those who elected free choice to differ from the Church. According to Thomas Aquinas and canon law, heresy constituted religious error held in willful and persistent opposition to the truth after it had been defined and declared by the Church in an authoritative manner.[72] The corollary function of the Inquisition was to see that the heretics were exposed and destroyed. "Faith must be persuaded to men," said Saint Bernard of Clairvaux (1091-1153), but he hastened to add: "Yet it would be better that they were coerced by the sword of that [magistrate] who beareth not the sword in vain, than they should be suffered to bring many others into their own error." [73]

In 1184 Pope Lucius III (in his bull *Ad abolendam*) ordered the bishops to make systematic inquiry (or an *inquisitio*) into deviations from the official teaching of the Church. Any persons "found branded by suspicion only" had to prove their innocence, or else on relapse be punished as heretics by the civil authorities; all law officers had to "help the Church faithfully and efficaciously against the heretics" or suffer excommunication.[74]

These local inquiries proving inadequate, however, Pope Innocent III appointed his own *inquisitores* directly from the Vatican, with absolute authority to override the bishops. The decree, later part of canon law, establishing the Holy Office, better known as the Roman Inquisition, came as a bull (March 25, 1199) to the town of Viterbo. It might be noted how interested the Inquisition was from the outset in expropriation of property following execution:

> For, seeing that the laws, when men are condemned to death for high treason, confiscate their goods and reserve a livelihood for their children only as an act of mercy, how much more should those who, straying from the Faith, offend against Jesus Christ, God and Son of God, be cut off by ecclesiastical rigour from our Head, who is Christ, and be despoiled of their earthly goods, since it is far more grievous to sin against the eternal than against an earthly Majesty.[75]

In a later decree, Pope Innocent III reinforced his earlier orders, demanding the civil authorities take a public oath to "strive in good faith, to the utmost of their power, to exterminate from the lands subject to their obedience all heretics who have been marked by the Church." [76] Five years later, in 1220, Holy Roman Emperor Frederick II incorporated this demand in civil law; and later ecclesiastical and civil codes reaffirmed the principle.[77]

The Inquisition burgeoned in the early thirteenth century because of the mounting insecurity, weakness, and corruption of the Roman church, manifested by the apostasy of the most civilized parts of Europe, especially southern France and the rich cities of central France and the Rhineland. At the end of the twelfth century, the monk Pierre des Vaux de Cernay wrote in his chronicle that "almost all the barons of Provence had become harbourers and defenders of heretics." [78]

The heretics whom the barons of Provence were harboring were the Albigensians, so called from their prevalence at Albi (and in other southern towns like Toulouse and Carcassonne). The Albigensians apparently believed in a dualistic universe, a God of good in heaven and a God of evil who ruled the earth. Their most serious offense, however, was their rejection of the Catholic sacerdotal system. Pacification failing, Pope Innocent III directed a "crusade" (1200-1229) against the southern barons.[79] The barons were either crushed or bribed into silence, but the heresy itself survived among their peoples. To root out the heretics, the newly organized Inquisition was brought in, and within a hundred years, by about 1300, all the Albigensian heretics had been burned.[80]

After the crushing of the Albigensians, the Inquisition had little reason to continue as a major organization. About 1320, says the *Encyclopaedia Britannica*, "the persecution [in southern France] stopped for lack of an object." [81] About 1360, the famous Inquisitor Nicholas Eymeric (1330-1393), who wrote the classic manual for inquisitors,[82] was lamenting: "In our days there are no more rich heretics; so that princes, not seeing much money in prospect, will not put themselves to any expenses; it is a pity that so salutary an institution as ours should be so uncertain of its future." [83] George Lincoln Burr summarized the situation thus:

> But when, in the lands where the Inquisition had found entrance, heresy was at last utterly rooted out,—when the souls of the faithful were safe and the hands of the inquisitors idle,—then, as was natural, the hungry organization cast its eyes about for other victims.[84]

The Inquisition consequently set about to invent a new heresy, one with so broad a base that the supply of victims would never dry up. The new heresy was called "witchcraft." [85] Its base was magic or sorcery, but, in order to take it away from

Introduction

the jurisdiction of the civil courts, which hitherto had the sole authority to try such evildoing, the Inquisition decided that magic and sorcery were thenceforward to be ascribed to the power of the devil. The expedient of the devil (and the pact) turned simple magic into not so simple heresy, and the same expedient turned everyone living into a potential witch, a potential heretic, and in addition a potential source of income to the inquisitors. It is not surprising that the celebrated Dutch Protestant theologian Balthasar Bekker, quoted by Felix Brähm (1709), stated that the theory of witchcraft was invented by the papacy to "warm the fires of Purgatory and to fill the pockets of the clergy."[86] And the Roman Catholic de Cauzons, in his *Histoire de l'Inquisition* (1909), said bluntly that the Inquisition had "invented the crime of witchcraft and relied on torture as a means of proving it."[87]

Two tasks were incumbent upon the promoters of the new heresy: first, the inculcation of the doctrine that all sorcery was heresy, and consequently that all sorcerers were heretics; and second, the circumvention of the previously established position of the Church (defined in the Canon Episcopi and accepted into canon law) that belief in sorcery was heresy and the establishing of a totally opposite view that *disbelief* in sorcery was heresy.

As the trial of Joan of Arc had shown, it was easier to prove heresy than sorcery, inasmuch as no overt act was necessary in determining heresy.[88] The emphasis in the manuals and in the trials therefore focused on the pact with the devil to do evil. While the speculative basis for the equation of sorcery with heresy had been discussed by theologians ranging from Archbishop Guillaume d'Auvergne of Paris (died 1249), through his student Thomas Aquinas (died 1274) and Duns Scotus (died 1308), to Pierre de Palude (died 1342) and Gabriel Biel (died 1495), the equation was actually put into force mainly by papal decrees and bulls, often requested by the Inquisition.

From 1257 the Inquisition had been trying to extend the field of heresy to include sorcery. This novel request was refused by Pope Alexander IV (*Quod super non nullis*), unless sorcery savored manifestly of heresy.[89] The ordinary ecclesiastical courts, Pope Alexander held, were competent to deal with simple sorcery, and the Inquisition should let them do it. Then in 1320, Pope John XXII empowered the Inquisition at Carcassonne to investigate magic and sorcery, especially worship of demons.[90] Pope Eugenius IV in 1434 and other years [91] and Pope Nicholas V in 1451 allowed the Inquisition control over sorcery even when heresy was not involved ("etiam si haerisim non sapiant manifeste").[92] This latitude was thereafter frequently reaffirmed.

The second task was turning the Canon Episcopi on its head, for most of the opposition to the new doctrine, apart from a few theologians and lawyers who objected to the legal processes of the trials, rested on accepting the canon. Although ascribed to the Synod of Ancyra of 314, it was really composed at the end of the ninth century, and included by Abbot Regino of Prüm about 906 in "a compilation of regulations ... to guide bishops in the visitation of their dioceses."[93] The canon stated flatly that the acts of *sceleratae mulieres*, such as

transvection, transmogrification, and intercourse with animals, were all illusions or fantasies originating in dreams (*talia phantasmata mentibus*): "Whoever believes such things loses the faith, and he who has not the right faith in God is not of God but of him in whom he believes, that is, the Devil." [94]

This tenet had to be discarded before witch hunts could occur. The canon was circumvented by various theses, such as:

1. Present-day witches were not the same as those mentioned in the Canon; and the new witches could do everything the Inquisition imputed to them (advanced by theologians like Vivetus, Jacquier, Prierias, Dodo, Grillandus, and Ciruelo).[95]
2. The Canon Episcopi was not approved by a General Council and therefore was not binding (Jacquier, Mamoris, Prierias, Spina).[96]
3. Even if a witch only dreamed about her activities, nevertheless her recollection of her dream made her guilty (advocated by Jacquier, Visconti, and Jordanus de Bergamo) [97]—a casuistry that cropped up later on the lips of the materialist Thomas Hobbes in his *Leviathan*.[98]
4. Supporting the canon interfered with getting rid of witches, as Jacquier, a Dominican inquisitor in northern France, honestly put it.[99]
5. Later, Bernard de Como and Spina, in massive attacks, added a fifth argument: the canon was not authentic (in that it was erroneously attributed to the fourth century).[100]

Thus the theory of the theologians supported the practice of the papal decrees, and witchcraft slowly spread.

Throughout these early centuries, while the new theory of the heresy of sorcery (that is, witchcraft) was being formulated,[101] some inquisitors and judges were unsure of its validity, and some very few others opposed it. For example, an influential lawyer, Paulus Grillandus (about 1525), devoted many pages of his *Tractatus de hereticis et sortilegiis* to the problem of evil—the first edition of 1536 is to be found in the Witchcraft Collection.[102] God allowed the devil certain powers, such as to tempt people to sin, to know the nature of things, and to cure disease. Asking help of the devil to do these "permitted" acts was sorcery, asking the devil to do other acts which God reserved for himself was heresy. Such confusion, honest doubt, and even disagreement were not surprising, for the Catholic church had its own tradition of sorcery and tended to view man against a backdrop of magic.[103] Before 1550 it was possible to question the doctrine; after 1550 and for the next century, opponents were silenced, by fear or by death. Among the early opponents of the delusion may be included the French physician Symphorien Champier (about 1500), who urged that doctors treat the alleged witches; [104] the Franciscan Samuel de Cassini (1505), who called the inquisitors themselves heretics; [105] the Milanese lawyer Andreas Alciatus (about 1514), who suggested herbs as a cure for deluded women; [106] and the eminent Florentine lawyer Gianfrancesco Ponzinibio (about 1520), who, though believing in natural magic, utterly rejected both witchcraft and Inquisition.[107]

Of these four skeptics, a scholar would find only Champier missing from the

Witchcraft Collection, but he could read extracts in Hansen. He would find one of the three copies known to exist of Samuel de Cassini's *Questione de le Strie* (1505). He would find the *Parergon juris* of Alciatus in his *Opera* (1581), housed in the Department of Rare Books, not listed in this Catalogue because it is considered primarily a law book, and he would find the *Tractatus de lamiis* of Ponzinibio, not the first edition of 1563, but the second edition of 1580.

Not only was there some intellectual opposition to the Inquisition; there was considerable popular opposition, about which inquisitors frequently complained. Johannes Nider,[108] a professor, and Johannes Vivetus, the inquisitor at Carcassonne, said "many" disbelieved in the incubus demon. The Witchcraft Collection has the second edition (1484) of Nider's *Formicarius*, and the *Tractatus contra demonum invocatores* of Vivetus (written about 1450), published at Cologne in 1487—a work apparently not known to Lea, who in his *Materials toward a History of Witchcraft* abstracts it very briefly from the selections in Hansen.[109] Jacquier, another inquisitor, said that "many" opposed the investigators;[110] Inquisitor Girolamo Visconti said that "many" believed the confessions were only extracted during torture (and so Visconti wrote a book to refute them).[111]

Cornell has the 1581 edition of Jacquier's *Flagellum haereticorum fascinariorum* and is fortunate to possess the second part of Visconti's manuscript dedicated to Francesco Sforza, written before 1465, as well as the complete *Lamiarum sive striarum opusculum*, printed in 1490 in Milan. It is not available in English, and Lea's summary is much abbreviated. The very influential Bartolommeo Spina, "Master of the Sacred Palace," likewise had to write his *Quaestio de strigibus* against disbelievers.[112] Thomas Murner, a learned Franciscan professor, best known for his satire against Luther, accused some theologians of explaining misfortunes by natural causes rather than by witchcraft, but his *De pythonico contractu*, printed in 1499, receives only a bare mention in Lea.[113] And Andreas Alciatus, the skeptic lawyer, said the peasants in the subalpine valleys broke into rebellion at the wholesale burning by the local inquisitor.[114]

If any one key date were needed to establish the coming of age of the heresy of witchcraft it would be December 5, 1484, when the bull of Pope Innocent VIII removed all uncertainties and hesitations.[115] The Canon Episcopi was abandoned. Thenceforward, to doubt the reality of witchcraft was heretical. "It fastened on European jurisprudence for nearly three centuries," wrote the eminent German historian of witchcraft Joseph Hansen, "the duty of combating the Devil and saving mankind from his clutches. . . . It served as justification for pitiless persecution."[116]

This bull (*Summis desiderantes affectibus*) received its prominence from its inclusion in a printed book, the *Malleus maleficarum* (1486), without doubt "the most important and most sinister work on demonology ever written. It crystallized into a fiercely stringent code previous folklore about black magic with church dogma on heresy, and, if any one work could, opened the floodgates of the inquisitorial hysteria."[117] It showed how to make effective the biblical command of Exodus XXII. 18: "Thou shalt not suffer a witch to live." It was the poisoned

source, inspiration, and mine for all subsequent treatises on witchcraft. This how-to book for witch hunters went through at least thirteen editions to 1520 (six of them before 1500), and was revived in another sixteen between 1547 and 1669. At least sixteen of these editions were German, eleven French, two Italian, and at least six English.[118] Although Charles Williams called this work "almost of the first order," [119] Henry Charles Lea on the other hand summed up its intellectual caliber thus: "The divagations [are] endless and perplexing, representing a wandering mind, unused to concentration of thought and diverted to following every intrusive idea." [120]

The *Malleus maleficarum* owed its authority and pride of place over other contemporary works to several factors. First was the reputation of its two authors, both Dominicans, Jakob Sprenger (dean of Cologne University) and Prior Heinrich Institoris (sometimes rendered in German as Krämer); second, the inclusion of the papal bull of 1484 which Institoris obtained from Pope Innocent VIII to silence opposition to the witch hunts; and third, the detailed procedure for conducting witchcraft trials, "in order, then, that the Judges both ecclesiastical and civil may have a ready knowledge of the methods of trying, judging and sentencing." [121]

Though written by inquisitors primarily for the use of other inquisitors, the *Malleus maleficarum* rapidly spread into civil law, and was constantly quoted by nearly all writers on witchcraft for the next two or three centuries. Its provisions were incorporated by 1509 into Ulric Tengler's *Layenspiegel*, the first book in German showing how to convict witches. Cornell does not have this first edition, but has the second edition (Augsburg, 1511) which has an enlarged section on witchcraft.[122] Joost Damhouder's *Praxis rerum criminalis* of 1544 was but a secularization of the *Malleus maleficarum* into criminal law, and was adopted throughout the lower Rhineland.[123] When the Jesuits introduced witchcraft into Bavaria in 1590, their guide was the *Malleus maleficarum*.[124] More surprising was its use by Protestants, who so vehemently rejected other aspects of Catholicism—for example, by Benedict Carpzov, "the law giver of Saxony," who in 1635 compiled his *Practica rerum criminalium*.[125] A century later, in 1728, Carpzov's work still served to send a poor woman, Anna Maria Rosenthal, to her death; the attorney general of Westphalia relied for his decision on Carpzov, "the celebrated criminalist," who in turn had relied on the *Malleus maleficarum*.[126] How right was George Lincoln Burr when he recalled Andrew Dickson White, in 1878, displaying his newly acquired incunabulum of the *Malleus maleficarum* to "his shuddering class," and telling the students it had "caused more suffering than any other [work] written by human pen." [127]

After 1500, apart from trials involving priests and other religious, the Inquisition generally deferred to the state courts in prosecuting witches. But although no longer in active command, its influence was mighty:

> And bicause it may appeare unto the world what trecherous and faithlesse dealing, what extreame and intollerable tyrannie, what grosse and fond absurdities, what unnaturall and uncivil discourtisie, what cancred and spitefull malice, what outragious and barbarous crueltie... what abhominable and divelish inventions, and what flat and plaine

> knaverie is practised against these old women, I will set downe the whole order of the inquisition, to the everlasting, inexcusable, and apparent shame of all witchmoongers.[128]

The Inquisition continued to provide the intellectual and religious sanction for judicial murder, and issued many manuals on witch hunting throughout the seventeenth century. Most of these authors have now limited appeal—Carena, Alberghini, Bergamo, Bordoni, Salelles, and Delbene—but in their time they were influential.[129] The ideas of these theoreticians were incorporated into civil law, as in the witch instructions drawn up by Volpert Mozel, attorney general of Innsbruck in 1637, and by a law professor (and rector) of Innsbruck, Johann Frölich, in 1696.[130] And what kinds of procedures were these scholars advocating? Throughout the second half of the seventeenth century, the works of Bordoni were circulating and being reprinted: Bordoni was writing that if an impotent bridegroom recovered his virility by making water through the wedding ring, he was to denounce the person who suggested the cure as a witch. Bordoni believed that an *indicium* sufficing for torture was a conversation overheard between a witch and a devil, when the devil was not visible. And Bordoni reaffirmed the old belief that physical deformity or ugliness merited torture to prove witchcraft.[131]

By 1550 the weight of learned opinion accepted the Inquisition's view that witchcraft was a heresy, to be extirpated with all ruthlessness. Nearly all these early works were written in Latin, but vernacular presentations soon spread the new theory to the lay public: German in 1517, Italian in 1524, and Spanish in 1539. The Witchcraft Collection has a first edition of Geiler von Kaisersberg, *Die Emeis* (Strassburg, 1517), a second edition of Pico della Mirandola, *Strega* (Pescia, 1555), and an early edition of Pedro Ciruelo, *Reprobacion* (Medina da Campo, 1551).

Since over ninety percent of European witchcraft trials took place after the beginning of the sixteenth century, a student might tend to hurry over the development of heresy by the early writers on witchcraft. Yet it is impossible to understand the final form of witchcraft without considering its evolution, especially as it relates to the trials, for without the trials witchcraft would have commanded no more attention than that devoted to any aspect of folklore. The later centuries inherited from the earlier six approaches to the conduct of the trials:

1. The legal rationalization whereby an alleged physical act (*maleficium*) was or was not considered "heretical" (and thereby warranting execution) depending on the intention or motives of the accused as determined by the investigating court.
2. The assumption that there existed an organized cult, sect, or religion of the witches—an assumption natural enough, for the thinking of the Inquisition had previously been geared exclusively to organized groups (such as the Albigensians), being itself unable to conceive of any person proposing an alternative pattern to the Catholic church *not* being organized. That legacy was expanded by the classic demonologists in their description of the sabbat.
3. The codification and unification of questions to be asked of a witch. Standard

sets of questions or interrogatories are found in inquisitional manuals and in the instructions to judges, and (later) in "guides to jurymen," and in other directives promulgated by official legal authorities.

4. Ascribing shocking crimes (like killing babies and intercourse with animals) to the accused in an effort to gain popular support for the condemning authorities. The classic examples are the allegations against the Knights Templar and against Gilles de Rais.
5. The continued use of the twin powers of the Inquisition, namely, torture and confiscation. There were some trials no doubt where torture was not employed, but by and large these were the exceptions that prove the rule; furthermore, there are large areas where, as the seventeenth century advanced, confiscation was modified. But in most witchcraft trials, torture was *always* used and confiscation of property used very frequently.
6. The necessity for the accused to reveal his accomplices at the alleged witch gathering, to name names, to identify his associates. On this aspect, George Lincoln Burr wrote: "A record of confessions kept by one local court during the space of seven years—you may still read the document for yourself—contains some six thousand accusations from about three hundred witches: that is to say, an average of twenty apiece. Under such circumstances you can see how the witch-trials must go on multiplying, when once the ball was set rolling." [132]

Of the many early writers on witchcraft up to 1550, there are very few not represented in the Witchcraft Collection at Cornell University either by first editions or else by early, near contemporary editions.[133] Yet apart from the *Malleus maleficarum* and several others, few have been given a modern critical edition, and not one—the *Malleus maleficarum* excepted—has been translated into English.

THE CLASSIC DEMONOLOGISTS

After the early writers on witchcraft had established the main features of the heresy of witchcraft and their principles had filtered down to local judges, the theory was refined and deepened from about 1580 by various writers, frequently trial judges, in voluminous compendiums. These "demonologists" might better be called "witchologists," for they were more concerned with the crimes of witches than with the wiles of devils. All harked back to the *Malleus maleficarum*, which continued to hold a prominent position even after the later demonologists had written their textbooks and so partly replaced it as an authority.

The most famous of the classic demonologists include the following: Jean Bodin, *De la Demonomanie des sorciers* (1580); Nicolas Remi, *Daemonolatreiae* (1595); Martin Antoine Del Rio, *Disquisitionum magicarum* (1599); Henri Bo-

guet, *Discours des sorciers* (1602); Francesco Maria Guazzo, *Compendium maleficarum* (1608); Pierre de L'Ancre, *Tableau de l'inconstance des mauvais anges* (1612).

These and similar books mark a complete break from earlier works. As a group they are composed by secular trial judges rather than inquisitors or theologians; several are written originally in the vernacular, implying a desire to reach a broader and less educated audience. Even more than the earlier works, they draw on the confessions of witches the judge-authors had themselves sentenced; they are on this account easier to read, since they present the illusion of reality through an eye-witness account rather than through advocacy of a dogma. They are more self-confident of the acceptance of their views; their accounts of the nefarious acts of witches become more and more shrill and culminate in lurid detailed expositions of the witches' sabbat. Their influence was guaranteed by the high social and political status of their authors as practicing lawyers and judges. It is noteworthy that these French works correspond with the main outbreak of mass witchcraft trials in France between 1580 and 1610, the peak of "the great days of witchcraft," and are doubtless both cause and effect.

Jean Bodin (1529-1596) was a professor of law at the University of Toulouse for twelve years, and in 1561 went to Paris in the service of the king. Falling into disfavor because of his advanced political views—he argued that the royal domain was vested in the people and (less dangerously, since it had never been practiced in France) against the principle of slavery [134]—he married the daughter of a king's prosecutor in 1576, and lived for some twenty years thereafter in Laon as a public prosecutor. Although forming but a small part of Bodin's works (commonly treatises on polity, of which the *République* is the best known), the *Demonomanie des sorciers* (1580) rapidly became one of the most celebrated books on the theory and techniques of witch hunting (especially in its fourth book).[135] Bodin was spurred to write his book by the reprinting of Johann Wier's *De praestigiis daemonum* at Basel in 1578, against whom he added an appendix to the *Demonomanie*, "Refutation des opinions de Jean Wier." Apart from the occasions when Bodin's professional training kept him within legal bounds—"I confess it is far better to absolve the guilty than condemn the innocent" [136]—as a rule he shows himself as intolerant as the authors of the *Malleus maleficarum*: children are to be forced to confess against their parents; suspicion is sufficient ground for torture, for popular rumor is almost never unfounded.[137] Witchcraft must be extirpated: "One must not adhere to the ordinary rules of prosecution," he wrote, "for proof of such evil is so obscure and difficult that not one out of a million witches would be accused or punished, if regular legal procedure were followed." [138]

Bodin published his work first in French, but in the following year (1581) he translated it into Latin as *De magorum daemonomania*, which George Lincoln Burr believed was more widely read, although the Latin text had only a few editions in comparison to the numerous French editions.[139] The Witchcraft Collection is exceptionally rich in copies: the Latin translations of 1581 (Basel), 1590 (Frankfurt), and 1603 (Frankfurt); the French texts of 1580 (Paris), 1582 (Paris),

1587 (Paris), 1598 (Paris), and the posthumous revised edition retitled *Le Fleav des demons et sorciers* (Nyort, 1615).[140] There are four German editions at Cornell: 1581, 1586, 1591, and 1698, this last expanded to include an attack on Bekker (born 38 years after the death of Bodin);[141] and an Italian translation of 1592. The collection of Bodin, of course, is not exhaustive.

Nicolas Remi (1530-1612), slightly junior to Bodin and in fact his student at Toulouse, held more influential official positions than Bodin, and as attorney general of Lorraine was probably able to sway more judges to follow his lead. His *Daemonolatreiae libri tres* was similarly bolstered by his vividly related experiences from 1581 to 1591 with witch trials,[142] in which he boasted (on the title page) of having condemned 900 witches to be burned, and quoted cases by name involving 128 condemned witches.[143] The work was written in Latin [144] and was never published in French,[145] though it was translated into German. It had several editions before 1600, when it was apparently displaced by the popularity of Del Rio.[146] The Witchcraft Collection has two copies of the first edition of 1595 (Lyons) as well as the second edition (Frankfurt, 1596), and two German translations, the 1693 reprinting of the 1598 Frankfurt version and a 1698 edition printed in Hamburg.[147]

"Among them that have lately written of Daemons and Spirits," wrote Meric Causabon in 1668, "and their instruments, men and women, Witches and Sorcerers, Bodinus and Remigius are most known, I think, and read, learned men both." [148] Like Bodin's, the last section of Remi's work concentrated on practical directions in dealing with witches, and this valuable section no doubt encouraged its use by judges. Like Bodin's, too, the work is loosely organized—a compilation of impressions, lecture notes, anecdotes, court records, and quotations from authorities (allegedly over 800 of them)—it jumps from incident to incident, discussing sabbat dances, torture and confessions, use of corpses, power of witches, werewolves, *maleficia*, legal methods of condemning witches, and the manner of their execution.

The third of the great classic French demonologists, Henri Boguet (ca. 1550-1619), chief judge at Saint Claude in Burgundy, also became an authority through his *Discours des sorciers*, first published in 1602, which went through about twelve editions in a few years.[149] It is very similar in scope to the others, and refers extensively to the *Malleus maleficarum*, to Bodin and to Remi, as well as to Binsfeld, Grillandus, and the earlier Bartolommeo Spina (who had been reprinted in 1576). Like Bodin and Remi, the *Discours* too originated in Boguet's interrogation of a witchcraft suspect, a woman who had sent five devils into an eight-year-old girl. He uses this trial, which he reports quite fully, as a starting point to discuss the ramifications of witchcraft. While admitting that "in a criminal process justice demands that the proofs should be clearer than daylight," [150] nevertheless Boguet hoped that "if effect could be given to my wish, the earth would be immediately cleared of [witches]; for I would that they should all be united in one single body, so that they might all be burned in a single fire." [151] Like the others, too, Boguet burned children of tender years, believing that since their crime was

so horrible, they could seldom be reformed.[152] It is difficult to say which of these Classic demonologists wielded the greatest influence. Lea [153] considered Remi and Del Rio the most important. Summers, on the other hand, believed that "after the great *Malleus maleficarum*, there is perhaps no treatise more authoritative, and certainly no treatise more revelatory of the human side of trials for witchcraft and of the psychology of those involved in such trials than the *Discours des sorciers*." [154] Boguet made explicit what others suggested, and the vogue of his work was helped by his appendix of ninety-one articles on "The Manner of Procedure of a Judge in a Case of Witchcraft," which neatly codified existing statutes and court methods.

Pierre de Rosteguy, sieur de L'Ancre (1553-1631), the last of the great witch hunters in early seventeenth-century France, was also a trial judge and boasted of burning six hundred witches. Trained as a lawyer in Italy and Bohemia, in 1582 he became a lawyer for the parliament of Bordeaux, and in 1609 was commissioned to investigate witchcraft in the Pays de Labourd, a Basque-speaking territory in southeastern Guienne. L'Ancre's experiences here—he found the entire population of 30,000, including the priests, to be infected by witchcraft—formed the basis for his *Tableau de l'inconstance des mauvais anges*.[155] In addition, he devotes some 150 pages to lycanthropy. Although enmired in almost unbelievable credulity, L'Ancre's first book has great value as a detailed account of a mass witch hunt. About the trials as a whole, Lea commented: "To a mind not wholly prejudiced in advance the extracts which he gives from the depositions would have led to the conclusion that the culprits were seeking merely to invent stories that would satisfy their judges." [156]

But to those who might question the activities of the witches, L'Ancre presented an incontrovertible argument:

> Let us add that the Catholic, Apostolic and Roman Church, which cannot err, punishes [witches] with death. Now it would err grievously to treat them so severely if they were only witches and criminals in fantasy. It is necessary therefore to infer that whosoever believes that the transvection of witches is only a false imagination, a dream, and an illusion, sins against the Church, which does not punish debatable, secret and non-manifest crimes, and which punishes as heretics only those who really do commit these acts, not just in dreams and illusions.[157]

Later, in his retirement, L'Ancre wrote two other works on witchcraft, *L'Incredvlité et mescreance dv sortilege* (1622) and *Du Sortilege* (1627).[158]

The works of the other major demonologists outside France are comparable in scope and attitude. Martin Antoine Del Rio (1551-1608) published his *Disquisitiones magicarum libri sex* at Louvain in 1599, with an abridged French translation appearing in 1611.[159] In many ways Del Rio was the most exhaustive of all these writers, and perhaps the most learned—he could read Hebrew and Aramaic, and wrote fifteen books. Born in Antwerp of a distinguished Castilian father and a wealthy Aragonese mother, at age twenty-four he was appointed by the king of Spain as attorney general for Brabant. Five years later (1580) he became a Jesuit and taught at many of the Jesuit colleges throughout Europe. Much of Del Rio's

reportage was taken from the annual reports (especially those from Louvain) circulated within the order.[160] The *Disquisitiones magicarum* was reprinted thirteen times to its final edition in 1747. The Cornell Witchcraft Collection is especially rich in Del Rio: it has the first edition of 1599, the 1604, 1608, and 1612 editions from Lyons, the 1612 and 1624 Mainz editions, the Cologne edition of 1678, as well as the French translation of 1611.[161] There has never been an English translation.

Francesco Maria Guazzo was a Milanese friar—his exact dates are not known—who served as assessor in witch trials. His *Compendium maleficarum* (1608) was written at the request of the bishop of Milan to expose and confute the practices of witchcraft.[162] Guazzo borrowed heavily from his predecessors, quoting in all from 322 authorities,[163] especially Remi and Del Rio. A second edition appeared in 1626; both editions contain many illustrations.

The anecdotes, the verbatim reporting of the trials, the personal experiences of the authors, the often vivid style, along with the detailed practical instructions on how to convict witches, assured the popularity of these works. Their influence was increased by reprintings and by continued borrowings by lesser demonologists.[164] During the height of the witchcraft hysteria, many similar works were published, but few attained the authoritative status of the major French writers. Some of the representative minor "promoters of the delusion" (as Lea called them),[165] not all French, not all Catholic, include the following:

Ludwig Lavater (1527-1586), *De spectris, lemuribus, et magis* (Geneva, 1570); [166]
Lambert Daneau (ca. 1530-1596), *Les Sorciers* (Geneva, [1574]); [167]
Pierre Nodé, *Declamation contre l'erreur execrable des maleficiers* (Paris, 1578); [168]
Giovanni Lorenzo Anania, *De natura demonum* (Venice, 1581); [169]
Pierre Le Loyer (1550-1634), *Quatre Livres des spectres ou apparitions et visions d'esprits* (Angers, 1586); [170]
F. Pierre Crespet (1543-1594), *De la Hayne de Sathan et malins esprits contre l'homme* (Paris, 1590); [171]
Petrus Thyraeus (1546-1601), *De daemoniacis* (Cologne, 1594); [172]
Henning Grosse (1553-1621), *Magica* (Eisleben, 1597); [173]
Jacques d'Autun (ca. 1608-1678), *L'Incredvlité scavante et la credvlité ignorante: au sujet des magiciens et des sorciers* (Lyons, 1671).[174]

Synopses of most of these works are given in Lea's *Materials toward a History of Witchcraft*, as indicated in the appropriate notes. Some of the French writers were translated into English soon after their publication in France.[175]

Clearly, most of the works of these minor demonologists are not well known, and in fact copies are not always easy to find. There is no question that Bodin and Del Rio, for example, are of prime importance in any history of witchcraft; there is, however, considerable question about Guazzo. After all, his book went through only one reprinting. Yet his *Compendium maleficarum* is read and quoted among English-speaking students—largely, I believe, because it is available in English. The work of Sinistrari (1622-1701), *De daemonialitate et incubis et succubis*, lay

for nearly two centuries in manuscript until its discovery in 1872 in a London bookshop; so obviously it exercised no influence whatsoever on its contemporaries. It first appeared in a French translation in 1876, and in an English translation in 1879. Then in 1927 it was reintroduced in Montague Summers' translation, and even though published in a limited edition of 1,200 copies, nevertheless it was widely read—no doubt the subject matter helped its exposure.[176] Scholars of the Elizabethan period have at least heard of the English versions of Le Loyer or Daneau, for example, and these texts, because they are in English, find their way into bibliographies.

And this is the glory of the Witchcraft Collection at Cornell: it has the original texts. Not every work of every minor writer is there, of course. The Collection lacks, for example, two interesting believers in witchcraft, Anhorn and Levenwald—who receive very brief mention in Lea—and there only from notes in Hauber's *Bibliotheca magica*.[177] But the Witchcraft Collection has copies of rare works which even the encyclopedic Lea knew only at second hand (from Diefenbach or Hauber), such as David Meder, whose *Acht Hexenpredigten von des Teufels Mordtkindern* was first printed in 1605, and reprinted in 1615, 1646, and 1675.[178] There is Jean de Filesac, who "reflects the extremest superstition of his time"; the first edition of his *De idolatria magica* (Paris, 1609) is at Cornell.[179] There is Heinrich Nicolai, who "accepts all the beliefs as to Sabbat, Incubi, etc.," whose *De magibus actionibus* (Danzig, 1649) is at Cornell.[180] And there is also Christian Stridtbeckh, whose *De sagis* was published at the very end of the seventeenth century (Leipzig, 1690), and reprinted in 1723, a most amazing university dissertation parroting the views of Grillandus, Del Rio, Carpzov, as well as the *Malleus maleficarum*.[181]

To scholars, the fact that the Witchcraft Collection has these works, and others similar, is of greater intellectual significance than that Cornell has fourteen editions of the *Malleus maleficarum*; and in my opinion it is to these works (and even more to the works of their opponents, in which the Witchcraft Collection, through the ingenuity of White and Burr, is especially blessed) that students of witchcraft could most profitably direct their attention.

For some considerable time the classic demonologists reinforced the pervasiveness of the witchcraft delusion, copying from each other as if repetition could establish veracity. For example, Sinistrari (1700), the last of the demonologists who stressed the sexual aspects of witchcraft, gave a succinct description of the witch's mark.[182] Said Sinistrari: "Character uero non est semper euisdem formae, aut figurae; aliquando enim est simile lepori, aliquando pedi bufonis, aliquando araneae, uel catello, uel glori." And Sinistrari continued, describing its location on the body: "Imprimitur autem in locis corporis magis occultis: uiris quidem aliquando sub palpebris, aliquando sub axillis, aut labiis, aut humeris, aut sede ima, aut alibi; mulieribus autem plerumque in mammis, seu locis muliebribus."[183]

But Sinistrari borrowed this account from Guazzo (1608),[184] who in turn had borrowed it from Boguet (1602),[185] who in turn had borrowed it from Del Rio (1599): "Non eadem est forma signi: aliquando est simile leporis uestigio, ali-

quando bufonis pedi, aliquando araneae; uel catello, uel gliri. In uirorum enim corpore saepe uisitur sub palpebris, sub labiis, sub axillis, in humeris, in sede ima; feminis etiam, in mammis uel muliebribus locis."[186] And Del Rio (1599) had borrowed it from Binsfeld (1589),[187] who in turn had borrowed it from Bodin (1580):

> Mais ie suis bien de l'aduis de Dagneau, qui dict que les plus grands Sorciers ne sont point marqués, ou bien en lieu si secret, qu'il est quasi impossible de les descouurir. Car i'ay sceu d'vn Gentil-homme de Vallois, qu'il y en a de marques par le Diable soubz le paupiere de l'oeil, soubz la leure, et mesmes au fondement. Mais Trois-eschelles disoit, que ceux qui estoient marqués auoyent comme vne piste, ou pied de lieure, et que l'endroict estoit insensible, encores qu'on y mist vne aiguille iusques aux os. Ce seroit bien vne presomption tres-violente, et suffizante auecques d'autres indices, pour proceder à la condamnation.[188]

In 1629, a law professor at the University of Cologne, Peter Ostermann, assembled all the stories of the witch's mark into a learned dissertation, *Commentarius juridicus... in quo de variis speciebus signaturarum... imprimis vero Antichristi et de illorum quae sagas inusta deprehenduntur*.[189] Since by this time the witchcraft craze was beginning to slacken, Ostermann was answered the following year (1630) by Johann Jordanaeus, a Protestant pastor, in his *Disputatio de proba stigmatica*.[190] The Cornell University Library does not possess a copy of Ostermann, but has a copy of the more scarce *Disputatio*.

Boguet in 1602 repeated a scandalous story from Bodin (1580) about the bestiality practiced by the nuns of a convent in Hesse with "certain dogs found on the beds of the nuns."[191] But Bodin himself[192] had taken this story from Wier's *De praestigiis* (1568).[193] L'Ancre (1612) relied heavily on earlier authorities: on one page of his *Tableau de l'inconstance*, he quotes Remi that witches add sacrilege to sorcery, and Del Rio that the devil works by himself in abducting infants; on another, describing the pact with the devil made with the blood of the witch, he quotes Bodin, Del Rio, and Boguet; and of course L'Ancre frequently quotes the *Malleus maleficarum*.[194]

From the works of the early writers before 1550 slowly emerges the witches' sabbat, a concept created in the interrogatories devised by misogynic and celibate inquisitors. The ensuing confessions forced from the accused then provided the basis for further elaboration by succeeding questioners. One can watch the idea developing and spreading, as lay inquisitors circulated their manuals and extended their heresy hunts.[195]

But the French demonologists, about 1600, expanded the concept of the sabbat, becoming more and more detailed. The French demonologists always used the word *sabbat*; German demonologists, on the other hand, preferred the word dance, dance place (*Tanz, Tanzplatz, zauberisch Tanzplatz*), or simply gathering (*Gesellschaft*).

Elsewhere I have described the five major parts of the classical sabbat: (1) assembly; (2) homage; (3) banquet; (4) dancing; and (5) intercourse. All that is called for at this point, therefore, is a very brief summation.[196] The demonologists devoted considerable attention to the sexual orgies in which the sabbat was sup-

posed to culminate. "The curiosity of the judges was insatiable to learn all the possible details as to sexual intercourse," wrote Lea, "and their industry in pushing the examination was rewarded by an abundance of foul imaginations."[197]

Just as the earliest accounts of the banquet had depicted it as giving pleasure, so did the first accounts of diabolic intercourse. The inquisitor Nicolas Jacquier, writing in 1458, said it was *"inordinate carnaliter,"* and that many witches "for several days afterward remain worn out" (*afflicti et debilitati*).[198] Early Italian accounts generally concurred: Grillandus reported confessions by women who enjoyed the devil *"maxima cum voluptata."* [199] William of Paris in his *De universo* said the devil could delude women into thinking that relations performed only once or twice were repeated fifty to sixty times a night.[200] But most later descriptions stressed the pain and terror of intercourse: a demonologist could not permit a witch to have pleasure. Boguet reported from Franche-Comté: "Thievenne Paget said, moreover, that when Satan coupled with her she had as much pain as a woman in travail."[201] Remi reported likewise from Lorraine: "Claudia Fellet said she herself had experienced something forced into her, swollen to such a size, that no matter how capacious a woman might be, she would not be able to contain it without extreme pain."[202] Adding a few further particulars of his own, L'Ancre gave the sworn testimony of sixteen-year-old Jeannette d'Abadie of Siboro:

> At the coupling, she deposed she had seen every one mix incestuously and in violation of the laws of nature ... she blamed herself for having been deflowered by Satan and carnally known an infinity of times by one of her relatives and others who vouchsafed to go in unto her. She said she put off intercourse with the devil, because his member was scaly and caused extreme pain; furthermore his semen was extremely cold, so cold that she had never become pregnant by him.[203]

Little Jeannette was a useful informant, for L'Ancre quoted her confession quite frequently.[204] Her confession was, of course, given under torture, in response to leading questions posed by an insatiable judge, and later written up in its final form by the court notary.

One of the few novel variants to these relations was that made by the inquisitor Sebastian Michaelis, to whom Sister Madeleine Bavoux had confessed that every time she went to a sabbat there was a different form of sexual activity: "Finally, they committed vncleannesse one with another: Vpon Sundaies they pollute themselves by their filthy copulation with Diuels, that are Succubi and Incubi: Vpon Thursdayes they contaminate themselves with Sodomy: Vpon Saturdaies they doe prostitvte themselves to abominable bestiality; Vpon other daies they use the ordinary course which nature prompteth vnto them."[205]

From the confession of one accused woman brought before him, Bodin builds up a composite account of the activites of a sabbat, starting with preparations for transvection and finishing with copulation:

> Marguerite Brement, wife of Noel Lavaret, deposed that last Monday, after dusk, she had been with her mother Marion at a gathering, near the mill of Franquis de Longny in a meadow. Her mother had taken a broom between her thighs, and, saying words she

did not understand, they were both suddenly carried through the air to the said place, where they found Jeanne Robert, Jeanne Guillemin, Marie the wife of Simon d'Agneau, and Guillemette wife of a man named Le Gras, and each one had her own broomstick. In this place there were also six devils, in the form of men, but very ugly to look on. When the dancing was done, the devils slept with them and enjoyed their company. One of them, who was her partner in the dancing, took her and kissed her twice, and cohabited with her for the period of over half an hour; but his emission was extremely icy. Jeanne Guillemin likewise deposed about this matter, and said the two of them were joined together for a good half hour, and that her devil discharged very cold semen.[206]

Of course, Marguerite Brement, Jeanne Guillemin, and the rest of the women were burned as witches.

From about 1430, the Inquisition, while not yet making it a major feature of the witchcraft trials, prosecuted women for relations with the devil. By 1600, whether in church or state courts, diabolic intercourse had become mandatory for every person accused of witchcraft, from young children of three to old women of eighty. At Würzburg in January, 1628, three children, Anna Rausch, Sybille Lutz, and Mürchin, all confessed to sexual relations with incubi. Twelve-year-old Anna declared she had intercourse six times with Master Hamerlin ("Jack Catch the devil"); the court records noted "this copulation the child has *formalissime* described." Eleven-year-old Sybille copulated with Master "Federlein." Little eight-year-old Mürchin testified *formaliter* she had *coitus cum demone*. Little Mürchin was not put to death.[207]

Because some of the demonologists are available in English translations (such as Remi, Boguet, Guazzo, and Sinistrari) and make highly sensational reading, the classic demonologists have been a major factor in forming the current popular misconceptions of witchcraft. Even academicians often accept these accounts of witchcraft, in view of the high prestige of the demonologists as leaders in state and church, as trustworthy evidence. This is an example of a pseudohistorical methodology, which accepts the words but ignores the circumstances in which the words were uttered. A scholar cannot end his investigations with this group, but must push forward and examine the writings of the penologists, the records of the trials, and the contemporary exposés of the eyewitness opponents.

THE PENOLOGISTS

Most "classic" demonologists included accounts of the trials at which they had presided, and gave in full the confessions of the witches they had sentenced. Some, Bodin and Boguet among others, appended sets of instructions to judges how to find and convict witches.[208] Bodin, for example, writing with the experience of an official prosecutor, considered a single eligible witness sufficient to warrant torture of an accused witch—and "eligible" witnesses included "infa-

mous" persons.[209] Boguet added to his *Discours des sorciers* ninety-one articles advising a judge how to take action against witches to secure confessions. One article, for example, recommended strict confinement: "If the Judge can draw no confession from the accused, he must confine him in a very narrow and dark cell; for it has been proved that the hardship of prison very often impels witches to confess, especially when they are young." [210]

Boguet recommended too that the "Judge must avoid torture as much as possible," [211] but wound up advising that "a witch's confession is warrant enough for the employment of torture against his accomplice, if such confession is substantiated by some other presumption or indication." [212] And Boguet added another article, a kind of escape clause to justify any actions by the judge: "The aforementioned threats [by the Judge], if they are followed by any effect, are enough to justify the resort to torture." [213] In case of retraction, Boguet advised that the witch "must be again exposed to the torture. This the Judge may do three times, but no more." [214] To a local and uneducated justice of the peace who had seldom taken part in a witch trial, these instructions of procedure would be invaluable. By recording their personal encounters with witches, these French demonologists were, I think, despite their practical advice, trying primarily to alert public opinion to the enormities of witchcraft.

On these enormities, another group of demonologists agreed without any question; but this group, the penologists, wrote about the mechanics of getting rid of the witches. One might take L'Ancre as a typical representative of the former, and Binsfeld of the latter school. L'Ancre concentrated on the lurid content of the confessions, Binsfeld on the lurid means which produced those confessions.[215]

Peter Binsfeld (1540-1598), trained by the Jesuits at Rome, was suffragan bishop of Trier; by virtue of his book he became a leading authority on trial procedure for Protestants as well as Catholics for many decades.[216] In his *Tractatus de confessionibus maleficorum et sagarum* the Witchcraft Collection is rich.[217] Binsfeld had in fact been preceded in time by Ulric Tengler, who, relying on the *Malleus maleficarum*, wrote his *Layenspiegel* in 1509, the first vernacular handbook to include procedures against witches.[218]

From time to time Binsfeld gives the air of moderation. For example, he recommends that judges avoid new and unusual torture: "And in this crime of sorcery it is inhuman for judges, forgetting that they are dealing with men, to employ dire, tyrannous and cruel methods, such as burning the flesh with candles or pouring hot oil." [219] The highly efficient strappado satisfied Binsfeld. Disagreeing with Daneau and Bodin, he is not convinced that witch's marks or physical ugliness are strong indications (*indicia*) of witchcraft; [220] no matter, there are plenty of others. But in practice, the *Tractatus* and the *Commentarius* encourage a judge to do all he can to convict. Apparently many doubted the validity of the evidence employed to secure further convictions, namely, denunciation of a person as an alleged accomplice by a "witch" under torture.[221] Binsfeld had a firm answer for the likes of these: "To exclude the denunciations of accomplices is to render impossible the extirpation of this crime and to preclude inquest, trial and

punishment of the leaders of this wickedness, which it would be most absurd to concede."[222] In the *Commentarius* appended to later editions, Binsfeld gives comprehensive instructions on the use of torture to secure confessions, and how to stay within the letter of the law:

> Experienced judges, when they order torture to cease, should order the notary to record that they do so with the intention of repeating it, and this is rather to be termed continuing it, even if there is an interval of some days.
>
> When the first *indicia* are very urgent and manifest, then, although by law torture cannot be repeated, nevertheless by custom it is repeated and such is the practice.
>
> The most efficacious tortures are those which can be prolonged without serious bodily injury, and that of sleeplessness is highly to be recommended as almost infallible.
>
> In this and other atrocious crimes, persistent denial under torture does not prevent condemnation when there is other sufficient proof.[223]

Thus despite the cautions against "excessive" torture, Binsfeld's disapprobation of judges who insist on so many indications of witchcraft that no one will denounce anyone,[224] his demand, "Fire for *malefici*, fire for *sagae*, fire for *magi*,"[225] would encourage most local judges to make sure of convicting those brought before them: "Although in other crimes when there is doubt it is safer to absolve the guilty than to condemn the innocent, yet in heresy and matters of the faith every one is presumed to be a heretic. And this is applicable to sorcery with greater strength, since it is the most atrocious of all crimes, destructive to religion and bringing many evils on the Republic."[226] Binsfeld must be accounted one of the most determined promoters of the witchcraft delusion.

Binsfeld's influence was spread in at least two handbooks for judges, not much more than translated paraphrases of the *Tractatus:* Diedrich Gramineau, *Inductio sive directorum: das ist: Anleitung oder Vnderweizung,* published in Cologne in 1594, and Franciscus Agricola, *Gründtlicher Bericht, ob Zauberey die argste vnd grewlichste sünd auff Erden sey* (Cologne, 1597).[227]

In 1653, some fifty years after Binsfeld, a Protestant professor at Leipzig, Benedict Carpzov (1595-1666), published his *Practica rerum criminalium,*[228] the *Malleus maleficarum* of Protestantism. By 1723 it had been reprinted nine times. Its importance was proportional to its author; whereas Binsfeld was largely restricted to dominating Trier, Carpzov exercised a continuing influence for many decades over Saxony, a very large part of Germany. Carpzov drew on all the recognized Catholic authorities—the *Malleus maleficarum* itself, Grillandus, Remi, Del Rio, Bodin, and Binsfeld—and was as credulous as any of them. In addition, he also drew on the more severe Saxon code of the Elector Augustus of 1579, which had been substituted for the more tolerant Catholic code.[229] Thus, at a period in history when other jurists and theologians were starting to explore the legality of the *crimen exceptum,* wherein the judge could in practice set his own rules to secure a conviction, Carpzov bolstered and kept alive this whole sinister system.[230] In his *Materials,* Lea devotes nearly fifty pages to summarizing Carpzov, and every student of witchcraft has to study the *Practica* very carefully. The following extracts illustrate only a few of Carpzov's opinions on securing confessions:

> The denunciation of an accomplice, without other presumptions, is insufficient to start an inquiry, especially if he is "infected" with other crimes—though there are authorities who hold it suffices in atrocious crimes.... But a complaint of accusation by an accomplice justifies summoning and examining the accused, when, if he varies, he gives grounds for suspicion which may justify arrest.
>
> If [the accused's] answers are evasive and ambiguous, the questions must be repeated until he replies clearly and categorically. If he will not do so or will not answer, he can be tortured, for his evasiveness is a sufficient *indicium*.
>
> In excepted crimes where the *indicia* are urgent, candles are applied to slowly burn parts of the body, or wooden wedges are driven under the nails and then set on fire.
>
> It not infrequently happens that [the witch] revokes his confession, alleging that it was extorted by torture. If this were admitted, crime would be unpunished for all would do so. It is necessary then to torture him again.
>
> So too in heresy one may be convicted solely on intention, even if there is no other proof, and these are considered as heretics who make pact with the devil.[231]

Carpzov's *Practica rerum criminalium* is not short—some four hundred pages, about half of which (pages 153-329) are given over to detailed instructions on torture, "a collection of horrors," said Lea, with a list of seventeen different kinds, "not to mention a hundred others."[232] At the end, Carpzov added thirty-six decisions of the Leipzig Supreme Court (from 1558 to 1622), of which he was a member. These decisions, "each one more bloody than the rest," were continually quoted in later witchcraft trials to justify sentencing.[233] By such methods Carpzov was able to boast he had sentenced twenty thousand witches to be burned.[234]

Most penologists were themselves concerned about the extreme measures taken to secure confessions, but they were so accustomed to believing in witchcraft that they were unwilling to stop the trials solely on grounds of legal misconduct. Johann Georg Godelmann (1559-1611) for example, professor of law at the University of Rostock,[235] tried to distinguish, without success, different kinds of witches—some guilty and some less guilty—claiming that those most often executed were really deluded old women (*lamiae*).[236] Their stories of sex and sabbat resulted from delusions sent by the devil or from the hallucinatory effects of their ointments. Yet Godelmann never doubted that what he termed *magi* and *venefici* could actually work *maleficia* (ligature at least)[237] through the pact they had made with the devil. The judges at the witch trials, however, did not distinguish between *lamiae* (deluded old women) and *magi* and *venefici* (the signers of the pact), and furthermore judges held delusions equally culpable as acts.[238] The importance of Godelmann is not only his revelation of the intellectual turmoil when honest doubts about the methods of finding witches clashed with credulous acceptance of a belief in witches, but even more in his depiction of what went on in the witch courts. Nearly all of the deluded women burned as witches pleaded their innocence to their confessors; the only evidence against them, said Godelmann, was their own confessions. But these very confessions were "extorted by insufferable torment." He addressed himself to their judges: "You would doubtless cease, if you saw the boiling oil poured upon the legs, the burning candles applied to the arm-pits and the infinite barbarities exercised on decrepit old women, as we have seen."[239]

Throughout Germany many inexperienced judges and assessors disregarded

the laws and the constitution, "and consigned [women] to the flames, without discrimination and without legitimate proofs." [240] Godelmann's *De magis, veneficis et lamiis recte cognoscendia et punienda* was first published in 1591 at Frankfurt, with a German translation appearing in 1592.[241]

The lesser penologists, the counterpart of the minor demonologists, included both Catholics and Protestants, many connected with the law faculties of German universities. Some, such as Binsfeld and Godelmann, cautioned against the disregard of even the slight protection the Carolina Code afforded those accused of witchcraft.[242] These cautions came from trained legal minds, and the very fact that they had to be made (as the writers frequently deplored) indicates not only that the majority of judges overlooked strict legal procedure (like the prohibition against the renewal of torture),[243] but also that the majority of witches were convicted on disregard of even the rules applicable to a *crimen exceptum*. The penologists listed below, all German, have been selected primarily for their intrinsic importance and secondarily because their works are conveniently abstracted in Lea's *Materials toward a History of Witchcraft*:

Johann Zanger, *Tractatus duo: de exceptionibus et quaestionibus seu torturis reorum* (1592); [244]
Artwig von Dassell, *Responsum juris in causa poenali maleficarum Winsiensium* (1597); [245]
Ernst Cothmann, *Responsum juris* (1597); [246]
David Meder, *Acht Hexenpredigten von des Teufels Mordtkindern* (1605); [247]
Melchior Goldast, *Rechtliches Bedencken von Confiscation der Zauberer und Hexen-Güther* (1629); [248]
Hermann Goehausen, *Processus juridicus contra sagas et veneficos; Das ist; Rechtlicher Process* (1630); [249]
Wolffgang Hildebrand, *Goêtia, vel theurgia, sive praestigiarum magicarum descriptio* (1631); [250]
Justus Oldekop, *Observationes criminales practicae* (1640); [251]
Nicolaus Brandt, *Disputatio de legitima maleficos et sagas investigandi et convincendi ratione* (1662).[252]

In expressing his opposition to the more extreme techniques of torture, Oldekop suggested that when the torturer searched for the witch's mark he practiced deceit: "Many people have scars or birthmarks, less sensitive than other places. May not also the exquisite torment of the patient hanging in the torture when the needle is thrust in prevent its pain from being felt? What prevents the executioner from using a deceiving stylus, magic and enchanted, or one, like the juggler's knives, which can either enter really or only apparently, as the torturer wishes?" [253] Deceit, or at the best stupidity, could also be found in the court room. Oldekop continued:

> There are some scriveners and actuaries and even commissioners of criminal justice, as experience shows, so inexpert that they very often, to the great danger of the accused, neglect necessary procedure, especially in the difficult points of torture, *indicia* and

confession. Some customarily, in order to conform with custom, frame protocols in which they enter their own opinions to the great disadvantage of the accused, or they make marginal notes on the records to make his case worse.[254]

What had originally been intended as a safeguard to protect the accused witch against a bigoted judge—that since (as Godelmann wrote) [255] "the proof of torture and even of unjust torture is easy, the presumption is in favor of the accused and the judge must prove the justification"—in practice had quite the opposite effect. Faced with the possibility of charges of unjust torture, the judge exerted himself by even more cruel torture to obtain a confession.[256] Later, some of the victims and opponents of witchcraft made this very point: that judges (and torturers) boasted they always obtained convictions.[257] One recalls the letter of Burgomaster Johannes Junius of Bamberg (in 1627) relating how the torturer advised him: "Sir, I beg you, for God's sake, confess something, whether it be true or not. Invent something, for you cannot endure the torture to which you will be subjected, and, even if you bear it all, you will not escape, even if you were a count, but one torture will follow another until you say you are a witch." [258]

Increasing the severity of the torture to produce the confession was actually recommended by some penologists. Artwig von Dassell published his opinions on torture, in answer to a brief submitted him by a lower court at Winsen in Lower Saxony, in 1597. Dassell gave complete freedom to the judge to repeat torture:

> We would not hasten to condemn, but try various methods to obtain confession, even by repetition of torture, for, though all the doctors say that new *indicia* are requisite for repetition, yet they commonly admit that, if torture has been insufficient, it may be repeated and, if we consider the custom of some judges, they repeat it indifferently without new *indicia*. Some authorities hold that, when the *indicia* are very urgent, torture can be repeated, and, however this may be, the judge in the present case cannot err in repeating the torture, for the witches seem not to have been sufficiently tortured and the *indicia* are very vehement.[259]

If the confused witch did not know what was expected of him, although the interrogatories were standard and several typical lists of specific topics were provided by the penologists, such as Godelmann and Brandt,[260] then the accused would be told what to say. Goldast, though a believer in witchcraft and the power of witches, warned against the abuse of suggesting the contents of confessions:

> And it is a great abuse among the common, ignorant country judges who have the barbarous custom not to condemn to death the criminal, however full and free his confession may be, without confirming it with torture. And it is much to be desired that in some places more caution and delay were used with the poor women and not so swiftly proceeded to torture on a simple denunciation. Especially should it be kept in view that many innocent persons, under unendurable torture, confess what they have never thought, much less put into action. Particularly as I have in some places seen with much disturbance of spirit and have abolished, where articles [of accusation] are read to the accused before torture, leading poor weak women in the torture to repeat and affirm what they have thus been told.[261]

Of all these technical manuals on the use of torture to extract confessions from the witches, I think two should be singled out for special notice, for both are

almost unknown except for a brief description in Robbins' *Encyclopedia*. (Both works are in the Witchcraft Collection.) The first is *Les Manières admirables pour décovvrir tovtes sortes de crimes et sortilèges avec l'instrvction solide povr bien ivger vn ɥ.ocez criminal,* printed in Paris in 1659, by Le Sieur Bouvet, provost general of the French armies in Italy.[262] Bouvet draws on his own experiences in the courtroom and torture chamber—"a whole volume would not suffice to relate them"—noting when the prisoner should shriek out with pain and when the judge should harden his heart.[263] Chapter 18 explains "How a good judge should superintend the torture, and how he should interrogate the accused, and what he should watch out for during the proceedings":

> The judge should have the accused shaved and bound, and then, unemotionally and composedly, have him tortured until he believes the prisoner can stand no more. The judge must proceed neither too lightly nor too severely, always show mercy and moderation, and take into account either the extreme age or tender youth of the accused, and his good or bad reputation. The judge must not desist on account of the cries and shrieks that will be made during the torture, lest feeling too much pity he lose the chance to find out the truth. His rules are not those of his own heart, but those of the civil and ecclesiastical law.[264]

In such grotesque yet homely fashion, the *Manières* is perhaps the most inhumanly human of all the manuals for secular judges.[265]

The second work is completely inhuman, and surely warrants Burr's grim comment, written on the back flyleaf of this small quarto volume of more than five hundred pages, each headed "Clementissime Jesu, illumina intellectum meum":

> This book is, to my thinking, the most gruesome in all the gruesome literature of witch-persecution; and there is good ground for suspecting it of being the only copy now surviving. It is a handbook for the pursuit and the conviction of witches, written by an expert who had succeeded and prospered, and is, I think, at the same time the most pious and the most cruel of all such handbooks.[266]

Eine aussfürliche Instrvction wie in Inqvisition Sachen des grewlichen Lasters der Zauberey . . . zu procediren was written by Heinrich von Schultheis and published in Cologne in 1634 at the author's expense. Schultheis was a doctor of both civil and ecclesiastical law and a secretary to several witch hunting bishops, including Peter Ostermann, "Aulic Councilor of the Archbishop and Prince-Elector of Mainz," who had in 1629 published his book on the reliability of the witch's mark.[267] Schultheis was provoked into writing his instructions, demanding the extermination of witches, by the works of Tanner and Spee, the two Jesuits who opposed the inquisitorial techniques of the trials. In turn Schultheis was himself answered by Hermann Löher, whose work survives in a sole copy.

The *Instrvction* was written in the form of a "friendly discourse" between a doctor (Schultheis himself) and a mythical baron (Freyherr) named Philadelphus, "who had communicated with me in sincerity all doubtful points in the procedure against witches." [268] Burr notes how "there were brought also into the dialogue the accused themselves, whose examinations—their denials and evasions, their very shrieks under the torture—are reproduced in full." [269] Forming an

appropriate summation of the works of these penologists are the words of Schultheis himself to a witch he has just condemned: "With the same, in fact with even greater indifference do I regard torturing you than I do bending this reed out of my path with my stick; for by so doing I earn nothing. But when I have you tortured, and by the severe means afforded by the law I bring you to confession, then I perform a work pleasing in God's sight, and it profiteth me." [270]

COURT RECORDS OF TRIALS

The court records of the trials of witches form the hard core of the source materials for the study of witchcraft. The documents must be examined against the background of demonologists and penologists—intellectual, establishing witchcraft as a *crimen exceptum* abrogating all legal procedures; and practical, establishing torture as the customary, even required, method to extract confessions of making a pact with the devil and of naming accomplices at witches' gatherings. Confiscation, general in witchcraft trials, did not receive very much attention from the witchologists, probably because in trials for treason it was seldom questioned, and witchcraft was treason against God.

Since my own studies impressed on me the correctness of the White-Burr position that witchcraft lies within the domain of theology—Christian theology—I was somewhat surprised when in 1960 a review of my *Encyclopedia* suggested I might be underplaying the importance of ideology (especially dualism) and overstressing the actual trials.[271] But nearly two decades of further research have only strengthened my original conclusions that of the various source materials the trial records (with the exposés of the confessors) are of utmost importance for the overall history of witchcraft.

Even in trials (after 1500) of priests and nuns, conducted by the Inquisition itself, where presumably the question of orthodoxy or nonorthodoxy would be paramount, I have never found any concern by the inquisitors for religious beliefs. For example, in the trial of Father Dominic Gordel, a parish priest in Lorraine, indicted by the bishop of Sitie acting as vicar-general of the cardinal of Lorraine "of witchcraft and other crimes and black art," the questioning dealt with the impious use of exorcism, the pact with the devil, attendance at the sabbat, and naming accomplices. Nary a word about theology.[272] In an earlier trial by the Inquisition of a married woman in Luxeuil, Franchez Comté, in 1529, the charges (which she admitted in strappado) are about the devil's promises to her, making hailstorms, flying through the air on a stick, dancing at the sabbat, copulation with the devil ("froid comme glace"), poisoning cattle, and naming her accomplices at the *sabbats et sinagogues des diables*.[273] Yet she was burned for renouncing the Catholic faith and committing the crime of heresy. Witchcraft was

not even mentioned in her sentence. Heresy had come to mean admitting to the five parts of the sabbat. In the very late trial in 1749 (of which the Witchcraft Collection has many unpublished manuscripts) of Sister Maria Renata, subprioress of the Convent of Unterzell near Würzburg, conducted with all formality and publicity by the Inquisition, there is not one question about doctrine; all the questions concern Sister Maria Renata's accomplices and her physical relations with the devil at the sabbat.[274] Her execution is one of the last in Europe and occasioned a considerable controversy, but the controversy was about the trial itself, not about her heretical beliefs.[275]

If the Inquisition, whose function it was to inquire into matters of faith, ignored doctrinal questions in favor of interrogations on sexual misconduct, how much more prone would the secular courts be to ignore the niceties of belief; and in the lower courts judges and assessors would be neither trained lawyers nor trained theologians. Nor was there any need; when a Catholic sin became a state crime, it was very easy for a state crime to become a Protestant sin. But the emphasis was always on the crime.

The sabbat, as gloatingly described by the French demonologists, is removed from actuality by the prurient stress on fantasies of sexual license. The reports are extracted, carefully selected, and screened. How the young girls' confessions—as reported by Bodin, Boguet, L'Ancre, and the rest—were obtained is seldom indicated in detail. But certainly the girls never gave those accounts voluntarily.[276]

Most students of witchcraft know of the trials through the words of the demonologists, for verbatim court records are hard to find.[277] A few court records, however, are available in English translation. Robbins' *Encyclopedia*, for example, covered the trial in 1590 of Rebecca Lemp of Nordlingen, wife of a well-educated accountant, who tried to sneak out a note to her husband after she had been tortured five times until she confessed. The note was intercepted and incorporated as part of the court records:

> O thou, the chosen of my heart, must I be parted from thee, though entirely innocent? If so, may God be followed throughout eternity by my reproaches. They force one and make one confess; they have so tortured me, but I am as innocent as God in heaven. If I know the least thing about such matters, may God shut the door of heaven against me! O thou, dearly beloved Husband, my heart is nearly broken! Alas, alas! My poor dear children orphaned! Husband, send me something that I may die, or I must expire under the torture; if thou canst not today, do it tomorrow. Write to me directly. R. L.

And on the verso: "Oh, Husband of thine innocent Rebecca, they take me from thee by force! How can God suffer it? If I am a witch, may God show no pity to me. Oh, what wrong is done me! Why will not God hear me? Send me something, else may I peril even my soul." [278]

Another example from the *Encyclopedia* is the trial in Bailleul in 1659 of Thomas Looten, an old man who went to the local court to clear himself of gossip that he was a witch. From the court records (in Flemish) can be reconstructed the progress of his condemnation:

> November 2, 1659. Looten is put to torture by the garrote, "seated in a wooden chair with his arms stretched out, his feet twisted under another chair and tightly bound,"

and his neck enclosed in an iron collar which could be tightened with screws. He affirms that in Jean Boone's tavern one Robert Beicqué said that Jean Merkinck had said Looten was a witch; that he had given plums to many children, including Adam Wycaert's child; and that he had heard that this child had become sick and died a few days later. Asked why he had not complained to the judge about such accusations, he replied that he had and that was the reason he was in prison. The torture is to continue until further notice.

November 4. The torture is continued, the torturer testifying that the constitution of the prisoner is such that he can stand much more rigorous torture.... At eight o'clock in the evening, Looten breaks down and confesses.

His confession is a stereotype: all the well-known crimes are listed and a few local names are inserted for verisimilitude. Looten says he has been a sorcerer for eight years, that he had signed a pact with the devil in blood "drawn from his right thumb," and had been marked on the shoulder, and that the devil, called Harlakyn, appeared to him dressed in green and with a deformed foot. Then Looten gives a list of places where he had attended the sabbat, always in the company of three or four beautiful women, with one of whom he always had intercourse, and says he had feasted on beer and hard cider and veal (but without salt). He had received green ointments from the devil so that he could fly wherever he wished. The devil had endured in his stead the pains of torture, and given him large sums of money to buy cows and horses for resale. He had given Wycaert's child "three plums on which he had previously spat, for which he received five coins from the devil." [279]

Then there is the verbatim report of the trial in 1637 of an unknown woman at Eichstatt. In this trial, the procedure follows every approved cliché of witchdom: the accused first denies, then is tortured; she invents what she thinks the judges want; then, released from the torture, she recants her confession, and straightway is tortured again. Soon she becomes half-demented and winds up believing herself a witch. None of the crimes of which she was accused—night rides, sabbat banquets, storm-raising, passing through locked doors—was real or possible of proof; nor was any proof offered. Once faced with fifteen denunciations—probably made by other simple persons themselves under torture, or even taken from a stock interrogatory—she was doomed. The judges, as this record shows, were interested only in extorting a confession of guilt and securing the names of alleged accomplices, who sooner or later would be subjected to similar procedure. During this time, the accused was allowed no legal aid; she was not confronted by witnesses, and only after her sentencing was she permitted a priest.[280]

The foregoing trials (and several others) are given in considerable detail in the pages of the *Encyclopedia.* Elsewhere I have translated further trials.[281] Attention might be drawn to two, both typical trials of the seventeenth century, one in the Vosges and the other, forty years later, in Belgium.

The first is a trial of a husband and wife and her widowed sister in Remirémont, near Nancy. The trio were apprehended on the basis of common report, and great care was taken with legal niceties. For example, the local municipal court officials went to other villages to collect depositions; confrontation of the witnesses was permitted; and the evidence collected was forwarded to the attorney general of Mirecourt for advice. Six weeks after the case opened, torture was commenced:

> We did then interrogate her on the matter with which she is charged, namely touching the said crime of witchcraft, on which matter she declined to say anything else but that

she was a good Christian; for this reason, she was ordered to be taken by the torturer who immediately led her to the torture chamber, made her sit on the rack, and undressed her and took off her shoes, then shaved her all over and in this state applied the thumbscrews. She cried out, "Saint Nicholas and Jesus!" When she confessed nothing, we ordered the torturer to compress and tighten them, but she still called to Saint Nicholas and prayed that Jesus be with her, denying all accusations. But when the thumbscrews were applied to her toes, she began to cry louder than before, "Jesus!" together with great exclamations, and tried to weep, yet without shedding a single tear, still denying everything on her sworn oath. Upon our order the torturer tightened the said thumbscrews; she cried out as before but without saying or confessing anything. When we ordered the thumbscrews applied to two other fingers and tightened, she went on crying and exclaiming as before, denying everything and saying only, "Jesus! how much it hurts, Provost! I have no other master but the good Lord Jesus!" insisting that she was being done great wrong. After she had been left in this condition for about a quarter of an hour, the torturer released the thumbscrews a little, and placed her, naked in her shift, on the rack, tied her feet to it and bound her hands with ropes to the pulleys. As she was thus stretched out, he placed the triangular piece of wood under her back. Having been stretched a little, she immediately screamed "Jesus!" and "Provost!" together with other exclamations to the effect that she would tell the truth if they loosened her a little. But when she was loosened a little, she refused to say anything. Having been stretched half a turn, she feigned death, then, interrogated, began to say that great wrong was done to her, denying everything by her faith, and saying that her accusers were wicked men. Being stretched another half turn, she started to grimace like a person being strangled, but on being questioned, still denied the charges. Left alone for a while, she continued contorting her features, then suddenly, opening her eyes, which by now had become bloodshot, she begged in a low voice to be released.

She was encouraged to tell the truth.

She said she spoke the truth and knew no evil.

Seeing that she was not going to say anything, we gave her a violent jolt by releasing the ropes; at which she was so frightened that she believed the devil was carrying her away. When the torturer wished to stretch her again, she begged to be put close to the fire [to recover somewhat], saying that at last she would confess.

She said she killed a calf, but she did not know to whom it belonged.

Asked where she was for the first time seduced and tempted.

She said she had forgotten.

Asked how her master called himself.

She said his name was Master Robin.

Charged with not telling the truth.

She asked to be taken off the rack, and said she would reveal everything.

Entreated to say truthfully what her master was called.

She said that he was the devil.

Pressed to reveal his name, she said that his name was Master Robin.

Asked where she was seduced and how the said Master Robin was dressed.

She said that he was dressed in black, and that she was seduced in a field.

She was released from the rack, led to the fire, and there interrogated. . . .

Upon which we ordered the torturer to put her back on the rack, which he did, feigning to tie her down while she was being interrogated on her accomplices; she positively identified those she had named before, saying she would maintain this to her death.

Upon this, we had her taken away under guard.[282]

Another trial in 1657 at Sugny in Belgium saw a sixty-seven-year-old woman, Jeannette Huart, accused by some ninety witnesses (an unusually high figure) of evildoing dating back at least thirty years. But under torture she was not ques-

tioned about any evildoing but on the traditional sabbat acts expected of all witches:

1. Whether the devil marked them by a sign, how he did it, and where the sign is.
2. Whether the familiar devils, whose names they are to reveal, made them renounce God and baptism.
3. Whether they had copulation with them on repeated occasions.
4. Where they held their dances; whether the devil came to seek them at night or whether they applied ointment on themselves to go there.
5. How they danced; whether they ate there, whether they drank there; where the food and drink came from; and all that is done there; and whether the devil gave them an ointment or powder.
6. How many people and animals they had killed.
7. Where they placed their ointment or powder, and whether there still is any in their houses.
8. Whether their devils came to see them since their imprisonment, what they told and counseled them.

Of course, Jeannette Huart confessed to all these brand new charges of pact and sabbat, and only at the confirmation of her confession the next day was she questioned about the original accusations of *maleficia*. Soon after, she was "strangled at the stake and her body reduced to ashes."[283]

I wish to give a few extracts from one final trial report, a typical classic trial at Arnstadt, in Thuringia, in 1667.[284] This report is longer than most, some twenty thousand words. It concerns a poor farm laborer, a "fodder-cutter," Barbara Elisabeth Schulz, against whom two basic charges were alleged: afflicting or bewitching two epileptic lads and infesting a man's coat with lice. The preliminary investigation started in April, 1667, and twenty-six witnesses were heard. After this, the local court at Arnstadt submitted its records to Leipzig, which extrapolated a list of thirty-seven questions, with opportunity for cross-examination.

At her questioning, Barbara gave firm denials. Accordingly the court recommended that since she did not want to give her confession voluntarily, "she might well be turned over to the torturer to pull her up, lead her undressed to the ladder, show her the instruments of torture, attach the thumbscrews and tighten them, and if this were not productive, to begin with the rope."

As soon as the torture started, with Barbara Elisabeth Schulz facing the instruments, the tenor of the trial underwent a complete reversal. The questions no longer concerned afflicting epileptic lads or keeping dragons[285] or fireballs in her house, or infecting coats with lice, but went to the theoretical heart of witchcraft:

> Article 1. Is it true that ten years ago the devil came to her on the Ritterstein, and led her behind a fence and committed acts of lewdness with her.
> Article 2. Is it true that the accused then made a pact with the devil and promised to obey him and follow him at all times.
> Article 3. Is it true that she herself verily renounced the dear Lord and let herself be rebaptized by the devil.

Article 4. Is it true that the devil baptized the accused in his name, and gave her another name, and that she was named "Devil's Liesa."

Article 6. Is it true that at various times the accused went along to the dance on the Brockelsberg, worshiped the devil, embraced and kissed him, and who else went along to the witches' dance.

Only one question (Article 5) recalled the months of interrogation about *maleficia*, that about her infesting a man's coat with lice.

Under quite severe torture, Barbara persisted in her denials. The judicial assessors left the torture chamber, and "one good quarter of an hour after that," the chief magistrate and assistant magistrate also left. The letter of the law had been followed.

However, one assessor, the torturer, and his assistants remained with the accused in the torture chamber. There is no record of what happened, except that an hour or two later, about eleven in the morning, Assessor Sonnenbecker reported to the chief magistrate that the accused wished to speak with him and reveal something:

> Ten years ago [she started to confess], it happened that the devil, in the guise of a man in black clothing, and a hat with a plume of black feathers, and instead of feet he had the talons of a rooster, and his face was very black, came to her on the Ritterstein at the bottom of the vineyards and introduced himself; his name was Hans, and he led her behind a fence, slept with her, but everything was ice cold what he did to her. In return, he promised to stand by her and take care of her. . . . In return she promised the devil to obey his commands and follow him, raising her fingers and renouncing the dear Lord. When this was done, the devil himself rebaptized her in his name at a crossroad, and called her "Devil's Liesa." . . . She also avers a few times on Walpurgis Night she went along to the Brockelsberg to the dance, they got there quickly, and it seemed to [her] as if they rode there on piebald horses. At first they danced, then they dined, after that they knelt before the goat, worshiped him and kissed him, and each one of them had her lover with her, with whom she committed lewdness. . . .

Here she named eight neighbors, seven women and one man. Her confession duplicates exactly, almost in the same words, the articles of interrogation.[286] Immediately afterward, Barbara Elisabeth Schulz was led outside the place of torture and again forced to give the same answers to the final articles she had just admitted. Three days later, yet once again, the same questions were put to her in a room of the Court's Commission. Again she admitted everything. She was condemned but begged for the mercy of execution by the sword.

All these trials follow a similar pattern: an open trial in court of the allegations of evildoing, often with minute examination of the witnesses, and (as the seventeenth century wore on) even opportunity for confrontation. The accused denies responsibility for any such evildoing or unusual occurrences. Then, since the accused will not confess she is a witch, the scene moves to the torture chamber, and *maleficia* is now relegated to the background and the questioning turns to relations with the devil. At this point, questioning becomes The Question, and to be "put to the question" means to be tortured. The accused, under torture, confesses and is condemned; often the original charges that led to her apprehension are never brought up again after the initial open court trial. It might be

observed that the witch trials in England, since torture was not sanctioned, end with the first part (that usually conducted in public), with the charges largely restricted to actual physical acts of harm.

Perhaps the best summation to conclude this discussion of the court records, the fourth area of source materials, is by George Lincoln Burr:

> There are not wanting still good people who marvel at what they call the "agreement" in the testimony of the witches. To such may be commended the prescribed lists of interrogatories, which from more than one "Instruction to judges" are now making their way to light. And, even where these were not used, leading questions were the rule, and the victim had little more to do than answer yes or no. Only here and there in the trials do we find some poor quivering woman begging her judges to tell her what she must confess. The confession was a criterion, not of the guilt of the witch, but of the learning of her inquisitors. It is rather a marvel that there should ever be disagreement, when the victim not only had such prompters, but must herself time and again have heard just such confessions read, as the custom was, to the crowd gathered about the stake.
>
> And if any are puzzled that the confessions should be persisted in after the torture and in the face of death (which, in countless cases, they were *not*), they should remember that persistence in confession was long a condition of that "forbearance of the Court" which suffered the prisoner to be first strangled or beheaded, instead of being burned alive. Only the *Church* always burned alive.[287]

Few manuscripts of witch trials are to be found in America, and the Witchcraft Collection is probably the sole repository to contain many original documents. With the exception of a partial copying of the voluminous Neuerburg trials, all are untranscribed and unpublished. In addition, some German and French trials have appeared in print (in their original language or dialect) in minor out-of-the-way antiquarian or regional books and periodicals.[288] The Witchcraft Collection is more fortunate than most parallel collections, for European scholars developed the habit of personally sending to White or Burr reprints of their articles on the trials.[289] Consequently a good part of the laborious work of examining file after file of local journals, even when they are available, has already been done by others. But personal perusal of every likely volume is still essential.

THE OPPONENTS

The fifth area of source materials for the study of witchcraft is the smallest, some half-dozen brave books written by humanitarians with actual knowledge of what really went on at the trials and the executions. As well as being the smallest, it is the most ignored; yet these few works are essential for any understanding of heretical sorcery or witchcraft. They are the most rare of the Collection's many treasures, precious jewels not to be found, or found only with difficulty, outside the Witchcraft Collection.

These exposés distill the first-hand experience of priests and pastors who accompanied the witches to the stake and heard their last words, of law officials and law professors who examined and adjudicated the records. Many others in similar positions had identical experiences; only a handful had the courage to try to make public their sense of outrage. The Witchcraft Collection possesses the following works of protest:

Cornelius Loos (1546-1595), *De vera et falsa magia* (1592);

Hermann Witekind [Augustin Lercheimer] (1522-1603), *Christlich Bedencken vnnd Erinnerung von Zauberey* [1585];

Michael Stapirius, *Brillentractat* [1628];

Friedrich von Spee (1591-1635), *Cautio criminalis* (1631);

Johann Matthäus Meyfart (1590-1642), *Christliche Erinnerung* (1636);

Hermann Löher (1595–ca. 1676), *Hochnötige unterthänige wemütige Klage der frommen Unschültigen* (1676).

These outspoken opponents were not entirely alone, and the way had been prepared for them by several prominent figures who expressed their dissent in various discrete ways, and by other lesser skeptics more closely identified with the eyewitness confessors such as Spee. A small stream of expressed opposition to the witchcraft beliefs had always existed, though for long periods it ran underground or appeared infrequently. Even during the formative years when the whole theory was evolving, it developed in the writings of men such as Cassini (1505), Alciatus (1514), or Ponzinibio (1520).[290]

Before noting the works of these eyewitness opponents, I shall mention the formal theoretical attacks on the delusion by Wier, Bekker, and Thomasius, excellently represented at Cornell. Johann Wier (1515-1588) was personal physician to Duke William of Cleves and Juliers-Berg.[291] The duke accepted Wier's moderating views on witchcraft so that the duchy became a relative haven of sanity in a Germany increasingly given to witch hunting. Wier actually went no further than trying to distinguish old women charged as working with Satan from magicians who really conspired with the devil—not really an effective argument.[292] Motivated by pity rather than by logic, Wier, by his doubt about the legitimacy of torture to produce confessions, struck a practical note that continued to be sounded by his successors.

Soon after the second edition of his *De praestigiis daemonum et incantationibus ac veneficiis* [293]—in a response to Johann Brenz (1499-1570), who argued that the devil influenced witches to produce hailstorms—Wier reinforced his earlier argument:

> [Alleged witches] confess many things, especially when subject to enormous tortures, which are mere fables, trifles, lies, which are not and never were, nor could be in the nature of things. Nor should more faith be given to that part of the confession in which they say that they are consecrated to the devil in this or that way and therefore have assented to his will and evil acts, than where they freely confess that they have disturbed the air, caused hailstorms, destroyed harvests and vines or have perpetrated any other evil. . . . When there is no other proof but the confession of an old woman crazed

> with prison and torture, to whom in many things we refuse faith, why not in all when nothing certain is to be derived from the erroneous confession of a demoniacally deluded old woman.[294]

Of Wier's first book on witchcraft, *De praestigiis,* the Witchcraft Collection possesses five Latin editions (including the first, 1563), the German translation, and both French translations.[295] Fourteen years later, in 1577, Wier, seeing a revival of witch persecutions, wrote an abridged and revised edition which he entitled *De lamiis.*[296] Of this, the Witchcraft Collection has three editions, as well as two copies of Wier's *Opera omnia* (1660).[297]

Wier wrote his famous book several decades before the hysteria climaxed; yet he was forced into exile after its publication, when it was placed on the *Index.*[298] Famous later opponents such as Bekker and Thomasius were writing at the very end of the seventeenth century, by which time it was relatively safe to say "Halt!" Nevertheless, on August 21, 1692, Pastor Balthasar Bekker (1634-1698) was unfrocked by the Dutch Reformed church for refusing to recant his views, especially on demoniacal possession.[299] The Amsterdam magistrates blocked a public burning of his book, and indeed continued to pay his ministerial stipend.[300] Bekker attacked the belief in witchcraft on the only logical basis possible. "Spirits, either good or bad (the existence of which Bekker did not deny), could exercise no influence over human affairs; nor should seemingly paranormal effects be attributed to witchcraft. Since the belief in the influence of spirits had crept into Christianity from paganism, . . . there was no reason to credit the pact between the witch and the devil, the core of the theory."[301]

At the time Bekker was writing (1691), burning of witches had almost ceased—in Holland it ceased in 1610—and the battle about the theory of the *crimen exceptum* (justifying torture) had largely been won. The need to attack the conduct of the trials, therefore, had shifted to the need to attack the philosophical basis of a belief in witchcraft. Thus the later writers could discuss the existence and influence of spirits, a theological question, as did the early writers on witchcraft.

The Witchcraft Collection has a huge holding in Bekker, especially his *De Betoverde Weerold* (1691),[302] or *The World Bewitch'd,* as the first English edition was translated. The main Dictionary Catalog in the Olin Library at Cornell has 182 separate entries on Bekker; this Catalogue prints 525 cards (many entries of course run over into a second or third card and many items appear several times under different headings, but the quantity is still impressive).[303] Yet despite the tremendous amount of material available, not a single article, let alone book, about Bekker and witchcraft has been written in English in modern times.

Just as Bekker received the torch from Wier, so Christian Thomasius (1655-1728) carried it forward from Bekker. Thomasius also derived from Wier, but naturally reflected the more liberal thinking of the period he lived in. At first, as a university referee in a witchcraft trial, in opposition to the majority view, he opted for torture for an accused witch. Thomasius then reconsidered his stand, found the evidence weak, and came to disbelieve in a personal devil.[304] Under

theological pressure, he modified his position to admit the existence of some witches, but denied the possibility of a pact.[305] He was particularly opposed to Carpzov and to the classic demonologists such as Bodin and Remi. As a famous law professor at the newly founded University of Halle, he was able to influence his students, some of whom wrote dissertations skeptical of witchcraft, such as those by Martinus Bernardi [306] and Johann Paul Ipsen.[307] About Thomasius' major work, *De crimine magiae,* translated into German as *Kurtze Lehr-Sätze von dem Laster der Zauberey* (1704), there is some question concerning the part played by his student Johann Reiche in helping write it.[308] Reiche was active in opposing the theory and practice of witchcraft, and in 1703 published a very useful compendium of the *Malleus judicum,* Spee's *Cautio criminalis,* Meyfart's *Christliche Erinnerung,* and a remarkable collection of *Hexen-Acta.*[309] Like Bekker, Thomasius aroused controversy: on the one hand, he was supported by cautious skeptics such as Brunneman (1708) [310] and Meinders (1716); [311] on the other hand, he was opposed by believers, who nonetheless wanted far stricter and fairer rules for the trials, such as Romanus (1703),[312] Goldschmidt (1705),[313] Schack (1706),[314] and Bruckner (1723).[315] The Witchcraft Collection has copies of the work of all these writers, and offers extensive materials for research in this later period. An edition and translation of the four works collected by Reiche in *Unterschiedliche Schrifften* would in itself help start a needed reorientation in witchcraft studies.

The works of protest about to be discussed—the exposés of the eyewitness confessors—were made at the very height of the witchcraft mania. Their being written put their authors' lives in peril. Löher waited forty years before he dared write his book; Loos was tortured and banished; even Spee was imprisoned. These works differ from the more academic, less engagé attacks (such as those of Wier and Scot and Thomasius), because they are written from personal knowledge by men who saw the trials from the victim's point of view. Some of their authors (Spee and Meyfart, for example) had served, not as judges, but as confessors to the condemned witches. While officially, as clergymen or professors or assessors, all were members of the Establishment, these men still had the humanity to see the other side, the nonofficial version of what happened to men and women accused as witches. One need only compare the writings of Schultheis and Löher.[316] No other source materials present the detailed revelations of dozens and dozens of executions that appear in Loos, Löher, Stapirius, Meyfart, or Spee. Thanks to the wide knowledge of Burr and the collector's instinct of White, a few books of this nature found their way to the Witchcraft Collection. They form an effective, if small, counterbalance to the writings of the classic demonologists, who were all—as these men were not—"hanging" judges. It is my belief that when these exposés on the fabrication of confessions—on the fabrication of witchcraft, indeed—are better known, the trend of witchcraft studies will drastically change, for the whole interpretation of witchcraft, rationalist or occultist, stands or falls on the veracity of the confessions.

A bridge exists from the trial records to these exposés—as is also true for the demonologists and penologists—for these works are likewise based on witchcraft

trials, and it is possible to parallel the official court records of how the accused shrieked out to the torturer with the secret admissions the accused told her confessor. The difference lies in the emotional shock value of the falsity of confessions and the distortion of legality in the witch trials, when presented by men who recoiled in horror at what they saw.

One could turn back to Rebecca Lemp's letter to her husband, a letter that must be taken at face value.[317] But the most famous of all smuggled letters is the missive of Johannes Junius, burgomaster of Bamberg, to his daughter Veronica on July 24, 1628. Taking several days to write it, because his fingers had been smashed in the thumbscrews, Johannes Junius demolishes the entire structure and superstructure of witchcraft; the trumped-up charges made by people like himself under intense torture; the loaded court seeking not justice but his confession and names of "accomplices"; and the formulaic admission to pact and sabbat put together from bits of folklore, time-old superstitions, and scraps of perversions forced from previous heretics. The letter is quite long, but the opening and closing paragraphs should be quoted here, and the entire letter read and reread:

> Many hundred thousand good nights, dearly beloved daughter Veronica. Innocent have I come into prison, innocent have I been tortured, innocent must I die. For whosoever comes into the Witch House must become a witch or be tortured until he invents something out of his head and—God pity him—bethinks him of something. I will tell you how it has gone with me.... Now, my dearest child, here you have all my acts and confession, for which I must die. And it is all sheer lies and inventions, so help me God. For all this I was forced to say through dread of torture beyond what I had already endured. For they never cease the torture till one confesses something; be he ever so pious, he must be a witch. Nobody escapes, though he were a count. If God send no means of bringing the truth to light, our whole kindred will be burned. From the outset, each man must openly confess what he really doesn't have knowledge of, as I had to do. God in heaven knows that I have not the slightest knowledge of this. I die innocent and as a martyr.[318]

Perhaps the first man in Germany (after Wier) to write against the witch hunts was a celebrated theologian, Cornelius Loos (1546-1595).[319] He started out as a conservative Catholic; he hated Luther, opposed Ponzinibio, and abjured heretics.[320] For his later defiance, "more daring than his predecessor Wier or his contemporary Godelmann," [321] this Jesuit-trained scholar was tortured and banished. Born in Gouda in 1546, Loos distinguished himself at several universities and soon accepted a professorship at the Catholic College of Mainz, and later at Trier. At that time Trier was a center of the witch persecution—between 1587 and 1594, in twenty villages belonging to the abbey of Saint Maximin, three hundred persons were burned.[322] The sights he witnessed horrified Loos, but he was just as horrified by the writings of Binsfeld. Loos, influenced by Wier,[323] determined to try to halt them. He approached the civil and ecclesiastical authorities without result. So he took to writing a tract, *De vera et falsa magia* (1592).[324] Going beyond Wier and anticipating Spee, Loos was especially vehement against the use of torture to produce confessions: "Wretched creatures are compelled by the severity of the torture to confess things they have never done, and so by the cruel butchery innocent lives are taken and by a new alchemy gold and silver coined

from human blood."[325] He was also equally vehement against the *Malleus maleficarum*, which he saw revivified in Binsfeld, blaming it for introducing persecution into Germany. Loos was one of the first to say that "witchcraft was a delusion."[326]

Word got out about his projected book, and by order of the Papal Nuncio the polemic was suppressed, and Father Loos jailed in the dungeons of the local Benedictine abbey of Saint Maximin. After a long imprisonment, during which his health was broken, on Monday, March 15, 1593, publicly kneeling before a swarm of dignitaries, Loos made his recantation (actually written for him by his opponent, Peter Binsfeld, the suffragan bishop of Trier), which was printed by the Jesuit demonologist Del Rio.[327] These were the two demonologists who were most hostile to Loos. Father Loos was banished, found a curacy in Brussels, but refused to keep silent. He was seized as a relapsed heretic, imprisoned but surprisingly not burned, and later set free. He died on February 3, 1595, avoiding death by burning, for he was about to be apprehended a third time.

For almost three hundred years his work was thought to have been destroyed at the time the Inquisition raided the Protestant printshop in Cologne, where Loos in 1592 had secretly sent his manuscript. What was known about it came through the words of his opponents. In 1886, by a stroke of great good fortune, two of the four books of *De vera et falsa magia* were found in manuscript by George Lincoln Burr at the Jesuit College in Trier, the same college where Spee spent his novitiate.[328] A few printed pages (completed before the raid) are in the City Library at Cologne. The Witchcraft Collection has a handwritten facsimile of the original manuscript and of the printed fragments.[329] Loos still awaits publication.

Hermann Witekind (1522-1603), under the pseudonym of Augustin Lercheimer,[330] wrote *Christlich Bedencken vnnd Erinnerung von Zauberey*, the first edition in 1585, the second in 1586 at Strassburg.[331] In one of his inimitable and useful little annotations, Burr wrote on the inside cover: "One of the most remarkable books in the history of witchcraft. It is a bold and startlingly eloquent protest against the worst features of the persecution." Witekind was a professor at Heidelberg and a friend of Melanchthon, and wrote with a refreshing freedom of thought. The title page of the second edition has an engraving of witches and devils in a ring dance, apparently a ploy to dispel suspicion (that the book was actually opposing witchcraft) until the reader should confront the arguments.

Another opponent was Michael Stapirius, a pastor of Hirschberg, Paderborn, who had been chaplain to many persons condemned as witches in Westphalia in 1626.[332] In righteous indignation, he wrote a little *Brillentractat* (about 1628), which today is known only by the extracts given by Hermann Löher.[333] It is no wonder it has not survived. Like other confessors, such as Father Friedrich von Spee, Father Kircher of Mamburg, and Pastor Weynhart Hartmann of Rheinbach, Pastor Stapirius reported many last testaments, all revealing how evidence had been wrested from accused by torture. When Stapirius pleaded with the condemned to recant and save their souls from perjury, he met with such answers as

this: "I was tortured, and I was asked, 'What do you know about so-and-so and so-and-so who live by the cemetery?' I was asked so often that I could not help seeing what people he [the inquisitor] wanted me to denounce. So I mentioned the names of the persons about whom people had been whispering. But I really don't know anything bad about them. . . . I begged the commissioner to strike out their names, but he answered that if I should declare them innocent I should be tortured again." [334]

Of all works attacking the witchcraft persecutions, however, the best known is undoubtedly the *Cautio criminalis* (1631) of Father Friedrich von Spee (1591-1635), a Jesuit professor at Würzburg in 1627, and a minor German lyric poet.[335] It was a major attempt to stem the tidal wave of terror against ordinary men and women accused as witches. Schwickerath, a modern Jesuit scholar, believed "this book is the boldest, most thorough and most enlightened work on the subject which appeared before the eighteenth century." [336] Spee's summary of the nightmarish legal proceedings deserves careful attention, coming from a trained theologian who had lived through the horrors of those accused. It exposes the whole sleazy fabric of the delusion. The philosopher Leibniz reported an earlier conversation when Spee told him he had personally and diligently investigated many prosecutions, but after considering the charges and confessions, never once had he found anything about the accused that would make them guilty of witchcraft.[337]

Spee's attack was as head-on as was possible at the time. He concentrated on the general disregard of even those thin legal safeguards allowed the accused and on the universal use of torture. These were the twin evils that the penologists deplored, but Spee was writing in 1631: "The innocent zealots [who encourage witch hunts] should bear in mind that, as the tortured must denounce some people and the processes thus continue to spread, the time must come when it will reach them and there can be no end until all are burned." [338]

Spee portrays a vividly ugly picture of the common practices in witch trials. Inquisitors and judges assume guilt in anyone calumniated by "common fame." They made it their business to prove guilt, holding it a disgrace if any one were acquitted. For this work they were paid well, four or five thalers a head. The accused was generally held incommunicado, allowed no counsel, frequently not informed of the specific charges or witnesses, and tortured until confessing guilt—in words suggested by the interrogators. Moreover, writes Spee: "A single innocent person, compelled by torture to confess guilt, is forced to denounce others of whom she knows nothing; it is the same with them, and thus there is scarce an end of accusers and accused, and, as none dares to revoke, all are marked for death." [339]

Yet on such forced confessions the opinions of all the classic demonologists and many modern authorities are based; Spee especially refutes the *Malleus maleficarum*, and the demonologists Binsfeld, Remi, and Del Rio. Spee concludes: "Hitherto it never came into my mind to doubt that there were many witches in the world; now, when I closely examine the public judgments, I find myself gradually led to doubt whether there are scarce any." [340]

One statement by Spee is valuable for its explanation of the inevitability of torture to produce confessions. Torture was so general that it was recorded in the court records only when exceptionally severe or causing death (neck broken by the devil):

> There is a frequent phrase used by judges [wrote Spee], that the accused has confessed without torture and thus is undeniably guilty. I wondered at this and made inquiry and learned that in reality they were tortured, but only in an iron press with sharp-edged channels over the shins, in which they are pressed like a cake, bringing blood and causing intolerable pain, and this is technically called without torture, deceiving those who do not understand the phrases of the inquisitors.[341]

While the immediate impact of Spee may have been limited, nevertheless his work influenced Thomasius,[342] who because of Spee switched from approving the witch-hunting Carpzov to becoming one of the most humane opponents of the delusion.

A Protestant counterpart to Spee, but not so well known, was the Lutheran professor of theology at Erfurt, Johann Matthäus Meyfart, and his *Christliche Erinnerung* (1636) confirms Spee's *Cautio criminalis* (1631).[343] Like Spee, Meyfart exposed the dilemmas used by judges to prove guilt of the accused. If their reputation was bad, they were clearly witches; if good, equally so, for witches always tried to appear virtuous. If on arrest the suspects were frightened, then they were surely witches—fearing merited punishment; if resolute, they were no less witches, because witches always pretended innocence. Meyfart becomes very bitter and angry; he hates the witch judges.

Meyfart tells how the accused had to name other witches. One victim, after three days of torture, confronted a burgher's wife of irreproachable character. She pleaded: "I have never seen you at a sabbat, but to end the torture I had to accuse some one. You came into my mind because, as I was being led to prison, you met me and said you would never have believed it of me. I beg forgiveness, but were I tortured again, again I would accuse you." [344] Thereupon the judges returned her to the torture to make her repeat her charges; the burgher's wife was prosecuted and burned. Many would have withdrawn their accusations, Meyfart reported, had they not feared a repetition of torture. "Oh God," they cried, "it would be unendurable." [345]

The last figure in this small group of opponents is Hermann Löher, whose *Hochnötige unterthänige wemütige Klage der frommen Unschültigen* is preserved in a unique print at Löher's birthplace at Münstereifel.[346] A 608-page handwritten copy by Graf von Carnap in 1896 is in the Witchcraft Collection.[347] Löher's book is not completely unknown; it was mentioned in 1828 and 1886, and was the topic of a doctoral dissertation and of an ensuing brilliant article.[348]

Löher [349] was a former burgomaster and an official of the law court at Rheinbach [350] near Bonn during the two fantastic waves of persecution in 1631 and 1636, which killed one person out of every two families. In the preceding hundred years, the village had not known one case warranting imprisonment, let alone execution.[351] But things changed with the visitation of a special itinerant judge,

Franz Buirmann.[352] Löher, as one of the court's seven assessors, saw terror grip the village, and contributed to a common bribe to get the judge to go elsewhere. Buirmann went, but returned five years later in 1636. Löher then joined the mayor and one other official in opposing Buirmann, but they received little support; Löher, having quietly liquidated as much of his property as he could (the rest was confiscated by Buirmann), barely escaped with his family to Amsterdam. He became a Dutch citizen, set up business again, and lived to be over eighty.

Löher felt impelled to record his own experiences "to lay bare the injustice of the 'witch' judges," and "to enlighten the authorities for justice in a uniform criminal procedure among humble folk in small towns and villages."[353] He knew what was happening at first hand: "But the person who has witnessed the torture of the innocent and heard their cries of anguish can speak with conviction that is quite out of the question to one who, seated in a cool garden, undertakes to work and dream about the way one ought to imprison, torture, and burn so-called witches."[354]

In a memorable passage, Löher describes Buirmann raging at the accused witch in the torture chamber:

> You apostate, you witch, you dumb dog! Confess your witchery; reveal the names of your accomplices! You miserable whore, the devil's annointed, you caterpillar-maker, you dumb toad! Speak and confess in God's name! Swallow the holy salt! Drink the holy water! Tell who it was that taught you witchcraft, and whom you saw and recognized at the witches' sabbat. Then you will not be tortured any more, but have eternal life.[355]

Löher stressed three points: (1) innocent people who are tried in the witch courts are tortured and die innocent; (2) victims lie when tortured; (3) all victims can be forced to confess anything, especially when the torture is repeated.[356] "The early Christian martyrs were falsely accused of grievous crimes," wrote Löher, "but in our day Christian witches are far more unjustly accused of mortal sins that they have not committed—and that they could not possibly commit."[357]

Although he started collecting his material when he came to Amsterdam, Löher did not publish his work until 1676 when he was eighty-one, delaying forty years for fear of reprisals from the authorities: "Who would assume such a dangerous task? Should anyone undertake it out of Christian charity, then people would somehow manage to prevent him from being heard; and if he were heard, then those who began the unjust 'witch' burnings would cry out, they mistrust that he is a 'witch patron.'"[358] It is something of a miracle that even one copy remains.[359]

I have devoted considerable space to these protestors because they are all barely known, their books unread and difficult of access, and because I think an awareness of what they say would radically change the current views about witchcraft. Arthur Howland, when he came to edit Lea's notes, realized the importance of this submerged group:

> One topic not yet adequately dealt with, a topic that has never received due attention from any scholar interested in the field, is the undercurrent of opposition, existing in all periods, to the methods of witch persecution and even to the whole theory of witch-

craft. A few men, such as Wier, Spee, and Laymann, had the courage to express their views more or less openly. Careful investigation would probably correct some of our conclusions as to the universality of the witch delusion even at the period of its widest acceptance.[360]

The six confessor opponents I have presented here are but representative examples. Here are a few of the other opponents—and some were staunch believers in a personal devil—who each in his own way protested the delusion:

Jo. Ewich (1525-1588), *De sagarvm (qvos vvlgo veneficas appellant) natvra* (1584); [361]

Johannes Jordanaeus, *Disputatio brevis et categorica de proba stigmatica* (1598); [362]

Adam Tanner (1572-1632), *Tractatus theologicus de processu adversus crimina excepta, ac speciatim adversus crimen veneficii* (1617); [363]

Johann Grevius (b. ca. 1584), *Tribunal reformatum* (1622); [364]

Paul Laymann (1574-1635), *Tractatus theologicus de sagis et veneficis* (1625); [365]

Malleus judicum, das ist Gesetz-Hammer der unbarmherzigen Hexenrichter [1626]; [366]

Anton Praetorius, *Gründlicher Bericht von Zauberey und Zauberern* (1629); [367]

Abraham Palingh, *'t Afgerukt Momaansight der Tooverye* (1659); [368]

Augustin Nicolas (1622-1695) *Si la torture est un moyen seur* (1681).[369]

The Witchcraft Collection has some three thousand volumes. No one scholar could know them all, even slightly—not even Lea or Burr, who came very close to becoming "universal doctors" of witchcraft. In drawing attention to the types of source materials this wonderful Collection contains, I feel like a prospector telling his friends there is gold at Ithaca. Almost any book you read will not be generally known; perhaps even a majority of these books have never been read by an English-speaking person. Select at random any card, study the book fetched, and you will be able to make a valuable contribution to the study of witchcraft—perhaps to the study of man.

NOTES

1. Jane Moress, "Andrew Dickson White and George Lincoln Burr: The Building of an Historical Library," B.A. paper, Cornell University, April 1954, p. 60. In 1926, however, about the White Library as a whole, Burr was cautioning that "it would be wise to avoid exaggeration as to the treasures of our library. ... President White, to whom the form of our older descriptive publication was largely due, was an enthusiastic, sanguine man who saw things large" (Moress, p. 78).

2. *George Lincoln Burr: His Life* by Roland H. Bainton, *Selections from His Writings*, ed. Lois Oliphant Gibbons (Ithaca: Cornell Univ. Press, 1943), p. 88 (hereafter Bainton and Gibbons, *Burr*).

3. Edward S. Bradley, *Henry Charles Lea* (Philadelphia: Univ. of Pennsylvania Press, 1931). The correspondence continued; see box 38 of Burr Papers in Cornell University Archives.

4. Henry Charles Lea, *Materials toward a History of Witchcraft*, ed. Arthur C. Howland, intro. George Lincoln Burr (Philadelphia: Univ. of Pennsylvania Press, 1939; rpt. New York: Yoseloff, 1957), I. xxiv, xxii.

5. Moress, "Historical Library," p. 60.

6. Lea, *Materials*, I. xxiv. In his later years Burr was able to help the Lea Library by giving it a surplus copy of the very important work by Albizzi (see n. 39). See also Henry Charles Lea, *Minor Historical Writings*, ed. Arthur C. Howland (1942; rpt. Port Washington, N.Y.: Kennikat Press, 1971), p. 4 (n. by Burr).

7. Jeffrey Burton Russell, *Witchcraft in the Middle Ages* (Ithaca: Cornell Univ. Press, 1972), p. 31, concurs: "still the finest collection of printed materials relating to witchcraft in the world." E. William Monter states in "The Historiography of European Witchcraft: Progress and Prospects," *Journal of Interdisciplinary History*, 2 (1972), 436: "perhaps the world's best collection of witchcraft literature."

8. Russell, *Witchcraft in the Middle Ages*, p. 299, n. 9, believes the Witchcraft Collection "has little that is not elsewhere available on the medieval period." But the Collection possesses the holograph of Visconti's tract (1460), which differs from the incunabulum of 1490; the rare editio princeps of Alphonsus de Spina's *Fortalitium fidei* (ca. 1470), of which the only other copies are in Trier and the University of Glasgow; and Samuel de Cassini's *Questione de le strie* (1505), of which the only other copies extant are in Milan and Glasgow. The Witchcraft Collection has three manuscripts written before 1500, and seventeen incunabula. Of the early writers up to 1550 abstracted in Lea, *Materials*, I, missing only are Johannes Nider, *Praeceptorium divinae legis* (ca. 1470), Lea, I. 264; Symphorien Champier, *Dialogus* (ca. 1500), Lea. I. 354; and a separate publication of the manuscript tract, *La Vauderye de Lyonois en brief*, Lea, I. 292,

trans. into French by Johann Tinctor from *De secta Vaudensium*, accessible in Joseph Hansen, *Quellen und Untersuchungen zur Geschichte des Hexenwahns und der Hexenverfolgung im Mittelalter* (Bonn, 1901; rpt. Hildesheim: Georg Olms, 1963), p. 186—hereafter Hansen, *Quellen*. The original manuscript is unpublished, in the Bibliothèque royale, Brussels; an illustration of the worship of the goat is in Robbins, *Encyclopedia*, p. 31 (see n. 191). But the Witchcraft Collection possesses a copy of Martín de Arles y Androsilla, *Tractatus de superstitionibus* (1559), described by Lea (*Materials*, I. 297) from its later printing with Jacquier.

9. Contrariwise, a few books in the open stacks are listed here for practical convenience, such as Hugo Zwetsloot, *Friedrich Spee und die Hexenprozesse* (Trier, 1954), the standard work on Spee's *Cautio criminalis*.

10. Lévi, *Dogme et rituel de la haute magie* (Paris, 1861), and nine other works. To be added to the works listed under Constant is *The Magical Ritual of the Sanctum Regnum Interpreted by the Tarot Trumps*, trans. W. Wynn Westcott (London, 1896).

11. Of the printed books, the following is a breakdown by centuries: 1401-1500, 17; 1501-1600, 204; 1601-1700, 625; 1701-1800, 547; 1801-1900, 726; after 1900, 536; no date, 4. By language: Dutch, 185; English, 755; French, 400; German, 711; Italian, 61; Latin, 459; Spanish, 17; Portuguese, 3. Of the manuscripts: 1401-1500, 3; 1501-1600, 28; 1601-1700, 96; classified by language: Dutch, 20, English, 48; French, 9; German, 119; Latin, 15.

12. In 1856 White was writing to his mother from Paris about the "most choice little German and French library of 700 volumes seen in a long time—a perfect gem" (*The Diaries of Andrew Dickson White*, ed. Robert Morris Ogden [Ithaca: Cornell Univ. Library, 1959], p. 142).

13. Andrew Dickson White, *Autobiography* (New York: Century, 1906), I. 375.

14. Bainton and Gibbons, *Burr*, p. 39; other examples, p. 38.

15. Cornell Univ. Archives, 13/3/705, No. 6599.

16. White, *Autobiography*, I. 440, 381.

17. Cornell Univ. Archives, 13/6/m.794.

18. Bainton and Gibbons, *Burr*, pp. 190-233.

19. The books bought by Notestein from Pickering & Co. came to £30 (or $146.64).
For lists of the extensive pamphlet literature on individual trials of English witches, see Wallace Notestein, *A History of Witchcraft in England from 1558 to 1718* (1911; rpt. New York: Thomas Y. Crowell, 1968), pp. 346-383, 384-420; Montague Summers, *The History of Witchcraft and Demonology* (1926; rpt. New York: University Books, 1956), pp. 329-338; and Barbara Rosen, *Witchcraft* (London: Edward Arnold, 1969), pp. 386-388. The Witchcraft Collection is only average in its holdings in this area.
Of the 27 notable books on the witchcraft controversy in England listed in my *Encyclopedia of Witchcraft and Demonology* (New York: Crown Publishers, 1959; 13th ed., 1975), p. 167, all are included in the Witchcraft Collection. In addition, further books not mentioned in that list are also found at Cornell, including the following:
1583 Pierre Viret, trans. T. Stocker, *The World Possessed with Devils*;
1596 Ludwig Lavater, trans. Robert Harrison, *Of Ghostes and Spirites*;
1605 Pierre Le Loyer, trans. Zachary Jones, *A Treatise of Specters or Straunge Sights*;
1612 John Mason, *The Anatomie of Sorcerie*;
1616 Alexander Roberts, *A Treatise of Witchcraft*;
1657 Gabriel Naudé, trans. J. Davies, *The History of Magic*;
1657 George Fox, *A Declaration of the Ground of Error*;
1658 Thomas Bramhall, ed. and trans., *Treatise of Specters, or An History of Apparitions* (Cornell has editions of 1670 and 1672);
1668 Meric Casaubon, *Treatise Proving Spirits*;
1678 Thomas Hickes, *Ravillac Redivivus*;
1678 Benjamin Camfield, *A Theological Discourse of Angels and Their Ministries*;
1685 George Sinclair, *Satan's Invisible World Discovered*;
1688 Nathaniel Crouch, *The Kingdom of Darkness*;
1691 Richard Baxter, *Certainty of the World of Spirits*;
1695 Balthasar Bekker, trans. B. B., *The World Bewitch'd* (reissued as *The World Turn'd Upside Down*, 1700).
The Witchcraft Collection does not have a copy of the very early and scarce Lambert Daneau, *A Dialogue of Witches* (1575), but a

copy is in the New York Public Library. On the other hand, the Witchcraft Collection contains many curiosa, such as the annual sermons preached at All Saints Church, Huntington, on March 25, 1792-3-4-5, by the Rev. M. J. Naylor on the anniversary of the Warboys Trial of 1593 (see Robbins, *Encyclopedia*, pp. 527-530). By this time, however, instead of preaching "against the detestable practice, sin, and offense of witchcraft" (for which the sermons had been funded), these sermons were preached against the superstition of witchcraft. The sermons came to an end in 1812. *A Sermon against Witchcraft* (London, 1808), delivered by Isaac Nicholson in Great Paxton, Huntingdonshire, on July 17, 1800, also is on these shelves. One of the very few books on witchcraft by an Englishman written in Latin is *De praestigiis et incantationibus daemonum* (Basel, 1568), the source of Caliban's speech in *The Tempest*, I, 2. Its author was Ricardus Argentinus or Richard Silver, a physician and priest from Ipswich and Exeter. He is listed in *DNB* under Argentine, alias Sexten.

20. White used "Inter folia fructa" as well as a logo, ADW, with "Discipulis est prioris posterior dies."

21. Cornell Univ. Archives has materials on books purchased by the *Warfare of Science* fund, e.g., in 1897, John Hale, *Modest Inquiry* (Boston, 1702); Riezler, *Hexenprozesse in Bayern* (Stuttgart, 1896); and Dennler, *Ein Hexenprozess im Elsass* (Zabern, 1896). J. Reuchlin, *Defensio* (Tübingen, 1513), mentioned under this year, is apparently not located. In 1897 White rejoiced that the royalties had "netted for the Library thus far nearly 1,500 dollars" (*Diaries*, p. 348).

22. Andrew Dickson White, *A History of the Warfare of Science with Theology in Christendom* (New York: Appleton, 1896), I. viii.

23. White's position did not go unchallenged: see Robert Schwickerath, S. J., "Dr. White on Witchcraft," *The Messenger*, 43 (June, 1905), 593-605. The tone is mild, but with the author's main contention White and Burr and many others would totally disagree: "The causes of the witch persecutions are quite different. The main source was the popular belief in witchcraft, which was a remnant of paganism" (pp. 604-605). The debate was to some degree a continuation of the controversy between Soldan and the Jesuits on one hand and Riezler and Father Bernhard Duhr on the other over the general attitude of the Jesuits.

So far as the persecution at Trier goes, one may rely on Burr (in his discussion of Flade in 1890, rpt. Bainton and Gibbons, *Burr*, pp. 190-233) that the Jesuits were the most ardent promoters of persecutions. The situation may have been different at Mainz and Coblenz.

24. A major acquisition promoting this view was the purchase of the library of the prominent rationalist Henry Thomas Buckle, in 1863. For Buckle's essay "History of Witchcraft," see his *Miscellaneous and Posthumous Works* (London, 1872), I. 418-426. Other essays by nineteenth-century rationalists include William Edward Hartpole Lecky, "Magic and Witchcraft," in *History of the Rise and Influence of the Spirit of Rationalism in Europe* (London, 1872), I. 1-138; Charles Mackay, "The Witch Mania," *Memoirs of Extraordinary Popular Delusions* (London, 1852), II. 101-191. Lecky clearly stated his position: "The prosecutions for witchcraft ... represent the action of undiluted superstition more faithfully than probably any others that could be named."

25. Heinrich Schneider, "Die Hexenliteratur-Sammlung der Cornell Universität in Ithaca, New York," *Hessische Blätter für Volkskunde*, 41 (1950), 201.

26. George Lyman Kittredge, *Witchcraft in Old and New England* (Cambridge: Harvard Univ. Press, 1929; rpt. New York: Russell and Russell, 1956). Earlier, "Notes on Witchcraft," *American Antiquarian Society Proceedings*, 18 (1907), 148-212; rpt. *Notes on Witchcraft* (Worcester, Mass.: Davis Press, 1907).

27. See Ian MacPhail, "The Mellon Collection of Alchemy and the Occult," *Ambix*, 14 (1967), 198-202, announcing the *Catalogue* (New Haven: Yale Univ. Press, 1968), 2 vols. The Interim Report of the Witchcraft Collection, October, 1972, TS for internal circulation, warned: "Cornell's special collection on witchcraft is designed for the historian ... at home in Latin as in German and other modern tongues ... not the dabbler in charms and cults" (Barbara Kauber).

28. Burr's part is told by Bainton and Gibbons, *Burr*, pp. 48-58 (which includes some of Burr's letters).

29. *Diaries*, p. 173.

30. White, *Autobiography*, I. 425. Originally published in one volume, *The Warfare of Science* (New York: Appleton, 1876).

31. White, *Autobiography*, I.

32. White, *Warfare of Science*, I. v. Today the conflict would be expressed in terms of experience versus authority. Cf. Sir George N. Clark, *The Seventeenth Century*, 2d ed. (Oxford: Clarendon Press, 1947), p. 246: "In one of the great controversies where the new spirit met the old ... about magic and witchcraft, one of the decisive encounters between science and authority."

33. Cornell Univ. Archives, 13/3/705. Bainton and Gibbons (*Burr*, p. 40) suggest somewhat later, in 1879.

34. Bainton and Gibbons, *Burr*, p. 167.

35. Bainton and Gibbons, *Burr*, p. 41.

36. Bainton and Gibbons, *Burr*, p. 42.

37. Bainton and Gibbons, *Burr*, p. 43. See also Moress, "Historical Library," p. 74 (letter to White, October 23, 1889).

38. Moress, "Historical Library," p. 74, quoting Librarian's Report, 1920-1921.

39. Burr's commentary should be committed to posterity here; it differs from his brief note in Lea, *Materials*, II. 951n. It is written in his not-too-easy hand on the cover:

"Perhaps the only printed copy existing of an official paper of very great interest for the history of witchcraft. It is the official *Instruction* of the Roman Inquisition to the prosecution, issued near the middle of the 17th century (1657), and shows the changed and changing attitude of the Curia.

"This *Instruction* was printed, enriched with a commentary, by the jurist Carena, at the end of his *Tractatus de officio sanctissimae inquisitionis* (ed. of Bologna, 1668, pp. 435-449).

"The printed edition seems to have been sent out on 4 September 1657 (see Delacroix, *Les Procès de sorcellerie au XVIIe siècle*, p. 249). The present copy is the very one reprinted by Horst, in Book III (pp. 115 ff.) of his *Zauber-Bibliothek*. (See Paulus, *Hexenwahn und Hexenprozess*, p. 275, n. 2). Horst mentions (p. 83) its bearing Messen's name, and says he himself borrowed it from Wyttenbach, librarian at Trier.

"Cardinal [Francesco] Albizzi in his *De inconstantia in jure* [*admittenda vel non*] (at pp. 350-353) reprints this *Instructio* from the impression of 1657, and says that the Suprema had of those printed and sent, with a circular letter, to the judicium fidei. Already (in 1650) Gastaldine, he says, had printed it in his *De potentia angelorum et daemonorum*.

"Gastaldus (or Castaldus), whose work we now have, in printing this instruction at length, ascribes it to an official of the Inquisition, a very dear friend of his own; and Quétif and Échard, s.v. Scaglia (II, p. 501) quote Rovotha (d. 1691), who in turn quotes Rivaline (? d. 1669) as ascribing such an instruction, "De modo formandi processione in causis strigum atque necrologicorum" to the pen of Cardinal Scalia (Scaglia). That he was its author is altogether probable. From 1616 to 1621 he was the Commissioner-General of the Inquisition at Rome. He was then made a Cardinal and till 1626 held a bishopric, but was in 1626 called back by the Pope to Rome, and till his death in 1639 had special care of the work of the Inquisition. Geo. L. Burr."

This *Instructio* was probably inspired by the Bull of Gregory XV (1623). An article by Ralph Brown, "Examination of an Interesting Roman Document: Instructio pro Formandis Processionibus in Causis Strigum," *Jurist*, 25 (April, 1964), 169-191, is somewhat tendentious. For description and facsimile of text see Robbins, *Encyclopedia*, pp. 269, 272. See note 369.

40. George Lincoln Burr, "The Literature of Witchcraft," *Papers of the American Historical Association*, 4 (1890), 37-66; "A Witch Hunter in the Bookshops," *Bibliographer*, 1 (1902), 431-446; both rpt. Bainton and Gibbons, *Burr*, pp. 166-189, 294-308.

41. *Bibliographer*, I. 434. I know of no collection so imbued with the spirit of its founders as this Witchcraft Collection is permeated by White and Burr. For example, on the cover of an obscure pamphlet by Gerhard Hennen, printed at Saint Wendel (1887), acquired by the President White Library in 1891, Burr wrote: "It was the MS volume containing this trial which cost me a Sunday tramp through mud and rain to the village of Ober-Fell, eight miles over the hills from Treves, in the autumn of 1885. Frau Nieser, the peasant woman who owned it, virtually sold it to me. And I yielded it to Prof. Dr. Reuse."

42. An extended summary of this material, "A Seventeenth Century Humanitarian: Hermann Löher," was included by Gibbons in *Persecution and Liberty: Essays in Honor of George Lincoln Burr*, ed. Lois Oliphant Gibbons (New York: Century, 1931), pp. 335-359. The Merritt M.A. thesis transcribes the trials in Ban de la Roche or Steinthal, Vosges Mountains, near Strassburg. Mrs. Merritt was a na-

tive of Alsace; her thesis consists of box 1, rough drafts and notes; box 2, typescript and notes; box 3, more transcript and notes. The thesis deserves careful editing and a posthumous publication.

43. Schneider, p. 196: "Sie ist weder sehr bekannt noch oft benutzt worden."

44. Burr, "Literature of Witchcraft," Bainton and Gibbons, *Burr*, p. 189. Burr continued: "and may it aid in making clear to future generations why the literature of witchcraft belongs not to folk-lore, but to theology."

45. Kittredge, *Notes on Witchcraft*, p. 65. Quoted by Burr, intro. to Lea, *Materials*, I. xl.

46. Henry Guerlac, "George Lincoln Burr," *Isis*, 35 (Spring, 1944), pt. 2, 149.

47. *Proceedings of the American Antiquarian Society*, October, 1911, pp. 3-35; rpt. Bainton and Gibbons, *Burr*, pp. 352-377.

48. Alan Macfarlane, *Witchcraft in Tudor and Stuart England* (London: Routledge & Kegan Paul, 1970), p. 312.

49. Keith Thomas, *Religion and the Decline of Magic* (New York: Scribner's, 1971), p. ix.

50. Thomas, *Religion*, p. 464. The anthropological distinction, of course, ignores the Christian devil. See Robbins' review of Thomas in *Renaissance Quarterly*, 26 (1973), 70-72.

51. Mircea Eliade, *Occultism, Witchcraft, and Cultural Fashions* (Chicago: Univ. of Chicago Press, 1976), p. 71.

52. Bainton and Gibbons, *Burr*. For an extended discussion of witchcraft as heresy see Russell, *Witchcraft in the Middle Ages*, p. 16.

53. Eliade, *Occultism*, p. 71; see Robbins' review in *Thought* (1977). An otherwise thoughtful article, "Recent Witch Hunting Research, or Where Do We Go from Here?" *Papers of the Bibliographical Society of America*, 62 (1968), 373-425—basically a bibliography of books and articles from 1940 to 1967—by H. C. Erik Midelfort, attacks the "prejudices" of the White-Burr position: "Evidently there is enough wrong with the Burr school to demand revision" (p. 376). Despite an attack on Burr (p. 17), Midelfort's *Witch Hunting in Southwestern Germany 1562-1684* (Stanford: Stanford Univ. Press, 1972) is an important major study because it is the first work in English based on original local records, with extensive bibliography, pp. 261-300.

54. Geoffrey Parrinder, *Witchcraft in Europe and Africa* (Harmondsworth, Middlesex: Penguin Books, 1958), p. 12.

55. Also to be remarked are Burr's two papers, "The Fate of Dietrich Flade," *Papers of the American Historical Association*, 5 (1891), no. 3, 3-57; rpt. Bainton and Gibbons, *Burr*, pp. 190-233; and "On the Loos Manuscript," Bainton and Gibbons, *Burr*, pp. 147-155. Since the source materials on which they based their conclusions were similar, to Burr's papers should be linked Henry Charles Lea, "The Witch Persecutions in Transalpine Europe" in *Minor Historical Writings*, pp. 6-55. Burr annotated this essay (pp. 3-6).

56. George Lincoln Burr, ed., *Narratives of the Witchcraft Cases 1648-1706* (1914; rpt. New York: Barnes & Noble, 1968), p. xi.

57. Norman Cohn, for example, notes the "stereotype of witch as old woman had existed for centuries before the witch-hunt began" (review in *Times Literary Supplement*, July 23, 1976, p. 902). True enough, but that old woman was *not* the object of witch-hunters.

58. Reginald Scot, *Discoverie of Witchcraft* (1584), bk. 1, chap. 3; ed. Montague Summers (London: J. Rodker, 1930), p. 4.

59. Samuel Harsnett, *A Declaration of Egregious Popish Impostures* (1605), p. 136. See further Robbins, *Encyclopedia*, p. 243.

As observed throughout this introduction and in the notes (e.g., n. 39), a valuable fringe benefit of the Witchcraft Collection consists of Burr's annotations to the books. Since these may be passed over, perhaps one more quotation might be reproduced here. On the flyleaf of *A Declaration* (London, 1605, impression of 1603 ed., with only title page reset), Burr wrote:

"The author of this book, Samuel Harsnet (1561-1631), was one of the most rational men of his time. At the time of its production he was only Chaplain to the Bishop of London (Dr. Bancroft, afterward Archbishop of Canterbury, whose friend and protegé he seems always to have remained) and Rector of St. Margaret's, 'Fishstones' (London); but became successively Master of Pembroke Hall, Vice-Chancellor of Cambridge, Bishop of Chichester, Bishop of Norwich, and Archbishop of

York. In a sermon at St. Paul's Cross in 1584 (he was then but twenty-three, and had just attained his Master's degree) he attacked with remarkable boldness, sense, and eloquence, the horrible doctrine of 'absolute predestination,' declaring the opinion 'monstrous' that 'saith that not one or two, but millions of men should fry in hell, and that [God] made them for no other purpose.' But in this outspoken career he was stopped (as Harsnet later himself tells us in his defence against the charges of the Puritans) by Archbishop Whitgift.

"It was in 1599, as it seems, that he first took ground against the Anglican exorcist, John Darrell, whom he virtually drove from the realm. The present 'Declaration of Popish Impostures,' written against the Jesuit Edmunds (or Weston) and his exorcisms, appeared in 1603. This original edition, though rare, is often cited; but of the present reprint [1605] I can nowhere find mention; and know no copy save this, which I buy for the White Library. In this work Harsnet shows himself a thorough-going disciple of Reginald Scot (whom he cites) and scoffs openly at the whole body of witchcraft superstition, declaring it delusion and humbug. . . . Geo. L. Burr. London, 30 June 1888."

60. Trans. from Friedrich Leitschuh, *Beiträge zur Geschichte des Hexenwesens in Franken* (Bamberg, 1883), pp. 17-19, by George Lincoln Burr, *The Witch-Persecutions*, Translations and Reprints from the Original Sources of European History, III (Department of History, Univ. of Pennsylvania, Philadelphia, 1903), 29. Burr has annotated Leitschuh's book in the Witchcraft Collection: "An extremely valuable contribution to the literature of the witch-persecution. The documents here brought forward are among the most important and instructive yet published."

61. Jean Bodin, *De la Demonomanie des sorciers* (1580), p. 1 (and similarly p. 41 verso): "celuy qui par moyens Diaboliques sciemment s'efforce de paruenir à quelque chose." A useful summary of Bodin's views on witchcraft is to be found in an anonymous article, "Quatrième centenaire Jean Bodin," *Province d'Anjou*, 4e Année, no. 20 (Nov./Dec., 1929). See also notes 134-141.

62. Martin Del Rio, *Disqvisitionum magicarvm libri sex* (1599), lib. 1, c. 2: "Ars qua vi pacti cum Daemonibus initi mira quaedam communem hominum captum superantia efficiuntur"; trans. Sir Robert Filmer, *An Advertisement to the Jury-men of England Touching Witches* (1653), p. 3. For Del Rio see *Biographie nationale de Belgique* (Brussels, 1875), V, and Robbins, *Encyclopedia*, p. 546.

63. William Perkins, *A Discourse of the Damned Art of Witchcraft* (1608), cap. 1, pp. 3-4; also quoted by Filmer, *Advertisement*, p. 3. For Perkins, see Robbins, *Encyclopedia*, p. 382. See also *Discourse*, p. 167: "A witch is a magician, who either by open or secret league, wittingly and willingly consenteth to use the aide and assistance of the Deuill, in the working of wonders."

64. Cotton Mather, *Memorable Providences relating to Witchcrafts and Possessions* (Boston, 1689), p. 4. Similar sentiments in *The Wonders of the Invisible World*, ed. George Lincoln Burr, *Narratives of the Witchcraft Cases 1648-1706*, p. 246.

65. Perkins, *Discourse*, p. 185. The same position was held by Thomas Cooper in his *Mystery of Witchcraft* (1617).

66. Thomas Fuller, *Holy and Profane State* (1642), p. 352.

67. *Statutes of the Realm* (London, 1819), 4, pt. 2, 1028-1029. Easily accessible in Robbins, *Encyclopedia*, pp. 280-281.

68. The Chelmsford trials of 1645 are described by their instigators, Matthew Hopkins, *The Discovery of Witches* (1647), p. 2, and John Stearne, *A Confirmation and Discovery of Witchcraft* (1648), pp. 14-16; as well as in *A True and exact Relation of the severall Informations, Examinations, and Confessions of the late Witches, Arraigned and Executed in the County of Essex* (1645). See Notestein, *History of Witchcraft*, pp. 166-174.

69. George Gifford, *A Dialogue concerning Witches and Witchcraft* (1593), n. pag.; rpt. Percy Society, 8 (1843), 95 (from 1603 ed.); and ed. Beatrice White (London: Shakespeare Association, 1931), l. k3. See James Hitchcock, "George Gifford and Puritan Witch Beliefs," *Archiv für Reformationsgeschichte*, 58 (1967), 90-99.

70. Burr, "Loos Manuscript," Bainton and Gibbons, *Burr*, p. 147. Unless a student accepts this definition, he will in effect find the Witchcraft Collection at Cornell of little use, and, one might add, unless that student is proficient in Latin, German, and French, the Collection will not easily reveal its secrets. Russell is in general agreement with me "that witchcraft and heresy are closely united." See

his "Medieval Witchcraft and Medieval Heresy," in *On the Margin of the Visible*, ed. Edward A. Tiryakian (New York: Wiley, 1974), pp. 179-189.

71. For a short general summary see Robbins, *Encyclopedia*, pp. 244-245, 266-274.

72. Burr, "Literature of Witchcraft," p. 46, rpt. Bainton and Gibbons, *Burr*, p. 173, commented on the role of Thomas Aquinas in the witchcraft delusion: "Now, it is these human allies and servants of Satan, thus postulated into existence by the brain of a monkish logician, whom history knows as 'witches.'" Similarly, Charles Edward Hopkin, in a doctoral dissertation, *The Share of Thomas Aquinas in the Growth of the Witchcraft Delusion* (Philadelphia, 1940): "It is clear that Thomas, directly or indirectly, afforded both explanation and support for the witchcraft delusion" (p. 179). For a Dominican apologist, see Gallus M. Manser, "Thomas von Aquin und der Hexenwahn," *Jahrbuch für Philosophie und spekulative Theologie*, ser. 2, vol. 9, pt. 1 (1922), 81-110. Also Sister Antoinette Marie Pratt, *The Attitude of the Catholic Church towards Witchcraft* (Washington, 1915, diss. Catholic Univ.), acknowledges help from Burr and the Witchcraft Collection (p. 4).

73. Quoted in G. G. Coulton, *The Inquisition* (London: Ernest Benn, 1929), pp. 35-36.

74. Trans. G. G. Coulton, *The Death Penalty for Heresy from 1184 to 1921* (London: Simpkin, Marshall, 1924), pp. 49-50; rpt. Jeffrey Burton Russell, *Religious Dissent in the Middle Ages* (New York: Wiley, 1971), pp. 127-128. For Pope Lucius III see also Henry Charles Lea, *History of the Inquisition of the Middle Ages* (New York: Harper, 1888; rpt. New York: Russell & Russell, 1955), I. 126; reprinted with introduction by Walter Ullmann, *The Inquisition of the Middle Ages* (London: Eyre & Spottiswoode, 1963), p. 63; A. S. Turberville, *Mediaeval Heresy and the Inquisition* (1920; rpt. Hamden, Conn.: Archon Books, 1964), p. 211; Walter L. Wakefield and Austin P. Evans, ed., *Heresies of the High Middle Ages* (New York: Columbia Univ. Press, 1969), p. 33; Russell, *Witchcraft in the Middle Ages*, p. 154; Walter L. Wakefield, *Heresy, Crusade, and Inquisition in Southern France, 1100-1250* (Berkeley: Univ. of California Press, 1974), p. 86.

75. Coulton, *Inquisition*, p. 22.

76. Decree, "*Excommunicamus*," to the Fourth Lateran Council, 1215, quoted by Coulton, *Inquisition*, p. 37; trans. Henry J. Schroeder, O.P., *Disciplinary Decrees of the General Councils* (St. Louis: Herder, 1937); rpt. Colman J. Barry, *Readings in Church History* (Westminster, Md.: Newman Press, 1960), I. 440-442; rpt. Russell, *Religious Dissent*, pp. 128-131. See Jacques Madaule, *The Albigensian Crusade* (1961), trans. Barbara Wall (London: Burns & Oates, 1967), pp. 75-78.

77. See G. G. Coulton, *Inquisition and Liberty* (London: William Heineman, 1938), p. 111; Lea, *History*, I. 321-323; rpt. Russell, *Religious Dissent*, pp. 135-137.

78. G. G. Coulton, *Inquisition and Liberty*, p. 92, translating *Hystoria albigensis*, ed. Pascal Guébin and Ernest Lyon (Paris, 1926-1929), chap. 1.

79. Madaule, *Albigensian Crusade*, pp. 56-63.

80. For recent studies see Madaule, *Albigensian Crusade*; Joseph R. Strayer, *The Albigensian Crusade* (New York: Dial Press, 1971); Wakefield, *Heresy, Crusade, and Inquisition*, with extensive bibliography, pp. 259-276.

81. Eleventh ed., 14. 592, article by Paul Daniel Alphandéry, professor of the History of Dogma at the Sorbonne (1910).

82. *Directorium Inquisitorum*, ed. Francis Pegna (Rome, 1585; Venice, 1607). See Burr, "Literature of Witchcraft," p. 50, rpt. Bainton and Gibbons, *Burr*, p. 176. Eymeric is abstracted by Lea, *Materials*, I. 209-213.

83. Trans. Coulton, *Inquisition*, p. 47, from *Directorium Inquisitorum* (1585), p. 204.

84. Burr, "Literature of Witchcraft," p. 48; rpt. Bainton and Gibbons, *Burr*, p. 174.

85. Burr, "Literature of Witchcraft," p. 39; rpt. Bainton and Gibbons, *Burr*, p. 167, points out that although the early Dominican inquisitors, such as Eymeric and Jacquier, believed they were proving witchcraft "was as old as mankind," it was actually a "new theme." See Lea, *Materials*, III. 1449: "In the early days of the witchcraft craze, while the Canon Episcopi was recognized as an authority, the effort of the demonologists was to prove that witchcraft was a new heretical sect and therefore not subject to its animadversions; while, after demonologists had argued the canon away,

they labored to show that witchcraft was known to the ancients, and that the cruel imperial laws were directed against it." For a summary of inquisitorial procedure see Robbins, "The Heresy of Witchcraft," *The South Atlantic Quarterly*, 65 (1966), 532-543.

86. Felix Martinus Brähm, *Disputatio inaugurensis de fallacibus indiciis magia* (Halle, 1709) as translated and abstracted by Lea, *Materials*, III. 1407. See n. 310. A parallel attack was made by Christian Thomasius, *Kurtze Lehr-Sätze von dem Laster der Zauberey* (Halle, 1703) as translated and abstracted by Lea, *Materials*, III. 1403: "In a word, I hold that the witch-process is worthless, that the bodily horned devil with his pitch-ladle and his mother is a pure invention of the papist priests, of whom he is the grand arcanum to frighten people into paying money for soul-masses and inveigle them into giving rich properties and foundations for convents or other pious causes and cast suspicion on the innocent who say *Papa quid facis* as though they were sorcerers. Christ did not convert the sinners with such a devil, nor did the apostles make of him a corner-stone, the removal of which would ruin the building. Then it was said, 'Who denies Christ, denies God;' now the cry is, 'Who denies the horned devil, denies God.' Were such absurdities heard, even in the darkest papacy?" For Thomasius see n. 308.

87. Thomas de Cauzons [pseud.], *Histoire de l'Inquisition en France* (Paris, 1909, 1913), II. 178: "inventé le délit de sorcellerie et imposé la torture comme moyen de preuve." Excellent material and documentation on the trials by the Inquisition is provided by L. Tanon, *Histoire des tribunaux de l'Inquisition en France* (Paris, 1893); see pp. 160-217 for detailed accounts of inquisitors' manuals (esp. Gui); and by A. S. Turberville, *Mediaeval Heresy and the Inquisition* (London, 1920).

The concept of witchcraft as a crime worthy of death was superimposed by the Catholic church and later by the secular states on a reluctant and hostile populace. After the Inquisition had caused to be burned many "notable persons, as well as lesser folk, crazy women, and others," at Arras in 1459-1460, their property to be confiscated, the Parlement of Paris investigated the whole affair and in 1461 officially declared the Inquisition had acted "in error and against the order and dignity of justice—a false trial and one conducted without due process." Furthermore, it condemned the "inhuman and cruel interrogation and tortures of the Inquisition, like *capellet*, putting the soles of the feet in the fire, and making the accused swallow oil and vinegar." See Georges Raviart, *Sorcières et possédées: La démonomanie dans le Nord de la France* (Lille, 1939, ltd. ed.). See further, Robbins, *Encyclopedia*, pp. 29-32.

88. The literature on Joan of Arc is voluminous, probably now amounting to some four thousand items. There is a valuable collection in Columbia University Library. The New York Public Library catalogues some 700 items, but only one, a minor magazine article, mentions witchcraft by name (Herbert Thurston, "Was She a Witch after all?" *Month* [London, 1922], vol. 139. Works on Joan of Arc are not included in this Catalogue. "It is often supposed that Joan of Arc was condemned as a witch. This is inaccurate. She was popularly bruited a sorceress and originally alleged a witch; but she was officially condemned as a heretic and legally burned as a relapsed heretic" (Robbins, *Encyclopedia*, p. 282; basic bibliography, p. 559).

89. Excerpted by Hansen, *Quellen*, p. 1. See Lea, *Inquisition*, III. 434; Russell, *Witchcraft in the Middle Ages*, pp. 156, 171.

90. Printed in Hansen, *Quellen*, pp. 4-5; Lea, *Inquisition*, III. 660. See Lea, *Materials*, I. 221; Russell, *Witchcraft in the Middle Ages*, p. 173. The decree was repealed in 1333. It should be noted that before the publication of Norman Cohn, *Europe's Inner Demons: An Enquiry Inspired by the Great Witch Hunt* (London: Chatto, Heinemann, 1975), pp. 128-138, and Richard Kieckhefer, *European Witch Trials: Their Foundations in Popular and Learned Culture, 1300-1500* (Berkeley: Univ. of California Press, 1976), pp. 16-18, 21, 37, all scholars accepted the authenticity of the documents on the mass executions of witches at Toulouse and Carcassonne between 1320 and 1350 (practicing advanced witchcraft procedures standard by the sixteenth century). The sources of this information were printed by Etienne-Léon, baron de Lamothe-Langon, *Histoire de l'Inquisition en France* (Paris, 1829), III. 211-307, and by Hansen, *Quellen*, pp. 449-456. They are in fact forgeries. All histories of witchcraft have to be emended accordingly; see esp. Kieckhefer, *Witch Trials*, p. 157, n. 27.

91. See Hansen, *Quellen*, p. 17; Lea, *Materials*, I. 224; other decrees in 1437, 1440, 1445; see Hansen, *Quellen*, pp. 17-19; Lea, *Inquisi-*

tion, III. 502, 512; Lea, *Materials*, I. 224-245; Russell, *Witchcraft in the Middle Ages*, pp. 220-229.

92. Hansen, *Quellen*, p. 19; Lea, *Inquisition*, III. 512; Lea, *Materials*, I. 225.

93. Russell, *Witchcraft in the Middle Ages*, p. 76. Latin text in Hansen, *Quellen*, pp. 38-39; Migne, *Patrologia Latina*, 132. 252-253; and cf. 160. 831; Russell, *Witchcraft in the Middle Ages*, pp. 291–293 (discussion, see esp. pp. 75-79, 234-235). Trans. in Lea, *Materials*, I. 178-180; Robbins, *Encyclopedia*, pp. 75-77; Russell, *Witchcraft in the Middle Ages*, pp. 76-77. See also Joseph Hansen, *Zauberwahn, Inquisition, und Hexenprozess im Mittelalter* (1900; rpt. Munich: Scientia Verlag Aalen, 1964), pp. 78-88.

94. Lea, *Materials*, I. 179.

95. For references see Lea, *Materials*, thus: Vivetus (in Lea, Vineti), I. 272; Jacquier, I. 277; Prierias, I. 354, 359; Dodo, I. 367; Grillandus, I. 401, 406; Ciruelo, I. 414.

96. Lea, *Materials*: Jacquier, I. 277; Mamoris, I. 298; Prierias, I. 358; Spina, I. 390.

97. Lea, *Materials*: Jacquier, I. 284; Visconti, I. 296; Jordanus, I. 303.

98. Thomas Hobbes, *Works* (London, 1889), III. 9 (*Leviathan*, 1561, pt. 2, chap. 2): "For as for witches, I think not that their witchcraft is any real power, but yet that they are justly punished for the false belief they have that they can do such a mischief, joined with their purpose to do it if they can, their trade being nearer to a new religion than to a craft or science."

99. Lea, *Materials:* Jacquier, I. 282-283.

100. Lea, *Materials:* Bernard, I. 372; Spina, I. 390.

101. Lea, *Materials*, I. 206, observes: "The connection between sorcery and heresy, including devil worship, was growing during the thirteenth century."

102. Lea, *Materials*, I. 408-409. Lea comments, *Materials*, I. 395: "Few writers are more frequently referred to in subsequent works and his little book unquestionably did its share in establishing the belief in witchcraft."

103. Thomas, *Religion and Decline of Magic*, pp. 25, 50.

104. Lea, *Materials*, I. 354, summarizes extracts from Hansen, *Quellen*, pp. 256-258.

105. Lea, *Materials*, I. 366, summarizes extracts from Hansen, *Quellen*, pp. 262-273. Cassini was answered by Vincente Dodo, *Apologia pro inquisitoribus* (Pavia, 1506), who in his dedication says "he is pursuing Cassini with a brandished sword" (Lea, *Materials*, I. 367). Not in the Witchcraft Collection, but in the Ferguson Collection of the Hunterian Library, University of Glasgow. In this Catalogue, Cassini is entered under Samuel, Cassinensis.

106. Lea, *Materials*, I. 375, summarizes extracts from Hansen, *Quellen*, pp. 310-312. Another interested in herbs was Andres a Laguna, a prominent physician, who resided in various European cities. In *Pedacio Dioscorides Anazarbio, cerca de la materia medicinal* (Salamanca, 1566), he discussed the use of nightshade to produce hallucinations of attendance at sabbat. See Harry Friedenwald, "Andres a Laguna, a Pioneer in His Views on Witchcraft," *Bulletin of the History of Medicine*, 7 (1939), 1037-1047. See also Laurent Catelan, *Rare et curieux discours de la plante appelée Mandragore, et ses especes, vertus et usages* (Paris, 1638).

107. Lea, *Materials*, I. 382. Lea abstracts from the 1592 Frankfurt edition of Ponzinibio, *Materials*, I. 377-381.

108. Lea, *Materials*, I. 264.

109. Lea, *Materials*, I. 272.

110. Lea, *Materials*, I. 278.

111. Lea, *Materials*, I. 295. Entire summary (*Materials*, I. 295-296) relying on Hansen, *Quellen*, pp. 201-204.

112. Abstracted in Lea, *Materials*, I. 385-395, from the 1576 edition.

113. Lea, *Materials*, I. 365.

114. Lea, *Materials*, I. 374.

115. Latin text in *Bullarum diplomaticum et privilegiorum sanctorum Romanorum pontificum*, V. 296-298; Hansen, *Quellen*, pp. 24-30; Wilhelm Römer, *Die Hexenbulle* (Schaffhau-

sen, 1889)—Latin with German trans.; convenient English trans. in Burr, *Witch-Persecutions*, pp. 8-10; Montague Summers, trans. and ed., *Malleus maleficarum* (1928; rpt. New York: Anglobooks, 1951; rpt. London: Hogarth Press, 1969), pp. xix-xxi; Robbins, *Encyclopedia*, pp. 264-266 (with plate). See also Hansen, *Zauberwahn*, pp. 467-475; Johann G. Sauter, *Zur Hexenbulle 1484* (Ulm, 1884); Charles Williams, *Witchcraft* (London: Faber, 1941) p. 173; Russell, *Witchcraft in the Middle Ages*, pp. 229-230. The importance of this bull is minimized by Herbert Thurston in the *Catholic Encyclopedia* (New York: Appleton, 1912), XV. 676. It followed the bulls of Sixtus IV in 1473, 1478, and 1483, a pope who was perhaps the first to equate sorcery and black magic positively with heresy—see Lea, *Materials*, I. 226. There is a useful chapter on papal bulls in Montague Summers, *The Geography of Witchcraft* (1927; rpt. Evanston, Ill: University Books, 1958), who also includes a translation of *Summis desiderantes affectibus*, pp. 533-536.

116. Hansen, *Zauberwahn*, trans. Lea, *Materials*, I. 365.

117. Robbins, *Encyclopedia*, p. 337. Detailed summary in Lea, *Materials*, I. 306-336. Valuable summary of a scarce paper by Hansen in Lea, *Materials*, I. 336-347.

118. The Witchcraft Collection has fourteen Latin editions: the very scarce first edition "before April 14, 1487," then editions of 1490/1491, 1494, 1519 (Lyons), 1519 (Nuremberg), 1520, 1580, 1582, 1584, 1588, 1598, 1604, 1620, 1669. One remarks the multiplicity of editions after 1580, when the delusion was rapidly spreading. For the first edition see Frederick R. Goff, "The Library of Congress Copy of the *Malleus maleficarum*, 1487," *Libri*, 13 (1963), 137-141. Russell, *Witchcraft in the Middle Ages*, p. 336, n. 12, says the *Malleus maleficarum* was first translated into English in 1584, but I have not come across any copy of this. In addition to the commentaries listed in this Catalogue under Institoris, see also J. W. R. Schmidt, *Malleus Maleficarum. Der Hexenhammer, verfasst von den beiden Inquisitoren J. Sprenger und H. Institoris* (Berlin, 1906), 3 vols.; Fritz Byloff, "Hexenglaube und Hexenverfolgung in den österreichischen Alpenländern," *Quellen zur deutschen Volkskunde*, 6 (1934), 30 ff.; G. Bonomo, "Il Malleus maleficarum," *Annali del Museo Pitrè*, 1 (1950), 120-147; H. C. Erik Midelfort, *Witch Hunting in Southwestern Germany 1562-1684*, pp. 20-24, and passim.

119. Williams, *Witchcraft*, p. 129.

120. Lea, *Materials*, I. 347.

121. Summers, *Malleus maleficarum*, p. 204. Much of its argument derived from Johannes Nider, *Formicarius* (1435) and *Praeceptorium* (1470)—Lea, *Materials*, I. 260-265, 265-272.

122. Noted in Lea, *Materials*, I. 374.

123. Abstracted in Lea, *Materials*, I. 754-761. Damhouder refers his readers to Grillandus, Martin de Arles, and the *Malleus maleficarum*. The need for modern editions of works such as these is underscored by Lea's note, *Materials*, II. 761: "The views held at this period by an eminent jurist have seemed to me to throw so much light on the opinion of intelligent and cultured men as to sorcery that I have given them thus at length, thinking that, if space allowed, it might be well to embody them as a whole."

124. Lea, *Materials*, III. 1125, quoting Sigmund Riezler, *Geschichte der Hexenprozesse* (Stuttgart, 1896), p. 188. See Robbins, *Encyclopedia*, pp. 42-44.

125. Abstracted in Lea, *Materials*, II. 813-850; and see III. 1083-1084. Like Damhouder, Carpzov relied on the older authorities such as Grillandus, Binsfeld, Remi, Del Rio, and especially Bodin—Georg Längin, *Religion und Hexenprozesse* (Leipzig, 1888), p. 211. See also Wilhelm Gottlieb Soldan, rev. Heinrich L. J. Heppe, rev. Max Bauer, *Geschichte der Hexenprozesse aus der Quellen dargestellt* (Munich, 1912), II. 212; "He stands entirely on the basis of the *Malleus*." Carpzov was reprinted nine times to 1723. See notes 228, 229, 230.

126. Soldan-Heppe, rev. Bauer, *Hexenprozesse*, I. 214. See Robbins, *Encyclopedia*, p. 79.

127. Cf. Burr, "Literature of Witchcraft," p. 54; rpt. Bainton and Gibbons, *Burr*, p. 179.

128. Scot, *Discoverie* (1584), bk. 1, chap. 9; ed. Summers, p. 10.

129. These authors (and some others) are abstracted in Lea, *Materials*: Carena, II. 942-950; Alberghini, II. 966-971; Bergamo, II. 971-979; Bordoni, II. 991-1000; Salelles, II. 1009-1017; and Delbene, II. 1017-1034.

130. See Lea, *Materials*, III. 1092, 1094, abstracting Ludwig Rapp, *Die Hexenprozesse*

und ihre Gegner aus Tirol (Innsbruck, 1874).

131. Lea, *Materials*, II. 993, 1009; II. 997; II. 1007. The ligature cure was widely circulated; see, e.g., Henri Boguet, *Discours des sorciers (1602)*, trans. E. A. Ashwin, *An Examen of Witches*, intro. by Montague Summers (1929; rpt. New York: Barnes & Noble, 1971), p. 302, note to p. 107, "Wedding Ring."

132. George Lincoln Burr, "Loos Manuscript," Bainton and Gibbons, *Burr*, p. 149.

133. For convenient charts listing the chief early writers up to 1550, see Robbins, *Encyclopedia*, pp. 145, 146, and 147. Copies of the works cited of all these writers are to be found in the Witchcraft Collection with the following exceptions: (p. 145) *Errores Gazariorum*, *La Vauderye de Lyonnois*, Bergamo, and Vincenti (all four available in extracts in Hansen, *Quellen*); (p. 146) Champier; (p. 147) Pirandola's *Strix*, and Vitoria. To the list on p. 146 might be added Thomas Murner, *De pythonico contractu* (1499), available in the Witchcraft Collection, and Vincenti Dodo, *Apologia Dodo* (1506), not at Cornell. Thus of these 37 major writers, only 8 are not to be found in the Witchcraft Collection, and 6 of these 8 are available extracted in Hansen, *Quellen*.

A valuable collection of 13 early works is appended in two volumes to the 1620 edition of the *Malleus maleficarum*, reprinted in the 1669 ed., which adds a fourth volume on exorcists. The Witchcraft Collection has other individual copies of Anania, Bernardus Comensis, Alfonso de Castro, [Gerson], Grillandus, Molitor, Murner, Nider, Bartolommeo Spina; but, though available in the large *Malleus maleficarum* editions, no separate editions of Bernado Basin, *Tractatus de magicis artibus* (mentioned in Lea, *Materials*, I. 304, only from Hansen, *Quellen*); Joannes Franciscus Leo, *Libellus de sortilegis*; Jacobus Simancas, *Titulus vnicus de lamiis*; Ambrosius de Vignate, *Tractatus de haereticis* (abstracted, Lea, *Materials*, I. 299-301). The fourth volume of the 1669 ed. contains Henricus de Gorchen, *Tractatus de superstitiosis*. These two late editions of the *Malleus maleficarum* do for the earlier authorities what Hauber's *Bibliotheca, acta, et scripta magica* (1738-1744) does for the later writers.

134. *De la République* (Paris, 1578): "la seruitude est droictement contre nature" (p. 35).

135. Abstracted in Lea, *Materials*, II. 555-574. For Bodin, see Robbins, *Encyclopedia*, pp. 53-56. The Witchcraft Collection has several offprints cross-referenced under Bodin, e.g., Köhler and Molinier, and Georges Marchand, "Bodin et les sorciers," entered in the Catalogue under *Province d'Anjou* (periodical). Another article, not in this Catalogue, is Harold Elmer Mantz, "Jean Bodin and the Sorcerers," *Romanic Review*, 15 (1924), 153-178 (good references, p. 154, n. 5); F. von Bezold, "Jean Bodin als Okkultist und seine *Demonomanie*," *Historische Zeitschrift*, 105 (1910), 1-64; Ursula Lange, *Untersuchungen zur Bodins Demonomanie* (Frankfurt [1970], diss. Cologne), with bibliography, pp. 165-172 (not in Witchcraft Collection, but available in Olin Library); J. Scheible, "Von Zauberern, Teufelsbeschwörern durch Joh. Bodin," *Das Kloster* (Stuttgart, 1846), II. 218-232; Roger Chauviré, *Jean Bodin, auteur de la République* (Paris, 1914; rpt. Geneva: Skatline Reprints, 1969), pp. 69-73; P. Collinet, "J. Bodin et la S. Barthélemy. Documents inédits sur sa vie, de juillet 1572 à mars 1573," *Nouvelle Revue historique de droit français et étranger*, 32 (1908), 752-756; and Henri Baudrillart, *J. Bodin et son temps* (Paris, 1853).

136. "Je confesse bien qu'il vaut mieux absouldre le coulpable que de condamner l'innocent." Elsewhere Bodin advocates quite different legal standards for proving witchcraft: "en crimes si occultes... la presomption et la preuue coniectural suffist" (*Demonomanie*, 1580, p. 175 verso).

137. Children confessing against parents: "Et faut ouyr la fille contre la mere en ce crime de Sorcellerie" (*Demonomanie*, p. 178 verso). "Il ne faut donc pas s'arrester aux voyes ordinaires que deffendent d'ouyr en tesmoignage le fils contre le pere, ny le pere contre le fils: car ce crime passe tous les autres" (*Demonomanie*, p. 179). Similarly Boguet, *Discours*, art. 66; Ashwin, *Examen*, p. 224. Common rumor is grounds for torture: "Car c'est vne presomption tres-violente quand vne femme a bruit d'estre Sorciere, qu'elle est telle, et qui suffit pour la condamner à la question auec quelques indices ionts au bruict commun" (*Demonomanie*, p. 188 verso). Followed by Boguet, *Examen*, p. 222 (art. 32).

138. "D'autant que la preuve de telles meschancetés est si cachee et si difficile qu'il n'y auroit iamais personne accusé n'y puni d'un million de Sorciers qu'il y a, si les parties estoyent reglees en proces ordinaire par faute de preuue" (*Demonomanie*, p. 216 verso).

In Laon in 1566 a woman was mistakenly burned alive; the executioner forgot to strangle her first and then afterward burn the dead

body. Bodin does not cry out at this miscarriage of "justice." Instead, he rationalizes: "not a mistake—it is better to say the just judgment of God, who thus reminds us... there is no crime more worthy of burning." "Une sorcière qui fut condamnée à estre estranglée, puys bruslée, et qui neantmoins fut bruslée viue par la faute du bourreau, ou pour mieux dire par le iuste iugement de Dieu, qui fist cognoistre qu'il faut discerner la peine selon la grandeur du forfaict, et qu'il n'y a point de meschanceté plus digne du feu." Story told by Boguet, *Examen*, p. 131 (chap. 45). Elsewhere, Bodin (p. 165 verso) writes: "Il y faut appliquer les cauteres et fers chaux, et couper les parties putrifiees: combien que à dire verité quelque punition qu'on ordonne contre eux à rostir, et brusler les Sorciers à petit feu, si est ce que ceste peine là n'est pas à beaucoup pres si grande que celle que Sathan leur fait souffrir en ce monde, sans parler des peines eternelles qui leur font preparees, car le feu ne peut durer vne heure voire demie, que les Sorciers ne soyent morts."

139. Bainton and Gibbons, *Burr*, p. 184, n. 73.

140. Other French editions include 1581 (Strassburg), 1586 (Anvers), 1593 (Paris), 1593 (Antwerp), 1593 (Lyons), 1598 (Lyons), 1604 (Rouen). Title page of first edition reproduced in Robbins, *Encyclopedia*, p. 55.

141. The early German translation was made by Johann Fischart: *De magorum daemonomania. Vom aussgelassnen wütigen Teuffelsheer allerhand Zauberern*; this has been edited by Hans Biedermann (Graz, 1973). The 1698 (Hamburg) copy has a different version: *Daemonomania: oder Auszführliche Erzehlung des wütenden Teuffels*; it added an account of the Salem witches. The Italian translation was first published in Venice, 1587; second edition, 1589.

142. For dating of work and trials see George Lincoln Burr, "The Fate of Dietrich Flade," Bainton and Gibbons, *Burr*, p. 195, n. 15.

143. Lucien Dintzner, *Nicolas Remy et son oeuvre démonologique* (Lyons, 1936), p. 33. The name is frequently spelled Remy; the Witchcraft Catalogue uses Remi.

144. Extracted in Lea, *Materials*, II. 604-624. For a death warrant signed by Remi see Laurent Leclerc, *Notice sur Nicolas Remy, procureur général de Lorraine* (Nancy, 1869), rpt. from article in *Mémoires de l'Academie de Stanislas, 1868*; text only in Dintzner, *Remy*, p. 37; facsimile and translation in Robbins, *Encyclopedia*, p. 409. Not in the Witchcraft Collection are the following: two detailed articles by Christian Pfister, "Nicolas Remy et la sorcellerie de Lorraine à la fin du xvie siècle," *Revue historique*, 93 (1907), 225-239, 94 (1907), 28-44 (with bibliographies, passim); A. Fournier, "Une Épidémie de sorcellerie en Lorraine," *Annales de l'Est* (1891), 256-258; Etienne Delcambre, *Le Concept de la sorcellerie dans le Duché de Lorraine aux xvie et xviie siècles* (Nancy, 1949-1951), 3 vols.; J. Levron, "La Sorcellerie en Lorraine," *Mercure de France*, 310 (1950), 180-184; Etienne Delcambre, "Les Procès de sorcellerie en Lorraine, psychologie des juges," *Tijdschrift voor Rechtsgeschiedenis (Revue d'histoire du droit)*, 21 (1953), 389-419. Emile Badel, *D'une Sorcière qu'aultrefois on brusla dans Sainct-Nicholas* (Nancy, 1869), gives an embellished but seemingly authentic account of a trial in 1582. Delcambre, *Concept*, notes (inter alia) that in court records details of copulation are rare, unlike the trials conducted by Remi.

145. For possible French version, see Dintzner, *Remy*, pp. 58-60.

146. Lea, *Materials*, I. 605.

147. Another Latin ed. 1596 (Cologne). The German titles vary: 1598, *Von Unholden und Zauber Geisten*; 1693, *Daemonolatria*. Modern English translation, by E. A. Ashwin, with introduction by Montague Summers (London, 1930; rpt. New York: Barnes & Noble, 1970). Facsimile of title page of added second part of 1693 German translation in Robbins, *Encyclopedia*, p. 407; portrait of Remi, p. 408.

148. Meric Casaubon, *Of Credulity and Incredulity* (1668), p. 169. For popularity of Remi see Reginald Trevor Davies, *Four Centuries of Witch Beliefs* (London: Methuen, 1947), p. 45.

149. Not abstracted in Lea, *Materials*. An exact bibliography of the *Discours* is hard to assemble; some editions are scarce, perhaps because (according to the story) his family bought up copies and destroyed them. There is reputedly a first edition in 1590 (Lyons), but the editio princeps is 1602 (Lyons), which itself was expanded in 1603 (Lyons), and this is the edition generally used. Because the *Discours* was being pirated (e.g., Paris, 1603), this 1603 Lyons edition was protected by a "Privilege du Roy" of King Henry IV against any other printers issuing the book. The Witch-

craft Collection has the 1602 and 1603 copies, the generally found 1606 (Rouen) edition (*Discours execrable des sorciers*, similarly entitled in the 1603 Rouen edition), and the 1608 (Lyons) edition. There is also an edition of 1610 (Lyons). There are no Latin or German translations; a modern English translation by E. A. Ashwin, with introduction by Montague Summers, *An Examen of Witches*, was published in London (1929; rpt. New York: Barnes & Noble, 1971). Like Bodin, Boguet wrote a legal work, a textbook, *In consuetudines generales comitatus Burgundiae observationes* (Lyons, 1604; Besançon, 1725). For Boguet see Aristide Dey, *Histoire de la sorcellerie au comté de Burgogne* (Vesoul, 1861), esp. pp. 48-57; also Jean Francais, *L'Eglise et la sorcellerie* (Paris, 1910), pp. 115-119; and an important work by Francis Bavoux, *Les Procès inédits de Boguet en matière de sorcellerie* (Dijon, 1958). Also, for Franche-Comté, see Francis Bavoux, *La Sorcellerie au pays de Quingey* (Besançon, 1947); Robert Mandrou, *Magistrats et sorciers en France au xvii*ᵉ *siècle* (Paris, 1968).

150. *Discours*, chap. 4; Ashwin, *Examen*, p. 6.

151. *Discours*, dedication; Ashwin, *Examen*, pp. xxxvi-xxxvii.

152. *Discours*, chap. 52; Ashwin, *Examen*, pp. 169-170.

153. Lea, *Materials*, II. 604.

154. Summers in Ashwin, *Examen*, pp. v-vi. For the historical background of these four French jurists and the decline of witchcraft see Mandrou, *Magistrats et sorciers*.

155. *Tableau de l'inconstance des mauvais anges* (Paris, 1612), p. 40; (Paris, 1613), pp. 38, 56. The Witchcraft Collection also possesses *L'Incredvlité et mescreance dv sortilege* (Paris, 1622). There is a German translation of the *Tableau: Wunderbarliche Geheimnüsse der Zauberey* (1630). The *Tableau* is abstracted by Lea, *Materials*, III. 1292-1304. The 1613 edition is notable for the double spread engraving of a witches' sabbat (reproduced in Robbins, *Encyclopedia*, p. 300) by the Polish engraver, Jan Ziarnko; unfortunately this engraving is missing in the Cornell copy, as in most others. This picture was satirized, as indeed was the entire *Tableau*, in Laurent Bordelon, *L'Histoire de Monsieur Oufle* (Amsterdam, 1710). "Oufle" is an anagram for "le fou." "There is such an ample and very particular description of all that passes at the Sabbath, that I don't believe I should be better informed concerning it if I had been there myself." See Robbins, *Encyclopedia*, p. 57; and monograph by Jacqueline de la Harpe, *L'Abbé Laurent Bordelon et la lutte contre la superstition en France entre 1680 et 1730*, Univ. of California *Publications in Modern Philology*, XXI (1942).

There is considerable secondary literature on L'Ancre; not all is available in the Witchcraft Collection. See V. Lespy, "Les Sorcières dans le Béarn 1393-1672," *Bulletin de la société des sciences, lettres et arts de Pau*, 2ᵉ sér., vol. 4 (1875), 5-72; Hilarion Barthely, *La Sorcellerie en Béarn et dans le Pays Basque* (Paris, 1879), dealing with magic, folklore, and legends; Jean Bernou, *La Chasse aux sorcières dans la Labourde 1609* (Agen, 1897)—a sort of index to L'Ancre; [anon.] *Sorciers et loups-garous dans les Landes* (Auch, 1904); Jules Vinson, "La Sorcellerie dans la Labourd," *Revue de linguistique et de philologie comparée*, 47 (1913), 153-160; Henri Carré, "Quelques mots sur la sorcellerie dans les provinces de l'Ouest au xviᵉ et xviiᵉ siècles," *Société des antiquaires de l'Ouest: Bulletin*, 3ᵉ sér., vol. 7 (Poitiers, 1927), 631-674; [W. Boissell,] "Le Conseiller Pierre de Lancre," *Bulletin du Musée Basque*, No. 14 (Bayonne, 1937), 225-233; No. 15 (1938), 133-203—No. 14 gives a description of eighteen modern paintings by Jean de la Peña in the Musée illustrating the *Tableau*, and in fact forming a description of the book's contents; in No. 15 are three selections from the *Tableau* (bk. 1, Discours 2; 3, 4; 5, 3) with introduction by Boissell. One of these pictures, "La Toilette pour le sabbat" (no. 3), is reproduced in Robbins, *Encyclopedia*, p. 41. For an account of witchcraft among the Basques in Spain, see Julio Caro Baroja, trans. Nigel Glendinning, *The World of Witches* (London: Weidenfeld and Nicolson, 1968), pp. 143-155, and (among Basques in France, quoting L'Ancre), pp. 156-170. Baroja finds Lea's position "futile" (p. 253). Pfister, *Revue historique*, 93. 226, n. 5, gives first ed. of *Tableau* as Paris, 1610.

156. Lea, *Materials*, III. 1295.

157. *Tableau* (1612), p. 104: "adioustons que l'Eglise Catholique Apostolique et Romaine, qui ne peut errer, les punit de mort; Or elle erreroit grandement d'en vser si seuerement s'ils n'estoient sorciers et criminels que par songe. Il faut donc necessairement inferer que quiconque croit que les transports sont seulement prestiges, songes, et illusions, peche contre l'eglise laquelle ne punit de crimes incertains, occultes et non manifestes, et ne

punit comme Heretiques que ceux qui le font veritablement et non par songe et illusion." This circular argument was common enough: so in *Malleus maleficarum*, Sylvester Prierias, and Bernard da Como, all quoted in Lea, *Materials*, II. 643.

158. *Du Sortilege* (1627), which Montague Summers, *The History of Witchcraft* (1926; rpt. New York: University Books, 1956), p. 318, says is "the rarest of De Lancre's books, and very little known," is not at Cornell.

159. Abstracted in Lea, *Materials*, II. 640-647. See Robbins, *Encyclopedia*, pp. 121-123, with reproduction of elaborate title page of 1604 ed.

160. Burr, "Fate of Dietrich Flade," Bainton and Gibbons, *Burr*, p. 200, n. 32.

161. Lea, *Materials*, II. 605, quotes Grässe (p. 47) listing later editions in 1603 (Mainz, enlarged), 1608 (Lyons), 1612 (Lyons and Mainz), 1617 (Mainz), 1624 (Mainz), 1633 (Cologne), 1657 (Cologne), 1679 (Cologne), and 1746 (Venice). Other editions include 1604 (Lyons), 1606 (Mainz). Burr, "Literature of Witchcraft," p. 60, n. 7, rpt. Bainton and Gibbons, *Burr*, p. 184, n. 81, says Grässe's citation of an edition of 1593 is a "myth." Burr refers to having seen a draft dated 1596, entitled "De superstitione et malis artibus." Burr gives the last ed. as 1747 (Venice), but Hodder gives the last ed. as 1749. There is a French translation by André Duschesne, *Les Controverses et recherches magiques* (1611), and a modern Italian translation by J. K. Huysmans, *Le Disquisizione magiche* (rpt. Naples, 1960). A useful bibliography appears in Robert Schwickerath, "The Attitude of the Jesuits in Trials for Witchcraft," *American Catholic Quarterly Review*, 27 (July, 1902), 490-516.

162. Briefly noted in Lea, *Materials*, II. 489-490, 918-919. See Robbins, *Encyclopedia*, pp. 236-237.

163. Lea, *Materials*, II. 489. Lea comments (II. 490): "The whole book is a prodigious collection of marvels, drawn from all sources, showing to what incredible lengths human credulity can extend."

164. Robbins, *Encyclopedia*, pp. 123-126.

165. Lea, *Materials*, I. xiii.

166. Lavater abstracted in Lea, *Materials*, II. 547-553. "The numerous editions show that it must have exercised a wide and lasting influence. Lavater was a Protestant pastor in Zurich" (II. 547). In some areas a skeptic, Lavater dismissed ghosts but replaced them with devils. The work was first published in German (Zurich, 1569; later eds., 1578, 1670), and translated by Lavater into Latin in 1570 (Zurich), with later editions in 1575 (Geneva), 1580 (Geneva), 1659 (Leiden), 1670 (Geneva), 1687 (Leiden), 1683 (Gorinchen), 1683 (Wittenberg), and one other (n.p., n.d.). English translation, 1572, 1590, and a modern edition by J. Dover Wilson (Oxford, 1929); Dutch translation, 1681; French translation, 1571 (Paris), 1571 (Geneva), 1581 (Zurich). See Lea, *Materials*, II. 547. The Witchcraft Collection has seven editions.

167. Daneau noted in Lea, *Materials*, II. 545-547. Also 1579 (Geneva); translations into Latin, *De veneficis*, 1574 ([Geneva]), 1575 (Cologne); into German, 1576 (Cologne). Lea, *Materials*, II. 545, says "first edition is in French, Geneva, 1564"—the date looks like a printing error. Daneau was a Calvinist.

168. Nodé noted in Lea, *Materials*, II. 553-554.

169. Anania noted in Lea, *Materials*, II. 463-465. Anania is included in the omnibus editions of the *Malleus maleficarum* of 1620 and of 1669. Editions not at Cornell: 1582 (Venice), 1620 (Lyons), 1651 (Rome).

170. Of Le Loyer the Witchcraft Collection has the first edition, and the revised editions (1605 and 1608, Paris), and the English translation (1605).

171. Of Crespet the Witchcraft Collection has two copies.

172. Thyraeus' *De daemoniacis* (Cologne, 1594) was expanded and retitled *Daemoniaci: de obsessis et spiritibus daemoniorvm hominibvs* (Cologne, 1598; Lyons, 1603; Cologne, 1604; Cologne, 1627). Lea, *Materials*, II. 624-627, briefly summarizes *De spirituum apparitionibus* (Cologne, 1594); the Witchcraft Collection has two copies of this work (Cologne, 1594) entitled *De variis tam spiritvvm*, and of its expanded revision, *De apparitionibvs spirituum tractatus duo* (Cologne, 1600). The Witchcraft Collection has several copies of the *Loca infesta* (Cologne, 1598, two copies; Lyons, 1599; Cologne, 1604; Cologne, 1627). Brief note on Thyraeus appears in Robbins, *Encyclopedia*, p. 498. Peter's elder brother

Notes

Hermann was also a distinguished Jesuit professor.

173. Grosse abstracted in Lea, *Materials*, II. 627-640. The Witchcraft Collection has the 1656 Leiden edition. Of one story, Lea comments (II. 639): "This is one of the most extraordinary jumbles of superstition that I have met."

174. Jacques d'Autun is noted (from Hauber, *Bibliotheca magica*) by Lea, *Materials*, II. 748. It is a very late defense of witchcraft and replies to Gabriel Naudé, *Apologie pour les grands hommes soupconnez de magie* (Paris, 1625). The Witchcraft Collection has the edition of 1679 (Lyons); it comprises 1172 pages (first ed. 1671; second, 1674).

175. Daneau trans. by Thomas Twyne, *A Dialogue of Witches* (1575); Viret by T. Stocker, *The World Possessed with Devils* (1583); Le Loyer by Zachary Jones, *A Treatise of Specters* (1605); Michaelis by W. B., *The Admirable History of the Possession and Conversion of a Penitent Woman* (1613); Naudé by J. Davies, *The History of Magic by Way of Apology for All the Wise Men Who Have Unjustly Been Reputed Magicians* (1657); Perrault by Peter du Moulin, *The Devill of Mascon* (1658).

176. *De la Démonialité et des animaux incubes et succubes*, trans. Isidore Liseux (Paris, 1876); *Demoniality: or Incubi and Succubi*, with the Latin text (Paris, 1879); *Demoniality*, trans. Montague Summers (London: Fortune Press [1927]).

177. Bartholomäus Anhorn, *Magiologia: Christliche Warnung für den Aberglauben und Zauberey* (Basel, 1674), noted in Lea, *Materials*, II. 747. Adam von Levenwald, *Tractätel von des Teufels List und Betrug* (Salzburg, 1680), noted in Lea, *Materials*, II. 748.

178. Meder noted in Lea, *Materials*, II. 647.

179. Filesac noted in Lea, *Materials*, II. 647 (later ed. Frankfurt, 1670).

180. Nicolai noted in Lea, *Materials*, II. 743.

181. Stridtbeckh abstracted in Lea, *Materials*, II. 749-754, from the German translation of Frankfurt, 1723, under the name of Valentin Albrecht.

182. Some demonologists distinguished the devil's mark—a birthmark, supposedly a sort of branding to indicate allegiance to the devil—and the witch's mark—any little protuberance on the body on which the witch's "familiar" demons could suck. See Robbins, *Encyclopedia*, pp. 551-553. Witch's mark is used here to indicate the scar or birthmark allegedly insensitive to pricking. See further, *Encyclopedia*, pp. 399-401.

183. Sinistrari, *De daemonialitate* (par. 23), trans. Summers, pp. 10-11: "That mark, moreover, is not always of the same shape or figure: sometimes it is the likeness of a hare, sometimes a toad's foot, sometimes a spider, a puppy, a dormouse. It is imprinted on the most hidden parts of the body; with men, under the eye-lids, or it may be under the armpits, or on the lips, on the shoulder, the fundament, or somewhere else; with women, it is usually on the breasts or the privy parts." Latin also in Summers, *History of Witchcraft*, p. 71. Sinistrari briefly abstracted in Lea, *Materials*, II. 919-922. "The *De Daemonialitate* is almost certainly a body of paragraphs cut by an ecclesiastical censor from an unfinished draft of Sinistrari's treatise on crimes and penalties" (Lea, II. 919).

184. *Compendium maleficarum* (1608), bk. I, vi, p. 17.

185. *Discours des sorciers*, trans. Ashwin, *Examen of Witches*, pp. 128-129: "For all witches have a mark on the shoulder, some on the eyelid, some on the tongue or lip, and others on the shameful parts.... Now the mark of a witch is generally some sort of blemish or hare's foot, or some such thing."

186. *Disquisitionum magicarum* (1599), I, pt. V, iv. 2, trans. Summers, *History of Witchcraft*, p. 71: The shape of the mark varies: sometimes it is like "the slot of a hare, the foot of a frog, a spider, a deformed whelp, or a mouse. In men it may often be seen under the eyelids, under the lips, on the shoulders, on the fundament; in women, moreover, on the breast or on the pudenda."

187. *Commentarius ... de maleficis* (Cologne, 1623), p. 607, listing twenty *indicia* of witchcraft, no. 14. But Binsfeld tends to dismiss this indication. See Lea, *Materials*, II. 599-600.

188. *Demonomanie* (1580), p. 193: "Mais ie suis bien de l'aduis de Dagneau, qui dict que les grands Sorciers ne sont point marqués, ou bien en lieu si secret, qu'il est quasi impossible de les descouurir. Car i'ay sceu d'vn Gen-

til-homme de Vallois, qu'il y en a de marques par le Diable soubz la paupiere de l'oeil, soubz la leure, et mesmes au fondement. Mais Trois-eschelles disoit, que ceux qui estoient marqués auoyent comme vne piste, ou pied de lieure, et que l'endroict estoit insensible, encores qu'on y mist vne aiguille iusques aux os. Ce seroit bien vne presomption tres-violente, et suffizante auecques d'autres indices, pour proceder à la condamnation."

Other descriptions of the witch's mark like a hare's foot occur in Oldekop, *Observationes criminales practicae* (1640), tit. 4, obs. 15, f. 6; and Brandt, *Disputatio de legitima maleficos et sagas investigandi* (1662), pars 1, thesis 1, n. 23 (Lea, *Materials*, II. 867). Elsewhere, Lea, *Materials*, II. 896, quotes from Nehing, *De iudiciis* (Jena, 1714), similarly. See notes 251, 252.

189. Abstracted in Lea, *Materials*, II. 889-892.

190. Ostermann was refuted by Johannes Jordanaeus, whose *Disputatio de proba stigmatica* (see n. 362), Burr says (Lea, *Materials*, II. 892), is at Cornell, but I have not seen it.

191. *Discours des sorciers*, trans. Ashwin, *Examen of Witches*, p. 34: "For we know that he [the devil] has at different times assumed the shape of a dog for the same purpose, and we have two remarkable examples of this: one of a dog, said to be a demon, which used to lift up the robes of the nuns in a convent in the diocese of Cologne in order to abuse them; the other, of certain dogs found on the beds of the nuns of a convent on Mount Hesse in Germany."

192. *Demonomanie* (1580), pp. 162-162 verso: "Il se peut bien faire aussi que Sathan soit enuoyé de Dieu, comme il est certain que toute punition vient de luy par ses moyens ordinaires, ou sans moyen, pour vanger vne telle vilanie: comme il aduint au Monastere du Mont de Hesse en Allemaigne, que les Religieuses furent demoniaques: et voyoit on sur leurs licts des chiens, qui attentoyent impudiquement celles qui estoient suspects d'en auoir abuzé, et commis le peché, qu'ils appellent le peché muet." In *De magorum daemonomania* (1579), p. 309.

193. *De praestigiis* (1568), IV, cap. 10. So Lea, *Materials*, II. 510: "The nuns of Hessimons (Nimeguen) tormented by demons, one of whom in shape of a dog leaped into the bed of a nun 'in quam muti peccati, quod vocant, cadebat suspicio.' So, in a prominent nunnery of Cologne, a demon in shape of a dog ran and got under the clothing of nuns when movements of the garments gave indications 'spuriae velitationis.' " Nuns were supposedly especially prone to this type of temptation; see E. Murisier, *Les Maladies du sentiment religieux* (Paris, 1901), p. 49.

194. *Tableau de l'inconstance des mauvais anges* (1612), p. 120: Remi, *Daemonolatreia*, II. 9; Del Rio, *Disquisitiones*, III. 9, 5; Bodin, *Demonomanie* (1580), III. 2; Del Rio, *Disquisitionum*, VI. 2, sect. 3, q. 3; Boguet, *Discours*, cap. 50; *Malleus maleficarum*, passim.

195. Russell, *Witchcraft in the Middle Ages*, p. 24: "The sabbat appears in medieval witchcraft only at the end of the fifteenth century; the coven and the black mass simply did not exist and are in no way a part of medieval witchcraft." For early developments see writers cited by Lea, *Materials*, I. 170-198; Russell (s.v. Demons, worship of; Devils, worship of; Flight; Kiss; Orgies; Pact; Ride; Sabbat; Sexual intercourse); Richard Kieckhefer, *European Witch Trials*, esp. "Calendar of Witch Trials," pp. 106-147. Walter Mapes, about 1182, was probably the first to describe a proto-sabbat as a "synagogue"; see Wakefield and Evans, *Heresies of the High Middle Ages*, p. 254. The evidence for "sabbat" in the 1335 trials must now be dismissed as forgery; see references in note 90. Other trials described only in Lamothe-Langnon should similarly be discarded. In the *Encyclopedia* (p. 415) I suggested the first use of the word "apparently by Inquisitor Jacquier about 1458." It also appears in 1460 (*La Vauderye de Lyonois*). Russell cites "sabbat" in trials in 1470 at Dijon and in 1475 at Bressuire. Martin le France, *Champion des dames* (ca. 1440) contains the first illustration of witches flying on broomsticks, and the anonymous French tract, *Errores Gazariorum* (ca. 1450) has further account of "synagogue." See Hansen, *Quellen*, pp. 99-104, briefly noted by Lea, *Materials*, I. 177; illustration in Robbins, *Encyclopedia*, p. 30.

196. Robbins, *Encyclopedia*, pp. 414-424.

197. Lea, *Materials*, II. 916.

198. Quoted in Lea, *Materials*, I. 276.

199. Quoted in Lea, *Materials*, I. 405.

200. See Robbins, *Encyclopedia*, p. 465. Accounts of the sabbat in *Encyclopedia*, pp. 254-259, 461-468, 490-492.

201. *Discours des sorciers,* trans. Ashwin, *Examen of Witches,* p. 31. So L'Ancre, *Tableau* (1612), III. 5, par. 8 (p. 225), confessed by fifteen-year-old Marie de Marigrane: "Qu'il les fait crier comme des femmes qui sont en mal d'enfant."

202. *Daemonolatreia,* I. 6, trans. Ashwin, *Demonolatry,* p. 14: "Claudia Fellaea expertam esse se saepius instar fusi in tantam vastitatem turgentis ut sine magno dolore contineri a quantumvis capace muliere non posset."

203. *Tableau* (1612), II. 4, par. 6 (p. 134): "Pour l'accouplement, qu'elle a veu tout le monde se mesler incestueusement et contre tout ordre de nature, comme nous auons dict cy deuant, s'accusant elle mesme d'auoir esté depucellee par Satan et cognue vne infinité de fois par vn sien parent et autres qui l'en daignoient semondre: qu'elle fuyoit l'accouplement du Diable, à cause qu'ayant son membre faict en escailles il fait souffrir vne extreme douleur; outre que sa semence est extremement froide." Later she added (III. 5, par. 8, pp. 223-224): "Dict d'auantage que lors que le Diable les cognoist charnellement elles souffrent vne extresme douleur, les ayant ouyes crier, et au sortir de l'acte, les ayant veues reuenir au sabbat toutes sanglantes, se plaignant de douleur, laquelle vient de ce que le membre du Demon estant faict à escailles comme vn poisson, elles se referrent en entrant, et se leuent et piquent en sortant: c'est pourquoy elles fuyent semblables rencontres."

204. E.g., p. 94.

205. From the English translation, *The Admirable History of the Possession of a Penitent Woman* (1613), p. 333.

206. Bodin, *Demonomanie* (1580), pp. 104 verso-105: "Marguerite Bremont femme de Nouël Laueret a dict que Lundy dernier, aprez iour failly, elle fut auec Marion sa mere à vne assemblee, prez le moulin Franquis de Longny en vn pré, et auoit sa dite mere vn ramon entre ses iambes disant, Ie ne mettray point les mots, et soudain elles furent transportees toutes deux audict lieu, ou elles trouuerent Ian Robert, Ianne Guillemin, Marie femme de Symon d'Agneau, et Guillemette femme d'vn nommé le Gras, qui auoyent chacun vn Ramon: Se trouuerent aussi en ce lieu six Diables, qui estoyent en forme humaine, mais fort hideux à voir etc. apres la danse finie les Diables se coucherent auecques elles, et eurent leur compagnie; et l'vn d'eux qui l'auoit menee danser la print, et la baisa par deux fois, et habita auecques elle l'espace de plus de demye heure: mais delaissa aller la semence bien fort froide. Ienne Guillemin se rapporte aussi au dire celle-cy, et dict qu'ilz furent bien demye heure ensemble, et qu'il lacha de la semence bien fort froide." The Latin text has this passage at p. 201.

207. Lea, *Materials,* III. 1185, abstracting Diefenbach, *Der Hexenwahn,* p. 123. Also (fuller) in Robbins, *Encyclopedia,* p. 462. In addition to Sinistrari, special attention is given to the sexual activities of the sabbat by Gottfried Voigt, *De conventu sagarum ad sua sabbata* (Wittenberg, 1667); Johannes Henricus Pott, *Specimen juridicum de nefando lamiarum cum diabolo coitu* (Jena, 1689), abstracted by Lea, *Materials,* II. 922-929; Johann Klein, *Examen juridicum judicialis lamiarum confessionis se ex nefando cum Satana coitu prolem suscipisse humanum* (Rostock, 1698), abstracted in Lea, *Materials,* II. 929-933. Also important for the sabbat is Jean le Normant, *Histoire veritable et memorable de ce qvi c'est passé sovs l'exorcisme de trois filles... en la descouuerte et confession de Marie de Sains* (Paris, 1623); Johannes Andreas Rinneberg, *Commentation de pactis hominum cum diabolo* (1716), new ed., Leipzig, 1741. Secondary material includes Hans Freimark, *Okkultismus u. Sexualität* (Leipzig, n.d.); Théophile Louise, *De la Sorcellerie et de la justice criminelle à Valenciennes* (Valenciennes, 1861); Jules Delassus, *Les Incubes et les succubes* (Paris, 1897), somewhat credulous and lacking documentation; Désiré Magloire Bourneville and E. Tenturier, *Le Sabbat des sorciers* (Paris, 1882); Jules Baissac, *Les Grands Jours de la sorcellerie* (Paris, 1890), pp. 94-125; Dr. Cabanès, *Moeurs intimes du passé; le sabbat* (Paris, 1931); Jean Vartier, *Sabbat, juges et sorciers, quatre siècles de superstitions dans la France de l'Est* (Paris, 1968).

208. Bodin, *Demonomanie* (1580), esp. pp. 165-180 verso (methods of entrapment), 187-194 verso ("presomptions qui peuvent seruir à la preuue et punition des Sorciers").

209. Bodin, *Demonomanie* (1580), p. 176 verso: normally "vn bon tesmoing sans reproche" or "homme de bien et sans reproche," but in witchcraft, evidence admissable from "les personnes infames de faict et de droict en tesmoignage contre les Sorciers."

210. Boguet, *Discours,* "Instruction pour vn Iuge en faict de Sorcelerie" (at end, pp. 1-32, separate pagination); trans. *Examen,* pp. 212-

238. *Examen*, p. 217 (art. xvi), *Discours*, art. xxiii: "Si le Iuge ne peut rien tirer de l'accusé, il le doit faire referrer en vne prison fort obscure et estroicte, parce que lon a experimenté que la rigeur de la prison constraint le plus souuent les Sorciers de venir à confession, et lors principalement qu'ils sont ieunes gens."

211. Boguet, *Discours*, art. xxix: "Le Iuge doit euiter la torture autant qu'il luy est possible."

212. Boguet, *Examen*, p. 221 (art. xxviii); *Discours*, art. xxxv: "Secondement la confession d'vn Sorcier est vn indice suffisant pour paruenir à la torture contre son complice, si elle est assistée de quelque autre presomption et indice."

213. Boguet, *Examen*, p. 221 (art. xxx); *Discours*, art. xxxvii: "En quatriesme lieu les menaces precedentes, suiuies de l'effect, sont suffisantes pour faire que l'on passe à la torture."

214. Boguet, *Examen*, p. 225 (art. xliv); *Discours*, art. lvii: "Que s'il se retracte il le faut de nouueau applicquer à la torture, ce que le Iuge peut faire iusques à trois fois, et non plus." So Carpzov; see note 232.

215. Remi, for example, who inevitably condoned torture in Lorraine, agrees on its desirability; nevertheless he does not overemphasize its importance, and seems more concerned with preventing witches from opposing their cunning to that of the executioner (*Demonolatry*, trans. Ashwin, p. 168).

In assembling the Witchcraft Collection in one location, the Cornell cataloguers for rare books had the problem of excluding or including legal works which dealt with witchcraft only secondarily. Consequently, a number of books not in the Witchcraft Collection but housed in the Department of Rare Books are significant for the conduct of the trials, for example: Tranquillo Ambrosino, *Processus informativus sive de modo formandi* (1614); *De malefico convicto* (1732); *Josephi Hals-Gerichts-Ordnung*; and *Bambergische Halsgerichts Ordnung*.

216. Probably the best-informed account of Binsfeld is the unpublished dissertation of Mabel Elisabeth Hodder (Ithaca, 1911), "Peter Binsfeld and Cornelius Loos," pp. 1-41. Lea gives extended abstracts of the *Tractatus* in *Materials*, II. 576-590, as well as of the *Commentarius* (*Materials*, II. 590-600), which was first added to the 1491 Trier edition, and retained in all the following revised editions. Robbins, *Encyclopedia*, pp. 49-50, has a brief note and reproduction of the title page of the first (1591) German translation.

217. In one copy of the first edition, A. D. White has written: "This is the book written by Binsfeld, and which brought such terrible suffering to Flade and torture and death to Loos." Actually, the first edition was written with the trial of Flade in mind, and the second edition extended to include a similar refutation against Loos. Binsfeld also introduced an attack on Wier (*Tractatus*, 1591, p. 23). In the fuller editions, several *indicia* indirectly point to Flade, e.g., (6) irreprehensible exterior, (7) flight before legal action commenced, (10) no denial of rumors. The 1625 edition has a note by Burr: "This was, I think, the last impression of Binsfeld's work. It is merely a reprint of the 4th ed.—that of 1596—the last edited by Binsfeld himself." The Witchcraft Collection also possesses both editions of the German translation, 1590 (Trier) and 1591 (Munich): *Tractat von Bekanntnuss der Zauberer vnd Hexen*. Binsfeld was conscious of the continuing antipathy against belief in witchcraft contained in the Canon Episcopi: "Ex dicti praeludio infero haereticum esse, et a fide Christiana alienum, qui cum pertinacia asserit maleficia nihil aliud esse, quam somnia et imaginatione" (*Tractatus*, p. 3; Lea, *Materials*, II. 578).

218. See Robbins, *Encyclopedia*, pp. 494-496.

219. Lea, *Materials*, II. 594; *Commentarius* (1622), pp. 555-556. But Binsfeld opposed the slight mercy of prior strangulation before burning—*Tractatus* (1589), p. 169.

220. Lea, *Materials*, II. 599; Indicia 13 and 14, *Commentarius*, pp. 606, 607.

221. Lea, *Materials*, II. 577-578; *Tractatus*, Epistola Dedicatoria: "I have wished the principal scope of my treatise to be the question whether faith is to be put in the confessions of witches against their accomplices." See Hodder, "Binsfeld and Loos," p. 9.

222. Lea, *Materials*, II. 587; *Tractatus*, pp. 276, 277.

223. Lea, *Materials*, II. 595, 597, 598; *Tractatus*, pp. 559, 560, 571, 583. Damhouder had recommended enforced sleeplessness in *Rerum criminalis praxis*, cap. 37, noted in Lea,

Materials, II. 900. It was a method used by the infamous "Witch Finder General," Matthew Hopkins, in 1645 against Parson John Lowes (see Robbins, *Encyclopedia*, p. 251).

224. Lea, *Materials*, II. 585; *Tractatus*, p. 249.

225. Lea, *Materials*, II. 578; *Tractatus*, Epistola dedicatoria.

226. Lea, *Materials*, II. 586; *Tractatus*, pp. 354-355.

227. Neither book noted by Lea. There is a third edition (Würzburg, 1627) of Agricola, in the Cornell Department of Rare Books. The significance of these two books lies in their being written in German.

228. First ed., Wittenberg, 1635. Abstracted at length (from the 1670 Wittenberg ed.) in Lea, *Materials*, II. 813-850. Brief article in Robbins, *Encyclopedia*, pp. 78-79. In this Catalogue there is only one secondary reference to Carpzov: Nicolaus Paulus, "Der sächsische Kriminalist Carpzov und seine 20,000 Todesurteile," an offprint. Other standard references include Malblanc, *Geschichte der peinlichen Halsgerichtsordnung Kaiser Karls V* (Nuremberg, 1783); R. von Strinzing, *Geschichte der deutschen Rechtswissenschaft* (Munich, 1884); Johann Diefenbach, *Wetzer und Welte*, 5 (1898-1899); Nicolaus Paulus, *Hexenwahn und Hexenprozess* (Freiburg, 1910).

229. Melchior Goldast, whose *Rechtliches Bedencken* was probably written about 1630 (printed Bremen, 1661, p. 82), explains how the Carolina Code was superseded by stricter Saxon laws introduced by the Elector Augustus, who "decreed that sorcerers and witches who renounce God and bind themselves to the devil are to be burnt whether they have wrought injuries or not" (Lea, *Materials*, II. 805). For the Carolina Code see the edition by J. Kohler and Willy Schiel, *Die peinliche Gerichtsordnung Kaiser Karls V: Constitutio criminalis Carolina 1532* (Halle, 1900). See also note 242.

230. Lea, *Materials*, II. 815, 816, 817, 819, 825, 828.

231. These extracts in Lea, *Materials*, II; pages in *Practica*, 1670, in parentheses, as follows: 816 and 818 (73 and 99), 819 (126), 823 (156), 829 (227), 845 (324).

232. Lea, *Materials*, II. 829.

233. Soldan-Heppe, rev. Bauer, *Hexenprozesse*, II. 120: "eines immer bluttriefender als das andere."

234. First mentioned by his admirer, Andreas Oldenburger, *Thesaurus rerum publicum* (Geneva, 1675), IV. 824, quoted in Soldan-Heppe, rev. Bauer, *Hexenprozesse*, II. 212.

235. *De magis* abstracted in Lea, *Materials*, II. 761-786. Brief note in Robbins, *Encyclopedia*, pp. 226-227.

236. And therefore should be pardoned. Lea, *Materials*, II. 771; *De magis*, II. 2, nn. 14-21. Others were making the same point, e.g., *Malleus judicum*, (ca. 1626)—Lea, *Materials*, II. 690.

237. Lea, *Materials*, II. 766; *De magis*, I. 6, nn. 1-28.

238. Lea, *Materials*, II. 788, neatly summarizes Godelmann's ineffectiveness: "All very well and very humane, but to what does it amount? How many were there of those who confessed to his impossibilities—that is to the Sabbat—who were not also compelled under torture to confess to some injury inflicted on person or property? Even had he succeeded in obtaining the adoption of his views, the saving of life would have been imperceptible. Still it was something in those days, however illogical the attempt, to deny the higher absurdities of the current delusions, and it required some independence to proclaim his disbelief, but of course his influence was trivial. He admitted too much and his opponents could reasonably ask what reason he could allege for drawing the line where he did between the possible and the impossible."

239. Lea, *Materials*, II. 771; *De magis*, II. 2, nn. 14-21.

240. Lea, *Materials*, II. 775; *De magis*, III. 1, n. 19.

241. A very late Latin edition (Nuremberg, 1676) is not in the Witchcraft Collection, but is to be found in the German Baroque Collection at Yale (No. 1248).

242. Binsfeld, *Tractatus* (1623), p. 231; Lea, *Materials*, II. 584. Godelmann, *De magis*, III. 10, nn. 9-26, Lea, *Materials*, II. 784-785. Goldast, *Rechtliches Bedencken*, p. 82, con-

demned the Carolina Code as too lenient; Lea, *Materials*, II. 805. See also note 229.

243. The rule was circumvented by a specious word play: torture could not be renewed for the same *indicium*, but it could be continued.

244. Zanger. A Protestant law professor at Wittenberg; work written in 1591. Abstracted from later edition (Frankfurt, 1730) in Lea, *Materials*, II. 788-793. Not in the Witchcraft Collection, but in Cornell Rare Books (Frankfurt, 1617, and Wittenberg, 1694).

245. Dassell. First edition (Hamburg, 1597); abstracted from later edition (Frankfurt on Oder, 1698) in Lea, *Materials*, II. 793-799.

246. Cothmann. Available in Hauber, *Bibliotheca magica*, II. 217-255; Lea, *Materials*, II. 799-804. Cothmann was a law professor at Rostock, and died in 1624.

247. Meder. First edition (Leipzig, 1605); second edition (Leipzig, 1615). Brief note from Diefenbach in Lea, *Materials*, II. 647.

248. Goldast. First edition (Bremen, 1661); written in 1629 and published posthumously; Lea, *Materials*, II. 804-811.

249. Goehausen. Goehausen's work is based on a text with the same title published in 1629, falsely ascribed to Paul Laymann (see n. 365). Burr, however (in Lea, *Materials*, II. 811) relying on Duhr (*Materials*, II. 688), ascribes this 1629 *Processus juridicus* to Johannes Jordanaeus (see n. 362), with perhaps Goehausen having a hand in it. Goehausen's work is relatively mild and favors Tanner (see n. 363), and Goehausen is clearly worried; but on the whole, and even as a professor at Rinteln adjudicating trials, he accepts the necessity of burning witches. Lea, *Materials*, II. 811-813.

250. Hildebrand. Written in German, a handbook for judges with emphasis on the pact, illustrated by excerpts from authorities.

251. Oldekop. Original (briefer) version, *Cautelarum criminalium* (Brunswick, 1633) in Witchcraft Collection; expanded version, ca. 1640 (Bremen, 1654). Lea, *Materials*, II. 850-864, from Frankfurt on Oder (1698) edition.

252. Brandt. Lea, *Materials*, II. 864-881.

253. Oldekop, *Observationes*; Lea, *Materials*, II. 855-857. Oldekop was not the only one to suspect trickery. Friedrich von Spee, the great opponent of the delusion, in his *Cautio criminalis*, a few years earlier in 1631, had written (Dubium 43): "More than all, the torturer should be closely watched to see that no fraud is performed, for many are vile and seek their pay, as one recently only pretended to prick and then cried out that he had found the mark; nor should he be allowed to use cheating pricks, whether magic and charmed, or so made that at pleasure they enter and wound or only seem to do so by sliding back into themselves" (Lea, *Materials*, II. 718). For "magic bodkin" see Pamela Reilly, "Friedrich von Spee's Belief in Witchcraft," *Modern Language Review*, 54 (1959), 54-55. For an illustration of false bodkins used by jugglers see Scot, *Discoverie of Witchcraft*, ed. Summers, p. 201. For pricking see Robbins, *Encyclopedia*, pp. 399-401.

254. Oldekop, *Observationes*; Lea, *Materials*, II. 850-851.

255. Godelmann, *De magis*, III. 9, n. 54; Lea, *Materials*, II. 786.

256. Elliott P. Currie, "Crimes without Criminals," *Law and Society*, 3 (1968-1969), 15, n. 35, refers to a contemporary view quoted by Adhémar Esmein, *A History of Continental Criminal Procedure* (Boston: Little, Brown, 1913), p. 130: "If by torture he will say nothing nor confess, and is not convicted by witnesses ... he should be released at the discretion of the judge on pain of being attainted and convicted of the matters with which he is charged and of which he is presumed guilty ... for if he be freed absolutely, *it would seem that he had been held prisoner without charge.*"

257. Oldekop, *Observationes*; Lea, *Materials*, II. 854: "Those who think it a disgrace if any prisoner escapes, when they cannot get *indicia* sufficient, keep them in squalid dungeons, perishing with hunger and cold until in desperation they confess." Lea himself emphasized this danger in his summary of the section on torture, *Materials*, II. 901-902: "All doubts were resolved by resort to torture, both of the accused and of witnesses. It is true that careful and minute prescriptions were current as to what justified torture, but in discussing them the conclusion is reached that in the end everything is left to the discretion of the judge. It is the same with the severity, duration and repetition of torture. It is described as almost equivalent to death and worse than the amputation of both hands, but there was prac-

tically no limit to its severity except that if it killed the accused the judge was subject to investigation. Theoretically it was admitted that a confession extorted by illegal torture did not condemn the accused, but in practice this was illusory, for to admit it condemned the judge, and there was no one to pronounce it illegal."

258. Leitschuh, *Beiträge zur Geschichte des Hexenwesens in Franken*, p. 51; App., pp. i-viii. Translated by Burr, *Witch Persecutions*, p. 27; Robbins, *Encyclopedia*, pp. 292-293; and cf. pp. 35-37, 222, 289-293, 555-557; abstracted by Lea, *Materials*, III. 1175. Facsimile of letter (now in Staatliche Bibliothek Bamberg RB misc. 134, no. 30) in Soldan-Heppe, rev. Bauer, *Hexenprozesse*, II, between pp. 6 and 7; rpt. Robbins, *Encyclopedia*, p. 291. For documentation and revised translation see Robbins, "Yellow Cross and Green Fagot," *Cornell Library Journal*, no. 10 (Winter, 1970). p. 32, n. 13.

259. Dassell, *Responsum juris*, n. 63; Lea, *Materials*, II. 797.

260. Godelmann, *De magis*, III. 8, n. 34; Lea, *Materials*, II. 781. Brandt, *Disputatio*; Lea, *Materials*, II. 869, 870, 878.

261. Goldast, *Rechtliches Bedencken*, pp. 105-106; Lea, *Materials*, II. 806. Similarly Oldekop, *Observationes*; Lea, *Materials*, II. 856: "He says he has very often seen examinations committed to inexperienced and ignorant scriveners and others, who can scarce abstain from suggestions, which is forbidden by Carolina [Code]." Similarly Brandt; Lea, *Materials*, II. 869: "The judge must strictly abstain from suggesting circumstances in his interrogatories, as provided in Carolina, c. 56, as the accused may be led to assent to them." Brandt, himself a believer in witchcraft, succinctly describes the typical routine of a trial for witchcraft, including the leading questions, in a late dissertation, *Disputatio de legitimata maleficos et sagas investigandi et convincendi ratione* (1622). It is significant because it is so dependent on authorities, and thereby indicates the traditional methods employed in trials for witchcraft (Lea, *Materials*, II. 868-869):

"To conduct properly the examination articles of interrogation should be drawn up, which should be interrogative and not, as some notaries do, be assertive of guilt. In most courts this is presented by the fiscal, who appears as the accuser, and he gives a long and detailed formula for it. This commences by the fiscal demanding that the accused answer each article with her own mouth and without a defender and, if necessary to extort the truth, that she be subjected to torture. The articles follow, commencing with pact, then that her mother and kindred were suspect of witchcraft, then that she was herself suspect, then that she had uttered threats in quarrel which were effective; that she consorted with suspicious persons or with so and so who was burnt and she had pots with toads; that three accomplices, N, N, and N, had testified and ratified to having seen her on the Blocksberg with her incubus named N, where they passed the night in the Zauber-Tantz; that she had boasted to N and N that the incubus had marked her under the hair of the back of the head, in virtue of which she could not under torture be forced to weep or to confess; that when her neighbor's daughter N was married, during the ceremony she had knotted a leather string, so that the husband was rendered impotent for six months until she untied it; that recently when the gaoler brought her food she said she would be burnt and so would other witches whom she could name, for the most certain proof of witchcraft according to Bodin is when one condemns herself before she is accused. The fiscal concludes by petitioning that the accused be declared to have committed great offenses against spiritual and secular law and to have thereby incurred vehement suspicion and, if not to be severely punished in body and life, at least to be sharply tortured to extort the truth, and then to be condemned."

262. Robbins, *Encyclopedia*, pp. 58-59.

263. Bouvet, *Manières*, p. 196: "vn volume ne suffiroit pas pour les rapporter."

264. Bouvet, *Manières*, pp. 164-166: "De la maniere avec laquelle le bon Iuge doit proceder à la question, et ce qu'il doit dire et obseruer pendant icelle.... Il le fera depouiller, lier, et appliquer à la question, et la fera continuer sans aucune émotion, auec un Iugement tranquille, iusques à ce qu'il conoisse que le questionné n'en puisse souffrir d'auantage, le Iuge prendra garde en cette occasion de ne point proceder legerement, ou trop seuerement, qu'il port tousiours la misericorde et la moderation, qu'il ait égard à la vieillesse extréme, ou trop basse ieunesse de l'accusé, la bonne ou la mauuaise disposition, et ce que les forces peuuent porter, il ne doit s'arrester aux cris et exclamations, qu'il fera pendant la question, afin que vsant de trop de commiseration, il laissast échapper le moyen de découurir la verité, aussi il ne suiura pas les

regles de son imagination, mais celles des Lois, et des Canons, il ne doit non plus exercier de tirannie, seulement ce que la Iustice desire."

265. Since Bouvet is so rare, a few more excerpts may prove useful. It was quite simple for this provost general to secure a confession from those who refused to answer questions: "Et quand l'accusé a subi la question pour sa desobeissance faite au Iuge de luy répondre, apres qu'il a obey, on peut de nouueau le faire reapliquer à la question pour le faire répondre sur le délit, particulierement quand il denie de l'auoir commis" (p. 92). And it was just as simple to get the names of the accomplices: if the accused was taciturn, the torture was heightened, and the judge went on questioning the witch: "parmi les cris qu'il poura faire ... on le peut encore interroger de ses companons et complices pour scauoir s'ils ont participé au délit" (p. 164). If an accused feigned illness, because of fear of the trial, then boiling water should be thrown under the armpits; the invalid, says Bouvet, will get back his vigor "en sorte que cela paroistra comme vn miracle" (p. 201). And Bouvet had a special dual-purpose treatment: "et quand ils ont la maladie venerienne, il faudra leur faire approcher le feu aux plantes des pieds qui leur causera vne sueur par tout le corps, en sorte que les eaux qui en couleront leur causera la guerison de leurs maux, tandis qu'ils seront constraints par la voye de ce tourment de dire la verité" (p. 202).

266. Burr's note in Lea, *Materials*, II. 727; Burr has brief note, pp. 726-727. Article in Robbins, *Encyclopedia*, pp. 451-452 (with portrait). Also discussed in Gibbons, "Rhenish Foes," passim. Noted by Hauber, *Bibliotheca magica*, III. 505-507. The dispute on witchcraft swayed back and forth: Binsfeld (1589) was answered by Loos (1592); Spee (1631) was answered by Schultheis (1634), who was answered by Löher (though his work was not printed until 1676); Spee (1631) was also answered by the fanatic witch hater, Heinrich Rimphof (1599-1655; Rinteln, 1647); who quotes Schultheis. Burr, in a note in Lea, *Materials*, II. 728, says Pastor Rimphof's *Drachen-König* is almost as rare as Schultheis. A copy is in the Witchcraft Collection.

267. Ostermann, *Commentarius juridicus ad L. Stigmata C. de Fabricansibus* (Cologne, 1629), is abstracted by Lea, *Materials*, II. 889-892. See note 190.

268. Schultheis, *Instrvction*, p. 10.

269. Burr's note in Lea, *Materials*, II. 727; chapter on torture in *Instrvction*, pp. 283-321.

270. Schultheis, *Instrvction*, p. 247, trans. Gibbons, "Rhenish Foes," p. 5.

271. Arthur Freeman, *Journal of American Folklore*, 73 (1960), 172-174. But the same conclusion was reached by Georgene Webber Davis, *The Inquisition at Albi 1299-1300* (New York: Columbia Univ. Press, 1948): "They [the inquisitors] seem interested, not in a careful sifting of all evidence, still less in the problems of Catharan dogma and religious speculation, but in the practical task of obtaining confession and abjuration as promptly as possible" (p. 36). Similarly Bernd Moeller, "Frömmigkeit in Deutschland um 1500," trans. *Pre-Reformation Germany*, ed. Gerald Strauss (New York: Harper & Row, 1972), p. 15: "heretical ideas no longer inflamed men's minds."

272. Robbins, *Encyclopedia*, pp. 310-312. This heart-rending document was first printed by F. de Chanteau, *Notes pour servir à l'histoire du chapitre de Saint-Dié: Les sorciers à Saint Dié et dans le val de Galilée* (Nancy, 1877), rpt. Docteur Cabanès, *Moeurs intimes du passé: Le sabbat a-t-il existé* (Paris, 1935), pp. 99-102. Looten died under torture ("suffocated by the devil himself"), was burned, and the remains exhibited for public spectacle on the wheel. The court of the nearby lordship of Cassel, hearing of the work of the torturer while at Bailleul, asked for and received the names of its six residents said by Looten to have been with him at the sabbat. The Looten trial record includes the costs.

273. Robbins, *Encyclopedia*, pp. 323-324. Verbatim transcripts of the secret evidence and ensuing trial in Francis Bavoux, *Hantises et diableries dans la terre abbatiale de Luxeuil d'un procès de l'inquisition (1529) à l'épidémie démoniaque de 1628-1630* (Monaco [1956], ltd. ed.).

274. Robbins, *Encyclopedia*, pp. 408-413, with reproductions of two manuscripts in the Witchcraft Collection. The literature of Sister Maria Renata is extensive; a short basic bibliography is given in *Encyclopedia*, s.v. Renata, p. 500. In the Witchcraft Collection the manuscripts and critiques are listed under Sänger; Burr has made a few annotations.

275. The controversy was set off by Father Georg Gaar and answered by Girolamo Tartar-

otti, and continued by their adherents. See Lea, *Materials*, III. 1453-1456. The minutes of the trial are printed in Johannes Scherr, *Hammerschläge und Historien* (Zurich, 1878), and in Anton Memminger, *Das verhexte Kloster* (Würzburg, 1904, rev. 1908). Extracts from the trial conveniently given in Soldan-Heppe, rev. Bauer, *Hexenprozesse*, II. 286-290.

276. "It mattered nothing whether [the accused witch] now confessed or not: she was tortured until she did" (Burr, "Loos Manuscript," Bainton and Gibbons, *Burr*, p. 149).

277. Lea, *Materials*, abstracts (often at length) accounts of trials given by nineteenth-century German (and French) historians, e.g., III. 1098-1112 (Mathias Perger), from Ignaz Zingerle, *Barbara Pachlerin und Mathias Perger* (Innsbruck, 1858); III. 1137-1140 (Ann Käserin), from Otto Snell, *Hexenprozesse und Geistesstörung* (Munich, 1891); III. 1143-1148 (Eva Vetter), from Frank Volk, *Hexen in der Landvogtei Ortenau und Reichsstadt Offenburg* (Lahr, 1882).

278. Robbins, *Encyclopedia*, pp. 303-305, which prints the three other smuggled letters, equally pathetic. Documentation in Jean Balthasar Guth, *Das Ries wie es war, und wie es ist. Eine historisch-statistische Zeitschrift*, VI (Nördlingen); Johann Friedrich Weng, *Die Hexen-Prozesse der ehemaligen Reichsstadt Nördlingen in den Jahren 1590-94* (Nördlingen, [1838]); also related in Jules Baissac, *Les Grands Jours de la sorcellerie* (Paris, 1890), p. 623.

279. Robbins, *Encyclopedia*, pp. 310-312. This trial, from a Flemish manuscript in his possession, was translated into French and printed by Cabanès, *Moeurs intimes*, pp. 103-125. See note 272.

280. Court report printed *in extenso* in Robbins, *Encyclopedia*, pp. 148-156, from which this account is taken. The scarce *Abdruck aktenmässiger Hexenprozesse* (Eichstatt, 1811) has been reprinted in Hugo Zwetsloot, *Friedrich Spee und die Hexenprozesse* (Trier, 1954). "For any reader who wants to understand what is witchcraft, this record gives a very clear introduction" (*Encyclopedia*, p. 149).

281. "Yellow Cross and Green Fagot," *Cornell Library Journal*, no. 10 (Winter, 1970), 3-33.

282. *Cornell Library Journal*, no. 10, pp. 8-13. Court records in Paul Thiacourt, *La Sorcellerie au Ban de Ramonchamp au xvie siècle* (Remirémont, 1908), pp. 11-39.

283. *Cornell Library Journal*, no. 10, pp. 12-13. Records in Théodore Delogne, *L'Ardenne meridonal belge... suivi du procès des sorciers de Sugny en 1637* (Brussels, 1914), pp. 225-250.

284. Described in my paper, "The Structure of the Witchcraft Trials," delivered at SUNY Binghamton, May 4, 1973; University of California, Riverside, February 13, 1974; and University of California, Davis, February 16, 1974. Publication delayed. Trial records in Reinhold Stade, *Barbara Elisabeth Schulzin: Ein Arnstädter Hexenprozess vom Jahre 1669* (Arnstadt, 1904), pp. 1-75.

285. The *draco volans* appears frequently; it looks like a folk belief incorporated into demonology. One of the earliest tracts is *De draconibus* ascribed to John of Damascus. See references in Lea, *Materials*, II, 896; III, 1411, 1425, 1428.

286. See note 261.

287. Burr, "Literature of Witchcraft," p. 51, n. 2, rpt. Bainton and Gibbons, *Burr*, p. 177, n. 27. Another great summation by Burr occurs in "Loos Manuscript," Bainton and Gibbons, *Burr*, pp. 151-152: "Perhaps you know something of the nature of those confessions. They are so much alike that one could half believe that the witch must have learned it by heart before coming to the torture—a unanimity which, however mysterious then has ceased to be so to us who know that the questions were prescribed beforehand and that the witch did little more than to answer yes or no. She confessed that she had met the Devil in person; that he had persuaded her to renounce her allegiance to God and his angels and to do homage to himself, whereupon he had scratched the chrism from her forehead and had given her his own private mark; she had then received from him a deadly ointment for her incantations, by the aid of which she worked all sorts of evil to her neighbors, their flocks and their fields; at stated intervals she had ridden through the air to take part in the horrid orgies of the witch-sabbats. And in all this she had had accomplices, whom she knew and must identify." See further, Robbins, *Encyclopedia*, pp. 100-109 (with reproductions of the trial manuscripts from the Witchcraft Collection).

288. Perhaps the most important manuscript

in the Witchcraft Collection is the "Minutes of the Trial for Witchcraft" of Dietrich Flade, a city judge and rector (in 1586) of the University of Trier. The manuscript was acquired by White in 1883. Burr wrote a meticulous study, "The Fate of Dietrich Flade," rpt. Bainton and Gibbons, *Burr*, pp. 190-233: "Though two centuries of witch-burning followed, Dietrich Flade remains today its most eminent victim in the land of its greatest thoroughness" (p. 190). See E. Zenz, "Dr. Dietrich Flade, ein Opfer des Hexenwahns," *Kurtrierisches Jahrbuch*, 2 (1962), 41-69. Name only in Lea, *Materials*, III. 1195. With the exception of the trials in the *Encyclopedia* and papers cited, and the summaries in Lea (see n. 277), there is no English literature on the trials. Scheduled for early publication is my *Witchcraft Trials in Western Europe 1390-1753*, thirty representative witch trials translated in full. George Lincoln Burr made a useful "List of Unpublished Witch-trials and Documents belonging to Witch-trials in the President White Library." A recent, very thorough study of the trials, is H. C. Erik Midelfort, *Witch Hunting in Southwestern Germany 1562-1684*.

289. I select the following examples (which go beyond the trials) at random: Peter Paul Beck, "Hexenprozesse aus dem Fränkischen," five offprints from *Württembergische Vierteljahrshefte für Landesgeschichte*, 6 and 7 (1883-1885); Edward Payson Evans, "Ein Trierer Hexenprozess," *Beilage zur Allgemeinen Zeitung*, (1892), no. 86, pp. 5-7; Herzog Johann Casimirs, "Gerichts-Ordnung die Hexerei betrf.... 1629," *Verein für Sachsen-Meiningische Geschichte und Landeskunde, Meiningen. Schriften*, 29 (1898), 99-122; Marcel Théaux, "Pages d'histoire judiciaire: Le crime de sorcellerie," *La Revue du palais*, 7 (1897), 103-135. A few offprints are not even yet identified: thus, [Louis Léon Théodore] Gosselin, "Les Petits Sorciers du xviie siècle et la torture avant l'exécution," appears on pages 80-104 of some unknown French periodical probably about 1865. It was acquired for the Witchcraft Collection on May 17, 1911. Another waif (J. Trefftz) has only recently been identified; see this Catalogue. To assemble a bibliography of these and similar articles today would in my opinion be impossible. And the completed assembly of diverse and ephemeral articles in one location is one of the great attractions of the Witchcraft Collection at Cornell.

290. Andreas Alciatus, *Parergon juris* (Basel, 1558), primarily a legal text, is in Cornell Rare Books. Cassini is entered in the Catalogue as Samuel, Cassinensis; see notes 105 and 106.

291. Robbins, *Encyclopedia*, pp. 538-540, with illustration of title page of the first edition of *De praestigiis daemonum*. The Catalogue prefers the spelling Wier, on which point see Carl Binz, "Wier oder Weyer, Nachträgliches über den ersten Bekämpfer des Hexenwahns in Deutschland," *Beiträge zur Geschichte des Niederrheins*, (1877) [p. 11]; also "Doctor Johann Weyer: Eine Nächlese," *Zeitschrift des Bergischen Geschichtvereins* (1887: offprint; Düsseldorf, 1889) [pp. 36]. Standard works and articles on Wier include: Alexandre Axenfeld, *Jean Wier et la sorcellerie* (Paris, 1866); Carl Binz, *Doctor Johann Weyer* (Bonn, 1885; Dusseldorf, 1889; rev. ed. Berlin, 1896, rpt. Wiesbaden, 1969); J. J. Cobben, *Johannes Wier* (Assen, 1960); Leonard Dooren, *Doctor Johannes Wier: Leven en Werken* (Aalten, 1940); Dr. H. Eschbach, "Dr. Med. Johannes Wier... Ein Beitrag zur Geschichte der Hexenprozesse," *Düsseldorfer Jahrbücher Beiträge zur Geschichte des Niederrheins*, 1 (1886), 57-174; Edward Theodore Withington, "Dr. John Weyer and the Witch Mania," in *Studies in the History and Method of Science*, ed. Charles Singer (Oxford: Clarendon Press, 1917-1921), [I], 189-224. Gregory Zilboorg, "Johann Weyer, the Founder of Modern Psychiatry," *The Medical Man and the Witch during the Renaissance* (Baltimore: Johns Hopkins Univ. Press, 1935), pp. 109-297.

Wier was opposed by Bodin who appended a "Réfutation des opinions de Jean Wier" to his *Demonomanie* (1593, pp. 522-604), and in his *Fleav des demons et sorciers* (1616, pp. 476-556).

I think it worth remarking that in a very popular work by Montague Summers, *A History of Witchcraft* (1926, and often rpt.), not one of the opponents noted here is even mentioned. It is inevitable that Summers' history is highly distorted. Burr reviewed this book, and three others by Summers, in *American Historical Review*, 34(1928-29), 321-325, rpt. Bainton and Gibbons, *Burr*, pp. 491-495. Having noted the "omissions and blunders" in his bibliographies, Burr concluded: "Real study he has given only to the demonologists, and his narrative is a tissue of their old-wives' tales" (p. 322, on *Geography of Witchcraft*). There is a little-known memoir on Summers by Joseph Jerome (London: Celia and Amelea Woolf, 1965, ltd. ed.).

292. Lea (*Materials*, II. 495): "Weyer's reform evidently only extended to shielding ignorant old women." This view was propounded by others, such as Godelmann; see note 236.

293. Extensively abstracted by Lea, *Mate-*

rials, II. 490-532, from the third edition; see also II. 574. White mentions Wier in *Warfare of Science*, II. 132.

294. *Liber apologeticus* in *Opera omnia* (Amsterdam, 1660), p. 584; trans. Lea, *Materials*, II. 544. See Nicolaus Paulus, "Johann Brenz und die Hexenfrage," *Wissenschaftliche Beilage zur Germania*, 26 (1909), 201-204.

295. *De praestigiis daemonum*: Basel, 1563; Basel, 1564; Basel, 1568 (enlarged; acquisition from Seligmann Collection); Basel, 1577 (with *Liber apologeticus*). Lea did not list the (fifth) 1577 edition. The Witchcraft Collection lacks the third edition of 1566, but has the revised one of 1583 (with *Liber apologeticus*), that used by Binsfeld and Loos. This edition is bound with *De lamiis* (Basel, 1582). German translation, *Von Teuffelsgespenst, Zauberern und Gifftbereytern, Schwartzkünstlern, Hexen vnd Vnholden* (Frankfurt, 1586); French translation, *Cinq Livres de l'imposture et tromperie des diables*, by Jacques Grévin (Paris, 1567; another ed., Paris, 1569, with note by Burr); another translation, *Histoires, disputes et discours, des illusions et impostures des diables... en six livres* ([Geneva], 1579; rpt., Paris, 1885).

296. Abstracted in Lea, *Materials*, II. 532-544.

297. *De lamiis*: Basel, 1577; Basel, 1582; German translation by Henricus Petrus Rebenstock, *De lamiis. Das ist: Von Teuffelsgespenst, Zauberern, vnd Gifftbereytern kurtzer doch gründtlicher Bericht* (Frankfurt, 1586).

298. F. H. Reusch, *Der Index der verbotenen Bücher* (Bonn: M. Cohn, 1883-1885), I. 44.

299. Adriaan J. Barnouw, *The Pageant of Netherlands History* (New York: Longmans Green, 1952), pp. 225-226, astutely comments: "The ministers saw too clearly that readers who were influenced by Bekker's reasoning would be ready to call the very authority of the Scriptures in question. They protected the survival of superstitions of the pagan past in order to save the future from losing faith in the revealed word of God. The danger was greater because all through the seventeenth century doubting Thomases had been undermining the power of the Calvinist church in so-called *Collegia*, conventicles where anyone might address the meeting. The first Collegiants were Remonstrants who had been ousted from the established Church.... Members of the most diverse sects began to swell the ranks of the Collegiants: Calvinists, Baptists, Lutherans, Catholics, Jews, all of them pious souls who were dissatisfied with their traditional beliefs."

300. A detailed account of Bekker's controversy with the Classis is given by Guilielmus Henricus Beckher, *Schediasma critico litterarium de controversiis praecipius Balthasari Bekkero quondam motis* (Leipzig, 1717, 1721), abstracted by Lea, *Materials*, III. 1385-1392; see esp. III. 1387-1389.

301. Robbins, *Encyclopedia*, pp. 45-46, with portrait.

302. Lea did not abstract Bekker (cf. *Materials*, III. 1382), but highlighted scarce and valuable works arising out of the "Bekker controversy" in *Materials*, III. 1382-1392 (Binet and Bremer, opposed; Beckher, supportive).

303. The Witchcraft Collection has all the first editions as well as many others, and various defenses and tracts by Bekker—plus a vast selection of the books he provoked, for or against. It also has an especially large holding of his opponent, Jacobus Schuts. For bibliographical reference see Burr's note in Lea, *Materials*, III. 1394.

304. Related in his *Gedancken und Erinnerungen*, retold from Hauber, *Bibliotheca magica*, by Lea, *Materials*, III. 1404. See the quotation in note 86.

305. Robbins, *Encyclopedia*, pp. 496-497; with satirical frontispiece of witches' sabbat from *Kurtze Lehr-Sätze* ([Leipzig], 1612). Thomasius received a chapter in Andrew Dickson White, *Seven Great Statesmen* (New York: Century, 1910), pp. 131-161, with good bibliography.

306. Bernardi, *Disputatio inauguralis juridica de tortura* (Halle, 1705).

307. Ipsen, *Disputatio juris canonici de origine ac progressu processus inquisitorii contra sagas* (Halle, 1712). Burr assigns this to Thomasius, citing a habit of professors to use students' names to veil their own identity. See Burr, "Literature of Witchcraft," p. 64, n. 1, rpt. Bainton and Gibbons, *Burr*, p. 188, n. 97.

308. *Kurtze Lehr-Sätze* abstracted by Lea, *Materials*, III. 1394-1405; see also I. 416-417, III. 1284-1285. On authorship, see Lea, *Materials*, III. 1391, 1405; in 1701 Reiche supposedly submitted his Latin dissertation, and

Thomasius praised it highly. However, in 1704 Thomasius in the *Kurtze Lehr-Sätze* called the *Disputatio de crimine magiae* (1701) his own; but so does Reiche in 1703. See Lea, *Materials*, III. 1415, and Burr, "Literature of Witchcraft," p. 63, n. 8, rpt. Bainton and Gibbons, *Burr*, p. 187, who accepts Thomasius as author. See also note 86.

309. *Unterschiedliche Schrifften von Unfug des Hexen-Processes* (Halle, 1703, 1704), noted in Lea, *Materials*, III. 1415-1416. Lea abstracts the *Malleus judicum oder Gesetz-Hammer* (III. 1415-1416), *Cautio criminalis* (II. 697-729), *Christliche Erinnerung* (II. 729-743), *Viereley Sorten Hexen-Acta* (III. 1236-1251). From this fourth part I have drawn the articles in my *Encyclopedia* for the terrifying trials of Althe Ahlers and Elsche Nelselings ("Mousemaker," pp. 351-352) and Chatrina Blanckenstein (pp. 52-53).

310. Jacob Brunneman [Aloysius Charitinus], *Discours von betrüglichen Kennzeichen der Zauberey* (Halle, 1727); abstracted by Lea, *Materials*, III. 1427-1430. Apparently based on Felix Martinus Brähm's dissertation, *De fallacibus indiciis magiae* (1701, 1709), it is a remarkably strong attack on the delusion. But Brähm demurred at Bekker's attack on the papacy (see n. 86). Abstracted by Lea, *Materials*, III. 1406-1411.

311. Hermann Adolph Meinders, *Unvorgreifliche Gedanken und Monita... mit denen Hexen-Processen und der Inquisition wegen der Zauberey* (Lengo, 1716), abstracted in Lea, *Materials*, III. 1431-1435.

312. Carolus Fridericus Romanus, *Commentatio polemica*, noted in Lea, *Materials*, III. 1416. Romanus tried to base a belief in witchcraft on reason.

313. Peter Goldschmidt, *Verworffener Hexen- und Zauberer-Advocat* (Hamburg, 1705).

314. Johann Schack, *Disputatio juridica* (Greifswald, 1706, first ed.); noted in Lea, *Materials*, III. 1421.

315. Wilhelm Hieronymus Bruckner, *De magicis personis et artibvs... Von zauberischen Leuten und Künsten* (Jena, 1723), noted in Lea, *Materials*, III. 1417-1418. Bruckner followed Romanus and was completely credulous.

316. See notes 266-270 for Schultheis, note 348 for Löher.

317. See note 278.

318. See note 258 for documentation.

319. Robbins, *Encyclopedia*, pp. 309-310. Brilliant dissertation by Hodder, "Binsfeld and Loos," pp. 126-152, and passim. Burr, "Loos Manuscript," Bainton and Gibbons, *Burr*, pp. 147-155, a highly significant essay on witchcraft with a good bibliography. Burr's paper was originally delivered at Cornell University, Oct. 6, 1886; introduced by President C[harles] K. Adams, with a summation of Burr, "A Manuscript and a Man," in *The Nation*, 43 (Nov. 11, 1886), 388-390. Brief mention by Sigmund Riezler, *Hexenprozesse*, (Stuttgart, 1896), pp. 244-246; Soldan-Heppe, rev. Bauer, *Hexenprozesse*, II. 22-24. Note the correction by Burr in 1938, in Lea, *Materials*, II. 604, to his original paper (*Burr*, p. 153) that only the corrections are in the hand of Loos, not the whole manuscript. See note 324.

320. *Ecclesiae venatus* (Cologne, 1588). For Ponzinibio see note 107.

321. Howland's note in Lea, *Materials*, II. 603.

322. "Two villages were absolutely blotted from the map, and in two others only two women were left alive"—"Cornelius Loos" (introduction by President Charles K. Adams to summation of Burr's paper, *New York Evening Post*, Nov. 13, 1886; later, more fully, in *The Nation*, 43 (Nov. 11, 1886), 388-390. Burr's revised manuscript was printed in Bainton and Gibbons, *Burr*, pp. 147-155. For Burr's note on Alphonsus de Spina's *Fortalicium fidei*, which he got from the Benedictine abbey of Saint Maximin, see Robbins, *Encyclopedia*, pp. 26-27 (with illustration).

323. Loos got a copy of Wier; cf. Carl Binz, *Doctor Johann Weyer* (Berlin, 1896).

324. Lea did not know of Burr's discovery of the Loos manuscript; thus he abstracts only the statements of Del Rio (attacking Loos) in *Disquisitio magiae* in *Materials*, II. 601-604.

The contents of Books 1 and 2 are listed in Robbins, *Encyclopedia*, p. 310. The chapter heads of the lost third and fourth books are as follows. Book 3: 1. Appearance of Spirits; 2. Haunting of Places; 3. Casting out of Devils; 4. Operation of Devils; 5. Spectres and Visions; 6. Bodies of the Dead; 7. Various Points

about Magic; 8. Causes of Magic; 9. Attendant Devils; 10. Functions of Devils; 11, Miraculous Works; 12. Transmutation. Book 4: 1. Assembly of Demons; 2. Deeds of Magicians; 3. Transportation of Bodies.

325. Quoted in *New York Evening Post*; see note 322.

326. "Loos manuscript," Bainton and Gibbons, *Burr*, p. 151.

327. Del Rio, *Disquisitio magiae*, bk. 5, app. 1. See Hodder, "Binsfeld and Loos," chap. 3 (pp. 126-152), chap. 4 (pp. 153-192), chap. 5 (pp. 193-243). Burr prints entire confession in English translation from Del Rio in *Witch Persecutions*, pp. 14-18.

328. This manuscript is of such significance and the name of Loos so important that I wish to record here the account of its discovery in the words of Burr himself, for finds like this come so seldom to the earnest laborer in the fields of scholarship as to be intoxicating. Furthermore, the collection of Burr's essays by Bainton and Gibbons is not available in all libraries: "His book, I say, was never heard from. It *had* never been heard from till two or three months ago. It had occurred to me that, inasmuch as both Binsfeld and Delrio expressed so much anxiety lest a copy of the manuscript might be at large in their day, it was not impossible that one might still be in existence—for I had had occasion to notice how very far from fully exploited are the manuscript treasuries of Europe. I made search for it, therefore, in various libraries and archives of Germany, Austria, Switzerland, Italy, France, England, Holland; but in vain. Of course I had looked especially at Treves, but there, too, to no purpose. Now it so happened that on my return from what was to be my last visit to that city I had the misfortune to lose a portfolio containing nearly all the notes and memoranda of many months [actually his doctoral dissertation]. After seeking it long in vain, I went sadly back to Treves to replace my papers; but, with a natural dread of taking up again work already carefully done, I gladly turned my hand to things before neglected; and one day it occurred to me to read through the rich manuscript catalogue in course. I did so, and came unexpectedly upon an imperfect description of a manuscript which might possibly be the lost book of Loos. Gaining the kind librarian's aid, I sought with him the dusty shelves, and soon unearthed the little volume. It lacked cover and title-page; but a moment's inspection convinced me that it was indeed the long-lost treatise.... I was permitted to make a facsimile of the whole book, and this now lies beside me." [*Burr*, p. 153]

329. Stadtbibliothek Trier. In the Witchcraft Collection are four typed pages copying the fragments surviving from the abortive edition of Cologne, 1592.

330. Witekind's real name was Wilcke. See brief note in Robbins, *Encyclopedia*, p. 424. See also Anton Birlinger and Carl Binz, *Augustin Lercheimer (Witekind) und seine Schrift wider den Hexenwahn* (Strassburg, 1888), which includes the 1597 text of *Christlich Bedencken*; Fritz Hauss, "Augustin Lercheimer," *Die Religion in Geschichte und Gegenwart*, 4 (1960), 324.

331. The Witchcraft Collection has the edition of 1593, Basel, with the woodcut; Burr appended a commentary on the front inside cover. The Collection has also *Theatrvm de veneficis: Das ist: Von Teuffelsgespenst Zauberern vnd Gifftbereitern* (Frankfurt, 1586), which gives it to Lercheimer; from this edition it was reprinted by J. Scheible, *Das Kloster* (Stuttgart, 1846), V. 263-347. The *Theatrum* includes German translations of many neglected works, such as Molitor, Layman, Lavater, Daneau, Ewich, and Wier. Binz printed a modern edition in 1888; see note 330.

332. Robbins, *Encyclopedia*, pp. 485-486. See also *Encyclopedia*, pp. 14, 105, 501. Also Gibbons, "Rhenish Foes," passim.

333. See Gibbons, "Rhenish Foes," p. 351, with references to Stapirius in Löher, *Hochnötige wemütige Klage*, pp. 11, 15, 102, 126, 374, 420.

334. Gibbons, "Rhenish Foes," p. 99, quoting Löher.

335. *Cautio criminalis* is abstracted in considerable detail in Lea, *Materials*, II. 697-726; Robbins, *Encyclopedia*, pp. 479-484, including Dubium 51. For biographical material see Hermann Cardauns, "Friedrich Spee," *Frankfurter zeitgemässe Broschüren*, N.F. 5, pt. 4 (1884), 103-133; Isabelle Rüttenauer, *Friedrich von Spee: Ein lebender Märtyrer* (Freiburg, 1951). Spee's part in witchcraft is treated by T. Ebner, "Friedrich von Spee und die Hexenprozesse seiner Zeit" (Hamburg, 1898, rpt. from *Sammlung gemeinverständlicher wissenschaftlicher Vorträge*, N.F. 13, Heft 291); and in modern studies by Theodorus Cornelis van

Stockum, *Friedrich von Spee in de hexen processen* (Amsterdam, 1949), and Huge Zwetsloot, S. J., *Friedrich von Spee und die Hexenprozesse* (Trier, 1954), with bibliography. See also Johannes Diel's life, extensively revised by Bernard Duhr, *Friedrich Spe* [sic] (Freiburg, 1901). A short but informative article, "The German Witches and Their Apostle," by J. M. Stone, occurs in the Roman Catholic *Month*, 100 (1902), 40-57; a longer, well-informed review article (unsigned) in the Anglican *Church Quarterly Review*, 57 (1904), 318-337; and a scholarly note by Pamela Reilly, "Spee's Belief in Witchcraft," in *Modern Language Review*, 54 (1959), 51-55. See also Pamela Reilly, "Some Notes on... 'Cautio Criminalis,'" *Modern Language Review*, 51 (1956), 536-543, and Charles Williams, *Witchcraft* (London: Faber, 1941), pp. 261-280, one of the few modern English writers to mention Spee. Question (Dubium) 51 is translated (with some omissions) by Burr, *Witch Persecutions*, pp. 14-18. Robert Schwickerath, S. J. translated some of the *Cautio* as summarized by Diel-Duhr in "The Attitude of Jesuits in Trials for Witchcraft," *American Catholic Quarterly*, 27 (1902), 475-516. An early M.A. thesis, "Friedrich Spee: A Biographical Sketch" by William Grant Godwin (Cornell, 1890), is available on microfilm only. The Catalogue of the Witchcraft Collection gives further references. The Collection owns the rare first edition of the *Cautio* (Rinteln, 1631), and the second edition (Frankfurt, 1632), used for the modern edition by Joachim Friedrich Ritter (Weimar, 1939), available in Olin Library; and later Latin editions of 1649 and 1703; with two German editions by Hermann Schmidt (Frankfurt, 1649; Halle, 1703), and the French translation by Frédéric Bouvot [pseud. F. B. de Vellédor], *Advis aux criminalistes* (Lyons, 1660). The Ferguson Collection at Glasgow University has a different translation in French, unpublished.

336. Robert Schwickerath, S. J., "Dr. White on Witchcraft," *The Messenger*, 43 (June, 1905), 601.

337. Spee said his hair had gone grey. The story of Leibniz occurs in his *Théodicée* (pars. 96, 97) and is quoted by Leitschuh, *Beiträge zur Geschichte des Hexenwesens in Francken* (see n. 60). See also Frederick W. C. Lieder, "Friedrich Spee and the Theodicee of Leibniz," *Journal of English and Germanic Philology*, 11 (1912). Spee mentions the anecdote in his *Cautio*, pp. 23-24, noted in Lea, *Materials*, II. 697.

338. *Cautio*, Dubium 15; Lea, *Materials*, II. 701.

339. *Cautio*, Dubium 20; Lea, *Materials*, II. 707.

340. *Cautio*, Dubium 48; Lea, *Materials*, II. 721-722. Cf. Dubium 21; Lea, II. 708.

341. *Cautio*, Dubium 20; Lea, *Materials*, II. 706.

342. Robert Schwickerath, S. J., "Dr. White on Witchcraft," p. 603.

343. Robbins, *Encyclopedia*, pp. 346-348. The *Christliche Erinnerung* was reprinted in Johann Reiche, *Unterschiedliche Schrifften* (Magdeburg, 1703), pp. 357-584, from which text Lea gives a detailed summary in *Materials*, II. 729-743.

344. Lea, *Materials*, II. 735-736, quoting from Reiche, p. 470. Lea comments (*Materials*, II. 734): "On the whole I am much impressed with the hearty earnestness of this work, in spite of its florid verbosity and pulpit eloquence." Lea also enjoyed the "rude and hearty eloquence" of Spee, "evidently a man of education and training" (*Materials*, II. 696).

345. Lea, *Materials*, II. 742, quoting from Reiche, p. 571.

346. Bibliothek des Kge. Gymnasiums zu Münstereifel bei Bonn.

347. In Carnap's transcription, pages 607-638 contain an extensive bibliography. Burr has a note at the end of the manuscript.

348. Jacobus Scheltema, *Geschiedenis der heksenprocessen* (Haarlem, 1828); Johann Diefenbach, *Der Hexenwahn vor und nach der Glaubensspaltung in Deutschland* (Mainz, 1886), pp. 118-123; Lois Oliphant Gibbons, "Some Rhenish Foes of Cruelty and Superstition" (diss., Cornell, 1920); Lois Oliphant Gibbons, "A Seventeenth Century Humanitarian: Hermann Löher," in *Persecution and Liberty*, pp. 335-359; Burr has a brief note in Lea, *Materials*, II. 728-729. Reproductions of some of the original plates in Bernard Duhr, *Geschichte des Jesuiten in den Ländern deutscher Zunge* (Freiburg im Breisgau, 1913), p. 482 (two); Hugo Zwetsloot, *Friedrich Spee und die Hexenprozesse* (Trier, 1954); and more accessibly in Robbins, *Encyclopedia*, pp. 60, 61 (two), 219, 309, 480. Some of these plates were used by Abraham Palingh, *'t Afge-*

rukt momaansight der tooverye (Amsterdam, 1725); see Gibbons, "Löher," p. 339, n. 11.

349. See Robbins, *Encyclopedia*, pp. 308-309.

350. Court records of five trials at Rheinbach are printed by G. Eckertz, "Hexenprozesse," *Annalen des historischen Vereins für den Niederrhein insbesondere die alte Erzdiöcese Köln*, 9-10 (1861), 136-181. The original manuscripts are now in the Witchcraft Collection.

351. Gibbons, "Löher," p. 338.

352. References and documentation for Buirmann in Gibbons, "Löher," pp. 336, n. 4, and 337. See entry in Robbins, *Encyclopedia*, pp. 59-60. Details in J. B. Dornbusch, "Aus dem Leben und Treiben einer alten Siegstadt im 15., 16. und 17. Jahrhundert," *Annalen des historischen Vereins für den Niederrhein*, 30 (1876).

353. Löher, *Hochnötige wemütige Klage*, p. 16; Gibbons, "Löher," p. 347; also Löher, p. 5; Gibbons, p. 349.

354. Löher, *Hochnötige wemütige Klage*, p. 5; Gibbons, "Löher," p. 349.

355. Löher, *Hochnötige wemütige Klage*, p. 503; Gibbons, "Löher," p. 350. The original German might be reproduced here: "O! O! Was lasterliche Worte und Reden müssen die unschultige Leute (den Fürsten unbekannt) vor Zucker essen, oder vor bittere Gall ... indem sie sagen du Gottesverleugner, ... du Wettermacher, du stummer Hund, bekenne dein Zauberlaster, besage deine Complices, ... du alte garstige Hur, du Teuffelsbuhlin, ... du Rupffenmachersche, du stumme Krotte rede und bekenne in Gottes Namen, nim ein das gesegent Salz, trinke das gesegent Wasser ... sage welche dich das Zauberen gelehrt haben, und welche du am Zaubertanz gesehen und gekent hast, dan soltu nicht mehr gepeiniget werden, sondern ein Kind des ewigen Lebens werden. Von diesen Manieren und fragen beschultigen, forteren und peinigen sie."

356. Löher, *Hochnötige wemütige Klage*, p. 247; Gibbons, "Löher," pp. 351-352.

357. Löher, *Hochnötige wemütige Klage*, p. 66; Gibbons, "Löher," p. 351.

358. Löher, *Hochnötige wemütige Klage*, pp. 550-551; Gibbons, "Löher," p. 348.

359. Gibbons, "Löher," p. 348, n. 47, thinks that about a thousand copies may have been printed, but loss could easily have occurred because of suppression (buying copies for destruction or outright confiscation), or because of loss by fire, overuse, and so forth. Gibbons remarks that editions of 30,000 copies of some books have completely disappeared (p. 358, n. 96).

360. Howland's note in Lea, *Materials*, I. vii. To these, of course, should be added the "Sadducees" in France and England; see, for example, the chart in Robbins, *Encyclopedia*, p. 167, and additional writers cited in note 19; and the classification of promoters and opponents in *Encyclopedia*, pp. 123-126. Nor is mention made here of the great Spanish opponent of witchcraft trials, Alonzo Salazar de Frias, who is not represented in the Witchcraft Collection. See Robbins, *Encyclopedia*, pp. 427-429, and comprehensive and fully documented article by Gustav Henningsen, "The Papers of Alonso de Salazar Frias: A Spanish Witchcraft Polemic 1610-14," *Temenos*, 5 (1969), 85-106.

361. Ewich mentioned in Lea, *Materials*, III. 1087, quoting Georg Längin, *Religion und Hexenprozess* (Leipzig, 1888), p. 269 (giving first ed., Bonn, 1585, which if correct has masculine genders throughout—*Sagorum quos*). The Witchcraft Collection has the first edition (Bremen, 1584, which has feminine genders—*Sagarum quas*). It has also the German translation in *Theatrum de veneficis* (1586). Ewich was answered by Wilhelm Scribonius, who favored the water ordeal, *De sagarum natura et potestate* (1588). Scribonius also opposed Hermann Neuwaldt (whom he listed on his title page along with Ewich), who himself had already refuted Scribonius in *Examinis sagarum super aquam frigidiam proiectarum* (1584). This was reprinted in Hauber, *Bibliotheca magica* (1739), I. 567-579, with German translation, I. 580-591, which had appeared in 1584 as *Bericht von Erforschung Prob vnd Erkentnis der Zauberinnen durchs kalte Wasser*. Scribonius was also attacked by Otto Meleander, *Resolutio praecipuarum quaestimum* (1597). The Witchcraft Collection has several other tracts on this topic, such as Gerhard Grave (1640—Carnap's manuscript copy), and Georg Adam Struve (1683). The water ordeal had a surprisingly wide acceptance as a folk test adopted by the courts; see Lea, *Materials*, III. 1271 (Hungary); also III. 1425.

362. Jordanaeus, a canon of Bonn who opposed the witch's mark, refuted Ostermann, a friend of Schultheis (see Lea, *Materials*, II.

889-892). See Soldan-Heppe, rev. Bauer, *Hexenprozesse*, I. 346. See note 190.

363. Tanner's *Tractatus theologicus de processu adversus crimina excepta et speciatim adversus crimen venificii* (extracted from *Disputationes theologicae*, 1617), abstracted in Lea, *Materials*, II. 647-662; *Disputatio angelis* (also extracts from *Disputationes*), abstracted in Lea, *Materials*, II. 662-670. See also Lea, III. 1096, 1163. Both tracts published in *Diversi tractatus* (Cologne, 1629). For Tanner see Ludwig Rapp, *Die Hexenprozesse und ihre Gegner aus Tirol* (Innsbruck, 1874), pp. 47-70, and (Brixen, 1891), pp. 65-84; and Wilhelm Lurz, *Adam Tanner und die Gradenstreitigkeiten des 17. Jahrhunderts* (Breslau, 1932).

364. Grevius named in Lea, *Materials*, III. 1088, from Längin, *Religion und Hexenprozess*, p. 282. Mentioned in Gibbons, "Rhenish Foes," p. 6, quoting his opposition to torture: "This loosener of the tongue which drags the wandering mind into guilt; how cruel and inhuman it is to expiate by such severe pains of torture." First edition is Hamburg, 1622; later, Wolfenbüttel, 1727. Supposedly partially translated into Dutch by Daniel Jonctys, *De Pynpbank wedersproken* (which actually gives More's *Utopia* on the title page as source).

365. Laymann's *Theologia moralis* (1625), abstracted in Lea, *Materials*, II. 670-687, 689, who lists various editions (last in 1733). The section on witchcraft, *Tractatus theologicus de sagis et veneficis*, was printed in the *Diversi tractatus* (Cologne, 1629). The *Processvs ivridicvs contra sagas et veneficos: das ist, Ein rechtlicher Process* (1629) is catalogued under Laymann in the Witchcraft Collection, and cross-referenced; but Burr (Lea, *Materials*, II. 688) ascribes it to Jordanaeus (see n. 362). The 1629 tract also appeared as *Aurea enucleatio*. The precise relationship between the numerous editions, revisions, expansions, and ascriptions needs clarification.

366. *Malleus judicum*, abstracted in Lea, *Materials*, II. 690-696. Available in the Witchcraft Collection in Reiche, *Unterschiedliche Schrifften* (1703); it discusses a warning to wicked judges, the horrors of prisons, and the abuse of torture.

367. Praetorius is mentioned in Gibbons, "Rhenish Foes," p. 343; and Soldan-Heppe, rev. Bauer, *Hexenprozesse*, I. 397. Early editions are 1598, 1602, 1613 (Heidelberg); the Witchcraft Collection also has his *Blockes-Berges Verrichtung: oder Ausführlicher geographischer Bericht* (Leipzig, 1668).

368. For Palingh see Gibbons, "Rhenish Foes," p. 339. The Witchcraft Collection has the 1725 edition (Amsterdam), with plates. Palingh discusses sorcery and possession, in a dramatic debate by three sorcerers named Tymon, Eusebus, and Mantus. It has many engravings (two taken from Löher's *Hochnötige wemütige Klage*—see n. 348).

369. Nicolas, a lawyer, protested against the use of torture. The Latin text of 1697 includes the Inquisition's "Instructio pro formandis processibus in causis strygum." See note 39.

It is fitting that this introduction conclude with a list of the opponents of the witchcraft delusion. Whoever writes a descriptive introduction to the Witchcraft Collection inevitably describes the aims of Andrew Dickson White and George Lincoln Burr in assembling it. That these aims were rational, humanitarian, skeptical, and moral becomes ever more clear the longer a scholar studies the books these two men collected. Their aims are now generally neglected in the allegedly unbiased approach to what happened in the past, with the consequent disregard of any lessons the past can offer the present and the future. ("Such memories are the world's best inspiration," said Burr.) And since the Witchcraft Collection is a memorial to them, I think it fitting that the last words here be those of Burr ("Loos Manuscript," Bainton and Gibbons, *Burr*, p. 150) on the attitudes of contemporaries to witchcraft: "Did all men believe in it? No: I think it can be distinctly shown that there never was a time when there were not plenty of men who doubted in their hearts whether there was any such thing as witchcraft or who at least suspected that the matter was vastly exaggerated. And such men were often the most learned and honored of their respective communities. The defenders of witchcraft are forever lamenting the skepticism of the learned on this subject. But they dared not speak out their convictions: they found it more prudent *not* to be convinced. How, then, shall we honor those who did speak?"

CATALOGUE

CATALOGUE OF THE CORNELL WITCHCRAFT COLLECTION

A

A**.

Witchcraft
BF
1583
Z7
1722
 Ausführliche Erzählung des Verhörs und der Hinrichtung des im Jahre 1722 der Hexerey beschuldigten Georg Pröls von Pfettrach in Baiern. Herausgezogen aus den Gerichts-Akten, und begleitet mit kritischen Anmerkungen zur Baierns Aufklärung. [n. p.] 1806.
 271, [3] p. 18cm.
 Vorrede signed: A**.
 1. Trials (Witchcraft)--Bavaria. 2. Pröls, Georg, d. 1722. I. A**.

8

A., F.

Witchcraft
BF
1582
Z7
1599
 Discours sommaire des sortilges [sic], venefices & idolatreries [sic], tiré des procez criminels iugez au siège royal de Montmorillon en Poictou, la présente année, 1599. A M. l'official en l'euesché de Poictiers. [Montmorillon, France? 1599?]
 51 p. 16cm.

 Epistle dedicatory signed: F. A.

A., J.

Witchcraft
BF
1575
W69
1869
 [Willard, Samuel] 1640-1707.
 Some miscellany observations on our present debates respecting witchcrafts, in a dialogue between S. & B. By P. E. and J. A. [pseud.] Philadelphia, Printed by W. Bradford, for H. Usher. 1692. Boston, 1869.
 24 p. 23cm. ("Congregational quarterly" reprint, no. 1)

 No. 6 of an edition of 100 copies.

 1. Witchcraft. I. E., P. II. A., J III. Title.

A., J. N.

Witchcraft
BF
1565
S19
 Samuel and the witch of Endor; or, The sin of witchcraft. [Battle Creek, Mich.] Seventh-Day Adventist Pub. Association, 18--.
 32 p. 18cm.

 Caption title.
 Signed: J. N. A.

 1. Witchcraft. I. Title: The sin of witchcraft. II. A., J. N. III. J. N. A.

A. T.

Witchcraft
BF
1410
B42
Z56
v.2
no.8
 Copy van een brief geschreeve aan een heer, woonende tusschen Rotterdam en Dort. Raakende het gepasseerde in de saak van Dr. B. Bekker; door een liefhebber van vreede en waarheid. Dord, Gedrukt by G. Abramsz, 1692.
 18 p. 19-20 blank; title vignette. 19 x 15cm.
 4°: A-B⁴, C².
 Signed: A. T.
 Van der Linde 48; 64.
 No. 8 in vol. lettered Bekker II.
 (Continued on next card)

8

A. v. M.

WITCHCRAFT
BF
1583
A2
N48
 Neuester Hexenprozess aus dem aufgeklärten heutigen Jahrhundert; oder, So dumm liegt mein bayrisches Vaterland noch unter dem Joch der Mönche und des Aberglaubens. Von A. v. M. [n.p.] 1786.
 36 p. 16cm.

 1. Superstition. 2. Witchcraft--Bavaria. 3. Trials (Witchcraft)--Bavaria. I. M., A.v. II. A. v. M.

8
NIC

A. W. S. K.

Witchcraft
BX
9479
B42
B11
no.8
 Het Woord Sitna verklaard, Gen. 26: 21. Met een vertoog, dat het woord Satan daar van afkomstig is. Waar by gevoegd word een verklaaring over 2 Sam. 24: 1, en 1 Chron. 21: 1. Door A. W. S. K. Amsterdam, By J. Roman, boekverkoper, 1699.
 13 p. [p. 14 blank] title and end page vignettes, illus. initial. 20 x 15cm.
 4°: A-B⁴(-B4)
 Black letter.
 No. 8 in vol. lettered B. Bekkers sterfbed en andere tractaten.
 (Continued on next card)

Aalst, Johannes, 1660-1712.
Zedige aanmerkingen.

Witchcraft
BF
1410
B42
Z56
v.1
no.7
 Bekker, Balthasar, 1634-1698. Brief van Balthasar Bekker S. T. D. en predikant tot Amsterdam. Aan twee eerwaardige predikanten D. Joannes Aalstius tot Hoornaar, ende D. Paulus Steenwinkel tot Schelluinen, over derselver Zedige aanmerkingen op een deel des tweeden boex van sijn werk genaamd De betoverde weereld. Amsterdam, By D. vanden Dalen, boekverkoper, 1693.
 11 p. [p. 12 blank] title vignette, illus. initial. 19 x 16cm.

8 (Continued on next card)

Aalst, Johannes, 1660-1712.

Witchcraft
BF
1410
B42
Z56
v.1
no.7
 Bekker, Balthasar, 1634-1698. Brief van Balthasar Bekker S. T. D. en predikant tot Amsterdam. Aan twee eerwaardige predikanten D. Joannes Aalstius tot Hoornaar, ende D. Paulus Steenwinkel tot Schelluinen, over derselver Zedige aanmerkingen op een deel des tweeden boex van sijn werk genaamd De betoverde weereld. Amsterdam, By D. vanden Dalen, boekverkoper, 1693.
 11 p. [p. 12 blank] title vignette, illus. initial. 19 x 16cm.

8 (Continued on next card)

Aalst, Johannes, 1660-1712.

Witchcraft
BF
1410
B42
Z56
v.1
no.7
 Bekker, Balthasar, 1634-1698. Brief van Balthasar Bekker ... aan ... Joannes Aalstius ... 1693. (Card 2)
 4°: A⁴, B².
 Letter autographed by Bekker.
 Van der Linde 72.
 No. 7 in vol. lettered Bekker I.
 1. Aalst, Johannes, 1660-1712. Zedige aanmerkingen. I. Aalst, Johannes, 1660-1712. II. Steenwinkel, Paulus, d. 1740. III. Title.

8

Aalstius, Joannes, 1660-1712.

see

Aalst, Johannes, 1660-1712.

Aanleydinge, om klaar te konnen uytvinden waneer men in de H. Schriftuur van duyvel, Satan, boose geest, &c. in ons Nederduyts leest, hoe het selve te verstaan zy.

Witchcraft
BX
9479
B42
B11
no.10
 [Bouman, Herman] Aanleydinge, om klaar te konnen uytvinden wanneer men in de H. Schriftuur van duyvel, Satan, boose geest, &c. in ons Nederduyts leest, hoe het selve te verstaan zy. Waar na volgt, een korte verklaring over Matth. 8: 28-31. ... Ook zijn hier bygevoegt vier brieven, waar in over en weder gehandelt, word van de versoekinge des Saligmakers Jesu Christi, van den hemel, de engelen, &c. 2. verm. druk. Amsterdam, By R. Blokland, boekverkoper, 1700.

 Continued on next card)

Aanleydinge, om klaar te konnen uytvinden waneer men in de H. Schriftuur van duyvel, Satan, boose geest, &c. ...

Witchcraft
BX
9479
B42
B11
no.10
 [Bouman, Herman] Aanleydinge ... 1700. (Card 2)
 2 p. l., 78 [i. e., 80] p. title vignette, illus. initials. 20 x 15cm.
 4°: *², A-K⁴.
 Black letter (except introduction and letters)
 Introduction signed: H. Bouman.
 Two letters are signed: N. N. [i. e., Jacobus Schuts]

 (Continued on next card)

Aanleydinge, om klaar te konnen uytvinden waneer men in de H. Schriftuur van duyvel, Satan, boose geest, &c. ...

Witchcraft
BX
9479
B42
B11
no.10
 [Bouman, Herman] Aanleydinge ... 1700. (Card 3)
 Van der Linde 81.
 No. 10 in vol. lettered B. Bekkers sterfbed en andere tractaten.

 1. Devil. 2. Spirits. 3. Bible. N. T. Matthew VIII, 28-31--Criticism, interpretation, etc. I. Schuts, Jacobus. II. Title.

8

1

CATALOGUE OF THE CORNELL WITCHCRAFT COLLECTION

Witchcraft
BF
1410
B42
1691a
no.4

Aanmerkinge op de handelingen der twee laatste noordhollandsche synoden, in de sake van B. Bekker ...
Bekker, Balthasar, 1634-1698.
Aanmerkinge op de handelingen der twee laatste noordhollandsche synoden, in de sake van B. Bekker, ten opsighte van sijn boek genaamd De betoverde weereld; nu versch t' Enkhuisen gedrukt. En de verschoninge derselve gemaakt in de voorrede daar voor, mitsgaders het reqvest der gedeputeerden van 't voorleden jaar daar achter by gevoegd. [Amsterdam? 1692]
16 p. 20 x 16cm.
4°: A-B⁴.
Caption title

8 (Continued on next card)

Witchcraft
BF
1410
B42
1691a
no.4

Aanmerkinge op de handelingen der twee laatste noordhollandsche synoden, in de sake van B. Bekker ...
Bekker, Balthasar, 1634-1698. Aanmerkinge op de handelingen der twee laatste noordhollandsche synoden ... [1692] (Card 2)
In autograph on p. 16: a. 13. Octob. 1692. Bekker.
Van der Linde 52.
No. 4 in vol. lettered B. Bekker. Betoverde weereld.
1. Nederlandse Hervormde Kerk. Synode van Noordholland, Edam, 1691. Acten ofte handelingen van de Noord-Hollandsche Synodus, gehouden binnen Edam en Alcmaar. I. Title.

8

Witchcraft
BF
1410
B42
Z56
v.3
no.12

Aanmerkinge op de handelingen der twee laatste noordhollandsche synoden.
Bekker, Balthasar, 1634-1698.
Drie resolutien des Classis van Amsterdam, by deselve genomen op den 22. Jan. 8. April en 21. July deses jaars, in de sake van Balthasar Bekker predikant tot Amsterdam, betreffende sijn boek De betoverde weereld. Waar by gevoegt zijn enige reflexien van onbekende hand den Auteur daar over toegesonden. Amsterdam, By D. van den Dalen, boekverkoper, 1692.
16, 16 p. title and end page vignettes.
19 x 15cm.

(Continued on next card)

Witchcraft
BF
1410
B42
Z56
v.3
no.12

Aanmerkinge op de handelingen der twee laatste noordhollandsche synoden.
Bekker, Balthasar, 1634-1698. Drie resolutien des Classis van Amsterdam ... 1692. (Card 2)
4°: A-B⁴, A-B⁴.
"Aanmerkinge op de handelingen der twee laatste noordhollandsche synoden, in de sake van B. Bekker, ten opsighte van sijn boek genaamd De betoverde weereld; nu versch t' Enkhuisen gedrukt:" 16 p.
Last p. autographed by Bekker, dated 2/13 Octob. 1692.

8 (Continued on next card)

Witchcraft
BF
1410
B42
Z56
v.3
no.12

Aanmerkinge op de handelingen der twee laatste noordhollandsche synoden.
Bekker, Balthasar, 1634-1698. Drie resolutien des Classis van Amsterdam ... 1692. (Card 3)
In the first section, Bekker quotes the resolutions which he discusses.
Van der Linde 44, 52.
No. 12 in vol. lettered Bekker III.
1. Bekker, Balthasar, 1634-1698. De betoverde weereld. I. Nederlandse Hervormde Kerk. Classes. Amsterdam. II. Title. III. His Aanmerkinge

8 (Continued on next card)

Witchcraft
BX
9479
B42
B11
no.11

Aanmerkinge over de woorden van den Evangelist Lucas...
[Bouman, Herman]
Aanmerkinge over de woorden van den Evangelist Lucas, beschreven in sijn H. Evangelium cap. 4: vs. 1-14. Daar verhaalt word hoe den Saligmaker Jesus Christus is versogt van den duyvel, en aangethoond wat voor een duyvel deselve kan geweest zyn; als mede, wat voor engelen de Heere Jesus na de versoekinge konnen gedient hebben. Amsterdam, By R. Blokland, boekverkooper, 1699.
47 p. [p. 48 blank] title vignette, illus. initia 1s. 20 x 15cm.

8 (Continued on next card)

Witchcraft
BX
9479
B42
B11
no.11

Aanmerkinge over de woorden van den Evangelist Lucas...
[Bouman, Herman] Aanmerkinge over de woorden van den Evangelist Lucas ... 1699. (Card 2)
4°: A-F⁴.
Black letter (except introduction)
Introduction signed: H. Bouman.
No. 11 in vol. lettered B. Bekkers sterfbed en andere tractaten.
1. Bible. N. T. Luke IV, 1-14--Criticism, interpretation, etc. 2. Jesus Christ--Temptation. 3. Devil. I. Title.

8

Witchcraft
BF
1410
B42
Z56
v.3
no.15

Aanmerkingen van eenige rechtzinnige broederen over de Articulen van satisfactie, waar op men met D. B. Bekker een verdrag gemaakt heeft. Leyden, By F. Haring, boekverkooper, 1692.
22, [1] p. [p. 24 blank] title vignette.
20 x 15cm.
4°: A-C⁴.
Consists of two letters, a short one signed N. N. [i. e., Jacobus Schuts], and one of 18 p. signed B. C.

8 (Continued on next card)

Witchcraft
BF
1410
B42
Z56
v.3
no.15

Aanmerkingen van eenige rechtzinnige broederen ... 1692. (Card 2)
Van der Linde 38.
No. 15 in vol. lettered Bekker III.
1. Bekker, Balthasar, 1634-1698. Articulen tot satisfactie aan de Eerw. Classis van Amsterdam. I. Schuts, Jacobus. II. B. C. III. C., B.

Witchcraft
BF
1410
B42
Z69
no.2

Aanmerkingen van Haggébher Philaleethees, op de invoegselen van Do. Balthasar Bekker.
[Hooght, Everard van der] d. 1716. Aanmerkingen van הגבר Φιλαληθης Haggébher Philaleethees, op de invoegselen van Do. Balthasar Bekker, voor zoo veel de zelve betreffen de stellingen, die reeds in sijne brieven tot noch toe zyn verhandelt, zynde een aanhangsel van den vyfden brief. Amsterdam, G. Borstius, 1691.
124-134 p. 21cm.
Signatures: 4°: A⁴, B².

NIC (Continued on next card)

Witchcraft
BF
1410
B42
Z69
no.2

Aanmerkingen van Haggébher Philaleethees, op de invoegselen van Do. Balthasar Bekker.
[Hooght, Everard van der] d. 1716. Aanmerkingen van ... Haggébher Philaleethees ... 1691. (Card 2)
Black letter.
Van der Linde 102.
No. 2 in a Collection of tracts against Balthasar Bekker and his Betoverde weereld.
1. Bekker, Balthasar, 1634-1698. De betoverde weereld. 2. Jesus Christ--Temptation. 3. Bible. O.T. Job. I. Title.

NIC

Witchcraft
BF
1410
B42
Z92

Aardige duyvelary, voorvallende in dese dagen.
[Walten, Ericus] 1663-1697.
Aardige duyvelary, voorvallende in dese dagen. Begrepen in een brief van een heer te Amsterdam, geschreven aan een van sijn vrienden te Leeuwaerden, in Vriesland. [Amsterdam, 1691]
45 p. [p. 46-48 blank] illus. initial.
19 x 16cm.
4°: A-F⁴.
Defense of B. Bekker and his book De betoverde weereld.

8 (Continued on next card)

Witchcraft
BF
1410
B42
Z92

Aardige duyvelary, voorvallende in dese dagen.
[Walten, Ericus] 1663-1697. Aardige duyvelary, voorvallende in dese dagen. [1691] (Card 2)
Van der Linde 170.
Stamped: Koninkl. bibliothek te 's Hage.
With this is bound Bekker, Balthasar, 1634-1698. Eenige extracten uyt Dr. Bekkers Betooverder weerelt, tweede deel. [n. p.] 1691.
1. Bekker, Balthasar, 1634-1698. De betoverde weereld. I. Title.

8

Aban, Pierre d'.

see

Abano, Pietro d', 1250-1315?

Witchcraft
BF
1598
A27
O2
1567

Abano, Pietro d', 1250-1316.
Heptameron.
Agrippa von Nettesheim, Heinrich Cornelius, 1486?-1535.
Henrici Cor. Agrippae ab Nettesheym, De occvlta philosophia libri III. Qvibvs accesservnt, Spurius Agrippae Liber de ceremonijs magicis. Heptameron Petri de Albano [sic]. Ratio compendiaria magiae naturalis, e Plinio desumpta. Disputatio de fascinationibus. Epistola de incantatione & adjuratione, collid; suspensione. Iohannis Tritemij opuscula quaedam huius argumenti. Parisiis, Ex officina Iacobi Dupuys, 1567.

8 (Continued on next card)

Witchcraft
BF
1598
A27
O2
1567

Abano, Pietro d', 1250-1316.
Heptameron.
Agrippa von Nettesheim, Heinrich Cornelius, 1486?-1535. Henrici Cor. Agrippae ab Nettesheym, De occvlta philosophia libri III. 1567. (Card 2)
16 p. l., 668, [1] p. illus., tables, diagrams (3 fold. in back) 20cm.
Binding: contemporary blind stamped pigskin with clasps (hinges wanting)
I. Abano, Pietro d', 1250-1316. Heptameron. II. De fascinationibus disputatio. III. De incantatione et adiuratione.

8

WITCHCRAFT
BF
1410
L69
1655

Abano, Pietro d', 1250-1315?, supposed author.
Heptameron, or Magical elements.
Henry Cornelius Agrippa's Fourth book of occult philosophy, and geomancy. Magical elements of Peter de Abano. Astronomical geomancy [by Gerardus Cremonensis]. The nature of spirits [by Georg Pictorius]: and Arbatel of magick. Translated into English by Robert Turner Philomathées. London, 1655.
9 p. l., [5]-266 [i.e., 286], [4] p. illus. 19cm.
Neither Agrippa nor Abano wrote the work

8 (Continued on next card)

WITCHCRAFT
BF
1410
L69
1655

Abano, Pietro d', 1250-1315?, supposed author.
Heptameron, or Magical elements.
Henry Cornelius Agrippa's Fourth book of occult philosophy, and geomancy ... 1655. (Card 2)
here ascribed to them; the Heptameron, or Magical elements also was ascribed to Agrippa under the title: Les oeuvres magiques, with Abano as translator (!)
Translation of a work variously titled Liber de ceremonijs magicis; and his De occulta philosophia, liber quartus.

8 (Continued on next card)

2

CATALOGUE OF THE CORNELL WITCHCRAFT COLLECTION

WITCHCRAFT
BF
1602
O29
1830

Abano, Pietro d', 1250-1315?, supposed author.
   Heptameron.
   Les Oeuvres magiques de Henri-Corneille Agrippa, mises en français par Pierre d'Aban, avec des secrets occultes, notamment celui de la Reine des Mouches velues. Rome, 1744. [Lille, Impr. de Bloquel, ca. 1830]
   112 p. port., illus. (1 fold.) 14cm.
   Caption title: Heptameron, ou Les éléments magiques de Pierre d'Aban, philosophe, disciple de Henri Corneille Agrippa.
   Has nothing to do either with Agrip-

8   (Continued on next card)

Witchcraft
BL
65
C8
R24

Der Aberglaube als weltgeschichtliche Macht.
   Raupach, Ernst Benjamin Salomon, 1784-1852.
   Der Aberglaube als weltgeschichtliche Macht. Vortrag im wissenschaftlichen Verein am 14. Februar 1852 von Dr. E. Raupach. Mit dem Bildnisse Raupach's aus früheren Jahren. Berlin [Druckerei von F. W. Gubitz] 1852.
   27 p. port. 21cm.

   1. Religion and culture. 2. Supernatural. I. Title.

8

Witchcraft
BL
490
A14

Aberglaube, Zauberei und Sympathie. Von einem Geistlichen. Hamburg, Agentur des Rauhen Hauses, 1884.
   v, 38 p. 18cm.

   1. Superstition. 2. Magic. I. Ein Geistlicher.

WITCHCRAFT
BF
1602
O29
1830

Abano, Pietro d', 1250-1315?, supposed author.
   Heptameron.
   Les Oeuvres magiques de Henri-Corneille Agrippa ... [1830] (Card 2)

pa or with Pietro d'Abano, who predeceased him by 2 centuries.
   Copy 1 has list of similar items for sale, e.g., Le veritable dragon rouge, Enchiridion Leonis papae, Secrets merveilleux de la magie naturelle du Petit Albert ...

   1. Occult sciences. 2. Magic. 3. Charms.

8   (Continued on next card)

WITCHCRAFT
BF
1425
S33

Der Aberglaube des Mittelalters.
   Schindler, Heinrich Bruno, 1797-1859.
   Der Aberglaube des Mittelalters. Ein Beitrag zur Culturgeschichte. Breslau, W. G. Korn, 1858.
   xxiv, 359 p. 23cm.

   Bibliography: p. [xi]-xxii.

8
NIC

WITCHCRAFT
BF
1555
M94
O29
no.4

Abfertigung der neuen Geister und alten Irtümer.
   Semler, Johann Salomo, 1725-1791.
   D. Joh. Salomo Semlers ... Abfertigung der neuen Geister und alten Irtümer in der Lohmannischen Begeisterung zu Kemberg nebst theologischem Unterricht von dem Ungrunde der gemeinen Meinung von leiblichen Besitzungen des Teufels und Bezauberungen der Christen. Halle, Bey J. J. Gebauer, 1760.
   40, 328 p. 18cm.
   Dedication and "Vorrede" comprise the first numbering.

8
NIC   (Continued on next card)

BF
1410
L69
1921

Abano, Pietro d', 1250-1315?
   Heinrich Cornelius Agrippa's von Nettesheim Magische Werke : sammt den geheimnissvollen Schriften des Petrus von Abano, Pictorius von Villingen, Gerhard von Cremona, Abt Tritheim von Spanheim, dem Buche Arbatel, der sogenannten Heil. Geist-Kunst und verschiedenen anderen zum ersten Male vollständig in's Deutsche übersetzt : vollständig in fünf Theilen, mit einer Menge Abbildungen. -- 4. Aufl. -- Berlin : H. Barsdorf, 1921.
   5 v. in 3. : ill. ; 17 cm. -- (Geheime Wissenschaften ; 10-14)

   (Continued on next card)

WITCHCRAFT
GR
90
M61

Der Aberglaube des Mittelalters und der nächstfolgenden Jahrhunderte.
   Meyer, Karl Remigius, 1842-
   Der Aberglaube des Mittelalters und der nächstfolgenden Jahrhunderte. Von Carl Meyer. Basel, F. Schneider, 1884.
   viii, 382 p. 23cm.

8

WITCHCRAFT
BF
1555
M94
O29
no.4

Abfertigung der neuen Geister und alten Irtümer.
   Semler, Johann Salomo, 1725-1791. ...
   Abfertigung der neuen Geister ... 1760. (Card 2)

   "Anhang. Auszug aus der Chaufepiee [sic] Nouveau dictionnaire historique et critique, von dem Artikel Balthas. Bekker": p. 317-328.
   No. 4 in vol. lettered Oesfeld u. a. ... 1. Lohmannin, Anna Elisabeth. 2. Müller, Gottlieb. Gründlicher Nachricht von einer begeisterten Weibesperson. 3. Devil. 4. Bekker, Balthasar, 1634-1698.

8
NIC   (Continued on next card)

WITCHCRAFT
BF
1775
M945
1886

Der Aberglaube.
   Mühe, Ernst.
   Der Aberglaube. Eine biblische Beleuchtung der finstern Gebiete der Sympathie, Zauberei, Geisterbeschwörung &c. 2. verm. und verb. Aufl. Leipzig, G. Böhme, 1886.
   48 p. 21cm.

8
NIC   1. Superstition.

Witchcraft
BL
490
F29

Der Aberglaube und die katholische Kirche des Mittelalters.
   Fehr, Joseph.
   Der Aberglaube und die katholische Kirche des Mittelalters; ein Beitrag zur Kultur- und Sittengeschichte. Stuttgart, Scheitlin, 1857.
   iv, 164 p. 20cm.

   1. Superstition. I. Title.

MSS
Bd.
WITCHCRAFT
HV
G77

Abgenötigte Rettung und Erklärung, zweyer zu Rinteln, jüngsthin, gedruckter Sendbrieffe.
   Grave, Gerhard, 1598-1675.
   Abgenötigte Rettung und Erklärung, zweyer zu Rinteln, jüngsthin, gedruckter Sendbrieffe, so mit Arrest sind hieselbst befangen: in welchen wird gehandelt: Von der Wasser Prob oder vermeint Hexenbaden ... Durch M. Gerhardum Graven ... Rinteln an der Weser, Gedruckt durch Petrum Lucium, 1640 [ca. 1900].
   157 p. 24cm.
   Carnap's manuscript copy.
   "Originaldruck in der Stadtbiblio-
   (Continued on next card)

Witchcraft
BF
1505
F52

Aberglaube aller Zeiten.
   Fischer, Wilhelm.
   Aberglaube aller Zeiten. Stuttgart, Strecker & Schröder [1906-07]
   5 v. in 1. illus. 19cm.

   Contents.--[1] Die Geschichte des Teufels.--[2] Die Geschichte der Buhlteufel und Dämonen.--[3] Dämonische Mittelwesen, Vampir, und Werwolf in Geschichte und Sage.--[4] Die Geschichte der Teufelsbündnisse, der Besessenheit, des Hexensabbats und der
   (Continued on next card)

WITCHCRAFT
BF
1775
L82
1897

Aberglaube und Strafrecht.
   Löwenstimm, August.
   Aberglaube und Strafrecht. Autorisierte Übersetzung aus dem Russischen. Mit einem Vorwort von J. Kohler. Berlin, J. Räde, 1897.
   xv, 232 p. 19cm.

8
NIC   1. Superstition. I. Title.

MSS
Bd.
WITCHCRAFT
HV
G77

Abgenötigte Rettung und Erklärung, zweyer zu Rinteln, jüngsthin, gedruckter Sendbrieffe.
   Grave, Gerhard, 1598-1675. Abgenötigte Rettung ... 1640 [ca. 1900] (Card 2)

thek zu Braunschweig im Samelbande 900.C. 794. 157 Seiten in 4° u. 6 Bl. Register."
   Numerals in the margins indicate pagination of the original.

   1. Trials (Witchcraft) 2. Torture. 3. Water (in religion, folk-lore, etc.) I. Title.

Witchcraft
BF
1505
F52

Aberglaube aller Zeiten.
   Fischer, Wilhelm. Aberglaube aller Zeiten. [1906-07] (Card 2)

   Contents--Continued.
Satansanbetung.--[5] Der verbrecherische Aberglaube und die Satansmessen im 17. Jahrhundert.

   1. Superstition. 2. Demonology. I. Title.

WITCHCRAFT
BF
1038
D18
L52
1908

Aberglaube und Zauberei von den ältesten Zeiten an.
   Lehmann, Alfred Georg Ludvig, 1858-1921.
   Aberglaube und Zauberei von den ältesten Zeiten an bis in die Gegenwart. Deutsche autorisierte Übersetzung von Dr. Petersen I. 2. umgearbeitete und erweiterte Auflage. Stuttgart, F. Enke, 1908.
   xii, 665 p. illus., facsims. 24cm.

   Translation of Overtro og trolddom.

   I. His Overtro og trolddom--German. II. Petersen, Dominikus. III. Title.

Witchcraft
BF
1565
C12

Abhandlung von Erscheinung der Geister.
   Cäsar, Aquilin Julius.
   Abhandlung von Erscheinung der Geister. [München] 1789.
   39 p. 18cm.

   Bound with his Ist die Nichtigkeit der Zauberey ganz erwiesen? München, 1789.

   1. Ghosts. 2. Apparitions. I. Title.

3

CATALOGUE OF THE CORNELL WITCHCRAFT COLLECTION

```
                    Abhandlungen vom physikalischen aberglauben
                        und der magie.
Witchcraft    Eberhard, Johann Peter, 1727-1779.
BF              D. Johann Peter Eberhards ... abhandlungen vom physika-
1413          lischen aberglauben und der magie. Halle im Magdeburgi-
E16           schen, Renger, 1778.
                7 p. l., 144 p. front. 20½ᶜᵐ.


                1. Superstition.  2. Magic.  I. Title: Abhandlungen vom physika-
              lischen aberglauben und der magie.
                                                              34-13015
                                                       [159.9611]  133
```

```
              Abus des divins.
Witchcraft   Massé, Pierre.
BF             De l'impostvre et tromperie des diables,
1410         devins, enchantevrs, sorciers, novevrs d'es-
M41          guillettes, cheuilleurs, necromanciens, chi-
             romanciens, & autres qui par telle inuoca-
             tion diabolique, ars magiques & supersti-
             tions abusent le peuple. Par Pierre Massé
             du Mans, aduocat. Paris, Chez Iean Poupy,
             1579.
               various pagings. 17cm.
8              Printer's           device on t. p.
                          (Continued on next card)
```

```
              Abus des divins.
Witchcraft   Massé, Pierre.  De l'impostvre et tromperie
BF             des diables ... 1579.         (Card 2)
1410
M41            Title on spine: Massé. Abus des divins.
             Text preceeded by Petit fragment cate-
             chistic d'vne plvs ample catechese de la
             magie ... de M. René Benoist Angevin ...;
             and followed by Benoist's Traicté enseignant
             en bref les cavses des malefices, sortileges
             et enchanteries... with special t. p.
             Declamation contre l'errevr execrable des
8                        (Continued on next card)
```

```
              Abus des divins.
Witchcraft   Massé, Pierre. De l'impostvre et tromperie
BF             des diables ... 1579.         (Card 3)
1410
M41          maleficiers ... par F. Pierre Nodé minime,
             has special t. p. with imprint Paris, Chez
             Iean du Carroy imprimeur, 1578, and is paged
             separately.
               Trois sermons de S. Avgvstin ... traduits
             en françois par M. René Benoist, has special
             t. p. with imprint Paris, Chez Iean Poupy,
             1579, and unnum    bered pages.
8                        (Continued on next card)
```

```
              Academische Abhandlung von den Hexen.
Witchcraft   Alberti, Valentin, 1635-1697, praeses.
BF             ... Academische Abhandlung von den Hexen
1565         und dem Bündniss so sie mit dem Teuffel ha-
A33          ben. Darinnen ... nebst Erörterung einiger
1723         andern curieusen Fragen, ob die bekannte Pu-
             celle d'Orleans, ingleichen das rasende Weib,
             das den Attilam erschrecket, eine Hexe ge-
             wesen sei? Franckfurt und Leipzig, 1723.
               [56] p. front. 21cm.
               Translation of his Dissertatio academica,
             De sagis, C. Stridtbeckh, respondent, Witte-
             bergae, 1690.
8                        (Continued on next card)
```

```
                    An account of the daemoniacks, and of the
                        power of casting out daemons.
Witchcraft   Whiston, William, 1667-1752.
BS             An account of the daemoniacks, and of the
2545         power of casting out daemons, both in the
D5           New Testament, and in the four first cen-
T97          turies. Occasioned by a late pamphlet [by
no.9         A. A. Sykes] intituled, An enquiry into the
             meaning of daemoniacks in the New Testament
             ... Added, an appendix, concerning the
             tythes and oblations paid by Christians ...
             London, Printed for J. Whiston, 1737.
               88 p. 21cm.
                          (Continued on next card)
```

```
                    An account of the daemoniacks, and of the
                        power of casting out daemons.
Witchcraft   Whiston, William, 1667-1752.  An account
BS             of the daemoniacks, and of the power of
2545         casting out daemons ... 1737.    (Card 2)
D5
T97            No. 9 in vol. lettered: Twells, Whiston,
no.9         etc. Tracts on the demoniacs in the New
             Testament. London, 1738-1775.

               1. Demoniac possession. 2. Bible. N.T.
             --Commentaries. 3. Tithes.  I. Title.
             Sykes, Arthur       Ashley, 1684?-1756.
             An enquiry into     the meaning of daemoniacs
             in the New Tes                tament.
```

```
              An account of the life and character of the
                  Rev. Samuel Parris.
Witchcraft   Fowler, Samuel P[age] 1800-1888.
BF             An account of the life and character of the Rev. Sam-
1575         uel Parris, of Salem village, and of his connection with
D76          the witchcraft delusion of 1692. By Samuel P. Fowler,
v.3          esq.  (In Drake, S. G. The witchcraft delusion in New
             England ... Roxbury, Mass., 1866. 21½ᶜᵐ. v. 3, p.
             198-222)
                Reprinted from Proceedings of the Essex institute, v. 2, 1856-60, Salem,
             1862, p. 49-68.

                Subject entries: 1. Parris, Samuel, 1653-1720.  2. Witchcraft—New Eng-
             land.  I. Title.
                                                               2-13716
                Library of Congress, no.
```

```
                   An account of the life, character, &c.,
                       of the Rev. Samuel Parris.
Witchcraft   Fowler, Samuel Page, 1800-1888.
F              An account of the life, character, &c.,
74           of the Rev. Samuel Parris, of Salem village
S1           and of his connection with the witchcraft
P26          delusion of 1692. Read before the Essex
             Institute, Nov'r 14, 1856. Salem, W. Ives
             and G. W. Pease, printers, 1857.
                20 p. 24cm.

               Cover title.
                 1. Parris, Samuel, 1658-1720. 2. Witch-
             craft--Salem,      Mass.
```

```
Witchcraft
BF             An account of the trial, confession & con-
1581         demnation of six witches, at Maidstone, in
Z7           the county of Kent, at the assizes held
1652         there July 1652, before Sir Peter Warbur-
             ton ... To which is added the trial,
             examination and execution of three witches
             executed at Faversham, in the same county,
             September 1645. London, 1837.
               vi, 11, 9 p. 22cm.
               Two hundred       copies reprinted verbatim
             from the ori       ginal editions.
                          (Continued on next card)
```

```
Witchcraft
BF             An account of the trial, confession & con-
1581         demnation of six witches... 1837.  (Card 2)
Z7
1652           Includes reprints of original title-pages,
             "A prodigious & tragicall history of the
             arraignment, tryall, confession, and con-
             demnation of six witches at Maidstone, in
             Kent ... London, Printed for R. Harper,
             1652"; and "The examination, confession,
             triall, and execution of Joane Williford,
             Joan Cariden and Jane Hott: who were exe-
             cuted at Faversham, in Kent, for being
                          (Continued on next card)
```

```
Witchcraft
BF             An account of the trial, confession & con-
1581         demnation of six witches ... 1837.
Z7                                             (Card 3)
1652         witches ... 1645 ... London, Printed
             for J. G., October 2, 1645."


                 1. Witchcraft--England.
```

```
Witchcraft
BF             An Account of the tryal and examination of
1563         Joan Buts, for being a common witch and
W81++        inchantress ... March 27, 1682.  London,
no.21        Printed for S. Gardener, 1682. [London,
             at the British Museum, 1923]
                [2] p. 27cm.
                Photocopy (negative)  2 p. on 2 l.  20 x
             32cm.
                No. 21 in vol. lettered: Witchcraft tracts,
             chapbooks and broadsides, 1579-1704; roto-
             graph copies.
                1. Witch-            craft--England.  2. Buts,
             Joan.
```

```
                An account of the tryals, examination and
                    condemnation, of Elinor Shaw and Mary
Witchcraft         Phillip's (two notorious witches).
BF          [Davis, Ralph]
1581          An account of the tryals, examination
A2          and condemnation, of Elinor Shaw and Mary
W81         Phillip's (two notorious witches,) at North-
1866a       ampton assizes, on Wednesday the 7th of
no.2        March 1705. ... London, Printed for F.
            Thorn [1705]  [Northampton, Taylor, 1866]
              8 p. 22cm.
              No. 2 in box lettered Witchcraft in
            Northamptonshire.
                1. Trials        (Witchcraft)--Northamp-
8           tonshire, En        gland.  I. Title.
```

```
                   An account of the "witch" murder trial,
                     York, Pa., January 7-9, 1929.
Witchcraft  Blymyer, John H       defendant.
BF            An account of the "witch" murder trial,
1578        York, Pa., January 7-9, 1929. Commonwealth of Pennsylvania vs. John Blymyer,
B66         et al. By A. Monroe Aurand, jr. ... Harrisburg, Pa., Priv.
            print. by the Aurand press, 1929.
              31 p. 23½ᶜᵐ.


               1. Rehmeyer, Nelson D., 1868-1928.  2. Witchcraft--Pennsylvania.  I.
            Aurand, Ammon Monroe, 1895-        II. Title: "Witch" murder trial,
            York, Pa., January 7-9, 1929.  III. Title.
               Library of Congress                      29-23242
               ——————  Copy 2.
               Copyright A 4228                   [2]
```

```
                  Acht Hexenpredigten, darinnen von des
WITCHCRAFT        Teuffels Mordtkindern, der Hexen, ...
BF          Meder, David.
1565          Acht Hexenpredigten darinnen von des
M48         Teuffels Mordtkindern, der Hexen, Unholde
            Zauberischen, Drachenleuten, Milchdieben
            gethan durch Davidem Mederum... Leipzig
            Gedruckt bey Valentins am Ende Erben, in
            Versetzung Bartholomei Voigts, 1615.
              119 l. 20cm.


8
NIC            1. Witchcraft. 2. Devil.  I. Title.
```

```
Witchcraft  Ackermann, Theodor, bookseller, Munich.
Z             Geheime Wissenschaften. 1-          ,
6880        1926-
Z9A18       München.
              v. 21cm. (His Katalog 594-



               1. Occult sciences--Bibliography--
            Catalogs.  I.        Title.
```

```
Witchcraft  Ackermann, Theodor, bookseller, Munich.
Z             Okkultismus und Verwandtes.  Muenchen
6880        [1933?]
Z9            10 p. 29 x 23cm. (Sonderliste, Nr. 58)
A181+



               1. Occult sciences--Bibl.--Catalogs.
               I. Title.
```

CATALOGUE OF THE CORNELL WITCHCRAFT COLLECTION

Rare
BR
304
A18
1631

Aconcio, Giacomo, 1492?-1566?
　Stratagematvm Satanae, libri octo. Editio iterata & emendata. Oxonii, G. Webb, 1631.
　426 p.　15cm.

"Iacobvs Acontivs Iohanni Wolfio": [26] p. at end.
Engr. t.p.
STC 93
1. Christianity--16th cent. 2. Creeds-- Hist. & Crit.　I.　Wolf, Johann, 1522-1571. II. Title.

Witchcraft
BF
1583
Z7
1689

Acta inquisitionalia contra Annen Marien Braunin in puncto Verdächtiger Hexerei.
　Braunin, Anna Maria, d. 1689, defendant.
　Acta inquisitionalia contra Annen Marien Braunin in puncto Verdächtiger Hexerey, Ambt Ostrau, 1689.
　(In Thüringisch-Sächsischen Verein für Erforschung des vaterländischen Alterthums und Erhaltung seiner Denkmale. Neue Mittheilungen aus dem Gebiet historisch-antiquarischer Forschungen. Halle. 22cm. Bd. 9 (1857) p. [76]-189)

"Nachschrift": signed Dr. Boehlau, p. 174-189.

Witchcraft
BF
1410
B42
1691a
no.3

Acten ofte handelingen van de Noord-Hollandsche Synodus, gehouden binnen Edam en Alcmaar, anno 1691 en 1692.
　Nederlandse Hervormde Kerk. Synode van Noordholland, Edam, 1691.
　Acten ofte handelingen van de Noord-Hollandsche Synodus, gehouden binnen Edam en Alcmaar, anno 1691. en 1692. Rakende Dr. Balthazar Bekker, en sijn boek De betoverde wereld, met alle de documenten daar toe behoorende, waar onder ook eenige, die in het synodale acten-boek niet en staan uyt-gedrukt; met een voor-reden, strekkende tot weder-legging van Dr. Bekkers Remonstrantie en verdere exceptien tegen de competentie van den Synodus. Enchuysen, Gedrukt by J. D. Kuyper, 1692.　(Continued on next card)

8

F
410
42
.691a
no.3

Acten ofte handelingen van de Noord-Hollandsche Synodus, gehouden binnen Edam en Alcmaar, anno 1691 en 1692.
　Nederlandse Hervormde Kerk. Synode van Noordholland, Edam, 1691. Acten ofte handelinge van de Noord-Hollandsche Synodus, gehouden binnen Edam en Alcmaar ... 1692.　(Card 2)

30 p. l., 102 p.　title and end page vignettes, illus. initials.　20 x 16cm.
4°: *-7*⁴, 8*², A-N⁴(-N4)
Remonstrantie, by Bekker: p. 73-83.
Van der Linde　51.
No. 3 in　vol. lettered B. Bekker.
Betoverde wee　reld.
(Continued on next card)

ITCHCRAFT
D
91
2
57
342

Actenmässige Darstellung der Theilnahme der Kalenbergischen Landstände an den ... Missverständnissen.
　Möhlmann, J　H　D
　Actenmässige Darstellung der Theilnahme der Kalenbergischen Landstände an den durch angeschuldigte Zauberei und Giftmischerei zwischen dem Landesherrn Erich dem Jungern und seiner Gemahlinn Sidonia veranlassten Missverständnissen.
　(In: Historischer Verein für Niedersachsen. Zeitschrift [under earlier title, Vaterländisches Archiv] Hannover. 19cm. 1842. p. 303-323)
(Continued on next card)

Witchcraft
BF
1583
R23+

Actenmässige Nachrichten von Hexenprozessen und Zaubereien in der Mark Brandenburg vom sechszehnten bis ins achtzehnte Jahrhundert.
　Raumer, Georg Wilhelm von, 1800-1856.
　Actenmässige Nachrichten von Hexenprozessen und Zaubereien in der Mark Brandenburg vom sechszehnten bis ins achtzehnte Jahrhundert.
　(In Märkische Forschungen (Verein für Geschichte der Mark Brandenburg) Berlin. 26cm. 1. Bd. (1841), p. [236]-265)

1. Witchcraft--Germany. 2. Trials (Witchcraft)--Germany. I. Märkische Forschungen (Verein für Geschichte der Mark Brandenburg) II. Title.

8

Witchcraft
GR
830
W4
A18

Acxtelmeier, Stanislaus Reinhard.
　Misantropus Audax; das ist: Der alles anbellende Menschen-Hund. Wider die Fehler, Irrthümer, Missbräuche, und aberglaubische, Gottes-lästerliche, teuffelische Zauber-Wercke, und andere Laster, welche leider, heutiges Tages häuffig im Schwung gehen, durch untadelhafftigen Tadel denen Irrgehenden zu Gemüth geleget, und im Reisen zusammen getragen.　Augspurg, L. Kop, 1710.
[3], 289 p.　16cm.
I. Title: anbellende Me　II. Title: Der alles nschen-Hund.

WITCHCRAFT
BF
1565
H77

Ad Reuerendissimū dñm dñm Philippū sancte ecclesie Coloniensis archiepm. Tractat' magistralis declarans quam graviter peccent querentes auxilium.
　Hoogstraten, Jacobus van, ca. 1460-1527.
　Ad Reuerendissimū dñm dñm Philippū sancte ecclesie Coloniensis archiepm. Tractat' magistralis declarans q̄ grauiter peccēt q̄rentes auxiliū a maleficis cōpilat' ab eximio sacre theologie professore & artiū magistro necnō heretice prauitatis inq̄sitore magistro Jacobo Hoechstrassen ordinis Predicatorū priore ꝯuentus Coloniensis. [Colonie, Impressum per Martinum de Werdena, 1510]

8　(Continued on next card)

WITCHCRAFT
BF
1565
H77

Ad Reuerendissimū dñm dñm Philippū sancte ecclesie Coloniensis archiepm. Tractat' magistralis declarans quam graviter peccent querentes auxilium.
　Hoogstraten, Jacobus van, ca. 1460-1527.
　Ad Reuerendissimū dñm dñm Philippū sancte ecclesie Coloniensis archiepm ... [1510]
(Card 2)

[16] p.　illus.　18cm.
Woodcut illus. on p. [16].
Running title: Contra petentes remedia a maleficis.

1. Witchcraft. I. Title: Tractatus magistralis declarans quam graviter peccent querentes auxilium a maleficis. II. Title: Contra petentes remedia a maleficis.

8

Witchcraft
BF
1445
D61
no.10

Ad scriptores aliqvot Roman. veteres, De apparitionibus spectror. & spirituum.
　Kirchmayer, Georg Caspar, 1635-1700, praeses.
　Ad scriptores aliqvot Roman. veteres, De apparitionibus spectror. & spirituum, sub corpor. inprimis human. schemate, nec non visionibus naturae probabilibus, adversus atheos inprimis, dissertatio, sub moderamine ... Dn. Georgii Casparis Kirchmajeri, à Johanne Gottlieb Stoltzen ... ventilationi publicae exposita, die 27. Juliii, anno 1692. Wittebergae, Typis Christiani Schrödteri [1692]

8　(Continued on next card)

Witchcraft
BF
1445
D61
no.10

Ad scriptores aliqvot Roman. veteres, De apparitionibus spectror. & spirituum.
　Kirchmayer, Georg Caspar, 1635-1700, praeses. Ad scriptores ... De apparitionibus spectror. & spirituum ... [1692]　(Card 2)

32, [2] p. 18cm. (bound in 21cm. vol.)
No. 10 in vol. lettered Dissertationes de spectris. 1646-1753.
1. Apparitions. I. Stoltze, Johann Gottlob, respondent. II. Title: De apparitionibus spectrorum et spirituum.

8

Witchcraft
BF
231
C18

Adami, Tobias.
　Campanella, Tommaso, 1568-1639.
　De sensv rervm et magia, libri quatuor, pars mirabilis occvltae philosophiae ... Tobias Adami recensvit, et nunc primum evulgauit. Francofvrti, Apud Egenolphvm Emmelivm, Impensis Godefridi Tampachij, 1620.
8 p. l., 371 p.　22cm.
Between p. 370 and 371 are bound in duplicates of p. [1]-[4] of the dedicatory epistle.
Ex libris Caspar Melchior Fuch.
With this are bound his Astrologicorum libri VII. Francofurti, 1630; and his Prodromus philosophiae instaurandae. Francofurti, 1617.

8

WITCHCRAFT
BF
1584
I8
Z7+
1623

Adamo, Orazio di.
　Millunzi, Gaetano.
　Un processo di stregoneria nel 1623 in Sicilia, pubblicato e illustrato dal Can. Gaetano Millunzi e da Salvatore Salomone-Marino.
　(In: Archivio storico siciliano. Palermo. 28cm. nuov. ser., anno 25, fasc. 3-4, 1901, p. [253]-379)

1. Trials (Witchcraft)--Sicily. 2. Adamo, Orazio di.　3. Cabala. 4. Occult sciences.　I. Salomone-Marino, Salvatore, 1847-1916.

8
NIC

Witchcraft
BF
1581
A22

Adams, William Henry Davenport, 1828-1891.
　Witch, warlock, and magician. Historical sketches of magic and witchcraft in England and Scotland, by W. H. Davenport Adams ... London, Chatto & Windus, 1889.
vi p. 1 l. 428 p. 23ᶜᵐ.

1. Magic. 2. Witchcraft--Gt. Brit. I. Title.

11-21968

Library of Congress　　　BF1581.A4

Witchcraft
F
67
N87
A2

Address before the Essex bar association.
　Northend, William Dummer, 1823-1902.
　Address before the Essex bar association. December 8. 1885. By William D. Northend ... Salem. Printed at the Salem press. 1885.
59 p. 22½ᶜᵐ.
"From the Historical collections of the Essex Institute, vol. xxii."
"Members of the bar": p. [55]-59.

1. Law--Massachusetts--Hist. & crit. 2. Courts--Massachusetts. 3. Lawyers--Essex co., Mass.　I. Title.

34-8901

Library of Congress　　[2]

Witchcraft
BF
1410
A23

Adelung, Johann Christoph, 1732-1806.
　Gallerie der neuen Propheten.
　[Adelung, Johann Christoph] 1732-1806.
　Geschichte der menschlichen Narrheit; oder, Lebensbeschreibungen berühmter Schwarzkünstler, Goldmacher, Teufelsbanner, Zeichen- und Liniendeuter, Schwärmer, Wahrsager, und anderer philosophischer Unholden.　Leipzig, Weygand, 1785-89.
7 v. in 3.　18cm.

Title vignette.

8　(Continued on next card)

Witchcraft
BF
1410
A23

Adelung, Johann Christoph, 1732-1806.
　Gallerie der neuen Propheten.
　[Adelung, Johann Christoph] 1732-1806.
　Geschichte der menschlichen Narrheit ... 1785-89.　(Card 2)

Witchcraft
BF
1410
A23
Suppl.

---Gallerie der neuen Propheten, apokalyptischen Träumer, Geisterseher und Revolutionsprediger. Ein Beytrag zur Geschichte der menschlichen Narrheit. Leipzig, Weygand, 1799.
3 p. l., 487, [3] p. 20cm.

8　(Continued on next card)

Witchcraft
BF
1410
A23

Adelung, Johann Christoph, 1732-1806.
　Gallerie der neuen Propheten.
　[Adelung, Johann Christoph] 1732-1806.
　Geschichte der menschlichen Narrheit; oder, Lebensbeschreibungen berühmter Schwarzkünstler, Goldmacher, Teufelsbanner, Zeichen- und Liniendeuter, Schwärmer, Wahrsager, und anderer philosophischer Unholden.　Leipzig, Weygand, 1785-89.
7 v. in 3.　18cm.

Title vignette.

8　(Continued on next card)

5

CATALOGUE OF THE CORNELL WITCHCRAFT COLLECTION

Witchcraft
BF
1410   [Adelung, Johann Christoph] 1732-1806.
A23   Geschichte der menschlichen Narrheit ...
       1785-89.   (Card 2)

Witchcraft
BF
1410   ---Gallerie der neuen Propheten, apokalyp-
A23   tischen Träumer, Geisterseher und Revolu-
Suppl. tionsprediger. Ein Beytrag zur Geschichte
       der menschlichen Narrheit. Leipzig, Weygand, 1799.
          3 p. l., 487, [3] p. 20cm.
8   (Continued on next card)

Witchcraft
BF
1410   [Adelung, Johann Christoph] 1732-1806.
A23   Geschichte der menschlichen Narrheit ...
       1785-89.   (Card 3)

       1. Occult sciences. 2. Alchemy--
    Hist. I. Title. II. His Gallerie
    der neuen Propheten. III. Title: Gal-
    lerie der neuen Propheten.

8

            Adjurationen, Exorcismen und Benedictio-
            nen, vorzüglich zum Gebrauch bei Gottes-
Witchcraft gerichten.
BX
2340   Runge, Heinrich, 1817-1886, ed.
R94++   Adjurationen, Exorcismen und Benedictio-
       nen, vorzüglich zum Gebrauch bei Gottesge-
       richten. Ein Rheinauer Codex des eilften
       Jahrhunderts. Zürich, In Commission bei
       Meyer und Zeller, 1859.
          [179]-203 p. facsim. 31cm. (Mittheilungen der antiquarischen Gesellschaft (der
       Gesellschaft für vaterländische Alterthümer)
       in Zürich. Bd. XII. Heft 5)
8   Imprint cover ed by bookseller's label.
                    (Continued on next card)

            The admirable history of the possession
            and conversion of a penitent woman.
WITCHCRAFT
BF
1517   Michaelis, Sebastien, 1543?-1618.
F5   The admirable history of the possession
M62   and conversion of a penitent woman. Se-
1613   dvced by a magician that made her to become
       a witch, and the princesse of sorcerers in
       the country of Prouince, who was brought to
       S. Baume to bee exorcised, in the yeere 161
       ... Wherevnto is annexed a pnevmology, or
       Discourse of spirits ... reuewed, corrected
       and enlarged ... Translated into English
       by W. B. Lon   don, Imprinted for Wil-
8   (Continued on next card)

            The admirable history of the possession
            and conversion of a penitent woman.
WITCHCRAFT
BF
1517   Michaelis, Sebastien, 1543?-1618. The admirable history of the possession ... of a
F5   penitent woman ... [1613]   (Card 2)
M62
1613   liam Aspley [1613]
          24 p. l., 418, [10], 154, [34] p. 20cm.
          Differs from another issue only in t. p.
       (lacks date; some spellings different)
          Translation of Histoire admirable de la
       possession ... d'vne penitente, and of Dis-
       covrs des esp   rits.
8   "A discov   rse of spirits" has spe-
       cial t. p.   and separate paging.
                    (Continued on next card)

            The admirable history of the possession
            and conversion of a penitent woman.
WITCHCRAFT
BF
1517   Michaelis, Sebastien, 1543?-1618. The admirable history of the possession ... of a
F5   penitent woman ... [1613]   (Card 3)
M62
1613   STC 17854.
          1. Palud, Magdeleine de la. 2. Gau-
       fridi, Louis, 1572-1611. 3. Loudun, France.
       Ursuline convent. 4. Demoniac possession.
       5. Exorcism. I. His Histoire admirable
       de la possession ... d'une penitente. Eng-
       lish. II. His   Discours des esprits.
       English.   III. Title. IV. W. B.,
8   tr. V. B.,   W., tr.

WITCHCRAFT   [Admirable vertu des saincts exorcismes]
BF
1517   Pichard, Remy.
F5   Admirable vertu des saincts exorcismes
P59   sur les princes d'enfer possédants réelle-
       ment vertueuse demoiselle Elisabeth de
       Ranfaing, avec ses justifications contre
       les ignorances et les calomnies de F. Claude
       Pithoys. Nancy, Par Sébastien Philippe,
       1622.
          674, 105 p. 14cm.

          T.p. lacking. Handwritten t.p. substi-
8   tuted.
NIC   Bound in   after chapter 17 are
                    (Continued on next card)

            [Admirable vertu des saincts exorcismes..]
WITCHCRAFT
BF
1517   Pichard, Remy. [Admirable vertu des
F5   saincts exorcismes...1622]   (Card 2)
P59
       what appear to be the preface and table of
       contents of Stimuli virtutum adolescentiae
       Christianae, by Guglielmo Baldesano [con-
       sidered by Bibliothèque nationale to be the
       pseudonym of Bernardino Rosignolo] The
       work itself is not in the vol.
          The 105 pages at end consist of a reprint
       of Claude Pi   thois' La descouverture
       des faux pos   sédez...la conférence
                    (Continued on next card)

            [Admirable vertu des saincts exorcisms..]
WITCHCRAFT
BF
1517   Pichard, Remy. [Admirable vertu des
F5   saincts exorcismes...1622]   (Card 3)
P59
       ...touchant la prétendue possédée de Nancy
       [the work to which Pichard is replying]
       and chapter 18 of the Admirable vertu des
       saincts exorcismes.
          1. Demoniac possession. 2. Exorcism. 3.
       Ranfaing, Elisabeth de, 1592-1649. 4. Pi-
       thois, Claude, 1587-1676. [La descouverture
       des faux possé   dez... I. Pithois,
       Claude, 1587-   1676. La descouverture
       des faux pos   sédez... II. Title.

            Les admirables secrets d'Albert le Grand.
Witchcraft
BF
1598   Albertus Magnus, Saint, bp. of Ratisbon,
A33   1193?-1280. Spurious and doubtful works.
A2   Les admirables secrets d'Albert le Grand.
1770   Contenant plusieurs traités sur la concep-
       tion des femmes, des vertus des herbes, des
       pierres précieuses, & des animaux ... Lyon,
       Chez les Héritiers de Beringos Fratres, 1770.
          291 p. illus. 14cm.
          With autograph of J. Tickell.
          Attributed also to Albertus de Saxonia.
          With this is bound Albertus, Lucius,
       Parvus, pseud.   Secrets merveilleux de
       la magie   naturelle ... Lyon
       [1729] in vol.   lettered: Tracts.

            Admonitio de superstitionibus magicis
WITCHCRAFT vitandis.
BF
1565   Hemmingsen, Niels, 1513-1600.
H48   Admonitio de svperstitionibvs magicis
       vitandis, in gratiam sincerae religionis
       amantium, scripta a Nicolao Hemmingio.
       Esaiae 8. Ad legem et testimonivm. [Haf-
       niae, Excvdebant Iohannes Stockelman & An-
       dreas Guterwitz] 1575.
          [220] p. 16cm.
          With colophon.
          1. Witchcraft. 2. Superstition. I.
       Title: Admon   itio de superstitionibus
8   magicis vita   ndis.

       Adolphsz, Joan, pseud.

            see

       Webbers, Zacharias.

Witchcraft The Adversary, his person, power, and
BF   purpose.
1548   Matson, William A.
M43   The Adversary, his person, power, and
1891   purpose; a study in satanology. [2d ed.]
       New York, W. B. Ketcham [c1891]
          xi, 238 p. 20cm.

          1. Devil. 2. Demonomania. I. Title.

            Adversus fallaces et superstitiosas artes.
Witchcraft
BF
1600   Pereira, Benito, ca. 1535-1610.
P43   Benedicti Pererii Valentini ... Adversvs
1592   fallaces & superstitiosas artes, id est, De
       magia, de observatione somniorum, &, de di-
       uinatione astrologica. Libri tres. Vene-
       tiis, Apud Ioan. Baptistam Ciottum, senensem,
       1592.
          3 p. l., 256, [8] p. 15cm.
          First published 1591.
          Later editions have title: De magia, de
       observatione so   mniorum, et de divinati-
8   one astrologi   ca.
                    (Continued on next card)

            Adversus fallaces et superstitiosas artes.
Witchcraft
BF
1600   Pereira, Benito, ca. 1535-1610. Benedicti
P43   Pererii Valentini ... Adversus fallaces ...
1592   1592.   (Card 2)

          Stamp of S. Michele in Bosco on cover.

          1. Magic. 2. Dreams. 3. Astrology. I.
       Title: Adversus fallaces et superstitiosas
8   artes.

            Adversus fallaces et superstitiosas
WITCHCRAFT artes.
BF
1600   Pereira, Benito, ca. 1535-1610.
P43   Benedicti Pererii Valentini ... Adversvs
1603   fallaces et superstitiosas artes, id est, De
       magia, de observatione somniorum, & de di-
       uinatione astrologica. Libri tres. Et à
       mendis quae anteà irrepserant accuratissimè
       repurgatus. Lvgdvni, Apvd Horativm Cardon,
       1603.
          5 p. l., 253, [8] p. 18cm.
          Title in red and black.
          1. Magic.   2. Dreams. 3. Astrolo-
8   gy. I. Tit   le: Adversus fallaces
       et superstiti   osas artes.

            An advertisement to the jury-men of
            England touching witches.
Witchcraft
BF
1565   [Filmer, Sir Robert] d. 1653.
F48   An advertisement to the jury-men of Englan
       touching witches. Together with a difference
       between an English and [an] Hebrew vvitch.
       London, Printed by I. G. for R. Royston, 1653
          24 p. 20cm.

          Ex libris Joseph Beard.

          1. Witchcraf   t. I. Title.

            An advertisement to the jury-men of
            England, touching witches.
Rare   Filmer, Sir Robert, d. 1653.
JC   The free-holders grand inquest,
153   touching our sovereign lord the King
F48F8 and his parliament. To which are added
1679   Observations upon forms of government.
       Together with Directions for obedience
       to governours in dangerous and doubtful
       times ... London, 1679.
          88, 76, 72, 257-346 p. 19cm.

          Contents.--The free-holders grand
                    (Continued on next card)

CATALOGUE OF THE CORNELL WITCHCRAFT COLLECTION

```
                An advertisement to the jury-men of
                  England, touching witches.
Rare      Filmer, Sir Robert, d. 1653.  The free-
JC          holders grand inquest ... 1679.
153         (Card 2)
F48F8
1679      inquest.--Observations upon Aristotle's
        politiques, touching forms of government.
        --Observations concerning the original
        of government, upon Mr. Hobs his Leviathan,
        Mr. Milton against Salmasius, H. Grotius
        De jure belli, Mr. Hunton's Treatise of
        monarchy.--The anarchy of a limited or
        mixed monarchy.--An advertisement to the

                    (Continued on next card)
```

```
                An advertisement to the jury-men of
                  England, touching witches.
Rare      Filmer, Sir Robert, d. 1653.  The free-
JC          holders grand inquest ... 1679.
153         (Card 3)
F48F8
1679      jury-men of England, touching witches.


          I. Title.  II. Title: An advertisement
        to the jury-men of England, touching
        witches.
```

```
                Advis aux criminalistes sur les abus.
Witchcraft
BF      ₍Spee, Friedrich von₎ 1591-1635.
1583        Advis avx criminalistes svr les abvs
A2S74   qvi se glissent dans les proces de sor-
1660    celerie.  Dediés avx magistrats d'Alle-
        magne.  Liure tres necessaire en ce temps
        icy, à tous iuges, conseillers, confes-
        seurs ... inquisiteurs, predicateurs, ad-
        uocats, & mêmes aux medecins. Par le P.
        N. S. I. theologian romain.  Imprimé en
        Latin pour la seconde fois à Francfort en
        l'année 1632.  Et mis en françois par F.
        B. de Velledor ₍pseud.₎ M.A.D.  Lyon,
                    (Continued on next card)
```

```
Witchcraft  Advis aux criminalistes sur les abus.
BF       ₍Spee, Friedrich von₎ 1591-1635.  Advis
1583        avx criminalistes ...  (Card 2)
A2S74
1660      Aux dépens de l'autheur: Et se vend chez
        Clavde Prost, 1660.
          ₍48₎, 336 p.  18cm.

          Translation of Cautio criminalis.

          I. His Cautio criminalis. French.
        II. Bouvot, Frédéric, tr. III. Title.
```

```
                Ein Advocat.
WITCHCRAFT
BF        Das Bezauberte Bauermägdgen: oder Geschichte
1555    von dem anjetzo in Kemberg bey Wittenberg
M94     sich aufhaltenden Landmägdchen Johanna
029     Elisabethen Lohmannin; aufgesetzet durch
no.2    einen vom Vorurtheil Befreyeten, und mit
        Anmerkungen eines Rechtsgelahrten verse-
        hen.  Breslau, Bey J. E. Meyer, 1760.
          167 p.  18cm.
          No. 2 in vol. lettered Oesfeld u. a. ...
        "Eines Advocatens Ehrenrettung wider
        Herrn Gottlieb    Müllers Beschuldigung":
-8      p. 51-162.
NIC                 (Continued on next card)
```

```
Witchcraft
BF        Ady, Thomas.
1565        A candle in the dark; or, A treatise con-
A24     cerning the nature of witches & witchcraft.
        Being advice to judges, sheriffes, justices
        of the peace, and grand-jury-men, what to do,
        before they passe sentence on such as are ar-
        raigned for their lives as witches.  London,
        Printed for R. I., to be sold by T. Newberry,
        1656.
          172 ₍i.e. 164₎ p.  19cm.
          Imperfect: p. 153-154 incorrectly numbered
        161-162; p. 163-   166 lacking; p. 155-164
        numbered 167-    172.
                    (Continued on next card)
```

```
Witchcraft  Ady, Thomas.  A candle in the dark.  1656.
BF          (Card 2)
1565
A24       Title vignette.
          Issued also under title: A perfect discovery
        of witches ...


          1. Witchcraft.  I. Title.  II. Ady, Thomas.
        ₍A perfect discovery of witches.
```

```
              Ady, Thomas.
Witchcraft   A perfect discovery of witches.
BF       ₍Ady, Thomas₎
1565        A perfect discovery of witches, shewing
A24     the divine cause of distractions of this
1661    kingdome, and also of the Christian world.
        London, 16--₎
          ₍140₎ p.  20cm.
          Imperfect: lacks t.p. and all before p. 9,
        also p. 107-110; p. 9-18, 139-140 mutilated;
        page numbers and part of text lacking; t.p.
        in ms. supplied.
          First ed.    published in 1656 under
        title: A candle   in the dark.
          I. Title.       II. His A candle in the
        dark.
```

```
Witchcraft
BT       ₍Ady, Thomas₎
980         The doctrine of devils, proved to be the
A24     grand apostacy of these later times.  An essay
        tending to rectifie those undue notions and
        apprehensions men have about daemons and evil
        spirits.  London, Printed for the author,
        1676.
          ₍8₎, 205 p.  17cm.


          1. Devil.  2. Demonology.  I. Title.
```

```
Witchcraft
BF       ₍Ady, Thomas₎
1565        A perfect discovery of witches, shewing
A24     the divine cause of distractions of this
1661    kingdome, and also of the Christian world.
        London, 16--₎
          ₍140₎ p.  20cm.
          Imperfect: lacks t.p. and all before p. 9,
        also p. 107-110; p. 9-18, 139-140 mutilated;
        page numbers and part of text lacking; t.p.
        in ms. supplied.
          First ed.    published in 1656 under
        title: A candle   in the dark.
          I. Title.       II. His A candle in the
        dark.
```

```
             Ady, Thomas.
Witchcraft  A perfect discovery of witches.
BF        Ady, Thomas.  A candle in the dark.  1656.
1565        (Card 2)
A24
          Title vignette.
          Issued also under title: A perfect discovery
        of witches ...


          1. Witchcraft.  I. Title.  II. Ady, Thomas.
        ₍A perfect discovery of witches.
```

```
             Ady, Thomas, supposed author.
Witchcraft
BT       ₍Orchard, N   ₎, supposed author.
980         The doctrine of devils, proved to be the
064     grand apostacy of these later times.  An es-
1676    say tending to rectifie those undue notions
        and apprehensions men have about daemons and
        evil spirits.  London, Printed for the au-
        thor, 1676.
          205 p.  17cm.

          Also attributed to Thomas Ady.

                 Devil.      2. Demonology.  I. Title.
        II. ¹Ady, Thomas, supposed author.
```

```
             Ady, Thomas, supposed author.
Witchcraft
BT       ₍Orchard, N    ₎, supposed author.
980         De leeringe der duyvelen, beweezen te zyn
064     de groote afval deezer laatste tyden.  Of een
1691    proeve, strekkende om die onbehoorlyke kun-
        digheden en bevattingen, welke de menschen van
        de demons en quaade geesten hebben, te verbé-
        teren.  In 't engelsch geschreeven door N.
        Orchard ... En volgens de copy, gedrukt tot
        Londen in 't jaar 1676, vertaald door Wm.
        Séwel.  t'Amsterdam, J. Broers, 1691.
          100 p.  21cm.

                    (Continued on next card)
```

```
             Ady, Thomas, supposed author.
Witchcraft
BT       ₍Orchard, N   ₎, supposed author.  De
980         leeringe der duyvelen ...  1691.  (Card 2)
064
1691      Translation of his The doctrine of devils
        ...
          Also attributed to Thomas Ady.

          1. Devil.  2. Demonology.  I. Title.  II.
        Orchard, N      supposed author.  The
        doctrine of devils--Dutch.  III. Ady, Thomas,
        supposed author.
```

```
             Aenmerckingen op De betoverde werelt van
Witchcraft    Dr. Balthazar Bekker ...
BF        Verrijn, Johannes, d. 1698.
1410        Aenmerckingen op De betoverde werelt
B42     van Dr. Balthazar Bekker, nopende de
Z88     geesten, en hun vermogen, en byzonderlijck
        den staet, en magt des duyvels.  Door J.
        Verryn.  Amsterdam, By G. Slaats, boek-
        verkoper, 1692.
          4 p. l., 136 p.  title and end page
        vignettes, illus. initials.  22 x 17cm.
          4°: *4, A-R4.
          Black letter.
          Van der       Linde 150.
                    (Continued on next card)
```

```
               L'affaire des poisons.
WITCHCRAFT
BF        Albe, Edmond, 1861-
1582        Autour de Jean XXII: Hugues Géraud, évèque
Z7      de Cahors, l'affaire des poisons et des en-
1317    voûtements en 1317.  Cahors, J. Girma, 1904.
          206 p.  25cm.
          "Extrait du Bulletin de la Société des
        Études littéraires, Scientifiques et Artis-
        tiques du Lot, t. XXIX."
          1. Géraud, Hugues, bp. of Cahors, fl. 1317.
        2. Joannes XXII, pope, d. 1334.  I. Title.
        II. Title: L'affaire des poisons.
```

```
               't Afgerukt mom-aansight der tooverye.
Witchcraft
BF        Palingh, Abraham.
1565        't Afgerukt mom-aansight der tooverye: daar
P16     in het bedrogh der gewaande toverye, naakt ont-
1725    dekt, en met gezonde redenen en exempelen dezer
        eeuwe aangewezen wort ...  Den tweeden Druk ...
        Amsterdam, By Andries van Damme, 1725.
          ₍16₎, 429, ₍10₎ p.  plates.  16cm.

          Title vignette, engraved.

          1. Witchcraft.  2. Magic.  I. Title.
```

CATALOGUE OF THE CORNELL WITCHCRAFT COLLECTION

Witchcraft
PN
3441
G92
A2
    Agnes.
    Günthert, Julius Ernst von.
        Agnes; eine Hexengeschichte aus dem 16. Jahrhundert. Stuttgart, A. Bonz, 1887.
        253 p. 19cm.

    1. Witchcraft. I. Title.

Witchcraft
BF
1565
A27
1597
    Agricola, Franciscus.
        Gründtlicher Bericht, ob Zauberey die argste vnd grewlichste sünd auff Erden sey. ...Zu Cölln, H. Falckenburg, 1597.
        231 p. 16cm.

    Colophon: Gedruckt bey Lambrecht Andreae.

Witchcraft
BF
1565
A27
1613
    Agricola, Franciscus.
        Gründtlicher Bericht, ob Zauber- vnd Hexerey die argste vnd grewlichste sünd auff Erden sey. Zum andern, ob die Zauberer noch Büsz thün vnd selig werden mögen. Zum dritten, ob die hohe Obrigkeit, so lieb ihr Gott vnd ire Seligkeit ist die Zauberer vnd Hexen am Leib vnd Leben zu straffen schuldig. Mit Ableinung allerley Einreden ... Dilingen, G. Hänlin, 1613.
        353 p. 16cm.

(Continued on next card)

Witchcraft
BF
1565
A27
1613
    Agricola, Franciscus. Gründtlicher Bericht ... 1613. (Card 2)
        Imperfect: lacks p. 207-222; p. 175-190 are repeated in their place.

    1. Witchcraft. 2. Magic. I. Title.

Agrippa Von Nettesheim

Witchcraft
B
781
A3
1600
    Agrippa von Nettesheim, Heinrich Cornelius, 1486?-1535.
        Opera omnia, in dvos tomos concinne digesta, & nunc denuò sublatis omnibus mendis, in φιλομούσων gratiam accuratissimè recusa. Qvibvs post omnivm editiones de nouo accessit Ars notoria ... Lvgdvni, Per Beringos Fratres, 1600.
        2 v. illus., diagrs., tables (part fold.) 18cm.
        Title vignette: printer's device.

Witchcraft
B
781
A3
1700
    Agrippa von Nettesheim, Heinrich Cornelius, 1486?-1535.
        Opera. In dvos tomos concinne digesta, et nunc denuò, sublatis omnibus mendis, in φιλομούσων gratiam accuratissimè recusa. Qvibvs post omnium editiones de novo accessit Ars notoria ... Lugduni, Per Beringos Fratres [ca. 1700?]
        2 v. illus., diagrs., tables (part fold.) 18cm.
        Title vignette.
        Vol. 2 has title: Opervm pars posterior.

(Continued on next card)

Witchcraft
B
781
A33A6
1605
    Agrippa von Nettesheim, Heinrich Cornelius, 1486?-1535.
        Appendix apologetica Henrici Cornelii Agrippae ab Nettesheym ... pertinens ad secvndam eivs opervm Lvgdvni editorum partem ... Lvgdvni, Per Beringos Fratres, 1605.
        262 p. 17cm.
        Page [135] is a special t. p. to the succeeding portions of the book: De beatissimae Annae monogamia, ac vnico pverperio propositiones abbreuiatae & articulatae ..

(Continued on next card)

B
781
A3
1630
    Agrippa von Nettesheim, Heinrich Cornelius, 1486?-1535.
        Opera, in dvos tomos concinne digesta, et nunc denuò sublatis omnibus mendis, in φιλομούσων gratiam accuratissimè recusa. Qvibvs post omnivm editiones de novo accessit Ars notoria ... Lvgdvni, Per Beringos Fratres [1630?]
        2 v. illus., diagrs., tables (part fold.) 19cm.
        Title vignette.

(Continued on next card)

Witchcraft
B
781
A3
1700
    Agrippa von Nettesheim, Heinrich Cornelius, 1486?-1535. Opera ... [ca. 1700?] (Card 2)
        Imprint probably fictitious.--Cf. Brit. Mus. Cat.

    1. Philosophy. 2. Occult sciences. 3. Science--Early works to 1800.

Witchcraft
B
781
A33A6
1605
    Agrippa von Nettesheim, Heinrich Cornelius, 1486?-1535. Appendix apologetica ... 1605. (Card 2)
        Defensio propositionvm praenarratarvm ... Argentorati, Impensis Lazari Zetzneri, 1605.

    I. Title.

B
781
A3
1630
    Agrippa von Nettesheim, Heinrich Cornelius, 1486?-1535. Opera ... [1630?] (Card 2)
        Vol. 2 has title: Opervm pars posterior. Imprint probably fictitious.--Cf. Brit. Mus. Cat.

    1. Philosophy. 2. Occult sciences. 2. Science--Early works to 1800.

Witchcraft
B
781
A33I32
1533
    Agrippa von Nettesheim, Heinrich Cornelius, 1486?-1535.
        Apologia aduersus calumnias propter Declamationem de Vanitate scientiarum, & excellentia uerbi Dei, sibi per aliquos Louanienses theologistas intentatas. Qverela svper calvmnia, ob eandem Declamationem, sibi per aliquot sceleratissimos sycophantas, apud Caesaream Maiest. nefarie ac proditorie illata. [Coloniae] 1533.
        [96] l. 17cm.
        Signatures: A-M^8.

(over)

Lavoisier
B
781
A33I3
1550
    Agrippa von Nettesheim, Heinrich Cornelius, 1486?-1535.
        Henrici Cornelii Agrippae ab Nettesheym De incertitudine et vanitate scientiarum declamatio invectiva, denuo ab autore recognita, et marginalibus annotationibus aucta [n.p., 1550?]
        1 v. (unpaged) 16cm.
        Title vignette: author's portrait.

    1. Learning and scholarship. 2. Scholasticism. 3. Science--Early works to 1800.

CATALOGUE OF THE CORNELL WITCHCRAFT COLLECTION

Witchcraft
B
781
A33I3
1584

Agrippa von Nettesheim, Heinrich Cornelius, 1486?-1535.
De incertitudine et vanitate scientiarum atque artium declamatio invectiua, ex ultima [recte] authoris recognitione. Coloniae, Apud Theodorum Baumium, 1584.
[311] l. 13cm.
Signatures: A-Z¹², Aa-Bb¹², Cc¹¹.
T. p. mutilated; missing letters and words supplied in manuscript.
Title vignette: author's portrait.

Witchcraft
781
33I3
609

Agrippa von Nettesheim, Heinrich Cornelius, 1486?-1535.
De incertitudine et vanitate omnium scientiarum & artium liber ... Accedunt dvo eivsdem avctoris libelli; quorum unus est de Nobilitate & praecellentia foeminei sexus, eiusdemq[ue] supra virilem eminentia. Alter de matrimonio seu coniugio ... [n.p.] 1609.
[264] l. 12cm.
Title vignette: author's portrait.
(Continued on next card)

Witchcraft
81
33I3
609

Agrippa von Nettesheim, Heinrich Cornelius, 1486?-1535. De incertitvdine ... 1609. (Card 2)
Contains only the first work.

1. Learning and scholarship. 2. Scholasticism. 3. Science—Early works to 1800. I. Title: De incertitudine et vanitate omnium scientiarum et artium liber.

Witchcraft
B
781
A33I3
1643

Agrippa von Nettesheim, Heinrich Cornelius, 1486?-1535.
De incertitudine & vanitate omnium scientiarum & artium liber ... Cum adiecto indice capitum. Accedunt duo ejusdem auctoris libelli; quorum unus est de Nobilitate & praecellentia foeminei sexus, ejusdemque supra virilem eminentiam; alter de matrimonio seu coniugio ... Lvgdvni Batavorvm, Excudebat Severinvs Matthaei, pro Officinis Abrahami Commelini & Davidis Lopes de Haro, 1643.
[16], 359 p. 14cm.
(Continued on next card)

Witchcraft
B
781
A33I3
1643

Agrippa von Nettesheim, Heinrich Cornelius, 1486?-1535. De incertitudine & vanitate omnium scientiarum ... 1643. (Card 2)
Title vignette.
Added t. p., engraved; dated: 1644.

1. Learning and scholarship. 2. Scholasticism. 3. Science—Early works to 1800. 4. Woman. 5. Marriage. I. Title. II. Title: De nobilitate et praecellentia foeminei sexus. III. Title: De matrimonio seu conjugio.

Witchcraft
B
781
A33I32
1533

Agrippa von Nettesheim, Heinrich Cornelius, 1486?-1535.
Apologia aduersus calumnias propter Declamationem de Vanitate scientiarum, & excellentia uerbi Dei, sibi per aliquos Louanienses theologistas intentatas. Qverela svper calvmnia, ob eandem Declamationem, sibi per aliquot sceleratissimos sycophantas, apud Caesaream Maiest. nefarie ac proditorie illata. [Coloniae] 1533.
[96] l. 17cm.
Signatures: A-M⁸.

Witchcraft
B
781
A33I3
1569

Agrippa von Nettesheim, Heinrich Cornelius, 1486?-1535. De incertitudine et vanitate—English.
Agrippa von Nettesheim, Heinrich Cornelius, 1486?-1535.
Of the vanitie and vncertaintie of artes and sciences, Englished by Ja. San., gent. ... London, Imprinted by Henry Wykes, 1569.
[8], 187 l. illus. 19cm.
First edition.
Translated by James Sandford.
Title within ornamental border.
Running title: Cornelius Agrippa of the vanities of sciences.
(Continued on next card)

Witchcraft
B
781
A33I3
1569

Agrippa von Nettesheim, Heinrich Cornelius, 1486?-1535. De incertitudine et vanitate—English.
Agrippa von Nettesheim, Heinrich Cornelius, 1486?-1535. Of the vanitie and vncertaintie of artes and sciences ... 1569. (Card 2)
Translation of De incertitudine et vanitate scientiarum atque artium declamatio invectiva.
Imperfect copy: leaf 185 wanting.

I. His De incertitudine et vanitate scientiarum. English. II. Sandford, James, fl. 1567, tr. III. Title.

Witchcraft
B
781
A33I3
1694

Agrippa von Nettesheim, Heinrich Cornelius, 1486?-1535. De incertitudine et vanitate—English.
Agrippa von Nettesheim, Heinrich Cornelius, 1486?-1535.
The vanity of arts and sciences ... London, Printed by R. Everingham for R. Bentley, and Dan. Brown, 1694.
[18], 368 p. 19cm.
Prefixed: The life of Henry Cornelius Agrippa; His epitaph; On the learned author ... (verse, signed: S. S.)
Translation of De incertitudine et vanitate scientiarum atque artium declamatio invectiva.

WITCHCRAFT
B
781
A33
I3
1582

Agrippa von Nettesheim, Heinrich Cornelius, 1486?-1535.
De incertitudine et vanitate omnium scientiarum et artium liber. French.
Agrippa von Nettesheim, Heinrich Cornelius, 1486?-1535.
Declamation svr l'incertitvde, vanité, et abvs des sciences, traduite en françois du latin de Henry Corneille Agr. ... Paris, Par Iean Dvrand, 1582.
8 p. l., 551 p. 17cm.
First edition in French, of De incertitudine et vanitate omnium scientiarum et artium liber.
"Trad. par Louis de Mayerne Turquet. C'est la seule traduction qui n'a pas
(Continued on next card)

WITCHCRAFT
B
781
A33
I3
1582

Agrippa von Nettesheim, Heinrich Cornelius, 1486?-1535.
De incertitudine et vanitate omnium scientiarum et artium liber. French.
Agrippa von Nettesheim, Heinrich Cornelius, 1486?-1535. Declamation svr l'incertitvde ... des sciences ... 1582. (Card 2)
été mutilée": in 17th century hand on flyleaf.
Gold stamped citron morocco binding with date 1695 on front and back covers.

1. Learning and scholarship. 2. Scholasticism. 3. Science—Early works to 1800. I. His De incertitudine et vanitate omnium scientiarum et artium liber. French. II. Mayerne, Louis Turquet de, d. 1618. III. Title.

WITCHCRAFT
B
781
A32
F8
1726

Agrippa von Nettesheim, Heinrich Cornelius, 1486?-1535.
De incertitudine et vanitate—French.
Agrippa von Nettesheim, Heinrich Cornelius, 1486?-1535.
Sur la noblesse, & excellence du sexe feminin, de sa preeminence sur l'autre sexe, & du sacrement du mariage. Avec le traitté sur l'incertitude, aussi bien que la vanité des sciences & des arts ... traduit par M. de Guedeville. Leiden, Chez Theodore Haak, 1726.
3 v. front., port. 17cm.
Vols. 2-3 have title: Sur l'in-
(Continued on next card)

Witchcraft
B
781
A32
F8
1726

Agrippa von Nettesheim, Heinrich Cornelius, 1486?-1535.
De incertitudine et vanitate scientiarum et artium—French.
Agrippa von Nettesheim, Heinrich Cornelius, 1486?-1535.
Sur la noblesse, & excellence du sexe feminin ... 1726. (Card 2)
certitude, aussi bien que la vanité des sciences & des arts.
Translation of De nobilitate et praecellentia foeminei sexus, and De incertitudine et vanitate scientiarum et artium.

1. Woman. 2. Marriage. 3. Learning and scholarship. 4. Scholasticism. I.
(Continued on next card)

WITCHCRAFT
B
781
A32
F8
1726

Agrippa von Nettesheim, Heinrich Cornelius, 1486?-1535.
De nobilitate et praecellentia—French.
Agrippa von Nettesheim, Heinrich Cornelius, 1486?-1535.
Sur la noblesse, & excellence du sexe feminin, de sa preeminence sur l'autre sexe, & du sacrement du mariage. Avec le traitté sur l'incertitude, aussi bien que la vanité des sciences & des arts ... traduit par M. de Guedeville. Leiden, Chez Theodore Haak, 1726.
3 v. front., port. 17cm.
Vols. 2-3 have title: Sur l'in-
(Continued on next card)

WITCHCRAFT
B
781
A32
F8
1726

Agrippa von Nettesheim, Heinrich Cornelius, 1486?-1535.
De nobilitate et praecellentia—French.
Agrippa von Nettesheim, Heinrich Cornelius, 1486?-1535.
Sur la noblesse, & excellence du sexe feminin ... 1726. (Card 2)
certitude, aussi bien que la vanité des sciences & des arts.
Translation of De nobilitate et praecellentia foeminei sexus, and De incertitudine et vanitate scientiarum et artium.

1. Woman. 2. Marriage. 3. Learning and scholarship. 4. Scholasticism. I.
(Continued on next card)

Agrippa von Nettesheim, Heinrich Cornelius, 1486?-1535, supposed author.
De occulta philosophia, liber quartus.

see

Liber de ceremoniis magicis.

Witchcraft
BF
1598
A27
O2++
1533

Agrippa von Nettesheim, Heinrich Cornelius, 1486?-1535.
Henrici Cornelii Agrippae ab Nettesheym à consiliis & archiuis inditiarii sacrae Caesareae Maiestatis: De occulta philosophia libri tres. Henricvs Cornelivs Agrippa ... [Coloniae, 1533]
6 p. l., ccclxii p. incl. illus., tables, diagrs. 31cm.
Title vignette: colored woodcut portrait of the author; initials; cabalistic characters, astronomical signs, figures and alphabets.
Dedication dated: ex Mechlinia, 1531. First published Antwerp, J. Grapheus, 1531.

1. Occult sciences. I. Title: De occulta philosophia.
20—7812
Library of Congress BF1598.A3O4 1533
[36b1]

Witchcraft
BF
1598
A27
O2
1567

Agrippa von Nettesheim, Heinrich Cornelius, 1486?-1535.
Henrici Cor. Agrippae ab Nettesheym, De occvlta philosophia libri III. Qvibvs accesservnt, Spurius Agrippae Liber de ceremonijs magicis. Heptameron Petri de Albano [sic]. Ratio compendiaria magiae naturalis, ex Plinio desumpta. Disputatio de fascinationibus. Epistola de incantatione & adjuratione, collig[e]; suspensione. Iohannis Tritemij opuscula quaedam huius argumenti. Parisiis, Ex officina Iaco[bi] bi Dupuys, 1567.
(Continued on next card)

CATALOGUE OF THE CORNELL WITCHCRAFT COLLECTION

Witchcraft
BF 1598 A27 O2 1567
Agrippa von Nettesheim, Heinrich Cornelius, 1486?-1535. Henrici Cor. Agrippae ab Nettesheym, De occvlta philosophia libri III. 1567. (Card 2)
16 p. l., 668, [1] p. illus., tables, diagrams (3 fold. in back) 20cm.
Binding: contemporary blind stamped pigskin with clasps (hinges wanting)
I. Abano, Pietro d', 1250-1316. Heptameron. II. De fascinationibus disputatio. III. De incantatione et adiuratione.
8

BF 1598 A27 O2++ 1967
Agrippa von Nettesheim, Heinrich Cornelius, 1486?-1535. De occulta philosophia. Hrsg. und erläutert von Karl Anton Nowotny. Graz, Akademische Druck- und Verlagsanstalt, 1967.
viii, 915 p. illus. 35cm.
At head of title: Henricus Cornelius Agrippa ab Nettesheim.
Facsimile of the 1533 ed.

Witchcraft
BF 1598 A27 O2 1651
Agrippa von Nettesheim, Heinrich Cornelius, 1486?-1535. De occulta philosophia—English.
Agrippa von Nettesheim, Heinrich Cornelius, 1486?-1535.
Three books of occult philosophy ... Translated out of the Latin into the English tongue, by J. F[reake]. London, Printed by R. W. for Gregory Moule, and are to be sold at the Sign of the three Bibles neer the West-end of Pauls, 1651.
[26], 583, [12] p. port., illus., tables, diagrs. 19cm.
Imprint of copy 3 varies slightly: London,
(Continued on next card)

Witchcraft
BF 1598 A27 O2 1651
Agrippa von Nettesheim, Heinrich Cornelius, 1486?-1535. De occulta philosophia—English.
Agrippa von Nettesheim, Heinrich Cornelius, 1486?-1535.
Three books of occult philosophy ... 1651. (Card 2)
Printed by R. W. for Gregory Moule, and are to be sold neer the West-end of Pauls, 1651.
Copy 1 lacks portrait; copy 2 lacks "An encomium on the three Books of Cornelius Agrippa, by Eugenius Philalethes." (sig.a2)
Portrait in copy 3 mounted.
Translation of De occulta philosophia libri tres.
I. His De occulta philosophia libri tres. English. II. Freake, J., tr. III. Title.

Witchcraft
BF 1598 A27 O2 1727
Agrippa von Nettesheim, Heinrich Cornelius, 1486?-1535. De occulta philosophia—French.
Agrippa von Nettesheim, Heinrich Cornelius, 1486?-1535.
La philosophie occulte. Divisée en trois livres, et traduite du Latin. La Haye, R. Chr. Alberts, 1727.
2 v. in 1. illus. 19cm.
Title vignettes, engraved.
"Apologie pour Agrippa, par Mr. G. Naudé": v. 1, p. [3]-[21] (From his Apologie pour les grands hommes soupçonnez de magie.)
Translation of De occulta philosophia.

BF 1410 L69 1921
Agrippa von Nettesheim, Heinrich Cornelius, 1486?-1535. De occulta philosophia libri tres. German.
Heinrich Cornelius Agrippa's von Nettesheim Magische Werke : sammt den geheimnissvollen Schriften des Petrus von Abano, Pictorius von Villingen, Gerhard von Cremona, Abt Tritheim von Spanheim, dem Buche Arbatel, der sogenannten Heil. Geist-Kunst und verschiedenen anderen zum ersten Male vollständig in's Deutsche übersetzt : vollständig in fünf Theilen, mit einer Menge Abbildungen. -- 4. Aufl. -- Berlin : H. Barsdorf, 1921.
5 v. in 3. : ill. ; 17 cm. -- (Geheime Wissenschaften ; 10-14)
(Continued on next card)

WITCHCRAFT
B 781 A33 I3 1582
Agrippa von Nettesheim, Heinrich Cornelius, 1486?-1535.
Declamation svr l'incertitvde, vanité, et abvs des sciences, traduite en françois du latin de Henry Corneille Agr. ... [Paris] Par Iean Dvrand, 1582.
8 p. l., 551 p. 17cm.
First edition in French, of De incertitudine et vanitate omnium scientiarum et artium liber.
"Trad. par Louis de Mayerne Turquet. C'est la seule traduction qui n'a pas
8 (Continued on next card)

WITCHCRAFT
B 781 A33 I3 1582
Agrippa von Nettesheim, Heinrich Cornelius, 1486?-1535. Declamation svr l'incertitvde ... des sciences ... 1582. (Card 2)
été mutilée": in 17th century hand on fly-leaf.
Gold stamped citron morocco binding with date 1695 on front and back covers.
1. Learning and scholarship. 2. Scholasticism. 3. Science—Early works to 1800. I. His De incertitudine et vanitate omnium scientiarum et artium liber. French. II. Mayerne, Louis Turquet de, d. 1618. III. Title.

WITCHCRAFT
BF 1410 L69 1655
Agrippa von Nettesheim, Heinrich Cornelius, 1486?-1535, supposed author.
Fourth book of occult philosophy.
Henry Cornelius Agrippa's Fourth book of occult philosophy, and geomancy. Magical elements of Peter de Abano. Astronomical geomancy [by Gerardus Cremonensis]. The nature of spirits [by Georg Pictorius]: and Arbatel of magick. Translated into English by Robert Turner. Philomathées. London, 1655.
9 p. l., [5]-266 [i.e., 286], [4] p. illus. 19cm.
8 Neither Agrippa nor Abano wrote the works
(Continued on next card)

WITCHCRAFT
BF 1410 L69 1655
Agrippa von Nettesheim, Heinrich Cornelius, 1486?-1535, supposed author.
Fourth book of occult philosophy.
Henry Cornelius Agrippa's Fourth book of occult philosophy, and geomancy ... 1655. (Card 2)
here ascribed to them; the Heptameron, or Magical elements also was ascribed to Agrippa under the title: Les oeuvres magiques, with Abano as translator (!)
Translation of a work variously titled Liber de ceremonijs magicis; and his De occulta philosophia, liber quartus.
8 (Continued on next card)

Agrippa von Nettesheim, Heinrich Cornelius, 1486?-1535, supposed author.
Liber de ceremoniis magicis.
see
Liber de ceremoniis magicis.

WITCHCRAFT
BF 1602 O29 1830
Agrippa von Nettesheim, Heinrich Cornelius, 1486?-1535, supposed author.
Les oeuvres magiques.
Les Oeuvres magiques de Henri-Corneille Agrippa, mises en français par Pierre d'Aban, avec des secrets occultes, notamment celui de la Reine des Mouches velues. Rome, 1744. [Lille, Impr. de Bloquel, ca. 1830]
112 p. port., illus. (1 fold.) 14cm.
Caption title: Heptameron, ou Les éléments magiques de Pierre d'Aban, philosophe, disciple de Henri Corneille Agrippa.
Has nothing to do either with Agrip-
8 (Continued on next card)

WITCHCRAFT
BF 1602 O29 1830
Agrippa von Nettesheim, Heinrich Cornelius, 1486?-1535, supposed author.
Les oeuvres magiques.
Les Oeuvres magiques de Henri-Corneille Agrippa ... [1830] (Card 2)
pa or with Pietro d'Abano, who predeceased him by 2 centuries.
Copy 1 has list of similar items for sale, e.g., Le veritable dragon rouge, Enchiridion Leonis papae, Secrets merveilleux de la magie naturelle du Petit Albert ...
1. Occult sciences. 2. Magic.
8 3. Charms. (Continued on next card)

Witchcraft
B 781 A33I3 1569
Agrippa von Nettesheim, Heinrich Cornelius, 1486?-1535.
Of the vanitie and vncertaintie of artes and sciences, Englished by Ja. San., gent. ... London, Imprinted by Henry Wykes, 1569.
[8], 187 l. illus. 19cm.
First edition.
Translated by James Sandford.
Title within ornamental border.
Running title: Cornelius Agrippa of the vanities of sciences.
(Continued on next card)

Witchcraft
B 781 A33I3 1569
Agrippa von Nettesheim, Heinrich Cornelius, 1486?-1535. Of the vanitie and vncertaintie of artes and sciences ... 1569. (Card 2)
Translation of De incertitudine et vanitate scientiarum atque artium declamatio invectiva.
Imperfect copy: leaf 185 wanting.
I. His De incertitudine et vanitate scientiarum. English. II. Sandford, James, fl. 1567, tr. III. Title.

Witchcraft
BF 1598 A27 O2 1727
Agrippa von Nettesheim, Heinrich Cornelius, 1486?-1535.
La philosophie occulte. Divisée en trois livres, et traduite du Latin. La Haye, R. Chr. Alberts, 1727.
2 v. in 1. illus. 19cm.
Title vignettes, engraved.
"Apologie pour Agrippa, par Mr. G. Naudé": v. 1, p. [3]-[21] (From his Apologie pour les grands hommes soupçonnez de magie.)
Translation of De occulta philosophia.
(over)

WITCHCRAFT
B 781 A32 F8 1726
Agrippa von Nettesheim, Heinrich Cornelius, 1486?-1535.
Sur la noblesse, & excellence du sexe feminin, de sa preeminence sur l'autre sexe & du sacrement du mariage. Avec le traitte sur l'incertitude, aussi bien que la vanité des sciences & des arts ... traduit par M. de Guedeville. Leiden, Chez Theodore Haak, 1726.
3 v. front., port. 17cm.
Vols. 2-3 have title: Sur l'in-
8 (Continued on next card)
NIC

WITCHCRAFT
B 781 A32 F8 1726
Agrippa von Nettesheim, Heinrich Cornelius, 1486?-1535. Sur la noblesse, & excellence du sexe feminin ... 1726. (Card 2)
certitude, aussi bien que la vanité des sciences & des arts.
Translation of De nobilitate et praecellentia foeminei sexus, and De incertitudine et vanitate scientiarum et artium.
1. Woman. 2. Marriage. 3. Learning and scholarship. 4. Scholasticism. I.
8 (Continued on next card)
NIC

10

CATALOGUE OF THE CORNELL WITCHCRAFT COLLECTION

WITCHCRAFT
B 781 A32 F8 1726

Agrippa von Nettesheim, Heinrich Cornelius, 1486?-1535. Sur la noblesse, & excellence du sexe feminin ... 1726. (Card 3)

His De nobilitate et praecellentia foeminei sexus. French. II. His De incertitudine et vanitate scientiarum et artium. French. III. Gueudeville, Nicolas, ca. 1654-ca. 1721, tr. IV. Title. V. Title: Sur l'incertitude, aussi bien que la vanité des sciences & des arts.

8
NIC

Witchcraft
BF 1598 A27 O2 1651

Agrippa von Nettesheim, Heinrich Cornelius, 1486?-1535.
Three books of occult philosophy ... Translated out of the Latin into the English tongue, by J. F[reake] London, Printed by R. W. for Gregory Moule, and are to be sold at the Sign of the three Bibles neer the West-end of Pauls, 1651.
[26], 583, [12] p. port., illus., tables, diagrs. 19cm.
Imprint of copy 3 varies slightly: London,
(Continued on next card)

Witchcraft
BF 1598 A27 O2 1651

Agrippa von Nettesheim, Heinrich Cornelius, 1486?-1535. Three books of occult philosophy ... 1651. (Card 2)
Printed by R. W. for Gregory Moule, and are to be sold neer the West-end of Pauls, 1651.
Copy 1 lacks portrait; copy 2 lacks "An encomium on the three Books of Cornelius Agrippa, by Eugenius Philalethes." (sig.a2)
Portrait in copy 3 mounted.
Translation of De occulta philosophia libri tres.
I. His De occulta philosophia libri tres. English. II. Freake, J., tr. III. Title.

BF 1598 A27 O2 1898

Agrippa von Nettesheim, Heinrich Cornelius, 1486?-1535.
Three books of occult philosophy or magic. Book one--Natural magic; which includes the early life of Agrippa, his seventy-four chapters on natural magic, new notes, illustrations, index and other original and selected matter. Ed. by Willis F. Whitehead. By direction of the Brotherhood of magic: The magic mirror, a message to mystics, containing full instructions on its make and use. Chicago, Hahn & Whitehead, 1898.
288 p. front. (port.) illus, plates, facsim. 25cm.
Includes extracts from Henry Morley's "Life of Cornelius Agrippa."

Witchcraft
B 781 A3313 1684

Agrippa von Nettesheim, Heinrich Cornelius, 1486?-1535.
The vanity of arts and sciences. London, Printed by R. E. for R. B. and are to be sold by C. Blount, 1684.
[14], 368 p. 17cm.
"The life of Henry Cornelius Agrippa, knight and judge of the Supreme Court": p. [7]-[10]. "On the learned author ...," poem signed S.S.: p. [11]-[12].
Wing A 791.

Witchcraft
B 781 A3313 1694

Agrippa von Nettesheim, Heinrich Cornelius, 1486?-1535.
The vanity of arts and sciences ... London, Printed by R. Everingham for R. Bentley, and Dan. Brown, 1694.
[18], 368 p. 19cm.
Prefixed: The life of Henry Cornelius Agrippa; His epitaph; On the learned author ... (verse, signed: S. S.)
Translation of De incertitudine et vanitate scientiarum atque artium declamatio invectiva.

(over)

BF 1410 L69 1970?

Agrippa von Nettesheim, Heinrich Cornelius, 1486?-1535, supposed author.
Liber de ceremoniis magicis. Italian. 1970?
Le cerimonie magiche. Prima traduzione italiana dal testo latino preceduta da una introduzione. Roma, All'insegna della corona dei magi, [1970?].
78 p. illus. 22cm.
At head of title: Enrico Cornelio Agrippa.
1. Occult sciences. I. Agrippa von Nettesheim, Heinrich Cornelius, 1486?-1535, supposed author. II. Title. III. Title: De occulta philosophia liber quartus. Italian.

NIC JAN 30,'74 COOxc

Witchcraft
B 781 A34 M86

Agrippa von Nettesheim, Heinrich Cornelius, 1486?-1535.
Morley, Henry, 1822-1894.
The life of Henry Cornelius Agrippa von Nettesheim, doctor and knight, commonly known as a magician. London, Chapman and Hall, 1856.
2 v. 21cm.
Title vignettes.
At head of title: Cornelius Agrippa.
1. Agrippa von Nettesheim, Heinrich Cornelius, 1486?-1535. I. Title.

Witchcraft
BF 1598 A27 O76

Agrippa von Nettesheim, Heinrich Cornelius, 1486?-1535.
Orsier, Joseph.
... Henri Cornélis Agrippa, sa vie et son œuvre d'après sa correspondance (1486-1535) Paris, Chacornac, 1911.
142 p., 1 l. 25½cm.
CONTENTS.—1. ptie. La vie et l'œuvre d'Agrippa.—2. ptie. Extraits, annotés et traduits pour la première fois du latin, de la correspondance d'Agrippa avec ses amis et les personnages de son temps.

I. Agrippa von Nettesheim, Heinrich Cornelius, 1486?-1535. I. Title.
13-1681

Witchcraft
BF 1598 A27 P96

Agrippa von Nettesheim, Heinrich Cornelius, 1486?-1535.
Prost, Auguste, 1817-1896.
Les sciences et les arts occultes au XVIe siècle. Corneille Agrippa, sa vie et ses oeuvres... Paris, Champion, 1881-82.
2 v. 23cm.
1. Agrippa von Nettesheim, Heinrich Cornelius, 1486?-1535. 2. Occult sciences. I. Title.

Witchcraft
BF 1565 S83 no.1

Akademische Rede von dem gemeinen Vortheil der wirkenden und thätigen Hexerey.
Sterzinger, Ferdinand, 1721-1786.
Akademische Rede von dem gemeinen Vortheil der wirkenden und thätigen Hexerey, welche an Sr. Churfürstl. Durchleucht in Baiern, &c. &c. &c. höchsterfreulichen Namensfeste abgelesen worden von P. Don Ferdinand Sterzinger ... Den 13. October 1766. München, Gedruckt bey M. M. Mayrin, Stadtbuchdruckerin [1766]
22 p. 20cm. (bound in 23cm. vol.)
No. 1 in vol. lettered Sterzinger über Hexerei, 1766- 1767.
8
1. Witchcraft. I. Title.

DQ 3 Q3 v.22

Die Akten des Jetzerprozesses nebst dem Defensorium.
Steck, Rudolf, 1842-1924, ed.
Die Akten des Jetzerprozesses nebst dem Defensorium. Basel, Verlag der Basler Buch- und Antiquariatshandlung vormals A. Geering, 1904.
xl, 679 p. illus. 23cm. (Quellen zur Schweizer Geschichte, 22. Bd.)
1. Jetzer, Johann, ca. 1483-ca. 1515. 2. Dominicans in Switzerland. 3. Bern--Church history--Sources. I. Title.

Aktienmässige Nachrichten von Hexenprozessen und Zaubereien im ehemaligen Herzogtum Pommern.
Witchcraft
CB 3 Z481

Stojentin, Max von.
Aktienmässige Nachrichten von Hexenprozessen und Zaubereien im ehemaligen Herzogtum Pommern.
(In Beiträge zur Kulturgeschichte. Weimar. 25cm. 2. Heft (1898), p. [18]-44)

1. Witchcraft--Germany. I. Title.

8

WITCHCRAFT
BF 1582 Z7 1317

Albe, Edmond, 1861-
Autour de Jean XXII: Hugues Géraud, évêque de Cahors, l'affaire des poisons et des envoûtements en 1317. Cahors, J. Girma, 1904.
206 p. 25cm.
"Extrait du Bulletin de la Société des Études littéraires, Scientifiques et Artistiques du Lot, t. XXIX."
1. Géraud, Hugues, bp. of Cahors, fl. 1317. 2. Jo annes XXII, pope, d. 1334. I. Title. II. Title: L'affaire des poisons.

Witchcraft
BX 1710 A32 1642

Alberghini, Giovanni, 1574-1644.
Manvale qvalificatorvm sanctiss. Inqvisitionis, in qvo omnia, qvae ad illvd tribvnal, ac haeresum censuram pertinent, breui methodo adducuntur ... Cum duplici indice ... Panormi, Apud Decium Cyrillum, 1642.
[24], 405, [3] p. 18cm.
Added t. p., engraved.

1. Inquisition. 2. Witchcraft. I. Title.

Witchcraft
BF 1548 A33

Albers, Johann Heinrich, 1840-
Die Lehre vom Teufel, allgemein fasslich dargestellt für liberale Protestanten aus dem Volk. Eine Preisschrift. Strassburg, J. Schneider, 1878.
58 p. 20cm.

1. Devil. I. Title.

Witchcraft
BF 1520 A33

Alberti, Michael, 1682-1757, praeses.
Dissertatio inauguralis medica, de potestate diaboli in corpus humanum, qvam ... praeside Dn. D. Michaele Alberti ... ventilationi subjiciet respondens Johannes Fridericus Corvinus ... [Halle] Typis Jo: Christian Hendel [1725]
52 p. 21cm.
Diss.--Halle (J. F. Corvinus, respondent)
1. Demonology. 2. Diseases--Causes and theories of causation. I. Corvinus, Johann Friedrich, of Halle, respondent. II. Title: De po testate diaboli in corpus humanum. III. Title.

HIST SCI
R 133 A33

Alberti, Michael, 1682-1757, praeses.
Dissertatio inauguralis medica De superstitione medica, quam...praeside Dn. D. Michaele Alberti...publicae ventilationi submittet David Godofred. Kletschke. Halae Magdeburgicae, Typis Ioanni Christiani Hendelii [1720]
40 p. 21 cm.

Diss.--Halle (D.G. Kletschke, respondent)
1. Medical delusions. 2. Folk medicine. 3. Medicine, popular. I. Kletschke David Gottfr ied, respondent. II. Title.

CATALOGUE OF THE CORNELL WITCHCRAFT COLLECTION

HIST SCI
R
128
.7
A1
A33
no.22
    Alberti, Michael, 1682-1757, praeses.
      Dissertatio inauguralis medica De superstitione medica, quam...praeside Dn. D. Michaele Alberti...publicae ventilationi submittet David Godofred. Kletschke. Halae Magdeburgicae, Typis Ioanni [sic] Christiani Hendelii [1720]
      40 p. 20cm.

      Diss.--Halle (D.G. Kletschke, respondent)
      No.22 in a vol. of dissertations for which Alberti acted as praeses. (Vol. lettered: Dispvtationvm medicarvm volumen LVI)
      (Continued on next card)

Witchcraft
BF
1565
D62
no.10
    Alberti, Valentin, 1635-1697, praeses.
      Dissertatio academica, De sagis, sive foeminis, commercium cum malo spiritu habentibus, e christiana pnevmatologia desumpta, & sub praesidio ... Dn. D. Valentini Alberti ... publicae proposita ventilationi ab autore Christiano Stridtbeckh ... Lipsiae, Typis Christoph. Fleischeri [1690]
      [52] p. illus. 20cm.
      No.10 in vol. lettered Dissertationes de sagis. 1636-1714.
      (Continued on next card)

Rare
BX
890
A33
1651++
    Albertus Magnus, Saint, Bp. of Ratisbon, 1193?-1280.
      ... Opera ... in lucem edita, studio & labore ... Petri Iammy. Lygdvni, Sumpt. Claudii Prost, Petri & Claudii Rigaud [etc], 1651.
      21v. front. (v.1) 35cm.
      Contents.--v.1. Logica.--v.2. Physica. De caelo & mundo. De generatione &
      (Continued on next card)

HIST SCI
R
128
.7
A1
A33
no.22
    Alberti, Michael, 1682-1757, praeses. Dissertatio inauguralis medica De superstitione medica...[1720]   (Card 2)

      1. Medical delusions. 2. Folk medicine. 3. Medicine, Popular. I. Kletschke, David Gottfried, respondent. II. Title.

Witchcraft
BF
1565
D62
no.10
    Alberti, Valentin, 1635-1697, praeses.
      Dissertatio academica, De sagis ... [1690]   (Card 2)

      1. Witchcraft. 2. Jeanne d'Arc, Saint, 1412-1431. 3. Attila, d. 453. I. Stridtbeckh, Christian, respondent. II. Title: De sagis. III. Dissertatio academica, De sagis.

Rare
BX
890
A33
1651++
    Albertus Magnus, Saint, Bp. of Ratisbon, 1193?-1280. Opera ... 1651. (Card 2)
      Contents: (cont'd)
    Politicorum Aristotelis commentarii.--v.5. Parva natvralia.--v.6. De animalibvs.--v.7. Commentarii in Psalmos.--v.8. Commentarii in Threnos Ieremiae, in Baruch, in Danielem, in 12 proph. minores.--v.9. Commentarii in Matthaeum, in Marcum.--v.10. Commentarii in Lvcam.--v.11. Commentarii in Ioannem, in Apocalypsim.--v.12
      (Continued on next card)

HIST SCI
R
133
A33
D6
    Alberti, Michael, 1682-1757, praeses.
      Dissertatio inauguralis medica medicinam pseudo-miraculosam aperiens, quam...in Alma Regia Fridericiana, praeside...Michaele Alberti...pro gradu doctoris summisque in medicina honoribus et privilegiis doctoralibus legitime...impetrandis, anno MDCCLIII. d. Maii...publicae...eruditorum ventilationi subjiciet auctor Georgius Heck... Halae Magdeburgicae, Typis Joh. Christiani Hendelii [1753]
      43, [5] p. 21cm.
      (Continued on next card)

Witchcraft
BF
1565
A33
1723
    Alberti, Valentin, 1635-1697, praeses.
      ... Academische Abhandlung von den Hexen und dem Bündniss so sie mit dem Teuffel haben. Darinnen ... nebst Erörterung einiger andern curieusen Fragen, ob die bekannte Pucelle d'Orleans, ingleichen das rasende Weib, das den Attilam erschrecket, eine Hexe gewesen sei? Franckfurt und Leipzig, 1723.
      [56] p. front. 21cm.
      Translation of his Dissertatio academica, De sagis, C. Stridtbeckh, respondent, Wittebergae, 1690.
      (Continued on next card)

Rare
BX
890
A33
1651++
    Albertus Magnus, Saint, Bp. of Ratisbon, 1193?-1280. Opera ... 1651. (Card 3)
      Contents: (cont'd)
    Sermones de tempore, de sanctis, de eucharista. Orationes super Evangelia dominicalia totius anni. de muliere forti liber.--v.13. Commentarij in D. Dionysium Compendij theologicae veritatis lib. VII. v.14-16. Commentarii in I.-IV. lib. Sententiarvm.--v.17-18. Svmma thologia.
      (Continued on next card)

HIST SCI
R
133
A33
D6
    Alberti, Michael, 1682-1757, praeses.
      Dissertatio inauguralis medica...1753.   (Card 2)

      Diss. inaug.--Halle (G. Heck, respondent)

      1. Medical delusions. 2. Medicine, Magic, mystic, and spagiric. I. Heck, Georg, respondent. II. Title.

BS
2545
D5A33
    Albertinus, Alexander
      Mallevs demonvm. Siuè quatuor experimentatissimi exorcismi, ex Euangelijs collecti ... Veronae, Typis Bartholomaei Merli, 1620.
      347 p. 17cm.
      Imprint of colophon: Veronae, Typis Bartholomaei Meruli, 1621.

      1. Demoniac possession. 2. Exorcism. I. Title.

Rare
BX
890
A33
1651++
    Albertus Magnus, Saint, Bp. of Ratisbon, 1193?-1280. Opera ... 1651. (Card 4)
      Contents: (cont'd)
    v.19. Svmma de creatvris.--v.20. Super missus. De laudibus Beatae Mariae. Biblia Mariana.--v.21. Philosophia pauperum.

      I. Jammy, Petrus, ed.

Witchcraft
BF
1565
A33
1723
    Alberti, Valentin, 1635-1697, praeses.
      ... Academische Abhandlung von den Hexen und dem Bündniss so sie mit dem Teuffel haben. Darinnen ... nebst Erörterung einiger andern curieusen Fragen, ob die bekannte Pucelle d'Orleans, ingleichen das rasende Weib, das den Attilam erschrecket, eine Hexe gewesen sei? Franckfurt und Leipzig, 1723.
      [56] p. front. 21cm.
      Translation of his Dissertatio academica, De sagis, C. Stridtbeckh, respondent, Wittebergae, 1690.
      (Continued on next card)

WITCHCRAFT
BF
1525
O85
1602
    Albertinus, Aegidius, 1560-1620, tr.
    Osuna, Francesco de, d. ca. 1540.
      Flagellum diaboli; oder, Dess Teufels Gaissl. Darinn ... gehandlet wirt: Von der Macht und Gewalt dess bösen Feindts. Von den Effecten und Wirckungen der Zauberer, Unholdter uñ Hexenmaister... Durch...Franciscum de Ossuna in spanischer Sprach ausgangen, und durch Egidium Albertinum...verteuscht. München, Getruckt bey Adam Berg, 1602.
      78 (i.e.76) 1. 19cm.
      1.Devil. 2.Demonology. 3.Witchcraft. I. Albertinus, Aegidius, 1560-1620, tr. II. Title.

Witchcraft
BF
1598
A33
A2
1770
    Albertus Magnus, Saint, bp. of Ratisbon, 1193?-1280. Spurious and doubtful works.
      Les admirables secrets d'Albert le Grand. Contenant plusieurs traités sur la conception des femmes, des vertus des herbes, des pierres précieuses, & des animaux ... Lyon, Chez les Héritiers de Beringos Fratres, 1770.
      291 p. illus. 14cm.
      With autograph of J. Tickell.
      Attributed also to Albertus de Saxonia.
      With this is bound Albertus, Lucius, Parvus, pseud. Secrets merveilleux de la magie naturelle ... Lyon [1729] in vol. lettered: Tracts. (Over)

Witchcraft
BF
1598
A33
A2
1770
    Albertus de Saxonia, d. 1390, supposed author.
    Albertus Magnus, Saint, bp. of Ratisbon, 1193?-1280. Spurious and doubtful works.
      Les admirables secrets d'Albert le Grand. Contenant plusieurs traités sur la conception des femmes, des vertus des herbes, des pierres précieuses, & des animaux ... Lyon, Chez les Héritiers de Beringos Fratres, 1770.
      291 p. illus. 14cm.
      With autograph of J. Tickell.
      Attributed also to Albertus de Saxonia.
      With this is bound Albertus, Lucius, Parvus, pseud. Secrets merveilleux de la magie naturelle ... Lyon [1729] in vol. lettered: Tracts.

Witchcraft
BF
1582
Z7
1675
    Albertus Magnus, saint, bp. of Ratisbon, 1193?-1280. Spurious and doubtful works. Les admirables secrets d'Albert le Grand
    Hautefeuille, lawyer.
      Plaidoyez svr les magiciens et svr les sorciers, tenus en la cour de Liege, le 16. Decembre 1675. Ov on montre clairement qu'il n'y peut avoir de ces sortes de gens. Par les sieurs de Havte Feüille & Santevr advocats. Svr l'imprimé a Liege, Chez Iacqves Persois imprimeur, 1676.
      120 p. 14cm.
      "Le livre d'Albert le Grand, leqvel traite des merveilles du monde," p. [77]-
      (Continued on next card)

CATALOGUE OF THE CORNELL WITCHCRAFT COLLECTION

Witchcraft
BF
1582
Z7
1675
8

Albertus Magnus, saint, bp. of Ratisbon, 1193?-1280. Spurious and doubtful works.
Les admirables secrets d'Albert le Grand.
Hautefeuille, lawyer. Plaidoyez svr les magiciens ... 1676. (Card 2)
120, has special t. p. with imprint: Lyon, Par Iean Hvgvetan, 1616. Text is taken from Les admirables secrets d'Albert le Grand.
1. Witchcraft. 2. Magic. 3. Sillieux, Sulpice, fl. 1675. I. Santeur, lawyer. II. Albertus Magnus, saint, bp. of Ratisbon, 1193?-1280. Spurious and doubtful works. Les admirables secrets d'Albert le Grand. III. Title: Plaidoyez sur les magiciens. IV. Title: Le livre d'Albert le Grand.

WITCHCRAFT
BF
1405
L85
1673
8

Albertus Magnus, bp. of Ratisbon, 1193?-1280, supposed author.
De virtutibus quarundam herbarum, lapidum et animalium.
Longinus, Caesar, ed.
Trinum magicum, sive Secretorum magicorum opus ... Editum à Caesare Longino philos. Francofurti, Sumptibus Jacobi Gothofredi Seyleri, 1673.
12 p. l., 498 p. 14cm.
Contents.--Marci Antonii Zimarae Tractatus magicus.--Appendix, De mirandis quibusdam naturali magia factis operationibus. Ex lib. 2. Mag. nat. Ioan. Bapt. Port.--Tractatvs De virtutibus quarundam herbarum,
(Continued on next card)

WITCHCRAFT
BF
1405
L85
1673
8

Albertus Magnus, bp. of Ratisbon, 1193?-1280, supposed author.
De virtutibus quarundam herbarum, lapidum et animalium.
Longinus, Caesar, ed. Trinum magicum ... 1673. (Card 2)
lapidum & animalium. A. M. A.--Commentatio De magnetica curatione vulnerum citra svperstitionem ... Authore R. G. M. D.--Logia, sive Oracvla Zoroastri ex Platonicorum libris collecta.--Tractatus De proprii cujusqve nati daemonis inqvisitione.
Layout of text corresponds to that of Frankfurt, 1630 ed. (C. Eifrid, printer)
(Continued on next card)

Witchcraft
BF
1602
A33
1743

Albertus Parvus, Lucius, pseud.
Libellus de mirabilibus naturae arcanis-- French.
Albertus Parvus, Lucius, pseud.
Secrets merveilleux de la magie naturelle & cabalistique du Petit Albert, traduits exactement sur l'original latin, intitulé Alberti Parvi Lucii Libellus de mirabilibus naturae arcanis. Enrichi de figures mistérieuses, & de la manière de les faire. Nouvelle edition corrigée & augmentée. Lion, Chez les Héritiers de Beringos Fratres, 1743.
[12], 252 p. illus., plates (part fold.) 15cm.
(Continued on next card)

Albertus Parvus, Lucius, pseud.
Witchcraft Libellus de mirabilibus naturae arcanis--
BF French.
1602 Albertus Parvus, Lucius, pseud.
A33 Secrets merveilleux de la magie naturelle & cabalistique du Petit Albert, traduits exactement sur l'original latin, intitulé Alberti Parvi Lucii Libellus de mirabilibus naturae arcanis. Enrichi de figures mistérieuses, & de la manière de les faire. Nouvelle edition corrigée & augmentée. Lion, Chez les Héritiers de Beringos Fratres, 1743.
[12], 252 p. illus., plates (part fold.) 15cm.

Witchcraft
BF
1602
A33
1800
8

Albertus Parvus, Lucius, pseud.
Secrets merveilleux de la magie naturelle et cabalistique du Petit Albert. Traduits sur l'original latin intitulé: Alberti parvi Luci Libellus de mirabilibus naturae arcanis. Nouv. éd. Nouvelle-Orléans, Martin, frère [1800?]
222 p. illus. 13cm.
1. Magic. 2. Charms. 3. Medicine, Magic, mystic, and spagiric. I. His Libellus de mirabilibus naturae arcanis--Fren ch. II. Title.

Witchcraft
BF
1602
A33
1700

Albertus Parvus, Lucius, pseud.
Secrets merveilleux de la magie naturelle et cabalistique du petit Albert, traduits exactement sur l'original latin, intitulé: Alberti Parvi Lucii Libellus de mirabilibus naturæ arcanis. Enrichis de figures mystérieuses; & le maniere de les faire. Nouv. éd., cor. & augm. Lyon, Héritiers de Beringos fratres, 6516 [17--?]
216 p. illus, plates (part fold.) 14cm.
Imperfect copy: p. 9-10 wanting.
1. Magic. 2. Charms. 3. Medicine, Magic, mystic, and spagiric.

11-15974

Witchcraft
BF
1602
A33
1743

Albertus Parvus, Lucius, pseud.
Secrets merveilleux de la magie naturelle & cabalistique du Petit Albert, traduits exactement sur l'original latin, intitulé Alberti Parvi Lucii Libellus de mirabilibus naturae arcanis. Enrichi de figures mistérieuses, & de la manière de les faire. Nouvelle edition corrigée & augmentée. Lion, Chez les Héritiers de Beringos Fratres, 1743.
[12], 252 p. illus., plates (part fold.) 15cm.
(Continued on next card)

Witchcraft
BF
1602
A33
1743

Albertus Parvus, Lucius, pseud. Secrets merveilleux ... 1743. (Card 2)
1. Magic. 2. Charms. 3. Medicine, Magic, mystic, and spagiric. I. Albertus Parvus, Lucius, pseud. Libellus de mirabilibus naturae arcanis--French. II. Title.

Witchcraft
BF
1598
A33
A2
1770

Albertus Parvus, Lucius, pseud.
Secrets merveilleux de la magic naturelle et cabalistique du Petit Albert, traduit exactement sur l'original latin intitulé: Alberti Parvi Lucii Libellus de mirabilibus naturae arcanis ... Nouv. éd., corr. et augm. Lion, Chez les Héritiers de Beringos Fratres, 1729.
252 p. illus. 14cm.
With autograph of J. Tickell.
Bound with Albertus Magnus, Saint. Les admirables secrets ... Lyon, 1770.
Vol. lettered Tracts.

WITCHCRAFT
BF
1602
A33
1788
8

Albertus Parvus, Lucius, pseud.
Secrets merveilleux de la magie naturelle et cabalistique du Petit Albert, traduits exactement sur l'original latin intitulé: Alberti Parvi Lucii, Libellus de mirabilibus naturae arcanis. Enrichi de figures mystérieuses, & la manière de les faire. Nouv. ed., corr. & augm. Lyon, Chez les héritiers de Beringos fratres, 1788.
245, [6] p. illus. (part fold.) 15cm.

Witchcraft
BF
1602
A33
1800
8

Albertus Parvus, Lucius, pseud.
Secrets merveilleux de la magie naturelle et cabalistique du Petit Albert. Traduits sur l'original latin intitulé: Alberti parvi Luci Libellus de mirabilibus naturae arcanis. Nouv. éd. Nouvelle-Orléans, Martin, frère [1800?]
222 p. illus. 13cm.
1. Magic. 2. Charms. 3. Medicine, Magic, mystic, and spagiric. I. His Libellus de mirabilibus naturae arcanis--Fren ch. II. Title.

WITCHCRAFT
PA
4220
L3
A4+
1516
8

Albinus.
De doctrina Platonis liber.
Jamblichus, of Chalcis.
[De mysteriis. Latin]
Iamblichus De mysteriis Aegyptiorum, Chaldaeorum, Assyriorum. Proclus In Platonicum Alcibiadem de anima, atq. demone. Proclus De sacrificio, & magia. Porphyrius De diuinis, atq. daemonibus. Synesius Platonicus De somniis. Psellus De daemonibus. Expositio Prisciani, & Marsilii in Theophrastum De sensu, phantasia, & intellectu. Alcinoi Platonici philoso phi, Liber de doctrina
(Continued on next card)

WITCHCRAFT
PA
4220
L3
A4+
1516
8

Albinus.
De doctrina Platonis liber.
Jamblichus, of Chalcis. [De mysteriis. Latin] [1516] (Card 2)
Platonis. Speusippi Platonis discipuli, Liber de Platonis definitionibus. Pythagorae philosophi Aurea uerba. Symbola Pithagorae philosophi. Xenocratis philosophi platonici, Liber de morte. Mercurii Trismegisti Pimander. Euisdem Asclepius. Marsilii Ficini De triplici uita lib. II. Eiusdem Liber de uoluptate. Eiusdem
(Continued on next card)

WITCHCRAFT
PA
4220
L3
A4+
1516
8

Albinus.
De doctrina Platonis liber.
Jamblichus, of Chalcis. [De mysteriis. Latin] [1516] (Card 3)
De sole & lumine libri. II. Apologia eiusdem in librum suum de lumine. Eiusdem Libellus de magis. Quod necessaria sit securitas, & tranquillitas animi. Praeclarissimarum sententiarum huius operis breuis annotatio. [Venetiis, In aedibvs Aldi, et Andreas soceri, 1516]
177 [i.e., 175] numbered leaves.
29cm.
(Continued on next card)

WITCHCRAFT
PA
4220
L3
A4+
1516
8

Albinus.
De doctrina Platonis liber.
Jamblichus, of Chalcis. [De mysteriis.] Latin. [1516] (Card 4)
At head of title: Index eorvm, qvas hoc in libro habentvr.
With colophon.
Provenance: Bibliotec: SS. Me. Novelle.
Translations by M. Ficino.
1. Occult sciences. 2. Philosophy, Ancient--Collections. I. Proclus Diadochus. In Platonicum Alcibiadem. II. Proclus Diadoch us. De sacrificio. III.
(Continued on next card)

Albinus Platonicus.

see

Albinus.

Witchcraft
BF
1565
A34

Albrecht, Bernhard.
Magia; das ist, Christlicher Bericht von der Zauberey vnd Hexerey ins gemein, vnd dero zwölfferley Sorten vnd Arten insonderheit ... Aus heiliger göttlicher Schrifft vnd andern bewährten Historien gestellet. Leipzig, G. Grosse, gedruckt durch J. A. Mintzeln, 1628.
314 p. 20cm.
1. Witchcraft. 2. Magic. I. Title.

Witchcraft
BF
1414
B73

Alchimia e satanismo.
Borrelli, P.
Alchimia e satanismo. Con illustrazioni di Edoardo Calandra. Napoli, Società Editrice Partenopea [1914]
xiv, 326 p. 20cm.

1. Demonology. 2. Alchemy. I. Title.

CATALOGUE OF THE CORNELL WITCHCRAFT COLLECTION

    Alcinous Platonicus.
        see
    Albinus.

Witchcraft
BS
2545
D5
A37

Alexander, William Menzies.
    Demonic possession in the New Testament; its relations historical, medical, and theological.   Edinburgh, T. & T. Clark, 1902.
    xii, 291 p. 22cm.

    1. Demoniac possession. 2. Bible. N.T.--Commentaries. I. Title.

    Alexicacon hoc est De maleficiis, ac morbis maleficis cognoscendis.

Witchcraft
BF
1555
B86
1714

Brognolo, Candido.
    Alexicacon hoc est De maleficiis, ac morbis maleficis cognoscendis. Opus tam exorcistis, quam medicis, ac theologis, confessariis, parochis, inquisitoribus, ac in quacunque necessitate constitutis, utilissimum.
Venetiis, Apud Nicolaum Pezzana, 1714.
    2 v. 24cm.

    With this is bound the author's Manuale exorcistarum, ac parochorum. Venetiis, 1714.

    Alexicacon hoc est Opus de maleficiis, ac morbis maleficis.

Witchcraft
BF
1555
B86++
1668

Brognolo, Candido.
    Alexicacon hoc est Opvs de maleficiis, ac morbis maleficis. Dvobvs tomis distribvtvm. Quorum alter quatuor de eorum cognitione disput. continet. Quorum alter totidem de eorum curatione disput. continet ... In qvarvm calce qvae sint partes exorcistae, quaeue medici, in eis cognoscendis, ac curandis, concluditur ... Prodit qvinqve indicibvs locvpletatvm.
Venetiis, Typis Io: Baptistae Catanei, 1668.
        (Continued on next card)

    Alexicacon hoc est Opus de maleficiis, ac morbis maleficis.

Witchcraft
BF
1555
B86++
1668

Brognolo, Candido. Alexicacon ... 1668.
        (Card 2)

    2 v. in 1. 34cm.

    Added general t. p., engraved. Each vol. has also special t. p.

    1. Demoniac possession. 2. Demonomania.
3. Witchcraft. 4. Exorcism. I. Title.

    Alexicacus.

Witchcraft
BF
1565
F28

Faye, Barthélemy, seigneur d'Espeisses, 16th cent.
    Bartholomęi Faij, regij in senatv Parisiensi consiliarij, ac Inquisitionum praesidis Energvmenicvs. Eiusdem Alexicacvs, cū liminari, vt vocant ad vtrūque librum epistola. Lvtetiae, Apud Sebastianum Niuellium, 1571.
    2 p. l., 397 p. 17cm.
    Alexicacvs, p. 167-397, has special t. p.
    1. Witchcraft. 2. Lord's Supper. 3. Christian life.
I. Title: En ergumenicus. II. Title: Alexicacus.

    Alexiterium.

Witchcraft
RA
1201
W43

Weiss, Georg Franz.
    Alexiterium; sive Opusculum continens remedia adversus venena et maleficia auctore Georgio Francisco Weiss, philosophiae & medicinae doctore urbis Marcoduranae physico ... Coloniae Agrippinae, Typis Petri Theodori Hilden, 1698.
    7 p. l., 172, [1] p. 16cm.
    Provenance: Bibl. Buxheim (Carthusian convent).
    1. Poisons. 2. Toxicology. I. Title.

Witchcraft
BF
1576
A42
2 copies

Allen, Rowland Hussey.
    The New-England tragedies in prose ... I. The coming of the Quakers. II. The witchcraft delusion. Boston, Nichols and Noyes, 1869.
    156 p. 19cm.

    I. Title.

    Der alles anbellende Menschen-Hund.

Witchcraft
GR
830
W4
A18

Acxtelmeier, Stanislaus Roinhard.
    Misantropus Audax; das ist: Der alles anbellende Menschen-Hund. Wider die Fehler, Irzthumer, Missbräuche, und aberglaubische, Gottes-lästerliche, teuffelische Zauber-Wercke, und andere Laster, welche leider, heutiges Tages häuffig im Schwung gehen, durch untadelhafftigen Tadel denen Irrgehenden zu Gemūth geleget, und im Reisen zusammen getragen. Augspurg, L. Kop, 1710.
    [3] 289 p. 16cm.
    I. Title. II. Title: Der alles anbellende Menschen-Hund.

Witchcraft
BF
1584
V9
A43

Allgäuer, Emil.
    Zeugnisse zum Hexenwahn des 17. Jahrh. (Ein Beitrag zur Volkskunde Vorarlbergs) Salzburg, Gedruckt bei R. Kiesel, 1914.

    Accompanies Programm--K.K. Staats-Gymnasium, Salzburg.

    1. Witchcraft--Vorarlberg. I. Title

    Allier, Elisabeth, fl. 1649.

WITCHCRAFT
BF
1582
Z7
1649a

Farconnet, François.
    Relation véritable contenant ce qui s'est passé aux exorcismes d'une fille appellée Elisabeth Allier, natife de la coste S. André en Dauphiné, possédée depuis vingt ans par deux démons nommez Orgueüil et Bonifarce et l'heureuse délivrance d'icelle fille après six exorcismes faits au couvent des F. F. Prescheurs de Grenoble. Avec quelques raisons pour obliger à croire la possession & la délivrance. Jouxte la coppie [sic] imprimée à Grenoble. Paris, P. Sevestre, 1649 [repr. Lyon, 1875]
    29 p. 23 cm.
    Title. Allier, Elisabeth, fl. 1649. I. Title.

Witchcraft
BF
1569
M62
1958

Michelet, Jules, 1798-1874.
    Satanism and witchcraft, a study in medieval superstition. Translated by A. R. Allinson. London, Arco Publications [1958]
    xx, 332 p. 21cm.

    Translation of La sorcière.

    1. Witchcraft. 2. Demonomania. 3. Civilization, Medieval. I. Allinson, Alfred Richard, tr. II. Michelet, Jules, 1798-1874. La sorcière.--English. III. Title.

Witchcraft
BF
1598
C13
A44

Alméras, Henri d', 1861-1938.
    ... Cagliostro (Joseph Balsamo) La franc-maçonnerie et l'occultisme au XVIIIe siècle. D'après des documents inédits. Paris, Société française d'imprimerie et de librairie, 1904.
    2 p. l., 386 p. front. (port.) 19[mm]. (Les romans de l'histoire)
    "Les sources": p. 1–22.

    1. Cagliostro, Alessandro, conte di, assumed name of Giuseppe Balsamo, 1743–1795.

Library of Congress   5-24040

    Aloysii Charitini Discurs von trüglichen Kennzeichen der Zauberey.

Witchcraft
BF
1583
A2
B89

[Brunneman, Jacob] d. 1735.
    Aloysii Charitini [pseud.] Discurs von trüglichen Kennzeichen der Zauberey, worinnen viel aberglaubische Meinungen vernunfftmässig untersucht und verworffen; wie auch Carpzovii, Berlichii, Crusii, und anderer so woll päbstischer, als protestantischer Jure Consultorum. Missliche und leichtglaubige Lehr-Sätze von der Zauberey erwogen und beleuchtet worden ... Stargard, E. und J. M. Jenisch [1708]
    94 p. 19 cm.

    1. Witchcr aft. I. Title.

    Aloysius Charitinus.
        see
    Brunneman, Jacob, d. 1735.

Rare
BT
1100
A45++
1471

Alphonsus de Spina, Bp. of Orense, d. 1469.
    Fortalitium fidei. [Strassburg, Johann Mentelin, not after 1471]
    [240] l. 40cm.

    Leaf [1a] (ms., red): Incipit phemiũ ī q[uo] laudes dine ānotāt[9] z mitit[ur] qrela añ thronũ maiestatis dei z põt īten[s] sebetis,
    Below (printed): [T]vrris fortitudinis a facie inimici ...
    Leaf [232a] (End): Tibi bone ihu q[u] es tu[...]
        (Continued on next ca[rd])

Rare
BT
1100
A45++
1471

Alphonsus de Spina, Bp. of Orense, d. 1469.
    Fortalitium fidei ... [not after 1471]
        (Card 2)

ris fortitudīs a facie īimici sit honor et gloria bñdictio & gracia[ȝ] actio sine fine Amen.
    Leaf [232b] blank.
    Leaf [233a]: [T]abula fortalicij fidei i[n]cipit ... Ends leaf [240b].
    This copy lacks the eight additional leaves containing the rubrics.
        (Continued on next ca[rd])

Rare
BT
1100
A45++
1471

Alphonsus de Spina, Bp. of Orense, d. 1469.
    Fortalitium fidei ... [not after 1471]
        (Card 3)

    Signatures: unsigned [a-d10, e-f8, g6, h-o10, p-q8, r-z10, A8, B6; *8].
    One- to eight-line spaces for capitals, other spaces for rubrics. Large capitals illuminated, smaller capitals, paragraphmarks, initial strokes and rubrics supplied in red.
    Hain. Repertorium (with Copinger's Sup[p.])
        (Continued on next ca[rd])

CATALOGUE OF THE CORNELL WITCHCRAFT COLLECTION

Rare
BT
1100
A45++
1471

Alphonsus de Spina, Bp. of Orense, d. 1469.
  Fortalitium fidei ... [not after 1471]
                                        (Card 4)

plement) *872 = Hain, 873; Proctor, 210; Brit. Mus. Cat. (XV cent.) I, p. 55 (IC. 542); Gesamtkat. d. Wiegendr., 1574; Goff. Third census, A-539.
  Manuscript note on second fly-leaf: Codex monasterij Sancti maximini extra muros treueren Continens tractatū dictū fortalitiū fidei. Manuscript notes on leaf [1a]: Ex
                    (Continued on next card)

Rare
BT
1100
A45++
1471

Alphonsus de Spina, Bp. of Orense, d. 1469.
  Fortalitium fidei ... [not after 1471]
                                        (Card 5)

libris Imperialis Monasterij S. Maximinj; and Bibl. publ. Trev.
  Contemporary binding: wooden boards covered with leather, without spine; metal corners and traces of metal bosses.

  1. Apologetics--Middle Ages. 2. Heresy. 3. Judaism--Controversial works. 4. Saracens. 5. Demonology. I. Title.

Rare
BT
1100
A45+
1487

Alphonsus de Spina, Bp. of Orense, d. 1469.
  Fortalitium fidei. [Lyons, Guillaume Balsarin] 22 May, 1487.
  [250] l. 1 illus. 28cm.

  Leaf [1] and [250] blank. Leaf [250] wanting in this copy.
  Leaf [2a]: [T]Abula fortalicii fidei Incipit.
  Leaf [249b] (Colophon): Anno incarnatōis dñice. M.ccccxxxvij. die. xxij. mensis maij. Below colophon device of G. Balsarin.
                    (Continued on next card)

Rare
BT
1100
A45+
1487

Alphonsus de Spina, Bp. of Orense, d. 1469.
  Fortalitium fidei ... 1487. (Card 2)

  Signatures: a8, a-r8, s-v6, A-L8.
  Capital spaces, some with guide-letters.
  The woodcut on leaf [10a] represents the "Fortalitium fidei," with its various enemies (heretics, Jews, Saracens, demons).
  Hain. Repertorium (with Copinger's Supplement) *874; Pellechet, 564; Proctor, 8575; Brit. Mus. Cat. (XV cent.) VIII, p. 277 (IB. 41763); Gesamtkat. d. Wiegendr.,
                    (Continued on next card)

Rare
BT
1100
A45+
1487

Alphonsus de Spina, Bp. of Orense, d. 1469.
  Fortalitium fidei ... 1487. (Card 3)

1577; Goff. Third census, A-542.
  Contents.--De armatura omnium fidelium.-- De bello hereticorum.--De bello Iudeorum.-- De bello Saracenorum.--De bello demonum.

  1. Apologetics--Middle Ages. 2. Heresy. 3. Judaism--Controversial works. 4. Saracens 5. Demonology. I. Title.

        Alt-Regensburgs gerichtsverfassung, strafverfahren und strafrecht bis zur Carolina.
  Knapp, Hermann, 1859-
    Alt-Regensburgs gerichtsverfassung, strafverfahren und strafrecht bis zur Carolina. Nach urkundlichen quellen dargestellt von dr. Hermann Knapp. Berlin, J. Guttentag, 1914.
    x, 275, [1] p. 23½ᶜᵐ.
    "Quellen und litteratur": p. [1]-3.
    Bound with the author's Das alte Nürnberger Kriminalrecht... Berlin, 1896.

  1. Courts--Ratisbon. 2. Criminal procedure--Ratisbon--Hist. 3. Criminal law--Ratisbon--Hist. I. Title.

                                39-23476
Library of Congress   [2]

        Das alte Nürnberger kriminalrecht.
Witchcraft
K
K665

Knapp, Hermann, 1859-
  Das alte Nürnberger kriminalrecht. Nach rats-urkunden erlautert [!] von dr. jur. Hermann Knapp ... Berlin, J. Guttentag, 1896.
  xviii, 307, [1] p. 23½ᶜᵐ.
  "Quellen": p. [xiii]-xiv; "Litteratur": p. [xv]-xvi.
  With this is bound the author's Alt-Regensburgs Gerichtsverfassung, Strafverfahren und Strafrecht bis zur Carolina... Berlin, 1914.

  I. Title.

Library of Congress   20-4178

        Ein altes Loosbuch.
Witchcraft
BF
1584
T9
Z59

Zingerle, Ignaz Vincenz, Edler von Summersberg, 1825-1892, ed.
  Barbara Pachlerin, die Sarnthaler Hexe, und Mathias Perger, der Lauterfresser. Zwei Hexenprozesse, hrsg. von Dr. Ignaz Zingerle. Innsbruck, Wagner, 1858.
  xii, 84 p. 19cm.
  Contents.--Barbara Pachlerin, die Sarnthaler Hexe.--Der Lauterfresser.--Anhang. Ein altes Loosbuch.

8   Each item has special t. p.
                    (Continued on next card)

        Die altevangelischen Gemeinden und der Hexenglaube.
WITCHCRAFT
BF
1555
K29

Keller, Ludwig, 1849-1915.
  Die altevangelischen Gemeinden und der Hexenglaube.
  (In [Geisteskultur;] Monatshefte der Comenius-Gesellschaft [für Geisteskultur und Volksbildung] Berlin, 1892-1934. 25cm. 8. Bd., 1. und 2. Heft (1899), p. [30]-35)

  Bibliographical footnotes.

8   1. Demoniac possession. 2. Waldenses. 3. Comenius, Johann Amos, 1592-
NIC   1670. I. Title.

Witchcraft
BF
1550
A46

Althamer, Andreas, ca. 1500-1539.
  Eyn [i. e., ein] Predig von dem Teüffel, das er alles Vnglück in der Welt anrichte. [Nuremberg, J. Gutknecht] 1532.
  [14] p. 21cm.

  1. Devil. I. Title: Ein Predig von dem Teüffel.

8

BF
1584
N6
A47

Alver, Bente Gullveig, 1941-
  Heksetro og trolldom. Et studie i norsk heksevæsen. Oslo, Universitetsforlaget, 1971.
  232 p., 4 l. of plates. illus. 24 cm. kr44.50   N 71-50
  Bibliography: p. 223-[226]

3   1. Witchcraft--Norway. 2. Trolls. I. Title.

BF1584.N6A79   72-887909
Library of Congress   72 [2]

        Amavero, Francone dell', pseud.
            see
        Sterzinger, Ferdinand, 1721-1786.

Witchcraft
PT
2430
M35
M3
1861

        The amber witch.
Meinhold, Wilhelm, 1797-1851.
  The amber witch. The most romantic and extraordinary case of witchcraft extant. London, W. Tinsley, 1861.
  168 p. 17cm.

  Translation of his Maria Schweidler, die Bernsteinhexe.
  "The extraordinary romance upon which W. Vincent Wallace has founded his ... opera, 'The amber witch.'" --cover.
  I. Title. II. His Maria Schweidler, die Bernsteinhexe--English. III. Wallace, William Vincent, 1813-1865.

Witchcraft
PT
2430
M35
M3
1895

        The amber witch.
Meinhold, Wilhelm, 1797-1851.
  The amber witch, a romance. Translated by Lady Duff Gordon. Edited, with an introd. by Joseph Jacobs, and illustrated by Philip Burne-Jones. London, D. Nutt, New York, Scribner, 1895.
  xxxviii, 221 p. illus. 20cm.

  Translation of his Maria Schweidler, die Bernsteinhexe.
  I. Title. II. Jacobs, Joseph, 1854-1916, ed. III. His Maria Schweidler, die Bernsteinhexe--English.

Witchcraft
PT
2430
M35
M3
1844

        The amber witch.
Meinhold, Wilhelm, 1797-1851.
  Mary Schweidler, the amber witch. The most interesting trial for witchcraft ever known. Printed from an imperfect manuscript by her father, Abraham Schweidler, the pastor of Coserow, in the island of Usedom. Translated from the German by Lady Duff Gordon. London, J. Murray, 1844.
  xi,171 p. 19cm.

  Translation of his Maria Schweidler, die Bernsteinhexe.

WITCHCRAFT
BF
1559
K62

        Amling, Wolfgang, 1542-1606.
Kittelman, Christian
  Von dem Exorcismo; das ist, Von den Wor[t]en: Fahre aus du unreiner Geist, unnd gib Raum dem heiligen Geist, etc. Gründlich und bestendiger Bericht. [Vor]aus zu ersehen, das er[melter] Exorcismus inn unsern Kirchen [billich] behalten werde, unnd das M. Wolffgang Amling keine erhebliche Ursachen gehabt, darumb er denselben zu Zerbst, und anderswo im Fürstenthumb Anhalt, abgeschafft. [Von] Christianus Kittelman ... [n. p.]
8   1591.
NIC   (Continued on next card)

WITCHCRAFT
BF
1559
K62

        Amling, Wolfgang, 1542-1606.
Kittelman, Christian
  Von dem Exorcismo...1591. (Card 2)

  Preface dated: Newemarckt, vor Halle, ... anno 1590.
  Imperfect copy: t. p. mutilated. Missing words and letters supplied from The National union catalog, pre-1956 imprints.
  "Consilium D. D. Martini Miri, amico cuidam priuatim communicatum, super abrogatione Exorcismi": [18] manuscript pages bound at end.
                    (Continued on next card)

Witchcraft
BF
1775
A51

Ammann, Franz Sebastian.
  Die Trübe Quelle des Aberglaubens an dem Volksglauben und den Wundererscheinungen, namentlich an der Blutschwitzerin in Zug nachgewiesen. Zürich, Leuthy, 1850.
  viii, 152 p. 23cm.

  1. Superstition. I. Title.

15

CATALOGUE OF THE CORNELL WITCHCRAFT COLLECTION

WITCHCRAFT
BX
2340
T35

Ammann, Franz Sebastian, tr.
Die Teufelsbeschwörungen, Geisterbannereien, Weihungen und Zaubereien der Kapuziner. Aus dem lateinischen Benedictionale übersetzt. [Bern?] ca. 1840?
48 p. 17cm.
Kayser's Bücher-Lexikon lists an edition of this item with much longer title, giving F. Ammann as translator and the imprint as: Bern, Jenni, Sohn, 1841.
1. Exorci sm. 2. Benediction.
I. Ammann, Franz Sebastian, tr. II. Catholic Church. Liturgy and ritual. Benedictional.

8
NIC

Witchcraft
BF
1584
T9
A51

Ammann, Hartmann.
Die Hexenprozesse im Fürstentum Brixen. Innsbruck, Wagner, 1914.
64 p. 23cm.
"Sonderabdruck aus den 'Forschungen und Mitteilungen zur Geschichte Tirols und Vorarlbergs', XI. Jahrgang."

1. Trials (Witchcraft)--Tyrol. I. Title.

Witchcraft
BF
1584
A93
Z7
1485

Ammann, Hartmann.
Der Innsbrucker Hexenprocess von 1485. [Innsbruck, 1890]
1-87 p. 23cm.
Detached from Zeitschrift des Ferdinandeums für Tirol und Vorarlberg, 3. Folge, 34. Heft, 1890.

1. Trials (Witchcraft)--Tyrol. I. Title.

8

Witchcraft
BT
980
A52

[Amsweer, Doede van]
Spieghel der aenvechtinghe des Sathans en ware proeve des Gheloofs; daer in ons de streydt des bleesches teghen den Gheest die alle Christen in tyde van Cruyce ende teghenspoet in sich gevoelen levendich wort voor oogen ghestelt ... Door D. van A. Groeninghen, Ghedruckt by H. S. Boeckdrucker, 1612.
1 v. (unpaged) 15cm.

1. Devil. I. Title.

WITCHCRAFT
BF
1555
F11

An adaemonismus cum fide et pietate Christiana conciliari possit?
Faber, Johann Gottlieb, 1717-1779, praeses.
Disqvisitio academica An adaemonismvs cvm fide et pietate Christiana conciliari possit? Qvam praeside ... Ioanne Gottlieb Faber ... svbmittit avctor defendens Martinvs Schvllervs ... Tvbingae, Literis Cottae et Revsii [1763]
42 p. 21cm.
Running title: De inflvxv adaemonismi in pietatem Christianam.
1. Demoni ac possession. I. Schuller, Ma rtin, respondent. II. Title: An adaemonismus cum fide et pietate Chr istiana conciliari possit?

8
NIC

WITCHCRAFT
BX
2340
L99

An das Consistorium zu Leipzig: Drey unterschiedliche Schreiben.
Lysthenius, Georgius.
An das Consistorium zu Leipzig: Drey unterschiedliche Schreiben als nemlich eine Recusatio, Protestatio, Eefutatio [i.e. Refutatio] M. Georgii Lysthenii wegen des jtzigen newen Wittenberger Theologen ihme und andern Superintendenten von oberwehntem Consistorio zugeschickten recht Zwinglischen und gut Caluinischen bedencken von Abschaffung des Exorcismi bey der heiligen Tauffe. Magdeburg, Bey Johan Francken, 1592.
[37] p. 20cm.

8
NIC
(Continued on next card)

Witchcraft
BF
1445
D61
no.17

An dentur spectra magi et sagae.
Romanus, Carl Friedrich.
Schediasma polemicum expendens qvaestionem an dentur spectra magi et sagae; vulgo Ob warhafft Gespenster, Zauberer und Hexen seyn? Una cum recensione historica plurimarum hac de re opinionum auctore Carolo Friderico Romano. Lipsiae, Literis & sumpt. Andreae Martini Schedii, 1717.
73 p. 21cm.
First published 1703?
No. 17 in vol. lettered Dissertationes de spectris. 1646-1753.

8
(Continued on next card)

Witchcraft
HV
8593
N63
1697

An quaestione per tormenta criminum.
Nicolas, Augustin, 1622-1695.
An quaestione per tormenta criminum veritas elucescat, dissertatio moralis et juridica, quâ ordo & series instrumenti capitalis judicii, praesertim in causis sortilegii serio discutitur, & ad saniorem divinarum legum & juris antiqui usum revocatur ... Auctore Augustino Nicolao ... Argentorati, Sumptibus Joh. Friderici Spoor, 1697.
289, 80, [5] p. 17cm.

(Continued on next card)

Witchcraft
HV
8593
N63
1697

An quaestione per tormenta criminum.
Nicolas, Augustin, 1622-1695. An quaestione per tormenta criminum veritas elucescat, dissertatio ... 1697. (Card 2)

"Instructio pro formandis processibus in causis strygum, sortilegorum & maleficorum": p. 271-289.
"Paradoxon de tortura in Christiana republica non exercenda ... à Jacobo Schallero": 80 p. at end.
I. Schaller, Jacob, 1604-1676. Paradoxon de tortura in Christiana republica non exercenda. II. Tit le.

Witchcraft
BX
2050
A1
B49

Anacephalaeosis.
Berg, Vincent von, comp.
Enchiridium quadripartitum P. Vincentii von Berg Franciscani conventualis. Pars prima exhibet varias, selectas, exquisitissimasque benedictiones rerum omnigenarum approbatas ... Pars secunda tractat de regulis artis exorcisticae cum suis exorcismis ... Pars tertia agit de archi-confraternitate ... Pars quarta praescribit modum aegros, agonizantesque adjuvandi; agendi cum obstinatis, haereticis converten-

8
(Continued on next card)

Witchcraft
BX
2050
A1
B49

Anacephalaeosis.
Berg, Vincent von, comp. Enchiridium quadripartitum ... 1743. (Card 2)

dis, sagis examinandis ... Accedit horum Anacephalaeosis in germanismo. In hanc commodissimam formam redactum, iconibus illustratum, indicéque alphabetico instructum. Coloniae, Typis J. C. Gussen, 1743.
8 p. l., 342, [10], 144 p. illus. 17cm.
Part 3 includes some German text.
Anacephalae osis; das ist, Kurtze

8
(Continued on next card)

Witchcraft
BX
2050
A1
B49

Anacephalaeosis.
Berg, Vincent von, comp. Enchiridium quadripartitum ... 1743. (Card 3)

Wiederholung zu Teutsch, vorstellend die Weiss [sic] und Manier mit den Krancken und Sterbenden umbzugehen has special t. p. and is paged separately.
Title in red and black.
Ex libris Lud. Parren.
1. Catholic Church--Prayer-books and devotions. 2. Exorcism. I. Title.
II. His An acephalaeosis. III. Title: Anace phalaeosis.

8

WITCHCRAFT
R
133
P43+

Anacephaleosis medico-theologica, magica juridica, moral, e politica.
Pereyra, Bernardo.
Anacephaleosis medico-theologica, magica, juridica, moral, e politica na qual ... se mostra a infalivel certeza de haver qualidades maleficas ... e se descreve a cura assim em geral, como em particular, de que se devem valer nos achaques procedidos das dittas qualidades maleficas, e demoniacas, chamadas vulgarmente feitiços, obra necessaria para os medicos, e muito preciza para os exorcistas. Coimbra, Na officina de

8
(Continued on next card)

WITCHCRAFT
R
133
P43+

Anacephaleosis medico-theologica, magica juridica, moral, e politica.
Pereyra, Bernardo. Anacephaleosis medico-theologica ... 1734. (Card 2)

Francisco de Oliveyra, 1734.
30 p. l., 432 p. 29cm.

1. Medicine, Magic, mystic, and spagyric. 2. Magic. 3. Diseases--Causes and theories of causation. I. Title.

8

Anagni, Givanni Lorenzo d'.

see

Anania, Giovanni Lorenzo d'.

Witchcraft
BF
1611
O49

An analysis of magic & witchcraft.
Olliver, Charles Wolfran, 1895-
An analysis of magic & witchcraft, a retrospective introduction to the study of modern metapsychics, by C. W. Olliver .. London, Rider & co. [1928]
xi, 244 p. front., illus., plates, diagrs. 24cm.
Bibliography: p. 235-244.

1. Magic. 2. Witchcraft. 3. Phallicism. I. Title.

Library of Congress   BF1611.O5   29-24487 Revised
[r42d2]

Witchcraft
BT
980
S42

An analytical investigation of the scriptural claims of the devil.
Scott, Russell, Unitarian.
An analytical investigation of the scriptural claims of the devil: To which is added, an explanation of the terms Sheol, Hades, and Gehenna, as employed by the scripture writers: In a series of lectures delivered at Portsmouth. London, Sold by Rowland Hunter [etc., etc.] 1822.
xxiv, 646 p. 22cm.

1. Devil. I. Title.

Witchcraft
BF
1520
A53
1581

Anania, Giovanni Lorenzo d'.
De natvra daemonvm libri IIII. Io. Lavrentii Ananiae ... Venetiis, 1581.
[21], 211 p. 15cm.

Title vignette.

1. Demonology. I. Title: De natura daemonum.

CATALOGUE OF THE CORNELL WITCHCRAFT COLLECTION

WITCHCRAFT
BF
1520
A53
1589

Anania, Giovanni Lorenzo d'.
  De natvra daemonvm, Io. Lavrentii Ananiae tabernatis theologi libri quatuor ... Venetiis, Apvd Aldum, 1589.
  6 p. l., 211 p. 17cm.
  With this is bound Vairo, Leonardo. De fascino libri tres. Venetiis, 1589.

  1. Demonology. I. Title: De natura daemonum.

8

Anania, Giovanni Lorenzo d'.
  De natura daemonum.

Witchcraft
BF
1520
A53
D2
1654

Anania, Giovanni Lorenzo d'.
  De Svbstantiis separatis. Opvsculvm primvm [-secvndvm] De natvra daemonvm et occultis eorum operationibus. Avthore Io:Lavrentio Anania. Romae, Typis Iacobi Dragondelli, 1654.
  2 v. in 1. 22cm.
  Vol. 2 has special t. p.: De svbstantiis separatis. Opvsculvm secvndvm. De natvra angelorvm et occultis eorum operationibus.
  Vol. 1 also published separately
  (Continued on next card)

8

Anania, Giovanni Lorenzo d'.
  De natura daemonum.

Witchcraft
BF
1520
A53
D2
1654

Anania, Giovanni Lorenzo d'. De Svbstantiis separatis. 1654. (Card 2)

  with title: De natvra daemonvm.

  1. Demonology. 2. Angels. I. Title: De substantiis separatis. II. Title: De natura angelorum. III. His De natura daemonum.

8

Witchcraft
BF
1520
A53
D2
1654

Anania, Giovanni Lorenzo d'.
  De Svbstantiis separatis. Opvsculvm primvm [-secvndvm] De natvra daemonvm et occultis eorum operationibus. Avthore Io:Lavrentio Anania. Romae, Typis Iacobi Dragondelli, 1654.
  2 v. in 1. 22cm.
  Vol. 2 has special t. p.: De svbstantiis separatis. Opvsculvm secvndvm. De natvra angelorvm et occultis eorum operationibus.
  Vol. 1 also published separately
  (Continued on next card)

8

Witchcraft
BF
1520
A53
D2
1654

Anania, Giovanni Lorenzo d'. De Svbstantiis separatis. 1654. (Card 2)

  with title: De natvra daemonvm.

  1. Demonology. 2. Angels. I. Title: De substantiis separatis. II. Title: De natura angelorum. III. His De natura daemonum.

8

Anania, Ioannes Laurentius.
  see
Anania, Giovanni Lorenzo d'.

The anatomie of sorcerie.

WITCHCRAFT
BF
1565
M39

Mason, James, M.A.
  The anotomie [sic] of sorcerie. Wherein the wicked impietie of charmers, inchanters, and such is discovered and confuted. London, Printed by John Legatt and are to be sold by Simon Waterson, 1612.
  103 p. 19cm.

  1. Witchcraft. 2. Occult sciences.
I. Title.   II. Title: The anatomie of sorcerie.

8
NIC

Witchcraft
BF
1410
B42
Z912

[Andala, Ruardus] 1665-1727.
  Balthazar Bekkers en insonderheyd sijner voedsterlingen onkunde, onbescheidentheyd en dwalingen, kort en klaar ontdekt door een discipel van de Heer J. vander Waeyen en voedsterling van de Academie van Friesland. Franeker, Gedrukt by H. Gyzelaar, ordinaris drukker der Eed. Mog. Heeren Staten, en der Academie van Friesland, 1696.
  2 p. l., 107 p. [p. 108 blank] title and end page vignettes, illus. initials. 21 x 17cm.
  (Continued on next card)

8

Witchcraft
BF
1410
B42
Z912

[Andala, Ruardus] 1665-1727. Balthazar Bekkers en insonderheyd sijner voedsterlingen onkunde ... 1696. (Card 2)

  4°: *², A-N⁴, O².
  Black letter.
  Van der Linde 165.
  Bound with Andala, Ruardus, 1665-1727. Uiterste verleegentheid van Doctor Balt. Bekker. Franeker, 1696.
  1. Bekker, Balthasar, 1634-1698. I. Title.

8

Witchcraft
BX
9479
B42
B11
no.18

Andala, Ruardus, 1665-1727.
  Gansch desperaate en verlooren saake van D. Balthazar Bekker, getoont uit de nasnikken en genoegsaame bekentenisse van onmagt en verleegentheid van sijn voesterling ... Tot een volstrekt bewijs, dat D. Bekker deese schrijver afte danken, en een beter, in de geestkunde bet geoefent, aan 't werk te stellen, of selve de hand aan de ploeg te slaan, of sijn sake ten besten te geven, genootsaakt is. Franeker, Gedrukt by
  (Continued on next card)

8

Witchcraft
BX
9479
B42
B11
no.18

Andala, Ruardus, 1665-1727. Gansch desperaate en verlooren saake.... 1698. (Card 2)

  H. Gyzelaar, ordinaris drukker der Eed. Mog. Heeren Staten, en der Academie van Friesland, 1698.
  35 p. [p. 36 blank] title and other vignettes, illus. initials. 20 x 15cm.
  4°: A-D⁴, E².
  Apparently refers to a work titled
  (Continued on next card)

8

Witchcraft
BX
9479
B42
B11
no.18

Andala, Ruardus, 1665-1727. Gansch desperaate en verlooren saake ... 1698. (Card 3)

  Den professor J. van der Waeyen, ongelukkig en scandaleus verdeedigt van twee predikanten, voormaals zijne discipulen, pub. 1697.
  No. 18 in vol. lettered B. Bekkers sterfbed en andere tractaten.
  1. Den Professor J. van der Waeyen, ongelukkig en scandaleus verdeedigt van twee predikanten. 2. Bekker, Balthasar, 1634-1698. De betoverde weerelde. 3. Devil. I. Title.

8

Witchcraft
BF
1410
B42
Z912

[Andala, Ruardus] 1665-1727.
  Uiterste verleegentheid van Doctor Balt. Bekker. Duidelijk aangeweesen door wederlegginge van alle sijne aanmerkingen ende naleesingen gevoegt bi het slordige mengelmoes van sijn E. Voedsterlingen. Uitgegeeven door een discipel van de Heer J. vander Waeyen en voedsterling van de Academie van Friesland. Franeker, By H. Gyzelaar, ordinaris drukker der Eed. Mog. Heeren Staten, en der Academie van Friesland, 1696.
  4 p. l., 234, [6] p. title and
  (Continued on next card)

8

Witchcraft
BF
1410
B42
Z912

[Andala, Ruardus] 1665-1727. Uiterste verleegentheid van Doctor Balt. Bekker. 1696. (Card 2)

  other vignettes, illus. initials. 22 x 17cm.
  4°: *⁴, A-2G⁴.
  Van der Linde 166.
  Criticizes Bekker's critique of Waaijen's De betoorde weereld van D. Balthasar Bekker ondersogt en weederlegt.
  With this is bound Andala, Ruardus, 1665-1727. Balthazar Bekkers en
  (Continued on next card)

8

Witchcraft
BF
1410
B42
Z912

[Andala, Ruardus] 1665-1727. Uiterste verleegentheid van Doctor Balt. Bekker. 1696. (Card 3)

  insonderheyd sijner voedsterlingen onkunde... Franeker, 1696.
  1. Bekker, Balthasar, 1634-1698. De betoverde weereld. 2. Waaijen, Johannes van der, 1639-1701. De betoverde weereld van D. Balthasar Bekker ondersogt en weederlegt. I. Title.

Andala, Ruardus, 1665-1727.

Witchcraft
BX
9479
B42
B11
no.13

Beknopte aanmerkingen over de korte opening van de plaatsen van 2 Pet. 2: 4 en Jud. v. 6. Voorgestelt aan R. A. predikant tot B. Als mede over de brief aan de selve. Waar in de bewysen over de gemelden plaatsen naarstiglyk ondersogt, en wederlegt werden. Door een liefhebber der waarheyt. Amsterdam, Gedrukt voor den autheur, 1697.
  4 p. l., 19 p. [p. 20 blank] title and other vignettes, illus. initials. 20 x 15cm.
  (Continued on next card)

8

Andala, Ruardus, 1665-1727.

Witchcraft
BX
9479
B42
B11
no.13

Beknopte aanmerkingen over de korte opening van de plaatsen van 2 Pet. 2: 4 en Jud. v. 6. 1697. (Card 2)

  4°: A-C⁴, D².
  Black letter (except introduction)
  Supports Ruardus Andala in his controversy with Balthasar Bekker over Biblical spirits.
  No. 13 in vol. lettered B. Bekkers sterfbed en andere tractaten.
  1. Devil. 2. Bible. N. T. 2 Peter, II, 4--Criticism, interpretation, etc.
  (Continued on next card)

8

Ander Theil ... von den Gespensten.

WITCHCRAFT
BF
1565
W16

Waldschmidt, Bernhard.
  Pythonissa Endorea, das ist: Acht vnd zwantzig Hexen- vnd Gespenstpredigten, genommen auss der Histori von der Zauberinn zu Endor ... Gehalten in der Kirchen zun Barfüssern in Franckfurt, vnd nunmehr mit nützlichen, auss vornehmer Theologorum vnd anderer berühmten Autorum Schrifften genommenen Anmerckungen vermehret ... Franckfurt, Johann-Wilhelm Ammon vnd Wilhelm Serlin, Gedruckt durch Hieronymum Polich, 1660.
  (Continued on next card)

8

17

CATALOGUE OF THE CORNELL WITCHCRAFT COLLECTION

Ander Theil ... von den Gespensten.

WITCHCRAFT
BF
1565
W16
    Waldschmidt, Bernhard. Pythonissa Endorea ... 1660. (Card 2)

16 p. l., 690, [26] p. port. 22cm.
Added engr. t. p. facing portrait.
"Ander Theil ... von den Gespensten ..." has special t. p.
Title in red and black.
1. Witchcraft. 2. Witchcraft in the Bible. 3. Ghosts. 4. Endor, Witch of (Biblical character) I. Title. II. Title: Ander Theil ... von den Gespensten.

8

Andreä, Erdmann Friedrich.

WITCHCRAFT
BF
1583
H73
    Hollenbach, Wilhelm.
Bilder aus Thüringen. I. Tragikomische Geisterbeschwörung auf dem Galgenberge bei Jena in der Christnacht des Jahres 1715. Nach den Originalquellen wahrheitsgetreu dargestellt ... Mit interessanten Bruchstücken der Streitschrift des Jenaischen Arztes Andreä und den Gutachten der theologischen und juristischen Fakultät zu Leipzig. Jena, F. Mauke (A. Schenk), 1885.
iv, 56 p. 21cm.
No more published?
(Continued on next card)

Witchcraft
BF
1555
A55
no.1
    Andreae, Tobias, 1633-1685.
Exercitationes philosophicae duae de angelorum malorum potentia in corpora. Amstelodami, Apud Samuelem Eickenbergium, 1691.
82 p. 14cm.
Each part has caption title beginning: Exercitationum physicarum.
Also published as: Wijsgeerige oefeningen betrekkelijk het vermogen van de kwade engelen op het menschlijk ligchaam.
No. 1 in vol. lettered Andreae. De angelorum ...
(Continued on next card)

Witchcraft
BF
1555
A55
no.1
    Andreae, Tobias, 1633-1685. Exercitationes philosophicae ... 1691. (Card 2)

1. Demoniac possession. 2. Angels. I. Title. II. Title: De angelorum malorum potentia in corpora.

8

Angelographia.

Witchcraft
BT
965
C33
    Casmann, Otto, d. 1607.
Othonis Casmanni Angelographia; sive Commentationum disceptationumque physicarum prodromvs problematicvs, de angelis sev creatis spiritibvs a corporvm consortio abiunctis, ex Dei verbo, S. Patrvm monumentis, dd. scholasticis & physicis; cum veteribus, tum recentioribus, concinnatus, & in duas partes distinctus. ... Francofurti, In officina Palthenii typographi, 1605.
2 v. in 1. 15cm.
(Continued on next card)

8

Angelographia.

Witchcraft
BT
965
C33
    Casmann, Otto, d. 1607. Othonis Casmanni Angelographia ... 1605. (Card 2)

Consecutively paged: 8 p. l., 672 p.
Vol. 2 has title: Othonis Casmanni Angelographiae, hoc est, descriptionis angelicae ... pars altera. Francofurti, Ex officina Zachariae Palthenii, 1605.

1. Angels. 2. Demonology. 3. Devil. I. Title: Angelographia.

8

Angelographía sive Pneumata leiturgika.

Witchcraft
BT
965
S25
    [Saunders, Richard] d. 1692.
Ἀγγελογραφία sive Πνεύματα λειτυργικά, Πνευματολογία: or, A discourse of angels: their nature and office, or ministry ... Also something touching devils and apparitions and impulses. With ... doctrine of angels ... London, Printed for T. Parkhurst, 1701.
314, [2] p. 21cm.
Preface signed: Geo. Hamond.
Publisher's advertisement: p. [315-316]
Title transliterated: Angelographía sive Pneumata leiturgika ...

8

Angelorum natura, proprietates, ac diversi status.

Witchcraft
BT
965
B95
    Burghaber, Adam, 1608-1687, praeses.
Angelorvm natvra, proprietates, ac diversi statvs qvos ... praeside Adamo Bvrghaber ... pvblice proposvit ... D. Iodocvs Bvelman ... Lucernae, Typis Dauidis Hautt, 1650.
2 p. l., 253, [5] p. 14cm.

1. Angels. 2. Devil. I. Büelman, Jodocus, respondent. II. Title: Angelorum natura, proprietates, ac diversi status.

8

Anhaltische Hexenprozesse.

WITCHCRAFT
BF
1583
S35
    Schmidt, W
Anhaltische Hexenprozesse.
(In Unser Anhaltland. Dessau. 32cm. (folded to 24cm.) 2. Jahrg., Nr. 1-2 (1902), p. [1]-5, [13]-17)

Subtitle: I. In Stadt und Amt Dessau.
In envelope.
1. Trials (Witchcraft)--Saxony. 2. Trials (Witchcraft)--Dessau. I. Title.

8
NIC

Anhang zu denen Thomasischen gemischten Händeln.

Witchcraft
B
2605
V5
    Thomasius, Christian, 1655-1728.
Vernünfftige und christliche aber nicht scheinheilige Thomasische Gedancken und Erinnerungen über allerhand gemischte philosophische und juristische Händel. Halle im Magdeburg, In der Rengerischen Buchhandlung, 1723-25.
3 v. front. 18cm.
Title of v. 1 in red and black.
"Es folget ... jetzo der fünffte Theil der Juristischen Händel [1720-21], jedoch
(Continued on next card)

8

Anhang zu denen Thomasischen gemischten Händeln.

Witchcraft
B
2605
V5
    Thomasius, Christian, 1655-1728. Vernünfftige und christliche aber nicht scheinheilige Thomasische Gedancken ... 1723-25. (Card 2)

mit einiger Änderung."--Vorrede, 1. Bd.

Witchcraft
B
2605
V5
suppl.
    ---Anhang zu denen Thomasischen gemischten Händeln. Halle im Magdeburgischen, In der Rengerischen Buchhandlung, 1726.
224 p. 18cm.
(Continued on next card)

Anhang zu denen Thomasischen gemischten Händeln.

Witchcraft
B
2605
V5
suppl.
    Thomasius, Christian, 1655-1728. Vernünfftige und christliche aber nicht scheinheilige Thomasische Gedancken ... 1723-25. (Card 3)

Bound with v. 2.

1. Philosophers, German--Correspondence, reminiscences, etc. 2. Witchcraft. I. His Ernsthaffte aber doch muntere ... Gedancken ... über ... juristische Händel. II. His Anhang zu denen Thomasischen gemischten Händeln. III. Title.

8

Anhang zu der Abfertigung der Lohmannischen Begeisterung.

WITCHCRAFT
BF
1555
M94
O29
no.5
    Semler, Johann Salomo, 1725-1791.
D. Joh. Salomo Semlers Anhang zu der Abfertigung der Lohmannischen Begeisterung, worin fernere historische Umstände gesamlet worden. Halle, Bey J. J. Gebauer, 1760.
112 p. 18cm.
Title of the original work reads: Abfertigung der neuen Geister und alten Irtümer der Lohmannischen Begeisterung. Halle, 1760.
No. 5 in vol. lettered Oesfeld u. a.
(Continued on next card)

8 NIC

Anhang zu der Anno 1720. ergangenen ... Brandenburg-Onolzbachischen Peinlichen Gerichts-Ordnung.

WITCHCRAFT
K
B816++
1582
    Brandenburg-Ansbach (Principality) Laws, statutes, etc.
Anhang zu der Anno 1720. ergangenen Hoch-Fürstl. Brandenburg-Onolzbachischen Peinlichen Gerichts-Ordnung, wie solcher von der Ober-Vormundschafftlichen Geheimen-Regierung Anno 1725 verfasst und beyzudrucken befohlen worden. Onolzbach, Gedruckt bey J. V. Lüders [1725]
10 p. 31cm.
Bound with Brandenburg (Electorate)
(Continued on next card)

8 NIC

Anhang zu der Anno 1720. ergangenen ... Brandenburg-Onolzbachischen Peinlichen Gerichts-Ordnung.

WITCHCRAFT
K
B816++
1582
    Brandenburg-Ansbach (Principality) Laws, statutes, etc. Anhang zu der Anno 1720. ergangenen ... Gerichts-Ordnung ... [1725] (Card 2)

Laws, statutes, etc. Peinlichen Halssgerichts-Ordnung. [Ansbach?] 1582.

1. Criminal procedure--Brandenburg-Ansbach (Principality) I. Title: Anhang zu der Anno 1720. ergangenen ... Brandenburg-Onolzbachische Peinlichen Gerichts-Ordnung. II. Its Neue Ordnung des Durchlauchti gsten Fürsten ...

8 NIC

Animal fascination, or charming.

Witchcraft
BF
1411
B63
    Blakeman, Rufus.
A philosophical essay on credulity and superstition; and also on animal fascination, or charming. By Rufus Blakeman ... New York, D. Appleton & co.; New Haven, S. Babcock, 1849.
206 p. 18cm.
CONTENTS.--Mental origin of credulity and superstition, and its influence on ancient society.--Witchcraft.--Dreams.--Ghosts.--Ecstacy, trance.--Empiricism and quackery.--Homœopathy.--Mesmerism.--Essay on animal fascination or charming.
1. Occult sciences. 2. Medical delusions. I. Title. II. Title: Animal fascination, or charming.

18-121

Animavversioni critiche sopra il Notturno congresso delle lammie.

Witchcraft
BF
1565
T19
B71
    [Bonelli, Benedetto] 1704-1783.
Animavversioni critiche sopra il Notturno congresso delle lammie, per modo di lettera indiritte ad un letterato. S'aggiugne il discorso del P. Gaar sulla strega d' Erbipoli, la Risposta dello stesso alle note, il Ragguaglio sulla strega di Salisburgo, e il Compendio storico della stregheria. Venezia, Presso Simone Occhi, 1751.
6 p. l., 188 p. 25cm.
(Continued on next card)

8

Animavversioni critiche sopra il Notturno congresso delle lammie.

Witchcraft
BF
1565
T19
B71
    [Bonelli, Benedetto] 1704-1783. Animavversioni critiche ... 1751. (Card 2)

Attributed to Bonelli by Melzi.
Each of the added items has special t. p. except the last, which has caption title.
1. Tartarotti, Girolamo, 1706-1761. Del congresso notturno delle lammie. 2. Witchcraft. I. Title. II. Gaar, Georg, b. 1702. Ragionamento ... fatto avanti al rogo di Maria Renata.

8

CATALOGUE OF THE CORNELL WITCHCRAFT COLLECTION

BF 1584 S9 A61
Ankarloo, Bengt, 1935–
Trolldomsprocesserna i Sverige. Stockholm, Nordiska bokhandeln (distr.), 1971.
355 p. illus. 24 cm. (Skrifter utg. av Institutet för rättshistorisk forskning. Serien 1: Rättshistoriskt bibliotek, bd. 17) kr47.05
S 72-5/6
Thesis--Lund.
Summary in English.
Bibliography: p. 344-354.
1. Trials (Witchcraft)--Sweden. I. Title. II. Series: Institutet för rättshistorisk forskning, Stockholm. Skrifter. Serien 1: Rättshistoriskt bibliotek bd. 17.
72-308069
Library of Congress   72 [2]

Witchcraft
BF 1583 Z7 1749b
Anna Renata Singer v. Mossau ... 1849. (Card 3)
1. Sänger, Maria Renata von Mossau, ca. 1680-1749. 2. Trials (Witchcraft)--Germany. 3. Witchcraft--Hist. I. Gaar, Georg, b. 1702. Christliche Anred nächst dem Scheiter-Hauffen. II. Siebdrat, Gustav Albert. Ein sächsischer Hexenprozess aus dem 17. Jahrhundert. III. Title: Ein sächsischer Hexenprozess aus dem 17. Jahrhundert.
8

Witchcraft
BF 1815 J62 S28 1570
Anselmo, Saint, bp. of Marsico, d. 1210.
Scalichius, Paulus von Lika, count, 1534-1575.
... Primi tomi Miscellaneorvm ... effigies ... (Card 2)
ta explanatio. Coloniae Agrippinae, Ex Officina Typographica Theodori Graminaei, 1570.
[12], 152 p. illus. 21cm.
Title vignette.

Witchcraft
BF 1583 A2 G74
Anleitung oder Unterweisung, wie ein Richter in Criminal ... Sachen die Zauberer und Hexen belangendt, sich zu verhalten.
Gramnaeus, Theodor, b. ca. 1530.
Indvctio sive directorivm: das ist: Anleitung oder Vnderweisung, wie ein Richter in Criminal vnd peinlichen Sachen die Zauberer vnd Hexen belangendt, sich zuverhalten, vnd der Gebür danit zuverfahren haben soll, in zwey Theil getheilet, als wie von Amptsswegen, vnd sonst, so der Kläger Recht begert, zuverfahren ... Cölln, H. Falckenburg, 1594.
[8], 157 p. 15cm.
I. Title. II. Title: Anleitung oder Unterweisung, wie ein Richter in Criminal ... Sach belangendt, si ch zuverhalten ... haben soll.

Witchcraft
BF 1576 D76
Annals of witchcraft in New England, and elsewhere in the United States, from their first settlement.
Drake, Samuel Gardner, 1798-1875.
Annals of witchcraft in New England, and elsewhere in the United States, from their first settlement. Drawn up from unpublished and other well authenticated records of the alleged operations of witches and their instigator, the devil. By Samuel G. Drake. Boston, W. E. Woodward, 1869.
liii, [55]-306 p. front. (port.) 22 x 18cm. (Woodward's historical series. no. VIII)
An edition of two hundred and seventy-five copies printed.
1. Witchcraft--New England.

Witchcraft
BS 2545 D5 T97 no.3
An answer to the Enquiry into the meaning of demoniacks in the New Testament.
Twells, Leonard, d. 1742.
An answer to the Enquiry into the meaning of demoniacks in the New Testament: shewing that the demons therein spoken of were fallen angels; and that the demoniacks were persons really possessed. In a letter to the author ... London, Printed for R. Gosling, 1737.
74 p. 21cm.
No. 3 in vol. lettered: Twells, Whiston, etc. Tracts on the demoniacs in the New Testament. London, 1738-1775.

WITCHCRAFT
BF 1555 T35
Anmerkungen über den Teufel zu Seefeld in Tirol.
Der Teufel zu Seefeld, noch 1783. Aus "Anmerkungen über den Teufel zu Seefeld in Tirol," Verfasst von einem geistlichen Ganser der ExKlarisserinnen. Auf Unkosten der St. Monica Brüderschaft zu Seefeld. 1783, 8, 80 Seiten.
(In Stats-Anzeigen. Göttingen. 20cm. 6. Bd., Heft 23 (1784), p. 274-294)
At head of title: 30.
1. Seiberin, Johanna, fl. 1782. 2. Demoniac possession. I. Title: Anmerkungen über den Teufel zu Seefeld in Tirol.
8

WITCHCRAFT
BF 1565 M39
The anotomie [sic] of sorcerie.
Mason, James, M.A.
The anotomie [sic] of sorcerie. Wherein the wicked impietie of charmers, inchanters, and such is discovered and confuted. London, Printed by John Legatt and are to be sold by Simon Waterson, 1612.
103 p. 19cm.
1. Witchcraft. 2. Occult sciences.
I. Title. II. Title: The anatomie of sorcerie.
8 NIC

Witchcraft
BS 2545 D5 T97 no.6
An answer to the Further enquiry into the meaning of demoniacks in the New Testament
Twells, Leonard, d. 1742.
An answer to the Further enquiry into the meaning of demoniacks in the New Testament. Wherein the arguments to prove that the demons of the New Testament were fallen angels are defended; and the objections against the scheme of the Enquiry are made good. In a second letter to the author. London, Printed for R. Gosling, 1738.
92 p. 21cm.
(Continued on next card)

WITCHCRAFT
BF 1583 Z7 1592
Anna, eine Hexengeschichte.
Pflug, Walther.
Anna, eine Hexengeschichte. Dessau, M. Salzmann, 1929. (Aus der Vergangenheit unserer Heimat, Heft 4)
23 p. 23cm.
Subtitle on cover: eine Hexengeschichte aus Mosigkau.
1. Witchcraft--Dessau. 2. Trials (Witchcraft)--Dessau. I. Title.
8 NIC

Witchcraft
BF 1584 A93 A61
Anpreisung der allergnädigsten Landesverordnung Ihrer kaiserl. königl. apostolischen Majestät, wie es mit dem hexenprocesse zu halten sey, nebst einer vorrede, in welcher die Kurze vertheidigung der hex- und zauberey, die herr pater Angelus März der Akademischen rede des herrn p. don Ferdinand Sterzingers über das vorurtheil der hexerey entgegengesetzet, beantwortet wird von einem gottesgelehrten. München, Akademische buchhandlung, 1767.
4 p. l., 282, [2] p. 23cm.
(Continued on next card)
42-40824
8   [2]

Witchcraft
BS 2545 D5 T97 no.6
An answer to the Further enquiry into the meaning of demoniacks in the New Testmament
Twells, Leonard, d. 1742.   An answer to the Further enquiry into the meaning of demoniacks in the New Testament... 1738. (Card 2)
No. 6 in vol. lettered: Twells, Whiston, etc. Tracts on the demoniacs in the New Testament. London, 1738-1775.
1. Sykes, Arthur Ashley, 1684?-1756. A further enquiry into the meaning of demoniacks in the New Testament. I. Title.

Witchcraft
BF 1583 Z7 1749b
Anna Renata Singer v. Mossau, die letzte deutsche Hexe. Ein Geschichtsbild, dargestellt zur Erinnerung an den nunmehr hundertjährigen Niedergang eines langen und grauenvollen Irrwahns und an die Befreiung von der Schmach wälscher Inquisition in Deutschland. Nebst einem Abriss der Geschichte der Hexenprocesse im Allgemeinen und beiliegenden Actenstücken sowie einem sächsischen Hexenprocesse aus dem siebzehnten Jahrhun-
(Continued on next card)

Witchcraft
BF 1584 A93 A61
Anpreisung der allergnädigsten Landesverordnung Ihrer kaiserl. königl. apostolischen Majestät ... 1767. (Card 2)
Variously ascribed to Jordan Simon and Andreas Ulrich Mayer.
"Sr. kaiserlich-königlich-apostolischen Majestät allergnädigste Landesordnung, wie es mit dem Hexenprocesse zu halten sey, mit kurzen Anpreisungen für den gemeinen Mann erkläret," p. [3]-62, has special t. p.
1. Witchcraft--Austria. 2. März, Angelus, 1731-1784. Kurze Vertheidigung der thätigen Hex- und Zauberey. 3. Sterzinger, Ferdinand, 1721-1786. Akademische Rede von dem gemeinen Vorurtheile der Hexerey. I. Simon, Jordan, pater, 1719-1776, supposed ed. II. Mayer, Andreas Ulrich, 1732-1802, supposed ed. III. Austria. Laws, statutes, etc. IV. Ein Gottesgelehrter.
Library of Congress   BF1584.A8A5   42-40824
8   [2]

WITCHCRAFT
BF 1558 P79
Anten, Conradus ab.
(Gynaikolousis) Γυναικόλουσις; sev, Mvliervm lavatio, qvam pvrgationem per aqvam frigidam vocant. Item vulgaris de potentia lamiarum opinio, quod vtraq; Deo, natvrae omni iuri et probatae consvetvdini sit contraria. Candida breuis & dilucida oratio. Autore Conrado ab Anten. Lvbecae, In officina typographica Asswer Crögeri, 1590.
[102] p. 17cm.
A small portion of the text is (Continued on next card)
8 NIC

Witchcraft
BF 1583 Z7 1749b
Anna Renata Singer v. Mossau ... 1849. (Card 2)
dert. [Leipzig, Bei F. Serig] 1849.
142 p. 22cm.
"Kurzer Abriss der Geschichte des Hexentums" and the four Beilagen each have special t. p.
Includes Rede am Scheiterhaufen, von G. Gaar, and Ein sächsischer Hexenprozess, von G. A. Siebdrat.
8
(Continued on next card)

Witchcraft
BF 1815 J62 S28 1570
Anselmo, Saint, bp. of Marsico, d. 1210.
Scalichius, Paulus von Lika, count, 1534-1575.
Pavli principis de la Scala ... Primi tomi Miscellaneorvm, de rervm caussis & successibus atque secretiori methodo meditanda, effigies ac exemplar, nimirum, vaticiniorum & imaginum Ioachimi Abbatis Florensis Calabriae, & Anselmi Episcopi Marsichani, super statu summorum Pontificum Rhomanae Ecclesiae, contra falsam, iniquam, vanam, conficatm & seditiosam cuiusdam Pseudomagi, quae nuper nomine Theophrasti Paracelsi in lucem prodijt, pseudomagicam expositionem, vera, certa, & indubita-
(Continued on next card)

WITCHCRAFT
BF 1558 P79
Anten, Conradus ab. (Gynaikolousis) Γυναικόλουσις...1590. (Card 2)
in German.
Bound with: Pomponazzi, Pietro, 1462-1524. De naturalium effectuum causis. Basileae, 1556.
1. Witchcraft. 2. Trials (Witchcraft) I. Title. II. Title: Mulierum lavatio.

CATALOGUE OF THE CORNELL WITCHCRAFT COLLECTION

Witchcraft
BF 1042 A62

Anti-Canidia: or, Superstition detected and exposed. In a confutation of the vulgar opinion concerning witches, spirits, demons, magick, divination, omens, prognostications, dreams, augurys, charms, amulets, incantations, astrology, oracles, &c. ... London, R. and J. Dodsley [1762?]
64 p. 20½ cm.

1. Psychical research. 2. Occult sciences.

Library of Congress — 11-2587
— Copy 2. BF1042.A6

Anti-Satan.

WITCHCRAFT
BF 1555 E74 O78

Ottokar, Amadeus.
Anti-Satan. Sendschreiben an Professor Eschenmayer betreffend dessen Entgegnung auf die Schrift: "Entdeckung eines Complots wider Religion und Christenthum etc." Nürnberg, Bauer und Raspe, 1838.
24 p. 21cm.

1. Devil. 2. Eschenmayer, Carl Adolph von, 1770?-1852. / Karakteristik des Unglaubens... I. Eschenmayer, Carl Adolph von, 1770?-1852. II. Title.

8 NIC

Antidämoniacus.

WITCHCRAFT
BF 1555 M94 B66

[Bobbe, Johann Benjamin Gottlieb]
Vermischte Anmerkungen über Sr. Hochehrwürden des Herrn Probstes und Superintendentens in Kemberg Herrn Gottlieb Müllers Gründlichen Nachricht und deren Anhang von einer begeisterten Weibesperson Annen Elisabeth Lohmännin, mitgetheilet von Antidämoniacus. Bernburg, Bey C. G. Cörner, 1760.
134 p. 18cm.
Attribution by Holzmann.

8 (Continued on next card)

Witchcraft
BF 1522 P45

L'antidemon de Mascon.
Perrault, François, 1572 or 77-1657.
Demonologie ov Traitte des demons et sorciers: de leur puissance et impuissance: par Fr. Perrevad. Ensemble L'Antidemon de Mascon, ou Histoire veritable de ce qu'un demon a fait & dit, il y a quelques années, en la maison dudit S^r. Perreaud à Mascon ... Geneve, Chez Pierre Aubert, 1653.
2 pts. in 1 v. 15cm.

1. Demonology. I. Title. II. Title: L'Antidemon de Mascon.

L'antidemon historial.

WITCHCRAFT
BF 1547 S48

Serclier, Jude, b. ca. 1568.
L'antidemon historial, où les sacrileges, larcins, ruses, & fraudes du Prince des tenebres, pour vsurper la Diuinité, sont amplement traictez, tant par le tesmoignage des S. Escritures, peres & docteurs de l'Eglise, qu'aussi par le rapport des historiens sacrez & profanes ... Lyon, Chez Pierre Rigavd, 1609.
10 p. l., 552, [15] p. 16cm.
Imperfect: last p. wanting.
1. Devil. 2. Gods. 3. Witchcraft. I. Title.

8 NIC

Antidotario contro li demonii; nel qvale si tratta, come entrano ne'corpi humani,...

WITCHCRAFT
BF 1555 P83

Porri, Alessio.
Antidotario contro li demonii; nel qvale si tratta, come entrano ne'corpi humani, oue in quelli stiano, come da quelli si scacciano, & altre cose degne di sapersi ... In Venetia, Appresso R. Megietti, 1601.
291 p. 20cm.

1. Demoniac possession. 2. Exorcism. I. Title.

8 NIC

Witchcraft
BF 1538 D9 G29

De antieke daemonolgie en Augustinus' geschrift De divinatione daemonum.
Geerlings, Hermanus Jacob
De antieke daemonologie en Augustinus' geschrift De divinatione daemonum.
's-Gravenhage, 1953.
191 p. 24 cm.

Diss.—Amsterdam.

1. Augustinus, Aurelius, Saint, Bp. of Hippo. [De divinatione daemonum. 2. Demonology. I. Title.

Antipalus maleficiorum.

WITCHCRAFT
BF 1565 T83 1605

Trithemius, Johannes, 1462-1516.
Antipalus maleficiorvm Iohannis Tritemii Spanhemensis ... qvatvor libris comprehensvs. Mogvntiae, Apud Balthasarum Lippium, 1605.
275-861 p. 19cm.
According to a note by G. L. Burr inside front cover, this is detached from Paralipomena opusculorum Petri Blesensis, Joannes Trithemii, Hincmari, aliorumque, compiled and edited by Jean Buys.

8 NIC (Continued on next card)

Antipalus maleficiorum.

WITCHCRAFT
BF 1565 T83 1605

Trithemius, Johannes, 1462-1516. Antipalvs maleficiorvm ... 1605. (Card 2)

Contents.—Antipalus maleficiorum.—Liber octo quaestionum, quas illi dissolvenda proposuit Maximilianus Caesar.—De laudibus ordinis Fratrum Carmelitarum.—Tractatus, De laudibus Sanctissimae Matris Annae.—Index Graecorum voluminum Ioannis Trithemii.—Hincmari Rhemensis ... Epistolae duae.—Hymni de solemnitate S. Wigberti.
Binding: 17th cent. blind stamped pig skin, with clasps.
(Continued on next card)

Witchcraft
BF 1581 Z7 1821

Antipas; a solemn appeal to the right reverend the archbishops and bishops of the united churches of England and Ireland; with reference to several bills passed, or passing through the imperial Parliament; especially that concerning witchcraft and sorcery. London, W. Stockdale, 1821.
43 p. 21cm.

1. Witchcraft—England.

11-15844
Library of Congress BF1581.Z7 1821

Anton Moses el Arradsch.

WITCHCRAFT
BF 1405 S41 no.6

Der Wahrhaftige feurige Drache; oder, Herrschaft über die himmlischen und höllischen Geister und über die Mächte der Erde und Luft ... Nebst den geheimen Mitteln, sich die schwarze Henne mit den goldnen Eiern zu verschaffen ... Nach einem in Frankreich aufgefundenen Manuscript von 1522. Nebst einem Postscriptum aus dem grossen Buche von König Salomo, mit einigen köstlichen Recepten, gefunden bei Peter Michel, dem letzten

8 NIC (Continued on next card)

Anton Moses el Arradsch.

WITCHCRAFT
BF 1405 S41 no.6

Der Wahrhaftige feurige Drache ... [ca. 1880] (Card 2)
Karthäuser zu Erfurt. [Berlin, E. Bartels, ca. 1880]
125 p. illus. 17cm.
Translation of Le véritable dragon rouge, which was published under a variety of titles, the best-known being Grimoire du Pape Honorius.
Erstes Buch, erstes Kapitel signed: Rab-

8 NIC (Continued on next card)

Anton Moses el Arradsch.

WITCHCRAFT
BF 1405 S41 no.6

Der Wahrhaftige fuerige Drache ... [ca. 1880] (Card 3)
bi Anton Moses el Arradsch.
No. 6 in vol. lettered Der schwarze Raabe.

1. Incantations. 2. Magic. I. Anton Moses el Arradsch. II. Le véritable dragon rouge. German. III. Grimoire du Pape Honorius. German.

8 NIC

Antonii de Haen ... De magia liber.

Witchcraft
BF 1565 H13 1775

Haen, Anton de, 1704?-1776.
Antonii de Haen ... De magia liber.
Lipsiae, Svmptibvs I. P. Kravs, 1775.
xxviii, 316, [1] p. 22cm.

1. Witchcraft. 2. Magic. I. Title: De magia liber.

8

Antonii van Dale ... De oraculis veterum ethnicorum.

WITCHCRAFT
BF 1761 D13 1700

Dale, Antonius van, 1638-1708.
Antonii van Dale ... De oraculis veterum ethnicorum dissertationes duae, quarum nunc prior agit de eorum origine atque auctoribus; secunda de ipsorum duratione & interitu. Editio secunda plurimum adaucta cui de novo accedunt dissertatiunculae I. De statua Simoni Mago ... II. De actis Pilati disseritur ... III. Schediasma de consecrationibus ... Amstelodami, Apud Henricum & vid uam Theodori Boom, 1700.

8 (Continued on next card)

Antonii van Dale ... De oraculis veterum ethnicorum.

WITCHCRAFT
BF 1761 D13 1700

Dale, Antonius van, 1638-1708. ... De oraculis veterum ethnicorum dissertatione duae ... 1700. (Card 2)
12 p. l., 694, [14] p. 8 fold. plates. 22cm.
Title in red and black.
First published 1683 under title: ... De oraculis ethnicorum.

1. Oracles. II. Title: De oraculis veterum ethnicorum.

8

Antonín Peter Příchovský, Abp. of Prague, 1707-1793.

see

Příchovský, Antonín Peter, Abp. of Prague, 1707-1793.

Antoninus, Saint, abp. of Florence, 1389-1459.

Witchcraft
BV 639 W7 C94+

Summa theologica.
Crohns, Hjalmar, 1862-1946.
Die Summa Theologica des Antonin von Florenz und die Schätzung des Weibes im Hexenhammer. [Helsingforsiae, ex Officina typographica Societatis litterariae fennicae, 1906]
1 p. l., 23 p. 28cm. ([Finska vetenskaps-societeten, Helsingfors] Acta Societatis scientiarum fennicae. t. xxxii, no 4)

8

20

CATALOGUE OF THE CORNELL WITCHCRAFT COLLECTION

Witchcraft
BF
1583
C94

Antoninus, Saint, abp. of Florence, 1389-1459.
  Crohns, Hjalmar, 1862-1946.
  Zwei Förderer des Hexenwahns und ihre Ehrenrettung durch die ultramontane Wissenschaft. Stuttgart, Strecker & Schröder, 1905.
    62 p. 20cm.

  1. Institoris, Henricus, d. 1508.
  2. Antoninus, Saint, abp. of Florence, 1389-1459. 3. Witchcraft. 4. Ultramontanism. I. Title.

Witchcraft
BF
1410
B42
256
v.3
no.26

Antwoord van Everardus van der Hooght, aan den eerwaarden, godzaligen, hooggeleerden heere, Do. Balthasar Bekker ...
  Hooght, Everard van der, d. 1716.
  Antwoord van Everardus van der Hooght, aan den eerwaarden, godzaligen, hooggeleerden heere, Do. Balthasar Bekker, S. Theologiae Doctor, yverig predikant tot Amsterdam. Amsterdam, By G. Borstius, boekverkoper, 1691.
    1 p. l., 8, [2] p. title vignette, illus. initial. 19 x 15cm.
    4°: π1, A⁴, [B]1.
    Black letter.
    Letter dated 29. Sept. 1691; postscript, 1 Oct. 1691.

        (Continued on next card)

Witchcraft
BF
1410
B42
256
v.3
no.26

Antwoord van Everardus van der Hooght, aan den eerwaarden, godzaligen, hooggeleerden heere, Do. Balthasar Bekker ...
  Hooght, Everard van der, d. 1716. Antwoord ... aan ... Do. Balthasar Bekker ... 1691. (Card 2)

  Van der Linde 106.
  No. 26 in vol. lettered Bekker III.

  1. Bekker, Balthasar, 1634-1698. Brief van den schrijver des boeks De betoverde weereld. I. Bekker, Balthasar, 1634-1698. II. Title.

Witchcraft
BF
1559
G25

Antwort auf die Anmerkungen, welche in dem Münchnerischen Intelligenzblat ... gemacht worden.
  Gassner, Johann Joseph, 1727-1779.
  Joseph Gassners ... Antwort auf die Anmerkungen, welche in dem Münchnerischen Intelligenzblat vom 12. Nov. wider seine Gründe und Weise zu exorciren, wie auch von der deutschen Chronik, und andern Zeitungsschreibern gemacht worden. Augsburg, Bey J. Wolff, 1774.
    48 p. 16cm. (bound in 19cm. vol.)
    With this is bound Gründlicher Beweiss ... von einem Vertheidiger der Wahrheit ... Augsburg, 1775.

        (Continued on next card)

Aperçu médico-légal sur la magie et la sorcellerie, avec leurs influences actuelles sur le développement des maladies mentales.
  Fanjoux, J M Joseph.
  Aperçu médico-légal sur la magie et la sorcellerie, avec leurs influences actuelles sur le développement des maladies mentales. Lyon, A. Rey, 1909.
    108 p. 25cm.

  1. Medicine, Magic, mystic and spagiric. I. Title.

Aperçus historiques et critiques sur la vie et les travaux de Jean Bodin.
  Molinier, Victor, 1799-1887.
  Aperçus historiques et critiques sur la vie et les travaux de Jean Bodin, sur sa Démonomanie des sorciers, et sur les procès pour sorcellerie au seizième et au dix-septième siècle. Montpellier, Impr. typographique de Gras, 1867.
    35 p. 28cm.

  "Extrait de la Revue judiciaire du Midi, Cahiers de janvier et de février 1867."
  1. Bodin, Jean, 1530-1596. De la démonomanie des sorciers. I. Title.

Witchcraft
BF
1566
B61

Apologetische Versuche in der Geschichtsschreibung der Hexenprozesse.
  Binz, Carl, 1832-1913.
  Apologetische Versuche in der Geschichtsschreibung der Hexenprozesse, von Karl Binz. [Berlin, 1901]
    9 p. 23cm.

  "Sonderabdruck aus Zeitschrift für Kulturgeschichte. VIII.Band, Heft 2 und 3."

  1. Trials (Witchcraft)--Hist. I. Title.

Witchcraft
B
781
A33I32
1533

Apologia aduersus calumnias propter Declamationem de Vanitate scientiarum ...
  Agrippa von Nettesheim, Heinrich Cornelius, 1486?-1535.
  Apologia aduersus calumnias propter Declamationem de Vanitate scientiarum, & excellentia uerbi Dei, sibi per aliquos Louanienses theologistas intentata. Qverela svper calvmnia, ob eandem Declamationem, sibi per aliquot scelerastissimos sycophantas, apud Caesaream Maiest. nefarie ac proditorie illata. [Coloniae] 1533.
    [96] l. 17cm.
    Signatures: A-M⁸.

Witchcraft
BF
1565
T192+

Apologia del Congresso notturno delle lammie.
  Tartarotti, Girolamo, 1706-1761.
  Apologia del Congresso notturno delle lammie, o sia risposta di Girolamo Tartarotti all' Arte magica dileguata del Sig. March. Scipione Maffei, ed all' opposizione del Sig. Assessore Bartolommeo Melchiori. S'aggiunge una lettera del Sig. Clemente Baroni di Cavalcabò. Venezia, Presso Simone Occhi, 1751.
    4 p. l., 268 p. 26cm.
    1. His Del congresso nottur-
        (Continued on next card)

Witchcraft
BF
1565
T192+

Apologia del Congresso notturno delle lammie.
  Tartarotti, Girolamo, 1706-1761. Apologia del Congresso notturno delle lammie ... 1751. (Card 2)

no delle lammie. 2. Maffei, Francesco Scipione, marchese, 1675-1755. Arte magica dileguata. 3. Melchiori, Bartolommeo. I. Baroni Cavalcabò, Clemente, 1726-1796. Lettera ... ad un giornalista oltrammontano, sopra il Congresso notturno delle lammie. II. Title.

Witchcraft
BF
1565
D62
no.1

Apologia principum, in qua processus in causa sagarum continetur, et maleficorum argumenta refutantur.
  Hofmann, Johann.
  Apologia principum, in qua processus in causa sagarum continetur, et maleficorum argumenta refutantur a Johanne Hofmanno culmbacensi ... & authoris sumtibus in lucem edita. Erfurti, Typis Friderici Melchioris Dedekindi, 1636.
    [47] p. 20cm.
    No. 1 in vol. lettered Dissertationes de sagis. 1636-1714.
    1. Trials (Witchcraft). I. Title.
    II. Title: Processus in causa sagarum.

Witchcraft
BF
1565
B73

Apologia pro exorcistis, energumenis, maleficiatis, & ab incubis daemonibus molestatis.
  Borre, Nicolas de, ca. 1590-1670.
  Apologia pro exorcistis, energumenis, maleficiatis, & ab incubis daemonibus molestatis, in qvatvor partes divisa. In qua demonstratur fuisse omni aevo, & ubique, modòq; esse, etiam apud nos, plurimos omnis aetatis & conditionis energumenos, maleficiatos, & ab incubis daemonibus molestatos. Contra quosdam incredulos, obtrectatores, & temerarios exorcistarum censores ... Lovanij, Typis Georgii Lipsii, 1660.
        (Continued on next card)

Witchcraft
BF
1565
B73

Apologia pro exorcistis, energumenis, maleficiatis, & ab incubis daemonibus molestatis.
  Borre, Nicolas de, ca. 1590-1670. Apologia pro exorcistis ... 1660. (Card 2)

    8 p. l., 236, [3] p. 19cm.
    Imperfect: t. p. and text of dedication partially destroyed by book-worms.
    With this is bound his Examen profani exorcismi primi contra daemonem mendacii. Lovanij, 1660.
    1. Witchcraft. 2. Witchcraft in the Bible. 3. Exorcism. I. Title.

WITCHCRAFT
BF
1589
N29
1669

Apologie des grands hommes accusez de magie.
  Naudé, Gabriel, 1600-1653.
  Apologie pour tous les grands hommes, qui ont esté accusez. de magie. Par Mr. Naudé. Paris, Chez François Eschart, 1669.
    12 p. l., 502 p. 15cm.
    First published 1625 under title: Apologie pour tous les grands personnages qui ont esté faussement soupçonnez de magie.
    Half title: Apologie des grands hommes accusez de magie.
    Imperfect copy: p. 493-502 (end of Table des matieres) badly mutilated.
    I. Title. II. Title: Apologie des grands hommes accusez de magie.

WITCHCRAFT
BF
1589
N29
1712

Apologie pour les grands hommes soupçonnez de magie.
  Naudé, Gabriel, 1600-1653.
  Apologie pour les grands hommes soupçonnez de magie. Dernière éd. où l'on a ajouté quelques remarques. Amsterdam, Chez Jean Frédéric Bernard, 1712.
    470 p. front. 16cm.
    First published in 1625 with title: Apologie pour tous les grands personnages qui ont esté faussement soupçonnez de magie.
    NIC Ex libris: Guillaume Doubigny.

WITCHCRAFT
BF
1589
N29
1669

Apologie pour tous les grands hommes, qui ont esté accusez. de magie.
  Naudé, Gabriel, 1600-1653.
  Apologie pour tous les grands hommes, qui ont esté accusez. de magie. Par Mr. Naudé. Paris, Chez François Eschart, 1669.
    12 p. l., 502 p. 15cm.
    First published 1625 under title: Apologie pour tous les grands personnages qui ont esté faussement soupçonnez de magie.
    Half title: Apologie des grands hommes accusez de magie.
    Imperfect copy: p. 493-502 (end of Table des matieres) badly mutilated.
    I. Title. II. Title: Apologie des grands hommes accusez de magie.

WITCHCRAFT
BF
1589
N29

Apologie pour tous les grands personnages qui ont esté faussement soupçonnez de magie.
  Naudé, Gabriel, 1600-1653.
  Apologie povr tovs les grands personnages qui ont esté faussement soupçonnez de magie. Par G. Navdé paris. Paris, Chez François Targa, 1625.
    12 p. l., 615 [i.e., 649], [23] p. 17cm.
    Page 641-649 incorrectly numbered 607-615.
    First edition.
    1. Magic--History. 2. Learning and scholarship--History. I. Title: Apologie pour tous les grands personnages qui ont esté faussement soupçonnez de magie.

Witchcraft
BF
1555
E13

An appeal to the public respecting George Lukins.
  Easterbrook, Joseph.
  An appeal to the public respecting George Lukins (called the Yatton demoniac), containing an account of his affliction and deliverance, together with variety of circumstances which tend to exculpate him from the charge of imposture. Nottingham, Printed and sold by W. Gray [1788?]
    23 p. 20cm.

  1. Demoniac possession. 2. Lukins, George, fl. 1788. I. Title.

CATALOGUE OF THE CORNELL WITCHCRAFT COLLECTION

```
                An appeal to the public respecting
                   George Lukins.
WITCHCRAFT    Easterbrook, Joseph.
BF               An appeal to the public respecting
1555          George Lukins, (called the Yatton demoni-
E13           ac,) containing an account of his afflic-
1788          tion and deliverance; together with a vari-
              ety of circumstances which tend to excul-
              pate him from the charge of imposture ...
              Bristol, Printed for T. Mills [1788]
                 31 p.  22cm.

                 1. Demoniac possession. 2. Lukins,
              George, fl.1788.    I.Title.
8
```

```
              Appendix apologetica Henrici Cornelii
Witchcraft       Agrippae ab Nettesheym.
B             Agrippa von Nettesheim, Heinrich Cornelius,
781              1486?-1535.
A33A6            Appendix apologetica Henrici Cornelii
1605          Agrippae ab Nettesheym ... pertinens ad se-
              cvndam eivs opervm Lvgdvni editorvm partem
              ... Lvgdvni, Per Beringos Fratres, 1605.
                 262 p. 17cm.

                 Page [135] is a special t. p. to the
              succeeding portions of the book: De beatis-
              simae Annae monogamia, ac vnico pverperio
              propositiones abbreuiatae & articulatae ...
                         (Continued on next card)
```

```
              Appendix apologetica Henrici Cornelii
Witchcraft       Agrippae ab Nettesheym.
B             Agrippa von Nettesheim, Heinrich Cornelius,
781              1486?-1535.  Appendix apologetica ...
A33A6          1605.              (Card 2)
1605
              Defensio propositionvm praenarratarvm ...
              Argentorati, Impensis Lazari Zetzneri, 1605.

                 I. Title.
```

```
              Apuleius Madaurensis, tr.
WITCHCRAFT      Hermes Trismegistus.
BF                [Poemander. Latin]
1598             Mercvrii Trismegisti Pymander, De potes-
H55           tate et sapientia Dei. Eivsdem Asclepivs,
A1            De uoluntate Dei. Opuscula sanctissimis
1532          mysterijs, ac uere coelestibus oraculis il-
              lustrissima. Iamblichvs De mysterijs Aegyp-
              tiorum, Chaldaeorum, & Assyriorū. Proclvs
              In Platonicum Alcibiadem, de anima & daemo-
              ne. Idem De sacrificio & magia. Quae omnia
8             solerti cura     repurgata, ac suo tandem
                      (Continued on next card)
```

```
              Apuleius Madaurensis, tr.
WITCHCRAFT      Hermes Trismegistus.   [Poemander. Latin]
BF            1532.                    (Card 2)
1598
H55           candori restituta sunt. Basileae [Per
A1            Mich. Isingrinivm] 1532.
1532             480, [3] p. 16cm.
                 With colophon.
              The Asclepius translated by Apuleius
              Madaurensis; the rest by Marsilio Ficino.
                 I. Jamblichus, of Chalcis. De myste-
              riis. Latin.    II. Proclus Diadochus.
              III. Apulei    us Madaurensis, tr. IV.
              Ficino, Mars   ilio, 1433-1499, tr. V.
8             His Asclep     ius.
```

```
              Arbatel of magick.
BF            Heinrich Cornelius Agrippa's von Nettesheim
1410             Magische Werke : sammt den geheimnissvollen
L69           Schriften des Petrus von Abano, Pictorius
1921          von Villingen, Gerhard von Cremona, Abt
              Tritheim von Spanheim, dem Buche Arbatel,
              der sogenannten Heil. Geist-Kunst und
              verschiedenen anderen zum ersten Male
              vollständig in's Deutsche übersetzt :
              vollständig in fünf Theilen, mit einer
              Menge Abbildungen. -- 4. Aufl. -- Berlin :
              H. Barsdorf, 1921.
                 5 v. in 3. : ill. ; 17 cm. -- (Geheime
              Wissenschaft        en ; 10-14)
                        (Continued on next card)
```

```
              Arbatel of magick.
WITCHCRAFT    Henry Cornelius Agrippa's Fourth book of
BF               occult philosophy, and geomancy. Magi-
1410          cal elements of Peter de Abano. Astro-
L69           nomical geomancy [by Gerardus Cremonen-
1655          sis]. The nature of spirits [by Georg
              Pictorius]: and Arbatel of magick.
              Translated into English by Robert Turner.
              Philomathées.   London, 1655.
                 9 p. l., [5]-266 [i.e., 286], [4] p.
              illus.  19cm.
8                Neither Agrippa nor Abano wrote the works

                         (Continued on next card)
```

```
              Arbatel of magick.
WITCHCRAFT    Henry Cornelius Agrippa's Fourth book of
BF               occult philosophy, and geomancy ...
1410          1655.                 (Card 2)
L69
1655          here ascribed to them; the Heptameron, or
              Magical elements also was ascribed to Agrip-
              pa under the title: Les oeuvres magiques,
              with Abano as translator (!)
                 Translation of a work variously titled
              Liber de ceremonijs magicis; and his De oc-
              culta philosophia, liber quartus.
8
                         (Continued on next card)
```

```
Rare          [Arbuckle, James] 1700-1734?
PR               Hibernicus's letters: or, A philosophical
1365          miscellany. Containing (among many others)
H6            essays on the following useful and entertain-
1734          ing subjects, viz. Of happiness ... Of wit-
              ches and apparitions ... Interspersed with
              several original poems and translations.
              Written by several eminent hands in Dublin.
              The 2d ed., with a compleat alphabetical in-
              dex.   London, Printed for J. Clark, 1734.
                 2 v.  21cm.

                         (Continued on next card)
```

```
Rare          [Arbuckle, James] 1700-1734?   Hibernicus's
PR               letters ... 1734.    (Card 2)
1365
H6            "Chiefly the work of Arbuckle, though Fran-
1734          cis Hutchison, Samuel Boyse, and the poet Par-
              nell made a few contributions. This collec-
              tion of papers, which first appeared in a
              Dublin journal, came to be known under the
              pen-name of the main contributor."--Cf. Hal-
              kett and Laing: Dictionary of anonymous and
              pseudonymous English literature, v. 3, p. 36.

                 I. Title.
```

```
              L'Ardenne méridionale belge.
Witchcraft    Delogne, Théodore.
GR               L'Ardenne méridionale belge: une page
185           de son histoire et son folklore, suivis
D36           du procès des sorcières de Sugny en 1657.
              Bruxelles, H. Lamertin, 1914.
                 273, vi p.  22cm.
```

```
              Ardoino, Ubbidente dell'Osa, pseud.

                 see

              Simon, Jordan, pater, 1719-1776.
```

```
Witchcraft    Arend, Johannes Pieter, 1796-1855.
BX               Verhandeling, over Balthasar Bekker.
9479          Door J. P. Arend, Lector in de hoogduitsche
B42           en engelsche talen en letterkunde aan de
A68           doorluchtige school te Deventer.
                 (In Vaderlandsche letteroefeningen.
              Mengelwerk, tot fraaije letteren, konsten
              en weetenschappen, betrekkelyk. Amsterdam.
              23cm.  no. 16 (1829), p. [713]-743)
                 8°:  3A-3B⁸, 3B⁶.
                 This issue        paged: [713]-756.

                         (Continued on next card)
```

```
Witchcraft    Arend, Johannes Pieter, 1796-1855. Ver-
BX               handeling, over Balthasar Bekker. 1829.
9479          B42                    (Card 2)
B42
A68           [1. Bekker Balthasar, 1634-1698. I.
              Title. II. Vaterlandsche letteroefeningen.
              Mengelwerk. No. 16. 1829.



8
```

```
Witchcraft    Arend, Johannes Pieter, 1796-1855.
BX               Verhandeling, over Balthasar Bekker.
9479          Door J. P. Arend, Lector in de hoogduitsche
B42           en engelsche talen en letterkunde aan de
L65           doorluchtige school te Deventer.  [Amster-
              dam] 1829.
                 [713]-743 p.  23 x 14cm.
                 8°:  3A-3B⁸, 3B⁶.
                 Detached from Vaderlandsche letteroef-
              eningen. Mengelwerk, tot fraaije letteren,
              konsten en weetenschappen, betrekkelyk. No.

                         (Continued on next card)
```

```
Witchcraft    Arend, Johannes Pieter, 1796-1855. Ver-
BX               handeling, over Balthasar Bekker. 1829.
9479                                  (Card 2)
B42
L65           16, 1829, Amsterdam.
                 Bound with Het Leven, de leer en lotge-
              vallen van Balthazar Bekker beschouwd in
              twee redevoeringen. [Amsterdam] 1804.



8
```

```
WITCHCRAFT    Argentine, Richard, d. 1568.
BF               De praestigiis et incantationibvs daemo-
1520          nvm et necromaticorvm liber singularis nun
A69           qàm [sic] antè hac aeditus. Auctore Ricar
1568          Argentino Anglo, medico.  Basilaeae, 1568.
                 216, [22] p. 16cm.
              "At pages 111-112 are accounts of Magel-
              lan's meeting in America with spirits call
              Setebi. Shakespeare ... makes Caliban say
              'His art is of such power, it would control
              my dam's god, Setebos'."--Bookseller's note
8             pasted inside       front cover.
NIC              1. Demono       logy. 2. Witchcraft.
              3. Witchcraf    t in the Bible. I. Ti
```

```
              Argentinus, Ricardus, d. 1568.

                 see

              Argentine, Richard, d. 1568.
```

22

CATALOGUE OF THE CORNELL WITCHCRAFT COLLECTION

Witchcraft
BR 135
A72
1559

Arles y Androsilla, Martín de.
Tractatvs de superstitionibus, contra maleficia sev sortilegia qvae hodie vigent in orbe terrarum. In lucem nuperrime editus. Auctore D. Martino de Arles: in sacra theologia professore: ac canonico & archidiacono Pamp̄. Romae, Apud Vincentium Luchinum, 1559.
1 p. l., 71 numbered l. 15cm.
Woodcut on t. p.
Colophon: Romae apvd Vincentivm Lvcrinvm 1560.

8 (Continued on next card)

Witchcraft
BR 135
A72
1559

Arles y Androsilla, Martín de. Tractatvs de superstitionibus ... 1559. (Card 2)

1. Superstition. I. Title: Tractatus de superstitionibus.

8

WITCHCRAFT
BF 1565
J19

Arles y Androsilla, Martín de.
Tractatus de superstitionibus.
Jacquier, Nicolas.
Flagellvm haereticorvm fascinariorvm, avtore Nicolao Iaqverio. His accesservnt Lamberti Danaei de veneficis dialogi, Ioachimi Camerarii in Plutarchi de oraculorum defectu epistola, Martini de Arles de superstitionibus tractatvs, Ioannis Trithemii de reprobis atq; maleficiis qvaestiones III, Thomae Erasti de strigibus liber. Studio Ioan. Myntzenbergij edita. Francofvrti ad Moenvm [Impressvm apud N. Bassaeum] 1581.
604 p. 17 cm.

8 (Continued on next card)
NIC

WITCHCRAFT
BX 2340
S87
1757

Armamentarium ecclesiasticum complectens arma spiritualia fortissima ad insultus diabolicos elidendos, & feliciter superandos.
Stoiber, Ubaldus.
Armamentarium ecclesiasticum complectens arma spiritualia fortissima ad insultus diabolicos elidendos, & feliciter superandos ... Editio quarta ... Pedeponti, Sumptibus Joan. Gastl, 1757.
2 v. in 1. illus., diagrs, part folded. 18cm.
Contents.--Pars prima. Complectens materiam de energumenis liberandis.--Pars secunda. Materiam de maleficiis curandis, & domibus aliis que locis à spectris infestatis, ex purgandis, continens.
1. Exorcism. 2. Witchcraft. 3. Demonology. I. Title.

8
NIC

Arne Magnússon, 1663-1730.

see

Árni Magnússon, 1663-1730.

WITCHCRAFT
BF 1584
D4
Z7
1698a

Árni Magnússon, 1663-1730.
Kort og sandfærdig beretning om den vidtudraabte besættelse udi Thisted. Til alles efterretning af original-akter og troværdige dokumenter uddragen og sammenskreven (af Arne Magnussen [sic]) Paany udgiven af Alfred Ipsen. København, J. Gjellerups Forlag, 1891.
112 p. 18cm.
Reprinted from ed. of 1699.
1. Bjørn, Ole, b.1648. 2. Trials (Witchcraft)--Thisted, Denmark. I. Ipsen, Alfred, 1852-1922, ed. II. Title.

8
NIC

Árni Magnússon, 1663-1730.

WITCHCRAFT
BF 1584
D4
C552

Christensen, Christian Villads, 1864-1922.
Besættelsen i Thisted.
(In: Samlinger til Jydsk historie og topografi. København. 22cm. ser.3, v.3, no.3. 1902. p.206-219)
With this, in same issue, is: Bang, Vilhelm. Tilføjelser til efterretningerne om hexeforfølgelserne i Ribe.
1. Witchcraft--Thisted, Denmark. 2. Demoniac possession. 3. Bjørn, Ole, b.1648. 4. Árni Magnússon, 1663-1730.

8
NIC

Arnold, Johann Jacob, respondent.

RARE
HV 8593
D611
no.2

Wildvogel, Christian, 1644-1728, praeses.
Dissertationem juridicam inauguralem De arbitrio judicis circa torturam, quam... sub praesidio Dn. Christiani Wildvogelii... submittit Iohann Iacob Arnold. Jenae, Litteris Müllerianis [1710]
54 p. 21cm.
Diss.--Jena (J. J. Arnold, respondent)
No. 2 in a vol. lettered: Dissertationes de tortura, 1697-1770.
1. Torture. I. Arnold, Johann Jacob, respondent. II. Title.

8
NIC

BX 1538
W95
Q3
v.23

Arnold, Klaus.
Johannes Trithemius (1462-1516) Würzburg, Kommissionsverlag F. Schöningh, 1971.
xi, 319 p. ports. 23cm. (Quellen und Forschungen zur Geschichte des Bistums und Hochstifts Würzburg, Bd. 23)
Originally presented as the author's thesis, Würzburg.
Bibliography: p. 282-306.
1. Trithemius, Johannes, 1462-1516. I. Title.

WITCHCRAFT
BF 1565
H97
1726

Arnold, Theodor, 1683-1771, ed. and tr.
Hutchinson, Francis, bp. of Down and Connor, 1660-1739.
Francisci Hutchinsons ... Historischer versuch von der hexerey, in einem gespräch zwischen einem geistlichen, einem schottländischen advocaten und englischen geschworen; worinnen über wurcklich geschehene dinge vernünfftige anmerckungen gemachet, die hieher gehörigen stellen aus der Heil. Schrifft richtig erkläret und die gemeinen irrthümer aufs bescheidenlichste widerleget werden. Nebst zwey vortrefflichen predigten, die erste zum beweiss der wahrheit christl. religion, die andere, von guten und bösen engeln; und einer vorrede des herrn geheimbden raths Thomasii. Aus
(Continued on next card)
32-6507

8

WITCHCRAFT
BF 1565
H97
1726

Arnold, Theodor, 1683-1771, ed. and tr.
Hutchinson, Francis, bp. of Down and Connor, 1660-1739.
Francisci Hutchinsons ... Historischer versuch von der hexerey ... (Card 2)
dem englischen ins teutsche übersetzt, auch mit kurtzen summarien und vollständigen registern versehen von Theodoro Arnold. Leipzig, J. C. Martini, 1726.
[50], 332, [23] p. front. 22 cm.
Head-pieces and initials.
"Verzeichniss derer in diesem werck nur teutsch angeführten englischen autorum": p. [1]-[4] at end.
With copies 1 and 2 are bound Saint André, F. de. Lesenswürdige Briefe ... über die Materie von der Zauberey. Leipzig, 1727. 32-6507
Library of Congress
——— Copy 2. (Continued on next card)

8

WITCHCRAFT
BF 1565
H97
1726

Arnold, Theodor, 1683-1771, tr.
Saint André, François de.
Mr. de St. André ... Lesenswürdige Briefe an einige seiner Freunde über die Materie von der Zauberey, den Ubelthaten, so dadurch angestifftet werden, und von den Zauberern und Hexen insbesondere; worinnen er die wunderbarsten Würckungen, die man gemeiniglich den Teuffeln zuschreibet, deutlich erkläret, und dabey zeiget, dass diese Geister offt
(Continued on next card)

8

Arnold, Theodor, 1683-1771, tr.

WITCHCRAFT
BF 1565
H97
1726

Saint André, François de. Mr. de St. André ... Lesenswürdige Briefe ... 1727. (Card 2)
nicht den geringsten Antheil daran haben ... Statt eines Suplements zum Hutchinson aus dem Französischen ins Teutsche übersetzt ... von Theodoro Arnold. Leipzig, Bey J. C. Martini, 1727.
10 p. l., 204, [9] p. 22cm.
Translation of Lettres ... à quelques-uns de ses amis, pub. 1725.
(Continued on next card)

8

Arnold, Theodor, 1683-1771, tr.

WITCHCRAFT
BF 1565
H97
1726

Saint André, François de. Mr. de St. André ... Lesenswürdige Briefe ... 1727. (Card 3)
Title in red and black.
Bound with Hutchinson, F. Historischer Versuch von der Hexerey. Leipzig, 1726.
1. Witchcraft. 2. Magic. I. His Lettres ... à quelques-uns de ses amis. German. II. Hutchinson, Francis, bp. of Down and Connor, 1660-1739. Historischer Versuch von der Hexerey. III. Arnold, Theodor, 1683-1771, tr. IV. Title: Lesenswürdige Briefe ... über die Materie von der Zauberey.

8

Witchcraft
K
A76+

Arnot, Hugo, 1749-1786, ed.
A collection and abridgement of celebrated criminal trials in Scotland from A. D. 1536 to 1784. With historical and critical remarks. Edinburgh, Printed for the author by W. Smellie, 1785.
xxiii, 400 p. 28cm.

Ex libris Joseph Goodall.

1. Trials-- Scotland. I. Title.

Law

Arnot, Hugo.
A collection and abridgment of celebrated criminal trials in Scotland, from A. D. 1536 to 1784. With historical and critical remarks. Glasgow, Napier, 1812.
x, 440 p.

WITCHCRAFT
BF 1583
Z7
1669

Ein Arnstädter Hexenprozess vom Jahre 1669.
Schulze, Barbara Elisabeth, fl. 1669, defendant.
Barbara Elisabeth Schulzin. Ein Arnstädter Hexenprozess vom Jahre 1669. Nach den Originalprozessakten herausgegeben von Reinhold Stade. Arnstadt, Fürstl. Buchdruckerei von E. Protscher, 1904.
75 p. 22cm.
1. Trials (Witchcraft)--Germany. 2. Trials (Witchcraft)--Arnstadt, Germany. I. Stade, Reinhold, 1848-, ed. II. Title. III. Title: Ein Arnstädter Hexenprozess vom Jahre 1669.

8
NIC

---

ar X
1962

Arrest de la cour du Parlement, qui juge que le crime de sortilege n'est pas cas royal.
France. Parlement (Paris)
Arrest de la cour du Parlement, qui juge que le crime de sortilege n'est pas cas royal, du 2 décembre 1611. Extrait des registres du Parlement. [Paris, C. Girard, 1738]
3 p. 27cm.
Caption title.

1. Witchcraft--Laws and legislation--France. I. Title.

Arrest de mort donne' contre Urbain Grandier prestre.
WITCHCRAFT
BF 1517 F5 G75 1634
Grandier, Urbain, 1590-1634.
Arrest de mort donne' contre Vrbain Grandier prestre, curé de la ville de Loudun, attaint & conuaincu de sortilege & magie. Riom , Chez la vefue Costeravste, 1634.
6, [1] p. 17cm.
"Suiuant la copie imprimée à Blois par Iacques & Michel Cortereau imprimeur du roy & de la ville."
"Cedvle," p. 6, is Grandier's pact with Lucifer.
I. France. Conseil du Roi. II. Title.
8

Arrhenius, Claudius, 1627-1695.
see
Ornhielm, Claudius Arrhenius, 1627-1695.

WITCHCRAFT
BF 1558 G86 1750
L'Art de commander les esprits célestes, aëriens, terrestres & infernaux. Suivi du Grand grimoire, de la magie noire et des forces infernales, du docteur J. Karter, La clavicule de Salomon, &c. Avec le vrai secret de faire parler les morts, pour découvrir tous les trésors caches, &c. &c. [Paris?] 1421 [i.e., ca. 1750?] iv, 5-108 [i. e., 118], [2] p. illus. 16cm.
Title in red and black.
8
(Continued on next card)

WITCHCRAFT
BF 1558 G86 1750
L'Art de commander les esprits ... [1750?] (Card 2)
Published also under other titles: Grimoire du Pape Honorius [best-known]; Le dragon rouge; and Le véritable dragon rouge.
1. Incantations. 2. Magic. I. Karter, J. II. Title: Le grand grimoire. III. Title: Grimoire du Pape Honorius. IV. Title: Le dragon rouge. V. Title: Le véritable dragon rouge. VI. Title: La clavicule de Salomon.
8

L'art de commander les esprits.
WITCHCRAFT
BF 1558 G86 1823
Le Dragon rouge, ou l'art de commander les esprits célestes, aériens, terrestres, infernaux, avec le vrai secret de faire parler les morts, de gagner toutes les fois qu'on met aux loteries, de découvrir les trésors cachés, etc., etc. Imprimé sur un manuscrit de 1522. Nismes, Chez Gaude, 1823.
108 p. illus. 15cm.
Published also under other titles: Grimoire du Pape Honorius [best-known];
8
(Continued on next card)

L'art de commander les esprits.
WITCHCRAFT
BF 1558 G86 1823
Le Dragon rouge ... 1823. (Card 2)
Le véritable dragon rouge; and L'art de commander les esprits.
Chapter 1 signed: Antonio Venitiana, del Rabbina.
1. Incantations. 2. Magic. I. Venitiana, Antonio, del Rabbina. II. Title: Grimoire du Pape Honorius. III. Title: Le véritable dragon rouge. IV. Title: L'art de commander les esprits.
8

L'art de commander les esprits.
WITCHCRAFT
BF 1558 G86 1800a
Le Véritable dragon rouge, ou l'Art de commander les esprits célestes, aériens, terrestres et infernaux, avec le secret de faire parler les morts; de gagner toutes les fois qu'on met aux loteries; de découvrir les trésors cachés; etc., etc.; suivi de La poule noire, cabale qui était restée inconnue jusqu'ici. [Lille, Imprimerie de Blocquel] 1521 [i.e., 18--]
140 p. illus. 16cm.
8
(Continued on next card)

L'art de commander les esprits.
WITCHCRAFT
BF 1558 G86 1800a
Le Véritable dragon rouge ... [18--] (Card 2)
Title in red and black.
Chapter 1 signed: J. Karter, Venetiana.
Published also under other titles: Grimoire du Pape Honorius [best-known]; Le dragon rouge; and L'art de commander les esprits.
1. Incantations. 2. Magic. I. Karter, J. II. Title: Grimoire du Pape Honorius. III. Title: Le dragon rouge. IV. Title: L'art de commander les esprits. V. Title: La poule noire.
8

Art magic.
Witchcraft
BF 1251 B86 A7
[Britten, William] *supposed author.*
Art magic; or, Mundane, sub-mundane and super-mundane spiritism. A treatise in three parts and twenty-three sections: descriptive of art magic, spiritism, the different orders of spirits in the universe known to be related to, or in communication with man; together with directions for invoking, controlling, and discharging spirits, and the uses and abuses, dangers and possibilities of magical art ... New York, The author, 1876.
2 p. l., 467 p. front., illus. (incl. ports.) plates. 22½cm.
Copyrighted by William Britten.
Ed. by Emma Hardinge Britten.
1. Spiritualism. 2. Magic. I. Britten, Mrs. Emma (Hardinge) ed. II. Title.
Library of Congress BF1251.B83 10-34683

Arte magica annichilata.
Witchcraft
BF 1604 M18 1754
[Maffei, Francesco Scipione, *marchese*] 1675-1755.
Arte magica annichilata. Libri tre. Con un' appendice. Verona, A. Andreoni, 1754.
5 p. l., 328, [6] p. 25cm.
Author's name appears in the dedication.
The fifth preliminary leaf bound in back of vol.
Work inspired by the controversy about G. Tartarotti's Del congresso notturno delle lammie.
1. Magic. 2. Witchcraft. 3. Tartarotti, Girolamo, 1706-1761. Del congresso notturno delle lammie. I. Title.
8
Copy 2.

Arte magica dileguata.
Witchcraft
BF 1565 T19 M18+
Maffei, Francesco Scipione, marchese, 1675-1755.
Arte magica dileguata: lettera del Signor Marchese Maffei al Padre Innocente Ansaldi ... Verona, Per Agostino Carattoni, 1749.
51 p. 26cm.
With this are bound his Tre lettere. Verona, 1748; and Benvenuti, Giuseppe, 1728-ca. 1770. De daemoniacis dissertatio. Lucae, 1775.
8
~~(Continued on next card)~~

L'arte magica dimostrata.
Witchcraft
BF 1604 P92
Preati, Bartolommeo.
L'arte magica dimostrata. Dissertazione di Bartolammeo Preati, Vicentino, contra l'opinione del Signor Marchese Maffei. Venezia, Stamperia Remondini, 1751.
95 p. 21cm.
1. Magic. 2. Maffei, Francesco Scipione, marchese, 1675-1755. I. Title.
8

Arte magica distrutta.
Witchcraft
BF 1565 T19 M183
Fiorio, Antonio.
Arte magica distrutta. Risposta di Don Antonio Fiorio Veronese. Trento, Per G. A. Brunati, 1750.
47 p. 24cm.
"As is pointed out on p. 4 of the Replica bound in these same covers, this imprint "In Trento per G. A. Brunati" is stamped in by hand. Melzi, ii, p. 418, ascribes the pamphlet to Maffei himself." --Note of George Lincoln Burr on t. p.
8
(Continued on next card)

Arte magica distrutta.
Witchcraft
BF 1565 T19 M183
Fiorio, Antonio. Arte magica distrutta. 1750. (Card 2)
With this is bound Replica alla risposta intitolata Arte magica distrutta. Verona, 1751.
1. Maffei, Francesco Scipione, marchese 1675-1755. Arte magica dileguata. 2. Magic. I. Maffei, Francesco Scipione, marchese, 1675-1755, supposed author. II. Title.
8

Witchcraft
BL 305 A79
Articles on mythology, etc. [v.p., 1871-1880]
1 v. (various pagings) 25cm.
Cover-title.
Articles reprinted from Contemporary review and Nineteenth century, with one from Once a week.
Contents.--On the philosophy of mythology, by Max Müller.--Germanic mythology, by Karl Blind.--The first sin, by François Lenormant. --The myths of the sea and the river of
(Continued on next card)
(Over)

Witchcraft
BL 305 A79
Articles on mythology, etc. 1871-1880. (Card 2)
Contents--Continued.
death, by C. F. Keary.--Wind myths, by C. F. Keary.--Forest and field myths, by W. R. S. Ralston.--Cinderella, by W. R. S. Ralston.--Demonology of the New Testament, by J. J. Owen. --Demoniacal possession in India, by W. Knighton.--Demonolatry, devil-dancing, and demoniacal possession, by R. C. Caldwell --Witchcraft in Devon.

Articulen tot satisfactie aan de Eerw. Classis van Amsterdam.
Witchcraft
BF 1410 B42 Z85 no.2
Bekker, Balthasar, 1634-1698.
Articulen tot satisfactie aan de Eerw. Classis van Amsterdam, van Do. Balthasar Bekker, overgeleverd den 22 January 1692. Wegens syn uytgegeven boek, genaamd De betoverde wereld. Amsterdam, By G. Borstius, boekverkoper, 1692.
11 p. [p. 12 blank] title vignette, illus. initial. 19 x 16cm.
4o: A^4, $[B^2]$
Van der Linde 32.
(Continued on next car
8

Articulen tot satisfactie aan de Eerw. Classis van Amsterdam.
Witchcraft
BF 1410 B42 Z85 no.2
Bekker, Balthasar, 1634-1698. Articulen tot satisfactie aan de Eerw. Classis van Amsterdam ... 1692. (Card 2)
No. 2 in vol. lettered Stukken betrekkelijk Bekker.
1. His De betoverde weereld. I. Nederlandse Hervormde Kerk. Classes. Amsterdam. II. Title.
8

CATALOGUE OF THE CORNELL WITCHCRAFT COLLECTION

Witchcraft
BF
1521
A82
[Ashdowne, William]
An attempt to prove that the opinion concerning the Devil, or Satan, as a fallen angel, and that he tempts men to sin, hath no real foundation in Scripture. Being a supplement to a pamphlet published about the year 1770, entituled, An enquiry into the Scripture meaning of the word Satan. 2d ed. with considerable additions... Canterbury, Printed and sold by W. Bristow, 1794.
63 p. 22cm.

(Continued on next card)

Witchcraft
BF
1521
A82
[Ashdowne, William] An attempt to prove that the opinion concerning the Devil... 1794. (Card 2)

Bound with his An inquiry into the Scripture meaning of the word Satan... London, 1772.
With autograph of M. H. Black.

1. Devil. I. Title. II. His An enquiry into the Scripture meaning of the word Satan.

Witchcraft
BF
1521
A82
[Ashdowne, William]
An inquiry into the Scripture meaning of the word Satan and its synonymous terms, the Devil, or the Adversary, and the Wicked-One. Wherein also the notions concerning devils or demons, are brought down to the standard of Scripture ... London, Printed for J. Wheble, 1772.
iii, 40, 77 p. 22cm.

With this is bound his An attempt to prove that the opinion concerning the Devil

(Continued on next card)

Witchcraft
BF
1521
A82
[Ashdowne, William] An inquiry ... Satan ... 1772. (Card 2)
... Canterbury, 1794.

With autographs of M. H. Black, Von Carnap, William Kite, William Ashdowne.
Interleaved, with ms. additions by author.

1. Devil. I. Title.

Witchcraft
BF
1521
A82
Ashdowne, William.
An inquiry into the Scripture meaning of the word Satan.
[Ashdowne, William]
An attempt to prove that the opinion concerning the Devil, or Satan, as a fallen angel, and that he tempts men to sin, hath no real foundation in Scripture. Being a supplement to a pamphlet published about the year 1770, entituled, An enquiry into the Scripture meaning of the word Satan. 2d ed. with considerable additions... Canterbury, Printed and sold by W. Bristow, 1794.
63 p. 22cm.

(Continued on next card)

Witchcraft
BF
1521
A82
Ashdowne, William.
An inquiry into the Scripture meaning of the word Satan.
[Ashdowne, William] An attempt to prove that the opinion concerning the Devil... 1794. (Card 2)

Bound with his An inquiry into the Scripture meaning of the word Satan... London, 1772.
With autograph of M. H. Black.

1. Devil. I. Title.

HIST SCI
QD
25
A82
Ashmole, Elias, 1617-1692, comp.
Theatrum chemicum britannicum. Containing severall poeticall pieces of our famous English philosophers, who have written the hermetique mysteries in their owne ancient language. Faithfully collected into one volume, with annotations thereon, by Elias Ashmole, esq., qui est Mercuriophilus anglicus. The first part. London, Printed by J. Grismond for N. Brooke, 1652.
8 p.l., 486 [8] p. illus. 19cm.

(Continued on next card)

HIST SCI
QD
25
A82
Ashmole, Elias, 1617-1692, comp. Theatrum chemicum britannicum ... London, 1652. (Card 2)

No more published.
Title vignette.
Contains the Ordinall of alchemie by Thomas Norton, the Compound of alchemie by George Ripley, the Chanon's yeoman's tale by Chaucer, Sir Edward Kelley's Worke, Doctor John Dee's Testament, Secreta secretorum by John Lydgate, and other works.
Wing A3987.
1. Alchemy. I. Title.

Witchcraft
BF
1581
A82
Ashton, John, 1834-
The devil in Britain and America ...
[London] Ward and Downey, 1896.
x, 363 p. illus. 23cm.

I. Title.

Ashwin, E Allen, tr.
Witchcraft
BF
1582
A2
B67
1929
Boguet, Henri, d. 1619.
An examen of witches, drawn from various trials of many of this sect in the district of Saint Oyan de Joux, commonly known as Saint Claude in the county of Burgundy, including the procedure necessary to a judge in trials for witchcraft. Tr. by E. Allen Ashwin, ed. by the Rev. Montague Summers. [London] J. Rodker, 1929.
liii, 328 p. 19cm.
"Edition limited to 1275 copies; this copy is number 290."

8

Witchcraft
BF
1505
A84
[Assier, Alexander] 1821-
Le diable en Champagne. Par l'auteur des Champenois à travers les siècles...
Paris, Dumoulin, 1869.
59 p. illus. 19cm.

1. Demonology. I. Title.

Witchcraft
PQ
4253
A6A85
1660
Astolfi, Giovanni Felice.
Cento avenimenti meravigliosi, stvpendi, e rari ... Ne'qvali sono compresi distruggimenti di oracoli, insidie, maleficij, e tradimenti. Atti magnanimi di huomini fortissimi, caste, e costanti donne, et fanciulli animosi ... Vittorie singolari contro demonij, mondo, carne, et huomini rei. Venetia, A instanza delli Turrini, 1660.
[12], 154 p. 22cm.

Title vignette: printer's device.

I. Title.

WITCHCRAFT
BF
1775
S38
1757
Astral-Geist.
Schütze, Heinrich Carl, 1700-1781.
Vernunft- und schriftmässige Abhandlung von Aberglauben. Nebst einem Anhange von Astral-Geist. Wernigerode, J. G. Struck, 1757.
9 p. l., 496, [16] p. front. 17cm.

1. Superstition. 2. Occult sciences.
I. Title. II. Title: Astral-Geist.

8
NIC

Witchcraft
BF
1718
B63
Astrological practice of physick.
Blagrave, Joseph, 1610-1682.
Astrological practice of physick. Discovering the true way to cure all kinds of diseases and infirmities which are naturally incident to the body of man. Being performed by such herbs and plants which grow within our own nation, directing the way to distil and extract their virtues and making up of medicines. Also, a discovery of some notable philosophical secrets worthy our knowledge, relating to a discovery of all kinds of evils, whet her natural or such
(Continued on next card)

Witchcraft
BF
1718
B63
Astrological practice of physick.
Blagrave, Joseph, 1610-1682. Astrological practice of physick ... 1689. (Card 2)

which come from sorcery or witchcraft, or by being possessed of an evil spirit; directing how to cast forth the said evil spirit out of any one which is possessed, with sundry examples thereof. London, Printed for O. Blagrave, 1689.
139 p. 17cm.

Wing B 3114.

Witchcraft
QB
36
K38
K38
Astronom Kepler und seine Zeit.
Keppler, Gustav, ed.
Familiengeschichte Keppler, bearb. und hrsg. von Oberpostinspector Gustav Keppler, Stuttgart. 2. Bd. Görlitz, Verlag für Sippenforschung und Wappenkunde C. A. Starke, 1930.
864 p. port., plates. 15cm.
Added t. p.: Astronom Kepler und seine Zeit, mit Schilderung des Hexenprozesses gegen seine Mutter.
Band 1 apparently not published.

8
(Continued on next card)

Witchcraft
BF
1521
A82
[Ashdowne, William]
An attempt to prove that the opinion concerning the Devil, or Satan, as a fallen angel, and that he tempts men to sin, hath no real foundation in Scripture. Being a supplement to a pamphlet published about the year 1770, entituled, An enquiry into the Scripture meaning of the word Satan. 2d ed. with considerable additions... Canterbury, Printed and sold by W. Bristow, 1794.
63 p. 22cm.

(Continued on next card)

Witchcraft
BF
1521
A82
[Ashdowne, William] An attempt to prove that the opinion concerning the Devil... 1794. (Card 2)

Bound with his An inquiry into the Scripture meaning of the word Satan... London, 1772.
With autograph of M. H. Black.

1. Devil. I. Title.

25

CATALOGUE OF THE CORNELL WITCHCRAFT COLLECTION

Attila, d. 453.

Witchcraft
BF
1565
A33
1723

Alberti, Valentin, 1635-1697, praeses.
... Academische Abhandlung von den Hexen und dem Bündniss so sie mit dem Teuffel haben. Darinnen ... nebst Erörterung einiger andern curieusen Fragen, ob die bekannte Pucelle d'Orleans, ingleichen das rasende Weib, das den Attilam erschrecket, eine Hexe gewesen sei? Franckfurt und Leipzig, 1723.
[56] p. front. 21cm.
Translation of his Dissertatio academica, De sagis, C. Stridtbeckh, respondent, Wittebergae, 1690.

8   (Continued on next card)

Attila, d. 453.

Witchcraft
BF
1565
D62
no.10

Alberti, Valentin, 1635-1697, praeses.
Dissertatio academica, De sagis, sive foeminis, commercium cum malo spiritu habentibus, e christiana pnevmatologia desumpta, & sub praesidio ... Dn. D. Valentini Alberti ... publicae proposita ventilationi ... ab autore Christiano Stridtbeckh ... Lipsiae, Typis Christoph. Fleischeri [1690]
[52] p. illus. 20cm.
No.10 in vol. lettered Dissertationes de sagis.   1636-1714.

8   (Continued on next card)

The attitude of Origen and Augustine toward magic.

Witchcraft
BF
1601
T49

Thorndike, Lynn, 1882-
The attitude of Origen and Augustine toward magic. [Chicago, 1908]
[46]-66 p. 23cm.

Reprinted from The monist, v.18, Jan. 1908.

1. Origenes. Contra Celsum. 2. Augustinus Aurelius, Saint, bp. of Hippo. De civitate Dei. 3. Magic. I. Title.

The attitude of the Catholic Church towards witchcraft and the allied practices.

Witchcraft
BF
1566
P91

Pratt, Sister Antoinette Marie, 1878-
The attitude of the Catholic Church towards witchcraft and the allied practices of sorcery and magic. Washington, D. C. [National Capital Press, Inc.] 1915.
138 p. 23cm.

Thesis (Ph. D.)--Catholic University of America.

1. Witchcraft. 2. Magic. 3. Catholic Church--Hist.   I. Title.

The attitude of the Catholic church towards witchcraft and the allied practices.

ar W
48249
no.4

Pratt, Sister Antoinette Marie, 1878-
The attitude of the Catholic church towards witchcraft and the allied practices of sorcery and magic, by Sister Antoinette Marie Pratt ... Washington, D. C. [National capital press, inc.] 1915.
138 p. 23cm.
Thesis (PH. D.)—Catholic university of America, 1915.
Vita.
Bibliography: p. 125-132.

1. Witchcraft. 2. Magic. 3. Catholic church—Hist. I. Title.

Library of Congress   BF1566.P7
Catholic Univ. of America   Libr.
                                    15-21989

Attitude of the Jesuits in the trials for witchcraft.

WITCHCRAFT
PQ
4416
C237

Schwickerath, Robert.
Attitude of the Jesuits in the trials for witchcraft.
(In The American Catholic quarterly review. Philadelphia. 25cm. v. 27, no. 107 (1902), p. 475-516)

8
NIC

1. Jesuits--Controversial literature. 2. Witchcraft--History. I. Title.

DC
611
P952
A67
v.1

Aubenas, Roger.
La sorcière et l'inquisiteur; épisode de l'Inquisition en Provence, 1439. Aix-en-Provence, La Pensée universitaire, 1956.
x, 81 p. facsims. 25 cm. (Archives de Provence, 1)
Bibliography: p. 79-80.

1. Malavesse, Catherine (David) fl. 1439. 2. Inquisition. Provence. I. Title. (Series)

BF1582.Z7   1439   57-36238
Library of Congress   [3]

WITCHCRAFT
BL
820
S3
A89

Aubignac, François Hédelin, abbé d', 1604-1676.
Des satyres brvtes, monstres et demons. De levr natvre et adoration. Contre l'opinion de ceux qui ont estimé les satyres estre vne espece d'hommes distincts & separez des Adamicques ... Par F. Hedelin, aduocat en Parlement ... Paris, Chez Nicolas Bvon, 1627.
12 p. l., 236 p. 17cm.

8   I. Title.   II. Les satyres.

Witchcraft
BF
1517
F5
A89

[Aubin, Nicolas] b. ca. 1655.
The cheats and illusions of Romish priests and exorcists. Discovered in the history of the devils of Loudun: being an account of the pretended possession of the Ursuline nuns, and of the condemnation and punishment of Urban Grandier, a parson of the same town ... London, Printed for W. Turner and R. Bassett, 1703.
4 p. l., 331 p. 20cm.
Translation of Histoire des diables de Loudun.
Attributed also to M. Des Niau.
1. Loudun, France. Ursuline Convent. 2. Grandier, Urbain, 1590-1634. I. Des Niau,   , supposed author. II. Title.

Witchcraft
BF
1517
F5
A892
1716

[Aubin, Nicolas] b. ca. 1655.
Cruels effets de la vengeance du Cardinal de Richelieu, ou Histoire des diables de Loudun, de la possession des religieuses ursulines, et de la condamnation et du suplice [sic] d'Urbain Grandier, curé de la même ville. Amsterdam, E. Roger, 1716.
[10], 5-378 p. front. 17cm.

Published also under titles: Histoire des diables de Loudun, ou, De la possession des religieuses ursu   lines ... Amsterdam, 1694;
(Continued on next card)

Witchcraft
BF
1517
F5
A892
1716

[Aubin, Nicolas] b. ca. 1655. Cruels effets de la vengeance du Cardinal de Richelieu ... 1716.   (Card 2)

and Histoire d'Urbain Grandier, condamné comme magicien ... Amsterdam, 1735.

1. Loudun, France. Ursuline convent. 2. Grandier, Urbain, 1590-1634. 3. Demoniac possession. I. Title. II. Title: Histoire des diables de Loudun. III. Title: Les diables de Loudun.

Witchcraft
BF
1517
F5
A893
1737

Aubin, Nicolas, b. ca. 1655.
Cruels effets de la vengeance du Cardinal de Richelieu.
[Aubin, Nicolas] b. ca. 1655. Histoire des diables de Loudun, ou De la possession des religieuses ursulines, et de la condamnation & du suplice d'Urbain Grandier, curé de la même ville. Amsterdam, aux de'pens de la Compagnie, 1737.
378 p. front. 17cm.

"Published   also under titles:
(Continued on next card)

Witchcraft
BF
1517
F5
A893
1737

Aubin, Nicolas, b. ca. 1655.
Cruels effets de la vengeance du Cardinal de Richelieu.
[Aubin, Nicolas] b. ca. 1655. Histoire des diables de Loudun ... 1737. (Card 2)

Histoire d'Urbain Grandier, condamné comme magicien ... Amsterdam, 1735, and Cruels effets de la vengeance du Cardinal de Richelieu; ou, Histoire des diables de Loudun ... Amsterdam, 1716."--L.C.

Witchcraft
BF
1517
F5
A893
1737

Aubin, Nicolas, b. ca. 1655. Histoire d'Urbain Grandier, condamné comme magicien.
[Aubin, Nicolas] b. ca. 1655.
Histoire des diables de Loudun, ou De la possession des religieuses ursulines, et de la condamnation & du suplice d'Urbain Grandier, curé de la même ville. Amsterdam, aux de'pens de la Compagnie, 1737.
378 p. front. 17cm.

"Published   also under titles:
(Continued on next card)

Witchcraft
BF
1517
F5
A893
1737

Aubin, Nicolas, b. ca. 1655. Histoire d'Urbain Grandier, condamné comme magicien.
[Aubin, Nicolas] b. ca. 1655. Histoire des diables de Loudun ... 1737. (Card 2)

Histoire d'Urbain Grandier, condamné comme magicien ... Amsterdam, 1735, and Cruels effets de la vengeance du Cardinal de Richelieu; ou, Histoire des diables de Loudun ... Amsterdam, 1716."--L.C.

Witchcraft
BF
1517
F5
A893
1694

[Aubin, Nicolas] b. ca. 1655.
Histoire des diables de Loudun, ou de la possession des religieuses ursulines, et de la condamnation & du suplice d'Urbain Grandier, curé de la même ville. Amsterdam, A. Vvolfgang, 1694.
473 p. 15cm.
With autograph of Du Coudray.

8
NIC

Lavoisier
BF
1517
F5
A893
1716

[Aubin, Nicolas] b. ca. 1655.
Histoire des diables de Loudun, ou De la possession des religieuses ursulines, et de la condamnation et du suplice d'Urbain Grandier, curé de la même ville. Amsterdam, Aux dépens d'Étienne Roger, 1716.
378 p. front. 16cm.

1. Demoniac possession. 2. Grandier, Urbain, 1590-1634. 3. Loudun, France. Ursuline convent. I. Title: Les diables de Loudun.

Witchcraft
BF
1517
F5
A893
1737

[Aubin, Nicolas] b. ca. 1655.
Histoire des diables de Loudun, ou De la possession des religieuses ursulines, et de la condamnation & du suplice d'Urbain Grandier, curé de la même ville. Cruels effets de la vengeance du Cardinal de Richelieu. Amsterdam, aux de'pens de la Compagnie, 1737.
378 p. front. 17cm.

"Published   also under titles:
(Continued on next card)

CATALOGUE OF THE CORNELL WITCHCRAFT COLLECTION

Witchcraft
BF
1517
F5
A893
1737
[Aubin, Nicolas] b. ca. 1655. Histoire des diables de Loudun ... 1737. (Card 2)

Histoire d' Urbain Grandier, condamné comme magicien ... Amsterdam, 1735, and Cruels effets de la vengeance du Cardinal de Richelieu; ou, Histoire des diables de Loudun ... Amsterdam, 1716."--L.C.

1. Demoniac possession. 2. Grandier, Urbain, 1590-1634. 3. Loudun, France. Ursuline convent. I. Title: Les diables de Loudun. II. Title.
(over)

Witchcraft
BF
1517
F5
A893
1740
[Aubin, Nicolas] b. ca. 1655. Histoire des diables de Loudun: ou, de la possession des religieuses Ursulines, et de la condamnation & du suplice d'Urbain Grandier, curé de la même ville. Cruels effets de la vengeance du Cardinal de Richelieu. Amsterdam, Aux dépens de la Compagnie, 1740.
378 p. front. 17cm.

8
NIC

Witchcraft
BF
1445
S595
[Simon, Jordan] pater, 1719-1776.
Nicht doch -- oder, Auflösung der kleinen Zweifel über zwey Berichte von einer Hexen- oder Studenten-Geschichte die sich in dem Jahre 1768. den 10. 11. 12. und 13. Junius zu Ingolstadt in Bayern soll zugetragen haben. Aus einem dritten Berichte des Herrn Directors gezogen. Gedruckt zu Berichtshausen. Mit klaren Schriften [i.e., Leipzig] 1769[?]
27 p. 21cm.

8
(Continued on next card)

Witchcraft
BF
1445
S595
Auflösung der kleinen Zweifel über zwey Berichte von einer Hexen- oder Studenten-Geschichte.
[Simon, Jordan] pater, 1719-1776. Nicht doch -- ... [1769?] (Card 2)

Attribution by Holzmann.
Continuation of his Nun, ja --. [Leipzig, 1769], with which this is bound.

1. Ghosts. 2. Witchcraft--Ingolstadt, Bavaria. I. His Nun, ja --. II. Title. III. Title: Auflösung der kleinen Zweifel über zwey Berichte von einer Hexen- oder Studenten-Geschichte.

8

Witchcraft
BF
1582
A92
[Augier, Adolphe Clovis]
Les grandes victimes de l'hystérie: Louis Gaufridi, curé des Accoules, et Magdeleine de la Palud. Relation historique et rationnelle d'un procès de sorcellerie. Paris, L. Michaud [1907]
313 p. 19cm.
At head of title: Raoul Gineste [pseud. of A. C. Augier].

1. Gaufridi, Louis, 1572-1611. 2. Palud, Magdeleine de la. 3. Witchcraft--Provence. I. Title.

8

Augsburg.
Kurzer Bericht Was alhier Malefiz-Recht gehalten wird, oder, Modius Procedendi in Malefiz Sachen wie auch ein richtige Verzeichnis aller und jeder Maleficanten, welche in der H: R: Statt Augsburg von anno 1353: bis zu disen unseren Zeitten ... [18th cent.?]
[6] l., 166 p. 20 x 16cm.
Manuscript, on paper, in five different hands. Hand-ruled frame on each page. The statement of court procedure, l. [1-6], and the list of court cases from
(Continued on next card)

MSS
Bd.
WITCHCRAFT
JS
A92
Augsburg. Kurzer Bericht Was alhier Malefiz-Recht gehalten wird. [18th cent.?] (Card 2)

1353 to 1747 are in one hand. Cases from 1747 to 1760 are recorded in four additional hands. Index, p. 147-163 again in the first hand. P. 139-146, 164-166 blank.
Bound in worn leather.
Ex libris: Xaverii Mösman.

1. Criminal procedure--Augsburg.
2. Criminal registers--Augsburg.
(Continued on next card)

MSS
Bd.
WITCHCRAFT
JS
A92
Augsburg. Kurzer Bericht Was alhier Malefiz-Recht gehalten wird. [18th cent.?] (Card 3)

3. Judgments, Criminal--Augsburg. 4. Sentences (Criminal procedure)--Augsburg. 5. Court records--Augsburg.

Witchcraft
BF
1601
T49
Augustinus, Aurelius, Saint, bp. of Hippo. De civitate Dei.
Thorndike, Lynn, 1882-
The attitude of Origen and Augustine toward magic. [Chicago, 1908]
[46]-66 p. 23cm.

Reprinted from The monist, v.18, Jan. 1908.

1. Origenes. Contra Celsum. 2. Augustinus, Aurelius, Saint, bp. of Hippo. De civitate Dei. 3. Magic. I. Title.

Witchcraft
BF
1538
D9
G29
Augustinus, Aurelius, Bp. of Hippo. De divinatione daemonum.
Geerlings, Hermanus Jacob
De antieke daemonologie en Augustinus' geschrift De divinatione daemonum.
's-Gravenhage, 1953.
191 p. 24 cm.

Diss.--Amsterdam.

1. Augustinus, Aurelius, Saint, Bp. of Hippo. De divinatione daemonum. 2. Demonology. I. Title.

Witchcraft
BF
1410
M41
Augustinus, Aurelius, Saint, Bp. of Hippo. Trois sermons.
Massé, Pierre.
De l'impostvre et tromperie des diables, devins, enchantevrs, sorciers, novevrs d'esguillettes, cheuilleurs, chiromanciens, necromanciens, & autres qui par telle inuocation diabolique, ars magiques & superstitions abusent le peuple. Par Pierre Massé du Mans, aduocat. Paris, Chez Iean Poupy, 1579.
various pagings. 17cm.
Printer's device on t. p.

8
(Continued on next card)

Witchcraft
BF
1410
M41
Augustinus, Aurelius, Saint, Bp. of Hippo. Trois sermons.
Massé, Pierre. De l'impostvre et tromperie des diables ... 1579. (Card 2)

Title on spine: Massé. Abus des divins.
Text preceeded by Petit fragment catechistic d'vne plvs ample catechese de la magie ... de M. René Benoist Angeuin ...; and followed by Benoist's Traicté enseignant en bref les cavses des maleficies, sortileges et enchanteries... with special t. p. Declamation contre l'errevr execrable des
(Continued on next card)

Witchcraft
BF
1410
M41
Augustinus, Aurelius, Saint, Bp. of Hippo. Trois sermons.
Massé, Pierre. De l'impostvre et tromperie des diables ... 1579. (Card 3)

maleficiers ... par F. Pierre Nodé minime, has special t. p. with imprint Paris, Chez Iean du Carroy imprimeur, 1578, and is paged separately.
Trois sermons de S. Avgvstin ... traduits en françois par M. René Benoist, has special t. p. with imprint Paris, Chez Iean Poupy, 1579, and unnumbered pages.
(Continued on next card)

R
133
A92
Aurand, Ammon Monroe, 1895-
The "pow-wow" book: a treatise on the art of "healing by prayer" and "laying on of hands", etc., practiced by the Pennsylvania-Germans and others: testimonials: remarkable recoveries: popular superstitions: and including an account of the famous "witch" murder trial, at York, Pa., by A. Monroe Aurand, jr. ... containing also the complete collection of remedies and cures in John George Hohman's "Pow-wows, or Long lost friend"; in popular use since 1820. Harrisburg, Pa., Priv. print. by The Aurand press, 1929.
x, 85, [1], xi, 13-64 p. incl. front., illus. 24cm.
(Continued on next card)

R
133
A92
Aurand, Ammon Monroe, 1895- The "pow-wow" book ... 1929. (Card 2)

"An account of the 'witch' murder trial" ... and "John George Hohman's Pow-wows; or, Long lost friend" have special title-pages and pagination.
"Pow-wows; or Long lost friend" was published in 1819 under title: Der lange verborgene freund, oder: Getreuer und christlicher unterricht für jedermann.
"This edition of the 'Pow-wow' book is limited to one thousand copies; one
(Continued on next card)

R
133
A92
Aurand, Ammon Monroe, 1895- The "pow-wow" book ... 1929. (Card 3)

hundred signed by the author. This is no.309."
Bibliography: p. vi.

1. Medicine, Magic, mystic, and spagiric.
2. Superstition. 3. Folklore--Pennsylvania.
4. Witchcraft--Pennsylvania. 5. Blymyer, John H.
6. Rehmeyer, Nelson D., 1868-1928.
I. Hohman, Johann Georg. II. Title. III. Title: "Witch" murder trial, York, Pa.

Witchcraft
BF
1578
B66
Aurand, Ammon Monroe, 1895-
Blymyer, John H defendant.
An account of the "witch" murder trial, York, Pa., January 7-9, 1929. Commonwealth of Pennsylvania vs. John Blymyer, et al. By A. Monroe Aurand, jr. ... Harrisburg, Pa., Priv. print. by the Aurand press, 1929.
31 p. 23[cm].

1. Rehmeyer, Nelson D., 1868-1928. 2. Witchcraft--Pennsylvania. I. Aurand, Ammon Monroe, 1895- II. Title: "Witch" murder trial, York, Pa., January 7-9, 1929. III. Title.

Library of Congress 29-23242
—————— Copy 2.
Copyright A 4228 [2]

Witchcraft
1559
A92
1892
[Aurelian, father, Capuchin]
Authentischer Bericht über die Teufelaustreibung welche am 13. und 14. Juli 1891 im Wemdinger Kapuzinerkloster stattgefunden hat. [Wemding, A. Hellmuth, 1892?]
12 p. 22cm.

No t. p.: caption title.
Originally published under title: Eine Teufelaustreibung in Baiern.

CATALOGUE OF THE CORNELL WITCHCRAFT COLLECTION

Witchcraft
BF
1559
A92
1892a
    [Aurelian, father, Capuchin]
      Authentischer Bericht über die Teufel-Austreibung, welche am 13. und 14. Juli 1891 im Wemdinger Kapuziner-Kloster stattgefunden hat. [Wemding, A. Hellmuth, 1892?]
      11 p. 20cm.
      Caption title.
      Originally published under title: Eine Teufelaustreibung in Baiern.

      1. Exorcism. I. Title. II. His Eine Teufelaustreibung in Bayern.

WITCHCRAFT
BT
1220
F67
W13
    Aurelian, father, Capuchin.
      Authentischer Bericht über die Teufelaustreibung.
    Aurelian, father, Capuchin.
      Die Teufelsaustreibung im Wemdinger Kapuzinerkloster.
      (In Wahrmund, Ludwig. Ultramontan. München, 1908. p. [20]-30)
      First published 1892 under titles: Eine Teufelaustreibung in Baiern; and Authentischer Bericht über die Teufelaustreibung.

      1. Exorcism. I. His Authentischer Bericht über die Teufelaustreibung. II. Title.

8

Witchcraft
BF
1559
A92
    Aurelian, father, Capuchin.
      Eine Teufelaustreibung in Baiern.
      (In Kölnische Zeitung. Köln. 22cm. Nr. 375 (1892) p. [1])

      Later eds. published under title: Authentischer Bericht über die Teufelaustreibung...
      1. Exorcism. I. Title.

    Aurelian, father, Capuchin.
      Eine Teufelaustreibung in Bayern.

Witchcraft
BF
1559
A92
1892a
    [Aurelian, father, Capuchin]
      Authentischer Bericht über die Teufel-Austreibung, welche am 13. und 14. Juli 1891 im Wemdinger Kapuziner-Kloster stattgefunden hat. [Wemding, A. Hellmuth, 1892?]
      11 p. 20cm.
      Caption title.
      Originally published under title: Eine Teufelaustreibung in Baiern.

      1. Exorcism. I. Title. II. His Eine Teufelaustreibung in Bayern.

WITCHCRAFT
BT
1220
F67
W13
    Aurelian, father, Capuchin.
      Die Teufelsaustreibung im Wemdinger Kapuzinerkloster.
      (In Wahrmund, Ludwig. Ultramontan. München, 1908. p. [20]-30)
      First published 1892 under titles: Eine Teufelaustreibung in Baiern; and Authentischer Bericht über die Teufelaustreibung.

      1. Exorcism. I. His Authentischer Bericht über die Teufelaustreibung. II. Title.

8

    Aus Dichtung und Sage.

PN
674
H57
    Hertz, Wilhelm, 1835-1902.
      Aus dichtung und sage; vorträge und aufsätze von Wilhelm Hertz. Hrsg. von Karl Vollmöller. Stuttgart und Berlin, J. G. Cotta nachfolger, 1907.
      x, 219, [1] p. 18½cm.
      Reprinted from different periodicals.
      CONTENTS.—Über den ritterlichen frauendienst.—Die Walküren.—Die Nibelungensage.—Altfranzösische volkslieder.—Beowulf, das älteste germanische epos.—Mythologie der schwäbischen volkssagen.—Die hexenprobe.—Mörikes "Feuerreiter."
      1. Literature, Medieval—Hist. & crit. 2. Witchcraft. 3. Folk-songs—France. 4. Mörike, Eduard Friedrich, 1804-1875. Der feuerreiter. 5. Folk literature—Swabia. I. Vollmöller, Karl Gustav, 1848-1922, ed. II. Title.

      32-10346

Library of Congress   PN674.H4   804

Witchcraft
BF
1583
H12
    Aus pommerschen Hexenprozessakten.
    Haas, Alfred Wilhelm Moritz Gottlieb, 1860-
      Aus pommerschen Hexenprozessakten: ein Beitrag zur Geschichte des pommerschen Volksglaubens. Stettin, F. Hessenland, 1896.
      18 p. 26cm.

      1. Witchcraft. 2. Trials (Witchcraft)—Germany. I. Title.

WITCHCRAFT
BF
1523
K78
no.2
    Auserlesene Bibliothek der neuesten deutschen Literatur. Beurtheilung der demüthigen Bitte.
    [Köster, Heinrich Martin Gottfried] 1734-1802.
      Belehrung des Verfassers der Demüthigen Bitte an die grossen Männer welche keinen Teufel glauben. Mit Anmerkungen des Verfassers. [n. p.] 1776.
      114 p. 18cm.
      "Beurtheilung der demüthigen Bitte u.s.s. in der Lemgoer auserlesenen Bibliotheck 8. Band, S. 549": p. [5]-54. With commentary.
      "Demüthigste Antwort eines geringen Land-

8   (Continued on next card)

WITCHCRAFT
BF
1523
K78
no.2
    Auserlesene Bibliothek der neuesten deutschen Literatur. Beurtheilung der demüthigen Bitte.
    [Köster, Heinrich Martin Gottfried] 1734-1802. Belehrung des Verfassers der Demüthigen Bitte ... 1776. (Card 2)

      geistlichen ... Mit Anmerkungen," p. [57]-114, has special t. p. Text of the "Antwort" itself not included.
      No. 2 in vol. lettered Ueber den Teufel.
      1. Bonnet, Johann Carl. Demüthigste Antwort eines geringen Landgeistlichen. 2. Devil. 3. His Demüthige Bitte um Belehrung. I. Auserlesene Bibliothek der neuesten deutschen Literatur. Beurtheilung der demüthigen Bitte. II. Title.

8

Witchcraft
BF
1583
Z7
1722
    Ausführliche Erzählung des Verhörs und der Hinrichtung des im Jahre 1722 der Hexerey beschuldigten Georg Pröls von Pfettrach in Baiern. Herausgezogen aus den Gerichts-Akten, und begleitet mit kritischen Anmerkungen zur Baierns Aufklärung. [n. p.] 1806.
      271, [3] p. 18cm.
      Vorrede signed: A**.
      1. Trials (Witchcraft)—Bavaria. 2. Pröls, Georg, d. 1722. I. A**.

8

WITCHCRAFT
BF
1559
K89
    Ausführliche Historie vom Exorcismo.
    Krafft, Johann Melchior, 1673-1751.
      Ausführliche Historie vom Exorcismo, oder von dem Gebrauch bey der Kinder-Taufe dem unreinen Geist zu gebieten auszufahren und ihn zu beschwören, welche aus der Kirchen- und Gelehrten-Geschichte, aus vielen raren gedruckten und ungedruckten Schriften, vom andern Jahrhundert an bis auf gegenwärtige Zeiten ausgeführet, auch wie solche bey der Reformation, und nachgehends, an vielen Orten unserer Evangeli-

8
NIC   (Continued on next card)

WITCHCRAFT
BF
1559
K89
    Krafft, Johann Melchior, 1673-1751.
      Ausführliche Historie vom Exorcismo... (Card 2)

      schen Kirchen abgeschaffet worden, gezeiget hat. Hamburg, C. W. Brandt, 1750.
      1042 p. 18cm.

      1. Exorcism. I. Title.

WITCHCRAFT
BF
1565
P89
2 copies
    Ausführlicher geographischer Bericht, von den hohen trefflich alt- und berühmten Blockes-Berge.
    Praetorius, Johannes, 1630-1680.
      Blockes-Berges Verrichtung; oder, Ausführlicher geographischer Bericht, von den hohen trefflich alt- und berühmten Blockes-Berge. Ingleichen von der Hexenfahrt, und Zauber-Sabbathe, so auff solchen Berge die Unholden aus gantz Teutschland, jährlich den 1. Maij in Sanct-Walpurgis Nachte anstellen sollen. Aus vielen autoribus abgefasset, und mit schönen Raritäten angeschmücket sampt zugehörigen Figuren ... Leipzig,
8
NIC   J. Scheiben, 1668.
      (Continued on next card)

WITCHCRAFT
BF
1565
P89
    Ausführlicher geographischer Bericht, von den hohen trefflich alt- und berühmten Blockes-Berge.
    Praetorius, Johannes, 1630-1680.
      Blockes-Berges Verrichtung... 1668. (Card 2)

      582 p. fold. front. 16cm.

      Copy 2 imperfect: pages trimmed too closely in binding.

      1. Witchcraft. I. Title. II. Title: Ausführlicher geographischer Bericht, von den hohen trefflich alt- und berühmten Blockes-Berge.

WITCHCRAFT
BF
1566
K78
    Ausgeburten des Menschenwahns im Spiegel der Hexenprozesse.
    König, Bruno Emil, 1833-1902.
      Ausgeburten des Menschenwahns im Spiegel der Hexenprozesse und der auto da fé's. Historische Schandsäulen des Aberglaubens. Eine Geschichte des After- und Aberglaubens bis auf die Gegenwart. Ein Volksbuch. Rudolstadt, A. Bock [1893]
      811 p. plates (part fold.) 19cm.

      Issued in 17 parts.

8
NIC   1. Witchcraft. 2. Superstition. I. Title.

WITCHCRAFT
BF
1565
S38
    Eine ausführliche Instruction, wie in Inquisition Sachen des grewlichen Laster der Zauberey ... zu procediren.
    Schultheis, Heinrich von.
      Eine ausführliche Instrvction, wie in Inqvisition Sachen des grewlichen Lasters der Zauberey gegen die Zaubere der göttlichen Majestät vnd der Christenheit Feinde ohn Gefahr der Vnschüldigen zu procediren ... In Form eines freundlichen Gesprächs gestelt ... Cölln, Bey Hinrich Berchem, Sumptibus authoris [gedruckt bey Gissbert Clemens] 1634.
      xiii, [7], 503 p. port.

8
NIC   (Continued on next card)

WITCHCRAFT
BF
1565
S38
    Eine ausführliche Instruction, wie in Inquisition Sachen des grewlichen Laster der Zauberey ... zu procediren.
    Schultheis, Heinrich von. Eine ausführliche Instrvction ... 1634. (Card 2)

      Refutation of A. Tanner, p. 367-436, in Latin.
      "This book is, to my thinking, the most gruesome in all the gruesome literature of witch-persecution; and there is good ground for suspecting it of being the only copy now surviving ..."—part of MS note by G. L. Burr tipped into back of vol.

8
NIC   (Continued on next card)

Rare
K
A923++
    Austria. Laws, statutes, etc.
      Constitutio criminalis Theresiana, oder Der Römisch-kaiserl. zu Hungarn und Böheim u. u. Königl. Apost. Majestät Mariä Theresiä, Erzherzogin zu Oesterreich, u. u., peinliche Gerichtsordnung. Wien, Gedruckt bey J. T. edlen von Trattnern, 1769.
      8 p.l., 282, lvi. p. incl. plates (part fold.) 35cm.
      Latin summary of paragraphs in margin.
      The plates (mostly printed on both

      (Continued on next card)

CATALOGUE OF THE CORNELL WITCHCRAFT COLLECTION

Rare K A923++

Austria. Laws, statutes, etc. Constitutio criminalis Theresiana ... 1769. (Card 2)

sides) are illustrations of instruments of torture and their application.
List of members of the commission entrusted with the elaboration of the code: p. lv-lvi.
Note in manuscript on p. ₍₂₎ of cover: Sehr selten, da die Exemplare unterdrückt wurden.

(Continued on next card)

Rare K A923++

Austria. Laws, statutes, etc. Constitutio criminalis Theresiana...1769. (Card 3)

1. Criminal law--Austria. 2. Criminal procedure--Austria. 3. Torture. I. Austria. Sovereigns, etc., 1740-1780 (Maria Theresia) II. Title. III. Title: Peinliche Gerichtsordnung.

Rare K A923++

Austria. Sovereigns, etc., 1740-1780 (Maria Theresia)
Austria. Laws, statutes, etc.
Constitutio criminalis Theresiana, oder Der Römisch-kaiserl. zu Hungarn und Böheim u. u. Königl. Apost. Majestät Mariä Theresiä, Erzherzogin zu Oesterreich, u. u., peinliche Gerichtsordnung. Wien, Gedruckt bey J. T. edlen von Trattnern, 1769.
8 p.l., 282, lvi p. incl. plates (part fold.) 35cm.
Latin summary of paragraphs in margin.
The plates (mostly printed on both

(Continued on next card)

Rare K A923++

Austria. Sovereigns, etc., 1740-1780 (Maria Theresia)
Austria. Laws, statutes, etc. Constitutio criminalis Theresiana ... 1769. (Card 2)

sides) are illustrations of instruments of torture and their application.
List of members of the commission entrusted with the elaboration of the code: p. lv-lvi.
Note in manuscript on p. ₍₂₎ of cover: Sehr selten, da die Exemplare unterdrückt wurden.

(Continued on next card)

Die Auswirkungen der Cautio criminalis.

ar W 25683

Geilen, Heinz Peter, 1933-
Die Auswirkungen der Cautio criminalis von Friedrich von Spee auf den Hexenprozess in Deutschland. ₍Köln, G. Wasmund, 1963₎
xviii, 92 p. 21cm.

Inaug.-Diss.--Bonn.

Ausführliche Erzehlung des wütenden Teuffels.

Witchcraft
BF 1520 B66 1698

Bodin, Jean, 1530-1596.
Daemonomania; oder, Ausführliche Erzehlung des wütenden Teuffels in seinen damahligen rasenden Hexen und Hexenmeistern dero Bezauberungen, Beschwerungen, Vergifftungen, Gauckel- und Possen-Wercke... Welches der andere Theil Nicolai Remigii Daemonolatria. Wobey gleichfalls angehänget: Vielerhand warhaftige und erschreckliche Geschichte besessener Leute...nebst noch einigen betrieglichen und von Menschen

(Continued on next card)

Ausführliche Erzehlung des wütenden Teuffels.

Witchcraft
BF 1520 B66 1698

Bodin, Jean, 1530-1596. Daemonomania. 1698. (Card 2)

practicirten kurtzweiligen Begenheiten. Hamburg, Gedruckt bey T. von Wiering, 1698.
2 v. in 1. plates. 18cm.

"Wiederlegung nebst der Schrifft des Hn. Weyer": v. 1, p. ₍400₎-465.
Translation of De la démonomanie.

Auszug der Frankfurter gelehrten Anzeigen Nro. 38 und 39 den 12. May 1775.

Witchcraft
BF 1559 G25 Z63 no.7

Lavater, Johann Caspar, 1741-1801.
Auszug der Frankfurter gelehrten Anzeigen Nro. 38 und 39 den 12. May 1775. Beytrag zur gelehrten Geschichte unserer Zeit. ₍Zürich, 1775₎
₍8₎ p. 17cm.

No. 7 in vol. lettered Gassneriana.

1. Gassner, Johann Joseph, 1727-1779. I. Title. II. Title: Beytrag zur gelehrten Geschichte unserer Zeit.

8

Autentyke copye van de articulen die van het Eerwaarde Consistorie van Amsterdam. den 23 Aug. 1691. opgestelt zyn.

Witchcraft
BF 1410 B42 Z56 v.2 no.1

Nederlandse Hervormde Kerk. Classes. Amsterdam. Consistorie.
Autentyke copye van de articulen die van het Eerwaarde Consistorie van Amsterdam. den 23 Aug. 1691. opgestelt zyn om voor te houden aen Do. B. Bekker en de aenbieding die Do. B. Bekker daar op gedaen heeft den 30 Augusti 1691. Amsterdam, Gedrukt by G. Borstius, boekverkooper ₍1691₎
₍8₎ p. title vignette. 19 x 15cm.
4°: A⁴.

(Continued on next card)

8

Autentyke copye van de articulen die van het Eerwaarde Consistorie van Amsterdam. den 23 Aug. 1691. opgestelt zyn.

Witchcraft
BF 1410 B42 Z56 v.2 no.1

Nederlandse Hervormde Kerk. Classes. Amsterdam. Consistorie. Autentyke copye van de articulen van ... den 23 Aug. 1691. ... ₍1691₎ (Card 2)

Aenbieding van Do. B. Bekker: p. ₍7₎-₍8₎
Van der Linde 30.
No. 1 in vol. lettered Bekker II.
1. Nederlandse Hervormde Kerk--Doctrinal and controversial works. I. Bekker, Balthasar, 1634-1698. II. Title.

8

An authenticated history of the famous Bell witch.

Witchcraft
BF 1578 B4 I54

Ingram, M V
An authenticated history of the famous Bell witch, the wonder of the 19th century, and unexplained phenomenon of the Christian era. The mysterious talking goblin that terrorized the west end of Robertson County, Tennessee, tormenting John Bell to his death. The story of Betsy Bell, her lover and the haunting sphinx. Clarksville, Tenn., 1894.
316 p. illus. 17cm.

Imprint covered by label: Setliff & Co., Nashville, Tenn.

Authentischer Bericht über die Teufel-Austreibung.

Witchcraft
BF 1559 A92 1892a

₍Aurelian, father, Capuchin₎
Authentischer Bericht über die Teufel-Austreibung, welche am 13. und 14. Juli 1891 im Wemdinger Kapuziner-Kloster stattgefunden hat. ₍Wemding, A. Hellmuth, 1892?₎
11 p. 20cm.

Caption title.
Originally published under title: Eine Teufelaustreibung in Baiern.

1. Exorcis. I. Title. II. His Eine Teufelaustreibung in Bayern.

The author of the History of the wars of England.

WITCHCRAFT
BF 1501 C95

₍Crouch, Nathaniel₎ 1632?-1725?
Wonderful prodigies of judgment and mercy: discovered in above three hundred memorable histories, containing I. Dreadful judgments upon atheists, perjured wretches, blasphemers ... II. The miserable ends of divers magicians, witches, conjurers, &c. with several strange apparitions. III. Remarkable presages of approaching death ... IV. The wicked lives, and woful deaths of wretched popes, apostates, and desperate

(Continued on next card)

8

The author of the History of the wars of England.

WITCHCRAFT
BF 1501 C95

₍Crouch, Nathaniel₎ 1632?-1725? Wonderful prodigies of judgment and mercy ... 1682. (Card 2)

persecutors. V. Fearful judgments upon cruel tyrants, murderers, &c. ... VI. Admirable deliverances from imminent dangers ... VII. Divine goodness to penitents, with the dying thoughts of several famous men concerning a future state after this life. Impartially collected from antient

(Continued on next card)

8

The author of the History of the wars of England.

WITCHCRAFT
BF 1501 C95

₍Crouch, Nathaniel₎ 1632?-1725? Wonderful prodigies of judgment and mercy ... 1682. (Card 3)

and modern authors ... By R. B. author of the History of the wars of England, and the Remarks of London, etc. London, Printed for Nath. Crouch, 1682.
2 p. l., 233, ₍3₎ p. illus. 15cm.
With added engr. t. p.
With armorial book plate: Hugh Cecil Earl of Lonsdale.

(Continued on next card)

8

The author of the History of the wars of England.

WITCHCRAFT
BF 1501 C95

₍Crouch, Nathaniel₎ 1632?-1725? Wonderful prodigies of judgment and mercy ... 1682. (Card 4)

Wing C7361.

1. Devil--Collections. 2. Reward (Theology) 3. Marvelous, The. I. The author of the History of the wars of England. II. R. B. III. B., R. IV. Title.

8

The author of The impossibility of witchcraft.

WITCHCRAFT
BF 1581 Z7 1712aa

The Impossibility of witchcraft further demonstrated, both from scripture and reason, wherein several texts of scripture relating to witches are prov'd to be falsly translated, with some cursory remarks on two trifling pamphlets in defence of the existence of witches. By the author of The impossibility of witchcraft, &c. London, Printed for J. Baker, 1712.
xv, 30, ₍2₎ p. 18cm.

(Continued on next card)

8

The author of The impossibility of witchcraft.

WITCHCRAFT
BF 1581 Z7 1712aa

The Impossibility of witchcraft further demonstrated ... 1712. (Card 2)

Bound with The impossibility of witchcraft. 2d ed. London, 1712.

1. Witchcraft. 2. Witchcraft in the Bible. 3. Bragge, Francis, b. 1690. Witchcraft farther display'd. I. The author of The impossibility of witchcraft.

8

29

CATALOGUE OF THE CORNELL WITCHCRAFT COLLECTION

The autobiography of Satan.

Witchcraft
BT Beard, John Relly, 1800-1876.
980   The autobiography of Satan. Edited
B36 [i.e. written] by John R. Beard. London,
      Williams and Norgate, 1872.
         xii, 418 p. front. 19cm.

1. Devil. I. Title.

Autour de Jean XXII: Hugues Géraud.

WITCHCRAFT
BF Albe, Edmond, 1861-
1582   Autour de Jean XXII: Hugues Géraud,
Z7   évêque de Cahors, l'affaire des poisons
1317 et des envoûtements en 1317. Cahors,
     J. Girma, 1904.
        206 p. 25cm.
        "Extrait du Bulletin de la Société des
     Études littéraires, Scientifiques et Artis-
     tiques du Lot, t. XXIX."
        1. Géraud, Hugues, bp. of Cahors, fl.
     1317. 2. Jo   annes XXII, pope, d.
     1334. I.   Title. II. Title:
     L'affaire des poisons.

Aux prises avec Satan.

BF Gaquère, François, 1888-
1555   Les possédés d'Illfurth, de Natal et de
G21 Phat-Diem (1868-1906-1925) Genval, Éditions
     "Marie-Mediatrice" [1956]
        125 p. illus. 18cm.
        At head of title: P. Sutter [et] François
     Gaquère. Aux prises avec Satan.
        Although Sutter's name appears first (left
     top of the t.p.) the work is presumably chiefly
     (or only) by Gaquère. Cf. "Avant-propos" and
     cover.
        1. Demoniac possession. I. His Aux prises
     avec Satan. II.   Sutter, P   III.
     Title. IV. Titl   e: Aux prises avec Satan.

Auxiliante summo numine specimen inaugurale
    theologicum De theologia daemonum.

Witchcraft
BF Krakevitz, Albert Joachim von, 1674-1734,
1520   praeses.
K89   Facultatis theologicae ad hunc actum de-
     canus Albertus Joach. de Krakevitz, ... suo
     & collegii theologici nomine ad disputatio-
     nem inauguralem ... Dn. M. Fridemanni Andreae
     Zulichii, Jenens. De theologia daemonum ...
     invitat. Rostochii, Litteris J. Wepplingi,
     Sereniss. Princ. & univ. typogr. [1715]
        10 p. l., 68 p. 21cm.
8   The first se   ction is a curriculum
                         (Continued on next card)

Auxiliante summo numine specimen inaugurale
    theologicum De theologia daemonum.

Witchcraft
BF Krakevitz, Albert Joachim von, 1674-1734,
1520   praeses. ...De theologia daemonum ...
K89   [1715]   (Card 2)

vitae.
        The dissertation proper has special t. p.:
     Auxiliante summo numine specimen inaugurale
     theologicum De theologia daemonum ...
        Diss.--Rostock (F. A. Zulich, respondent)
        1. Demonology. 2. Devil. I. Zulich,
     Fridemann Andre
     II. His Spe   cimen inaugurale theologi-
8   cum De theolog ia daemonum. III. Title:
     De theologia   daemonum.

Auxonne, France. Ursuline convent.

Witchcraft
BF Garnier, Samuel.
1517   Barbe Buvée, en religion soeur Sainte-
F5   Colombe, et la prétendue possession des
G23 ursulines d'Auxonne (1658-1663) Étude his-
     torique et médicale d'après des manuscrits
     de la Bibliothèque nationale et des archives
     de l'ancienne province de Bourgogne. Pré-
     face de M. le Dr. Bourneville. Paris,
     F. Alcan, 1895.
        93 p. 23cm. (Bibliothèque diabolique.
     (Collection Bourneville))

Avano, Peter de.

see

Abano, Pietro d', 1250-1315?

Witchcraft
BX Avertanus à S. Elia, Carmelite Prior at
1070   Ravensburg.
A95   Rettung der Catholischen Ehr vnd Wahr-
     heit, auff etlich vnd zwantzig Fragen,
     vnder andern, ob von Silvestro II. biss
     auff Gregorium den VII. alle Päbst Zau-
     berer gewesen? Wider die Lutherische Præ-
     dicanten daselbsten ... Ravenspurg, J. J.
     Wehrlin, 1669.
        iiij l., 120 p. 16cm.
        I. Title.

Ayres, Harry Morgan, tr.

PT Mariken van Nimmegen.
5443   A marvelous history of Mary of Nimmegen,
M33 who for more than seven year lived and had
1924 ado with the devil. Translated from the
     Middle Dutch by Harry Morgan Ayres. With an
     introd. by Adriaan J. Barnouw. The Hague,
     M. Nijhoff, 1924.
        xxv, 78 p. 17cm. (The Dutch library.
     v. 3)
        "The Engli   sh and the Dutch
                       (Continued on next card)

Ayres, Harry Morgan, tr.

PT   Mariken van Nimmegen.   A marvelous his-
5443   tory of Mary of Nimmegen ... 1924.
M33   (Card 2)
1924
     versions are undated, but from the type and
     the printing devices used both are assigned
     to 1518-19. Hence a question has arisen as
     to the priority of the two versions. Some
     scholars regard the English version as an
     adaptation of the Dutch play, and others
     claim that both   are based on a now lost
     Dutch prose   original." Introd. of
     1932 facsimil   ed.
        I. Ayres, Harry Morgan, tr.

Azevedo, Alonso María de.
    De reorum absolutione.
Rare
HV Castro, Pedro de, *canon of Seville*.
8599   Defensa de la tortura y leyes patrias que la establecieron: e
S8   inpugnacion del tratado que escribio contra ella el doctor d.
C35 Alfonso Maria de Acevedo: su autor, don pedro de Castro ...
     Madrid, M. Escribano, 1778.
        xxviii, 256 p. 21 cm.

        1. Torture. 2. Azevedo, Alonso María de. [De reorum absolutione ...
     I. Title.

     Library of Congress   HV8599.S8C3   45-42238
                               [3]

CATALOGUE OF THE CORNELL WITCHCRAFT COLLECTION

B

B----, Abbot.

Witchcraft
PQ
1957
B67
A64
1711

[Bordelon, Laurent] 1653-1730.
A history of the ridiculous extravagancies of Monsieur Oufle; occasion'd by his reading books treating of magick, the black-art, daemoniacks, conjurers, witches ... With notes containing a multitude of quotations out of those books, which have either caused such extravagant imaginations, or may serve to cure them. Written originally in French, by the Abbot B----; and now translated into English. London, Printed

8   (Continued on next card)

B----, Abbot.

Witchcraft
PQ
1957
B67
A64
1711

[Bordelon, Laurent] 1653-1730. A history of the ridiculous extravagancies of Monsieur Oufle ... 1711. (Card 2)
for J. Morphew, 1711.
4 p. l., 303 [i.e., 319] p. 20cm.
Translation of Histoire des imaginations extravagantes de Monsieur Oufle.
Gathering G, between p. 96 and 97, incorrectly paged 81-96.
1. Occult sciences. 2. Apparitions.

8   (Continued on next card)

B***, Monsieur, 17th cent.

    see

Binet, Benjamin, 17th cent.

B., F. S.

Witchcraft
BF
1445
D61
no.1

M. F. S. B. jurium studiosi recentissimum monimentum De spectris ad ... dominvm Christophorum Schonbeck ... Lugduni Batavorum, Typis Marsianis, 1646.
22, [2] p. 18cm. (bound in 21cm. vol.)

No. 1 in vol. lettered Dissertationes de spectris. 1646-1753.

1. Apparitions. I. B., F. S. II. F. S. B. III. Schonbeck, Christoph. IV. Title: De spectris.

8

WITCHCRAFT B., H. A.
BF
1583
A2
I43

Informatio ivris, in causa poenali; vtrvm tres mvlieres maleficii, et veneficii, cevreae, delatae capi, & torqueri potuerint, necne? Qvad. Caroli V. imp. constitvtio criminalis aliqvot in locis declaratur. Rechtliches Bedencken, in Malefitzsachen; ob drey Weiber, der Zauberey halber angegeben, in gefängliche Verhafft angenommen, und peinlich befragt werden können, oder nicht? Darinnen Keyser Carols, dess Fünfften, hochlöblichister Gedächtnuss Peinliche, oder Halss-

8
NIC   (Continued on next card)

WITCHCRAFT B., H. A.
BF
1583
A2
I43

Informatio ivris, in causa poenali... (Card 2)

gerichtsordnunge in etlichen Articuln erkläret wirdt. Per H. A. B. V. I. D. Franckf[urt a. M.] Bey C. Egen[olffs] Erben, 1590.
68 l. 16cm.
1. Witchcraft--Germany. 2. Torture--Germany. I. B., H. A. II. H. A. B. III. Karl V, Emperor of Germany, 1500-1558. IV. Title: Recht liches Bedencken, in Malefitzsach en.

B., J. F.

Witchcraft
BD
428
B54

Bertram, Johann Friedrich, 1699-1741.
Ob die Thiere Teufel seyn? wird durch Veranlassung dess von einem Französischen Jesuiten P. Bonjeau unlängst ans Licht gestellten neuen Lehr-Begriffs von den Seelen der Thiere genannt: Amusements philosophiques sur le langage des bestes; oder: Philosophische Zeit-Vertreib über die Thier-Sprache; in welchen sie zu Teufeln gemachet werden; nach Schrifft und Vernunfft untersuchet und beantwortet, von J.F.
B.   [Bremen]   S. Pomarius [1740]
[15], 94 p.   16cm.

B., M.

Witchcraft
PS
991
A1
P54

Philip English's two cups. "1692."
New York, A. D. F. Randolph, 1869.
109 p. 19cm.

Dedication signed: M. B.

1. Witchcraft--Salem, Mass.--Fiction.
I. B., M.

B., R.

WITCHCRAFT
BF
1501
C95

[Crouch, Nathaniel] 1632?-1725?
Wonderful prodigies of judgment and mercy: discovered in above three hundred memorable histories, containing I. Dreadful judgments upon atheists, perjured wretches, blasphemers ... II. The miserable ends of divers magicians, witches, conjurers, &c. with several strange apparitions. III. Remarkable presages of approaching death ... IV. The wicked lives, and woful deaths of wretched popes, apostates, and desperate

8   (Continued on next card)

B., R.

WITCHCRAFT
BF
1501
C95

[Crouch, Nathaniel] 1632?-1725? Wonderful prodigies of judgment and mercy ... 1682.
(Card 2)

persecutors. V. Fearful judgments upon cruel tyrants, murderers, &c. ... VI. Admirable deliverances from imminent dangers ... VII. Divine goodness to penitents, with the dying thoughts of several famous men concerning a future state after this life. Imparti ally collected from antient

8   (Continued on next card)

B., R.

WITCHCRAFT
BF
1501
C95

[Crouch, Nathaniel] 1632?-1725? Wonderful prodigies of judgment and mercy ... 1682.
(Card 3)

and modern authors ... By R. B. author of the History of the wars of England, and the Remarks of London, etc. London, Printed for Nath. Crouch, 1682.
2 p. l., 233, [3] p. illus. 15cm.
With added engr. t. p.
With armorial book plate: Hugh Cecil Earl of Lons dale.

8   (Continued on next card)

B., R.

WITCHCRAFT
BF
1501
C95

[Crouch, Nathaniel] 1632?-1725? Wonderful prodigies of judgment and mercy ... 1682.
(Card 4)

Wing C7361.

1. Devil--Collections. 2. Reward (Theology) 3. Marvelous, The. I. The author of the History of the wars of England. II. R. B. III. B., R. IV. Title.

8

B., W., tr.

WITCHCRAFT
BF
1517
F5
M62
1613

Michaelis, Sebastien, 1543?-1618.
The admirable history of the possession and conversion of a penitent woman. Sedvced by a magician that made her to become a witch, and the princesse of sorcerers in the country of Prouince, who was brought to S. Baume to bee exorcised, in the yeere 1610 ... Wherevnto is annexed a pnevmology, or Discourse of spirits ... reuewed, corrected, and enlarged ... Translated into English by W. B. Lon don, Imprinted for Wil-

8   (Continued on next card)

B., W., tr.

WITCHCRAFT
BF
1517
F5
M62
1613

Michaelis, Sebastien, 1543?-1618. The admirable history of the possession ... of a penitent woman ... [1613] (Card 2)
liam Aspley [1613]
24 p. l., 418, [10], 154, [34] p. 20cm.
Differs from another issue only in t. p. (lacks date; some spellings different)
Translation of Histoire admirable de la possession ... d'vne penitente, and of Discovrs des esp rits.
"A discovrse of spirits" has special t. p. and separate paging.

8   (Continued on next card)

B., W., tr.

WITCHCRAFT
BF
1517
F5
M62
1613

Michaelis, Sebastien, 1543?-1618. The admirable history of the possession ... of a penitent woman ... [1613] (Card 3)

STC 17854.
1. Palud, Magdeleine de la. 2. Gaufridi, Louis, 1572-1611. 3. Loudun, France. Ursuline convent. 4. Demoniac possession. 5. Exorcism. I. His Histoire admirable de la possession ... d'une penitente. English. II. His Discours des esprits. English. III. Title. IV. W. B., tr. V. B., W., tr.

8

31

CATALOGUE OF THE CORNELL WITCHCRAFT COLLECTION

Witchcraft
BF 1410 B42 Z56 v.3 no.15

B. C.
Aanmerkingen van eenige rechtzinnige broederen over de Articulen van satisfactie, waar op men met D. B. Bekker een verdrag gemaakt heeft. Leyden, By F. Haring, boekverkooper, 1692.
22, [1] p. [p. 24 blank] title vignette. 20 x 15cm.
4°: A-C⁴.
Consists of two letters, a short one signed N. N. [i. e., Jacobus Schuts], and one of 18 p. signed B. C.

(Continued on next card)

Witchcraft
BF 1410 B42 Z56 v.3 no.15

B. C.
Aanmerkingen van eenige rechtzinnige broederen ... 1692. (Card 2)
Van der Linde 38.
No. 15 in vol. lettered Bekker III.

1. Bekker, Balthasar, 1634-1698. Articulen tot satisfactie aan de Eerw. Classis van Amsterdam. I. Schuts, Jacobus. II. B. C. III. C., B.

Witchcraft
K B111

Baader, Joseph.
Eine bayerische Verordnung gegen Zauberer, Hexen und Wahrsager v. J. 1611.
[n. p., 1873]
[92]-102 p. 23cm.
Extract from Deutsche Kulturgeschichte. Neue Folge. 1873.

1. Witchcraft—Laws and legislation—Bavaria. I. Title.

BX 9339 P44 B11

Baarsel, Jan Jacobus van.
William Perkins: eene bijdrage tot de kennis der religieuse ontwikkeling in Engeland, ten tijde van Koningin Elisabeth. 's-Gravenhage, H. P. de Swart [1912]
321 p. illus. 25cm.

1. Perkins, William, 1558-1602. I. Title.

Witchcraft
BF 1584 S9 B11

Bååth, Albert Ulrik, 1853-1912.
Några ord om trolldomsväsendet i Swerige på 1600-talet. [Stockholm, 1887]
[195]-205 p. 21cm.
Caption title.
Detached from Läsning för folket, 1887.

1. Witchcraft—Sweden. 2. Witchcraft—Dalecarlia, Sweden. I. Title. II. Läsning för svenska folket.

Witchcraft
BF 1583 Z7+ 1613

Bacmeister, Dr., archivist.
Zur Geschichte der Hexenprozesse. Concept Bedenkens über die zu Niedernhaal um Hexerei und Zauberei willen in verhaft liegende Susann, Michel Lunge's Weib, derem Aussage, und noch weiters angebene Personen. [Würtemberg, 1886]
282-292 p. 30cm.
Caption title.
Detached from Württembergische Vierteljahrsheft für Landesgeschichte, IX, 1886.

(Continued on next card)

Witchcraft
BF 1583 Z7+ 1613

Bacmeister, Dr., archivist. Zur Geschichte der Hexenprozesse. (Card 2)
In pamphlet binder with Bossert, Gustav. Frankisches Gemeinderecht. [Würtemberg, 1886]

1. Lunge, Susann, fl. 1613. 2. Witchcraft—Germany. I. Title.

WITCHCRAFT
BF 1555 S44

Baddeley, Richard, fl. 1621.
The boy of Bilson.
The Second part of the Boy of Bilson: or, a true and particular relation of the impostor, Susanna Fowles ... who pretended her self possess'd with the Devil ... The whole being writ and attested by Robert Howson, clerk; Captain John Bonsey, and Mr. Nicholas Wade ... London, Printed by E. Whitlock, 1698.
24 p. 20cm.

1. Fowles, Susanna, fl. 1698. 2. Demoniac possession. I. Howson, Robert. II. Baddeley, Richard, fl. 1621. The boy of Bilson.

Rare AC 14 C18+ 1621

Baddeley, Richard, fl. 1621, ed.
Camerarius, Philipp, 1537-1624.
The living librarie; or, Meditations and observations historical, natvral, moral, political, and poetical. Written in Latin by P. Camerarivs. And done into English by Iohn Molle, esquire. London, Printed by Adam Islip, 1621.

I. Molle, John, fl. 1621, tr. II. Molle, H., fl. 1625, tr. III. Baddeley, Richard, fl. 1621, ed. IV. Title.

Witchcraft
BF 1582 Z7 1582

Badel, Émile, 1867-
D'une sorcière qu'aultrefois on brusla dans Sainct-Nicholas. Le tout habillé d' ymaiges [sic] par J. Jacquot. Nancy, Berger-Levrault, 1891.
227 p. illus. 22cm.

1. Nigal, Nicolle, d. 1582. 2. Witchcraft—France. I. Title.

Witchcraft
BF 1445 D61 no.19

Bäckerström, Andreas, respondent.
Waller, Nicolai, praeses.
Theoria spectrorum philosophica, quam ... praeside ... Dn. Nicolao Wallerio, ... publico bonorum examini modeste offert ... Andreas Bäckerström ... Upsaliae, Excud. L. M. Höjer [1753]
13, [1] p. 21cm.
Imperfect copy: t. p. and other pages badly torn.
No. 19 in vol. lettered Dissertationes de spectris. 1646-1753.

1. Apparitions. 2. Demonology. I. Bäckerström, Andreas, respondent. II. Title.

Witchcraft
BF 1584 D4B13

Bæksted, Anders.
Besaettelsen i Tisted, 1696-98. København, Munksgaard, 1959-60.
2 v. illus. 23 cm. (Danmarks folkeminder, nr. 69-70)
Summary in English.
Bibliography: v. 2, p. [365]-370.

1. Witchcraft—Thisted, Denmark. (Series) II. Title.
BF1584.A2D44
Illinois. Univ. Librar
for Library of Congress
A 61-5352

DL 103 .5 D18+ no.69-70

Baeksted, Anders.
Besaettelsen i Tisted, 1696-98. København, Munksgaard, 1959-60.
2 v. illus. 23cm. (Danmarks folkeminder, nr. 69-70)
Summary in English

1. Witchcraft—Thisted, Denmark.

DL 103 .5 D18+ no.61

Baeksted, Anders.
Brunsmand, Johan, 1637-1707.
Køge huskors. Med indledning og noter ved Anders Baeksted. København, E. Munksgaard, 1953.
320 p. illus. 22cm. (Danmarks folkeminder, nr. 61)
Includes reproduction of the title page of the original edition published in 1674, with title: Et forfaerdeligt huus-kaars.

1. Witchcraft—Denmark. I. Baeksted, Anders. II. His Et forfaerdeligt huus-kaars. III. Title.

WITCHCRAFT
BF 1584 N6 B14

[Baetzmann, Frederik] 1841-1913.
Hexevaesen og troldskab i Norge. Meddelt til laesning for menigmand. Christiania, B. M. Bentzen, 1865.
80 p. 16cm.

1. Witchcraft—Norway. I. Title.

Witchcraft
BF 1565 B16

Baissac, Jules, 1827-1898.
Les grands jours de la sorcellerie. Paris, C. Klincksieck, 1890.
v, 735 p. 25cm.
Sequel to his Histoire de la diablerie chrétienne.

1. Witchcraft—Hist. I. Title. II. His Histoire de la diablerie chrétienne. III. Title: Histoire de la diablerie chrétienne.

Witchcraft
BF 1549 B16

Baissac, Jules, 1827-1898.
Histoire de la diablerie chrétienne.
I. Le Diable; la personne du Diable, le personnel du Diable. Paris, M. Dreyfous [1882]
ix, 611 p. 24cm.
Title on spine: Le Diable.
The second vol. of the series, published in 1890 under title: Les grands jours de la sorcellerie, does not have the general title Histoire de la diablerie chrétienne.

1. Devil. I. Title: La diablerie chrétienne. II. Title. III. Title: Le Diable.

Witchcraft
BF 1565 B16

Baissac, Jules, 1827-1898.
Les grands jours de la sorcellerie. Paris, C. Klincksieck, 1890.
v, 735 p. 25cm.
Sequel to his Histoire de la diablerie chrétienne.

1. Witchcraft—Hist. I. Title.

CATALOGUE OF THE CORNELL WITCHCRAFT COLLECTION

Baker, Anne, d. 1618.

Witchcraft
BF
1563
T75
    The Wonderfvl discoverie of the witchcrafts of Margaret and Phillip[pa] Flower, daughters of Joan Flower neere Beuer Castle ... Together with the seuerall examinations and confessions of Anne Baker, Ioan Willimot, and Ellen Greene, witches in Leicestershire. London, Printed by G. Eld for I Barnes, 1619. [Greenwich, Reprinted by H. S. Richardson, ca. 1840]
    26 p. title   vignettes. 23cm.

8   (Continued on next card)

Baker, Anne, d. 1618.

Witchcraft
BF
1563
T75
    The Wonderfvl discoverie of the witchcrafts of Margaret and Phillip[pa] Flower ... [1840]   (Card 2)

    The examinations of Anne Baker, Ioanne Willimot, and Ellen Greene has special t. p. No. 4 in vol. lettered Tracts on witchcraft.

Balbontín Moreno, Manuel G
    Brujos y hechicerías [por] Manuel G. Balbontín. Santiago de Chile, Ediciones Arco [1965]
    95 p. illus. 19cm.

6

1. Witchcraft--Hist. 2. Witchcraft--Chile. I. Title.

Witchcraft
BF
1583
B17
    Baldi, Alexander.
    Die Hexenprozesse in Deutschland und ihr hervorragendster Bekämpfer; eine kulturhistorische Abhandlung. Würzburg, Stahel, 1874.
    42 p. 24cm.

1. Trials (Witchcraft)--Germany. 2. Spee, Friedrich von, 1591-1635. I. Title.

Baldwin, Mary, b. 1690.

Witchcraft
GR
142
H6
A3
no.10
    A short rehearsal of the sad condition of three of the children of John Baldwin of Sarret in the county of Hertford, and also the manner of their deliverance, 1717. The parents' evidence together with a summary of the testimonies of the children and friends and a brief introductory note by W. B. Gerish. Bishops' Stortford, 1915.
    19 p. 21½cm. [Hertfordshire folk lore. no. 10]

1. Baldwin, Rebecca, 1688-1713. 2. Baldwin, Mary, b. 1690. 3. Essex, Mrs. Anne (Baldwin) b. 1686. I. Gerish, William Blyth, ed.

16-25743

Library of Congress   GR142.H6A3 no. 17

Baldwin, Rebecca, 1688-1713.

Witchcraft
GR
142
H6
A3
no.10
    A short rehearsal of the sad condition of three of the children of John Baldwin of Sarret in the county of Hertford, and also the manner of their deliverance, 1717. The parents' evidence together with a summary of the testimonies of the children and friends and a brief introductory note by W. B. Gerish. Bishops' Stortford, 1915.
    19 p. 21½cm. [Hertfordshire folk lore. no. 10]

1. Baldwin, Rebecca, 1688-1713. 2. Baldwin, Mary, b. 1690. 3. Essex, Mrs. Anne (Baldwin) b. 1686. I. Gerish, William Blyth, ed.

16-25743

Library of Congress   GR142.H6A3 no. 17

Ballerini, Antonio, supposed author.

Witchcraft
BF
1565
T19
M183
    Replica alla risposta intitolata Arte magica distrutta, di un dottore e sacerdote Veronese. Verona, Nella stamperia Vescovile del seminario per Angelo Targa, 1751.
    68, [1] p. 24cm.
    Ascribed to P. Antonio Ballerini in a contempory hand on t. p. and in another hand on p. [69]
    "Melzi (II, p. 430) ascribes this to P. Andrea Lugiato, despite its praise of him;

8   (Continued on next card)

Ballerini, Antonio, supposed author.

Witchcraft
BF
1565
T19
M183
    Replica alla risposta intitolata Arte magica distrutta ... 1751.   (Card 2)

    but Melzi knows nothing of the ascription to Ballerini."--Note of George Lincoln Burr on t. p.
    Bound with Fiorio, Antonio. Arte magica distrutta. Trento, 1750.
    1. Fiorio, Antonio. Arte magica distrutta. 2. Lugiato, Andrea. Osservazzioni sopra ... Arte magica dileguata.

8   (Continued on next card)

Balthasar Bekker. Bibliografie.

Witchcraft
Z
8086
.8
L74+
    Linde, Antonius van der, 1833-1897.
    Balthasar Bekker. Bibliografie door Dr. A. van der Linde ... 's Gravenhage, M. Nijhoff, 1869.
    2 p. l. 57 p. 26cm.

1. Bekker, Balthasar, 1634-1698--Bibl. I. Title.

8-7359

Library of Congress   Z8086.8.L5

Balthasar Bekker de bestrijder van het bijgeloof.

Witchcraft
BX
9479
B42
K74
    Knuttel, Willem Pieter Cornelis, 1854-1921.
    Balthasar Bekker de bestrijder van het bijgeloof. 'S Gravenhage, M. Nijhoff, 1906.
    3 p. l., 368 p. port. 25cm.

1. Bekker, Balthasar, 1634-1698--Biog. I. Title.

Balthasar Bekker in Amsterdam.

Witchcraft
BX
9479
B42
L872
    Lorgion, Everardus Jan Diest, 1812-1876.
    Balthasar Bekker in Amsterdam. Een portret uit de zeventiende eeuw. Door Dr. E. J. Diest Lorgion, schrijver van Balthasar Bekker in Franker. Groningen, H. R. Roelfsema, 1851.
    2 v. title vignette (port.) 24 x 15cm.
    8°: v. 1: π3, 1-19⁸, 20 1; v. 2: π², 1-17⁸, 18⁴.
    Title page on special paper, inserted.
    Van der Linde   228.
    1. Bekker, Balthasar, 1634-1698 --Biog. I. Title.

8

Balthazar Bekker in Franeker.

Witchcraft
BX
9479
B42
L87
    [Lorgion, Everardus Jan Diest] 1812-1876.
    Balthazar Bekker in Franeker. Een portret uit de zeventiende eeuw. Groningen, H. R. Roelfsema, 1848.
    4 p. l., 264 p. front. 23 x 14cm.
    8°: π⁴, 1-16⁸, 17⁴.
    Prefaced signed: L--N.
    Van der Linde 227.
    1. Bekker, Balthasar, 1634-1698--Biog. I. Title.

8

Balthazar Bekkers en insonderheyd sijner voedsterlingen onkunde, onbescheidentheyd en dwalingen, kort en klaar ontdekt.

Witchcraft
BF
1410
B42
Z912
    [Andala, Ruardus] 1665-1727.
    Balthazar Bekkers en insonderheyd sijner voedsterlingen onkunde, onbescheidentheyd en dwalingen, kort en klaar ontdekt door een discipel van de Heer J. vander Waeyen en voedsterling van de Academie van Friesland. Franeker, Gedrukt by H. Gyzelaar, ordinaris drukker der Eed. Mog. Heeren Staten, en der Academie van Friesland, 1696.
    2 p. l., 107 p. [p. 108 blank] title and end page vignettes, illus. initials. 21 x 17cm.

8   (Continued on next card)

Balthazar Bekkers en insonderheyd sijner voedsterlingen onkunde, onbescheidentheyd en dwalingen, kort en klaar ontdekt.

Witchcraft
BF
1410
B42
Z912
    [Andala, Ruardus] 1665-1727. Balthazar Bekkers en insonderheyd sijner voedsterlingen onkunde ... 1696.   (Card 2)
    4°: *², A-N⁴, O².
    Black letter.
    Van der Linde 165.
    Bound with Andala, Ruardus, 1665-1727. Uiterste verleegentheid van Doctor Balt. Bekker. Franeker, 1696.
    1. Bekker, Balthasar, 1634-1698. I. Title.

8

Witchcraft
BF
1761
F682
    Baltus, Jean François, 1667-1743.
    Réponse à l'histoire des oracles, de Mr. de Fontenelle. Dans laquelle on réfute le systeme de Mr. Van-Dale, sur les auteurs des oracles du paganisme, sur la cause & le temps de leur silence; & où l'on établit le sentiment des Pères de l'Église sur le même sujet. Strasbourg, J. R. Doulssecker, 1707.
    [42], 374, [13] p. front. 18cm.

1. Fontenelle, Bernard Le Bovier de, 1657-1757. Histoire des oracles. 2. Oracles. 3. Dale, Antonius van, 1638-1708. De oraculis ethnicorum. I. Title.

Witchcraft
BF
1583
B19
    Balzer, Eugen.
    Die Bräunlinger Hexenprozesse.
    (In Alemannia. Freiburg im Breisgau. 23cm. 3. Folge, Bd. 2 (1910) p. 1-42)

1. Trials (Witchcraft)--Germany. I. Title.

AS
283
N86H6+
stiania, I
1901
no.1
    Bang, Anton Christian, 1840-1913.
    ... Norske hexeformularer og magiske opskrifter ... Kristiania, I commission hos J. Dybwad, 1901-02.
    xxxii, 761 p. 27½cm. (Videnskabs-selskabet i Christiania. Skrifter II. Historisk-filosofisk klasse, no. 1)
    "Udgivet for Hans A. Benneches fond."
    "Fremlagt i den Historisk-filosofisk klasse 19. jan. 1900."

I. Title.

3--24333

Library of Congress   AS283.O57 1901 no. 1
    [a35b1]

Witchcraft
BF
1584
D4
B21
    Bang, Vilhelm.
    Hexevaesen og hexelforfølgelser isaer i Danmark. Kjøbenhavn, J. Frimodt, 1896.
    138 p. 22cm.

1. Witchcraft. 2. Witchcraft--Denmark. I. Title. II. Hexelforfølgelser isaer i Danmark.

CATALOGUE OF THE CORNELL WITCHCRAFT COLLECTION

WITCHCRAFT
BF
1584
D4
C552

Bang, Vilhelm.
Tilføjelser til efterretningerne om hexeforfølgelserne i Ribe.
(In: Samlinger til Jydsk historie of topografi. København. 22cm. ser.3, v.3, no.3. 1902. p.271-272)

With, in same issue: Christensen, Christian Villads. Besaettelsen i Thisted.

8
NIC
1. Witchcraft--Denmark. 2. Witchcraft--Ribe, Denmark. I. Title.

Witchcraft
BX
9479
B42
B11
no.20

Banningh, Jacob.
Eenvoudig verhaal van de proceduuren gepleegt, in de waaterlandse doopsgesinde gemeentens tot Wormer en Jisp, over het doen ophouden van een haarer leeraaren, in sijn predikdienst ... veroorsaakt door het zoo genaamde nieuw gevoelen der geesten, engelen ende duyvelen, met de disputatien in voorvallen soo alse in deselve zyn geschiet, na waarheyd verhaalt door de zelve leeraar, Jacob Banningh. Amsterdam, by A. van Damme, boekverkooper, 1698.

8
(Continued on next card)

Witchcraft
BX
9479
B42
B11
no.20

Banningh, Jacob. Eenvoudig verhaal van de proceduuren gepleegt ... tot Wormer en Jisp ... 1698. (Card 2)

44 p. title and other vignettes, illus. initials. 20 x 15cm.
4°: A-E⁴, F².
Black letter (except introduction and post scriptum)
Local development of the controversy over Balthasar Bekkers De betoverde weereld.

8
(Continued on next card)

Witchcraft
BX
9479
B42
B11
no.20

Banningh, Jacob. Eenvoudig verhaal van de proceduuren gepleegt ... tot Wormer en Jisp ... 1698. (Card 3)

No. 20 in vol. lettered B. Bekkers sterfbed en andere tractaten.

1. Nederlandse Hervormde Kerk--Doctrinal and controversial works. 2. Bekker, Balthasar, 1634-1698. De betoverde weereld. I. Title.

RARE
HV
8593
B21

Banniza von Bazan, Joseph Leonhard, 1733-1800.
Disquisitio de tortura nec ex integro reprobata, nec ex integro adprobata. Oeniponti, Typis Joann. Thomae nob. de Trattnern, 1774.
94 p. 20cm.

8
NIC
1. Torture. I. Title.

Witchcraft
BF
1582
B22+

Bapst, Edmond, 1858-
Les sorcières de Bergheim; épisode de l'histoire d'Alsace. Paris, A. Lahure, 1929.
179 p. front. 30cm.

1. Witchcraft--Germany--Bergheim. I. Title.

Baptistae Codronchi ... De morbis veneficis, ac veneficijs.

Witchcraft
RA
1201
C67
1618

Codronchi, Giovanni Battista, fl. 1620.
Baptistae Codronchi ... De morbis veneficis, ac veneficijs. Libri qvattvor, in quibus non solum certis rationibus veneficia dari demonstratur, sed eorum species, caußae, signa, & effectus noua methodo aperiuntur. Postremo de eorum curatione ac praeseruatione exactè tractatur ... Qd opus alias editū, nuperrimè fuit ab auctore emēdatū ... Mediolani, Apud Io. Bapt. Bidelliū, 1618.
15 p.l., 248, [25] p. 19cm.

8
(Continued on next card)

Baptistae Codronchi ... De morbis veneficis, ac veneficijs.

Witchcraft
RA
1201
C67
1618

Codronchi, Giovanni Battista, fl. 1620. ...
De morbis veneficis ... 1618. (Card 2)

Added t. p., engraved.

1. Toxicology. 2. Poisons. I. Title: De morbis veneficis, ac veneficiis.

8

Barbara Elisabeth Schulzin.

WITCHCRAFT
BF
1583
Z7
1669

Schulze, Barbara Elisabeth, fl. 1669, defendant.
Barbara Elisabeth Schulzin. Ein Arnstädter Hexenprozess vom Jahre 1669. Nach den Originalprozessakten herausgegeben von Reinhold Stade. Arnstadt, Fürstl. Buchdruckerei von E. Protscher, 1904.
75 p. 22cm.

1. Trials (Witchcraft)--Germany. 2. Trials (Witchcraft)--Arnstadt, Germany. I. Stade, Reinhold, 1848- , ed. II. Title. III. Title: Ein Arnstädter Hexenprozess vom Jahre 1669.

8
NIC

Barbara Pachlerin, die Sarnthaler Hexe.

Witchcraft
BF
1584
T9
Z59

Zingerle, Ignaz Vincenz, Edler von Summersberg, 1825-1892, ed.
Barbara Pachlerin, die Sarnthaler Hexe, und Mathias Perger, der Lauterfresser. Zwei Hexenprozesse, hrsg. von Dr. Ignaz Zingerle. Innsbruck, Wagner, 1858.
xii, 84 p. 19cm.
Contents.--Barbara Pachlerin, die Sarnthaler Hexe.--Der Lauterfresser.--Anhang. Ein altes Loosbuch.
Each item has special t. p.

8
(Continued on next card)

Witchcraft
BF
1517
F5
G23

Barbe Buvée, en religion soeur Sainte-Colombe.

Garnier, Samuel.
Barbe Buvée, en religion soeur Sainte-Colombe, et la prétendue possession des ursulines d'Auxonne (1658-1663) Étude historique et médicale d'après des manuscrits de la Bibliothèque nationale et des archives de l'ancienne province de Bourgogne. Préface de M. le Dr. Bourneville. Paris, F. Alcan, 1895.
93 p. 23cm. (Bibliothèque diabolique. (Collection Bourneville))

Barber, Mary, d. 1612.

Witchcraft
BF
1581
A2
W81
1866a
no.1

The Witches of Northamptonshire. Agnes Browne. Ioane Vaughan. Arthur Bill. Hellen Ienkinson. Mary Barber. Witches. Who were all executed at Northampton the 22. of Iuly last. 1612. London, Printed by Thos Purfoot, for Arthur Iohnson, 1612. [Northampton, England, Taylor & son, 1866]
[28] p. 22cm.
No. 1 in box lettered Witchcraft in Northamptonshire.

8
1. Witchcraft--Northamptonshire, England. I. Title: Witchcraft in Northamptonshire.

Witchcraft
BF
1598
C13
B23

[Barberi]
Compendio della vita, e delle gesta di Giuseppe Balsamo, denominato il conte Cagliostro, che si è estratto dal processo contro di lui formato in Roma l'anno 1790, e che può servire di scorta per conoscere l'indole delle setta de' Liber muratori. Roma, nella Stampa. della Rev. Camera Apostolica, 1791.
141 p. 21cm.

1. Cagliostro, Alessandro, conte di, assumed name of Giuseppe Balsamo, 1743-1795. 2. Freemasons. I. Title.

Witchcraft
BF
1598
C13
B23
1791b

[Barberi,]
Compendio della vita, e delle gesta di Giuseppe Balsamo, denominato il conte Cagliostro, che si è estratto dal processo contro di lui formato in Roma l'anno 1790. E che può servire di scorta per conoscere l'indole della setta de' Liberi muratori. Roma, Stamp. della Rev. Camera apostolica, 1791.
189 p. front. (ports.) 19cm.

1. Cagliostro, Alessandro, conte di, assumed name of Giuseppe Balsamo, 1743-1795. 2. Freemasons. I. Title.

Library of Congress   BF1598.C2B3 1791
CA 7—7324 Unrev'd

Witchcraft
BF
1598
C13
B23
1791

[Barberi]
Compendio della vita e delle gesta di Giuseppe Balsamo--French.
Vie de Joseph Balsamo, connu sous le nom de comte Cagliostro. Extraite de la procédure instruite contre lui à Rome en 1790. Traduite d'après l'original italien, imprimé à la Chambre apostolique. Enrichie de notes curieuses, et ornée de son portrait. 2. éd. Paris, Onfroy, 1791.
xxvi, 239 p. front. (port.) 19cm.

Translation of Compendio della vita e delle gesta di Giuseppe Balsamo.
(Continued on next card)

Witchcraft
BF
1598
C13
B23
1791

[Barberi,]
Compendio della vita e delle gesta di Giuseppe Balsamo--French.
Vie de Joseph Balsamo ... 1791. (Card 2)

With this is bound Goupil, P. E. A. Essai historiques sur ... Marie Antoinette. Londres, 1789.

1. Cagliostro, Alessandro, conte di, assumed name of Giuseppe Balsamo, 1743-1795. I. Barberi. Compendio della vita e delle gesta di Giuseppe Balsamo--French. II. Title.

Witchcraft
BF
1598
C13
B23
1791d

[Barberi,]
Compendio della vita, e delle gesta di Giuseppe Balsamo--German.
Kurzgefasste Beschreibung des Lebens und der Thaten des Joseph Balsamo, oder sogenannten Grafen Kagliostro, gezogen aus dem wider ihn zu Rom 1790; angestellten Prozesse: zur Beleuchtung der wahren Beschaffenheit der Freymaurersekte. Aus dem Italiänischen ins Deutsche übersetzt. Augsburg, J. N. Styx, 1791.
86, 40, 112, 23 p. 17cm.
(Continued on next card)

Witchcraft
BF
1598
C13
B23
1791d

[Barberi,] Compendio della vita, e delle gesta di Giuseppe Balsamo--German.
Kurzgefasste Beschreibung des Lebens und der Thaten des Joseph Balsamo ... 1791. (Card 2)

Translation of Compendio della vita, e delle gesta di Giuseppe Balsamo.

1. Cagliostro, Alessandro, conte di, assumed name of Giuseppe Balsamo, 1743-1795. 2. Freemasons. I. His Compendio della vita, e delle gesta di Giuseppe Balsamo--German. II. Title. III. Autograph-- Dumont, Paul.

CATALOGUE OF THE CORNELL WITCHCRAFT COLLECTION

Witchcraft
[Barberi,
Compendio della vita e delle gesta di
[Barberi, Giuseppe Balsamo--German]
Leben und Thaten des Joseph Balsamo,
sogenannten Grafen Cagliostro. Nebst
einigen Nachrichten über die Beschaffenheit und den Zustand der Freymaurersekten.
Aus den Alten des 1790 in Rom wider ihn
geführten Prozesses gehoben, und aus dem
in der päbstlichen Kammerdruckerey erschien-
en italienischen Originale übersetzt.
Zürich, Orell, Gessner, Füssli, 1791.
xii, 171 p. 20cm.
Translation of Compendio della
vita e delle gesta di Giuseppe
Balsamo.

Witchcraft
BF
1598
C13
B23
1791d
[Barberi,]
Kurzgefasste Beschreibung des Lebens
und der Thaten des Joseph Balsamo, oder
sogenannten Grafen Kagliostro, gezogen aus
dem wider ihn zu Rom 1790; angestellten
Prozesse: zur Beleuchtung der wahren
Beschaffenheit der Freymaurersekte. Aus
dem Italiänischen ins Deutsche übersetzt.
Augsburg, J. N. Styx, 1791.
86, 40, 112, 23 p. 17cm.
(Continued on next card)

Witchcraft
BF
1598
C13
B23
1791d
[Barberi,] Kurzgefasste Beschreibung
des Lebens und der Thaten des Joseph
Balsamo ... 1791. (Card 2)

Translation of Compendio della vita, e
delle gesta di Giuseppe Balsamo.

1. Cagliostro, Alessandro, conte di,
assumed name of Giuseppe Balsamo, 1743-
1795. 2. Freemasons. I. His Compendio
della vita, e delle gesta di Giuseppe
Balsamo--German. II. Title.
III. Autograph-- Dumont, Paul.

Witchcraft
[Barberi,]
Leben und Thaten des Joseph Balsamo,
sogenannten Grafen Cagliostro. Nebst
einigen Nachrichten über die Beschaffenheit und den Zustand der Freymaurersekten.
Aus den Alten des 1790 in Rom wider ihn
geführten Prozesses gehoben, und aus dem
in der päbstlichen Kammerdruckerey erschien-
en italienischen Originale übersetzt.
Zürich, Orell, Gessner, Füssli, 1791.
xii, 171 p. 20cm.
Translation of Compendio della
vita e delle gesta di Giuseppe
Balsamo. (Over)

Witchcraft
[Barberi]
Vie de Joseph Balsamo, connu sous le nom
de comte Cagliostro. Extraite de la procédure
instruite contre lui à Rome en 1790. Traduite
d'après l'original italien, imprimé à la
Chambre apostolique. Enrichie de notes curieuses, et ornée de son portrait. 2. éd. Paris,
Onfroy, 1791.
xxvi,239 p. front. (port.) 19cm.

Translation of Compendio della vita e delle
gesta di Giuseppe Balsamo.
(Continued on next card)

Witchcraft
[Barberi] Vie de Joseph Balsamo
... 1791. (Card 2)

With this is bound Goupil, P. E. A. Essais
historiques sur ... Marie Antoinette. Londres,
1789.
1. Cagliostro, Alessandro, conte di, assumed
name of Giuseppe Balsamo, 1743-1795. I.
Barberi. Compendio della vita e delle gesta de
Giuseppe Balsamo--French. II. Title.

Witchcraft
BF
1598
C13
B23
1791a
[Barberi,]
Vie de Joseph Balsamo, connu seus le
nom de Comte Cagliostro; extraite de la
Procédure instruite contre lui à Rome, en
1790. Traduite d'après l'original italien,
imprimé à la Chambre Apostolique, enrichie
de notes curieuses, et ornée de son portrait.
2. éd. Paris, Onfroy, 1791.
xxvj, 239 p. port. 20cm.

Translation of Compendio della vita e
delle geste de Giuseppe Balsamo.
Ex libris Arthur Flower-Ellis.
I. Ex Libris-- Flower-Ellis, Arthur.

Witchcraft
BS
2545
D5
B25
Barker, Thomas, 1722-1809.
The nature and circumstances of the
demoniacks in the Gospels, stated and
methodized, and considered in the several
particulars. London, Printed for B.
White, 1783.
vi, 54 p. 22cm.

Witchcraft
BT
355
F23
1768
Barker, Thomas, 1722-1809.
The nature and circumstances of the demoniacks in the Gospels, stated and methodized,
and considered in the several particulars.
... London, Printed for B. White, 1783.
vi,56 p. 22cm.

Bound with c.1 of Farmer, Hugh. An inquiry into the nature and design of Christ's
temptation in the wilderness. London [1768?]

1. Demoniac possession. 2. Bible.
N.T.--Commenta ries. I. Title.

Barnouw, Adriaan Jacob, 1877-

PT
5443
M33
1924
Mariken van Nimmegen.
A marvelous history of Mary of Nimmegen,
who for more than seven year lived and had
ado with the devil. Translated from the
Middle Dutch by Harry Morgan Ayres. With an
introd. by Adriaan J. Barnouw. The Hague,
M. Nijhoff, 1924.
xxv,78 p. 17cm. (The Dutch library.
v. 3)

"The English and the Dutch
(Continued on next card)

Barnouw, Adriaan Jacob, 1877-

PT
5443
M33
1924
Mariken van Nimmegen. A marvelous history of Mary of Nimmegen ... 1924.
(Card 2)

versions are undated, but from the type and
the printing devices used both are assigned
to 1518-19. Hence a question has arisen as
to the priority of the two versions. Some
scholars regard the English version as an
adaptation of the Dutch play, and others
claim that both are based on a now lost
Dutch prose original." Introd. of
1932 facsimile ed.
I. Ayres, Harry Morgan, tr.

Baroni Cavalcabò, Clemente, 1726-1796.
Lettera ... ad un giornalista oltram-
montano sopra il Congresso notturno delle
Witchcraft lammie.
BF Tartarotti, Girolamo, 1706-1761.
1565 Apologia del Congresso notturno delle
T192+ lammie, o sia risposta di Girolamo Tarta-
rotti all' Arte magica dileguata del Sig.
March. Scipione Maffei, ed all' opposizione
del Sig. Assessore Bartolommeo Melchiori.
S'aggiunge una lettera del Sig. Clemente
Baroni di Cavalcabò. Venezia, Presso
Simone Occhi, 1751.
4 p. l., 268 p. 26cm.
1. His Del congresso nottur-
8 (Continued on next card)

Barskier, Anne Hans.

Witchcraft
BF
1555
A55
no.2
Brunsmand, Johan, 1637-1707.
Johannis Brunsmanni Energumeni Coagienses, sive Admirabilis historia, de horrenda
cacodaemonis tentatione, quacum in Selandia
Daniae, ejusque urbe Coagio familia civis,
& vita honestissimi & fama integerrimi, per
annorum aliquot spatium est conflictata:
primum sermone Danico aliquoties edita &
impressa: nunc vero in exterorum gratiam
Latine interpretata & cum duplici auctario
edita. Editio altera Latina, auctior
8 (Continued on next card)

Barskier, Anne Hans.

Witchcraft
BF
1555
A55
no.2
Brunsmand, Johan, 1637-1707. ... Energumeni
Coagienses ... 1695. (Card 2)

& correctior Leidensi. Lipsiae, Apud Joh.
Melchior Lieben, 1695.
4 p. l., 156 p. 14cm.
First published 1674 with title: Et
forfaerdeligt huus-kaars.
Attributed by British Museum to A. H.
Barskier, whose narrative makes up first
part of work (p. 1-73)
8 (Continued on next card)

Barskier, Anne Hans.

Witchcraft
BF
1555
A55
no.2
Brunsmand, Johan, 1637-1707. ...Energumeni
Coagienses ... 1695. (Card 3)

No. 2 in vol. lettered Andreae. De angelorum...

1. Witchcraft--Denmark. 2. Bartholin,
Thomas, 1616-1680. 3. Bekker, Balthasar,
1634-1698. I. Barskier, Anne Hans. II.
His Et forfaerdeligt huus-kaars--Latin.
III. Title: Energumeni Coagienses.

Bartelius, Peter, respondent.

Witchcraft
BF
1445
D61
no.12
Cameen, Sven, praeses.
Dissertatio philosophica De spectris,
quam ... sub moderamine celeberrimi viri
Dni. Svenonis Cameen ... pro laurea magisterii reportanda publicae bonorum ventilationi subjicit ... Petrus Bartelius ...
Dorpati, Excudit Johannes Brendeken [1693]
[24] p. 19cm. (bound in 21cm. vol.)
Diss.---Dorpat (P. Bartelius, respondent)
No. 12 in vol. lettered Dissertationes
de spectris. 1646-1753.
1. Demono logy. I. Bartelius,
Peter, respon dent. II. Title: De
8 spectris.

Witchcraft
BF
1582
B28
Barthety, Hilarion.
La sorcellerie en Béarn et dans le pays
Basque. Conférence publique à la mairie de
Pau, suivie des pratiques de sorcellerie et
superstitions populaires du Béarn. Pau,
L. Ribaut, 1879.
87 p. 25cm.

1. Witchcraft--Béarn, France. 2. Witch-
craft--Basque provinces. I. Title.

Bartholin, Thomas, 1616-1680.

Witchcraft
BF
1555
A55
no.2
Brunsmand, Johan, 1637-1707.
Johannis Brunsmanni Energumeni Coagienses, sive Admirabilis historia, de horrenda
cacodaemonis tentatione, quacum in Selandia
Daniae, ejusque urbe Coagio familia civis,
& vita honestissimi & fama integerrimi, per
annorum aliquot spatium est conflictata:
primum sermone Danico aliquoties edita &
impressa: nunc vero in exterorum gratiam
Latine interpretata & cum duplici auctario
edita. Editio altera Latina, auctior
8 (Continued on next card)

CATALOGUE OF THE CORNELL WITCHCRAFT COLLECTION

Bartholin, Thomas, 1616-1680.

Witchcraft
BF 1555 A55 no.2

Brunsmand, Johan, 1637-1707. ... **Energumeni Coagienses** ... 1695.   (Card 2)

& correctior Leidensi. Lipsiae, Apud Joh. Melchior Lieben, 1695.
4 p. l., 156 p. 14cm.
First published 1674 with title: Et forfaerdeligt huus-kaars.
Attributed by British Museum to A. H. Barskier, whose narrative makes up first part of work   (p. 1-73)
      (Continued on next card)

8

Bartholin, Thomas, 1616-1680.

Witchcraft
BF 1555 A55 no.2

Brunsmand, Johan, 1637-1707. ...Energumeni Coagienses ... 1695.   (Card 3)

No. 2 in vol. lettered Andreae. De angelorum...

1. Witchcraft--Denmark. 2. Bartholin, Thomas, 1616-1680. 3. Bekker, Balthasar, 1634-1698. I. Barskier, Anne Hans. II. His Et forfaerdeligt huus-kaars--Latin. III. Title: Energumeni Coagienses.

8

Bartholomei Faij ... Energumenicus.

Witchcraft
BF 1565 F28

Faye, Barthélemy, seigneur d'Espeisses, 16th cent.
Bartholomei Faij, regij in senatv Parisiensi consiliarij, ac Inquisitionum praesidis Energvmenicvs. Eiusdem Alexicacvs, cū liminari, vt vocant ad vtrūque librum epistola. Lvtetiae, Apud Sebastianum Niuellium, 1571.
2 p. l., 397 p. 17cm.
Alexicacvs, p. 167-397, has special t. p.
1. Witchcra   ft. 2. Lord's Supper--Bread and win   e. 3. Christian life.
I. Title: En   ergumenicus. II. Title: Alexicacus.

8

BF 1565 B29

Baschwitz, Kurt, 1886-
Hexen und Hexenprozesse; die Geschichte eines Massenwahns und seiner Bekämpfung. München, Rütten & Loening ₁1963₎
480 p. illus., plates. 21cm.

1. Witchcraft. 2. Trials (Witchcraft) 3. Magic. I. Title.

Baskin, Wade, ed. and tr.

Witchcraft
BF 1503 C69 1965

Collin de Plancy, Jacques Albin Simon, 1794-1881.
Dictionary of demonology. Edited and translated by Wade Baskin. New York, Philosophical Library ₁1965₎
177 p. 22 cm.
Selections from Dictionnaire infernal.

1. Demonology--Dictionaries.   I. Baskin, Wade, ed. and tr.
II. Title.   III. His   Dictionnaire infernal--English.
BF1503.C613   133.4   65-11952
Library of Congress   ₍8₎

Die Basler Hexenprozesse in dem 16ten und 17ten Jahrhundert.

Witchcraft
BF 1584 S97 H14+

Hagenbach, Karl Rudolf, 1801-1874.
Die Basler Hexenprozesse in dem 16ten und 17ten Jahrhundert. Einladungsschrift zu der Rede des zeit. Rector magn., K. R. Hagenbach, welche Donnerstags, den 24. September 1840, Morgens 10 Uhr in der Aula gehalten werden wird, von Fr. Fischer. Basel, Schweighauser'sche Universitätsbuchdruckerei ₁1840?₎
23 p. 26cm.

1. Trials (Wit   chcraft)--Basel. I. Title. II. Fis   cher, Friedrich, 1801-1853.

Bassaeus, Nicolaus, d. 1599.

Witchcraft
BF 1520 W64 P8++ 1586

Theatrvm ₍i. e., Theatrum₎ de veneficis. Das ist: Von Teuffelsgespenst, Zauberern vnd Gifftbereitern, Schwartzkünstlern, Hexen vnd Vnholden, vieler fürnemmen Historien vnd Exempel ... Sampt etlicher hingerichteten zäuberischer Weiber gethaner Bekanntnuß, Examination, Prob, Vrgicht ₍sic₎ vnd Straff ... Allen Vögten, Schuldtheissen, Amptleuthen deß weltlichen Schwerdts, &c. sehr nützlich vnd dienstlich zu wiss   en, vnd keines wegs zu
      (Continued on next card)

8

Bassaeus, Nicolaus, d. 1599.

Witchcraft
BF 1520 W64 P8++ 1586

Theatrvm ₍i. e., Theatrum₎ de veneficis. 1586.   (Card 2)

verachten. Franckfurt am Mayn, Gedruckt durch Nicolaum Basseum, 1586.
6 p. l., 396, ₍9₎ p. 34cm.
Title in red and black.
Preface signed: Nicolaus Bassaeus.
Bound with Wier, Johann, 1515-1588. De praestigiis daemonum. Von Teuffelsgespenst, Zauberern, vnd   Gifftbereytern.
      (Continued on next card)

8

Bassaeus, Nicolaus, d. 1599.

Witchcraft
BF 1520 W64 P8++ 1586

Theatrvm ₍i. e., Theatrum₎ de veneficis. 1586.   (Card 3)

Franckfurt am Mayn, 1586.
Contents.--Warhafftige Zeittung von gottlosen Hexen, by R. Lutz.--Ein Gespräch von Zäuberern, welche man lateinisch Sortilegos oder Sortiarios nennet, by L. Daneus.--Von Zäuberern, Hexen, vnd Vnholden, by J. Vallick.--Von Hexen vnd Vnholden, by V. Molitoris, tr.   by C. Lautenbach.--
      (Continued on next card)

8

Bassaeus, Nicolaus, d. 1599.

Witchcraft
BF 1520 W64 P8++ 1586

Theatrvm ₍i. e., Theatrum₎ de veneficis. 1586.   (Card 4)

Contents--Continued.

Ein christlich vnd nothwendig Gespräch, von den bösen abtrünnigen Engeln, by A. Rheynmannus.--Von Gespensten, Vngehewren, Fällen, oder Poltern, vnd anderen wunderbaren Dingen, by L. Lavater.--Bedencken, was er von Exorcisterey halte, by L. Thurneysser.--Eine   kurtze, trewe Warnung,
      (Continued on next card)

8

Bassaeus, Nicolaus, d. 1599.

Witchcraft
BF 1520 W64 P8++ 1586

Theatrvm ₍i. e., Theatrum₎ de veneficis. 1586.   (Card 5)

Contents--Continued.

... ob auch zu dieser vnser Zeit vnder vns Christen, Hexen, Zäuberer vnd Vnholden vorhanden, by A. Sawr.--Von deß Teuffels Nebelkappen, das ist: ein kurtzer Begriff, den gantzen Handel von der Zäuberey belangend, by P. Frisius.--Bericht von Erforschung, Prob vnd Erkän   ntniß der Zäuberinnen
      (Continued on next card)

8

Bassaeus, Nicolaus, d. 1599.

Witchcraft
BF 1520 W64 P8++ 1586

Theatrvm ₍i. e., Theatrum₎ de veneficis. 1586.   (Card 6)

Contents--Continued.

durchs kalte Wasser, by H. Neuwalt, tr. by H. Meybaum.--Ein christlich Bedencken vnnd Erjnnerung von Zauberey, by A. Lercheimer.--Wider die schwartzen Künst, by H. Bullinger.--Ware Entdeckung vnnd Erklärung aller fürnembster Artickel der Zauberey, by J. Freyherr von   Liechtenberg.--Von
      (Continued on next card)

8

Bassaeus, Nicolaus, d. 1599.

Witchcraft
BF 1520 W64 P8++ 1586

Theatrvm ₍i. e., Theatrum₎ de veneficis. 1586.   (Card 7)

Contents--Continued.

der Hexen, die man gemeiniglich Zauberin nennet, by J. Ewich.--Antwort auff etliche Fragen ... von ...Keyser Maximiliano, by J. Trithemius.--Consilia vnd Bedencken etlicher zu vnsern Zeiten rechtsgelehrten Juristen, von Hexen vnd Vnholden.
      (Continued on next card)

8

Bassaeus, Nicolaus, d. 1599.

Witchcraft
BF 1520 W64 P8++ 1586

Theatrvm ₍i. e., Theatrum₎ de veneficis. 1586.   (Card 8)

Binding: blind stamped pigskin, with clasps (one wanting); front cover initialed A K A S H and dated 1589.
1. Demonology. 2. Witchcraft. 3. Magic. I. Bassaeus, Nicolaus, d. 1599. II. Title: Von Teuffelsgespenst, Zauberern und Gifftbereytern.

8

Basson, Govert, tr.

Witchcraft
BF 1565 S42 1638

Scot, Reginald, 1538?-1599.
Ontdecking van tovery, beschreven int Engels door Reinald Scot, verduyscht by Th. en G. Basson. Beverwyck, Gedruckt by Frans Pels, 1638.
15 p. l., 351, ₍17₎ p. 15cm.
With engraved t. p., depicting a witch.
Abridgment and translation of Discoverie of witchcraft.
To this are appended: Historie van 't ghene gheschiet   is in 't Graefschap van
      (Continued on next card)

8

Basson, Govert, tr.

Witchcraft
BF 1565 S42 1638

Scot, Reginald, 1538?-1599. Ontdecking van tovery ... 1638.   (Card 2)

Artoys ..., door J. DuClercq, with special t. p.; Extract uyt 't playdoye van M. L. Servin; Historie van de Maegt van Orleans ... Extract uyt J. P. van Bergamo; and various poems.
1. Witchcraft. 2. Magic. 3. Demonology. I. His Discoverie of witchcraft. Dutch. II. DuClercq, Jacques, seigneur
      (Continued on next card)

8

Basson, Thomas, 1555-1613, tr.

Witchcraft
BF 1565 S42 1638

Scot, Reginald, 1538?-1599.
Ontdecking van tovery, beschreven int Engels door Reinald Scot, verduyscht by Th. en G. Basson. Beverwyck, Gedruckt by Frans Pels, 1638.
15 p. l., 351, ₍17₎ p. 15cm.
With engraved t. p., depicting a witch.
Abridgment and translation of Discoverie of witchcraft.
To this are appended: Historie van 't ghene gheschiet   is in 't Graefschap van
      (Continued on next card)

8

Basson, Thomas, 1555-1613, tr.

Witchcraft
BF 1565 S42 1638

Scot, Reginald, 1538?-1599. Ontdecking van tovery ... 1638.   (Card 2)

Artoys ..., door J. DuClercq, with special t. p.; Extract uyt 't playdoye van M. L. Servin; Historie van de Maegt van Orleans ... Extract uyt J. P. van Bergamo; and various poems.
1. Witchcraft. 2. Magic. 3. Demonology. I. His Discoverie of witchcraft. Dutch. II. DuClercq, Jacques, seigneur
      (Continued on next card)

8

CATALOGUE OF THE CORNELL WITCHCRAFT COLLECTION

Bateman, Mary (Harker) 1768-1809.

Witchcraft
BF
1581
Z7
1809
 Extraordinary life and character of Mary Bateman, the Yorkshire witch; traced from the earliest thefts of her infancy through a most awful course of crimes and murders, till her execution at the New Drop, near the castle of York, on Monday, the twentieth of March, 1809. 6th ed. Leeds, Printed by E. Baines, for J. Davies [1810?]
56 p. front. (port.) 23cm.
 1. Bateman, Mary (Harker) 1768-1809. 2. Witchcraft-- England.

Witchcraft
BF
1410
B33
 Battista, Giovanni.
 Del vero stvdio christiano contra l'arte planetaria, notoria, cabalistica, lunaria, clauicula di Salomone, Paulina, reuelata da spiriti mali, & altri superstitiosi modi vsati per imparare supernaturalmente, & voler sapere più de gli altri superbamente. Opera novamente composta dal R. P. Don Gio. Battista Segni da Bologna ... Ferrara, Appresso Benedetto Mammarello, 1592.
8 p. l., 153 , [15] p. 2 illus. 15cm.
 (Continued on next card)

Witchcraft
BF
1410
B33
 Battista, Giovanni. Del vero stvdio christiano ... 1592. (Card 2)

 1. Occult sciences. 2. Magic. 3. Christian life. I. Title: Del vero studio christiano.

8

WITCHCRAFT
BX
2340
V82
1643
 Baucio, Carlo de.
 Modus interrogandi daemonem ab exorcista.
 Visconti, Zaccaria.
 Complementvm artis exorcisticae: cui simile nunquam visum est: cvm litaniis, benedictionibvs, & doctrinis nouis, exorcismis efficacissimis, ac remediis copiosis in maleficiatis expertis. Nuper correctum, & in tres partes diuisum. Qvarvm prima dicitvr doctrinalis. Secunda benedictionalis. Tertia exorcismalis. Cui addita est Oratio supra febricitantes. Avthore Fr. Zacharia Vicecomite ... Cui nupperrimè in hac
8 (Continued on next card)

WITCHCRAFT
BX
2340
V82
1643
 Baucio, Carlo de.
 Modus interrogandi daemonem ab exorcista.
 Visconti, Zaccaria. Complementvm artis exorcisticae ... 1643. (Card 2)
postrema editione veneta. Pro vberiori complemento, additus est tractatus de Modo interrogandi daemonem ab exorcista ... Avthore Carolo de Bavcio ... Venetiis, Apud Turrinum, 1643.
8 p. l., 359, 85 p. 17cm.
 "Modvs interrogandi daemonem ab exorcista," by Carlo de Baucio, has special t. p.
8 (Continued on next card)

WITCHCRAFT
BF
1565
W37
S347
 Bauer, Friedrich.
 Gedanken eines Landpfarrers über den Ungrund des Hexenglaubens.
 [Schmid, Franz Josef]
 Und der Satz: Teuflische Magie existirt, besteht noch. In einer Antwort des katholischen Weltmannes auf die von einem Herrn Landpfarrer herausgegebene Apologie der Professor Weberschen Hexenreformation. Augsburg, Bey J. N. Styx, 1791.
xxiv, 350 p. 19cm.
 1. Bauer, Friedrich. Gedanken eines Landpfarrers über den Ungrund des Hexenglaubens. 2. Weber, Joseph, 1753-1831.
8 (Continued on next card)

Witchcraft
BF
1583
B34
 Baumgarten, Paul Maria, 1860-
 Die deutschen Hexenprozesse. Frankfurt a.M., A. F. Nachfolger, 1883.
[115]-154 p. 23cm.

 Detached from Frankfurter zeitgemäsze Broschüren. Neue Folge, Bd. IV, Heft 5.

 1. Trials (Witchcraft)--Germany. I. Title.

MSS
Bd.
WITCHCRAFT
JS
B35+
 Bavaria.
 Instruction. Wie sich in denen Landten zu Bayen [sic] die Pfleger, Landtrichter, Pflegs Comisary, unnd Anwalten, auch Gerichtsschreiber, und andere Bediente in Malefizsachen in ain: und andern zu verhalten. Was sy wegen der Inquisition, Incarceration, in: und bey dem Examen Einhaltung der Erfahrungen: Vornemhung der Inspection, Confrontation: Tortur: Erstattung der Berichten, bei dem Leben Abthundten, gegen denen begleitten: in Verfassung der Ur gichten: unnd bey
 (Continued on next card)

MSS
Bd.
WITCHCRAFT
JS
B35+
 Bavaria. Instruction. Wie sich in denen Landten zu Bayen [sic] ... in Malefizsachen ... zu verhalten ... [17th cent.] (Card 2)
 Exequierung diser, und einer Urtls zu thunn: unnd zu observieren haben. [17th cent.]
83, [4] l. 30 x 21cm.
 Manuscript, on paper in a seventeenth century German hand. Index on last 4 leaves. Bound in boards with vellum spine. On spine: Instruction für Beamte.
 1. Criminal procedure--Bavaria. 2. Criminal justice, Administration of-- Bavaria.

Witchcraft
BF
1583
A2
B35+
 Bavaria. Laws, statutes, etc.
 Der Churfürstl. Durchleucht Herzogs Maximilian Joseph in Bayern &c. &c. ... erneuerte Land-Gebott, wider die Aberglauben, Zauberey, Hexerey, und andere straffliche Teuffels-Künsten. München, Gedruckt bey Johann Jacob Vötter, 1746.
[18] p. 29cm.
 1. Witchcraft--Germany. 2. Superstition. I. Bavaria. Sovereigns, etc., 1745-1777 (Maximilian III Joseph) II. Title: Erneuerte Land-Gebott wider die Aberglauben, Zauberey. III. Title.
8

Bavent, Madeleine, ca. 1608-1647.

Witchcraft
BF
1582
Z7
1647
 Desmarets, oratorien.
 Histoire de Madeleine Bavent, religieuse du monastère de Saint-Louis de Louviers. Réimpression textuelle sur l'édition rarissime de 1652. Précédée d'une notice bio-bibliographique, et suivie de plusieurs pièces supplémentaires. Orné d'un front. et d'une vue de l'ancien couvent de Saint-Louis ... Rouen, J. Lemonnyer, 1878.
xl, vii, 169 p. illus. 21cm.
 No. 141 of 177 copies printed.
 (Continued on next card)

Witchcraft
BF
1582
Z7
1647
 Desmarets, oratorien. Histoire de Madeleine Bavent ... 1878. (Card 2)
 Original t.p. reads: Historie de Magdelaine Bavent, religieuse du monastère de Saint Louis de Louviers, avec sa confession générale & testamentaire, où elle déclare les abominations, impietez, & sacrilèges qu'elle a pratiqué & veu pratiquer, tant ledit monastere, qu'au sabat, & les personnes qu'il y a rema rquées. Ensemble l'arrest
 (Continued on next card)

Witchcraft
BF
1582
Z7
1647
 Desmarets, oratorien. Histoire de Madeleine Bavent ... 1878. (Card 3)
donné contre Mathurin Picard, Thomas Boullé & ladite Bavent, tous convaincus du crime de magie. Dedie'e à Mme. la Dvchesse d'Orleans. Paris, J. Le Gentil, 1652.

 1. Bavent, Madeleine, ca.1608-1647. I. Title. II. Title: Historie de Magdelaine Bavent.

Bavent, Madeleine, ca. 1608-1647.

WITCHCRAFT
BF
1555
E77
2 copies
 Esprit du Bosroger, Capuchin.
 La pieté affligee; ov, Discovrs historiqve & theologique de la possession des religieuses dittes de Saincte Elizabeth de Lovviers. Divisé en trois parties. Roven, Chez Iean le Bovlenger, 1652.
[30], 458, 8 p. front. 23cm.
 Copy 1 imperfect: front. wanting. Inserted at end of copy 1: 6 p. of ms.
 1. Demoniac possession. 2. Bavent, Madeleine, 1608-1647. 3. Louviers, France. St. Louis (Convent) 4. Witchcraft. I. Title.

Bavent, Madeleine, ca. 1608-1647.

MSS
Bd.
WITCHCRAFT
BF
L37
 Laugeois, Antoine, d. 1674.
 L'innocence opprimee; ou, Défense de Mathurin Picard, curé de Mesnil-Jourdain ... Par M. Laugois, successeur immédiat dudit Picard - dans la cure de Mesnil-Jourdain. Ouvrage qui n'a jamais été imprimé et extrait sur l'original, par M. Chemin curé de Tourneville. [n. p. 17th cent.]
x, 102 p. title vignette. 18cm.
Manuscript, on paper.
Preface signed M. du Passeur (Gabriel), curé de Vironvay.
 (Continued on next card)

Bavent, Madeleine, ca. 1608-1647.

MSS
Bd.
WITCHCRAFT
BF
L37
 Laugeois, Antoine, d. 1674. L'innocence opprimee... [17th cent.] (Card 2)
Notes by G. L. Burr inside front cover discuss history and provenance of the manuscript.
Bound in boards.
 1. Demoniac possession. 2. Picard, Mathurin, d. 1647. 3. Bavent, Madeleine, ca. 1608-1647. 4. Louviers, France. St. Louis (Convent) 5. Witchcraft. I. Chemin, J B , 1725 -1781, ed. II. Title. III. Title: Défense de Mathurin Picard.

Bavent, Madeleine, ca. 1608-1647.

WITCHCRAFT
BF
1555
P61
 Piérart, Z J
 Le magnétisme, le somnambulisme et le spiritualisme dans l'histoire. Affaire curieuse des possédées de Louviers... Paris, Au Bureau du Journal du magnétisme, 1858.
39 p. 23cm.
 Extract from Journal du magnétisme.
 1. Demoniac possession. 2. Louviers, France. St. Louis (Convent) 3. Bavent, Madeleine, ca. 1608-1647. 4 Picard, Mathurin, d.1647. 5. Boullé, Thomas.
8
NIC

Bavent, Madeleine, ca. 1608-1647.

WITCHCRAFT
BF
1555
R31
 Recueil de pièces sur les possessions des religieuses de Louviers. Rouen [Imprimerie L. Deshays] 1879.
2 v. in l. 25cm.
 Title page and prefatory material bound following v. 1.
 Contents.--[1] Histoire de Magdelaine Bavent, religieuse du monastere de Saint Loüis de Louviers (1652)--[2] I. Examen de la possession des religieuses de Louviers, par le Docteur Yvelin (1643)
 (Continued on next card)
8
NIC

CATALOGUE OF THE CORNELL WITCHCRAFT COLLECTION

WITCHCRAFT
BF
1555
R31

Bavent, Madeleine, ca. 1608-1647.
  Recueil de pièces sur les possessions des religieuses de Louviers...1879. (Card 2)

  Contents--continued.
  II. Response à l'Examen de la possession des religieuses de Louviers (1643) III. Censure de l'Examen de la possession des religieuses de Louviers (1643) IV. Apologie pour l'autheur de l'Examen de la possession des religieuses de Louviers, attribuée au Docteur Yvelin (1643)   V. Responce à l'Apologie de l'Exa   men du sieur Yvelin
          (Continued on next card)

WITCHCRAFT
BF
1555
R31

Bavent, Madeleine, ca. 1608-1647.
  Recueil de pièces sur les possessions des religieuses de Louviers...1879. (Card 3)

  Contents--continued.
  (1644) VI. Recit veritable de ce qui s'est fait & passé à Louviers, touchant les religieuses possedées (1643) VII. Recit veritable de ce qui s'est fait & passé aux exorcismes de plusieurs religieuses de la ville de Louviers (1643) VIII. La deffense de la verité   touchant la possession des religieu   ses de Louvier, par
          (Continued on next card)

WITCHCRAFT
BF
1555
R31

Bavent, Madeleine, ca. 1608-1647.
  Recueil de pièces sur les possessions des religieuses de Louviers...1879. (Card 4)

  Contents--continued.
  Jean Le Breton (1643) IX. Attestation de messieurs les commissaires envoyez par sa Majesté pour prendre connoissance, avec monseigneur l'evesque d'Evreux, de l'estat des religieuses qui paroissent agitées au monastere de Saint Louys & Sainte Elizabeth de Louviers   (1643?) X. Procés verbal de   Monsieur le Peniten-
          (Continued on next card)

WITCHCRAFT
BF
1555
R31

Bavent, Madeleine, ca. 1608-1647.
  Recueil de pièces sur les possessions des religieuses de Louviers...1879. (Card 5)

  Contents--continued.
  tier d'Evreux, de ce qui luy est arrivé dans la prison, interrogeant & consolant Magdelaine Bavent, magicienne, à une heureuse conversion & repentance, par Delangle (1643) XI. Lettre adressée à Monsieur D. L. V., medicin du Roy, & doyen de la Faculté de Paris, sur   l'Apologie du sieur Yvelin, medi   cin, attribuée au doc-
          (Continued on next card)

WITCHCRAFT
BF
1555
R31

Bavent, Madeleine, ca. 1608-1647.
  Recueil de pièces sur les possessions des religieuses de Louviers...1879. (Card 6)

  Contents--continued.
  teur Maignart (1644) XII. Traicté des marques des possedez & la preuve de la veritable possession des religieuses de Louviers, par P. M., esc. d. en m. (attribué à Simon Pietre; 1644) XIII. Copie en forme de recueil de ce qui se fait de jour en jour dans le monastere   des filles relligieuzes Saint Louis   (1643) XIV. Pièces dé-
          (Continued on next card)

WITCHCRAFT
BF
1555
R31

Bavent, Madeleine, ca. 1608-1647.
  Recueil de pièces sur les possessions des religieuses de Louviers...1879. (Card 7)

  Contents--continued.
  tachées extraites du manuscrit H. F. n° 34 de la Bibliothèque Ste Geneviève, formant suite à la pièce précédente. XV. Notice sur la Mere Françoise, superieure des religieuses de la Place royale, au sujet de l'histoire des possedées de Louviers.

) (Continued on next card)

WITCHCRAFT
BF
1569
T37

8
NIC

Bavent, Madeleine, ca. 1608-1647.
  Théaux, Marcel.
    Pages d'histoire judiciaire. Le crime de sorcellerie.
      (In La revue du palais. Paris. 25cm. 1. année, no. 7 (1897), p. [103]-135)

    In envelope.

    1. Witchcraft--History. 2. Devil. 3. Bavent, Madeleine, ca. 1608-1647. I. Title. II.   Title: Le crime de sorcellerie.

BF
1582
B35H2

Bavoux, Francis, 1896-
  Hantises et diableries dans la terre abbatiale de Luxeuil; d'un procès de l'Inquisition (1529) à l'épidémie démoniaque de 1628-1630. Préface de Lucien Febvre. Monaco, Editions du Rocher [1956]
  vii,200 p. illus., maps. 24cm.
  (Folklore)

  1. Witchcraft--France--Luxeuil. I. Title.

WITCHCRAFT
BF
1075
B81

8
NIC

Baxter, Andrew, 1686?-1750.
  An enquiry into the nature of human soul.
  Branch, Thomas, fl. 1753.
    Thoughts on dreaming. Wherein the notion of the sensory, and the opinion that it is shut up from the inspection of the soul in sleep, and that spirits supply us with all our dreams, are examined by revelation and reason. Occasioned by an essay on the phenomenon of dreaming, in a book, entitled, An enquiry into the nature of the human soul; wherein the im   materiality of the
          (Continued on next card)

WITCHCRAFT
BF
1075
B81

8
NIC

Baxter, Andrew, 1686?-1750.
  An enquiry into the nature of human soul.
  Branch, Thomas, fl. 1753. Thoughts on dreaming... (Card 2)

  soul is evinced from the principles of reason and philosophy. By Tho. Branch. London, Printed for R. Dodsley [etc.] 1738.
  96 p. 21cm.
  1. Dreams. 2. Soul. 3. Baxter, Andrew, 1686?-1750. An enquiry into the nature of human soul. I. Title.

BF
1445
B35

Baxter, Richard, 1615-1691.
  The certainty of the world of the spirits. Fully evinced by the unquestionable histories of apparitions, operations, witchcrafts, voices, &c. Proving the immortality of souls, the malice and misery of the devils, and the damned, and the blessedness of the justified. Written for the conviction of Sadduces & infidels. London, Printed for T. Parkhurst, and J. Salusbury, 1691.
  [16], 252 p. 17cm.

Witchcraft
BF
1445
B35
1840

Baxter, Richard, 1615-1691.
  The certainty of the world of spirits fully evinced. To which is added, The wonders of the invisible world, by Cotton Mather. The former taken from the edition published by Mr. Baxter, 1691, the latter from the Ecclesiastical history of New England, published 1702. With a preface by the editor. London, H. Howell, 1840.
  245 p. 11cm.

  The second part is not The wonders of the
          (Continued on next card)

Witchcraft
BF
1445
B35
1840

Baxter, Richard, 1615-1691. The certainty of the world of spirits fully evinced ... 1840.   (Card 2)

  invisible world but only passages from Mather's Magnalia; or, Ecclesiastical history of New England.

  I. Mather, Cotton, 1663-1728. Magnalia Christi americana. II. Title.

Witchcraft
K
B111

Eine bayerische Verordnung gegen Zauberer, Hexen und Wahrsager v. J. 1611.
  Baader, Joseph.
    Eine bayerische Verordnung gegen Zauberer, Hexen und Wahrsager v. J. 1611. [n. p., 1873]
    [92]-102 p. 23cm.

    Extract from Deutsche Kulturgeschichte. Neue Folge. 1873.

    1. Witchcraft--Laws and legislation--Bavaria. I. Title.

Witchcraft
BF
1555
B35

Bayle, François.
  Relation de l'état de quelques personnes pretenduës possedées. Faite d'autorite' du Parlement de Toulouse, par Me. François Bayle & Me. Henri Grangeron ... Toulouse, Chez la veuve Pouchac & Bely, 1682.
  118 p. 14cm.

  1. Demoniac possession. I. Grangeron, Henri. II.   Title.

Rare
PQ
1714
B3++
1727

Bayle, Pierre, 1647-1706.
  Oeuvres diverses, contenant tout ce que cet auteur a publié sur des matières de Théologie, de philosophie, de critique, d'histoire & de littérature; excepté son Dictionnaire historique et critique. La Haye, P. Husson, 1727-31.
  4 v. illus. 41 cm.

  Edited by Pierre Desmaizeaux.

  For contents see Rare main card.

  I. Desmaizeaux, Pierre, 1673?-1745, ed.

WITCHCRAFT
BF
1565
M498

8
NIC

Bayle, Pierre, 1647-1706.
  Réponse aux questions d'un provincial.
  Meinders, Hermann Adolph.
    Unvorgreifliche Gedancken und Monita, wie ohne blinden Eyfer und Übereilung mit denen Hexen-Processen und der Inquisition wegen der Zauberey, an Seiten des Richters so wol als des Königlichen Fiscalis und Defensoris in denen Königl. Preussischen und Cuhrfürstlichen [sic] Brandenburgischen Landen ohnmassgeblich zu verfahren. Auf Königlichen Special-Befehl laut Edicti vom 13 Decembris   1714 zusammen getragen
          (Continued on next card)

WITCHCRAFT
BF
1565
M498

Bayle, Pierre, 1647-1706.
  Réponse aux questions d'un provincial.
  Meinders, Hermann Adolph. Unvorgreifliche Gedancken und Monita...1716. (Card 2)

  und aufgesetzet von...Hermann Adolph Meinders. Lemgo, Druckts und verlegts Henrich Wilhelm Meyer, 1716
  152 p. 22cm.

  Collection of extracts from various sources concerning witchcraft, magic and trials for witchcraft.
  The most   extensive extract is
          (Continued on next card)

38

CATALOGUE OF THE CORNELL WITCHCRAFT COLLECTION

WITCHCRAFT
BF
1565
M498
Bayle, Pierre, 1647-1706.
Réponse aux questions d'un provincial.
Meinders, Hermann Adolph. Unvorgreifliche
Gedancken und Monita...1716. (Card 3)

that from Pierre Bayle's Réponse aux questions d'un provincial. (in the original
French, p. 12-93)

1. Witchcraft. 2. Trials(Witchcraft)
3. Magic. I. Bayle, Pierre, 1647-1706.
Réponse aux questions d'un provincial.
II. Title: Unvorgreifliche Gedancken und
Monita, wie ...mit denen Hexen-Pro-
cessen...zu verfahren.

Witchcraft
BF
1565
S83
M69
Beantwortete Frage: Ob man die Ausfahrt
der Hexen zulassen könne?
Model, Johann Michael
Johann Michael Models, J. U. Lic. beantwortete Frage: Ob man die Ausfahrt der Hexen
zulassen könne? Wider den heutigen Hexenstürmer P. Ferdinand Sterzinger. München,
Bey J. A. Crätz, 1769.
36 p. 18cm.
1. Sterzinger, Ferdinand, 1721-1786.
2. Witchcraft. I. Title: Beantwortete
Frage: Ob man die Ausfahrt der Hexen zulassen könne? II. Title: Frage, Ob
man die Ausfahrt der Hexen zulassen
könne?

8

WITCHCRAFT
DD
801
06
L83

8
NIC
Bearbeitung von Birkenfelder Kirchen-
büchern.
Lohmeyer, Heinrich Karl, 1832-1909.
Bearbeitung von Birkenfelder Kirchen-
büchern. Teil I. Die geschichtlichen, kul-
tur- und volkskundlichen Beziehungen.
Birkenfeld, F. Fillmann, 1909.
123 p. 22cm.

"Spuren des Hexenglaubens": p.27-41.

1. Birkenfeld (Landkreis) 2. Witchcraft
--Birkenfeld (Landkreis) 3. Trials
(Witchcraft) --Birkenfeld (Landkreis)

Witchcraft
BF
1576
B36
Beard, George Miller, 1839-1883.
The psychology of the Salem witchcraft excitement of
1692, and its practical application to our own time; by
George M. Beard ... New York, G. P. Putnam's sons,
1882.
xx, 112 p. incl. front. 17½ᶜᵐ.
Largely a comparison of the witchcraft trials with those of Cadet Whit-
taker and Charles Guiteau.

1. Witchcraft — Salem, Mass. 2. Guiteau, Charles Julius, 1841-1882.
3. Insanity—Jurisprudence. I. Title.
11-8994
Library of Congress   BF1576.B3

Witchcraft
BT
980
B36
Beard, John Relly, 1800-1876.
The autobiography of Satan. Edited
[i.e. written] by John R. Beard. London,
Williams and Norgate, 1872.
xii, 418 p. front. 19cm.

1. Devil. I. Title.

Witchcraft
BF
1445
B37
Beaumont, John, d. 1731.
An historical, physiological and theological treatise of spirits,
apparitions, witchcrafts, and other magical practices ... With
a refutation of Dr. Bekker's World bewitch'd; and other authors that have opposed the belief of them. By John Beaumont
... London, Printed for D. Browne [etc.], 1705.
8 p. l., 400 p. front. 20cm.

1. Occult sciences. 2. Ghosts. 3. Apparitions. 4. Bekker, Balthasar,
1634-1698. De betoverde weereld. I. Title.
41-30604
Library of Congress   BF1445.B4
[2]

Witchcraft
BF
1582
B38
Beaune, Henri, 1833-1907.
Les sorciers de Lyon: episode judiciaire
du XVIIIe siècle. [n.p., 18--]
[65]-154 p. 22cm.

Caption title.

1. Trials (Witchcraft)--Lyon, France.
I. Title.

MSS
Bd.
WITCHCRAFT
GR
B38
Beauvois de Chauvincourt, sieur de.
Discovrs de la lycantropie ou de la trans-
mutation des hommes en loups: par le Sieur
de Beauvoys de Chauvincourt; gentil-homme
Angevin. Paris, chez Jacques Rezé, 1599
[ca. 1900]
[8], 31, [1] p. title vignette, illus.
initial. 19cm.
Signatures: A-E⁴.
Carnap's manuscript copy.
"Original i. d. Grossherz. H. Bib-
liothek zu Darmstadt."
(Continued on next card)

MSS
Bd.
WITCHCRAFT
GR
B38
Beauvois de Chauvincourt, sieur de. Dis-
covrs de la lycantropie ... 1599 [ca.
1900]   (Card 2)

"Die Seiten-zahlen dieser Abschrift
stimmen mit denjenigen der Originaldruckschrift überein."

1. Werwolves. 2. Metamorphosis (in
religion, folk- lore, etc.) I. Title.

Beauvoys de Chauvincourt, sieur de.

see

Beauvois de Chauvincourt, sieur de.

Bebel, Heinrich, 1472-ca. 1516, ed.
Witchcraft
BF
1520
P71
Plantsch, Martinus, ca. 1460-1533.
Opusculum de sagis maleficis ... [Phor-
ce, In Aedibus Thome Anshelmi impensisque Si-
gismundi Stir, 1507]
[49] l. 20cm.
Signatures: a-e⁸, f⁴, g⁵.
Edited by Heinrich Bebel.

1. Demonology. 2. Divination. 3. Magic.
I. Bebel, Heinrich, 1472-ca. 1516, ed. II.
Title: De sagis maleficis. III. Title.

WITCHCRAFT
K
B378
1717
Bechmann, Johann Volkmar, 1624-1689, praeses.
Discursus juridicus de crimine maleficii,
vulgo Von Zauberey, sub praesidio Joh. Volk.
Bechmanns, submittit Joach. Ernst. Kober.
Nunc recusa. Jenae, 1717.
30 p. 20cm.
Originally published as dissertation, Jena,
1678 (Joachim Ernst Kober, respondent)

8
NIC
1. Witchcraft. I. Kober, Joachim Ernst,
respondent. II. Title. III. Title:
Von Zauberey.

Witchcraft
BF
1583
B39+
Beck, Peter Paul.
Hexenprozesse aus dem Fränkischen.
[Stuttgart, 1883-1885]
various pagings. 28cm.

Five parts, extracted from Württembergische Vierteljahrshefte für Landesgeschichte, Jahrg. vi, vii (1883-1885).
At head of title: Historischer Verein
für das Württembergische Franken.
1. Trials (Witchcraft)--Franconia. I.
Title. II. Württembergische Vierteljahrshefte für Landesgeschichte.

8

Becker, Andreas, 1634-1698, respondent.
Witchcraft
BF
1445
S92
1738
Stryk, Joannes Samuel, 1668-1715, praeses.
Dispvtatio ivridica inavgvralis, De
ivre spectrorvm qvam ... praeside Dn. Io.
Samvele Strykio ... svbmittit Andreas
Becker. Halae Magdebvrgicae, Literis
Ioh. Christ. Grvnerti, 1738.
43, [1] p. 21cm.
Diss.--Halle (A. Becker, respondent)
German terms in black letter.
1. Ghosts. 2. Devil. 3. Witchcraft
--Germany. I. Becker, Andreas, 1634-
1698, respondent. II. Title:
De iure spectrorum.

8

Becker, Balthasar, 1634-1698.

see

Bekker, Balthasar, 1634-1698.

Witchcraft
BF
1410
B42
Z55
Beckher, Wilhelm Heinrich.
Schediasma critico-litterarivm de controversiis praecipvis Balthasari Bekkero, theologo batavo qvondam motis, ob librvm cvi
titvlvm fecit: Die bezauberte Welt. Adiecta in fine avctorvm farragine, qvi vel Bekkeri scriptvm refvtarvnt, vel asseclarvm
more illvd defendervnt. Regiomonti ac Lipsiae, Impensis J. P. Hasii, 1721.
47 p. [p. 48 blank] title (port.), caption and end page vignettes. 19 x 16cm.

8
(Continued on next card)

Witchcraft
BF
1410
B42
Z55
Beckher, Wilhelm Heinrich. Schediasma
critico-litterarivm de controversiis prae-
cipvis Balthasari Bekkero ... 1721.
(Card 2)

4°: A-F⁴.
At head of title: M. Gvlielmi Henrici
Beckher, Regiom. Prvssi.
Van der Linde 215.

1. Bekker, Balthasar, 1634-1698. De betoverde weereld. I. Title.

8

Bedford, Arthur, 1668-1745.
Witchcraft
BF
1581
Z7
1762
Durbin, Henry.
A narrative of some extraordinary things that hap-
pened to Mr. Richard Giles's children at the Lamb, with-
out Lawford's-Gate, Bristol, supposed to be the effect of
witchcraft. By the late Mr. Henry Durbin ... To which
is added, a letter from the Rev. Mr. Bedford ... to the
Bishop of Glocester, relative to one Thomas Perks, of
Mangotsfield, who had dealings with familiar spirits.
Bristol, Printed and sold by R. Edwards, 1800.
60 p. 21ᶜᵐ.

1. Witchcraft. 2. Demonology. I. Bedford, Arthur, 1668-1745.

A 11-136
Title from Harvard Univ.   Printed by L. C.

CATALOGUE OF THE CORNELL WITCHCRAFT COLLECTION

Bedford, Jaquetta of Luxembourg, duchess of.

Witchcraft
BF 1581 A2 W81 1866a no.5

Wright, Thomas, 1810-1877, ed. Curious account of the remarkable case of the Duchess of Bedford, in the reign of Edward IV., who was charged with having by witchcraft fixed the love of the king on her daughter Queen Elizabeth. Furnished by the rolls of Parliament of 9th Edward IV. Northampton, J. Taylor, 1867.
  8 p. 22cm.
  "In the Proceedings against Dame Alice Kyteler, for the Camden Society."

8   (Continued on next card)

Bedford, Jaquetta of Luxembourg, duchess of.

Witchcraft
BF 1581 A2 W81 1866a no.5

Wright, Thomas, 1810-1877, ed. Curious account of the remarkable case of the Duchess of Bedford ... 1867. (Card 2)
  No. 5 in box lettered Witchcraft in Northamptonshire.

  1. Bedford, Jaquetta of Luxembourg, duchess of. 2. Edward IV, King of England, 1442-1483. I. Title.

8

Witchcraft
BF 1555 B41

Beer, Johann Christoph, 1690-1760.
  Der höllische Intelligenz-Zettul; das ist, Merckwürdige Betrachtungen über die dermahlige Verwirrung der gantzen Welt: verursachet durch vile tausend, von höllischen Geistern heimlich, und in der Still besessene Menschen. ... Augspurg, J. J. Mauracher [1753]
  8 p. l., 472, [16] p. 18cm.

  1. Demoniac possession. I. Title. II. Title: Merckwürdige Betrachtungen über die dermahlige Verwirrung der gantzen Welt.

8

Witchcraft
BF 1581 B42 1864

Beigel, Hermann, 1830-1879, ed.
  The examination and confession of certain witches at Chelmsford in the county of Essex ... [London, Philobiblon Society, pref. 1864]
  49 p. 23cm.

  A reprint of two pamphlets in the library of Lambeth Palace, respectively entitled: The examination and confession of certaine wytches at Chensforde ... 1556 [i.e. 1566] ..." and

                         (Continued on next card)

Witchcraft
BF 1581 B42 1864

Beigel, Hermann, 1830-1879, ed. The examination and confession of certain witches ... [1864]   (Card 2)
  The second examination of mother Agnes Waterhouse ... 1566 ...
  Offprint from Miscellanies of the Philobiblon Society, v. 8, 1863-63.

  1. Witchcraft—England. 2. Waterhouse, Agnes. I. Title. II. Title: The second examination of mother Agnes Waterhouse.

Beiträge zur deutschen Geschichte.

K W12

Wächter, Carl Georg von, 1797-1880.
  Beiträge zur deutschen Geschichte, insbesondere zur Geschichte des deutschen Strafrechts. [Von] Karl Georg von Wächter. Neudr. d. Ausg. Tübingen 1845. Aalen, Sciencia-Verl., 1970.
  viii, 331 p. 22 cm. DM50.00   GDB 70-A39-128
  Includes bibliographical references.

3   1. Law — Germany — History and criticism. 2. Criminal law — Germany — History. 3. Fehmic courts. 4. Witchcraft — Germany. I. Title.

ISBN 3-511-00425-X   75-583846
Library of Congress   71 [2]

Beiträge zur Erklärung des volkstümlichen Hexenglaubens in Schlesien.

Witchcraft
BF 1583 K96

Kurtz, Oswald Amand, 1889-
  Beiträge zur Erklärung des volkstümlichen Hexenglaubens in Schlesien. Anlam, R. Poettke, 1916.
  vi, 150 p. 23cm.

  Diss.—Greifswald.

  1. Witchcraft—Silesia. I. Title.

Beiträge zur Geschichte des Hexenglaubens und des Hexenprocesses in Siebenbürgen.

WITCHCRAFT
BF 1584 T77 M94

Müller, Friedrich.
  Beiträge zur Geschichte des Hexenglaubens und des Hexenprocesses in Siebenbürgen. Braunschweig, C. A. Schwetschke, 1854.
  77 p. 22cm.

8 NIC   1. Witchcraft—Transylvania. 2. Trials (Witchcraft)—Transylvania.

Beiträge zur Geschichte des Hexenwesens in Franken.

WITCHCRAFT
BF 1583 L53

Leitschuh, Friedrich, 1837-1898.
  Beiträge zur Geschichte des Hexenwesens in Franken. Bamberg, C. Hübischer, 1883.
  62, xviii, 11 p. 22cm.

  Note inside front cover by G.L. Burr: An extremely valuable contribution to the literature of the witch-persecution.

8 NIC   1. Witchcraft—Franconia. 2. Trials (Witchcraft)—Franconia.

Ein Beitrag zu den Hexenprozessen in Tirol im 17. Jahrhundert.

Witchcraft
BF 1584 T9 Z7 1644

Zingerle, Ignaz Vincenz, Edler von Summersberg, 1825-1892, ed.
  Ein Beitrag zu den Hexenprozessen in Tirol im 17 Jahrhundert. Von Ignaz V. Zingerle. [Innsbruck, 1882]
  [183]-189 p. 23cm.
  Reprint from Zeitschrift des Ferdinandeum, 3. Folge, 26. Heft, 1882.

  1. Pozza, Juliana de, fl. 1644. 2. Trials (Witchcraft)—Tyrol. I. Title: Die Hexenprozesse in Tirol im 17. Jahrhundert.

8

Beitrag zur Dämonologie.

WITCHCRAFT
BT 980 M54

[Menke, Karl F]
  Beitrag zur Dämonologie, oder, Widerlegung der exegetischen Aufsätze des Herrn Professor's Grimm. Von einem Geistlichen. Frankfurt und Leipzig, 1793.
  174 p. 17cm.

  With autograph: W. Wirbel?

8 NIC   1. Devil. 2. Demonology. 3. Grimm, Heinrich Adolph, 1754-1813. I. Title.

Ein Beitrag zur Geschichte der Hexenprocesse.

WITCHCRAFT
BF 1566 S68 B4

Soldan, Wilhelm Gottlieb, d. 1869.
  Ein Beitrag zur Geschichte der Hexenprocesse.
  (In Zeitschrift für deutsches Strafverfahren. Karlsruhe. 22cm. 3. Bd. (1843) p. [355]-378)
  At head of title: XXIII.
  1. Trials (Witchcraft)—Germany. I. His Geschichte der Hexenprocesse. II. Title.

8 NIC

Bekker, Balthasar

Bekker, Balthasar, 1634-1698.
  Aan Frouk Fullenia.

Witchcraft
BF 1410 B42 Z56 v.3 no.18

Brief van Do. Balthasar Bekker aan zijn huisvrouw, Frouk Fullenia, benevens een antwoord van de christelijke gemeente t'Amsterdam, op de selve: mitsgaders den fameusen antwoorder rustigh afgeslagen: waar by gevoeghd, een antwoord op de naam van deselve Frouk Fullenia. [n. p.] Gedrukt na de copy tot Uytrecht by J. Michielsz [1692?]
  [12] p. title vignette. 19 x 15cm.
  4°: A⁴, B².

8   Continued on next card

Bekker, Balthasar, 1634-1698.
  Aan Frouk Fullenia.

Witchcraft
BF 1410 B42 Z56 v.3 no.18

Brief van Do. Balthasar Bekker aan zijn huisvrouw, Frouk Fullenia ... [1692?]   (Card 2)
  Four poems. The first, by Bekker, appears in vol. 1 of his De betoverde weereld. The others are signed L. B. v. W., L. v. D., and S. T. v. W.
  Van der Linde 195.
  No. 18 in vol. lettered Bekker III.
  1. Bekker, Balthasar, 1634-1698. De betoverde weereld. I. Bekker, Balthasar, 1634-1698. Aan Frouk Fullenia.

3

Witchcraft
BF 1410 B42 1691a no.4

Bekker, Balthasar, 1634-1698.
  Aanmerkinge op de handelingen der twee laatste noordhollandsche synoden, in de saak van B. Bekker, ten opsighte van sijn boek genaamd De betoverde weereld; nu versch t Enkhuisen gedrukt. En de verschoninge de selve gemaakt in de voorrede daar voor, mitsgaders het reqvest der gedeputeerden 't voorleden jaar daar achter by gevoegd. [Amsterdam? 1692]
  16 p. 20 x 16cm.
  4°: A-B⁴.
  Caption title   (Continued on next ca

8

CATALOGUE OF THE CORNELL WITCHCRAFT COLLECTION

Witchcraft
BF Bekker, Balthasar, 1634-1698. Aanmerkinge
1410 op de handelingen der twee laatste noord-
B42 hollandsche synoden ... [1692] (Card 2)
1691a
no.4 In autograph on p. 16: a. 13. Octob.
 1692. Bekker.
 Van der Linde 52.
 No. 4 in vol. lettered B. Bekker. Betoverde wereld.
 1. Nederlandse Hervormde Kerk. Synode
 van Noordholland, Edam, 1691. Acten ofte
 handelingen van de Noord-Hollandsche
 Synodus, gehou den binnen Edam en Alcmaar. I. Tit le.
8

 Bekker, Balthasar, 1634-1698.
 Aanmerkinge op de handelingen der twee
Witchcraft laatste noordhollandsche synoden.
BF [Bekker, Balthasar,] 1634-1698.
1410 Drie resolutien des Classis van Amsterdam,
B42 by deselve genomen op den 22. Jan. 8. April
Z56 en 21. July deses jaars, in de sake van Bal-
v.3 thasar Bekker predikant tot Amsterdam, be-
no.12 treffende sijn boek De betoverde weereld.
 Waar by gevoegt zijn enige reflexien van onbekende hand den Auteur daar over toegesonden.
 Amsterdam, By D. van den Dalen, boekverkoper,
 1692.
 16, 16 p. title and end page vignettes.
 19 x 15cm.
8 (Continued on next card)

 Bekker, Balthasar, 1634-1698.
 Aanmerkinge op de handelingen der twee
Witchcraft laatste noordhollandsche synoden.
BF [Bekker, Balthasar,] 1634-1698. Drie
1410 resolutien des Classis van Amsterdam ...
B42 1692. (Card 2)
Z56
v.3 4°: A-B⁴, A-B⁴.
no.12 "Aanmerkingen op de handelingen der twee
 laatste noordhollandsche synoden, in de sake
 van B. Bekker, ten opsighte van sijn boek
 genaamd De betoverde weereld; nu versch t'
 Enkhuisen gedrukt:" 16 p.
 Last p. autographed by Bekker, dated 2/13
 Octob. 1692.
8 (Continued on next card)

 Bekker, Balthasar, 1634-1698.
 Aanmerkinge op de handelingen der twee
Witchcraft laatste noordhollandsche synoden.
BF [Bekker, Balthasar,] 1634-1698. Drie
1410 resolutien des Classis van Amsterdam ...
B42 1692. (Card 3)
Z56
v.3 In the first section, Bekker quotes the
no.12 resolutions which he discusses.
 Van der Linde 44, 52.
 No. 12 in vol. lettered Bekker III.
 1. Bekker, Balthasar, 1634-1698. De
 betoverde weereld. I. Nederlandse Her-
 vormde Kerk. Classes. Amsterdam.
 II. Title. III. His Aanmerkinge
8 (Continued on next card)

Witchcraft
BF Bekker, Balthasar, 1634-1698.
1410 Articulen tot satisfactie aan de Eerw.
B42 Classis van Amsterdam, van Do. Balthasar
Z85 Bekker, overgeleverd den 22 January 1692.
no.2 Wegens syn uytgegeven boek, genaamd De
 betoverde wereld. Amsterdam, By G. Borstius, boekverkoper, 1692.
 11 p. [p. 12 blank] title vignette,
 illus. initial. 19 x 16cm.
 4°: A⁴, [B²]
 Van der Linde 32.
8 (Continued on next card)

Witchcraft
BF Bekker, Balthasar, 1634-1698. Articulen
1410 tot satisfactie aan de Eerw. Classis van
B42 Amsterdam ... 1692. (Card 2)
Z85
no.2 No. 2 in vol. lettered Stukken betrekkelijk Bekker.
 1. His De betoverde weereld. I.
 Nederlandse Hervormde Kerk. Classes. Amsterdam. II. Title.
8

Witchcraft
BF Bekker, Balthasar, 1634-1698.
1410 Articulen tot satisfactie aan de Eerw.
B42 Classis van Amsterdam, van Do. Balthasar
Z86 Bekker, overgeleverd den 22 January 1692.
no.7 Wegens syn uytgegeven boek, genaamd De
 betoverde wereld. Amsterdam, By G. Borstius, boekverkoper, 1692.
 11 p. [p. 12 blank] title vignette,
 illus. initial. 19 x 15cm.
 4°: A⁴, [B²]
 Verso of t. p. autographed: Bern: Homoet.
8 (Continued on next card)

Witchcraft
BF Bekker, Balthasar, 1634-1698. Articulen
1410 tot satisfactie aan de Eerw. Classis van
B42 Amsterdam ... 1692. (Card 2)
Z86
no.7 Van der Linde 32.
 No. 7 in vol. lettered Tractaten voor
 en tegen B. Bekker.
8

Witchcraft
BF Bekker, Balthasar, 1634-1698.
1410 Articulen tot satisfactie aan de Eerw.
B42 Classis van Amsterdam, van Do. Balthasar
Z56 Bekker, overgeleverd den 22 January 1692.
v.2 Wegens syn uytgegeven boek, genaamd De
 betoverde wereld. Amsterdam, By G. Borstius, boekverkoper, 1692.
 11 p. [p. 12 blank] title vignette,
 illus. initial. 19 x 15cm.
 4°: A⁴, [B²]
 Van der Linde 32.
8 No. 2 in vol. lettered Bekker II.

 Bekker, Balthasar, 1634-1698.
 Articulen tot satisfactie aan de Eerw.
Witchcraft Classis van Amsterdam.
BF Aanmerkingen van eenige rechtzinnige broe-
1410 deren over de Articulen tot satisfactie,
B42 waar op men met D. B. Bekker een verdrag
Z56 gemaakt heeft. Leyden, By F. Haring,
v.3 boekverkooper, 1692.
no.15 22, [1] p. [p. 24 blank] title vignette.
 20 x 15cm.
 4°: A-C⁴.
 Consists of two letters, a short one signed
 N. N. [i. e., Jacobus Schuts], and one of 18
 p. signed B. C.
8 (Continued on next card)

 Bekker, Balthasar, 1634-1698.
 Articulen tot satisfactie aan de Eerw.
Witchcraft Classis van Amsterdam.
BF Aanmerkingen van eenige rechtzinnige broe-
1410 deren ... 1692. (Card 2)
B42
Z56
v.3 Van der Linde 38.
no.15 No. 15 in vol. lettered Bekker III.
 1. Bekker, Balthasar, 1634-1698. Articulen tot satisfactie aan de Eerw. Classis
 van Amsterdam. I. Schuts, Jacobus. II.
 B. C. III. C., B.
8

 Bekker, Balthasar, 1634-1698.
 Articulen tot satisfactie aan de
Witchcraft Eerw. Classis van Amsterdam.
BF [Walten, Ericus,] 1663-1697.
1410 Brief aan een regent der Stad Amsterdam.
B42 Behelsende een regtsinnige uytlegginge, en
Z82 redenmatige verklaringe, van de articulen
no.1 die D. Balthasar Bekker op den 22 Januarij
 1692 heeft overgeleverd aan de Classis van
 Amsterdam, wegens sijn uytgegeven boek, genaamd, De betoverde wereld; met eenige philosophische redeneringen, seer nut en dienstig,
 om verscheidene dingen in 't selve boek wel
 te verstaan; en een kort verhaal van den uytslag der kerke lijke proceduyren, daar
8 (Continued on next card)

 Bekker, Balthasar, 1634-1698.
 Articulen tot satisfactie aan de Eerw.
Witchcraft Classis van Amsterdam.
BF [Walten, Ericus,] 1663-1697. Brief aan een
1410 regent der Stad Amsterdam. 1692.
B42 (Card 2)
Z82
no.1 over gehouden. ... Gravenhage, By M. Uyt-
 werf, boekverkoper, 1692.
 135 p. [p. 136 blank] title vignette.
 19 x 15cm.
 4°: A-R⁴.
 Signed: Ericus Walten. 18. Mey 1692.
 Van der Linde 41.
 No. 1 in vol. lettered Over Bek-
8 kers Betoverde wereld. 1692.
 (Continued on next card)

Witchcraft
BF Bekker, Balthasar, 1634-1698.
1410 De betoverde weereld, zynde een grondig
B42 ondersoek van 't gemeen gevoelen aangaande
1691 de geesten, derselver aart en vermogen, bewind
 en bedrijf: als ook 't gene de menschen door
 derselver kraght en gemeenschap doen. In
 vier boeken ondernommen... Amsterdam, By
 D. van den Dalen, boekverkoper, 1691-1693.
 4 v. in 2. title vignettes, illus., illus.
 initials. 21 x 17cm.
 Vol. 1: 4°: π², *-2*⁴, A-R⁴, S².
8 (Continued on next card)

Witchcraft
BF Bekker, Balthasar, 1634-1698. De betoverde
1410 weereld ... 1691-1693. (Card 2)
B42
1691
 Vol. 2: 4°: 2*⁴, 2A-3K⁴.
 Vol. 3: 4°: *⁴, a-d⁴, A-2A⁴.
 Vol. 4: 4°: *⁴, A-2E⁴, 2E*⁴, 2E2*⁴, 2F-
 2M⁴.
 Vols. 2-4 have separate t. p.
 Black letter.
 Each vol. autographed by Bekker.
 Van der Lin de 16, 17, 19, 20.
8 (Continued on next card)

Witchcraft
BF Bekker, Balthasar, 1634-1698. De betoverde
1410 weereld ... 1691-1693. (Card 3)
B42
1691
 1. Demonology. 2. Angels. 3. Magic.
 4. Witchcraft. I. Title.
8

Witchcraft
BF Bekker, Balthasar, 1634-1698. De betoverde
1410 weereld, zynde een grondig
B42 ondersoek van 't gemeen gevoelen aangaande
1691a de geesten, derselver aart en vermogen,
no.1- bewind en bedryf: als ook 't gene de men-
2 schen door derselver kraght en gemeenschap
 doen. In vier boeken ondernomen van Balthasar Bekker ... Amsterdam, By D. van
 den Dalen, boekverkoper, 1691-1693.
 4 v. in . title vignettes, illus. initials. 20 x 16cm.
8 (Continued on next card)

Witchcraft
BF Bekker, Balthasar, 1634-1698. De betoverde
1410 weereld ... 1691-1693. (Card 2)
B42
1691a Vol. 1: 4°: *⁴, 2-2*⁴, A-R⁴, S1, *3.
no.1- Vol. 2: 4°: 2*⁴, 2A-3K⁴.
2 Black letter.
 Incomplete: vol. 1-2 only.
 Both vols. autographed by Bekker.
 Variant of van der Linde 16: extra gathering at end; van der Linde 17.
 Nos. 1 and 2 in vol. lettered B.
8 Bekker. Beto verde wereld.

41

CATALOGUE OF THE CORNELL WITCHCRAFT COLLECTION

```
Witchcraft
BF      Bekker, Balthasar, 1634-1698.
1410      De betoverde weereld, zynde een grondig
B42     ondersoek van 't gemeen gevoelen aangaande
1739    de geesten, derselver aart en vermogen, be-
        wind en bedryf: als ook 't gene de menschen
        door derselver kraght en gemeenschap doen.
        In vier boeken ondernomen van Balthasar Bek-
        ker, S. T. D. predikant tot Amsterdam. Dee-
        sen druk, volgens des autheurs eigen hand,
        merkelyk vermeerdert, en van drukfeilen ge-
        suivert. Deventer, By M. de Vries, boek-
        drukker en ver              kooper, 1739.

8                    (Continued on next card)
```

```
Witchcraft
BF      Bekker, Balthasar, 1634-1698.  De betover-
1410      de weereld ... 1739.            (Card 2)
B42
1739      4 v. in 1. front., fold. port, title
        vignettes, illus. initials. 20 x 16cm.
          Vol. 1: 4°: †-2†3, a-d4, e2, *-2*4,
        A-S4, T2.
          Vol. 2: 4°: *3, A-2M4, N2.
          Vol. 3: 4°:   *4, A-2B4, C2.
          Vol. 4: 4°:   *3, A-2Q4, R2.

8                    (Continued on next card)
```

```
Witchcraft
BF      Bekker, Balthasar, 1634-1698.  De betover-
1410      de weereld ... 1739.            (Card 3)
B42
1739      Black letter.
          Variant of van der Linde 24: dated 1739,
        not 1736; and t. p. of vol. 2 wanting.

          1. Demonology. 2. Angels. 3. Magic.
        4. Witchcraft. I. Title.

8
```

```
        Bekker, Balthasar, 1634-1698.
        De betoverde weereld.
Witchcraft
BF      Bekker, Balthasar, 1634-1698.
1410      Eenige extracten uyt Dr. Beckers Betoo-
B42     verder weerelt, tweede deel. Daer beneffens
Z92     een extract uyt de synode, gehouden den 10.
        Augusti 1691. tot Edam. Raakende Dr. Beckers
        Betooverde weerelt. Beneffens desselfs ver-
        oordeeling. [n. p.] 1691.
          7 p. [p. 8 blank] title and end page
        vignettes, illus. initials. 19 x 16cm.
          4°: A4.
          Black letter.
          Van der Li         nde 29.

8                    (Continued on next card)
```

```
        Bekker, Balthasar, 1634-1698.
        De betoverde weereld.
Witchcraft
BF      Bekker, Balthasar, 1634-1698.  Eenige
1410    extracten uyt Dr. Beckers Betooverder
B42     weerelt, tweede deel. 1691. (Card 2)
Z92
          Bound with Walten, Ericus, 1663-1697.
        Aardige duyvelary, voorvallende in dese
        dagen.

          I. Bekker, Balthasar, 1634-1698. De
        betoverde weereld. II. Nederlandse Her-
        vormde Kerk. Synode, Edam, 1691. III.
        Title.

8
```

```
        Bekker, Balthasar, 1634-1698.
        De betoverde weereld.
Witchcraft
BF      Bekker, Balthasar, 1634-1698.
1410      Kort begrip van de twee boeken der
B42     Betoverde weereld, in 't ligt gebragt
1691b   door den heere Balthazar Bekker, S. T. D.
        en predikant te Amsterdam, zeer dienstig
        tot het recht verstaan (en teffens strek-
        kende voor een bondig register) van dat
        vermaarde werk, opgesteld door een reden-
        lievenden hater van bygeloof. Rotterdam,
        By I. van Ruynen, boekverkooper, 1691.
          2 p. l., 39 p. [p. 40 is blank] title

8                    (Continued on next card)
```

```
        Bekker, Balthasar, 1634-1698.
Witchcraft  De betoverde weereld.
BF      Bekker, Balthasar, 1634-1698.  Kort begrip
1410    van de twee boeken der Betooverde weereld
B42     ... 1691.                       (Card 2)
1691b
        vignette, illus. initials.  20 x 16cm.
          4°: π2, A-E4.
          Black letter.
          Preface signed: I. van Ruynen.
          Van der Linde 18.

          1. Demonology. 2. Angels. 3. Magic.
        4. Witchcraft. I. His  De betoverde wee-
        reld. II. Ti        tle. III. Ruynen, I.
        van. IV. Ee         n redenlievende hater
        van bygeloof.
8
```

```
        Bekker, Balthasar, 1634-1698.
        De betoverde weereld.
Witchcraft
BF      Bekker, Balthasar, 1634-1698.
1410      Naakte uitbeeldinge van alle de vier
B42     boeken der Betooverde weereld, uitgegeven
Z86     door Baltasar Bekker, S. S. Th. Dr. predi-
no.1    kant tot Amsterdam. Vertonende het oogmerk
        van den schryver, de schikkinge van 't werk
        en sijn eigentlyk gevoelen daar in voorge-
        steld en voorgestaan; tot wechneeminge van
        vooroordeelen, en een kort begryp des gan-
        schen werx. Ingesteld door den selfen
        auteur. Amsterdam, By D. van den Dalen,
        boekverkoper,         1693.

                     (Continued on next card)
```

```
        Bekker, Balthasar, 1634-1698.
        De betoverde weereld.
Witchcraft
BF      Bekker, Balthasar, 1634-1698.  Naakte uit-
1410    beeldinge van alle de vier boeken der Beto-
B42     verde weereld ... 1693.         (Card 2)
Z86
no.1      2 p. l., 32 p. title and end page vi-
        gnettes, illus. initials. 19 x 15cm.
          4°: *2, a-d4.
          Black letter.
          Introduction autographed by Bekker.
          Van der Linde 21.
          No. 1 in vol.      lettered Tractaten voor
        en tegen B.        Bekker.

                     (Continued on next card)
```

```
        Bekker, Balthasar, 1634-1698.
        De betoverde weereld--English.
Witchcraft
BF      Bekker, Balthasar, 1634-1698.
1410      The world bewitch'd; or, An examination
B42     of the common opinions concerning spirits:
1695    their nature, power, administration, and
        operations. As also, the effects men are
        able to produce by their communication.
        Divided into IV parts. By Balthazar Bekker,
        D. D. and pastor at Amsterdam. Vol. I.
        Translated from a French copy, approved of
        and subscribed by the author's own hand.
        [London] Printed for R. Baldwin, 1695.

                     (Continued on next card)
```

```
        Bekker, Balthasar, 1634-1698.
        De betoverde weereld--English.
Witchcraft
BF      Bekker, Balthasar, 1634-1698.  The world
1410    bewitch'd ... 1695.             (Card 2)
B42
1695      41 p. l., 264 p. 17 x 10cm.
          12°: a6(-a1), b-d12, B-M12.
          No more published.
          Half title: The world bewitch'd, &c.
        Vol. I.
          Translation of vol. 1 of Le monde enchanté,
        Amsterdam, 1694, which is a translation of
        his De betoverde weereld, Amsterdam, 1691-93.

                     (Continued on next card)
```

```
        Bekker, Balthasar, 1634-1698.
        De betoverde weereld--English.
Witchcraft
BF      Bekker, Balthasar, 1634-1698.  The world
1410    bewitch'd ... 1695.             (Card 3)
B42
1695      Reissued in 1700 under title: The world
        turn'd upside down.
          Autograph on t. p.: Ch. Whittuck.
          Wing B 1781.
          Variant of van der Linde 28: 12°, not 8°.
          1. Demonology. 2. Angels. 3. Magic.
        4. Witchcraft. I. Title. II. His  De
        betoverde weereld--English. III. His Le
        monde enchanté     --English.
```

```
        Bekker, Balthasar, 1634-1698.
        De betoverde weereld--English.
Witchcraft
BF      [Bekker, Balthasar] 1634-1698.  The world
1410      turn'd upside down: or, A plain
B42     detection of errors, in the common or vulgar
1700    belief, relating to spirits, spectres or
        ghosts, daemons, witches, &c. In a due and
        serious examination of their nature, power,
        administration, and operation. In what form
        or shape incorporeal spirits appear to men,
        by what means, and of what elements they take
        to themselves, and form appearances of bodies
        visible to mort           al eyes; why they

                     (Continued on next card)
```

```
        Bekker, Balthasar, 1634-1698.
        De betoverde weereld--English.
Witchcraft
BF      [Bekker, Balthasar] 1634-1698.  The world
1410      turn'd upside down ... 1700.  (Card 2)
B42
1700    appear, and what frights and force of imag-
        ination often delude us into the appre-
        hensions of supposed phantasms, through the
        intimidation of the mind, &c. Also what evil
        tongues have power to produce of hurt of man-
        kind, or irational [sic] creatures; and the
        effects men and       women are able to produce
        by their commun      ication with good or evil

                     (Continued on next card)
```

```
        Bekker, Balthasar, 1634-1698.
        De betoverde weereld--English.
Witchcraft
BF      [Bekker, Balthasar] 1634-1698.  The world
1410      turn'd upside down ... 1700.  (Card 3)
B42
1700    spirits, &c. Written at the request of a
        person of honour, by B. B., a Protestant min-
        ister for publick information. London,
        Printed for E. Harris, 1700.
          37 p. l., 264 p. 16cm.
          12°: π1, b-d12, B-M12.
          With two old prints of devils inserted at
        front and back of book.

                     (Continued on next card)
```

```
        Bekker, Balthasar, 1634-1698.
        De betoverde weereld--English.
Witchcraft
BF      [Bekker, Balthasar] 1634-1698.  The world
1410      turn'd upside down ... 1700.  (Card 4)
B42
1700      Title on spine: Bekker's World bewitch'
          First published in 1695 with title: The
        world bewitch'd. This is same, with new
        t. p. and lacking the dedication.
          Translation of Book 1 of his Le monde en-
        chanté, which is a translation of De beto-
        verde weereld.
          Variant of van der Linde 28.

                     (Continued on next card)
```

```
        Bekker, Balthasar, 1634-1698.
        De betoverde weereld--French.
Witchcraft
BF      Bekker, Balthasar, 1634-1698.
1410      Le monde enchanté; ou, Examen des communs senti-
B42     mens touchant les esprits, leur nature, leur pouvoir, leur
1694    administration, & leurs opérations. Et touchant les éfets
        que les hommes sont capables de produire par leur com-
        munication & leur vertu, divisé en quatre parties, par Ba-
        thasar Bekker ... Tr. du hollandois. Amsterdam, P. Rot-
        terdam, 1694.
          4 v. plates, port., title and other vignettes, illus.
        initials. 14cm.
          Translation of his De betoverde weereld.
          Dedication, to M. Feyo Jean Winter, autograph
        by Bekker.                              10-33805

        Library of Congress    (Continued on next card)
```

```
        Bekker, Balthasar, 1634-1698.
        De betoverde weereld--French.
Witchcraft
BF      Bekker, Balthasar, 1634-1698.  Le monde
1410      enchanté ... 1694.            (Card 2)
B42
1694      12°: vol. 1: *8, 2*-6*12, A-Q12, R4,
        vol. 2: *12, A-2F12; vol. 3: *12, 2*6,
        A-V12, X4; vol. 4: *12, 2*4, A-2O12, H7.
          Van der Linde 27.

          1. Demonology. 2. Angels. 3. Magic.
        4. Witchcraft. I. Title. II. His  De
        betoverde weere          ld.
```

CATALOGUE OF THE CORNELL WITCHCRAFT COLLECTION

Witchcraft
BF
1410
B42
1693

Bekker, Balthasar, 1634-1698.
De betoverde weereld--German.
Bekker, Balthasar, 1634-1698.
Die bezauberte Welt: oder Eine gründliche Untersuchung des allgemeinen Aberglaubens, betreffend, die arth und das Vermögen, Gewalt und Wirckung des Satans und der bösen Geister über den Menschen, und was diese durch derselben Krafft und Gemeinschafft thun: so aus natürlicher Vernunfft und H. Schrifft in 4 Büchern zu bewehren sich unternommen hat Balthasar Bekker, S. Theol. Doct. und Prediger zu Amsterdam. Nebenst des

(Continued on next card)

Witchcraft
BF
1410
B42
1693

Bekker, Balthasar, 1634-1698.
De betoverde weereld--German.
Bekker, Balthasar, 1634-1698. Die bezauberte Welt ... 1693. (Card 2)

Autoris generale Vorrede über diese seine 4 Bücher: wie und welcher Gestalt dieselbe zu lesen, der Zweck seines Vorhabens, und dann die Ordnung, so er darinnen gehalten. Aus dem Holländischen nach der letzten vom Autore vermehrten Edition. Amsterdam, gedruckt bey D. von Dahlen, 1693.
39, [1], 136, 270, [2], 195, [3], 308, [4] p. Title vignette (port.), plate. 23 x 17cm. (Continued on next card)

Witchcraft
BF
1410
B42
1693

Bekker, Balthasar, 1634-1698.
De betoverde weereld--German.
Bekker, Balthasar, 1634-1698. Die bezauberte Welt ... 1693. (Card 3)

4°: a-e⁴, A-S⁴, A-2K⁴, A-2A⁴, A-2P⁴.
Black letter.
Translation of De betoverde weereld.
Van der Linde 25.
1. Demonology. 2. Angels. 3. Magic. 4. Witchcraft. I. Title. II. His De betoverde weereld--German.

Witchcraft
BF
1410
B42
1781

Bekker, Balthasar, 1634-1698.
De betoverde weereld--German.
Bekker, Balthasar, 1634-1698. D. [i. e., Doktor] Balthasar Bekkers reformierten Predigers in Amsterdam bezauberte Welt. Neu übersetzt von Johann Moritz Schwager, Pastor zu Jöllenbeck; durchgesehen und vermehrt von D. Johann Salomo Semler. Leipzig, In der Weygandschen Buchhandlung, 1781.
3 v. title vignette (port.), fold. plate. 20cm.

(Continued on next card)

Witchcraft
BF
1410
B42
1781

Bekker, Balthasar, 1634-1698.
De betoverde weereld--German.
Bekker, Balthasar, 1634-1698. D. Balthasar Bekkers ... bezauberte Welt. 1781. (Card 2)

⁸(-8), A-2F⁸, G⁴; vol. 3: *⁸(-*1, *8), A-2Y6.
Translation of his De betoverde weereld.

1. Demonology. 2. Angels. 3. Magic. 4. Witchcraft. I. Title. II. Title:

(Continued on next card)

Witchcraft
BX
9479
B42
B11
no.18

Bekker, Balthasar, 1634-1698.
De betoverde weereld.
Andala, Ruardus, 1665-1727. Gansch desperaate en verlooren saake van D. Balthasar Bekker, getoont uit de nasnikken en genoegsaame bekentenisse van onmagt en verleegentheid van sijn voesterling ... Tot een volstrekt bewijs, dat D. Bekker deese schrijver afdedanken, en een beter, in de geestkunde meer geoefent, aan 't werk te stellen, of selve de hand aan de ploeg te slaan, of sijn sake ten besten te geven, genootsaakt is. Franeker, Gedrukt by

(Continued on next card)

Witchcraft
BX
9479
B42
B11
no.18

Bekker, Balthasar, 1634-1698.
De betoverde weereld.
Andala, Ruardus, 1665-1727. Gansch desperaate en verlooren saake.... 1698. (Card 2)

H. Gyzelaar, ordinaris drukker der Eed. Mog. Heeren Staten, en der Academie van Friesland, 1698.
35 p. [p. 36 blank] title and other vignettes, illus. initials. 20 x 15cm.
4°: A-D⁴, E².
Apparently refers to a work titled

(Continued on next card)

Witchcraft
BX
9479
B42
B11
no.18

Bekker, Balthasar, 1634-1698.
De betoverde weereld.
Andala, Ruardus, 1665-1727. Gansch desperaate en verlooren saake ... 1698. (Card 3)

Den professor J. van der Waeyen, ongelukkig en scandaleus verdeedigt van twee predikanten, voormaals zijne discipulen, pub. 1697.
No. 18 in vol. lettered B. Bekkers sterfbed en andere tractaten.
1. Den Professor J. van der Waeyen, ongelukkig en scandaleus verdeedigt van twee predikanten. 2. Bekker, Balthasar, 1634-1698. De betoverde weereld. 3. Devil. I. Title.

Witchcraft
BF
1410
B42
Z912

Bekker, Balthasar, 1634-1698.
De betoverde weereld.
[Andala, Ruardus] 1665-1727. Uiterste verleegentheid van Doctor Balt. Bekker. Duidelijk aangeweesen door wederlegginge van alle sijne aanmerkingen en naleesingen gevoegt bi het slordige mengelmoes van sijn E. Voedsterlingen. Uitgegeeven door een discipel van de Heer J. vander Waeyen en voedsterling van de Academie van Friesland, Franeker, By H. Gyzelaar, ordinaris drukker der Eed. Mog. Heeren Staten, en der Academie van Friesland, 1696.
4 p. l., 234, [6] p. title and

(Continued on next card)

Witchcraft
BF
1410
B42
Z912

Bekker, Balthasar, 1634-1698.
De betoverde weereld.
[Andala, Ruardus] 1665-1727. Uiterste verleegentheid van Doctor Balt. Bekker. 1696. (Card 2)

other vignettes, illus. initials. 22 x 17cm.
4°: *⁴, A-2G⁴.
Van der Linde 166.
Criticizes Bekker's critique of Waaijen's De betoverde weereld van D. Balthasar Bekker ondersogt en weederlegt.
With this is bound Andala, Ruardus, 1665-1727. Balthazar Bekkers en

(Continued on next card)

Witchcraft
BF
1410
B42
Z912

Bekker, Balthasar, 1634-1698.
De betoverde weereld.
[Andala, Ruardus] 1665-1727. Uiterste verleegentheid van Doctor Balt. Bekker. 1696. (Card 3)

insonderheyd sijner voedsterlingen onkunde... Franeker, 1696.
1. Bekker, Balthasar, 1634-1698. De betoverde weereld. 2. Waaijen, Johannes van der, 1639-1701. De betoverde weereld van D. Balthasar Bekker ondersogt en weederlegt. I. Title.

Witchcraft
BX
9479
B42
B11
no.20

Bekker, Balthasar, 1634-1698.
De betoverde weereld.
Banningh, Jacob. Eenvoudig verhaal van de proceduuren gepleeght, in de waaterlandse doopsgesinde gemeentens tot Wormer en Jisp, over het doen ophouden van een haarer leeraaren, in sijn predikdienst ... veroorsaakt door het zoo genaamde nieuw gevoelen der geesten, engelen ende duyvelen, met de disputatien en voorvallen soo alse in deselve zyn geschiet, na waarheyd verhaalt door de zelve leeraar, Jacob Banningh. Amsterdam, by A. van Damme, boekverkooper, 1698.

(Continued on next card)

Witchcraft
BX
9479
B42
B11
no.20

Bekker, Balthasar, 1634-1698.
De betoverde weereld.
Banningh, Jacob. Eenvoudig verhaal van de proceduuren gepleeght ... tot Wormer en Jisp ... 1698. (Card 2)

44 p. title and other vignettes, illus. initials. 20 x 15cm.
4°: A-E⁴, F².
Black letter (except introduction and post scriptum)
Local development of the controversy over Balthasar Bekkers De betoverde weereld.

(Continued on next card)

Witchcraft
BX
9479
B42
B11
no.20

Bekker, Balthasar, 1634-1698.
De betoverde weereld.
Banningh, Jacob. Eenvoudig verhaal van de proceduuren gepleeght ... tot Wormer en Jisp ... 1698. (Card 3)

No. 20 in vol. lettered B. Bekkers sterfbed en andere tractaten.
1. Nederlandse Hervormde Kerk--Doctrinal and controversial works. 2. Bekker, Balthasar, 1634-1698. De betoverde weereld. I. Title.

Witchcraft
BF
1445
B37

Bekker, Balthasar, 1634-1698.
De betoverde weereld.
Beaumont, John, d. 1731.
An historical, physiological and theological treatise of spirits, apparitions, witchcrafts, and other magical practices ... With a refutation of Dr. Bekker's World bewitch'd; and other authors that have opposed the belief of them. By John Beaumont ... London, Printed for D. Browne, etc., 1705.
8 p. l., 400 p. front. 20cm.

1. Occult sciences. 2. Ghosts. 3. Apparitions. +Bekker, Balthasar, 1634-1698. De betoverde weereld.

Library of Congress   BF1447.B4
                                  41-27994

Witchcraft
BF
1410
B42
Z55

Bekker, Balthasar, 1634-1698.
De betoverde weereld.
Beckher, Wilhelm Heinrich.
Schediasma critico-litterarivm de contoversiis praecipvis Balthasari Bekkero, theologo batavo qvondam motis, ob librvm cvi titvlvm fecit: Die bezauberte Welt. Adiecta in fine avctorvm farragine, qvi vel Bekkeri scriptvm refvtarvnt, vel asseclarvm more illvd defendervnt. Regiomonti ac Lipsiae, Impensis J. P. Hasii, 1721.
47 p. [p. 48 blank] title (port.), caption and end page vignettes. 19 x 16cm.

(Continued on next card)

Witchcraft
BF
1410
B42
Z55

Bekker, Balthasar, 1634-1698.
De betoverde weereld.
Beckher, Wilhelm Heinrich. Schediasma critico-litterarivm de controversiis praecipvis Balthasari Bekkero ... 1721. (Card 2)

4°: A-F⁴.
At head of title: M. Gvilielmi Henrici Beckher, Regiom. Prvssi.
Van der Linde 215.

1. Bekker, Balthasar, 1634-1698. De betoverde weereld. I. Title.

Witchcraft
BF
1410
B42
Z85
no.2

Bekker, Balthasar, 1634-1698.
Bekker, Balthasar, 1634-1698.
Articulen tot satisfactie aan de Eerw. Classis van Amsterdam, van Do. Balthasar Bekker, overgeleverd den 22 January 1692. Wegens syn uytgegeven boek, genaamd De betoverde wereld. Amsterdam, By G. Borstius, boekverkoper, 1692.
11 p. [p. 12 blank] title vignette, illus. initial. 19 x 16cm.
4°: A⁴, B²]
Van der Linde 32.

(Continued on next card)

43

CATALOGUE OF THE CORNELL WITCHCRAFT COLLECTION

Witchcraft
BF
1410
B42
285
no.2

Bekker, Balthasar, 1634-1698.
  De betoverde weereld.
Bekker, Balthasar, 1634-1698. Articulen tot satisfactie aan de Eerw. Classis van Amsterdam ... 1692.   (Card 2)

No. 2 in vol. lettered Stukken betrekkelijk Bekker.
  1. His De betoverde weereld. I. Nederlandse Hervormde Kerk. Classes. Amsterdam. II. Title.

8

Witchcraft
BF
1410
B42
Z56
v.3
no.12

Bekker, Balthasar, 1634-1698.
  De betoverde weereld.
[Bekker, Balthasar] 1634-1698. Drie resolutien des Classis van Amsterdam ... 1692.   (Card 3)

In the first section, Bekker quotes the resolutions which he discusses.
Van der Linde 44, 52.
No. 12 in vol. lettered Bekker III.
  1. Bekker, Balthasar, 1634-1698. De betoverde weereld. I. Nederlandse Hervormde Kerk. Classes. Amsterdam. II. Title. III. His Aanmerkinge
  (Continued on next card)

8

Witchcraft
BF
1410
B42
Z56
v.1
no.1

Bekker, Balthasar, 1634-1698.
  De betoverde weereld.
Bekker, Balthasar, 1634-1698. Nodige bedenkingen op de niewe beweegingen ... [1692?]   (Card 2)

Dated at end: den 9. July 1692.
Van der Linde 42.
No. 1 in vol. lettered Bekker I.
  1. Nederlandse Hervormde Kerk. Kerkenraden. Rotterdam. Circulaire brief ... wegens de saake van Dr. Balthasar Bekker. 2. Nederlandse Hervormde Kerk--Doctrinal and controversial works. 3. Bekker, Balthasar, 1634-1698.   betoverde weereld. I. Title.

8

Witchcraft
BF
1410
B42
Z86
no.2

Bekker, Balthasar, 1634-1698.
  De betoverde weereld.
Bekker, Balthasar, 1634-1698. Brief van Balthasar Bekker, S. Th. Dr. predikant tot Amsterdam. Aan den Heer Joannes vander Waeyen, S. Theol. Dr. en professor in de loffelike en vermaarde Universiteit tot Franeker. In antwoord op desselven brief, waarmede hy hem sijn boek tegen De betoverde weereld onlangs uitgegeven, heeft toegesonden. [Amsterdam? 1693]
  8 p. illus. initial. 19 x 15cm.

8   (Continued on next card)

Witchcraft
BF
1410
B42
Z56
v.1
no.2

Bekker, Balthasar, 1634-1698.
  De betoverde weereld.
Bekker, Balthasar, 1634-1698.
  Kort beright van Balthasar Bekker S. T. D. predikant tot Amsterdam. Aangaande alle de schriften, welke over sijn boek De betoverde weereld enen tijd lang heen en weder verwisseld zijn. De tweede druk met enige stukken vermeerdert. Amsterdam, By D. vanden Dalen, boekverkoper [1692]
  80, 8 p. title vignette, illus. initials.
  19 x 16cm.
  4°: A-K⁴, A⁴.
  Black lett   er.

8   (Continued on next card)

Witchcraft
BF
1410
B42
1691a
no.7

Bekker, Balthasar, 1634-1698.
  De betoverde weereld.
Bekker, Balthasar, 1634-1698.
  Ondersoek en antwoord van Balthasar Bekker, S.S.Th.D. predikant tot Amsterdam, op 't request door de gedeputeerden der Noordhollandsche Synode tot Edam, in den herfst des jaars 1691. ingegeven aan de Ed. Gr. Mog. Heeren Staten van Holland en West Friesland tegen sijn boek De betoverde weereld. ... Amsterdam, By D. vanden Dalen, boekverkoper, 1693.
  2 p. l., 98 p. title vignette, illus. initials. 20   x 16cm.

8   (Continued on next card)

Witchcraft
BF
1410
B42
Z86
no.2

Bekker, Balthasar, 1634-1698.
  De betoverde weereld.
Bekker, Balthasar, 1634-1698. Brief ... aan den Heer Joannes vander Waeyen ... [1693]   (Card 2)

  4°: A⁴.
  Caption title.
  Dated: Amsterdam den 8 Augusty 1693.
  Van der Linde 157.
  No. 2 in vol. lettered Tractaten voor en tegen B. Bekker.
  1. His De betoverde weereld. I. Waaijen, Johannes van der, 1639-1701. II. Title.

8

Witchcraft
BF
1410
B42
Z56
v.1
no.2

Bekker, Balthasar, 1634-1698.
  De betoverde weereld.
Bekker, Balthasar, 1634-1698. Kort beright ... [1692]   (Card 2)

Dated Franeker den 21/31 Jul. 1692.
Variant of van der Linde 76: t. p. includes statement De tweede druk...
No. 2 in vol. lettered Bekker I.
  1. Bekker, Balthasar, 1634-1698. De betoverde weereld. I. Title.

8

Witchcraft
BF
1410
B42
1691a
no.7

Bekker, Balthasar, 1634-1698.
  De betoverde weereld.
Bekker, Balthasar, 1634-1698. Ondersoek en antwoord ... 1693.   (Card 2)

  4°: *², A-M⁴, N1.
  Black letter.
  Prefatory letter autographed by Bekker.
  Van der Linde 53.
  No. 7 in vol. lettered B. Bekker. Betoverde weereld.
  1. Nederlandse Hervormde Kerk. Synode van Noordholland, Edam, 1691. 2. Bekker, Balthasar, 1634-1698. De betoverde weereld. I. Netherlands (United Provinces, 1581-1795) Staten General. II. Title.

8

Witchcraft
BF
1410
B42
Z56
v.3
no.27

Bekker, Balthasar, 1634-1698.
  De betoverde weereld.
[Bekker, Balthasar] 1634-1698.
  Brief van den schrijver des boeks De betoverde weereld genaamd, aan den eerwaardigen heere Everhard van der Hooght, yverigen leeraar van 's heeren gemeente tot Niewendam. Amsterdam, By G. Borstius, boekverkoper [1691]
  11 p. [p. 12 is blank] title vignette, illus. initial.
  4°: A⁴, [B²]
  Van der Linde 105.
  No. 27 in vol. lettered Bekker III.
  (Continued on next card)

8

Witchcraft
BF
1410
B42
Z56
v.1
no.5

Bekker, Balthasar, 1634-1698.
  De betoverde weereld.
Bekker, Balthasar, 1634-1698.
  Kort en waarachtig verhaal van 't gebeurde tsederd den 31. Mey 1691. tot den 21. Aug. 1692. In den Kerkenraad en Classis van Amsterdam, en de Synode van Noord-Holland. In de sake van Balthasar Bekker, S. S. Th. Dr. en predikant tot Amsterdam; over sijn boek genaamd De betoverde weereld. Amsterdam, By D. van den Dalen, boekverkoper, 1692.
  2 p. l., 30 p. [p. 31-32 blank] title vignette, illus.   initials.
  (Continued on next card)

8

Witchcraft
BF
1410
B42
Z56
v.3
no.28

Bekker, Balthasar, 1634-1698.
  De betoverde weereld.
Bekker, Balthasar, 1634-1698.
  Twee brieven van Balthasar Bekker predikant tot Amsterdam, aan Everhardus vander Hooght predikant tot Niewendam. D'eerste voor desen uitgegeven van den 25. September 1691, uit Amsterdam. D'andere nu daar by gevoegd, van den 3/13 Juny 1692, uit Franeker. Beide over het boek genaamd De betoverde weereld, en 't gene daar ontrent is voorgevallen. Met een kort beright over de voorrede van seker Opstel van aanmerkingen
  (Continued on next card)

8

Witchcraft
BF
1410
B42
Z56
v.3
no.12

Bekker, Balthasar, 1634-1698.
  De betoverde weereld.
[Bekker, Balthasar] 1634-1698.
  Drie resolutien des Classis van Amsterdam, by deselve genomen op den 22. Jan. 8. April en 21. July deses jaars, in de sake van Balthasar Bekker predikant tot Amsterdam, betreffende sijn boek De betoverde weereld. Waar by gevoegt zijn enige reflexien van onbekende hand den Auteur daar over toegesonden. Amsterdam, By D. van den Dalen, boekverkoper, 1692.
  16, 16 p. title and end page vignettes.
  19 x 15cm.
                (Continued on next card)

8

Witchcraft
BF
1410
B42
Z56
v.1
no.5

Bekker, Balthasar, 1634-1698.
  De betoverde weereld.
Bekker, Balthasar, 1634-1698. Kort en waarachtig verhaal ... 1692.   (Card 2)

  19 x 16cm.
  4°: π², *-4⁴.
  Introductory letter autographed by Bekker.
  Van der Linde 47.
  No. 5 in vol. lettered Bekker I.
  1. Nederlandse Hervormde Kerk. 2. Bekker, Balthasar, 1634-1698. De betoverde weereld. I. Title.

8

Witchcraft
BF
1410
B42
Z56
v.3
no.28

Bekker, Balthasar, 1634-1698.
  De betoverde weereld.
Bekker, Balthasar, 1634-1698. Twee brieven ... aan Everhardus vander Hooght ... 1692.   (Card 2)

gemaakt door J. J. F. B. en tot Leewarden by Hero Nauta gedrukt. Franeker, By Leonardus Strik, boekverkoper, 1692.
  2 p. l., 32 p. title vignette, illus. initials. 19 x 15cm.
  4°: π², A-D⁴.
  Back of t. p. autographed by Bekker.

8   (Continued on next card)

Witchcraft
BF
1410
B42
Z56
v.3
no.12

Bekker, Balthasar, 1634-1698.
  De betoverde weereld.
[Bekker, Balthasar] 1634-1698. Drie resolutien des Classis van Amsterdam ... 1692.   (Card 2)

  4°: A-B⁴, A-B⁴.
  "Aanmerkinge op de handelingen der twee laatste noordhollandsche synoden, in de sake van B. Bekker, ten opsighte van sijn boek genaamd De betoverde weereld; nu versch t' Enkhuisen gedrukt:" 16 p.
  Last p. autographed by Bekker, dated 2/13 Octob. 1692.

8   (Continued on next card)

Witchcraft
BF
1410
B42
Z56
v.1
no.1

Bekker, Balthasar, 1634-1698.
  De betoverde weereld.
Bekker, Balthasar, 1634-1698.
  Nodige bedenkingen op de niewe beweegingen, onlangs verwekt door den circulairen brief en andere middelen, tegen den auteur van 't boek De betoverde weereld, door Balthasar Bekker, predikant tot Amsterdam. Amsterdam, Gedruckt by D. vanden Dalen, boekverkoper [1692?]
  1 p. l., 62, [1] p. [p. 64 blank] title vignette, illus. initial. 19 x 16cm.
  4°: π1, A-H⁴.
  Preface auto   graphed by Bekker.
                (Continued on next card)

8

Witchcraft
BF
1410
B42
Z56
v.3
no.28

Bekker, Balthasar, 1634-1698.
  De betoverde weereld.
Bekker, Balthasar, 1634-1698. Twee brieven ... aan Everhardus vander Hooght ... 1692.   (Card 3)

Variant of van der Linde 107: has p. 31-32.
No. 28 in vol. lettered Bekker III.
  1. Bekker, Balthasar, 1634-1698. De betoverde weereld. 2. Opstel van enige aanmerkingen op het boek van B. Bekker. I. Hooght, Everard van der, d. 1716. II. Title.

8

44

CATALOGUE OF THE CORNELL WITCHCRAFT COLLECTION

Bekker, Balthasar, 1634-1698.
  De betoverde weereld.

Witchcraft
  Bekker, Balthasar, 1634-1698.
  Viervoudige beantwoordinge van beswaarnissen, voorgesteld aan Balthasar Bekker, S. S. Th. Dr. predikant tot Amsterdam, over sijn boek, genaamd De betoverde weereld. ... Amsterdam, By D. van den Dalen, boekverkoper, 1692.
  3 p. l., 74, 95, [1] p. title vignette, illus. initials. 21 x 17cm.
  4°: *⁴, A-J⁴, K1, a-m⁴.

  (Continued on next card)

Bekker, Balthasar, 1634-1698.
  De betoverde weereld.

Witchcraft
  Bekker, Balthasar, 1634-1698. Viervoudige beantwoordinge van beswaarnissen ... 1692.
  (Card 2)

  Black letter.
  Preface autographed by Bekker.
  Includes actions taken by the church.
  Variant of van der Linde 49: four final gatherings wanting.
    1. Bekker, Balthasar, 1634-1698. De betoverde weereld. I. Nederlandse Hervormde Kerk. II. Title.

Bekker, Balthasar, 1634-1698.
  De betoverde weereld.

Witchcraft
  Bekker door Bekker overtuygt. Uytgewerckt in een brief hem schriftelijk toegesonden in welke vertoont wort dat Do. Bekker, en uyt Gods woort, en ook uyt sijn eygen grond regels en belydenis; van de valscheyt sijnes gevoelens, aengaende de goede en quade geesten, moetover tuygt sijn. Neffens. Een korte aenmerking over twee geschrifte in faveur van Do. Bekker in 't ligt gebracht, her [sic] eerste geschreven aen een heer tot Uytrecht, en het andere genaemt de Aerdige duyvelarye.

  (Continued on next card)

Witchcraft
BF
1410
B42
v.3
no.7
  Bekker, Balthasar, 1634-1698.
  De betoverde weereld.
  Bekker door Bekker overtuygt. 1692.
  (Card 2)

  Gravenhage, By B. Beek, konst-en boekverkooper, 1692.
  5 p. l., 18 p. title and other vignettes, illus. initials. 20 x 16cm.
  4°: π1, *⁴, A-B⁴, C1.
  Black letter (second numbering only)
  Van der Linde 173.
  No. 7 in vol. lettered Bekker III.

  (Continued on next card)

Witchcraft
BF
1410
B42
Z57
1708
  Bekker, Balthasar, 1634-1698.
  De betoverde weereld.
  [Berns, Michael] Gründliche und völlige Wiederlegung der Bezauberten Welt Balthasar Beckers, D. Aus der Heil. Schrifft gezogen. Wobey zugleich unzählige curioese Antiquitaeten erläutert und zum rechten Gebrauch angewendet werden; und andere rare auch zu dieser Zeit höchstnöthige Materien. Nebst einem Anhange vom Licht und Recht der Natur. Mit völligen Registern versehen. Von M. Hamburg, S. Heyl und J. Liebezeit, 1708.

  (Continued on next card)

Witchcraft
BF
1410
B42
Z57
1708
  Bekker, Balthasar, 1634-1698.
  De betoverde weereld.
  [Berns, Michael] Gründliche und völlige Wiederlegung der Bezauberten Welt ... 1708.
  (Card 2)

  3 p. l., 958, [11] p. [p. [2] blank] title and other vignettes, illus. initials. 21 x 17cm.
  4°:)(3, A-I⁴, A-6D⁴, 6E3, 6F⁴, 6G².
  Black letter.
  According to J. G. T. Grässe, Bibliotheca magica et pneumatica, 1843, this work

  (Continued on next card)

Witchcraft
BF
1410
B42
Z57
1708
  Bekker, Balthasar, 1634-1698.
  De betoverde weereld.
  [Berns, Michael] Gründliche und völlige Wiederlegung der Bezauberten Welt ... 1708.
  (Card 3)

  first appeared in 1697 with title: Die dreifache Welt als der Christen, Phantasten und Bezauberten, in dreyen Büchern abgefasst.
    1. Bekker, Balthasar, 1634-1698. De betoverde weereld. 2. Christian life. 3. Millennialism. 4. Spirits. I. Title. II. M., pseud. III. His Die dreifache Welt als der Christen, Phantasten und Bezauberten.

Witchcraft
BF
1410
B42
Z56
v.2
no.7
  Bekker, Balthasar, 1634-1698.
  De betoverde weereld.
  Beschryvinge van een vremd nagt-gezigte, vertoont aan een toehoorder der predikatie, die door den remonstrantsche leeraer Ds. Johannes Molinaeus voor 't vermogen des duivels, en tegen den aucteur van 't boek De betoverde weereld, onlangs te Rotterdam gedaan is. Logoochoorion, Gedrukt by den drukker van Haar Majesteit Krisis [1692]
  2 p. l., 12 p. title vignette, illus. initial. 19 x 15cm.

  (Continued on next card)

Witchcraft
BF
1410
B42
Z56
v.2
no.7
  Bekker, Balthasar, 1634-1698.
  De betoverde weereld.
  Beschryvinge van een vremd nagt-gezigte ... [1692]
  (Card 2)

  4°: π², A⁴, B².
  Black letter.
  Van der Linde 132.
  No. 7 in vol. lettered Bekker II.
    1. Molinaeus, Johannes, d. 1702. De betoverde werelt van D. Balthazar Bekker. 2. Bekker, Balthasar, 1634-1698. De betoverde weereld. I. Title: Een vremd nagt-gezigt.

Witchcraft
BF
1508
B61
1699
  Bekker, Balthasar, 1634-1698.
  De betoverde weereld.
  [Binet, Benjamin] 17th cent. Idée generale de la theologie payenne, servant de refutation au systeme de Mr. Bekker. Touchant l'existence & l'operation des demons. Ou Traitté [sic] historique des dieux du paganisme. Par Mr. B***. Amsterdam, Chez J. du Fresne, 1699.
  6 p. l., 227 p. 26cm.
  12: *⁶, A-I¹², K⁶.
  First published 1696 with title Traité historique des dieux et des demons du paganisme.

  (Continued on next card)

Witchcraft
BF
1508
B61
1699
  Bekker, Balthasar, 1634-1698.
  De betoverde weereld.
  [Binet, Benjamin] 17th cent. Idée generale de la theologie payenne ... 1699.
  (Card 2)

  Ex libris cabalisticis Kurt Seligmann.
    1. Paganism. 2. Demonology. 3. Bekker, Balthasar, 1634-1698. De betoverde weereld. I. Title. II. His Traité historique des dieux et des demons du paganisme.

Witchcraft
BF
1410
B42
Z82
no.3
  Bekker, Balthasar, 1634-1698.
  De betoverde weereld.
  Blyenbergh, Willem van, 17th cent. Klaare en beknopte verhandeling van de natuur en werkinge der menschelijke zielen, engelen en duivelen, vervat in gewisselde brieven tusschen de heer Willem van Blyenbergh en Willem Deurhoff. Amsterdam, By J. ten Hoorn, boekverkooper, 1692.
  64 p. title vignette, illus. initials. 20 x 15cm.
  4°: A-H⁴.
  Discussion of questions raised in the contemporary controversy over Bal-

  (Continued on next card)

Witchcraft
BF
1410
B42
Z82
no.3
  Bekker, Balthasar, 1634-1698.
  De betoverde weereld.
  Blyenbergh, Willem van, 17th cent. Klaare en beknopte verhandeling van de natuur en werkinge der menschelijke zielen ... 1692.
  (Card 2)

  thasar Bekker's De Betoverde weereld.
  Van der Linde 77.
  No. 3 in vol. lettered Over Bekkers Betoverde wereld. 1692.
    1. Soul. 2. Spirits. 3. Bekker, Balthasar. De betoverde weereld. I. Deurhoff, Willem, 1650-1717. II. Title.

Witchcraft
BX
9479
B42
B11
no.14
  Bekker, Balthasar, 1634-1698.
  De betoverde weereld.
  Brief, aan een heer, waar in uyt de H. Schrift getoond werd, dat'er is een quade geest, die een redelijk schepsel is buyten de ziel des mensche. Met eenige aenmerkinge voor het boek, De ware oorspronk, voort en ondergank des Satans. Door I. W. Amsterdam, By J. de Veer gedrukt, 1696.
  64 p. title vignette, illus. initial. 20 x 15cm.
  4°: A-H⁴.
  Probably by Joannes van Wijk.

  (Continued on next card)

Witchcraft
BX
9479
B42
B11
no.14
  Bekker, Balthasar, 1634-1698.
  De betoverde weereld.
  Brief, aan een heer, waar in uyt de H. Schrift getoond werd, dat'er is een quade geest ... 1696.
  (Card 2)

  Supports Balthasar Bekker in the controversy over his De betoverde weereld.
  No. 14 in vol. lettered B. Bekkers sterfbed en andere tractaten.
    1. Devil. 2. Webbers, Zacharias. De waare oorspronk, voort- en ondergank des Satans. 3. Bekker, Balthasar, 1634-1698. De betoverde weereld. I. Wijk, Joannes van, supposed author. II. I. W. III. W., I.

Witchcraft
BX
9479
B42
B11
no.19
  Bekker, Balthasar, 1634-1698.
  De betoverde weereld.
  Brief, aan een predikant, noopens den tegenwoordigen staat des geschils, over den duivel. Amsterdam, By J. de Veer gedrukt, 1696.
  28 p. title vignette, illus. initial. 20 x 15cm.
  4°: A-C⁴, D².
  Signed: N. N. [not Jacobus Schuts]
  On the controversy over Balthasar Bekker's De betoverde weereld.
  No. 19 in vol. lettered B. Bekkers sterfbed en andere tractaten.

  (Continued on next card)

Witchcraft
BF
1410
B42
Z56
v.2
no.9
  Bekker, Balthasar, 1634-1698.
  De betoverde weereld.
  Brief, geschreven van Uitregt, aan een vriend tot Amsterdam, over het boek genaamd De betoverde weereld. Als mede wat daar omtrent is voorgevallen. [Amsterdam? 1691?]
  19 p. [p. 20 blank] 19 x 15cm.
  4°: A-B⁴, C².
  Dated: Uitregt 2/12 September 1691.
  Van der Linde 57.
  No. 9 in vol. lettered Bekker II.
    1. Bekker, Balthasar, 1634-1698. De betoverde weereld.

Witchcraft
BF
1410
B42
Z56
v.3
no.18
  Bekker, Balthasar, 1634-1698.
  De betoverde weereld.
  Brief van Do. Balthasar Bekker aan zijn huisvrouw, Frouk Fullenia, benevens een antwoord van de christelijke gemeente t'Amsterdam, op de selve: mitsgaders den fameusen antwoorder rustigh afgeslagen: waar by gevoeghd, een antwoord op de naam van deselve Frouk Fullenia. [n. p.] Gedrukt na de copy tot Uytrecht by J. Michielsz [1692?]
  [12] p. title vignette. 19 x 15cm.
  4°: A⁴, B².

  (Continued on next card)

45

CATALOGUE OF THE CORNELL WITCHCRAFT COLLECTION

Witchcraft
BF
1410
B42
Z56
v.3
no.18

Bekker, Balthasar, 1634-1698.
De betoverde weereld.
Brief van Do. Balthasar Bekker aan zijn huisvrouw, Frouk Fullenia ... [1692?] (Card 2)

Four poems. The first, by Bekker, appears in vol. 1 of his De betoverde weereld. The others are signed L. B. v. W., L. v. D., and S. T. v. W.
Van der Linde 195.
No. 18 in vol. lettered Bekker III.
1. Bekker, Balthasar, 1634-1698. De betoverde weereld. I. Bekker, Balthasar, 1634-1698. Aan Frouk Fullenia.

Witchcraft
BF
1410
B42
Z56
v.3
no.1

Bekker, Balthasar, 1634-1698.
De betoverde weereld.
[Costerus, Florentius] fl. 1654-1703. De gebannen duyvel weder in-geroepen, ofte het vonnis van Doctor Bekker over den duyvel gevelt, in revisie gebraght. Den tweede druck, vermeerdert met twee gedigten. Hoorn, Gedruckt by S. J. Kortingb [sic] en J. J. Beets, boek-verkoopers, 1691.
42 p. title and end page vignettes. 21 x 16cm.
4°: A-E⁴, F1.
Black letter.
(Continued on next card)

Witchcraft
BF
1410
B42
Z56
v.3
no.1

Bekker, Balthasar, 1634-1698.
De betoverde weereld.
[Costerus, Florentius] fl. 1654-1703. De gebannen duyvel weder in-geroepen ... 1691. (Card 2)

Signed: Bloemardus Thusius.
Variant of van der Linde 87: 2d., enl. printing.
No. 1 in vol. lettered Bekker III.
1. Bekker, Balthasar, 1634-1698. De betoverde weereld. I. Title.

Witchcraft
BF
1410
B42
Z56
v.3
no.5

Bekker, Balthasar, 1634-1698.
De betoverde weereld.
Daillon, Benjamin de. Omstandig bewys, dat de daemones overgeset duyvelen, geen quade geesten, maar zielen van menschen geweest zijn de welke op de werelt rechtvaardigh geleeft hadden, en dat de selve naar het gevoelen van d'oude heydenen, hare woonsteede in 't oppersche en zuyverste deel van de lucht gehadt hebben, en ook middelaars tusschen de goden en menschen geweest zijn. Als ook datter maar eene duyvel of Satan is. Welk gevoelen met dat van d'Heer Predikant Bekker, in sijn boek De betoverde
(Continued on next card)

Witchcraft
BF
1410
B42
Z56
v.3
no.5

Bekker, Balthasar, 1634-1698.
De betoverde weereld.
Daillon, Benjamin de. Omstandig bewys, dat de daemones overgeset duyvelen ... 1692. (Card 2)

wereld genaamt vervat, over een stemt. Getrokken uyt de schriften van d'Heer Daillon frans predikant. Gravenhage, By M. Uytwerf, boekverkooper, 1692.
2 p. l., 43 p. [p. 44 blank] title vignette, illus. initial. 21 x 15cm.
4°: π², A-E⁴, E².
(Continued on next card)

Witchcraft
BF
1410
B42
Z56
v.3
no.5

Bekker, Balthasar, 1634-1698.
De betoverde weereld.
Daillon, Benjamin de. Omstandig bewys, dat de daemones overgeset duyvelen ... 1692. (Card 3)

Black letter.
Translation of selections from his Examen de l'opression des reformez en France ... avec l'explication de la doctrine des demons. Amsterdam, 1691.
Selections chosen to support Bekker's views in De betoverde weereld.
Van der Linde 74.
(Continued on next card)

Witchcraft
BF
1410
B42
Z56
v.3
no.5

Bekker, Balthasar, 1634-1698.
De betoverde weereld.
Daillon, Benjamin de. Omstandig bewys, dat de daemones overgeset duyvelen ... 1692. (Card 4)

No. 5 in vol. lettered Bekker III.
1. Devil. 2. Bekker, Balthasar, 1634-1698. De betoverde weereld. I. His Examen de l'opression des reformez en France ... Selections--Dutch. II. Title.

Witchcraft
BF
1410
B42
Z56
v.2
no.14

Bekker, Balthasar, 1634-1698.
De betoverde weereld.
Dale, Antonius van, 1638-1708. Lasteringen van Jakob Koelman, in zijn zoo genaamde wederlegging van B. Bekkers Betooverde wereld, zedighlijk aangewesen in een brief van Antony van Dale, med. doctor. Aan zijnen vrind. Rotterdam, By I. van Ruynen, boekverkooper, 1692.
15, [1] p. title vignette, illus. initial. 19 x 15cm.
4°: A-B⁴.
Van der Linde 124.
No. 14 in vol. lettered Bekker II.
(Continued on next card)

Witchcraft
BF
1410
B42
Z69
no.22

Bekker, Balthasar, 1634-1698.
De betoverde weereld.
Dialogue ofte zamen-spraek, tusschen een theologant, advocaat, militair en koopman, over den tegenwoordigen staat van land en kerke. Beschreven door I.S. [n.p., 1693?].
15 p. 21cm.
Signatures: 4°: A-B⁴.
Not in Van der Linde.
No t.p.; half-title only.

1. Jurisdiction. 2. Bekker, Balthasar, 1634-1698. De betoverde weereld.

Witchcraft
BF
1410
B42
Z56
v.3
no.23

Bekker, Balthasar, 1634-1698.
De betoverde weereld.
Eenige originele brieven geschreven aan Do. Balthasar Bekker, over sijn boek De betoverde wereld. Door Do. Jacobus Koelman. En andere bekende, en onbekende persoonen. Amsterdam, By D. van den Dalen, boekverkooper, 1692.
1 p. l., 8 p. title and end page vignettes. 19 x 15cm.
4°: π1, ⁴.
Four letters: one from Koelman, one from Pieter Hessels, and two signed N. N. (but
(Continued on next card)

Witchcraft
BF
1410
B42
Z56
v.3
no.23

Bekker, Balthasar, 1634-1698.
De betoverde weereld.
Eenige originele brieven geschreven aan Do. Balthasar Bekker ... 1692. (Card 2)

same person.)
Variant of van der Linde 123: lacks second numbering (sign. A-C)
No. 23 in vol. lettered Bekker III.
1. Bekker, Balthasar, 1634-1698. De betoverde weereld. I. Koelman, Jacobus, b. 1632.

Witchcraft
BF
1410
B42
Z56
v.2
no.3

Bekker, Balthasar, 1634-1698.
De betoverde weereld.
Eenvoudig aanmerkinge, over 't geene in de saak van Do. B. Bekker en sijn boek is gepasseert, vergeleeken met de handelingen der roomsche geestelijkheyd hier in overeenkomende: dat men moet gelooven wat de kerk gelooft, en den ketters geen woord houden. Amsterdam, 1692.
8 p. title vignette, illus. initial. 19 x 15cm.
4°: A⁴.
Van der Linde 60.
No. 3 in vol. lettered Bekker II.
(Continued on next card)

MSS
Bd.
WITCHCRAFT
BF
E61

Bekker, Balthasar, 1634-1698.
De betoverde weereld.
Der entlarvte Teuffel oder denkwürdige Geschichte von vielen warhaftig Besessenen, welche dieses Feindes Grausamkeit heftig erfahren, entlich aber durch den mächtigen Finger Gottes wieder erlediget worden. Zu mehrer Bekräftigung der von Doct. Beckern, in seiner verzauberten Welt, zweiffelhaft gemachten Kögischen Geschichte ... Zusammen getragen von M. J. J. L. Leipzig, Johann Melchior Liebe, 1697 [ca. 1900]
(Continued on next card)

MSS
Bd.
WITCHCRAFT
BF
E61

Bekker, Balthasar, 1634-1698.
De betoverde weereld.
Der entlarvte Teuffel ... 1697 [ca. 1900] (Card 2)

77 p. 19cm.
Carnap's manuscript copy.
"Originaldruck in der Königl. öff. Bibliothek zu Dresden, 98 pag. Seiten in 8°."
"Diese Schrift bildet gewissermassen die Fortsetzung zu: 'Das geängstigte Köge oder Eine warhaffte und denkwürdige Historie, von einer entsetzlichen Versuchung des leidigen Satans zu Köge in
(Continued on next card)

MSS
Bd.
WITCHCRAFT
BF
E61

Bekker, Balthasar, 1634-1698.
De betoverde weereld.
Der entlarvte Teuffel ... 1697 [ca. 1900] (Card 3)

Seeland" wo in deutscher Sprache durch denselben Verfasser ... i. J. 1695 herausgegeben. Hierrus erklärt es sich, dass diese Schrift mit " die dritte Zugabe" anfängt, da "das geängstigte Köge mit der zweiten Zugabe abschliesst."
Marginal numerals and signatures indicate paginations ans signatures of the original.
(Continued on next card)

MSS
Bd.
WITCHCRAFT
BF
E61

Bekker, Balthasar, 1634-1698.
De betoverde weereld.
Der entlarvte Teuffel ... 1697 [ca. 1900] (Card 4)

Printed copy not in Van der Linde.

1. Demoniac possession. 2. Devil. 3. Bekker, Balthasar, 1634-1698. De betoverde weereld. I. Das geängstigte Köge. II. M. J. J. L. III. L., M. J. J.

Witchcraft
BF
1520
F17

Bekker, Balthasar, 1634-1698.
De betoverde weereld.
Falck, Nathanael, 1663-1693. Nathanaelis Falcken ... Dissertationes quatuor, De daemonologia recentiorum autorum falsa, Anno 1692. Wittebergae habitae, nunc verò praefixis literis Schomerianis ibidem recusae. [Wittebergae] Typis Martini Schultzii, 1694.
92 p. illus. initials. 20 x 16cm.
4°: A², B-M⁴, N².
Contents.--De falsa recentiorum autorum daemonologia ... respondente Joh.
(Continued on next card)

Witchcraft
BF
1520
F17

Bekker, Balthasar, 1634-1698.
De betoverde weereld.
Falck, Nathanael, 1663-1693. Nathanaelis Falcken ... Dissertationes quatuor ... 1694. (Card 2)

Contents--Continued.
Isaaco Trempenau.--Dissertatio II. Ortum daemonologiae falsae & progressum historicè declarans, respondente Johanne Furmann.--Dissertatio III. De daemonologia Hobbesii & Spinozae, respondente Jac. Friderico Hollero.--Dissertatio IV. De daemonolo-
(Continued on next card)

46

CATALOGUE OF THE CORNELL WITCHCRAFT COLLECTION

Bekker, Balthasar, 1634-1698.
    De betoverde weereld.
Falck, Nathanael, 1663-1693. Nathanaelis
    Falcken ... Dissertationes quatuor ...
    1694.   (Card 3)

gia Bekkeri & aliorum, respondente Georg.
Abrahamo Wolf.
    1. Demonology. 2. Hobbes, Thomas,
1588-1679. Elementa philosophica de cive.
3. Spinoza, Benedictus de, 1632-1677.
Tractatus theologico-politicus. 4. Bekker, Balthasar, 1634-1698. De betoverde weereld. I. Title: De daemonologia recentiorum autorum falsa.

Bekker, Balthasar, 1634-1698.
    De betoverde weereld.
De Geharpoende muys. Of staatkundige consideratien, over zeekere arabische vertaalinge, uyt een turkx leeraar Hamets Sidach Effendi. Raakende het gewoel, over Do. Balthasar Bekkers Betooverde weereld. Beneffens Minerva, en Mercurius; aan de betooverde schriftgeleerden. [Amsterdam?]
1691.
    12 p. title vignette. 19 x 15cm.
    4°: A⁴, B².
Published also in Verscheyde gedichten,

    (Continued on next card)

Bekker, Balthasar, 1634-1698.
    De betoverde weereld.
De Geharpoende muys. 1691.   (Card 2)

so voor, als tegen het boek, genaamt: De
betoverde weereld.
    No. 12 in vol. lettered Bekker II.

    1. Vertaeling uit seker arabisch schryver. 2. Bekker, Balthasar, 1634-1698. De Betoverde weereld. I. Minerva met Mercurius. Aan de betooverde schrift-geleerden.

Bekker, Balthasar, 1634-1698.
    De betoverde weereld.
Groenewegen, Hendrik.
    Pneumatica; ofte, Leere van de geesten,
zijnde denkende en redelike wesens ... uytgegeven by gelegentheyd van 't boek De betooverde wereld, geschreven door Balthazar Bekker ..., Enchuysen, H. van Straalen,
1692.
    88, 126, 56 p. 20cm.

    1. Ghosts. 2. Bekker, Balthasar, 1634-1698. De betoverde weereld. I. Title. II. Title: Leere van de geesten.

Bekker, Balthasar, 1634-1698.
    De betoverde weereld.
Haak, Arent, ed.
    Liefdelooze achterhoudinge van Do. Everhardus van der Hooght predikant tot Nieuwendam. Gebleeken in zijn schriftelyke onderhandelinge met Arent Haak. Amsterdam, By
D. van den Dalen, boekverkooper, 1693.
    32 p. title and end page vignettes, illus.
initial. 20 x 15cm.
    4°: A-D⁴.
    Introduction by Haak: p. 3-9. The rest
consists of letters exchanged by van
der Hooght and Haak (in black letter),

    (Continued on next card)

Bekker, Balthasar, 1634-1698.
    De betoverde weereld.
Haak, Arent, ed. Liefdelooze achterhoudinge
    van Do. Everhardus van der Hooght ... 1693.
                                       (Card 2)
on Balthasar Bekker's De betoverde weereld.
    Van der Linde 118.
    No. 29 in vol. lettered Bekker III.

    1. Bekker, Balthasar, 1634-1698. De betoverde weereld. I. Hooght, Everard van der,
d. 1716. II. Title.

Witchcraft
BF
1410
B42
Z56
v.3
no.22

Bekker, Balthasar, 1634-1698.
    De betoverde weereld.
[Hamer, Petrus] 1646-1716.
    Den swadder, die E. W. op Cartesianen en
Coccejanen geworpen heeft, in sijn twee deelen van Aardige duivelarye zuiver af-gevaagt,
met een het geschil dat Dr. Bekker ongegrond
opwerpt, als of daimoon, &c. niet wel duivel
overgezet wierd, kortelijk voldongen, en in
staat van wijzen gebracht, door Iiratiel Leetsosoneus. Amsterdam, By G. Borstius, boekverkooper, 1692.
    2 p. l., 42 p. title and other vignettes,
illus. initia 1s. 20 x 15cm.

    (Continued on next card)

Witchcraft
BF
1410
B42
Z56
v.3
no.22

Bekker, Balthesar, 1634-1698.
    De betoverde weereld.
[Hamer, Petrus] 1646-1716. Den swadder, die
    E. W. op Cartesianen en Coccejanen geworpen
    heeft ... 1692.   (Card 2)

    4°: *², A-E⁴, F1.
    Van der Linde 172.
    No. 22 in vol. lettered Bekker III.
    1. Walten, Ericus, 1663-1697. Aardige
duyvelary. 2. Bekker, Balthasar, 1634-1698.
De betoverde weereld. I. Title.

8

Witchcraft
BF
1410
B42
Z82
no.2

Bekker, Balthasar, 1634-1698.
    De betoverde weereld.
Hamer, Petrus, 1646-1716.
    Voorlooper tot de volstrekte wederlegginge
van het gene de heeren, Orchard, Daillon en
Bekker hebben aen het licht gebragt; aengaende de werken, en macht der geesten: en
met name der duivelen. Door Petrus Hamer,
dienaer Jesus Christi in Numansdorp. Uitgegeven na kerken-ordre. Met belofte refutatoir van zekeren Brief aen een regent van
Amsteldam. Dato 18 Maij 1692. Dordrecht,
By C. Wilgaarts, boekverkooper, 1692.
    4 p. l., 40 p. title vignette, illus.

    (Continued on next card)

8

Witchcraft
BF
1410
B42
Z82
no.2

Bekker, Balthasar, 1634-1698.
    De betoverde weereld.
Hamer, Petrus, 1646-1716. Voorlooper tot
    de volstrekte wederleggingevan... Orchard,
    Daillon en Bekker ... 1692.   (Card 2)
    initials. 20 x 15cm.
    4°: *⁴, A-E⁴.
    Van der Linde 95.
    No. 2 in vol. lettered Over Bekkers Betoverde wereld. 1692.
    1. Orchard, N   , supposed author.
The doctrine of   devils. 2. Daillon,
Benjamin de.   Examen de l'opression

    (Continued on next card)

8

Witchcraft
BF
1410
B42
Z85
no.3

Bekker, Balthasar, 1634-1698.
    De betoverde weereld.
[Holy, Nikolaas Muys van] 1654-
    Overweging van het hooftpoint in Do.
Bekkers boek, genaamt De betoverde weereld,
te weten, of de duyvel op een mensch
werken kan. [Amsterdam, By P. Rotterdam,
boekverkooper, 1692]
    8 p. 19 x 16cm.
    4°: A⁴.
    Caption title.
    Signed: Nicolaes Muys van Holy.
    No. 3 in vol. lettered Stukken betrekkelijk Bekker.

    (Continued on next card)

8

Witchcraft
BF
1410
B42
Z69
no.2

Bekker, Balthasar, 1634-1698.
    De betoverde weereld.
[Hooght, Everard van der] d. 1716.
    Aanmerkingen van הגבר Φιλαληθης
Haggébher Philaleethees, op de invoegselen
van Do. Balthasar Bekker, voor zoo veel de
zelve betreffen de stellingen, die reeds in
sijne brieven tot noch toe zyn verhandelt,
zynde een aanhangsel van den vyfden brief.
Amsterdam, G. Borstius, 1691.
    124-134 p. 21cm.

    Signatures: 4°: A⁴, B².

NIC   (Continued on next card)

Witchcraft
BF
1410
B42
Z69
no.2

Bekker, Balthasar, 1634-1698.
    De betoverde weereld.
[Hooght, Everard van der], d. 1716. Aanmerkingen van ... Haggébher Philaleethees
    ... 1691.   (Card 2)

    Black letter.
    Van der Linde 102.
    No. 2 in a Collection of tracts against
Balthasar Bekker and his Betoverde weereld.

    1. Bekker, Balthasar, 1634-1698. [De betoverde weereld. 2. Jesus Christ
--Tempta   tion. 3. Bible. O.T.
Job. I.   Title.

NIC

Witchcraft
BF
1410
B42
Z69
no.3

Bekker, Balthasar, 1634-1698.
    De betoverde weereld.
[Hooght, Everard van der], d. 1716.
    Eerste briev van הגבר Φιλαληθης
Haggébher Philaleethees, geschreeven aan
zynen vriend N. N. over den persoon en het
boek van Do. Balthasar Bekker. In opzicht
van de gudheyd, ende het gewichte zyner
dwaling; nevens sijne onkunde in de godtgeleertheyd ende in de gronden van de Hebreeusche tale; demonstratiiv beweesen, uyt zyne
verklaring van Gen. 18. ende Job 1. en 2.
Amsterdam,   G. Borstius, 1691.
    20 p.   21cm.

NIC   (Continued on next card)

Witchcraft
BF
1410
B42
Z69
no.3

Bekker, Balthasar, 1634-1698.
    De betoverde weereld.
[Hooght, Everard van der], d. 1716. Eerste
    briev van ... Haggébher Philaleethees...
    1691.   (Card 2)

    Signatures: 4°: A-B⁴, C¹.
    Black letter.
    N. N. is thought to be Jacobus Schuts.
    Van der Linde 97.
    No. 3 in a Collection of tracts against
Balthasar Bekker and his Betoverde weereld.

NIC   (Continued on next card)

Witchcraft
BF
1410
B42
Z56
v.3
no.24

Bekker, Balthasar, 1634-1698.
    De betoverde weereld.
[Hooght, Everard van der], d. 1716.
    Tweede brief van הגבר [Haggébher]
ΦΙΛΑΛΗΘΗΣ [philaleethees], geschreeven
aan zynen vriend N. N. over de ordentelyke
kerkelyke proceduuren, gehouden tegen den
persoon ende het boek van Do. Balthasar
Bekker, by zyn E. geintituleert De betoverde
wereld. Met eenige ecclesiastique, theologische, philosophische ende philologische
aanmerkingen over de zelve. Amsterdam, By
G. Borstius, boekverkoper, 1691.
    [19]-40 p.   title vignette, illus.
initial. 19 x 15cm.

8   (Continued on next card)

Witchcraft
BF
1410
B42
Z56
v.3
no.24

Bekker, Balthasar, 1634-1698.
    De betoverde weereld.
[Hooght, Everard van der], d. 1716. Tweede
    brief ... aan zynen vriend N. N. ... 1691.
                                       (Card 2)
    4°: π1, A-B⁴, C².
    Black letter.
    The friend N. N. is Jacobus Schuts?
    Van der Linde 98.
    No. 24 in vol. lettered Bekker III.
    1. Bekker, Balthasar, 1634-1698. 2.
Bekker, Balthasar, 1634-1698. De betoverde
weereld. 3.   Nederlandse Hervormde
Kerk. I. Sc   huts, Jacobus. II.
Title.

8

Witchcraft
BF
1410
B42
Z69
no.6

Bekker, Balthasar, 1634-1698.
    De betoverde weereld.
[Hooght, Everard van der], d. 1716.
    Vierde briev van הגבר Φιλαληθης
Haggébher Philaleethees, geschreeven aan
zynen vriend N. N. over het weesen, denken,
willen, vermoogen, ende de plaats der engelen
in het gemeen, ende der quade geesten, in
het byzonder. Item, van des menschen ziele,
en harewerking, het zy afgesondert, ofte ook
vereenigt met her lichaam; ende hoe verre de
quade geesten op de selve konnen werken. Met
een onder   soek of D. Bekker wel kan
seggen, dat

NIC   (Continued on next card)

47

CATALOGUE OF THE CORNELL WITCHCRAFT COLLECTION

Witchcraft
BF
1410
B42
Z69
no.6

Bekker, Balthasar, 1634-1698.
   De betoverde weereld.
    [Hooght, Everard van der] d. 1716. Vierde briev van ... Haggebher Philaleethees ... (Card 2)
    de authoriteyt van Gods woord, ende de eere des alderhoogsten. Amsterdam, G. Borstius, 1691.
    59-96 p. 21cm.
    Signatures: 4°: ¶1, A-C⁴, D².
    Black letter.
    Van der Linde 100.

NIC   No. 6 in a Collection of tracts
(Continued on next card)

Witchcraft
BF
1410
B42
Z69
no.6

Bekker, Balthasar, 1634-1698.
   De betoverde weereld.
    [Hooght, Everard van der] d. 1716. Vierde briev van ... Haggebher Philaleethees ... 1691. (Card 3)
    against Balthasar Bekker and his Betoverde weereld.
    N. N. is thought to be Jacobus Schuts.

    1. God--Omnipotence. 2. Schaak, Petrus, fl. 1691. 3. Bekker, Balthasar, 1634-1698. De betoverde weereld.
NIC   I. Title. II. Schuts, Jacobus.

Witchcraft
BF
1410
B42
Z69
no.7

Bekker, Balthasar, 1634-1698.
   De betoverde weereld.
    [Hooght, Everard van der] d. 1716. Vyfde briev van הנבר Φιλαλήθης Haggebher Philaleethees, geschreeven aan zynen vriend N. N. over de versoekinge Christi in de woestyne, tot wederlegging van het 18 (ofte 20) capp. in het boek van D. Balthasar Bekker, genaamt de Betoverde wereld. Item, over de classicale proceduuren, &c. Amsterdam, G. Borstius, 1691.
    99-123 p. 21cm.
    Signatures: 4°: ¶1, A-C⁴, D¹.
    Black letter.
NIC   (Continued on next card)

Witchcraft
BF
1410
B42
Z69
no.7

Bekker, Balthasar, 1634-1698.
   De betoverde weereld.
    [Hooght, Everard van der] d. 1716. Vyfde briev van ... Haggebher Philaleethees ... 1691. (Card 2)
    Van der Linde 101.
    No. 7 in a Collection of tracts against Balthasar Bekker and his Betoverde weereld.
    The friend N. N. is thought to be Jacobus Schuts.

NIC   (Continued on next card)

Witchcraft
BF
1410
B42
Z56
v.2
no.23

Bekker, Balthasar, 1634-1698.
   De betoverde weereld.
    Hooght, Everard van der, d. 1716. Zeedig ondersoek van het boek, door den autheur, Balthasar Bekker, genaamt de Betoverde weereld. In het welke dat tweede boek, van vooren tot achteren, door alle de capittelen en paragraaphen, ordentelijk werd wederlegt. Door Everardus van der Hooght ... Welke achter dit werk gevoegt heeft; drie-der-ley registers; te weeten I. Van Bekkers valsche citatien. II. Een van de texten, ende III. Een van de verhandelde saaken, de welke in dit boek of, in de seven brieven, zijn verhandelt, met des
    (Continued on next card)

Witchcraft
BF
1410
B42
Z56
v.2
no.23

Bekker, Balthasar, 1634-1698.
   De betoverde weereld.
    Hooght, Everard van der, d. 1716. Zeedig ondersoek van ... de Betoverde weereld. (Card 2)
    autheurs antwoort op de brieven van B. Bekker. t'Amsterdam, By Dirk Boeteman [1692]
    4 p. l., 229, [1] p. [p. 231-232 blank] title and other vignettes, illus. initials. 19 x 15cm.
    4°: *⁴, A-2P⁴.
    Black letter.
    Autograph on back of t. p.: Ev. van der Hooght.
    (Continued on next card)

Witchcraft
BF
1410
B42
Z56
v.2
no.23

Bekker, Balthasar, 1634-1698.
   De betoverde weereld.
    Hooght, Everard van der, d. 1716. Zeedig ondersoek van ... de Betoverde weereld. (Card 3)
    Van der Linde 114.
    No. 23 in vol. lettered Bekker II.

Witchcraft
BF
1410
B42
Z69
no.8

Bekker, Balthasar, 1634-1698.
   De betoverde weereld.
    Een klaare uytlegginge, over de versoekinge des Heere Jesu Christi in de woestyne. In antwoord op de vijfde brief van Philaleethees. t'Amsterdam, Voor den autheur gedrukt, en zijn volt te bekomen by P. Rotterdam [169-?]
    24 p. 21cm.
    Signatures: 4°, a², A-C⁴.
    Black letter.
    Van der Linde 110.
    No. 8 in a Collection of tracts against Balthasar Bekker and his Betoverde weereld.
NIC   (Continued on next card)

Witchcraft
BF
1410
B42
Z76
1692

Bekker, Balthasar, 1634-1698.
   De betoverde weereld.
    Leydekker, Melchior, 1642-1721. Historische en theologische Redeneringe, over het onlangs uitgegeve Boek van ... Balthasar Bekker, strekkende tot bevestinge der Waarheit en Authoriteit van de H. Schriftuur. Uit het Latijn overgebragt, engeschikt na het begrip van den Nederduitschen Leser. Waar achter gevoegt is een Brief van de Hr. D'Aillon, wegens sijn gevoelen van de Eenheit des Duyvels, geschreven uit London, den 16 Decemb.
NIC   (Continued on next card)

Witchcraft
BF
1410
B42
Z76
1692

Bekker, Balthasar, 1634-1698.
   De betoverde weereld.
    Leydekker, Melchior, 1642-1721. Historische en theologische Redeneringe ... (Card 2)
    1691. Utregt, By de Weduwe van W. Clerck, 1692.
    64, 8 p. 20cm.
    Van der Linde 127.

NIC   (Continued on next card)

Witchcraft
BF
1410
B42
Z69
no.27, 28

Bekker, Balthasar, 1634-1698.
   De betoverde weereld.
    Leydekker, Melchior, 1642-1721. Historische en theologische Redeneringe, over het onlangs uitgegeve Boek van ... Balthasar Bekker, strekkende tot bevestinge der Waarheit en Authoriteit van de H. Schriftuur. Uit het Latijn overgebragt, engeschikt na het begrip van den Nederduitschen Leser. Waar achter gevoegt is een Brief van de Hr. D'Aillon, wegens sijn gevoelen van de Eenheit des Duyvels, geschreven uit London, den 16 Decemb.
NIC   (Continued on next card)

Witchcraft
BF
1410
B42
Z69
no.27, 28

Bekker, Balthasar, 1634-1698.
   De betoverde weereld.
    Leydekker, Melchior, 1642-1721. Historische en theologische Redeneringe ... (Card 2)
    1691. Utregt, By de Weduwe van W. Clerck, 1692.
    64, 8 p. 21cm.
    Van der Linde 127, 75.
    No. 28 has half-title only.
    No. 27, 28 in a Collection of tracts against Balthasar Bekker and his Betoverde weereld.
NIC   (Continued on next card)

WITCHCRAFT
BF
1583
A2
M39

Bekker, Balthasar, 1634-1698.
   De betoverde weereld.
    Masecovius, Thomas.
    Warhaffte und umbständliche Beschreibung der wunderbahren Geschichte, so sich mit einer angefochtenen Jungfer in dem 1683ten und folgenden Jahren zu Königsberg in Preussen... Nebst einer Vorrede D. Bernhard von Sanden...gerichtet wider die Bezauberte Welt D. Balthasar Beckers. Königsb., In Verlegung Heinrich Boye, Druckts Johann Zacharias Etoile, 1695.
    363 p. 17cm.
    1. Witchcraft. 2. Witchcraft--Germany. 3. Bekker, Balthasar, 1634-1698. De betoverde weereld. I. Sanden, Bernhard von.
NIC

Witchcraft
BF
1410
B42
Z86
no.6

Bekker, Balthasar, 1634-1698.
   De betoverde weereld.
    Missive van M. D. E. P. aan een vrind, over de zaak van Do. B: Bekker, en het boek van de Heer Professor M. Leydekker. Rotterdam, By J. Gysen, 1692.
    8 p. l. title vignette, illus. initial.
    19 x 15cm.
    4°: A-B⁴.
    Incomplete: second gathering wanting.
    Van der Linde 129.
    No. 6 in vol. lettered Tractaten voor en tegen B. Bekker.
    (Continued on next card)

Witchcraft
BF
1410
B42
Z86
no.5

Bekker, Balthasar, 1634-1698.
   De betoverde weereld.
    Molinaeus, Johannes, d. 1702.
    De betoverde werelt van D. Balthazar Bekker handelende van den aert en 't vermogen, van 't bewind en bedrijf der goede en quade engelen, onderzogt en wederleydt: in twee predikaetien; d' eerste van 't gebruik en misbruyk der philosophie; de tweede van den aert en 't bedrijf der goede engelen. En laetstelik in een verhandelige van de booze geesten, of van den Duyvel en zijne engelen. Rotterdam, By B. Bos, boekverkooper, 1692.
8   (Continued on next card)

Witchcraft
BF
1410
B42
Z86
no.5

Bekker, Balthasar, 1634-1698.
   De betoverde weereld.
    Molinaeus, Johannes, d. 1702. De betoverde werelt van D. Balthazar Bekker ... 1692. (Card 2)
    6 p. l., 104 p. title vignette, illus. initials. 19 x 15cm.
    4°: *⁴, 2*², A-N⁴.
    Black letter (except for introduction)
    Variant of van der Linde 131: 2*², N⁴ wanting in van der Linde copy.
    No. 5 in vol. lettered Tractaten voor en tegen B. Bekker.
8   (Continued on next card)

Witchcraft
BF
1410
B42
Z56
v.3
no.13

Bekker, Balthasar, 1634-1698.
   De betoverde weereld.
    Nederlandse Hervormde Kerk.
    Brieven van eenige kerkenraden buyten de Provintie van Holland, namentlijk van 't Eerw. Classis van Walcheren, van de Eerwaerdige Kerkenraden van Middelburg, Utrecht, Leeuwaarden, Groningen, aen de Eerwaerdige Kerkenraad van Rotterdam, tot antwoord op haren Circulaire brief, rakende de sake van Dr. B. Bekker. Rotterdam, By R. van Doesburg, boekverkooper, 1692.
    16 p. title vignette, illus. initials. 19 x 15cm.
8   (Continued on next card)

Witchcraft
BF
1410
B42
Z56
v.3
no.13

Bekker, Balthasar, 1634-1698.
   De betoverde weereld.
    Nederlandse Hervormde Kerk. Brieven van eenige kerkenraden ... 1692. (Card 2)
    4°: A-B⁴.
    Van der Linde 36.
    No. 13 in vol. lettered Bekker III.
    1. Bekker, Balthasar, 1634-1698. De betoverde weereld. 2. Nederlandse Hervormde Kerk. Kerkenraden. Rotterdam. Circulair brief ... wegens de saake van Dr. Balthasar Bekker. I. Nederlandse Hervormde Kerk. Kerkenraden. Rotterdam. II. Title
8

CATALOGUE OF THE CORNELL WITCHCRAFT COLLECTION

Bekker, Balthasar, 1634-1698.
   De betoverde weereld.

Witchcraft
BF
1410
B42
Z56
v.3
no.16

Nederlandse Hervormde Kerk. Kerkenraden. Rotterdam.
   Circulaire brief van de Eerwaarde Kerkenraad van Rotterdam, geschreven aan de respective kerken-raden van Zuyd ende Noord Holland; misgaders aan de voornaamste steden van de verdere geünieerde provincien, wegens de saake van D Balthasar Bekker, en syn boek De betooverde weereld. [Rotterdam? 1692]
   [4] p. 20 x 15cm.
   4°: π⁴
   Caption title.

(Continued on next card)

Bekker, Balthasar, 1634-1698.
   De betoverde weereld.

Witchcraft
F
410
42
56
.3
no.16

Nederlandse Hervormde Kerk. Kerkenraden. Rotterdam. Circulaire brief ... [1692] (Card 2)

   Van der Linde 33.
   No. 16 in vol. lettered Bekker III.

   1. Bekker, Balthasar, 1634-1698. De betoverde weereld. I. Nederlandse Hervormde Kerk. Kerkenraden. II. Title.

Bekker, Balthasar, 1634-1698.
   De betoverde weereld.

Witchcraft
BF
1410
B42
1691a
no.3

Nederlandse Hervormde Kerk. Synode van Noordholland, Edam, 1691.
   Acten ofte handelingen van de Noord-Hollandsche Synodus, gehouden binnen Edam en Alcmaar, anno 1691. en 1692. Rakende Dr. Balthazar Bekker, en sijn boek De betoverde wereld, met alle de documenten daar toe behoorende, waar onder ook eenige, die in het synodale acten-boek niet en staan uyt-gedrukt; met een voor-reden, strekkende tot weder-legging van Dr. Bekkers Remonstrantie en verdere exceptien tegen de competentie van de Synodus. Enchuysen, Gedrukt by J. D. Kuyper, 1692. (Continued on next card)

8

Bekker, Balthasar, 1634-1698.
   De betoverde weereld.

Witchcraft
F
410
42
1691a
no.3

Nederlandse Hervormde Kerk. Synode van Noordholland, Edam, 1691. Acten ofte handelingen van de Noord-Hollandsche Synodus, gehouden binnen Edam en Alcmaar ... 1692. (Card 2)

   30 p. 1., 102 p. title and end page vignettes., illus. initials. 20 x 16cm.
   4°: *-7*⁴, 8*², A-N⁴(-N4)
   Remonstrantie, by Bekker: p. 73-83.
   Van der Linde 51.
   No. 3 in vol. lettered B. Bekker. Betoverde weereld.
(Continued on next card)

Bekker, Balthasar, 1634-1698.
   De betoverde weereld.

Witchcraft
BF
1410
B42
Z56
v.2
no.6

Nodige aanmerkinge omtrent eenige woorden gesprooken van D. Johannes Visscherus, in een catechisatie, over den 34 Sondag des Catechismus. Dog bysonderlijk over de 94 vrage, enz. voorgevallen op Sondag den 24 Augusty 1692. Door T. S. Amsterdam, By D. vanden Dalen, boekverkoper, 1692.
   7 p. [p. 8 blank] title vignette. 19 x 15cm.
   4°: A⁴.

(Continued on next card)

8

Bekker, Balthasar, 1634-1698.
   De betoverde weereld.

Witchcraft
BF
1410
B42
Z56
v.2
no.6

Nodige aanmerkinge omtrent eenige woorden gesprooken van D. Johannes Visscherus ... 1692. (Card 2)

   Black letter.
   Response to Visscher's attack on Balthasar Bekker.
   No. 6 in vol. lettered Bekker II.
   1. Visscher, Johannes, 1617?-1694. 2. Bekker, Balthasar, 1634-1698. De betoverde weereld. I. T. S. II. S., T.

8

Bekker, Balthasar, 1634-1698.
   De betoverde weereld.

Witchcraft
BF
1410
B42
Z56
v.2
no.22

Noomtjins, Zalomon.
   Spiegel voor den verwarden, en warzoekende Haggebher Philaleethees. Waar in, uit zyne 6 brieven, enz. getoond word, syne onkunde, en verwarring, zoo in taal, als in zaaken. Ofte een briev van Zalomon Noomtjins, tot Amsteldam. Geschreven aan zynen vriend C. S. S. tot Buiksloot. Inhoudende (neevens andere zaaken) voornaamelijk, eenige aanmerkingen, over den perzoon, en de 6 brieven, enz. van Haggebher Philaleethees. Als meede over de briev, en perzoon van Everardus
(Continued on next card)

Bekker, Balthasar, 1634-1698.
   De betoverde weereld.

Witchcraft
BF
1410
B42
Z56
v.2
no.22

Noomtjins, Zalomon. Spiegel voor den verwarden, en warzoekende Haggebher Philaleethees. 1692. (Card 2)

van der Hooght, en daar by ook over zyne Aanmerkingen, over de ordre van een welgestelde predikatie. Mitsgaders d'ontdekking, der lasteringen van Brink. Amsterdam, By D. van den Dalen. boekverkooper, 1692.
   33, [1] p. title and other vignettes. 19 x 15cm.

(Continued on next card)

Bekker, Balthasar, 1634-1698.
   De betoverde weereld.

Witchcraft
BF
1410
B42
Z56
v.2
no.22

Noomtjins, Zalomon. Spiegel voor den verwarden, en warzoekende Haggebher Philaleethees. 1692. (Card 3)

   4°: A-D⁴, E1.
   Black letter (except for introduction)
   Attacks critics of Balthasar Bekker's De betoverde weereld.
   G. L. Burr suggests Noomtjins may be a pseudonymn for Bekker.
   Haggebher is a pseudonym of E. van der Hooght.

(Continued on next card)

8

Bekker, Balthasar, 1634-1698.
   De betoverde weereld.

Witchcraft
BF
1410
B42
Z56
v.2
no.22

Noomtjins, Zalomon. Spiegel voor den verwarden, en warzoekende Haggebher Philaleethees. 1692. (Card 4)

   Van der Linde 111.
   No. 22 in vol. lettered Bekker II.
   1. Hooght, Everard van der, d. 1716. 2. Brink, Hendrik, 1645-1723. De godslasteringen van den amsterdamschen predikant Bekker. 3. Bekker, Balthasar, 1634-1698. De betoverde weereld. I. Title. II. Bekker, Balthasar, 1634-1698, supposed author.

8

Bekker, Balthasar, 1634-1698.
   De betoverde weereld.

Witchcraft
BF
1410
B42
Z56
v.2
no.18

Overdenkinge op het boek Den Satan in zijn weesen, aard-bedryf, en guigelspel, &c. beschreven door Simon de Vries. Amsterdam, By D. van den Dalen, boekverkooper, 1691.
   15 p. [p. 16 blank] title vignette, illus. initial. 19 x 15cm.
   4°: A-B⁴.
   Black letter (except for introduction)
   Plea for tolerance in the controversy over Balthasar Bekker's De betoverde weereld.

(Continued on next card)

8

Bekker, Balthasar, 1634-1698.
   De betoverde weereld.

Witchcraft
BF
1410
B42
Z56
v.2
no.18

Overdenkinge op het boek Den Satan in zijn weesen ... 1691. (Card 2)

   Van der Linde 154.
   No. 18 in vol. lettered Bekker II.
   1. Vries, Simon de, 1630- . De Satan in syn wesen, aart, bedryf en guychelspel. 2. Bekker, Balthasar, 1634-1698. De betoverde weereld.

Bekker, Balthasar, 1634-1698.
   De betoverde weereld.

Witchcraft
BF
1410
B42
Z69
no.17,
18

Den predikant D. Balthasar Becker, seediglyk ondersogt so in zyn persoon als Schriften, ofhy die derst voorgeven, buyten hem alleen, de gantsche werelt betovert te zyn, selfs hier af wel vry is, ende dat daar en boven op hem niet soude werken, de geest van hovaardye en dwalinge tot ergernisse en van de kleine, en van de arme, en van de verslagene van geest, en die beeven voor Godts woort. By een missive den 19 January 1692, door H.v.G. van Amsterdam geschreven aan

NIC
(Continued on next card)

Bekker, Balthasar, 1634-1698.
   De betoverde weereld.

Witchcraft
BF
1410
B42
Z69
no.17,
18

Den predikant D. Balthasar Becker ... (Card 2)

D. T. S. de Jonge tot Uytrecht. Met zyn Andtwoord provisioneel tot nader berigt daar op gevolgt, den 4. February desselven jaars. Uytregt, Gedrukt by W. Jansz, 1692.
   32, 36 p. 21cm.

   Signatures: 4°: A-D⁴. 4°: A-D⁴, E2.
   The Provisioneel Antwoord has special half-title and separate

NIC
(Continued on next card)

Bekker, Balthasar, 1634-1698.
   De betoverde weereld.

Witchcraft
BF
1410
B42
Z69
no.17,
18

Den predikant D. Balthasar Becker ... 1692. (Card 3)

paging.
   Van der Linde 63, 61.
   "Extracten van ... De betoverde werelt, uytgetrokken en t'samengestelt door N. N.": p. 17-28 of the Provisioneel Antwoord; "Extract van 'tgepasseerde des Synodi tot Edam, 10. Aug. 1691. rakende D. Balthasar Bekker ...": p. 28-29; "Articulen voor te stellen aan Do. B. Bekker" signed Leonardus

NIC
(Continued on next card)

Bekker, Balthasar, 1634-1698.
   De betoverde weereld.

Witchcraft
BF
1410
B42
Z69
No.17,
18

Den predikant D. Balthasar Becker ... 1692. (Card 4)

Groenewegen: p. 29-31; "Eerste aanbieding van D. B. Bekker, op den 30. Aug. 1691": p. 31; "Articulen tot satisfactie aan de Eerw. Classis van Amsterdam, van Do. Balthasar Bekker ... wegens ... de Betoverde wereld ...": p. 32-36.
   Nos. 17 & 18 in a Collection of tracts against Balthasar Bekker and his Betoverde weereld.

NIC
(Continued on next card)

Bekker, Balthasar, 1634-1698.
   De betoverde weereld.

Witchcraft
BF
1445
D61
no.17

Romanus, Carl Friedrich.
   Schediasma polemicum expendens qvaestionem an dentur spectra magi et sagae; vulgo Ob wahrhafft Gespenster, Zauberer und Hexen seyn? Una cum recensione historica plurimarum hac de re opinionum auctore Carolo Friderico Romano. Lipsiae, Literis & sumpt. Andreae Martini Schedii, 1717.
   73 p. 21cm.
   First published 1703?
   No. 17 in vol. lettered Dissertationes de spectris. 1646-1753.

8
(Continued on next card)

Bekker, Balthasar, 1634-1698.
   De betoverde weereld.

Witchcraft
BF
1410
B42
Z69
no.16

[Schuts, Jacobus]
   De betoverde Bekker, ofte een overtuygent bewijs dat het boek vande Heer Bekker, genaemt de Betoverde weerelt, doorsaeyt is met de onredelijkste redenering, notoirste Onwaarheeden en andere schadelijke gevolgen; waar door de waare reeden verlogent, de waarheyt vervalst, en de deught ontsenuwt wert. De Saduceen seggen datter geen Opstanding en is, noch Engel, noch Geest, maer de Fariseen gelooven het beyde Act VIII: vers 23. In 's Gravenhage,

NIC
(Continued on next card)

CATALOGUE OF THE CORNELL WITCHCRAFT COLLECTION

Bekker, Balthasar, 1634-1698.
De betoverde weereld.

Witchcraft
BF
1410
B42
Z69
no.16

[Schuts, Jacobus] De betoverde Bekker ... (Card 2)
By B. Beek, 1691.
[4] p. 21cm.

Signatures: 4°: A3.
Consists of the printer's letter to the reader only; followed by text of his Seedige aanmerkinge over ... De Godslasteringe van ... Dr. Bekker, of which the t.p. and first 8 p. form no. 20 in this vol.

NIC   (Continued on next card)

Bekker, Balthasar, 1634-1698.
De betoverde weereld.

Witchcraft
BF
1410
B42
Z69
no.30

[Schuts, Jacobus] Tweede missive aen d'Heer Balthasar Bekker ... 1692. (Card 2)
D. Brink. Met den korten inhoud van de eerste Missive. D'Opdragt toont, dat Ericus Walten, in sijn Brief aan een Regent van Amsteldam, ydelijk voorgeest, dat het voor den Staat dezer Landen gevaarlijk is, de zaak van Dr. Bekker verder, in synoden, of andersins, te laten verhandelen of Deciderien. 's Gravenhage, By B. Beek en M. Uitwerf, 1692.
[24] 72 p.   21cm.
(Continued on next card)

Bekker, Balthasar, 1634-1698.
De betoverde weereld.

Witchcraft
BX
9479
B42
B11
no.6

[Silvius, J   ] Consideratien over het boek van de Heer Doctor Balthasar Bekker, genaamt De betoverde weereld, voorgestelt door J. S. Amsterdam, By G. Borstius, boekverkoper, 1691.
20 p. title vignette, illus. initials.
20 x 15cm.

4°: π1, A-B⁴, C1.
Black letter (except for introduction)
Ascribed to J. Silvius by Doorninck.
Variant of   van der Linde 149:

8   (Continued on next card)

Bekker, Balthasar, 1634-1698.
De betoverde weereld.

Witchcraft
BF
1410
B42
Z69
no.16

[Schuts, Jacobus] De betoverde Bekker ... 1691.   (Card 3)

No. 16 in a Collection of tracts against Balthasar Bekker and his Betoverde weereld.
Van der Linde 146.

1. Bekker, Balthasar, 1634-1698. De betoverde   weereld. I. Title.

NIC

Bekker, Balthasar, 1634-1698.
De betoverde weereld.

Witchcraft
BF
1410
B42
Z69
no.30

[Schuts, Jacobus] Tweede missive aen d'Heer Balthasar Bekker ... 1692.   (Card 3)

Signatures: 4°: †-3†⁴. A-I⁴, (Leaf I² is mis-signed as H²)
Van der Linde 148.

Bekker, Balthasar, 1634-1698.
De betoverde weereld.

Witchcraft
BX
9479
B42
B11
no.6

[Silvius, J   ] Consideratien over het boek van de Heer Doctor Balthasar Bekker ... 1691.   (Card 2)

only 20, instead of 22 p.
No. 6 in vol. lettered B. Bekkers sterf-bed en andere tractaten.

1. Bekker, Balthasar, 1634-1698. De betoverde weereld. I. Title. II. J. S. III. S., J.

Bekker, Balthasar, 1634-1698.
De betoverde weereld.

Witchcraft
BF
1410
B42
Z56
v.3
no.6

[Schuts, Jacobus] Missive, aen D. Balthazar Bekker, in 't korte ontdekkende de gronden van sijn mis-grepen, begaen in sijn drie tractaten De betoverde weereld, over den prophete Daniel, en van de cometen. Waer in N. Orchard, in sijn Leeringe der duivelen den grooten afval der Christenen, ende den spotterigen Philo-pater in sijn leven, ook hare voldoeninge konnen krygen. Tot Nederlands waerschouwinge en onderricht der Joden. Gravenhage, By B. Beek, konst- en boekverkoper, 1692.

8   (Continued on next card)

Bekker, Balthasar, 1634-1698.
De betoverde weereld.

Witchcraft
BX
9479
B42
S39

Schwager, Johann Moritz.
Beytrag zur Geschichte der Intoleranz; oder Leben, Meynungen und Schicksale des ehemaligen Doct. der Theologie und refor-mierten Predigers in Amsterdam Balthasar Bekkers, meist nach kirchlichen Urkunden. ... Mit einer Vorrede Hrn. Doct. Joh. Salomo Semlers von einer unter dessen Aufsicht nächstens herauskommenden verbesserten Auflage der bezauberten Welt. Leipzig, In der Weygandschen Buchhandlung, 1780.
10, LXXXXII. 190 p. 18 x 11cm.

8   (Continued on next card)

Bekker, Balthasar, 1634-1698.
De betoverde weereld.

Witchcraft
BF
1410
B42
Z56
v.2
no.16

Den verkeerden duyvel van den throon geschopt en den rechten weder hervoort gebragt, ver-handelende van engelen en duyvelen, hare macht ende werkinge, waar in besonderlyk getoont wort wat den duyvel is, schrift-matigh voorgestelt, waar in de swaarste stukken van die materie worden opgelost, noch noyt zoo voortgebracht. Door K. A. H. Amsterdam, By N. Holbeex, boekverkoper, 1692.
2 p. l., 36 p. title and end page vignettes, illus. initials. 19 x 15cm.

(Continued on next card)

Bekker, Balthasar, 1634-1698.
De betoverde weereld.

Witchcraft
BF
1410
B42
Z56
v.3
no.6

[Schuts, Jacobus] Missive, aen D. Baltha-zar Bekker ... 1692.   (Card 2)

10 p. l., 69 p. [p. 70-72 blank] title and other vignettes, illus. initials. 20 x 15cm.
4°: a-b⁴, c², A-I⁴.
Black letter.
Signed and dated at end: N. N. Den 22 November 1691.
Neither Orchard nor Philopater is mentioned in the   text.

8   (Continued on next card)

Bekker, Balthasar, 1634-1698.
De betoverde weereld.

Witchcraft
BX
9479
B42
S39

Schwager, Johann Moritz. Beytrag zur Geschichte der Intoleranz ... 1780. (Card 2)

8°: a-g⁸, A-M⁸.

Van der Linde 217.

1. Bekker, Balthasar, 1634-1698--Biog.
2. Bekker, Balthasar, 1634-1698. De be-toverde weereld. I. Semler, Johann Salomo, 1725-1791. II. Title.

8

Bekker, Balthasar, 1634-1698.
De betoverde weereld.

Witchcraft
BF
1410
B42
Z56
v.2
no.16

Den verkeerden duyvel van den throon geschopt ... 1692.   (Card 2)

4°: *², A-D⁴, E².
Black letter (except for introduction)
Modeled on Balthasar Bekker's De betoverde weereld, but not always supporting it.
Van der Linde 66.
No. 16 in vol. lettered Bekker II.
1. Demonology. 2. Angels. 3. Magic. 4. Witchcraft. 5. Bekker, Balthasar, 1634-1698. De betoverde weereld.
I. Title. II. K. A. H. III. H., K. A.

8

Bekker, Balthasar, 1634-1698.
De betoverde weereld.

Witchcraft
BF
1410
B42
Z56
v.3
no.6

[Schuts, Jacobus] Missive, aen D. Baltha-zar Bekker ... 1692.   (Card 3)

Van der Linde 147.
No. 6 in vol. lettered Bekker III.
1. Bekker, Balthasar, 1634-1698. De betoverde weereld. 2. Bekker, Balthasar, 1634-1698. Ondersoek van de betekeninge der kometen. 3. Bekker, Balthasar, 1634-1698. Uitlegginge van den prophet Daniel. I. Title.

8

Bekker, Balthasar, 1634-1698.
De betoverde weereld.

Witchcraft
BF
1410
B42
Z69
no.14

[Seegen, Charinus van]
Oogmerck van Everardus van der Hoogt in sijn Brabbelen teegen het boek De Betoverde wereld genoeemd. Sulx blijktuit de groote opheff, om D. Becker eens voor al, wel ter deegen, swart te maken ... t'Amsterdam, By D. van den Dalen, 1691.
16 p. 21cm.

Signatures: 4°: A-B⁴.
Black letter.

(Continued on next card)

Bekker, Balthasar, 1634-1698.
De betoverde weereld.

Witchcraft
BF
1410
B42
Z88

Verrijn, Johannes, d. 1698.
Aenmerckingen op De betoverde werelt van Dr. Balthasar Bekker, nopende de geesten, en hun vermogen, en byzonderlijck den staet, en magt des duyvels. Door J. Verryn. Amsterdam, By G. Slaats, boekverkoper, 1692.
4 p. l., 136 p. title and end page vignettes, illus. initials. 22 x 17cm.
4°: *4, A-R⁴.
Black letter.
Van der   Linde 150.
(Continued on next card)

Bekker, Balthasar, 1634-1698.
De betoverde weereld.

Witchcraft
BF
1410
B42
Z69
no.30

[Schuts, Jacobus]
Tweede missive aen d'Heer Balthasar Bekker, over sijn Betoverde weereld, Daniel, en den 2den druk van de Cometen. Waer in benessens Orchards, en Philopaters genoegdoeninge, Daillions wederlegginge ook aangeroert word; en getoont, dat het woord Daimones met alle vereischte wettelijkheid vertaalt word Duivelen. Ende in het stuk van de Prophetien, en de Cometen word de saak eenigermate betrekkelijk gemaakt, op de Schriften van D. Koelman en
(Continued on next card)

Bekker, Balthasar, 1634-1698.
De betoverde weereld.

Witchcraft
BF
1410
B42
Z69
no.14

[Seegen, Charinus van] Oogmerck van Everardus van der Hoogt ... 1691.   (Card 2)

Signed: Charinus van Seegen.
Van der Linde 108.
No. 14 in a Collection of tracts against Balthasar Bekker and his Betoverde weereld.

Bekker, Balthasar, 1634-1698.
De betoverde weereld.

Witchcraft
BF
1410
B42
Z89

Verscheyde gedichten, so voor, als tegen het boek, genaamt: De betoverde weereld. [Amsterdam?] Gedrukt voor de liefhebbers 1691.
1 p. l., 12, 9-32 p. title vignettes, illus. initials. 20 x 15cm.

4°: π1, A⁶, B-D⁴.
First poem has own t. p. with title: Gestroojde zeegen-palmen, op het doorwrogte werk van de Heer Balthasar Bekker...genaamt De betoverde   weereld. [Van der Linde 188]

8   (Continued on next card)

50

CATALOGUE OF THE CORNELL WITCHCRAFT COLLECTION

Bekker, Balthasar, 1634-1698.
De betoverde weereld.

Witchcraft
BF
1410
B42
Z89

Verscheyde gedichten, so voor, als tegen het boek, genaamt: De betoverde weereld. 1691. (Card 2)

Includes other works published separately: De betoverde predikant Dr. Balthasar Bekker [van der Linde 189]; Verta[e]ling uit seker arabisch schryver; De geharpoende muys. Van der Linde 197.
1. Bekker, Balthasar, 1634-1698. De betoverde weereld. I. Gestroojde zeegen-

(Continued on next card)

Bekker, Balthasar, 1634-1698.
De betoverde weereld.

Witchcraft
BF
1410
B42
Z56
v.2
no.11

Vertaeling uit seker arabisch schryver. Hamets Sidach Effendi, voornaem turks leeraer, verhaelt in syne wederlegginge van 't gevoelen der Sadduceen, een parabel of gelykeni/se, die, hoewel Mahometans, echter in dese tyden met vrucht onder de Christenen kan gelesen werden. [Amsterdam, By P. Rotterdam, 1692]
4 p. illus. initial. 19 x 15cm.
4°: A².
Caption title.

(Continued on next card)

Bekker, Balthasar, 1634-1698.
De betoverde weereld.

Witchcraft
BF
1410
B42
Z56
v.2
no.11

Vertaeling uit seker arabisch schryver. [1691] (Card 2)

"Redenering over de nuttigheid der fabelen": p. 3-4.
Parable itself published also in Verscheyde gedichten, so voor, als tegen het boek, genaamt: De betoverde weereld. No. 11 in vol. lettered Bekker II.
1. Parables. 2. Bekker, Balthasar, 1634-1698. De betoverde weereld.

Bekker, Balthasar, 1634-1698.
De betoverde weereld.

Witchcraft
BF
1410
B42
Z892

Vervolg van Verscheyde gedigten, &c. So voor als tegen het boek tegen De betoverde werelt. [Amsterdam?] Gedrukt voor de liefhebbers, 1692.
1 p. l., 54 p. title vignette, illus. initial. 20 x 16cm.
4°: π1, A-F⁴, G3.
Contains prose as well as poems.
First poem has own t. p. with title: Verklaeringe van een turkse parabel ... door Mr. Gratianus de Bly...

(Continued on next card)

Bekker, Balthasar, 1634-1698.
De betoverde weereld.

Witchcraft
BF
1410
B42
Z892

Vervolg van Verscheyde gedigten, &c. 1692. (Card 2)

Klinkende bel; of uytroep om den verloorenen duyvel: P. 17-19. [Van der Linde 194]
Variant of van der Linde 198: signatures differ (but not paging).
1. Bekker, Balthasar, 1634-1698. De betoverde weer eld. I. Verscheyde

(Continued on next card)

Bekker, Balthasar, 1634-1698.
De betoverde weereld.

Witchcraft
BF
1410
B42
Z56
v.3
no.20

De Volmaakte kragt Godts verheerlykt. Nevens eenige aanmerkinge over de drie predikatien van Do. Petrus Schaak. Gedaan over Psal. 72: v. 18. Gen. 18: v. 1,2... en Gen. 32: v. 24, 25. In haar eigen gronden ondersogt, en met de waarheid vergeleken. En eenige andere aanmerkingen daar by gevoegd. Amsterdam, By D. van den Dalen, boekverkooper, 1691.
47 p. [p. 48 blank] title and other vignettes, illus. initial. 19 x 15cm.

(Continued on next card)

Bekker, Balthasar, 1634-1698.
De betoverde weereld.

Witchcraft
BF
1410
B42
Z56
v.3
no.20

De Volmaakte kragt Godts verheerlykt. 1691. (Card 2)

4: A-F⁴.
Black letter.
Preface signed: J:P. L: R.
Supports B. Bekker against Schaak's attacks on Bekker's De betoverde weereld.
Van der Linde 145.
No. 20 in vol. lettered Bekker III.

Bekker, Balthasar, 1634-1698.
De betoverde weereld.

Witchcraft
BF
1528
D9
V98
1692

Vries, Simon de, b. 1630.
De Satan, in sijn weesen, aert, bedryf, en guychel-spel, vertoond in een historische verhandelingh van duyvelen, gesigten, spoocken, voorseggingen, voorteeckenen, droomen, toveryen, betoveringen, beseetenheyd, en wat noch voorts deese stof aenhangigh is. Nevens afweeringh van 't geen daer tegens ingebraght werd met meenighvuldige verwringingen der H. Schrift, en tegenspraeck der geduerige ondervindingh.

(Continued on next card)

Bekker, Balthasar, 1634-1698.
De betoverde weereld.

Witchcraft
BF
1528
D9
V98
1692

Vries, Simon de, b. 1630. De Satan ... 1692. (Card 2)

Door S. de Vries. Utrecht, By A. Schouten, Boeckverkooper, 1692.
20 p. l., 571, [57] p. title and other vignettes, illus. initials. 17 x 11cm.
8°: *-2*⁸, 3*⁴, A-2Q⁸, 2R⁴.
First published 1691.
In part a refutation of Balthasar Bekker's De betoverde weereld.

(Continued on next card)

Bekker, Balthasar, 1634-1698.
De betoverde weereld.

Witchcraft
BF
1528
D9
V98
1692

Vries, Simon de, b. 1630. De Satan ... 1692. (Card 3)

ker's De betoverde weereld.
Van der Linde 153.
1. Devil. 2. Demonology. 3. Bekker, Balthasar, 1634-1698. De betoverde weereld. II. Title.

Bekker, Balthasar, 1634-1698.
De betoverde weereld.

Witchcraft
BF
1410
B42
Z91

Waaijen, Johannes van der, 1639-1701.
De betoverde weereld van D. Balthasar Bekker ondersogt en weederlegt door Johannes vander Waeyen. Franeker, By L. Strik en J. Horreus, boekverkoopers, 1693.
1 p. l., VIII, 3-16, 651, [11] p. title vignette, illus. initials. 20 x 16cm.
4°: π1, *⁴, *²-2*⁴, A-K⁴, L3, M-O⁴, P².
Black letter.
Van der Linde 156.
1. Bekker, Balthasar, 1634-1698. De betoverde weereld. I. Title.

Bekker, Balthasar, 1634-1698.
De betoverde weereld.

Witchcraft
BF
1410
B42
Z92

[Walten, Ericus] 1663-1697.
Aardige duyvelary, voorvallende in dese dagen. Begrepen in een brief van een heer te Amsterdam, geschreven aan een van sijn vrienden te Leeuwaerden, in Vriesland. [Amsterdam, 1691]
45 p. [p. 46-48 blank] illus. initial. 19 x 15cm.
4°: A-F⁴.
Defense of B. Bekker and his book De betoverde weereld.

(Continued on next card)

Bekker, Balthasar, 1634-1698.
De betoverde weereld.

Witchcraft
BF
1410
B42
Z92

[Walten, Ericus] 1663-1697. Aardige duyvelary, voorvallende in dese dagen. [1691] (Card 2)

Van der Linde 170.
Stamped: Koninkl. bibliothek te 's Hage.
With this is bound Bekker, Balthasar, 1634-1698. Eenige extracten uyt Dr. Bekkers Betooverder weerelt, tweede deel. [n. p.] 1691.
1. Bekker, Balthasar, 1634-1698. De betoverde weereld. I. Title.

Bekker, Balthasar, 1634-1698.
De betoverde weereld.

Witchcraft
BF
1410
B42
Z82
no.1

[Walten, Ericus] 1663-1697.
Brief aan een regent der Stad Amsterdam. Behelsende een regtsinnige uytlegginge, en redenmatige verklaringe, van de articulen die D. Balthasar Bekker op den 22 Januarij 1692 heeft overgelevert aan de Classis van Amsterdam, wegens sijn uytgegeven boek, genaamt, De betoverde weereld; met eenige philosophische redeneringen, seer nut en dienstig, om verscheidene dingen in 't selve boek wel te verstaan; en een kort verhaal van den uytslag der kerke lijke proceduyren, daar

(Continued on next card)

Bekker, Balthasar, 1634-1698.
De betoverde weereld.

Witchcraft
BF
1410
B42
Z82
no.1

[Walten, Ericus] 1663-1697. Brief aan een regent der Stad Amsterdam. 1692. (Card 2)

over gehouden. ... Gravenhage, By M. Uytwerf, boekverkooper, 1692.
135 p. [p. 136 blank] title vignette. 19 x 15cm.
4°: A-R⁴.
Signed: Ericus Walten. 18. Mey 1692.
Van der Linde 41.
No. 1 in vol. lettered Over Bekkers Betoverde weereld. 1692.

(Continued on next card)

Bekker, Balthasar, 1634-1698.
De betoverde weereld.

Witchcraft
BF
1410
B42
Z69
no.12

[Webbers, Zacharias]
In antwoort op het jonghste post scriptum van de VI. brief van Haggebher Philaleethees tegens eene van de (soo hem dunkt) schaddyke helpers van Do. B. Bekker, raakende desselfs aanmerkinge over de predicatie van Do. Adrianus van Weesel, 's Sondags by sijn eerw. in de Wester Kerk den 25 Novemb. over Math. IV. 5,6,7. Van der versoekinge onses saligmakers door den Duyvel, gedaan. Dienende dit tot kraghtiger bewijs, dat deselve niet eygentlijk, maar by forme van een

(Continued on next card)

Bekker, Balthasar, 1634-1698.
De betoverde weereld.

Witchcraft
BF
1410
B42
Z69
no.12

[Webbers, Zacharias] In antwoort op het jonghste post scriptum ... (Card 2)

gesighte, en in den geest geschiet zy: door den zelven S. W. S. F. t'Amsterdam, by D. van den Dalen, 1692.
16 p. 21cm.
Signatures: 4°: A-B⁴.
Black letter.
No. 12 in a Collection of tracts against Balthasar Bekker and his Betoverde weereld.

(Continued on next card)

Bekker, Balthasar, 1634-1698.
De betoverde weereld.

Witchcraft
BF
1410
B42
Z69
no.12

[Webbers, Zacharias] In antwoort op het jonghste post scriptum ... 1692. (Card 3)

Attributed to Webbers by Aa, A. J. van der. Biographisch woordenboek der Nederlanden. Haarlem, 1852-78, and by Doorninck, J. I. van. Vermonde en naamlooze schrijvers ... Leiden, 1883-85.
Van der Linde 113.

(Continued on next card)

CATALOGUE OF THE CORNELL WITCHCRAFT COLLECTION

```
                Bekker, Balthasar, 1634-1698.
                   De betoverde weereld.
Witchcraft
BF        [Webbers, Zacharias]
1528          De waare oorspronk, voort- en onder-gank
D9        des Satans: behelzende, een buitengewoone,
W37       edog klare verhandeling, van de voornaamste
1729      plaatsen der Heilige Schrift, welke zyn
          spreekende van den Duivel. Dienende voor
          een inleiding tot de Bybelsche Godgeleerd-
          heid, en het waare Christendom. Door Joan
          Adolphsz. 4. druk. Van nieuws overzien.
          Amsterdam, By Jacob Graal, boekverkooper,
8         1729.
                        (Continued on next card)
```

```
                Bekker, Balthasar, 1634-1698.
                  De betoverde weereld.
Witchcraft
BF        [Webbers, Zacharias]  De waare oorspronk,
1528      voort- en onder-gank des Satans ... 1729.
D9                                       (Card 2)
W37       7 p. l., 418, 3 p.  17cm.
1729        8°: *8 (-*1), A-2C8, 2D3.
            Black letter; title in red and black.
            "De uitgever tot den leezer" signed:
          N. N. (i. e., Jacobus Schuts)
            First edition 1695.
8
                        (Continued on next card)
```

```
                Bekker, Balthasar, 1634-1698.
                  De betoverde weereld.
Witchcraft
BF        Zeedige overweeging op de praedikatie van
1410      d'Hr. Petrus Schaak, gedaan in d'Oude
B42       Kerk op den 30 September 1691.  Amster-
Z56       dam, By A. Hendriksz [1691]
v.3         7 p. [p. 8 blank] title vignette, illus.
no.3      initial.  20 x 16cm.
            4°:  A4.
            Schaak's sermon was against De betoverde
          weereld, by Balthasar Bekker.
            Van der Linde 143.
            No. 3 in vol.       lettered Bekker III.
                        (Continued on next card)
```

```
                Bekker, Balthasar, 1634-1698.
                   De betoverde weereld.
Witchcraft
BF        Zobel, Enoch, 1653-1697.
1429          Declaratio apologetica, das ist: Schutz-
G62       schriftliche und fernere Erklärung, uber [sic]
1704      die St. Annabergische Gespensts-Historie,
          wider Herrn Balthasar Bekker ... heraus-ge-
          gebenes Buch, genannt Die bezauberte Welt,
          abgefasset von M. Enoch Zobeln, Archi-Diac.
          zu St. Annaberg.  Leipzig, Verlegt von den
          Lanckischen Erben, 1695.
            7 p. l., 174, [1] p. [p. 176 blank]
          front., vignettes.  17 x 10cm.
                        (Continued on next card)
```

```
                Bekker, Balthasar, 1634-1698.
                  De betoverde weereld.
Witchcraft
BF        Zobel, Enoch, 1653-1697.  Declaratio apo-
1429      logetica ... 1695.            (Card 2)
G62         8°: X8 (-)(8), A-L8.
1704        Black letter.
            At head of title:  B. C. D.
            Autograph on p. [176]: Adolph Gerhard
          Eduard Grovermann.
            Bound with Goldschmidt, P.  Höllischer
          Morpheus.  Hamburg, 1704.
            1. Ghosts--Germany.  2. Bekker, Baltha-
                        (Continued on next card)
```

```
Witchcraft
BF        Die bezauberte Welt: oder Eine gründliche
1410      Untersuchung des allgemeinen Aberglaubens,
B42       betreffend, die arth und das Vermögen, Ge-
1693      walt und Wirckung des Satans und der bösen
          Geister über den Menschen, und was diese
          durch derselben Krafft und Gemeinschafft
          thun: so aus natürlicher Vernunfft und H.
          Schrifft in 4 Büchern zu bewehren sich unter-
          nommen hat Balthasar Bekker, S. Theol. Doct.
          und Prediger zu Amsterdam.  Nebenst des
                        (Continued on next card)
```

```
Witchcraft
BF        Bekker, Balthasar, 1634-1698.  Die bezau-
1410          berte Welt ... 1693.       (Card 2)
B42
1693        Autoris generale Vorrede über diese seine 4
          Bücher: wie und welcher Gestalt dieselbe zu
          lesen, der Zweck seines Vorhabens, und dann
          die Ordnung, so er darinnen gehalten.  Aus
          dem Holländischen nach der letzten vom Au-
          tore vermehrten Edition.  Amsterdam, ge-
          druckt bey D. von Dahlen, 1693.
            39, [1], 136, 270, [2], 195, [3], 308,
          [4] p.  Title     vignette (port.), plate.
          23 x 17cm.          (Continued on next card)
```

```
Witchcraft
BF        Bekker, Balthasar, 1634-1698.  Die bezau-
1410          berte Welt ... 1693.       (Card 3)
B42
1693        4°: a-e4, A-S4, A-2K4, A-2A4, A-2P4.
            Black letter.
            Translation of De betoverde weereld.
            Van der Linde 25.
            1. Demonology.  2. Angels.  3. Magic.
          4. Witchcraft.  I. Title.  II. His   De
          betoverde weereld--German.
```

```
Witchcraft
BF        Bekker, Balthasar, 1634-1698.
1410          Brief van Baltasar [sic] Bekker, S. T. D.
B42       predikant tot Amsterdam, aan de Heeren
Z86       Joost de Smeth, Willem Weyer, en Nikolaas
no.3      vander Hagen, so tegenwoordig dienende als
          meermaals gediend hebbende ouderlingen der
          Gereformeerde Kerk aldaar.  Tot antwoord
          op den brief van den Professor vander
          Waeyen aan deselven, gesteld voor sijn
          boek genaamd De betoverde weereld van B. B.
          ondersocht en wederleid.  Hier achter is
                        (Continued on next card)
```

```
Witchcraft
BF        Bekker, Balthasar, 1634-1698.  Brief ...
1410          aan de Heeren Joost de Smeth, Willem
B42           Weyer, en Nikolaas vander Hagen ... 1693.
Z86                                      (Card 2)
no.3        bygevoegd d'Opdraght-brief desselfden pro-
          fessors aan sijne Vorst. Doorl. den Prinsse
          van Nassaw Stadhouder &c. en d'Ed. Mog.
          Heeren Gedeputeerde Staten van Friesland,
          voor het selfde boek, met een antwoord op
          den selven.  Amsterdam, By D. van den
                        (Continued on next card)
```

```
Witchcraft
BF        Bekker, Balthasar, 1634-1698.  Brief ...
1410          aan de Heeren Joost de Smeth, Willem
B42           Weyer, en Nikolaas vander Hagen ... 1693.
Z86                                      (Card 3)
no.3        Dalen, boekverkoper, 1693.
            16, 15*-16*, 17-24 p.  title vignette,
          illus. initial.  19 x 15cm.
            4°:  A-B4, B*1, C4.
            Van der Linde 159.
            No. 3 in vol. lettered Tractaten voor
          en tegen B. Be      kker.
                        (Continued on next card)
```

```
Witchcraft
BF        Bekker, Balthasar, 1634-1698.  Brief ...
1410          aan de Heeren Joost de Smeth, Willem
B42           Weyer, en Nikolaas vander Hagen ... 1693.
Z86                                      (Card 4)
no.3
            1. Waaijen, Johannes van der, 1639-1701.
          De betoverde weereld van D. Balthasar Bekker
          ondersogt en weederlegt.  I. Smeth, Joost
          de.  II. Title.  III. His  Brief ... aan
          den Doorlugtigen Hooghgeboorenen Prinsse
          Hendrik Kasimir.
```

```
                Bekker, Balthasar, 1634-1698.
                  Brief ... aan den Doorlugtigen Hooghge-
Witchcraft    boorenen Prinsse Hendrik Kasimir.
BF        Bekker, Balthasar, 1634-1698.
1410          Brief van Baltasar [sic] Bekker, S. T. D.
B42       predikant tot Amsterdam, aan de Heeren
Z86       Joost de Smeth, Willem Weyer, en Nikolaas
no.3      vander Hagen, so tegenwoordig dienende als
          meermaals gediend hebbende ouderlingen der
          Gereformeerde Kerk aldaar.  Tot antwoord
          op den brief van den Professor vander
          Waeyen aan deselven, gesteld voor sijn
          boek genaamd De betoverde weereld van B. B.
          ondersocht en wederleid.  Hier achter is
                        (Continued on next card)
```

```
                Bekker, Balthasar, 1634-1698.
                  Brief ... aan den Doorlugtigen Hooghge-
Witchcraft    boorenen Prinsse Hendrik Kasimir.
BF        Bekker, Balthasar, 1634-1698.  Brief ...
1410          aan de Heeren Joost de Smeth, Willem
B42           Weyer, en Nikolaas vander Hagen ... 1693.
Z86                                      (Card 2)
no.3        bygevoegd d'Opdraght-brief desselfden professors
          aan sijne Vorst. Doorl. den Prinsse
          van Nassaw Stadhouder &c.
          Heeren Gedeputeerde Staten van Friesland,
          voor het selfde boek, met een antwoord op
          den selven.  Amsterdam, By D. van den
                        (Continued on next card)
```

```
                Bekker, Balthasar, 1634-1698.
                  Brief ... aan den Doorlugtigen Hooghge-
Witchcraft    boorenen Prinsse Hendrik Kasimir.
BF        Bekker, Balthasar, 1634-1698.  Brief ...
1410          aan de Heeren Joost de Smeth, Willem
B42           Weyer, en Nikolaas vander Hagen ... 1693.
Z86                                      (Card 3)
no.3        Dalen, boekverkoper, 1693.
            16, 15*-16*, 17-24 p.  title vignette,
          illus. initial.  19 x 15cm.
            4°:  A-B4, B*1, C4.
            Van der Linde 159.
            No. 3 in vol. lettered Tractaten voor
          en tegen B. Be      kker.
                        (Continued on next card)
```

```
Witchcraft
BF        Bekker, Balthasar, 1634-1698.
1410          Brief van Balthasar Bekker, S. Th. Dr.
B42       predikant tot Amsterdam.  Aan den Heer
Z86       Joannes vander Waeyen, S. Theol. Dr. en
no.2      professor in de loffelike en vermaarde
          Universiteit tot Franeker.  In antwoord
          op desselven brief, waarmede hy hem sijn
          boek tegen De betoverde weereld onlangs
          uitgegeven, heeft toegesonden.  [Amster-
          dam? 1693]
            8 p.  illus. initial.  19 x 15cm.
                        (Continued on next card)
```

```
Witchcraft
BF        Bekker, Balthasar, 1634-1698.  Brief ...
1410          aan de Heer Joannes vander Waeyen ...
B42           [1693]                     (Card 2)
Z86
no.2        4°:  A4.
            Caption title.
            Dated:  Amsterdam den 8 Augusty 1693.
            Van der Linde 157.
            No. 2 in vol. lettered Tractaten voor
          en tegen B. Bekker.
            1. His   De betoverde weereld.  I.
          Waaijen, Johannes van der, 1639-
          1701.  II. T                itle.
```

```
Witchcraft
BF        Bekker, Balthasar, 1634-1698.
1410          Brief van Balthasar Bekker S. T. D.
B42       predikant tot Amsterdam.  Aan twee eer-
Z56       waardige predikanten D. Joannes Aalstius
v.1       tot Hoornaar, ende D. Paulus Steenwinkel
no.7      tot Schelluinen, over derselver Zedige
          aanmerkingen op een deel des tweeden boeks
          van sijn werk genaamd De betoverde weere
          Amsterdam, By D. vanden Dalen, boekverko
          1693.
            11 p. [p. 12 blank] title vignette,
          illus. initi      al.  19 x 16cm.
                        (Continued on next card
```

52

CATALOGUE OF THE CORNELL WITCHCRAFT COLLECTION

Witchcraft
BF 1410 B42 Z56 v.1 no.7

Bekker, Balthasar, 1634-1698. Brief van Balthasar Bekker ... aan ... Joannes Aalstius ... 1693. (Card 2)

4°: A⁴, B².
Letter autographed by Bekker.
Van der Linde 72.
No. 7 in vol. lettered Bekker I.
I. Aalst, Johannes, 1660-1712. Zedige aanmerkingen. I. Aalst, Johannes, 1660-1712. II. Steenwinkel, Paulus, d. 1740. III. Title.

8

Witchcraft
BF 1410 B42 Z56 v.3 no.27

[Bekker, Balthasar] 1634-1698.
Brief van den schrijver des boeks De betoverde weereld genaamd, aan den eerwaardigen heere Everhard van der Hooght, yverigen leeraar van 's heeren gemeente tot Niewendam. Amsterdam, By G. Borstius, boekverkoper [1691]
11 p. [p. 12 is blank] title vignette, illus. initial.
4°: A⁴, [B²]
Van der Linde 105.
No. 27 in vol. lettered Bekker III.

(Continued on next card)

8

Witchcraft
BF 1410 B42 Z56 v.3 no.27

[Bekker, Balthasar] 1634-1698. Brief van den schrijver des boeks De betoverde weereld genaamd ... [1691] (Card 2)

I. Bekker, Balthasar, 1634-1698. De betoverde weereld. I. Hooght, Everard van der, d. 1716. II. Title.

8

Witchcraft
BF 1410 B42 Z56 v.3 no.26

Hooght, Everard van der, d. 1716.
Brief van den schrijver des boeks De betoverde weereld.
Antwoord van Everardus van der Hooght, aan den eerwaarden, godzaligen, hoog-geleerden heere, Do. Balthasar Bekker, S. Theologiae Doctor, yverig predikant tot Amsterdam. Amsterdam, By G. Borstius, boekverkoper, 1691.
1 p. l., 8, [2] p. title vignette, illus. initial. 19 x 15cm.
4°: π1, A⁴, [B]1.
Black letter.
Letter dated 29. Sept 1691; postscript, 1 Oct. 1691.

(Continued on next card)

8

Witchcraft
BF 1410 B42 Z56 v.3 no.26

Hooght, Everard van der, d. 1716. Antwoord ... aan ... Do. Balthasar Bekker ... 1691. (Card 2)

Van der Linde 106.
No. 26 in vol. lettered Bekker III.
1. Bekker, Balthasar, 1634-1698. Brief van den schrijver des boeks De betoverde weereld. I. Bekker, Balthasar, 1634-1698. II. Title.

8

Witchcraft
BF 1410 B42 1781

Bekker, Balthasar, 1634-1698.
D. [i. e., Doktor] Balthasar Bekkers reformierten Predigers in Amsterdam bezauberte Welt. Neu übersetzt von Johann Moritz Schwager, Pastor zu Jöllenbeck; durchgesehen und vermehrt von D. Johann Salomo Semler. Leipzig, In der Weygandschen Buchhandlung, 1781.
3 v. title vignette (port.), fold. plate. 20cm.
8°: vol. 1: a⁸, b², A-2F⁸; vol. 2:

(Continued on next card)

8

Witchcraft
BF 1410 B42 1781

Bekker, Balthasar, 1634-1698. D. Balthasar Bekkers ... bezauberte Welt. 1781. (Card 2)

⁸(- 8), A-2F⁸, G⁴; vol. 3: *⁸(-*1, *8), A-2Y6.
Translation of his De betoverde weereld.
1. Demonology. 2. Angels. 3. Magic. 4. Witchcraft. I. Title. II. Title:

(Continued on next card)

Witchcraft
BF 1410 B42 1781

Bekker, Balthasar, 1634-1698. D. Balthasar Bekkers ... bezauberte Welt. 1781. (Card 3)

Die bezauberte Welt. III. Schwager, Johann Moritz, tr. IV. Semler, Johann Salomo, 1725-1791, ed. V. His De betoverde weereld--German.

8

Witchcraft
BF 1410 B42 Z56 v.3 no.12

[Bekker, Balthasar] 1634-1698.
Drie resolutien des Classis van Amsterdam, by deselve genomen op den 22. Jan. 8. April en 21. July deses jaars, in de sake van Balthasar Bekker predikant tot Amsterdam, betreffende sijn boek De betoverde weereld. Waar by gevoegt zijn enige reflexien van onbekende hand van den auteur daar over toegesonden. Amsterdam, By D. van den Dalen, boekverkoper, 1692.
16, 16 p. title and end page vignettes. 19 x 15cm.

(Continued on next card)

8

Witchcraft
BF 1410 B42 Z56 v.3 no.12

[Bekker, Balthasar] 1634-1698. Drie resolutien des Classis van Amsterdam ... 1692. (Card 2)

4°: A-B⁴, A-B⁴.
"Aanmerkinge op de handelingen der twee laatste noordhollandsche synoden, in de sake van B. Bekker, ten opsighte van sijn boek genaamd De betoverde weereld; nu versch t' Enkhuisen gedrukt:" 16 p.
Last p. autographed by Bekker, dated 2/13 Octob. 1692.

(Continued on next card)

8

Witchcraft
BF 1410 B42 Z56 v.3 no.12

[Bekker, Balthasar] 1634-1698. Drie resolutien des Classis van Amsterdam ... 1692. (Card 3)

In the first section, Bekker quotes the resolutions which he discusses.
Van der Linde 44, 52.
No. 12 in vol. lettered Bekker III.
1. Bekker, Balthasar, 1634-1698. De betoverde weereld. I. Nederlandse Hervormde Kerk. Classes. Amsterdam. II. Title. III. His Aanmerkinge

(Continued on next card)

8

Witchcraft
BF 1410 B42 Z56 v.3 no.12

[Bekker, Balthasar] 1634-1698. Drie resolutien des Classis van Amsterdam ... 1692. (Card 4)

op de handelingen der twee laatste noordhollandsche synoden. IV. Title: Aanmerkinge op de handelinge der twee laatste noordhollandsche synoden.

Witchcraft
BF 1410 B42 Z92

Bekker, Balthasar, 1634-1698. Eenige extracten uyt Dr. Beckers Betooverder weerelt, tweede deel. Daer beneffens een extract uyt de synode, gehouden den 10. Augusti 1691. tot Edam. Raakende Dr. Beckers Betooverde weerelt. Beneffens desselfs veroordeeling. [n. p.] 1691.
7 p. [p. 8 blank] title and end page vignettes, illus. initials. 19 x 16cm.
4°: A⁴.
Black letter.
Van der Linde 29.

(Continued on next card)

8

Witchcraft
BF 1410 B42 Z92

Bekker, Balthasar, 1634-1698. Eenige extracten uyt Dr. Beckers Betoverder weerelt, tweede deel. 1691. (Card 2)

Bound with Walten, Ericus, 1663-1697. Aardige duyvelary, voorvallende in dese dagen.
I. Bekker, Balthasar, 1634-1698. De betoverde weereld. II. Nederlandse Hervormde Kerk. Synode, Edam, 1691. III. Title.

8

Witchcraft
BF 1581 A2 B43

Bekker, Balthasar, 1634-1698.
Engelsch verhaal van ontdekte tovery wederleid door Balthasar Bekker S. T. D. predikant tot Amsterdam. Amsterdam, By D. van den Dalen, boekverkooper, 1689. Met privilegie.
28 p. title vignette, illus. initial. 21 x 16cm.
4°: A-C⁴, D².
Van der Linde 13.
1. Witchcraft--England. I. Title.

8

Witchcraft
BF 1410 B42 1691b

Bekker, Balthasar, 1634-1698.
Kort begrip van de twee boeken der Betoverde weereld, in 't ligt gebragt door den heere Balthazar Bekker, S. T. D. en predikant te Amsterdam, zeer dienstig tot het recht verstaan (en teffens strekkende voor een bondig register) van dat vermaarde werk, opgesteld door een redenlievenden hater van bygeloof. Rotterdam, By I. van Ruynen, boekverkooper, 1691.
2 p. l., 39 p. [p. 40 is blank] title

(Continued on next card)

8

Witchcraft
BF 1410 B42 1691b

Bekker, Balthasar, 1634-1698. Kort begrip van de twee boeken der Betooverde weereld ... 1691. (Card 2)

vignette, illus. initials. 20 x 16cm.
4°: π², A-E⁴.
Black letter.
Preface signed: I. van Ruynen.
Van der Linde 18.
1. Demonology. 2. Angels. 3. Magic. 4. Witchcraft. I. His De betoverde weereld. II. Title. III. Ruynen, I. van. IV. Een redenlievende hater van bygeloof.

8

Witchcraft
BF 1410 B42 Z56 v.1 no.2

Bekker, Balthasar, 1634-1698.
Kort beright van Balthasar Bekker S. T. D. predikant tot Amsterdam. Aangaande alle de schriften, welke over sijn boek De betoverde weereld enen tijd lang heen en weder verwisseld zijn. De tweede druk met enige stukken vermeerderd. Amsterdam, By D. vanden Dalen, boekverkoper [1692]
80, 8 p. title vignette, illus. initials. 19 x 16cm.
4°: A-K⁴, A⁴.
Black letter.

(Continued on next card)

8

53

CATALOGUE OF THE CORNELL WITCHCRAFT COLLECTION

Witchcraft
BF   Bekker, Balthasar, 1634-1698. Kort bericht
1410   ... [1692]   (Card 2)
B42
Z56   Dated Franeker den 21/31 Jul. 1692.
v.1   Variant of van der Linde 76: t. p. in-
no.2   cludes statement De tweede druk...
     No. 2 in vol. lettered Bekker I.

     1. Bekker, Balthasar, 1634-1698. De
betoverde weereld. I. Title.

8

Witchcraft
BF   Bekker, Balthasar, 1634-1698.
1410   Kort en waarachtig verhaal van 't gebeurde
B42   tsederd den 31. Mey 1691. tot den 21. Aug.
Z56   1692. In den Kerkenraad en Classis van
v.1   Amsterdam, en de Synode van Noord-Holland.
no.5   In de sake van Balthasar Bekker, S. S. Th. Dr.
     en predikant tot Amsterdam; over sijn boek
     genaamd De betoverde weereld. Amsterdam, By
     D. van den Dalen, boekverkoper, 1692.
     2 p. l., 30 p. [p. 31-32 blank] title
vignette, illus. initials.
     (Continued on next card)

Witchcraft
BF   Bekker, Balthasar, 1634-1698. Kort en
1410   waarachtig verhaal ... 1692. (Card 2)
B42
Z56   19 x 16cm.
v.1 $4°: \pi^2, *-4*^4$.
no.5 Introductory letter autographed by Bekker.
   Van der Linde 47.
   No. 5 in vol. lettered Bekker I.

   1. Nederlandse Hervormde Kerk. 2.
Bekker, Balthasar, 1634-1698. De
betoverde weereld. I. Title.

8

Witchcraft
BF   Bekker, Balthasar, 1634-1698.
1410   Kort en waarachtig verhaal van 't
B42   gebeurde tsederd den 31. Mey 1691. tot
Z56   den 21. Aug. 1692. In den Kerkenraad
v.2   en Classis van Amsterdam, en de Synode
no.17 van Noord-Holland. In de sake van Bal-
    thasar Bekker, S. S. Th. Dr. en predikant
    tot Amsterdam; over sijn boek genaamd De
    betoverde weereld. Amsterdam, By D. van
    den Dalen, boekverkoper, 1692.
    2 p. l., 30 p. [p. 31-32 blank]
title vignette, illus. initials.

8   (Continued on next card)

Witchcraft
BF   Bekker, Balthasar, 1634-1698. Kort en
1410   waarachtig verhaal ... 1692. (Card 2)
B42
Z56   19 x 15cm.
v.2 $4°: \pi^2, *-4*^4$.
no.17 Introductory letter autographed by Bekker.
   Van der Linde 47.
   No. 17 in vol. lettered Bekker II.

8

Witchcraft
BX   [Bekker, Balthasar] 1634-1698.
9479   Kort en waarachtig verhaal van 't ge-
B42   beurde tsederd den 31. Mey 1691. tot den
B11   21. Aug. 1692. In den Kerkenraad en Classis
no.5 van Amsterdam, en de Synode van Noord-Holland.
    In de sake van Balthasar Bekker, S. S. Th.
    Dr. en predikant tot Amsterdam; over sijn
    boek genaamd De betoverde weereld. Amster-
    dam, By D. van den Dalen, boekverkoper, 1692.
    2 p. l. 30 p. title vignette, illus.
initials. 20 x 16cm.

8   (Continued on next card)

Witchcraft
BX   [Bekker, Balthasar] 1634-1698. Kort en
9479   waarachtig verhaal ... 1692. (Card 2)
B42
B11 $4°: \pi^2, *-4*^4 (-4*4)$.
no.5 Introductory letter autographed by Bekker.
   Van der Linde 47.
   No. 5 in vol. lettered B. Bekker's sterf-
bed en andere tractaten.

8

Witchcraft
BF   **Bekker, Balthasar, 1634-1698.**
1410   Le monde enchanté; ou, Examen des communs senti-
B42   mens touchant les esprits, leur nature, leur pouvoir, leur
1694 administration, & leurs opérations. Et touchant les éfets
    que les hommes sont capables de produire par leur com-
    munication & leur vertu, divisé en quatre parties, par Bal-
    thasar Bekker ... Tr. du hollandois. Amsterdam, P. Rot-
    terdam, 1694.
    4 v. plates, port., title and other vignettes, illus.
initials. 14cm.
    Translation of his De betoverde weereld.
    Dedication, to M. Feyo Jean Winter, autographed
by Bekker. 10-33805
Library of Congress   (Continued on next card)

Witchcraft
BF   Bekker, Balthasar, 1634-1698. Le monde
1410   enchanté ... 1694. (Card 2)
B42
1694 $12°$: vol. 1: $*^8, 2*-6*^{12}, A-Q^{12}, R^4$;
    vol. 2: $*^{12}, A-2F^{12}$; vol. 3: $*^{12}, 2*^6$,
    $A-V^{12}, X^4$; vol. 4: $*^{12}, 2*^4, A-2G^{12}, H^7$.
    Van der Linde 27.

    1. Demonology. 2. Angels. 3. Magic.
4. Witchcraft. I. Title. II. His De
betoverde weereld.--French.

Witchcraft Bekker, Balthasar, 1634-1698.
BF   Le monde enchanté--English.
1410   Bekker, Balthasar, 1634-1698.
B42   The world bewitch'd; or, An examination
1695 of the common opinions concerning spirits:
    their nature, power, administration, and
    operations. As also, the effects men are
    able to produce by their communication.
    Divided into IV parts. By Balthazar Bekker,
    D. D. and pastor at Amsterdam. Vol. I.
    Translated from a French copy, approved of
    and subscribed by the author's own hand.
    [London] Printed for R. Baldwin, 1695.

    (Continued on next card)

Witchcraft Bekker, Balthasar, 1634-1698.
BF   Le monde enchanté--English.
1410   Bekker, Balthasar, 1634-1698. The world
B42   bewitch'd ... 1695. (Card 2)
1695
    41 p. l., 264 p. 17 x 10cm.
    $12°$: $a^6(-a1), b-d^{12}, B-M^{12}$.
    No more published.
    Half title: The world bewitch'd, &c.
    Vol. I.
    Translation of vol. 1 of Le monde enchanté,
    Amsterdam, 1694, which is a translation of
    his De betoverde weereld, Amsterdam, 1691-93.

    (Continued on next card)

Witchcraft Bekker, Balthasar, 1634-1698.
BF   Le monde enchanté--English.
1410   Bekker, Balthasar, 1634-1698. The world
B42   bewitch'd ... 1695. (Card 3)
1695
    Reissued in 1700 under title: The world
    turn'd upside down.
    Autograph on t. p.: Ch. Whittuck.
    Wing B 1781.
    Variant of van der Linde 28: $12°$, not $8°$.
    1. Demonology. 2. Angels. 3. Magic.
4. Witchcraft. I. Title. II. His De
betoverde weereld--English. III. His Le
monde enchanté --English.

    Bekker, Balthasar, 1634-1698.
Witchcraft Le monde enchanté--English.
BF   [Bekker, Balthasar] 1634-1698.
1410   The world turn'd upside down: or, A plain
B42   detection of errors, in the common or vulgar
1700 belief, relating to spirits, spectres or
    ghosts, daemons, witches, &c. In a due and
    serious examination of their nature, power,
    administration, and operation. In what form
    or shape incorporeal spirits appear to men,
    by what means, and of what elements they take
    to themselves, and form appearances of bodies
    visible to mortal eyes; why they

    (Continued on next card)

    Bekker, Balthasar, 1634-1698.
Witchcraft Le monde enchanté--English.
BF   [Bekker, Balthasar] 1634-1698. The world
1410   turn'd upside down ... 1700. (Card 2)
B42
1700 appear, and what frights and force of imag-
    ination often delude us into the appre-
    hensions of supposed phantasms, through the
    intimidation of the mind, &c. Also what evil
    tongues have power to produce of hurt of man-
    kind, or irrational [sic] creatures; and the
    effects men and women are able to produce
    by their communication with good or evil

    (Continued on next card)

    Bekker, Balthasar, 1634-1698.
Witchcraft Le monde enchanté--English.
BF   [Bekker, Balthasar] 1634-1698. The world
1410   turn'd upside down ... 1700. (Card 3)
B42
1700 spirits, &c. Written at the request of a
    person of honour, by B. B., a Protestant min-
    ister for publick information. London,
    Printed for E. Harris, 1700.
    37 p. l., 264 p. 16cm.
    $12°$: $\pi 1, b-d^{12}, B-M^{12}$.
    With two old prints of devils inserted at
front and back of book.

    (Continued on next card)

    Bekker, Balthasar, 1634-1698.
Witchcraft Le monde enchanté--English.
BF   [Bekker, Balthasar] 1634-1698. The world
1410   turn'd upside down ... 1700. (Card 4)
B42
1700 Title on spine: Bekker's World bewitch'd.
    First published in 1695 with title: The
    world bewitch'd. This is same, with new
    t. p. and lacking the dedication.
    Translation of Book 1 of his Le monde en-
    chanté, which is a translation of De beto-
    verde weereld.
    Variant of van der Linde 28.

    (Continued on next card)

Witchcraft
BF   Bekker, Balthasar, 1634-1698.
1410   Naakt verhaal van alle de kerkelike
B42   handelingen, voorgevallen in den Kerken-
1691a raad en de Classis van Amsterdam, alsmede
no.5 in de Synoden van Noord-Holland, tsedert
    den 31. May 1691. tot den 21. Aug. 1692,
    na vervolg des tijds uit de eigene acten
    en bygevoegde stukken der voornoemde kerk-
    like vergaderingen tsaamgesteld, en met
    aantekeningen van den auteur over verschei-
    dene omstandigheden breder verklaard. Am-
    sterdam, By D. vanden Dalen, boekver-
kooper, 1692.
    (Continued on next card)

Witchcraft
BF   Bekker, Balthasar, 1634-1698. Naakt
1410   verhaal van alle de kerkelike handelingen
B42   ... 1692. (Card 2)
1691a
no.5 6 p. l., 80, 40, 78 p. [p. 79-80 blank]
    title vignette, illus. initials. 20 x 16cm.
    $4°: *^4, 2*^2, A-C^4, D^2, E-K^4, L^2, 2A-2I^4$,
$3A-3K^4$.
    Black letter.
    Introduction autographed by Bekker.
    Variant of van der Linde 50:

8   (Continued on next card)

CATALOGUE OF THE CORNELL WITCHCRAFT COLLECTION

Witchcraft
BF
1410
B42
1691a
no.5

Bekker, Balthasar, 1634-1698. Naakt verhaal van alle de kerkelike handelingen ... 1692. (Card 3)

Nader beright, p. 73-78, added.
No. 5 in vol. lettered B. Bekker. Betoverde weereld.
I. Nederlandse Hervormde Kerk. Classes. Amsterdam. II. Nederlandse Hervormde Kerk. Synode van Noordholland, Edam, 1691. III. Title.

8

Witchcraft
BF
1410
B42
Z56
v.1
no.1

Bekker, Balthasar, 1634-1698. Nodige bedenkingen op de niewe beweegingen, onlangs verwekt door den circulairen brief en andere middelen, tegen den auteur van 't boek De betoverde weereld, door Balthasar Bekker, predikant tot Amsterdam. Amsterdam, Gedruckt by D. vanden Dalen, boekverkooper [1692?]
1 p. l., 62, [1] p. [p. 64 blank] title vignette, illus. initial. 19 x 16cm.
4°: π1, A-H⁴.
Preface autographed by Bekker.

(Continued on next card)

Witchcraft
BX
9479
B42
B11
no.4

Bekker, Balthasar, 1634-1698. Nodige bedenkingen op de niewe beweegingen, onlangs verwekt door den circulairen brief en andere middelen, tegen den auteur van 't boek De betoverde weereld, door Balthasar Bekker, predikant tot Amsterdam. Amsterdam, Gedruckt by D. vanden Dalen, boekverkooper [1692?]
1 p. l., 62 p. title vignette, illus. initial. 20 x 16cm.
4°: π1, A-H⁴.

(Continued on next card)

8

Witchcraft
BF
1410
B42
Z56
v.1
no.6

Bekker, Balthasar, 1634-1698. Naakt verhaal van alle de kerkelike handelingen, voorgevallen in den Kerkenraad en de Classis van Amsterdam, alsmede in de Synoden van Noord-Holland, tsedert den 31. May 1691. tot den 21. Aug. 1692. Na vervolg des tijds uit de eigene acten en bygevoegde stukken der voornoemde kerklike vergaderingen tsaamgesteld, en met aantekeningen van den auteur over verscheidene omstandigheden breder verklaard. Amsterdam, By D. vanden Dalen, boekverkooper, 1692.

(Continued on next card)

8

Witchcraft
BF
1410
B42
Z56
v.1
no.1

Bekker, Balthasar, 1634-1698. Nodige bedenkingen op de niewe beweegingen ... [1692?] (Card 2)

Dated at end: den 9. July 1692.
Van der Linde 42.
No. 1 in vol. lettered Bekker I.
1. Nederlandse Hervormde Kerk. Kerkenraden. Rotterdam. Circulaire brief ... wegens de saake van Dr. Balthasar Bekker. 2. Nederlandse Hervormde Kerk--Doctrinal and controversial works. 3. Bekker, Balthasar, 1634-1698. De betoverde weereld. I. Title.

8

Witchcraft
BX
9479
B42
B11
no.4

Bekker, Balthasar, 1634-1698. Nodige bedenkingen op de niewe beweegingen ... [1692?] (Card 2)

Preface autographed by Bekker.
Dated: Amsterdam den 9. July 1692.
Incomplete copy: final signature wanting.
Van der Linde 42.
No. 4 in vol. lettered B. Bekker's sterfbed en andere tractaten.

8

Witchcraft
BF
1410
B42
Z56
v.1
no.6

Bekker, Balthasar, 1634-1698. Naakt verhaal van alle de kerkelike handelingen ... 1692. (Card 2)

6 p. l., 80, 40, 71 p. [p. 72 blank] title vignette, illus. initials. 19 x 16cm.
4°: *⁴, 2*², A-C⁴, D², E-K⁴, L², 2A-2E⁴, 3A-3J⁴.
Black letter.
Introduction autographed by Bekker.
Van der Linde 50.
No. 6 in vol. lettered Bekker I.

Witchcraft
BF
1410
B42
Z56
v.2
no.5

Bekker, Balthasar, 1634-1698. Nodige bedenkingen op de niewe beweegingen, onlangs verwekt door den circulairen brief en andere middelen, tegen den auteur van 't boek De betoverde weereld, door Balthasar Bekker, predikant tot Amsterdam. Amsterdam, Gedruckt by D. vanden Dalen, boekverkooper [1692?]
1 p. l., 62, [1] p. [p. 64 blank] title vignette, illus. initial. 19 x 16cm.
4°: π1, A-H⁴.
Preface autographed by Bekker.

(Continued on next card)

8

Witchcraft
BF
1410
B42
1691a
no.8

Bekker, Balthasar, 1634-1698. Omstandig beright, van Balthasar Bekker, S. T. D. predikant tot Amsterdam, van sijne particuliere onderhandelinge met D. Laurentius Homma, sal. ged. in sijn leven mede predikant aldaar. Beneffens d'ontdekte lagen van Everhardus van der Hooght, en Jakob Lansman tegen denselven. Amsterdam, By D. vanden Dalen, boekverkooper, 1693.
1 p. l., 22 p. title and end page vignettes, illus. initials. 20 x 16cm.
4°: π1, A-C⁴ (-C4)

(Continued on next card)

8

Witchcraft
BF
1410
B42
Z86
no.1

Bekker, Balthasar, 1634-1698. Naakte uitbeeldinge van alle de vier boeken der Betoverde weereld, uitgegeven door Baltasar Bekker, S. S. Th. Dr. predikant tot Amsterdam. Vertonende het oogmerk van den schryver, de schikkinge van 't werk en sijn eigentlyk gevoelen daar in voorgesteld en voorgestaan; tot wechneeminge van vooroordeelen, en een kort begryp des ganschen werx. Ingesteld door den selften auteur. Amsterdam, By D. van den Dalen, boekverkooper, 1693.

(Continued on next card)

Witchcraft
BF
1410
B42
Z56
v.2
no.5

Bekker, Balthasar, 1634-1698. Nodige bedenkingen op de niewe beweegingen ... [1692?] (Card 2)

Dated at end: den 9. July 1692.
Van der Linde 42.
No. 5 in vol. lettered Bekker II.

8

Witchcraft
BF
1410
B42
1691a
no.8

Bekker, Balthasar, 1634-1698. Omstandig beright ... 1693. (Card 2)

Black letter.
"Bedekte lagen van Everhard van der Hooght, predikant tot Nieuwendam, en Jakob Lansman, procureur en notaris tot Amsterdam: ontdekt aan Balthasar Bekker ...:" p. 17-22.
Van der Linde 117.
No. 8 in vol. lettered B. Bekker. Betoverde weereld.
1. Hooght, Everard van der, d. 1716. 2. Lansman, Jakob. 3. Homma, Laurentius, d. 1681. II. Title.

8

Witchcraft
BF
1410
B42
Z86
no.1

Bekker, Balthasar, 1634-1698. Naakte uitbeeldinge van alle de vier boeken der Betoverde weereld ... 1693. (Card 2)

2 p. l., 32 p. title and end page vignettes, illus. initials. 19 x 15cm.
4°: *², a-d⁴.
Black letter.
Introduction autographed by Bekker.
Van der Linde 21.
No. 1 in vol. lettered Tractaten voor en tegen B. Bekker.

(Continued on next card)

Witchcraft
BF
1410
B42
Z56
v.3
no.11

Bekker, Balthasar, 1634-1698. Nodige bedenkingen op de niewe beweegingen, onlangs verwekt door den circulairen brief en andere middelen, tegen den auteur van 't boek De betoverde weereld, door Balthasar Bekker, predikant tot Amsterdam. Amsterdam, Gedruckt by D. vanden Dalen, boekverkoper [1692?]
1 p. l., 62, [1] p. [p. 64 blank] title vignette, illus. initial. 19 x 15cm.
4°: π1, A-H⁴.
Preface autographed by Bekker.

(Continued on next card)

Witchcraft
BF
1410
B42
Z56
v.1
no.8

Bekker, Balthasar, 1634-1698. Omstandig beright, van Balthasar Bekker, S. T. D. Predikant tot Amsterdam, van sijne particuliere onderhandelinge met D. Laurentius Homma, sal. ged. in sijn leven mede predikant aldaar. Beneffens d'ontdekte lagen van Everhardus van der Hooght, en Jakob Lansman tegen denselven. Amsterdam, By D. vanden Dalen, boekverkooper, 1693.
1 p. l., 22 p. title and end-page vignettes, illus. initials. 19 x 16cm.

(Continued on next card)

8

Witchcraft
BF
1410
B42
Z86
no.1

Bekker, Balthasar, 1634-1698. Naakte uitbeeldinge van alle de vier boeken der Betoverde weereld ... 1693. (Card 3)

1. His De betoverde weereld. II. Title.

Witchcraft
BF
1410
B42
Z56
v.3
no.11

Bekker, Balthasar, 1634-1698. Nodige bedenkingen op de niewe beweegingen ... [1692?] (Card 2)

Dated at end: den 9. July 1692.
Van der Linde 42.
No. 11 in vol. lettered Bekker III.

8

Witchcraft
BF
1410
B42
Z56
v.1
no.8

Bekker, Balthasar, 1634-1698. Omstandig beright ... 1693. (Card 2)

4°: π1, A-C⁴(-C4)
Black letter.
"Bedekte lagen van Everhard van der Hooght, predikant tot Nieuwendam, en Jakob Lansman, procureur en notaris tot Amsterdam: ontdekt aan Balthasar Bekker ...:" p. 17-22.
Van der Linde 117.
No. 8 in vol. lettered Bekker I.

CATALOGUE OF THE CORNELL WITCHCRAFT COLLECTION

Witchcraft
BF
1410
B42
1691a
no.7

Bekker, Balthasar, 1634-1698.
    Ondersoek en antwoord van Balthasar Bekker, S.S.Th.D. predikant tot Amsterdam, op 't request door de gedeputeerden der Noordhollandsche Synode tot Edam, in den herfst des jaars 1691. ingegeven aan de Ed. Gr. Mog. Heeren Staten van Holland en West Friesland tegen sijn boek De betoverde weereld. ... Amsterdam, By D. vanden Dalen, boekverkoper, 1693.
    2 p. l., 98 p. title vignette, illus. initials. 20 x 16cm.

8   (Continued on next card)

Witchcraft
BF
1410
B42
Z56
v.3
no.6

[Schuts, Jacobus] Missive, aen D. Balthazar Bekker ... 1692.   (Card 3)

    Van der Linde 147.
    No. 6 in vol. lettered Bekker III.
    1. Bekker, Balthasar, 1634-1698. De betoverde weereld. 2. Bekker, Balthasar, 1634-1698. Ondersoek van de betekeninge der kometen. 3. Bekker, Balthasar, 1634-1698. Uitlegginge van den prophet Daniel. I. Title.

8

Witchcraft
BF
1410
B42
Z56
v.3
no.28

Bekker, Balthasar, 1634-1698.
    Twee brieven van Balthasar Bekker predikant tot Amsterdam, aan Everhardus van der Hooght predikant tot Niewendam. D'eerste voor desen uitgegeven van den 25. September 1691, uit Amsterdam. D'andere nu daar by gevoegd, van den 3/13 Juny 1692, uit Franeker. Beide over het boek genaamd De betoverde weereld, en 't gene daar ontrent is voorgevallen. Met een kort berigt over voorrede van seker Opstel van aanmerkingen

8   (Continued on next ca[rd])

Witchcraft
BF
1410
B42
1691a
no.7

Bekker, Balthasar, 1634-1698. Ondersoek en antwoord ... 1693.   (Card 2)

    4°: *², A-M⁴, N1.
    Black letter.
    Prefatory letter autographed by Bekker.
    Van der Linde 53.
    No. 7 in vol. lettered B. Bekker. Betoverde weereld.
    1. Nederlandse Hervormde Kerk. Synode van Noordholland, Edam, 1691. 2. Bekker, Balthasar, 1634-1698. De betoverde weereld. I. Netherlands (United Provinces, 1581-1795) Staten General. II. Title.

8

Witchcraft
BX
9476
N8
B42++

Bekker, Balthasar, 1634-1698.
    Protest van Balthasar Bekker, S. S. T. D. en predikant tot Amsterdam, ter Synode van Noordholland binnen Alkmaar ingeleverd, den 7 Aug. 1692. Alkmaar, 1692.
    broadside. illus. initial. 32 x 20cm.
    Van der Linde 46.
    With this is bound De betoverde weereld van den hooggeleerden heer, Dr. Balthasar Bekker... [poem. n. p., 169-]
    1. Nederlandse Hervormde Kerk. Synode van Noordholland, Alkmaar, 1692. 2. Nederlandse Hervormde Kerk. Classes. Amsterdam. I. Title.

8

Witchcraft
BF
1410
B42
Z56
v.3
no.28

Bekker, Balthasar, 1634-1698. Twee brieven ... aan Everhardus vander Hooght ... 1692.   (Card 2)

    gemaakt door J. J. F. B. en tot Leewarden by Hero Nauta gedrukt. Franeker, By Leonardus Strik, boekverkoper, 1692.
    2 p. l., 32 p. title vignette, illus. initials. 19 x 15cm.
    4°: π², A-D⁴.
    Back of t. p. autographed by Bekker.

8   (Continued on next car[d])

Witchcraft
BF
1410
B42
Z56
v.1
no.4

Bekker, Balthasar, 1634-1698.
    Ondersoek en antwoord van Balthasar Bekker, S.S.Th.D. predikant tot Amsterdam, op 't request door de gedeputeerden der Noordhollandsche Synode tot Edam, in den herfst des jaars 1691. ingegeven aan de Ed. Gr. Mog. Heeren Staten van Holland en West Friesland tegen sijn boek De betoverde weereld. ... Amsterdam, By D. vanden Dalen, boekverkoper, 1693.
    2 p. l., 98 p. title vignette, illus. initials. 20 x 16cm.

                (Continued on next card)

Witchcraft
BF
1410
B42
Z56
v.3
no.9

[Bekker, Balthasar] 1634-1698.
    Remonstrantie in de Eerw. Synode van Noord-Holland, jegenwoordig vergaderd tot Alkmaar, ingediend by ofte van wegen Balthasar Bekker, S.S.Th.Dr. ende predikant tot Amsterdam, op den 5. Aug. 1692. [Alkmaar? 1692]
    8 p. illus. initial. 20 x 15cm.
    4°: A⁴.
    Caption title.
    Signed: Balthasar Bekker.

8   (Continued on next card)

Witchcraft
BF
1410
B42
Z56
v.3
no.28

Bekker, Balthasar, 1634-1698. Twee brieven ... aan Everhardus vander Hooght ... 1692.   (Card 3)

    Variant of van der Linde 107: has p. 32.
    No. 28 in vol. lettered Bekker III.
    1. Bekker, Balthasar, 1634-1698. De betoverde weereld. 2. Opstel van enige aanmerkingen op het boek van B. Bekker. I. Hooght, Everard van der, d. 1716. II. Title.

8

Witchcraft
BF
1410
B42
Z56
v.1
no.4

Bekker, Balthasar, 1634-1698. Ondersoek en antwoord ... 1693.   (Card 2)

    4°: *², A-M⁴, N1.
    Black letter.
    Prefatory letter autographed by Bekker.
    Imperfect: p. 31-32 sliced out.
    Van der Linde 53.
    No.4 in vol. lettered Bekker I.

8

Witchcraft
BF
1410
B42
Z56
v.3
no.9

[Bekker, Balthasar] 1634-1698. Remonstrantie in de Eerw. Synode van Noord-Holland ... [1692]   (Card 2)

    Describes Bekker's relations with the Classis of Amsterdam.
    Van der Linde 45.
    No. 9 in vol. lettered Bekker III.
    1. Nederlandse Hervormde Kerk. Classes. Amsterdam. I. Nederlandse Hervormde Kerk. Synode, Alkmaar, 1692. II. Title.

8

Witchcraft
BF
1410
B42
Z56
v.2
no.23

Bekker, Balthasar, 1634-1698.
    Twee brieven ... aan Everhardus vande[r] Hooght.
Hooght, Everard van der, d. 1716.
    Zeedig ondersoek van het boek, door den autheur, Balthasar Bekker, genaamt de Betoverde weereld. In het welke dat tweede boek, van vooren tot achteren, door alle de capittelen paragraaphen, ordentelijk werd wederlegt. Door Everardus van der Hooght ... Welke achter dit werk gevoegd heeft; drie-der-ley register te weeten I. Van Bekkers valsche citatien. II. Een van de texten, ende III. Een van verhandelde saaken, de welke of in dit boek

                (Continued on next ca[rd])

Witchcraft
BF
1410
B42
Z56
v.3
no.6

Bekker, Balthasar, 1634-1698.
    Ondersoek van de betekeninge der kometen.
[Schuts, Jacobus]
    Missive, aen D. Balthazar Bekker, in 't korte ontdekkende de gronden van sijn misgrepen, begaen in sijn drie tractaten De betooverde weereld, van den prophete Daniel, en van de cometen. Waer in N. Orchard, in sijn Leeringe der duivelen den grooten afval der Christenen, ende den spotterigen Philopater in sijn leven, ook hare voldoeninge krygen. Tot Nederlands waerschouwinge en onderricht der Joden. Gravenhage, By B. Beek, konst- en boekverkoper, 1692.

8   (Continued on next card)

Witchcraft
BF
1410
B42
1691a
no.3

Bekker, Balthasar, 1634-1698.
    Remonstrantie in de Eerw. Synode van Noord-Holland ... op den 5. Aug. 1692.
Nederlandse Hervormde Kerk. Synode van Noordholland, Edam, 1691.
    Acten ofte handelingen van de Noord-Hollandsche Synodus, gehouden binnen Edam en Alcmaar, anno 1691. en 1692. Rakende Dr. Balthasar Bekker, en sijn boek De betoverde wereld, met alle de documenten daar toe behoorende, waar onder ook eenige, die in het synodale acten-boek niet en staan uyt-gedrukt; met een voor-reden, strekkende tot weder-legging van Dr. Bekkers Remonstrantie en verdere exceptien tegen de competentie van de Synodus. Enchuysen, Gedrukt by J. D. Kuyper, 1692.

8   (Continued on next card)

Witchcraft
BF
1410
B42
Z56
v.2
no.23

Bekker, Balthasar, 1634-1698.
    Twee brieven ... aan Everhardus vander Hooght.
Hooght, Everard van der, d. 1716. Zeedig ondersoek van ... de Betoverde weereld ... [1692?]   (Card 2)

    of, in de seven brieven, zijn verhandelt, des autheurs antwoort op de brieven van B. Bekker. t'Amsterdam, By Dirk Boeteman [1692]
    4 p. l., 229, [1] p. [p. 231-232 blank], title and other vignettes, illus. initials.

                (Continued on next card)

Witchcraft
BF
1410
B42
Z56
v.3
no.6

Bekker, Balthasar, 1634-1698.
    Ondersoek van de betekeninge der kometen.
[Schuts, Jacobus] Missive, aen D. Balthazar Bekker ... 1692.   (Card 2)

    10 p. l., 69 p. [p. 70-72 blank], title and other vignettes, illus. initials. 20 x 15cm.
    4°: a-b⁴, c², A-I⁴.
    Black letter.
    Signed and dated at end: N. N. Den 22 November 1691.
    Neither Orchard nor Philopater is mentioned in the text.

8   (Continued on next card)

Witchcraft
BF
1410
B42
1691a
no.3

Bekker, Balthasar, 1634-1698.
    Remonstrantie in de Eerw. Synode van Noord-Holland ... op den 5. Aug. 1692.
Nederlandse Hervormde Kerk. Synode van Noordholland, Edam, 1691. Acten ofte handelingen van de Noord-Hollandsche Synodus, gehouden binnen Edam en Alcmaar ... 1692.   (Card 2)

    30 p. l., 102 p. title and end page vignettes., illus. initials. 20 x 16cm.
    4°: *-7⁴, 8*², A-N⁴(-N4)
    Remonstrantie, by Bekker: p. 73-83.
    Van der Linde 51.
    No. 3 in vol. lettered B. Bekker. Betoverde weereld.

8   (Continued on next card)

Witchcraft
BF
1410
B42
Z56
v.2
no.23

Bekker, Balthasar, 1634-1698.
    Twee brieven ... aan Everhardus vande[r] Hooght.
Hooght, Everard van der, d. 1716. Zeedig ondersoek van ... de Betoverde weereld... [1692?]   (Card 3)

    19 x 15cm.
    4°: *⁴, A-2F⁴.
    Black letter.
    Autograph on back of t. p.: Ev. van der Hooght.
    Van der Linde 114.
    No. 23 in vol. lettered Bekker II.

8   (Continued on next ca[rd])

CATALOGUE OF THE CORNELL WITCHCRAFT COLLECTION

Witchcraft
BF
1410
B42
Z56
v.3
no.6

Bekker, Balthasar, 1634-1698.
  Uitlegginge van den prophet Daniel.
  [Schuts, Jacobus]
    Missive, aen D. Balthazar Bekker, in 't korte ontdekkende de gronden van sijn misgrepen, begaen in sijn drie tractaten De betooverde weereld, over den prophete Daniel, en van de cometen. Waer in N. Orchard, in sijn Leeringe der duivelen den grooten afval der Christenen, ende den spotterigen Philopater in sijn leven, ook hare voldoeningen konnen krygen. Tot Nederlands waerschouwinge en onderricht der Joden. Gravenhage, By B. Beek, konst- en boekverkoper, 1692.

8 (Continued on next card)

Witchcraft
BF
1410
B42
Z56
v.3
no.6

Bekker, Balthasar, 1634-1698.
  Uitlegginge van den prophet Daniel.
  [Schuts, Jacobus] Missive, aen D. Balthazar Bekker ... 1692. (Card 2)
    10 p. l., 69 p. [p. 70-72 blank] title and other vignettes, illus. initials. 20 x 15cm.
    4°: a-b⁴, c², A-I⁴.
    Black letter.
    Signed and dated at end: N. N. Den 22 November 1691.
    Neither Orchard nor Philopater is mentioned in the text.

8 (Continued on next card)

Witchcraft
BF
1410
B42
Z56
v.3
no.6

Bekker, Balthasar, 1634-1698.
  Uitlegginge van den prophet Daniel.
  [Schuts, Jacobus] Missive, aen D. Balthazar Bekker ... 1692. (Card 3)
    Van der Linde 147.
    No. 6 in vol. lettered Bekker III.
    1. Bekker, Balthasar, 1634-1698. De betoverde weereld. 2. Bekker, Balthasar, 1634-1698. Ondersoek van de betekeninge der kometen. 3. Bekker, Balthasar, 1634-1698. Uitlegginge van den prophet Daniel. I. Title.

8

Witchcraft
BF
1410
B42
1691a
no.6

Bekker, Balthasar, 1634-1698.
    Viervoudige beantwoordinge van beswaarnissen, voorgesteld aan Balthasar Bekker, S. S. Th. Dr. predikant tot Amsterdam, over sijn boek, genaamd De betoverde weereld. ... Amsterdam, By D. van den Dalen, boekverkoper, 1692.
    3 p. l., 74, [110, i. e., 112], [8] p. title vignette, illus. initials. 20 x 16cm.
    4°: *3, A-J⁴, K1, a-o⁴, 2*⁴.
    Black letter.

8 (Continued on next card)

Witchcraft
BF
1410
B42
1691a
no.6

Bekker, Balthasar, 1634-1698. Viervoudige beantwoordinge van beswaarnissen ... 1692. (Card 2)
    Includes actions taken by the church.
    Preface autographed by Bekker.
    In second numbering, p. 94-95 repeated.
    Variant of van der Linde 49: signatures of third numbering differ.
    No. 6 in vol. lettered B. Bekker. Betoverde weereld.

8

Witchcraft
BF
1410
B42
Z56
v.1
no.3

Bekker, Balthasar, 1634-1698. Viervoudige beantwoordinge van beswaarnissen, voorgesteld aan Balthasar Bekker, S. S. Th. Dr. predikant tot Amsterdam, over sijn boek, genaamd De betoverde weereld. ... Amsterdam, By D. van den Dalen, boekverkoper, 1692.
    3 p. l., 74, 95, [1] p. title vignette, illus. initials. 19 x 17.
    4°: *⁴, A-J⁴, K1, a-m⁴.

8 (Continued on next card)

Witchcraft
BF
1410
B42
Z56
v.1
no.3

Bekker, Balthasar, 1634-1698. Viervoudige beantwoordinge van beswaarnissen ...1692. (Card 2)
    Black letter.
    Preface autographed by Bekker.
    Includes actions taken by the church.
    Variant of van der Linde 49: four final gatherings wanting.
    No. 3 in vol. lettered Bekker I.

8

Witchcraft
BF
1410
B42
1695

Bekker, Balthasar, 1634-1698.
    The world bewitch'd; or, An examination of the common opinions concerning spirits: their nature, power, administration, and operations. As also, the effects men are able to produce by their communication. Divided into IV parts. By Balthazar Bekker, D. D. and pastor at Amsterdam. Vol. I. Translated from a French copy, approved of and subscribed by the author's own hand. [London] Printed for R. Baldwin, 1695.

  (Continued on next card)

Witchcraft
BF
1410
B42
1695

Bekker, Balthasar, 1634-1698. The world bewitch'd ... 1695. (Card 2)
    41 p. l., 264 p. 17 x 10cm.
    12°: a⁶(-a1), b-d¹², B-M¹².
    No more published.
    Half title: The world bewitch'd, &c. Vol. I.
    Translation of vol. 1 of Le monde enchanté, Amsterdam, 1694, which is a translation of his De betoverde weereld, Amsterdam, 1691-93.

  (Continued on next card)

Witchcraft
BF
1410
B42
1695

Bekker, Balthasar, 1634-1698. The world bewitch'd ... 1695. (Card 3)
    Reissued in 1700 under title: The world turn'd upside down.
    Autograph on t. p.: Ch. Whittuck.
    Wing B 1781.
    Variant of van der Linde 28: 12°, not 8°.
    1. Demonology, 2. Angels. 3. Magic. 4. Witchcraft. I. Title. II. His De betoverde weereld—English. III. His Le monde enchanté—English.

Witchcraft
BF
1410
B42
1700

Bekker, Balthasar, 1634-1698.
    The world bewitch'd.
    [Bekker, Balthasar] 1634-1698. The world turn'd upside down: or, A plain detection of errors, in the common or vulgar belief, relating to spirits, spectres or ghosts, daemons, witches, &c. In a due and serious examination of their nature, power, administration, and operation. In what forms or shape incorporeal spirits appear to men, by what means, and of what elements they take to themselves, and form appearances of bodies, visible to mortal eyes; why they

  (Continued on next card)

Witchcraft
BF
1410
B42
1700

Bekker, Balthasar, 1634-1698.
    The world bewitch'd.
    [Bekker, Balthasar] 1634-1698. The world turn'd upside down ... 1700. (Card 2)
    appear, and what frights and force of imagination often delude us into the apprehensions of supposed phantasms, through the intimidation of the mind, &c. Also what evil tongues have power to produce of hurt of mankind, or irational [sic] creatures; and the effects men and women are able to produce by their communication with good or evil

  (Continued on next card)

Witchcraft
BF
1410
B42
1700

Bekker, Balthasar, 1634-1698.
    The world bewitch'd.
    [Bekker, Balthasar] 1634-1698. The world turn'd upside down ... 1700. (Card 3)
    spirits, &c. Written at the request of a person of honour, by B. B., a Protestant minister for publick information. London, Printed for E. Harris, 1700.
    37 p. l., 264 p. 16cm.
    12°: π1, b-d¹², B-M¹².
    With two old prints of devils inserted at front and back of book.

  (Continued on next card)

Witchcraft
BF
1410
B42
1700

Bekker, Balthasar, 1634-1698.
    The world bewitch'd.
    [Bekker, Balthasar] 1634-1698. The world turn'd upside down ... 1700. (Card 4)
    Title on spine: Bekker's World bewitch'd.
    First published in 1695 with title: The world bewitch'd. This is same, with new t. p. and lacking the dedication.
    Translation of Book 1 of his Le monde enchanté, which is a translation of De betoverde weereld.
    Variant of van der Linde 28.

  (Continued on next card)

Witchcraft
BF
1410
B42
1700

Bekker, Balthasar, 1634-1698.
    The world turn'd upside down: or, A plain detection of errors, in the common or vulgar belief, relating to spirits, spectres or ghosts, daemons, witches, &c. In a due and serious examination of their nature, power, administration, and operation. In what forms or shape incorporeal spirits appear to men, by what means, and of what elements they take to themselves, and form appearances of bodies, visible to mortal eyes; why they

  (Continued on next card)

Witchcraft
BF
1410
B42
1700

[Bekker, Balthasar] 1634-1698. The world turn'd upside down ... 1700. (Card 2)
    appear, and what frights and force of imagination often delude us into the apprehensions of supposed phantasms, through the intimidation of the mind, &c. Also what evil tongues have power to produce of hurt of mankind, or irational [sic] creatures; and the effects men and women are able to produce by their communication with good or evil

  (Continued on next card)

57

CATALOGUE OF THE CORNELL WITCHCRAFT COLLECTION

Witchcraft
BF
1410
B42
1700

[Bekker, Balthasar] 1634-1698. The world turn'd upside down ... 1700. (Card 3)

spirits, &c. Written at the request of a person of honour, by B. B., a Protestant minister for publick information. London, Printed for E. Harris, 1700.
37 p. l., 264 p. 16cm.
12°: π1, b-d¹², B-M¹²
With two old prints of devils inserted at front and back of book.

(Continued on next card)

Witchcraft
BF
1410
B42
1700

[Bekker, Balthasar] 1634-1698. The world turn'd upside down ... 1700. (Card 4)

Title on spine: Bekker's World bewitch'd.
First published in 1695 with title: The world bewitch'd. This is same, with new t. p. and lacking the dedication.
Translation of Book 1 of his Le monde enchanté, which is a translation of De betoverde weereld.
Variant of van der Linde 28.

(Continued on next card)

Witchcraft
BF
1410
B42
1700

[Bekker, Balthasar] 1634-1698. The world turn'd upside down ... 1700. (Card 5)

1. Demonology. 2. Angels. 3. Magic. 4. Witchcraft. I. Title. II. His Le monde enchanté--English. III. His De betoverde weereld--English. IV. His The world bewitch'd.

Bekker, Balthasar, 1634-1698.
Witchcraft
BF
1410
B42
Z56
v.3
no.26

Hooght, Everard van der, d. 1716.
Antwoord van Everardus van der Hooght, aan den eerwaarden, godzalige, hoog-geleerden heere, Do. Balthasar Bekker, S. Theologiae Doctor, yverig predikant tot Amsterdam. Amsterdam, By G. Borstius, boekverkoper, 1691.
1 p. l., 8, [2] p. title vignette, illus. initial. 19 x 15cm.
4°: π1, A⁴, [B]1.
Black letter.
Letter dated 29. Sept. 1691; postscript, 1 Oct. 1691.

(Continued on next card)

Bekker, Balthasar, 1634-1698.
Witchcraft
BF
1410
B42
Z56
v.3
no.26

Hooght, Everard van der, d. 1716. Antwoord ... aan ... Do. Balthasar Bekker ... 1691. (Card 2)

Van der Linde 106.
No. 26 in vol. lettered Bekker III.

1. Bekker, Balthasar, 1634-1698. Brief van den schrijver des boeks De betoverde weereld. I. Bekker, Balthasar, 1634-1698. II. Title.

Bekker, Balthasar, 1634-1698.
Witchcraft
BF
1410
B42
Z85
no.1

Nederlandse Hervormde Kerk. Classes. Amsterdam.
Vermeerderde articulen voor te stellen aen Do. B: Bekker. [Amsterdam, 1691]
[4] p. 19 x 16cm.
4°: π².
Caption title.
Text given also in its Autentyke copye van de articulen die ... den 23 Aug. 1691 opgestelt zyn. [Van der Linde 34]
No. 1 in vol. lettered Stukken betrekkelijk Bekker.

8
(Continued on next card)

Bekker, Balthasar, 1634-1698, supposed author.
Witchcraft
BF
1410
B42
Z56
v.2
no.22

Noomtjins, Zalomon.
Spiegel voor den verwarden, en warzoekende Haggebher Philaleethees. Waar in, uit zyne 6 brieven, enz. getoond word, syne onkunde, en verwarring, zoo in taal, als in zaaken. Ofte een briev van Zalomon Noomtjins, tot Amstelddam. Geschreeven aan zynen vriend C. S. S. tot Buiksloot. Inhoudende (neevens andere zaaken) voornaamelijk, eenige aanmerkingen, over den persoon, en de 6 brieven, enz. van Haggebher Philaleethees. Als meede over de briev, en persoon van Everardus

(Continued on next card)

Bekker, Balthasar, 1634-1698, supposed author.
Witchcraft
BF
1410
B42
Z56
v.2
no.22

Noomtjins, Zalomon. Spiegel voor den verwarden, en warzoekende Haggebher Philaleethees. 1692. (Card 2)

van der Hooght, en daar by ook over zyne Aanmerkingen, over de ordre van een welgestelde predikatie. Mitsgaders d'ontdekking, der lasteringen van Brink. Amsterdam, By D. van den Dalen, boekverkooper, 1692.
33, [1] p. title and other vignettes. 19 x 15cm.

(Continued on next card)

Bekker, Balthasar, 1634-1698, supposed author.
Witchcraft
BF
1410
B42
Z56
v.2
no.22

Noomtjins, Zalomon. Spiegel voor den verwarden, en warzoekende Haggebher Philaleethees. 1692. (Card 3)

4°: A-D⁴, E1.
Black letter (except for introduction)
Attacks critics of Balthasar Bekker's De betoverde weereld.
G. L. Burr suggests Noomtjins may be a pseudonym for Bekker.
Haggebher is a pseudonym of E. van der Hooght.

8
(Continued on next card)

Bekker, Balthasar, 1634-1698, supposed author.
Witchcraft
BF
1410
B42
Z56
v.2
no.22

Noomtjins, Zalomon. Spiegel voor den verwarden, en warzoekende Haggebher Philaleethees. 1692. (Card 4)

Van der Linde 111.
No. 22 in vol. lettered Bekker II.
1. Hooght, Everard van der, d. 1716. 2. Brink, Hendrik, 1645-1723. De godslasteringen van den amsterdamschen predikant Bekker. 3. Bekker, Balthasar, 1634-1698. De betoverde weereld. I. Title. II. Bekker, Balthasar, 1634-1698, supposed author.

8

Bekker, Balthasar, 1634-1698.
Witchcraft
BF
1410
B42
Z69
no.17,
18

Den predikant D. Balthasar Becker, seediglyk ondersogt so in zyn persoon als Schriften, of in die derst voorgeven, buyten hem alleen, de gantsche werelt betovert te zyn, selfs hier af wel vry is, ende dat daar en boven op hem niet soude werken, de geest van hovaardye en dwalinge tot ergernisse en van de kleine, en van de arme, en van de verslagene van geest, en die beeven voor Godts woort. By een missive den 19 January 1692, door H.v.G. van Amsterdam geschreven aan

NIC
(Continued on next card)

Bekker, Balthasar, 1634-1698.
Witchcraft
BF
1410
B42
Z69
no.17,
18

Den predikant D. Balthasar Becker ... (Card 2)

D. T. S. de Jonge tot Uytrecht. Met zyn Andtwoord provisioneel tot nader berigt daar op gevolgt, den 4. February desselven jaars, 1692.
Uytregt, Gedrukt by W. Jansz, 1692.
32, 36 p. 21cm.

Signatures: 4°: A-D⁴. 4°: A-D⁴, E2.
The Pro visioneel Antwoord has
special half-title and separate

NIC
(Continued on next card)

Bekker, Balthasar, 1634-1698.
Witchcraft
BF
1410
B42
Z69
no.17,
18

Den predikant D. Balthasar Becker ... 1692. (Card 3)

paging.
Van der Linde 63, 61.
"Extracten van ... De betoverde werelt, uytgetrokken en t'samengestelt door N. N.": p. 17-28 of the Provisioneel Antwoord; "Extract van 'tgepasseerde des Synodi tot Edam, 10. Aug. 1691. rakende D. Bekker ...": p. 28-29; "Articulen voor te stellen aan Do. B. Bekker" signed Leonardus

NIC
(Continued on next card)

Bekker, Balthasar, 1634-1698.
Witchcraft
BF
1410
B42
Z69
No.17,
18

Den predikant D. Balthasar Becker ... 1692. (Card

Groenewegen: p. 29-31; "Eerste aanbieding D. B. Bekker, op den 30. Aug. 1691": p. 31 "Articulen tot satisfactie aan de Eerw. Classis van Amsterdam, van Do. Balthasar Bekker ... wegens ... de Betoverde wereld ...": p. 32-36.
Nos. 17 & 18 in a Collection of tracts against Balthasar Bekker and h Betoverde weereld.

NIC
(Continued on next card)

Bekker, Balthasar, 1634-1698.
Witchcraft
BF
1410
B42
Z912

[Andala, Ruardus] 1665-1727.
Balthazar Bekkers en insonderheyd sijner voedsterlingen onkunde, onbescheidentheyd en dwalingen, kort en klaar ontdekt door een discipel van de Heer J. vander Waeyen en voedsterling van de Academie van Friesland. Franeker, Gedrukt by H. Gyzelaar, ordinaris drukker der Eed. Mog. Heeren Staten, en der Academie van Friesland, 1696.
2 p. l., 107 p. [p. 108 blank] title and end page vignettes, illus. initials. 21 x 17cm.

8
(Continued on next card)

Bekker, Balthasar, 1634-1698.
Witchcraft
BF
1410
B42
Z912

[Andala, Ruardus] 1665-1727. Balthazar Bekkers en insonderheyd sijner voedsterlingen onkunde ... 1696. (Card 2)

4°: *², A-N⁴, O².
Black letter.
Van der Linde 165.
Bound with Andala, Ruardus, 1665-1727. Uiterste verleegentheyd van Doctor Balt. Bekker. Franeker, 1696.
1. Bekker, Balthasar, 1634-1698. I. Title.

8

Bekker, Balthasar, 1634-1698.
Witchcraft
BX
9479
B42
A68

Arend, Johannes Pieter, 1796-1855.
Verhandeling, over Balthasar Bekker. Door J. P. Arend, Lector in de hoogduitsche en engelsche talen en letterkunde aan de doorluchtige school te Deventer.
(In Vaderlandsche letteroefeningen. Mengelwerk, tot fraaije letteren, konsten en weetenschappen, betrekkelyk. Amsterdam. 23cm. no. 16 (1829), p. [713]-743)
8°: 3A-3B⁸, 3B⁶.
This issue paged: [713]-756.

(Continued on next card)

Bekker, Balthasar, 1634-1698.
Witchcraft
BX
9479
B42
B11
no.13

Beknopte aanmerkingen over de korte opening van de plaatsen van 2 Pet. 2: 4 en Jud. v. 6. Voorgestelt aan R. A. predikant tot B. Als mede over de brief aan de selve. Waar in de bewysen over de geme den plaatsen naarstiglyk ondersogt, en wederlegt werden. Door een liefhebber der waarheyt. Amsterdam, Gedrukt voor den autheur, 1697.
4 p. l., 19 p. [p. 20 blank] title a other vignettes, illus. initials. 20 x 15cm.

(Continued on next ca

58

CATALOGUE OF THE CORNELL WITCHCRAFT COLLECTION

Witchcraft
BX 9479 B42 B11 no.13

Bekker, Balthasar, 1634-1698.
    Beknopte aanmerkingen over de korte opening van de plaatsen van 2 Pet. 2: 4 en Jud. v. 6. 1697.   (Card 2)

    4°: A-C^4, D^2.
    Black letter (except introduction)
    Supports Ruardus Andala in his controversy with Balthasar Bekker over Biblical spirits.
    No. 13 in vol. lettered B. Bekkers sterfbed en andere tractaten.
    1. Devil. 2. Bible. N. T. 2 Peter, II, 4--Criticism, interpretation, etc.

8   (Continued on next card)

Witchcraft
BF 1555 A55 no.2

Bekker, Balthasar, 1634-1698.
    Brunsmand, Johan, 1637-1707.
    Johannis Brunsmanni Energumeni Coagienses, sive Admirabilis historia, de horrenda cacodaemonis tentatione, quacum in Selandia Daniae, ejusque urbe Coagio familia civis, & vita honestissimi & fama integerrimi, per annorum aliquot spatium est conflictata: primum sermone Danico aliquoties edita & impressa: nunc vero in exterorum gratiam Latine interpretata & cum duplici auctario edita. Editio   altera Latina, auctior

8   (Continued on next card)

Witchcraft
BF 1410 B42 Z56 v.3 no.25

Bekker, Balthasar, 1634-1698.
    [Hooght, Everard van der] d. 1716.
    Derde briev van הגבר [Haggebher] ΦΙΛΑΛΗΘΗΣ [Philaleethees] geschreeven aan zynen vriend N. N. over het vervolg van de kerkelyke proceduuren tegen den persoon van Do. Balthasar Bekker; nevens de aan-merkingen over de gereformeerde confessie, ende het gevoelen van de gesonde gereformeerde godsgeleerden, nopende het hooft-stuk van de natuure ende de werkingen der engelen. Amsterdam, By G. Borstius, boekverkoper, 1691.

8   (Continued on next card)

Witchcraft
BX 9476 N8 B42++

Bekker, Balthasar, 1634-1698.
    De Betoverde weereld van den hooggeleerden heer, Dr. Balthasar Bekker, door de geestelykheit bevogten. [poem. n. p., 169-]
    broadside. 21 x 20cm.

    Bound with Bekker, Balthasar, 1634-1698. Protest ... ter Synode van Noordholland ... Alkmaar, 1692.

    1. Bekker, Balthasar, 1634-1698.

8

Witchcraft
BF 1555 A55 no.2

Bekker, Balthasar, 1634-1698.
    Brunsmand, Johan, 1637-1707. ... Energumeni Coagienses ... 1695.   (Card 2)

    & correctior Leidensi. Lipsiae, Apud Joh. Melchior Lieben, 1695.
    4 p. l., 156 p. 14cm.
    First published 1674 with title: Et forfaerdeligt huus-kaars.
    Attributed by British Museum to A. H. Barskier, whose narrative makes up first part of work   (p. 1-73)

8   (Continued on next card)

Witchcraft
BF 1410 B42 Z56 v.3 no.25

Bekker, Balthasar, 1634-1698.
    [Hooght, Everard van der] d. 1716. Derde briev ... aan zynen vriend N. N. ... 1691.   (Card 2)

    [39]-58 p. title vignette, illus. initial. 19 x 15cm.
    4°: π1, A-B^4, C1.
    Black letter.
    The friend N. N. is Jacobus Schuts?
    Van der Linde 99.
    No. 25 in vol. lettered Bekker III.

    (Continued on next card)

Witchcraft
BF 1410 B42 Z56 v.3 no.2

Bekker, Balthasar, 1634-1698.
    Bly, Gratianus de
    Verklaeringe van een turkse parabel: of Voorbeeld der mahumetaense kerktucht: in rijm gesteld door Mr. Gratianus de Bly, volgens de vertaelinge uit seker arabisch schrijver. ... [Amsterdam?] By J. Rieuwertsz, boekverkoper, 1691.
    54 p. end page vignette, illus. initial. 19 x 15cm.
    4°: A-G^4(-G4)
    A collection   of satirical verse and prose, other   authors included, in

8   (Continued on next card)

Witchcraft
BF 1555 A55 no.2

Bekker, Balthasar, 1634-1698.
    Brunsmand, Johan, 1637-1707. ... Energumeni Coagienses ... 1695.   (Card 3)

    No. 2 in vol. lettered Andreae. De angelorum...

    1. Witchcraft--Denmark. 2. Bartholin, Thomas, 1616-1680. 3. Bekker, Balthasar, 1634-1698. I. Barskier, Anne Hans. II. His   Et forfaerdeligt huus-kaars--Latin. III. Title: Energumeni Coagienses.

8

Witchcraft
BF 1410 B42 Z69 no.9

Bekker, Balthasar, 1634-1698.
    [Hooght, Everard van der] d. 1716.
    Sesde briev van הגבר Φιλαλήθης Haggebher Philaleethees, geschreeven aan zynen vriend N. N. vervattende: I. Een afwysing van vyfderlei gewaande voorspraaken van D. Bekker. Ende II. een verhandeling van de De Daimonia, na hare beteekenisse voor, in, ende na de tyden Christi. Volgens het welke uyt het Hebreeusch Griekich en Syrisch klaar te sien is, dat De Daimonia zedert   Christi tyden niet anders zyn, dan   de Duyvelen. Amsterdam,

NIC   (Continued on next card)

Witchcraft
BF 1410 B42 Z56 v.3 no.2

Bekker, Balthasar, 1634-1698.
    Bly, Gratianus de   Verklaeringe van een turkse parabel ... 1691.   (Card 2)

    defense of Balthasar Bekker.
    Gratianus de Bly is possibly a pseudonym.
    No. 2 in vol. lettered Bekker III.
    1. Bekker, Balthasar, 1634-1698. I. Title.

Witchcraft
BF 1410 B42 Z56 v.2 no.8

Bekker, Balthasar, 1634-1698.
    Copy van een brief geschreeve aan een heer, woonende tusschen Rotterdam en Dort. Raakende het gepasseerde in de saak van Dr. B. Bekker; door een liefhebber van vreede en waarheid. Dord, Gedrukt by G. Abramsz, 1692.
    18 p. [p. 19-20 blank] title vignette. 19 x 15cm.
    4°: A-B^4, C^2.
    Signed: A. T.
    Van der Lin   de 48; 64.
    No. 8 in   vol. lettered Bekker II.

8   (Continued on next card)

Witchcraft
BF 1410 B42 Z69 no.9

Bekker, Balthasar, 1634-1698.
    [Hooght, Everard van der] d. 1716. Sesde briev van ... Haggebher Philaleethees ...   (Card 2)

    G. Borstius, 1691.
    135-176 p. 21cm.
    Signatures: 4°: π1, A-E^4, F1.
    Black letter.
    The friend N.N. may be Jacobus Schuts.
    Van der Linde 103.
    No. 9 in   a Collection of tracts against   Balthasar Bekker and his betoverde   weereld.

NIC   (Continued on next card)

Witchcraft
BX 9479 B42 B11 no.17

Bekker, Balthasar, 1634-1698.
    Brief van L. P. aan Herman Bouman; eerst in 't bysonder aan hem geschreeven, en nu door hem, met verlof van den autheur, gemeen gemaakt: behelsende sommige redenen waarom hy de soo genaamde Sleutel der geesten enz. van M. van Diepen, en J. Hubener niet, ofte niet zoodanig alse daar ligt, behoorde te beantwoorden; en teffens een volstrekte omkeering van de gronden van dat woest geschrift. Amsterdam, By   R. Blokland, boekverkoper, 1699.

8   (Continued on next card)

Witchcraft
BX 9479 B42 B11 no.3

Bekker, Balthasar, 1634-1698.
    Do. [i. e., doctor] B. Bekkers Sterf-bedde verdeedigt, tegens de zoo genaamde Nodige aanmerkingen over het zelve: vervat in een brief aan den schryver; behelzende een openbaar bewijs zijner onkunde in de geschillen, en verdere ongegronde redeneeringen: tot wegschuiminge van zijn alderhaatelijkste beschryving en veroor-deeling van den overledene. Door M. G. Amsterdam, By R. Blokland, boekverkooper, 1699.
    1 p. l.,   16 p. title and end

8   (Continued on next card)

Witchcraft
BF 1410 B42 Z69 no.10

Bekker, Balthasar, 1634-1698.
    [Hooght, Everard van der] d. 1716.
    Sevende briev van Φιλαλήθης geschreeven aan den E. Heer C. E. over den oorspronk, voortgang, ende het gebruyk der talen in het gemeen. Ende, in het byzonder, van de Duyvelen in het Oude Testament, onder de woorden scheedhijm, ende segnirijm, cap. 8. Item, een vertooning, dat de Heere Jesus ons de geheele Gods-geleertheyd in zijne dagen heest geleert, na de waarheyd der saake, ende   nooit, tegen de waarheyd, na de   dwaling des volks. cap. 9. Ende dat de   beseetene ofte beduyvelde

NIC   (Continued on next card)

Witchcraft
BX 9479 B42 B11 no.17

Bekker, Balthasar, 1634-1698.
    Brief van L. P. aan Herman Bouman ... 1699.   (Card 2)

    2 p. l., 12 p. title and end page vignettes, illus. initials. 20 x 15cm.
    4°: π^2, A^4, B^2.
    Written by a supporter of Balthazar Bekker, whom Diepen and Hubener attacked.
    No. 17 in vol. lettered B. Bekkers sterfbed en andere tractaten.
    1. Diepen,   Marcus van. De sleutel der geesten.   2. Bekker, Balthasar,

    (Continued on next card)

Witchcraft
BX 9479 B42 B11 no.3

Bekker, Balthasar, 1634-1698.
    Do. [i. e., doctor] B. Bekkers Sterf-bedde verdeedigt ... 1699.   (Card 2)

    page vignettes, illus. initial. 20 x 16 cm.
    4°: π1, A-B^4.
    Van der Linde 207.
    No. 3 in vol. lettered B. Bekkers sterf-bed en andere tractaten.
    1. Bekker, Balthasar, 1634-1698. 2. Bekker, Johannes Henricus, fl. 1698-1737. Sterf-bedde van   ... Do. Balthazar Bekker.

    (Continued on next card)

Witchcraft
BF 1410 B42 Z69 no.10

Bekker, Balthasar, 1634-1698.
    [Hooght, Everard van der] d. 1716. Sevende briev van ...   (Card 2)

    sijn geplaagt geworden van den Duyvel, als de naaste oorsaak van hare siektens, cap. 10. Nevens een klaar vertoog, dat het niet de minste eygenschap en heeft, om zoo veele texten in Gods woord, alwaar de Satan, als een werker, benoemt word, alleen te willen betrekken op den Duyvel, voor soo veel hy geweest is   de oorsaak van de eerste verleyding   des menschen, cap. 11.

NIC   (Continued on next card)

CATALOGUE OF THE CORNELL WITCHCRAFT COLLECTION

Witchcraft
BF
1410
B42
Z69
no.10

Bekker, Balthasar, 1634-1698.
⌞Hooght, Everard van der⌟, d. 1716. Sevende brief van ...   (Card 3)
Waar by koomen eenige invoegselen tegens sommige misduydingen, in het Post-scriptum. Met het vervolg der kerkelijke proceduuren tegen D. B. Bekker. t'Amsterdam, By G. Borstius, 1692.
179-235 p. 21cm.
Signatures: 4°: π1, A-G⁴, H¹.
Black letter.

NIC   (Continued on next card)

Witchcraft
BF
1410
B42
Z56
v.3
no.10

Bekker, Balthasar, 1634-1698.
Klinkende bel; of Uytroep om den verlorenen duyvel, door last van sijn liefhebbers. Rotterdam, Gedrukt by P. van Veen, boekdrukker, 1691.
8 p. title vignette. 20 x 15cm.
4°: A⁴.
Poem supporting Balthasar Bekker against the Synode van Noordholland.
"De duyvel roepende uyt sijn kerker, tot antwoord van den Uytroper:" p. 7-8. (Poem)
Van der Linde 194.

8   (Continued on next card)

Witchcraft
BF
1410
B42
Z56
v.2
no.1

Bekker, Balthasar, 1634-1698.
Nederlandse Hervormde Kerk. Classes. Amsterdam. Consistorie. Autentyke copye van de articulen van ... den 23 Aug. 1691. ... ⌞1691⌟   (Card 2)
Aenbieding van Do. B. Bekker: p. ⌞7⌟-⌞8⌟.
Van der Linde 30.
No. 1 in vol. lettered Bekker II.
1. Nederlandse Hervormde Kerk--Doctrinal and controversial works. I. Bekker, Balthasar, 1634-1698. II. Title.

8

Witchcraft
BF
1410
B42
Z69
no.10

Bekker, Balthasar, 1634-1698.
⌞Hooght, Everard van der⌟, d. 1716. Sevende briev van ... 1692.   (Card 4)
Van der Linde 104.
No. 10 in a collection of tracts against Balthasar Bekker and his Betoverde weereld.
1. Language and languages. 2. Devil. 3. Bekker, Balthasar, 1634-1698. I. Title.

NIC

Witchcraft
BF
1410
B42
Z56
v.3
no.10

Bekker, Balthasar, 1634-1698.
Klinkende bel; of Uytroep om den verlorenen duyvel ... 1691.   (Card 2)
No. 10 in vol. lettered Bekker III.
1. Bekker, Balthasar, 1634-1698. 2. Nederlandse Hervormde Kerk. Synode van Noordholland, Edam, 1691. I. De duyvel roepende uyt sijn kerker. ⌞poem⌟

8

Witchcraft
BX
9477
U92

Bekker, Balthasar, 1634-1698.
Nederlandse Hervormde Kerk. Classes. Utrecht.
Briev van de Eerwaerde Classis van Utrecht aan de Eerwaerde Classis van Amsterdam. Daer toe dienende, dat Dr. Bekker autheur van de fameuse boek, De betoverde werelt genaemt, niet wederom tot de bedieninge van het predikampt in de Gereformeerde Kerck toegelaten de. Gedruckt na de copy tot Utrecht. Amsterdam, By A. D. Oossaan, boekverkooper, 1692.

8   (Continued on next card)

Witchcraft
BF
1410
B42
Z56
v.3
no.24

Bekker, Balthasar, 1634-1698.
Tweede brief van ⌞הבר הבר⌟ ⌞Haggébher⌟ ΦΙΛΑΛΗΘΗΣ ⌞philaleethees⌟, geschreeven aan zynen vriend N. N. over de ordentelyke kerkelyke proceduuren, gehouden tegen den persoon ende het boek van Do. Balthasar Bekker, by zyn E. geintituleert De betoverde wereld. Met eenige ecclesiastique, theologische, philosophische ende philologische aanmerkingen over de zelve. Amsterdam, By G. Borstius, boekverkoper, 1691.
⌞19⌟-40 p. title vignette, illus. initial. 19 x 15cm.

8   (Continued on next card)

Witchcraft
BF
1410
B42
Z56
v.3
no.31

Bekker, Balthasar, 1634-1698.
Eine Medaille, auf den weltberühmten Teufels-Banner, D. Balthasar Bekker, von A. 1692.
(In Wöchentliche historische Münz-Belustigung. Bremen? 21cm. 44. Stück (1736), p. 345-352)
4°: 2X⁴.
Both sides of coin are depicted.
No. 31 in vol. lettered Bekker III.
1. Bekker, Balthasar, 1634-1698.

8

Witchcraft
BX
9477
U92

Bekker, Balthasar, 1634-1698.
Nederlandse Hervormde Kerk. Classes. Utrecht. Briev ... aan de Eerwaerde Classis van Amsterdam. 1692.   (Card 2)
6 p. ⌞p. 7-8 blank⌟ title vignette, illus. initial. 22 x 17cm.
4°: A⁴.
Dated: 18 Martii ... 1692.
Van der Linde 34.
1. Bekker, Balthasar, 1634-1698. I. Nederlandse Hervormde Kerk. Classes. Amsterdam. II. Title.

Witchcraft
BF
1410
B42
Z56
v.3
no.24

Bekker, Balthasar, 1634-1698.
⌞Hooght, Everard van der⌟, d. 1716. Tweede brief ... aan zynen vriend N. N. ... 1691.   (Card 2)
4°: π1, A-B⁴, C².
Black letter.
The friend N. N. is Jacobus Schuts?
Van der Linde 98.
No. 24 in vol. lettered Bekker III.
1. Bekker, Balthasar, 1634-1698. 2. Bekker, Balthasar, 1634-1698. De betoverde weereld. 3. Nederlandse Hervormde Kerk. I. Schuts, Jacobus. II. Title.

8

Witchcraft
BF
1410
B42
Z56
v.3
no.4

Bekker, Balthasar, 1634-1698.
⌞Molinaeus, Johannes⌟, d. 1702.
Paraenesis; ofte ernstige aenspraek aen den siender van Een vremt nagtgesigt. Rotterdam, By B. Bos, 1692.
1 p. l., 10 p. title vignette, illus. initial. 20 x 16cm.
4°: π1, A⁴, B1.
Black letter.
Signed: J:M.
Defense of the author's attack on Balthasar Bekker and De betoverde weereld.

8   (Continued on next card)

Witchcraft
BF
1410
B42
Z56
v.3
no.14

Bekker, Balthasar, 1634-1698.
Nederlandse Hervormde Kerk. Kerkenraden. Utrecht.
Briev van de Eerwaerde Kerkenraad van Utrecht, aan de Eerw. Kerkenraad van Amsterdam, daer toe tendeerende dat de autheur van het boek, De betoverde wereld genaamt, niet wederom tot de bedieninge van het predikampt in de Gereformeerde Kerke mach werden toegelaten. ⌞Amsterdam, 1692?⌟
4 p. 20 x 15cm.
4°: A².

8   (Continued on next card)

Witchcraft
B
3998
K43

Bekker, Balthasar, 1634-1698.
Kettner, Friedrich Ernst.
De duobus impostoribus, Benedicto Spinosa et Balthasare Bekkero. Lipsiae, Stanno Immanuelis Titii ⌞1694⌟.
⌞17⌟ p. 20cm.
Diss.--Leipzig.
1. Spinoza, Benedictus de, 1632-1677. 2. Bekker, Balthasar, 1634-1698. I. Title.

Witchcraft
BF
1410
B42
Z56
v.3
no.4

Bekker, Balthasar, 1634-1698.
⌞Molinaeus, Johannes⌟, d. 1702. Paraenesis ... 1692.   (Card 2)
Van der Linde 134.
No. 4 in vol. lettered Bekker III.
1. Bekker, Balthasar, 1634-1698. 2. Beschryvinge van een vremd nagt-gezigte. I. Title.

Witchcraft
BF
1410
B42
Z56
v.3
no.14

Bekker, Balthasar, 1634-1698.
Nederlandse Hervormde Kerk. Kerkenraden. Utrecht. Briev ... aan de Eerw. Kerkenraad van Amsterdam ... ⌞1692?⌟   (Card 2)
Caption title.
"Gedrukt na de copie van Johannes Dale. Variant of van der Linde 43, which is the printing by Johannes Dalé.
No. 14 in vol. lettered Bekker III.
1. Bekker, Balthasar, 1634-1698. I. Nederlandse Hervormde Kerk. Kerkenraden. Amsterdam. II. Title.

8

Witchcraft
BF
1410
B42
Z56
v.3
no.8

Bekker, Balthasar, 1634-1698.
Een Keuning-kaarsje voor den siender van Een vremt nagtgesigte, om te dienen tot ophelderinge van syn St. Niklaas-droom. Ezelenburg, Gedrukt in de Gulde Schoolplak ⌞1692⌟
8 p. illus. initial. 20 x 15cm.
4°: A⁴.
Black letter.
Defending Molinaeus, and against Bekker.
Van der Linde 133.
No. 8 in vol. lettered Bekker III.

8   (Continued on next card)

Witchcraft
BF
1410
B42
Z56
v.2
no.1

Bekker, Balthasar, 1634-1698.
Nederlandse Hervormde Kerk. Classes. Amsterdam. Consistorie.
Autentyke copye van de articulen die van het Eerwaerde Consistorie van Amsterdam. den 23 Aug. 1691. opgestelt zyn om voor te houden aan Do. B. Bekker en de aenbieding die Do. B. Bekker daar op gedaen heeft den 30 Augusti 1691. Amsterdam, Gedrukt by G. Borstius, boekverkooper ⌞1691⌟
⌞8⌟ p. title vignette. 19 x 15cm.
4°: A⁴.

8   (Continued on next card)

Witchcraft
BF
1410
B42
Z56
v.3
no.21

Bekker, Balthasar, 1634-1698.
Rabus, Petrus, 1660-1702.
Ernstige en zedige verantwoording van P. Rabus, tegen de lasteringen des remonstrantschen predigers J. Molinaeus. Rotterdam, By P. Boekenes, boekverkooper, 16
1 p. l., 24 p. title and end page vignettes, illus. initial. 20 x 16cm.
4°: π1, A-C⁴.
Black letter.
In defense of Balthasar Bekker.
Van der Linde 135.
No. 21 in vol. lettered Bekker

8   (Continued on next card)

CATALOGUE OF THE CORNELL WITCHCRAFT COLLECTION

Bekker, Balthasar, 1634-1698.

Witchcraft
BF
1410
B42
v.5
no.4

Request aan de Eerwaarde Kerkenraad van Amsterdam, overgelevert den 20 Maart 1692. Ten eynde de suspensie van Do. Balthasar Bekker mochte werden gecontinueert. Amsterdam, By G. Borstius, boekverkooper [1692]
11 p. [p. 12 blank] title vignette, illus. initial. 19 x 16cm.
4°: A⁴, [B²]
Van der Linde 39.
No. 4 in vol. lettered Stukken betrekkelijk Bekker.

(Continued on next card)

Bekker, Balthasar, 1634-1698.

Witchcraft
BX
9479
B42
B11
no.2

[Schuts, Jacobus]
Nodige aanmerking over het Sterf-bedde van Balthasar Bekker. Vertonende de openbare valsheyt van dat syn gevoelen, dat hy op syn dood-bedde segt hem voor paart en wagen verstrekt te hebben om hem te voeren na den hemel. Gravenhage, By P. van Tol, boekverkooper, 1698.
13 p. [p. 14 blank] title vignette, illus. initial. 20 x 16cm.
4°: A-B⁴(-B4)

(Continued on next card)

Bekker, Balthasar, 1634-1698.

Witchcraft
BX
9479
B42
B11
no.2

[Schuts, Jacobus] Nodige aanmerking over het Sterf-bedde van Balthasar Bekker. 1698. (Card 2)
Black letter.
Ascribed to Schuts by van der Linde.
Van der Linde 206.
No. 2 in vol. lettered B. Bekkers sterf-bed en andere tractaten.
1. Bekker, Balthasar, 1634-1698. 2. Bekker, Johannes Henricus, fl. 1698-1737. Sterf-bedde van ... Do. Balthazar Bekker. I. Title.

Bekker, Balthasar, 1634-1698.

Witchcraft
BF
1410
B42
Z56
v.2
no.19

[Schuts, Jacobus]
Seedige aanmerkinge over de voorreden, genaamt: De godtslasteringe van den amsterdamsche predikant Dr. Bekker, ter waarschouwinge van alle vroome in den lande wederleyt, in de voorreden voor de toetsteen der waarheyt, ende der meyninge, door Henrikus Brink, &c. Door N. N. Amsterdam, By D. van den Dalen, boekverkooper, 1691.
8, 88 p. title vignette, illus. initial. 19 x 15cm.

(Continued on next card)

Bekker, Balthasar, 1634-1698.

Witchcraft
BF
1410
B42
Z56
v.2
no.19

[Schuts, Jacobus] Seedige aanmerkinge over de voorreden ... 1691. (Card 2)
4°: A⁴, A-L⁴.
Black letter.
Signed on back of t. p.: J: C:
Incomplete: all after first gathering wanting.
Van der Linde 84.
No. 19 in vol. lettered Bekker II.
1. Brink, Hendrik, 1645-1723.

(Continued on next card)

Bekker, Balthasar, 1634-1698.

WITCHCRAFT
BF
1555
M94
029
no.4

Semler, Johann Salomo, 1725-1791.
D. Joh. Salomo Semlers ... Abfertigung der neuen Geister und alten Irtümer in der Lohmannischen Begeisterung zu Kemberg nebst theologischem Unterricht von dem Ungrunde der gemeinen Meinung von leiblichen Besitzungen des Teufels und Bezauberungen der Christen. Halle, Bey J. J. Gebauer, 1760.
40, 328 p. 18cm.
Dedication and "Vorrede" comprise the first numbering.

8
NIC
(Continued on next card)

Bekker, Balthasar, 1634-1698.

WITCHCRAFT
BF
1555
M94
029
no.4

Semler, Johann Salomo, 1725-1791. ...
Abfertigung der neuen Geister ... 1760. (Card 2)
"Anhang. Auszug aus des Chaufepiee [sic] Nouveau dictionnaire historique et critique, von dem Artikel Balthas. Bekker": p. 317-328.
No. 4 in vol. lettered Oesfeld u. a.
1. Lohmannin, Anna Elisabeth. 2. Müller, Gottlieb. Gründlicher Nachricht von einer begeisterten Weibesperson. 3. Devil. 4. Bekker, Balthasar, 1634-1698.

8
NIC
(Continued on next card)

Bekker, Balthasar, 1634-1698.

Witchcraft
BF
1410
B42
Z56
v.2
no.13

Den triumpheerenden duyvel spookende omtrent den Berg van Parnassus, en beginnende, na sijn gedaane triumph-spokery, te maalen, over seekere hem nog in de weg sijnde swarigheden; gelijk meede over seekere nu in 't ligt gekomene medailje of penning, verbeeldende de duyvelisten en der selver doen; van welke medailje de beschrijvinge en uytlegginge hier agter gevoegd is.
[Middelburg, By G. Horthemels, boekverkooper, 1692]
24 p. 19 x 15cm.

(Continued on next card)

Bekker, Balthasar, 1634-1698.

Witchcraft
BF
1410
B42
Z56
v.2
no.13

Den triumpheerenden duyvel spookende omtrent den Berg van Parnassus ... [1692] (Card 2)
4°: A-C⁴.
Satire defending Balthasar Bekker against the Reformed Church.
Van der Linde 185.
No. 13 in vol. lettered Bekker II.

1. Devil—Fiction. 2. Bekker, Balthasar, 1634-1698. 3. Nederlandse Hervormde Kerk.

8

Bekker, Balthasar, 1634-1698.

Witchcraft
BF
1410
B42
1691a
no.9

't Voorgevallene in de catechisatie, by Do. Adrianus van Wesel, op Sondagh den 28sten December. Ao. 1692. in de Oudezijds Kapel, opgesteld door een toehoorder. Amsterdam, By D. vanden Dalen, boekverkooper, 1693.
8 p. title vignette. 20 x 16cm.
4°: A⁴.
Black letter.
Van der Linde 177.
Argues for tolerance of views held by Balthasar Bekker and his followers.

8
(Continued on next card)

Bekker, Balthasar, 1634-1698.

Witchcraft
BF
1410
B42
1691a
no.9

't Voorgevallene in de catechisatie, by Do. Adrianus van Wesel ... 1693. (Card 2)
No. 9 in vol. lettered B. Bekker. Betoverde weereld.

1. Nederlandse Hervormde Kerk—Doctrinal and controversial works. 2. Wesel, Adrianus van, d. 1710. 3. Bekker, Balthasar, 1634-1698. I. Een toehoorder, pseud.

8

Bekker, Balthasar, 1634-1698.

Witchcraft
BF
1410
B42
Z56
v.2
no.4

Walten, Ericus, 1663-1697.
Brief aan sijn Excellentie, de Heer Graaf van Portland, &c. &c. Rakende de persoon en het gevoelen van Dr. B. Bekker, en 't geen tegen hem, by eenige van sijn partyen, word verwagt, en uytgestrooyd, ten opsigte van sijn Koninglijke Majesteyt van Groot Britanjen. ... Door Ericus Walten ... Gedrukt voor den auteur. Gravenhage, By Meyndert Uytwerf, boekverkooper, 1692.
80 p. title vignette, illus. initial. 19 x 15cm.

4
(Continued on next card)

Bekker, Balthasar, 1634-1698.

Witchcraft
BF
1410
B42
Z56
v.2
no.4

Walten, Ericus, 1663-1697. Brief aan sijn Excellentie, de Heer Graaf van Portland ... 1692. (Card 2)
4°: A-K⁴.
Van der Linde 174.
No. 4 in vol. lettered: Bekker II.

1. Bekker, Balthasar, 1634-1698. 2. Devil. I. Portland, William Bentinck, 1st earl of, 1649-1709. II. William III, King of Great Britain, 1649-1709. III. Title.

8

Bekker, Balthasar, 1634-1698—Bibliography.

Witchcraft
Z
8086
.8
L74+

Linde, Antonius van der, 1833-1897.
Balthasar Bekker. Bibliografie door Dr. A. van der Linde ... 's Gravenhage, M. Nijhoff, 1869.
2 p. l., 57 p. 26 cm.

1. Bekker, Balthasar, 1634-1698—Bibl. I. Title.

8-7359

Library of Congress   Z8086.8.L5

Bekker, Balthasar, 1634-1698—Biography.

Witchcraft
BX
9479
B42
B11
no.1

Bekker, Johannes Henricus, fl. 1698-1737.
Sterf-bedde, van den eerwaarden, godsaligen en seer geleerden, Do. Balthazar Bekker: in sijn leeven S. T. D. en predikant tot Amsterdam. Ofte een oprecht bericht hoe hy sich gedurende sijne siekte gedragen heeft; voornamentljik [sic] voorgestelt uit sijn redenen tegens verscheidene menschen; en sulks na een voor af-gaande kort ontwerp van sijn leeven, volgens sijn eigen handschrift, gevonden onder sijne nagelatene papieren. Te samen, tot stuitinge

3
(Continued on next card)

Bekker, Balthasar, 1634-1698—Biography.

Witchcraft
BX
9479
B42
B11
no.1

Bekker, Johannes Henricus, fl. 1698-1737.
Sterf-bedde van ... Do. Balthazar Bekker ... [1698] (Card 2)
van valsche geruchten, uytgegeven door sijn soon Joannes Henricus Bekker ... Amsterdam, By D. vanden Dalen, boekverkooper [1698]
3 p. l., 26 p. title vignette, illus. initials. 20 x 15cm.
4°: *3, A-C⁴, D1.
Black letter   (except for introduction)

8
(Continued on next card)

Bekker, Balthasar, 1634-1698—Biography.

Witchcraft
BX
9479
B42
B11
no.1

Bekker, Johannes Henricus, fl. 1698-1737.
Sterf-bedde van ... Do. Balthazar Bekker ... [1698] (Card 3)
No. 1 in vol. lettered B. Bekkers sterf-bed en andere tractaten.

1. Bekker, Balthasar, 1634-1698—Biog. I. Title.

8

Bekker, Balthasar, 1634-1698—Biography.

Witchcraft
BX
9479
B42
K74

Knuttel, Willem Pieter Cornelis, 1854-1921.
Balthasar Bekker de bestrijder van het bijgeloof. 'S Gravenhage, M. Nijhoff, 1906.
3 p. l., 368 p. port. 25cm.

1. Bekker, Balthasar, 1634-1698—Biog. I. Title.

CATALOGUE OF THE CORNELL WITCHCRAFT COLLECTION

```
                Bekker, Balthasar, 1634-1698--Biography.
Witchcraft
BX          Het Leven, de leer en lotgevallen var.
9479          Balthazar Bekker beschouwd in twee
B42           redevoeringen. [Amsterdam] 1804.
L65           3 pts. in 1. 23 x 14cm.

              Detached from Vaderlandsche letteroefe-
            ningen. Mengelwerk, tot fraaije letteren,
            konsten en weetenschappen, betrekkelyk.
            Nos. 2-4, 1804, Amsterdam, p. [49]-66, [97]-
            112, [145]-158.

8                              (Continued on next card)
```

```
                Bekker, Balthasar, 1634-1698--Biography.
Witchcraft
BX          Het Leven, de leer en lotgevallen van Bal-
9479          thazar Bekker ... 1804.       (Card 2)
B42
L65           With this is bound Arend, Johannes Pieter,
            1796-1855. Verhandeling, over Balthasar
            Bekker. [Amsterdam] 1829.
              1. Bekker, Balthasar, 1634-1698--Biog.
            I. Vaderlandsche letteroefeningen. Mengel-
            werk. Nos. 2-4. 1804.

8
```

```
                Bekker, Balthasar, 1634-1698--Biography.
Witchcraft
BX          Lorgion, Everardus Jan Diest, 1812-1876.
9479          Balthazar Bekker in Amsterdam. Een
B42         portret uit de zeventiende eeuw. Door
L872        Dr. E. J. Diest Lorgion, schrijver van
            Balthasar Bekker in Franker. Groningen,
            H. R. Roelfsema, 1851.
              2 v. title vignette (port.) 24 x 15cm.
              8°: v. 1: π3, 1-19⁸, 20 1; v. 2: π²,
            1-17⁸, 18⁴.
              Title page on special paper, inserted.
              Van der Linde 228.
              1. Bekker,       Balthasar, 1634-1698
8           --Biog. I.   Title.
```

```
                Bekker, Balthasar, 1634-1698--Biography.
Witchcraft
BX          [Lorgion, Everardus Jan Diest] 1812-1876.
9479          Balthazar Bekker in Franeker. Een por-
B42         tret uit de zeventiende eeuw. Groningen,
L87         H. R. Roelfsema, 1848.
              4 p. l., 264 p. front. 23 x 14cm.
              8°: π⁴, 1-16⁸, 17⁴.
              Prefaced signed: L--N.
              Van der Linde 227.
              1. Bekker, Balthasar, 1634-1698--Biog.
            I. Title.

8
```

```
                Bekker, Balthasar, 1634-1698--Biography.
Witchcraft
BX          Schwager, Johann Moritz.
9479          Beytrag zur Geschichte der Intoleranz;
B42         oder Leben, Meynungen und Schicksale des
S39         ehemaligen Doct. der Theologie und refor-
            mierten Predigers in Amsterdam Balthasar
            Bekkers, meist nach kirchlichen Urkunden.
            ... Mit einer Vorrede Hrn. Doct. Joh. Salo-
            mo Semlers von einer unter dessen Aufsicht
            nächstens herauskommenden verbesserten Auf-
            lage der bezauberten Welt. Leipzig, In der
            Weygandschen Buchhandlung, 1780.
              10, LXXXXII. 190 p. 18 x 11cm.

8                              (Continued on next card)
```

```
                Bekker, Balthasar, 1634-1698--Biography.
Witchcraft
BX          Schwager, Johann Moritz. Beytrag zur Ge-
9479          schichte der Intoleranz ... 1780. (Card 2)
B42
S39           8°: a-g⁸, A-M⁸.

              Van der Linde 217.

              1. Bekker, Balthasar, 1634-1698--Biog.
            2. Bekker, Balthasar, 1634-1698. De be-
            toverde weereld. I. Semler, Johann Salomo,
            1725-1791. II. Title.

8
```

```
                Bekker, Balthasar, 1634-1698--Fiction.
Witchcraft
BF          Curieuse Gespräche im Reiche derer Todten,
1410          zwischen dem bekandten Auctore der be-
C97         zauberten Welt, und ehemahligen Prediger
            in Holland Balthasar Beckern, der bey nahe
            wenig vom Teufel geglaubet; und zwischen
            dem in gantz Teutschland berühmten Theo-
            logo Christian Scrivern, der einen Menschen
            zurecht gebracht, so einen Pact mit dem
            Teufel gemacht; ... Leipzig und Braun-
            schweig, 1731-[1734]
              4 v. in 1. (208 p.) 4 plates, vi-
            gnettes.       21 x 17cm.
8                              (Continued on next card)
```

```
                Bekker, Balthasar, 1634-1698--Fiction.
Witchcraft
BF          Curieuse Gespräche im Reiche derer Todten,
1410          zwischen .. Balthasar Beckern .. und ..
C97         Christian Scrivern ... 1731-[1734]
                                          (Card 2)

              4°: A-P⁴, P3, Q-2C⁴.
              Black letter.
              Sometimes ascribed to David Fassmann.
              Title of v. 2: Zweyte Unterredung oder
            Gespräche im Reiche der Todten ...; of v. 3:

                               (Continued on next card)
```

```
                Bekker, Balthasar, 1634-1698--Fiction.
Witchcraft
BF          Curieuse Gespräche im Reiche derer Todten,
1410          zwischen .. Balthasar Beckern .. und ..
C97         Christian Scrivern ... 1731-[1734]
                                          (Card 3)

              Besonderes curieses [sic] Gespräche im
            Reiche derer Todten ...; of v. 4: Curieuses
            Gespräche in dem Reiche derer Todten ...
              With this is bound Curieuses Gespräche
            im Reiche der Todten, zwischen .. Johann
            Friedrich Mayern .. und Johann Wilhelm
            Petersen ... [Leipzig] 1732.
8                              (Continued on next card)
```

```
Witchcraft
BX          Bekker, Johannes Henricus, fl. 1698-1737.
9479          Sterf-bedde, van den eerwaarden, godsa-
B42         ligen en seer geleerden, Do. Balthazar Bek-
B11         ker: in sijn leeven S. T. D. en predikant
no.1        tot Amsterdam. Ofte een oprecht bericht hoe
            hy sich gedurende sijne siekte gedragen
            heeft; voornamentlijk [sic] voorgestelt uit
            sijne redenen tegens verscheidene gebruikt:
            en sulks in sijn voor af-gaande kort ontwerp
            van sijn leeven, volgens sijn eigen hand-
            schrift, gevonden onder sijne nagelatene pa-
            pieren. Te      samen, tot stuitinge
8                              (Continued on next card)
```

```
Witchcraft
BX          Bekker, Johannes Henricus, fl. 1698-1737.
9479          Sterf-bedde van ... Do. Balthazar Bekker
B42           ... [1698]                    (Card 2)
B11
no.1        van valsche geruchten, uytgegeven door sijn
            soon Joannes Henricus Bekker ... Amsterdam,
            By D. vanden Dalen, boekverkooper [1698]
              3 p. l., 26 p. title vignette, illus.
            initials. 20 x 15cm.
              4°: *3, A-C⁴, D1.
              Black letter    (except for introduction)

8                              (Continued on next card)
```

```
Witchcraft
BX          Bekker, Johannes Henricus, fl. 1698-1737.
9479          Sterf-bedde van ... Do. Balthazar Bekker
B42           ... [1698]                    (Card 3)
B11
no.1          No. 1 in vol. lettered B. Bekkers sterf-
            bed en andere tractaten.

              1. Bekker, Balthasar, 1634-1698--Biog.
            I. Title.

8
```

```
Witchcraft
BF          Bekker, Johannes Henricus, fl. 1698-1737.
1410          Sterf-bedde, van den eerwaarden, godsali-
B42         gen en seer geleerden, Do. Balthazar Bekker:
Z56         in sijn leeven S. T. D. en predikant tot Am-
v.3         sterdam. Ofte een oprecht bericht hoe hy
no.30       sich gedurende sijne siekte gedragen heeft;
            voornamentljjk voorgestelt uit sijne redenen
            tegens verscheidene gebruikt: en sulks in sijn
            voor af-gaande kort ontwerp van sijn leeven,
            volgens sijn eigen hand-schrift, gevonden on-
            der sijne nagelatene papieren. Te samen, tot
            stuitinge van          valsche geruchten, uyt-
8                              (Continued on next card)
```

```
Witchcraft
BF          Bekker, Johannes Henricus, fl. 1698-1737.
1410          Sterf-bedde van ... Do. Balthazar Bekker
B42           ...                           (Card 2)
Z56
v.3         gegeven door sijn soon Joannes Henricus Bek-
no.30       ker S. S. Theol. & Math. Stud. Amsterdam,
            By D. vanden Dalen, boekverkooper [1698]
              3 p. l., 26 p. title vignette, illus.
            initials. 20 x 15cm.
              4°: *1, A-C⁴, D1.
              Black letter (except for introduction)
              Introduction dated 1698.
              Van der Linde 205.
              No. 30 in      vol. lettered Bekker II
8
```

```
                Bekker, Johannes Henricus, fl. 1698-1737.
                 Sterf-bedde van ... Do. Balthazar Bekke
Witchcraft
BX          Do. [i. e., doctor] B. Bekkers Sterf-bedde
9479          verdeedigt, tegens de zoo genaamde Nodi-
B42         ge aanmerkingen over het zelve: vervat
B11         in een brief aan den schryver; behelzende
no.3        een openbaar bewijs zijner onkunde in de
            geschillen, en verdere ongegronde rede-
            neeringen: tot wegschuiminge van zijn
            alderhaatelijkste beschryving en veroor-
            deeling van den overledene. Door M. G.
            Amsterdam, By R. Blokland, boekverkooper,
            1699.
              1 p. l.,       16 p. title and end
8                              (Continued on next card)
```

```
                Bekker, Johannes Henricus, fl. 1698-1737.
                 Sterf-bedde van ... Do. Balthazar
Witchcraft   Bekker.
BX          Do. [i. e., doctor] B. Bekkers Sterf-bedde
9479          verdeedigt ... 1699.          (Card 2)
B42
B11         page vignettes, illus. initial. 20 x 16 cm.
no.3          4°: π1, A-B⁴.
              Van der Linde 207.
              No. 3 in vol. lettered B. Bekkers sterf-
            bed en andere tractaten.
              1. Bekker, Balthasar, 1634-1698. 2.
            Bekker, Johannes Henricus, fl. 1698-1737.
            Sterf-bedde van    ... Do. Balthazar Bekke
                               (Continued on next card)
```

```
                Bekker, Johannes Henricus, fl. 1698-173
                 Sterf-bedde van ... Do. Balthazar
Witchcraft   Bekker.
BX          [Schuts, Jacobus]
9479          Nodige aanmerking over het Sterf-bedde
B42         van Balthasar Bekker. Vertonende de open-
B11         bare valsheyt van dat syn gevoelen, dat hy
no.2        op syn dood-bedde segt hem voor paart en
            wagen verstrekt te hebben om hem te voeren
            na den hemel. Gravenhage, By P. van Tol,
            boekverkooper, 1698.
              13 p. [p. 14 blank] title vignette,
            illus. initial. 20 x 16cm.
              4°: A-B⁴(-B4)

8                              (Continued on next card)
```

```
                Bekker, Johannes Henricus, fl. 1698-173
                 Sterf-bedde van ... Do. Balthazar
Witchcraft   Bekker.
BX          [Schuts, Jacobus] Nodige aanmerking over
9479          het Sterf-bedde van Balthasar Bekker.
B42           1698.                         (Card 2)
B11
no.2          Black letter.
              Ascribed to Schuts by van der Linde.
              Van der Linde 206.
              No. 2 in vol. lettered B. Bekkers sterf-
            bed en andere tractaten.
              1. Bekker, Balthasar, 1634-1698. 2.
            Bekker, Johannes Henricus, fl. 1698-1737.
            Sterf-bedde             van ... Do. Balthazar
            Bekker. I.         Title.
8
```

CATALOGUE OF THE CORNELL WITCHCRAFT COLLECTION

Witchcraft
BF 1410 B42 Z56 v.3 no.7
Bekker door Bekker overtuygt. Uytgewerckt in een brief hem schriftelijk toegesonden in welke vertoont wort dat Do. Bekker, en uyt Gods woort, en ook uyt sijn eygen grond regels en belydenis; van de valscheyt sijnes gevoelens, aengaende de goede en quade geesten, moetover tuygt sijn. Neffens. Een korte aenmerking over twee geschrifte in faveur van Do. Bekker in 't ligt gebracht, her [sic] eerste geschreven aen een heer tot Uytrecht, en het andere genaemt de Aerdige duyvelarye.

8 (Continued on next card)

Witchcraft
BX 9479 B42 B11 no.13
Beknopte aanmerkingen over de korte opening van de plaatsen van 2 Pet. 2: 4 en Jud. v. 6. Voorgestelt aan R. A. predikant tot B. Als mede over de brief aan de selve. Waar in de bewysen over de gemelden plaatsen naarstiglyk ondersogt, en wederlegt werden. Door een liefhebber der waarheyt. Amsterdam, Gedrukt voor den autheur, 1697.
4 p. l., 19 p. [p. 20 blank] title and other vignettes, illus. initials. 20 x 15cm.

8 (Continued on next card)

Belahatehem (The word)

Witchcraft
BF 1565 S69
Sonnenfels, Aloysius von Sendschreiben des hochedelgebohrnen Herrn Aloysius von Sonnenfels ... an den hochgelehrten P. don Ferdinand Sterzinger, ... Über zwey hebräische Wörter chartumim und belahatehem: nachmals zur nothwendigen Belehrung des sogenannten Liebhabers der Wahrheit, und seines lateinischen Eutychii Benjamin Transalbini in ihrem Zauber- und Hexerey Streite zum Drucke befördert, von einem Verenrer des Ster[...]ngerischen Namens.

8 (Continued on next card)

Witchcraft
BF 1410 B42 Z56 v.3 no.7
Bekker door Bekker overtuygt. 1692. (Card 2)
Gravenhage, By B. Beek, konst-en boekverkooper, 1692.
5 p. l., 18 p. title and other vignettes, illus. initials. 20 x 16cm.
4°: π1, *4, A-B4, C1.
Black letter (second numbering only)
Van der Linde 173.
No. 7 in vol. lettered Bekker III.

8 (Continued on next card)

Witchcraft
BX 9479 B42 B11 no.13
Beknopte aanmerkingen over de korte opening van de plaatsen van 2 Pet. 2: 4 en Jud. v. 6. 1697. (Card 2)
4°: A-C4, D2.
Black letter (except introduction)
Supports Ruardus Andala in his controversy with Balthasar Bekker over Biblical spirits.
No. 13 in vol. lettered B. Bekkers sterfbed en andere tractaten.
1. Devil. 2. Bible. N. T. 2 Peter, II, 4--Criticism, interpretation, etc.

8 (Continued on next card)

Belahatehem (The word)

Witchcraft
BF 1565 S69
Sonnenfels, Aloysius von ... Sendschreiben ... 1768. (Card 2)
Wjen, Gedruckt mit schulzischen Schriften, 1768.
30, [1] p. 21cm.
1. Witchcraft in the Bible. 2. Bible. O.T.--Criticism, Textual. 3. Hartumim (The word) 4. Belahatehem (The word) 5. Durych, Fortunat, 1730-1802. Eutychii Beniamin Transalbini Dissertatio philologica... 6. März, Agnellus, 1726-1784.

8

Witchcraft
BF 1410 B42 Z56 v.3 no.7
Bekker door Bekker overtuygt. 1692. (Card 3)
1. Bekker, Balthasar, 1634-1698. De betoverde weereld. 2. Walten, Ericus, 1663-1697. Aardige duyvelary.

8

Witchcraft
BX 9479 B42 B11 no.13
Beknopte aanmerkingen over de korte opening van de plaatsen van 2 Pet. 2: 4 en Jud. v. 6. 1697. (Card 3)
3. Bible. N. T. Jude, 6--Criticism, interpretation, etc. 4. Andala, Ruardus, 1665-1727. 5. Bekker, Balthasar, 1634-1698. I. Een liefhebber der waarheyt.

Belcier, Jeanne de, 1602-1665.

see

Jeanne des Anges, mère, 1602-1665.

WITCHCRAFT
BF 1410 B42 Z69 no.23
Bekker door Bekker overtugt. Uytgewerckt in een brief hem schriftelijk toegesonden in welke vertoont wort dat Do. Bekker, en uyt Gods woort, en ook uyt sijn eygen grond regels en belydenis; van de valscheyt sijnes gevoelens, aengaende de goede en quade geesten, moetover tuygt sijn. Neffens. Een korte aenmerking over twee geschrifte in faveur van Do. Bekker in 't ligt gebracht, her [sic] eerste geschreven aen een heer tot Uytrecht, en het andere genaemt de Aerdige duyvelarye.   Gravenhage, By B. Beek,
8 NIC (Continued on next card)

[Bel, Jean Jacques] 1693-1738.
Le nouveau Tarquin.
Witchcraft
BF 1582 G51R3 1731c
Girard, Jean Baptiste, 1680-1733, defendant.
Recueil général des pièces concernant le procez entre la Demoiselle Cadière de la ville de Toulon, et le père Girard, jesuite ... La Haye, Swart, 1731.
8 v. 17cm.

The trials were held before the Parlement of Aix.
A collection of items originally published separately; there is a general title
(Continued on next card)

Belehrung des Verfassers der Demüthigen Bitte an die grossen Männer welche keinen Teufel glauben.
WITCHCRAFT
BF 1523 K78 no.2
[Köster, Heinrich Martin Gottfried] 1734-1802.
Belehrung des Verfassers der Demüthigen Bitte an die grossen Männer welche keinen Teufel glauben. Mit Anmerkungen des Verfassers. [n. p.] 1776.
114 p. 18cm.
"Beurtheilung der demühtigen Bitte u.s.s. in der Lemgoer auserlesenen Bibliotheck 8. Band, S. 549": p. [5]-54. With commentary.
"Demüthigste Antwort eines geringen Land-
8 (Continued on next card)

WITCHCRAFT
BF 1410 B42 Z69 no.23
Bekker door Bekker overtuygt... (Card 2)
konst-en boekverkooper, 1692.
5 p. l., 18 p. title and other vignettes, illus. initials. 21cm.
4°: π1, *4, A-B4, C1.
Black letter (second numbering only)
Van der Linde 173.
No. 23 in a Collection of tracts against Balthasar Bekker and his Betoverde weereld.
8 NIC (Continued on next card)

Witchcraft
BF 1582 G51R3 1731c
Girard, Jean Baptiste, 1680-1733, defendant.
Recueil général des pièces concernant le procez ... 1731. (Card 2)
page and a table of contents for each vol. Bound with v.8 is Le nouveau Tarquin, usually attributed to Jean Jacques Bel.

I. Cadière, Catherine, b. 1709.
II. France. Parlement (Aix) III. Title.
IV. [Bel, Jean Jacques] 1693-1738. Le nouveau Tarquin. V. Title: Le nouveau Tarquin.

WITCHCRAFT
BF 1523 K78 no.2
Belehrung des Verfassers der Demüthigen Bitte an die grossen Männer welche keinen Teufel glauben.
[Köster, Heinrich Martin Gottfried] 1734-1802. Belehrung des Verfassers der Demüthigen Bitte ... 1776. (Card 2)
geistlichen ... Mit Anmerkungen," p. [57]-114, has special t. p. Text of the "Antwort" itself not included.
No. 2 in vol. lettered Ueber den Teufel.
1. Bonnet, Johann Carl. Demühtigste Antwort eines geringen Landgeistlichen. 2. Devil. 3. His Demühtige Bitte um Belehrung. I. Auserlesene Bibliotheck der neuesten deutschen Literatur. Beurtheilung der demühtigen Bitte. II. Title.

WITCHCRAFT
BF 1410 B42 Z69 no.23
Bekker door Bekker overtuygt...1692. (Card 3)
1. Bekker, Balthasar, 1634-1698. De betoverde weereld. 2. Walten, Ericus, 1663-1697. Aardige duyvelary.

8 NIC

Belahatehem (The word)
Witchcraft
BF 1565 D96
[Durych, Fortunat] 1730-1802.
Eutychii Beniamin Transalbini Dissertatio philologica De vocibus hhartymmim et belahatehem Exod. VII. 2. [Vindobonae?] 1767.
20 p. 21cm.
"Opusculi inscripti: Gedanken über die Werke des Liebhabers der Wahrheit von der Hexerey."
1. Witchcraft in the Bible. 2. Bible. O.T.--Criticism, Textual. 3. Hartumim
8 (Continued on next card)

A belief in witchcraft unsupported by scripture.
WITCHCRAFT
BF 1566 P29
Paterson, James, minister of the Associated Congregation, Midmar.
A belief in witchcraft unsupported by scripture; an essay. Aberdeen, Printed by D. Chalmers, for A. Brown, 1815.
vi, 134 p. 20cm.

1. Witchcraft. 2. Witchcraft in the Bible. I. Title.
8 NIC

63

CATALOGUE OF THE CORNELL WITCHCRAFT COLLECTION

WITCHCRAFT
BF
1581
Z7
1712f

The Belief of witchcraft vindicated: proving, from Scripture, there have been witches; and, from reason, that there may be such still. In answer to a late pamphlet, intituled, The impossibility of witchcraft: plainly proving, from Scripture and reason that there never was a witch, &c. By G. R., A.M. London, Printed for J. Baker, 1712.
40 p. 19cm.
Sometimes attributed to F. Bragge.

8   (Continued on next card)

WITCHCRAFT
BF
1581
Z7
1712f

The Belief of witchcraft vindicated ...
1712.   (Card 2)

1. Witchcraft. 2. Witchcraft in the Bible. 3. The impossibility of witchcraft. I. Bragge, Francis, b. 1690, supposed author. II. G. R., M.A. III. R., G., M.A.

8

Witchcraft
BF
1578
B4
I54

Bell family.
Ingram, M V
An authenticated history of the famous Bell witch, the wonder of the 19th century, and unexplained phenomenon of the Christian era. The mysterious talking goblin that terrorized the west end of Robertson County, Tennessee, tormenting John Bell to his death. The story of Betsy Bell, her lover and the haunting sphinx. Clarksville, Tenn., 1894.
316 p. illus. 17cm.
Imprint covered by label: Setliff & Co., Nashville, Tenn.

Witchcraft
BF
1578
B4
I54

The Bell witch.
Ingram, M V
An authenticated history of the famous Bell witch, the wonder of the 19th century, and unexplained phenomenon of the Christian era. The mysterious talking goblin that terrorized the west end of Robertson County, Tennessee, tormenting John Bell to his death. The story of Betsy Bell, her lover and the haunting sphinx. Clarksville, Tenn., 1894.
316 p. illus. 17cm.
Imprint covered by label: Setliff & Co., Nashville, Tenn.

Witchcraft
BF
1555
B44
1616

Bell'Haver, Giovanni Battista, fl. 1580-1623.
Theorica, e pratica per la vera intelligenza et cognitione intorno à gli spiriti maligni ch' entrano ne'corpi humani et anco intorno all'arte essorcistica per discacciarli da essi ... Et vi si raccolgono poi alcuni più notabili casi scielti da graui autori con nuoui vtili documenti, et acute inuentioni fruttuosissime. Venetia, G. B. Combi, 1616.
[32], 277 p. 16cm.
I. Title.

Witchcraft
BF
1410
S83
1785

Bemühung den Aberglaube zu stürzen.
Sterzinger, Ferdinand, 1721-1786.
Don Ferdinand Sterzingers Bemühung den Aberglaube zu stürzen. München, Bey J. Lentner, 1785.
6 p. l., 187 p. 21cm.
Table of contents bound by mistake between p. 186-187.
First published 1784, according to Kayser.

1. Occult sciences. 2. Superstition. I. Title: Bemühung den Aberglaube zu stürzen.
8

Witchcraft
BF
1584
I8
G49

I benandanti.
Ginzburg, Carlo.
I benandanti; ricerche sulla stregoneria e sui culti agrari tra Cinquecento e Seicento. [Torino] G. Einaudi [c1966]
xvii, 197 p. illus. 22cm. (Biblioteca di cultura storica, 89)

1. Witchcraft--Italy. I. Title.

Witchcraft
BF
1598
H55A4
1548

Benci, Tommaso, tr.
Hermes Trismegistus.
[Poemander. Italian]
Il Pimandro di Mercurio Trismegisto, tradotto da Tommaso Benci in lingua fiorentina. Firenze [L. Torrentino] 1548.
[24], 119, [14] p. 18cm.
Title vignette.
Edited by Carlo Lenzoni.

I. Benci, Tommaso, tr. II. Lenzoni, Carlo, d. 1551, ed.

Witchcraft
BF
1600
P43
1612

Benedicti Pererii ... De magia, de observatione somniorum et de divinatione astrologica.
Pereira, Benito, ca. 1535-1610.
Benedicti Pererii ... De magia, de observatione somniorvm et de divinatione astrologica libri tres. Adversvs fallaces, et superstitiosas artes. Coloniae Agrippinae, Apud Ioannem Gymnicum, 1612.
324, [8] p. 13cm.
First published 1591 under title: ... Adversus fallaces et superstitiosas artes.

1. Magic. 2. Dreams. 3. Astrology. I. His ... Adversus fallaces et superstitiosas artes. II. Title: De magia, de observatione somniorum, et de divinatione astrologica.
8

Witchcraft
BF
1600
P43
1592

Benedicti Pererii Valentini ... Adversus fallaces et superstitiosas artes.
Pereira, Benito, ca. 1535-1610.
Benedicti Pererii Valentini ... Adversvs fallaces & superstitiosas artes, id est, De magia, de observatione somniorum, &, de diuinatione astrologica. Libri tres. Venetiis, Apud Ioan. Baptistam Ciottum, senensem, 1592.
3 p. l., 256, [8] p. 15cm.
First published 1591.
Later editions have title: De magia, de observatione somniorum, et de divinatione astrologica.
(Continued on next card)

Witchcraft
BF
1600
P43
1592

Benedicti Pererii Valentini ... Adversus fallaces et superstitiosas artes.
Pereira, Benito, ca. 1535-1610. Benedicti Pererii Valentini ... Adversus fallaces ... 1592.   (Card 2)
Stamp of S. Michele in Bosco on cover.

1. Magic. 2. Dreams. 3. Astrology. I. Title: Adversus fallaces et superstitiosas artes.
8

Witchcraft
BX
2340
F89

Benedictio numismatum crucis.
Freyschmid, Joseph Caspar.
Thesaurus sacer benedictionum veterum, ac novarum, ex sanctae ecclesiae ritibus, sanctorum virorum scriptis, probatis authoribus, & approbatissimo temporum usu collectus ... dicatus, dedicatus, consecratus a Josepho Casparo Freyschmid. Lincij, 1708.
6 p. l., 725, [27] p. 14cm.
Title in red and black.
Benedictio numismatum crucis: Sancti Patris Benedicti has special t. p.
(Continued on next card)

Witchcraft
BX
2340
F89

Benedictio numismatum crucis.
Freyschmid, Joseph Caspar. Thesaurus sacer benedictionum ... 1708. (Card 2)
with imprint: Lincij, Typis Caspari Josephi Freyschmid, 1708, and is unpaged.

1. Exorcism. 2. Benediction. I. Title. II. Title: Benedictio numismatum crucis.
8

Witchcraft
BX
2045
B4
1856

Benedictionale Constantiense, jussu et authoritate.
Catholic Church. Liturgy and ritual. Benedictional. Constance.
Benedictionale Constantiense, jussu et authoritate ... Maximiliani Christophori, Dei gratia Episcopi Constantiensis ... juxta normam ritualis Romani reformatum, approbatum et editum. Denuo impressum cum licentia ... Josephi, ... Episcopi Rottenburgensis. Biberaci, Sumtibus F. Haller, 1856.
xiv, 314 p. 22cm.
1. Benediction. 2. Exorcism. I. Title.
8

Witchcraft
BF
1555
P96
1883

Bénet, Armand Eugène, 1858-
Procès verbal fait povr délivrer vne fille possédée par le malin esprit à Lovviers. Publié d'après le manuscrit original et inédit de la Bibliothèque Nationale par Armand Benet ... précédé d'une introduction par B. de Moray. Paris, Aux bureaux du Progrès médical, 1883.
cxiv, 98 p. 22cm. (Bibliothèque diabolique)
1. Fontaine, Françoise, fl. 1591. 2. Demoniac possession. I. Moray, B de. II. Bénet, Armand Eugène, 1858-
8 NIC

Witchcraft
BF
1410
M41

Benoist, René, 1521-1608.
Petit fragment catechistic.
Massé, Pierre.
De l'impostvre et tromperie des diables, devins, enchantevrs, sorciers, novevrs d'esguillettes, cheuilleurs, necromanciens, chiromanciens, & autres qui par telle inuocation diabolique, ars magiques & superstitions abusent le peuple. Par Pierre Massé du Mans, aduocat. Paris, Chez Iean Poupy, 1579.
various pagings. 17cm.
Printer's device on t. p.
(Continued on next card)

Witchcraft
BF
1410
M41

Benoist, René, 1521-1608.
Petit fragment catechistic.
Massé, Pierre. De l'impostvre et tromperie des diables ... 1579. (Card 2)
Title on spine: Massé. Abus des divins.
Text preceeded by Petit fragment catechistic d'vne plvs ample catechese de la magie ... de M. René Benoist Angevin ...; and followed by Benoist's Traicté enseignant en bref les cavses des malefices, sortileges et enchanteries... with special t. p. Declamation contre l'errevr execrable des
(Continued on next card)

Witchcraft
BF
1410
M41

Benoist, René, 1521-1608.
Petit fragment catechistic.
Massé, Pierre. De l'impostvre et tromperie des diables ... 1579. (Card 3)
maleficiers ... par F. Pierre Nodé minime. has special t. p. with imprint Paris, Chez Iean du Carroy imprimeur, 1578, and is paged separately.
Trois sermons de S. Avgvstin ... traduit en françois par M. René Benoist ... has spec. t. p. with imprint Paris, Chez Iean Poupy, 1579, and unnumbered pages.
(Continued on next card)

64

CATALOGUE OF THE CORNELL WITCHCRAFT COLLECTION

Benoist, René, 1521-1608.
  Traicté enseignant en bref les causes
Witchcraft des maleficés.
BF   Massé, Pierre.
1410   De l'imposture et tromperie des diables,
M41 devins, enchanteurs, sorciers, noueurs d'esguillettes, cheuilleurs, necromanciens, chiromanciens, & autres qui par telle inuocation diabolique, ars magiques & superstitions abusent le peuple. Par Pierre Massé
  du Mans, aduocat. Paris, Chez Iean Poupy,
  1579.
    various pagings. 17cm.
8   Printer's device on t. p.
        (Continued on next card)

Benoist, René, 1521-1608.
  Traicté enseignant en bref les causes
Witchcraft des maleficés.
BF   Massé, Pierre. De l'imposture et tromperie
1410   des diables ... 1579.   (Card 2)
M41
    Title on spine: Massé. Abus des divins.
    Text preceeded by Petit fragment cate-
  chistic d'une plus ample catechese de la
  magie ... de M. René Benoist Angeuin ...;
  and followed by Benoist's Traicté enseignant
  en bref les causes des maleficés, sortileges
  et enchanteries... with special t. p.
    Declamation contre l'erreur execrable des
8   (Continued on next card)

Benoist, René, 1521-1608.
  Traicté enseignant en bref les causes
Witchcraft des maleficés.
BF   Massé, Pierre. De l'imposture et tromperie
1410   des diables ... 1579.   (Card 3)
M41
  maleficiers ... par F. Pierre Nodé minime,
  has special t. p. with imprint Paris, Chez
  Iean du Carroy imprimeur, 1578, and is paged
  separately.
    Trois sermons de S. Avgustin ... traduits
  en françois par M. René Benoist, has special
  t. p. with imprint Paris, Chez Iean Poupy,
  1579, and unnum bered pages.
8   (Continued on next card)

Benoît, René, 1521-1608.

  see

Benoist, René, 1521-1608.

Witchcraft Benvenuti, Giuseppe, 1728-ca. 1770.
BF   Josephi Benvenuti ... De daemoniacis
1565 dissertatio. Lucae, Typis Joannis Ric-
T19   comini, 1775.
M18+   lxxxiv p. 26cm.

    Bound with Maffei, Francesco Scipione,
  marchese, 1675-1755. Arte magica dileguata.
  Verona, 1749.

8   1. Demonolo gy. 2. Haen, Anton de,
  1704?-1776.   I. Title: De daemoniacis disser tatio.

Benvenuti, Joseph, 1728-ca. 1770.

  see

Benvenuti, Giuseppe, 1728-ca. 1770.

Witchcraft Berbiguier de Terre-Neuve du Thym, Alexis
BF   Vincent Charles, 1765?-1851.
1552   Les farfadets, ou Tous les démons ne sont
B48   pas de l'autre monde ... Paris Chez l'auteur [et] P. Gueffier, 1821.
    3 v. plates. 21cm.

    1. Fairies. 2. Spirits. 3. Demonology.
  4. Superstition. I. Title. II. Title:
  Tous les démons ne sont pas de l'autre
  monde.

  Berg, Adam, d. 1610.
WITCHCRAFT
BF   Warhafft: vnd gründtlicher Bericht, sehr
1555 wunderlich: vnnd gleichsam vnerhörter Ge-
H67   schichten, so sich vnlangst zu Bergen
1589 [i.e., Mons] in Henogau, Ertzbisthumbs
  Cambrai, mit einer besessnen, vnd hernach
  widerledigten Closterfrawen verloffen.
  Auss frantzösischer Sprach, in Hochteutsch
  gebracht. [München, Gedruckt bey Adam
  Berg] 1589.
    4 p. l., 47 numbered l. 19cm.
8   Illustrati ve title vignette.
    With colo phon.
        (Continued on next card)

  Berg, Adam, d. 1610.
WITCHCRAFT
BF   Warhafft: vnd gründtlicher Bericht, sehr
1555   wunderlich ... 1589.   (Card 2)
H67
1587 Translation of Histoire admirable et
  veritable des choses advenues a l'endroict
  d'une religieuse professe ... pub. 1586.
  Preface by Adam Berg.
    1. Demoniac possession. 2. Fery,
  Jeanne, fl. 1584. I. Histoire admirable
  et veritable des choses advenues a l'endroict d'une religieuse professe.
8 German. II. Berg, Adam, d. 1610.

  Berg, Vincent von.
    Anacephalaeosis.
Witchcraft
BX   Berg, Vincent von, comp.
2050   Enchiridium quadripartitum P. Vincentii
A1   von Berg Franciscani conventualis. Pars
B49   prima exhibet varias, selectas, exquisitissimasque benedictiones rerum omnigenarum
  approbatas ... Pars secunda tractat de
  regulis artis exorcisticae cum suis exorcismis ... Pars tertia agit de archi-confraternitate ... Pars quarta praescribit
  modum aegros, agonizantesque adjuvandi; a-
  gendi cum obstinatis, haereticis converten-
8   (Continued on next card)

  Berg, Vincent von.
    Anacephalaeosis.
Witchcraft
BX   Berg, Vincent von, comp. Enchiridium quad-
2050   ripartitum ... 1743.   (Card 2)
A1
B49   dis, sagis examinandis ... Accedit horum
  Anacephalaeosis in germanismo. In hanc com-
  modissimam formam redactum, iconibus illus-
  tratum, indicéque alphabetico instructum.
  Coloniae, Typis J. C. Gussen, 1743.
    8 p. l., 342, [10], 144 p. illus. 17cm.
  Part 3 includes some German text.
    Anacephalae osis; das ist, Kurtze
8   (Continued on next card)

  Berg, Vincent von.
    Anacephalaeosis.
Witchcraft
BX   Berg, Vincent von, comp. Enchiridium quad-
2050   ripartitum ... 1743.   (Card 3)
A1
B49   Wiederholung zu Teutsch, vorstellend die
  Weiss [sic] und Manier mit den Krancken
  und Sterbenden umbzugehen has special t. p.
  and is paged separately.
    Title in red and black.
    Ex libris Lud. Parren.
    1. Catholic Church--Prayer-books and
  devotions. 2. Exorcism. I. Title.
  II. His An acephalaeosis. III.
  Title: Anace phalaeosis.

Witchcraft
BX   Berg, Vincent von, comp.
2050   Enchiridium quadripartitum P. Vincentii
A1   von Berg Franciscani conventualis. Pars
B49   prima exhibet varias, selectas, exquisitissimasque benedictiones rerum omnigenarum
  approbatas ... Pars secunda tractat de
  regulis artis exorcisticae cum suis exorcismis ... Pars tertia agit de archi-confraternitate ... Pars quarta praescribit
  modum aegros, agonizantesque adjuvandi; a-
  gendi cum obstinatis, haereticis converten-
8   (Continued on next card)

Witchcraft
BX   Berg, Vincent von, comp. Enchiridium quad-
2050   ripartitum ... 1743.   (Card 2)
A1
B49   dis, sagis examinandis ... Accedit horum
  Anacephalaeosis in germanismo. In hanc com-
  modissimam formam redactum, iconibus illus-
  tratum, indicéque alphabetico instructum.
  Coloniae, Typis J. C. Gussen, 1743.
    8 p. l., 342, [10], 144 p. illus. 17cm.
  Part 3 includes some German text.
    Anacephalae osis; das ist, Kurtze
8   (Continued on next card)

Witchcraft
BX   Berg, Vincent von, comp. Enchiridium quad-
2050   ripartitum ... 1743.   (Card 3)
A1
B49   Wiederholung zu Teutsch, vorstellend die
  Weiss [sic] und Manier mit den Krancken
  und Sterbenden umbzugehen has special t. p.
  and is paged separately.
    Title in red and black.
    Ex libris Lud. Parren.
    1. Catholic Church--Prayer-books and
  devotions. 2. Exorcism. I. Title.
  II. His An acephalaeosis. III.
  Title: Anace phalaeosis.

WITCHCRAFT
BF   Berg, W
1003   Die Wahrheit im Zauber- und Hexenwesen.
U22+
v.24 (In: Die Übersinnliche Welt. Leipzig.
  26cm. v.24 (1916) p. [249]-271, 287-310,
  331-337, 356-367)

8   1. Witchcraft. 2. Magic. 3. Occult
NIC   sciences. I. Title.

Bergamo, Jacobus Philippus.

  see

Foresti, Jacopo Filippo, da Bergamo, 1434-
  1520.

Bergamo, Jacopo Filippo Foresti, da.

  see

Foresti, Jacopo Filippo, da Bergamo, 1434-
  1520.

CATALOGUE OF THE CORNELL WITCHCRAFT COLLECTION

Bergmann, Ernest Wilhelm, respondent.

Witchcraft
BF
1520
B98
    Buttner, Christophorus Andreas, praeses.
      Diiudicatio iudicii De non-existentia diaboli quam ... praeside M. Christophoro Andrea Buttnero ... defendet Ernestus Wilhelm. Bergmann. Halae Magdeburgicae, Litteris Ioh. Friderici Grunerti [1734]
    24 p. 24cm.
    Diss.--Halle (E. W. Bergmann, respondent)
    1. Devil. 2. Demonology. I. Bergmann, Ernest Wilhelm, respondent. II. Title: De non-existentia diaboli.

8

WITCHCRAFT
BF
1405
B51
    Berlinische Monatsschrift.
      [Extracts from the periodical, concerning witchcraft and related subjects.]
    Berlin, 1783-96.
    44 items. 18cm.

    Some of the extracts are manuscript copies by Carnap.

    1. Witchcraft. 2. Witchcraft--Germany. 3. Occult sciences. 4. Trials (Witchcraft)--Germany.

8
NIC

Witchcraft
BF
1581
A2B52
    Bernard, Richard, 1568-1641.
      A gvide to grand ivry men, divided into two bookes: In the first, is the authors best aduice to them what to doe, before they bring in a Billa vera in cases of witchcraft ... In the second, is a treatise touching witches good and bad ... London, Printed by Felix Kingston for Ed. Blackmore, 1627.
    267 p. 15cm.
    1. Witchcraft. I. Title.

Witchcraft
BT
1313
B52
    Bernardus Comensis.
      Lucerna inquisitorum haereticae pravitatis R. P. F. Bernardi Comensis... et eiusdem Tractatus de strigibus, cum annotationibus Francisci Pegnae... Additi sunt in hac impressione duo tractatus Joannis Gersoni... Roma, ex officina Bartholomaei Grassi, 1584.
    [4] l., 184, [28] p. 22cm.
    1. Heresies and heretics. I. Pegna, Francesco, ed. II. Gerson, Joannes, 1363-1429. III. Title.

Der Berner Jetzerprozess (1507-1509) in neuer Beleuchtung.

WITCHCRAFT
BX
3545
S9
S81
    Steck, Rudolf, 1842-1924.
      Der Berner Jetzerprozess (1507-1509) in neuer Beleuchtung nebst Mitteilungen aus den noch ungedruckten Akten. Bern, Schmid & Francke, 1902.
    87 p. illus. 24cm.
    "Separat-Abdruck aus der 'Schweizerischen theolog. Zeitschrift' (Verlag von August Frick, Zürich II)."
    Greatly expanded in his Die Akten des Jetzerprozesses nebst dem Defensorium. Basel, 1904.

8
NIC
    (Continued on next card)

Der Berner Jetzerprozess (1507-1509) in neuer Beleuchtung.

WITCHCRAFT
BX
3545
S9
S81
    Steck, Rudolf, 1842-1924. Der Berner Jetzerprozess ... 1902. (Card 2)
    Stamped on cover: A. Francke, Verlags-Cto. vormals Schmid & Francke, Bern.
    1. Jetzer, Johann, ca. 1483-ca. 1515. 2. Dominicans in Switzerland. 3. Bern--Church history--Sources. I. His Die Akten des Jetzerprozesses nebst dem Defensorium. II. Title.

8
NIC

Bernhardi, Martinus, respondent.

RARE
HV
8593
T46
    Thomasius, Christian, 1655-1728, praeses.
      Disputatio inauguralis juridica De tortura ex foris Christianorum proscribenda, quam...praeside Dn. Christiano Thomasio... discussioni submittit Martinus Bernhardi. Halae Magdeburgicae, Typis Christoph. Andreae Zeitleri [1705]
    38 p. 19cm.

    Diss.--Halle (M. Bernhardi, respondent)
    With this is bound the edition of 1759 of the diss. with title as: Tractatio juridica De tortura ex foris Christianor um proscribenda.

8
NIC
    (Continued on next card)

Bernhardi, Martinus, respondent.

RARE
HV
8593
T46
1743
    Thomasius, Christian, 1655-1728, praeses.
      Dissertatio juridica De tortura ex foris Christianorum proscribenda...quam praeside Christiano Thomasio...respondendo propugnavit Martinus Bernhardi. Halae Salicae, Ex officina Hendeliana, 1743.
    37 p. 20cm.

    Diss.--Halle, 1705 (M. Bernhardi, respondent)
    Originally published in 1705 with title: Disputatio inauguralis juridica De tortura ex foris Christianorum proscribenda.

8
NIC
    (Continued on next card)

Bernhardi, Martinus, respondent.

RARE
HV
8593
T46
    Thomasius, Christian, 1655-1728.
      Tractatio juridica De tortura ex foris Christianorum proscribenda. Halae Magdeburgicae, Typis Io. Christ. Grunerti, 1759.
    38 p. 19cm.

    Originally issued in 1705 as diss. with M. Bernhardi as respondent, with title: Disputatio inauguralis juridica De tortura ex foris Christianorum proscribenda.
    Bound with the 1705 ed.

8
NIC
    (Continued on next card)

Witchcraft
BF
1582
B52
    Bernou, Jean.
      La chasse aux sorcières dans le Labourd (1609), étude historique ... Agen, Calvet et Célérie, 1897.
    414 p. 25cm.

    1. Witchcraft--Labourd, France. I. Title.

Berns, Michael.
Die dreifache Welt als der Christen, Phantasten und Bezauberten.

Witchcraft
BF
1410
B42
Z57
1708
    [Berns, Michael] Gründliche und völlige Wiederlegung der Bezauberten Welt Balthasar Beckers, D. Aus der Heil. Schrifft gezogen. Wobey zugleich unzählige curioese Antiqvitaeten erläutert und zum rechten Gebrauch angewendet werden; und andere rare auch zu dieser Zeit höchstnöthige Materien. Nebst einem Anhange vom Licht und Recht der Natur. Mit völligen Registern versehen. Von M. Hamburg, S. Heyl und J. Liebezeit, 1708.

    (Continued on next card)

Berns, Michael.
Die dreifache Welt als der Christen, Phantasten und Bezauberten.

Witchcraft
BF
1410
B42
Z57
1708
    [Berns, Michael] Gründliche und völlige Wiederlegung der Bezauberten Welt ... 1708. (Card 2)

    3 p. l., 958, [11] p. [p. 12 blank] title and other vignettes, illus. initials. 21 x 17cm.
    4°:)(3, A-I⁴, A-6D⁴, 6E3, 6F⁴, 6G².
    Black letter.
    According to J. G. T. Grässe, Bibliotheca magica et pneumatica, 1843, this work

8
    (Continued on next card)

Berns, Michael.
Die dreifache Welt als der Christen, Phantasten und Bezauberten.

Witchcraft
BF
1410
B42
Z57
1708
    [Berns, Michael] Gründliche und völlige Wiederlegung der Bezauberten Welt ... 1708. (Card 3)

    first appeared in 1697 with title: Die dreifache Welt als der Christen, Phantasten und Bezauberten, in dreyen Büchern abgefasst.

    1. Bekker, Balthasar, 1634-1698. De betoverde weereld. 2. Christian life. 3. Millennialism. 4. Spirits. I. Title. II. M., pseud. III. His Die dreifache Welt als der Christen, Phantasten und Bezauberten.

8

Witchcraft
BF
1410
B42
Z57
1708
    [Berns, Michael] Gründliche und völlige Wiederlegung der Bezauberten Welt Balthasar Beckers, D. Aus der Heil. Schrifft gezogen. Wobey zugleich unzählige curioese Antiqvitaeten erläutert und zum rechten Gebrauch angewendet werden; und andere rare auch zu dieser Zeit höchstnöthige Materien. Nebst einem Anhange vom Licht und Recht der Natur. Mit völligen Registern versehen. Von M. Hamburg, S. Heyl und J. Liebezeit, 1708.

    (Continued on next card)

Witchcraft
BF
1410
B42
Z57
1708
    [Berns, Michael] Gründliche und völlige Wiederlegung der Bezauberten Welt ... 1708. (Card 2)

    3 p. l., 958, [11] p. [p. 12 blank] title and other vignettes, illus. initials. 21 x 17cm.
    4°:)(3, A-I⁴, A-6D⁴, 6E3, 6F⁴, 6G².
    Black letter.
    According to J. G. T. Grässe, Bibliotheca magica et pneumatica, 1843, this work

8
    (Continued on next card)

Witchcraft
BF
1410
B42
Z57
1708
    [Berns, Michael] Gründliche und völlige Wiederlegung der Bezauberten Welt ... 1708. (Card 3)

    first appeared in 1697 with title: Die dreifache Welt als der Christen, Phantasten und Bezauberten, in dreyen Büchern abgefasst.

    1. Bekker, Balthasar, 1634-1698. De betoverde weereld. 2. Christian life. 3. Millennialism. 4. Spirits. I. Title. II. M., pseud. III. His Die dreifache Welt als der Christen, Phantasten und Bezauberten.

8

Bersmann, Adam Nicolaus, respondent.

Witchcraft
BF
1583
A2
M94
    Müller, Johannes, praeses.
      De conventu sagarum in monte Bruckterorum, nocte ante Calendas Maji, disputatio, quam ... praeside ... Dno. M. Johanne Müllern ... exponit Adamus Nicolaus Bersmannus ... Wittebergae, Ex typotheteo Hakiano [1675]
    [16] p. 19cm.

    1. Witchcraft--Brocken, Germany. 2. Walpurgisnacht. I. Bersmann, Adam Nicolaus, respondent. II. Title.

Witchcraft
BD
428
B54
2 copies
    Bertram, Johann Friedrich, 1699-1741.
      Ob die Thiere Teufel seyn? wird durch Veranlassung dess von einem Französischen Jesuiten P. Bonjeau unlängst ans Licht gestellten neuen Lehr-Begriffs von den Seelen der Thiere genannt: Amusements philosophiques sur le langage des bestes; oder: Philosophischer Zeit-Vertreib über die Thier-Sprache; in welchen sie zu Teufeln gemachet werden; nach Schrifft und Vernunfft untersuchet und beantwortet, von J.F. B. [Bremen] S. Pomarius [1740]
    [15], 94 p. 16cm.
    (over)

CATALOGUE OF THE CORNELL WITCHCRAFT COLLECTION

Witchcraft
BF 1582
B54
1905
 Bertrand, Isidore.
  Les possédées de Loudun, et Urbain Grandier. Étude historique. Paris, Bloud [1905?]
  61 p. 18cm. (Science et religion: études pour le temps présent)

  Includes bibliography (5 p.)
  Bound with his La sorcellerie.

  1. Demoniac possession. 2. Grandier, Urbain, 1590-1634. 3. Loudun, France. Ursuline Convent. I. Title.

8

Witchcraft
BF 1582
B54
1905
 Bertrand, Isidore.
  La sorcellerie. 6. éd. Paris, Bloud [1905?]
  62 p. 18cm. (Science et religion: études pour le temps présent)

  With this is bound his Les possédées de Loudun et Urbain Grandier. Paris [1905?]

  1. Witchcraft. I. Title.

WITCHCRAFT
BF 1584
S7
B55+
 Berzunza, Julio, 1896-
  Miscellaneous notes on witchcraft and alcahuetería. [Lancaster, Pa., Lancaster Press, 1928]
  141-150 p. 26cm.

  Title on cover: Notes on witchcraft and alcahuetería.
  Reprinted from the Romanic review, v.19, no.2, Apr.-June 1928.

  1. Witchcraft --Spain. I. His Notes on witchcraft and alcahuetería. I. Title.

8
NIC

 Berzunza, Julio, 1896-
  Notes on witchcraft and alcahuetería.

WITCHCRAFT
BF 1584
S7
B55+
 Berzunza, Julio, 1896-
  Miscellaneous notes on witchcraft and alcahuetería. [Lancaster, Pa., Lancaster Press, 1928]
  141-150 p. 26cm.

  Title on cover: Notes on witchcraft and alcahuetería.
  Reprinted from the Romanic review, v.19, no.2, Apr.-June 1928.

  1. Witchcraft --Spain. I. His Notes on witchcraft and alcahuetería.

8
NIC

 Besaettelsen i Thisted.

WITCHCRAFT
BF 1584
D4
C552
 Christensen, Christian Villads, 1864-1922.
  Besaettelsen i Thisted.

  (In: Samlinger til Jydsk historie og topografi. København. 22cm. ser.3, v.3, no.3. 1902. p.206-219)
  With this, in same issue, is: Bang, Vilhelm. Tilføjelser til efterretningerne om hexeforfølgelserne i Ribe.

  1. Witchcraft--Thisted, Denmark. 2. Demoniac possession. 3. Bjørn, Ole, b.1648. 4. Arni Magnússon, 1663-1730.

Witchcraft Besaettelsen i Tisted, 1696-98.
BF 1584
D4B13
 Bæksted, Anders.
  Besaettelsen i Tisted, 1696-98. København, Munksgaard, 1959-60.
  2 v. illus. 23 cm. (Danmarks folkeminder, nr. 69-70)
  Summary in English.
  Bibliography: v.2, p. [365]-370.

  1. Witchcraft--Thisted, Denmark. (Series) II. Title.
  BF1584.A2D44 A 61-5352
  Illinois. Univ. Library for Library of Congress

 Beschreyen und Verzaubern.

Witchcraft
BF 1565
G57
 Gockel, Eberhard, 1636-1703.
  Tractatus polyhistoricus magico-medicus curiosus, oder Ein kurtzer, mit vielen verwunderlichen Historien untermengter Bericht von dem Beschreyen und Verzaubern, auch denen darauss entspringenden Kranckheiten und zauberischen Schäden ... Alles aus berühmter Alter und Neuer Medicorum Scriptis, auch auss eigner Erfahrung und 42jähriger Praxi zusammen getragen und hervor gegeben von Eberhardo Gockelio ... Franckfurt und

8 (Continued on next card)

 Beschreyen und Verzaubern.

Witchcraft
BF 1565
G57
 Gockel, Eberhard, 1636-1703. Tractatus polyhistoricus ... 1699. (Card 2)

  Leipzig, Im Verlag Lorentz Kronigers, und Gottlieb Göbels sel. Erben Buchhändl. in Augspurg, 1699.
  4 p. l., 182 p. 17cm.
  "Mantissa oder ... Geheime Artzney. Mittel wider die zauberische Schäden und Kranckheiten," p. [134]-182, has special t. p.

  1. Witchcraft. 2. Medicine, Magic, mystic, and spagiric. 3. Medicine--Formulae, receipts, prescriptions. I. Title.

8

Witchcraft
BF 1410
B42
Z56
v.2
no.7
 Beschryvinge van een vremd nagt-gezigte, vertoont aan een toehoorder der predikatie, die door den remonstrantsche leeraer Ds. Johannes Molinaeus voor 't vermogen des duivels, en tegen den aucteur van 't boek De betooverde weereld, onlangs te Rotterdam gedaan is. Logoochoorion, Gedrukt by den drukker van Haar Majesteit Krisis [1692]
  2 p. l., 12 p. title vignette, illus. initial. 19 x 15cm.

  (Continued on next card)

Witchcraft
BF 1410
B42
Z56
v.2
no.7
 Beschryvinge van een vremd nagt-gezigte ... [1692] (Card 2)

  4°: π², A⁴, B².
  Black letter.
  Van der Linde 132.
  No. 7 in vol. lettered Bekker II.
  I. Molinaeus, Johannes, d. 1702. De betoverde werelt van D. Balthazar Bekker. 2. Bekker, Balthasar, 1634-1698. De betoverde weereld. I. Title: Een vremd nagt-gezigt.

3

Witchcraft
BF 1410
B42
Z69
no.25
 Beschryvinge van een vremd nagt-gezigte, vertoont aan een toehoorder der predikatie, die door den remonstrantsche leeraer Ds. Johannes Molinaeus voor 't vermogen des duivels, en tegen den aucteur van 't boek De betooverde weereld, onlangs te Rotterdam gedaan is. Logoochoorion, Gedrukt by den drukker van Haar Majesteit Krisis [1692]
  2 p. l., 12 p. title vignette, illus. initial. 21cm.

  (Continued on next card)

Witchcraft
BF 1410
B42
Z69
no.25
 Beschryvinge van een vremd nagt-gezigte ... [1692] (Card 2)

  4°: π², A⁴, B².
  Black letter.
  Van der Linde 132.
  No. 25 in a Collection of tracts against Balthasar Bekker and his Betoverde weereld.

3

 Beschryvinge van een vremd nagt-gezigte.

Witchcraft
BF 1410
B42
Z56
v.3
no.8
 Een Keuning-kaarsje voor den siender van Een vremt nagtgezigte, om te dienen tot ophelderinge van syn St. Niklaas-droom. Ezelenburg, Gedrukt in de Gulde Schoolplak [1692]
  8 p. illus. initial. 20 x 15cm.
  4°: A⁴.
  Black letter.
  Defending Molinaeus, and against Bekker.
  Van der Linde 133.
  No. 8 in vol. lettered Bekker III.

8 (Continued on next card)

 Beschryvinge van een vremd nagt-gezigte.

Witchcraft
BF 1410
B42
Z56
v.3
no.4
 [Molinaeus, Johannes] d. 1702.
  Paraenesis; ofte ernstige aenspraek aen den siender van Een vremt nagtgezigt. Rotterdam, By B. Bos, 1692.
  1 p. l., 10 p. title vignette, illus. initial. 20 x 16cm.
  4°: π 1, A⁴, B1.
  Black letter.
  Signed: J:M.
  Defense of the author's attack on Balthasar Bekker and De betoverde weereld.

  (Continued on next card)

 Beschryvinge van een vremd nagt-gezigte.

Witchcraft
BF 1410
B42
Z56
v.3
no.4
 [Molinaeus, Johannes] d. 1702. Paraenesis ... 1692. (Card 2)

  Van der Linde 134.
  No. 4 in vol. lettered Bekker III.

  1. Bekker, Balthasar, 1634-1698. 2. Beschryvinge van een vremd nagt-gezigte. I. Title.

 Die Besessenen im Neuen Testamente.

WITCHCRAFT
BF 1555
N19
 Nanz, Carl Friedrich.
  Die Besessenen im Neuen Testamente. Ein exegetischer Versuch mit Rücksicht auf Dr. Strauss Leben Jesu. Reutlingen, J. C. Marcken, 1840.
  ii, 42 p. 21cm.

  I. Strauss, David Friedrich, 1808-1874. Das Leben Jesu. 2. Demoniac possession. 3. Bible. N.T.--Criticism, interpretation, etc. 4. Jesus Christ.

8
NIC

 Die Besessenheit.

WITCHCRAFT
BF 1555
O292
 Oesterreich, Traugott Konstantin, 1880-1949.
  Die Besessenheit. Langensalza, Wendt & Klauwell, 1921.
  vii, 403 p. 25cm.

  Bibliographical notes: p. [387]-401.

  1. Demoniac possession.

8
NIC

 Die Besessenheit (Dämonomanie)

WITCHCRAFT
BF 1003
U22+
v.24
 Langner, Fritz.
  Die Besessenheit (Dämonomanie)

  (In: Die Übersinnliche Welt. Leipzig. 26cm. v.24 (1916) p. 118-130, 169-171, 212-215, 240-248)

8
NIC 1. Demoniac possession. 2. Demonomania.

CATALOGUE OF THE CORNELL WITCHCRAFT COLLECTION

WITCHCRAFT
BF 1555 L53

Leistle, David.
  Die Besessenheit mit besonderer Berücksichtigung der Lehre der hl. Väter.
  Dillingen, L. Keller's Witwe [1886]
  178 p. 23cm.

  Programm--Dillingen.

  1. Demoniac possession. 2. Devil. 3. Demonology.

8
NIC

Witchcraft
BF 1411 D55

Diefenbach, Johann.
  Besessenheit, Zauberei und Hexenfabeln. Eine Studie, veranlasst durch die Teufelaustreibung zu Wemding. Frankfurt a. M., A. F. Nachfolger, 1893.
  56 p. 24cm.

  1. Demoniac possession. 2. Magic. I. Title.

Witchcraft
BF 1410 B42 Z91

Waaijen, Johannes van der, 1639-1701.
  De betoverde weereld van D. Balthasar Bekker ondersogt en weederlegt door Johannes vander Waeyen. Franeker, By L. Strik en J. Horreus, boekverkoopers, 1693.
  1 p. l., VIII, 3-16, 651, [1] p. title vignette, illus. initials. 20 x 16cm.
  4°: π1, *⁴, *2-2*⁴, A-K⁴, L3, M-O⁴, P².
  Black letter.
  Van der Linde 156.

  1. Bekker, Balthasar, 1634-1698. De betoverde weereld. I. Title.

Witchcraft
BF 1410 B42 Z89

Verscheyde gedichten, so voor, als tegen het boek, genaamt: De betoverde weereld. [Amsterdam?] Gedrukt voor de liefhebbers, 1691.
  1 p. l., 12, 9-32 p. title vignettes, illus. initials. 20 x 15cm.
  4°: π1, A⁶, B-D⁴.
  First poem has own t. p. with title: Gestroojde zeegen-palmen, op het doorwrogte werk van de Heer Balthasar Bekker ...genaamd De betoverde weereld. [Van der Linde 188]

  (Continued on next card)

8

Witchcraft
BF 1410 B42 Z89

De betoverde predikant Dr. Balthasar Bekker.
  Verscheyde gedichten, so voor, als tegen het boek, genaamt: De betoverde weereld. 1691. (Card 2)

  Includes other works published separately: De betoverde predikant Dr. Balthasar Bekker [van der Linde 189]; Verta[e]ling uit seker arabisch schryver; De geharpoende muys. Van der Linde 197.

  1. Bekker, Balthasar, 1634-1698. De betoverde weereld. I. Gestroojde zeegen-
  (Continued on next card)

8

Witchcraft
BF 1410 B42 1691

Bekker, Balthasar, 1634-1698.
  De betoverde weereld, zynde een grondig ondersoek van 't gemeen gevoelen aangaande de geesten, derselver aart en vermogen, bewind en bedryf: als ook 't gene de menschen door derselver kragt en gemeenschap doen. In vier boeken ondernommen... Amsterdam, By D. van den Dalen, boekverkoper, 1691-1693.
  4 v. in 2. title vignettes, illus., illus. initials. 21 x 17cm.
  Vol. 1: 4°: π², *-2*⁴, A-R⁴, S².

  (Continued on next card)

Witchcraft
BF 1410 B42 1691

De betoverde weereld.
  Bekker, Balthasar, 1634-1698. De betoverde weereld ... 1691-1693. (Card 2)

  Vol. 2: 4°: 2*⁴, A-3K⁴.
  Vol. 3: 4°: *⁴, a-d⁴, A-2A⁴.
  Vol. 4: 4°: *⁴, A-2E⁴, 2E*⁴, 2E2*⁴, 2F-2M⁴.
  Vols. 2-4 have separate t. p.
  Black letter.
  Each vol. autographed by Bekker.
  Van der Linde 16, 17, 19, 20.

  (Continued on next card)

Witchcraft
BF 1410 B42 1739

Bekker, Balthasar, 1634-1698.
  De betoverde weereld, zynde een grondig ondersoek van 't gemeen gevoelen aangaande de geesten, derselver aart en vermogen, bewind en bedryf: als ook 't gene de menschen door derselver kragt en gemeenschap doen. In vier boeken ondernommen van Balthasar Bekker, S. T. D. predikant tot Amsterdam. Deesen druk, volgens des autheurs eigen hand, merkelijk vermeerdert, en van drukfeilen gesuivert. Deventer, By M. de Vries, boekdrukker en verkooper, 1739.

8 (Continued on next card)

Witchcraft
BF 1410 B42 1739

De betoverde weereld.
  Bekker, Balthasar, 1634-1698. De betoverde weereld ... 1739. (Card 2)

  4 v. in 1. front., fold. port, title vignettes, illus. initials. 20 x 16cm.
  Vol. 1: 4°: †-2†3, a-d⁴, e², *-2*⁴, A-S⁴, T².
  Vol. 2: 4°: *3, A-2M⁴, N².
  Vol. 3: 4°: *⁴, A-2B⁴, C².
  Vol. 4: 4°: *3, A-2Q⁴, R².

  (Continued on next card)

8

Witchcraft
BF 1410 B42 1739

De betoverde weereld.
  Bekker, Balthasar, 1634-1698. De betoverde weereld ... 1739. (Card 3)

  Black letter.
  Variant of van der Linde 24: dated 1739, not 1736; and t. p. of vol. 2 wanting.

  1. Demonology. 2. Angels. 3. Magic. 4. Witchcraft. I. Title.

8

Witchcraft
BX 9476 N8 B42++

De Betoverde weereld van den hooggeleerden heer, Dr. Balthasar Bekker, door de geestelykheit bevogten. [poem. n. p., 169-]
  broadside. 21 x 20cm.

  Bound with Bekker, Balthasar, 1634-1698. Protest ... ter Synode van Noordholland ... Alkmaar, 1692.

  1. Bekker, Balthasar, 1634-1698.

8

Witchcraft
BF 1410 B42 Z86 no.5

Molinaeus, Johannes, d. 1702.
  De betoverde werelt van D. Balthazar Bekker handelende van den aert en 't vermogen, van 't bewind en bedrijf der goede en quade engelen, ondersogt en wederleydt: in twee predikaetien; d' eerste van 't gebruik en misbruyk der philosophie; de tweede van den aert en 't bedrijf der goede engelen. En laetstelik in een verhandelinge van de booze geesten, of van den Duyvel en zijne engelen. Rotterdam, By B. Bos, boekverkooper, 1692.

8 (Continued on next card)

Witchcraft
BF 1410 B42 Z86 no.5

De betoverde werelt van D. Balthazar Bekker handelende van den aert en 't vermogen, van 't bewind en bedrijf...
  Molinaeus, Johannes, d. 1702. De betoverde werelt van D. Balthazar Bekker ... 1692. (Card 2)

  6 p. l., 104 p. title vignette, illus. initials. 19 x 15cm.
  4°: *⁴, 2*², A-N⁴.
  Black letter (except for introduction)
  Variant of van der Linde 131: 2*², H-N⁴ wanting in van der Linde copy.
  No. 5 in vol. lettered Tractaten voor en tegen B. Bekker.

8 (Continued on next card)

Witchcraft
BF 1565 S83 S83

Sterzinger, Ferdinand, 1721-1786.
  Betrügende Zauberkunst und träumende Hexerey, oder Vertheidigung der akademischen Rede, von dem gemeinen Vorurtheile der wirkenden und thätigen Hexerey, wider das Urtheil ohne Vorurtheil &c. ... München, In der akademischen Buchhandlung, 1767.
  4 p. l., 96, [2] p. 21cm.
  1. His Akademische Rede von dem gemeinen Vorurtheile der Hexerey. 2. Witchcraft. 3. März, Agnellus, 1726-1784. Urtheil ohne Vorurtheil über die wirkend- und thätige Hexerey. I. Title.

8

Witchcraft
BT 980 G87 1744

Gross, Johann Matthias.
  Beweissthum der grossen Macht und Ohnmacht des Fürsten der Finsterniss ... Nürnberg [J. L. Montag] 1744.
  [20] 46 [26] 818, 64 [40] p. illus. 19cm.

  Added t. p. on two leaves: Die grosse Macht und Ohnmacht des Fürsten der Finsterniss. Leipzig, J. L. Montag, 1734.

  1. Devil. I. Title. II. Title: Die grosse Macht und Ohnmacht des Fürsten der Finsternis.

Witchcraft
BF 1555 B57

[Bewerlein, Sixtus]
  Erschröckliche gantz warhafftige Geschicht welche sich mit Apolonia, Hannsen Geißlbrechts Burgers zu Spalt inn dem Lystätter Bistumb, Haußfrawen, so den 20. Octobris, Anno 82. von dem bösen Feind gar hart besessen, vnnd doch den 24. gedachten Monats widerumb durch sein gnädige Hilff, auß solcher grossen Pein vnn Marter entlediget worden, verlauffen hat. Allen gottlosen, zänckischen, vbelfluchenden Eheleuten, vnnd andern zu sonderer Warnung Truck gegeben. Durch M. Sixtum Agrico

8 (Continued on next card)

Witchcraft
BF 1555 B57

[Bewerlein, Sixtus] Erschröckliche gantz warhafftige Geschicht ... 1584. (Card

  lam [pseud.] ... vnd dann D. Georgium Witmerum ... Ingolstatt, Getruckt durch Wolffgang Eder, 1584.
  3 p. l., 49 p. 20cm.
  Title in red and black.

  1. Demoniac possession. 2. Exorcism. 3. Geisslbrecht, Anna, fl. 1584. I. Witmer, Georg, joint author. II. Title.

8

Witchcraft
BF 1583 B57

Beyer, Conrad.
  Kulturgeschichtliche Bilder aus Mecklenburg. Berlin, W. Süsserott, 1903.
  131 p. 24cm. (Mecklenburgische Geschichte in Einzeldarstellungen. Heft 6)

  Contents.--Zauberei und Hexenprozesse im evangelischen Mecklenburg.--Unter den Elenden und Ehrlosen.

  1. Magic--Germany--Mecklenburg. 2. Trials (Witchcraft)--Mecklenburg, Ger. I. Title: Zauberei und Hexenprozesse im evangelischen Mecklenburg. II. Tit

68

CATALOGUE OF THE CORNELL WITCHCRAFT COLLECTION

Witchcraft
BF
1559
G25
Z63
no.7

Beytrag zur gelehrten Geschichte unserer Zeit.
Lavater, Johann Caspar, 1741-1801.
Auszug der Frankfurter gelehrten Anzeigen Nro. 38 und 39 den 12. May 1775. Beytrag zur gelehrten Geschichte unserer Zeit. [Zürch, 1775]
[8] p. 17cm.

No. 7 in vol. lettered Gassneriana.

1. Gassner, Johann Joseph, 1727-1779. I. Title. II. Title: Beytrag zur gelehrten Geschichte unserer Zeit.

8

Witchcraft
BX
9479
B42
S39

Beytrag zur Geschichte der Intoleranz ...
Schwager, Johann Moritz.
Beytrag zur Geschichte der Intoleranz; oder Leben, Meynungen und Schicksale des ehemaligen Doct. der Theologie und reformierten Predigers in Amsterdam Balthasar Bekkers, meist nach kirchlichen Urkunden. ... Mit einer Vorrede Hrn. Doct. Joh. Salomo Semlers von einer unter dessen Aufsicht nächstens herauskommenden verbesserten Auflage der bezauberten Welt. Leipzig, In der Weygandschen Buchhandlung, 1780.
10, LXXXXII, 190 p. 18 x 11cm.

8 (Continued on next card)

Witchcraft
BX
9479
B42
S39

Beytrag zur Geschichte der Intoleranz ...
Schwager, Johann Moritz. Beytrag zur Geschichte der Intoleranz ... 1780. (Card 2)

8°: a-g⁸, A-M⁸.

Van der Linde 217.

1. Bekker, Balthasar, 1634-1698--Biog. 2. Bekker, Balthasar, 1634-1698. De betoverde weereld. I. Semler, Johann Salomo, 1725-1791. II. Title.

8

WITCHCRAFT
BF
1555
M94
029
no.2

Das Bezauberte Bauermägdgen: oder Geschichte von dem anjetzo in Kemberg bey Wittenberg sich aufhaltenden Landmägdgen Johannen Elisabethen Lohmannin; aufgesetzt durch einen vom Vorurtheil Befreyeten, und mit Anmerkungen eines Rechtsgelahrten versehen. Breslau, Bey J. E. Meyer, 1760.
167 p. 18cm.
No. 2 in vol. lettered Oesfeld u. a. ...
"Eines Advocatens Ehrenrettung wider ... Herrn Gottlieb Müllers Beschuldigung": p. 51-162.

8
NIC (Continued on next card)

WITCHCRAFT
BF
1555
M94
029
no.2

Das Bezauberte Bauermägdgen ... 1760. (Card 2)

1. Lohmannin, Anna Elisabeth. 2. Müller, Gottlieb. Gründlicher Nachricht von einer begeisterten Weibesperson. 3. Demoniac possession. I. Ein vom Vorurtheil Befreyter. II. Ein Rechtgelahrter. III. Ein Advocat.

8
NIC

Witchcraft
BF
1410
B42
1693

Die bezauberte Welt.
Bekker, Balthasar, 1634-1698.
Die bezauberte Welt: oder Eine gründliche Untersuchung des allgemeinen Aberglaubens, betreffend, die arth und das Vermögen, Gewalt und Würckung des Satans und der bösen Geister über den Menschen, und was diese durch derselben Krafft und Gemeinschafft thun: so aus natürlicher Vernunfft und H. Schrifft in 4 Büchern zu bewehren sich unternommen hat Balthasar Bekker, S. Theol. Doct. und Prediger zu Amsterdam. Nebenst des

(Continued on next card)

Witchcraft
BF
1410
B42
1693

Die bezauberte Welt.
Bekker, Balthasar, 1634-1698. Die bezauberte Welt ... 1693. (Card 2)

Autoris generale Vorrede über diese seine 4 Bücher: wie und welcher Gestalt dieselbe zu lesen, der Zweck seines Vorhabens, und dann die Ordnung, so er darinnen gehalten. Aus dem Holländischen nach der letzten vom Autore vermehrten Edition. Amsterdam, gedruckt bey D. von Dahlen, 1693.
39, [1], 136, 270, [2], 195, [3], 308, [4] p. Title vignette (port.), plate. 23 x 17cm. (Continued on next card)

Witchcraft
BF
1410
B42
1693

Die bezauberte Welt.
Bekker, Balthasar, 1634-1698. Die bezauberte Welt ... 1693. (Card 3)

4°: a-e⁴, A-S⁴, A-2K⁴, A-2A⁴, A-2P⁴.
Black letter.
Translation of De betoverde weereld.
Van der Linde 25.

1. Demonology. 2. Angels. 3. Magic. 4. Witchcraft. I. Title. II. His De betoverde weereld--German.

Witchcraft
BF
1410
B42
1781

Die bezauberte Welt.
Bekker, Balthasar, 1634-1698.
D. [i. e., Doktor] Balthasar Bekkers reformierten Predigers in Amsterdam bezauberte Welt. Neu übersetzt von Johann Moritz Schwager, Pastor zu Jöllenbeck; durchgesehen und vermehrt von D. Johann Salomo Semler. Leipzig, In der Weygandschen Buchhandlung, 1781.
3 v. title vignette (port.), fold. plate. 20cm.
8°: vol. 1: a⁸, b2, A-2F⁸; vol. 2:

(Continued on next card)

Witchcraft
BF
1410
B42
1781

Die bezauberte Welt.
Bekker, Balthasar, 1634-1698. D. Balthasar Bekkers ... bezauberte Welt. 1781. (Card 2)

8 (-8), A-2F⁸, G⁴; vol. 3: *⁸ (-*1, *8), A-2Y6.
Translation of his De betoverde weereld.

1. Demonology. 2. Angels. 3. Magic. 4. Witchcraft. I. Title. II. Title:

(Continued on next card)

WITCHCRAFT
BF
1555
M61+

Die Beziehungen der Geisteskranken zu den Besessenen und Hexen.
Meyer, Ludwig.
Die Beziehungen der Geisteskranken zu den Besessenen und Hexen.

(In: Westermann's illustrirte deutsche Monatshefte. Wiesbaden. 26cm. No.57, June 1861. p. 258-264)

8
NIC
1. Demoniac possession. 2. Witchcraft.

WITCHCRAFT
BF
1517
G3
K58

Beziehungen des Dämonen- und Hexenwesens zur deutschen Irrenpflege.
Kirchhoff, Theodor, 1853-1922.
Beziehungen des Dämonen- und Hexenwesens zur deutschen Irrenpflege, von Dr. Kirchhoff.
(In Allgemeine Zeitschrift für Psychiatrie und ihre Grenzgebiete. Berlin, 1844-1949. 23cm. 44. Bd., 4. u. 5. Heft (1888), p. [329]-398)
Caption title.
Bibliographical footnotes.
1. Demonology. 2. Mental illness--Germany. 3. Mental illness (in religion, folk-lore, etc.) I. Title.

8
NIC

Witchcraft
BF
1429
B57
1845

Bianco, Filippo.
Lessicomanzia; ovvero, Dizionario degli esseri, dei personaggi, dei libri, dei fatti e delle cose, che riferisconsi alle apparizioni, alla divinazione, alla magia ec. Per servere di corredo alla storia degli scorsi secoli, con aggiunte interessanti in questa ed. Siena, Tipografia dell'Ancora, 1845.
xlix, 660 p. illus. 16cm.

1. Occult sciences--Dict. I. Title.

Witchcraft
BF
1445
B57

Bianor, pseud.
Curieuse Winter-Discourse einer gewissen Compagnie bestehende in etlichen raren Fragen und deren Beantwortung hrsg. von Einem aus dieser Compagnie, welcher sich nennet Bianor. Jena, J. Bielcken, 1704.
149 p. 16cm.

1. Devil. I. Title.

WITCHCRAFT
BF
1566
P33
B5++

Bibel und protestantische Hexenverfolgung.
Paulus, Nicolaus, 1853-1930.
Bibel und protestantische Hexenverfolgung.
(In Wissenschaftliche Beilage zur Germania. Blätter für Literatur, Wissenschaft und Kunst. Berlin. 31cm. Jahrg. 1907, Nr. 44 (1907), p. [345]-349)
In columns.
In broadside box.

1. Witchcraft--History. 2. Witchcraft in the Bible. I. Title.

8
NIC

Witchcraft
Z
6878
W8
F35

Bibliographical notes on the witchcraft literature of Scotland.
Ferguson, John, 1837-1916.
Bibliographical notes on the witchcraft literature of Scotland.
(In The Edinburgh Bibliographical Society. [Publications] Session 1896-97. Edinburgh. 25cm. v. 3 (1897) p. [37]-124)

WITCHCRAFT
Z
6878
W8
M82
1888

Bibliographical notes on witchcraft in Massachusetts.
Moore, George Henry, 1823-1892.
Bibliographical notes on witchcraft in Massachusetts. Worcester, Printed for the author, 1888.
31 p. 25cm.

Read before the American Antiquarian Society, Apr. 25, 1888.
Originally appeared in the Proceedings of the American Antiquarian Society, new ser., v.5, pt. 2, Apr.1888, p.245-273, with title: Notes on the bibliography of witchcraft in Massachusetts.

8
NIC (Continued on next card)

Witchcraft
Z
6876
J86

Bibliographie occultiste et maçonnique.
Jouin, Ernest.
Bibliographie occultiste et maçonnique. Répertoire d'ouvrages imprimés et manuscrits relatifs à la franc-maçonnerie, les sociétés secrètes, la magie, etc. publié d'après les fiches recueillies par A.-Peeters Baertsoen et avec des notes historiques et bibliographiques. Tome I. Jusqu'à l'année 1717. Paris, Revue internationale des sociétés secrètes, 1930.
653 p. 25cm.

At head of title: Mgr E. Jouin et V. Descreux.
No more published? --

69

CATALOGUE OF THE CORNELL WITCHCRAFT COLLECTION

Witchcraft   Bibliotheca, acta et scripta magica.
BF
1547   Hauber, Eberhard David, 1695-1765.
H36   Bibliotheca, acta et scripta magica. Gründliche Nachrichten und Urtheile von solchen Büchern und Handlungen, welche die Macht des Teufels in leiblichen Dingen betreffen ... Lemgo, Gedruckt bey J. H. Meyer, 1738-45.
     36 pts. in 3 v. plates (part fold.) ports. 18cm.

     Vol.[1]: 1. Stück. 2. und verbesserter Druck. 1739.
     For detailed contents see J. G. T. Grässe:
         (Continued on next card)

Witchcraft   Bibliotheca, acta et scripta magica.
BF
1547   Hauber, Eberhard David, 1695-1765. Bibliotheca, acta et scripta magica ... 1738-
H36   45.   (Card 2)

     Bibliotheca magica, p. 118-130.

     1. Devil. 2. Devil--Bibl. 3. Witchcraft. 4. Witchcraft--Bibl. 5. Occult sciences. I. Title.

     Bibliotheca diabolica; being a choice selection of the most valuable books relating to the Devil.
Witchcraft
Z
5761   [Kernot, Henry] 1806-1874.
K39   Bibliotheca diabolica; being a choice selection of the most valuable books relating to the Devil; his origin, greatness, and influence. Comprising the most important works on the devil, Satan, demons, hell, hell-torments, magic, witchcraft ... with some curious volumes on dreams and astrology. In two parts, pro and con, serious and humorous ... [New York] On sale by Scribner, Welford & Armstrong, 1874.
     40 p. illus. 25cm.

Witchcraft   Bibliotheca esoterica, catalogue annoté et illustré de 6707 ouvrages anciens et modernes.
Z
6880   Dorbon aîné, bookseller, Paris.
Z9   Bibliotheca esoterica, catalogue annoté et illustré de 6707 ouvrages anciens et modernes
D69   ... comme aussi des sociétés secrètes ... En vente à la Librairie Dorbon-aîné. Paris [1940]
     2 p. l., 656 p., 2 l. illus. (incl. music) plates, facsims. 25cm.

     1. Occult sciences--Bibl.--Catalogs. 2. Secret societies--Bibl.--Catalogs. I. Title.
     Library of Congress   Z6880.Z9D6   43-36450
         [3]   016.133

Witchcraft   Bibliotheca magica et pneumatica.
Z
6876   Grässe, Johann Georg Theodor, 1814-1885.
G73   Bibliotheca magica et pneumatica; oder, Wissenschaftlich geordnete bibliographie der wichtigsten in das gebiet des zauber-, wunder-, geister- und sonstigen aberglaubens vorzüglich älterer zeit einschlagenden werke. Mit angabe der aus diesen wissenschaften auf der Königl. Sächs. oeff. bibliothek zu Dresden befindlichen schriften. Ein beitrag zur sittengeschichtlichen literatur. Zusammengestellt und mit einem doppelten register versehen. Leipzig, W. Engelmann, 1843.
     iv, 175 p. 22cm.
     Copy 1 interleaved.
     Manuscript notes, copy 1.
     1. Occult sciences--Bibl. I. Title.

Witchcraft   Bibliotheca magica et pneumatica.
Z
6880   Rosenthal, J., firm, booksellers, Munich.
Z9R81   Bibliotheca magica et pneumatica. Geheime Wissenschaften. Sciences occultes. Occult
1903   sciences. Folk-lore. München [1903]
     48, 680 p. 24cm. (Its Kataloge 31-35)

     Issued in parts.

     1. Occult sciences--Bibl.--Catalogs. 2. Folk-lore--Bibl.--Catalogs. 3. Curiosa--Bibl. I. Title.

     Bibliotheca magica et pneumatica.
Witchcraft
Z
6880   Rosenthal, Ludwig, Munich.
Z9C35   Bibliotheca magica et pneumatica. Geheime Wissenschaften, Magie, gute und böse Geister,
no.1   Gespenster, Volksaberglauben; Hexen und Hexenprocesse ... Ellwangen, L. Weil [188-?]
     148 p. 23cm.

     "Katalog 45."
     No. 1 in vol. lettered: Catalogues of books on magic and witchcraft.

     Bibliotheca magica et pneumatica.
Witchcraft
Z
6880   Teubner, Franz, bookseller, Bonn.
Z9   Bibliotheca magica et pneumatica. [Abth.] I[-III, VI] Antiquaritäts-Katalog
T35   No. 49[-Nr. 51, 54. Bonn, 189-]
     v. in . 22cm.
     Abth. II and III in 1 vol.
     At head of title, vol. I: Franz Teubner's Antiquariat (vorm. Antiquariat der Firma Paul Neubner in Köln)
     1. Occult sciences--Bibl.--Catalogs. 2. Magic--Bibl.--Catalogs. I. Title.

     Bibliotheca occulta et philosophica; Sammlung Baron C. Du Prel, und kleine andere Beiträge.
Witchcraft
Z
6880   Du Prel, Karl Ludwig August Friedrich Maximilian Alfred, Freiherr, 1839-1899.
Z9   Bibliotheca occulta et philosophica; Sammlung Baron C. Du Prel, und kleine andere
D94   Beiträge (Inhaltsverzeichnis umstehend) Mit Vorwort von H. L. Held. München, E. Hirsch [193-]
     104 p. 22cm.
     Katalog 58.
     1. Occult sciences--Bibliography--Catalogs. I. Held, Hans Ludwig, 1885- II. Hirsch, Emil, bookseller, Munich. III. Title.

Rare
BX
8011   Bidembach, Felix, 1564-1612, ed.
B58   Consiliorum theologicorum decades VIII. Das ist: Achtzig theologischer Bedencken,
1612   Bericht, oder Antwort auff mancherley (in Glaubens, Gewissens vnd andern mehr sachen) zutragende Fälle, vnnd vorfallende Fragen, oder Handelungen gerichtet, vnnd mehrern Theils vor viel Jahren gestellet: durch etliche Hochgelehrte vnnd vortreffliche Theologos ... Itzo zum andern mahl auffs New in Truck verfertiget. Wittenberg, A. Rüdingern, 1612-14.
        (Continued on next card)

Rare
BX
8011   Bidembach, Felix, 1564-1612, ed. Consiliorum theologicorum decades ... 1612-14.
B58   (Card 2)
1612

     3 v. in 1. 20cm.

     Vols. [2]-[3] have title: Consiliorum theologicorum decas IX[-X]. Der neundte [-zehende] Theil theologischer Bedencken, Bericht, oder Antwort ... Franckfurt am Mayn, Getruckt bey Erasmo Kempffern, in Verlegung Johann Berners, 1614.
     1. Theology--Collections--Lutheran authors. I. Title.

     Biedermann, Hans, fl. 1968- ed.
BF
1520   Bodin, Jean, 1530-1596.
B66+   Vom aussgelasnen wütigen Teuffelsheer. Übers. v. Johann Fischart. (Um ein neues Vorw. verm.
1973   Nachdr. d. Ausg. Strassburg 1591.) Vorw.: Hans Biedermann. Graz, Akadem. Druck- u. Verlagsanst., 1973.
     vii p., 372 p. of facsims. 28cm.

     Translation of De la démonomanie des sorciers.
     Bibliography: p. vii.

Witchcraft   Bieler, Benjamin, 1693-1772.
BS
1325   ... Richtige Auslegung der Unterredung
B59   Sauls mit der Zauberin und mit einem Gespenste zu Endor. 1. B. Sam. XXVIII. Auf Veranlassung eines gelehrten Mannes zur Vertheydigung seiner in der fortgesetzten Sammlung 1748 ans Licht gestellten schriftmässigen Betrachtung herausgegeben. Leipzig und Wittenberg, J. F. Schlomach, 1752.
     126 p. 18cm.

8   (Continued on next card)

Witchcraft
BS
1325   Bieler, Benjamin, 1693-1772. Richtige Auslegung der Unterredung Sauls mit der Zauberin ... 1752.   (Card 2)
B59

     1. Schmersahl, Elias Friedrich, 1719-1775. Natürliche Erklärung der Geschichte Sauls mit der Betrügerin zu Endor. 2. Bible. O.T. 1 Samuel XXVIII--Criticism, interpretation, etc. 3. Witchcraft in the Bible. I. Title.

     Biermann, Gottlieb, 1824- , supposed author.
Witchcraft
BF
1584   Zwei Hexenprocesse zu Braunau.
B6   (In Verein für Geschichte der Deutschen
Z68   in Böhmen. Mittheilungen. Prag. 23cm. 33. Jahrg., Nr. 3 (1895), p. 285-292)
     An editorial, probably by G. Biermann.

     1. Trials (Witchcraft)--Bohemia. I. Biermann, Gottlieb, 1824- , supposed author.

     Bijdrage tot de geschiedenis der heksenprocessen in de Provincie Groningen.
Witchcraft
BF
1584   Feith, Hendrik Octávius, 1813-1895.
N4   Bijdrage tot de geschiedenis der heksenprocessen in de Provincie Groningen, door
F31   Mr. H. O. Feith. [n. p., ca. 1850?]
     26 p. 25cm.
     "Eene voorlezing, gehouden in het Gron. genootschap Pro excolendo jure patrio."
     Reprint from Nieuwe Bijdragen voor vaderlandsche Geschiedenis en Oudheidkunde, i, according to G. L. Burr.
     Caption title.
     1. Trials (Witchcraft)--Netherlands. I. Title.

     Bijdrage tot de geschiedenis der heksenprocessen, in Gelderland.
WITCHCRAFT
BF
1584   Molhuysen, Philip Christiaan, 1870-1944.
N4   Bijdrage tot de geschiedenis der heksenprocessen, in Gelderland. [n.p., n.d.]
M71   16 p. 24cm.

     Extract from Nieuwe bijdragen voor vaderl. geschiedenis en oudheidkunde, v.1, p.43-68
     With this is bound: Weerwolven. n.d.
8
NIC   1. Trials (Witchcraft)--Gelderland.

Witchcraft   Bila, Constantin.
BF
1595   ... La croyance à la magie au XVIIIe siècle en France dans les contes, romans & traités ... Paris, J. Gamber, 192[?]
B59
     158 p., 1 l. 23cm.
     Thèse--Univ. de Paris.
     "Errata": 1 leaf laid in.
     "Bibliographie": p. [151]-158.

     1. Magic. 2. French literature--18th cent.--Hist. & crit. I. Title.
                                        26-16744

     Library of Congress   BF1595.B5

CATALOGUE OF THE CORNELL WITCHCRAFT COLLECTION

Bilder aus der deutschen Vergangenheit.

chcraft
    Freytag, Gustav, 1816-1895.
        Bilder aus der deutschen Vergangenheit.
    Der deutsche Teufel im 16. Jahrhundert.
    (In Die Grenzboten. Leipzig, 1858)
    XVII. Jahrg. (1858) p. [363]-386)

    1. Devil. II. Title. III. Title: Der deutsche Teufel im 16. Jahrhundert.

Bilder aus Thüringen.

TCHCRAFT
    Hollenbach, Wilhelm.
83
3
        Bilder aus Thüringen. I. Tragikomische Geisterbeschwörung auf dem Galgenberge bei Jena in der Christnacht des Jahres 1715. Nach den Originalquellen wahrheitsgetreu dargestellt ... Mit interessanten Bruchstücken der Streitschrift des Jenaischen Arztes Andreä und den Gutachten der theologischen und juristischen Fakultät zu Leipzig. Jena, F. Mauke (A. Schenk), 1885.
    iv, 56 p.   21cm.
    No more   published?
    (Continued on next card)

Bill, Arthur, d. 1612.

chcraft
    The Witches of Northamptonshire. Agnes Browne. Ioane Vaughan. Arthur Bill. Hellen Ienkinson. Mary Barber. Witches.
6a
1
    Who were all executed at Northampton the 22. of Iuly last. 1612. London, Printed by Tho: Purfoot, for Arthur Iohnson, 1612. [Northampton, England, Taylor & son, 1866]
    [28] p.   22cm.
    No. 1 in box lettered Witchcraft in Northamptonshire.

    1. Witchcraft--Northamptonshire, England. I. Title: Witchcraft in Northamptonshire.

---

chcraft
    Billengren, Ehrenfried.
        Om trolldomswäsendet i Dalarne under Karl XI:s regering.
    (In Läsning för folket. Stockholm. 21cm. 7e Bandet, 2a Häftet (1875), p. 97-139)
    Caption title.
    1. Witchcraft--Sweden. 2. Witchcraft-- Dalecarlia, Sweden. I. Title. II. Läsning för svenska folket.

Binder, Nicolaus.

    Drey warhafftige grundtliche Zeitungen, die erste von ettlichen Hexen und Zauberin welche hin und wider in Ungern und Teutschland grossen Schaden angericht haben... Beschriben durch den hochgelerten Herrn Nicolaum Binder... Die ander von einem Burger und Thuchmacher der in grosser Unzucht ein zeitlang gelebt ... unnd wie er durch dess Teufels Eingebung 3. Kinder und sein Weib jämmerlicher weiss ermördet... Die dritte   von Erscheinung zweyer
HCRAFT
    (Continued on next card)

Binder, Nicolaus.

    Drey warhafftige grundtliche Zeitungen ...
    1610 [ca. 1900]   (Card 2)

HCRAFT
    Engel... Beschriben durch den ehrwürdigen Herrn Joannem Röseler diser Zeit Pfarrern daselbsten. Erstlich Getruckt zu Tirnau in Ungern nachmals aber zu Freyburg, bey Georg Hofmann, 1610 [ca. 1900]
    [7] l.   24cm.

    T. p. added by scribe: [Kerpffen]
    (Continued on next card)

Binder, Nicolaus.

MSS
Bd.
WITCHCRAFT
BF
D77
    Drey warhafftige grundtliche Zeitungen ...
    1610 [ca. 1900]   (Card 3)

    Drey warhafftige Zeitungen. Die erste von etlichen Hexen in Ungern, den 11. October 1609. Beschriben durch Nicolaus Binder. &c. 1610.
    Carnap's manuscript copy.
    "Originaldruck in der Stadtbibliothek zu Zürich. 4 Bl. in 4°."
    Numerals in the margins indicate the paginati on of the original.
    (Continued on next card)

Binder, Nicolaus.

MSS
Bd.
WITCHCRAFT
BF
D77
    Drey warhafftige grundtliche Zeitungen ...
    1610 [ca. 1900]   (Card 4)

    In verse.

    1. Witchcraft. 2. Apparitions. 3. Prock, Hans, d. 1610. I. Binder, Nicolaus. II. Röseler, Joannes.

Witchcraft
BF
1508
B61
1699
    [Binet, Benjamin] 17th cent.
        Idée generale de la theologie payenne, servant de refutation au systeme de Mr. Bekker. Touchant l'existence & l'operation des demons. Ou Traitté [sic] historique des dieux du paganisme. Par Mr. B***. Amsterdam, Chez J. du Fresne, 1699.
    6 p. l., 227 p.   26cm.
    12: *6, A-I12, K6.
    First published 1696 with title Traité historique des dieux et des demons du paganisme.
8   (Continued on next card)

Witchcraft
BF
1508
B61
1699
    [Binet, Benjamin] 17th cent. Idée generale de la theologie payenne ... 1699.   (Card 2)

    Ex libris cabalisticis Kurt Seligmann.

    1. Paganism. 2. Demonology. 3. Bekker, Balthasar, 1634-1698. De betoverde weereld. I. Title. II. His Traité historique des dieux et des demons du paganisme.
8

Binet, Benjamin, 17th cent.
Traité historique des dieux et des demons du paganisme.
Witchcraft
BF
1508
B61
1699
    [Binet, Benjamin] 17th cent.
        Idée generale de la theologie payenne, servant de refutation au systeme de Mr. Bekker. Touchant l'existence & l'operation des demons. Ou Traitté [sic] historique des dieux du paganisme. Par Mr. B***. Amsterdam, Chez J. du Fresne, 1699.
    6 p. l., 227 p.   26cm.
    12: *6, A-I12, K6.
    First published 1696 with title Traité historique des dieux et des demons du paganisme.
8   (Continued on next card)

Binet, Benjamin, 17th cent.
Traité historique des dieux et des demons du paganisme.
Witchcraft
BF
1508
B61
1699
    [Binet, Benjamin] 17th cent. Idée generale de la theologie payenne ... 1699.   (Card 2)

    Ex libris cabalisticis Kurt Seligmann.

    1. Paganism. 2. Demonology. 3. Bekker, Balthasar, 1634-1698. De betoverde weereld. I. Title. II. His Traité historique des dieux et des demons du paganisme.
8

Witchcraft
DC
102
.8
R2
V77
    Binns, Clare, joint author.
    Vincent, Louis, 1876–
        Gilles de Rais: the original Bluebeard, by A. L. Vincent & Clare Binns, introduction by M. Hamblin Smith ... London, A. M. Philpot, ltd., 1926.
    2 p. l., 3-221, [1] p. illus., plates, 2 port. (incl. front.) 19½cm.
    "Genealogy of Gilles de Rais": p. 199-202.
    "List of works consulted": p. 217-221.

    1. Rais, Gilles de Laval, seigneur de, 1404-1440. I. Binns, Clare, joint author. II. Title.   27-18294 Revised
8   Library of Congress   DC102.8.R2V6
        [r31c2]

Binsfeld, Peter.

    see

Binsfeld, Pierre, ca. 1540-1598.

Witchcraft
BF
1565
B61
1590
    Binsfeld, Pierre, ca. 1540-1598.
        Tractat von Bekantnuss der Zauberer vnnd Hexen. Ob vnd wie viel denselben zu glauben. Anfänglich durch den hochwürdigen Herrn Petrum Binsfeldium ... in Latein beschrieben. Jetzt aber allen Liebhabern der Warheit vnd Gerechtigkeit zu gutem verteutscht. Trier, Getruckt bey Heinrich Bock, 1590.
    8 p. l., 154 (i.e. 308), [9] p. 16cm.
    Title in red and black.
8   (Continued on next card)

Witchcraft
BF
1565
B61
1590
    Binsfeld, Pierre, ca. 1540-1598. Tractat von Bekantnuss der Zauberer vnnd Hexen. 1590.   (Card 2)

    Translation of Tractatus de confessionibus maleficorum & sagarum, made by H. Bock.
    "Monastery Weingartensis Anº 1620": in ms. on t. p.

    I. Bock, Heinrich, tr.
8

Witchcraft
BF
1565
B61
1591a
    Binsfeld, Pierre, ca. 1540-1598.
        Tractat von Bekantnuss der Zauberer vnd Hexen. Ob vnd wie viel denselben zu glauben. Anfänglich durch den hochwürdigen Herrn Petrum Binsfeldium ... in Latein beschrieben. Jetzt aber der Warheit zu stewr in vnser teutsche Sprach vertiert durch ... Bernhart Vogel ... München, Gedruckt bey Adam Berg, 1591.
    4 p. l., 75 (i.e. 150), [6] p. 20cm.
    Title in red and black.
8   With colophon.
    (Continued on next card)

Witchcraft
BF
1565
B61
1591a
    Binsfeld, Pierre, ca. 1540-1598. Tractat von Bekanntnuss der Zauberer vnd Hexen. 1591.   (Card 2)

    Translation of Tractatus de confessionibus maleficorum & sagarum.
    Title vignette shows witches and devils.
    1. Witchcraft. 2. Demonology. I. His Tractatus de confessionibus maleficorum & sagarum--German. II. Vogel, Bernhard, tr. III. Title: Tractat von Bekanntnuss der Zauberer und Hexen.
8

CATALOGUE OF THE CORNELL WITCHCRAFT COLLECTION

```
Witchcraft
BF      Binsfeld, Pierre, ca. 1540-1598.
1565       Tractatvs de confessionibvs maleficorum
B61     & sagarum, an, et qvanta fides ijs adhiben-
        da sit. Avgvstae Trevirorvm, Excudebat
        Henricus Bock, 1589.
           8 p. l., 196, [17] p. 16cm.
           First edition, according to the Deutsche
        Biographie and G. L. Burr.
           "This is the book written by Binsfeld,
        & wh. brought such terrible suffering to
        Flade & torture    & death to Loos. See
   8
                      (Continued on next card)
```

```
Witchcraft
BF      Binsfeld, Pierre, ca. 1540-1598. Tracta-
1565    tvs de confessionibvs maleficorum & sagarum
B61     ... 1589.                    (Card 2)

        Soldan et al. [Signed] AD White": in ms.
        on flyleaf of copy 1.
           With copy 2 is bound Kreitman, Martinus.
        Histori von dem fürtreffenlichen Ritter vnd
        ansehlichen Martyr S. Castl. München, 1589.

   8
```

```
Witchcraft
BF      Binsfeld, Pierre, ca. 1540-1598.
1565       Tractatvs de confessionibvs maleficorum
B61     et sagarvm recognitus & auctus. An, et
1591    qvanta fides ijs adhibenda sit. ... Ac-
        cessit de nouo, eodem auctore, Commentarius
        in titulum Codicis lib. 9. de maleficis &
        mathematicis ... Avgvstae Trevirorvm,
        Excudebat Henricus Bock, 1591.
           8 p. l., 633, [14] p. 17cm.
           Commentarivs in titvlvm codicis lib. IX.
        de maleficis et           mathematicis, p. [365]-
   8    633, has spe         cial t. p.
```

```
Witchcraft
BF      Binsfeld, Pierre, ca. 1540-1598.
1565       Tractatvs de confessionibvs maleficorum
B61     et sagarvm, secvndò recognitus, & auctior
1596    redditus. An, & quanta fides ijs adhiben-
        da sit? Avctore Petro Binsfeldio ... 
        Adiungitur Commentarius, eodem auctore, in
        tit. c. lib. 9. de malefic. & mathematicis
        ... In fine adijciuntur bullae & extrava-
        gantes pontificum ... contra astrologos,
        diuinatores, magos, maleficos & alios super-
        stitiosos. Av        gvstae Trevirorvm, Ex
   8
                      (Continued on next card)
```

```
Witchcraft
BF      Binsfeld, Pierre, ca. 1540-1598. Tracta-
1565    tvs de confessionibvs maleficorum et sa-
B61     garum ... 1596.              (Card 2)
1596
        officina typographica Henrici Bock, 1596.
           8 p. l., 795, [18] p. 17cm.
           Commentarivs in titvlvm codicis lib. IX.
        de maleficis et mathematicis, p. 407-758,
        has special t. p.
           Extravagantes et bvllae apostolicae di-
        versorvm pontif     icum ...: p. 759-795.
   8       Binding:             contemporary blind
        stamped pigsk         in, with clasps.
```

```
Witchcraft
BF      Binsfeld, Pierre, ca. 1540-1598.
1565       Tractatvs de confessionibvs maleficorvm et sagarvm,
B61     secvndò recognitvs, & auctior redditus. An, et quanta
1605    fides ijs adhibenda sit?  Avctore Petro Binsfeldio ...
        Adiungitur Commentarius, eodem auctore, in tit. c. lib.
        9. de malefic. et mathematicis, theologiæ & iuris scientiæ
        ... accommodatus, jam primum reuisus et auctus. In fine
        adijciuntur bullæ & extrauagantes pontificum ... contra
        astrologos, diuinatores, magos, maleficos & alios super-
        stitiosos. Avgvstæ Trevirorvm, ex officina typographica
        Henrici Bock, 1605.
           7 p. l., 767, [17] p. 17cm.
           The "Commentarius" has    special t. p.
   8    Binding: contem       porary blind stamped
        pigskin.
        Library of Congress, no.
```

```
Witchcraft
BF      Binsfeld, Pierre, ca. 1540-1598.
1565       Tractatvs de confessionibvs maleficorum
B61     et sagarvm.  An & quanta fides ijs adhi-
1623    benda sit?  Auctore Petro Binsfeldio ...
        Accedit eiusdem auctoris Commentarius in
        tit. cod. lib. 9. de malefic. & mathematic.
        ... Item bvllae & extrauagantes pontifi-
        cum, &c.  Editio quarta correctior & auc-
        tior.  Coloniae Agrippinae, Sumptib. Pe-
        tri Henningij, 1623.
           8 p. l.,        638, [17] p. 16cm.
   8
                      (Continued on next card)
```

```
Witchcraft
BF      Binsfeld, Pierre, ca. 1540-1598. Tracta-
1565    tvs de confessionibvs maleficorvm et sa-
B61     garvm. 1623.                  (Card 2)
1623
           Commentarivs in titvlvm codicis lib. IX.
        de maleficis et mathematicis, p. 329-611,
        has special t. p.
           Extravagantes et bvllae apostolicae di-
        versorvm pontificum: p. 612-638.
           "This was, I think, the last impression
        of Binsfeld's work.  It is merely a reprint
        of the 4th ed.         --that of 1596--the
   8
                      (Continued on next card)
```

```
Witchcraft
BF      Binsfeld, Pierre, ca. 1540-1598. Tracta-
1565    tvs de confessionibvs maleficorvm et sa-
B61     garvm. 1623.                  (Card 3)
1623
        last edited by himself. [Signed] G. L.
        B[urr]" in ms. inside front cover.
           1. Witchcraft. 2. Demonology.  I.
        Title: Tractatus de confessionibus malefi-
        corum et sagarum.  II. Title: De confes-
        sionibus malef    icorum et sagarum. III.
   8    Title: Comme          ntarius in titulum ...
        de maleficis          et mathematicis.
```

```
                Binsfeld, Pierre, ca. 1540-1598.
                  Tractatus de confessionibus maleficorum
                & sagarum--German.
Witchcraft
BF      Binsfeld, Pierre, ca. 1540-1598.
1565       Tractat von Bekanntnuss der Zauberer vnd
B61     Hexen. Ob wo wie viel denselben zu glau-
1591a   ben. Anfänglich durch den hochwürdigen
        Herrn Petrum Binsfeldium ... in Latein be-
        schrieben.  Jetzt aber der Warheit zu stewr
        in vnser teutsche Sprach vertiert durch ...
        Bernhart Vogel ... München, Gedruckt bey
        Adam Berg, 1591.
           4 p. l., 75 (i.e. 150), [6] p. 20cm.
           Title in red      and black.
   8       With coloph       on.
                      (Continued on next card)
```

```
                Binsfeld, Pierre, ca. 1540-1598.
                  Tractatus de confessionibus maleficorum
                & sagarum--German.
Witchcraft
BF      Binsfeld, Pierre, ca. 1540-1598. Tractat
1565    von Bekanntnuss der Zauberer vnd Hexen.
B61     1591.                         (Card 2)
1591a
           Translation of Tractatus de confessioni-
        bus maleficorum & sagarum.
           Title vignette shows witches and devils.
           1. Witchcraft. 2. Demonology. I.
        His   Tractatus de confessionibus malefi-
        corum & sagarum--German.  II. Vogel, Bern-
        hard, tr.  III.   Title: Tractat von
   8    Bekanntnuss           der Zauberer und Hexen.
```

```
Thesis  Hodder, Mabel Elisabeth.
1911      Peter Binsfeld and Cornelius Loos,
338     an episode in the history of witchcraft.
        Ithaca, N. Y., 1911.
           228 l. 29cm.

           Thesis (Ph. D.)--Cornell University,
        1911.

           1. Binsfeld, Pierre, ca.1540-1598. 2. Loos,
        Cornelius, 1546-1595. 3. Witchcraft.
```

```
             Binsfeldius, Petrus.

                see

             Binsfeld, Pierre, ca. 1540-1598.
```

```
Witchcraft
BF      Binz, Carl, 1832-1913.
1566       Apologetische Versuche in der Geschichts-
B61     schreibung der Hexenprozesse, von Karl Binz.
        [Berlin, 1901]
           9 p. 23cm.

           "Sonderabdruck aus Zeitschrift für
        Kulturgeschichte. VIII. Band, Heft 2 und 3."

           1. Trials (Witchcraft)--Hist. I. Title.
```

```
Witchcraft
R       Binz, Carl, 1832-1913.
512        Doctor Johann Weyer. (1515-1588) Eine
W64     Nachlese. [Düsseldorf, Gedruckt bei E. Voss]
B612    1889.
           36 p. facsim. 23cm.
           "Sonderabdruck aus dem 24. Band der Zeit-
        schrift des Bergischen Geschichtsvereins."
           Includes further discussion of the question
        raised in his Wier oder Weyer? [Düsseldorf,
        1887]
           1. Weir, Johann, 1515-1588. 2. His Weir oder
        Weyer? I. Title.
```

```
Witchcraft
R       Binz, Carl, 1832-1913.
512        Doctor Johann Weyer: ein rheinischer
W64     Arzt, der erste Bekämpfer des Hexenwahns.
B61     Ein Beitrag zur deutschen Kulturgeschichte
        des 16. Jahrhunderts. Mit den Bildnissen
        Weyers und seines Lehrers Agrippa. Bonn,
        A. Marcus, 1885.
           vii, 167 p. 2 ports. 22cm.
           Commentary in ms. by G. L. Burr on front
        end-paper and on p. 167.
           "Sonderabdruck aus dem 21. Band der Zeit
   8    schrift des           Bergischen Geschichts
        vereins."
```

```
Witchcraft
R       Binz, Carl, 1832-1913.
512        Doctor Johann Weyer: ein rheinischer
W64     Arzt, der erste Bekämpfer des Hexenwahns.
B61     Ein Beitrag zur Geschichte der Aufklärung
1896    und der Heilkunde. 2., umgearb. u. verm.
        Aufl. Mit dem Bildnisse Johann Weyers.
        Berlin, A. Hirschwald, 1896.
           vii, 189 p. port. 24cm.

           1. Wier, Johann, 1515-1588.  I. Title.

   8
```

```
                Binz, Carl, 1832-1913.
                  Doctor Johann Weyer.
Witchcraft
BF      Die ersten Bekämpfer des Hexenwahns.
1563    München, C. Wolf, 1897.
E92++      [321]-323, [329]-331, 338-339 p. 32cm.
no. 4-6  (Deutscher Merkur, 28. Jahrg., No. 41-43)

           A review of Binz. Doktor Johann Weyer,
        der erste Bekämpfer des Hexenwahns.
```

CATALOGUE OF THE CORNELL WITCHCRAFT COLLECTION

---

ar W
53168

Binz, Carl, 1832-1913.
Miscellen. Pater P. Laymann, S. J., und die Hexenprocesse. Zur weiteren Ausklärung. [München, 190-]
[290]-292 p. 22cm.

"Sonderabzug aus der Historischen Zeitschrift."

1. Laymann, Paul, 1574-1635.

Witchcraft
R
512
W64
B618

Binz, Carl, 1832-1913.
Wier oder Weyer? Nachträgliches über den ersten Bekämpfer des Hexenwahns in Deutschland. [Düsseldorf, 1877]
11 p. 23cm.
"Sonderabdruck aus: Beiträge zur Geschichte des Niederrheins, Band II."
In ms. on t. p.: Sent me by Dr. Binz himself, Nov. 1890. G. L. B[urr]
1. Wier, Johann, 1515-1588. I. Title.

8

Binz, Carl, 1832-1913.
Wier oder Weyer?

tchcraft

Binz, Carl, 1832-1913.
Doctor Johann Weyer. (1515-1588) Eine Nachlese. [Düsseldorf, Gedruckt bei E. Voss] 1889.
36 p. facsim. 23cm.
"Sonderabdruck aus dem 24. Band der Zeitschrift des Bergischen Geschichtvereins."
Includes further discussion of the question raised in his Wier oder Weyer? [Düsseldorf, 1887]

Binz, Carl, 1832-1913, ed.

Witchcraft
BF
1583
A2
W82
1888

Witekind, Hermann, 1522-1603.
Augustin Lercheimer (Professor H. Witekind in Heidelberg) und seine Schrift wider den Hexenwahn. Lebensgeschichtliches und Abdruck der letzten vom Verfasser besorgten Ausgabe von 1597. Sprachlich bearbeitet durch Anton Birlinger. Hrsg. von Carl Binz. Strassburg, J. H. E. Heitz (Heitz und Mündel) 1888.
xxxii, 188 p. 21cm.

(Continued on next card)

Binz, Carl, 1832-1913, ed.

Witchcraft
BF
1583
A2
W82
1888

Witekind, Hermann, 1522-1603. Augustin Lercheimer ... und seine Schrift wider den Hexenwahn. 1888. (Card 2)
Includes reprint of original t.p.: Christlich bedencken vnd Erinnerung von Zauberey.
Contents.--Mitteilungen über die Person und die Schriften des Professors H. Witekind.--Text.--Sprachliches, Wort- und Sachbestand, Textesunterschiede.--Vilmar über Witekind.
Ex libris Fri   d. Zarncke.

WITCHCRAFT
BF
1559
B61
1618

Birette, Sanson.
Refvtation de l'errevr dv vvlgaire, tovchant les responces des diables exorcizez. Par Frere Sanson Birette religieux cu Conuent des Augustins de Barfleu ... Rouen, Chez Iacques Besongne, 1618.
12 p. l., 319, [12] p. 14cm.

First published 1612.

8

Witchcraft
BF
1559
B61
1618a

Birette, Sanson.
Refvtation de l'errevr dv vvlgaire tovchant les responces des diables exorcizez ... Constances, I. le Carrel imprimeur, 1618.
143 numb. l. 15cm.

"Explication dv canon episcopi, 26. quest. 5.": verso l. 126-verso l. 139.
Imperfect: l. 11 mutilated; part of text missing.

1. Exorcism.   2. Demoniac possession.
I. Title.

Witchcraft
BF
1439
B61

Birlinger, Anton, 1834-1891.
Der Teufelskratz oder Hexenmal.

(In Im neuen Reich. Leipzig. 24cm. no. 32 (1879) p. 193-210)

I. Title.

Birlinger, Anton, 1834-1891.

Witchcraft
BF
1583
A2
W82
1888

Witekind, Hermann, 1522-1603.
Augustin Lercheimer (Professor H. Witekind in Heidelberg) und seine Schrift wider den Hexenwahn. Lebensgeschichtliches und Abdruck der letzten vom Verfasser besorgten Ausgabe von 1597. Sprachlich bearbeitet durch Anton Birlinger. Hrsg. von Carl Binz. Strassburg, J. H. E. Heitz (Heitz und Mündel) 1888.
xxxii, 188 p. 21cm.

(Continued on next card)

Birlinger, Anton, 1834-1891.

Witchcraft
BF
1583
A2
W82
1888

Witekind, Hermann, 1522-1603. Augustin Lercheimer ... und seine Schrift wider den Hexenwahn. 1888. (Card 2)
Includes reprint of original t.p.: Christlich bedencken vnd Erinnerung von Zauberey.
Contents.--Mitteilungen über die Person und die Schriften des Professors H. Witekind.--Text.--Sprachliches, Wort- und Sachbestand, Textesunterschiede.--Vilmar über Witekind.
Ex libris Fri   d. Zarncke.

Witchcraft
BF
1413
B62+
1859

Bischof, Ferdinand.
Zur Geschichte des Glaubens an Zauberer, Hexen, und Vampyre in Mähren und Oesterr. Schlesien. Von Ferdinand Bischof und Christian d'Elvert. Brünn, Buchdruckerei von R. Rohrer's Erben, 1859.
164 p. 26cm.

"Aus dem XII. Bande der Schriften der historisch-statistischen Sektion der k. k. mähr. schles. Gesellschaft zur Beförderung des Ackerbaues, der Natur- und Landeskunde besonders abgedruckt."
(over)

Witchcraft
BX
2340
B62
D2
1858

Bischofberger, Theobald.
De benedictionibus et exorcismis ecclesiae catholicae libri duo. Liber secundus de exorcismis, Scripsit Theobaldus Bischofberger. Ed. 2ª. Monachii, In libraria Lentneriana (E. Stahl), 1858.
103, [1], 22 p. 15cm.
Books 1 and 2 consecutively paged; to this is added an appendix titled De jurisdictione exorcista commentatio juridica

8   (Continued on next card)

Witchcraft
BX
2340
B62
D2
1858

Bischofberger, Theobald. De benedictionibus et exorcismis ecclesiae catholicae ... 1858. (Card 2)
et moralis, which is lacking in the first edition of the work. (cf. Kayser)
Book 2 and appendix each have special t. p.
Colophon, p. [104]: Typis Halbergerianis Stuttgartiae.
1. Exorcism. 2. Benediction.
I. Title. II. His De jurisdictione exorcista. III. Title: De jurisdictione exorcista.

8

Bischofberger, Theobald.
De jurisdictione exorcista.

Witchcraft
BX
2340
B62
D2
1858

Bischofberger, Theobald.
De benedictionibus et exorcismis ecclesiae catholicae libri duo. Liber primus de benedictionibus. [Liber secundus de exorcismis] Scripsit Theobaldus Bischofberger. Ed. 2ª. Monachii, In libraria Lentneriana (E. Stahl), 1858.
103, [1], 22 p. 15cm.
Books 1 and 2 consecutively paged; to this is added an appendix titled De jurisdictione exorcista commentatio juridica

8   (Continued on next card)

Bischofberger, Theobald.
De jurisdictione exorcista.

Witchcraft
BX
2340
B62
D2
1858

Bischofberger, Theobald. De benedictionibus et exorcismis ecclesiae catholicae ... 1858. (Card 2)
et moralis, which is lacking in the first edition of the work. (cf. Kayser)
Book 2 and appendix each have special t. p.
Colophon, p. [104]: Typis Halbergerianis Stuttgartiae.
1. Exorcism. 2. Benediction.
I. Title. II. His De jurisdictione exorcista. III. Title: De jurisdictione exorcista.

8

Witchcraft
BX
2340
B62
1893

Bischofberger, Theobald.
Die Verwaltung des Exorcistats nach Massgabe des römischen Benediktionale. 2. verm. und verb. Aufl. Neue Ausg. Stuttgart, J. Roth, 1893.
57 p. 18cm.

1. Exorcism. 2. Benedictionals. I. Title.

Witchcraft
BF
1559
B62

Bischoff, Wilhelm Friedrich.
Die Geisterbeschwörer im neunzehnten Jahrhunderte; oder die Folgen des Glaubens an Magie aus Untersuchungs-Acten dargestellt. Neustadt a. b. Orla, J. K. G. Wagner [pref. 1823]
viii, 264 p. fold. pl. 18cm.

1. Exorcism. I. Title.

Witchcraft
BF
1532
B62

Bizouard, Joseph, b. 1797.
Des rapports de l'homme avec le démon; essai historique et philosophique, par Joseph Bizouard ... Paris, Gaume frères et J. Duprey, 1863-64.
6 v. 23cm.

1. Demonology. I. Title.

34-10142

Library of Congress   BF1532.B5   [159.961409] 133.409

CATALOGUE OF THE CORNELL WITCHCRAFT COLLECTION

Witchcraft
BF 1584
S9
B62
    Björlin, Gustaf, 1845–
        Fordomdags; kulturhistoriska utkast och berättelser. Stockholm, H. Geber [1885]
        196 p. 20cm.

    "Trolldomsväsendet i Stockholm 1676": p. 67–130.

    1. Witchcraft—Stockholm. I. Title.

WITCHCRAFT
BF 1584
D4
Z7
1698a
    Bjørn, Ole, b. 1648.
    Arni Magnússon, 1663–1730.
        Kort og sandfærdig beretning om den vidtudraabte besættelse udi Thisted. Til alles efterretning af original-akter og troværdige dokumenter uddragen og sammenskreven (af Arne Magnussen [sic]) Paany udgiven af Alfred Ipsen. København, J. Gjellerups Forlag, 1891.
        112 p. 18cm.

    Reprinted from ed. of 1699.
    1. Bjørn, Ole, b.1648. 2. Trials (Witchcraft)—Thisted, Denmark. I. Ipsen, Alfred, 1852–1922, ed. II. Title.

8 NIC

WITCHCRAFT
BF 1584
D4
C552
    Bjørn, Ole, b. 1648.
    Christensen, Christian Villads, 1864–1922.
        Besættelsen i Thisted.

    (In: Samlinger til Jydsk historie og topografi. København. 22cm. ser.3, v.3, no.3. 1902. p.206–219)

    With this, in same issue, is: Bang, Vilhelm. Tilføjelser til efterretningerne om hexeforfølgelserne i Ribe.
    1. Witchcraft—Thisted, Denmark. 2. Demoniac possession. 3. Bjørn, Ole, b.1648. 4. Arni Magnússon, 1663–1730.

8 NIC

Witchcraft
BF 1555
H18
    Bjørn, Ole, b. 1648.
    Hallager, Frederik, 1816–1876.
        Magister Ole Bjørn og de besatte i Thisted. København, Dansk Sundhedstidendes Forlag, 1901.
        188 p. 21cm.

    1. Bjørn, Ole, b. 1648. 2. Demonology. 3. Exorcism. I. Title.

PT 8834
B63
1914
    Blaafjeld.
    Bull, Jacob Breda, 1853–1930.
        ... Blaafjeld: et folkelivsbillede fra hekseprocessenes tid. Kristiania og København, Gyldendal, 1914.
        2 p. l., [7]–190 p. 20cm.

    At head of title: Jacob B. Bull.

    I. Title.

Library of Congress   PT8834.B6 1914   839.8236

32-2409

Witchcraft
BF 1581
B62+
1938
    Black, George Fraser, 1866–
    A calendar of cases of witchcraft in Scotland, 1510–1727, compiled by George F. Black, PH. D. New York, The New York public library, 1938.
    102 p. front. 25½ᶜᵐ.

    "Reprinted from the Bulletin of the New York public library of November-December 1937 and January 1938."

    1. Witchcraft—Scotland. I. Title.

Library of Congress

38-13909

Witchcraft
BF 1581
B62
S6+
1941
    Black, George Fraser, 1866– ed.
        Some unpublished Scottish witchcraft trials; transcribed and annotated by Dr. George F. Black. New York, The New York public library, 1941.
    50 p. 25ᶜᵐ.

    "The following Scottish witchcraft trials were copied in 1894–1895 from a manuscript abridgment of the Books of adjournal in the library of the Society of antiquaries of Scotland. This abridgment ... contains records ... of the Court of Justiciary from 5th February, 1584, to 8th July, 1728."—p. 3.
    "Reprinted from the Bulletin of the New York public library of April-May-August-September 1941."

    1. Witchcraft—Scotland. I. Title: Scottish witchcraft trials. II. Title.

New York. Public library   A 42-700
for Library of Congress

Witchcraft
Z 6878
W8
N531+
1908
    Black, George Fraser, 1866–
    New York. Public library.
        List of works in the New York public library relating to witchcraft in the United States. Comp. by George F. Black, of the Lenox staff. [New York, 1908]
    18 p. 26ᶜᵐ.

    Caption title.
    "Reprinted from the Bulletin, November, 1908."
    At end: 40 titles of works not in the library.

    1. Witchcraft—U. S.—Bibl. I. Black, George Fraser, 1866– II. Title.

Library of Congress   Z6878.W8N6

CA 9–2852 Unrev'd

Witchcraft
Z 6878
W8
N53+
1911
    Black, George Fraser, 1866–
    New York. Public library.
        ... List of works relating to witchcraft in Europe. New York, 1911.
    31 p. 26½ᶜᵐ.

    "Reprinted at the New York public library from the Bulletin, December, 1911."
    Comp. by George F. Black.

    1. Witchcraft—Bibl. I. Black, George Fraser, 1866– II. Title.

Library of Congress   Z6878.W8N5

Witchcraft
BF 1718
B63
    Blagrave, Joseph, 1610–1682.
        Astrological practice of physick. Discovering the true way to cure all kinds of diseases and infirmities which are naturally incident to the body of man. Being performed by such herbs and plants which grow within our own nation, directing the way to distil and extract their virtues and making up of medicines. Also, a discovery of some notable philosophical secrets worthy our knowledge, relating to a   discovery of all kinds of evils, whet   her natural or such

(Continued on next card)

Witchcraft
BF 1718
B63
    Blagrave, Joseph, 1610–1682.   Astrological practice of physick ... 1689. (Card 2)

    which come from sorcery or witchcraft, or by being possessed of an evil spirit; directing how to cast forth the said evil spirit out of any one which is possessed, with sundry examples thereof. London, Printed for O. Blagrave, 1689.
    139 p. 17cm.

    Wing B 3114.
    I. Title.

Witchcraft
BF 1775
B63
    Blair, George.
        The holocaust; or, The witch of Monzie, a poem illustrative of the cruelties of superstition. Lays of Palestine and other poems. To which is prefixed, Enchantment disenchanted; or, A treatise on superstition. ... London, J. F. Shaw, 1845.
    xii,277 p. 20cm.

    1. Superstition. I. Title. II. Title: The witch of Monzie. III. Title: Lays of Palestine. IV. Title: Enchantment disenchanted.

Witchcraft
BF 1411
B63
    Blakeman, Rufus.
        A philosophical essay on credulity and superstition and also on animal fascination, or charming. By Rufus Blakeman ... New York, D. Appleton & co.; New Haven S. Babcock, 1849.
    206 p. 18ᶜᵐ.

    CONTENTS.—Mental origin of credulity and superstition, and its influence on ancient society.—Witchcraft.—Dreams.—Ghosts.—Ecstacy, trance, &c.—Empiricism and quackery.—Homœopathy.—Mesmerism.—Essay on animal fascination or charming.

    1. Occult sciences. 2. Medical delusions. I. Title. II. Title: Animal fascination, or charming.

18-12143

BF 1566
B64
    Blankenship, Roberta.
        Escape from witchcraft. Grand Rapids, Zondervan Pub. House [1972]
    114 p. port. 18 cm. (Zondervan books) $0.95

4 NIC
    1. Witchcraft. 2. Conversion. 3. Blankenship, Roberta. I. Title.

BF1566.B54   133.4'092'4 [B]   72-8556 MARC

Library of Congress   73 [4]

BF 1566
B64
    Blankenship, Roberta.
    Blankenship, Roberta.
        Escape from witchcraft. Grand Rapids, Zondervan Pub. House [1972]
    114 p. port. 18 cm. (Zondervan books) $0.95

4 NIC
    1. Witchcraft. 2. Conversion. 3. Blankenship, Roberta. I. Title.

BF1566.B54   133.4'092'4 [B]   72-855 MA

Library of Congress   73 [4]

Witchcraft
BF 1584
I8
B64
    Blasio, Abele de.
        Inciarmatori, maghi e streghe di Benevento. Con prefazione di Enrico Morselli e proemio di G. Nicolucci. Napoli, L. Pierro, 1900.
    249 p. illus. 20cm.

    1. Witchcraft—Benevento, Italy. I. Title.

Witchcraft
DC 801
L87
B64
    Bleau, Alphonse.
        Précis d'histoire sur la ville et les possédées de Loudun. Poitiers, Typograph de H. Oudin, 1877.
    246 p. 18cm.

    1. Loudun, France—Hist. 2. Loudun, France. Ursuline Convent. 3. Grandier, Urbain, 1590–1634. 4. Demoniac possession. I. Title.

WITCHCRAFT
BX 2340
P33
    Bleick, Anna.
    Keussen, Hermann, 1862–
        Zwei Hexenprozesse aus der Crefelder Gegend.

    (In: Historischer Verein für den Niederrhein. Annalen. Köln. 23cm. No.63 (1 p. 111–119)

    With, in the same issue: Pauls, Emil. Exorcismus an Herzog Johann Wilhelm von Jülich in den Jahren 1604 und 1605.
    1. Trials (Witchcraft)—Krefeld, Ger. 2. Hagh, Catharina. 3. Blex, Sibilla. 4. Bleick, Anna.

8 NIC

CATALOGUE OF THE CORNELL WITCHCRAFT COLLECTION

Witchcraft
BF
1555
B64
    Blendec, Charles.
        Cinq histoires admirables, esqvelles est monstre' comme miraculeusement par la vertu & puissance du S.-Sacrement de l' Autel, a esté chassé Beelzebub, Prince des diables, auec plusieurs autres demons, qui se disoiét estre de ses subiects, hors des corps de quatre diuerses personnes. Et le tout aduenu en ceste presente année 1582. en la ville & diocese de Soissons ... Paris, G. Chaudiere, 1582.
    125 p. 17cm.

(Continued on next card)

Witchcraft
BF
1555
B64
    Blendec, Charles. Cinq histoires admirables ... 1582. (Card 2)
    Bound in full polished calf, gilt extra, by C. Smith.

1. Demoniac possession. I. Title.

WITCHCRAFT
BX
2340
P33
    Blex, Sibilla.
    Keussen, Hermann, 1862-
      Zwei Hexenprozesse aus der Crefelder Gegend.
    (In: Historischer Verein für den Niederrhein. Annalen. Köln. 23cm. No.63 (1897) p. 111-119)
    With, in the same issue: Pauls, Emil. Der Exorcismus an Herzog Johann Wilhelm von Jülich in den Jahren 1604 und 1605.

8
NIC
    1.Trials (Witchcraft)--Krefeld, Ger. 2.Hagh, Catharina. 3. Blex, Sibilla. 4. Bleick, Anna.

Blockberger, F. N., pseud.
    see
Mayer, Andreas Ulrich, 1732-1802.

WITCHCRAFT
BF
1565
P89
2 copies
    Blockes-Berges Verrichtung.
    Praetorius, Johannes, 1630-1680.
      Blockes-Berges Verrichtung; oder, Ausführlicher geographischer Bericht, von den hohen trefflich alt- und berühmten Blockes-Berge. Ingleichen von der Hexenfahrt, und Zauber-Sabbathe, so auff solchen Berge die Unholden aus gantz Teutschland, jährlich den 1. Maij in Sanct-Walpurgis Nachte anstellen sollen. Aus vielen autoribus abgefasset, und mit schönen Raritäten angeschmücket sampt zugehörigen Figuren ... Leipzig, J. Scheiben, 1668.

8
NIC
(Continued on next card)

WITCHCRAFT
BF
1565
P89
    Blockes-Berges Verrichtung.
    Praetorius, Johannes, 1630-1680.
    Blockes-Berges Verrichtung...1668. (Card 2)
    582 p. fold. front. 16cm.
    Copy 2 imperfect: pages trimmed too closely in binding.

1. Witchcraft. I. Title. II. Title: Ausführlicher geographischer Bericht, von den hohen trefflich alt- und berühmten Block es-Berge.

Witchcraft
BF
1040
I72
miniature
    The Blocksberg tryst.
    Irwin, Frank.
      The Blocksberg tryst. Franklin, N. H., Hillside Press, 1963.
    70 p. illus. 60 mm.
    "310 numbered copies ... Number 205."
    Contents.--The Blocksberg tryst.--Peyote and pomades.--Magic under duress.--The Hexenhammer.--Dimensions beyond time.

1. Psychical research. 2. Witchcraft. I. Title.

BF1040.I7   63-3827
Library of Congress   [1]

WITCHCRAFT
BF
1566
K72
    Blocksbergspuk, Hexen, Teufel und.
    Knortz, Karl, 1841-1918.
      Hexen, Teufel und Blocksbergspuk in Geschichte, Sage und Literatur. Annaberg, Sachsen, Grasers Verlag (R. Liesche) [1913?]
    169 p. 19cm.
    Bibliographical footnotes.

8
NIC
1. Witchcraft. 2. Demonology. 3. Supernatural in literature. I. Title. II. Title: Blocksbergspuk, Hexen, Teufel und.

BF
1503
B65
1971
    Blocquel, Simon, 1780-1863.
      Le triple vocabulaire infernal: manuel du démonomane; ou, Les ruses de l'enfer dévoilées, par Frinellan, démonographe. Paris, N. Bussière [1971?]
    319 p. illus. 15 cm. 22.50F
    "Réimpression photomécanique."
    Frinellan, pseud. of Simon Blocquel.

4
1. Demonology--Dictionaries--French. 2. Occult sciences--Dictionaries--French. I. Title.

BF1503.B48 1971   74-875408
Library of Congress   71 [2]

Bloemardus Thusius, pseud.
    see
Costerus, Florentius, fl. 1654-1703.

Witchcraft
N
8140
E33
    Blomberg, Hugo, Freiherr von, 1820-1871.
      Der Teufel und seine Gesellen in der bildenen Kunst. Berlin, C. Duncker, 1867.
    133 p. 24cm. (Added t.p.: Studien zur Kunstgeschichte und Aesthetik. I.)

1. Devil--Art. I. Title. II. Title: Studien zur Kunstgeschichte und Aesthetik. I.

Rare
PR
3318
B89
    Blount, Charles, 1654-1693.
      Miscellaneous works. To which is prefixed the life of the author, and an account and vindication of his death. [London] 1695.
    1 v. (various pagings) 16cm.
    Each item of contents has special t.p. and seperate paging.
    Contents.--I. The oracles of reason, &c.--2. Anima mundi.--III. Great is Diana of the Ephesians.--IV. An appeal from the country to the city for the preservation
(Continued on next card)

Rare
PR
3318
B89
    Blount, Charles, 1654-1693. Miscellaneous works. 1695. (Card 2)
    Contents--continued
of His Majesties person, liberty and property, and the Protestant religion.-- V. A just vindication of learning, and of the liberty of the press.--VI. A supposed dialogue betwixt the late King James and King William on the banks of the Boyne, the day before that famous victory.

BR
520
B65
    The blue laws of Connecticut; taken from the code of 1650 and the public records of the colony of Connecticut previous to 1655, as printed in a compilation of the earliest laws and orders of the General court of Connecticut, and from Dr. Lewis's book on Sunday legislation; also an extract from the constitution or civil compact adopted by the towns of Hartford, Windsor and Wethersfield in 1838-9, showing the Biblical basis of the colony legislation; with an account of the persecution of witches and Quakers in New England and some

(Continued on next card)   99-160 Revised
[r89b2]

BR
520
B65
    The blue laws of Connecticut ... (Card 2)
extracts from the blue laws of Virginia. New York, The Truth seeker company [c.1898]
88 p. front., 1 illus., plates. 19cm.

1. Law--Connecticut (Colony). 2. Law-- Virginia (Colony). 3. Witchcraft--New England. 4. Friends, Society of. New England. I. Connecticut (Colony) Laws, statutes, etc.

Witchcraft
BF
1410
B42
Z56
v.3
no.2
    Bly, Gratianus de
      Verklaeringe van een turkse parabel: of Voorbeeld der mahumetaense kerktucht: in rijm gesteld door Mr. Gratianus de Bly, volgens de vertaelinge uit seker arabisch schrijver. ... [Amsterdam?] By J. Rieuwertsz, boekverkooper, 1691.
    54 p. end page vignette, illus. initial. 19 x 15cm.
    4°: A-G⁴(-G4)
    A collection of satirical verse and prose, other authors included, in

8
(Continued on next card)

Witchcraft
BF
1410
B42
Z56
v.3
no.2
    Bly, Gratianus de   Verklaeringe van een turkse parabel ... 1691. (Card 2)
defense of Balthasar Bekker.
Gratianus de Bly is possibly a pseudonym. No. 2 in vol. lettered Bekker III.
1. Bekker, Balthasar, 1634-1698. I. Title.

8

Witchcraft
BF
1410
B42
Z892
    Bly, Gratianus de.
      Verklaeringe van een turkse parabel.
    Vervolg van Verscheyde gedigten, &c. So voor als tegen het boek genaamt De betoverde werelt. [Amsterdam?] Gedrukt voor de liefhebbers, 1692.
    1 p. l., 54 p. title vignette, illus. initial. 20 x 16cm.
    4°: π1, A-F⁴, G3.
    Contains prose as well as poems.
    First poem has own t. p. with title: Verklaeringe van een turkse parabel ... door Mr. Gratianus de Bly...

8
(Continued on next card)

CATALOGUE OF THE CORNELL WITCHCRAFT COLLECTION

Bly, Gratianus de.
Verklaeringe van een turkse parabel.

Witchcraft
BF
1410   Vervolg van Verscheyde gedigten, &c. 1692.
B42   (Card 2)
Z892
       Klinkende bel; of uytroep om den verloo-
       renen duyvel: P. 17-19. [Van der Linde
       194]
       Variant of van der Linde 198: signatures
       differ (but not paging).

       1. Bekker, Balthasar, 1634-1698. De
       betoverde wereld. I. Verscheyde

                    (Continued on next card)

Witchcraft
BF   Blyenbergh, Willem van, 17th cent.
1410   Klaare en beknopte verhandeling van de
B42   natuur en werkinge der menschelijke zielen,
Z82   engelen en duivelen, vervat in gewisselde
no.3   brieven tusschen de heer Willem van Blyen-
          bergh en Willem Deurhoff. Amsterdam, By
          J. ten Hoorn, boekverkooper, 1692.
              64 p. title vignette, illus. initials.
          20 x 15cm.
              4°: A-H⁴.
              Discussion of questions raised in the
          contemporary   controversy over Bal-

                    (Continued on next card)

Witchcraft
BF   Blyenbergh, Willem van, 17th cent. Klaare
1410   en beknopte verhandeling van de natuur en
B42   werkinge der menschelijke zielen ... 1692.
Z82   (Card 2)
no.3
thasar Bekker's De Betoverde weereld.
Van der Linde 77.
No. 3 in vol. lettered Over Bekkers
Betoverde wereld. 1692.
    1. Soul. 2. Spirits. 3. Bekker, Bal-
thasar. De betoverde weereld. I. Deurhoff,
Willem, 1650-   1717. II. Title.

8

Witchcraft
BF   Blymyer, John H   defendant.
1578   An account of the "witch" murder trial, York, Pa., January
B66   7-9, 1929. Commonwealth of Pennsylvania vs. John Blymyer,
       et al. By A. Monroe Aurand, jr. ... Harrisburg, Pa., Priv.
       print. by the Aurand press, 1929.
          31 p. 23½ᶜᵐ.

       1. Rehmeyer, Nelson D., 1868-1928. 2. Witchcraft—Pennsylvania. I.
       Aurand, Ammon Monroe, 1895-   II. Title: "Witch" murder trial,
       York, Pa., January 7-9, 1929. III. Title.
       Library of Congress   29-23242
       ——— Copy 2.
       Copyright A 4228   [2]

R   Blymyer, John H.
133   Aurand, Ammon Monroe, 1895-
A92   The "pow-wow" book: a treatise on the art of
       "healing by prayer" and "laying on of hands",
       etc., practiced by the Pennsylvania-Germans and
       others; testimonials; remarkable recoveries;
       popular superstitions; etc., including an account
       of the famous "witch" murder trial, at York, Pa,
       by A. Monroe Aurand, jr. ... containing also the
       complete collection of remedies and cures in
       John George Hohman's "Pow-wows, or Long lost
       friend"; in popular use since 1820. Harrisburg,
       Pa., Priv. print. by The Aurand press, 1929.
          x, 85, [1], 34,   [1], xi, 13-64 p. incl.
       front., illus.   24cm.
                    (Continued on next card)

       Blymyer, John H.
R   Aurand, Ammon Monroe, 1895-   The "pow-wow"
133   book ... 1929.   (Card 2)
A92
       "An account of the 'witch' murder trial" ...
       and "John George Hohman's Pow-wows; or, Long
       lost friend" have special title-pages and
       pagination.
       "Pow-wows; or Long lost friend" was published
       in 1819 under title: Der lange verborgene freund
       oder: Getreuer und christlicher unterricht für
       jedermann.
       "This edition of the 'Pow-wow' book is limit-
       ed to one thousand copies; one hundred signed
       by the author. This is no. 309."
          Bibliography: p. vi.

         Boaistuau, Pierre, d. 1566.
              Histoires prodigieuses.
Witchcraft
AG   [Boaistuau, Pierre] d. 1566.
241   Qvatorze histoires prodigievses de nov-
B66   ueau adioustées aux precedentes, recueil-
1567   lies par Claude de Tesserant Parisien.
         Paris, Chez Iean de Bordeaux [1567]
            4 p. l., 278 [i.e. 557] p. illus. 12cm.
         Tesserant's fourteen tales, p. 217-278,
         have caption title: Avtres histoires pro-
         digievses ...
            The illustrations are reduced copies of
         those in author 's Histoires prodigievses,
                    (Continued on next card)

         Boaistuau, Pierre, d. 1566.
              Histoires prodigieuses.
Witchcraft
AG   [Boaistuau, Pierre] d. 1566. Qvatorze
241   histoires prodigievses ... [1567]
B66   (Card 2)
1567
         published 1560 by V. Sertenas, Paris.
         Introductory letter signed Lyon, 1567,
         by Claude de Tesserant.

         1. Wonders. 2. Monsters. I. His
         Histoires prodigieuses. II. Tesserant,
         Claude de. III. Title: Quatorze
8   histoires pro   digieuses.

Witchcraft
AG   [Boaistuau, Pierre] d. 1566.
241   Qvatorze histoires prodigievses de nov-
B66   ueau adioustées aux precedentes, recueil-
1567   lies par Claude de Tesserant Parisien.
         Paris, Chez Iean de Bordeaux [1567]
            4 p. l., 278 [i.e. 557] p. illus. 12cm.
         Tesserant's fourteen tales, p. 217-278,
         have caption title: Avtres histoires pro-
         digievses ...
            The illustrations are reduced copies of
         those in author 's Histoires prodigievses,
                    (Continued on next card)

Witchcraft
AG   [Boaistuau, Pierre] d. 1566. Qvatorze
241   histoires prodigievses ... [1567]
B66   (Card 2)
1567
         published 1560 by V. Sertenas, Paris.
         Introductory letter signed Lyon, 1567,
         by Claude de Tesserant.

         1. Wonders. 2. Monsters. I. His
         Histoires prodigievses. II. Tesserant,
         Claude de. III. Title: Quatorze
8   histoires pro   digieuses.

WITCHCRAFT
BF   [Bobbe, Johann Benjamin Gottlieb]
1555   Vermischte Anmerkungen über Sr. Hoch-
M94   ehrwürden des Herrn Probstes und Superin-
B66   tendentens in Kemberg Herrn Gottlieb Müllers
         Gründlichen Nachricht und deren Anhang von
         einer begeisterten Weibesperson Annen Eli-
         sabeth Lohmännin, mitgetheilet von Antidä-
         moniacus. Bernburg, Bey C. G. Cörner,
         1760.
            134 p. 18cm.
            Attribution by Holzmann.

8   (Continued on next card)

WITCHCRAFT
BF   [Bobbe, Johann Benjamin Gottlieb] Ver-
1555   mischte Anmerkungen über ... Gottlieb
M94   Müllers Gründlichen Nachricht ... 1760.
B66   (Card 2)

         1. Müller, Gottlieb. Gründlicher
         Nachricht von einer begeisterten Weibes-
         person. 2. Lohmannin, Anna Elisabeth.
         3. Demoniac possession. I. Title: Vermischte
         Anmerkungen   über ... Gottlieb
8   Müllers Grü   ndlichen Nachricht.

WITCHCRAFT
BF   [Bobbe, Johann Benjamin Gottlieb]
1555   Vermischte Anmerkungen über Sr. Hochehr-
M94   würden des Herrn Probstes und Superintenden-
O29   tens in Kemberg Herrn Gottlieb Müllers
no.3   Gründlichen Nachricht und deren Anhang von
         einer begeisterten Weibesperson Annen Eli-
         sabeth Lohmännin, mitgetheilet von Antidä-
         moniacus. Bernburg, Bey C. G. Cörner,
         1760.
            134 p. 18cm.
            No. 3 in vol. lettered Oesfeld u. a. ...

8
NIC

         Bock, Heinrich, tr.
Witchcraft
BF   Binsfeld, Pierre, ca. 1540-1598.
1565   Tractat von Bekantnuss der Zauberer vnnd
B61   Hexen. Ob vnd wie viel denselben zu glau-
1590   ben. Anfänglich durch den hochwürdigen
         Herrn Petrum Binsfeldium ... in Latein be-
         schrieben. Jetzt aber allen Liebhabern der
         Warheit vnd Gerechtigkeit zu gutem ver-
         teutscht. Trier, Getruckt bey Heinrich
         Bock, 1590.
            8 p. l., 154 (i.e. 308), [9] p. 16cm.
            Title in red   and black.

8   (Continued on next card)

         Bock, Heinrich, tr.
Witchcraft
BF   Binsfeld, Pierre, ca. 1540-1598. Tractat
1565   von Bekantnuss der Zauberer vnnd Hexen.
B61   1590.   (Card 2)
1590
         Translation of Tractatus de confessioni-
         bus maleficorum & sagarum, made by H. Bock.
         "Monastery Weingartensis Anᵒ 1620": in
         ms. on t. p.

         I. Bock, Heinrich, tr.

8

Witchcraft
BF   Bode, Heinrich von, 1652-1720, praeses.
1565   Disputatio inauguralis De fallacibus in-
B66   diciis magiae, qvam ... praeside Dn. Henri-
         co Bodino ... die 22. Octobris A. C. 1701
         ... submittit Felix Martinus Brühm. Halae
         Magdebvrgicae, Literis C. Henckelii, typogr.
         [1701]
            50 p. 20cm.
            Diss.--Halle (F. M. Brühm, respondent)
            Supports Balthasar Bekker.

8   (Continued on next card)

Witchcraft
BF   Bode, Heinrich von, 1652-1720, praeses.
1565   Disputatio inauguralis De fallacibus indi-
B66   ciis magiae ... [1701]   (Card 2)

         1. Witchcraft--Addresses, essays, lec-
         tures. 2. Magic--Addresses, esays, lectu
         3. Bekker, Balthasar, 1634-1698. I. Brü
         Felix Martin, respondent. II. Title. II
         Title: De fallacibus indiciis magiae.

8

RARE
HV   Bode, Heinrich von, 1652-1720, praeses.
8593   Tractatio juridica De usu & abusu tor
B66   rae...quam...MDCXCVII habuit Heinricus
1726   Boden [sic] Editio novissima. Halae
         Magdeb., sumtu Hendeliano, 1726.
            38 p. 21cm.
            Diss.--Halle (M. J. Sassen, responden
         1697.

8   1. Torture. I. Sassen, Meint Johann,
NIC   spondent. II. Title.

76

CATALOGUE OF THE CORNELL WITCHCRAFT COLLECTION

```
RARE            Bode, Heinrich von, 1652-1720.
HV                 Tractatio juridica De usu & abusu tortu-
8593            rae...quam...habuit Heinricus de Boden. Edi-
D512            tio novissima.  Halae Magdeb., Sumtu Hen-
no.8            deliano, 1735.
                   40 p.  22cm.

                   Originally issued as diss., 1697, with
                M. J. Sassen as respondent.
                   No.8 in a vol. lettered: Dissertation[e]s
                de tortura,              1721-92.
  8                1.Torture.    I. Sassen, Meint Jo-
NIC             hann, respo      ndent. II. Title.
```

```
                Bodenham, Anne.
Witchcraft
BF              Bower, Edmond.
1581               Doctor Lamb revived; or, Witchcraft
A2              condemn'd in Anne Bodenham, a servant of
B78             his, who was arraigned and executed the
                Lent assizes last at Salisbury, before ...
                Baron Wild,   judge of the assise..Where-
                in is set forth her strange and wonderful
                diabolical usage of a maid, servant to Mr.
                Goddard, as also her attempt against his
                daughters ...   London, Printed by T. W.
                for R. Best and     J. Place, 1653.
                   44 p.  20   cm.
```

Bodin, Jean

```
Witchcraft
BF              Bodin, Jean, 1530-1596.
1520               Daemonomania; oder, Auszführliche
B66             Erzehlung des wütenden Teuffels in seinen
1698            damahligen rasenden Hexen und Hexenmeistern
                dero Bezauberungen, Beschwerungen, Vergifftun-
                gen, Gauckel- und Possen-Wercke... Welches
                der andere Theil Nicolai Remigii Daemonolatria.
                Wobey gleichfalls angehänget: Vielerhand
                warhaftige und erschreckliche Geschichte
                besessener Leute...nebst noch einigen
                betrieglichen          und von Menschen
                                    (Continued on next card)
                                         (over)
```

```
Witchcraft
BF              Bodin, Jean, 1530-1596.
1520               De la demonomanie des sorciers ... Reueu,
B66             corr. & augm. d'vne grande partie.   Paris,
1587            I. dv-Pvys, 1587.
                   276 numb. 1.  23cm.

                "Refvtation des opinions de Jean VVier":
                l. 238 verso-276 verso.
                With book-plate of Sidney Edward Bouverie
                Bouverie-Pusey.
```

```
                Bodin, Jean, 1530-1596.
                   De la démonomanie des sorciers.
WITCHCRAFT
BF              Bodin, Jean, 1530-1596.
1520               Le fleav des demons et sorciers, par
B66             I. B. angevin. Reueu & corrigé de plu-
1616            sieurs fautes qui s'estoyent glissees és
                precedentes impressions ... Derniere ed.
                Nyort, Par Dauid du Terroir, 1616.
                   2 p. l., 38, 556, [21] p.  17cm.
                   Title in ornamental woodcut border.
                   First published under title: De la
                daemonomanie.
                   "Refvtation des opinions de Iean VVier":
  8             p. 476-556.       (Continued on next card)
```

```
Witchcraft
BF              Bodin, Jean, 1530-1596.  Daemonomania.
1520               1698.                    (Card 2)
B66
1698            practicirten kurtzweiligen Begenheiten.
                Hamburg, Gedruckt bey T. von Wiering, 1698.
                   2 v. in 1. plates. 18cm.

                   "Wiederlegung nebst der Schrifft des Hn.
                Weyer":  v. 1, p. [400]-465.
                   Translation of De la démonomanie.
```

```
Witchcraft
BF              Bodin, Jean, 1530-1596.
1520               De la demonomanie des sorciers.  A
B66             Monseignevr M. Chrestofle de Thou ...
1593            Seigneur de Coeli ... Par I. Bodin Angevin.
                Lyon, Povr P. Frellon et A. Cloqvemin, 1593.
                   604 p.  17cm.

                   "Réfutation des opinions de Jean Wier":
                p. 522-604.

                   1. Wier,    Johann, 1515-1588.
                   II. Title.
```

```
                Bodin, Jean, 1530-1596.
                   De la démonomanie des sorciers--German.
Witchcraft
BF              Bodin, Jean, 1530-1596.
1520               Daemonomania; oder, Auszführliche
B66             Erzehlung des wütenden Teuffels in seinen
1698            damahligen rasenden Hexen und Hexenmeistern
                dero Bezauberungen, Beschwerungen, Vergifftun-
                gen, Gauckel- und Possen-Wercke... Welches
                der andere Theil Nicolai Remigii Daemonolatria.
                Wobey gleichfalls angehänget: Vielerhand
                warhaftige und erschreckliche Geschichte
                besessener Leute...nebst noch einigen
                betrieglichen          und von Menschen
                                     (Continued on next card)
```

```
itchcraft
F               Bodin, Jean, 1530-1596.
520                De la demonomanie des sorciers ...
66              Paris, I. du Puys, 1580.
                   252 numb. 1.  24cm.

                   "Réfutation des opinions de Jean Wier":
                l. 218-252.
```

```
                Bodin, Jean, 1530-1596.
WITCHCRAFT         De la démonomanie des sorciers.
BF              Bodin, Jean, 1530-1596.
1520               La demonomanie des sorciers.  Par I. Bo-
B66             din angevin.  Reueuë & corrigee d'vne infi-
1598            nité de fautes qui se sont passees és pre-
                cedentes impressions.  Auec vn indice des
                choses les plus remarquables contenuës en
                ce liure.  Edition derniere.  Paris, Chez
                Estienne Prevosteav, 1598.
                   604, [31] p.  15cm.
                   "Refvtation des opinions de Iean Wier":
                p. 523-604.
  8                              (Continued on next card)
```

```
                Bodin, Jean, 1530-1596.
Witchcraft         De la démonomanie des sorciers--German.
BF              Bodin, Jean, 1530-1596.
1520               1698.                     (Card 2)
B66
1698            practicirten kurtzweiligen Begenheiten.
                Hamburg, Gedruckt bey T. von Wiering, 1698.
                   2 v. in 1. plates. 18cm.

                   "Wiederlegung nebst der Schrifft des Hn.
                Weyer":  v. 1, p. [400]-465.
                   Translation of De la démonomanie.
```

```
itchcraft
BF              Bodin, Jean, 1530-1596.
1520               De la demonomanie des sorciers ...  Paris,
B66             Chez Iacques du Puys, 1582.
1582               [12], 251 l.  22cm.

                   Title vignette


                   1. Demonomania. 2. Witchcraft. 3. Magic.
                4. Wier, Johann, 1515-1588. I. Title.
```

```
                Bodin, Jean, 1530-1596.
WITCHCRAFT         De la démonomanie des sorciers.
BF              Bodin, Jean, 1530-1596.  La demonomanie
1520               des sorciers ...  1598.   (Card 2)
B66
1598               First published under title: De la de-
                monomanie des sorciers.

                   1. Demonomania. 2. Witchcraft. 3.
                Magic. 4. Wier, Johann, 1515-1588. I.
                His  De la démonomanie des sorciers. II.
  8             Title.
```

```
                Bodin, Jean, 1530-1596.
                   De la démonomanie des sorciers. German.
BF              Bodin, Jean, 1530-1596.
1520               Vom aussgelasnen wütigen Teuffelsheer. Übers.
B66+            v. Johann Fischart.  (Um ein neues Vorw. verm.
1973            Nachdr. d. Ausg. Strassburg 1591.)  Vorw.:
                Hans Biedermann.  Graz, Akadem. Druck- u.
                Verlagsanst., 1973.
                   vii p., 372 p. of facsims.  28cm.

                   Translation of De la démonomanie des sorciers
                   Bibliography: p. vii.
```

CATALOGUE OF THE CORNELL WITCHCRAFT COLLECTION

WITCHCRAFT
BF 1520 B66 1592

Bodin, Jean, 1530-1596.
De la démonomanie des sorciers. Italian.
Bodin, Jean, 1530-1596.
    Demonomania de gli stregoni, cioè Fvrori, et malie de' demoni, col mezo de gl'hvomini: Diuisa in libri IIII. Di Gio. Bodino Francese, tradotta dal K.r Hercole Cato ... Di nuouo purgata, & ricorretta. Venetia, Presso Aldo, 1592.
    26 p. l., 419 p. 22cm.
    "Confvtatione delle opinioni di Giovanni VVier": p. [360]-419.
    Translation of De la démonomanie.

8   (Continued on next card)

Witchcraft
BF 1520 B66 1586

Bodin, Jean, 1530-1596. De magorvm daemonomania ... (Card 2)
    Fischart ... auss Frantzösischer sprach ... in Teutsche gebracht, vnd nun zum andernmal an vielen enden vermehrt vnd erklärt ... Strassburg, B. Jobin, 1586.
    [16], 767 p. 18cm.

    Bound in blind stamped pigskin, dated: 1597.

8

WITCHCRAFT
BF 1520 B66 1592

Bodin, Jean, 1530-1596. Demonomania de gli stregoni ... 1592. (Card 2)

    1. Demonomania. 2. Witchcraft. 3. Magic. 4. Wier, Johann, 1515-1588. I. His De la démonomanie des sorciers. Italian. II. Cato, Ercole, tr. III. Title.

8

Witchcraft
BF 1520 B66 1590

Bodin, Jean, 1530-1596.
De la démonomanie des sorciers--Latin.
Bodin, Jean, 1530-1596.
    De magorvm daemonomania, sev Detestando lamiarum ac magorum cum Satana commercio, libri IV. Recens recogniti, & multis in locis à mendis repurgati. Accessit eiusdem Opinionum Ioan. Vieri confutatio non minùs docta quam pia. Francofvrti, Ex Officina Typographica Nicolai Bassaei, 1590.
    798 p. 16cm.

    Title vignette.

    I. Title. II. Title: Detestando lamiarum ac magnorum cum Satana commercio. III. His De la demonomanie--Latin.

Witchcraft
BF 1520 B66 1590

Bodin, Jean, 1530-1596.
    De magorvm daemonomania, sev Detestando lamiarum ac magorum cum Satana commercio, libri IV. Recens recogniti, & multis in locis à mendis repurgati. Accessit eiusdem Opinionum Ioan. Vieri confutatio non minùs docta quam pia. Francofvrti, Ex Officina Typographica Nicolai Bassaei, 1590.
    798 p. 16cm.

    Title vignette.

    I. Title. II. Title: Detestando lamiarum ac magnorum cum Satana commercio. III. His De la demonomanie--Latin.

8

WITCHCRAFT
BF 1520 B66 1598

Bodin, Jean, 1530-1596.
    La demonomanie des sorciers. Par I. Bodin angevin. Reueuë & corrigee d'vne infinité de fautes qui se sont passees és precedentes impressions. Auec vn indice des choses les plus remarquables contenuës en ce liure. Edition derniere. Paris, Chez Estienne Prevosteav, 1598.
    604, [31] p. 15cm.
    "Refvtation des opinions de Iean Wier": p. 523-604.

8   (Continued on next card)

Witchcraft
BF 1520 B66 M72+

Bodin, Jean, 1530-1596.
De la démonomanie des sorciers.
Molinier, Victor, 1799-1887.
    Aperçus historiques et critiques sur la vie et les travaux de Jean Bodin, sur sa Démonomanie des sorciers, et sur les procès pour sorcellerie au seizième et au dix-septième siècle. Montpellier, Impr. typographique de Gras, 1867.
    35 p. 28cm.

    "Extrait de la Revue judiciaire du Midi, Cahiers de janvier et de février 1867."
    1. Bodin, Jean, 1530-1596. De la démonomanie des sorciers. I. Title.

Witchcraft
BF 1520 B66++ 1591

Bodin, Jean, 1530-1596.
    De magorvm daemonomania. Vom aussgelasnen wütigen Teuffelssheer allerhand Zauberern, Hexen vnnd Hexermeistern... Gegen des Herrn Doctor J. Wier Buch von der Geister verfuhrungen durch den edlen... Herrn Johann Bodin ... Und nun erstmals durch ... Johann Fischart ... auss frantzösischer Sprach ... in Teutsche gebracht vnd ... vermehrt vnd erklärt. Strassburg, Getruckt bei B. Jobin, 1591.
    336 p. 32cm.
    (Continued on next card)

WITCHCRAFT
BF 1520 B66 1598

Bodin, Jean, 1530-1596. La demonomanie des sorciers ... 1598. (Card 2)

    First published under title: De la demonomanie des sorciers.

    1. Demonomania. 2. Witchcraft. 3. Magic. 4. Wier, Johann, 1515-1588. I. His De la démonomanie des sorciers. II. Title.

8

Witchcraft
BF 1520 B66 P99+

Bodin, Jean, 1530-1596.
De la démonomanie des sorciers.
[Puymaigre, Théodore Joseph Boudet, comte de,] 1816-1901.
    Traité de la démonomanie contre les sorciers, par Jean Bodin. [Metz, ca. 1838]
    [169]-184, [236]-256, [307]-324 p. 26cm.
    Extracted from Revue de l'Austrasie, according to the Bibliothèque Nationale.
    1. Bodin, Jean, 1530-1596. De la démonomanie. 2. Witchcraft--France. 3. Witchcraft. I. Title.

8

Witchcraft
BF 1520 B66++ 1591

Bodin, Jean, 1530-1596. De magorvm daemonomania ... 1591. (Card 2)

    Translation of De la démonomanie.
    "Widerlegung der Meynungen vnd Opinionen Johannis Weyer": p. 258-297.

    1. Demonomania. 2. Witchcraft. 3. Magic. 4. Wier, Johann, 1515-1588. I. Bodin, Jean, 1530-1596. De la démonomanie--German. II. Title.

WITCHCRAFT
BF 1520 B66 1616

Bodin, Jean, 1530-1596.
    Le fleav des demons et sorciers, par I. B. angevin. Reueu & corrigé de plusieurs fautes qui s'estoyent glissees és precedentes impressions ... Derniere ed. Nyort, Par Dauid du Terroir, 1616.
    2 p. l., 38, 556, [21] p. 17cm.
    Title in ornamental woodcut border.
    First published under title: De la daemonomanie.
    "Refvtation des opinions de Iean VVier": p. 476-556.

8   (Continued on next card)

WITCHCRAFT
BF 1520 B66 1581

Bodin, Jean, 1530-1596.
    Io. Bodini Andegavensis De magorvm daemonomania libri IV. Nvnc primvm e Gallico in Latinum translati per Lotarivm Philoponvm. Basileae, Per Thomam Guarinum, 1581.
    16 p. l., 488 p. 21cm.
    Translation of his De la démonomanie.

    I. Junius, Franciscus, 1545-1602, tr.

8

WITCHCRAFT
BF 1520 B66 1603

Bodin, Jean, 1530-1596.
    Ioannis Bodini, Andegavensis, De magorvm daemonomania, sev Detestando lamiarum ac magorum cum Satana commercio, libri IV. Recens recogniti, et mvltis in locis à mendis repurgati. Accessit eivsdem Opinionvm Ioannis Wieri confutatio, non minus docta quam pia. Francofvrti, Typis Wolffgangi Richteri, impensis omnium haeredum Nicolai Bassaei, 1603.
    557 p. 17cm.
    Translation of De la démonomanie des sorciers.

8

WITCHCRAFT
BF 1520 B66 1616

Bodin, Jean, 1530-1596. Le fleav des demons et sorciers ... 1616. (Card 2)

    1. Demonomania. 2. Witchcraft. 3. Magic. 4. Wier, Johann, 1515-1588. De lamiis. I. His De la daemonomania. II. Title.

8

Witchcraft
BF 1520 B66 1586

Bodin, Jean, 1530-1596.
    De magorvm daemonomania. Vom aussgelassnen wütigen Teuffelssheer allerhand Zauberern, Hexen vnd Hexermeistern, Vnholden, Teuffelsbeschwereren, Warsagern, Schwartzkünstlern, Vergifftern, Augenverblendern, etc. Wie die vermög aller Recht erkant, eingetrieben, gehindert, erkündt, erforscht, peinlich ersucht vnd gestrafft werden sollen. Gegen des Herrn Doctor J. Wier Buch von der Geister verführungen, durch ... Johann Bodin ... aussgegangen. Vnd nun erstmals durch ... Johann
    (Continued on next card)

WITCHCRAFT
BF 1520 B66 1592

Bodin, Jean, 1530-1596.
    Demonomania de gli stregoni, cioè Fvrori, et malie de' demoni, col mezo de gl'hvomini: Diuisa in libri IIII. Di Gio. Bodino Francese, tradotta dal K.r Hercole Cato ... Di nuouo purgata, & ricorretta. Venetia, Presso Aldo, 1592.
    26 p. l., 419 p. 22cm.
    "Confvtatione delle opinioni di Giovanni VVier": p. [360]-419.
    Translation of De la démonomanie.

8   (Continued on next card)

BF 1520 B66+ 1973

Bodin, Jean, 1530-1596.
    Vom aussgelasnen wütigen Teuffelsheer. Ut. v. Johann Fischart. (Um ein neues Vorw. verm. Nachdr. d. Ausg. Strassburg 1591.) Vorw.: Biedermann. Graz, Akadem. Druck- u. Verlags. 1973.
    vii p. 372 p. of facsims. 28cm.

    Translation of De la démonomanie des sorciers.
    Bibliography: p. vii.
    1. Witchcraft. 2. Magic. 3. Demonology. I. Fischart, Johann, 1550 (ca.)-1590?, tr. II. Biedermann, Hans, fl. 1968- ed. III. Title. IV. His De la démonomanie des sorciers. German.

CATALOGUE OF THE CORNELL WITCHCRAFT COLLECTION

Bodin, Jean, 1530-1596.

WITCHCRAFT
JC
139
B66
K79
    Kohler, Josef, 1849-1919.
        Bodinus und die Hexenverfolgung.
    (In Archiv für Strafrecht und Strafprozess. Berlin, 1853-1933. 25cm. 66. Bd., 1. Heft (1918), p. 39-57)

    Caption title.
    Bibliographical footnotes.

    1. Bodin, Jean, 1530-1596. 2. Witchcraft. I. Title.

WITCHCRAFT
BF
1565
N99
    Bodin, Jean, 1530-1596.
        Nynauld, J de
        De la lycanthropie, transformation, et extase des sorciers... Avec la refutation des argumens contraires que Bodin allegue au 6. chap. de sa Demonomanie... Paris, Chez Iean Millot, 1615.
    109 p. 16cm.

8
NIC
    1. Witchcraft. 2. Demonomania. 3. Werwolves. 4. Bodin, Jean, 1530-1596. ¿ De la démonomanie des sorciers. I. Title.

Bodin, Jean, 1530-1596.

itchcraft
81
3
96
    Province d'Anjou (periodical)
        IVe [i. e. Quatrième] centenaire Jean Bodin, 10 et 11 novembre 1929. [Angers, Société anonyme des Editions de l'Ouest, 1929]
    [359]-478 p. port. 25cm.

    Issued as 4. année, no. 20.

    1. Bodin, Jean, 1530-1596. I. Title.

---

itchcraft
380
B66
    Bodin, Lucien, bookseller, Paris.
        Catalogue de livres d'occasion anciens et modernes relatifs aux sciences occultes et philosophiques. Paris.
    nos. 24cm.

    √ 1. Occult sciences--Bibl.--Catalogs.
    √ 2. Witchcraft-- Bibl.--Catalogs.
    √ I. Title.

Bodinus und die Hexenverfolgung.

ITCHCRAFT
9
6
79
    Kohler, Josef, 1849-1919.
        Bodinus und die Hexenverfolgung.
    (In Archiv für Strafrecht und Strafprozess. Berlin, 1853-1933. 25cm. 66. Bd., 1. Heft (1918), p. 39-57)

    Caption title.
    Bibliographical footnotes.

    1. Bodin, Jean, 1530-1596. 2. Witchcraft. I. Title.

Boehlau, Hugo.

Witchcraft
BF
1583
Z7
1689
    Braunin, Anna Maria, d. 1689, defendant.
        Acta inquisitionalia contra Annen Marien Braunin in puncto Verdächtiger Hexerey, Ambt Ostrau, 1689.
    (In Thüringisch-Sächsischen Verein für Erforschung des vaterländischen Alterthums und Erhaltung seiner Denkmale. Neue Mittheilungen aus dem Gebiet historisch-antiquarischer Forschungen. Halle. 22cm. Bd. 9 (1857) p. [76]-189)

    "Nachschrift": signed Dr. Boehlau, p. 174-189.

Witchcraft
BV
5080
B67
1682
    Böhme, Jakob, 1575-1624.
        Alle theosophische Wercken. Darinnen alle tieffe Geheimnüsse Gottes, der ewigen und zeitlichen Natur und Creatur, samt dem wahren Grunde christlicher Religion und der Gottseeligkeit, nach dem apostolischen Gezeugnüss offenbahret werden. Theils aus des Authoris eigenen Originalen, theils aus den ersten und nachgesehenen besten Copyen auffs fleissigste corrigiret, und in Beyfügung etlicher Clavium so vorhin noch nie gedruckt, nebenst
    (Continued on next card)

Witchcraft
BV
5080
B67
1682
    Böhme, Jakob, 1575-1624. Alle theosophische Wercken ... 1682. (Card 2)
    einem zweyfachen Register. Amsterdam, 1682.
    10 v. illus. (part fold.) 16cm.

    Contents.--t.1. Gründlich und wahrhaffter Bericht von dem Leben und Abscheid des in Gott seelig-ruhenden Jacob Böhmens. Zwey Register über alle Jacob Böhms seel. Schrifften.-- t.2. Morgenröte im Auf-
    (Continued on next card)

Witchcraft
BV
5080
B67
1682
    Böhme, Jakob, 1575-1624. Alle theosophische Wercken ... 1682. (Card 3)
    gang.--t.3. Beschreibung der drey Principien göttliches Wesens.--t.4. Hohe und tieffe Gründe von dem dreyfachen Leben des Menschen. Von Christi Testamenten zwey Büchlein.--t.5. Der Weeg zu Christo. Von der Menschwerdung Jesu Christi.--t.6. Viertzig Fragen von der Seelen Urstand. Von der Genaden-Wahl.--t.7. Von sechs Puncten. Theosophische Send-
    (Continued on next card)

Witchcraft
BV
5080
B76
1682
    Böhme, Jakob, 1575-1624. Alle theosophische Wercken ... 1682. (Card 4)
    Contents--Continued.
    Briefe.--t.8. Mysterium magnum.--t.9. Bedencken über Esaiae Stiefels Büchlein: Von dreyerley Zustand des Menschen, und dessen newen Gebuhrt.--t.10. De signatura rerum. Clavis oder Schlüssel etlicher vornehmen Puncten und Wörter. Tabula principiorum, von Gott und vor der grossen und kleinen Welt. Betrachtung göttlicher Offenbahrung.

Die bösen Geister im Alten Testament.

Witchcraft
BS
1199
D4
D87
    Duhm, Hans.
        Die bösen Geister im Alten Testament. Tübingen, P. Siebeck, 1904.
    iv, 68 p. 24cm.

    1. Bible and spiritualism. 2. Legends, Jewish. 3. Devil--Biblical teaching.

Witchcraft
BF
1582
A2
B67
    Boguet, Henri, d. 1619.
        Discovrs des sorciers. Tiré de quelques procez, faicts dez deux ans en ça à plusieurs de la mesme secte, en la terre de S. Oyan de Ioux, dicte de S. Claude au Comté de Bourgongne. Auec vne Instruction pour vn iuge, en faict de sorcelerie. Lyon, Par Iean Pillehotte, 1602.
    8 p. l., 191, [30] p. 17cm.
    First edition.
8   Ex libris   Herman Le Roy Edgar.

Witchcraft
BF
1582
A2
B67
1603
    Boguet, Henri, d. 1619.
        Discovrs des sorciers. Tiré de quelques procez, faicts dez deux ans en ça à plusieurs de la mesme secte, en la terre de S. Oyan de Ioux, dicte de S. Claude au Comté de Bourgongne. Auec vne Instruction povr vn iuge en faict de sorcelerie. 2. ed. augmentee et enrichie par l'autheur de plusieurs autres procez, histoires et chapitres. Lyon, Par Iean Pillehotte, 1603.
8   12 p. l., 252, [28] p. 17cm.
    Ex libris Cabalisticis Kurt Seligmann.

Witchcraft
BF
1582
A2
B67
1608
    Boguet, Henri, d. 1619.
        Discovrs des sorciers, avec six advis advis en faict de sorcelerie. Et vne instrvction povr vn iuge en sembable matiere ... 2. ed. Lyon, Chez Pierre Rigavd, 1608.
    1 v. (various pagings) 18cm.
    Six advis, en faict de sorcelerie, has special t. p.

    1. Witchcraft--France. 2. Demonology, French. 3. Criminal law--France. 4. Criminal procedure--France. I. Title: Discours des sorciers.

Boguet, Henri, d. 1619.
    Discours des sorciers.

Witchcraft
BF
1582
A2
B67
1606
    Boguet, Henri, d. 1619.
        Discovrs execrable des sorciers. Ensemble leur procez, faits depuis 2. ans en ça, en diuers endroicts de la France. Auec vne Instruction pour vn iuge, en faict de sorcelerie. Rovеn, Chez Iean Osmont, 1606.
    6 p. l., 445, [6] p. 15cm.
    First published 1602 under title: Discovrs des sorciers.
8   Ex libris   Cabalisticis Kurt Seligmann.
    (Continued on next card)

Boguet, Henri, d. 1619.
    Discours des sorciers--English.

Witchcraft
BF
1582
A2
B67
1929
    Boguet, Henri, d. 1619.
        An examen of witches, drawn from various trials of many of this sect in the district of Saint Oyan de Joux, commonly known as Saint Claude in the county of Burgundy, including the procedure necessary to a judge in trials for witchcraft. Tr. by E. Allen Ashwin, ed. by the Rev. Montague Summers. [London] J. Rodker, 1929.
    liii, 328 p. 19cm.
8   "Edition limited to 1275 copies; this copy is number 290."

Witchcraft
BF
1582
A2
B67
1606
    Boguet, Henri, d. 1619.
        Discovrs execrable des sorciers. Ensemble leur procez, faits depuis 2. ans en ça, en diuers endroicts de la France. Auec vne Instruction pour vn iuge, en faict de sorcelerie. Rovеn, Chez Iean Osmont, 1606.
    6 p. l., 445, [6] p. 15cm.
    First published 1602 under title: Discovrs des sorciers.
8   Ex libris   Cabalisticis Kurt Seligmann.
    (Continued on next card)

Witchcraft
BF
1582
A2
B67
1606
    Boguet, Henri, d. 1619. Discovrs execrable des sorciers. 1606. (Card 2)

    1. Witchcraft--France. 2. Demonology, French. 3. Criminal law--France. 4. Criminal procedure--France. I. Title: Discours execrable des sorciers. II. His Discours des sorciers.

8

CATALOGUE OF THE CORNELL WITCHCRAFT COLLECTION

Witchcraft
BF 1582 A2 B67 1929
Boguet, Henri, d. 1619.
An examen of witches, drawn from various trials of many of this sect in the district of Saint Oyan de Joux, commonly known as Saint Claude in the county of Burgundy, including the procedure necessary to a judge in trials for witchcraft. Tr. by E. Allen Ashwin, ed. by the Rev. Montague Summers. London, J. Rodker, 1929.
liii, 328 p. 19cm.
8
"Edition limited to 1275 copies; this copy is number 290."
(over)

BF 1582 A2 B67 1929a
Boguet, Henri, d. 1619.
An examen of witches (Discours des sorciers) by Henri Boguet, New York, Barnes & Noble, 1971.
liii, 328 p. 20 cm.
A facsimile of the 1929 ed.

4
1. Witchcraft — France. 2. Demonology, French. 3. Criminal law—France. 4. Criminal procedure—France. I. Title. II. His Discours des sorciers—English.
71-27506 MARC
Library of Congress 71 [4]

Witchcraft
BF 1549 B68
Bois, Jules, 1871–
... Le satanisme et la magie, avec une étude de J.-K. Huysmans; illustrations de Henry de Malvost. Paris, L. Chailley, 1895.
xxvii, 427 p. incl. illus., plates. 22½ cm.

1. Satanism. 2. Magic. I. Huysmans, Joris Karl, 1848-1907. II. Title.
11-9026 Revised
Library of Congress   BF1549.B6

Witchcraft
BF 1549 B68 1897
Bois, Jules, 1871–
Le satanisme et la magie. Avec une étude de J.-K. Huysmans. Paris, Flammarion [1897].
xxvii, 339 p. 19cm.

With book-plate of Theodore Stanton.

1. Satanism. 2. Magic. I. Huysmans, Joris Karl, 1848-1907. II. Title.

WITCHCRAFT
BF 1750 B68++
2 copies
Boissard, Jean Jacques, 1528-1602.
Tractatus posthumus Jani Jacobi Boissardi Vesvntini de divinatione et magicis praestigiis, quarum veritas ac vanitas solidè exponitur per descriptionem deorum fatidecorum qui olim responsa dederunt; eorundemque prophetarum, sacerdotum, phoebadum, sibyllarum & divinorum, qui priscis temporibus celebres oracula exstiterunt. Adjunctis ... effigiebus, ab ipso autore ... delineatis; jam ... aeri incisis per Joh. Theodor de Bry. Oppenheimii,
8
(Continued on next card)

WITCHCRAFT
BF 1750 B68++
Boissard, Jean Jacques, 1528-1602. Tractatus posthumus Jani Jacobi Boissardi Vesvntini de divinatione et magicis praestigiis ... (Card 2)
typis H. Galleri [1616?]
14 p. l., 358, [1] p. illus., ports. 32cm.
Engr. t.-p.
Engraving on p. 151 (Nicostrata) is different in the two copies.
8 (Continued on next card)

WITCHCRAFT
BF 1750 B68++
Boissard, Jean Jacques, 1528-1602. Tractatus posthumus Jani Jacobi Boissardi Vesvntini de divinatione et magicis praestigiis ... [1616?]   (Card 3)

8
1. Occult sciences. 2. Oracles. 3. Divination. 4. Magic. I. Bry, Johann Theodor de, 1561-1623? II. Title. III. Title: De divinatione et magicis praestigiis.

Witchcraft
BF 1602 S13 B68
Boissier, A.
Recueil de lettres au sujet des maléfices et du sortilège: servant de réponse aux Lettres du Sieur de Saint-André, medecin à Coutances, sur le même sujet. Avec la scavante remontrance du Parlement de Rouen faite au roy Louis XIV, au sujet du sortilege, du maléfice, des sabats, & autres effets de la magie, pour la perfection du procez dont il est parlé dans ces Lettres. Paris, Brunet fils, 1731.
xiii, 387 p. 17cm.

1. Saint-André, François de. Lettres au sujet de la magie. 2. Witchcraft. 3. Sorcery. I. Title.

WITCHCRAFT
BF 1508 P97 1838
Boissonade, Jean François, 1774-1857, ed.
Psellus, Michael.
Michael Psellus De operatione daemonum cum notis Gaulmini curante Jo. Fr. Boissonade. Accedunt inedita opuscula Pselli. Norimbergae, Apud F. N. Campe, 1838.
xxvii, 348 p. 21cm.
At head of title: Ψελλος.
Greek text only: Peri energeias daimōnōn dialogos, with notes in Latin.
1. Demonology. I. His Peri energeias daimonōn dialogos. II. Gaulmin, Gilbert, 1585-1665, ed. III. Boissonade, Jean François, 1774-1857, ed.
8 NIC

RARE K S2545 1599
Bolognini, Ludovico, 1447 (ca.)-1508.
Suzaria, Guido de.
Tractatus II [i.e. duo] perutiles & quotidiani De indiciis, quaestionibus et tortura ...Guidonis de Suzaria & Pauli Grillandi de Castilione, una cum additionib. Ludovici Bolognini...geordnet durch Ioannem Guörnerum de Vineca. Ursellis, Apud Nicolaum Henricum, sumptibus Cornelij Suterij, 1597.
291 p. 16cm.
Bound with: Saur, Abraham. Notarien Spiegel. Franckfort am Mayn, 1599.
8 NIC (Continued on next card)

Bombast von Hohenheim, Philipp Aureolus Theophrastus, known as Paracelsus.
see
Paracelsus, 1493-1541.

Witchcraft
BF 1815 C2D31 1720
Bond, William, d. 1735, supposed author.
[Defoe, Daniel] 1660?-1731.
The history of the life and adventures of Mr. Duncan Campbell, a gentleman, who tho' deaf and dumb, writes down any stranger's name at first sight: with their future contingencies of fortune. Now living in Exeter-Court over-against the Savoy in the Strand ... 2d ed. cor. London, Printed for E. Curll, and sold by W. Mears [etc.], 1720.
xix, [4], 320 p. front. (port.) 4 pl. 19cm.
Authorship disputed; probably by Defoe, though ascribed also to William Bond under whose name it appeared in 1728, with new title: The supernatural philosopher; or, The mysteries of magick ... unfolded by William Bond. cf. Dict. nat. biog.; Camb. hist. Eng. lit., v. 9; Dottin's "Daniel DeFoe et ses romans" (1924) p. 261.
Frontispiece wanting.
28-19517
8 (Continued on next card)

Witchcraft
BF 1815 C2 D31 1742
Bond, William, d. 1735, supposed author.
[Defoe, Daniel] 1660?-1731.
Der Übernatürliche Philosoph, oder Die Geheimnisse der Magie, nach allen ihren Arten deutlich erkläret ... aus den bewährtesten Autoribus zusammen getragen und durch das Exempel und Leben des Herrn Duncan Campbells, des tauben und stummen Edelmanns, erörtert. Nebst D. Wallis Methode, taube und stumme lesen, schreiben und jede Sprache verstehen zu lernen, von W. Bond ... Aus dem Englischen
8 (Continued on next card)

Witchcraft
BF 1815 C2 D31 1742
Bond, William, d. 1735, supposed author.
[Defoe, Daniel] 1660?-1731. Der Übernatürliche Philosoph ... 1742. (Card 2)
ins Deutsche übersetzt und mit einigen nöthigen und dienlichen Anmerckungen versehen ... Berlin, J. A. Rüdiger, 1742.
[92], 432 p. front. (port.), 4 fold. plates. 17cm.
First published 1720 anonymously with title: The history of the life and adventures of Mr. Duncan Campbell. Reissued 1728 with some additions as: The super
3 (Continued on next card)

Witchcraft
BF 1815 C2 D31 1742
Bond, William, d. 1735, supposed author.
[Defoe, Daniel] 1660?-1731. Der Übernatürliche Philosoph ... 1742. (Card 3)
natural philosopher, or, The mysteries of magick ... unfolded by William Bond, from which this is translated.
Authorship disputed; probably by Daniel Defoe with the assistance of William Bond and possibly of Eliza Haywood.
Imperfect: plate to p. [72] wanting.

Witchcraft
BF 1565 T19 B71
[Bonelli, Benedetto] 1704-1783.
Animavversioni critiche sopra il Notturno congresso delle lammie, per modo di lettera indiritte ad un letterato. S'aggiungon il discorso del P. Gaar sulla strega d'Erbipoli, la Risposta dello stesso alle note, il Ragguaglio sulla strega di Salisburgo, e il Compendio storico della stregheria. Venezia, Presso Simone Occhi, 1751.
6 p. l., 188 p. 25cm.
8 (Continued on next card)

Witchcraft
BF 1565 T19 B71
[Bonelli, Benedetto] 1704-1783. Animavversioni critiche ... 1751. (Card 2)
Attributed to Bonelli by Melzi.
Each of the added items has special t. except the last, which has caption title.
1. Tartarotti, Girolamo, 1706-1761. Del congresso notturno delle lammie. 2. Witchcraft. I. Title. II. Gaar, Georg, b. 1702. Ragionamento ... fatto avanti al rogo di Maria Renata.
8

Witchcraft
BF 1566 B71
Bonilla García, Luis.
Historia de la hechicería y de las brujas. Madrid, Biblioteca Nueva, 1962.
301 p. illus. 23 cm.
Includes bibliography.

1. Witchcraft—Hist. I. Title.
BF1566.B6   62-6533
Library of Congress

CATALOGUE OF THE CORNELL WITCHCRAFT COLLECTION

Witchcraft
BD
+28
354

Bonjeau, P
    Amusements philosophiques sur le langage des bestes.
Bertram, Johann Friedrich, 1699-1741.
    Ob die Thiere Teufel seyn? wird durch Veranlassung dess von einem Französischen Jesuiten P. Bonjeau unlängst ans Licht gestellten neuen Lehr-Begriffs von den Seelen der Thiere genannt: Amusements philosophiques sur le langage des bestes; oder: Philosophischer Zeit-Vertreib über die Thier-Sprache; in welchen sie zu Teufeln gemachet werden; nach Schrifft und Vernunfft untersuchet und beantwortet, von J.F. B. [Bremen] S. Pomarius [1740]
    [15], 94 p.   16cm.

Witchcraft
BF
1584
I8
B71

Bonomo, Giuseppe.
    Caccia alle streghe. La credenza nelle streghe dal sec. XIII al XIX con particolare riferimento all'Italia. [Palermo], Palumbo, 1971.
    548 p. plates. 24½ cm. L6000   It 72-Jan
    Bibliography: p. [477]-534.

9

1. Witchcraft—Italy.   I. Title.

BF1584.I 8B64   72-316181

Library of Congress   72 [2]

Witchcraft
PQ
1957
B67
A64
1754

[Bordelon, Laurent] 1653-1730.
    L'histoire des imaginations extravagantes de M. Oufle [pseud.] Servant de preservatif contre la lecture des livres qui traitent de la magie, du grimoire, des démoniaques, sorciers ... Avec un tresgrand nombre de nottes [sic] curieuses, qui rapportent fidellement les endroits des livres qui ont causé ces imaginations, & qui les combattent ... Paris, Duchesne, 1754.
    5 v. in 2. illus. 17cm.
    Imperfect: p. 3-24 of Part V are incorrectly bound between p. 4-25 of Part IV.
    1. Occult sciences. 2. Apparitions. 3. Demonology.   I. Title.

8

WITCHCRAFT
BF
1523
V19
no.5

[Bonnet, Johann Carl]
    Demüthigste Antwort eines geringen Landgeistlichen auf die Demüthige Bitte um Belehrung an die grossen Männer, welche keinen Teufel glauben. In Deutschland, 1776.
    54 p. 17cm.
    Attribution by Holzmann.
    No. 5 in vol. lettered Varia scripta demonolog.
    1. Köster, Heinrich Martin Gottfried, 1734-1802. Demüthige Bitte um Belehrung. 2. Devil.   I. Ein geringer Landgeistlicher.   II. Title.

8

BF
1584
I8
B71

Bonomo, Giuseppe.
    Caccia alle streghe. La credenza nelle streghe dal sec. XIII al XIX con particolare riferimento all'Italia. [Palermo], Palumbo, 1971.
    548 p. plates. 25cm.
    Bibliography: p. [477]-534.

1. Witchcraft—Italy.   I. Title

NIC DEC 20,'74   COOxc   72-316181

Witchcraft
PQ
1957
B67
A64
1793

Bordelon, Laurent, 1653-1730.
    Histoire de M. Oufle, par abbé Bordelon [retouchée et réduite par M. G.] et la Description du sabbat. Paris, Gay & Gide, 1793.
    360 p. 20cm.

"...C'est un nouveau roman, mais ... nous sommes redevables néanmoins à l'abbé Bordelon...": p. 5-6.
"Description du sabbat" is not by Bordelon.

WITCHCRAFT
BF
1523
K78
no.2

Bonnet, Johann Carl.
    Demüthigste Antwort eines geringen Landgeistlichen.
[Köster, Heinrich Martin Gottfried] 1734-1802.
    Belehrung des Verfassers der Demüthigen Bitte an die grossen Männer welche keinen Teufel glauben. Mit Anmerkungen des Verfassers. [n. p.] 1776.
    114 p. 18cm.
    "Beurtheilung der demüthigen Bitte u.s.s. in der Lemgoer auserlesenen Bibliotheck 8. Band, S. 549": p. [5]-54. With commentary.
    "Demüthigste Antwort eines geringen Land-
8   (Continued on next card)

Witchcraft
PQ
1957
B67
A64
1710

[Bordelon, Laurent] 1653-1730.
    L'histoire des imaginations extravagantes de Monsieur Oufle, causées par la lecture des livres qui traitent de la magie, du grimoire, des démoniaques, sorciers ... des fées, ogres ... phantômes & autres revenans, des songes, de la pierre philosophale, de l'astrologie judiciaire ... Le tout enrichi de figures, & accompagné d'un tres-grand nombre de nottes curieuses, qui rapportent fidellement les endroits des livres, qui ont causé ses imaginations extravagantes, ou qui peuvent servir pour les combattre. Amsterdam, E. Roger, P. Humbert, P. de Coup, & les frères Chatelain, 1710.
    2 v. in 1. illus. 17cm.
                   13-20382

Library of Congress   PQ1957.B   1710

Witchcraft
PQ
1957
B67
A64
1711

Bordelon, Laurent, 1653-1730.
    Histoire des imaginations extravagantes de Monsieur Oufle--English.
[Bordelon, Laurent] 1653-1730.
    A history of the ridiculous extravagancies of Monsieur Oufle; occasion'd by his reading books treating of magick, the black-art, daemoniacks, conjurers, witches ... With notes containing a multitude of quotations out of those books, which have either caused such extravagant imaginations, or may serve to cure them. Written originally in French, by the Abbot B----; and now translated into English. London, Printed
8   (Continued on next card)

Witchcraft
BF
1523
K78
no.2

Bonnet, Johann Carl.
    Demüthigste Antwort eines geringen Landgeistlichen.
[Köster, Heinrich Martin Gottfried] 1734-1802. Belehrung des Verfassers der Demüthigen Bitte ... 1776.   (Card 2)
geistlichen ... Mit Anmerkungen," p. [57]-114, has special t. p. Text of the "Antwort" itself not included.
    No. 2 in vol. lettered Ueber den Teufel.
    1. Bonnet, Johann Carl. Demüthigste Antwort eines geringen Landgeistlichen. 2. Devil. 3. His Demüthige Bitte um Belehrung. I. Auserlesene Bibliothek der neuesten deutschen Literatur. Beurtheilung der demüthigen Bitte. II. Title.

8

WITCHCRAFT
PQ
1957
B67
A64
1710

[Bordelon, Laurent] 1653-1730.
    L'histoire des imaginations extravagantes de Monsieur Oufle, causées par la lecture des livres qui traitent de la magie, du grimoire, des démoniaques, sorciers ... des fées, ogres ... phantômes & autres revenans, des songes, de la pierre philosophale, de l'astrologie judiciaire. Le tout enrichi de figures, & accompagné d'un tres-grand nombre de nottes curieuses, qui rapportent
8   (Continued on next card)
NIC

Witchcraft
PQ
1957
B67
A64
1711

[Bordelon, Laurent] 1653-1730. A history of the ridiculous extravagancies of Monsieur Oufle ... 1711.   (Card 2)
    for J. Morphew, 1711.
    4 p. l., 303 [i.e., 319] p. 20cm.
    Translation of Histoire des imaginations extravagantes de Monsieur Oufle.
    Gathering G, between p. 96 and 97, incorrectly paged 81-96.
    1. Occult sciences. 2. Apparitions.

8   (Continued on next card)

Witchcraft
BF
1555
B71

Bonnhöfer, Johann Friedrich.
    ... Erbauliche Abhandlung von dem erschröcklichen und Jammer-vollen Zustand der geist- und leiblichen Besitzung des Teuffels. In zweyen Betrachtungen aus Heil. Schrifft erwiesen und mit historischen Exempeln erleutert ... mit einer Vorrede Gustav Georg Zeltners, D. worinnen er seine Gedancken vom Binden des Satans, Offenb. 20, 2. eröffnet. Nürnberg, Bey J. W. Rönnagel, 1733.
    26 p. l., 884, [36] p. port. 17cm.

8   (Continued on next card)

WITCHCRAFT
PQ
1957
B67
A64
1710a

[Bordelon, Laurent] 1653-1730.
    L'Histoire des imaginations extravagantes de Monsieur Oufle, causées par la lecture des livres qui traitent de la magie, du grimoire, des démoniaques, sorciers ... des fées, ogres ... phantômes & autres revenans, des songes, de la pierre philosophale, de l'astrologie judiciaire. Le tout enrichi de figures, & accompagné d'un tres-grand nombre de nottes curieuses, qui rapportent
8   (Continued on next card)
NIC

Witchcraft
PQ
1957
B67
A64
1711

[Bordelon, Laurent] 1653-1730.
    A history of the ridiculous extravagancies of Monsieur Oufle; occasion'd by his reading books treating of magick, the black-art, daemoniacks, conjurers, witches ... With notes containing a multitude of quotations out of those books, which have either caused such extravagant imaginations, or may serve to cure them. Written originally in French, by the Abbot B----; and now translated into English. London, Printed
8   (Continued on next card)

Witchcraft
BF
1555
B71

Bonnhöfer, Johann Friedrich. Erbauliche Abhandlung ... 1733.   (Card 2)

    1. Demoniac possession. 2. Devil. I. Zeltner, Gustav Georg, 1672-1738. II. Title.

8

WITCHCRAFT
PQ
1957
B67
A64
1710a

[Bordelon, Laurent] 1653-1730. L'histoire des imaginations extravagantes de Monsieur Oufle...   (Card 2)
fidellement les endroits des livres, qui ont causé ses imaginations extravagantes, ou qui peuvent servir pour les combattre. Paris, N. Gosselin [etc.] 1710.
    2 v. illus. (1 fold.) 18cm.

8
NIC

Witchcraft
PQ
1957
B67
A64
1711

[Bordelon, Laurent] 1653-1730. A history of the ridiculous extravagancies of Monsieur Oufle ... 1711.   (Card 2)
    for J. Morphew, 1711.
    4 p. l., 303 [i.e., 319] p. 20cm.
    Translation of Histoire des imaginations extravagantes de Monsieur Oufle.
    Gathering G, between p. 96 and 97, incorrectly paged 81-96.
    1. Occult sciences. 2. Apparitions.

8   (Continued on next card)

CATALOGUE OF THE CORNELL WITCHCRAFT COLLECTION

Witchcraft
PQ 1957 B67 A64 1711
[Bordelon, Laurent] 1653-1730. A history of the ridiculous extravagancies of Monsieur Oufle ... 1711. (Card 3)

3. Demonology. I. His Histoire des imaginations extravagantes de Monsieur Oufle. English. II. B----, Abbot. III. Title. IV. Title: Oufle, Monsieur, A history of.

8

Rare BX 1710 B72++ 1665
Bordoni, Francesco, 1580-1654.
Operum tomus primus, quo continetvr Sacrvm tribvnal ivdicvm in cavsis sanctae fidei ... Lvgdvni, sumptibus Ioannis-Antonii Hvgvetan & Marci-Antonii Ravavd, 1665.
561 p. 36cm.

1. Inquisition.

Rare BX 1939 H4 B72++
Bordoni, Francesco, 1595-1671.
... Francisci Bordoni... Opus posthumum, de recenti primo in lucem proditur, quod consistit in duas appendices ad Manuale consultorum in causis Sancti Officii contra haereticam pravitatem occurrentibus ...in prima diffuse ostenditur quasi omnem excogitabilem blasphemiam... In secunda vero explicantur essentia, qualitates, ac diversitatum genus omnium sortilegiorum... Ad cujus calcem subsequitur nova reimpressio Tractatus de legatis ejusdem auctoris
(Continued on next card)

Rare BX 1939 H4 B72++
Bordoni, Francesco, 1595-1671. ... Opus posthumum... (Card 2)

denuò revisus, ac ...correctus ...industria ...Francisci Odoardi Mancini... Parmae, Typis Pauli Montj, 1703.
[3], 669 p. 37cm.

1. Heresy (Canon law) 2. Inquisition. 3. Catholic Church--Clergy. 4. Ecclesiastical benefices.

Born, Jacobus Henricus, 1717-1775
see
Born, Jakob Heinrich, 1717-1775

Born, Jakob Heinrich, 1717-1775.

WITCHCRAFT
BF 1598 S53 S35
Schmutzer, Joannes Gottfried.
De Michaele Scoto veneficii inivste damnato disserit ... Iacobo Henrico Bornio ... qvvm is senator Lipsiensis in solemni Senatvs lectione ... nasceretvr hanc dignitatem gratvlatvrvs Ioannes Gottfried. Schmvtzervs. Lipsiae, Ex officina Langenhemiana [1739]
xvi p. 22cm.
1. Scott, Michael, 1175?-1234? 2. Witchcraft. 3. Born, Jakob Heinrich, 1717-1775. I. Title.

8 NIC

Bornius, Jacobus Henricus, 1717-1775
see
Born, Jakob Heinrich, 1717-1775

Witchcraft
BF 1565 B73
Borre, Nicolas de, ca. 1590-1670.
Apologia pro exorcistis, energumenis, maleficiatis, & ab incubis daemonibus molestatis, in qvatvor partes divisa. In qua demonstratur fuisse omni aevo, & ubique, modòq; esse, etiam apud nos, plurimos omnis aetatis & conditionis energumenos, maleficiatos, & ab incubis daemonibus molestatos. Contra quosdam incredulos, obtrectatores, & temerarios exorcistarum censores ... Lovanij, Typis Georgii Lipsii, 1660.

8
(Continued on next card)

Witchcraft
BF 1565 B73
Borre, Nicolas de, ca. 1590-1670. Apologia pro exorcistis ... 1660. (Card 2)

8 p. l., 236, [3] p. 19cm.
Imperfect: t. p. and text of dedication partially destroyed by book-worms.
With this is bound his Examen profani exorcismi primi contra daemonem mendacii. Lovanij, 1660.
1. Witchcraft. 2. Witchcraft in the Bible. 3. Exorcism. I. Title.

8

Witchcraft
BF 1565 B73
Borre, Nicolas de, ca. 1590-1670.
Examen profani Exorcismi primi contra daemonem mendacii sub ementito Lamberti Dicaei theologi medici nomine in lucem nuper emissi, nec non inepti & ridiculi ipsius Cataplasmatis &c. In quo duae & triginta imposturae deteguntur, omnium oculis exponuntur, & solidè refutantur. Lovanij, Typis Georgii Lipsii, 1660.
73 p. 19cm.
Bound with his Apologia pro exorcistis. Lovanij, 1660.

8
(Continued on next card)

Witchcraft
BF 1565 B73
Borre, Nicolas de, ca. 1590-1670. Examen profani Exorcismi primi ... 1660. (Card 2)

1. Dicaeus, Lambertus, pseud. Exorcismus primus contra daemonem mendacii. 2. Dicaeus, Lambertus, pseud. Cataplasma contra inflammationem cerebri. 3. Exorcism. I. Title.

8

Witchcraft
BF 1414 B73
Borrelli, P.
Alchimia e satanismo. Con illustrazioni di Edoardo Calandra. Napoli, Società Editrice Partenopea [1914]
xiv, 326 p. 20cm.

1. Demonology. 2. Alchemy. I. Title.

BF 1412 B74
Bosc, Ernest, 1837-
Petite encyclopédie synthétique des sciences occultes. Éd. de la curiosité. Nice, Bureau de la Curiosité, 1904.
xiii, 285 p. 18cm.

At head of title: Ernest Bosc de Vèze.

1. Occult sciences--Dictionaries. I. Title

HIST SCI R 133 P74
Bose, Ernst Gottlob, 1723-1788.
Pohl, Johann Ehrenfried, 1746-1800, praes De medico exorcista...praeside Iohanne Ehrenfried Pohl...disputabit auctor ac respondens Iohannes Godofredus Iancke... Lipsiae, Ex officina Sommeria [1788]
26, xv p. 21cm.

Diss.--Leipzig (J. G. Jancke, respondens "Procancellarius D. Ernestus Gottlob Bo Panegyrin medicam...indicit. De phantasi laesa, gravium morborum matre.": xv p. at end.

8 NIC
(Continued on next card)

Bosheit und Wahnglaube.

WITCHCRAFT
PT 2376 K12 B7
Keller, Karl, of Bunzlau.
Bosheit und Wahnglaube; oder, Der Hexenprozess. Sittengemälde aus der Mitte des 17ten Jahrhunderts. Bunzlau, Appun, 18__
239 p. 19cm.

8 NIC
I. Title.

Witchcraft
BF 1589 B76 1960
Bouisson, Maurice.
Magic: its rites and history. Translated from the French by G. Almayrac. London, Rider [1960]
319 p. illus. 24 cm.
Includes bibliography.

Translation of La magie; ses grands rites, son histoire.

1. Magic—Hist. I. Title. II. His La magi ses grands rites, son histoire—English.
BF1589.B653   133.409   60-51858
Library of Congress   [2]

Bouisson, Maurice.
La magie; ses grands rites, son histoire. English

BF 1589 B76 1960
Bouisson, Maurice.
Magic: its rites and history. Translated from the French by G. Almayrac. London, Rider [1960]
319 p. illus. 24 cm.
Includes bibliography.

Translation of La magie; ses grands rites, son histoire.

1. Magic—Hist. I. Title. II. His La magi ses grands rites, son histoire--English.
BF1589.B653   133.409   60-51858
Library of Congress   [2]

Witchcraft
BF 1582 Z7 1566
Boulaese, Jehan
Le manvel de l'admirable victoire dv corps de Dieu svr l'esprit maling Beelzebub obtenue à Laon, 1566 ... Liège, H. Hou 1598.
392 p. 14cm.

Four pages of dedication bound between 24-25.
Colophon has date: M.D.IVC.

1. Witchcraft--France. I. Title

CATALOGUE OF THE CORNELL WITCHCRAFT COLLECTION

WITCHCRAFT
BF
1555
P61

Boullé, Thomas.

Piérart, Z J
Le magnétisme, le somnambulisme et le spiritualisme dans l'histoire. Affaire curieuse des possédées de Louviers... Paris, Au Bureau du Journal du magnétisme, 1858.
39 p. 23cm.

Extract from Journal du magnétisme.

8
NIC

1. Demoniac possession. 2. Louviers, France. St. Louis (Convent) 3. Bavent, Madeleine, ca. 1608-1647. 4 Picard, Mathurin, d.1647. 5. Boullé, Thomas.

WITCHCRAFT
BF
1555
R31

Boullé, Thomas.

Recueil de pièces sur les possessions des religieuses de Louviers. Rouen ₁Imprimerie L. Deshays₎ 1879.
2 v. in 1. 25cm.

Title page and prefatory material bound following v. 1.

Contents.--₁₁₎ Histoire de Magdelaine Bavent, religieuse du monastere de Saint Loüis de Louviers (1652)--₂₂₎ I. Examen de la possession des religieuses de Louviers, par le Docteur Yvelin (1643)

8
NIC

(Continued on next card)

WITCHCRAFT
BF
1555
R31

Boullé, Thomas.

Recueil de pièces sur les possessions des religieuses de Louviers...1879. (Card 2)

Contents--continued.

II. Response à l'Examen de la possession des religieuses de Louviers (1643) III. Censure de l'Examen de la possession des religieuses de Louviers (1643) IV. Apologie pour l'autheur de l'Examen de la possession des religieuses de Louviers, attribuée au Docteur Yvelin (1643) V. Responce à l'Apologie de l'Examen du sieur Yvelin

(Continued on next card)

WITCHCRAFT
BF
1555
R31

Boullé, Thomas.

Recueil de pièces sur les possessions des religieuses de Louviers...1879. (Card 3)

Contents--continued.

(1644) VI. Recit veritable de ce qui s'est fait & passé à Louviers, touchant les religieuses possedées (1643) VII. Recit veritable de ce qui s'est fait & passé aux exorcismes de plusieurs religieuses de la ville de Louviers (1643) VIII. La deffense de la verité touchant la possession des religieuses de Louvier, par

(Continued on next card)

WITCHCRAFT
BF
1555
R31

Boullé, Thomas

Recueil de pièces sur les possessions des religieuses de Louviers...1879. (Card 4)

Contents--continued.

Jean Le Breton (1643) IX. Attestation de messieurs les commissaires envoyez par sa Majesté pour prendre connoissance, avec monseigneur l'evesque d'Evreux, de l'estat des religieuses qui paroissent agitées au monastere de Saint Louys & Sainte Elizabeth de Louviers (1643?) X. Procés verbal de Monsieur le Penitentier

(Continued on next card)

WITCHCRAFT
BF
1555
R31

Boullé, Thomas.

Recueil de pièces sur les possessions des religieuses de Louviers...1879. (Card 5)

Contents--continued.

tier d'Evreux, de ce qui luy est arrivé dans la prison, interrogeant & consolant Magdelaine Bavent, magicienne, à une heureuse conversion & repentance, par Delangle (1643) XI. Lettre adressée à Monsieur D. L. V., medicin du Roy, & doyen de la Faculté de Paris, sur l'Apologie du sieur Yvelin, medicin, attribuée au doc-

(Continued on next card)

WITCHCRAFT
BF
1555
R31

Boullé, Thomas.

Recueil de pièces sur les possessions des religieuses de Louviers...1879. (Card 6)

Contents--continued.

teur Maignart (1644) XII. Traicté des marques des possedez & la preuve de la veritable possession des religieuses de Louviers, par P. M., esc. d. en m. (attribué à Simon Pietre; 1644) XIII. Copie en forme de recueil de ce qui se fait de jour en jour dans le monastere des filles relligieuses Saint Louis (1643) XIV. Pièces dé-

(Continued on next card)

WITCHCRAFT
BF
1555
R31

Boullé, Thomas.

Recueil de pièces sur les possessions des religieuses de Louviers...1879. (Card 7)

Contents--continued.

tachées extraites du manuscrit H. F. n° 34 de la Bibliothèque Ste Geneviève, formant suite à la pièce précédente. XV. Notice sur la Mere Françoise, superieure des religieuses de la Place royale, au sujet de l'histoire des possedées de Louviers.

(Continued on next card)

Witchcraft
BF
1410
B76C7

₁Boulton, Richard₎ fl. 1697-1724.
A compleat history of magick, sorcery, and witchcraft ... London, Printed for E. Curll, J. Pemberton; and W. Taylor, 1715-16.
2 v. in 1. front. 17cm.

Copy 2: 2 v.

1. Magic. 2. Witchcraft. I. Title.

Witchcraft
BF
1410
B76P8

Boulton, Richard, fl. 1697-1724.
A compleat history of magick, sorcery, and witchcraft.

Boulton, Richard, fl. 1697-1724.
The possibility and reality of magick, sorcery, and witchcraft, demonstrated. Or, A vindication of A compleat history of magick, sorcery, and witchcraft. In answer to Dr. Hutchinson's Historical essay ... In two parts ... London, Printed for J. Roberts, 1722.
xvi, ₍4₎, 184 p. 17cm.

Witchcraft
BF
1410
B76P8

Boulton, Richard, fl. 1697-1724.
The possibility and reality of magick, sorcery, and witchcraft, demonstrated. Or, A vindication of A compleat history of magick, sorcery, and witchcraft. In answer to Dr. Hutchinson's Historical essay ... In two parts ... London, Printed for J. Roberts, 1722.
xvi, ₍4₎, 184 p. 17cm.

(over)

Witchcraft
BF
1505
D13

Boulton, Richard, fl. 1699-1724.
The possibility and reality of magick.

Daillon, Jacques, ca. 1634-1726. Δαιμονολογία; or, A treatise of spirits. Wherein several places of Scripture are expounded, against the vulgar errors concerning witchcraft, apparitions, &c. To which is added, an appendix, containing some reflections on Mr. Boulton's answer to Dr. Hutchinson's Historical essay; entitled The possibility and reality of magick, sorcery and witchcraft demonstrated. London,

Title transliterated:
Daimonología.
(Continued on next card)

Witchcraft
BF
1505
D13

Boulton, Richard, fl. 1699-1724.
The possibility and reality of magick.

Daillon, Jacques, ca. 1634-1726. Δαιμονολογία. (Card 2)

Printed for the author, 1723.
182 p. 19cm.
Ex libris Lord Hill.
A Preface, consisting of eight pages, numbered iii-x, is inserted between the t.p. and p. v.
With this is bound his The ax laid to the root of popery. ₍London? 1721?₎

Witchcraft
BX
9479
B42
B11
no.10

₁Bouman, Herman₎
Aanleydinge, om klaar te konnen uytvinden wanneer men in de H. Schriftuur van duyvel, Satan, boose geest, &c. in ons Nederduyts leest, hoe het selve te verstaan zy. Waar na volgt, een korte verklaring over Matth. 8: 28-31. ... Ook zijn hier bygevoegt vier brieven, waar in over en weder gehandelt, word van de versoekinge des Saligmakers Jesu Christi, van den hemel, de engelen, &c. 2. verm. druk. Amsterdam, By R. Blokland, boekverkoper, 1700.

(Continued on next card)

Witchcraft
BX
9479
B42
B11
no.10

₁Bouman, Herman₎ Aanleydinge ... 1700. (Card 2)

2 p. l., 28 ₍i. e., 80₎ p. title vignette, illus. initials. 20 x 15cm.
4°: *², A-K⁴.
Black letter (except introduction and letters)
Introduction signed: H. Bouman.
Two letters are signed: N. N. ₍i. e., Jacobus Schuts₎

(Continued on next card)

Witchcraft
BX
9479
B42
B11
no.10

₁Bouman, Herman₎ Aanleydinge ... 1700. (Card 3)

Van der Linde 81.
No. 10 in vol. lettered B. Bekkers sterfbed en andere tractaten.

1. Devil. 2. Spirits. 3. Bible. N. T. Matthew VIII, 28-31--Criticism, interpretation, etc. I. Schuts, Jacobus. II. Title.

8

Witchcraft
BX
9479
B42
B11
no.11

₁Bouman, Herman₎
Aanmerkinge over de woorden van den Evangelist Lucas, beschreven in sijn H. Evangelium cap. 4: vs. 1-14. Daar verhaalt word hoe den Saligmaker Jesus Christus is versogt van den duyvel, en aangetoond wat voor een duyvel deselve kan geweest zyn; als mede, wat voor engelen de Heere Jesus na de versoekinge konnen gedient hebben. Amsterdam, By R. Blokland, boekverkooper, 1699.
4° p. ₍p. 48 blank₎ title vignette, illus. initia ls. 20 x 15cm.

(Continued on next card)

Witchcraft
BX
9479
B42
B11
no.11

₁Bouman, Herman₎ Aanmerkinge over de woorden van den Evangelist Lucas ... 1699. (Card 2)

4°: A-F⁴.
Black letter (except introduction)
Introduction signed: H. Bouman.
No. 11 in vol. lettered B. Bekkers sterfbed en andere tractaten.

1. Bible. N. T. Luke IV, 1-14--Criticism, interpretation, etc. 2. Jesus Christ--Temptation. 3. Devil. I. Title.

CATALOGUE OF THE CORNELL WITCHCRAFT COLLECTION

Witchcraft
BF
1410
B42
Z56
v.2
no.24
   Bouman, Herman.
      Brief van Lambert Joosten, met een antwoord op de selve, van Herman Bouman, waar in gehandelt word van de engelen en geesten, &c. En welk laatste een zedige verantwoordinge beheltt, van de swaare gevolgen, of besluyten, die den autheur des briefs, uyt het gevoelen van H: B: tracht te maaken. Amsterdam, By A. van Damme, boekverkoper, 1696.
      42 p. title vignette, illus. initial.
   19 x 15cm.

(Continued on next card)

Witchcraft
BF
1410
B42
Z56
v.2
no.24
   Bouman, Herman. Brief van Lambert Joosten, met een antwoord op de selve ... 1696.
                        (Card 2)

    4°: A-B⁴, F1.
    Black letter (except for introduction)
    Bouman divides Joosten's letter into sentences, and gives a refutation after each.
    Van der Linde 80.
    No. 24 in vol. lettered Bekker II.
    1. Angels.   2. Spirits.   I. Joosten, Lambert.   II. Title.

8

Witchcraft
BX
9479
B42
B11
no.15
   Bouman, Herman, ed.
      Disputatio van verscheyde saaken, raakende de wonderwerken, en of een schepsel die doen kan: item van de engelen, duyvelen, &c. Voorgevallen in de Menniste Kerk, het Lam genaamd, terwijl het oeffening was, den 7 Augustus, en den 29 Mey te vooren, deses jaars 1695. Door verscheyde broeders van deselve societeyt, die tegenwoordig waren, opgestelt, en nagesien van H: Bouman, die ook een kleyne voor-reden voor, en weynig aanmerkingen achter heeft bygevoegd.

(Continued on next card)

8

Witchcraft
BX
9479
B42
B11
no.15
   Bouman, Herman, ed. Disputatio van verscheyde saaken ... 1695.   (Card 2)
    Amsterdam, By J. Smets en P. Dibbits, boekdrukkers, 1695.
    23 p. [p. 24 blank] title vignette, illus. initials. 20 x 15cm.
    4°: A-C⁴.
    Black letter (except introduction and letters at end)
    Letters of Bouman and N. N. [i. e,

(Continued on next card)

Witchcraft
BX
9479
B42
B11
no.15
   Bouman, Herman, ed. Disputatio van verscheyde saaken ... 1695.   (Card 3)
   Jacobus Schuts]: p. 22-23.
    Van der Linde 78.
    No. 15 in vol. lettered B. Bekkers sterfbed en andere tractaten.
    1. Miracles--Early works to 1800.   2. Spirits.   I. Schuts, Jacobus.   II. Title.

8

Witchcraft
BX
9479
B42
B11
no.17
   Bouman, Herman.
      Brief van L. P. aan Herman Bouman; eerst in 't bysonder aan hem geschreeven, en nu door hem, met verlof van den autheur, gemeen gemaakt: behelsende sommige redenen waarom hy de soo genaamde Sleutel der geesten enz. van M. van Diepen, en J. Hubener niet, ofte niet zoodanig alse daar ligt, behoorde te beantwoorden; en teffens een volstrekte omkeering van de gronden van dat woest geschrift. Amsterdam, By R. Blokland, boekverkoper, 1699.

(Continued on next card)

8

Witchcraft
BX
9479
B42
B11
no.17
   Bouman, Herman.
      Brief van L. P. aan Herman Bouman ... 1699.   (Card 2)
    2 p. l., 12 p. title and end page vignettes, illus. initials. 20 x 15cm.
    4°: π², A⁴, B².
    Written by a supporter of Balthazar Bekker, whom Diepen and Hubener attacked.
    No. 17 in vol. lettered B. Bekkers sterfbed en andere tractaten.
    1. Diepen, Marcus van. De sleutel der geesten.   2. Bekker, Balthasar,

(Continued on next card)

Witchcraft
BX
9479
B42
B11
no.16
   Bouman, Herman.
      Kuyk, J van.
      Disputatie over den duyvel, of dezelve is een geschaapen geest, buyten de zielen der menschen, dewelke afgevallen en boos geworden is, ofte niet? Voorgevallen tusschen J. van Kuyk, krankbesoeker, ter eenre, en H. Bouman, ter andere zyde ... op den 26 December, 1694. Door een liefhebber der waarheyt, soo daar tegenwoordig was, opgestelt. Hier is noch by gevoegd een brief, aan geseyde J. van Kuyk ... den 27 January, 1693.

(Continued on next card)

8

Witchcraft
BX
9479
B42
B11
no.16
   Bouman, Herman.
      Kuyk, J van. Disputatie over den duyvel ... 1695.   (Card 2)
   aldaar bestelt; met redenen, waarom deselve nu eerst door den druk gemeen gemaakt wort. Amsterdam, By E. Webber, boekverkooper, 1695.
    16 p. title and end page vignettes. 20 x 15cm.
    4°: A-B⁴.
    Black letter (except introduction)
    Letter and Na-reeden, p. 10-16,

(Continued on next card)

8

Witchcraft
BX
9479
B42
B11
no.16
   Bouman, Herman.
      Kuyk, J van. Disputatie over den duyvel ... 1695.   (Card 3)
   signed: Z. W. [i. e., Zacharias Webbers]
    Van der Linde 79.
    No. 16 in vol. lettered B. Bekkers sterfbed en andere tractaten.
    1. Devil.   I. Bouman, Herman.   II. Webbers, Zacharias.   III. Een liefhebber der waarheyt.   IV. Title.

8

Witchcraft
BF
1566
B77
   Bourneville, [Désiré Magloire] 1840-
      Le Sabbat des sorciers, par Bourneville et E. Teinturier. Paris, Aux Bureaux du Progrès médical; Delahaye et Lecrosnier, 1882.
    38 p. illus. 22cm. (Bibliothèque diabolique)

    1. Witchcraft.   I. Teinturier, E.   II. Title.

Witchcraft
BF
1555
H67
1886
   Bourneville, Désiré Magloire, 1840-1909, ed.
      La Possession de Jeanne Fery, religieuse professe du couvent des soeurs noires de la ville de Mons (1584) Paris, Aux bureaux du Progrès médical, 1886.
    v, 109 p. 23cm. (Bibliothèque diabolique; Collection Bourneville)
    Reprint of Histoire admirable et veritable des choses advenues a l'endroict d'une religieuse professe ..., pub. 1586.
    Edited by D. B. Bourneville.
    With facsimile of original t. p.

(Continued on next card)

8

Witchcraft
HV
6025
B78
   Bouvet, prévost général des armées du roy en Italie.
      Les manières admirables povr de'covrir tovtes sortes de crimes et sortilèges. Avec l'instrvction solide povr bien ivger vn procez criminel. Ensemble l'espèce des crimes, & la punition d'iceux, suiuant les loix, ordonnances, canons, & arrests ... Paris, I. de la Caille, 1659.
    342 p. 17cm.

    1. Crime and criminals.   I. Title.

Witchcraft
BF
1583
A2S74
1660
   Bouvot, Frédéric, tr.
      [Spee, Friedrich von] 1591-1635.
      Advis avx criminalistes svr les abvs qvi se glissent dans les proces de sorcelerie. Dediés aux magistrats d'Allemagne. Liure tres necessaire en ce temps icy, à tous iuges, conseillers, confesseurs ... inquisiteurs, predicateurs, aduocats, & mêmes aux medecins. Par le P. N. S. I. theologien romain. Imprimé en Latin pour la seconde fois à Francfort en l'année 1632. Et mis en françois par F. B. de Velledor [pseud.] M.A.D. Lyon,

(Continued on next card)

Witchcraft
BF
1583
A2S74
1660
   Bouvot, Frédéric, tr.
      [Spee, Friedrich von] 1591-1635. Advis avx criminalistes ... (Card 2)
    Aux dépens de l'autheur: Et se vend chez Clavde Prost, 1660.
    [48], 336 p. 18cm.

    Translation of Cautio criminalis.

    I. His Cautio criminalis. French.   II. Bouvot, Frédéric, tr.   III. Title.

Witchcraft
BF
1565
B78
   Bovet, Richard, b. ca. 1641.
      Pandaemonium: or, The Devil's cloyster. Being a further blow to modern Sadduceism, proving the existence of witches and spirits. In a discourse deduced from the fall of the angels, the propagation of Satans kingdom before the flood ... With an account of the lives and transactions of several ... witches. Also a collection of several authentic relations of strange apparitions of daemons and specters, and fascinations of witches ...

(Continued on next card)

Witchcraft
BF
1565
B78
   Bovet, Richard, b. ca. 1641. Pandaemonium ... 1684.   (Card 2)
    London, Printed for J. Walthoe, 1684.
    239 p. 16cm.

    I. Title.

BF
1565
B78
1951
   Bovet, Richard, b. ca. 1641.
      Pandaemonium, 1684. With an introduction and notes by Montague Summers. Aldington, Kent, The Hand and Flower Press, 1951.
    xxvii, 191 p. 23cm.

    1. Witchcraft.   I. Summers, Montague, 1880-   II. Title.

CATALOGUE OF THE CORNELL WITCHCRAFT COLLECTION

Bower, Edmond.
Doctor Lamb revived; or, Witchcraft condemn'd in Anne Bodenham, a servant of his, who was arraigned and executed the Lent assizes last at Salisbury, before ... Baron Wild, judge of the assise. Wherein is set forth her strange and wonderful diabolical usage of a maid, servant to Mr. Goddard, as also her attempt against his daughters ... London, Printed by T. W. for R. Best and J. Place, 1653.
44 p. 20 cm.
1. Bodenham, Anne. I. Title.

Witchcraft
BF
1566
B79

Bracelin, Jack L
Gerald Gardner: witch. [London] Octagon Press [1960]
224 p. illus. 22 cm.

1. Gardner, Gerald Brosseau, 1884- 2. Witchcraft. I. Title.
BF1566.B7   920.91334   61-34293
Library of Congress

Witchcraft
BF
1581
Z7
1712c

Bragge, Francis, b. 1690.
A defense of the proceedings against Jane Wenham, wherein the possibility and reality of witchcraft are demonstrated from Scripture, and the concurrent testimonies of all ages. In answer to two pamphlets, entituled, I. The impossibility of witchcraft, &c. II. A full confutation of witchcraft. By Francis Bragge ... London, Printed for E. Curll, 1712.
2 p. l., 36 p. 18½ cm.

1. Wenham, Jane, d. 1730. 2. Witchcraft--England. I. Title.
Library of Congress   BF1518.Z7 1712   11-14486

Bowman, Frank Paul.
Eliphas Lévi; visionnaire romantique. Préface et choix de textes par Frank Paul Bowman. Paris, Presses Universitaires de France, 1969.
242 p. 19cm. ("A la découverte")
At head of title: Publications du Département de langues romanes de l'Université de Princeton.

1. Constant, Alphonse Louis, 1810-1875. I. Title. II. Series: Princeton University. Princeton publications in modern languages.

MSS
Bd.
WITCHCRAFT
BF
B81

Bradwell, Stephan, fl. 1594-1636.
Marie Glovers late woefull case, together wth her joyfull deliverance written upon occasion of Dr. Jordens Discourse of the mother... With a defence of the truthe against D. J. his scandalous impugnations. [n.p.] 1603.
171 l. 20 x 29cm.
Photostatic copy of Sloan MSS 831 in the British Museum.
Second treatise, beginning on l. 42,
(Continued on next card)

Witchcraft
BF
1581
Z7
1712

[Bragge, Francis] b. 1690.
A full and impartial account of the discovery of sorcery and witchcraft, practis'd by Jane Wenham of Walkerne in Hertfordshire, upon the bodies of Anne Thorn, Anne Street, &c. The proceedings against her from her being first apprehended, till she was committed to gaol by Sir Henry Chavncy. Also her tryal at the assizes at Hertford before Mr. Justice Powell, where she was found guilty of felony and witchcraft, and receiv'd sen-
(Continued on next card)

Boyer, Paul S
Salem possessed: the social origins of witchcraft [by] Paul Boyer and Stephen Nissenbaum. Cambridge, Mass., Harvard University Press, 1974.
xxi, 231 p. illus. 25 cm.
Includes bibliographical references.

1. Witchcraft--Salem, Mass. 2. Porter family. 3. Putnam family. I. Nissenbaum, Stephen, joint author. II. Title

C MAY 22,'74   CCCxc   73-84399

MSS
Bd.
WITCHCRAFT
BF
B81

Bradwell, Stephan, fl. 1594-1636.   Marie Glovers late woefull case...1603. (Card 2)

has caption title: A defence of the publique sentence of lawe, and of the iudgment, of certayne phisitions, ^y averred Marie Glouers case to be supernaturall: againste D. Jordens slie, but scandalous impugnations of bothe.
Bound in maroon buckram.
1. Glover, Mary, fl. 1603. 2. Demoniac possession. 3. Witchcraft--
(Continued on next card)

Witchcraft
BF
1581
Z7
1712

[Bragge, Francis]   A full and impartial account of the discovery of sorcery and witchcraft ... 1712.   (Card 2)

tence of death for the same, March 4.1711-12... London, Printed for E. Curll, 1712.
2 p. l., 36 p. 19cm.

1. Wenham, Jane, d. 1730. 2. Witchcraft--England. I. Title.

Boyer, Paul S
Salem possessed: the social origins of witchcraft [by] Paul Boyer and Stephen Nissenbaum. Cambridge, Mass., Harvard University Press, 1974.
xxi, 231 p. illus. 25 cm.
Includes bibliographical references.

1. Witchcraft--Salem, Mass. 2. Porter family. 3. Putnam family. I. Nissenbaum, Stephen, joint author. II. Title

C JUL 28,'75   COOUxc   73-84399

MSS
Bd.
WITCHCRAFT
BF
B81

Bradwell, Stephan, fl. 1594-1636.   Marie Glovers late woefull case...1603. (Card 3)

England. 4. Jorden, Edward. A briefe discourse of a disease called suffocation of the mother. I. Title.

Witchcraft
BF
1581
Z7
1712d

Bragge, Francis, b. 1690.
A full and impartial account of the discovery of sorcery...
The witch of Walkerne. Being, I. A full and impartial account of the discovery of sorcery and witchcraft, practis'd by Jane Wenham of Walkerne in Hertfordshire ... II. Witchcraft farther display'd. Containing an account of the witchcraft practis'd by Jane Wenham, since her condemnation, etc. ... III. A defense of the proceedings against Jane Wenham ... In answer to two pamphlets, entituled, 1. The impossibility of witchcraft. 2. A full confutation of
(Continued on next card)

---

witchcraft
BF
1581
Z7
1699

Boys, James, d. 1725.
The case of witchcraft at Coggeshall, Essex, in the year 1699, being the narrative of the Rev. J. Boys, minister of that parish. Printed from his manuscript in the possession of the publisher. London, A. R. Smith, 1901.
23, [1] p. 23¼ cm.
[Hazlitt tracts, v. 53, no. 14]
"Only 50 copies printed."
"A brief account of the indisposition of the widow Coman ... penned down by the aforesaid divine ... and afterwards transcribed (by the same person) from loose leaf papers in the year 1712": p. [3]

1. Witchcraft--England. 2. Coggeshall, Eng. I. Title.

Library of Congress   AC911.H3 vol. 53, no. 14   23-4835
[2]

Brähm, Felix Martin, respondent.

Witchcraft
BF
1565
B66

Bode, Heinrich von, 1652-1720, praeses.
Disputatio inauguralis De fallacibus indiciis magiae, qvam ... praeside Dn. Henrico Bodino ... die 22. Octobris A. C. 1701 ... submittit Felix Martinus Brähm. Halae Magdebvrgicae, Literis C. Henckelii, typogr. [1701]
50 p. 20cm.
Diss.--Halle (F. M. Brähm, respondent)
Supports Balthasar Bekker.

8   (Continued on next card)

Witchcraft
BF
1581
Z7
1712d

Bragge, Francis.   A full and impartial account of the discovery of sorcery...
The witch of Walkerne ... (Card 2)

witchcraft. IV. A general preface to the whole. 5th ed. London, Printed for E. Curll, 1712.
3 pts. in 1 v. 20cm.

Parts 2 and 3 have special title pages.

1. Witchcraft--England. 2. Wenham, Jane, d. 1730. I. Title.

Bozzano, Ernesto, 1862-1943.
Übersinnliche Erscheinungen bei Naturvölkern. Mit einem Nachwort und einem Register von Gastone De Boni. Bern, A. Francke [1948]
323 p. 18cm. (Sammlung DALP)

Bibliography: p. 299-301.

1. Occult sciences. 2. Witchcraft. I. Title.

Witchcraft
BF
1583
B19

Die Bräunlinger Hexenprozesse.

Balzer, Eugen.
Die Bräunlinger Hexenprozesse.
(In Alemannia. Freiburg im Breisgau. 23cm. 3. Folge, Bd. 2 (1910) p. 1-42)

1. Trials (Witchcraft)--Germany. I. Title.

Witchcraft
BF
1581
Z7
1712e

[Bragge, Francis] b. 1690.
A full and impartial account of the discovery of sorcery and witchcraft, practis'd by Jane Wenham.
The case of the Hertfordshire witchcraft consider'd. Being an examination of a book, entitl'd, A full and impartial account of the discovery of sorcery & witchcraft, practis'd by Jane Wenham of Walkern, upon the bodies of Anne Thorne, Anne Street, &c. London, Printed for J. Pemberton, 1712.
3 p. l., vi, 86 p. 20 cm.

With copy 1 is bound [Bragge, Francis] Witchcraft farther display'd. London, 1712.

85

CATALOGUE OF THE CORNELL WITCHCRAFT COLLECTION

WITCHCRAFT
BF
1581
Z7
1712aa

Bragge, Francis, b. 1690.
A full and impartial account of the discovery of sorcery and witchcraft...
The impossibility of witchcraft, plainly proving, from Scripture and reason, that there never was a witch; and that it is both irrational and impious to believe there ever was. In which the depositions against Jane Wenham, lately try'd and condemn'd for a witch, at Hertford, are confuted and expos'd. 2d ed. London, Printed and sold by J. Baker, 1712.
4 p. l.,   36 p. 18cm.
Imperfect copy: p. 17-24

8
NIC
(Continued on next card)

WITCHCRAFT
BF
1581
Z7
1712aa

Bragge, Francis, b. 1690.
A full and impartial account of the discovery of sorcery and witchcraft...
The impossiblity of witchcraft... 1712. (Card 2)
erroneously numbered 25-32.
With this is bound The impossiblity of witchcraft further demonstrated. London, 1712.

1. Witchcraft--England. 2. Wenham, Jane, d. 1730. 3. Bragge, Francis, b. 1690. A full and impartial account of the discovery of sorcery and witchcraft.

8
NIC

BF
1581
Z7
1712d

Bragge, Francis, b. 1690.
The witch of Walkerne. Being, I. A full and impartial account of the discovery of sorcery, practis'd by Jane Wenham of Walkerne in Hertfordshire ... II. Witchcraft farther display'd. Containing an account of the witchcraft practis'd by Jane Wenham, since her condemnation, etc. ... III. A defense of the proceedings against Jane Wenham ... In answer to two pamphlets, entituled, 1. The impossibility of witchcraft. 2. A full confutation of
(Continued on next card)

Witchcraft
BF
1581
Z7
1712d

Bragge, Francis. The witch of Walkerne ... (Card 2)
witchcraft. IV. A general preface to the whole. 5th ed. London, Printed for E. Curll, 1712.
3 pts. in 1 v. 20cm.
Parts 2 and 3 have special title pages.

1. Witchcraft--England. 2. Wenham, Jane, d. 1730. I. Title. II. His A full and impartial account of the discovery of sorcery ...

WITCHCRAFT
BF
1581
Z7
1712b

[Bragge, Francis] b. 1690.
Witchcraft farther display'd. Containing I. An account of the witchcraft practis'd by Jane Wenham of Walkerne, in Hertfordshire, since her condemnation, upon the bodies of Anne Thorn and Anne Street. II. An answer to the most general objections against the being and power of witches: with some remarks upon the case of Jane Wenham in particular, and on Mr. Justice Powel's procedure therein. To which are added, the tryals of Florence

8
(Continued on next card)

WITCHCRAFT
BF
1581
Z7
1712b

[Bragge, Francis] Witchcraft farther display'd ... (Card 2)
Newton, a famous Irish witch, at the assizes held at Cork, anno 1661; as also of two witches at assizes held at Bury St. Edmonds in Suffolk, anno 1664, before Sir Matthew Hale ... who were found guildty and executed. London, Printed for E. Curll, 1712.
2 p. l., 39 p. 19cm.
Introduction signed: F. B.
Bound with A Full confutation of witchcraft. London, 1712.
(Continued on next card)

WITCHCRAFT
BF
1581
Z7
1712b

[Bragge, Francis] Witchcraft farther display'd ... 1712. (Card 3)

8
1. Wenham, Jane, d. 1730. 2. Witchcraft--England. I. Title.

Witchcraft
BF
1581
Z7
1712e

[Bragge, Francis] b. 1690.
Witchcraft farther display'd. Containing I. An account of the witchcraft practis'd by Jane Wenham of Walkerne, in Hertfordshire, since her condemnation, upon the bodies of Anne Thorn and Anne Street ... II. An answer to the most general objections against the being and power of witches: with some remarks upon the case of Jane Wenham in particular, and on Mr. Justice Powel's procedure therein. To which are added, the tryals of Florence Newton, a famous Irish witch, at the assizes
(Continued on next card)

Witchcraft
BF
1581
Z7
1712e

[Bragge, Francis] Witchcraft farther displayed ... (Card 2)
held at Cork, anno 1661; as also of two witches at the assizes held at Bury St. Edmonds in Suffolk, anno 1664, before Sir Matthew Hale ... who were found guilty and executed ... London, Printed for E. Curll, 1712.
[4], 39 p. 20cm.
Introduction signed: F. B.
Bound with The case of the Hertfordshire witchcraft consi der'd. London, 1712.

WITCHCRAFT
BF
1581
Z7
1712aa

Bragge, Francis, b. 1690.
Witchcraft farther display'd.
The Impossibility of witchcraft further demonstrated, both from scripture and reason, wherein several texts of scripture relating to witches are prov'd to be falsly translated, with some cursory remarks on two trifling pamphlets in defence of the existence of witches. By the author of The impossibility of witchcraft, &c. London, Printed for J. Baker, 1712.
xv, 30, [2] p. 18cm.

8
(Continued on next card)

WITCHCRAFT
BF
1581
Z7
1712aa

Bragge, Francis, b. 1690.
Witchcraft farther display'd.
The Impossibility of witchcraft further demonstrated ... 1712. (Card 2)
Bound with The impossibility of witchcraft. 2d ed. London, 1712.

1. Witchcraft. 2. Witchcraft in the Bible. 3. Bragge, Francis, b. 1690. Witchcraft farther display'd. I. The author of The impossibility of witchcraft.

8

WITCHCRAFT
BF
1581
Z7
1712f

Bragge, Francis, b. 1690, supposed author.
The Belief of witchcraft vindicated: proving, from Scripture, there have been witches; and, from reason, that there may be such still. In answer to a late pamphlet, intituled, The impossibility of witchcraft: plainly proving, from Scripture and reason, that there never was a witch, &c. By G. R., A.M. London, Printed for J. Baker, 1712.
40 p. 19cm.
Sometimes attributed to F. Bragge.

8
(Continued on next card)

WITCHCRAFT
BF
1589
B81
1852

Braid, James, 1795?-1860.
Magic, witchcraft, animal magnetism, hypnotism, and electro-biology ... 3d ed. greatly enl., embracing observations on J. C. Colquhon's "History of magic" ... London, J. Churchill, 1852.
122 p. 19cm.

1. Magic. 2. Witchcraft. 3. Animal magnetism. 4. Colquhon, John Campbell, 1785-1854. An history of magic. I. Title.

8
NIC

WITCHCRAFT
BF
1075
B81

Branch, Thomas, fl. 1753.
Thoughts on dreaming. Wherein the notion of the sensory, and the opinion that it is shut up from the inspection of the soul in sleep, and that spirits supply us with all our dreams, are examined by revelation and reason. Occasioned by an essay on the phenomenon of dreaming, in a book, entitled, An enquiry into the nature of the human soul; wherein the im materiality of the

8
NIC
(Continued on next card)

WITCHCRAFT
BF
1075
B81

Branch, Thomas, fl. 1753. Thoughts on dreaming... (Card 2)
soul is evinced from the principles of reason and philosophy. By Tho. Branch. London, Printed for R. Dodsley [etc.] 1738.
96 p. 21cm.

1. Dreams. 2. Soul. 3. Baxter, Andrew 1686?-1750. An enquiry into the nature of human soul. I. Title.

8
NIC

Witchcraft
K
B816++
1582

Brandenburg (Electorate) Laws, statutes, etc.
Peinliche Halssgerichts-Ordnung, des Durchleuchtigen Hochgebornen Fürsten vnnd Herren, Herrn Georg Friderichen Marggrauen zu Brandenburg ... Welcher massen in J. F. G. Landen vnd Fürstenthumen in peinlichen Sachen einzuziehen, zufragen, zurichten, z straffen, vnd zuuolfahren &c. Jtzo auff ein Newe wider vbersehen, gemehrt vnd verbessert sampt einer Vor rede &c. [Ansbach?]
(Continued on next card)

8

Witchcraft
K
B816++
1582

Brandenburg (Electorate) Laws, statutes, etc. Peinliche Halssgerichts-Ordnung ... 1582. (Card 2)
druckt zum Hoff durch Mattheum Pfeilschmid 1582.
3 p. l., lxii numbered, 11 unnumbered l. 31cm.
Interleaved, with ms. notes in contemporary hand; 7 l. appended at end.
With colophon.
Title in red and black, armorial device.
(Continued on next card)

8

Witchcraft
K
B816++
1582

Brandenburg (Electorate) Laws, statutes, etc. Peinliche Halssgerichts-Ordnung ... (Card 3)
With this are bound Brandenburg-Ansbach (Principality) Laws, statutes, etc. Ne Ordnung ... Onolzbach, 1720; and Brandenburg-Ansbach (Principality) Laws, statutes, etc. Anhang zu der Anno 1720. ergangenen ... Gerichts-Ordnung. Onolzbach [1725]
1. Criminal procedure--Brandenburg (Electorate). I. Georg Friedrich, Margrave of Brandenburg, 1539-1603. II. Title.

8
NIC

86

CATALOGUE OF THE CORNELL WITCHCRAFT COLLECTION

WITCHCRAFT
K
B816++
1582
    Brandenburg-Ansbach (Principality) Laws, statutes, etc.
      Anhang zu der Anno 1720. ergangenen Hoch-Fürstl. Brandenburg-Onolzbachischen Peinlichen Gerichts-Ordnung, wie solcher von der... Ober-Vormundschafftlichen Geheimen-Regierung Anno 1725 verfasst und beyzudrucken befohlen worden. Onelzbach, Gedruckt bey J. V. Lüders [1725]
      10 p. 31cm.
8 NIC
    Bound with Brandenburg (Electorate)
    (Continued on next card)

WITCHCRAFT
K
B816++
1582
    Brandenburg-Ansbach (Principality) Laws, statutes, etc. Anhang zu der Anno 1720. ergangenen ... Gerichts-Ordnung ... [1725]
    (Card 2)
    Laws, statutes, etc. Peinlichen Halssgerichts-Ordnung. [Ansbach?] 1582.
      1. Criminal procedure--Brandenburg-Ansbach (Principality) I. Title: Anhang zu der Anno 1720. ergangenen ... Brandenburg-Onolzbachischen Peinlichen Gerichts-Ordnung. II. Its Neue Ordnung des Durchlauchtigsten Fürsten ...
8 NIC

WITCHCRAFT
K
B816++
1582
    Brandenburg-Ansbach (Principality) Laws, statutes, etc.
      Neue Ordnung des Durchläuchtigsten Fürsten und Herrn, Herrn Wilhelm Friederich, Marggrafens zu Brandenburg ... Wie es in Criminal- und peinl. Sachen mit denen gültlichen und peinlichen Verhören, und inquisitorialischen Untersuchungen ... und sonsten mit denen Verurtheilten in dem Brandenburg-Onolzbachischen Fürstenthum und Landen des Burggrafthums Nürnberg unterhalb Gebürgs
8 NIC
    (Continued on next card)

WITCHCRAFT
K
B816++
1582
    Brandenburg-Ansbach (Principality) Laws, statutes, etc. Neue Ordnung ... 1720.
    (Card 2)
    gehalten werden solle. Onolzbach, Gedruckt bey J. V. Lüders, 1720.
      34 p. 31cm.
    Bound with Brandenburg (Electorate) Laws, statutes, etc. Peinliche Halssgerichts-Ordnung. Ansbach? 1582.
8 NIC
    (Continued on next card)

    Brandenburg-Ansbach (Principality). Laws, statutes, etc.
    Neue Ordnung des Durchlauchtigsten Fürsten
WITCHCRAFT
K
B816++
1582
    Brandenburg-Ansbach (Principality) Laws, statutes, etc.
      Anhang zu der Anno 1720. ergangenen Hoch-Fürstl. Brandenburg-Onolzbachischen Peinlichen Gerichts-Ordnung, wie solcher von der... Ober-Vormundschafftlichen Geheimen-Regierung Anno 1725 verfasst und beyzudrucken befohlen worden. Onelzbach, Gedruckt bey J. V. Lüders [1725]
      10 p. 31cm.
8 NIC
    Bound with Brandenburg (Electorate)
    (Continued on next card)

    Brandenburg-Ansbach (Principality) Laws, statutes, etc.
    Neue Ordnung des Durchlauchtigsten Fürsten.
WITCHCRAFT
K
B816++
1582
    Brandenburg-Ansbach (Principality) Laws, statutes, etc. Anhang zu der Anno 1720. ergangenen ... Gerichts-Ordnung ... [1725]
    (Card 2)
    Laws, statutes, etc. Peinlichen Halssgerichts-Ordnung. [Ansbach?] 1582.
      1. Criminal procedure--Brandenburg-Ansbach (Principality) I. Title: Anhang zu der Anno 1720. ergangenen ... Brandenburg-Onolzbachischen Peinlichen Gerichts-Ordnung. II. Its Neue Ordnung des Durchlauchtigsten Fürsten ...
8 NIC

Witchcraft
BV 4627
A8
B81
    Brandmüller, Johann.
      Vom Geitz Teuffel. Ein christliche und heilsame Predig, gethan zů Basel, unnd hernach auss Bitt eines christenlichen Bruders auch geschrieben. Durch Johansen Brandmüllern. Basel, P. Perna, 1579.
      30 p. 17cm.
      1. Avarice. 2. Devil. 3. Sermons, Swiss. I. Title.

Witchcraft
BF 1413
B82
    Brauchitsch, C von
      Zauberei und Hexerei.
      (In Die Grenzboten. Zeitschrift für Politik, Literatur und Kunst. Leipzig. 25cm. Jahrg. 36 (1877) p. [281]-294)
      1. Occult sciences. I. Title.

    Braun, Heinrich, 1732-1792, supposed author.
Witchcraft
BF 1565
S83
no.3
      Drey Fragen zur Vertheidigung der Hexerey. I. Ob P. Angelus März die Rede des P. Don Ferdinand Sterzingers gründlich, und II. bescheiden widerleget habe? III. Und ob wohl diese akademische Rede dem heiligen Kreutze von Scheyrn in der That nachtheilig sey? Mit einem sichern Ja beantwortet, und dem P. Angelus März selbst dedicirt von J. F. Z. ...
      [München?] 1767.
      28 p. 23cm.
8
    (Continued on next card)

    Braun, Heinrich, 1732-1792, supposed author.
Witchcraft
BF 1565
S83
no.3
      Drey Fragen zur Vertheidigung der Hexerey ... 1767. (Card 2)
      "In spite of the initials J. F. Z. (Johann Felix Zech) in the dedication, the work is probably by H. Braun. See Fieger, H. P. Don Ferdinand Sterzinger, 1907."--Note by G. L. Burr on his ms. catalog slip for this item.
      No. 3 in vol. lettered Sterzinger über Hexerei, 1766-1767.
8
    (Continued on next card)

Witchcraft
BF 1583
Z7
1689
    Braunin, Anna Maria, d. 1689, defendant.
      Acta inquisitionalia contra Annen Marien Braunin in puncto Verdächtiger Hexerey, Ambt Ostrau, 1689.
      (In Thüringisch-Sächsischen Verein für Erforschung des vaterländischen Alterthums und Erhaltung seiner Denkmale. Neue Mittheilungen aus dem Gebiet historisch-antiquarischer Forschungen. Halle. 22cm. Bd. 9 (1857) p. [76]-189)
      "Nachschrift": signed Dr. Boehlau, p. 174-189.
    (over)

Witchcraft
BF 1583
Z7
1689
    Braunin, Anna Maria, d. 1689, defendant.
      Acta inquisitionalia contra Annen Marien Braunin in puncto Verdächtiger Hexerey, Ambt Ostrau, 1689.
      (In Thüringisch-Sächsischen Verein für Erforschung des vaterländischen Alterthums und Erhaltung seiner Denkmale. Neue Mittheilungen aus dem Gebiet historisch-antiquarischer Forschungen. Halle. 22cm. Bd. 9 (1857) p. [76]-189)
      "Nachschrift": signed Dr. Boehlau, p. 174-189.

    Braunschweig-und-Lüneburg, Erich II, Herzog zu.
WITCHCRAFT
DD 491
H2
H67
1842
    Möhlmann, J   H   D
      Actenmässige Darstellung der Theilnahme der Kalenbergischen Landstände an den durch angeschuldigte Zauberei und Giftmischerei zwischen dem Landesherrn Erich dem Jungern und seiner Gemahlinn Sidonia veranlassten Missverständnissen.
      (In: Historischer Verein für Niedersachsen. Zeitschrift [under earlier title, Vaterländisches Archiv] Hannover. 19cm. 1842. p. 303- 323)
8 NIC
    (Continued on next card)

    Braunschweig-und Lüneburg, Erich II, Herzog zu.
WITCHCRAFT
DD 491
H2
H67
1842
    Havemann, Wilhelm, 1800-1869.
      Sidonia, Herzogin zu Braunschweig-Lüneburg, geborene Herzogin von Sachsen.
      (In: Historischer Verein für Niedersachsen Zeitschrift [under earlier title, Vaterländisches Archiv] Hannover. 19cm. 1842. p. 278-303)
      1. Braunschweig-und-Lüneburg, Sidonia, Herzogin zu. 2. Braunschweig-und-Lüneburg, Erich II,   Herzog zu.
8 NIC

    Braunschweig-und-Lüneburg, Sidonia, Herzogin zu.
WITCHCRAFT
DD 491
H2
H67
1842
    Möhlmann, J   H   D
      Actenmässige Darstellung der Theilnahme der Kalenbergischen Landstände an den durch angeschuldigte Zauberei und Giftmischerei zwischen dem Landesherrn Erich dem Jungern und seiner Gemahlinn Sidonia veranlassten Missverständnissen.
      (In: Historischer Verein für Niedersachsen. Zeitschrift [under earlier title, Vaterländisches Archiv] Hannover. 19cm. 1842. p. 303- 323)
8 NIC
    (Continued on next card)

    Braunschweig-und-Lüneburg, Sidonia, Herzogin zu.
WITCHCRAFT
DD 491
H2
H67
1842
    Havemann, Wilhelm, 1800-1869.
      Sidonia, Herzogin zu Braunschweig-Lüneburg, geborene Herzogin von Sachsen.
      (In: Historischer Verein für Niedersachsen Zeitschrift [under earlier title, Vaterländisches Archiv] Hannover. 19cm. 1842. p. 278-303)
      1. Braunschweig-und-Lüneburg, Sidonia, Herzogin zu. 2. Braunschweig-und-Lüneburg, Erich II,   Herzog zu.
8 NIC

WITCHCRAFT
BF 1627
B82
    Brazil. Biblioteca Nacional. Divisão de Publicações e Divulgação.
      A magia no mundo; catálogo da exposição. [Rio de Janeiro] 1971.
      79 p. illus. 23cm.
      1. Magic--Exhibitions--Catalogs.
NIC9
    I. Title.

Witchcraft
BF 1581
B82
    Brechin, Scotland. (Presbytery)
      Extracts from the records of the presbytery of Brechin, from 1639 to 1660. Dundee, W. Kidd, 1876.
      64 p. 17cm.
      1. Witchcraft--Scotland. I. Title.

CATALOGUE OF THE CORNELL WITCHCRAFT COLLECTION

Breck, Robert, 1713-1784.

BX 9321 B99 1896a
Byington, Ezra Hoyt, 1828-1901.
　　The Puritan in England and New England. By Ezra Hoyt Byington ... With an introduction by Alexander McKenzie ... London, S. Low, Marston & co., ltd., 1896.
　　xl, 406 p. 21½ᶜᵐ.
　　"List of authorities referred to": p. ₍xxv₎-xxix.

1. Puritans. 2. Witchcraft. 3. Pynchon, William, 1590?-1662. 4. Breck, Robert, 1713-1784. I. Title.

Library of Congress　　　　　　　16-9631

Witchcraft
BF 1520 S32
　　Breithaupt, Christian, 1689-1749, praeses.
　　　Commentatio secvnda De existentia daemonvm, qvam ... praeside Christiano Breithavpto ... pvblicae litteratorvm dispvtationi svbmittit avtor Iacobvs Fridericvs Ditmar ... Helmstadii, Exscripsit Herm. Dan. Hammivs ₍1722₎
　　4 p. l., 18, ₍2₎ p. 19cm. (bound in 21cm. vol.)
　　Bound with Schwerzer, Johann Adam, praeses. Daemonologia. Lipsiae, 1672.

8　　　　　　　　　(Continued on next card)

Witchcraft
BF 1520 S32
　　Breithaupt, Christian, 1689-1749, praeses.
　　　Commentatio secvnda ... ₍1722₎ (Card 2)

　　In vol. lettered Dissertationes de daemonibus. 1672-1722.

1. Demonology. I. Ditmar, Jacob Friedrich, respondent. II. Title: De existentia daemonum. III. Commentatio secvnda De existentia dae monvm.

8

Brenz, Johann, 1499-1570.

WITCHCRAFT
BR 350 B83 P33++
　　Paulus, Nicolaus, 1853-1930.
　　　Johann Brenz und die Hexenfrage.
　　(In Wissenschaftliche Beilage zur Germania. Blätter für Literatur, Wissenschaft und Kunst. Berlin. 31cm. Jahrg. 1909, Nr. 26 (1909), p. ₍201₎-204)
　　In double columns.
　　In broadside box.
　　1. Brenz, Johann, 1499-1570. 2. Witchcraft--Germany--History. I. Title.

8
NIC

Witchcraft
BF 1549 B84
　　Brévannes, Roland.
　　　L'orgie satanique à travers les siècles. Paris, C. Offenstadt, 1904.
　　268 p. illus. 19cm.

1. Demonology. I. Title.

BT 97 B84 1884
　　Brewer, Ebenezer Cobham, 1810-1897.
　　　A dictionary of miracles, imitative, realistic, and dogmatic ... by the Rev. E. Cobham Brewer ... Philadelphia, J. B. Lippincott company, 1884.
　　xliv, 582 p. illus. 21cm.

I. Title.

WITCHCRAFT
BF 1042 B84 1842
　　Brewster, Sir David, 1781-1868.
　　　Letters on natural magic, addressed to Sir Walter Scott, bart ... 5th ed. London, J. Murray, 1842.
　　viii, 351 p. illus., diagrs. 16cm.
　　₍Family library. Murray ed. v. 1₎

1. Scientific recreations. I. Title. II. Title: Natural magic. III. Scott, Sir Walter, bart., 1771-1832.

8
NIC

Witchcraft
PQ 2309 H4 L111
　　Bricaud, Joanny.
　　　J.-K. Huysmans et le satanisme, d'après des documents inédits. Paris, Bibliothèque Chacornac, 1913.
　　77 p. 17cm.

Inscribed by the author to "Monsieur J. Brien."

1. Huysmans, Joris Karl, 1848-1907. Là-bas. 2. Devil. I. Title.

Witchcraft
BX 9479 B42 B11 no.14
　　Brief, aan een heer, waar in uyt de H. Schrift getoond werd, dat'er is een quade geest, die een redelijk schepsel is buyten de ziel des mensche. Met eenige aanmerkinge over het boek, De ware oorspronk, voort en ondergank des Satans. Door I. W. Amsterdam, By J. de Veer gedrukt, 1696.
　　64 p. title vignette, illus. initial.
　　20 x 15cm.
　　4°: A-H⁴.
　　Probably by　　　　Joannes van Wijk.

3　　　　　　　(Continued on next card)

Witchcraft
BX 9479 B42 B11 no.14
　　Brief, aan een heer, waar in uyt de H. Schrift getoond werd, dat'er is een quade geest ... 1696.　　(Card 2)

　　Supports Balthasar Bekker in the controversy over his De betoverde weereld.
　　No. 14 in vol. lettered B. Bekkers sterfbed en andere tractaten.
　　1. Devil. 2. Webbers, Zacharias. De waare oorspronk, voort- en onder-gank des Satans. 3. Bekker, Balthasar, 1634-1698. De betoverde weereld. I. Wijk, Joannes van, supposed author. II. I. W. III. W., I.

8

Witchcraft
BX 9479 B42 B11 no.19
　　Brief, aan een predikant, noopens den tegenwoordigen staat des geschils, over den duivel. Amsterdam, By J. de Veer gedrukt, 1696.
　　28 p. title vignette, illus. initial.
　　20 x 15cm.
　　4°: A-C⁴, D².
　　Signed: N. N. ₍not Jacobus Schuts₎
　　On the controversy over Balthasar Bekker's De betoverde weereld.
　　No. 19 in vol. lettered B. Bekkers sterfbed en andere tractaten.

8　　　　　　　(Continued on next card)

Witchcraft
BX 9479 B42 B11 no.19
　　Brief, aan een predikant, noopens den tegenwoordigen staat des geschils, over den duivel. 1696.　　(Card 2)

1. Bekker, Balthasar, 1634-1698. De betoverde weereld. 2. Devil. I. N. N. II. N., N.

3

Brief aan een regent der Stad Amsterdam.

Witchcraft
BF 1410 B42 Z82 no.1
　　₍Walten, Ericus₎ 1663-1697.
　　　Brief aan een regent der Stad Amsterdam. Behelsende een regtsinnige uytlegginge, en redenmatige verklaringe, van de articulen die D. Balthasar Bekker op den 22 Januarij 1692 heeft overgeleverd aan de Classis van Amsterdam, wegens sijn uytgegeven boek, genaamd, De betoverde wereld; met eenige philosophische redeneringen, seer nut en dienstig om verscheiden dingen in 't selve boek wel te verstaan; en een kort verhaal van den uytslag der kerke　　lijke proceduyren, daa

　　　　　　(Continued on next card)

Brief aan een regent der Stad Amsterdam.

Witchcraft
BF 1410 B42 Z82 no.1
　　₍Walten, Ericus₎ 1663-1697. Brief aan een regent der Stad Amsterdam. 1692.　　(Card 2)

　　over gehouden. ... Gravenhage, By M. Uytwerf, boekverkooper, 1692.
　　135 p. ₍p. 136 blank₎ title vignette.
　　19 x 15cm.
　　4°: A-R⁴.
　　Signed: Ericus Walten. 18. Mey 1692.
　　Van der Linde　41.
　　No. 1 in　　vol. lettered Over Bekkers Betoverde　　wereld. 1692.

8　　　　　　(Continued on next card)

Brief aan sijn Excellentie, de Heer Graaf van Portland, &c. &c. Rakende de persoon en het gevoelen van Dr. B. Bekker

Witchcraft
BF 1410 B42 Z56 v.2 no.4
　　Walten, Ericus, 1663-1697.
　　　Brief aan sijn Excellentie, de Heer Graaf van Portland, &c. &c. Rakende de persoon en het gevoelen van Dr. B. Bekker, en 't geen tegen hem, by eenige van sijn partyen, word verwagt, en uytgestrooyd, te opsigte van sijn Koninglijke Majesteyt van Groot Britanjen. ... Door Ericus Walten ... Gedrukt voor den auteur. Gravenhage By Meyndert Uytwerf, boekverkoper, 1692.
　　80 p. title vignette, illus. initial.
　　19 x 15cm.

4　　　　　　(Continued on next card

Brief aan sijn Excellentie, de Heer Graaf van Portland, &c. &c. Rakende de persoon en het gevoelen van Dr. B. Bekker

Witchcraft
BF 1410 B42 Z56 v.2 no.4
　　Walten, Ericus, 1663-1697. Brief aan sijn Excellentie, de Heer Graaf van Portland ... 1692.　　(Card
　　4°: A-K⁴.
　　Van der Linde 174.
　　No. 4 in vol. lettered: Bekker II.

1. Bekker, Balthasar, 1634-1698. 2. Devil. I. Portland, William Bentinck, earl of, 1649-　　1709. II. William III, King of Great　　Britain, 1649-1709. III. Title.

8

Witchcraft
BF 1410 B42 Z56 v.2 no.9
　　Brief, geschreven van Uitregt, aan een vriend tot Amsterdam, over het boek genaamd De betoverde wereld. Als mede wat daar omtrent is voorgevallen. ₍Amsterdam? 1691?₎
　　19 p. ₍p. 20 blank₎ 19 x 15cm.
　　4°: A-B⁴, C².
　　Dated: Uitregt 2/12 September 1691.
　　Van der Linde 57.
　　No. 9 in vol. lettered Bekker II.
　　1. Bekker,　　Balthasar, 1634-1698. De betoverde　　weereld.

3

Witchcraft
BF 1410 B42 Z86 no.4
　　Brief, geschreven van Uitregt, aan een vriend tot Amsterdam, over het boek genaamd De betoverde wereld. Als mede wat daar omtrent is voorgevallen. ₍Amsterdam? 1691?₎
　　19 p. ₍p. 20 blank₎ 20 x 16 cm.
　　4°: A-B⁴, C².
　　Van der Linde 57.
　　No. 4 in vol. lettered Tractaten voor en tegen B. Bekker.

8

CATALOGUE OF THE CORNELL WITCHCRAFT COLLECTION

Witchcraft
BF
1581
A2
W81
1866a
no.4

A brief history of witchcraft, with especial reference to the witches of Northamptonshire.
[Marshall, F]
A brief history of witchcraft, with especial reference to the witches of Northamptonshire. Collected in great part from original sources. Northampton, J. Taylor, 1866.
18 p. illus. 22cm.
No.4 in box lettered Witchcraft in Northamptonshire.
1. Witchcraft—History. 2. Witchcraft—Northamptonshire, England. I. Title.

8

Witchcraft
BF
1410
B42
Z86
no.3

Brief van Baltasar [sic] Bekker, S. T. D. predikant tot Amsterdam, aan de Heeren Joost de Smeth, Willem Weyer ...
Bekker, Balthasar, 1634-1698.
Brief van Baltasar [sic] Bekker, S. T. D. predikant tot Amsterdam, aan de Heeren Joost de Smeth, Willem Weyer, en Nikolaas vander Hagen, so tegenwoordig dienende als meermaals gediend hebbende ouderlingen der Gereformeerde Kerk aldaar. Tot antwoord op den brief van den Professor vander Waeyen aan deselven, gesteld voor sijn boek genaamd De betoverde weereld van B. B. ondersocht en wederleid. Hier achter is

(Continued on next card)

8

Witchcraft
BF
1410
B42
Z86
no.3

Brief van Baltasar [sic] Bekker, S. T. D. predikant tot Amsterdam, aan de Heeren Joost de Smeth, Willem Weyer ...
Bekker, Balthasar, 1634-1698. Brief ... aan de Heeren Joost de Smeth, Willem Weyer, en Nikolaas vander Hagen ... 1693. (Card 2)
bygevoegd d'Opdraght-brief desselfden professors aan sijne Vorst. Doorl. den Prinsse van Nassau Stadhouder &c. en d'Ed. Mog. Heeren Gedeputeerde Staten van Friesland, voor het selfde boek, met een antwoord op den selven. Amsterdam, By D. van den

(Continued on next card)

8

Witchcraft
BF
1410
B42
Z86
no.3

Brief van Baltasar [sic] Bekker, S. T. D. predikant tot Amsterdam, aan de Heeren Joost de Smeth, Willem Weyer ...
Bekker, Balthasar, 1634-1698. Brief ... aan de Heeren Joost de Smeth, Willem Weyer, en Nikolaas vander Hagen ... 1693. (Card 3)
Dalen, boekverkoper, 1693.
16, 15*-16*, 17-24 p. title vignette, illus. initial. 19 x 15cm.
4°: A-B^4, B*^{1}, C^4.
Van der Linde 159.
No. 3 in vol. lettered Tractaten voor en tegen B. Bekker.

(Continued on next card)

8

Witchcraft
BF
1410
B42
Z86
no.2

Brief van Balthasar Bekker, S. Th. Dr. predikant tot Amsterdam. Aan den Heer Joannes vander Waeyen.
Bekker, Balthasar, 1634-1698.
Brief van Balthasar Bekker, S. Th. Dr. predikant tot Amsterdam. Aan den Heer Joannes vander Waeyen, S. Theol. Dr. en professor in de loffelike en vermaarde Universiteit tot Franeker. In antwoord op desselven brief, waarmede hy hem sijn boek tegen De betoverde weereld onlangs uitgegeven, heeft toegesonden. [Amsterdam? 1693]
8 p. illus. initial. 19 x 15cm.

(Continued on next card)

8

Witchcraft
BF
1410
B42
Z86
no.2

Brief van Balthasar Bekker, S. Th. Dr. predikant tot Amsterdam. Aan den Heer Joannes vander Waeyen.
Bekker, Balthasar, 1634-1698. Brief ... aan den Heer Joannes vander Waeyen ... [1693] (Card 2)
4°: A^4.
Caption title.
Dated: Amsterdam den 8 Augusty 1693.
Van der Linde 157.
No. 2 in vol. lettered Tractaten voor en tegen B. Bekker.
1. His De betoverde weereld. I. Waaijen, Johannes van der, 1639-1701. II. Title.

8

Witchcraft
BF
1410
B42
Z56
v.1
no.7

Brief van Balthasar Bekker ... aan ... twee eerwaardige predikanten D. Joannes Aalstius ... ende D. Paulus Steenwinkel ...
Bekker, Balthasar, 1634-1698.
Brief van Balthasar Bekker S. T. D. en predikant tot Amsterdam. Aan twee eerwaardige predikanten D. Joannes Aalstius tot Hoornaar, ende D. Paulus Steenwinkel tot Schelluinen, over derselver Zedige aanmerkingen op een deel des tweeden boex van sijn werk genaamd De betoverde weereld. Amsterdam, By D. vanden Dalen, boekverkoper, 1693.
11 p. [p. 12 blank] title vignette, illus. initial. 19 x 16cm.

(Continued on next card)

8

Witchcraft
BF
1410
B42
Z56
v.1
no.7

Brief van Balthasar Bekker ... aan ... twee eerwaardige predikanten D. Joannes Aalstius ... ende D. Paulus Steenwinkel ...
Bekker, Balthasar, 1634-1698. Brief van Balthasar Bekker ... aan ... Joannes Aalstius ... 1693. (Card 2)
4°: A^4, B^2.
Letter autographed by Bekker.
Van der Linde 72.
No. 7 in vol. lettered Bekker I.
1. Aalst, Johannes, 1660-1712. Zedige aanmerkingen. I. Aalst, Johannes, 1660-1712. II. Steenwinkel, Paulus, d. 1740. III. Title.

8

Witchcraft
BF
1410
B42
Z56
v.3
no.14

Brief van de Eerwaarde Kerkenraad van Utrecht, aan de Eerw. Kerkenraad van Amsterdam.
Nederlandse Hervormde Kerk. Kerkenraden. Utrecht.
Briev van de Eerwaarde Kerkenraad van Utrecht, aan de Eerw. Kerkenraad van Amsterdam, daar toe tendeerende dat de autheur van het boek, De betoverde weereld genaamt, niet wederom tot de bediening in de Gereformeerde Kerke mach werden toegelaten. [Amsterdam, 1692?]
4 p. 20 x 15cm.
4°: A^2.

(Continued on next card)

8

Witchcraft
BF
1410
B42
Z56
v.3
no.14

Brief van de Eerwaarde Kerkenraad van Utrecht, aan de Eerw. Kerkenraad van Amsterdam.
Nederlandse Hervormde Kerk. Kerkenraden. Utrecht. Briev ... aan de Eerw. Kerkenraad van Amsterdam ... [1692?] (Card 2)
Caption title.
"Gedrukt na de copie van Johannes Dale."
Variant of van der Linde 43, which is the printing by Johannes Dalé.
No. 14 in vol. lettered Bekker III.
1. Bekker, Balthasar, 1634-1698. I. Nederlandse Hervormde Kerk. Kerkenraden. Amsterdam. II. Title.

8

Witchcraft
BF
1410
B42
Z56
v.3
no.27

Brief van den schrijver des boeks De betoverde weereld genaamd, aan den eerwaardigen heere Everhard van der Hooght ...
[Bekker, Balthasar,] 1634-1698.
Brief van den schrijver des boeks De betoverde weereld genaamd, aan den eerwaardigen heere Everhard van der Hooght, yverigen leeraar van 's heeren gemeente tot Niewendam. Amsterdam, By G. Borstius, boekverkoper [1691]
11 p. [p. 12 is blank] title vignette, illus. initial.
4°: A^4, [B^2]
Van der Linde 105.
No. 27 in vol. lettered Bekker III.

(Continued on next card)

8

Witchcraft
BF
1410
B42
Z56
v.3
no.18

Brief van Do. Balthasar Bekker aan zijn huisvrouw, Frouk Fullenia, benevens een antwoord van de christelijke gemeente t'Amsterdam, op de selve: mitsgaders den fameusen antwoorder rustigh afgeslagen: waar by gevoeghd, een antwoord op de naam van deselve Frouk Fullenia. [n. p.] Gedrukt na de copy tot Uytrecht by J. Michielsz [1692?]
[12] p. title vignette. 19 x 15cm.
4°: A^4, B^2.

(Continued on next card)

8

Witchcraft
BF
1410
B42
Z56
v.3
no.18

Brief van Do. Balthasar Bekker aan zijn huisvrouw, Frouk Fullenia ... [1692?] (Card 2)
Four poems. The first, by Bekker, appears in vol. 1 of his De betoverde weereld. The others are signed L. B. v. W., L. v. D., and S. T. v. W.
Van der Linde 195.
No. 18 in vol. lettered Bekker III.
1. Bekker, Balthasar, 1634-1698. De betoverde weereld. I. Bekker, Balthasar, 1634-1698. Aan Frouk Fullenia.

8

Witchcraft
BX
9479
B42
B11
no.17

Brief van L. P. aan Herman Bouman; eerst in 't bysonder aan hem geschreeven, en nu door hem, met verlof van den autheur, gemeen gemaakt: behelsende sommige redenen waarom hy de soo genaamde Sleutel der geesten enz. van M. van Diepen, en J. Hubener niet, ofte niet zoodanig alse daar ligt, behoorde te beantwoorden; en teffens een volstrekte omkeering van de gronden van dat woest geschrift. Amsterdam, By R. Blokland, boekverkoper, 1699

(Continued on next card)

8

Witchcraft
BX
9479
B42
B11
no.17

Brief van L. P. aan Herman Bouman ... 1699. (Card 2)
2 p. l., 12 p. title and end page vignettes, illus. initials. 20 x 15cm.
4°: π^2, A^4, B^2.
Written by a supporter of Balthazar Bekker, whom Diepen and Hubener attacked.
No. 17 in vol. lettered B. Bekkers sterfbed en andere tractaten.
1. Diepen, Marcus van. De sleutel der geesten. 2. Bekker, Balthasar,

(Continued on next card)

8

Witchcraft
BX
9479
B42
B11
no.17

Brief van L. P. aan Herman Bouman ... 1699. (Card 3)
1634-1698. I. Bouman, Herman. II. L. P. III. . P., L.

8

Witchcraft
BF
1410
B42
Z56
v.2
no.24

Brief van Lambert Joosten, met een antwoord op de selve, van Herman Bouman ...
Bouman, Herman.
Brief van Lambert Joosten, met een antwoord op de selve, van Herman Bouman, waar in gehandelt word van de engelen en geesten, &c. En welk laatste een zedige verantwoordinge behelft, van de swaare gevolgen, of besluyten, die den autheur des briefs, uyt het gevoelen van H: B: tracht te maaken. Amsterdam, By A. van Damme, boekverkoper, 1696.
42 p. title vignette, illus. initial. 19 x 15cm.

(Continued on next card)

8

Witchcraft
BF
1410
B42
Z56
v.2
no.24

Brief van Lambert Joosten, met een antwoord op de selve, van Herman Bouman ...
Bouman, Herman. Brief van Lambert Joosten, met een antwoord op de selve ... 1696. (Card 2)
4°: A-E^4, F1.
Black letter (except for introduction)
Bouman divides Joosten's letter into sentences, and gives a refutation after each.
Van der Linde 80.
No. 24 in vol. lettered Bekker II.
1. Angels. 2. Spirits. I. Joosten, Lambert. II. Title.

8

CATALOGUE OF THE CORNELL WITCHCRAFT COLLECTION

Witchcraft
BF 1711 B85
A Briefe description of the notoriovs life of Iohn Lambe, otherwise called Doctor Lambe, together with his ignominiovs death. Amsterdam, Printed, 1628.
21 p. 22cm.

Witchcraft
BF 1711 B85 1730
A briefe description of the notoriovs life of Iohn Lambe, otherwise called Doctor Lambe, together with his ignominiovs death. Amsterdam, Printed 1628. [London] Barker, printer [173-]

Facsimile reprint.

1. Lambe, John, d. 1628.

Witchcraft
BF 1563 W81++ no.8
Jorden, Edward.
A briefe discourse of a disease called the suffocation of the mother.
A briefe discovrse of a disease called the suffocation of the mother. Written vppon occasion which hath beene of late taken thereby, to suspect possession of an euill spirit, or some such like supernaturall power. Wherin is declared that diuers strange actions and passions of the body of man, which in the common opinion, are imputed to the Diuell, haue their true naturall causes, and do accompanie this disease. London, Printed by J. Windet, 1603. [London, at the British Museum, 1923]
(Continued on next card)

Witchcraft
BF 1563 W81++ no.8
Jorden, Edward. A briefe discovrse of a disease... 1603. [1923] (Card 2)
[58] p. 17cm.
Signatures: A-G⁴, H¹.
Photocopy (negative) 58 p. on 26 l. 20 x 32cm.
No. 8 in vol. lettered: Witchcraft tracts, chapbooks and broadsides, 1579-1704; rotograph copies.
1. Glover, Mary, fl. 1603.
2. Exorcism.

Witchcraft
BF 1052 B85 1853
Brierre de Boismont, Alexandre Jacques François, 1798-1881.
Des hallucinations.
Hallucinations: or, The rational history of apparitions, visions, dreams, ecstasy, magnetism, and somnambulism. By A. Brierre de Boismont ... 1st American, from the 2d enl. and improved Paris ed. Philadelphia, Lindsay and Blakiston, 1853.
xx, [17]-553 p. 20ᶜᵐ.

1. Hallucinations and illusions. I. Title.
20-8491
Library of Congress   BF1052.B8 1853   [28b1]

Witchcraft
BF 1052 B85 1853
Brierre de Boismont, Alexandre Jacques François, 1798-1881.
Hallucinations: or, The rational history of apparitions, visions, dreams, ecstasy, magnetism, and somnambulism. By A. Brierre de Boismont ... 1st American, from the 2d enl. and improved Paris ed. Philadelphia, Lindsay and Blakiston, 1853.
xx, [17]-553 p. 20ᶜᵐ.

1. Hallucinations and illusions. I. Title. II. Title: The rational history of apparitions. III. His Des hallucinations.
20-8491
Library of Congress   BF1052.B8 1853   [28b1]

Witchcraft
BX 9477 U92
Briev van de Eerwaerde Classis van Utreht, aan de Eerwaerde Classis van Amsterdam.
Nederlandse Hervormde Kerk. Classes. Utrecht.
Briev van de Eerwaerde Classis van Utreht, aan de Eerwaerde Classis van Amsterdam. Daer toe dienende, dat Dr. Bekker autheur van dat fameuse boek, De betoverde werelt genaamt, niet wederom tot de bedieninge van het predikampt in de Gereformeerde Kerck toegelaten werde. Gedruckt na de copy tot Utrecht. Amsterdam, By A. D. Oossaan, boekverkooper, 1692.
(Continued on next card)
8

Witchcraft
BX 9477 U92
Briev van de Eerwaerde Classis van Utreht, aan de Eerwaerde Classis van Amsterdam.
Nederlandse Hervormde Kerk. Classes. Utrecht. Briev ... aan de Eerwaerde Classis van Amsterdam. 1692. (Card 2)
6 p. [p. 7-8 blank] title vignette, illus. initial. 22 x 17cm.
4°: A⁴.
Dated: 18 Martii ... 1692.
Van der Linde 34.
1. Bekker, Balthasar, 1634-1698. I. Nederlandse Hervormde Kerk. Classes. Amsterdam. II. Title.

Witchcraft
BF 1410 B42 Z56 v.3 no.13
Brieven van eenige kerkenraden buyten de Provintie van Holland.
Nederlandse Hervormde Kerk.
Brieven van eenige kerkenraden buyten de Provintie van Holland, namentlijk van 't Eerw. Classis van Walcheren, van de Eerwaardige Kerkenraden van Middelburg, Utrecht, Leeuwaarden, Groningen, aen de Eerwardige Kerkenraad van Rotterdam, tot antwoord op haren Circulaire brief, rakende de sake van Dr. B. Bekker. Rotterdam, By R. van Doesburg, boekverkooper, 1692.
16 p. title vignette, illus. initials. 19 x 15cm.
(Continued on next card)
8

Witchcraft
BF 1410 B42 Z56 v.3 no.13
Brieven van eenige kerkenraden buyten de Provintie van Holland.
Nederlandse Hervormde Kerk. Brieven van eenige kerkenraden ... 1692. (Card 2)
4°: A-B⁴.
Van der Linde 36.
No. 13 in vol. lettered Bekker III.
1. Bekker, Balthasar, 1634-1698. De betoverde weereld. 2. Nederlandse Hervormde Kerk. Kerkenraden. Rotterdam. Circulaire brief ... wegens de saake van Dr. Balthasar Bekker. I. Nederlandse Hervormde Kerk. Kerkenraden. Rotterdam. II. Title.
8

Witchcraft
BF 1581 B85 1962
Briggs, Katharine Mary.
Pale Hecate's team; an examination of the beliefs on witchcraft and magic among Shakespeare's contemporaries and his immediate successors. London, Routledge and K. Paul [1962]
viii, 291 p. illus. 23 cm.

1. Witchcraft—Gt. Brit. 2. Magic. 3. Folk-lore—Gt. Brit. I. Title.
BF1581.B7   133.40942   62-6110 ‡
Library of Congress   [2]

Briggs, Katharine Mary.
BF 1566 W81
The Witch figure; folklore essays by a group of scholars in England honouring the 75th birthday of Katharine M. Briggs. Edited by Venetia Newall. London, Boston, Routledge & Kegan Paul [1973]
xiii, 239 p. illus. 23 cm.
Includes bibliographical references.
CONTENTS.—Michaelis-Jena, R. Katharine M. Briggs.—Blacker, C. Animal witchcraft in Japan.—Davidson, H. R. E. Hostile magic in the Icelandic sagas.—Dean-Smith, M. The ominous wood.—Grinsell, L. V. Witchcraft at some prehistoric sites.—Hole, C. Some instances of image-magic in Great Britain.—Newall, V. The Jew as a witch figure.—Parrinder, G. The witch as vict im.—Ross, A. The
NIC   COOdc See next card

Briggs, Katharine Mary.
BF 1566 W81
The Witch figure; ... [1973] (Card 2)
divine hag of the pagan Celts.—Simpson, J. Olaf Tryggvason versus the powers of darkness.—White, B. Cain's kin.—Widdowson, J. The witch as a frightening and threatening figure.—Publications by Katharine M. Briggs (p. 221)

NIC   COOdc   73-8307

Briggs, Katharine Mary.
BF 1566 W81
The Witch figure; folklore essays by a group of scholars in England honouring the 75th birthday of Katharine M. Briggs. Edited by Venetia Newall. London, Boston, Routledge & Kegan Paul [1973]
xiii, 239 p. illus. 23 cm.
Includes bibliographical references.
CONTENTS.—Michaelis-Jena, R. Katharine M. Briggs.—Blacker, C. Animal witchcraft in Japan.—Davidson, H. R. E. Hostile magic in the Icelandic sagas.—Dean-Smith, M. The ominous wood.—Grinsell, L. V. Witchcraft at some prehistoric sites.—Hole, C. Some instances of image-magic in Great Britain.—Newall, V. The Jew as a witch figure.—Parrinder, G. The witch as vict im.—Ross, A. The
NIC   COOdc See next card

Briggs, Katharine Mary.
BF 1566 W81
The Witch figure; ... [1973] (Card 2)
divine hag of the pagan Celts.—Simpson, J. Olaf Tryggvason versus the powers of darkness.—White, B. Cain's kin.—Widdowson, J. The witch as a frightening and threatening figure.—Publications by Katharine M. Briggs (p. 221)

NIC   COOdc   73-83

Brinck, Hendrik, 1645-1723.
see
Brink, Hendrik, 1645-1723.

Witchcraft
BF 1410 B42 Z56 v.2 no.22
Brink, Hendrik, 1645-1723.
De godslasteringen van den amsterdamsche predikant Bekker.
Noomtjins, Zalomon.
Spiegel voor den verwarden, en warzoekende Haggebher Philaleethees. Waar in, uit zyne brieven, enz. getoond word, zyne onkunde, en verwarring, zoo in taal, als in zaaken. Of een briev van Zalomon Noomtjins, tot Amstel Geschreeven als zynen vriend C. S. S. tot Buiksloot. Inhoudende (neevens andere zaake voornaamelijk, eenige aanmerkingen, over de persoon, en de 6 brieven, enz. van Haggebher Philaleethees. Als meede over de briev, en
(Continued on next card)

Brink, Hendrik, 1645-1723.
De godslasteringen van den amsterdamschen predikant Bekker.
Witchcraft
BF 1410 B42 Z56 v.2 no.22
Noomtjins, Zalomon. Spiegel voor den verw. en warzoekende Haggebher Philaleethees. 1 (Card 2)
perzoon van Everardus van der Hooght, en d by ook over zyne Aanmerkingen, over de ord een welgestelde predikatie. Mitsgaders d'ontdekking, der lasteringen van Brink. Amste By D. van den Dalen, boekverkooper, 1692.
33, [1] p. title and other vignettes. 19 x 15cm.
(Continued on next c

CATALOGUE OF THE CORNELL WITCHCRAFT COLLECTION

Witchcraft
BF
1410
B42
Z56
v.2
no.22

Brink, Hendrik, 1645-1723.
De godslasteringen van den amsterdamschen predikant Bekker.
Noomtjins, Zalomon. Spiegel voor den verwarden, en warzoekende Haggebher Philaleethees. 1692. (Card 3)

4°: A-D⁴, E1.
Black letter (except for introduction)
Attacks critics of Balthasar Bekker's De betoverde weereld.
G. L. Burr suggests Noomtjins may be a pseudonym for Bekker.
Haggebher is a pseudonym of E. van der Hooght.

(Continued on next card)

Witchcraft
BF
1410
B42
Z56
v.2
no.22

Brink, Hendrik, 1645-1723.
De godslasteringen van den amsterdamschen predikant Bekker.
Noomtjins, Zalomon. Spiegel voor den verwarden, en warzoekende Haggebher Philaleethees. 1692. (Card 4)

Van der Linde 111.
No. 22 in vol. lettered Bekker II.
1. Hooght, Everard van der, d. 1716. 2. Brink, Hendrik, 1645-1723. De godslasteringen van den amsterdamschen predikant Bekker. 3. Bekker, Balthasar, 1634-1698. De betoverde weereld. I. Title. II. Bekker, Balthasar, 1634-1698, supposed author.

Witchcraft
BF
1410
B42
Z56
v.2
no.19

Brink, Hendrik, 1645-1723.
De godslasteringen van den amsterdamschen predikant Bekker.
[Schuts, Jacobus]
Seedige aanmerkinge over de voorreden, genaamt: De godtslasteringe van den amsterdamsche predikant Dr. Bekker, ter waarschouwinge van alle vroome in den lande wederleyt, in de voorreden voor de toetsteen der waarheyt, ende der meyninge, door Henrikus Brink, &c. Door N. N. Amsterdam, By D. van den Dalen, boekverkooper, 1691.
8, 88 p. title vignette, illus. initial. 19 x 15cm.

(Continued on next card)

Witchcraft
BF
1410
B42
Z56
v.2
no.19

Brink, Hendrik, 1645-1723.
De godslasteringen van den amsterdamschen predikant Bekker.
[Schuts, Jacobus] Seedige aanmerkinge over de voorreden ... 1691. (Card 2)

4°: A⁴, A-L⁴.
Black letter.
Signed on back of t. p.: J: C:
Incomplete: all after first gathering wanting.
Van der Linde 84.
No. 19 in vol. lettered Bekker II.
1. Brink, Hendrik, 1645-1723.

(Continued on next card)

Brink, Henrikus, 1645-1723.
see
Brink, Hendrik, 1645-1723.

Witchcraft

Brinley, John.
A discovery of the impostures of witches and astrologers... London, Printed for J. Wright, and sold by E. Milward, 1680.
127 p. 15cm.

Part 2 has special t. p.: "The second part, being a discourse of the impostures practised in judicial astrology. London, Printed in the year 1680."
1. Witchcraft. 2. Astrology. I. Title.

BF
1553
B85

Brisset, Joseph Mathurin, 1792-1856.
Le mauvais oeil, tradition dalmate, suivi d'une nouvelle française. Paris, U. Canel, 1833.
303 p. 22cm.

1. Evil eye. 2. Superstition. I. Title.

Witchcraft
BF
1251
B86
A7

Britten, Mrs. Emma (Hardinge) ed.
[Britten, William] supposed author.
Art magic; or, Mundane, sub-mundane and super-mundane spiritism. A treatise in three parts and twenty-three sections: descriptive of art magic, spiritism, the different orders of spirits in the universe known to be related to, or in communication with man; together with directions for invoking, controlling, and discharging spirits, and the uses and abuses, dangers and possibilities of magical art ... New York, The author, 1876.
2 p. l., 467 p. front. (incl. ports.) plates. 22½ cm.
Copyrighted by William Britten.
Ed. by Emma Hardinge Britten.
1. Spiritualism. 2. Magic. I. Britten, Mrs. Emma (Hardinge) ed. II. Title.

Library of Congress   BF1251.B83
                                10-34683

Witchcraft
BF
1251
B86
A7

[Britten, William] supposed author.
Art magic; or, Mundane, sub-mundane and super-mundane spiritism. A treatise in three parts and twenty-three sections: descriptive of art magic, spiritism, the different orders of spirits in the universe known to be related to, or in communication with man; together with directions for invoking, controlling, and discharging spirits, and the uses and abuses, dangers and possibilities of magical art ... New York, The author, 1876.
2 p. l., 467 p. front. (incl. ports.) plates. 22½ cm.
Copyrighted by William Britten.
Ed. by Emma Hardinge Britten.
1. Spiritualism. 2. Magic. I. Britten, Mrs. Emma (Hardinge) ed. II. Title. III. Title: Mundane, sub-mundane and super-mundane spiritism.

Library of Congress   BF1251.B83

Witchcraft
BF
1581
B86

Brodie-Innes, John William, 1848-
Scottish witchcraft trials. By J. W. Brodie-Innes, master of the rolls to the Sette of odd volumes ... London, Imprinted at the Chiswick press, 1891.
66 p. 1 l. 14 x 11½ cm. (Half-title: Privately printed opuscula. Issued to members of the Sette of odd volumes. no. xxv)
"This edition is limited to 245 copies, and is imprinted for private circulation only. no. 145."
"Read before the Sette at a meeting held at Limmer's hotel, on Friday, 7th November, 1890."
Lists of club's publications and members: p. [51]-66.

1. Witchcraft—Scotland. I. Title.

                                                17-17243
Library of Congress   AC1.S5 no.25

Witchcraft
BF
1555
B86++
1668

Brognolo, Candido.
Alexicacon hoc est Opvs de maleficiis, ac morbis maleficis. Dvobvs tomis distribvtvm. Quorum alter quatuor de eorum cognitione disput. continet. Quorum alter totidem de eorum curatione disput. continet ... In qvarvm calce qvae sint partes exorcistae, quaeue medici, in eis cognoscendis, ac curandis, concluditur ... Prodit qvinqve indicibvs locvpletatvm. Venetiis, Typis Io: Baptistae Catanei, 1668.

(Continued on next card)

Witchcraft
BF
1555
B86++
1668

Brognolo, Candido. Alexicacon ... 1668. (Card 2)

2 v. in 1. 34cm.
Added general t. p., engraved. Each vol. has also special t. p.

1. Demoniac possession. 2. Demonomania. 3. Witchcraft. 4. Exorcism. I. Title.

Witchcraft
BF
1555
B86
1714

Brognolo, Candido.
Alexicacon hoc est De maleficiis, ac morbis maleficis cognoscendis. Opus tam exorcistis, quam medicis, ac theologis, confessariis, parochis, inquisitoribus, ac in quacunque necessitate constitutis, utilissimum. Venetiis, Apud Nicolaum Pezzana, 1714.
2 v. 24cm.

With this is bound the author's Manuale exorcistarum, ac parochorum. Venetiis, 1714.

I. Title.

Witchcraft
BX
2340
B86
1725

Brognolo, Candido.
Brognolo recopilado, e substanciado com addictamentos, de gravissimos authores. Methodo mais breve, muy suave, e utilissimo de exorcizar, expelindo Demonios, e desfazendo feytiços: segundo os dictames do Sagrado Evangelho ... Collegido, rezumido, e tradusido da lingua Latina, Italiana, e Hespanhola na Portugueza para clareza dos Exorcistas, e bem dos Exorcizados. Por Fr. Joseph de Jesus Maria Ullyssiponense ... Lisboa Oriental, Na Officina Ferreyriana, 1725.

(Continued on next card)

Witchcraft
BX
2340
B86
1725

Brognolo, Candido. Brognolo recopilado ... 1725. (Card 2)

[24], 347 p. 15cm.

Translation of Manuale exorcistarum.

1. Exorcism. I. Brognolo, Candido. Manuale exorcistarum--Portuguese. II. Joseph de Jesus Maria, tr. III. Title.

Witchcraft
BX
2340
B86
1658

Brognolo, Candido.
Manvale exorcistarvm, ac parochorvm, hoc est Tractatvs de cvratione, ac protectione divina, in quo, variis reprobatis erroribus, verus, certus, securus, Catholicus, Apostolicus, & Euangelicus eiiciendi daemones ab hominibus, & è rebus ad homines spectantibus: curandi infirmos: ab inimicis se tuendi: Deúmque in cunctis necessitatibus propitium habendi modus traditur ... Prodit quatuor Indicibus locupletatum. Lvgdvni, Apud Joannem Radisson, 1658.

(Continued on next card)

Witchcraft
BX
2340
B86
1658

Brognolo, Candido. Manvale exorcistarvm ... 1658. (Card 2)

[24], 452, [40] p. 24cm.

1. Exorcism. I. Title: Manuale exorcistarum.

Witchcraft
BF
1555
B86
1714

Brognolo, Candido.
Manuale exorcistarum, ac parochorum: hoc est Tractatus de curatione ac protectione divina; in quo reprobatis erroribus, verus, certus, securus, catholicus, apostolicus, & evangelicus eiiciendi daemones ab hominibus, & è rebus ad homines spectantibus: curandi infirmos: ab inimicis se tuendi: Deumque in cunctis necessitatibus propitium habendi modus traditur ... Venetiis, Apud Nicolaum Pezzana, 1714.
[22], 352, [24] p. 24cm.

(Continued on next card)

CATALOGUE OF THE CORNELL WITCHCRAFT COLLECTION

Witchcraft
BF 1555 B86 1714
Brognolo, Candido. Manuale exorcistarum ... 1714. (Card 2)

Bound with the author's Alexicacon. Venetiis, 1714.

1. Exorcism. I. Title. II. Title: Tractatus de curatione ac protectione divina.

Witchcraft
BX 2340 B86 1725
Brognolo, Candido.
Manuale exorcistarum--Portugese.
Brognolo, Candido.
Brognolo recopilado, e substanciado com addictamentos, de gravissimos authores. Methodo mais breve, muy suave, e utilissimo de exorcizar, expelindo Demonios, e desfazendo feytiços: segundo os dictames do Sagrado Evangelho ... Collegido, rezumido, e tradusido da lingua Latina, Italiana, e Hespanhola na Portugueza para clareza dos Exorcistas, e bem dos Exorcizados. Por Fr. Joseph de Jesus Maria Ullyssiponense ... Lisboa Oriental, Na Officina Ferreyriana, 1725.

(Continued on next card)

Witchcraft
BX 2340 B86 1725
Brognolo, Candido.
Manuale exorcistarum--Portugese.
Brognolo, Candido. Brognolo recopilado ... 1725. (Card 2)

[24], 347 p. 15cm.

Translation of Manuale exorcistarum.

1. Exorcism. I. Brognolo, Candido. Manuale exorcistarum--Portugese. II. Joseph de Jesus Maria, tr.

Witchcraft
BX 2340 B86 1725
Brognolo recopilado, e substanciado com addictamentos, de gravissimos authores.
Brognolo, Candido.
Brognolo recopilado, e substanciado com addictamentos, de gravissimos authores. Methodo mais breve, muy suave, e utilissimo de exorcizar, expelindo Demonios, e desfazendo feytiços: segundo os dictames do Sagrado Evangelho ... Collegido, rezumido, e tradusido da lingua Latina, Italiana, e Hespanhola na Portugueza para clareza dos Exorcistas, e bem dos Exorcizados. Por Fr. Joseph de Jesus Maria Ullyssiponense ... Lisboa Oriental, Na Officina Ferreyriana, 1725.

(Continued on next card)

Witchcraft
BX 2340 B86 1725
Brognolo recopilado, e substanciado com addictamentos, de gravissimos authores.
Brognolo, Candido. Brognolo recopilado ... 1725. (Card 2)

[24], 347 p. 15cm.

Translation of Manuale exorcistarum.

1. Exorcism. I. Brognolo, Candido. Manuale exorcistarum--Portugese. II. Joseph de Jesus Maria, tr.

WITCHCRAFT
BF 1552 H47
Broke, Johannes Georgius de, b. 1698.
Heister, Lorenz, 1683-1758, praeses.
Lavrentivs Heistervs ... programmate avspicali qvo demonstrat infantes pro a diabolo svppositis habitos qvos vvlgo Wechselbälge appellarvnt rhachiticos fvisse ad clarissima medicinae candidati Io. Georgii de Broke ... dispvtationem inavgvralem invitat. Helmstadii, Literis Schnorrianis, 1725.

[16] p. 21cm.

8

(Continued on next card)

Witchcraft
BF 1445 B86+
[Bromhall, Thomas] ed. and tr.
Treatise of specters; or, An history of apparitions, oracles ... with dreams, visions ... Collected out of sundry authours and delivered into English by T.B. Annexed, a learned treatise, confuting the opinions of Sadduces [sic] and epicures ... Written in French and now rendred [sic] into English. London, Printed by J. Streater, 1658.

367 p. 28cm.

With autograph: William Jones.

1. Apparitions. I. Title. II. Title: An history of apparitions.

Bromley, Sir Edward, fl. 1612.
Witchcraft
BF 1581 P87
Potts, Thomas, fl. 1612-1618.
Pott's Discovery of witches in the county of Lancaster, reprinted from the original ed. of 1613. With an introduction and notes, by James Crossley ... [Manchester] Printed for the Chetham society, 1745 [i.e. 1845]

3 p. l., [iii]-lxxix, [190] p. 1 l., 51, 6 p. illus. 23 x 18cm. (Added t.-p.: Remains, historical & literary, connected with the palatine counties of Lancaster and Chester, pub. by the Chetham society. vol. VI)

(Continued on next card)

Bromley, Sir Edward, fl. 1612.
Witchcraft
BF 1581 P87
Potts, Thomas, fl. 1612-1618. Pott's Discovery of witches in the county of Lancaster. (Card 2)

With reproduction of original t.-p.: The Wonderfvll Discoverie Of Witches In The Countie Of Lancaster ... Together with the arraignement and triall of Iennet Preston, at the assizes holden at the Castle of Yorke ... London, 1613. "The arraignement and triall of Iennet Preston" has special t.-p. with imprint: London, 1612.

Revised by Sir Edward Bromley.

Bromley, Sir Edward, fl. 1612.
Witchcraft
BF 1581 P87T8 1929
Potts, Thomas, fl. 1612-1618.
The trial of the Lancaster witches A. D. MDCXII, edited with an introduction by G. B. Harrison. London. P. Davies, 1929.

xlvi p., 1 l., 188 p. 1 illus. 21½cm.

With reproduction of original t.-p.: The wonderfvll discoverie of witches in the covntie of Lancaster ... Together with the arraignement and triall of Iennet Preston, at the assizes holden at the Castle of Yorke ... By Thomas Potts ... London, 1613.

"The arraignement and triall of Iennet Preston" has special t.-p. with imprint: London, 1612.

Revised by Sir Edward Bromley.

1. Witchcraft--Lancashire, Eng. 2. Preston, Jennet, d. 1612. I. Bromley, Sir Edward, fl. 1612. II. Harrison, George Bagshawe, ed. III. Title.

Library of Congress   BF1581.P65   30-9994
                              [3]   133.4

Witchcraft
PR 1259 W81 H62+
Broome, Richard, d. 1622?
The late Lancashire witches.
Heywood, Thomas, d. 1641.
The poetry of witchcraft illustrated by copies of the plays on the Lancashire witches by Heywood and Shadwell. Reprinted under the direction of James O. Halliwell. Brixton Hill, Printed for priv. circ. only, 1853.

238 p. 29cm.

Eighty copies printed.
Each play has also separate t.p.

(Continued on next card)

Witchcraft
PR 1259 W81 H62+
Broome, Richard, d. 1622?
The late Lancashire witches.
Heywood, Thomas, d. 1641. The poetry of witchcraft... 1853. (Card 2)

Contents.--The Lancashire witches and Tegue o Divelly, the Irish priest, by Thomas Shadwell.--The late Lancashire witches, by Thomas Heywood and Richard Broome.

I. Halliwell-Phillipps, James Orchard, 1820-1889. II. Shadwell, Thomas, 1642?-1692. The Lancashire witches and Tegue o Divelly. III. His The late Lancashire witches. IV. Broome, Richard, d. 1622? The late Lancashire witches V. Title.

Thesis
Film 1894 48
Brown, Harriet Chedie (Connor), 1872-
An inquiry into the extent of the witch persecutions in Germany. Ithaca, N. Y., 1894.

151 l. 27cm.

Thesis (A. B.)--Cornell University, 1894.
Microfilm. Ithaca, N. Y., Photo Science, Cornell University, 1974. part of reel. 35mm.

14
NIC
I. Title.

Witchcraft
Q 143 S42 B87
Brown, James Wood.
An enquiry into the life and legend of Michael Scot. Edinburgh, David Douglas, 1897.

xvi, 281 p. front. 23cm.

1. Scott, Michael, 1175?-1234? I. Title.

Witchcraft
BF 1251 B88
Brown, Robert, of Barton-upon-Humber.
Demonology and witchcraft, with especial reference to modern "spiritualism," so-called, and the "doctrines of demons." London, J. F. Shaw, 1889.

354 p. 19cm.

1. Spiritualism. 2. Demonology. I. Title

Witchcraft
BT 980 B88
Brown, Robert, of Barton-upon-Humber.
The personality and history of Satan. London, S. W. Partridge, 1887.

232 p. (p. [217]-232 advertisements) 19cm.

1. Devil. I. Title.

Browne, Agnes, d. 1612.
Witchcraft
BF 1581 A2 W81 1866a no.1
The Witches of Northamptonshire. Agnes Browne. Ioane Vaughan. Arthur Bill. Hellen Ienkinson. Mary Barber. Witches Who were all executed at Northampton the 22. of July last. 1612. London, Printed by Tho: Purfoot, for Arthur Iohnson, 1612. [Northampton, England, Taylor & son, 1866]

[28] p. 22cm.

No. 1 in box lettered Witchcraft in Northamptonshire.

8

1. Witchcraft--Northamptonshire, England. I. Title: Witchcraft in Northamptonshire.

Witchcraft
BF 1589 B88
Bruckner, Wilhelm Hieronymus.
De magicis personis et artibvs disserit, et eas omnino dari ostendit. Von zauberischen Leuten und Künsten, das solche warhafftig anzutreffen und nicht in einer blossen Einbildung bestehen, occasione legis 6. c. de malef. & mathem. a nobilissimo jurium candidato Jo. Reinhardo Wegelino ... solemni lectione ... explicandae die IX. Maji M DCC XII ... [Jena?] 1723.

28 p. 20cm.

1. Magic. I. Wegelin, Johann Reinhard.

CATALOGUE OF THE CORNELL WITCHCRAFT COLLECTION

Witchcraft
BF 1587 D61 no.15
   Bruckner, Wilhelm Hieronymus.
     De magicis personis et artibvs disserit, et eas omnino dari ostendit. Von zauberischen Leuten und Künsten, dass solche warhafftig anzutreffen, und nicht in einer blossen Einbildung bestehen, occasione legis 6. c. de malef. & mathem. a nobilissimo jurium candidato Jo. Reinhardo Wegelino ... solemni lectione ... explicandae die IX. Maji M DCC XII ... [Jenae?] 1723.
     28 p. 21cm.
     No. 15 in vol. lettered Dissertationes de magia. 1623- 1723.

8

Bruers, Antonio, 1887-   ed.

BF 231 C18 1925
   Campanella, Tommaso, 1568-1639.
     ... Del senso delle cose e della magia; testo inedito italiano con le varianti dei codici e delle due edizioni latine, a cura di Antonio Bruers. Bari, G. Laterza & figli, 1925.
     xxix, [1] p. 1 l., 348 p. 21½ᵐ. (Half-title: Classici della filosofia moderna ... a cura di B. Croce e G. Gentile. xxiv)

     1. Senses and sensations. 2. Magic. I. Bruers, Antonio,1887- ed. II. Campanella, Tommaso, 1568-1639. De sensu rerum et magia. III.Title. 26-11842
Library of Congress   BF253.C3
     [2]

Witchcraft
BX 1735 B89
   La Bruja; the witch; or, A picture of the court of Rome; found among the manuscripts of a respectable theologian, a great friend of that court. Translated from the Spanish by Markophrates [pseud.] London, J. Hatchard, 1840.
     188 p. 19cm.

     Added t. p. engr.

     1. Rome--Hist. 2. Inquisition.
     I. Title: The court of Rome.
     II. Markophrates, pseud., trans.

Brujos y hechicerías.

566
17
   Balbontín Moreno, Manuel G
     Brujos y hechicerías [por] Manuel G. Balbontín. Santiago de Chile, Ediciones Arco [1965]
     95 p. illus. 19cm.

     1. Witchcraft--Hist. 2. Witchcraft--Chile. I. Title.

Witchcraft
BF 1583 A2 B89 1727
   Brunnemann, Jacob, d. 1735.
     Discours von betrüglichen Kennzeichen der Zauberey, worinnen viel abergläubische Meinungen freymüthig untersuchet und verworffen, wie auch Carpzovii, Berlichii, Crusii ... missliche und leichtgläubige Lehr-Sätze von der Zauberey erwogen, zugleich J. J. Weidnerii Gegensätze wider diesen Discours kurtz und bescheidentlich beantwortet werden ... Halle, J. E. Fritsch, 1727.
     [32], 228, [16] p. 22cm.
         (Continued on next card)

Witchcraft
BF 1583 A2 B89 1727
   Brunnemann, Jacob, d. 1735.   Discours von betrüglichen Kennzeichen der Zauberey ... 1727.   (Card 2)
     With this is bound Weidner, J. J. Christ-bescheidentliche Gegen-Erinnerungen. Rostock, 1730.

     1. Witchcraft. 2. Trials (Witchcraft)-- Germany. I. Weidner, Johann Joachim, 1672-1732. II. Title.

Witchcraft
BF 1583 A2 B89
   [Brunneman, Jacob] d. 1735.
     Aloysii Charitini [pseud.] Discurs von trüglichen Kennzeichen der Zauberey, worinnen viel abergläubische Meinungen vernunfftmässig untersucht und verworffen; wie auch Carpzovii, Berlichii, Crusii, und anderer so woll päbstischer, als protestantischer Jure Consultorum. Missliche und leichtgläubige Lehr-Sätze von der Zauberey erwogen und beleuchtet worden ... Stargard, E. und J. M. Jenisch [1708]
     94 p. 19 cm.

     1. Witchcraft. I. Title. II. Title: Discurs von trüglichen Kennzeichen.

Brunnemann, Jacob, d. 1735.

Witchcraft
BF 1583 A2 B89 1727
   Weidner, Johann Joachim, 1672-1732.
     Christ-bescheidentliche Gegen-Erinnerungen, worinnen der teuffelischen Wirckungen halber, umständliche Nachricht geschehen, und zugleich Jacobi Brunnemanni Anmerckungen, mit guten Grunde und nach Gottes Wort geprüfet und hingeleget seyn ... Rostock, Kissner, 1730.
     143, [1] p. 22cm.
     Bound with Brunnemann, Jacob. Discours von betrüglichen Kennzeichen Halle, 1727.

Witchcraft
BF 1555 A55 no.2
   Brunsmand, Johan, 1637-1707.
     Johannis Brunsmanni Energumeni Coagienses, sive Admirabilis historia, de horrenda cacodaemonis tentatione, quacum in Selandia Daniae, ejusque urbe Coagio familia civis, & vita honestissimi & fama integerrimi, per annorum aliquot spatium est conflictata: primum sermone Danico aliquoties edita & impressa: nunc vero in exterorum gratiam Latine interpretata & cum duplici auctario edita. Editio altera Latina, auctior
         (Continued on next card)

Witchcraft
BF 1555 A55 no.2
   Brunsmand, Johan, 1637-1707.   ...Energumeni Coagienses ... 1695.   (Card 2)
     & correctior Leidensi. Lipsiae, Apud Joh. Melchior Lieben, 1695.
     4 p. l., 156 p. 14cm.
     First published 1674 with title: Et forfaerdeligt huus-kaars.
     Attributed by British Museum to A. H. Barskier, whose narrative makes up first part of work   (p. 1-73)
         (Continued on next card)

Witchcraft
BF 1555 A55 no.2
   Brunsmand, Johan, 1637-1707.   ...Energumeni Coagienses ... 1695.   (Card 3)
     No. 2 in vol. lettered Andreae. De angelorum...

     1. Witchcraft--Denmark. 2. Bartholin, Thomas, 1616-1680. 3. Bekker, Balthasar, 1634-1698. I. Barskier, Anne Hans. II. His Et forfaerdeligt huus-kaars--Latin. III. Title: Energumeni Coagienses.

DL 103 .5 D18+ no.61
   Brunsmand, Johan, 1637-1707.
     Køge huskors. Med indledning og noter ved Anders Bæksted. København, E. Munksgaard, 1953.
     320 p. illus. 22cm. (Danmarks folkeminder, nr. 61)

     Includes reproduction of the title page of the original edition published in 1674, with title: Et forfaerdeligt huus-kaars.

     1. Witchcraft--Denmark. I. Bæksted, Anders. II. His Et forfaerdeligt huus-kaars. III. Title.

Brunsmand, Johan, 1637-1707.
   Et forfaerdeligt huus-kaars--Latin.

Witchcraft
BF 1555 A55 no.2
   Brunsmand, Johan, 1637-1707.
     Johannis Brunsmanni Energumeni Coagienses, sive Admirabilis historia, de horrenda cacodaemonis tentatione, quacum in Selandia Daniae, ejusque urbe Coagio familia civis, & vita honestissimi & fama integerrimi, per annorum aliquot spatium est conflictata: primum sermone Danico aliquotis edita & impressa: nunc vero in exterorum gratiam Latine interpretata & cum duplici auctario edita. Editio altera Latina, auctior
         (Continued on next card)

Brunsmand, Johan, 1637-1707.
   Et forfaerdeligt huus-kaars--Latin.

Witchcraft
BF 1555 A55 no.2
   Brunsmand, Johan, 1637-1707.   ...Energumeni Coagienses ... 1695.   (Card 2)
     & correctior Leidensi. Lipsiae, Apud Joh. Melchior Lieben, 1695.
     4 p. l., 156 p. 14cm.
     First published 1674 with title: Et forfaerdeligt huus-kaars.
     Attributed by British Museum to A. H. Barskier, whose narrative makes up first part of work   (p. 1-73)
         (Continued on next card)

Witchcraft
BF 1555 A55 no.2
   Brunsmand, Johan, 1637-1707.   ...Energumeni Coagienses ... 1695.   (Card 3)
     No. 2 in vol. lettered Andreae. De angelorum...

     1. Witchcraft--Denmark. 2. Bartholin, Thomas, 1616-1680. 3. Bekker, Balthasar, 1634-1698. I. Barskier, Anne Hans. II. His Et forfaerdeligt huus-kaars--Latin. III. Title: Energumeni Coagienses.

DL 103 .5 D18+ no.61
   Brunsmand, Johan, 1637-1707.
     Køge huskors. Med indledning og noter ved Anders Bæksted. København, E. Munksgaard, 1953.
     320 p. illus. 22cm. (Danmarks folkeminder, nr. 61)

     Includes reproduction of the title page of the original edition published in 1674, with title: Et forfaerdeligt huus-kaars.

     1. Witchcraft--Denmark. I. Bæksted, Anders. II. His Et forfaerdeligt huus-kaars. III. Title.

Brunsmann, Johannes, 1637-1707.
   see
Brunsmand, Johan, 1637-1707.

Bry, Johann Theodor de, 1561-1623?

WITCHCRAFT
BF 1750 B68+
   Boissard, Jean Jacques, 1528-1602.
     Tractatus posthumus Jani Jacobi Boissardi Vesvntini de divinatione et magicis praestigiis, quarum veritas ac vanitas solide exponitur per descriptionem deorum fatidicorum qui olim responsa dederunt; eorundemque prophetarum, sacerdotum, phoebadum, sibyllarum & divinorum, qui priscis temporibus celebres oraculis exstiterunt. Adjunctis ... effigiebus, ab ipso autore ... delineatis; jam ... aeri incisis per Joh. Theodor de Bry. Oppenheimii,
         (Continued on next card)

2 copies

CATALOGUE OF THE CORNELL WITCHCRAFT COLLECTION

Bry, Johann Theodor de, 1561-1623?

WITCHCRAFT
BF
1750
B68++
 Boissard, Jean Jacques, 1528-1602. Tractatus posthumus Jani Jacobi Boissardi Vesvntini de divinatione et magicis praestigiis ... (Card 2)
 typis H. Galleri [1616?]
 14 p. l., 358, [11] p. illus., ports. 32cm.
 Engr. t.-p.
 Engraving on p. 151 (Nicostrata) is different in the two copies.

8 (Continued on next card)

Buch, Georg, respondent.

Witchcraft
BF
1587
D61
no.4
 Buch, Philipp, 1639-1696, praeses.
 Disputatio physica De magia et magicis prima, quam praeside Dn.M. Philippo Buchio ... respondens Georgius Buchius ... publicè tuebitur. Francofurti ad Oderam, Typis Becmanianus, 1666.
 [40] p. 21cm.
 Caption title: Sectio I. De magia licita. (No other sections follow)
 No 4 in vol. lettered Dissertationes de magia. 1623- 1723.

8 (Continued on next card)

Witchcraft
BF
1587
D61
no.4
 Buch, Philipp, 1639-1696, praeses.
 Disputatio physica De magia et magicis prima, quam praeside Dn.M. Philippo Buchio ... respondens Georgius Buchius ... publicè tuebitur. Francofurti ad Oderam, Typis Becmanianus, 1666.
 [40] p. 21cm.
 Caption title: Sectio I. De magia licita. (No other sections follow)
 No 4 in vol. lettered Dissertationes de magia. 1623- 1723.

8 (Continued on next card)

Witchcraft
BF
1587
D61
no.4
 Buch, Philipp, 1639-1696, praeses. Disputatio physica De magia et magicis prima ... 1666. (Card 2)
 1. Physics--Early works to 1800--Addresses, essays, lectures. 2. Magic--Addresses, essays, lectures. I. Buch, Georg, respondent. II. Title: De magia et magicis. III. Title: De magia licita. IV. Title.

8

Das Buch vom Aberglauben.

Witchcraft
BF
1775
F52
 [Fischer, Heinrich Ludwig, d. 1820?]
 Das Buch vom Aberglauben. Leipzig, Im Schwickertschen Verlage, 1790.
 3 p. l., 359, [3] p. illus. 18cm.
 Ex libris T. G. Mättig.

 1. Superstition. 2. Folk-lore--Germany. 3. Magic. I. Title.

HT
913
B91
 Buchmann, Jakob.
 Die unfreie und die freie Kirche in ihren Beziehungen zur Sclaverei, zur Glaubens- und Gewissenstyrannei und zum Dämonismus. Breslau, A. Gosohorsky, 1873.
 xvi, 331 p. 22cm.

 1. Slavery and the church. 2. Demonology. I. Title.

Witchcraft
BF
1413
B91
 Buchner, Eberhard, 1877- ed.
 Medien, Hexen und Geisterseher; kulturhistorisch interessante Dokumente aus alten deutschen Zeitungen und Zeitschriften (16. bis 18. Jahrhundert) München, A. Langen, 1926.
 359 p. 20cm.

 1. Occult sciences--Germany. I. Title.

BF
1555
B92
 Bucke (R. M.) Memorial Society.
 Trance and possession states, edited by Raymond Prince. Proceedings [of the] second annual conference, R. M. Bucke Memorial Society, 4-6 March 1966, Montreal. [Montreal, R. M. Bucke Memorial Society, c1968]
 xii, 200 p. illus. 23cm.

 1. Demoniac possession--Addresses, essays, lectures. 2. Trance--Addresses, essays, lectures. I. Prince, Raymond, ed. II. Title.

Büching, Godofredus, respondent.

WITCHCRAFT
R
133
H71
 Hoffmann, Friedrich, 1660-1742, praeses.
 Disputatio inauguralis medico-philosophica De potentia diaboli in corpora, quam ... praeside DN. Friderico Hoffmanno ... publico ... examini submittit Godofredus Büching. Halae, Typis Ioannis Gruneri [1703]
 [39] p. 21cm.

8
NIC Diss.--Halle (G. Büching, respondent)

Büelman, Jodocus, respondent.

Witchcraft
BT
965
B95
 Burghaber, Adam, 1608-1687, praeses.
 Angelorvm natvra, proprietates, ac diversi statvs qvos ... praeside Adamo Bvrghaber ... pvblice proposvit ... D. Iodocvs Bvelman ... Lucernae, Typis Dauidis Hautt, 1650.
 2 p. l., 253, [5] p. 14cm.

 1. Angels. 2. Devil. I. Büelman, Jodocus, respondent. II. Title: Angelorum natura, proprietates, ac diversi status.

8

Bündnisse der Menschen mit dem Teufel bey dem Schatz-Graben.

Witchcraft
BF
1547
F65
1741
 Förtsch, Michael, 1654-1724.
 Commentatio de pactis hominvm cvm diabolo circa abditos in terra thesavros effodiendos et acqvirendos, ad casvm illvm tragicvm, qvi anno MDCCXV. in vigiliis festi Nativitatis Christi in agro Ienensi institvta. Von denen Bündnissen der Menschen mit dem Teufel bey dem Schatz-Graben. Editio novissima. Lipsiae, Apvd Christian. Schroetervm, 1741.
 61, [2] p. 22cm.

A new edition of a dissertation at Jena,
(Continued on next card)

Bündnisse der Menschen mit dem Teufel bey dem Schatz-Graben.

Witchcraft
BF
1547
F65
1741
 Förtsch, Michael, 1654-1724. Commentatio de pactis hominvm cvm diabolo ... 1741. (Card 2)

with Michael Förtsch as praeses and Johannes Andreas Rinneberg as respondent, published Jena, 1716.

 1. Devil. 2. Treasure-trove. I. Rinneberg, Johannes Andreas, respondent. II. Title: De pactis hominum cum diabolo circa abditos in terra thesauros effodiendos. III. Title: Bündnisse der Menschen mit dem Teufel bey dem Schatz-Graben.

Witchcraft
BF
1587
D61
no.11
 Büttner, Daniel, 1642-1696, praeses.
 Magiologia seu Disputatio de magia licita et illicita qvam ... praeside Dn. Daniele Büttnero ... disquisitionis submittit Albertus zum Felde ... Hamburgi, Literis Conradi Neumanni [1693]
 26, [6] p. 18cm. (bound in 21cm. vol.)
 No. 11 in vol. lettered Dissertationes de magia. 1623-1723.
 1. Magic--Addresses, essays, lectures. I. Felde, Albert zum, 1672-1720, respondent. II. Title. III. Title: De magia licita et illicita. IV. Disputatio de magia licita et illicita.

8

Büttner, Georg Wilhelm, respondent.

RARE
HV
8593
D611
no.12
 Leyser, Augustin, Reichsfreiherr von, 1683-1752, praeses.
 De officio iudicis circa tormenta, praeside Augustino a Leyser...disputabit Georgius Guilielm..Büttnerus. Vitembergae, Typis Schlomachianis [1740]
 28 p. 21cm.
 Diss.--Wittenberg (G. W. Büttner, respondent)
 No. 12 in a vol. lettered: Dissertationes de tortura, 1697-1770.
 1. Torture. 2. Criminal procedure. I. Büttner, Georg Wilhelm, respondent. II. Title.

8
NIC

Witchcraft
BF
1587
D61
no.6
 Bugges, Laurentius, praeses.
 Disputatio physica qva magiam doemoniacam [sic] ceu illicitam, & naturalem ceu licitam, in electorali ad albim academia explicabunt praeses M. Laurentius Bugges, ... respondens Samuel Porath ... Wittebergae, Typis Johannis Haken, 1667.
 [12] p. 18cm. (bound in 21cm. vol.)
 No. 6 in vol. lettered Dissertationes de magia. 1623-1723.
 1. Magic--Addresses, essays, lectures. I. Porath, Samuel, respondent. II. Title: Disputatio physica qua magiam ... explicabunt...

8

PT
8834
B63
1914
 Bull, Jacob Breda, 1853-1930.
 ... Blaafjeld: et folkelivsbillede fra hekseprocesserne i Kristiania og København, Gyldendal, 1914.
 2 p. l., [1]-190 p. 20cm.
 At head of title: Jacob B. Bull.

 I. Title.
              32-2409
Library of Congress PT8834.B6 1914 839.8

Burchard, Christoph Martin, 1680-1742, respondent.

WITCHCRAFT
BF
1572
M4
S32
 Schelhammer, Günther Christoph, 1649-1716, praeses.
 Disputatio inauguralis medica De morbis magicis quam ... sub praesidio ... Gunth. Christophori Schelhammeri ... submittet Christoph. Martinus Burchardus ... Kil., Literis B. Reutheri [1704]
 40, [1] p. 20cm.

 1. Witchcraft. 2. Diseases--Causes and theories of causation. I. Burchard, Christoph Martin, 1680-1742, respondent. II. Title: De morbis magicis.

8

Bure, Johan, 1568-1652.

WITCHCRAFT
BF
1584
S9
L66
 Levin, Herman, 1862-
 Forna tiders mörker och vidskepelse.
 (In: Läsning för svenska folket. Stockholm. 20cm. 1909. p. 43-67, 92-115, 210-226)

 1. Witchcraft--Sweden. 2. Witchcraft Scandinavia. 3. Trials (Witchcraft)--Sweden. 4. Bure, Johan, 1568-1652. 5. Magnus, Olaus, abp. of Uppsala, 1490-1558. I. Läsning för svenska folket. II. Title.

8
NIC

94

CATALOGUE OF THE CORNELL WITCHCRAFT COLLECTION

Witchcraft
BT 965 B95

Burghaber, Adam, 1608-1687, praeses.
Angelorvm natvra, proprietates, ac diversi statvs qvos ... praeside Adamo Bvrghaber ... pvblice proposvit ... D. Iodocvs Bvelman ... Lucernae, Typis Dauidis Hautt, 1650.
2 p. l., 253, [5] p. 14cm.

1. Angels. 2. Devil. I. Büelman, Jodocus, respondent. II. Title: Angelorum natura, proprietates, ac diversi status.

8

WITCHCRAFT
BF 1483 S89

Burgiss, Elizabeth, fl. 1681.
Strange and wonderful news from Yowel [sic] in Surry; giving a true and just account of one Elizabeth Bvrgiss, who was most strangely bewitched and tortured ... As, also, how great stones ... were thrown at her ...; and after she came to her fathers house, the throwing of the pewter-dishes, candlesticks, and other clattering of houshold goods at her ... West-Smithfield, Printed for F. Clarke, seignior, 1681.
6 p. illus. 19cm.
(Continued on next card)

8

WITCHCRAFT
BF 1483 S89

Burgiss, Elizabeth, fl. 1681.
Strange and wonderful news from Yowel [sic] in Surry ... 1681. (Card 2)

Wing S5869b.
Illustrations are 5 woodcuts printed on verso of t. p.

1. Burgiss, Elizabeth, fl. 1681. 2. Ghosts--Ewell, Surrey, England. 3. Ghosts--England. 4. Witchcraft--England.

8

Burr, George Lincoln

Witchcraft
BF 1583 B96 1891

Burr, George Lincoln, 1857-1938.
The fate of Dietrich Flade. New York, London, G. P. Putnam's Sons, 1891.
57 p. 24cm.

"Reprinted from the Papers of the American Historical Association, vol. V, no. 3, July, 1891."

1. Flade, Dietrich, 1534-1589. 2. Witchcraft--Germany. I. Title.

Witchcraft
BF 1573 A2 B96

Burr, George Lincoln, 1857-1938, ed.
Narratives of the witchcraft cases ... 1914. (Card 2)
Contents.--From "An essay for the recording of illustrious providences" ... by Increase Mather, 1684.--The New York cases of Hall and Harrison, 1665, 1670.--"Lithobolia, or The stone-throwing devil", by Richard Chamberlain, 1698.--The Pennsylvania cases of Mattson, Hendrickson, and Guard, 1684, 1701.--"Memorable providences, relating to witchcrafts
(Continued on next card)

Witchcraft
BF 1576 B96

Burr, George Lincoln, 1857-
... New England's place in the history of witchcraft, by George Lincoln Burr ... Worcester, Mass., The Society, 1911.
35 p. 25cm.

At head of title: American antiquarian society.
"Reprinted from the Proceedings of the American antiquarian society for October, 1911."

1. Witchcraft. 2. Witchcraft--New England. I. Title.

15-3X17

Library of Congress   BF1566.B8

Witchcraft
BF 1581 B96

Burr, George Lincoln, 1857-1938.
[Letter] to the editor of The nation [about witch-burning in England]
(In the Nation. New York. 17cm. v. 49 (1889) p. 71)

With, in envelope, his Woman-burning in England. 1889.

1. Witchcraft--England.

Witchcraft
BF 1573 A2 B96

Burr, George Lincoln, 1857-1938.
Narratives of the witchcraft cases ... 1914. (Card 3)
Contents--Continued.
and possessions", by Cotton Mather, 1689.--"A brief and true narrative of witchcraft at Salem village", by Deodat Lawson, 1692.--Letter of Thomas Brattle, F.R.S., 1692.--Letters of Governor Phips to the home government, 1692, 1693.--From "The wonders of the invisible world", by Cotton Mather, 1693.--"A brand pluck'd out of the burning", by Cotton Mather, 1693.--
(Continued on next card)

Witchcraft
Z 987 B96

Burr, George Lincoln, 1857-1938.
A witch-hunter in the book-shops.
(In The bibliographer. New York. 25cm. v.1(1902) p. 431-446)

Witchcraft
Z 6879 W8 B96 1890

Burr, George Lincoln, 1857-1938.
The literature of witchcraft. New York, Putnam, 1890.
37-66 p. 24cm.

Double paging.
"Reprinted from the papers of the American Historical Association," vol. IV, p. 237-266.
Annoted by the author; copy 2 detailed annotations.

I. Title.

Witchcraft
BF 1573 A2 B96

Burr, George Lincoln, 1857-1938, ed.
Narratives of the witchcraft cases... 1914. (Card 4)
Contents--Continued.
From "More wonders of the invisible world", by Robert Calef.--From "A modest inquiry into the nature of witchcraft", by John Hale, 1702.--The Virginia case of Grace Sherwood, 1706.

1. Witchcraft. 2. Witchcraft--New England. I. Title.

Witchcraft
Z 987 B96 1902

Burr, George Lincoln, 1857-1938.
A witch-hunter in the book-shops. [n.p., 1902]
[16] p. facsims. 25cm.

"Reprinted from The bibliographer, December 1902."

1. Book collecting. 2. Libraries, Private. 3. Witchcraft--Bibl. I. Title.

Witchcraft
BF 1573 A2 B96

Burr, George Lincoln, 1857-1938, ed.
Narratives of the witchcraft cases, 1648-1706, ed. by George Lincoln Burr ... with three facsimiles. New York, C. Scribner's sons, 1914.
xviii, 467 p. 3 facsim. 23cm. (Original narratives of early American history)

Inscribed to President A.D. White by the author, (c.1); with manuscript notes by the editor (c.2).
(Continued on next card)

BF 1573 A2 B96 1972

Burr, George Lincoln, 1857-1938, comp.
Narratives of the witchcraft cases, 1648-1706. New York, Barnes & Noble [1972]
xiv, 465 p. (Original narratives of early American history)

Reprint of the 1914 ed.

1. Witchcraft. 2. Witchcraft--New England. I. Title.

4

Witchcraft
BF 1565 B96

Burr, George Lincoln, 1857-1938.
The witch-persecutions. Philadelphia, Dept. of History, Univ. of Pennsylvania, 1897.
cover-title, 36 p. 22cm. (Translations and reprints from the original sources of European history, v. III, no. 4, [1896])

With this is bound a revised ed. of the above, 1903.

1. Witchcraft--Hist. I. Title.

CATALOGUE OF THE CORNELL WITCHCRAFT COLLECTION

ARCHIVES   14/17/22

Burr, George Lincoln, 1857-1938.
Pamphlet, 1897.

"The Witch-Persecutions" translations and reprints from the original sources of European history, edited by Burr, published by the University of Pennsylvania. 36pp.

ARCHIVES   14/17/22

Burr, George Lincoln, 1857-1938.
Papers, 1862-1938.

Translations and reprints from the original sources of European History, v. III, no. 4: The witch persecutions, ed. by G. L. Burr. Department of History, University of Pennsylvania, 1897.
(In Box 38: Witchcraft material collected by Burr and Charles H. Lea.)

Witchcraft
BF
1581
B96

Burr, George Lincoln, 1857-1938.
Woman-burning in England [letter] (In the Nation. New York. 17cm. v. 49 (1889) p. 169)

With, in envelope, his [Letter] to the editor of the Nation [about witch-burning in England] 1889.

1. Witchcraft--England. I. Title.

MSS
Bd.
WITCHCRAFT
BF
L86
1592a

Burr, George Lincoln, 1857-1938.
Extracts from the De vera et falsa magia of Cornelius Loos. (Made from the Ms. at Trier and verified by the printed fragment at Köln in July, 1912.) Köln, 1912.
4, 1-6, [1], 7-15, [1], 16-48 l. 20cm.

Manuscript, in small notebook of graph paper, in the hand of G. L. Burr. P. 41-48 are Notes on the printed fragment at Cologne, by G. L. Burr.
Four loose typewritten leaves of the Latin text are inserted inside
(Continued on next card)

MSS
Bd.
WITCHCRAFT
BF
L86
1592a

Burr, George Lincoln, 1857-1938.
Loos, Cornelius, 1546-1595. Extracts from the De vera et falsa magia ... 1912. (Card 2)
front cover.
In marbled case with his [De vera et falsa magia. Trier, 1592; 1886]

1. Demonology. 2. Witchcraft. 3. His De vera et falsa magia. I. Burr, George Lincoln, 1857-1938.

Witchcraft
B
1201
B73E7
1694

Burthogge, Richard, 1638?-ca. 1700.
An essay upon reason, and the nature of spirits. By Richard Burthogge, M. D. London, Printed for J. Dunton, 1694.
3 p. l., 280 p. diagr. 18cm.

1. Knowledge, Theory of. 2. Supernatural. I. Title.

10-29068†

Library of Congress   B1201.B73E6 1694

Witchcraft
BF
1563
W81++
no.21

Buts, Joan.
An Account of the tryal and examination of Joan Buts, for being a common witch and inchantress ... March 27, 1682. London, Printed for S. Gardener, 1682. [London, at the British Museum, 1923]
[2] p. 27cm.
Photocopy (negative) 2 p. on 2 l. 20 x 32cm.
No. 21 in vol. lettered: Witchcraft tracts, chapbooks and broadsides, 1579-1704; rotograph copies.

Witchcraft
BF
1520
B98

8

Buttner, Christophorus Andreas, praeses.
Diiudicatio iudicii De non-existentia diaboli quam ... praeside M. Christophoro Andrea Buttnero ... defendet Ernestus Wilhelm. Bergmann. Halae Magdeburgicae, Litteris Ioh. Friderici Grunerti [1734]
24 p. 24cm.
Diss.--Halle (E. W. Bergmann, respondent)
1. Devil. 2. Demonology. I. Bergmann, Ernest Wilhelm, respondent. II. Title: De non-existentia diaboli. III. Diiudicatio iudicii De non-existentia diaboli.

Witchcraft
BF
1587
D61
no.14

8

Butzow, Henricus Olai, respondent.
Lunde, Nicolaus Johann, praeses.
Theses de magis, volente Deo, publicè tuebimur Nicolaus Joh. Lunde praeses & Henricus Olai Butzow respondens ... Havniae, Ex Reg. Majest. & universit. typographéo [1709]
8 p. 18cm. (bound in 21cm. vol.)
No. 14 in vol. lettered Dissertationes de magia. 1623-1723.
1. Witchcraft--Addresses, essays, lectures. I. Butzow, Henricus Olai, respondent. II. Title.

BX
9321
B99
1896a

Byington, Ezra Hoyt, 1828-1901.
The Puritan in England and New England. By Ezra Hoyt Byington ... With an introduction by Alexander McKenzie ... London, S. Low, Marston & co., ltd., 1896.
xl, 406 p. 21½cm.
"List of authorities referred to": p. [xxv]-xxix.
1. Puritans. 2. Witchcraft. 3. Pynchon, William, 1590?-1662. 4. Breck, Robert, 1713-1784. I. Title.

16-9631

Library of Congress

Witchcraft
K
B99
V4

Byloff, Fritz, 1875-
Das Verbrechen der Zauberei (crimen magiae) Ein Beitrag zur Geschichte der Strafrechtspflege in Steiermark. Graz, Leuschner & Lubensky, 1902.
440 p. 24cm.

1. Criminal law--Styria. 2. Witchcraft--Styria. I. Title.

Witchcraft
BF
1584
A93
B991

Byloff, Fritz, 1875-
Volkskundliches aus strafprozessen der österreichischen penländer, mit besonderer berücksichtigung der zauberei-hexenprozesse 1455 bis 1850; gesammelt, hrsg. und mit anmerkungen versehen von Fritz Byloff. Berlin und Leipzig, de Gruyter & co., 1929.
68 p. 24½cm. (Added t.-p.: Quellen zur deutschen volkskunde 3. hft.)
"Literaturverzeichnis": p. [59]-60.

1. Folk-lore--Austria. 2. Witchcraft--Austria. 3. Trials--Austria. I. Title.

36-66

Library of Congress

BF
1581
B99

Byrne, Patrick F
Witchcraft in Ireland, by Patrick F. Byrne. Cork, Mercier Press [1967]
75 p. 18cm. (A Mercier original paperback)

1. Witchcraft--Ireland. I. Title.

CATALOGUE OF THE CORNELL WITCHCRAFT COLLECTION

C., B.

Witchcraft
BF
1410   Aanmerkingen van eenige rechtzinnige broe-
B42   deren over de Articulen van satisfactie,
Z56   waar op men met D. B. Bekker een verdrag
v.3   gemaakt heeft.   Leyden, By F. Haring,
no.15   boekverkooper, 1692.
           22, [1] p. [p. 24 blank] title vignette.
           20 x 15cm.
           4°: A-C⁴.
           Consists of two letters, a short one signed
        N. N. [i. e., Jacobus Schuts], and one of 18
        p. signed B. C.

8   (Continued on next card)

C., B.

Witchcraft
BF
1410   Aanmerkingen van eenige rechtzinnige broe-
B42   deren ... 1692.   (Card 2)
Z56
v.3   Van der Linde 38.
no.15 No. 15 in vol. lettered Bekker III.

       1. Bekker, Balthasar, 1634-1698. Arti-
       culen tot satisfactie aan de Eerw. Classis
       van Amsterdam. I. Schuts, Jacobus. II.
       B. C. III. C., B.

C. P., bibliophile.

WITCHCRAFT
BT
980   Le Diable et ses métamorphoses; étude his-
D53   torique par le bibliophile C. P. Paris,
          Sandoz et Thuillier, 1882.
          100 p. 19cm.

          1. Devil. 2. Devil in literature.
8   I. P., C., bibliophile. II. C. P., biblio-
NIC   phile.

Caccia alle streghe.

Witchcraft
BF
1584   Bonomo, Giuseppe.
I8   Caccia alle streghe. La credenza nelle streghe dal sec.
B71   XIII al XIX con particolare riferimento all'Italia. [Pa-
          lermo], Palumbo, 1971.
          548 p. plates. 24½ cm. L6000   It 72-Jan
          Bibliography: p. [477]-534.

9   1. Witchcraft—Italy.   I. Title.

          BF1584.I8B64   72-316181

          Library of Congress   72 [2]

Caccia alle streghe nell'America puritana.

BF
1576   Vivan, Itala.
V85   Caccia alle streghe nell'America puritana. Milano, Riz-
          zoli, 1972.
          751 p. illus. 20½ cm. (Nuova collana) L7500   It 72-June
          Includes bibliographical references.

9
NIC   1. Witchcraft—New England.   I. Title.

          BF1576.V58   72-340534

          Library of Congress   72 [2]

Cadière, Catherine

WITCHCRAFT
BF
1582   Cadière, Catherine, b. 1709.
G51   Interrogatoires, recollement et confron-
P96   tation du P. Girard, Jesuite, et de la
v.1   Demoiselle Cadière; avec des Observations.
no.8   Ensemble la revocation de la variation de
          ladite Demoiselle Cadière, & la confronta-
          tion mutuelle avec le Père Nicolas, prieur
          des Carmes de Toulon. [s.l., 173-?]
          128 p. 17cm.

8   No. 8 in vol. lettered: Procès de Girard.
NIC   [v.1]

                       (Continued on next card)

WITCHCRAFT
BF
1582   Cadière, Catherine, b. 1709. Interroga-
G51   toires ... [173-?]   (Card 2)
P96
v.1
no.8

8   √ Girard, Jean Baptiste, 1680-1733. √
NIC   Girard, Jean Baptiste, 1680-1733. II.
          Title.

WITCHCRAFT
BF
1582   Cadière, Catherine, b. 1709, complainant.
G51   Mémoire instructif pour Demoiselle Ca-
P96   therine Cadière, de ... Toulon, querellante
v.1   & decretée. Contre le Père Jean Baptiste
no.2   Girard, Jesuite, querellé; & encore M. le
          Procureur Général du Roy. [s.l., 173-?]
          38 p. 17cm.

          No. 2 in vol. lettered: Procès de Girard.
          [v.1]

8   √ I. Girard,   Jean Baptiste, 1680-
NIC   1733,   respondent.

WITCHCRAFT
BF
1582   Cadière, Catherine, b. 1709, appellant.
G51   Mémoire instructif, pour Demoiselle
P96   Catherine Cadière de ... Toulon, appelante
v.2   comme d'abus de la procédure faite par
no.3   l'official en l'evêché de la même ville, à
          la requête du promoteur & par appel simple
          de la procédure faite contr'elle par MM.
          les Commissaires du Parlement, du décret
          d'ajournement personnel contr'elle laxe, &
          à minimâ du décret d'assigné par eux rendu,
8   demanderesse   en Lettres Royaux inci-
NIC   dentes de   restitution, du 19 mai
                       (Continued on next card)

WITCHCRAFT
BF
1582   Cadière, Catherine, b. 1709, appellant.
G51   Mémoire instructif ...   (Card 2)
P96
v.2   1731, & au principal querellante en enchante-
no.3   ment, rapt, inceste spirituel, avortement
          & subornation de témoins. Contre le Père
          Jean Baptiste Girard, Jesuite ... intimé en
          appel à minimâ & querellé, & ... Mr. le
          P.G. du Roy, intimé aux autres appels: &
          tous deux défendeurs aux Lettres Royaux.
          [s.l., 173-?]
8   172 p.   17cm.
NIC
                       (Continued on next card)

WITCHCRAFT
BF
1582   Cadière, Catherine, b. 1709, appellant.
G51   Mémoire instructif ... [173-?] (Card 3)
P96
v.2   No. 3 in vol. lettered: Procès de Girard.
no.3   [v.2]

8   √1. Girard, Jean Baptiste, 1680-1733,
NIC   appellee.   √I. Title.

97

CATALOGUE OF THE CORNELL WITCHCRAFT COLLECTION

WITCHCRAFT
BF Cadière, Catherine, b. 1709, complainant.
1582 Précis des charges, pour Demoiselle
G51 Catherine Cadière, de ... Toulon, querel-
P96 lante en inceste spirituel, & autres crimes.
v.1 Contre le Père Jean Baptiste Girard, Jesu-
no.4 ite, querellé. [s.l., 173-?]
     51 p. 17cm.

No. 4 in vol. lettered: Procès de Girard. [v.1]

8   I. Girard, Jean Baptiste, 1680-
NIC 1733, respondent.

WITCHCRAFT
BF Cadière, Catherine, b. 1709, complainant.
1582 Réponse à la seconde partie du Second
G51 Mémoire du Père Girard. [s.l., 173-?]
P96 106 p. 17cm.
v.1
no.3 No. 3 in vol. lettered: Procès de Girard. [v.1]

8   I. Girard, Jean Baptiste, 1680-1733, re-
NIC spondent. II. Title

WITCHCRAFT
BF Cadière, Catherine, b. 1709, appellant.
1582 Réponse au Mémoire instructif du Père
G51 J. B. Girard, Jesuite. Pour Demoiselle
P96 Catherine Cadière, de la ville de Toulon,
v.2 appellante à minimâ de decret d'assigné
no.2 rendu par MM. les commissaires du Parlement,
     le 23. fév. dernier, & au principal querel-
     lante en inceste spirituel, & autres crimes.
     Contre ledit Père Girard, intimé & querellé.
     [s.l., 1731?]
8   191 p.   17cm.
NIC No. 2 in vol. lettered: Procès
     de Girard.   [v.2]
                (Continued on next card)

WITCHCRAFT
BF Cadière, Catherine, b. 1709, appellant.
1582 Réponse au Mémoire instructif ... du Père J. B.
G51 Girard ... [1731?] (Card 2)
P96
v.2
no.2

8   I. Girard, Jean Baptiste, 1680-1733,
NIC appellee.

WITCHCRAFT
BF Cadière, Catherine, b. 1709, complainant.
1582 Réponse au Second Mémoire instructif du
G51 Père Girard, Jesuite, pour Demoiselle
P96 Catherine Cadière, de ... Toulon, querel-
v.1 lante en crimes d'enchantement, d'inceste
no.1 spirituel, d'avortement, & de subornation
     de témoins. Contre ledit Père Girard,
     querellé. [s.l., 173-?]
     104 p. 17cm.

8   Signed: Catherine Cadière. Chaudron,
NIC avocat.   Aubin, procurateur.
     De Ville   neuve d'Ansous, raporteur
                (Continued on next card)

WITCHCRAFT
BF Cadière, Catherine, b. 1709, complainant.
1582 Réponse au Second Mémoire ... du Père
G51 Girard. [173-?]   (Card 2)
P96
v.1
no.1 [sic]
     No. 1 in vol. lettered: Procès de Girard. [v.1]

8   I. Girard, Jean Baptiste, 1680-1733,
NIC respondent. II. Title.

Cadière, Catherine, b.1709.
Witchcraft
BF Girard, Jean Baptiste, 1680-1733, defendant.
1582 A compleat translation of the Memorial of
G51M5 the Jesuit Father John Baptist Girard, rector
1732 of the Royal Seminary of the Chaplains of the
     Navy, in the city of Toulon, against Mary
     Catherine Cadière and the atorney [sic] gen-
     eral, plaintiff.   London, Printed for J.
     Millan, 1732.
     172, 143 p. 17cm.

"A collection   of the letters of Father
Girard and Mary   Catherine Cadière, the
                (Continued on next card)

Cadière, Catherine, b. 1709.
Witchcraft
BF Girard, Jean Baptiste, 1680-1733, defendant.
1582 A compleat translation of the Memorial of
G51M5 the Jesuit Father John Baptist Girard ...
1732 1732.   (Card 2)

originals whereof were produced in court": 143 p. at end.

1. Cadière, Catherine, b. 1709.
I. Girard, Jean Baptiste, 1680-1733. Mémoire
instructif.....   English. II. Cadière,
     Catherine,   b. 1709. III. Title.

Cadière, Catherine, b. 1709.
Witchcraft
BF Girard, Jean Baptiste, 1680-1733, defendant.
1582 A compleat translation of the Sequel
G51 of the Proceedings of Mary Catherine Cadiere,
S9   against the Jesuit Father John Baptist
1732a Girard. Containing many curious pieces
     ... 2d ed. London, Printed for J.
     Millan, 1732.
     255, [1] p. 17cm.

Publisher's advertisement: p. [256]
I. Cadière, Catherine, b. 1709.
II. Title.

Cadière, Catharine, b. 1709.
Witchcraft
BF Girard, Jean Baptiste, 1680-1733, defendant.
1582 The defence of F. John Baptist Girard,
G51 Jesuit, and rector of the Royal Seminary
D3   of Chaplains of the Navy in the city of
1732 Toulon; against the accusation of Mary
     Catharine Cadière. London, Printed for
     and sold by J. Roberts, 1731-32 [pt. 1,
     1732]
     3 pts. in 1 v. 21cm.

Parts 1-2: 3d ed.

I. Cadière,   Catharine,
b. 1709.   II. Title.

Cadière, Catherine, b. 1709..
Witchcraft
BF [Girard, Jean Baptiste] 1680-1733, defendant.
1582 Memoir [sic] du P. et de la Cadier [sic]
G51 [Aix, etc., De l'imprimerie de la veuve
M48++ de Joseph Senez, etc., 1731]
     various pagings. 32cm.
     Cover title.
     Contents.--Mémoire instructif, pour Mes-
     sire François Cadiere.--Observations sur le
     memoire manuscrit distribué par le P. Girard.
     --Memoire du Pere Girard.--Memoire instruc-
     tif, pour le Pere Nicolas de S. Joseph.--
8   (Continued on next card)

Witchcraft
BF [Girard, Jean Baptiste] 1680-1733, defendant.
1582 Memoir du P. et de la Cadier. [1731]
G51   (Card 2)
M48++
     Contents--Continued.
     Reflexions sur la recrimination en pretendu
     complot imputé au Pere Estienne Thomas Ca-
     diere.--Observations sur les reponses per-
     sonnelles du P. Girard.--Second mémoire pour
     le Pere Girard.--Reponse a l'ecrit, qui a
     pour titre: Memoire des faits qui se
8   (Continued on next card)

Cadière, Catherine, b. 1709.
Witchcraft
BF [Girard, Jean Baptiste] 1680-1733, defendant.
1582 Memoir du P. et de la Cadier. [1731]
G51   (Card 3)
M48++
     Contents--Continued.
     sont passez sur les yeux de M. l'Evêque de
     Toulon.--A nosseigneurs de Parlement [par
     Estienne-Thomas Cadiere]--A nosseigneurs de
     Parlement [par Catherine Cadiere]--A nos-
     seigneurs de Parlement [par Catherine Ca-
8   diere]
                (Continued on next card)

Cadière, Catherine, b. 1709.
Witchcraft
BF Girard, Jean Baptiste, 1680-1733.
1582 Mémoire instructif pour le père Jean-
G51M5 Baptiste Girard, jesuite ... contre Marie-
1731 Catherine Cadière; et encore M. le procur-
     eur général du roy, querellant.   La Haye,
     H. Scheurleer, sur la copie imprimée à Paris,
     chez Gissey & Bordelet, 1731.
     284 p. 20cm.

"Recueil des lettres du Père Girard et de
la demoiselle Cadière, dont les ori-
                (Continued on next card)

Cadière, Catherine, b. 1709.
Witchcraft
BF Girard, Jean Baptiste, 1680-1733. Mémoire
1582 instructif pour le père Jean-Baptiste
G51M5 Girard ... 1731.   (Card 2)
1731

originaux ont été produits au procès": p. [141]-284.

1. Cadière, Catherine, b. 1709.
I. Cadière, Catherine, b. 1709. II.
Title.

Cadière, Catherine, b. 1709.
Witchcraft
BF Girard, Jean Baptiste, 1680-1733, defendant.
1582 Procedure sur laquelle le pere Jean
G51 Baptiste Girard, jesuite, Catherine Cadiere,
P9++ le pere Estienne Thomas Cadiere, dominicain,
     Mre. François Cadiere, prêtre, et le pere
     Nicolas de S. Joseph Carme Dechaussé, ont
     e'te' jugez par arrêt du parlement de
     Provence du 10. octobre 1731 ... Aix,
     Chez J. David, 1733.
     422 p. 36cm.

With this   is bound Montvalon,
A. B. de.   Motifs des juges du
parlement de   Provence qui ont été
                (Continued on next card)

Witchcraft Cadière, Catherine, b. 1709..
BF Girard, Jean Baptiste, 1680-1733, defendant.
1582 Procedure ... 1733.   (Card 2)
G51
P9++ d'avis de condamner le p. Jean Baptiste
     Girard ... [Aix?] 1733.

I. France. Parlement (Aix) II. Cadière,
     Catherine, b. 1709. III. Cadière,
     Estienne Thomas, fl. 1730. IV. Cadière,
     François, fl. 1730. V. Dechaussé, Nicolas
     de S. Joseph Carme, fl. 1730. VI. Title:
     Procedure sur laquelle le pere Jean Baptist
     Girard ... [est   été jugez.

Cadière, Catherine, b. 1709.
WITCHCRAFT
BF Girard, Jean Baptiste, 1680-1733.
1582 Recueil des lettres du Père Girard & de
G51 la Demoiselle Cadière, dont les originaux
P96 ont été produits au procès. Réflexions
v.1 générales sur ces lettres. [s.l., 173-?]
no.5 147 p. 17cm.

No. 5 in vol. lettered: Procès de Girard. [v.1]

8   I. Cadière, Catherine, b. 1709.
NIC

98

CATALOGUE OF THE CORNELL WITCHCRAFT COLLECTION

Cadière, Catherine, b. 1709.

Witchcraft
BF
1582 Girard, Jean Baptiste, 1680-1733, defendant.
G51R3   Recueil général des pièces concernant le
1731c procez entre la Demoiselle Cadière de la
       ville de Toulon, et le père Girard, jesuite
       ... La Haye, Swart, 1731.
         8 v. 17cm.

   The trials were held before the Parlement
of Aix.
   A collection of items originally published
separately; th   ere is a general title
                       (Continued on next card)

Cadière, Catherine, b. 1709..

Witchcraft
BF
1582 Girard, Jean Baptiste, 1680-1733, defendant.
G51R3   Recueil général des pièces concernant le
1731c procez ... 1731.   (Card 2)

page and a table of contents for each vol.
Bound with v.8 is Le nouveau Tarquin, usually
attributed to Jean Jacques Bel.

   I. Cadière,   Catherine, b. 1709.
   II. France. Parlement (Aix) III. Title.
   IV. [Bel, Jean   Jacques] 1693-1738.
Le nouveau Tar   quin. V. Title: Le
nouveau Tarquin.

Cadière,   Catherine, b. 1709.

itchcraft
F
582   Girard, Jean Baptiste, 1680-1733, defendant.
51R3   Recueil général des pièces contenues au
731b procez du Père Jean Baptiste Girard, Jesuite
      ... & de Demoiselle Catherine Cadière, querel-
      lante. Aix, J. David, 1731.
        6 v. fronts. 17cm.

   A collection of items originally published
separately. There is a general title page
and a table of contents for each vol. except
vol. 6. Bound   with v. 6 is Le nouveau
                      (Continued on next card)

Cadière,   Catherine, b. 1709.

itchcraft
F
582   Girard, Jean Baptiste, 1680-1733, defendant.
51R3   Recueil général des pièces contenues au
731b procez ... 1731.   (Card 2)

Tarquin, usually attributed to Jean Jacques
Bel.

   I. Cadière,   Catherine, b. 1709.
   II. Title.

WITCHCRAFT   Cadière, Catherine, b. 1709.
BF
1582   Recueil des premières requestes de la
G51   Demoiselle Cadière, du Père Estienne
P96   Thomas Cadière, Jacobin, et du Père
v.3   Nicolas, prieur des Carmes de Toulon.
       [s.l., 173-?]
         1 v. (various pagings) 17cm.
       Binder's title: Procès de Girard. [v.3]

      1. Girard, Jean Baptiste, 1680-1733. I.
   Cadière, Catherine, b. 1709. II. Cadière,
8 Estienne   Thomas, fl. 1730. III.
NIC Nicolas de   Saint Joseph, fl. 1730.

WITCHCRAFT   Cadière, Catherine, b. 1709.
BF
1582   Cadière, François, fl. 1730, appellant.
G51   Mémoire instructif, pour Messire François
P96   Cadière, prêtre de la ville de Toulon, ap-
v.2   pellant du decret d'assigné contre lui ren-
no.1   du le 23. fév. dernier, & de ce qui s'en
       est ensuivi, & demandeur en requête d'ad-
       hérance à l'appel comme d'abus relevé par
       la Demoiselle Cadière, sa soeur, de la pro-
       cedure faite à la requête du promoteur en
       l'evêché de Toulon.   Contre M. le procu-
       reur général   du Roy, intimé & défen-
       deur.   [s.l., 1731?]
8   131 p.   17cm.
NIC   (Continued on next card)

WITCHCRAFT   Cadière, Catherine, b. 1709.
BF
1582   Cadière, François, fl. 1730, appellant.
G51   Mémoire instructif ... [1731?] (Card 2)
P96
v.2   Signed: François Cadière. Bourgarel,
no.1   avocat. Simon, procureur.
          No. 1 in vol. lettered: Procès de Girard.
       [v.2]

8   1. Girard, Jean Baptiste, 1680-1733. 2.
NIC   Cadière,   Catherine, b. 1709.

Witchcraft   Cadière, Catherine, b. 1709.
BF
1582   Girard, Jean Baptiste, 1680-1733, defendant.
G51   The case of Mrs. Mary Catharine Cadiere,
C33   against the Jesuit Father John Baptist Gi-
1732   rard. In a memorial presented to the Par-
       liament of Aix. Wherein he is accused of
       seducing her, by the abominable doctrines
       of quietism, into the most criminal ex-
       cesses of lewdness, and under an appearance
       of the highest mystical devotion, deluding
       into the same vices six other females, who
       had put their   consciences under his
8   (Continued on next card)

Witchcraft   Cadière, Catherine, b. 1709.
BF
1582   Girard, Jean Baptiste, 1680-1733, defendant.
G51   The case of Mrs. Mary Catharine Cadiere ...
C33   1732.   (Card 2)
1732
       direction. With a preface by the publisher
       ... 10th ed. corr. London, Printed for
       and sold by J. Roberts, 1732.
         vi, 96 p. 23cm.
       "This memorial was originally drawn up
       by that eminent lawyer ... Chaudon ... the
       following piece   is not a bare transla-
8   tion ..." p. ii   (Continued on next card)

Witchcraft   Cadière, Catherine, b. 1709.
BF
1582   Girard, Jean Baptiste, 1680-1733, defendant.
G51M5   A compleat translation of the Memorial of
1732   the Jesuit Father John Baptist Girard, rector
       of the Royal Seminary of the Chaplains of the
       Navy, in the city of Toulon, against Mary
       Catherine Cadière and the atorney [sic] gen-
       eral, plaintiff. London, Printed for J.
       Millan, 1732.
         172, 143 p. 17cm.

       "A collection   of the letters of Father
       Girard and Mary   Catherine Cadière, the
                             (Continued on next card)

Witchcraft   Cadière, Catherine, b. 1709.
BF
1582   Girard, Jean Baptiste, 1680-1733, defendant.
G51M5   A compleat translation of the Memorial of
1732   the Jesuit Father John Baptist Girard ...
       1732.   (Card 2)

originals whereof were produced in court":
143 p. at end.

    1. Cadière,   Catherine, b. 1709.
I. Girard, Jean Baptiste, 1680-1733. Mémoire
instructif... --   English. II. Cadière,
    Catherine,   b. 1709. III. Title.

Witchcraft   Cadière, Catherine, b. 1709.
BF
1582   [Girard, Jean Baptiste] 1680-1733, defendant.
G51   Memoir [sic] du P. et de la Cadier [sic]
M48++   [Aix, etc., De l'imprimerie de la veuve
        de Joseph Senez, etc., 1731]
          various pagings. 32cm.
        Cover title.
        Contents.--Mémoire instructif, pour Mes-
        sire François Cadière.--Observations sur le
        memoire manuscrit distribué par le P. Girard.
        --Memoire du Pere Girard.--Memoire instruc-
        tif, pour le Pere Nicolas de S. Joseph.--
8   (Continued on next card)

Cadière, Catherine, b. 1709.

Witchcraft
BF
1582   [Girard, Jean Baptiste] 1680-1733, defendant.
G51   Memoir du P. et de la Cadier. [1731]
M48++   (Card 2)

       Contents--Continued.
    Reflexions sur la recrimination en pretendu
complot imputé au Pere Estienne Thomas Cadiere.--Observations sur les reponses per-
sonnelles du P. Girard.--Second mémoire pour
le Pere Girard.--Reponse a l'ecrit, qui a
pour titre: Me   moire des faits qui se
8   (Continued on next card)

Cadière, Catherine, b. 1709.

Witchcraft
BF
1582   [Girard, Jean Baptiste] 1680-1733, defendant.
G51   Memoir du P. et de la Cadier. [1731]
M48++   (Card 3)

       Contents--Continued.
sont passez sous les yeux de M. l'Evêque de
Toulon.--A nosseigneurs de Parlement [par
Estienne-Thomas Cadière]--A nosseigneurs de
Parlement [par Catherine Cadiere]--A nosseigneurs de Parlement [par Catherine Ca-
diere]
8   (Continued on next card)

Cadière, Catherine, b. 1709.

WITCHCRAFT
BF
1582   Girard, Jean Baptiste, 1680-1733, respondent
G51   Mémoire instructif, pour le Père Jean
P96   Baptiste Girard, Jesuite, recteur du Se-
v.2   minaire Royal de la Marine de la ville de
no.4   Toulon. Contre Marie Catherine Cadière,
        & encore M. le Procureur Général du Roi,
        querellant.   [s.l., 173-?]
          144 p. 17cm.

        No. 4 in vol. lettered: Procès de Girard.
        [v.2]

8
NIC   1. Cadière,   Catherine, b. 1709.

Cadière, Catherine, b. 1709..

Witchcraft
BF
1582   Girard, Jean Baptiste, 1680-1733.
G51M5   Mémoire instructif pour le père Jean-
1731   Baptiste Girard, jesuite ... contre Marie-
        Catherine Cadière; et encore M. le procur-
        eur général du roy, querellant. La Haye,
        H. Scheurleer, sur la copie imprimée à Paris,
        chez Gissey & Bordelet, 1731.
          284 p. 20cm.

        "Recueil des lettres du Père Girard et de
la demoiselle Ca   dière, dont les ori-
                      (Continued on next card)

Cadière, Catherine, b. 1709.

Witchcraft
BF
1582   Girard, Jean Baptiste, 1680-1733. Mémoire
G51M5   instructif pour le père Jean-Baptiste
1731   Girard ... 1731.   (Card 2)

       originaux ont été produits au procès": p.
[141]-284.

       1. Cadière,   Catherine, b. 1709.
I. Cadière,   Catherine,   II.
Title.

Cadière, Catherine, b. 1709.

Witchcraft
BF
1582   Girard, Jean Baptiste, 1680-1733, defendant.
G51R3   [Recueil des pièces concernant le procez
1731d   entre le père Girard, jesuite, et la Demoi-
        selle Cadière. n.p., 1731?]
          1 v. (various pagings) 17cm.

        Cover-title: Procès de Girard. Tom. II.
        Contents.--1. Mémoire instructif pour le
        p. Nicolas de Saint Joseph.--2. Thorame, Paz-
        ery. Second mémoire pour le p. Girard. Jes-
        uite.--3. Ca   dière, M. C. Justi-
                                (Continued on next card)

CATALOGUE OF THE CORNELL WITCHCRAFT COLLECTION

Cadière, Catherine, b. 1709.
Witchcraft
BF   Girard, Jean Baptiste, 1680-1733, defendant.
1582   ₍Recueil des pièces concernant le procez
G51R3   ... n.p., 1731?₎   (Card 2)
1731d
             Contents--Continued.
          fication.--4. Premières actes et contrat
          protestatifs de la Demoiselle Cadière.--5.
          Mémoire des faits qui se sont passez sous les
          yeux de M. l'évêque de Toulon.--6. Cadière,
          M. C. Réponse à l'écrit de M. l'évêque de
          Toulon.--7. Cadière, François. Second
                        (Continued on next card)

Cadière, Catherine, b. 1709.
Witchcraft
BF   Girard, Jean Baptiste, 1680-1733, defendant.
1582   ₍Recueil des pièces concernant le procez
G51R3   ... n.p., 1731?₎   (Card 3)
1731d
             Contents--Continued.
          mémoire par M. Cadière, prêtre.--8. Cadière,
          E. T. Réponse au second mémoire imprimé sous
          le nom du p. Girard, jesuite.
             I. Cadière, Catherine, b. 1709.
             II. Title.

Cadière, Catherine, b. 1709.
Witchcraft
BF   Girard, Jean Baptiste, 1680-1733, defen-
1582   dant.
G51   The tryal of Father John Baptist Girard
T8   on an accusation of quietism, sorcery, in-
          cest, abortion and subornation, before the
          great chamber of Parlement at Aix, at the
          instance of Miss Mary Catherine Cadiere
          ... London, Printed for J. Isted, 1732.
             48 p. 23cm.
             Bound in sprinkled calf gilt by W. Pratt.
             1. Cadière, Catherine, b.
          1709.   I. Title.

Cadiere, Catherine, b. 1709.
WITCHCRAFT
BF   Memoirs of Miss Mary-Catherine Cadiere,
1582   and Father Girard, Jesuit, containing
G51   an exact account of that extraordinary
M53   affair; interspers'd with letters and
          other original papers relating thereto,
          and which have hitherto been unknown to
          the publick. In an epistle from a per-
          son of quality at Paris to his corre-
          spondent in London. London, Printed
          for J. Isted, 1731.
             32 p. 20cm.
          1. Cadiere, Catherine, b.1709. 2.
8   Girard, Jean Baptiste, 1680-1733.
NIC   I. A Person of quality at Paris.

WITCHCRAFT
BF   ₍Cadière, Estienne Thomas₎ fl. 1730.
1582   Observations sur le Mémoire manuscrit,
G51   attribué par le Père Girard, dans le cours
P96   de la plaidoirie de M. l'Avocat Général.
v.1   ₍s.l., 173-?₎
no.7   28 p. 17cm.
             Signed: P. Etienne Thomas Cadière.
             No. 7 in vol. lettered: Procès de Girard.
          ₍v.1₎
8   I. Girard, Jean Baptiste, 1680-1733.
NIC   II. Girard, Jean Baptiste, 1680-1733.
             III. Title.

WITCHCRAFT
BF   Cadière, Estienne Thomas, fl. 1730.
1582   Réflexions sur la récrimination en pré-
G51   tendu complot, imputé au Père Estienne
P96   Thomas Cadière ... par le P. Jean Baptiste
v.1   Girard ... ₍s.l., 173-?₎
no.6   144 p. 17cm.
             No. 6 in vol. lettered: Procès de Girard.
          ₍v.1₎
8   I. Girard, Jean Baptiste, 1680-1733.
NIC   II. Title.

Cadière, Estienne Thomas, fl. 1730.
Witchcraft
BF   ₍Girard, Jean Baptiste₎ 1680-1733, defendant.
1582   Memoir ₍sic₎ du P. et de la Cadier ₍sic₎
G51   ₍Aix, etc., De l'imprimerie de la veuve
M48++   de Joseph Senez, etc., 1731₎
             various pagings. 32cm.
             Cover title.
             Contents.--Mémoire instructif, pour Mes-
          sire François Cadiere.--Observations sur le
          memoire manuscrit distribué par le P. Girard.
          --Memoire du Pere Girard.--Memoire instruc-
          tif, pour le Pere Nicolas de S. Joseph.--
8   (Continued on next card)

Cadière, Estienne Thomas, fl. 1730.
Witchcraft
BF   ₍Girard, Jean Baptiste₎ 1680-1733, defendant.
1582   Memoir du P. et de la Cadier. ₍1731₎
G51   (Card 2)
M48++
             Contents--Continued.
          Reflexions sur la recrimination en pretendu
          complot imputé au Pere Estienne Thomas Ca-
          diere.--Observations sur les reponses per-
          sonnelles du P. Girard.--Second mémoire pour
          le Pere Girard.--Reponse a l'ecrit, qui a
          pour titre: Memoire des faits qui se
8   (Continued on next card)

Cadière, Estienne Thomas, fl. 1730.
Witchcraft
BF   ₍Girard, Jean Baptiste₎ 1680-1733, defendant.
1582   Memoir du P. et de la Cadier. ₍1731₎
G51   (Card 3)
M48++
             Contents--Continued.
          sont passez sour les yeux de M. l'Evêque de
          Toulon.--A nosseigneurs de Parlement ₍par
          Estienne-Thomas Cadière₎--A nosseigneurs de
          Parlement ₍par Catherine Cadière₎--A nos-
          seigneurs de Parlement ₍par Catherine Ca-
          diere₎
8   (Continued on next card)

Cadière, Estienne Thomas, fl. 1730.
Witchcraft
BF   Girard, Jean Baptiste, 1680-1733, defendant.
1582   Procedure sur laquelle le pere Jean
G51   Baptiste Girard, jesuite, Catherine Cadiere,
P9++   le pere Estienne Thomas Cadiere, dominicain,
          Mre. François Cadiere, prêtre, et le pere
          Nicolas de S. Joseph Carme Dechaussé, ont
          e'te' jugez par arrêt du parlement de
          Provence du 10. octobre 1731 ... Aix,
          Chez J. David, 1733.
             422 p. 36cm.
             With this is bound Montvalon,
          A. B. de.   Motifs des juges du
          parlement de   Provence qui ont été
                        (Continued on next card)

Witchcraft   Cadière, Estienne Thomas, fl. 1730.
BF   Girard, Jean Baptiste, 1680-1733, defendant.
1582   Procedure ... 1733.   (Card 2)
G51
P9++   d'avis de condamner le p. Jean Baptiste
          Girard ... ₍Aix?₎ 1733.
             I. France. Parlement (Aix) II. Cadière,
             Catherine, b. 1709. III. Cadière,
             Estienne Thomas, fl. 1730. IV. Cadière,
             François, fl. 1730. V. Dechaussé, Nicolas
             de S. Joseph Carme, fl. 1730. VI. Title:
             Procedure sur laquelle le pere Jean Baptiste
             Girard ... est été jugez.

WITCHCRAFT   Cadière, Estienne Thomas, fl. 1730.
BF   Recueil des premières requestes de la
1582   Demoiselle Cadière, du Père Estienne
G51   Thomas Cadière, Jacobin, et du Père
P96   Nicolas, prieur des Carmes de Toulon.
v.3   ₍s.l., 173-?₎
             1 v. (various pagings) 17cm.
             Binder's title: Procès de Girard. ₍v.3₎
             1. Girard, Jean Baptiste, 1680-1733. I.
          Cadière, Catherine, b. 1709. II. Cadière,
8   Estienne Thomas, fl. 1730. III.
NIC   Nicolas de Saint Joseph, fl. 1730.

WITCHCRAFT   Cadière, François, fl. 1730, appellant.
BF   Mémoire instructif, pour Messire François
1582   Cadière, prêtre de la ville de Toulon, ap-
G51   pellant du decret d'assigné contre lui ren-
P96   du le 23. fév. dernier, & de ce qui s'en
v.2   est ensuivi, & demandeur en requête d'ad-
no.1   hérance à l'appel comme d'abus relevé par
          la Demoiselle Cadière, sa soeur, de la pro-
          cedure faite à la requête du promoteur en
          l'evêché de Toulon. Contre M. le procu-
          reur général du Roy, intimé & défen-
          deur.   ₍s.l., 1731?₎
8   131 p. 17cm.
NIC   (Continued on next card)

WITCHCRAFT   Cadière, François, fl. 1730, appellant.
BF   Mémoire instructif ... ₍1731?₎ (Card 2)
1582
G51   Signed: François Cadière. Bourgarel,
P96   avocat. Simon, procureur.
v.2   No. 1 in vol. lettered: Procès de Girard.
no.1   ₍v.2₎

8   I. Girard, Jean Baptiste, 1680-1733. II.
NIC   Cadière, Catherine, b. 1709.
             I. Title.

Cadière, François, fl. 1730.
Witchcraft
BF   ₍Girard, Jean Baptiste₎ 1680-1733, defendant.
1582   Memoir ₍sic₎ du P. et de la Cadier ₍sic₎
G51   ₍Aix, etc., De l'imprimerie de la veuve
M48++   de Joseph Senez, etc., 1731₎
             various pagings. 32cm.
             Cover title.
             Contents.--Mémoire instructif, pour Mes-
          sire François Cadiere.--Observations sur le
          memoire manuscrit distribué par le P. Girard.
          --Memoire du Pere Girard.--Memoire instruc-
          tif, pour le Pere Nicolas de S. Joseph.--
8   (Continued on next card)

Cadière, François, fl. 1730.
Witchcraft
BF   ₍Girard, Jean Baptiste₎ 1680-1733, defendant.
1582   Memoir du P. et de la Cadier. ₍1731₎
G51   (Card 2)
M48++
             Contents--Continued.
          Reflexions sur la recrimination en pretendu
          complot imputé au Pere Estienne Thomas Ca-
          diere.--Observations sur les reponses per-
          sonnelles du P. Girard.--Second mémoire pour
          le Pere Girard.--Reponse a l'ecrit, qui a
          pour titre: Memoire des faits qui se
8   (Continued on next card)

Cadière, François, fl. 1730.
Witchcraft
BF   ₍Girard, Jean Baptiste₎ 1680-1733, defendant.
1582   Memoir du P. et de la Cadier. ₍1731₎
G51   (Card 3)
M48++
             Contents--Continued.
          sont passez sour les yeux de M. l'Evêque de
          Toulon.--A nosseigneurs de Parlement ₍par
          Estienne-Thomas Cadière₎--A nosseigneurs de
          Parlement ₍par Catherine Cadière₎--A nos-
          seigneurs de Parlement ₍par Catherine Ca-
          diere₎
8   (Continued on next card)

Cadière, François, fl. 1730.
Witchcraft
BF   Girard, Jean Baptiste, 1680-1733, defendant.
1582   Procedure sur laquelle le pere Jean
G51   Baptiste Girard, jesuite, Catherine Cadiere,
P9++   le pere Estienne Thomas Cadiere, dominicain,
          Mre. François Cadiere, prêtre, et le pere
          Nicolas de S. Joseph Carme Dechaussé, ont
          e'te' jugez par arrêt du parlement de
          Provence du 10. octobre 1731 ... Aix,
          Chez J. David, 1733.
             422 p. 36cm.
             With this is bound Montvalon,
          A. B. de.   Motifs des juges du
          parlement de   Provence qui ont été
                        (Continued on next card)

CATALOGUE OF THE CORNELL WITCHCRAFT COLLECTION

Witchcraft   Cadière, François, fl. 1730.
BF   Girard, Jean Baptiste, 1680-1733, defendant.
1582   Procedure ... 1733.   (Card 2)
G51
P9++   d'avis de condamner le p. Jean Baptiste
     Girard ... [Aix?] 1733.

     I. France. Parlement (Aix) II. Cadière,
     Catherine, b. 1709. III. Cadière,
     Estienne Thomas, fl. 1730. IV. Cadière,
     François, fl. 1730. V. Dechaussé, Nicolas
     de S. Joseph Carme, fl. 1730. VI. Title:
     Procedure sur laquelle le pere Jean Baptiste
     Girard ... [est été jugez.

Cadière, Marie Catherine, b. 1709.

see

Cadière, Catherine, b. 1709.

Cadière, Mary Catherine, b. 1709.

see

Cadière, Catherine, b. 1709.

Witchcraft   Cäsar, Aquilin Julius.
BF   Abhandlung von Erscheinung der Geister.
1565   [München] 1789.
C12   39 p. 18cm.

     Bound with his Ist die Nichtigkeit der
     Zauberey ganz erwiesen? München, 1789.

     1. Ghosts.   2. Apparitions.
     I. Title.

Witchcraft   Cäsar, Aquilin Julius.
BF   Ist die Nichtigkeit der Zauberey ganz
1565   erwiesen? [München] 1789.
C12   56 p. 18cm.

     With this are bound his Abhandlung von
     Erscheinung der Geister. München, 1789,
     and his Meine Bedenken von den Besessenen
     der Welt vorgelegt. München, 1789.

     1. Witchcraft.   I. Title.

Witchcraft   Cäsar, Aquilin Julius.
BF   Meine Bedenken von den Besessenen der
1565   Welt vorgelegt. [München] 1789.
C12   56 p. 18cm.

     Bound with his Ist die Nichtigkeit der
     Zauberey ganz erwiesen? München, 1789.

     1. Demonology.   I. Title.

Witchcraft   Cagliostro, Alessandro, conte di, assumed
BF   name of Giuseppe Balsamo, 1743-1795, de-
1598   fendant.
C13   Procès de Joseph Balsamo, surnommé le
A2   comte Cagliostro. Commencé devant le Tri-
1791   bunal de la Ste. Inquisition en décembre
     1790, & jugé définitivement par le pape le 7
     avril 1791. Avec des éclaircissemens sur la
     vie de Cagliostro, & sur les différentes
     sectes de Francs-Maçons. Ouvrage traduit

     (Continued on next card)

Witchcraft
BF   Cagliostro, Alessandro, conte di, assumed
1598   name of Giuseppe Balsamo, 1743-1795, de-
C13   fendant. Procès de Joseph Balsamo, surnommé
A2   le comte Cagliostro. 1791.   (Card 2)
1791

     sur l'original publié à Rome... Liège, J.
     J. Tutot, 1791.
     iv, 295 p. 17cm.

     Ex libris Arthur Flower-Ellis.

     1. Freemasons.   I. Title.
     II. Inquisition. Italy.

Witchcraft   Cagliostro, Alessandro, conte di, assumed
BF   name of Giuseppe Balsamo, 1743-1795.
1598   Alméras, Henri d', 1861-1938.
C13   ... Cagliostro (Joseph Balsamo) La franc-maçonnerie
A44   et l'occultisme au XVIIIe siècle. D'après des documents
     inédits. Paris, Société française d'imprimerie et de
     librairie, 1904.

     2 p. l., 386 p. front. (port.) 19cm. (Les romans de l'histoire)
     "Les sources": p. 1–22.

     1. Cagliostro, Alessandro, conte di, assumed name of Giuseppe Balsamo, 1743-1795.

     Library of Congress   5-24040

Witchcraft   Cagliostro, Alessandro, conte di, assumed
BF   name of Giuseppe Balsamo, 1743-1795.
1598   [Barberi,]
C13   Compendio della vita, e delle gesta di Giuseppe Bal-
B23   samo, denominato il conte Cagliostro, che si è estratto dal
1791b   processo contro di lui formato in Roma l'anno 1790.
     E che può servire di scorta per conoscere l'indole della
     setta de' Liberi muratori. Roma, Stamp. della Rev. Ca-
     mera apostolica, 1791.

     189 p. front. (ports.) 19cm.

     1. Cagliostro, Alessandro, conte di, assumed name of Giuseppe Balsamo,
     1743-1795. 2. Freemasons. I. Title.
     Library of Congress   BF1598.C2B3 1791   CA 7—7324 Unrev'd

---

Witchcraft.   Cagliostro, Alessandro, conte di, assumed
BF   name of Giuseppe Balsamo, 1743-1795.
1598   [Barberi,]
C13   Kurzgefasste Beschreibung des Lebens
B23   und der Thaten des Joseph Balsamo, oder
1791d   sogenannten Grafen Kagliostro, gezogen aus
     dem wider ihn zu Rom 1790; angestellten
     Prozesse: zur Beleuchtung der wahren
     Beschaffenheit der Freymaurersekte. Aus
     dem Italiänischen ins Deutsche übersetzt.
     Augsburg, J. N. Styx, 1791.
     86, 40, 112, 23 p. 17cm.

     (Continued on next card)

Witchcraft   Cagliostro, Alessandro, conte di, assumed
BF   name of Giuseppe Balsamo, 1743-1795.
1598   [Barberi,] Kurzgefasste Beschreibung
C13   des Lebens und der Thaten des Joseph
B23   Balsamo ... 1791.   (Card 2)
1791d

     Translation of Compendio della vita, e
     delle gesta di Giuseppe Balsamo.

     1. Cagliostro, Alessandro, conte di,
     assumed name of Giuseppe Balsamo, 1743-
     1795. 2. Freemasons. I. His Compendio
     della vita, e delle gesta di Giuseppe
     Balsamo--German. II. Title.
     III. Autograph-- Dumont, Paul.

Witchcraft   Cagliostro, Alessandro, conte di, assumed
BF   name of Giuseppe Balsamo, 1743-1795.
1598   [Barberi,]
C13   Vie de Joseph Balsamo, connu sous le nom
B23   de comte Cagliostro. Extraite de la procédure
1791   instruite contre lui à Rome en 1790. Traduite
     d'après l'original italien, imprimé à la
     Chambre apostolique. Enrichie de notes curieu-
     ses, et ornée de son portrait. 2. éd.   Paris,
     Onfroy, 1791.
     xxvi, 239 p. front. (port.) 19cm.

     Translation of Compendio della vita e delle
     gesta di Giuseppe Balsamo.

     (Continued on next card)

Witchcraft   Cagliostro, Alessandro, conte di, assumed
BF   name of Giuseppe Balsamo, 1743-1795.
1598   [Barberi,]   Vie de Joseph Balsamo
C13   ... 1791.   (Card 2)
B23
1791   With this is bound Goupil, P. E. A. Essais
     historiques sur ... Marie Antoinette. Londres,
     1789.

     1. Cagliostro, Alessandro, conte di, assumed
     name of Giuseppe Balsamo, 1743-1795. I.
     Barberi. Compendio della vita e delle gesta di
     Giuseppe Balsamo--French. II. Title.

Cagliostro, Alessandro, conte di,
     assumed name of Giuseppe Balsamo, 1743-
WITCHCRAFT   1795.
DC   [Luchet, Jean Pierre Louis de la Roche du
137   Maine, marquis de] 1740-1792.
.15   Memoir authentique pour servir à l'his-
L93   toire du comte de Cagliostro. Nouv. ed.
1786a   Strasbourg, 1786.
     iv, 36 p. 22cm.

     1. Diamond necklace affair. 2. Cag-
     liostro, Alessandro, conte di, assumed name
     of Giuseppe Balsamo, 1743-1795. I.
8   Title.

Witchcraft   Cagliostro, Alessandro, conte di, assumed
BF   name of Giuseppe Balsamo, 1743-1795.
1598   [Lucia] pseud.
C13   The life of the Count Cagliostro ... dedi-
L93   cated to Madame la Comtesse de Cagliostro.
1787   2d ed.   London, Printed for the author, and
     sold by T. Hookham, 1787.
     viii, xxxii, 127 p. 22cm.

     Dedication signed: Lucia.

     1. Cagliostro, Alessandro, conte di, assum-
     ed name of Giuseppe Balsamo, 1743-1795. I.
     Title.

WITCHCRAFT   Cagliostro, Alessandro, conte di, assumed
BF   name of Giuseppe Balsamo, 1743-1795.
1408   Sierke, Eugen, 1845-
S57   Schwärmer und Schwindler zu Ende des
     achtzehnten Jahrhunderts. Leipzig, S.
     Hirzel, 1874.
     vi, 462 p. 21cm.
     1. Occult sciences--Biography. 2.
     Superstition. 3. Swedenborg, Emanuel,
     1688-1772. 4. Mesmer, Franz Anton, 1734-
     1815. 5. Gassner, Johann Joseph, 1727-
     1779. 6. Schrepfer, Johann Georg, 1730?-
8   1774. 7.   Cagliostro, Alessandro,
NIC   conte de, as sumed name of Giuseppe
     Balsamo, 1743 -1795. I. Title.

Witchcraft   Cahagnet, Louis Alphonse, 1809-1885.
BF   Magie magnétique; ou, Traité historique
1412   et pratique de fascinations, miroirs caba-
C13   listiques, apports, suspensions, pactes,
1858   talismans ... 2. éd., corr. et augm.
     Paris, G. Baillière, 1858.
     516 p. 18cm.
     First published 1854.

     1. Occult sciences--Hist. I. Title.
     II. Title: Traité historique et pratique
8   des fascinations.

CATALOGUE OF THE CORNELL WITCHCRAFT COLLECTION

Witchcraft
Z 6876 C13
Caillet, Albert Louis, 1869–
... Manuel bibliographique des sciences psychiques ou occultes ... Paris, L. Dorbon, 1912.
3 v. fold. tab. 25½ cm.
Covers dated 1913.
"Réunion de plusieurs bibliographies partielles et de catalogues, célèbres mais peu communs, fondus en un seul corps aussi homogène que possible."—Pref.
11,648 entries.

1. Occult sciences—Bibl. I. Title.
Z6876.C25   13–10632
Library of Congress   (53c1)

Witchcraft
BF 1600 C14 1658++
Caldera de Heredia, Gaspar.
Tribunal magicvm, quo omnia quae ad magiam spectant, accurate tranctantur & explanantur, seu Tribunalis medici [pars secunda] Lugduni Batavorum, apud Johannem Elsevirium, 1658.
194 p. 37cm.

I. Title.

Caldwell, R   C
Demonolatry, devil-dancing, and demoniacal possession.
Witchcraft
BL 305 A79
Articles on mythology, etc. [v.p.], 1871-1880.
1 v. (various pagings) 25cm.

Cover-title.
Articles reprinted from Contemporary review and Nineteenth century, with one from Once a week.
Contents.--On the philosophy of mythology, by Max Müller.--Germanic mythology, by Karl Blind.--The first sin, by François Lenormant.--The myths of the sea and the river of
(Continued on next card)

Caldwell, R   C
Demonolatry, devil-dancing, and demoniacal possession.
Witchcraft
BL 305 A79
Articles on mythology, etc. 1871-1880.
(Card 2)

Contents--Continued.
death, by C. F. Keary.--Wind myths, by C. F. Keary.--Forest and field myths, by W. R. S. Ralston.--Cinderella, by W. R. S. Ralston.--Demonology of the New Testament, by J. J. Owen.--Demoniacal possession in India, by W. Knighton.--Demonolatry, devil-dancing, and demoniacal possession, by R. C. Caldwell.--Witchcraft in Devon.

Calef, Robert

Witchcraft
BF 1575 C14
Calef, Robert, 1648-1719, comp.
More wonders of the invisible world: or, The wonders of the invisible world, display'd in five parts ... To which is added a Postscript relating to a book intitled, The life of Sir William Phips. London, Printed for N. Hillar and Jos. Collyer, 1700.
156 p. 17cm.
Ex libris Brinley.
Bound in full crimson crushed levant, gilt extra, all edges gilt, by W. Pratt.

Witchcraft
BF 1575 D76 v.2-3
Calef, Robert, 1648-1719.
More wonders of the invisible world: or, The wonders of the invisible world, display'd in five parts. Part I. An account of the sufferings of Margaret Rule, written by the Reverend Mr. C. M. P. II. Several letters to the author, &c. And his reply relating to witchcraft. P. III. The differences between the inhabitants of Salem village, and Mr. Parris their minister, in New-England. P. IV. Letters of a gentleman uninterested, endeavouring to prove the received opinions about witchcraft to be orthodox. With short essays to their answers. P. v. A short historical accout [!] of matters of fact in that affair. To
(Continued on next card)
[r31e2]   2-13714 rev.

Witchcraft
BF 1575 D76 v.2-3
Calef, Robert, 1648-1719. More wonders of the invisible world ... (Card 2)
which is added, a postscript relating to a book intitled, The life of Sir William Phips. Collected by Robert Calef, merchant, of Boston in New-England ... London, Printed for N. Hillar and J. Collyer, 1700.
Reprint. (In Drake, S. G. The witchcraft delusion in New England ... Roxbury, Mass., 1866. 21½cm. v. 2, p. 1-212; v. 3, p. 3-167)
Woodward's historical series. no. VI-VII.
Prefatory: by the editor: p. [v]-x. Pedigree of Calef: 1 fold. leaf.
Memoir of Robert Calef: p. [xi]-xxix.
The text, here annotated, is that of the 1st edition, 1700. "It is given as exactly like the original as a much better type can be made to imitate an old type of 166 years ago."—Pref. by the editor. p. vi.
(Continued on next card)
[r31e2]   2-13714 rev.

Witchcraft
BF 1575 D76 v.2-3
Calef, Robert, 1648-1719. More wonders of the invisible world ... 1700. (Card 3)
Appendix: I. Examination of Giles Cory.--II. Giles Corey and Goodwyfe Corey. A ballad of 1692. III. Testimony of William Beale, of Marblehead, against Mr. Philip English of Salem, given Aug. 2d. 1692.--IV. [Examination of the Indian woman belonging to Mr. Parris's family]--V. The examination of Mary Clark of Haverhill.--VI. An account of the life and character of the Rev.
(Continued on next card)

Witchcraft
BF 1575 D76 v.2-3
Calef, Robert, 1648-1719. More wonders of the invisible world ... 1700. (Card 4)
Samuel Parris, of Salem village, and of his connection with the witchcraft delusion of 1692. By Samuel P. Fowler.

1. Mather, Cotton, 1663-1728. The wonders of the invisible world. 2. Mather, Cotton, 1663-1728 Pietas in patriam. The life of Sir W. Phips.
(Continued on next card)

Witchcraft
BF 1575 D76 v.2-3
Calef, Robert, 1648-1719. More wonders of the invisible world ... 1700. (Card 5)
3. Phips, Sir William, 1651-1695. 4. Rule, Margaret. 5. Parris, Samuel, 1653-1720. 6. Corey, Giles, 1611?-1692. 7. English, Philip, 1650-1734. 8. Clark, Mrs. Mary, of Haverhill. 9. Witchcraft--New England. I. Title.

BF 1575 D76 v.2-3
Calef, Robert, 1648-1719.
More wonders of the invisible world: or, The wonders of the invisible world, display'd in five parts. Part I. An account of the sufferings of Margaret Rule, written by the Reverend Mr. C. M. P. II. Several letters to the author, &c. And his reply relating to witchcraft. P. III. The differences between the inhabitants of Salem village, and Mr. Parris their minister, in New-England. P. IV. Letters of a gentleman uninterested, endeavouring to prove the received opinions about witchcraft to be orthodox. With short essays to their answers. P. v. A short historical accout [!] of matters of fact in that affair. To
(Continued on next card)
[r31e2]   2-13714 rev.

BF 1575 D76 v.2-3
Calef, Robert, 1648-1719.   More wonders of the invisible world ... (Card 2)
which is added, a postscript relating to a book intitled, The life of Sir William Phips. Collected by Robert Calef, merchant, of Boston in New-England ... London, Printed for N. Hillar and J. Collyer, 1700.
Reprint. (In Drake, S. G. The witchcraft delusion in New England ... Roxbury, Mass., 1866. 21½cm. v. 2, p. 1-212; v. 3, p. 3-167)
Woodward's historical series. no. VI-VII.
Prefatory: by the editor: p. [v]-x. Pedigree of Calef: 1 fold. leaf.
Memoir of Robert Calef: p. [xi]-xxix.
The text, here annotated, is that of the 1st edition, 1700. "It is given as exactly like the original as a much better type can be made to imitate an old type of 166 years ago."—Pref. by the editor. p. vi.
(Continued on next card)
[r31e2]   2-13714 rev.

BF 1575 D76 v.2-3
Calef, Robert, 1648-1719. More wonders of the invisible world ... 1700. (Card 3)
Appendix: I. Examination of Giles Cory.--II. Giles Corey and Goodwyfe Corey. A ballad of 1692. III. Testimony of William Beale, of Marblehead, against Mr. Philip English of Salem, given Aug. 2d. 1692.--IV. [Examination of the Indian woman belonging to Mr. Parris's family]--V. The examination of Mary Clark of Haverhill.--VI. An account of the life and character of the Rev. Samuel Parris, of Salem village, and of his connection with the witchcraft delusion of 1692. By Samuel P. Fowler.

CATALOGUE OF THE CORNELL WITCHCRAFT COLLECTION

WITCHCRAFT
BF
1575
C14
1796

Calef, Robert, 1648-1719.
More wonders of the invisible world: or, The wonders of the invisible world, displayed in five parts ... To which is added a postscript ... Printed in London in the year 1700. Salem, Mass., Printed by W. Carlton, 1796.
318 p. 18cm.

Title on spine: Salem witchcraft.
In case.

8

Witchcraft
BF
1575
C14
1823

Calef, Robert, 1648-1719.
More wonders of the invisible world, or The wonders of the invisible world displayed. In five parts. Part I.—An account of the sufferings of Margaret Rule, written by the Rev. Cotton Mather. Part II.—Several letters to the author, &c. and his reply relating to witchcraft. Part III.—The differences between the inhabitants of Salem village, and Mr. Parris, their minister, in New-England. Part IV.—Letters of a gentleman uninterested, endeavouring to prove the received opinions about witchcraft to be orthodox. With short essays to their answers. Part V.—A short historical account of matters of
(Continued on next card)
[31e2]   2-13712 rev.

Witchcraft
BF
1575
C14
1823

Calef, Robert, 1648-1719.   More wonders of the invisible world ... (Card 2)
fact in that affair. To which is added a postscript [!] relating to a book entitled "The life of Sir Wm. Phips". Collected by Robert Calef, Merchant, of Boston, in New-England. Printed in London, 1700. Salem, Re-printed by J. D. & T. C. Cushing, jr. for Cushing and Appleton, 1823.
312 p. 18½ cm.
Appended: Giles Cory [a report of his examination, taken from the witchcraft records]: p. 310-312.
(Continued on next card)
[31e2]   2-13712 rev.

Witchcraft
1575
14
323

Calef, Robert, 1648-1719. More wonders of the invisible world ... 1823.   (Card 3)

"The second Salem edition appears to have been copied from the first [Salem edition] that of 1796. In some instances slight departures are made from the copy ... such departures are also departures from the original [London edition of 1700]"—S. G. Drake, pref. to ed. of 1866.

1. Mather, Cotton, 1663-1728. The wonders of the invisible world. 2. Mather, Cotton, 1663-
(Continued on next card)

Witchcraft
75
4
23

Calef, Robert, 1648-1719. More wonders of the invisible world ... 1823.   (Card 4)

1728. Pietas in patriam. The life of Sir W. Phips. 3. Phips, Sir William, 1651-1695. 4. Rule, Margaret. 5. Parris, Samuel, 1653-1720. 6. Witchcraft—New England. 7. Corey, Giles, 1611?-1692. I. Title.

Witchcraft
BF
1575
C14
1865

Calef, Robert, 1648-1719.
More wonders of the invisible world.
Salem witchcraft: comprising More wonders of the invisible world, collected by Robert Calef; and Wonders of the invisible world, by Cotton Mather; together with notes and explanations by Samuel P. Fowler. Boston, William Veazie, 1865.
450 p. 22cm.

Witchcraft
BF
1575
C14
1828

Calef, Robert, 1648-1719.
More wonders of the invisible world.
Wonders of the invisible world, or, Salem witchcraft. In five parts. Boston, T. Bedlington [1828]
333 p. front. 14cm.

A reply to Cotton Mather's "Wonders of the invisible world."
First ed. published in 1700 under title: More wonders of the invisible world displayed.
(Continued on next card)

Witchcraft
BF
1575
C14
1828

Calef, Robert, 1648-1719.   Wonders of the invisible world ... [1828]   (Card 2)

Contents.—Part 1. An account of the sufferings of Margaret Rule, by Cotton Mather.—Part 2. Several letters from the author to Mr. Mather and others, relating to witchcraft.—Part 3. Account of the differences in Salem village between the villagers and their minister, Mr. Parris.—Part 4. Letters of a gentleman uninter-
(Continued on next card)

Witchcraft
BF
1575
C14
1828

Calef, Robert, 1648-1719.   Wonders of the invisible world ... [1828]   (Card 3)

ested, endeavouring to prove the received opinions about witchcraft to be orthodox.—Part 5. An impartial account of the most memorable matters of fact touching the supposed witchcraft in New-England.—Postscript, relating to Cotton Mather's life of Sir William Phips.—Giles Cory: a report of his examination, taken from the witchcraft files.

Witchcraft
BF
1575
D76

Calef, Robert, 1648-1719.
More wonders of the invisible world.
Drake, Samuel Gardner, 1798-1875, comp.
The witchcraft delusion in New England; its rise, progress, and termination, as exhibited by Dr. Cotton Mather, in The wonders of the invisible world; and by Mr. Robert Calef, in his More wonders of the invisible world. With a preface, introduction, and notes, by Samuel G. Drake ... Roxbury, Mass., Printed for W. E. Woodward, 1866.
3 v. 21½ x 17cm. (Half-title: Woodward's historical series. no. V-VII)
(Continued on next card)

Witchcraft
BF
1575
D76

Calef, Robert, 1648-1719.
More wonders of the invisible world.
Drake, Samuel Gardner, 1798-1875, comp. The witchcraft delusion in New England. 1866. (Card 2)

No. 89 of an "edition in this size" of 280 copies.
Includes reprints of original title-pages.
Contents.—v.1. The wonders of the invisible world ... By Cotton Mather. v.2-3. More wonders of the invisible world ... Collected by Robert Calef.

Witchcraft
BF
1575
C23
H75

Calef, Robert, 1648-1719.
More wonders of the invisible world.
Holmes, Thomas James, 1874-
The surreptitious printing of one of Cotton Mather's manuscripts, by Thomas J. Holmes ... Cambridge [Mass, Printed at the Harvard university press] 1925.
1 p. l., 12 p. 25cm.
"Reprinted from Bibliographical essays; a tribute to Wilberforce Eames."
With this is bound his Cotton Mather and his writings on witchcraft. [1926]
1. Calef, Robert, 1648-1719. More wonders of the invisible world. 2. Mather, Cotton, 1663-1728. 3. Witchcraft—New England. I. Title.
Library of Congress   BF1575.C23H6
41-38390

Witchcraft
BF
1575
C14
1861

Calef, Robert, 1648-1719.
Salem witchcraft; comprising More wonders of the invisible world. Collected by Robert Calef; and Wonders of the invisible world, by Cotton Mather: together with notes and explanations by Samuel P. Fowler. Salem, Mass. [H. P. Ives and A. A. Smith] 1861.
450 p. 20cm.

First published 1700 under title: More wonders of the invisible world displayed.
"G. M. Whipple & A. A. Smith" pasted over imprint.

8

Witchcraft
BF
1575
C14
1865

Calef, Robert, 1648-1719.
Salem witchcraft; comprising More wonders of the invisible world, collected by Robert Calef; and Wonders of the invisible world; together with notes and explanations by Samuel P. Fowler. Boston, William Veazie, 1865.
450 p. 22cm.

(over)

Witchcraft
BF
1575
C14
1828

Calef, Robert, 1648-1719.   Wonders of the invisible world, or, Salem witchcraft. In five parts. Boston, T. Bedlington [1828]
333 p. front. 14cm.

A reply to Cotton Mather's "Wonders of the invisible world."
First ed. published in 1700 under title: More wonders of the invisible world displayed.
(Continued on next card)
(over)

Witchcraft
BF
1575
C14
1828

Calef, Robert, 1648-1719.   Wonders of the invisible world ... [1828]   (Card 2)

Contents.—Part 1. An account of the sufferings of Margaret Rule, by Cotton Mather.—Part 2. Several letters from the author to Mr. Mather and others, relating to witchcraft.—Part 3. Account of the differences in Salem village between the villagers and their minister, Mr. Parris.—Part 4. Letters of a gentleman uninter-
(Continued on next card)

Witchcraft
BF
1575
C14
1828

Calef, Robert, 1648-1719.   Wonders of the invisible world ... [1828]   (Card 3)

ested, endeavouring to prove the received opinions about witchcraft to be orthodox.—Part 5. An impartial account of the most memorable matters of fact touching the supposed witchcraft in New-England.—Postscript, relating to Cotton Mather's life of Sir William Phips.—Giles Cory: a report of his examination, taken from the witchcraft files.

Witchcraft
BF
1575
C14
H31+

Calef, Robert, 1648-1719.
Harris, William Samuel, 1861-
Robert Calef, "Merchant, of Boston, in New England."
(In Granite monthly. Manchester, N. H. 26cm. v. 39 (1907) p. [157]-163])

1. Calef, Robert, 1648-1719. I. Title.

CATALOGUE OF THE CORNELL WITCHCRAFT COLLECTION

A calendar of cases of witchcraft in Scotland, 1510-1727.

Witchcraft
BF
1581
B62+
1938
Black, George Fraser, 1866–
  A calendar of cases of witchcraft in Scotland, 1510-1727, compiled by George F. Black, ph. d. New York, The New York public library, 1938.
  109 p. front. 25½ᶜᵐ.
  "Reprinted from the Bulletin of the New York public library of November-December 1937 and January 1938."

  1. Witchcraft—Scotland. I. Title.
                                              38-13999
Library of Congress   [0]

Callidius, Cornelius, pseud.
  see
Loos, Cornelis, 1546-1595.

Witchcraft
BF
1412
C16
  Calmet, Augustin, 1672-1757.
    Dissertations sur les apparitions des anges, des démons & des esprits, et sur les revenans et vampires de Hongrie, de Bohême, de Moravie & de Silesie. Paris, Chez de Bure l'aîné, 1746.
    xxxvi, 500 p. 17cm.
    Published also under title: Traité sur les apparitions des esprits ... Paris, 1751 [etc.]
    "Dissertation sur ce qu'on doit penser
                         (Continued on next card)
8

Witchcraft
BF
1412
C16
  Calmet, Augustin, 1672-1757. Dissertations sur les apparitions des anges ... 1746. (Card 2)
  de l'apparition des esprits, a l'occasion de l'avanture arrivée a Saint Maur. Paris, 1707: p. [467]-500, has special t. p., and is attributed to F. Poupart by the Bibliothèque Nationale.
  1. Demonology. 2. Apparitions. I. Poupart, François. Dissertation sur ce qu'on doit penser... II. Title. III. Title: Dissertation de l'apparition des esprits.
8

Witchcraft
BF
1412
C16
1759
  Calmet, Augustin, 1672-1757.
    Dissertations sur les apparitions.
  Calmet, Augustin, 1672-1757.
    Traité sur les apparitions des esprits, et sur les vampires, ou les revenans de Hongrie, de Moravie, &c. Nouv. éd., rev., corr., & augm. Senones, Chez Joseph Pariset, 1759.
    2 v. 17cm.
    Later ed. of Dissertations sur les apparitions
    "Lettre de M. le Marquis Maffei sur la magie": v. 2, p. 325-393.
    I. Maffei, Francesco Scipione, marchese, 1675-1755. II. Title. III. His Dissertations sur les apparitions.

Witchcraft
BF
1412
C16
1850
  Calmet, Augustin, 1672-1757.
    Dissertations sur les apparitions--English.
  Calmet, Augustin, 1672-1757.
    The phantom world; or, The philosophy of spirits, apparitions, etc. Edited with an introd. and notes by Henry Christmas. London, R. Bentley, 1850.
    2 v. 20cm.
    Translation of Dissertations sur les apparitions des anges, des démons & des esprits ... which was also published under title: Traité sur les apparitions des esprits et sur les vamp ires ...

Calmet, Augustin, 1672-1757.
  Dissertations sur les apparitions.

Witchcraft
BF
1445
L56
  Lenglet Dufresnoy, [Nicolas] 1674-1755.
    Traité historique et dogmatique sur les apparitions les visions & les révélations particulières. Avec des observations sur les Dissertations du r. p. Dom Calmet abbé de Sénones, sur les apparitions & les revenans Par M. l'abbé Lenglet Dufresnoy. Avignon & Paris, Chez J. M. Leloup, 1751.
    2 v. pl. 18cm.
                                              2-11834
  1. Apparitions. 2. Calmet, Augustin, 1672-1757. Dissertations sur les apparitions. I. Title
Library of Congress, no.

Witchcraft
BF
1412
C16
1850
  Calmet, Augustin, 1672-1757.
    The phantom world; or, The philosophy of spirits, apparitions, etc. Edited with an introd. and notes by Henry Christmas. London, R. Bentley, 1850.
    2 v. 20cm.
    Translation of Dissertations sur les apparitions des anges, des démons & des esprits ... which was also published under title: Traité sur les apparitions des esprits et sur les vamp ires ...
                              (over)

Witchcraft
BF
1412
C16
1751
  Calmet, Augustin, 1672-1757.
    Traité sur les apparitions des esprits, et sur les vampires, ou les revenans de Hongrie, de Moravie, &c. Nouv. éd., rev., corr., & augm. par l'auteur. Paris, Chez Debure l'aîné, 1751.
    2 v. 17cm.
    "Lettre de M. le Marquis Maffei, sur la magie": v. 2, p. 383-469.

Witchcraft
BF
1412
C16
1759
  Calmet, Augustin, 1672-1757.
    Traité sur les apparitions des esprits, et sur les vampires, ou les revenans de Hongrie, de Moravie, &c. Nouv. éd., rev., corr., & augm. Senones, Chez Joseph Pariset, 1759.
    2 v. 17cm.
    Later ed. of Dissertations sur les apparitions
    "Lettre de M. le Marquis Maffei sur la magie": v. 2, p. 325-393.
    I. Maffei, Francesco Scipione, marchese, 1675-1755. VII. Title. III. His Dissertations sur les apparitions.

Witchcraft
BF
1412
C16
1850
  Calmet, Augustin, 1672-1757.
    Traité sur les apparitions des esprits--English.
  Calmet, Augustin, 1672-1757.
    The phantom world; or, The philosophy of spirits, apparitions, etc. Edited with an introd. and notes by Henry Christmas. London, R. Bentley, 1850.
    2 v. 20cm.
    Translation of Dissertations sur les apparitions des anges, des démons & des esprits ... which was also published under title: Traité sur les apparitions des esprits et sur les vamp ires ...

Witchcraft
BF
1445
D61
no.12
  Cameen, Sven, praeses.
    Dissertatio philosophica De spectris, quam ... sub moderamine celeberrimi viri Dni. Svenonis Cameen ... pro laurea magisterii reportanda publicae bonorum ventilationi subjicit ... Petrus Bartelius ... Dorpati, Excudit Johannes Brendeken [1693]
    [24] p. 19cm. (bound in 21cm. vol.)
    Diss.--Dorpat (P. Bartelius, respondent)
    No. 12 in vol. lettered Dissertationes de spectris. 1646-1753.
    1. Demonology. I. Bartelius, Peter, respondent. II. Title: De spectris. III. Dissertatio philoso-
8   phica De spectris

WITCHCRAFT
R
133
C173
  Camerarius, Elias, 1672-1734, praeses.
    Magici morbi historia attentius pensitata. Hanc...praeside Elia Camerario...examini publico submittit Christianus Neufferus... Tubingae, Typis Georgii Friderici Pelickii [1724]
    31 p. 20cm.
    Diss.--Tübingen (C. Neuffer, respondent)
    1. Medicine, Magic, mystic and spagiric.
8   2. Demonology. I. Neuffer, Christian, respondent. II. Title.
NIC

Witchcraft
R
708
C18
T2
  Camerarius, Elias, 1672-1734.
    Temerarii circa magica judicii exemplum. ... praeside Elia Camerario ... In dispvtatione inavgvrali pro summis in medicina honoribus obtendis ... publice defendet Johannes Dannenberger ... Tubingae, Literis Josephi Sigmundi [1729]
    18 p. 20cm.
    Diss.--Tübingen (J. Dannenberger, respondent)
    1. Medicine-- Addresses, essays, lectures. 2. Magic. I. Dannenberger, Johannes, respondent. II. Title.
8

WITCHCRAFT
BF
1565
J19
  Camerarius, Joachim, 1500-1574.
    Procemium in libellum Plutarchi de defectu oraculorum.
  Jaquier, Nicolas.
    Flagellvm haereticorvm fascinariorvm, avtore Nicolao Iaqverio. His accesservnt Lamberti Danaei de veneficiis dialogi, Ioachimi Camerarii in Plutarchi de oraculorum defectu epistola, Martini de Arles de superstitionibus tractatvs, Ioannis Trithemii de reprobis atq; maleficiis qvaestiones III, Thomae Erasti de strigibus liber. Studio Ioan. Myntzenbergii edita. Francofvrti ad Moenvm [Impressvm apud N. Bassaeum] 1581.
8   604 p. 17 cm.   (Continued on next card)
NIC

Rare
AC
14
C18+
1621
  Camerarius, Philipp, 1537-1624.
    The living librarie; or, Meditations and observations historical, natvral, moral, political, and poetical. Written in Latin by P. Camerarivs. And done into English by Iohn Molle, esquire. London, Printed by Adam Islip, 1621.
    I. Molle, John, fl. 1621, tr. II. Molle, H., fl. 1625, tr. III. Baddeley, Richard, fl. 1621, ed. IV. Title.

Witchcraft
BT
965
C18
  Camfield, Benjamin.
    A theological discourse of angels and their ministries. Wherein their existence, nature, number, order and offices are modestly treated of: with the character of those for whose benefit especially they are commissioned and such practical inferences deduced as are most proper to the premises. Also an appendix containing some reflections upon Mr. Webster's Displaying supposed witchcraft. London, Printed by R. E. for H. Brome, 1678.
    214 p. 19cm.
                              (Continued on next card)

Witchcraft
BT
965
C18
  Camfield, Benjamin. A theological discourse of angels and their ministries ... 1678.
                                            (Card 2)
  "Appendix..." has separate t.p.
  Wing C 388.

  1. Angels. 2. Witchcraft. 3. Webster, John, 1610-1682. The displaying of supposed witchcraft. I. Title.

104

CATALOGUE OF THE CORNELL WITCHCRAFT COLLECTION

Witchcraft
BF
231
C18
    Campanella, Tommaso, 1568-1639.
    De sensv rervm et magia, libri qvatuor, pars mirabilis occvltae philosophiae ... Tobias Adami recensvit, et nunc primum evulgauit. Francofvrti, Apud Egenolphvm Emmelivm, Impensis Godefridi Tampachij, 1620.
    8 p. l., 371 p. 22cm.
    Between p. 370 and 371 are bound in duplicates of p. [1]-[4] of the dedicatory epistle.
    Ex libris Caspar Melchior Fuch.
    With this are bound his Astrologicorum libri VII. Francofurti, 1630; and his Prodromus philosophiae instaurandae. Francofurti, 1617. (Over)

Witchcraft
BF
231
C18
1637
    Campanella, Tommaso, 1568-1639.
    ... De sensv rervm, et magia. Libros qvatvor... Correctos et defensos à stupidorum incolarum mundi calumniis per argumenta & testimonia Diuinorum Codicum, naturae, [etc.] ... dedicat consecratqve. Parisiis, Apud Ioannem dv Bray, 1637.
    8 p. l., 92, 229 p. 22cm.
    "Defensio libri svi De sensv rervm" preceeds text of De sensu rerum.
    1. Senses and sensation--Early works to 1800. 2. Magic. I. Title: De sensu rerum et magia.

Campanella, Tommaso, 1568-1639.
De sensu rerum et magia.
BF
231
C18
1925
    ... Del senso delle cose e della magia; testo inedito italiano con le varianti dei codici e delle due edizioni latine, a cura di Antonio Bruers. Bari, G. Laterza & figli, 1925.
    xxix, [1] p., 1 l., 348 p. 21½cm. (Half-title: Classici della filosofia moderna ... a cura di B. Croce e G. Gentile. XXIV)

    1. Senses and sensations. 2. Magic. I. Bruers, Antonio, 1887- ed. II. Campanella, Tommaso, 1568-1639. De sensu rerum et magia.
    Library of Congress   BF233.C3   26-11842
     [2]

Campanella, Tommaso, 1568-1639.
    ... Del senso delle cose e della magia; testo inedito italiano con le varianti dei codici e delle due edizioni latine, a cura di Antonio Bruers. Bari, G. Laterza & figli, 1925.
    xxix, [1] p., 1 l., 348 p. 21½cm. (Half-title: Classici della filosofia moderna ... a cura di B. Croce e G. Gentile. XXIV)

    1. Senses and sensations. 2. Magic. I. Bruers, Antonio, 1887- ed. II. Campanella, Tommaso, 1568-1639. De sensu rerum et magia. III. Title.

Witchcraft
    Campbell, Duncan, 1680?-1730.
BF
15
D31
20
    [Defoe, Daniel] 1660?-1731.
    The history of the life and adventures of Mr. Duncan Campbell, a gentleman, who tho' deaf and dumb, writes down any stranger's name at first sight: with their future contingencies of fortune. Now living in Exeter-Court over-against the Savoy in the Strand ... 2d ed. cor. London, Printed for E. Curll, and sold by W. Mears [etc.], 1720.
    xix, [4], 320 p. front. (port.) 4 pl. 19cm.
    Authorship disputed; probably by Defoe, though ascribed also to William Bond under whose name it appeared in 1728, with new title: The supernatural philosopher; or, The mysteries of magick ... unfolded by William Bond. cf. Dict. nat. biog.; Camb. hist. Eng. lit., v. 9; Dottin's "Daniel DeFoe et ses romans" (1924) p. 261.
    Frontispiece wanting.
     28-19517
    (Continued on next card)

    Campbell, Duncan, 1680?-1730.
Witchcraft
BF
1815
C2
D31
1742
    [Defoe, Daniel] 1660?-1731.
    Der übernatürliche Philosoph, oder Die Geheimnisse der Magie, nach allen ihren Arten deutlich erkläret ... aus den bewährtesten Autoribus zusammen getragen und durch das Exempel und Leben des Herrn Duncan Campbell, des tauben und stummen Edelmanns, erörtert. Nebst D. Wallis Methode, taube und stumme lesen, schreiben und jede Sprache verstehen zu lernen, von W. Bond ... Aus dem Englischen
    (Continued on next card)

    Campbell, Duncan, 1680?-1730.
Witchcraft
BF
1815
C2
D31
1742
    [Defoe, Daniel] 1660?-1731. Der übernatürliche Philosoph ... 1742. (Card 2)
    ins Deutsche übersetzt und mit einigen nöthigen und dienlichen Anmerckungen versehen ... Berlin, J. A. Rüdiger, 1742.
    [92], 432 p. front. (port.), 4 fold. plates. 17cm.
    First published 1720 anonymously with title: The history of the life and adventures of Mr. Duncan Campbell. Reissued 1728 with some additions as: The super-
    (Continued on next card)

    Campbell, Duncan, 1680?-1730.
Witchcraft
BF
1815
C2
D31
1742
    [Defoe, Daniel] 1660?-1731. Der übernatürliche Philosoph ... 1742. (Card 3)
    natural philosopher, or, The mysteries of magick ... unfolded by William Bond, from which this is translated.
    Authorship disputed; probably by Daniel Defoe with the assistance of William Bond and possibly of Eliza Haywood.
    Imperfect: plate to p. [72] wanting.

Witchcraft
BF
1581
C18
    Campbell, John Gregorson, 1836-1891.
    Witchcraft & second sight in the Highlands & islands of Scotland; tales and traditions collected entirely from oral sources. Glasgow, J. MacLehose, 1902.
    xii, 314 p. 21cm.

    1. Witchcraft. 2. Second sight. 3. Folk-lore--Scotland. I. Title.

BF
1581
C18
    Campbell, John Gregorson, 1836-1891.
    Witchcraft & second sight in the Highlands & islands of Scotland; tales and traditions collected entirely from oral sources by the late John Gregorson Campbell ... Glasgow, J. MacLehose and sons, 1902.
    xii, 314 p., 1 l. 20½cm.

    1. Witchcraft. 2. Second sight. 3. Folk-lore--Scotland. I. Title.
     3--3747
    Library of Congress   BF1581.C2
     [a37g1]

DS
42
M85
v.21
    Canaan, Taufik.
    Dämonenglaube im Lande der Bibel ... Leipzig, J. C. Hinrichs, 1929.
    iv, 64 p. 25cm. (Morgenland; Darstellungen aus Geschichte und Kultur des Ostens. Hft. 21)

    1. Demonology. 2. Folk-lore--Palestine. I. Title.

A candle in the dark.
Witchcraft
BF
1565
A24
    Ady, Thomas.
    A candle in the dark; or, A treatise concerning the nature of witches & witchcraft. Being advice to judges, sheriffes, justices of the peace, and grand-jury-men, what to do, before they passe sentence on such as are arraigned for their lives as witches. London, Printed for R. I., to be sold by T. Newberry, 1656.
    172 [i.e. 164] p. 19cm.
    Imperfect: p. 153-154 incorrectly numbered 161-162; p. 163-166 lacking; p. 155-164 numbered 167-172.
    (Continued on next card)

A candle in the dark.
Witchcraft
BF
1565
A24
    Ady, Thomas. A candle in the dark. 1656. (Card 2)
    Title vignette.
    Issued also under title: A perfect discovery of witches ...

    1. Witchcraft. I. Title. II. Ady, Thomas. A perfect discovery of witches.

Canidia.
Witchcraft
BF
1565
G29
    Gebhard, Johann.
    Canidia, hoc est, Venefica, fetura cacodaemonis spurcissimi ex creaturis praepotentiae divinae pulcerrimis nobilissimisq, facta spurcissimarum omnium spurcissima; non peniculo pigmentario, sed vivo vocis charactere ex lyrici Venusini Epodis V. & XVII adumbrata, inq; theatro Gymnasii Vratislaviensium Elisabetani publico ad contemplandum ... proponenda, curante Johanne Gebhardo ... Wratislaviae, Typis Baumannianis, Per
    (Continued on next card)

Canidia.
Witchcraft
BF
1565
G29
    Gebhard, Johann. Canidia ... [1651] (Card 2)
    Gottfridum Grunderum [1651]
    [8] p. 20cm.

    1. Witchcraft. I. Title. II. Title: Venefica.

Canisius, Petrus, Saint, 1521-1597.
Catechismus.
Witchcraft
BF
1583
D55
Z3
    Diefenbach, Johann.
    Der Zauberglaube des sechzehnten Jahrhunderts nach den Katechismen Dr. Martin Luthers und des P. Canisius. Mit Berücksichtigung der Schriften Pfarrers Längin-Karlsruhe und des Professors Riezler-München. Mainz, F. Kirchheim, 1900.
    xii, 209 p. 23cm.
    1. Witchcraft--Germany. 2. Theology, Doctrinal--16th century. 3. Canisius, Petrus, Saint, 1521-1597. Catechismus.
    (Continued on next card)

Witchcraft
BF
1584
B4C22
    Cannaert, Joseph Bernard, 1768-1848.
    Olim. Procès des sorcières en Belgique sous Philippe II et le gouvernement des archiducs. Tirés d'actes judiciaires et de documens inédits. Gand, C. Annoot-Braeckman, 1847.
    155 p. illus. 24cm.

    1. Witchcraft--Belgium. I. Title. II. Title: Procès des sorcières en Belgique.

WITCHCRAFT
PT
1792
C26
    Cardauns, Hermann, 1847-1925.
    Friedrich Spee. Frankfurt a. M., A. Foesser Nachf., 1884.
    [103]-133 p. 23cm. (Frankfurter zeitgemässe Broschüren. N. F., Bd. 5, Heft 4)

    1. Spee, Friedrich von, 1591-1635. 2. Spee, Friedrich von, 1591-1635. Cautio criminalis. I. Series. II. Title.

8
NIC

CATALOGUE OF THE CORNELL WITCHCRAFT COLLECTION

Witchcraft
BX 1711 C26

Cardew, *Sir* Alexander Gordon, 1861–
A short history of the inquisition, by Sir Alexander G. Cardew ... London, Watts & co. [1933]
viii, 115 p. 19ᶜᵐ.
"Mainly based on the exhaustive works of ... Dr. Henry Charles Lea—namely, Superstition and force, A history of the inquisition in the middle ages, and A history of the inquisition in Spain."—Pref.
"First published April, 1933."

1. Inquisition—Hist. I. Lea, Henry Charles, 1825–1909. II. Title.

Library of Congress — BX1711.C3 — 34-7592
[3] — 272.2

Witchcraft
BX 2340 C26

Cardi, Paolo Maria, frater.
Ritualis Romani documenta de exorcizandis obsessis a daemonio comentariis ex SS. patribus, & Ecclesiasticis Scriptoribus potissimum depromptis, illustrata per Fr. Paulum Mariam Cardi ... Venetiis, Apud Josephum Corona, 1733.
8 p. l., 504 p. 18cm.

1. Exorcism. 2. Demonology. I. Catholic Church. Liturgy and ritual. II. Title.

8

Witchcraft
BX 1710 C27 T7

Carena, Cesare, fl. 1645.
Tractatvs de modo procedendi in cavsis S. Officii, Caesaris Carenae Cremonensis I. C. ... Auditoris, consultoris, & adu. fiscalis Sancti Officij, opus omnibus episcopis, inquisitoribus, & eorum ministris, ac etiam confessarijs perutile, & necessarium. Cremonae, Apud Marc'Ant. Belp.erum, 1636.
26 p. l., 385, [2] p. 20cm.
Later published as part 2 of his Trac-
(Continued on next card)

8

Witchcraft
BX 1710 C27 T7

Carena, Cesare, fl. 1645. Tractatvs de modo procedendi ... 1636. (Card 2)

tatvs de officio Sanctissimae Inqvisitonis.

1. Inquisition. 2. Heresy (Canon law) 3. Witchcraft. I. Title: Tractatus de modo procedendi in causis S. Officii. II. His Tractatus de officio Sanctissimae Inquisitionis.

8

Witchcraft
BX 1710 C27 T7

Carena, Cesare, fl. 1645.
Tractatus de officio Sanctissimae Inquisitionis.
Carena, Cesare, fl. 1645.
Tractatvs de modo procedendi in cavsis S. Officii, Caesaris Carenae Cremonensis I. C. ... Auditoris, consultoris, & adu. fiscalis Sancti Officij, opus omnibus episcopis, inquisitoribus, & eorum ministris, ac etiam confessarijs perutile, & necessarium. Cremonae, Apud Marc'Ant. Belp.erum, 1636.
26 p. l., 385, [2] p. 20cm.
Later published as part 2 of his Trac-
(Continued on next card)

8

Witchcraft
BX 1710 C27 T7

Carena, Cesare, fl. 1645.
Tractatus de officio Sanctissimae Inquisitionis.
Carena, Cesare, fl. 1645. Tractatvs de modo procedendi ... 1636. (Card 2)

tatvs de officio Sanctissimae Inqvisitonis.

1. Inquisition. 2. Heresy (Canon law) 3. Witchcraft. I. Title: Tractatus de modo procedendi in causis S. Officii. II. His Tractatus de officio Sanctissimae Inquisitionis.

8

Witchcraft
BF 1563 T86

Cariden, Joan, d. 1645.
The examination, confession, triall, and execution, of Joane Williford, Joan Cariden, and Jane Hott, who were executed at Feversham in Kent, for being witches, on Munday the 29 of September 1645... Taken by the major of Feversham and jurors for the said inquest. With the examination and confession of Elizabeth Harris, not yet executed. All attested under the hand of Robert Greenstreet, major of Feversham. London, Printed for J. G., 1645.
(Continued on next card)

Witchcraft
BF 1563 T86

Cariden, Joan, d. 1645.
The examination, confession, triall, and execution ... 1645. (Card 2)
6 p. 19cm.
No. 5 in vol. lettered: Tracts of witches.

1. Witchcraft. 2. Williford, Joane, d. 1645. 3. Cariden, Joan, d. 1645. 4. Hott, Jane, d. 1645. 5. Harris, Elizabeth, d. 1645.

Witchcraft
BF 1520 C27

Caristinio, Dominico.
... Exercitatio per saturam, sive Diatriba theologico-critica daemonologiae elementa complectens, cui accedunt Meditationes philosophicae theologico morales super eodem subjecto, auctore Bernardo Maria Marsicani ... Neapoli, Typis Dominici Pianese, 1788.
11 p. l., 207 p. 21cm.
Marsicani's work not included; but dedication includes letter by and to him.

1. Demonology. I. Marsicani, Bernardo Maria. II. Title. III. Title: Diatriba theologico-critica daemonologiae.

8

Witchcraft
BF 1565 T19

Carli, Giovanni Rinaldo, conte, 1720–1795.
Lettera ... al signor Girolamo Tartarotti, intorno all' origine, e falsità della dottrina de' Maghi.
Tartarotti, Girolamo, 1706–1761. Del congresso notturno delle lammie, libri tre di Girolamo Tartarotti Roveretano. S'aggiungono due dissertazioni epistolari sopra l'arte magica... Rovereto, A spese di Giambatista Pasquali in Venezia, 1749.
xxxii, 460 p. 24cm.
Letter from Gianrinaldo Carli dated Padua, 1745, p. [317]-350, has special t. p.
(Continued on next card)

8

Witchcraft
BF 1565 T19

Carli, Giovanni Rinaldo, conte, 1720–1795.
Lettera ... al signor Girolamo Tartarotti, intorno all' origine, e falsità della dottrina de' Maghi.
Tartarotti, Girolamo, 1706–1761. Del congresso notturno delle lammie ... 1749. (Card 2)

Letter of Tartarotti dated Roverete, 1746, p. [351]-447, has special t. p.

1. Witchcraft. 2. Magic. I. Carli, Giovanni Rinaldo, conte, 1720–1795. Lettera ... al signor Girolamo Tartarotti, intorno all' origine, e falsità della dottrina de' Maghi. II. Title.

8

Witchcraft
BF 1531 C28

Carlisle, William.
An essay on evil spirits; or, Reasons to prove their existence. In opposition to a lecture delivered by the Rev. N. T. [i.e. N.S.] Heineken, in the Unitarian Chapel, Bradford. ... Bradford, Printed for the Author, and sold by T. Inkersley [pref. 1825]
170 p. 20cm.

Witchcraft
BF 1531 C28 1825

Carlisle, William.
An essay on evil spirits; or, Reasons to prove their existence: in opposition to a lecture, delivered by the Rev. N. T. (i. e. S.) Heineken in the Unitarian chapel, Bradford. By William Carlisle. 2d ed., enl. and cor. London, Printed for the author, and sold by Hamilton, Adams and co.; [etc., etc.] 1825.
2 p. l., x p., 1 l., [13]-176 p. 19cm.

1. Demonology. 2. Heineken, Nicholas Samuel.

Library of Congress — BF1531.C2 — 11-9195

Witchcraft
BF 1531 C28 1827

Carlisle, William.
An essay on evil spirits; or, Reasons to prove their existence. In opposition to a lecture delivered by the Rev. N. T. [i.e. N.S.] Heineken, in the Unitarian Chapel, Bradford. 3d ed., enl. and corr. ... London, Printed for the Author, and sold by Hamilton, Adams, 1827.
176 p. 20cm.

1. Demonology. 2. Heineken, Nicholas Samuel. I. Title.

WITCHCRAFT
BF 1531 C28 H46

Carlisle, William.
An essay on evil spirits.
Heineken, Nicholas Samuel.
A discourse, on the supposed existence of an evil spirit, called the devil; and also, a reply to the observations of Mr. William Carlisle, ... the ostensible author of an "Essay on evil spirits," written in opposition to the discourse which was delivered in the Unitarian Chapel, Bradford. By the Rev. N. T. [i.e., N. S.] Heineken, London, R. Hunter [1825?]
iv, 139 p. 23cm.

1. Carlisle, William. An essay on evil spirits. 2. Demonology.

8

Witchcraft
PB 1645 C28 1928

Carmichael, Alexander, 1832–1912, comp. and tr.
Carmina gadelica; hymns and incantations with illustrative notes on words, rites, and customs, dying and obsolete: orally collected in the Highlands and islands of Scotland and translated into English. Edinburgh, Oliver and Boyd, 1928–
v. fronts. (v. 1,3, ports.) 24cm.

Gaelic and English on opposite pages.
Initials from Gaelic mss.
Half-title: Carmina gadelica; ortha nan Gaidheal. (Continued on next card)

Witchcraft
PB 1645 C28 1928

Carmichael, Alexander, 1832–1912, comp. and tr.
Carmina gadelica. 1928– (Card 2)

Vols. 1-2 first issued in a limited ed. 1900 2d ed. edited by Mrs. Elizabeth Carmichael Watson, 1928. Vols. 3-4 a continuation of the work, translated and edited by James Carmichael Watson from the author's unfinished manuscripts published 1940-1941. Vol. 5 edited by Angus Matheson—cf. L.C.

I. Title.

BF 1521 J28 1924

Carmichael, James, d. 1628, supposed author.
James I, king of Great Britain, 1566-1625.
King James, the First: Daemonologie (1597). Newes from Scotland, declaring the damnable life and death of Doctor Fian, a notable sorcerer who was burned at Edenbrough in Ianuary last (1591) London, J. Lane; New York, Dutton [1924]
xv, 81, 29 p. illus. 19cm. (The Bodley head quartos, no. 9)
With facsimiles of original title pages.
Newes from Scotland has been ascribed to James Carmichael, minister of
(Continued on next card)

106

CATALOGUE OF THE CORNELL WITCHCRAFT COLLECTION

BF 1521 J28 1924

Carmichael, James, d. 1628, supposed author.
James I, king of Great Britain, 1566-1625.
King James, the First: Daemonologie...
[1924]   (Card 2)

Haddington. Cf. Sir James Melville, Memories, p. 195, and D. Webster, Collection of tracts on witchcraft, etc., 1820, p. 38.
1. Demonology. 2. Magic. 3. Witchcraft--Scotland. 4. Fian, John, d. 1591. I. Harrison, George Bagshawe, 1894- ed. II. Carmichael, James, d. 1628, supposed author. III. Title: Daemonologie. IV. Title: Newes from Scotland.

Witchcraft PB 1645 C28 1928

Carmina gadelica.
Carmichael, Alexander, 1832-1912, comp. and tr.
Carmina gadelica; hymns and incantations with illustrative notes on words, rites, and customs, dying and obsolete: orally collected in the Highlands and islands of Scotland and translated into English.   Edinburgh, Oliver and Boyd, 1928-
v. fronts. (v. 1,3, ports.) 24cm.

Gaelic and English on opposite pages.
Initials from Gaelic mss.
Half-title: Carmina gadelica; ortha nan Gaidheal.   (Continued on next card)

Witchcraft PB 1645 C28 1928

Carmina gadelica.
Carmichael, Alexander, 1832-1912, comp. and tr.
Carmina gadelica. 1928-   (Card 2)

Vols. 1-2 first issued in a limited ed. 1900; 2d ed. edited by Mrs. Elizabeth Carmichael Watson, 1928. Vols. 3-4 a continuation of the work, translated and edited by James Carmichael Watson from the author's unfinished manuscripts, published 1940-1941. Vol. 5 edited by Angus Matheson--cf. L.C.

Witchcraft BF 1566 C29

Caro Baroja, Julio.
Las brujas y su mundo--English.
Caro Baroja, Julio.
The world of the witches. Translated by O. N. V. Glendinning. [Chicago] University of Chicago Press [1964]
xiv, 313 p. illus. 22 cm. (The Nature of human society series)
Translation of Las brujas y su mundo.
Bibliographical references included in "Notes" (p. 259-306)

1. Witchcraft. 2. Magic. I. Title. II. Series: The Nature of human society. III. His Las brujas y su mundo--English.   64-15829

Library of Congress

Witchcraft BF 1595 C29

Caro Baroja, Julio, 1914-
Vidas magicas e Inquisición. Madrid, Taurus, 1967.
2 v. 24cm.

1. Witchcraft--Spain. 2. Magic--Spain. I. Inquisition. Spain. II. Title.

Witchcraft BF 1566 C29

Caro Baroja, Julio.
The world of the witches. Translated by O. N. V. Glendinning. [Chicago] University of Chicago Press [1964]
xiv, 313 p. illus. 22 cm. (The Nature of human society series)
Translation of Las brujas y su mundo.
Bibliographical references included in "Notes" (p. 259-306)

1. Witchcraft. 2. Magic. I. Title. II. Series: The Nature of human society. III. His Las brujas y su mundo--English.   64-15829

Library of Congress

Rare K C287 P8++ 1658

Carpzov, Benedict, 1595-1666.
Practicae novae imperialis Saxonicae rerum criminalium pars I.[-III.] ... Editio quarta correctior, cum indice rerum et verborum priore multum locupletiore. Francofurti et Wittebergae, Sumptibus Haeredum D. Tobiae Mevii, & Elerdi Schumacheri, Typis Balthasari Christophori Wustij, 1658.
3 v. 35cm.

For contents see Rare card.

(Continued on next card)

Rare K C287 P8++ 1658

Carpzov, Benedict, 1595-1666. Practicae novae imperialis Saxonicae...1658. (Card 2)

1. Criminal procedure--Holy Roman Empire. 2. Criminal law--Holy Roman Empire. 3. Criminal procedure--Saxony. 4. Criminal law--Saxony. 5. Criminal law (Roman law) I. Title: Practica nova imperialis Saxonica rerum criminalium.

WITCHCRAFT HV 8551 P33++

Carpzov, Benedict, 1595-1666.
Paulus, Nicolaus, 1853-1930.
Der sächsische Kriminalist Carpzov und seine 20 000 Todesurteile. [Köln, 1907]
1 column. 58 cm. (folded to 34cm.)

Detached from the Kölnische Volkszeitung und Handels-Blatt for February 18, 1907.
In broadside box.

1. Carpzov, Benedict, 1595-1666. 2. Capital punishment--Germany. I. Title.

8 NIC

Witchcraft BF 1582 C31

Carré, Henri, 1850-
Quelques mots sur la sorcellerie dans les provinces de l'Ouest au XVIe et au XVIIe siècles.
(In Société des antiquaires de l'Ouest. Bulletin. Poitiers. 24cm. sér. 3, t. 7 (1927) p. [631]-674)

1. Witchcraft--France--Hist. I. Title.

Witchcraft BF 1548 C32+

Carus, Paul, 1852-1919.
The history of the devil and the idea of evil, from the earliest times to the present day. Chicago, The Open Court Publishing Co.; [etc., etc.,] 1900.
xvi, 496 p. illus. 28cm.

1. Devil. 2. Demonology. 3. Good and evil. I. Title.

Witchcraft BF 773 C33

Casaubon, Meric, 1599-1671.
Of credulity and incredulity; in things divine & spiritval: wherein, (among other things) a true and faithful account is given of the Platonick philosophy, as it hath reference to Christianity: as also the business of witches and witchcraft, against a late writer, fully argued and disputed. By Merick Casaubon ... and one of the prebends of Christ-Church, Canturbury. London, Printed by T. N. for Samuel Lownds, 1670.
2 p. l., 208 p. 17cm.

8   (Continued on next card)

BF 773 C33

Casaubon, Meric, 1599-1671. Of credulity and incredulity ... 1670. (Card 2)

A continuation of his Of credulity and incredulity; in things natural, civil and divine, first published 1688 without the third part on the divine.
1. Credulity. 2. Christianity--Philosophy. 3. Plato. 4. Witchcraft. 5. Wagstaffe, John, 1633-1677. The question of witchcraft debated. I. His Of credulity and incredulity; in things natural, civil and divine. II. Title: Of credulity and incredulity; in things divine & spiritual.

8

Witchcraft BF 773 C33

Casaubon, Meric, 1599-1671.
Of credulity and incredulity; in things natural, civil and divine.
Casaubon, Meric, 1599-1671.
Of credulity and incredulity; in things divine & spiritval: wherein, (among other things) a true and faithful account is given of the Platonick philosophy, as it hath reference to Christianity: as also the business of witches and witchcraft, against a late writer, fully argued and disputed. By Merick Casaubon ... and one of the prebends of Christ-Church, Canturbury. London, Printed by T. N. for Samuel Lownds, 1670.
2 p. l., 208 p. 17cm.

8   (Continued on next card)

Witchcraft BF 773 C33

Casaubon, Meric, 1599-1671. Of credulity and incredulity ... 1670. (Card 2)

A continuation of his Of credulity and incredulity; in things natural, civil and divine, first published 1688 without the third part on the divine.
1. Credulity. 2. Christianity--Philosophy. 3. Plato. 4. Witchcraft. 5. Wagstaffe, John, 1633-1677. The question of witchcraft debated. I. His Of credulity and incredulity; in things natural, civil and divine. II Title: Of credulity and incredulity; in things divine & spiritual.

8

Witchcraft BF 773 C33 O3 1672

Casaubon, Meric, 1599-1671.
Of credulity and incredulity; in things natural, civil and divine.
Casaubon, Meric, 1599-1671.
A treatise proving spirits, witches, and supernatural operations by pregnant instances and evidences. Together with other things worthy of note. London, Printed for B. Aylmer, 1672.
316 p. 18cm.
Caption title: Of credulity and incredulity in things natural and civil.
First ed.   published in 1668 under title: of credulity and incredulity;
(Continued on next card)

Witchcraft BF 773 C33 O3 1672

Casaubon, Meric, 1599-1671. A treatise proving spirits, witches, and supernatural operations by pregnant instances and evidences ... 1672. (Card 2)

in things natural, civil and divine.
"Reissue of first ed."--British Museum catalogue.
Contains a preface "To the reader" dated 1688, which explains that the author was unable to write the third part mentioned in the title. The third part
(Continued on next card)

Witchcraft BF 773 C33 O3 1672

Casaubon, Meric, 1599-1671. A treatise proving spirits, witches, and supernatural operations by pregnant instances and evidences ... 1672. (Card 3)

was published in 1670 under title: Of credulity and incredulity in things divine & spiritual ...
1. Credulity. 2. Witchcraft. I. Title. II. His Of credulity and incredulity; in things natural, civil and divine. III. Title: Of credulity and incredulity in things natural and civil.

CATALOGUE OF THE CORNELL WITCHCRAFT COLLECTION

Rare
BF
575
E6 C33
1656
2 copies

Casaubon, Meric, 1599-1671
　A treatise concerning enthusiasme, as it is an effect of nature: but is mistaken by many for either divine inspiration, or diabolicall possession. By Meric Casaubon, D.D. 2d ed.: rev., and enl. ... London, Printed by Roger Daniel, and are to be sold by Thomas Johnson, 1656.
　10 p. l., 297 p.　17cm.
　1. Enthusiasm.　I. Title.

Witchcraft
BF
773
C33
O3
1672

Casaubon, Meric, 1599-1671.
　A treatise proving spirits, witches, and supernatural operations by pregnant instances and evidences. Together with other things worthy of note.　London, Printed for B. Aylmer, 1672.
　316 p.　18cm.
　Caption title: Of credulity and incredulity in things natural and civil.
　First ed. published in 1668 under
(Continued on next card)

Witchcraft
BF
773
C33
O3
1672

Casaubon, Meric, 1599-1671. A treatise proving spirits, witches, and supernatural operations by pregnant instances and evidences ... 1672.　(Card 2)
　title: Of credulity and incredulity; in things natural, civil and divine.
　"Reissue of first ed."--British Museum catalogue.
　Contains a preface "To the reader" dated 1668, which　　explains that the author was unable to　write the third part
(Continued on next card)

Witchcraft
BF
773
C33
O3
1672

Casaubon, Meric, 1599-1671. A treatise proving spirits, witches, and supernatural operations by pregnant instances and evidences ... 1672.　(Card 3)
　mentioned in the title. The third part was published in 1670 under title: Of credulity and incredulity in things divine & spiritual ...
　1. Credulity. 2. Witchcraft. I. Title. II. His Of credulity and incredulity; in things natural, civil and divine. III. Title: Of credulity and incredulity in things natural and civil.

Witchcraft
BF
1582
G51
C33
1732

The case of Mrs. Mary Catharine Cadiere, against the Jesuit Father John Baptist Girard.
Girard, Jean Baptiste, 1680-1733, defendant.
　The case of Mrs. Mary Catharine Cadiere, against the Jesuit Father John Baptist Girard. In a memorial presented to the Parliament of Aix. Wherein he is accused of seducing her, by the abominable doctrines of quietism, into the most criminal excesses of lewdness, and under an appearance of the highest mystical devotion, deluding into the same vices six other females, who had put their　　consciences under his
8　　(Continued on next card)

Witchcraft
BF
1582
G51
C33
1732

The case of Mrs. Mary Catharine Cadiere, against the Jesuit Father John Baptist Girard.
Girard, Jean Baptiste, 1680-1733, defendant. The case of Mrs. Mary Catharine Cadiere ... 1732.　(Card 2)
　direction. With a preface by the publisher ... 10th ed. corr. London, Printed for and sold by J. Roberts, 1732.
　vi, 96 p. 23cm.
　"This memorial was originally drawn up by that eminent lawyer ... Chaudon ... the following piece　　is not a bare translation ..." p. ii
8　　(Continued on next card)

Witchcraft
BF
1555
S53
1807

The case of Saul.
Sharp, Granville, 1735-1813.
　The case of Saul, shewing that his disorder was a real spiritual possession, and proving (by the learned researches and labours of a strenuous promoter even of the contrary doctrine(that actual possessions of spirits were generally acknowledged by the ancient writers among the heathens as well as among the Jews and Christians. ... To which is added a short tract, wherein the influence of demons are further illustrated by Remarks on 1. Timothy iv, 1-3.　London,　　Printed by W. Calvert for Vernor and　　Hood, 1807.
(Continued on next card)

Witchcraft
BF
1555
S53
1807

The case of Saul.
Sharp, Granville, 1735-1813. The case of Saul ... 1807. (Card 2)
　187, xv p. 19cm.
　The "Remarks on 1. Timothy ..." has separate t.p.

Witchcraft
BS
2545
D5
L32

The case of the demoniacs mentioned in the New Testament.
Lardner, Nathaniel, 1684-1768.
　The case of the demoniacs mentioned in the New Testament: four discourses upon Mark V. 19. With an appendix for farther illustrating the subject. London, Printed for C. Henderson ... sold also by J. Buckland, 1758.
　156 p. 21cm.

Witchcraft
BF
1581
Z7
1712e

The case of the Hertfordshire witchcraft consider'd. Being an examination of a book, entitl'd, A full and impartial account of the discovery of sorcery & witchcraft, practis'd by Jane Wenham of Walkern, upon the bodies of Anne Thorne, Anne Street, &c. London, Printed for J. Pemberton, 1712.
　3 p. l., vi, 86 p.　20cm.
　With copy 1 is bound [Bragge, Francis] Witchcraft farther display'd. London, 1712.
　1. Wenham, Jane, d. 1730. 2. [Bragge, Francis] A full and impartial account of the discovery of sorcery and witchcraft, practis'd by Jane Wenham.
11-14482

Witchcraft
BF
1581
Z7
1699

The case of witchcraft at Coggeshall, Essex, in the year, 1699.
Boys, James, d. 1725.
　The case of witchcraft at Coggeshall, Essex, in the year, 1699, being the narrative of the Rev. J. Boys, minister of that parish. Printed from his manuscript in the possession of the publisher. London, A. R. Smith, 1901.
　23, [1] p. 23⁴ᵐ.
　[Hazlitt tracts, v. 53, no. 14]
　"Only 50 copies printed."
　"A brief account of the indisposition of the widow Coman ... penned down by the aforesaid divine ... and afterwards transcribed (by the same person) from loose leaf papers in the year 1712": p. [3]
　1. Witchcraft—England. 2. Coggeshall, Eng. I. Title.
Library of Congress　　AC911.H3 vol. 53, no. 14　23-4835
(2)

Witchcraft
BF
1575
M427
C3

Cases of conscience concerning evil spirits.
Mather, Increase, 1639-1723.
　Cases of conscience concerning evil spirits personating men, witchcrafts, infallible proofs of guilt in such as are accused of that crime. All considered according to the Scriptures, history, experience, and the judgment of many learned men... Boston, Printed and sold by B. Harris, 1693.
　67 p. 15cm.
　With autographs of John Dodge, 1692, Ebenezer Parker, John Temple, and Rebekah Temple.　(Continued on next card)

Witchcraft
BF
1575
M427
C3

Cases of conscience concerning evil spirits.
Mather, Increase, 1639-1723.　Cases of conscience concerning evil spirits personating men ... 1693.　(Card 2)
　With book-plate of Matt. B. Jones. Seventeenth century binding. Original calf in full brown crushed levant solander case by Rivière & Son.
　One of 2 known copies with inscription dated 1692 (December 13)
　Holmes: I.　M. #22; Wing M 1193.
　1. Witchcraft. I. Title.

Witchcraft
BT
965
C33

Casmann, Otto, d. 1607.
　Othonis Casmanni Angelographia; sive Commentationum disceptationumque physicarum prodromvs problematicvs, de angelis sev creatis spiritibvs a corporvm consortio abiunctis, ex Dei verbo, S. Patrvm monumentis, dd. scholasticis & physicis; cum veteribus, tum recentioribus, concinnatus, & in duas partes distinctus. ... Francofurti, In officina Palthenii typographi, 1605.
　2 v. in 1.　　　15cm.
8　　(Continued on next card)

Witchcraft
BT
965
C33

Casmann, Otto, d. 1607. Othonis Casmanni Angelographia ... 1605.　(Card 2)
　Consecutively paged: 8 p. l., 672 p.
　Vol. 2 has title: Othonis Casmanni Angelographiae, hoc est, descriptionis angelicae ... pars altera. Francofurti, Ex officina Zachariae Palthenii, 1605.
　1. Angels. 2. Demonology. 3. Devil. I. Title: Angelographia. VII. Othonis
8　　Casmanni Angelographia.

WITCHCRAFT
BS
2545
D5
S473

Caspari, Joannes Burckhardus, respondent.
Müller, Joannes Stephanus.
　De daemoniacis Semlerianis in duabus dissertationibus theologicis commentatur D. Ioannes Steph. Müllerus. Francofurti et Lipsiae, Apud Theodor. Vilhelm. Ern. Güthium, 1763.
　95, 102 p. 23cm.
　Each dissertation has separate t.p. (reprints of original title pages) No.1: Notionem δαιμονίου sive δαίμονος olim et inprimis　　Christi tempore non hoc
8
NIC　　(Continued on next card)

WITCHCRAFT
BS
2545
D5
S473

Caspari, Joannes Burckhardus, respondent.
Müller, Joannes Stephanus. De daemoniacis Semlerianis...1763.　(Card 2)
　involuisse vi anima mortui daemon esse crederetur...demonstrat et...praeside...Ioann Stephano Müllero...defendet Ioann. Burckhard. Caspari. Ienae [1761] No.2: Notio illa animam mortui esse et dici in evangeliis daemonem opinioni debetur...praeside ...Ioanne Stephano Müllero...defendere conatur Georg.　　Christ. Wagenbronner. Ienae [1762]
(Continued on next card)

Witchcraft
BF
1563
E92++
no. 7.

Cassel, Clemens, 1850-1925.
　Eine Hexenprozess-Akte vom Jahre 1547. Hannover, 1899.
　131-132 p. 32cm. (Hannoversche Geschichtsblätter, 2. Jahrg., No. 17)
　1. Witchcraft. 2. Trials (Witchcraft) --Germany. I. Title.

CATALOGUE OF THE CORNELL WITCHCRAFT COLLECTION

Witchcraft
T
65
34++
    Castaldi, Giovanni Tommaso, d. 1655.
      De potestate angelica sive De potentia motrice, ac mirandis operibvs angelorvm atqve doemonvm, dissertatio ... Romae, Ex Typographia Francisci Caballi, 1650-52.
      3 v. 34cm.

      Engraved title vignettes.
      T. p. of v. 2 reads: ... daemonvm ...

      1. Angels—Early works to 1800. 2. Demonology. I. Title. II. Title: De potentia motrice.

Rare
HV
8599
S8
C35
    Castro, Pedro de, canon of Seville.
      Defensa de la tortura y leyes patrias que la establecieron: e inpugnacion del tratado que escribio contra ella el doctor d. Alfonso Maria de Acevedo: su autor, don pedro de Castro ... Madrid, M. Escribano, 1778.
      xxviii, 256 p. 21cm.

      1. Torture. 2. Azevedo, Alonso Maria de. De reorum absolutione ... I. Title.

DC
119
.8
D31
    Catherine de Médicis, ses astrologues et ses magiciens-envoûteurs.
    Defrance, Eugène, 1874-
      ... Catherine de Médicis, ses astrologues et ses magiciens-envoûteurs. Documents inédits sur la diplomatie et les sciences occultes du XVIe siècle; avec vingt illustrations. Paris, Mercvre de France, 1911.
      306 p., 3 l. incl. front., illus. (incl. ports., facsim.) 19cm.

BF
1572
D4
C34
    Castellani, Carlo, 1822-1897.
      Le donne e il diavolo. Milano, Longanesi [c1963]
      238 p. illus. 20cm. (Il Cammeo, v. 183)
      1. Witchcraft. 2. Devil. I. Title.
                NUC65-31256

HS
368
C37
    Catalogue d'une précieuse collection de livres anciens manuscrits et imprimés de documents originaux, etc., sur les francs-maçons, les rose-croix, le mesmérisme, la magie, l'alchimie, les sciences occultes, les prophéties, les miracles, etc. Dont la vente se fera jeudi 23, février 1860, et jours suivants, à 7 heures du soir, Maison Silvestre. Paris, Librairie Tross, 1860.
      111 p. 23 cm.
      1. Freemasons—Catalogs. 2. Secret societies—Catalogs.

WITCHCRAFT
BX
1935
N42

8
NIC
    Catholic Church.
      Codex iuris canonici.
      Neller, Georg Christoph, praeses.
      ...Conatus exegeticus in cap. Eam te 7 De rescriptis, quem una cum parergis, ex omni jure, nec non ex re monetaria, tum biblico-canonica, tum Treverensi delibatis ...praeside...Georgio Christoph. Neller... publicae disputationi pro admissione ad tentamen graduandorum supposuit...Carolus Josephus Embden. Augustae Treviorum, Typis Eschermannianis [1779].
      48 p. front., plate. 22cm.

      Burr's note inside front cover:
                (Continued on next card)

Witchcraft
Z
6880
Z9B66
    Catalogue de livres d'occasion anciens et modernes relatifs aux sciences occultes.
    Bodin, Lucien, bookseller, Paris.
      Catalogue de livres d'occasion anciens et modernes relatifs aux sciences occultes et philosophiques. Paris.
      nos. 24cm.

      1. Occult sciences—Bibl.—Catalogs. 2. Witchcraft— Bibl.—Catalogs. I. Title.

WITCHCRAFT
BX
1935
N42
    Catholic Church.
      Codex iuris canonici.
      Neller, Georg Christoph, praeses. Conatus exegeticus in cap. Eam te 7 De rescriptis ...[1779] (Card 2)

      "This book is valuable in containing a... letter of the Elector, Johann VII of Treves asking the advice of the University theological faculty at Treves as to the trial of Dr. Dietrich Flade for witchcraft. (See pp. 32-35) It is to be noted that this student, writing under the eye of the eminent jurist Neller in 1779, still believes in witchcraft..."
                (Continued on next card)

Witchcraft
BF
1775
C35
    [Castillon, Jean Louis, 1720-ca. 1793.
      Essai sur les erreurs et les superstitions. Par m. L. C... Amsterdam, Arckée & Merkus, 1765.
      411 [i.e. 481] 18cm.

      Page 481 incorrectly numbered 411.
      Ex libris René Amédée Choppin.
      I. Title.

Witchcraft
Z
6878
W8
G64
    Catalogue of the private library of the late Abner C. Goodell.
    Goodell, Abner Cheney, 1831-1914.
      ... Catalogue of the private library of the late Abner C. Goodell, Salem, Mass. ... Pt. II, P to Z and witchcraft collection, including Prince Society publications, Prynne's tracts, rare Quaker tracts ... valuable collection of books relating to witchcraft and demonology... Boston, C. F. Libbie, book and art auctioneers, 1918.
      [93]-174 p. illus., facsims. 25cm.
      At head of title: Auction sale: ... March 12th, 1918 ...
      1. Witchcraft—Bibl.—Cat. I. Libbie, firm, auctioners, Boston. II. Title.

WITCHCRAFT
BX
2340
E96

8
NIC
    Catholic Church. Liturgy and ritual.
      Exorcismus in Satanam et angelos apostaticos, jussu Leonis XIII P. M. editus. [Romae, Typ. S. C. De Propaganda Fide, 1890]
      9 p. 15cm.

      With autograph: A. D. White.

      1. Exorcism. I. Catholic Church. Pope, 1878-1903 (Leo XIII) II. Catholic Church. Liturgy and ritual.

Witchcraft
BF
1775
C35
1766
    Castillon, Jean Louis, 1720-ca. 1793.
      Essai sur les erreurs et les superstitions anciennes & modernes. Par m. L. Castilhon. Nouv. éd., rev., corr. & considérablement augm. Francfort, Knoe & Eslinger, 1766.
      2 v. 21cm.

      1. Superstition. I. Title.

Witchcraft
Z
6880
Z91697
    Catalogue périodique d'ouvrages anciens et modernes, neufs et d'occasion relatifs à l'étude des phénomènes et des sciences occultes.
    Librairie du Merveilleux, Paris.
      Catalogue périodique d'ouvrages anciens et modernes, neufs et d'occasion relatifs à l'étude des phénomènes et des sciences occultes, franc-maçonnerie & sociétés secretes. [no.] -15, -1911? Paris.
      nos. 24cm.

      No. 15 has title: Catalogue general de liquidation.
      No more published?
      1. Occult Sciences. 2. Secret Societies. I. Title.

WITCHCRAFT
BX
2340
L81
1680

8
NIC
    Catholic Church. Liturgy and ritual.
      Locatellus, Petrus.
      Exorcismi potentissimi, & efficaces, ad expellendas aëreas tempestates, a daemonibus per se, sive ad nutum cujusvis diabolici ministri excitatas... ... Petro Locatello... Editio altera correctior. Labaci, Typis & impensis Joannis Bapt. Mayr, 1680.
      188 p. 14cm.

      Published earlier with title: Conjurationes potentissimae et efficaces ad expellendas ...aëreas tempestates...
                (Continued on next card)

Witchcraft
    Caston, Alfred de
      Les marchands de miracles: histoire de la superstition humaine, par Alfred de Caston. Paris, E. Dentu, 1864.
      338 p. 20cm.

      1. Superstition. 2. Occult sciences. I. Title.

DC
119
.8
D31
    Catherine de Médicis, queen consort of Henry II, king of France, 1519-1589.
    Defrance, Eugène, 1874-
      ... Catherine de Médicis, ses astrologues et ses magiciens-envoûteurs. Documents inédits sur la diplomatie et les sciences occultes du XVIe siècle; avec vingt illustrations. Paris, Mercvre de France, 1911.
      306 p., 3 l. incl. front., illus. (incl. ports., facsim.) 19cm.

WITCHCRAFT
BX
2340
L81
1680
    Catholic Church. Liturgy and ritual.
      Locatellus, Petrus. Exorcismi potentissimi, & efficaces...1680. (Card 2)

      With this is bound: Preces et coniurationes contra aëreas tempestates... Campidonae, 1667.

      1. Exorcism. I. Catholic Church. Liturgy and ritual. II. His Conjurationes potentissimae et efficaces... III. Title. IV. Title: Conjurationes potentissimae et efficaces...

Rare
BT
1313
.C35
    Castro, Alfonso de, d.1558.
      ...De iusta haereticorum punitione libri tres, nunc recens accurate recogniti...Venetiis, ad signum Spei, 1549.

      1. Heresies and heretics. I. Title.

109

CATALOGUE OF THE CORNELL WITCHCRAFT COLLECTION

WITCHCRAFT
BX
2045
B4
1671

Catholic Church. Liturgy and ritual.
Manuale exorcismorum et benedictionum selectorum pro exorcistarum, parochorum, et aliorum quorumvis curatorum commodiori usu collectorum. ₍Einsiedeln₎ Typis Einsidlensibus, per Nicolaum Wagenmann & Josephum Reymann, 1671.
171 p. 13cm.
Bound with: Catholic Church. Liturgy and ritual. Benedictional. Constance. Manuale benedictionum et rituum. 1671.

8
NIC

1. Exorcism.   I. Catholic Church. Liturgy and ritual.

Witchcraft
BX
2045
B4
1856

Catholic Church. Liturgy and ritual. Benedictional. Constance.
Benedictionale Constantiense, jussu et authoritate ... Maximiliani Christophori, Dei gratia Episcopi Constantiensis ... juxta normam ritualis Romani reformatum, approbatum et editum. Denuo impressum cum licentia ... Josephi, ... Episcopi Rottenburgensis. Biberaci, Sumtibus F. Haller, 1856.
xiv, 314 p. 22cm.
1. Benediction. 2. Exorcism. I. Title.

8

WITCHCRAFT
BX
2045
B4
1671

Catholic Church. Liturgy and ritual. Benedictional. Constance.
Manuale benedictionum et rituum, qui saepius extra ecclesias exercendi occurrunt, ex rituali Romano, Constantiensi, aliisque collectum. ₍Einsiedeln₎ Typis Monasterij Einsidlensis, per Nicolaum Wagenmann & Iosephum Reymann, 1671.
114 p. 13cm.
Includes rites for exorcism.
With this is bound: Manuale exorcismorum et benedictionum...1671.

8
NIC

1. Benediction. 2. Exorcism. I. Title.

WITCHCRAFT
BX
2045
B4
1849

Catholic Church. Liturgy and ritual. Benedictional. Passau.
Manuale benedictionum. Accedunt processiones variae publicis necessitatibus congruentes. Commodo animarum pastorum usui adaptavit Severinus Lueg... Editio secunda. Passavii, Elsässer & Waldbauer, 1849.
xix, 401 p. 17cm.
"Additio. I. Benedictio a daemonio vexatorum. II. Exorcismus pro exorcizandis obsessis.": xix p. at beginning.

8
NIC

1. Benediction. 2. Exorcism. I. Lueg, Severinus, ed. II. Title.

Witchcraft
BX
2045
B4
1872

Catholic Church. Liturgy and ritual. Regensburg.
Collectio benedictionum, instructionum et precum Sanctae apostolicae sedis auctoritate approbatarum aut indultarum quae tamen in rituali Romano non sunt receptae. Editio Ratisbonensis prima ... Ratisbonae, Sumtibus F. Pustet, 1872.
156 p. 22cm.
Title and text in red and black.
1. Benediction. I. Title.

8

WITCHCRAFT
BF
1565
C36
1889

Catholic Church. Pope, 1484-1492 (Innocentius VIII) Summis desiderantes affectibus (9 Dec. 1484)
Die Hexenbulle, nebst Auszügen aus dem "Hexenhammer." Aus dem Lateinischen ins Deutsche übers. und mit erläuternden Anmerkungen versehen ... 2. Aufl., von Wilhelm Römer. Schaffhausen (Schweiz) 1889.
32 p. 21cm.

8
NIC

"Zum 400jährigen Jubiläum des 'Hexenhammers.'"
(Continued on next card)

WITCHCRAFT
BF
1565
C36
1889

Catholic Church. Pope, 1484-1492 (Innocentius VIII) Summis desiderantes affectibus (9 Dec. 1484)
Die Hexenbulle...1889.   (Card 2)

Each page of the Hexenbulle has Latin text at the top, followed by German translation below.

1. Witchcraft. I. Institoris, Henricus, d. 1508. Malleus maleficarum. German. II. Römer, Wilhelm, ed. & tr. III. Title.

WITCHCRAFT
BF
1565
C36
1905

Catholic Church. Pope, 1484-1492 (Innocentius VIII) Summis desiderantes affectibus (9 Dec. 1484)
Die Hexenbulle Papst Innocens' VIII. Summis desiderantes; aus dem Bullarium magnum. Übertragen und hrsg. von Paul Friedrich. Leipzig, J. Zeitler, 1905.
15 p. 25cm.

1. Witchcraft. I. Title.

WITCHCRAFT
BF
1569
S26

Catholic Church. Pope, 1484-1492 (Innocentius VIII) Summis desiderantes affectibus (9 Dec. 1484)
Sauter, Johann G
Zur Hexenbulle 1484. Die Hexerei, mit besonderer Berücksichtigung Oberschwabens. Eine culturhistorische Studie. Ulm, J. Ebner, 1884.
82 p. 21cm.

8
NIC

1. Witchcraft--History. 2. Witchcraft--Swabia. 3. Catholic Church. Pope, 1484-1492 (Innocent VIII) Summis desiderantes affectibus (9 Dec. 1484) I. Title.

WITCHCRAFT
BX
2340
E96

Catholic Church. Pope, 1878-1903 (Leo XIII)
Exorcismus in Satanam et angelos apostaticos, jussu Leonis XIII P. M. editus. ₍Romae₎ Typ. S. C. De Propaganda Fide, 1890.
9 p. 15cm.
With autograph: A. D. White.

8
NIC

1. Exorcism. I. Catholic Church. Pope, 1878-1903 (Leo XIII) II. Catholic Church. Liturgy and ritual.

WITCHCRAFT
BF
1520
B66
1592

Cato, Ercole, tr.
Bodin, Jean, 1530-1596.
Demonomania de gli stregoni, cioè Fvrori, et malie de' demoni, col mezo de gl'hvomini: Diuisa in libri IIII. Di Gio. Bodino Francese, tradotta dal F. Hercole Cato ... Di nuouo purgata, & ricorretta. Venetia, Presso Aldo, 1592.
26 p. l., 419 p. 22cm.
"Confvtatione delle opinioni di Giovanni VVier": p. ₍360₎-419.
Translation of De la démonomanie.

8

(Continued on next card)

Cato, Hercole.

see

Cato, Ercole.

WITCHCRAFT
BF
1524
P59
1555

Cattani da Diacceto, Francesco, bp. of Fiesole, d. 1595.
Discorso del reverendo M. Francesco de Cattani da Diacceto ... sopra la svperstizzione dell'arte magica. Fiorenza, Appresso Valente Panizzi & Marco Peri C., 1567.
4 p. l., 36 numb. l. 23cm.
Bound with Pico della Mirandola, G. F. Dialogo intitolata La strega. Pescia, 1555.

8

1. Witchcraft. I. Title: La superstizzione dell'arte magica. II. Title.

Rare
HV
6211
G28
1734

Causes célèbres et interessantes.
Gayot de Pitaval, François, 1673-1743.
Causes célèbres et interessantes, avec les jugemens qui les ont décidées. La Haye, J. Neaulme, 1734-1751.
22 v. in 12. 17cm.
Imprint varies: v.1-2, Paris, J. de Nully. Vol. 1-2 published under pseud. "M. ***, avocat au Parlement."

1. Crime and criminals. 2. Trials. I. La Ville, Jean Claude de, b. 1735. II. Title.

Witchcraft
BF
1583
A2S74
1632

Cautelarum criminalium sylloge practica.
Oldekop, Justus
Cautelarum criminalium sylloge practica. Consiliarijs, maleficiorum judicibus, advocatis, inquisitoribus & actuarijs utilissima & pernecessaria ... Brunsvigae, Typis & sumptibus Gruberianis, 1633.
₍12₎, 363, ₍37₎ p. 17cm.
Bound with ₍Spee, Friedrich von₎ Cautio criminalis. Editio secunda. Francofvrti, 1632.
I. Title.

Witchcraft
BF
1583
A2S74
1695

Cautio criminalis.
₍Spee, Friedrich von₎ 1591-1635.
Cautio criminalis, seu De processibus contra sagas liber, inquisitoribus Germaniae hoc tempore summè necessarius, praeprimis consiliariis et confessariis Principum, inquisitoribus, judicibus, advocatis, confessoribus reorum, concionatoribus, aliisque lectu utilissimus. Solisbaci, Sumpt. Martini Endteri, 1695.
₍22₎, 407, ₍1₎ p. 15cm.
1. Witchcraft. 2. Witchcraft--Germany. I. Title.

Witchcraft
BF
1583
A2S74
1703

Cautio criminalis.
₍Spee, Friedrich von₎ 1591-1635.
... Cautio criminalis; sev, De processibus contra sagas liber. Das ist: Peinliche Warschauung von Anstell- und Führung des Processes gegen die angegebene Zauberer, Hexen und Unholden ... ins Teutsch treulich übersetzt ... ₍Halle im Magdeburg, 1703₎
₍49₎-356 p. 21cm.
Imperfect: p. 89-218 wanting.
Translated by Hermann Schmidt.

(Continued on next card)

Witchcraft
BF
1583
A2S74
1703

Cautio criminalis.
₍Spee, Friedrich von₎ 1591-1635.
Cautio criminalis ... ₍1703₎ (Card 2)

From Unterschiedliche Schrifften von Unfug des Hexen-Processes, by Johann Reiche.

1. Witchcraft. 2. Witchcraft--Germany. I. Title. II. Title: De processus contra sagas liber. III. Schmidt, Hermann, tr.

CATALOGUE OF THE CORNELL WITCHCRAFT COLLECTION

Cauz, Constantinus Franciscus de, 1735-1797.

see

Kauz, Constantin Franz Florian Anton von, 1735-1797.

BF 1410 L69 1970

Le cerimonie magiche.
Liber de ceremoniis magicis. Italian. 1970?
Le cerimonie magiche. Prima traduzione italiana dal testo latino preceduta da una introduzione. Roma, All'insegna della corona dei magi, [1970?].
78 p. illus. 22cm.
At head of title: Enrico Cornelio Agrippa.

1. Occult sciences. I. Agrippa von Nettesheim, Heinrich Cornelius, 1486?-1535, supposed author. II. Title III. Title: De occulta philosophia liber quartus. Italian.

NIC   JAN 30,'74   COOxc

Witchcraft
BF 1576 C43

Chadwick, John White, 1840-1904.
Witches in Salem and elsewhere. [n.p., 1885?]
[63]-82 p. 24cm.

Caption title.

1. Witchcraft--New England. I. Title.

Witchcraft
BF 1434 F8 C37

Cauzons, Thomas de, pseud.
La magie et la sorcellerie en France ... par Th. de Cauzons ... Paris, Dorbon-aîné [1910-11?]
4 v. 20½cm.

CONTENTS.--I. Origine de la sorcellerie. Ce qu'on racontait des sorcières. Opinions diverses à leur sujet.--II. Poursuite et châtiment de la magie jusqu'à la réforme protestante. Le procès des Templiers. Mission et procès de Jeanne d'Arc.--III. La sorcellerie de la réforme à la révolution. Les couvents possédées. La franc-maçonnerie. Le magnétisme animal.--IV. La magie contemporaine. Les transformations du magnétisme. Psychoses et névroses. Les esprits des vivants. Les esprits des morts. Le diable de nos jours. Le merveilleux populaire.

1. Occult sciences. 2. Magic. 3. Superstition. I. Title.

Library of Congress   BF1434.F8C3   12-23102 Revised
                       [r34b2]

Witchcraft
BF 1445 B35 1840

The certainty of the world of spirits fully evinced.
Baxter, Richard, 1615-1691.
The certainty of the world of spirits fully evinced. To which is added, The wonders of the invisible world, by Cotton Mather. The former taken from the edition published by Mr. Baxter, 1691, the latter from the Ecclesiastical history of New England, published 1702. With a preface by the editor. London, H. Howell, 1840.
245 p. 11cm.

The second part is not The wonders of the

(Continued on next card)

PQ 2625 A437 T8

Chantraine, Anne de--Fiction.
Mallet-Joris, Françoise, 1930-
Trois âges de la nuit, histoires de sorcellerie [par] Françoise Mallet-Joris. Paris, B. Grasset, 1968.
377 p. 21cm.

1. Chantraine, Anne de--Fiction. 2. Ranfaing, Élisabeth de, 1592-1649--Fiction. 3. Harvilliers, Jeanne--Fiction. I. Title.

Witchcraft
PQ 1961 C5A64 1845
2 copies

Cazotte, Jacques, 1719-1792--Biography.
Cazotte, Jacques. 1719-1792.
Le diable amoureux, roman fantastique par J. Cazotte; précédé de sa vie, de son procès, et de ses prophéties et révélations, par Gérard de Nerval. Illustré de 200 dessins par Édouard de Beaumont. Paris, L. Ganivet, 1845.
2 p. l., xc p., 1 l., 192 p. front. (port.) illus., 6 pl. 19½cm.

1. Devil--Fiction. 2. Cazotte, Jacques, 1719-1792--Biog.

I. Gérard de Nerval, Gerard Labrunie, known as, 1808-1855. II. Beaumont, Édouard de, 1821-1888, illus. III. Title.

17-8449

Library of Congress   PQ1961.C5.\64

Witchcraft
BF 1445 B35 1840

Baxter, Richard, 1615-1691. The certainty of the world of spirits fully evinced ... 1840.   (Card 2)

invisible world but only passages from Mather's Magnalia; or, Ecclesiastical history of New England.

I. Mather, Cotton, 1663-1728. Magnalia Christi americana.

Witchcraft
BF 1555 C46+

Charcot, Jean Martin, 1825-1893.
Les démoniaques dans l'art, par J. M. Charcot et Paul Richer. Paris, A. Delahaye et E. Lecrosnier, 1887.
116 p. 67 illus. 30cm.

(over)

MSS Bd. WITCHCRAFT BF C39

Celichius, Andreas, d. 1599.
Notwendige Errinnerung. Vonn des Sathans letzten Zornsturm, und was es auff sich habe und bedeute, das nu zu dieser Zeit so viel Menschen an Leib und Seel vom Teuffel besessen werden durch Andream Celichium... Wittenberg, Zacharias Lehman, 1594 [ca. 1900]
59 p. 23cm.
Carnap's manuscript copy.
"Original dr   uck in der Kgl.
(Continued on next card)

BF 1517 F5 C41

Certeau, Michel de.
La possession de Loudun, présentée par Michel de Certeau. [Paris, Julliard, 1970]
347 p. plates. 19 cm. (Collection Archives, 37) 9.00F F***
Includes bibliographical references.

4   1. Demoniac possession. 2. Loudun, France. Ursuline convent. 3. Grandier, Urbain, 1590-1634. I. Title.

BF1517.F5C47   76-575412
Library of Congress   71 [2]

HIST SCI
BF 1556 C47

Chardulliet, Melchior.
Dissertatio medica inauguralis De incubo, quam...examini submittit Melchior Chardulliet ... Argentorati, Typis Johannis Henrici Heitzii [1734]
24 p. 19cm.

Diss.--Strasbourg.

1. Medicine, Magic, mystic, and spagiric. 2. Demonology. 3. Medical delusions. I. Title.

8

MSS Bd. WITCHCRAFT BF C39

Celichius, Andreas, d. 1599. Notwendige Errinnerung...1594 [ca. 1900] (Card 2)
Universit. Bibliothek zu Leipzig, 113 S. in 4°."
Title in red and black.
Numerals and signatures in the margins indicate pagination and signatures of the original.

1. Demoniac possession. 2. Exorcism. I. Title.

History of Science
QL 666 O6 A11

Cesalpino, Andrea, 1519-1603.
Daemonum investigatio peripatetica. In qua explicatur locus Hippocratis Progn. Siquid diuinum in morbis habetur. Florentiae, Apud Iuntas, 1580.
24 l. 22cm.

Title vignette: Giunta's device; repeated at end in variant form.
Bound with Abati, Baldo Angelo. De admirabili viperae natvra ... Vrbini, 1589.
1. Demonol   ogy. 2. Hippocrates. Prognostica.   I. Title: Daemonum investigatio peripatetica.

Charitinus, Aloysius

see

Brunneman, Jacob, d. 1735.

---

chcraft
3 85 0

Astolfi, Giovanni Felice.
Cento avenimenti meravigliosi, stupendi, e rari.
Cento avenimenti meravigliosi, stvpendi, e rari ... Ne'qvali sono compresi distruggimenti di oracoli, insidie, maleficij, e tradimenti. Atti magnanimi di huomini fortissimi, caste, e costanti donne, et fanciulli animosi ... Vittorie singolari contro demonij, mondo, carne, et huomini rei. Venetia, A instanza delli Turrini, 1660.
[12], 154 p. 22cm.

Title vigne   tte: printer's device.

Witchcraft
BF 1566 C42

Chabloz, Fritz.
Les sorcières neuchateloises ... Neuchatel, Imprimerie de J. Attinger, 1868.
512 p. 19cm.

1. Witchcraft--Hist. I. Title.

Witchcraft
BF 1582 B52

La chasse aux sorcières dans le Labourd (1609)
Bernou, Jean.
La chasse aux sorcières dans le Labourd (1609); étude historique ... Agen, Calvet et Célérie, 1897.
414 p. 25cm.

1. Witchcraft--Labourd, France. I. Title.

CATALOGUE OF THE CORNELL WITCHCRAFT COLLECTION

Witchcraft
BF 1761
C61

Châteillon, Sébastien, 1515-1563.
Clasen, Daniel, 1623-1678.
De oraculis gentilium et in specie de vaticiniis sibyllinis libri tres, autore Daniele Clasen ... In fine adivncta svnt carmina sibyllina è versione Sebastiani Castalionis. Vt et Onuphrii Panvinii tractatvs de sibyllis. Helmstadii, apud H. Mullerum, 1673.
8 p. l., 824, [8], 104, [43] p. 20cm.
"Sibyllina oracula" has special t.-p. and separate paging.

1. Oracles. I. Oracula sibyllina. II. Châteillon, Sébastien, 1515-156 III. Panvinio, Onofrio, 1529-1568.

Library of Congress   BF1761.C6   11-14022

WITCHCRAFT
BF 1584
S97
Z7
1652

Chauderon, Michée, defendant.
Procès criminel de la dernière sorcière brulée à Genève le 6 avril 1652, publié d'après des documents inédits et originaux conservés aux Archives de Genève (N° 3465) par le d^r Ladame. Paris, Aux Bureaux du Progrès médical, 1888.
xii, 52 p. 24cm. (Bibliothèque diabolique (Collection Bourneville))

8 NIC

Running title: Procès criminel de Michée Chauderon.
(Continued on next card)

WITCHCRAFT
BF 1584
S97
Z7
1652

Chauderon, Michée, defendant.
Procès criminel de la dernière sorcière brulée à Genève...1888. (Card 2)

1. Trials (Witchcraft)—Geneva. I. Geneva. Conseil général. II. Ladame, Paul Louis, 1842-1919. III. Title. IV. Title: Procès criminel de Michée Chauderon.

Witchcraft
BF 1582
G51
C33
1732

Chaudon, lawyer.
Girard, Jean Baptiste, 1680-1733, defendant.
The case of Mrs. Mary Catharine Cadiere, against the Jesuit Father John Baptist Girard. In a memorial presented to the Parliament of Aix. Wherein he is accused of seducing her, by the abominable doctrines of quietism, into the most criminal excesses of lewdness, and under an appearance of the highest mystical devotion, deluding into the same vices six other females, who had put their consciences under his

8   (Continued on next card)

Witchcraft
BF 1582
G51
C33
1732

Chaudon, lawyer.
Girard, Jean Baptiste, 1680-1733, defendant.
The case of Mrs. Mary Catharine Cadiere ... 1732. (Card 2)
direction. With a preface by the publisher ... 10th ed. corr. London, Printed for and sold by J. Roberts, 1732.
vi, 96 p. 23cm.
"This memorial was originally drawn up by that eminent lawyer ... Chaudon ... the following piece is not a bare translation ..." p. ii

8   (Continued on next card)

WITCHCRAFT
BF 1555
M94
029
no.4

Chauffepié, Jacques Georges de, 1702-1786.
Nouveau dictionnaire historique et critique.
Semler, Johann Salomo, 1725-1791. ... D. Joh. Salomo Semlers ... Abfertigung der neuen Geister und alten Irtümer in der Lohmannischen Begeisterung zu Kemberg nebst theologischem Unterricht von dem Ungrunde der gemeinen Meinung von leiblichen Besitzungen des Teufels und Bezauberungen der Christen. Halle, Bey J. J. Gebauer, 1760.
40, 328 p. 18cm.
Dedication and "Vorrede" comprise the first numbering.

8 NIC   (Continued on next card)

WITCHCRAFT
BF 1555
M94
029
no.4

Chauffepié, Jacques Georges de, 1702-1786.
Nouveau dictionnaire historique et critique.
Semler, Johann Salomo, 1725-1791. ...
Abfertigung der neuen Geister ... 1760. (Card 2)
"Anhang. Auszug aus des Chaufepiee [sic] Nouveau dictionnaire historique et critique, von dem Artikel Balthas. Bekker": p. 317-328.
No. 4 in vol. lettered Oesfeld u. a. ...
1. Lohmannin, Anna Elisabeth. 2. Müller, Gottlieb. Gründlicher Nachricht von einer begeisterten Weibesperson. 3. Devil. 4. Bekker, Balthasar, 1634-1698.

8 NIC   (Continued on next card)

Chauvincourt, de Beauvoys, sieur de.

see

Beauvois de Chauvincourt, sieur de.

Witchcraft
BF 1517
F5
A89

The cheats and illusions of Romish priests and exorcists.
[Aubin, Nicolas] b. ca. 1655.
The cheats and illusions of Romish priests and exorcists. Discovered in the history of the devils of Loudun: being an account of the pretended possession of the Ursuline nuns, and of the condemnation and punishment of Urban Grandier, a parson of the same town ... London, Printed for W. Turner and R. Bassett, 1703.
4 p. l., 331 p. 20cm.
Translation of Histoire des diables de Loudun Attributed also to M. Des Niau.
1. Loudun, France. Ursuline Convent. 2. Grandier, Urbain, 1590-1634. I. Des Niau, , supposed author. II. Title

---

MSS Bd.
WITCHCRAFT
BF L37

Chemin, J B , 1725-1781, ed.
Laugeois, Antoine, d. 1674.
L'innocence opprimee; ou, Défense de Mathurin Picard, curé de Mesnil-Jourdain ... Par M. Laugois, successeur immédiat dudit Picard - dans la cure de Mesnil-Jourdain. Ouvrage qui n'a jamais été imprimé et extrait sur l'original, par M. Chemin curé de Tourneville. [n. p. 17th cent.]
x, 102 p. title vignette. 18cm.
Manuscript, on paper.
Preface signed M. du Passeur (Gabriel), curé de Vironvay.
(Continued on next card)

MSS Bd.
WITCHCRAFT
BF L37

Chemin, J B , 1725-1781, ed.
Laugeois, Antoine, d. 1674. L'innocence opprimee... [17th cent.] (Card 2)
Notes by G. L. Burr inside front cover discuss history and provenance of the manuscript.
Bound in boards.
1. Demoniac possession. 2. Picard, Mathurin, d. 1647. 3. Bavent, Madeleine, b. 1607. 4. Louviers, France. St. Louis (Convent) 5. Witchcraft. I. Chemin, J B , 1725 -1781, ed. II. Title. III. Title: Défense de Mathurin Picard.

Witchcraft
PS 1292
C86
C7

Child, Frank Samuel, 1854–
A colonial witch; being a study of the black art in the colony of Connecticut, by Frank Samuel Child ... New York, The Baker & Taylor co. [1897]
307 p. 18½cm.

1. Witchcraft—Conn.—Fiction. I. Title.

Library of Congress   PZ3.C436C   6-20984†

BF 1581
S49
C5

Children against witches.
Seth, Ronald.
Children against witches. New York, Taplinger Pub. Co. [1969]
190 p. illus. 23 cm. 4.95

1. Witchcraft—England. I. Title.
BF1581.S35 1969   133.4'0942   71-83294 MARC
Library of Congress   69 [2]

Witchcraft
BF 1598
C53

Chiozzi, Bartolomeo, 1671-1741.
Chiozzini, ossia La magia. Ferrara, Alla Pace. Tipi Negri, 1842.
42 p. front. 16cm.

1. Chiozzi, Bartolomeo, 1671-1741.

Witchcraft
BF 1598
C53

Chiozzini, ossia La magia. Ferrara, Alla Pace. Tipi Negri, 1842.
42 p. front. 16cm.

1. Chiozzi, Bartolomeo, 1671-1741.

Witchcraft
ML 50
W19
A4

Chorley, Henry Fothergill, 1808-1872.
The amber witch.
Wallace, William Vincent, 1812-1865.
[The amber witch. Libretto. English]
The amber witch: a romantic opera in four acts. The words by Henry F. Chorley, the music by W. Vincent Wallace. First represented at Her Majesty's Theatre, on Thursday, Feb. 28, 1861. London, Cramer, Beale & Chappell [1861?]
48 p. 18cm.
Based on the novel Maria Schweidler, die Bernstein Hexe, by Wilhelm Meinhold.

NIC   (Continued on next card)

Witchcraft
BF 1583
A2
B89
1727

Christ-bescheidentliche Gegen-Erinnerungen.
Weidner, Johann Joachim, 1672-1732.
Christ-bescheidentliche Gegen-Erinnerungen, worinnen der teuffelischen Wirckungen halber, umständliche Nachricht geschehen, und zugleich Jacobi Brunnemanni Anmerckungen, mit guten Grunde und nach Gottes Wort geprüfet und hingeleget seyn ... Rostock, Kissner, 1730.
143, [1] p. 22cm.
Bound with Brunnemann, Jacob. Discours von betrüglichen Kennzeichen Halle, 1727.

Witchcraft
BF 1565
T46
1717a

Christ. Thomasii Kurtze Lehr-Sätze von dem Laster der Zauberey.
Thomasius, Christian, 1655-1728.
Christ. Thomasii Kurtze Lehr-Sätze von dem Laster der Zauberey, mit dessen eigenen Vertheidigung vermehret. Worbey Johann Kleins ... Juristische Untersuchung, was von der Hexen Bekäntniss zu halten, dass solche aus schändlichem Beyschlaff mit dem Teuffel Kinder gezeuget. Beydes aus dem Lateinischen ins Teutsche übersetzt. Franckfurth und Leipzig, 1717.
134 p. front. 19cm.

8   (Continued on next card)

112

CATALOGUE OF THE CORNELL WITCHCRAFT COLLECTION

Witchcraft
BF
1565
T46
1717a
Christ. Thomasii Kurtze Lehr-Sätze von dem Laster der Zauberey.
Thomasius, Christian, 1655-1728. Christ. Thomasii Kurtze Lehr-Sätze von dem Laster der Zauberey ... 1717. (Card 2)
Translation of his Dissertatio de crimine magiae, J. Reiche, respondent; and of Meditatio academica, exhibens examen juridicum judicialis, by J. Klein (N. Putter, respondent.)
Johann Kleins Juristische Untersuchung, p. [79]-134, has special t. p.
(Continued on next card)

Witchcraft
BF
1565
T46
1717a
Christ. Thomasii Kurtze Lehr-Sätze von dem Laster der Zauberey.
Thomasius, Christian, 1655-1728. Christ. Thomasii Kurtze Lehr-Sätze von dem Laster der Zauberey ... 1717. (Card 3)
With this are bound Ludovici, Gottfried, 1670-1724. ... Theologicum novae... Coburgi [1718] and Sturm, Johann Christoph, 1635-1703. ... Wahrhaffte und gründliche Vorstellung von der lügenhafften Stern-Wahrsagerey. Coburg, 1722.
1. Witchcraft. I. His Dissertatio de crimine magiae.-- German. II.
(Continued on next card)

WITCHCRAFT
BF
1584
D4
C552
Christensen, Christian Villads, 1864-1922. Besaettelsen i Thisted.
(In: Samlinger til Jydsk historie og topografi. København. 22cm. ser.3, v.3, no.3. 1902. p.206-219)
With this, in same issue, is: Bang, Vilhelm. Tilføjelser til efterretningerne om hexeforfølgelserne i Ribe.
1. Witchcraft--Thisted, Denmark. 2. Demoniac possession. 3. Björn, Ole, b.1648. 4. Arni Magnússon, 1663-1730. I. Title.

Witchcraft
BF
1584
D4
C55
Christensen, Christian Villads, 1864-1922. Hekseprocesser fra Midtjylland (Viborg-Skive Egnen) af Villads Christensen.
(In Samlinger til jydsk historie og topografi. København. 22cm. 3. raekke, 6. bind (1908-10), p. [313]-378)
1. Witchcraft--Denmark. 2. Trials (Witchcraft)--Denmark. I. Title. II. Samlinger til jydsk historie og topografi.

WITCHCRAFT
BF
1584
D4
C551
Christensen, Christian Villads, 1864-1922. Hvorledes en hekseproces kommer i gang. En fortaelling fra Agernaes Birk.
(In: Fra arkiv og museum, København. 23cm. v.1, no.2, 1900. p. [109]-134)
1. Trials (Witchcraft)--Denmark. 2. Witchcraft--Denmark. I. Title.

WITCHCRAFT
DL
271
T44
H67
1919
Christensen, Severin, 1867-
Om heksetroen og om heksene i Thy og V. Hanherred.
(In: Historisk aarbog for Thisted Amt. København. 23cm. 1919. p. [3]-30)
Continuation of an article in the 1917 issue.
1. Witchcraft--Denmark. 2. Trials (Witchcraft)--Denmark. I. Title.

Christensen, Villads, 1864-1922.
see
Christensen, Christian Villads, 1864-1922.

Witchcraft
BF
1584
D4
J172
Christenze Kruckow. En adelig Troldkvinde fra Chr. IV's Tid.
Jacobsen, Jørgen Carl, 1916-
Christenze Kruckow. En adelig Troldkvinde fra Chr. IV's Tid. [Af] J. C. Jacobsen. København, Gad, 1972.
8, 96 p. 25cm.
1. Kruckow, Christence, d. 1621. 2. Trials (Witchcraft)--Denmark. I. Title.

Witchcraft
BF
1523
E35
Christian Thomasii Gelehrte Streitschrift von dem Verbrechen der Zauber- und Hexerey.
Thomasius, Christian, 1655-1728.
Christian Thomasii Gelehrte Streitschrift von dem Verbrechen der Zauber- und Hexerey. Aus dem Lateinischen übersetzt, und bey Gelegenheit der Gassnerischen Wunderkuren zum Besten des Publikums herausgegeben. [Leipzig?] 1775.
95 p. 18cm.
Bound with Einziger von Einzing, Johann Martin Maximilian, 1725-1798. Dämonologie. [Leipzig?] 1775.
(Continued on next card)

Witchcraft
BF
1523
E35
Christian Thomasii Gelehrte Streitschrift von dem Verbrechen der Zauber- und Hexerey.
Thomasius, Christian, 1655-1728. Christian Thomasii Gelehrte Streitschrift von dem Verbrechen der Zauber- und Hexerey ... 1775. (Card 2)
Translation of Dissertatio de crimine magiae.
1. Witchcraft. I. His Dissertatio de crimine magiae. German. II. Title: Streitschrift von dem Verbrechen der Zauber- und Hexerey.

Witchcraft
B
2605
Z7
N63
Christian Thomasius. Ein Beitrag zur Geschichte der Aufklärung.
Nicoladoni, Alexander.
Christian Thomasius. Ein Beitrag zur Geschichte der Aufklärung. Dresden, Hönsch & Tiesler [1888]
vi, 140 p. port. 22cm.
1. Thomasius, Christian, 1655-1728-- Biog.

Witchcraft
PT
1793
T4
W13+
Christian Thomasius; ein Beitrag zur Würdigung seiner Verdienste um die deutsche Literatur.
Wagner, B. A
Christian Thomasius; ein Beitrag zur Würdigung seiner Verdienste um die deutsche Literatur. Berlin, W. Weber, 1872.
26 p. 27cm.

Witchcraft
B
2605
Z7
K64
Christian Thomasius, ein Vorkämpfer der Volksaufklärung.
Klemperer, Prediger zu Landsberg a. W.
Christian Thomasius, ein Vorkämpfer der Volksaufklärung. Vortrag, gehalten vom Prediger Dr. Klemperer im Vereins-Verband für öffentliche Vorträge zu Landsberg a. W. am 15. Februar 1877. Landsberg a. W., Druck von F. Striewing, 1877.
43 p. 21cm.
1. Thomasius, Christian, 1655-1728 --Biog.

Witchcraft
B
2605
Z7
L94
Christian Thomasius, nach seinen Schicksalen und Schriften dargestellt.
Luden, Heinrich, 1778?-1847.
Christian Thomasius, nach seinen Schicksalen und Schriften dargestellt, von H. Luden. Mit einer Vorrede von Johann von Müller ... Berlin, Bei J. F. Unger, 1805.
xvi, 311 p. 17cm.
1. Thomasius, Christian, 1655-1728-- Biog. I. Müller, Johannes von, 1752-1809.

Witchcraft
BF
1581
A2C55
Christie, John, comp.
Witchcraft in Kenmore, 1730-57: extracts from the kirk session records of the parish. Aberfeldy, D. Cameron, 1893.
19 p. 19cm.
1. Witchcraft--Kenmore (Scotland) I. Church of Scotland. Presbytery of Kenmore. II. Title.

Witchcraft
BF
1583
A2
W82
1593
Christlich Bedencken unnd Erinnerung von Zauberey.
Witekind, Hermann, 1522-1603.
Christlich Bedencken unnd Erinnerung von Zauberey, woher, was, vnd wie vielfältig sie sey, wem sie schaden könne oder nicht, wie diesem Laster zu wehren, vnd die so damit behafft, zu bekehren, oder auch zu straffen seyn. Beschrieben durch Augustin Lercheimer [pseud.] von Steinfelden. Aut assentire his, aut meliora doce. Jetzund auffs new gemehret vnd gebessert. Basel, Getruckt durch Sebastianum Henricpetri [1593]
(Continued on next card)

Witchcraft
BF
1583
A2
W82
1593
Christlich Bedencken unnd Erinnerung von Zauberey.
Witekind, Hermann, 1522-1603. Christlich Bedencken vnnd Erinnerung von Zauberey ... [1593] (Card 2)
280, [3] p. 17cm.
With colophon and printer's device. Woodcut of a witches' sabbath on t. p. Commentary by G. L. Burr on front inside cover.
1. Witchcraft. 2. Trials (Witchcraft) --Germany. I. Title: Christlich Bedencken und Erinnerung von Zauberey.

Witchcraft
BF
1583
Z7
1749
Christliche Anred nächst dem Scheiter-Hauffen, worauf der Leichnam Mariae Renatae.. verbrennet worden.
Gaar, Georg, b. 1702.
Christliche Anred nächst dem Scheiter-Hauffen, worauf der Leichnam Mariae Renatae, einer durchs Schwerdt hingerichteten Zauberin, den 21. Junii anno 1749 ausser der Stadt Wirtzburg verbrennet worden, an ein zahlreich-versammletes Volck gethan, und hernach aus gnädigstem Befehl einer Hohen Obrigkeit in offentlichen Druck gegeben. [Würzburg] M. A. Engmann [1749?]
[12] p. 21cm.
(Continued on next card)

CATALOGUE OF THE CORNELL WITCHCRAFT COLLECTION

WITCHCRAFT
BF
1565
M61

Christliche Erinnerung an gewaltige Regenten ...
Meyfart, Johann Matthäus, 1590-1642.
Christliche Erinnerung an gewaltige Regenten und gewissenhaffte Praedicanten wie das abscheuliche Laster der Hexerey mit Ernst ausszurotten... Schleusingen, Gedruckt bey Peter Schmiden, 1636.
272 p. 20cm.

8
NIC

1. Witchcraft. 2. Trials (Witchcraft) I. Title.

Witchcraft
BF
1412
C16
1850

Christmas, Henry, 1811-1868, tr.
Calmet, Augustin, 1672-1757.
The phantom world; or, The philosophy of spirits, apparitions, etc. Edited with an introd. and notes by Henry Christmas. London, R. Bentley, 1850.
2 v. 20cm.

Translation of Dissertations sur les apparitions des anges, des démons & des esprits ... which was also published under title: Traité sur les apparitions des esprits et sur les vampires ...

Witchcraft
BF
1583
A2
B35+

Der Churfürstl. Durchleucht Herzogs Maximilian Joseph in Bayern &c. &c. ...
Bavaria. Laws, statutes, etc.
Der Churfürstl. Durchleucht Herzogs Maximilian Joseph in Bayern &c. &c. ... erneuerte Land-Gebott, wider die Aberglauben, Zauberey, Hexerey, und andere straffliche Teuffels-Künsten. München, Gedruckt bey Johann Jacob Vötter, 1746.
[18] p. 29cm.

8

1. Witchcraft—Germany. 2. Superstition. I. Bavaria. Sovereigns, etc., 1745-1777 (Maximilian III Joseph) II. Title: Erneuerte Landglauben, Zauberey. Gebott wider die Aberrey.

WITCHCRAFT
BF
1555
S32

Christliche Erinnerung, bey der Historien von jüngst beschehener Erledigung einer Junckfrawen.
Scherer, Georg, 1539-1605.
Christliche Erinnerung, bey der Historien von jüngst bescheener Erledigung einer Junckfrawen, die mit zwölfftausent sechs hundert zwey und fünffzig Teufel besessen gewesen. Geprediget zu Wien in Oesterreich Anno 1583 ... Jngolstatt, Getruckt durch David Sartorivm, 1584.
4 p. l., 63 p. 21cm.
Title in red and black.

8
NIC

1. Demoniac possession. 2. Exorcism. 3. Schultter bäwrin, Anna, fl. 1583. I. Title.

Witchcraft
BF
1575
L42
1704

Christ's fidelity the only shield against Satan's malignity.
Lawson, Deodat.
Christ's fidelity the only shield against Satan's malignity. Asserted in a sermon deliver'd at Salem-village the 24th of March, 1692. Being lecture-day there, and a time of publick examination, of some suspected for witchcraft. By Deodat Lawson ... 2d ed. ... Printed at Boston in New-England, and Reprinted in London, by R. Tookey for the Author; and are to be sold by T. Parkhurst, at the Bible and Three Crowns in Cheapside; and J. Lawrence, at the Angel in the Poultry, 1704.
6 p. l., 120 p. 16cm.

(Continued on next card) 25-13271

Witchcraft
BF
1520
C57
1605

Cigogna, Strozzi.
Del palagio de gl'incanti, et delle gran merauiglie de gli spiriti, & di tutta la natura loro. Diuiso in libri XXXXV. & in III. prospettiue, Spirituale, Celeste, & Elementare ... Brescia, Appresso il Buozzola, 1605.
[40], 623 p. 17cm.

Title vignette: device of G. B. Bozola.
Contains only "Prospettiva prima, libro primo-quarto." No more published.

1. Demonology. 2. Incantations. I. Title.

Witchcraft
BV
5083
G59

Die christliche Mystik.
Görres, Johann Joseph von, 1776-1848.
Die christliche Mystik. Regensburg, G. J. Manz, 1836-42.
4 v. in 3. 21cm.
Contents.—1. Buch. Natürliche Unterlage der Mystik.—2. Buch. Der religiöse und kirchliche Grund der Mystik.—3. Buch. Die reinigende Mystik.—4. Buch. Eintritt in die Kreise höheren Zuges und Triebes, so wie höherer Erleuchtung.—5. Buch. Fortstreben zum Ziele in Liebe und höherer Erleuchtung durch die Ecstase.—6. Buch. Die historische,

8 (Continued on next card)

Witchcraft
BF
1575
L42
1704

Christ's fidelity the only shield against Satan's malignity.
Lawson, Deodat. Christ's fidelity the only shield against Satan's malignity. 1704. (Card 2)

Appendix (p. 93-120): "Brief account of the amazing things which occasioned that discourse to be delivered."

1. Witchcraft—Salem, Mass. I. Title.

Witchcraft
BF
1520
C57
1607

Cigogna, Strozzi.
Magiæ omnifariæ, vel potius, Vniversæ natvræ theatrvm: in qvo a primis rervm principiis arcessita disputatione, vniuersa spiritvvm & incantationvm natura, &c. explicatur. Auctore d. Strozzio Cigogna ... ex italico latinitati donatum opera & studio Caspari Ens ... Coloniæ, sumptibus C. Butgenij, 1607.
4 p. l., 568 p. 16cm.

1. Demonology. 2. Exorcism. I. Ens, Gaspar, 1570-1636?, tr. II. Title.
11-9698

Witchcraft
BV
5083
G59

Die christliche Mystik.
Görres, Johann Joseph von, 1776-1848. Die christliche Mystik ... 1836-42. (Card 2)

Contents—Continued.
sagenhafte, physische und psychische Begründung der dämonischen Mystik.—7. Buch. Die dämonische Vorbereitung und Ascese.—8. Buch. Die Besessenheit.—9. Buch. Das Hexen- und Zauberwesen.
Introduction and table of contents to vol. 4 is bound in between books 8 and 9.
Each book has special t. p.

8

Witchcraft
BS
2545
D5
C56

[Church, Thomas]
An essay towards vindicating the literal sense of the demoniacks in the New Testament. In answer to a late Enquiry into the meaning of them [by A.A. Sykes] ... London, Printed by J. Bettenham, and sold by J. Roberts, 1737.
118 p. 19cm.

1. Demoniac possession. 2. Bible. N.T.—Commentaries. 3. Sykes, Arthur Ashley, 1684?-1756. [An enquiry into the meaning of demoniacks in the New Testament. I. Title.

Witchcraft
BX
2340
C57
1733

Cilia, Gelasius di.
Locupletissimus thesaurus continens varias & selectissimas benedictiones, conjurationes, exorcismos, absolutiones ... ad utilitatem Christi fidelium, & commodiorem usum parochorum, omniúmque sacerdotum, tam saecularium, quàm religiosorum curam habentium, ex diversis ritualibus & probatissimis authoribus. Locupletior & correctior redditus a Gelasio di Cilia ... Ed. 4ª. Augustae Vindelicorum, Expensis F. A. Strötter, 1733.

8 (Continued on next card)

Witchcraft
BX
1750
C98
1645

Christliche Zuchtschul, in welcher gründliche unnd warhafftige Resolution ... fürgebracht wird.
Cusanus, Nicolaus, 1574-1635.
Christliche Zuchtschul, in welcher gründliche unnd warhafftige Resolution und Aufflösung aller schwähren Fragstück so in jedem weltlichen Standt, Wandel und Handel mögen fürfallen, wie auch der fürnembsten streitigen Articklen Erklärung kürtzlich fürgebracht wird; allen Seelsorgern und dem gemeinen Mann sehr nutzlich ... Lucern, D. Hautten, 1645.
8 l., 731 p. 17cm.

Added t. p. engraved.

Witchcraft
BS
2545
D5
T97
no.4

[Church, Thomas]
An essay towards vindicating the literal sense of the demoniacks in the New Testament. In answer to a late Enquiry into the meaning of them ... London, Printed by J. Bettenham and sold by J. Roberts, 1737.
123 p. 21cm.

No. 4 in vol. lettered: Twells, Whiston, etc. Tracts on the demoniacs in the New Testament. London, 1738-1775.

Witchcraft
BX
2340
C57
1733

Cilia, Gelasius di. Locupletissimus thesaurus ... 1733. (Card 2)

774, [10] p. 17cm.

1. Exorcism. 2. Benediction. 3. Prayers. I. Catholic Church. Liturgy and ritual. II. Title.

8

Witchcraft
BR
115
M2
G87

Christlicher Bericht von und wieder Zauberey.
Gross, Christianus.
Christlicher Bericht von und wieder Zauberey, was solche schröckliche Sünde sey, wo sie herkomme, und wie man in allen Ständen derselben steuren und wehren könne und solle; auss Gottes Wort verfasset und Erfür gegeben. Colberg, J. Kusen, 1661.
[16] 68 p. 15cm.

1. Witchcraft. I. Title.

Witchcraft
BS
2545
D5
T97
no.5

Church, Thomas.
An essay towards vindicating the literal sense of the demoniacks in the New Testament. [Sykes, Arthur Ashley, 1684?-1756.
A further enquiry into the meaning of demoniacks in the New Testament. Wherein the Enquiry is vindicated against the objections of ... Mr. Twells, and of the author of the Essay in answer to it [i.e. Thomas Church] ... London, Printed for J. Roberts, 1737.
116 p. 21cm.

No. 5 in vol. lettered: Twells, Whiston, etc. Tracts on the demoniacs in the New Testament. London, 1737-1775.

WITCHCRAFT
BF
1555
P84

Cinexis, Rosa.
Portal, Placido, 1793-1843.
Demonomania con commozione celebrale senza stravaso; osservazione fatta nel mese di novembre dell'anno 1833 nella R. Casa de' Matti in Palermo. Palermo, Dalla Tipografia del Giorn. letterario, 1834.
25, [4] p. port. 20cm.

"Autopsia cadaverica della demonomoniaca [sic] Rosa Cinexis ...": [4] p. at end.
Includes bibliographical references.

8
NIC

(Continued on next card)

CATALOGUE OF THE CORNELL WITCHCRAFT COLLECTION

Witchcraft
BF
1555
B64

Cinq histoires admirables, esqvelles est monstre' comme miraculeusement par la vertu & puissance du S.-Sacrement de Blendec, Charles.   l'Autel.
Cinq histoires admirables, esqvelles est monstre' comme miraculeusement par la vertu & puissance du S.-Sacrement de l' Autel, a esté chassé Beelzebub, Prince des diables, auec plusieurs autres demons, qui se disoiét estre de ses subiects, hors des corps de quatre diuerses personnes. Et le tout aduenu en ceste presente année 1582, en la ville & diocese de Soissons ... Paris, G. Chaudiere,   1582.
125 p. 17cm.

Witchcraft
BF
1520
W64
P8
1569

Cinq livres de l'imposture et tromperie des diables: des enchantements et sorcelleries.
Wier, Johann, 1515-1588.
Cinq livres de l'imposture et tromperie des diables: des enchantements et sorcelleries. Pris du latin de Iean Uvier et faits françois par Iaques Gréuin de Clermont en Beauuoisis, médicin à Paris. Paris, Iaques du Puys, 1569.
468, [79] p. 16cm.
Incomplete: t. p. and all before p. 1 wanting.
Title taken   from Yve-Plessis, Ro-
(Continued on next card)

Witchcraft
F
520
64
8
569

Cinq livres de l'imposture et tromperie des diables: des enchantements et sorcelleries.
Wier, Johann, 1515-1588. Cinq livres de l'imposture et tromperie des diables ...
1569.   (Card 2)
bert. Essai d'une bibliographie ... de la sorcellerie, p. 104, no. 832.
A t. p. in G. L. Burr's hand indicates this edition of the work; however, a long note by Burr on facing page claims the edition agrees with no. 833 in Yve-Plessis. But no. 833 co   nsists of 6 books, not 5.   (Continued on next card)

Witchcraft
520
64
8
569

Cinq livres de l'imposture et tromperie des diables: des enchantements et sorcelleries.
Wier, Johann, 1515-1588. Cinq livres de l'imposture et tromperie des diables ...
1569.   (Card 3)
Translation of his De praestigiis daemonum.
1. Demonology. 2. Witchcraft. 3. Magic. 4. Fasting. I. Grévin, Jacques, 1538?-1570, tr. II. His De praestigiis daemonum--French. III. Title. IV. Title: De l'imposture et tromperie des diables.

Witchcraft
410
42
56
3
.16

Circulaire brief van de Eerwaarde Kerkenraad van Rotterdam, geschreven aan de respective kerken-raden.
Nederlandse Hervormde Kerk. Kerkenraden. Rotterdam.
Circulaire brief van de Eerwaarde Kerkenraad van Rotterdam aan de respective kerken-raden van Zuyd ende Noord Holland; misgaders aan de voornaamste steden van de verdere geunieerde provincien, wegens de saake van D Balthasar Bekker, en syn boek De betooverde weereld. [Rotterdam? 1692]
[4] p. 20 x 15cm.
4°: π².
Caption ti   tle.
(Continued on next card)

Witchcraft
10
2
5
3
.16

Circulaire brief van de Eerwaarde Kerkenraad van Rotterdam, geschreven aan de respective kerken-raden.
Nederlandse Hervormde Kerk. Kerkenraden. Rotterdam. Circulaire brief ... [1692]
(Card 2)
Van der Linde 33.
No. 16 in vol. lettered Bekker III.
1. Bekker, Balthasar, 1634-1698. De betoverde weereld. I. Nederlandse Hervormde Kerk. Kerkenraden. II. Title.

Witchcraft
BF
1565
C57
R4
1551

Ciruelo, Pedro, 1470 (ca.)-1560.
Reprobacion de las svpersticiones y hechizerias. Libro muy vtil, y necessario a todos los buenos christianos. ... Medina del Campo, Fue impresso en casa de Guillermo de millis, 1551.
62 [i.e., 124] p. 20cm.
Title vignette (printer's device)
Imperfect: t. p. somewhat mutilated.
8   I. Title.

Witchcraft
BF
1565
C57R4
1952

Ciruelo, Pedro, 1470 (ca.)-1560.
Reprobación de las supersticiones y hechicerías.   Madrid, 1952.
xliii, 147 p. 26cm. (Colección Joyas bibliograficas, 7)
"Número 73."
1. Witchcraft. I. Series.

Witchcraft
BF
1581
A2
W81
1866a
no.6

Clark, G
Relation of a memorable piece of witchcraft, at Welton, near Daventry, in Northamptonshire. ... Contained in a letter of Mr. G. Clark to Mr. M. T.   Northampton, Taylor, 1867.
8 p. 22cm.
Letter dated 1658.
"Reprinted from Glanvil's Sadducismus triumphatus. London, 1681."
No. 6 in box   lettered Witchcraft in Northamptonshi   re.
8   1. Ghosts.   I. Title.

Clark, Mrs. Mary, of Haverhill.
Witchcraft
BF
1575
D76
v.2-3
Calef, Robert, 1648-1719. More wonders of the invisible world: or, The wonders of the invisible world, display'd in five parts. Part I. An account of the sufferings of Margaret Rule, written by the Reverend Mr. C. M. P. II. Several letters to the author, &c. And his reply relating to witchcraft. P. III. The differences between the inhabitants of Salem village, and Mr. Parris their minister, in New-England. P. IV. Letters of a gentleman uninterested, endeavouring to prove the received opinions about witchcraft to be orthodox. With short essays to their answers. P. v. A short historical accout [!] of matters of fact in that affair. To
(Continued on next card)
2-18714 rev.
[r31e2]

Clark, Mrs. Mary, of Haverhill.
Witchcraft
BF
1575
D76
v.2-3
Calef, Robert, 1648-1719. More wonders of the invisible world ... (Card 2)
which is added, a postscript relating to a book intitled, The life of Sir William Phips. Collected by Robert Calef, merchant, of Boston in New-England ... London, Printed for N. Hillar and J. Collyer, 1700.
Reprint. (In Drake, S. G. The witchcraft delusion in New England ... Roxbury, Mass. 1866. 21cm. v. 1, p. 1-212; v. 3, p. 3-167) Woodward's historical series. no. VI-VII.
Prefatory: by the editor: p. [v]-x. Pedigree of Calef: 1 fold. leaf.
Memoir of Robert Calef: p. [xi]-xxix.
The text, here annotated, is that of the 1st edition, 1700. "It is given as exactly like the original as a much better type can be made to imitate an old type of 166 years ago."--Pref. by the editor. p. vi.
(Continued on next card)
2-18714 rev.
[r31e2]

Clark, Mrs. Mary, of Haverhill.
Witchcraft
BF
1575
D76
v.2-3
Calef, Robert, 1648-1719. More wonders of the invisible world ... 1700.   (Card 3)
Appendix: I. Examination of Giles Cory.-- II. Giles Corey and Goodwyfe Corey. A ballad of 1692.--III. Testimony of William Beale, of Marblehead, against Mr. Philip English of Salem, given Aug. 2d. 1692.--IV. Examination of the Indian woman belonging to Mr. Parris's family]-- V. The examination of Mary Clark of Haverhill.-- VI. An account of the life and character of the Rev. Samuel Parr is, of Salem village, and of his connection with the witchcraft delusion of 1692. By Samuel P. Fowler.

Clark, Samuel, 1675-1729.
see
Clarke, Samuel, 1675-1729.

F
5
C59

Clarke, Helen Archibald, d. 1926.
Longfellow's country, by Helen Archibald Clarke ... New York, The Baker and Taylor company, 1909.
6 p. l., 252 p. front. (port.) 31 pl. 24cm. $2.50
Illus. end-papers.
CONTENTS.--Along the coast of New England.--Under the shadow of Blomidon.--Idyls from history.--The New England tragedies.--The lore of Hiawatha.--In Cambridge.
1. Longfellow, Henry Wadsworth, 1807-1882. 2. New England--Descr. & trav. 3. Acadians. 4. Revere, Paul, 1735-1818. 5. Pilgrim fathers. 6. Friends, Society of--Massachusetts. 7. Witchcraft--New England. 8. Indians of North America--Folk-lore. 9. Cambridge, Mass.--Descr.
I. Title.   9-27937
Library of Congress   F5.C59
Copy 2.
© Oct. 18, 1909; 2c. Oct. 19, 1909; A 248662; Baker & Taylor co., New York, N. Y.

WITCHCRAFT
BT
97
A2
S48

Clarke, Samuel, 1675-1729.
A discourse concerning the being and attributes of God.
Serces, Jaques, 1695-1762.
Traité sur les miracles. Dans lequel on prouve que le diable n'en sauroit faire pour confirmer l'erreur ... et où l'on examine le système opposé, tel que l'a établi le Dr. Samuel Clarke, dans le chap. XIX. du II. vol. de son Traité sur la religion naturelle & chrétienne ... Amsterdam, Chez P. Humbert, 1729.
21 p. l., 371 p. 16cm.
8
NIC
Serces takes   issue with Samuel
(Continued on next card)

WITCHCRAFT
BT
97
A2
S48

Clarke, Samuel, 1675-1729.
A discourse concerning the being and attributes of God.
Serces, Jaques, 1695-1762. Traité sur les miracles ... 1729.   (Card 2)
Clarke's A discourse concerning the being and attributes of God, translated by P. Ricotier as De l'existence et des attributs de Dieu, Amsterdam, 1717. [See RARE B 1365 D32 F8 1717]
1. Miracles--Early works to 1800. 2. Clarke, Samuel, 1675-1729. A discourse concerning the being and attributes of God. 3. Magic. I.   Title.
8
NIC

Witchcraft
BF
1761
C61

Clasen, Daniel, 1623-1678.
De oraculis gentilium et in specie de vaticiniis sibyllinis libri tres, autore Daniele Clasen ... In fine adivncta svnt carmina sibyllina è versione Sebastiani Castalionis. Vt et Onuphrii Panvinii tractatvs de sibyllis. Helmstadii, apud H. Mullerum, 1673.
8 p. l., 824, [8], 104, [43] p. 20cm.
"Sibyllina oracula" has special t.-p. and separate paging.
1. Oracles. I. Oracula sibyllina. II. Chateillon, Sébastien, 1515-1563. III. Panvinio, Onofrio, 1529-1568. IV. Title.

La clavicule de Salomon.
WITCHCRAFT
BF
1558
G86
1750
L'Art de commander les esprits célestes, aëriens, terrestres & infernaux. Suivi du Grand grimoire, de la magie noire et des forces infernales, du docteur J. Karter, La clavicule de Salomon, &c. Avec le vrai secret de faire parler les morts, pour découvrir tous les trésors caches, &c. &c. [Paris?] 1421 [i.e., ca. 1750?]
iv, 5-108 [i. e., 118], [2] p. illus.
16cm.
Title in red and black.
8
(Continued on next card)

CATALOGUE OF THE CORNELL WITCHCRAFT COLLECTION

La clavicule de Salomon.

WITCHCRAFT
BF
1558
G86
1750

L'Art de commander les esprits ... [1750?] (Card 2)

Published also under other titles: Grimoire du Pape Honorius [best-known]; Le dragon rouge; and Le véritable dragon rouge.

1. Incantations. 2. Magic. I. Karter, J. II. Title: Le grand grimoire. III. Title: Grimoire du Pape Honorius. IV. Title: Le dragon rouge. V. Title: Le véritable dragon rouge. VI. Title: La clavicule de Salomon.

8

Witchcraft
BF
1505
G94

La clef de la magie noire.

Guaita, Stanislas de, 1860–1897.
... Le serpent de la Genèse ... par Stanislas de Guaita. Paris, Librairie du merveilleux, 1891–

v. front., plates, ports. 23 cm. (His Essais de sciences maudites II)

Books 1-2 only

Books 1 and 2 only.
Vol. 2 has imprint: Bibliothèque Chacornac, 1897. Date on cover: 1902.
Vol. 1 has subtitle: Le temple de Satan.
Vol. 2 has subtitle: La clef de la magie noire.
Ex libris, vol. 2: Arthur Edward Waite.

1. Demonology. I. Title. II. His Essais de sciences maudites. III. Title: Le temple de Satan. IV. Title: La clef de la magie noire.

Library of Congress   BF1405.G8 vol. 2

WITCHCRAFT
BF
1557
C64
1708

Clodius, Johann, 1645–1733, praeses.
De spiritibus familiaribus vulgo sic dictis, praeside Johanne Clodio, disseret Jo. Christophorus Rudingerus. Vitembergae, C. Schroedter, 1708.
[32] p. 20cm.

Originally issued as dissertation, Wittenberg, 1693 (J. C. Rudinger, respondent)

8   1. Demonology. I. Rudinger, J.C.
NIC   II. Title.

Cochem, Martin von, pater, 1634?–1712.

see

Martin von Cochem, pater, 1634?–1712.

Cochemensis, Martin, 1634?–1712.

see

Martin von Cochem, pater, 1634?–1712.

Codronchi, Baptista, fl. 1620.

see

Codronchi, Giovanni Battista, fl. 1620.

Witchcraft
RA
1201
C67
1618

Codronchi, Giovanni Battista, fl. 1620.
Baptistae Codronchi ... De morbis veneficis, ac veneficijs. Libri qvattvor, in quibus non solum certis rationibus veneficia dari demonstratur, sed eorum species, caußae, signa, & effectus noua methodo aperiuntur. Postremo de eorum curatione ac praeseruatione exactè tractatur ... Qd opus alias editū, nuperrimè fuit ab auctore emēdatū ... Mediolani, Apud Io. Bapt. Bidelliū, 1618.
15 p.l., 248, [25] p. 19cm.

8   (Continued on next card)

Witchcraft
RA
1201
C67
1618

Codronchi, Giovanni Battista, fl. 1620. ...
De morbis veneficis ... 1618. (Card 2)
Added t. p., engraved.

1. Toxicology. 2. Poisons. I. Title: De morbis veneficis, ac veneficiis. II. Baptistae Codronchi ... De morbis veneficis; ac veneficijs.

8

WITCHCRAFT
BF
1501
D12
no.2

Cölln, Ludwig Friedrich August von, tr.
Farmer, Hugh, 1714–1787.
Hugo Farmers Versuch über die Dämonischen des Neuen Testamentes. Aus dem Englischen übersetzt von L. F. A. von Cölln. Nebst einer Vorrede D. Joh. Sal. Semlers. Bremen und Leipzig, Bey J. H. Cramer, 1776.
38, 327 p. 17cm.

Translation of An essay on the demoniacs of the New Testament.
No. 2 in vol. lettered Dämonologische Schriften.

8   (Continued on next card)

WITCHCRAFT
BX
2340
V94

Coler, Jacob, 1537–1612.
Vom Exorcismo bey der Taufe.
Vom Exorcismo. Das dieser ohne Verletzung des Gewissens bey der Tauffe wol mag gebraucht vnd behalten werden: etliche Tractetlein. I. Iusti Menij. II. Lutheri Vorrede vber das Tauffbüchlein. III. Die gewöhnliche Gebet bey der Tauffe im Stifft vnd der Thumkirchen zu Cölln an der Sprew. IIII. Aus dem Appendice D. Vrbani Regij. V. Zwo Episteln Tilemanni Heshusij. VI. Eine Epistel Philippi Melanchton is. VII. D. Iacobi Co-

8   (Continued on next card)

WITCHCRAFT
BX
2340
V94

Coler, Jacob, 1537–1612.
Vom Exorcismo ... 1591. (Card 2)
leri Büchlein. Alles zu guter Nachrichtung den einfeltigen Leyen zum besten zusammen bracht. [Franckfurt an der Oder] In Verlegung Johan vnd Friderich Hartmans, 1591.
[269] p. 17cm.
Title in red and black.
With colophon: Gedruckt zu Franckfurt an der Oder, durch Nicolaum Voltzen, 1591.

8   (Continued on next card)

WITCHCRAFT
BX
2340
V94

Coler, Jacob, 1537–1612.
Vom Exorcismo bey der Taufe.
Vom Exorcismo ... 1591. (Card 3)
Vom Exorcismo, oder Von dem Beschweren der Kinder bey der Tauffe. Drey Sendbriefe deren zwene D. Tilemannvs Heshvsivs: den dritten Herr Philippvs Melanchton geschrieben ... Verdeutscht durch Heinrich Rätel, has special t. p. with date 1590.
Vom Exorcismo bey der Tauffe ... durch Jacobum Colerum D. has special t. p., no date.

8   (Continued on next card)

Witchcraft
BX
2045
B4
1872

Collectio benedictionum et precum Sanctae apostolicae.
Catholic Church. Liturgy and ritual. Regensburg.
Collectio benedictionum, instructionum et precum Sanctae apostolicae sedis auctoritate approbatarum aut indultarum quae tamen in rituali Romano non sunt receptae. Editio Ratisbonensis prima ... Ratisbonae, Sumtibus F. Pustet, 1872.
156 p. 22cm.
Title and text in red and black.
1. Benediction. I. Title.

8

WITCHCRAFT
BX
2340
S22
1761

Collectio, sive Apparatus absolutionum.
Sannig, Bernhard.
Collectio, sive Apparatus absolutionum, benedictionum, conjurationum, exorcismorum, rituum, & ceremoniarum ecclesiasticarum, ac administrationis sacramentorum ... Coordinatum A. R. P. Bernardo Sannig. Venetiis, Apud J. B. Recurti, 1761.
xii, 466 p. 15cm.

8   1. Exorcism 2. Benediction. I.
NIC   Catholic Church. Liturgy and ritual. II. Title.

Witchcraft
K
A76+

A collection and abridgement of celebrated criminal trials in Scotland from A. D. 1536 to 1784.
Arnot, Hugo, 1749–1786, ed.
A collection and abridgement of celebrated criminal trials in Scotland from A. D. 1536 to 1784. With historical and critical remarks. Edinburgh, Printed for the author by W. Smellie, 1785.
xxiii, 400 p. 28cm.

Ex libris Joseph Goodall.

1. Trials—Scotland. I. Title.

Witchcraft
BF
1563
H16

A collection of modern relations of matter of fact, concerning witches and witchcraft.
Hale, Sir Matthew, 1609–1676.
A collection of modern relations of matter of fact, concerning witches & witchcraft upon the persons of people. To which is prefixed a meditation concerning the mercy of God, in preserving us from the malice and power of evil angels. Written ... upon occasion of a trial of several witches ... Part I. London, Printed for J. Harris, 1693.
64 p. 20cm.
Wing H224.
No more published?
1. Witchcraft—England. I. Title.

Witchcraft
BF
1581
W37

A collection of rare and curious tracts on witchcraft and the second sight.
[Webster, David]
A collection of rare and curious tracts on witchcraft and the second sight; with an original essay on witchcraft. Edinburgh, Printed for D. Webster, 1820.
iv, 183 p. 20cm.

1. Witchcraft—Scotland. 2. Second sight. I. Title.

Rare
DA
300
S69+
1809

A collection of scarce and valuable tracts ... [on] the history ... of these kingdoms.
Somers, John Somers, baron, 1651–1716.
A collection of scarce and valuable tracts ... [on] the history and constitution of these kingdoms ... 2d ed., rev., augm., and arr. by Walter Scott. London, Printed for T. Cadell and W. Davies, 1809–1815.
13 v. 30cm.

Ex libris Henry Thomas Buckle.

1. Gt. Brit.—History—Modern period, 14 —Sources. 2. Pamphlets—Bibliography. I. Scott, Sir Walter, bart., 1771–183 ed. II. Title.

116

CATALOGUE OF THE CORNELL WITCHCRAFT COLLECTION

Collin de Plancy, Jacques Albin Simon, 1794–1881.
Le diable peint par lui même, ou Galerie de petits romans, de contes bizarres, d'anecdotes prodigieuses, sur les aventures des démons ... et les services qu'ils ont pu rendre aux mortels ... Extrait et traduit des démonomanes, des théologiens, des légendes, et des diverses chroniques du sombre empire. Paris, P. Mongie aîné, 1819.
xl, 258 p. front. 21cm.

(over)

BL 31 M63+ v.48-49

[Collin de Plancy, Jacques Albin Simon] 1794–1881. Dictionnaire des sciences occultes ... 1860–61. (Card 2)
Fifth edition of Collin de Plancy's "Dictionnaire infernal", first published in 1818. cf. G. Vicaire, Manuel de l'amateur de livres; and R. Yve-Plessis, Essai d'une bibliographie française ... de la sorcellerie et de la possession démoniaque, 1900, p. 4.
In double columns, numbered.

1. Occult sciences—Dictionaries. I. Title.
[Name originally: Jacques Albin Simon Collin]
6-22420 Revised
Library of Congress   BF1025.C7
——— Copy 2.   BL31.M5
[r33b2]

Witchcraft
BF 1503 C69 1965

Collin de Plancy, Jacques Albin Simon, 1794–1881. Dictionnaire infernal—English.
Dictionary of demonology. Edited and translated by Wade Baskin. New York, Philosophical Library [1965]
177 p. 22 cm.
Selections from Dictionnaire infernal.

1. Demonology—Dictionaries. I. Baskin, Wade, ed. and tr. II. Title. III. His Dictionnaire infernal—English.
BF1508.C613   133.4   65-11952
Library of Congress   [8]

Witchcraft
[Collin de Plancy, Jacques Albin Simon] 1794–1881.
Le diable peint par lui-même—German.
Geschichten vom Teufel.   Quedlinburg und Leipzig, G. Basse, 1821.
179 p. 17cm.
"... nach dem Werke: 'Le diable peint par lui même, par Collin de Plancy' zusammengestellt." Vorwort, p. 9.
Considerably shortened and simplified.
1. Devil. 2. Occult sciences. I. His Le diable peint par lui-même—German. II. Title

---

Witchcraft
BF 1503 C69

Collin de Plancy, Jacques Albin Simon, 1794–1881.
Dictionnaire infernal; ou, Recherches et anecdotes, sur les démons, les esprits, les fantômes, les spectres, les revenants, les loups-garoux, les possédés, les sorciers, le sabbat, les magiciens, les salamandres, les sylphes, les gnomes, etc., les visions, les songes, les prodiges, les charmes, les maléfices, les secrets merveilleux, les talismans, etc.; en un mot, sur tout ce qui tient
(Continued on next card)

WITCHCRAFT
BF 1503 C69 S61

8 NIC

Collin de Plancy, Jacques Albin Simon, 1794–1881.
Dictionnaire infernal.
[Simonnet, P. B.]
Réalité de la magie et des apparitions, ou Contrepoison du Dictionnaire infernal. Ouvrage dans lequel on prouve, par une multitude de faits et d'anecdotes authentiques ... l'existence des sorciers, la certitude des apparitions, la foi due aux miracles, la vérité des possessions, etc., ... précédé d'une Histoire très-précise de la magie ... Paris, P. Mongie aîné, 1819.
xxii, 152 p. 21cm.
Ascription   by Barbier.
(Continued on next card)

Witchcraft
BF 1503 C69 1965

Collin de Plancy, Jacques Albin Simon, 1794–1881.
Dictionary of demonology. Edited and translated by Wade Baskin. New York, Philosophical Library [1965]
177 p. 22 cm.
Selections from Dictionnaire infernal.

1. Demonology—Dictionaries. I. Baskin, Wade, ed. and tr. II. Title. III. His Dictionnaire infernal—English.
BF1508.C613   133.4   65-11952
Library of Congress   [8]

Witchcraft
BF 1503 C69 1825

Collin de Plancy, Jacques Albin Simon, 1794–1881.
Dictionnaire infernal, ou Bibliothèque universelle, sur les êtres, les personnages, les livres, les faits et les choses qui tiennent aux apparitions, à la magie, au commerce de l'enfer, aux divinations, aux sciences secrètes, aux grimoires, aux prodiges, aux erreurs et aux préjugés, aux traditions et aux contes populaires, aux superstitions diverses, et généralement à toutes les croyances mer-
(Continued on next card)

Witchcraft
BF 1549 C69 1821

[Collin de Plancy, Jacques Albin Simon] 1794–1881.
Geschichten vom Teufel.   Quedlinburg und Leipzig, G. Basse, 1821.
179 p. 17cm.
"... nach dem Werke: 'Le diable peint par lui même, par Collin de Plancy' zusammengestellt." Vorwort, p. 9.
Considerably shortened and simplified.
1. Devil. 2. Occult sciences. I. His Le diable peint par lui-même—German. II. Title

---

[Collin de Plancy, Jacques Albin Simon] 1794–1881.
Dictionnaire des sciences occultes ... ou, Répertoire universel des êtres, des personnages, des livres, des faits et des choses qui tiennent aux apparitions, aux divinations, à la magie, au commerce de l'enfer, aux démons, aux sorciers, aux sciences occultes ... et généralement à toutes les fausses croyances, merveilleuses, surprenantes, mystérieuses ou surnaturelles; suivi du Traité historique des dieux et des démons du paganisme, par Binet; et de la Réponse à l'Histoire des oracles de Fontenelle, par Baltus. Publié par m. l'abbé Migne ... Paris, Chez l'éditeur, 1848.
2 v. 28cm. (Added t.-p.: Encyclopédie théologique, ou Série de dictionnaires sur chaque branche de la science religieuse ... pub. par m. l'abbé Migne ...   t. 48-49)
(Continued on next card)   6-22420 Revised
[r33b2]

Witchcraft
BF 1503 C69 1825

Collin de Plancy, Jacques Albin Simon, 1794–1881. Dictionnaire infernal ...   (Card 2)
veilleuses, surprenantes, mystérieuses et surnaturelles. 2. éd., entièrement refondue ...   Paris, P. Mongie, aîné, 1825-26.
4 v. plates, facsims. 21cm.

1. Occult sciences—Dictionaries. 2. Magic—Dictionaries. 3. Superstition. I. Title.

Witchcraft
BF 1552 C69

Collin de Plancy, Jacques Albin Simon, 1794–1881.
Légendes infernales. Relations et pactes des hotes de l'enfer avec l'espèce humaine. Paris, H. Plon [1862]
395 p. col. front. 22cm.

Bound with his Légendes des esprits ... Paris [1864]

I. Title

[Collin de Plancy, Jacques Albin Simon] 1794–1881. Dictionnaire des sciences occultes ... 1848. (Card 2)
Fifth edition of Collin de Plancy's "Dictionnaire infernal", first published in 1818. cf. G. Vicaire, Manuel de l'amateur de livres; and R. Yve-Plessis, Essai d'une bibliographie française ... de la sorcellerie et de la possession démoniaque, 1900, p. 4.
In double columns, numbered.
Added t. p. of v.1 dated: 1846.

1. Occult sciences—Dictionaries. I. Title.
[Name originally: Jacques Albin Simon Collin]
6-22420 Revised
Library of Congress   BF1025.C7
——— Copy 2.   BL31.M5
[r33b2]

[Collin de Plancy, Jacques Albin Simon] 1794–1881.
Dictionnaire des sciences occultes ... ou, Répertoire universel des êtres, des personnages, des livres, des faits et des choses qui tiennent aux apparitions, aux divinations, à la magie, au commerce de l'enfer, aux démons, aux sorciers, aux sciences occultes ... et généralement à toutes les fausses croyances, merveilleuses, surprenantes, mystérieuses ou surnaturelles; suivi du Traité historique des dieux et des démons du paganisme, par Binet; et de la Réponse à l'Histoire des oracles de Fontenelle, par Baltus. Publié par m. l'abbé Migne ... Paris, Chez l'éditeur, 1860–61.
2 v. 28cm. (Added t.-p.: Encyclopédie théologique, ou Série de dictionnaires sur chaque branche de la science religieuse ... pub. par m. l'abbé Migne ...   t. 48-49)
(Continued on next card)   6-22420 Revised
[r33b2]

Witchcraft
BF 1503 C69+ 1863

Collin de Plancy, Jacques Albin Simon, 1794–1881.
Dictionnaire infernal. Répertoire universel des etres, des personnages, des livres, des faits et des choses qui tiennent aux esprits, aux démons, aux sorciers ... et généralement à toutes les fausses croyances merveilleuses, surprenantes, mystérieuses et surnaturelles. 6. éd., augm. et illustrée ... par M. L. Breton.   Paris, H. Plon, 1863.
723 p. illus., ports. 27cm.

1. Occult sciences—Dictionaries.
2. Magic—Dictionaries. I. Title.

A colonial witch.

Witchcraft
PS 1292 C86 C7

Child, Frank Samuel, 1854–
A colonial witch; being a study of the black art in the colony of Connecticut, by Frank Samuel Child ...   New York, The Baker & Taylor co. [1897]
307 p. 18½cm.

1. Witchcraft—Conn.—Fiction. I. Title.

Library of Congress   PZ3.C436C   6-20984†

CATALOGUE OF THE CORNELL WITCHCRAFT COLLECTION

Witchcraft
BF 1589 C72
Colquhoun, John Campbell, 1785-1854.
An history of magic, witchcraft, and animal magnetism. By J. C. Colquhoun ... London, Longman, Brown, Green, & Longmans; [etc., etc.] 1851.
2 v. 19cm.

1. Magic. 2. Witchcraft. 3. Animal magnetism. I. Title.
11—14510
Library of Congress   BF1589.C7

Colquhon, John Campbell, 1785-1854.

WITCHCRAFT
BF 1589 B81 1852
Braid, James, 1795?-1860.
Magic, witchcraft, animal magnetism, hypnotism, and electro-biology ... 3d. ed., greatly enl., embracing observations on J. C. Colquhon's "History of magic" ... London, J. Churchill, 1852.
122 p. 19cm.

1. Magic. 2. Witchcraft. 3. Animal magnetism. 4. Colquhon, John Campbell, 1785-1854. An history of magic. I. Title.

8
NIC

Witchcraft
BF 1785 C73 1665
[Comenius, Johann Amos] 1592-1670, comp.
Lux e tenebris, novis radiis aucta. Hoc est: solemnissimae divinae revelationes, in usum seculi nostri factae ... Per immissas visiones, & angelica divinaqve alloqvia, facta I. Christophoro Kottero silesio, ab anno 1616, ad 1624. II. Christinae Poniatoviae bohemae, annis 1627, 1628, 1629, III. Nicolao Drabicio moravo, ab anno 1638, ad 1664 ... [Amstelodami] 1665.
various pagings. illus., ports. 21cm.
Added engr. t. p.

8   (Continued on next card)

Witchcraft
BF 1785 C73 1665
[Comenius, Johann Amos] 1592-1670, comp.
Lux e tenebris ... 1665.   (Card 2)

"Voluminis prophetici," first item, has special t. p. with imprint 1667.
"Revelationes Christophoro Kottero" and "Revelationes Christinae Poniatoviae" each have special t. p. with imprint 1664.
"Revelationes Nicolao Drabicio" has special t. p. without imprint.
First published 1657 with title: Lux in tenebris.

8   (Continued on next card)

Witchcraft
BF 1785 C73 1665
[Comenius, Johann Amos] 1592-1670, comp.
Lux e tenebris ... 1665.   (Card 3)

1. Prophecies. 2. Mysticism—Bohemia. 3. Prophets. I. Kotter, Christoph, 17th cent. II. Poniatowska, Krystyna, 1610-1644. III. Drabik, Mikuláš, 1588-1671. IV. Title.

8

Comenius, Johann Amos, 1592-1670.

WITCHCRAFT
BF 1555 K29
Keller, Ludwig, 1849-1915.
Die altevangelischen Gemeinden und der Hexenglaube.
(In [Geisteskultur;] Monatshefte der Comenius-Gesellschaft [für Geisteskultur und Volksbildung] Berlin, 1892-1934. 25cm. 8. Bd., 1. und 2. Heft (1899), p. [30]-35)

Bibliographical footnotes.

1. Demoniac possession. 2. Waldenses. 3. Comenius, Johann Amos, 1592-1670. I. Title.

8
NIC

Witchcraft
BT 965 O23+ 1739
Ode, Jacobus, 1698-1751.
Commentarius de angelis. Trajecti ad Rhenum, Apud Matthaeum Visch, 1739.
[38], 1068, [46] p. 26cm.

Engraved title vignette.
Added t. p., engraved.

1. Angels—Early works to 1800. 2. Demonology. I. Title.

8

Commentarius, de praecipuis divinationum generibus.

WITCHCRAFT
BF 1410 P51 1593
Peucer, Kaspar, 1525-1602.
Commentarivs, de praecipvis divinationvm generibvs, in qvo a prophetiis, avthoritate diuina traditis, & à physicis coniecturis, discernuntur artes & imposturae diabolicae, atque obseruationes natae ex superstitione, & cum hac coniunctae: et monstrantur fontes ac causae physicarum praedictionum diabolicae verò ac superstitiosae confutatae damnantur, ea serie, quam tabella praefixa ostendit. Recognitus vltimò, & auctus, ab avthore ipso Casparo Pevcer   o D. Addita, singulis

8   (Continued on next card)

Commentarius, de praecipuis divinationum generibus.

WITCHCRAFT
BF 1410 P51 1593
Peucer, Kaspar, 1525-1602. Commentarivs, de praecipvis divinationvm generibvs ... 1593.   (Card 2)

voculis & sententiis Graecis, sua interpretatione. Francofvrti, Apud Andreae Wecheli heredes, Claudium Marnium, & Ioan. Aubrium, 1593.
16 p. l., 738, [51] p. 2 fold. tables. 18cm.

First published 1553.
1. Divination. 2. Prophecies. 3. Magic. 4. Witchcraft. I. Title.

8

Commentarius in titulum ... de maleficis et mathematicis.

Witchcraft
BF 1565 B61 1623
Binsfeld, Pierre, ca. 1540-1598.
Tractatvs de confessionibvs maleficorvm et sagarvm. An & quanta fides ijs adhibenda sit? Auctore Petro Binsfeldio ... Accedit eiusdem auctoris Commentarius in tit. cod. lib. 9. de malefic. & mathematic. ... Item bvllae & extravagantes pontificum, &c. Editio quarta correctior & auctior. Coloniae Agrippinae, Sumptib. Petri Henningij, 1623.
8 p. l., 638, [17] p. 16cm.

8   (Continued on next card)

Commentarius in titulum ... de maleficis et mathematicis.

Witchcraft
BF 1565 B61 1623
Binsfeld, Pierre, ca. 1540-1598. Tractatvs de confessionibvs maleficorvm et sagarvm. 1623.   (Card 2)

Commentarivs in titvlvm codicis lib. IX. de maleficis et mathematicis, p. 329-611, has special t. p.
Extravagantes et bvllae apostolicae diversorvm pontificum: p. 612-638.
"This was, I think, the last impression of Binsfeld's work. It is merely a reprint of the 4th ed."   —that of 1596—the

8   (Continued on next card)

Commentarius in titulum ... de maleficis et mathematicis.

Witchcraft
BF 1565 B61 1623
Binsfeld, Pierre, ca. 1540-1598. Tractatvs de confessionibvs maleficorvm et sagarvm. 1623.   (Card 3)

last edited by himself. [Signed] G. L. B[urr]" in ms. inside front cover.

1. Witchcraft. 2. Demonology. I. Title: Tractatus de confessionibus maleficorum et sagarum. II. Title: De confessionibus maleficorum et sagarum. III. Title: Commentarius in titulum ... de maleficis et mathematicis.

8

Commentatio de crimine conivrationis spirituum.

Witchcraft
BF 1600 F62
Floercke, Johann Ernst von, 1695-1762.
Io. Ernesti Floerckii I. V. D. Commentatio de crimine conivrationis spirituvm eivs processv et poenis praemissis nonnvllis ad magiam svpernatvralem divinam daemoniacam et hvmanam nec non thevrgiam cabbalam et theologiam mysticam pertinentibvs ... Ienae, Apvd Io. Felic. Bielckivm, 1721.
8 p. l., 522, [33] p. 21cm.
Title in red and black.
1. Magic. 2. Witchcraft. 3. Trials (Witchcraft) I. Title: De crimine conjurationis spirituum.

8

Commentatio de daemoniacis.

Witchcraft
BF 1555 G89
Gruner, Christian Gottfried, 1744-1815.
Christiani Godofredi Grvner ... Commentatio de daemoniacis a Christo Sospitatore percvratis. Accedit Danielis Wilhelmi Trilleri ... Exercitatio medico-philologica De mirando lateris cordisqve Christi vvlnere atqve effvso inde largo sangvinis et aqvae proflvvio. Ienae, Litteris et impensis I. C. Stravssii, 1775.
6 p. l., 64, [3] p. 18cm.
1. Demoniac possession. 2. Jesus

8   (Continued on next card)

Commentatio de daemoniacis quorum in N. T. fit mentio.

WITCHCRAFT
BS 2545 D5 S47 1769
Semler, Johann Salomo, 1725-1791.
Ioannis Salomonis Semleri ... Commentatio de daemoniacis qvorvm in N. T. fit mentio. Editio avctior. Halae Magdebvrgicae, Impensis I. C. Hendelii, 1769.
62 p. 21cm.

First published 1760 under title: De daemoniacis, quorum in Evangeliis fit mentio. (Title from Kayser)
1. Demoniac possession. 2. Bible. N. T.—Commentaries. I. His De daemoniacis, quorum in Evangeliis fit mentio. II. Title: De daemoniacis quorum in N. T. fit mentio.

8

Commentatio de pactis hominvm cvm diabolo circa abditos in terra thesavros effodiendos

Witchcraft
BF 1547 F65 1741
Förtsch, Michael, 1654-1724.
Commentatio de pactis hominvm cvm diabolo circa abditos in terra thesavros effodiendos et acqvirendos, ad casvm illvm tragicvm, qvi anno MDCCXV. in vigiliis festi Nativitatis Christi in agro Ienensi institvta. Von denen Bündnissen der Menschen mit dem Teufel bey dem Schatz-Graben. Editio novissima. Lipsiae, Apvd Christian. Schroetervm, 1741.
61, [2] p. 22cm.

A new edition of a dissertation at Jena,

8   (Continued on next card)

Commentatio de pactis hominvm cvm diabolo circa abditos in terra thesavros effodiend[os]

Witchcraft
BF 1547 F65 1741
Förtsch, Michael, 1654-1724. Commentatio de pactis hominvm cvm diabolo ... 1741.   (Card 2)

with Michael Förtsch as praeses and Johannes Andreas Rinneberg as respondent, published Jena, 1716.

1. Devil. 2. Treasure-trove. I. Rinneberg, Johannes Andreas, respondent. II. Title: De pactis hominum cum diabolo circa abditos in terra thesauros effodiendos. III. Title: Bündnisse der Menschen mit dem Teufel bey dem Schatz-Graben.

8

Commentatio iuridica De coniugibus incantatis.

WITCHCRAFT
HQ 822 H33 1741
Hartmann, Johann Zacharias.
Io. Zachariae Hartmanni ... Commentatio ivridica De conivgibvs incantatis eorvmqv separatione. Von bezauberten Ehe-Leuten, durch Nesselknüpfen, Schloss zuschnappen &c. und derselben Scheidung. Jenae, Ex officina Schilliana, 1741.
40, 16 p. 22cm.

Programma D. Ioh. Zach. Hartmanni ... Dispvtationi ivridicae has special t. p., and is paged separately.
1. Marriage—Annulment. 2. Spells. I. Title: De conjugibus incantatis.

8

CATALOGUE OF THE CORNELL WITCHCRAFT COLLECTION

Commentatio secvnda De existentia daemonvm.

Witchcraft
BF
520
32
    Breithaupt, Christian, 1689-1749, praeses.
        Commentatio secvnda De existentia daemonvm, qvam ... praeside Christiano Breithavpto ... pvblicae litteratorvm dispvtationi svbmittit avtor Iacobvs Fridericvs Ditmar ... Helmstadii, Exscripsit Herm. Dan. Hammivs [1722]
    4 p. l., 18, [2] p. 19cm. (bound in 21cm. vol.)
    Bound with Schwerzer, Johann Adam, praeses. Daemonologia. Lipsiae, 1672.

(Continued on next card)

Commentatio secvnda De existentia daemonvm.

Witchcraft
BF
520
32
    Breithaupt, Christian, 1689-1749, praeses.
        Commentatio secvnda ... [1722] (Card 2)

    In vol. lettered Dissertationes de daemonibus. 1672-1722.

    1. Demonology. I. Ditmar, Jacob Friedrich, respondent. II. Title: De existentia daemonum.

Commentationem ad titulum codicis De mathematicis maleficis et ceteris similibus.

Witchcraft
BF
1565
M53
    Mencken, Lüder, praeses.
        Commentationem ad titulum codicis De mathematicis maleficis et ceteris similibus praeside Lüdero Menckenio ... excutiendam publice proponet auctor et respondens Jacob. Benedictus Wincklerus ... Lipsiae, Literis I. Titii [1725]
    72 p. 20cm.

    1. Witchcraft. 2. Trials (Witchcraft) I. Winckler, Jacob Benedict, respondent. II. Title: De mathematicis maleficis et ceteris similibus.

8

Compendiaria et facillima ratio rite exorcizandi.

WITCHCRAFT
BX
2340
T83
    Triumphus artis exorcisticae seu Compendiaria, et facillima ratio rite exorcizandi; benedictionis conficiendae super aegros, et aliarum cum suis exorcismis benedictionum; parochis utile, & exorcistis opusculum perutile. Lugani, Typis Agnelli, & soc., 1766.
    xvi, 267 p. 18cm.

    1. Exorcism. I. Title: Compendiaria, et facillima ratio rite exorcizandi.

8
NIC

Compendio dell' arte essorcistica.

WITCHCRAFT
BF
1524
M54
1582
    Menghi, Girolamo, d. 1610.
        Compendio dell' arte essorcistica, et possibilita delle mirabili, et stvpende operationi delli demoni, et dei malefici. Con li rimedij opportuni alle infirmità maleficiali. Del R. P. F. Girolamo Menghi da Viadana ... Bologna, Nella stamperia di Giouanni Rossi, 1582.
    10 p. l., 614, [58] p. 15cm.
    Title in red and black.
    First published 1580.
8   1. Demonology. 2. Witchcraft. 3. Exorcism. I. Title.

Compendio della vita, e delle gesta di Giuseppe Balsamo.

itchcraft
[Barberi]
98
3
3
91b
    Compendio della vita, e delle gesta di Giuseppe Balsamo, denominato il conte Cagliostro, che si è estratto dal processo contro di lui formato in Roma l'anno 1790. E che può servire di scorta per conoscere l'indole della setta de' Liberi muratori. Roma, Stamp. della Rev. Camera apostolica, 1791.
    189 p. front. (ports.) 19cm.

    1. Cagliostro, Alessandro, conte di, assumed name of Giuseppe Balsamo, 1743-1795. 2. Freemasons. I. Title.
    CA 7—7324 Unrev'd
Library of Congress   BF1598.C2B3 1791

Compendivm maleficarvm.

Witchcraft
BF
1559
G91
    Guazzo, Francesco Maria.
        Compendivm maleficarvm in tres libros distinctum ex plvribvs avthoribvs per fratrem Franciscvm Mariam Gvaccivm ... Mediolani, Apud Haeredes August. Tradati, 1608.
    8 p. l., 245, [1] p. illus. 21cm.
    First edition.
    Colophon: Mediolani, Apud Bernardinum Lantonum, 1608.
    Copy 1 has autograph commentary by G. L. Burr inside cover.
    Copy 2: ex libris cabalisticis
8   Kurt Seligmann. (Continued on next card)

Compendium Miraculorum.

Witchcraft
BF
1413
M21
1620
    Maier, Michael, 1568?-1622.
        Compendium Miraculorum, das ist: Kurtze, jedoch klare Beschreibung vnterschiedtlicher Wunderwercken vnd Geschichten: Insonderheit der Gänse, so in den Orcadischen Insuln auff Bäumen wachsen: Dessgleichen von Vrsprung vnd Geburt etlicher sehr frembden Vegetabilien, Menschen vnd Thier: wie auch dem Vogel Phoenix, Wehrwölffen, Geniis, Waldtgöttern, Lamiis, Hexen, vnd anderer Gedächtnusswürdiger Sachen Erörterung. Von H. Michael Mayern ... Lateinisch beschrieben, vnd an jetzo ins
(Continued on next card)

Compendium Miraculorum.

Witchcraft
BF
1413
M21
1620
    Maier, Michael, 1568?-1622. Compendium miraculorum ... (Card 2)

    Teutsche vbersetzt, durch M. Georgivm Beatvm ... Franckfurt, Getruckt in Verlegung Lucae Jennis, 1620.
    [16], 142 p. 17cm.

    1. Occult sciences. 2. Marvelous, The. 3. Miracles--Early works to 1800. I. Title.

[Compendium of folklore and popular beliefs of the seventeenth century. n.p. late 17th - early 18th cent.]

MSS.
Bd.
WITCHCRAFT
AG
C73
    [389] l. illus. 23cm.
    Manuscript, on paper, in an 18th century German hand.
    Text rubricated in red and green. Richly illustrated with colored drawings, charts, calendars and astrological tables.
    Bound in vellum.
    Ex libris: Kurt Seligmann.
    1. Folk-lore--Collections. 2. Occult sciences--Collections.

A compleat history of magick, sorcery, and witchcraft.

Witchcraft
BF
1410
B76C7
2 copies
    [Boulton, Richard] fl. 1697-1724.
        A compleat history of magick, sorcery, and witchcraft ... London, Printed for E. Curll, J. Pemberton; and W. Taylor, 1715-16.
    2 v. in 1. front. 17cm.

    Copy 2: 2 v.

    1. Magic. 2. Witchcraft. I. Title.

A compleat history of the most remarkable providences.

Rare
BL
230
T95++
1697
    Turner, William, 1653-1701.
        A compleat history of the most remarkable providences, both of judgment and mercy, which have happened in this present age; extracted from the best writers ... to which is added whatever is curious in the works of nature and art ... being a work set on foot thirty years ago by the Reverend Mr. Pool ... London, John Dunton, 1697.
    1v. (various pagings) 35cm.

    I. Title.

A compleat translation of the Memorial of the Jesuit Father John Baptist Girard.

Witchcraft
BF
1582
G51M5
1732
    Girard, Jean Baptiste, 1680-1733, defendant.
        A compleat translation of the Memorial of the Jesuit Father John Baptist Girard, rector of the Royal Seminary of the Chaplains of the Navy, in the city of Toulon, against Mary Catherine Cadière and the atorney [sic] general, plaintiff. London, Printed for J. Millan, 1732.
    172, 143 p. 17cm.

    "A collection of the letters of Father Girard and Mary Catherine Cadière, the
(Continued on next card)

A compleat translation of the Memorial of the Jesuit Father John Baptist Girard.

Witchcraft
BF
1582
G51M5
1732
    Girard, Jean Baptiste, 1680-1733, defendant.
        A compleat translation of the Memorial of the Jesuit Father John Baptist Girard ... 1732. (Card 2)

    originals whereof were produced in court": 143 p. at end.

    1. Cadière, Mary Catherine, fl. 1730. I. Girard, Jean Baptiste, 1680-1733. Mémoire instructif ... — English. II. Cadière, Mary Catherine, fl. 1730. III. Title.

A compleat translation of the Sequel of the Proceedings of Mary Catherine Cadiere.

Witchcraft
BF
1582
G51
S9
1732a
    Girard, Jean Baptiste, 1680-1733, defendant.
        A compleat translation of the Sequel of the Proceedings of Mary Cathe Cadiere, against the Jesuit Father John Baptist Girard. Containing many curious pieces ... 2d ed. London, Printed for J. Millan, 1732.
    255, [1] p. 17cm.

    Publisher's advertisement: p. [256]
    I. Cadière, Catherine, b. 1709. II. Title.

The Compleat wizzard.

Witchcraft
BF
1565
C73
    The Compleat wizzard; being a collection of authentic and entertaining narratives of the real existence and appearance of ghosts, demons, and spectres: together with several wonderful instances of the effects of witchcraft. To which is prefixed an account of haunted houses, and subjoined a treatise on the effects of magic. ... London, Printed for T. Evans, 1770.
    304 p. 21cm.

    1. Apparitions. 2. Witchcraft. 3. Magic.

Complementum artis exorcisticae.

WITCHCRAFT
BX
2340
V82
1643
    Visconti, Zaccaria.
        Complementvm artis exorcisticae: cui simile nunquam visum est: cvm litaniis, benedictionibvs, & doctrinis nouis, exorcismis efficacissimis, ac remedijs copiosis in maleficiatis expertis. Nuper correctum, & in tres partes diuisum. Qvarvm prima dicitvr doctrinalis. Secunda benedictionalis. Tertia exorcismalis. Cui addita est Oratio supra febricitantes. Avthore Fr. Zacharia Vicecomite ... Cui nupperrimè in hac
8   (Continued on next card)

Complementum artis exorcisticae.

WITCHCRAFT
BX
2340
V82
1643
    Visconti, Zaccaria. Complementvm artis exorcisticae ... 1643. (Card 2)

    postrema editione veneta. Pro vberiori complemento, additus est tractatus de Modo interrogandi daemonem ab exorcista ... Avthore Carolo de Bavcio ... Venetiis, Apud Turrinum, 1643.
    8 p. l., 359, 85 p. 17cm.

    "Modvs interrogandi daemonem ab exorcista," by Carlo de Baucio, has special t. p.
8   (Continued on next card)

CATALOGUE OF THE CORNELL WITCHCRAFT COLLECTION

WITCHCRAFT
BX
1935
N42

Conatus exegeticus in cap. Eam te 7 De rescriptis.
Neller, Georg Christoph, praeses.
...Conatus exegeticus in cap. Eam te 7 De rescriptis, quem una cum parergis, ex omni jure, nec non ex re monetaria, tum biblico-canonica, tum Trevirensi delibatis ...praeside...Georgio Christoph. Neller... publicae disputationi pro admissione ad tentamen graduandorum supposuit...Carolus Josephus Embden. Augustae Trevirorum, Typis Eschermannianis [1779]
48 p. front., plate. 22cm.

8
NIC   Burr's   note inside front cover:
(Continued on next card)

WITCHCRAFT
BX
1935
N42

Conatus exegeticus in cap. Eam te 7 De rescriptis.
Neller, Georg Christoph, praeses. Conatus exegeticus in cap. Eam te 7 De rescriptis ...[1779]   (Card 2)

"This book is valuable in containing a... letter of the Elector, Johann VII of Treves asking the advice of the University theological faculty at Treves as to the trial of Dr. Dietrich Flade for witchcraft. (See pp. 32-35) It is to be noted that this student, writing under the eye of the eminent jurist   Neller in 1779, still believes in   witchcraft... "
(Continued on next card)

Witchcraft
BF
1582
D34

Le concept de la sorcellerie dans le duché de Lorraine au XVIe et au XVIIe siècle.
Delcambre, Étienne.
Le concept de la sorcellerie dans le duché de Lorraine au XVIe et au XVIIe siècle ... Nancy, Société d'archéologie Lorraine, 1948.
v. 22cm. (Half-title: Recueil de documents sur l'histoire de Lorraine)

Contents.--fasc. 1. L'initiation à la sorcellerie et le sabbat.

1. Witchcraft--Lorraine--Hist. I. Title.

DC
123
.9
C6
M74

Concini, Leonora (Dori) called Galigaï, d.1617.
Mongrédien, Georges, 1901-
Léonora Galigaï. Un procès de sorcellerie sous Louis XIII. [Paris,] Hachette, 1968.
234 p. 21 cm. (L'Envers de l'histoire)   16.50 F
Illustrated cover.   (F***)
Bibliography: p. [223]-232.

1. Concini, Leonora (Dori) called Galigaï, d. 1617. 2. Trials (Witchcraft)--France. I. Title.

DC123.9.C62M6   68-134611
Library of Congress   [1]

BR
334
A2
C6
1875

La conférence entre Luther et le diable.
Luther, Martin, 1483-1546.
La conférence entre Luther et le diable au sujet de la messe; raconté par Luther lui-même. Trad. nouv. du latin par Isidore Liseux, avec les remarques et annotations des abbés de Cordemoy et Lenglet-Dufresnoy. Paris, 1875.
viii, 91 p. 16cm.

From Luther's tractate De missa privata atque sacerdotum unctione. Latin text parallel with   French translation.
(Continued on next card)

Witchcraft
BF
1581
P69
C7

Confessions of witches under torture.
Pitts, John Linwood.
Confessions of witches under torture. MDCXVII. Edinburgh, E. & G. Goldsmid, 1886.
15 p. 20cm. (In 25cm. envelope)
"This ... is taken from Mr. J. L. Pitt's [sic] Witchcraft and Devil-Lore in the Channel Islands." --Introduction, signed E. G.
"This edition is limited to 120 copies."

1. Witchcraft--Guernsey. I. His Witchcraft and devil lore in the Channel Islands. II.   Title.

8

Witchcraft
BF
1581
S79

A confirmation and discovery of witch-craft.
Stearne, John.
A confirmation and discovery of witch-craft containing these severall particulars; that there are witches called bad witches, and witches untruely called good or white witches, and what manner of people they be, and how they may bee knowne, with many particulars thereunto tending. Together with the confessions of many of those executed since May 1645, in the severall counties hereafter mentioned. As also some objections answered. London, Printed by W.   Wilson, 1648.
61 p. 19cm.   (Continued on next card)

Witchcraft
BF
1581
S79

A confirmation and discovery of witch-craft.
Stearne, John.   A confirmation and discovery of witch-craft containing these severall particulars ... 1648.   (Card 2)

Binding by Douglas Cockerell, full brown niger, blind tooled, spine gilt, dated 1902.

1. Witchcraft. I. Title.

WITCHCRAFT
BF
1555
E74
C7

Conflict zwischen Himmel und Hölle.
Eschenmayer, Carl Adolph von, 1770?-1852.
Conflict zwischen Himmel und Hölle, an dem Dämon eines besessenen Mädchens beobachtet von C. A. Eschenmayer in Kirchheim unter Teck. Nebst einem Wort an Dr. Strauss. Tübingen, Buchhandlung Zu-Guttenberg, 1837.
xvi, 215 p. 17cm.

1. Demoniac possession. 2. Stadebauer, Caroline. I.   Title.

8
NIC

Witchcraft
BX
2340
C75
1495

Coniuratio malignorum spirituum.
Coniuratio malignorum spirituum. [Venice, Manfredus de Bonellis, about 1495]
[8] l. woodcut; illus. 14cm.

Leaf [1a] (Title): Coniuratio malignorum spirituum in corporibus hominum existentium: prout fit in sancto Petro.
Signatures: a8.
Sander. Livre à fig. italien, 2095: Gesamtkat. d. Wiegendr., 7388 (Coniuratio daemonum); Goff. Third census, C-830.

1. Exorcism.

WITCHCRAFT
BX
2340
D66

Conjurationes potentissimae, ad fugandas tempestates a daemonibus.
Dominicus Domesticus, pseud.
Conjurationes potentissimae, ad fugandas tempestates a daemonibus, seu ab eorum ministris excitatas: unà cum imprecationibus, & maledictionibus, contra animalia, fructus, ac fruges vastantia: ac etiam, cum agrorum, vinearum &c: ac seminis bombicum: & super aegrotantes benedictionibus in fine additis ... Auctore M.R.D.P. Dominico Domestico exorcista pleb. alliati. Brixiae, Sumptibus Caroli Gromi, 1726.
84 p. 13cm.
1. Exorcism.   2. Weather-lore. I. Title.

8

WITCHCRAFT
BX
2340
L81
1680

Conjurationes potentissimae et efficaces...
Locatellus, Petrus.
Exorcismi potentissimi, & efficaces, ad expellendas aëreas tempestates, a daemonilici ministri excitatas... a ...Petro Locatello... Editio altera correctior. Labaci, Typis & impensis Joannis Bapt. Mayr, 1680.
188 p 14cm.

Published earlier with title: Conjurationes potentiss   imae et efficaces ad expellendas   ...aëreas tempestates...
(Continued on next card)

8
NIC

WITCHCRAFT
BX
2340
L81
1680

Conjurationes potentissimae et efficaces..
Locatellus, Petrus. Exorcismi potentissimi, & efficaces...1680.   (Card 2)

With this is bound: Preces et coniurationes contra aëreas tempestates... Campidonae 1667.

1. Exorcism. I. Catholic Church. Liturgy and ritual. II. His Conjurationes potentissimae et   efficaces... III.Title: Conjurationes potentissimae et eff   icaces...
IV. Title:

BR
520
B65

Connecticut (Colony) Laws, statutes, etc.
The blue laws of Connecticut; taken from the code of 1650 and the public records of the colony of Connecticut previous to 1655, as printed in a compilation of the earliest laws and orders of the General court of Connecticut, and from Dr. Lewis' book on Sunday legislation; also an extract from the constitution or civil compact adopted by the towns of Hartford Windsor and Wethersfield in 1838-9, showing the Biblical basis of the colony legislation; with an account of the persecution of witches and Quakers in New England and some
(Continued on next card)
[1892]   99-180 Revised

BR
520
B65

Connecticut (Colony) Laws, statutes, etc.
The blue laws of Connecticut ... (Card 2)

extracts from the blue laws of Virginia. New York, The Truth seeker company [c1898]
88 p. front., 1 illus., plates. 19cm.

Witchcraft
BF
1587
D61
no.5

Conradi, Elias, respondent.
Ziegra, Constantinus, praeses.
Disputatio physica exhibens I. Doctrinam de magia. II. Theoremata miscellanea ex parte tùm generali tùm speciali physicae. Qvam sub praesidio ... Dn. Constantini Ziegra ... ventilationi subjicit M. Elias Conradi ... aut. & resp. Wittebergae, Typis Jobi Wilhelmi Fincelii, 1661.
[36] p. 21cm.
No. 5 in vol. lettered Dissertationes de magia. 1623-   1723.

8   1. Occult sciences--Addresses, essays, lectures. I. Conradi, Elias, respondent.

Witchcraft
BX
9479
B42
B11
no.6

Consideratien over het boek van de Heer Doctor Balthasar Bekker, genaamt De betoverde weereld.
[Silvius, J]
Consideratien over het boek van de Heer Doctor Balthasar Bekker, genaamt De betoverde weereld, voorgestelt door J. S. Amsterdam, By G. Borstius, boekverkoper, 1691.
20 p. title vignette, illus. initials. 20 x 15cm.
4°: π1, A-B4, C1.
Black letter (except for introduction)
Ascribed to J. Silvius by Doorninck.
Variant of   van der Linde 149:

8   (Continued on next card)

Witchcraft
BX
9479
B42
B11
no.6

Consideratien over het boek van de Heer Doctor Balthasar Bekker, genaamt De betoverde weereld.
[Silvius, J]   Consideratien over het boek van de Heer Doctor Balthasar Bekker ... 1691.   (Card 2)

only 20, instead of 22 p.
No. 6 in vol. lettered B. Bekkers sterfbed en andere tractaten.

1. Bekker, Balthasar, 1634-1698. De betoverde weereld. I. Title. II. J. S. III. S., J.

CATALOGUE OF THE CORNELL WITCHCRAFT COLLECTION

Consiliorum theologicorum decades VIII.

Rare
BX
3011
B58
1612

Bidembach, Felix, 1564-1612, ed.
Consiliorum theologicorum decades VIII. Das ist: Achtzig theologischer Bedencken, Bericht, oder Antwort auff mancherley (in Glaubens, Gewissens vnd andern mehr sachen) zutragende Fälle, vnnd vorfallende Fragen, oder Handelungen gerichtet, vnnd mehrern Theils vor viel Jahren gestellet: durch etliche Hochgelehrte vnnd vortreffliche Theologos ... Itzo zum andern mahl auffs New in Truck verfertiget. Wittenberg, A. Rüdingern, 1612-14.
(Continued on next card)

Consiliorum theologicorum decades VIII.

Rare
BX
3011
B58
1612

Bidembach, Felix, 1564-1612, ed. Consiliorum theologicorum decades ... 1612-14. (Card 2)

3 v. in 1. 20cm.

Vols. [2]-[3] have title: Consiliorum theologicorum decas IX[-X]. Der neundte [-zehende] Theil theologischer Bedencken, Bericht, oder Antwort ... Franckfurt am Mayn, Getruckt bey Erasmo Kempffern, in Verlegung Joh ann Berners, 1614.
1. Theology-- Collections--Lutheran authors. I. Title.

Consilis, responsa ac deductiones juris variae, cumprimis vero processum contra sagas concernentia.

WITCHCRAFT
BF
1583
A2
L52

Leib, Johann, 1591-1666.
Consilia, responsa ac deductiones juris variae, cumprimis vero processum contra sagas concernentia. Opus non tantum jurisconsultis et advocatis, sed & adsessoribus, iudicibus, aliisque apprime utile ac necessarium. ...wie und welcher Gestalt der Process wider die Zauberer und Hexen anzustellen und hierinnen verantwortlich zuverfahren. Mit beygefügten underschiedlicher Universitäten über verschiedene schwere Fälle, Bedencken und Informationen...
(Continued on next card)

8
NIC

Consilis, responsa ac deductiones juris variae, cumprimis vero processum contra sagas concernentia.

WITCHCRAFT
BF
1583
A2
L52

Leib, Johann, 1591-1666. Consilia, responsa ac deductiones juris variae...1666. (Card 2)

Francofurti, Apud Hermannum à Sande, 1666. 540 p. 21cm.

Text in Latin or German.

1 Witchcraft--Germany. 2. Trials (Witchcraft)--Germ any. 3. Torture--Germany. I. Title.

Consolatio peccatorum.

Rare
...

Palladinus, Jacobus, de Theramo, Bp. of Spoleto, 1349-1417.
Consolatio peccatorum, seu Processus Belial. [Strassburg, Heinrich Knoblochtzer] 1484.
[94] l. 30cm.

Leaves [1], [93b] and [94] blank.
Leaf [2a]: Reuerendi patris domini Iacobi de Theramo Compendium pbreue Consolatio peccatorum nun cupatū. Et apud nonnullos Belial vocitatū ad papā Vrbanum
(Continued on next card)

Consolatio peccatorum.

Rare
...

Palladinus, Jacobus, de Theramo, Bp. of Spoleto, 1349-1417. Consolatio peccatorum ... 1484. (Card 2)

sextum conscriptum. Incipit feliciter.
Leaf [93a] (Colophon): Explicit liber belial nūcupat' al's peccatorum consolatio. Anno dñi Mº.ccccclxxxiiij.
Signatures: a-b⁸, c-d⁶, e-k⁸.⁶, 1-n⁸.
Capital spaces, mostly with guide-letters.
Copinger. Supplement to Hain's Repertorium, 5793; Proctor, 373;
(Continued on next card)

Consolatio peccatorum.

Rare
BT
980
P16+
1484

Palladinus, Jacobus, de Theramo, Bp. of Spoleto, 1349-1417. Consolatio peccatorum ... 1484. (Card 3)

Brit. Mus. Cat. (SV cent.) I, p. 89 (IB. 1091; Javobus [Palladinus] de Theramo); Goff. Third census, J-70 (Jacobus de Theramo).

1. Devil. I. Title: Consolatio peccatorum. II. Ti tle: Processus Belial.

Witchcraft
BF
1775
C75

Constable, Henry Strickland, 1821-
Observations suggested by the cattle plague, about witchcraft, credulity, superstition, parliamentary reform, and other matters. By H. Strickland Constable ... London, Dalton & Lucy, 1866.
99 p. 21cm.

1. Rinderpest. 2. Superstition. I. Title.

Witchcraft
BF
1517
F5C75
1863

Constans, Augustin.
Relation sur une épidémie d'hystéro-démonopathie en 1861. 2. éd. Paris, A. Delahaye, 1863.
viii, 130 p. 24cm.

1. Demoniac possession. 2. Witchcraft--Morzines, France. I. Title: Une épidémie d' hystéro-démonopathie en 1861. II. Title.

[Constant, Alphonse Louis] 1810?-1875.

BF
1612
C75
1861

Dogme et rituel de la haute magie, par Éliphas Lévi [pseud.] 2. éd. très augmentée. Paris, G. Baillière; New York, H. Baillière, 1861.
2 v. illus. 22cm.

Contents.--t. 1. Dogme.--t. 2. Rituel.

1. Magic. I. Title.

Witchcraft
BF
1612
C75
1930

[Constant, Alphonse Louis] 1810?-1875.
Dogme et rituel de la haute magie, par Éliphas Lévi [pseud.] Nouvelle édition. Paris, Chacornac Frères, 1930.
2 v. illus. 22cm.

Contents.--t. 1. Dogme.--t. 2. Rituel.

1. Magic. I. Title. II. Ex Libris--Seligmann, Kurt.

Constant, Alphonse Louis, 1810-1875.
Dogme et rituel de la haute magie--English.

Witchcraft
BF
1612
C75
1938

[Constant, Alphonse Louis] 1810?-1875.
Transcendental magic, its doctrine and ritual, by Eliphas Levi [pseud.] translated, annotated and introduced by Arthur Edward Waite. New and rev. ed. New York, E. P. Dutton & company, inc. [1938]
xxxiii p., 1 l., 521, [1] p. front. (port.) illus., plates. 22½cm.
Printed in Great Britain.
Translation of Dogme et rituel de la haute magie.
Imperfect: front. wanting.

Witchcraft
BF
1589
C75

[Constant, Alphonse Louis] 1810?-1875.
Histoire de la magie, avec une exposition claire et précise de ses procédés, de ses rites et de ses mystères, par Éliphas Lévi [pseud.] ... Avec 18 planches représentant 90 figures. Paris, G. Baillière; Londres et New-York, H. Baillière; [etc., etc.] 1860.
xvi, 560 p. front., plates. 22½cm.

1. Magic. I. Title.

Library of Congress   BF1589.C75   11-14511

Witchcraft
BF
1589
C75
1949

Constant, Alphonse Louis, 1810-1875.
Histoire de la magie--English.
The history of magic, including a clear and precise exposition of its procedure, its rites and its mysteries, by Éliphas Lévi (Alphonse Louis Constant) Tr., with a preface and notes, by Arthur Edward Waite. Los Angeles, Borden Pub. Co. [1949]
384 p. illus. 22cm.
Translation of Histoire de la magie.

1. Magic. I. Waite, Arthur Edward, 1857-1942, tr. II. Ti tle. III. His Histoire de la magie --English.

Witchcraft
BF
1589
C75
1949

Constant, Alphonse Louis, 1810-1875.
The history of magic, including a clear and precise exposition of its procedure, its rites and its mysteries, by Éliphas Lévi (Alphonse Louis Constant) Tr., with a preface and notes, by Arthur Edward Waite. Los Angeles, Borden Pub. Co. [1949]
384 p. illus. 22cm.
Translation of Histoire de la magie.

1. Magic. I. Waite, Arthur Edward, 1857-1942, tr. II. Ti tle. III. His Histoire de la magie --English.

Witchcraft
BF
1612
C75
M9

[Constant, Alphonse Louis] 1810?-1875.
The mysteries of magic: a digest of the writings of Éliphas Lévi [pseud.] With biographical and critical essay, by Arthur Edward Waite ... London, G. Redway, 1886.
xliii, 349 p. 22½cm.

1. Magic. I. Waite, Arthur Edward, 1857-1942. II. Title.

11—14358

Witchcraft
BF
1412
C75

[Constant, Alphonse Louis] 1810-1875.
La science des esprits; révélation du dogme secret des kabbalistes esprit occulte des évangiles, appréciation des doctrines et des phénomènes spirites, par Éliphas Lévi [pseud.] Paris, Germer Baillière, 1865.
507 p. 23cm. (His Philosophie occulte. 2. série)

1. Occult sciences. 2. Spiritualism. I. Title.

Witchcraft
BF
1612
C75
1938

[Constant, Alphonse Louis] 1810-1875.
Transcendental magic, its doctrine and ritual, by Eliphas Levi [pseud.] translated, annotated and introduced by Arthur Edward Waite. New and rev. ed. New York, E. P. Dutton & company, inc. [1938]
xxxiii p., 1 l., 521, [1] p. front. (port.) illus., plates. 22½cm.
Printed in Great Britain.
Translation of Dogme et rituel de la haute magie.
Imperfect: front. wanting.

1. Magic. 2. Waite, Arthur Edward, 1857- ed. and tr. II. Title.
II. His Dogme et rituel de la haute magie--English.   BF1612.C72 1988
[159.9614]   133.1

121

CATALOGUE OF THE CORNELL WITCHCRAFT COLLECTION

Witchcraft

BF
1612
C75
1958

Constant, Alphonse Louis, 1810?-1875.
Transcendental magic, its doctrine and ritual [by] Éliphas Lévi [pseud.] Translated, annotated and introduced by Arthur Edward Waite. London, Rider [1958]
xxxi, 438 p. illus. 24cm.

"First published 1896."
Translation of Dogme et rituel de la haute magie.

Constant, Alphonse Louis, 1810-1875.

BF
1598
C75
B78

Bowman, Frank Paul.
Éliphas Lévi; visionnaire romantique. Préface et choix de textes par Frank Paul Bowman. Paris, Presses Universitaires de France, 1969.
242 p. 19cm. ("A la découverte")
At head of title: Publications du Département de langues romanes de l'Université de Princeton.

1. Constant, Alphonse Louis, 1810-1875. I. Title. II. Series: Princeton University. Princeton publications in modern languages.

Constantini Francisci de Cauz ... De cultibus magicis.

Witchcraft
BF
1565
K21
1771

Kauz, Constantin Franz Florian Anton von, 1735-1797.
Constantini Francisci de Cauz ... De cultibus magicis eorumque perpetuo ad ecclesiam et rempublicam habitu libri duo. ... Editio II. Aucta et emendata. Vindobonae, Literis Trattnerianis, 1771.
18 p.l., 400, [6] p. 22cm.
"ΕΠΙΜΕΤΡΟΝ. De ritu ignis natali Joannis Baptistae die accensi dissertatio," p. [377]-400, has special t. p. (First printed 1759)

(Continued on next card)

Constitutio criminalis Theresiana.

Rare
K
A923++

Austria. Laws, statutes, etc.
Constitutio criminalis Theresiana, oder Der Römisch-kaiserl. zu Hungarn und Böheim u. u. Königl. Apost. Majestät Mariä Theresiä, Erzherzogin zu Oesterreich, u. u., peinliche Gerichtsordnung. Wien, Gedruckt bey J. T. edlen von Trattnern, 1769.
8 p.l., 282, lvi p. incl. plates (part fold.) 35cm.
Latin summary of paragraphs in margin.
The plates (mostly printed on both

(Continued on next card)

Constitutio criminalis Theresiana.

Rare
K
A923++

Austria. Laws, statutes, etc. Constitutio criminalis Theresiana ... 1769. (Card 2)

sides) are illustrations of instruments of torture and their application.
List of members of the commission entrusted with the elaboration of the code: p. lv-lvi.
Note in manuscript on p. [2] of cover: Sehr selten, da die Exemplare unterdrückt wurden.

(Continued on next card)

A contemporary narrative of the proceedings against Dame Alice Kyteler.

Witchcraft
BF
1581
Z7
1324

Kyteler, Alice, fl. 1324, defendant.
A contemporary narrative of the proceedings against Dame Alice Kyteler, prosecuted for sorcery in 1324, by Richard de Ledrede, bishop of Ossory. Edited by Thomas Wright ... London, Printed for the Camden society, by J. B. Nichols and son, 1843.
2 p. l., xlii p., 1 l., 61, [1] p. 21x17cm.
[Camden society. Publications. no. XXIV]
Text in Latin.
Printed from Harleian ms., no. 641. cf. Introd.

Conti, Francesco.

Witchcraft
BX
1710
M39
1730

[Masini, Eliseo] brother, 17th cent.
Sacro arsenale, ovvero Pratica dell'Uffizio della Santa Inquisizione; coll'inserzione di alcune regole fatte dal p. inquisitore Tommaso Menghini ... e di diverse annotazioni del dottore Gio: Pasqualone ... In questa 4. impressione aggiuntavi la Settima Denunzia fatta dal suddetto padre per li sponte comparenti, impressa in Ferrara 1687. e corretta in alcune cose la parte decima degli avvertimenti ... Roma, Nella Stamperia di

(Continued on next card)
Secular name: Cesare Masini]

Conti, Francesco.

Witchcraft
BX
1710
M39
1730

[Masini, Eliseo] brother, 17th cent. Sacro arsenale ... (Card 2)
S. Michele a Ripa, 1730.
[6], 506, [54] p. 23cm.

Edited by Luigi and Francesco Conti.

1. Inquisition. I. Menghini, Tommaso, 17th cent. II. Pasqualone, Giovanni. III. Conti, Luigi. IV. Conti, Francesco. V. Title. VI. Title: Pratica dell'Uffizio della Santa Inquisizione.

Conti, Luigi.

Witchcraft
BX
1710
M39
1730

[Masini, Eliseo] brother, 17th cent.
Sacro arsenale, ovvero Pratica dell'Uffizio della Santa Inquisizione; coll'inserzione di alcune regole fatte dal p. inquisitore Tommaso Menghini ... e di diverse annotazioni del dottore Gio: Pasqualone ... In questa 4. impressione aggiuntavi la Settima Denunzia fatta dal suddetto padre per li sponte comparenti, impressa in Ferrara 1687. e corretta in alcune cose la parte decima degli avvertimenti ... Roma, Nella Stamperia di

(Continued on next card)
Secular name: Cesare Masini]

Conti, Luigi.

Witchcraft
BX
1710
M39
1730

[Masini, Eliseo] brother, 17th cent. Sacro arsenale ... (Card 2)
S. Michele a Ripa, 1730.
[6], 506, [54] p. 23cm.

Edited by Luigi and Francesco Conti.

1. Inquisition. I. Menghini, Tommaso, 17th cent. II. Pasqualone, Giovanni. III. Conti, Luigi. IV. Conti, Francesco. V. Title. VI. Title: Pratica dell'Uffizio della Santa Inquisizione.

Contra daemonum invocatores.

Witchcraft
BF
1520
V85
1487

Vivetus, Johannes, fl. 1450.
Contra daemonum invocatores ... [Cologne, Ludwig von Renchen, about 1487]
[42] l. 20cm.

Leaf [1a] (Title): Tractatus contra demonū inuocatores
Leaf [1b]-[2b]: Tabula.
Leaf [3a]: Incipit tractatus ɔtra demonū inuocatores ɔpilatus per sacre theologie pfessorē fratrem Johannē viueti. ordinis predicatoɣ inquisitorem apostolicū Carcassone.

(Continued on next card)

Contra daemonum invocatores.

Witchcraft
BF
1520
V85
1487

Vivetus, Johannes, fl. 1450. Contra daemonum invocatores ... [about 1487] (Card 2)

Leaf [41b] (End): Finit tractatus cōtra demonū inuocatores.
Leaf [42] blank; wanting in this copy. Signatures: a-d⁸, e¹⁰.
Capital spaces. Capitals, paragraph-marks, initial-strokes and underlines supplied in red.
Copinger. Supplement to Hain's Repertorium, 6273-6274; Proctor, 1282; Brit. Mus.

(Continued on next card)

Witchcraft
BF
1520
V85
1487

Contra daemonum invocatores.
Vivetus, Johannes, fl. 1450. Contra daemonum invocatores ... [about 1487] (Card 3)
Cat (XV cent.) I, p. 269 (IA. 4514; author's name: Johannes, Vineti); Goff. Third census, V-310.
With a few manuscript marginal notes.

1. Demonology. 2. Magic. 3. Witchcraft. I. Title. II. His Tractatus contra demonum inuocatores. III. Title: Tractatus contra demonum inuocatores.

Contra las brujas.

BF
1566
T46

Thót, László, d. 1935.
Contra las brujas; procesos al demonio, la magia, y misas negras [por] Ladislao Thot. Buenos Aires, Ediciones La Sirena [1969]
80 p. 20 cm.

LACAP 69-8168

Bibliographical footnotes.

1. Witchcraft. I. Title.

BF1566.T47   133.4   74-427132
Library of Congress   69 [4]

Contra petentes remedia a maleficis.

WITCHCRAFT
BF
1565
H77

Hoogstraten, Jacobus van, ca. 1460-1527.
Ad Reuerendissimū dm̄m dm̄m Philippū sancte ecclesie Coloniensis archiepm. Tractat⁹ magistralis declarans q̄ grauiter peccēt q̄rentes auxiliū a maleficis cōpilat⁹ ab eximio sacre theologie professore & artiū magistro necnō heretice prauitatis inq̄sitore magistro Jacobo Hoechstrassen ordinis Predicatorū priore Ɔuentus Coloniensis. [Colonie, Impressum per Martinum de Werdena 1510]

8

(Continued on next card)

Contra petentes remedia a maleficis.

WITCHCRAFT
BF
1565
H77

Hoogstraten, Jacobus van, ca. 1460-1527.
Ad Reuerendissimū dm̄m dm̄m Philippū sancte ecclesie Coloniensis archiepm ... [1510] (Card 2)
[16] p. illus. 18cm.
Woodcut illus. on p. [16].
Running title: Contra petentes remedia a maleficis.

1. Witchcraft. I. Title: Tractatus magistralis declarans quam graviter peccent querentes au xilium a maleficis. II. Title: Contra petentes remedia a maleficis.

8

Contrepoison du Dictionnaire infernal.

WITCHCRAFT
BF
1503
C69
S61

[Simonnet, P. B.]
Réalité de la magie et des apparitions, ou Contrepoison du Dictionnaire infernal. Ouvrage dans lequel on prouve, par une multitude de faits et d'anecdotes authentiques ... l'existence des sorciers, la certitude des apparitions, la foi due aux miracles, la vérité des possessions, etc., ... précédé d'une Histoire très-précise de la magie ... Paris, P. Mongie aîné, 1819.
xxii, 152 p. 21cm.

8
NIC   Ascription by Barbier.

(Continued on next card)

Die Controverse über den Hexenhammer und seine Kölner Approbation vom Jahre 14...

WITCHCRAFT
DD
741
W52
v.27
no.2/3

Hansen, Joseph, 1862-1943.
Die Kontroverse über den Hexenhammer und seine Kölner Approbation vom Jahre 1487.
(In: Westdeutsche Zeitschrift für Geschichte und Kunst. Trier. 24cm. v.27 (1908) no.2/3. p.366-372)

8
NIC

1. Institoris, Henricus, d.1508. Malleus maleficarum. I. Title.

CATALOGUE OF THE CORNELL WITCHCRAFT COLLECTION

Witchcraft
BF
1600
D36
1611

Les controverses et recherches magiqves.
Del Rio, Martin Antoine, 1551-1608.
    Les controverses et recherches magiqves ... Divisees en six livres, ausquels sont exactement & doctement confutees les sciences curieuses, les vanitez, & superstitions de toute la magie. Avec qves la maniere de proceder en iustice contre les magiciens et sorciers, accommodee à l'instruction des confesseurs ... Traduit et abregé du Latin par André dv Chesne. Paris, Chez Iean Petit-Pas, 1611.
    [32], 1024 (i.e. 1104), [54] p. 19cm.
    Errors in paging: 1100-1104 numbered 1101,
        (Continued on next card)

Witchcraft
BF
1600
D36
1611

Les controverses et recherches magiqves.
Del Rio, Martin Antoine, 1551-1608. Les controverses et recherches magiqves ... 1611.   (Card 2)
    1102, 1002, 1003 and 1024 respectively.
    Translation of Disquisitionum magicarum libri sex.

    1. Magic. 2. Witchcraft. I. Del Rio, Martin Antoine, 1551-1608. Disquisitionum magicarum libri sex--French. II. Duchesne, André, 1584-1640, tr. III. Title.

Conway, Moncure Daniel, 1832-1907.
    Demonology and devil-lore. London, Chatto and Windus, 1879.
    2 v. illus. 23cm.

Conway, Moncure Daniel, 1832-1907.
    Demonology and devil-lore. New York, H. Holt and Co., 1879.
    2 v. illus. 23cm.

    Author's autograph presentation copy.

    1. Demonology. 2. Mythology. I. Title.

Witchcraft
BF
1581
A2
C77

Cooper, Thomas, fl. 1598-1626.
    The mystery of witch-craft, discovering the truth, nature, occasions, growth and power therof; together with the detection and punishment of the same. As also, the seuerall stratagems of Sathan ... London, N. Okes, 1617.
    [368] p. 14cm.

    Later ed., 1622, has title: Sathan transformed into an angell of light.
    1. Witchcraft. I. Title.

Cooper, Thomas, fl. 1598-1626.
    The mystery of witchcraft.
Cooper, Thomas, fl. 1598-1626.
    Sathan transformed into an angell of light, expressing his dangerous impostures vnder glorious shewes. Emplified specially in the doctrine of witch-craft, and such sleights of Satan as are incident thereunto. Very necessary to discerne the speci-plague (sic) raging in these dayes, and so to hide our selues from the snare thereof. London, B. Alsop, 1622.
    368 p. 15cm.

    Originally published in 1617 under title: The mystery of witch-craft.

Witchcraft
BF
1581
A2
C77
1622

Cooper, Thomas, fl. 1598-1626.
    Sathan transformed into an angell of light, expressing his dangerous impostures vnder glorious shewes. Emplified specially in the doctrine of witch-craft, and such sleights of Satan as are incident thereunto. Very necessary to discerne the speci-plague (sic) raging in these dayes, and so to hide our selues from the snare thereof. London, B. Alsop, 1622.
    368 p. 15cm.

    Originally published in 1617 under title: The mystery of witch-craft.   (over)

WITCHCRAFT
BF
1517
F5
C78
1634

Coppie d'v procez verbal faict le vingt & deuxiesme d'aoust mil six cens trente & quatre. Par Monsieur de Laubardemont conseller du roy en ses conseils d'estat & priué, sur le miracle fait dans la ville de Loudun. Poictiers, Par René Allain, 1634.
    9 p. 17cm.

    1. Loudun, France. Ursuline Convent. 2. Exorcism. I. Laubardemont, Jean Martin de.

Witchcraft
BF
1410
B42
Z56
v.2
no.8

Copy van een brief geschreeve aan een heer, woonende tusschen Rotterdam en Dort. Raakende het gepasseerde in de saak van Dr. B. Bekker; door een liefhebber van vreede en waarheid. Dord, Gedrukt by G. Abramsz, 1692.
    18 p. [p. 19-20 blank] title vignette. 19 x 15cm.
    4°: A-B⁴, C².
    Signed: A. T.
    Van der Linde 48; 64.
    No. 8 in vol. lettered Bekker II.
    (Continued on next card)

Witchcraft
BF
1410
B42
Z56
v.2
no.8

Copy van een brief geschreeve aan een heer, woonende tusschen Rotterdam en Dort. 1692.   (Card 2)

    1. Bekker, Balthasar, 1634-1698. 2. Nederlandse Hervormde Kerk. Classes. Amsterdam. 3. Nederlandse Hervormde Kerk. Kerkenraden. Amsterdam. I. A. T. II. T., A. III. Een liefhebber van vreede en waarheid.

Cordemoy, Géraud de, d. 1684, ed.

BR
334
A2
C6
1875

Luther, Martin, 1483-1546.
    La conférence entre Luther et le diable au sujet de la messe; raconté par Luther lui-même. Trad. nouv. du latin par Isidore Liseux, avec les remarques et annotations des abbés de Cordemoy et Lenglet-Dufresnoy. Paris, 1875.
    viii, 91 p. 16cm.

    From Luther's tractate De missa privata atque sacerdotum unctione. Latin text parallel with French translation.

Witchcraft
BF
1575
D76
v.2-3

Corey, Giles, 1611?-1692.
Calef, Robert, 1648-1719.
    More wonders of the invisible world: or, The wonders of the invisible world, display'd in five parts. Part I. An account of the sufferings of Margaret Rule, written by the Reverend Mr. C. M. P. II. Several letters to the author, &c. And his reply relating to witchcraft. P. III. The differences between the inhabitants of Salem village, and Mr. Parris their minister, in New-England. P. IV. Letters of a gentleman uninterested, endeavouring to prove the received opinions about witchcraft to be orthodox. With short essays to their answers. P. v. A short historical account [!] of matters of fact in that affair. To
    (Continued on next card)
    [31e2]
    2-18714 rev.

Witchcraft
BF
1575
D76
v.2-3

Corey, Giles, 1611?-1692.
    Calef, Robert, 1648-1719. More wonders of the invisible world ... (Card 2)

which is added, a postscript relating to a book intitled, The life of Sir William Phips. Collected by Robert Calef, merchant, of Boston in New-England ... London, Printed for N. Hillar and J. Collyer, 1700.
    Reprint. (In Drake, S. G. The witchcraft delusion in New England ... Roxbury, Mass., 1866. 21½cm. v. 2, p. 1-212; v. 3, p. 3-167)
    Woodward's historical series. no. VI-VII.
    Prefatory: by the editor: p. [v]-x. Pedigree of Calef: 1 fold. leaf. Memoir of Robert Calef: p. [xi]-xix.
    The text, here annotated, is that of the 1st edition, 1700. "It is given as exactly like the original as a much better type can be made to imitate an old type of 166 years ago."--Pref. by the editor, p. vi.
    (Continued on next card)
    [31e2]
    2-18714 rev.

Witchcraft
BF
1575
D76
v.2-3

Corey, Giles, 1611?-1692.
    Calef, Robert, 1648-1719. More wonders of the invisible world ... 1700. (Card 3)

    Appendix: I. Examination of Giles Cory.--II. Giles Corey and Goodwyfe Corey. A ballad of 1692.--III. Testimony of William Beale, of Marblehead, against Mr. Philip English of Salem, given Aug. 2d. 1692.--IV. [Examination of the Indian woman belonging to Mr. Parris's family]--V. The examination of Mary Clark of Haverhill.--VI. An account of the life and character of the Rev. Samuel Parris, of Salem village, and of his connection with the witchcraft delusion of 1692. By Samuel P. Fowler.

Witchcraft
BF
1575
C14
1823

Corey, Giles, 1611?-1692.
    Calef, Robert, 1648-1719. More wonders of the invisible world, or The invisible world displayed. In five parts. Part I.--An account of the sufferings of Margaret Rule, written by the Rev. Cotton Mather. Part II.--Several letters to the author, &c. and his reply relating to witchcraft. Part III.--The differences between the inhabitants of Salem village, and Mr. Parris, their minister, in New-England. Part IV.--Letters of a gentleman uninterested, endeavouring to prove the received opinions about witchcraft to be orthodox.
    (Continued on next card)

Witchcraft
BF
1575
C14
1823

Corey, Giles, 1611?-1692.
    Calef, Robert, 1648-1719. More wonders of the invisible world ... 1823. (Card 2)

With short essays to their answers. Part V.--A short historical account of matters of fact in that affair. To which is added a postcript [!] relating to a book entitled "The life of Sir Wm. Phips". Collected by Robert Calef. Merchant, of Boston, in New-England. Printed in London, 1700. Salem, Reprinted by J.D. & T.C. Cushing, jr. for Cushing and Appleton, 1823.
    312 p. 18½cm.
    (Continued on next card)

Witchcraft
BF
1575
C14
1823

Corey, Giles, 1611?-1692.
    Calef, Robert, 1648-1719. More wonders of the invisible world ... 1823. (Card 3)

    Appended: Giles Cory [a report of his examination, taken from the witchcraft records]: p. 310-312.

    "The second Salem edition appears to have been copied from the first [Salem edition] that of 1796. In some instances slight departures are made from the copy ... such departures are also departures from the original [London edition of 1700]"--S. G. Drake, pref. to ed. of 1866.

Witchcraft
BF
1575
C14
1828

Corey, Giles, 1611?-1692.
    Calef, Robert, 1648-1719.
    Wonders of the invisible world, or, Salem witchcraft. In five parts. Boston, T. Bedlington [1828]
    333 p. front. 14cm.

    A reply to Cotton Mather's "Wonders of the invisible world."
    First ed. published in 1700 under title: More wonders of the invisible world displayed.
    (Continued on next card)

123

CATALOGUE OF THE CORNELL WITCHCRAFT COLLECTION

Corey, Giles, 1611?-1692.

Witchcraft
BF 1575 C14 1828
    Calef, Robert, 1648-1719. Wonders of the invisible world ... [1828] (Card 2)

    Contents.--Part 1. An account of the sufferings of Margaret Rule, by Cotton Mather.--Part 2. Several letters from the author to Mr. Mather and others, relating to witchcraft.--Part 3. Account of the differences in Salem village between the villagers and their minister, Mr. Parris.--Part 4. Letter s of a gentleman uninter-

(Continued on next card)

Corey, Giles, 1611?-1692.

Witchcraft
BF 1575 C14 1828
    Calef, Robert, 1648-1719. Wonders of the invisible world ... [1828] (Card 3)

    ested, endeavouring to prove the received opinions about witchcraft to be orthodox.--Part 5. An impartial account of the most memorable matters of fact touching the supposed witchcraft in New-England.--Postscript, relating to Cotton Mather's life of Sir William Phips.--Giles Cory: a report of his examinati on, taken from the witchcraft files.

Corvinus, Johann Friedrich, of Halle, respondent.

Witchcraft
BF 1520 A33
    Alberti, Michael, 1682-1757, praeses. Dissertatio inauguralis medica, de potestate diaboli in corpus humanum, qvam ... praeside Dn. Michaele Alberti ... ventilationi subjiciet respondens Johannes Fridericus Corvinus ... [Halle] Typis Jo: Christian Hendel [1725]
    52 p. 21cm.
    Diss.--Halle (J. F. Corvinus, respondent)
    1. Demonology. 2. Diseases--Causes and theories of causation. I. Corvinus, Johann Friedrich, of Halle, respondent. II. Title: De po testate diaboli in corpus humanum.

8

Witchcraft
CB 151 C83
    Costadau, Alphonse.
    Traité historique et critique des principaux signes dont nous nous servons pour manifester nos pensées. Avec quantité de planches en taille-douce. Lyon, Chez la veuve de J. B. Guillimin & T. l'Abbé [etc.] 1717-20.
    7 v. plates. 19cm.
    Vols. 5-7 have title: Traité historique et critique des principaux signes qui servent a manifester les pensées, ou le com-

8 (Continued on next card)

Witchcraft
CB 151 C83
    Costadau, Alphonse. Traité historique et critique des principaux signes ... 1717-20. (Card 2)

    merce des esprits. Seconde partie. Qui contient les signes superstitieux & diaboliques, par lesquels certains hommes s'entendent avec les demons, & les demons avec certains hommes. Lyon, Chez les freres Bruyset, 1720.
    Ex libris Congault.

8 (Continued on next card)

Witchcraft
CB 151 C83
    Costadau, Alphonse. Traité historique et critique des principaux signes ... 1717-20. (Card 3)

    1. Civilization. 2. Signs and symbols. 3. Occult sciences. I. Title.

8

Costard, George, 1710-1782, supposed author.

Witchcraft
BT 980 S97
    [Swinton, John] 1703-1777.
    A critical dissertation concerning the words ΔAIMΩN and ΔAIMONION. Occasion'd by two late enquiries [by Arthur Ashley Sykes] into the meaning of demoniacs in the New Nestament. In a letter to a friend. By a Gentleman of Wadham College, Oxford. London, Printed for J. Crokatt; and sold by J. Roberts, 1738.
    29 p. 20cm.
    Also attributed to George Costard.
    Letter sig ned: Philalethes.

8 (Continued on next card)

Witchcraft
BF 1410 B42 Z56 v.3 no.1
    [Costerus, Florentius] fl. 1654-1703.
    De gebannen duyvel weder in-geroepen, ofte het vonnis van Doctor Bekker over den duyvel gevelt, in revisie gebraght. Den tweede druck, vermeerdert met twee gedigten. Hoorn, Gedruckt by S. J. Kortingb [sic] en J. J. Beets, boek-verkoopers, 1691.
    42 p. title and end page vignettes. 21 x 16cm.
    4°: A-E⁴, F1.
    Black letter.

(Continued on next card)

Witchcraft
BF 1410 B42 Z56 v.3 no.1
    [Costerus, Florentius] fl. 1654-1703. De gebannen duyvel weder in-geroepen ... 1691. (Card 2)

    Signed: Bloemardus Thusius.
    Variant of van der Linde 87: 2d., enl. printing.
    No. 1 in vol. lettered Bekker III.

    1. Bekker, Balthasar, 1634-1698. De betoverde weereld. I. Title.

8

Witchcraft
BF 1410 B42 Z56 v.2 no.21
    [Costerus, Florentius] fl. 1654-1703.
    De gebannen duyvel weder in-geroepen, ofte het vonnis van Doctor Bekker over den duyvel gevelt, in revisie gebraght. Den tweede druck, vermeerdert met twee gedigten. Hoorn, Gedruckt by S. J. Kortingb [sic] en J. J. Beets, boek-verkoopers, 1691.
    42 p. title and end page vignettes. 19 x 15cm.
    4°: A-E⁴, F1.
    Black letter.

8 (Continued on next card)

Witchcraft
BF 1410 B42 Z56 v.2 no.21
    [Costerus, Florentius] fl. 1654-1703. De gebannen duyvel weder in-geroepen ... 1691. (Card 2)

    Signed: Bloemardus Thusius.
    Variant of van der Linde 87: 2d., enl. printing.
    No. 21 in vol. lettered Bekker II.

8

Witchcraft
BF 1410 B42 Z86 no.9
    [Costerus, Florentius] fl. 1654-1703. De gebannen duyvel weder in-geroepen, ofte het vonnis van Doctor Bekker over den duyvel gevelt, in revisie gebraght. Den tweede druck, vermeerdert met twee gedigten. Hoorn, Gedruckt by S. J. Kortingb [sic] en J. J. Beets, boek-verkoopers, 1691.
    42 p. title and end page vignettes. 19 x 15cm.
    4°: A-E⁴, F1.
    Black letter.

8 (Continued on next card)

Witchcraft
BF 1410 B42 Z86 no.9
    [Costerus, Florentius] fl. 1654-1703. De gebannen duyvel weder in-geroupen ... 1691. (Card 2)

    Signed: Bloemardus Thusius.
    Variant of van der Linde 87: 2d., enl. printing.
    No. 9 in vol. lettered Tractaten voor en tegen B. Bekker.

8

Witchcraft
BF 1410 B42 Z69 no.21
    [Costerus, Florentius] fl. 1654-1703. De gebannen Duyvel weder in geroepen, ofte het vonnis van Doctor Bekker over den Duyvel bevelt, in revisie gebraght. [n.p.] Gedruckt by W. van Vreden [1691?]
    37 p. 21cm.
    Signatures: 4°: ∏1, A-D⁴, E3.
    Black letter.
    Signed: Bloemardus Thusius.
    Van der Linde 87.
    No. 21 in a Collection of tracts against Balthasar Bekker and his
NIC Betoverde weereld.

Witchcraft
BF 1565 C84 1624
    Cotta, John, 1575?-1650?
    The infallible trve and assvred vvitch; or, The second edition of The tryall of witch-craft. Shevving the right and trve methode of the discoverie; with a confvtation of erroneovs vvaies, carefvlly reviewed and more fully cleared and augmented. London, Printed by I. L. for R. Higginbotham, 1624.
    155 p. 19cm.

    STC 5837.
    I. Title. II. His The tryall of witch-craft.

Witchcraft
BF 1565 C84 1625
    Cotta, John, 1575?-1650?
    The infallible trve and assvred vvitch; or, the second edition of The tryall of witch-craft, shevving the right and trve methode of the discoverie. With a confvtation of erroneous waies, carefvlly reviewed and more fully cleared and augm. London, Printed by I. L. for R. H., and are to be sold at the signe of the Greyhound in Pauls church-yard, 1625.
    155 p. 18cm.

Witchcraft
BF 1565 C84 1616
    Cotta, John, 1575?-1650?
    The triall of witch-craft, shewing the trve and right methode of the discouery: with a confutation of erroneous wayes. London, Printed by George Pvrslowe for Samvel Rand, 1616.
    [8], 128 p. 19cm.

    1. Witchcraft. 2. Demonology. 3. Criminal procedure. I. Title.

Witchcraft
BF 1563 T86
    Cotta, John, 1575?-1650.
    The triall of witch-craft, shewing the trve and right methode of the discouery: with a confusation of erroneous wayes. London, Printed by G. Pvrslowe for S. Rand, 1616.
    128 p. 19cm.

    No. 2 in vol. lettered: Tracts of witches.

    1. Witchcraft.

124

CATALOGUE OF THE CORNELL WITCHCRAFT COLLECTION

Cotta, John, 1575?-1650?
  The tryall of witch-craft.

Witchcraft
BF   Cotta, John, 1575?-1650?
1565   The infallible trve and assvred vvitch;
C84   or, The second edition of The tryall of
1624   witch-craft. Shevving the right and trve
       methode of the discoverie; with a confvta-
       tion of erroneovs vvaies, carefvlly reviewed
       and more fully cleared and augmented. Lon-
       don, Printed by I. L. for R. Higginbotham,
       1624.
         155 p. 19cm.

       STC 5837.
       ✓I. Title.   "II. His The tryall of
       witch-craft.

Cotton Mather and his writings on witchcraft.

Witchcraft
BF   Holmes, Thomas James, 1874-
1575   Cotton Mather and his writings on witch-
C23   craft. [Chicago, Univ. of Chicago Press,
H75   1926]
         29 p. 25cm.

       "Reprinted for private distribution from
       Papers of the Bibliographical Society of
       America, vol. XVIII, Parts 1 and 2."
         Bound with his The surreptitious printing
       of one of Cotton Mather's manuscripts.
         1. Mather,   Cotton, 1663-1728--Bibl.
         2. Witchcraft   --Bibl. I. Title.

Cotton Mather and Salem witchcraft.

Witchcraft
BF   Poole, William Frederick, 1821-1894.
1576   Cotton Mather and Salem witchcraft. By William
P82   Frederick Poole. ⟨Reprinted from the North American
       review for April, 1869.⟩ Boston [University press] 1869.
         63 p. 24cm.
       "One hundred copies printed."

         1. Witchcraft—Salem, Mass. 2. Mather, Cotton, 1663-1728. I. Title.
         3. Upham, Charles   Wentworth, 1802-1875.
         Salem witchcraft;   with an account of   A-15947
         Salem village.
       Library of Congress   BF1576.P83

Cotton Mather and witchcraft.

Witchcraft
BF   Poole, William Frederick, 1821-1894.
1576   Cotton Mather & witchcraft; two notices of Mr. Upham,
P82   his reply. Boston, T. R. Marvin & son; [etc., etc.] 1870.
U676   30 p. 17cm.

         1. Witchcraft—Salem, Mass. 2. Mather, Cotton, 1663-1728. 3. Upham,
       Charles Wentworth, 1802-1875.   I. Title.
                                                       11--9001
       Library of Congress   BF1576.P8

The court of Rome.

Witchcraft
BX   La Bruja; the witch; or, A picture of the
1735   court of Rome; found among the manu-
B89   scripts of a respectable theologian, a
       great friend of that court. Translated
       from the Spanish by Markophrates [pseud.]
       London, J. Hatchard, 1840.
         188 p. 19cm.

       Added t. p. engr.
         1. Rome—Hist. 2. Inquisition.
         I. Title: The court of Rome.

WITCHCRAFT
BF   Courtilz, Gatien de, sieur de Sandras,
1547   1644?-1772. Les fredaines du diable; ou, Recueil de
C86   morceaux épars, pour servir à l'histoire
1797   du diable et de ses suppôts; tirés d'auteurs
       dignes de foi, par feu M. Sandras, avocat
       en Parlement; mis en nouveau style et pub-
       liés par J. Fr. N. D. L. R. [i.e., Jean
       François Née de la Rochelle] Paris, Chez
       Merlin, 1797.
         216 p. 17 cm.
8
NIC   (Continued on next card)

WITCHCRAFT
BF   Courtilz, Gatien de, sieur de Sandras,
1547   1644?-1772. Les fredaines du diable ...
C86   1797.   (Card 2)
1797
       Ascription by BM, Biographie universelle;
       and BN for entry under Née de la Rochelle
       as editor.
       Author entry in BN: Sandras,   ,
       advocat au Parlement.
8
NIC   ✓ 1. Devil. 2. Devil--Bibliography.
       I. Sandras,   , advocat au Parlement,
       supposed aut   her. II. Née de la Ro-
       ✓chelle, Jean   François, 1751-1838, ed.
       III. Title.

Courtilz de Sandras, Gatien de, 1644?-
  1712.
  see
Courtilz, Gatien de, sieur de Sandras,
  1644?-1712.

Witchcraft
BF   Coxe, Francis.
1563   A short treatise declaringe the detestable
W81++ wickednesse of magicall sciences, as necro-
no.4   mancie, coniurations of spirites, curiouse
       astrologie and such lyke ... [London, 1561.
       London, at the British Museum, 1923]
         [30] p. 14cm.
         Signatures: A⁸, B⁷.
         Photocopy (negative) 30 p. on 15 l. 20 x
       32cm.
         No. 4 in vol. lettered: Witchcraft tracts,
       chapbooks and   broadsides, 1579-1704;
       rotograph   copies.
         ✓I. Title.

Witchcraft
BF   Coynart, Charles de, 1863-
1582   ... Une sorcière au XVIIIᵉ siècle, Marie-Anne de La
L41   Ville, 1680-1725, avec une préface de Pierre de Ségur.
C88   Paris, Hachette et cⁱᵉ, 1902.
         2 p. l., iv, 286 p., 1 l. 19ᶜᵐ.

         1. La Ville, Marie Anne de, b. 1680. 2. Witch-
       craft--France. ✓I. Title.

Library of Congress, no.

RARE
HV   Cramer, Wilhelm Zacharias, praeses.
8593   Dissertatio iuridica De tortura eiusque
C88   usu et effectibus...praeside Wilhelmo Za-
       charia Cramero respondente Io. Christopho-
       ro Goetzio pro loco in Facultate Iuridica
       rite obtinendo...habenda... Lipsiae, Lit-
       teris Breitkopfianis [1742]
         85 p. 23cm.

         "An magi et sagae sint torquendi?" : p.
       57-66.
8   1. Torture.   ✓I. Goetz, Johann Chris-
NIC   toph, respo   ndent. ✓II. Title.

Witchcraft
BF   [Cranz, August Friedrich] 1737-1801.
1523   Gallerie der Teufel, bestehend in einer
C89   auserlesenen Sammlung von Gemählden mora-
       lisch politischer Figuren, deren Originale
       zwischen Himmel und Erden anzutreffen sind,
       nebst einigen bewährten Recepten gegen die
       Anfechtungen der bösen Geister, von Pater
       Gassnern dem Jüngern [pseud] nach Art perio-
       discher Schriften stückweise hrsg. Frank-
       furt, 1777-78.
         5 v. in 1. 18cm.
         1. Devil.   ✓I. Title.

Crause, Rudolph Wilhelm.
  see
Krause, Rudolf Wilhelm, 1642-1719.

Crausius, Rudolphus Guilielmus,
  1642-1719.
  see
Krause, Rudolf Wilhelm, 1642-1719.

Crausius, Rudolphus Wilhelmus,
  1642-1718.
  see
Krause, Rudolf Wilhelm, 1642-1719.

Credulity as it concerns the medical man.

ar W   Diller, Theodore, 1863-
7956   Credulity as it concerns the medical man.
       Chicago, American Medical Association Press,
       1930.
         18 p. illus., facsims. 21cm.

       "Reprinted from the Transactions of the
       American Neurological Association, 1929, pp.
       489-497."

         1.Credulity. 2.Witchcraft.   I. Title.

Witchcraft
BF   Cremer, Tillmann.
1583   Eine Hexenverbrennung in der Eifel; Kul-
Z7   turbild aus der Zeit des dreissigjährigen
1627a Krieges. Bonn, P. Hanstein, 1904.
         342-346, 380-383 p. 23cm. (Rheinische
       Geschichtsblätter, 7. Jahrg., No. 11-12)

         1. Trials (Witchcraft)--Germany. 2. Exe-
       cutions and exe   cutioners. ✓I. Title.

Witchcraft
BF   Crespet, Pierre, 1543-1594.
1522   Devx livres de la hayne de Sathan et ma-
C92   lins esprits contre l'homme, & de l'homme
       contre eux. Ou sont par notables discours
2 copies & curieuses recherches expliquez les arts,
       ruses, & moyens, qu'ils prattiquent pour
       nuyre à l'homme par charmes, obsessions, ma-
       gie, sorcellerie, illusions, phantosmes, im-
       postures, & autres estranges façons, auec
       les remedes conuenables pour leur resister
       suyuant l'vsage qui se pratique en l'Eglise.

                      (Continued on next card)

CATALOGUE OF THE CORNELL WITCHCRAFT COLLECTION

Witchcraft
BF 1522 C92
Crespet, Pierre, 1543-1594. Devx livres de la hayne de Sathan ... (Card 2)
Auec la table bien ample des matieres y contenues. Paris, Chez Guillaume de la Nouë, 1590.
[26], 428, [22] l. 17cm.
Errors in paging.
Copy 1 bound in two volumes.
Copy 2 with Robert Southey's autograph.
I. Title. II. Title: La hayne de Sathan et malins esprits contre l'homme.

Creusé, Pierre, b. 1614.
WITCHCRAFT
BF 1555 H678 1881
Histoire admirable de la maladie prodigieuse de Pierre Creusé, arrivée en la ville de Niort en 1628. Avec une introduction par L. Favre. Niort, Typ. de L. Favre, 1881.
iii, 84 p. 22cm.
Half title: Maladie prodigieuse de Pierre Creusé.
Includes reprint of the original t. p., whose title includes: "... auec vn plaidoyé de l'ad uocat du Roy de ladite
8 (Continued on next card)

Creusé, Pierre, b. 1614.
WITCHCRAFT
BF 1555 H678 1881
Histoire admirable de la maladie prodigieuse de Pierre Creusé ... 1881. (Card 2)
ville sur le subjet de ladite maladie, & la sentence interuenue sur ledit plaidoyé: ensemble les certificats de medecins & chirurgiens dudit lieu. Niort, 1631."
1. Demoniac possession. 2. Creusé, Pierre, b. 1614. I. Favre, Léopold, 1817-1890, ed. II. Title: Maladie prodigieuse de Pierre Creusé.
8

Le crime de sorcellerie.
WITCHCRAFT
BF 1569 T37
Théaux, Marcel.
Pages d'histoire judiciaire. Le crime de sorcellerie.
(In La revue du palais. Paris. 25cm.
1. année, no. 7 (1897), p. [103]-135)
In envelope.
1. Witchcraft--History. 2. Devil. 3. Bavent, Madeleine, ca. 1608-1647. I. Title. II. Title: Le crime de sorcellerie.
8 NIC

Criminal-Prozess gegen Besessene ... 1664 und 1666.
Witchcraft
BF 1555 W65
Wigand, Paul, 1786-1866.
Epidemie der vom Teufel Besessenen. 44. Criminal-Prozess gegen Besessene, und Untersuchung, ob sie wirklich vom Teufel besessen seien, oder nicht. 1664 und 1666. [Leipzig, S. Hirzel, 1854]
[320]-339 p. 23cm.
Caption title.
Detached from Denkwürdigkeiten, Kap. XI.
1. Demoniac possession. 2. Witchcraft --Germany. I. Title.
8

Criminal trials in Scotland.
K P674+
Pitcairn, Robert, comp., 1793-1835.
Criminal trials in Scotland, from A. D. 1488 to A. D. 1624, embracing the entire reigns of James IV. and V., Mary Queen of Scots, and James VI. Compiled from the original records and MSS., with historical notes and illustrations. Edinburgh, W. Tait, 1833.
3 v. in 4. 30cm.
Also published under title: Ancient criminal trial s in Scotland.
(Continued on next card)

Criminal trials in Scotland.
K P674+
Pitcairn, Robert, comp., 1793-1835. Criminal trials in Scotland ... 1833. (Card 2)
Contents.--v.1, pt. 1. 1488-1568.--v.1, pt. 2. 1568-1592.--v.2 1596-1609--v.3 1609-1624.
1. Trials--Scotland. I. Title.

Criminal-Verfahren vorzüglich bei Hexenprozessen im ehemaligen Bissthum Bamberg.
WITCHCRAFT
BF 1583 L22
Lamberg, G von
Criminal-Verfahren vorzüglich bei Hexenprozessen im ehemaligen Bissthum Bamberg während der Jahre 1624 bis 1630. Aus actenmässigen Urkunden gezogen von G. v. Lamberg. Nürnberg, Kiegel und Wiessner [1835]
39, 28 p. 19cm.
8 NIC
1. Trials (Witchcraft)--Bamberg (Diocese) I. Title.

A critical dissertation concerning the words DAIMON and DAIMONION.
Witchcraft
BT 980 S97
[Swinton, John] 1703-1777.
A critical dissertation concerning the words ΔΑΙΜΩΝ and ΔΑΙΜΟΝΙΟΝ. Occasion'd by two late enquiries [by Arthur Ashley Sykes] into the meaning of demoniacs in the New Nestament. In a letter to a friend. By a Gentleman of Wadham College, Oxford. London, Printed for J. Crokatt; and sold by J. Roberts, 1738.
29 p. 20cm.
Also attributed to George Costard.
Letter sig ned: Philalethes.
8 (Continued on next card)

Witchcraft
BV 639 W7 C94+
Crohns, Hjalmar, 1862-1946.
Die Summa Theelogica des Antonin von Florenz und die Schätzung des Weibes im Hexenhammer. [Helsingforsiae, ex Officina typographica Societatis litterariae fennicae, 1906]
1 p. l., 23 p. 28cm. ([Finska vetenskaps-societeten, Helsingfors] Acta Societatis scientiarum fennicae. t. xxxii, no. 4)
8 (over)

Q 60 F508+ v. 32 no. 4
Crohns, Hjalmar, 1862-
... Die Summa theologica des Antonin von Florenz und die schätzung des weibes im Hexenhammer, von dr. Hjalmar Crohns ... [Helsingforsiae, ex Officina typographica Societatis litterariae fennicae, 1906]
1 p. l., 23 p. 28 x 23½cm. ([Finska vetenskaps-societeten, Helsingfors] Acta Societatis scientiarum fennicae. t. XXXII, no. 4)
Bibliographical foot-notes.
(Continued on next card)

Q 60 F508+ v. 32 no. 4
Crohns, Hjalmar, 1862- ... Die Summa theologica des Antonin von Florenz ... 1906. (Card 2)
1. Antoninus, Saint, abp. of Florence, 1389-1459. Summa theologica. 2. Institoris, Henricus, d. 1508. Malleus maleficarum. 3. Women in literature.
[Full name: Hjalmar Johannes Crohns]

Witchcraft
BF 1583 C94
Crohns, Hjalmar, 1862-1946.
Zwei Förderer des Hexenwahns und ihre Ehrenrettung durch die ultramontane Wissenschaft. Stuttgart, Strecker & Schröder, 1905.
62 p. 20cm.
1. Institoris, Henricus, d. 1508. 2. Antoninus, Saint, abp. of Florence, 1389-1459. 3. Witchcraft. 4. Ultramontanism. I. Title.

Witchcraft
BF 1548 C95
Cross, William.
The Devil: a myth... London, E. Truelove, 1872.
16 p. 20cm.
1. Devil. I. Title.

Witchcraft
BF 1581 P87
Crossley, James, 1800-1883, ed.
Potts, Thomas, fl. 1612-1618.
Pott's Discovery of witches in the county of Lancaster, reprinted from the original ed. of 1613. With an introduction and notes, by James Crossley ... [Manchester] Printed for the Chetham society, 1745 [i.e. 1845]
3 p. l., (iii)-lxxix, [190] p. 1 l., 51, 6 p. illus. 23x18cm. (Added t.-p.: Remains, historical & literary, connected with the palatine counties of Lancaster and Chester, pub. by the Chetham society. vol. VI)
(Continued on next card)

Witchcraft
BF 1581 P87
Crossley, James, 1800-1883, ed.
Potts, Thomas, fl. 1612-1618. Pott's Discovery of witches in the county of Lancaster. (Card 2)
With reproduction of original t.-p.: The Wonderfvll Discoverie Of Witches In The Covntie Of Lancaster ... Together with the arraignement and triall of Iennet Preston, at the assizes holden at the Castle of Yorke ... London, 1613
"The arraignement and triall of Iennet Preston" has special t.-p. with imprint: London, 1612
Revised by Sir Edward Bromley.

Witchcraft
BF 1565 C95
[Crouch, Nathaniel] 1632?-1725?
The kingdom of darkness: or, The history of daemons, specters, witches, apparitions, possessions, disturbances, and other wonderful and supernatural delusions, mischievous feats and malicious impostures of the Devil. ... By R. B. [pseud.] ... London, Printed for N. Crouch, 1688.
169, [9] p. illus. 15cm.
Publisher's catalogue: [9] p. at end.
1. Witchcraft--Hist. VI. Title.

WITCHCRAFT
BF 1501 C95
[Crouch, Nathaniel] 1632?-1725?
Wonderful prodigies of judgment and mercy: discovered in above three hundred memorable histories, containing I. Dreadful judments upon atheists, perjured wretches, blphemers ... II. The miserable ends of divers magicians, witches, conjurers, &c. wi several strange apparitions. III. Remarkable presages of approaching death ... IV The wicked lives, and woful deaths of wretched popes, apostates, and desperate
8 (Continued on next card)

126

CATALOGUE OF THE CORNELL WITCHCRAFT COLLECTION

```
WITCHCRAFT
BF        [Crouch, Nathaniel] 1632?-1725?  Wonderful
1501         prodigies of judgment and mercy ...  1682.
C95                                          (Card 2)

          persecutors.  V. Fearful judgments upon
          cruel tyrants, murderers, &c. ...  VI. Ad-
          mirable deliverances from imminent dangers
          ...  VII. Divine goodness to penitents,
          with the dying thoughts of several famous
          men concerning a future state after this
          life.  Imparti    ally collected from antient
  8
                    (Continued on next card)
```

```
WITCHCRAFT
BF        [Crouch, Nathaniel] 1632?-1725?  Wonderful
1501         prodigies of judgment and mercy ...  1682.
C95                                          (Card 3)

          and modern authors ...  By R. B. author of
          the History of the wars of England, and the
          Remarks of London, etc.  London, Printed
          for Nath. Crouch, 1682.
              2 p. l., 233, [3] p. illus. 15cm.
              With added engr. t. p.
              With armorial book plate: Hugh Cecil
          Earl of Lons         dale.
  8
                    (Continued on next card)
```

```
WITCHCRAFT
BF        [Crouch, Nathaniel] 1632?-1725?  Wonderful
1501         prodigies of judgment and mercy ...  1682.
C95                                          (Card 4)

          Wing C7361.

              1. Devil--Collections.  2. Reward
          (Theology)  3. Marvelous, The.  I. The
          author of the History of the wars of Eng-
          land.  II. R. B.  III. B., R.  IV. Title.
  8
```

```
          Crowther, Patricia.
581           Witchcraft in Yorkshire. [Clapham,
95         Yorkshire], Dalesman, 1973.
              72 p. illus., facsims., map. 21 cm.




              1. Witchcraft--Yorkshire, Eng.
              I. Title

   C  MAR 21,'74       COOxc     73-168514
```

```
          La croyance à la magie au XVIIIe siècle en
             France dans les contes, romans & traités.
Witchcraft
BF        Bila, Constantin.
1595         ... La croyance à la magie au XVIIIe siècle en France dans
B59         les contes, romans & traités ...  Paris, J. Gamber, 1925.
              158 p., 1 l. 23cm.
              Thèse--Univ. de Paris.
              "Errata": 1 leaf laid in.
              "Bibliographie": p. [151]-158.


           1. Magic.  2. French literature--18th cent.--Hist. & crit.  I. Title.
                                                  26-16744

    Library of Congress          BF1595.B5
```

```
          Cruels effets de la vengeance du Cardinal
             de Richelieu.
tchcraft
          [Aubin, Nicolas] b. ca. 1655.
17           Cruels effets de la vengeance du Cardinal de
          Richelieu, ou Histoire des diables de Loudun,
92        de la possession des religieuses ursulines, et
16        de la condamnation et du suplice [sic] d'Urbain
          Grandier, curé de la même ville.  Amsterdam,
          E. Roger, 1716.
              [10], 5-378 p. front. 17cm.

              Published also under titles: Histoire des
          diables de Loudun, ou, De la possession des
                    (Continued on next card)
```

```
          Cruels effets de la vengeance du Cardinal de
             Richelieu.
Witchcraft
BF        [Aubin, Nicolas] b. ca. 1655.  Cruels effets de
1517         la vengeance du Cardinal de Richelieu ...
F5           1716.                             (Card 2)
A892
1716      religieuses ursulines ...  Amsterdam, 1694; and
          Histoire d'Urbain Grandier, condamné comme
          magicien ...  Amsterdam, 1735.
```

```
MSS       Cudius, Hans.
Bd.           Newe Zeitung und ware Geschicht, dieses
WITCHCRAFT 76. Jars geschehen im Breissgaw, wie man da
BF         in etlichen Stätten und Flecken, in die 55.
C96        Unhulden gefangen und verbrent hat, auch
           wie sie schröckliche ding bekent haben ...
           Gestellt und gemacht durch Hans Cudium.
              [n.p.] 1576 [ca. 1900]
                  4 l. 19cm.
              Carnap's manuscript copy.
              "Originaldr     uck in der Stadtbiblio-
          thek zu Zür         ich, 8 Seiten in 8°."
                    (Continued on next card)
```

```
MSS       Cudius, Hans.  Newe Zeitung ...  1576
Bd.       [ca. 1900]                        (Card 2)
WITCHCRAFT
BF            Notations in the margins indicate folia-
C96       tion of the original.
              In verse.

              1. Witchcraft--Germany.  I. Title.
```

```
          Cullender, Rose, fl. 1664.
Witchcraft
BF        Hale, Sir Matthew, 1609-1676.
1581          Trial of witches, at the Bury assizes,
Z7        March 10, 1762 [i.e. 1664] before Sir Matthew
1664a     Hale ... Rose Cullender and Amy Duny, ... were
          severally indicted for bewitching Elizabeth and
          Anne Durent ... and ... pleaded not guilty.
              [n.p., 1762?]
                  57-64 p. 21cm.
              Reprinted from the original ed. of 1682;
          evidently detach       ed from a periodical
                    (Continued on next card)
```

```
          Cullender, Rose, fl. 1664.
Witchcraft
BF        Hale, Sir Matthew, 1609-1676.
1581          Trial of witches ... [1762?]    (Card 2)
Z7
1664a     (printed 1762?) but has no identification
          except paging and "Vol. III" at bottom of
          p. 57.

              1. Cullender, Rose, fl. 1664.  2. Duny,
          Amy, fl. 1664.  I. Title.
```

```
          Cullender, Rose, fl. 1664.
Witchcraft
BF        Hale, Sir Matthew, 1609-1676.
1563          A tryal of witches, at the assizes held
T75       at Bury St. Edmonds for the county of Suf-
          folk; on the tenth day of March, 1664, be-
          fore Sir Matthew Hale ... Reprinted verba-
          tim from the original edition of 1682.
          With an appendix by C. Clark, esq., of Great
          Totham, Essex.  London, J. R. Smith, 1838.
              28 p. 23cm.
              No. 3 in vol. lettered Tracts on witch-
  8       craft.
              1. Trials    (Witchcraft)--England.
              I. Title.
```

```
          Culmination of the Puritan theocracy.
Witchcraft
F         Horton, Edward Augustus, 1843-
7             The culmination of the Puritan theocracy,
H82       by Edward A. Horton.  Boston, J.S. Lockwood,
          1900.
              32 p. 24½cm.


              I. Title.
```

```
WITCHCRAFT Culturgeschichte, Curiosa, Facetiae.
Z         Kirchhoff & Wigand, Leipzig.
6880          Culturgeschichte, Curiosa, Facetiae,
Z9C35     ältere deutsche etc. Literatur, Vermischtes
no.3      ... enthaltend auch die alten Sammlungen des
          ... Nationalökonomen Johann Georg Büsch über
          Hexen, Dämonologie, Alchemie und Geheime
          Wissenschaften im allgemeinen.  New-York,
          G.E. Stechert [1885]
              72 p. 23cm.
              At head of            title: Nr. 743.
              No. 3 in              vol. lettered:
                       (Continued on next card)
```

```
WITCHCRAFT Culturgeschichte, Curiosa, Facetiae.
Z         Kirchhoff & Wigand, Leipzig.  Culturge-
6880         schichte, Curiosa, Facetiae, ältere
Z9C35        deutsche etc. Literatur, Vermischtes ...
no.3      [1885]                            (Card 2)

          Catalogues of books on magic and witchcraft.

              1. Bibliography--Rare books.  2. Occult
          sciences--Bibl.--Catalogs.  3. Witchcraft--
          Bibl.--Catalogs.  I. Title.
```

```
          Culturgeschichte und Curiositäten in
             Druckschriften, fliegenden Blättern ...
Witchcraft
Z         Heberle, J     M
6880          Culturgeschichte und Curiositäten in
Z9        Druckschriften, fliegenden Blättern,
C35       Bildern, Autographen und Monumenten.  Aus
no.2      den Sammlungen von Heinrich Lempertz...
          Zu beigesetzten Preisen vorräthig auf dem
          Bücher- und Kunstlager von J. M. Heberle
          (H. Lempertz' Söhne) in Cöln.  Abth. E:
          Physiognomik, Phrenologie, Mimik, natürliche
          Magie, Kunststücke, Alchymie, etc. ... Abth.
          F: Zauberei         und Hexerei, Faust,
          Cagliostro,         Teufelswesen und
                    (Continued on next card)
```

```
          Culturgeschichte und Curiositäten in
             Druckschriften, fliegenden Blättern ...
Witchcraft
Z         Heberle, J     M
6880          Culturgeschichte und Curiositäten...
Z9        [1874?]                           (Card 2)
C35
no.2      Beschwörungen, Besessensein, etc. ...
          Cöln, Steven's Druckerei [1874?]
              64 p. 23cm.
              At head of title: Nro. 74.
              No. 2 in vol. lettered: Catalogues of
          books on magic and witchcraft.
              1. Occult       sciences--Bibl.--
          Catalogs.           2. Witchcraft--Bibl.--
          Catalogs.           3. Magic--Bibl.--
                              Catalogs.
```

```
          Culturhistorische Bilder aus Böhmen.

DB        Svátek, Josef, 1835-
200           Culturhistorische Bilder aus Böhmen.
.5        Von Josef Svátek ...  Wien, W. Braumüller,
S96       1879.
              vi p., 2 l., [3]-311 p. 23cm.
              Contents.--Hexenprocesse in Böhmen.--Die
          Alchemie in Böhmen.--Adamiten und Deisten in
          Böhmen.--Ein griechischer Abenteurer in Prag.
          --Die Guillotine in Böhmen.--Bauern-Rebellio-
          nen in Böhmen.--Schiller in Böhmen.--Die Ru-
          dolfinische Kunstkammer in Prag.--Die Zigeu-
          ner in Böhmen.

              I. Title.
```

CATALOGUE OF THE CORNELL WITCHCRAFT COLLECTION

Witchcraft
PT
2445
P3709
1883
    Culturhistorische Bilder aus den Zeiten des Wahns.
    Culturhistorische Bilder aus den Zeiten des Wahns. Bd. 1. Das Marile. Eine Geschichte aus der Zeit des Hexenwahns. Hamburg, Seelig & Ohmann, 1883.
    vi, 184 p. 21cm.

    No more published?

    I. Title. II. Title: Marile.

WITCHCRAFT
BF
1565
H33
1634
    Cunradi Hartz ... Tractatus criminalis theorico-practicus, De reorum, inprimisque veneficarum, inquisitione:
    Hartz, Konrad.
    Cunradi Hartz ... Tractatvs criminalis theorico-practicus, De reorum, inprimisque veneficarum, inquisitione juridice instituenda, in foro haud minus, quam scholis apprimè utilis & jucundus. Nunc primùm in lucem editus ... cum notis ... anonymi cujusdam in Hassia LL. D. Marpvrgi, Typis & sumptibus Nicolai Hampelii, 1634.
    189, [13] p. 20cm.
    1. Trials (Witchcraft) 2. Witchcraft. I. Title: De reorum, inprimisque veneficarum, inquisitione ...

8

Witchcraft
BF
1410
C97
    Curieuse Gespräche im Reiche derer Todten, zwischen dem bekandten Auctore der bezauberten Welt, und ehemahligen Prediger in Holland Balthasar Beckern, der bey nahe wenig vom Teufel geglaubet; und zwischen dem in gantz Teutschland berühmten Theologo Christian Scrivern, der einen Menschen zurecht geducht, so einen Pact mit dem Teufel gemacht; ... Leipzig und Braunschweig, 1731-[1734]
    4 v. in 1. (208 p.) 4 plates, vignettes. 21 x 17cm.
    (Continued on next card)

8

Witchcraft
BF
1410
C97
    Curieuse Gespräche im Reiche derer Todten, zwischen .. Balthasar Beckern .. und .. Christian Scrivern ... 1731-[1734]
    (Card 2)

    4°: A-P⁴, P3, Q-2C⁴.
    Black letter.
    Sometimes ascribed to David Fassmann.
    Title of v. 2: Zweyte Unterredung oder Gespräche im Reiche derer Todten ...; of v. 3:

    (Continued on next card)

Witchcraft
BF
1410
C97
    Curieuse Gespräche im Reiche derer Todten, zwischen .. Balthasar Beckern .. und .. Christian Scrivern ... 1731-[1734]
    (Card 3)

    Besonderes curieuses [sic] Gespräche im Reiche derer Todten ...; of v. 4: Curieuses Gespräche in dem Reiche derer Todten ...
    With this is bound Curieuses Gespräche im Reiche der Todten, zwischen .. Johann Friedrich Mayern .. und Johann Wilhelm Petersen ... [Leipzig] 1732.

    (Continued on next card)

8

Witchcraft
BF
1410
C97
    Curieuse Gespräche im Reiche derer Todten, zwischen ... Balthasar Beckern ... und ... Christian Scrivern ... 1731-[1734]
    (Card 4)

    1. Demonology. 2. Bekker, Balthasar, 1634-1698--Fiction. 3. Scriver, Christian, 1629-1693--Fiction. I. Fassmann, David, 1683-1744, supposed author.

8

Witchcraft
BF
1445
B57
    Curieuse Winter-Discourse einer gewissen raren Fragen und deren Beantwortung.
    Bianor, pseud.
    Curieuse Winter-Discourse einer gewissen Compagnie bestehende in etlichen raren Fragen und deren Beantwortung, hrsg. von Einem aus dieser Compagnie, welcher sich nennet Bianor. Jena, J. Bielcken, 1704.
    149 p. 16cm.

Witchcraft
BF
1410
C97
    Curieuses Gespräche im Reiche derer Todten, zwischen zweyen hochberühmten Männern, Johann Friedrich Mayern, ... und Johann Wilhelm Petersen ... Darinnen nechst dieser beyder hochberühmten Männer Lebens-Particularitäten, von vielen curieusen und zu unserer Zeit strittig gewordenen Glaubens-Lehren, pro & contra gestritten wird. [Leipzig] 1732.
    2 v. in 1. (128 p.) 2 plates, vignettes. 21 x 17cm.

    (Continued on next card)

8

Witchcraft
BF
1410
C97
    Curieuses Gespräche im Reiche derer Todten, zwischen ... Johann Friedrich Mayern, ... und Johann Wilhelm Petersen ... 1732.
    (Card 2)

    4°: A3, B-H⁴, J3, K-Q⁴.
    Black letter.
    Vol. 2 has title: Gespräche im Reiche derer Todten ...
    Bound with Curieuse Gespräche im Reiche derer Todten, zwischen ... Balthasar Beckern ... und ... Christian Scrivern ... 1731-[1734]

    (Continued on next card)

Witchcraft
BF
1410
C97
    Curieuses Gespräche im Reiche derer Todten, zwischen ... Johann Friedrich Mayern,... und Johann Wilhelm Petersen ... 1732.
    (Card 3)

    1. Lutheran Church--Doctrinal and controversial works. 2. Mayer, Johann Friedrich, 1650-1712--Fiction. 3. Petersen, Friedrich Wilhelm--Fiction.

8

Curiosa--bibliography.
Witchcraft
Z
6880
Z9R81
1903
    Rosenthal, J., firm, booksellers, Munich.
    Bibliotheca magica et pneumatica. Geheime Wissenschaften. Sciences occultes. Occult sciences. Folk-lore. München [1903]
    48, 680 p. 24cm. (Its Kataloge 31-35)

    Issued in parts.

Witchcraft
BF
1429
C97
    Curiose Erwegung der Worte Mosis Gen. VI, 2 ... Da sahen die Söhne Gottes, wie die Töchter der Menschen schön waren, und nahmen ihnen Weiber, auss allen die sie erwehleten &c. Amsterdam, 1700.
    48 p. 13cm.

    1. Demonology.

WITCHCRAFT
BR
135
L14
    Curiosités de l'histoire des croyances populaires au moyen âge.
    Lacroix, Paul, 1806-1884.
    Curiosités de l'histoire des croyances populaires au moyen âge, par P. L. Jacob [pseud.] Paris, A. Delahays, 1859.
    323 p. 17cm.

    Running title: Histoire des moeurs.
    Includes bibliographies.
    Contents.--Superstitions et croyances populaires.--Le juif-errant.--Les blasphé-

8
NIC
    (Continued on next card)

WITCHCRAFT
BR
135
L14
    Curiosités de l'histoire des croyances populaires au moyen âge.
    Lacroix, Paul, 1806-1884.
    Curiosités de l'histoire des croyances populaires...1859. (Card 2)

    Contents--continued.
    mateurs.--Les démons de la nuit.--Les sorciers et le sabbat.--Le boeuf gras.--Origines du mal de Naples.

    1. Superstition. I. Title. II. Title: Histoire des moeurs.

WITCHCRAFT
BF
1532
L14
    Curiosités infernales.
    Lacroix, Paul, 1806-1884.
    Curiosités infernales, par P. L. Jacob [pseud.] Paris, Garnier frères, 1886.
    ii, 396 p. 19cm.

    Bibliographical footnotes.
    Contents.--Les diables.--Les bons anges.--Le royaume des fées.--Nature troublée.--Monde des esprits.--Prodiges.--Empire des morts.--Présages.

8
NIC
    1. Demonology. I. Title.

Witchcraft
BF
1581
A2
W81
1866a
no.5
    Curious account of the remarkable case of the Duchess of Bedford.
    Wright, Thomas, 1810-1877, ed.
    Curious account of the remarkable case of the Duchess of Bedford, in the reign of Edward IV., who was charged with having by witchcraft fixed the love of the king on her daughter Queen Elizabeth. Furnished by the rolls of Parliament of 9th Edward IV. Northampton, J. Taylor, 1867.
    8 p. 22cm.
    "In the Proceedings against Dame Alice Kyteler, for the Camden Society."

8
    (Continued on next card)

Witchcraft
BF
1581
A2
W81
1866a
no.5
    Curious account of the remarkable case of the Duchess of Bedford.
    Wright, Thomas, 1810-1877, ed. Curious account of the remarkable case of the Duchess of Bedford ... 1867. (Card 2)

    No. 5 in box lettered Witchcraft in Northamptonshire.

    1. Bedford, Jaquetta of Luxembourg, duchess of. 2. Edward IV, King of England, 1442-1483. I. Title.

8

Witchcraft
BX
1750
C98
1645
    Cusanus, Nicolaus, 1574-1635.
    Christliche Zuchtschul, in welcher gründliche unnd warhafftige Resolution und Aufflösung aller schwähren Fragstück so in jedem weltlichen Standt, Wandel und Handel mögen fürfallen, wie auch der fürnembsten streitigen Artickeln Erklärung kürtzlich fürgebracht wird; allen Seelsorgern und dem gemeinen Mann sehr nutzlich ... Lucern, D. Hautten, 1645.
    8 l., 731 p. 17cm.

    Added t. p. engraved.
    I. Title.

CATALOGUE OF THE CORNELL WITCHCRAFT COLLECTION

Cyprianus, of Antioch. Legend.

WITCHCRAFT
BF
1565
S76   Spitzel, Gottlieb, 1639-1691.
　　Die gebrochne Macht der Finsternüss, oder Zerstörte teuflische Bunds- und Buhl-Freundschafft mit den Menschen: das ist Gründlicher Bericht, wie und welcher Gestalt die abscheuliche und verfluchte Zauber-Gemeinschafft mit den bösen Geistern angehe; wie dieselbe zu- und fortgehe; ob und auf was Art und Weise sie widerum zergehe ... allen Heyl- und Gnaden-begierigen und vom leydigen Satan schänd　　　lich-berückten und ver-

NIC　　　　　(Continued on next card)

Cyprianus, of Antioch. Legend.

WITCHCRAFT
BF
1565
S76   Spitzel, Gottlieb, 1639-1691.　Die gebrochne Macht der Finsternüss ...　1687.
　　　　　　　　　　　　　　　　(Card 2)
strickten Seelen zum nothwendigen Unterricht und heylsamer Widerkehrung beschrieben ... Augspurg, In Verlegung Gottlieb Göbels seel. Wittib, Gedruckt bey Jacob Koppmayer, 1687.
　24 p. l., 813, [18] p. 17cm.
　　With added engr. t. p. for whole work and each of the　three Abtheilungen.

8
NIC　　　　　(Continued on next card)

Cyprianus, of Antioch. Legend.

WITCHCRAFT
BF
1565
S76   Spitzel, Gottlieb, 1639-1691.　Die gebrochne Macht der Finsternüss ...　1687.
　　　　　　　　　　　　　　　　(Card 3)
　Title in red and black.
　Cyprianvs magvs ... oder dess zu Christe wunderbarlich bekehrten Ertz-Zauberers Cypriani von Antiochia hertzliche Buss und Bekehrung: p. 778-813.
　1. Witchcraft. 2. Devil. 3. Salvation--Early works to 1800. I. Cyprianus, of Antioch. L　egend. II. Title.

8
NIC

CATALOGUE OF THE CORNELL WITCHCRAFT COLLECTION

D

Witchcraft
BF
1582
Z7
1631

D., J.
La sorcière de Munster ₍Catherine Huger₎: sa torture à Wihr-au-Val et son exécution à Gunsbach, MDCXXXI. Colmar, E. Barth, 1869.
15 p. 23cm.

Signed: J. D.

1. Huger, Catherine, d. 1631. 2. Witchcraft. I. D., J. II. J. D.

Witchcraft
BF
1410
B42
1781

D. Balthasar Bekkers reformierten Predigers in Amsterdam bezauberte Welt.
Bekker, Balthasar, 1634-1698.
D. ₍i.e., Doktor₎ Balthasar Bekkers reformierten Predigers in Amsterdam bezauberte Welt. Neu übersetzt von Johann Moritz Schwager, Pastor zu Jöllenbeck; durchgesehen und vermehrt von D. Johann Salomo Semler. Leipzig, In der Weygandschen Buchhandlung, 1781.
3 v. title vignette (port.), fold. plate. 20cm.
8°: vol. 1: a⁸, b2, A-2F⁸; vol. 2:
(Continued on next card)

Witchcraft
BF
1410
B42
1781

D. Balthasar Bekkers reformierten Predigers in Amsterdam bezauberte Welt.
Bekker, Balthasar, 1634-1698. D. Balthasar Bekkers ... bezauberte Welt. 1781.
(Card 2)

8 (- 8), A-2F⁸, G⁴; vol. 3: *⁸ (-*1, *8), A-2Y6.
Translation of his De betoverde weereld.

1. Demonology. 2. Angels. 3. Magic. 4. Witchcraft. I. Title. II. Title:
(Continued on next card)

WITCHCRAFT
BF
1565
T68
1678

D. D. Francisci Torreblanca Cordubensis ... Epitome delictorum, sive De magia.
Torreblanca Villalpando, Francisco.
D. D. Francisci Torreblanca Cordubensis ... Epitome delictorum, sive De magia: in qva aperta vel occvlta invocatio daemonis intervenit. Editio novissima innvmeris mendis expvrgata, necnon indice rerum & verborum copiosissimo nunc primvm locupletata. Lugduni, Sumpt. Joannis Antonij Huguetan, & Soc., 1678.
4 p. l., 576, ₍107₎ p. 23cm.
Title in red and black.
First published 1618 under title: Daemonologia sive De magia ...
(Continued on next card)

8

WITCHCRAFT
BF
1555
M94
029
no.4

D. Joh. Salomo Semlers ... Abfertigung der neuen Geister und alten Irtümer.
Semler, Johann Salomo, 1725-1791.
D. Joh. Salomo Semlers ... Abfertigung der neuen Geister und alten Irtümer in der Lohmannischen Begeisterung zu Kemberg nebst theologischem Unterricht von dem Ungrunde der gemeinen Meinung von leiblichen Besitzungen des Teufels und Bezauberungen der Christen. Halle, Bey J. J. Gebauer, 1760.
40, 328 p. 18cm.
Dedication and "Vorrede" comprise the first numbering.

8
NIC
(Continued on next card)

WITCHCRAFT
BF
1555
M94
029
no.4

D. Joh. Salomo Semlers ... Abfertigung der neuen Geister und alten Irtümer.
Semler, Johann Salomo, 1725-1791.
Abfertigung der neuen Geister ... 1760.
(Card 2)
"Anhang. Auszug aus des Chaufepiee ₍sic₎, Nouveau dictionnaire historique et critique, von dem Artikel Balthas. Bekker": p. 317-328.
No. 4 in vol. lettered Oesfeld u. a. ...
1. Lohmannin, Anna Elisabeth. 2. Müller, Gottlieb. Gründlicher Nachricht von einer begeisterten Weibesperson. 3. Devil. 4. Bekker, Balthasar, 1634-1698.

8
NIC
(Continued on next card)

WITCHCRAFT
BF
1555
M94
029
no.5

D. Joh. Salomo Semlers Anhang zu der Abfertigung der Lohmannischen Begeisterung.
Semler, Johann Salomo, 1725-1791.
D. Joh. Salomo Semlers Anhang zu der Abfertigung der Lohmannischen Begeisterung, worin fernere historische Umstände gesamlet worden. Halle, Bey J. J. Gebauer, 1760.
112 p. 18cm.
Title of the original work reads: Abfertigung der neuen Geister und alten Irtümer der Lohmannischen Begeisterung. Halle, 1760.
No. 5 in vol. lettered Oesfeld u. a. ...
(Continued on next card)

8 NIC

WITCHCRAFT
BS
2545
D5
S472

D. Joh. Salomo Semlers ... Umständliche Untersuchung der dämonischen Leute oder sogenannten Besessenen.
Semler, Johann Salomo, 1725-1791.
D. Joh. Salomo Semlers ... Umständliche Untersuchung der dämonischen Leute oder sogenannten Besessenen, nebst Beantwortung einiger Angriffe. Halle, Bey J. I. Gebauer, 1762.
24 p. l., 272 p. 18cm.
Contents.--Auszug und Erleuterung der Dissertation: De daemoniacis, qvorvm in Evangeliis fit mentio.--Auszug und Beantwortung der jenaischen Disputation.--Antwort
(Continued on next card)

8

WITCHCRAFT
BS
2545
D5
S472

D. Joh. Salomo Semlers ... Umständliche Untersuchung der dämonischen Leute oder sogenannten Besessenen.
Semler, Johann Salomo, 1725-1791. ...Umständliche Untersuchung der dämonischen Leute ... 1762. (Card 2)

auf die unbillige Recension in den Auszügen aus Dispvtationibvs.
1. Demoniac possession. 2. His De daemoniacis, quorum in Evangeliis fit mentio. 3. Bible. N. T.--Commentaries. I. Title: Umständliche Untersuchung der dämonischen Leute oder sogenannten Besessenen.

8

Witchcraft
BF
1413
E16

D. Johann Peter Eberhards ... Abhandlungen vom physikalischen Aberglauben und der Magie.
Eberhard, Johann Peter, 1727-1779.
D. Johann Peter Eberhards ... abhandlungen vom physikalischen aberglauben und der magie. Halle im Magdeburgischen, Renger, 1778.
7 p. l., 144 p. front. 20½ cm.

1. Superstition. 2. Magic. I. Title: Abhandlungen vom physikalischen aberglauben und der magie.

34-13015
Library of Congress   BF1413.E3   ₍159.961₎ 133

WITCHCRAFT
RC
340
W53
1707

D. Johannis-Caspari VVestphali, academici curiosi, Pathologia daemoniaca.
Westphal, Johann Caspar.
D. Johannis-Caspari VVestphali, academici curiosi, Pathologia daemoniaca, id est Observationes & meditationes physiologico-magico-medicae circa daemonomanias, similesque morbos convulsivos â fascino ortos, daemonibus olim Graecorum ethnicorum ac Judaeorum aëreis, hodiè verò obsessioni aliisque diaboli infernalis tentationibus & operationibus superstitiosè adscriptos ... Nunc verò philiatrorum desiderio & adhortationi-
(Continued on next card)

8

WITCHCRAFT
RC
340
W53
1707

D. Johannis-Caspari VVestphali, academici curiosi, Pathologia daemoniaca.
Westphal, Johann Caspar. ... Pathologia daemoniaca ... 1707. (Card 2)

bus revisae, & variis annotatis illustriores redditae. Quibus accedent Judicium physiologico-magico-medicum de viva jumentorum contagio infectorum contumulatione, & Observationes atque experimenta chymico-physica de prodigiis sanguinis, falsò hactenus proclamatis. Lipsiae, Apud haeredes F. Lanckisii, 1707.
6 p. l., 148, ₍16₎ p. 22cm.
(Continued on next card)

8

WITCHCRAFT
RC
340
W53
1707

D. Johannis-Caspari VVestphali, academici curiosi, Pathologia daemoniaca.
Westphal, Johann Caspar. ... Pathologia daemoniaca ... 1707. (Card 3)

The first section, subtitled Historia morbi & species facti, is German and Latin in double columns.

1. Nervous system--Diseases. 2. Demonomania. 3. Epilepsy. 4. Hysteria. I. Title: Pathologia daemoniaca.

8

Witchcraft
BF
1410
B42
Z69
no.17,
18

D. T. S. jr.
Den predikant D. Balthasar Becker, seediglyk ondersogt so in zyn persoon als Schriften, ofhy die derst voorgeven, buyten hem alleen, de gantsche werelt betovert te zyn, selfs hier af wel vry is, ende dat daar en boven op hem niet soude werken, de geest van hovaardye en dwalinge tot ergernisse en van de kleine, en van de arme, en van de verslagene van geest, en die beeven voor Godts woort. By een missive den 19 January 1692, door H.v.G. van Amsterdam geschreven aan
NIC
(Continued on next card)

Witchcraft
BF
1410
B42
Z69
no.17,
18

D. T. S. jr.
Den predikant D. Balthasar Becker ...
(Card 2)

D. T. S. de Jonge tot Uytrecht. Met zyn Andtwoord provisioneel tot nader berigt daar op gevolgt, den 4. February desselv jaars. Uytregt, Gedrukt by W. Jansz, 1692.
32, 36 p. 21cm.

Signatures: 4°: A-D4. 4°: A-D4, E2.
The Provisioneel Antwoord has
special half-title and separate
NIC (Continued on next card

130

CATALOGUE OF THE CORNELL WITCHCRAFT COLLECTION

D. T. S., jr.

Witchcraft
BF
1410
B42
Z69
no.17,
18

Den predikant D. Balthasar Becker ... 1692. (Card 3)

paging.
Van der Linde 63, 61.
"Extracten van ... De betoverde werelt, uytgetrokken en t'samengesteld door N. N.": p. 17-28 of the Provisioneel Antwoord; "Extract van 'tgepasseerde des Synodi tot Edam, 10. Aug. 1691. rakende D. Bekker ...": p. 28-29; "Articulen voor te stellen aan Do. B. Bekker" signed Leonardus

NIC

(Continued on next card)

D. T. S. jr.

Witchcraft
BF
1410
B42
Z69
No.17,
18

Den predikant D. Balthasar Becker ... 1692. (Card 4)

Groenewegen: p. 29-31; "Eerste aanbieding van D. B. Bekker, op den 30. Aug. 1691": p. 31; "Articulen tot satisfactie aan de Eerw. Classis van Amsterdam, van Do. Balthasar Bekker ... wegens ... de Betoverde wereld ...": p. 32-36.
Nos. 17 & 18 in a Collection of tracts against Balthasar Bekker and his Betoverde weereld.

NIC

(Continued on next card)

D'une sorcière qu'aultrefois on brusla dans Sainct-Nicholas.

Witchcraft
F
2582
7
N582

Badel, Émile, 1867-
D'une sorcière qu'aultrefois on brusla dans Sainct-Nicholas. Le tout habillé d'ymaiges [sic] par J. Jacquot. Nancy, Berger-Levrault, 1891.
227 p. illus. 22cm.

1. Nigal, Nicolle, d. 1582. 2. Witchcraft--France. I. Title.

D'Aban, Pierre.
see
Abano, Pietro d', 1250-1315?

D'Abano, Pietro, 1250-1315?
see
Abano, Pietro d', 1250-1315?

Dachselt, Michael, respondent.

HIST SCI
F
445
85

Posner, Caspar, praeses.
Diatribe physica De virunculis metallicis, quam...praeside...Casparo Posnero...publice ventilandam exhibet Michael Dachselt...Jenae, Literis Krebsianis, 1662.
[30] p. 20cm.

Diss.--Jena (M. Dachselt, respondent)

1. Apparitions. 2. Demonology. 3. Occult sciences. I. Dachselt, Michael, respondent. II. Title.

NIC

Die Dämonen und ihre Abwehr im Alten Testament.

WITCHCRAFT
BT
975
J61

Jirku, Anton, 1885-
Die Dämonen und ihre Abwehr im Alten Testament. Leipzig, A. Deichert, 1912.
viii, 99 p. 22cm.

"Literatur": p. [vii]-viii.

1. Demonology--Biblical teaching. I. Title.

8
NIC

Dämonenglaube im Lande der Bibel.

DS
42
M85
v.21

Canaan, Taufik.
Dämonenglaube im Lande der Bibel ... Leipzig, J. C. Hinrichs, 1929.
iv, 64 p. 25cm. (Morgenland; Darstellungen aus Geschichte und Kultur des Ostens. Hft. 21)

1. Demonology. 2. Folk-lore--Palestine. I. Title.

Daemones an sint.

Witchcraft
BF
1520
D94

Durastante, Giano Matteo, 16th cent.
Problemata Iani Matthaei Durastantis ... I. Daemones an sint, & an morborum sint causae, pro theologorum, philosophorum, & medicorum sententiis. II. An uirium imbecillitati iuncta cacochymia per epicrasim curanda sit. III. Et, an rhabarbarum ob lienterian, dysenterian, & astrictionem sit comburendum. Venetijs, Ex officina Stellae, Iordani Ziletti, 1567.
140 numb. l. 15cm.

8

(Continued on next card)

Daemones an sint.

Witchcraft
BF
1520
D94

Durastante, Giano Matteo, 16th cent. Problemata Iani Matthaei Durastantis ... 1567. (Card 2)

Printer's device on t. p. and verso of t. p.
With this is bound his De aceti scillini ... compositione. Venetiis, 1567.

1. Demonology. 2. Diseases--Causes and theories of causation. 3. Medicine--Early works to 1800. I. Title.

8

WITCHCRAFT
BF
1555
T54
1603

Daemoniaci.
Thyraeus, Pierre, 1546-1601.
Daemoniaci, hoc est: De obsessis a spiritibvs daemoniorvm hominibvs, liber vnvs. In qvo daemonvm obsidentivm conditio: obsessorum hominum status ... et his similia, discutiuntur et explicantur, denuò omnia repurgata et aucta. Avctore Petro Thyraeo ... Lvgdvni, Apvd Ioannem Pillehotte, 1603.
324, [4] p. 17cm.

Title vignette (device of J. Pillehotte)

WITCHCRAFT
BF
1555
T54
1627

Daemoniaci cum Locis infestis.
Thyraeus, Pierre, 1546-1601.
Daemoniaci cvm Locis infestis et terricvlamentis noctvrnis. Id est, libri tres, qvibvs spiritvvm homines obsidentium atque infestantium genera, conditiones, &, quas adferunt, molestiae, molestiarumq; causae atque modi explicantur ... Coloniae Agrippinae, Ex officina Choliniana, Sumptibus Petri Cholini, 1627.
20 p. l., 164, 356 p. 21cm.
Loca infesta also published separately.

8
NIC

(Continued on next card)

WITCHCRAFT
BF
1555
T54
1627

Daemoniaci cum Locis infestis.
Thyraeus, Pierre, 1546-1601. Daemoniaci cum Locis infestis et terricvlamentis noctvrnis ... 1627. (Card 2)

Daemoniaci first published 1694 under title: De daemoniacis.
1. Demoniac possession. 2. Demonology. 3. Apparitions. 4. Ghosts. I. His De daemoniacis. II. His Loca infesta. III. Title. IV. Title: Loca infesta.

8
NIC

Daemoniacs.

Witchcraft
BF
1565
F31
2 copies

Fell, John, 1735-1797.
Daemoniacs. An enquiry into the heathen and the Scripture doctrine of daemons. In which the hypotheses of the Rev. Mr. Farmer, and others on this subject, are particularly considered ... London, Printed for Charles Dilly, 1779.
xv, 432 p. 21cm.

1. Demoniac possession. 2. Farmer, Hugh, 1714-1787. I. Title.

Daemonis mimica, in magiae progressu.

WITCHCRAFT
BT
980
M77

Monteacuto, Henricus a.
Daemonis mimica, in magiae progressu, tum in sectis errorum quorum author est... Parisiis, Apud Claudium Rigaud, 1612.
410 p. 15cm.

8
NIC

1. Devil. 2. Oracles. 3. Magic. 4. Occult sciences. I. Title.

Das Dämonische.

WITCHCRAFT
BJ
1408
T57

Tillich, Paul, 1886-1965.
Das Dämonische. Ein Beitrag zur Sinndeutung der Geschichte. Tübingen, J. C. B. Mohr (P. Siebeck), 1926.
44 p. 24cm. (Sammlung gemeinverständlicher Vorträge und Schriften aus dem Gebiet der Theologie und Religionsgeschichte, 119)
"... [ein] Aufsatz, der zwei Vorträge und einiges sonstige Material vereinigt ..."
1. Good and evil. 2. History--Philosophy. I. Title.

8
NIC

Dämonische Besessenheit.

WITCHCRAFT
BS
2545
D5
T12

Taczak, Teodor, 1878-
Dämonische Besessenheit. Ein Kapitel aus der katholischen Lehre von der Herrschaft des Fursten der Sünde und des Todes. Von Theodor Taczak, Priester der Erzdiözese Gnesen-Posen. Münster i. W., Druck der Westfälischen Vereinsdruckerei [1903]
61, [4] p. 23cm.
Inaug.-diss.--Münster.
Contents.--Begriff und Tatsache der dämonischen Besessenheit.--Stellung der pro-

8
NIC

(Continued on next card)

Dämonische Besessenheit.

WITCHCRAFT
BS
2545
D5
T12

Taczak, Teodor, 1878- . Dämonische Besessenheit ... [1903] (Card 2)

Contents--Continued.
testantischen Theologie zur Besessenheit.--Besessenheit und Besessenheitswahn.

1. Demoniac possession. 2. Devil. 3. Theology, Doctrinal. I. Title.

8
NIC

CATALOGUE OF THE CORNELL WITCHCRAFT COLLECTION

Das Dämonische in Jahwe.

WITCHCRAFT
BM
610
V94

Volz, Paul, 1871-
Das Dämonische in Jahwe ... Vortrag auf dem Alttestamentlertag in München. Tübingen, J. C. B. Mohr (P. Siebeck), 1924.
41 p. 24cm. (Sammlung gemeinverständlicher Vorträge und Schriften aus dem Gebiet der Theologie und Religionsgeschichte 110)
1. God (Judaism) 2. God--Attributes. I. Title.

8

Die Dämonischen des Neuen Testaments.

Witchcraft
BS
2545
D5
H13

Hafner, Georg.
Die Dämonischen des Neuen Testaments. Ein Vortrag gehalten und dem Verein der Deutschen Irrenärzte gewidmet. Frankfurt a. M., K. Brechert, 1894.
33 p. 22cm.

1. Demoniac possession. 2. Bible. N. T.--Commentaries. 3. Bible--Psychology. I. Title.

Die dämonistischen Krankheiten im finnischen Volksaberglauben.

WITCHCRAFT
R
133
M28

Manninen, Ilmari, 1894-1935.
Die dämonistischen Krankheiten im finnischen Volksaberglauben; vergleichende volksmedizinische Untersuchung. Akademische Abhandlung. Loviisa, Loviisan Sanomain Osakeyhtion Kirjapaino, 1922.
253 p. 22cm.

Bibliography: p. 228-251.

1. Medicine, Magic, mystic and spagiric. 2. Folk medicine--Finland. 3. Demonology.

8
NIC

Daemonolatreiae libri tres.

Witchcraft
BF
1520
R38
1596

Remi, Nicolas, 1530-1612.
Daemonolatreiae libri tres. Nicolai Remigii... ex iudiciis capitalibus DCCCC. plus minus hominum, qui sortilegii crimen intra annos XV. in Lotharingia capite luerunt. Miris ac iucundis narrationibus, variarum naturalium quaestionum ac mysteriorum daemonicorum discussionibus, valde suaues & grati, adque sales mouendos inprimis apti. Francofvrti, in officina Palthenii, 1596.
12 p. l., 407 p. 14½cm.
First edition. Lugduni, 1595.

Daemonolatria, oder: Beschreibung von Zauberern und Zauberinnen.

Witchcraft
BF
1520
R38
1693

Remi, Nicolas, 1530-1612.
Nicolai Remigii Daemonolatria, oder: Beschreibung von Zauberern und Zauberinnen. Mit wunderl. Erzehlungen, vielen natürlichen Fragen und teuflis. Geheimnissen vermischet. 1. Theil. Der ander Theil hält in sich: Wunder-seltzame Historien von des Teuffels Hinterlist, Betrug, Falschheit und Verführungen, an, bey und umb den Menschen ... Mit einem Anhange. Von falschen, erdichteten ... gespenstischen Begebenheiten.

8 (Continued on next card)

Daemonolatria, oder: Beschreibung von Zauberern und Zauberinnen.

Witchcraft
BF
1520
R38
1693

Remi, Nicolas, 1530-1612. Daemonolatria, oder: Beschreibung von Zauberern und Zauberinnen. 1693. (Card 2)

Hamburg, Gedruckt bey T. von Wiering, 1693.
5 p. l., 288, 544, 96 p. 8 plates. 18cm.
Part 2 has title: Der bösen Geister und Gespenstes wunder-seltzame Historien ...
Part 3 has title: Der Gespensten Gauckel-Wercks dritter Theil ...

8 (Continued on next card)

Daemonolatria, oder: Beschreibung von Zauberern und Zauberinnen.

Witchcraft
BF
1520
R38
1693

Remi, Nicolas, 1530-1612. Daemonolatria, oder: Beschreibung von Zauberern und Zauberinnen. 1693. (Card 3)

Translation of his Daemonolatreiae libri tres.

1. Demonology. 2. Witchcraft--Lorraine. I. Title: Daemonolatria, oder: Beschreibung von Zauberern und Zauberinnen. II. His Dae monolatreiae libri tres --German.

8

Daemonologia.

WITCHCRAFT
BF
1555
E33

Ehinger, Christoph.
Daemonologia; oder, Etwas Neues vom Teufel. Das ist: Wahrhaffter historischer Bericht, von einem sonder- und wunderbaren Casu, Anfechtungs-Fall, und satanischer Versuchung, mit welcher, auss Gottes Verhängnuss, ein Burger, und Schuhmacher in Augspurg, etliche Jahr yexiret, und geplaget worden ... Augspurg, In Verlegung Gottlieb Göbels, Druckts Jacob Koppmayr, 1681.
12 p. l., 208 p. 16cm.

1. Demoniac possession. 2. Devil. I. Title.

8

Daemonologia.

Witchcraft
BF
1520
S32

Scherzer, Johann Adam, praeses.
Daemonologia sive Duae disputationes theologicae de malis angelis ... praeside ... Dno. Joh. Adamo Scherzero ... nunc vero conjunctim editae à M. Christiano Trautmanno ... Lipsiae, Literis Spörelianis, 1672.
[64] p. 19cm. (bound in 21cm. vol.)
With this are bound Schwartz, Johann Conrad, 1677-1747. Dissertatio theologica De usu et praestantia daemonum. Altdorfii

8 (Continued on next card)

Daemonologia.

Witchcraft
BF
1520
S32

Scherzer, Johann Adam, praeses. Daemonologia ... 1672. (Card 2)

Noric. [1715], and Breithaupt, Christian, 1689-1749, praeses. Commentatio secunda De existentia daemonum. Helmstadii [1722]
In vol. lettered Dissertationes de daemonibus. 1672-1722.

1. Demonology. 2. Angels. I. Trautmann, Christian, respondent. II. Title.

8

Daemonologia.

WITCHCRAFT
BF
1565
T68
1623

Torreblanca Villalpando, Francisco.
Daemonologia sive De magia natvrali, daemoniaca, licita, & illicita, deq; aperta & occulta, interuentione & inuocatione daemonis libri quatuor ... Avctore Don Francisco Torreblanca Villalpando Cordvbensi ... Nunc cum summariis capitum, rerumq́ indice iuris publici facti. Mogvntiae, Impensis Ioh. Theowaldi Schönwetteri, 1623.
12 p. l., 632, [42], 76 p. 22cm.

8 (Continued on next card)

Daemonologia.

WITCHCRAFT
BF
1565
T68
1623

Torreblanca Villalpando, Francisco. Daemonologia sive De magia ... 1623. (Card 2)

"Defensa en favor de los libros catolicos de la magia" separately paged.
Title in engraved illustrated border.
Provenance: Monast. S. Michaelis Archang. Bamberg.
Binding: contemporary blind stamped pigskin.

8 (Continued on next card)

Daemonologia: a discourse on witchcraft.

BF
1581
F16
1882

Fairfax, Edward, d. 1635.
Daemonologia: a discourse on witchcraft as it was acted in the family of Mr. Edward Fairfax, of Fuyston, in the county of York, in the year 1621; along with the only two eclogues of the same author known to be in existence. With a biographical introduction, and notes topographical & illustrative. By William Grainge. Harrogate, R. Ackrill, 1882.
2 p. l., v p., 1 l., [9]-189 p. 21cm.

Daemonologia sacra.

Witchcraft
BF
1546
G48

[Gilpin, Richard]
Daemonologia sacra: or, A treatise of Satans temptations ... By R. G. ... London, Printed by J. D. for R. Randel and P. Maplisden, 1677.
3 pts. in 1 v. 20cm.

1. Devil. I. Title. II. Title: Satans temptations. III. G., R. IV. R. G.

Dämonologie.

Witchcraft
BF
1523
E35

Einzinger von Einzing, Johann Martin Maximilian, 1725-1798.
Dämonologie; oder, Systematische Abhandlung von der Natur und Macht des Teufels, von den Kennzeichen, eine verstellte oder eingebildete Besitznehmung des Teufels von einer wahren am leichtesten zu unterscheiden, sammt den natürlichsten Mitteln, die meisten Gespenster am sichersten zu vertreiben, dem Gassnerischen Teufelssysteme entgegengesetzt. [Leipzig?] 1775.

(Continued on next card)

Dämonologie.

Witchcraft
BF
1523
E35

Einzinger von Einzing, Johann Martin Maximilian, 1725-1798. Dämonologie. [Leipzig?] 1775. (Card 2)

140 p. 18cm.

With this is bound Thomasius, C. Gelehrte Streitschrift von dem Verbrechen der Zauber- und Hexerey. Leipzig, 1775.

1. Gassner, Johann Joseph, 1727-1779. I. Title.

Dämonologie.

BF
1521
J28
1924

James I, king of Great Britain, 1566-1625.
King James, the First: Daemonologie (1597). Newes from Scotland, declaring the damnable life and death of Doctor Fian, a notable sorcerer who was burned at Edenbrough in Ianuary last (1591) London, J. Lane; New York, Dutton [1924]
xv, 81, 29 p. illus. 19cm. (The Bodley head quartos, no. 9)
With facsimiles of original title pages.
Newes from Scotland has been ascribed to James Carmichael, minister of

(Continued on next card)

Dämonologie.

BF
1521
J28
1924

James I, king of Great Britain, 1566-1625. King James, the First: Daemonologie. [1924] (Card 2)

Haddington. Cf. Sir James Melville, Memories, p. 195, and D. Webster, Collection of tracts on witchcraft, etc., 1820, p. 38.

1. Demonology. 2. Magic. 3. Witchcraft--Scotland. 4. Fian, John, d. 1591. I. Harrison, George Bagshawe, 1894- ed II. Carmichael, James, d. 1628, supposed author. III. Title: Daemonologi IV. Title: Newes from Scotland.

CATALOGUE OF THE CORNELL WITCHCRAFT COLLECTION

Daemonologie and theologie.

Witchcraft
BF
1517
H7
76

Homes, Nathaniel.
Daemonologie and theologie. The first, the malady, demonstrating the diabolicall arts, and devillish hearts of men. The second, the remedy, demonstrating God, a rich supply of all good. London, Printed by T. Roycroft, and are to be sold by J. Martin and J. Ridley, 1650.
208, 31 p. 15cm.

The second part has special t.p.
With bookplate of Sir William Grace, bart.
I. Title.

Daemonologische fragmenten of byvoegzels tot de Oudheid- en geneeskundige verhandeling.

Witchcraft
BF
528
R9
58

Rütz, Franz Georg Christoph.
Daemonologische fragmenten of byvoegzels tot de Oudheid- en geneeskundige verhandeling van den heer professor Theod. Gerhard Timmermann, over de daemonische menschen, waarvan in de geschiedverhaalen der Evangelien gewaagd wordt. Opgesteld en in 't licht gegeeven door F. G. C. Rütz ... Haarlem, By Plaat en Loosjes, 1789-90.
2 v. in 1. 22cm.

Vol. 2 has imprint: 'sGravenhage, by J. C. Leeuwestyn, 1790.

(Continued on next card)

Daemonomagia.

Witchcraft
BF
520
E42

Elich, Philipp Ludwig.
Daemonomagia; siue Libellvs ἐρωτηματικός, de daemonis caeurgia, cacomagorum et lamiarum energiâ... Francoforti, Prelo Richteriano, Impensâ verò Conradi Nebenii, 1607.
213, [6] p. 17cm.

Device of C. Nebenius on t. p. and on recto of last leaf.
Colophon: Francoforti, Ex Typographeio Wolfgangi Richteri, Sumptibus verò
(Continued on next card)

Daemonomagia.

Witchcraft
BF
1520
E42

Elich, Philipp Ludwig. Daemonomagi... 1607. (Card 2)

Conradi Nebenii.
Armorial bookplate: Ex Bibliotheca Gerardi Schimmelpfenninck Jani. F.

1. Demonology. 2. Demonomania. 3. Magic. 4. Witchcraft. I. Title.

Dämonomagie.

Witchcraft
BF
523
H1

Horst, Georg Conrad, 1767-1838?
Dämonomagie, oder Geschichte des Glaubens an Zauberei und dämonische Wunder, mit besonderer Berücksichtigung des Hexenprocesses seit den Zeiten Innocentius des Achten. Nebst einer ausführlichen, nach Inquisitionsacten bearbeiteten Beschreibung des Hexenthurms zu Lindheim in der Wetterau ... Mit Kupfern. Frankfurt am Main, bei den Gebrüdern Wilmans, 1818.
2 v. fold. plates. 20cm.
I. Title. II. Title: Geschichte des Glaubens an Zauberei und dämonische Wunder.

Daemonomania.

Witchcraft
BF
1520
B66
1698

Bodin, Jean, 1530-1596.
Daemonomania; oder, Ausführliche Erzehlung des wütenden Teuffels in seinen damahligen rasenden Hexen und Hexenmeistern dero Bezauberungen, Beschwerungen, Vergifftungen, Gauckel- und Possen-Wercke... Welches der andere Theil Nicolai Remigii Daemonolatria. Wobey gleichfalls angehänget: Vielerhand warhaftige und erschreckliche Geschichte besessener Leute...nebst noch einigen betrieglichen und von Menschen
(Continued on next card)

Daemonomania.

Witchcraft
BF
1520
B66
1698

Bodin, Jean, 1530-1596. Daemonomania. 1698. (Card 2)

practicirten kurtzweiligen Begenheiten. Hamburg, Gedruckt bey T. von Wiering, 1698.
2 v. in 1. plates. 18cm.

"Wiederlegung nebst der Schrifft des Hn. Weyer": v. 1, p. [400]-465.
Translation of De la démonomanie.

Daemonomania Pistoriana.

Witchcraft
BF
1520
P67

Pistorius, Johann, 1546-1608.
Daemonomania Pistoriana. Magica et cabalistica morborum curandorum ratio, à Ioanne Pistorio Niddano ... ex lacunis iudaicis ac gentilitiis hausta, post christianis proprinata. Cum antidoto prophylactico Iacobi Heilbronneri... Lauingae, typis Palatinis, 1601.
26 p. l., 1934 p. 16½cm.

Daemonum investigatio peripatetica.

History of Science
QL
666
.06A11

Cesalpino, Andrea, 1519-1603.
Daemonvm investigatio peripatetica. In qua explicatur locus Hippocratis Progn. Si quid diuinum in morbis habetur. Florentiae, Apud Iuntas, 1580.
24 l. 21cm.

Title vignette: Giunta's device; repeated at end in variant form.
Bound with Abati, Baldo Angelo. De admirabili viperae natvra ... Vrbini, 1589.

Witchcraft
BF
1520
D12

Daemonvrgia [i.e. daemonurgia] theologice expensa, sev De potestate daemonvm in rebvs hvmanis, deqve potestate in daemones a Christo ecclesiae relicta. [n. p.] 1776.
4 p. l., 232, [8] p. 24cm.

Printed in England?

1. Demonology. 2. Exorcism. 3. Witchcraft. I. Title: De potestate daemonum in rebus humanis.

8

Witchcraft
BF
1566
D13

Dahl, Jürgen.
Nachtfrauen und Galsterweiber; eine Naturgeschichte der Hexe. [Ebenhausen bei München] Langewiesche-Brandt [1960]
96 p. illus. 19 cm.

1. Witchcraft. I. Title.

Michigan. State Univ. Library
for Library of Congress
A 61-2068

Witchcraft
BF
1584
D4
D13

Dahlerup, Verner, 1859-1938.
Hexe og Hexeprocesser i Danmark. Et Foredrag holdt i Foreningen til Oplysningens Fremme blandt Kjøbenhavns Arbejdere. Kjobenhavn, Studentersamfundets Forlag, 1888.
22 p. 22cm. (Studentersamfundets Smaaskrifter, Nr. 80)

1. Witchcraft--Denmark. 2. Trials (Witchcraft)--Denmark. I. Title. II. Series: Studentersamfundet, Copenhagen. Skrifter. Nr. 80.

Daillon, Benjamin de.

Witchcraft
BF
1410
B42
Z76
1692

Brief ... over sijn gevoelen van de eenheit des duyvels.
Leydekker, Melchior, 1642-1721.
Historische en theologische Redeneringe, over het onlangs uitgegeve Boek van ... Balthasar Bekker, strekkende tot bevestinge der Waarheit en Authoriteit van de H. Schriftuur. Uit het Latijn overgebragt, engeschikt na het begrip van den Nederduitschen Leser. Waar achter gevoegt is een Brief van de Hr. D'Aillon, wegens sijn gevoelen van de Eenheit des Duyvels, geschreven uit London, den 16 Decemb.

NIC (Continued on next card)

Daillon, Benjamin de.

Witchcraft
BF
1410
B42
Z76
1692

Brief ... over sijn gevoelen van de eenheit des duyvels.
Leydekker, Melchior, 1642-1721. Historische en theologische Redeneringe ... (Card 2)

1691. Utregt, By de Weduwe van W. Clerck, 1692.
64, 8 p. 20cm.

Van der Linde 127.

NIC (Continued on next card)

Daillon, Benjamin de.

Witchcraft
BF
1410
B42
Z69
no.27, 28

Brief ... over sijn gevoelen van de eenheit des duyvels.
Leydekker, Melchior, 1642-1721.
Historische en theologische Redeneringe, over het onlangs uitgegeve Boek van ... Balthasar Bekker, strekkende tot bevestinge der Waarheit en Authoriteit van de H. Schriftuur. Uit het Latijn overgebragt, engeschikt na het begrip van den Nederduitschen Leser. Waar achter gevoegt is een Brief van de Hr. D'Aillon, wegens sijn gevoelen van de Eenheit des Duyvels, geschreven uit London, den 16 Decemb.

NIC (Continued on next card)

Daillon, Benjamin de.

Witchcraft
BF
1410
B42
Z69
no.27, 28

Brief ... over sijn gevoelen van de eenheit des duyvels.
Leydekker, Melchior, 1642-1721. Historische en theologische Redeneringe ... (Card 2)

1691. Utregt, By de Weduwe van W. Clerck, 1692.
64, 8 p. 21cm.

Van der Linde 127, 75.
No. 28 has half-title only.
No. 27, 28 in a Collection of tracts against Balthasar Bekker and his Betoverde weereld.

NIC (Continued on next card)

Daillon, Benjamin de.

Witchcraft
BF
1410
B42
Z56
v.3
no.5

Examen de l'opression des reformez en France--Selections--Dutch.
Daillon, Benjamin de.
Omstandig bewys, dat de daemones overgeset duyvelen, geen quade geesten, maar zielen van menschen geweest zijn de welke op de werelt rechtvaardigh geleeft hadden, en dat de selve naar het gevoelen van d'oude heydenen, hare woonsteede in 't oppersste en zuyverste deel van de lucht gehadt hebben, en ook middelaars tusschen de goden en menschen geweest zijn. Als ook datter maar eene duyvel of Satan is. Welk gevoelen met dat van d'Heer Predikant Bekker, in sijn boek De betoverde

8 (Continued on next card)

Daillon, Benjamin de.

Witchcraft
BF
1410
B42
Z56
v.3
no.5

Examen de l'opression des reformez en France--Selections--Dutch.
Daillon, Benjamin de. Omstandig bewys, dat de daemones overgeset duyvelen ... 1692. (Card 2)

wereld genaamt vervat, over een stemt. Getrokken uyt de schriften van d'Heer Daillon frans predikant. Gravenhage, By M. Uytwerf, boekverkooper, 1692.
2 p. l., 43 p. [p. 44 blank] title vignette, illus. initial. 21 x 15cm.
4°: π², A-E⁴, E².

8 (Continued on next card)

CATALOGUE OF THE CORNELL WITCHCRAFT COLLECTION

Witchcraft
BF
1410
B42
Z56
v.3
no.5

Daillon, Benjamin de.
  Examen de l'opression des reformez en
  France--Selections--Dutch.
  Daillon, Benjamin de. Omstandig bewys, dat
    de daemones overgeset duyvelen ... 1692.
                                            (Card 3)

  Black letter.
  Translation of selections from his Examen
de l'opression des reformez en France ... avec
l'explication de la doctrine des demons.
Amsterdam, 1691.
  Selections chosen to support Bekker's
views in De betoverde weereld.
  Van der Lin   de 74.

8   (Continued on next card)

Witchcraft
BF
1410
B42
Z56
v.3
no.5

Daillon, Benjamin de.
  Examen de l'opression des reformez en
  France--Selections--Dutch.
  Daillon, Benjamin de. Omstandig bewys, dat
    de daemones overgeset duyvelen ... 1692.
                                            (Card 3)

  Black letter.
  Translation of selections from his Examen
de l'opression des reformez en France ... avec
l'explication de la doctrine des demons.
Amsterdam, 1691.
  Selections chosen to support Bekker's
views in De betoverde weereld.
  Van der Lin   de 74.

8   (Continued on next card)

Witchcraft
BF
1505
D13

Daimonologia.
  Daillon, Jacques, ca. 1634-1726. Δαιμονο-
    λογία.   (Card 2)

  Printed for the author, 1723.
    182 p. 19cm.
    Ex libris Lord Hill.
  A Preface, consisting of eight pages,
numbered iii-x, is inserted between the
t.p. and p. v.
  With this is bound his The ax laid to
the root of popery. [London? 1721?]

Witchcraft
BF
1410
B42
Z56
v.3
no.5

Daillon, Benjamin de.
  Examen de l'opression des reformez en
  France--Selections--Dutch.
  Daillon, Benjamin de. Omstandig bewys, dat
    de daemones overgeset duyvelen ... 1692.
                                            (Card 4)

  No. 5 in vol. lettered Bekker III.

  1. Devil. 2. Bekker, Balthasar, 1634-
1698. De betoverde weereld. I. His
Examen de l'opression des reformez en France
...Selections--Dutch. II. Title.

8

Witchcraft
BF
1410
B42
Z56
v.3
no.5

Daillon, Benjamin de.
  Examen de l'opression des reformez en
  France--Selections--Dutch.
  Daillon, Benjamin de. Omstandig bewys, dat
    de daemones overgeset duyvelen ... 1692.
                                            (Card 4)

  No. 5 in vol. lettered Bekker III.

  1. Devil. 2. Bekker, Balthasar, 1634-
1698. De betoverde weereld. I. His
Examen de l'opression des reformez en France
...Selections--Dutch. II. Title.

8

Witchcraft
BF
1611
D75

Daimonomageia.
  [Drage, William] 1637?-1669.
    Daimonomageia. A small treatise of
  sicknesses and diseases from witchcraft
  and supernatural causes. Never before,
  at least in this comprised order and general manner, was the like published. Being
  useful to others besides physicians, in
  that it confutes atheistical, sadducistical,
  and sceptical principles and imaginations.
  London, Printed by J. Dover, 1665.
    [43] p. 20cm.

                     (Continued on next card)

Witchcraft
BF
1410
B42
Z82
no.2

Daillon, Benjamin de.
  Examen de l'opression des reformez en
  France ...
  Hamer, Petrus, 1646-1716.
    Voorlooper tot de volstrekte wederlegginge
  van het gene de heeren, Orchard, Daillon en
  Bekker hebben aen het licht gebragt; aengaende de werken, en macht der geesten: en
  met name der duivelen. Door Petrus Hamer,
  dienaer Jesus Christi in Numansdorp. Uitgegeven na kerken-ordre. Met belofte refutatoir van zekeren Brief aen een regent van
  Amsteldam. Dato 18 Maij 1692. Dordrecht,
  By C. Wilgaarts,   boekverkooper, 1692.
    4 p. l., 40   p. title vignette, illus.

8   (Continued on next card)

Witchcraft
BF
1505
D13

  Daillon, Jacques, ca. 1634-1726.
    Δαιμονολογία; or, A treatise of
  spirits. Wherein several places of Scripture are expounded, against the vulgar errors concerning witchcraft, apparitions, &c.
  To which is added, an appendix, containing
  some reflections on Mr. Boulton's answer to
  Dr. Hutchinson's Historical essay; entitled
  The possibility and reality of magick, sorcery and witchcraft demonstrated. London,

                  Title transliterated:
                     Daimonología.
                 (Continued on next card)

Witchcraft
BF
1611
D75

Daimonomageia.
  [Drage, William] 1637?-1669. Daimonomageia.
    1665.   (Card 2)

  Imperfect: lacks all after p. 32.
  Wing D 2117.
  Bound with his A physical nosonomy.
London, 1664.

  1. Medicine, Magic, mystic and spagiric.
I. Title.

Witchcraft
BF
1410
B42
Z82
no.2

Daillon, Benjamin de.
  Examen de l'opression des reformez en
  France ...
  Hamer, Petrus, 1646-1716. Voorlooper tot
  de volstrekte wederlegginge van... Orchard,
  Daillon en Bekker ... 1692. (Card 2)

  initials. 20 x 15cm.
  4°: *⁴, A-E⁴.
  Van der Linde 95.
  No. 2 in vol. lettered Over Bekkers Beto-
verde wereld. 1692.
  1. Orchard, N   , supposed author.
The doctrine of   devils. 2. Daillon,
Benjamin de.   Examen de l'opression

8   (Continued on next card)

Witchcraft
BF
1505
D13

  Daillon, Jacques, ca. 1634-1726. Δαιμονο-
    λογία.   (Card 2)

  Printed for the author, 1723.
    182 p. 19cm.
    Ex libris Lord Hill.
  A Preface, consisting of eight pages,
numbered iii-x, is inserted between the
t.p. and p. v.
  With this is bound his The ax laid to
the root of popery. [London? 1721?]

                     (Continued on next card)

Witchcraft
BF
1761
D13

  Dale, Antonius van, 1638-1708.
    Antonii van Dale M. D. De oraculis ethnicor
  dissertationes duae: quarum prior de ipsorum
  duratione ac defectu, posterior de eorundem
  auctoribus. Accedit et schediasma de consecrationibus ethnicis. Amstelaedami, apud Henricum
  & viduam Theodori Boom, 1683.
    16 p. l., 510, [15] p. fold. pl. 17cm.

  Added t.-p. engr.
  1. Oracles. I. Title.

Witchcraft
BF
1410
B42
Z56
v.3
no.5

  Daillon, Benjamin de.
    Omstandig bewys, dat de daemones overgeset
  duyvelen, geen quade geesten, maar zielen van
  menschen geweest zijn de welke op de werelt
  rechtvaardigh geleeft hadden, en dat de selve
  naar het gevoelen van d'oude heydenen, hare
  woonsteede in 't opperste en zuyverste deel
  van de lucht gehadt hebben, en ook middelaars
  tusschen de goden en menschen geweest zijn.
  Als ook datter maar eene duyvel of Satan is.
  Welk gevoelen met dat van d'Heer Predikant
  Bekker, in si   jn boek De betoverde

8   (Continued on next card)

Witchcraft
BF
1505
D13

  Daillon, Jacques, ca. 1634-1726. Δαιμονολογία.
    1723.   (Card 3)

  1. Boulton, Richard, fl. 1699-1724. The
possibility and reality of magick. 2.
Hutchinson, Francis, bp. of Down and Connor,
1660-1739. An historical essay concerning
witchcraft. I. Title. II. Title: A treatise
of spirits.

                 (Continued on next card)

WITCHCRAFT
BF
1761
D13
1700

Dale, Antonius van, 1638-1708.
  De oraculis ethnicorum.
  Dale, Antonius van, 1638-1708.
    Antonii van Dale ... De oraculis vete-
  rum ethnicorum dissertationes duae, quarum
  nunc prior agit de eorum origine atque auctoribus; secunda de ipsorum duratione &
  interitu. Editio secunda plurimum adaucta;
  cui de novo accedunt dissertatiunculae I.
  De statua Simoni Mago ... II. De actis
  Pilati disseritur ... III. Schediasma de
  consecrationibus ... Amstelodami, Apud
  Henricum & vid   uam Theodori Boom, 1700.

8   (Continued on next card)

Witchcraft
BF
1410
B42
Z56
v.3
no.5

  Daillon, Benjamin de. Omstandig bewys, dat
    de daemones overgeset duyvelen ... 1692.
                                            (Card 2)

  wereld genaamt vervat, over een stemt. Getrokken uyt de schriften van d'Heer Daillon
frans predikant. Gravenhage, By M. Uytwerf,
boekverkooper, 1692.
  2 p. l., 43 p. [p. 44 blank] title
vignette, illus. initial. 21 x 15cm.
  4°: π², A-E⁴, E².

8   (Continued on next card)

Witchcraft
BF
1505
D13

Daimonologia.
  Daillon, Jacques, ca. 1634-1726.
    Δαιμονολογία; or, A treatise of
  spirits. Wherein several places of Scripture are expounded, against the vulgar errors concerning witchcraft, apparitions, &c.
  To which is added, an appendix, containing
  some reflections on Mr. Boulton's answer to
  Dr. Hutchinson's Historical essay; entitled
  The possibility and reality of magick, sorcery and witchcraft demonstrated. London,

                  Title transliterated:
                     Daimonología.
                 (Continued on next card)

WITCHCRAFT
BF
1761
D13
1700

Dale, Antonius van, 1638-1708.
  De oraculis ethnicorum.
  Dale, Antonius van, 1638-1708. ... De
  oraculis veterum ethnicorum dissertationes
  duae ... 1700.   (Card 2)

    12 p. l., 694, [14] p. 8 fold. plates.
22cm.
  Title in red and black.
  First published 1683 under title: ... De
oraculis ethnicorum.
  1. Oracles. II. Title: De oraculis
veterum ethni   corum.

8

CATALOGUE OF THE CORNELL WITCHCRAFT COLLECTION

```
           Dale, Antonius van, 1638-1708.
             De oraculis ethnicorum.
WITCHCRAFT
BF       Fontenelle, Bernard Le Bovier de, 1657-1757.
1761       Histoire des oracles. Nouvelle édition
F68      augmentée.  Londres, Aux depens de Paul &
1707     Isaak Vaillant, 1707.
           119, [1] p. front. 17cm.
           Title in red and black.
           Rifacimento of A. van Dale's De oraculis
         ethnicorum dissertationes duae, Amstelaeda-
         mi, 1683.
           I. Dale, Antonius van, 1638-1708. De
         oraculis ethnicorum. II. Title.
```

```
           Dale, Antonius van, 1638-1708.
             De oraculis ethnicorum.
WITCHCRAFT
BF       Fontenelle, Bernard Le Bovier de, 1657-1757.
1761       The history of oracles, in two disserta-
F68      tions. Wherein are proved, I. That the ora-
1753     cles were not given out by daemons ... II.
         That the oracles did not cease at the com-
         ing of Jesus Christ ... Translated from
         the best edition of the original French.
         Glasgow, Printed by R. Urie, 1753.
           x, 144, [2] p. 17cm.
           Translation of Histoire des oracles, a
         rifacimento of A. van Dale's De oraculis
         ethnicorum           dissertationes duae, Am-
         stelaedami,          1683.
```

```
           Dale, Antonius van, 1638-1708.
             De oraculis ethnicorum.
BF       Baltus, Jean François, 1667-1743.
1761       Réponse à l'histoire des oracles, de Mr.
F682     de Fontenelle. Dans laquelle on réfute le
         système de Mr. Van-Dale, sur les auteurs des
         oracles du paganisme, sur la cause & le temps
         de leur silence; & où l'on établit le senti-
         ment des Pères de l'Eglise sur le même sujet.
         Strasbourg, J. R. Doulssecker, 1707.
           [42], 374, [13] p. front. 18cm.

           1. Fontenelle, Bernard Le Bovier de, 1657-
         1757. Histoire    des oracles. 2. Oracles.
         3. Dale, Anto   nius van, 1638-1708.
         De oraculis ethnicorum.
```

```
WITCHCRAFT
BF       Dale, Antonius van, 1638-1708.
1761       Antonii van Dale ... De oraculis vete-
D13      rum ethnicorum dissertationes duae, quarum
1700     nunc prior agit de eorum origine atque auc-
         toribus; secunda de ipsorum duratione &
         interitu. Editio secunda plurimum adaucta;
         cui de novo accedunt dissertatiunculae I.
         De statua Simoni Mago ... II. De actis
         Pilati disseritur ... III. Schediasma de
         consecrationibus ... Amstelodami, Apud
         Henricum & vid    uam Theodori Boom, 1700.

8                  (Continued on next card)
```

```
WITCHCRAFT
BF       Dale, Antonius van, 1638-1708.  ... De
1761     oraculis veterum ethnicorum dissertationes
D13      duae ... 1700.             (Card 2)
1700
           12 p. l., 694, [14] p. 8 fold. plates.
         22cm.
           Title in red and black.
           First published 1683 under title: ... De
         oraculis ethnicorum.
           1. Oracles.   II. Title: De oraculis
         veterum ethni      corum. III. Title.
         IV. His De or   aculis ethnicorum.
```

```
         Dale, Antonius van, 1638-1708.
           Antonii van Dale ... Dissertationes de
         origine ac progressu idololatriae et super-
         stitionum: de vera ac falsa prophetia; uti
         et de divinationibus idololatricis judaeorum.
         Amstelodami, Apud H. & viduam T. Boom,
         1696.
           26 p. l., 762, [13] p. 22cm.
           Parts 2 and 3 have own half titles.
           With armorial bookplate of Francesco Var-
         gas Macciucca.
                             (Continued on next card)
```

```
Witchcraft
BL       Dale, Antonius van, 1638-1708. Antonii
75       van Dale ... Dissertationes de origine
D13      ac progressu idololatriae ...  1696.
                                       (Card 2)

           1. Superstition. 2. Idols and images
         --Worship. 3. Prophets. 4. Divination.
         I. Title: Dissertationes de origine ac
         progressu idololatriae.

8
```

```
Witchcraft
BF       Dale, Antonius van, 1638-1708.
1410       Lasteringen van Jakob Koelman, in zijn
B42      zoo genaamde wederlegging van B. Bekkers Be-
Z56      tooverde wereld, zediglijk aangewesen in een
v.2      brief van Antony van Dale, med. doctor. Aan
no.14    zijnen vrind. Rotterdam, By I. van Ruynen,
         boekverkooper, 1692.
           15, [1] p. title vignette, illus. initial.
         19 x 15cm.
           4°: A-B⁴.
           Van der Lin       de 124.
           No. 14 in          vol. lettered Bekker II.

8                       (Continued on next card)
```

```
Witchcraft
BF       Dale, Antonius van, 1638-1708.  Lasteringen
1410     van Jakob Koelman ... 1692.    (Card 2)
B42
Z56        1. Koelman, Jacobus, 1632-1695. Weder-
v.2      legging van B. Bekkers Betoverde wereldt.
no.14    2. Bekker, Balthasar, 1634-1698. De beto-
         verde wereld. I. Title.
```

```
WITCHCRAFT
BF       Dale, Antonius van, 1638-1708.
1410       Lasteringen van Jakob Koelman, in zijn zoo
B42      genaamde wederlegging van B. Bekkers Be-
Z69      tooverde wereld, zediglijk aangewesen in een
no.32    brief van Antony van Dale, med. doctor. Aan
         zijnen vrind.  Rotterdam, By I. van Ruynen,
         boekverkooper, 1692.
           15, [1] p. title vignette, illus.
         initial. 21cm.

           No. 32 in a Collection of tracts against
         Balthasar Bek     ker and his Betoverde
8        weereld.
NIC                     (Continued on next card)
```

```
WITCHCRAFT
BF       Dale, Antonius van, 1638-1708.  Lasteringen
1410     van Jakob Koelman...1692.   (Card 2)
B42
Z69        1. Koelman, Jacobus, 1632-1695. Weder-
no.32    legging van B. Bekkers Betoverde wereldt.
         2. Bekker, Balthasar, 1634-1698. De beto-
         verde wereld. I. Title.


8
NIC
```

```
             Dalmas, Jean Baptiste.
               Géologie et astronomie.
Witchcraft
BF       Dalmas, Jean Baptiste.
1582       Les sorcières du Vivarais devant les
D14      inquisiteurs de la foi.  Privas, Typo-
         graphie et lithographie de Ph. Guiremand,
         1865.
           251 p. port. 22cm.
           Bound in at end "Géologie et astronomie",
         signed by Dalmas, 8 p.
           1. Witchcraft--Vivarais, France.  I.
         Title. II. His            Géologie et astronomie.
         III. Géologie et          astronomie.
```

```
Witchcraft
BF       Dalmas, Jean Baptiste.
1582       Les sorcières du Vivarais devant les
D14      inquisiteurs de la foi.  Privas, Typo-
         graphie et lithographie de Ph. Guiremand,
         1865.
           251 p. port. 22cm.
           Bound in at end "Géologie et astronomie",
         signed by Dalmas, 8 p.
           1. Witchcraft--Vivarais, France.  I.
         Title. II. His            Géologie et astronomie.
         III. Géologie et          astronomie.
```

```
Witchcraft
BF       Dalyell, Sir John Graham, 6th bart., 1775-1851.
1434       The darker superstitions of Scotland.
S3       Glasgow, Printed for R. Griffin, 1835.
D15        vii, 700 p. 22cm.

           1. Superstition. 2. Scotland--Social life
         and customs. I. Title.
```

```
         Danaeus, Lambertus, 1530 (ca.)-1595?

           see

         Daneau, Lambert, 1530 (ca.)-1595?
```

```
WITCHCRAFT
BF       Dandolo, Tullio, conte, 1801-1870.
1584       La signora di Monzi e le streghe del
I8       Tirolo, processi famosi del secolo decimo-
D17      settimo per la prima volta cavati dalle
         filze originali.  Milano, E. Besozzi,
         1855.
           259 p. port., facsims. 23cm.
           1. Witchcraft--Tyrol. 2. Leyva, Mari-
         anna de, known as Signora di Monza, 1575-
         1650. 3. Man      zoni, Alessandro, 1785-
8        1873. I pro      messi sposi. I. Title.
```

```
Witchcraft
BF       Daneau, Lambert, ca. 1530-1595?
1565       De veneficis, qvos olim sortilegos, nvnc
D17      autem vulgò sortiarios vocant, dialogvs: in
         qvo qvae de hoc argumento quaeri solent,
         breuiter & commodè explicantur.  Tractatus
         propter varias et controuersas de hac quaes-
         tione hominum sententias vtilissimus, & re-
         rum capitalium iudicibus maximè necessarius.
         Per Lambertum Danaeum.  [Genevae] Apvd
         Evstathivm Vignon, 1574.
           127 p. 18cm.
8          Title vign      ette ( E. Vignon's
         device)           (Continued on next card)
```

```
Witchcraft
BF       Daneau, Lambert, ca. 1530-1595?  De venefi-
1565     cis ... 1574.              (Card 2)
D17


           1. Witchcraft. 2. Demonology. I.
         Title: De veneficis, quos olim sortilegos
         ... vocant.

8
```

CATALOGUE OF THE CORNELL WITCHCRAFT COLLECTION

Witchcraft Daneau, Lambert, 1530 (ca.)-1595?
BF   De veneficis, qvos olim sortilegos, nvnc
1569   avtem vvlgo sortiarios vocant: dialogvs, in quo
A2   quae de hoc argumento quaeri solent, breuiter &
I59   commode explicantur. Tractatus propter varias &
1519   controuersas de hac quaestione hominum senten-
       tias vtilissimus, & rerum capitalium iudicibus
       maxime necessarius. Per Lambertum Danaeum.
       Coloniae Agrippinae, apud Ioannem Gymnicum,
       1575.
         118 p. 15cm. [With Institoris, Henricus]
       Mallevs maleficarvm. Lugduni, 1519.
         Title vignette: device of Joannes Gymnicus.
         Imperfect: p. 97-112 wanting.

         Daneau, Lambert, ca. 1530-1595?
           De veneficis, quos olim sortilegos ...
WITCHCRAFT   vocant.
BF   Jacquier, Nicolas.
1565   Flagellvm haereticorvm fascinariorvm,
J19   avtore Nicolao Iaqverio. His accesservnt
       Lamberti Danaei de veneficis dialogi, Ioa-
       chimi Camerarii in Plutarchi de oraculorum
       defectu epistola, Martini de Arles de super-
       stitionibus tractatvs, Ioannis Trithemii de
       reprobis atq; maleficis qvaestiones III,
       Thomae Erasti de strigibus liber. Studio
       Ioan. Myntzenbergii edita. Francofvrti ad
       Moenvm [Impressvm apud N. Bassaeum] 1581.
8   604 p. 17   cm.
NIC   (Continued on next card)

         Daneau, Lambert, ca. 1530-1595.
           De veneficis, quos olim sortilegos ...
FILM   vocant. English.
470   Daneau, Lambert, ca. 1530-1595.
reel   A dialogue of witches in foretime named lot-
283   tellers, and novv commonly called sorcerers ...
       Written in Latin by Lambertus Danaeus. And now
       translated into English. [London] Printed by
       R. W[atkins] 1575.
         The translation is sometimes attributed to
       Thomas Twyne. cf. Short-title catalogue.
         Translation of De veneficis, quos olim sor-
       tilegos ... vocant.
         University microfilms no. 12047 (case 48,
       carton 283)
         Short-title   catalogue no. 6226.
                    (Continued on next card)

         Daneau, Lambert, ca. 1530-1595?
           De veneficis, quos olim sortilegos ...
Witchcraft vocant--French.
BF   Daneau, Lambert, ca. 1530-1595?
1565   Devx traitez novveavx, tres-vtiles povr ce
D17   temps. Le premier tovchant les sorciers, auquel
1579   ce qui se dispute auiourd'huy sur cete matiere,
       est bien amplement resolu & augmenté de deux
       proces extraicts des greffes pour l'esclair-
       cissement & confirmation de cet argument. Le
       second contient vne breue Remonstrance sur les
       ieux de cartes & de dez. Reu. & augm. par
       l'auteur M. Lambert Daneau. [Geneve?] Par
       Jaqves Bavmet, 1579.
         160 p. 15cm.
                (Continued on next card)

         Daneau, Lambert, ca. 1530-1595?
           De veneficis, quos olim sortilegos ...
Witchcraft   vocant--French.
BF   Daneau, Lambert, ca. 1530-1595? Devx traitez
1565   nouveavx. 1579.   (Card 2)
D17
1579   "Dialogve des sorciers ov eriges" is transla-
       tion of most of his De veneficis, qvos olim
       sortilegos ... vocant.

         Daneau, Lambert, ca. 1530-1595?
           De veneficis, quos olim sortilegos ...
Witchcraft vocant--German.
BF   Daneau, Lambert, ca. 1530-1595.
1565   Von den Zauberern, Hexen, vnd Vnholden,
D17   drei christliche verscheidene [sic], vnnd
1576   zu diesen vnsern vngefärlichen Zeiten not-
       wendige Bericht ... Durch die hoch vnd
       wohlgelehrte Herren, Lambertvm Danaeuvm,
       Iacobvm Vallick, vnnd Vlricvm Molitoris.
       ... Cölln, Gedruckt durch Johannem Gym-
       nicum, 1576.
         2 v. in 1. 16cm.
         "Der ander Tractat von Zauberern, Hexen,
       vnd Vnholden,   durch J. Vallick, p.
8   Continued on next card

         Daneau, Lambert, ca. 1530-1595?
           De veneficis, quos olim sortilegos ...
Witchcraft   vocant--German.
BF   Daneau, Lambert, ca. 1530-1595. Von den
1565   Zauberern, Hexen, vnd Vnholden... 1576
D17   (Card 2)
1576   157-222 of v. 1, has special t. p.
         Translation of De veneficis, quos olim
       sortilegos ... vocant, by L. Daneau; of an
       unidentified work by J. Vallick; and of
       De lamiis et phitonicis mulieribus, by
       U. Molitor.
         1. Witchcraft. 2. Demonology. I. His
8   De veneficis, quos olim sortigelos ... vo-
                (Continued on next card)

Witchcraft
BF   Daneau, Lambert, ca. 1530-1595?
1565   Devx traitez novveavx, tres-vtiles povr ce
D17   temps. Le premier tovchant les sorciers, auquel
1579   ce qui se dispute auiourd'huy sur cete matiere,
       est bien amplement resolu & augmenté de deux
       proces extraicts des greffes pour l'esclaircissement
       & confirmation de cet argument. Le second
       contient vne breue Remonstrance sur les ieux de
       cartes & de dez. Reu. & augm. par l'auteur M.
       Lambert Daneau. [Geneve?] Par Jaqves Bavmet,
       1579.
         160 p. 15cm.
                (Continued on next card)

Witchcraft
BF   Daneau, Lambert, ca. 1530-1595? Devx traitez
1565   novveavx. 1579.   (Card 2)
D17
1579   "Dialogve des sorciers ov eriges" is transla-
       tion of most of his De veneficis, qvos olim
       sortilegos ... vocant.

         Daneau, Lambert, ca. 1530-1595?
Witchcraft   Dialogue des sorciers ou eriges.
BF   Daneau, Lambert, ca. 1530-1595?
1565   Devx traitez novveavx, tres-vtiles povr ce
D17   temps. Le premier tovchant les sorciers, auquel
1579   ce qui se dispute auiourd'huy sur cete matiere,
       est bien amplement resolu & augmenté de deux
       proces extraicts des greffes pour l'esclaircissement
       & confirmation de cet argument. Le second
       contient vne breue Remonstrance sur les ieux de
       cartes & de dez. Reu. & augm. par l'auteur M.
       Lambert Daneau. [Geneve?] Par Jaqves Bavmet,
       1579.
         160 p. 15cm.
                (Continued on next card)

         Daneau, Lambert, ca. 1530-1595?
Witchcraft   Dialogue des sorciers ou eriges.
BF   Daneau, Lambert, ca. 1530-1595? Devx traitez
1565   novveavx. 1579.   (Card 2)
D17
1579   "Dialogve des sorciers ov eriges" is transla-
       tion of most of his De veneficis, qvos olim
       sortilegos ... vocant.

FILM
470   Daneau, Lambert, ca. 1530-1595.
reel   A dialogue of witches in foretime named lot-
283   tellers, and novv commonly called sorcerers ...
       Written in Latin by Lambertus Danaeus. And now
       translated into English. [London] Printed by
       R. W[atkins] 1575.
         The translation is sometimes attributed to
       Thomas Twyne. cf. Short-title catalogue.
         Translation of De veneficis, quos olim sor-
       tilegos ... vocant.
         University microfilms no. 12047 (case 48,
       carton 283)
         Short-title   catalogue no. 6226.
                (Continued on next card)

FILM
470   Daneau, Lambert, ca. 1530-1595. A dialogue
reel   of witches ... 1575.   (Card 2)
283

         1. Witches. 2. Demonology. I. His
       De veneficis, quos olim sortilegos ... vo-
       cant. English. II. Twyne, Thomas, 1543-
       1613, supposed tr. III. Title.

         Daneau, Lambert, ca. 1530-1595?
Witchcraft   Remonstrance sur les jeux de sort.
BF   Daneau, Lambert, ca. 1530-1595?
1565   Devx traitez novveavx, tres-vtiles povr ce
D17   temps. Le premier tovchant les sorciers, auquel
1579   ce qui se dispute auiourd'huy sur cete matiere,
       est bien amplement resolu & augmenté de deux
       proces extraicts des greffes pour l'esclaircis-
       ment & confirmation de cet argument. Le second
       contient vne breue Remonstrance sur les ieux de
       cartes & de dez. Reu. & augm. par l'auteur M.
       Lambert Daneau. [Geneve?] Par Jaqves Bavmet,
       1579.
         160 p. 15cm.
                (Continued on next card)

         Daneau, Lambert, ca. 1530-1595?
Witchcraft   Remonstrance sur les jeux de sort.
BF   Daneau, Lambert, ca. 1530-1595? Devx traitez
1565   novveavx. 1579.   (Card 2)
D17
1579   "Dialogve des sorciers ov eriges" is transla-
       tion of most of his De veneficis, qvos olim
       sortilegos ... vocant.

Witchcraft
BF   Daneau, Lambert, ca. 1530-1595?
1565   Von den Zauberern, Hexen, vnd Vnholden,
D17   drei christliche verscheidene [sic], vnnd
1576   zu diesen vnsern vngefärlichen Zeiten not-
       wendige Bericht ... Durch die hoch vnd
       wohlgelehrte Herren, Lambertvm Danaeuvm,
       Iacobvm Vallick, vnnd Vlricvm Molitoris.
       ... Cölln, Gedruckt durch Johannem Gym-
       nicum, 1576.
         2 v. in 1. 16cm.
         "Der ander Tractat von Zauberern, Hexen,
       vnd Vnholden,   durch J. Vallick, p.
8   Continued on next card

Witchcraft
BF   Daneau, Lambert, ca. 1530-1595? Von den
1565   Zauberern, Hexen, vnd Vnholden... 1576
D17   (Card 2)
1576   157-222 of v. 1, has special t. p.
         Translation of De veneficis, quos olim
       sortilegos ... vocant, by L. Daneau; of an
       unidentified work by J. Vallick; and of
       De lamiis et phitonicis mulieribus, by
       U. Molitor.
         1. Witchcraft. 2. Demonology. I. H
8   De veneficis, quos olim sortigelos ... vo-
                (Continued on next car

CATALOGUE OF THE CORNELL WITCHCRAFT COLLECTION

Witchcraft
F
565
17
576
    Daneau, Lambert, ca. 1530-1595? Von den Zauberern, Hexen, vnd Vnholden... 1576. (Card 3)

cant.-- German. II. Vallick, Jacob. Ein Dialogus oder Gesprech von Zäuberey. III. Molitor, Ulrich, fl. 1470-1501. Von Hexen unnd Unholden. IV. Molitor, Ulrich, fl. 1470-1501. De lamiis et phitonicis mulieribus.-- German. V. Title. VI. Title: Von Hexen unnd Unholden.

Witchcraft
490
51+
    Danforth, Elliot.
    Henkels, firm, auctioneers, Philadelphia.
    The extraordinary collection of autograph letters belonging to the late Hon. Elliot Danforth ... To be sold ... Dec. 11, 1913, and ... Dec. 12, 1913 ... Stan. V. Henkels, auction commission merchant. Philadelphia, [M. H. Power, printer, 1913?]
    135 p. facsims. 28cm.

Catalogue no. 1074, Part 3.
(Continued on next card)

Witchcraft
490
51+
    Danforth, Elliot.
    Henkels, firm, auctioneers, Philadelphia. The extraordinary collection of autograph letters... [1913?] (Card 2)

Contains facsimile of a letter signed by some of her neighbors, certifying that Winnefred Holman was not guilty of witchery.

1. Autographs--Collections. 2. Danforth, Elliot. 3. Holman, Winnefred.

Dannenberger, Johannes, respondent.
Witchcraft
R
708
18
2
    Camerarius, Elias, 1672-1734.
    Temerarii circa magica judicii exemplum. ... praeside Elia Camerario ... In dispvtatione inavgvrali pro summis in medicina honoribus obtendis ... publice defendet Johannes Dannenberger ... Tubingae, Literis Josephi Sigmundi [1729]
    18 p. 20cm.
Diss.--Tübingen (J. Dannenberger, respondent)

1. Medicine--Addresses, essays, lectures. 2. Magic. I. Dannenberger, Johannes, respondent. II. Title.

Witchcraft
5
    Dannhauer, Johann Conrad, 1603-1666.
    Scheid - vnd- Absag-Brieff einem vngenanten Priester auss Cöllen auff sein Antworts-Schreiben an einen seiner ... Freunde über das zu Strassburg (also titulirte) vom Teuffel besessene adeliche Jungfräwlin gegeben ... Strassburg, J. Städel, 1667.
    396 p. 17cm.

The priest's letter is given in Latin and German.

1. Demoniac possession. I. Title.

Danske Domme i Trolddomssager i øverste Instans.
Jacobsen, Jørgen Carl, 1916-
    Danske Domme i Trolddomssager i øverste Instans. Indledning og kommentar, af J. C. Jacobsen. [København] I kommission: G. E. C. Gad, 1966.
    20, 309 p. 24 cm. 48.- dkr
    Bibliography: p. xi-xx. (D 66-16)

1. Witchcraft--Denmark. I. Title.

66-66095
Library of Congress [2]

Witchcraft
BF
1589
D19
    Danzel, Theodor Wilhelm, 1886-
    Magie und Geheimwissenschaft in ihrer Bedeutung für Kultur und Kulturgeschichte. Stuttgart, Strecker und Schröder, 1924.
    xv, 213 p. front. 22cm.

1. Magic. I. Title.

Witchcraft
BF
1566
D21
    Daraul, Arkon.
    Witches and sorcerers. London, F. Muller [1962]
    270 p. illus. 23 cm.

1. Witchcraft. I. Title.

BF1566.D3   62-59797
Library of Congress [1]

Darcy, Justice, fl. 1582, supposed author.
Witchcraft
BF
1563
W81++
no. 3
    A True and iust recorde of the information, examination and confession of all the witches taken at S. Oses in ... Essex; whereof some were executed, and other some entreated according to ... lawe. ... Written orderly as the cases were tryed by euidence, by W. W. [pseud.] London, Imprinted by T. Dawson, 1582. [London, at the British Museum, 1923]
    [121] p. 14cm.
    Signatures: A⁴, A-G⁸, χ¹.
(Continued on next card)

Darcy, Justice, fl. 1582, supposed author.
Witchcraft
BF
1563
W81++
no. 3
    A true and iust recorde of ... witches ... at S. Oses ... 1582 [1923] (Card 2)

"Dedicated to Justice Darcy; and ... evident that it was written by the judge himself."--Cf. Notestein, Wallace. A history of witchcraft in England from 1558 to 1718, p. 348.

Photocopy (negative) 121 p. on 53 l. 20 x 32cm.

No. 3 in vol. lettered: Witchcraft tracts, chapbooks and broadsides, 1579-1704; rotograph copies.

Witchcraft
BF
1581
M29
    The dark world of witches.
    Maple, Eric
    The dark world of witches. London, R. Hale [1962]
    192 p. illus. 23cm.

1. Witchcraft--Gt. Brit. I. Title.

The darker superstitions of Scotland.
Witchcraft
BF
1434
S3
D15
    Dalyell, Sir John Graham, 6th bart., 1775-1851.
    The darker superstitions of Scotland. Glasgow, Printed for R. Griffin, 1835.
    vii, 700 p. 22cm.

Witchcraft
BF
1581
H32D61
    [Darrell, John] fl. 1562-1602.
    A detection of that sinnfvl shamfvl lying and ridicvlovs discovrs, of Samvel Harshnet, entitvled: A discoverie of the fravvdvlent practises of Iohn Darrell. Wherein is manifestly and apparantly shewed in the eyes of the world, not only the vnlikelihoode, but the flate impossibilitie of the pretended counterfayting of William Somers, Thomas Darling, Kath. Wright, and Mary Couper; togeather with the other 7. in Lancashire, and the
(Continued on next card)

Witchcraft
BF
1581
H32D61
    [Darrell, John] fl. 1562-1602. A detection of ... discovrs of Samvel Harshnet ... (Card 2)

supposed teaching of them by the saide Iohn Darrell. [London?] 1600.
    208, [3] p. 19cm.

1. Harsnett, Samuel, abp. of York, 1561-1631. A discovery of the fraudulent practises of John Darrell. 2. Witchcraft--Lancashire. I. Title.

WITCHCRAFT
BF
1555
D22
    Darrell, John, fl. 1562-1602.
    The replie of Iohn Darrell, to the answer of Iohn Deacon, and Iohn Walker, concerning the doctrine of the possession and dispossession of demoniakes. [London?] 1602.
    50, [8] p. 18cm.

1. Deacon, John, preacher. A summarie answere. 2. Walker, John, preacher. 3. His A true narration of the strange and grevous vexation by the Devil. I. Title.

Witchcraft
BF
1555
D22T8
    Darrell, John, fl. 1562-1602.
    A trve narration of the strange and grevous vexation by the Devil of 7. persons in Lancashire and VVilliam Somers of Nottingham. Wherein the doctrine of possession and dispossession of demoniakes ovt of the word of God is particularly applyed vnto Somers, and the rest of the persons controuerted, togeather with the use we are to make of these workes of God. [London?] 1600.
    24 [i.e. 23], 106 p. 19cm.

1. Demoniac possession. 2. Somers, William, fl. 1600. I. Title.

WITCHCRAFT
BF
1555
D22
    Darrell, John, fl. 1562-1602.
    A true narration of the strange and grevous vexation by the Devil.
    Darrell, John, fl. 1562-1602.
    The replie of Iohn Darrell, to the answer of Iohn Deacon, and Iohn Walker, concerning the doctrine of the possession and dispossession of demoniakes. [London?] 1602.
    50, [8] p. 18cm.

1. Deacon, John, preacher. A summarie answere. 2. Walker, John, preacher. 3. His A true narration of the strange and grevous vexation by the Devil. I. Title.

Darrell, John, fl. 1562-1602.
Witchcraft
BF
1581
H32D6
    [Harsnett, Samuel] archbishop of York, 1561-1631.
    [A discovery of the fraudulent practises of John Darrell, bacheler of artes, in his proceedings concerning the pretended possession and dispossession of William Somers at Nottingham; of Thomas Darling, the boy of Burton at Caldwell; and of Katherine Wright at Mansfield, and Whittington; and of his dealings with one Mary Couper at Nottingham, detecting in some sort the deceitful trade in these latter dayes of casting out deuils.
(Continued on next card)

CATALOGUE OF THE CORNELL WITCHCRAFT COLLECTION

Witchcraft   Darrell, John, fl. 1562-1602.
BF
1581   [Harsnett, Samuel] archbishop of York, 1561-
H32D6   1631. [A discovery of the fraudulent
     practises of John Darrell ... [1599]
                                     (Card 2)

     London, 1599]
     [328] p. 18cm.
     Epistle to the reader signed: S. H.
     Imperfect: t.-p. mounted, part of it
     missing; title taken from Halkett & Laing;
     pages cropped; numbers missing from 324-
     [328]

Witchcraft   Dassell, Artwig von.
BF
1583   Hardevvici à Dassell j.c. Responsvm ju-
A2   ris, in causa poenali maleficarum VVinsien-
D23   sium. Pro defensione innoxiarvm, et con-
     demnatione nocentum; ne quisquam ante ju-
     dicium injuste innocentere condemnetur; ad
     requisitionem quorundam Dominorum & amico-
     rum, juris justitiaeq; amantium, conscriptum
     ... Hamburgi, Theodosius VVolderus, 1597.
     [96] p. 17cm.
     Title in red and black.
8   1. Trials (Witchcraft)--Germany.
   I. Title: Responsum juris, in causa
poenali maleficarum Winsiensium. (Over

Witchcraft
BF
1602   [Daugis, Antoine Louis]
D23   Traité sur la magie, le sortilege, les possessions, obsessions
     et malefices, où l'on en démontre la verité & la réalité; avec
     une methode sûre & facile pour les discerner; & les reglemens
     contre les devins, sorciers, magiciens, &c. Ouvrage très-utile
     aux ecclesiastiques, aux medecins, & aux juges. Par m. D***.
     Paris, P. Prault, 1732.
     2 p. l., xxiv, [4], 304, 18 p. 17cm.

     1. Magic. 2. Witchcraft.   I. Title.   II. D***.

     Library of Congress   BF1602.D2   11-14490 Revised
                       [r35b2]

     Daurer, Christophorus, respondent.
Witchcraft
BF   Mauritius, Erich, 1631-1692, praeses.
1565   Dissertatio inauguralis, De denuntia-
M45   tione sagarum, iisque quae ad eam recte
     intelligendam faciunt. Qvam ... praeside
     Erico Mauritio ... submittit Christophorus
     Daurer, Hamburg. Tubingae, Excudit Gre-
     gorius Kerner, 1664.
     96 p. 20cm.
     Diss.--Tübingen (C. Daurer, respondent)
     1. Witchcraft. 2. Trials (Witchcraft)
   I. Daurer, Christophorus, respondent. II.
8   Title: De denuntiatione sagarum.

     Daurer, Christophorus, respondent.
WITCHCRAFT
K   Mauritius, Erich, 1631-1692.
M452   Dissertationes et opuscula de selectis
     jurispublici, feudalis & privati vati ar-
     gumentis conscripta, & seorsim antehac di-
     versis locis edita, jam...in unum volumen
     collecta. Accessit praefatio Dn. Joannis
     Nicolai Hertii... Francofurti ad Moenum,
     Sumptibus Christophori Olfen, 1692.
     1256 p. 21cm.
     "De denuntiatione sagarum dissertatio":
8   p.1035-1138.   Followed by an appendix
NIC   containing   Mauritius' opinion
                     (Continued on next card)

     Daurer, Christophorus, respondent.
WITCHCRAFT
K   Mauritius, Erich, 1631-1692. Dissertatio-
M452   nes et opuscula...1692.   (Card 2)
     in a witchcraft case. The dissertation
     was originally published at Tübingen in
     1664 with title: Dissertatio inauguralis
     De denuntiatione sagarum. (Respondent: C.
     Daurer)
     1. Law--Addresses, essays, lectures. 2.
     Witchcraft. 3. Trials (Witchcraft) I.His
   Dissertatio   inauguralis De denuntia-
   tione sagaru   m. II. Daurer, Christo-
   phorus, resp   ondent. III.Title: De
   denuntiatio   ne sagarum. IV. Hertius,
   Johann Nikol   aus,1651-1710, ed.

Witchcraft
BF   [Davenport, John] ed.
1581   The witches of Hvntingdon, their examina-
Z7   tions and confessions; exactly taken by His
1646   Majesties justices of peace for that county.
     Whereby will appeare how craftily and danger-
     ously the Devill tempeth and seizeth on poore
     soules ... London, Printed by W. Wilson for
     R. Clutterbuck, 1646.
     15 p. 19cm.
     With book-plate of Herman Le Roy Edgar.
     Bound in full 19th century diced red roan,
   triple gilt   fillets on covers, spine
gilt extra.
     I. Title.

     Davidson, Isabel, d. 1676.
Witchcraft
BF   Two witchcraft trials [of Janet Trall, of
1581   Perth, in 1623, and of Isabel Davidson
T97   of Aberdeenshire, in 1676]
1676   (In North British advertiser & ladies'
     journal. Edinburgh. 25cm. v. 70 (1896)
     p. 2.)
     "Reprinted from the preface to the 'Pres-
     bytery book of Strathbogie.'"

     1. Witchcraft--Scotland. 2. Trall, Janet,
     d. 1623. 3.   Davidson, Isabel, d.
     1676.

WITCHCRAFT
BF   Davidson, Thomas Douglas, 1911-   comp.
1581   Rowan tree and red thread. A Scottish witchcraft mis-
D248   cellany of tales, legends, and ballads; together with a de-
     scription of the witches' rites and ceremonies. Edinburgh,
     Oliver and Boyd, 1949.
     x, 286 p. front. 23 cm.
     Bibliography: p. 271-275.
     With autograph: Joseph Foster.

8   1. Witchcraft—Scotland.   I. Title.
NIC   BF1581.D28   133.40941   50–32379

     Davies, John, 1625-1693, tr.
WITCHCRAFT
BF   Naudé, Gabriel, 1600-1653.
1589   The history of magick by way of apology,
N29   for all the wise men who have unjustly been
1657   reputed magicians, from the creation, to
     the present age. Written in French, by G.
     Naudaeus ... Englished by J. Davies.
     London, Printed for John Streater, 1657.
     8 p. l., 306, [2] p. 18cm.
     Publisher's catalog p. [307]-[308]
     Translation of Apologie pour tous les
     grands personnages qui ont esté faussement
     soupçonnez de   magie (1625).
8   Wing N246.   (Continued on next card)

WITCHCRAFT
BF   Davies, Reginald Trevor.
1581   Four centuries of witch-beliefs, with special reference
D25   to the Great Rebellion, by R. Trevor Davies. New York,
1972   B. Blom, 1972.
     xii, 222 p. 24 cm. $12.50
     Reprint of the 1947 ed.
     Bibliography: p. 204-212.

     1. Witchcraft—England.   I. Title.
4   BF1581.D3 1972   133.4'0942   74-180026
   Library of Congress   72 [4]   MARC

Witchcraft
BF   Davies, Thomas Witton, 1851-1923.
1591   Magic, divination, and demonology among
D25   the Hebrews and their neighbours, including an
1898   examination of biblical references and of the
     biblical terms.   London, J. Clarke [pref.
     1898]
     xvi,130 p. 20cm.
     "This treatise was presented to the Univer-
     sity of Leipzig [for the degree of doctor of
     philosophy] July 1897."--Pref.
     Without thesis statement on t.p.
   I. Title.

Witchcraft
BF   Davis, H   P.
1576   Exposé of Newburyport eccentricities, witches and
D26   witchcraft. The murdered boy, and apparition of the
     Charles-street school-house. [n. p., c1873]
     24 p. illus. 24cm.
                             1-10144-M 2

     I. Title.

Witchcraft
BF   [Davis, Ralph]
1581   An account of the tryals, examination
A2   and condemnation, of Elinor Shaw and Mary
W81   Phillip's (two notorious witches,) at North-
1866a   ampton assizes, on Wednesday the 7th of
no.2   March 1705. ... London, Printed for F.
     Thorn [1705] [Northampton, Taylor, 1866]
     8 p. 22cm.
     No. 2 in box lettered Witchcraft in
     Northamptonshire.
     1. Trials (Witchcraft)--Northamp-
8   tonshire, En   gland. 2. Shaw, Elinor,
   d. 1705. 3.   Phillips, Mary, d. 1705.
                                    (Over)

Witchcraft
BF   [Davis, Ralph]
1581   The Northamptonshire witches. Being a
A2   true and faithful account of the births,
W81   educations, lives, and conversations, of
1866a   Elinor Shaw, and Mary Phillips, (the two
no.3   notorious witches) that were executed at
     Northampton on Saturday, March the 17th,
     1705, for bewitching a woman and two child-
     ren to death. ... London, Printed for
     F. Thorn [1705] [Northampton, Taylor, 1866]
     8 p. 22cm.
8
                           (Continued on next card)

Witchcraft
BF   [Davis, Ralph] The Northamptonshire
1581   witches ... [1866]   (Card 2)
A2
W81   No. 3 in box lettered Witchcraft in
1866a   Northamptonshire.
no.3
     1. Witchcraft--Northamptonshire, Eng-
     land. I. Title. 2. Shaw, Elinor, d. 1705.
     3. Phillips, Mary, d. 1705.

8

     De angelis malis ex lum. nat. demonstra-
WITCHCRAFT   bilibus.
BT   Ohm, Gottfried, praeses.
960   De angelis malis ex lum. nat. demonstra-
O38   bilibus, quam...disputatione publica...
     examini submittet praeses M. Godofredus
     Ohm respondente Joh. Georg. Linkio.
     Lipsiae, Literis Brandenburgerianis [1704]
     [28] p. 19cm.

8   1. Devil. 2. Demonology.   I. Link, Jo-
NIC   hann Georg, respondent.

     De angelis tractatus tertius.
WITCHCRAFT
BT   Oregio, Agostino, cardinal, 1577-1635.
965   De angelis tractatus tertius, auctore
O66   Augustino Oregio. Romae, Ex typographi
     Vaticana, 1632.
     216 p. 24cm.

     Third in his series of theological tra-
     tates.
     With this is bound his De opere sex di-
8   rum tractatus quartus. 1632.
NIC   1. Angels--Early works to 1800.

CATALOGUE OF THE CORNELL WITCHCRAFT COLLECTION

WITCHCRAFT
BT
966
R98

De angelorum existentia, natura, negotiis et in hominum vitae conditionem vel laetam vel tristem influxu.
Rutta, Carl.
   De angelorum existentia, natura, negotiis et in hominum vitae conditionem vel laetam vel tristem influxu. Auctore Carolo Rutta. Wirceburgi, C. G. Becker, 1823.
   46 p. 21cm.

   Inauguralis dissertatio--Würzburg.

8
N IC

   1. Angels. I. Title.

WITCHCRAFT
BF
1445
T54
D2
1600

De apparitionibus spirituum tractatus duo.
Thyraeus, Pierre, 1546-1601.
   Reverendi patris Petri Thyraei ... De apparitionibvs spirituum tractatus duo: quorum prior agit de apparitionibvs omnis generis spirituvm, Dei, angelorvm, daemonvm, et animarum humanarum libro vno ... Posterior continet divinarvm sev Dei in Veteri Testamento apparitionum & locutionum tam externarum, quam internarum libros quatuor nunc primum editos. Coloniae Agrippinae, Ex officina Mater. Cholini, sumptibus Gosuini Cholini.   1600.

8
   (Continued on next card)

Witchcraft
BR
135
H46
1473

De celebratione festorum.
Heinrich von Gorkum, 1386 (ca.)-1431.
   De superstitiosis quibusdam casibus. De celebratione festorum. [Esslingen, Conrad Fyner, not after 1473]
   [18] l. 21cm.

   Leaf [1a]: Incipit tractatus de supsticiosis quibusdā casibꝰ ꝓpilatꝰ in alma vnivesitate studij Colonienſ ꝑ veñabilem mgͫ Heinricū de Gorīhem sacre theo. ꝓfessoreɜ eximium.
   Leaf [9b]: Explicit Tractatꝰ de supsticiosis quibusdam casit--

   (Continued on next card)

De angelorum malorum potentia in corpora.
Andreae, Tobias, 1633-1685.
   Exercitationes philosophicae duae de angelorum malorum potentia in corpora. Amstelodami, Apud Samuelem Eickenbergium, 1691.
   82 p. 14cm.
   Each part has caption title beginning: Exercitationum physicarum.
   Also published as: Wijsgeerige oefeningen betrekkelijk het vermogen van de kwade engelen op het menschlijk ligchaam.
   No. 1 in vol. lettered Andreae. De angelorum ...

WITCHCRAFT
BF
1445
T54
D2
1600

De apparitionibus spirituum tractatus duo.
Thyraeus, Pierre, 1546-1601. ... De apparitionibvs spirituum tractatus duo ... 1600.
   (Card 2)
   8 p. l., 486 p. 21cm.
   Revised and expanded version of his De variis tam spirituum, quam vivorum hominum prodigiosis apparitionibus ... libri tres.
   Binding: contemporary blind stamped pigskin, with clasps.
   With this is bound his De prodigiosis. Wircebvrgi [1591?]
   1. Apparitions. 2. Ghosts. I. His De variis tam spirituum, quam vivorum hominum ... apparitionibus ... libri tres. II. Title: De apparitionibus spirituum tractatus duo.

WITCHCRAFT
BR
135
H46
1473

De celebratione festorum.
Heinrich von Gorkum, 1386 (ca.)-1431. De superstitiosis quibusdam casibus ... [not after 1473]
   (Card 2)
   Leaf [10a]: Incipit tractatus de Celebratōne festoꝝ.
   Leaf [18b]: Explicit Tractatus cuiꝰ supra de Celebratōne festoꝝ.
   Signatures: unsigned [a⁸, b¹⁰].
   Capital spaces; capitals, initial-strokes, paragraph-marks and underlines supplied in red.

   (Continued on next card)

WITCHCRAFT
BL
25
R3805
v.7
no.3

De antiquorum daemonismo.
Tambornino, Julius.
   De antiquorum daemonismo. Giessen, A. Töpelmann, 1909.
   112 p. 23cm. (Religionsgeschichtliche Versuche und Vorarbeiten, VII. Bd. 3. Heft)
   "Kap. II und III sind auch gesondert als Dissertation aus Münster 1909 unter dem Titel De antiquorum daemonismo capita duo erschienen."
   1. Demoniac possession. 2. Occult sciences. 3. Classical literature (Selections: extracts, etc.) I. Title.

8
NIC

WITCHCRAFT
BV
810
G68

De baptismo diabolico.
[Gottwald, Johannes Petrus]
   Programma de baptismo diabolico. [Cobvrgi, Typis I. N. Monachi, 1702]
   [8] p. 21cm.

   Introduction to an oral dissertation.

   1. Baptism--Early works to 1800. I. Title. II. Title: De baptismo diabolico.

8
NIC

WITCHCRAFT
BR
135
H46
1473

De celebratione festorum.
Heinrich von Gorkum, 1386 (ca.)-1431. De superstitiosis quibusdam casibus ... [not after 1473]
   (Card 3)
   Hain. Repertorium (with Copinger's Supplement) *7807; Proctor, 2462; Brit. Mus. Cat. (XV cent.) II, p. 521 (IA. 8923; variant); Goff. Third census, H-24 (Under Henricus de Gorichen).

   1. Superstition. 2. Fasts and feasts--Catholic Church. I. Heinrich von Gorkum, 1386 (ca.)-1431. celebratione festorum. I. Title. II. De celebratione festo--

---

WITCHCRAFT
BT
980
M51

De apparitionibus daemonum exercitationem antipontificam.
Meisner, Johann, praeses.
   De apparitionibus daemonum exercitationem antipontificam praeside...Johanne Meisnero ...publico...examini...sistet M. Carolus Ortlob. [Wittebergae] Excudebatur literis Röhnerianis [1654]
   [78] p. 20cm.

   Diss.--Wittenberg (K. Ortlob, respondent)

8
NIC

   1. Devil 2. Demonology. 3. Apparitions. I. Ortlob, Karl,   respondent.

Witchcraft
BV
30
G83

De benedictionibus.
Gretser, Jacob, 1560-1625.
   Jacobi Gretseri ... Libri dvo De benedictionibvs, et tertivs De maledictionibvs ... Ingolstadii, Ex typographeo Ederiano, apud Elisabetham Angermariam, viduam, Impensis Ioannis Hertsroi, 1615.
   14 p. l., 288, [43] p. 20cm.
   Bound with his De festis Christianorum libri duo. Ingolstadii, 1612.
   1. Benediction. 2. Exorcism. 3. Blessing and cursing. I. Title: De benedictionibus. II. Title: De maledictionibus.

8

Witchcraft
BF
1520
W64
P8+
1582

De commentitiis ieiuniis.
Wier, Johann, 1515-1588.
   De lamiis liber: item De commentitiis ieivniis. Cum rerum ac uerborum copioso indice ... Basileae, Ex Officina Ooriniana, 1582.
   138 columns, [7] p. illus., port. 26cm.
   Title vignette: device of J. Oporinus.
   First published 1577, as an epitome of his De praestigiis daemonum. Cf. Allgemeine deutsche Biographie, v. 42, p. 267.

8
   (Continued on next card)

Witchcraft
BF
1445
D61
no.10

De apparitionibus spectrorum et spirituum.
Kirchmayer, Georg Caspar, 1635-1700, praeses.
   Ad scriptores aliqvot Roman. veteres, De apparitionibus spectror. & spirituum, sub corpor. inprimis human. schemate, nec non visionibus naturae probabilibus, adversus atheos inprimis, dissertatio, sub moderamine ... Dn. Georgii Casparis Kirchmajeri, à Johanne Gottlieb Stoltzen ... ventilationi publicae exposita, die 27. Julii, anno 1692. Wittebergae, Typis Christiani Schrödteri [1692]
8
   (Continued on next card)

Witchcraft
BX
2340
B62
D2
1858

De benedictionibus et exorcismis ecclesiae catholicae libri duo.
Bischofberger, Theobald.
   De benedictionibus et exorcismis ecclesiae catholicae libri duo. Liber primus de benedictionibus. [Liber secundus de exorcismis] Scripsit Theobaldus Bischofberger. Ed. 2ᵃ. Monachii, In libraria Lentneriana (E. Stahl), 1858.
   103, [1], 22 p. 14cm.
   Books 1 and 2 consecutively paged; to this is added an appendix titled De jurisdictione exorcista commentatio juridica
8
   (Continued on next card)

Witchcraft
BF
1520
W64
P8+
1582

De commentitiis ieiuniis.
Wier, Johann, 1515-1588. De lamiis liber ... 1582.
   (Card 2)
   With this is bound his De praestigiis daemonum. Basileae, 1583.
   Binding: blind stamped pigskin; front cover initialed B P I and dated 1588.
   1. Demonology. 2. Witchcraft. 3. Magic. 4. Fasting. I. His De praestigiis daemonum. II. Title: De lamiis. III. Title: De commentitiis ieiuniis.

8

Witchcraft
BF
1445
D61
no.10

De apparitionibus spectrorum et spirituum.
Kirchmayer, Georg Caspar, 1635-1700, praeses. Ad scriptores ... De apparitionibus spectror. & spirituum ... [1692]
   (Card 2)
   32, [2] p. 18cm. (bound in 21cm. vol.)
   No. 10 in vol. lettered Dissertationes de spectris. 1646-1753.
   1. Apparitions. I. Stoltze, Johann Gottlob, respondent. II. Title: De apparitionibus spectrorum et spirituum.

8

Witchcraft
BX
2340
B62
D2
1858

De benedictionibus et exorcismis ecclesiae catholicae libri duo.
Bischofberger, Theobald. De benedictionibus et exorcismis ecclesiae catholicae ... 1858.
   (Card 2)
   et moralis, which is lacking in the first edition of the work. (cf. Kayser)
   Book 2 and appendix each have special t. p.
   Colophon, p. [104]: Typis Halbergerianis Stuttgartiae.
   1. Exorcism. 2. Benediction. I. Title. II. His De jurisdictione exorcista. III. Title: De jurisdictione exorcista.

8

Witchcraft
BF
1565
B61
1623

De confessionibus maleficorum et sagarum.
Binsfeld, Pierre, ca. 1540-1598.
   Tractatvs de confessionibvs maleficorvm et sagarum. An & quanta fides ijs adhibenda sit? Auctore Petro Binsfeldio ... Accedit eiusdem auctoris Commentarius in tit. cod. lib. 9. de malefic. & mathematic. ... Item bvllae & extravagantes pontificum, &c. Editio quarta correctior & auctior. Coloniae Agrippinae, Sumptib. Petri Henningij, 1623.
   8 p. l., 638, [17] p. 16cm.

8
   Continued on next card

CATALOGUE OF THE CORNELL WITCHCRAFT COLLECTION

De confessionibus maleficorum et sagarum.

Witchcraft
BF 1565 B61 1623

Binsfeld, Pierre, ca. 1540-1598. Tractatvs de confessionibvs maleficorvm et sagarvm. 1623. (Card 2)

Commentarivs in titvlvm codicis lib. IX. de maleficis et mathematicis, p. 329-611, has special t. p.
Extravagantes et bvllae apostolicae diversorvm pontificum: p. 612-638.
"This was, I think, the last impression of Binsfeld's work. It is merely a reprint of the 4th ed.--that of 1596--the

8 (Continued on next card)

De confessionibus maleficorum et sagarum.

Witchcraft
BF 1565 B61 1623

Binsfeld, Pierre, ca. 1540-1598. Tractatvs de confessionibvs maleficorvm et sagarvm. 1623. (Card 3)

last edited by himself. [Signed] G. L. B[urr]," in ms. inside front cover.

1. Witchcraft. 2. Demonology. I. Title: Tractatus de confessionibus maleficorum et sagarum. II. Title: De confessionibus malef icorum et sagarum. III. Title: Comme ntarius in titulum ... de maleficis et mathematicis.

8

De conjugibus incantatis.

WITCHCRAFT
HQ 822 H33 1741

Hartmann, Johann Zacharias.
Io. Zachariae Hartmanni ... Commentatio ivridica De conivgibvs incantatis eorvmqve separatione. Von bezauberten Ehe-Leuten, durch Nesselknüpfen, Schloss zuschnappen &c. und derselben Scheidung. Jenae, Ex officina Schilliana, 1741.
40, 16 p. 22cm.
Programma D. Ioh. Zach. Hartmanni ... Dispvtationi ivridicae has special t. p., and is paged separately.
1. Marri age--Annulment. 2. Spells. I. Title: De conjugibus incantatis.

8

De conjugibus incantatis eorumque separatione.

Witchcraft
HQ 822 H33 1731

Hartmann, Johann Zacharias, praeses.
Dispvtatio inavgvralis ivridica De conivgibvs incantatis eorvmqve separatione, Germanice: Von bezauberten Ehe-Leuten und derselben Scheidung, qvam ... svb praesidio ... Io. Zachariae Hartmanni ... pvblico ervditorvm examini svbiicit avctor Ioannes Helvigivs Zielinski ... Ienae, Recvsa per I. B. Hellervm, 1731.
38, [2] p. 21cm.
Diss.--Jena (J. H. Zielinski, respondent, 1727)

8 (Continued on next card)

De continuatione torturae interruptae.

RARE
HV 8593 D611 no.14

Hoffmann, Gottfried Daniel, 1719-1780, praeses.
De continuatione torturae interruptae.. praeside Godofredo Daniele Hoffmanno...disputabit Burcardus Fridericus Mauchart. Tubingae, Formis Erhardianis [1757]
48 p. 21cm.
Diss.--Tübingen (B. F. Mauchart, respondent)
No. 14 in a vol. lettered: Dissertationes de tortura, 1697-1770.
1. Torture. 2. Criminal procedure. I. Mauchart, Burcard Friedrich, respondent. II. Title.

8
NIC

De conventu sagarum ad sua sabbata, qvae vocant.

Witchcraft
BF 1565 D62 no.8

Mirus, Adam Erdmann, 1656-1727, praeses.
De conventu sagarum ad sua sabbata, qvae vocant, dissertationem, ... praeside M. Adamo Erdmann Miro ... exhibebit respondens Johannes Niessner ... Wittenbergae, Typis Matthaei Henckelii [1682]
[16] p. 20cm.
No. 8 in vol. lettered Dissertationes de sagis. 1636-1714.
1. Witchcraft. 2. Devil. I. Niessner, Johann, respondent. II. Title.

8

De conventu sagarum ad sua sabbata, qvae vocant.

Witchcraft
BF 1565 D62 no.2

Voigt, Gottfried, 1644-1682, praeses.
De conventu sagarum ad sua sabbata, qvae vocant ... praeside ... Dn. M. Gothofredo Voigt ... responsurus Philipp. David Fuhrmann ... Wittebergae, Typis Johannis Borckardi [1667]
[16] p. 20cm.
No. 2 in vol. lettered Dissertationes de sagis. 1636-1714.
1. Witchcraft. I. Fuhrmann, Philipp David, respondent. II. Title.

8

De conventu sagarum in monte Bruckterorum, nocte ante Calendas Maji, disputatio.

Witchcraft
BF 1583 A2 M94

Müller, Johannes, praeses.
De conventu sagarum in monte Bruckterorum, nocte ante Calendas Maji, disputatio, quam ... praeside ... Dno. M. Johanne Müllern ... exponit Adamus Nicolaus Bersmannus ... Wittebergae, Ex typotheteo Hakiano [1675]
[16] p. 19cm.

De crimine conjurationis spirituum.

Witchcraft
BF 1600 F62

Floercke, Johann Ernst von, 1695-1762.
Io. Ernesti Floerckii I. V. D. Commentatio de crimine conivrationis spirityvm eivs processv et poenis praemissis nonnvllis ad magiam svpernatvralem divinam daemoniacam et hvmanam nec non thevrgiam cabbalam et theologiam mysticam pertinentibvs ... Ienae, Apvd Io. Felic. Bielckivm, 1721.
8 p. l., 522, [33] p. 21cm.
Title in red and black.
1. Magic. 2. Witchcraft. 3. Trials (Witch craft) I. Title: De crimine conju rationis spirituum.

8

De crimine magiae.

Witchcraft
BF 1565 T46

Thomasius, Christian, 1655-1728, praeses.
Theses inavgvrales, De crimine magiae, qvas ... praeside D. Christiano Thomasio ... svbmittit M. Iohannes Reiche ... Halae Magdebvrgicae, Literis Christoph. Salfeldii [1701]
40 p. 21cm.
Diss.--Halle (J. Reiche, respondent)
Also known as Dissertatio de crimine magiae.
1. Witchc raft. I. Reiche, Johann, respond ent. II. His Dissertatio de c rimine magiae. III. Title: De cr imine magiae.

8

De cultibus magicis.

Witchcraft
BF 1565 K21 1771

Kauz, Constantin Franz Florian Anton von, 1735-1797.
Constantini Francisci de Cauz ... De cultibus magicis eorumque perpetuo ad ecclesiam et rempublicam habitu libri duo. ... Editio II. Aucta et emendata. Vindobonae, Literis Trattnerianis, 1771.
18 p. l., 400, [6] p. 22cm.
"ΒΙΙΙΜΕΤΡΟΝ. De ritu ignis natali Joannis Baptistae die accensi dissertatio," p. [377]-400, has special t. p. (First printed 1759)

8 (Continued on next card)

De daemoniacis a Christo Sospitatore percuratis.

Witchcraft
BF 1555 G89

Gruner, Christian Gottfried, 1744-1815.
Christiani Godofredi Grvner ... Commentatio de daemoniacis a Christo Sospitatore percvratis. Accedit Danielis Wilhelmi Trilleri ... Exercitatio medico-philologica De mirando lateris cordisqve Christi vvlnere atqve effvso inde largo sangvinis et aqvae proflvvio. Ienae, Litteris et impensis I. C. Stravssii, 1775.
6 p. l., 64, [3] p. 18cm.
1. Demoniac possession. 2. Jesus

8 (Continued on next card)

De daemoniacis dissertatio.

Witchcraft
BF 1565 T19 M18+

Benvenuti, Giuseppe, 1728-ca. 1770.
Josephi Benvenuti ... De daemoniacis dissertatio. Lucae, Typis Joannis Riccomini, 1775.
lxxxiv p. 26cm.
Bound with Maffei, Francesco Scipione, marchese, 1675-1755. Arte magica dileguata. Verona, 1749.

8 1. Demonolo gy. 2. Haen, Anton de, 1704?-1776. I. Title: De daemoniacis disser tatio.

De daemoniacis Evangeliorum.

WITCHCRAFT
BS 2545 D5 T58

Timmermann, Theodor Gerhard, 1727-1792.
Theodor. Gerhard. Timmermann ... Diatribe antiqvario-medica De daemoniacis Evangeliorvm. Rintelii, Apvd Ant. Henr. Boesendahl, 1786.
90 p. 24cm.

1. Demoniac possession. 2. Bible. N. T.--Commentaries. I. Title: De daemoniacis Evan geliorum.

8
NIC

De daemoniacis in historia Evangelica.

WITCHCRAFT
BS 2545 D5 S64

Smit, Johannes.
De daemoniacis in historia Evangelica. Dissertatio exegetico-apologetica ... Romae, Sumptibus Pontificii Instituti Biblici, 1913.
xxii, 590 p. 25cm. (Rome (City) Pontificio Istituto Biblico. Scripta.)

1. Demoniac possession. 2. Bible. N.T.--Commentaries. 3. Bible--Psychology. I. Title. II. Series.

8
NIC

De daemoniacis quorum in N. T. fit mentio.

WITCHCRAFT
BS 2545 D5 S47 1769

Semler, Johann Salomo, 1725-1791.
Ioannis Salomonis Semleri ... Commentatio de daemoniacis qvorvm in N. T. fit mentio. Editio avctior. Halae Magdebvrgicae, Impensis I. C. Hendelii, 1769.
62 p. 21cm.
First published 1760 under title: De daemoniacis, quorum in Evangeliis fit mentio. (Title from Kayser)
1. Demoniac possession. 2. Bible. N. T.--Commentaries. I. His De daemoni acis, quorum in Evangeliis fit ment II. Title: De daemoniacis quorum in N. T. fit mentio.

8

De daemoniacis Semlerianis in duabus dissertationibus theologicis commentatur.

WITCHCRAFT
BS 2545 D5 S473

Müller, Joannes Stephanus.
De daemoniacis Semlerianis in duabus dissertationibus theologicis commentatur D. Ioannes Steph. Müllerus. Francofurti et Lipsiae, Apud Theodor. Vilhelm. Ern. Güthium, 1763.
95, 102 p. 23cm.
Each dissertation has separate t. p. (reprints of original title pages) No.1: Nonem δαιμονίου sive δαίμονος olim et inprimis Christi tempore non h (Continued on next ca

8
NIC

De daemoniacis Semlerianis in duabus dissertationibus theologicis commentat

WITCHCRAFT
BS 2545 D5 S473

Müller, Joannes Stephanus. De daemoniac Semlerianis...1763. (Card 2)

involuisse vi anima mortui daemon esse c deretur...demonstrat et...praeside...Ioa Stephano Müllero...defendet Ioann. Burck hard. Caspari. Ienae [1761], No. 2: Noti illa animam mortui esse et dici in evang liis daemonem opinioni debetur...praesid ...Ioanne Stephano Müllero...defendere c natur Georg. Christ. Wagenbronner Ienae [1762] (Continued on next ca

140

CATALOGUE OF THE CORNELL WITCHCRAFT COLLECTION

De daemonibus.

Witchcraft
BF
1520
R2

Rabener, Justus Gotthart, respondent.
   Dissertatio philologica secunda de daemonibus, quam ... defendet M. Justus Gotthart Rabener ... Lipsiae, Literis Christiani Goezi [1707]
   [40] p. 21cm.

   First Dissertatio philologica de daemonibus published 1706.

   1. Demonology. 2. De potentia, operationibus & cultus daemonum. I. Title. II. Title: De daemonibus.

HIST SCI
BF
1533
.G77

De daemonibus morbisque daemoniacis medica arte.
   Dresde, Fridericus Guilielmus.
   De daemonibus morbisque daemoniacis medica arte tollendis disserit et fratri dulcissimo Ioanni Eliae Dresdio doctori artis medicae recens creato honores novos gratulatur Fridericus Guilielmus Dresde. Lipsiae, Ex officina Langenhemia [1763]
   40 p. 19cm.

   1. Medicine, Magic, mystic, and spagiric. 2. Demonology. I. Dresde, Joannes Elias. II. Title.

De daemonologia in sacris Novi Testamenti libris proposita. Commentatio prima.

Witchcraft
BF
1530
.W79

Winzer, Julius Friedrich.
   De daemonologia in sacris Novi Testamenti libris proposita. Commentatio prima. Scripsit ... pro licentia svmmos in theologia honores capessendi ... sine praeside ... pvblice defendet Ivlivs Fridericvs Winzer ... Vitebergae, Literis C. H. Graessleri [1812]
   57 p. 22cm.
   Diss.--Wittenberg.
   With this is bound his De daemonologia ... Commentatio secvnda. Vitebergae [1813]

   1. Demonology. 2. Bible. N.T.--Theology. I. Title.

De daemonologia in sacris Novi Testamenti libris proposita. Commentatio secunda.

Witchcraft
BF
1530
.W79

Winzer, Julius Friedrich.
   De daemonologia in sacris Novi Testamenti libris proposita. Commentatio secvnda. Qva ad aviendam orationem aditialem ... recitandam hvmanissime invitat D. Ivlivs Fridericvs Winzer ... Vitebergae, Literis C. H. Graessleri [1813]
   22 p. 22cm.
   Bound with his De daemonologia ... Commentatio prima. Viteborgae [1812]
   1. Demonology. 2. Bible--N.T.--Theology. I. Title.

De daemonologia recentiorum autorum falsa.

Witchcraft
BF
1520
F17

Falck, Nathanael, 1663-1693.
   Nathanaelis Falcken ... Dissertationes quatuor, De daemonologia recentiorum autorum falsa, Anno 1692. Wittebergae habitae, nunc vero praefixis literis Schomerianis ibidem recusae. [Wittebergae] Typis Martini Schultzii, 1694.
   92 p. illus. initials. 20 x 16cm.
   4°: A², B-M⁴, N².
   Contents.--De falsa recentiorum auctorum daemonologia ... respondente Joh.
(Continued on next card)

De daemonologia recentiorum autorum falsa.

Witchcraft
BF
1520
F17

Falck, Nathanael, 1663-1693. Nathanaelis Falcken ... Dissertationes quatuor ... 1694. (Card 2)

   Contents--Continued.
   Isaaco Trempenau.--Dissertatio II. Ortum daemonologiae falsae & progressum historice declarans, respondente Johanne Furmann.--Dissertatio III. De daemonologia Hobbesii & Spinozae, respondente Jac. Friderico Mollero.--Dissertatio IV. De daemonolo-
(Continued on next card)

De daemonologia recentiorum autorum falsa.

Witchcraft
BF
1520
F17

Falck, Nathanael, 1663-1693. Nathanaelis Falcken ... Dissertationes quatuor ... 1694. (Card 3)

gia Bekkeri & aliorum, respondente Georg. Abrahamo Wolf.
   1. Demonology. 2. Hobbes, Thomas, 1588-1679. Elementa philosophica de cive. 3. Spinoza, Benedictus de, 1632-1677. Tractatus theologico-politicus. 4. Bekker, Balthasar, 1634-1698. De betoverde weereld. I. Title: De daemonologia recentiorum autorum falsa.

De daemonologie van het Oude Testament.

WITCHCRAFT
BF
1508
V83

Visser, Johannes Theodoor de, 1857?-1932.
   De daemonologie van het Oude Testament ... Utrecht, A. F. Blanche, 1880.
   x, 177 p. 24cm.

   Diss.--Utrecht.

   1. Demonology. 2. Devil. 3. Bible. O.T.--Criticism, interpretation, etc. I. Title.

De daemonum distinctione.

MSS
Bd.
WITCHCRAFT
BT
M24

Maldonado, Juan, 1534-1583.
   Eruditissimi domini Joannis Maldonati ... Disputatio De daemonum distinctione et de praestigiis hoc est de potestate, actione et fallacia eorundem. Paris, 1572.
   [30] l. 23cm.

   Manuscript, on paper.
   The second part of a treatise which was never printed in the original Latin. A French translation of the entire work was published in 1605, 1616, 1617, 1619 with title: Traicté des anges et
(Continued on next card)

De daemonum distinctione.

MSS
Bd.
WITCHCRAFT
BT
M24

Maldonado, Juan, 1534-1583. Eruditissimi domini Joannis Maldonati ... Disputatio De daemonum distinctione ... 1572. (Card 2)

demons.
   Signed: Sebastianus Hamelius.
   Notes inside front cover of vol. discuss history and provenance of the manuscript. Originally the vol. was in the Lamoignon library, then passed to library of Prof. E. Dowden.
   With this ms. are bound three printed works: Nicaise, Claude. De
(Continued on next card)

De daemonum distinctione.

MSS
Bd.
WITCHCRAFT
BT
M24

Maldonado, Juan, 1534-1583. Eruditissimi domini Joannis Maldonati ... Disputatio De daemonum distinctione ... 1572. (Card 3)

nummo pantheo Hadriani imperatoris. Lugduni, 1690. Patin, Charles. Commentarius Caroli Patini in tres inscriptiones Graecas. Patavii, 1685. Rigord, Jean Pierre. Dissertation historique sur une medaille d'Herodes Antipas. Paris, 1689.
   1. Demonology. 2. Devil. I. His Traicté des anges et demons. II. Title: Disputatio De daemonum distinctione. III. Title: De daemonum distinctione.

De delictis, et poenis tractatus.

Rare
K
S61++

Sinistrari, Luigi Maria, 1622-1701.
   ... De delictis, et poenis tractatus ... Venetiis, Apud Hieronymum Albriccium, 1700.
   676 p. 34cm.

De denuntiatione sagarum.

Witchcraft
BF
1565
M45

Mauritius, Erich, 1631-1692, praeses.
   Dissertatio inauguralis, De denuntiatione sagarum, iisque quae ad eam recte intelligendam faciunt. Qvam ... praeside Erico Mauritio ... submittit Christophorus Daurer, Hamburg. Tubingae, Excudit Gregorius Kerner, 1664.
   96 p. 20cm.
   Diss.--Tübingen (C. Daurer, respondent)
   1. Witchcraft. 2. Trials (Witchcraft) I. Daurer, Christophorus, respondent. II. Title: De denuntiatione sagarum.

De denuntiatione sagarum.

WITCHCRAFT
K
M452

Mauritius, Erich, 1631-1692.
   Dissertationes et opuscula de selectis jurispublici, feudalis & privati vati argumentis conscriptae, & seorsim antehac diversis locis edita, jam ... in unum volumen collecta. Accessit praefatio Dn. Joannis Nicolai Hertii ... Francofurti ad Moenum, Sumptibus Christophori Olfen, 1692.
   1256 p. 21cm.
   "De denuntiatione sagarum dissertatio": p. 1035-1138. Followed by an appendix containing Mauritius' opinion
(Continued on next card)

De denuntiatione sagarum.

WITCHCRAFT
K
M452

Mauritius, Erich, 1631-1692. Dissertationes et opuscula ... 1692. (Card 2)

in a witchcraft case. The dissertation was originally published at Tübingen in 1664 with title: Dissertatio inauguralis De denuntiatione sagarum. (Respondent: C. Daurer)
   1. Law--Addresses, essays, lectures. 2. Witchcraft. 3. Trials (Witchcraft) I. His Dissertatio inauguralis De denuntiatione sagarum. II. Daurer, Christophorus, respondent. III. Title: De denuntiatione sagarum. IV. Hertius, Johann Nikolaus, 1651-1710, ed.

De diaboli potentia in corpora.

WITCHCRAFT
R
133
H71
1725

Hoffmann, Friedrich, 1660-1742.
   Friderici Hoffmanni ... De diaboli potentia in corpora, dissertatio physico-medica curiosa. Emendatior jam edita. Halae Magdeburgicae, Typis Joh. Gruneri, 1725.
   [39] p. 21cm.
   First published 1703 under title: Disputatio inauguralis medico-philosophica De potentia diaboli in corpora.
   1. Medicine, Magic, mystic, and spagiric. 2. Devil. I. His Disputatio inauguralis medico-philosophica De potentia diaboli in corpora.

De divinatione et magicis praestigiis.

WITCHCRAFT
BF
1750
B68++

Boissard, Jean Jacques, 1528-1602.
   Tractatus posthumus Jani Jacobi Boissardi Vesvntini de divinatione et magicis praestigiis, quarum veritas ac vanitas solide exponitur per descriptionem deorum fatidecorum qui olim responsa dederunt; eorundemque prophetarum, sacerdotum, phoebadum, sibyllarum & divinorum, qui priscis temporibus celebres oracula exstiterunt. Adjunctis ... effigiebus, ab ipso autore ... delineatis; jam ... aeri incisis per Joh. Theodor de Bry. Oppenheimii,
(Continued on next card)

De divinatione et magicis praestigiis.

WITCHCRAFT
BF
1750
B68++

Boissard, Jean Jacques, 1528-1602. Tractatus posthumus Jani Jacobi Boissardi Vesvntini de divinatione et magicis praestigiis ... (Card 2)

typis H. Galleri [1616?]
   14 p. l., 358, [11] p. illus., ports. 32cm.
   Engr. t.-p.
   Engraving on p. 151 (Nicostrata) is different in the two copies.
(Continued on next card)

CATALOGUE OF THE CORNELL WITCHCRAFT COLLECTION

De doctrina daemoniorum.

WITCHCRAFT
BS
2745
.3
M39

Masius, Hector Gottfried, 1653-1709.
Hectoris Gothofr. Masii ... Disputatio theologica De doctrina daemoniorum ex I. Timoth. IV. v. 1 & seq. In abstinentiâ ab esu carnis potissimum monstratâ. Qvam respondente M. Severino Winthero, publicae disquisitioni exposuit ad 3. April. 1699. Wittebergae, Sumptibus A. Haeberi, 1709.
39 p. 20cm.
1. Bible. N.T. 1 Timothy IV--Criticism, interpretation, etc. 2. Heresy.
I. Wintherus, Severinus, respondent.
II. Title: De doctrina daemoniorum.

8

De duobus impostoribus, Benedicto Spinosa et Balthasare Bekkero.

Witchcraft
B
3998
K43

Kettner, Friedrich Ernst.
De duobus impostoribus, Benedicto Spinosa et Balthasare Bekkero. Lipsiae, Stannô Immanuelis Titii [1694]
[17] p. 20cm.

Diss.--Leipzig.

1. Spinoza, Benedictus de, 1632-1677.
2. Bekker, Balthasar, 1634-1698. I. Title.

De Ebraeorum veterum arte medica, de daemone, et daemoniacis.

WITCHCRAFT
R
135
L74

Lindinger, Johann Simon.
De Ebraeorum veterum arte medica, de daemone, et daemoniacis. Servestae et Leucoreae, Apud Sam. Godofr. Zimmermannum, 1774.
188 p. 20cm.

1. Medicine, Ancient. 2. Demonology.
3. Demoniac possession.

8
NIC

De existentia corporum angelicorum.

Witchcraft
BT
965
G59

Göde, Carolus Fridericus.
Demonstrationes philosophicae De existentia corporvm angelicorvm non nvllisqve ad ea pertinentibvs per Carol. Frider. Goede. Halae Magdebvrgicae, Impensis Carol. Herm. Hemmerde, 1744.
6 p. l., 116 p. 18cm.

1. Angels--Early works to 1800. 2. Supernatural. I. Title: De existentia corporum angelicorum.

De existentia daemonum.

Witchcraft
BF
1520
S32

Breithaupt, Christian, 1689-1749, praeses.
Commentatio secvnda De existentia daemonvm, qvam ... praeside Christiano Breithavpto ... pvblicae litteratorvm dispvtationi svbmittit avtor Iacobvs Fridericvs Ditmar ... Helmstadii, Exscripsit Herm. Dan. Hammivs [1722]
4 p. l., 18, [2] p. 19cm. (bound in 21cm. vol.)
Bound with Schwerzer, Johann Adam, praeses. Daemonologia. Lipsiae, 1672.

(Continued on next card)

8

De existentia daemonum.

Witchcraft
BF
1520
S32

Breithaupt, Christian, 1689-1749, praeses.
Commentatio secvnda ... [1722] (Card 2)

In vol. lettered Dissertationes de daemonibus. 1672-1722.

1. Demonology. I. Ditmar, Jacob Friedrich, respondent. II. Title: De existentia daemonum.

8

De fallacibus indiciis magiae.

Witchcraft
BF
1565
B66

Bode, Heinrich von, 1652-1720, praeses.
Disputatio inauguralis De fallacibus indiciis magiae, qvam ... praeside Dn. Henrico Bodino ... die 22. Octobris A. C. 1701 ... submittit Felix Martinus Brähm. Halae Magdebvrgicae, Literis C. Henckelii, typogr. [1701]
50 p. 20cm.
Diss.--Halle (F. M. Brähm, respondent)
Supports Balthasar Bekker.

Witchcraft
BF
1565
F93

De fascinatione.
Frommann, Johann Christian, b. ca. 1640.
Tractatus de fascinatione novus et singularis, in quo fascinatio vulgaris profligatur, naturalis confirmatur, & magica examinatur ... Norimbergae, Sumtibus Wolfgangi Mauritii Endteri, & Johannis Andreae Endteri Haeredum, 1675.
[78], 1067, [45] p. 21cm.

Added t. p., engraved, dated: 1674.
Manuscript note on t. p.: Bibliotheca Scholar: Piar: 1783. Colleg. Loevenburgh.

(Continued on next card)

Witchcraft
BF
1565
F93

De fascinatione.
Frommann, Johann Christian, b. ca. 1640.
Tractatus de fascinatione ... 1675. (Card 2)

Copy 2 has super exlibris: C[omes], W. G. V[on], N[rostitz]; autograph on t. p.: Jos. Bernhardt Graff von Herberstein; and 17th century vellum binding, with supra libros: I[oseph] B[ernhard] G[raf] V[on] H[erberstein] 1681.

1. Witchcraft. 2. Magic. 3. Superstition. I. Title. II. Title: De fascinatione.

De fascinationibus disputatio.

Witchcraft
BF
1598
A27
O2
1567

Agrippa von Nettesheim, Heinrich Cornelius, 1486?-1535.
Henrici Cor. Agrippae ab Nettesheym, De occvlta philosophia libri III. Qvibvs accesservnt, Spurius Agrippae Liber de ceremonijs magicis. Heptameron Petri de Albano [sic] Ratio compendiaria magiae naturalis, ex Plinio desumpta. Disputatio de fascinationibus. Epistola de incantatione & adjuratione, collid; suspensione. Iohannis Tritemij opuscula quaedam huius argumenti. Parisiis, Ex officina Iacobi Dupuys, 1567.

(Continued on next card)

8

De fascinationibus disputatio.

Witchcraft
BF
1598
A27
O2
1567

Agrippa von Nettesheim, Heinrich Cornelius, 1486?-1535.
Henrici Cor. Agrippae ab Nettesheym, De occvlta philosophia libri III. 1567. (Card 2)

16 p. l., 668, [1] p. illus., tables, diagrams (3 fold. in back) 20cm.

Binding: contemporary blind stamped pigskin with clasps (hinges wanting).
I. Abano, Pietro d', 1250-1316. Heptameron. II. De fascinationibus disputatio. III. De incantatione et adiuratione.

8

Witchcraft
BF
840
N66

De fascino.
Gutiérrez, Juan Lazaro, 17th cent.
Ioannis Lazari Gvtierrii ... Opvscvlvm de fascino ... Lvgdvni, Sumpt. Philip. Borde, Lavr. Arnavd, & Cl. Rigavd, 1653.
[8], 210, [15] p. 24cm.

Engraved title vignette: publishers' device.
Bound with Nicquet, Honorat. Physiognomia hvmana. Lvgdvni, 1648.

1. Magic. 2. Witchcraft. I. Title: De fascino. II. Title. III. Title: Opusculum de fascino.

De fascino et incantatione.

WITCHCRAFT
BF
1565
T16

Tandler, Tobias.
Dissertatio de fascino & incantatione, sub auspicio praelectionum publ. habita, à Tobia Tandlero philos. & medicin. doctore, ac math. profess. 24. Octobris, anno 1606 ... VVitebergae, Sumptibus Clementis Bergeri, Excudebat Johann. Schmidt, 1606.
8 p. l., 142 p. 16cm.
Title in ornamental border.
1. Witchcraft. 2. Evil eye.
3. Magic. I. Title: De fascino et incantatione.

8
NIC

Witchcraft
BF
1565
V13
1589

De fascino libri tres.
Vairo, Leonardo, Bp., ca. 1540-1603.
De fascino libri tres. In quibus omnes fascini species, & causae optima methodo describuntur, & ex philosophorum ac theologorum sententijs eleganter explicantur: nec non contra praestigias, imposturas, allusionesque daemonum, cautiones & amuleta praescribuntur: ac denique nugae, quae de ijsdem narrari solent, dilucidè confutantur. Cum gemino indice ... Venetiis, Apud Aldum, 1589.
[16], 375, [42] p. 17cm.

Aldine device on t. p.

De generatione diaboli cum sagis.

Witchcraft
BF
1565
D62
no.11

Panecius, Nicolaus, praeses.
Dissertatio De generatione diaboli cum sagis, qvam ... sub praesidio M. Nicol. Panecii ... submittit autor respondens Georg. Christoph. Kranzius ... Wittebergae, Literis Johannis Wilckii [1693]
[16] p. 20cm.
No. 11 in vol. lettered Dissertationes de sagis. 1636-1714.
1. Witchcraft. 2. Devil. I. Kranz, Georg Christoph, respondent. II. Title: De generatione diaboli cum sagis.

8

De hereticis et sortilegiis.

Witchcraft
BF
1565
G85
1536

Grillando, Paolo.
Paulus Grillädus. Tractat' de hereticis: z sortilegiis omnifariam coitu: eorumq; penis. Itē de questionibus: z tortura: ac de relaxatione carceratorum Domini Pauli Grillandi Castilionei: vltima hac impressione summa cura castigat': additis vbilibet sūmariis: prepositoq; perutili reptorio speciales sentētias aptissime continente. Veneūt Lugd., Apud Jacobū Giūcti, 1536.
16 p. l., cxxviii l. 17cm.

8 (Continued on next card)

De hereticis et sortilegiis.

Witchcraft
BF
1565
G85
1536

Grillando, Paolo. ... Tractat' de hereticis ... 1536. (Card 2)

Title in red and black, with woodcut border.
Printed in double columns.

1. Witchcraft. 2. Heresy. 3. Torture. I. Title: De hereticis et sortilegiis.

8

De horrenda et miserabili Satanae obsessione.

Witchcraft
BF
1555
D71
1743

Dorsch, Johann Georg, 1597-1659, praeses.
Dispvtatio theologica De horrenda et miserabili Satanae obsessione eivsdemqve ex obsessis expvlsione, von leibl. Besitzungen. Svb praesidio Dn. Io. Georg. Dorschei ...a. 1656 d. 23. Avg. pvblico ervditorvm examini svbmissa ab avtore et respondente Daniel Springsgut ... Vitembergae, Ex officina Scheffleriana, 1743.
48 p. 20cm.

8 (Continued on next card)

CATALOGUE OF THE CORNELL WITCHCRAFT COLLECTION

De horrenda et miserabili Satanae obsessione.

Witchcraft
 Dorsch, Johann Georg, 1597-1659, praeses.
  Summi theologi D. Joh. Georgii Dorschei, dissertatio De horrenda & miserabili Satanae obsessione, ejusdemqve ex obsessis expulsione, multorum votis expetita, juventutis studiosae commodo iterum prodit. Rostochii, Typis Johannis Richelii, 1667.
  [24] p. 20cm.
  Presented August 23, 1656, with D. Springinsgut as respondent, and title: Disputatio theologica De horrenda et miserabili Satanae obsessione.

(Continued on next card)

De incantationibus sev ensalmis.

Witchcraft
BF
1558
V18+
 Valle de Moura, Emanuel, fl. 1620.
  De incantationibus sev ensalmis ... Eborae, Typis Laurentij Crasbeeck, 1620.
  [6], 11 l., 12-609, [1] p. 28cm.

  Title vignette.

  1. Magic. 2. Incantations. I. Title.

De incubo eiusque medela.

ar W
36018
 Kutsche, Joseph.
  De incubo eiusque medela. Berolini [1842]
  32 p. 21cm.

  1. Spirits. I. Title.

De hydromantia.

Witchcraft
 Hering, Johannes Ernst, praeses.
  Disputatio physica De hydromantia, qvoad sagas probandas per aqvam frigidam, qvam ... sub praesidio M. Johannis Ernesti Herings ... publicè ventilandam sistit respondens Gabriel Kartnerus reichenbergâ ... Wittebergae, In officina Finceliana exscribebat Michael Meyer [1667]
  [20] p. 18cm. (bound in 20cm. vol.)
  No. 15 in vol. lettered Dissertationes de sagis. 1636-1714.

(Continued on next card)

De incantatis.

Witchcraft
BF
1565
K91
 Krause, Rudolph Wilhelm, 1642-1719, praeses.
  Dissertatio medica inavgvralis De incantatis, qvam ... svb praesidio Rvdolffi VVilhelmi Cravsii ... subjicit Iohannes Ernestvs Rauschelbach ... Ienae, Literis Krebsianis [1701]
  28 p. 20cm.
  Diss.--Jena (J. E. Rauschelbach, respondent)
  1. Witchcraft. 2. Personality, Disorders of. I. Rauschelbach, Johann Ernst, respondent. II. Title.

De indiciis cui annectitur quaestio de proba per aquam frigidam sagarum.

Witchcraft
BF
1565
D62
no.16
 Struve, Georg Adam, 1619-1692, praeses.
  Disputatio juridica De indiciis cui annectitur quaestio de proba per aquam frigidam sagarum. Von der Wasser-Prob der Hexen ... sub praesidio Dn. Georgii Adami Struven ... publicè proposita à Joh. Christoph. Nehringio ... Jenae, Typis Pauli Ehrichii, 1714.
  52 p. 20cm.
  No. 16 in vol. lettered Dissertationes de sagis. 1636-1714.

(Continued on next card)

De idololatria magica, dissertatio.

Witchcraft
 Filesac, Jean, ca. 1550-1638.
  De idololatria magica, dissertatio, Ioannis Filesaci theologi parisiensis. Parisiis, Ex officina Nivelliana, Apud Sebastianvm Cramoisy, 1609.
  8 p. l., 73 numbered leaves. 17cm.

  1. Demonology. 2. Witchcraft. 3. Magic. I. Title.

De incertitudine & vanitate omnium scientiarum & artium liber.

Witchcraft
B
781
A33I3
1643
 Agrippa von Nettesheim, Heinrich Cornelius, 1486?-1535.
  De incertitudine & vanitate omnium scientiarum & artium liber ... Cum adiecto indice capitum. Accedunt duo ejusdem auctoris libelli; quorum unus est de Nobilitate & praecellentia foeminei sexus, ejusdemque supra virilem eminentia; alter de matrimonio seu conjugio ... Lvgdvni Batavorvm, Excudebat Severinvs Matthaei, pro Officinis Abrahami Commelini & Davidis Lopes de Haro, 1643.
  [16], 359 p. 14cm.

(Continued on next card)

De indiciis et proba per aquam frigidam sagarum.

Witchcraft
BF
1565
S92
1683
 Struve, Georg Adam, 1619-1692, praeses.
  Disputatio juridica De indiciis & proba per aquam frigidam sagarum. Wasser-Prob der Hexen. Sub praesidio Dn. Georgii Adami Struven ... publicè proposita à Johanne Christophoro Nehringio ... [Jenae?], Literis Müllerianis, 1683.
  [54] p. 20cm.
  First published 1666 with title: Disputatio juridica De indiciis cui annectitur quaestio de proba per aquam frigidam sagarum.

De illorum daemonum qui sub lunari collimitio versantur.

Witchcraft
 Pictorius, Georg.
  De illorvm daemonvm qvi svb lvnari collimitio uersantur ... Basileae, Per Henricvm Petri, 1563.
  80 p. 16cm.

  Bound with his Παντοπωλίον.

  1. Magic. I. Title.

De incertitudine & vanitate omnium scientiarum & artium liber.

Witchcraft
B
781
A33I3
1643
 Agrippa von Nettesheim, Heinrich Cornelius, 1486?-1535. De incertitudine & vanitate omnium scientiarum ... 1643. (Card 2)

  Title vignette.
  Added t. p., engraved; dated: 1644.

  1. Learning and scholarship. 2. Scholasticism. 3. Science--Early works to 1800. 4. Woman. 5. Marriage. I. Title. II. Title: De nobilitate et praecellentia foeminei sexus. III. Title: De matrimonio seu conjugio.

De influxu adaemonismi in pietatem Christianam.

WITCHCRAFT
BF
1555
F11
 Faber, Johann Gottlieb, 1717-1779, praeses.
  Disqvisitio academica An adaemonismvs cvm fide et pietate Christiana conciliari possit? Qvam praeside ... Ioanne Gottlieb Faber ... svbmittit avctor defendens Martinvs Schvllervs ... Tvbingae, Literis Cottae et Revsii [1763]
  42 p. 21cm.
  Running title: De inflvxv adaemonismi in pietatem Christianam.
  1. Demoniac possession. I. Schuller, Martin, respondent. II. Title: An adaemonismus cum fide et pietate Christiana conciliari possit?

De incantatione et adiuratione.

Witchcraft
 Agrippa von Nettesheim, Heinrich Cornelius, 1486?-1535.
  Henrici Cor. Agrippae ab Nettesheym, De occvlta philosophia libri III. Qvibvs accesservnt, Spurius Agrippae Liber de ceremonijs magicis. Heptameron Petri de Albano [sic]. Ratio compendiaria magiae naturalis, ex Plinio desumpta. Disputatio de fascinationibus. Epistola de incantatione & adjuratione, colliq; suspensione. Iohannis Tritemij opuscula quaedam huius argumenti. Parisiis, Ex officina Iacobi Dupuys, 1567.

(Continued on next card)

De incubo.

WITCHCRAFT
RC
547
T26
 Teichmeyer, Hermann Friedrich, 1685-1746, praeses.
  Dissertatio inavgvralis medica De incvbo qvam ... svb praesidio Herm. Frider. Teichmeyeri ...svbmittit Daniel Textoris ... Ienae, Litteris Wertherianis [1740]
  26 [i.e., 28] p. 21cm.
  Diss.--Jena (D. Textoris, respondent)
  1. Sleep--Addresses, essays, lectures. 2. Folk-lore, German. I. Textoris, Daniel, respondent. II. Title: De incubo.

Witchcraft
HQ
1024
D27
 De injuriis, qvae haud raro novis nuptis, I. Per sparsionem dissectorum culmorum frugum Germ., durch das Herckerling-[sic] Streuen; II. Per injustam interpellationem ulterioris proclamationis, durch ungebührlichen Einspruch; III. Per ligationes magicas, durch das Nestel-Knüpfen, inferri solent, qvas adjectis summariis & indice, per varias qvaestiones practicas tractavit, examinavit, & praejudiciis hinc inde illustravit Patronus

(Continued on next card)

De incantatione et adiuratione.

Witchcraft
 Agrippa von Nettesheim, Heinrich Cornelius, 1486?-1535. Henrici Cor. Agrippae ab Nettesheym, De occvlta philosophia libri III. 1567. (Card 2)

  16 p. l., 668, [1] p. illus., tables, diagrams (3 fold. in back) 20cm.

  Binding: contemporary blind stamped pigskin with clasps (hinges wanting)
  I. Abano, Pietro d', 1250-1316. Heptameron. II. De fascinationibus disputatio. III. De incantatione et adiuratione.

De incubo.

Witchcraft
RC
547
W39
 Wedel, Georg Wolfgang, 1645-1721, praeses.
  Dissertatio medica De incvbo, ex epitome praxeos clinicae Georgii Wolffgangi Wedelii ... eodem praeside, pvblicae ... disqvisitioni svbiecta a Christophoro Lvdovico Göckelio ... Ienae, Litteris Krebsianis [1708]
  20 p. 21cm.

  Diss.--Jena (C. L. Göckelius, respondent)

Witchcraft
HQ
1024
D27
 De injuriis, qvae haud raro novis nuptis ... inferri solent ... 1699. (Card 2)

  Nupturientium. Qvedlinburg, Sumptibus Gottlob Ernesti Strunzi, 1699.
  123, [16] p. 21cm.

  Title in red and black.

  1. Marriage (Canon law) 2. Marriage customs and rites. 3. Charms. I. Patronus nupturientium.

CATALOGUE OF THE CORNELL WITCHCRAFT COLLECTION

De iure spectrorum.

Witchcraft
BF 1445 S92 1738
   Stryk, Joannes Samuel, 1668-1715, praeses.
     Dispvtatio ivridica inavgvralis, De ivre spectrorvm qvam ... praeside Dn. Io. Samvele Strykio ... svbmittit Andreas Becker. Halae Magdebvrgicae, Literis Ioh. Christ. Grvnerti, 1738.
     43, [1] p. 21cm.
     Diss.--Halle (A. Becker, respondent)
     German terms in black letter.
     1. Ghosts. 2. Devil. 3. Witchcraft--Germany. I. Becker, Andreas, 1634-1698, respondent. II. Title: De iure spectrorum.

8

De iusta haereticorum punitione.

Rare
BT 1313 C35
   Castro, Alfonso de, d. 1558.
     ...De iusta haereticorum punitione libri tres, nunc recens accurate recogniti... Venetiis, ad signum Spei, 1549.

De jurisdictione exorcista.

Witchcraft
BX 2340 B62 D2 1858
   Bischofberger, Theobald.
     De benedictionibus et exorcismis ecclesiae catholicae libri duo. Liber primus de benedictionibus; Liber secundus de exorcismis; Scripsit Theobaldus Bischofberger. Ed. 2ª. Monachii, In libraria Lentneriana (E. Stahl), 1858.
     103, [1], 22 p. 15cm.
     Books 1 and 2 consecutively paged; to this is added an appendix titled De jurisdictione exorcista commentatio juridica

8   (Continued on next card)

De jurisdictione exorcista.

Witchcraft
BX 2340 B62 D2 1858
   Bischofberger, Theobald. De benedictionibus et exorcismis ecclesiae catholicae ... 1858. (Card 2)
     et moralis, which is lacking in the first edition of the work. (cf. Kayser)
     Book 2 and appendix each have special t. p.
     Colophon, p. [104]: Typis Halbergerianis Stuttgartiae.
     1. Exorcism. 2. Benediction. I. Title. II. His De jurisdictione exorcista. III. Title: De jurisdictione exorcista.

8

De l'horrible et épouvantable sorcellerie de Louis Goffredy.

Witchcraft
PQ 1914 R6 A72 1701
   Rosset, François de, b. ca. 1570.
     De l'horrible & épouvantable sorcellerie de Louis Goffredy, prêtre beneficié de Marseille.
     (In his Les histoires tragiques de nostre temps. Dernière éd. Lyon, 1701. 18cm. p. 27-56)

     1. Gaufridi, Louis, 1572-1611. I. Title.

De l'imposture et tromperie des diables.

Witchcraft
BF 1410 M41
   Massé, Pierre.
     De l'impostvre et tromperie des diables, devins, enchantevrs, sorciers, novevrs d'esguillettes, cheuilleurs, necromanciens, chiromanciens, & autres qui par telle inuocation diabolique, ars magiques & superstitions abusent le peuple. Par Pierre Massé du Mans, aduocat. Paris, Chez Iean Poupy, 1579.
     various pagings. 17cm.
     Printer's device on t. p.

8   (Continued on next card)

De l'imposture et tromperie des diables.

Witchcraft
BF 1410 M41
   Massé, Pierre. De l'impostvre et tromperie des diables ... 1579. (Card 2)
     Title on spine: Massé. Abus des divins.
     Text preceeded by Petit fragment catechistic d'vne plvs ample catechese de la magie ... de M. René Benoist Angeuin ...; and followed by Benoist's Traicté enseignant en bref les cavses des malefices, sortileges et enchanteries ... with special t. p. Declamation contre l'errevr execrable des

8   (Continued on next card)

De l'imposture et tromperie des diables.

Witchcraft
BF 1410 M41
   Massé, Pierre. De l'impostvre et tromperie des diables ... 1579. (Card 3)
     maleficiers ... par F. Pierre Nodé minime, has special t. p. with imprint Paris, Chez Iean du Carroy imprimeur, 1578, and is paged separately.
     Trois sermons de S. Avgvstin ... traduits en françois par M. René Benoist, has special t. p. with imprint Paris, Chez Iean Poupy, 1579, and unnumbered pages.

8   (Continued on next card)

De l'imposture et tromperie des diables.

Witchcraft
BF 1520 W64 P8 1569
   Wier, Johann, 1515-1588.
     Cinq livres de l'imposture et tromperie des diables: des enchantements et sorcelleries. Pris du latin de Iean Uvier et faits françois par Iaques Gréuin de Clermont en Beauuoisis, médicin à Paris. Paris, Iaques du Puys, 1569.
     468, [79] p. 16cm.
     Incomplete: t. p. and all before p. 1 wanting.
     Title taken from Yve-Plessis, Ro-

8   (Continued on next card)

De l'imposture et tromperie des diables.

Witchcraft
BF 1520 W64 P8 1569
   Wier, Johann, 1515-1588. Cinq livres de l'imposture et tromperie des diables ... 1569. (Card 2)
     bert. Essai d'une bibliographie ... de la sorcellerie, p. 104, no. 832.
     A t. p. in G. L. Burr's hand indicates this edition of the work; however, a long note by Burr on facing page claims the edition agrees with no. 833 in Yve-Plessis. But no. 833 consists of 6 books, not 5.

8   (Continued on next card)

De l'imposture et tromperie des diables.

Witchcraft
BF 1520 W64 P8 1569
   Wier, Johann, 1515-1588. Cinq livres de l'imposture et tromperie des diables ... 1569. (Card 3)
     Translation of his De praestigiis daemonum.
     1. Demonology. 2. Witchcraft. 3. Magic. 4. Fasting. I. Grévin, Jacques, 1538?-1570, tr. II. His De praestigiis daemonum--French. III. Title. IV. Title: De l'imposture et tromperie des diables.

8

De la démonialité et des animaux incubes et succubes.

WITCHCRAFT
BF 1556 S61 1876
   Sinistrari, Luigi Maria, 1622-1701.
     De la démonialité et des animaux incubes et succubes ... par le R. P. Louis Marie Sinistrari d'Ameno ... Publié d'après le manuscrit original découvert à Londres en 1872 et traduit du Latin par Isidore Liseux. 2. éd. Paris, I. Liseux, 1876.
     xix, 267 p. 15cm.
     Title in red and black.
     Latin and French.
     1. Demonology. I. Liseux, Isidore, 1835- , tr. II. His De daemonialitate et incubis. III. His De daemonialitate et incubis et succubis. IV. Title.

8
NIC   De daemonialibis. French.

De la demonomanie des sorciers.

Witchcraft
BF 1520 B66 1593
   Bodin, Jean, 1530-1596.
     De la demonomanie des sorciers. A Monseignevr M. Chrestofle de Thou ... Seigneur de Coeli ... Par I. Bodin Angevin. Lyon, Povr P. Frellon et A. Cloqvemin, 1593.
     604 p. 17cm.

     "Réfutation des opinions de Jean Wier": p. 522-604.

     1. Wier, Johann, 1515-1588. II. Title.

8

De la lycanthropie, transformation, et extase des sorciers.

WITCHCRAFT
BF 1565 N99
   Nynauld, J de
     De la lycanthropie, transformation, et extase des sorciers... Avec la refutation des argumens contraires que Bodin allegue au 6. chap. de sa Demonomanie... Paris, Chez Iean Millot, 1615.
     109 p. 16cm.

     1. Witchcraft. 2. Demonomania. 3. Werwolves. 4. Bodin, Jean, 1530-1596. ∠De la démonomanie des sorciers. I. Title.

8
NIC

De la sorcellerie, des sorciers et de leurs juges.

BF 1566 P18
   Palou, Jean.
     De la sorcellerie, des sorciers & de leurs juges. Pref. de Robert Amadou. Sazeray, Indre, France, Presses des Mollets [1972]
     16, x, 132 p. illus. 24cm. (Fondation Jean Palou. Publications. Série Recherches, 1)

     1. Witchcraft. 2. Witchcraft--France. I. Title. II. Series

NIC   MAY 03,'74   CCCxc

De la sorcellerie et de la justice criminelle à Valenciennes.

WITCHCRAFT
BF 1582 L88
   Louise, Théophile, b. 1822.
     De la sorcellerie et de la justice criminelle à Valenciennes (XVIe et XVIIe siècles) Valenciennes, Typ. de E. Prignet, 1861.
     iii, xix, 214 p. 6 plates. 22cm.

     Pages 165-166 omitted in paging.

     1. Witchcraft--France. 2. Trials (Witchcraft)--France. 3. Witchcraft.

8
NIC

De lacrymis sagarum.

Witchcraft
BF 1565 D62 no.5
   Wolf, Johann, praeses.
     De lacrymis sagarum. Disputationem physicam ... praeside Dn. M. Johanne Wolfio ... exponit Christianus Stegmann ... VVittebergae, Typis Christiani Schrödteri [1676]
     [16] 20cm.
     No. 5 in vol. lettered Dissertationes de sagis. 1636-1714.
     1. Witchcraft. 2. Crying. I. Stegmann, Christian, respondent. II. Title.

8

De lamiis.

Witchcraft
BF 1850 G85 1592
   Grillando, Paolo.
     Tractatvs dvo: Vnus De sortilegiis D. Pavli Grillandi ... Alter De lamiis et excellentia iuris vtrivsque D. Ioannis Francisci Ponzinibij Florentini ... Olim qvidem in lvcem editi; nunc verò recogniti, & ab innumeris passim mendis vindicati: adiecto indice locupletissimo. Francoforti ad Moenvm [Apvd Martinvm Lechlervm, Impensis Haeredvm Christiani Egenolphi] 1592.
     16 p. l., 299 [1] p. 17cm.
     With colophon.

8   (Continued on next card)

CATALOGUE OF THE CORNELL WITCHCRAFT COLLECTION

De lamiis.

chcraft
Schröter, Ernst Friedrich, 1621-1676, praeses.
    Dissertatio juridica De lamiis earumqve processu criminali, quam ... sub praesidio ... Dn. Ernesti Friderici Schröter ... publicae eruditorum censurae subjicit, Michael Paris Walburger ... Jenae, Literis Joh. Jacobi Bauhoferi, 1690.
    149, [3] p. 20cm.
    No. 3 in vol. lettered Dissertationes de sagis. 1636-1714.
    1. Witchcr... aft. 2. Trials (Witchcraft) I. Wa... lburger, Michael Paris, respondent. II. Title: De lamiis.

De lamiis.

chcraft
Wier, Johann, 1515-1588.
    De lamiis liber: item De commentitiis ieivniis. Cum rerum ac uerborum copioso indice ... Basileae, Ex Officina Oporiniana, 1582.
    138 columns, [7] p. illus., port. 26cm.
    Title vignette: device of J. Oporinus.
    First published 1577, as an epitome of his De praestigiis daemonum. Cf. Allgemeine deutsche Biographie, v. 42, p. 267.

    (Continued on next card)

De lamiis.

tchcraft
    Wier, Johann, 1515-1588. De lamiis liber ... 1582.   (Card 2)

    With this is bound his De praestigiis daemonum. Basileae, 1583.
    Binding: blind stamped pigskin; front cover initialed B P I and dated 1588.
    1. Demonology. 2. Witchcraft. 3. Magic. 4. Fasting. I. His De praestigiis daemonum. II. Title: De lamiis. III. Title: De commentitiis ieiuniis.

De lamiis et phitonicis mulieribus.

Molitor, Ulrich, fl. 1470-1501.
    De lamiis et phitonicis mulieribus. [Strassburg, Johann Prüss, not before 10 Jan., 1489]
    [28] l. illus. (woodcuts) 21cm.
    Leaf [1a] (Title): De lamiis z phitonicis mulieribus.
    Leaf [2a]: Tractat⁹ ad illustrissimū prīcipem dm̄ Sigismundum archiducem austrie. Stirie carinthie tc. de lanijs z phitonicis mulieribus per Ulricum molitoris de constan-
    (Continued on next card)

De lamiis et phitonicis mulieribus.

Molitor, Ulrich, fl. 1470-1501. De lamiis et phitonicis mulieribus ... [not before 10 Jan., 1489]   (Card 2)

tia. studij papiensis. decretorum doctorem z curie constantieñ. causarum patronum. ad honorē eiusdē pñcipis ac sub sue celsitudinis emēdatōe scriptis.
    Leaf [27b] (End): Ex constañ. anno dñi. m.cccc.lxxxix. die decima ianuarij. Tue celsitudinis humilis cōsiliarius z seruulus vlricus molitoris de constātia decre-
    (Continued on next card)

De lamiis et phitonicis mulieribus.

Molitor, Ulrich, fl. 1470-1501. De lamiis et phitonicis mulieribus ... [not before 10 Jan., 1489]   (Card 3)

tom doctor.
    Leaf [28] blank; wanting in this copy.
    Signatures: a-b⁸, c-d⁶.
    Capital space on leaf [2a].
    Six woodcuts (and a repeat) measuring about 120x75 mm., designed for the book, with a larger one (135x92 mm.) of a procession for exorcism from "De miseria cu-
    (Continued on next card)

Witchcraft
BF 1569 A2M72 1489

De lamiis et phitonicis mulieribus.
Molitor, Ulrich, fl. 1470-1501. De lamiis et phitonicis mulieribus ... [not before 10 Jan., 1489]   (Card 4)

ratorum (on leaf [1b])."
    Hain. Repertorium, *11535; Schramm. Bilderschmuck d. Frühdr., v.20, p. 27; Proctor, 562; Brit. Mus. Cat. (XV cent) I, p. 126 (IA. 1723; dated [about 1488-93]); Goff. Third census, M-794.

    1. Witchcraft. 2. Demonology. I. Title.

Witchcraft
BF 1569 A2M72 1493

De lamiis et phitonicis mulieribus.
Molitor, Ulrich, fl. 1470-1501.
    De lamiis et phitonicis mulieribus. German. [Strassburg, Johann Prüss, about 1493]
    [30] l. 7 woodcuts. 19cm.
    Leaf [1a] (Title): Von den unholdē oder hexen.
    Leaf [2a]: Tractatus von denn bosen wiber die man nennet die hexen &c. durch doctor vlrichen molitoris zu latin. vnd ouch czu tutsch gemacht. vnd dem durchleuchtigistē Ertzhertzog Sigmund von osterrich als dem
    (Continued on next card)

Witchcraft
BF 1569 A2M72 1493

De lamiis et phitonicis mulieribus.
Molitor, Ulrich, fl. 1470-1501. De lamiis et phitonicis mulieribus. German ... [about 1493]   (Card 2)

loblichen eren fursten zu corrigirē czu gesant.
    Leaf [29b]: Datū zu costentz anno dñi. m.cccc.lxxxix. &c. Diner erhochsten furstlichen gnaden. demutiger raut vnd diener vlricus molitoris von costentz in den rechtenn doctor &c.
    Leaf [30] blank.
    (Continued on next card)

Witchcraft
BF 1569 A2M72 1493

De lamiis et phitonicis mulieribus.
Molitor, Ulrich, fl. 1470-1501. De lamiis et phitonicis mulieribus. German ... [about 1493]   (Card 3)

    Signatures: A-F⁴, G⁶.
    Hain. Repertorium, 11539; Polain (B), 2767; Schramm, XX, p. 27; Goff. Third census, M-806.
    With manuscript marginal notes.

    1. Witchcraft. I. Title. II. Title: Von den Unholden oder Hexen.

Witchcraft
BF 1569 A2M72 1500

De lamiis et phitonicis mulieribus.
Molitor, Ulrich, fl. 1470-1501.
    De lamiis et phitonicis mulieribus. [Paris, Georg Mittelhus?, about 1500]
    [32] l. 14cm.
    Leaf [1a] (Title): Tractatus utilis et necessarius per viā dyalogi ymmo trilogi. De Phitonicis mulieribus. Unacum quodā paruo tractatulo doctissimi et acutissimi in sacra pagina doctoris Johānis de gersono cancellarii parisiensis De probatione spirituum.
    Leaf [1a-b]: Tabula et capitula presentis
    (Continued on next card)

Witchcraft
BF 1569 A2M72 1500

De lamiis et phitonicis mulieribus.
Molitor, Ulrich, fl. 1470-1501. De lamiis et phitonicis mulieribus ... [about 1500]   (Card 2)

tractatus.
    Leaf [2]: Epistola ... ad illustrissimū principē dominū Sigismundū archiducē Austrie Stirie Carinthie etc.
    The dialogue begins at the bottom of leaf [2b] and ends on leaf [27a].
    "Johānis de gersonno ... tractatulus ... de probatione spirituum ...": leaf [27b]-
    (Continued on next card)

Witchcraft
BF 1569 A2M72 1500

De lamiis et phitonicis mulieribus.
Molitor, Ulrich, fl. 1470-1501. De lamiis et phitonicis mulieribus ... [about 1500]   (Card 3)

[32b] (Colophon): Explicit tractatus de laniis [sic] et phitonicis mulieribus vna cū tractatu de probatiōe spūum venerabilis mgrī iohānis de gersono cācellarij parisiēsis.
    Signatures: a-d⁸.
    Copinger. Supplementum, 4341; Polain
    (Continued on next card)

Witchcraft
BF 1569 A2M72 1500

De lamiis et phitonicis mulieribus.
Molitor, Ulrich, fl. 1470-1501. De lamiis et phitonicis mulieribus ... [about 1500]   (Card 4)

(B), 2763; Goff. Third census, M-805.

    1. Witchcraft. 2. Demonology. 3. Visions. I. Gerson, Joannes, 1363-1429. De probatione spirituum. II. Title. III. Title: De probatione spirituum.

Witchcraft
BF 1569 A2M72 1926

De lamiis et phitonicis mulieribus.
Molitor, Ulrich, fl. 1470-1501.
    Des sorcières et des devineresses par Ulric Molitor reproduit en fac-simile d'après l'édition latine de Cologne 1489 et traduit pour la première fois en français. Paris, E. Nourry, 1926.
    vii p., facsim. ([56] p. illus.), 84 p. 25cm. (Bibliothèque magique des XVe et XVIe siècles, 1)
    Original t. p.: De lamiis et phitonicis mulieribus. (p. [1])
    "Tirage limité a 500 exemplaires sur vélin a la cuve. N⁰ 100.
    I. Title. II. Title: De lamiis et Phitonicis mulieribus.

WITCHCRAFT
BF 1569 A2 M72 1561

De lamiis et pythonicis.
Molitor, Ulrich, fl. 1470-1501.
    Tractatvs De lamiis et pythonicis, autore Vlrico Molitore Constantiensi, ad Sigismundum Archiducem Austriae, anno 1489. Parisiis, Apud Aegidium Corrozet, 1561.
    40 numbered l. 17cm.
    First published under title: De laniis [sic] et phitonicis mulieribus.
    Imperfect copy: l. 38-40 damaged, some text of l. 40 wanting.
    1. Witchcraft. 2. Demonology. 3. Visions. I. His De laniis [sic] et phitonicis mulieribus. II. Title.
8

De magia.

Witchcraft
BF 1587 D61 no.10

Ürnhielm, Claudius Arrhenius, 1627-1675, praeses.
    Dissertatio philosophica De magia qvam ... sub moderamine ... Dn. Claudii Arrhenii ... examinandam proponit ... Andreas Torselius ... Holmiae, Excudit Nicolaus Wankif [1679]
    2 p. l., 41 p. 21cm.
    Imperfect: p. 3-6 wanting.
    No. 10 in vol. lettered Dissertationes de magia. 1623-1723.

8   (Continued on next card)

De magia.

Witchcraft
BF 1587 D61 no.7

Schütze, Bartholomaeus, praeses.
    Disputatio physica De magia, quam ... exhibent praeses M. Bartholomaeus Schütze, ... & respondens Heino Meyer ... Rostochii, Typis Johannis Killi [1669]
    [24] p. 18cm. (bound in 21cm. vol.)
    No. 7 in vol. lettered Dissertationes de magia. 1623-1723.
    1. Magic--Addresses, essays, lectures. I. Meyer, Heino, respondent. II. Title: De magia.
8

CATALOGUE OF THE CORNELL WITCHCRAFT COLLECTION

De magia.

WITCHCRAFT
BF
1565　Torreblanca Villalpando, Francisco.
T68　　　D. D. Francisci Torreblanca Cordubensis
1678　... Epitome delictorum, sive De magia: in
qva aperta vel occvlta invocatio daemonis
intervenit. Editio novissima innvmeris
mendis expvrgata, necnon indice rerum &
verborum copiosissimo nunc primùm locupletata. Lugduni, Sumpt. Joannis Antonij
Huguetan, & Soc., 1678.
4 p. l., 576, [107] p. 23cm.
Title in red and black.
8　　First published 1618 under title:
Daemonologia sive De magia ...
(Continued on next card)

De magia daemoniaca disquisitio physica.

Witchcraft
BF
1587　Werger, Johann, praeses.
D61　　　De magia daemoniaca disquisitio physica,
no.3　quam ... praeside M. Johanne VVerger Lubec.
... exponit ... Nicolaus Schmidt Lubec.
... Wittebergae, Literis Oelschlegelianis
[1657]
[16] p. 21cm.
No. 3 in vol. lettered Dissertationes de
magia. 1623-1723.
1. Occult sciences--Addresses, essays,
8　lectures. I. Schmidt, Nicolaus, of
Lübeck, respondent. II. Title.

De magia, de observatione somniorum, et
de divinatione astrologica.

Witchcraft
BF
1600　Pereira, Benito, ca. 1535-1610.
P43　　　Benedicti Pererii ... De magia, de ob-
1612　servatione somniorvm et de divinatione astrologica libri tres. Adversvs fallaces, et
superstitiosas artes. Coloniae Agrippinae,
Apud Ioannem Gymnicum, 1612.
324, [8] p. 13cm.
First published 1591 under title: ...
Adversus fallaces et superstitiosas artes.
1. Magic. 2. Dreams. 3. Astrology. I.
His ... Adversus fallaces et superstitiosas artes. II. Title: De magia,
8　de observatione somniorum, et de divinatione astrologica.

De magia diabolica, et magorum prodigiis.

Witchcraft
BF
1565　Planch, Alexius M , praeses.
P71+　　　Dissertatio critico-scripturistica de
magia diabolica, et magorum prodigiis
Exod. 7. coram Pharaone patratis. Una cum
conclusionibus ex utroque testamento desumptis, quas praeside P. Alexio M. Planch
defendendas suscepere P. P. Chrysostomus
M. Ennemoser, et Joan. Evang. M. Püchler
... [Oeniponti?] Litteris Wagnerianis
[1767]
8　6 p. l., 66, [9] p. 28cm.
(Continued on next card)

De magia diabolica, et magorum prodigiis.

Witchcraft
BF
1565　Planch, Alexius M , praeses. Disser-
P71+　tatio critico-scripturistica de magia diabolica ... [1767]　　(Card 2)

Diss.--Innsbruck (C. M. Ennemoser and
J. E. M. Püchler, respondents)

1. Witchcraft in the Bible. 2. Witchcraft. 3. Magic. I. Ennemoser, Chrysostomus M., respondent. II. Püchler, Johann
Evangelica M., respondent. III. Ti-
8　tle: De magia diabolica, et magorum
prodigiis.

De magia disputatio ex cap. 7. Exo.

WITCHCRAFT
BF
1565　Heerbrand, Jacob, 1521-1600, praeses.
H45　　　De magia dispvtatio ex cap. 7. Exo.
... Praeside reverendo ... Iacobo Heerbrando, ... Nicolavs Falco Salueldensis
respondere conabitur. Tubingae, 1570.
17 p. 21cm.

1. Witchcraft in the Bible. 2. Bible.
O.T. Exodus VII--Criticism, interpretation,
etc. I. Falco, Nicolaus, respondent.
8　II. Title.

De magia et magicis.

Witchcraft
BF
1587　Buch, Philipp, 1639-1696, praeses.
D61　　　Disputatio physica De magia et magicis
no.4　prima, quam praeside Dn.M. Philippo Buchio
... respondens Georgius Buchius ... publicè
tuebitur. Francofurti ad Oderam, Typis
Becmanianus, 1666.
[40] p. 21cm.
Caption title: Sectio I. De magia licita. (No other sections follow)
No 4 in vol. lettered Dissertationes de
magia. 1623-1723.
8　(Continued on next card)

De magia illicita.

WITCHCRAFT
BF
1565　Rüdinger, Johannes
R91　　　De magia illicita, decas concionum; zehen
mühtliche Predigten von der Zauber- vnd
Hexenwerck aus Anleitung heiliger Schrifft
vnd bewehrter Autorum rationibus nach dem
bekanten Schul-Vers Quis? Quid? Ubi? vnd
folgends andern Vmbstenden gehalten. Darinnen auff die von dieser Materia fürnembsten
Fragen geantwortet, etliche darüber vngleí-
che Meynung erzehlet vnd dieselben kürtz-
8　lich wiederleget werden, durch
NIC
(Continued on next card)

De magia illicita.

WITCHCRAFT
BF
1565　Rüdinger, Johannes
R91　　　De magia illicita...　　(Card 2)

Johannem Rüdinger. Jehna, In Verlegung J.
Reiffenberger, 1630.
406 p. 20cm.

1. Witchcraft--Sermons. I. Title. II.
Title: Zehen mühtliche Predigten von der
Zauber- und Hexenwerck. III. Title: Von der
Zauber- und Hexenwerck.

De magia liber.

Witchcraft
BF
1565　Haen, Anton de, 1704?-1776.
H13　　　Antonii de Haen ... De magia liber.
1775　Lipsiae, Svmptibvs I. P. Kravs, 1775.
xxviii, 316, [1] p. 22cm.

1. Witchcraft. 2. Magic. I. Title:
De magia liber.

8

De magia licita.

Witchcraft
BF
1587　Buch, Philipp, 1639-1696, praeses.
D61　　　Disputatio physica De magia et magicis
no.4　prima, quam praeside Dn.M. Philippo Buchio
... respondens Georgius Buchius ... publicè
tuebitur. Francofurti ad Oderam, Typis
Becmanianus, 1666.
[40] p. 21cm.
Caption title: Sectio I. De magia licita. (No other sections follow)
No 4 in vol. lettered Dissertationes de
magia. 1623-1723.
8　(Continued on next card)

De magia licita et illicita.

Witchcraft
BF
1587　Büttner, Daniel, 1642-1696, praeses.
D61　　　Magiologia seu Disputatio de magia lici-
no.11　ta et illicita qvam ... praeside Dn. Daniele
Büttnero ... disquisitioni submittit Albertus zum Felde ... Hamburgi, Literis Conradi Neumanni [1693]
26, [6] p. 18cm. (bound in 21cm. vol.)
No. 11 in vol. lettered Dissertationes
de magia. 1623-1723.
1. Magic--Addresses, essays, lectures.
I. Felde, Albert zum, 1672-1720, respond-
8　ent. II. Title. III. Title: De
magia licita et illicita.

De magia naturali, daemoniaca, licita
& illicita.

WITCHCRAFT
BF
1565　Torreblanca Villalpando, Francisco.
T68　　　Daemonologia sive De magia natvrali,
1623　daemoniaca, licita, & illicita, deq; ape[rta]
& occulta, interuentione & inuocatione
daemonis libri quatuor ... Avctore Don
Francisco Torreblanca Villalpando Cordvbensi ... Nunc cum summariis capitum, rerumq[ue] indice iuris publici facti. Mogvntiae, Impensis Ioh. Theowaldi Schönwette[ri]
1623.
12 p. l., 632, [42], 76 p. 22cm
8　(Continued on next card)

De magia naturali, daemoniaca, licita
& illicita.

WITCHCRAFT
BF
1565　Torreblanca Villalpando, Francisco. Dae-
T68　monologia sive De magia ... 1623.
1623　　　　　　　　　　　　　　　　　(Card 2)

"Defensa en favor de los libros catoli-
cos de la magia" separately paged.
Title in engraved illustrated border.
Provenance: Monast. S. Michaelis Arc[h].
Bamberg.
Binding: contemporary blind stamped
skin.
8　(Continued on next card)

De magia theses theologicae.

Witchcraft
BF
1520　Hunger, Albert, 1545?-1604, praeses.
H93　　　De magia theses theologicae, ... per re-
querendum & eruditum virum M. Hectorem VVey-
man ... pro impetrando licentiae gradu, ac
publicam disputationem propositae: praesi[de]
reuerendo & clarissimo viro Alberto Hvnge[ro]
... Ingolstadii, Ex officina VVeissenho[r]-
niana [1574]
[23] p. 20cm.
In MS at bottom of t. p.: Rdo dno M. C[...]
8　paro Boos ddt H. W.
(Continued on next card)

De magiae vanitate.

WITCHCRAFT
R
133　Plaz, Anton Wilhelm, 1708-1784.
P72　　　Procancellarius D. Antonius Guilielmu[s]
Plaz Panegyrin medicam...indicit et de ma-
giae vanitate iterum disserit. [Lipsi[ae],
Ex officina Langenhemia, 1777]
xvi p. 24cm.

Introductory to a diss. for which Geh[...]
acted as praeses Wildenhayn as responde[nt]
De praeceptore medico.
Bound with his: Procancellarius
8　Antonius Gui- lielmus Plaz Panegyr[in]
NIC　medicam...in dicit et de magiae
tate prolusi one prima praefatur.
(Continued on next card)

De magiae vanitate.

WITCHCRAFT
R
133　Plaz, Anton Wilhelm, 1708-1784.
P72　　　Procancellarius D. Antonius Guilielm[us]
Plaz Panegyrin medicam...indicit et de ma-
giae vanitate prolusione prima praefat[ur]
[Lipsiae, Ex officina Langenhemia, 1777]
xvi p. 24cm.

Introductory to a diss. for which Ge[...]
acted as praeses, Hendrich as responde[nt]
De oleosis pinguibus rancidis.
With this is bound his: Procancellar[ius]
D. Antonius Guilielmus Plaz Pa[...]
8　rin medicam ...indicit et de m[agiae]
NIC　vanitate it erum disserit. 177[7]
(Continued on next card)

De magica morborum curatione.

WITCHCRAFT
R
133　Ziegra, Christian Samuel, praeses.
Z66　　　Disputatio physica De magica morboru[m]
curatione, qvam ... exponit praeses M.
Christianus Samuel Ziegra ... responden[s]
M. Johanne Georgio Spiess ... [Witte-
bergae,] Typis Matthaei Henckelii [1681]
[24] p. 19cm.

1. Medicine, Magic, mystic, and spagiric. 2. Witchcraft. 3. Folk medic[ine]
I. Spiess, Johannes Georg, respondent.
8　II. Title: De magica morborum c[u-]
NIC　ratione.

146

CATALOGUE OF THE CORNELL WITCHCRAFT COLLECTION

De magicis actionibus earumque probationibus.

Witchcraft
BF
1587
M.1
.1
    Martini, Jacob, metaphysician, praeses.
    ΔΙΑΣΚΕΨΙΣ [i.e., diaskepsis] philosophica, De magicis actionibus earumque probationibus, ... praeside Jacobo Martini, ... respondente Henrico Nicolai. Ed. 2. [Wittebergae] Typis Christiani Tham, 1623.
    [24] p. 21cm.
    No. 1 in vol. lettered Dissertationes de magia. 1623-1723.
    1. Magic--Addresses, essays, lectures. 2. Witchcraft-- Addresses, essays, lectures. I. Nicolai, Heinrich, 1605-1665, respondent. I. Title: Diaskepsis philosophica, De magicis actionibus.

De magicis actionibus tractatus.

Witchcraft
BF
1600
N63
    Nicolai, Heinrich, 1605-1665.
    De magicis actionibus tractatus singularis philosophico-theologicus & historicus, existentiam, definitionem, qvalitatem, cognitionem, probationem, averrionem, & remedia magicarum actionum discutens ... Exercitationibus quibusdam in Gymnasio Gedanensi percursus. Dantisci, E typographejo viduae G. Rhetii, 1649.
    [8], 252 p. 19cm.

    1. Magic.   I. Title.

De magicis affectibus lib. VI.

Witchcraft
BF
1610
P6
35
    Piperno, Pietro.
    De magicis affectibus lib. VI. medice, stratagemmatice, divine, cum remediis electis, exorcismis, phisicis, ac curiosis, & De nuce Beneventana maga... [Neapoli, Typis Io. Dominici Montanati, 1635]
    208, 24 p. 21cm.

De magis tempestates cientibus.

Witchcraft
BF
1565
.2
.6
    Müller, Johannes, praeses.
    Disputatio physica De magis tempestates cientibus, qvam ... sub praesidio ... Dn. M. Johannis Mülleri ... publicè pro virili defendet Gottlob Freygang ... Wittenbergae, Literis Matthaei Henckelii [1676]
    [16] p. 20cm.
    No. 6 in vol. lettered Dissertationes de sagis. 1636-1714.
    1. Witchcraft. 2. Weather-lore. I. Freygang, Gottlob, respondent. II. Title: De magis tempestates cientibus.

De magnetica curatione vulnerum.

WITCHCRAFT
BF
1405
L85
1673
    Longinus, Caesar, ed.
    Trinum magicum, sive Secretorum magicorum opus ... Editum à Caesare Longino philos. Francofurti, Sumptibus Jacobi Gothofredi Seyleri, 1673.
    12 p. l., 498 p. 14cm.
    Contents.--Marci Antonii Zimarae Tractatus magicus.--Appendix, De mirandis quibusdam naturali magia factis operationibus. Ex lib. 2. Mag. nat. Ioan. Bapt. Port.--Tractatvs De virtutibus quarundam herbarum,

    (Continued on next card)

De magnetica curatione vulnerum.

WITCHCRAFT
BF
1405
L85
1673
    Longinus, Caesar, ed. Trinum magicum ... 1673.   (Card 2)

    lapidum & animalium. A. M. A.--Commentatio De magnetica curatione vulnerum citra svperstitionem ... Authore R. G. M. D.--Logia, sive Oracvla Zoroastri ex Platonicorum libris collecta.--Tractatus De proprii cujusqve nati daemonis inqvisitione.
    Layout of text corresponds to that of Frankfurt, 1630 ed. (C. Eifrid, printer)

    (Continued on next card)

De magorvm daemonomania, sev Detestando lamiarum ac magorum cum Satana commercio...

Witchcraft
BF
1520
B66
1590
    Bodin, Jean, 1530-1596.
    De magorvm daemonomania, sev Detestando lamiarum ac magorum cum Satana commercio, libri IV. Recens recogniti, & multis in locis à mendis repurgati. Accessit eiusdem Opinionum Ioan. Vieri confutatio non minùs docta quam pia. Francofvrti, Ex Officina Typographica Nicolai Bassaei, 1590.
    798 p. 16cm.

    Title vignette.

    I. Title. II. Title: Detestando lamiarum ac magnorum cum Satana commercio. III. His De la demonomanie--Latin.

De maledictionibus.

Witchcraft
BV
30
G83
    Gretser, Jacob, 1560-1625.
    Jacobi Gretseri ... Libri dvo De benedictionibvs, et tertivs De maledictionibvs ... Ingolstadii, Ex typographeo Ederiano, apud Elisabetham Angermariam, viduam, Impensis Ioannis Hertsroi, 1615.
    14 p. l., 288, [43] p. 20cm.
    Bound with his De festis Christianorum libri duo. Ingolstadii, 1612.
    1. Benediction. 2. Exorcism. 3. Blessing and cursing. I. Title: De benedictionibus. II. Title: De maledictionibus.

De maleficis et sagis.

Witchcraft
BF
1565
F13
    Fachinei, Andrea, d. ca. 1607, praeses.
    Dispvtatio jvridica, De maleficis et sagis, vt vocant, in theses aliqvot coniecta: qvas ... svb praesidio ... Andreae Fachinei ... tvebitvr Ioannes Christophorvs Ficlervs ... Ingolstadii, Ex officina typographica Wolfgangi Ederi, 1592.
    4 p. l., 36 p.
    On inside cover, long note by G. L. Burr on J. Christoph and J. Baptist Fickler.
    1. Witchcraft. I. Fickler, Johann Christoph, respondent. II. Title: De maleficis et sagis.

De malis angelis.

Witchcraft
BF
1520
S32
    Scherzer, Johann Adam, praeses.
    Daemonologia sive Duae disputationes theologicae de malis angelis ... praeside ... Dno. Joh. Adamo Scherzero ... nunc vero conjunctim editae à M. Christiano Trautmanno ... Lipsiae, Literis Spörelianis, 1672.
    [64] p. 19cm. (bound in 21cm. vol.)
    With this are bound Schwartz, Johann Conrad, 1677-1747. Dissertatio theologica De usu et praestantia daemonum. Altdorfii

    (Continued on next card)

De malis angelis.

Witchcraft
BF
1520
S32
    Scherzer, Johann Adam, praeses. Daemonologia ... 1672.   (Card 2)

    Noric. [1715], and Breithaupt, Christian, 1689-1749, praeses. Commentatio secunda De existentia daemonum. Helmstadii [1722]
    In vol. lettered Dissertationes de daemonibus. 1672-1722.

    1. Demonology. 2. Angels. I. Trautmann, Christian, respondent. II. Title.

De mancipiis diaboli sive sagis.

Witchcraft
BF
1565
D62
no.14
    Fischer, Daniel, 1695-1745.
    Tentamen pnevmatologico physicvm De mancipiis diaboli sive sagis. Avthore Daniele Fischero kesmarkiensi-hvngaro. Med. cvlt. Vitembergae, Ex officina Krevsigiana, 1716.
    24 p. 20cm.
    No. 14 in vol. lettered Dissertationes de sagis. 1636-1714.
    1. Witchcraft. I. Title: De mancipiis diaboli sive sagis. II. Title: De sagis.

De masticatione mortuorum.

Witchcraft
BF
1556
R73
    Rohr, Philipp, praeses.
    Dissertatio historico-philosophica De masticatione mortuorum, quam ... sistent praeses M. Philippus Rohr ... & respondens Benjamin Frizschius ... Lipsiae, Typis Michaelis Vogtii [1679]
    [24] p. 21cm.

    1. Vampires. 2. Devil. I. Fritzsch, Benjamin, respondent. II. Title: De masticatione mortuorum.

De mathematicis maleficis et ceteris similibus.

Witchcraft
BF
1565
M53
    Mencken, Lüder, praeses.
    Commentationem ad titulum codicis De mathematicis maleficis et ceteris similibus praeside Lüdero Menckenio ... excutiendam publice proponet auctor et respondens Jacob. Benedictus Wincklerus ... Lipsiae, Literis I. Titii [1725].
    72 p. 20cm.

    1. Witchcraft. 2. Trials (Witchcraft) I. Winckler, Jacob Benedict, respondent. II. Title: De mathematicis maleficis et ceteris similibus.

De matrimonio seu conjugio.

Witchcraft
B
781
A33I3
1643
    Agrippa von Nettesheim, Heinrich Cornelius, 1486?-1535.
    De incertitudine & vanitate omnium scientiarum & artium liber ... Cum adiecto indice capitum. Accedunt duo ejusdem auctoris libelli; quorum unus est de Nobilitate & praecellentia foeminei sexus, ejusdemque supra virilem eminentia; alter de matrimonio seu conjugio ... Lvgdvni Batavorvm, Excudebat Severinvs Matthaei, pro Officinis Abrahami Commelini & Davidis Lopes de Haro, 1643.
    [16], 359 p. 14cm.

    (Continued on next card)

De matrimonio seu conjugio.

Witchcraft
B
781
A33I3
1643
    Agrippa von Nettesheim, Heinrich Cornelius, 1486?-1535. De incertitudine & vanitate omnium scientiarum ... 1643. (Card 2)

    Title vignette.
    Added t. p., engraved; dated: 1644.

    1. Learning and scholarship. 2. Scholasticism. 3. Science--Early works to 1800. 4. Woman. 5. Marriage. I. Title. II. Title: De nobilitate et praecellentia foeminei sexus. III. Title: De matrimonio seu conjugio.

De medico exorcista.

HIST SCI
R
133
P74
    Pohl, Johann Ehrenfried, 1746-1800, praeses.
    De medico exorcista...praeside Iohanne Ehrenfried Pohl...disputabit auctor ac respondens Iohannes Godofredus Iancke... Lipsiae, Ex officina Sommeria [1788]
    26, xv p. 21cm.

    Diss.--Leipzig (J. G. Jancke, respondent)
    "Procancellarius D. Ernestus Gottlob Bose Panegyrin medicam...indicit. De phantasia laesa, gravium morborum matre.": xv p. at end.

    (Continued on next card)

De Michaele Scoto veneficii iniuste damnato.

WITCHCRAFT
BF
1598
S53
S35
    Schmutzer, Joannes Gottfried.
    De Michaele Scoto veneficii inivste damnato disserit ... Iacobo Henrico Bornio ... qvvm is senator Lipsiensis in solemni Senatvs lectione ... nasceretvr hanc dignitatem gratvlatvrvs Ioannes Gottfried. Schmvtzervs. Lipsiae, Ex officina Langenhemiana [1739]
    xvi p. 22cm.

    1. Scott, Michael, 1175?-1234? 2. Witchcraft. 3. Born, Jakob Heinrich, 1717-1775. I. Title.

CATALOGUE OF THE CORNELL WITCHCRAFT COLLECTION

De miraculis liber.

Witchcraft
BT 97 A2 H13 1778
Haen, Anton de, 1704?-1776.
... De miraculis liber. Parisiis, Apud P. F. Didot juniorem, 1778.
xx, 144 [i. e., 148] p. 18cm.

First published in Frankfurt, 1776.
J. J. Gassner's methods discussed in chapter 5.

1. Miracles—Early works to 1800. 2. Gassner, Johann Joseph, 1727-1779. I. Title.

8

De mirando lateris cordisque Christi vulnere.

Witchcraft
BF 1555 G89
Gruner, Christian Gottfried, 1744-1815.
Christiani Godofredi Grvner ... Commentatio de daemoniacis a Christo Sospitatore percvratis. Accedit Danielis Wilhelmi Trilleri ... Exercitatio medico-philologica De mirando lateris cordisqve Christi vvlnere atqve effvso inde largo sangvinis et aqvae proflvvio. Ienae, Litteris et impensis I. C. Stravssii, 1775.
6 p. l., 64, [3] p. 18cm.
1. Demoniac possession. 2. Jesus

8

(Continued on next card)

De mirando lateris cordisque Christi vulnere.

Witchcraft
BF 1555 G89
Gruner, Christian Gottfried, 1744-1815. ...
Commentatio de daemoniacis ... 1775. (Card 2)

Christ—Miracles. 3. Jesus Christ—Passion. I. Triller, Daniel Wilhelm, 1695-1782. Exercitatio medico-philologica De mirando lateris cordisque Christi vulnere. II. Title: De daemonia cis a Christo Sospitatore percuratis.

8

De morbis a spectrorum apparitione oriundis.

History of Science
BF 1471 D47
Detharding, Georg Christoph, 1671-1747, praeses.
Scrutinium medicum De morbis a spectrorum apparitione oriundis, Von Gespenstern, wie weit solche durch ihre Erscheinung Kranckheiten verursachen, id qvod ... praeside ... Georgio Dethardingio ... pro gradu doctorali summisque in arte medica honoribus insignibus ac privilegiis rite obtinendis, ... ad diem 27. Octobr. An. 1729. publico examini offert Georgius Erhard von Gehren... Rostochii, Typis Io. Iacob. Adleri [1729]

(Continued on next card)

De morbis a spectrorum apparitione oriundis.

History of Science
BF 1471 D47
Detharding, Georg Christoph, 1671-1747, praeses. Scrutinium medicum ... [1729] (Card 2)
38 p. 20cm.

Diss.—Rostock (G. E. von Gehren, respondent)

1. Apparitions. 2. Ghosts. 3. Medicine—15th-18th centuries. I. Gehren, Georg Erhard von, respondent. II. Title: De morbis a spectrorum apparitione oriundis.

De morbis magicis.

WITCHCRAFT
BF 1572 M4 S32
Schelhammer, Günther Christoph, 1649-1716, praeses.
Disputatio inauguralis medica De morbis magicis quam ... sub praesidio ... Guntheri Christophori Schelhammeri ... submittet Christoph. Martinus Burchardus ... Kiloni, Literis B. Reutheri [1704]
4⁰, [1] 20cm.

1. Witchcraft. 2. Diseases—Causes and theories of causation. I. Burchard, Christoph Martin, 1680-1742, respondent. II. Title: De morbis magicis.

8

De morbis veneficis, ac veneficiis.

Witchcraft
RA 1201 C67 1618
Codronchi, Giovanni Battista, fl. 1620.
Baptistae Codronchi ... De morbis veneficis, ac veneficijs. Libri qvattvor, in quibus non solum certis rationibus veneficia dari demonstratur, sed eorum species, caußae, signa, & effectus noua methodo aperiuntur. Postremo de eorum curatione ac praeseruatione exactè tractatur ... Qd opus alias editū, nuperrimè fuit ab auctore emē-datū ... Mediolani, Apud Io. Bapt. Bidelliū, 1618.
15 p.l., 248, [25] p. 19cm.

8

(Continued on next card)

De morbis veneficis, ac veneficiis.

Witchcraft
RA 1201 C67 1618
Codronchi, Giovanni Battista, fl. 1620. ...
De morbis veneficis ... 1618. (Card 2)
Added t. p., engraved.

1. Toxicology. 2. Poisons. I. Title: De morbis veneficis, ac veneficiis.

8

De natura angelorum.

Witchcraft
BF 1520 A53 D2 1654
Anania, Giovanni Lorenzo d'.
De Svbstantiis separatis. Opvsculvm primvm [-secvndvm] De natvra daemonvm et occultis eorum operationibus. Avthore Io:Lavrentio Anania. Romae, Typis Iacobi Dragondelli, 1654.
2 v. in 1. 22cm.
Vol. 2 has special t. p.: De svbstantiis separatis. Opvscvlvm secvndvm. De natvra angelorvm et occultis eorum operationibus.
Vol. 1 also published separately

8

(Continued on next card)

De natura angelorum.

Witchcraft
BF 1520 A53 D2 1654
Anania, Giovanni Lorenzo d'. De Svbstantiis separatis. 1654. (Card 2)
with title: De natvra daemonvm.

1. Demonology. 2. Angels. I. Title: De substantiis separatis. II. Title: De natura angelorum. III. His De natura daemonum.

8

De natura daemonum.

Witchcraft
BF 1520 A53 1581
Anania, Giovanni Lorenzo d'.
De natvra daemonvm libri IIII. Io. Lavrentii Ananiae ... Venetiis, 1581.
[21], 211 p. 15cm.

Title vignette.

1. Demonology. I. Title: De natura daemonum.

De natura daemonum.

WITCHCRAFT
BF 1520 A53 1589
Anania, Giovanni Lorenzo d'.
De natvra daemonvm, Io. Lavrentii Ananiae tabernatis theologi libri quatuor ... Venetiis, Apvd Aldum, 1589.
6 p. l., 211 p. 17cm.
With this is bound Vairo, Leonardo. De fascino libri tres. Venetiis, 1589.

1. Demonology. I. Title: De natura daemonum.

8

De naturalium effectuum causis.

WITCHCRAFT
BF 1558 P79
Pomponazzi, Pietro, 1462-1524.
De naturalium effectuum causis, siue de incantationibus, opvs abstrvsioris philosophiae plenvm, & breuissimis historijs illustratum atq; ante annos xxxv compositum, nunc primum vero in lucem fideliter editum. Adiectis breuibus scholijs à Gulielmo Gratarolo. Basileae [per Henrichvm Petri, 1556.]
349 p. 17cm.

8 NIC

(Cont'd on next card)

De naturalium effectuum causis.

WITCHCRAFT
BF 1558 P79
Pomponazzi, Pietro, 1462-1524. De naturalium effectuum causis ... [1556.] (Card 2)

Autograph on flyleaf: Gerardus Vossius, 1577-1649.
With this are bound: Landi, Bassiano. De incremento. Venetiis, 1556; Erastus, Thomas. Dispvtatio de avro potabili. Basileae, 1578; Anten, Conradus ab. (Gynaikolousis) seu mvliervm lavatio. Lvbecae, 1590.
1. Demonology. I. Grataroli, Guglielmo, 1516-1568, ed.

De nefando lamiarum cum diabolo coitu.

Witchcraft
BF 1565 D62 no.9
Pott, Johann Heinrich.
Specimen juridicum, De nefando lamiarum cum diabolo coitu, von der Hexen schändlichen Beyschlaff mit dem bösen Feind, in quo abstrusissima haec materia dilucidè explicatur, quaestiones inde emergentes curatè resolvuntur, variisque non injucundis exemplis illustrantur, publicâ luce donatum à Johanne Henrico Pott ... Jenae, Prostat apud Tobiam Oehrlingium, 1689.
72 p. 20cm.

8

(Continued on next card)

De nefando lamiarum cum diabolo coitu.

Witchcraft
BF 1565 D62 no.9
Pott, Johann Heinrich. Specimen juridicum ... 1689. (Card 2)

"Pacta und Gelübdnüss einer ... hohen Person, so dieselbe mit dem leydigen Satan soll haben getroffen," p. [69]-72, has special t. p.
No. 9 in vol. lettered Dissertationes de sagis. 1636-1714.
1. Witchcraft. 2. Devil. I. Title: De nefando lamiarum cum diabolo coitu. II. Title: Pacta und Gelübdnüss einer ... hohen Person.

8

De nobilitate et praecellentia foeminei sexus.

Witchcraft
B 781 A33I3 1643
Agrippa von Nettesheim, Heinrich Cornelius 1486?-1535.
De incertitudine & vanitate omnium scientiarum & artium liber ... Cum adiecto indi capitum. Accedunt duo ejusdem auctoris libli; quorum unus est de Nobilitate & praecellentia foeminei sexus, ejusdemque supra vi lem eminentia; alter de matrimonio seu congio ... Lvgdvni Batavorvm, Excudebat Serinvs Matthaei, pro Officinis Abrahami Comlini & Davidis Lopes de Haro, 1643.
[16], 359 p. 14cm.

(Continued on next car

De nobilitate et praecellentia foeminei sexus.

Witchcraft
B 781 A33I3 1643
Agrippa von Nettesheim, Heinrich Cornelius 1486?-1535. De incertitudine & vanita omnium scientiarum ... 1643. (Card

Title vignette.
Added t. p., engraved; dated: 1644.

1. Learning and scholarship. 2. Scholaticism. 3. Science—Early works to 1800. Woman. 5. Marriage. I. Title. II. Titl De nobilitate et praecellentia foeminei se III. Title: De matrimonio seu conjugio.

148

CATALOGUE OF THE CORNELL WITCHCRAFT COLLECTION

De non-existentia diaboli.

Witchcraft
F
520
98
    Buttner, Christophorus Andreas, praeses.
        Diiudicatio iudicii De non-existentia diaboli quam ... praeside M. Christophoro Andrea Buttnero ... defendet Ernestus Wilhelm.Bergmann. Halae Magdeburgicae, Litteris Ioh. Friderici Grunerti [1734]
        24 p. 24cm.
        Diss.--Halle (E. W. Bergmann, respondent)
        1. Devil. 2. Demonology. I. Bergmann, Ernest Wilhelm, respondent. II. Title: De non-   existentia diaboli.

De nuce maga Beneventana.

WITCHCRAFT
F
1410
66
635
    Piperno, Pietro.
        De magicis affectibus lib. VI. medice, stratagemmatice, divine, cum remediis electis, exorcismis, phisicis, ac curiosis, & De nuce Beneventana maga... [Neapoli, Typis Io. Dominici Montanati, 1635]
        208, 24 p. 21cm.
        The De nuce Beneventana maga has separate t.p. (title as: De nuce maga Beneventana) and pagination.
        1.Occult   sciences. 2.Demonology. 3.Medicine,   Magic,mystic and spagiric. I.Title: De   nuce maga Beneventana. II.His / De   nuce maga Beneventana.

NIC

De obsessione eademque spuria.

WITCHCRAFT
C
33
47
724
    Detharding, Georg Christoph, 1671-1747, praeses.
        Dissertatio medica inauguralis De obsessione eademque spuria, von Besessenen und vor besessen gehaltenen Menschen, qvam ... sub praesidio ... Georgii Dethardingii publice examinandam proponit Christ. Frider. Stever ... Rostochii, Recusa typis Io. Ioacob. Adleri [1724?]
        [102] p. 19cm.
        Diss.--Rostock (C. F. Stever, respondent)

NIC

De obsessis a spiritibus daemoniorum hominibus.

WITCHCRAFT
BF
1555
T54
1603
    Thyraeus, Pierre, 1546-1601.
        Daemoniaci, hoc est: De obsessis a spiritibvs daemoniorvm hominibvs, liber vnvs. In qvo daemonvm obsidentivm conditio: obsessorum hominum status ... et his similia, discutiuntur et explicantur, denuò omnia repurgata et aucta. Avctore Petro Thyraeo ... Lvgdvni, Apvd Ioannem Pillehotte, 1603.
        324, [4] p. 17cm.

    Title vignette (device of J. Pillehotte)

De obsessis a spiritibus daemoniorum hominibus.

WITCHCRAFT
F
555
54
627
    Thyraeus, Pierre, 1546-1601.
        Daemoniaci cvm Locis infestis et terricvlamentis noctvrnis. Id est, libri tres, qvibvs spiritvvm homines obsidentium atque infestantium genera, conditiones, &, quas adferunt, molestiae, molestiarumq; causae atque modi explicantur ... Coloniae Agrippinae, Ex officina Choliniana, Sumptibus Petri Cholini, 1627.
        20 p. l., 164, 356 p. 21cm.
        Loca infesta also published separately.
        (Continued on next card)

NIC

De obsessis a spiritibus daemoniorum hominibus.

WITCHCRAFT
F
555
54
627
    Thyraeus, Pierre, 1546-1601. Daemoniaci cum Locis infestis et terricvlamentis noctvrnis ... 1627. (Card 2)

    Daemoniaci first published 1694 under title: De daemoniacis.
        1. Demoniac possession. 2. Demonology. 3. Apparitions. 4.Ghosts. I. His De daemoniacis. II. His Loca infesta. III. Title. IV. Title: Loca infesta.

C

De obsessis falsis atque veris.

HIST SCI
BF
1555
W82
    Witt, Joannes Michael.
        De obsessis falsis atque veris...disserit Joannes Michael Witt... Erfordiae, Prelo Heringiano [1739]
        32 p. 21cm.

    Diss.--Erfurt.

8
        1. Demoniac possession. 2. Obsessive-compulsive neuroses. I. Title.

De occulta philosophia liber quartus. Italian.

BF
1410
L68
1970
    Liber de ceremoniis magicis. Italian. 1970?
        Le cerimonie magiche. Prima traduzione italiana dal testo latino preceduta da una introduzione. Roma, All'insegna della corona dei magi, [1970?]
        78 p. illus. 22cm.
        At head of title: Enrico Cornelio Agrippa.

        1. Occult sciences. I. Agrippa von Nettesheim, Heinrich Cornelius, 1486?-1535, supposed author. II. Title III. Title: De occulta philosophia liber quartus. Italian.

NIC   JAN 30, '74   COOxc

De officio iudicis circa tormenta.

RARE
HV
8593
D611
no.12
    Leyser, Augustin, Reichsfreiherr von, 1683-1752, praeses.
        De officio iudicis circa tormenta, praeside Augustino A Leyser...disputabit Georgius Guilielm..Büttnerus. Vitembergae, Typis Schlomachianis [1740]
        28 p. 21cm.
        Diss.--Wittenberg (G. W. Büttner, respondent)
        No. 12 in a vol. lettered: Dissertationes de tortura, 1697-1770.

8
NIC
        1. Torture. 2. Criminal procedure. I. Büttner,   Georg Wilhelm, respondent II. Title.

De officio s. inquisitionis circa haeresim.

Rare
BX
1710
D34++
1680
    Delbene, Thomas.
        De officio s. inquisitionis circa haeresim, cum bullis tam veteribus quam recentioribus ad eandem materiam, seu ad idem officium spectantibus & locis theologicis in ordine ad qualificandas propositiones. Ed. altera accurate emendata. Lugduni sumptibus Laurentii Arnaud, Petri Borde, Ioannis & Petri Arnaud, 1680.
        2 vol. in 1. 38 cm.

        1. Inquisition. I. Title.

De operatione daemonum.

WITCHCRAFT
BF
1508
P97
1838
    Psellus, Michael.
        Michael Psellus De operatione daemonum cum notis Gaulmini curante Jo. Fr. Boissonade. Accedunt inedita opuscula Psellii. Norimbergae, Apud F. N. Campe, 1838.
        xxvii, 348 p. 21cm.
        At head of title: Ψελλος.
        Greek text only: Peri energeias daimōnōn dialogos, with notes in Latin.
        1. Demonology. I. His Peri energeias daimōnōn dialogos. II. Gaulmin, Gilbert, 1585-1665, ed. III. Boissonade, Jean François, 1774-1857, ed.

8
NIC

De operatione daemonum dialogus.

WITCHCRAFT
BF
1508
P97
1688
    Psellus, Michael.
        [Michaelou tou Psellou Peri energeias daimōnōn dialogos] Μιχαήλου του Ψέλλου Περὶ ἐνέργειας δαιμόνων διαλόγος. Michaelis Pselli De operatione daemonum dialogus. Gilbertus Gaulminus Molinensis primus Graecè edidit & notis illustravit. È museo Dan. Hasenmülleri. Kiloni, Sumtibus Joh. Sebastiani Richelii, 1688.
        6 p. l., 166 p. 15cm.

8
NIC   (Continued on next card)

De operatione daemonum dialogus.

WITCHCRAFT
BF
1508
P97
1688
    Psellus, Michael. [Michaelou tou Psellou Peri energeias daimōnōn dialogos] 1688. (Card 2)

    Latin and Greek on facing pages, with notes by Gaulmin at bottom of page.
    Latin translation by Petrus Morellus, "illius qui & Nicetae Thesaurum orthodoxae fidei de Graeco Latinum fecit."

8
NIC
        1. Demonology. I. Gaulmin, Gilbert, 1585-1665, ed. II. Morellus, Petrus, Turonensis, tr. III. Hasenmüller, (Continued on next card)

De oraculis ethnicorum.

Witchcraft
BF
1761
D13
    Dale, Antonius van, 1638-1708.
        Antonii van Dale M.D. De oraculis ethnicorum dissertationes duae: quarum prior de ipsorum duratione ac defectu, posterior de eorundem auctoribus. Accedit et schediasma de consecrationibus ethnicis. Amstelaedami, apud Henricum & viduam Theodori Boom, 1683.
        16 p. l., 510, [15] p. fold. pl. 17cm.
        Added t.-p., engr.

De oraculis gentilium et in specie de vaticiniis sibyllinis.

Witchcraft
BF
1761
C61
    Clasen, Daniel, 1623-1678.
        De oraculis gentilium et in specie de vaticiniis sibyllinis libri tres, autore Daniele Clasen ... In fine adivncta svnt carmina sibyllina è versione Sebastiani Castalionis. Vt et Onuphrii Panvinii tractatvs de sibyllis. Helmstadii, apud H. Mullerum, 1673.
        8 p. l., 824, [8], 104, [43] p. 20cm.
        "Sibyllina oracula" has special t.-p. and separate paging.

De oraculis veterum ethnicorum.

WITCHCRAFT
BF
1761
D13
1700
    Dale, Antonius van, 1638-1708.
        Antonii van Dale ... De oraculis veterum ethnicorum dissertationes duae, quarum nunc prior agit de eorum origine atque auctoribus; secunda de ipsorum duratione & interitu. Editio secunda plurimum adaucta; cui de novo accedunt dissertatiunculae I. De statua Simoni Mago ... II. De actis Pilati disseritur ... III. Schediasma de consecrationibus ... Amstelodami, Apud Henricum & vid   uam Theodori Boom, 1700.

8   (Continued on next card)

De oraculis veterum ethnicorum.

WITCHCRAFT
BF
1761
D13
1700
    Dale, Antonius van, 1638-1708. ... De oraculis veterum ethnicorum dissertationes duae ... 1700. (Card 2)

    12 p. l., 694, [14] p. 8 fold. plates. 22cm.
    Title in red and black.
    First published 1683 under title: ... De oraculis ethnicorum.

8
        1. Oracles. II. Title: De oraculis veterum ethnicorum.

De origine ac progressu processus inquisitorii contra sagas.

Witchcraft
BF
1565
T461
1729
    Thomasius, Christian, 1655-1728, praeses.
        Disputatio juris canonici De origine ac progressu processus inquisitorii contra sagas, quam ... praeside Dn. Christiano Thomasio ... subiicit die XXX. Aprilis A. M DCC XII ... Johannes Paulus Ipsen ... Halae Magdeburgicae, Apud J. C. Hendelium, 1729.
        68 [i.e. 76] p. 23cm.
        Pages 73-76 numbered 65-68.
        Diss.--Halle (J. P. Ipsen, respondent)

8   (Continued on next card)

CATALOGUE OF THE CORNELL WITCHCRAFT COLLECTION

De origine et progressu officii Sanctae Inquisitionis.

Rare
BX
1710
P22+
1598

Paramo, Luis de, 1545-1619.
De origine et progressv officii Sanctae Inqvisitionis, eiúsque dignitate & vtilitate, de Romani Pontificis potestate & delegata inquisitorum: edicto Fidei, & ordine iudiciario Sancti Officij, quaestiones decem. Libri tres. Autore Ludouico a Paramo ... Matriti, Ex Typographia Regia, 1598.
[118], 887 p. 30cm.

De pactis hominum cum diabolo circa abditos in terra thesauros effodiendos.

Witchcraft
BF
1547
F65
1741

Förtsch, Michael, 1654-1724.
Commentatio de pactis hominvm cvm diabolo circa abditos in terra thesavros effodiendos et acqvirendos, ad casvm illvm tragicvm, qvi anno MDCCXV. in vigiliis festi Nativitatis Christi in agro Ienensi institvta. Von denen Bündnissen der Menschen mit dem Teufel bey dem Schatz-Graben. Editio novissima. Lipsiae, Apvd Christian. Schroetervm, 1741.
61, [2] p. 22cm.

A new edition of a dissertation at Jena,
(Continued on next card)

De pactis hominum cum diabolo circa abditos in terra thesauros effodiendos.

Witchcraft
BF
1547
F65
1741

Förtsch, Michael, 1654-1724. Commentatio de pactis hominvm cvm diabolo ... 1741.
(Card 2)

with Michael Förtsch as praeses and Johannes Andreas Rinneberg as respondent, published Jena, 1716.

1. Devil. 2. Treasure-trove. I. Rinneberg, Johannes Andreas, respondent. II. Title: De pactis hominum cum diabolo circa abditos in terra thesauros effodiendos. III. Title: Bündnisse der Menschen mit dem Teufel bey dem Schatz-Graben.

De panurgia lamiarum, sagarum, strigum ac veneficarum.

WITCHCRAFT
BF
1523
M51

Meigerius, Samuel.
De panurgia lamiarum, sagarum, strigum ac veneficarum, totiusque cohortis magicae cacodaemonia libri tres... Hamborch, [Gedrückt durch Hans Binder] 1587.
[438] p. 21cm.

Text in Low German.

8
NIC

1. Demonology. 2. Witchcraft. 3. Magic.

De potentia diaboli in corpora.

WITCHCRAFT
R
133
H71

Hoffmann, Friedrich, 1660-1742, praeses.
Disputatio inauguralis medico-philosophica De potentia diaboli in corpora, quam ... praeside DN. Friderico Hoffmanno ... publico ... examini submittit Godofredus Büching. Halae, Typis Ioannis Gruneri [1703]
[39] p. 21cm.

8
NIC

Diss.--Halle (G. Büching, respondent)

De potentia diaboli in sensus.

Witchcraft
BF
1520
S38

Schubart, Christoph, praeses.
Dissertatio De potentia diaboli in sensus, quam ... sub praesidio M. Joh. Christophori Schubarti, die 23. April hor. 8. placidae eruditorum ventilationi in acroaterio philosophorum submittet respondens Paulus Nicolaus Einert ... Erfordiae, Literis Limprechtianis [1707]
[14] p. 20cm.

8

1. Devil. I. Einert, Paul Nicolaus, respondent. II. Title: De potentia diaboli in sensus.

De potentia motrice.

Witchcraft
BT
965
C34++

Castaldi, Giovanni Tommaso, d. 1655.
De potestate angelica sive De potentia motrice, ac mirandis operibvs angelorvm atqve doemonvm, dissertatio ... Romae, Ex Typographia Francisci Caballi, 1650-52.
3 v. 34cm.

Engraved title vignettes.
T. p. of v. 2 reads: ... daemonvm ...

1. Angels--Early works to 1800. 2. Demonology. I. Title.

De potentia, operationibus & cultus daemonum.

Witchcraft
BF
1520
R12

Rabener, Justus Gotthart, respondent.
Dissertatio philologica secunda de daemonibus, quam ... defendet M. Justus Gotthart Rabener ... Lipsiae, Literis Christiani Goezi [1707]
[40] p. 21cm.

First Dissertatio philologica de daemonibus published 1706.

8

1. Demonology. 2. De potentia, operationibus & cultus daemonum. I. Title. II. Title: De daemonibus.

De potestate angelica.

Witchcraft
BT
965
C34++

Castaldi, Giovanni Tommaso, d. 1655.
De potestate angelica sive De potentia motrice, ac mirandis operibvs angelorvm atqve doemonvm, dissertatio ... Romae, Ex Typographia Francisci Caballi, 1650-52.
3 v. 34cm.

Engraved title vignettes.
T. p. of v. 2 reads: ... daemonvm ...

1. Angels--Early works to 1800. 2. Demonology. I. Title.

De potestate daemonum, arte magica, superstitionibus ...

MSS
Bd.
RARE
B
J17

Jacobus, of Jüterbogk, 1381-1465.
[Treatises. s.l., 1762-65]
10 pts. in 1 v. ([257] l.) 21cm.

Copies of the original manuscripts, made 1762-65.
Bound in boards with parchment back and corners.
Contents.--Colloquium hominis ad animam suam.--De conflictu inter amorem dei & mundi.--De statibus mundi.--De VII statibus Ecclesiae in Apocalypsi descriptis, & De authorita te Ecclesiae ac eiusdem
(Continued on next card)

8
NIC

De potestate daemonum, arte magica, superstitionibus ...

MSS
Bd.
RARE
B
J17

Jacobus, of Jüterbogk, 1381-1465. [Treatises. 1762-65] (Card 2)

reformatione.--De statu securiori incedendi in hac vita.--De partitione redditu[s] inter religiosos.--De receptione & proventibus monialium & aliorum religiosorum deque propietate.--De contractibus & redemptionibus.--De indulgentiis anni jubilei.--De potestate daemonum, arte magica, superstitionibus & illusionibus eorundem.
(Continued on next card)

De potestate daemonum in rebus humanis.

Witchcraft
BF
1520
D12

Daemonvrgia [i.e. daemonurgia] theologice expensa, sev De potestate daemonvm in rebvs hvmanis, deqve potestate in daemones a Christo ecclesiae relicta. [n. p.] 1776.
4 p. l., 232, [8] p. 24cm.

Printed in England?

8

1. Demonology. 2. Exorcism. 3. Witchcraft. I. Title: De potestate daemonum in rebus humanis.

De potestate diaboli in corpus humanum.

Witchcraft
BF
1520
A33

Alberti, Michael, 1682-1757, praeses.
Dissertatio inauguralis medica, de potestate diaboli in corpus humanum, qvam ... praeside Dn. D. Michaele Alberti ... ventilationi subjiciet respondens Johannes Fridericus Corvinus ... [Halle] Typis Jo: Christian Hendel [1725]
52 p. 21cm.

Diss.--Halle (J. F. Corvinus, respondent)
1. Demonology. 2. Diseases--Causes and theories of causation. I. Corvinus, Johann Friedrich, of Halle, respondent. II. Title: De potestate diaboli in corpus humanum.

8

De praestigiis daemonvm, et incantationibus, ac ueneficijs, libri V.

Witchcraft
BF
1520
W64
P8
1563

Wier, Johann, 1515-1588.
De praestigiis daemonvm, et incantationibus, ac ueneficijs, libri V ... Basileae, Per Ioannem Oporinum, 1563.
479 p. 18cm.

Contemporary binding: fragment of a German manuscript on vellum, partly covered with blind stamped pigskin.

1. Demonology. 2. Magic. 3. Witchcraft. I. Title.

De praestigiis daemonum, et incantationibus, ac ueneficijs, libri V.

Witchcraft
BF
1520
W64
P8
1564

Wier, Johann, 1515-1588.
De praestigiis daemonvm, et incantationibus ac ueneficijs, libri V. recogniti, & ualde aucti ... Acceßit index amplißimus. Basileae, Per Ioannem Oporinum, 1564.
565, [58] p. 18cm.

Ex libris Benno Loewy.

8

De praestigiis daemovm, et incantationibus ac ueneficijs libri sex, aucti & recogniti.

Witchcraft
BF
1520
W64P8
1568

Wier, Johann, 1515-1588.
Ioannis VVieri De præstigiis dæmonvm, et incantationibus ac ueneficijs libri sex, aucti & recogniti. Accessit rerum & uerborum copiosus index ... Basileæ, ex officina Oporiniana, 1568.
697, [55] p. 20cm.

1. Demonology. 2. Magic. 3. Witchcraft. I. Title.

11-9703

Library of Congress   BF1520 W64

De praestigiis daemonum, & incantationibus ac ueneficiis libri sex, postrema editione sexta aucti & recogniti.

Witchcraft
BF
1520
W64
P8+
1582

Wier, Johann, 1515-1588.
De praestigiis daemonum, & incantationibus ac ueneficiis libri sex, postrema editione sexta aucti & recogniti. Accessit Liber apologeticus, et Pseudomonarchia daemonum. Cum rerum ac uerborum copioso indice. Basileae, Ex Officina Oporiniana, 1583.
934 columns, [35] p. illus., port. 26cm.

Contents of De praestigiis daemonum are
(Continued on next card)

8

De praestigiis daemonum, & incantationibus ac ueneficiis libri sex, postrema editione sexta aucti & recogniti.

Witchcraft
BF
1520
W64
P8+
1582

Wier, Johann, 1515-1588. De praestigiis daemonum ... 1583. (Card 2)

same as in 5th ed., 1577. Cf. Allgemeine deutsche Biographie, v. 42, p. 267.
Liber apologeticus, and Pseudomonarchia daemonum each with special t. p.
Colophon: Basileae, Ex Officina Oporiniana, per Balthasarvm Han, et Hieronymvm Gemvsaeum, Anno Salutis humanae M. D. LXXXIII mense Augusto.

(Continued on next card)

CATALOGUE OF THE CORNELL WITCHCRAFT COLLECTION

De praestigiis daemonum, & incantationibus ac ueneficiis libri sex, postrema editione sexta aucti & recogniti.

Wier, Johann, 1515-1588. De praestigiis daemonum ... 1583. (Card 3)

Bound with his De lamiis liber. Basileae, 1582.
Binding: blind stamped pigskin; front covered initialed B P I and dated 1588.
1. Demonology. 2. Witchcraft. 3. Magic. 4. Fasting. I. Title. II. His Liber apologeticus. III. His Pseudomonarchia daemonum. IV. Title: Liber apologeticus. V. Title: Pseudomonarchia daemonum.

De praestigiis et incantationibus daemonum et necromaticorum.

WITCHCRAFT
BF
1520
A69
1568

Argentine, Richard, d. 1568.
De praestigiis et incantationibvs daemonvm et necromaticorvm liber singularis nunqām [sic] antè hac aeditus. Auctore Ricardo Argentino Anglo, medico. Basilaeae, 1568.
216, [22] p. 16cm.
"At pages 111-112 are accounts of Magellan's meeting in America with spirits called Setebi. Shakespeare ... makes Caliban say, 'His art is of such power, it would control my dam's god, Setebos!'"--Bookseller's note pasted inside front cover.
1. Demonology. 2. Witchcraft. 3. Witchcraft in the Bible. I. Title.

De probatione criminis magiae.

Witchcraft

Schack, Johann, praeses.
Disputatio juridica ordinaria De probatione criminis magiae, qvam sub praesidio D. Johannis Schackii ... publicè defendet Martinus von Normann ... Gryphiswaldiae, Typis Danielis Benjaminis Starckii [1706?]
26 p. 18cm. (bound in 21cm. vol.)
Pages 1-8 are bound between p. 72 & 73 of no. 12; rest of text follows no. 12.
No. 13 in vol. lettered Dissertationes de magia. 1623-1723.
1. Witchcraft--Addresses, essays, lectures. 2. Trials (Witchcraft) I. Normann, Martin, respondent. II. Title: De probatione criminis magiae.

De probatione spirituum.

Molitor, Ulrich, fl. 1470-1501.
De lamiis et phitonicis mulieribus. [Paris, Georg Mittelhus?, about 1500] [32] l. 14cm.
Leaf [1a] (Title): Tractatus utilis et necessarius per viā dyalogi ymmo trilogi. De Phitonicis mulieribus. Unacum quodā paruo tractatulo doctissimi et acutissimi in sacra pagina doctoris Johānis de gersono cancellarii parisiensis De probatione spirituum.
Leaf [1a-b]: Tabula et capitula presentis
(Continued on next card)

De probatione spirituum.

Molitor, Ulrich, fl. 1470-1501. De lamiis et phitonicis mulieribus ... [about 1500] (Card 2)

tractatus.
Leaf [2]: Epistola ... ad illustrissimū principē dominū Sigismundū archiducē Austrie Stirie Carinthie etc. ...
The dialogue begins at the bottom of leaf [2b] and ends on leaf [27a].
"Johānis de gersonno ... tractatulus ... de probatione spirituum ...": leaf [27b]-
(Continued on next card)

De probatione spirituum.

Molitor, Ulrich, fl. 1470-1501. De lamiis et phitonicis mulieribus ... [about 1500] (Card 3)

[32b]
Leaf [32b] (Colophon): Explicit tractatus de laniis [sic] et phitonicis mulieribus vna cū tractatulo de probatiōe spūum venerabilis mgr̄i iohānis de gersono cācellarij parisiēssis.
Signatures: a-d8.
Copinger. Supplementum, 4341; Polain
(Continued on next card)

De probatione spirituum.

Witchcraft
BF
1569
A2M72
1500

Molitor, Ulrich, fl. 1470-1501. De lamiis et phitonicis mulieribus ... [about 1500] (Card 4)

(B), 2763; Goff. Third census, M-805.

1. Witchcraft. 2. Demonology. 3. Visions. I. Gerson, Joannes, 1363-1429. De probatione spirituum. II. Title. III. Title: De probatione spirituum.

De processus contra sagas liber.

Witchcraft
BF
1583
A2S74
1703

[Spee, Friedrich von] 1591-1635.
... Cautio criminalis; sev, De processus contra sagas liber. Das ist: Peinliche Warschauung von Anstell- und Führung des Processes gegen die angegebene Zauberer, Hexen und Unholden ... ins Teutsch treulich übersetzt ... [Halle im Magdeburg, 1703]
[49]-356 p. 21cm.

Imperfect: p. 89-218 wanting.
Translated by Hermann Schmidt.

(Continued on next card)

De processus contra sagas liber.

Witchcraft
BF
1583
A2S74
1703

[Spee, Friedrich von] 1591-1635.
Cautio criminalis ... [1703] (Card 2)

From Unterschiedliche Schrifften von Unfug des Hexen-Processes, by Johann Reiche.

1. Witchcraft. 2. Witchcraft--Germany. I. Title. II. Title: De processus contra sagas liber. III. Schmidt, Hermann, tr.

De prodigiosis viuorum hominum apparitionibus.

WITCHCRAFT
BF
1445
T54
D2
1600

Thyraeus, Pierre, 1546-1601, praeses.
De prodigiosis viuorum hominum apparitionibus. Dispvtatio theologica bipartita: et priori qvidem explicantvr illae, in quibus se viui sub propria forma, nunc vigilantibus, nunc dormientibus exhibent; posteriori verò, in quibus ijdem, sub brutorum animantium varijs formis conspiciuntur... Pro gradv responsvrvs est ... Ioannes Henricvs Sylvivs ... praeside P. Petro Thyraeo ... Wircebvrgi, Ex officina typographica Henri-
(Continued on next card)

De prodigiosis viuorum hominum apparitionibus.

WITCHCRAFT
BF
1445
T54
D2
1600

Thyraeus, Pierre, 1546-1601, praeses. De prodigiosis ... [1591?] (Card 2)

ci Aquensis [1591?]
[80] p. 21cm.
Title in ornamental border.
Binding: contemporary blind stamped pigskin, with clasps.
Bound with his De apparitionibus spirituum tractatus duo. Coloniae Agrippinae, 1600.
1. Apparitions. 2. Ghosts. I. Sylvius, Joannes Henricus, respondent. II. Title.

De proprii cujusque nati daemonis inquisitione.

WITCHCRAFT
BF
1405
L85
1673

Longinus, Caesar, ed.
Trinum magicum, sive Secretorum magicorum opus ... Editum à Caesare Longino philos. Francofurti, Sumptibus Jacobi Gothofredi Seyleri, 1673.
12 p. l., 498 p. 14cm.
Contents.--Marci Antonii Zimarae Tractatus magicus.--Appendix, De mirandis quibusdam naturali magia factis operationibus. Ex lib. 2. Mag. nat. Ioan. Bapt. Port.--Tractatvs De virtutibus quarundam herbarum,
(Continued on next card)

De proprii cujusque nati daemonis inquisitione.

WITCHCRAFT
BF
1405
L85
1673

Longinus, Caesar, ed. Trinum magicum ... 1673. (Card 2)

lapidum & animalium. A. M. A.--Commentatio De magnetica curatione vulnerum citra svperstitionem ... Authore R. G. M. D.--Logia, sive Oracvla Zoroastri ex Platonicorum libris collecta.--Tractatus De proprii cujusqve nati daemonis inqvisitione.
Layout of text corresponds to that of Frankfurt, 1630 ed. (C. Eifrid, printer)
(Continued on next card)

De pyn-bank wedersproken.

RARE
HV
8593
J76
1736

Jonctys, Daniel, 1600-1654.
De pyn-bank wedersproken, en bematigt, door Dan. Jonktys [sic]... Amsterdam, By Salomon Schouten, 1736.
268, [62] p. 16cm.
Added t.p. engr.
"Gevoelen van Thomas Morus, dat dievery met de dood niet behoort gestraft te werden...uyt zijn boek...Utopia": 14 p. after p. 268.
1. Torture. I. More, Sir Thomas, 1478-1535. Utopia. II. Title.

De pythonico contractu.

Witchcraft
BF
1569
A2
M97
1499

Murner, Thomas, 1475-1537.
De pythonico contractu. [N. p., n. pr., after 2 Oct., 1499]
[12] l. 22cm.
Leaf [1a] (Title): Tractatus perutilis de phitonico contractu fratris Thome murner liberaliū artium magistri ordinis minorum Ad instantiam Generosi domini Iohannis Wörnher de Mörsperg compilatus.
Leaf [12a]: Ex vniuersitate Friburgeñ. Sole in .xvij. gradu libre gradiente. M.cccc.-xcix.
(Continued on next card)

De pythonico contractu.

Witchcraft
BF
1569
A2
M97
1499

Murner, Thomas, 1475-1537. De pythonico contractu ... after 2 Oct., 1499. (Card 2)

Signatures: a-b6.
Ornamental capital I on leaf [2a].
Hain. Repertorium (with Copinger's Supplement) *11647; Proctor, 3212; Brit. Mus. Cat. (XV cent.) III, 692 (IA. 14018); Goff. Third census, M-877.
Brit. Mus. Catalog. gives as place and printer: Kirchheim in Elsass, Printer of
(Continued on next card)

De pythonico contractu.

Witchcraft
BF
1569
A2
M97
1499

Murner, Thomas, 1475-1537. De pythonico contractu ... after 2 Oct., 1499. (Card 3)

Sankt Brandons Leben or Strassburg, Matthias Hupfuff.
49 blank sheets bound in at end.

1. Witchcraft. I. Title.

De quaestione quae fuerit artium magicarum origo.

Witchcraft
BF
1565
T56

Tiedemann, Dietrich, 1748-1803.
... Dispvtatio de qvaestione qvae fverit artivm magicarvm origo, qvomodo illae ab Asiae popvlis ad Graecos, atqve Romanos, et ab his ad ceteras gentes sint propagatae, qvibvsqve rationibvs advcti fverint ii qvi ad nostra vsqve tempora easdem vel defenderent, vel oppvgnarent? ... Marbvrgi, In nova officina libraria academica, 1787.
158 p. 25cm.
With this is bound Ad Adonai, 3 leaves in MSS, in Latin in a German hand.
(Continued on next card)

151

CATALOGUE OF THE CORNELL WITCHCRAFT COLLECTION

De qualitatibus vulgò dictis occultis.

Witchcraft
BF
1775
G88

Grube, Hermann, praeses.
Disputatio physica De qvalitatibus vulgò dictis occultis, quam ... sub praesidio ... Dn. Hermanni Gruben ... publico eruditorum examini exponet Zacharias Hermannus ... Jenae, Praelo Nisiano [1665?]
[28] p. 18cm.
1. Superstition--Addresses, essays, lectures. 2. Science--Early works to 1800. I. Hermann, Zacharias, respondent. II. Title: De qualitatibus vulgò dictis occultis.

8

De reorum, inprimisque veneficarum, inquisitione.

WITCHCRAFT
BF
1565
H33
1634

Hartz, Konrad.
Cunradi Hartz ... Tractatvs criminalis theorico-practicus, De reorum, inprimisque veneficarum, inquisitione juridice instituenda, in foro haud minus, quam scholis apprimè utilis & jucundus. Nunc primùm in lucem editus ... cum notis ... anonymi cujusdam in Hassia LL. D. Marpvrgi, Typis & sumptibus Nicolai Hampelii, 1634.
189, [13] p. 20cm.
1. Trials (Witchcraft) 2. Witchcraft. I. Title: De reorum, inprimisque veneficarum, inquisitione ...

8

De retractu consanguinitatis.

Witchcraft
HD
1239
G2
R37
1662

Reinking, Dietrich, 1590-1664.
Theodori Reinkingk ... Tractatus synopticus De retractu consangvinitatis ... in certas quaestiones collectus. Editio secunda priori correctior. Huic accessit ejusdem auctoris Responsum juris accuratè elaboratum de processu contra sagas et maleficos &c. Hactenus suppresso nomine editum. Gissae Hassorvm, Sumptibus Hermanni Velstenii, 1662.
16 p. l., 420, [58] p. 14cm.
Added engrav   ed t. p.
(Continued on next card)

8

De retractu consanguinitatis.

Witchcraft
HD
1239
G2
R37
1662

Reinking, Dietrich, 1590-1664. Theodori Reinkingk ... Tractatus synopticus De retractu consangvinitatis ... 1662. (Card 2)

Incomplete: Responsum juris ... wanting.
With this in slipcase is his Responsum juris ... Gissae Hassorvm, 1662, detached from another copy of Tractatus synopticus.
1. Pre-emption--Germany. 2. Pre-emption (Roman law) I. Title: De retractu consanguinitatis.

8

De sagarum natura et potestate, deque his recte cognoscendis et puniendis physiologia.

WITCHCRAFT
BF
1565
S43
1588

Scribonius, Wilhelm Adolf, 16th cent.
De sagarvm natura et potestate, deque his recte cognoscendis et pvniendis physiologia Gulielmi Adolphi Scribonii Marpurgensis. Vbi de pvrgatione earvm per aquam frigidam. Contra Joannem Evvichium ... & Her. Nevvvaldum ... doctores medicos & professores ... Marpurgi, typis Pauli Egenolphi, 1588.
[8], 132 l. 17cm.
In copy 2, contents in MS on 1 [8b].
Title on spi   ne of copy 1:
Scribonius.   Witchcraft pamphlets.
(Continued on next card)

8

De sagarum natura et potestate, deque his recte cognoscendis et puniendis physiologia.

WITCHCRAFT
BF
1565
S43
1588

Scribonius, Wilhelm Adolf, 16th cent. De sagarvm natura ... 1588. (Card 2)

With copy 1 are bound Ignotus Patronus Veritatis, pseud. Examen epistolae et partis physiologiae de examine sagarum ([Francofurti, 1589]); Scribonius, W. A. Responsio ad examen Ignoti Patroni Veritatis (Francofurdi, 1590); and Ignotus Patronus Veritatis, pseud. Refvtatio responsionis Gvlielmi-Adolphi Scribonii (Herbornae, 1591).
1. Witchcraft   2. Ewich, Johann, 1525-1588. 3. Neuwa   ldt, Hermann. I. Title: De sagarum na   tura.

8

De sagarum (quas vulgò veneficas appellant) natura...

Witchcraft
BF
1565
E95

Ewich, Johann, 1525-1588.
De sagarvm (qvas vvlgò veneficas appellant) natvra, arte, viribvs & factis: Item de notis indicijsq́; quibus agnoscantur: et poena, qua afficiendae sint, censura aequa & moderata D. Joann: Evvich ... Bremae, Ex officina typographica Theodori Glvichstein, 1584.
[93] p. 17cm.
With this are bound Neuwaldt, Hermann. Exegesis purgationis. Helmstadii, 1584.
(Continued on next card)

8

De sagarum (quas vulgò veneficas appellant) natura...

Witchcraft
BF
1565
E95

Ewich, Johann, 1525-1588. De sagarvm ... 1584. (Card 2)

and Ad frivolas calumnias, et cavillationes sophisticas Danielis Hoffmanni. Bremae, 1583.

1. Witchcraft. I. Title: De sagarum (quas vulgò veneficas appellant) natura...

8

De sagis.

Witchcraft
BF
1565
D62
no.10

Alberti, Valentin, 1635-1697, praeses.
Dissertatio academica, De sagis, sive foeminis, commercium cum malo spiritu habentibus, e christiana pnevmatologia desumpta, & sub praesidio ... Dn. D. Valentini Alberti ... publicae proposita ventilationi ... ab autore Christiano Stridtbeckh ... Lipsiae, Typis Christoph. Fleischeri [1690].
[52] p. illus. 20cm.
No.10 in vol. lettered Dissertationes de sagis. 1636-1714.
(Continued on next card)

8

De sagis.

Witchcraft
BF
1565
D62
no.14

Fischer, Daniel, 1695-1745.
Tentamen pnevmatologico physicvm De mancipiis diaboli sive sagis. Avthore Daniele Fischero kesmarkiensi-hvngaro. Med. cvlt. Vitembergae, Ex officina Krevsigiana, 1716.
24 p. 20cm.
No. 14 in vol. lettered Dissertationes de sagis. 1636-1714.
1. Witchcraft. I. Title: De mancipiis diaboli sive sagis. II. Title: De sagis.

8

De sagis maleficis.

Witchcraft
BF
1520
P71

Plantsch, Martinus, ca. 1460-1533.
Opusculum de sagis maleficis ... [Phorce, In Aedibus Thomę Anshelmi impensisque Sigismundi Stir, 1507]
[49] l. 20cm.
Signatures: a-e⁸, f⁴, g⁵.
Edited by Heinrich Bebel.

1. Demonology. 2. Divination. 3. Magic. I. Bebel, Heinrich, 1472-ca. 1516, ed. II. Title: De sagis maleficis. III. Title.

De saxis, acubus, ferreis vitreisque frustis, non exiguae molis, variae superficiei et figura.

WITCHCRAFT
BF
1555
V14

Valcarenghi, Paolo.
De saxis, acubus, ferreis vitreisque frustis, non exiguae molis, variae superficiei & figurae, aliisque plurimis rebus, plerumque per vomitum, aliquando etiam per inferiores partes ejectis, tum & de miris animi & corporis morbosis affectionibus, quibus identidem per plures annos Cremonensis virgo quaedam obnoxia fuit, dissertatio epistolaris ... Cremonae, Apud P. Ricchini, 1746.
v-xx, 172 p. 23cm.

8
NIC

1. Demo   niac possession. 2. Medicine--   15th-18th centuries. I. Title.

De sensv rervm, et magia.

Witchcraft
BF
231
C18
1637

Campanella, Tommaso, 1568-1639.
... De sensv rervm, et magia. Libros qvatvor... Correctos et defensos à stupidorum incolarum mundi calumniis per argumenta & testimonia Diuinorum Codicum, naturae, [etc.] ... dedicat consecratqve. Parisiis, Apud Ioannem dv Bray, 1637.
8 p. l., 92, 229 p. 22cm.
"Defensio libri svi De sensv rervm" preceeds text of De sensu rerum.
1. Senses and sensation--Early works to 1800. 2. Ma   gic. I. Title: De sensu rerum et   magia.

8

De sortilegiis.

Witchcraft
BF
1850
G85
1592

Grillando, Paolo.
Tractatvs dvo: Vnus De sortilegiis D. Pavli Grillandi ... Alter De lamiis et excellentia iuris vtriusque D. Ioannis Francisci Ponzinibij Florentini ... Olim qvidem in lvcem editi; nunc verò recogniti, & ab innumeris passim mendis vindicati: adiecto indice locupletissimo. Francoforti ad Moenvm [Apvd Martinvm Lechlervm, Impensis Haeredvm Christiani Egenolphi, 1592.
16 p. l., 299 [1] p. 17cm.
With colop   hon.
(Continued on next card)

8

De spectris.

Witchcraft
BF
1445
D61
no.12

Cameen, Sven, praeses.
Dissertatio philosophica De spectris, quam ... sub moderamine celeberrimi viri Dni. Svenonis Cameen ... pro laurea magisterii reportanda publicae bonorum ventilationi subjiciet ... Petrus Bartelius ... Dorpati, Excudit Johannes Brendeken [1693]
[24] p. 19cm. (bound in 21cm. vol.)
Diss.--Dorpat (P. Bartelius, respondent)
No. 12 in vol. lettered Dissertationes de spectris. 1646-1753.
1. Demono   logy. I. Bartelius, Peter, respon   dent. II. Title: De spectris.

8

De spectris.

Witchcraft
BF
1445
D61
no.9

Donati, Christian, praeses.
Disputatio de spectris, quam sub praesidio Dn. Christiani Donati ... publicae ventilationi sistit Johann. Gottlieb Frimel ... Wittenbergae, Typis Christiani Schrödteri [1688]
[34] p. 18cm. (bound in 21cm. vol.)
No. 9 in vol. lettered Dissertationes de spectris. 1646-1753.
1. Spirits. I. Frimel, Johann Gottlieb, respondent. II. Title: De spectris.

8

De spectris.

Witchcraft
BF
1445
D61
no.1

M. F. S. B. jurium studicsi recentissimum monimentum De spectris ad ... dominvm Christophorum Schonbeck ... Lugduni Batavorum, Typis Marsianis, 1646.
22, [2] p. 18cm. (bound in 21cm. vol.)

No. 1 in vol. lettered Dissertationes de spectris. 1646-1753.

1. Apparitions. I. B., F. S. II. F. S. B. III. Schonbeck, Christoph. IV. Title: De sp   ectris.

8

De spectris.

Witchcraft
BF
1445
D61
no.5

Rechenberg, Adam, 1642-1721, praeses.
De spectris, incl. facult. philosoph. annuente, praeside Dominc M. Adamo Rechenberg, ... publicè disputabit ... Johannes Gabriel Drechsslar, ... A. & R. ... Lipsiae, Literis Johannis Erici Hahnii [1668]
[20] p. 19cm. (bound in 21cm. vol.)

No. 5 in vol. lettered Dissertationes de spectris. 1646-1753.

1. Apparit   ions. I. Drechssler, Johann Gabriel, d. 1677, respondent. Title.

8

CATALOGUE OF THE CORNELL WITCHCRAFT COLLECTION

De spectris.

WITCHCRAFT
BF
1445
S327
  Scherertz, Sigismund, 1584-1639.
    Libellus consolatorius De spectris, hoc est, apparitionibus & illusionibus daemonum. Pio studio conscriptus per Sigismundum Scherertzium ... Wittebergae, Typis Augusti Boreck, Sumptibus Pauli Helvvigij, 1621.
    [158] p. 16cm.

8
NIC
    1. Ghosts. 2. Spirits. 3. Demonology. I. Title. II. Title: De spectris.

De spectris.

.chcraft
...5
..11
  Schlosser, Philipp Casimir, praeses.
    Disputatio inauguralis philosophica De spectris. Quam ... praeside ... M. Philippo Casimiro Schlossero ... pro lauru magisteriali rite & legitime impetranda, publice defendendam conscripsit, ac omnibus sobrie & candide philosophantibus subjicit A. & R. Johannes Philippus Hechler ... Gissae Hassorvm, Typis Christoph. Hermanni Kargeri [1693]
    46 p. 21cm.

  (Continued on next card)

De spectris.

tchcraft
.45
1
.11
  Schlosser, Philipp Casimis, praeses. Disputatio inauguralis philosophica De spectris ... [1693]   (Card 2)

    Diss.--Giessen (J. P. Hechler, respondent)
    No. 11 in vol. lettered Dissertationes de spectris. 1646-1753.
    1. Apparitions. 2. Demonology. I. Hechler, Johann Philipp, respondent. II. Title: De spectris.

De spectris.

itchcraft
?
445
61
o.13
  Wedel, Georg Wolfgang, 1645-1721, praeses.
    Dissertatio medica De spectris, praeside Georgio Wolffgango VVedelio ... proposita ab Ernesto Henrico Wedelio ... Editio secunda. Jenae, Litteris Krebsianis, 1698.
    39, [1] p. 19cm. (bound in 21cm. vol.)

    Diss.--Jena (E. H. Wedel, respondent)
    No. 13 in vol. lettered Dissertationes de spectris. 1646-1753.

De spectris, disputationem II.

Witchcraft
BF
1445
D61
no.6
  Drechssler, Johann Gabriel, d. 1677, praeses.
    De spectris, disputationem II. Inclut. facultat. philosoph. Lipsiensis consensu P. P. praeses M. Johannes Gabriel Drechssler ... et respondens Christianus Michelmann ... Lipsiae, Literis Johannis Erici Hahnii [1669]
    [12] p. 21cm.
    No. 6 in vol. lettered Dissertationes de spectris. 1646-1753.
    1. Rechenberg, Adam, 1642-1721, praeses. De spectris. 2. Apparitions. 3. Devil. I. Michelmann, Christian, respondent. II. Title.

De spectris, & in specie eorum depulsione, disputationem III.

Witchcraft
BF
1445
D61
no.7
  Drechssler, Johann Gabriel, d. 1677, praeses.
    De spectris, & in specie eorum depulsione, disputationem III. Inclut. facultatis philosoph. Lipsiensis indultu, sub praesidio M. Johannis Gabrielis Drechsslers, ... publice defendet respondens Jacobus Friedrich Müller ... Lipsiae, Excudebat Samuel Spörel [1670]
    [20], p. illus. 21cm.
    No. 7 in vol. lettered Dissertationes de spectris. 1646-1753.

  (Continued on next card)

WITCHCRAFT
BF
1445
L39
1659
  De spectris, lemuribus et magnis atque insolitis fragoribus.
    De spectris, lemuribus et magnis atque insolitis fragoribus, variisque praesagitionibus, quae plerunque obitum hominum, magnas clades, mvtationesque Imperiorum praecedunt. Liber vnvs. In tres partes distributus ... Authore Ludov. Lavatero Tigurino. Editio secunda priori multo emendatior. Lvgd. Batavorvm, Apud Henr. Verbiest, 1659.
    [18], 245 p. 13cm.

  (Continued on next card)

WITCHCRAFT
BF
1445
L39
1659
  De spectris, lemuribus et magnis atque insolitis fragoribus.
    Lavater, Ludwig, 1527-1586. De spectris ... 1659.   (Card 2)

    Added t. p., engraved.
    Error in paging: 244 numbered 144.
    Colophon: Lvgd. Batav., Ex Typogr. Joh. Z. Baron, 1659.

    1. Apparitions. 2. Ghosts. 3. Demonology. I. Title.

De spiritibus familiaribus vulgo sic dictis.

WITCHCRAFT
BF
1557
C64
1708
  Clodius, Johann, 1645-1733, praeses.
    De spiritibus familiaribus vulgo sic dictis, praeside Johanne Clodio, disseret Jo. Christophorus Rudingerus. Vitembergae, C. Schroedter, 1708.
    [32] p. 20cm.

    Originally issued as dissertation, Wittenberg, 1693 (J. C. Rudinger, respondent)
    1. Demonology. I. Rudinger, J.C. II. Title.

8
NIC

De stigmatiis.

WITCHCRAFT
HV
8609
S76
  Spitz, Erhard, fl. 1712-1716.
    De stigmatiis ... sine praeside dispvtabit ... Erhardus Spitz Altdorfinus. [Altdorfii] Literis Kohlesii [ca. 1715?]
    50 p. 20cm.

    1. Punishment--History. 2. Cicatrices. 3. Birthmarks. 4. Witchcraft. I. Title.

8
NIC

De strigimagarum daemonumque mirandis.

WITCHCRAFT
BF
1565
M47
1575
  Mazzolini, Silvestro, da Prierio, 1456-1523.
    Reverendi Patris F. Silvestri Prieriatis ... De strigimagarvm, daemonumque mirandis, libri tres ... Romae, In aedibus Po[r]puli, Ro[m]ani, 1575.
    12 p. l., 262 p. 23cm.
    With colophon.
    With this is bound Spina, Bartolommeo. ... Quaestio de strigibus. Romae, 1576.

8
NIC
    1. Witch craft. 2. Demonology. I. Title: De strigimagarum... mirandis.

De substantiis separatis.

Witchcraft
BF
1520
A53
D2
1654
  Anania, Giovanni Lorenzo d'.
    De Svbstantiis separatis. Opvscvlvm primvm [-secvndvm]. De natvra daemonvm et occultis eorum operationibus. Avthore Io:Lavrentio Anania. Romae, Typis Iacobi Dragondelli, 1654.
    2 v. in 1. 22cm.
    Vol. 2 has special t. p.: De svbstantiis separatis. Opvscvlvm secvndvm. De natvra angelorvm et occultis eorum operationibus.
    Vol. 1 also published separately

  (Continued on next card)

De substantiis separatis.

Witchcraft
BF
1520
A53
D2
1654
  Anania, Giovanni Lorenzo d'. De Svbstantiis separatis. 1654.   (Card 2)
    with title: De natvra daemonvm.

    1. Demonology. 2. Angels. I. Title: De substantiis separatis. II. Title: De natura angelorum. III. His De natura daemonum.

8

De superstitiosis quibusdam casibus.

Witchcraft
BR
135
H46
1473
  Heinrich von Gorkum, 1386 (ca.)-1431.
    De superstitiosis quibusdam casibus. De celebratione festorum. [Esslingen, Conrad Fyner, not after 1473]
    [18] l. 21cm.

    Leaf [1a]: Incipit tractatus de supsticiosis quibusda casib[9] ppilat[9] in alma vniveśitate studij Colonien[s] [p] venabilem mgrm Heinricū de Gorihem sacre theo. [p]fessore[m] eximium.
    Leaf [9b]: Explicit Tractat[9] de supsticiosis quibusdam casib[9].

  (Continued on next card)

De superstitiosis quibusdam casibus.

Witchcraft
BR
135
H46
1473
  Heinrich von Gorkum, 1386 (ca.)-1431. De superstitiosis quibusdam casibus ... [not after 1473]   (Card 2)

    Leaf [10a]: Incipit tractatus de Celebratōne festor[u].
    Leaf [18b]: Explicit Tractatus cui[9] supra de Celebratōne festor[u].
    Signatures: unsigned [a8, b10].
    Capital spaces; capitals, initial-strokes, paragraph-marks and underlines supplied in red.

  (Continued on next card)

De superstitiosis quibusdam casibus.

Witchcraft
BR
135
H46
1473
  Heinrich von Gorkum, 1386 (ca.)-1431. De superstitiosis quibusdam casibus ... [not after 1473]   (Card 3)

    Hain. Repertorium (with Copinger's Supplement) *7807; Proctor, 2462; Brit. Mus. Cat. (XV cent.) II, p. 521 (IA. 8923; variant); Goff. Third census, H-24 (Under Henricus de Gorichen).

    1. Superstition. 2. Fasts and feasts--Catholic Church. I. Heinrich von Gorkum, 1386 (ca.)-1431. De celebratione festorum. I. Title. II. De celebratione festorum.

De theologia daemonum.

Witchcraft
BF
1520
K89
  Krakevitz, Albert Joachim von, 1674-1734, praeses.
    Facultatis theologicae ad hunc actum decanus Albertus Joach. de Krakevitz, ... suo & collegii theologici nomine ad disputationem inauguralem ... Dn. M. Fridemanni Andreae Zulichii, Jenens. De theologia daemonum ... invitat. Rostochii, Litteris J. Wepplingi, Sereniss. Princ. & univ. typogr. [1715]
    10 p. l., 68 p. 21cm.
    The first section is a curriculum

  (Continued on next card)

De theologia daemonum.

Witchcraft
BF
1520
K89
  Krakevitz, Albert Joachim von, 1674-1734, praeses. ...De theologia daemonum ... [1715]   (Card 2)

    vitae.
    The dissertation proper has special t. p.: Auxiliante summo numine specimen inaugurale theologicum De theologia daemonum ...
    Diss.--Rostock (F. A. Zulich, respondent)
    1. Demonology. 2. Devil. I. Zulich, Fridemann Andreas, b. 1687, respondent. II. His Specimen inaugurale theologicum De theologia daemonum. III. Title: De theologia daemonum.

153

CATALOGUE OF THE CORNELL WITCHCRAFT COLLECTION

WITCHCRAFT
QC
859
H82

De tonitru et tempestate.
Hossmann, Abraham, d. 1617.
De tonitru et tempestate, das ist: Nohtwendiger Bericht, von Donnern vnd Hagel-Wettern, wannen vnd woher sich dieselben verursachen, ob sie natürlich: Item, ob Teufel vnd Zäuberer auch Wetter machen können ... Neben Erzehlung etlicher seltzamen Fälle ... in Druck gegeben durch Abrahamum Hosmanum ... Leipzig, In Verlegung Henning Grossn den Ältern Buchhändl. ₍Typis Beerwaldin, durch Jacobum Popporeich₎ 1612.
123, ₍1₎ p. 20cm.

8
NIC
(Continued on next card)

WITCHCRAFT
QC
859
H82

De tonitru et tempestate.
Hossmann, Abraham, d. 1617. De tonitru & tempestate ... 1612. (Card 2)
Title in red and black, within ornamental border.
With colophon.

1. Meteorology--Early works to 1800. 2. Folk-lore, German. 3. Witchcraft. I. Title. II. Title: Von Donnern und Hagel-Wettern.

8
NIC

Witchcraft
BL
325
M45
T46

De transformatione hominum in bruta.
Thomasius, Jacob, 1622-1684, praeses.
De transformatione hominum in bruta, dissertationem philosophicam priorem, inclytae facultatis philosophicae permissu & authoritate sub praesidio ... Dn. M. Jacobi Thomasii ... ventilationi subjicit ... Fridericus Tobias Moebius ... ₍Lipsiae?₎ Typis Joh. Wittigau ₍1667₎
₍20₎ p. 19cm.
Diss.--Leipzig (F. T. Moebius, respondent)
1. Metamorphosis (in religion, folk-lore, etc.) 2. Magic. I. Moebius, Friedrich Tobias, respondent. II. Title.

8

Witchcraft
BF
1520
S32

De usu et praestantia daemonum.
Schwartz, Johann Conrad, 1677-1747.
Dissertatio theologica De vsv et praestantia daemonvm ad demonstrandam natvram Dei, qvam ... tvebitvr Io. Conradvs Schwartz ... Altdorfi Noric., Literis Iodoci Gvilielmi Kohlesii ₍1715₎
26 p. 21cm.
Bound with Scherzer, Johann Adam, praeses. Daemonologia. Lipsiae, 1672.
In vol. lettered Dissertationes de daemonibus. 1672- 1722.
1. God. 2. Demonology. I. Title: De usu et praestantia daemonum.

8

MSS
Bd.
WITCHCRAFT
BF
D27

De vampiri vnico trattato. In cui si dimostra che l'apparizioni di spettri, larve, fantasme, e dette con altri termini, larve, lenture, mani, lari, genij, ó siano fale, monacchi, incubi non sono altro che imagini formate dall 'vmana fantasia alterate, e guasta... ₍n.p. after 1738₎
112 p. 22cm.
Manuscript, on paper, in an Italian hand. Note on fly-leaf by a former owner states that the manuscript was never printed. Bound in vellum.
1. Vampires. 2. Apparitions.

WITCHCRAFT
BF
1445
T54
D2

De variis tam spirituum, quam vivorum hominum ... apparitionibus ... libri tres.
Thyraeus, Pierre, 1546-1601.
Reverendi P. Petri Thyraei ... De variis tam spiritvvm, qvam vivorvm hominvm prodigiosis apparitionibus, & nocturnis infestationibus libri tres. Quorum contenta pagina versa demonstrabit ... Coloniae Agrippinae, Ex officina Mater. Cholini, sumptibus Gosuini Cholini, 1594.
8 p. l., 159 p. 21cm.
1. Apparitions. 2. Ghosts. I. Title: De variis tam spirituum, quam vivorum hominum ... apparitionibus ... libri tres.

8

WITCHCRAFT
BF
1565
H33
1639

De veneficarum inquisitione.
Hartz, Konrad.
Tractatvs criminalis De veneficarum inquisitione Cunradi Hartz ... Editio secunda, priori longè auctiori & emendatiori. Rintelii ad Visvrgim, Typis exscripsit Petrus Lucius typog. acad., 1639.
394, ₍40₎ p. 15cm.
Published earlier as his Tractatus ... De reorum, inprimisque veneficarum, inquisitione juridice instituenda.
1. Trials (Witchcraft) 2. Witchcraft. I. His Tractatus ... De reorum, in primisque veneficarum, inquisitione ... II. Title: De venefica rum inquisitione.

8

WITCHCRAFT
BF
1565
J19

De veneficis.
Jacquier, Nicolas.
Flagellvm haereticorvm fascinariorvm, avtore Nicolao Iaqverio. His accesservnt Lamberti Danaei de veneficis dialogi, Ioachimi Camerarii in Plutarchi de oraculorum defectu epistola, Martini de Arles de superstitionibus tractatvs, Ioannis Trithemii atq; maleficis qvaestiones III, Thomae Erasti de strigibus liber. Studio Ioan. Myntzenbergii edita. Francofvrti ad Moenvm ₍Impressvm apud N. Bassaeum₎ 1581.
604 p. 17 cm.

8
NIC
(Continued on next card)

Witchcraft
BF
1565
D17

De veneficis, qvos olim sortilegos, nvnc autem vulgò sortiarios vocant, dialogvs.
Daneau, Lambert, ca. 1530-1595.
De veneficis, qvos olim sortilegos, nvnc autem vulgò sortiarios vocant, dialogus: in qvo qvae de hoc argumento quaeri solent, breuiter & commodè explicantur. Tractatus propter varias et controuersas de hac quaestione hominum sententias vtilissimus, & rerum capitalium iudicibus maximè necessarius. Per Lambertum Danaeum. ₍Genevae₎ Apvd Evstathivm Vignon, 1574.
127 p. 18cm.
Title vignette (E. Vignon's device)

8
(Continued on next card)

MSS
Bd.
WITCHCRAFT
BF
L86
1592b

De vera et falsa magia.
Loos, Cornelius, 1546-1595.
₍De vera et falsa magia. Köln? 1592? ca. 1900₎
₍1₎, 96, ₍1₎, 89, ₍1₎ p.; 15 blank l., ₍1₎ p. 15cm.
Signatures: A-F⁸. (p. 1-96 only)
Carnap's manuscript copy of a printed fragment, according to G. L. Burr, probably as much as had been completed before seizure by the Inquisition.
"Das Original befindet sich in der Stadtbibliothek zu Köln ... 6 Bogen
(Continued on next card)

MSS
Bd.
WITCHCRAFT
BF
L86
1592b

De vera et falsa magia.
Loos, Cornelius, 1546-1595. ₍De vera et falsa magia. 1592? ca. 1900₎ (Card 2)
in Kl. 8°. Ein Titelblatt ist nicht vorhanden."
The second part, p. 1-89 consists of bibliographical citations and excerpts from articles concerning Loos and his work.

1. Demonology. 2. Witchcraft. 3. His De vera et falsa magia. I. Title.

Witchcraft
PA
8555
N59F7
1692

De visionibus ac revelationibus.
Nider, Johannes, d. 1438.
De visionibus ac revelationibus opus rarissimum Historiis Germaniae refertissimum, Anno 1517. Argentinae editum. Auspiciis... Rudolphi Augusti, Brunsvicens. ac Luneburg. Ducis, luci & integritati restitutum, recensente Hermanno von der Hardt ... Helmestadii, Impensis Pauli Zeisingii, Typis Salomonis Schnorrii, 1692.
₍30₎, 669 p. front. 17cm.
A reprint, under a new title, of Nider's
(Continued on next card)

Witchcraft
PA
8555
N59F7
1692

De visionibus ac revelationibus.
Nider, Johannes, d. 1438. De visionibus ... 1692. (Card 2)
Formicarius.
"Liber quintus: De maleficis & eorum deceptionibus": p. 514-669.
Ex libris Kurt Seligmann.

1. Conduct of life. 2. Christian life. 3. Witchcraft. 4. Demonology. I. Hardt, Hermann von der, 1660-1746, ed. II. Nider, Johannes, d. 1438. Formicarius. III. Title. IV. Title: Formicarius.

Witchcraft
BF
1565
D96

De vocibus hhartymmim et belahatehem.
₍Durych, Fortunat₎ 1730-1802.
Eutychii Beniamin Transalbini Dissertatio philologica De vocibus hhartymmim et belahatehem Exod. VII. 2. ₍Vindobonae?₎ 1767.
20 p. 21cm.
"Opusculi inscripti: Gedanken über die Werke des Liebhabers der Wahrheit von der Hexerey."

1. Witchcraft in the Bible. 2. Bible. O.T.--Criticism, Textual. 3. Hartumim

8
(Continued on next card)

Witchcraft
BF
1565
D96

De vocibus hhartymmim et belahatehem.
₍Durych, Fortunat₎ 1730-1802. Eutychii Beniamin Transalbini Dissertatio philologica De vocibus hhartymmim ... 1767. (Card 2)

(The word) 4. Belahatehem (The word) 5. März, Agnellus, 1726-1784. I. Title: Dissertatio philologica De vocibus hhartymmim et belahatehem.

8

De Abano, Peter.
see
Abano, Pietro d', 125C-1315?

Witchcraft
BF
1565
D27
2 Copies

Deacon, John, Preacher.
Dialogicall discourses of spirits and divels, declaring their proper essence, natures, dispositions, and operations, and dispossessions: with other the appendantes ... By John Deacon ₍and₎ John Walker ... Londini, G. Bishop, 1601.
356 p. 20cm.

1. Witchcraft. I. Walker, John, Preacher, joint author. II. Title.

WITCHCRAFT
BF
1555
D22

Deacon, John, preacher.
A summarie answere.
Darrell, John, fl. 1562-1602.
The replie of Iohn Darrell, to the answer of Iohn Deacon, and Iohn Walker, concerning the doctrine of the possessio and dispossession of demoniakes. ₍London?₎ 1602.
50, ₍8₎ p. 18cm.

1. Deacon, John, preacher. A summarie answere. 2. Walker, John, preacher. His A true narration of the strange and grevous vexation by the Devil. I. Title.

154

CATALOGUE OF THE CORNELL WITCHCRAFT COLLECTION

Witchcraft

[Deane, Charles] 1813–1889.
... Spurious reprints of early books. Boston [Cambridge, University press] 1865.
19 p. 25ᶜᵐ. (Bibliographical tracts. no. 1)
Signed at end "Delta".
"From the Boston Daily advertiser of March 24, 1865. With additions and corrections. One hundred and thirty-one copies printed."
"This reprint was not made by Mr. Deane."—Sabin.
A review of "Salem witchcraft: comprising More wonders of the invisible world, collected by Robert Calef; and Wonders of the invisible world, by Cotton Mather. Together with notes and explanations by Samuel P. Fowler. Boston, W. Veazie, 1865" [reissue from the stereotyped plates of the Salem, 1861, edition]

1. Fowler, Samuel Page, 1800-1888, ed. [Salem witchcraft ... Boston, 1865.] I. Title. II. Delta, pseud.

Library of Congress   Z1001.D28   2—13743
.33d1.

Death by enchantment.

Witchcraft
BF 1566
F83 1971

Franklyn, Julian.
Death by enchantment; an examination of ancient and modern witchcraft. [1st American ed.] New York, Putnam [1971]
x, 244 p. illus. 22 cm. $6.95
Includes bibliographical references.

1. Witchcraft.   I. Title.
BF1566.F7 1971   133.4   78-152769 MARC
Library of Congress   71 [4]

Witchcraft
BF 1410
D28 1883

Debay, Auguste, 1802-1890.
Histoire des sciences occultes depuis l'antiquité jusqu'à nos jours. 3. éd. ...
Paris, E. Dentu, 1883.
536 p. 18cm.

1. Occult sciences—Hist.   I. Title.

De Beauvoys de Chauvincourt, sieur.

see

Beauvois de Chauvincourt, sieur de.

Decas qvaestionum ex magiae illicitae materia.

Witchcraft
F 587
61 o.9

Schultze, Georg, fl. 1671-1682, praeses.
Decas qvaestionum ex magiae illicitae materia ... ventilationi propositarum â praeside M. Georg Schultzen ... respondente filio Christiano Schultzen, Halâ-Saxone ... [Lipsiae?] Typis viduae Joh. Wittigau [1677]
[16] p. 21cm.
No. 9 in vol. lettered Dissertationes de magia. 1623-1723.

1. Magic—Addresses, essays, lectures.
I. Schultze, Christian, respondent.
II. Title: Decas quaestionum ex magiae illici tae materia.

Witchcraft
BF 1582
G51 P9++

Dechaussé, Nicolas de S. Joseph Carme, fl. 1730.
Girard, Jean Baptiste, 1680-1733, defendant.
Procedure sur laquelle le pere Jean Baptiste Girard, jesuite, Catherine Cadiere, le pere Estienne Thomas Cadiere, dominicain, Mre. François Cadiere, prêtre, et le pere Nicolas de S. Joseph Carme Dechaussé, ont e'te' jugez par arrêt du parlement de Provence du 10. octobre 1731 ... Aix, Chez J. David, 1733.
422 p. 36cm.

With this ... is bound Montvalon, A. B. de. Motifs des juges du parlement de Provence qui ont été
(Continued on next card)

Witchcraft
BF 1582
G51 P9++

Dechaussé, Nicolas de S. Joseph Carme, fl. 1730.
Girard, Jean Baptiste, 1680-1733, defendant.
Procedure ... 1733. (Card 2)
d'avis de condamner le p. Jean Baptiste Girard ... [Aix?] 1733.

I. France. Parlement (Aix) II. Cadière, Mary Catherine, fl. 1730. III. Cadière, Estienne Thomas, fl. 1730. IV. Cadière, François, fl. 1730. V. Dechaussé, Nicolas de S. Joseph Carme, fl. 1730. VI. Title: Procedure sur laquelle le pere Jean Baptiste Girard ... [est   été jugez.

De Chauvincourt, de Beauvoys, sieur.

see

Beauvois de Chauvincourt, sieur de.

Witchcraft
BF 1445
D29

Decker, Johann Heinrich, 1665-1707.
Spectrologia; h. e. Discursus ut plurimum philosophicus de spectris; brevibus & succinctis thesibus illorum existentiam, essentiam, qualitatem, ὡς, varias apparitionum formas, & fallacias exhibens. Hamburgi, Apud Gothofr. Liebernickel, Literis Brendekii, 1690.
10 p. l., 197, [18] p. 14cm.
Added engraved t. p.
1. Apparitions. 2. Ghosts. I. Title.
8

Witchcraft
BX 1711
D29

Deckert, Joseph.
Inquisition und Hexenprocesse. "Greuel der katholischen Kirche." Wien, "Sendboten des heil. Joseph" in Commission bei H. Kirsch, 1896.
34 p. 21cm.

"Separat-Abdruck aus dem 'Sendboten des heil. Joseph.'"

1. Inquisition.   2. Trials (Witchcraft)
I. Title.

Declamation sur l'incertitude, vanité, et abus des sciences.

WITCHCRAFT
B 781
A33 I3 1582

Agrippa von Nettesheim, Heinrich Cornelius, 1486?-1535.
Declamation svr l'incertitvde, vanité, et abvs des sciences, traduite en françois du latin de Henry Corneille Agr. ...
[Paris] Par Iean Dvrand, 1582.
8 p. l., 551 p. 17cm.
First edition in French, of De incertitudine et vanitate omnium scientiarum et artium liber.
"Trad. par Louis de Mayerne Turquet. C'est la seule   traduction qui n'a pas
8   (Continued on next card)

Declamation sur l' incertitude, vanité, et abus des sciences.

WITCHCRAFT
B. 781
A33 I3 1582

Agrippa von Nettesheim, Heinrich Cornelius, 1486?-1535. Declamation svr l'incertitvde ... des sciences ... 1582. (Card 2)
été multilée": in 17th century hand on flyleaf.
Gold stamped citron morocco binding with date 1695 on front and back covers.

1. Learning and scholarship. 2. Scholasticism. 3. Science—Early works to 1800. I. His De incertitudine et vanitate omnium scientiarum et artium liber, French. II. Mayerne, Louis Turquet, d. 1618. III. Title.

Declaratio apologetica.

Witchcraft
BF 1429
G62 1704

Zobel, Enoch, 1653-1697.
Declaratio apologetica, das ist: Schutzschriftliche und fernere Erklärung, uber [sic] die St. Annabergische Gespensts-Historie, wider Herrn Balthasar Bekkers ... herausgebenes Buch, genannt Die bezauberte Welt, abgefasset von M. Enoch Zobeln, Archi-Diac. zu St. Annaberg. Leipzig, Verlegt von den Lanckischen Erben, 1695.
7 p. l., 174, [1] p. [p. 176 blank] front., vignettes. 17 x 10cm.

(Continued on next card)

Declaratio apologetica.

Witchcraft
BF 1429
G62 1704

Zobel, Enoch, 1653-1697. Declaratio apologetica ... 1695. (Card 2)
8°:)(⁸ (-)(8), A-L⁸.
Black letter.
At head of title: B. C. D.
Autograph on p. [176]: Adolph Gerhard Eduard Grovermann.
Bound with Goldschmidt, P. Höllischer Morpheus. Hamburg, 1704.

1. Ghosts—Germany. 2. Bekker, Baltha-
(Continued on next card)

Witchcraft
BF 1581
Z7 1652a

A Declaration in answer to several lying pamphlets concerning the witch of Wapping.
Being a more perfect relation of the arraignment, condemnation, and suffering of Jone Peterson, who was put to death on Munday the 12 of April, 1652. Shevving the bloudy plot and wicked conspiracy of one Abraham Vandenbemde, Thomas Crompton, Thomas Collet, and others. London, Printed in the year 1652.
11 p. 20cm.

(Continued on next card)

Witchcraft
BF 1581
Z7 1652a

A Declaration in answer to several lying pamphlets concerning the witch of Wapping... 1652. (Card 2)

Bound with The witch of Wapping. London, 1652.
With bookplate of Francis Freeling.

1. Peterson, Joan, d. 1652.

A declaration of egregious Popish impostures.

Witchcraft
BF 1581
H32 1605

[Harsnett, Samuel] archbishop of York, 1561-1631.
A declaration of egregious Popish impostures, to with-draw the harts of His Maiesties subiects from their allegeance, and from the truth of Christian religion professed in England, vnder the pretence of casting out of deuils. Practised by Edmunds, alias VVeston, a Iesuit, & diuers Romish priestes his vvicked associates. Where-vnto are annexed the copies of the confessions, & examinations of the parties themselues,   which were pretended to
(Continued on next card)

A declaration of egregious Popish impostures.

Witchcraft
BF 1581
H32 1605

[Harsnett, Samuel] archbishop of York, 1561-1631. A declaration of egregious Popish impostures ... 1605.   (Card 2)
be possessed and dispossessed: taken vppon oath before His Maiesties commissioners, for causes ecclesiasticall. Barbican [London] Newly printed by Ia. Roberts, 1605.
284 p. 19cm.

Epistle "To the sedvced Catholiques of England" signed: S.H.
1. Edmond s, William, 1550?-1616.
I. Title.

155

CATALOGUE OF THE CORNELL WITCHCRAFT COLLECTION

Witchcraft | A declaration of the ground of error & errors, blasphemy, blasphemers, and blasphemies.
BV 4617 B6 F79 | [Fox, George], 1624-1691.
A declaration of the ground of error & errors, blasphemy, blasphemers and blasphemies: and the ground of inchantings and seducing spirits and the doctrine of devils, the sons of sorcerers and the seed of the adulterer, and the ground of nicromancy, which doth defile witches and wizards ... By G. F. London, Printed for G. Calvert, 1657.
41 p. 18cm.

I. F., G.   II. . G. F. III. Title.

WITCHCRAFT
BF 1598 D31 A3++ 1659 | Dee, John, 1527-1608.
A true & faithful relation of what passed for many yeers between Dr. John Dee ... and some spirits: tending (had it succeeded) to a general alteration of most states and kingdomes in the world. His private conferences with Rodolphe Emperor of Germany, Stephen K. of Poland, and divers other princes about it. The particulars of his cause, as it was agitated in the Emperors Court; by the Popes intervention: his banishment, and restoration in part.   As also the letters of
(Continued on next card)

WITCHCRAFT
BF 1598 D31 A3++ 1659 | Dee, John, 1527-1608. A true and faithful relation...1659.   (Card 2)
sundry great men and princes ... to the said D. Dee. Out of the original copy, written with Dr. Dees own hand: kept in the library of Sir Tho. Cotton ... With a preface confirming the reality ... of this relation ... by Meric. Casaubon. London, Printed by D. Maxwell, for T. Gartwait, 1659.
[78], 448, 45 p. front., 3 tables (1 fold.) 34 cm.
I. Title.

Witchcraft
BF 1582 G51 D3 1732 | The defence of F. John Baptist Girard.
Girard, Jean Baptiste, 1680-1733, defendant.
The defence of F. John Baptist Girard, Jesuit, and rector of the Royal Seminary of Chaplains of the Navy in the city of Toulon; against the accusation of Mary Catharine Cadiere. London, Printed for and sold by J. Roberts, 1731-32 [pt. 1, 1732]
3 pts. in 1 v. 21cm.

Parts 1-2: 3d ed.

I. Cadière, Catharine, b. 1709.   II. Title.

Rare HV 8599 S8 C35 | Defensa de la tortura y leyes patrias que la establecieron.
Castro, Pedro de, canon of Seville.
Defensa de la tortura y leyes patrias que la establecieron: e inpugnacion del tratado que escribio contra ella el doctor d. Alfonso Maria de Acevedo: su autor, don pedro de Castro ... Madrid, M. Escribano, 1778.
xxviii, 256 p. 21cm.

1. Torture. 2. Azevedo, Alonso María de. [De reorum absolutione ...
I. Title.

Library of Congress   HV8599.S8C3   45-42238
[3]

MSS Bd. WITCHCRAFT BF L37 | Défense de Mathurin Picard.
Laugeois, Antoine, d. 1674.
L'innocence opprimee; ou, Défense de Mathurin Picard, curé de Mesnil-Jourdain ... Par M. Laugois, successeur immédiat dudit Picard - dans la cure de Mesnil-Jourdain. Ouvrage qui n'a jamais été imprimé et extrait sur l'original, par M. Chemin curé de Tourneville. [n. p. 17th cent.]
x, 102 p. title vignette. 18cm.
Manuscript, on paper.
Preface signed M. du Passeur (Gabriel), curé de Vironvay.
(Continued on next card)

MSS Bd. WITCHCRAFT BF L37 | Défense de Mathurin Picard.
Laugeois, Antoine, d. 1674. L'innocence opprimee...[17th cent.]   (Card 2)
Notes by G. L. Burr inside front cover discuss history and provenance of the manuscript.
Bound in boards.
1. Demoniac possession. 2. Picard, Mathurin, d. 1647. 3. Bavent, Madeleine, b. 1607. 4. Louviers, France. St. Louis (Convent) 5. Witchcraft. I. Chemin, J B   , 1725   -1731, ed. II. Title. III. Title: Défense de Mathurin Picard.

Witchcraft
BF 1581 Z7 1712c | A defense of the proceedings against Jane Wenham.
Bragge, Francis.
A defense of the proceedings against Jane Wenham, wherein the possibility and reality of witchcraft are demonstrated from Scripture and the concurrent testimonies of all ages. In answer to two pamphlets, entituled, I. The impossibility of witchcraft, &c. II. A full confutation of witchcraft. By Francis Bragge ... London, Printed for E. Curll, 1712.
2 p. l., 36 p. 18½cm.

Witchcraft
BF 1584 I8D31 1783 | Defeza de Cecilia Faragó, accusada do crime de feiticeria: obra util para desabusar as pessoas preoccupadas da arte magica, e seus pertendidos effeitos. Lisboa, Na Officina da Academia das Sciencias, 1783.
[6], 149 p. 14cm.

Signed at end: Napoles 26 de Março de 1770. José Rafael.

1. Faragó, Cecilia. 2. Witchcraft—Italy.

Defoe, Daniel

Witchcraft
BF 1445 D31 | [Defoe, Daniel] 1660-1731.
An essay on the history and reality of apparitions. Being an account of what they are, and what they are not; whence they come, and whence they come not. London, J. Roberts, 1727.
6 p.l., 395 p. front., plates. 19 1/2cm.

I. Title.

Witchcraft
BF 1445 D31 1770 | Defoe, Daniel, 1660-1731.
An essay on the history and reality of apparitions.
[Defoe, Daniel] 1660-1731. The secrets of the invisible world laid open; or, A general history of apparitions, sacred and prophane, whether angelical, diabolical, or departed souls. Shewing I. Their various returns to this world; with sure rules to know if they are good or evil. II. An enquiry into the scriptural doctrine of spirits. III. The different species of apparitions, with their real existence. IV. The nature of seeing ghosts, before
(Continued on next card)

Witchcraft
BF 1445 D31 1770 | Defoe, Daniel, 1660-1731.
An essay on the history and reality of apparitions.
[Defoe, Daniel] 1660-1731. The secrets of the invisible world laid open. 1770.   (Card 2)
and after death. V. The effects of fancy, vapours, dreams, hyppo, and the difference between real or imaginary appearances. VI. A collection of the most authentic relations of apparitions, particularly that surprizing one attested by the learned Dr. Scott. Likewise Mrs. Veal's appearance to
(Continued on next card)

Witchcraft
BF 1445 D31 1770 | Defoe, Daniel, 1660-1731.
An essay on the history and reality of apparitions.
[Defoe, Daniel] 1660-1731. The secrets of the invisible world laid open. 1770.   (Card 3)
Mrs. Bargrave, Sir George Villers to the duke of Buckingham, &c. &c. Also the notions of the heathens concerning apparitions. Being the most entertaining and, in quantity, the cheapest book of the kind. London, Printed for the Author and sold by D. Steel, 1770.
(Continued on next card)

Witchcraft
BF 1445 D31 1770 | Defoe, Daniel, 1660-1731.
An essay on the history and reality of apparitions.
[Defoe, Daniel] 1660-1731. The secrets of the invisible world laid open. 1770.   (Card 4)
4, v, 252 p. 17cm.

The first ed. was published anonymously, in 1727, under title: An essay on the history and reality of apparitions.

1. Apparitions. I. Title. II. Defoe, Daniel, 1660-   1731. An essay on the history and   reality of apparitions.

Witchcraft
PR 3404 H5 1733 | [Defoe, Daniel] 1660-1731.
Geschichte des Teuffels; aus dem Englischen übersetzet, in zwey Theilen. Franckfurt am Mayn, 1733.
532 p. port. 18cm.

Translation of The political history of the devil.
Also published under title: Gründliche historische Nachricht vom Teuffel.

I. His   The political history of the devil. German.   II. Title. III. His Gründliche his   torische Nachricht vom Teuffel.

CATALOGUE OF THE CORNELL WITCHCRAFT COLLECTION

Defoe, Daniel, 1660-1731.
    Geschichte des Teuffels.

Witchcraft
PR
3404   [Defoe, Daniel] 1660-1731.
H5   Gründliche historische Nachricht vom Teuffel,
1748   darinnen die Siege, so der Teuffel über das
         menschliche Geschlechte von Eva an, bis auf
         unsere Zeiten erhalten hat, klar und deutlich
         erwiesen. Erster und anderer Theil. Aus dem
         Englischen und Französischen in das Teutsche
         übersetzet. Cöthen, J.C. Cörner, 1748.
            184 p. 17cm.

            Translation of   The political history of
                           (Continued on next card)

    Defoe, Daniel, 1660-1731.
        Geschichte des Teuffels.

Witchcraft
PR
3404   [Defoe, Daniel] 1660-1731. Gründliche
H5   historische Nachricht vom Teuffel ...
1748   1748.   (Card 2)

    the devil.
        Also published under title: Geschichte des
    Teufels.

    1. Devil. I. Title. II. Defoe, Daniel,
    1660-1731. The   political history of the
    devil--German.   III. Defoe, Daniel,
    1660-1731. Ges   chichte des Teuffels.

Witchcraft
PR
3404   [Defoe, Daniel] 1660-1731.
H5   Gründliche historische Nachricht vom Teuffel,
1748   darinnen die Siege, so der Teuffel über das
         menschliche Geschlechte von Eva an, bis auf
         unsere Zeiten erhalten hat, klar und deutlich
         erwiesen. Erster und anderer Theil. Aus dem
         Englischen und Französischen in das Teutsche
         übersetzet. Cöthen, J.C. Cörner, 1748.
            184 p. 17cm.

            Translation of   The political history of
                           (Continued on next card)

Witchcraft
PR
3404   [Defoe, Daniel] 1660-1731. Gründliche
H5   historische Nachricht vom Teuffel ...
1748   1748.   (Card 2)

    the devil.
        Also published under title: Geschichte des
    Teufels.

    1. Devil. I. Title. II. Defoe, Daniel,
    1660-1731. The   political history of the
    devil--German.   III. Defoe, Daniel,
    1660-1731. Ges   chichte des Teuffels.

        Defoe, Daniel, 1660-1731.
            Gründliche historische Nachricht vom
Witchcraft Teuffel.
PR   [Defoe, Daniel] 1660-1731.
3404   Geschichte des Teuffels; aus dem
H5   Englischen übersetzet, in zwey Theilen.
1733   Franckfurt am Mayn, 1733.
            532 p. port. 18cm.

            Translation of The political history
         of the devil.
            Also published under title: Gründliche
         historische Nachricht vom Teuffel.

            I. His   The political history of the
         devil. German.   II. Title.

WITCHCRAFT
PR
3404   [Defoe, Daniel] 1660-1731.
H5   Histoire du diable, traduite de l'ang-
1745a   lois. Tome premier, contenant un détail
         des circonstances, où il s'est trouvé, de-
         puis son bannissement du ciel ... Tome
         second, qui traite de la conduite qu'il a
         tenue jusqu'à-present ... Amsterdam, Aux
         dépens de la compagnie, 1729.
            302 p. illus. 17cm.
            Title in red and black.
            Translation   of The political history
         of the devil.
                        (Continued on next card)

WITCHCRAFT
PR
3404   [Defoe, Daniel] 1660-1731. Histoire du
H5   diable ... 1729.   (Card 2)
1745a

            1. Devil. I. His The political
         history of the devil. French. II. Title.

Witchcraft
PR
3404   [Defoe, Daniel] 1660-1731.
H5   The history of the Devil, as well ancient
1727   as modern. In two parts. Part I. Containing
         a state of the Devil's circumstances, and the
         various turns of his affairs; from his expul-
         sion out of heaven to the creation of man; with
         remarks on the several mistakes concerning the
         reason and manner of his fall. Also his
         proceedings with mankind ever since Adam, to
         the first planting of the Christian religion in
         the world. Part   II. Containing his more
                        (Continued on next card)

Witchcraft
PR
3404   [Defoe, Daniel] 1660-1731. The history of
H5   the Devil ... 1727.   (Card 2)
1727   private conduct, down to the present times: his
         government, his appearances, his manner of
         working, and the tools he works with. The 2d
         ed. London, Printed for T. Warner, 1727.
            408 p. front. 20cm.

            First ed. published 1726 under title: The
         political histor   y of the Devil.

Witchcraft
PR
3404   [Defoe, Daniel] 1660-1731.
H5   The history of the Devil, as well ancient
1745   as modern. In two parts. Part I. Containing
         a state of the Devil's circumstances, and the
         various turns of his affairs, from his expul-
         sion out of heaven, to the creation of man;
         with remarks on the several mistakes concerning
         the reason and manner of his fall. Also his
         proceedings with mankind ever since Adam, to
         the first planting of the Christian religion
         in the world.   Part II. Containing his
                        (Continued on next card)

Witchcraft
PR
3404   [Defoe, Daniel] 1660-1731. The history of
H5   the Devil ... 1745.   (Card 2)
1745   more private conduct, down to the present
         times; his government, his appearances, his
         manner of working, and the tools he works
         with... 4th ed. Dublin, Printed by and
         for T. Agrippa, 1745.
            331 p. 17cm.

            First publi   shed (London, 1726) as
         Political hist   ory of the Devil.

Witchcraft
PR
3404   [Defoe, Daniel] 1660-1731.
H5   The history of the Devil, ancient and mod-
1780   ern. In two parts. Part I. Containing a
         state of the Devil's circumstances, from his
         expulsion out of heaven to the creation; with
         remarks on the several mistakes concerning his
         fall. Part II. Containing his more private
         conduct down to the present times: his govern-
         ment, his appearance, his manner of working,
         and the tools he works with. In which is in-
         cluded a description of the Devil's dwelling.
         London,   Printed for G. Hay, 1780.
            viii, 340 p. 17cm.
                        (Continued on next card)

Witchcraft
PR
3404   [Defoe, Daniel] 1660-1731. The history of
H5   the Devil ... 1780.   (Card 2)
1780
            First ed. published in 1726 under title:
         The political history of the Devil.

            I. Title: The history of the Devil.
            II. His   the political history of the
         devil.

Witchcraft
PR
3404   The history of the Devil, ancient and modern. In two parts
H5   ... With a description of the devil's dwelling ... London,
1793   A. Law, W. Millar, and R. Cater, 1793.
            viii, 304 p. 17cm.

            CONTENTS.—pt. I. Containing a state of the devil's circumstances, from
         his expulsion out of heaven to the creation.—pt. II. Containing his more
         private conduct down to the present times.

            First ed. published 1726 under title: The
         political history of the Devil.

         Library of Congress   PR3404.H5 1793   2-11079
                                                         [a28c1]

PR
3404   Defoe, Daniel, 1660?-1731.
H5   History of the Devil: ancient & modern, in two parts.
1972   With a new introd. by Richard G. Landon. Totowa, N. J.,
         Rowman and Littlefield [1972]
            xiv, 431 p. illus. 22 cm. $7.75

            Reprint of the 1819 ed., which was originally published under
         title: The political history of the Devil.

            1. Devil—History of doctrines.   I. Title.   II. His The
         political history of the Devil.
         PR3404.H5 1972   828'.5'07   72-171011
4   ISBN 0-87471-102-9   MARC
NIC
         Library of Congress   72 [4]

Witchcraft
BF
1815   [Defoe, Daniel] 1660-1731.
C2   The history of the life and adventures of Mr. Duncan
D31   Campbell, a gentleman, who, tho' deaf and dumb, writes down
         any stranger's name at first sight; with their future contingen-
         cies of fortune. Now living in Exeter Court over-against the
         Savoy in the Strand ...   London, Printed for E.
         Curll, and sold by W. Mears [etc.] 1720.
            xix, [4], 320 p. front. (port.)   19cm.
            Authorship disputed; probably by Defoe, though ascribed also to Wil-
         liam Bond under whose name it appeared in 1728, with new title: The
         supernatural philosopher; or, The mysteries of magick ... unfolded by
         William Bond. cf. Dict. nat. biog.; Camb. hist. Eng. lit., v. 9; Dottin's
         "Daniel DeFoe et ses romans" (1924) p. 261.

                [31b1]   28-19517

Witchcraft
BF
1815   [Defoe, Daniel] 1660?-1731.
C2D31   The history of the life and adventures of
1720   Mr. Duncan Campbell, a gentleman, who tho' deaf
         and dumb, writes down any stranger's name at
         first sight: with their future contingencies of
         fortune. Now living in Exeter-Court over-against
         the Savoy in the Strand ... 2d ed. cor. London,
         Printed for E. Curll, and sold by W. Mears [etc.]
         1720.
            xix, [4], 320 p. front. (port.) 4 pl. 19cm.
            Authorship disputed; probably by Defoe,
         though ascribed also to William Bond under whose
                        (Continued on next card)

Witchcraft
BF
1815   [Defoe, Daniel] 1660?-1731. The history of the
C2D31   life and adventures of Mr. Duncan Campbell ...
1720   1720.   (Card 2)

         name it appeared in 1728, with new title: The
         supernatural philosopher; or, The mysteries of
         magick ... unfolded by William Bond. cf. Dict.
         nat. biog.; Camb. hist. Eng. lit., v. 9;
         Dottin's "Daniel DeFoe et ses romans" (1924)
         p. 261.
            Frontispiece wanting.
                                    (Continued on next card)

CATALOGUE OF THE CORNELL WITCHCRAFT COLLECTION

Witchcraft
BF
1815
C2D31
1720

[Defoe, Daniel] 1660?-1731. The history of the life and adventures of Mr. Duncan Campbell ... 1720. (Card 3)

1. Campbell, Duncan, 1680?-1730. I. Bond, William, d. 1735, supposed author. II. Title.

Rare
PR
3404
H5
1726

[Defoe, Daniel] 1660-1731.
The political history of the devil, as well ancient as modern: in two parts ... London, Printed for T. Warner, 1726.
[4] l., 408 p. 19cm.

1. Devil. I. Title.

Rare
PR
3404
H5
1734

Defoe, Daniel, 1660-1731.
The political history of the devil ... The whole interspers'd with many of the devil's adventures ... The third edition ... Westminster, Printed for J. Brindley, O. Payne [etc.] 1734.
408 p. front. 21cm.

1. Devil. I. Title.

Witchcraft
PR
3404
H5
1739

[Defoe, Daniel] 1660-1731.
The political history of the Devil. Containing: his original; a state of his circumstances; his conduct [sic] publick and private; the various turns of his affairs from Adam down to this present time; the various methods he takes to converse with mankind; with the manner of his making witches, wizards, and conjurers, and how they sell their souls to him, &c. &c. The whole interspers'd with many of the Devil's
(Continued on next card)

Witchcraft
PR
3404
H5
1739

[Defoe, Daniel] 1660-1731. The political history of the Devil ... 1739. (Card 2)

adventures. To which is added, a description of the Devil's dwelling, vulgarly call'd hell. The 4th ed. London, Printed for J. Fisher, 1739.
351 p. 18cm.

I. Title.

Witchcraft
PR
3404
H5
1780

Defoe, Daniel, 1660-1731.
The political history of the devil.
[Defoe, Daniel] 1660-1731.
The history of the Devil, ancient and modern. In two parts. Part I. Containing a state of the Devil's circumstances, from his expulsion out of heaven to the creation; with remarks on the several mistakes concerning his fall. Part II. Containing his more private conduct down to the present times; his government, his appearance, his manner of working, and the tools he works with. In which is included a description of the Devil's dwelling.
London, Printed for G. Hay, 1780.
viii, 340 p. 17cm.
(Continued on next card)

Witchcraft
PR
3404
H5
1780

Defoe, Daniel, 1660-1731.
The political history of the devil.
[Defoe, Daniel] 1660-1731. The history of the Devil ... 1780. (Card 2)

First ed. published in 1726 under title: The political history of the Devil.

I. Title: The history of the Devil.
II. His the political history of the devil.

Witchcraft
PR
3404
H5
1817

Defoe, Daniel, 1660-1731.
The political history of the Devil.
[Defoe, Daniel] 1660-1731.
Satan's devices; or, The political history of the Devil, ancient and modern. In two parts. Part I. His original; a state of his circumstances; his conduct, public and private; the various turns of his affairs, from Adam down to this present time. Part II. The various methods he takes to converse with mankind; with the manner of his making witches, wizards, and conjurers; and how they sell their souls to him. The whole inter-
(Continued on next card)

Witchcraft
PR
3404
H5
1817

Defoe, Daniel, 1660-1731.
The political history of the Devil.
[Defoe, Daniel] 1660-1731. Satan's devices ... 1817. (Card 2)

spersed with many of the Devil's adventures. To which is added, a description of the Devil's dwelling, vulgarly called hell. A new ed., with engravings. London, T. Kelly, sold by W. Davies, 1817.
431 p. front. 21cm.

Added t.p. engr., with title The
(Continued on next card)

Witchcraft
PR
3404
H5
1817

Defoe, Daniel, 1660-1731. Satan's devices ... 1817. (Card 3)

history of the Devil, ancient and modern, and imprint: Exeter, Davies & Eldridge, 1815.
First ed. published 1726 under title: The political history of the Devil.

1. Devil. I. Title. II. Defoe, Daniel, 1660-1731. The political history of the Devil.

WITCHCRAFT
PR
3404
H5
1745a

Defoe, Daniel, 1660-1731.
The political history of the devil. French.
[Defoe, Daniel] 1660-1731.
Histoire du diable, traduite de l'anglois. Tome premier, contenant un détail des circonstances, où il s'est trouvé, depuis son bannissement du ciel ... Tome second, qui traite de la conduite qu'il a tenue jusqu'à-present ... Amsterdam, Aux dépens de la compagnie, 1729.
302 p. illus. 17cm.
Title in red and black.
Translation of The political history of the devil.
(Continued on next card)

Witchcraft
PR
3404
H5
1733

Defoe, Daniel, 1660-1731.
The political history of the devil--German.
[Defoe, Daniel] 1660-1731.
Geschichte des Teuffels; aus dem Englischen übersetzet, in zwey Theilen. Franckfurt am Mayn, 1733.
532 p. port. 18cm.

Translation of The political history of the devil.
Also published under title: Gründliche historische Nachricht vom Teuffel.

I. His The political history of the devil. German. II. Title.

Witchcraft
PR
3404
H5
1748

Defoe, Daniel, 1660-1731.
The political history of the devil--German.
[Defoe, Daniel] 1660-1731.
Gründliche historische Nachricht vom Teuffel, darinnen die Siege, so der Teuffel über das menschliche Geschlechte von Eva an, bis auf unsere Zeiten erhalten hat, klar und deutlich erwiesen. Erster und anderer Theil. Aus dem Englischen und Französischen in das Teutsche übersetzet. Cöthen, J.C. Cörner, 1748.
184 p. 17cm.

Translation of The political history of
(Continued on next card)

Witchcraft
PR
3404
H5
1748

Defoe, Daniel, 1660-1731.
The political history of the devil--German.
[Defoe, Daniel] 1660-1731. Gründliche historische Nachricht vom Teuffel ... 1748. (Card 2)

the devil.
Also published under title: Geschichte des Teufels.

1. Devil. I. Title. II. Defoe, Daniel, 1660-1731. The political history of the devil--German. III. Defoe, Daniel, 1660-1731. Ges chichte des Teuffels.

Witchcraft
PR
3404
H5
1817

[Defoe, Daniel] 1660-1731.
Satan's devices; or, The political history of the Devil, ancient and modern. In two parts. Part I. His original; a state of his circumstances; his conduct, public and private; the various turns of his affairs, from Adam down to this present time. Part II. The various methods he takes to converse with mankind; with the manner of his making witches, wizards, and conjurers; and how they sell their souls to him. The whole inter-
(Continued on next card)

Witchcraft
PR
3404
H5
1817

[Defoe, Daniel] 1660-1731. Satan's devices ... 1817. (Card 2)

spersed with many of the Devil's adventures. To which is added, a description of the Devil's dwelling, vulgarly called hell. A new ed., with engravings. London, T. Kelly, sold by W. Davies, 1817.
431 p. front. 21cm.

Added t.p. engr., with title The
(Continued on next card)

Witchcraft
PR
3404
H5
1817

[Defoe, Daniel] 1660-1731. Satan's devices ... 1817. (Card 3)

history of the Devil, ancient and modern, and imprint: Exeter, Davies & Eldridge, 1815.
First ed. published 1726 under title: The political history of the Devil.

1. Devil. I. Title. II. Defoe, Daniel, 1660-1731. The political history of the Devil.

Witchcraft
BF
1445
D31
1729

[Defoe, Daniel] 1660-1731.
The secrets of the invisible world disclos'd: or, An universal history of apparitions sacred and prophane, under all denominations; whether, angelical, diabolical, or human-souls departed ... By Andrew Moreton, esq. [pseud.] ... London, Printed for J. Clarke, A. Millar, and J. Green, 1729.
[6], 395 p. 20cm.
The first edition was published anonymously, under title: An essay on the history and reality of apparitions.

CATALOGUE OF THE CORNELL WITCHCRAFT COLLECTION

Witchcraft
BF 1445 D31 1735

[Defoe, Daniel] 1660-1731.
 The secrets of the invisible world disclos'd: or, An universal history of apparitions sacred and profane under all denominations; whether angelical, diabolical, or human souls departed ... By Andrew Moreton [pseud.] ... 2d ed. London, Printed for J. Watts, and sold by T. Worral, 1735.
 395 p. front. 20cm.
 The first ed. was published
 (Continued on next card)

Witchcraft
BF 1445 D31 1735

[Defoe, Daniel] 1660-1731. The secrets of the invisible world disclos'd ... 1735. (Card 2)
anonymously in 1727 under title: An essay on the history and reality of apparitions.

Witchcraft

[Defoe, Daniel] 1660-1731.
 The secrets of the invisible world disclosed: or, An universal history of apparitions sacred and prophane, under all denominations; whether angelical, diabolical, or human souls departed... By Andrew Moreton [pseud.] ... The third edition. London, Printed for J. Clarke, A. Millar, and J. Brindley, 1738.
 395 p. front., plates. 20cm.
 (Continued on next card)

Witchcraft

[Defoe, Daniel] 1660-1731. The secrets of the invisible world disclosed. 1738. (Card 2)
The first edition was published anonymously, under title: An essay on the history and reality of apparitions.
 1. Apparitions. I. Title.

Witchcraft
BF 1445 D31 1770

[Defoe, Daniel] 1660-1731.
 The secrets of the invisible world laid open; or, A general history of apparitions, sacred and prophane, whether angelical, diabolical, or departed souls. Shewing I. Their various returns to this world; with sure rules to know if they are good or evil. II. An enquiry into the scriptural doctrine of spirits. III. The different species of apparitions, with their real existence. IV. The nature of seeing ghosts, before
 (Continued on next card)

Witchcraft
BF 1445 D31 1770

[Defoe, Daniel] 1660-1731. The secrets of the invisible world laid open. 1770. (Card 2)
and after death. V. The effects of fancy, vapours, dreams, hyppo, and the difference between real or imaginary appearances. VI. A collection of the most authentic relations of apparitions, particularly that surprizing one attested by the learned Dr. Scott. Likewise Mrs. Veal's appearance to
 (Continued on next card)

Witchcraft
BF 1445 D31 1770

[Defoe, Daniel] 1660-1731. The secrets of the invisible world laid open. 1770. (Card 3)
Mrs. Bargrave, Sir George Villers to the duke of Buckingham, &c. &c. Also the notions of the heathens concerning apparitions. Being the most entertaining, and, in quantity, the cheapest book of the kind. London, Printed for the Author and sold by D. Steel, 1770.
 (Continued on next card)

Witchcraft
BF 1445 D31 1770

[Defoe, Daniel] 1660-1731. The secrets of the invisible world laid open. 1770. (Card 4)
 4,v,252 p. 17cm.
 The first ed. was published anonymously, in 1727, under title: An essay on the history and reality of apparitions.
 1. Apparitions. I. Title. II. Defoe, Daniel, 1660-1731. An essay on the history and reality of apparitions.

Defoe, Daniel, 1660.-1731.
 The supernatural philosopher--German.

Witchcraft
BF 1815 C2 D31 1742

[Defoe, Daniel] 1660?-1731.
 Der Übernatürliche Philosoph, oder Die Geheimnisse der Magie, nach allen ihren Arten deutlich erkläret ... aus den bewährtesten Autoribus zusammen getragen und durch das Exempel und Leben des Herrn Duncan Campbells, des tauben und stummen Edelmanns, erörtert. Nebst D. Wallis Methode, taube und stumme lesen, schreiben und jede Sprache verstehen zu lernen, von W. Bond ... Aus dem Englischen
 (Continued on next card)

Defoe, Daniel, 1660.-1731.
 The supernatural philosopher--German.

Witchcraft
BF 1815 C2 D31 1742

[Defoe, Daniel] 1660?-1731. Der Übernatürliche Philosoph ... 1742. (Card 2)
ins Deutsche übersetzt und mit einigen nöthigen und dienlichen Anmerckungen versehen ... Berlin, J. A. Rüdiger, 1742.
 [92], 432 p. front. (port.), 4 fold. plates. 17cm.
 First published 1720 anonymously with title: The history of the life and adventures of Mr. Duncan Campbell. Reissued 1728 with some additions as: The super-
 (Continued on next card)

Defoe, Daniel, 1660.-1731.
 The supernatural philosopher--German.

Witchcraft
BF 1815 C2 D31 1742

[Defoe, Daniel] 1660?-1731. Der Übernatürliche Philosoph ... 1742. (Card 3)
natural philosopher, or, The mysteries of magick ... unfolded by William Bond, from which this is translated.
 Authorship disputed; probably by Daniel Defoe with the assistance of William Bond and possibly of Eliza Haywood.
 Imperfect: plate to p. [72] wanting.

Witchcraft
BF 1601 D31

[Defoe, Daniel] 166 0-1731.
 A system of magick; or, A history of the black art. Being an historical account of mankind's most early dealing with the devil; and how the acquaintance on both sides first began ... London, Printed: and sold by J. Roberts, MDCCXXVII.
 6 p. l., 403 p. incl. front. 20cm.
 First edition.
 1. Magic. I. Title.
 Library of Congress BF1601.D3 1727
 [42b1] [159.9614] 133.4
 35—19190

Witchcraft
BF 1601 D31 1840

[Defoe, Daniel] 1660-1731.
 A system of magic. In one volume. Oxford, Printed by D. A. Talboys, for T. Tegg, 1840.
 xvii, 396 p. 18cm.
 Reprint of the London ed. of 1728 with a new t. p.
 1. Magic. I. Title.

PR 3404 S98 1727a

[Defoe, Daniel] 1660-1731.
 A system of magick; or, A history of the black art. Being an historical account of mankind's most early dealing with the Devil; and how the acquaintance on both sides first began. London, J. Roberts, 1727.
 403 p. front.
 Moore no. 487.
 Photocopy of original in British Museum. London, University Microfilms [1966?]
 403 p. (on double leaves) 18cm.
 1. Magic. I. Title.

Witchcraft
BF 1815 C2 D31 1742

[Defoe, Daniel] 1660-1731.
 Der Übernatürliche Philosoph, oder Die Geheimnisse der Magie, nach allen ihren Arten deutlich erkläret ... aus den bewährtesten Autoribus zusammen getragen und durch das Exempel und Leben des Herrn Duncan Campbells, des tauben und stummen Edelmanns, erörtert. Nebst D. Wallis Methode, taube und stumme lesen, schreiben und jede Sprache verstehen zu lernen, von W. Bond ... Aus dem Englischen
 (Continued on next card)

Witchcraft
BF 1815 C2 D31 1742

[Defoe, Daniel] 1660-1731. Der Übernatürliche Philosoph ... 1742. (Card 2)
ins Deutsche übersetzt und mit einigen nöthigen und dienlichen Anmerckungen versehen ... Berlin, J. A. Rüdiger, 1742.
 [92], 432 p. front. (port.), 4 fold. plates. 17cm.
 First published 1720 anonymously with title: The history of the life and adventures of Mr. Duncan Campbell. Reissued 1728 with some additions as: The super-
 (Continued on next card)

Witchcraft
BF 1815 C2 D31 1742

[Defoe, Daniel] 1660-1731. Der Übernatürliche Philosoph ... 1742. (Card 3)
natural philosopher, or, The mysteries of magick ... unfolded by William Bond, from which this is translated.
 Authorship disputed; probably by Daniel Defoe with the assistance of William Bond and possibly of Eliza Haywood.
 Imperfect: plate to p. [72] wanting.
 1. Campbell, Duncan, 1680?-1730. I. Bond, William, d. 1735, supposed author. II. Title. III. His The supernatural philosopher--German.

DC 119 .8 D31

Defrance, Eugène, 1874–
 ... Catherine de Médicis, ses astrologues et ses magiciens-envoûteurs. Documents inédits sur la diplomatie et les sciences occultes du XVIe siècle; avec vingt illustrations. Paris, Mercvre de France, 1911.
 306 p., 3 l. incl. front., illus. (incl. ports., facsim.) 19cm.
 1. Catherine de Médicis, queen consort of Henry II, king of France, 1519-1589. 2. Astrology--Hist. 3. Witchcraft--France. 4. Superstition. I. Title.

CATALOGUE OF THE CORNELL WITCHCRAFT COLLECTION

de Franchillon, Charles.

see

Franchillon, Charles de, d. 1626.

BF 231 C18 1925
Del senso delle cose e della magia.
Campanella, Tommaso, 1568-1639.
... Del senso delle cose e della magia; testo inedito italiano con le varianti dei codici e delle due edizioni latine, a cura di Antonio Bruers. Bari, G. Laterza & figli, 1925.
xxix, [1] p., 1 l., 348 p. 21½cm. (Half-title: Classici della filosofia moderna ... a cura di B. Croce e G. Gentile. XXIV)

Witchcraft
BT 980 D33 1890
Delaporte, Albert, b. 1829.
The Devil: does he exist? And what does he do? Translated from the sixth French ed., rev. and corr. by the author, by Mrs. James Sadlier. New York, D. & J. Sadlier [c1890]
202 p. 18cm. (Sadliers' household library, no. 11)

Cover has date: 1878.
Translation of: Le diable, existe-t-il, et que fait-il?
I. His   Le diable, existe-t-il, et que fait-il?   English. II. Title.

BT 981 D32
DeHaan, Richard W
Satan, satanism, and witchcraft, by Richard W. Dehaan with Herbert Vander Lught. Grand Rapids, Mich., Zondervan Pub. House [1972]
125 p. 18 cm. (Zondervan books) $0.95
Bibliography: p. 123-125.

4
1. Devil. 2. Christianity and occult sciences. I. Vander Lught, Herbert, joint author. II. Title.
BT981.D44   235'.47   72-81786
Library of Congress   '72 [4]   MARC

Witchcraft
BF 1410 B33
Del vero stvdio christiano contra l'arte planetaria, notoria, cabalistica ...
Battista, Giovanni.
Del vero stvdio christiano contra l'arte planetaria, notoria, cabalistica, lunaria, clauicula di Salomone, Paulina, reuelata da spiriti mali, & altri superstitiosi modi vsati per imparare supernaturalmente, & voler sapere più de gli altri superbamente. Opera novamente composta dal R. P. Don Gio. Battista Segni da Bologna ... Ferrara, Appresso Benedetto Mammarello, 1592.
8 p. l., 153 , [15] p. 2 illus.
8   15cm.
(Continued on next card)

Delaporte, Albert, b. 1829.
Le diable, existe-t-il, et que fait-il? English.
Witchcraft
BT 980 D33 1890
Delaporte, Albert, b. 1829.
The Devil: does he exist? And what does he do? Translated from the sixth French ed., rev. and corr. by the author, by Mrs. James Sadlier. New York, D. & J. Sadlier [c1890]
202 p. 18cm. (Sadliers' household library, no. 11)

Cover has date: 1878.
Translation of: Le diable, existe-t-il, et que fait-il?
I. His   Le diable, existe-t-il, et que fait-il?   English. II. Title.

De Harbach, Laurentio.

see

Harbach, Laurentio de

Witchcraft
BF 1571 D33
Delacroix, Frédéric.
Les procès de sorcellerie au XVII. siècle. Paris, Librairie de La Nouvelle Revue, 1894.
328 p. 19cm.

1. Trials (Witchcraft) I. Title.

De la Rochelle, Jean François Née, 1751-1838.

see

Née de la Rochelle, Jean François, 1751-1838.

Witchcraft
BF 1565 T19
Del congresso notturno delle lammie.
Tartarotti, Girolamo, 1706-1761.
Del congresso notturno delle lammie, libri tre di Girolamo Tartarotti Roveretano. S'aggiungono due dissertazioni epistolari sopra l'arte magica... Rovereto, A spese di Giambatista Pasquali in Venezia, 1749.
xxxii, 460 p. 24cm.
Letter from Gianrinaldo Carli dated Padua, 1745, p. [317]-350, has special t. p.

8
(Continued on next card)

De la Haye, Maria Francisca.

MSS Bd. WITCHCRAFT BF W275 Z55
Warhaffter Bericht und denckwürdiger Verlauff, welcher Gestalten in dem 1664. Jahr den 3. Tag Jenners, durch die Barmhertzigkeit Gottes auff Anruffung dess H. Francisci Xaverii ... die wol-edle und tugendreiche Junckfraw Anna Elisabetha Susanna, nunmehr aber Maria Francisca de la Haye von den bösen Geistern, so sie besessen und verfolgt, in unser Frauen Kirchen ... wunderbarlich ist erlediget worden. St raubing, Bey Magdalena Haanin, 16   65 [ca. 1900]
(Continued on next card)

Witchcraft
BF 1556 D33
Delassus, Jules.
Les incubes et les succubes ... Paris, Société dv Mercvre de France [1897]
62 p. 19cm.

1. Demonology. I. Title.

Witchcraft
BF 1565 T19 1749
Del congresso notturno delle lammie.
Tartarotti, Girolamo, 1706-1761. Del congresso notturno delle lammie ... (Card 2)

Letter of Tartarotti dated Rovereto, 1746, p. [351]-447, has special t. p.

1. Witchcraft. 2. Magic. I. Carli, Giovanni Rinaldo, conte, 1720-1795. Lettera ... al signor Girolamo Tartarotti, intorno all' or   igine, e falsità della dottrina de'   Maghi. II. Title.

8

De la Haye, Maria Francisca.

MSS Bd. WITCHCRAFT BF W275 Z55
Warhaffter Bericht und denckwürdiger Verlauff ... 1665 [ca. 1900]   (Card 2)
97 p. 19cm.
Carnap's manuscript copy.
"Originaldruck in der Königlichen u. Staats-Bibliothek zu München, VIII + 83 S. S. in 8°."
Numerals in the margins indicate pagination of the original.
1. Demoniac   possession. 2. De la Haye, Maria   Francisca.

Rare BX 1710 D34++ 1680
Delbene, Thomas.
De officio s. inquisitionis circa haeresim, cum bullis tam veteribus quam recentioribus ad eandem materiam, seu ad idem officium spectantibus & locis theologicis in ordine ad qualificandas propositiones. Ed. altera accurate emendata. Lugduni sumptibus Laurentii Arnaud, Petri Borde, Ioannis & Petri Arnaud, 1680.
2 vol. in 1. 38 cm.

1. Inquisi   tion. I. Title.

Witchcraft
BF 1520 C57 1605
Del palagio de gl'incanti, et delle gran merauiglie de gli spiriti.
Cigogna, Strozzi.
Del palagio de gl'incanti, et delle gran merauiglie de gli spiriti, & di tutta la natura loro. Diuiso in libri XXXXV. & in III. prospettiue, Spirituale, Celeste, & Elementare ... Brescia, Appresso il Bozzola, 1605.
[40], 623 p. 17cm.
Title vignette: device of G. B. Bozola.
Contains only "Prospettiva prima, libro primo-quarto." No more published.
1. Demonology. 2. Incantations. I. Title.

De la Palud, Magdeleine.

see

Palud, Magdeleine de la.

Witchcraft
BF 1582 D34
Delcambre, Étienne.
Le concept de la sorcellerie dans le duché de Lorraine au XVIe et au XVIIe siècle ... Nancy, Société d'archéologie Lorraine, 1948.
v. 22cm. (Half-title: Recueil de documents sur l'histoire de Lorraine)

Contents.--fasc. 1. L'initiation à la sorcellerie et le sabbat.
1. Witchcraft--Lorraine--Hist. I. Title. II. Title: L'initiation à la sorcellerie et le sabbat.

CATALOGUE OF THE CORNELL WITCHCRAFT COLLECTION

GN 1 L311 B5 v.39 L2200

Delfino, Giuseppe.
   Stregoneria, magia, credenze e superstizioni a Genova e in Liguria. Firenze, L. S. Olschki, 1973.
   iv, 87 p. illus., plates. 21 cm. (Biblioteca di "Lares," v. 39)
                          It 73-Aug

At head of title: Giuseppe Delfino, Aldano Schmuckher.
Bibliography: p. 81-84.

9 NIC ✓ 1. Occult sciences—Genoa. 2. Occult sciences—Liguria. I. Schmuckher, Aldano, joint author. II. Title.

BF1434.I 8D44   73-339982

Library of Congress   73 [2]

Deliciae physicae.

WITCHCRAFT QL 50 V89

Voigt, Gottfried, 1644-1682.
   Gothofrei Voigtii ... Deliciae physicae ΕΠΙΔΙΕΣΚΕΥΑΣΜΕΝΑΙ, de stillicidio sanguinis ex interemti hominis cadavere praesente occisore, lacrymis crocodili, catulis ursarum, amore ovis et lupi, piscibus fossilibus et volatilibus, conventu sagarum ad sua sabbata, infantibus supposititiis, cornu cervi, et stellis cadentibus accurata methodo conscr   iptae. Rostochii, Im-

8   (Continued on next card)

Deliciae physicae.

WITCHCRAFT QL 50 V89

Voigt, Gottfried, 1644-1682. ...Deliciae physicae ... 1671.   (Card 2)

primebat Johannes Kilius, 1671.
   7 p. l., 369, [1] p. 17cm.
   Title in red and black.

   1. Natural history—Curiosa and miscellany. 2. Animal lore. 3. Witchcraft. I. Title: Deliciae physicae.

8

Dell, Mrs. Annis, d. 1606.

Witchcraft GR 142 H6 A3 no.17

A **Hertfordshire** miracle. The most cruell and bloody murther, committed by an inkeeper's wife, called Annis Dell, and her sonne George Dell, four yeeres since, on the bodie of a childe called Anthony James in Bishop's Hatfield in the countie of Hartford, and now most miraculously revealed by the sister of the said Anthony, who at the time of the murther had her tongue cut out, and four yeares remaynes dumme, and speechless, and now perfectly speaketh, revealing the murther, having no
      (Continued on next card)   16-25741

Dell, Mrs. Annis, d. 1606.

Witchcraft GR 142 H6 A3 no.17

A **Hertfordshire** miracle ... (Card 2)
tongue to be seen. Who were executed at Hartford the 4 of August last past 1606. Reprinted, with an introductory by W. B. Gerish. Bishop's Stortford, 1913.
   27 p. 22cm. [Hertfordshire folk lore. no.
   The original pamphlet is in 2 parts and is entitled: The most cruell and bloody murther committed by ... Annis Dell ... With the severall witchcrafts and most damnable practises of one Johane Harrison and her daughter ... London, Printed for W. Ferebrand and J. Wright, 1606.
   1. Crime and criminals—England—Hertfordshire. 2. Dell, Mrs. Annis, d. 1606. 3. Dell, George, d. 1606. I. Gerish, William Blyth, ed. II. Title: The most cruell and bloody murther ...

Library of Congress   GR142.H6A3 no. 13

Dell, Mrs. Annis, d. 1606.

Witchcraft BF 1563 W81++ no.9

The Most crvell and bloody mvrther committed by ... Annis Dell and her sonne George Dell, foure yeeres since, on ... Anthony Iames ... and now most miraculously reuealed by the sister of the said Anthony ... With the seuerall vvitch-crafts and most damnable practises of one Iohane Harrison and her daughter vpon seuerall persons ... who were all executed ... the 4 of August last past ... London, Pr   inted for W. Firebrand
     (Continued on next card)

Dell, Mrs. Annis, d. 1606.

Witchcraft BF 1563 W81++ no.9

The Most crvell and bloody mvrther... 1606. [1923]   (Card 2)

   and J. Wright, 1606. [London, at the British Museum, 1923]
   [24] p. 17cm.

   Signatures: A-C⁴.
   Photocopy (negative) 24 p. on 13 l. 20 x 32cm.
   No. 9 in vol. lettered: Witchcraft tracts chapbooks and   broadsides, 1579-1704; rotograph   copies.

Dell, George, d. 1606.

Witchcraft GR 142 H6 A3 no.17

A **Hertfordshire** miracle. The most cruell and bloody murther, committed by an inkeeper's wife, called Annis Dell, and her sonne George Dell, four yeeres since, on the bodie of a childe called Anthony James in Bishop's Hatfield in the countie of Hartford, and now most miraculously revealed by the sister of the said Anthony, who at the time of the murther had her tongue cut out, and four yeares remaynes dumme, and speechless, and now perfectly speaketh, revealing the murther, having no
     (Continued on next card)   16-25741

Dell, George, d. 1606.

Witchcraft GR 142 H6 A3 no.17

A **Hertfordshire** miracle ... (Card 2)
tongue to be seen. Who were executed at Hartford the 4 of August last past 1606. Reprinted, with an introductory by W. B. Gerish. Bishop's Stortford, 1913.
   27 p. 22cm. [Hertfordshire folk lore. no.
   The original pamphlet is in 2 parts and is entitled: The most cruell and bloody murther committed by ... Annis Dell ... With the severall witchcrafts and most damnable practises of one Johane Harrison and her daughter ... London, Printed for W. Ferebrand and J. Wright, 1606.
   1. Crime and criminals—England—Hertfordshire. 2. Dell, Mrs. Annis, d. 1606. 3. Dell, George, d. 1606. I. Gerish, William Blyth, ed. II. Title: The most cruell and bloody murther ...

Library of Congress   GR142.H6A3 no. 13

Dell, George, d. 1606.

Witchcraft BF 1563 W81++ no.9

The Most crvell and bloody mvrther committed by ... Annis Dell and her sonne George Dell, foure yeeres since, on ... Anthony Iames ... and now most miraculously reuealed by the sister of the said Anthony ... With the seuerall vvitch-crafts and most damnable practises of one Iohane Harrison and her daughter vpon seuerall persons ... who were all executed ... the 4 of August last past ... London, Pr   inted for W. Firebrand
     (Continued on next card)

Dell, George, d. 1606.

Witchcraft BF 1563 W81++ no.9

The Most crvell and bloody mvrther... 1606. [1923]   (Card 2)

   and J. Wright, 1606. [London, at the British Museum, 1923]
   [24] p. 17cm.

   Signatures: A-C⁴.
   Photocopy (negative) 24 p. on 13 l. 20 x 32cm.
   No. 9 in vol. lettered: Witchcraft tracts chapbooks and   broadsides, 1579-1704; rotograph   copies.

Della Porta, Giovanni Battista, 1535?-1615.

   see

Porta, Giovanni Battista della, 1535?-1615.

Dell'Osa, Ardoino Ubbidente, pseud.

   see

Simon, Jordan, pater, 1719-1776.

Witchcraft GR 185 D36

Delogne, Théodore
   L'Ardenne méridionale belge: une page de son histoire et son folklore, suivis du procès des sorcières de Sugny en 1657. Bruxelles, H. Lamertin, 1914.
   273, vi p. 22cm.

✓ I. Title.

Delphina, Maria Augusta, fl. 1848.

MSS Bd. WITCHCRAFT BF E69

Erledigung der ehrw. Klosterfrau Maria Augusta Delphina, im Frauenkloster zu Stanz, den 28. März 1848 durch P. Anizet Regli, Guardian zu Stanz. [n.p.] Nach einem Original-Manuskripte getreu abgedruckt, 1848 [ca. 1900]
   9 l. 19cm.
   Carnap's manuscript copy.
   "Originaldruck i. d. Stadtbibliothek zu Zürich. 13 S. in 8°."
   Numerals i   n the margins indicate pagination of   the original.
      (Continued on next card)

Delphina, Maria Augusta, fl. 1848.

WITCHCRAFT BF 1555 L65

[Leu, Josef Burkard] 1808-1865.
   Die Teufels-Beschwörung in Stans; oder, Gutachten über die Broschüre: Erledigung der ehrw. Klosterfrau Maria Augusta Delphina im Frauenkloster zu Stans den 28. März 1848 durch P. Anizet Regli... Luzern, X. Meyer, 1848.
   15 p. 20cm.

   1. Demoniac possession. 2. Devil. 3. Exorcism. 4. Delphina, Maria Augusta, fl. 1848. 5. Regli, Anizet,   fl. 1848. 6. Erledigung der   ehrw. Klosterfrau Maria Augusta Delp   hina. I. Title.

8 NIC

Witchcraft BF 1600 D36 1611

Del Rio, Martin Antoine, 1551-1608.
   Les controverses et recherches magiqves. Divisees en six livres, ausquels sont exactement & doctement confutees les sciences curieuses, les vanitez, & superstitions de toute la magie. Avec qves la maniere de proceder en iustice contre les magiciens et sorciers, accommodee à l'instruction des confesseurs ... Traduit et abregé du Latin par André dv Chesne. Paris, Chez Iean Petit-Pas, 1611.
   [32], 1024 (i.e. 1104), [54] p. 19cm.

   Errors in paging: 1100-1104 numbered 1101,
      (Continued on next card)

Witchcraft BF 1600 D36 1611

Del Rio, Martin Antoine, 1551-1608. Les controverses et recherches magiqves ... 1611.   (Card 2)

1102, 1002, 1003 and 1024 respectively.
Translation of Disquisitionum magicarum libri sex.

   1. Magic. 2. Witchcraft. ✓ I. Del Rio, Martin Antoine, 1551-1608. Disquisitionum magicarum libri sex—French. ✓ II. Duchesne, André, 1584-1640, tr. ✓ III. Title.

CATALOGUE OF THE CORNELL WITCHCRAFT COLLECTION

BF 1600 D36D6 1960
Del Rio, Martin Antoine, 1551-1608.
  Le disquisizioni magiche: magia e stregoneria, i patti col diavolo, incubi e succubi, fatture e filtri d'amore e di morte, le statuette di cera, messe nere, le profezie, ecc. ₍Con uno studio sul "Satanismo" ai nostri giorni di J. K. Huysmans₎ Napoli, G. Rocco ₍1960?₎
  124 p. 19cm.
  First published in Latin in 1599.
  1. Magic. 2. Witchcraft. 3. Satanism. I. Huysmans, Joris Karl, 1848-1907. II. Title.

WITCHCRAFT
BF 1600 D36
Del Rio, Martin Antoine, 1551-1608.
  Disqvisitionvm magicarvm libri sex, in tres tomos partiti. Auctore Martino Delrio. Lovanii, ex officina Gerardi Rivii, 1599-1600.
  3 v. in 1. 22cm.
  Colophon of vol. 3 dated 1601.

8 NIC

Witchcraft
BF 1600 D36 1604
Del Rio, Martin Antoine, 1551-1608.
  Disqvisitionvm magicarvm libri sex. In tres tomos partiti ... Nvnc secvndis cvris avctior longè, additionibus multis passim insertis: correctior quoque mendis sublatis. Lvgdvni, Apud Io: Pillehotte, 1604.
  3 pts. in 1 v. 25cm.
  Engraved t. p.
  1. Magic. 2. Witchcraft. I. Title.

Witchcraft
BF 1600 D36++ 1608
Del Rio, Martin Antoine, 1551-1608.
  Disqvisitionvm magicarvm libri sex: quibus continetur accurata curiosarum artium, & vanarum superstitionum confutatio, vtilis theologis, iurisconsultis, medicis, philologis ... Prodit opus vltimis curis longe et auctius & castigatius. Lvgdvni, Apvd Ioannem Pillehotte, 1608.
  ₍24₎, 553 p. 36cm.
  Engraved t. p.

Witchcraft
BF 1600 D36++ 1612
Del Rio, Martin Antoine, 1551-1608.
  Disqvisitionvm magicarvm libri sex: quibus continetur accurata curiosarum artium, & vanarum superstitionum confutatio ... Editio postrema, quae vt auctior castigatiorque coeteris, sic & indicibus pernecessariis prodit hodie illustrior. Lvgdvni, Apud Horativm Cardon, 1612.
  ₍52₎, 468, ₍55₎ p. 36cm.
  Engraved t. p.

Witchcraft
BF 1600 D36 1612a
Del Rio, Martin Antoine, 1551-1608.
  Disqvisitionvm magicarvm libri sex. Quibus continetur accurata curiosarum artium, et vanarum superstitionum confutatio, vtilis theologis, iurisconsultis, medicis, philologis. Prodit opus vltimis curis longe et auctius et castigatius. Mogvntiae, Apud Johannem Albinvm, 1612.
  ₍24₎, 1070 p. 25cm.
  17th century stamped pigskin binding; traces of metal clasps.

Witchcraft
BF 1600 D36 1624
Del Rio, Martin Antoine, 1551-1608.
  Disqvisitionvm magicarvm libri sex, qvibvs continetvr accvrata cvriosarvm artivm, et vanarvm svperstitionvm confutatio vtilis theologis, iurisconsultis, medicis, philologis. Auctore Martino Delrio ... Prodit opus vltimis curis longe & auctius & castigatius. Mogvntiae, sumptibus P. Hennigii, 1624.
  12 p. l., 1070 p. 24cm.
  1. Magic. 2. Witchcraft. I. Title.

Witchcraft
BF 1600 D36 1679
Del Rio, Martin Antoine, 1551-1608.
  Disqvisitionvm magicarvm libri sex, qvibvs continetvr accvrata cvriosarvm artivm et vanarum superstitionum confutatio, utilis theologis, jurisconsultis, medicis, philologis. Prodit opus vltimis curis longe accuratius ac castigatius. Coloniae Agrippinae, Sumptibus Hermanni Demen, 1679.
  ₍16₎, 1221, ₍48₎ p. 22cm.
  Engraved t. p.
  I. Title.

Witchcraft
BF 1600 D36 1611
Del Rio, Martin Antoine, 1551-1608.
  Disqvisitionum magicarum libri sex--French
Del Rio, Martin Antoine, 1551-1608.
  Les controverses et recherches magiqves. Divisees en six livres, ausquels sont exactement & doctement confutees les sciences curieuses, les vanitez, & superstitions de toute la magie. Avec qves la maniere de proceder en iustice contre les magiciens et sorciers, accommodee à l'instruction des confesseurs ... Traduit et abregé du Latin par André dv Chesne. Paris, Chez Iean Petit-Pas, 1611.
  ₍32₎, 1024 (i.e. 1104), ₍54₎ p. 19cm.
  Errors in paging: 1100-1104 numbered 1101, (Continued on next card)

Witchcraft
BF 1600 D36 1611
Del Rio, Martin Antoine, 1551-1608.
  Disqvisitionum magicarum libri sex--French.
Del Rio, Martin Antoine, 1551-1608. Les controverses et recherches magiqves ... 1611. (Card 2)
  1102, 1002, 1003 and 1024 respectively. Translation of Disquisitionum magicarum libri sex.
  1. Magic. 2. Witchcraft. I. Del Rio, Martin Antoine, 1551-1608. Disquisitionum magicarum libri sex--French. II. Duchesne, André, 1584-1640, tr. III. Title.

  Delta, pseud.
Witchcraft
Z 1001 D28 1865
₍Deane, Charles₎ 1813-1889.
  ... Spurious reprints of early books. Boston, ₍Cambridge, University press₎ 1865.
  19 p. 25cm. (Bibliographical tracts, no.1)
  Signed at end "Delta."
  "From the Boston Daily advertiser of March 24, 1865. With additions and corrections. One hundred and thirty-one copies printed."
  "This reprint was not made by Mr. Deane."--Sabin.
  A review of "Salem witchcraft: comprising More wonders of the invisible world, (Continued on next card)

  Delta, pseud.
Witchcraft
Z 1001 D28 1865
₍Deane, Charles₎ 1813-1889. ...Spurious reprints of early books. 1865. (Card 2)
  collected by Robert Calef; and Wonders of the invisible world, by Cotton Mather. Together with notes and explanations by Samuel P. Fowler. Boston, W. Veazie, 1865" ₍reissue from the stereotyped plates of the Salem, 1861, edition₎

WITCHCRAFT
BF 1582 L86
Demandolx, Madeleine de, 1593?-1670.
Lorédan, Jean, 1853-
  Un grand procès de sorcellerie au XVIIe siècle: l'abbé Gaufridy et Madeleine de Demandolx (1600-1670) d'après des documents inédits. Ouvrage orné de 9 gravures et de 2 fac-similés. Paris, Perrin, 1912.
  xiv, 436 p. illus. 21cm.
  1. Witchcraft--France 2. Trials (Witchcraft)--France. 3. Gaufridi, Louis, 1572-1611. 4. Demandolx, Madeleine de, 1593?-1670. I. Title.

8 NIC

  Le démon.
Witchcraft
BT 975 L44+
Le Blant, Edmond Frédéric, 1818-1897.
  Les premiers chrétiens et le démon. Memoria del Socio Edmondo Le Blant, letta nella seduta del 22 gennaio 1888. ₍Roma, 1887₎
  161-168 p. 30cm.
  Caption title.
  Detached from Accademia nazionale dei Lincei, Rome. Classe di scienze morali storiche, critiche e filologiche. Memorie, ser. IV, v. 3.
  1. Demonology. 2. Church history--Primitive and early church. I. Title.

8

  Demoni, streghe a guaritori.
BF 1555 P34
Pazzini, Adalberto.
  Demoni, streghe a guaritori. ₍Milano₎ V. Bompiani, 1951.
  290 p. illus. 21cm. (Avventure del pensiero, v. 80)

  Demoniacal possession, its nature and cessation.
Witchcraft
BF 1555 W89
Woodward, Thomas.
  Demoniacal possession, its nature and cessation. An essay. London, J. Masters, 1849.
  60 p. 22cm.
  1. Demoniac possession. I. Title.

Witchcraft
BS 2545 D5 D38
Demoniacal possessions. Reasons for the credibility of their reality, not only as recorded, but as exhibited, in the New Testament. ₍London₎ Printed for J. Nunn, 1817.
  143 p. 20cm.
  Marginal notes in ms. By the author, in preparation for a new ed.?
  1. Demoniac possession.

Witchcraft
BF 1547 V81 1583
  The demoniacke worlde.
₍Viret, Pierre₎ 1511-1571.
  The second part of The demoniacke vvorlde, or, Worlde possessed with diuels, conteining three dialogues: 1. Of familiar diuels. 2. Of lunaticke diuels. 2. Of the coniuring of diuels. Translated out of French into Engli by T. S. ₍i.e. Thomas Stocker₎ London, Imprinted for I. Perin, and are to be sold i Paules church-yard at the signe of the Angel 1583.
  1 v. (unpaged) 15cm.
  Bound with his The worlde possesse with deuils. London, 1583.

CATALOGUE OF THE CORNELL WITCHCRAFT COLLECTION

Demoniality.

Witchcraft
BF
1556
S61
1879
 Sinistrari, Luigi Maria, 1622-1701.
  Demoniality; or Incubi and succubi. A treatise wherein is shown that there are in existence on earth rational creatures besides man ... Published from the original Latin manuscript discovered in London in the year 1872, and translated into French by Isidore Liseux. Now first translated into English. With the Latin text. Paris, I. Liseux, 1879.
  xvi, 251, [1] p. 17cm.

8   (Continued on next card)

Demoniality.

Witchcraft
BF
1556
S61
1927
 Sinistrari, Luigi Maria, 1622-1701.
  Demoniality. Translated into English from the Latin (with introd. and notes) by Montague Summers. London, Fortune Press [1927]
  xliii, 127 p. 23cm.

  No. 237 of 1200 copies.

  1. Demonology. I. Summers, Montague, 1880-1948, tr. II. Title. II. His De daemoniali tate et incubis et succubis--English.

Les démoniaques dans l'art.

Witchcraft
BF
1555
C46+
 Charcot, Jean Martin, 1825-1893.
  Les démoniaques dans l'art, par J. M. Charcot et Paul Richer. Paris, A. Delahaye et E. Lecrosnier, 1887.
  116 p. 67 illus. 30cm.

Demonic possession in the New Testament.

Witchcraft
BS
2545
A5
A37
 Alexander, William Menzies.
  Demonic possession in the New Testament; its relations historical, medical, and theological. Edinburgh, T. & T. Clark, 1902.
  xii, 291 p. 22cm.

  1. Demoniac possession. 2. Bible. N.T.--Commentaries. I. Title.

Demonolatry.

Remi, Nicolas, 1530-1612.
 Demonolatry. In 3 books; translated by E. A. Ashwin, edited with introd. and notes by Montague Summers. Drawn from the capital trials of 900 persons, more or less, who within the last fifteen years have in Lorraine paid the penalty of death for the crime of witchcraft. London, J. Rodker, 1930.
 xliii, 188 p. 27cm.

 French original first published, Lyon, 1595.

Demonologia; or Natural knowledge revealed.

[Forsyth, J S]
 Demonologia; or, Natural knowledge revealed; being an exposé of ancient and modern superstitions, credulity, fanaticism, enthusiasm, & imposture, as connected with the doctrine, caballa, and jargon, of amulets, apparitions, astrology, charms, demonology ... witchcraft, &c. ... By J. S. F. ... London, J. Bumpus, 1827.
 1 p. l., [v]-xvi, 438 p. front. 19cm.
 By J. S. Forsyth. cf. Halkett and Laing, Dict. anon. and pseud., new ed., 1926, v.2, p.37.

Demonologie.

Witchcraft
BF
1522
P45
 Perrault, François, 1572 or 77-1657.
  Demonologie ov Traitte des demons et sorciers: de leur puissance et impuissance: par Fr. Perreavd. Ensemble L'Antidemon de Mascon, ou Histoire veritable de ce qu'un demon a fait & dit, il y a quelques années, en la maison dudit S[r]. Perreaud à Mascon ... Geneve, Chez Pierre Aubert, 1653.
  2 pts. in 1 v. 15cm.

  1. Demonology. I. Title. II. Title: L'Antidemon de Mascon.

La démonologie de Michel Psellos.

WITCHCRAFT
BF
1508
P97
S97
 Swoboda, Karl Maria, 1889-
  La démonologie de Michel Psellos (Démonologie Michala Psella) Brno, V komisi knihkupectví A. Piša, 1927.
  60 p. 24cm. (Brno. Universita. Filosofícka faculta. Spisy. 22)

  At head of title: K. Svoboda.
  With summary in Czech.

8
NIC
  1. Psellus, Michael. Peri energeias daimonon dia logos. 2. Demonology. I. Title.

Witchcraft Demonology--Dictionaries--English.
BF
1503
R63+
 Robbins, Rossell Hope, 1912-
  The encyclopedia of witchcraft and demonology. New York, Crown Publishers [1959]
  571 p. illus. 26 cm.

  Includes bibliography.

  1. Witchcraft--Dictionaries--English. 2. Demonology--Dictionaries--English. I. Title.

BF1503.R6   133.403   59-9155 ‡

Library of Congress   [80]

Demonology--Dictionaries--French.

BF
1503
B65
1971
 Blocquel, Simon, 1780-1863.
  Le triple vocabulaire infernal: manuel du démonomane; ou, Les ruses de l'enfer dévoilées, par Frinellan, démonographe. Paris, N. Bussière [1971]
  319 p. illus. 15 cm. 22.50F   F***

  "Réimpression photomécanique."
  Frinellan, pseud. of Simon Blocquel.

4

  1. Demonology--Dictionaries--French. 2. Occult sciences--Dictionaries--French. I. Title.

BF1503.B48 1971   74-875408

Library of Congress   71 [2]

Demonology--Dictionaries--French.

BF
1503
T66
 Tondriau, Julien L
  Dictionnaire du diable et de la démonologie [par] J. Tondriau & R. Villeneuve. (Verviers, Gérard & Co., 1968).
  333 p. illus., facsims., ports. 18 cm. (Marabout université, v. 154) bfr 80.--   (Be 68-3086)

  Bibliography: p. [827]-830.

  1. Demonology--Dictionaries--French. I. Villeneuve, Roland, 1922- joint author. II. Title.

BF1503.T6   133.4'2'03   78-365611

Library of Congress   69 [1]

Demonology.

Witchcraft
BT
975
Y73
 Young, Joseph.
  Demonology: or, The Scripture doctrine of devils. Edinburgh, T. Grant, 1856.
  xviii, 460 p. 18cm.

  1. Devil. I. Title: The Scripture doctrine of devils. II. Title: Demonology.

Demonology and devil-lore.

Witchcraft
BF
1505
C76
1879
 Conway, Moncure Daniel, 1832-1907.
  Demonology and devil-lore. New York, H. Holt and Co., 1879.
  2 v. illus. 23cm.

  Author's autograph presentation copy.

  1. Demonology. 2. Mythology. I. Title.

Demonology and witchcraft, with especial reference to modern "spiritualism," so-called, and the "doctrines of demons."

Witchcraft
BF
1251
B88
 Brown, Robert, of Barton-upon-Humber.
  Demonology and witchcraft, with especial reference to modern "spiritualism," so-called, and the "doctrines of demons." London, J. F. Shaw, 1889.
  354 p. 19cm.

  1. Spiritualism. 2. Demonology. I. Title.

Demonology, sympathetic magic and witchcraft.

Witchcraft
BF
1531
F91
 Friend, John Albert Newton, 1881-
  Demonology, sympathetic magic and witchcraft; a study of superstition as it persists in man and affects him in a scientific age. London, C. Griffin [1961]
  173 p. illus. 20 cm.

  Includes bibliography.

  1. Demonology. 2. Witchcraft. I. Title: Sympathetic magic.

BF1531.F7   133.4   61-66183 ‡

Library of Congress   [2]

Demonomania con commozione celebrale ...

WITCHCRAFT
BF
1555
P84
 Portal, Placido, 1793-1843.
  Demonomania con commozione celebrale senza stravaso; osservazione fatta nel mese di novembre dell'anno 1833 nella R. Casa de' Matti in Palermo. Palermo, Dalla Tipografia del Giorn. letterario, 1834.
  25, [4] p. port. 20cm.

  "Autopsia cadaverica della demonomoniaca [sic] Rosa Cinexis ...": [4] p. at end.
8
NIC
  Includes bibliographical references.

   (Continued on next card)

Demonomania de gli stregoni.

WITCHCRAFT
BF
1520
B66
1592
 Bodin, Jean, 1530-1596.
  Demonomania de gli stregoni, cioè Fvrori, et malie de' demoni, col mezo de gl'hvomini: Diuisa in libri IIII. Di Gio. Bodino Francese, tradotta dal K.[r] Hercole Cato ... Di nuouo purgata, & ricorretta. Venetia, Presso Aldo, 1592.
  26 p. l., 419 p. 22cm.
  "Confvtatione delle opinioni di Giovanni VVier": p. [360]-419.
8 Translation of De la démonomanie.

   (Continued on next card)

La demonomanie des sorciers.

WITCHCRAFT
BF
1520
B66
1598
 Bodin, Jean, 1530-1596.
  La demonomanie des sorciers. Par I. Bodin angevin. Reueuë & corrigee d'vne infinité de fautes qui se sont passees és precedentes impressions. Auec vn indice des choses les plus remarquables contenuës en ce liure. Edition derniere. Paris, Chez Estienne Prevosteav, 1598.
  604, [31] p. 15cm.
  "Refvtation des opinions de Iean Wier": p. 523-604.

8   (Continued on next card)

CATALOGUE OF THE CORNELL WITCHCRAFT COLLECTION

La demonomanie des sorciers.

WITCHCRAFT
BF
1520
B66
1598

Bodin, Jean, 1530-1596. La demonomanie des sorciers ... 1598. (Card 2)

First published under title: De la demonomanie des sorciers.

1. Demonomania. 2. Witchcraft. 3. Magic. 4. Wier, Johann, 1515-1588. I. His De la démonomanie des sorciers. II. Title.

8

Witchcraft
BF
1582
D39

Denis, Albert.
La sorcellerie à Toul aux XVIe & XVIIe siècles. Étude historique. Toul, T. Lemaire, 1888.
191 p. 19cm.

1. Witchcraft--Toul, France. 2. Witchcraft--France. 3. Trials (Witchcraft) --France. I. Title.

8

Der im Alten und Neuen Testament unterschiedene, auch ungleich eingesehene Dienst der guten Engel.

WITCHCRAFT
BT
960
O61

Oporin, Joachim.
Der im Alten und Neuen Testament unterschiedene, auch ungleich eingesehene Dienst der guten Engel, nebst augenscheinlicher Rache des Messiae an dem Teufel. Das ist, Die erläuterte Lehre der Hebraeer und Christen von guten und bösen Engeln. Zamburg, Bey T. C. Felginers Wittwe gedruckt, 1735.
359p. 17cm.

8
NIC

1. Angels--Early works to 1800. 2. Devil.

Demonstrationes philosophicae De existentia corporum angelicorum.

Witchcraft
BT
965
G59

Göde, Carolus Fridericus.
Demonstrationes philosophicae De existentia corporvm angelicorvm non nvllisqve ad ea pertinentibvs per Carol. Frider. Goede. Halae Magdebvrgicae, Impensis Carol. Herm. Hemmerde, 1744.
6 p. l., 116 p. 18cm.

1. Angels--Early works to 1800. 2. Supernatural. I. Title: De existentia corporum angeli corum.

Witchcraft
BF
1411
D39

Denis, Ferdinand, 1798-1890.
Tableau historique, analytique, et critique des sciences occultes, où l'on examine l'origine, le développement, l'influence et le caractère de la divination, de l'astrologie, des oracles ... Précédé d'une introduction et suivi d'une biographie, d'une bibliographie et d'un vocabulaire ... Paris, L'Encyclopédie portative, 1830.
xii, 296 p. front. 13cm.
(Continued on next card)

Der in die katholische Schule geführte Fragensteller über den Katechismus von der Geisterlehre.

Witchcraft
BF
1603
S83
no.3

[Sterzinger, Ferdinand] 1721-1786.
Der in die katholische Schule geführte Fragensteller über den Katechismus von der Geisterlehre. [München?] 1775.
29 p. 17cm.

Ascribed to Sterzinger by British Museum.
No. 3 in vol lettered Francone dell' Amavero (Sterzinger) Untersuchung [etc.]

8

1. Frage, ob der Katechismus von der Geisterlehre e in katholischer Katechismus sey? 2. Magic. I. Title.

Demüthige Bitte um Belehrung an die grossen Männer.

WITCHCRAFT
BF
1523
V19
no.2

[Köster, Heinrich Martin Gottfried] 1734-
Demüthige Bitte um Belehrung an die grossen Männer, welche keinen Teufel glauben. 3. rechtmässige Aufl. In Deutschland, 1775.
56 p. 17cm.

Attribution by Holzmann, Jocher, et al.
No. 2 in vol. lettered Varia scripta demonolog.
1. Devil. 2. Devil--Biblical teaching. I. Title.

8

Witchcraft
BF
1411
D39

Denis, Ferdinand, 1798-1890. Tableau historique ... des sciences occultes ... 1830. (Card 2)

Half-title: Encyclopédie portative; ou, Résumé universel des sciences, des lettres et des arts, en une collection de traités séparés. Par une société de savans et de gens de lettres ...
Ex-libris Frédéric de Sevillia.

1. Occult sciences--Hist. I. Title. II. Title: Encyclopédie portative.

Der mit allerhand Staats-Friedens-Kriegs-Hof-Literatur- und Religions- wie auch Privat-Affairen ... Secretarius

WITCHCRAFT
BF
1555
S93

[Stübel, Andreas] 1653-1725.
Der mit allerhand Staats-Friedens-Kriegs-Hof-Literatur- und Religions- wie auch Privat-Affairen beschäfftige Secretarius ... Freyburg [1709-21]
various pagings. illus. (part fold.) 17cm.

Attribution by Holzmann.
Incomplete: detached sections dealing with supposed cases of demoniac possession. In form of "Expeditionen;" running

8
NIC
(Continued on next card)

Demüthiges Danksagungsschreiben an den grossen Mann.

WITCHCRAFT
BF
1523
K78
K513

[Köster, Heinrich Martin Gottfried] 1734-1802.
Emanuel Swedenborgs demüthiges Danksagungsschreiben an den grossen Mann, der die Nonexistenz des Teufels demonstrirt hat. Frankfurt und Leipzig, 1778.
46 p. 17cm.
Attribution by Holzmann.
1. Kindleben, Christian Wilhelm, 1748-1785. Ueber die Non-Existenz des Teufels. 2. Devil. I. Swedenborg, Emanuel, 1688-1772, supposed author. II. Title. III. Title: Demüthiges Danksagungsschre iben an den grossen Mann.

8

Witchcraft
BF
1583
Z7
1616

Dennler, J.
Ein Hexenprozess im Elsass vom Jahre 1616. Ein Beitrag zur Kulturgeschichte des Elsasses. Nach dem Rotbuch von Enzheim. Zabern, A. Fuchs, 1896.
28 p. 21cm.

1. Trials (Witchcraft)--Alsace. I. Title.

Witchcraft
BF
1555
S93

[Stübel, Andreas] 1653-1725. Der mit allerhand Staats-Friedens-Kriegs-Hof-Literatur- ... Affairen beschäfftige Secretarius ... [1709-21] (Card 2)

title reads: Des beschäfftige Secretarii erste [zweite, dritte, u. s. w.] Expedition. Includes excerpts from Expedition 1, 5, 8, 10, 12, 18, 20, 24, 27, 28, 37-39, 42, 44, 45.
Pages consecutively numbered in MS, and Register in MS bound in at end.

8
NIC
(Continued on next card)

Demüthigste Antwort eines geringen Landgeistlichen auf die Demüthige Bitte um Belehrung.

WITCHCRAFT
BF
1523
V19
no.5

[Bonnet, Johann Carl]
Demüthigste Antwort eines geringen Landgeistlichen auf die Demüthige Bitte um Belehrung an die grossen Männern, welche keinen Teufel glauben. In Deutschland, 1776.
54 p. 17cm.
Attribution by Holzmann.
No. 5 in vol. lettered Varia scripta demonolog.
1. Köster, Heinrich Martin Gottfried, 1734-1802. Demüthige Bitte um Belehrung. 2. Devil. I. Ein geringer Landgeistlicher. II. Title.

8

Der heiligen Jungfrauen ... Gertraud himmlische Anmuthungen.

Witchcraft
BF
1775
W13
1800

Der Wahre geistliche Schild. 2. Th. Oder: Heiliger Segen aller heil. Apostel und Jünger Jesu Christi ..., um alle unheilbaren Krankheiten der Menschen zu vertreiben, und alle Anfälle des Satans abzuwenden. Sammt dem wunderthätigen Gertrauden-Büchlein, das ist: Der heil. Jungfrau und Abtissin Gertraud himmlische Anmuthungen und Gebete um zeitliche und ewige Güter. Salzburg, 1667. [n. p., 18--] 148 p. illus. 16cm.

8
(Continued on next card)

Der Teufeleien des achtzehnten Jahrhunderts letzter Akt.

WITCHCRAFT
BF
1523
K78
K516

Kindleben, Christian Wilhelm, 1748-1785.
Der Teufeleien des achtzehnten Jahrhundert letzter Akt, worinn des Emanuel Schwedenborg demüthiges Danksagungsschreiben kürzlich beantwortet, der ganze bisher geführte Streit friedlich beygelegt, und in dem Büchlein über die Nonexistenz des Teufels zurückgenommen, ergänzt und berichtiget wird ... Leipzig, Bey C. F. Schneider, 1779.
63 p. 20cm.

8
NIC
(Continued on next card)

---

ar W
37205

Dendy, Walter Cooper, 1794-1871.
The philosophy of mystery. London, Longman, Orme, Brown, Green, & Longmans, 1841.
xii, 443 p. 23cm.

1. Psychical research. I. Title.

Der heiligen Jungfrauen ... Gertraud himmlische Anmuthungen.

Witchcraft
BF
1775
W13
1800

Der Wahre geistliche Schild ... [18--] (Card 2)

Heiliger Segen aller heiligen Apostel ... has special t. p.
Der heiligen Jungfrauen und Abtissin Gertraud himmlische Anmuthungen und Gebeter has special t. p. and imprint Cöln, 1506.
1. Charms. 2. Prayers. I. Gertrude, Saint, surnamed the Great, 1256-1302? supposed author. II. Title: Heiliger Segen aller heiligen Apostel. III. Title: Der heiligen Jungfrauen ...Gertraud himmlische An muthungen.

8

Witchcraft
BF
1603
S83
no.4

Der von seinem unglücklich gewählten Schüler abgefertigte Schulmeister. [n. p.] 1775.
80 p. 17cm.

No. 4 in vol. lettered Francone dell' Amavero (Sterzinger) Untersuchung [etc.]

1. Sterzinger, Ferdinand, 1721-1786. Katekismus von der Geisterlehre. 2. Sterzinger, Ferdin and, 1721-1786. Der in die kathol ische Schule geführte Fragensteller.

8

CATALOGUE OF THE CORNELL WITCHCRAFT COLLECTION

Witchcraft
BF
1410
B42
Z56
v.3
no.25

Derde briev van Haggébher Philaleethees geschreeven aan zynen vriend N. N. ...
[Hooght, Everard van der] d. 1716.
Derde briev van הגבר [Haggébher] ΦΙΛΑΛΗΘΗΣ [Philaleethees] geschreeven aan zynen vriend N. N. over het vervolg van de kerkelyke procedueren tegen den persoon van Do. Balthasar Bekker; nevens de aan-merkingen over de gereformeerde confessie, ende over het gevoelen van de gesonde gereformeerde godsgeleerden, nopende het hooft-stuk van de natuure ende de werkingen der engelen. Amsterdam, By G. Borstius, boekver koper, 1691.
(Continued on next card)

8

Witchcraft
BF
1410
B42
Z56
v.3
no.25

Derde briev van Haggébher Philaleethees geschreeven aan zynen vriend N. N. ...
[Hooght, Everard van der] d. 1716. Derde briev ... aan zynen vriend N. N. ... 1691. (Card 2)
[39]-58 p. title vignette, illus. initial. 19 x 15cm.
4°: π1, A-B⁴, C1.
Black letter.
The friend N. N. is Jacobus Schuts?
Van der Linde 99.
No. 25 in vol. lettered Bekker III.
(Continued on next card)

Witchcraft
AZ
999
S16

Des erreurs et des préjugés répandus dans la société.
Salgues, Jacques Barthélemy, 1760 (ca.)-1830.
Des erreurs et des préjugés répandus dans la société ... Paris, Chez F. Buisson, 1810-15.
3 v. 20cm.
Vol. 2: "2. éd., revue et augmentée", with title: Des erreurs et des préjugés répandus dans les diverses classes de la société. Paris, Lepetit, 1815.
Imprint of vol. 1 is partly covered by a bookplate.

ar W
37210

Des erreurs et des préjugés répandus dans les dix-huitième et dix-neuvième siècles.
Salgues, Jacques Barthélemy, 1760 (ca.)-1830.
Des erreurs et des préjugés répandus dans les dix-huitième et dix-neuvième siècles. Paris, J. G. Dentu, 1828.
2 v. 22cm.

1. Superstition. I. Title.

Des grossen Wasserguss.
Wetz, Ambrosius.
Warhafftige und ein erschröckliche newe Zeitung, des grossen Wasserguss, so den 15. May diss lauffenden 78. Jahrs, zu Horb geschehen ... wie man hernach alda etlich Unhulden verbrent hatt, wie sie schröcklich Ding bekendt haben ... durch Ambrosium Wetz ... [n.p., 1578? ca. 1900]
4 l. 19cm.
Carnap's manuscript copy.
"Originaldr uck in der Stadtbibliothek zu Züri ch, 8 Seiten in 8°."
(Continued on next card)

Des grossen Wasserguss.
Wetz, Ambrosius. Warhafftige und ein erschröckliche newe Zeitung, des grossen Wasserguss ... [1578? ca. 1900] (Card 2)
Annotations in the margins indicate foliation of the original.
In verse.

1. Witchcraft--Austria. I. Title.
II. Title: Des grossen Wasserguss.

Witchcraft
BF
1582
Z7
1611a

Des marqves des sorciers et de la reelle possession que le diable prend sur le corps des hommes.
Fontaine, Jacques, d. 1621.
Des marqves des sorciers et de la reelle possession que le diable prend sur le corps des hommes. Sur le subiect du proces de l'abominable & detestable sorcier Louys Gaufridy ... Lyon, Par Claude Larjot, 1611 [Arras, 1865]
45, [1] p. 21cm.

8

1. Trials (Witchcraft)--France. 2. Gaufridi, Louis, 1572-1611. 3. Witchcraft.
I. Title.

Witchcraft
BF
1532
B62

Des rapports de l'homme avec le démon.
Bizouard, Joseph, b. 1797.
Des rapports de l'homme avec le démon; essai historique et philosophique, par Joseph Bizouard ... Paris, Gaume frères et J. Duprey, 1863-64.
6 v. 23cm.

1. Demonology. I. Title.

34-10142

Library of Congress   BF1532.B5   [159.961409]   133.409

Des satyres brutes, monstres et demons.
WITCHCRAFT
BL
820
S3
A89

Aubignac, François Hédelin, abbé d', 1604-1676.
Des satyres brvtes, monstres et demons. De levr natvre et adoration. Contre l'opinion de ceux qui ont estimé les satyres estre vne espece d'hommes distincts & separez des Adamicqves ... Par F. Hedelin, aduocat en Parlement ... Paris, Chez Nicolas Bvon, 1627.
12 p. l., 236 p. 17cm.

8

Witchcraft
BF
1569
A2M72
1926

Des sorcières et des devineresses.
Molitor, Ulrich, fl. 1470-1501.
Des sorcières et des devineresses par Ulric Molitor reproduit en fac-simile d'après l'édition latine de Cologne 1489 et traduit pour la première fois en français. Paris, E. Nourry, 1926.
vii p., facsim. ([56] p. illus.), 84 p. 25cm. (Bibliothèque magique des XVe et XVIe siècles, 1)
Original t. p.: De lamiis et phitonicis mulieribus. (p. [1])
"Tirage limité a 500 exemplaires sur vélin a la cuve. N° 100.
I. Title.   II. Title: De lamiis et phithonicis mulieribus.

Des sorciers aux XVme et XVIme siècles.
WITCHCRAFT
BF
1582
L16

La Fons, Alexandre de, baron de Mélicocq.
Des sorciers aux XVme et XVIme siècles. [Abbeville, 1843]
[435]-448 p. 24cm.
Extract from Mémoires de la Société d'Abbeville, 1841-43.

8
NIC

1. Witchcraft--France. 2. Witchcraft--History.

Witchcraft
Z
6876
J86

Descreux, V., joint author.
Jouin, Ernest.
Bibliographie occultiste et maçonnique. Répertoire d'ouvrages imprimés et manuscrits relatifs à la franc-maçonnerie, les sociétés secrètes, la magie, etc. publié d'après les fiches recueillies par A.-Peeters Baertsoen et avec des notes historiques et bibliographiques. Tome I. Jusqu'à l'année 1717. Paris, Revue internationale des sociétés secrètes, 1930.
653 p. 25cm.
At head of title: Mgr E. Jouin et V. Descreux.
No more publi shed?

Witchcraft
PQ
1957
B67
A64
1793

Description du sabbat.
Bordelon, Laurent, 1653-1730.
Histoire de M. Oufle, par abbé Bordelon [retouchée et réduite par M. G.] et la Description du sabbat. Paris, Gay & Gide, 1793.
360 p. 20cm.
"...C'est ... un nouveau roman, mais ... nous sommes redevables néanmoins à l'abbé Bordelon...": p. 5-6.
"Descripti on du sabbat" is not by Bordelon.

Rare
PQ
1714
B3++
1727

Desmaizeaux, Pierre, 1673?-1745, ed.
Bayle, Pierre, 1647-1706.
Oeuvres diverses, contenant tout ce que cet auteur a publié sur des matières de Théologie, de philosophie, de critique, d'histoire & de litterature; excepté son Dictionnaire historique et critique. La Haye, P. Husson, 1727-31.
4 v. illus. 41 cm.
Edited by Pierre Desmaizeaux.
For contents see Rare main card.

I. Desmaizea ux, Pierre, 1673?-1745, ed.

Witchcraft
BF
1582
Z7
1647

Desmarets,   oratorien.
Histoire de Madeleine Bavent, religieuse du monastère de Saint-Louis de Louviers. Réimpression textuelle sur l'édition rarissime de 1652. Précédée d'une notice bio-bibliographique, et suivie de plusieurs pièces supplémentaires. Orné d'un front. et d'une vue de l'ancien couvent de Saint-Louis ... Rouen, J. Lemonnyer, 1878.
xl, vii, 169 p. illus. 21cm.
No. 141 of 177 copies printed.
(Continued on next card)

Witchcraft
BF
1582
Z7
1647

Desmarets,   oratorien. Histoire de Madeleine Bavent ... 1878. (Card 2)
Original t.p. reads: Historie de Magdelaine Bavent, religieuse du monastère de Saint Louis de Louviers, avec sa confession générale & testamentaire, où elle déclare les abominations, impietez, & sacrilèges qu'elle a pratiqué & veu pratiquer, tant ledit monastere, qu'au sabat, & les personnes qu'elle y a rema rquées. Ensemble l'arrest
(Continued on next card)

Witchcraft
BF
1582
Z7
1647

Desmarets,   oratorien. Histoire de Madeleine Bavent ... 1878. (Card 3)
donné contre Mathurin Picard, Thomas Boullé & ladite Bavent, tous convaincus du crime de magie. Dedie'e à Mme. la Dvchesse d'Orleans. Paris, J. Le Gentil, 1652.

1. Bavent, Madeleine, ca.1608-1647.
I. Title. II. Title: Historie de Magdelaine Bavent.

Witchcraft
BF
1517
F5
D46
1887

[Des Niau, ---]
The history of the devils of Loudun, the alleged possession of the Ursuline nuns, and the trial and execution of Urbain Grandier, told by an eye-witness. Translated from the original French, and edited by Edmund Goldsmid. Edinburg, Priv. Print., 1887-88.
3 v. 18cm. (Collectanea Adamantaea, XXI.)
Contains facsimile of original French t.p.: La véritable historie des diables de Loudun ... Poitiers, J Thoreau, 1634.
(Over)

CATALOGUE OF THE CORNELL WITCHCRAFT COLLECTION

Witchcraft
BF
1517
F5
D46
1887

Des Niau, ---.
　La véritable histoire des diables de Loudun.-- English.
　[Des Niau, ---]
　　The history of the devils of Loudun, the alleged possession of the Ursuline nuns, and the trial and execution of Urbain Grandier, told by an eye-witness. Translated from the original French, and edited by Edmund Goldsmid. Edinburg, Priv. Print., 1887-88.
　　3 v. 18cm. (Collectanea Adamantaea, XXI.I)
　　Contains facsimile of original French t.p.: La véritable historie des diables de Loudun ... Poitiers, J. Thoreau, 1634.

Witchcraft
BF
1517
F5
A89

Des Niau, ___, supposed author.
[Aubin, Nicolas] b. ca. 1655.
　The cheats and illusions of Romish priests and exorcists. Discovered in the history of the devils of Loudun: being an account of the pretended possession of the Ursuline nuns, and of the condemnation and punishment of Urban Grandier, a parson of the same town ... London, Printed for W. Turner and R. Bassett, 1703.
　4 p. l., 331 p. 20cm.
　Translation of Histoire des diables de Loudun Attributed also to M. Des Niau.
　1. Loudun, France. Ursuline Convent. 2. Grandier, Urbain, 1590-1634. I. Des Niau, ___, supposed author. II.Title

WITCHCRAFT
BF
1555
R47

Destaing, count of Lyons.
Rhodes, ___, de.
　Lettre en forme de dissertation de M^r. de Rhodes escuyer docteur en mededine, aggregé au college des medecins de Lyon. A monsievr Destaing comte de Lyon; au sujet de la prétenduë possession de Marie Volet de la parroisse de Pouliat en Bresse, dans laquelle il est traité des causes naturelles de ses accidens, & de sa guérison. Lyon, Chez Thomas Amaulry, 1691.
　4 p. l., 75 p. 18cm.

8　　　　　Continued on next card)

WITCHCRAFT
BF
1555
R47

Destaing, count of Lyons.
Rhodes, ___, de. Lettre en forme de dissertation ... 1691. (Card 2)
　Imperfect copy: p. 1-2 (second t. p.?) wanting.
　With this is bound Sentimens d'Eudoxe et d'Aristée, sur le dialogue satirique de Mystagogue et de Neophile. 1691.
　1. Demoniac possession. 2. Volet, Marie, fl. 1690. I. Title. II. Title: La prétenduë possession de Marie Volet.

8

Witchcraft
BF
1563
W81++
no.2

A Detection of damnable driftes, practized by three vvitches arraigned at Chelmisforde in Essex ... April 1579. ...
　London, Imprinted for E. White [1579? London, at the British Museum, 1923]
　[19] p. 14cm.
　Photocopy (negative) [19] p. on 9 l. 20 x 32cm.
　No. 2 in vol. lettered: Witchcraft tracts, chapbooks and broadsides, 1579-1704; rotograph copies.
　1. Witchcraft--England.

FILM
470
reel
417

A detection of damnable driftes, practized by three vvitches arraigned at Chelmisforde in Essex, at the last assises there holden, whiche were executed in Apiill. 1579 ... Imprinted at London for Edward White ... [1579]
　University microfilms no. 11704 (case 70, carton 417)
　Short-title catalogue no. 5115.
　1. Witchcraft--England.

Witchcraft
BF
1563
T75

A detection of damnable driftes.
　Witchcraft at Maldon, Essex, in 1579.
　[Great Totham, Essex, Printed at C. Clark's private press, ca. 1840]
　2 numbered leaves. 23cm.

　Caption title.
　Extract from A detection of damnable driftes ...
　No. 2 in vol. lettered Tracts on witchcraft.

8　　1. Smithe, Elleine. I. A detection of damnable driftes.

Witchcraft
BF
1581
H32D61

A detection of that sinnfvl shamfvl lying and ridicvlovs discovrs, of Samvel Harshnet.
[Darrell, John] fl. 1562-1602.
　A detection of that sinnfvl shamfvl lying and ridicvlovs discovrs, of Samvel Harshnet, entitvled: A discoverie of the fravvdvlent practises of Iohn Darrell. Wherein is manifestly and apparantly shewed in the eyes of the world, not onely the vnlikelihoode, but the flate impossibilitie of the pretended counterfayting of William Somers, Thomas Darling, Kath. Wright, and Mary Couper; togeather with the other 7. in Lancashire, and the (Continued on next card)

Witchcraft
BF
1581
H32D61

A detection of that sinnfvl shamfvl lying and ridicvlovs discovrs, of Samvel Harshnet.
[Darrell, John] fl. 1562-1602. A detection of ... discovrs of Samvel Harshnet ... (Card 2)
　supposed teaching of them by the saide Iohn Darrell. [London] 1600.
　208, [3] p. 19cm.

　1. Harsnett, Samuel, abp. of York, 1561-1631. A discovery of the fraudulent practices of John Darrell. 2. Witchcraft--Lancashire. I. Title.

Witchcraft
BF
1520
B66
1590

Detestando lamiarum ac magnorum cum Satana commercio.
Bodin, Jean, 1530-1596.
　De magorvm daemonomania, sev Detestando lamiarum ac magorum cum Satana commercio, libri IV. Recens recogniti, & multis in locis à mendis repurgati. Accessit eiusdem Opinionum Ioan. Vieri confutatio non minùs docta quam pia. Francofvrti, Ex Officina Typographica Nicolai Bassaei, 1590.
　798 p. 16cm.

　Title vignette.
　I. Title. II. Title: Detestando lamiarum ac magnorum cum Satana commercio. III. His De la demonomanie--Latin.

WITCHCRAFT
RC
533
D47
1724

Detharding, Georg Christoph, 1671-1747, praeses.
　Dissertatio medica inauguralis De obsessione eademque spuria, von Besessenen und vor besessen gehaltenen Menschen, qvam ... sub praesidio ... Georgii Dethardingii ... publice examinandam proponit Christ. Frider. Stever ... Rostochii, Recusa typis Io. Ioacob. Adleri [1724?]
　[102] p. 19cm.
　Diss.--Rostock (C. F. Stever, respondent)
　I. Stever, Christianus, respondent)
8　II. Title. III. Title: De obsessione eadeque spuria.

History of Science
BF
1471
D47

Detharding, Georg Christoph, 1671-1747, praeses.
　Scrutinium medicum De morbis a spectrorum apparitione oriundis, Von Gespenstern, wie weit solche durch ihre Erscheinung Kranckheiten verursachen, ed qvod ... praeside ... Georgio Dethardingio ... pro gradu doctorali summisque in arte medica honoribus insignibus ac privilegiis rite obtinendis, ... ad diem 27. Octobr. An. 1729. publico examini offert Georgius Erhard von Gehren...
(Continued on next card)

History of Science
BF
1471
D47

Detharding, Georg Christoph, 1671-1747, praeses. Scrutinium medicum ... [1729] (Card 2)
　Rostochii, Typis Io. Iacob. Adleri [1729] 38 p. 20cm.
　Diss.--Rostock (G. E. von Gehren, respondent)
　1. Apparitions. 2. Ghosts. 3. Medicine--15th-18th centuries. I. Gehren, Georg Erhard von, respondent. II. Title: De morbis a spectrorum apparitione oriundis. III. Title.

De Torre, Ludovicus.
　see
Torre, Luis de, d. 1635.

Witchcraft
BF
1584
S97
D48

Dettling, Alois.
　Die Hexenprozesse im Kanton Schwyz. Schwyz, Buchdruckerei von C. Triner, 1907.
　115 p. illus. 24cm.

　1. Trials (Witchcraft)--Schwyz. I. Title.

Witchcraft
BF
1410
B42
Z82
no.3

Deurhoff, Willem, 1650-1717.
Blyenbergh, Willem van, 17th cent.
　Klaare en beknopte verhandeling van de natuur en werkinge der menschelijke zielen, engelen en duivelen, vervat in gewisselde brieven tusschen de heer Willem van Blyenbergh en Willem Deurhoff. Amsterdam, By J. ten Hoorn, boekverkooper, 1692.
　64 p. title vignette, illus. initials. 20 x 15cm.
　4°: A-H⁴.
　Discussion of questions raised in the contemporary controversy over Bal-
(Continued on next card)

Witchcraft
BF
1410
B42
Z82
no.3

Deurhoff, Willem, 1650-1717.
Blyenbergh, Willem van, 17th cent. Klaare en beknopte verhandeling van de natuur en werkinge der menschelijke zielen ... 1692. (Card 2)
　thasar Bekker's De Betoverde weereld. Van der Linde 77.
　No. 3 in vol. lettered Over Bekkers Betoverde wereld. 1692.
　1. Soul. 2. Spirits. 3. Bekker, Balthasar. De betoverde weereld. I. Deurhoff, Willem, 1650-1717. II. Title.

8

WITCHCRAFT
BF
1325
H81

Deuteroskopie.
Horst, Georg Conrad, 1767-1838?
　Deuteroskopie, oder Merkwürdige psychische und physiologische Erscheinungen und Probleme aus dem Gebiete der Pneumatologie Für Religionsphilosophen, Psychologen, und denkende Aerzte. Eine nöthige Beilage zur Dämonomagie, wie zur Zauber-Bibliothek. Frankfurt am Main, H. Wilmans, 1830.
　2 v. in 1. 21cm.
　1. Second sight. 2. Visions. I. His Dämonomagie. II. His Zauber-Bibliothek. III. Title.

CATALOGUE OF THE CORNELL WITCHCRAFT COLLECTION

Deutliche Vorstellung der Nichtigkeit der Zauberey.

Witchcraft
F
565
2

Franck, Johannes Christophorus, fl. 1717.
  Gottfried Wahrliebs [pseud.] Deutliche vorstellung der nichtigkeit derer vermeynten hexereyen und des ungegründeten hexen-processes. Nebst einer Gründlichen beantwortung der unter dem nahmen eines nach Engelland reisenden passagiers unlängst herausgekommenen Untersuchung vom kobold, darinnen die falschen auflagen / mit welchen derselbe so wohl den hrn. geheimbd. rath Thomasivm als Iohann Webstern ohne allen grund zu diffamiren gesucht. deutlich
  (Continued on next card)

Deutliche Vorstellung der Nichtigkeit der Zauberey.

Witchcraft
F
565
82

Franck, Johannes Christophorus, fl. 1717.
  Gottfried Wahrliebs [pseud.] Deutliche Vorstellung der nichtigkeit derer vermeynten hexereyen... [pref. 1720]   (Card 2)

entdecket, wie auch die Thomasische, Lehrsätze vom laster der zauberey wieder dessen ungegründete einwürfe zulänglich behauptet werden. Amsterdam, Nach erfindung der hexerey im dritten seculo, und nach einführung des hexenprocesses im Jahr 236 [pref. 1720]
    172, 78 p.   front.   22cm.
  (Continued on next card)

Deutliche Vorstellung der Nichtigkeit der Zauberey.

WITCHCRAFT
BF
1565
F82

Franck, Johannes Christophorus, fl. 1717.
  Gottfried Wahrliebs [pseud.] Deutliche vorstellung der nichtigkeit derer vermeynten hexereyen... [pref. 1720]   (Card 3)

"Gründliche beantwortung der ... Untersuchung vom kobold" has separate paging and special t. p. with imprint: Amsterdam, 1720.

  (Continued on next card)

Deutsche Segen, Heil- und Bannsprüche.

Losch, Friedrich, comp.
  Deutsche Segen, Heil- und Bannsprüche; nach gedruckten, schriftlichen und mündlichen Quellen zusammengestellt und hrsg. [Stuttgart, W. Kohlhammer, 1890]
    157-259 p.   29cm.

Detached from Württembergische Vierteljahrshefte für Landesgeschichte, Jahrg. 13, Heft 3.

  1. Incantations. 2. Exorcism. I. Title.

Der deutsche Teufel im 16. Jahrhundert.

Witchcraft
BF
550
89

Freytag, Gustav, 1816-1895.
  Bilder aus der deutschen Vergangenheit. Der deutsche Teufel im 16. Jahrhundert. (In Die Grenzboten. Leipzig. 24cm. XVII. Jahrg. (1858) p. [365]-386)

  1. Devil. II. Title. III. Title: Der deutsche Teufel im 16. Jahrhundert.

Der deutsche Volksaberglaube in seinem Verhältnis zum Christentum.

BL
490
89

Freybe, Albert.
  Der deutsche Volksaberglaube in seinem Verhältnis zum Christentum und im Unterschiede von der Zauberei. Gotha, F. A. Perthes, 1910.
    xv, 194 p.   22cm.

  1. Superstition. I. Title.

Die deutschen Hexenprozesse.

Witchcraft
BF
1583
B34

Baumgarten, Paul Maria, 1860-
  Die deutschen Hexenprozesse.   Frankfurt a.M., A. F. Nachfolger, 1883.
    [115]-154 p.   23cm.

Detached from Frankfurter zeitgemäsze Broschüren. Neue Folge, Bd. IV, Heft 5.

  1. Trials (Witchcraft)--Germany. I. Title.

Devx livres de la hayne de Sathan et malins esprits contre l'homme.

Witchcraft
BF
1522
C92
2 copies

Crespet, Pierre, 1543-1594.
  Devx livres de la hayne de Sathan et malins esprits contre l'homme, & de l'homme contre eux. Ou sont par notables discours & curieuses recherches expliquez les arts, ruses, & moyens, qu'ils prattiquent pour nuyre à l'homme par charmes, obsessions, magie, sorcellerie, illusions, phantosmes, impostures, & autres estranges façons, auec les remedes conuenables pour leur resister suyuant l'vsage qui se pratique en l'Eglise.
  (Continued on next card)

Devx livres de la hayne de Sathan et malins esprits contre l'homme.

Witchcraft
BF
1522
C92

Crespet, Pierre, 1543-1594. Devx livres de la hayne de Sathan ...   (Card 2)

Auec la table bien ample des matieres y contenues. Paris, Chez Guillaume de la Noüe, 1590.
    [26], 428, [22] l.   17cm.

Errors in paging.
Copy 1 bound in two volumes.
Copy 2 with Robert Southey's autograph.
  I. Title.

Devx traitez novveavx, tres-vtiles povr ce temps.

Witchcraft
BF
1565
D17
1579

Daneau, Lambert, ca. 1530-1595?
  Devx traitez novveavx, tres-vtiles povr ce temps. Le premier tovchant les sorciers, auquel ce qui se dispute auiourd'huy sur cete matiere, est bien amplement resolu & augmenté de deux proces extraicts des greffes pour l'esclaircissement & confirmation de cet argument. Le second contient vne breue Remonstrance sur les ieux de cartes & de dez. Reu. & augm. par l'auteur M. Lambert Daneau. [Geneve?] Par Jaqves Bavmet, 1579.
    160 p.   15cm.
  (Continued on next card)

Devx traitez novveavx, tres-vtiles povr ce temps.

Witchcraft
BF
1565
D17
1579

Daneau, Lambert, ca. 1530-1595? Devx traitez novveavx, tres-vtiles povr ce temps. 1579.   (Card 2)

"Dialogve des sorciers ov eriges" is translation of most of his De veneficis, qvos olim sortilegos ... vocant.

Devil--Bibliography.

Witchcraft
BF
1547
H36

Hauber, Eberhard David, 1695-1765.
  Bibliotheca, acta et scripta magica. Gründliche Nachrichten und Urtheile von solchen Büchern und Handlungen, welche die Macht des Teufels in leiblichen Dingen betreffen ... Lemgo, Gedruckt bey J. H. Meyer, 1738-45.
    36 pts. in 3 v. plates (part fold.) ports.   18cm.

Vol.[1]: 1. Stück. 2. und verbesserter Druck. 1739.
For detailed contents see J. G. T. Grässe:
  (Continued on next card)

Devil--Bibliography.

Witchcraft
BF
1547
H36

Hauber, Eberhard David, 1695-1765. Bibliotheca, acta et scripta magica ... 1738-45.   (Card 2)

Bibliotheca magica, p. 118-130.

  1. Devil. 2. Devil--Bibl. 3. Witchcraft. 4. Witchcraft--Bibl. 5. Occult sciences. I. Title.

Devil--Bibliography.

Witchcraft
Z
5761
K39

[Kernot, Henry] 1806-1874.
  Bibliotheca diabolica; being a choice selection of the most valuable books relating to the Devil; his origin, greatness, and influence. Comprising the most important works on the devil, Satan, demons, hell, hell-torments, magic, witchcraft ... with some curious volumes on dreams and astrology. In two parts, pro and con, serious and humerous ... [New York] On sale by Scribner, Welford & Armstrong, 1874.
    40 p. illus   25cm.

Devil--Bibliography.

WITCHCRAFT
BF
1523
K78
no.4

[Köster, Heinrich Martin Gottfried] 1734-1802.
  Teufeleien des achtzehnten Jahrhunderts, von dem Verfasser der Demüthigen Bitte um Belehrung an die grossen Männer welche keinen Teufel glauben. 1. rechtmässige Aufl. Leipzig, Bey C. F. Schneidern, 1778.
    142 p.   18cm.
  No. 4 in vol. lettered Ueber den Teufel.
  1. His Demüthige Bitte um Belehrung.
  2. Devil--Bibl. I. Title.

The Devil: a myth...

Witchcraft
BF
1548
C95

Cross, William.
  The Devil: a myth...   London, E. Truelove, 1872.
    16 p.   20cm.

  1. Devil. I. Title.

The Devil amongst us.

Witchcraft
BF
1576
T77

Trask, Richard B
  The Devil amongst us; a history of the Salem village parsonage, 1681-1784. Danvers, Mass., Danvers Historical Society, 1971.
    12 p. illus.   23cm.

  1. Witchcraft--Salem, Mass. I. Title.
  II. Title: The Salem village parsonage, 1681-1784.

The devil; an historical, critical and medical study.

Witchcraft
BT
980
G21
1929

Garçon, Maurice.
  The devil; an historical, critical and medical study. London, V. Gollancz, 1929.
    288 p.   22cm.

At head of title: Maurice Garçon & Jean Vinchon, translated by Stephen Haden Guest from the sixth French edition.

  1. Devil. 2. Demonomania. 3. Demonology.
  I. Vinchon, Jean, 1884-   joint author. II. Garçon, Maurice. Le diable.--English. III. Title.

CATALOGUE OF THE CORNELL WITCHCRAFT COLLECTION

The devil and all his works.

BF 1411 W55+
Wheatley, Dennis, 1897–
 The devil and all his works. New York, American Heritage Press [1971]
 302 p. illus. (part col.), maps, ports. 29 cm. $14.95

4

1. Occult sciences. 2. Psychical research. I. Title.

BF1411.W45 1971   133   79-145620
ISBN 0-07-089501-6   MARC
Library of Congress   71 [10-2]

The Devil, demonology, and witchcraft.

BT 975 K29
Kelly, Henry Ansgar.
 The Devil, demonology, and witchcraft; the development of Christian beliefs in evil spirits. Garden City, N. Y., Doubleday, 1968.
 vi, 187 p. 22 cm. (A Scott & Collins book) $4.95
 Bibliographical footnotes.

1. Demonology. I. Title.

BT975.K42   235'.4   68-24838
Library of Congress   [3]

The Devil: does he exist? And what does he do?

Witchcraft
BT 980 D33 1890
Delaporte, Albert, b. 1829.
 The Devil: does he exist? And what does he do? Translated from the sixth French ed., rev. and corr. by the author, by Mrs. James Sadlier. New York, D. & J. Sadlier [c1890]
 202 p. 18cm. (Sadliers' household library, no. 11)
 Cover has date: 1878.
 Translation of: Le diable, existe-t-il, et que fait-il?
 I. His   Le diable, existe-t-il, et que fait-il? English. II. Title.

The devil his origin, greatness and decadence.

Witchcraft
BF 1548 R45 1871
Réville, Albert, 1826-1906.
 The devil his origin, greatness and decadence. London, Williams and Norgate, 1871.
 xvi, 72 p. 18cm.
 "Translator's prefatory notes", p. [v]-x, signed H. A. [i. e. Henry Attwell]
 1. Devil. I. Réville, Albert, 1826-1906. Histoire du diable, ses origines, sa grandeur et sa décadence--English. II. Attwell, Henry, 1834–   tr. III. Title.

The devil in Britain and America.

Witchcraft
BF 1581 A82
Ashton, John, 1834–
 The devil in Britain and America ... [London] Ward and Downey, 1896.
 x, 363 p. illus. 23cm.

I. Title.

The devil in Lancashire.

Witchcraft
BF 1548 W78
Winterbottom, Vera.
 The devil in Lancashire. With drawings and cover design by Barbara Tomlinson. [Stockport, Heaton Mersey, Eng., Cloister Press, 1962]
 87 p. illus. 23cm.

1. Devil. 2. Witchcraft--Lancashire, Eng. I. Title.

The devil in Massachusetts.

BF 1576 S79 1961
Starkey, Marion Lena
 The devil in Massachusetts; a modern inquiry into the Salem witch trials. Garden City, N. Y., Doubleday [1961]
 310 p. 19cm. (Dolphin Books)

1. Witchcraft--Salem, Mass. I. Title.

Witchcraft
PR 2610 A16 1905
The devil is an ass.
 Jonson, Ben, 1573?-1637.
 The devil is an ass. Edited with introduction, notes, and glossary by William Savage Johnson. New York, Henry Holt and Co., 1905.
 lxxix, 252 p. 24cm. (Yale studies in English, 29)

I. Johnson, William Savage, ed. II. Title.

Witchcraft
BF 1548 D49
Devil or no devil: job or no job. By an Old Sunday School teacher. Birmingham, William H. Davis, Printer, 1821.
 102 p. 19cm.

1. Devil.

The Devill of Mascon.

Witchcraft
BF 1555 P45 1658
Perrault, François, 1572 or 77-1657.
 The Devill of Mascon; or, A true relation of the chiefe things which an vncleane spirit did, and said, at Mascon in Burgundy, in the house of Mr. Francis Perreand [sic] ... Published in French lately by himself; and now made English by one that hath a particular knowledge of the truth of this story [i.e. Peter Du Moulin. With a letter from the Hon. R. Boyle to the translator] Oxford, Printed by H. Hall, for R. Davis, 1658.
 46 p. 15cm.   (Continued on next card)

The Devill of Mascon.

Witchcraft
BF 1555 P45 1658
Perrault, François, 1572 or 77-1657. The Devill of Mascon ... 1658.   (Card 2)
 Translation of his L'Antidémon de Mascon ...

1. Demonology. I. Title. II. Perrault, François, 1572 or 77-1657. L'Antidémon de Mascon--English.

The devils of Loudun.

WITCHCRAFT
BF 1517 F5 H98
Huxley, Aldous Leonard, 1894–
 The devils of Loudun. London, Chatto & Windus, 1952.
 376 p. illus., facsims. 21cm.

Les devins.

WITCHCRAFT
BF 1410 P51 1584a
Peucer, Kaspar, 1525-1602.
 Les devins, ov Commentaire des principales sortes de devinations: distingué en quinze liures, esquels les ruses & impostures de Satan sont descouuertes, solidement refutees, & separees d'auec les sainctes propheties & d'auec les predictions naturelles. Escrit en latin par M. Gaspar Peucer, ... nouuellement tourné en françois par S. G. S. [i.e., Simon Goulart, Senlisien] ... Anvers, Par Hevdrik Connix, 1584

8   (Continued on next card)

Les devins.

WITCHCRAFT
BF 1410 P51 1584a
Peucer, Kaspar, 1525-1602. Les devins, ov Commentaire des principales sortes de devinations ... 1584.   (Card 2)
 6 p. l., 653, [24] p. 24cm.
 Translation of Commentarius de praecipuis generibus divinationum.
 1. Divination. 2. Prophecies. 3. Magic. 4. Witchcraft. I. His Commentarius de praecipuis generibus divinationum. II. Goulart, Simon, 1543-1628, tr. III. Title.

8

De Visser, Johannes Theodoor, 1857?-1932.

see

Visser, Johannes Theodoor de, 1857?-1932.

Devonshire witches.

WITCHCRAFT
BF 1581 K18
Karkeek, Paul Quick.
 Devonshire witches, by Paul Q. Karkeek. (Read at Teignmouth, July, 1874) ... [London? 1874?]
 30 p. 21cm.
 "Reprinted from the Transactions of the Devonshire Association for the Advancement of Science, Literature, and Art. 1874."
 With this are bound the author's Recent cases of supposed witchcraft in Devonshire. [London? 1875?] and the au-

8   (Continued on next card)
NIC

Devonshire witches.

WITCHCRAFT
BF 1581 K18
Karkeek, Paul Quick. Devonshire witches... [1874?]   (Card 2)
 thor's A budget of witch stories. [London? 1882?]

1. Witchcraft--Devonshire, Eng. 2. Trials (Witchcraft)--Devonshire, Eng. I. Title.

DA 670 G9 G93 no. 3
Dewar, Stephen.
 Witchcraft and the evil eye in Guernsey. Guernsey, Toucan P., 1968.
 12 p. illus. 19 cm. (Guernsey historical monographs, no. 3)
 2/6   (B 68-1425)
 Bibliography: p. 12.

1. Witchcraft--Guernsey. 2. Evil eye. I. Title.

DA670.G9G85 no. 3   133.4   72-3544
Library of Congress   69 [1]

168

CATALOGUE OF THE CORNELL WITCHCRAFT COLLECTION

Witchcraft
BF
1582
D52

Déy, Aristide, 1807-
Histoire de la sorcellerie au comté de Bourgogne. Vesoul, Typographie de L. Suchaux, 1861.
124 p. 22cm.

1. Witchcraft--Burgundy, France--Hist. I. Title.

WITCHCRAFT
BT
980
D53

Le Diable et ses métamorphoses; étude historique par le bibliophile C. P. Paris, Sandoz et Thuillier, 1882.
100 p. 19cm.

1. Devil. 2. Devil in literature. I. P., C., bibliophile. II. C. P., bibliophile.

8
NIC

Witchcraft
BF
1517
F5
A893
1737

Les diables de Loudun.
[Aubin, Nicolas] b. ca. 1655.
Histoire des diables de Loudun, ou De la possession des religieuses ursulines, et de la condamnation & du suplice d'Urbain Grandier, curé de la même ville. Cruels effets de la vengeance du Cardinal de Richelieu. Amsterdam, aux de'pens de la Compagnie, 1737.
378 p. front. 17cm.

"Published also under titles:
(Continued on next card)

Witchcraft
BF
1549
B16

Le Diable.
Baissac, Jules, 1827-1898.
Histoire de la diablerie chrétienne.
I. Le Diable; la personne du Diable, le personnel du Diable. Paris, M. Dreyfous [1882]
ix, 611 p. 24cm.
Title on spine: Le Diable.
The second vol. of the series, published in 1890 under title: Les grands jours de la sorcellerie, does not have the general title Histoire de la diablerie chrétienne.

Witchcraft
BF
1549
C69

Le diable peint par lui même.
Collin de Plancy, Jacques Albin Simon, 1794-1881.
Le diable peint par lui même, ou Galerie de petits romans, de contes bizarres, d'anecdotes prodigieuses, sur les aventures des démons ... et les services qu'ils ont pu rendre aux mortels. Extrait et traduit des démonomanes, des théologiens, des légendes, et des diverses chroniques du sombre empire. Paris, P. Mongie aîné, 1819.
xl, 258 p. front. 21cm.

Witchcraft
BF
1517
F5
A893
1737

Les diables de Loudun.
[Aubin, Nicolas] b. ca. 1655. Histoire des diables de Loudun ... 1737. (Card 2)
Histoire d' Urbain Grandier, condamné comme magicien ... Amsterdam, 1735, and Cruels effets de la vengeance du Cardinal de Richelieu; ou, Histoire des diables de Loudun ... Amsterdam, 1716."--L.C.

1. Demoniac possession. 2. Grandier, Urbain, 1590- 1634. 3. Loudun, France. Ursuline convent. I. Title: Les diables de Loudun.

WITCHCRAFT
BF
1511
V48

Le diable dans la vie des saints.
Verdun, Paul, 1861-
Le diable dans la vie des saints. Paris, Delhomme et Briguet [1897]
2 v. 18cm.

Contents.--T. 1. Du Xe au XIVe siècle. --T. 2. Du XVe au XIXe siècle.

1. Demonology. 2. Devil. 3. Exorcism. 4. Demoniac possession. 5. Saints--Biog. I. Title.

WITCHCRAFT
BF
1555
T61

Le diable qui n'y voit goutte.
Tissot, Claude-Joseph, 1801-1876.
Les possédées de Morzine, ou Le diable qui n'y voit goutte. Par M. J. Tissot. Paris, Didier, 1865.
32 p. 24cm.

"Extrait de la Revue moderne, du 1er mai 1865."

1. Demoniac possession. 2. Morzine, France--History. I. Title. II. Title: Le diable qui n'y voit goutte.

8
NIC

WITCHCRAFT
BF
1517
F5
L22

Diables de Loudun.
La Menardaye, Jean Baptiste de.
Examen et discussion critique de l'histoire des diables de Loudun, de la possession des religieuses Ursulines, et de la condamnation d'Urbain Grandier. Paris, Chez Debure l'aîné, 1747.
xxix, 521 p. 17cm.

1. Demoniac possession. 2. Grandier, Urbain, 1590-1634. 3. Loudun, France. Ursuline convent. I. Title: Histoire des diables de Loudun. II. Title: Diables de Loudun.

8
NIC

Witchcraft

Le diable en Champagne.
[Assier, Alexander] 1821-
Le diable en Champagne. Par l'auteur des Champenois à travers les siècles... Paris, Dumoulin, 1869.
59 p. illus. 19cm.

1. Demonology. I. Title.

Witchcraft
BF
1555
M72
1873

Le Diable révolutionnaire.
[Molinier, Jean Baptiste] 1835-
Le Diable révolutionnaire; ou, Histoire d'une possédée encore vivante. Traduite de l'espagnol, avec introd. et conclusion sur les oeuvres diaboliques en général et sur les oeuvres diaboliques modernes en particulier, suivie d'un résumé en forme d'épilogue, ou catéchisme de Satan sur les principaux devoirs et les principales vérités du christianisme ... Par le comte Reinilom de Sneruab [pseud.] Toulouse, L. Hébrail, Durand & Delpuech, 1873.
133 p. 17cm.

1. Demoniac possession. 2. Trasfi, Carmette. I. Title.

WITCHCRAFT
BF
1517
F5
P75

Les diables de Loudun.
Poitiers, Jean de.
Les diables de Loudun. Paris, Ghio, 1876.
271 p. 17cm.

1. Demoniac possession. 2. Grandier, Urbain, 1590-1634. 3. Loudun, France. Ursuline convent. I. Title.

8
NIC

Najean, Henry.
Le diable et les sorcières chez les Vosgiens.
Le Diable et les sorcières chez les Vosgiens. 88 Saint-Dié, impr. Loos, 11, rue de Robache, 1970.
187 p. plates. 22cm.
Bibliography: p. [183]-[184]

1. Witchcraft--Vosges Mountains. 2. Demonology. I. Title

MAR 21.'74   COOxc   73-309027

Witchcraft
BF
1549
B16

La diablerie chrétienne.
Baissac, Jules, 1827-1898.
Histoire de la diablerie chrétienne.
I. Le Diable; la personne du Diable, le personnel du Diable. Paris, M. Dreyfous [1882]
ix,611 p. 24cm.

The second vol. of the series, published in 1890 under title: Les grands jours de la sorcellerie, does not have the general title Histoire de la diablerie chrétienne.

1. Devil. I. Title: La diablerie chrétienne. II. Title.

BF
1535
G92

O diabo sem preconceitos.
Gueiros, José Alberto.
O diabo sem preconceitos / José Alberto Gueiros ; capa e ilustrações de Benicio. Rio de Janeiro : Editora Monterrey : distribuido por F. Chinaglia, 1974.
190 p. : ill. ; 21 cm.

1. Demonology. I. Title.

WITCHCRAFT

Le diable et les sorciers.
Surbled, Georges, 1855-
Le diable et les sorciers. Arras, Impr. Sueur-Charruey, 1898.
23 p. 25cm.

"Extrait de la Science Catholique, XIIe année, Août 1898."

1. Witchcraft--History. I. Title.

Witchcraft
BF
1517
F5
A892
1716

Les diables de Loudun.
[Aubin, Nicolas] b. ca. 1655.
Cruels effets de la vengeance du Cardinal de Richelieu, ou Histoire des diables de Loudun, de la possession des religieuses ursulines, et de la condamnation et du suplice [sic] d'Urbain Grandier, curé de la même ville. Amsterdam, E. Roger, 1716.
[10], 5-378 p. front. 17cm.

Published also under titles: Histoire des diables de Loudun, ou, De la possession des religieuses ursulines ... Amsterdam, 1694; and Histoire d'Urbain Grandier, condamné comme magicien ... Amsterdam, 1735.

WITCHCRAFT
BF
1555
L68
1963a

Diabolical possession, true and false.
Lhermitte, Jacques Jean, 1877-
Diabolical possession, true and false. [This translation was made by P. J. Hepburne-Scott.] London, Burns & Oates [1963]
127 p. 20cm. (Faith and fact books, 57)

Translation of Vrais et faux possédés.

CATALOGUE OF THE CORNELL WITCHCRAFT COLLECTION

Dialogi und Gespräch von der Lycanthropia, oder der Menschen in Wölff-Verwandlung.

Witchcraft
GR
830
W4
L36

Laube, Theophilus.
Dialogi und Gespräch von der Lycanthropia, oder der Menschen in Wölff-Verwandlung, darinnen vier gelehrte Personen, eine geistliche, eine rechts-gelehrte, eine arzney-verständige, und welt-weise von dieser Materi und andern merckwürdigen Sachen viel curieuses discuriren ... Auch durchgehends mit Kupffern aussgefertigt durch Theophilum Lauben. Franckfurt, Bey Arnold Heyl, 1686.
6 p. l., 175 p. 9 plates. 13cm.
(Continued on next card)

Dialogicall discourses of spirits and divels.

Witchcraft
BF
1565
D27
2 copies

Deacon, John, Preacher.
Dialogicall discourses of spirits and divels, declaring their proper essence, natures, dispositions and operations, and dispossessions: with other the appendantes ... By John Deacon [and] John Walker ... Londini, G. Bishop, 1601.
356 p. 20cm.

1. Witchcraft. I. Walker, John, Preacher, joint author. II. Title.

Dialogo intitolato La strega.

WITCHCRAFT
BF
1524
P59
1555

Pico della Mirandola, Giovanni Francesco, 1470-1533.
Dialogo intitolato La strega, overo De gli inganni de demoni dell' illustre Signor Giouan Francesco Pico conte de la Mirandola. Tradotto in lingva toscana per il Signor abate Turino Turini da Pescia ... In Pescia, 1555.
5 p. l., [17]-126 p., 1 l. 21½cm.
Title within ornamental border.
At end: Stampato in Pescia, appresso Lorenzo Torrentino, stampator ducale, MDLV.
Translation of Strix, sive De ludificatione daemonum dialogi tres.
With this is bound Cattani da Diacceto, F. Discorso ... sopra la superstizione dell' arte magica. Fiorenza, 1567. 11-9699

8 ————— Copy 2. (Continued on next card)

A dialogue concerning witches & witchcrafts.

WITCHCRAFT
BF
1565
G45
1842

Gifford, George, d. 1620.
A dialogue concerning witches & witchcrafts, by George Gifford. Reprinted from the edition of 1603. London, Printed for the Percy society [by T. Richards] 1842.
viii, v, [7]-119 p. 20cm.

With reproduction of the t.-p. of the London edition of 1603.
Edited by Thomas Wright.

1. Witchcraft. I. Wright, Thomas, 1810-1877, ed. II. Title.

Dialogve de la lycanthropie ...

WITCHCRAFT
GR
830
W4
P95

Prieur, Claude.
Dialogve de la lycanthropie, ov transformation d'hommes en lovps, vulgairement dits loups-garous, & si telle se peut faire; auquel en discourant est traicté de la maniere de se contregarder des enchantemens & sorcelleries, ensemble de plusieurs abus & superstitions, lesquelles se commettent en ce temps. Lovvain, I. Maes, 1596.
72 l. 15cm.

8
NIC

1. Werwolves. I. Title.

Dialogue des sorciers ou eriges.

Witchcraft
BF
1565
D17
1579

Daneau, Lambert, ca. 1530-1595?
Devx traitez novveavx, tres-vtiles povr ce temps. Le premier tovchant les sorciers, auquel ce qui se dispute auiourd'huy sur cete matiere, est bien amplement resolu & augmenté de devx proces extraicts des greffes pour l'esclaircissement & confirmation de cet argument. Le second contient vne breue Remonstrance sur les ieux de cartes & de dez. Reu. & augm. par l'auteur M. Lambert Daneau. [Geneve?] Par Jaqves Bavmet, 1579.
160 p. 15cm.

(Continued on next card)

Dialogue des sorciers ou eriges.

Witchcraft
BF
1565
D17
1579

Daneau, Lambert, ca. 1530-1595? Devx traitez novveavx, tres-vtiles povr ce temps. 1579.
(Card 2)

"Dialogve des sorciers ov eriges" is translation of most of his De veneficis, qvos olim sortilegos ... vocant.

A dialogue of witches.

FILM
470
reel
283

Daneau, Lambert, ca. 1530-1595.
A dialogue of witches in foretime named lottellers, and novv commonly called sorcerers ... Written in Latin by Lambertus Danaeus. And now translated into English. [London] Printed by R. W[atkins] 1575.
The translation is sometimes attributed to Thomas Twyne. cf. Short-title catalogue.
Translation of De veneficis, quos olim sortilegos ... vocant.
University microfilms no. 12047 (case 48, carton 283)
Short-title catalogue no. 6226.
(Continued on next card)

Witchcraft
BF
1410
B42
Z69
no.22

Dialogue ofte zamen-spraek, tusschen een theologant, advocaat, militair en koopman, over den tegenwoordigen staat van land en kerke. Beschreven door I.S. [n.p., 1693?]
15 p. 21cm.
Signatures: 4°: A-B⁴.
Not in Van der Linde.
No t.p.; half-title only.

1. Juris diction. 2. Bekker, Balthasar, 1634-1698. [De betoverde weereld.
NIC

Diaskepsis philosophica, De magicis actionibus.

Witchcraft
BF
1587
D61
no.1

Martini, Jacob, metaphysician, praeses.
ΔIAΣKEΨIS [i.e., diaskepsis] philosophica, De magicis actionibus earumque probationibus, ... praeside Jacobo Martini, ... respondente Henrico Nicolai. Ed. 2. [Wittebergae] Typis Christiani Tham, 1623.
[24] p. 21cm.
No. 1 in vol. lettered Dissertationes de magia. 1623-1723.
1. Magic—Addresses, essays, lectures. 2. Witchcraft—Addresses, essays, lectures. I. Nicolai, Heinrich, 1605-1665, respondent. I. Title: Diaskepsis philosophica, De magicis actionibus.

Diatriba theologico-critica daemonologiae.

Witchcraft
BF
1520
C27

Caristinio, Dominico.
... Exercitatio per saturam, sive Diatriba theologico-critica daemonologiae elementa complectens, cui accedunt Meditationes philosophicae theologico morales super eodem subjecto, auctore Bernardo Maria Marsicani ... Neapoli, Typis Dominici Pianese, 1788.
11 p. l., 207 p. 21cm.
Marsicani's work not included; but dedication includes letter by and to him.
1. Demonology. I. Marsicani, Bernardo Maria. II. Title. III. Title: Diatriba theologico-critica daemonologiae.

Diatribe antiquario-medica De daemoniacis Evangeliorum.

WITCHCRAFT
BS
2545
D5
T58

Timmermann, Theodor Gerhard, 1727-1792.
Theodor. Gerhard. Timmermann ... Diatribe antiqvario-medica De daemoniacis Evangeliorvm. Rintelii, Apvd Ant. Henr. Boesendahl, 1786.
90 p. 24cm.

1. Demoniac possession. 2. Bible. N. T.—Commentaries. I. Title: De daemoniacis Evangeliorum.

8
NIC

Diatribe physica De virunculis metallicis.

HIST SCI
BF
1445
P85

Posner, Caspar, praeses.
Diatribe physica De virunculis metallicis, quam...praeside...Casparo Posnero...publice ventilandam exhibet Michael Dachselt... Jenae, Literis Krebsianis, 1662.
[30] p. 20cm.
Diss.—Jena (M. Dachselt, respondent)

1. Apparitions. 2. Demonology. 3. Occult sciences. I. Dachselt, Michael, respondent. II. Title.

8
NIC

Il diavolo.

Witchcraft
BT
980
G73
1890

Graf, Arturo, 1848-1913.
Il diavolo. 3. ed. Milano, Fratelli Treves, 1890.
viii, 463 p. 20cm.

I. Title.

Il diavolo ad Issime.

BF
1517
I8
F22
1970

Fabretti, Ariodante, 1816-1894.
Il diavolo ad Issime. Il più sensazionale processo del Seicento. Torino, Piemonte in bancarella, 1970.
99 p. illus. 18cm.
At head of title: A. Fabretti and P. Vayra.
Includes bibliographical references.

1. Demonology. I. Vayra, Pietro, 1838- II. Title

NIC APR 25,   xc 72-33387

Il diavolo e le streghe.

Witchcraft
BF
1566
Z29

Zangolini, Asclepiade.
Il diavolo e le streghe, ossia il pregiudizio popolare delle malie ragionamento del dottore Asclepiade Zangolini ... coll' aggiunta di alcuni racconti piacevoli del medesimo. Livorno, G. B. Rossi, 1864.
272 p. 13cm. (Biblioteca enciclopedica popolare)
Contents.—Il diavolo e le streghe.—Racconti piacevoli.—Epigrammi editi ed inediti e novellette inedite del dottore
(Continued on next card)

Il diavolo e le streghe.

Witchcraft
BF
1566
Z29

Zangolini, Asclepiade. Il diavolo e le streghe ... 1864. (Card 2)

Filippo Pananti.
Racconti and Epigrammi each have special t. p.

1. Witchcraft. 2. Devil. I. His Racconti piacevoli. II. Pananti, Filippo, 1766-1837. III. Title.

Witchcraft
PQ
1947
A1D5
1730

Il diavolo storico, critico, politico, esposto sotto la figura del diavolo guercio, in lega col diavolo zoppo, contro 'l diavolo gobbo Trattonimento curioso e morale di venti e una sera; ricavato dal francese. Venezia, C. Zane, 1730.
216 p. 16cm.

1. Devil.

CATALOGUE OF THE CORNELL WITCHCRAFT COLLECTION

Witchcraft
BF
1565
B73
    Dicaeus, Lambertus, pseud.
      Cataplasma contra inflammationem cerebri.
  Borre, Nicolas de, ca. 1590-1670.
    Examen profani Exorcismi primi contra daemonem mendacii sub ementito Lamberti Dicaei theologi medici nomine in lucem nuper emissi, nec non inepti & ridiculi ipsius Cataplasmatis &c. In quo duae & triginta imposturae deteguntur, omnium oculis exponuntur, & solidè refutantur. Lovanij, Typis Georgii Lipsii, 1660.
    73 p. 19cm.
    Bound with his Apologia pro exorcistis. Lovanij, 1660.
8   (Continued on next card)

Witchcraft
BF
1565
B73
    Dicaeus, Lambertus, pseud.
      Exorcismus primus contra daemonem mendacii.
  Borre, Nicolas de, ca. 1590-1670.
    Examen profani Exorcismi primi contra daemonem mendacii sub ementito Lamberti Dicaei theologi medici nomine in lucem nuper emissi, nec non inepti & ridiculi ipsius Cataplasmatis &c. In quo duae & triginta imposturae deteguntur, omnium oculis exponuntur, & solidè refutantur. Lovanij, Typis Georgii Lipsii, 1660.
    73 p. 19cm.
    Bound with his Apologia pro exorcistis. Lovanij, 1660.
8   (Continued on next card)

Witchcraft
BF
1566
M68
    Dickie, John, joint author.
  Mitchell, John, 1786-1856.
    The philosophy of witchcraft. By J. Mitchell and Jn. Dickie. Paisley, Murray and Stewart [etc., etc.] 1839.
    viii, 424 p. illus. 17cm.

    1. Witchcraft. I. Dickie, John, joint author. II. Title.

    Dictionary of demonology.
  Collin de Plancy, Jacques Albin Simon, 1794-1881.
    Dictionary of demonology. Edited and translated by Wade Baskin. New York, Philosophical Library [1965]
    177 p. 22cm.

    Selections from Dictionnaire infernal.

    A dictionary of miracles.
  Brewer, Ebenezer Cobham, 1810-1897.
    A dictionary of miracles, imitative, realistic, and dogmatic ... by the Rev. E. Cobham Brewer ... Philadelphia, J. B. Lippincott company, 1884.
    xliv, 582 p. illus. 21cm.

    I. Title.

    Dictionnaire des sciences occultes.
  [Collin de Plancy, Jacques Albin Simon] 1794-1881.
    Dictionnaire des sciences occultes ... ou, Répertoire universel des êtres, des personnages, des livres, des faits et des choses qui tiennent aux apparitions, aux divinations, à la magie, au commerce de l'enfer, aux démons, aux sorciers, aux sciences occultes ... et généralement à toutes les fausses croyances, merveilleuses, surprenantes, mystérieuses ou surnaturelles; suivi du Traité historique des dieux et des démons du paganisme. par Binet;
    (Continued on next card)

Witchcraft
BF
1503
C69+
1848
    Dictionnaire des sciences occultes.
  [Collin de Plancy, Jacques Albin Simon] 1794-1881. Dictionnaire des sciences occultes ... 1848. (Card 2)

    et de la Réponse à l'Histoire des oracles de Fontenelle, par Baltus. Publié par m. l'abbé Migne ... Paris, Chez l'éditeur, 1848.
    2 v. 28cm. (Added t.-p.: Encyclopédie théologique, ou Série de dictionnaires sur chaque branche de la science religieuse ... pub. par m. l'abbé Migne ... t. 48-49)

    (Continued on next card)

Witchcraft
BF
1503
C69+
1848
    Dictionnaire des sciences occultes.
  [Collin de Plancy, Jacques Albin Simon] 1794-1881. Dictionnaire des sciences occultes ... 1848. (Card 3)

    Fifth edition of Collin de Plancy's "Dictionnaire infernal", first published in 1818. cf. G. Vicaire, Manuel de l'amateur de livres; and R. Yve-Plessis, Essai d'une bibliographie francaise ... de la sorcellerie et de la possession démoniaque, 1900, p. 4.
    In double columns, numbered.
    Added t. p. of v.1. dated: 1846.

    Dictionnaire du diable et de la démonologie.
BF
1503
T66
  Tondriau, Julien L
    Dictionnaire du diable et de la démonologie [par] J. Tondriau & R. Villeneuve. (Verviers, Gérard & Co., 1968).
    333 p. illus., facsims., ports. 18 cm. (Marabout université, v. 154) bfr 80.-
    Bibliography: p. [327]-330.
    (Be 68-3086)

    1. Demonology--Dictionaries--French. I. Villeneuve, Roland, 1922- joint author. II. Title.

BF1503.T6   133.4'2'03   78-365611
Library of Congress   69 [1]

Witchcraft
BF
1503
C69+
1863
    Dictionnaire infernal.
  Collin de Plancy, Jacques Albin Simon, 1794-1881.
    Dictionnaire infernal. Répertoire universel des etres, des personnages, des livres, des faits et des choses qui tiennent aux esprits, aux démons, aux sorciers ... et généralement a toutes les fausses croyances merveilleuses, surprenantes, mystérieuses et surnaturelles. 6. éd., augm. et illustrée ... par M. L. Breton. Paris, H. Plon, 1863.
    723 p. illus., ports. 27cm.

    1. Occult sciences--Dictionaries. 2. Magic--Dictionaries. I. Title.

MSS
Bd.
WITCHCRAFT
BF
F93
    Die auss Gottes Zulass... leiblichbesessene ... Susanna Raabin.
  Fronmüller, Johann Christoph.
    Die auss Gottes Zulass von dem abgesagten Gottes und Menschen-Feind, dem leidigen Teuffel eine geraume Zeit leiblich-besessene, und übel-geklagte, allein durch Gottes Gnade auf fleissiges Gebet vieler fromm Christen von der leiblichen Besitzung widerum befreydte ... Susanna Raabin. ...Theils auss den Actis, theils aber auss der Erfahrung selbsten zusamm getragen von Johann Christoff Fronmüller. 1696-[1703]
    [1] l., 116 p. 18cm.
    (Continued on next card)

MSS
Bd.
WITCHCRAFT
BF
F93
    Die auss Gottes Zulass... leiblichbesessene ... Susanna Raabin.
  Fronmüller, Johann Christoph. Die auss Gottes Zulass ... leiblich-besessene ... Susanna Raabin. 1696-[1703] (Card 2)

    Manuscript, on paper, in a German hand.
    Added leaf before t. p.: "Die Kÿrchendiener, welche auf Verordnung der hohen Obrigkeit die Susanna Raabin besuchten sind folgende ..."
    Line frame on each page.
    Bound in marbled boards.
    1. Raabin, Susanna, b. 1666. 2. Demoniac possession. I. Title: Die auss Gottes Zulass... leiblichbesessene ... Susanna Raabin.

Witchcraft
BF
1411
D55
  Diefenbach, Johann.
    Besessenheit, Zauberei und Hexenfabeln. Eine Studie, veranlasst durch die Teufelaustreibung zu Wemding. Frankfurt a.M. A. F. Nachfolger, 1893.
    56 p. 24cm.

    1. Demoniac possession. 2. Magic. I. Title.

Witchcraft
BF
1583
D55
  Diefenbach, Johann.
    Der Hexenwahn vor und nach der Glaubensspaltung in Deutschland. Mainz, F. Kirchheim, 1886.
    viii, 360 p. 23cm.

    1. Witchcraft--Germany. I. Title.

Witchcraft
BF
1583
D55
Z3
  Diefenbach, Johann.
    Der Zauberglaube des sechzehnten Jahrhunderts nach den Katechismen Dr. Martin Luthers und des P. Canisius. Mit Berücksichtigung der Schriften Pfarrers Längin-Karlsruhe und des Professors Riezler-München. Mainz, F. Kirchheim, 1900.
    xii, 209 p. 23cm.
    1. Witchcraft--Germany. 2. Theology, Doctrinal--16th century. 3. Canisius, Petrus, Saint, 1521-1597. Catechismus.
8   (Continued on next card)

Witchcraft
BF
1583
D55
Z3
  Diefenbach, Johann. Der Zauberglaube des sechzehnten Jahrhunderts ... 1900. (Card 2)

    4. Luther, Martin, 1483-1546. Catechismus. 5. Längin, Georg, 1827-1897. Religion und Hexenglaube. 6. Riezler, Sigmund, Ritter von, 1843-1927. Geschichte der Hexenprozesse in Bayern. I. Title.

WITCHCRAFT
PT
1792
D56
1901
  Diel, Johannes Baptista, 1843-1875.
    Friedrich Spe. Von Johannes Diel. 2., umgearb. Aufl. von Barnhard Duhr. Freiburg i. B., Herder, 1901.
    viii, 147 p. port., facsim. 20cm. (Sammlung historischer Bildnisse. [IX])
    First published 1872 under title: Friedrich von Spee.
    Very extensively revised.
    1. Spee, Friedrich von, 1591-1635. I. Duhr, Bernhard, 1852-1930. II. Title.
8 NIC

WITCHCRAFT
PT
1792
D56
  Diel, Johannes Baptista, 1843-1875.
    Friedrich von Spee. Eine biographische und literarhistorische Skizze. Von J. B. M. Diel. Freiburg i. Br., Herder, 1872.
    119 p. port. 19cm. (Sammlung historischer Bildnisse. IX)
    Includes as "Beilage" selections from Spee's Trutznachtigall, in German and Latin.
    1. Spee, Friedrich von, 1591-1635. I. Spee, Friedrich von, 1591-1635. Trutz-Nachtigall. Selections. German and Latin. II. Title.
8 NIC

CATALOGUE OF THE CORNELL WITCHCRAFT COLLECTION

Diepen, Marcus van.
De sleutel der geesten.

Witchcraft
BX
9479
B42
B11
no.17
Brief van L. P. aan Herman Bouman; eerst in 't bysonder aan hem geschreeven, en nu door hem, met verlof van den autheur, gemeen gemaakt: behelsende sommige redenen waarom hy de soo genaamde Sleutel der geesten enz. van M. van Diepen, en J. Hubener niet, ofte niet zoodanig alse daar ligt, behoorde te beantwoorden; en teffens een volstrekte omkeering van de gronden van dat woest geschrift. Amsterdam, By R. Blokland, boekverkoper, 1699.

8 (Continued on next card)

Diepen, Marcus van.
De sleutel der geesten.

Witchcraft
BX
9479
B42
B11
no.17
Brief van L. P. aan Herman Bouman ... 1699. (Card 2)
2 p. l., 12 p. title and end page vignettes, illus. initials. 20 x 15cm.
4°: π², A⁴, B².
Written by a supporter of Balthazar Bekker, whom Diepen and Hubener attacked.
No. 17 in vol. lettered B. Bekkers sterfbed en andere tractaten.
1. Diepen, Marcus van. De sleutel der geesten. 2. Bekker, Balthasar,
(Continued on next card)

Diest Lorgion, Everardus Janus, 1812-1876.
see
Lorgion, Everardus Jan Diest, 1812-1876.

Witchcraft
BF
1505
D56
Diestel, Ernst.
Der Teufel als Sinnbild des Bösen im Kirchenglauben, in den Hexenprozessen und als Bundesgenosse der Freimaurer. Berlin, A. Unger, 1921.
45 p. port. 22cm. (Comenius-Schriften zur Geistesgeschichte. Beihefte der Zeitschrift der Comenius-Gesellschaft "Geisteskultur und Volksbildung," 3. Heft)
1. Devil. I. Title.

Di Francesco, Matteuccia, fl. 1420.

DG
975
T65
R42
no.8
Mammoli, Domenico.
Processo alla strega Matteuccia di Francesco. 20 marzo 1428. Todi, 1969.
57 p. illus. 24cm. (Res Tudertinae. 8)
9

1. Di Francesco, Matteuccia, fl. 1420. I. Title.

Diiudicatio iudicii De non-existentia diaboli.

Witchcraft
BF
1520
B98
Buttner, Christophorus Andreas, praeses.
Diiudicatio iudicii De non-existentia diaboli quam ... praeside M. Christophoro Andrea Buttnero ... defendet Ernestus Wilhelm.Bergmann. Halae Magdeburgicae, Litteris Ioh. Friderici Grunerti [1734]
24 p. 24cm.
Diss.--Halle (E. W. Bergmann, respondent)
1. Devil. 2. Demonology. I. Bergmann, Ernest Wilhelm, respondent. II. Title: De non- existentia diaboli.
8

---

ar W
7956
Diller, Theodore, 1863-
Credulity as it concerns the medical man. Chicago, American Medical Association Press, 1930.
18 p. illus., facsims. 21cm.
"Reprinted from the Transactions of the American Neurological Association, 1929, pp. 489-497."
1.Credulity. 2.Witchcraft. I. Title.

Dillingen, Germany. Stadtgericht.

WITCHCRAFT
BF
1583
Z7
1587
Haussmännen, Walpurga, d. 1587, defendant.
Vrgicht vnd Verzaichnuss, so Walpurga Haussmännen zu Dillingen, inn ihrer peinlichen Marter bekandt hatt, was sy für Vbels vnd Jamers mit jhrer Hexerey, so sy biss in die 30. Jar getrüben, angericht vnd gestüfft hat, mit Hilff vnd Raht jhres Bülteüffels, so ihr darzu geholffen: welche Walburga Anno 1587. Jar, den 24. October, verbrandt vnd gericht ist worden, &c. [Dillingen?] 1588.
8 [20] p. 20cm. (Continued on next card)

WITCHCRAFT
BF
1520
R38
D58
Dintzer, Lucien.
Nicolas Remy et son oeuvre démonologique. Lyon, L'imprimerie de Lyon, 1936.
148 p. 25cm.
Thèse--Lyons.
At head of title: Université de Lyon, Faculté des lettres.
Bibliography: p. [135]-143.
1. Remi, Nicolas, 1530-1612. Daemonolatreiae libri tres. 2. Demonology. 3. Witchcraft. I. Title.
8
NIC

Rare
BX
1710
E97++
1578
Directorium inquisitorum.
Eymerich, Nicolás, 1320-1399.
Directorivm inqvisitorvm ... denvo ex collatione plvrivm exemplarium emendatum, et accessione multarum literarum Apostolicarum, officio Sanctae Inquisitionis deseruientium, locupletatum, cvm scholiis sev annotationibvs ... Francisci Pegnae Hispani, ... Accessit rerum & verborum ... index. Romae, In aedibvs Pop. Rom., 1578.
3 pts. in 1 v. 34cm.
Title vignette.
Colophon of pt. 3 dated: 1579.

Witchcraft
BF
1582
'59
Diricq, Édouard.
Maléfices et sortilèges: procès criminels de l'ancien évêché de Bâle pour faits de sorcellerie (1549-1670) Lausanne, Payot, 1910.
240 p. 18cm.

1. Witchcraft--Basel (Diocese)--History. I. Title.

Witchcraft
BF
1563
W81++
no.6
The Disclosing of a late counterfeyted possession by the Deuyl in two maydens within the citie of London. London, Printed by R. Watkins [1574. London, at the British Museum, 1923]
[44] p. 14cm.
Signatures: A-B⁸, C⁶.
Photocopy (negative) 44 p. on 23 l. 20 x 32cm.
No. 6 in vol. lettered: Witchcraft tracts, chapbooks and broadsides, 1579-1704; rotograph copies.
1. Demoniac possession.

Discorso del reverendo M. Francesco de Cattani da Diacceto ... sopra la superstizzione dell'arte magica.

WITCHCRAFT
BF
1524
P59
1555
Cattani da Diacceto, Francesco, bp. of Fiesole, d. 1595.
Discorso del reverendo M. Francesco de Cattani da Diacceto ... sopra la svperstizione dell'arte magica. Fiorenza, Appresso Valente Panizzi & Marco Feri C., 1567.
4 p. l., 36 numb. l. 23cm.
Bound with Pico della Mirandola, G. F. Dialogo intitolata La strega. Pescia, 1555.
1. Witchcraft. I. Title: La superstizzione de ll'arte magica.
8

Discorso dell' eccellentiss. filosofo M. Francesco de' Vieri ... Intorno a' dimonii.

WITCHCRAFT
BT
960
V66
Vieri, Francesco de, called Il Verino Secondo.
Discorso dell' eccellentiss. filosofo M. Francesco de' Vieri cognominato il Secondo Verino. Intorno a' dimonii, volgarmente chiamati spiriti... Fiorenza, Appresso Bartolomeo Sermartelli, 1576.
8 p. l., 108, [1] p. 17cm.
1. Spirits. 2. Demonology. 3. Witchcraft. I. Title: Intorno a' dimonii.
8

WITCHCRAFT
BF
1582
Z7
1623
Discovrs admirable d'vn magicien de la ville de Moulins, qui auoit vn demon dans vne phiole, condemné d'estre bruslé tout vif par arrest de la Cour de Parlement. Paris, Chez Antoine Vitray, 1623.
15 p. 16cm.
1. Witchcraft--Moulins, France. I. France. Parlement (Moulin) 2. Michel, d. 1623.
8

Witchcraft
BT
97
A2
D61
1876
Discours d'une histoire et miracle advenu en la ville de Montfort à cinq lieues près Rennes en Bretagne: avec une oraison à Nostre Dame de Lyesse. Rennes, 1588 [Lyon, Imprimerie L. Perrin, 1876]
13 p. 23cm.

1. Miracles--Early works to 1800.

Discovrs des sorciers.

Witchcraft
BF
1582
A2
B67
1608
Boguet, Henri, d. 1619.
Discovrs des sorciers, avec six advis advis en faict de sorcelerie. Et vne instrvction povr vn juge en semblable matiere ... 2. ed. Lyon, Chez Pierre Rigavd, 1608.
1 v. (various pagings) 18cm.
Six advis, en faict de sorcelerie, has special t. p.
1. Witchcraft--France. 2. Demonology, French. 3. Criminal law--France. 4. Criminal procedure--France. I. Title: Discours des sorciers.
8

Discours des spectres, ou visions.

WITCHCRAFT
BF
1445
L54
1608
Le Loyer, Pierre, sieur de La Brosse, 1550-1634.
Discovrs des spectres, ov visions et apparitions d'esprits, comme anges, demons, et ames, se monstrans visibles aux hommes, où sont rapportez les argvmens et raisons de cevx qui revocquent en doute ce qui se dit sur ce subiect ... Le tovt en hvict livres ... 2. ed. reveve et avgmentee. Paris, Chez Nicolas Bvon, 1608.
12 p. l., 979, [43] p. 24cm.
8 (Continued on next card)

CATALOGUE OF THE CORNELL WITCHCRAFT COLLECTION

Discours des spectres, ou visions.

WITCHCRAFT
BF
1445
L54
1604

Le Loyer, Pierre, sieur de La Brosse, 1550-1634. Discovrs des spectres ... 1608.
(Card 2)

Title in red and black.
First published 1586 under title: IIII. Livres des spectres ou apparitions.

1. Apparitions. 2. Demonology. I. His IIII. (Quatre) livres des spectres ou apparitions. II. Title: Discours des spectres, ou visions.

8

Witchcraft
BF
1522
D61

Discours dogmatiques et moraux sur les tentations du demon, où l'on fait voir par l'Ecriture & les Peres de l'Eglise quelle est la force, l'étendue & la durée du pouvoir des Esprits de tenebres: l'excez de leur fureur, & leurs differens artifices contre les hommes, & les moyens sûrs de s'en garantir. Rouen, François Vaultier, 1717.
2 v. in 1. 18cm.

-3/10/65
-3/18/65

WITCHCRAFT
BF
1445
L54
1605

Discours, et histoires des spectres.
Le Loyer, Pierre, sieur de La Brosse, 1550-1634.
Discovrs, et histoires des spectres, visions et apparitions des esprits, anges, demons, et ames, se monstrans visibles aux hommes. Divisez en hvict livres. Esqvels par les visions merveillevses, & prodigieuses apparitions avenuës en tous siecles, tirees & recueillies des plus celebres autheurs tant sacrez que prophanes, est manifestee la certitude des spectres & visions des esprits: &
(Continued on next card)

WITCHCRAFT
BF
1445
L54
1605

Discours, et histoires des spectres.
Le Loyer, Pierre, sieur de la Brosse, 1550-1634. Discovrs, et histoires des spectres ... (Card 2)

sont baillees les causes des diverses sortes d'apparitions d'iceux, leurs effects, leurs differences, & les moyens pour recognoistre les bons & les mauuais, & chasser les demons. Avssi est traicté des extases et rauissemens: de l'essence, nature, et origine des ames, et de leur estat apres le deceds de leurs corps:
(Continued on next card)

Witchcraft
BF
1445
L54
1605

Discours, et histoires des spectres.
Le Loyer, Pierre, sieur de La Brosse, 1550-1634. Discovrs, et histoires des spectres ... (Card 3)

plus des magiciens et sorciers, de leur communication auec les malins esprits: ensemble des remedes pour se preseruer des illusions et impostures diaboliques. Paris, Chez Nicolas Bvon, 1605.
[26], 976, [39] p. 23cm.

2d ed. of IIII. livres des spectres.
I. His IIII. (Quatre) livres des spectres. II. Title.

Discours execrable des sorciers.

Witchcraft
BF
1582
A2
B67
1606

Boguet, Henri, d. 1619.
Discovrs execrable des sorciers. Ensemble leur procez, faits depuis 2. ans en çà, en diuers endroicts de la France. Auec vne Instruction pour vn iuge, en faict de sorcelerie. Roven, Chez Iean Osmont, 1606.
6 p. l., 445, [6] p. 15cm.

First published 1602 under title: Discovrs des sorciers.
Ex libris Cabalisticis Kurt Seligmann.
(Continued on next card)

8

WITCHCRAFT
BF
1582
Z7
1610c

Discovrs prodigievx et espouuentable, de trois Espaignols & vne Espagnolle, magiciens & sorciers, qui se faisoient porter par les diables, de ville en ville, auec leurs declarations d'auoir fait mourir plusieurs personnes & bestail par leurs sorcilleges, & aussi d'auoir fait plusieurs degats aux biens de la terre. Ensemble l'arrest prononcé contre eux par la Cour de Parlement de Bourdeaux, le samedy 10. iour de mars, 1610. Paris [1623]
(Continued on next card)

8

WITCHCRAFT
BF
1582
Z7
1610c

Discovrs prodigievx et espouuantable, de trois Espaignols ... [1623] (Card 2)

16 p. 17cm.

"Iouxte la coppie imprimee à Bourdeaux."

1. Witchcraft--France. I. France. Parlement (Bordeaux)

8

Witchcraft
BF
1582
Z7
1610a

Discovrs prodigievx et espouvantable du thresorier & bāquier du diable & son fils, qui ont esté bruslés à Vesouz en la Frāche Comté, le 18. janvier 1610, après avoir confessé vne infinité des maleficies & sorceleries par eux cōmises. Ensemble le moyen comme ils furent descouvres. Avec la copie de l'arrest du parlement de Dole. Lyon, I. Doret, Prins sur la copie imprimée à Dole [1610] Paris, L. Willem, 1871]
15 p. 17cm.
Facsim. of copy in B. N.
Edition limited to 150 copies.

Witchcraft
BF
1582
Z7
1599

Discours sommaire des sortilges [sic], venefices & idolatreries [sic], tiré des procez criminels iugez au siège royal de Montmorillon en Poictou, la présente année, 1599. A M. l'official en l'euesché de Poictiers. [Montmorillon, France? 1599?]
51 p. 16cm.

Epistle dedicatory signed: F. A.

1. Trials(Witchcraft)--France. I. A., F.

MSS
Bd.
WITCHCRAFT
BF
D61

Discours sur la mort et condemnation de Charles de Franchillon, Baron de Chenevières, exécuté en la place de Grève, par arrest de la Cour de Parlement de Paris pour crime de sortilege et de magie, du jeudy 14. may 1626. Paris, chez P. Mettayer, 1626 [1901]
6 l. 19cm.

Carnap's manuscript copy.
"Originald ruck in der Bibliothèque Nationale zu Paris (Imprimés Ln 27.
(Continued on next card)

MSS
Bd.
WITCHCRAFT
BF
D61

Discours sur la mort et condemnation de Charles de Franchillon ... 1626 [1901] (Card 2)

4768.) Copie davon genomen durch Mr. Herviant - Paris im Mai 1901, wonach die vorliegende gemacht. (pet. in 4° de 16 pp.)"
Numerals in margin indicate pagination of the original.

1. Witchcraft--France. 2. Franchillon, Charles de, d. 1626.

Witchcraft
BF
1582
Z7
1609a

Discours véritable d'un sorcier nommé Gimel Truc, natif de Léon en Bretaigne, surprins en ses charmes et sorcelleries au pays de Vivarois. Ensemble les receptes pour guarir le bestail que par sa subtil poison avait mis sur les champs. En l'année 1609. Paris, jouxte la coppie imprimée à Lyon, par H. Bottet, 1609 [1875]
13 p. 23cm.

1. Witchcraft--Léon, France. 2. Truc, Gimel, d. 1609

Witchcraft
BF
1582
Z7
1606a

Discours véritable de l'execution faicte de cinquante tant sorciers que sorcières exécutez en la ville de Douay. Paris, J. Pillou, jouxte la copie imprimée à Mons-en-Hainault, 1606 [Lyon, Perrin, 1876]
6 p. 23cm.

1. Witchcraft--Douay, France.

Witchcraft
BF
1583
A2
B89
1727

Discours von betrüglichen Kennzeichen der Zauberey ...
Brunnemann, Jacob, d. 1735.
Discours von betrüglichen Kennzeichen der Zauberey, worinnen viel abergläubische Meinungen freymüthig untersuchet und verworffen, wie auch Carpzovii, Berlichii, Crusii ... missliche und leichtgläubige Lehr-Sätze von der Zauberey erwogen, zugleich J. J. Weidnerii Gegensätze wider diesen Discours kurtz und bescheidentlich beantwortet werden ... Halle, J. E. Fritsch, 1727.
[32], 228, [16] p. 22cm.
(Continued on next card)

Witchcraft
BF
1583
A2
B89
1727

Discours von betrüglichen Kennzeichen der Zauberey ...
Brunnemann, Jacob, d. 1735. Discours von betrüglichen Kennzeichen der Zauberey ... 1727. (Card 2)

With this is bound Weidner, J. J. Christbescheidentliche Gegen-Erinnerungen. Rostock, 1730.

1. Witchcraft. 2. Trials (Witchcraft)--Germany. I. Weidner, Johann Joachim, 1672-1732.

WITCHCRAFT
BT
125
P68

A discourse concerning the trial of spirits.
Pittis, Thomas, 1636-1687.
A discourse concerning the trial of spirits. Wherein inquiry is made into mens pretences to inspiration for publishing doctrines, in the name of God, beyond the rules of the Sacred Scriptures. In opposition to some principles and practices of papists and fanaticks; as they contradict the doctrines of the Church of England, defined in her Articles of religion, established by her ecclesiastical canons, and confirmed by acts of Parliament. By Thomas Pittis ... London, E. Vize, 1683.
4 p. l., 359 p. 18½cm.
Wing P2313.
1. Inspiration. 2. Church of England--Doctrinal and controversial works. I. Title. II. Title: Trial of spirits.
Library of Congress   BT125.P6
8   40-24455
[2]   231.74

Witchcraft
BT
965
S25

A discourse of angels.
[Saunders, Richard] d. 1692.
Ἀγγελογραφία sive Πνεύματα λειτουργικά, Πνευματολογία: or, A discourse of angels: their nature and office, or ministry ... Also something touching devils and apparitions and impulses. With ... doctrine of angels ... London, Printed for T. Parkhurst, 1701.
314, [2] p. 21cm.
Preface signed: Geo. Hamond.
Publisher's advertisement: p. [315-316]

Title transliterated: Angelographia sive Pneumata leiturgika ...

173

CATALOGUE OF THE CORNELL WITCHCRAFT COLLECTION

Witchcraft
BF
1565
P45++
1631
   A discourse of the damned art of witchcraft.
   Perkins, William, 1558-1602.
     A discovrse of the damned art of witchcraft. So farre forth as it is revealed in the scriptvres, and manifested by true experience. Framed and delivered by Master William Perkins, in his ordinary course of preaching, and published by Thomas Pickering. London, Printed for Iames Boler, 1631.
     [10], 607-652 p. 33cm.
     Signatures: A111-Oooo⁶.
     Imperfect: last leaf mutilated.
     From the author's Works? Cf. signatures and pagination. (Continued on next card)

Witchcraft
BF
1565
P45++
1631
   A discourse of the damned art of witchcraft
   Perkins, William, 1558-1602. A discovrse of the damned art of witchcraft ... 1631. (Card 2)
     With this is bound the author's A resolvtion to the countrey-man ... 1631.

     1. Witchcraft. I. Pickering, Thomas. II. Title.

WITCHCRAFT
BF
1565
G45
D5

8
NIC
   A discourse of the subtill practises of deuilles by vvitches and sorcerers.
   Gifford, George, d. 1620.
     A discourse of the subtill practises of deuilles by vvitches and sorcerers. By which men are and haue been greatly deluded: the antiquitie of them: their diuers sorts and names. With an answer vnto diuers friuolous reasons which some doe make to prooue that the deuils did not make those aperations in any bodily shape. By G. Gyfford. London, Imprinted for Toby Cooke, 1587.
     [66] p. 18cm.
     Title page in ornamental border.
     (Continued on next card)

WITCHCRAFT
BF
1565
G45
D5

8
NIC
   A discourse of the subtill practises of deuilles by vvitches and sorcerers.
   Gifford, George, d. 1620. A discourse of the subtill practises of deuilles ... 1587. (Card 2)
     Printed at the press of George Robinson, d. 1586 or 1587, whose widow soon afterward married Thomas Orwin.

     1. Witchcraft. 2. Devil. I. Title.

WITCHCRAFT
BF
1531
C28
H46

8
   A discourse, on the supposed existence of an evil spirit, called the devil.
   Heineken, Nicholas Samuel.
     A discourse, on the supposed existence of an evil spirit, called the devil; and also, a reply to the observations of Mr. William Carlisle, ... the ostensible author of an "Essay on evil spirits," written in opposition to the discourse which was delivered in the Unitarian Chapel, Bradford. By the Rev. N. T. [i.e., N. S.] Heineken. London, R. Hunter [1825?]
     iv, 139 p. 23cm.
     1. Carli... sle, William. An essay on evil spir... its. 2. Demonology.

Witchcraft
BF
1565
D61
   A discourse on witchcraft. Occasioned by a bill now depending in Parliament, to repeal the statute made in the first year of the reign of King James I, intituled, An act against conjuration, witchcraft, and dealing with evil and wicked spirits... London, Printed for J. Read, 1736.
     47 p. 21cm.

     1. Witch... craft.

Witchcraft
BF
1565
S42+
1965
   The discoverie of witchcraft.
   Scot, Reginald, 1538?-1599.
     The discoverie of witchcraft. Introduced by Hugh Ross Williamson. Carbondale, Southern Illinois University Press [1965, ᶜ1964]
     400 p. illus. 26 cm. (Centaur classics)

     1. Witchcraft. 2. Magic. 3. Demonology. I. Title. II. Ross Williamson, Hugh, 1901-
     BF1565.S4 1965   133.4   64-18551

Witchcraft
BF
1581
H32D6
   A discovery of the fraudulent practises of John Darrell.
   [Harsnett, Samuel] archbishop of York, 1561-1631.
     [A discovery of the fraudulent practises of John Darrell, bacheler of artes, in his proceedings concerning the pretended possession and dispossession of William Somers at Nottingham; of Thomas Darling, the boy of Burton at Caldwell; and of Katherine Wright at Mansfield, and Whittington; and of his dealings with one Mary Couper at Nottingham, detecting in some sort the deceitful trade in these latter day... es of casting out deuils.
     (Continued on next card)

Witchcraft
BF
1581
H32D6
   A discovery of the fraudulent practises of John Darrell.
   [Harsnett, Samuel] archbishop of York, 1561-1631. [A discovery of the fraudulent practises of John Darrell ... [1599] (Card 2)
     London, 1599]
     [328] p. 18cm.
     Epistle to the reader signed: S. H.
     Imperfect: t.-p. mounted, part of it missing; title taken from Halkett & Laing; pages cropped; numbers missing from 324-[328].
     1. Darrell, John, fl. 1562-1602. I. Title. II. S. H. III. H., S.

Witchcraft
BF
1565
B85
   A discovery of the impostures of witches and astrologers.
   Brinley, John.
     A discovery of the impostures of witches and astrologers... London, Printed for J. Wright, and sold by E. Milward, 1680.
     127 p. 15cm.
     Part 2 has special t. p.: "The second part, being a discourse of the impostures practised in judicial astrology. London, Printed in the year 1680."

     1. Witchcraft. 2. Astrology. I. Title.

Witchcraft
BF
1565
S42+
1930
   The discovery of witchcraft.
   Scot, Reginald, 1538?-1599.
     The discoverie of witchcraft, by Reginald Scot; with an introduction by the Rev. Montague Summers. [London] J. Rodker, 1930.
     xxxvii, 282, [1] p. illus. 30cm.
     "This edition ... is limited to 1275 copies ... This copy is no. 462."
     "The spelling ... is that of the edition of 1584."
     "A bibliographical note upon Scot's 'Discouerie'": p. xxxiii-xxxvii.

Witchcraft
BF
1581
S95
   The discovery of witches: a study of Master Matthew Hopkins commonly call'd witch finder generall.
   Summers, Montague, 1880-1948.
     The discovery of witches: a study of Master Matthew Hopkins commonly call'd witch finder generall, together with a reprint of The discovery of witches, from the rare original of 1647. London, Cayme Press, 1928.
     61 p. illus. 22cm. (Cayme Press pamphlet, no. 7)

     With facsimile of t.p. of original ed.

Witchcraft
BF
1563
T75

8
   The discovery of witches: in answer to severall queries, lately delivered to the judges of assize for the county of Norfolk.
   Hopkins, Matthew, d. 1647.
     The discovery of witches: in answer to severall queries, lately delivered to the judges of assize for the county of Norfolk. And now published by Mathew Hopkins, witchfinder, for the benefit of the whole kingdome ... Reprinted verbatim from the original edition of 1647. Only 100 copies printed. Great Totham, Essex, Printed at C. Clark's private press, 1837.
     11 numbered leaves. port. 23cm.
     No. 1 in vo... 1. lettered Tracts on witches.

Witchcraft
BF
1583
A2
B89
   Discurs von trüglichen Kennzeichen der Zauberey.
   [Brunneman, Jacob] d. 1735.
     Aloysii Charitini [pseud.] Discurs von trüglichen Kennzeichen der Zauberey, worinnen viel abergläubische Meinungen vernunfftmässig untersucht und verworffen, wie auch Carpzovii, Berlichii, Crusii, und anderer so woll päbstischer, als protestantischer Jure Consultorum. Missliche und leichtgläubige Lehr-Sätze von der Zauberey erwogen und beleuchtet worden ... Stargard, E. und J. M. Jenisch [1708]
     94 p. 19 cm.

     1. Witchcraft. I. Title.

WITCHCRAFT
K
B378
1717

8
NIC
   Discursus juridicus de crimine maleficii.
   Bechmann, Johann Volkmar, 1624-1689, praeses.
     Discursus juridicus de crimine maleficii, vulgo Von Zauberey, sub praesidio Joh. Volk. Bechmanns, submittit Joach. Ernst. Kober. Nunc recusa. Jenae, 1717.
     30 p. 20cm.
     Originally published as dissertation, Jena, 1678 (Joachim Ernst Kober, respondent)

     1. Witchcraft. I. Kober, Joachim Ernst, respondent. II. Title. III. Title: Von Zauberey.

WITCHCRAFT
BF
1559
P76

8
NIC
   Dispersio daemonvm.
   Polidoro, Valerio.
     [Practica exorcistarum ... ad daemones et maleficia de Christifidelibus ejiciendum. Patavii, Apud Paulum Meietum, 1587.
     2 v. in 1. 15cm.
     Title page for vol. 1 lacking; title obtained from British Museum. Dept. of Printed Books. General catalogue of printed books. London, 1963. Running title: Expvlsio daemonvm.
     Title for vol. 2: Dispersio daemonvm qvae (Cont'd on next card)

WITCHCRAFT
BF
1559
P76
   Dispersio daemonvm.
   Polidoro, Valerio. [Practica exorcistarum ...1587] (Card 2)
     secvnda pars est practice exorcistarum. Additional exorcisms in ms. (16 p.) inserted.

     1. Exorcism. I. Title. II. Title: Expvlsio daemonvm. III. Dispersio daemonvm.

Witchcraft
BF
1565
W38+
   The displaying of supposed witchcraft.
   Webster, John, 1610-1682.
     The displaying of supposed witchcraft. Wherein is affirmed that there are many sorts deceivers and impostors, and divers persons under a passive delusion of melancholy and far... But that there is a corporeal league made betw... the devil and the witch, or that he sucks on t... witches body ... or the like, is utterly denie... and disproved. Wherein also is handled, the existence of angels and spirits, the truth of apparitions ... the force of charms, and philters; with other abstruse matters. By John Webster ... London, Printed by J.M., 167...
     (Continued on next card)

CATALOGUE OF THE CORNELL WITCHCRAFT COLLECTION

tchcraft
65
8+
    The displaying of supposed witchcraft.
        Webster, John, 1610-1682. The displaying of supposed witchcraft. 1677.   (Card 2)

        7 p. l., 346, [4] p. 30cm.

        1. Witchcraft. I. Title.

MSS
Bd.
WITCHCRAFT
BT
M24
    Disputatio De daemonum distinctione.
        Maldonado, Juan, 1534-1583. Eruditissimi domini Joannis Maldonati...Disputatio De daemonum distinctione...1572.   (Card 3)

      nummo pantheo Hadriani imperatoris. Lugduni, 1690. Patin, Charles. Commentarius Caroli Patini in tres inscriptiones Graecas. Patavii, 1685. Rigord, Jean Pierre. Dissertation historique sur une medaille d'Herodes Antipas. Paris, 1689.
        1. Demonology. 2. Devil. I. His Traicté des anges et demons. II. Title: Disputatio De daemonum distinctione. III. Title: De daemonum distinctione.

    Disputatio inauguralis De spectris.
Witchcraft
BF
1445
D61
no.11
        Schlosser, Philipp Casimir, praeses.
      Disputatio inauguralis philosophica De spectris. Quam ... praeside ... M. Philippo Casimiro Schlossero ... pro lauru magisteriali ritè & legitimè impetranda, publicè defendendam conscripsit, ac omnibus sobriè & candidè philosophantibus subjicit A. & R. Johannes Philippus Hechler ... Gissae Hassorvm, Typis Christoph. Hermanni Kargeri [1693]
        46 p. 21cm.

8   (Continued on next card)

---

itchcraft
X
479
42
11
o.16
    Disputatie over den duyvel, of dezelve is een geschaapen geest ...
      Kuyk, J   van.
      Disputatie over den duyvel, of dezelve is een geschaapen geest, buyten de zielen der menschen, dewelke afgevallen en boos geworden is, ofte niet? Voorgevallen tusschen J. van Kuyk, krankbesoeker, ter eenre, en H. Bouman, ter andere zyde ... op den 26 December, 1694. Door een liefhebber der waarheyt, soo daar tegenwoordig was, opgesteld. Hier is noch by gevoegt een brief, aan geseyde J. van Kuyk ... den 27 January, 1693.

      (Continued on next card)

WITCHCRAFT
BF
1565
J19
    Disputatio de lamiis, seu strigibus.
      Jacquier, Nicolas.
      Flagellvm haereticorvm fascinariorvm, avtore Nicolao Iaqverio. His accesservnt Lamberti Danaei de veneficis dialogi, Ioachimi Camerarii in Plutarchi de oraculorum defectu epistola, Martini de Arles de superstitionibus tractatvs, Ioannis Trithemii de reprobis atq; maleficis qvaestiones III, Thomae Erasti de strigibus liber. Studio Ioan. Myntzenbergii edita. Francofvrti ad Moenvm [Impressvm apud N. Bassaeum, 1581.
8   604 p. 17   cm.
NIC   (Continued on next card)

    Disputatio inauguralis De spectris.
Witchcraft
BF
1445
D61
no.11
        Schlosser, Philipp Casimis, praeses. Disputatio inauguralis philosophica De spectris ... [1693]   (Card 2)

      Diss.---Giessen (J. P. Hechler, respondent)
      No. 11 in vol. lettered Dissertationes de spectris. 1646-1753.
      1. Apparitions. 2. Demonology. I. Hechler, Johann Philipp, respondent. II. Title: De spectris.

8

---

itchcraft
X
479
42
11
o.16
    Disputatie over den duyvel, of dezelve is een geschaapen geest ...
      Kuyk, J   van. Disputatie over den duyvel ... 1695.   (Card 2)

      aldaar besteld; met redenen, waarom deselve nu eerst door den druk gemeen gemaakt wort. Amsterdam, By E. Webber, boekverkooper, 1695.
      16 p. title and end page vignettes. 20 x 15cm.
      4°: A-B⁴.
      Black letter (except introduction)
      Letter and   Na-reeden, p. 10-16,

      (Continued on next card)

Witchcraft
BF
1587
D61
no.11
    Disputatio de magia licita et illicita.
      Büttner, Daniel, 1642-1696, praeses.
      Magiologia seu Disputatio de magia licita et illicita qvam ... praeside Dn. Daniele Büttnero ... disquisitioni submittit Albertus zum Felde ... Hamburgi, Literis Conradi Neumanni [1693]
      26, [6] p. 18cm. (bound in 21cm. vol.)
      No. 11 in vol. lettered Dissertationes de magia. 1623-1723.
      1. Magic--Addresses, essays, lectures. I. Felde, Albert zum, 1672-1720, respondent. II. Title. III. Title: De magia licita et illicita.

8

    Disputatio inauguralis iuridica De coniugibus incantatis eorumque separatione.
Witchcraft
HQ
822
H33
1731
      Hartmann, Johann Zacharias, praeses.
      Dispvtatio inavgvralis ivridica De conivgibvs incantatis eorvmqve separatione, Germanice: Von bezauberten Ehe-Leuten und derselben Scheidung, qvam ... svb praesidio ... Io. Zachariae Hartmanni ... pvblico ervditorvm examini svbiicit avctor Ioannes Helvigivs Zielinski ... Ienae, Recvsa per I. B. Hellervm, 1731.
      38, [2] p. 21cm.
      Diss.---Jena   (J. H. Zielinski, respondent, 1727)
8   (Continued on next card)

Witchcraft
BX
9479
B11
no.16
    Disputatie over den duyvel, of dezelve is een geschaapen geest ...
      Kuyk, J   van. Disputatie over den duyvel ... 1695.   (Card 3)

      signed: Z. W. [i. e., Zacharias Webbers]
      Van der Linde 79.
      No. 16 in vol. lettered B. Bekkers sterfbed en andere tractaten.
      1. Devil. I. Bouman, Herman. II. Webbers, Zacharias. III. Een liefhebber der waarheyt. IV. Title.

Witchcraft
BF
1565
T56
    Disputatio de quaestione quae fuerit artium magicarum origo.
      Tiedemann, Dietrich, 1748-1803.
      ... Dispvtatio de qvaestione qvae fverit artivm magicarvm origo, qvomodo illae ab Asiae popvlis ad Graecos, atqve Romanos, et ab his ad ceteras gentes sint propagatae, qvibvsqve rationibvs addvcti fverint ii qvi ad nostra vsqve tempora easdem vel defenderent, vel oppvgnarent? ... Marbvrgi, In nova officina libraria academica, 1787.
      158 p. 25cm.
      With this is   bound Ad Adonai, 3 leaves
8   in MSS, in La   tin in a German hand.
      (Continued on next card)

    Disputatio inauguralis juridica De tortura ex foris Christianorum proscribenda.
RARE
HV
8593
T46
      Thomasius, Christian, 1655-1728, praeses.
      Disputatio inauguralis juridica De tortura ex foris Christianorum proscribenda, quam...praeside Dn. Christiano Thomasio... discussioni submittit Martinus Bernhardi. Halae Magdeburgicae, Typis Christoph. Andreae Zeitleri [1705]
      38 p. 19cm.

8   Diss.---Halle (M. Bernhardi, respondent)
NIC   With this is bound the edition of 1759 of the diss.   with title as: Tractatio juridica   De tortura ex foris Christianor   vm proscribenda.
      (Continued on next card)

MSS
d.
ITCHCRAFT
T
24
    Disputatio De daemonum distinctione.
      Maldonado, Juan, 1534-1583.
      Eruditissimi domini Joannis Maldonati... Disputatio De daemonum distinctione et de praestigiis hoc est de potestate, actione et fallacia eorundem.   Paris, 1572.
      [30] l. 23cm.

      Manuscript, on paper.
      The second part of a treatise which was never printed in the original Latin. A French translation of the entire work was published in   1605, 1616, 1617, 1619
3   with title: Traicté des anges et
NIC   (Continued on next card)

Witchcraft
BF
1445
D61
no.9
    Disputatio de spectris.
      Donati, Christian, praeses.
      Disputatio de spectris, quam sub praesidio Dn. Christiani Donati ... publicae ventilationi sistit Johann. Gottlieb Frimel ... Wittenbergae, Typis Christiani Schrödteri [1688]
      [34] p. 18cm. (bound in 21cm. vol.)
      No. 9 in vol. lettered Dissertationes de spectris. 1646-1753.
      1. Spirits. I. Frimel, Johann Gottlieb, respondent. II. Title: De spectris.

8

WITCHCRAFT
BF
1572
M4
S32
    Disputatio inauguralis medica De morbis magicis.
      Schelhammer, Günther Christoph, 1649-1716, praeses.
      Disputatio inauguralis medica De morbis magicis quam ... sub praesidio ... Guntheri Christophori Schelhammeri ... submittit Christoph. Martinus Burchardus ... Kiloni, Literis B. Reutheri [1704]
      40, [1] p. 20cm.

      1. Witchcraft. 2. Diseases--Causes and theories of causation. I. Burchard, Christoph Ma   rtin, 1680-1742, respondent. II. T   Title: De morbis magicis.

8

MSS
d.
ITCHCRAFT
T
24
    Disputatio De daemonum distinctione.
      Maldonado, Juan, 1534-1583. Eruditissimi domini Joannis Maldonati...Disputatio De daemonum distinctione...1572. (Card 2)

    demons.
      Signed: Sebastianus Hamelius.
      Notes inside front cover of vol. discuss history and provenance of the manuscript. Originally the vol. was in the Lamoignon library, then passed to library of Prof. E. Dowden.
      With this   ms. are bound three printed works:
      Nicaise, Claude. De
      (Continued on next card)

Witchcraft
BF
1565
B66
    Disputatio inauguralis De fallacibus indiciis magiae.
      Bode, Heinrich von, 1652-1720, praeses.
      Disputatio inauguralis De fallacibus indiciis magiae, qvam ... praeside Dn. Henrico Bodino ... die 22. Octobris A. C. 1701 ... submittit Felix Martinus Brühm. Halae Magdeburgicae, Literis C. Henckelii, typogr. [1701]
      50 p. 20cm.
      Diss.---Halle (F. M. Brühm, respondent)
      Supports Balthasar Bekker.

8   (Continued on next card)

WITCHCRAFT
R
133
H71
    Disputatio inauguralis medico-philosophica De potentia diaboli in corpora.
      Hoffmann, Friedrich, 1660-1742, praeses.
      Disputatio inauguralis medico-philosophica De potentia diaboli in corpora, quam ... praeside DN. Friderico Hoffmanno ... publico ... examini submittit Godofredus Büching. Halae, Typis Ioannis Gruneri [1703]
      [39] p. 21cm.

8   Diss.---Halle (G. Büching, respondent)
NIC

CATALOGUE OF THE CORNELL WITCHCRAFT COLLECTION

Witchcraft
BF
1445
S92
1738

Disputatio iuridica inauguralis, De iure spectrorum.
   Stryk, Joannes Samuel, 1668-1715, praeses.
     Dispvtatio ivridica inavgvralis, De ivre spectrorvm qvam ... praeside Dn. Io. Samvele Strykio ... svbmittit Andreas Becker. Halae Magdebvrgicae, Literis Ioh. Christ. Grvnerti, 1738.
     43, [1] p. 21cm.
     Diss.--Halle (A. Becker, respondent)
     German terms in black letter.
     1. Ghosts. 2. Devil. 3. Witchcraft--Germany. I. Becker, Andreas, 1634-1698, respondent. II. Title: De iure spectrorum.

8

Witchcraft
BF
1565
D62
no.16

Disputatio juridica De indiciis cui annectitur quaestio de proba per aquam frigidam sagarum.
   Struve, Georg Adam, 1619-1692, praeses.
     Disputatio juridica De indiciis cui annectitur quaestio de proba per aquam frigidam sagarum. Von der Wasser-Prob der Hexen ... svb praesidio Dn. Georgii Adami Struven ... publicè proposita à Joh. Christoph. Nehringio ... Jenae, Typis Pauli Ehrichii, 1714.
     52 p. 20cm.
     No. 16 in vol. lettered Dissertationes de sagis. 1636-1714.
     (Continued on next card)

8

Witchcraft
BF
1565
S92
1683

Disputatio juridica De indiciis et proba per aquam frigidam sagarum.
   Struve, Georg Adam, 1619-1692, praeses.
     Disputatio juridica De indiciis & proba per aquam frigidam sagarum. Wasser-Prob der Hexen. Sub praesidio Dn. Georgii Adami Struven ... publicè proposita à Johanne Christoph Nehringio ... [Jenae?] Literis Müllerianis, 1683.
     [54] p. 20cm.
     First published 1666 with title: Disputatio juridica De indiciis cui annectitur quaestio de proba per aquam frigidam sagarum.

8

Witchcraft
BF
1565
F13

Dispvtatio jvridica, De maleficis et sagis.
   Fachinei, Andrea, d. ca. 1607, praeses.
     Dispvtatio jvridica, De maleficis et sagis, vt vocant, in theses aliqvot coniecta: qvas ... svb praesidio ... Andreae Fachinei ... tvebitvr Ioannes Christophorvs Ficlervs ... Ingolstadii, Ex officina typographica Wolfgangi Ederi, 1592.
     4 p. l., 36 p.
     On inside cover, long note by G. L. Burr on J. Christoph and J. Baptist Fickler.
     1. Witchcraft. I. Fickler, Johann Christoph, respondent. II. Title: De maleficis et sagis.

8

RARE
HV
8593
D61
no.16

Disputatio juridica De quaestionibus et torturis.
   Martini, Werner Theodor, praeses.
     Disputatio juridica De quaestionibus et torturis, quam ... sub praesidio ... Werneri Theodori Martini .. publico examini subjicit autor Johannes Valerianus Fischer ... [Wittebergae] Typis Matthaei Henckelii, 1668.
     [28] p. 21cm.
     Diss.--Wittenberg (J. V. Fischer, respondent)
     No. 16 in a vol. lettered: Dissertationes de trotura, 1667-1787.
     1. Torture. I. Fischer, Johann Valerian, respondent. II. Title.

8
NIC

Witchcraft
BF
1587
D61
no.13

Disputatio juridica ordinaria De probatione criminis magiae.
   Schack, Johann, praeses.
     Disputatio juridica ordinaria De probatione criminis magiae, qvam sub praesidio D. Johannis Schackii ... publicè defendet Martinus von Normann ... Gryphiswaldiae, Typis Danielis Benjaminis Starckii [1706?]
     26 p. 18cm. (bound in 21cm. vol.)
     Pages 1-8 are bound between p. 72 & 73 of no. 12; rest of text follows no. 12.
     No. 13 in vol. lettered Dissertationes de magia. 1623-1723.
     1. Witchcraft--Addresses, essays, lectures. 2. Trials (Witchcraft)
I. Normann, Martin, respondent. II. Title: De probatione criminis magiae.

8

Witchcraft
BF
1565
T461
1729

Disputatio juris canonici De origine ac progressu processus inquisitorii contra sagas.
   Thomasius, Christian, 1655-1728, praeses.
     Disputatio juris canonici De origine ac progressu processus inquisitorii contra sagas, quam ... praeside Dn. Christiano Thomasio ... subiicit die XXX. Aprilis A. M DCC XII ... Johannes Paulus Ipsen ... Halae Magdeburgicae, Apud J. C. Hendelium, 1729.
     68 [i.e. 76] p. 23cm.
     Pages 73-76 numbered 65-68.
     Diss.--Halle (J. P. Ipsen, respondent)
     (Continued on next card)

8

WITCHCRAFT
BF
1556
P47

Disputatio medica De ephialte seu incubo.
   Petermann, Andreas, 1649-1703, praeses.
     Disputatio medica De ephialte seu incubo, quam ... sub praesidio ... Andr. Petermanni ... publico ... examini subjicit Johannes Müller ... Lipsiae, Typis Christophori Fleischeri [1688]
     [40] p. 20cm.
     Diss.--Leipzig (J. Müller, respondent)
     1. Medicine, Magic, mystic and spagiric. 2. Demonology. 3. Diseases--Causes and theories of causation. I. Müller, Johannes, of Stargard, respondent.

8
NIC

WITCHCRAFT
BF
1559
S85

Disputatio philosophica. Examinans quaestionem, Utrum sonus campanarum ingruentem tonitruum ... tempestatem ... abigere queat.
   Spinaeus, Godofredus, praeses.
     Disputatio philosophica. Examinans quaestionem, Utrvm sonvs campanarvm ingruentem tonitruum ac fulminum tempestatem, pruinas item, nec non spectra ac diabolum, depellere & abigere queat? Quam ... praeside ... D. Godofredo Spinaeo ... Exercitationis ergo, publico subjicit examini, Joh. Iacobus Wagnerus ... Steinfvrti, Typis Cornelij Wellenberg, 1661.
     20 p. 19cm.
     (Continued on next card)

8

WITCHCRAFT
BF
1559
S85

Disputatio philosophica. Examinans quaestionem, Utrum sonus campanarum ingruentem tonitruum ... tempestatem ... abigere queat.
   Spinaeus, Godofredus, praeses. Disputatio philosophica ... 1661. (Card 2)
     Diss.--Steinfurt (J. J. Wagner, respondent)
     1. Bells (in religion, folk-lore, etc.) 2. Demonology. 3. Weather-lore. I. Wagner, Johann Jacob, respondent. II. Title: Utrum sonus campanarum ingruentem tonitruum ... tempestatem ... abigere queat.

8

Witchcraft
BF
1565
D62
no.15

Disputatio physica De hydromantia.
   Hering, Johannes Ernst, praeses.
     Disputatio physica De hydromantia, qvoad sagas probandas per aqvam frigidam, qvam ... sub praesidio M. Johannis Ernesti Herings ... publicè ventilandam sistit respondens Gabriel Kartnerus reichenbergâ ... [Wittebergae] In officina Finceliana exscribebat Michael Meyer [1667]
     [20] p. 18cm. (bound in 20cm. vol.)
     No. 15 in vol. lettered Dissertationes de sagis. 1636-1714.
     (Continued on next card)

8

Witchcraft
BF
1587
D61
no.7

Disputatio physica De magia.
   Schütze, Bartholomaeus, praeses.
     Disputatio physica De magia, quam ... exhibent praeses M. Bartholomaeus Schütze, ... & respondens Heino Meyer ... Rostochii, Typis Johannis Kilii [1669]
     [24] p. 18cm. (bound in 21cm. vol.)
     No. 7 in vol. lettered Dissertationes de magia. 1623-1723.
     1. Magic--Addresses, essays, lectures. I. Meyer, Heino, respondent. II. Title: De magia.

8

Witchcraft
BF
1587
D61
no.4

Disputatio physica De magia et magicis prima.
   Buch, Philipp, 1639-1696, praeses.
     Disputatio physica De magia et magicis prima, quam praeside Dn. M. Philippo Buchio ... respondens Georgius Buchius ... publicè tuebitur. Francofurti ad Oderam, Typis Becmanianus, 1666.
     [40] p. 21cm.
     Caption title: Sectio I. De magia licita. (No other sections follow)
     No 4 in vol. lettered Dissertationes de magia. 1623-1723.
     (Continued on next card)

8

WITCHCRAFT
R
133
Z66

Disputatio physica De magica morborum curatione.
   Ziegra, Christian Samuel, praeses.
     Disputatio physica De magica morborum curatione, qvam ... exponit praeses M. Christianus Samuel Ziegra ... respondente M. Johanne Georgio Spiess ... [Wittebergae] Typis Matthaei Henckelii [1681]
     [24] p. 19cm.
     1. Medicine, Magic, mystic, and spagiric. 2. Witchcraft. 3. Folk medicine. I. Spiess, Johannes Georg, respondent. II. Title: De magica morborum curatione.

8
NIC

Witchcraft
BF
1565
D62
no.6

Disputatio physica De magis tempestates cientibus.
   Müller, Johannes, praeses.
     Disputatio physica De magis tempestates cientibus, qvam ... sub praesidio ... Dn. M. Johannis Mülleri ... publicè pro virili defendet Gottlob Freygang ... Wittenbergae, Literis Matthaei Henckelii [1676]
     [16] p. 20cm.
     No. 6 in vol. lettered Dissertationes de sagis. 1636-1714.
     1. Witchcraft. 2. Weather-lore. I. Freygang, Gottlob, respondent. II. Title: De magis tempestates cientibus.

8

Witchcraft
BF
1775
G88

Disputatio physica De qvalitatibus vulgò dictis occultis.
   Grube, Hermann, praeses.
     Disputatio physica De qvalitatibus vulgò dictis occultis, quam ... sub praesidio ... Dn. Hermanni Gruben ... publico eruditorum examini exponet Zacharias Hermannus ... Jenae, Praelo Nisiano [1665?]
     [28] p. 18cm.
     1. Superstition--Addresses, essays, lectures. 2. Science--Early works to 1800. I. Hermann, Zacharias, respondent. II. Title: De qualitatibus vulgò dictis occultis.

8

Witchcraft
BF
1587
D61
no.5

Disputatio physica exhibens I. Doctrinam de magia.
   Ziegra, Constantinus, praeses.
     Disputatio physica exhibens I. Doctrinam de magia. II. Theoremata miscellanea ex parte tùm generali tùm speciali physicae Qvam sub praesidio ... Dn. Constantini Ziegra ... ventilationi subjicit M. Elias Conradi ... aut. & resp. Wittebergae, Typis Jobi Wilhelmi Fincelii, 1661.
     [36] p. 21cm.
     No. 5 in vol. lettered Dissertationes de magia. 1623-1723.
     1. Occult sciences--Addresses, essays, lectures. I. Conradi, Elias, respondent.

8

Witchcraft
BF
1587
D61
no.6

Disputatio physica qua magiam ... explicabunt.
   Bugges, Laurentius, praeses.
     Disputatio physica qva magian doemoniacam [sic] ceu illicitam, & naturalem ceu licitam, in electorali ad albim academia explicabunt praeses M. Laurentius Bugges, ... respondens Samuel Porath ... Wittebergae, Typis Johannis Haken, 1667.
     [12] p. 18cm. (bound in 21cm. vol.)
     No. 6 in vol. lettered Dissertationes de magia. 1623-1723.
     1. Magic--Addresses, essays, lectures. I. Porath, Samuel, respondent. II. Title: Disputatio physica qua magiam ... explicabunt...

8

CATALOGUE OF THE CORNELL WITCHCRAFT COLLECTION

Disputatio theologica De doctrina daemoniorum.

WITCHCRAFT
BS
2745
.3
M39

Masius, Hector Gottfried, 1653-1709.
Hectoris Gothofr. Masii ... Disputatio theologica De doctrina daemoniorum ex I. Timoth. IV. v. 1 & seq. In abstinentiâ ab esu carnis potissimùm monstratâ. Qvam respondente M. Severino Winthero, publicae disquisitioni exposuit ad 3. April. 1699. Wittebergae, Sumptibus A. Haeberi, 1709.
39 p. 20cm.
1. Bible. N.T. 1 Timothy IV—Criticism, interpretation, etc. 2. Heresy. I. Wintherus, Severinus, respondent. II. Title: De doctrina daemoniorum.

Disputatio theologica De horrenda et miserabili Satanae obsessione.

Witchcraft
F
555
71
743

Dorsch, Johann Georg, 1597-1659, praeses.
Dispvtatio theologica De horrenda et miserabili Satanae obsessione eivsdemqve ex obsessis expvlsione, von leibl. Besitzungen. Svb praesidio Dn. Io. Georg. Dorschei ...a. 1656 d. 23. Avg. pvblico ervditorvm examini svbmissa ab avtore et respondente Daniel Springinsgut ... Vitembergae, Ex officina Scheffleriana, 1743.
48 p. 20cm.

(Continued on next card)

Disputatio van verscheyde saaken, raakende de wonderwerken, en of een schepsel die doen kan...

Witchcraft
BX
9479
.B42
B11
no.15

Bouman, Herman, ed.
Disputatio van verscheyde saaken, raakende de wonderwerken, en of een schepsel die doen kan: item van de engelen, duyvelen, &c. Voorgevallen in de Menniste Kerk, het Lam genaamd, terwijl het oeffening was, den 7 Augustus, en den 29 Mey te vooren, deses jaars 1695. Door verscheyde broeders van deselve societeyt, die tegenwoordig waren, opgesteld, en nagesien van H: Bouman, die ook een kleyne voor-reden voor, en weynig aanmerkingen achter heeft bygevoegd.
(Continued on next card)

Disputatio van verscheyde saaken, raakende de wonderwerken, en of een schepsel die doen kan...

Witchcraft
BX
9479
.B42
B11
no.15

Bouman, Herman, ed. Disputatio van verscheyde saaken ... 1695. (Card 2)
Amsterdam, By J. Smets en P. Dibbits, boekdrukkers, 1695.
23 p. [p. 24 blank] title vignette, illus. initials. 20 x 15cm.
4°: A–C⁴.
Black letter (except introduction and letters at end)
Letters of Bouman and N. N. [i.e.,
(Continued on next card)

Disputatio van verscheyde saaken, raakende de wonderwerken, en of een schepsel die doen kan...

Witchcraft
BX
9479
.B42
B11
no.15

Bouman, Herman, ed. Disputatio van verscheyde saaken ... 1695. (Card 3)
Jacobus Schuts]; p. 22-23.
Van der Linde 78.
No. 15 in vol. lettered B. Bekkers sterfbed en andere tractaten.
1. Miracles—Early works to 1800. 2. Spirits. I. Schuts, Jacobus. II. Title.

Disputatione prima existentiam spectrorum ... demonstrabit ... Pistori.

Witchcraft
F
445
61
.15

Pistori, Gustav Friedrich, praeses.
... Dispvtatione prima existentiam spectrorvm, praesertim ex sagarum veneficarumque pactis cum diabolo sancitis, benevolo facultatis philosophicae indultu demonstrabit praeses M. Gvstav. Frider. Pistori, ... et respondens Io. Gerhardvs Pagendarm ... Vitembergae, Praelo Christiani Gerdesii [ca. 1700]
[16] p. 18cm. (bound in 21cm. vol.)
No. 15 in vol. lettered Dissertationes de spectris. 1646-1753.
(Continued on next card)

Disputatione secunda existentiam spectrorum.

Witchcraft
BF
1445
D61
no.16

Pistori, Gustav Friedrich, praeses.
... Dispvtatione secvnda existentiam spectrorvm, ex sagarum veneficarumque pactis cum daemone sancitis, declarabunt praeses M. Gvstavvs Fridericvs Pistori ... et respondens Ioannes Beniamin. Horn ... Vitembergae, Prelo Gerdesiano [1703]
[16] p. 19cm. (bound in 21cm. vol.)
No. 16 in vol. lettered Dissertationes de spectris. 1646-1753.
1. Spirits. 2. Witchcraft. I.
(Continued on next card)

8

Disputationem De lykanthrōpia.

WITCHCRAFT
GR
830
W4
M94

Müller, Jacobus Friedrich, praeses.
Disputationem De λυκανθρωπία [lykanthrōpia], seu transmutatione hominum in lupos...examini sistunt publice praeses M. Jacobus Friedrich Müller et respondens Johan. Christoph. Pezelius... Lipsiae, Typis Viduae Joh. Wittigau [1673]
[20] p. 19cm.
Diss.—Leipzig (J. C. Pezelius, respondent.
8   1. Werwolves. I. Pezelius, Johann
NIC Christoph, respondent.

Disputationem...inauguralem juridicam De quaestionibus seu torturis reorum.

RARE
HV
8593
D61
no.9

Lang, Johann Philibert.
Disputationem...inauguralem juridicam De quaestionibus seu torturis reorum...disquisitioni...subjiciet Joh. Philibertus Lang. Ob argumenti praestantiam denuo typis expressa. Basileae et Lipsiae, 1747.
80 p. 21cm.
Diss.—Basel, 1661.
No. 9 in a vol. lettered: Dissertationes de tortura, 1667-1787.
1. Torture.   2. Criminal procedure.
I. Title.

8 NIC

Disputationem physicam, evelventem qv. Num daemon cum sagis generare possit.

Witchcraft
BF
1565
D62
no.7

Wolf, Johann, praeses.
Disputationem physicam, evolventem qv. Num daemon cum sagis generare possit, ... sub praesidio Dn. M. Johannis Wolfii ... submittit Johann. Paulus Reineccius ... Wittebergae, Typis Christiani Schrödteri [1676]
[16] p. 20cm.
No. 7 in vol. lettered Dissertationes de sagis. 1636-1714.
1. Witchcraft. 2. Devil. I. Reineck, Johann Paul, respondent. II. Title: Num daemon cum sagis generare possit.

Disquisitio academica An adaemonismus cum fide et pietate Christiana conciliari possit?

WITCHCRAFT
BF
1555
F11

Faber, Johann Gottlieb, 1717-1779, praeses.
Disquisitio academica An adaemonismvs cvm fide et pietate Christiana conciliari possit? Qvam praeside ... Ioanne Gottlieb Faber ... svbmittit avctor defendens Martinvs Schvllervs ... Tvbingae, Literis Cottae et Revsii [1763]
42 p. 21cm.
Running title: De inflvxv adaemonismi in pietatem Christianam.
1. Demoni ac possession. I. Schuller, Martin, respondent. II. Title: An adaemonismus cum fide et pietate Christiana conciliari possit?

8 NIC

Disquisitio de magia divinatrice & operatrice ...

WITCHCRAFT
BT
960
M73

Monceaux, François de.
Disquisitio de magia divinatrice & operatrice... Auctore Francisco Moncaejo. Francofurti et Lipsiae, Sumtibus Joh. Christiani Wohlfarti 1683.
184 p. 19cm.
Date trimmed off by binder.
Note by G.L. Burr: Is Monceaus a pseud. of Joh. Praetorius? See Rosenthal, Cat. 83, no. 204.
1. Supernatural. 2. Spirits. 3. Magic.
I. Praetorius, Johannes, 1630-1680, supposed author. II. Title.

8 NIC

Disquisitio de tortura nec ex integro reprobata, nec ex integro adprobata.

RARE
HV
8593
B21

Banniza von Bazan, Joseph Leonhard, 1733-1800.
Disquisitio de tortura nec ex integro reprobata, nec ex integro adprobata. Oeniponti, Typis Joann. Thomae nob. de Trattnern, 1774.
94 p. 20cm.

8 NIC
1. Torture.   I. Title.

Disqvisitionvm magicarvm libri sex.

Witchcraft
BF
1600
D36
1679

Del Rio, Martin Antoine, 1551-1608.
Disqvisitionvm magicarvm libri sex, qvibvs continetvr accvrata cvriosarvm artivm et vanarum superstitionum confutatio, utilis theologis, juristconsultis, medicis, philologis. Prodit opus vltimis curis longe accuratius ac castigatius. Coloniae Agrippinae, Sumptibus Hermanni Demen, 1679.
[16], 1221, [48] p. 22cm.

Engraved t. p.
I. Title.

Le disquisizioni magiche.

BF
1600
D36D6
1960

Del Rio, Martin Antoine, 1551-1608.
Le disquisizioni magiche: magia e stregoneria, i patti col diavolo, incubi e succubi, fatture e filtri d'amore e di morte, le statuette di cera, messe nere, le profezie, ecc. [Con uno studio sul "Satanismo" ai nostri giorni di J. K. Huysmans] Napoli, G. Rocco [1960?]
124 p. 19cm.

Witchcraft
BF
1505
D61
1885

Disselhoff, August.
Ueber die Geschichte des Teufels. Vortrag. 4. Aufl. Berlin N, Deutsche Evangelische Buch- und Tractat Gesellschaft, 1885.
32 p. 19cm.

1. Devil.   I. Title.

Dissertatio academica, De sagis.

Witchcraft
BF
1565
D62
no.10

Alberti, Valentin, 1635-1697, praeses.
Dissertatio academica, De sagis, sive foeminis, commercium cum malo spiritu habentibus, e christiana pnevmatologia desumpta, & sub praesidio ... Dn. D. Valentini Alberti ... publicae proposita ventilationi ... ab autore Christiano Stridtbeckh ... Lipsiae, Typis Christoph. Fleischeri [1690]
[52] p. illus. 20cm.
No. 10 in vol. lettered Dissertationes de sagis. 1636-1714.
(Continued on next card)

Dissertatio critico-scripturistica de magia diabolica, et magorum prodigiis.

Witchcraft
BF
1565
P71+

Planch, Alexius M   , praeses.
Dissertatio critico-scripturistica de magia diabolica, et magorum prodigiis Exod. 7. coram Pharaone patratis. Una cum conclusionibus ex utroque testamento desumptis, quas praeside P. Alexio M. Planch defendendas suscepere P. P. Chrysostomus M. Ennemoser, et Joan. Evang. M. Püchler ... [Oeniponti?] Litteris Wagnerianis [1767]
6 p. l., 66, [9] p. 28cm.
(Continued on next card)

8

177

CATALOGUE OF THE CORNELL WITCHCRAFT COLLECTION

Dissertatio critico-scripturistica de magia diabolica, et magorum prodigiis.

Witchcraft
BF 1565 P71+

Planch, Alexius M , praeses. Dissertatio critico-scripturistica de magia diabolica ... [1767] (Card 2)
Diss.--Innsbruck (C. M. Ennemoser and J. E. M. Püchler, respondents)
1. Witchcraft in the Bible. 2. Witchcraft. 3. Magic. I. Ennemoser, Chrysostomus M., respondent. II. Püchler, Johann Evangelica M., respondent. III. Title: De magia diabolica, et magorum prodigiis.

8

Dissertatio de fascino & incantatione.

WITCHCRAFT
BF 1565 T16

Tändler, Tobias.
Dissertatio de fascino & incantatione, sub auspicio praelectionum publ. habita, à Tobia Tandlero philos. & medicin. doctore, ac math. profess. 24. Octobris, anno 1606 ... VVitebergae, Sumptibus Clementis Bergeri, Excudebat Johann. Schmidt, 1606.
8 p. l., 142 p. 16cm.
Title in ornamental border.
1. Witchcraft. 2. Evil eye. 3. Magic. I. Title: De fascino et incantatione.

8 NIC

Dissertatio De generatione diaboli cum sagis.

Witchcraft
BF 1565 D62 no.11

Panecius, Nicolaus, praeses.
Dissertatio De generatione diaboli cum sagis, qvam ... sub praesidio M. Nicol. Panecii ... submittit autor respondens Georg. Christoph. Kranzius ... Wittebergae, Literis Johannis Wilckii [1693]
[16] p. 20cm.
No. 11 in vol. lettered Dissertationes de sagis. 1636-1714.
1. Witchcraft. 2. Devil. I. Kranz, Georg Christoph, respondent. II. Title: De generatione diaboli cum sagis.

8

Dissertatio de magia.

Witchcraft
BF 1600 R55

Riegger, Paul Joseph, Ritter von, 1705-1775.
Dissertatio de magia ... Vindobonae, Typis Ioan. Thomae nob. de Trattnern, 1773.
104 p. 20cm.
Title vignette: J. T. Trattner's device.

1. Magic. I. Title.

Dissertatio De potentia diaboli in sensus.

Witchcraft
BF 1520 S38

Schubart, Christoph, praeses.
Dissertatio De potentia diaboli in sensu$, quam ... sub praesidio M. Joh. Christophori Schubarti, die 23. April hor. 8. placidae eruditorum ventilationi in acroaterio philosophorum submittet respondens Paulus Nicolaus Einert ... Erfordiae, Literis Limprechtianis [1707]
[14] p. 20cm.
1. Devil. I. Einert, Paul Nicolaus, respondent. II. Title: De potentia diaboli in sensus.

8

Dissertatio historico-philosophica De masticatione mortuorum.

Witchcraft
BF 1556 R73

Rohr, Philipp, praeses.
Dissertatio historico-philosophica De masticatione mortuorum, quam ... sistent praes M. Philippus Rohr ... & respondens Benjamin Frizschius ... Lipsiae, Typis Michaelis Vogtii [1679]
[24] p. 21cm.
1. Vampires. 2. Devil. I. Fritzsch, Benjamin, respondent. II. Title: De masticatione mortuorum.

8

Dissertatio inauguralis, De denuntiatione sagarum.

Witchcraft
BF 1565 M45

Mauritius, Erich, 1631-1692, praeses.
Dissertatio inauguralis, De denuntiatione sagarum, iisque quae ad eam recte intelligendam faciunt. Qvam ... praeside Erico Mauritio ... submittit Christophorus Daurer, Hamburg. Tubingae, Excudit Gregorius Kerner, 1664.
96 p. 20cm.
Diss.--Tübingen (C. Daurer, respondent)
1. Witchcraft. 2. Trials (Witchcraft)
I. Daurer, Christophorus, respondent. II. Title: De denuntiatione sagarum.

8

Dissertatio inauguralis medica De incubo.

WITCHCRAFT
RC 547 T26

Teichmeyer, Hermann Friedrich, 1685-1746, praeses.
Dissertatio inavgvralis medica De incvbo .qvam ... svb praesidio Herm. Frider. Teichmeyeri ...svbmittit Daniel Textoris ... Ienae, Litteris Wertherianis [1740]
26 [i.e., 28] p. 21cm.
Diss.--Jena (D. Textoris, respondent)
1. Sleep--Addresses, essays, lectures. 2. Folk-lore, German. I. Textoris, Daniel, respondent. II. Title: De incubo.

8

Dissertatio inauguralis medica, de potestate diaboli in corpus humanum.

Witchcraft
BF 1520 A33

Alberti, Michael, 1682-1757, praeses.
Dissertatio inauguralis medica, de potestate diaboli in corpus humanum, qvam ... praeside Dn. D. Michaele Alberti ... ventilationi subjiciet respondens Johannes Fridericus Corvinus ... [Halle] Typis Jo: Christian Hendel [1725]
52 p. 21cm.
Diss.--Halle (J. F. Corvinus, respondent)
1. Demonology. 2. Diseases--Causes and theories of causation. I. Corvinus, Johann Friedrich, of Halle, respondent. II. Title: De potestate diaboli in corpus humanum.

8

Dissertatio inauguralis medica De superstitione medica.

HIST SCI
R 133 A33

Alberti, Michael, 1682-1757, praeses.
Dissertatio inauguralis medica De superstitione medica, quam...praeside Dn. D. Michaele Alberti...publicae ventilationi submittet David Godofred. Kletschke. Halae Magdeburgicae, Typis Ioanni Christiani Hendelii [1720]
40 p. 21 cm.
Diss.--Halle (D.G. Kletschke, respondent)
1. Medical delusions. 2. Folk medicine. 3. Medicine, popular. I. Kletschke, David Gottfried, respondent. II. Title.

Dissertatio inauguralis medica De superstitione medica.

HIST SCI
R 128 .7 A1 A33 no.22

Alberti, Michael, 1682-1757, praeses.
Dissertatio inauguralis medica De superstitione medica, quam...praeside Dn. D. Michaele Alberti...publicae ventilationi submittet David Godofred. Kletschke. Halae Magdeburgicae, Typis Ioanni [sic] Christiani Hendelii [1720]
40 p. 20cm.
Diss.--Halle (D.G. Kletschke, respondent)
No. 22 in a vol. of dissertations for which Alberti acted as praeses. (Vol. lettered: Dispvtationvm medicarvm volumen LVI)

Dissertatio inauguralis medica medicinam pseudo-miraculosam aperiens.

History of Science
R 133 A33 D6

Alberti, Michael, 1682-1757, praeses.
Dissertatio inauguralis medica medicinam pseudo-miraculosam aperiens, quam ... in Alma Regia Fridericiana, praeside ... Michaele Alberti ... progradu doctoris summisque in medicina honoribus et privilegiis doctoralibus legitime ... impetrandis, anno MDCCLIII. d. Maii ... publicae ... eruditorum ventilationi subjiciet auctor Georgius Heck ... Halae Magdeburgicae, Typis Joh. Christiani Hendelii [1753]
43,[5] p. 21cm.
Diss. inaug.-- Halle (G. Heck, respondent)

Dissertatio iuridica De tortura eiusque usu et effectibus.

RARE
HV 8593 C88

Cramer, Wilhelm Zacharias, praeses.
Dissertatio iuridica De tortura eiusque usu et effectibus...praeside Wilhelmo Zacharia Cramero respondente Io. Christophoro Goetzio pro loco in Facultate Iuridica rite obtinendo...habenda... Lipsiae, Litteris Breitkopfianis [1742]
85 p. 23cm.
"An magi et sagae sint torquendi?" : p. 57-66.
1. Torture. I. Goetz, Johann Christoph, respondent. II. Title.

8 NIC

Dissertatio juridica De lamiis.

Witchcraft
BF 1565 D62 no.3

Schröter, Ernst Friedrich, 1621-1676, praeses.
Dissertatio juridica De lamiis earumqve processu criminali, quam ... sub praesidio ... Dn. Ernesti Friderici Schröter ... publicae eruditorum censurae subjicit, Michael Paris Walburger ... Jenae, Literis Joh. Jacobi Bauhoferi, 1690.
149, [3] p. 20cm.
No. 3 in vol. lettered Dissertationes de sagis. 1636-1714.
1. Witchcraft. 2. Trials (Witchcraft) I. Walburger, Michael Paris, respondent. II. Title: De lamiis.

8

Dissertatio juridica De tortura ex foris Christianorum proscribenda.

RARE
HV 8593 T46 1743

Thomasius, Christian, 1655-1728, praeses.
Dissertatio juridica De tortura ex foris Christianorum proscribenda...quam praeside Christiano Thomasio...respondendo propugnavit Martinus Bernhardi. Halae Salicae, Ex officina Hendeliana, 1743.
37 p. 20cm.
Diss.--Halle, 1705 (M. Bernhardi, respondent)
Originally published in 1705 with title: Disputatio inauguralis juridica tortura ex foris Christianorum proscribenda. (Continued on next card)

8 NIC

Dissertatio medica De incubo.

Witchcraft
RC 547 W39

Wedel, Georg Wolfgang, 1645-1721, praeses.
Dissertatio medica De incvbo, ex epitome praxeos clinicae Georgii Wolffgangi Wedelii ... eodem praeside, pvblicae ... disqvisitioni svbiecta a Christophoro Lvdovico Göckelio ... Ienae, Litteris Krebsianis [1708]
20 p. 21cm.
Diss.--Jena (C. L. Göckelius, respondent)

8

Dissertatio medica De spectris.

Witchcraft
BF 1445 D61 no.13

Wedel, Georg Wolfgang, 1645-1721, praeses.
Dissertatio medica De spectris, praeside Georgio Wolffgango VVedelio ... proposita ab Ernesto Henrico Wedelio ... Editio secunda. Jenae, Litteris Krebsianis, 1698.
39, [1] p. 19cm. (bound in 21cm. vol.)
Diss.--Jena (E. H. Wedel, respondent)
No. 13 in vol. lettered Dissertationes de spectris. 1646-1753.

8

Dissertatio medica inavgvralis De incartatis.

Witchcraft
BF 1565 K91

Krause, Rudolph Wilhelm, 1642-1719, praeses.
Dissertatio medica inavgvralis De incartatis, qvam ... svb praesidio Rvdolffi VVilhelmi Cravsii ... subjicit Iohannes Ernestvs Rauschelbach ... Ienae, Literi Krebsianis [1701]
28 p. 20cm.
Diss.--Jena (J. E. Rauschelbach, respondent)
1. Witchcraft. 2. Personality Disorders of. I. Rauschelbach, Johann Ernst, respondent. II. Title.

8

178

CATALOGUE OF THE CORNELL WITCHCRAFT COLLECTION

Dissertatio medica inauguralis De incubo.

T SCI
 Chardulliet, Melchior.
6   Dissertatio medica inauguralis De incubo,
    quam...examini submittit Melchior Chardulliet
    ... Argentorati, Typis Johannis Henrici
    Heitzii [1734]
      24 p. 19cm.
      Diss.--Strasbourg.

      1. Medicine, Magic, mystic, and spagiric.
    2. Demonology. 3. Medical delusions.
    I. Title.

Dissertatio medica inauguralis De obsessione eademque spuria.

CHCRAFT
 Detharding, Georg Christoph, 1671-1747,
   praeses.
.4   Dissertatio medica inauguralis De obses-
    sione eademque spuria, von Besessenen und
    vor besessen gehaltenen Menschen, qvam ...
    sub praesidio ... Georgii Dethardingii ...
    publice examinandam proponit Christ. Fri-
    der. Stever. ...   Rostochii, Recusa typis
    Io. Ioacob. Adleri [1724?]
      [102] p. 19cm.
      Diss.--Rostock (C. F. Stever, respondent)

Dissertatio philologica De vocibus hhartymmim et belahatehem.

chcraft
 [Durych, Fortunat] 1730-1802.
5   Eutychii Beniamin Transalbini Disserta-
    tio philologica De vocibus hhartymmim et
    belahatehem Exod. VII. 2. [Vindobonae?]
    1767.
      20 p. 21cm.
      "Opusculi inscripti: Gedanken über die
    Werke des Liebhabers der Wahrheit von der
    Hexerey."
      1. Witchcraft in the Bible. 2. Bible.
    O.T.--Criticism, Textual. 3. Hartumim
        (Continued on next card)

Dissertatio philologica secunda de daemonibus.

chcraft
 Rabener, Justus Gotthart, respondent.
0   Dissertatio philologica secunda de
    daemonibus, quam ... defendet M. Justus
    Gotthart Rabener ... Lipsiae, Literis
    Christiani GoeziI [1707]
      [40] p. 21cm.
      First Dissertatio philologica de daemo-
    nibus published 1706.

      1. Demonology. 2. De potentia, opera-
    tionibus & cul   tus daemonum. I. Title.
    II. Title: De daemonibus.

Dissertatio philosophica De magia.

chcraft
 Örnhielm, Claudius Arrhenius, 1627-1675,
7   praeses.
10   Dissertatio philosophica De magia qvam
    ... sub moderamine ... Dn. Claudii Arrhenii
    ... examinandam proponit ... Andreas Torse-
    lius ...   Holmiae, Excudit Nicolaus Wankif
    [1679]
      2 p. l., 41 p. 21cm.
      Imperfect: p. 3-6 wanting.
      No. 10 in vol. lettered Dissertationes de
    magia. 1623-1723.
        (Continued on next card)

Dissertatio philosophica De spectris.

chcraft
 Cameen, Sven, praeses.
5   Dissertatio philosophica De spectris,
12   quam ... sub moderamine celeberrimi viri
    Dni. Svenonis Cameen ... pro laurea magi-
    sterii reportanda publicae bonorum ventila-
    tioni subjicit ... Petrus Bartelius ...
    Dorpati, Excudit Johannes Brendeken [1693]
      [24] p. 19cm. (bound in 21cm. vol.)
      Diss.--Dorpat (P. Bartelius, respondent)
      No. 12 in vol. lettered Dissertationes
    de spectris. 1646-1753.
      1. Demono   logy. I. Bartelius,
    Peter, respon   dent. II. Title: De
    spectris.

Dissertatio philosophica de superstitione.

Witchcraft
BF   Eberhard, Johann August, 1739-1809, praeses.
1775   Dissertatio philosophica de superstiti-
E16 one, quam praeside ... Ioanne Augusto Eber-
    hard ... A. D. 16 April 1801 publice defen-
    det auctor Henricus Christianus Millies.
    Halis Saxonum, Typis Schimmelpfennigianis
    [1801]
      51 p. 21cm.
      Imperfect: t. p. badly worn.
      Diss.--Halle (H. C. Millies, respondent)
      1. Superstition. 2. Occult sciences.
    I. Millies,   Henricus Christianus,
8   fl. 1801, res   pondent. II. Title.

Dissertatio theologica De usu et praestantia daemonum.

Witchcraft
BF   Schwartz, Johann Conrad, 1677-1747.
1520   Dissertatio theologica De vsv et prae-
S32 stantia daemonvm ad demonstrandam natvram
    Dei, qvam ... tvebitvr Io. Conradvs Schwartz
    ... Altdorfii Noric., Literis Iodoci Gvi-
    lielmi Kohlesii [1715]
      26 p. 21cm.
      Bound with Scherzer, Johann Adam, prae-
    ses. Daemonologia. Lipsiae, 1672.
      In vol. lettered Dissertationes de dae-
    monibus. 1672-   1722.
      1. God.   2. Demonology. I.
8   Title: De usu   et praestantia daemonum.

A dissertation on the demoniacs in the Gospels.

Witchcraft
BS   A dissertation on the demoniacs in the
2545   Gospels.   London, Printed for J. and
L5   F. Rivington, 1775.
T759   63 p. 20cm.
no.5
      No. 5 in vol. lettered: Tracks [sic] of
    demoniacks.

      1. Demoniac possession. 2. Bible. N.T.--
    Commentaries.

A dissertation on the demoniacs in the Gospels.

Witchcraft
BS   [Newton, Thomas, bp. of Bristol] 1704-1782.
2545   A dissertation on the demoniacs in the
D5   Gospels. London, Printed for J. and F.
T97   Rivington, 1775.
no.1   63 p. 21cm.

      No. 1 in vol. lettered: Twells, Whiston,
    etc. Tracts on the demoniacs in the New
    Testament. London, 1738-1775.

      1. Demoniac   possession. 2. Bible.
    N.T.--Commen   taries. I. Title.

A dissertation on the Gospel Daemoniacs.

MSS
Bd.   [Young, Arthur] 1693-1759.
WITCHCRAFT A dissertation on the Gospel Daemoniacs,
BS   occasioned by the Bp. of St. David's
Y68   answer to Mr. Woolston. [n.p., before
    1760]
      64 l. 23cm.
      Manuscript, on paper, with gilt edges.
      "...This dissertation ... was printed in
    1760... It is not improbable that this is
    the author's autograph": G. L. Burr's note
    at beginning.
      Bound in gi   lt-stamped black leather.
      1. Demoniac   possession. 2. Bible.
    N. T.--Commen   taries. I. Title.

Dissertation sur ce qu'on doit penser de l'apparition des esprits.

Witchcraft
BF   Calmet, Augustin, 1672-1757.
1412   Dissertations sur les apparitions des
C16   anges, des démons & des esprits, et sur
    les revenans et vampires de Hongrie, de
    Bohème, de Moravie & de Silesie. Paris,
    Chez de Bure l'aîné, 1746.
      xxxvi, 500 p. 17cm.
      Published also under title: Traité sur
    les apparitions des esprits ... Paris, 1751
    [etc.]
      "Dissertation sur ce qu'on doit penser
8   (Continued on next card)

Dissertation sur ce qu'on doit penser de l'apparition des esprits.

Witchcraft
BF   Calmet, Augustin, 1672-1757. Dissertations
1412   sur les apparitions des anges ... 1746.
C16   (Card 2)

    de l'apparition des esprits, a l'occasion de
    l'aventure arrivée a Saint Maur. Paris,
    1707: p. [467]-500, has special t. p., and
    is attributed to F. Poupart by the Biblio-
    thèque Nationale.
      1. Demonology. 2. Apparitions. I.
    Poupart, François. Dissertation sur ce qu'on
    doit penser...   II. Title. III. Title:
8   Dissertation   sur ce qu'on doit penser
    de l'apparition   des esprits.

Dissertation sur les maléfices et les sorciers.

WITCHCRAFT
BF   [Valmont, de]
1582   Dissertation sur les maléfices et les
V18   sorciers selon les principes de la théolo-
1752a gie et de la physique, ou l'on examine en
    particulier l'état de la fille de Tourcoing.
    Tourcoing, 1752.   Lille, Leleu, 1862.
      85 p. 16cm.
      Title in red and black.
      "Réimpression sur l'original à deux cents
    exemplaires."
      Note in back of text claims Barbier at-
8   tributed this   item to the Abbé Valle-
        (Continued on next card)

Dissertation sur les maléfices et les sorciers.

WITCHCRAFT
BF   [Valmont, de] Dissertation sur les
1582 maléfices et les sorciers ... 1862.
V18   (Card 2)
1752a
    mont. However, the Abbé died 1721, and the
    introductory letter is dated 1751.

      1. Witchcraft. I. Vallemont, Pierre
    Le Lorrain, abbé de, 1649-1721, supposed
    author. II.   Title.

Dissertationem inauguralem De confessione tormentis extorta.

RARE
HV   Dondorff, Christoph, 1667-1737.
8593   Dissertationem inauguralem De confessione
D67   tormentis extorta...publico examini sub-
    mittit M. Christophorus Dondorff...
    Lipsiae, Typis Joh. Christoph. Brandenbur-
    geri [1693]
      [58] p. 20cm.

8   Diss.--Leipzig.
NIC   1. Torture. 2. Confession (Law)
    I. Title.

Dissertationem juridicam inauguralem De arbitrio judicis circa torturam.

RARE
HV   Wildvogel, Christian, 1644-1728, praeses.
8593   Dissertationem juridicam inauguralem De
D611 arbitrio judicis circa torturam, quam...
no.2 sub praesido Dn. Christiani Wildvogelii...
    submittit Iohann Iacob Arnold. Jenae,
    Litteris Müllerianis [1710]
      54 p. 21cm.
      Diss.--Jena (J. J. Arnold, respondent)
      No. 2 in a vol. lettered: Dissertationes
8   de tortura. 1697-1770.
NIC   1. Torture.   I. Arnold, Johann Jacob,
    respondent.   II. Title.

Dissertationem medicam inauguralem De incubo.

WITCHCRAFT
BF   Krause, Rudolf Wilhelm, 1642-1719, praeses.
1556   Dissertationem medicam inauguralem De in-
K91   cubo...praeside Dn. Rudolfo Wilhelmo Krauss
    ...publicae...disquisitioni submittit
    Daniel Christophorus Meineke... Jenae,
    Typis Viduae Samuelis Krebsii [1683]
      [26] p. 20cm.

8   Diss.--Jena (D. C. Meineke, respondent)
NIC
      1. Medicine, Magic, mystic and spagiric.
    2. Medical delu   sions. I. Meineke,
    Daniel Chris   tophorus, respondent.

CATALOGUE OF THE CORNELL WITCHCRAFT COLLECTION

Dissertationes de origine ac progressu idololatriae.

Witchcraft
BL   Dale, Antonius van, 1638-1708.
75   Antonii van Dale ... Dissertationes de
D13   origine ac progressu idololatriae et super-
        stitionum: de vera ac falsa prophetia; uti
        et de divinationibus idololatricis judaeorum.
        Amstelodami, Apud H. & viduam T. Boom,
        1696.
            26 p. l., 762, [13] p. 22cm.
            Parts 2 and 3 have own half titles.
            With armorial bookplate of Francesco Var-
        gas Macciucca.
8   (Continued on next card)

Dissertationes quatuor, De daemonologia recentiorum autorum falsa.

Witchcraft
BF   Falck, Nathanael, 1663-1693.
1520   Nathanaelis Falcken ... Dissertationes
F17   quatuor, De daemonologia recentiorum auto-
        rum falsa, Anno 1692. Wittebergae habitae,
        nunc vero praefixis literis Schomerianis
        ibidem recusae. [Wittebergae] Typis Mar-
        tini Schultzii, 1694.
            92 p. illus. initials. 20 x 16cm.
            4°: A², B-M⁴, N².
            Contents.--De falsa recentiorum aucto-
        rum daemonolog   ia ... respondente Joh.
8   (Continued on next card)

Dissertationes quatuor, De daemonologia recentiorum autorum falsa.

Witchcraft
BF   Falck, Nathanael, 1663-1693.   Nathanaelis
1520   Falcken ... Dissertationes quatuor ...
F17   1694.   (Card 2)

            Contents--Continued.
        Isaaco Trempenau.--Dissertatio II. Ortum
        daemonologiae falsae & progressum historicè
        declarans, respondente Johanne Furmann.--
        Dissertatio III. De daemonologia Hobbesii
        & Spinozae, respondente Jac. Friderico Mol-
        lero.--Dissert   atio IV. De daemonolo-
8   (Continued on next card)

Dissertationes quatuor, De daemonologia recentiorum autorum falsa.

Witchcraft
BF   Falck, Nathanael, 1663-1693.   Nathanaelis
1520   Falcken ... Dissertationes quatuor ...
F17   1694.   (Card 3)

        gia Bekkeri & aliorum, respondente Georg.
        Abrahamo Wolf.
            1. Demonology. 2. Hobbes, Thomas,
        1588-1679. Elementa philosophica de cive.
        3. Spinoza, Benedictus de, 1632-1677.
        Tractatus theologico-politicus. 4. Bek-
        ker, Balthasar, 1634-1698. De beto-
        verde weereld.   I. Title: De daemo-
        nologia recen   tiorum autorum falsa.
8

Dissertations sur les apparitions des anges, des démons & des esprits, et sur les re- venans et vampires de Hongrie, de Boheme, de Moravie & de Silesie.

Witchcraft
BF   Calmet, Augustin, 1672-1757.
1412   Dissertations sur les apparitions des
C16   anges, des démons & des esprits, et sur
        les revenans et vampires de Hongrie, de
        Boheme, de Moravie & de Silesie. Paris,
        Chez de Bure l'aîné, 1746.
            xxxvi, 500 p. 17cm.
            Published also under title: Traité sur
        les apparitions des esprits ... Paris, 1751
        [etc.]
            "Dissertation   sur ce qu'on doit penser
8   (Continued on next card)

Dissertations sur les apparitions des anges, des démons & des esprits, et sur les re- venans et vampires de Hongrie, de Boheme, de Moravie & de Silesie.

Witchcraft
BF   Calmet, Augustin, 1672-1757. Dissertations
1412   sur les apparitions des anges ... 1746.
C16   (Card 2)

        de l'apparition des esprits, a l'occasion de
        l'avanture arrivée a Saint Maur. Paris,
        1707: p. [467]-500, has special t. p., and
        is attributed to F. Poupart by the Biblio-
        thèque Nationale.
            1. Demonology. 2. Apparitions. I.
        Poupart, François. Dissertation sur ce qu'on
        doit penser...   II. Title. III. Title:
        Dissertation   sur ce qu'on doit penser
8   de l'apparition   des esprits.

Dissertations theologiques et dogmatiques.

Witchcraft
BT   [Duguet, Jacques Joseph] 1649-1732.
15   Dissertations theologiques et dogmatiques,
D86   I. Sur les exorcismes & les autres céré-
        monies du batême. II. Sur l'eucharistie.
        III. Sur l'usure.   Paris, J. Estienne,
        1727.
            3 pts. in 1 v. 17cm.

            Parts 2 and 3 paged continuously.

            1. Exorcism.   2. Lord's Supper. 3.
        Interest and   usury.   I. Title.

Dissertazione circa la stregheria con apendice della magia diabolica. [Milan?

MSS   early 18th cent.]
Bd.   26 l. 22 x 16cm.
WITCHCRAFT
BX   Manuscript, in an eighteenth century
D61   Italian hand, on paper.
no.2   Bound in gray boards.
            No. 2 in vol. of anonymous dissertations
        on theology and witchcraft.

            1. Witchcraft.   2. Magic.

8

Dissertazione in cui si investiga quali sieno le operazioni che dependono dalla magia diabolica.

Witchcraft
BF   Grimaldi, Costantino, 1667-1750.
1604   Dissertazione in cui si investiga quali
G86+   sieno le operazioni che dependono dalla ma-
        gia diabolica e quali quelle che derivano
        dalle magie artificiale e naturale e qual
        cautela si ha da usare nella malagevolezza
        di discernerle. Roma, Nella Stamperia di
        Pallade, Appresso Niccolò, e Marco Pagliari-
        ni, 1751.
            [8], 139 p.   port. 16cm.
            Engraved ti   tle vignette.
8   Edited by   Ginesio Grimaldi.

Dissertazione intorno a veri, e falsi

MSS   miracoli. [n.p. early 18th cent.]
Bd.   15 l. 22 x 16cm.
WITCHCRAFT
BX   Manuscript, in an eighteenth century
D61   Italian hand, on paper.
no.3   Bound in gray boards.
            No. 3 in a vol. of anonymous dissertations
        on theology and witchcraft.

            1. Witchcraft.   2. Magic. 3. Miracles.

Diszes Wonder, auch erschricklic Zaychen

MSS   ist durch Zulassung Gottesz warhafftig
Bd.   unnd thadlich gesehen in der Stat von
WITCHCRAFT
BF   Gent in Flandren, auff den XVIII. Augustii
D613   in Jaer, MDLXXXVI bey dem bossen Gayst
        unnd seinnesz Wercks, seer erschrocklich
        ist unnb zu leessen.   Anntorff, By Paulus
        Brackfeldt, 1586 [ca. 1900]
            4 l. illus. 23cm.
            Carnap's manuscript copy.
            "Original   druck i. d. Gust. Frey-
        tag Biblioth   ek, jetzt i. d. Stadt-
                       (Continued on next card)

Diszes Wonder, auch erschricklic Zaychen ...

MSS   1586 [ca. 1900]   (Card 2)
Bd.
WITCHCRAFT
BF   bibliothek zu Frankfurt a/M. 4 Bl. 4°."
D613   A letter received by D. H. V. W.
        At end: "Ghetranslateert durch M. Carel
        Strutberger."
        Numerals and signatures in the margins
        indicate pagination and signatures of the
        original.
            1. Apparit   ions. 2. Devil.   I.
        W., D. H. V.   II. Strutberger, Carel,
        tr.

Ditmar, Jacob Friedrich, respondent.

Witchcraft
BF   Breithaupt, Christian, 1689-1749, praeses.
1520   Commentatio secvnda De existentia dae-
S32   monvm, qvam ... praeside Christiano Breit-
        havpto ... pvblicae litteratorvm dispvta-
        tioni svbmittit avtor Iacobvs Fridericvs
        Ditmar ... Helmstadii, Exscripsit Herm.
        Dan. Hammivs [1722]
            4 p. l., 18, [2] p. 19cm. (bound in
        21cm. vol.)
            Bound with Schwerzer, Johann Adam, prae-
8   ses. Daemonolo   gia. Lipsiae, 1672.
                           (Continued on next card)

Ditmar, Jacob Friedrich, respondent.

Witchcraft
BF   Breithaupt, Christian, 1689-1749, praeses.
1520   Commentatio secvnda ... [1722] (Card 2)
S32
            In vol. lettered Dissertationes de dae-
        monibus. 1672-1722.

            1. Demonology.   I. Ditmar, Jacob Fried-
        rich, respondent. II. Title: De existen-
        tia daemonum.

8

Witchcraft
BF   The Divels delvsions; or, A faithfull re-
1563   lation of John Palmer and Elizabeth Knott
W81++   two notorious vvitches lately condemned
no.15   ... St. Albans ... executed July 16. All
        their accusations of severall witches in
        ... the county of Hartford.   London,
        Printed for R. Williams, 1649. [London,
        at the British Museum, 1923]
            6 p. 16cm.

                           (Continued on next card)

Witchcraft
BF   The Divels delvsions... [1923] (Card 2)
1563
W81++   Photocopy (negative) 6 p. on 5 l. 20 x
no.15   32cm.
            No. 15 in vol. lettered: Witchcraft
        tracts, chapbooks and broadsides, 1579-1704
        rotograph copies.

            1. Witchcraft--England. 2. Palmer, John,
        d. 1649. 3. Knott, Elizabeth, d. 1649.

The divel's delusions.

Witchcraft
GR   [Misodaimon, B.] pseud.
142   The divel's delusions; or, A faithful relation of John
H6   Palmer and Elizabeth Knott, two notorious vvitches
A3   lately condemned at the sessions of Oyer and Terminer
no.18   in St. Albans. Together with the confession of the afore-
        said John Palmer and Elizabeth Knott, executed July 16.
        Also their accusations of severall witches in Hitchen,
        Norton, and other places in the county of Hartford. Lon-
        don, Printed for Richard Williams, stationer, at St. Al-
        bans, anno Dom, 1649. Reprinted with an introduction
        by W. B. Gerish. Bishop's Stortford, 1914.
            13, (1) p. 21½ᶜᵐ. [Hertfordshire folk lore. no. 18]
            Signed: "B. Misodaimon."
            1. Witchcraft--England. 2. Palmer, John, d. 1649. 3. Knott,
        Elizabeth, d. 1649. I. Gerish, William Blyth, ed. II. Title.
                                                        16-25733
        Library of Congress   GR530.M55

Witchcraft
BF   Diversi tractatvs: De potestate ecclesia-
1563   stica coercendi daemones circa energu-
D61   menos & maleficiatos, de potentia ac
        viribus daemonum. De modo procedendi a
        versvs crimina excepta; praecipuè contra
        sagas & maleficos ... Ex diversis jis-
        qve celeberrimis huius aeui scriptoribus
        ... disputantur. Coloniae Agrippinae,
        Sumptibus Constantini Munich bibliopola,
        1629.
            8, 236,   166 p. 20cm.
8   (Continued on next card)

180

CATALOGUE OF THE CORNELL WITCHCRAFT COLLECTION

Witchcraft
BF Diversi tractatvs ... 1629. (Card 2)
1563
D61   Contents.--Tractatvs de potestate ecclesiae coercendi daemones circa obsessos &
maleficiatos, vnà cum praxi exorcistica, a
R. della Torre.--Tractatvs theologicvs de
processv adversvs crimina excepta, ac speciatim adversvs crimen veneficij, a A. Tanner.--Tractatvs alter theologicus de sagis
et veneficis, a P. Laymanni.--Consilium de
sagis, a M. A. Peregrini.

(Continued on next card)

Witchcraft
BF Diversi tractatvs ... 1629. (Card 3)
1563
D61   Title in red and black.
In double columns except for t. p., dedication, and titles of first, second, and
fourth works.
 1. Witchcraft. 2. Trials (Witchcraft)
3. Exorcism. I. Torre, Raffaelle della.
Tractatus de potestate ecclesiae coercendi
daemones. II. Tanner, Adam, 1572-1632.
Tractatus theologicus de processu adversus

(Continued on next card)

Witchcraft
F Diversi tractatvs ... 1629. (Card 4)
563
61   crimina excepta. III. Laymann, Paul, 1574-
1635. Tractatus de sagis et veneficis. IV.
Peregrinus, Marcus Antonius, 1530-1616.
Consilium de sagis. V. Munich, Constantinus.

Divina quatuor energumenorum liberatio.
WITCHCRAFT
BF Gervais de Tournai, Martin, b. 1515.
1555   Divina qvatvor energvmenorvm liberatio,
338 facta apvd Suessiones, anno Domini millesimo
quingentesimo octogesimo secundo. In qua
sacrosanctae Eucharistiae vis & veritas pla-
nè elucet. Eam scripsit Geruasius Tornacensis ... Parisiis, Apud Guillelmum Chaudiere, 1583.
 111 numb. l., [3] p. 17cm.
 Contents.--1. Laurentius.--2. Nicolea.
--3. Margarita.--4. Nicolaus.--Appendix

(Continued on next card)

Divina quatuor energumenorum liberatio.
WITCHCRAFT
F Gervais de Tournai, Martin, b. 1515. Di-
555 vina qvatvor energvmenorvm liberatio ...
38 (Card 2)

de Astarotho daemone fugitiuo.
Copy two imperfect: t. p., l. 1-8 and
all after l. 109 mutilated.

 1. Demoniac possession. 2. Devil.
I. Title: Divina quatuor energumenorum
liberatio.

Witchcraft
    Divination, witchcraft, and mesmerism.
     [New York, 1852]
     198-213 p. 26cm.

    Signed: S. F.
    Detached from the International monthly
magazine of literature, science, and art.
v. 5.

 1. Divination. 2. Witchcraft.
3. Mesmerism. I. F., S. II. S. F.

Witchcraft
BX Do. [i. e., doctor] B. Bekkers Sterf-bedde
9479 verdeedigt, tegens de zoo genaamde Nodi-
B42 ge aanmerkingen over het zelve: vervat
B11 in een brief aan den schryver; behelzende
no.3 een openbaar bewijs zijner onkunde in de
geschillen, en verdere ongegronde redeneeringen; tot wegschuiminge van zijn
alderhaatelijkste beschryving en veroordeeling van den overledene. Door M. G.
Amsterdam, By R. Blokland, boekverkooper,
1699.
 1 p. l., 16 p. title and end

(Continued on next card)

Witchcraft
BX Do. [i. e., doctor] B. Bekkers Sterf-bedde
9479 verdeedigt ... 1699. (Card 2)
B42
B11 page vignettes, illus. initial. 20 x 16 cm.
no.3 4°: π1, A-B⁴.
Van der Linde 207.
No. 3 in vol. lettered B. Bekkers sterf-
bed en andere tractaten.
 1. Bekker, Balthasar, 1634-1698. 2.
Bekker, Johannes Henricus, fl. 1698-1737.
Sterf-bedde van ... Do. Balthazar Bekker.

(Continued on next card)

Witchcraft
BX Do. [i. e., doctor] B. Bekkers Sterf-bedde
9479 verdeedigt ... 1699. (Card 3)
B42
B11 3. Schuts, Jacobus. Nodige aanmerking
no.3 over het Sterf-bedde van Balthasar Bekker.
 I. M. G. II. G., M.

Doctor Johann Weyer: ein rheinischer
Arzt, der erste Bekämpfer des Hexenwahns.
Witchcraft
R Binz, Carl, 1832-1913.
512   Doctor Johann Weyer: ein rheinischer
W64 Arzt, der erste Bekämpfer des Hexenwahns.
B61 Ein Beitrag zur Geschichte der Aufklärung
1896 und der Heilkunde. 2., umgearb. u. verm.
Aufl. Mit dem Bildnisse Johann Weyers.
Berlin, A. Hirschwald, 1896.
 vii, 189 p. port. 24cm.

Doctor Johann Weyer. (1515-1588) Eine
Nachlese.
Witchcraft
R Binz, Carl, 1832-1913.
512   Doctor Johann Weyer. (1515-1588) Eine
W64 Nachlese. [Düsseldorf, Gedruckt bei E. Voss]
B612 1889.
 36 p. facsim. 23cm.
 "Sonderabdruck aus dem 24. Band der Zeit-
schrift des Bergischen Geschichtvereins."
 Includes further discussion of the question
raised in his Wier oder Weyer?
[Düsseldorf, 1887]

 1. Weir, Johann, 1515-1588. 2. His Weir
oder Weyer? I. Title.

Doctor Lamb revived.
Witchcraft
BF Bower, Edmond.
1581   Doctor Lamb revived; or, Witchcraft
A2 condemn'd in Anne Bodenham, a servant of
B78 his, who was arraigned and executed the
Lent assizes last at Salisbury, before ...
Baron Wild, judge of the assise. Where-
in is set forth her strange and wonderful
diabolical usage of a maid, servant to Mr.
Goddard, as also her attempt against his
daughters ... London, Printed by T. W.
for R. Best and J. Place, 1653.
 44 p. 20 cm.

The doctrine of devils, proved to be the
grand apostacy of these later times.
Witchcraft
BT [Ady, Thomas]
980   The doctrine of devils, proved to be the
A24 grand apostacy of these later times. An essay
tending to rectifie those undue notions and
apprehensions men have about daemons and evil
spirits. London, printed for the author,
1676.
 [8], 205 p. 17cm.

The doctrine of devils, proved to be the
grand apostacy of these later times.
Witchcraft
BT [Orchard, N], supposed author.
980   The doctrine of devils, proved to be the
O64 grand apostacy of these later times. An essay tending to rectifie those undue notions
and apprehensions men have about daemons and
evil spirits. London, Printed for the author, 1676.
 205 p. 17cm.

 Also attributed to Thomas Ady.

 1. Devil. 2. Demonology. I. Title.
II. Ady, Thomas, supposed author.

Un documento de la Inquisición sobre
brujería en Navarra.
WITCHCRAFT
BF Idoate, Florencio, 1912-
1584   Un documento de la Inquisición sobre
S7 brujería en Navarra. Pamplona, Editorial
I21 Aranzadi, 1972.
 193 p. illus. (part fold.) 24cm.

 1. Witchcraft--Navarre (Kingdom) 2.
Inquisition. Spain. 3. Witchcraft--
Spain. I. Title.

Documents inédits sur un procès de
magie en Provence.
WITCHCRAFT
BF Mouan, J L G
1582   Documents inédits sur un procès de magie
Z7 en Provence. (1318) Paris, Impr. impéri-
1318 ale, 1869.
 [169]-182 p. 25cm.

 Extract from the Mémoires lus à la Sorbonne dans les séances extraordinaires du
Comité impérial des travaux historiques et
des sociétés savantes tenues les 14, 15, 16
et 17 avril 1868. Histoire, philologie et
sciences morales.
 1. Trials (Witchcraft)--Aix,France.
2. Robert de Mauvoisin, abp. of Aix.

Documents pour servir à l'histoire des
possédées de Loudun.
WITCHCRAFT
BF Legué, Gabriel, d. 1913.
1517   Documents pour servir à l'histoire des
F5 possédées de Loudun. Paris, A. Delahaye,
L52 1874.
1874   90 p. 22cm.

 Issued also as diss.--Paris.

 1. Loudun, France. Ursuline Convent.
2. Demoniac possession. 3. Grandier, Urbain,
1590-1634.

BV Dölger, Franz Josef, 1879-1940.
803   Der Exorzismus im altchristlichen Tauf-
D65 ritual; eine religionsgeschichtliche Studie.
1967 Paderborn, F. Schöningh, 1909. New York,
Johnson Reprint Corp. [1967]
 xi, 175 p. 23cm. (Studien zur Geschichte und Kultur des Altertums, 3. Bd.,
1.-2. Heft)

 1. Baptism--Hist.--Early church. 2.
Exorcism. I. Title. II. Series.

CATALOGUE OF THE CORNELL WITCHCRAFT COLLECTION

Rare K D65 1693

Döpler, Jacob, 17th cent.
Theatrum poenarum, suppliciorum et executionum criminalium. Oder Schau-Platz, derer Leibes und Lebens-Straffen, welche nicht allein von alters bey allerhand Nationen und Völckern in Gebrauch gewesen, sondern auch noch heut zu Tage in allen vier Welt-Theilen üblich sind. Darinnen zugleich der gantze Inquisitions-Process, Captur, Examination, Confrontation, Tortur ... enthalten ... Anbei mit unterschiedlichen Protocollen, sonderlich bei den Zauber- und Hexen-Torturen..
(Continued on next card)

Rare K D65 1693

Döpler, Jacob, 17th cent. Theatrum poenarum ... 1693-97. (Card 2)
Sondershausen, In Verlegung des Autoris, Druckts Ludwig Schönermarck, 1693-97.
2 v. in 1. 21cm.
Vol. 2 has special t. p.: Theatri poenarum, suppliciorum et executionum criminalium, Oder Schau-Platzes derer Leibes- und Lebens-Strafen anderer Theil ... Leipzig, In Verlegung Friedrich Lanckischen Erben, 1697.
I. Title.

Dogme et rituel de la haute magie.

Witchcraft BF 1612 C75 1861

[Constant, Alphonse Louis] 1810?-1875.
Dogme et rituel de la haute magie, par Éliphas Lévi [pseud.] 2. éd. très augmentée. Paris, G. Baillière; New York, H. Baillière, 1861.
2 v. illus. 22cm.
Contents.--t. 1. Dogme.--t. 2. Rituel.
1. Magic. I. Title.

WITCHCRAFT BF 1584 D4 Z7 1621

Dom over Christence Kruchow for troldom, 1621.
(In: Nye danske magazin. Kjøbenhaven. 24cm. [ser.2] v.1, no.12, 1794, p.378-391)

8 NIC

1. Kruckow, Christence, d.1621. 2.Trials (Witchcraft)--Denmark.

Domesticus, Dominicus, pseud.
see
Dominicus Domesticus, pseud.

Witchcraft BX 2340 D66

Dominicus Domesticus, pseud.
Conjurationes potentissimae, ad fugandas tempestates a daemonibus, seu ab eorum ministris excitatas: unà cum imprecationibus, & maledictionibus, contra animalia, fructus, ac fruges vastantia: ac etiam, cum agrorum, vinearum &c: ac seminis bombicum: & super aegrotantes benedictionibus in fine additis ... Auctore M.R.D.P. Dominico Domestico exorcista pleb. alliati. Brixiae, Sumptibus Caroli Gromi, 1726.
84 p. 13cm.

8

1. Exorcism. 2. Weather-lore. I. Title.

Don Ferdinand Sterzingers Bemühung den Aberglaube zu stürzen.

Witchcraft BF 1410 S83 1785

Sterzinger, Ferdinand, 1721-1786.
Don Ferdinand Sterzingers Bemühung den Aberglaube zu stürzen. München, Bey J. Lentner, 1785.
6 p. l., 187 p. 21cm.
Table of contents bound by mistake between p. 186-187.
First published 1784, according to Kayser.

8

1. Occult sciences. 2. Superstition. I. Title: Bemühung den Aberglaube zu stü rzen.

Don Ferdinand Sterzingers Geister- und Zauberkatekismus.

Witchcraft BF 1603 S83 G3

Sterzinger, Ferdinand, 1721-1786.
Don Ferdinand Sterzingers Geister- und Zauberkatekismus. München, Bey J. N. Fritz, 1783.
72 p. 17cm.
Expansion of his Katekismus von der Geisterlehre, first published 1775 in his Untersuchung, ob es eine Festigkeit gebe, and again in his Die aufgedeckten Gassnerischen Wunderkuren, 1775.

8

1. Magic. 2. Witchcraft. 3. Spirits. I. Title: Geister- und Zauberkateki smus.

Witchcraft BF 1445 D61 no.9

Donati, Christian, praeses.
Disputatio de spectris, quam sub praesidio Dn. Christiani Donati ... publicae ventilationi sistit Johann. Gottlieb Frimel ... Wittenbergae, Typis Christiani Schrödteri [1688]
[34] p. 18cm. (bound in 21cm. vol.)
No. 9 in vol. lettered Dissertationes de spectris. 1646-1753.
1. Spirits. I. Frimel, Johann Gottlieb, respondent. II. Title: De spectris.

8

III. Disputatio de spectris.

Donatus, Christian.
see
Donati, Christian.

RARE HV 8593 D67

Dondorff, Christoph, 1667-1737.
Dissertationem inauguralem De confessione tormentis extorta...publico examini submittit M. Christophorus Dondorff... Lipsiae, Typis Joh. Christoph. Brandenburgeri [1693]
[58] p. 20cm.

8 NIC

Diss.--Leipzig.
1. Torture. 2. Confession (Law) I. Title.

Le donne e il diavolo.

BF 1572 D4 C34

Castellani, Carlo, 1822-1897.
Le donne e il diavolo. Milano, Longanesi [c1963]
238 p. illus. 20cm. (Il Cammeo, v. 183)
1. Witchcraft. 2. Devil. I. Title.
NUC65-31256

Witchcraft Z 6880 Z9 D69

Dorbon aîné, bookseller, Paris.
Bibliotheca esoterica, catalogue annoté et illustré de 6707 ouvrages anciens et modernes, qui traitent des sciences occultes ... comme aussi des sociétés secrètes ... En vente à la Librairie Dorbon-aîné. Paris [1940]
2 p. l., 656 p., 2 l. illus. (incl. music) plates, facsims. 25cm.

1. Occult sciences--Bibl.--Catalogs. 2. Secret societies--Bibl.--Catalogs. I. Title.
Library of Congress   Z6880.Z9D6   43-36450
[3]   016.13

Witchcraft Z 6880 Z9 D685

Dorbon, bookseller, Paris.
Catalogue ... de livres et manuscrits relatifs aux sciences occultes ... Provenant de la bibliothèque de feu Stanislaus de Guaita ... En vente aux prix marqués à la Librairie Dorbon. Paris, 1898-1899.
4 nos. 22cm. (Its Catalogue 180, 182, 184, 186)
In envelope.
1. Occult sciences--Bibl.--Catalogs. I. Guaita, Stanislaus de, 1860-1897.

8

Witchcraft GR 166 D69 1750

Das Dorfconvent, welches allerley Gespräche von Hexen, Gespenstern, Schätzgräbern, und Naturerscheinungen enthält. Hrsg. vom Schulmeister zu Glücksfeld. Ganz neu gedruckt. [n. p., 1750?]
64 p. illus. 16cm.

1. Folk-lore, German. I. Der Schulmeister zu Glücksfeld, pseud.

Witchcraft BX 1710 M39 1679

Doriguzzi, Natale, ed.
[Masini, Eliseo] brother, 17th cent.
Sacro arsenale, ouero Prattica dell'Officio della Santa Inqvisitione. Di nuouo corretto, & ampliato ... Bologna, Per Gioseffo Longhi, 1679.
[14], 528 p. 17cm.
Edited by Natale Doriguzzi.
I. Doriguzzi, Natale, ed. II. Title.
[Secular name: Cesare Masini]

Witchcraft BF 1555 D71 1743

Dorsch, Johann Georg, 1597-1659, praeses.
Dispvtatio theologica De horrenda et miserabili Satanae obsessione eivsdemqve ex obsessis expvlsione, non leibl. Besitzungen. Svb praesidio Dn. Io. Georg. Dorschei ...a. 1656 d. 23. Avg. pvblico ervditorvm examini svbmissa ab avtore et respondente Daniel Springinsgut ... Vitembergae, Ex officina Scheffleriana, 1743.
48 p. 20cm.

8

Continued on next card)

Witchcraft BF 1555 D71 1743

Dorsch, Johann Georg, 1597-1659, praeses.
Dispvtatio theologica De horrenda et miserabili Satanae obsessione ... 1743. (Card 2)

1. Demoniac possession. 2. Exorcism. I. Springinsgut, Daniel, respondent. II. Title: De horrenda et miserabili Satanae obsessione. III. Disputatio theologica De horrenda et mis erabili Satanae obsess

CATALOGUE OF THE CORNELL WITCHCRAFT COLLECTION

```
                Dorsch, Johann Georg, 1597-1659, praeses.
                   Disputatio theologica De horrenda et
                miserabili Satanae obsessione.
Witchcraft
BF           Dorsch, Johann Georg, 1597-1659, praeses.
1555            Summi theologi D. Joh. Georgii Dorschei,
D71          dissertatio De horrenda & miserabili Sata-
1667         nae obsessione, ejusdemqve ex obsessis ex-
             pulsione, multorum votis expetita, juven-
             tutis studiosae commodo iterum prodit.
             Rostochii, Typis Johannis Richelii, 1667.
                [24] p.  20cm.
                Presented August 23, 1656, with D.
             Springinsgut as respondent, and title:
             Disputatio theo    logica De horrenda et
 8           miserabili Sa             tanae obsessione.
                           (Continued on next card)
```

```
Witchcraft
BF           Dorsch, Johann Georg, 1597-1659, praeses.
1555            Summi theologi D. Joh. Georgii Dorschei,
D71          dissertatio De horrenda & miserabili Sata-
1667         nae obsessione, ejusdemqve ex obsessis ex-
             pulsione, multorum votis expetita, juven-
             tutis studiosae commodo iterum prodit.
             Rostochii, Typis Johannis Richelii, 1667.
                [24] p.  20cm.
                Presented August 23, 1656, with D.
             Springinsgut as respondent, and title:
             Disputatio theo    logica De horrenda et
 8           miserabili Sa             tanae obsessione.
                           (Continued on next card)
```

```
Witchcraft
BF           Dorsch, Johann Georg, 1597-1659, praeses.
1555            Summi theologi ... 1667.   (Card 2)
D71
1667
             1. Demoniac possession.  2. Exorcism.
             I.  Springinsgut, Daniel, respondent.  II.
             His  Disputatio theologica De horrenda et
             miserbili Satanae obsessione.  III. Title:
             De horrenda et miserabili Satanae obsessione.
             IV. Summi theologi D. Joh. Georgii Dorschei,
             dissertatio De horrenda & miserabili Satanae
 8           obsessione.
```

```
                Die Doruchower Hexenverbrennung vom
WITCHCRAFT   Jahre 1775.
BF              Pietsch, Paul.
1584            Die Doruchower Hexenverbrennung vom Jahre
P6           1775.
P62             (In: Historische Gesellschaft für die
             Provinz Posen.  Zeitschrift. Posen. 24cm.
             v.14, no. 3/4, July/Dec. 1899. p. 336-339)

                1. Witchcraft--Posen (Province) 2.Trials
 8           (Witchcraft)       --Posen (Province)
NIC          I. Title.
```

```
Witchcraft
BL           Doughty, Henry Montagu,
490             Witchcraft and Christianity.  [Edinburgh,
D73          1898]
                378-397 p.  24cm.

                Extract from Blackwood's Edinburgh
             magazine, vol. 163, March 1898.

                1. Superstition.  I. Title.
```

```
             Dr. Dietrich Flade, ein Opfer des Hexenwahnes.
BF              Zenz, Emil
1583            Dr. Dietrich Flade, ein Opfer des Hexen-
F56          wahnes.  Trier, J. Lintz, 1962.
                41-69 p. 24cm.

                Caption title.
                "Kurtrierisches Jahrbuch. Jahrgang 2,
             1962. Sonderabdruck."

               1. Flade, Dietrich, 1534-1589.  2. Witch-
             craft--Germany.   I. Title.
```

```
             Dr. Hartlieb's Buch aller verbotenen
MSS            Kunst.
Bd.             Hartlieb, Johann, fl. 1450.
WITCHCRAFT      Dr. Hartlieb's Buch aller verbotenen Kunst,
BF           Unglaubens und der Zauberei.  [n.p. 1456;
H32          1896]
                153 p.  23cm.
                Carnap's manuscript copy.
                "Wörtlich genaue Abschrift der Handschrift
             ... in der Herzoglichen Bibliothek zu
             Wolfenbüttel."
                Numerals in the margins indicate foliation
             of the origin        al.
                         (Continued on next card)
```

```
             Dr. Hartlieb's Buch aller verbotenen
MSS            Kunst.
Bd.             Hartlieb, Johann, fl. 1450.  Buch aller
WITCHCRAFT   verbotenen Kunst ...  [1456; 1896]  (Card 2)
BF
H32             Between pages 134 and 135 are inserted
             5 unnumbered leaves of "Erläuterungen".
             P. 135-153 are copies of short articles on
             the original work.

                1. Magic.  2. Witchcraft.  3. Devil.
             I. Title.
```

```
             Dr. med. Johannes Wier, der Leibarzt des
Witchcraft     Herzogs Wilhelm III. von Cleve-Jülich-Berg.
BF              Eschbach, H
1520            Dr. med. Johannes Wier, der Leibarzt des
W64          Herzogs Wilhelm III. von Cleve-Jülich-Berg.
P83          Ein Beitrag zur Geschichte der Hexenprozesse.
                (In Düsseldorfer Jahrbuch. Beiträge zur
             Geschichte des Niederrheins. Düsseldorf. 23cm.
             1. Band (1886), p. [57]-174)
                1. Wier, Johann, 1515-1588. De praestigiis
             demonum. 2. Wier, Johann, 1515-1588. 3. Witch-
             craft--Germany.  I. Title.  II. Düsseldorfer
             Jahrbücher. Beiträge zur Geschichte des
             Niederrheins.
```

```
             Dr. White on witchcraft.
Witchcraft
BF              Schwickerath, Robert.
1566            Dr. White on witchcraft.
S41             (In The Messenger. New York, N. Y.
             25cm.  v. 43, no. 6 (1905), p. 593-605)

                With MS annotations by A. D. White.

                1. White, Andrew Dickson, 1832-1918.
             Seven great statesmen in the warfare of
             humanity with unreason. 2. Witchcraft.
             I. Title.
```

```
             Drabik, Mikuláš, 1588-1671.
Witchcraft
BF              [Comenius, Johann Amos] 1592-1670, comp.
1785            Lux e tenebris, novis radiis aucta.  Hoc
C73          est: solemnissimae divinae revelationes, in
1665         usum seculi nostri factae ... Per immissas
             visiones, & angelica divináqve alloqvia,
             facta I.  Christophoro Kottero silesio, ab
             anno 1616, ad 1624.  II. Christinae Ponia-
             toviae bohemae, annis 1627, 1628, 1629,
             III. Nicolao Drabicio moravo, ab anno 1638,
             ad 1664 ...  Amstelodami, 1665.
                various pagings.  illus., ports. 21cm.
                Added engr.    t. p.
 8                         (Continued on next card)
```

```
             Drabik, Mikuláš, 1588-1671.
Witchcraft
BF              [Comenius, Johann Amos] 1592-1670, comp.
1785            Lux e tenebris ...  1665.   (Card 2)
C73
1665            "Voluminis prophetici," first item, has
             special t. p. with imprint 1667.
                "Revelationes Christophoro Kottero" and
             "Revelationes Christinae Poniatoviae" each
             have special t. p. with imprint 1664.
                "Revelationes Nicolao Drabicio" has
             special t. p. without imprint.
                First published 1657 with title: Lux
 8           in tenebris.       (Continued on next card)
```

```
             Drachen-König.
WITCHCRAFT      Rimphoff, Hinrich, 1599-1655.
BF              Drachen-König; das ist: Warhafftige, deut-
1583         liche, christliche, vnd hochnothwendige
A2           Beschreybunge, dess grawsamen, hochvermale-
R567         deyten Hexen, vnd Zauber Teuffels, welcher
             durch Gottes sonderbahre direction, Schi-
             kunge vnd Gnade, an diesem Ort bald fürm
             Jahr, durch ein neunjähriges Mägdelein,
             wieder aller Menschen Gedancken manifestirt,
             vnd gantz wunderbarlich aus Liecht gebracht.
 8           Zu Salvir,         vnd Rettunge vieler
NIC          christlicher,      vnschuldiger, frommer
                            (Continued on next card)
```

```
             Drachen-König
WITCHCRAFT      Rimphoff, Hinrich, 1599-1655.
BF              Drachen-König...           (Card 2)
1583
A2              Hertzen dieses Orts, auch zur Warnunge aller
R567         Hexen Patronen, Adhaerenten, Vorfechteren
             vnd leichtfertigen Calumnianten.  Sampt
             einem Appendice wider Johan Seiferten von
             Ulm ...  Auss hoher Noth öffentlich in den
             Druck gegeben, durch Heinricum Rimphof.
             Rinteln, Druckts P. Lucius, 1647.
                566 p.  16        cm.

                               (Continued on next card)
```

```
Witchcraft
BF           [Drage, William] 1637?-1669.
1611            Daimonomageia. A small treatise of
D75          sicknesses and diseases from witchcraft
             and supernatural causes. Never before,
             at least in this comprised order and gen-
             eral manner, was the like published. Being
             useful to others besides physicians, in
             that it confutes atheistical, sadducistical,
             and sceptical principles and imaginations.
             London, Printed by J. Dover, 1665.
                [43] p.  20cm.

                               (Continued on next card)
```

```
Witchcraft
BF           [Drage, William] 1637?-1669. Daimonomageia.
1611            1665.   (Card 2)
D75
                Imperfect: lacks all after p. 32.
                Wing D 2117.
                Bound with his A physical nosonomy.
             London, 1664.


                1. Medicine, Magic, mystic and spagiric.
             I. Title.
```

```
Witchcraft
GR           Drage, William, 1637?-1669.
142             A relation of Mary Hall of Gadsden, reputed to be
H6           possessed of two devils, 1664, from "A small treatise of
A3           sicknesses and diseases from witchcraft," appended to
no.15        "Physical experiments," by William Drage, London.
             Printed for Miller at the Star next the George in Little
             Britain [1668]  With an introductory by W. B. Gerish.
             Bishop's Stortford, 1912.
                28 p.  22cm.  [Hertfordshire folk lore. no. 15]

                1. Demonomania.  2. Hall, Mary, fl. 1664.  I. Gerish, William Blyth, ed.
             II. Title.                                          16-25740
```

```
WITCHCRAFT   Le Dragon rouge, ou l'art de commander les
BF              esprits célestes, aériens, terrestres,
1558         infernaux, avec le vrai secret de faire
G86          parler les morts, de gagner toutes les
1823         fois qu'on met aux loteries, de décou-
             vrir les trésors cachés, etc., etc.
             Imprimé sur un manuscrit de 1522.
             Nismes, Chez Gaude, 1823.
                108 p.  illus.  15cm.
                Published also under other titles: Gri-
 8           moire du Pape       Honorius [best-known];
                              (Continued on next card)
```

CATALOGUE OF THE CORNELL WITCHCRAFT COLLECTION

WITCHCRAFT
BF 1558 G86 1823
Le Dragon rouge ... 1823. (Card 2)
Le véritable dragon rouge; and L'art de commander les esprits.
Chapter 1 signed: Antonio Venitiana, del Rabbina.

1. Incantations. 2. Magic. I. Venitiana, Antonio, del Rabbina. II. Title: Grimoire du Pape Honorius. III. Title: Le véritable dragon rouge. IV. Title: L'art de commander les esprits.

8

Le dragon rouge.

WITCHCRAFT
BF 1558 G86 1750
L'Art de commander les esprits célestes, aëriens, terrestres & infernaux. Suivi du Grand grimoire, de la magie noire et des forces infernales, du docteur J. Karter, La clavicule de Salomon, &c. Avec le vrai secret de faire parler les morts, pour découvrir tous les trésors caches, &c. &c. [Paris?] 1421 [i.e., ca. 1750?] iv, 5-108 [i. e., 118], [2] p. illus. 16cm.
Title in red and black.

8
(Continued on next card)

Le dragon rouge.

WITCHCRAFT
BF 1558 G86 1750
L'Art de commander les esprits ... [1750?] (Card 2)
Published also under other titles: Grimoire du Pape Honorius [best-known]; Le dragon rouge; and Le véritable dragon rouge.

1. Incantations. 2. Magic. I. Karter, J. II. Title: Le grand grimoire. III. Title: Grimoire du Pape Honorius. IV. Title: Le dragon rouge. V. Title: Le véritable dragon rouge. VI. Title: La clavicule de Salomon.

8

Le dragon rouge.

WITCHCRAFT
BF 1558 G86 1800a
Le Véritable dragon rouge, ou l'Art de commander les esprits célestes, aériens, terrestres et infernaux, avec le secret de faire parler les morts; de gagner toutes les fois qu'on met aux loteries; de découvrir les trésors cachés; etc., etc.; suivi de La poule noire, cabale qui était restée inconnue jusqu'ici. [Lille, Imprimerie de Blocquel] 1521 [i.e., 18--] 140 p. illus. 16cm.

8
(Continued on next card)

Le dragon rouge.

WITCHCRAFT
BF 1558 G86 1800a
Le Véritable dragon rouge ... [18--] (Card 2)
Title in red and black.
Chapter 1 signed: J. Karter, Venetiana.
Published also under other titles: Grimoire du Pape Honorius [best-known]; Le dragon rouge; and L'art de commander les esprits.

1. Incantations. 2. Magic. I. Karter, J. II. Title: Grimoire du Pape Honorius. III. Title: Le dragon rouge. IV. Title: L'art de commander les esprits. V. Title: La poule noire.

8

Witchcraft
BF 1576 D76
Drake, Samuel Gardner, 1798-1875.
Annals of witchcraft in New England, and elsewhere in the United States, from their first settlement. Drawn up from unpublished and other well authenticated records of the alleged operations of witches and their instigator, the devil. By Samuel G. Drake. Boston, W. E. Woodward, 1869.
liii, [55]-306 p. front. (port.) 22x17½cm. (half-title: Woodward's historical series, no. VIII)
An edition of two hundred and seventy-five copies printed.
1. Witchcraft--New England. I. Title.

8

Witchcraft
BF 1575 D76
Drake, Samuel Gardner, 1798-1875, *comp.*
The witchcraft delusion in New England; its rise, progress, and termination, as exhibited by Dr. Cotton Mather, in The wonders of the invisible world; and by Mr. Robert Calef, in his More wonders of the invisible world. With a preface, introduction, and notes, by Samuel G. Drake ... Roxbury, Mass., Printed for W. E. Woodward, 1866.
3 v. 21½ x 17 cm. (Half-title: Woodward's historical series, no. V-VII)
No. 89 of an "edition in this size" of 280 copies.
Includes reprints of original title-pages.
CONTENTS.--v. 1. The wonders of the invisible world ... By Cotton Mather.--v. 2-3. More wonders of the invisible world ... Collected by Robert Calef.
1. Witchcraft--New England. I. Mather, Cotton, 1663-1728. II. Calef, Robert, 1648-1719. III. Title.
BF1575.D75   11—9005
Library of Congress

BF 1575 D76
Drake, Samuel Gardner, 1798-1875, *comp.*
The witchcraft delusion in New England; its rise, progress, and termination, as exhibited by Dr. Cotton Mather, in The wonders of the invisible world; and by Mr. Robert Calef, in his More wonders of the invisible world. With a preface, introduction, and notes, by Samuel G. Drake ... Roxbury, Mass., Printed for W. E. Woodward, 1866.
3 v. 21½ x 17 cm. (Half-title: Woodward's historical series, no. V-VII)
No. 89 of an "edition in this size" of 280 copies.
Includes reprints of original title-pages.
CONTENTS.--v. 1. The wonders of the invisible world ... By Cotton Mather.--v. 2-3. More wonders of the invisible world ... Collected by Robert Calef.
1. Witchcraft--New England. I. Mather, Cotton, 1663-1728. II. Calef, Robert, 1648-1719. III. Title.
BF1575.D75   11—9005
Library of Congress

Drechsler, Johann Gabriel, d. 1677.

see

Drechssler, Johann Gabriel, d. 1677.

Witchcraft
BF 1445 D61 no.6
Drechssler, Johann Gabriel, d. 1677, praeses.
De spectris, disputationem II. Inclut. facultat. philosoph. Lipsiensis consensu P. P. praeses M. Johannes Gabriel Drechssler ... et respondens Christianus Michelmann ... Lipsiae, Literis Johannis Erici Hahnii [1669] [12] p. 21cm.
No. 6 in vol. lettered Dissertationes de spectris. 1646-1753.
1. Rechenberg, Adam, 1642-1721, praeses. De spectris. 2. Apparitions. 3. Devil. I. Michelmann, Christian, respondent. II. Title.

8

Drechssler, Johann Gabriel, d. 1677, praeses.

Witchcraft
BF 1445 D61 no.7
Drechssler, Johann Gabriel, d. 1677, praeses.
De spectris, & in specie eorum depulsione, disputationem III. Inclut. facultatis philosoph. Lipsiensis indultu, sub praesidio M. Johannis Gabrielis Drechsslers, ... publicè defendet respondens Jacobus Friedrich Müller ... Lipsiae, Excudebat Samuel Spörel [1670] [20] p. illus. 21cm.
No. 7 in vol. lettered Dissertationes de spectris. 1646-1753.

8
(Continued on next card)

Witchcraft
BF 1445 D61 no.7
Drechssler, Johann Gabriel, d. 1677, praeses.
De spectris, & in specie eorum depulsione, disputationem III. Inclut. facultatis philosoph. Lipsiensis indultu, sub praesidio M. Johannis Gabrielis Drechsslers, ... publicè defendet respondens Jacobus Friedrich Müller ... Lipsiae, Excudebat Samuel Spörel [1670] [20] p. illus. 21cm.
No. 7 in vol. lettered Dissertationes de spectris. 1646-1753.

8
(Continued on next card)

Witchcraft
BF 1445 D61 no.7
Drechssler, Johann Gabriel, d. 1677, praeses.
De spectris, & in specie eorum depulsione ... [1670] (Card 2)

1. Exorcism. 2. His De spectris, disputationem II. 3. Demonology. I. Müller, Jacobus Friedrich, respondent. II. Title.

8

Drechssler, Johann Gabriel, d. 1677, respondent.

Witchcraft
BF 1445 D61 no.5
Rechenberg, Adam, 1642-1721, praeses.
De spectris, incl. facult. philosoph. annuente, praeside Domino M. Adamo Rechenberg, ... publicè disputabit ... Johannes Gabriel Drechssler, ... A. & R. ... Lipsiae, Literis Johannis Erici Hahnii [1668] [20] p. 19cm. (bound in 21cm. vol.)
No. 5 in vol. lettered Dissertationes de spectris. 1646-1753.
1. Apparitions. I. Drechssler, Johann Gabriel, d. 1677, respondent. II. Title.

8

Drei Hexenverbrennungen zu Ulm.

WITCHCRAFT
BF 1583 S33+
Schilling, A
Drei Hexenverbrennungen zu Ulm. [Stuttgart, 1883] 137-141 p. 28cm.
Detached from Sitzungsberichte (?) of the Württembergischer Altertumsverein.

1. Trials (Witchcraft)--Ulm, Germany. 2. Witchcraft--Germany. I. Title.

8
NIC

HIST SCI R 133 D77
Dresde, Fridericus Guilielmus.
De daemonibus morbisque daemoniacis medica arte tollendis disserit et fratri dulcissimo Ioanni Eliae Dresdio doctori artis medicae recens creato honores novos gratulatur Fridericus Guilielmus Dresde. Lipsiae, Ex officina Langenhemia [1763] 40 p. 19cm.

1. Medicine, Magic, mystic and spagiric. 2. Demonology. I. Dresde, Joannes Elias. II. Title.

8
NIC

Dresde, Joannes Elias.

HIST SCI R 133 D77
Dresde, Fridericus Guilielmus.
De daemonibus morbisque daemoniacis medica arte tollendis disserit et fratri dulcissimo Ioanni Eliae Dresdio doctori artis medicae recens creato honores novos gratulatur Fridericus Guilielmus Dresde. Lipsiae, Ex officina Langenhemia [1763] 40 p. 19cm.

1. Medicine, Magic, mystic and spagiric. 2. Demonology. I. Dresde, Joannes Elias. II. Title.

8
NIC

Witchcraft
BF 1565 S83 no.3
Drey Fragen zur Vertheidigung der Hexerey. I. Ob P. Angelus März die Rede des P. Don Ferdinand Sterzingers gründlich, und II. bescheiden widerlegt habe? III. Und ob wohl diese akademische Rede dem heiligen Kreutze von Scheyrn in der That nachtheilig sey? Mit einem sichern Ja beantwortet, und dem P. Angelus März selbst dedicirt von J. F. Z. ... [München?] 1767. 28 p. 23cm.

8
(Continued on next card)

CATALOGUE OF THE CORNELL WITCHCRAFT COLLECTION

Witchcraft

Drey Fragen zur Vertheidigung der Hexerey ... 1767. (Card 2)

"In spite of the initials J. F. Z. (Johann Felix Zech) in the dedication, the work is probably by H. Braun. See Fieger, H. P. Don Ferdinand Sterzinger, 1907."--Note by G. L. Burr on his ms. catalog slip for this item.

No. 3 in vol. lettered Sterzinger über Hexerei, 1766-1767.

(Continued on next card)

Witchcraft

Drey Fragen zur Vertheidigung der Hexerey ... 1767. (Card 3)

1. März, Angelus, 1731-1784. Kurze Vertheidigung der thätigen Hex- und Zauberey. 2. Sterzinger, Ferdinand, 1721-1786. Akademische Rede von dem gemeinen Vorurtheile der Hexerey. 3. Witchcraft. I. Zech, Johann Nepomuk Felix, supposed author. II. Braun, Heinrich, 1732-1792, supposed author. III.   J. F. Z. IV. Z., J. F.

Drey warhafftige grundtliche Zeitungen, die erste von etlichen Hexen und Zauberin welche hin und wider in Ungern und Teutschland grossen Schaden angerichtet haben... Beschriben durch den hochgelerten Herrn Nicolaum Binder... Die ander von einem Burger und Thuchmacher der in grosser Unzucht ein zeitlang gelebt ... unnd wie er durch dess Teufels Eingebung 3. Kinder und sein Weib jämmerlicher weiss ermördet... Die dritte   von Erscheinung zweyer

(Continued on next card)

Drey warhafftige grundtliche Zeitungen ... 1610 [ca. 1900] (Card 2)

Engel... Beschriben durch den ehrwürdigen Herrn Joannem Röseler diser Zeit Pfarrern daselbsten. Erstlich Getruckt zu Tirnau in Ungern nachmals aber zu Freyburg, bey Georg Hofmann, 1610 [ca. 1900] [7] l. 24cm.

T. p. added by scribe: [Kerpffen]
(Continued on next card)

Drey warhafftige grundtliche Zeitungen ... 1610 [ca. 1900] (Card 3)

Drey warhafftige Zeitungen. Die erste von etlichen Hexen in Ungern, den 11. October 1609. Beschriben durch Nicolaus Binder. &c. 1610.
Carnap's manuscript copy.
"Originaldruck in der Stadtbibliothek zu Zürich. 4 Bl. in 4°."
Numerals in the margins indicate the paginati   on of the original.
(Continued on next card)

Drey warhafftige grundtliche Zeitungen ... 1610 [ca. 1900] (Card 4)

In verse.

1. Witchcraft. 2. Apparitions. I. Prock, Hans, d. 1610. II. Binder, Nicolaus. III. Röseler, Joannes.

Witchcraft
BF 1565
D77

Drey wichtige Fragen über das Hexen-System von einem gesunden, unverruckten Kopf disseits der Donau. [n. p.] 1767.
24 p. 21cm.
H. Fieger, in P. Don Ferdinand Sterzinger, attributes this work to one "Premb, Weltpriester."
1. Witchcraft. 2. Sterzinger, Ferdinand, 1721-1786. Akademische Rede von dem gemeinen Vorurtheile der ... Hexerey. I. Premb,   , supposed author. II. Ein gesunder, unverruckter Kopf disseits der Donau.

Drie resolutien des Classis van Amsterdam...

Witchcraft
BF 1410
B42
Z56
v.3
no.12

[Bekker, Balthasar] 1634-1698.
Drie resolutien des Classis van Amsterdam, by deselve genomen op den 22. Jan. 8. April en 21. July deses jaars, in de sake van Balthasar Bekker predikant tot Amsterdam, betreffende sijn boek De betoverde weereld. Waar by gevoegt zijn enige reflexien van onbekende hand den Auteur daar over toegesonden. Amsterdam, By D. van den Dalen, boekverkooper, 1692.
16, 16 p. title and end page vignettes. 19 x 15cm.

(Continued on next card)

Drie resolutien des Classis van Amsterdam.

Witchcraft
BF 1410
B42
Z56
v.3
no.12

[Bekker, Balthasar] 1634-1698. Drie resolutien des Classis van Amsterdam ... 1692. (Card 2)

4°: A-B⁴, A-B⁴.
"Aanmerkinge op de handelingen der twee laatste noordhollandsche synoden, in de sake van B. Bekker, ten opsighte van sijn boek genaamd De betoverde weereld; nu versch t' Enkhuisen gedrukt:" 16 p.
Last p. autographed by Bekker, dated 2/13 Octob. 1692.

(Continued on next card)

Drie resolutien des Classis van Amsterdam..

Witchcraft
BF 1410
B42
Z56
v.3
no.12

[Bekker, Balthasar] 1634-1698. Drie resolutien des Classis van Amsterdam ... 1692. (Card 3)

In the first section, Bekker quotes the resolutions which he discusses.
Van der Linde 44, 52.
No. 12 in vol. lettered Bekker III.
1. Bekker, Balthasar, 1634-1698. De betoverde weereld. I. Nederlandse Hervormde Kerk. Classes. Amsterdam.
II. Title.   III. His   Aanmerkinge

(Continued on next card)

Witchcraft
BF 1600
D36
1611

Duchesne, André, 1584-1640, tr.
Del Rio, Martin Antoine, 1551-1608. Les controverses et recherches magiques. Divisees en six livres, ausquels sont exactement & doctement confutees les sciences curieuses, les vanitez, & superstitions de toute la magie. Avec qves la maniere de proceder en iustice contre les magiciens et sorciers, accommodee à l'instruction des confesseurs ... Traduit et abregé du Latin par André dv Chesne. Paris, Chez Iean Petit-Pas, 1611.
[32], 1024 (i.e. 1104), [54] p. 19cm.
Errors in paging: 1100-1104 numbered 1101,

(Continued on next card)

Witchcraft
BF 1600
D36
1611

Duchesne, André, 1584-1640, tr.
Del Rio, Martin Antoine, 1551-1608. Les controverses et recherches magiques ... 1611. (Card 2)

1102, 1002, 1003 and 1024 respectively.
Translation of Disquisitionum magicarum libri sex.

1. Magic. 2. Witchcraft. I. Del Rio, Martin Antoine, 1551-1608. Disquisitionum magicarum libri sex--French. II. Duchesne, André 1584-1640, tr. III. Title.

Witchcraft
BF 1565
S42
1638

DuClercq, Jacques, seigneur de Beauvoir en Ternois, b. 1420.
Scot, Reginald, 1538?-1599. Ontdecking van tovery, beschreven int Engels door Reinald Scot, verduyscht by Th. en G. Basson. Beverwyck, Gedruckt by Frans Pels, 1638.
15 p. l., 351, [17] p. 15cm.
With engraved t. p., depicting a witch. Abridgment and translation of Discoverie of witchcraft.
To this are appended: Historie van 't ghene gheschiet   is in 't Graefschap van

(Continued on next card)

Witchcraft
BF 1565
S42
1638

DuClercq, Jacques, seigneur de Beauvoir en Ternois, b. 1420.
Scot, Reginald, 1538?-1599. Ontdecking van tovery ... 1638. (Card 2)
Artoys ..., door J. DuClercq, with special t. p.; Extract uyt 't playdoye van M. L. Servin; Historie van de Maegt van Orleans ... Extract uyt J. P. van Bergamo; and various poems.
1. Witchcraft. 2. Magic. 3. Demonology. I. His Discoverie of witchcraft. Dutch. II. DuClercq, Jacques, seigneur
(Continued on next card)

Dudouet, Dr.

WITCHCRAFT
BF 1555
P827

Porée, Charles Gabriel.
Le pour et contre de la possession des filles de la parroisse de Landes, diocése de Bayeux [par C.-G. Porée et Dudouet, médicin] ... A Antioche, Chez les Héritiers de la bonne foy, 1738.
275 p. 19cm.

1. Demoniac possession. I. Dudouet, Dr. III. Title.

Witchcraft
PT 2430
M35
M3
1844

Duff-Gordon, Lucie (Austin), lady, 1821-1869, tr.
Meinhold, Wilhelm, 1797-1851.
Mary Schweidler, the amber witch. The most interesting trial for witchcraft ever known. Printed from an imperfect manuscript by her father, Abraham Schweidler, the pastor of Coserow, in the island of Usedom. Translated from the German by Lady Duff Gordon. London, J. Murray, 1844.
xi,171 p. 19cm.

Translation of his Maria Schweidler, die Bernsteinhexe.

WITCHCRAFT
PT 2430
M35
S5
1894

Duff-Gordon, Lucie (Austin) lady, 1821-1869, tr.
Meinhold, Wilhelm, 1797-1851.
Sidonia, the sorceress, the supposed destroyer of the whole reigning ducal house of Pomerania, translated by Lady Wilde; Mary Schweidler, the amber witch... London, Reeves and Turner, 1894.
2 v. 20cm.

Translation of Sidonia von Bork, die Klosterhexe, and Maria Schweidler, die Bernsteinhexe.

(Continued on next card)

Witchcraft
PT 2430
M35
S5
1894

Duff-Gordon, Lucie (Austin) lady, 1821-1869, tr.
Meinhold, Wilhelm, 1797-1851. Sidonia, the sorceress... 1894. (Card 2)

"Mary Schweidler" translated by Lady Duff Gordon.

1. Witchcraft--Pomerania. I. Meinhold, Wilhelm, 1797-1851. Sidonia von Bork, die Klosterhexe--English. II. Meinhold, Wilhelm, 1797-1851. Maria Schweidler, die Bernsteinhexe--English. III. Wilde, Jane Francesca (Elgee) lady, 1826-1896, tr. IV. Duff-Gordon, Lucie (Austin) lady, 1821-1869, tr. V. Title: Sidonia, the sorceress. VI. Title: Mary Schweidler, the amber witch.

CATALOGUE OF THE CORNELL WITCHCRAFT COLLECTION

Dugdale, Richard.

Witchcraft
BF
1555
J75V7

[Jollie, Thomas] 1629-1703.
A vindication of the Surey demoniack as no impostor: or, A reply to a certain pamphlet publish'd by Mr. Zach. Taylor, called The Surey impostor. With a further clearing and confirming of the truth as to Richard Dugdale's case and cure. By T. J., one of the ministers who attended upon that affair from first to last ... To which is annexed a brief narrative of the Surey demoniack, drawn up by the same author, for the satisfaction of such who have not
(Continued on next card)

Dugdale, Richard.

Witchcraft
BF
1555
J75V7

[Jollie, Thomas] 1629-1703. A vindication of the Surey demoniack ... 1698.   (Card 2)

seen the former narrative... London, Printed for N. Simmons, and sold by G. Conyers, 1698.
80 p. 21cm.

Wing J 889.

1. Dugdale, Richard. 2. Taylor, Zachary. The Surey imposter, being an answer to ... The surey demoniack. I. Title.

Witchcraft
BT
15
D86

[Duguet, Jacques Joseph] 1649-1732.
Dissertations theologiques et dogmatiques, I. Sur les exorcismes & les autres céremonies du batême. II. Sur l'eucharistie. III. Sur l'usure. Paris, J. Estienne, 1727.
3 pts. in 1 v. 17cm.

Parts 2 and 3 paged continuously.

1. Exorcism. 2. Lord's Supper. 3. Interest and usury. I. Title.

Witchcraft
BS
1199
D4
D87

Duhm, Hans.
Die bösen Geister im Alten Testament.
Tübingen, P. Siebeck, 1904.
iv, 68 p. 24cm.

1. Bible and spiritualism. 2. Legends, Jewish. 3. Devil--Biblical teaching. I. Title.

Witchcraft
PT
1792
D87

Duhr, Bernhard, 1852-1930.
Neue Daten und Briefe zum Leben des P. Friedrich Spe.
(In Görres-Gesellschaft zur Pflege der Wissenschaft im katholischen Deutschland, Bonn. Historisches Jahrbuch. München. 24cm. 21. Bd., 2. u. 3. Heft (1900), p. [328]-352)

1. Spee, Friedrich von, 1591-1635. 2. Witchcraft--Germany. I. Title. II. Görres-Gesellschaft zur Pflege der Wissenschaft im katholischen Deutschland, Bonn. Historisches Jahrbuch.

8

Witchcraft
BF
1565
L42
D87

Duhr, Bernhard, 1852-1930.
Paul Laymann und die Hexenprozesse.
(In Zeitschrift für katholische Theologie. Innsbruck. 23cm. 23. Bd., 4. Heft (1899), p. 733-745)

1. Laymann, Paul, 1574-1635. Processus juridicus contra sagas et veneficos. 2. Trials (Witchcraft)--Germany. I. Title. II. Zeitschrift für katholische Theologie.

8

Witchcraft
BF
1583
D87

Duhr, Bernhard, 1852-1930.
Die Stellung der Jesuiten in den deutschen Hexenprozessen. Köln, J.P. Bachem, 1900.
92 p. 25cm. (Görres-Gesellschaft zur Pflege der Wissenschaft im katholischen Deutschland, Bonn. Schriften, 1900, 1)

1. Witchcraft--Germany. 2. Jesuits. I. Series. II. Title.

BF
1583
D87

Duhr, Bernhard, 1852-1930.
Die Stellung der Jesuiten in den deutschen Hexenprozessen. Köln, J.P. Bachem, 1900.
92 p. 25cm. (Görres-Gesellschaft zur Pflege der Wissenschaft im katholischen Deutschland, Bonn. Schriften, 1900, 1)

1. Witchcraft--Germany. 2. Jesuits. I. Series.

Duhr, Bernhard, 1852-1930.

WITCHCRAFT
PT
1792
D56
1901

Diel, Johannes Baptista, 1843-1875.
Friedrich Spe. Von Johannes Diel. 2., umgearb. Aufl. von Barnhard Duhr. Freiburg i. B., Herder, 1901.
viii, 147 p. port., facsim. 20cm. (Sammlung historischer Bildnisse. [IX])
First published 1872 under title: Friedrich von Spee.
Very extensively revised.
1. Spee, Friedrich von, 1591-1635. I. Duhr, Bernhard, 1852-1930.

8
NIC

Witchcraft
BF
1411
D88

Dumcke, Julius, 1867-
Zauberei und Hexenprozess. Berlin, A. Scherl [1912]
323 p. 17cm.

1. Occult sciences. I. Title.

Duns, Joannes, Scotus, 1265?-1308?

WITCHCRAFT
BX
2340
M66

Ministerium exorcisticum, quo exorcista possessos, obsessos, & maleficiatos a daemonijs...liberare potest. Cum annexis thesibus theologicis ad mentem...Joannis Duns-Scoti ex tribus libris sententiarum, quas...publice defendendas susceperunt praeside M. R. P. Adolpho Medelsky... Franciscus Solanus Monschmidt & ...Gelasius Stoephel .. Oppaviae, Typis Joannis W. Schindler [1738]
99 p. 17cm.
Apparently a cooperative undertaking of the Franciscan Fathers in Moravia.
(Continued on next card)

8
NIC

Duny, Amy, fl. 1664.

Witchcraft
BF
1581
z7
1664a

Hale, Sir Matthew, 1609-1676.
Trial of witches, at the Bury assizes, March 10, 1762 [i.e. 1664] before Sir Matthew Hale ... Rose Cullender and Amy Duny, ... were severally indicted for bewitching Elizabeth and Anne Durent ... and ... pleaded not guilty. [n.p., 1762?]
57-64 p. 21cm.

Reprinted from the original ed. of 1682; evidently detached from a periodical
(Continued on next card)

Duny, Amy, fl. 1664.

Witchcraft
BF
1581
z7
1664a

Hale, Sir Matthew, 1609-1676.
Trial of witches ... [1762?]   (Card 2)

(printed 1762?) but has no identification except paging and "Vol. III" at bottom of p. 57.

1. Cullender, Rose, fl. 1664. 2. Duny, Amy, fl. 1664. I. Title.

Duny, Amy, fl. 1664.

Witchcraft
BF
1563
T75

Hale, Sir Matthew, 1609-1676.
A tryal of witches, at the assizes held at Bury St. Edmonds for the county of Suffolk; on the tenth day of March, 1664, before Sir Matthew Hale ... Reprinted verbatim from the original edition of 1682. With an appendix by C. Clark, esq., of Great Totham, Essex. London, J. R. Smith, 1838.
28 p. 23cm.
No. 3 in vol. lettered Tracts on witchcraft.
1. Trials (Witchcraft)--England. I. Title.

8

Witchcraft
BT
960
D93
1628

Dupont, René.
La philosophie des esprits, divisee en cinq livres,& generaux discours Chrestiens, specifiez en la page suiuante. Recueillie & mise en lumiere par F. M. Le Heurt ... 3. ed. Roven, R. Feron, 1628.
[8], 257 [i.e. 267], [5] l. 17cm.

1. Spirits. I. Le Heurt, Matthieu, ed. II. Title.

Witchcraft
Z
6880
Z9
D94

Du Prel, Karl Ludwig August Friedrich Maximilian Alfred, Freiherr, 1839-1899.
Bibliotheca occulta et philosophica; Sammlung Baron C. Du Prel, und kleine andere Beiträge (Inhaltsverzeichnis umstehend) Mit Vorwort von H. L. Held. München, E. Hirsch [193-]
104 p. 22cm.
Katalog 58.
1. Occult sciences--Bibliography--Catalog I. Held, Hans Ludwig, 1885- II. Hirsch, Emil, bookseller, Munich. III. Title.

8

Witchcraft
BF
1413
D94

Du Prel, Karl Ludwig August Friedrich Maximilian Alfred, Freiherr, 1839-1899.
Studien aus dem Gebiete der Geheimwissenschaften. Erster Theil: Thatsachen und Probleme. Leipzig, W. Friedrich, 1890.
vii, 252 p. 22cm.

No more published?

1. Occult sciences. I. Title.

Witchcraft
BF
1520
D94

Durastante, Giano Matteo, 16th cent.
Problemata Iani Matthaei Durastantis ... I. Daemones an sint, & an morborum sint causae, pro theologorum, philosophorum,& medicorum sententiis. II. An uirium imbecillitati iuncta cacochymia per epicrasim curanda sit. III. Et, an rhabarbarum ob lienterian, dysenterian, & astrictionem sit comburendum. Venetijs, Ex officina Stellae, Iordani Ziletti, 1567.
140 numb. l. 15cm.

8
(Continued on next card)

CATALOGUE OF THE CORNELL WITCHCRAFT COLLECTION

Witchcraft
BF
1520
D94
    Durastante, Giano Matteo, 16th cent. Problemata Iani Matthaei Durastantis ... 1567.   (Card 2)
    Printer's device on t. p. and verso of t. p.
    With this is bound his De aceti scillini ... compositione. Venetiis, 1567.
    1. Demonology. 2. Diseases--Causes and theories of causation. 3. Medicine--Early works to 1800. I. Title. II. Title: Daemones an sint.

Durastantes, Janus Matthaeus.
    see
Durastante, Giano Matteo, 16th cent.

Witchcraft
BF
1581
D7
762
    Durbin, Henry.
    A narrative of some extraordinary things that happened to Mr. Richard Giles's children at the Lamb, without Lawford's-Gate, Bristol, supposed to be the effect of witchcraft. By the late Mr. Henry Durbin ... To which is added, a letter from the Rev. Mr. Bedford ... to the Bishop of Glocester, relative to one Thomas Perks, of Mangotsfield, who had dealings with familiar spirits. Bristol, Printed and sold by R. Edwards, 1800.
    60 p. 21cm.
    1. Witchcraft. 2. Demonology. I. Bedford, Arthur, 1668-1745. 3. Perks, Thomas. II. Title.   A 11-136
    Title from Harvard Univ.   Printed by L. C.

Durich, Fortunat
    see
Durych, Fortunat, 1730-1802

Witchcraft
BF
1565
D96
    [Durych, Fortunat] 1730-1802.
    Eutychii Beniamin Transalbini Dissertatio philologica De vocibus hhartymmim et belahatehem Exod. VII. 2. [Vindobonae?] 1767.
    20 p. 21cm.
    "Opusculi inscripti: Gedanken über die Werke des Liebhabers der Wahrheit von der Hexerey."
    1. Witchcraft in the Bible. 2. Bible. O.T.--Criticism, Textual. 3. Hartumim
    (Continued on next card)

Witchcraft
BF
1565
D96
    [Durych, Fortunat] 1730-1802. Eutychii Beniamin Transalbini Dissertatio philologica De vocibus hhartymmim ... 1767.   (Card 2)
    (The word) 4. Belahatehem (The word) 5. März, Agnellus, 1726-1784. I. Title: Dissertatio philologica De vocibus hhartymmim et belahatehem. II. Title: De vocibus hhartymmim et belahatehem. III. Title.

Witchcraft
BF
1565
S69
    Durych, Fortunat, 1730-1802.
    Eutychii Beniamin Transalbini Dissertatio philologica ...
    Sonnenfels, Aloysius von
    Sendschreiben des hochedelgebohrnen Herrn Aloysius von Sonnenfels ... an den hochgelehrten P. don Ferdinand Sterzinger, ... Über zwey hebräische Wörter chartumim und belahatehem: nachmals zur nothwendigen Belehrung des sogenannten Liebhabers der Wahrheit, und seines lateinischen Eutychii Benjamin Transalbini in ihrem Zauber- und Hexerey Streite zum Drucke befördert, von einem Verehrer des Ster[n]ingerischen Namens.
    (Continued on next card)

Witchcraft
BF
1565
S69
    Durych, Fortunat, 1730-1802.
    Eutychii Beniamin Transalbini Dissertatio philologica ...
    Sonnenfels, Aloysius von   Sendschreiben ... 1768.   (Card 2)
    Wjen, Gedruckt mit schulzischen Schriften, 1768.
    30, [1] p. 21cm.
    1. Witchcraft in the Bible. 2. Bible. O.T.--Criticism, Textual. 3. Hartumim (The word) 4. Belahatehem (The word) 5. Durych, Fortunat, 1730-1802. Eutychii Beniamin Transalbini Dissertatio philologica ... 6. März, Agnellus, 1726-1784.

Dutch Reformed Church, Netherlands.
    see
Nederlandse Hervormde Kerk.

MSS
Bd.
WITCHCRAFT
BF
D97
    Du Triez, Robert.
    Livre des ruses, finesses et impostures des esprits malins, oeuvre fort utile & delectable par un chacun a cause de la verité des choses estranges contenue en iceluy: Mis en lumiere par Robert du Triez. Cambray, Nicolas Lombart, 1563 [ca. 1900]
    92 [i.e. 183], [14] p. illus. 19cm.
    Signatures: A-Z⁴, AA-BB².
    Carnap's manuscript copy.
    "Die Seiten dieser Abschrift
    (Continued on next card)

MSS
Bd.
WITCHCRAFT
BF
D97
    Du Triez, Robert. Livre des ruses, finesses et impostures ... 1563 [ca. 1900]   (Card 2)
    stimmen mit denjenigen der Originaldruckschrift überein."
    1. Demonology. 2. Occult sciences. I. Title.

Witchcraft
BF
1582
D98
    Duval, César, comp.
    Procès de sorciers a Viry, bailliage de Ternier de 1534 à 1548. Documents inédits. Avec introduction par Eloy Duboin. [Genève, 1880]
    [299]-515 p. 23cm.
    From Institut national genevois. Bulletin, v. 24, 1880.
    1. Trials (Witchcraft)--Viry, France. I. Title.

Witchcraft
BF
1584
B4
D98
    Duverger, Arthur.
    La vauderie dans les états de Philippe le Bon. Arras, Imprimerie J. Moullé, 1885.
    131 p. 19cm.
    At head of title: Le premier grand procès de sorcellerie aux Pays-Bas.
    1. Witchcraft--Belgium. I. Title. II. Title: Le premier grand procès de sorcellerie aux Pays-Bas.

Witchcraft
BF
1410
B42
Z56
v.3
no.10
    De duyvel roepende uyt sijn kerker. [poem]
    Klinkende bel; of Uytroep om den verlorenen duyvel, door last van sijn liefhebbers. Rotterdam, Gedrukt by P. van Veen, boekdrukker, 1691.
    8 p. title vignette. 20 x 15cm.
    4°: A⁴.
    Poem supporting Balthasar Bekker against the Synode van Noordholland.
    "De duyvel roepende uyt sijn kerker, tot antwoord van den Uytroper:" p. 7-8. (Poem)
    Van der Linde 194.
    (Continued on next card)

Witchcraft
BF
1410
B42
Z56
v.3
no.10
    De duyvel roepende uyt sijn kerker. [poem]
    Klinkende bel; of Uytroep om den verlorenen duyvel ... 1691.   (Card 2)
    No. 10 in vol. lettered Bekker III.
    1. Bekker, Balthasar, 1634-1698. 2. Nederlandse Hervormde Kerk. Synode van Noordholland, Edam, 1691. I. De duyvel roepende uyt sijn kerker. [poem]

CATALOGUE OF THE CORNELL WITCHCRAFT COLLECTION

E

E., H. W. B.

Witchcraft
BX
9479
B42
B11
no.9

Een der gezigten van Zacharias, waar in de Satan vertoond word, staande ter regterhand van de engel des Heeren. Uyt Zach. III: 1-8. Door H. W. B. E. Amsterdam, By J. Roman, boekverkooper, 1699.
16 p. title and one page vignettes, illus. initial. 20 x 15cm.
4°: A-B⁴.
Black letter.
No. 9 in vol. lettered B. Bekkers sterfbed en andere tractaten.

8

E., P.

Witchcraft
BF
1575
W69
1869

[Willard, Samuel] 1640-1707.
Some miscellany observations on our present debates respecting witchcrafts, in a dialogue between S. & B. By P. E. and J. A. [pseud.] Philadelphia, Printed by W. Bradford, for H. Usher. 1692. Boston, 1869.
24 p. 23cm. ("Congregational quarterly" reprint, no. 1)
No. 6 of an edition of 100 copies.
1. Witchcraft. I. E., P. II. A., J. III. Title.

Witchcraft
BF
1555
E13

Easterbrook, Joseph.
An appeal to the public respecting George Lukins (called the Yatton demoniac), containing an account of his affliction and deliverance, together with variety of circumstances which tend to exculpate him from the charge of imposture. Nottingham, Printed and sold by W. Gray [1788?]
23 p. 20cm.
1. Demoniac possession. 2. Lukins, George, fl. 1788. I. Title.

WITCHCRAFT
BF
1555
E13
1788

Easterbrook, Joseph.
An appeal to the public respecting George Lukins, (called the Yatton demoniac,) containing an account of his affliction and deliverance; together with a variety of circumstances which tend to exculpate him from the charge of imposture ... Bristol, Printed for T. Mills [1788]
31 p. 22cm.
1. Demoniac possession. 2. Lukins, George, fl.1788. I.Title.

8

Easterbrook, Joseph.

WITCHCRAFT
BF
1555
N23
1788

A Narrative of the extraordinary case, of Geo. Lukins, of Yatton, Somersetshire, who was possessed of evil spirits for near eighteen years, also an account of his remarkable deliverance ... extracted from the manuscripts of several persons who attended. To which is prefixed a letter from the Rev. W. R. W. With the Rev. Mr. Easterbrook's letter annex'd ... 2d ed. Bristol, Printed by Bulgin and Rosser, and sold by W. Bulgin [etc.] 1788.

8   (Continued on next card)

Easterbrook, Joseph.

WITCHCRAFT
BF
1555
N23
1788

A Narrative of the extraordinary case, of Geo. Lukins ... 1788. (Card 2)

gin [etc] 1788.
24 p. 21cm.
1. Demoniac possession. 2. Exorcism. 3. Lukins, George, fl. 1788. I. W. R. W. II. W., R. W. III. Easterbrook, Joseph.

8

Die ebenthürliche [sic] Beschreibung des Gespenstes ...

Witchcraft
BF
1483
Z84
1692

Zobel, Enoch, 1653-1697.
Die ebenthürliche [sic] Beschreibung des Gespenstes, welches in einem Hause zu St. Annaberg, im abgelegten 1691 Jahr 2 Monath lang, viel Schrecken, Furcht und wunderseltzame Schau-Spiele angerichtet. Beschrieben von des Hauses Eigenthumbs-Herrn, M. Enoch Zobeln, Arch. Diac. daselbst. Hamburg, Zu bekommen bey T. von Wiering [1692]
[24] p. 18cm.
Reproduces p. [1]-48 of the author's

(Continued on next card)

Die ebenthürliche [sic] Beschreibung des Gespenstes ...

Witchcraft
BF
1483
Z84
1692

Zobel, Enoch, 1653-1697. Die ebenthürliche Beschreibung des Gespenstes ... [1692]
(Card 2)

Historische und theologische Vorstellung des ebenteuerlichen Gespenstes ... Leipzig, 1692.

1. Ghosts--Germany. I. Title. II. His Historische und theologische Vorstellung des ebenteuerlichen Gespenstes.

Witchcraft
BF
1775
E16

Eberhard, Johann August, 1739-1809, praeses.
Dissertatio philosophica de superstitione, quam praeside ... Ioanne Augusto Eberhard ... A. D. 16 April 1801 publice defendet auctor Henricus Christianus Millies. Halis Saxonum, Typis Schimmelpfennigianis [1801]
51 p. 21cm.
Imperfect: t. p. badly worn.
Diss.--Halle (H. C. Millies, respondent)
1. Superstition. 2. Occult sciences.
I. Millies, Henricus Christianus, fl. 1801, respondent. II. Title.

8

Witchcraft
BF
1413
E16

Eberhard, Johann Peter, 1727-1779.
D. Johann Peter Eberhards ... abhandlungen vom physikalischen aberglauben und der magie. Halle im Magdeburgischen, Renger, 1778.
7 p. l., 144 p. front. 20½cm.

1. Superstition. 2. Magic. I. Title: Abhandlungen vom physikalischen aberglauben und der magie. II. Title.

34-13015

Library of Congress   BF1413.E3   [159.9611] 133

AC
30
S18
n.s.
no.291

Ebner, Theodor.
Friedrich von Spee und die Hexenprozesse seiner Zeit. Hamburg, Verlagsanstalt und Druckerei A.-G. (vormals J. F. Richter) 1898.
47 p. 21cm. (Sammlung gemeinverständlicher wissenschaftlicher Vorträge, n.F., 13. Ser., Heft 291)
1. Spee, Friedrich von, 1591-1635. 2. Witchcraft--Germany. I. Title.

Edit du Roi, pour la punition de différens crimes, notamment des empoisonneurs...

Witchcraft
BF
1582
F81+
1776

France. Sovereigns, etc., 1643-1715 (Louis XIV)
Edit du Roi, pour la punition de différens crimes, notamment des empoisonneurs, ceux qui se disent divins, magiciens & enchanteurs; & portant reglement pour les epiciers & apothicaires. Donné à Versailles, au mois de Juillet 1682. [Paris, Chez Prault, imprimeur du Roi, 1776]
7 p. 28cm.
Caption title.

8   (Continued on next card)

Edmonds, William, 1550?-1616.

Witchcraft
BF
1581
H32
1605

[Harsnett, Samuel] archbishop of York, 1561-1631.
A declaration of egregious Popish impostures, to with-draw the harts of His Maiesties subiects from their allegeance, and from the truth of Christian religion professed in England, vnder the pretence of casting out of deuils. Practised by Edmunds, alias VVeston, a Iesuit, & diuers Romish priestes his vvicked associates. Where-vnto are annexed the copies of the confessions, & examinations of the parties themselues, which were pretended to
(Continued on next card)

Edmonds, William, 1550?-1616.

Witchcraft
BF
1581
H32
1605

[Harsnett, Samuel] archbishop of York, 1561-1631. A declaration of egregious Popish impostures ... 1605. (Card 2)

be possessed and dispossessed: taken vppon oath before His Maiesties commissioners, for causes ecclesiasticall. Barbican [London] Newly printed by Ia. Roberts, 1605.
284 p. 19cm.
Epistle "To the sedvced Catholiques of England" signed: S.H.
1. Edmonds, William, 1550?-1616. I. Title.

Edward IV, King of England, 1442-1483.

Witchcraft
BF
1581
A2
W81
1866a
no.5

Wright, Thomas, 1810-1877, ed.
Curious account of the remarkable case of the Duchess of Bedford, in the reign of Edward IV., who was charged with having by witchcraft fixed the love of the king on her daughter Queen Elizabeth. Furnished by the rolls of Parliament of 9th Edward IV. Northampton, J. Taylor, 1867.
8 p. 22cm.
"In the Proceedings against Dame Alice Kyteler, for the Camden Society."

8   (Continued on next card)

CATALOGUE OF THE CORNELL WITCHCRAFT COLLECTION

Edward IV, King of England, 1442-1483.
Witchcraft
BF
1581
A2
W81
1866a
no.5

Wright, Thomas, 1810-1877, ed. Curious account of the remarkable case of the Duchess of Bedford ... 1867. (Card 2)

No. 5 in box lettered Witchcraft in Northamptonshire.

1. Bedford, Jaquetta of Luxembourg, duchess of. 2. Edward IV, King of England, 1442-1483. I. Title.

8

Edwards, Susanna, d. 1682.
Witchcraft
BF
1581
T86

A true and impartial relation of the informations against three witches, viz.: Temperance Lloyd, Mary Trembles, and Susanna Edwards. Who were indicted, arraigned, and convicted, at the assizes holden for the county of Devon at the castle of Exon, Aug. 14, 1682. ... As also, their speeches, confessions, and behaviour, at the time and place of execution ... London, Printed by F. Collins, and are to be sold by T. Benskin and C. Yeo, 1682.
40 p. 21cm.

(Continued on next card)

Edwards, Susanna, d. 1682.
Witchcraft
BF
1581
T86

A true and impartial relation of the informations against three witches ... 1682. (Card 2)

With this is bound Stephens, Edward. A plain relation of the late action at sea ... London, 1690.

1. Lloyd, Temperance, d. 1682. 2. Trembles, Mary, d. 1682. 3. Edwards, Susanna, d. 1682.

Witchcraft
BX
9479
B42
B11
no.9

Een der gezigten van Zacharias, waar in de Satan vertoond word, staande ter regterhand van de engel des Heeren. Uyt Zach. III: 1-8. Door H. W. B. E. Amsterdam, By J. Roman, boekverkooper, 1699.
16 p. title and end page vignettes, illus. initial. 20 x 15cm.
4°: A-B⁴.
Black letter.
No. 9 in vol. lettered B. Bekkers sterfbed en andere tractaten.

(Continued on next card)

Witchcraft
BX
9479
B42
B11
no.9

Een der gezigten van Zacharias, waar in de Satan vertoond word ... 1699. (Card 2)

1. Devil. 2. Bible. O. T. Zacharias III, 1-8--Criticism, interpretation, etc. I. H. W. B. E. II. E., H. W. B.

Eenige extracten uyt Dr. Beckers Betooverder weerelt, tweede deel.
Witchcraft
BF
1410
Z92

Bekker, Balthasar, 1634-1698. Eenige extracten uyt Dr. Beckers Betooverder weerelt, tweede deel. Daer beneffens een extract uyt de synode, gehouden den 10. Augusti 1691. tot Edam. Raakende Dr. Beckers Betoverde weerelt. Beneffens desselfs veroordeelinge. [n. p.] 1691.
7 p. [p. 8 blank] title and end page vignettes, illus. initials. 19 x 16cm.
Black letter.
Van der Linde 29.

(Continued on next card)

8

Eenige extracten uyt Dr. Beckers Betooverder weerelt, tweede deel.
Witchcraft
BF
1410
B42
Z92

Bekker, Balthasar, 1634-1698. Eenige extracten uyt Dr. Beckers Betooverder weerelt, tweede deel. 1691. (Card 2)

Bound with Walten, Ericus, 1663-1697. Aardige duyvelary, voorvallende in dese dagen.

I. Bekker, Balthasar, 1634-1698. De betoverde weerelt. II. Nederlandse Hervormde Kerk. Synode, Edam, 1691. III. Title.

8

Witchcraft
BF
1410
B42
Z56
v.3
no.23

Eenige originele brieven geschreven aan Do. Balthasar Bekker, over sijn boek De betoverde werelt. Door Do. Jacobus Koelman. En andere bekende, en onbekende persoonen. Amsterdam, By D. van den Dalen, boekverkooper, 1692.
1 p. l., 8 p. title and end page vignettes. 19 x 15cm.
4°: π1, *⁴.
Four letters: one from Koelman, one from Pieter Hessels, and two signed N. N. (but not, apparently, by the

(Continued on next card)

Witchcraft
BF
1410
B42
Z56
v.3
no.23

Eenige originele brieven geschreven aan Do. Balthasar Bekker ... 1692. (Card 2)

same person.)
Variant of van der Linde 123: lacks second numbering (sign. A-C)
No. 23 in vol. lettered Bekker III.
1. Bekker, Balthasar, 1634-1698. De betoverde weerelt. I. Koelman, Jacobus, b. 1632.

Witchcraft
BF
1410
B42
Z69
no.31

Eenige originele brieven geschreven aan Do. Balthasar Bekker, over sijn boek De betoverde werelt. Door Do. Jacobus Koelman. En andere bekende, en onbekende persoonen. Amsterdam, By D. van den Dalen, boekverkooper, 1692.
1 p.l., 8, 18 p. 21cm.
Signatures: 4°: π1, *⁴, A-B⁴, C¹.
Six letters: one from Koelman, one from Pieter Hessels, three signed N. N. (but

NIC   (Continued on next card)

Witchcraft
BF
1410
B42
Z69
no.31

Eenige originele brieven geschreven aan Do. Balthasar Bekker ... 1692. (Card 2)

not, apparently, by the same person) and one signed: Palaeologus Alethaeus.
Van der Linde 123.
No. 31 in a Collection of tracts against Balthasar Bekker and his Betoverde weerelt.

NIC

Witchcraft
BF
1410
B42
Z56
v.2
no.3

Eenvoudig aanmerkinge, over 't geene in de saak van Do. B. Bekker en sijn boek is gepasseert, vergeleeken met de handelingen der roomsche geestelijkheyd hier in overeenkomende: dat men moet gelooven wat de kerk gelooft, en den ketters geen woord houden. Amsterdam, 1692.
8 p. title vignette, illus initial.
19 x 15cm.
4°: A⁴.
Van der   Linde 60.
No. 3 in   vol. lettered Bekker II.

(Continued on next card)

8

Eenvoudig aanmerkinge, over 't geene in de saak van Do. B. Bekker ... 1692. (Card 2)
Witchcraft
BF
1410
B42
Z56
v.2
no.3

1. Bekker, Balthasar, 1634-1698. De betoverde weerelt. 2. Nederlandse Hervormde Kerk.

8

Eenvoudig verhaal van de proceduuren gepleeght ... tot Wormer en Jisp ...
Witchcraft
BX
9479
B42
B11
no.20

Banningh, Jacob. Eenvoudig verhaal van de proceduuren gepleeght, in de waaterlandse doopsgesinde gemeentens tot Wormer en Jisp, over het doen ophouden van een haarer leeraaren, in sijn predikdienst ... veroorsaakt door het zoo genaamde nieuw gevoelen der geesten, engelen ende duyvelen, met de disputatien en voorvallen soo alse in deselve zyn geschiet, na waarheyd verhaalt door de zelve leeraar, Jacob Banningh. Amsterdam, by A. van Damme, boekver   kooper, 1698.

(Continued on next card)

8

Eenvoudig verhaal van de proceduuren gepleeght ... tot Wormer en Jisp ...
Witchcraft
BX
9479
B42
B11
no.20

Banningh, Jacob. Eenvoudig verhaal van de proceduuren gepleeght ... tot Wormer en Jisp ... 1698. (Card 2)

44 p. title and other vignettes, illus. initials. 20 x 15cm.
4°: A-E⁴, F².
Black letter (except introduction and post scriptum)
Local development of the controversy over Balthasar Bekk   ers De betoverde weerelt.

(Continued on next card)

8

Eenvoudig verhaal van de proceduuren gepleeght ... tot Wormer en Jisp ...
Witchcraft
BX
9479
B42
B11
no.20

Banningh, Jacob. Eenvoudig verhaal van de proceduuren gepleeght ... tot Wormer en Jisp ... 1698. (Card 3)

No. 20 in vol. lettered B. Bekkers sterfbed en andere tractaten.

1. Nederlandse Hervormde Kerk--Doctrinal and controversial works. 2. Bekker, Balthasar, 1634-1698. De betoverde weerelt. I. Title.

8

Eerste briev van ... Haggébher Philaleethees, geschreeven aan zynen vriend N. N.
Witchcraft
BF
1410
B42
Z69
no.3

[Hooght, Everard van der] d. 1716.
Eerste briev van יבבה Φιλαληθης Haggébher Philaleethees, geschreeven aan zynen vriend N. N. over den persoon en het boek van Do. Balthasar Bekker. In opzicht van de gudheyd, ende het gewichte zyner dwaling; nevens sijne onkunde in de godtgeleertheyd ende in de gronden van de Hebreeusche tale; demonstratiiv beweesen, uyt zyne verklaring van Gen. 18. ende Job 1. en 2. Amsterdam,   G. Borstius, 1691.
20 p.   21cm.

NIC   (Continued on next card)

Eerste briev van ... Haggébher Philaleethees, geschreeven aan zynen vriend N. N.
Witchcraft
BF
1410
B42
Z69
no.3

[Hooght, Everard van der] d. 1716. Eerste briev van ... Haggébher Philaleethees ... 1691. (Card 2)

Signatures: 4°: A-B⁴, C¹.
Black letter.
N. N. is thought to be Jacobus Schuts.
Van der Linde 97.
No. 3 in a Collection of tracts against Balthasar Bekker and his Betoverde weerelt.

NIC   (Continued on next card)

189

CATALOGUE OF THE CORNELL WITCHCRAFT COLLECTION

Witchcraft
BF 1583 Z7 1583
Effroyable histoire arrivée cette année 1583 dans la ville et hors la ville de Hambourg, ou l'on a pris quarante-trois esprits ou sorcières; ce qu'elles ont avoué avoir fait; les premières révélations des crimes; jugées le 20 mai, et brulées. Hambourg, Imprimé par J. Grunsblatt, 1583 [Lille, Imprimerie de Horemans, 186-?]
8 p. 23cm.

1. Witchcraft--Hamburg, Germany.

L'Église et la sorcellerie.

Witchcraft
BF 1566 F81
Français, J.
L'Église et la sorcellerie. Précis historique, suivi des documents officiels, des textes principaux, et d'un procès inédit. Paris, E. Nourry, 1910.
263 p. 19cm. (Bibliothèque de critique religieuse)

1. Catholic Church--Doctrinal and controversial works. 2. Witchcraft. I. Title.

WITCHCRAFT
BF 1555 E33
Ehinger, Christoph.
Daemonologia; oder, Etwas Neues vom Teufel. Das ist: Wahrhaffter historischer Bericht, von einem sonder- und wunderbaren Casu, Anfechtungs-Fall, und satanischer Versuchung, mit welcher, auss Gottes Verhängnuss, ein Burger, und Schuhmacher in Augspurg, etliche Jahr yexiret, und geplaget worden ... Augspurg, In Verlegung Gottlieb Göbels, Druckts Jacob Koppmayr, 1681.
12 p. l., 208 p. 16cm.
8   1. Devil. 2. Demoniac possession. I. Title. 3. Heinrich N., shoemaker of Augsburg, fl. 1667-1681.

Witchcraft
BF 1522 E34
Eigentliche Fürstellung der arglistigen satanischen Erscheinung, welche sich jüngsthin am 17. Julii, war der 4. Sonntag nach dem Fest der H. Dreyeinigkeit, mit Hanss Grunern, einem Einwohner zu Mellingen, warhafftig begeben, jedermann zur Warnung und Schrecken, aus des Mannes eigener Schrifft- und mündlichen Erzehlung entworffen, und auff vielfältiges Ansuchen und Begehren ans Licht gestellet. Pirna, G. B. Ludewig, 1698.
16 p. fold. pl. 20cm.
I. Gruner, Hans, fl. 1698.

Ein nach Engelland reisender Passagier.

WITCHCRAFT
BF 1552 K96
Kurtze Untersuchung von Kobold, in so ferne gewisse phaenomena unter diesem Nahmen dem Teuffel zugeschrieben werden, auf Veranlassung einer besondern Begebenheit wobey überhaupt von denen sichtbaren Würckungen des Teuffels in und durch die natürlichen Cörper gehandelt. Auch hiernächst gezeiget wird wie der Herr autor derer Lehr-Sätze von dem Laster der Zauberey etliche hieher gehörige Schrifft-Stellen zur Ungebühr verdrehet und überdis seine
8 NIC
(Continued on next card)

Ein nach Engelland reisender Passagier.

WITCHCRAFT
BF 1552 K96
Kurtze Untersuchung von Kobold... (Card 2)
gantze Meynung de pacto auf unbündige paralogismos gegründet. Von einen nach Engelland reisenden Passagier. Roterdam, 1719.
108 p. front. 17cm.

1. Demonology. 2. Witchcraft. 3. Thomasius, Christian, 1655-1728. Kurtze Lehr-Sätze vom Laster der Zauberey. I. Ein nach Engelland reisender Passagier.

Ein vom Vorurtheil Befreyter.

WITCHCRAFT
BF 1555 M94 029 no.2
Das Bezauberte Bauermägdgen: oder Geschichte von dem anjetzo in Kemberg bey Wittenberg sich aufhaltenden Landmägdchen Johannen Elisabethen Lohmannin; aufgesetzt durch einen vom Vorurtheil Befreyeten, und mit Anmerkungen eines Rechtsgelahrten versehen. Breslau, Bey J. E. Meyer, 1760.
167 p. 18cm.
No. 2 in vol. lettered Oesfeld u. a. ...
"Eines Advocatens Ehrenrettung wider ... Herrn Gottlieb Müllers Beschuldigung": p. 51-162.
8 NIC
(Continued on next card)

Einert, Paul Nicolaus, respondent.

Witchcraft
BF 1520 S38
Schubart, Christoph, praeses.
Dissertatio De potentia diaboli in sensus, quam ... sub praesidio M. Joh. Christophori Schubarti, die 23. April hor. 8. placidae eruditorum ventilationi in acroaterio philosophorum submittet respondens Paulus Nicolaus Einert ... Erfordiae, Literis Limprechtianis [1707]
[14] p. 20cm.

8   1. Devil. I. Einert, Paul Nicolaus, respondent. II. Title: De potentia diaboli in sensus.

Eines Anonymi Gutachten von dem mit Herrn D. Thomasio erregten Streit über einige freye Meynungen.

Witchcraft
BF 1565 T46 E358
Das Wohl-meritirte und wohlverdiente Ehren-Kleid dem Anonymo und Autori des Gutachten von dem mit Herrn Doct. Thomasio erregten Streit über einige freye Meynungen in einem teutschen Programmate, und von Herrn D. Strykii Disputation de jure Sabbathi, zum Recompens vor die Mühe praesentiret von einem Liebhaber der Wahrheit und Feind der Calumnien. Freystatt, 1703.
24 p. 18cm.
8   (Continued on next card)

Witchcraft
BF 1559 G25 Z63 no.6
Eines redlichen Protestantens aufrichtige Erinnerung an den Verfasser des Exorcisten in seiner Blösse, den Prager Hirtenbrief betreffend. Frankfurt und Leipzig, 1776.
45 p. 17cm.
No. 6 in vol. lettered Gassneriana.
1. Gassner, Johann Joseph, 1727-1779.
2. Příchovský, Antonín Peter, Abp. of Prague, 1707-1793. Hirtenbrief ... 1775. 3. Der Exorcist in seiner Blösse. I. Ein redlicher Protestant.

Einwirkung guter und böser Geister in die Menschen.

WITCHCRAFT
BF 1555 M94 029 no.1
Oesfeld, Gotthelf Friedrich.
Gedanken von der Einwirkung guter und böser Geister in die Menschen. Nebst beygefügter Beurtheilung eines neuern Beyspiels einer vermeynten leiblichen Besitzung, herausgegeben von M. Gotthelf Friedrich Oesfeld ... Wittenberg, J. J. Ahlfeld, 1760.
110 p. 18cm.
No. 1 in vol. lettered Oesfeld u. a. ...
1. Spirits. 2. Demoniac possession. 3. Lohmann, Anna Elisabeth. I. Title. II. Title: Einwirkung guter und böser Geister in die Menschen.
8 NIC

Witchcraft
BF 1523 E35
Einzinger von Einzing, Johann Martin Maximilian, 1725-1798.
Dämonologie; oder, Systematische Abhandlung von der Natur und Macht des Teufels, von den Kennzeichen, eine verstellte oder eingebildete Besitznehmung des Teufels von einer wahren am leichtesten zu unterscheiden, sammt den natürlichsten Mitteln, die meisten Gespenster an sich selbsten zu vertreiben, dem Gassnerischen Teufelssysteme entgegengesetzt. [Leipzig?] 1775.
(Continued on next card)

Witchcraft
BF 1523 E35
Einzinger von Einzing, Johann Martin Maximilian, 1725-1798. Dämonologie. [Leipzig?] 1775. (Card 2)
140 p. 18cm.
With this is bound Thomasius, C. Gelehrte Streitschrift von dem Verbrechen der Zauber- und Hexerey. Leipzig, 1775.

1. Gassner, Johann Joseph, 1727-1779. I. Title.

Witchcraft
PA 19 S98 suppl. v.20
Eitrem, Samson, 1872-
Some notes on the demonology in the New Testament, by S. Eitrem. 2d ed., rev. and enl. Osloae, In Aedibus Universitetsforlaget, 1966.
78 p. 25cm. (Symbolae Osloenses Fasc. Supplet., 20)

1. Demonology. 2. Bible. N.T.--Theology. I. Title.

Eliae Henrici Henckelii ... Ordo et methodus cognoscendi & curandi energumenos.

WITCHCRAFT
BF 1555 H49
Henckel, Elias Heinrich von, fl. 1654-1688.
Eliae Henrici Henckelii ... Ordo et methodus cognoscendi & curandi energumenos seu à Stygio cacodaemone obsessos. Antehac à nemine, quantum sunt, qui de obsessis scripserunt, tradita. Francofurti & Lipsiae, Sumptibus Nicolai Försteri, 1689.
7 p. l., 240, [16] p. 17cm.
Title in red and black.
1. Demoniac possession. 2. Medicine --15th-18th centuries. I. Title: Ordo et methodus cognoscendi & curandi energumenos.
8

Witchcraft
BF 1520 E42
Elich, Philipp Ludwig.
Daemonomagia; siue Libellvs ἐρωτηματικός, de daemonis cacurgia, cacomagorum et lamiarum energiâ ... Francoforti, Prelo Richteriano, Impensâ verò Conradi Nebenii, 1607.
213, [6] p. 17cm.

Device of C. Nebenius on t. p. and on recto of last leaf.
Colophon: Francoforti, Ex Typographeio Wolfgangi Richteri, Sumptibus verò Conradi
(Continued on next card)

Witchcraft
BF 1520 E42
Elich, Philipp Ludwig. Daemonomagia ... 1607. (Card 2)
Nebenii.
Armorial bookplate: Ex Bibliotheca Gerardi Schimmelpfenninck Jani. F.

1. Demonology. 2. Demonomania. 3. Magic. 4. Witchcraft. I. Title.

Eliphas Lévi; visionnaire romantique.

BF 1598 C75 B78
Bowman, Frank Paul.
Eliphas Lévi; visionnaire romantique. Préface et choix de textes par Frank Paul Bowman. Paris, Presses Universitaires de France, 1969.
242 p. 19cm. ("A la découverte")
At head of title: Publications du Département de langues romanes de l'Université de Princeton.

1. Constant, Alphonse Louis, 1810-1875. I. Title. II. Series: Princeton University. Princeton publications in modern language

190

CATALOGUE OF THE CORNELL WITCHCRAFT COLLECTION

Elizabethan demonology.

tchcraft
Spalding, Thomas Alfred, 1850-
    Elizabethan demonology. An essay in
illustration of the belief in the existence
of devils, and the powers possessed by them,
as it was generally held during the period
of the Reformation, and the times immediately
succeeding; with special reference to
Shakspere and his works. London, Chatto and
Windus, 1880.
    xii,151 p. 20cm.

1. Demonolo   gy. 2. Shakespeare,
William--Super   natural element.
I. Title.

---

itchcraft
F   Ellinger, Johann.
565   Hexen Coppel; das ist, Vhralte Ankunfft
46   vnd grosse Zunfft des vnholdseligen Vn-
        holden oder Hexen, welche in einer Coppel
        von einem gantzen Dutzet auff die Schaw vnd
        Muster und geführet ... Franckfurt am
        Mayn, J. C. Onckels, 1629.
           59 p. 19cm.

1. Witchcraft. ✓ I. Title.

Witchcraft
BF   Elliott, Charles Wyllys, 1817-1883.
1411   Mysteries; or, Glimpses of the
E46   supernatural, containing accounts of
2 copies the Salem witchcraft, the Cock-lane
        ghost, the Rochester rappings, the
        Stratford mysteries, oracles, astrology,
        dreams, demons, ghosts, spectres, &c.
        ... New York, Harper & Brothers, 1852.
           273 p. illus. (plan) 20cm.

✓ I. Title.

Witchcraft
BF   Elvert, Christian, Ritter d', 1803-1896.
583   Das Zauber- und Hexenwesen, dann der
51+   Glauben an Vampyre in Mähren und Oesterr.
859   Schlesien. ₍Brunn, 1859₎
           319-₍421₎ p. 26cm. (Schriften der
        Historisch-Statistischen Section der
        Mähr.-Schles. Gesellschaft zur Beförde-
        rung der Natur- und Landeskunde, Bd. 12)

1. Witchcraft. 2. Vampires. ✓ I. Title.

Witchcraft
BF   Bischof, Ferdinand.
1413   Zur Geschichte des Glaubens an Zauberer,
862+   Hexen, und Vampyre in Mähren und Oesterr.
1859   Schlesien. Von Ferdinand Bischof und Christ-
        ian d'Elvert. Brünn, Buchdruckerei von R.
        Rohrer's Erben, 1859.
           164 p. 26cm.

"Aus dem XII. Bande der Schriften der
historisch-statistischen Sektion der k. k.
mähr. schles. Gesellschaft zur Beförderung
des Ackerbaues,   der Natur- und Landeskunde besonders   abgedruckt."

        Elvert, Christian, Ritter d', 1803-
        1896, supposed author.
chcraft   Zur Geschichte des Hexenwesens in Mähren
        und Schlesien. ₍Brunn? 1865₎
           395-424 p. 26cm. (Schriften der
        historisch- statistischen Section der
        mährschlesischen Gesellschaft zur Beför-
        derung des Ackerbaues, der Natur- u. Lan-
        deskunde, 4)

1. Witchcraft. 2. Trials (Witchcraft)--
Germany. I. Elvert, Christian, Ritter d',
1803-1896, supp   osed author.

        Emanuel Swedenborgs demüthiges Dank-
        sagungsschreiben an den grossen Mann.

WITCHCRAFT
BF   ₍Köster, Heinrich Martin Gottfried₎ 1734-
1523   1802.
K78   Emanuel Swedenborgs demüthiges Danksa-
K513   gungsschreiben an den grossen Mann, der die
        Nonexistenz des Teufels demonstrirt hat.
        Frankfurt und Leipzig, 1778.
           46 p. 17cm.
        Attribution by Holzmann.
        1. Kindleben, Christian Wilhelm, 1748-
        1785. Ueber die Non-Existenz des Teufels.
        2. Devil. I.   Swedenborg, Emanuel,
                        1688-1772,   supposed author. II.
8   Title. III.   Title: Demüthiges Dank-
        sagungsschre   iben an den grossen Mann.

        Embden, Carolus Josephus, respondent.

WITCHCRAFT
BX   Neller, Georg Christoph, praeses.
1935   ...Conatus exegeticus in cap. ₸am te 7
N42   De rescriptis, quem una cum parergis, ex
        omni jure, nec non ex re monetaria, tum
        biblico-canonica, tum Trevirensi delibatis
        ...praeside...Georgio Christoph. Neller...
        publicae disputationi pro admissione ad
        tentamen graduandorum supposuit...Carolus
        Josephus Embden. Augustae Trevirorum,
        Typis Eschermannianis ₍1779₎
           48 p. front., plate. 22cm.

8   Burr's   note inside front cover:
NIC   (Continued on next card)

        Embden, Carolus Josephus, respondent.
WITCHCRAFT
BX   Neller, Georg Christoph, praeses. Conatus
1935   exegeticus in cap. ₸am te 7 De rescriptis
N42   ...₍1779₎   (Card 2)

        This book is valuable in containing a...
        letter of the Elector, Johann VII of
        Treves asking the advice of the University
        theological faculty at Treves as to the
        trial of Dr. Dietrich Flade for witchcraft.
        (See pp. 32-35) It is to be noted that this
        student, writing under the eye of the emi-
        nent jurist   Neller in 1779, still
        believes in   witchcraft..."
                           (Continued on next card)

        Die emeis.
Witchcraft
BX   Geiler, Johannes, von Kaisersberg, 1445-
890   1510.
G31   Die emeis. Dis ist das bůch von der omeis-
E5+   sen, vnnd auch Herr der künnig ich diente
1517   gern. Vnd sagt von eigentschafft der omeis-
        sen. Vñ gibt vnderweisung von den vnholden
        oder hexen, vnd von gespenst der geist, vnd
        von dem wütenden heer wunderbarlich vnd nütz-
        lich zewissen, was man daruon glauben vnd hal-
        ten soll. Vnd ist von dem hoch gelertẽ doc-
8   (Continued on next card)

        Die emeis.
Witchcraft
BX   Geiler, Johannes, von Kaisersberg, 1445-
890   1510. Die emeis ... ₍1517₎ (Card 2)
G31
E5+   tor Johãnes Geiler võ Keisersperg ... in
1517   eim quadragesimal geprediget worden alle son-
        tag in der fasten ... ₍Strassburg, Johan-
        nes Grienniger, 1517₎
           xc ₍i.e. lxxxviii₎ l. illus. 29cm.
        Title and parts of text in red and black.
        Leaves v and vi not wanting; printer
        skipped numbers.

8   (Continued on next card)

        Die emeis.
Witchcraft
BX   Geiler, Johannes, von Kaisersberg, 1445-
890   1510. Die emeis ... ₍1517₎ (Card 3)
G31
E5+   Colophon at end of first section, Die
1517   emeis, reads Grienninger instead of Grien-
        niger.
           "Her d'küng ich diente gern", l. ₍lxvii₎-
        xc, has special t. p.
        1. Sermons, German--Middle High German.
        2. Folk-lore, German. 3. Magic. I. His
        Her der küng ich diente gern. II. Title.
8   III. Title: Her der küng ich dien-
        te gern.

        The emphatical prophecy of Pedan.

Witchcraft
BF   Macleod, Malcolm.
1566   History of witches &c. The majesty of
M16   darkness discovered: in a series of tremendous
        tales ... of apparitions, witches,augers, ma-
        gicians ... in confirmation of a future state,
        & the superintendency of a Divine Providence,
        by the agency of spirits & angels. With The
        prophecy of Pedan; or, The Caledonian apocalypse
        of the last century; sublimely adumbrating the
        awful events which now amaze and alarm all
        Europe. Lon   don, Printed by and for
                          (Continued on next card)

        The emphatical prophecy of Pedan.
Witchcraft
BF   Macleod, Malcolm. History of witches &c...
1566   ₍1793₎   (Card 2)
M16
        I. Roach ₍1793₎
           97 p. front. 17cm.

        Title vignette.

        I. Title. II. Title: The majesty of dark-
        ness discovered. III. Title: The emphatical
        prophecy of Pedan.

        Enchantment disenchanted.
Witchcraft
BF   Blair, George.
1775   The holocaust; or, The witch of Monzie, a
B63   poem illustrative of the cruelties of super-
        stition. Lays of Palestine and other poems.
        To which is prefixed, Enchantment disenchanted;
        or, A treatise on superstition. ... London,
        J. F. Shaw, 1845.
           xii,277 p. 20cm.

        1. Superstition. I. Title. II. Title: The
        witch of Monzie.   III. Title: Lays of
        Palestine. IV.   Title: Enchantment dis-
        enchanted.

        Enchiridion.
WITCHCRAFT
BF   Viglioni, Giovanni Battista.
1068   Jo: Baptistae Viglioni ... Enchiridion
V67   quatuor tractatus complectens de somniis,
1734   cabalis, cacodaemonibus, et ludo in genere.
        Ad excellentiss. principem Julium Visconti
        Borromeum ... Nova editio. Neapoli, 1734.
           xvi, 188, 51, 188-231 p. 23cm.
        1. Sleep--Early works to 1800. 2.
        Dreams. 3. Cabala. 4. Demonology. 5.
        Games--Early works to 1800. I. Title:
8   Enchiridion.

        Enchiridion exorcisticum.
WITCHCRAFT
BF   Pizzurini, Gervasio.
1559   Enchiridion exorcisticum; compendiosissi-
P69   me continens diagnosim, prognosim, ac the-
        rapiam medicam et divinam affectionum ma-
        gicarum. Lugduni, Apud Antonium Valançol,
        1668.
           133 p. 17cm.

8   1. Exorcism. 2. Medicine, Magic, mystic
NIC   and spagiric. I. Title.

        Enchiridium quadripartitum.
Witchcraft
BX   Berg, Vincent von, comp.
2050   Enchiridium quadripartitum P. Vincentii
A1   von Berg Franciscani conventualis. Pars
B49   prima exhibet varias, selectas, exquisitis-
        simasque benedictiones rerum omnigenarum
        approbatas ... Pars secunda tractat de
        regulis artis exorcisticae cum suis exor-
        cismis ... Pars tertia agit de archi-con-
        fraternitate ... Pars quarta praescribit
        modum aegros, agonizantesque adjuvandi; a-
8   gendi cum obstinatis, haereticis converten-
                          (Continued on next card)

CATALOGUE OF THE CORNELL WITCHCRAFT COLLECTION

Enchiridium quadripartitum.

Witchcraft
BX
2050   Berg, Vincent von, comp.   Enchiridium quad-
A1   ripartitum ...   1743.   (Card 2)
B49
       dis, sagis examinandis ... Accedit horum
     Anacephalaeosis in germanismo. In hanc com-
     modissimam formam redactum, iconibus illus-
     tratum, indicéque alphabetico instructum.
       Coloniae, Typis J. C. Gussen, 1743.
         8 p. l., 342, [10], 144 p. illus. 17cm.
         Part 3 includes some German text.
         Anacephalaeosis; das ist, Kurtze
8
                    (Continued on next card)

Enchiridium quadripartitum.

Witchcraft
BX
2050   Berg, Vincent von, comp.   Enchiridium quad-
A1   ripartitum ...   1743.   (Card 3)
B49
       Wiederholung zu Teutsch, vorstellend die
     Weiss [sic], und Manier mit den Krancken
     und Sterbenden umbzugehen has special t. p.
     and is paged separately.
       Title in red and black.
       Ex libris Lud. Parren.
       1. Catholic Church--Prayer-books and
     devotions.   2.   Exorcism. I. Title.
8   II. His   An   acephalaeosis. III.
     Title: Anace   phalaeosis.

An encyclopaedia of occultism.

BF
1025   Spence, Lewis, 1874- 1955.
S74+   An encyclopædia of occultism; a compendium of infor-
1920   mation on the occult sciences, occult personalities, psychic
       science, magic, demonology, spiritism and mysticism, by
       Lewis Spence. London, G. Routledge & sons, ltd., 1920.
         3 p. l., ix-xii, [2], 451 p. illus., plates, ports. 25½ x 20½ cm.
         "Select bibliography": [2] p. after p. xii.

         1. Occult sciences—Dictionaries.   I. Title.

       Library of Congress   BF1025.S7   20-7507
                                   [4]

Witchcraft   The encyclopedia of witchcraft and demonol-
BF   ogy.
1503   Robbins, Rossell Hope, 1912-
R63+   The encyclopedia of witchcraft and demonology. New
       York, Crown Publishers [1959]
         571 p. Illus. 26 cm.
         Includes bibliography.

         1. Witchcraft—Dictionaries—English.   2. Demonology—Diction-
       aries—English.   I. Title.

       BF1503.R6   133.403   59-9155 ‡
       Library of Congress   [30]

Encyclopédie portative.

Witchcraft
BF
1411   Denis, Ferdinand, 1798-1890.
D39   Tableau historique, analytique, et cri-
       tique des sciences occultes, où l'on examine
       l'origine, le développement, l'influence et
       le caractère de la divination, de l'astro-
       logie, des oracles ... Précédé d'une intro-
       duction et suivi d'une biographie, d'une
       bibliographie et d'un vocabulaire ... Paris,
       L'Encyclopédie portative, 1830.
         xii, 296 p. front. 13cm.
                          (Continued on next card)

Encyclopédie portative.

Witchcraft
BF
1411   Denis, Ferdinand, 1798-1890. Tableau his-
D39   torique ... des sciences occultes ...
         1830.   (Card 2)
         Half-title: Encyclopédie portative; ou,
       Résumé universel des sciences, des lettres
       et des arts, en une collection de tratiés
       séparés ... Par une société de savans et de
       gens de lettres ...
         Ex-libris Frédéric de Sevillia.

         1. Occult   sciences--Hist.

The endemoniadas of Queretaro.

Witchcraft
BF
1555   [Lea, Henry Charles] 1825-1909.
L43   The endemoniadas of Queretaro.   [Phila-
       delphia, 1890]
         33-38 p. 25cm.

         Detached from the Journal of American
       folklore, v. 3, no. 8, 1890.

         1. Inquisition.   Mexico.   2. Demoniac
       possession.   I. Title.

Endor, Witch of (Biblical character)

Witchcraft
BF
1445   Gerhard, Johann Ernst, 1621-1668, praeses.
D61   Spectrum Endoreum, ex I. Sam. 28. Aus-
no.8   pice numine summo, sub praesidio ... Johan-
       nis Eernesti Gerhardi ... Publicae erudi-
       torum disquisitioni expositum, ab autore &
       respondente Benedicto Hahn ... ed. tertia
       auctior & emendatior. Jenae, Literis Jo-
       hannis Nisii, 1684.
         112 p. 21cm.
         No. 8 in vol. lettered Dissertationes
       de spectris. 1646-1753.
8   (Continued on next card)

Endor, Witch of (Biblical character)

WITCHCRAFT
BS
1325   Lathrop, Joseph, 1731-1820.
L35   Illustrations and reflections on the
       story of Saul's consulting the witch of
       Endor. A discourse delivered at West-
       Springfield.   Springfield, Mass., Henry
       Brewer, printer, 1806.
         20 p. 21cm.

         1. Endor, Witch of. (Biblical character)
       2. Saul, king of Israel.   3. Bible. O.T.
8   1. Samuel XXVIII--Criticism, interpretation,
NIC   etc.   4.   Witchcraft in the
       Bible.

Endor, Witch of (Biblical character)

WITCHCRAFT
BF
1565   Waldschmidt, Bernhard.
W16   Pythonissa Endorea, das ist: Acht vnd
       zwantzig Hexen- vnd Gespenstpredigten, ge-
       nommen auss der Histori von der Zauberinn
       zu Endor ... Gehalten in der Kirchen zun
       Barfüssern in Franckfurt, vnd nunmehr mit
       nützlichen, auss vornehmer Theologorum vnd
       anderer berühmten Autorum Schrifften genom-
       menen Anmerckungen vermehret ...   Franck-
       furt, Johann-Wilhelm Ammon vnd Wilhelm
       Serlin, Gedruck t durch Hieronymum Polich,
       1660.
8   (Continued on next card)

Endor, Witch of (Biblical character)

WITCHCRAFT
BF
1565   Waldschmidt, Bernhard.   Pythonissa Endorea
W16   ... 1660.   (Card 2)
         16 p. l., 690, [26] p. port. 22cm.
         Added engr. t. p. facing portrait.
         "Ander Theil ... von den Gespensten ..."
       has special t. p.
         Title in red and black.
         1. Witchcraft.   2. Witchcraft in the
       Bible.   3. Ghosts.   4. Endor, Witch of
       (Biblical char   acter) I. Title. II.
       Title: Ander   Theil ... von den Ge-
8   spensten.

Energumeni Coagienses.

Witchcraft
BF
1555   Brunsmand, Johan, 1637-1707.
A55   Johannis Brunsmanni Energumeni Coagien-
no.2   ses, sive Admirabilis historia, de horrenda
       cacodaemonis tentatione, quacum in Selandia
       Daniae, ejusque urbe Coagio familia civis,
       & vita honestissimi & fama integerrimi, per
       annorum aliquot spatium est conflictata:
       primum sermone Danico aliquoties edita &
       impressa: nunc vero in exterorum gratiam
       Latine interpretata & cum duplici auctario
       edita.   Editio   altera Latina, auctior
8   (Continued on next card)

Energumeni Coagienses.

Witchcraft
BF
1555   Brunsmand, Johan, 1637-1707.   ... Energumeni
A55   Coagienses ...   1695.   (Card 2)
no.2
       & correctior Leidensi.   Lipsiae, Apud Joh.
       Melchior Lieben, 1695.
         4 p. l., 156 p. 14cm.
         First published 1674 with title: Et
       forfaerdeligt huus-kaars.
         Attributed by British Museum to A. H.
       Barskier, whose narrative makes up first
       part of work   (p. 1-73)
8   (Continued on next card)

Energumeni Coagienses.

Witchcraft
BF
1555   Brunsmand, Johan, 1637-1707.   ...Energumeni
A55   Coagienses ...   1695.   (Card 3)
no.2
         No. 2 in vol. lettered Andreae. De ange-
       lorum...

         1. Witchcraft--Denmark.   2. Bartholin,
       Thomas, 1616-1680.   3. Bekker, Balthasar,
       1634-1698. I. Barskier, Anne Hans.   II.
       His   Et forfaerdeligt huus-kaars--Latin.
8   III. Title: Energumeni Coagienses.

Energumenicus.

Witchcraft
BF
1565   Faye, Barthélemy, seigneur d'Espeisses,
F28   16th cent.
         Bartholomei Faij, regij in senatv Pari-
       siensi consiliarij, ac Inquisitionum prae-
       sidis Energvmenicvs. Eiusdem Alexicacvs,
       cū liminari, vt vocant ad vtrūque librum
       epistola.   Lvtetiae, Apud Sebastianum
       Niuellium, 1571.
         2 p. l., 397 p. 17cm.
         Alexicacvs, p. 167-397, has special t. p.
         1. Witchcra   ft.   2. Lord's Supper--
       Bread and win   e.   3. Christian life.
8   I. Title: En   ergumenicus. II. Title:
       Alexicacus.

MSS
Bd.   Engelhard, Elsa, defendant.
WITCHCRAFT   Inquisitions-acta contra Elsa und Mar-
BF   greta Engelhardin, Geschwister zu Cabartz
E46++ und Klein Cabartz w.gn. verdächtiger Hexerei.
       [Reinhardsbrunn? 1686]-87.
         94 l. 34cm.
         Manuscript, on paper, in various 17th
       century hands.
         2 extra leaves inserted between l. 91, 92
       and 93, 94 form one sheet and are a frag-
       ment of anoth   er court document
       having noth   ing to do with the
                          (Continued on next card)

MSS
Bd.   Engelhard, Elsa, defendant.   Inquisitions-
WITCHCRAFT   acta ...   [1686]-87.   (Card 2)
BF
E46++ trial.
         Note by G. L. Burr inside front cover
       discusses the trial.
         Bound in gray marbled boards with vellum
       spine. On spine: Trial for witchcraft of
       Elsa and Margaret Engelhardt. 1687.
         1. Trials (Witchcraft)--Saxony.   2. Witch-
       craft--Saxony.   I. Engelhard, Margreta
       defendant.

Engelhard, Margreta, defendant.

MSS
Bd.   Engelhard, Elsa, defendant.
WITCHCRAFT   Inquisitions-acta contra Elsa und Mar-
BF   greta Engelhardin, Geschwister zu Cabartz
E46++ und Klein Cabartz w.gn. verdächtiger Hexerei
       [Reinhardsbrunn? 1686]-87.
         94 l. 34cm.
         Manuscript, on paper, in various 17th
       century hands.
         2 extra leaves inserted between l. 91, 92
       and 93, 94 form one sheet and are a frag-
       ment of anoth   er court document
       having noth   ing to do with the
                          (Continued on next card

CATALOGUE OF THE CORNELL WITCHCRAFT COLLECTION

Engelhard, Margreta, defendant.
    Engelhard, Elsa, defendant. Inquisitions-
acta ... [1686]-87.   (Card 2)
    trial.
    Note by G. L. Burr inside front cover
discusses the trial.
    Bound in gray marbled boards with vellum
spine. On spine: Trial for witchcraft of
Elsa and Margaret Engelhardt. 1687.
    1. Trials (Witchcraft)--Saxony. 2. Witch-
craft--Saxony. I. Engelhard, Margreta,
defendant.

Engelsch verhaal van ontdekte tovery
    wederleid door Balthasar Bekker.
Witchcraft
BF   Bekker, Balthasar, 1634-1698.
1581   Engelsch verhaal van ontdekte tovery
A2   wederleid door Balthasar Bekker S. T. D.
343   predikant tot Amsterdam. Amsterdam, By
D. van den Dalen, boekverkooper, 1689.
Met privilegie.
    28 p. title vignette, illus. initial.
21 x 16cm.
    4°: A-C⁴, D².
    Van der Linde 13.
    1. Witchcraft--England. I.
Title.

Witchcraft
BF   Englert, Anton, ed.
1583   Eine gereimte Zeitung über den Hexenbrand
Z7   in Dieburg im Jahre 1627. [Leipzig] 1913.
1627   199-204 p. 23cm.
    "Sonderabdruck aus Hessische Blätter für
Volkskunde 1913, Band XII, Heft 3."
    1. Witchcraft--Dieburg, Germany. I.
Title.

Witchcraft
BF   Englert, Anton, 1855-
1583   Ein kleiner Beitrag zur Geschichte der
Z7   Hexenprozesse.
1629   (In Hessische Blätter für Volkskunde.
Leipzig. 24cm. Bd. 5 (1906), p. [65]-
71)
    1. Witchcraft--Dieburg, Germany. 2.
Fleischbein, Hans, d. 1632. I. Title.
8

Witchcraft
BF   English, Philip, 1650-1734.
1575   Calef, Robert, 1648-1719.
D76   More wonders of the invisible world: or, The wonders of the
v.2-3   invisible world, display'd in five parts. Part I. An account of
the sufferings of Margaret Rule, written by the Reverend Mr.
C. M. P. II. Several letters to the author, &c. And his reply
relating to witchcraft. P. III. The differences between the inhabitants of Salem village, and Mr. Parris their minister, in
New-England. P. IV. Letters of a gentleman uninterested,
endeavouring to prove the received opinions about witchcraft
to be orthodox. With short essays to their answers. P. v. A
short historical accout [!] of matters of fact in that affair. To
(Continued on next card)   2-13714 rev.
[r31e2]

English, Philip, 1650-1734.
    Calef, Robert, 1648-1719.   More wonders of the invisible
world ... (Card 2)
which is added, a postscript relating to a book intitled, The
life of Sir William Phips. Collected by Robert Calef, merchant, of Boston in New-England ... London, Printed for
N. Hillar and J. Collyer, 1700.
    Reprint. (In Drake, S. G. The witchcraft delusion in New England
... Roxbury, Mass., 1866. 21½ᶜᵐ. v. 3, p. 3-167)
    Woodward's historical series. no. VI-VII.
    Prefatory: by the editor: p. [v]-x.
    Pedigree of Calef: 1 fold. leaf.
    Memoir of Robert Calef: p. [xi]-xxix.
    The text, here annotated, is that of the 1st edition, 1700. "It is given
as exactly like the original as a much better type can be made to imitate an old type of 166 years ago."--Pref. by the editor. p. vi.
(Continued on next card)   2-13714 rev.
[r31e2]

English, Philip, 1650-1734.
Witchcraft
BF   Calef, Robert, 1648-1719.   More wonders of the
1575   invisible world ... 1700.   (Card 3)
D76
v.2-3   Appendix: I. Examination of Giles Cory.--
II. Giles Corey and Goodwyfe Corey. A ballad of
1692.--III. Testimony of William Beale, of
Marblehead, against Mr. Philip English of Salem
given Aug. 2d. 1692.--IV. [Examination of the
Indian woman belonging to Mr. Parris's family]--
V. The examination of Mary Clark of Haverhill.--
VI. An account of the life and character of the
Rev. Samuel Parris, of Salem village, and of
his connection with the witchcraft delusion
of 1692. By Samuel P. Fowler.

The English opponents of the witch
    persecution.
Thesis
1903   Stowell, Roy Sherman.
463   The English opponents of the witch
persecution. Ithaca, N. Y., 1903.
[4], iv, 192 l. 28cm.
    Thesis (A. M.)--Cornell University, June,
1903.
    1. Witchcraft--England. I. Title.

English witchcraft and James the First.
Witchcraft
BF   Kittredge, George Lyman, 1860-1941.
1581   English witchcraft and James the First, by George
K62   Lyman Kittredge; from Studies in the history of reli-
1912   gions presented to Crawford Howell Toy, by pupils, colleagues and friends. New York, The Macmillan company, 1912.
    cover-title, 65 p. 23½ᶜᵐ.
    With this is bound his King James I and The
Devil is an ass.
    Cover has initials of author (G.L.K.) and
donor (J. M. H., i.e. J. M. Hart)
Library of Congress   BF1581.K5
    13-11912

Ennemoser, Chrysostomus M., respondent.
Witchcraft
BF   Planch, Alexius M, praeses.
1565   Dissertatio critico-scripturistica de
P71+   magia diabolica, et magorum prodigiis
Exod. 7. coram Pharaone patratis. Una cum
conclusionibus ex utroque testamento de-
sumptis, quas praeside P. Alexio M. Planch
defendendas suscepere P. P. Chrysostomus
M. Ennemoser, et Joan. Evang. M. Püchler
... [Oeniponti?] Litteris Wagnerianis
[1767]
8   6 p. l., 66, [9] p. 28cm.
(Continued on next card)

Ennemoser, Chrysostomus M., respondent.
Witchcraft
BF   Planch, Alexius M, praeses. Disser-
1565   tatio critico-scripturistica de magia dia-
P71+   bolica ... [1767]   (Card 2)
    Diss.--Innsbruck (C. M. Ennemoser and
J. E. M. Püchler, respondents)
    1. Witchcraft in the Bible. 2. Witch-
craft. 3. Magic. I. Ennemoser, Chrysostomus M., respondent. II. Püchler, Johann
Evangelica M., respondent. III. Ti-
8   tle: De magia diabolica, et magorum
prodigiis.

BF   Ennemoser, Joseph, 1787-1854.
1589   Geschichte der Magie. (Neudruck der Ausgabe von
E59   1844) Wiesbaden, Sändig (1966)
1966   xlviii, 1001 p. 21 cm. DM 98.-
    (GDNB 66-A18-405)
    1. Magic. 2. Occult sciences. I. Title.
BF1589.E58 1966   66-75303
Library of Congress   [2]

Ennemoser, Joseph, 1787-1854.
WITCHCRAFT   Geschichte der Magie. English.
BF   Ennemoser, Joseph, 1787-1854.
1589   The history of magic. Translated from
E59   the German by William Howitt. To which is
1854   added an appendix of the most remarkable
and best authenticated stories of apparitions, dreams, second sight, somnambulism,
predictions, divination, witchcraft, vampires, fairies, table-turning, and spirit-
rapping. Selected by Mary Howitt. London,
Henry G. Bohn, 1854.
    2 v. 19cm. (Bohn's scientific library)
    Translation of Geschichte der Magie.
(Continued on next card)

Witchcraft
BF   Ennemoser, Joseph, 1787-1854.
1589   The history of magic. Translated from the
E59   German by William Howitt. To which is added an
1854   appendix of the most remarkable and best
authenticated stories of apparitions, dreams,
second sight ... and spirit-rapping. Selected by
Mary Howitt. London, H. G. Bohn, 1854.
    2 v. 19cm. (Bohn's scientific library)
    Translation of Die Geschichte der Magie.
    I. His Geschichte der Magie. English.
II. Howitt, William, 1792-1879, tr. III. Howitt,
Mrs. Mary (Botham) 1799-1888, ed. IV. Title.

Enquiries into the meaning of demoniacks
    in the New Testament.
WITCHCRAFT
BF   Some thoughts on the miracles of Jesus; with
1559   an introduction to that of His casting
S69   out devils, which is particularly discuss'd. Occasioned by two late tracts,
intitled, Enquiries into the meaning of
demoniacks in the New Testament. By an
Impartial Hand. London, Printed for
John Clarke; and sold by J. Roberts, 1738.
69 p. 20cm.
    1. Exorcism. 2. Demonology. 3. En-
8   quiries into the meaning of demoniacks in
the New Testament. I. An Impartial
Hand.

An enquiry into the life and legend of
    Michael Scot.
Witchcraft
Q   Brown, James Wood.
143   An enquiry into the life and legend
S42   of Michael Scot. Edinburgh, David
B87   Douglas, 1897.
    xvi, 281 p. front. 23cm.
    1. Scott, Michael, 1175?-1234? I.
Title.

An enquiry into the meaning of demoniacks
Witchcraft   in the New Testament.
BS   [Sykes, Arthur Ashley] 1684?-1756.
2545   An enquiry into the meaning of demoniacks
D5   in the New Testament. ... By T.P.A.P.O.A.B.
T97   I.T.C.O.S. 2d ed., corr. and amended. Lon-
no.2   don, Printed for J. Roberts, 1737.
79 p. 21cm.
    No. 2 in vol. lettered: Twells, Whiston,
etc. Tracts on the demoniacs in the New Testament. London, 1738-1775.
    1. Demoniac possession. 2. Bible. N.T.--
Commentaries. I. Title.

Ens, Gaspar, 1570-1636?, tr.
Witchcraft
BF   Cigogna, Strozzi.
1520   Magiæ omnifariæ, vel potius, Vniversæ natvræ thea-
C57   trvm: in qvo a primis rervm principiis arcessita disputa-
1607   tione, vniuersa spiritvvm & incantationvm natura, &c.
explicatur. Auctore d. Strozzio Cigogna ... ex italico
latinitati donatum opera & studio Caspari Ens ... Coloniæ, sumptibus C. Butgenij, 1607.
    4 p. l., 568 p. 16ᶜᵐ.
    1. Demonology. 2. Exorcism. I. Ens, Gaspar, 1570-1636?, tr.
II. Title.
    11-9698

CATALOGUE OF THE CORNELL WITCHCRAFT COLLECTION

MSS Bd.
WITCHCRAFT
BF
E61
    Der entlarvte Teuffel oder denkwürdige Geschichte von vielen warhaftig Besessenen, welche dieses Feindes Grausamkeit heftig erfahren, entlich aber durch den mächtigen Finger Gottes wieder erlediget worden. Zu mehrer Bekräftigung der von Doct. Beckern, in seiner verzauberten Welt, zweiffelhaft gemachten Kögischen Geschichte ... Zusammen getragen von M. J. J. L. Leipzig, Johann Melchior Liebe, 16 97 [ca. 1900]
    (Continued on next card)

MSS Bd.
WITCHCRAFT
BF
E61
    Der entlarvte Teuffel ... 1697 [ca. 1900] (Card 2)
    77 p. 19cm.
    Carnap's manuscript copy.
    "Originaldruck in der Königl. öff. Bibliothek zu Dresden, 98 pag. Seiten in 8°."
    "Diese Schrift bildet gewissermassen die Fortsetzung zu: "Das geängstigte Köge oder Eine warhaffte und denkwürdige Historie, von einer ent setzlichen Versuchung des leidigen Satans zu Köge in
    (Continued on next card)

MSS Bd.
WITCHCRAFT
BF
E61
    Der entlarvte Teuffel ... 1697 [ca. 1900] (Card 3)
    Seeland" wo in deutscher Sprache durch denselben Verfasser ... i. J. 1695 herausgegeben. Hieraus erklärt es sich, dass diese Schrift mit " die dritte Zugabe" anfängt, da "das geängstigte Köge mit der zweiten Zugabe abschliesst."
    Marginal numerals and signatures indicate paginati on ans signatures of the original.
    (Continued on next card)

MSS Bd.
WITCHCRAFT
BF
E61
    Der entlarvte Teuffel ... 1697 [ca. 1900] (Card 4)
    Printed copy not in Van der Linde.

    1. Demoniac possession. 2. Devil. 3. Bekker, Balthasar, 1634-1698. De betoverde weere ld. I. Das geängstigte Köge. II. M. J. J. L. III. L., M. J. J.

Un envoutement en Gévaudan en l'année 1347.
Witchcraft
BF
1582
Z7
1347
    Falgairolle, Edmond.
    Un envoutement en Gévaudan en l'année 1347. Nîmes, Catélan, 1892.
    117 p. 19cm.

    Contains the complete proceedings of the trial of Etienne Pépin in Latin, and an abridged version in French.

    1. Pépin, Étienne, fl. 1347. I. Title.

Une épidémie d'hystéro-démonopathie en 1861.
Witchcraft
BF
1517
F5C75
1863
    Constans, Augustin.
    Relation sur une épidémie d'hystéro-démonopathie en 1861. 2. éd. Paris, A. Delahaye, 1863.
    viii, 130 p. 24cm.

    1. Demoniac possession. 2. Witchcraft--Morzines, France. I. Title: Une épidémie d'hystéro-démonopathie en 1861. II. Title.

Epidemie der vom Teufel Besessenen.
Witchcraft
BF
1555
W65
    Wigand, Paul, 1786-1866.
    Epidemie der vom Teufel Besessenen. 44. Criminal-Prozess gegen Besessene, und Untersuchung, ob sie wirklich vom Teufel besessen seien, oder nicht. 1664 und 1666. [Leipzig, S. Hirzel, 1854]
    [320]-339 p. 23cm.
    Caption title.
    Detached from Denkwürdigkeiten, Kap. XI.
    1. Demoniac possession. 2. Witchcraft--Germany. I. Title.
8

Epimetron. De ritu ignis.
Witchcraft
BF
1565
K21
1771
    Kauz, Constantin Franz Florian Anton von, 1735-1797.
    Constantini Francisci de Cauz ... De cultibus magicis eorumque perpetuo ad ecclesiam et rempublicam habitu libri duo. ... Editio II. Aucta et emendata. Vindobonae, Literis Trattnerianis, 1771.
    18 p. l., 400, [6] p. 22cm.
    "ΕΠΙΜΕΤΡΟΝ. De ritu ignis natali Joannis Baptistae die accensi dissertatio," p. [377]-400, has special t. p. (First printed 1759)
8   (Continued on next card)

Epistolarum familiarium libri duo ad diversos Germaniae principes.
Witchcraft
PA
8585
T85E6
1536
    Trithemius, Johannes, 1462-1516.
    Epistolarum familiarium libri duo ad diuersos Germaniae principes, episcopos, ac eruditione praestantes uiros ... Haganoae, Ex Officina Petri Brubachij, 1536.
    [16], 344 p. 20cm.
    Title vignette.
    Ex libris Frid. Zarncke.
    I. Ex Libris--Zarncke, Friderich. II. Title.

Epitome delictorum, sive De magia.
WITCHCRAFT
BF
1565
T68
1678
    Torreblanca Villalpando, Francisco.
    D. D. Francisci Torreblanca Cordubensis ... Epitome delictorum, sive De magia: in qva aperta vel occvlta invocatio daemonis intervenit. Editio novissima innvmeris mendis expvrgata, necnon indice rerum & verborum copiosissimo nunc primùm locupletata. Lugduni, Sumpt. Joannis Antonij Huguetan, & Soc., 1678.
    4 p. l., 576, [107] p. 23cm.
    Title in red and black.
    First pub lished 1618 under title: Daemonologia sive De magia ...
8   (Continued on next card)

Erastus, Thomas, 1524-1583. Dispvtatio de lamiis, sev strigibvs.
WITCHCRAFT
BF
1565
J19
    Jacquier, Nicolas.
    Flagellvm haereticorvm fascinariorvm, avtore Nicolao Iaqverio. His accesservnt Lamberti Danaei de veneficis dialogi, Ioachimi Camerarii in Plutarchi de oraculorum defectu epistola, Martini de Arles de superstitionibus tractatvs, Ioannis Trithemii de reprobis atq; maleficis qvaestiones III, Thomae Erasti de strigibus liber. Studio Ioan. Myntzenbergii edita. Francofvrti ad Moenvm [Impressvm apud N. Bassaeum] 1581.
8
NIC   604 p. 17 cm.
    (Continued on next card)

Witchcraft
BF
1565
E65
    Erastus, Thomas, 1524-1583.
    Repetitio dispvtationis de lamiis sev strigibvs: in qua plenè, solidè, & perspicuè, de arte earum, potestate, itémque poena disceptatur ... Basileae, Apud Petrum Pernam [1578]
    7 p. l., 127 p. 16cm.

    1. Witchcraft. I. Title.
8

Erastus, Thomas, 1524-1583.
Witchcraft
BF
1520
W64P8
1579
    Wier, Johann, 1515-1588.
    Histoires, dispvtes et discovrs, des illusions et impostures des diables, des magiciens infames, sorcieres & empoisonneurs: Des ensorcelez & demoniaques, & de la guerison d'iceux: Item de la punition que meritent les magiciens, les empoisonneurs, & les sorcieres. Le tout comprins en six livres ... Devx dialogves de Thomas Erastvs ... touchant le pouuoir des sorcieres: & de la punition qu'elles meritent. Auec deux indices ... [Genève, Povr Iaqves Chovet, 1579.
    (Continued on next card)

Erastus, Thomas, 1524-1583.
Witchcraft
BF
1520
W64P8
1579
    Wier, Johann, 1515-1588. Histoires, dispvtes et discovres, des illusions et impostures des diables ... 1579. (Card 2)
    [32], 875, [39] p. 18cm.
    Translation of the author's De praestigiis daemonum.
    "Devx dialogves de Thomas Erastvs" has special t. p.

Erastus, Thomas Lieber.
    see
Erastus, Thomas, 1524-1583.

Erbauliche Abhandlung von dem erschröcklichen und Jammer-vollen Zustand der geist- und leiblichen Besitzung des T[euffels]
Witchcraft
BF
1555
B71
    Bonnhöfer, Johann Friedrich.
    ... Erbauliche Abhandlung von dem erschröcklichen und Jammer-vollen Zustand der geist- und leiblichen Besitzung des Teuffe In zweyen Betrachtungen aus Heil. Schrifft erwiesen und mit historischen Exempeln erleutert ... mit einer Vorrede Gustav Georg Zeltners, D. worinnen er seine Gedancken vom Binden des Satans, Offenb. 20, 2. eröffnet. Nürnberg, Bey J. W. Rönnagel, 1733.
    26 p. l., 884, [36] p. port. 17cm.
8   (Continued on next card)

Erdmann, Adam, 1656-1727.
    see
Mirus, Adam Erdmann, 1656-1727.

Erklärungsversuch einiger französischen, auf das Hexenwesen des Mittelalters bezüglichen Ausdrücke.
WITCHCRAFT
BF
1569
P52+
    Pfannenschmid, Heino, 1828-1906.
    Erklärungsversuch einiger französischen, auf das Hexenwesen des Mittelalters bezüglichen Ausdrücke: Genot, Genocherie, Criage

    (In: La Revue nouvelle d'Alsace-Lorraine. Colmar. 26cm. v.4, no.1, June 1884. p. 36-47)
8
NIC   1. Witchcraft--Hist. 2. Witchcraft--France.

CATALOGUE OF THE CORNELL WITCHCRAFT COLLECTION

MSS   Erledigung der ehrw. Klosterfrau Maria
Bd.   Augusta Delphina, im Frauenkloster zu
WITCHCRAFT   Stanz, den 28. März 1848 durch P.
BF   Anizet Regli, Guardian zu Stanz. [n.p.]
169   Nach einem Original-Manuskripte getreu
    abgedruckt, 1848 [ca. 1900]
    9 l. 19cm.
    Carnap's manuscript copy.
    "Originaldruck i. d. Stadtbibliothek zu
Zürich. 13 l. in 8°."
    Numerals in the margins indicate
pagination of   the original.
    (Continued on next card)

MSS   Erledigung der ehrw. Klosterfrau Maria
Bd.   Augusta Delphina ... 1848 [ca. 1900]
WITCHCRAFT   (Card 2)
BF
169

    1. Demoniac possession. 2. Delphina,
Maria Augusta, fl. 1848. I. Regli,
Anizet, fl. 1848.

WITCHCRAFT   Erledigung der ehrw. Klosterfrau Maria
BF   Augusta Delphina.
1555   [Leu, Josef Burkard] 1808-1865.
L65   Die Teufels-Beschwörung in Stans; oder,
    Gutachten über die Broschüre: Erledigung
    der ehrw. Klosterfrau Maria Augusta Del-
    phina im Frauenkloster zu Stans den 28.
    März 1848 durch P. Anizet Regli... Luzern,
    X. Meyer, 1848.
    15 p. 20cm.
    1.Demoniac possession. 2. Devil. 3. Ex-
orcism. 4.Delphina, Maria Augusta,fl.1848.
5.Regli,Anizet,   fl. 1848. 6. Erledigung der   ehrw. Klosterfrau Maria
8   Augusta Delp   hina. I. Title.
NIC

    Erneuerte Land-Gebott wider die Aber-
    glauben, Zauberey ...
Witchcraft
BF   Bavaria. Laws, statutes, etc.
1583   Der Churfürstl. Durchleucht Herzogs Maxi-
A2   milian Joseph in Bayern &c. &c. ... erneu-
B35+   erte Land-Gebott, wider die Aberglauben,
    Zauberey, Hexerey, und andere straffliche
    Teuffels-Künsten. München, Gedruckt bey
    Johann Jacob Vötter, 1746.
    [18] p. 29cm.
    1. Witchcraft--Germany. 2. Superstit-
tion. I. Bavaria. Sovereigns, etc., 1745-
1777 (Maximilian   III Joseph) II. Title:
Erneuerte Land-   Gebott wider die Aber-
8   glauben, Zaube   rey.

BX   **Ernst, Cécile.**
2340   Teufelaustreibungen; die Praxis der katholischen Kirche
E71   im 16. und 17. Jahrhundert. Bern, H. Huber [c1972]
    147 p. 23 cm.
    Bibliography: p. 135-141.

    1. Exorcism.   I. Title.
BX2340.E75   265'.9   73-188553
ISBN 3-456-00262-3
NIC   Library of Congress   72 [2]

    Ernsthaffte aber doch muntere und ver-
    nünfftige Thomasische Gedancken u. Er-
    rinnerungen.
Witchcraft
K   Thomasius, Christian, 1655-1728.
T463   Ernsthaffte aber doch muntere und ver-
E7   nünfftige Thomasische Gedancken u. Errinne-
    rungen über allerhand ausserlesene juris-
    tische Händel. Halle im Magdeburgischen,
    In der Rengerischen Buchhandlung, 1720-21.
    4 v. in 2. front. 22cm.
    Title of v. 1 in red and black.
    List of Thomasius' works in MS, from
S. Calvary & co., Berlin, tipped in before
t. p.
    Continued on next card)

    Ernsthaffte aber doch muntere und ver-
    nünfftige Thomasische Gedancken u. Er-
Witchcraft   rinnerungen.
K   Thomasius, Christian, 1655-1728. Ernst-
T463   haffte aber doch muntere und vernünfftige
E7   Thomasische Gedancken ... 1720-21.
    (Card 2)
    Continued by his Vernünfftige und christ-
liche aber nicht scheinheilige Thomasische
Gedancken, 1723-25.
    1. Law reports, digests, etc.--Germany.
I. His   Vernünfftige und christliche ...
Gedancken. II.   Title.

    Ernstige en zedige verantwoording van P.
    Rabus, tegen de lasteringen des remon-
Witchcraft   strantschen predigers J. Molinaeus.
BF   Rabus, Petrus, 1660-1702.
1410   Ernstige en zedige verantwoording van
B42   P. Rabus, tegen de lasteringen des remon-
Z56   strantschen predigers J. Molinaeus. Rot-
v.3   terdam, By P. Boekenes, boekverkooper, 1692.
no.21   1 p. l., 24 p. title and end page vi-
    gnettes, illus. initial. 20 x 16cm.
    4°: π1, A-C^4.
    Black letter.
    In defense of Balthasar Bekker.
    Van der Linde   135.
    No. 21 in   vol. lettered Bekker III.
    (Continued on next card)

Witchcraft   Eros and evil.
BF
1556   Masters, R   E   L
M42   Eros and evil; the sexual psychopathology of witchcraft.
    New York, Julian Press, 1962.
    xviii, 322 p. 24 cm.
    Bibliography: p. [309]-313.

    1. Witchcraft. 2. Sexual perversion. 3. Demonology. I. Title.
BF1556.M35   62-19302
Library of Congress   2

    Erric, prince of Lorraine, bp. of
    Verdun, d. 1623.
WITCHCRAFT
BF   Langlois, Ernest, 1857-1924.
1582   Un évêque de Verdun, prince de Lorraine,
Z7   ensorcelé, marié et condamné par le tribu-
1605   nal de l'inquisition. [Nancy, Impr. Ber-
    ger-Levrault, 1895]
    23 p. 20cm.
    Concerning Erric, prince of Lorraine,
bishop of Verdun.
    Extract from Annales de l'est, Apr. 1895.
    1. Erric, prince of Lorraine, bp. of Ver-
8   dun, d.1623.   I. Title.
NIC

MSS   Erschreckliche newe Zeitung, welche sich be-
Bd.   geben und zugetragen in diesem 1650.
WITCHCRAFT   Jahr, in der Osternacht, im Schweitzer
BF   Gebirge, bey der Stadt Dillhofen auff
E733   einem Dorffe Dinndurff genandt, in welchem
    drey Hexen gewohnet ... Dilhofen,
    Matthias Hammer, 1650 [ca. 1900]
    [6] p. 19cm.
    Carnap's manuscript copy.
    "Originaldruck in der Königl. Bibliothek
zu Berlin, (Me   usebach'sche Samlung),
4 Bl. in 16°."   (Continued on next card)

MSS   Erschreckliche newe Zeitung ... 1650 [ca.
Bd.   1900]   (Card 2)
WITCHCRAFT
BF   In verse.
E733

    1. Witchcraft--Switzerland.

MSS   Ein Erschröcklich Geschicht vom Tewfel und
Bd.   einer Unhulden, beschehen zu Schilta bey
WITCHCRAFT   Rotweil in der Karwochen MDXXXIII. Jar.
BF   [n.p., 1533? ca. 1900]
E735   2 l. 19cm.

    Carnap's manuscript copy.
    "Originaldruck in der Stadtbibliothek zu
Zürich. 1 Bl. Fol."
    At end: Steffan hamer, Briefmaler.
    1. Exempla.   2. Devil. I. Hamer,
Steffan.

MSS   Erschröckliche doch warhaffte Geschicht,
Bd.   die sich in der spanischen Statt, Madri-
WITCHCRAFT   leschos genannt, mit einer verheurafen
BF   Weibss-person zugetragen, welche von
E736   einer gantzen Legion Teuffel siben Jar
Z55   lang besessen gewest. Und durch Patrem
    Ludovicum de Torre ... widerumb erlediget
    worden. München, Durch Nicolaum Hen-
    ricum, 1608 [ca. 1900]
    11 l. illus. 24cm.
    Carnap's man   uscript copy.
    (Continued on next card)

MSS   Erschröckliche doch warhaffte Geschicht,
Bd.   die sich in der spanischen Statt ... zu-
WITCHCRAFT   getragen ... 1608 [ca. 1900] (Card 2)
BF
E736   "Originaldruck in der Kgl. u. Staats-
Z55   Bibliothek zu München. 8 Bl. in 4°. Sig.
    A^2-B^3."
    Numerals in the margins indicate pagina-
tion of the original.
    May have been written by De Torre himself.
    1. Demoniac possession. 2. Exorcism.
3. Witchcraft--Spain. 4. Garcia de Rodriguez
de Gutierrez,   Maria, b. 1564. I.
Torre, Luis   de, d. 1635, supposed
author.

    Erschröckliche gantz warhafftige Geschicht,
    welche sich mit Apolonia ... verlauffen
Witchcraft   hat.
BF   [Bewerlein, Sixtus]
1555   Erschröckliche gantz warhafftige Geschicht,
B57   welche sich mit Apolonia, Hannsen Geißlbrechts
    Burgers zu Spalt inn dem Lystätter Bistumb,
    Hauβfrawen, so den 20. Octobris, Anno 82. von
    dem bösen Feind gar hart besessen, vnnd doch
    den 24. gedachten Monats widerumb durch Gottes
    gnädige Hilff, auβ solcher grossen Pein vnnd
    Marter entlediget worden, verlauffen hat.
    Allen gottlosen, zänckischen, vbelfluchenden
    Eheleuten, vnnd andern zu sonderer Warnung in
8   Truck gegeben.   Durch M. Sixtum Agrico-
    (Continued on next card)

    Erschröckliche gantz warhafftige Geschicht,
Witchcraft   welche sich mit Apolonia ... verlauffen
BF   hat.
1555   [Bewerlein, Sixtus] Erschröckliche gantz
B57   warhafftige Geschicht ... 1584. (Card 2)

    lam [pseud.] ... vnd dann D. Georgium Witme-
rum ... Ingolstatt, Getruckt durch Wolffgang Eder, 1584.
    3 p. l., 49 p. 20cm.
    Title in red and black.
    1. Demoniac possession. 2. Exorcism.
3. Geisslbrecht, Anna, fl. 1584. I.
Witmer, Georg, joint author. II. Title.
8

Witchcraft
BF   Die ersten Bekämpfer des Hexenwahns.
1563   München, C. Wolf, 1897.
E92++   [321]-323, [329]-331, 338-339 p. 32cm.
no. 4-6   (Deutscher Merkur, 28. Jahrg., No. 41-43)

    A review of Binz. Doktor Johann Weyer,
der erste Bekämpfer des Hexenwahns.

    1. Wier, Johann, 1515-1588. 2. Binz,
Carl, 1832-1913. Doctor Johann Weyer.

OVER

195

CATALOGUE OF THE CORNELL WITCHCRAFT COLLECTION

Ertappter Briefwechsel von der Zauberey.

Witchcraft
BF 1432
E73
   Erzstein, pseud., ed.
      Ertappter Briefwechsel von der Zauberey, Schröpfers Künsten, Nativitätstellen, Sympathie, Gespenstern u.d.g., gesammlet von einem Juristen, Mediciner, Philosophen und Theologen, und hrsg. von Erzstein. Leipzig, C. G. Huscher, 1777.
      282 p. 18cm.

      1. Schrepfer, Johann Georg, 1730?-1774. I. Title.

MSS
Bd.
WITCHCRAFT
BF
E738
   Erweytterte Unholden Zeyttung. Kurtze Erzelung wie viel der Unholden hin und wider, sonderlich inn dem Obern Teutschland, gefänglich eingezogen: was für grossen Schaden sie den Menschen, vermög ihrer Urgicht, zugefüget, und wieviel ungefährlich deren, inn disem 1590. Jar, biss auff den 21. Julij, von dem Leben zum Todt hingerichtet und verbrandt worden seyen. [Ulm, 1590? ca. 1900]
      6 l. illus., end vignette. 24cm.
      Carnap's manuscript copy.
      (Continued on next card)

MSS
Bd.
WITCHCRAFT
BF
E738
   Erweytterte Unholden Zeyttung. [1590? ca. 1900] (Card 2)
      "Originaldruck i. d. Kgl. Bibliothek zu Berlin, 6 Bl. in 4°. Sig. Aij--Bij."
      Numerals and signatures in the margins indicate pagination and signatures of the original.

      1. Witchcraft. 2. Trials (Witchcraft)--Germany.

Witchcraft
BF 1559
E73
   Erzählung einer vom Bischof Laurent in Luxemburg bewirkten Teufels-Austreibung. Aus dem Holländischen wörtlich übers. Luxemburg, G. Michaelis, 1843.
      23 p. 18cm.

      1. Exorcism. 2. Demonology. 3. Devil.

Witchcraft
BF 1432
E73
   Erzstein, pseud., ed.
      Ertappter Briefwechsel von der Zauberey, Schröpfers Künsten, Nativitätstellen, Sympathie, Gespenstern u.d.g., gesammlet von einem Juristen, Mediciner, Philosophen und Theologen, und hrsg. von Erzstein. Leipzig, C. G. Huscher, 1777.
      282 p. 18cm.

      1. Schrepfer, Johann Georg, 1730?-1774. I. Title.

Escape from witchcraft.

BF 1566
B64
   Blankenship, Roberta.
      Escape from witchcraft. Grand Rapids, Zondervan Pub. House [1972]
      114 p. port. 18cm. (Zondervan books)

Witchcraft
BF 1520
W64
P83
   Eschbach, H
      Dr. med. Johannes Wier, der Leibarzt des Herzogs Wilhelm III. von Cleve-Jülich-Berg. Ein Beitrag zur Geschichte der Hexenprozesse. (In Düsseldorfer Jahrbuch. Beiträge zur Geschichte des Niederrheins. Düsseldorf. 23cm.
      1. Band (1886), p. [57]-174)

      1. Wier, Johann, 1515-1588. De praestigiis daemonum. 2. Wier, Johann, 1515-1588. 3. Witchcraft--Germany. I. Title. II. Düsseldorfer Jahrbücher. Beiträge zur Geschichte des Niederrheins.

WITCHCRAFT
BF 1555
E74
C7
   Eschenmayer, Carl Adolph von, 1770?-1852.
      Conflict zwischen Himmel und Hölle, an dem Dämon eines besessenen Mädchens beobachtet von C. A. Eschenmayer in Kirchheim unter Teck. Nebst einem Wort an Dr. Strauss. Tübingen, Buchhandlung Zu-Guttenberg, 1837.
      xvi, 215 p. 17cm.

8
NIC
      1. Demoniac possession. 2. Stadebauer, Caroline. I. Title.

WITCHCRAFT
BF 1555
K39
   Eschenmayer, Carl Adolph von, 1770?-1852.
   Einige Reflexionen über Besitzung und Zauber.
   Kerner, Justinus Andreas Christian, 1786-1862.
      Geschichten Besessener neuerer Zeit; Beobachtungen aus dem Gebiete kakodämonisch-magnetischer Erscheinungen. Nebst Reflexionen von C. A. Eschenmayer über Besessenseyn und Zauber. Stuttgart, Druck von J. Wachendorf, 1834.
      vi, 195 p. 19cm.

8
NIC
      1. Demoniac possession. I. Eschenmayer, Carl Adolph von, 1770?-1852. Einige Reflexionen über Besitzung und Zauber. II. Title.

Witchcraft
BF 1555
E74
   Eschenmayer, Carl Adolph von, 1770?-1852.
      Karakteristik des Unglaubens, Halbglaubens und Vollglaubens, in Beziehung auf die neuern Geschichten besessener Personen. Nebst Beleuchtung der Kritik im Christenboten. Tübingen, Verlag der Buchhandlung Zu-Guttenberg, 1838.
      110 p. 20cm.

      1. Demoniac possession. I. Title.

WITCHCRAFT
BF 1555
E74
O78
   Eschenmayer, Carl Adolph von, 1770?-1852.
   Ottokar, Amadeus.
      Anti-Satan. Sendschreiben an Professor Eschenmayer betreffend dessen Entgegnung auf die Schrift: "Entdeckung eines Complots wider Religion und Christenthum etc." Nürnberg, Bauer und Raspe, 1838.
      24 p. 21cm.

8
NIC
      1. Devil. 2. Eschenmayer, Carl Adolph von, 1770?-1852. Karakteristik des Unglaubens... I. Eschenmayer, Carl Adolph von, 1770?-1852. II. Title.

WITCHCRAFT
BF 1555
E74
O78
   Eschenmayer, Carl Adolph von, 1770?-1852.
   Ottokar, Amadeus.
      Anti-Satan. Sendschreiben an Professor Eschenmayer betreffend dessen Entgegnung auf die Schrift: "Entdeckung eines Complots wider Religion und Christenthum etc." Nürnberg, Bauer und Raspe, 1838.
      24 p. 21cm.

8
NIC
      1. Devil. 2. Eschenmayer, Carl Adolph von, 1770?-1852. Karakteristik des Unglaubens... I. Eschenmayer, Carl Adolph von, 1770?-1852. II. Title.

Esorcismi e magia nell'Italia del Cinquecento e del Seicento.

BF 1559
P49
   Petrocchi, Massimo.
      Esorcismi e magia nell'Italia del Cinquecento e del Seicento. Napoli, Libreria scientifica editrice, 1957.
      52 p. 20cm. (Collana di storia religiosa 3)

      1. Exorcism. 2. Witchcraft--Italy. I. Title.

WITCHCRAFT
BF 1555
E77
   Esprit du Bosroger, Capuchin.
      La pieté affligee; ov, Discovrs historiqve & theologique de la possession des religieuses dittes de Saincte Elizabeth de Louuiers. Divisé en trois parties. Roven, Chez Iean le Boulenger, 1652.
      [30], 458, 8 p. front. 23cm.
      Copy 1 imperfect: front. wanting.
      Inserted at end of copy 1: 6 p. of ms.
      2 copies
      1. Demoniac possession. 2. Bavent, Madeleine, ca. 1608-1647. 3. Louviers, France. St. Louis (Convent) 4. Witchcraft. I. Title.

Essai d'une bibliographie française méthodique & raisonnée de la sorcellerie et de la possession démoniaque...

Witchcraft
Z 6878
W8
Y98
   ...Essai d'une bibliographie francaise méthodique & raisonnée de la sorcellerie et de la possession démoniaque; pour servir de suite et de complément à la Bibliotheca magica de Graesse, aux catalogues Sépher, Ouvaroff, D'Ourches et Guldenstubbe, S. de Guaita et aux divers travaux partiels publiés sur cette matière. Préface par Albert de Rochas. Paris, Bibliothèque Chacornac, 1900.
      xiv p., 1 l., 254, [1] p. front., facsims., plates. 25cm.
      "Il a été tiré de cet ouvrage: 10 exemplaires sur papier de Hollande et 500 exemplaires sur papier ordinaire, tous numérotés et paraphés. No. 13."
      1,793 titles, classified.
      1. Witchcraft--Bibl. 2. Occult sciences--Bibl.
I. Grässe, Johann Georg Theodor, 1814-1885. Bibliotheca magica et pneumatica. II. Title.
   Library of Congress, no. Z6878.W8Y8.

Essai médico-historique sur les possédés de Loudun.

WITCHCRAFT
BF 1517
F5
S26+
   Sauzé, J.-Charles, 1815-
      Essai médico-historique sur les possédés de Loudun. Paris, Impr. Rignoux, 1839.
      59 p. 26cm.

      Thèse--Paris.
      "Questions sur diverses branches des sciences médicales": p. [51]-59.

8
NIC
      1. Loudun, France. Ursuline convent. 2. Demoniac possession. 3. Psychical research. I. Title: Les possédés de Loudun.

Essai sur le satanisme et la superstition au moyen age.

WITCHCRAFT
BF 1549
J41
   Jaulmes, Alfred.
      Essai sur le satanisme et la superstition au moyen age, précédé d'une introduction sur leurs origines. Étude historique. Montauban, Imprimerie typo-lithographique J. Granié, 1900.
      110 p. 22cm.

      Bibliography: p. [7]-8.
      Imprint stamped on t. p.: Paris, Librairie Fischbacher.

8
NIC
      1. Satanism. I. Title.

Essai sur les erreurs et les superstitions

Witchcraft
BF 1775
C35
   Castillon, Jean Louis, 1720-ca. 1793.
      Essai sur les erreurs et les superstitions. Par m. L. C... Amsterdam, Arckée & Merkus, 1765.
      411 [i.e. 481] p. 18cm.

      Page 481 incorrectly numbered 411.
      Ex libris René Amédée Choppin.
      I. Title.

CATALOGUE OF THE CORNELL WITCHCRAFT COLLECTION

Witchcraft
BF
1775
C35
1766
    Essai sur les erreurs et les superstitions anciennes & modernes.
    Castillon, Jean Louis, 1720-ca. 1793.
        Essai sur les erreurs et les superstitions anciennes & modernes. Par m. L. Castillon. Nouv. éd., rev., corr. & considérablement augm. Francfort, Knoe & Eslinger, 1766.
        2 v. 21cm.

    1. Superstition.   I. Title.

Witchcraft
BF
1775
G96
    Essai sur les superstitions.
    Guillois, Ambroise, 1796-1856.
        Essai sur les superstitions, par M. l'Abbé Guillois. Lille, L. Lefort, 1836.
        144 p. 16cm.

8   1. Superstition. 2. Occult sciences.

Witchcraft
BF
1411
T35
    An essay on demonology, ghosts, and apparitions, and popular superstitions.
    Thacher, James, 1754-1844.
        An essay on demonology, ghosts, and apparitions, and popular superstitions. Also, an account of the witchcraft delusion at Salem in 1692 ... Boston, Carter and Hendee, 1831.
        234 p. 18cm.

    1. Demonology. 2. Apparitions. 3. Witchcraft--Salem, Mass. 4. Superstition. I. Title.

Witchcraft
BF
1531
28
1827
    An essay on evil spirits.
    Carlisle, William.
        An essay on evil spirits; or, Reasons to prove their existence. In opposition to a lecture delivered by the Rev. N. T. [i.e. N.S.] Heineken, in the Unitarian Chapel, Bradford. 3d ed., enl. and corr. ... London, Printed for the Author, and sold by Hamilton, Adams, 1827.
        176 p. 20cm.

    1. Demonology.   2. Heineken, Nicholas Samuel. I. Title.

WITCHCRAFT
BS
2545
D5
F23
1805
    An essay on the demoniacs of the New Testament.
    Farmer, Hugh, 1714-1787.
        An essay on the demoniacs of the New Testament. 2d ed. London, Printed by R. Taylor and sold by J. Johnson, and W. Vidler, 1805.
        xii, 264 p. 18cm.

    With copy 2 is bound his An inquiry into the nature and design of Christ's temptation in the wilderness. 4th ed. London, 1805.

8
NIC

Witchcraft
[Defoe, Daniel] 1660-1731.
    Essay on the history and reality of apparitions.
    An essay on the history and reality of apparitions. Being an account of what they are, and what they are not; whence they come, and whence they come not. London, J. Roberts, 1727.
    6 p.l., 395 p. front., plates. 19 1/2cm.

    I. Title.

Witchcraft
BS
2545
D5
C56
    An essay towards vindicating the literal sense of the demoniacks in the New Testament
    [Church, Thomas]
        An essay towards vindicating the literal sense of the demoniacks in the New Testament. In answer to a late Enquiry into the meaning of them [by A.A. Sykes] ... London, Printed by J. Bettenham, and sold by J. Roberts, 1737.
        118 p. 19cm.

    1. Demoniac possession. 2. Bible. N.T.--Commentaries. 3. Sykes, Arthur Ashley, 1684?-1756. [An enquiry into the meaning of demoniacks in the New Testament. I. Title.

WITCHCRAFT
BF
1555
E78
    An Essay upon demoniacs; with remarks upon the existence and influence of fallen spirits. By Plain Truth [pseud.] Amherst, Mass., J.S. & C. Adams, printers, 1833.
    34 p. 19cm.

8
NIC
    1. Demoniac possession. 2. Demonology.
    I. Plain Truth, pseud.

Witchcraft
B
1201
B73E7
1694
    An essay upon reason, and the nature of spirits.
    Burthogge, Richard, 1638?-ca.1700.
        An essay upon reason, and the nature of spirits. By Richard Burthogge, M.D. London, Printed for J. Dunton, 1694.
        3 p. l., 280 p. diagr. 18cm.

Witchcraft
B
1201
G53
S2
1665
    Essays on several important subjects in philosophy and religion.
    Glanvill, Joseph, 1636-1680.
        Essays on several important subjects in philosophy and religion. By Joseph Glanvill ... London, Printed by J. D. for J. Baker and H. Mortlock, 1676.
        [340] p. 20cm.
        Various paging.
        CONTENTS.--Against confidence in philosophy.--Of scepticism, and certainty.--Modern improvements of knowledge.--The usefulness of philosophy to theology.--The agreement of reason, and religion.--Against modern Sadducism, in the matter of witches and apparitions.--Anti-fanatical religion and free philosophy. In a continuation of the New Atlantis. Wing G809.
        Bound with his Scepsis scientifica. London, 1665.
    1. Philosophy and religion.
    I. Title.

Witchcraft
GR
142
H6
A3
no.10
    Essex, Mrs. Anne (Baldwin) b. 1686.
    A short rehearsal of the sad condition of three of the children of John Baldwin of Sarret in the county of Hertford, and also the manner of their deliverance, 1717. The parents' evidence together with a summary of the testimonies of the children and friends and a brief introductory note by W. B. Gerish. Bishops' Stortford, 1915.
    19 p. 21½cm. (Hertfordshire folk lore. no. 10)

    1. Baldwin, Rebecca, 1688-1713. 2. Baldwin, Mary, b. 1690. 3. Essex, Mrs. Anne (Baldwin) b. 1686. I. Gerish, William Blyth, ed. II. Title.

                    16-25743
    Library of Congress   GR142.H6A3 no. 17

Witchcraft
BF
1583
R43
    Ettenheimer Hexenprozesse im 17. Jahrhundert.
    Rest, Josef, 1884-
        Ettenheimer Hexenprozesse im 17. Jahrhundert.
        (In Die Ortenau. Mitteilungen des historischen Vereins für Mittelbaden. Offenburg i. B. 25cm. 3. Heft (1912), p. [38]-56)
        Includes transcripts of records.
        1. Trials (Witchcraft)--Ettenheim, Germany. 2. Trials (Witchcraft)--Alsace. I. Title. II. Die Ortenau.

Witchcraft
BF
1566
R15
    Étude sur la sorcellerie.
    Raiponce, Léon.
        Étude sur la sorcellerie. Dour, Typographie A. Vaubert, 1894.
        105, [1] p. 19cm.

    1. Witchcraft. 2. Witchcraft--France. I. Title.

WITCHCRAFT
BF
1582
S14
    Étude sur le merveilleux au XVe siècle.
    Saint-Olive, Pierre.
        Étude sur le merveilleux au XVe siècle. Un miracle à St.-Genis-d'Aoste. Une affaire de sorcellerie aux Avenières. Belley, Impr. L. Chaduc, 1912.
        15 p. illus. 23cm.
        "Extrait de la revue 'Le Bugey' Octobre 1911. Tiré à 80 exemplaires. N°. 0014."
    1. Witchcraft--France. 2. Witchcraft--Avenières, France. I. Title: Le merveilleux au XVe siècle. II. Title: Un miracle à St.-Genis-d'Aoste.

Witchcraft
BF
1582
G52
N8
    Étude sur les procès de sorcellerie en Normandie.
    Giraud, Albert.
        Étude sur les procès de sorcellerie en Normandie. Discours de réception de M. le Dr. Giraud. Rouen, Imprimerie Cagniard (L. Gy, successeur), 1897.
        54 p. 24cm.

    At head of title: Académie des sciences, belles-lettres et arts de Rouen.

    1. Trials (Witchcraft)--Normandy. I. Title.

WITCHCRAFT
RC
532
R52
1885
    Études cliniques sur la grande hystérie ou hystéro-épilepsie.
    Richer, Paul Marie Louis Pierre, 1849-1933.
        Études cliniques sur la grande hystérie ou hystéro-épilepsie. 2. éd., rev. et considérablement augmentée. Paris, A. Delahaye et E. Lecrosnier, 1885.
        xv, 975 p. illus. 25cm.

    Imprint covered by label: Paris, O. Doin.
    1. Hysteria. 2. Hypnotism. I. Title. II. Title: La grande hystérie.

WITCHCRAFT
BF
1591
G87+
    Études sur la sorcellerie.
    Groff, William N
        Études sur la sorcellerie; ou, Le rôle que la Bible a joué chez les sorciers. Le Caire, 1897.
        [337]-415 p. 29cm. (Institut égyptien, Cairo. Mémoires, t.3, fasc. 4)

    Includes detailed description of a papyrus, containing notes of a sorcerer, probably of the second century A.D.

    1. Magic--Hist. 2. Witchcraft--Hist. 3. Cabala. 4. Witchcraft in the Bible. I. Series.

WITCHCRAFT
BF
1517
F5
L61
    Études sur les possessions en général et sur celle de Loudun en particulier.
    Leriche, Pierre Ambroise.
        Études sur les possessions en général et sur celle de Loudun en particulier. Précédées d'une lettre adressée à l'auteur par Ventura de Raulica. Paris, H. Plon, 1859.
        x, 258 p. 17cm.

    1. Demoniac possession. 2. Loudun, France. Ursuline Convent. 3. Grandier, Urbain, 1590-1634.

CATALOGUE OF THE CORNELL WITCHCRAFT COLLECTION

Witchcraft
BF 1583
R24

Etwas Näheres über die Hexen-Prozesse der Vorzeit.
Rautert, Fr , ed.
Etwas Näheres über die Hexen-Prozesse der Vorzeit, aus authentischer Quelle von Fr. Rautert. Essen, Gedruckt bei G. D. Bädeker, 1827.
4 p. l., 79, [1] p. 22cm.
"Die Zeichnung für den Umschlag [ist] nach alten Holzschnitten aus dem 15ten und 16ten Jahrhundert."
Caption title: Hexen-Prozesse der Vorzeit.
8   1. Trials (Witchcraft)--Germany. I. Title. II. Title: Hexen-Prozesse der Vorzeit.

Witchcraft
BF 1569
E86

Eubel, Conrad, 1842-1923.
Vom Zaubereiunwesen anfangs des 14. Jahrhunderts (Mit urkundlichen Beilagen) München, Herder, 1897.
608-631 p. 24cm. (Historisches Jahrbuch der Görres-Gesellschaft, 18. Bd., 3. Heft)

1. Witchcraft. I. Title.

Witchcraft
BF 1565
D96

Eutychii Beniamin Transalbini Dissertatio philologica De vocibus hhartymmim et belahatehem.
[Durych, Fortunat] 1730-1802.
Eutychii Beniamin Transalbini Dissertatio philologica De vocibus hhartymmim et belahatehem Exod. VII. 2. [Vindobonae?] 1767.
20 p. 21cm.
"Opusculi inscripti: Gedanken über die Werke des Liebhabers der Wahrheit von der Hexerey."
1. Witchcraft in the Bible. 2. Bible. O.T.--Criticism, Textual. 3. Hartumim
8   (Continued on next card)

Eutychius Transalpinus, Benjamin, pseud.
see
Durych, Fortunat, 1730-1802

Witchcraft
BF 1563
E92++
no. 1.

Evans, Edward Payson, 1831-1917.
Ein Trierer Hexenprocess. München, J. G. Cotta, 1892.
5-7 p. 32cm. (Beilage zur Allgemeinen Zeitung, Nr. 86)
No. 1 in vol. lettered Evans: Ein Trierer Hexenprocess, etc.

1. Witchcraft. 2. Trials (Witchcraft)--Germany. I. Title.

Evans, John.
Witchcraft
BF 1555
H44
1822

Heaton, James.
The extraordinary affliction and gracious relief of a little boy [John Evans]; supposed to be the effects of spiritual agency. Carefully examined and faithfully narrated with Observations on demoniac possession and animadversions on superstition. 2d ed. improved and enl. ... Plymouth [Eng.] Printed and sold for the Author by J. Williams, 1822.
156, 114 p. 20cm.
"Farther observations on demoniac
(Continued on next card)

Evans, John.
Witchcraft
BF 1555
H44
1822

Heaton, James. The extraordinary affliction and gracious relief of a little boy [John Evans] ... 1822. (Card 2)

possession..." has separate t.p. and paging.
First ed. published in 1820 under title: The demon expelled; or, The influence of Satan ...

1. Evans, John. 2. Demoniac possession. 3. Superstition. I. Heaton, James. The demon expelled ... II. Heaton, James. Farther observations on demoniack possession, and ... superstition. III. Title.

Witchcraft
BF 1582
Z7
1605

Un évêque de Verdun, prince de Lorraine, encorcelé, marié et condamné par le tribunal.
Langlois, Ernest, 1857-1924.
Un évêque de Verdun, prince de Lorraine, ensorcelé, marié et condamné par le tribunal de l'inquisition. [Nancy, Impr. Berger-Levrault, 1895]
23 p. 20cm.
Concerning Erric, prince of Lorraine, bishop of Verdun.
Extract from Annales de l'est, Apr. 1895.
8   1. Erric, prince of Lorraine, bp. of Verdun, d.1623. I. Title.
NIC

Witchcraft
BS 2655
A5
E93

Everling, Otto.
Die paulinische Angelologie und Dämonologie: ein biblisch-theologischer Versuch. Göttingen, Vandenhoeck und Ruprecht, 1888.
126 p. 24cm.

1. Bible. N.T. Epistles of Paul--Theology. 2. Angels. 3. Demonology. I. Title.

WITCHCRAFT
BF 1581
Z7
1605

Ewen, Cecil Henry L'Estrange, 1877-
A noted case of witchcraft at North Moreton, Berks, in the early 17th century. [London] 1936.
7 p. 23cm.
"Reprinted from the Berkshire archaeological journal, vol. 40, no.2."
8   1. Gunter, Anne, fl. 1605. 2. Witchcraft--Berkshire, England. I. Title.

---

ar W
12307

Ewen, Cecil Henry L'Estrange, 1877-
A noted case of witchcraft at North Moreton, Berks., in the early 17th century. [London] 1936.
7 p. 22cm.
Cover title.
"Reprinted from the Berkshire archaeological journal, vol. 40, no. 2, 1936."
No. 3 in a vol. lettered: Ewen. Miscellaneous pamphlets, 1934-1938.

Pamphlet
GR 1

Ewen, Cecil Henry L'Estrange, 1877-
Séances and statutes. Devon, C. L. Ewen, 1948.
17 p. 22cm.

1. Witchcraft. I. Title.

WITCHCRAFT
BF 1581
Z7
1645

Ewen, Cecil Henry L'Estrange, 1877-
The trials of John Lowes, clerk. [London] 1937.
7 p. 23cm.

1. Lowes, John, clerk, d. 1645. 2. Trials (Witchcraft)--Great Britain. I. Title.
8

---

ar W
12307

Ewen, Cecil Henry L'Estrange, 1877-
The trials of John Lowes, clerk. [London] 1937.
7 p. 23cm.
Cover title.
No. 6 in a vol. lettered: Ewen. Miscellaneous pamphlets, 1934-1938.

1. Lowes, John, clerk, d. 1645.

BF 1581
E94W8
1929

Ewen, Cecil Henry L'Estrange, 1877- ed.
Witch hunting and witch trials; the indictments for witchcraft from the records of 1373 assizes held for the home circuit A. D. 1559-1736, collected and edited by C. L'Estrange Ewen, with an introduction. London, K. Paul, Trench, Trubner & co., ltd., 1929.
xiii, 345 p. front., plates, facsims., diagrs. 23cm.
"Appendix I. Essex gaol delivery roll, summer 1645": 1 folded leaf inserted.
"Volumes relating to witchcraft in England ... most useful for reference": p. ix-x.
1. Witchcraft. 2. Criminal law--Gt. Brit. 3. Criminal procedure--Gt. Brit. I. Gt. Brit. Courts of assize and nisi prius. II. Title.
Library of Congress   BF1581.E8   30-12056

Witchcraft
BF 1581
E94
W8
1929

Ewen, Cecil Henry L'Estrange, 1877- ed.
Witch hunting and witch trials; the indictments for witchcraft from the records of 1373 assizes held for the home circuit A. D. 1559-1736, collected and edited by C. L'Estrange Ewen, with an introduction. New York, L. MacVeagh, The Dial Press, 1929.
xiii, 345 p. front., plates, facsims., diagrs. 23cm.
"Appendix I. Essex gaol delivery roll, summer 1645": 1 folded leaf inserted.
"Volumes relating to witchcraft in England ... most useful for reference": p. ix-x.
1. Witchcraft. 2. Criminal law--Gt. Brit. 3. Criminal procedure--Gt. Brit. I. Gt. Brit. Courts of assize and nisi prius. II. Title.
Library of Congress   BF1581.E8   30-12056

BF 1581
E94
W8
1971

Ewen, Cecil Henry L'Estrange, 1877- comp.
Witch hunting and witch trials; the indictments for witchcraft from the records of 1373 assizes held for the Home Circuit A.D. 1559-1736. Collected and edited by C. L'Estrange Ewen. London, K. Paul, Trench, Trubner, 19 [New York, Barnes & Noble, 1971]
xiii, 345 p. illus. 23 cm.

1. Witchcraft--England. 2. Criminal law--Great Britain. 3. Criminal procedure--Great Britain. I. Great Britain. Courts of Assize and Nisi Prius. II. Title

NIC   SEP 30,'75   COOOxc   76-2

Witchcraft
BF 1581
E94

Ewen, Cecil Henry L'Estrange, 1877-
Witchcraft and demonianism; a concise account derived from sworn depositions and confessions obtained in the courts of England and Wales, by C. L'Estrange Ewen ... with contemporary illustrations. London, Heath, Cranton, limited, 1933.
495 p. front., plates, port., facsims., fold. tab. 22½cm.
With autograph: Geo. L. Burr.
1. Witchcraft. 2. Demonology. I. Title.
Library of Congress   BF1581.E83   34-54
[3]   [159.9614]

CATALOGUE OF THE CORNELL WITCHCRAFT COLLECTION

Witchcraft
BF
1581
E84
    Ewen, Cecil Henry L'Estrange, 1877–
       Witchcraft in the Star chamber, by C. L'Estrange Ewen ..
    [London] The author, 1938.
       68 p. 23cm.

    1. Witchcraft—England. 2. Gt. Brit. Court of Star chamber.
    I. Title.

    Library of Congress   BF1581.E84   39–23888
    ———— Copy 2.   [2]   [159.961140942] 133.4094₂

Witchcraft
BF
1565
E95
    Ewich, Johann, 1525-1588.
       De sagarvm (qvas vvlgò veneficas appel-
lant) natvra, arte, viribvs & factis: Item
de notis indicijsq[;], quibus agnoscantur:
et poena, qua afficiendae sint, censura
aequa & moderata D. Joann: Evvich ...
Bremae, Ex officina typographica Theodori
Glvichstein, 1584.
    [93] p. 17cm.
    With this are bound Neuwaldt, Hermann.
Exegesis purgationis. Helmstadii, 1584.
    (Continued on next card)

Witchcraft
BF
1565
E95
    Ewich, Johann, 1525-1588. De sagarvm ...
1584.   (Card 2)

and Ad frivolas calumnias, et cavillationes
sophisticas Danielis Hoffmanni. Bremae,
1583.

    1. Witchcraft. I. Title: De sagarum
(quas vulgò veneficas appellant) natura...

8

    Ewich, Johann, 1525-1588.
WITCHCRAFT
BF
1565
S43
1588
    Scribonius, Wilhelm Adolf, 16th cent.
       De sagarvm natura et potestate, deque his
recte cognoscendis et pvniendis physiologia
Gulielmi Adolphi Scribonii Marpurgensis. Vbi
de pvrgatione earvm per aquam frigidam. Contra Joannem Evvichium ... & Her. Neuvvaldum
... doctores medicos & professores ...
Marpurgi, typis Pauli Egenolphi, 1588.
    [8], 132 l. 17cm.

    In copy 2, contents in MS on 1 [8b],
    Title on spine of copy 1:
8   Scribonius.   Witchcraft pamphlets.
    (Continued on next card)

    Ewich, Johann, 1525-1588.
WITCHCRAFT
BF
1565
S43
1588
    Scribonius, Wilhelm Adolf, 16th cent. De
sagarvm natura ... 1588.   (Card 2)

    With copy 1 are bound Ignotus Patronus
Veritatis, pseud. Examen epistolae et partis
physiologiae de examine sagarum ([Francofurti],
1589); Scribonius, W. A. Responsio ad examen
Ignoti Patroni Veritatis (Francofurdi, 1590);
and Ignotus Patronus Veritatis, pseud. Refvtatio responsionis Gvlielmi-Adolphi Scribonii
(Herbornae, 1591).
    1. Witchcraft   2. Ewich, Johann, 1525-
1588. 3. Neuwaldt, Hermann. I. Title:
8   De sagarum natura.

    Ewichius, Joannes, 1525-1588.
       see
    Ewich, Johann von, 1525-1588.

WITCHCRAFT
BF
1565
S43
1588
    Examen epistolae et partis physiologiae de
       examine sagarum per aquam frigidam.
    Ignotus Patronus Veritatis, pseud.
       Examen epistolae et partis physiologiae de
examine sagarum per aquam frigidam; à Gvilhelmo Adolpho Scribonio, medicinae et philosophiae
doctore, diuersis temporibus in lucem editarum
concinnatum à quodam Ignoto Patrono Veritatis.
Epistola Scribonij, quae examinatur, in fine
adiecta est.   [Francofurti?], 1589.
    78 p. 17cm.

    "De examine et pvrgatione sagarvm per aqvam
    (Continued on next card)

WITCHCRAFT
BF
1565
S43
1588
    Examen epistolae et partis physiologiae de
       examine sagarum per aquam frigidam.
    Ignotus Patronus Veritatis, pseud. Examen
epistolae ... 1589.   (Card 2)
frigidam epistola ... (with special t. p.):
p. [51]-65.
    Bound with Scribonius, Wilhelm Adolf. De
sagarvm natvra. Marpurgi, 1588.

    1. Scribonius, Wilhelm Adolf, 16th cent.
De sagarum natura. 2. Witchcraft. I. Scribonius, Wilhelm Adolf, 16th cent.

    Examen juridicum judicialis lamiarum
       confessionis.
Witchcraft
BF
1572
D4
K64
1752
    Klein, Johann, 1659-1732, praeses.
       Meditatio academica exhibens examen
ivridicvm ivdicialis lamiarvm confessionis
se ex nefando cvm Satana coitv prolem svscepisse hvmanam. Was von dem Bekenntniss
der Hexen zu halten, dass sie aus schändlichem Beyschlaf mit dem Teufel Kinder gezeuget? Praeside Domino Ioanne Klein ...
svbmittit Nicolavs Pvtter ... Vitembergae, Apvd Io. Christoph. Tzschiedrich, 1752.
    48 p. 21cm.
8   First published 1698.
    (Continued on next card)

    An examen of witches, drawn from various
       trials of many of this sect in the dis-
       trict of Saint Oyan de Joux ...
Witchcraft
BF
1582
A2
B67
1929
    Boguet, Henri, d. 1619.
       An examen of witches, drawn from various
trials of many of this sect in the district
of Saint Oyan de Joux, commonly known as
Saint Claude in the county of Burgundy, including the procedure necessary to a judge
in trials for witchcraft. Tr. by E. Allen
Ashwin, ed. by the Rev. Montague Summers.
[London] J. Rodker, 1929.
    liii, 328 p. 19cm.
8   "Edition limited to 1275 copies; this
copy is number 290."

    Examen profani Exorcismi primi contra
       daemonem mendacii.
Witchcraft
BF
1565
B73
    Borre, Nicolas de, ca. 1590-1670.
       Examen profani Exorcismi primi contra
daemonem mendacii sub ementito Lamberti
Dicaei theologi medici nomine in lucem nuper emissi, nec non inepti & ridiculi ipsius Cataplasmatis &c. In quo duae & triginta imposturae deteguntur, omnium oculis
exponuntur, & solidè refutantur. Lovanij,
Typis Georgii Lipsii, 1660.
    73 p. 19cm.
    Bound with his Apologia pro exorcistis.
8   Lovanij, 1660.
    (Continued on next card)

    The examination and confession of certain
       witches at Chelmsford.
Witchcraft
BF
1581
B42
1864
    Beigel, Hermann, 1830-1879, ed.
       The examination and confession of certain
witches at Chelmsford in the county of Essex
... [London, Philobiblon Society, pref.
1864]
    49 p. 23cm.

    A reprint of two pamphlets in the library
of Lambeth Palace, respectively entitled: The
examination and confession of certaine wytches
at Chensforde ...   1556 [i.e. 1566] ..." and
    (Continued on next card)

    The examination and confession of certain
       witches at Chelmsford.
Witchcraft
BF
1581
B42
1864
    Beigel, Hermann, 1830-1879, ed. The exami-
nation and confession of certain witches
... [1864]   (Card 2)

    The second examination of mother Agnes
Waterhouse ... 1566 ...
    Offprint from Miscellanies of the Philo-
biblon Society, v. 8, 1863-63.

    1. Witchcraft—England. 2. Waterhouse,
Agnes. I. Title. II. Title: The second
examination of mother Agnes Waterhouse.

Witchcraft
BF
1563
T86
    The examination, confession, triall, and
execution, of Joane Williford, Joan Cariden,
and Jane Hott, who were executed at Feversham in Kent, for being witches, on Munday the 29
of September 1645... Taken by the major of
Feversham and jurors for the said inquest.
With the examination and confession of Elizabeth Harris, not yet executed. All attested
under the hand of Robert Greenstreet, major
of Feversham.   London, Printed for J. G.,
1645.
    (Continued on next card)

Witchcraft
BF
1563
T86
    The examination, confession, triall, and
execution ... 1645.   (Card 2)

    6 p. 19cm.

    No. 5 in vol. lettered: Tracts of
witches.

    1. Witchcraft. 2. Williford, Joane, d.
1645. 3. Cariden, Joan, d. 1645. 4. Hott,
Jane, d. 1645.   5. Harris, Elizabeth,
d. 1645.

Witchcraft
BF
1563
W81++
no.5
    The Examination of John Walsh, before Master
Thomas Williams ... upon certayne interrogatories touchyng wytchcrafte and sor-
cerye, in the presence of diuers gentle-
men and others, the XX. of August, 1566.
London, Imprinted by J. Awdely, 1566.
[London, at the British Museum, 1923]
    [16] p. 14cm.

    Signature: A⁸.

    (Continued on next card)

Witchcraft
BF
1563
W81++
no.5
    The Examination of John Walsh ...   1566.
[1923]   (Card 2)

    Photocopy (negative) 16 p. on 9 l. 20 x
32cm.
    No. 5 in vol. lettered: Witchcraft tracts,
chapbooks and broadsides, 1579-1704; rotograph copies.

    1. Witchcraft—England. 2. Walsh, John.

    An examination of the Enquiry into the
       meaning of demoniacs in the New
       Testament.
Witchcraft
BS
2545
D5
T75
no.6
    Pegge, Samuel, 1704-1796.
       An examination of the Enquiry into the
meaning of demoniacs in the New Testament.
In a letter to the author.   Wherein it is
shewn, that the word demon does not signify
a departed soul, either in the classics or
the Scriptures; and consequently, that the
whole of the Enquiry is without foundation.
London, Printed for F. Gyles, 1739.
    86 p. 20cm.

    No. 6 in vol. lettered: Tracts on
demoniacks.   1737.

CATALOGUE OF THE CORNELL WITCHCRAFT COLLECTION

Excorcismarium, in duos libros dispositum.

Witchcraft
BF
1559
N66

Nicuesa, Hilarius.
Excorcismarivm, in duos libros dispositum qvorvm annvale altervm, altervm sanctvarivm dicimvs conivrationvm. Qvibvs pro totivs anni feriis ... ex sacra scriptura & sancti patribus apposita materia ... exorcistae non deest. Venice, Iunta, 1639.
414 p. 23cm.

1. Exorcism. I. Title.

Exercitationes philosophicae duae de angelorum malorum potentia in corpora.

Witchcraft
BF
1555
A55
no.1

Andreae, Tobias, 1633-1685.
Exercitationes philosophicae duae de angelorum malorum potentia in corpora. Amstelodami, Apud Samuelem Eickenbergium, 1691.
82 p. 14cm.

Each part has caption title beginning: Exercitationum physicarum.
Also published as: Wijsgeerige oefeningen betrekkelijk het vermogen van de kwade engelen op het menschlijk ligchaam.
No. 1 in vol. lettered Andreae. De angelorum ...

Exorcismo.

Rare
BX
2340
F22

Farinerio, Bonaventura.
Exorcismo. Mirabile da disfari ogni sorte di maleficii, e da cacciare li demoni, & è prouato. Et per il Reveren. P. Frate Bonaventvra Farinerio, inquisitor reuisto, corretto & ristampato. Venetia [Francesco Rampazetto] 1560.
[56] p. 16cm.

1. Exorcism. I. Title.

Exécutions de sorciers et sorcières en 1615, dans les possessions de Murbach et le Haut-Mundat.

Witchcraft
BF
1582
F52

Fischer, Dagobert.
Exécutions de sorciers et sorcières en 1615, dans les possessions de Murbach et le Haut-Mundat.
(In Revue d'Alsace. Colmar. 25cm.
New ser., v.1 (1870) p. [324]-327)

1. Witchcraft--Alsace. I. Title.

An exhibition of books on witchcraft and demonology.

Witchcraft
Z
6878
W8G54+

Glasgow. University. Hunterian Library.
An exhibition of books on witchcraft and demonology. January-March, 1966.
[Glasgow? 1966]
24 p. 26cm.

1. Witchcraft--Exhibitions.
2. Witchcraft--Bibl. I. Title.

Der Exorcismus an Herzog Johann Wilhelm von Jülich.

WITCHCRAFT
BX
2340
P33

Pauls, Emil.
Der Exorcismus an Herzog Johann Wilhelm von Jülich in den Jahren 1604 und 1605.
(In: Historischer Verein für den Niederrhein. Annalen. Köln. 23cm. No.63 (1897) p. [27]-53)

With this, in the same issue, is: Keussen, Hermann. Zwei Hexenprozesse aus der Crefelder Gegend.
1. Exorcism. 2. Medicine, Magic, mystic and spagiric. 3. Johann Wilhelm, Herzog von Jüli ch-Kleve-Berg, 1562-1609.

8
NIC

Exegesis purgationis.

Witchcraft
BF
1565
E95

Neuwaldt, Hermann.
Exegesis pvrgationis sive Examinis sagarum super aquam frigidam proiectarum: in qua refutata opinione Guilhelmi Adolphi Scribonij, de huius purgationis & aliarum similium origine, natura, & veritate agitur: omnibus ad rerum gubernacula sedentibus maximè necessaria ... Helmstadii, Excudebat Iacobus Lucius, 1584.
[120] p. 17cm.
Bound with Ewich, Johann, 1525-1588.

8 (Continued on next card)

The existence of evil spirits proved.

Witchcraft
BF
1531
S432

Scott, Walter, Pres. of Airedale College.
The existence of evil spirits proved; and their agency, particularly in relation to the human race, explained and illustrated. London, Jackson and Walford, 1853.
xx, 368 p. 20cm. (The Congregational lecture, ninth series)

"New and uniform edition."

1. Demonology. 2. Devil. I. Title.

Der Exorcismus im Herzogtum Braunschweig.

WITCHCRAFT
BF
1559
K81
1893

Koldewey, Friedrich, 1866-
Der Exorcismus im Herzogtum Braunschweig seit den Tagen der Reformation; eine kirchenhistorische Studie. Wolfenbüttel, J. Zwissler, 1893.
50 p. 24cm.

Originally published as the author's dissertation, Jena.

8
NIC

1. Exorci sm. I. Title.

Exegesis purgationis.

Witchcraft
BF
1565
E95

Neuwaldt, Hermann. Exegesis pvrgationis ... 1584. (Card 2)

De sagarum ... natura. Bremae, 1584.

1. Scribonius, Wilhelm Adolf, 16th cent. De sagarum natura. 2. Witchcraft. I. Title: Exegesis purgationis.

8

Les exorcismes en Lozère en 1792.

Witchcraft
BF
1559
F18

Falgairolle, Edmond.
Les exorcismes en Lozère en 1792. Paris, Chamuel, 1894.
38 p. 25cm.

1. Exorcism. I. Title.

WITCHCRAFT
BX
2340
E96

Exorcismus in Satanam et angelos apostaticos, jussu Leonis XIII P. M. editus. [Romae, Typ. S. C. De Propaganda Fide, 1890]
9 p. 15cm.

With autograph: A. D. White.

1. Exorcism. I. Catholic Church. Pope, 1878-1903 (Leo XIII) II. Catholic Church. Liturgy and ritual.

8
NIC

Exercitatio medico-philologica De mirando lateris cordisque Christi vulnere.

Witchcraft
BF
1555
G89

Gruner, Christian Gottfried, 1744-1815.
Christiani Godofredi Grvner ... Commentatio de daemoniacis a Christo Sospitatore percvratis. Accedit Danielis Wilhelmi Trilleri ... Exercitatio medico-philologica De mirando lateris cordisqve Christi vvlnere atqve effvso inde largo sangvinis et aqvae proflvvio. Ienae, Litteris et impensis I. C. Stravssii, 1775.
6 p. l., 64, [3] p. 18cm.
1. Demoniac possession. 2. Jesus

8 (Continued on next card)

Exorcismi potentissimi, & efficaces.

WITCHCRAFT
BX
2340
L81
1680

Locatellus, Petrus.
Exorcismi potentissimi, & efficaces, ad expellendas aëreas tempestates, a daemonibus per se, sive ad nutum cujusvis diabolici ministri excitatas... a ...Petro Locatello... Editio altera correctior. Labaci, Typis & impensis Joannis Bapt. Mayr, 1680.
188 p. 14cm.

Published earlier with title: Conjurationes potentiss imae et efficaces ad expellendas ...aëreas tempestates...

8
NIC (Continued on next card)

Der Exorcist in seiner Blösse. [n. p.] 1776.

Witchcraft
BF
1559
G25
Z63
no.1

40 p. port. 17cm.
No. 1 in vol. lettered Gassneriana.

1. Gassner, Johann Joseph, 1727-1779.
2. Exorcism. 3. Příchovský, Antonín Peter, Abp. of Prague, 1707-1793. Hirtenbrief ... 1775.

8

Exercitatio per saturam.

Witchcraft
BF
1520
C27

Caristinio, Dominico.
... Exercitatio per saturam, sive Diatriba theologico-critica daemonologiae elementa complectens, cui accedunt Meditationes philosophicae theologico morales super eodem subjecto, auctore Bernardo Maria Marsicani ... Neapoli, Typis Dominici Pianese, 1788.
11 p. l., 207 p. 21cm.
Marsicani's work not included; but dedication includes letter by and to him.
1. Demono logy. I. Marsicani, Bernardo Mar ia. II. Title. III. Title: Diatri ba theologico-critica daemonologiae.

8

Exorcismi potentissimi, & efficaces.

WITCHCRAFT
BX
2340
L81
1680

Locatellus, Petrus. Exorcismi potentissimi, & efficaces...1680. (Card 2)

With this is bound: Preces et coniurationes contra aëreas tempestates... Campidonae, 1667.

1. Exorcism. I. Catholic Church. Liturgy and ritual. II. His Conjurationes potentissimae et efficaces... III. Title. IV. Title: Conjurationes potentis simae et eff icaces...

Der Exorcist in seiner Blösse.

Witchcraft
BF
1559
G25
Z63
no.6

Eines redlichen Protestantens aufrichtige Erinnerung an den Verfasser des Exorcisten in seiner Blösse, den Prager Hirtenbrief betreffend. Frankfurt und Leipzig, 1776.
45 p. 17cm.
No. 6 in vol. lettered Gassneriana.
1. Gassner, Johann Joseph, 1727-1779.
2. Příchovský, Antonín Peter, Abp. of Prague, 1707-1793. Hirtenbrief ... 1775. 3. Der Exorcist in sei ner Blösse. I. Ein redlicher Prot estant.

8

CATALOGUE OF THE CORNELL WITCHCRAFT COLLECTION

WITCHCRAFT
BF
1559
P64

Exorcista rite' edoctus, seu Accurata methodus omne maleficiorum genus probe ac prudenter curandi.
    Pinamonti, Giovanni Pietro, 1632-1703.
      Exorcista rite' edoctus; seu, Accurata methodus omne maleficiorum genus probe ac prudenter curandi. Exposita a quodam religioso, & in lucem edita a quodam sacerdote ... Lucae, Typis Marescandoli, 1705.
    154 p. 14cm.

"Formula exorcismi": p. 127-154.

8
NIC

    1. Exorcism. 2. Witchcraft. 3. Demoniac possession. I. Title.

WITCHCRAFT
BF
1559
P64
1737

Exorcista rite' edoctus, seu Accurata methodus omne maleficiorum genus probe ac prudenter curandi.
    Pinamonti, Giovanni Pietro, 1632-1703.
      Exorcista rite' edoctus; seu, Accurata methodus omne maleficiorum genus probe ac prudenter curandi. Auctore R. P. Jo. Petro Pinamonti. Editio tertia. Venetiis, Ex Leonardo Pittono, 1737.
    96 p. port. 16cm.

"Exorcismi": p. 88-91. (Abridged from the section, "Formula exorcismi" at the end of first ed., 1705)

8
NIC

    1. Exorcism. 2. Witchcraft. 3. Demoniac possession. I. Title.

BV
303
D65
1967

Der Exorzismus im altchristlichen Taufritual.
    Dölger, Franz Josef, 1879-1940.
      Der Exorzismus im altchristlichen Taufritual; eine religionsgeschichtliche Studie. Paderborn, F. Schöningh, 1909. New York, Johnson Reprint Corp. [1967].
    xi, 175 p. 23cm. (Studien zur Geschichte und Kultur des Altertums, 3. Bd., 1.-2. Heft)

    1. Baptism--Hist.--Early church. 2. Exorcism. I. Title. II. Series.

Witchcraft
BF
1576
D26

Exposé of Newburyport eccentricities, witches and witchcraft.
    Davis, H P.
      Exposé of Newburyport eccentricities, witches and witchcraft. The murdered boy, and apparition of the Charles-street school-house. [n. p., °1873]
    24 p. illus. 24cm.

    I. Title.

WITCHCRAFT
BF
1559
P76

Expvlsio daemonvm.
    Polidoro, Valerio.
      [Practica exorcistarum ... ad daemones et maleficia de Christifidelibus ejiciendum. Patavii, Apud Paulum Meietum, 1587]
    2 v. in 1. 15cm.
    Title page for vol. 1 lacking; title obtained from British Museum. Dept. of Printed Books. General catalogue of printed books. London, 1963. Running title: Expvlsio daemonvm.

8
NIC

    Title for vol. 2: Dispersio daemonvm qvae
    (Cont'd on next card)

WITCHCRAFT
BF
1559
P76

Expvlsio daemonvm.
    Polidoro, Valerio. [Practica exorcistarum ...1587] (Card 2)

secvnda pars est practice exorcistarum. Additional exorcisms in ms. (16 p.) inserted.

    1. Exorcism. I. Title. II. Title: Expvlsio daemonvm. III. Dispersio daemonvm.

Witchcraft
BF
1581
B82

Extracts from the records of the presbytery of Brechin, from 1639-1660.
    Brechin, Scotland. (Presbytery)
      Extracts from the records of the presbytery of Brechin, from 1639 to 1660. Dundee, W. Kidd, 1876.
    64 p. 17cm.

    1. Witchcraft--Scotland. I. Title.

Witchcraft
BF
1517
F5
F81

Extraict des registres de la Commission ordonnée par le Roy povr le ivgement ...
    France. Commission pour le jugement du procez criminel fait a l'encontre de Maistre Urbain Grandier & ses complices.
      Extraict des registres de la Commission ordonnée par le Roy povr le ivgement ... Poictiers, Par I. Thoreav & la vefue d'A. Mesnier, 1634.
    25 p. 16cm.

Witchcraft
BF
1555
H44
1822

The extraordinary affliction and gracious relief of a little boy.
    Heaton, James.
      The extraordinary affliction and gracious relief of a little boy [John Evans]; supposed to be the effects of spiritual agency. Carefully examined and faithfully narrated with Observations on demoniac possession and animadversions on superstition. 2d ed. improved and enl. ... Plymouth [Eng.] Printed and sold for the Author by J. Williams, 1822.
    156, 114 p. 20cm.

"Farther observations on demoniac
(Continued on next card)

Witchcraft
BF
1555
H44
1822

The extraordinary affliction and gracious relief of a little boy.
    Heaton, James. The extraordinary affliction and gracious relief of a little boy [John Evans] ... 1822. (Card 2)

possession..." has separate t.p. and paging.
First ed. published in 1820 under title: The demon expelled; or, The influence of Satan ...

    1. Evans, John. 2. Demoniac possession. 3. Superstition. I. Heaton, James. The demon expelled ... II. Heaton, James. Farther observations on demoniack possession, and ... superstition. III. Title.

Witchcraft
BF
1581
Z7
1809

Extraordinary life and character of Mary Bateman, the Yorkshire witch; traced from the earliest thefts of her infancy through a most awful course of crimes and murders, till her execution at the New Drop, near the castle of York, on Monday, the twentieth of March, 1809. 6th ed. ... Leeds, Printed by E. Baines, for J. Davies [1810?]
    56 p. front. (port.) 23cm.

    1. Bateman, Mary (Harker) 1768-1809.
    2. Witchcraft--England.

Rare
BX
1710
E97++
1578

Eymerich, Nicolás, 1320-1399.
    Directorivm inqvisitorvm ... denvo ex collatione plvrivm exemplarium emendatum, et accessione multarum literarum Apostolicarum, officio Sanctae Inquisitionis deseruientium, locupletatum, cvm scholiis sev annotationibvs ... Francisci Pegnae Hispani ... Accessit rerum & verborum ... index. ... Romae, In aedibvs Pop. Rom., 1578.
    3 pts. in 1 v. 34cm.

Title vignette.
Colophon of pt. 3 dated: 1579.
    1. Inquisition. I. Peña, Francisco, 1540?-1612, ed. II. Title: Directorium inquisitorum.

Witchcraft
BX
2340
E97
1626

Eynatten, Maximilian van, d. 1631.
    Manvale exorcismorvm: continens instrvctiones, & exorcismos ad eiiciendos è corporibus obsessis spiritus malignos, & ad quaeuis maleficia depellenda, & ad quascumque infestationes daemonum reprimendas ... Antverpiae, Ex officina Plantiniana, Apud Balthasarem Moretum, & Viduam Ioannis Moreti, & Io. Meursium, 1626.
    8 p. l., 314 p., 1 l.
    Title in red and black.
    With colophon.

WITCHCRAFT
BX
2340
E97
1709

Eynatten, Maximilian van, d. 1631.
    Manuale exorcismorum, continens instructiones, et exorcismos ad ejiciendos è corporibus obsessis spiritus malignos, & ad quaevis maleficia depellenda, & ad quascumque infestationes daemonum reprimendas ... Antverpiae, Apud H. & C. Verdussen, 1709.
    6 p. l., 291, [1] p. 17cm.

    1. Exorcism. I. Title.

WITCHCRAFT
BF
1559
T41
1626

Eynatten, Maximilian van, d. 1631.
Manuale exorcismorum.
    Thesavrvs exorcismorvm atqve conivrationvm terribilivm, potentissimorum, efficacissimorum cum practica probatissima: qvibvs spiritvs maligni, dæmones maleficiaque omnia de corporibus humanis obsessis, tanquam flagellis, fustibusque fugantur, expelluntur, doctrinis refertissimus atqꝫ uberrimus: ad maximam exorcistarum commoditatem nunc vltimo plenariè in lucem editus & recusus: cuius authores, vt & singuli tractatus sequente pagellà consignati, inueniuntur. Cum indice capitum, rerum & verborum ... Coloniæ, sumptibus hæredum Lazari Zetzneri, 1626.
    12 p. l., 1232, [39] p. 18 ᵐ.
(Continued on next card)

WITCHCRAFT
BF
1559
T41
1626

Eynatten, Maximilian van, d. 1631.
Manuale exorcismorum.
    Thesavrvs exorcismorvm atqve conivrationvm terribilivm ... 1626. (Card 2)
Previously published at Cologne in 1608.
Contents.--F. Valerii Polydori ... Practica exorcistarum ad dæmones & malefícia de Christi fidelibus pellendum, pars prima ... [et] secunda ... R. p. f. Hieronymi Mengi ... Flagellum dæmonum.--Eivsdem Fvstis dæmonvm.--F. Zacharie Vicecomitis ... Complementum artis exorcisticæ.--Petri Antonii Stampæ ... Fuga Satanæ.--R. d. Maximiliani ab Eynatten ... Manuale exorcismorum.
    1. Exorcism. 2. Demonomania. 3. Witchcraft. I. Polidoro, Valerio. Practica exorcistarum. II. Menghi, Girolamo, d. 1610. Flagellum daemonum. III. Visconti, Zaccaria. Complementum artis exorcisticae. IV. Stampa, Pietro Antonio. Fuga Satanae. V. Eynatten, Maximilian van, d. 1631. Manuale exorcismorum.

CATALOGUE OF THE CORNELL WITCHCRAFT COLLECTION

F

Witchcraft F., G.
BV   [Fox, George] 1624-1691.
4617   A declaration of the ground of error &
B6   errors, blasphemy, blasphemers, and blas-
F79   phemies: and the ground of inchantings and
       seducing spirits and the doctrine of devils,
       the sons of sorcerers and the seed of the
       adulterer, and the ground of nicromancy,
       which doth defile witches and wizards ...
       By G. F.   London, Printed for G. Calvert,
       1657.
          41 p. 18cm.

          I. F., G.   II. G. F.   III. Title.

Witchcraft F., H.
BF   A Prodigious & tragicall history of the ar-
1563   raignment, tryall, confession, and condem-
W81++ nation of six witches at Maidstone in Kent,
no.18 ... July ... 1652 ... Collected from the
       observations of E. G., Gent. (a learned per-
       son, present at their conviction and con-
       demnation) and digested by H. F., Gent. To
       which is added a true relation of one Mrs.
       Atkins ... who was strangely carried away
       from her house in July last, and hath not
       been heard of since. London, Printed for
       R. Harper, 1652. [London, at the British
       Museum, 1923]
          8 p. 16cm.   (Continued on next card)

Witchcraft F., H.
BF   A Prodigious & tragicall history of ... six
1563   witches at Maidstone ... 1652. (Card 2)
W81++
no.18   Photocopy (negative) 8 p. on 5 l. 20 x
       32cm.
          No. 18 in vol. lettered: Witchcraft tracts,
       chapbooks and broadsides, 1579-1704; roto-
       graph copies.

          1. Witchcraft--England. I. G., E. II.
       F., H.

                 F., H.
Witchcraft
BF
1563   A true and exact relation of the severall
T86   informations, examinations, and confessions
       of the late witches, arraigned and executed
       in the county of Essex. Who were arraigned
       and condemned at the late sessions, holden at
       Chelmesford before the Rt. Hon. Robert, earle
       of Warwicke, and severall of His Majesties
       justices of peace, the 29 of July, 1645...
       London, Printed by M. S. for H. Overton,
       1645.
          36 p.   19cm.
                           (Continued on next card)

                 F., H.
Witchcraft
BF
1563   A true and exact relation of the severall
T86   informations, examinations, and confessions
       of the late witches ... 1645. (Card 2)

          Preface signed H. F.
          No. 1 in vol. lettered: Tracts of witches.

          1. Witchcraft. I. F., H.   II. H.F.

Witchcraft F., J. S.
BF   [Forsyth, J   S   ]
1411   Demonologia; or, Natural knowledge revealed; being an
F73   exposé of ancient and modern superstitions, credulity, fanati-
1827   cism, enthusiasm, & imposture, as connected with the doctrine,
       caballa, and jargon, of amulets, apparitions, astrology,
       charms, demonology ... witchcraft, &c. ... By J. S. F. ...
       London, J. Bumpus, 1827.
          1 p. l., [v]-xvi, 488 p. front. 19cm.
          By J. S. Forsyth. cf. Halkett and Laing, Dict. anon. and pseud.,
       new ed., 1926, v. 2, p. 87.

          1. Superstition. 2. Demonology. 3. Witchcraft.   I. F., J. S.
       II. J. S. F. III. Title.
                                                  11-9203 rev.
       Library of Congress   BF1411.F6 1827
                                          133

             F., S.
Witchcraft
BF   Divination, witchcraft, and mesmerism.
1152   [New York, 1852]
D61+   198-213 p. 26cm.

          Signed: S. F.
          Detached from the International monthly
       magazine of literature, science, and art.
       v. 5.

          1. Divination. 2. Witchcraft.
       3. Mesmerism.   I. F., S. II. S. F.

             F. S. B.
Witchcraft
BF   M. F. S. B. jurium studiosi recentissimum
1445   monimentum De spectris ad ... dominvm
D61   Christophorum Schonbeck ... Lugduni
no.1   Batavorum, Typis Marsianis, 1646.
          22, [2] p. 18cm. (bound in 21cm. vol.)

          No. 1 in vol. lettered Dissertationes
       de spectris. 1646-1753.

          1. Apparitions. I. B., F. S. II.
       F. S. B. III. Schonbeck, Christoph. IV.
8   Title: De spectris.

Witchcraft
BF   Fabart, Félix.
1412   Histoire philosophique et politique de
F11   l'occulte: magie, sorcellerie, spiritisme;
       avec une préface de Camille Flammarion.
       Paris, C. Marpon et E. Flammarion
       [1885?]
          xx, 346 p. 19cm.

          1. Occult sciences--Hist. I. Flam-
       marion, Camille, 1842-1925. II.
       Title.

Witchcraft
BL   Faber, Daniel.
820   Die höllische Zauberin Circe, in ihren
C6   vermaledeyten Töchtern und verdammten
F12   Schwestern abgemahlet. Auch alle Obrig-
       keiten und Richter der Welt zu ernstlicher
       Bestraffung derselben treuhertzig erinnert
       und angemahnet. Magdeburg, C. Seidel, 1699.
          253 p. illus. 18cm.

          1. Circe.   2. Witchcraft.
       I. Title.

WITCHCRAFT
BF   Faber, Johann Gottlieb, 1717-1779, praeses.
1555   Disqvisitio academica An adaemonismvs cvm
F11   fide et pietate Christiana conciliari pos-
       sit? Qvam praeside ... Ioanne Gottlieb Fa-
       ber ... svbmittit avctor defendens Martinvs
       Schvllervs ... Tvbingae, Literis Cottae
       et Revsii [1763]
          42 p. 21cm.
          Running title: De inflvxv adaemonismi
       in pietatem Christianam.
          1. Demoniac possession. I.
8   Schuller, Martin, respondent. II.
NIC   Title: An adaemonismus cum fide et
       pietate Christiana conciliari possit?
       (Over)

WITCHCRAFT
BF   Faber, Johann Gottlieb, 1717-1779, praeses.
1555   Dissertatio academica de daemoniacis,
F11   adversvs Wetstenivm. Tvbingae, literis
D6   Cottae et Revsii, 1763.
          28 p. 21cm.
          Diss.--Tubingen (C. F. Renz, respondent)

          1. Demoniac possession. I. Renz, Carolus
       Friedrich, resp. II. Wettstein, Johann
8   Jakob, 1693-1754.
NIC

BF   Fabretti, Ariodante, 1816-1894.
1517   Il diavolo ad Issime. Il piu
F22   sensazionale processo del Seicento.
1970   Torino, Piemonte in bancarella, 1970.
          88 p. illus. 18cm.
          At head of title: A Fabretti and F.
       Vayra.
          Includes bibliographical references.

          1. Demonology. I. Vayra, Pietro,
       1838-   II. Title

NIC APR 25, '72   COxc   72-333875

                    Fabricius, Joannes, Rosravia-Hungarus.
WITCHCRAFT
GR   Heucher, Johann Heinrich, 1677-1747.
780   Magic plants; being a translation of a
H59   curious tract entitled De vegetalibus ma-
1886   gicis, written by M. J. H. Heucher. (1700.)
       Edited by Edmund Goldsmid. Edinburgh
       [Printed by E. & G. Goldsmid] 1886.
          39 p. 23cm. (Bibliotheca curiosa)
          Title in red and black.
          "This edition is limited to 275 small-
       paper copies ..."
          Translation of Ex historia naturali
8   (Continued on next card)

                    Fabricius, Joannes, Rosravia-Hungarus.
WITCHCRAFT
GR   Heucher, Johann Heinrich, 1677-1747.
780   Magic plants ... 1886. (Card 2)
H59
1886   de vegetalibus magicis generatim, by Heucher
       and J. Fabricius.
          "I have given, as an Appendix, a transla-
       tion from the Official records of the Royal
       Court of Guernsey, of the trials of three
       women for witchcraft in 1617. This transla-
       tion is taken from Mr. J. L. Pitt's Witch-
       craft and Devil-Lore in the Channel Islands.
8   --ed.
                     (Continued on next card)

CATALOGUE OF THE CORNELL WITCHCRAFT COLLECTION

Witchcraft
BF 1565 F13
   Fachinei, Andrea, d. ca. 1607, praeses.
     Dispvtatio jvridica, De maleficis et sagis, vt vocant, in theses aliqvot coniecta: qvas ... svb praesidio ... Andreae Fachinei ... tvebitvr Ioannes Christophorvs Ficlervs ... Ingolstadii, Ex officina typographica Wolfgangi Ederi, 1592.
    4 p. l., 36 p.
    On inside cover, long note by G. L. Burr on J. Christoph and J. Baptist Fickler.
    1. Witchcraft. I. Fickler, Johann Christoph, respondent. II. Title: De maleficis et sagis.
(Over)

Witchcraft
F 520 .89
   Krakevitz, Albert Joachim von, 1674-1734, praeses.
    Facultatis theologicae ad hunc actum decanus Albertus Joach. de Krakevitz ... ad disputationem ... De theologia daemonum ... invitat.
    Facultatis theologicae ad hunc actum decanus Albertus Joach. de Krakevitz, ... suo & collegii theologici nomine ad disputationem inauguralem ... Dn. M. Fridemanni Andreae Zulichii, Jenens. De theologia daemonum ... invitat. Rostochii, Litteris J. Wepplingi, Sereniss. Princ. & univ. typogr. [1715]
    10 p. l., 68 p. 21cm.
    The first section is a curriculum
(Continued on next card)

Witchcraft
F 520 .89
   Facultatis theologicae ad hunc actum decanus Albertus Joach. de Krakevitz ... ad disputationem ... De theologia daemonum ... invitat.
   Krakevitz, Albert Joachim von, 1674-1734, praeses. ...De theologia daemonum ... [1715] (Card 2)
vitae.
    The dissertation proper has special t. p.: Auxiliante summo numine specimen inaugurale theologicum De theologia daemonum ...
    Diss.--Rostock (F. A. Zulich, respondent)
    1. Demonology. 2. Devil. I. Zulich, Fridemann Andreas, b. 1687, respondent. II. His Specimen inaugurale theologicum De theologia daemonum. III. Title: De theologia daemonum.

Faggin, Giuseppe, 1906–
   Le streghe. Milano, Longanesi [1959]
   305 p. illus. 19cm. (I Marmi, v. 24)

   1. Witchcraft. I. Title.

BF 1584 .9 F15
Fahlgren, Karl.
   Till Blåkulla. Trolldomsväsendet i Västerbotten 1675-1677. Umeå, Botnia, 1966.
   115 p. 23 cm. 17.50 skr (unb. 9.50 skr)   (S 66-49)
   Bibliographical references included in "Källor, litteratur och anmärkningar" (p. 109-115)

   1. Witchcraft—Västerbotten, Sweden. I. Title.
                      67-81566
Library of Congress   [2]

F 581 16 882
Fairfax, Edward, d. 1635.
   Daemonologia: a discourse on witchcraft as it was acted in the family of Mr. Edward Fairfax, of Fuyston, in the county of York, in the year 1621; along with the only two eclogues of the same author known to be in existence. With a biographical introduction, and notes topographical & illustrative. By William Grainge. Harrogate, R. Ackrill, 1882.
   2 p. l., v p., 1 l., [9]-189 p. 21cm.

   1. Witchcraft. I. Grainge, William, ed. II. Title.

WITCHCRAFT
BF 1555 P51 1693
   A faithful narrative of the wonderful and extraordinary fits which Mr. Tho. Spatchet ... was under by witchcraft.
   Petto, Samuel, 1624?-1711.
    A faithful narrative of the wonderful and extraordinary fits which Mr. Tho. Spatchet (late of Dunwich and Cookly) was under by witchcraft: or, a mysterious providence in his even unparallel'd fits ... London, Printed for John Harris, 1693.
    2 p. l., 31, [1] p. 19cm.
    Also issued London, 1693, without printer or bookseller named.
    Wing P1897.
    1. Spatchet, Thomas, 1614– 2. Demoniac possession. 3. Convulsions. I. Title.

Faiths that healed.

RZ 400 M23
Major, Ralph Hermon, 1884–
   Faiths that healed, by Ralph H. Major ... New York, London, D. Appleton-Century company, incorporated, 1940.
   x p., 1 l., 290 p. incl. plates. front., plates, ports. 21½ᶜᵐ.

   1. Medicine, Magic, mystic, and spagiric. 2. Faith-cure. 3. Witchcraft. I. Title.
Library of Congress   RZ405.M3   40-5965

Witchcraft
BF 1520 F17
   Falck, Nathanael, 1663-1693.
    Nathanaelis Falcken ... Dissertationes quatuor, De daemonologia recentiorum autorum falsa, anno 1692. Wittebergae habitae, nunc vero praefixis literis Schomerianis ibidem recusae. [Wittebergae] Typis Martini Schultzii, 1694.
    92 p. illus. initials. 20 x 16cm.
    4°: A², B-M⁴, N².
    Contents.--De falsa recentiorum auctorum daemonologia ... respondente Joh.
(Continued on next card)

Witchcraft
BF 1520 F17
   Falck, Nathanael, 1663-1693. Nathanaelis Falcken ... Dissertationes quatuor ... 1694.   (Card 2)
   Contents--Continued.
Isaaco Trempenau.--Dissertatio II. Ortum daemonologiae falsae & progressum historice declarans, respondente Johanne Furmann.--Dissertatio III. De daemonologia Hobbesii & Spinozae, respondente Jac. Friderico Mollero.--Dissertatio IV. De daemonologia
(Continued on next card)

Witchcraft
BF 1520 F17
   Falck, Nathanael, 1663-1693. Nathanaelis Falcken ... Dissertationes quatuor ... 1694.   (Card 3)
gia Bekkeri & aliorum, respondente Georg. Abrahamo Wolf.
    1. Demonology. 2. Hobbes, Thomas, 1588-1679. Elementa philosophica de cive. 3. Spinoza, Benedictus de, 1632-1677. Tractatus theologico-politicus. 4. Bekker, Balthasar, 1634-1698. De betoverde weereld. I. Title: De daemonologia recentiorum autorum falsa.
(Over)

Falco, Nicolaus, respondent.

WITCHCRAFT
BF 1565 H45
   Heerbrand, Jacob, 1521-1600, praeses.
    De magia dispvtatio ex cap. 7. Exo. ... Praeside reverendo ... Iacobo Heerbrando, ... Nicolavs Falco Salueldensis respondere conabitur. Tubingae, 1570.
    17 p. 21cm.

   1. Witchcraft in the Bible. 2. Bible. O.T. Exodus VII--Criticism, interpretation, etc. I. Falco, Nicolaus, respondent. II. Title.

Witchcraft
BF 1582 Z7 1347
   Falgairolle, Edmond.
    Un envoutement en Gévaudan en l'année 1347. Nîmes, Catélan, 1892.
    117 p. 19cm.

   Contains the complete proceedings of the trial of Etienne Pépin in Latin, and an abridged version in French.

   1. Pépin, Étienne, fl. 1347. I. Title.

Witchcraft
BF 1559 F18
   Falgairolle, Edmond.
    Les exorcismes en Lozère en 1792. Paris, Chamuel, 1894.
    38 p. 25cm.

   1. Exorcism. I. Title.

Familiengeschichte Keppler.

Witchcraft
QB 36 K38 K38
   Keppler, Gustav, ed.
    Familiengeschichte Keppler, bearb. und hrsg. von Oberpostinspektor Gustav Keppler, Stuttgart. 2. Bd. Görlitz, Verlag für Sippenforschung und Wappenkunde C. A. Starke, 1930.
    864 p. port., plates. 15cm.
    Added t. p.: Astronom Kepler und seine Zeit, mit Schilderung des Hexenprozesses gegen seine Mutter.
    Band 1 apparently not published.
(Continued on next card)

Witchcraft
BF 1612 F21
   Fanjoux, J M Joseph.
    Aperçu médico-légal sur la magie et la sorcellerie, avec leurs influences actuelles sur le développement des maladies mentales. Lyon, A. Rey, 1909.
    108 p. 25cm.

   1. Medicine, Magic, mystic and spagiric. I. Title.

Faragó, Cecilia.

Witchcraft
BF 1584 I8D31 1783
   Defeza de Cecilia Faragó, accusada do crime de feiticeria: obra util para desabusar as pessoas preoccupadas da arte magica, e seus pertendidos effeitos. Lisboa, Na Officina da Academia das Sciencias, 1783.
    [6], 149 p. 14cm.

   Signed at end: Napoles 26 de Março de 1770. José Rafael.
    1. Faragó, Cecilia. 2. Witchcraft--Italy.

WITCHCRAFT
BF 1582 Z7 1649a
   Farconnet, François.
    Relation véritable contenant ce qui s'est passé aux exorcismes d'une fille appellée Élisabeth Allier, natifve de la coste S. André en Dauphiné, possédée depuis vingt ans par deux démons nommez Orgueuil et Boniface et l'heureuse délivrance d'icelle fille après six exorcismes faits au couvent des F. F. Prescheurs de Grenoble. Avec quelques raisons pour obliger à croire la possession & la délivrance. Jouxte la coppie [sic] imprimée à Grenoble. Paris, P. Sevestre, 1649 [repr. Lyon, 1875]
    29 p. 23 cm.
    1. Allier, Elisabeth, fl. 1649. I. Title.

CATALOGUE OF THE CORNELL WITCHCRAFT COLLECTION

Witchcraft
BF
1552
B48
    Les farfadets.
    Berbiguier de Terre-Neuve du Thym, Alexis
Vincent Charles, 1765?-1851.
      Les farfadets, ou Tous les démons ne sont
pas de l'autre monde ... Paris Chez l'auteur ₍et₎ P. Gueffier, 1821.
      3 v. plates. 21cm.

    1. Fairies. 2. Spirits. 3. Demonology.
4. Superstition. I. Title.

Witchcraft
BV
5090
F22
    Farges, Albert, 1848-1926.
      Les phénomènes mystiques distingués de
leurs contrefaçons humaines et diaboliques.
Traité de théologie mystique a l'usage des
séminaires, du clergé et des gens du monde.
Paris ₍1920₎
      640 p. 20cm.

    1. Mysticism--Catholic church. I.
Title.

Rare
K
F22T7
1619
++
    Farinacci, Prospero, 1554-1618.
      Tractatus de haeresi, qui est Opervm
criminalivm pars VIII ... Prostat
Francofvrti ad Moenum, Sumptibus Haeredum
D. Zachariae Palthenij, 1619.

    1. Heresy. 2. Canon law. I. Title.

Rare
BX
2340
F22
    Farinerio, Bonaventura.
      Exorcismo. Mirabile da disfari ogni
sorte de maleficii, e da cacciare li demoni,
& è prouato. Et per il Reveren. P. Frate
Bonaventvra Farinerio, inquisitor reuisto,
corretto & ristampato. Venetia ₍Francesco
Rampazetto₎ 1560.
      ₍56₎ p. 16cm.

    1. Exorcism. I. Title.

WITCHCRAFT
BS
2545
D5
F23
1805
    Farmer, Hugh, 1714-1787.
      An essay on the demoniacs of the New
Testament. 2d ed. London, Printed by
R. Taylor and sold by J. Johnson, and W.
Vidler, 1805.
      xii, 264 p. 18cm.

2 copies

      With copy 2 is bound his An inquiry
into the nature and design of Christ's
temptation in the wilderness. 4th ed.
London, 1805.

8
NIC
    I. Title.

BS
2545
D5F23
1805
    Farmer, Hugh, 1714-1787.
      An essay on the demoniacs of the New
Testament. 2d ed. London, Printed by
R. Taylor and Co., and sold by J. Johnson,
and W. Vidler, 1805.
      xii, 264 p. 18cm.

    1. Demoniac possession. 2. Demonology.

WITCHCRAFT
BF
1501
D12
no.2
    Farmer, Hugh, 1714-1787.
      An essay on the demoniacs of the New
Testament. German.
      Hugo Farmers Versuch über die Dämonischen
des Neuen Testamentes. Aus dem Englischen
übersetzt von L. F. A. von Cölln. Nebst
einer Vorrede D. Joh. Sal. Semlers. Bremen und Leipzig, Bey J. H. Cramer, 1776.
      38, 327 p. 17cm.
      Translation of An essay on the demoniacs
of the New Testament.
      No. 2 in vol. lettered Dämonologische
Schriften.

8   (Continued on next card)

WITCHCRAFT
BF
1501
D12
no.2
    Farmer, Hugh, 1714-1787.
      Hugo Farmers Versuch über die Dämonischen
des Neuen Testamentes. Aus dem Englischen
übersetzt von L. F. A. von Cölln. Nebst
einer Vorrede D. Joh. Sal. Semlers. Bremen und Leipzig, Bey J. H. Cramer, 1776.
      38, 327 p. 17cm.
      Translation of An essay on the demoniacs
of the New Testament.
      No. 2 in vol. lettered Dämonologische
Schriften.

8   (Continued on next card)

WITCHCRAFT
BF
1501
D12
no.2
    Farmer, Hugh, 1714-1787. Hugo Farmers
Versuch über die Dämonischen des Neuen
Testamentes ... 1776. (Card 2)

    1. Demoniac possession. 2. Demonology. I. His An essay on the demoniacs
of the New Testament. German. II. Cölln,
Ludwig Friedrich August von, tr. III.
Semler, Johann Salomo, 1725-1791. IV.
Title: Versuch über die Dämonischen
des Neuen Testamentes. V. Title.

Witchcraft
BF
1565
F31
2 copies
    Fell, John, 1735-1797.
      Daemoniacs. An enquiry into the
heathen and the Scripture doctrine of
daemons. In which the hypotheses of
the Rev. Mr. Farmer, and others on this
subject, are particularly considered
... London, Printed for Charles Dilly,
1779.
      xv, 432 p. 21cm.

    1. Demoniac possession. 2. Farmer,
Hugh,   I. Title.

Witchcraft
BF
1565
F23
    ₍Farnworth, Richard₎
      Witchcraft cast out from the religious
seed and Israel of God. And the black art of
nicromancery, inchantments, sorcerers,
wizards ... Also some things to clear the
truth from reproaches, lies and slanders ...
occasioned by Daniel Bott... Written in
Warwickshire, the ninth moneth, 1654. As a
judgement upon witchcraft, and a deniall,
testimony and declaration against witchcraft,
from those   that the world
      (Continued on next card)

Witchcraft
BF
1565
F23
    ₍Farnworth, Richard₎ Witchcraft cast out
from the religious seed and Israel of God.
1655.   (Card 2)

reproachfully calleth Quakers. London,
Printed for G. Calvert, 1655.
    20 p. 20cm.

    With book-plate of Francis Freeling.

    1. Witchcraft. I. Title.

Witchcraft
BX
2340
F24
    Fasciculus triplex exorcismorum, et benedictionum, in Romano-Catholica Ecclesia
usitatarum, ex variis authoribus approbatis collectus, & historiis, ac exemplis subinde illustratus, cum adnexo
Tractatu de indulgentiis, et jubilaeo,
ac resolutionibus moralibus ... Tyrnaviae, Typis academicis, 1739.
      2 p. l., 148, 78, ₍7₎ p. 21cm.
      "Thesaurus ecclesiasticus ... de indulgentiis ...," has special t. p. and
separate paging.
      (Continued on next card)

Witchcraft
BX
2340
F24
    Fasciculus triplex exorcismorum, et benedictionum ... 1739.   (Card 2)

    1. Exorcism. 2. Benediction. 3. Indulgences. I. Catholic Church. Liturgy
and ritual. II. Title: Thesaurus ecclesiasticus ... de indulgentiis.

La fascinación en España.

WITCHCRAFT
BF
1566
S16
    Salillas, Rafael.
      La fascinación en España. Estudio
hecho con la información promovida por
la Sección de Ciencias morales y políticas del Ateneo de Madrid. Madrid,
Imprenta á cargo de E. Arias, 1905.
      107 p. 24cm.

    Subtitle on cover: Erujas--brujerías
--amuletos.

8
NIC
    1. Witchcraft--Spain. 2.
Amulets.   I. Title.

MSS
Bd.
WITCHCRAFT
BF
F24
    Fassiculus ₍sic₎ artis exorcisticae ex varijs
authorib. collectus. Ad omnes infirmitates tam maleficiales quam demoniacas manifestandas, ac propulsandas vtilis, ac
per necessarius. ₍n.p.₎ 16th cent?₎
      150 l. illus. 21cm.
      Manuscript, on paper, in a Latin hand.
The illustrations and illustrated initials have been cut out of printed works and
pasted in. Line borders on each page.
      Bound in brown boards.
    1. Exorcism.

Fassmann, David, 1683-1744, supposed author

Witchcraft
BF
1410
C97
    Curieuse Gespräche im Reiche derer Todten,
zwischen dem bekandten Auctore der bezauberten Welt, und ehemahligen Prediger
in Holland Balthasar Beckern, der bey nahe
wenig vom Teufel geglaubet; und zwischen
dem in gantz Teutschland berühmten Theologo Christian Scrivern, der einen Menschen
zurecht gebracht, so einen Pact mit dem
Teufel gemacht; ... Leipzig und Braunschweig, 1731-₍1734₎
      4 v. in 1. (208 p.) 4 plates, vignettes.   21 x 17cm.
      (Continued on next card)

Fassmann, David, 1683-1744, supposed author

Witchcraft
BF
1410
C97
    Curieuse Gespräche im Reiche derer Todten,
zwischen .. Balthasar Beckern .. und ..
Christian Scrivern ... 1731-₍1734₎
      (Card 2)

    4°: A-P⁴, P3, Q-2C⁴.
    Black letter.
    Sometimes ascribed to David Fassmann.
    Title of v. 2: Zweyte Unterredung oder
Gespräche im Reiche derer Todten ...; of v. 3:

    (Continued on next card)

CATALOGUE OF THE CORNELL WITCHCRAFT COLLECTION

Witchcraft
BF
1410
C97

Fassmann, David, 1683-1744, supposed author.
    Curieuse Gespräche im Reiche derer Todten, zwischen .. Balthasar Beckern .. und .. Christian Scrivern ... 1731-₁1734₎
                        (Card 3)
    Besonderes curieuses ₍sic₎ Gespräche im Reiche derer Todten ...; of v. 4: Curieuses Gespräche in dem Reiche derer Todten ...
    With this is bound Curieuses Gespräche im Reiche der Todten, zwischen .. Johann Friedrich Mayern .. und Johann Wilhelm Petersen ... ₍Leipzig₎ 1732.
              (Continued on next card)

The fate of Dietrich Flade.

Witchcraft
BF
1583
B96
1891

Burr, George Lincoln, 1857-1938.
    The fate of Dietrich Flade. New York, London, G. P. Putnam's Sons, 1891.
    57 p. 24cm.
    "Reprinted from the Papers of the American Historical Association, vol. V, no. 3, July, 1891."

Witchcraft
BF
1582
F26

Faure-Biguet, Albert.
    Recherches sur les procès de sorcellerie au XVIe siècle. Valence, Imprimerie de Chenevier, 1877.
    45 p. 23cm.

1. Trials (Witchcraft) I. Title.

WITCHCRAFT
BF
1555
H678
1881

Favre, Léopold, 1817-1890, ed.
    Histoire admirable de la maladie prodigieuse de Pierre Creusé, arrivée en la ville de Niort en 1628. Avec une introduction par L. Favre. Niort, Typ. de L. Favre, 1881.
    iii, 84 p. 22cm.
    Half title: Maladie prodigieuse de Pierre Creusé.
    Includes reprint of the original t. p., whose title includes: "... auec vn plaidoyé de l'ad uocat du Roy de ladite
              (Continued on next card)

WITCHCRAFT
BF
1555
H678
1881

Favre, Léopold, 1817-1890, ed.
    Histoire admirable de la maladie prodigieuse de Pierre Creusé ... 1881.   (Card 2)
    ville sur le subjet de ladite maladie, & la sentence interuenue sur ledit plaidoyé: ensemble les certificats de medecins & chirurgiens dudit lieu. Niort, 1631."

1. Demoniac possession. 2. Creusé, Pierre, b. 1614. I. Favre, Léopold, 1817-1890, ed. II. Title: Maladie prodigieuse de Pierre Creusé.

Witchcraft
BF
1565
F28

Faye, Barthélemy, seigneur d'Espeisses, 16th cent.
    Alexicacus.
    Faye, Barthélemy, seigneur d'Espeisses, 16th cent.
    Bartholomęi Faij, regij in senatv Parisiensi consiliarij, ac Inquisitionum praesidis Energvmenicvs. Eiusdem Alexicacvs, cū liminari, vt vocant ad vtrūque librum epistola. Lvtetiae, Apud Sebastianum Niuellium, 1571.
    2 p. l., 397 p. 17cm.
    Alexicacvs, p. 167-397, has special t. p.
    1. Witchcraft. 2. Lord's Supper--Bread and win e. 3. Christian life. I. Title: En ergumenicus. II. Title: Alexicacus.

Witchcraft
BF
1565
F28

Faye, Barthélemy, seigneur d'Espeisses, 16th cent.
    Bartholomęi Faij, regij in senatv Parisiensi consiliarij, ac Inquisitionum praesidis Energvmenicvs. Eiusdem Alexicacvs, cū liminari, vt vocant ad vtrūque librum epistola. Lvtetiae, Apud Sebastianum Niuellium, 1571.
    2 p. l., 397 p. 17cm.
    Alexicacvs, p. 167-397, has special t. p.
    1. Witchcra ft. 2. Lord's Supper--Bread and win e. 3. Christian life. I. Title: En ergumenicus. II. Title: Alexicacus.   (Over)

Witchcraft
BF
1511
F29

Fehr, Hans Adolf, 1874-
    Gottesurteil und Folter: eine Studie zur Dämonologie des Mittelalters und der neueren Zeit. Berlin, W. de Gruyter, 1926.
    24 p. plate. 23cm.
    Pages also numbered ₍231₎-254.
    "Sonderausgabe aus Festgabe für Rudolf Stammler zum 70. Geburtstage."
    1. Demonology. I. Title. II. Stammler, Rudolf, 1856-   1938.

Witchcraft
BL
490
F29

Fehr, Joseph.
    Der Aberglaube und die katholische Kirche des Mittelalters; ein Beitrag zur Kultur- und Sittengeschichte. Stuttgart, Scheitlin, 1857.
    iv, 164 p. 20cm.

1. Superstition. I. Title.

Witchcraft
BF
1584
N4
F31

Feith, Hendrik Octavius, 1813-1895.
    Bijdrage tot de geschiedenis der heksenprocessen in de Provincie Groningen, door Mr. H. O. Feith. ₍n. p., ca. 1850?₎
    26 p. 25cm.
    "Eene voorlezing, gehouden in het Gron. genootschap Pro excolendo jure patrio."
    Reprint from Nieuwe Bijdragen voor vaderlandsche Geschiedenis en Oudheidkunde, 1, according to G. L. Burr.
    Caption title.
    1. Trials (Witchcraft)--Netherlands. I. Title.

Felde, Albert zum, 1672-1720, respondent.

Witchcraft
BF
1587
D61
no.11

Büttner, Daniel, 1642-1696, praeses.
    Magiologia seu Disputatio de magia licita et illicita qvam ... praeside Dn. Daniele Büttner ... disquisitioni submittit Albertus zum Felde ... Hamburgi, Literis Conradi Neumanni ₍1693₎
    26, ₍6₎ p. 18cm. (bound in 21cm. vol.)
    No. 11 in vol. lettered Dissertationes de magia. 1623-1723.
    1. Magic--Addresses, essays, lectures. I. Felde, Albert zum, 1672-1720, respondent. II. Title. III. Title: De magia licita et illicita.

Witchcraft
BF
1565
F31
2 copies

Fell, John, 1735-1797.
    Daemoniacs. An enquiry into the heathen and the Scripture doctrine of daemons. In which the hypotheses of the Rev. Mr. Farmer, and others on this subject, are particularly considered ... London, Printed for Charles Dilly, 1779.
    xv, 432 p. 21cm.
    1. Demoniac possession. 2. Farmer, Hugh, 1714-17 87. I. Title.

Femgericht und Hexenprozesse.

WITCHCRAFT
JN
3269
T36

Thamm, Melchior, 1860-
    Femgericht und Hexenprozesse. Leipzig und Wien, Bibliographisches Institut ₍1903₎
    179 p. 15cm. (Meyers Volksbücher. Nr. 1345-1347)

1. Femic courts. 2. Witchcraft--History--Germany. I. Title.

Fenderlyn, Giles, d. 1652.

Witchcraft
BF
1563
W81++
no.17

The Tryall and examination of Mrs. Joan Peterson ... for her supposed witchcraft, and poysoning of the lady Powel ... together with her confession ... Also, the tryal, examination and confession of Giles Fenderlyn, who had made a convenent with the Devil for 14 years... London, Printed for G. Horton, 1652. ₍London, at the British Museum, 1923₎
    8 p. 16cm.

(Continued on next card)

Fenderlyn, Giles, d. 1652.

Witchcraft
BF
1563
W81++
no.17

The Tryall and examination of Mrs. Joan Peterson... ₍1923₎   (Card 2)

    Photocopy (negative) 8 p. on 7 l. 20 x 32cm.
    No. 17 in vol. lettered: Witchcraft tracts, chapbooks and broadsides, 1579-1704; rotograph copies.

1. Witchcraft--England. 2. Peterson, Joan, d.1652. 3. Fenderlyn, Giles, d. 1652.

BF
1566
F35

Ferguson, Ian.
    The philosophy of witchcraft, by Ian Ferguson ... London ₍etc.₎ G. G. Harrap & co. ltd. ₍1924₎
    218, ₍1₎ p. 19½ cm.
    Bibliography: p. 217-218, ₍1₎

1. Witchcraft. I. Title.

BF1566.F4   25—9421
Library of Congress   ₍53h1₎

Witchcraft
BF
1566
F35
1925

Ferguson, Ian.
    The philosophy of witchcraft. New York, D. Appleton, 1925.
    218 p. 20cm.

1. Witchcraft. I. Title.

Witchcraft
Z
6878
W8
F35

Ferguson, John, 1837-1916.
    Bibliographical notes on the witchcraft literature of Scotland.
    (In The Edinburgh Bibliographical Society. ₍Publications₎ Session 1896-97. Edinburgh. 25cm. v.3 (1897) p. ₍37₎-124)

1. Witchcraft --Scotland--Bibl. I. Title.

CATALOGUE OF THE CORNELL WITCHCRAFT COLLECTION

Fernerer Unfug der Zauberey.

WITCHCRAFT
BF 1565 R34

Reiche, Johann, ed.
Herrn D. Christian Thomasii ... Kurtze Lehr-Sätze von dem Laster der Zauberey, nach dem wahren Verstande des lateinischen Exemplars ins Deutsche übersetzet, und aus den berühmten Theologi D. Meyfarti, Naudaei, und anderer gelehrter Männer Schrifften erleutert ... nebst einigen Actis magicis heraus gegeben von Johann Reichen. Halle im Magdeburgischen, Im Rengerischen Buchladen, 1704.
2 v. in 1. 21cm.

8 NIC (Continued on next card)

Fernerer Unfug der Zauberey.

WITCHCRAFT
BF 1565 R34

Reiche, Johann, ed. Herrn D. Christian Thomasii ... Kurtze Lehr-Sätze ... 1704. (Card 2)

Vol. 1 has special t. p.: Fernerer Unfug der Zauberey. Halle im Magdeburgischen, 1704.
Vol. 2 has special t. p.: Unterschiedliche Schrifften von Unfug des Hexen-Processes. Halle im Magdeburg., 1703.
Contents.--[1. Bd.] Gabriel Naudaei

8 NIC (Continued on next card)

Fernerer Unfug der Zauberey.

WITCHCRAFT
BF 1565 R34

Reiche, Johann, ed. Herrn D. Christian Thomasii ... Kurtze Lehr-Sätze ... 1704. (Card 3)

Contents.--Continued.
Schutz-Schrifft [tr. of Apologie pour tous les grands hommes]--Geschichte der Teuffel zu Lodün.--Trauer-Geschichte von der greulichen Zauberey Ludwig Goffredy [tr. of De l'horrible et épouvantable sorcellerie de Louis Goffredy, author F. de Rosset]--D. Christian Thomasii ... Kurtze Lehr-Sätze von

8 NIC (Continued on next card)

Fernerer Unfug der Zauberey.

WITCHCRAFT
BF 1565 R34

Reiche, Johann, ed. Herrn D. Christian Thomasii ... Kurtze Lehr-Sätze ... 1704. (Card 4)

Contents--Continued.
dem Laster der Zauberey [tr. of Dissertatio de crimine magiae, J. Reiche, respondent]. [2. Bd.] Malleus judicum oder Gesetz-Hammer der unbarmhertzigen Hexen-Richter.--Cautio criminalis [von F. Spee]--D. Johann Matthäus Meyfarths Christliche Erinnerung an Regenten.-- Viererley Sorten Hexen-Acta. (Continued on next card)

8 NIC

BF 1584 I8 F36

Ferraioni, Francesco
Le streghe e l'Inquisizione; superstizioni e realtà. Roma, Tipografia sallustiana, 1955.
132, 6 p. illus. 21cm.

1. Witchcraft--Italy. 2. Inquisition. Italy. I. Title.

Ferrier, Auger, 1513-1588.
Des jugements astronomiques sur les nativitez.

WITCHCRAFT
BF 51 S33

Schindler, Heinrich Bruno, 1797-1859.
Das magische Geistesleben. Ein Beitrag zur Psychologie. Breslau, W. G. Korn, 1857.
xvi, 356 p. 24cm.

1. Psychology, Religious. 2. Occult sciences--Psychology. I. Title.

8 NIC

Fery, Jeanne, fl. 1584.

Witchcraft
BF 1555 H67 1886

La Possession de Jeanne Fery, religieuse professe du couvent des soeurs noires de la ville de Mons (1584) Paris, Aux bureaux du Progrès médical, 1886.
v, 109 p. 23cm. (Bibliothèque diabolique; Collection Bourneville)
Reprint of Histoire admirable et veritable des choses advenues a l'endroict d'une religieuse professe ..., pub. 1586.
Edited by D. B. Bourneville.
With facsimile of original t. p.

8 (Continued on next card)

Fery, Jeanne, fl. 1584.

WITCHCRAFT
BF 1555 H67 1589

Warhafft: vnd gründtlicher Bericht, sehr wunderlich: vnnd gleichsam vnerhörter Geschichten, so sich vnlangst zu Bergen [i.e., Mons] in Henogau, Ertzbisthumbs Cambrai, mit einer besessnen, vnd hernach widerledigten Closterfrawen verloffen. Auss frantzösischer Sprach, in Hochteutsch gebracht. [München, Gedruckt bey Adam Berg] 1589.
4 p. l., 47 numbered l. 19cm.
Illustrati ve title vignette.
With colo phon.

8 (Continued on next card)

Fery, Jeanne, fl. 1584.

WITCHCRAFT
BF 1555 H67 1587

Warhafft: vnd gründtlicher Bericht, sehr wunderlich ... 1589. (Card 2)

Translation of Histoire admirable et veritable des choses advenues a l'endroict d'une religieuse professe ... pub. 1586.
Preface by Adam Berg.
1. Demoniac possession. 2. Fery, Jeanne, fl. 1584. I. Histoire admirable et veritable des choses advenues a l'endroict d'une religieuse professe.
8 German. II. Berg, Adam, d. 1610.

GR 535 F41

Feslikenian, Franca.
I maghi. Storie vere di magie, riti e sortilegi. Milano, G. De Vecchi, 1970.
195 p. plates. 20½ cm. L2500   It 71-Feb

1. Witchcraft--Italy.   I. Title.

9   GR535.F4   73-594798

Library of Congress   71 [2]

Feyerabend, Sigmund, ca. 1527-ca. 1590.

Witchcraft
BF 1603 T37++ 1575

Theatrvm diabolorum, das ist: Warhaffte eigentliche vnd kurtze Beschreibung allerley grewlicher, schrecklicher vnd abschewlicher Laster ... Getruckt zu Franckfurt am Mayn, durch Peter Schmid [in Verlägung Sigismund Feyrabendt] 1575.
568 l. 35cm.

Foreword signed: Sigmund Feyrabend, Buchhandler.
I. Feyer   abend, Sigmund, ca.
1527-ca. 15   90.

BF 1521 J28 1924

James I, king of Great Britain, 1566-1625.
King James, the First: Daemonologie (1597). Newes from Scotland, declaring the damnable life and death of Doctor Fian, a notable sorcerer who was burned at Edenbrough in Ianuary last (1591) London, J. Lane; New York, Dutton [1924]
xv, 81, 29 p. illus. 19cm. (The Bodley head quartos, no. 9)
With facsimiles of original title pages.
Newes from Scotland has been ascribed to James Carmichael, minister of Haddington. Cf. Sir James Melville, Memories, p. 195, and D. Webster, Collection of   tracts on witchcraft, etc., 1820, p. 38.

Witchcraft
BF 1602 F44 1803

Fiard, Jean Baptiste, 1736-1818.
La France trompée par les magiciens et démonolatres du dix-huitième siècle, fait démontré par des faits. Paris, Grégoire, 1803.
200 p. 22cm.

Bound with his Lettres philosophiques sur la magie. Paris, 1803.

1. Magic.   I. Title.

Fiard, Jean Baptiste, 1736-1818.
Lettres magique, ou, Lettres sur le diable.

Witchcraft
BF 1602 F44 1803

[Fiard, Jean Baptiste] 1736-1818.
Lettres philosophiques sur la magie. Ed. corr. et augm. Paris, Grégoire, 1803.
130 p. 22cm.

First ed., Paris, 1791, had title: Lettres magiques, ou, Lettres sur le diable.
With this is bound his La France trompée par les magiciens ... Paris, 1803.

1. Magic. I.   Title. II. Fiard, Jean Baptiste, 1736-   1818. Lettres magique, ou, Lettres sur   le diable.

Witchcraft
BF 1602 F44 1803

[Fiard, Jean Baptiste] 1736-1818.
Lettres philosophiques sur la magie. Ed. corr. et augm. Paris, Grégoire, 1803.
130 p. 22cm.

First ed., Paris, 1791, had title: Lettres magiques, ou, Lettres sur le diable.
With this is bound his La France trompée par les magiciens ... Paris, 1803.

1. Magic. I.   Title. II. Fiard, Jean Baptiste, 1736-   1818. Lettres magique, ou, Lettres sur   le diable.

Ficino, Marsilio, 1433-1499, tr.

WITCHCRAFT
BF 1598 H55 A1 1532

Hermes Trismegistus.
[Poemander. Latin]
Mercvrii Trismegisti Pymander, De potestate et sapientia Dei. Eivsdem Asclepivs, De uoluntate Dei. Opuscula sanctissimis mysterijs, ac uerè coelestibus oraculis illustrissima. Iamblichvs De mysterijs Aegyptiorum, Chaldaeorum, & Assyriorū. Proclvs In Platonicum Alcibiadem, de anima & daemone. Idem De sacrificio & magia. Quae omni solerti cura   repurgata, ac suo tandem

8 (Continued on next card)

Ficino, Marsilio, 1433-1499, tr.

WITCHCRAFT
BF 1598 H55 A1 1532

Hermes Trismegistus. [Poemander. Latin]
1532.   (Card 2)

candori restituta sunt. Basileae [Per Mich. Isingrinivm] 1532.
480, [3] p. 16cm.
With colophon.
The Asclepius translated by Apuleius Madaurensis; the rest by Marsilio Ficino.
I. Jamblichus, of Chalcis. De mysteriis. Latin.   II. Proclus Diadochus.
8   III. Apulei   us Madaurensis, tr. IV.
Ficino, Mars   ilio, 1433-1499, tr. V.
His Asclep   ius.

Ficino, Marsilio, 1433-1499.

WITCHCRAFT
PA 4220 L3 A4+ 1516

Jamblichus, of Chalcis.
[De mysteriis. Latin]
Iamblichus De mysteriis Aegyptiorum, Chaldaeorum, Assyriorum. Proclus In Platonicum Alcibiadem de anima, atq. demone. Proclus sacrificio, & magia. Porphyrius De diuini atq. daemonibus. Synesius Platonicus De so niis. Psellus De daemonibus. Expositio Prisciani, & Marsilii in Theophrastum De su, phantasia, & intellectu. Alcinoi Pla
8   nici philoso   phi, Liber de doctrina
(Continued on next card)

206

CATALOGUE OF THE CORNELL WITCHCRAFT COLLECTION

Ficino, Marsilio, 1433-1499.

WITCHCRAFT
PA 4220 L3 A44 1516

Jamblichus, of Chalcis. [De mysteriis. Latin.] [1516.]   (Card 2)

Platonis. Speusippi Platonis discipuli, Liber de Platonis definitionibus. Pythagorae philosophi Aurea uerba. Symbola Pithagorae philosophi. Xenocratis philosophi platonici, Liber de morte. Mercurii Trismegisti Pimander. Euisdem Asclepius. Marsilii Ficini De triplici uita lib. II. Eiusdem Liber de uoluptate. Eiusdem

8

(Continued on next card)

Ficino, Marsilio, 1433-1499.

WITCHCRAFT
PA 4220 L3 A44 1516

Jamblichus, of Chalcis. [De mysteriis. Latin.] [1516.]   (Card 3)

De sole & lumine libri. II. Apologia eiusdem in librum suum de lumine. Eiusdem Libellus de magis. Quod necessaria sit securitas, & tranquillitas animi. Praeclarissimarum sententiarum huius operis breuis annotatio. [Venetiis, In aedibvs Aldi, et Andreae soceri, 1516.]
177 [i.e., 175] numbered leaves.
8   29cm.   (Continued on next card)

Ficino, Marsilio, 1433-1499.

WITCHCRAFT
PA 4220 L3 A44 1516

Jamblichus, of Chalcis. [De mysteriis.] Latin. [1516.]   (Card 4)

At head of title: Index eorvm, qvae hoc in libro habentvr.
With colophon.
Provenance: Bibliotec: SS. Me. Novelle.
Translations by M. Ficino.
1. Occult sciences. 2. Philosophy, Ancient--Collections. I. Proclus Diadochus. In Platonicum Alcibiadem. II. Proclus Diadoch us. De sacrificio. III.

8   (Continued on next card)

Witchcraft
PA 4220 L3 A4 1577

Ficino, Marsilio, 1433-1499, tr.
Jamblichus, of Chalcis.
[De mysteriis. Latin.]
Iamblichvs De mysteriis Ægyptiorvm, Chaldæorum, Assyriorum. Proclvs in Platonicum Alcibiadem de anima, atque dæmone. Idem De sacrificio & magia. Porphyrivs De diuinis atq; dæmonib. Psellvs De dæmonibus. Merevrii Trismegisti Pimander. Eiusdem Asclepius. Lvgdvni, apvd Ioan. Tornaesivm, 1577.
543, [1] p. 13cm.
Title vignette (printer's mark)
"Marsilvs Ficinvs ... se commendat": p. 3.

(2)   25-19681

Fickler, Johann Baptist, 1533-1610.

Witchcraft
BF 1565 F13

Fachinei, Andrea, d. ca. 1607, praeses.
Dispvtatio jvridica, De maleficis et sagis, vt vocant, in theses aliqvot coniecta: qvas ... svb praesidio ... Andreae Fachinei ... tvebitvr Ioannes Christophorvs Ficlervs ... Ingolstadii, Ex officina typographica Wolfgangi Ederi, 1592.
4 p. l., 36 p.
On inside cover, long note by G. L. Burr on J. Christoph and J. Baptist Fickler.
1. Witchcr aft. I. Fickler, Johann Christop h, respondent. II.
8   Title: De ma leficis et sagis.

Fickler, Johann Christoph, respondent.

Witchcraft
BF 1565 F13

Fachinei, Andrea, d. ca. 1607, praeses.
Dispvtatio jvridica, De maleficis et sagis, vt vocant, in theses aliqvot coniecta: qvas ... svb praesidio ... Andreae Fachinei ... tvebitvr Ioannes Christophorvs Ficlervs ... Ingolstadii, Ex officina typographica Wolfgangi Ederi, 1592.
4 p. l., 36 p.
On inside cover, long note by G. L. Burr on J. Christoph and J. Baptist Fickler.
1. Witchcr aft. I. Fickler, Johann Christop h, respondent. II.
8   Title: De ma leficis et sagis.

Ficlerus, Johannes Christophorus.

see

Fickler, Johann Christoph.

Witchcraft
BF 1595 F45

Fiedler, Hermann.
Zauberei und Aberglaube. Eine kulturhistorische und kritische Beleuchtung dieser Erscheinungen. Bernburg, J. Bacmeister [1884.]
37 p. 21cm.

1. Magic. 2. Superstition. I. Title.

Witchcraft
BX 4705 S832 F45 1907

Fieger, Hans, 1857-
P. Don Ferdinand Sterzinger, Lector der Theatiner in München, Director der historischen Klasse der kurbayerischen Akademie der Wissenschaften, Bekämpfer des Aberglaubens und Hexenwahns und der Pfarrer Gassnerschen Wunderkuren. Ein Beitrag zur Geschichte der Aufklärung in Bayern unter Kurfürst Maximilian III. Joseph. München, R. Oldenbourg, 1907.
xi, 275 p. 2 tables. 23cm.

8   (Continued on next card)

Witchcraft
BX 4705 S832 F45 1907

Fieger, Hans, 1857-   . P. Don Ferdinand Sterzinger ...   1907.   (Card 2)

Inaug.-diss.--München.
Expansion of a Programmschrift: Pater Don Ferdinand Sterzingers Leben und Schriften, München, 1907.

1. Sterzinger, Ferdinand, 1721-1786.
2. Bavaria--Hist.--Maximilian III Joseph (1745-1777).   I. Title.   II. His
8   Pater Don Ster zingers Leben und Schriften.

Witchcraft
BX 4705 S832 F45

Fieger, Hans, 1857-
Pater Don Sterzingers Leben und Schriften. Ein Beitrag zur Geschichte der Aufklärungsepoche in Bayern. München, Druck von C. Gerber [1896.]
48 p. 2 tables (1 fold.) 24cm.
Programmschrift--Königl. Ludwigs-Kreisrealschule, München.
1. Sterzinger, Ferdinand, 1721-1786.
2. Bavaria--Hist.--Maximilian III Joseph (1745-1777). I. Title.

Fieger, Hans, 1857-
Pater Don Sterzingers Leben und Schriften.

Witchcraft
BX 4705 S832 F45

Fieger, Hans, 1857-   . P. Don Ferdinand Sterzinger ...   1907.   (Card 2)

Inaug.-diss.--München.
Expansion of a Programmschrift: Pater Don Ferdinand Sterzingers Leben und Schriften, München, 1907.

1. Sterzinger, Ferdinand, 1721-1786.
2. Bavaria--Hist.--Maximilian III Joseph (1745-1777).   I. Title.

Figuier, Guillaume Louis.

see

Figuier, Louis, 1819-1894.

Witchcraft
BF 1412 F47 1860

Figuier, Louis, 1819-1894.
Histoire du merveilleux dans les temps modernes, par Louis Figuier ... Paris, L. Hachette et cⁱᵉ, 1860-61.
4 v. 18½ᶜᵐ.
Vols. 1-2, 2. édition.
CONTENTS.--t. 1. Introduction. Les diables de Loudun. Les convulsionnaires jansénistes.--t. 2. La baguette divinatoire. Les prophètes protestants.--t. 3. Le magnétisme animal.--t. 4. Les tables tournantes. Les médiums et les esprits.

1. Demonomania. 2. Divination. 3. Animal magnetism. 4. Spiritualism.   I. Title.
[Full name: Guillaume Louis Figuier]
11-20783 Revised
Library of Congress   BF1412.F4

Witchcraft
BF 1412 F47 M9+

Figuier, Louis, 1819-1894.
Les mystères de la science, par Louis Figuier ... Paris, Librairie illustrée [1887.]
2 v. plates. 28½ᶜᵐ.
CONTENTS.--[1] Autrefois. Introduction. Les diables de Loudun. Les convulsionnaires jansénistes. Les prophètes protestants. La baguette divinatoire.--[2] Aujourd'hui. Les prodiges de Cagliostro. Le magnétisme animal. Les magnétiseurs mystiques. La fille électrique. Les escargots sympathiques. Les esprits frappeurs. Les tables tournantes et les médiums. Les spirites. L'hypnotisme.

1. Occult sciences.   I. Title.
[Full name: Guillaume Louis Figuier]
33-32826

Witchcraft
BF 1520 F48

Filesac, Jean, ca. 1550-1638.
De idololatria magica, dissertatio, Ioannis Filesaci theologi parisiensis. Parisiis, Ex officina Nivelliana, Apud Sebastianvm Cramoisy, 1609.
8 p. l., 73 numbered leaves. 17cm.

1. Demonology. 2. Witchcraft. 3. Magic. I. Title.

8

Witchcraft
BF 1565 F48

[Filmer, Sir Robert] d. 1653.
An advertisement to the jury-men of England touching witches. Together with a difference between an English and [an] Hebrew vvitch. London, Printed by I. G. for R. Royston, 1653.
24 p. 20cm.

Ex libris Joseph Beard.

1. Witchcraf t. I. Title.

CATALOGUE OF THE CORNELL WITCHCRAFT COLLECTION

```
Rare        Filmer, Sir Robert, d. 1653.
JC            The free-holders grand inquest,
153         touching our sovereign lord the King
F48F8       and his parliament. To which are added
1679        Observations upon forms of government.
            Together with Directions for obedience
            to governours in dangerous and doubtful
            times ... London, 1679.
                88,76,72,257-346 p. 19cm.

                Contents.--The free-holders grand

                          (Continued on next card)
```

```
Rare        Filmer, Sir Robert, d. 1653. The free-
JC            holders grand inquest ... 1679.
153           (Card 2)
F48F8
1679        inquest.--Observations upon Aristotle's
            politiques, touching forms of government.
            --Observations concerning the original
            of government, upon Mr. Hobs his Leviathan,
            Mr. Milton against Salmasius, H. Grotius
            De jure belli, Mr. Hunton's Treatise of
            monarchy.--The anarchy of a limited or
            mixed monarchy.--An advertisement to the

                          (Continued on next card)
```

```
Rare        Filmer, Sir Robert, d. 1653. The free-
JC            holders grand inquest ... 1679.
153           (Card 3)
F48F8
1679        Jury-men of England, touching witches.


                I. Title.  II. Title: An advertisement
            to the jury-men of England, touching
            witches.
```

```
            Final notes on witchcraft in Massachusetts ...
Witchcraft
BF          Moore, George Henry, 1823-1892.
1576          Final notes on witchcraft in Massachusetts: a summary
M822+       vindication of the laws and liberties concerning attain-
            ders with corruption of blood, escheats, forfeitures for
            crime, and pardon of offenders, in reply to "Reasons,"
            etc., of Hon. Abner C. Goodell, jr. ... By George H.
            Moore ... New York, Printed for the author, 1885.
                120 p. 25¹ᶜᵐ.
            "Pamphlets hitherto issued in this discussion": p. [2].
            Autographed presentation copy from the author.
                1. Witchcraft--Massachusetts. 2. Goodell, Abner Cheney, 1831-1914.
8           Reasons for concluding that the act of 1711 ...
            became a law.  I.  Title.         11-13449

            Library of Congress          BF1579.M8
```

```
Witchcraft
BF          [Finot, Jules] 1842-1908?
1582          Procès de sorcellerie au bailliage de
F51         Vesoul de 1606 à 1636. [Vesoul, 1875]
                71 p. 23cm.

                Extract from Société d'agriculture,
            sciences et arts du département de la
            Haute-Saône, Vesoul. Bulletin. 3. sér.,
            v. 3, 1875.

                1. Trials (Witchcraft)--Vesoul, France.
            I. Title.
```

```
Witchcraft
BF          Fiorio, Antonio.
1565          Arte magica distrutta. Risposta di
T19         Don Antonio Fiorio Veronese. Trento,
M183        Per G. A. Brunati, 1750.
                47 p. 24cm.
                "As is pointed out on p. 4 of the Repli
            ca bound in these same covers, this imprint
            'In Trento per G. A. Brunati' is stamped in
            by hand. Melzi, ii, p. 418, ascribes the
            pamphlet to Maffei himself."--Note of
            George Lincoln Burr on t. p.

8                         (Continued on next card)
```

```
Witchcraft
BF          Fiorio, Antonio.  Arte magica distrutta.
1565          1750.                     (Card 2)
T19
M183            With this is bound Replica alla risposta
            intitolata Arte magica distrutta.  Verona,
            1751.
                1. Maffei, Francesco Scipione, marchese,
            1675-1755. Arte magica dileguata.  2.
            Magic.  I. Maffei, Francesco Scipione, mar-
            chese, 1675-1755, supposed author.  II.
            Title.

8
```

```
            Fiorio, Antonio.
                  Arte magica distrutta.
Witchcraft
BF          Replica alla risposta intitolata Arte magi-
1565          ca distrutta, di un dottore e sacerdote
T19         Veronese.  Verona, Nella stamperia
M183        Vescovile del seminario per Angelo Targa,
            1751.
                68, [1] p. 24cm.
                Ascribed to P. Antonio Ballerini in a
            contempory hand on t. p. and in another
            hand on p. [69]
                "Melzi (II, p. 430) ascribes this to P.
            Andrea Lugiato, despite its praise of him;
8                         (Continued on next card)
```

```
            Fiorio, Antonio.
                  Arte magica distrutta.
Witchcraft
BF          Replica alla risposta intitolata Arte magi-
1565          ca distrutta ... 1751.  (Card 2)
T19
M183        but Melzi knows nothing of the ascription
            to Ballerini."--Note of George Lincoln Burr
            on t. p.
                Bound with Fiorio, Antonio.  Arte magica
            distrutta.  Trento, 1750.
                1. Fiorio, Antonio. Arte magica dis-
            trutta.  2. Lugiato, Andrea. Osservazzi-
            oni sopra ...       Arte magica dileguata.
8                         (Continued on next card)
```

```
            Fischart, Johann, 1550(ca.)-1590?, tr.
BF          Bodin, Jean, 1530-1596.
1520          Vom aussgelasnen wütigen Teuffelsheer. Übers.
B66+        v. Johann Fischart. (Um ein neues Vorw. verm.
1973        Nachdr. d. Ausg. Strassburg 1591) Vorw.: Hans
            Biedermann. Graz, Akadem. Druck- u. Verlagsanst.,
            1973.
                vii p., 372 p. of facsims. 28cm.
                Translation of De la démonomanie des sorciers.
                Bibliography: p. vii.
```

```
Witchcraft
BF          [Fischer, Dagobert]
1582          Exécutions de sorciers et sorcières
F52         en 1615, dans les possessions de Murbach
            et le Haut-Mundat.
                (In Revue d'Alsace. Colmar. 25cm.
            New ser., v.1 (1870) p. [324]-327)



                1. Witchcraft--Alsace.  I. Title.
```

```
Witchcraft
BF          Fischer, Daniel, 1695-1745.
1565          Tentamen pnevmatologico physicvm De
D62         mancipiis diaboli sive sagis.  Avthore
no.14       Daniele Fischero kesmarkiensi-hvngaro.
            Med. cvlt. Vitembergae, Ex officina
            Krevsigiana, 1716.
                24 p. 20cm.
                No. 14 in vol. lettered Dissertationes
            de sagis. 1636-1714.
                1. Witchcraft.  I. Title: De manci-
            piis diaboli sive sagis.  II. Title: De
8           sagis.  III.     Title: Tentamen pnevma-
            tologico phy         sicvm De mancipiis
            diaboli sive         sagis.
```

```
Witchcraft
BF          Fischer, E
1566          Die Licht- und Schattenseiten der
F52         Inquisition; nebst einer Geschichte der
            Hexenprocesse und historischen Rück-
            blicken auf die Geisselgesellschaften.
            Aus geschichtlichen Quellen geschöpft
            und parteilos. Wien, A. A. Benedikt
            [1881]
                310 p. 4 plates. 17cm.

                1. Inquisition.  2. Trials (Witchcraft)
            I. Title.
```

```
            Fischer, Friedrich, 1801-1853.
Witchcraft
BF          Hagenbach, Karl Rudolf, 1801-1874.
1584          Die Basler Hexenprozesse in dem 16ten und
S97         17ten Jahrhundert.  Einladungsschrift zu der
H14+        Rede des zeit. Rector magn., K. R. Hagenbach,
            welche Donnerstags, den 24. September 1840,
            Morgens 10 Uhr in der Aula gehalten werden
            wird, von Fr. Fischer. Basel, Schweighau-
            ser'sche Universitätsbuchdruckerei [1840?]
                23 p. 26cm.

                1. Trials (Wit    chcraft)--Basel.  I.
            Title.  II. Fis   cher, Friedrich, 1801-
            1853.
```

```
Witchcraft
BF          [Fischer, Heinrich Ludwig] d. 1820?
1775          Das Buch vom Aberglauben.  Leipzig,
F52         Im Schwickertschen Verlage, 1790.
                3 p. l., 359, [3] p. illus. 18cm.

                Ex libris T. G. Mättig.


                1. Superstition.  2. Folk-lore--Ger-
            many.  3. Magic.  I. Title.
```

```
            Fischer, Johann Valerian, respondent.
RARE        Martini, Werner Theodor, praeses.
HV            Disputatio juridica De quaestionibus et
8593        torturis, quam ... sub praesidio ... Werneri
D61         Theodori Martini .. publico examini subjic
no.16       autor Johannes Valerianus Fischer...
            [Wittebergae] Typis Matthaei Henckelii, 16
                [28] p. 21cm.
                Diss.--Wittenberg (J. V. Fischer, respo
            dent)
                No. 16 in a vol. lettered: Dissertation
            de trotura,         1667-1787.
8               1.Torture.    I. Fischer, Johann Va
NIC         rian, respon      dent. II. Title.
```

```
Witchcraft
BF          Fischer, Wilhelm.
1505          Aberglaube aller Zeiter. Stuttgart,
F52         Strecker & Schröder [1906-07]
                5 v. in 1. illus. 19cm.

                Contents.--[1] Die Geschichte des Teu-
            fels.--[2] Die Geschichte der Buhlteufel un
            Dämonen.--[3] Dämonische Mittelwesen, Vampi
            und Werwolf in Geschichte und Sage.--[4] Di
            Geschichte der Teufelsbündnisse, der Besess
            heit, des Hexe      nsabbats und der
                          (Continued on next ca
```

```
Witchcraft
BF          Fischer, Wilhelm.  Aberglaube aller Zeiten.
1505          [1906-07]                 (Card 2)
F52
                Contents--Continued.
            Satansanbetung.--[5] Der verbrecherische
            Aberglaube und die Satansmessen im 17.
            Jahrhundert.

                1. Superstition.  2. Demonology.
            I. Title.
```

CATALOGUE OF THE CORNELL WITCHCRAFT COLLECTION

Fiske, John, 1842-1901.
    Witchcraft in Salem village, by John Fiske ... Boston and New York, Houghton Mifflin company, 1923.
    2 p. l., 60 p. illus. (incl. ports., facsims.) 19½ᶜᵐ.
    "This account ... is reprinted from the author's 'New France and New England'."

1. Witchcraft—Salem, Mass.   I. Title.

Library of Congress   BF1576.F5   23-13030
    [3]

Flade, Dietrich

Flade, Dietrich, 1534-1589, defendant.
WITCHCRAFT
    [Minutes of the trial for witchcraft of Dr. Dietrich Flade of Trier, 1589. Trier, 1589]
    127 l. 34cm.
    Manuscript, on paper, in a 16th century German hand.
    Title page supplied by G. L. Burr.
    The first leaf is detached and badly mutilated. A transcription of it in a 19th century German hand has been added.
    (Continued on next card)

Flade, Dietrich, 1534-1589, defendant.
WITCHCRAFT
    [Minutes of the trial for witchcraft ... 1589]   (Card 2)
    L. 2 is missing and supplied in transcript by G. L. Burr from the fragment at Trier. L. 105-106 are blank, and represent a lacuna.
    Bound in brown boards with leather spine.
    On spine: Hexenprozesse 1589.
    1. Trials (Witchcraft)—Trier. 2. Witchcraft—Trier.

Flade, Dietrich, 1534-1589.
Witchcraft
    Burr, George Lincoln, 1857-1938.
    The fate of Dietrich Flade. New York, London, G. P. Putnam's Sons, 1891.
    57 p. 24cm.
    "Reprinted from the Papers of the American Historical Association, vol. V, no. 3, July, 1891."

Flade, Dietrich, 1534-1589.
WITCHCRAFT
    Neller, Georg Christoph, praeses.
    ...Conatus exegeticus in cap. Eam te 7 De rescriptis, quem una cum parergis, ex omni jure, nec non ex re monetaria, tum biblico-canonica, tum Trevirensi delibatis ...praeside...Georgio Christoph. Neller... publicae disputationi pro admissione ad tentamen graduandorum supposuit...Carolus Josephus Embden. Augustae Trevirorum, Typis Eschermannianis [1779]
    48 p. front., plate. 22cm.
    Burr's note inside front cover:
    (Continued on next card)

Flade, Dietrich, 1534-1589.
WITCHCRAFT
BX
1935
N42
    Neller, Georg Christoph, praeses. Conatus exegeticus in cap. Eam te 7 De rescriptis ...[1779]   (Card 2)
    "This book is valuable in containing a... letter of the Elector, Johann VII of Treves asking the advice of the University theological faculty at Treves as to the trial of Dr. Dietrich Flade for witchcraft. (See pp. 32-35) It is to be noted that this student, writing under the eye of the eminent jurist Neller in 1779, still believes in witchcraft..."
    (Continued on next card)

Flade, Dietrich, 1534-1589.
Witchcraft
BF
1583
Z56
    Zenz, Emil
    Dr. Dietrich Flade, ein Opfer des Hexenwahnes. Trier, J. Lintz, 1962.
    41-69 p. 24cm.
    Caption title.
    "Kurtrierisches Jahrbuch. Jahrgang 2, 1962. Sonderabdruck."

BR
141
S93
v.9
pt.1
    Flade, Paul, 1860-1921.
    Das römische inquisitionsverfahren in Deutschland bis zu den hexenprozessen, dargestellt von lic. theol. Paul Flade ... Leipzig, Dietrich, 1902.
    4 p. l., [v]-x, 122 p. 22cm. (Added t.-p.: Studien zur geschichte der theologie und der kirche. 9. bd., hft. 1)
    1. Inquisition.   I. Title.

Flagellum daemonum.
WITCHCRAFT
BX
2340
M54
1589
    Menghi, Girolamo, d. 1610.
    Flagellvm daemonvm. Exorcismos terribiles, potentissimos, et efficaces ... complectens ... Accessit postremò pars secunda, quae Fustis daemonum inscribitur. Quibus novi exorcismi, & alia nonnulla, quae prius desiderabantur, superaddita fuerunt. Auctore R. P. F. Hieronymo Mengo Vitellianensis ... Bononiae, Apud Ioannem Rossium, 1589.
    8 p. l., 247, [16], 350, 102, [2] p. 15cm.
    Title in red and black.
    (Continued on next card)

Flagellum daemonum.
WITCHCRAFT
BX
2340
M54
1589
    Menghi, Girolamo, d. 1610.   Flagellvm daemonvm ... 1589.   (Card 2)
    "Fvstis daemonvm" has special t. p. and separate paging.
    "Remedia efficacissima in malignos spiritvs expellendos," with caption title, is appended to "Fvstis daemonvm" and has separate paging.
    1. Exorcism. 2. Demonology. I. His Fustis daemonum. II. His Remedia efficacissima in malignos spiritus expellendos. III. Title: Flagellum daemonum. IV. Title: Remedia efficacissima.

Flagellum daemonum.
WITCHCRAFT
BX
2340
M54
1727
    Menghi, Girolamo, d. 1610.
    Flagellum daemonum. Exorcismos terribiles, potentissimos, & efficaces ... complectens ... Accessit postremo pars secunda, quae Fustis daemonum inscribitur. Quibus novi exorcismi, & alia nonnulla, quae prius desiderabantur, super addita fuerunt. Auctore R. P. F. Hieronymo Mengo, Vitellianensi ... [Mediolani] 1727.
    7 p. l., 309, [3], [16], 308, [1] p. 18cm.
    "Fustis daemonum" has special t. p. and separate paging.
    (Continued on next card)

Flagellum diaboli; oder, Dess Teufels Gaissl.
WITCHCRAFT
BF
1525
O85
1602
    Osuna, Francesco de, d. ca. 1540.
    Flagellum diaboli; oder, Dess Teufels Gaissl. Darinn ...gehandlet wirt: Von der Macht und Gewalt dess bösen Feindts. Von den Effecten und Wirckungen der Zauberer, Unholdter uñ Hexenmaister... Durch...Franciscum de Ossuna in spanischer Sprach aussgangen, und durch Egidium Albertinum...verteuscht. München, Getruckt bey Adam Berg, 1602.
    78 (i.e. 76) l. 19cm.
    1. Devil. 2. Demonology. 3. Witchcraft. I. Albertinus, Aegidius, 1560-1620, tr. II. Title.

Flagellum haereticorum fascinariorum.
WITCHCRAFT
BF
1565
J19
    Jacquier, Nicolas
    Flagellvm haereticorvm fascinariorvm, avtore Nicolao Iaqverio. His accesservnt Lamberti Danaei de veneficis dialogi, Ioachimi Camerarii in Plutarchi de oraculorum defectu epistola, Martini de Arles de superstitionibus tractatvs, Ioannis Trithemii de reprobis atq; maleficis qvaestiones III, Thomae Erasti de strigibus liber. Studio Ioan. Myntzenbergii edita. Francofvrti ad Moenvm [Impressvm apud N. Bassaeum] 1581.
    604 p. 17 cm.
    (Continued on next card)

CATALOGUE OF THE CORNELL WITCHCRAFT COLLECTION

        Flagellum maleficorum.

WITCHCRAFT
BF 1569 A2 M26 1621

Mamoris, Petrus.
   Flagellum maleficorum, authore M. Petro Mamoris. Cum indicibus. [Lugduni] 1621.
   82 p. 18cm.

   First published in Lyons about 1490. Later included in v.3 of 1669 ed. of Institoris' Malleus maleficarum.
   "Tractatus de superstitiosis quibusdam casibus, compilatus...per...Henricum de Gorchen.": p. 71-82.
   1. Witchcraft. 2. Demonology. 3. Superstition. I. Heinrich von Gorkum, 1386 (ca.)-1431. II. Title.

8
NIC

      Flammarion, Camille, 1842-1925.

Witchcraft
BF 1412 F11

Fabart, Félix.
   Histoire philosophique et politique de l'occulte: magie, sorcellerie, spiritisme; avec une préface de Camille Flammarion. Paris, C. Marpon et E. Flammarion [1885?]
   xx, 346 p. 19cm.

   1. Occult sciences--Hist.

      Le fleau des demons et sorciers.

WITCHCRAFT
BF 1520 B66 1616

Bodin, Jean, 1530-1596.
   Le fleav des demons et sorciers, par I. B. angevin. Reueu & corrigé de plusieurs fautes qui s'estoyent glissees és precedentes impressions ... Derniere ed. Nyort, Par Dauid du Terroir, 1616.
   2 p. l., 38, 556, [21] p. 17cm.
   Title in ornamental woodcut border.
   First published under title: De la daemonomanie.
   "Refvtation des opinions de Iean VVier": p. 476-556. (Continued on next card)

8

      Fleischbein, Hans, d. 1632.

Witchcraft
BF 1583 Z7 1629

Englert, Anton, 1855-
   Ein kleiner Beitrag zur Geschichte der Hexenprozesse.
   (In Hessische Blätter für Volkskunde. Leipzig. 24cm. Bd. 5 (1906), p. [65]-71)

   1. Witchcraft--Dieburg, Germany. 2. Fleischbein, Hans, d. 1632. I. Title.

8

Witchcraft
BF 1600 F62

Floercke, Johann Ernst von, 1695-1762.
   Io. Ernesti Floerckii I. V. D. Commentatio de crimine conivrationis spiritvvm eivs processv et poenis praemissis nonnvllis ad magiam svpernatvralem divinam daemoniacam et hvmanam nec non thevrgiam cabbalam et theologiam mysticam pertinentibvs ... Ienae, Apvd Io. Felic. Bielckivm, 1721.
   8 p. l., 522, [33] p. 21cm.
   Title in red and black.
   1. Magic. 2. Witchcraft. 3. Trials (Witchcraft) I. Title: De crimine conjurationis spirituum. (Over)

8

      Floerckius, Johannes Ernestus, 1695-1762.

      see

      Floercke, Johann Ernst von, 1695-1762.

      Floerke, Johann Ernst, 1695-1762.

      see

      Floercke, Johann Ernst von, 1695-1762.

      Flower, Margaret, d. 1618.

Witchcraft
BF 1563 T75

   The Wonderfvl discoverie of the witchcrafts of Margaret and Phillip[pa] Flower, daughters of Joan Flower neere Beuer Castle ... Together with the seuerall examinations and confessions of Anne Baker, Ioan Willimot, and Ellen Greene, witches in Leicestershire. London, Printed by G. Eld for I Barnes, 1619. [Greenwich, Reprinted by H. S. Richardson, ca. 1840]
   26 p. title vignettes. 23cm.

8
      (Continued on next card)

      Flower, Margaret, d. 1618.

Witchcraft
BF 1563 T75

   The Wonderfvl discoverie of the witchcrafts of Margaret and Phillip[pa] Flower ... [1840] (Card 2)

   The examinations of Anne Baker, Ioanne Willimot, and Ellen Greene has special t. p. No. 4 in vol. lettered Tracts on witchcraft.

8

      Flower, Philippa, d. 1618.

Witchcraft
BF 1563 T75

   The Wonderfvl discoverie of the witchcrafts of Margaret and Phillip[pa] Flower, daughters of Joan Flower neere Beuer Castle ... Together with the seuerall examinations and confessions of Anne Baker, Ioan Willimot, and Ellen Greene, witches in Leicestershire. London, Printed by G. Eld for I Barnes, 1619. [Greenwich, Reprinted by H. S. Richardson, ca. 1840]
   26 p. title vignettes. 23cm.

8
      (Continued on next card)

      Flower, Philippa, d. 1618.

Witchcraft
BF 1563 T75

   The Wonderfvl discoverie of the witchcrafts of Margaret and Phillip[pa] Flower ... [1840] (Card 2)

   The examinations of Anne Baker, Ioanne Willimot, and Ellen Greene has special t. p. No. 4 in vol. lettered Tracts on witchcraft.

8

Witchcraft
BF 1547 F65 1741

Förtsch, Michael, 1654-1724.
   Commentatio de pactis hominvm cvm diabolo circa abditos in terra thesavros effodiendos et acqvirendos, ad casvm illvm tragicvm, qvi anno MDCCXV. in vigiliis festi Nativitatis Christi in agro Ienensi institvta. Von denen Bündnissen der Menschen mit dem Teufel bey dem Schatz-Graben. Editio novissima. Lipsiae, Apvd Christian. Schroetervm, 1741.
   61, [2] p. 22cm.

   A new edition of a dissertation at Jena,
      (Continued on next card)

Witchcraft
BF 1547 F65 1741

Förtsch, Michael, 1654-1724. Commentatio de pactis hominvm cvm diabolo ... 1741. (Card 2)

   with Michael Förtsch as praeses and Johannes Andreas Rinneberg as respondent, published Jena, 1716.
   1. Devil. 2. Treasure-trove. I. Rinneberg, Johannes Andreas, respondent. II. Title: De pactis hominum cum diabolo circa abditos in terra thesauros effodiendos. III. Title: Bündnisse der Menschen mit dem Teufel bey dem Schatz-Graben. IV. Title.

Witchcraft
BF 1547 F65

Förtsch, Michael, 1654-1724, praeses.
   Exercitatio theologica De pactis hominvm cvm diabolo circa additos in terra thesavros effodiendos et acqvirendos, ad casvm illvm tragicvm, qvi anno priori exevnte in vigiliis festi Nativitatis Christi in agro Ienensi contigit, institvta, qvam ... moderatore ... Michaele Foertschio ... ad d. IV. Ivlii MDCCXVI, ... ervditorvm examini svbiicit avctor et respondens Ioannes Andreas Rinneberg ... Ienae, Apvd Werthervm [1716]
   [4], 76 p. 21cm.

      (Continued on next card)

Witchcraft
BF 1547 F65

Förtsch, Michael, 1654-1724, praeses. Exercitatio theologica De pactis hominvm cvm diabolo ... [1716] (Card 2)

   Diss.--Jena (J. A. Rinneberg, respondent)

   1. Devil. 2. Treasure-trove. I. Rinneberg, Johannes Andreas, respondent. II. Title: De pactis hominum cum diabolo circa additos in terra thesauros effodiendos.

Witchcraft
BF 1582 F66

[Foix, Vincent M.]
   Sorcières et loups-garous dans les Landes. Auch, Imprimerie centrale, 1904.
   72 p. 25cm.

   Caption title: Folklore. Glossaire de la sorcellerie landaise.

   1. Witchcraft--France--Dictionaries. 2. Werwolves--Dictionaries. I. Title. II. Title: Glossaire de la sorcellerie landaise.

8

      Folk-doctor's island.

GR 153 M3 T25 1964

Teare, T Denys G
   Folk-doctor's island, by T. D. G. Teare. [2d ed.] Douglass, Isle of Man, Times Press [1964]
   222 p. illus. 19cm.

   1. Folk-lore, Manx. 2. Witchcraft--Man, Isle of. I. Title.

      Folk-lore--Bibliography--Catalogs.

Witchcraft
Z 6880 Z9R81 1903

Rosenthal, J., firm, booksellers, Munich.
   Bibliotheca magica et pneumatica. Geheime Wissenschaften. Sciences occultes. Occult sciences. Folk-lore. München [1903]
   48, 680 p. 24cm. (Its Kataloge 31-35)

   Issued in parts.

CATALOGUE OF THE CORNELL WITCHCRAFT COLLECTION

craft
    The folk-lore of Hertfordshire.
  Gerish, William Blyth.
    The folk-lore of Hertfordshire; a brief list of material collected and classified by W. B. Gerish ... Bishop's Stortford, 1911.
    16 p. 22ᶜᵐ. (Hertfordshire folk lore. no. 11)

1. Folk-lore—England—Hertfordshire. I. Title.
                      17-20382
Library of Congress   GR142.H6A3 no. 11

    Fontaine, Françoise, fl. 1591.
ITCHCRAFT
55
6
83
    Procès verbal fait povr délivrer vne fille possédée par le malin esprit à Lovviers. Publié d'après le manuscrit original et inédit de la Bibliothèque Nationale par Armand Benet ... précédé d'une introduction par B. de Moray. Paris, Aux bureaux du Progrès médical, 1883.
    cxiv, 98 p. 22cm. (Bibliothèque diabolique)
    1. Fontaine, Françoise, fl. 1591. 2. Demoniac possession. I. Moray, B. de. II. Bénet, Armand Eugène, 1858-

---

chcraft
    Fontaine, Jacques, d. 1621.
2
    Des marqves des sorciers et de la reelle possession que le diable prend sur le corps des hommes. Sur le subiect du proces de l'abominable & detestable sorcier Lovys Gaufridy ... Lyon, Par Claude Larjot, 1611
1a
    [Arras, 1865]
    45, [1] p. 21cm.

1. Trials (Witchcraft)--France. 2. Gaufridi, Louis, 1572-1611. 3. Witchcraft. I. Title.

TCHCRAFT
    Fontenelle, Bernard Le Bovier de, 1657-1757.
61
8
07
    Histoire des oracles. Nouvelle édition augmentée. Londres, Aux depens de Paul & Isaak Vaillant, 1707.
    119, [1] p. front. 17cm.
    Title in red and black.
    Rifacimento of A. van Dale's De oraculis ethnicorum dissertationes duae, Amstelaedami, 1683.
    I. Dale, Antonius van, 1638-1708. De oraculis ethnicorum. II. Title.

    Fontenelle, Bernard Le Bovier de, 1657-1757.
    ... Histoire des oracles. Édition critique publiée par Louis Maigron. Paris, E. Cornély et cⁱᵉ, 1908.
    2 p. l., a-k, x, 217, [2] p. 19cm.
    At head of title: Société des textes français modernes. Fontenelle.
    Rifacimento of Antonius van Dale's De oraculis ethnicorum dissertationes duae ... Amstelaedami, 1683. Reprint of the first edition, pub. anonymously, Paris, 1686.

CHCRAFT
    Fontenelle, Bernard Le Bovier de, 1657-1757.
51
    Histoire des oracles. English.
    Fontenelle, Bernard Le Bovier de, 1657-1757.
3
    The history of oracles, in two dissertations. Wherein are proved, I. That the oracles were not given out by daemons ... II. That the oracles did not cease at the coming of Jesus Christ ... Translated from the best edition of the original French. Glasgow, Printed by R. Urie, 1753.
    x, 144, [2] p. 17cm.
    Translation of Histoire des oracles, a rifacimento of A. van Dale's De oraculis ethnicorum dissertationes duae, Amstelaedami, 1683.

Witchcraft   Fontenelle, Bernard Le Bovier de, 1657-1757. Histoire des oracles.
BF
1761
F682
    Baltus, Jean François, 1667-1743.
    Réponse à l'histoire des oracles, de Mr. de Fontenelle. Dans laquelle on réfute le système de Mr. Van-Dale, sur les auteurs des oracles du paganisme, sur la cause & le temps de leur silence; & où l'on établit le sentiment des Pères de l'Eglise sur le même sujet. Strasbourg, J. R. Doulssecker, 1707.
    [42], 374, [13] p. front. 18cm.

1. Fontenelle, Bernard Le Bovier de, 1657-1757. Histoire des oracles. 2. Oracles. 3. Dale, Antonius van, 1638-1708. De oraculis ethnicorum.

WITCHCRAFT
BF
1761
F68
1753
    Fontenelle, Bernard Le Bovier de, 1657-1757.
    The history of oracles, in two dissertations. Wherein are proved, I. That the oracles were not given out by daemons ... II. That the oracles did not cease at the coming of Jesus Christ ... Translated from the best edition of the original French. Glasgow, Printed by R. Urie, 1753.
    x, 144, [2] p. 17cm.
    Translation of Histoire des oracles, a rifacimento of A. van Dale's De oraculis ethnicorum dissertationes duae, Amstelaedami, 1683.
    I. His Histoire des oracles. English. II. Dale, Antonius van, 1638-1708. De oraculis ethnicorum. III. Title.

PS
3511
O64M6
    Forbes, Esther.
    A mirror for witches in which is reflected the life, machinations, and death of famous Doll Bilby, who, with a more than feminine perversity, preferred a demon to a mortal lover. Here is also told how and why a righteous and most awfull judgement befell her, destroying both corporeal body and immortal soul. By Esther Forbes, with woodcuts by Robert Gibbings. Boston and New York, Houghton Mifflin company, 1928.
    4 p. l., 3-213, [1] p. front., illus., plates. 23½cm.

1. Witchcraft—Salem, Mass. I. Title.   28—12074
Library of Congress   PZ3.F7418Mi
——— Copy 2.
Copyright A 1074255   [28e3]

Witchcraft
K
F688
    Forcadel, Étienne, 1534-1579.
    Necyomantia ivrisperiti. Mira magiae descriptio, per quam euocati iurisconsulti, innumeros iuris ciuilis locos disertissimè declarant. Stephano Forcatvlo blyterensi ivriscos. avtore. Lvgdvni, Apvd Seb. Gryphivm, 1544.
    142 p. 19cm.

1. Roman law--Interpretation and criticism. 2. Magic. I. Title.

8

    Forcatulus, Stephanus, 1534-1579.

    see

Forcadel, Étienne, 1534-1579.

    Fordomdags; kulturhistoriska utkast och berättelser.
Witchcraft
BF
1584
S9
B62
    Björlin, Gustaf, 1845-
    Fordomdags; kulturhistoriska utkast och berättelser. Stockholm, H. Geber [1885]
    196 p. 20cm.

    "Trolldomsväsendet i Stockholm 1676": p. 67-130.

1. Witchcraft--Stockholm. I. Title.

Witchcraft   Foresti, Jacopo Filippo, da Bergamo, 1434-1520.
BF
1565
S42
1638
    Scot, Reginald, 1538?-1599.
    Ontdecking van tovery, beschreven int Engels door Reinald Scot, verduyscht by Th. en G. Basson. Beverwyck, Gedruckt by Frans Pels, 1638.
    15 p. l., 351, [17] p. 15cm.
    With engraved t. p., depicting a witch.
    Abridgment and translation of Discoverie of witchcraft.
    To this are appended: Historie van 't ghene gheschiet is in 't Graefschap van
    (Continued on next card)

    Foresti, Jacopo Filippo, da Bergamo, 1434-1520.
Witchcraft
BF
1565
S42
1638
    Scot, Reginald, 1538?-1599. Ontdecking van tovery ... 1638. (Card 2)
    Artoys ..., door J. DuClercq, with special t. p.; Extract uyt 't playdoye van M. L. Servin; Historie van de Maegt van Orleans ... Extract uyt J. P. van Bergamo; and various poems.

1. Witchcraft. 2. Magic. 3. Demonology. I. His Discoverie of witchcraft. Dutch. II. DuClercq, Jacques, seigneur
8   (Continued on next card)

Witchcraft   Formicarius.
PA
8555
N59F7
1692
    Nider, Johannes, d. 1438.
    De visionibus ac revelationibus opus rarissimum Historiis Germaniae refertissimum, Anno 1517. Argentinae editum. Auspiciis... Rudolphi Augusti, Brunsvicens. ac Luneburg. Ducis, luci & integritati restitutum, recensente Hermanno von der Hardt ... Helmestadii, Impensis Pauli Zeisingii, Typis Salomonis Schnorrii, 1692.
    [30], 669 p. front. 17cm.

    A reprint, under a new title, of Nider's
    (Continued on next card)

Witchcraft   Formicarius.
PA
8555
N59F7
1692
    Nider, Johannes, d. 1438. De visionibus ... 1692. (Card 2)
    Formicarius.
    "Liber quintus: De maleficis & eorum deceptionibus": p. 514-669.
    Ex libris Kurt Seligmann.

1. Conduct of life. 2. Christian life. 3. Witchcraft. 4. Demonology. I. Hardt, Hermann von der, 1660-1746, ed. II. Nider, Johannes, d. 1438. Formicarius. III. Title. IV. Title: Formicarius.

    Forna tiders mörker och vidskepelse.
WITCHCRAFT
BF
1584
S9
L66
    Levin, Herman, 1862-
    Forna tiders mörker och vidskepelse.
    (In: Läsning för svenska folket. Stockholm. 20cm. 1909. p. 43-67, 92-115, 210-226)

1. Witchcraft--Sweden. 2. Witchcraft--Scandinavia. 3. Trials (Witchcraft)--Sweden. 4. Bure, Johan, 1568-1652. 5. Magnus, Olaus, abp. of Uppsala, 1490-1558. I.
8
NIC   folket. II. Läsning för svenska Title.

    Fornari, ed.
Witchcraft
BF
1412
G51
1849
    Giraldo, Mathias de, pseud.
    Histoire curieuse et pittoresque des sorciers, devins, magiciens, astrologues, voyants, revenants, ames en peine, vampires, spectres, fantomes, apparitions, visions, gnomes, lutins, esprits malins, sorts jetés, exorcismes, etc. ... depuis l'antiquité jusqu'à nos jours, par le révérend père dominicain Mathias de Giraldo, ancien exorciste de l'Inquisition, rev. et augm. par M. Fornari, professeur de philosophie hermétique à Milan. Paris, Chez tous les libraires marchandˢ de nouveautés [1849]
    315 p. 4 fold. plates. 24cm.
    Half-title: Histoire des sorciers.

CATALOGUE OF THE CORNELL WITCHCRAFT COLLECTION

Witchcraft
BF   Forner, Friedrich, Bp. of Hebron, d. 1630.
1520   Panoplia armatvrae Dei, adversus omnem
F72   svperstitionvm, divinationvm, excantationvm,
1626   daemonolatriam, et vniversas magorvm, vene-
         ficorum, & sagarum, & ipsiusmet Sathanae
         insidias, praestigias & infestationes.
         Concionibvs ... instructa ... atq; inscripta
         a Friderico Fornero ...   Ingolstadii, Typis
         Gregorii Haenlini, 1626.
            20 p. l., 292 p. 20cm.
8   1. Demonol   ogy. 2. Witchcraft. I.
         Title: Panopl   ia armaturae Dei.

Witchcraft
BT   Forner, Friedrich, Bp. of Hebron, d. 1630.
608   Panoplia armatvrae Dei, adversvs omnem
F72   svperstitionvm, divinationvm, excantationvm,
         daemonolatriam, et vniversas magorvm, vene-
         ficorum, & sagarum, & ipsiusmet Sathanae in-
         sidias, praestigias & infestationes. ...
         Ingolstadii, Typis Gregorii Haenlini, 1626.
            20 p. l., 292 p. 21cm.
            Bound with his Sermones tricesimales de
         felicissimo ... Virginis Mariae. Ingolsta-
         dii, 1627.
8

                Forner, Friedrich, Bp. of Hebron, d. 1630.
Witchcraft
BF   New, unerhörte, erschröckliche, warhafftige
1584   Wundergeschicht, so sich in der Statt
N4   Edam in Holland den 24. Tag Hornung diss
Z7   lauffenden 1602. Jahrs zugetragen ...
1602a   Erstlich in flandrischer Sprache getruckt
         zu Brüssel ... Mit sampt einem Bader-
         bornensischem Sendschreiben. Item: Dess
         ehrwürdigen hochgelehrten Herr Friderich
         Forner ... Sendtschreiben von erschröck-
         lichem Vntergang sechs ketzerischen Per-
         sonen ... in   Francken bey Bamberg ...
8   (Continued on next card)

            Forner, Friedrich, Bp. of Hebron, d. 1630.
Witchcraft
BF   New, unerhörte, erschröckliche, warhafftige
1584   Wundergeschicht ... 1602.   (Card 2)
N4
Z7   jm Jahr 1601. Auss dem Latein ins Teutsch
1602a   gebracht. Ingolstadt, Getruckt in der
         Ederischen Truckerey durch Andream Anger-
         mayer, 1602.
            17 p. 21cm.
            1. Witchcraft--Netherlands. 2. Witch-
         craft--Germany. I. Forner, Friedrich, Bp.
8   of Hebron, d.   1630.

WITCHCRAFT
BF   En forskreckelig oc sand bescriffuelse om
1583   mange troldfolck; som ere forbrende for
H82   deris misgierninger skyld, fra det aar
1921   1589... København ₍Bianco Lunos
         bogtrykkeri₎ 1921.
            ₍25₎ p. illus. 21cm. (Bianco Lunos
         bibliofiludgaver)
            Added t.-p.: Gammel dansk folkelitteratur.
            Flyveskrift første gang trykt i Köln paa
         Caspar Schumans af Eefurts bekostning og
         derefter i Kø   benhavn af Laurentz
8
NIC   (Continued on next card)

WITCHCRAFT
BF   En forskrechelig oc sand bescriffuelse om
1583   mange troldfolck... 1921.   (Card 2)
H82
1921   Benedicht, 1591.
            According to G. L. Burr, a translation
         of "Hort an new schrecklich abenthewr ...
         ₍Köln, 1589?₎.
            "Efter et gammelt flyveblad, der nu op-
         bevares paa det Kongelige bibliotek i
         København ... paany ... udgivet ... efter
         ... modernise   rede udkast."
8
NIC   (Continued on next card)

WITCHCRAFT
BR   En forskreckelig oc sand bescriffeulse om
1583   mange troldfolck... 1921.   (Card 3)
H82
1921   "Stumme Peders graffschrift ... 1589":
         p. ₍14₎.
            "Oplysninger," af Emil Selmar p. ₍15₎-
         ₍23₎ has special t. p.
            "Bogen er trykt i 500 ... ekspl. ... nr.
         58."
8   1. Witchcraft--Germany. 2. Witchcraft--
NIC   Denmark. 3.   Printing--History--
         Europe. II. Luno, Bianco, ed.
         ₍schrecklich   ₎ Emil. III. Hort an new
                          abentewr.

Witchcraft
BF   ₍Forsyth, J   S   ₎
1411   Demonologia; or, Natural knowledge revealed; being an
F73   exposé of ancient and modern superstitions, credulity, fanati-
1827   cism, enthusiasm, & imposture, as connected with the doctrine,
         caballa, and jargon, of amulets, apparitions, astrology,
         charms, demonology ... witchcraft, &c. ... By J. S. F. ...
         London, J. Bumpus, 1827.
            1 p. l., ₍v₎-xvi, 438 p. front. 19cm.
            By J. S. Forsyth. cf. Halkett and Laing, Dict. anon. and pseud.,
         new ed., 1926, v. 2 p. 87.
            1. Superstition. 2. Demonology. 3. Witchcraft. I. F., J. S.
         II. J. S. F. III. Title.
                                                     11-9203 rev.
         Library of Congress   BF1411.F6 1827
                                          ₃₎   133

Witchcraft
BF   ₍Forsyth, J   S   ₎
1411   Demonologia; or, Natural knowledge revealed;
F73   being an exposé of ancient and modern supersti-
1831   tions, credulity, fanaticism, enthusiasm, &
         imposture, as connected with the doctrine,
         caballa, and jargon, of amulets, apparitions,
         astrology, charms, demonology ... witchcraft, &c.
         ... By J.S.F. London, printed for A.K. Newman
         and co., 1831.
            xvi, 438 p. 20cm.

                Fortalitium fidei.
Rare
BT   Alphonsus de Spina, Bp. of Orense, d. 1469.
1100   Fortalitium fidei. ₍Lyons, Guillaume
A45+   Balsarin₎ 22 May, 1487.
1487   ₍250₎ l. 1 illus. 28cm.

            Leaf ₍1₎ and ₍250₎ blank. Leaf ₍250₎
         wanting in this copy.
            Leaf ₍2a₎: ₍T₎Abula fortalicii fidei In-
         cipit.
            Leaf ₍249b₎ (Colophon): Anno incarnatōis
         dñice. M.ccccLxxxvij. die. xxij. mensis maij.
         Below colophon device of G. Balsarin.
                         (Continued on next card)

                Fortalitium fidei.
Rare
BT   Alphonsus de Spina, Bp. of Orense, d. 1469.
1100   Fortalitium fidei ... 1487.   (Card 2)
A45+
1487   Signatures: a8, a-r8, s-v6, A-L8.
            Capital spaces, some with guide-letters.
         The woodcut on leaf ₍10a₎ represents the
         "Fortalitium fidei," with its various ene-
         mies (heretics, Jews, Saracens, demons).
            Hain. Repertorium (with Copinger's Sup-
         plement) *874; Pellechet, 564; Proctor,
         8575; Brit. Mus. Cat. (XV cent.) VIII, p.
         277 (IB. 41763)₅G   samtkat.d. Wiegendr.,
                         (Continued on next card)

                Fortalitium fidei.
Rare
BT   Alphonsus de Spina, Bp. of Orense, d. 1469.
1100   Fortalitium fidei ... 1487.   (Card 3)
A45+
1487   1577; Goff. Third census, A-542.
            Contents.--De armatura omnium fidelium.--
         De bello hereticorum.--De bello Iudeorum.--
         De bello Saracenorum.--De bello demonum.

            1. Apologetics--Middle Ages. 2. Heresy.
         3. Judaism--Controversial works. 4. Saracens
         5. Demonology. I. Title.

         Foster, Ann, d. 1674.
Witchcraft
BF   A Full and true relation of the tryal, con-
1581   demnation, and execution of Ann Foster,
A2   (who was arrained for a witch) on Sat-
W81   urday the 22th ₍sic₎ of this instant
1866a   August, at the place of execution
no.9   at Northampton. ... London, Printed
         for D. M., 1674. ₍Northampton, Re-
         printed by Taylor, 1873₎
            8 p. 22cm.
            No. 9 in box lettered Witchcraft in
         Northamptonshire.
8   1. Foster,   Ann, d. 1674. 2.
         Witchcraft--   Northamptonshire, Eng-
         land.

Witchcraft
BF   Foucault, Maurice.
1582   Les procès de sorcellerie dans l'ancien-
F76   ne France devant les jurisdictions sécu-
         lières. Paris, Bonvalot-Jouve, 1907.
            362 p. 25cm.

            1. Trials (Witchcraft)--France. I.
         Title.

         Four centuries of witch-beliefs.
WITCHCRAFT
BF   Davies, Reginald Trevor.
1581   Four centuries of witch-beliefs, with special reference
D25   to the Great Rebellion, by R. Trevor Davies. New York,
1972   B. Blom, 1972.
            xii, 222 p. 24 cm. $12.50
            Reprint of the 1947 ed.
            Bibliography: p. 204-212.

            1. Witchcraft—England.   Title.

         4   BF1581.D3 1972   133.4'0942   74-180026
         Library of Congress   72 ₍4₎   MARC

         Fourth book of occult philosophy, and
WITCHCRAFT geomancy.
BF   Henry Cornelius Agrippa's Fourth book of
1410   occult philosophy, and geomancy. Magi-
L69   cal elements of Peter de Abano. Astro-
1655   nomical geomancy ₍by Gerardus Cremonen-
         sis₎. The nature of spirits ₍by Georg
         Pictorius₎: and Arbatel of magick.
         Translated into English by Robert Turner
         Philomathées.   London, 1655.
            9 p. l., ₍5₎-266 ₍i.e., 286₎, ₍4₎ p.
         illus. 19cm.
8   Neither Agrippa nor Abano wrote the wor
                         (Continued on next card)

            Fourth book of occult philosophy, and
WITCHCRAFT geomancy.
BF   Henry Cornelius Agrippa's Fourth book of
1410   occult philosophy, and geomancy ...   (Card 2)
L69   1655.
1655
            here ascribed to them; the Heptameron, or
         Magical elements also was ascribed to Agri
         pa under the title: Les oeuvres magiques,
         with Abano as translator (!)
            Translation of a work variously titled
         Liber de ceremonijs magicis; and his De oc
         culta philosophia, liber quartus.
8
                         (Continued on next card)

         Fowkes, Thomas.
Witchcraft
HV   A Magazine of scandall; or, A heape of wicke
6248   nesse of two infamous ministers, consorts,
F76   one named Thomas Fowkes of Earle Soham in
         Suffolk, convicted by law for killing a ma
         and the other named Iohn Lowes of Brandest
         who hath beene arraigned for witchcraft, a
         convicted by law for a common barretor.
         Together with the manner how my lord of
         Canterbury would put and keep them in the
         ministery, notwithstanding the many peti-
         tions and cer   tificates from their
                         (Continued on next car

CATALOGUE OF THE CORNELL WITCHCRAFT COLLECTION

Fowkes, Thomas.

itchcraft A Magazine of scandall ... 1642.
48   (Card 2)
3
parishioners, and others... and against
whom .. the county of Suffolke have [sic]
petitioned to the Parliament ... because
... one of these scandalous ministers have
[sic] abused the authority of the lords in
Parliament ... London, Printed for R. H.,
1642.
[12] p. 20cm.
1. Fowkes, Thomas. 2. Lowes, John,
clerk, d. 1645.

Fowler, Samuel P[age] 1800-1888.
5   An account of the life and character of the Rev. Samuel Parris, of Salem village, and of his connection with the witchcraft delusion of 1692. By Samuel P. Fowler, esq. (In Drake, S. G. The witchcraft delusion in New England ... Roxbury, Mass., 1866. 21½ cm. v. 3. p. 198-222)
Reprinted from Proceedings of the Essex institute, v. 2, 1856-60, Salem, 1862, p. 49-68.
Subject entries: 1. Parris, Samuel, 1653-1720. 2. Witchcraft—New England. I. Title.
2-13716
Library of Congress, no.

Fowler, Samuel P[age] 1800-1888.
5   An account of the life and character of the Rev. Samuel Parris, of Salem village, and of his connection with the witchcraft delusion of 1692. By Samuel P. Fowler, esq. (In Drake, S. G. The witchcraft delusion in New England ... Roxbury, Mass., 1866. 21½ cm. v. 3. p. 198-222)
Reprinted from Proceedings of the Essex institute, v. 2, 1856-60, Salem, 1862, p. 49-68.
Subject entries: 1. Parris, Samuel, 1653-1720. 2. Witchcraft—New England. I. Title.
2-13716
Library of Congress, no.

Witchcraft
F   Fowler, Samuel Page, 1800-1888.
74   An account of the life, character, &c., of the Rev. Samuel Parris, of Salem village and of his connection with the witchcraft delusion of 1692. Read before the Essex Institute, Nov'r 14, 1856. Salem, W. Ives and G. W. Pease, printers, 1857.
S1
P26   20 p. 24cm.
Cover title.
1. Parris, Samuel, 1653-1720. 2. Witchcraft--Salem, Mass. I. Title.

itchcraft Fowler, Samuel Page, 1800-1888, ed.
         Salem witchcraft ... Boston, 1865.
[Deane, Charles] 1813-1889.
01 ... Spurious reprints of early books. Boston [Cambridge, University press] 1865.
3
65 19 p. 25cm. (Bibliographical tracts. no. 1)
Signed at end "Delta".
"From the Boston Daily advertiser of March 24, 1865. With additions and corrections. One hundred and thirty-one copies printed."
"This reprint was not made by Mr. Deane."—Sabin.
A review of "Salem witchcraft: comprising More wonders of the invisible world, collected by Robert Calef; and Wonders of the invisible world, by Cotton Mather. Together with notes and explanations by Samuel P. Fowler. Boston. W. Veazie, 1865" [reissue from the stereotyped plates of the Salem, 1861 edition]
1. Fowler, Samuel Page, 1800-1888, ed. [Salem witchcraft ... Boston, 1865. I. Title.
2-13743
Library of Congress   Z1001.D28
[3501]

Fowles, Susanna, fl. 1698.
ITCHCRAFT
F   The Second part of the Boy of Bilson: or,
555 a true and particular relation of the
44   impostor, Susanna Fowles ... who pretended her self possess'd with the Devil ... The whole being writ and attested by Robert Howson, clerk; Captain John Bonsey, and Mr. Nicholas Wade ... London, Printed by E. Whitlock, 1698.
24 p. 20cm.
1. Fowles, Susanna, fl. 1698. 2. Demoniac possession. I. Howson, Robert. II. Baddeley, Richard, fl. 1621. The boy of Bilson.

Witchcraft
BV   [Fox, George] 1624-1691.
4617   A declaration of the ground of error &
B6   errors, blasphemy, blasphemers, and blas-
F79   phemies; and the ground of inchantings and seducing spirits and the doctrine of devils, the sons of sorcerers and the seed of the adulterer, and the ground of nicromancy, which doth defile witches and wizards ... By G. F.   London, Printed for G. Calvert, 1657.
41 p. 18cm.
I. F., G.   II. G. F.   III. Title.

Witchcraft
BF   Fox, Paul.
1563
F86   Strange and fearfull newes from Plaisto, in the parish of West-Ham, neere Bow, foure miles from London, in the house of one Paul Fox, a silke-weaver where is dayly to be seene throwing of stones, bric-bats, oystershels, bread, cutting his worke in peeces, breaking his windowes, stones of fifty wayt comming up the stayers, a sword flying about the roome, books going up and down the house ...   London, Printed by I. H. [1645]
(Continued on next card)

Witchcraft
BF   Fox, Paul.
1563
T86   Strange and fearfull newes from Plaisto ... [1645]   (Card 2)
8 p. 19cm.
No. 8 in vol. lettered: Tracts of witches
1. Witchcraft.   2. Fox, Paul.

KFM   Fox, Sanford J
2478   Science and justice; the Massachusetts witchcraft trials [by] Sanford J. Fox. Baltimore, Johns Hopkins Press [1968]
.8
W5
F79   xix, 121 p. Illus. 24 cm. $6.95
Bibliographical footnotes.

1. Witchcraft—Massachusetts.   2. Medical jurisprudence—Massachusetts.   I. Title.

KFM2478.8.W5F6   340'.6'09744   68-18771
Library of Congress   [7]

Fra hexenes tid.
WITCHCRAFT
DL   Klitgaard, Carl, 1868-
271   Fra hexenes tid. I. Hexeprocesser fra
R2   Randers Amt. II. Hexene paa Mariageregnen.
R19
1915-16   (In: Randers Amts Historiske Samfund. Aarbog. Randers. 23cm. v.9 (1915) p. [97]-140; v.10 (1916) p. [86]-106)

1 Witchcraft--Randers, Denmark. 2.Witchcraft--Denmark. 3. Trials (Witchcraft)--Randers, Denmark. 4. Trials (Witchcraft)--Denmark.
8
NIC

Fra hexernes tid.
WITCHCRAFT
BF   [Holm, Viggo Valdemar] 1855-1899.
1584   Fra Hexernes Tid. Kuriøse Historier
D4   af Woldemar [pseud.]   Kjøbenhavn, P. G.
H742   Philipsen, 1887.
100, [4] p. 17cm.
Contents.--Hexerne.--Geworben.--Skielmen.--Dend brølendis Basune.--Margalitha.--Udi Linnehuuset.

1. Witchcraft--Denmark.   I. Title.
8

Witchcraft
BF   Frage, ob der Katechismus von der Geister-
1603   lehre ein katholischer Katechismus sey?
S83   [Augsburg?] 1775.
no.2   45 p. 17cm.
No. 2 in vol. lettered Francone dell' Amavero (Sterzinger) Untersuchung [etc.]
1. Sterzinger, Ferdinand, 1721-1786. Katekismus von der Geisterlehre.   2. Miracles--Early works to 1800.
8

Frage, ob der Katechismus von der Geisterlehre ein katholischer Katechismus sey?
Witchcraft
BF   [Sterzinger, Ferdinand] 1721-1786.
1603   Der in die katholische Schule geführte
S83   Fragensteller über den Katechismus von der
no.3   Geisterlehre. [München?] 1775.
29 p. 17cm.
Ascribed to Sterzinger by British Museum.
No. 3 in vol lettered Francone dell' Amavero (Sterzinger) Untersuchung [etc.]
1. Frage, ob der Katechismus von der Geisterlehre e in katholischer Katechismus sey? 2.   Magic. I. Title.
8

Frage, Ob man die Ausfahrt der Hexen zulassen könne?
Witchcraft
BF   Model, Johann Michael
1565   Johann Michael Models, J. U. Lic. beant-
S83   wortete Frage: Ob man die Ausfahrt der Hexen
M69   zulassen könne? Wider den heutigen Hexenstürmer P. Ferdinand Sterzinger. München, Bey J. A. Crätz, 1769.
36 p. 18cm.
1. Sterzinger, Ferdinand, 1721-1786. 2. Witchcraft. I. Title: Beantwortete Frage: Ob man die Ausfahrt der Hexen zulassen könne? II. Title: Frage, Ob man die Ausfa hrt der Hexen zulassen könne?
8

Fragments d'histoire de la folie.
Witchcraft
BF   Giraud, Albert.
1582   Fragments d'histoire de la folie; la
G52   sorcellerie au moyen-âge, une épidémie de délire de nos jours. [Bar-le-Duc, Impr. Contant-Laguerre, 1883]
24 p. 24cm.
Extract from Mémoires de la Société des lettres, sciences, et arts de Bar-le-Duc, t. 2, 2. série, 1883.
1. Witchcraft--France.   I. Title.

Witchcraft
BF   Français, J.
1566   L'Église et la sorcellerie. Précis historique, suivi des documents officiels, des textes
F81   principaux, et d'un procès inédit. Paris, E. Nourry, 1910.
263 p. 19cm. (Bibliothèque de critique religieuse)
1. Catholic Church--Doctrinal and controversial works. 2. Witchcraft. I. Title.

Witchcraft
BF   France. Commission pour le jugement du procez
1517   criminel fait a l'encontre de Maistre Urbain
F5   Grandier & ses complices.
F81   Extraict des registres de la Commission ordonnée par le Roy povr le ivgement ... Poictiers, Par I. Thoreav & la vefue d'A. Mesnier, 1634.
25 p. 16cm.
1. Grandier, Urbain, 1590-1634. 2. Loudun, France. Ursuline convent. I. Title.

CATALOGUE OF THE CORNELL WITCHCRAFT COLLECTION

ar X France. Parlement (Paris)
1962 Arrest de la cour du Parlement, qui juge que le crime de sortilege n'est pas cas royal, du 2 décembre 1611. Extrait des registres du Parlement. ₍Paris, C. Girard, 1738₎
3 p. 27cm.
Caption title.

1. Witchcraft--Laws and legislation--France.
I. Title.

France. Parlement (Rennes)
WITCHCRAFT
BF Parfouru, Paul, 1846-1905.
1582 Un procès de sorcellerie au Parlement de
Z7+ Bretagne. La condamnation de l'abbé Poussi-
1642 nière, Mathurin Trullier, known as l'abbé.
Roy, 1893.
11 p. 26cm.
"Extrait de la revue L'Hermine."

1. Trials (Witchcraft)--Rennes. 2. Poussinière, Mathurin Trullier, known as l'abbé.
8 3. Marais, Isaac. 4. France. Parle-
NIC ment (Rennes)

Witchcraft
BF France. Sovereigns, etc., 1643-1715
1582 (Louis XIV)
F81+ Edit du Roi, pour la punition de dif-
1776 férens crimes, notamment des empoisonneurs, ceux qui se disent divins, magiciens & enchanteurs; & portant reglement pour les epiciers & apothicaires. Donné à Versailles, au mois de Juillet 1682. ₍Paris, Chez Prault, imprimeur du Roi, 1776₎
7 p. 28cm.
8 Caption title.
(Continued on next card)

Witchcraft
BF France. Sovereigns, etc., 1643-1715
1582 (Louis XIV) Edit du Roi ... ₍1776₎
F81+ (Card 2)
1776

1. Witchcraft--France. 2. Poisoning--France. 3. Drugs--Laws and legislation--France. I. Title. II. France. Laws, statutes, etc., 1643-1715 (Louis XIV)

8

La France trompée par les magiciens et démonolâtres du dix-huitième siècle, fait
Witchcraft démontré par des faits.
BF Fiard, Jean Baptiste, 1736-1818.
1602 La France trompée par les magiciens et
F44 démonolâtres du dix-huitième siècle, fait
1803 démontré par des faits. Paris, Grégoire, 1803.
200 p. 22cm.
Bound with his Lettres philosophiques sur la magie. Paris, 1803.

1. Magic. I. Title.

Franchillon, Charles de, d. 1626.
MSS Discours sur la mort et condemnation de
Bd. Charles de Franchillon, Baron de
WITCHCRAFT Chenevières, exécuté en la place de
BF Grève, par arrest de la Cour de Parle-
D61 ment de Paris pour crime de sortilege et de magie, du jeudy 14. may 1626.
Paris, chez P. Mettayer, 1626 ₍1901₎
6 l. 19cm.
Carnap's manuscript copy.
"Originald   ruck in der Bibliothèque
Nationale zu   Paris (Imprimés Ln 27.
(Continued on next card)

Franchillon, Charles de, d. 1626.
MSS Discours sur la mort et condemnation de
Bd. Charles de Franchillon ... 1626 ₍1901₎
WITCHCRAFT (Card 2)
BF
D61 4768.) Copie davon genomen durch M^r.
Herviant - Paris im Mai 1901, wonach die vorliegende gemacht. (pet. in 4° de 16 pp.)"
Numerals in margin indicate pagination of the original.

1. Witchcraft--France. 2. Franchillon, Charles de,   d. 1626.

Witchcraft
BF Francisci, Erasmus, 1627-1694.
1445 Der höllische Proteus, oder tausendkün-
F82 stige Versteller, vermittelst Erzehlung der
1695 vielfältigen Bild-Verwechslungen erscheinender Gespenster, werffender und poltrender Geister ... wie auch andrer abentheurlicher Händel ... und von theils gelehrten, für den menschlichen Lebens-Geist irrig-angesehenen Betriegers, (nebst vorberichtlichem Grund-Beweis der Gewissheit, dass es würcklich Gespenster gebe) ... Nürnberg, In Ver-
8 (Continued on next card)

Witchcraft
BF Francisci, Erasmus, 1627-1694. Der höl-
1445 lische Proteus ... 1695. (Card 2)
F82
1695 legung Wolfgang Moritz Endters, 1695.
23 p. l., 1120, ₍46₎ p. front. 18cm.
First published 1690.

1. Ghosts. 2. Demonology. 3. Ghost
8 stories. I. Title.

Francisci de Cordva Schrifft- und vernunfftmässige Gedancken vom Schatzgraben und Beschwörung der Geister.
Witchcraft
BF Franciscus de Cordua, pseud.
1523 ... Schrifft- und vernunfftmässige Ge-
F81 dancken vom Schatz-graben und Beschwerung der Geister, aus dem Lateinischen ins Teutsche übersetzet. Hamburg, Bey Zacharias Schotken, 1716.
141 p. 17cm.
According to the "Vorrede," the author is French; however, the work exists only in German.
1. Demonology. 2. Occult sciences.
8 I. Title.

WITCHCRAFT Francisci Hutchinsons ... Historischer
BF Versuch von der Hexerey.
1565 Hutchinson, Francis, bp. of Down and Connor, 1660-1739.
H97 Francisci Hutchinsons ... Historischer versuch von der hexe-
1726 rey, in einem gespräch zwischen einem geistlichen, einem schottländischen advocaten und englischen geschwornen; worinnen über würcklich geschehene dinge vernünfftige anmerckungen gemachet, die hieher gehörigen stellen aus der Heil. Schrifft richtig erkläret und die gemeinen irrthümer aufs bescheidentlichste widerleget werden. Nebst zwey vortrefflichen predigten, die erste zum beweiss der wahrheit christl. religion, die andere, von guten und bösen engeln; nebst einer vorrede des herrn geheimbden raths Thomasii. Aus
(Continued on next card)
8   32-6507

Francisci Hutchinsons ... Historischer
WITCHCRAFT Versuch von der Hexerey.
BF Hutchinson, Francis, bp. of Down and Connor, 1660-1739.
1565 Francisci Hutchinsons ... Historischer versuch von der
H97 hexerey ... (Card 2)
1726 dem englischen ins teutsche übersetzt, auch mit kurtzen summarien und vollständigen registern versehen von Theodoro Arnold. Leipzig, J. C. Martini, 1726.
₍50₎, 332, ₍23₎ p. front. 22 cm.
Head-pieces and initials.
"Verzeichniss derer in diesem werck nur teutsch angeführten englischen autorum": p. ₍1₎-₍4₎ at end.
With copies 1 and 2 are bound Saint André, F. de. Lesenswürdige Briefe ... über die Materie von der Zauberey. Leipzig, 1727.   32-6507
8 Library of Congress
— Copy 2.   (Continued on next card)

Witchcraft
BF Franciscus de Cordua, pseud.
1523 ... Schrifft- und vernunfftmässige Ge-
F81 dancken vom Schatz-graben und Beschwerung der Geister, aus dem Lateinischen ins Teutsche übersetzet. Hamburg, Bey Zacharias Schotken, 1716.
141 p. 17cm.
According to the "Vorrede," the author is French; however, the work exists only in German.
1. Demonology. 2. Occult sciences.
8 I. Title. II. Title: Francisci de Cordva Schrifft-   und vernunfftmässige Gedancken vom Sch   atz-graben und Beschwör
der Geister.

Franciscus de Cordua, pseud.
Schrifft- und vernunfftmässige Gedanck vom Schatzgraben.
Witchcraft
BF Ludovici, Gottfried, 1670-1724.
1565 Godofredi Ludovici ... Theologicvm novae
T46 novi avtoris Francisci de Cordva anthropo-
1717a logiae et daemonologiae examen, nouitates vti alias, ab hoc in Schrifft- und Vernunfft mässigen Gedanken vom Schatzgraben und Beschwerung der Geister propositas ... Coburgi, Sumptu Pauli Güntheri Pfotenhaueri ₍1718
134 p. 19cm.
Bound with Thomasius, Christian, 1655-
8 1728. ... Kurt ze Lehr-Sätze von dem
(Continued on next card)

Franciscus de Cordua, pseud.
Schrifft- und vernunfftmässige Gedanck vom Schatzgraben.
Witchcraft Ludovici, Gottfried, 1670-1724. Godofredo
BF Ludovici ... Theologicvm novae ... anthro-
1565 pologiae ... examen ... ₍1718₎ (Card 2)
T46
1717a Laster der Zauberey. Franckfurth, 1717.

1. Franciscus de Cordua, pseud.
Schrifft- und vernunfftmässige Gedancken vom Schatzgraben. 2. Demonology. I.
Title: Theologicum novae ... anthropologiae ... examen.

8

Witchcraft
BF Franck, Archivrath in Donaueschingen.
1583 Der Hexenprozess gegen den Fürsten-
Z7 bergischen Registrator Obervogteiverweser un
1632 Notar Mathias Tinctorius und Consorten zu Hüfingen. Ein Sittenbild aus den 1630er Jahren. Freiburg im Breisgau, F. X. Wangler 1870.
42 p. 21cm.

1. Tinctorius, Mathias, d. 1632. I. Title

Witchcraft
BF Franck, Johannes, 1854-
1583 Geschichte des Wortes Hexe. Bonn, C.
F82 Georgi, 1901.
59 p. 24cm.
"Sonder-Abdruck aus Hansen: Quellen und Untersuchungen zur Geschichte des Hexenwahn und der Hexenverfolgung im Mittelalter."

I. Title.

Witchcraft Franck, Johannes, 1854-
BF Hansen, Joseph, 1862-1943.
1569 Quellen und Untersuchungen zur Geschichte
H24 des Hexenwahns und der Hexenverfolgung im Mittelalter. Mit einer Untersuchung der Geschichte des Wortes Hexe, von Johannes Franck. Bonn, C. Georgi, 1901.
xi, 703 p. illus. 24cm.

I. Franck, Johannes, 1854- II. Title.

CATALOGUE OF THE CORNELL WITCHCRAFT COLLECTION

hcraft
    Franck, Johannes Christophorus, fl. 1717.
        Gottfried Wahrliebs [pseud.] Deutliche vor-
    stellung der nichtigkeit derer vermeynten
    hexereyen und des ungegründeten hexen-processes.
    Nebst einer Gründlichen beantwortung der unter
    dem nahmen eines nach Engelland reisenden
    passagiers unlängst heraus gekommenen Untersuch-
    ung vom kobold, darinnen die falschen auflagen /
    mit welchen derselbe so wohl den hrn. geheimbd.
    rath Thomasivm als Iohann Webstern ohne allen
    grund zu diffamiren gesucht. deutlich entdecket.
             (Continued on next card)

hcraft
    Franck, Johannes Christophorus, fl. 1717.
        Gottfried Wahrliebs [pseud.] Deutliche vor-
    stellung der nichtigkeit derer vermeynten
    hexereyen ... [pref. 1720]   (Card 2)
    wie auch die Thomasische, Lehr-sätze vom laster
    der zauberey wieder dessen ungegründete
    einwürffe zulänglich behauptet werden.
    Amsterdam, Nach erfindung der hexerey im dritten
    seculo, und nach einführung des hexen-processes
    im jahr 236 [pref. 1720]
        172, 78 p.   front. 22cm.
             (Continued on next card)

ITCHCRAFT
F
565
82
    Franck, Johannes Christophorus, fl. 1717.
        Gottfried Wahrliebs [pseud.] Deutliche
    vorstellung der nichtigkeit derer vermeyn-
    ten hexereyen...[pref. 1720]   (Card 3)
    "Gründliche beantwortung der ... Unter-
    suchung vom kobold" has separate paging and
    special t. p. with imprint: Amsterdam, 1720.

             (Continued on next card)

ITCHCRAFT
F
565
82
    Franck, Johannes Christophorus, fl. 1717.
        Gottfried Wahrliebs [pseud.] Deutliche
    vorstellung der nichtigkeit derer vermeyn-
    ten hexereyen...[pref. 1720]   (Card 4)
    1. Witchcraft. 2. Kurtze Untersuchung von
    Kobold. 3. Webster, John, 1610-1682. The
    displaying of supposed witchcraft. 4. Thoma-
    sius, Christian, 1655-1728. Kurtze Lehr-sätze
    von dem Laster der Zauberey. I. Title:
    Deutliche Vo   rstellung der Nichtig-
    keit der Zau   berey. II. Title:
    Gründliche   Beantwortung der ...
    Untersuchung   vom Kobold.

    Francke, Johann Christoph, fl. 1717.
        see
    Franck, Johannes Christophorus, fl. 1717.

    Francone dell' Amavero Untersuchung ob
      es eine Festigkeit gebe.
Witchcraft
BF
1603
S83
no.1
    [Sterzinger, Ferdinand] 1721-1786.
        ... Untersuchung ob es eine Festigkeit
    gebe dabey viele andere aberglaubische Irr-
    thümer wiederleget werden nebst beygefügtem
    Katechismus von der Geisterlehre. München,
    W. Schwarzkopf, Buchhändler in Nürnberg,
    1775.
        200 p. 17cm.
        At head of title: Francone dell' Ama-
    vero [pseud. of F. Sterzinger]
        No. 1 in vol. lettered Francone dell'
    Amavero (Ster   zinger) Untersuchung
8   [etc.]   (Continued on next card)

    Francone dell' Amavero Untersuchung ob
      es eine Festigkeit gebe.
Witchcraft
BF
1603
S83
no.1
    [Sterzinger, Ferdinand] 1721-1786. ... Un-
    tersuchung ob es eine Festigkeit gebe ...
    1775.   (Card 2)
        Attributed by British Museum and Kayser
    to A. U. Mayer.
        1. Magic. 2. Spells. I. His Kate-
    kismus von der Geisterlehre. II. Title.
    III. Mayer, Andreas Ulrich, 1732-1802, sup-
    posed author.   IV. Title: Katekismus
8   von der Geist   erlehre.

BF
1566
F83
1971
    Franklyn, Julian.
        Death by enchantment; an examination of ancient and
    modern witchcraft. [1st American ed.] New York, Put-
    nam [1971]
        x, 244 p. illus. 22 cm. $6.95
        Includes bibliographical references.

        1. Witchcraft. I. Title.
4
    BF1566.F7 1971   133.4   78-152769
                            MARC
    Library of Congress   71 [4]

WITCHCRAFT
BF
1583
F83+
    Franz, Heinrich.
        Der Hexenglaube in Hessen.
        (In: Hessenland. Kassel. 27cm. v.30
    (1916) p. 2-3, 17-19, 39-41, 145-149,
    161-164, 273-276)

8
NIC   1. Witchcraft--Hesse. I. Title.

    Frau Holle.
WITCHCRAFT
BF
1583
S37
    Schrader, Ludwig Wilhelm.
        Die Sage von den Hexen des Brockens und
    deren Entstehen in vorchristlicher Zeit
    durch die Verehrung des Melybogs und der
    Frau Holle. Historisch bearbeitet ...
    Quedlinburg und Leipzig, G. Basse, 1839.
        48 p. 19cm.
        Sent to L. Freytag and published through
    him.
        1. Walpurgisnacht. 2. Witchcraft--
    Thuringia. 3. Folk-lore--Thuringia.
8   4. Melybog. 5. Frau Holle. I.
NIC Title.

Witchcraft
BF
1598
A27
O2
1651
    Freake, J., tr.
    Agrippa von Nettesheim, Heinrich Cornelius,
    1486?-1535.
        Three books of occult philosophy ...
    Translated out of the Latin into the English
    tongue, by J. F[reake] London, Printed by
    R. W. for Gregory Moule, and are to be sold
    at the Sign of the three Bibles neer the
    West-end of Pauls, 1651.
        [26], 583, [12] p. port., illus., tables,
    diagrs. 19cm.
        Imprint of copy 3 varies slightly: London,
             (Continued on next card)

Witchcraft
BF
1598
A27
O2
1651
    Freake, J., tr.
    Agrippa von Nettesheim, Heinrich Cornelius,
    1486?-1535. Three books of occult phi-
    losophy ... 1651.   (Card 2)
    Printed by R. W. for Gregory Moule, and are
    to be sold neer the West-end of Pauls, 1651.
    Copy 1 lacks portrait; copy 2 lacks "An
    encomium on the three Books of Cornelius
    Agrippa, by Eugenius Philalethes." (sig.a2)
    Portrait in copy 3 mounted.
        Translation of De occulta philosophia
    libri tres.
        I. His   De occulta philosophia
    libri tres.   English. II. Freake,
    J., tr. III.   Title.

    Les fredaines du diable.
WITCHCRAFT
BF
1547
C86
1797
    Courtilz, Gatien de, sieur de Sandras,
    1644?-1772.
        Les fredaines du diable; ou, Recueil de
    morceaux épars, pour servir à l'histoire
    du diable et de ses suppôts; tirés d'auteurs
    dignes de foi, par feu M. Sandras, avocat
    en Parlement; mis en nouveau style et pub-
    liés par J. Fr. N. D. L. R. [i.e., Jean
    François Née de la Rochelle] Paris, Chez
    Merlin, 1797.
        216 p. 17 cm.
8
NIC   (Continued on next card)

    Les fredaines du diable.
WITCHCRAFT
BF
1547
C86
1797
    Courtilz, Gatien de, sieur de Sandras,
    1644?-1772. Les fredaines du diable ...
    1797.   (Card 2)
        Ascription by BM, Biographie universelle;
    and BN for entry under Née de la Rochelle
    as editor.
        Author entry in BN: Sandras, ,
    advocat au Parlement.
        1. Devil. 2. Devil--Bibliography.
8   I. Sandras,   , advocat au Parlement,
NIC supposed aut   her. II. Née de la Ro-
    chelle, Jean   François, 1751-1838, ed.
    III. Title.

    The free-holders grand inquest.
Rare
JC
153
F48F8
1679
    Filmer, Sir Robert, d. 1653.
        The free-holders grand inquest,
    touching our sovereign lord the King
    and his parliament. To which are added
    Observations upon forms of government.
    Together with Directions for obedience
    to governours in dangerous and doubtful
    times ... London, 1679.
        88,76,72,257-346 p. 19cm.
        Contents.--The free-holders grand

             (Continued on next card)

    The free-holders grand inquest.
Rare
JC
153
F48F8
1679
    Filmer, Sir Robert, d. 1653. The free-
      holders grand inquest ... 1679.
      (Card 2)
    inquest.--Observations upon Aristotle's
    politiques, touching forms of government.
    --Observations concerning the original
    of government, upon Mr. Hobs his Leviathan,
    Mr. Milton against Salmasius, H. Grotius
    De jure belli, Mr. Hunton's Treatise of
    monarchy.--The anarchy of a limited or
    mixed monarchy.--An advertisement to the

             Continued on next card)

    The free-holders grand inquest.
Rare
JC
153
F48F8
1679
    Filmer, Sir Robert, d. 1653. The free-
      holders grand inquest ... 1679.
      (Card 3)
    Jury-men of England, touching witches.

        I. Title. II. Title: An advertisement
    to the jury-men of England, touching
    witches.

Witchcraft
BF
1413
F86
    Freimark, Hans, 1881-
        Okkultismus u. Sexualität. Beiträge zur
    Kulturgeschichte der Vergangenheit u. Gegen-
    wart. Leipzig, Leipziger Verlag [1909]
        xvi, 433 p. 24cm.

        1. Occult sciences. 2. Sex. 3. Sexual
    perversion. 4. Psychical research. I.
    Title.

CATALOGUE OF THE CORNELL WITCHCRAFT COLLECTION

Rare K T8116+ — The French impostors: or, An historical account of some very extraordinary criminal cases brought before the Parliament of France ... To which is prefixed a copious Preface, in relation to the laws and constitution of France. London, Printed by J. Applebee, for J. Hazard [etc.] 1737.
xliii, 306, [8] p. 17cm.
Publishers' Catalogues: p. [307]-[314]
Lacks p. i-xii.
In box lettered: Trials.
1. Impostors and imposture.

Witchcraft
BF 1555 F88 — Frese, Jürgen, 1623-
Umständlicher Bericht, von dem Unlängst in Hamburg vom leidigen Satan besessenen Mägdlein, wie auch Beantwortung einiger Fragen von der Universität Kiel, nebst des Autore Lebens-Lauf, worin gemeldet werden die Wunder von dem glühenden Rink und Kohlen, und noch beygefüget, eine Trostschrift an einige betrübte Herzen. [Hamburg?] 1692.
112 p. 17cm.
1. Grambecken, Catharina, fl. 1692. I. Title.

BF 1565 F879 1924 — Freud, Sigmund, 1856-1939.
Eine Teufelsneurose im siebzehnten Jahrhundert. Leipzig, Internationaler Psychoanalytischer Verlag, 1924.
41 p. 23cm.
Published first in Imago, Bd. 9, Heft 1.
1. Witchcraft--17th cent. 2. Neuroses. I. Title.

Witchcraft
BF 1565 F88 1671 — Freudius, Michael.
Gewissens-Fragen oder Gründlicher Bericht von Zauberey und Zauberern, von Mitteln wider dieselbe, und was für einen Process christliche Obrigkeit wider die Zauberer gebrauchen solle. Benebenst einem Anhang von Geist- und leiblicher Besitzung und Austreibung dess bösen Geistes ... Franckfurt am Mayn, Drucks und Verlags Balth. Christoph Wusts, 1671.
[54], 714, [144, 46] 88, [10] p. 21cm.
Added t. p., engraved.
I. Title.

Ein Freund der Wahrheit.
WITCHCRAFT
BT 980 M26 — Man muss auch dem Teufel nicht zu viel aufbürden. Bey Gelegenheit der Brochüre: Sollte der Teufel wirklich ein Unding seyn? etc. Beherziget von einem Freunde der Wahrheit ... Bremen, J. H. Cramer, 1776.
xxxii, 426 p. 16cm.
Attributed by various sources to C. H. Runge; cf. Holzmann, Michael. Deutsches Anonymenlexikon (Weimar, 1902-28)
8 NIC
(Continued on next card)

Freundschaftliche und vertrauliche Briefe den so genannten sehr berüchtigten Hexenhandel zu Glarus betreffend.
WITCHCRAFT
BF 1584 S97 Z7 1782a — Lehmann, Heinrich Ludwig.
Freundschaftliche und vertrauliche Briefe den so genannten sehr berüchtigten Hexenhandel zu Glarus betreffend. Zürich, Bey Johann Caspar Füessin, 1783.
2 v. in 1. plate. 19cm.
No more published.
1. Trials (Witchcraft)--Glarus (Canton) 2. Göldi, Anna. 3. Tschudi, Anna Maria.
8 NIC

BL 490 F89 — Freybe, Albert.
Der deutsche Volksaberglaube in seinem Verhältnis zum Christentum und im Unterschiede von der Zauberei. Gotha, F. A. Perthes, 1910.
xv, 194 p. 22cm.
1. Superstition. I. Title.

Freygang, Gottlob, respondent.
Witchcraft
BF 1565 D62 no.6 — Müller, Johannes, praeses.
Disputatio physica De magis tempestates cientibus, qvam ... sub praesidio ... Dn. M. Johannis Mülleri ... publicè pro virili defendet Gottlob Freygang ... Wittenbergae, Literis Matthaei Henckelii [1676]
[16] p. 20cm.
No. 6 in vol. lettered Dissertationes de sagis. 1636-1714.
1. Witchcraft. 2. Weather-lore. I. Freygang, Gottlob, respondent. II. Title: De magis tempestates cientibus.
8

Witchcraft
BX 2340 F89 — Freyschmid, Joseph Caspar.
Thesaurus sacer benedictionum veterum, ac novarum, ex sanctae ecclesiae ritibus, sanctorum virorum scriptis, probatis authoribus, & approbatissimo temporum usu collectus ... dicatus, dedicatus, consecratus a Josepho Casparo Freyschmid. Lincij, 1708.
6 p. l., 725, [27] p. 14cm.
Title in red and black.
Benedictio numismatum crucis: Sancti Patris Benedicti has special t. p.
(Continued on next card)

Witchcraft
BX 2340 F89 — Freyschmid, Joseph Caspar. Thesaurus sacer benedictionum ... 1708. (Card 2)
with imprint: Lincij, Typis Caspari Josephi Freyschmid, 1708, and is unpaged.
1. Exorcism. 2. Benediction. I. Title. II. Title: Benedictio numismatum crucis.

Witchcraft
BF 1550 F89 — Freytag, Gustav, 1816-1895.
Bilder aus der deutschen Vergangenheit. Der deutsche Teufel im 16. Jahrhundert. (In Die Grenzboten. Leipzig. 24cm. XVII. Jahrg. (1858) p. [363]-386)
1. Devil. II. Title. III. Title: Der deutsche Teufel im 16. Jahrhundert.

Friderici Hoffmanni ... De diaboli potentia in corpora.
WITCHCRAFT
R 133 H71 1725 — Hoffmann, Friedrich, 1660-1742.
Friderici Hoffmanni ... De diaboli potentia in corpora, dissertatio physico-medica curiosa. Emendatior jam edita. Halae Magdeburgicae, Typis Joh. Gruneri, 1725.
[39] p. 21cm.
First published 1703 under title: Disputatio inauguralis medico-philosophica De potentia diaboli in corpora.
1. Medicine, Magic, mystic, and spagiric. 2. Devil. I. His Disputatio inauguralis medico-philosophica De potentia diaboli in corpora.

Friedrich Spe.
WITCHCRAFT
PT 1792 D56 1901 — Diel, Johannes Baptista, 1843-1875.
Friedrich Spe. Von Johannes Diel. 2., umgearb. Aufl. von Bernhard Duhr. Freiburg i. B., Herder, 1901.
viii, 147 p. port., facsim. 20cm.
(Sammlung historischer Bildnisse. [IX])
First published 1872 under title: Friedrich von Spee.
Very extensively revised.
1. Spee, Friedrich von, 1591-1635. I. Duhr, Bernhard, 1852-1930.
8 NIC

Friedrich Spee.
WITCHCRAFT
PT 1792 C26 — Cardauns, Hermann, 1847-1925.
Friedrich Spee. Frankfurt a. M., A. Foesser Nachf., 1884.
[103]-133 p. 23cm. (Frankfurter zeitgemässe Broschüren. N. F., Bd. 5, Heft 4)
1. Spee, Friedrich von, 1591-1635. 2. Spee, Friedrich von, 1591-1635. Cautio criminalis. I. Series.
8 NIC

Friedrich Spee und die Hexenprozesse.
PT 1792 Z97 — Zwetsloot, Hugo.
Friedrich Spee und die Hexenprozesse; die Stellung u. Bedeutung der Cautio criminalis in der Geschichte d. Hexenverfolgungen. Trier, Paulinus-Verlag, 1954.
345 p. illus., port. 24 cm.
Bibliography: p. 323-328.
"Ausgaben und Übersetzungen der Cautio criminalis": p. 329-3
1. Spee, Friedrich von, 1591-1635. Cautio criminalis. 2. Tri (Witchcraft)--Germany. I. Title.
56-333

Friedrich Spee von Langenfeld. Sein Leben und seine Schriften.
Witchcraft
PT 1792 H69+ — Hölscher, Otto.
Friedrich Spee von Langenfeld. Sein Leben und seine Schriften. Düsseldorf, Gedruckt von L. Boss [1871]
16 p. 27cm.
Accompanies "Programm" (zu den öffentlichen Prüfungen am 28., 29. und 30 August 1871)--Realschule erster Ordnung, Düsseldorf.
Pages 13-16 give poems by Spee.
1. Spee, Friedrich von, 1591-1635. I. Title.

Friedrich von Spee. Eine biographische und literarhistorische Skizze.
WITCHCRAFT
PT 1792 D56 — Diel, Johannes Baptista, 1843-1875.
Friedrich von Spee. Eine biographische und literarhistorische Skizze. Von J. B. M. Diel. Freiburg i. Br., Herder, 1872.
119 p. port. 19cm. (Sammlung historischer Bildnisse. IX)
Includes as "Beilage" selections from Spee's Trutznachtigall, in German and Latin.
1. Spee, Friedrich von, 1591-1635. I. Spee, Friedrich von, 1591-1635. Trutz-Nachtigall. Selections. German and Latin.
8 NIC

Friedrich von Spee und die Hexenprozesse seiner Zeit.
AC 30 S18 n.s. no.291 — Ebner, Theodor.
Friedrich von Spee und die Hexenprozesse seiner Zeit. Hamburg, Verlagsanstalt u. Druckerei A.-G. (vormals J. F. Richter) 18
47 p. 21cm. (Sammlung gemeinverständlicher wissenschaftlicher Vorträge, n.F., 13. Ser., Heft 291)
1. Spee, Friedrich von, 1591-1635. 2. Witchcraft--Germany. I. Title.

CATALOGUE OF THE CORNELL WITCHCRAFT COLLECTION

Witchcraft
BF
1531
F91
    Friend, John Albert Newton, 1881-
        Demonology, sympathetic magic and witchcraft; a study of superstition as it persists in man and affects him in a scientific age. London, C. Griffin [1961]
        173 p. illus. 20 cm.
        Includes bibliography.

        1. Demonology. 2. Witchcraft. I. Title: Sympathetic magic. II. Title.
        BF1531.F7   133.4   61-66183 ‡
    Library of Congress   [2]

    Fries, Ellen, 1855-1900.
        ... Sverges sista häxprocess i Dalarne 1757-1763, efter handlingarna i målet tecknad av Ellen Fries. Uppsala, Almqvist & Wicksells boktr.-aktiebolag, 1893.
        73 p. 23½ cm. ([Nyare] bidrag till kännedom om de svenska landsmålen ock svenskt folkliv XIII. 6)
        Forms 50. hft. of the whole series.

        1. Witchcraft—Sweden. I. Title.   23—2440
    Library of Congress   PD5001.S9   50. hft., XIII. 6
        [38b1]

    Frimel, Johann Gottlieb, respondent.

Witchcraft
BF
1445
D61
no.9
    Donati, Christian, praeses.
        Disputatio de spectris, quam sub praesidio Dn. Christiani Donati ... publicae ventilationi sistit Johann. Gottlieb Frimel ... Wittenbergae, Typis Christiani Schrödteri [1688]
        [34] p. 18cm. (bound in 21cm. vol.)
        No. 9 in vol. lettered Dissertationes de spectris. 1646-1753.
        1. Spirits. I. Frimel, Johann Gottlieb, respondent. II. Title: De spectris.

8

Witchcraft
BF
1558
F91
    Frischbier, Hermann Karl, 1823-1891.
        Hexenspruch und Zauberbann; ein Beitrag zur Geschichte des Aberglaubens in der Provinz Preussen. Berlin, T. C. F. Enslin, 1870.
        x, 167 p. 19cm.

        1. Incantations. 2. Magic. I. Title.

    Fritzsch, Benjamin, respondent.

Witchcraft
BF
1556
R73
    Rohr, Philipp, praeses.
        Dissertatio historico-philosophica De masticatione mortuorum, quam ... sistent praeses M. Philippus Rohr ... & respondens Benjamin Frizschius ... Lipsiae, Typis Michaelis Vogtii [1679]
        [24] p. 21cm.

        1. Vampires. 2. Devil. I. Fritzsch, Benjamin, respondent. II. Title: De masticatione mortuorum.

Witchcraft
BX
2048
B5
F92
    Friz, Joannes Chrysostomus.
        Manuale selectissimarum benedictionum, conjurationum, exorcismorum, absolutionum, rituum. Ad commodiorem usum parochorum, omniumque sacerdotum tam saecularium, quàm religiosorum. Ex diversis ritualibus et probatissimis auctoribus collectum, & novissime auctum per P.F. Joannem Chrysostomum Friz, Ord. Min. S. P. Francisci Reformat. Provinciae Tyrolensis. [Campidonae] Per Andream Stadler, 1737.
        (Continued on next card)

8

Witchcraft
BX
2048
B5
F92
    Friz, Joannes Chrysostomus. Manuale selectissimarum benedictionum ... 1737.
        (Card 2)
        9 p. l., 657 p. 17cm.

        1. Benediction. 2. Exorcism. I. Title.

8

Witchcraft
BF
1520
F92
    Frobes, Johann Nikolaus, 1701-1756.
        Mysterivm de daemonibvs sive geniis atqve intelligentiis philosophicvm strictim et fideliter revelatvm. Helmstadii, Ex Officina Schnorriana, 1748.
        lxxv p. 22cm.

        1. Demonology. 2. Spirits. 3. Angels. I. Title: Mysterium de daemonibus sive geniis atque intelligentiis philosophicum revelatum.

    Frölin, Barbara, 1637-1654.

MSS
Bd.
WITCHCRAFT
BF
W275
Z88
    Warhaffter sumarisch-aussführlicher Bericht und Erzehlung. Was die in dess heyligen Röm- Reichsstatt Augspurg etlich Wochen lang in Verhafft gelegne zwo Hexen, benandtlich Barbara Frölin von Rieden unnd Anna Schäflerin von Eringen, wegen ihrer Hexereyen gut- und peinlich bekent ... und wie endtlich dise beede Unholden ihrem Verdienst nach, auff Sambstag den 18. Aprill diss 1654 Jahrs hingericht worden. Augspurg,   Durch Andream Aperger, 1654 [ca.   1900]
        (Continued on next card)

    Frölin, Barbara, 1637-1654.

MSS
Bd.
WITCHCRAFT
BF
W275
Z88
    Warhaffter sumarisch-aussführlicher Bericht und Erzehlung ... 1654 [ca. 1900] (Card 2)
        8 l. 24cm.
        Carnap's manuscript copy.
        "Originaldruck in der Gustav Freytag Biblioth. jetzt in der Stadtbibliothek zu Frankfurt a/M. 6 Blatt in 4°. Sig. Aij-B."
        Numerals in the margins indicate pagination of the original.
        1. Witchcraft --Augsburg. 2. Demoniac possession.   3. Frölin, Barbara, 1637-1654.   4. Schäfler, Anna, 1590-1654.

    Frohertz, Anna Traute.

WITCHCRAFT
BF
1583
Z7
1652
    Könnecke, Max
        Zwei Hexenprozesse aus der Grafschaft Mansfeld.
        (In Mansfelder Blätter. Eisleben, 1887-1940? 23cm. 10. Jahrg. (1896), p. [32]-65)
        Caption title.
        "Inquisitionsakten wider die Pfarrwitwe Anna Kluge zu Ahlsdorf in Sachen beschuldigter Hexerei, 1652 und 1655": p. 34-51.
        "Inquisitionsakten wider Anna Traute Frohertzin und Marie Grösseln in Gerbstedt wegen beschuldigter Hexerei, 1689": p. 52-65.

8
NIC
        (Continued on next card)

    From the history of human folly.

Witchcraft
BF
1418
H9
R23
1963
    Ráth Végh, István, 1870-1959.
        From the history of human folly. [Translated from the Hungarian by Zsuzsanna Horn. Budapest] Corvina [1963]
        288, [1] p. 21cm.
        Translation of his Az emberek butításának történetéből.
        "The translation has been revised by Elisabeth West."

        (Continued on next card)

8

Witchcraft
BF
1565
F93
    Frommann, Johann Christian, b. ca. 1640.
        Tractatus de fascinatione novus et singularis, in quo fascinatio vulgaris profligatur, naturalis confirmatur, & magica examinatur ... Norimbergae, Sumtibus Wolfgangi Mauritii Endteri, & Johannis Andreae Endteri Haeredum, 1675.
        [78], 1067, [45] p. 21cm.
        Added t. p., engraved, dated: 1674.
        Manuscript note on t. p.: Bibliotheca Scholar: Piar: 1783. Colleg. Loevenburgh.
        (Continued on next card)

Witchcraft
BF
1565
F93
    Frommann, Johann Christian, b. ca. 1640.
        Tractatus de fascinatione ... 1675.
        (Card 2)

        Copy 2 has super exlibris: C[omes], W. G. V[on] N[ostitz]; autograph on t. p.: Jos. Bernhardt Graff von Herberstein; and 17th century vellum binding, with supra libros: I[oseph] B[ernhard] G[raf] V[on] H[erberstein], 1681.

        1. Witchcraft. 2. Magic. 3. Superstition. I. Title. II. Title: De fascinatione.

    Fronmüller, Johann Christoff.
        see
    Fronmüller, Johann Christoph.

MSS
Bd.
WITCHCRAFT
BF
F93
    Fronmüller, Johann Christoph.
        Die auss Gottes Zulass von dem abgesagten Gottes und Menschen-Feind, dem leidigen Teuffel eine geraume Zeit leiblich-besessene, und übel-geklagte, allein durch Gottes Gnade auf fleissiges Gebet vieler fromm Christen von der leiblichen Besitzung widerum befreÿdte ... Susanna Raabin. ...Theils auss den Actis, theils aber auss der Erfahrung selbsten zusamm getragen von Johann Christoff Fronmüller. 1696-[1703]
        [1] l., 116   p. 18cm.
        (Continued on next card)

MSS
Bd.
WITCHCRAFT
BF
F93
    Fronmüller, Johann Christoph. Die auss Gottes Zulass ... leiblich-besessene ... Susanna Raabin...1696-[1703] (Card 2)
        Manuscript, on paper, in a German hand.
        Added leaf before t. p.: "Die Kyrchendiener, welche auf Verordnung der hohen Obrigkeit die Susanna Raabin besuchten sind folgende ...
        Line frame on each page.
        Bound in marbled boards.
        1. Raabin, Susanna, b. 1666. 2. Demoniac possession. I. Title: Die auss Gottes Zulass... leiblich-besessene ... Susanna Raabin.

Witchcraft
BF
1583
Z7
1663
    Fuchs, Hugo.
        Ein Hexenprozess in Schleusingen aus dem Jahre 1663. Meiningen, Keyssner, 1889.
        13 p. 25cm.

        1. Witchcraft. 2. Trials (Witchcraft) --Germany. I. Title.

CATALOGUE OF THE CORNELL WITCHCRAFT COLLECTION

Fünff Predigten von den Hexen.

Witchcraft
BF 1565 Z44
8

Zehner, Joachim, 1566-1612.
Fünff Predigten von den Hexen, ihren Anfang, Mittel vnd End in sich haltend vnd erklärend. Aus heiliger göttlicher Schrifft vnd vornembsten alten Kirchenlehrern zusammen getragen vnd vor dessen gehalten in der Pfarrkirchen zu Schleusingen durch Ioachimum Zehner ... Leipzig, In Verlegung Thomae Schürers Buchhändlers [Gedruckt durch Michael Lantzenbergers Erben] 1613.
3 p. l., 90, [2] p. 20cm.
(Continued on next card)

Fünff Predigten von den Hexen.

Witchcraft
BF 1565 Z44
8

Zehner, Joachim, 1566-1612. Fünff Predigten von den Hexen ... 1613. (Card 2)

Title in woodcut border.
With colophon.

1. Witchcraft. 2. Witchcraft in the Bible. I. Title.

WITCHCRAFT
K M4769 no.3
8 NIC

Fürstl. Mecklenb. Erweiterte Verordnung welcher massen es mit der befragunge der Zaubereyhalber eingezogenen Persohnen...zu...
Mecklenburg. Laws, statutes, etc.
Fürstl. Mecklenb. Erweiterte Verordnung welcher massen es mit der befragunge der Zaubereyhalber eingezogenen Persohnen sonderlich mittelst adhibirter Tortur, wegen Ihrer complicum, zuhalten. Güstrow, Gedruckt durch Johann Spierling, 1683.
[7] p. 21cm.

No.3 in a vol. of ordinances of Mecklenburg concerning witchcraft.
1. Witchcraft--Laws and legislation--Mecklenburg. 2. Trials (Witchcraft)--Mecklenburg. I. Title.

WITCHCRAFT
K M4769 no.2
8 NIC

Fürstl. Mecklenb. Verordnung wie nach diesem die der Zauberey halber gefänglich...
Mecklenburg. Laws, statutes, etc.
Fürstl. Mecklenb. Verordnung wie nach diesem die der Zauberey halber gefänglich ein gezogene Personen bewahret werden sollen. Güstrow, Gedruckt durch Johann Spierling, 1682.
[6] p. 21cm.

No. 2 in a vol. of ordinances of Mecklenburg concerning witchcraft.
1. Witchcraft--Laws and legislation--Mecklenburg. 2. Trials (Witchcraft)--Mecklenburg. I. Title.

WITCHCRAFT
K M4769 no.4
8 NIC

Fürstl. Mecklenburg Anderweite Instruction und Verordnung.
Mecklenburg. Laws, statutes, etc.
Fürstl. Mecklenburg Anderweite Instruction und Verordnung, [wie von denen Beampten E. E. Ritterschafft Gerichts-Verwaltern Bürgermeistern Richtern und Räthen und ins gemein andern Gerichts-vorwesern wieder die dess Zauberlasters und abergläubischen Dinge berüchtigte Persohnen und deren Complices zuverfahren sey. Güstrow, Gedruckt durch Johann Spierling, 1683.
[12] p. 21 cm.
No.4 in a vol. of ordinances of Mecklenburg concerning witchcraft.
(Continued on next card)

WITCHCRAFT
BF 1569 A2 I59 1604
8 NIC

Fuga Satanae.
Stampa, Pietro Antonio.
Fuga Satanae. Exorcismvs ex sacrarum litterarum fontibus, pióque sacros. Ecclesiae instituto exhaustus. Cum indice ad oram libri annexo. Lvgdvni, Svmptibvs Petri Landry, 1610.
112 [i.e. 88], [5] p. 18cm.

Many errors in paging.
Bound with v. 2-3 of Institoris, Henricus. Malleus maleficarvm. Lvgdvni, 1604.

1. Exorcism. I. Title.

Fuhrmann, Philipp David, respondent.

Witchcraft
BF 1565 D62 no.2
8

Voigt, Gottfried, 1644-1682, praeses.
De conventu sagarum ad sua sabbata, qvae vocant ... praeside ... Dn. M. Gothofredo Voigt ... responsurus Philipp. David Fuhrmann ... Wittebergae, Typis Johannis Borckardi [1667]
[16] p. 20cm.
No. 2 in vol. lettered Dissertationes de sagis. 1636-1714.
1. Witchcraft. I. Fuhrmann, Philipp David, respondent. II. Title.

Fuldaer Anekdotenbüchlein.

WITCHCRAFT
DD 901 F9 M25

Malkmus, Georg Joseph.
Fuldaer Anekdotenbüchlein. Fulda, Druck der Fuldaer Aktienbuchdr., 1875.
viii, 151 p. 17cm.

"Eine Teufelsaustreibung.": p. 93-95.
"Noch eine Teufelsaustreibung.": p. 95-97.
"Ein Hexenrichter.": p.101-151. An account, based on documents, of Balthasar Nuss and the witch trials in Fulda.

1. Fulda, Ger. 2. Trials (Witchcraft)--Fulda, Ger. 3. Nuss, Balthasar. 4. Demoniac possession. I. Title.

8 NIC

Witchcraft
BF 1581 Z7 1712

A full and impartial account of the discovery of sorcery and witchcraft, practis'd by Jane Wenham of Walkerne in Hertfordshire.
[Bragge, Francis]
A full and impartial account of the discovery of sorcery and witchcraft, practis'd by Jane Wenham of Walkerne in Hertfordshire, upon the bodies of Anne Thorn, Anne Street, &c. The proceedings against her from her being first apprehended, till she was committed to gaol by Sir Henry Chavncy. Also her tryal at the assizes at Hertford before Mr. Justice Powell, where she was found guilty of felony and witchcraft, and receiv'd sen-
(Continued on next card)

Witchcraft
BF 1581 Z7 1712

A full and impartial account of the discovery of sorcery and witchcraft, practis'd by Jane Wenham of Walkerne of Hertfordshire.
[Bragge, Francis] A full and impartial account of the discovery of sorcery and witchcraft ... 1712. (Card 2)

tence of death for the same, March 4.1711-12... London, Printed for E. Curll, 1712.
2 p. l., 36 p. 19cm.

1. Wenham, Jane, d. 1730. 2. Witchcraft--England.

Witchcraft
BF 1563 W81++ no.22

A Full and true account of the discovering, apprehending and taking of a notorious witch ... on Sunday, July the 23. Together with her examination and committment to Bridewel, Clerkenwel. London, Printed by H. Hills [1704. London, at the British Museum, 1923]
[1] p. 27cm.

Photocopy (negative) 1 p. 20 x 32cm.
No. 22 in vol. lettered: Witchcraft tracts, chapbooks and broadsides, 1579-1704; rotograph copies.

Witchcraft
BF 1581 A2 W81 1866a no.9

A Full and true relation of the tryal, condemnation, and execution of Ann Foster, (who was arrained for a witch) on Saturday the 22th [sic] of this instant August, at the place of execution at Northampton. ... London, Printed for D. M., 1674. [Northampton, Reprinted by Taylor, 1878]
8 p. 22cm.
No. 9 in box lettered Witchcraft in Northamptonshire.
1. Foster, Ann, d. 1674. 2. Witchcraft--Northamptonshire, England.

8

Witchcraft
BF 1581 Z7 1712b

A full confutation of witchcraft: more particularly of the depositions against Jane Wenham, lately condemned for a witch; at Hertford. In which the modern notions of witches are overthrown, and the ill consequences of such doctrines are exposed by arguments; proving that, witchcraft is priestcraft ... In a letter from a physician in Hertfordshire, to his friend in London. London, Printed for J. Baker, 1712.
48 (i. e. 40) p. 18cm.
With this is bound [Bragge, Francis] Witchcraft farther display'd. London, 1712.

1. Witchcraft. 2. Wenham, Jane, d. 1730.

11-14484 rev. 2
Library of Congress   BF1581.Z7 1712
[r36c2]

Witchcraft
BF 1575 M427

A further account of the tryals of the New-England witches.
Mather, Increase, 1639-1723.
A further account of the tryals of the New-England witches. With the observations of a person who was upon the place several days when the suspected witches were first taken into examination. To which is added Cases of conscience concerning witchcrafts and evil spirits personating men. Written at the request of the ministers of New England. By Increase Mather, president Harvard colledge ... London, Printed for J. Dunton 1693.
(Continued on next card)
5-33455†

Witchcraft
BF 1575 M427

A further account of the tryals of the New-England witches.
Mather, Increase, 1639-1723. A further account of the tryals of the New-England witches ... 1693. (Card 2)
1 p. l., 10 p., 1 l., [2], 39, [5] p. 20cm.
Title within double line border.
After year of imprint: Of whom may be had the third edition of Mr. Cotton Mather's first Account of the tryals of the New-England witches. Printed on the same size with this last account that they may bind up together.
"Cases of conscience" has special t.-p. and separate paging. (Continued on next card)

Witchcraft
BF 1575 M427

A further account of the tryals of the New-England witches.
Mather, Increase, 1639-1723. A further account of the tryals of the New-England witches ... 1693. (Card 3)

"A true narrative of some remarkable passages relating to sundry persons afflicted by witchcraft at Salem village in New-England, which happened from the 19th. of March to the 5th. of April, 1692. Collected by Deodat Lawson":p.1-
"A further account of the tryals of the New England witches, sent in a letter from the ... to a gentleman in London": p. 9-10.
Wing M 1213.

Witchcraft
BS 2545 D5 T97 no.5

A further enquiry into the meaning of demoniacks in the New Testament.
[Sykes, Arthur Ashley], 1684?-1756.
A further enquiry into the meaning of demoniacks in the New Testament. Wherein the Enquiry is vindicated against the objections of ... Mr. Twells, and of the author of the Essay in answer to it [i.e. Thomas Church] ... London, Printed for J. Roberts, 1737.
116 p. 21cm.

No. 5 in vol. lettered: Twells, Whiston, etc. Tracts on the demoniacs in the New Testament. London, 1737-1775.

WITCHCRAFT
BF 1576 M82 G64+

[Further notes on the history of witchcraft in Massachusetts]
Goodell, Abner Cheney, 1831-1914.
[Further notes on the history of witchcraft in Massachusetts]
(In: Massachusetts Historical Society. Proceedings. Boston. 26cm. June 1883. p. 280-326)

Running title: Witch-trials in Massachusetts.
Reply to George Henry Moore's Notes on the history of witchcraft in Massachusetts.
(Continued on next card)

8 NIC

CATALOGUE OF THE CORNELL WITCHCRAFT COLLECTION

WITCHCRAFT
BF
1576
M82
G64+
1884
3 copies

Further notes on the history of witchcraft in Massachusetts.
Goodell, Abner Cheney, 1831-1914.
Further notes on the history of witchcraft in Massachusetts, containing additional evidence of the passage of the Act of 1711, for reversing the attainders of the witches; also affirming the legality of the Special Court of Oyer and Terminer of 1692... Cambridge, J. Wilson, 1884.
52 p. facsim. 26cm.

Reprinted, with slight alterations, from the Proceedings of the Massachusetts Historical Society, June 1883.
(Continued on next card)

NIC

WITCHCRAFT
BF
1576
M82
G64+
1884

Further notes on the history of witchcraft in Massachusetts.
Goodell, Abner Cheney, 1831-1914. Further notes on the history of witchcraft... 1884. (Card 2)

Caption title of this reprint, and running title of the original article: Witch-trials in Massachusetts.
Reply to George Henry Moore's Notes on the history of witchcraft in Massachusetts.

1. Witchcraft--Massachusetts. 2. Moore, George Henry, 1823-1892. Notes on the history of witchcraft in Massachusetts. I. His Witch-trials in Massachusetts. II. Title. III. Title: Witch-trials in Massachusetts.

WITCHCRAFT
BX
2340
M54
1589

Fustis daemonum.
Menghi, Girolamo, d. 1610.
Flagellvm daemonvm. Exorcismos terribiles, potentissimos, et efficaces ... complectens ... Accessit postremò pars secunda, quae Fustis daemonum inscribitur. Quibus noui exorcismi, & alia nonnulla, quae prius desiderabantur, superaddita fuerunt. Auctore R. P. F. Hieronymo Mengo Vitellianensis ... Bononiae, Apud Ioannem Rossium, 1589.
8 p. l., 247, [16], 350, 102, [2] p. 15cm.
Title in red and black.
(Continued on next card)

WITCHCRAFT
BX
2340
M54
1589

Fustis daemonum.
Menghi, Girolamo, d. 1610. Flagellvm daemonvm ... 1589. (Card 2)

"Fvstis daemonvm" has special t. p. and separate paging.
"Remedia efficacissima in malignos spiritvs expellendos," with caption title, is appended to "Fvstis daemonvm" and has separate paging.

1. Exorcism. 2. Demonology. I. His Fustis daemonum. II. His Remedia efficacissima in malignos spiritus expellendos. III. Title: Flagellum daemonum. IV. Title: Remedia efficacissima.

WITCHCRAFT
BX
2340
M54
1727

Fustis daemonum.
Menghi, Girolamo, d. 1610.
Flagellum daemonum. Exorcismos terribiles, potentissimos, & efficaces ... complectens ... Accessit postremo pars secunda, quae Fustis daemonum inscribitur. Quibus novi exorcismi, & alia nonnulla, quae prius desiderabantur, super addita fuerunt. Auctore R. P. F. Hieronymo Mengo, Vitellianensi ... [Mediolani] 1727.
7 p. l., 309, [3], [16], 308, [1] p. 18cm.
"Fustis daemonum" has special t. p. and separate paging.
(Continued on next card)

Witchcraft
BF
1559
M54
F9

Fustis daemonum, adiurationes formidabile, potentissimas, & efficaces.
Menghi, Girolamo, d. 1610.
Fvstis daemonvm, adivrationes formidabiles, potentissimas, & efficaces in malignos spiritus fugandos de oppressis corporibus humanis. Ex sacre Apocalypsis fonte, varyque sanctorum patrum auctoritatibus haustas, complectens ... Venice, D. Maldura, 1606.
350 p. 15cm.

219

CATALOGUE OF THE CORNELL WITCHCRAFT COLLECTION

G

G., E.

Witchcraft
BF
1563
W81++
no.18

A Prodigious & tragicall history of the arraignment, tryall, confession, and condemnation of six witches at Maidstone in Kent, ... July ... 1652 ... Collected from the observations of E. G., Gent. (a learned person, present at their conviction and condemnation) and digested by H. F., Gent. To which is added a true relation of one Mrs. Atkins ... who was strangely carried away from her house in July last, and hath not been heard of since. London, Printed for R. Harper, 1652. [London, at the British Museum, 1923]
8 p. 16cm. (Continued on next card)

G., E.

Witchcraft
BF
1563
W81++
no.18

A Prodigious & tragicall history of ... six witches at Maidstone ... 1652. (Card 2)

Photocopy (negative) 8 p. on 5 l. 20 x 32cm.
No. 18 in vol. lettered: Witchcraft tracts, chapbooks and broadsides, 1579-1704; rotograph copies.

1. Witchcraft--England. I. G., E. II. F., H.

G., H. v.

Witchcraft
BF
1410
B42
Z69
no.17,
18

Den predikant D. Balthasar Becker, seediglyk ondersogt so in zyn persoon als Schriften, ofny die derst voorgeven, buyten hem alleen, de gantsche werelt betovert te zyn, selfs hier af wel vry is, ende dat daar en boven op hem niet soude werken, de geest van hovaardye en dwalinge tot ergernisse en van de kleine, en van de arme, en van de verslagene van geest, en die beeven voor Godts woort. By een missive den 19 January 1692, door H.v.G. van Amsterdam geschreven aan

NIC (Continued on next card)

G., H. v.

Witchcraft
BF
1410
B42
Z69
no.17,
18

Den predikant D. Balthasar Becker ... (Card 2)

D. T. S. de Jonge tot Uytrecht. Met zyn Andtwoord provisioneel tot nader berigt daar op gevolgt, den 4. February desselven jaars. Uytregt, Gedrukt by W. Jansz, 1692.
32, 36 p. 21cm.
Signatures: 4°: A-D⁴. 4°: A-D⁴, E2.
The Pro visioneel Antwoord has special half-title and separate
NIC (Continued on next card)

G., H. v.

Witchcraft
BF
1410
B42
Z69
no.17,
18

Den predikant D. Balthasar Becker ... 1692. (Card 3)

paging. Van der Linde 63, 61.
"Extracten van ... De betoverde werelt, uytgetrokken en t'samengestelt door N. N.": p. 17-28 of the Provisioneel Antwoord; "Extract van 'tgepasseerde des Synodi tot Edam, 10. Aug. 1691. rakende D. Bekker ...": p. 28-29; "Articu len voor te stellen aan Do. B. Bekker" signed Leonardus

NIC (Continued on next card)

G., H. v.

Witchcraft
BF
1410
B42
Z69
No.17,
18

Den predikant D. Balthasar Becker ... 1692. (Card 4)

Groenewegen: p. 29-31; "Eerste aanbieding van D. B. Bekker, op den 30. Aug. 1691": p. 31; "Articulen tot satisfactie aan de Eerw. Classis van Amsterdam, van Do. Balthasar Bekker ... wegens ... de Betoverde wereld ...": p. 32-36.
Nos. 17 & 18 in a Collection of tracts against Balthasar Bekker and his Betoverde weereld.
NIC (Continued on next card)

G., M.

Witchcraft
PQ
1957
B67
A64
1793

Bordelon, Laurent, 1653-1730.
Histoire de M. Oufle, par abbé Bordelon [retouchée et réduite par M. G.] et la Description du sabbat. Paris, Gay & Gide, 1793.
360 p. 20cm.

"...C'est ... un nouveau roman, mais ... nous sommes redevables néanmoins à l'abbé Bordelon ...": p. 5-6.
"Description du sabbat" is not by Bordelon.

G., M.

Witchcraft
BX
9479
B42
B11
no.3

Do. [i. e., doctor] B. Bekkers Sterf-bedde verdeedigt, tegens de zoo genaamde Nodige aanmerkingen over het zelve: vervat in een brief aan den schryver; behelzende een openbaar bewijs zijner onkunde in de geschillen, en verdere ongegronde redeneeringen: tot wegschuiminge van zijn alderhaatelijkste beschryving en veroordeeling van den overledene. Door M. G. Amsterdam, By R. Blokland, boekverkooper, 1699.
1 p. l., 16 p. title and end
8 (Continued on next card)

G., M.

Witchcraft
BX
9479
B42
B11
no.3

Do. [i. e., doctor] B. Bekkers Sterf-bedde verdeedigt ... 1699. (Card 2)

page vignettes, illus. initial. 20 x 16 cm.
4°: π1, A-B⁴.
Van der Linde 207.
No. 3 in vol. lettered B. Bekkers sterf-bed en andere tractaten.
1. Bekker, Balthasar, 1634-1698. 2. Bekker, Johannes Henricus, fl. 1698-1737. Sterf-bedde van ... Do. Balthazar Bekker.
8 (Continued on next card)

G., R.

Witchcraft
BF
1546
G48

[Gilpin, Richard]
Daemonologia sacra: or, A treatise of Satans temptations ... By R. G. ... London, Printed by J. D. for R. Randel and P. Maplisden, 1677.
3 pts. in 1 v. 20cm.

1. Devil. I. Title. II. Title: Satans temptations. III. G., R. IV. R. G.

G., R., M. D.

WITCHCRAFT
BF
1405
L85
1673

Longinus, Caesar, ed.
Trinum magicum, sive Secretorum magicorum opus ... Editum à Caesare Longino philos. Francofurti, Sumptibus Jacobi Gothofredi Seyleri, 1673.
12 p. l., 498 p. 14cm.
Contents.--Marci Antonii Zimarae Tractatus magicus.--Appendix, De mirandis quibusdam naturali magia factis operationibus. Ex lib. 2. Mag. nat. Ioan. Bapt. Port.--Tractatvs De virtutibus quarundam herbarum,
8 (Continued on next card)

G., R., M. D.

WITCHCRAFT
BF
1405
L85
1673

Longinus, Caesar, ed. Trinum magicum ... 1673. (Card 2)

lapidum & animalium. A. M. A.--Commentatio De magnetica curatione vulnerum citra svperstitionem ... Authore R. G. M. D.--Logia, sive Oracvla Zoroastri ex Platonicorum libris collecta.--Tractatus De proprii cujusqve nati daemonis inqvisitione.
Layout of text corresponds to that of Frankfurt, 1630 ed. (C. Eifrid, printer)
8 (Continued on next card)

G. F.

Witchcraft
BV
4617
B6
F79

[Fox, George] 1624-1691.
A declaration of the ground of error & errors, blasphemy, blasphemers, and blasphemies: and the ground of inchantings and seducing spirits and the doctrine of devils, the sons of sorcerers and the seed of the adulterer, and the ground of nicromancy, which doth defile witches and wizards ... By G. F. London, Printed for G. Calvert, 1657.
41 p. 18cm.

I. F., G. II. G. F. III. Title.

G. R., M. A.

WITCHCRAFT
BF
1581
Z7
1712f

The Belief of witchcraft vindicated: proving, from Scripture, there have been witches; and, from reason, that there may be such still. In answer to a late pamphlet, intituled, The impossibility of witchcraft: plainly proving, from Scripture and reason, that there never was a witch, &c. By G. R., A.M. London, Printed for J. Baker, 1712.
40 p. 19cm.
Sometimes attributed to F. Bragge.
8 (Continued on next card)

220

Gaar, Georg

Witchcraft / F 583 / 7 / 749
Gaar, Georg, b. 1702.
Christliche Anred nächst dem Scheiter-Hauffen, worauf der Leichnam Mariae Renatae, einer durchs Schwerdt hingerichteten Zauberin, den 21. junii anno 1749 ausser der Stadt Wirtzburg verbrennet worden, an ein zahlreich-versammletes Volck gethan, und hernach aus gnädigstem Befehl einer Hohen Obrigkeit in offentlichen Druck gegeben. [Würzburg] M. A. Engmann [1749?]
[12] p. 21cm.

(Continued on next card)

MSS Bd. WITCHCRAFT BF G12
Gaar, Georg, b. 1702.
Heylsame Lehr-Stück, und Zauberey betreffende Anmerckungen in der christlichen, nach Hinrichtung Mariae Renatae einer Zauberin, gehaltenen Anred, einiger Massen zwar angeregt, hernach aber ausführlicher erläutert ... An jetzo mit einem Zusatz vermehrt ... Wirtzburg, Marco Antonio Engman, 1750 [ca. 1900]
38 p. 22cm.
Carnap's manuscript copy.
"Originaldruck in der Kgl. Universitätsbiblio thek zu Würzburg,
(Continued on next card)

Witchcraft / BF 1583 / Z7 / 1749a
Gaar, Georg, b. 1702.
Ragionamento del padre Giorgio Gaar, della Compagnia di Gesu', fatto avanti al rogo di Maria Renata, strega abbruciata in Erbipoli a' 21. di Giugno del corrente anno 1749. Tradotto del Tedesco nell' Italiano dal Dr. F. A. T. [Girolamo Tartarotti] Con alcune annotazioni critiche. Verona, Per D. Ramanzini [1749]
23 p. 24cm.

(Continued on next card)

Witchcraft / F 583 / 7 / 1749
Gaar, Georg, b. 1702. Christliche Anred nächst dem Scheiter-Hauffen ... [1749]   (Card 2)

1. Witchcraft--Germany. 2. Sänger, Maria Renata von Mossau, ca. 1680-1749.
I. Title.

MSS Bd. WITCHCRAFT BF G12
Gaar, Georg, b. 1702. Heylsame Lehr-Stück ... 1750 [ca. 1900]   (Card 2)
44 S. in 4°."
Numerals in margins indicate pagination of the original.
In part a rebuttal of: Johann Christian Rinder. Eine Hexe nach ihrer gresslichen Gestalt und gerechter Strafe.
Provoked in answer: Johann Christian Rinder. Kurtze doch nachdrückliche Abfertigung an den ... Herrn Georg Gaar.
(Continued on next card)

Witchcraft / BF 1583 / Z7 / 1749a
Gaar, Georg, b. 1702. Ragionamento del padre Giorgio Gaar ... [1749]   (Card 2)

1. Witchcraft--Germany. 2. Sänger, Maria Renata von Mossau, ca. 1680-1749. I. Tartarotti, Girolamo, 1706-1761. II. Title. III. His ChristlicheAnred nächst dem Scheiter-Hauffen--Italian.

Witchcraft / F 583 / 7 / 749b
Gaar, Georg, b. 1702.
Christliche Anred nächst dem Scheiter-Hauffen.
Anna Renata Singer v. Mossau, die letzte deutsche Hexe. Ein Geschichtsbild, dargestellt zur Erinnerung an den nunmehr hundertjährigen Niedergang eines langen und grauenvollen Irrwahns und an die Befreiung von der Schmach wälscher Inquisition in Deutschland. Nebst einem Abriss der Geschichte der Hexenprocesse im Allgemeinen und beiliegenden Actenstücken sowie einem sächsischen Hexenprocesse aus dem siebzehnten Jahrhun-
(Continued on next card)

MSS Bd. WITCHCRAFT BF G12
Gaar, Georg, b. 1702. Heylsame Lehr-Stück ... 1750 [ca. 1900]   (Card 3)

1. Witchcraft--Germany. 2. Witchcraft--Sermons. 3. Rinder, Johann Christian. Eine Hexe nach ihrer gresslichen Gestalt und gerechter Strafe. I. Rinder, Johann Christian. Kurtze doch nachdrückliche Abfertigung an den ... Herrn Georg Gaar. II. Title.

Witchcraft / BF 1565 / T19 / B71
Gaar, Georg, b. 1702.
Ragionamento ... fatto avanti al rogo di Maria Renata.
[Bonelli, Benedetto] 1704-1783.
Animavversioni critiche sopra il Notturno congresso delle lammie, per modo di lettera indiritte ad un letterato. S'aggiugne il discorso del P. Gaar sulla strega d'Erbipoli, la Risposta dello stesso alle note, il Ragguaglio sulla strega di Salisburgo, e il Compendio storico della stregheria. Venezia, Presso Simone Occhi, 1751.
6 p. l., 188 p. 25cm.
8
(Continued on next card)

Witchcraft / F 583 / 7 / 749b
Gaar, Georg, b. 1702.
Christliche Anred nächst dem Scheiter-Hauffen.
Anna Renata Singer v. Mossau ... 1849.   (Card 2)

dert. [Leipzig, Bei F. Serig] 1849.
142 p. 22cm.
"Kurzer Abriss der Geschichte des Hexentums" and the four Beilagen each have special t. p.
Includes Rede am Scheiterhaufen, von G. Gaar, and Ein sächsischer Hexenprozess, von G. A. Siebdrat.
(Continued on next card)

MSS Bd. WITCHCRAFT BF G12 R57
Gaar, Georg, b. 1702.
Heylsame Lehrstück, und Zauberey betreffende Anmerckungen.
Rinder, Johann Christian.
Johann Christian Rinders ... Kurtze doch nachdrückliche Abfertigung an den würtzburgischen Pater Herrn Georg Gaar, Lojoliten, der ihn in einer öffentlichen und nun zum Druck gegebenen Canzelrede ... so gar mit Namen um der Wahrheit willen herum genommen, statt einer Franckfurter Messe dafür bey Gelegenheit derselben wie schuldig, übermacht. Jena, In der Cröckerischen Buchhandlung, 1750 [ca. 1900]
24 l. 23cm.
(Continued on next card)

Witchcraft / BF 1565 / T19 / B71
Gaar, Georg, b. 1702.
Ragionamento ... fatto avanti al rogo di Maria Renata.
[Bonelli, Benedetto] 1704-1783. Animavversioni critiche ... 1751.   (Card 2)
Attributed to Bonelli by Melzi.
Each of the added items has special t. p. except the last, which has caption title.
1. Tartarotti, Girolamo, 1706-1761. Del congresso notturno delle lammie. 2. Witchcraft. I. Title. II. Gaar, Georg, b. 1702. Ragionamento ... fatto avanti al rogo di Maria Renata.
8

Witchcraft / BF 1583 / Z7 / 1749a
Gaar, Georg, b. 1702.
Christliche Anred nächst dem Scheiter-Hauffen--Italian.
Gaar, Georg, b. 1702.
Ragionamento del padre Giorgio Gaar, della Compagnia di Gesu', fatto avanti al rogo di Maria Renata, strega abbruciata in Erbipoli a' 21. di Giugno del corrente anno 1749. Tradotto del Tedesco nell' Italiano dal Dr. F. A. T. [Girolamo Tartarotti] Con alcune annotazioni critiche. Verona, Per D. Ramanzini [1749]
23 p. 24cm.

(Continued on next card)

MSS Bd. WITCHCRAFT BF G12 R57
Gaar, Georg, b. 1702.
Heylsame Lehrstück, und Zauberey betreffende Anmerckungen.
Rinder, Johann Christian. ...Kurtze doch nachdrückliche Abfertigung ... 1750 [ca. 1900]   (Card 2)
Carnap's manuscript copy.
"Originaldruck in der Kgl. Hof u. Staats-Bibliothek zu München. 46 S. in 4°."
Numerals in the margins indicate pagination of the original.
A defense of his Eine Hexe nach ihrer gresslichen Gestalt und gerechter Strafe.
1. Witchcraft--Germany. 2. Gaar, Georg, b. 1702. Heylsame Lehrstück, und Zauberey betreffende Anmerckungen.
(Continued on next card)

Witchcraft / BF 1565 / G12
Gaar, Georg, b. 1702.
Ragionamento... fatto avanti al rogo di Maria Renata.
Gaar, Georg, b. 1702.
Responsa ad annotationes criticas D. F. A. T. [i.e. Girolamo Tartarotti] in sermonem de Maria Renata, saga supplicio addicta die 21. Junii Anno 1749. Herbipoli habitum, Veronae typis evulgatas, in lucem edita ab authore ejusdem sermonis P. Georgio Gaar, S.J. ... Wirceburgi, Typis M. A. Engman [1750?]
55 p. 20cm.
8
(Continued on next card)

CATALOGUE OF THE CORNELL WITCHCRAFT COLLECTION

Witchcraft
BF
1565
G12
Gaar, Georg, b. 1702.
    Ragionamento... fatto avanti al rogo di Maria Renata.
    Gaar, Georg, b. 1702. Responsa ad annotationes criticas D. F. A. T. in sermonem de Maria Renata ... [1750] (Card 2)

    His Ragionamento del padre Giorgio Gaar, p. [37]-55, has special t. p., facsimile of the Verona edition. This text includes Tartarotti's commentary.
    1. Tartarotti, Girolamo, 1706-1761. 2. His Ragionamento. 3. Witchcraft. 4. Sänger, Maria Renata von Mossau, ca. 1680-1749. I. His Ragionamento. II. Title.

8

Witchcraft
BF
1565
G12
Gaar, Georg, b. 1702.
    Ragionamento... fatto avanti al rogo di Maria Renata.
    Gaar, Georg, b. 1702.
    Responsa ad annotationes criticas D. F. A. T. [i.e. Girolamo Tartarotti] in sermonem de Maria Renata, saga supplicio addicta die 21. Junii Anno 1749. Herbipoli habitum, Veronae typis evulgatas, in lucem edita ab authore ejusdem sermonis P. Georgio Gaar, S.J. ... Wirceburgi, Typis M. A. Engman [1750?]
    55 p. 20cm.

8   (Continued on next card)

Witchcraft
BF
1565
G12
Gaar, Georg, b. 1702.
    Ragionamento... fatto avanti al rogo di Maria Renata.
    Gaar, Georg, b. 1702. Responsa ad annotationes criticas D. F. A. T. in sermonem de Maria Renata ... [1750] (Card 2)

    His Ragionamento del padre Giorgio Gaar, p. [37]-55, has special t. p., facsimile of the Verona edition. This text includes Tartarotti's commentary.
    1. Tartarotti, Girolamo, 1706-1761. 2. His Ragionamento. 3. Witchcraft. 4. Sänger, Maria Renata von Mossau, ca. 1680-1749. I. His Ragionamento. II. Title.

8

Witchcraft
BF
1565
G12
Gaar, Georg, b. 1702. Responsa ad annotationes criticas D. F. A. T. [i.e. Girolamo Tartarotti] in sermonem de Maria Renata, saga supplicio addicta die 21. Junii Anno 1749. Herbipoli habitum, Veronae typis evulgatas, in lucem edita ab authore ejusdem sermonis P. Georgio Gaar, S.J. ... Wirceburgi, Typis M. A. Engman [1750?]
    55 p. 20cm.

8   (Continued on next card)

Witchcraft
BF
1565
G12
Gaar, Georg, b. 1702. Responsa ad annotationes criticas D. F. A. T. in sermonem de Maria Renata ... [1750] (Card 2)

    His Ragionamento del padre Giorgio Gaar, p. [37]-55, has special t. p., facsimile of the Verona edition. This text includes Tartarotti's commentary.
    1. Tartarotti, Girolamo, 1706-1761. 2. His Ragionamento. 3. Witchcraft. 4. Sänger, Maria Renata von Mossau, ca. 1680-1749. I. His Ragionamento. II. Title.

8

Gablidone.
WITCHCRAFT
BF
1557
L39
    Lavater, Johann Caspar, 1741-1801.
    Protokoll über den Spiritus Familiaris Gablidone. Mit Beylagen und einem Kupfer. Frankfurth und Leipzig, 1787.
    84 p. plate. 19cm.

8
NIC   1. Spirits. 2. Demonology. 3. Talismans. I. Title. II. Title: Gablidone.

Gadelius, Bror, 1862-
    see
Gadelius, Bror Edvard, 1862-

Witchcraft
BF
1775
G12
Gadelius, Bror Edvard, 1862-
    Tro och öfvertro i gångna tider, af Bror Gadelius. Stockholm, H. Geber [1912-13]
    2 v. illus. 23cm.

    1. Superstition. 2. Occult sciences. 3. Folk-lore. I. Title.

8

Witchcraft
BV
4935
G66
G12
Gätschenberger, Stephan.
    Zwei Klostergeschichten des vorigen Jahrhunderts. Zum erstenmale nach den Inquisitions-Akten bearbeitet ... Leipzig, C. F. Fleischer, 1858.
    124 p. 18cm.
    Contents.--1. Graf James Gordon oder Pater Marianus.--2. Die letzte Hexe in Deutschland.
    1. Gordon, James, 1704-1734. 2. Conversion. 3. Sänger, Maria Renata von Mossau, ca. 1680-1749. 4. Witchcraft. 5. Martyrs. I. Title.

8

Witchcraft
PA
4220
A4++
1678
Gale, Thomas, 1635?-1702, ed.
    Jamblichus, of Chalcis.
    [De mysteriis. Greek & Latin]
    Ἰαμβλίχου Χαλκιδέως τῆς κοίλης Συρίας περὶ μυστηρίων λόγος. Iamblichi Chalcidensis ex Coele-Syria, de mysteriis liber. Præmittitur epistola Porphyrii ad Anebonem Ægyptium, eodem argumento. Thomas Gale Anglus græce nunc primum edidit, latine vertit, & notas adjecit. Oxonii, e theatro Sheldoniano, 1678.
    20 p. l., 316, [6] p., 1 l. 32cm.
    Title vignette.
    Greek and Latin in parallel columns.
    1. Mysteries, Religious. I. Porphyrius. II. Gale, Thomas, 1635?-1702, ed.   Title transliterated: Peri mysteriōn logos.

Library of Congress   [2]

Gallerie der neuen Propheten.
Witchcraft
BF
1410
A23
    [Adelung, Johann Christoph] 1732-1806.
    Geschichte der menschlichen Narrheit; oder, Lebensbeschreibungen berühmter Schwarzkünstler, Goldmacher, Teufelsbanner, Zeichen- und Liniendeuter, Schwärmer, Wahrsager, und anderer philosophischer Unholden. Leipzig, Weygand, 1785-89.
    7 v. in 3. 18cm.
    Title vignette.

8   (Continued on next card)

Gallerie der neuen Propheten.
Witchcraft
BF
1410
A23
    [Adelung, Johann Christoph] 1732-1806.
    Geschichte der menschlichen Narrheit ... 1785-89. (Card 2)

Witchcraft
BF
1410
A23
Suppl.
    ---Gallerie der neuen Propheten, apokalyptischen Träumer, Geisterseher und Revolutionsprediger. Ein Beytrag zur Geschichte der menschlichen Narrheit. Leipzig, Weygand, 1799.
    3 p. l., 487, [3] p. 20cm.

8   (Continued on next card)

Gallerie der Teufel.
Witchcraft
BF
1523
C89
    [Cranz, August Friedrich] 1737-1801.
    Gallerie der Teufel, bestehend in einer auserlesenen Sammlung von Gemählden moralisch politischer Figuren, deren Originale zwischen Himmel und Erden anzutreffen sind, nebst einigen bewährten Recepten gegen die Anfechtungen der bösen Geister, von Pater Gassnern dem Jüngern [pseud] nach Art periodischer Schriften stückweise hrsg. Frankfurt, 1777-78.
    5 v. in 1. 18cm.
    1. Devil. I. Title.

Die Gallerinn auf der Rieggersburg.
Witchcraft
PT
2290
H35
G2
1845
    [Hammer-Purgstall, Joseph, Freiherr von] 1774-1856.
    Die Gallerinn auf der Rieggersburg. Historischer Roman mit Urkunden. Von einem Steiermärker. Darmstadt, Carl Wilhelm Leske, 1845.
    3 v. fronts. 22cm.

    Contents.--1. T. Die Jungfrau und das Erbfräulein.--2. T. Die Huldigung und die Verschwörung.--3. T. Der Hexenprozess.
    I. Title.

BF
1622
18
G19
Ganci Battaglia, Giuseppe.
    Streghe, stregoni e stregonerie di Sicilia. Superstizione e magia, i misteri del mondo occulto, le avventure diaboliche del conte Cagliostro e della Vecchia dell'aceto. Palermo, D. Malato, [1972]
    218 p. plates. 21cm.
    Bibliography: p. 211-[219]

    1. Magic--Sicily. 2. Witchcraft--Sicily. I. Title

NIC   FEB 28, '74   COOxc   73-321911

Gansch desperaate en verlooren saake van D. Balthasar Bekker.
Witchcraft
BX
9479
B42
B11
no.18
    Andala, Ruardus, 1665-1727.
    Gansch desperaate en verlooren saake van D. Balthasar Bekker, getoont uit de nasnikken en genoegsaame bekentenisse van onmagt en verleegentheid van sijn voesterling ... Tot een volstrekt bewijs, dat D. Bekker deese schrijver aftedanken, en een beter, in de geestkunde bet geoefent, aan 't werk te stellen, of selve de hand aan de ploeg te slaan, of sijn sake ten besten te geven, genootsaakt is.   Franeker, Gedrukt by

3   (Continued on next card)

Gansch desperaate en verlooren saake van D. Balthasar Bekker.
Witchcraft
BX
9479
B42
B11
no.18
    Andala, Ruardus, 1665-1727. Gansch desperaate en verlooren saake.... 1698. (Card 2)

    H. Gyzelaar, ordinaris drukker der Eed. Mog. Heeren Staten, en der Academie van Friesland, 1698.
    35 p. [p. 36 blank] title and other vignettes, illus. initials. 20 x 15cm.
    4°: A-D⁴, E².
    Apparently   refers to a work titled

3   (Continued on next card)

Gansch desperaate en verlooren saake van D. Balthasar Bekker.
Witchcraft
BX
9479
B42
B11
no.18
    Andala, Ruardus, 1665-1727. Gansch desperaate en verlooren saake ... 1698. (Card 3)

    Den professor J. van der Waeyen, ongelukkig en scandaleus verdeedigt van twee predikanten, voormaals zijne discipulen, pub. 1697. No. 18 in vol. lettered B. Bekkers sterfbed en andere tractaten.
    1. Den Professor J. van der Waeyen, ongelukkig en scandaleus verdeedigt van tweus predikanten. 2. Bekker, Balthasar, 1634-1698. De beto   verde weereld. 3. Devil. I. Title.

8

CATALOGUE OF THE CORNELL WITCHCRAFT COLLECTION

Witchcraft
BF
1565
S83
G19
 [Ganser, Benno] 1728-1779?
  Sendschreiben an einen gelehrten Freund betreffend die heutige Streitschriften von der Hexerey. Vom Donau-Strohm [1767?]
  [12] p. 20cm.
  Attribution by Holzmann and British Museum (the latter gives Christian name as Brenno), Fieger, in his P. Don Ferdinand Sterzinger, p. 136, gives the name as B. Janser: a misprint?
  1. Sterzinger, Ferdinand, 1721-1786. 2. Witchcraft. I. Title. II. Janser, B , supposed author.

 Gaquère, François, 1888-
  Aux prises avec Satan.

Gaquère, François, 1888-
 Les possédés d'Illfurth, de Natal et de Phat-Diem (1868-1906-1925) Genval, Éditions "Marie-Mediatrice" [1956]
 125 p. illus. 18cm.
 At head of title: P. Sutter [et] François Gaquère. Aux prises avec Satan.
 Although Sutter's name appears first (left top of the t.p.) the work is presumably chiefly (or only) by Gaquère. Cf. "Avant-propos" and cover.
 1. Demoniac possession. I. His Aux prises avec Satan. II. Sutter, P III. Title. IV. Title: Aux prises avec Satan.

Gaquère, François, 1888-
 Les possédés d'Illfurth, de Natal et de Phat-Diem (1868-1906-1925) Genval, Éditions "Marie-Mediatrice" [1956]
 125 p. illus. 18cm.
 At head of title: P. Sutter [et] François Gaquère. Aux prises avec Satan.
 Although Sutter's name appears first (left top of the t.p.) the work is presumably chiefly (or only) by Gaquère. Cf. "Avant-propos" and cover.
 1. Demoniac possession. I. His Aux prises avec Satan. II. Sutter, P III. Title. IV. Title: Aux prises avec Satan.

Garcia de Rodriguez de Gutierrez, Maria, b. 1564.
 Erschröckliche doch warhaffte Geschicht, die sich in der spanischen Statt, Madrileschos genannt, mit einer verheuraten Weibss-person zugetragen, welche von einer gantzen Legion Teuffel siben Jar lang besessen gewest. Und durch Patrem Ludovicum de Torre ... widerumb erlediget worden. München, Durch Nicolaum Henricum, 1608 [ca. 1900]
 11 l. illus. 24cm.
 Carnap's manuscript copy.
  (Continued on next card)

Garcia de Rodriguez de Gutierrez, Maria, b. 1564.
 Erschröckliche doch warhaffte Geschicht, die sich in der spanischen Statt ... zugetragen ... 1608 [ca. 1900] (Card 2)
 "Originaldruck in der Kgl. u. Staats Bibliothek zu München. 8° Bl. in 4°. Sig. A²-B³."
 Numerals in the margins indicate pagination of the original.
 May have been written by De Torre himself.
 1. Demoniac possession. 2. Exorcism. 3. Witchcraft--Spain. 4. Garcia de Rodriguez de Gutierrez, Maria, b. 1564. I. Torre, Luis de, d. 1635, supposed author.

Witchcraft
BT
980
G21
1929
 Garçon, Maurice.
  The devil; an historical, critical and medical study. London, V. Gollancz, 1929.
  288 p. 22cm.
  At head of title: Maurice Garçon & Jean Vinchon, translated by Stephen Haden Guest from the sixth French edition.
  1. Devil. 2. Demonomania. 3. Demonology. I. Vinchon, Jean, 1884- joint author. II. Garçon, Maurice. Le diable.--English. III. Title.

Witchcraft
BT
980
G21
1926
 Garçon, Maurice.
  Le diable; étude historique, critique et médicale. 5. éd. Paris, Gallimard, 1926.
  251 p. 19cm. (Les Documents bleus. N° 26)
  At head of title: Maurice Garçon et Jean Vinchon.

Witchcraft
BT
980
G21
1929
 Garçon, Maurice. Le diable--English.
 Garçon, Maurice.
  The devil; an historical, critical and medical study. London, V. Gollancz, 1929.
  288 p. 22cm.
  At head of title: Maurice Garçon & Jean Vinchon, translated by Stephen Haden Guest from the sixth French edition.
  1. Devil. 2. Demonomania. 3. Demonology. I. Vinchon, Jean, 1884- joint author. II. Garçon, Maurice. Le diable.--English. III. Title.

Witchcraft
PQ
2613
A44
V6
1926
 Garçon, Maurice, 1899-
  ... La vie exécrable de Guillemette Babin, sorcière. Paris, H. Piazza [1926]
  viii, 151, [1] p., 2 l. plates. 21ᶜᵐ.
  "Exemplaire n° 220."

  I. Title.
 Library of Congress PQ2613.A44V5 1926
 Copyright A—Foreign 31061
  26-17655
  [2]

Rare
PQ
6437
T7A4
1618
 The garden of curious flowers.
 Torquemada, Antonio de, fl. 1553-1570.
  The Spanish Mandevile of myracles. Or The garden of curious flowers. Wherein are handled sundry points of humanity, philosophy, diuinity, and geography, beautified with many strange and pleasant histories: first written in Spanish by Anthonio de Torquemada, and translated out of that tongue into English. It is diuided into sixe treatises, composed in the manner of a dialogue ... London, Imprinted by Bernard Alsop, by the assigne of Richard Hawkins, 1618.
  (Continued on next card)

Rare
PQ
6437
T7A4
1618
 The garden of curious flowers.
 Torquemada, Antonio de, fl. 1553-1570. The Spanish Mandevile of myracles ... 1618.
  (Card 2)
 [6], 325, [3] p. 20cm.
 Translated by Lewis Lewkenor although the translation is usually attributed to Ferdinand Walker who published it.
 Translation of Jardin de flores curiosas.
 I. Lewkenor, Sir Lewis, tr. II. Walker, Ferdinand, fl. 1600, supposed tr. III. His Jardin de flores curiosas--English. IV. Title. V. Title: The garden of curious flowers.

Witchcraft
BF
1566
B79
 Gardner, Gerald Brosseau, 1884-
 Bracelin, Jack L
  Gerald Gardner: witch. [London] Octagon Press [1960]
  224 p. illus. 22 cm.

 1. Gardner, Gerald Brosseau, 1884- 2. Witchcraft. I. Title.
 BF1566.B7 920.91334 61-34293
 Library of Congress

Witchcraft
BF
1622
F7
G23
 Garinet, Jules, 1797-1877.
  Histoire de la magie en France depuis le commencement de la monarchie jusqu'a nos jours. Paris, Foulon, 1818.
  liii,363 p. front. 21cm.

  I. Title.

BF
1622
F7
G23
1965
 Garinet, Jules, 1797-1877.
  Histoire de la magie en France. Texte revu et présenté par Roland Villeneuve. Paris, Livre club du libraire, 1965.
  260 p. plates. 20 cm. 32 F. (F 66-340)

 1. Magic—France. I. Villeneuve, Roland, 1922- ed. II. Title.
 BF1622.F7G3 133.40944 66-72041
 Library of Congress [5]

BF
1622
F7
G232
1970
 Garinet, Jules, 1797-1877.
  La Sorcellerie en France, histoire de la magie jusqu'au XIXᵉ siècle. Paris, F. Beauval [1970].
  254 p. illus. plates (part col.) 20 cm. 9.90F F 72-7280
  Includes bibliographical references.

 1. Magic—France. 2. Demonology—History. I. Title.
 4
 NIC BF1622.F7G33 1970 72-357231
 Library of Congress 72 [2]

Witchcraft
PQ
1957
B67
A64
1793
 Garnier, Charles Georges Thomas, 1746-1795, ed.
 Bordelon, Laurent, 1653-1730.
  Histoire de M. Oufle, par abbé Bordelon [retouchée et réduite par M. G.] et la Description du sabbat. Paris, Gay & Gide, 1793.
  360 p. 20cm.
  "...C'est ... un nouveau roman, mais ... nous sommes redevables néamoins à l'abbé Bordelon ...": p. 5-6.
  "Description du sabbat" is not by Bordelon.

Witchcraft
BF
1517
F5
G23
 Garnier, Samuel.
  Barbe Buvée, en religion soeur Sainte-Colombe, et la prétendue possession des ursulines d'Auxonne (1658-1663) Étude historique et médicale d'après des manuscrits de la Bibliothèque nationale et des archives de l'ancienne province de Bourgogne. Préface de M. le Dr. Bourneville. Paris, F. Alcan, 1895.
  93 p. 23cm. (Bibliothèque diabolique. (Collection Bourneville))
  1. Auxonne, France. Ursuline convent. I. Title.

Witchcraft
AC
41
G24
1617
 Garzoni, Tommaso, 1549?-1589.
  Opere. Nvovamente in qvesta nostra impressione con somma diligenza ristampate, & da molti errori espurgate ... Venetia, Presso Giorgio Valentini, et Antonio Giuliani, 1613-17 (v.[5], 1613)
  5 v. in 2. 23cm.
  Title vignettes (printers' device)
  Vol. [5] has imprint: Venetia, Appresso Ambrosio, et Bartolomeo Dei, Fratelli, 1613.
  Vols. [2]-[5] have special title pages only. (Continued on next card)

CATALOGUE OF THE CORNELL WITCHCRAFT COLLECTION

Witchcraft
AC 41 G24 1617
Garzoni, Tommaso, 1549?-1589. Opere ... 1613-17 (v.[5], 1613]) (Card 2)
Edited by Bartolomeo Garzoni.
Contents.--[1] La piazza vniuersale di tutte le professioni del mondo.--[2] La sinagoga degl'ignoranti.--[3] Il theatro dei varii, & diuersi ceruelli mondani.--[4] L'hospidale de'pazzi incurabili.--[5] Il serraglio de gli stupori del mondo.

Witchcraft
PR 4712 G14 W8 1830
Gaspey, Thomas, 1788-1871.
The witch-finder; or, The wisdom of our ancestors. London, H. Lea [183-?]

I. Title. II. Title: The wisdom of our ancestors.

Gassner, der Jüngere, Pater, pseud.
see
Cranz, August Friedrich, 1737-1801.

Witchcraft
BF 583 G24
Gaspers, Josef.
Hexenglaube und Hexenwahn in Erkelenz. Erkelenz, im Selbstverlag des Vereins. Kommissionsverlag: J. Herle, 1921.
17 p. fold. pl. 19cm. (Erkelenzer Geschichts- und Altertumsverein. Heft 3)

1. Witchcraft--Erkelenz, Germany. I. Title.

Gassner, Johann Joseph

Witchcraft
BF 1559 G25
Gassner, Johann Joseph, 1727-1779.
Joseph Gassners ... Antwort auf die Anmerkungen, welche in dem Münchnerischen Intelligenzblat vom 12. Nov. wider seine Gründe und Weise zu exorciren, wie auch von der deutschen Chronik, und andern Zeitungsschreibern gemacht worden. Augsburg, Bey J. Wolff, 1774.
48 p. 16cm. (bound in 19cm. vol.)
With this is bound Gründlicher Beweiss ... von einem Vertheidiger der Wahrheit ... Augsburg, 1775.
8 (Continued on next card)

Witchcraft
BF 1559 G25
Gassner, Johann Joseph, 1727-1779. Joseph Gassners ... Antwort auf die Anmerkungen, welche in dem Münchnerischen Intelligenzblat ... gemacht worden ... 1774. (Card 2)

1. Exorcism. 2. Medicine, Magic, mystic, and spagiric. I. Title: Antwort auf die Anmerkungen, welche in dem Münchnerischen Intelligenzblat . gemacht worden. II. Title.
8

Witchcraft
BF 1559 G25 W4 1775
Gassner, Johann Joseph, 1727-1779.
Weise fromm und gesund zu leben, auch ruhig und gottseelig zu sterben: oder, Nützlicher Unterricht wider den Teufel zu streiten: durch Beantwortung der Fragen: 1. Kann der Teufel dem Leibe der Menschen schaden? II. Welchen am mehresten? III. Wie ist zu helfen? 8. verb. Aufl. und vermehrt von Herrn Verfasser selbsten. Augsburg gedruckt, zu finden bey J. G. Bullman, 1775.
40 p. front. 17cm.
1. Exorcism. I. Title. II. Title: Nützlicher Unterricht wider den Teufel zu streiten.

Gassner, Johann Joseph, 1727-1779, supposed author.
Witchcraft
BF 1559 G25 Z63 no.2
Unterricht für diejenigen, welche in ihren körperlichen Anliegenheiten, bey dem hochwürdigen Herrn Johann Joseph Gassner ... entweder Hülfe zu suchen gedenken, oder selbe schon gesucht, und gefunden haben. Als eine Fortsetzung des gründlichen Beweiss &c. von einem Vertheidiger der Wahrheit und aufrichtigem Menschenfreunde in öffentlichen Druck gegeben. Augsburg, Bey J. Wolff, 1775.
96 p. 17cm.
8 (Continued on next card)

Gassner, Johann Joseph, 1727-1779, supposed author.
Witchcraft
BF 1559 G25 Z63 no.2
Unterricht für diejenigen, welche ... Hülfe zu suchen gedenken ... 1775. (Card 2)
Attributed by British Museum to Gassner.
No. 2 in vol. lettered Gassneriana.

1. Faith-cure. 2. Exorcism. I. Gassner, Johann Joseph, 1727-1779, supposed author. II. Gründlicher Beweiss ... von einem Vertheidiger der Wahrheit und aufrichtigem Menschenfreunde.
8

Gassner, Johann Joseph, 1727-1779, supposed author.
Witchcraft
BF 1559 G25 Z92 1796
Das Vorurtheil, Glaub, und Unglaub, bey denen Gassnerischen Kuren, oder, Etwas für diejenigen, die keinen Teufel glauben. Nebst einem Verzeichniss von denen pro und contra herausgekommenen Schriften. [n. p.] 1796.
77 p. 18cm.
British Museum, whose edition has imprint Sulzbach, 1775, attributes work to Gassner.
1. Gassner, Johann Joseph, 1727-1779. 2. Exorcism. I. Gassner, Johann Joseph, 1727-1779, supposed author.
8

Gassner, Johann Joseph, 1727-1779.
Witchcraft
BF 1559 G25 Z63 no.6
Eines redlichen Protestantens aufrichtige Erinnerung an den Verfasser des Exorcisten in seiner Blösse, den Prager Hirtenbrief betreffend. Frankfurt und Leipzig, 1776.
45 p. 17cm.
No. 6 in vol. lettered Gassneriana.
1. Gassner, Johann Joseph, 1727-1779. 2. Přichovský, Antonín Peter, Abp. of Prag 1707-1793. Hirtenbrief ... 1775. 3. Der Exorcist in seiner Blösse. I. Ein redlicher Protestant.
8

Gassner, Johann Joseph, 1727-1779.
Witchcraft
BF 1523 E35
Einzinger von Einzing, Johann Martin Maximilian, 1725-1798.
Dämonologie; oder, Systematische Abhandlung von der Natur und Macht des Teufels, von den Kennzeichen, eine verstellte oder eingebildete Besitznehmung des Teufels von einer wahren am leichtesten zu unterscheiden, sammt den natürlichsten Mitteln, die meisten Gespenster am sichersten zu vertreiben, dem Gassnerischen Teufelssysteme entgegengesetzt. [Leipzig?] 1775.
(Continued on next

Gassner, Johann Joseph, 1727-1779.
Witchcraft
BF 1523 E35
Einzinger von Einzing, Johann Martin Maximilian, 1725-1798. Dämonologie. [Leipzig?] 1775. (Card 2)
140 p. 18cm.
With this is bound Thomasius, C. Gelehrte Streitschrift von dem Verbrechen der Zauber- und Hexerey. Leipzig, 1775.
1. Gassner, Johann Joseph, 1727-1779. I. Title.

CATALOGUE OF THE CORNELL WITCHCRAFT COLLECTION

Gassner, Johann Joseph, 1727-1779.
Witchcraft
BF   Der Exorcist in seiner Blösse. [n. p.]
1559   1776.
G25   40 p. port. 17cm.
Z63
no.1   No. 1 in vol. lettered Gassneriana.

  1. Gassner, Johann Joseph, 1727-1779.
  2. Exorcism. 3. Přichovský, Antonín Peter, Abp. of Prague, 1707-1793. Hirtenbrief ... 1775.

8

Gassner, Johann Joseph, 1727-1779.
Witchcraft
BF   Gründlicher Beweiss, dass die Art, mit welcher
1559   der nun in ganz Deutschland berühmte hochw.
G25   Herr Pfarrer zu Klösterl Johann
          Joseph Gassner die Krankheiten zu heilen
          pflegt, den evangelischen Grundsätzen und
          den Gesinnungen der allererersten Kirche
          ganz gleichförmig sey. Von einem Vertheidiger
          der Wahrheit und aufrichtigem Menschenfreunde
          in öffentlichen Druck gegeben. Augsburg, Bey J. Wolff, 1775.
8   93 p. 19cm.
                        (Continued on next card)

Gassner, Johann Joseph, 1727-1779.
Witchcraft
BF   Gründlicher Beweiss ... von einem Vertheidiger
1559   der Wahrheit ... 1775. (Card 2)
G25
          Bound with Gassner, Johann Joseph, 1727-1779. Antwort auf die Anmerkungen, welche in dem Münchnerischen Intelligenzblat ... gemacht worden. Augsburg, 1774.

  1. Gassner, Johann Joseph, 1727-1779.
  2. Exorcism. 3. Medicine, Magic, mystic, and spagiric. I. Ein Vertheidiger der Wahrheit und   aufrichtiger Menschenfreund.
8

Gassner, Johann Joseph, 1727-1779.
Witchcraft
         Haen, Anton de, 1704?-1776.
            ... De miraculis liber. Parisiis,
         Apud P. F. Didot juniorem, 1778.
            xx, 144 [i. e., 148] p. 18cm.

         First published in Frankfurt, 1776.
         J. J. Gassner's methods discussed in chapter 5.

  1. Miracles--Early works to 1800.
  2. Gassner,   Johann Joseph, 1727-
  1779. I. Ti   tle.

Gassner, Johann Joseph, 1727-1779.
Witchcraft
BF   Lavater, Johann Caspar, 1741-1801.
1559   Auszug der Frankfurter gelehrten Anzeigen
G25   Nro. 38 und 39 den 12. May 1775. Beytrag
Z63   zur gelehrten Geschichte unserer Zeit.
no.7   [Zürich, 1775]
            [8] p. 17cm.

         No. 7 in vol. lettered Gassneriana.

  1. Gassner, Johann Joseph, 1727-1779.
  I. Title.   II. Title: Beytrag
  zur gelehrten   Geschichte unserer
8 Zeit.

Gassner, Johann Joseph, 1727-1779.
Witchcraft
BF   Semler, Johann Salomo, 1725-1791, ed.
1559   Samlungen von Briefen und Aufsätzen über
G25   die Gassnerischen und Schröpferischen Geisterbeschwörungen,
Z87   mit eigenen vielen Anmerkungen hrsg. von Johann Salomo Semler ...
            Halle im Magdeburgischen, C. H. Hemmerde, 1776.
            2 v. in 1. 20cm.
  1. Gassner, Johann Joseph, 1727-1779.
  2. Schrepfer, Johann Georg, 1730?-1774. 3.
8 Exorcism. 4.   Faith-cure.

WITCHCRAFT   Gassner, Johann Joseph, 1727-1779.
BF   Sierke, Eugen, 1845-
1408   Schwärmer und Schwindler zu Ende des
S57   achtzehnten Jahrhunderts. Leipzig, S.
            Hirzel, 1874.
            vi, 462 p. 21cm.

  1. Occult sciences--Biography. 2.
  Superstition. 3. Swedenborg, Emanuel,
  1688-1772. 4. Mesmer, Franz Anton, 1734-
  1815. 5. Gassner, Johann Joseph, 1727-
8   1779. 6. Schrepfer, Johann Georg, 1730?-
NIC   1774. 7.   Cagliostro, Alessandro,
conte de, as   sumed name of Giuseppe
Balsamo, 1743   -1795. I. Title.

Gassner, Johann Joseph, 1727-1779.
Witchcraft
BF   Thomasius, Christian, 1655-1728.
1523   Christian Thomasii Gelehrte Streitschrift
E35   von dem Verbrechen der Zauber- und Hexerey.
            Aus dem Lateinischen übersetzt, und bey Gelegenheit
            der Gassnerischen Wunderkuren zum Besten des Publikums herausgegeben. [Leipzig?]
            1775.
            95 p. 18cm.
            Bound with Einziger von Einzing, Johann
8   Martin Maximilian, 1725-1798. Dämonologie.
        [Leipzig?] 1775.
                        (Continued on next card)

Gassner, Johann Joseph, 1727-1779.
Witchcraft
BF   Thomasius, Christian, 1655-1728. Christian
1523   Thomasii Gelehrte Streitschrift von
E35   dem Verbrechen der Zauber- und Hexerey ...
           1775.   (Card 2)

         Translation of Dissertatio de crimine magiae.
  1. Witchcraft. I. His   Dissertatio
  de crimine magiae. German. II. Title:
  Streitschrift von dem Verbrechen der Zauber-
8 und Hexerey.

Gassner, Johann Joseph, 1727-1779.
Witchcraft
BF   Das Vorurtheil, Glaub, und Unglaub, bey
1559   denen Gassnerischen Kuren, oder, Etwas
G25   für diejenigen, die keinen Teufel glauben.
Z92   Nebst einem Verzeichniss von denen
1796   pro und contra herausgekommenen Schriften.
           [n. p.] 1796.
           77 p. 18cm.
         British Museum, whose edition has imprint
         Sulzbach, 1775, attributes work to Gassner.
  1. Gassner, Johann Joseph, 1727-1779.
  2. Exorcism. I. Gassner, Johann
8 Joseph, 1727-   1779, supposed author.

Gassner, Johann Joseph, 1727-1779.
Witchcraft
BF   Was soll man an den Kuren des Herrn geistlichen
1559   Raths Gassner, die er bisher im
G25   Namen Jesu gemacht hat, noch untersuchen,
Z63   so nicht schon längst hundertmal ist untersucht worden? Frankfurt und Berlin,
no.3   1775.
           96 p. 17cm.
         No. 3 in vol. lettered Gassneriana.
  1. Gassner, Johann Joseph, 1727-1779.
  2. Faith-cure. 3. Politische Frage, ob
  ein ... Landes   fürst über die Gassnerischen Kuren   ... gleichgültig seyn
  kann. 4. Ste   rzinger, Ferdinand, 1721-
8 1786.

Gassner, Johann Joseph, 1727-1779.
Witchcraft
BF   [Zapf, Georg Wilhelm] 1747-1810.
1565   Zauberbibliothek. [München] 1776.
S83   91 p. 19cm.
Z97
         Based on annotated bibliography of the
         Gassner and Sterzinger controversies which
         first appeared in Allgemeine deutsche Bibliothek,
         Berlin, 1775-76. CUL holdings noted in ms. in text.
         [BF 1565 S83 Z98]
  1. Sterzinger, Ferdinand, 1721-1786. 2.
  Gassner, Johann Joseph, 1727-1779. 3.
  Witchcraft--   Bibl. I. Title.

Gassner, Johann Joseph, 1727-1779.
Witchcraft
BF   Zauberbibliothek. 1775-1776. [Berlin,
1565   1775-76]
S83   various pagings. 20cm.
Z98   Title from spine.
         Consists of three sections detached from
         Allgemeine deutsche Bibliothek, titled:
         Zauberey; Teufeleyen; and Teufeleyen. Eine
         Fortsetzung der vorigen.
  1. Sterzinger, Ferdinand, 1721-1786.
  2. Gassner, Johann Joseph, 1727-1779. 3.
8 Witchcraft--Bibl.

Gassner, Johann Joseph, 1727-1779.
Witchcraft
BX   Zimmermann, J   A
4705   Johann Joseph Gassner, der berühmte Exorzist.
G35406   Sein Leben und wundersames Wirken aus
Z74   Anlass seiner hundertjährigen Todesfeier
           neuerdings erzählt und gewürdigt von J. A.
           Zimmermann. Kempten, J. Kösel'sche Buchhandlung,
           1878.
           viii, 122 p. 19cm.

  1. Gassner, Johann Joseph, 1727-1779.
8 2. Exorcism.   3. Faith-cure.

Gaston Jean Baptiste, duke of Orléans, 1608-1660.
WITCHCRAFT
BF   Relation veritable de ce qvi s'est passé
1517   aux exorcismes des religieuses vrsulines
F5   possedees de Loudun, en la presence de
R38   Monsieur frere vnique du roy. Auec l'attestation
1635   des exorcistes. Paris, Chez
           Iean Martin, 1635.
           46 p. 17cm.

         "Iouxte la coppie imprimée à Poictiers."

  1. Loudun,   France. Ursuline Convent. 2.   Exorcism. I. Gaston
8 Jean Baptiste,   duke of Orléans, 1608-
1660.

Gaufrédy, Louis, 1572-1611.

         see

         Gaufridi, Louis, 1572-1611.

Gaufridi, Louis, 1572-1611.
Witchcraft
BF   [Augier, Adolphe Clovis]
1582   Les grandes victimes de l'hystérie: Louis
A92   Gaufridi, curé des Accoules, et Magdeleine
           de la Palud. Relation historique et rationnelle
           d'un procès de sorcellerie. Paris,
           L. Michaud [1907]
           313 p. 19cm.
         At head of title: Raoul Gineste [pseud.
         of A. C. Augier]
  1. Gaufridi, Louis, 1572-1611. 2.
  Palud, Magdeleine de la. 3. Witchcraft--
8 Provence. I.   Title.

Gaufridi, Louis, 1572-1611.
Witchcraft
BF   Fontaine, Jacques, d. 1621.
1582   Des marques des sorciers et de la reelle
Z7   possession que le diable prend sur le corps
1611a   des hommes. Sur le subiect du proces de
           l'abominable & detestable sorcier Louys
           Gaufridy ... Lyon, Par Claude Larjot, 1611
           [Arras, 1865]
           45, [1] p. 21cm.

  1. Trials (Witchcraft)--France. 2.
  Gaufridi, Louis, 1572-1611. 3. Witchcraft.
8 I. Title.

CATALOGUE OF THE CORNELL WITCHCRAFT COLLECTION

Witchcraft
BF
1563
T86

Gaufridi, Louis, 1572-1611.
    The life and death of Lewis Gaufredy: a priest of the Church of the Accoules in Marseilles in France, (who ... committed many most abhominable sorceries, but chiefly vpon two very faire young gentle-women ... hee was ... burnt aliue ... the last day of April, 1611. Together with the 53 articles of his confession ... Translated ... out of two French copies ... London, Printed by T. C. for R. Redmer, 1612.

(Continued on next card)

WITCHCRAFT
BF
1517
F5
M62

Gaufridi, Louis, 1572-1611.
    Michaelis, Sebastien, 1543?-1618.
    Histoire admirable de la possession et conversion d'vne penitente, seduite par vn magicien, la faisant sorciere & princesse des sorciers au pays de Prouence, conduite à la S. Baume pour y estre exorcizee l'an M.DC.X. au mois de Nouembre, soubs l'authorité du R. P. F. Sebastien Michaelis ... Commis par luy aux exorcismes & recueil des actes le R. P. F. François Domptivs ... Ensemble la Pneumalogie, ou Discours du

8   (Continued on next card)

WITCHCRAFT
BF
1508
P97
1688

Gaulmin, Gilbert, 1585-1665, ed.
    Psellus, Michael.
    [Michaelou tou Psellou Peri energeias daimōnōn dialogos] Μιχαήλου του Ψελλου Περὶ ἐνέργειας δαιμόνων διάλογος. Michaelis Pselli De operatione daemonum dialogus. Gilbertus Gaulminus Molinensis primus Graecè edidit & notis illustravit. E museo Dan. Hasenmülleri ... Kiloni, Sumtibus Joh. Sebastiani Richelii, 1688.
    6 p. l., 166 p. 15cm.

8
NIC   (Continued on next card)

Witchcraft
BF
1563
T86

Gaufridi, Louis, 1572-1611.
    The life and death of Lewis Gaufredy ... 1612.   (Card 2)

    [34] p. 19cm.

    No. 11 in vol. lettered: Tracts of witches.

    1. Witchcraft. 2. Gaufridi, Louis, 1572-1611.

WITCHCRAFT
BF
1517
F5
M62

Gaufridi, Louis, 1572-1611.
    Michaelis, Sebastien, 1543?-1618. Histoire admirable ... 1613.   (Card 2)

    susdit Pere Michaelis, reueu, corrigé, & augmenté par luy-mesme ... Paris, Chez Charles Chastellain, 1613.
    16 p. l., 352, 124, 196, [30] p. 17cm.
    "Actes recveillis ... par le reverend Pere Michaëlis" has separate paging.
    "Discovrs des esprits" has special t. p. with imprint Paris, 1512, and separate paging.

8   (Continued on next card)

WITCHCRAFT
BF
1508
P97
1688

Gaulmin, Gilbert, 1585-1665, ed.
    Psellus, Michael. [Michaelou tou Psellou Peri energeias daimōnōn dialogos] 1688.
    (Card 2)

    Latin and Greek on facing pages, with notes by Gaulmin at bottom of page.
    Latin translation by Petrus Morellus, "illius qui & Nicetae Thesaurum orthodoxae fidei ex Graeco Latinum fecit."
    1. Demonology. I. Gaulmin, Gilbert, 1585-1665, ed. II. Morellus, Petrus,
8   tr. III. Hasenmüller,
NIC   Turonensis, (Continued on next card)

WITCHCRAFT
BF
1582
L86

Gaufridi, Louis, 1572-1611.
    Lorédan, Jean, 1853-
    Un grand procès de sorcellerie au XVIIe siècle: l'abbé Gaufridy et Madeleine de Demandolx (1600-1670) d'après des documents inédits. Ouvrage orné de 9 gravures et de 2 fac-similés. Paris, Perrin, 1912.
    xiv, 436 p. illus. 21cm.

    1. Witchcraft--France. 2. Trials (Witchcraft)--France. 3. Gaufridi, Louis, 1572-
8   1611. 4. Demandolx, Madeleine de, 1593?-
NIC   1670. I. Title.

Witchcraft
PQ
1914
R6 A72
1701

Gaufridi, Louis, 1572-1611.
    Rosset, François de, b. ca. 1570.
    De l'horrible & épouvantable sorcellerie de Louis Goffredy, prêtre beneficié de Marseille.
    (In his Les histoires tragiques de nostre temps. Dernière éd. Lyon, 1701. 18cm. p. 27-56)

    1. Gaufridi, Louis, 1572-1611. I. Title.

MSS
Bd.
WITCHCRAFT
BF
G27++

Gause, Anna, defendant.
    Inquisitions Acten wider Anna Gausen, sel. Claus Zaumanns Witwe in puncto beschuldigter Zauberei. Wittenburg, 1689.
    29 l. 33cm.
    Manuscript, on paper, in the hands of the official notary, Joachim Ehler and other jurists.
    T. p. supplied by a former owner.
    At head of first leaf: "Protocollum gehalten Wittem burgk... In Inquisition Sachen wieder Anna Gausen,
    (Continued on next card)

WITCHCRAFT
BF
1517
F5
M62
1613

Gaufridi, Louis, 1572-1611.
    Michaelis, Sebastien, 1543?-1618.
    The admirable history of the possession and conversion of a penitent woman. Sedvced by a magician that made her to become a witch, and the princesse of sorcerers in the country of Prouince, who was brought to S. Baume to bee exorcised, in the yeere 1610 ... Wherevnto is annexed a pnevmology, or Discourse of spirits ... reuewed, corrected, and enlarged ... Translated into English by W. B. London, Imprinted for Wil-
8   (Continued on next card)

Gaufridy, Louys, 1572-1611.

see

Gaufridi, Louis, 1572-1611.

MSS
Bd.
WITCHCRAFT
BF
G27++

Gause, Anna, defendant. Inquisitions Acten...1689.   (Card 2)

    sehl. Claus Zaumans nachgelassene Witwen in pō. beschüldigter Zauberey."
    Slightly mutilated but mended.
    Bound in black boards.
    On spine: Hexenprocess-Akten 1689.

    1. Trials (Witchcraft)--Wittenburg.
    2. Witchcraft-- Wittenburg.

WITCHCRAFT
BF
1517
F5
M62
1613

Gaufridi, Louis, 1572-1611.
    Michaelis, Sebastien, 1543?-1618. The admirable history of the possession ... of a penitent woman ... [1613]   (Card 2)

    liam Aspley [1613]
    24 p. l., 418, [10], 154, [34] p. 20cm.
    Differs from another issue only in t. p. (lacks date; some spellings different)
    Translation of Histoire admirable de la possession ... d'vne penitente, and of Discovrs des esprits.
    "A discovrse of spirits" has special t. p. and separate paging.
8   (Continued on next card)

Witchcraft
BF
1565
G26

Gaule, John.
    Select cases of conscience touching witches and witchcrafts ... London, Printed by W. Wilson for R. Clutterbuck, 1646.
    208 p. 12cm.

    Contains a letter from Matthew Hopkins, called the witch-finder, announcing his intention of visiting Great Staughton (where Gaule was the preacher) "to search for evill disposed persons called witches."
    Has book-plate of Edwd. Place, and his autograph.
    I. Hopkins, Matthew, d. 1647. II. Title.

Rare
HV
6211
G28
1734

Gayot de Pitaval, François, 1673-1743.
    Causes célèbres et interessantes, avec les jugemens qui les ont décidées. La Haye, J. Neaulme, 1734-1751.
    22 v. in 12. 17cm.

    Imprint varies: v.1-2, Paris, J. de Nully.
    Vol. 1-2 published under pseud. "M. ***, avocat au Parlement."

    1. Crime and criminals. 2. Trials. I. La Ville, Jean Claude de, b. 1735. II. Title.

WITCHCRAFT
BF
1517
F5
M62
1613

Gaufridi, Louis, 1572-1611.
    Michaelis, Sebastien, 1543?-1618. The admirable history of the possession ... of a penitent woman ... [1613]   (Card 3)

    STC 17854.
    1. Palud, Magdeleine de la. 2. Gaufridi, Louis, 1572-1611. 3. Loudun, France. Ursuline convent. 4. Demoniac possession. 5. Exorcism. I. His Histoire admirable de la possession ... d'une penitente. English. II. His Discours des esprits. English. III. Title. IV. W. B.,
8   tr. V. B., W., tr.

WITCHCRAFT
BF
1508
P97
1838

Gaulmin, Gilbert, 1585-1665, ed.
    Psellus, Michael.
    Michael Psellus De operatione daemonum cum notis Gaulmini curante Jo. Fr. Boissonade. Accedunt inedita opuscula Pselli. Norimbergae, Apud F. N. Campe, 1838.
    xxvii, 348 p. 21cm.
    At head of title: Ψελλος.
    Greek text only: Peri energeias daimōnōn dialogos, with notes in Latin.
    1. Demonology. I. His Peri energeias daimōnōn dialogos. II. Gaulmin, Gilbert, 1585-1665, ed. III. Boissonade, Jean
8
NIC   François, 1774-1857, ed.

MSS
Bd.
WITCHCRAFT
BF
E61

Das geängstigte Köge.
    Der entlarvte Teuffel oder denkwürdige Geschichte von vielen warhaftig Besessenen, welche dieses Feindes Grausamke heftig erfahren, entlich aber durch de mächtigen Finger Gottes wieder erledig worden. Zu mehrer Bekräftigung der vo Doct. Beckern, in seiner verzauberten Welt, zweiffelhaft gemachten Kögischer Geschichte ... Zusammen getragen von M. J. J. L. Leipzig, Johann Melchior Liebe, 16 97 [ca. 1900]
    (Continued on next card)

CATALOGUE OF THE CORNELL WITCHCRAFT COLLECTION

Das geängstigte Köge.

Der entlarvte Teuffel ...   1697 [ca. 1900]
(Card 2)

77 p. 19cm.
Carnap's manuscript copy.
"Originaldruck in der Königl. öff. Bibliothek zu Dresden, 98 pag. Seiten in 8°."
"Diese Schrift bildet gewissermassen die Fortsetzung zu: "Das geängstigte Köge oder Eine warhaffte und denkwürdige Historie, von einer ent   setzlichen Versuchung des leidigen   Satans zu Köge in
(Continued on next card)

Das geängstigte Köge.

Der entlarvte Teuffel ...   1697 [ca. 1900]
(Card 3)

Seeland" wo in deutscher Sprache durch denselben Verfasser ... i. J. 1695 herausgegeben. Hieraus erklärt es sich, dass diese Schrift mit " die dritte Zugabe" anfängt, da "das geängstigte Köge mit der zweiten Zugabe abschliesst."
Marginal numerals and signatures indicate paginati   on ans signatures of the original.
(Continued on next card)

Das geängstigte Köge.

Der entlarvte Teuffel ...   1697 [ca. 1900]
(Card 4)

Printed copy not in Van der Linde.

1. Demoniac possession. 2. Devil. 3. Bekker, Balthasar, 1634-1698. De betoverde weere   ld. I. Das geängstigte Köge.   II. M. J. J. L. III. L., M. J. J.

De gebannen duyvel weder in-geroepen.

Witchcraft
BF 1410 B42 Z56 v.3 no.1

[Costerus, Florentius] fl. 1654-1703.
De gebannen duyvel weder in-geroepen, ofte het vonnis van Doctor Bekker over den duyvel gevelt, in revisie gebraght. Den tweede druck, vermeerdert met twee gedigten. Hoorn, Gedruckt by S. J. Kortingb [sic] en J. J. Beets, boek-verkoopers, 1691.
42 p. title and end page vignettes.
21 x 16cm.
4°: A-E⁴, F1.
Black letter.

(Continued on next card)

De gebannen duyvel weder in-geroepen.

Witchcraft
BF 1410 B42 Z56 v.3 no.1

[Costerus, Florentius] fl. 1654-1703. De gebannen duyvel weder in-geroepen ... 1691.
(Card 2)

Signed: Bloemardus Thusius.
Variant of van der Linde 87: 2d., enl. printing.
No. 1 in vol. lettered Bekker III.

1. Bekker, Balthasar, 1634-1698. De betoverde weereld. I. Title.

Witchcraft
BF 1565 G29

Gebhard, Johann.
Canidia, hoc est, Venefica, fetura cacodaemonis spurcissimi ex creaturis praepotentiae divinae pulcerrimis nobilissimisq[ue] facta spurcissimarum omnium spurcissima; non peniculo pigmentario, sed vivo vocis charactere ex lyrici Venusini Epodis V. & XVII adumbrata, inq[ue] theatro Gymnasii Vratislaviensium Elisabetani publico ad contemplandum ... proponenda, curante Johanne Gebhardo ... Vratislaviae, Typ   is Baumannianis, Per
(Continued on next card)

Witchcraft
BF 1565 G29

Gebhard, Johann. Canidia ...   [1651]
(Card 2)

Gottfridum Grunderum [1651]
[8] p. 20cm.

1. Witchcraft.   I. Title.   II. Title: Venefica.

Die gebrochne Macht der Finsternüss.

WITCHCRAFT
BF 1565 S76

Spitzel, Gottlieb, 1639-1691.
Die gebrochne Macht der Finsternüss, oder Zerstörte teuflische Bunds- und Buhl-Freundschafft mit den Menschen: das ist Gründlicher Bericht, wie und welcher Gestalt die abscheuliche und verfluchte Zauber-Gemeinschafft mit den bösen Geistern angehe; wie dieselbe zu- und fortgehe; ob und auf was Art und Weise sie widerum zergehe ... allen Heyl- und Gnaden-begierigen und vom leydigen Satan schänd   lich-berückten und ver-
(Continued on next card)

Die gebrochne Macht der Finsternüss.

WITCHCRAFT
BF 1565 S76

Spitzel, Gottlieb, 1639-1691. Die gebrochne Macht der Finsternüss ...   1687.
(Card 2)

strickten Seelen zum nothwendigen Unterricht und heylsamer Widerkehrung beschrieben ... Augspurg, In Verlegung Gottlieb Göbels seel. Wittib, Gedruckt bey Jacob Koppmayer, 1687.
24 p. l., 813, [18] p. 17cm.
With added engr. t. p. for whole work and each of the   three Abtheilungen.
(Continued on next card)

Die gebrochne Macht der Finsternüss.

WITCHCRAFT
BF 1565 S76

Spitzel, Gottlieb, 1639-1691. Die gebrochne Macht der Finsternüss ...   1687.
(Card 3)

Title in red and black.
Cyprianvs magvs ... oder dess zu Christe wunderbarlich bekehrten Ertz-Zauberers Cypriani von Antiochia hertzliche Buss und Bekehrung: p. 778-813.
1. Witchcraft. 2. Devil. 3. Salvation—Early works to 1800. I. Cyprianus, of Antioch. L   egend. II. Title.

Gedancken von Gespenstern.

Witchcraft
BF 1445 W41

[Wegner, Georg Wilhelm]
Gedancken von Gespenstern. Halle, C. H. Hemmerde, 1747.
47 p. 18cm.
Attributed to Wegner by Holzmann in v. 6 and 7 (correction of v. 2, which attributes the work to G. F. Meier)
Second printing, 1749, spells title: Gedanken von Gespenstern.
With this is bound Sucro, Johann Georg. Widerlegung der   Gedancken von Gespenstern. Halle, 1748.
(Continued on next card)

Gedanken eines Landpfarrers über den Ungrund des Hexenglaubens.

WITCHCRAFT
BF 1565 W37 S347

[Schmid, Franz Josef]
Und der Satz: Teuflische Magie existirt, besteht noch. In einer Antwort des katholischen Weltmannes auf die von einem Herrn Landpfarrer herausgegebene Apologie der Professor Weberschen Hexenreformation. Augsburg, Bey J. N. Styx, 1791.
xxiv, 350 p. 19cm.

1. Bauer, Friedrich. Gedanken eines Landpfarrers über den Ungrund des Hexenglaubens. 2. We   ber, Joseph, 1753-1831.

Gedanken über die Werke des Liebhabers der Wahrheit von der Hexerey.

Witchcraft
BF 1565 S83 M177

[Sterzinger, Ferdinand] 1721-1786.
Gedanken über die Werke des Liebhabers der Wahrheit von der Hexerey. München, Bey J. A. Crätz, 1767.
27, [1] p. 21cm.
Attributed to Sterzinger by Holzmann and British Museum.

1. März, Agnellus, 1726-1784. Urtheil ohne Vorurtheil über die wirkend- und thätige Hexerey. 2.   His Akademische Rede von dem gemein   en Vorurtheile der ... Hexerey. I.   Title.

Gedanken von Besessenen und Bezauberten.

WITCHCRAFT
BF 1555 K96

Kurella, Ernst Gottfried, 1725-1799.
Gedanken von Besessenen und Bezauberten. Halle im Magdeburgischen, C. H. Hemmerde, 1749.
64 p. 20cm.

1. Demoniac possession. I. Title.

Gedanken von der Einwirkung guter und böser Geister in die Menschen.

WITCHCRAFT
BF 1555 M94 O29 no.1

Oesfeld, Gotthelf Friedrich.
Gedanken von der Einwirkung guter und böser Geister in die Menschen. Nebst beygefügter Beurtheilung eines neuern Beyspiels einer vermeynten leiblichen Besitzung, herausgegeben von M. Gotthelf Friedrich Oesfeld ... Wittenberg, J. J. Ahlfeld, 1760.
110 p. 18cm.
No. 1 in vol. lettered Oesfeld u. a. ...
1. Spirits. 2. Demoniac possession. 3. Lohmanni   n, Anna Elisabeth. I. Title. II.   Title: Einwirkung guter und böser Ge   ister in die Menschen.

Gedanken von Gespenstern.

Witchcraft
BF 1445 W41

[Wegner, Georg Wilhelm]
Gedancken von Gespenstern. Halle, C. H. Hemmerde, 1747.
47 p. 18cm.
Attributed to Wegner by Holzmann in v. 6 and 7 (correction of v. 2, which attributes the work to G. F. Meier)
Second printing, 1749, spells title: Gedanken von Gespenstern.
With this is bound Sucro, Johann Georg. Widerlegung der   Gedancken von Gespenstern. Halle, 1748.

Witchcraft
BF 1538 D9 G29

Geerlings, Hermanus Jacob
De antieke daemonologie en Augustinus' geschrift De divinatione daemonum. 's-Gravenhage, 1953.
191 p. 24 cm.

Diss.—Amsterdam.

1. Augustinus, Aurelius, Saint, Bp. of Hippo. [De divinatione daemonum. 2. Demonology. I.   Title.

Witchcraft
BX 9479 B42 B11 no.12

De Geestelyke stryd; of Een gewapend-Christen, teegen de listige omleydinge des duyvels. Verstaanbaar verklaard, over de woorden Pauli; Ephes. 6: 11, 12, &c. Zyn de blaaden Josuas. Amsterdam, By A. van Damme, 1699.
14 p. title vignette, illus. initial.
20 x 15cm.
4°: A-B⁴(-B4)
Black letter.
No. 12 in   vol. lettered B. Bekkers sterfbed en   andere tractaten.
(Continued on next card)

CATALOGUE OF THE CORNELL WITCHCRAFT COLLECTION

Witchcraft
BX
9479
B42
B11
no.12
 De Geestelyke stryd ... 1699. (Card 2)
  1. Bible. N. T. Ephesians VI, 11-12--Criticism, interpretation, etc. 2. Devil. I. Title: Een gewapend-Christen, teegen de listige omleydinge des duyvels.

WITCHCRAFT
BF
1566
N71

8
NIC
 Die gegenwärtige Wiederbelebung des Hexenglaubens.
  Nippold, Friedrich Wilhelm Franz, 1838-
  Die gegenwärtige Wiederbelebung des Hexenglaubens. Mit einem literarisch-kritischen Anhang über die Quellen und Bearbeitungen der Hexenprozesse. Berlin, C.G. Lüderitz, 1875.
  95 p. 23cm. (Deutsche Zeit- und Streit-Fragen, Jahrg. 4, Heft 57/58)
  1. Witchcraft. 2. Witchcraft--Hist.

Witchcraft
BF
1410
B42
Z56
v.2
no.12
 De Geharpoende muys. Of staatkundige consideratien, over zeekere arabische vertaalinge, uyt een turkx leeraar Hamets Sidach Effendi. Raakende het gewoel, over Do. Balthasar Bekkers Betooverde weereld. Beneffens Minerva, en Mercurius; aan de betooverde schriftgeleerden. ₍Amsterdam?₎ 1691.
  12 p. title vignette. 19 x 15cm.
  4°: A⁴, B².
  Published also in Verscheyde gedichten,

(Continued on next card)

Witchcraft
BF
1410
B42
Z56
v.2
no.12
 De Geharpoende muys. 1691. (Card 2)
  so voor, als tegen het boek, genaamt: De betoverde weereld.
  No. 12 in vol. lettered Bekker II.
  1. Vertaeling uit seker arabisch schryver. 2. Bekker, Balthasar, 1634-1698. De Betooverde weereld. I. Minerva met Mercurius. Aan de betoverde schrift-geleerden.

Witchcraft
BF
1410
B42
Z89
 De geharpoende muys.
  Verscheyde gedichten, so voor, als tegen het boek, genaamt: De betoverde weereld. ₍Amsterdam?₎ Gedrukt voor de liefhebbers, 1691.
  1 p. l., 12, 9-32 p. title vignettes, illus. initials. 20 x 15cm.
  4°: π1, A⁶, B-D⁴.
  First poem has own t. p. with title: Gestroojde zeegen-palmen, op het doorwrogte werk van de Heer Balthasar Bekker ...genaamd De betoverde weereld. ₍Van der Linde 188₎

(Continued on next card)

Witchcraft
BF
1410
B42
Z89
 De geharpoende muys.
  Verscheyde gedichten, so voor, als tegen het boek, genaamt: De betoverde weereld. 1691. (Card 2)
  Includes other works published separately: De betoverde predikant Dr. Balthasar Bekker ₍van der Linde 189₎; Verta₍e₎ling uit seker arabisch schryver; De geharpoende muys. Van der Linde 197.
  1. Bekker, Balthasar, 1634-1698. De betoverde weereld. I. Gestroojde zeegen-

(Continued on next card)

Witchcraft
Z
6880
Z9A18
 Geheime Wissenschaften.
  Ackermann, Theodor, bookseller, Munich.
  Geheime Wissenschaften. 1- , 1926-
  München.
  v. 21cm. (His Katalog 594-)

  1. Occult sciences--Bibliography--Catalogs. I. Title.

Witchcraft
BF
1413
K47
G3
 Die geheimwissenschaften.
  Kiesewetter, Karl, 1854-1895.
  Die geheimwissenschaften. Von Karl Kiesewetter. Leipzig, W. Friedrich ₍1895₎
  iii-xxvii p., 1 l., 749, ₍1₎ p. illus., 2 port. 22ᶜᵐ.
  Added t. p.: Geschichte des Occultismus.
  Forms second part of the author's: Geschichte des neueren occultismus.
  CONTENTS.—Die alchymie.—Die astrologie und das divinationswesen.—Das hexenwesen und seinen erscheinungen.—Die weisse magie. Die theurgie. Die nekromantie.—Vergleichung der spiritistischen phänomene mit den geheimwissenschaftlichen.
  1. Occult sciences--Hist. I. His Geschichte des neueren Occultismus. II. His Geschichte des Occultismus. III. Title.

Library of Congress, no.   8-15781

History of Science
BF
1471
D47
 Gehren, Georg Erhard von, respondent.
  Detharding, Georg Christoph, 1671-1747, praeses.
  Scrutinium medicum De morbis a spectrorum apparitione oriundis, Von Gespenstern, wie weit solche durch ihre Erscheinung Krankheiten verursachen, id qvod ... praeside ... Georgio Dethardingio ... pro gradu doctorali summisque in arte medica honoribus insignibus ac privilegiis rite obtinendis, ... ad diem 27. Octobr. An. 1729. publico examini offert Georgius Erhard von Gehren... Rostochii, Typis Io. Iacob. Adleri ₍1729₎

(Continued on next card)

History of Science
BF
1471
D47
 Gehren, Georg Erhard von, respondent.
  Detharding, Georg Christoph, 1671-1747, praeses. Scrutinium medicum ... ₍1729₎ (Card 2)
  38 p. 20cm.
  Diss.--Rostock (G. E. von Gehren, respondent)
  1. Apparitions. 2. Ghosts. 3. Medicine--15th-18th centuries. I. Gehren, Georg Erhard von, respondent. II. Title: De morbis a spectrorum apparitione oriundis.

WITCHCRAFT
BF
1583
Z7
1587a
 Geiger, Lucia, fl. 1587.
  Her, , Rat.
  Ein Hexenprocess zu Schongau vom Jahre 1587. Aus den Originalacten geschichtlich dargestellt von Rath Her. München, Druck von G. Franz, 1849.
  19 p. 24cm.
  "Aus dem Oberbay. Archiv Bd. XI. Heft 1 besonders abgedruckt."
  1. Geiger, Lucia, fl. 1587. 2. Witchcraft--Bavaria. I. Title.

Rare
ar W
25683
 Geilen, Heinz Peter, 1933-
  Die Auswirkungen der Cautio criminalis von Friedrich von Spee auf den Hexenprozess in Deutschland. ₍Köln, G. Wasmund, 1963₎
  xviii, 92 p. 21cm.
  Inaug.-Diss.--Bonn.
  1. Spee, Friedrich von, 1591-1635. Cautio criminalis. 2. Witchcraft--Germany. I. Title.

Witchcraft
BX
890
G31
E5+
1517
 Geiler, Johannes, von Kaisersberg, 1445-1510.
  Die emeis. Dis ist das büch von der omeissen, vnnd auch Herr der künnig ich diente gern. Vnd sagt von eigentschafft der omeissen. Vn gibt vnderweisung von den vnholden oder hexen, vnd von gespenst der geist, vnd von dem witenden heer wunderbarlich vnd nützlich zewissen, was man daruon glauben vnd halten soll. Vnd ist von dem hoch gelertē doc-

(Continued on next card)

Witchcraft
BX
890
G31
E5+
1517
 Geiler, Johannes, von Kaisersberg, 1445-1510. Die emeis ... ₍1517₎ (Card 2)
  tor Johānes Geiler vō Keisersperg ... in eim quadragesimal gepredigt worden alle sontag in der fasten ... ₍Strassburg, Johannes Grienniger, 1517₎
  xc ₍i.e. lxxxviii₎ l. illus. 29cm.
  Title and parts of text in red and black.
  Leaves v and vi not wanting; printer skipped numbers.

(Continued on next card)

Witchcraft
BX
890
G31
E5+
1517
 Geiler, Johannes, von Kaisersberg, 1445-1510. Die emeis ... ₍1517₎ (Card 3)
  Colophon at end of first section, Die emeis, reads Grienninger instead of Grienniger.
  "Her d'küng ich diente gern", l. ₍lxvii₎-xc, has special t. p.
  1. Sermons, German--Middle High German. 2. Folk-lore, German. 3. Magic. I. His Her der küng ich diente gern. II. Title. III. Title: Her der küng ich diente gern.

Witchcraft
BX
890
G31
E5
1856
 Geiler, Johannes, von Kaisersberg, 1445-1510.
  Die Emeis.
  Zur Geschichte des Volks-Aberglaubens im Anfange des XVI. Jahrhunderts. Aus Dr. Joh. Geilers von Kaisersberg Emeis. Mit einer Einleitung, Erläuterung und sonstigen literarischen Nachweisungen herausgegeben von August Stöber ... Basel, Schweighauser, 1856.
  4 p. l., 92 p. 24cm.

Witchcraft
BX
890
G31
E5+
1517
 Geiler, Johannes, von Kaisersberg, 1445-1510.
  Her der küng ich direte gern.
  Die emeis. Dis ist das büch von der omeissen, vnnd auch Herr der künnig ich diente gern. Vnd sagt von eigentschafft der omeissen. Vn gibt vnderweisung von den vnholden oder hexen, vnd von gespenst der geist, vnd von dem witenden heer wunderbarlich vnd nützlich zewissen, was man daruon glauben vnd halten soll. Vnd ist von dem hoch gelertē doc-

(Continued on next card)

Witchcraft
BX
890
G31
E5+
1517
 Geiler, Johannes, von Kaisersberg, 1445-1510.
  Her der küng ich dinete gern.
  Die emeis ... ₍1517₎ (Card 2)
  tor Johānes Geiler vō Keisersperg ... in eim quadragesimal gepredigt worden alle sontag in der fasten ... ₍Strassburg, Johannes Grienniger, 1517₎
  xc ₍i.e. lxxxviii₎ l. illus. 29cm.
  Title and parts of text in red and black.
  Leaves v and vi not wanting; printer skipped numbers.

(Continued on next card)

CATALOGUE OF THE CORNELL WITCHCRAFT COLLECTION

Geiler, Johannes, von Kaisersberg, 1445-1510.
    Her der küng ich dinete gern.

Witchcraft
BX
890
G31
+
.517
    Geiler, Johannes, von Kaisersberg, 1445-1510. Die emeis ... [1517] (Card 3)

    Colophon at end of first section, Die emeis, reads Grienninger instead of Grienniger.
    "Her d'küng ich diente gern", l. [lxvii]-xc, has special t. p.
    1. Sermons, German—Middle High German. 2. Folk-lore, German. 3. Magic. I. His Her der küng ich diente gern. II. Title. III. Title: Her der küng ich diente gern.

Witchcraft
BX
890
G31
1856
    Geiler, Johannes, von Kaisersberg, 1445-1510.
    Zur Geschichte des Volks-Aberglaubens im Anfange des XVI. Jahrhunderts. Aus Dr. Joh. Geilers von Kaisersberg Emeis. Mit einer Einleitung, Erläuterung und sonstigen literarischen Nachweisungen herausgegeben von August Stöber ... Basel, Schweighauser, 1856.
    4 p. l., 92 p. 24cm.
    I. His Die Emeis. II. Stöber, August, 1808-1884, ed. III. Title.

8

Geiler, John, of Keisersberg, 1445-1510.
    see
Geiler, Johannes, von Kaisersberg, 1445-1510.

Geiler von Kaisersberg, Johannes, 1445-1510.
    see
Geiler, Johannes, von Kaisersberg, 1445-1510.

Geisslbrecht, Anna, fl. 1584.

Witchcraft
F
555
57
    [Bewerlein, Sixtus]
    Erschröckliche gantz warhafftige Geschicht, welche sich mit Apolonia, Hannsen Geißlbrechts Burgers zu Spalt inn dem Lystätter Bistumb, Haußfrawen, so den 20. Octobris, Anno 82. von dem bösen Feind gar hart besessen, vnnd doch den 24. gedachts Monats widerumb durch Gottes gnädige Hilff, auß solcher grossen Pein vnnd Marter entlediget worden, verlauffen hat. Allen gottlosen, zänckischen, vbelfluchenden Eheleuten, vnnd andern zu sonderer Warnung in Truck gegeben. Durch M. Sixtum Agrico-
    (Continued on next card)

Geisslbrecht, Anna, fl. 1584.

Witchcraft
F
555
57
    [Bewerlein, Sixtus] Erschröckliche gantz warhafftige Geschicht ... 1584. (Card 2)
    lam [pseud.] ... vnd dann D. Georgium Witmerum ... Ingolstatt, Getruckt durch Wolffgang Eder, 1584.
    3 p. l., 49 p. 20cm.
    Title in red and black.
    1. Demoniac possession. 2. Exorcism. 3. Geisslbrecht, Anna, fl. 1584. I. Witmer, Georg, joint author. II. Title.

Geist-Wunder-Hexen- und Zaubergeschichten, vorzüglich neuester Zeit.

Witchcraft
GR
580
W48
    Wenzel, Gottfried Immanuel, 1754-1809.
    Geist-Wunder-Hexen- und Zaubergeschichten, vorzüglich neuester Zeit. Erzählt und erklärt von Gottfried Immanuel Wenzel ... Prag und Leipzig, In der von Schönfeldschen Buchhandlung, 1793.
    4 p. l., 160 p. 20cm.
    Illustrative vignette on t. p.
    1. Ghost stories. 2. Magic. 3. Superstition. I. Title.

8

Geister- und Zauberkatekismus.

Witchcraft
BF
1603
S83
G3
    Sterzinger, Ferdinand, 1721-1786.
    Don Ferdinand Sterzingers Geister- und Zauberkatekismus. München, Bey J. N. Fritz, 1783.
    72 p. 17cm.
    Expansion of his Katekismus von der Geisterlehre, first published 1775 in his Untersuchung, ob es eine Festigkeit gebe, and again in his Die aufgedeckten Gassnerischen Wunderkuren, 1775.
    1. Magic. 2. Witchcraft. 3. Spirits. I. Title: Geister- und Zauberkatekismus.

8

Witchcraft
BF
1445
G31
    Geister, Zauber, Hexen- und Kobolds-Geschichten. Eisenach, Bey J. G. E. Wittelkinde, 1793.
    216 p. 16cm.
    Contents.--Graf H***s von F***a. Eine Geistergeschichte.--Der Wundervogel. Eine Zaubergeschichte.--Die Wachspuppen. Eine Hexengeschichte.--Der Schadenfroh. Eine Koboldsgeschichte.
    Each story has special t. p.
    1. Ghost stories. 2. Magic. 3. Folk-lore, German.

8

Die Geisterbeschwörer im neunzehnten Jahrhundert.

Witchcraft
BF
1559
B62
    Bischoff, Wilhelm Friedrich.
    Die Geisterbeschwörer im neunzehnten Jahrhunderte; oder die Folgen des Glaubens an Magie aus Untersuchungs-Acten dargestellt. Neustadt a. b. Orla, J. K. G. Wagner [pref. 1823]
    viii, 264 p. fold. pl. 18cm.

    1. Exorcism. I. Title.

Die Geisterwelt; eine Schatzkammer des Wunderglaubens.

BF
1613
G31
    Die Geisterwelt; eine Schatzkammer des Wunderglaubens. Berlin, H. Hollstein [1869]
    576 p. 22cm.

    1. Magic. 2. Occult sciences. 3. Witchcraft.

Ein Geistlicher.

Witchcraft
BL
490
A14
    Aberglaube, Zauberei und Sympathie. Von einem Geistlichen. Hamburg, Agentur des Rauhen Hauses, 1884.
    v, 38 p. 18cm.

MSS
Bd.
WITCHCRAFT
BF
G31
    Geistliches Zeug-Hauss in sich haltend starckhe und geistliche Waysen, die teuflische Anfäll glücklich zu yberwinden. [n.p. 17th cent.]
    473 p. 17cm.

    Manuscript, on paper, in a 17th century German hand.
    Bound in vellum.

    1. Demoniac possession. 2. Exorcism. 3. Witchcraft.

Gelehrte Streitschrift von dem Verbrechen der Zauber- und Hexerey.

Witchcraft
BF
1523
E35
    Thomasius, Christian, 1655-1728.
    Gelehrte Streitschrift von dem Verbrechen der Zauber- und Hexerey. Aus dem Lateinischen übers., und bey Gelegenheit der Gassnerischen Wunderkuren zum Besten des Publikums hrsg. [Leipzig?] 1775.
    95 p. 18cm.

    Bound with Einzinger von Einzing, J. M. M. Dämonologie. [Leipzig?] 1775.
    Translation of De crimine magiae

Witchcraft
BF
1576
G32
    Gemmill, William Nelson, 1860–
    The Salem witch trials, a chapter of New England history, by William Nelson Gemmill. Chicago, A. C. McClurg & co., 1924.
    2 p. l., iii p., 1 l., 240 p. front. 19½ cm.

    1. Witchcraft—Salem, Mass. I. Title.
    Library of Congress   BF1576.G4
    ———— Copy 2.   25—471
    Copyright A 814362   [s25c3]

BF
1576
G32
    Gemmill, William Nelson, 1860–
    The Salem witch trials, a chapter of New England history, by William Nelson Gemmill. Chicago, A. C. McClurg & co., 1924.
    2 p. l., iii p., 1 l., 240 p. front. 19½ cm.

    1. Witchcraft—Salem, Mass. I. Title.
    Library of Congress   BF1576.G4
    ———— Copy 2.   25—471
    Copyright A 814362   [s25c3]

Witchcraft
BD
444
G32
1880
    Gener, Pompeyo, 1846-1920.
    La mort et le diable; histoire et philosophie des deux négations suprêmes. Précédé d'une lettre à l'auteur de E. Littré. Paris, C. Reinwald, 1880.
    xl, 780 p. 24cm.

    At head of title: Contribution à l'étude de l'évolution des idées.

    1. Death. 2. Devil. 3. Good and evil. I. Title.

Geneva. Conseil général.

WITCHCRAFT
BF
1584
S97
Z7
1652
    Chauderon, Michée, defendant.
    Procès criminel de la dernière sorcière brulée à Genève le 6 avril 1652, publié d'après des documents inédits et originaux conservés aux Archives de Genève (N° 3465) par le d[r] Ladame. Paris, Aux Bureaux du Progrès médical, 1888.
    xii, 52 p. 24cm. (Bibliothèque diabolique (Collection Bourneville))

8
NIC
    Running title: Procès criminel de Michée Chauderon.
    (Continued on next card)

CATALOGUE OF THE CORNELL WITCHCRAFT COLLECTION

A Gentleman of Wadham College.

Witchcraft
BT 980 S97
[Swinton, John] 1703-1777.
A critical dissertation concerning the words ΔΑΙΜΩΝ and ΔΑΙΜΟΝΙΟΝ. Occasion'd by two late enquiries [by Arthur Ashley Sykes] into the meaning of demoniacs in the New Nestament. In a letter to a friend. By a Gentleman of Wadham College, Oxford. London, Printed for J. Crokatt; and sold by J. Roberts, 1738.
29 p. 20cm.
Also attributed to George Costard.
Letter signed: Philalethes.
8
(Continued on next card)

Witchcraft
BF 1566 S9503 1927
The geography of witchcraft.
Summers, Montague, 1880-1948.
The geography of witchcraft. New York, A. A. Knopf, 1927.
xi, 623 p. illus., facsim. 24cm. (The history of civilization. [Subject histories])

"The present work may be regarded as a complementary volume to, or even a second volume of, my History of witchcraft and demonology."--Introd.

Géologie et astronomie.

Witchcraft
BF 1582 D14
Dalmas, Jean Baptiste.
Les sorcières du Vivarais devant les inquisiteurs de la foi. Privas, Typographie et lithographie de Ph. Guiremand, 1865.
251 p. port. 22cm.

Bound in at end "Géologie et astronomie", signed by Dalmas, 8 p.

1. Witchcraft--Vivarais, France. I. Title. II. His Géologie et astronomie. III. Géologie et astronomie.

Georg Friedrich, Margrave of Brandenburg, 1539-1603.

Witchcraft
K B816++ 1582
Brandenburg (Electorate) Laws, statutes, etc.
Peinliche Halssgerichts-Ordnung, des Durchleuchtigen Hochgebornen Fürsten vnnd Herren, Herrn Georg Friderichen Marggrauen zu Brandenburg ... Welcher massen in J. F. G. Landen vnd Fürstenthumen in peinlichen Sachen einzuziehen, zufragen, zurichten, zustraffen, vnd zuuolfahren &c. Jtzo auff das Newe wider vbersehen, gemehrt vnd verbessert sampt einer Vorrede &c. [Ansbach?] Ge-
8   Continued on next card)

Georg Friedrich, Margrave of Brandenburg, 1539-1603.

Witchcraft
K B816++ 1582
Brandenburg (Electorate) Laws, statutes, etc. Peinliche Halssgerichts-Ordnung ... 1582.   (Card 2)

druckt zum Hoff durch Mattheum Pfeilschmidt, 1582.
3 p. l., lxii numbered, 11 unnumbered l. 31cm.
Interleaved, with ms. notes in contemporary hand; 7 l. appended at end.
With colophon.
Title in red and black, armorial device.
8   (Continued on next card)

Georg Friedrich, Margrave of Brandenburg, 1539-1603.

Witchcraft
K B816++ 1582
Brandenburg (Electorate) Laws, statutes, etc. Peinliche Halssgerichts-Ordnung ... 1582.   (Card 3)

With this are bound Brandenburg-Ansbach (Principality) Laws, statutes, etc. Neue Ordnung ... Onolzbach, 1720; and Brandenburg-Ansbach (Principality) Laws, statutes, etc. Anhang zu der Anno 1720. ergangenen ... Gerichts-Ordnung. Onolzbach [1725]
1. Criminal procedure--Brandenburg (Electorate). I. Georg Friedrich, Margrave of Brandenburg, 1539-1603. II. Title.
8 NIC

Georg Friedrich Meiers ... Philosophische Gedanken von den Würkungen des Teufels.

WITCHCRAFT
BF 1555 M94 029 no.6
Meier, Georg Friedrich, 1718-1777.
Georg Friedrich Meiers ... Philosophische Gedanken von den Würkungen des Teufels auf dem Erdboden. Halle, C. H. Hemmerde, 1760.
168 p. 18cm.

No. 6 in vol. lettered Oesfeld u. a. ...

1. Müller, Gottfried. Gründlicher Nachricht von einer begeisterten Weibesperson. 2. Devil. I. Title: Philosophische Gedanken von den Würkungen des Teufels.
8 NIC

Georg Wilhelm Wegners ... philosophische Abhandlung von Gespenstern.

Witchcraft
BF 1445 W41 P5
Wegner, Georg Wilhelm.
Philosophische Abhandlung von Gespenstern, worinn zugleich eine kurtze Nachricht von dem Wustermarckischen Kobold gegeben wird. Berlin, Zu haben bey A. Haude u. C. Spener, 1747.
80 p. 17cm.

1. Ghosts. I. Title.
8

Gerade Schweizer-Erklärung von Centralismus,

WITCHCRAFT
BF 1623 R7 012
Obereit, Jacob Hermann, 1725-1798.
Gerade Schweizer-Erklärung von Centralismus, [Exjesuiterey, Anecdotenjagd, Aberglauben, Maulglauben und Unglauben, gegen einen neuen Rosenkreuz-Bruder in der Berliner Monatsschrift vom August 1785... Berlin, Bei August Mylius, 1786.
viii, 94 p. 17cm.

1. Rosicrucians. 2. Mysticism. 3. Superstition. 4. Jesuits--Controversial literature. I. Zimmermann, Johann Georg, Ritter von, 1728-1795. II. Title. III. Title: Schweizer-Erklärung von Centralismus...
8 NIC

Gerald Gardner: witch.

Witchcraft
BF 1566 B79
Bracelin, Jack L
Gerald Gardner: witch. [London] Octagon Press [1960]
224 p. illus. 22 cm.

1. Gardner, Gerald Brosseau, 1884-   2. Witchcraft. I. Title.
BF1566.B7   920.91334   61-34293 ‡
Library of Congress

Gerardus (Cremonensis), of Sabbioneta, 13th cent.

BF 1410 L69 1921
Heinrich Cornelius Agrippa's von Nettesheim Magische Werke : sammt den geheimnissvollen Schriften des Petrus von Abano, Pictorius von Villingen, Gerhard von Cremona, Abt Tritheim von Spanheim, dem Buche Arbatel, der sogenannten Heil. Geist-Kunst und verschiedenen anderen zum ersten Male vollständig in's Deutsche übersetzt : vollständig in fünf Theilen, mit einer Menge Abbildungen. -- 4. Aufl. -- Berlin : H. Barsdorf, 1921.
5 v. in 3. : ill. ; 17cm. -- (Geheime Wissenschaften ; 10-14)

Gerardus (Cremonensis), of Sabbioneta, 13th cent.

WITCHCRAFT
BF 1410 L69 1655
Henry Cornelius Agrippa's Fourth book of occult philosophy, and geomancy. Magical elements of Peter de Abano. Astronomical geomancy [by Gerardus Cremonensis]. The nature of spirits [by Georg Pictorius]; and Arbatel of magick. Translated into English by Robert Turner. Philomathées. London, 1655.
9 p. l., [5]-266 [i.e., 286], [4] p. illus. 19cm.
Neither Agrippa nor Abano wrote the works
8
(Continued on next card)

Gerardus (Cremonensis), of Sabbioneta, 13th cent.

WITCHCRAFT
BF 1410 L69 1655
Henry Cornelius Agrippa's Fourth book of occult philosophy, and geomancy.
1655.   (Card 2)

here ascribed to them; the Heptameron, or Magical elements also was ascribed to Agrippa under the title: Les oeuvres magiques, with Abano as translator (!)
Translation of a work variously titled Liber de ceremonijs magicis; and his De occulta philosophia, liber quartus.
8   (Continued on next card)

Géraud, Hugues, bp. of Cahors, fl. 1317.

WITCHCRAFT
BF 1582 Z7 1317
Albe, Edmond, 1861-
Autour de Jean XXII: Hugues Géraud, évêque de Cahors, l'affaire des poisons et des envoûtements en 1317. Cahors, J. Girma, 1904.
206 p. 25cm.
"Extrait du Bulletin de la Société des Études littéraires, Scientifiques et Artistiques du Lot, t. XXIX."
1. Géraud, Hugues, bp. of Cahors, fl. 1317. 2. Johannes XXII, pope, d. 1334. I. Title. II. Title: L'affaire des poisons.

Gerbertsagnet; studie over middelalderlige djaevlekontrakthistorier.

WITCHCRAFT
BX 1158 M61
Meyer, Raphael Ludwig, 1869-1925.
Gerbertsagnet; studie over middelalderlige djaevlekontrakthistorier. København Det Nordiske Forlag, 1902.
170 p. 25cm.

8 NIC
1. Sylvester II, Pope, d. 1003. 2. Devil 3. Demonology. I. Title.

Der gerechte Folter-Banck.

RARE
HV 8593 W16
Waldkirch, Johann Rudolf von.
Der gerechte Folter-Banck; das ist, Ein rechtliche und gründliche Anweisung und Untersuchung ob, wie und wann eine christliche Obrigkeit die verdächtigen Maleficanten könne oder solle peinlich befragen Bern, Bey Daniel Tschiffeli, 1710.
95 p. 19cm.
"Von Zauberey": p. 74-77.
8 NIC
1. Torture. I. Title.

Eine gereimte Zeitung über den Hexenbra in Dieburg im Jahre 1627.

Witchcraft
BF 1583 Z7 1627
Englert, Anton, ed.
Eine gereimte Zeitung über den Hexenbrand in Dieburg im Jahre 1627. [Leipzig] 1913.
199-204 p. 23cm.
"Sonderabdruck aus Hessische Blätter für Volkskunde 1913, Band XII, Heft 3."
1. Witchcraft--Dieburg, Germany. I. Title.

Witchcraft
BL 795 D2 G36+
Gerhard, Eduard, 1795-1867.
Über Wesen, Verwandtschaft und Ursprung der Dämonen und Genien. Gelesen in der königl. Akademie der Wissenschaften zu Berlin am 13. Mai 1852. Berlin, In Commission der Besserschen Buchhandlung (W. Hertz) 1852.
[237]-266 p. 27cm.
Repr. from Akademie der Wissenschaften Berlin. Abhandlungen, v. 37 (1852) Philologische und historische Abhandlungen
8
1. Spirit. I. Title.

CATALOGUE OF THE CORNELL WITCHCRAFT COLLECTION

Witchcraft
BF 1445 D61 no.8

Gerhard, Johann Ernst, 1621-1668, praeses.
  Spectrum Endoreum, ex I. Sam. 28. Auspice numine summo, sub praesidio ... Johannis Eernesti Gerhardi ... Publicae eruditorum disquisitioni expositum, ab autore & respondente Benedicto Hahn ... ed. tertia auctior & emendatior. Jenae, Literis Johannis Nisii, 1684.
  112 p. 21cm.
  No. 8 in vol. lettered Dissertationes de spectris. 1646-1753.

8   (Continued on next card)

Witchcraft
BF 1445 D61 no.8

Gerhard, Johann Ernst, 1621-1668, praeses.
Spectrum Endoreum ... 1684. (Card 2)

  1. Bible. O.T. I Samuel XXVIII—Criticism, interpretation, etc. 2. Endor, Witch of (Biblical character) 3. Devil.
  I. Hahn, Benedict, respondent. II. Title.

8

Gerichts Teuffel.

WITCHCRAFT
GT 6260 W15

Wald, Georg am.
  Gerichts Teuffel, darin angezeigt vnd gehandlet wirt, wie vnnd in was massen der leidig Sathan bissweylen Vnordnung vnd Zerrüttung in Gerichten durch die Richter, Cleger, Beklagten, Aduocaten, Procuratoren, Zeugen vnd dergleichen Personen, so zu einem Gericht gehören, anrichten thut ... Zu End ist auch angehenckt der Gerichtlich Process ... Durch Georgen am Wald, der Rechten Lice   ntaten ... S. Gallen,
8   (Continued on next card)

Gerichts Teuffel.

WITCHCRAFT
GT 6260 W15

Wald, Georg am.   Gerichts Teuffel ...
1580.   (Card 2)

Gedruckt bey Leonhart Straub, 1580.
  [98] p. 20cm.
  Title in red and black.
  Gerichtlicher Process, wie er im gemeinen geschrionen bäpstlichen vnnd keyserlichen Rechten gegründet ... has special t. p., and is in verse.
  1. Germany—Social life and customs. 2. Procedur   e(Law)—Germany. 3. Trial practi   ce—Germany. I. His Gerichtliche   r Process. II. Title.

8

Das Gerichtswesen und die Hexenprozesse in Appenzell.

WITCHCRAFT
BF 1584 S97 S33

Schiess, Emil, 1394-
  Das Gerichtswesen und die Hexenprozesse in Appenzell. Trogen, Buchdr. O. Kübler, 1919.
  208 p. 20cm.
  Inaug.-Diss.—Bern.
  Anhang. Hexengeständnisse: p. [159]-204.
  1. Witchcraft—Switzerland. 2. Criminal procedure—Appenzell, Switzerland. I. Title.

8
NIC

Ein geringer Landgeistlicher.

WITCHCRAFT
BF 1523 V19 no.5

[Bonnet, Johann Carl]
  Demüthigste Antwort eines geringen Landgeistlichen auf die Demühige Bitte um Belehrung an die grossen Männer, welche keinen Teufel glauben. In Deutschland, 1776.
  54 p. 17cm.
  Attribution by Holzmann.
  No. 5 in vol. lettered Varia scripta demonolog.
  1. Köster, Heinrich Martin Gottfried, 1734-1802. Demühige Bitte um Belehrung. 2. Devil. I. Ein geringer Landgeistlicher. II. Title.

8

Witchcraft
GR 142 H6 A3 no.11

Gerish, William Blyth.
  The folk-lore of Hertfordshire; a brief list of material collected and classified by W. B. Gerish ... Bishop's Stortford, 1911.
  16 p. 22cm. [Hertfordshire folk lore. no. 11]

  1. Folk-lore—England—Hertfordshire. I. Title.
                                                  17-20382
Library of Congress   GR142.H6A3 no. 11

Witchcraft
GR 142 H6 A3 no.7

Gerish, William Blyth.
  A Hertfordshire witch; or, The story of Jane Wenham, the "wise woman" of Walkern, by W. B. Gerish. [Bishop's Stortford?] 1906]
  cover-title, 13 p. 23cm. [Hertfordshire folk lore. no. 7]
  With facsimile of the t.-p. of the Rev. Francis Bragge's pamphlet: A full and impartial account of the discovery of sorcery and witchcraft, practis'd by Jane Wenham ... 3d ed. London, 1712.

  1. Wenham, Jane, d. 1730. 2. Witchcraft—England. I. Title.
                                                  17-20384

Gerish, William Blyth, ed.
Witchcraft
GR 142 H6 A3 no.15

Drage, William, 1637?-1669.
  A relation of Mary Hall of Gadsden, reputed to be possessed of two devils, 1664, from "A small treatise of sicknesses and diseases from witchcraft," appended to "Physical experiments," by William Drage, London. Printed for Miller at the Star next the George in Little Britain [1668] With an introductory by W. B. Gerish. Bishop's Stortford, 1912.
  28 p. 22cm. [Hertfordshire folk lore. no. 15]

  1. Demonomania. 2. Hall, Mary, fl. 1664. I. Gerish, William Blyth, ed.
                                                  16-25740

Gerish, William Blyth, ed.
Witchcraft
GR 142 H6 A3 no.8

  The Hartfordshire wonder; or, Strange news from Ware. Being an exact and true relation of one Jane Stretton, the daughter of Thomas Stretton of Ware in the county of Herts, who hath been visited in a strange kind of manner by extraordinary and unusual fits, her abstaining from sustenance for the space of 9 months, being haunted by imps or devils in the form of several creatures here described, the parties adjudged of all by whom she was thus tormented and the occasion thereof ...

               (Continued on next card)   17-20383

Gerish, William Blyth, ed.
Witchcraft
GR 142 H6 A3 no.8

  The Hartfordshire wonder ... (Card 2)
London: printed for J. Clark ... 1669. Reprinted with an introductory note by W. B. Gerish. Bishop's Stortford, 1908.
  15 p. 22cm. [Hertfordshire folk lore. no. 8]
  Preface signed: M. J.

  1. Stretton, Jane, b. 1649. 2. Witchcraft—England. I. J., M. III. Gerish, William Blyth, ed.
                                                  17-20383
Library of Congress   GR142.H6A3 no. 5

Gerish, William Blyth, ed.
Witchcraft
GR 142 H6 A3 no.17

  A Hertfordshire miracle. The most cruell and bloody murther, committed by an inkeeper's wife, called Annis Dell, and her sonne George Dell, four yeeres since, on the bodie of a childe called Anthony James in Bishop's Hatfield in the countie of Hartford, and now most miraculously revealed by the sister of the said Anthony, who at the time of the murther had her tongue cut out, and four yeares remaynes dumme, and speechless, and now perfectly speaketh, revealing the murther, having no

               (Continued on next card)   16-25741

Gerish, William Blyth, ed.
Witchcraft
GR 142 H6 A3 no.17

  A Hertfordshire miracle ... (Card 2)
tongue to be seen. Who were executed at Hartford the 4 of August last past 1606. Reprinted, with an introductory by W. B. Gerish. Bishop's Stortford, 1913.
  27 p. 22cm. [Hertfordshire folk lore. no.]
  The original pamphlet is in 2 parts and is entitled: The most cruell and bloody murther committed by ... Annis Dell ... With the severall witchcrafts and most damnable practises of one Johane Harrison and her daughter ... London, Printed for W. Ferebrand and J. Wright, 1606.
  1. Crime and criminals—England—Hertfordshire. 2. Dell, Mrs. Annis, d. 1606. 3. Dell, George, d. 1606. I. Gerish, William Blyth, ed. II. Title: The most cruell and bloody murther ...
                                                  16-25741
Library of Congress   GR142.H6A3 no. 13

Gerish, William Blyth, ed.
Witchcraft
GR 142 H6 A3 no.18

  [Misodaimon, B.] pseud.
  The divel's delusions; or, A faithful relation of John Palmer and Elizabeth Knott, two notorious witches, lately condemned at the sessions of Oyer and Terminer in St. Albans. Together with the confession of the aforesaid John Palmer and Elizabeth Knott, executed July 16. Also their accusations of several witches in Hitchen, Norton, and other places in the county of Hartford. London, Printed for Richard Williams, stationer, at St. Albans, anno Dom, 1649. Reprinted with an introductory by W. B. Gerish. Bishop's Stortford, 1914.
  13, [1] p. 21½cm. [Hertfordshire folk lore. no. 18]
  Signed: "B. Misodaimon."
  1. Witchcraft—England. 2. Palmer, John, d. 1649. 3. Knott, Elizabeth, d. 1649. I. Gerish, William Blyth, ed. II. Title.
                                                  16-25733
Library of Congress   GR530.M55

Gerish, William Blyth, ed.
Witchcraft
GR 142 H6 A3 no.2

  The severall practices of Johane Harrison and her daughter, condemned and executed at Hartford for witchcraft, the 4th August last, 1606. Reprinted from the only known copy, with an introduction by W. B. Gerish. [Bishop's Stortford?] 1909.
  15 p. 22cm. [Hertfordshire folk lore. no. 2]

  The original pamphlet is in 2 parts and is entitled: The mo   st cruell and
               (Continued on next card)

Gerish, William Blyth, ed.
Witchcraft
GR 142 H6 A3 no.2

  The severall practices of Johane Harrison ... 1909. (Card 2)
bloody murther committed by ... Annis Dell ... With the several witchcrafts and most damnable practises of one Johane Harrison and her daughter ... London, Printed for W. Ferebrand and J. Wright, 1606.

Gerish, William Blyth, ed.
Witchcraft
GR 142 H6 A3 no.10

  A short rehearsal of the sad condition of three of the children of John Baldwin of Sarret in the county of Hertford, and also the manner of their deliverance, 1717. The parents' evidence together with a summary of the testimonies of the children and friends and a brief introductory note by W. B. Gerish. Bishops' Stortford, 1915.
  19 p. 21½cm. [Hertfordshire folk lore. no. 10]

  1. Baldwin, Rebecca, 1688-1713. 2. Baldwin, Mary, b. 1690. 3. Essex, Mrs. Anne (Baldwin) b. 1686. I. Gerish, William Blyth, ed.
                                                  16-25743
Library of Congress   GR142.H6A3 no. 17

Witchcraft
BF 1569 A2M72 1500

Gerson, Joannes, 1363-1429.
  De probatione spirituum.
Molitor, Ulrich, fl. 1470-1501.
  De lamiis et phitonicis mulieribus.
[Paris, Georg Mittelhus?, about 1500]
  [32] l. 14cm.

  Leaf [1a] (Title): Tractatus utilis et necessarius per viā dyalogi ymmo trilogi. De Phitonicis mulieribus. Unacum quodā paruo tractatulo doctissimi et acutissimi in sacra pagina doctoris Johānis de gersono cancellarii parisiensis De probatione spirituum.
  Leaf [1a-b]: Tabula et capitula presentis
               (Continued on next card)

231

CATALOGUE OF THE CORNELL WITCHCRAFT COLLECTION

Witchcraft
BF
1569
A2M72
1500
   Gerson, Joannes, 1363-1429.
     De probatione spirituum.
   Molitor, Ulrich, fl. 1470-1501. De lamiis et phitonicis mulieribus ... [about 1500] (Card 2)

tractatus.
   Leaf [2]: Epistola ... ad illustrissimū principē dominū Sigismundū archiducē Austrie Stirie Carinthie etc.
   The dialogue begins at the bottom of leaf [2b] and ends on leaf [27a].
   "Johānis de gersonno ... tractatulus ... de probatione spirituum ...": leaf [27b].
     (Continued on next card)

Witchcraft
BF
1569
A2M72
1500
   Gerson, Joannes, 1363-1429.
     De probatione spirituum.
   Molitor, Ulrich, fl. 1470-1501. De lamiis et phitonicis mulieribus ... [about 1500] (Card 3)

[32b]
   Leaf [32b] (Colophon): Explicit tractatus de laniis [sic] et phitonicis mulieribus vna cū tractatu de probatiōe spūm venerabilis mgīi iohānis de gersono cācellarij parisiēsis.
   Signatures: a-d8.
   Copinger. Supplementum, 4341; Polain
     (Continued on next card)

Witchcraft
BF
1569
A2M72
1500
   Gerson, Joannes, 1363-1429.
     De probatione spirituum.
   Molitor, Ulrich, fl. 1470-1501. De lamiis et phitonicis mulieribus ... [about 1500] (Card 4)

(B), 2763; Goff. Third census, M-805.

   1. Witchcraft. 2. Demonology. 3. Visions. I. Gerson, Joannes, 1363-1429. De probatione spirituum. II. Title. III. Title: De probatione spirituum.

Witchcraft
BT
1313
B52
   Gerson, Joannes, 1363-1429.
   Bernardus Comensis.
     Lucerna inquisitorum haereticae pravitatis R. P. F. Bernardi Comensis... et eiusdem Tractatus de strigibus, cum annotationibus Francisci Pegnae... Additi sunt in hac impressione duo tractatus Joannis Gersoni... Roma, ex officina Bartholomaei Grassi, 1584.
   [4] l., 184, [28] p. 22cm.
   1. Heresies and heretics. I. Pegna, Francesco, ed. II. Gerson, Joannes, 1363-1429. III. Title.

Witchcraft
BF
1775
W13
1800
   Gertrude, Saint, surnamed the Great, 1256-1302? supposed author.
   Der Wahre geistliche Schild. 2. Th. Oder: Heiliger Segen aller heil. Apostel und Jünger Jesu Christi ..., um alle unheilbaren Krankheiten der Menschen zu vertreiben, und alle Anfälle des Satans abzuwenden. Sammt dem wunderthätigen Gertrauden-Büchlein, das ist: Der heil. Jungfrau und Abtissin Gertraud himmlische Anmuthungen und Gebete um zeitliche und ewige Güter. Salzburg, 1667. [n. p., 18--]
   148 p. illus. 16cm.
8   (Continued on next card)

Witchcraft
BF
1775
W13
1800
   Gertrude, Saint, surnamed the Great, 1256-1302? supposed author.
   Der Wahre geistliche Schild ... [18--] (Card 2)
   Heiliger Segen aller heiligen Apostel ... has special t. p.
   Der heiligen Jungfrauen und Abtissin Gertraud himmlische Anmuthungen und Gebeter has special t. p. and imprint Cöln, 1506.
   1. Charms. 2. Prayers. I. Gertrude, Saint, surnamed the Great, 1256-1302? supposed author. II. Title: Heiliger Segen aller heiligen Apostel. III. Title: Der heiligen Jungfrauen ...Gertraud himmlische Anmuthungen.

WITCHCRAFT
BF
1555
G38
   Gervais de Tournai, Martin, b. 1515.
     Divina qvatvor energvmenorvm liberatio, facta apvd Suessiones, anno Domini millesimo quingentesimo octogesimo secundo. In qua sacrosanctae Eucharistiae vis & veritas planè elucet. Eam scripsit Geruasius Tornacensis. . . Parisiis, Apud Guillelmum Chaudiere, 1583.
   111 numb. l., [3] p. 17cm.
   Contents.--1. Laurentius.--2. Nicolea.--3. Margarita.--4. Nicolaus.--Appendix
8   (Continued on next card)

WITCHCRAFT
BF
1555
G38
   Gervais de Tournai, Martin, b. 1515. Divina qvatvor energvmenorvm liberatio ... (Card 2)

de Astarotho daemone fugitiuo.
Copy two imperfect: t. p., l. 1-8 and all after l. 109 mutilated.

   1. Demoniac possession. 2. Devil. I. Title: Divina quatuor energumenorum liberatio.

ar W
9788
   Gervasius, of Tilbury.
     Otia imperialia. In einer Auswahl neu hrsg. und mit Anmerkungen begleitet von Felix Liebrecht. Ein Beitrag zur deutschen Mythologie und Sagenforschung. Hannover, C. Rümpler, 1856.
   xxii, 274 p. 23cm.

   I. Liebrecht, Felix, 1812-1890, ed. II. Title.

Gervasius Tornacensis.
see
Gervais de Tournai, Martin, b. 1515.

Geschichte der Hexen und Hexenprozesse.
WITCHCRAFT
BF
1566
L56
   Lempens, Carl, 1839-
     Geschichte der Hexen und Hexenprozesse.. St. Gallen (Schweiz), H. Fuhrimann, 1880.
   80 p. 19cm.

8
NIC   1. Witchcraft--Hist. 2. Trials (Witchcraft)--Hist.

Geschichte der Hexenprozesse.
Witchcraft
BF
1566
S68
1912
   Soldan, Wilhelm Gottlieb, d. 1869.
     Geschichte der Hexenprozesse. Neu bearbeitet und hrsg. von Max Bauer. München, G. Müller [1912]
   2 v. illus. 22cm.
   At head of title: Soldan-Heppe.
   First ed. 1843; 2d ed., edited by Heinrich Heppe, published 1880. Cf. Allgemeine deutsche Biographie.

   1. Witchcraft. I. Heppe, Heinrich Ludwig Julius, 1820-1879 ed. II. Bauer, Max, 1861- ed. III. Title.

Geschichte der Hexenprozesse in Bayern.
Witchcraft
BF
1583
R56
   Riezler, Sigmund, Ritter von, 1843-1927.
     Geschichte der Hexenprozesse in Bayern. Im Lichte der allgemeinen Entwickelung dargestellt von Sigmund Riezler. Stuttgart, Verlag der J. G. Cotta'schen Buchhandlung Nachf., 1896.
   x, 340 p. 23cm.
   Includes excerpts from Johann Hartliebs Buch aller verbotenen Kunst.

Geschichte der Magie.
BF
1589
E59
1966
   Ennemoser, Joseph, 1787-1854.
     Geschichte der Magie. (Neudruck der Ausgabe von 1844) Wiesbaden, Sändig (1966)
   xlviii, 1001 p. 21 cm. DM 98.-
     (GDNB 66-A18-405)

   1. Magic. 2. Occult sciences. I. Title.

BF1589.E58 1966   66-75303
Library of Congress   [2]

Geschichte der menschlichen Narrheit.
Witchcraft
BF
1410
A23
   [Adelung, Johann Christoph] 1732-1806.
     Geschichte der menschlichen Narrheit; oder, Lebensbeschreibungen berühmter Schwarzkünstler, Goldmacher, Teufelsbanner, Zeichen- und Liniendeuter, Schwärmer, Wahrsager, und anderer philosophischer Unholden. Leipzig, Weygand, 1785-89.
   7 v. in 3. 18cm.
   Title vignette.
8   (Continued on next card)

Geschichte der menschlichen Narrheit.
Witchcraft
BF
1410
A23
   [Adelung, Johann Christoph] 1732-1806.
   Geschichte der menschlichen Narrheit ... 1785-89. (Card 2)

Witchcraft
BF
1410
A23
Suppl.
   ---Gallerie der neuen Propheten, apokalyptischen Träumer, Geisterseher und Revolutionsprediger. Ein Beytrag zur Geschichte der menschlichen Narrheit. Leipzig, Weygand, 1799.
   3 p. l., 487, [3] p. 20cm.
8   (Continued on next card)

WITCHCRAFT
BF
1405
G28
   Geschichte der Natur u. Kunst von 1717-1726 Ausschnitte. [Bresslau, etc. 1718-1728]
   1 v. (various pagings) illus. 21cm.
   Cover title.
   Extracts from Sammlung von Natur- und Medicin- wie auch hierzu gehörigen Kunst- und Literatur-Geschichten, and Supplementum I-III. Curieuser und nutzbarer Anmerckungen von Natur- und Kunst-Geschichten.
   Paged (635) and with Register in MS.
8
NIC   1. Occult sciences. 2. Curiosities and wonders. I. Sammlung von Natur- und Medicin- ... Geschichten

Geschichte der Psychiatrie in Polen.
WITCHCRAFT
RC
438
R84
   Rothe, A   von
     Geschichte der Psychiatrie in Polen, von A. v. Rothe. Leipzig, F. Deuticke, 1896.
   99 p. 23cm.
   Bibliographical footnotes.

   1. Psychiatry--Poland--History. 2. Demonology. I. Title.

CATALOGUE OF THE CORNELL WITCHCRAFT COLLECTION

Geschichte der spanischen Inquisition.

cW
9639
    Lea, Henry Charles, 1825-1909.
        Geschichte der spanischen Inquisition; deutsch bearb. von P. Müllendorff. Leipzig, Dyk, 1911-12.
        3 v. 25cm.

        Translation of History of the inquisition of Spain.

        I. Lea, Henry Charles, 1825-1909. History of the inquisition of Spain-- German. II. Title.

Geschichte des Glaubens an Zauberei.

Witchcraft
BF
1523
H81
    Horst, Georg Conrad, 1767-1838?
        Dämonomagie, oder Geschichte des Glaubens an Zauberei und dämonische Wunder, mit besonderer Berücksichtigung des Hexenprocesses seit den Zeiten Innocentius des Achten. Nebst einer ausführlichen, nach Inquisitionsacten bearbeiteten Beschreibung des Hexenthurms zu Lindheim in der Wetterau ... Mit Kupfern. Frankfurt am Main, bei den Gebrüdern Wilmans, 1818.
        2 v. fold. plates. 20cm.

        I. Title. II. Title: Geschichte des Glaubens an Zauberei und dämonische Wunder.

Geschichte des Hexenbrennens in Franken im siebzehnten Jahrhundert.

WITCHCRAFT
BF
1583
J22
    Jäger, Franz Anton, 1765-1835.
        Geschichte des Hexenbrennens in Franken im siebzehnten Jahrhundert, aus Original-Prozess-Akten, von Dr. Jäger, Pfarrer in Pföring an der Donau. Würzburg, 1834.
        72 p. 23cm.

        Caption title.
        Detached from Historischer Verein von Unterfranken und Aschaffenburg. Archiv. 2. Bd.

        1. Witchcraft--Franconia. I. Title.

Geschichte des neueren occultismus.

Witchcraft
    Kiesewetter, Karl, 1854-1895.
        Geschichte des neueren occultismus. Geheimwissenschaftliche systeme von Agrippa von Nettesheym bis zu Carl du Prel. Von Carl Kiesewetter ... Leipzig, W. Friedrich [1891]
        xiv, 799, [2] p. illus. 22cm.

        Half-title: Erster teil. Systeme und systematiker.
        Pt. 2 issued under title: Die geheimwissenschaften.

        1. Occult sciences--Hist. I. Title.

Library of Congress, no.

Geschichte des Teufels.

Witchcraft
    Roskoff, Gustav, 1814-1889.
        Geschichte des Teufels. Leipzig, F. A. Brockhaus, 1869.
        2 v. 23cm.

        1. Devil. 2. Witchcraft. I. Title.

Geschichte des Teuffels.

Witchcraft
PR
3404
    [Defoe, Daniel] 1660-1731.
1733
        Geschichte des Teuffels; aus dem Englischen übersetzet, in zwey Theilen. Franckfurt am Mayn, 1733.
        532 p. port. 18cm.

        Translation of The political history of the devil.
        Also published under title: Gründliche historische Nachricht vom Teuffel.

        I. His The political history of the devil. German. II. Title.

Geschichte des Wortes Hexe.

Witchcraft
BF
1583
F82
    Franck, Johannes, 1854-
        Geschichte des Wortes Hexe. Bonn, C. Georgi, 1901.
        59 p. 24cm.

        "Sonder-Abdruck aus Hansen: Quellen und Untersuchungen zur Geschichte des Hexenwahns und der Hexenverfolgung im Mittelalter."

        I. Title.

Geschichte einer merkwürdigen Teufels-Besitzung in Franken.

WITCHCRAFT
BF
1517
G3
M51
    Meiners, Christoph, 1747-1810.
        Geschichte einer merkwürdigen Teufels-Besitzung in Franken zwischen den Jahren 1740 und 1750. [Hannover, 1788]
        39 p. 20cm.

        Detached from Göttingisches historisches Magazin, v.2, 1788.

        1. Demoniac possession. 2. Witchcraft--Franconia. 3. Sänger, Maria Renata von Mossau, ca.1680-1749.

Geschichten Besessener neuerer Zeit.

WITCHCRAFT
BF
1555
K39
    Kerner, Justinus Andreas Christian, 1786-1862.
        Geschichten Besessener neuerer Zeit; Beobachtungen aus dem Gebiete kakodämonisch-magnetischer Erscheinungen. Nebst Reflexionen von C. A. Eschenmayer über Besessenseyn und Zauber. Stuttgart, Druck von J. Wachendorf, 1834.
        vi, 195 p. 19cm.

        1. Demoniac possession. I. Eschenmayer, Carl Adolph von, 1770?-1852. Einige Reflexionen über Besessenseyn und Zauber. II. Title.

Geschichten vom Teufel.

Witchcraft
BF
1549
C69
1821
    [Collin de Plancy, Jacques Albin Simon] 1794-1881.
        Geschichten vom Teufel. Quedlinburg und Leipzig, G. Basse, 1821.
        179 p. 17cm.

        "... nach dem Werke: 'Le diable peint par lui même, par Collin de Plancy' zusammengestellt:" Vorwort, p. 9.
        Considerably shortened and simplified.

        1. Devil. 2. Occult sciences. I. His Le diable peint par lui-même. German. II. Title.

Geschiedenis der heksenprocessen.

WITCHCRAFT
BF
1569
S32
    Scheltema, Jacobus, 1767-1835.
        Geschiedenis der heksenprocessen, eene bijdrage tot den roem des vaderlands. Door Mr. Jacobus Scheltema ... Haarlem, V. Loosjés, 1828.
        2 p. l., xvi, 312, 101, [5] p. 23cm.

        Engr. t-p., with portrait of J. Wier.
        "Aanteekeningen en ophelderingen" has special t. p. and separate paging.

        1. Witchcraft--History. 2. Trials (Witchcraft)--History. I. Title.

Library of Congress   BF1569.S3   11-9021

Die Gespenstererscheinungen, eine Phantasie oder Betrug, durch die Bibel, Vernunftlehre und Erfahrung bewiesen.

Witchcraft
BF
1445
S83
    Sterzinger, Ferdinand, 1721-1786.
        Die Gespenstererscheinungen, eine Phantasie oder Betrug, durch die Bibel, Vernunftlehre und Erfahrung bewiesen ... München, Bey J. Lentner, 1786.
        4 p. l., 123 p. 22cm.

        1. Ghosts. 2. Superstition. I. Title.

Gespräche von verschiedenem Innhalte unter einer muntern Fastnachtcompagnie, verfasset von einem Liebhaber einer anständigen Freyheit.

MSS
Bd
Witchcraft
BF
G38
        Gespräche von verschiedenem Innhalte unter einer muntern Fastnachtcompagnie, verfasset von einem Liebhaber einer anständigen Freyheit. Gedruckt vor baares Geld, im Jahr, als noch im Märze Fasching war. [München? 1677]
        16 p. 22cm.
        Carnap's manuscript copy.
        Concerns the Sterzinger-März controversy.

        1. Sterzinger, Ferdinand, 1721-1786. 2. Superstition. I. Ein Liebhaber ein er anständigen Freyheit.

Die Gestalten des Todes und des Teufels in der darstellenden Kunst.

Witchcraft
N
8217
D5
W51
    Wessely, Joseph Eduard, 1826-1895.
        Die Gestalten des Todes und des Teufels in der darstellenden Kunst. Von J. E. Wesseley. Mit 2 Radirungen des Verfassers und 21 Illustrationen in Holzschnitt. Leipzig, H. Vogel (früher R. Weigel) 1876.
        123 p. illus. (part col.) 23cm.
        Contents.--I. Iconographie des Todes.--II. Iconographie des Teufels.
        Each part has special t. p.

        1. Death--Art. 2. Devil--Art. I. Title.

Gestroojde zeegenpalmen.

Witchcraft
BF
1410
B42
Z89
        Verscheyde gedichten, so voor, als tegen het boek, genaamt: De betoverde weereld. [Amsterdam?] Gedrukt voor de liefhebbers, 1691.
        1 p. l., 12, 9-32 p. title vignettes, illus. initials. 20 x 15cm.
        4°: π1, A⁶, B-D⁴.
        First poem has own t. p. with title: Gestroojde zeegen-palmen, op het doorwrogte werk van de Heer Balthasar Bekker ... genaamd De betoverde weereld. [Van der Linde 188]

(Continued on next card)

Gestroojde zeegen-palmen.

Witchcraft
BF
1410
B42
Z89
        Verscheyde gedichten, so voor, als tegen het boek, genaamt: De betoverde weereld. 1691. (Card 2)

        Includes other works published separately: De betoverde predikant Dr. Balthasar Bekker [van der Linde 189]; Verta[e]ling uit seker arabisch schryver; De geharpoende muys. Van der Linde 197.

        1. Bekker, Balthasar, 1634-1698. De betoverde weereld. I. Gestroojde zeegen-

(Continued on next card)

Ein gesunder, unverruckter Kopf disseits der Donau.

Witchcraft
BF
1565
D77
        Drey wichtige Fragen über das Hexen-System von einem gesunden, unverruckten Kopf disseits der Donau. [n. p.] 1767.
        24 p. 21cm.

        H. Fieger, in P. Don Ferdinand Sterzinger, attributes this work to one "Premb, Weltpriester."

        1. Witchcraft. 2. Sterzinger, Ferdinand, 1721-1786. Akademische Rede von dem gemeinen Vorurtheil der ... Hexerey. I. Premb, , supposed author. II. Ein gesu nder, unverruckter Kopf disseits der Donau.

Den gevallen engel, weereloos.

Witchcraft
BF
1410
B42
Z56
v.2
no.15
    Gunst, Lucas van.
        Den gevallen engel, weereloos. En desselfs onmacht, en krachteloosheyd, klarlijck, vertoont uyt de H. Schriftuur, het geestelijck en wereldlijck recht, als mede uyt de historien. Door Mr. Lucas van Gunst, rechtsgeleerde. Amsterdam, Te koop by J. en G. Janssonius van Waesberge, 1692.
        2 p. l., 52 p. title vignette, illus. initials. 19 x 15cm.
        4°: π², A- F⁴, G².

(Continued on next card)

233

CATALOGUE OF THE CORNELL WITCHCRAFT COLLECTION

Den gevallen engel, weereloos.

Witchcraft
BF
1410
B42
Z56
v.2
no.15
    Gunst, Lucas van. Den gevallen engel, weereloos. 1692.   (Card 2)

    Black letter (except for introduction)
    Van der Linde 94.
    No. 15 in vol. lettered Bekker II.

    1. Devil. 2. Spirits. I. Title.

8

Gewalt und Wirckung des Teuffels.

WITCHCRAFT
R
133
H71
1704
    [Hoffmann, Friedrich] 1660-1742.
      Philosophische Untersuchung von Gewalt und Wirckung des Teuffels in natürlichen Körpern. Franckfurt und Leipzig, 1704.
      29 p. 20cm.

    Translation of Disputatio inauguralis medico-philosophica De potentia diaboli in corpora. Halae, 1703.

    1. Medicine, Magic, mystic, and spagiric 2. Devil. I. His Disputatio inauguralis medico-philosophica De potentia diaboli in corpora. German. II. Title.

8
NIC

Een gewapend-Christen, teegen de listige omleydinge des duyvels.

Witchcraft
BX
9479
B42
B11
no.12
    De Geestelyke stryd; of Een gewapend-Christen, teegen de listige omleydinge des duyvels. Verstaanbaar verklaard, over de woorden Pauli; Ephes. 6: 11, 12, &c. Zyn de blaaden Josuas. Amsterdam, By A. van Damme, 1699.
    14 p. title vignette, illus. initial. 20 x 15cm.
    4°: A-B⁴(-B4)
    Black letter.
    No. 12 in vol. lettered B. Bekkers sterfbed en andere tractaten.
    (Continued on next card)

8

Gewissens-Fragen oder Gründlicher Bericht von Zauberey und Zauberern.

Witchcraft
BF
1565
F88
1671
    Freudius, Michael.
      Gewissens-Fragen oder Gründlicher Bericht von Zauberey und Zauberern, von Mitteln wider dieselbe, und was für einen Process christliche Obrigkeit wider die Zauberer gebrauchen solle. Benebenst einem Anhang von Geist- und leiblicher Besitzung und Austreibung dess bösen Geistes ... Franckfurt am Mayn, Drucks und Verlags Balth. Christoph Wusts, 1671.
    [54], 714, [144, 46] 88, [10] p. 21cm.
    Added t. p., engraved.
    I. Title.

Geyssler, Valentin.

Witchcraft
BF
1555
G31
    Gründlicher vnnd warhaffter Bericht, was sich mit dem Mann, der sich Hanns Vatter von Mellingen, ausdem Landt zu Düringen genennt, vnnd ein zeytlang im Teutschlandt herumb gezogen, zur Buss geruffen, vnd bey den Leuten fürgegeben, als ob er vom Sathan gepunden vnnd geplagt würde, zu Nürnberg zugetragen vnnd verloffen hat. Nürnberg, Gedruckt bey Valentin Geyssler, 1562.
    [20] p. 20cm.

8   (Continued on next card)

Geyssler, Valentin.

Witchcraft
BF
1555
G31
    Gründlicher vnnd warhaffter Bericht, was sich mit ... Hanns Vatter ... zugetragen hat ... 1562.   (Card 2)

    "Meniglich zu warhafftem Bericht verloffner Handlungen inn Druck gegeben durch mich Valtin Geyssler Buchdrucker zu Nürmberg." Portrait of Vatter on t. p.

    1. Vatter, Hanns, von Mellingen. 2. Demoniac possession. I. Geyssler, Valentin.

8

Ghirlando, Paulus.

see

Grillando, Paolo.

Giffard, George.

see

Gifford, George, d. 1620.

Witchcraft
BF
1565
G45
1593a
    Gifford, George, d. 1620.
      ...A dialogue concerning witches and witchcraftes, 1593, by George Gifford; with an introduction by Beatrice White. [London] Pub. for the Shakespeare association by H. Milford, Oxford university press, 1931.
      x p., facsim. ([96] p.), 1 l. 23cm. (Shakespeare association. Facsimiles. no. 1)

    "From the copy of the first edition in the British museum (c. 57 e. 43)."
    With facsimile of original t.-p.
    Bibliography: p. x.

WITCHCRAFT
BF
1565
G45
1842
    Gifford, George, d. 1620.
      A dialogue concerning witches & witchcrafts, by George Gifford. Reprinted from the edition of 1603. London, Printed for the Percy society [by T. Richards] 1842.
      viii, v, [7]-119 p. 20cm.

    With reproduction of the t.-p. of the London edition of 1603.
    Edited by Thomas Wright.

    1. Witchcraft. I. Wright, Thomas, 1810-1877, ed. II. Title.

PR
1120
P43
v.8
    Gifford, George, d. 1620.
      A dialogue concerning witches & witchcrafts, by George Gifford. Reprinted from the edition of 1603. London, Printed for the Percy society [by T. Richards] 1842.
      viii, v, [7]-119 p. 20cm. (In Percy society. Early English poetry ... vol. VIII)

    With reproduction of the t.-p. of the London edition of 1603.
    Edited by Thomas Wright.
    No.2 in vol.

WITCHCRAFT
BF
1565
G45
D5
    Gifford, George, d. 1620.
      A discourse of the subtill practises of deuilles by vvitches and sorcerers. By which men are and haue been greatly deluded: the antiquitie of them: their diuers sorts and names. With an answer vnto diuers friuolous reasons which some doe make to prooue that the deuils did not make those aperations in any bodily shape. By G. Gyfford. London, Imprinted for Toby Cooke, 1587.
      [66] p. 18cm.
    Title page in ornamental border.
    (Continued on next card)

8
NIC

WITCHCRAFT
BF
1565
G45
D5
    Gifford, George, d. 1620. A discourse of the subtill practises of deuilles ... 1587.   (Card 2)

    Printed at the press of George Robinson, d. 1586 or 1587, whose widow soon afterward married Thomas Orwin.

    1. Witchcraft. 2. Devil. I. Title.

8
NIC

WITCHCRAFT
BF
1517
F5
J43
1886
    Gilles de la Tourette, Georges Albert Édouard Brutus, 1857-   ed.
      Jeanne des Anges, mère, 1602-1665.
      Soeur Jeanne des Anges, supérieure des Ursulines de Loudun (XVIIe siècle) Autobiographie d'une hystérique possédée, d'après le manuscrit inédit de la bibliothèque de Tours. Annoté et publié par les docteurs Gabriel Legué et Gilles de la Tourette. Préface de M. le professeur Charcot. Paris, Aux Bureaux du Progrès, 1886.
      xiv, 321 p. facsim. 24cm. (Bibliothèque diabolique [Collection Bourneville])
    (Continued on next card)

8
NIC

Gilles de Rais: the original Bluebeard.

Witchcraft
DC
102
.8
R2
V77
    Vincent, Louis, 1876–
      Gilles de Rais: the original Bluebeard, by A. L. Vincent & Clare Binns, introduction by M. Hamblin Smith ... London, A. M. Philpot, ltd., 1926.
      2 p. l., 3-221, [1] p. illus., plates, 2 port. (incl. front.) 19½ᶜᵐ.
    "Genealogy of Gilles de Rais": p. 199-202
    "List of works consulted": p. 217-221.

    1. Rais, Gilles de Laval, seigneur de, 1404-1440. I. Binns, Clare, joint author. II. Title.

                27-18294 Revised

8   Library of Congress   DC102.8.R2V6
                          [r31c2]

Witchcraft
BF
1546
G48
    [Gilpin, Richard]
      Daemonologia sacra: or, A treatise of Satan temptations ... By R. G. ... London, Printed by J. D. for R. Randel and P. Maplisden, 1677.
      3 pts. in 1 v. 20cm.

    1. Devil. I. Title. II. Title: Satans temptations. III. G., R. IV. R. G.

Gineste, Raoul, pseud.

see

Augier, Adolphe Clovis.

Witchcraft
BF
1584
I8
G49
    Ginzburg, Carlo.
      I benandanti; ricerche sulla stregoneria e sui culti agrari tra Cinquecento e Seicento. [Torino] G. Einaudi [c1966]
      xvii, 197 p. illus. 22cm. (Biblioteca di cultura storica, 89)

    1. Witchcraft--Italy. I. Title.

CATALOGUE OF THE CORNELL WITCHCRAFT COLLECTION

```
itchcraft    Giraldo, Mathias de, pseud.
 12           Histoire curieuse et pittoresque des sorciers,
             devins, magiciens, astrologues, voyants,
 49          revenants, ames en peine, vampires, spectres,
             fantomes, apparitions, visions, gnomes, lutins,
             esprits malins, sorts jetés, exorcismes, etc....
             depuis l'antiquité jusqu'à nos jours, par le
             révérend père dominicain Mathias de Giraldo,
             ancien exorciste de l'Inquisition, rev. et augm.
             par M. Fornari, professeur de philosophie
             hermétique à Milan.  Paris, Chez tous les
             libraires marchands de nouveautés [1849]
              315 p.  4 fold. plates.  24cm.
              Half-title: Histoire des sorciers.
                                   (Continued on next card)
```

```
Witchcraft
BF        Giraldo, Mathias de, pseud.   Histoire
1412        curieuse et pittoresque des sorciers ...
G51         [1849]                           (Card 2)
1849
              1. Occult sciences.  2. Superstition.
            I. Fornari,       ed.   II. Title.
            III. Title: Histoire des sorciers.

   8
```

Girard, Jean Baptiste

```
Witchcraft
        Girard, Jean Baptiste, 1680-1733, defendant.
1582      The case of Mrs. Mary Catharine Cadiere,
G51     against the Jesuit Father John Baptist Gi-
C33     rard.  In a memorial presented to the Par-
1732    liament of Aix.  Wherein he is accused of
        seducing her, by the abominable doctrines
        of quietism, into the most criminal ex-
        cesses of lewdness, and under an appearance
        of the highest mystical devotion, deluding
        into the same vices six other females, who
        had put their          consciences under his
                           (Continued on next card)
```

```
Witchcraft
BF        Girard, Jean Baptiste, 1680-1733, defendant.
1582        A compleat translation of the Memorial of
G51M5       the Jesuit Father John Baptist Girard ...
1732        1732.                            (Card 2)

        originals whereof were produced in court":
        143 p. at end.

           1. Cadière,       Catherine, b. 1709.
           I. Girard, Jean Baptiste, 1680-1733.  Mémoire
        instructif.... English.  II. Cadière,
           Catherine,       b. 1709.  III. Title.
```

```
Witchcraft
BF       [Girard, Jean Baptiste] 1680-1733, defendant.
1582        Memoir [sic] du P. et de la Cadier [sic]
G51         [Aix, etc., De l'imprimerie de la veuve
M48++    de Joseph Senez, etc., 1731]
           various pagings.  32cm.
           Cover title.
           Contents.--Mémoire instructif, pour Mes-
        sire François Cadière.--Observations sur le
        memoire manuscrit distribué par le P. Girard.
        --Memoire du Pere Girard.--Memoire instruc-
        tif, pour le Pere Nicolas de S. Joseph.--
   8                          (Continued on next card)
```

```
itchcraft
F         Girard, Jean Baptiste, 1680-1733, defendant.
582         The case of Mrs. Mary Catharine Cadiere ...
51          1732.                            (Card 2)
33
732     direction.  With a preface by the publisher
        ... 10th ed. corr.  London, Printed for
        and sold by J. Roberts, 1732.
           vi, 96 p. 23cm.
           "This memorial was originally drawn up
        by that eminent lawyer ... Chaudon ... the
        following piece  is not a bare transla-
        tion ..." p. ii
                           (Continued on next card)
```

```
Witchcraft
BF        Girard, Jean Baptiste, 1680-1733, defendant.
1582        A compleat translation of the Sequel
G51     of the proceedings of Mary Catherine Cadiere
S9      against the Jesuit Father John Baptist
1732    Girard...  London, Printed for J. Millan,
        1732.
           255, [1] p.  front. (port.)  17cm.

           Publisher's catalogue: p. [256]
           Ex libris I. R. Inge.
```

```
Witchcraft
BF       [Girard, Jean Baptiste] 1680-1733, defendant.
1582       Memoir du P. et de la Cadier.  [1731]
G51                                        (Card 2)
M48++
           Contents--Continued.
           Reflexions sur la recrimination en pretendu
        complot imputé au Pere Estienne Thomas Ca-
        diere.--Observations sur les reponses per-
        sonnelles du P. Girard.--Second mémoire pour
        le Pere Girard.--Reponse a l'ecrit, qui a
        pour titre: Memoire des faits qui se
   8                          (Continued on next card)
```

```
Witchcraft
BF         Girard, Jean Baptiste, 1680-1733, defendant.
1582         The case of Mrs. Mary Catharine Cadiere ...
G51          1732.                            (Card 3)
C33
1732        1. Cadière,       Catherine, b. 1709.
            2. Girard, Jean Baptiste, 1680-1733.  3.
        Witchcraft--France.  I. Chaudon,
        lawyer.  II. France. Parlement (Aix)  III.
        Title.


   8
```

```
Witchcraft
BF        Girard, Jean Baptiste, 1680-1733, defendant.
1582        A compleat translation of the Sequel
G51     of the Proceedings of Mary Catherine Cadiere,
S9      against the Jesuit Father John Baptist
1732a   Girard.  Containing many curious pieces
        ... 2d ed.  London, Printed for J.
        Millan, 1732.
           255, [1] p. 17cm.

           Publisher's advertisement: p. [256]
           I. Cadière,       Catherine, b. 1709.
           II. Title.
```

```
Witchcraft
BF       [Girard, Jean Baptiste] 1680-1733, defendant.
1582       Memoir du P. et de la Cadier.  [1731]
G51                                        (Card 3)
M48++
           Contents--Continued.
        sont passez sour les yeux de M. l'Evêque de
        Toulon.--A nosseigneurs de Parlement [par
        Estienne-Thomas Cadiere]--A nosseigneurs de
        Parlement [par Catherine Cadiere]--A nos-
        seigneurs de Parlement [par Catherine Ca-
                                              diere]
   8                          (Continued on next card)
```

```
itchcraft
F          Girard, Jean Baptiste, 1680-1733, defendant.
582          A compleat translation of the Memorial of
51M5     the Jesuit Father John Baptist Girard, rector
732      of the Royal Seminary of the Chaplains of the
         Navy, in the city of Toulon, against Mary
         Catherine Cadière and the attorney [sic] gen-
         eral, plaintiff.  London, Printed for J.
         Millan, 1732.
            172, 143 p. 17cm.

            "A collection     of the letters of Father
         Girard and Mary       Catherine Cadière, the
                           (Continued on next card)
```

```
Witchcraft
BF         Girard, Jean Baptiste, 1680-1733, defendant.
1582         The defence of F. John Baptist Girard,
G51      Jesuit, and rector of the Royal Seminary
D3       of Chaplains of the Navy, in the city of
1732     Toulon; against the accusation of Mary
         Catharine Cadiere.  London, Printed for
         and sold by J. Roberts, 1731-32 [pt. 1,
         1732]
            3 pts. in 1 v. 21cm.

            Parts 1-2: 3d ed.

            I. Cadière,      Catharine, b. 1709.  8
            II. Title.
```

```
Witchcraft
BF       [Girard, Jean Baptiste] 1680-1733, defendant.
1582       Memoir du P. et de la Cadier.  [1731]
G51                                        (Card 4)
M48++

           1. Cadière,       Catherine, b. 1709.
           2. Girard, Jean Baptiste, 1680-1733.  3.
        Witchcraft--France.  I. Cadière, François,
        fl. 1730.  II. Cadière,       Catherine, b.
        1709.  III. France. Parlement (Aix)  IV.
        Cadière, Estienne Thomas, fl. 1730.
        V. Title.
```

235

CATALOGUE OF THE CORNELL WITCHCRAFT COLLECTION

WITCHCRAFT
BF   Girard, Jean Baptiste, 1680-1733, respondent
1582   Mémoire instructif, pour le Père Jean
G51   Baptiste Girard, Jesuite, recteur du Sé-
P96   minaire Royal de la Marine de la ville de
v.2   Toulon. Contre Marie Catherine Cadière,
no.4   & encore M. le Procureur Général du Roi,
          querellant. [s.l., 173-?]
            144 p. 17cm.

            No. 4 in vol. lettered: Procès de Girard.
            [v.2]
8
NIC   1. Cadière, Catherine, b. 1709.

Witchcraft
BF   Girard, Jean Baptiste, 1680-1733.
1582   Mémoire instructif pour le père Jean-
G51M5   Baptiste Girard, jesuite ... contre Marie-
1731   Catherine Cadière; et encore M. le procur-
          eur général du roy, querellant. La Haye,
          H. Scheurleer, sur la copie imprimée à Paris,
          chez Gissey & Bordelet, 1731.
            284 p. 20cm.

            "Recueil des lettres du Père Girard et de
          la demoiselle Ca   dière, dont les ori-
                        (Continued on next card)

Witchcraft
BF   Girard, Jean Baptiste, 1680-1733. Mémoire
1582   instructif pour le père Jean-Baptiste
G51M5   Girard ... 1731.   (Card 2)
1731
          originaux ont été produits au procès": p.
          [141]-284.

            1. Cadière, Catherine, b. 1709.
            I. Cadière, Catherine, b. 1709. II.
            Title.

            Girard, Jean Baptiste, 1680-1733.
            Mémoire instructif...--English.
Witchcraft
BF   Girard, Jean Baptiste, 1680-1733, defendant.
1582   A compleat translation of the Memorial of
G51M5   the Jesuit Father John Baptist Girard, rector
1732   of the Royal Seminary of the Chaplains of the
          Navy, in the city of Toulon, against Mary
          Catherine Cadière and the atorney [sic] gen-
          eral, plaintiff. London, Printed for J.
          Millan, 1732.
            172, 143 p. 17cm.

            "A collection   of the letters of Father
          Girard and Mary   Catherine Cadière, the
                        (Continued on next card)

            Girard, Jean Baptiste, 1680-1733.
            Mémoire instructif...--English.
Witchcraft
BF   Girard, Jean Baptiste, 1680-1733, defendant.
1582   A compleat translation of the Memorial of
G51M5   the Jesuit Father John Baptist Girard ...
1732   1732.   (Card 2)

          originals whereof were produced in court":
          143 p. at end.

            1. Cadière, Catherine, b. 1709. Mémoire
          I. Girard, Jean Baptiste, 1680-1733. Mémoire
          instructif.....   English. II. Cadière,
          Catherine,   b. 1709.   III. Title.

Witchcraft
BF   Girard, Jean Baptiste, 1680-1733, defendant.
1582   Procedure sur laquelle le pere Jean
G51   Baptiste Girard, jesuite, Catherine Cadiere,
P9++   le pere Estienne Thomas Cadiere, dominicain,
          Mre. François Cadiere, prêtre, et le pere
          Nicolas de S. Joseph Carme Dechaussé, ont
          e'te' jugez par arrêt du parlement de
          Provence du 10. octobre 1731 ... Aix,
          Chez J. David, 1733.
            422 p. 36cm.

            With this   is bound Montvalon,
          A. B. de.   Motifs des juges du
          parlement de   Provence qui ont été
                        (Continued on next card)

Witchcraft
BF   Girard, Jean Baptiste, 1680-1733, defendant.
1582   Procedure ... 1733.   (Card 2)
G51
P9++   d'avis de condamner le p. Jean Baptiste
          Girard ... [Aix?] 1733.

            I. France. Parlement (Aix) II. Cadière,
          Catherine, b. 1709. III. Cadière,
          Estienne Thomas, fl. 1730. IV. Cadière,
          François, fl. 1730. V. Dechaussé, Nicolas
          de S. Joseph Carme, fl. 1730. VI. Title:
          Procedure sur laquelle le pere Jean Baptiste
          Girard ... [est   été jugez.

WITCHCRAFT
BF   Girard, Jean Baptiste, 1680-1733.
1582   Recueil des lettres du Père Girard & de
G51   la Demoiselle Cadière, dont les originaux
P96   ont été produits au procès. Réflexions
v.1   générales sur ces lettres. [s.l., 173-?]
no.5   147 p. 17cm.

            No. 5 in vol. lettered: Procès de Girard.
            [v.1]
8
NIC   1. Cadière, Catherine, b. 1709.
            II. Title.

Witchcraft
BF   Girard, Jean Baptiste, 1680-1733, defendant.
1582   [Recueil des pièces concernant le procez
G51R3   entre le père Girard, jesuite, et la Demoi-
1731d   selle Cadière. n.p., 1731?]
            1 v. (various pagings) 17cm.

            Cover-title: Procès de Girard. Tom. II.
            Contents.--1. Mémoire instructif pour le
          p. Nicolas de Saint Joseph.--2. Thorame, Paz-
          ery. Second mémoire pour le p. Girard, jes-
          uite.--3. Ca   dière, M. C. Justi-
                        (Continued on next card)

Witchcraft
BF   Girard, Jean Baptiste, 1680-1733, defendant.
1582   [Recueil des pièces concernant le procez
G51R3   ... n.p., 1731?]   (Card 2)
1731d
            Contents--Continued.
          fication.--4. Premières actes et contrat
          protestatifs de la Demoiselle Cadière.--5.
          Mémoire des faits qui se sont passez sous les
          yeux de M. l'évêque de Toulon.--6. Cadière,
          M. C. Réponse à l'écrit de M. l'évêque de
          Toulon.--7. Cadiè   re, François. Second
                        (Continued on next card)

Witchcraft
BF   Girard, Jean Baptiste, 1680-1733, defendant.
1582   [Recueil des pièces concernant le procez
G51R3   ... n.p., 1731?]   (Card 3)
1731d
            Contents--Continued.
          mémoire pour M. Cadière, prêtre.--8. Cadière,
          E. T. Réponse au second mémoire imprimé sous
          le nom du p. Girard, jesuite.
            I. Cadière, Catherine, b. 1709.
            II. Title.

Witchcraft
BF   Girard, Jean Baptiste, 1680-1733, defendant
1582   Recueil général des pièces concernant le
G51R3++   procez entre la Demoiselle Cadière de la ville
1731   de Toulon, et le père Girard, jesuite ...
          Actuellement pèndant au Parlement d'Aix en
          Provence.   [Aix, R. Adibert] 1731.
            3 v. 40cm.

            A collection of items originally published
          separately. Vols. 1 and 2 have a general title
          page; v.3 has   none.
            I. Cadière,   Catherine, b.
          1709. II. Title.

Witchcraft
BF   Girard, Jean Baptiste, 1680-1733, defendant.
1582   Recueil général des pièces concernant le
G51R3++   procez entre la Demoiselle Cadière, de la
1731a   ville de Toulon, et le père Girard, jesuite
          ... [Aix, R. Adibert] 1731.
            2 v. 38cm.

            A collection of items originally published
          separately; with a general t.p.
            Title page and table of contents of v.2
          have been suppl   ied in ms.; and all
                        (Continued on next card)

Witchcraft
BF   Girard, Jean Baptiste, 1680-1733, defendant.
1582   Recueil général des pièces concernant le
G51R3++   procez entre la Demoiselle Cadière ...
1731a   1731.   (Card 2)

          after the piece entitled Sentence de M.
          l'official de l'évêché de Toulon ... is also
          in ms.
            I. Cadière, Catherine, b. 1709.
            II. Title.

Witchcraft
BF   Girard, Jean Baptiste, 1680-1733, defendant.
1582   Recueil général des pièces concernant le
G51R3   procez entre la Demoiselle Cadière de la
1731c   ville de Toulon, et le père Girard, jesuite
          ... La Haye, Swart, 1731.
            8 v. 17cm.

            The trials were held before the Parlement
          of Aix.
            A collection of items originally published
          separately; th   ere is a general title
                        (Continued on next card)

Witchcraft
BF   Girard, Jean Baptiste, 1680-1733, defendant.
1582   Recueil général des pièces concernant le
G51R3   procez ... 1731.   (Card 2)
1731c
          page and a table of contents for each vol.
          Bound with v.8 is Le nouveau Tarquin, usually
          attributed to Jean Jacques Bel.
            I. Cadière, Catherine, b. 1709.
            II. France. Parlement (Aix) III. Title.
            IV. [Bel, Jean   Jacques] 1693-1738.
          Le nouveau Tar   quin. V. Title: Le
          nouveau Tarquin.

Witchcraft
BF   Girard, Jean Baptiste, 1680-1733, defendant.
1582   Recueil général des pièces contenues au
G51R3   procez du Père Jean Baptiste Girard, Jesuite
1731b   ... & de Demoiselle Catherine Cadière, querel-
          lante. Aix, J. David, 1731.
            6 v. fronts. 17cm.

            A collection of items originally published
          separately. There is a general title page
          and a table of contents for each vol. except
          vol. 6. Bound   with v. 6 is Le nouveau
                        (Continued on next card)

Witchcraft
BF   Girard, Jean Baptiste, 1680-1733, defendant.
1582   Recueil général des pièces contenues au
G51R3   procez ... 1731.   (Card 2)
1731b
          Tarquin, usually attributed to Jean Jacques
          Bel.
            I. Cadière, Catherine, b. 1709.
            II. Title.

236

CATALOGUE OF THE CORNELL WITCHCRAFT COLLECTION

```
Witchcraft
BF       Girard, Jean Baptiste, 1680-1733, defen-
1582       dant.
G51       The tryal of Father John Baptist Girard
P8     on an accusation of quietism, sorcery, in-
       cest, abortion and subornation, before the
       great chamber of Parlement at Aix, at the
       instance of Miss Mary Catherine Cadiere
       ... London, Printed for J. Isted, 1732.
       48 p. 23cm.

          Bound in sprinkled calf gilt by W. Pratt.

          1. Cadière, Catherine, b. 1709.
                     I. Title.
```

```
           Girard, Jean Baptiste, 1680-1733.
WITCHCRAFT
BF       Cadière, Catherine, b. 1709.
1582       Interrogatoires, recollement et confron-
G51    tation du P. Girard, Jesuite, et de la
P96    Demoiselle Cadière; avec des Observations.
v.1    Ensemble la revocation de la variation de
no.8   ladite Demoiselle Cadière, & la confronta-
       tion mutuelle avec le Père Nicolas, prieur
       des Carmes de Toulon.   [s.l., 173-?]
       128 p.  17cm.

8         No. 8 in vol. lettered: Procès de Girard.
NIC       [v.1]
                       (Continued on next card)
```

```
           Girard, Jean Baptiste, 1680-1733,
WITCHCRAFT         respondent.
BF       Cadière, Catherine, b. 1709, complainant.
1582       Mémoire instructif pour Demoiselle Ca-
G51    therine Cadière, de ... Toulon, querellante
P96    & decretée. Contre le Père Jean Baptiste
v.1    Girard, Jesuite, querellé; & encore M. le
no.2   Procureur Général du Roy.  [s.l., 173-?]
       38 p. 17cm.

          No. 2 in vol. lettered: Procès de Girard.
          [v.1]

8         I. Girard,        Jean Baptiste, 1680-
NIC    1733,                 respondent.
```

```
           Girard, Jean Baptiste, 1680-1733,
WITCHCRAFT         respondent.
BF       Cadière, Catherine, b. 1709, complainant.
1582       Précis des charges, pour    Demoiselle
G51    Catherine Cadière, de ... Toulon, querel-
P96    lante en inceste spirituel, & autres crimes.
v.1    Contre le Père Jean Baptiste Girard, Jesu-
no.4   ite, querellé.  [s.l., 173-?]
       51 p. 17cm.

          No. 4 in vol. lettered: Procès de Girard.
          [v.1]

8         I. Girard,       Jean Baptiste, 1680-
NIC    1733, re                  spondent.
```

```
           Girard, Jean Baptiste, 1680-1733,
WITCHCRAFT         respondent.
BF       Cadière, Catherine, b. 1709, complainant.
1582       Réponse à la seconde partie du Second
G51    Mémoire du Père Girard.  [s.l., 173-?]
P96    106 p. 17cm.
v.1
no.3      No. 3 in vol. lettered: Procès de Girard.
          [v.1]


8         I. Girard, Jean Baptiste, 1680-1733, re-
NIC    spondent.
```

```
           Girard, Jean Baptiste, 1680-1733,
WITCHCRAFT         respondent.
BF       Cadière, Catherine, b. 1709, complainant.
1582       Réponse au Second Mémoire instructif du
G51    Père Girard, Jesuite, pour Demoiselle
P96    Catherine Cadière, de ... Toulon, querel-
v.1    lante en crimes d'enchantement, d'inceste
no.1   spirituel, d'avortement, & de subornation
       de témoins. Contre ledit Père Girard,
       querellé.  [s.l., 173-?]
       104 p. 17cm.

8         Signed: Catherine Cadière. Chaudron,
          avocat.          Aubin, procurateur.
       De Ville neuve d'Ansous, raporteur
                       (Continued on next card)
```

```
           Girard, Jean Baptiste, 1680-1733,
WITCHCRAFT         respondent.
BF       Cadière, Catherine, b. 1709, complainant.
1582       Réponse au Second Mémoire ... du Père
G51    Girard.  [173-?]           (Card 2)
P96
v.1    [sic]
no.1      No. 1 in vol. lettered: Procès de Girard.
          [v.1]


8         1. Girard, Jean Baptiste, 1680-1733,
NIC    respondent.
```

```
           Girard, Jean Baptiste, 1680-1733.
WITCHCRAFT
BF       [Cadière, Estienne Thomas] fl. 1730.
1582       Observations sur le Mémoire manuscrit,
G51    attribué par le Père Girard, dans le cours
P96    de la plaidoirie de M. l'Avocat Général.
v.1    [s.l., 173-?]
no.7   28 p. 17cm.

          Signed: P. Etienne Thomas Cadière.
          No. 7 in vol. lettered: Procès de Girard.
          [v.1]

8         1. Girard,    Jean Baptiste, 1680-1733.
NIC    I. Girard,      Jean Baptiste, 1680-1733.
       II. Title.
```

```
           Girard, Jean Baptiste, 1680-1733.
WITCHCRAFT
BF       Cadière, Catherine, b. 1709.
1582       Interrogatoires, recollement et confron-
G51    tation du P. Girard, Jesuite, et de la
P96    Demoiselle Cadière; avec des Observations.
v.1    Ensemble la revocation de la variation de
no.8   ladite Demoiselle Cadière, & la confronta-
       tion mutuelle avec le Père Nicolas, prieur
       des Carmes de Toulon.  [s.l., 173-?]
       128 p. 17cm.

8         No. 8 in vol. lettered: Procès de Girard.
NIC       [v.1]
                       (Continued on next card)
```

```
           Girard, Jean Baptiste, 1680-1733,
WITCHCRAFT         appellee.
BF       Cadière, Catherine, b. 1709, appellant.
1582       Mémoire instructif, pour Demoiselle
G51    Catherine Cadière de ... Toulon, appelante
P96    comme d'abus de la procédure faite par
v.2    l'official en l'evêché de la même ville, à
no.3   la requête du promoteur & par appel simple
       de la procédure faite contr'elle par MM.
       les Commissaires du Parlement, du décret
       d'ajournement personnel contr'elle rendu, &
       à minima du décret d'assigné par eux rendu,
       demanderesse    en Lettres Royaux inci-
8      dentes de          restitution, du 19 mai
NIC                    (Continued on next card)
```

```
           Girard, Jean Baptiste, 1680-1733,
WITCHCRAFT         appellee.
BF       Cadière, Catherine, b. 1709, appellant.
1582       Mémoire instructif ...         (Card 2)
G51
P96    1731, & au principal querellante en enchante-
v.2    ment, rapt, inceste spirituel, avortement
no.3   & subornation de témoins. Contre le Père
       Jean Baptiste Girard, Jesuite ... intimé en
       appel à minima & querellé, & ... Mr. le
       P.G. du Roy, intimé aux autres appels: &
       tous deux défendeurs aux Lettres Royaux.
       [s.l., 173-?]
8      172 p.          17cm.
NIC                    (Continued on next card)
```

```
           Girard, Jean Baptiste, 1680-1733,
WITCHCRAFT         appellee.
BF       Cadière, Catherine, b. 1709, appellant.
1582       Mémoire instructif ...  [173-?] (Card 3)
G51
P96       No. 3 in vol. lettered: Procès de Girard.
v.2       [v.2]
no.3




8         1. Girard, Jean Baptiste, 1680-1733,
NIC    appellee.
```

```
           Girard, Jean Baptiste, 1680-1733,
WITCHCRAFT         appellee.
BF       Cadière, Catherine, b. 1709, appellant.
1582       Réponse au Mémoire instructif du Père
G51    J. B. Girard, Jesuite. Pour Demoiselle
P96    Catherine Cadière, de la ville de Toulon,
v.2    appellante à minima de decret d'assigné
no.2   rendu par MM. les commissaires du Parlement,
       le 23. fév. dernier, & au principal querel-
       lante en inceste spirituel, & autres crimes.
       Contre ledit Père Girard, intimé & querellé.
       [s.l., 1731?]
8      191 p.          17cm.
NIC       No. 2 in      vol. lettered: Procès
       de Girard.      [v.2]
                       (Continued on next card)
```

```
           Girard, Jean Baptiste, 1680-1733.
WITCHCRAFT
BF       [Cadière, Estienne Thomas] fl. 1730.
1582       Observations sur le Mémoire manuscrit,
G51    attribué par le Père Girard, dans le cours
P96    de la plaidoirie de M. l'Avocat Général.
v.1    [s.l., 173-?]
no.7   28 p. 17cm.

          Signed: P. Etienne Thomas Cadière.
          No. 7 in vol. lettered: Procès de Girard.
          [v.1]

8         1. Girard.    Jean Baptiste, 1680-1733.
NIC    I. Girard,      Jean Baptiste, 1680-1733.
       II. Title.
```

```
           Girard, Jean Baptiste, 1680-1733.
WITCHCRAFT
BF       Cadière, Estienne Thomas, fl. 1730.
1582       Réflexions sur la récrimination en pré-
G51    tendu complot, imputé au Père Estienne
P96    Thomas Cadière ... par le P. Jean Baptiste
v.1    Girard ...  [s.l., 173-?]
no.6   144 p. 17cm.


          No. 6 in vol. lettered: Procès de Girard.
          [v.1]

8         1. Girard,    Jean Baptiste, 1680-1733.
NIC
```

```
           Girard, Jean Baptiste, 1680-1733.
WITCHCRAFT
BF       Cadière, François, fl. 1730, appellant.
1582       Mémoire instructif, pour Messire François
G51    Cadière, prêtre de la ville de Toulon, ap-
P96    pellant du decret d'assigné contre lui ren-
v.2    du le 23. fév. dernier, & de ce qui s'en
no.1   est ensuivi, & demandeur en requête d'ad-
       hérance à l'appel comme d'abus relevé par
       la Demoiselle Cadière, sa soeur, de la pro-
       cedure faite à la requête du promoteur en
       l'evêché de Toulon. Contre M. le procu-
       reur général     du Roy, intimé & défen-
8      deur.            [s.l., 1731?]
NIC    131 p.           17cm.
                       (Continued on next card)
```

```
           Girard, Jean Baptiste, 1680-1733.
WITCHCRAFT
BF       Cadière, François, fl. 1730, appellant.
1582       Mémoire instructif ... [1731?] (Card 2)
G51
P96       Signed: François Cadière. Bourgarel,
v.2    avocat. Simon, procureur.
no.1      No. 1 in vol. lettered: Procès de Girard.
          [v.2]



8         1. Girard, Jean Baptiste, 1680-1733.  2.
NIC    Cadière,               Catherine, b. 1709.
```

```
           Girard, Jean Baptiste, 1680-1733.
Witchcraft
BF       Girard, Jean Baptiste, 1680-1733, defendant.
1582       The case of Mrs. Mary Catharine Cadiere,
G51    against the Jesuit Father John Baptist Gi-
C33    rard.  In a memorial presented to the Par-
1732   liament of Aix. Wherein he is accused of
       seducing her, by the abominable doctrines
       of quietism, into the most criminal ex-
       cesses of lewdness, and under an appearance
       of the highest mystical devotion, deluding
       into the same vices six other females, who
       had put their          consciences under his
8                     (Continued on next card)
```

237

CATALOGUE OF THE CORNELL WITCHCRAFT COLLECTION

Girard, Jean Baptiste, 1680-1733.

Witchcraft
BF   Girard, Jean Baptiste, 1680-1733, defendant.
1582   The case of Mrs. Mary Catharine Cadiere ...
G51   1732.   (Card 2)
C33
1732   direction. With a preface by the publisher
     ... 10th ed. corr. London, Printed for
     and sold by J. Roberts, 1732.
       vi, 96 p. 23cm.
       "This memorial was originally drawn up
     by that eminent lawyer ... Chaudon ... the
     following piece ... is not a bare transla-
8   tion ..." p. ii   (Continued on next card)

Girard, Jean Baptiste, 1680-1733.

Witchcraft
BF   [Girard, Jean Baptiste] 1680-1733, defendant.
1582   Memoir [sic] du P. et de la Cadier [sic]
G51   [Aix, etc., De l'imprimerie de la veuve
M48++   de Joseph Senez, etc., 1731]
       various pagings. 32cm.
       Cover title.
       Contents.--Mémoire instructif, pour Mes-
     sire François Cadiere.--Observations sur le
     memoire manuscrit distribué par le P. Girard.
     --Memoire du Pere Girard.--Memoire instruc-
     tif, pour le Pere Nicolas de S. Joseph.--
8   (Continued on next card)

Girard, Jean Baptiste, 1680-1733.

Witchcraft
BF   [Girard, Jean Baptiste] 1680-1733, defendant.
1582   Memoir du P. et de la Cadier.   [1731]
G51   (Card 2)
M48++
       Contents--Continued.
     Reflexions sur la recrimination en pretendu
     complot imputé au Pere Estienne Thomas Ca-
     diere.--Observations sur les reponses per-
     sonnelles du P. Girard.--Second mémoire pour
     le Pere Girard.--Reponse a l'ecrit, qui a
     pour titre: Memoire des faits qui se
8   (Continued on next card)

Girard, Jean Baptiste, 1680-1733.

Witchcraft
BF   [Girard, Jean Baptiste] 1680-1733, defendant.
1582   Memoir du P. et de la Cadier.   [1731]
G51   (Card 3)
M48++
       Contents--Continued.
     sont passez sous les yeux de M. l'Evêque de
     Toulon.--A nosseigneurs de Parlement [par
     Estienne-Thomas Cadiere]--A nosseigneurs de
     Parlement [par Catherine Cadiere]--A nos-
     seigneurs de Parlement [par Catherine Ca-
8   diere]   (Continued on next card)

Girard, Jean Baptiste, 1680-1733.

Witchcraft
BF   Memoirs of Miss Mary-Catherine Cadiere,
1582   and Father Girard, Jesuit, containing
G51   an exact account of that extraordinary
M53   affair; interspers'd with letters and
     other original papers relating thereto,
     and which have hitherto been unknown to
     the publick. In an epistle from a per-
     son of quality at Paris to his corre-
     spondent in London. London, Printed
     for J. Isted, 1731.
       32 p. 20cm.
       1. Cadiere, Catherine, b.1709. 2.
8   Girard, Jean Baptiste, 1680-1733.
NIC   I. A Person of quality at Paris.

Girard, Jean Baptiste, 1680-1733.

Witchcraft
BF   [Montvalon, André Barrigue de] 1678-1779.
1582   Motifs des juges du parlement de Provence
G51   qui ont été d'avis de condamner le p. Jean
P9++   Baptiste Girard, envoyez à M. le Chancel-
     lier, le 31. decembre 1731. Ensemble la
     lettre de ce magistrat à Mr. le Président
     de Maliverney; la réponse de ce juge, &
     celle des autres messieurs qui ont été de
     son opinion. 3. éd. avec des notes cri-
     tiques tirées de la Procedure & des lettres
     écrites d'Aix, servant de motifs aux juges
     de l'opinion contraire. On a cité
     ces lettres sur la premiere éd.
                 (Continued on next card)

Girard, Jean Baptiste, 1680-1733.

Witchcraft
BF   [Montvalon, André Barrigue de] 1678-1779.
1582   Motifs des juges ...   (Card 2)
G51
P9++   qui en a été faite à Aix.   [Aix?] 1733.
       67 p. 36cm.
       Bound with Girard, J. B. Procedure
     ... Aix, 1733.
       1. Girard, Jean Baptiste, 1680-1733.
     I. Title.

Girard, Jean Baptiste, 1680-1733.

WITCHCRAFT
BF   Recueil des premières requestes de la
1582   Demoiselle Cadière, du Père Estienne
G51   Thomas Cadière, Jacobin, et du Père
P96   Nicolas, prieur des Carmes de Toulon.
v.3   [s.l., 173-?]
       1 v. (various pagings) 17cm.
       Binder's title: Procès de Girard. [v.3]
       1. Girard, Jean Baptiste, 1680-1733. I.
     Cadière, Catherine, b. 1709. II. Cadière,
8   Estienne Thomas, fl. 1730. III.
NIC   Nicolas de Saint Joseph, fl. 1730.

Witchcraft
BF   Giraud, Albert.
1582   Etude sur les procès de sorcellerie en
G52   Normandie. Discours de réception de M. le
E8   Dr. Giraud. Rouen, Imprimerie Gagniard
     (L. Gy, successeur), 1897.
       54 p. 24cm.
       At head of title: Académie des sciences,
     belles-lettres et arts de Rouen.
       1. Trials (Witchcraft)--Normandy. I.
8   Title.

Witchcraft
BF   Giraud, Albert.
1582   Fragments d'histoire de la folie; la
G52   sorcellerie au moyen-âge, une épidémie de
     délire de nos jours.   [Bar-le-Duc, Impr.
     Contant-Laguerre, 1883]
       24 p. 24cm.
       Extract from Mémoires de la Société
     des lettres, sciences, et arts de Bar-le-
     Duc, t. 2, 2. série, 1883.
       1. Witchcraft--France. I.
     Title.

Glanvil, Joseph, 1635-1680.

see

Glanvill, Joseph, 1636-1680.

Glanvill, Joseph

Witchcraft
BF   [Glanvill, Joseph] 1636-1680.
1581   A blow at modern sadducism in some philosophical consid-
A2G54   erations about witchcraft. To which is added, the relation of
1668   the fam'd disturbance by the drummer, in the house of Mr.
     John Mompesson: with some reflections on drollery, and athe-
     isme [!] By a member of the Royal society. London. Print-
     ed by E. C. for J. Collins, 1668.
       8 p. l., 160 p. 16cm.
       In two parts, each part having special t-p.
              (Continued on next card)

Witchcraft
BF   [Glanvill, Joseph] 1636-1680. A blow at modern saddu-
1581   cism ... 1668. (Card 2)
A2G54
1668   CONTENTS.--[1] A philosophical endeavour in the defence of the being
     of witches and apparitions: with some things concerning the famous
     Greatrek's. Written in a letter to the much honoured Robert Hunt, esq.
     London, 1668.--[2] Palpable evidence of spirits and witchcraft: in an ac-
     count of the fam'd disturbance by the drummer, in the house of M.
     Mompesson. With another modern and certain relation. In two leteers
     [!], one to the Right Honourable William, Lord Brereton; the other, to
     the learned Dr. Henry More, D. D. London, 1668.
       1. Witchcraft.   I. Title.

Witchcraft
BF   Glanvill, Joseph, 1636-1680.
1581   A blow at modern sadducism in some philoso-
A2G54   cal considerations about witchcraft. And the
1668c   relation of the famed disturbance at the hous
     of M. Mompesson. With reflections on drollery
     and atheisme [!] 4th ed. corrected and inlar
     London, Printed by E. Cotes for James Collins
     1668.
       [28], 183, [10] p. 18cm.
       In three parts, each having special t.p.
                (Continued on next car

CATALOGUE OF THE CORNELL WITCHCRAFT COLLECTION

---

hcraft
Glanvill, Joseph, 1636-1680. A blow at modern sadducism ... 1668. (Card 2)

Contents.--₁₁ A philosophical endeavour in the defence of the being of witches and apparitions: with some things concerning the famous Greatrek's. Written in a letter to the much honoured Robert Hunt, esq. London, 1668.--₂₁ Palpable evidence of spirits and witchcraft: in an account of the fam'd disturbance by the drummer, in the house of M. Mompesson. With another modern and certain relation, in two
(Continued on next card)

WITCHCRAFT
BF 1581 A2 G55 1689

Glanvill, Joseph, 1636-1680.
Saducismus triumphatus: or, Full and plain evidence concerning witches and apparitions. In two parts. The first treating of their possibility; the second of their real existence. By Jos. Glanvil ... The third edition. The advantages whereof above the former, the reader may understand out of Dʳ H. More's account prefixed thereunto. With two authentick, but wonderful stories of certain Swedish witches, done

8   (Continued on next card)

Witchcraft
BF 1581 A2G55 1726

Glanvill, Joseph, 1636-1680.
Saducismus triumphatus: or, A full and plain evidence, concerning witches and apparitions. In two parts. The first treating of their possibility. The second of their real existence. By Joseph Glanvil ... The 4th ed., with additions. The advantages whereof, the reader may understand out of Dr. H. More's account prefixed hereunto. Also, two authentick, but wonderful stories of certain Swedish witches. Done into English by Dr. Horneck. With some account of Mr. Glanvil's life and writings. London, A. Bettesworth and J. Batley [etc.] 1726.
[510] p. front., illus., pl. 20ᶜᵐ.
Various paging.
1. Witchcraft. 2. Apparitions. I. More, Henry, 1614-1687. II. Horneck, Anthony, 1641-1697. III. Title.

---

hcraft
Glanvill, Joseph, 1636-1680. A blow at modern sadducism ... 1668. (Card 3)

Contents.--Continued.
letters, one to the Right Honourable William Lord Brereton; the other, to the learned Dr. Henry More, D.D. London, 1668.--₃₁ A whip for the droll, fidler to the atheist: being reflections on drollery & atheism. Sent, upon the occasion of the drummer of Tedworth, in a letter to the most learned Dr. Hen. More, D.D. London, 1668.

WITCHCRAFT
BF 1581 A2 G55 1689

Glanvill, Joseph, 1636-1680. Saducismus triumphatus ... 1689. (Card 2)

into English by A. Horneck. London, printed for S. L. and are to be sold by Anth. Baskervile, 1689.
597 p. illus. 19cm.

With added engr. t. p.
Part 2 has special t. p. with imprint: London, Printed for S. Lownds, 1688.

8

Glanvill, Joseph, 1636-1680.
Saducismus triumphatus.

Witchcraft
BF 1581 A2 G56

[Glanvill, Joseph] 1636-1680.
Some philosophical considerations touching the being of witches and witchcraft; written in a letter to Robert Hunt by J. G., a member of the Royal Society. London, Printed by E. C. for J. Collins, 1667.
62 p. 21cm.
Later incorporated into his Saducismus triumphatus.
I. His Saducismus triumphatus. II. Title.

---

hcraft
Glanvill, Joseph, 1636-1680.
Essays on several important subjects in philosophy and religion. By Joseph Glanvill ... London, Printed by J. D. for J. Baker and H. Mortlock, 1676.
[340] p. 20cm.
Various paging.
CONTENTS.--Against confidence in philosophy.--Of scepticism, and certainty.--Modern improvements of knowledge.--The usefulness of philosophy to theology.--The agreement of reason, and religion.--Against modern Sadducism, in the matter of witches and apparitions.--Anti-fanatical religion and free philosophy. In a continuation of the New Atlantis.
Wing G809.
Bound with his Scepsis scientifica.
London, 1665.
1. Philosophy and religion.
I. Title.

Witchcraft
BF 1581 A2 G55 1689a

Glanvill, Joseph, 1636-1680.
Saducismus triumphatus: or, Full and plain evidence concerning witches and apparitions (1689) A facsimile reproduction with an introd. by Coleman O. Parsons. Gainesville, Fla., Scholars' Facsimiles & Reprints, 1966.
xxiv, 597 p. illus. 23cm.

"Some twentieth century studies of Glanvill": p. xxiv.

WITCHCRAFT
BF 1581 A2 G551

Glanvill, Joseph, 1636-1680.
Saducismus triumphatus.
Prior, Moody Erasmus, 1901-
Joseph Glanvill, witchcraft, and seventeenth-century science... Chicago, 1932.
167-193 p. 25cm.

"A part of a dissertation submitted to ..., the University of Chicago, ...for the degree of Doctor of Philosophy."
Reprinted from Modern philology, v.30, no.2, 1932.
1. Glanvill, Joseph, 1636-1680. Saducismus triumphatus. 2. Hobbes, Thomas, 1588-1679. 3. Witchcraft.
8
NIC

Glanvill, Joseph, 1636-1680.
Saducismus triumphatus: or, Full and plain evidence concerning witches and apparitions. In two parts. The first treating of their possibility, the second of their real existence. With a letter of Dr. Henry More on the same subject. And an authentick, but wonderful story of certain Swedish witches; done into English by Anth. Horneck. London, Printed for J. Collins, and S. Lownds, 1681.
1 v. (various pagings) illus. 18cm.
Includes special title-pages.

Witchcraft
BF 1581 A2G55 1700
2 copies

Glanvill, Joseph, 1636-1680.
Saducismus triumphatus; or, Full and plain evidence concerning witches and apparitions. In two parts. The first treating of their possibility. The second of their real existence. 3d ed., with additions. The advantages whereof, above the former, the reader may understand out of Dr. H. More's account prefix'd thereunto. With two authentick, but wonderful stories of certain Swedish witches. Done into English by A. Horneck. London, Printed for A.L.
(Continued on next card)

Witchcraft
BF 1581 A2 G56

[Glanvill, Joseph] 1636-1680.
Some philosophical considerations touching the being of witches and witchcraft; written in a letter to Robert Hunt by J. G., a member of the Royal Society. London, Printed by E. C. for J. Collins, 1667.
62 p. 21cm.
Later incorporated into his Saducismus triumphatus.
I. His Saducismus triumphatus. II. Title.

Glanvill, Joseph, 1636-1680.
Saducismus triumphatus: or, Full and plain evidence concerning witches and apparitions. In two parts. The first treating of their possibility; the second of their real existence. 3d ed. The advantages whereof above the former, the reader may understand out of Dr. H. More's account prefixed thereunto. With two authentick, but wonderful stories of certain Swedish witches; done into English by Anth. Horneck.
(Continued on next card)

Witchcraft
BF 1581 A2G55 1700

Glanvill, Joseph, 1636-1680. Saducismus triumphatus ... (Card 2)

and sold by R. Tuckyr, 1700.
1 v. (various pagings) illus., diagrs. 20cm.

Added t. p., engraved.
Includes special title-pages.
Frontispiece of copy 2 wanting.

Witchcraft
Z 6878 W8G54+

Glasgow. University. Hunterian Library.
An exhibition of books on witchcraft and demonology. January-March, 1966. [Glasgow? 1966]
24 p. 26cm.

1. Witchcraft--Exhibitions.
✓2. Witchcraft--Bibl. ✓I. Title.

---

hcraft
581 2G55 688

Glanvill, Joseph, 1636-1680. Saducismus triumphatus ... (Card 2)

London, Printed for S. Lownds, 1688.
597 p. illus., diagrs. 19cm.

Includes special title-pages.

Witchcraft
BF 1429 G62 1704

Glanvill, Joseph, 1636-1680.
Saducismus triumphatus; oder, Vollkommener und klarer Beweiss von Hexen und Gespenstern oder Geister-Erscheinungen, in zween Theilen verfasset, deren ersterer die Möglichkeit vorstellet, oder dass sie seyn können; der andere beweiset, dass sie würcklich seyn ... Hamburg, G. Liebernickel, 1701.
2 v. in 1. illus. 18cm.

Bound with Goldschmidt, P. Höllischer Morpheus. Hamburg, 1704.

Witchcraft
BF 1413 B62+ 1859

Der Glaube an Zauberer, Hexen, und Vampyre in Mähren und Österr. Schlesien.
Bischof, Ferdinand.
Zur Geschichte des Glaubens an Zauberer, Hexen, und Vampyre in Mähren und Oesterr. Schlesien. Von Ferdinand Bischof und Christian d'Elvert. Brünn, Buchdruckerei von R. Rohrer's Erben, 1859.
164 p. 26cm.

"Aus dem XII. Bande der Schriften der historisch-statistischen Sektion der k. k. mähr. schles. Gesellschaft zur Beförderung des Ackerbaues, der Natur- und Landeskunde besonders abgedruckt."

CATALOGUE OF THE CORNELL WITCHCRAFT COLLECTION

Glaubrecht, O., pseud.
    see
Oeser, Rudolf, 1807-1859.

Glossaire de la sorcellerie landaise.

Witchcraft
BF
1582
F66
[Foix, Vincent M.]
    Sorcières et loups-garous dans les Landes. Auch, Imprimerie centrale, 1904.
    72 p. 25cm.
    Caption title: Folklore. Glossaire de la sorcellerie landaise.
    1. Witchcraft--France--Dictionaries.
    2. Werwolves--Dictionaries. I. Title.
    II. Title: Glossaire de la sorcellerie landaise.

8

Glover, Mary, fl. 1603.

MSS
Bd.
WITCHCRAFT
BF
B81
Bradwell, Stephan, fl. 1594-1636.
    Marie Glovers late woefull case, together wth her joyfull deliverance written upon occasion of Dr. Jordens Discourse of the mother.... With a defence of the truthe against D. J. his scandalous impugnations. [n.p.] 1603.
    171 l. 20 x 29cm.
    Photostatic copy of Sloan MSS 831 in the British Museum.
    Second treatise, beginning on l. 42,
    (Continued on next card)

Glover, Mary, fl. 1603.

MSS
Bd.
WITCHCRAFT
BF
B81
Bradwell, Stephan, fl. 1594-1636. Marie Glovers late woefull case...1603. (Card 2)
    has caption title: A defence of the publique sentence of lawe, and of the iudgment, of certayne phisitions, t^ averred Marie Glouers case to be supernaturall: against D. Jordens slie, but scandalous impugnations of bothe.
    Bound in maroon buckram.
    1. Glover, Mary, fl. 1603. 2. Demoniac possession. 3. Witchcraft--
    (Continued on next card)

Glover, Mary, fl. 1603.

Witchcraft
BF
1563
W81++
no.8
Jorden, Edward.
    A briefe discovrse of a disease called the suffocation of the mother. Written vppon occasion which hath beene of late taken thereby, to suspect possession of an euill spirit, or some such like supernaturall power. Wherin is declared that diuers strange actions and passions of the body of man, which in the common opinion, are imputed to the Diuell, haue their true naturall causes, and do accompanie this disease. London, Printed by J. Windet, 1603. [London, at the British Museum, 1923]
    (Continued on next card)

Glover, Mary, fl. 1603.

Witchcraft
BF
1563
W81++
no.8
Jorden, Edward. A briefe discovrse of a disease... 1603. [1923] (Card 2)
    [58] p. 17cm.
    Signatures: A-G^4, H^1.
    Photocopy (negative) 58 p. on 26 l. 20 x 32cm.
    No. 8 in vol. lettered: Witchcraft tracts, chapbooks and broadsides, 1579-1704; rotograph copies.
    1. Glover, Mary, fl. 1603.
    2. Exorcism.

Glover, Mary, fl. 1603.

Witchcraft
BF
1563
W81++
no.7
Swan, John.
    A trve and breife report of Mary Glovers vexation, and of her deliuerance by the meanes of fastinge and prayer. Performed by those whose names are sett downe in the next page. ... [London?] 1603. [London, at the British Museum, 1923]
    [88] p. 14cm.
    Signatures: A^4, A-K^4.
    Photocopy (negative) 88 p. on 44 l. 20 x 32cm.
    No. 7 in vol. lettered: Witchcraft tracts, chapbooks and broadsides, 1579-1704; rotograph copies.

Glückwünschungsschreiben an den Hochw. P. Angelus März, über seine Vertheidigung der Hex- und Zauberey.

Witchcraft
BF
1565
S83
M186
[Mayer, Andreas Ulrich] 1732-1802.
    Glückwünschungsschreiben an den Hochw. P. Angelus März, über seine Vertheidigung der Hex- und Zauberey, von F. N. Blocksberger, Beneficiaten zu T. [pseud.] Straubingen, 1767.
    [16] p. 22cm.
    1. März, Angelus, 1731-1784. ... Kurze Vertheidigung der thätigen Hex- und Zauberey. 2. Sterzinger, Ferdinand, 1721-1786. I. Title.

8

Witchcraft
BF
1565
G57
Gockel, Eberhard, 1636-1703.
    Tractatus polyhistoricus magico-medicus curiosus, oder Ein kurtzer, mit vielen verwunderlichen Historien untermengter Bericht von dem Beschreyen und Verzaubern, auch denen darauss entspringenden Kranckheiten und zauberischen Schäden ... Alles aus berühmter Alter und Neuer Medicorum Scriptis, auch auss eigner Erfahrung und 42jähriger Praxi zusammen getragen und hervor gegeben von Eberhardo Gockelio ... Franckfurt und
    (Continued on next card)

Witchcraft
BF
1565
G57
Gockel, Eberhard, 1636-1703. Tractatus polyhistoricus ... 1699. (Card 2)
    Leipzig, Im Verlag Lorentz Kronigers, und Gottlieb Göbels sel. Erben Buchhändl. in Augspurg, 1699.
    4 p. l., 182 p. 17cm.
    "Mantissa oder ... Geheime Artzney. Mittel wider die zauberische Schäden und Kranckheiten," p. [134]-182, has special t. p.
    1. Witchcraft. 2. Medicine, Magic, mystic, and spagiric. 3. Medicine--Formulae, receipts, prescriptions. I. Title. II. Title: Beschreyen und Verzaubern.

WITCHCRAFT
BF
1565
M51
Goclenius, Rudolph, 1547-1628.
Melander, Otto, 1571-1640.
    Resolutio praecipuarum quaestionum criminalis adversus sagas processus, cum refutatione nova tam juridica quam philosophica purgationis sagarum per aquam frigidam, adversus Guilielmum Adolphum Scribonium...Autore Otthone Melandro... Adjecta est ...Rodolphi Goclenii...Oratio...de natura sagarum in purgatione et examinatione per frigidam aquis innatantium. Lichae, Apud Nicolaum Erbenium, 1597.
    131 p. 17cm.
    (Continued on next card)

8
NIC

The god of the witches.

Witchcraft
BF
1566
M98
1933
Murray, Margaret Alice.
    The god of the witches, by Margaret Alice Murray ... London. S. Low, Marston & co., ltd. [1933]
    ix. 214 p. plates. facsims. 23cm.
    "References": p. 201-208.
    Review copy from the American historical review to George Lincoln Burr.

1. Witchcraft. 2. Demonology. 3. Magic. 4. Cultus. I. Title.

Library of Congress   BF1566.M8   34-41836

WITCHCRAFT
BF
1576
P82
U673
Goddard, Delano Alexander, 1831-1882.
    The Mathers weighed in the balances by Delano A. Goddard and found not wanting. Boston: Office of the Daily Advertiser; London: Office of H. Stevens, 1870.
    32 p. 16cm.
    2 copies
    Copy 1 is autograph presentation copy to A. D. White.
    1. Upham, Charles Wentworth, 1802-1875. Salem witchcraft and Cotton Mather. 2. Mather, Increase, 1639-1723. 3. Mather, Cotton, 1663-1728. I. Title.

8
NIC

Witchcraft
BF
1565
G58
Godelmann, Johann Georg, 1559-1611.
    Tractatvs de magis, veneficis et lamiis, deqve his recte cognoscendis et pvniendis ... publicè in Academia Rostochiana praelectus, & in tres libros distributus à Ioanne Georgio Godelmanno ... Francoforti, Ex officina typographica Nicolai Bassaei, 1591.
    3 v. in 1. 22cm.
    Vols. 2 and 3 each have special t. p. Vol. 2 has title: De lamiis. Vol. 3 has title: Qvomodo contra magos, veneficas, et lamias procedatur.

8

Witchcraft
BF
1565
G58
1601
Godelmann, Johann Georg, 1559-1611.
    Tractatvs de magis, veneficis et lamiis, deqve his recte cognoscendis et puniendis ... publicè in Academia Rostochiana olim praelectus, & in tres libros distributus, iam denuo recognitus, recensque allegationibus ab ipso contextu characterum diuersitate distinctis, editus à Ioanne Georgio Godelmanno ... Francoforti, Ex officina typographica Ioannis Saurii, Impensis Nicolai Bassaei, 1601.
    (Continued on next card)

8

Witchcraft
BF
1565
G58
1601
Godelmann, Johann Georg, 1559-1611. Tractatvs de magis, veneficis et lamiis ... 1601. (Card 2)
    3 v. in 1. 21cm.
    Vols. 2 and 3 each have special t. p. Vol. 2 has title: De lamiis. Vol. 3 has title: Qvomodo contra magos, veneficas et lamias procedatur.
    1. Witchcraft. 2. Demonology. 3. Trials (Witchcraft) I. Title: Tractatus de magis, veneficis et lamiis.

8

Godelmann, Johann Georg, 1559-1611.
    Tractatus de magis, veneficis et lamiis--German.

Witchcraft
BF
1565
G58
1592
Godelmann, Johann Georg, 1559-1611.
    Von Zäuberern Hexen vnd Vnholden, warhaffter vnd wolgegründter Bericht Herrn Georgii Gödelmanni ..., wie dieselbigen zuerkennen vnd zu straffen. Allen Beampten zu vnsern Zeiten von wegen vieler vngleicher vnd streittigen Meynung sehr nützlich vnnd nothwendig zuwissen ... verteutschet ... durch Georgium Nigrinum ... Franckfort am Mayn, Gedruckt durch Nicolaum Bassaeum, 1592.
    (Continued on next card)

8

Godelmann, Johann Georg, 1559-1611.
    Tractatus de magis, veneficis et lamiis--German.

Witchcraft
BF
1565
G58
1592
Godelmann, Johann Georg, 1559-1611. Von Zäuberern Hexen vnd Vnholden ... 1592. (Card 2)
    8 p. l., 483 p. illus. 20cm.
    Translation of Tractatus de magis, veneficis et lamiis.
    1. Witchcraft. 2. Demonology. 3. Trials (Witchcraft) I. His Tractatus de magis, veneficis et lamiis--German. II. Title: Von Zäuberern, Hexen und Unholden.

8

CATALOGUE OF THE CORNELL WITCHCRAFT COLLECTION

Witchcraft
BF
1565
G58
1592
    Godelmann, Johann Georg, 1559-1611.
      Von Zäuberern Hexen vnd Vnholden, warhaffter vnd wolgegründter Bericht Herrn Georgii Gödelmanni ..., wie dieselbigen zuerkennen vnd zu straffen. Allen Beampten zu vnsern Zeiten von wegen vieler vngleicher vnd streittigen Meynung sehr nützlich vnnd nothwendig zuwissen ... verteutschet ... durch Georgium Nigrinum ... Franckfort am Mayn, Gedruckt durch Nicolaum Bassaeum, 1592.
      (Continued on next card)

Witchcraft
BF
1565
G58
1592
    Godelmann, Johann Georg, 1559-1611. Von Zäuberern Hexen vnd Vnholden ... 1592.
                              (Card 2)

    8 p. l., 483 p. illus. 20cm.
    Translation of Tractatus de magis, veneficis et lamiis.
    1. Witchcraft. 2. Demonology. 3. Trials (Witchcraft) I. His Tractatus de magis, veneficis et lamiis. German. II. Title: V on Zäuberern, Hexen und Unholden.   (Over)

    Godofredi Ludovici ... Theologicum novae ... anthropologiae ... examen.

Witchcraft
BF
1565
L46
1717a
    Ludovici, Gottfried, 1670-1724.
      Godofredi Ludovici ... Theologicvm novae novi avtoris Francisci de Cordva anthropologiae et daemonologiae examen, nouitates vti alias, ab hoc in Schrifft- und Vernunfftmässigen Gedancken vom Schatzgraben und Beschwerung der Geister propositas ... Coburgi, Sumptu Pauli Güntheri Pfotenhaueri [1718]
    134 p. 19cm.
    Bound with Thomasius, Christian, 1655-1728. ... Kurtze Lehr-Sätze von dem
      (Continued on next card)

    Godofredi Ludovici ... Theologicum novae ... anthropologiae ... examen.

Witchcraft
BF
1565
L46
1717a
    Ludovici, Gottfried, 1670-1724. Godofredo Ludovici ... Theologicvm novae ... anthropologiae ... examen ... [1718]   (Card 2)

Laster der Zauberey. Franckfurth, 1717.

    1. Franciscus de Cordua, pseud. Schrifft- und vernunfftmässige Gedancken vom Schatzgraben. 2. Demonology. I. Title: Theologicum novae ... anthropologiae ... examen.

Witchcraft
    Godwin, William, 1756-1836.
      Lives of the necromancers. Or, An account of the most eminent persons in successive ages, who have claimed for themselves, or to whom has been imputed by others, the exercise of magical power ... New York, Harper & Brothers, 1835.
    xii, [25]-307 p. 19cm.

    1. Magic. 2. Witchcraft. I. Title.

BF
1597
G59
1876
    Godwin, William, 1756-1836.
      Lives of the necromancers; or, An account of the most eminent persons in successive ages who have claimed for themselves, or to whom has been imputed by others, the exercise of magical power ... London, Chatto and Windus, 1876.
    xvi, 282 p. 16cm.

    Göckelius, Christophorus Ludovicus, respondent.

Witchcraft
RC
547
W39
    Wedel, Georg Wolfgang, 1645-1721, praeses.
      Dissertatio medica De incvbo, ex epitome praxeos clinicae Georgii Wolffgangi Wedelii ... eodem praeside, pvblicae ... disqvisitioni svbiecta a Christophoro Lvdovico Göckelio ... Ienae, Litteris Krebsianis [1708]
    20 p. 21cm.

    Diss.--Jena (C. L. Göckelius, respondent)

8

Witchcraft
BT
965
G59
    Göde, Carolus Fridericus.
      Demonstrationes philosophicae De existentia corporvm angelicorvm non nvllisqve ad ea pertinentibvs per Carol. Frider. Goede. Halae Magdebvrgicae, Impensis Carol. Herm. Hemmerde, 1744.
    6 p. l., 116 p. 18cm.

    1. Angels--Early works to 1800. 2. Supernatural. I. Title: De existentia corporum angeli corum. II. Title.

    Gödelmann, Georg, 1559-1611

    see

    Godelmann, Johann Georg, 1559-1611

    Gödelmann, Johann Georg, 1559-1611

    see

    Godelmann, Johann Georg, 1559-1611

    Göehausen, Hermann.

    see

    Goehausen, Hermann.

    Goehausen, Hermann.
      Decisiones aliquot quaestionum.

Witchcraft
BF
1565
L42
1630
    [Laymann, Paul] 1574-1635, supposed author.
      Processus juridicus contra sagas & veneficos; das ist: Rechtlicher Proceß, wie man gegen Vnholdten vnd zauberische Personen verfahren soll. Mit erweglichen Exempeln vnd wunderbaren Geschichten, welche sich durch Hexerey zugetragen, außführlich erkläret. Vnàcum Decisionibus quaestionum ad hanc materiam pertinentium. Herman. Goehavsen ... edidit et recensuit. Rintelij ad Visurgim, Typis exscripsit Petrus Lucius, 1630.
      (Continued on next card)

    Goehausen, Hermann.
      Decisiones aliquot quaestionum.

Witchcraft
BF
1565
L42
1630
    [Laymann, Paul] 1574-1635, supposed author.
      Processus juridicus contra sagas & veneficos ... 1630.   (Card 2)

    8 p. l., 447, 188 (i. e., 288) p. 16cm.
    Title in red and black.
    Decisiones aliquot quaestionum ad hanc materiam ... avctore Herman: Göehausen [sic] has special t. p. and is paged separately.
    Each Titulus followed by commentary in Latin.
      (Continued on next card)

    Goehausen, Hermann.
      Decisiones aliquot quaestionum.

Witchcraft
BF
1565
L42
1630
    [Laymann, Paul] 1574-1635, supposed author.
      Processus juridicus contra sagas & veneficos ... 1630.   (Card 3)

    Also ascribed to Johann Jordanaeus (see G. L. Burr's note facing t. p.) and Goehausen. (See Duhr, Bernhard, 1852-1635. Paul Laymann und die Hexenprozesse, in Zeitschrift für katholische Theologie, Bd. 23 (1899), p. 733-745, on authorship question)
    I. Goehausen, Hermann, ed. II. Goehausen, Herman n. Decisiones aliquot quaestionum.

    Goehausen, Hermann, ed.

Witchcraft
BF
1565
L42
1630
    [Laymann, Paul] 1574-1635, supposed author.
      Processus juridicus contra sagas & veneficos; das ist: Rechtlicher Proceß, wie man gegen Vnholdten vnd zauberische Personen verfahren soll. Mit erweglichen Exempeln vnd wunderbaren Geschichten, welche sich durch Hexerey zugetragen, außführlich erkläret. Vnàcum Decisionibus quaestionum ad hanc materiam pertinentium. Herman. Goehavsen ... edidit et recensuit. Rintelij ad Visurgim, Typis exscripsit Petrus Lucius, 1630.
      (Continued on next card)

    Goehausen, Hermann, ed.

Witchcraft
BF
1565
L42
1630
    [Laymann, Paul] 1574-1635, supposed author.
      Processus juridicus contra sagas & veneficos ... 1630.   (Card 2)

    8 p. l., 447, 188 (i. e., 288) p. 16cm.
    Title in red and black.
    Decisiones aliquot quaestionum ad hanc materiam ... avctore Herman: Göehausen [sic] has special t. p. and is paged separately.
    Each Titulus followed by commentary in Latin.
      (Continued on next card)

    Goehausen, Hermann, ed.

Witchcraft
BF
1565
L42
1630
    [Laymann, Paul] 1574-1635, supposed author.
      Processus juridicus contra sagas & veneficos ... 1630.   (Card 3)

    Also ascribed to Johann Jordanaeus (see G. L. Burr's note facing t. p.) and Goehausen. (See Duhr, Bernhard, 1852-1635. Paul Laymann und die Hexenprozesse, in Zeitschrift für katholische Theologie, Bd. 23 (1899), p. 733-745, on authorship question)
    I. Goehausen, Hermann, ed. II. Goehausen, Herman n. Decisiones aliquot quaestionum.

    Göldi, Anna.

WITCHCRAFT
BF
1584
S97
Z7
1782a
    Lehmann, Heinrich Ludwig.
      Freundschaftliche und vertrauliche Briefe den so genannten sehr berüchtigten Hexenhandel zu Glarus betreffend. Zürich, Bey Johann Caspar Füessin, 1783.
    2 v. in 1. plate. 19cm.

    No more published.

    1. Trials (Witchcraft)--Glarus (Canton) 2. Göldi, Anna. 3. Tschudi, Anna Maria.

8 NIC

CATALOGUE OF THE CORNELL WITCHCRAFT COLLECTION

Göldi, Anna.

WITCHCRAFT
BF 1584
S97
Z7
1782
   Osenbrüggen, Eduard, 1809-1879.
   Der letzte Hexenprocess. [Leipzig, 1867]
   [513]-529 p. 24cm.

Extracted from Deutsches Museum, Nr. 17, Apr. 25, 1867.

1. Trials (Witchcraft)--Glarus (Canton) 2. Trials (Witchcraft)--Switzerland. 3. Göldi, Anna. 4. Tschudi, Anna Maria.

8 NIC

Witchcraft
BV 5083
G59
   Görres, Johann Joseph von, 1776-1848.
   Die christliche Mystik. Regensburg, G. J. Manz, 1836-42.
   4 v. in 3. 21cm.
   Contents.--1. Buch. Natürliche Unterlage der Mystik.--2. Buch. Der religiöse und kirchliche Grund der Mystik.--3. Buch. Die reinigende Mystik.--4. Buch. Eintritt in die Kreise höheren Zuges und Triebes, so wie höherer Erleuchtung.--5. Buch. Fortstreben zum Ziele in Liebe und höherer Erleuchtung durch die Ecstase.--6. Buch. Die historische,

8   (Continued on next card)

Witchcraft
BV 5083
G59
   Görres, Johann Joseph von, 1776-1848. Die christliche Mystik ... 1836-42. (Card 2)
   Contents--Continued.
   sagenhafte, physische und psychische Begründung der dämonischen Mystik.--7. Buch. Die dämonische Vorbereitung und Ascese.--8. Buch. Die Besessenheit.--9. Buch. Das Hexen- und Zauberwesen.
   Introduction and table of contents to vol. 4 is bound in between books 8 and 9.
   Each book has special t. p.
   I. Title.

8

Witchcraft
BV 5081
G59
1861
   Görres, Johann Joseph von, 1776-1848.
   La mystique divine, naturelle et diabolique; ouvrage traduit de l'allemand par M. Charles Sainte-Foi. 2. éd. Paris, Vme Poussielgue-Rusand, 1861-62.
   5 v. 18cm.
   Translation of Die christliche Mystik.

1. Mysticism. 2. Occult sciences. 3. Demonomania. I. Görres, Johann Joseph von, 1776-1848. Die christliche Mystik--French. II. Sainte-Foi, Charles, 1806-1861, tr. III. Title.

Witchcraft
BV 5081
G59
1861
   Görres, Johann Joseph von, 1776-1848.
   La mystique divine, naturelle et diabolique; ouvrage traduit de l'allemand par M. Charles Sainte-Foi. 2. éd. Paris, Vme Poussielgue-Rusand, 1861-62.
   5 v. 18cm.
   Translation of Die christliche Mystik.

1. Mysticism. 2. Occult sciences. 3. Demonomania. I. Görres, Johann Joseph von, 1776-1848. Die christliche Mystik--French. II. Sainte-Foi, Charles, 1806-1861, tr. III. Title.

WITCHCRAFT
PT 2631
L34
H61
   Goethe, Johann Wolfgang von, 1749-1832. Faust.
   Lobau, Richard.
   Spaziergänge mit Planitz, dessen Ideen und Ansichten über Faust und Hexe. Tagenbuchnotizen. Wittenberg, A.Piehler [1924]
   vii, 96, 12 p. 19cm.
   Includes passages from Planitz' Die Hexe von Goslar, with commentary.
   1. Planitz, Ernst Alfons, Edler von der, 1857- . 2.Witchcraft. 3.Goethe,Johann Wolfgang von,1749-1832. Faust. 4. Planitz, Ernst Alfons, Edler von der, 1857- . Die Hexe von Goslar. I.Planitz, Ernst Alfons, Edler von der, 1857- . II. Planitz,Ernst Alfons,Edler von der, 1857- . Die Hexe von Goslar. III. Title.

8 NIC

   Goêtia, vel Theurgia.

WITCHCRAFT
BF 1565
H64
1631
   Hildebrand, Wolffgang.
   Goêtia, vel Theurgia, sive Praestigiarum magicarum descriptio, revelatio, resolutio, inquisitio, & executio. Das ist, Wahre vnd eigentliche Entdeckunge, Declaration oder Erklärunge fürnehmer Articul der Zauberey. Vnd was von Zauberern, Vnholden, Hexen, deren Händel, Art, Thun ... vnd ihrer Machination ... Etwan durch den wolgebornen Herrn Jacob Freyherrn von Liechtenberg &c. ... erfahren, durch den hochgelahrten Herrn

8 NIC   (Continued on next card)

   Goêtia, vel Theurgia.

WITCHCRAFT
BF 1565
H64
1631
   Hildebrand, Wolffgang. Goêtia, vel Theurgia ... 1631. (Card 2)
   Jacob Weckern M. D. etwas weitleufftiger beschrieben. Nun aber an jetzo mit allem Fleisse revidiret ... durch Wolfgangum Hildebrandum ... Leipzig, In Verlegung Joh. Francken S. Erben vnd Samuel Scheiben Buchh., 1631.
   8 p. l., 342, [17] p. 18cm.
   Title in red and black.

8   (Continued on next card)

RARE
HV 8593
C88
   Goetz, Johann Christoph, respondent.
   Cramer, Wilhelm Zacharias, praeses.
   Dissertatio iuridica De tortura eiusque usu et effectibus...praeside Wilhelmo Zacharia Cramero respondente Io. Christophoro Goetzio pro loco in Facultate Iuridica rite obtinendo...habenda... Lipsiae, Litteris Breitkopfianis [1742]
   85 p. 23cm.
   "An magi et sagae sint torquendi?" : p. 57-66.

1. Torture. I. Goetz, Johann Christoph, respondent. II. Title.

8 NIC

Witchcraft
BF 1583
J65
Z6+
   Götze, Ludwig.
   Johanns VI., Grafen von Nassau-Dillenburg, Urteil über Hexenprocesse (1582) Mitgetheilt von Dr. L. Götze.
   (In Verein für Nassauische Altertumskunde und Geschichtsforschung, Wiesbaden. Nassauische Annalen. Wiesbaden. 27cm. 13. Bd. (1874), p. [327]-329)
   1. Johann VI, Count of Nassau-Dillenburg, 1535 or 6-1605 or 6. 2. Witchcraft--Nassau (Duchy) I. Verein für

8   (Continued on next card)

Witchcraft
BF 1583
J65
Z6+
   Götze, Ludwig. Johanns VI., Grafen von Nassau-Dillenburg, Urteil über Hexenprocesse (1582) 1874. (Card 2)
   Nassauische Altertumskunde und Geschichtsforschung, Wiesbaden. Nassauische Annalen. II. Johann VI, Count of Nassau-Dillenburg, 1535 or 6-1605 or 6.

8

Witchcraft
BF 1569
A2
I594
   Goff, Frederick Richmond, 1916-
   The Library of Congress copy of the Malleus maleficarum, 1487. Copenhagen, Munksgaard, 1963.
   [137]-141 p. facsim. 25cm.
   "Separatum" from Libri; international library review and IFLA-Communications-FIAB, vol. 13, no. 2, 1963.

1. Institoris, Henricus, d. 1508. Malleus maleficarum. I. Title.

Goffredy, Louis, 1572-1611.

see

Gaufridi, Louis, 1572-1611.

Goffridi, Louis, 1572-1611.

see

Gaufridi, Louis, 1572-1611.

Gofridi, Louis, 1572-1611.

see

Gaufridi, Louis, 1572-1611.

Witchcraft
BF 1565
G61
   Goldast, Melchior, 1578-1635.
   Rechtliches Bedencken, von Confiscation der Zauberer und Hexen-Güther. Ueber die Frage: Ob die Zauberer und Hexen, Leib und Guth mit und zugleich verwürcken, allso und dergestalt, dass sie nicht allein an Leib und Leben, sondern auch an Haab und Guth, können und sollen gestraffet werden? Sampt ein verliebtem kurtzem Bericht, von mancherley Arth der Zauberer und Hexen, underen ungleiche Bestraffung ... Bremen, A. Wessels, 1661.
   180 p. 21 cm.
   I. Title.

Witchcraft
BF 1429
G62
   Goldschmidt, Peter, d. 1713.
   Höllischer Morpheus, welcher Kund wird du die geschehene Erscheinungen derer Gespenste und Polter-Geister so bisshero zum Theil von keinen eintzigen Scribenten angeführet und bemercket worden sind ... Hamburg, G. Liebernickel, 1698.
   [14], 409, [37] p. illus. 17cm.

Witchcraft
BF 1429
G62
1704
   Goldschmidt, Peter, d. 1713.
   Höllischer Morpheus, welcher Kund wird durch die geschehene Erscheinungen derer Gespenster und Polter-Geister so bisshero zum Theil von keinen eintzigen Scribenten angeführet und bemercket worden sind ... Hamburg, G. Liebernickel, 1704.
   [14], 409, [37] p. illus. 18cm.
   With this are bound Glanvill, J. Sadducismus triumphatus. Hamburg. 1701. Zobel, E. Historische und theologische Vorstellung des ebentheuerlichen Gespenstes. Leipzig. 1692; and Declaratio apologetica. Leipzig. 1695.
   I. Title.

CATALOGUE OF THE CORNELL WITCHCRAFT COLLECTION

tchcraft

Goldschmidt, Peter, d. 1713.
Verworffener Hexen- und Zauberer-Advocat. Das ist: wolgegründete Vernichtung des thörichten Vorhabens Hn. Christiani Thomasii J. U. D. & Professoris Hallensis und aller derer, welche durch ihre super-kluge Phantasie-Grillen dem teufflischen Hexen-Geschmeiss das Wort reden wollen ... Hamburg, G. Liebernickel, 1705.
[13], 654, [19] p. illus. 18cm.
1. Thomasius, Christian, 1655-1728. I. Title.

Goldsmid, Edmund Marsden, ed. and tr.
[Des Niau, ---]
The history of the devils of Loudun, the alleged possession of the Ursuline nuns, and the trial and execution of Urbain Grandier, told by an eye-witness. Translated from the original French, and edited by Edmund Goldsmid. Edinburg, Priv. Print., 1887-88.
3 v. 18cm. (Collectanea Adamantaea, XXI.I)
Contains facsimile of original French t.p.: La véritable historie des diables de Loudun ... Poitiers, J. Thoreau, 1634.

Goldsmid, Edmund Marsden, ed. and tr.
Heucher, Johann Heinrich, 1677-1747.
Magic plants; being a translation of a curious tract entitled De vegetalibus magicis, written by M. J. H. Heucher. (1700.) Edited by Edmund Goldsmid. Edinburgh [Printed by E. & G. Goldsmid] 1886.
39 p. 23cm. (Bibliotheca curiosa)
Title in red and black.
"This edition is limited to 275 small-paper copies ..."
Translation of Ex historia naturali
(Continued on next card)

Goldsmid, Edmund Marsden, ed. and tr.
Heucher, Johann Heinrich, 1677-1747.
Magic plants ... 1886. (Card 2)
de vegetalibus magicis generatim, by Heucher and J. Fabricius.
"I have given, as an Appendix, a translation from the Official records of the Royal Court of Guernsey, of the trials of three women for witchcraft in 1617. This translation is taken from Mr. J. L. Pitt's Witchcraft and Devil-Lore in the Channel Islands." --ed.
(Continued on next card)

---

tchcraft

Goodcole, Henry.
The wonderfull discouerie of Elizabeth Sawyer, a witch, late of Edmonton, her conuiction and condemnation and death. Together with the relation of the Diuels accesse to her and their conference together. London, Printed for VV. Butler, 1621. [London, at the British Museum, 1923]
[32] p. 16cm.
Signatures: A-D⁴.
Photocopy (negative) 31 p. on 15 l. 20 x 32cm.
1. Sawyer, Elizabeth, d. 1621. I. Title.

ITCHCRAFT
BF
1576
M82
G641+

Goodell, Abner Cheney, 1831-1914.
[Additional considerations on the history of witchcraft in Massachusetts]
(In: Massachusetts Historical Society. Proceedings. Boston. 26cm. Jan./Mar.1884. p.65-71)
Running title: Witch-trials in Massachusetts.
With this, in same issue, are: Moore, George Henry. Supplementary notes on witchcraft in Massachusetts; and Goodell's Reasons for concluding that the act of 1711 became a law.
(Continued on next card)

WITCHCRAFT
BF
1576
M82
G641+

Goodell, Abner Cheney, 1831-1914. [Additional considerations on the history of witchcraft in Massachusetts,] 1884. (Card 2)
1. Witchcraft--Massachusetts. I. His Witch-trials in Massachusetts. II. Title: Witch-trials in Massachusetts.

Witchcraft
Z
6878
W8
G64

Goodell, Abner Cheney, 1831-1914.
... Catalogue of the private library of the late Abner C. Goodell, Salem, Mass. ... Pt. II, P to Z and witchcraft collection, including Prince Society publications, Prynne's tracts, rare Quaker tracts ... valuable collection of books relating to witchcraft and demonology... Boston, C. F. Libbie, book and art auctioneers, 1918]
[9]-174 p. illus., facsims. 25cm.
At head of title: Auction sale: ... March 12th, 1918 ...
1. Witchcraft--Bibl.--Cat. I. Libbie, firm, actioners, Boston. II. Title.

WITCHCRAFT
BF
1576
M82
G64+

Goodell, Abner Cheney, 1831-1914.
[Further notes on the history of witchcraft in Massachusetts]
(In: Massachusetts Historical Society. Proceedings. Boston. 26cm. June 1883. p. 280-326)
Running title: Witch-trials in Massachusetts.
Reply to George Henry Moore's Notes on the history of witchcraft in Massachusetts.
(Continued on next card)

8
NIC

WITCHCRAFT
BF
1576
M82
G64+

Goodell, Abner Cheney, 1831-1914. [Further notes on the history of witchcraft in Massachusetts]...1883. (Card 2)
1. Witchcraft--Massachusetts. 2. Moore, George Henry, 1823-1892. Notes on the history of witchcraft in Massachusetts. I. His Witch-trials in Massachusetts. II. Title. III. Title: Witch-trials in Massachusetts.

WITCHCRAFT
BF
1576
M82
G64+
1884
3 copies

Goodell, Abner Cheney, 1831-1914.
Further notes on the history of witchcraft in Massachusetts, containing additional evidence of the passage of the Act of 1711, for reversing the attainders of the witches; also affirming the legality of the Special Court of Oyer and Terminer of 1692... Cambridge, J. Wilson, 1884.
52 p. facsim. 26cm.
Reprinted, with slight alterations, from the Proceedings of the Massachusetts Historical Society, June 1883.
(Continued on next card)

8
NIC

WITCHCRAFT
BF
1576
M82
G64+
1884

Goodell, Abner Cheney, 1831-1914. Further notes on the history of witchcraft... 1884. (Card 2)
Caption title of this reprint, and running title of the original article: Witch-trials in Massachusetts.
Reply to George Henry Moore's Notes on the history of witchcraft in Massachusetts.
1. Witchcraft--Massachusetts. 2. Moore, George Henry, 1823-1892. Notes on the history of witchcraft in Massachusetts. I. His Witch-trials in Massachusetts. II.Title. III.Title: Witch-trials in Massachusetts.

WITCHCRAFT
BF
1576
M82
G641+

Goodell, Abner Cheney, 1831-1914.
Further notes on the history of witchcraft...
Moore, George Henry, 1823-1892. [Supplementary notes on witchcraft in Massachusetts]
(In: Massachusetts Historical Society. Proceedings. Boston. 26cm. Jan./Mar.1884. p.77-99)
With, in same issue: Goodell, Abner Cheney. Additional considerations on the history of witchcraft in Massachusetts.
Running title: History of witchcraft in Massachusetts.
Continues his Notes on the history (Continued on next card)

8
NIC

WITCHCRAFT
BF
1576
M82
G641+

Goodell, Abner Cheney, 1831-1914.
Further notes on the history of witchcraft...
Moore, George Henry, 1823-1892. [Supplementary notes on witchcraft...] 1884. (Card 2)
of witchcraft in Massachusetts. Continued by his Final notes on witchcraft in Massachusetts.
1. Witchcraft--Massachusetts. 2.Goodell, Abner Cheney, 1831-1914. Further notes on the history of witchcraft... I. Title. II. His History of witchcraft in Massachusetts. III. Title: History of witchcraft in Massachusetts.

WITCHCRAFT
BF
1576
M821+
1884

Goodell, Abner Cheney, 1831-1914.
Further notes on the history of witchcraft...
Moore, George Henry, 1823-1892. Supplementary notes on witchcraft in Massachusetts; a critical examination of the alleged law of 1711 for reversing the attainders of the witches of 1692. Cambridge, J. Wilson, 1884.
25 p. facsim. 26cm.
Reprinted from the Proceedings of the Massachusetts Historical Society, Mar.1884.
Caption title: Witchcraft in Massachusetts.
(Running title of original article: History of witchcraft in Massachusetts)
(Continued on next card)

8
NIC

WITCHCRAFT
BF
1576
M821+
1884

Goodell, Abner Cheney, 1831-1914. Further notes on the history of witchcraft...
Moore, George Henry, 1823-1892. Supplementary notes on witchcraft...1884. (Card 2)
Continues his Notes on the history of witchcraft in Massachusetts. Continued by his Final notes on witchcraft in Massachusetts.
1. Witchcraft--Massachusetts. 2.Goodell, Abner Cheney, 1831-1914. Further notes on the history of witchcraft... I.Title. II. His Witchcraft in Massachusetts. III. Title: Witchcraft in Massachusetts. IV. His History of witchcraft in Massachusetts. V. Title: History of witchcraft in Massachusetts.

WITCHCRAFT
BF
1576
M82
G641+

Goodell, Abner Cheney, 1831-1914.
History of witchcraft in Massachusetts.
Goodell, Abner Cheney, 1831-1914.
[Reasons for concluding that the act of 1711, reversing the attainders of the persons convicted of witchcraft in Massachusetts in the year 1692, became a law. Being a reply to Supplementary notes, etc. by George H. Moore.]
(In: Massachusetts Historical Society. Proceedings. Boston. 26cm. Jan./Mar.1884. p.99-118)
With, in same issue: his Additional considerations on the history (Continued on next card)

8
NIC

WITCHCRAFT
BF
1576
M82
G641+

Goodell, Abner Cheney, 1831-1914.
History of witchcraft in Massachusetts.
Goodell, Abner Cheney, 1831-1914. [Reasons for concluding that the act of 1711... became a law, 1884. (Card 2)
of witchcraft in Massachusetts.
Running title: History of witchcraft in Massachusetts.
1. Witchcraft--Massachusetts. 2. Moore, George Henry, 1823-1892. Supplementary notes on witchcraft... I. His History of witchcraft in Massachusetts. II. Title: History of witchcraft in Massachusetts. III. Title: Reasons for concluding that the act of 1711 became a law.

CATALOGUE OF THE CORNELL WITCHCRAFT COLLECTION

WITCHCRAFT
BF 1576 M82 G641+
Goodell, Abner Cheney, 1831-1914.
₍Reasons for concluding that the act of 1711, reversing the attainders of the persons convicted of witchcraft in Massachusetts in the year 1692, became a law. Being a reply to Supplementary notes, etc. by George H. Moore₎
(In:. Massachusetts Historical Society. Proceedings. Boston. 26cm. Jan./Mar.1884. p.99-118)
8 NIC
With, in same issue: his Additional cons iderations on the history
(Continued on next card)

WITCHCRAFT
BF 1576 M82 G641+
Goodell, Abner Cheney, 1831-1914. ₍Reasons for concluding that the act of 1711... became a law₎ 1884. (Card 2)
Running title: History of witchcraft in Massachusetts.
1. Witchcraft--Massachusetts. 2. Moore, George Henry, 1823-1892. Supplementary notes on witchcraft... I. His ⁄History of witchcraft in Massachusetts. II. Title: History of witchcraft in Massachusetts. III. Title: Reasons for concluding that the act of 1711 became a law.

WITCHCRAFT
BF 1576 M821 G64+ 1884
Goodell, Abner Cheney, 1831-1914.
Reasons for concluding that the act of 1711, reversing the attainders of the persons convicted of witchcraft in Massachusetts in the year 1692, became a law. Being a reply to Supplementary notes, etc. by George H. Moore. Cambridge, J. Wilson, 1884.
2 copies
21 p. 26cm.
Originally appeared in the Proceedings of the Massa chusetts Historical Society, Jan./ Mar.1884
8 NIC
(Continued on next card)

WITCHCRAFT
BF 1576 M821 G64+ 1884
Goodell, Abner Cheney, 1831-1914. Reasons for concluding that the act of 1711... became a law...1884. (Card 2)
Caption title: Witchcraft in Massachusetts. (Running title of original article: History of witchcraft in Massachusetts)
1. Witchcraft--Massachusetts. 2.Moore, George Henry, 1823-1892. Supplementary notes on witchcraft... I. His Witchcraft in Massachuse tts. II.Title: Witchcraft in Massachus etts. III.His⁄History of witchcraft in Massachusetts. IV. Title: Histo ry of witchcraft in Mas sachusetts. V. Title.

Witchcraft
BF 1576 M822+
Goodell, Abner Cheney, 1831-1914. Reasons for concluding that the act of 1711 ... became a law.
Moore, George Henry, 1823-1892.
Final notes on witchcraft in Massachusetts: a summary vindication of the laws and liberties concerning attainders with corruption of blood, escheats, forfeitures for crime, and pardon of offenders, in reply to "Reasons," etc., of Hon. Abner C. Goodell, jr. ... By George H. Moore ... New York, Printed for the author, 1885.
120 p. 25½cm.
"Pamphlets hitherto issued in this discussion": p. ₍2₎
Autographed presentation copy from the author.
1. Witchcraft--Massachusetts. 2. Goodell, Abner Cheney, 1831-1914. Reasons for concluding that the act of 1711 ... became a law. I. Title. 11-13449
8 Library of Congress BF1579.M8

WITCHCRAFT
BF 1576 M82 G641+
Goodell, Abner Cheney, 1831-1914.
₍Additional considerations on the history of witchcraft in Massachusetts₎
(In: Massachusetts Historical Society. Proceedings. Boston. 26cm. Jan./Mar.1884. p.65-71)
Running title: Witch-trials in Massachusetts.
With this, in same issue, are: Moore, George Henry. Supplementary notes on witchcraft in Mas sachusetts; and Goodell's Reasons for concluding that the act of 1711 became a law.
8 NIC
(Continued on next card)

WITCHCRAFT
BF 1576 M82 G64+
Goodell, Abner Cheney, 1831-1914.
Witch-trials in Massachusetts.
Goodell, Abner Cheney, 1831-1914.
₍Further notes on the history of witchcraft in Massachusetts₎
(In: Massachusetts Historical Society. Proceedings. Boston. 26cm. June 1883. p. 280-326)
Running title: Witch-trials in Massachusetts.
Reply to George Henry Moore's Notes on the history of witchcraft in Massachusetts.
8 NIC
(Continued on next card)

WITCHCRAFT
BF 1576 M821 G64+ 1884
Goodell, Abner Cheney, 1831-1914.
Witchcraft in Massachusetts.
Goodell, Abner Cheney, 1831-1914.
Reasons for concluding that the act of 1711, reversing the attainders of the persons convicted of witchcraft in Massachusetts in the year 1692, became a law. Being a reply to Supplementary notes, etc. by George H. Moore. Cambridge, J. Wilson, 1884.
21 p. 26cm.
Originally appeared in the Proceedings of the Massa chusetts Historical Society, Jan./ Mar.1884
8 NIC
(Continued on next card)

WITCHCRAFT
BF 1576 M821 G64+ 1884
Goodell, Abner Cheney, 1831-1914.
Witchcraft in Massachusetts.
Goodell, Abner Cheney, 1831-1914. Reasons for concluding that the act of 1711... became a law...1884. (Card 2)
Caption title: Witchcraft in Massachusetts. (Running title of original article: History of witchcraft in Massachusetts)
1. Witchcraft--Massachusetts. 2.Moore, George Henry, 1823-1892. Supplementary notes on witchcraft... I. His Witchcraft in Massachuse tts. II.Title: Witchcraft in Massachus etts. III.His⁄History of witchcraft in Massachusetts. IV. Title: Histo ry of witchcraft in Mas sachusetts. V. Title.

Witchcraft
BV 4935 G66 G12
Gordon, James, 1704-1734.
Gätschenberger, Stephan.
Zwei Klostergeschichten des vorigen Jahrhunderts. Zum erstenmale nach den Inquisitions-Akten bearbeitet ... Leipzig, C. F. Fleischer, 1858.
124 p. 18cm.
Contents.--1. Graf James Gordon oder Pater Marianus.--2. Die letzte Hexe in Deutschland.
1. Gordon, James, 1704-1734. 2. Conversion. 3. Sänger, Maria Renata von Mossau, ca. 1680-1749. 4. Witchcraft. 5. Martyrs. I. Title.
3

Witchcraft
BF 1582 G67
₍Gosselin, Louis Léon Théodore₎ 1857-1935.
Les petits sorciers du XVIIe siècle et la torture avant l'exécution. ₍Paris? 19--₎
₍80₎-104 p. 25cm.
Caption title.
Detached from a periodical.
1. Trials (Witchcraft)--France. 2. Torture--France. I. Title.
8

Witchcraft
BF 1548 G68 1871
Gostick, Jesse.
Who is the devil? (Twentieth thousand) London, Printed for the Trade ₍1871₎
12 p. 19cm.
1. Devil. I. Title.

WITCHCRAFT
QL 50 V89
Gothofrei Voigtii ... Deliciae physicae.
Voigt, Gottfried, 1644-1682.
Gothofrei Voigtii ... Deliciae physicae ΕΠΙΔΙΕΣΚΕΥΑΣΜΕΝΑΙ, de stillicidio sanguinis ex interemti hominis cadavere praesente occisore, lacrymis crocodili, catulis ursarum, amore ovis et lupi, piscibus fossilibus et volatilibus, conventu sagarum ac sua sabbata, infantibus supposititiis, cornu cervi, et stellis cadentibus accurata methodo conscr iptae. Rostochii, Im-
8
(Continued on next card)

WITCHCRAFT
QL 50 V89
Gothofrei Voigtii ... Deliciae physicae
Voigt, Gottfried, 1644-1682. ...Deliciae physicae ... 1671. (Card 2)
primebat Johannes Kilius, 1671.
7 p. l., 369, ₍1₎ p. 17cm.
Title in red and black.
1. Natural history--Curiosa and miscellany. 2. Animal lore. 3. Witchcraft. I. Title: Deliciae physicae.
8

Witchcraft
BF 1584 A93 A61
Ein Gottesgelehrter.
Anpreisung der allergnädigsten Landesverordnung Ihrer kaiserl. königl. apostolischen Majestät, wie es mit dem hexenprocesse zu halten sey, nebst einer vorrede, in welcher die Kurze vertheidigung der hex- und zauberey, die herr pater Angelus März der Akademischen rede des herrn p. don Ferdinand Sterzingers über das vorurtheil der hexerey entgegengesetzet, beantwortet wird von einem gottesgelehrten. München, Akademische buchhandlung, 1767.
4 p. l., 282, ₍2₎ p. 23cm.
(Continued on next card)
42-40824
8 ₍2₎

Witchcraft
BF 1511 F29
Gottesurteil und Folter: eine Studie zur Dämonologie des Mittelalters und der neueren Zeit.
Fehr, Hans Adolf, 1874-
Gottesurteil und Folter: eine Studie zur Dämonologie des Mittelalters und der neueren Zeit. Berlin, W. de Gruyter, 1926.
24 p. plate. 23cm.
Pages also numbered ₍231₎-254.
"Sonderausgabe aus Festgabe für Rudolf Stammler zum 70. Geburtstage."
1. Demonology. I. Title. II. Stammler, Rudolf, 1856- 1938.

WITCHCRAFT
BV 810 G68
₍Gottwald, Johannes Petrus₎
Programma de baptismo diabolico. ₍Co bvrgi, Typis I. N. Monachi, 1702₎
₍8₎ p. 21cm.
Introduction to an oral dissertation.
1. Baptism--Early works to 1800. I. Title. II. Title: De baptismo diabolico
8 NIC

Witchcraft
BF 1612 G69
Gougenot des Mousseaux, Henri Roger, 180-
Les hauts phénomènes de la magie précédés du spiritisme antique ... et quelques le addressées à l'auteur ... Paris, H. Plon, 1864.
xxxviii, 480 p. 23cm.
1. Magic. 2. Spiritualism. 3. Occult sciences. I. Title.
8

CATALOGUE OF THE CORNELL WITCHCRAFT COLLECTION

Witchcraft
Gougenot des Mousseaux, Henri Roger, 1805-1876.
Moeurs et pratiques des démons ou des esprits visiteurs, d'après les autorités de l'église, les auteurs païens, les faits contemporains, etc. Paris, H. Vrayet de Surcy, 1854.
xv, 404 p. 18cm.

Witchcraft
Gougenot des Mousseaux, Henri Roger, 1805-1876.
Moeurs et pratiques des démons ou des esprits visiteurs du spiritisme ancien et moderne ... Nouv. éd. entièrement refondue et fort augmentée. Paris, H. Plon, 1865.
xl, 436 p. 24cm.

1. Demonology. I. Title.

WITCHCRAFT
Goulart, Simon, 1543-1628.
Thresor d'histoires admirables et memorables de nostre temps. Recueilliies de plusieurs autheurs, memoires, et auis de diuers endroits. Mises en lvmiere par Simon Govlart Senlisien. [Genève?] Par Pavl Marceav, 1610.
2 v. in 1. ([16], 1117, [35] p.) 18cm.

Title vignette.
First published Paris, 1600.

I. Title.

WITCHCRAFT
BF 1410 P51 1584a
Goulart, Simon, 1543-1628, tr.
Peucer, Kaspar, 1525-1602.
Les devins, ov Commentaire des principales sortes de devinations: distingué en quinze liures, esquels les ruses & impostures de Satan sont descouuertes, solidement refutees, & separees d'auec les sainctes propheties & d'auec les predictions naturelles. Escrit en latin par M. Gaspar Pevcer, ... nouuellement tourné en françois par S. G. S. [i.e., Simon Goulart, Senlisien] ... Anvers, Par Hevdrik Connix, 1584.

(Continued on next card)

WITCHCRAFT
F 410 51 584a
Goulart, Simon, 1543-1628.
Peucer, Kaspar, 1525-1602. Les devins, ov Commentaire des principales sortes de devinations ... 1584. (Card 2)
6 p. l., 653, [24] p. 24cm.
Translation of Commentarius de praecipuis generibus divinationum.
1. Divination. 2. Prophecies. 3. Magic. 4. Witchcraft. I. His Commentarius de praecipuis generibus divinationum. II. Goulart, Simon, 1543-1628, tr. III. Title.

WITCHCRAFT
BF 1578 S55 A2 1894
Grace Sherwood, the Virginia witch.
Sherwood, Grace, defendant.
Grace Sherwood, the Virginia witch. Communicated by Edward W. James.
(In: William and Mary college quarterly historical magazine. Williamsburg, Va. 25cm. v.3, no.2, Oct. 1894, p. 96-101; v.3, no.3, Jan. 1895, p. 190-192)
Witchcraft Collection has only the first two of five articles. Cornell University Libr ary has complete file of
(Continued on next card)
8 NIC

Grace Sherwood, the Virginia witch.

WITCHCRAFT
BF 1578 S55 A2 1894
Sherwood, Grace, defendant. Grace Sherwood, the Virginia witch. 1894-1895. (Card 2)
the periodical (F221 W71)
Contains court records of prosecutions of Grace Sherwood for witchcraft, in Princess Anne County, Virginia.
1. Witchcraft--Princess Anne Co., Virginia. 2. Trials (Witchcraft)--Princess Anne Co., Virginia. I. James, Edward Wilson, d.1906, ed. II. Title.

Witchcraft
Z 6876 G73
Grässe, Johann Georg Theodor, 1814-1885.
Bibliotheca magica et pneumatica; oder, Wissenschaftlich geordnete bibliographie der wichtigsten in das gebiet des zauber-, wunder-, geister- und sonstigen aberglaubens vorzüglich älterer zeit einschlagenden werke. Mit angabe der aus diesen wissenschaften auf der Königl. Sächs. oeff. bibliothek zu Dresden befindlichen schriften. Ein beitrag zur sittengeschichtlichen literatur. Zusammengestellt und mit einem doppelten register versehen.
Leipzig, W. Engelmann, 1843.
iv, 175 p. 22cm.
Copy 1 interleaved.
Manuscript notes, copy 1.
1. Occult sciences--Bibl. I. Title.

Witchcraft
Z 6878 W8 Y98
Grässe, Johann Georg Theodor, 1814-1885.
Bibliotheca magica et pneumatica.
Yve-Plessis, R[obert]
...Essai d'une bibliographie française méthodique & raisonnée de la sorcellerie et de la possession démoniaque; pour servir de suite et de complément à la Bibliotheca magica de Græsse, aux catalogues Sépher, Ouvaroff, D'Ourches et Guldenstubbe, S. de Guaita et aux divers travaux partiels publiés sur cette matière. Préface par Albert de Rochas. Paris, Bibliothèque Chacornac, 1900.
xiv p., 1 l., 254, [1] p. front, facsims., plates. 25cm.
"Il a été tiré de cet ouvrage: 10 exemplaires sur papier de Hollande et 500 exemplaires sur papier ordinaire, tous numérotés et paraphés. No. 13".
1,793 titles, classified.
1. Witchcraft--Bibl. 2. Occult sciences--Bibl. I. Grässe, Johann Georg Theodor, 1814-1885. Bibliotheca magica et pneumatica. II. Title.
Library of Congress, no. Z6878.W8Y8.

Witchcraft
BF 1583 A2 G73
Graeter, M Jacob
Hexen oder Unholden Predigten. Darinnen zu zweyen vnderschiedlichen Predigten, auff das kürtzest vnnd ordenlichest angezeigt würdt, was in disen allgemeinen Landklagen, vber die Hexen vnd Vnholden, von selbigen warhafftig vnnd Gottseeliglich zuhalten. Tübingen, A. Hock, 1589.
[28] p. 20cm.

1. Witchcraft. I. Title.

Witchcraft
BT 980 G73 1890
Graf, Arturo, 1848-1913.
Il diavolo. 3. ed. Milano, Fratelli Treves, 1890.
viii, 463 p. 20cm.

I. Title.

Witchcraft
BT 980 G73 1931
Graf, Arturo, 1848-1913.
Il diavolo--English.
Graf, Arturo, 1848-1913.
The story of the devil, by Arturo Graf; translated from the Italian by Edward Noble Stone, with notes by the translator. New York, The Macmillan company, 1931.
xiv, 206 p. 22½cm.

Translation of Il diavolo.

Witchcraft
BT 980 G73 1889
Graf, Arturo.
Il diavolo--German.
Graf, Arturo.
Naturgeschichte des Teufels. Einzige vom Verfasser autorisierte deutsche Ausg. Aus dem Italienischen von R. Teuscher. Jena, H. Costenoble [1889]
xviii, 448 p. 18cm.

1. Devil. I. Graf, Arturo. Il diavolo--German. II. Title.

Witchcraft
BT 980 G73 1889
Graf, Arturo.
Naturgeschichte des Teufels. Einzige vom Verfasser autorisierte deutsche Ausg. Aus dem Italienischen von R. Teuscher. Jena, H. Costenoble [1889]
xviii, 448 p. 18cm.

1. Devil. I. Graf, Arturo. Il diavolo--German. II. Title.

Witchcraft
BT 980 G73 1931
Graf, Arturo, 1848-1913.
The story of the devil, by Arturo Graf; translated from the Italian by Edward Noble Stone, with notes by the translator. New York, The Macmillan company, 1931.
xiv, 206 p. 22½cm.

Translation of Il diavolo.

1. Devil. I. Stone, Edward Noble, 1870- tr. II. Graf, Arturo, 1848-1913. Il diavolo.--English. III. Title.

Witchcraft
BF 1581 F16 1882
Fairfax, Edward, d. 1635.
Daemonologia: a discourse on witchcraft as it was acted in the family of Mr. Edward Fairfax, of Fuyston, in the county of York, in the year 1621; along with the only two eclogues of the same author known to be in existence. With a biographical introduction, and notes topographical & illustrative. By William Grainge. Harrogate, R. Ackrill, 1882.
2 p. l., v p., 1 l., [9]-189 p. 21cm.

1. Witchcraft. I. Grainge, William, ed.

Witchcraft
BF 1555 F88
Grambecken, Catharina, fl. 1692.
Frese, Jürgen, 1623-
Umständlicher Bericht, von dem Unlängst in Hamburg vom leidigen Satan besessenen Mägdlein, wie auch Beantwortung einiger Fragen von der Universität Kiel, nebst des Autore Lebens-Lauf, worin gemeldet werden die Wunder von dem glühenden Rink und Kohlen, und noch beygefüget, eine Trostschrift an einige betrübte Herzen. [Hamburg?] 1692.
112 p. 17cm.

Witchcraft
BF 1583 A2 G74
Graminaeus, Theodor, b. ca. 1530.
Indvctio sive directorivm: das ist: Anleitung oder Vnderweisung, wie ein Richter in Criminal vnd peinlichen Sachen die Zauberer vnd Hexen belangendt, sich zuverhalten, vnd der Gebür damit zuverfahren haben soll, in zwey Theil getheilet, als wie von Amptsswegen, vnd sonst, so der Kläger Recht begert, zuverfahren ... Cölln, H. Falckenburg, 1594.
[8] 157 p. 15cm.

I. Title. II. Title: Anleitung oder Unterweisung, wie ein Richter in Criminal ... Sachen die Zauberer und Hexen belangendt, sich zuverhalten ... haben soll.

CATALOGUE OF THE CORNELL WITCHCRAFT COLLECTION

Le grand feu, tonnerre et foudre du ciel.

WITCHCRAFT
BF
1517
F5
V83
1620a

La Vision pvbliqve d'vn horrible & tres-espouuantable demon, sur l'Eglise Cathedralle de Quinpercorentin en Bretagne. Le premier iour de ce mois de feurier 1620. Lequel demon consomma vne pyramide par feu, & y suruint vn grand tonnerre & foudre du ciel. Paris, Chez Abraham-Saugrin, 1620. [Arras, Imprimerie de Rousseau-Leroy, ca. 1865]

8   8 p. 19cm. (bound in 23cm. vol.) (Portefeuille de l'ami des livres)

(Continued on next card)

Le grand feu, tonnerre et foudre du ciel.

WITCHCRAFT
BF
1517
F5
V83
1620a

La Vision pvbliqve d'vn horrible & tres-espouuantable demon ... [Ca. 1865] (Card 2)

Caption title reads: Le grand fev, tonnerre & foudre du ciel ..."
"Iouxte la copie imprimee à Rennes."

1. Demonology. 2. Quimper, France. Cathedrale. I. Title: Le grand feu, tonnerre & foudre du ciel.

Le grand grimoire.

WITCHCRAFT
BF
1558
G86
1750

L'Art de commander les esprits célestes, aëriens, terrestres & infernaux. Suivi du Grand grimoire, de la magie noire et des forces infernales, du docteur J. Karter, La clavicule de Salomon, &c. Avec le vrai secret de faire parler les morts, pour découvrir tous les trésors caches, &c. &c. [Paris?] 1421 [i.e., ca. 1750?] iv, 5-108 [i. e., 118], [2] p. illus. 16cm.

Title in red and black.

(Continued on next card)

Le grand grimoire.

WITCHCRAFT
BF
1558
G86
1750

L'Art de commander les esprits ... [1750?] (Card 2)

Published also under other titles: Grimoire du Pape Honorius [best-known]; Le dragon rouge; and Le véritable dragon rouge.

1. Incantations. 2. Magic. I. Karter, J. II. Title: Le grand grimoire. III. Title: Grimoire du Pape Honorius. IV. Title: Le dragon rouge. V. Title: Le véritable dragon rouge. VI. Title: La clavicule de Salomon.

Le grand grimoire.

Witchcraft
BF
1558
G86
1760a

Grimoire du Pape Honorius, avec un recueil des plus rares secrets. A Rome, 1760. [Avignon, Offray ainé, ca. 1880] 95 p. illus., 12 col. plates. 13cm. Title page is plate 2 (Pl. I in the numbering)

Added title page preceeding text has title: Le grand grimoire, avec La grande clavicule de Salomon.

1. Incantations. 2. Magic. I. Honorius III, Pope, d. 1227. Spurious and doubtful works. II. Title: Le grand grimoire.

Un grand procès de sorcellerie au XVIIe siècle.

WITCHCRAFT
BF
1582
L86

Lorédan, Jean, 1853-
Un grand procès de sorcellerie au XVIIe siècle: l'abbé Gaufridy et Madeleine de Demandolx (1600-1670) d'après des documents inédits. Ouvrage orné de 9 gravures et de 2 fac-similés. Paris, Perrin, 1912.
xiv, 436 p. illus. 21cm.

1. Witchcraft--France. 2. Trials (Witchcraft)--France. 3. Gaufridi, Louis, 1572-1611. 4. Demandolx, Madeleine de, 1593?-1670. I. Title.

8
NIC

La grande clavicule de Salomon.

Witchcraft
BF
1558
G86
1760a

Grimoire du Pape Honorius, avec un recueil des plus rares secrets. A Rome, 1760. [Avignon, Offray ainé, ca. 1880] 95 p. illus., 12 col. plates. 13cm. Title page is plate 2 (Pl. I in the numbering)

Added title page preceeding text has title: Le grand grimoire, avec La grande clavicule de Salomon.

1. Incantations. 2. Magic. I. Honorius III, Pope, d. 1227. Spurious and doubtful works. II. Title: Le grand grimoire.

La grande hystérie.

WITCHCRAFT
RC
532
R52
1885

Richer, Paul Marie Louis Pierre, 1849-1933.
Études cliniques sur la grande hystérie ou hystéro-épilepsie. 2. éd., rev. et considérablement augmentée. Paris, A. Delahaye et E. Lecroisier, 1885.
xv, 975 p. illus. 25cm.

Imprint covered by label: Paris, O. Doin.
1. Hysteria. 2. Hypnotism. I. Title. II. Title: La grande hystérie.

Les grandes victimes de l'hystérie.

Witchcraft
BF
1582
A92

[Augier, Adolphe Clovis]
Les grandes victimes de l'hystérie: Louis Gaufridi, curé des Accoules, et Magdeleine de la Palud. Relation historique et rationnelle d'un procès de sorcellerie. Paris, L. Michaud [1907]
313 p. 19cm.

At head of title: Raoul Gineste [pseud. of A. C. Augier]

1. Gaufridi, Louis, 1572-1611. 2. Palud, Magdeleine de la. 3. Witchcraft--Provence. I. Title.

Grandier, Urbain

WITCHCRAFT
BF
1517
F5
G75
1634

Grandier, Urbain, 1590-1634.
Arrest de mort donne' contre Vrbain Grandier prestre, curé de la ville de Loudun, attaint & conuaincu de sortilege & magie. Riom, Chez la vefue Costeravste, 1634.
6, [1] p. 17cm.
"Suiuant la copie imprimee à Blois par Iacques & Michel Cortereau imprimeur du roy & de la ville."
"Cedvle," p. 6, is Grandier's pact with Lucifer.
I. France. Conseil du Roi. II. Title.

Grandier, Urbain, 1590-1634.

Witchcraft
BF
1517
F5
A89

[Aubin, Nicolas] b. ca. 1655.
The cheats and illusions of Romish priests and exorcists. Discovered in the history of the devils of Loudun: being an account of the pretended possession of the Ursuline nuns, and of the condemnation and punishment of Urban Grandier, a parson of the same town ... London, Printed for W. Turner and R. Bassett, 1703.
4 p. l., 331 p. 20cm.

Attributed also to M. Des Niau.

Grandier, Urbain, 1590-1634.

Witchcraft
BF
1517
F5
A892
1716

[Aubin, Nicolas] b. ca. 1655.
Cruels effets de la vengeance du Cardinal de Richelieu, ou Histoire des diables de Loudun, de la possession des religieuses ursulines, et de la condamnation et du suplice [sic] d'Urbain Grandier, curé de la même ville. Amsterdam, E. Roger, 1716.
[10], 5-378 p. front. 17cm.

Published also under titles: Histoire des diables de Loudun, ou, De la possession des religieuses ursulines ... Amsterdam, 1694; and Histoire d'Urbain Grandier, condamné comme magicien... Amsterdam, 1735.

Grandier, Urbain, 1590-1634.

Witchcraft
BF
1517
F5
A893
1737

[Aubin, Nicolas] b. ca. 1655.
Histoire des diables de Loudun, ou De la possession des religieuses ursulines, et de la condamnation & du suplice d'Urbain Grandier, curé de la même ville. Cruels effets de la vengeance du Cardinal de Richelieu. Amsterdam, aux de'pens de la Compagnie, 1737.
378 p. front. 17cm.

"Published also under titles:

(Continued on next card)

Grandier, Urbain, 1590-1634.

Witchcraft
BF
1517
F5
A893
1737

[Aubin, Nicolas] b. ca. 1655. Histoire des diables de Loudun ... 1737. (Card 2)

Histoire d'Urbain Grandier, condamné comme magicien ... Amsterdam, 1735, and Cruels effets de la vengeance du Cardinal de Richelieu; ou, Histoire des diables de Loudun ... Amsterdam, 1716."--L.C.

1. Demoniac possession. 2. Grandier, Urbain, 1590-1634. 3. Loudun, France. Ursuline convent. I. Title: Les diables de Loudun.

Grandier, Urbain, 1590-1634.

Witchcraft
BF
1582
B54
1905

Bertrand, Isidore.
Les possédées de Loudun, et Urbain Grandier. Étude historique. Paris, Bloud [1905?]
61 p. 18cm. (Science et religion: études pour le temps présent)

Includes bibliography (5 p.)
Bound with his La sorcellerie.

1. Demoniac possession. 2. Grandier, Urbain, 1590-1634. 3. Loudun, France. Ursuline Convent. I. Title.

CATALOGUE OF THE CORNELL WITCHCRAFT COLLECTION

Grandier, Urbain, 1590-1634.
   Bleau, Alphonse.
     Précis d'histoire sur la ville et les possédées de Loudun. Poitiers, Typographie de H. Oudin, 1877.
     246 p. 18cm.

     1. Loudun, France--Hist. 2. Loudun, France. Ursuline Convent. 3. Grandier, Urbain, 1590-1634. 4. Demoniac possession. I. Title.

Grandier, Urbain, 1590-1634.
   Certeau, Michel de.
     La possession de Loudun, présentée par Michel de Certeau. [Paris, Julliard, 1970]
     347 p. plates. 19 cm. (Collection Archives, 37) 9.00F F***
     Includes bibliographical references.

     1. Demoniac possession. 2. Loudun, France. Ursuline convent. 3. Grandier, Urbain, 1590-1634. I. Title.

BF1517.F5C47   76-575412
Library of Congress   71 [2]

Grandier, Urbain, 1590-1634.
   [Des Niau, ---]
     The history of the devils of Loudun, the alleged possession of the Ursuline nuns, and the trial and execution of Urbain Grandier, told by an eye-witness. Translated from the original French, and edited by Edmund Goldsmid. Edinburg, Priv. Print., 1887-88.
     3 v. 18cm. (Collectanea Adamantaea, XXI.I)
     Contains facsimile of original French t.p.: La véritable historie des diables de Loudun ... Poitiers, J. Thoreau, 1634.

Grandier, Urbain, 1590-1634.
   France. Commission pour le jugement du procez criminel fait a l'encontre de Maistre Urbain Grandier & ses complices.
     Extraict des registres de la Commission ordonnée par le Roy povr le ivgement ... Poictiers, Par I. Thoreav & la vefue d'A. Mesnier, 1634.
     25 p. 16cm.

Grandier, Urbain, 1590-1634.
   Interrogatoire de Maistre Vrbain Grandier, Prestre, Curé de S. Pierre du marché de Loudun, & Chanoyne de l'Eglise Saincte Croix dudit lieu. Avec les confrontations des Religieuses possédées contre le dit Grandier. Ensemble la liste & les noms des Iuges deputez par sa Majesté. A Paris, Chez Estienne Hebert, & Iacqves Povllard, 1634.
     10 p. 16cm.
     1. Loudun, France. Ursuline Convent. 2. Grandier, Urbain, 1590-1634.

Grandier, Urbain, 1590-1634.
WITCHCRAFT
BF 1517 F5 J43 1886
   Jeanne des Anges, mère, 1602-1665.
     Soeur Jeanne des Anges, supérieure des Ursulines de Loudun (XVIIe siècle) Autobiographie d'une hystérique possédée, d'après le manuscrit inédit de la bibliothèque de Tours. Annoté et publié par les docteurs Gabriel Legué et Gilles de la Tourette. Préface de M. le professeur Charcot. Paris, Aux Bureaux du Progrès, 1886.
     xiv, 321 p. facsim. 24cm. (Bibliothèque diabolique [Collection Bourneville])
8 NIC   [Continued on next card]

Grandier, Urbain, 1590-1634.
WITCHCRAFT BF 1517 F5 L22
   La Menardaye, Jean Baptiste de.
     Examen et discussion critique de l'histoire des diables de Loudun, de la possession des religieuses Ursulines, et de la condamnation d'Urbain Grandier. Paris, Chez Debure l'aîné, 1747.
     xxix, 521 p. 17cm.

     1. Demoniac possession. 2. Grandier, Urbain, 1590-1634. 3. Loudun, France. Ursuline convent. I. Title: Histoire des diables de Loudun. II. Title: Diables de Loudun.
8 NIC

Grandier, Urbain, 1590-1634.
WITCHCRAFT BF 1517 F5 L52 1874
   Legué, Gabriel, d. 1913.
     Documents pour servir à l'histoire des possédées de Loudun. Paris, A. Delahaye, 1874.
     90 p. 22cm.

     Issued also as diss.--Paris.

     1. Loudun, France. Ursuline Convent. 2. Demoniac possession. 3. Grandier, Urbain 1590-1634.
8 NIC

Grandier, Urbain, 1590-1634.
WITCHCRAFT BF 1517 F5 L521 1884
   Legué, Gabriel, d. 1913.
     Urbain Grandier et les possédées de Loudun. Nouv. éd. revue et augmentée. Paris, Charpentier, 1884.
     xii, 348 p. 19cm.

     1. Grandier, Urbain, 1590-1634. 2. Loudun, France. Ursuline Convent. 3. Demoniac possession.
8 NIC

Grandier, Urbain, 1590-1634.
WITCHCRAFT BF 1517 F5 L61
   Leriche, Pierre Ambroise.
     Etudes sur les possessions en général et sur celle de Loudun en particulier. Précédées d'une lettre adressée à l'auteur par Ventura de Raulica. Paris, H. Plon, 1859.
     x, 258 p. 17cm.

     1. Demoniac possession. 2. Loudun, France. Ursuline Convent. 3. Grandier, Urbain, 1590-1634.
8 NIC

Grandier, Urbain, 1590-1634.
WITCHCRAFT BF 1517 F5 P75
   Poitiers, Jean de.
     Les diables de Loudun. Paris, Ghio, 1876
     271 p. 17cm.

     1. Demoniac possession. 2. Grandier, Urbain, 1590-1634. 3. Loudun, France. Ursuline convent. I. Title.
8 NIC

Grandier, Urbain, 1590-1634.
Witchcraft BF 1517 F5R29
   Recit veritable de ce qvi s'est passé à Lovdvn. Contre Maistre Vrbain Grandier, Prestre Curé de l'Eglise de S. Pierre de Loudun, attaint & convaincu du crime de Magie, malefice & possession, arriuée par son faict és personne d'aucunes des Religieuses Vrseline de la ville de Loudun. A Paris, De l'Imprimerie de Pierre Targa, 1634.
     15 p. 16cm.
     1. Loudun, France. Ursuline Convent 2. Grandier, Urbain, 1590-1634.

Grandier, Urbain, 1590-1634.
WITCHCRAFT BF 1517 F5 T77 1634a
   Tranquille de Saint-Rémi, capuchin.
     Veritable relation des ivstes procedvres observees av faict de la possession des Vrsulines de Loudun. Et au procez d'Vrbain Grandier. Auec les theses generales touchant les diables exorcisez. Par le R. P. Tranquille, Capucin. La Fleche, Chez George Griveav, imprimeur ordinaire du roy, 1634.
     80 p. 14cm.
     Expanded version of the Poictiers text.
     1. Loudun, France. Ursuline Convent. 2. Grandier, Urbain, 1590-1634. 3. Exorcism. I. Title.

Grandier, Urbain, 1590-1634.
WITCHCRAFT BF 1593 U57
   Unger, Franz, 1871-
     Die schwarze Magie: ihre Meister und ihre Opfer. Coethen, R. Schumann [1904]
     80 p. 20cm. (Collection rätselhafte Naturen Bd. VII)
     Contents.--Präludium: Das Problem des übernatürlichen Geschlechtsverkehrs.--Geschlechtsverkehr zwischen Menschen, Teufeln und Dämonen.--Urbain Grandier und die Besessenen von Loudun.--Werke des Teufels in alter Zeit.
     1. Magic. 2. Devil. 3. Grandier, Urbain, 1590-1634. I. Title.
8

Les grands jours de la sorcellerie.
Witchcraft BF 1565 B16
   Baissac, Jules, 1827-1898.
     Les grands jours de la sorcellerie. Paris, C. Klincksieck, 1890.
     v, 735 p. 25cm.

     Sequel to his Histoire de la diablerie chrétienne.

     1. Witchcraft--Hist. I. Title.

Grangeron, Henri.
Witchcraft BF 1555 B35
   Bayle, François.
     Relation de l'état de quelques personnes pretenduës possédées. Faite d'autorite' du Parlement de Toulouse, par Me. François Bayle & Me. Henri Grangeron ... Toulouse, Chez la veuve Pouchac & Bely, 1682.
     118 p. 14cm.

     1. Demoniac possession. I. Grangeron, Henri. II. Title.

Witchcraft BF 1411 G76
   Grant, James.
     The mysteries of all nations: rise and progress of superstition, laws against and trials of witches, ancient and modern delusions, together with strange customs, fables, and tales ... By James Grant. Leith, Reid & son; [etc., etc.], 1880.
     xxviii, 640 p. 23cm.
     Running title: The collected mysteries of all nations.

     1. Superstition. I. Title.

     15-13524
Library of Congress   BF1411.G7

Grataroli, Guglielmo, 1516-1568, ed.
WITCHCRAFT BF 1558 P79
   Pomponazzi, Pietro, 1462-1524.
     De naturalium effectuum causis, siue de incantationibus, opvs abstrvsioris philosophiae plenvm, & breuissimis historijs illustratum atq; ante annos xxxv compositum, nunc primum verò in lucem fideliter editum. Adiectis breuibus scholijs à Gulielmo Grataroli. Basileae [per Henrichvm Petri, 1556]
     349 p. 17cm.

8 NIC   (Cont'd on next card)

CATALOGUE OF THE CORNELL WITCHCRAFT COLLECTION

Grataroli, Guglielmo, 1516-1568, ed.

WITCHCRAFT
BF
1558
P79
    Pomponazzi, Pietro, 1462-1524. De naturalium effectuum causis... [1556]. (Card 2)

    Autograph on flyleaf: Gerardus Vossius, 1577-1649.
    With this are bound: Landi, Bassiano. De incremento. Venetiis, 1556; Erastus, Thomas. Dispvtatio de avro potabili. Basileae, 1578; Anten, Conradus ab. (Gynaikolousis) sev mvliervm lavatio. Lvbecae, 1590.
    1. Demonology. I. Grataroli, Guglielmo, 1516-1568, ed.

MSS
Bd.
WITCHCRAFT
HV
G77
    Grave, Gerhard, 1598-1675.
    Abgenötigte Rettung und Erklärung, zweyer zu Rinteln, jüngsthin, gedruckter Sendbrieffe, so mit Arrest sind hieselbst befangen: in welchen wird gehandelt: Von der Wasser Prob oder vermeintem Hexenbaden ... Durch M. Gerhardum Graven ... Rinteln an der Weser, Gedruckt durch Petrum Lucium, 1640 [ca. 1900]
    157 p. 24cm.
    Carnap's manuscript copy.
    "Originald ruck in der Stadtbiblio-
(Continued on next card)

MSS
Bd.
WITCHCRAFT
HV
G77
    Grave, Gerhard, 1598-1675. Abgenötigte Rettung ... 1640 [ca. 1900] (Card 2)

    thek zu Braunschweig im Samelbande 900.C.794. 157 Seiten in 4° u. 6 Bl. Register."
    Numerals in the margins indicate pagination of the original.

    1. Trials (Witchcraft) 2. Torture. 3. Water (in religion, folk-lore, etc.) I. Title.

Witchcraft
BF
1555
G77
    Eine Grawsame erschreckliche vnd wunderbarliche Geschicht oder newe Zeitung, welche warhafftig geschehen ist, in diesem M.D.LIX. Jar, zur Platten, zwo Meil weges vom Joachims Thal, Alda hat ein Schmid eine Tochter, die ist von bösen Feind dem Teufel eingenomen vnd besessen worden, der hat so wunderbarlich vnd seltzam Ding aus jr geredt, mit den Priestern, die teglich bey jr gewest sind... Witteberg, 1559.
    [9] p. 20cm.

Witchcraft
F
74
G88
G794
    Green, Samuel Abbott, 1830-1918.
    Groton in the witchcraft times. By Samuel A. Green, M. D. Groton, Mass. [J. Wilson and son, Cambridge] 1883.
    29 p. 24cm.
    "A briefe account of a strange & unusuall providence of God befallen to Elizabeth Knap of Groton, p me Sam^ll Willard": p. 7-21.

    I. Willard, Samuel, 1640-1707. II. Title.

F
74
G88
G79
no.6
    Green, Samuel A[bbott] 1830-1918.
    Groton in the witchcraft times. By Samuel A. Green, M.D. Groton, Mass. [J. Wilson and son, Cambridge] 1883.
    29 p. 25cm.
    "A briefe account of a strange & unusuall providence of God befallen to Elizabeth Knap of Groton, p me Sam^ll Willard": p. 7-21.

    1. Groton, Mass.--Hist.--Colonial period. 2. Witchcraft--Groton, Mass. I. Willard, Samuel, 1640-1707.

Greene, Ellen, d. 1618.

Witchcraft
BF
1563
T75
    The Wonderfvl discoverie of the witchcrafts of Margaret and Phillip[pa] Flower, daughters of Joan Flower neere Beuer Castle ... Together with the seuerall examinations and confessions of Anne Baker, Ioan Willimot, and Ellen Greene, witches in Leicestershire. London, Printed by G. Eld for I Barnes, 1619. [Greenwich, Reprinted by H. S. Richardson, ca. 1840]
    26 p. title vignettes. 23cm.
(Continued on next card)

Greene, Ellen, d. 1618.

Witchcraft
BF
1563
T75
    The Wonderfvl discoverie of the witchcrafts of Margaret and Phillip[pa] Flower ... [1840] (Card 2)

    The examinations of Anne Baker, Ioanne Willimot, and Ellen Greene has special t. p.
    No. 4 in vol. lettered Tracts on witchcraft.

Witchcraft
BF
1558
G86
1800
    Gremoire [sic] du Pape Honorius, avec un recueil des plus rares secrets. A Rome [i.e. Paris?] 1800.
    123 p. illus., 12 plates. 14cm.

    Text differs considerably from the Rome ed. of 1760.

    1. Incantations. 2. Magic. I. Honorius III, Pope, d. 1227. Spurious and doubtful works. II. Title: Grimoire du Pape Honorius.

Witchcraft
BV
30
G83
    Gretser, Jacob, 1560-1625.
    Jacobi Gretseri ... Libri dvo De benedictionibvs, et tertivs De maledictionibvs ... Ingolstadii, Ex typographeo Ederiano, apud Elisabetham Angermariam, viduam, Impensis Ioannis Hertsroi, 1615.
    14 p. l., 288, [43] p. 20cm.
    Bound with his De festis Christianorum libri duo. Ingolstadii, 1612.
    1. Benediction. 2. Exorcism. 3. Blessing and cursing. I. Title: De benedictionibus. II. Title: De maledictionibus. (Over)

Grévin, Jacques, 1538?-1570, tr.

Witchcraft
BF
1520
W64
P8
1569
    Wier, Johann, 1515-1588.
    Cinq livres de l'imposture et tromperie des diables: des enchantements et sorcelleries. Pris du latin de Iean Uvier et faits françois par Iaques Gréuin de Clermont en Beauuoisis, médicin à Paris. Paris, Iaques du Puys, 1569.
    468, [79] p. 16cm.
    Incomplete: t. p. and all before p. 1 wanting.
    Title taken from Yve-Plessis, Ro-
(Continued on next card)

Grévin, Jacques, 1538?-1570, tr.

Witchcraft
BF
1520
W64
P8
1569
    Wier, Johann, 1515-1588. Cinq livres de l'imposture et tromperie des diables ... 1569. (Card 2)

    bert. Essai d'une bibliographie ... de la sorcellerie, p. 104, no. 832.
    A t. p. in G. L. Burr's hand indicates this edition of the work; however, a long note by Burr on facing page claims the edition agrees with no. 833 in Yve-Plessis. But no. 833 consists of 6 books, not 5.
(Continued on next card)

Grévin, Jacques, 1538?-1570, tr.

Witchcraft
BF
1520
W64
P8
1569
    Wier, Johann, 1515-1588. Cinq livres de l'imposture et tromperie des diables ... 1569. (Card 3)

    Translation of his De praestigiis daemonum.
    1. Demonology. 2. Witchcraft. 3. Magic. 4. Fasting. I. Grévin, Jacques, 1538?-1570, tr. II. His De praestigiis daemonum--French. III. Title. IV. Title: De l'imposture et tromperie des diables.

Grillandi, Paolo.

see

Grillando, Paolo.

Grillando, Paolo.
    De sortilegiis.

WITCHCRAFT
K
Z695
1580
    Ziletti, Giovanni Battista, fl. 1559, ed.
    Volvmen praeclarissimvm ... omnivm tractatvvm criminalivm nvnc per D. Ioan. Baptistam Zilettum ab omnibus mendis expurgatum ac omnino correctum ... Venetiis, Apud Io. Antonium Bertanum, 1580.
    78 p. l., 473 numbered leaves. 21cm.
    Includes Tractatvs ... de lamijs ... Ioanni Francisci Ponzinibij, p. 89-99 v.; De sortilegiis tractatus Pauli Ghirlandi, l. 104 v.-138 v.
(Continued on next card)

Witchcraft
BF
1565
G85
1536
    Grillando, Paolo.
    Paulus Grillādus. Tractat' de hereticis z sortilegiis omnifariam coitu: eorumq̃ penī Itē de questionibus: z tortura: ac de relaxatione carceratorum Domini Pauli Grillandi Castilionei: vltima hac impressione summa cura castigat': additis vbilibet sūmariis: prepositoq̃ perutili reptorio speciales sentētias aptissime continente. Veneūt Lugd., Apud Jacobū Giūcti, 1536.
    16 p. l., cxxviii l. 17cm.
(Continued on next card)

Witchcraft
BF
1565
G85
1536
    Grillando, Paolo. ... Tractat' de hereticis ... 1536. (Card 2)

    Title in red and black, with woodcut border.
    Printed in double columns.

    1. Witchcraft. 2. Heresy. 3. Torture. I. Title: De hereticis et sortilegiis. II. Title. III. Title: Tractatus de hereticis et sortilegiis.

Witchcraft
BF
1850
G85
1592
    Grillando, Paolo.
    Tractatvs dvo: Vnus De sortilegiis D. Pavli Grillandi ... Alter De lamiis et excellentia iuris vtriusque D. Ioannis Francisci Ponzinibij Florentini ... Olim qvidem in lvcem editi; nunc verò recogniti, & ab innvmeris passim mendis vindicati: adiec to indice locupletissimo. Francoforti ad Moenvm [Apvd Martinvm Lechlervm, Impensis Haeredvm Christiani Egenolphi] 1592.
    16 p. l., 290 [1] p. 17cm.
    With colophon.
(Continued on next card)

CATALOGUE OF THE CORNELL WITCHCRAFT COLLECTION

:chcraft Grillando, Paolo.   Tractatvs dvo: Vnus De
50   sortilegiis ... 1592.   (Card 2)
5
92

1. Divination. 2. Witchcraft. 3.
Demonology. I. Ponzinibius, Joannes Fran-
ciscus. De lamiis. et excellentia. II.
Title: De sort   ilegiis. III. Title:
De lamiis.   (Over)

Grillando, Paolo.
  Suzaria, Guido de.
    Tractatus II [i.e. duo] perutiles & quoti-
RE diani De indiciis, quaestionibus et tortura
    ...Guidonis de Suzaria & Pauli Grillandi
545 de Castilione, una cum additionib. Ludovici
99 Bolognini...geordnet durch Ioannem Guórnerum
    de Vineca. Ursellis, Apud Nicolaum Henri-
    cum, sumptibus Cornelij Suterij, 1597.
      291 p. 16cm.
      Bound with: Saur, Abraham. Notarien Spie-
    gel. Franckf   ort am Mayn, 1599.
C   (Continued on next card)

Grillandus, Paulus.
   see
Grillando, Paolo.

Witchcraft
BF   Grillot de Givry, Émile Angelo, 1870-
1412   Le musée des sorciers, mages et alchi-
G85+ mistes, par Grillot de Givry. Paris, Li-
      brairies de France, 1929.
        4 p. l., 450 p. col. front., illus., col.
      plates, diagrs. 28cm.
        "Recueil iconographique de l'occultisme."
      --Préf.
8   1. Occult   sciences. I. Title.

Grillot de Givry, Émile Angelo, 1870-
   Le musée des sorciers, mages et
alchimistes--English.

:chcraft Grillot de Givry, Émile Angelo, 1870-
-12   A pictorial anthology of witchcraft,
85   magic & alchemy. Translated by J. Cour-
58   tenay Locke. New Hyde Park, N. Y., Uni-
      versity Books [1958]
        394 p. illus. 25cm.

      Translation of Le musée des sorciers,
      mages et alchimistes.

Grillot de Givry, Émile Angelo, 1870-
   Le musée des sorciers, mages et al-
chimistes--English.

:tchcraft Grillot de Givry, Émile Angelo, 1870-
F   Witchcraft, magic & alchemy, by Grillot
412   de Givry, translated by J. Courtenay Locke;
85+   with ten plates in colour and 366 illustra-
931   tions in the text. London, G. G. Harrap
       [1931]
         394 p. illus. (part col.) 29cm.
       "A collection of the iconography of oc-
       cultism."--Pref.
       Translation of Le musée des sorciers,
       mages et alchi mistes.
                        (Continued on next card)

Witchcraft
BF   Grillot de Givry, Émile Angelo, 1870-
1412   A pictorial anthology of witchcraft,
G85   magic & alchemy. Translated by J. Cour-
1958 tenay Locke. New Hyde Park, N. Y., Uni-
      versity Books [1958]
        394 p. illus. 25cm.

      Translation of Le musée des sorciers,
      mages et alchimistes.
        I. His Le musée des sorciers, mages et
      alchimistes--   English. II. Title.

Witchcraft
BF   Grillot de Givry, Émile Angelo, 1870-
1412   Witchcraft, magic & alchemy, by Grillot
G85+ de Givry, translated by J. Courtenay Locke;
1931 with ten plates in colour and 366 illustra-
      tions in the text. London, G. G. Harrap
      [1931]
        394 p. illus. (part col.) 29cm.
      "A collection of the iconography of oc-
      cultism."--Pref.
      Translation of Le musée des sorciers,
8   mages et alchi   mistes.
                     (Continued on next card)

Witchcraft
BF   Grillot de Givry, Émile Angelo, 1870-
1412   Witchcraft, magic & alchemy ... [1931]
G85+   (Card 2)
1931

      1. Occult sciences. I. Locke, J.
      Courtenay, tr. II. His Le musée des
      sorciers, mages et alchimistes. English.
8   III. Title.

Witchcraft
BF   Grimaldi, Costantino, 1667-1750.
1604   Dissertazione in cui si investiga quali
G86+ sieno le operazioni che dependono dalla ma-
      gia diabolica e quali quelle che derivano
      dalle magie artificiale e naturale e qual
      cautela si ha da usare nella malagevolezza
      di discernerle. Roma, Nella Stamperia di
      Pallade, Appresso Niccolò, e Marco Pagliari-
      ni, 1751.
        [8], 139 p.   port. 16cm.
8   Engraved ti   tle vignette.
        Edited by   Ginesio Grimaldi. (Over)

Grimaldi, Ginesio, ed.

Witchcraft
BF   Grimaldi, Costantino, 1667-1750.
1604   Dissertazione in cui si investiga quali
G86+ sieno le operazioni che dependono dalla ma-
      gia diabolica e quali quelle che derivano
      dalle magie artificiale e naturale e qual
      cautela si ha da usare nella malagevolezza
      di discernerle. Roma, Nella Stamperia di
      Pallade, Appresso Niccolò, e Marco Pagliari-
      ni, 1751.
        [8], 139 p.   port. 16cm.
        Engraved ti   tle vignette.
8   Edited by   Ginesio Grimaldi.

WITCHCRAFT Grimana.
K   Marsiliis, Hippolytus de, 1451-1529.
        Tractatus de quaestionibus nuperrime recognitus: in quo ma-
M375 terie maleficiorũ admodum diffuse subtili-
T7   terq̨, pertractant: cũ tabula ... per modũ nu-
1537 meri et alphabeti diligentissime distributa.
      Lugd[uni], Ueneunt apud Jacobum Giuncti, 1537.
        [27], cxliiij l. 18cm.

        Title within woodcut ornamental border;
      title vignette: author's portrait.
        Colophon (l. cxliiija): Hippolyti de Mar-
                        (Continued on next card)

WITCHCRAFT Grimana.
K   Marsiliis, Hippolytus de, 1451-1529.   ...
        Tractatus de quaestionibus ... 1537.
M375   (Card 2)
T7
1537   silijs ... Lectura super titu. ff. de questio-
      nib⁹ explicit Lugduni impressa p Benedictũ
      Bonyn impensis ... D. Jacobi .q. Frãcisci de
      Giuncta Florenti. ac sociorũ. Anno domini
      .M. CCCCXXXVI. Die vero xxiij. mensis Nouem-
      bris.
        Giunta's device on l. cxliiijb.
        Commentary on Digesta, lib. XLVIII, tit.
18.   (Continued on next card)

WITCHCRAFT Grimana.
K   Marsiliis, Hippolytus de, 1451-1529.   ...
        Tractatus de quaestionibus ... 1537.
M375   (Card 3)
T7
1537   From its dedication to Cardinal Grimani,
      the treatise bears, in some editions, the
      title Grimana.
        With this is bound the author's Singula-
      ria. Lugduni, 1546.

        1. Roman law. 2. Corpus juris civilis.
      Digesta. Lib. XLVIII, tit. 18. I. Title:
      Tractatus De quaestionibus. II. Title:
      Grimana.

             Grimm, Heinrich Adolph, 1754-1813.
WITCHCRAFT
BT   [Menke, Karl F]
980   Beitrag zur Dämonologie; oder, Widerle-
M54   gung der exegetischen Aufsätze des Herrn
      Professor's Grimm. Von einem Geistlichen.
      Frankfurt und Leipzig, 1793.
        174 p. 17cm.

        With autograph: W. Wirbel?

8   1. Devil. 2. Demonology. 3. Grimm,
NIC   Heinrich Adolph,   1754-1813. I. Title.

Witchcraft
BF   Grimoire; ou La magie naturelle. La Haye,
1603 Aux dépens de la Compagnie [ca. 1750]
H46   600 p. illus. 14cm.
1750
        "Traduction altérée d'un bizarre ouvrage
      allemand intitulé Heldenschutz"--Graesse,
      Trésor de livres rares et précieux.
        1. Magic. 2. Receipts--Early works to
      1800. 3. Handbooks, vade-mecums, etc. 4.
      Medicine--Formulae, receipts, prescriptions,
      etc.   I. Held   enschutz. French. VII.
8   Title: La mag   ie naturelle.

Witchcraft
BF   Grimoire du Pape Honorius, avec un recueil
1558   des plus rares secrets. A Rome, 1760.
G86   [Avignon, Offray ainé, ca. 1880]
1760a   95 p. illus., 12 col. plates. 13cm.
        Title page is plate 2 (Pl. I in the
      numbering)
        Added title page preceeding text has
      title: Le grand grimoire, avec La grande
      clavicule de Salomon.
        1. Incantations. 2. Magic. I. Hono-
      rius III, Pope,   d. 1227. Spurious and
8   doubtful works. II. Title: Le grand
      grimoire.   (Over)

            Grimoire du Pape Honorius.

WITCHCRAFT
BF   L'Art de commander les esprits célestes,
1558 aëriens, terrestres & infernaux. Suivi
G86   du Grand grimoire, de la magie noire et
1750 des forces infernales, du docteur J. Kar-
      ter, La clavicule de Salomon, &c. Avec
      le vrai secret de faire parler les morts,
      pour découvrir tous les trésors cachés,
      &c. &c. [Paris?] 1421 [i.e., ca. 1750?]
      iv, 5-108 [i. e., 118], [2] p. illus.
      16cm.
        Title in red and black.
8
                   (Continued on next card)

249

CATALOGUE OF THE CORNELL WITCHCRAFT COLLECTION

Grimoire du Pape Honorius.

WITCHCRAFT
BF 1558
G86
1750

L'Art de commander les esprits ... [1750?] (Card 2)

Published also under other titles: Grimoire du Pape Honorius [best-known]; Le dragon rouge; and Le véritable dragon rouge.

1. Incantations. 2. Magic. I. Karter, J. II. Title: Le grand grimoire. III. Title: Grimoire du Pape Honorius. IV. Title: Le dragon rouge. V. Title: Le véritable dragon rouge. VI. Title: La clavicule de Salomon.

8

Grimoire du Pape Honorius.

WITCHCRAFT
BF 1558
G86
1823

Le Dragon rouge, ou l'art de commander les esprits célestes, aériens, terrestres, infernaux, avec le vrai secret de faire parler les morts, de gagner toutes les fois qu'on met aux loteries, de découvrir les trésors cachés, etc., etc. Imprimé sur un manuscrit de 1522. Nismes, Chez Gaude, 1823.
108 p. illus. 15cm.
Published also under other titles: Grimoire du Pape Honorius [best-known];

8   (Continued on next card)

Grimoire du Pape Honorius.

WITCHCRAFT
BF 1558
G86
1823

Le Dragon rouge ... 1823. (Card 2)

Le véritable dragon rouge; and L'art de commander les esprits.
Chapter 1 signed: Antonio Venitiana, del Rabbina.

1. Incantations. 2. Magic. I. Venitiana, Antonio, del Rabbina. II. Title: Grimoire du Pape Honorius. III. Title: Le véritable dragon rouge. IV. Title: L'art de commander les esprits.

8

Grimoire du Pape Honorius.

Witchcraft
BF 1558
G86
1800

Gremoire [sic] du Pape Honorius, avec un recueil des plus rares secrets. A Rome [i.e. Paris?] 1800.
123 p. illus., 12 plates. 14cm.

Text differs considerably from the Rome ed. of 1760.

1. Incantations. 2. Magic. I. Honorius III, Pope, d. 1227. Spurious and doubtful works. II. Title: Grimoire du Pape Honorius.

8

Grimoire du Pape Honorius.

WITCHCRAFT
BF 1558
G86
1800a

Le Véritable dragon rouge, ou l'Art de commander les esprits célestes, aériens, terrestres et infernaux, avec le secret de faire parler les morts, de gagner toutes les fois qu'on met aux loteries; de découvrir les trésors cachés; etc., etc.; suivi de La poule noire, cabale qui était restée inconnue jusqu'ici. [Lille, Imprimerie de Blocquel] 1521 [i.e., 18--]
140 p. illus. 16cm.

8   (Continued on next card)

Grimoire du Pape Honorius.

WITCHCRAFT
BF 1558
G86
1800a

Le Véritable dragon rouge ... [18--] (Card 2)

Title in red and black.
Chapter 1 signed: J. Karter, Venetiana.
Published also under other titles: Grimoire du Pape Honorius [best-known]; Le dragon rouge; and L'art de commander les esprits.

1. Incantations. 2. Magic. I. Karter, J. II. Title: Grimoire du Pape Honorius. III. Title: Le dragon rouge. IV. Title: L'art de commander les esprits. V. Title: La poule noire.

8

Grimoire du Pape Honorius--German.

WITCHCRAFT
BF 1405
S41
no.6

Der Wahrhaftige feurige Drache; oder, Herrschaft über die himmlischen und höllischen Geister und über die Mächte der Erde und Luft ... Nebst den geheimen Mitteln, sich die schwarze Henne mit den goldnen Eiern zu verschaffen ... Nach einem in Frankreich aufgefundenen Manuscript von 1522. Nebst einem Postscriptum aus dem grossen Buche von König Salomo, mit einigen köstlichen Recepten, gefunden bei Peter Michel, dem letzten

8 NIC   (Continued on next card)

Grimoire du Pape Honorius--German.

WITCHCRAFT
BF 1405
S41
no.6

Der Wahrhaftige feurige Drache ... [ca. 1880] (Card 2)

Karthäuser zu Erfurt. [Berlin, E. Bartels, ca. 1880]
125 p. illus. 17cm.
Translation of Le véritable dragon rouge, which was published under a variety of titles, the best-known being Grimoire du Pape Honorius.
Erstes Buch, erstes Kapitel signed: Rab-

8 NIC   (Continued on next card)

Grimoire du Pape Honorius--German.

WITCHCRAFT
BF 1405
S41
no.6

Der Wahrhaftige fuerige Drache ... [ca. 1880] (Card 3)

bi Anton Moses el Arradsch.
No. 6 in vol. lettered Der schwarze Raabe.

1. Incantations. 2. Magic. I. Anton Moses el Arradsch. II. Le véritable dragon rouge. German. III. Grimoire du Pape Honorius. German.

8 NIC

Grimoires et secrets.

BF 1532
S33

Schindelholz, Georges.
Grimoires et secrets. Porrentruy, Éditions Jurassiennes, 1970.
199 p. illus. 23 cm. 18.00F
Bibliography: p. 97-101.
Sw 70-A-6944

9

1. Demonology. 2. Witchcraft—Jura Mountain region. 3. Magic. I. Title.

BF1532.S35   76-550819
Library of Congress   71 [2]

Witchcraft
BF 1445
G87

Groenewegen, Hendrik.
Pneumatica; ofte, Leere van de geesten, zijnde denkende en redelike wesens ... uytgegeven by gelegentheyd van 't boek De betoverde wereld, geschreven door Balthazar Bekker ... Enchuysen, H. van Straalen, 1692.
88, 126, 56 p. 20cm.

1. Ghosts. 2. Bekker, Balthasar, 1634-1698. De betoverde weereld. I. Title. II. Title: Leere van de geesten.

Witchcraft
BF 1410
B42
Z69
no.17,
18

Groenewegen, Leonardus.
Den predikant D. Balthasar Becker, seediglyk ondersogt so in zyn persoon als Schriften, ofhy die derst voorgeven, buyten hem alleen, de gantsche werelt betovert te zyn, selfs hier af wel vry is, ende dat daar en boven op hem niet soude werken, de geest van hovaardye en dwalinge tot ergernisse en van de kleine, en van de arme, en van de verslagene van geest, en die beeven voor Godts woort. By een missive den 19 January 1692, door H.v.G. van Amsterdam geschreven aan

NIC   (Continued on next card)

Groenewegen, Leonardus.

Witchcraft
BF 1410
B42
Z69
no.17,
18

Den predikant D. Balthasar Becker ... (Card 2)

D. T. S. de Jonge tot Uytrecht. Met zyn Andtwoord provisioneel tot nader berigt daar op gevolgt, den 4. February desselven jaars. Uytregt, Gedrukt by W. Jansz, 1692.
32, 36 p. 21cm.
Signatures: 4°: A-D4. 4°: A-D4, E2.
The Provisioneel Antwoord has special half-title and separate

NIC   (Continued on next card)

Groenewegen, Leonardus.

Witchcraft
BF 1410
B42
Z69
no.17,
18

Den predikant D. Balthasar Becker ... 1692. (Card 3)

paging.
Van der Linde 63, 61.
"Extracten van ... De betoverde werelt, uytgetrokken en t'samengestelt door N. N.": p. 17-28 of the Provisioneel Antwoord; "Extract van 'tgepasseerde des Synodi tot Edam, 10. Aug. 1691. rakende D. Bekker...": p. 28-29; "Articulen voor te stellen aan Do. B. Bekker" signed Leonardus

NIC   (Continued on next card)

Groenewegen, Leonardus.

Witchcraft
BF 1410
B42
Z69
No.17,
18

Den predikant D. Balthasar Becker ... 1692. (Card 4)

Groenewegen: p. 29-31; "Eerste aanbieding van D. B. Bekker, op den 30. Aug. 1691": p. 31; "Articulen tot satisfactie aan de Eerw. Classis van Amsterdam, van Do. Balthasar Bekker ... wegens ... de Betoverde wereld ...": p. 32-36.
Nos. 17 & 18 in a Collection of tracts against Balthasar Bekker and his Betoverde weereld.

NIC   (Continued on next card)

Witchcraft
BF 1584
D4
G87

Grönlund, David.
Historisk efterretning om de i Ribe bye for hexerie forfulgte og braendte mennesker. Viborg, C.E. Mangor, 1780.
250 p. 22cm.

1. Witchcraft. 2. Trials (Witchcraft)--Denmark. I. Title.

BF 1584
D4
G87
1973

Grønlund, David, 1716-1784.
Historisk efterretning om de i Ribe Bye for Hexerie forfulgte og braendte Mennesker. 2. udg. Genudg. ved Kirst Agerbæk. Ølgod, Historisk samfund f Ribe Amt. Eksp.: S. Manøe Hansen, 19
195 p. illus. 24 cm.
Bibliography: p. 192-193.

1. Witchcraft--Ribe, Denmark. I. Title

NIC APR 01,'75   200xc   74-314

Witchcraft
BF 1584
S9
Z7
1706

Grönwall, F W
En skånsk hexproces. Lund, E. Malms 1899.
18 p. 24cm.

"Särtryck ur Kulturhistoriska meddelan

1. Witchcraft. 2. Trials (Witchcraft)--Sweden. I. Title.

250

CATALOGUE OF THE CORNELL WITCHCRAFT COLLECTION

Grössel, Marie.

WITCHCRAFT
BF
1583
K
652

Könnecke, Max
　Zwei Hexenprozesse aus der Grafschaft Mansfeld.
　(In Mansfelder Blätter. Eisleben, 1887-1940? 23cm. 10. Jahrg. (1896), p. [32]-65)
　Caption title.
　"Inquisitionsakten wider die Pfarrwitwe Anna Kluge zu Ahlsdorf in Sachen, beschuldigter Hexerei, 1652 und 1655": p. 34-51.
　"Inquisitionsakten wider Anna Traute Frohertzin und Marie Grösseln in Gerbstedt wegen beschuldigter Hexerei, 1689": p. 52-65.

(Continued on next card)

WITCHCRAFT
BF
1591
G87+

Groff, William N
　Etudes sur la sorcellerie; ou, Le rôle que la Bible a joué chez les sorciers. Le Caire, 1897.
　[337]-415 p. 29cm. (Institut égyptien, Caire. Mémoires, t.3, fasc. 4)
　Includes detailed description of a papyrus, containing notes of a sorcerer, probably of the second century A.D.

8
NIC

1.Magic--Hist. 2. Witchcraft--Hist. 3. Cabala. 4. Witchcraft in the Bible. 2.Series. II. Title.

Witchcraft
BR
115
M2
G87

Gross, Christianus.
　Christlicher Bericht von und wieder Zauberey, was solche schröckliche Sünde sey, wo sie herkomme, und wie man in allen Ständen derselben steuren und wehren könne und solle; auss Gottes Wort verfasset und Erfur gegeben. Colberg, J. Kusen, 1661.
　[16] 68 p. 15cm.

1. Witchcraft. I. Title.

Witchcraft
BT
980
G87
1744

Gross, Johann Matthias.
　Beweissthum der grossen Macht und Ohnmacht des Fürsten der Finsterniss ... Nürnberg [J. L. Montag] 1744.
　[20] 46 [26] 818, 64 [40] p. illus. 19cm.
　Added t. p. on two leaves: Die grosse Macht und Ohnmacht des Fürsten der Finsterniss. Leipzig, J. L. Montag, 1734.

1. Devil. I. Title. II. Title: Die grosse Macht und Ohnmacht des Fürsten der Finsternis.

Witchcraft
BR
730
.8
G87

Gross, Wilibald.
　Sonder- und wunderbare, doch wahre Geschichte, wie der Teufel ††† sich einmal in der leiblichen Gestalt eines Esels auf dem Rathhause zu B...r im W..b..g..schen sehen liess; zu Frommen und Besserung der izigen, höchst unglaubigen Welt, auch zum Beweiss des, in unsern Tagen so sehr geläugneten Daseyns eines Teufels †††, in Reimen, nach der bekannten Melodie: Ein Ritter, wie die Chronik sagt & c. &c. Im Manuscript aufgefunden und ans Licht gestellt

(Continued on next card)

Witchcraft
BR
730
.8
G87

Gross, Wilibald. Sonder- und wunderbare, doch wahre Geschichte. Seefeld in Tyrol, 1786. (Card 2)
　auch mit Anmerkungen vers. von Paul Weisshammer. [Seefeld in Tyrol] Gedrukt auf Kosten des Klosters, 1786.
　29 p. 18cm.

I. Weisshammer, Paul, ed. II. Title.

Grosse, Henning, 1553-1621, ed.

WITCHCRAFT
BF
1520
M19
1656

Magica de spectris et apparitionibus spirituū, de vaticiniis, divinationibus, &c. Lugd.Batavorvm, apud Franciscum Hackium, 1656.
　12 p.l., 636, [33] p. 14cm.
　Engraved t.-p.
　First edition published under title: Magica; seu Mirabilium historiarum de spectris et apparitionibus spirituum ... libri II. Islebiae, typis et sumpt. Henningi Grosij, 1597.
　"Epistola dedicatoria" signed by the editor: Henningus Grosius.
　"Catalogus auctorum, e quibus historiae atque exempla ista congesta sunt": 11th -12th prelim. leaves.

Grosse, Henning, 1553-1621, comp.

Witchcraft
GT
6710
T76
1615

Tractatus tragicus De poenis omnium delictorum, quae adversus Deum aut homines admissa & mirabiliter vindicata sunt. Ex probatissimis omnium aetatum scriptoribus diligenter collectus ac libris duobus explicatus per Joannem Polycarium [pseud.?] [Islebiae?] Impensis Henningi Grosij, 1615.
　4 p. l., 667, [32] p. 20cm.
　With colophon.
　First published 1597 under title:

(Continued on next card)

Grosse, Henning, 1553-1621, comp.

Witchcraft
GT
6710
T76
1615

Tractatus tragicus De poenis omnium delictorum ... 1615. (Card 2)
　Tragica, seu tristium historiarum de poenis criminalibus, and with dedication signed Henningus Grosius [sic]; no mention of J. Polycarius on t. p. or elsewhere.
　This edition is the same printing as that of 1597, but with different t. p. and preliminary leaves.
　Book I has caption title: Tragicorvm,

(Continued on next card)

Grosse, Henning, 1553-1621, comp.

Witchcraft
GT
6710
T76
1615

Tractatus tragicus De poenis omnium delictorum ... 1615. (Card 3)
　seu sylvae tristivm, hoc est, Horribilium historiarum de poenis criminalibus.
　Grässe, Bibliotheca magica, attributes this edition to Polycarpus, Johannes.

1. Punishment. 2. Crime and criminals --Biog. I. Grosse, Henning, 1553-1621, comp. II. Polycarius, Johannes. III. Polycarpus, Johannes. IV. Johannes Polycarius. V. Title: Tragicorum, seu sylvae tristium.

Grosse, Henning, 1553-1621, comp.

Witchcraft
GT
6710
T76

Tragica, seu tristium historiarum de poenis criminalibvs et exitv horribili eorum qui impietate, blasphemia, contemptu & abnegatione Dei, haeresi, magia, execratione, maledicentia ... & omnis generis illicita atq; execrabili vitę turpitudine vltionem diuinam prouocarunt, & mirabiliter perpessi sunt. Libri II ... Islebiae, Procurante & sumptum faciente Henningo Grosio, 1597.
　8 p. l., 667, [32] p. 21cm.

(Continued on next card)

Grosse, Henning, 1553-1621, comp.

Witchcraft
GT
6710
T76

Tragica, seu tristium historiarum de poenis criminalibvs ... 1597. (Card 2)
　With colophon.
　Book I has caption title: Tragicorvm, seu sylvae tristivm, hoc est, Horribilium historiarum de poenis criminalibus.

1. Punishment. 2. Crime and criminals --Biog. I. Grosse, Henning, 1553-1621, comp. II. Title: Tragicorum, seu sylvae tristium.

Die grosse Macht und Ohnmacht des Fürsten der Finsterniss.

WITCHCRAFT
BT
980
G87
1744

Gross, Johann Matthias.
　Beweissthum der grossen Macht und Ohnmacht des Fürsten der Finsterniss ... Nürnberg [J. L. Montag] 1744.
　[20] 46 [26] 818, 64 [40] p. illus. 19cm.
　Added t. p. on two leaves: Die grosse Macht und Ohnmacht des Fürsten der Finsterniss. Leipzig, J. L. Montag, 1734.

1. Devil. I. Title. II. Title: Die grosse Macht und Ohnmacht des Fürsten der Finsternis.

Das grosse Welt-betrügende Nichts.

WITCHCRAFT
BF
1565
S59

[Simon, Jordan] pater, 1719-1776.
　Das grosse Welt-betrügende Nichts; oder, Die heutige Hexerey und Zauberkunst in zweyen Büchern, von Ardoino Ubbidente dell'Osa [pseud.] entworfen ... Wirtzburg, J. J. Stahel, 1761.
　4 p. l., 600 p. 17cm.
　Second edition published under title: Die Nichtigkeit der Hexerey und Zauberkunst. (cf. Kayser)

8
NIC

Contents.-- 1. Th. Die Gründe und

(Continued on next card)

Das grosse Welt-betrügende Nichts.

WITCHCRAFT
BF
1565
S59

[Simon, Jordan] pater, 1719-1776. Das grosse Welt-betrügende Nichts ... 1761. (Card 2)
　Beweisthümer aus der Göttlichen Schrift ... dass die heutige Hexerey oder Zauberkunst ein leeres Nichts seye.--2. Th. Die Widerlegung der aus der Göttlichen Schrift gezogenen Beweis-Gründen, dass es Hexerey oder Zauberkunst gebe.

1. Witchcraft. 2. Witchcraft in the Bible. 3. Superstition. I. Title. II. Title: Die heutige Hexerey und Zauberkunst.

Grosser Hexenprocess zu Schongau von 1589 bis 1592.

WITCHCRAFT
BF
1583
Z7
1587b

Her, Rat.
　Grosser Hexenprocess zu Schongau von 1589 bis 1592. Aus den Originalacten geschichtlich dargestellt von Rath Her. (In Oberbayerisches Archiv. München. 25cm. 11. Bd. (1850-51), p. [356]-380)
　At head of title: IX.
　Sequel to his Ein Hexenprocess zu Schongau vom Jahre 1587, published in the same vol. (1849), p. [128]-144.

1. Witchcraft--Bavaria. I. His Ein Hexenprocess zu Schongau vom Jahre 1587. II. Title.

Witchcraft
BF
1583
Z7
1612

Grote, Otto, Freiherr.
　Ortia Lindemann; oder, Der Zaubereiprocess zu Egeln 1612; mit Benutzung geschichtlicher Quellen bearb. Osterwieck a.H., A. W. Zickfeldt, 1877.
　62 p. 23cm.

1. Witchcraft. 2. Trials (Witchcraft) --Germany. 3. Lindemann, Ortia, fl. 1612. I. Title.

Groton in the witchcraft times.

Witchcraft
F
74
G88
G794

Green, Samuel Abbott, 1830-1918.
　Groton in the witchcraft times. By Samuel A. Green, M. D. Groton, Mass. [J. Wilson and son, Cambridge] 1883.
　29 p. 24cm.
　"A briefe account of a strange & unusuall providence of God befallen to Elizabeth Knap of Groton, p me Samll Willard": p. 7-21.

CATALOGUE OF THE CORNELL WITCHCRAFT COLLECTION

Witchcraft
BF 1775 G88
Grube, Hermann, praeses.
Disputatio physica De qvalitatibus vulgò dictis occultis, quam ... sub praesidio ... Dn. Hermanni Gruben ... publico eruditorum examini exponet Zacharias Hermannus ... Jenae, Praelo Nisiano [1665]
[28] p. 18cm.
1. Superstition--Addresses, essays, lectures. 2. Science--Early works to 1800. I. Hermann, Zacharias, respondent. II. Title: De qualitatibus vulgo dictis occultis. III. Title.

8

Gründlich ausgeführte Materie von der Hexerey.
WITCHCRAFT
BF 1565 W13 1711
Wagstaffe, John, 1633-1677.
Johann Wagstaffs Gründlich ausgeführte Materie von der Hexery, oder: Die Meynung derer jenigen so da glauben, dass es Hexen gebe; deutlich widerlegt und mit vernünfftigen Anmerckungen über jedes Capitel erläutert. Aus dem Englischen übersetzt. Halle in Megdeburgischen, Im Rengerischen Buchladen, 1711.
16 p. l., 152 p. 16cm.

8 (Continued on next card)

Gründlich ausgeführte Materie von der Hexerey.
WITCHCRAFT
BF 1565 W13 1711
Wagstaffe, John, 1633-1677. Johann Wagstaffs Gründlich ausgeführte Materie von der Hexerey ... 1711. (Card 2)
Translation of a revised version of The question of witchcraft debated.

1. Witchcraft. I. His The question of witchcraft debated. German. II. Title: Gründlich ausgeführte Materie von der Hexerey.

8

Gründliche Abfertigung der Unpartheyischen Gedancken eines ungenandten Auctoris.
Witchcraft
BF 1565 T46 U584
[Gundling, Nicolaus Hieronymus] 1671-1729.
Gründliche Abfertigung der Unpartheyischen Gedancken eines ungenandten Auctoris, die in Causa De crimine magiae, des hochberühmten Herrn D. Christiani Thomasii, neulichst heraus gegeben, gestellet von Hieronymo à sancta Fide. Franckfurth, 1703.
[48] p. 19cm.
Attribution by G. L. Burr.
1. Unpartheyischen Gedancken über die Kurze Lehr-Sätze von dem Laster der Zauberey. 2. Witchcraft. I. Hieronymus à sancta Fide. II. Title.

8

Gründliche Beantwortung der ... Untersuchung vom Kobold.
Witchcraft
BF 1565 F82
Franck, Johannes Christophorus, fl. 1717.
Gottfried Wahrliebs [pseud.] Deutliche vorstellung der nichtigkeit derer vermeynten hexereyen und des ungegründeten hexen-processes. Nebst einer gründlichen beantwortung der unter dem nahmen eines nach Engelland reisenden passagiers unlängst heraus gekommenen Untersuchung vom kobold, darinnen die falschen auflagen / mit welchen derselbe so wohl den hrn. geheimbd. rath Thomasivm als Iohann Webstern ohne allen grund zu diffamiren gesucht
(Continued on next card)

Gründliche Beantwortung der ... Untersuchung vom Kobold.
Witchcraft
BF 1565 F82
Franck, Johannes Christophorus, fl. 1717.
Gottfried Wahrliebs [pseud.] Deutliche vorstellung der nichtigkeit derer vermeynten hexereyen ... [pref. 1720] (Card 2)
deutlich entdecket, wie auch die Thomasische, Lehr-sätze von laster der zauberey wieder dessen ungegründete einwürffe zulänglich behauptet werden. Amsterdam, Nach erfindung der hexerey im dritten seculo, und nach einführung des hexen-processes im jahr 236 [pref. 1720]
172, 78 p. front. 22cm.
(Continued on next card)

Gründliche Beantwortung der ... Untersuchung vom Kobold.
WITCHCRAFT
BF 1565 F82
Franck, Johannes Christophorus, fl. 1717.
Gottfried Wahrliebs [pseud.] Deutliche vorstellung der nichtigkeit derer vermeynten hexereyen... [pref. 1720] (Card 3)
"Gründliche beantwortung der ... Untersuchung vom kobold" has separate paging and special t. p. with imprint: Amsterdam, 1720.

(Continued on next card)

Gründliche historische Nachricht vom Teuffel.
Witchcraft
PR 3404 H5 1748
[Defoe, Daniel] 1660-1731.
Gründliche historische Nachricht vom Teuffel, darinnen die Siege, so der Teuffel über das menschliche Geschlechte seit Eva an, bis auf unsere Zeiten erhalten hat, klar und deutlich erwiesen. Erster und anderer Theil. Aus dem Englischen und Französischen in das Teutsche übersetzet. Cöthen, J.C. Cörner, 1748.
184 p. 17cm.

Translation of The political history of
(Continued on next card)

Gründliche historische Nachricht vom Teuffel.
Witchcraft
PR 3404 H5 1748
[Defoe, Daniel] 1660-1731. Gründliche historische Nachricht vom Teuffel ... 1748. (Card 2)
the devil.
Also published under title: Geschichte des Teufels.

1. Devil. I. Title. II. Defoe, Daniel, 1660-1731. The political history of the devil--German. III. Defoe, Daniel, 1660-1731. Geschichte des Teuffels.

Gründliche und völlige Wiederlegung der Bezauberten Welt Balthasar Beckers, D.
Witchcraft
BF 1410 B42 Z57 1708
[Berns, Michael]
Gründliche und völlige Wiederlegung der Bezauberten Welt Balthasar Beckers, D. Aus der Heil. Schrifft gezogen. Wobey zugleich unzählige curioese Antiqvitaeten erläutert und zum rechten Gebrauch angewendet werden; und andere rare auch zu dieser Zeit höchstnöthige Materien. Nebst einem Anhange vom Licht und Recht der Natur. Mit völligen Registern versehen. Von M. Hamburg, S. Heyl und J. Liebezeit, 1708.
(Continued on next card)

Gründliche und völlige Wiederlegung der Bezauberten Welt Balthasar Beckers, D.
Witchcraft
BF 1410 B42 Z57 1708
[Berns, Michael] Gründliche und völlige Wiederlegung der Bezauberten Welt ... 1708. (Card 2)
3 p. l., 958, [11] p. [p. [12] blank] title and other vignettes, illus. initials. 21 x 17cm.
4°:)(3, A-I⁴, A-6D⁴, 6E3, 6F⁴, 6G².
Black letter.
According to J. G. T. Grässe, Bibliotheca magica et pneumatica, 1843, this work

8 (Continued on next card)

Gründliche und völlige Wiederlegung der Bezauberten Welt Balthasar Beckers, D.
Witchcraft
BF 1410 B42 Z57 1708
[Berns, Michael] Gründliche und völlige Wiederlegung der Bezauberten Welt ... 1708. (Card 3)
first appeared in 1697 with title: Die dreifache Welt als der Christen, Phantasten und Bezauberten, in dreyen Büchern abgefasst.

1. Bekker, Balthasar, 1634-1698. De betoverde weereld. 2. Christian life. 3. Millennialism. 4. Spirits. I. Title. II. M., pseud. III. His Die dreifache Welt als der Christen, Phantasten und Bezaub-
8   erten.

Gründliche vernunfft- und schrifftmässige Betrachtung von der Würckung ... des Teuffels.
WITCHCRAFT
R 133 H71 D2 1749
Hoffmann, Friedrich, 1660-1742.
D. Friedrich Hoffmanns ... Vernunfftmässige Abhandlung von dem heidnischen Fato, und der christlichen Providentz, in medicinisch und physicalischen Dingen. Sorau, Bey G. Hebold, 1749.
116 p. 17cm.
Translation of De fato physico et medico ejusque rationali explicatione disquisitio. Halae Magdeb., 1724.
Added t. p.: D. Friedrich Hoffmanns ...

8
NIC (Continued on next card)

Gründliche vernunfft- und schrifftmässige Betrachtung von der Würckung ... des Teuffels.
WITCHCRAFT
R 133 H71 D2 1749
Hoffmann, Friedrich, 1660-1742. ... Vernunfftmässige Abhandlung von dem heidnischen Fato ... 1749. (Card 2)
Gründliche vernunfft- und schrifftmässige Betrachtung von der Würckung, Macht und Gewalt des Teuffels in der Lufft und menschlichen Körpern [translation of Disputatio inauguralis medico-philosophica De potentia diaboli in corpora. Halae, 1703].
1. Medicine, Magic, mystic, and spagiric. 2. Fate and fatalism. 3. Medical delu-
8
NIC (Continued on next card)

Gründlicher Bericht von Zauberey vnd Zauberern.
WITCHCRAFT
BF 1565 P888 1629
Praetorius, Antonius.
Gründlicher Bericht von Zauberey vnd Zauberern; deren Vrsprung, Vnterscheid, Vermögen vnd Handlungen; auch wie einer christlichen Obrigkeit, solchem schändlichen Laster zu begegnen, dasselbige auffzuheben, zu hindern vnd zu straffen gebühre vnd wol müglich sey. Auss göttlichem vnd kayserlichem Recht kurtzlich vnd ordentlich gestellt vnd zusammen getragen. Männiglich, sonderlich aber den Hohen vnd Nidern Obrigkeiten
8
NIC   Richtern vnd Gerichten, zu nohtwen-
(Continued on next card)

Gründlicher Bericht von Zauberey vnd Zauberern.
WITCHCRAFT
BF 1565 P888 1629
Praetorius, Antonius.
Gründlicher Bericht von Zauberey vnd Zauberern... (Card 2)
diger Nachrichtung sehr dienlich vnd nutzlich zu lesen. Jetzo zum vierdtenmal in Truck gegeben, sampt einem vollkommenen Register. Franckfurt am Mayn, Getruckt durch J.-N. Stoltzenbergern; In Verlag J. C. Vnckels, 1629.
174 p. 20 cm.

(Continued on next card)

Gründlicher Bericht von Zauberey vnd Zauberern.
WITCHCRAFT
BF 1565 P888 1629
Praetorius, Antonius.
Gründlicher Bericht von Zauberey vnd Zauberern...1629. (Card 3)
Originally published under title: Von Zauberey und Zauberern, gründlicher Bericht.

1. Witchcraft. I. His Von Zauberey und Zauberern, gründlicher Bericht. II. Title.

Witchcraft
BF 1559 G25
Gründlicher Beweiss, dass die Art, mit welcher der nun in ganz Deutschland berühmte hochw. Herr Pfarrer zu Klösterl Johan Joseph Gassner die Krankheiten zu heilen pflegt, den evangelischen Grundsätzen und den Gesinnungen der allerersten Kirche ganz gleichförmig sey. Von einem Vertheidiger der Wahrheit und aufrichtigem Menschenfreunde in öffentlichen Druck gegeben. Augsburg, Bey J. Wolff, 1775.
93 p. 19cm.
8 (Continued on next card)

CATALOGUE OF THE CORNELL WITCHCRAFT COLLECTION

Witchcraft
F
559
25
    Gründlicher Beweiss ... von einem Vertheidiger der Wahrheit ... 1775. (Card 2)
        Bound with Gassner, Johann Joseph, 1727-1779. Antwort auf die Anmerkungen, welche in dem Münchnerischen Intelligenzblat ... gemacht worden. Augsburg, 1774.

    1. Gassner, Johann Joseph, 1727-1779. 2. Exorcism. 3. Medicine, Magic, mystic, and spagiric. I. Ein Vertheidiger der Wahrheit und aufrichtiger Menschenfreund.

8

    Gründlicher Beweiss ... von einem Vertheidiger der Wahrheit und aufrichtigem Menschenfreunde.

Witchcraft
BF
1559
G25
Z63
no.2
    Unterricht für diejenigen, welche in ihren körperlichen Anliegenheiten, bey dem hochwürdigen Herrn Johann Joseph Gassner ... entweder Hülfe zu suchen gedenken, oder selbe schon gesucht, und gefunden haben. Als eine Fortsetzung des gründlichen Beweiss &c. von einem Vertheidiger der Wahrheit und aufrichtigem Menschenfreunde in öffentlichen Druck gegeben. Augsburg, Bey J. Wolff, 1775. 96 p. 17cm.

    (Continued on next card)

    Gründlicher Beweiss ... von einem Vertheidiger der Wahrheit und aufrichtigem Menschenfreunde.

Witchcraft
BF
1559
G25
Z63
no.2
    Unterricht für diejenigen, welche ... Hülfe zu suchen gedenken ... 1775. (Card 2)

    Attributed by British Museum to Gassner. No. 2 in vol. lettered Gassneriana.

    1. Faith-cure. 2. Exorcism. I. Gassner, Johann Joseph, 1727-1779, supposed author. II. Gründlicher Beweiss ... von einem Vertheidiger der Wahrheit und aufrichtigem Menschenfreunde.

8

    Gründlicher und wahrhaftiger Bericht, was von der List, Macht und Wirckung des Satans ... zu halten sey.
    Reuter, Simon Henrich.
    (Sulṭān al-Ẓulmah)
    سلطان الظلمة
    das ist, Das mächtige, doch umschränckte Reich des Teufels; oder, Gründlicher und wahrhaftiger Bericht, was von der List, Macht und Wirckung des Satans und der bösen Geister zu halten sey, und was die Menschen durch derselben Kraft und Gemeinschaft wissen, thun und verrichten können ... Alles treulich aus Gottes Wort und vieler

    (Continued on next card)

    Gründlicher und wahrhaftiger Bericht, was von der List, Macht und Wirckung des Satans ... zu halten sey.
CHCRAFT
    Reuter, Simon Henrich.
    (Sulṭān al-Ẓulmah)... (Card 2)

    Gelehrten Bücher zusammen getragen, untersuchet und zur Warnung der glaubigen Kinder Gottes vorgestellet; auch mit einem nützlichen Register versehen. Lemgo, H. W. Meyer, 1716. 1293 p. 20cm.

    (Continued on next card)

Witchcraft
BF
1555
G31
    Gründlicher vnnd warhaffter Bericht, was sich mit dem Mann, der sich Hanns Vatter von Mellingen, ausdem Landt zu Düringen genennt, vnnd ein zeytlang im Teutschlandt herumb gezogen, zur Buss geruffen, vnd bey den Leuten fürgegeben, als ob er vom Sathan gepunden vnnd geplagt würde, zu Nürmberg zugetragen vnnd verloffen hat. Nürmberg, Gedruckt bey Valentin Geyssler, 1562.
    [20] p. 20cm.

    (Continued on next card)

Witchcraft
BF
1555
G31
    Gründlicher vnnd warhaffter Bericht, was sich mit ... Hanns Vatter ... zugetragen hat ... 1562. (Card 2)

    "Meniglich zu warhafftem Bericht verloffner Handlungen inn Druck gegeben durch mich Valtin Geyssler Buchdrucker zu Nürmberg." Portrait of Vatter on t. p.

    1. Vatter, Hanns, von Mellingen. 2. Demoniac possession. I. Geyssler, Valentin.

8

    Gründtlicher Bericht, die von Hexerey und Zauberey zu dieser Zeit, sehr nothwendige drey Hauptfragen betreffend.

WITCHCRAFT
BF
1565
H25
    Harbach, Laurentio de
    Gründtlicher Bericht, die von Hexerey vnd Zauberey zu dieser Zeit, sehr nothwendige drey Hauptfragen betreffend ... Mit gutem Bedacht zusammen getragen vnd der Welt Vrtheil heim gestellet, von Laurentio de Harbach ... [n. p.] 1630.
    [15] p. 19cm.

    1. Witchcraft. I. Title.

8

    Gründtlicher Bericht, ob Zauber- vnd Hexerey die argste vnd grewlichste sünd auff Erden sey.
Witchcraft
BF
1565
A27
1613
    Agricola, Franciscus.
    Gründtlicher Bericht, ob Zauber- vnd Hexerey die argste vnd grewlichste sünd auff Erden sey. Zum andern, ob die Zauberer noch Büsz vnnd selig werden mögen. Zum dritten, ob die hohe Obrigkeit, so lieb ihr Gott vnd ire Seligkeit ist die Zauberer vnd Hexen am Leib vnd Leben zu straffen schuldig. Mit Ableinung allerley Einreden ... Dilingen, G. Hänlin, 1613.
    353 p. 16cm.

    Imperfect: lacks p. 207-222; p. 175-190 are repeated in their place.

Witchcraft
BF
1555
G89
    Gruner, Christian Gottfried, 1744-1815.
    Christiani Godofredi Grvner ... Commentatio de daemoniacis a Christo Sospitatore percvratis. Accedit Danielis Wilhelmi Trilleri ... Exercitatio medico-philologica De mirando lateris cordisqve Christi vvlnere atqve effvso inde largo sangvinis et aqvae profluvio. Ienae, Litteris et impensis I. C. Stravssii, 1775.
    6 p. l., 64, [3] p. 18cm.
    1. Demoniac possession. 2. Jesus

8   (Continued on next card)

Witchcraft
BF
1555
G89
    Gruner, Christian Gottfried, 1744-1815. ... Commentatio de daemoniacis ... 1775. (Card 2)

    Christ--Miracles. 3. Jesus Christ--Passion. I. Triller, Daniel Wilhelm, 1695-1782. Exercitatio medico-philologica De mirando lateris cordisque Christi vulnere. II. Title: De daemoniacis a Christo Sospitatore percuratis. III. Title: Commentatio

8   (Over)

HIST SCI
RE
93
N63
G89
    Gruner, Christian Gottfried, 1744-1815.
    Decanus D. Christ. Godofredus Gruner... Dissertationem...Christiani Gottlob Rothe... indicit de daemoniacis a Christo Sospitatore percuratis breviter commentatus. Ienae, Litteris Fickelscherrii [1774]
    16 p. 20cm.

    Introductory to a diss. for which Nicolai acted as praeses, Rothe as respondent: Dissertatio inauguralis medica De nyctalopia ac hemeralopia visu simplici et duplici possession. 1.Demoniac 2.Rothe, Christian Gottlob, b.1750. 3.Nicolai, Ernst Anton,1722-1802,praeses. Dissertatio inauguralis medica De nyctalopia...

Witchcraft
BF
1522
E34
    Gruner, Hans, fl. 1698.
    Eigentliche Fürstellung der arglistigen satanischen Erscheinung, welche sich jüngsthin am 17. Julii, war der 4. Sonntag nach dem Fest der H. Dreyeinigkeit, mit Hanss Grunern, einem Einwohner zu Mellingen, warhafftig begeben, jedermann zur Warnung und Schrecken, aus des Mannes eigener Schrifft- und mündlichen Erzehlung entworffen, und auff vielfältiges Ansuchen und Begehren ans Licht gestellet. Pirna, G. B. Lude wig, 1698.
    16 p. fold. pl. 20cm.
    I. Gruner, Hans, fl. 1698.

8

RARE
HV
8593
G89
    Grupen, Christian Ulrich, 1692-1767.
    Observatio juris criminalis De applicatione tormentorum, insbesondere im Schnüren-Anfang, und in vollen Schnüren, mit einer dissertatione praeliminari von den tormentis Romanorum et Graecorum... Hannover, Bei Johann Christoph Richter, 1754.
    xii, 442 (i.e. 244) p. 4 plates. 21cm.

    With this is bound: Manipulus responsorum votorum ac de cendendi rationum... Ienae, 1726.

8
NIC   1. Torture. 2. Torture--Hist. I. Title.

Witchcraft
BF
1505
G94
    Essais de sciences maudites.
    Guaita, Stanislas de, 1860-1897.
    ... Le serpent de la Genèse ... par Stanislas de Guaita. Paris, Librairie du merveilleux, 1891-
    v. front., plates, ports. 23cm. (His Essais de sciences maudites II)

Books 1 and 2 only.
Vol. 2 has imprint: Bibliothèque Chacornac, 1897. Date on cover: 1902.
Vol. 1 has subtitle: Le temple de Satan.
Vol. 2 has subtitle: La clef de la magie noire.
Ex libris, vol. 2: Arthur Edward Waite.
1. Demonology. I. Title. II. His Essais de sciences maudites. III. Title: Le temple de Satan. IV. Title: La clef de la magie noire.
Library of Congress   BF1405.G8 vol. 2

Witchcraft
BF
1505
G94
    Guaita, Stanislas de, 1860-1897.
    ... Le serpent de la Genèse ... par Stanislas de Guaita. Paris, Librairie du merveilleux, 1891-
    v. front., plates, ports. 23cm. (His Essais de sciences maudites II)

Books 1 and 2 only.
Vol. 2 has imprint: Bibliothèque Chacornac, 1897. Date on cover: 1902.
Vol. 1 has subtitle: Le temple de Satan.
Vol. 2 has subtitle: La clef de la magie noire.
Ex libris, vol. 2: Arthur Edward Waite.
1. Demonology. I. Title. II. His Essais de sciences maudites. III. Title: Le temple de Satan. IV. Title: La clef de la magie noire.
Library of Congress   BF1405.G8 vol. 2

Witchcraft
Z
6880
G94
    Guaita, Stanislas de, 1860-1897.
    Stanislas de Guaita et sa bibliothèque occulte. Paris, Dorbon, 1899.
    1 p. l., vi p., 1 l., 299 p. front. (port.) plates, facsims. 24cm.

Preface by René Philipon.
A catalogue of 2,227 lots, offered for sale, with prices.
First issued in four parts, 1898-99, under title: Catalogue des livres et manuscrits relatifs aux sciences occultes.

    1. Occult sciences--Bibl. I. Title.   3-22281

Library of Congress, no.   Z6880.G9#

Witchcraft
Z
6880
Z9
D685
    Guaita, Stanislaus de, 1860-1897.
    Dorbon, bookseller, Paris.
    Catalogue ... de livres et manuscrits ... aux sciences occultes ... Provenant de la bibliothèque de feu Stanislaus de Guaita ... En vente aux prix marqués à la Librairie Dorbon. Paris, 1898-1899.
    4 nos. 22cm. (Its Catalogue 180, 182, 184, 186)
    In envelope.
    1. Occult sciences--Bibl.--Catalogs. I. Guaita, Stanislaus de, 1860-1897.

8

CATALOGUE OF THE CORNELL WITCHCRAFT COLLECTION

Witchcraft
BF 1559 G91

Guazzo, Francesco Maria.
Compendivm maleficarvm in tres libros distinctum ex plvribvs avthoribvs per fratrem Franciscvm Mariam Gvaccivm ... Mediolani, Apud Haeredes August. Tradati, 1608.
8 p. l., 245, [1] p. illus. 21cm.
First edition.
Colophon: Mediolani, Apud Bernardinum Lantonum, 1608.
Copy 1 has autograph commentary by G. L. Burr inside cover.
Copy 2: ex libris Cabalisticis Kurt Seligmann

8 (Continued on next card)

Witchcraft
BF 1559 G91

Guazzo, Francesco Maria. Compendivm maleficarvm in tres libros ... 1608. (Card 2)

1. Exorcism. 2. Demonology. 3. Witchcraft. I. Title.

Witchcraft
BF 1559 G91 1626

Guazzo, Francesco Maria.
Compendium maleficarum, ex quo nefandissima in genus humanum opera venefica, ac ad illa vitanda remedia conspiciuntur ... In hac autem secunda æditione ab eodem authore pulcherrimis doctrinis ditatum, exemplis auctum, & remedijs locupletatum. His additus est exorcismus potentissimus ad soluendum omne opus diabolicum; nec non modus curandi febricitantes ... Mediolani, ex Collegij Ambrosiani typographia, 1626.
8 p. l., 391 p. illus. 21cm.
Engr. t.-p.; head-piece; initials.
1. Exorcism. 2. Demonology. 3. Witchcraft. I. Title.

R-3/10/65
C-3/11/65
11-9016
Library of Congress BF1559.G8

BF 1559 G91+ 1929

Guazzo, Francesco Maria.
Compendium maleficarum, collected in three books from many sources, showing the iniquitous and execrable operations of witches against the human race, and the divine remedies by which they may be frustrated. Edited with notes by Montague Summers. Translated by E. A. Ashwin. London, J. Rodker, 1929.
xxi, 206 p. illus. 26cm.

Witchcraft
BF 1555 G92

Guden, Friedrich ed.
Schreckliche Geschichte teuflischer Besitzung; in 3 merckwürdigen Historien. Budissin, D. Richter, 1716.
[56], 188 p. 16cm.

1. Devil. 2. Exorcism. I. Title.

MSS Bd.
WITCHCRAFT
BF H33

Guden, Friedrich, ed.
Schreckliche Geschichte teuflischer Besitzung.
Hartmann, Andreas. Warhafftige und mit vielen glaubwürdigen Zeugen bewährte Relation was sich zu Döffingen, hoch-fürstl. württembergischer Herrschafft, und Böblinger Amts, mit zwey besessenen Weibs-Personen im Monat Decembr. 1714, mercklich zugetragen hat ... Ans Licht gebracht von M. Andreas Hartmann ... [n.p.] 1716 [ca. 1900]
14 l. 18cm.
Carnap's manuscript copy.
"Wörtliche Abschrift aus: Altes und Neues aus dem Reich Gottes und (Continued on next card)

MSS Bd.
WITCHCRAFT
BF H33

Guden, Friedrich, ed.
Schreckliche Geschichte teuflischer Besitzung.
Hartmann, Andreas. Warhafftige und mit vielen glaubwürdigen Zeugen bewährte Relation ... 1716 [ca. 1900] (Card 2)
der übrigen guten und bösen Geister, etc. hrsg. von J. J. Moser, 9ter Theil. Franckfurt u. Leipzig, 1734. 8°. S. 10-28."
"NB. Diese Besessenheitsgeschichte steht auch wörtlich in: Guden, Friedrich, Schreckliche Geschichte Teuflischer Besitzung, in 3 merkw. Historien, etc. Budissin, 1717. 8°. S. 159-188."
1. Demoniac possession. 2. Exorcism. (Continued on next card)

WITCHCRAFT
B 781 A32 F8 1726

Guedeville, Nicolas, ca. 1654-ca. 1721. tr.
Agrippa von Nettesheim, Heinrich Cornelius, 1486?-1535.
Sur la noblesse, & excellence du sexe feminin, de sa preeminence sur l'autre sexe, & du sacrement du mariage. Avec le traitté sur l'incertitude, aussi bien que la vanité des sciences & des arts ... traduit par M. de Guedeville. Leiden, Chez Theodore Haak, 1726.
3 v. front., port. 17cm.
Vols. 2-3 have title: Sur l'in-
8
NIC (Continued on next card)

WITCHCRAFT
B 781 A32 F8 1726

Guedeville, Nicolas, ca. 1654-ca. 1721, tr.
Agrippa von Nettesheim, Heinrich Cornelius, 1486?-1535. Sur la noblesse, & excellence du sexe feminin ... 1726. (Card 2)
certitude, aussi bien que la vanité des sciences & des arts.
Translation of De nobilitate et praecellentia foeminei sexus, and De incertitudine et vanitate scientiarum et artium.
1. Woman. 2. Marriage. 3. Learning and scholarship. 4. Scholasticism. I.
8
NIC (Continued on next card)

BF 1535 G92

Gueiros, José Alberto.
O diabo sem preconceitos / José Alberto Gueiros ; [capa e ilustrações de Benicio]. Rio de Janeiro : Editora Monterrey ; distribuido por F. Chinaglia, 1974.
190 p. : ill. ; 21 cm.

1. Demonology. I. Title

NIC JUL 31,'75 C000xc 75-562370

Witchcraft
BF 1583 Z7 1621

Günther, Louis, 1859-
Ein Hexenprozess; ein Kapitel aus der Geschichte des dunkelsten Aberglaubens. Giessen, A. Töpelmann, 1906.
xii, 112 p. 22cm.

1. Kepler, Katharina, 1547-1622. 2. Witchcraft. 3. Trials (Witchcraft)--Germany. I. Title.

Witchcraft
PN 3441 G92 A2

Günthert, Julius Ernst von.
Agnes; eine Hexengeschichte aus dem 16. Jahrhundert. Stuttgart, A. Bonz, 1887.
253 p. 19cm.

1. Witchcraft. I. Title.

WITCHCRAFT
DC 92 R56+

Guichard, Bp. of Troyes, d. 1317.
Rigault, Abel
Le procès de Guichard, évêque de Troyes (1308-1313) Paris, A. Picard, 1896.
xii, 313 p. illus., facsim. 26cm.
(Paris. École des chartes. Société de l'École des chartes. Mémoires et documents, 1)

Bibliographical footnotes.
1. Guichard, Bp. of Troyes, d. 1317. 2. France--History--Philip IV, 1285-1314. 3. Witchcraft--France. I. Title. II. Series.

8
NIC

A guide to grand iury men.

Witchcraft
BF 1581 A2B52

Bernard, Richard, 1568-1641.
A gvide to grand ivry men, divided into two bookes: In the first, is the authors best aduice to them what to doe, before they bring in a Billa vera in cases of witchcraft ... In the second, is a treatise touching witches good and bad ... London, Printed by Felix Kingston for Ed. Blackmore, 1627.
267 p. 15cm.

Witchcraft
BF 1775 G96

Guillois, Ambroise, 1796-1856.
Essai sur les superstitions, par M. l'Abbé Guillois. Lille, L. Lefort, 1836.
144 p. 16cm.

1. Superstition. 2. Occult sciences.
I. Title.

8

Witchcraft
BF 1576 B36

Guiteau, Charles Julius, 1841-1882.
Beard, George Miller, 1839-1883.
The psychology of the Salem witchcraft excitement of 1692, and its practical application to our own time; by George M. Beard ... New York, G. P. Putnam's sons, 1882.
xx, 112 p. incl. front. 17½cm.
Largely a comparison of the witchcraft trials with those of Cadet Whittaker and Charles Guiteau.

1. Witchcraft — Salem. Mass. 2. Guiteau, Charles Julius. 1841-1882. 3. Insanity—Jurisprudence. I. Title.

Library of Congress BF1576.B3
11-8994

Witchcraft
BF 1565 T46 U584

[Gundling, Nicolaus Hieronymus] 1671-1729.
Gründliche Abfertigung der Unpartheyischen Gedancken eines ungenandten Auctoris, die er von der Lehre De crimine magiae, des hochberühmten Herrn D. Christiani Thomasii, neulichst heraus gegeben, gestellet von Hieronymo à sancta Fide. Franckfurth, 1703.
[48] p. 19cm.
Attribution by G. L. Burr.
1. Unpartheyische Gedancken über die Kurze Lehr-Sätze von dem Laster der Zauberey. 2. Witchcraft. I. Hieronymus à sancta Fide. II. Title.

8

Witchcraft
BF 1410 B42 Z56 v.2 no.15

Gunst, Lucas van.
Den gevallen engel, weereloos. En desselfs onmacht, en krachteloosheyd, klarlijck, vertoont uyt de H. Schriftuur, het geestelijck en wereldlijck recht, als mede uyt de historien. Door Mr. Lucas van Gunst, rechtsgeleerde. Amsterdam, Te koop by J. en G. Janssonius van Waesberge, 1692.
2 p. l., 52 p. title vignette, illus. initials. 19 x 15cm.
4°: π², A- F⁴, G².

8 (Continued on next card)

CATALOGUE OF THE CORNELL WITCHCRAFT COLLECTION

.tchcraft
    Gunst, Lucas van. Den gevallen engel, weere-
-10   loos. 1692.   (Card 2)
-2
6   Black letter (except for introduction)
2   Van der Linde 94.
.15   No. 15 in vol. lettered Bekker II.

      1. Devil. 2. Spirits. I. Title.

    Gutierrez, Maria Garcia de Rodriguez de,
       b. 1564.

    see

    Garcia de Rodriguez de Gutierrez, Maria,
       b. 1564.

      Gunter, Anne, fl. 1605.

ITCHCRAFT
F   Ewen, Cecil Henry L'Estrange, 1877-
581   A noted case of witchcraft at North
7   Moreton, Berks, in the early 17th century.
605   [London] 1936.
      7 p. 23cm.

      "Reprinted from the Berkshire archaeo-
logical journal, vol. 40, no.2."

      1. Gunter, Anne, fl. 1605. 2. Witch-
craft--Berkshire, England. I. Title.

    Gyfford, George.

    see

    Gifford, George, d. 1620.

      Guörnerus, Joannes, ed.

RE   Suzaria, Guido de.
      Tractatus II [i.e. duo] perutiles & quoti-
545 diani De indiciis, quaestionibus et tortura
99   ...Guidonis de Suzaria & Pauli Grillandi
de Castilione, una cum additionib. Ludovici
Bolognini...geordnet durch Ioannem Guörnerum
de Vineca. Ursellis, Apud Nicolaum Henricum, sumptibus Cornelij Suterij, 1597.
     291 p. 16cm.

     Bound with: Saur, Abraham. Notarien Spie-
gel. Franckfort am Mayn, 1599.
C   (Continued on next card)

      Gynaikolousis
WITCHCRAFT
BF   Anten, Conradus ab.
1558   (Gynaikolousis) Γυναικόλουσις ; sev,
P79   Mvliervm lavatio, qvam pvrgationem per
aqvam frigidam vocant. Item vulgaris de
potentia lamiarum opinio, quod vtraq; Deo,
natvrae omni iuri et probatae consvetvdini sit contraria. Candida breuis & dilucida oratio. Autore Conrado ab Anten.
Lvbecae, In officina typographica Assweri
Crögeri, 1590.
     [102] p.   17cm.
8   A small   portion of the text is
NIC   (Continued on next card)

      Gutachten von dem mit Herrn D. Thomasio
         erregten Streit.
tchcraft
     Das Wohl-meritirte und wohlverdiente Ehren=
65   Kleid dem Anonymo und Autori des Gutach-
6   ten von dem mit Herrn Doct. Thomasio er-
58   regten Streit über einige freye Meynungen
in einem teutschen Programmate, und von
Herrn D. Strykii Disputation de jure Sabbathi, zum Recompens vor die Mühe praesentiret von einem Liebhaber der Wahrheit
und Feind der Calumnien. Freystatt,
1703.
     24 p. 18cm.

             (Continued on next card)

      Gynaikolousis
WITCHCRAFT
BF   Anten, Conradus ab. (Gynaikolousis)
1558   Γυναικόλουσις...1590.   (Card 2)
P79
    in German.
      Bound with: Pomponazzi, Pietro, 1462-1524.
De naturalium effectuum causis. Basileae,
1556.
      1. Witchcraft. 2. Trials (Witchcraft)
I. Title. II. Title: Mulierum lavatio.

      Guthramdaughter, Margaret, d. 1644.

itchcraft
     Trial of witches in Shetland, A. D. 1644.
581   Intent upon pannel Marion Peebles alias
7+   Pardone, spouse to Swene in Hildiswick.
44a   [Edinburgh? 1822?]
     10 p. 28cm.
     Caption title.
     Extract from Hibbert-Ware, Samuel, 1782-
1848. A description of the Shetland Islands. Edinburgh, 1822. "... the original
document was in the possession of a gentleman of Shetland,   lately deceased."

            (Continued on next card)

   Gutiérrez, Juan Lazaro, 17th cent.
     Ioannis Lazari Gvtierrii ... Opvscvlvm
de fascino ... Lvgdvni, Sumpt. Philip.
Borde, Lavr. Arnavd, & Cl. Rigavd, 1653.
   [8], 210, [15] p. 24cm.

   Engraved title vignette: publishers'
device.
   Bound with Nicquet, Honorat. Physiognomia
hvmana. Lvgdvni, 1648.

    1. Magic. 2. Witchcraft. I. Title: De
fascino. II. Title. III. Title:
Opusculum de fascino.

CATALOGUE OF THE CORNELL WITCHCRAFT COLLECTION

H

H., K. A.
Witchcraft
BF 1410 B42 Z56 v.2 no.16
Den verkeerden duyvel van den throon geschopt, en den rechten weder hervoort gebragt, verhandelende van engelen en duyvelen, hare macht ende werkinge, waar in besonderlyk getoont wort wat den duyvel is, schriftmatigh voorgestelt, waar in de swaarste stukken van die materie worden opgelost, noch noyt zoo voortgebracht. Door K. A. H. Amsterdam, By N. Holbeex, boekverkooper, 1692.
2 p. l., 36 p. title and end page vignettes, illus. initials. 19 x 15cm.
(Continued on next card)

H., K. A.
Witchcraft
BF 1410 B42 Z56 v.2 no.16
Den verkeerden duyvel van den throon geschopt ... 1692. (Card 2)
4°: *², A-D⁴, E².
Black letter (except for introduction)
Modeled on Balthasar Bekker's De betoverde weereld, but not always supporting it.
Van der Linde 66.
No. 16 in vol. lettered Bekker II.
1. Demonology. 2. Angels. 3. Magic. 4. Witchcraft. 5. Bekker, Balthasar, 1634-1698. De betoverde weereld.
I. Title. II. K. A. H. III. H., K. A.
8

H., S.
Witchcraft
BF 1581 H32D6
[Harsnett, Samuel] archbishop of York, 1561-1631.
[A discovery of the fraudulent practises of John Darrell, bacheler of artes, in his proceedings concerning the pretended possession and dispossession of William Somers at Nottingham; of Thomas Darling, the boy of Burton at Caldwell; and of Katherine Wright at Mansfield, and Whittington; and of his dealings with one Mary Couper at Nottingham, detecting in some sort the deceitful trade in these latter day es of casting out deuils.
(Continued on next card)

H., S.
Witchcraft
BF 1581 H32D6
[Harsnett, Samuel] archbishop of York, 1561-1631. [A discovery of the fraudulent practises of John Darrell ... 1599] (Card 2)
London, 1599]
[328] p. 18cm.
Epistle to the reader signed: S. H.
Imperfect: t.-p. mounted, part of it missing; title taken from Halkett & Laing; pages cropped; numbers missing from 324-[328]
1. Darrell, John, fl. 1562-1602. I. Title. II. S. H. III. H., S.

H. A. B.
WITCHCRAFT
BF 1583 A2 I43
Informatio ivris, in causa poenali; vtrvm tres mvlieres maleficii, et veneficii, cevreae, delatae capi, & torqueri potuerint, nécne? Qvad. Caroli V. imp. constitvtio criminalis aliqvot in locis declaratur. Rechtliches Bedencken, in Malefitzsachen; ob drey Weiber, der Zauberey halber angegeben, in gefängliche Verhafft angenommen, und peinlich befragt werden können, oder nicht? Darinnen Keyser Carols, dess Fünfften, hochlöblichister Gedächtnuss Peinliche, oder Halss-
8 NIC (Continued on next card)

H. A. B.
WITCHCRAFT
BF 1583 A2 I43
Informatio ivris, in causa poenali... (Card 2)
gerichtsordnunge in etlichen Articuln erkläret wirdt. Per H. A. B. V. I. D. Franckf[urt a. M.] Bey C. Egen[olffs] Erben, 1590.
68 l. 16cm.
1. Witchcraft--Germany. 2. Torture--Germany. I. B., H. A. II. H. A. B. III. Karl V, Emperor of Germany, 1500-1558. IV. Title: Recht liches Bedencken, in Malefitzsach en.

H.F.
Witchcraft
BF 1563 T86
A true and exact relation of the severall informations, examinations, and confessions of the late witches, arraigned and executed in the county of Essex. Who were arraigned and condemned at the late sessions, holden at Chelmesford before the Rt. Hon. Robert, earle of Warwicke, and severall of His Majesties justices of peace, the 29 of July, 1645... London, Printed by M. S. for H. Overton, 1645.
36 p. 19cm.
(Continued on next card)

H. F.
Witchcraft
BF 1563 T86
A true and exact relation of the severall informations, examinations, and confessions of the late witches ... 1645. (Card 2)
Preface signed H. F.
No. 1 in vol. lettered: Tracts of witches.
1. Witchcraft. I. F., H. II. H.F.

H. v. G.
Witchcraft
BF 1410 B42 Z69 no.17, 18
Den predikant D. Balthasar Becker, seediglyk ondersogt so in zyn persoon als Schriften, ofhy die derst voorgeven, buyten hem alleen, de gantsche werelt betovert te zyn, selfs hier af wel vry is, ende dat daar en boven op hem niet soude werken, de geest van hovaardye en dwalinge tot ergernisse en van de kleine, en van de arme, en van de verslagene van geest, en die beeven voor Godts woort. By een missive den 19 January 1692, door H.v.G. van Amsterdam geschreven aan
NIC (Continued on next card)

H. v. G.
Witchcraft
BF 1410 B42 Z69 no.17, 18
Den predikant D. Balthasar Becker ... (Card 2)
D. T. S. de Jonge tot Uytrecht. Met zyn Andtwoord provisioneel tot nader berigt daar op gevolgt, den 4. February desselven jaars. Uytregt, Gedrukt by W. Jansz, 1692.
32, 36 p. 21cm.
Signatures: 4°: A-D⁴. 4°: A-D⁴, E2.
The Pro visioneel Antwoord has special half-title and separate
NIC (Continued on next card)

H. v. G.
Witchcraft
BF 1410 B42 Z69 no.17, 18
Den predikant D. Balthasar Becker ... 1692. (Card 3)
paging.
Van der Linde 63, 61.
"Extracten van ... De betoverde werelt, uytgetrokken en t'samengestelt door N. N.": p. 17-28 of the Provisioneel Antwoord; "Extract van 't gepasseerde des Synodi tot Edam, 10. Aug. 1691. rakende D. Bekker ...": p. 28-29; "Articu len voor te stellen aan Do. B. Bekker" signed Leonardus
NIC (Continued on next card)

H. v. G.
Witchcraft
BF 1410 B42 Z69 No.17, 18
Den predikant D. Balthasar Becker ... 1692. (Card 4)
Groenewegen: p. 29-31; "Eerste aanbieding D. B. Bekker, op den 30. Aug. 1691": p. 31; "Articulen tot satisfactie aan de Eerw. Classis van Amsterdam, van Do. Balthasar Bekker ... wegens ... de Betoverde wereld ...": p. 32-36.
Nos. 17 & 18 in a Collection of tracts against Balthasar Bekker and his Betoverde weereld.
NIC (Continued on next card)

H. W. B. E.
Witchcraft
BX 9479 B42 B11 no.9
Een der gezigten van Zacharias, waar in de Satan vertoond word, staande ter regterhand van de engel des Heeren. Uyt Zach. III: 1-8. Door H. W. B. E. Amsterdam, By J. Roman, boekverkooper, 1699.
16 p. title and end page vignettes, illus. initial. 20 x 15cm.
4°: A-B⁴.
Black letter.
No. 9 in vol. lettered B. Bekkers sterfbed en andere tractaten.
(Continued on next card)

Witchcraft
BF 1410 B42 Z56 v.3 no.29
Haak, Arent, ed. Liefdelooze achterhoudinge van Do. Everhardus van der Hooght predikant tot Nieuwendam. Gebleeken in zijn schriftelyke onderhandelinge met Arent Haak. Amsterdam, By D. van den Dalen, boekverkooper, 1693.
32 p. title and end page vignettes, illus initial. 20 x 15cm.
4°: A-D⁴.
Introduction by Haak: p. 3-9. The rest consists of let ters exchanged by van der Hooght and Haak (in black letter).
8 (Continued on next card)

Witchcraft
BF 1410 B42 Z56 v.3 no.29
Haak, Arent, ed. Liefdelooze achterhoudinge van Do. Everhardus van der Hooght ... 1693. (Card 2)
on Balthasar Bekker's De betoverde weereld.
Van der Linde 118.
No. 29 in vol. lettered Bekker III.
1. Bekker, Balthasar, 1634-1698. De betoverde weereld. I. Hooght, Everard van der, d. 1716. II. Title.
8

CATALOGUE OF THE CORNELL WITCHCRAFT COLLECTION

BF Haan, Jean.
1566   Von Hexen und wildem Gejäg. Mit mittelalterlichen
H2   Holzschnitten und Kupferstichen sowie Zeichnungen von
   Félix Mersch, Gab Weis und Pit Weyer. Luxembourg,
   Edi-Centre, 1971.
     159 p. illus. 24 cm. (Am Sagenborn des Luxemburger Volkes,
   Bd. 3)
     Bibliography: p. 159.

     1. Witchcraft.   I. Title. II. Series.

BF1566.H3   70-594907
Library of Congress   71 [2]

Witchcraft
BF   Haas, Alfred Wilhelm Moritz Gottlieb,
1583   1860-
H12   Aus pommerschen Hexenprozessakten:
   ein Beitrag zur Geschichte des pommerschen Volksglaubens. Stettin, F. Hessenland, 1896.
     18 p. 26cm.

     1. Witchcraft. 2. Trials (Witchcraft)
   --Germany. I. Title.

Witchcraft
BF   Haas, Carl.
1583   Die Hexenprozesse: ein cultur-histori-
H122   scher Versuch nebst Dokumenten. Tübingen,
   Laupp & Siebeck, 1865.
     viii, 120 p. 18cm.

     1. Witchcraft. 2. Trials (Witchcraft)
   --Germany. I. Title.

WITCHCRAFT
BF   [Hacker, Franz Xavier] 1836-1894.
1583   Die Hexenrichter von Würzburg. Histo-
H11   rische Novelle von Franz von Seeburg [pseud.]
1894   3. Aufl. Regensburg [etc.], F. Pustet,
   1894.
     iv, 297 p. 17cm.

     1. Witchcraft--Fiction. 2. Witch-
   craft--Germany. 3. Spee, Friedrich von,
   1591-1635--Fiction. I. Title.

8
NIC

MSS   Haeberlin, Georg Heinrich, 1644-1727.
Bd.   Historische Relation, von denen in der
WITCHCRAFT Würtemb. wohlbenahmssten Ampts-
BF   und Handel-Stadt Calw einige Zeit her der
H13   Zauberey halber beschreyten Kindern, und
   andern Personen. Sambt einer christlichen
   Predigt, wie solchen und dergleichen satan-
   ischen Anläufften christlich zu begegnen...
   In öffentlicher Versammlung daselbsten ge-
   halten, und in Truck gegeben von Georg
   Heinrich Heberlin ... Stuttgart,
       Johann Gottfried Zubrodt,
   zu finden bey
              (Continued on next card)

MSS   Haeberlin, Georg Heinrich, 1644-1727.
Bd.   Historische Relation ... 1685 [ca. 1900]
WITCHCRAFT   (Card 2)
BF
H13   daselbst gedruckt bey Melchior Gerhard
   Lorbern, 1685 [ca. 1900]
     36 p. 23cm.
     Carnap's manuscript copy.
     "Originaldruck in der Königlichen öff.
   Bibliothek zu Stuttgart 40 pag. S. in 4°."
     Numerals in the margins indicate
   pagination of   the original.
               (Continued on next card)

MSS   Haeberlin, Georg Heinrich, 1644-1727.
Bd.   Historische Relation ... 1685 [ca. 1900]
WITCHCRAFT   (Card 3)
BF
H13
     1. Demoniac possession. 2. Witchcraft--
   Sermons. 3. Devil. I. Title: Historische
   Relation, von denen ... der Zauberey
   halber beschreyten Kindern.

     Hällwarth, Margarete, d. 1676.

WITCHCRAFT
BF   Trefftz, Johannes.
1583   Ein Hexenprozess aus dem Jahre 1676.
Z7   (In Verein für Thüringische Geschichte
1676   und Altertumskunde. Zeitschrift. Jena.
   23cm. 29. Bd. Heft 1 (1912), p. [171]-
   180)
     At head of title: IV.

     1. Trials (Witchcraft)--Thuringia.
   2. Hällwarth,   Margarete, d. 1676.
   I. Title.
8
NIC

Witchcraft
BF   Haen, Anton de, 1704?-1776.
1565   Antonii de Haen ... De magia liber.
H13   Lipsiae, Svmptibvs I. P. Kravs, 1775.
1775   xxviii, 316, [1] p. 22cm.

     1. Witchcraft. 2. Magic. I. Title:
   De magia liber. II. Title.

8

WITCHCRAFT
BF   Haen, Anton de, 1704?-1776.
1565   Antonii de Haen ... De magia liber.
H13   Parisiis, Apud P. Fr. Didot juniorem, 1777.
1777   xxiv, 220 p. 17cm.

     1. Witchcraft. 2. Magic. I. Title:
   De magia liber.

8

Witchcraft
BT   Haen, Anton de, 1704?-1776.
97   ... De miraculis liber. Parisiis,
A2   Apud P. F. Didot juniorem, 1778.
H13   xx, 144 [i. e., 148] p. 18cm.
1778
     First published in Frankfurt, 1776.
     J. J. Gassner's methods discussed in
   chapter 5.

     1. Miracles--Early works to 1800.
   2. Gassner,   Johann Joseph, 1727-
      1779. I. Title.
8

     Haen, Anton de, 1704?-1776.

Witchcraft
BF   Benvenuti, Giuseppe, 1728-ca. 1770.
1565   Josephi Benvenuti ... De daemoniacis
T19   dissertatio. Lucae, Typis Joannis Ric-
M18+   comini, 1775.
     lxxxiv p. 26cm.

     Bound with Maffei, Francesco Scipione,
   marchese, 1675-1755. Arte magica dileguata.
   Verona, 1749.

     1. Demonolo   gy. 2. Haen, Anton de,
8   1704?-1776.   I. Title: De daemoniacis disser   tatio.

     Häxboken.

WITCHCRAFT
BF   Isberg, Anders Ulrik Martin, 1867-1940.
1584   Häxboken; kulturhistoriska skildringar
B9   från det gamla Malmö, af A. U. Isberg. 1.
I76   delen. [Malmö, Bröderna Forssells bok-
   tryckeri, 1916]
     256 p. illus. 24cm.

     No more published?

     1. Witchcraft--Malmö, Sweden. I. Title.

8
NIC

     Häxeriet och häxeriprocesserna.

WITCHCRAFT
BF   Nyström, Anton Kristen, 1842-1931.
1566   Häxeriet och häxeriprocesserna. Stock-
N99   holm, A. Bonnier [1896]
     28 p. 22cm. (Studentföreningen Verdan-
   dis Småskrifter, 58)

8   1 Witchcraft--History. 2. Trials (Witch-
NIC   craft)--History. I. Title.

     Haxprocesser i norska Finnmarken.

PD   Rutberg, Hulda, 1884-
5001   Häxprocesser i norska Finnmarken, 1620-
S96   1692. Stockholm, P. A. Norstedt, 1918.
ser.1   109 p. 24cm. (Bidrag till kännedom om
v.16   svenska landsmålen ock svenskt folkliv. XVI.4)
no.4
     1. Witchcraft--Finmark, Norway. I. Title.

Witchcraft
BS   Hafner, Georg.
2545   Die Dämonischen des Neuen Testaments.
D5   Ein Vortrag gehalten und dem Verein der
H13   Deutschen Irrenärzte gewidmet. Frank-
   furt a. M., K. Brechert, 1894.
     33 p. 22cm.

     1. Demoniac possession. 2. Bible.
   N. T.--Commentaries. 3. Bible--Psychology.
   I. Title.

     Hafner, Gotthart, 1707-1767, ed.

Witchcraft
AG   Onomatologia cvriosa artificiosa et magica;
27   oder, Ganz natürliches zauber-lexicon, welches
O59   das nöthigste, nützlichste und angenehmste in
1764   allen realen wissenschaften überhaupt und besonders in der naturlehre, mathematick, der haus-
   haltungs- und naturhistorischen zauberkunst, und aller
   andern, vornemlich auch curieuser künsten deutlich
   und vollständig nach alphabethischer ordnung
   beschreibet ... 2. vielvermehrte a ufl. Nürnberg,
   Auf kosten der Raspischen handlung, 1764.
     3 p. l., 1648 col. front., diagrs.(1 fold.)
   21cm.
     In double col umns.
     Edited by Got   thart Hafner. cf. Meusel,
   J.G. Lexikon der vom jahr 1750 bis 1800 verstorbenen teutschen schriftsteller v.5, p. 36.

Witchcraft
BT   Hagen, Martin.
980   Der Teufel im Lichte der Glaubensquellen.
H14   Freiburg im Breisgau, Herder, 1899.
     v, 69 p. 20cm.

     1. Devil--Bible teaching. I. Title.

257

CATALOGUE OF THE CORNELL WITCHCRAFT COLLECTION

Witchcraft
BF 1584 S97 H14+
Hagenbach, Karl Rudolf, 1801-1874.
Die Basler Hexenprozesse in dem 16ten und 17ten Jahrhundert. Einladungsschrift zu der Rede des zeit. Rector magn., K. R. Hagenbach, welche Donnerstags, den 24. September 1840, Morgens 10 Uhr in der Aula gehalten werden wird, von Fr. Fischer. Basel, Schweighauser'sche Universitätsbuchdruckerei [1840?]
23 p. 26cm.

1. Trials (Witchcraft)--Basel. I. Title. II. Fischer, Friedrich, 1801-1853.

Haggebher Philaleethees, pseud.
see
Hooght, Everard van der, d. 1716.

Hagh, Catharina.
WITCHCRAFT
BX 2340 P33
Keussen, Hermann, 1862-
Zwei Hexenprozesse aus der Crefelder Gegend.
(In: Historischer Verein für den Niederrhein. Annalen. Köln. 23cm. No.63 (1897) p. 111-119)
With, in the same issue: Pauls, Emil. Der Exorcismus an Herzog Johann Wilhelm von Jülich in den Jahren 1604 und 1605.

8 NIC
1. Trials (Witchcraft)--Krefeld, Ger. 2. Hagh, Catharina. 3. Blex, Sibilla. 4. Bleick, Anna.

Hahn, Benedict, respondent.
Witchcraft
BF 1445 D61 no.8
Gerhard, Johann Ernst, 1621-1668, praeses.
Spectrum Endoreum, ex I. Sam. 28. Auspice numine summo, sub praesidio ... Johannis Eernesti Gerhardi ... Publicae eruditorum disquisitioni expositum, ab autore & respondente Benedicto Hahn ... ed. tertia auctior & ememdatior. Jenae, Literis Johannis Nisii, 1684.
112 p. 21cm.
No. 8 in vol. lettered Dissertationes de spectris. 1646-1753.

8   (Continued on next card)

Witchcraft
BF 1575 H16
Hale, John, 1636-1700.
A modest enquiry into the nature of witchcraft, and how persons guilty of that crime may be convicted: and the means used for their discovery discussed, both negatively and affirmatively, according to Scripture and experience. By John Hale, pastor of the Church of Christ in Beverley, anno Domini 1697 ... Boston in N.E., Printed by B. Green and J. Allen, for B. Eliot, 1702.
176 p. 15cm.
"An epistle to the reader," p. 3-7, signed: John Higginson, pastor of the church of Salem.
(Continued on next card)

Witchcraft
BF 1575 H16
Hale, John, 1636-1700. A modest enquiry into the nature of witchcraft, ... 1702. (Card 2)
Imperfect: t.p., 7 l. at beginning and 3 l. at end lacking; supplied in ms.

I. Title.

Hale, Sir Matthew

Witchcraft
BF 1563 H16
Hale, Sir Matthew, 1609-1676.
A collection of modern relations of matter of fact, concerning witches & witchcraft upon the persons of people. To which is prefixed a meditation concerning the mercy of God, in preserving us from the malice and power of evil angels. Written ... upon occasion of a trial of several witches ... Part I. London, Printed for J. Harris, 1693.
64 p. 20cm.
Wing H224.
No more published?
1. Witchcraft--England. I. Title.

Witchcraft
K H16P7 1716
Hale, Sir Matthew, 1609-1676.
Pleas of the crown: or, A methodical summary of the principal matters relating to that subject. By Sir Matthew Hale ... 5th ed. To which are now added, several hundred references, never before printed, to the ancient and modern books of the law. Also three other treatises by the same author; viz. Of the sheriff's accompts, Trial of witches, (before him) and Provisions for the poor. [London] in the Savoy, Printed by J. N., assignee of E. Sayer, for D. Brown, J. Walthoe [etc.] 1716.
9 p. l., 272, [8], 143 p. 19½cm.
(Continued on next card)   16-9199

Witchcraft
K H16P7 1716
Hale, Sir Matthew, 1609-1676.
Pleas of the crown: or, A methodical summary of the principal matters relating to that subject. By Sir Matthew Hale ... 5th ed. To which are now added, several hundred references, never before printed, to the ancient and modern books of the law. Also three other treatises by the same author; viz. Of the sheriff's accompts, Trial of witches, (before him) and Provisions for the poor. [London] in the Savoy, Printed by J. N., assignee of E. Sayer, for D. Brown, J. Walthoe [etc.] 1716.
9 p. l., 272, [8], 143 p. 19½cm.
(Continued on next card)   16-9199

Witchcraft
K H16P7 1716
Hale, Sir Matthew, 1609-1676. Pleas of the crown ... 1716. (Card 2)
Interleaved.
Each of the three treatises has special t.-p.

1. Pleas of the crown. I. Hale, Sir Matthew, 1609-1676. [A short treatise touching sheriffs accompts. II. Hale, Sir Matthew, 1609-1676. [A tryal of witches. III. Hale, Sir Matthew, 1609-1676. [A discourse touching provision for the poor.
16-9199
Library of Congress

Witchcraft
BF 1581 Z7 1664b
Hale, Sir Matthew, 1609-1676.
A short treatise touching sheriffs accompts. Written by the Honourable Sir Matthew Hale, kt. ... To which is added, A tryal of witches, at the assizes held at Bury St. Edmonds, for the county of Suffolk, on the 19th of March 1664, before the said Sir Matthew Hale, kt. London, Printed, and are to be sold by Will. Shrowsbery, 1683.
4 p. l., 110 p., 2 l., 59 p. 19cm.
Signatures: A⁴, B-H⁸ (last leaf blank) 2 leaves unsigned, B-D⁸, E⁶.
(Continued on next card)

Witchcraft
BF 1581 Z7 1664b
Hale, Sir Matthew, 1609-1676. A short treatise touching sheriffs accompts...1683... (Card 2)
"A tryal of witches, at the assizes held at Bury St. Edmonds ... London, Printed for William Shrewsbery, 1682" (with special t.-p.): 2 l., 59 p. at end.

1. Sheriffs--Gt. Brit. 2. Finance--Gt. Brit. Accounting. 3. Money--Gt. Brit. 4. Witchcraft--Gt. Brit. I. A tryal of witches, at the assizes held at Bury St. Edmonds for the county of Suffolk: on the tenth day of March, 1664... London, 1682. II. Title.
Wing H 260.

Witchcraft
BF 1581 Z7 1664a
Hale, Sir Matthew, 1609-1676.
Trial of witches, at the Bury assizes, March 10, 1762 [i.e. 1664] before Sir Matthew Hale ... Rose Cullender and Amy Duny ... were severally indicted for bewitching Elizabeth and Anne Durent ... and ... pleaded not guilty. [n.p., 1762?]
57-64 p. 21cm.
Reprinted from the original ed. of 1682; evidently detached from a periodical
(Continued on next card)

Witchcraft
BF 1581 Z7 1664a
Hale, Sir Matthew, 1609-1676.
Trial of witches ... [1762?] (Card 2)
(printed 1762?) but has no identification except paging and "Vol. III" at bottom of p. 57.

1. Cullender, Rose, fl. 1664. 2. Duny, Amy, fl. 1664. I. Title.

Witchcraft
BF 1581 Z7 1664
Hale, Sir Matthew, 1609-1676.
A tryal of witches, at the assizes held at Bury St. Edmonds for the county of Suffolk, on the tenth day of March, 1664, before Sir Matthew Hale Kt., then lord chief baron of His Majesties court of Exchequer. Taken by a person then attending the court. London, Printed for W. Shrewsbury, 1682.
59 p. 17cm.
Wing T 2240.

258

CATALOGUE OF THE CORNELL WITCHCRAFT COLLECTION

Witchcraft
BF
1563
T75
    Hale, Sir Matthew, 1609-1676.
       A tryal of witches, at the assizes held at Bury St. Edmonds for the county of Suffolk; on the tenth day of March, 1664, before Sir Matthew Hale ... Reprinted verbatim from the original edition of 1682. With an appendix by C. Clark, esq., of Great Totham, Essex. London, J. R. Smith, 1838.
       28 p. 23cm.
       No. 3 in vol. lettered Tracts on witchcraft.
       1. Trials (Witchcraft)--England.
       II. Cullender, Rose, fl. 1664.
       III. Duny, Amy, fl. 1664.

Hale, Sir Matthew, 1609-1676.
A tryal of witches.

Witchcraft
K
H16P7
1716
    Hale, Sir Matthew, 1609-1676.
       Pleas of the crown: or, A methodical summary of the principal matters relating to that subject. By Sir Matthew Hale ... 5th ed. To which are now added, several hundred references, never before printed, to the ancient and modern books of the law. Also three other treatises by the same author; viz. Of the sheriff's accompts, Trial of witches, (before him) and Provisions for the poor. London, in the Savoy, Printed by J. N., assignee of E. Sayer, for D. Brown, J. Walthoe [etc.] 1716.
       9 p. l., 272, [8], 143 p. 19¼cm.
       16-9199

Witchcraft
BF
1521
H17
    Hall, Frederic Thomas.
       The pedigree of the devil. ... London, Trübner, 1883.
       xv, 256 p. illus. 22cm.

       1. Devil. I. Title.

Hall, Mary, fl. 1664.

Witchcraft
R
42
6
3
no.15
    Drage, William, 1637?-1669.
       A relation of Mary Hall of Gadsden, reputed to be possessed of two devils, 1664, from "A small treatise of sicknesses and diseases from witchcraft," appended to "Physical experiments," by William Drage, London. Printed for Miller at the Star next the George in Little Britain [1668] With an introductory by W. B. Gerish. Bishop's Stortford, 1912.
       28 p. 22cm. [Hertfordshire folk lore. no. 15]

       1. Demonomania. 2. Hall, Mary, fl. 1664. I. Gerish, William Blyth, ed.
       16-25740

Witchcraft
F
1555
H8
    Hallager, Frederik, 1816-1876.
       Magister Ole Bjørn og de besatte i Thisted. København, Dansk Sundhedstidendes Forlag, 1901.
       188 p. 21cm.

       1. Bjørn, Ole, b. 1648. 2. Demonology. 3. Exorcism. I. Title.

Hallager, Morton, 1740-1803, tr.

Witchcraft
BF
1565
M54
1800
    Mentzel, Andreas.
       Om Hexemestere, Troldqvinder, Spøgelser, Gjengangere, Spaamaend, Forvarsler og Sandsigere. En Bog for Almuen ... Oversat af det Tydske ved M. Hallager. Kjøbenhavn, Malling, 1800.
       2 p. l., 39 p. 21cm.
       Translation of part of his Gespräche, Fabeln und Erzählungen für niedre Schulen.
       1. Witchcraft. 2. Occult sciences. I. His Gespräche, Fabeln und Erzählungen für niedre Schulen. II. Hallager, Morton, 1740-1803, tr. III. Title.

Witchcraft
PR
1259
W81
H62+
    Halliwell-Phillipps, James Orchard, 1820-1889.
       Heywood, Thomas, d. 1641.
       The poetry of witchcraft illustrated by copies of the plays on the Lancashire witches by Heywood and Shadwell. Reprinted under the direction of James O. Halliwell. Brixton Hill, Printed for priv. circ. only, 1853.
       238 p. 29cm.

       Eighty copies printed.
       Each play has also separate t.p.

       (Continued on next card)

Witchcraft
PR
1259
W81
H62+
    Halliwell-Phillipps, James Orchard, 1820-1889.
       Heywood, Thomas, d. 1641. The poetry of witchcraft... 1853. (Card 2)
       Contents.--The Lancashire witches and Tegue o Divelly, the Irish priest, by Thomas Shadwell.--The late Lancashire witches, by Thomas Heywood and Richard Broome.
       I. Halliwell-Phillipps, James Orchard, 1820-1889. II. Shadwell, Thomas, 1642?-1692. The Lancashire witches and Tegue o Divelly. III. His The late Lancashire witches. IV. Broome Richard, d. 1652? The late Lancashire witches. V. Title.

Hallucinations.

Witchcraft
BF
1052
B85
1853
    Brierre de Boismont, Alexandre Jacques François, 1798-1881.
       Hallucinations: or, The rational history of apparitions, visions, dreams, ecstasy, magnetism, and somnambulism. By A. Brierre de Boismont ... 1st American, from the 2d enl. and improved Paris ed. Philadelphia, Lindsay and Blakiston, 1853.
       xx, [17]-553 p. 20cm.

       1. Hallucinations and illusions. I. Title.
       Library of Congress   BF1052.B8 1853
       [28b1]   20-8491

Witchcraft
BF
1521
H19
    Hallywell, Henry, b. ca. 1630.
       Melampronoea: or, A discourse of the polity and kingdom of darkness. Together with a solution of the chiefest objections brought against the being of witches ... London, Printed for Walter Kettilby, 1681.
       [16], 118 p. 15cm.
       2 copies

       1. Demonology. 2. Witchcraft. I. Title. II. Title: The polity and kingdom of darkness.

Hamberger, Georg Erhard, 1697-1755, respondent.

WITCHCRAFT
BT
960
R53
    Richter, David, of Güstrow, praeses.
       Qvadriga dispp. [i.e. disputationum] magico-thevrgicarum de conciliatione spirituvm, oder: Von der Kunst sich mit Geistern bekant zu machen, qvam svb praesidio Davidis Richteri habvervnt Henr. Andr. Mätcke et Georg. Erhard. Hambergervs. Jena, J. B. Heller, 1716.
       86 p. 20cm.

       (Continued on next card)

Witchcraft
GR
825
H21
    Hamel, Frank.
       Human animals. London, W. Rider, 1915.
       xii, 301 p. 23cm.

       1. Animal lore. 2. Occult sciences. I. Title.

Witchcraft
BF
1410
B42
Z56
v.3
no.22
    [Hamer, Petrus] 1646-1716.
       Den swadder, die E. W. op Cartesianen en Coccejanen geworpen heeft, in sijn twee deelen van Aardige duivelarye zuiver af-gevaagt, met een het geschil dat Dr. Bekker ongegrond opwerpt, als of daimoon, &c. niet wel duivel overgezet wierd, kortelijk voldongen, en in staat van wijzen gebracht, door Iiratiel Leetsosoneus. Amsterdam, By G. Borstius, boekverkooper, 1692.
       2 p. l., 42 p. title and other vignettes, illus. initia 1s. 20 x 15cm.

       (Continued on next card)

Witchcraft
BF
1410
B42
Z56
v.3
no.22
    [Hamer, Petrus] 1646-1716. Den swadder, die E. W. op Cartesianen en Coccejanen geworpen heeft ... 1692. (Card 2)
       4°: *², A-E⁴, F1.
       Van der Linde 172.
       No. 22 in vol. lettered Bekker III.
       1. Walten, Ericus, 1663-1697. Aardige duyvelary. 2. Bekker, Balthasar, 1634-1698. De betoverde weereld. I. Title.

Witchcraft
BF
1410
B42
Z82
no.2
    Hamer, Petrus, 1646-1716. Voorlooper tot de volstrekte wederlegginge van het gene de heeren, Orchard, Daillon en Bekker hebben aen het licht gebragt; aengaende de werken, en macht der geesten: en met name der duivelen. Door Petrus Hamer, dienaer Jesus Christi in Numansdorp. Uitgegeven na kerken-ordre. Met belofte refutatoir van zekeren Brief aen een regent van Amsteldam. Dato 18 Maij 1692. Dordrecht, By C. Wilgaarts, boekverkooper, 1692.
       4 p. l., 40 p. title vignette, illus.
       (Continued on next card)

Witchcraft
BF
1410
B42
Z82
no.2
    Hamer, Petrus, 1646-1716. Voorlooper tot de volstrekte wederlegginge van... Orchard, Daillon en Bekker ... 1692. (Card 2)
       initials. 20 x 15cm.
       4°: *⁴, A-E⁴.
       Van der Linde 95.
       No. 2 in vol. lettered Over Bekkers Betoverde wereld. 1692.
       1. Orchard, N   , supposed author. The doctrine of devils. 2. Daillon, Benjamin de. Examen de l'opression
       (Continued on next card)

Witchcraft
BF
1410
B42
Z82
no.2
    Hamer, Petrus, 1646-1716. Voorlooper tot de volstrekte wederlegginge van ... Orchard, Daillon en Bekker ... 1692. (Card 3)
       des reformez en France. 3. Bekker, Balthasar, 1634-1698. De betoverde weereld. 4. Walten, Ericus, 1663-1697. Brief aan een regent der Stad Amsterdam. I. Title.

Witchcraft
BF
1410
B42
Z56
v.2
no.20
    Hamer, Petrus, 1646-1716. Voorlooper tot de volstrekte wederlegginge van het gene de heeren, Orchard, Daillon en Bekker hebben aen het licht gebragt; aengaende de werken, en macht der geesten: en met name der duivelen. Door Petrus Hamer, dienaer Jesus Christi in Numansdorp. Uitgegeven na kerken-ordre. Met belofte refutatoir van zekeren Brief aen een regent van Amsteldam. Dato 18 Maij 1692. Dordrecht, By C. Wilgaarts, Boekverkooper, 1692.
       4 p.l., 40 p. title vignette, illus.
       (Continued on next card)

CATALOGUE OF THE CORNELL WITCHCRAFT COLLECTION

Witchcraft
BF 1410 B42 Z56 v.2 no.20
Hamer, Petrus, 1646-1716. Voorlooper tot de volstrekte wederlegginge van... Orchard, Daillon en Bekker ... 1692. (Card 2)
initials. 19 x 15 cm.
4º: *⁴, A-E⁴.
Van der Linde 95.
No. 20 in vol. lettered Bekker II.

Hamer, Steffan.
MSS Bd. WITCHCRAFT BF E735
Ein Erschröcklich Geschicht vom Tewfel und einer Unhulden, beschehen zu Schilta bey Rotweil in der Karwochen MDXXXIII. Jar. [n.p., 1533? ca. 1900]
2 l. 19cm.
Carnap's manuscript copy.
"Originaldruck in der Stadtbibliothek zu Zürich. 1 Bl. Fol."
At end: Steffan hamer, Briefmaler.
1. Exempla.   2. Devil.   I. Hamer, Steffan.

Witchcraft
PT 2290 H35 G2 1845
[Hammer-Purgstall, Joseph, Freiherr von] 1774-1856.
Die Gallerinn auf der Rieggersburg. Historischer Roman mit Urkunden. Von einem Steiermärker. Darmstadt, Carl Wilhelm Leske, 1845.
3 v. fronts. 22cm.
Contents.--1. T. Die Jungfrau und das Erbfräulein.--2. T. Die Huldigung und die Verschwörung.--3. T. Der Hexenprozess.
I. Title.

Witchcraft
BF 1775 H22
[Hammond, Henry] 1605-1660.
Of svperstition. ... Oxford, Printed by Henry Hall, Printer to the Universitie, 1645.
25 p. 19cm.
Wing H 566.
1. Superstition.   I. Title.

Witchcraft
BT 965 S25
Hamond, George, ed.
Saunders, Richard, d. 1692.
Ἀγγελογραφία sive Πνεύματα λειτυργικά, Pneumatologia: or, A discourse of angels: their nature and office, or ministry ... Also something touching devils and apparitions and impulses. With ... doctrine of angels ... London, Printed for T. Parkhurst, 1701.
314, [2] p. 21cm.
Preface signed: Geo. Hamond.
Publisher's advertisement: p. [315-316]
Title transliterated: Angelographia sive Pneumata leitourgika ...

A handbook on witches.

Witchcraft
BF 1566 T58
Tindall, Gillian.
A handbook on witches. London, A. Barker [1965]
156 p. illus. 23cm.
1. Witchcraft.   I. Title.

Witchcraft
BF 1589 H23
Handschriftliche Schätze aus Kloster-Bibliotheken: Hauptwerke über Magie, verborgene Kräfte, Offenbarungen und geheimste Wissenschaften; ein Beitrag zum Aberglauben früherer Jahrhunderte. Köln, L. M. Glogau Sohn, 1734.
476 p. illus. 17cm.
1. Witchcraft.   2. Cabala.   3. Occult sciences.

BF 1576 H24
Hansen, Chadwick, 1926-
Witchcraft at Salem. New York, G. Braziller [1969]
xvii, 252 p. 22 cm. 6.95
Includes bibliographical references.
1. Witchcraft--Salem, Mass.   I. Title.
BF1576.H26   133.4   69-15825
Library of Congress   MARC

WITCHCRAFT
DD 741 W52 v.26 no.4
Hansen, Joseph, 1862-1943.
Der Hexenhammer, seine Bedeutung und die gefälschte Kölner Approbation vom Jahre 1487.
(In: Westdeutsche Zeitschrift für Geschichte und Kunst. Trier. 24cm. v.26 (1907) no.4. p. 372-404)
8 NIC
I. Institoris, Henricus, d.1508. Malleus maleficarum.   V. Title.

WITCHCRAFT
BF 1566 H24 I5
Hansen, Joseph, 1862-1943.
Inquisition und Hexenverfolgung im Mittelalter. [München, 1898]
[385]-432 p. 23cm.
Detached from Historische Zeitschrift, 81. Bd., 3. Heft (1898)
1. Witchcraft--History.   2. Inquisition.   I. Title.
8 NIC

WITCHCRAFT
DD 741 W52 v.27 no.2/3
Hansen, Joseph, 1862-1943.
Die Kontroverse über den Hexenhammer und seine Kölner Approbation vom Jahre 1487.
(In: Westdeutsche Zeitschrift für Geschichte und Kunst. Trier. 24cm. v.27 (1908) no.2/3. p.366-372)
8 NIC
I. Institoris, Henricus, d.1508. Malleus maleficarum.   V. Title.

WITCHCRAFT
DD 741 W52 v.17 no.2
Hansen, Joseph, 1862-1943.
Der Malleus maleficarum, seine Druckausgaben und die gefälschte Kölner Approbation vom J. 1487.
(In: Westdeutsche Zeitschrift für Geschichte und Kunst. Trier. 24cm. v.17 (1898) no.2. p. 119-168)
8 NIC
I. Institoris, Henricus, d.1508. Malleus maleficarum.   V. Title.

WITCHCRAFT
BF 1569 A2 I595
Hansen, Joseph, 1862-1943.
Der Malleus maleficarum, seine Druckausgaben und die gefälschte Kölner Approbation vom J. 1487. [Trier, 1898]
[119]-168 p. 23cm.
2 copies
Caption title.
"Sonder-Abdruck aus Westdeutsche Zeitschrift für Geschichte und Kunst." [Bd. 17, Heft 2, 1898]
8 NIC
1. Institoris, Henricus, d. 1508. Malleus maleficarum.   I. Title.

Witchcraft
BF 1569 H24
Hansen, Joseph, 1862-1943.
Quellen und Untersuchungen zur Geschichte des Hexenwahns und der Hexenverfolgung im Mittelalter. Mit einer Untersuchung der Geschichte des Wortes Hexe, von Johannes Franck. Bonn, C. Georgi, 1901.
xi, 703 p. illus. 24cm.
I. Franck, Johannes, 1854-   II. Title.

BF 1569 H24 1963
Hansen, Joseph, 1862-1943.
Quellen und Untersuchungen zur Geschichte des Hexenwahns und der Hexenverfolgung im Mittelalter. Mit einer Untersuchung der Geschichte des Wortes Hexe, von Johannes Franck. Hildesheim, G. Olms, 1963.
xi, 703 p. illus. 24cm.
"Reprografischer Nachdruck der Ausgabe Bonn 1901."
1. Witchcraft--Hist.   2. Magic--Hist.
I. Franck, Johannes, 1854-   II. Title.

WITCHCRAFT
BF 1566 H24
Hansen, Joseph, 1862-1943.
Zauberwahn, inquisition und hexenprozess im mittelalter und die entstehung der grossen hexenverfolgung. Von Joseph Hansen. München und Leipzig, R. Oldenbourg, 1900.
xv, 538 p. 22cm. (Historische bibliothek. 12. bd.)
1. Witchcraft--History.   2. Inquisition.
8 NIC   3. Trials (Witchcraft)--History.   I. Title.   II. Series.
Library of Congress, no.

BF 1582 B35H2
Hantises et diableries dans la terre abbatiale de Luxeuil.
Bavoux, Francis, 1896-
Hantises et diableries dans la terre abbatiale de Luxeuil; d'un procès de l'Inquisition (1529) à l'épidémie démoniaque de 1628-1630. Préface de Lucien Febvre. Monaco, Éditions du Rocher [1956]
vii, 200 p. illus., maps. 24cm. (Folklore)
1. Witchcraft--France--Luxeuil.   I. Title.

WITCHCRAFT
BF 1565 H25
Harbach, Laurentio de
Gründtlicher Bericht, die von Hexerey vnd Zauberey zu dieser Zeit, sehr nothwendige drey Hauptfragen betreffend ... Mit gutem Bedacht zusammen getragen vnd der Welt Vrtheil heim gestellet, von Laurentio de Harbach ... [n. p.,] 1630.
[15] p. 19cm.
1. Witchcraft.   I. Title.
8

CATALOGUE OF THE CORNELL WITCHCRAFT COLLECTION

Witchcraft
BF
1583
A2
D23

Hardevvici à Dassell j.c. Responsvm juris, in causa poenali maleficarum Winsiensium.

Dassell, Artwig von.
Hardevvici à Dassell j.c. Responsvm juris, in causa poenali maleficarum VVinsiensium. Pro defensione innoxiarvm, et condemnatione nocentum; ne quisquam ante judicium injuste innocenterq condemnetur; ad requisitionem quorundam Dominorum & amicorum, juris justitiaeq; amantium, conscriptum ... Hamburgi, Theodosius VVolderus, 1597.
[96] p. 17cm.
Title in red and black.
1. Trials (Witchcraft)--Germany. I. Title: Responsum juris, in causa poenali maleficarum Winsiensium.

8

Witchcraft
PA
8555
N59F7
1692

Hardt, Hermann von der, 1660-1746, ed.
Nider, Johannes, d. 1438.
De visionibus ac revelationibus opus rarissimum Historiis Germaniae refertissimum, Anno 1517. Argentinae editum. Auspiciis... Rudolphi Augusti, Brunsvicens. ac Luneburg. Ducis, luci & integritati restitutum, recensente Hermanno von der Hardt ... Helmestadii, Impensis Pauli Zeisingii, Typis Salomonis Schnorrii, 1692.
[30], 669 p. front. 17cm.
A reprint, under a new title, of Nider's
(Continued on next card)

Witchcraft
PA
8555
N59F7
1692

Hardt, Hermann von der, 1660-1746, ed.
Nider, Johannes, d. 1438. De visionibus ... 1692. (Card 2)
Formicarius.
"Liber quintus: De maleficis & eorum deceptionibus": p. 514-669.
Ex libris Kurt Seligmann.
1. Conduct of life. 2. Christian life. 3. Witchcraft. 4. Demonology. I. Hardt, Hermann von der, 1660-1746, ed. II. Nider, Johannes, d. 1438. Formicarius. III. Title. IV. Title: Formicarius.

DA
670
L2
H28

Harland, John, 1806-1868.
Lancashire legends, traditions, pageants, sports, etc., with an appendix containing a rare tract on the Lancashire witches, etc., etc., by J. Harland and T. T. Wilkinson. London, G. Routledge, 1873.
xxxv, 283 p. illus. 20cm.
1. Lancashire, Eng.--Soc. life & customs. 2. Folk-lore--England--Lancashire. I. Wilkinson, T T joint author. II. Title.

Witchcraft
BF
1563
H86

Harris, Elizabeth, d. 1645.
The examination, confession, triall, and execution, of Joane Williford, Joan Cariden, and Jane Hott, who were executed at Feversham in Kent, for being witches, on Munday the 29 of September 1645... Taken by the major of Feversham and jurors for the said inquest. With the examination and confession of Elizabeth Harris, not yet executed. All attested under the hand of Robert Greenstreet, major of Feversham. London, Printed for J. G., 1645.
(Continued on next card)

Witchcraft
BF
1563
H86

Harris, Elizabeth, d. 1645.
The examination, confession, triall, and execution ... 1645. (Card 2)
6 p. 19cm.
No. 5 in vol. lettered: Tracts of witches.
1. Witchcraft. 2. Williford, Joane, d. 1645. 3. Cariden, Joan, d. 1645. 4. Hott, Jane, d. 1645. 5. Harris, Elizabeth, d. 1645.

Witchcraft
BF
1575
C14
H31+

Harris, William Samuel, 1861-
Robert Calef, "Merchant, of Boston, in New England."
(In Granite monthly. Manchester, N. H. 26cm. v. 39 (1907) p. [157]-163])
1. Calef, Robert, 1648-1719. I. Title.

Witchcraft
GR
142
H6
A3
no.2

Harrison, Anne, d. 1606.
The severall practices of Johane Harrison and her daughter, condemned and executed at Hartford for witchcraft, the 4th August last, 1606. Reprinted from the only known copy, with an introduction by W. B. Gerish. [Bishop's Stortford?] 1909.
15 p. 22cm. [Hertfordshire folk lore. no. 2]
The original pamphlet is in 2 parts and is entitled: The most cruell and
(Continued on next card)

Witchcraft
GR
142
H6
A3
no.2

Harrison, Anne, d. 1606.
The severall practices of Johane Harrison ... 1909. (Card 2)
bloody murther committed by ... Annis Dell ... With the several witchcrafts and most damnable practises of one Johane Harrison and her daughter ... London, Printed for W. Ferebrand and J. Wright, 1606.

BF
1521
J28
1924

Harrison, George Bagshawe, 1894- ed.
James I, king of Great Britain, 1566-1625.
King James, the First: Daemonologie (1597). Newes from Scotland, declaring the damnable life and death of Doctor Fian, a notable sorcerer who was burned at Edenbrough in Ianuary last (1591) London, J. Lane; New York, Dutton [1924]
xv, 81, 29 p. illus. 19cm. (The Bodley Head quartos, no. 9)
With facsimiles of original title pages.
Newes from Scotland has been ascribed to James Carmichael, minister of Haddington. Cf. Sir James Melville, Memories, p. 195, and D. Webster, Collection of tracts on witchcraft, etc., 1820, p. 38.

Witchcraft
BF
1581
P87T8
1929

Harrison, George Bagshawe, 1894- , ed.
[Potts, Thomas] fl. 1612-1618.
The trial of the Lancaster witches A.D. MDCXII, edited with an introduction by G. B. Harrison. London, P. Davies, 1929.
xlvi p., 1 l., 188 p. 1 illus. 21½cm.
With reproduction of original t.-p.: The wonderfvll discoverie of witches in the covntie of Lancaster ... Together with the arraignement and triall of Iennet Preston, at the assizes holden at the Castle of Yorke ... By Thomas Potts ... London, 1613.
"The arraignement and triall of Iennet Preston" has special t.-p. with imprint: London, 1612.
Revised by Sir Edward Bromley.

Witchcraft
GR
142
H6
A3
no.2

Harrison, Johanna, d. 1606.
The severall practices of Johane Harrison and her daughter, condemned and executed at Hartford for witchcraft, the 4th August last, 1606. Reprinted from the only known copy, with an introduction by W. B. Gerish. [Bishop's Stortford?] 1909.
15 p. 22cm. [Hertfordshire folk lore. no. 2]
The original pamphlet is in 2 parts and is entitled: The most cruell and
(Continued on next card)

Witchcraft
GR
142
H6
A3
no.2

Harrison, Johanna, d. 1606.
The severall practices of Johane Harrison ... 1909. (Card 2)
bloody murther committed by ... Annis Dell ... With the several witchcrafts and most damnable practises of one Johane Harrison and her daughter ... London, Printed for W. Ferebrand and J. Wright, 1606.

BF
1566
H31

Harrison, Michael.
The roots of witchcraft. [London] Muller [1973]
278 p. illus. 24 cm.
Bibliography: p. 265-269.

1. Witchcraft--History. I. Title

NIC APR 11, '74 COOxc 74-152852

WITCHCRAFT
BF
1445
L39
1596

Harrison, Robert, d. 1585?, tr.
Lavater, Ludwig, 1527-1586.
Of ghostes and spirites, walking by night, and of strange noyses, crackes, and sundrie forewarnings, which commonly happen before the death of men: great slaughters, and alterations of kingdomes. One booke, written by Lewes Lauaterus of Tigurine. And translated into English by R. H. [i.e., Robert Harrison] London, Imprinted by Thomas Creede, 1596.
10 p. l., 220 p. 18cm.
(Continued on next card)

8

WITCHCRAFT
BF
1445
L39
1596

Harrison, Robert, d. 1585?, tr.
Lavater, Ludwig, 1527-1586. Of ghostes and spirites, walking by night ... 1596. (Card 2)
Imperfect copy: p. 217-220 wanting.
Translation of De spectris, lemuribus et magnis atque insolitis fragoribus.
STC 15321.
Armorial bookplate: Holland House.
1. Apparitions. 2. Ghosts. 3. Demonology. I. His De spectris, lemuribus et magnis atque insolitis fragoribus. English. II. Harrison, Robert, d. 1585?, tr. III. Title.

8

Witchcraft
BF
1581
H32
1605

[Harsnett, Samuel] archbishop of York, 1561-1631.
A declaration of egregious Popish impostures, to with-draw the harts of His Maiesties subiects from their allegeance, and from the truth of Christian religion professed in England, vnder the pretence of casting out of deuils. Practised by Edmunds, alias VVeston, a Iesuit, & diuers Romish priestes his vvicked associates. Where-vnto are annexed the copies of the confessions, & examinations of the parties themselues, which were pretended to
(Continued on next card)

Witchcraft
BF
1581
H32
1605

[Harsnett, Samuel] archbishop of York, 1561-1631. A declaration of egregious Popish impostures ... 1605. (Card 2)
be possessed and dispossessed: taken vppon oath before His Maiesties commissioners, for causes ecclesiasticall. Barbican [London] Newly printed by Ia. Roberts, 1605.
284 p. 19cm.
Epistle "To the sedvced Catholiques of England" signed: S.H.
1. Edmonds, William, 1550?-1616. I. Title.

261

CATALOGUE OF THE CORNELL WITCHCRAFT COLLECTION

Witchcraft
BF
1581
H32D6
  [Harsnett, Samuel] archbishop of York, 1561-1631.
  [A discovery of the fraudulent practises of John Darrell, bacheler of artes, in his proceedings concerning the pretended possession and dispossession of William Somers at Nottingham; of Thomas Darling, the boy of Burton at Caldwell; and of Katherine Wright at Mansfield, and Whittington; and of his dealings with one Mary Couper at Nottingham, detecting in some sort the deceitful trade in these latter dayes of casting out deuils.
  (Continued on next card)

Witchcraft
BF
1581
H32D6
  [Harsnett, Samuel] archbishop of York, 1561-1631. [A discovery of the fraudulent practises of John Darrell ... [1599]
  (Card 2)
  London, 1599]
  [328] p. 18cm.
  Epistle to the reader signed: S. H.
  Imperfect: t.-p. mounted, part of it missing; title taken from Halkett & Laing; pages cropped; numbers missing from 324-[328].
  1. Darrell, John, fl. 1562-1602. I. Title. II. S. H. III. H., S.

Witchcraft
BF
1581
H32D61
  Harsnett, Samuel, abp. of York, 1561-1631. A discovery of the fraudulent practices of John Darrell.
  [Darrell, John] fl. 1562-1602.
  A detection of that sinnfvl shamfvl lying and ridicvlovs discovrs, of Samvel Harshnet, entitvled: A discoverie of the fravvdvlent practises of Iohn Darrell. Wherein is manifestly and apparantly shewed in the eyes of the world, not only the vnlikelihoode, but the flate impossibilitie of the pretended counterfayting of William Somers, Thomas Darling, Kath. Wright, and Mary Couper; together with the other 7.   in Lancashire, and the
  (Continued on next card)

Witchcraft
BF
1581
H32D61
  Harsnett, Samuel, abp. of York, 1561-1631. A discovery of the fraudulent practices of John Darrell.
  [Darrell, John] fl. 1562-1602. A detection of ... discovrs of Samvel Harshnet ...
  (Card 2)
  supposed teaching of them by the saide Iohn Darrell. [London] 1600.
  208, [3] p. 19cm.
  1. Harsnett, Samuel, abp. of York, 1561-1631. A discovery of the fraudulent practices of John Darrell. 2. Witchcraft--Lancashire. I. Title.

BF
1566
H32
  Hart, Roger.
  Witchcraft. London, Wayland Publishers [1971]
  128 p. illus., facsims., port. 24 cm. Index. (The Wayland documentary history series)
  Bibliography: p. 123.
  B 72-14448
  1. Witchcraft. I. Title.
  BF1566.H37   133.4'094   73-539830
  ISBN 0-85340-150-0   MARC
  Library of Congress   71 [2]

Witchcraft
BF
1639
H32+
  Hart, William Henry, d. 1888.
  Observations on some documents relating to magic in the reign of Queen Elizabeth. Communicated to the Society of Antiquaries by W. H. Hart, esq. F.S.A. London, Printed by J. B. Nichols, 1867.
  9 p. 30cm.
  1. Alchemy. 2. Witchcraft--England. I. Society of Antiquaries of London. II. Title: Magic in the reign of Queen Elizabeth.
  8

Witchcraft
GR
142
H6
A3
no.8
  The **Hartfordshire** wonder; or, Strange news from Ware. Being an exact and true relation of one Jane Stretton, the daughter of Thomas Stretton of Ware in the county of Herts, who hath been visited in a strange kind of manner by extraordinary and unusual fits, her abstaining from sustenance for the space of 9 months, being haunted by imps or devils in the form of several creatures here described, the parties adjudged of all by whom she was thus tormented and the occasion thereof ...
  (Continued on next card)   17-20383

Witchcraft
GR
142
H6
A3
no.8
  The **Hartfordshire** wonder ... (Card 2)
  London: printed for J. Clark ... 1669. Reprinted with an introductory note by W. B. Gerish. Bishop's Stortford. 1908.
  15 p. 22cm. (Hertfordshire folk lore. no. 8)
  Preface signed: M. J.
  1. Stretton, Jane, b. 1649. 2. Witchcraft--England. I. J., M. II. M. J. III. Gerish, William Blyth, ed.
                                      17-20383
  Library of Congress   GR142.H6A3 no. 5

MSS
Bd.
WITCHCRAFT
BF
H32
  Hartlieb, Johann, fl. 1450.
  Dr. Hartlieb's Buch aller verbotenen Kunst, Unglaubens und der Zauberei. [n.p. 1456; 1896]
  153 p. 23cm.
  Carnap's manuscript copy.
  "Wörtlich genaue Abschrift der Handschrift ... in der Herzoglichen Bibliothek zu Wolfenbüttel."
  Numerals in the margins indicate foliation of the original.
  (Continued on next card)

MSS
Bd.
WITCHCRAFT
BF
H32
  Hartlieb, Johann, fl. 1450. Buch aller verbotenen Kunst ... [1456; 1896] (Card 2)
  Between pages 134 and 135 are inserted 5 unnumbered leaves of "Erläuterungen".
  P. 135-153 are copies of short articles on the original work.
  1. Magic. 2. Witchcraft. 3. Devil. I. Title.

Witchcraft
BF
1583
R56
  Hartlieb, Johann, fl. 1450. Buch aller verbotenen Kunst.
  Riezler, Sigmund, Ritter von, 1843-1927.
  Geschichte der Hexenprozesse in Bayern. Im Lichte der gleichzeitigen Entwickelung dargestellt von Sigmund Riezler. Stuttgart, Verlag der J. G. Cotta'schen Buchhandlung Nachf., 1896.
  x, 340 p. 23cm.
  Includes excerpts from Johann Hartliebs Buch aller verbotenen Kunst.

MSS
Bd.
WITCHCRAFT
BF
H33
  Hartmann, Andreas.
  Warhafftige und mit vielen glaubwürdigen Zeugen bewährte Relation was sich zu Döffingen, hoch-fürstl. würtembergischer Herrschafft, und Böblinger Amts, mit zwey besessenen Weibs-Personen im Monat Decembr. 1714, mercklich zugetragen hat ... Ans Licht gebracht von M. Andreas Hartmann ... [n.p.] 1716 [ca. 1900]
  14 l. 18cm.
  Carnap's manuscript copy.
  "Wörtliche   Abschrift aus: Altes und Neues aus   dem Reich Gottes und
  (Continued on next card)

MSS
Bd.
WITCHCRAFT
BF
H33
  Hartmann, Andreas. Warhafftige und mit vielen glaubwürdigen Zeugen bewährte Relation ... 1716 [ca. 1900] (Card 2)
  der übrigen guten und bösen Geister, etc. [hrsg. von J. J. Moser] 9ter Theil. Franckfurt u. Leipzig, 1734. 8°. S. 10-28."
  "NB. Diese Besessenheitsgeschichte steht auch wörtlich in: Guden, Friedrich, Schreckliche Geschichte Teuflischer Besitzung, in 3 merkw. Historien, etc. Budissin, 1717. 8°. S. 159-188."
  1. Demoniac   possession. 2. Exorcism
  (Continued on next card)

MSS
Bd.
WITCHCRAFT
BF
H33
  Hartmann, Andreas. Warhafftige und mit vielen glaubwürdigen Zeugen bewährte Relation ... 1716 [ca. 1900] (Card 3)
  I. Guden, Friedrich, ed. Schreckliche Geschichte teuflischer Besitzung. II. Moser, Johann Jacob, 1701-1785. Altes und Neues aus dem Reich Gottes. III. Title.

Witchcraft
HQ
822
H33
1741
  Hartmann, Johann Zacharias.
  Io. Zachariae Hartmanni ... Commentatio ivridica De conivgibvs incantatis eorvmqve separatione. Von bezauberten Ehe-Leuten, durch Nesselknüpfen, Schloss zuschnappen &c. und derselben Scheidung. Jenae, Ex officina Schilliana, 1741.
  40, 16 p. 22cm.
  Programma D. Ioh. Zach. Hartmanni ... Dispvtationi ivridicae has special t. p., and is paged   separately.
  1. Marri   age--Annulment. 2. Charms. I.   Title: De conjugibus incantatis. II. Title. III. Title: (Over
  8

Witchcraft
HQ
822
H33
1731
  Hartmann, Johann Zacharias, praeses.
  Dispvtatio inavgvralis ivridica De conivgibvs incantatis eorvmqve separatione, Germanice: Von bezauberten Ehe-Leuten und derselben Scheidung, qvam ... svb praesidio ... Io. Zachariae Hartmanni ... pvblico ervditorvm examini svbiicit avctor Ioannes Helvigivs Zielinski ... Ienae, Recvsa per I. B. Hellervm, 1731.
  38, [2] p. 21cm.
  Diss.--Jena   (J. H. Zielinski, respondent, 1727)
  8   (Continued on next card)

Witchcraft
HQ
822
H33
1731
  Hartmann, Johann Zacharias, praeses. Dispvtatio inavgvralis ivridica De conivgibvs incantatis ... 1731. (Card 2)
  1. Marriage--Annulment. 2. Witchcraft. I. Zielinski, Johann Helvigius, respondent. II. Title: De conjugibus incantatis eorumque separatione. III. Title.
  8

WITCHCRAFT
BF
1533
S18
  Hartmann, Peter, preacher.
  [Sambuga, Joseph Anton Franz Martin] 1752-1815.
  Der Teufel, ein Neujahrsgeschenk! Oder Prüfung des Glaubens an höllische Geister, nach der Lehre des hochwürdigen Herrn Peter Hartmann, Predigers zu Altenöting. [München] 1810.
  114 p. 21cm.
  Ascription by Holzmann and Kayser.
  1. Devil. 2. Hartmann, Peter, preach I. Title.
  8

CATALOGUE OF THE CORNELL WITCHCRAFT COLLECTION

DD 491 H34Q3 v.35
Hartmann, Wilhelm.
Die hexenprozesse in der stadt Hildesheim, von Wilhelm Hartmann. Hildesheim und Leipzig, A. Lax, 1927.
3 p. l., 107 p. 24½ᶜᵐ. (Added t.-p.: Quellen und darstellungen zur geschichte Niedersachsens ... bd. 35)

1. Witchcraft—Hildesheim. I. Title.

Library of Congress — DD491.H2Q4 bd.35 — 28-30893
[2]

Hartumim (The word)

Witchcraft
BF 1565 D96
[Durych, Fortunat] 1730-1802.
Eutychii Beniamin Transalbini Dissertatio philologica De vocibus hhartymmim et belahatehem Exod. VII. 2. [Vindobonae?] 1767.
20 p. 21cm.
"Opusculi inscripti: Gedanken über die Werke des Liebhabers der Wahrheit von der Hexerey."

1. Witchcraft in the Bible. 2. Bible. O.T.—Criticism, Textual. 3. Hartumim
8 (Continued on next card)

Hartumim (The word)

Witchcraft
BF 1565 S69
Sonnenfels, Aloysius von
Sendschreiben des hochedelgebohrnen Herrn Aloysius von Sonnenfels ... an den hochgelehrten P. don Ferdinand Sterzinger, ... Über zwey hebräische Wörter chartumim und belahatehem: nachmals zur nothwendigen Belehrung des sogenannten Liebhabers der Wahrheit, und seines lateinischen Eutychii Benjamin Transalbini in ihrem Zauber- und Hexerey Streite zum Drucke befördert, von einem Verehrer des Ster¨ngerischen Namens.
(Continued on next card)

Hartumim (The word)

Witchcraft
BF 1565 S69
Sonnenfels, Aloysius von — Sendschreiben ... 1768. (Card 2)
Wien, Gedruckt mit schulzischen Schriften, 1768.
30, [1] p. 21cm.

1. Witchcraft in the Bible. 2. Bible. O.T.—Criticism, Textual. 3. Hartumim (The word) 4. Belahatehem (The word) 5. Durych, Fortunat, 1730-1802. Eutychii Beniamin Transalbini Dissertatio philologica... 6. März, Agnellus, 1726-1784.
8

WITCHCRAFT
BF 1565 H33 1639
Hartz, Konrad.
Tractatvs criminalis De veneficarum inquisitione Cunradi Hartz ... Editio secunda, priori longe auctiori & emendatiori. Rintelii ad Visvrgim, Typis exscripsit Petrus Lucius typog. acad., 1639.
394, [40] p. 15cm.
Published earlier as his Tractatus ... De reorum, inprimisque veneficarum, inquisitione juridice instituenda.

1. Trials (Witchcraft) 2. Witchcraft. I. His Tractatus ... De reorum, in primisque veneficarum, inquisitio... II. Title: De venefica...rum inquisitione. (Over)
8

WITCHCRAFT
BF 1565 H33 1634
Hartz, Konrad.
Cunradi Hartz ... Tractatvs criminalis theorico-practicus, De reorum, inprimisque veneficarum, inquisitione juridice instituenda, in foro haud minus, quam scholis apprime utilis & jucundus. Nunc primum in lucem editus ... cum notis ... anonymi cujusdam in Hassia LL. D. Marpvrgi, Typis & sumptibus Nicolai Hampelii, 1634.
189, [13] p. 20cm.

1. Trials (Witchcraft) 2. Witchcraft. I. Title: De reorum, inprimisque vene...ficarum, inquisitione... II. Title: Tractatus criminalis theorico-practicus, De reorum, inprimisque (Over)
8

WITCHCRAFT
BF 1565 H33 1639
Hartz, Konrad.
Tractatus ... De reorum, in primisque veneficarum, inquisitione ...
Tractatvs criminalis De veneficarum inquisitione Cunradi Hartz ... Editio secunda, priori longe auctiori & emendatiori. Rintelii ad Visvrgim, Typis exscripsit Petrus Lucius typog. acad., 1639.
394, [40] p. 15cm.
Published earlier as his Tractatus ... De reorum, inprimisque veneficarum, inquisitione juridice instituenda.

1. Trials (Witchcraft) 2. Witchcraft. I. His Tractatus ... De primisque veneficarum, ...he II. Title: De venefica rum inquisitione.
8

Harvilliers, Jeanne—Fiction.

PQ 2625 A437 T8
Mallet-Joris, Françoise, 1930-
Trois âges de la nuit, histoires de sorcellerie [par] Françoise Mallet-Joris. Paris, B. Grasset, 1968.
377 p. 21cm.

1. Chantraine, Anne de—Fiction. 2. Ranfaing, Elisabeth de, 1592-1649—Fiction. 3. Harvilliers, Jeanne—Fiction. I. Title.

Hasenmüller, Daniel, 1651-1691.

WITCHCRAFT
BF 1508 P97 1688
Psellus, Michael.
[Michaelou tou Psellou Peri energeias daimōnōn dialogos] Μιχαήλου τοῦ Ψέλλου Περὶ ἐνεργείας δαιμόνων διάλογος. Michaelis Pselli De operatione daemonum dialogus. Gilbertus Gaulminus Molinensis primus Graecè edidit & notis illustravit. E museo Dan. Hasenmülleri ... Kiloni, Sumtibus Joh. Sebastiani Richelii, 1688.
6 p. l., 166 p. 15cm.
8 NIC (Continued on next card)

Hasenmüller, Daniel, 1651-1691.

WITCHCRAFT
BF 1508 P97 1688
Psellus, Michael. [Michaelou tou Psellou Peri energeias daimōnōn dialogos] 1688. (Card 2)
Latin and Greek on facing pages, with notes by Gaulmin at bottom of page.
Latin translation by Petrus Morellus, "illius qui & Nicetae Thesaurum orthodoxae fidei de Graeco Latinum fecit."

1. Demonology. I. Gaulmin, Gilbert, 1585-1665, ed. II. Morellus, Petrus, Turonensis, tr. III. Hasenmüller,
8 NIC (Continued on next card)

WITCHCRAFT
K H363 1754
Hathaway, Richard, fl. 1702, defendant.
The trial of Richard Hathaway, at Surrey assizes ... upon an information for being a cheat and impostor, and endeavouring to take away the life of Sarah Morduck, on a false accusation of witchcraft; in which is discovered the malicious designs of the said impostor, with an account of his pretended inchantments and witchcraft ... London, Printed for R. Griffiths, 1754.
92 p. 17cm.
8 (Continued on next card)

WITCHCRAFT
K H363 1754
Hathaway, Richard, fl. 1702, defendant. The trial of Richard Hathaway ... 1754. (Card 2)

1. Morduck, Sarah, fl. 1702. 2. Witchcraft—England. I. Title.
8

Witchcraft
K H363++
Hathaway, Richard, fl. 1702, defendant.
The tryal of Richard Hathaway, upon an information, for being a cheat and impostor, for endeavouring to take away the life of Sarah Morduck, for being a witch, at Surry assizes, begun and held in the burrough of Southwark, March the 24th, 1702. To which is added, a short account of the tryal of Richard Hathaway, Thomas Wellyn and Elizabeth his wife, and Elizabeth Willoughby, wife of Walter Willoughby, upon an information for a (Continued on next card)

Witchcraft
K H363++
Hathaway, Richard, fl. 1702, defendant. The tryal of Richard Hathaway. (Card 2)
riot and assault upon Sarah Morduck, the pretended witch, at the said assizes. London, Printed for I. Cleave, 1702.
1 p. l., 30 p. 31cm.

Rare
DA 430 T81++ no.12
Hathaway, Richard, fl. 1702.
The tryal of Richard Hathaway, upon an information, for being a cheat and impostor, for endeavouring to take away the life of Sarah Morduck, for being a witch, at Surry assizes, begun and held in the burrough of Southwark, March the 24th, 1702 ... To which is added, a short account of the tryal of Richard Hathaway, Thomas Wellyn and Elizabeth his wife, and Elizabeth Willoughby, wife of Walter Willoughby, upon an information for a (Continued on next card)

Rare
DA 430 T81++ no.12
Hathaway, Richard, fl. 1702. The tryal of Richard Hathaway. (Card 2)
riot and assault upon Sarah Morduck, the pretended witch, at the said assizes. London, Printed for I. Cleave, 1702.
1 p. l., 30 p. 31cm.
No. 12 in vol. lettered: Trials, 1685-1702.

1. Witchcraft— England.

Witchcraft
BF 1547 H36
Hauber, Eberhard David, 1695-1765.
Bibliotheca, acta et scripta magica. Gründliche Nachrichten und Urtheile von solchen Büchern und Handlungen, welche die Macht des Teufels in leiblichen Dingen betreffen ... Lemgo, Gedruckt bey J. H. Meyer, 1738-45.
36 pts. in 3 v. plates (part fold.) ports. 18cm.
Vol. [1]: 1. Stück. 2. und verbesserter Druck. 1739.
For detailed contents see J. G. T. Grässe: (Continued on next card)

Witchcraft
BF 1547 H36
Hauber, Eberhard David, 1695-1765. Bibliotheca, acta et scripta magica ... 1738-45. (Card 2)
Bibliotheca magica, p. 118-130.

1. Devil. 2. Devil—Bibl. 3. Witchcraft. 4. Witchcraft—Bibl. 5. Occult sciences. I. Title.

CATALOGUE OF THE CORNELL WITCHCRAFT COLLECTION

Witchcraft
BF
1547
R34
Hauber, Eberhard David, 1695-1765.
Bibliotheca, acta et scripta magica.
Reichard, Elias Caspar, 1714-1791.
Vermischte Beyträge zur Beförderung einer nähern Einsicht in das gesamte Geisterreich. Zur Verminderung und Tilgung des Unglaubens und Aberglaubens. Als eine Fortsetzung von D. David Eberhard Haubers Magischen Bibliothek herausgegeben. Helmstedt, Johann Heinrich Kühnlin, 1781-88.
2 v. 19cm.

Vol. 1 in 4 parts, each with special t.p.

Hausmännen, Walpurga, d. 1587.

see

Haussmännen, Walpurga, d. 1587.

Haute Feüille, lawyer.

see

Hautefeuille, lawyer.

WITCHCRAFT
BF
1523
H49
[Hempel, Christian Gottlob] 1748-
Von den bösen Geistern und der Zauberey: Ein Sendschreiben an den Herrn M. Haubold, Vesperprediger bei der Universitätskirche zu Leipzig, auf Veranlassung einer von demselben am letztverwichenen Michaelsfeste 1782 gehaltenen Nachmittagspredigt, von einem damals unter seinen Zuhörern gewesenen Messfremden. Sorau, 1783.
96 p. 19cm.
Attribution by Holzmann.
1. Demonology. 2. Witchcraft. I. Haubold, , preacher. II. Ein Messfremder. III. Title.

Haubold, , preacher.

8

Hausmann, Walpurga, d. 1587.

see

Haussmännen, Walpurga, d. 1587.

Witchcraft
BF
1582
Z7
1675
Hautefeuille, lawyer.
Plaidoyez svr les magiciens et svr les sorciers, tenus en la cour de Liege, le 16. Decembre 1675. Ov on montre clairement qu'il n'y peut avoir de ces sortes de gens. Par les sieurs de Havte Feüille & Santevr advocats. Sur l'imprimé a Liege, Chez Iacqves Persois imprimeur, 1676.
120 p. 14cm.
"Le livre d'Albert le Grand, leqvel traite des merveilles du monde," p. [77]—

4
(Continued on next card)

WITCHCRAFT
BF
1583
H36
Hauffen, Adolf, 1863-1930.
Der Hexenwahn. [Prag] 1897.
20 p. 22cm. (Sammlung gemeinnütziger Vorträge. No. 230)

Caption title.

1. Witchcraft--Germany. 2. Witchcraft--Austria. I. Title.

8

Haussmänne, Walpurga, d. 1587.

see

Haussmännen, Walpurga, d. 1587.

Witchcraft
BF
1582
Z7
1675
Hautefeuille, lawyer. Plaidoyez svr les magiciens ... 1676. (Card 2)

120, has special t. p. with imprint: Lyon, Par Iean Hvgvetan, 1616. Text is taken from Les admirables secrets d'Albert le Grand.
1. Witchcraft. 2. Magic. 3. Sillieux, Sulpice, fl. 1675. I. Santevr, lawyer. II. Albertus Magnus, saint, bp. of Ratisbon, 1193?-1280. Spurious and doubtful works. Les admirables secrets d'Albert le Grand. III. Title: Plaidoyez sur les magiciens. IV. Title: Le livre d'Albert le Grand.

8

Witchcraft
BF
1583
Z7
1705
Hausberg, Anna Martha, 1663-1705.
Schütz, W
Ein Hexenprocess vom Jahre 1705, mitgetheilt von Herrn Amtscommissär W. Schütz in Weimar. [Jena, 1853]
178-183 p. 23cm.
In "Miscellen," detached from the Zeitschrift of the Verein für thüringische Geschichte und Altertumskunde, Jena, 1. Bd., 2. Heft, and bound in vol. lettered Miscellen über Hexerei.
With this is bound Auen, Karl, Segen und Zauberformeln. [Jena, 1853]
8
(Continued on next card)

WITCHCRAFT
BF
1583
Z7
1587
Haussmännen, Walpurga, d. 1587, defendant.
Vrgicht vnd Verzaichnuss, so Walpurga Haussmännen zu Dillingen, inn ihrer peinlichen Marter bekandt hatt, was sy für Vbels vnd Jamers mit jhrer Hexerey, so sy biss in die 30. Jar getrüben, angericht vnd gestüfft hat, mit Hilff vnd Raht jhres Bültevffels, so ihr darzu geholffen: welche Walburga Anno 1587. Jar, den 24. October, verbrandt vnd gericht ist worden, &c. [Dillingen?] 1588.
[20] p. 20cm.

8
(Continued on next card)

Witchcraft
BF
1612
G69
Les hauts phénomènes de la magie précédés du spiritisme antique.
Gougenot des Mousseaux, Henri Roger, 1805-18
Les hauts phénomènes de la magie précédés du spiritisme antique ... et quelques lettres addressées à l'auteur. Paris, H. Plon, 1864.
xxxviii, 480 p. 23cm.

1. Magic. 2. Spiritualism. 3. Occult sciences. I. Title.

8

Witchcraft
Z
6880
Z9
H37+
Hauser, Lionel
Catalogue of the very extensive and important library of early books and manuscripts relating to alchemy & the occult & physical sciences, the property of M. Lionel Hauser... and of four important mediaeval manuscripts...which will be sold by auction by Messrs. Sotheby and Co...the 16th of April, 1934... London, Printed by J. Davy [1934]
ii, 68 p. illus. 26cm.
1. Alchemy --Bibl. 2. Occult sciences--Bibl. I. Sotheby, firm, auctioneers, London.

WITCHCRAFT
BF
1583
Z7
1587
Haussmännen, Walpurga, d. 1587, defendant.
Vrgicht vnd Verzaichnuss ... 1588. (Card 2)

1. Trials (Witchcraft)--Germany. I. Dillingen, Germany. Stadtgericht. II. Title: Urgicht und Verzaichnuss, so Walpurga Haussmännen ... bekandt hatt.

8

WITCHCRAFT
DD
491
H2
H67
1842
Havemann, Wilhelm, 1800-1869.
Sidonia, Herzogin zu Braunschweig-Lüneburg, geborene Herzogin von Sachsen.
(In: Historischer Verein für Niedersachs Zeitschrift [under earlier title, Vaterländisches Archiv] Hannover. 19cm. 1842 p. 278-303)
1. Braunschweig-und-Lüneburg, Sidonia, Herzogin zu. 2. Braunschweig-und-Lüneburg, Erich II, Herzog zu. I. Title.

8
NIC

Hausmänne, Walpurga, d. 1587.

see

Haussmännen, Walpurga, d. 1587.

Haussmann, Walpurga, d. 1587.

see

Haussmännen, Walpurga, d. 1587.

Witchcraft
BF
1576
H38
[Haven, Samuel Foster] 1806-1881.
[The Mathers and the witchcraft delusions. Boston, 1874]
14 p. 25cm.

Title on cover in ms.
"From the Proceedings of the meeting of the American Antiquarian Society in Boston, April 29, 1874. Report of the librarian."

1. Witchcraft-- New England. 2. Mather, Cotton, 1663- 1728. I. Title.

264

CATALOGUE OF THE CORNELL WITCHCRAFT COLLECTION

Witchcraft
BF
1522
C92
2 copies

La hayne de Sathan et malins esprits contre l'homme.
Crespet, Pierre, 1543-1594.
Devx livres de la hayne de Sathan et malins esprits contre l'homme, & de l'homme contre eux. Ou sont par notables discours & curieuses recherches expliquez les arts, ruses, & moyens, qu'ils practiquent pour nuyre à l'homme par charmes, obsessions, magie, sorcellerie, illusions, phantosmes, impostures, & autres estranges façons, avec les remedes conuenables pour leur resister suyuant l'vsage qui se pratique en l'Eglise.
(Continued on next card)

Witchcraft
BF
1522
C92

La hayne de Sathan et malins esprits contre l'homme.
Crespet, Pierre, 1543-1594. Devx livres de la hayne de Sathan ... (Card 2)
Auec la table bien ample des matieres y contenues. Paris, Chez Guillaume de la Noue, 1590.
[26], 428, [22] l. 17cm.
Errors in paging.
Copy 1 bound in two volumes.
Copy 2 with Robert Southey's autograph.
I. Title.

Witchcraft
BF
1815
S55
H43
1710

[Head, Richard] 1637?-1686?
The history of Mother Shipton: containing an account of her strange and unnatural conception, her birth, life, actions and death: the correspondence she held with the devil, and the many strange and wonderful things perform'd by her. Together with all the predictions and prophecies that have been made by her, and since fulfilled, from the reign of King Henry the Seventh, to the third year of our Sovereign Lady Queen Anne ... London, Printed by and for W. Onley [ca. 1710]
(Continued on next card)

Witchcraft
BF
1815
S55
H43
1710

[Head, Richard] 1637?-1686? The history of Mother Shipton ... [ca. 1710] (Card 2)
24 p. 21cm.
Title vignette (woodcut)
For authorship cf. Halkett & Laing. Dict. of anonymous and pseudonymous English lit., v. 3, p. 72.
First published 1684 (or 1677) under title: The life and death of Mother Shipton.
1. Shipton, Ursula. 2. Prophecies. I. Title. II. His The life and death of Mother Shipton.

Witchcraft
BF
1815
S55
H43
1687

[Head, Richard] 1637?-1686?
The life and death of Mother Shipton. Being not only a true account of her strange birth, the most important passages of her life, but also all her prophesies ... until this present year 1667. Containing the most important passages of state during the reigns of these kings and queens of England following: ... London, W. Harris, 1687.
30 p. front. 23cm.
1. Shipton, Ursula. 2. Prophecies. I. Title.

Witchcraft
BF
1815
S55
H43
1710

[Head, Richard] 1637?-1686?
The history of Mother Shipton: containing an account of her strange and unnatural conception, her birth, life, actions and death: the correspondence she held with the devil, and the many strange and wonderful things perform'd by her. Together with all the predictions and prophecies that have been made by her, and since fulfilled, from the reign of King Henry the Seventh, to the third year of our Sovereign Lady Queen Anne ... London, Printed by and for W. Onley [ca. 1710]
(Continued on next card)

Witchcraft
BF
1815
S55
H43
1710

Head, Richard, 1637?-1686?
The life and death of Mother Shipton.
[Head, Richard] 1637?-1686? The history of Mother Shipton ... [ca. 1710] (Card 2)
24 p. 21cm.
Title vignette (woodcut)
For authorship cf. Halkett & Laing. Dict. of anonymous and pseudonymous English lit., v. 3, p. 72.
First published 1684 (or 1677) under title: The life and death of Mother Shipton.
1. Shipton, Ursula. 2. Prophecies. I. Title. II. His The life and death of Mother Shipton.

Witchcraft
BF
1555
H44
1822

Heaton, James.
The demon expelled.
The extraordinary affliction and gracious relief of a little boy [John Evans]; supposed to be the effects of spiritual agency. Carefully examined and faithfully narrated with Observations on demoniac possession and animadversions on superstition. 2d ed. improved and enl. ... Plymouth [Eng.] Printed and sold for the Author by J. Williams, 1822.
156, 114 p. 20cm.
"Farther observations on demoniac
(Continued on next card)

Witchcraft
BF
1555
H44
1822

Heaton, James. The extraordinary affliction and gracious relief of a little boy [John Evans] ... 1822. (Card 2)
possession..." has separate t.p. and paging.
First ed. published in 1820 under title: The demon expelled; or, The influence of Satan ...
1. Evans, John. 2. Demoniac possession. 3. Superstition. I. Heaton, James. The demon expelled ... II. Heaton, James. Farther observations on demoniack possession, and ... supersti tion. III. Title.

Witchcraft
BF
1555
H44
1822

Heaton, James.
The extraordinary affliction and gracious relief of a little boy [John Evans]; supposed to be the effects of spiritual agency. Carefully examined and faithfully narrated with Observations on demoniac possession and animadversions on superstition. 2d ed. improved and enl. ... Plymouth [Eng.] Printed and sold for the Author by J. Williams, 1822.
156, 114 p. 20cm.
"Farther observations on demoniac
(Continued on next card)

Witchcraft
BF
1555
H44
1822

Heaton, James. The extraordinary affliction and gracious relief of a little boy [John Evans] ... 1822. (Card 2)
possession..." has separate t.p. and paging.
First ed. published in 1820 under title: The demon expelled; or, The influence of Satan ...
1. Evans, John. 2. Demoniac possession. 3. Superstition. I. Heaton, James. The demon expelled ... II. Heaton, James. Farther observations on demoniack possession, and ... supersti tion. III. Title.

Witchcraft
BF
1555
H44
1822

Heaton, James.
Farther observations on demoniack possession, and ... superstition.
The extraordinary affliction and gracious relief of a little boy [John Evans]; supposed to be the effects of spiritual agency. Carefully examined and faithfully narrated with Observations on demoniac possession and animadversions on superstition. 2d ed. improved and enl. ... Plymouth [Eng.] Printed and sold for the Author by J. Williams, 1822.
156, 114 p. 20cm.
"Farther observations on demoniac
(Continued on next card)

Witchcraft
BF
1555
H44
1822

Heaton, James.
Farther observations on demoniack possession, and ... superstition.
Heaton, James. The extraordinary affliction and gracious relief of a little boy [John Evans] ... 1822. (Card 2)
possession..." has separate t.p. and paging.
First ed. published in 1820 under title: The demon expelled; or, The influence of Satan ...
1. Evans, John. 2. Demoniac possession. 3. Superstition. I. Heaton, James. The demon expelled ... II. Heaton, James. Farther observations on demoniack possession, tion. III. Title.

Witchcraft
Z
6880
Z9
C35
no.2

Heberle, J M
Culturgeschichte und Curiositäten in Druckschriften, fliegenden Blättern, Bildern, Autographen und Monumenten. Aus den Sammlungen von Heinrich Lempertz. Zu beigesetzten Preisen vorräthig auf dem Bücher- und Kunstlager von J. M. Heberle (H. Lempertz' Söhne) in Cöln. Abth. E: Physiognomik, Phrenologie, Mimik, natürliche Magie, Kunststücke, Alchymie, etc. ... Abth. F: Zauberei und Hexerei, Faust, Cagliostro, Teufelswesen und
(Continued on next card)

Witchcraft
Z
6880
Z9
C35
no.2

Heberle, J M
Culturgeschichte und Curiositäten... [1874?] (Card 2)
Beschwörungen, Besessensein, etc. ... Cöln, Steven's Druckerei [1874?]
64 p. 23cm.
At head of title: Nro. 74.
No. 2 in vol. lettered: Catalogues of books on magic and witchcraft.
1. Occult sciences—Bibl.— Catalogs. 2. Witchcraft—Bibl.— Catalogs. 3. Magic—Bibl.— Catalogs. I. Title.

Witchcraft
BF
1445
D61
no.11

Hechler, Johann Philipp, respondent.
Schlosser, Philipp Casimir, praeses.
Disputatio inauguralis philosophica De spectris. Quam ... praeside ... M. Philippo Casimiro Schlossero ... pro lauru magisteriali rité & legitimè impetranda, publicè defendendam conscripsit, ac omnibus sobriè & candidè philosophantibus subjicit A. & R. Johannes Philippus Hechler ... Gissae Hassorvm, Typis Christoph. Hermanni Kargeri [1693]
46 p. 21cm.
8
(Continued on next card)

Witchcraft
BF
1445
D61
no.11

Hechler, Johann Philipp, respondent.
Schlosser, Philipp Casimis, praeses. Disputatio inauguralis philosophica De spectris ... [1693] (Card 2)
Diss.—Giessen (J. P. Hechler, respondent)
No. 11 in vol. lettered Dissertationes de spectris. 1646-1753.
1. Apparitions. 2. Demonology. I. Hechler, Johann Philipp, respondent. II. Title: De spectris.
8

History of Science
R
133
A33
D6

Heck, Georg, respondent.
Alberti, Michael, 1682-1757, praeses.
Dissertatio inauguralis medica medicinam pseudo-miraculosam aperiens, quam ... in Alma Regia Fridericiana, praeside ... Michaele Alberti ... pro gradu doctoris summisque in medicina honoribus et privilegiis doctoralibus legitime ... impetrandis, anno MDCCLIII. d. Maii ... publicae ... eruditorum ventilationi subjiciet auctor Georgius Heck ... Halae Magdeburgicae, Typis Joh. Christiani Hendelii [1753]
43, [5] p. 21cm.
Diss. inaug.— Halle (G. Heck, respondent)

265

CATALOGUE OF THE CORNELL WITCHCRAFT COLLECTION

Hédelin, François, 1604-1676.

see

Aubignac, François Hédelin, abbé d', 1604-1676.

Heiliger Segen.

Witchcraft
BF
1775
W132
1849

Der Wahre geistliche Schild, so vor 300 Jahren von dem heil. Papst Leo X. bestätigt worden, wider alle gefährliche böse Menschen sowohl als aller Hexerei und Teufelswerk entgegen gesetzt; darinnen sehr kräftige Segen und Gebete ... Nebst einem Anhang heiliger Segen ... [n. p.] 1617. [Erie? 1849?]
144, 35 p. illus. 12cm.
Contents.--Andächtige Weise, dem Amt der heiligen Messe nützlich beizuwohnen.--Ein

8   (Continued on next card)

WITCHCRAFT
BF
1531
C28
H46

Heineken, Nicholas Samuel.
A discourse, on the supposed existence of an evil spirit, called the devil; and also, a reply to the observations of Mr. William Carlisle, ... the ostensible author of an "Essay on evil spirits," written in opposition to the discourse which was delivered in the Unitarian Chapel, Bradford. By the Rev. N. T. [i.e. N. S.] Heineken. London, R. Hunter [1825?]
iv, 139 p.   23cm.

8   1. Carlisle, William. An essay on evil spirits. 2. Demonology. I. Title.

WITCHCRAFT
BF
1565
H45

Heerbrand, Jacob, 1521-1600, praeses.
De magia dispvtatio ex cap. 7. Exo.
... Praeside reverendo ... Iacobo Heerbrando, ... Nicolavs Falco Salueldensis respondere conabitur. Tubingae, 1570.
17 p. 21cm.

1. Witchcraft in the Bible. 2. Bible. O.T. Exodus VII--Criticism, interpretation, etc. I. Falco, Nicolaus, respondent.
8   II. Title.

Heiliger Segen.

Witchcraft
BF
1775
W132
1849

Der Wahre geistliche Schild ... [1849?]
(Card 2)
Contents--Continued.

schöner und wohlapprobirter heiliger Segen zu Wasser und Land wider alle seine Feinde. --Geistliche Schild-Wacht, darinnen der Mensch ihm für eine jegliche Stund ... einen besonderen Patron aus den Heiligen Gottes erwähltet [sic].--Anhang. Heiliger Segen ... um in allen Gefahren, worein sowohl Men-

8   (Continued on next card)

Heineken, Nicholas Samuel.

Witchcraft
BF
1531
C28
1827

Carlisle, William.
An essay on evil spirits; or, Reasons to prove their existence. In opposition to a lecture delivered by the Rev. N. T. [i.e. N.S.] Heineken, in the Unitarian Chapel, Bradford. 3d ed., enl. and corr. ... London, Printed for the Author, and sold by Hamilton, Adams, 1827.
176 p. 20cm.

1. Demonology.   2. Heineken, Nicholas Samuel. I. Title.

WITCHCRAFT
BF
1566
H46
1899

Heigl, Ferdinand.
Der Hexenglaube. Ein Rückblick als Perspektive für die Spiritisten unserer Zeit. Von Ferdinand Heigl, Verfasser der "Spaziergänge eines Atheisten." 2. Aufl. Bamberg, Handelsdruckerei Bamberg [1899]
2 v. in 1. 12cm. (Volksschriften zur Umwälzung der Geister, VII a, b)
Contents.--1. T. Der Hexenglaube.-- 2. T. Der Spiritismus.
1. Witchcraft--History. 2.
8   Spiritualism.   I. Title.

Heiliger Segen.

Witchcraft
BF
1775
W132
1849

Der Wahre geistliche Schild ... [1849?]
(Card 3)
Contents--Continued.

schen als Vieh oft gerathen, gesichert zu sein.
Each item has special t. p.
Geistliche Schild-Wacht has imprint 1840; the Anhang has imprint 1849 and is paged separately.
1. Charms.   2. Prayers. I. Leo X, Pope, 1475-15 21. II. Title: Heiliger Segen.

8

Z
2771
B58
fasc.5
pt.5
no.2

Heinemann, Franz, 1870-
Inquisition, Intoleranz, Exkommunikation, Interdikt, Index, Zensur. Sektenwesen, Hexenwahn und Hexenprozesse, Rechtsanschauungen. Bern, K. J. Wyss, 1908-09.
2 v. in 1. 22cm. (His Kulturgeschichte und Volkskunde (Folklore) der Schweiz, Heft 2)

Bibliographie der schweizerischen Landeskunde, Fasc. V5.
1. Witchcraft--Bibliography. I. Title.

BF
1584
F5
H46

Heikkinen, Antero
Paholaisen liittolaiset. Noita- ja magiakäsityksiä ja -oikeudenkäyntejä Suomessa 1600-luvun jälkipuoliskolla (n. 1640-1712) Helsinki, 1969.
394 p. map. 24cm. (Suomen Historiallinen Seura. Historiallisia tutkimuksia, 78)
Summary in English.
Yliopistollinen väitöskirja--Helsinki.
Extra t.p., with thesis statement, inserted.
(Continued on next card)

Heiliger Segen aller heiligen Apostel.

Witchcraft
BF
1775
W13
1800

Der Wahre geistliche Schild. 2. Th. Oder: Heiliger Segen aller heil. Apostel und Jünger Jesu Christi ..., um alle unheilbaren Krankheiten der Menschen zu vertreiben, und alle Anfälle des Satans abzuwenden. Sammt dem wunderthätigen Gertrauden-Büchlein, das ist: Der heil. Jungfrau und Abtissin Gertraud himmlische Anmuthungen und Gebete um zeitliche und ewige Güter. Salzburg, 1667. [n. p., 18--] 148 p. illus. 16cm.

8   (Continued on next card)

BF
1410
L69
1921

Heinrich Cornelius Agrippa's von Nettesheim Magische Werke : sammt den geheimnissvollen Schriften des Petrus von Abano, Pictorius von Villingen, Gerhard von Cremona, Abt Tritheim von Spanheim, dem Buche Arbatel, der sogenannten Heil. Geist-Kunst und verschiedenen anderen zum ersten Male vollständig in's Deutsche übersetzt : vollständig in fünf Theilen, mit einer Menge Abbildungen.-- 4. Aufl. -- Berlin : H. Barsdorf, 1921.
5 v. in 3. : ill. ; 17cm. -- (Geheime Wissenschaften : 10-14)
(Continued on next card)

BF
1584
F5
H46

Heikkinen, Antero. Paholaisen liittolaiset.
1969.   (card 2)

1. Witchcraft--Finland.   I. Title. II. Series: Suomen Historiallinen Seura, Helsingfors. Historiallisia tutkimuksia, 78.

Heiliger Segen aller heiligen Apostel.

Witchcraft
BF
1775
W13
1800

Der Wahre geistliche Schild ... [18--]
(Card 2)
Heiliger Segen aller heiligen Apostel ... has special t. p.
Der heiligen Jungfrauen und Abtissin Gertraud himmlische Anmuthungen und Gebete has special t. p. and imprint Cöln, 1506.
1. Charms. 2. Prayers. I. Gertrude, Saint, surnamed the Great, 1256-1302? supposed author. II. Title: Heiliger Segen aller heiligen Apostel. III. Title: Der heiligen Jungfrauen ...Gertraud himmlische Anmuthungen.

8

BF
1410
L69
1921

Heinrich Cornelius Agrippa's von Nettesheim Magische Werke... 1921.   (Card 2)

1. Occult sciences. 2. Magic. I. Trithemius, Johannes, 1462-1516. II. Abano, Pietro d', 1250-1315? III. Gerardus (Cremonensis), of Sabbioneta, 13th cent. IV. Pictorius, Georg. V. Series. VI. Agrippa von Nettesheim, Heinrich Cornelius, 1486?-1535. De occulta philosophia libri tres. German. VII. Liber de ceremoniis magicis. German. VIII. Arbatel of magick.

Heilbronner, Jacob, 1548-1618.

Witchcraft
BF
1520
P67

Pistorius, Johann, 1546-1608.
Daemonomania Pistoriana. Magica et cabalistica morborum curandorum ratio, à Ioanne Pistorio Niddano ... ex lacunis iudaicis ac gentilitiis hausta, post christianis proprinata. Cum antidoto prophylactico Iacobi Heilbronneri ... Lauingae, typis Palatinis, 1601.
26 p. l., 1934 p. 16½cm.

Heineken, N. T.

see

Heineken, Nicholas Samuel.

WITCHCRAFT
BF
1569
A2
I596

Heinrich Institoris, der Verfasser des Hexenhammers.
Müller, Karl Otto, 1884-
Heinrich Institoris, der Verfasser des Hexenhammers, und seine Tätigkeit als Hexeninquisitor in Ravensburg im Herbst 1484.
(In: Württembergische Vierteljahrshefte für Landesgeschichte. Stuttgart. 24cm. new ser. v.19, no.4. 1910. p. 397-417)

8   1. Institoris, Henricus, d.1508. 2.Trials
NIC   (Witchcraft)   --Ravensburg, Ger.

CATALOGUE OF THE CORNELL WITCHCRAFT COLLECTION

Heinrich N., shoemaker of Augsburg, fl. 1667-1681.

WITCHCRAFT
BF
1555
E33

Ehinger, Christoph.
  Daemonologia; oder, Etwas Neues vom Teufel. Das ist: Wahrhaffter historischer Bericht, von einem sonder- und wunderbaren Casu, Anfechtungs-Fall, und satanischer Versuchung, mit welcher, auss Gottes Verhängnuss, ein Burger, und Schuhmacher in Augspurg, etliche Jahr vexiret, und geplaget worden ... Augspurg, In Verlegung Gottlieb Göbels, Druckts Jacob Koppmayr, 1681.
  12 p. l., 208 p. 16cm.

8
  1. Demoniac possession. 2. Devil. I. Title.

Heinrich von Gorkum, 1386 (ca.)-1431.
  De celebratione festorum.

Witchcraft
R
135
H46
1473

Heinrich von Gorkum, 1386 (ca.)-1431.
  De superstitiosis quibusdam casibus. De celebratione festorum. [Esslingen, Conrad Fyner, not after 1473]
  [18] l. 21cm.

  Leaf [1a]: Incipit tractatus de supsticiosis quibusdā casibꝰ ꝓpilatꝰ in alma vniveŝitate studij Colonien̄ p venabilem mgr̄m Heinricū de Gorihem sacre theo. ꝓfessoreȝ eximium.
  Leaf [9b]: Explicit Tractatꝰ de supsticosis quibusdam casib—

(Continued on next card)

Heinrich von Gorkum, 1386 (ca.)-1431.
  De celebratione festorum.

Heinrich von Gorkum, 1386 (ca.)-1431. De superstitiosis quibusdam casibus ... [not after 1473] (Card 2)

  Leaf [10a]: Incipit tractatus de Celebratōne festoȝ.
  Leaf [18b]: Explicit Tractatus cuiꝰ supra de Celebratōne festoȝ.
  Signatures: unsigned [a8, b10].
  Capital spaces; capitals, initial-strokes, paragraph-marks and underlines supplied in red.

(Continued on next card)

Heinrich von Gorkum, 1386 (ca.)-1431.
  De celebratione festorum.

Heinrich von Gorkum, 1386 (ca.)-1431. De superstitiosis quibusdam casibus ... [not after 1473] (Card 3)

  Hain. Repertorium (with Copinger's Supplement) *7807; Proctor, 2462; Brit. Mus. Cat. (XV cent.) II, p. 521 (IA. 8923; variant); Goff. Third census, H-24 (Under Henricus de Gorichen).

  1. Superstition. 2. Fasts and feasts-- Catholic Church. I. Heinrich von Gorkum, 1386 (ca.)-1431. De celebratione festorum. I. Title. II. De celebratione festorum.

Heinrich von Gorkum, 1386 (ca.)-1431.
  De superstitiosis quibusdam casibus. De celebratione festorum. [Esslingen, Conrad Fyner, not after 1473]
  [18] l. 21cm.

  Leaf [1a]: Incipit tractatus de supsticiosis quibusdā casibꝰ ꝓpilatꝰ in alma vniveŝitate studij Colonien̄ p venabilem mgr̄m Heinricū de Gorihem sacre theo. ꝓfessoreȝ eximium.
  Leaf [9b]: Explicit Tractatꝰ de supsticosis quibusdam casib—

(Continued on next card)

WITCHCRAFT

Heinrich von Gorkum, 1386 (ca.)-1431. De superstitiosis quibusdam casibus ... [not after 1473] (Card 2)

  Leaf [10a]: Incipit tractatus de Celebratōne festoȝ.
  Leaf [18b]: Explicit Tractatus cuiꝰ supra de Celebratōne festoȝ.
  Signatures: unsigned [a8, b10].
  Capital spaces; capitals, initial-strokes, paragraph-marks and underlines supplied in red.

(Continued on next card)

WITCHCRAFT
BR
135
H46
1473

Heinrich von Gorkum, 1386 (ca.)-1431. De superstitiosis quibusdam casibus ... [not after 1473] (Card 3)

  Hain. Repertorium (with Copinger's Supplement) *7807; Proctor, 2462; Brit. Mus. Cat. (XV cent.) II, p. 521 (IA. 8923; variant); Goff. Third census, H-24 (Under Henricus de Gorichen).

  1. Superstition. 2. Fasts and feasts-- Catholic Church. I. Heinrich von Gorkum, 1386 (ca.)-1431. De celebratione festorum. II. Title. III. De celebratione festorum.

Heinrich von Gorkum, 1386(ca.)-1431.

WITCHCRAFT
BF
1569
A2
M26
1621

Mamoris, Petrus.
  Flagellum maleficorum, authore M. Petro Mamoris. Cum indicibus. [Lugduni] 1621.
  82 p. 18cm.

  First published in Lyons about 1490. Later included in v.3 of 1669 ed. of Institoris' Malleus maleficarum.
  "Tractatus de superstitiosis quibusdam casibus, compilatus...per...Henricum de Gorchen.": p. 71-82.

8
NIC
  1. Witchcraft. 2. Demonology. 3. Superstition. I. Heinrich von Gorkum,1386 (ca.)-1431. II. Title.

WITCHCRAFT
BF
1552
H47

Heister, Lorenz, 1683-1758, praeses.
  Lavrentivs Heistervs ... programmate avspicali qvo demonstrat infantes pro a diabolo svppositis habitos qvos vvlgo Wechselbälge appellarvnt rhachiticos fvisse ad clarissima medicinae candidati Io. Georgii de Broke ... dispvtationem inavgvralem invitat. Helmstadii, Literis Schnorrianis, 1725.
  [16] p. 21cm.

8

(Continued on next card)

WITCHCRAFT
BF
1552
H47

Heister, Lorenz, 1683-1758, praeses. Lavrentivs Heistervs ... programmate avspicali ... 1725. (Card 2)

  1. Fairies. 2. Children--Diseases. 3. Broke, Johannes Georgius de, b. 1698. I. Partial title: Wechselbälge. II. Title: Laurentius Heisterus ... programmate auspicali quo demonstrat infantes pro a diabolo suppositis habitos ... rhachiticos fuisse.

8

Heksenprocessen.

WITCHCRAFT
BF
1584
B4
L15+

Laenen, Joseph, 1871-1940.
  Heksenprocessen. Antwerpen, Algem. Katholieke Boekhandel "Veritas," 1914.
  77 p. 26cm.

  Bibliographical footnotes.

8
NIC
  1. Trials (Witchcraft)--Belgium. 2. Witchcraft--Belgium. I. Title.

De heksenprocessen.

WITCHCRAFT
BF
1584
N4
R78

Rooses, Max writer on witchcraft.
  De heksenprocessen; eene volksvoordracht. [n. p., 187-?]
  [60]-87 p. 21cm.

  Caption title.
  Signed: Max. Rooses.
  Detached copy.

8
NIC
  1. Trials (Witchcraft)--Netherlands. I. Title.

Heksenvervolging.

BF
1566
T73

Toussaint Raven, J E 1934-
  Heksenvervolging. [Door] J. E. Toussaint Raven. Bussum, Fibula-Van Dishoeck, 1972. [1973]
  135 p. with illus. 21cm. (Fibulareeks, 23)
  Bibliography: p. 109-114.

  1. Witchcraft. I. Title

NIC   MAY 03, '74   COOxc   73-343288

Hekseprocesser fra Midtjylland (Viborg-Skive Egnen)

Witchcraft
BF
1584
D4
C55

Christensen, Christian Villads, 1864-1922.
  Hekseprocesser fra Midtjylland (Viborg-Skive Egnen) af Villads Christensen. (In Samlinger til jydsk historie og topografi. København. 22cm. 3. raekke, 6. bind (1908-10), p. [313]-378)

8
  1. Witchcraft--Denmark. 2. Trials (Witchcraft)--Denmark. I. Title. II. Samlinger til jydsk historie og topografi.

WITCHCRAFT
BF
1584
D4
A2++

[Hekseprocesserne. Collection of extracts from Danish periodicals on witchcraft and witchcraft trials, chiefly in Denmark and Scandinavia. v.p., 1752-1929]
  34 items. 31cm.

8
NIC
  1. Witchcraft. 2. Trials (Witchcraft) 3. Witchcraft--Denmark. 4. Trials (Witchcraft)--Denmark.

Heksetro og trolddom.

BF
1584
N6
A47

Alver, Bente Gullveig, 1941-
  Heksetro og trolddom. Et studie i norsk heksevæsen. Oslo, Universitetsforlaget, 1971.
  282 p. 4 l. of plates. illus. 24 cm. kr44.50   N 71-50
  Bibliography: p. 223-[226]

3
  1. Witchcraft--Norway. 2. Trolls. I. Title.

BF1584.N6A79   72-887909
Library of Congress   72 [2]

Held, Hans Ludwig, 1885-

Witchcraft
Z
6880
Z9
D94

Du Prel, Karl Ludwig August Friedrich Maximilian Alfred, Freiherr, 1839-1899.
  Bibliotheca occulta et philosophica; Sammlung Baron C. Du Prel, und kleine andere Beiträge (Inhaltsverzeichnis umstehend) Mit Vorwort von H. L. Held. München, E. Hirsch [193-]
  104 p. 22cm.
  Katalog 58.

Heldenschutz--French.

Witchcraft
BF
1603
H46
1750

Grimoire; ou La magie naturelle. La Haye, Aux dépens de la Compagnie [ca. 1750]
  600 p. illus. 14cm.

  "Traduction altérée d'un bizarre ouvrage allemand intitulé Heldenschutz"--Graesse, Trésor de livres rares et précieux.

  1. Magic. 2. Receipts--Early works to 1800. 3. Handbooks, vade-mecums, etc. 4. Medicine--Formulae, receipts, prescriptions, etc. I. Heldenschutz. French. II.
8 Title: La magie naturelle.

CATALOGUE OF THE CORNELL WITCHCRAFT COLLECTION

Hellwig, Albert, 1880–

see

Hellwig, Albert Ernst Karl Max, 1880–

WITCHCRAFT
BF 1523 H49

[Hempel, Christian Gottlob] 1748–
Von den bösen Geistern und der Zauberey: Ein Sendschreiben an den Herrn M. Haubold, Vesperprediger bei der Universitätskirche zu Leipzig, auf Veranlassung einer von demselben am letztverwichenen Michaelsfeste 1782 gehaltenen Nachmittagspredigt, von einem damals unter seinen Zuhörern gewesenen Messfremden. Sorau, 1783.
96 p. 19cm.
Attribution by Holzmann.

8
1. Demonology. 2. Witchcraft. I. Haubold, ___, preacher. II. Ein Messfremder. III. Title.

WITCHCRAFT
AZ 999 H51

Henne am Rhyn, Otto, 1828–1914.
Eine Reise durch das Reich des Aberglaubens. Leipzig, M. Spohr [1893]
iv, 175 p. 22cm.

8
I. Title.

WITCHCRAFT
BF 1583 Z7 1907

Hellwig, Albert Ernst Karl Max, 1880– , ed.
Ein moderner Hexenprozess in Posen. Von Dr. Albert Hellwig.
(In Schlesische Gesellschaft für Volkskunde. Mitteilungen. Breslau. 25cm.
Bd. XII (1910), p. 191–215)

8
1. Witchcraft--Germany. I. Title.

WITCHCRAFT
DD 801 T4 T533 v.1–2

Hempel, Richard.
Hexenprozesse in Mühlhausen.
(In: Thüringer Monatshefte [under earlier title: Pflüger] Mühlhausen. 23cm. Jahrg.1 (1924) p. 164-169, 295-300; Jahrg. 2 (1925) p. 26-33, 116-122, 271-276, 343-348)

8
NIC
1. Witchcraft--Mühlhausen, Ger. (Thuringia) 2. Trials (Witchcraft)-- Mühlhausen, Ger. (Thuringia) I. Title.

WITCHCRAFT
BF 1566 H51

Henne am Rhyn, Otto, 1828–1914.
Der Teufels- und Hexenglaube, seine Entwickelung, seine Herrschaft und sein Sturz. Leipzig, M. Spohr, 1892.
vi, 159 p. 22cm.

8
1. Witchcraft--Hist. 2. Demonology. I. Title.

WITCHCRAFT
BF 1142 H48 1904

Hélot, Charles, 1830–
L'hypnose chez les possédés ... [3. éd.] Paris, Bloud, 1908.
125 p. 19cm. (Science et religion. Études pour le temps présent. 204-205) (Religions et sciences occultes)
Bound with his Le diable dans l'hypnotisme. Paris, 1904.

8
1. Demoniac possession. 2. Hysteria. 3. Hypnotism. I. Title.

WITCHCRAFT
BF 1555 H49

Henckel, Elias Heinrich von, fl. 1654–1688.
Eliae Henrici Henckelii ... Ordo et methodus cognoscendi & curandi energumenos seu à Stygio cacodaemone obsessos. Antehac à nemine, quantum sunt, qui de obsessis scripserunt, tradita. Francofurti & Lipsiae, Sumptibus Nicolai Försteri, 1689.
7 p. l., 240, [16] p. 17cm.
Title in red and black.

8
1. Demoniac possession. 2. Medicine --15th–18th centuries. I. Title: Ordo et methodus cognoscendi & curandi energumenos. II. Title.

WITCHCRAFT
BF 1583 Z7 1572

Hennen, Gerhardus.
Ein Hexenprozess aus der Umgegend von Trier aus dem Jahre 1572. Ein Beitrag zur Kulturgeschichte des Mosellandes von Dr. Hennen. St. Wendel, Druck von F. Maurer, 1887.
24 p. 25cm.

8
1. Trials (Witchcraft)--Germany. I. Title.

WITCHCRAFT
BF 1555 H48 1898

Hélot, Charles.
Névroses et possessions diaboliques. 2. éd. Paris, Bloud et Barral, 1898.
556 p. 22cm.
Contents.--1. ptie. Quelques faits à juger.--2. ptie. Le jugement de la science.--3. ptie. Jugement de l'Eglise.
1. Demoniac possession. 2. Hysteria. 3. Somnambulism. 4. Hypnotism. 5. Exorcism. I. Title.

8

Hendrich, Joannes Christianus Fridericus Aemilius, b. 1748.

WITCHCRAFT
R 133 P72

Plaz, Anton Wilhelm, 1708–1784.
Procancellarius D. Antonius Guilielmus Plaz Panegyrin medicam...indicit et de magiae vanitate prolusione prima praefatur. [Lipsiae, Ex officina Langenhemia, 1777]
xvi p. 24cm.
Introductory to a diss. for which Gehler acted as praeses, Hendrich as respondent: De oleosis pinguibus rancidis.
With this is bound his: Procancellarius D. Antonius Guilielmus Plaz Panegyrin medicam ...indicit et de magiaerum disserit. 1777.
(Continued on next card)

8
NIC

Witchcraft
BF 1523 H51

Henning, Max.
Der Teufel: sein Mythos und seine Geschichte im Christentum. Hamburg, P. Hartung [ca. 1910]
123 p. 20cm.

8
1. Devil. 2. Witchcraft. I. Title.

Hemming, Nicolaus, 1513–1600.

see

Hemmingsen, Niels, 1513–1600.

Witchcraft
Z 6490 H51+

Henkels, firm, auctioneers, Philadelphia.
The extraordinary collection of autograph letters belonging to the late Hon. Elliot Danforth ... To be sold ... Dec. 11, 1913, and ... Dec. 12, 1913 ... Stan. V. Henkels, auction commission merchant. Philadelphia, [M. H. Power, printer, 1913?]
135 p. facsims. 28cm.
Catalogue no. 1074, Part 3.
(Continued on next card)

Witchcraft
BF 1598 A27 O76

Henri Cornélis Agrippa, sa vie et son oeuvre d'après sa correspondance.
Orsier, Joseph.
... Henri Cornélis Agrippa, sa vie et son œuvre d'après sa correspondance (1486-1535) Paris, Chacornac, 19__
142 p., 1 l. 25½ᶜᵐ.
CONTENTS.--1. ptie. La vie et l'œuvre d'Agrippa.--2. ptie. Extraits, notés et traduits pour la première fois du latin, de la correspondance d'Agrippa avec ses amis et les personnages de son temps.

1. Agrippa von Nettesheim, Heinrich Cornelius, 1486?-1535. I. Title.
13-1681
Library of Congress

WITCHCRAFT
BF 1565 H48

Hemmingsen, Niels, 1513–1600.
Admonitio de svperstitionibvs magicis vitandis, in gratiam sincerae religionis amantium, scripta a Nicolao Hemmingio. Esaiae 8. Ad legem et testimonivm. [Hafniae, Excvdebant Iohannes Stockelman & Andreas Guterwitz] 1575.
[220] p. 16cm.
With colophon.
1. Witchcraft. 2. Superstition. I. Title: Admonitio de superstitionibus magicis vitandis.

8

Witchcraft
Z 6490 H51+

Henkels, firm, auctioneers, Philadelphia.
The extraordinary collection of autograph letters... [1913?] (Card 2)

Contains facsimile of a letter signed by some of her neighbors, certifying that Winnefred Holman was not guilty of witchery.

1. Autographs--Collections. 2. Danforth, Elliot. 3. Holman, Winnefred.

Henrici Kornmanni Opera curiosa.

WITCHCRAFT
AC 31 K84 1694

Kornmann, Heinrich, fl. 1607.
Henrici Kornmanni Opera curiosa in tractatus qvatuor distributa, qvorum I. Miracula vivorum; II. Miracula mortuorum ... Templum naturae historicum ... IV. Qvaestiones enucleatae de virginum statu ac ... Nunc in lucem edita. Francofurti Moenum, Ex officina Genschiana, 1694-96.
6 v. in 2. 17cm.
Vol. 3-6 have been bound in order: 5, 4, 3.

8
NIC
(Continued on next card)

268

CATALOGUE OF THE CORNELL WITCHCRAFT COLLECTION

```
                Henrici Kornmanni Opera curiosa.
WITCHCRAFT
AC          Kornmann, Heinrich, fl. 1607.    Henrici
31          Kornmanni Opera curiosa ...   1694-96.
K84                                        (Card 2)
1694
              Each vol. also has special t. p.; vol.
            5-6 also have special shared t. p.: Hen-
            rici Kornmanni tractatus duo ... qvorum
            prior Linea amoris ... posterior De annulo
            triplici ... with imprint 1696.
              Bound into copy 1 of vol. 5 is t. p. for
8           Opera curiosa    in 6 vols., with imprint
NIc         1696.
            1. Curio        sities and wonders.  I.
         Title: Oper      a curiosa.
```

```
WITCHCRAFT
BF          Henry Cornelius Agrippa's Fourth book of
1410          occult philosophy, and geomancy.  Magi-
L69           cal elements of Peter de Abano.  Astro-
1655          nomical geomancy by Gerardus Cremonen-
              sis.  The nature of spirits by Georg
              Pictorius: and Arbatel of magick.
              Translated into English by Robert Turner.
              Philomathées.   London, 1655.
              9 p. l., 5-266 i.e., 286, 4 p.
              illus. 19cm.

8             Neither Agrippa nor Abano wrote the works

                 (Continued on next card)
```

```
WITCHCRAFT
BF          Henry Cornelius Agrippa's Fourth book of
1410          occult philosophy, and geomancy ...
L69           1655.                          (Card 2)
1655
              here ascribed to them; the Heptameron, or
            Magical elements also was ascribed to Agrip-
            pa under the title: Les oeuvres magiques,
            with Abano as translator (!)
              Translation of a work variously titled
            Liber de ceremonijs magicis; and his De oc-
            culta philosophia, liber quartus.

8
                (Continued on next card)
```

```
WITCHCRAFT
BF          Henry Cornelius Agrippa's Fourth book of
1410          occult philosophy, and geomancy ...
L69           1655.                          (Card 3)
1655
              1. Occult sciences.  I. Agrippa von
            Nettesheim, Heinrich Cornelius, 1486?-1535,
            supposed author. Fourth book of occult
            philosophy.  II. Abano, Pietro d', 1250-
            1315?, supposed author. Heptameron, or
            Magical elements.  III. Gerardus (Cremo-
            nensis), of Sa       bbioneta, 13th cent.
8
                (Continued on next card)
```

```
WITCHCRAFT
BF          Henry Cornelius Agrippa's Fourth book of
1410          occult philosophy, and geomancy ...
L69           1655.                          (Card 4)
1655
              IV. Pictorius, Georg.  V. Arbatel of
            magick.  VI. Turner, Robert, fl. 1654-
            1655, tr.  VII. Liber de ceremoniis ma-
            gicis. English.  VIII. Title: Fourth
            book of occult philosophy, and geomancy.

8
```

```
              Heptameron, ou Les éléments magiques
                  de Pierre d'Aban.
WITCHCRAFT
BF          Les Oeuvres magiques de Henri-Corneille
1602          Agrippa, mises en français par Pierre
029           d'Aban, avec des secrets occultes, no-
1830          tamment celui de la Reine des Mouches
              velues. Rome, 1744. Lille, Impr. de
              Bloquel, ca. 1830
              112 p. port., illus. (1 fold.) 14cm.
              Caption title: Heptameron, ou Les élé-
            ments magiques de Pierre d'Aban, philosophe,
            disciple de Henri Cornelille Agrippa.
              Has nothing        to do either with Agrip-
8
                 (Continued on next card)
```

```
              Heptameron, ou Les éléments magiques
                  de Pierre d'Aban.
WITCHCRAFT
BF          Les Oeuvres magiques de Henri-Corneille
1602          Agrippa ...   1830         (Card 2)
029
1830         pa or with Pietro d'Abano, who predeceased
            him by 2 centuries.
              Copy 1 has list of similar items for
            sale, e.g., Le veritable dragon rouge,
            Enchiridion Leonis papae, Secrets merveil-
            leux de la magie naturelle du Petit Albert
            ...
              1. Occult         sciences.  2. Magic.
8           3. Charms.        (Continued on next card)
```

```
WITCHCRAFT
BF          Her,       , Rat.
1583          Grosser Hexenprocess zu Schongau von
Z7          1589 bis 1592. Aus den Originalacten ge-
1587b       schichtlich dargestellt von Rath Her.
              (In Oberbayerisches Archiv. München.
            25cm. 11. Bd. (1850-51), p. 356-380)
              At head of title: IX.
              Sequel to his Ein Hexenprocess zu Schon-
            gau vom Jahre 1587, published in the same
            vol. (1849), p. 128-144.
              1. Witchcr       aft--Bavaria.  I. His
8           Ein Hexenpro       cess zu Schongau vom
            Jahre 1587.       II. Title.
```

```
WITCHCRAFT
BF          Her,       , Rat.
1583          Ein Hexenprocess zu Schongau vom Jahre
Z7          1587.  Aus den Originalacten geschichtlich
1587a       dargestellt von Rath Her.  München, Druck
            von G. Franz, 1849.
              19 p.  24cm.
              "Aus dem Oberbay. Archiv Bd. XI. Heft 1
            besonders abgedruckt."
              1. Geiger, Lucia, fl. 1587.  2. Witch-
8           craft--Bavaria.  I. Title.
```

```
WITCHCRAFT
BF          Her,       , Rat.
1583          Ein Hexenprocess zu Schongau vom Jahre
Z7          1587.  Aus den Originalacten geschichtlich
1587b       dargestellt von Rath Her.
              (In Oberbayerisches Archiv. München.
            25cm. 11. Bd. (1849), p. 128-144)

              At head of title: III.
              Also published separately as a reprint.

8
```

```
              Her,       , Rat.
              Ein Hexenprocess zu Schongau vom
              Jahre 1587.
WITCHCRAFT
BF          Her,       , Rat.
1583          Grosser Hexenprocess zu Schongau von
Z7          1589 bis 1592. Aus den Originalacten ge-
1587b       schichtlich dargestellt von Rath Her.
              (In Oberbayerisches Archiv. München.
            25cm. 11. Bd. (1850-51), p. 356-380)
              At head of title: IX.
              Sequel to his Ein Hexenprocess zu Schon-
            gau vom Jahre 1587, published in the same
            vol. (1849), p. 128-144.
              1. Witcher       aft--Bavaria.  I. His
8           Ein Hexenpro       cess zu Schongau vom
            Jahre 1587.       II. Title.
```

```
              Her der küng ich dinete gern.
Witchcraft
BX          Geiler, Johannes, von Kaisersberg, 1445-
890         1510.
G31           Die emeis. Dis ist das buch von der omeis-
E5+         sen, vnnd auch Herr der künnig ich diente
1517        gern.  Vnd sagt von eigentschafft der omeis-
            sen.  Vn gibt vnderweisung von den vnholden
            oder hexen, vnd von gespenst der geist, vnd
            von dem wütenden heer wunderbarlich vnd nütz-
            lich zewissen, was man daruon glauben vnd hal-
            ten soll. Vnd ist von dem hoch gelertē doc-
                (Continued on next card)
```

```
              Her der küng ich dinete gern.
Witchcraft
BX          Geiler, Johannes, von Kaisersberg, 1445-
890         1510.   Die emeis ...   1517.    (Card 2)
G31
E5+         tor Johānes Geiler vō Keisersperg ... in
1517        eim quadragesimal gepredigt worden alle son-
            tag in der fasten  Strassburg, Johan-
            nes Grienniger, 1517
              xc i.e. lxxxviiii l. illus. 29cm.
              Title and parts of text in red and black
              Leaves v and vi not wanting; printer
            skipped numbers.
8
                (Continued on next card)
```

```
              Her der küng ich dinete gern.
Witchcraft
BX          Geiler, Johannes, von Kaisersberg, 1445-
890         1510.   Die emeis ...   1517.    (Card 3)
G31
E5+           Colophon at end of first section, Die
1517        emeis, reads Grienninger instead of Grien-
            niger.
              "Her d'küng ich diente gern", l. lxvii-
            xc, has special t. p.
              1. Sermons, German--Middle High German.
            2. Folk-lore, German. 3. Magic.  I. His
8           Her der küng ich diente gern.  II. Title.
            III. Title:        Her der küng ich dien-
                te gern.
```

```
              Hereditary chorea.
Witchcraft
BF          Vessie, Percy R., d. 1953.
1576          Hereditary chorea: St. Anthony's dance
V58+        and witchcraft in colonial Connecticut.
            n. p., 1939
              7 p. illus. 28cm.

              "Reprinted from Journal of the Connecti-
            cut State Medical Society, vol. 3, no. 11,
            November, 1939."

              1. Witchcraft--Connecticut.  2. Chorea.
            I. Title. II.       St. Anthony's dance and
            witchcraft in         colonial Connecticut.
```

```
              The heresy of witchcraft.
Witchcraft
BF          Robbins, Rossell Hope, 1912-
1565          The heresy of witchcraft. Durham, N. C.,
R63         1966
            532-543 p.  23cm.

              "Reprinted from The South Atlantic
            quarterly, vol. LXV, no. 4, Autumn 1966."
              Inscribed by the author.

              1. Witchcraft.  2. Heresy.  I. The South
            Atlantic quart       erly, vol. 65, no.
            4, Autumn 1966.      II. Title.
```

```
Witchcraft
BF          Hering, Johannes Ernst, praeses.
1565          Disputatio physica De hydromantia,
D62         qvoad sagas probandas per aqvam frigidam,
no.15       qvam ... sub praesidio M. Johannis Er-
            nesti Herings ... publice ventilandam
            sistit respondens Gabriel Kartnerus
            reichenbergâ ...  Wittebergae In offi-
            cina Finceliana exscribebat Michael
            Meyer 1667
              20 p. 18cm.  (bound in 20cm. vol.)
              No. 15 in vol. lettered Dissertationes
8           de sagis.              1636-1714.
                (Continued on next card)
```

```
Witchcraft
BF          Hering, Johannes Ernst, praeses. Dispu-
1565          tatio physica De hydromantia ...  1667
D62                                          (Card 2)
no.15

              1. Trials (Witchcraft)  I. Kartner,
            Gabriel, respondent.  II. Title: De
            hydromantia. III. Title.

8
```

269

CATALOGUE OF THE CORNELL WITCHCRAFT COLLECTION

WITCHCRAFT
BF
1583
Z7
1627b

Hermann, Ernst, 1837-1908.
   Die Hexen von Baden-Baden. Nach den Original-Akten des allgemeinen grossherzogl. Landes-Archivs in Karlsruhe. Karlsruhe, Macklot [1890].
   56 p. 18cm.

   1. Trials (Witchcraft)--Baden-Württemberg. I. Title.

8

Hermann, Zacharias, respondent.

Witchcraft
BF
1775
G88

Grube, Hermann, praeses.
   Disputatio physica De qvalitatibus vulgò dictis occultis, quam ... sub praesidio ... Dn. Hermanni Gruben ... publico eruditorum examini exponet Zacharias Hermannus ... Jenae, Praelo Nisiano [1665?]
   [28] p. 18cm.
   1. Superstition--Addresses, essays, lectures. 2. Science--Early works to 1800. I. Hermann, Zacharias, respondent. II. Title: De qualitatibus vulgò dictis occultis.

8

Hermes Trismegistus.
   Asclepius.

WITCHCRAFT
BF
1598
H55
A1
1532

Hermes Trismegistus.
   [Poemander. Latin]
   Mercvrii Trismegisti Pymander, De potestate et sapientia Dei. Eivsdem Asclepivs, De uoluntate Dei. Opuscula sanctissimis mysterijs, ac uerè coelestibus oraculis illustrissima. Iamblichvs De mysterijs Aegyptiorum, Chaldaeorum, & Assyriorū. Proclvs In Platonicum Alcibiadem, de anima & daemone. Idem De sacrificio & magia. Quae omnia solerti cura   repurgata, ac suo tandem
   (Continued on next card)

8

Hermes Trismegistus.
   Asclepius.

WITCHCRAFT
BF
1598
H55
A1
1532

Hermes Trismegistus. [Poemander. Latin]
1532.   (Card 2)
   candori restituta sunt. Basileae [Per Mich. Isingrinivm] 1532.
   480, [3] p. 16cm.
   With colophon.
   The Asclepius translated by Apuleius Madaurensis; the rest by Marsilio Ficino.
   I. Jamblichus, of Chalcis. De mysteriis. Latin. II. Proclus Diadochus.
   III. Apuleius Madaurensis, tr. IV. Ficino, Marsilio, 1433-1499, tr. V. His Asclepius.

8

Hermes Trismegistus.
   Asclepius.

WITCHCRAFT
PA
4220
L3
A4+
1516

Jamblichus, of Chalcis. [De mysteriis. Latin]
   Iamblichus De mysteriis Aegyptiorum, Chaldaeorum, Assyriorum. Proclus In Platonicum Alcibiadem de anima, atq; demone. Proclus De sacrificio, & magia. Porphyrius De diuinis, atq; daemonibus. Synesius Platonicus De somniis. Psellus De daemonibus. Expositio Prisciani, & Marsilii in Theophrastum De sensu, phantasia, & intellectu. Alcinoi Platonici philoso   phi, Liber de doctrina
   (Continued on next card)

8

Hermes Trismegistus.
   Asclepius.

WITCHCRAFT
PA
4220
L3
A4+
1516

Jamblichus, of Chalcis. [De mysteriis. Latin] [1516]   (Card 2)
   Platonis. Speusippi Platonis discipuli, Liber de Platonis definitionibus. Pythagorae philosophi Aurea uerba. Symbola Pithagorae philosophi. Xenocratis philosophi platonici, Liber de morte. Mercurii Trismegisti Pimander. Eiusdem Asclepius. Marsilii Ficini De triplici uita lib. II. Eiusdem Liber   de uoluptate. Eiusdem
   (Continued on next card)

8

Hermes Trismegistus.
   Asclepius.

WITCHCRAFT
PA
4220
L3
A4+
1516

Jamblichus, of Chalcis. [De mysteriis. Latin] [1516]   (Card 3)
   De sole & lumine libri. II. Apologia eiusdem in librum suum de lumine. Eiusdem Libellus de magis. Quod necessaria sit securitas, & tranquillitas animi. Praeclarissimarum sententiarum huius operis breuis annotatio. [Venetiis, In aedibvs Aldi, et Andreae soceri, 1516]
   177 [i.e.,   175] numbered leaves.
   29cm.
   (Continued on next card)

8

Hermes Trismegistus.
   Asclepius.

WITCHCRAFT
PA
4220
L3
A4+
1516

Jamblichus, of Chalcis. [De mysteriis. Latin] [1516]   (Card 4)
   At head of title: Index eorvm, qvae hoc in libro habentvr.
   With colophon.
   Provenance: Bibliotec: SS. Me. Novelle.
   Translations by M. Ficino.
   1. Occult sciences. 2. Philosophy, Ancient--Collections. I. Proclus Diadochus. In Platonicum Alcibiadem. II. Proclus Diadochus. De sacrificio. III.
   (Continued on next card)

8

Hermes Trismegistus.
   De potestate et sapientia Dei.

   see

Hermes Trismegistus.
   Poemander.

Witchcraft
BF
1598
H55A4
1548

Hermes Trismegistus.
   [Poemander. Italian]
   Il Pimandro di Mercurio Trismegisto, tradotto da Tommaso Benci in lingua fiorentina. Firenze [L. Torrentino] 1548.
   [24], 119, [14] p. 18cm.

   Title vignette.
   Edited by Carlo Lenzoni.
   I. Benci, Tommaso, tr. II. Lenzoni, Carlo, d. 1551, ed. III. Title.

WITCHCRAFT
BF
1598
H55
A1
1532

Hermes Trismegistus.
   [Poemander. Latin]
   Mercvrii Trismegisti Pymander, De potestate et sapientia Dei. Eivsdem Asclepivs, De uoluntate Dei. Opuscula sanctissimis mysterijs, ac uerè coelestibus oraculis illustrissima. Iamblichvs De mysterijs Aegyptiorum, Chaldaeorum, & Assyriorū. Proclvs In Platonicum Alcibiadem, de anima & daemone. Idem De sacrificio & magia. Quae omnia solerti cura   repurgata, ac suo tandem
   (Continued on next card)

8

WITCHCRAFT
BF
1598
H55
A1
1532

Hermes Trismegistus. [Poemander. Latin]
1532.   (Card 2)
   candori restituta sunt. Basileae [Per Mich. Isingrinivm] 1532.
   480, [3] p. 16cm.
   With colophon.
   The Asclepius translated by Apuleius Madaurensis; the rest by Marsilio Ficino.
   I. Jamblichus, of Chalcis. De mysteriis. Latin. II. Proclus Diadochus.
   III. Apuleius Madaurensis, tr. IV. Ficino, Marsilio, 1433-1499, tr. V. His Asclepius. VI. Title.

8

Hermes Trismegistus.
   Poemander. Latin.

WITCHCRAFT
PA
4220
L3
A4+
1516

Jamblichus, of Chalcis. [De mysteriis. Latin] [1516]
   Iamblichus De mysteriis Aegyptiorum, Chaldaeorum, Assyriorum. Proclus In Platonicum Alcibiadem de anima, atq; demone. Proclus De sacrificio, & magia. Porphyrius De diuinis, atq; daemonibus. Synesius Platonicus De somniis. Psellus De daemonibus. Expositio Prisciani, & Marsilii in Theophrastum De sensu, phantasia, & intellectu. Alcinoi Platonici philoso   phi, Liber de doctrina
   (Continued on next card)

8

Hermes Trismegistus.
   Poemander. Latin.

WITCHCRAFT
PA
4220
L3
A4+
1516

Jamblichus, of Chalcis. [De mysteriis. Latin] [1516]   (Card 2)
   Platonis. Speusippi Platonis discipuli, Liber de Platonis definitionibus. Pythagorae philosophi Aurea uerba. Symbola Pithagorae philosophi. Xenocratis philosophi platonici, Liber de morte. Mercurii Trismegisti Pimander. Eiusdem Asclepius. Marsilii Ficini De triplici uita lib. II. Eiusdem Liber   de uoluptate. Eiusdem
   (Continued on next card)

8

Hermes Trismegistus.
   Poemander. Latin.

WITCHCRAFT
PA
4220
L3
A4+
1516

Jamblichus, of Chalcis. [De mysteriis. Latin] [1516]   (Card 3)
   De sole & lumine libri. II. Apologia eiusdem in librum suum de lumine. Eiusdem Libellus de magis. Quod necessaria sit securitas, & tranquillitas animi. Praeclarissimarum sententiarum huius operis breuis annotatio. [Venetiis, In aedibvs Aldi, et Andreae soceri, 1516]
   177 [i.e.,   175] numbered leaves.
   29cm.
   (Continued on next card)

8

Hermes Trismegistus.
   Poemander. Latin.

WITCHCRAFT
PA
4220
L3
A4+
1516

Jamblichus, of Chalcis. [De mysteriis. Latin] [1516]   (Card 4)
   At head of title: Index eorvm, qvae hoc in libro habentvr.
   With colophon.
   Provenance: Bibliotec: SS. Me. Novelle.
   Translations by M. Ficino.
   1. Occult sciences. 2. Philosophy, Ancient--Collections. I. Proclus Diadochus. In Platonicum Alcibiadem. II. Proclus Diadochus. De sacrificio. I.
   (Continued on next card)

8

Witchcraft
PA
4220
L3
A4
1577

Hermes Trismegistus.
   Jamblichus, of Chalcis.
   [De mysteriis. Latin]
   Iamblichvs De mysteriis Ægyptiorvm, Chaldæorum, Assyriorum. Proclvs in Platon cum Alcibiadem de anima, atque dæmone. Idem De sacrificio & magia. Porphyrivs De diuinis atq; dæmonib. Psellvs De dæmonibus. Mercvrii Trismegisti Pimander. Eiusdem Asclepius. Lvgdvni, apvd Ioan. Tornaesivm, 1577.
   543, [1] p. 13cm.
   Title vignette (printer's mark)
   "Marsilivs Ficinvs ... se commendat": p. 3.

[2]   25-1968

Witchcraft
GR
142
H6
A3
no.17

A Hertfordshire miracle. The most cruell and bloody murther, committed by an inkeeper's wife, called Annis Dell, and her sonne George Dell, four yeeres since, on the bodie of a childe called Anthony James in Bishop's Hatfield in the countie of Hartford, and now most miraculously revealed by the sister of the said Anthony, who at the time of the murther had her tongue cut out, and four yeares remaynes dumme, and speechless, and now perfectly speaketh, revealing the murther, having ...
   (Continued on next card)

16-2574

tchcraft
A **Hertfordshire** miracle ... (Card 2)
2 tongue to be seen. Who were executed at Hartford the 4 of August last past 1606. Reprinted, with an introductory by W. B. Gerish. Bishop's Stortford, 1913.
.17 27 p. 22cm (Hertfordshire folk lore. no.
The original pamphlet is in 2 parts and is entitled: The most cruell and bloody murther committed by ... Annis Dell ... With the severall witchcrafts and most damnable practises of one Johane Harrison and her daughter ... London, Printed for W. Ferebrand and J. Wright, 1606.
1. Crime and criminals—England—Hertfordshire. 2. Dell, Mrs. Annis, d. 1606. 3. Dell, George, d. 1606. I. Gerish, William Blyth, ed. II. Title: The most cruell and bloody murther ...
16-25741
Library of Congress GR142.H6A3 no. 13

A Hertfordshire witch.
tchcraft
R 42 6 3 .7
Gerish, William Blyth.
A Hertfordshire witch; or, The story of Jane Wenham, the "wise woman" of Walkern, by W. B. Gerish. [Bishop's Stortford? 1906]
13 p. 23cm. [Hertford shire folk lore. no.7]

Hertius, Johann Nikolaus, 1651-1710, ed.
TCHCRAFT
52
Mauritius, Erich, 1631-1692.
Dissertationes et opuscula de selectis jurispublici, feudalis & privati vati argumentis conscripta, & seorsim antehac diversis locis edita, jam...in unum volumen collecta. Accessit praefatio Dn. Joannis Nicolai Hertii... Francofurti ad Moenum, Sumptibus Christophori Olfen, 1692.
1256 p. 21cm.
"De denuntiatione sagarum dissertatio": p.1035-1138. Followed by an appendix containing Mauritius' opinion
IC
(Continued on next card)

Hertius, Johann Nikolaus, 1651-1710, ed.
TCHCRAFT
52
Mauritius, Erich, 1631-1692. Dissertationes et opuscula...1692. (Card 2)
in a witchcraft case. The dissertation was originally published at Tübingen in 1664 with title: Dissertatio inauguralis De denuntiatione sagarum. (Respondent: C. Daurer)
1. Law--Addresses, essays, lectures. 2. Witchcraft. 3. Trials (Witchcraft) I. His Dissertatio inauguralis De denuntiatione sagarum. II. Daurer, Christophorus, respondent. III. Title: De denuntiatione sagarum. IV. Hertius, Johann Nikolaus, 1651-1710, ed.

Hertz, Wilhelm, 1835-1902.
Aus dichtung und sage; vorträge und aufsätze von Wilhelm Hertz. Hrsg. von Karl Vollmöller. Stuttgart und Berlin, J. G. Cotta nachfolger, 1907.
x, 219, [1] p. 18½cm.
Reprinted from different periodicals.
CONTENTS.—Über den ritterlichen frauendienst.—Die Walküren.—Die Nibelungensage.—Altfranzösische volkslieder.—Beowulf, das älteste germanische epos.—Mythologie der schwäbischen volkssagen.—Die hexenprobe.—Mörikes "Feuerreiter".
1. Literature, Medieval—Hist. & crit. 2. Witchcraft. 3. Folk-songs—France. 4. Mörike, Eduard Friedrich, 1804-1875. Der feuerreiter. 5. Folk literature—Swabia. I. Vollmöller, Karl Gustav, 1848-1922, ed. II. Title.
32-10346
Library of Congress PN674.H4 804

r W
460
Hertz, Wilhlem, 1835-1902.
Der Werwolf; Beitrag zur Sagengeschichte. Stuttgart, A. Kröner, 1862.
134 p. 22cm.
Bound with Rochholz, E. L. Gaugöttinnen: Walburg, Verena und Gertrud. Leipzig, 1870.
1. Werwolves. I. Title.

WITCHCRAFT
GR 200 H57
Hertzberg, Rafäel, 1845-1896.
Kulturbilder ur Finlands historia. Helsingfors, G. W. Edlund, 1885-88.
2 v. illus. 23cm.
Contents.--I. Skildringar och sägner från Finlands hednatid.--II. Hexprocesser på 1600 talet.
Incomplete: v. 2 lacking illus.
1. Folk-lore--Finland. 2. Witchcraft--Finland. I. Title.
8

Witchcraft
BF 1566 H58+
Herzog,
Hexe, Hexerei. [Leipzig, J. F. Gleditsch, 1830]
343-359 p. 28cm.
Detached from Allgemeine Encyclopädie der Wissenschaften und Künste [hrsg. von J. Ersch and J. G. Gruber], 2e Zection, Th. 7.
Article actually begins on p. 342.
P. 337-338 bound in front.
8
1. Witchcraft. I. Title.

Herzog Johann Casimirs "Gerichts-Ordnung die Hexerei betreffend."
Witchcraft
BF 1583 A2 S27+ 1898
Saxe-Coburg. Laws, statutes, etc.
Herzog Johann Casimirs "Gerichts-Ordnung die Hexerei betrf: Publiciret ahm 21. February 1629." Aus dem Hildburghäuser Ratsarchiv mitgeteilt von Dr. A. Human.
(In Verein für Sachsen-Meiningische Geschichte und Landeskunde, Meiningen. Schriften. Hildburghausen. 27cm. 29 (1898), p. 99-112)
8
~~(Continued on next card)~~

Heshusius, Tilemann, 1527-1588.
WITCHCRAFT
BX 2340 V94
Vom Exorcismo. Das dieser ohne Verletzung des Gewissens bey der Tauffe wol mag gebraucht vnd behalten werden: etliche Tractetlein. I. Iusti Menij. II. Lutheri Vorrede vber das Tauffbüchlein. III. Die gewöhnliche Gebet bey der Tauffe im Stifft vnd der Thumkirchen zu Cölln an der Sprew. IIII. Aus dem Appendice D. Vrbani Regij. V. Zwo Episteln Tilemanni Heshusij. VI. Eine Epistel Philippi Melanchton is. VII. D. Iacobi Co-
8
(Continued on next card)

Heshusius, Tilemann, 1527-1588.
WITCHCRAFT
BX 2340 V94
Vom Exorcismo ... 1591. (Card 2)
leri Büchlein. Alles zu guter Nachrichtung den einfeltigen Leyen zum besten zusammen bracht. [Franckfurt an der Oder] In Verlegung Johan vnd Friderich Hartmans, 1591.
[269] p. 17cm.
Title in red and black.
With colophon: Gedruckt zu Franckfurt an der Oder, durch Nicolaum Voltzen, 1591.
8
(Continued on next card)

Heshusius, Tilemann, 1527-1588.
WITCHCRAFT
BX 2340 V94
Vom Exorcismo ... 1591. (Card 3)
Vom Exorcismo, oder Von dem Beschweren der Kinder bey der Tauffe. Drey Sendbriefe deren zwene D. Tilemannvs Heshvsivs: den dritten Herr Philippvs Melanchton geschrieben ... Verdeutscht durch Heinrich Rätel, has special t. p. with date 1590.
Vom Exorcismo bey der Tauffe ... durch Jacobum Colerum D. has special t. p., no date.
8
~~(Continued on next card)~~

WITCHCRAFT
BF 1501 D12 no.1
[Hesse, Otto Justus Basilius] d. 1793.
Versuch einer biblischen Dämonologie, oder Untersuchung der Lehre der heil. Schrift vom Teufel und seiner Macht. Mit einer Vorrede und einem Anhang von D. Johann Salomo Semler. Halle im Magdeburgischen, C. H. Hemmerde, 1776.
28 p. l., 359 p. 17cm.
No. 1 in vol. lettered Dämonologische Schriften.
1. Devil. 2. Demonomania. 3. Bible--Criticism, interpretation, etc. I. Semler, Johann Salomo, 1725-1791. II. Title.
8

Hesse, Otto Justus Basilius, d. 1793.
WITCHCRAFT
BF 1523 V19 no.1
Untersuchung und Beleuchtung der sogenannten biblischen Dämonologie, die mit Herrn D. Semlers Anhange herausgekommen ist. Danzig, Bey J. H. Flörke, 1778.
348 p. 17cm.
No. 1 in vol. lettered Varia scripta demonolog.
1. Devil--Biblical teaching. 2. Hesse, Otto Justus Basilius, d. 1793. Versuch einer biblischen Dämonologie. 3. Demonology.
8

WITCHCRAFT
BF 1583 Z7 1630
Hesse, Werner.
Ueber einen Hexenprozess in München-Gladbach.
(In Rheinische Geschichtsblätter. Bonn. 23cm. 3. Jahrg., No. 8 (1897), p. [225]-232)
1. Trials (Witchcraft)--Germany. 2. Trials (Witchcraft)--München-Gladbach, Germany. I. Title.
8

WITCHCRAFT
BF 1583 Z7 1680
Hessler, Matthes, defendant.
Verhörsprotokoll über einen der Hexerei Angeklagten. Frötstedt, den 27. July 1680.
(In Aus der Heimath. Blätter der Vereinigung für Gothaische Geschichte und Alterthumsforschung. Gotha. 25cm. 1. Jahrg., Nr. 3 (1897), p. 41-43)
1. Trials (Witchcraft)--Germany. I. Title. II. Aus der Heimath.
8

Heucher, Johann Heinrich, 1677-1747.
Ex historia naturali de vegetalibus magicis. English.
WITCHCRAFT
GR 780 H59 1886
Heucher, Johann Heinrich, 1677-1747.
Magic plants; being a translation of a curious tract entitled De vegetalibus magicis, written by M. J. H. Heucher. (1700.) Edited by Edmund Goldsmid. Edinburgh [Printed by E. & G. Goldsmid] 1886.
39 p. 23cm. (Bibliotheca curiosa)
Title in red and black.
"This edition is limited to 275 small-paper copies ..."
Translation of Ex historia naturali
8
(Continued on next card)

Heucher, Johann Heinrich, 1677-1747.
Ex historia naturali de vegetalibus magicis. English.
WITCHCRAFT
GR 780 H59 1886
Heucher, Johann Heinrich, 1677-1747.
Magic plants ... 1886. (Card 2)
de vegetalibus magicis generatim, by Heucher and J. Fabricius.
"I have given, as an Appendix, a translation from the Official records of the Royal Court of Guernsey, of the trials of three women for witchcraft in 1617. This translation is taken from Mr. J. L. Pitt's Witchcraft and Devil-Lore in the Channel Islands." --ed.
8
~~(Continued on next card)~~

CATALOGUE OF THE CORNELL WITCHCRAFT COLLECTION

WITCHCRAFT
GR
780
H59
1886

Heucher, Johann Heinrich, 1677-1747.
Magic plants; being a translation of a curious tract entitled De vegetalibus magicis, written by M. J. H. Heucher. (1700.) Edited by Edmund Goldsmid. Edinburgh [Printed by E. & G. Goldsmid] 1886.
39 p. 23cm. (Bibliotheca curiosa)
Title in red and black.
"This edition is limited to 275 small-paper copies ..."

8   Translation of Ex historia naturali
(Continued on next card)

WITCHCRAFT
GR
780
H59
1886

Heucher, Johann Heinrich, 1677-1747.
Magic plants ... 1886. (Card 2)
de vegetalibus magicis generatim, by Heucher and J. Fabricius.
"I have given, as an Appendix, a translation from the Official records of the Royal Court of Guernsey, of the trials of three women for witchcraft in 1617. This translation is taken from Mr. J. L. Pitt's Witchcraft and Devil-Lore in the Channel Islands."
--ed.

8   (Continued on next card)

WITCHCRAFT
GR
780
H59
1886

Heucher, Johann Heinrich, 1677-1747.
Magic plants ... 1886. (Card 3)

1. Plants (in religion, folk-lore, etc.) 2. Magic. 3. Witchcraft--Guernsey. I. His Ex historia naturali de vegetalibus magicis. English. II. Fabricius, Joannes, Rosnavia-Hungarus. III. Goldsmid, Edmund Marsden, ed. and tr. IV. Pitts, John Linwood. Witchcraft and devil-lore in the Channel Islands. V. Title.

8

Die heutige Hexerey und Zauberkunst.
WITCHCRAFT
BF
1565
S59

[Simon, Jordan] pater, 1719-1776.
Das grosse Welt-betrügende Nichts; oder, Die heutige Hexerey und Zauberkunst in zweyen Büchern, von Ardoino Ubbidente dell'Osa [pseud.] entworfen ... Wirtzburg, J. J. Stahel, 1761.
4 p. l., 600 p. 17cm.
Second edition published under title: Die Nichtigkeit der Hexerey und Zauberkunst. (cf. Kayser)
Contents.-- 1. Th. Die Gründe und
(Continued on next card)

8
NIC

Die heutige Hexerey und Zauberkunst.
WITCHCRAFT
BF
1565
S59

[Simon, Jordan] pater, 1719-1776. Das grosse Welt-betrügende Nichts ... 1761. (Card 2)

Beweisthümer aus der Göttlichen Schrift ... dass die heutige Hexerey oder Zauberkunst ein leeres Nichts seye.--2. Th. Die Widerlegung der aus der Göttlichen Schrift ... gezogenen Beweis-Gründen, dass es Hexerey oder Zauberkunst gebe.
1. Witchcraft. 2. Witchcraft in the Bible. 3. Superstition. I. Title. II. Title: Die heutige Hexerey und Zauberkunst.

8
NIC

Hexe, Hexerei.
Witchcraft
BF
1566
H58+

Herzog,
Hexe, Hexerei. [Leipzig, J. F. Gleditsch, 1830]
343-359 p. 28cm.
Detached from Allgemeine Encyclopädie der Wissenschaften und Künste [hrsg. von J. Ersch and J. G. Gruber], 2e Zection, Th. 7.
Article actually begins on p. 342.
P. 337-338 bound in front.

8   1. Witchcraft. I. Title.

Eine Hexe nach ihrer greslichen Gestalt und gerechten Strafe...
WITCHCRAFT
BF
1583
A2
R57

Rinder, Johann Christian.
Eine Hexe nach ihrer greslichen Gestalt und gerechten Strafe, stellete auf das erschollene und sich weit ausbreitende Gerücht eines zu Apolda vermeintlich vorgegangenen Zauberwerks in nachmittäglicher Sonntags-Predigt den 17. Nov. 1748, aus einem besonders dazu erwehlten Text, 2 B. Mos. XXII, v. 18, Die Zauberinnen solt du nicht leben lassen, vor, und gabs nebst wahrhaftigem Bericht der ganzen Sache zum Druck. Jena, Im Verlag der Marggrafischen
(Continued on next card)

8
NIC

Eine Hexe nach ihrer greslichen Gestalt und gerechten Strafe...
WITCHCRAFT
BF
1583
A2
R57

Rinder, Johann Christian.
Eine Hexe nach ihrer greslichen Gestalt und gerechten Strafe... (Card 2)

Buchhandlung [175-?].
44 p. 22cm.

1. Witchcraft--Apolda, Ger. 2. Witchcraft--Sermons. I. Title.

Hexe og Hexeprocesser i Danmark.
Witchcraft
BF
1584
D4
D13

Dahlerup, Verner, 1859-1938.
Hexe og Hexeprocesser i Danmark. Et Foredrag holdt i Foreningen til Oplysningens Fremme blandt Kjøbenhavns Arbejdere. Kjøbenhavn, Studentersamfundets Forlag, 1888.
22 p. 22cm. (Studentersamfundets Smaaskrifter, Nr. 80)

Hexelforfølgelser isaer i Danmark.
Witchcraft
BF
1584
D4
B21

Bang, Vilhelm.
Hexevaesen og hexelforfølgelser isaer i Danmark. Kjøbenhavn, J. Frimodt, 1896.
138 p. 22cm.

1. Witchcraft. 2. Witchcraft--Denmark. I. Title.

Hexen Coppel.
Witchcraft
BF
1565
E46

Ellinger, Johann.
Hexen Coppel; das ist, Vhralte Ankunfft vnd grosse Zunfft des vnholdseligen Vnholden oder Hexen, welche in einer Coppel von einem gantzen Dutzet auff die Schaw vnd Musterund geführet. Franckfurt am Mayn, J. C. Onckels, 1629.
59 p. 19cm.

1. Witchcraft. I. Title.

Hexen in der Landvogtei Ortenau und Reichsstadt Offenburg.
WITCHCRAFT
BF
1583
V91

Volk, Franz.
Hexen in der Landvogtei Ortenau und Reichsstadt Offenburg. Ein Beitrag zur Sittengeschichte von Franz Volk, Bürgermeister in Offenburg. Lahr, M. Schauenburg, 1882.
154 p. 22cm.

1. Witchcraft--Baden. 2. Witchcraft--Germany. I. Title.

8

Die Hexen in und um Prenzlau.
WITCHCRAFT
BF
1583
O38+

Ohle, Rudolf, 1857-
Die Hexen in und um Prenzlau. Eine Untersuchung über Entstehung, Verlauf und Ausgang des Hexenwahnes.
(In Uckermärkischer Museums- und Geschichts-Verein, Prenzlau. Mitteilungen. Prenzlau. 26cm. 4. Bd., 1. Heft (1908), p. [1]-86)

1. Witchcraft--Prenzlau, Germany. 2. Witchcraft--Germany. I. Uckermärkischer Museums- und Geschichts-Verein, Prenzlau. II. Title.

8
NIC

Hexen Meysterey.
WITCHCRAFT
BF
1569
A2
M72
1545

Molitor, Ulrich, fl. 1470-1501.
Hexen Meysterey. Dess hochgebornen Fürsten, Hertzog Sigmunds von Osterreich mit D. Vlrich Molitoris vnd Herr Cunrad Schatz, weilandt Burgermeister zü Costentz, ein schön Gesprech von den Onholden, ob die selben bösen Weyber, Hagel, Reiffen, vnd ander Ongefell, den Menschen zuschaden, machen können. Auch sunst ihrem gantzen Hexen Handel, waher der kumpt, vnd was dauon zühalten sey, vnd zum letzsten, das sie auss R.

8   (Continued on next card)

Hexen Meysterey.
WITCHCRAFT
BF
1569
A2
M72
1545

Molitor, Ulrich, fl. 1470-1501. Hexen Meysterey ... 1545. (Card 2)

Rechten abzüthun seyen. &c. Weitleuffiger mit mer Exempeln der Alten, dann vor nie kains aussgangen. Nottwendig vnnd nutz aller Obergkeyt zūwissen. [Cölln?] 1545.
[32] l. illus. 20cm.
8 woodcuts (several repeated)
For place, see Grässe, Trésor (describes 1544 ed.)
Translation of De lamiis et phitonicis mulieribus.
(Continued on next card)

8

Hexen oder Unholden Predigten.
Witchcraft
BF
1583
A2
G73

Graeter, M Jacob
Hexen oder Unholden Predigten. Darinnen zu zweyen vnderschiedlichen Predigten, auff das kürtzest vnnd ordenlichest angezeigt würdt, was in disen allgemeinen Landklagen, vber die Hexen vnd Vnholden, von selbigen warhafftig vnnd Gottseeliglich zuhalten. Tübingen, A. Hock, 1589.
[28] p. 20cm.

1. Witchcraft. I. Title.

MSS
Bd.
WITCHCRAFT
BF
H61+

Hexen-Processe im Elsass. Vom Jahre 1615 bis 1635. [Hamburg] 1835 [ca. 1900]
5 l. 27cm.

Carnap's typewritten copy of an article in Die Börsen-Halle, no. 1092-1093, Hamburg, 1835.

1. Trials (Witchcraft)--Alsace.

Die Hexen-Prozesse der ehemaligen Reichsstadt Nördlingen in den Jahren 1590-94.
Witchcraft
BF
1583
Z7
1590

Weng, Johann Friedrich.
Die Hexen-Prozesse der ehemaligen Reichsstadt Nördlingen in den Jahren 1590-94. Aus den Kriminal-Akten des Nördlingischen Archives gezogen ... Nördlingen, C. H. Beck [1838]
60, 28 p. 22cm.
Aus der historisch-statistischen Zeitschrift: "Das Ries, wie es war und wie es ist" besonders abgedruckt.
1. Trials (Witchcraft)--Nördlingen. 2. Trials (Witchcraft)--Germany. I. Title.
Hollin, Maria, fl. 1594. I. Title.

8

CATALOGUE OF THE CORNELL WITCHCRAFT COLLECTION

Hexen-Prozesse der Vorzeit.

Witchcraft
BF
1583
.R24
    Rautert, Fr   , ed.
    Etwas Näheres über die Hexen-Prozesse der Vorzeit, aus authentischer Quelle von Fr. Rautert. Essen, Gedruckt bei G. D. Bädeker, 1827.
    4 p. l., 79, [1] p. 22cm.
    "Die Zeichnung für den Umschlag [ist] nach alten Holzschnitten aus dem 15ten und 16ten Jahrhundert."
    Caption title: Hexen-Prozesse der Vorzeit.
    1. Trials (Witchcraft)--Germany. I. Title. II. Title: Hexen-Prozesse der Vorzeit.

Hexen-Report.

    Seebacher-Mesaritsch, Alfred, 1925-
    Hexen-Report. Bericht über eine Massentragödie in d. Steiermark, 1425-1746. [Illustr.] Graz, Leykam (1972).
    272 p. illus. 21cm.
    Bibliography: p. 271.

    COOdc   73-321799

Hexen, Teufel und Blocksbergspuk.

WITCHCRAFT
    Knortz, Karl, 1841-1918.
    Hexen, Teufel und Blocksbergspuk in Geschichte, Sage und Literatur. Annaberg, Sachsen, Grasers Verlag (R. Liesche) [1913?]
    169 p. 19cm.
    Bibliographical footnotes.
    1. Witchcraft. 2. Demonology. 3. Supernatural in literature. I. Title. II. Title: Blocksbergspuk, Hexen, Teufel und.

Hexen und Hexenmeister.

WITCHCRAFT
    Pressel, Wilhelm, writer on witchcraft.
    Hexen und Hexenmeister; oder, Vollständige und getreue Schilderung und Beurtheilung des Hexenwesens. Stuttgart, C. Belser, 1860.
    iv, 102 p. 19cm.
    1. Witchcraft. I. Title. II. Title: Vollständige und getreue Schilderung und Beurtheilung des Hexenwesens.

Die Hexen und Hexenprocesse.

WITCHCRAFT
    Vollert, Anton, 1828-1897.
    Die Hexen und Hexenprocesse. Eine criminal-historische Skizze. Von Dr. A. Vollert, Herausgeber des "neuen Pitaval". [Leipzig? 1871]
    [595]-603 p. 23cm.
    Caption title.
    Extract from a periodical.
    Incomplete copy: part one only of 2.
    1. Witchcraft. 2. Trials (Witchcraft) I. Title.

WITCHCRAFT
    Hexen und Hexenprozesse. Leipzig, Verlag zur Kunst und Wissenschaft A. O. Paul [1904]
    48 p. 11cm. (Miniatur-Bibliothek. 632.)
    1. Witchcraft--Germany. 2. Trials (Witchcraft)--Germany.

Hexen und Hexenprozesse.

BF
1565
B29
    Baschwitz, Kurt, 1886-
    Hexen und Hexenprozesse; die Geschichte eines Massenwahns und seiner Bekämpfung. München, Rütten & Loening [1963]
    480 p. illus., plates. 21cm.
    1. Witchcraft. 2. Trials (Witchcraft) 3. Magic. I. Title.

Hexen und Hexenprozesse.

WITCHCRAFT
BF
1569
K77
1858
    Köppen, Karl Friedrich, 1808-1863.
    Hexen und Hexenprozesse. Zur Geschichte des Aberglaubens und des inquisitorischen Prozesses. Von K. F. Köppen. 2. Aufl. Leipzig, O. Wigand, 1858.
    119 p. 14cm.
    1. Witchcraft--History. 2. Trials (Witchcraft)--History. I. Title.

Hexen und Hexenprozesse im Wallis.

WITCHCRAFT
BF
1584
S97
K12
    Kämpfen, Peter Joseph
    Hexen & [i. e. und] Hexenprozesse im Wallis; nach bewährten Quellen bearb. und kritisch beleuchtet. Stans, C. von Matt, 1867.
    76 p. 19cm.
    1. Witchcraft--Valais (Canton) 2. Trials (Witchcraft)--Valais (Canton) I. Title.

Hexen und Hexenzauber.

WITCHCRAFT
BF
1583
K95
    Kühnau, Richard, 1858-1930.
    Hexen und Hexenzauber, nebst einem Anhang über Zauberer und Hexenmeister.
    (In Schlesische Gesellschaft für Volkskunde, Breslau. Mitteilungen. Breslau, 1894/96-1938. 25cm. [Bd. 7] Heft 13 (1905), p. 82-98)
    Caption title.
    1. Witchcraft--Germany. I. Title.

Die Hexen von Baden-Baden.

WITCHCRAFT
BF
1583
Z7
1627b
    Hermann, Ernst, 1837-1908.
    Die Hexen von Baden-Baden. Nach den Original-Akten des allgemeinen grossherzogl. Landes-Archivs in Karlsruhe. Karlsruhe, Macklot [1890]
    56 p. 18cm.
    1. Trials (Witchcraft)--Baden-Württemberg. I. Title.

Hexenaberglaube, Hexenprozesse und Zauberwahn in Dortmund.

WITCHCRAFT
BF
1583
R898
    Rübel, Carl, 1848-1916.
    Hexenaberglaube, Hexenprozesse und Zauberwahn in Dortmund, von Karl Rübel.
    (In Beiträge zur Geschichte Dortmunds und der Grafschaft Mark. Dortmund. 23cm. v. 22 (1913), p. [96]-117)
    Caption title.
    Bibliographical footnotes.
    1. Witchcraft--Dortmund. I. Title.

Hexenaberglaube in Schlesien.

Witchcraft
BF
1583
W83
    Wittig, Gregor Constantin.
    Hexenaberglaube in Schlesien.
    (In Psychische Studien. Leipzig. 23cm. 25. Jahrg., 9. Heft (1898), p. 443-450)
    In envelope.
    1. Witchcraft--Silesia. I. Title.

Hexenaberglaube und Hexenprozesse in Deutschland.

WITCHCRAFT
BF
1583
M94
    Müller, Curt.
    Hexenaberglaube und Hexenprozesse in Deutschland. Leipzig, P. Reclam Jun. [1893]
    172 p. 15cm. (Universal-Bibliothek, 3166-3167)
    1. Witchcraft--Germany. 2. Trials (Witchcraft)--Germany.

Die Hexenbulle.

WITCHCRAFT
BF
1565
C36
1889
    Catholic Church. Pope, 1484-1492 (Innocentius VIII) Summis desiderantes affectibus (9 Dec. 1484)
    Die Hexenbulle, nebst Auszügen aus dem "Hexenhammer." Aus dem Lateinischen ins Deutsche übers. und mit erläuternden Anmerkungen versehen ... 2. Aufl., von Wilhelm Römer. Schaffhausen (Schweiz) 1889.
    32 p. 21cm.
    "Zum 400jährigen Jubiläum des 'Hexenhammers.'"
    (Continued on next card)

Die Hexenbulle.

WITCHCRAFT
BF
1565
C36
1889
    Catholic Church. Pope, 1484-1492 (Innocentius VIII) Summis desiderantes affectibus (9 Dec. 1484)
    Die Hexenbulle...1889. (Card 2)
    Each page of the Hexenbulle has Latin text at the top, followed by German translation below.
    1. Witchcraft. I. Institoris, Henricus, d. 1508. Malleus maleficarum, German. II. Römer, Wilhelm, ed. & tr. III. Title.

Die Hexenbulle Papst Innocens' VIII.

WITCHCRAFT
BF
1565
C36
1905
    Catholic Church. Pope, 1484-1492 (Innocentius VIII) Summis desiderantes affectibus (9 Dec. 1484)
    Die Hexenbulle Papst Innocens' VIII. Summis desiderantes; aus dem Bullarium magnum. Übertragen und hrsg. von Paul Friedrich. Leipzig, J. Zeitler, 1905.
    15 p. 25cm.
    1. Witchcraft. I. Title.

Die Hexengerichte im Prättigau.

Witchcraft
BF
1584
S97
K97+
    Kuoni, Michael.
    Die Hexengerichte im Prättigau. Kulturhistorische Skizze aus dem 17. Jahrhundert.
    (In Alpenrosen. Ein schweizerisches Sonntagsblatt. Bern. 27cm. 15. Jahrg. (1885), p. 366-367, 372-373)
    Alpenrosen is a "Gratis-Beilage zum 'Intelligenzblatt der Stadt Bern'."
    1. Witchcraft--Switzerland. I. Title. II. Alpenrosen. Ein schweizerisches Sonntagsblatt.

CATALOGUE OF THE CORNELL WITCHCRAFT COLLECTION

Der Hexenglaube.

WITCHCRAFT
BF
1566
H46
1899

Heigl, Ferdinand.
  Der Hexenglaube. Ein Rückblick als Perspektive für die Spiritisten unserer Zeit. Von Ferdinand Heigl, Verfasser der "Spaziergänge eines Atheisten." 2. Aufl. Bamberg, Handelsdruckerei Bamberg [1899]
  2 v. in 1. 12cm. (Volksschriften zur Umwälzung der Geister, VII a, b)
  Contents.--1. T. Der Hexenglaube.--2. T. Der Spiritismus.
  1. Witchcraft--History. 2. Spiritualism. I. Title.

8

Der Hexenglaube bei den Jatrochemikern des 17. Jahrhunderts.

R
131
A1
Z94
n.s.
no.12

Minder, Robert.
  Der Hexenglaube bei den Jatrochemikern des 17. Jahrhunderts. Zürich, Juris-Verlag, 1963.
  26 p. illus. 23cm. (Zürcher medizingeschichtliche Abhandlungen, neue Reihe, Nr. 12)
  Issued also as thesis, Zürich.

  1. Medicine--15th-18th cent. 2. Witchcraft. I. Title.

Der Hexenglaube in Hessen.

WITCHCRAFT
BF
1583
F83+

Franz, Heinrich.
  Der Hexenglaube in Hessen.
  (In: Hessenland. Kassel. 27cm. v.30 (1916) p. 2-3, 17-19, 39-41, 145-149, 161-164, 273-276)

8
NIC   1. Witchcraft--Hesse.

Hexenglaube und Hexenprocesse, vornämlich in den braunschweigischen Landen.

WITCHCRAFT
BF
1583
R46

Rhamm, A.
  Hexenglaube und Hexenprocesse, vornämlich in den braunschweigischen Landen, von A. Rhamm. Wolfenbüttel, J. Zwissler, 1882.
  104 p. 20cm.

  Bibliographical footnotes.

  1. Witchcraft--Brunswick (Duchy) 2. Trials (Witchcraft)--Brunswick (Duchy) I. Title.

8
NIC

Hexenglaube und Hexenprozesse in unserer Heimat.

WITCHCRAFT
BF
1583
K21

Kausch, Friedrich.
  Hexenglaube und Hexenprozesse in unserer Heimat; ein Beitrag zur Geschichte der Provinz Sachsen und des Harzgebietes. Burg b. M., 1927.
  78 p. 19cm.

  1. Witchcraft--Saxony (Province) 2. Witchcraft--Harz Mountains. 3. Trials (Witchcraft)--Saxony (Province) 4. Trials (Witchcraft)--Harz Mountains. I. Title.

8
NIC

Hexenglaube und Hexenwahn in Erkelenz.

Witchcraft
BF
1583
G24

Gaspers, Josef.
  Hexenglaube und Hexenwahn in Erkelenz. Erkelenz, im Selbstverlag des Vereins. Kommissionsverlag: J. Herle, 1921.
  17 p. fold. pl. 19cm. (Erkelenzer Geschichts- und Altertumsverein. Heft 3)

  1. Witchcraft--Erkelenz, Germany. I. Title.

Der Hexenhammer.

Witchcraft
BF
1569
A2I59
1906

Institoris, Henricus, d. 1508.
  Malleus maleficarum. Der Hexenhammer, verfasst von den beiden Inquisitoren Jakob Sprenger und Heinrich Institoris. Zum ersten Male ins Deutsche übertragen und eingeleitet von J. W. R. Schmidt. Berlin, H. Barsdorf, 1906.
  3 v. 20cm.

  Translation of Malleus maleficarum.

Der Hexenhammer, seine Bedeutung und die gefälschte Kölner Approbation vom Jahre 1487.

WITCHCRAFT
DD
741
W52
v.26
no.4

Hansen, Joseph, 1862-1943.
  Der Hexenhammer, seine Bedeutung und die gefälschte Kölner Approbation vom Jahre 1487.
  (In: Westdeutsche Zeitschrift für Geschichte und Kunst. Trier. 24cm. v.26 (1907) no.4. p. 372-404)

8
NIC   1. Institoris, Henricus, d.1508. Malleus maleficarum. I. Title.

Die Hexenplätze der Rufacher Hexenurkunden.

WITCHCRAFT
BF
1583
W23

Walter, Theobald.
  Die Hexenplätze der Rufacher Hexenurkunden.
  (In Jahrbuch für Geschichte, Sprache und Litteratur Elsass-Lothringens. Strassburg. 24cm. 12. Jahrg. (1896), p. [40]-43)

8   1. Witchcraft--Alsace. I. Title.

Der Hexenprocess: ein Traum erzählt von einer unpartheyischen Feder.

Witchcraft
BF
1565
S83
S84

[Sterzinger, Joseph] 1746-1821.
  Der Hexenprocess: ein Traum erzählt von einer unpartheyischen Feder im Jahre 1767. [München?] 1767.
  18 p. 22cm.

  Attribution and dates from Fieger, Hans. P. Don Ferdinand Sterzinger, München, 1907, p. 144-45. (Accepted also by Holzmann)
  1. Sterzinger, Ferdinand, 1721-1786. Akademische Rede von dem gemeinen Vorurtheile der ... Hexer ey. 2. Witchcraft. I. Eine unpartheyische Feder. II. Title.

8

Hexenprocess -- und Glauben, Pfaffen und Teufel.

WITCHCRAFT
BF
1569
H69

Hössli, Heinrich.
  Hexenprocess -- und Glauben, Pfaffen und Teufel. Als Beitrag zur Cultur- und Sittengeschichte der Jahrhunderte. Leipzig, H. Barsdorf, 1892.
  80 p. 22cm.

  1. Witchcraft--History. 2. Superstition. I. Title.

8
NIC

Ein Hexenprocess, verhandelt bei dem Amtsgerichte zu Neustadt an der Dosse, im Jahre 1667.

WITCHCRAFT
BF
1583
Z7
1667

Riedel, Adolph Friedrich Johann, 1809-1872.
  Ein Hexenprocess, verhandelt bei dem Amtsgerichte zu Neustadt an der Dosse, im Jahre 1667; nach den Akten vom Geheimen Archivrathe Prof. Dr. Riedel. [Berlin, 18--]
  [106]-119 p. 25cm.

  Caption title.
  Detached from Märkische Forschungen.

8
NIC   1. Trials (Witchcraft)--Neustadt, Ger. (Brandenburg) 2. Müller, Maria (Rhinow) I. Title.

Ein Hexenprocess vom Jahre 1705.

Witchcraft
BF
1583
Z7
1705

Schütz, W
  Ein Hexenprocess vom Jahre 1705, mitgetheilt von Herrn Amtscommissär W. Schütz in Weimar. [Jena, 1853]
  178-183 p. 23cm.
  In "Miscellen," detached from the Zeitschrift of the Verein für thüringische Geschichte und Altertumskunde, Jena, 1. Bd., 2. Heft, and bound in vol. lettered Miscellen über Hexerei.
  With this is bound Auen, Karl, Segen und Zauberform ein. [Jena, 1853]
  (Continued on next card)

8

Ein Hexenprocess vor dem Criminalgericht zu Horn im Fürstenthum Lippe.

WITCHCRAFT
BF
1583
Z7
1554

Wigand, Paul, 1786-1866.
  Zur Geschichte der Hexenprocesse. 1) Ein Hexenprocess vor dem Criminalgericht zu Horn im Fürstenthum Lippe. 1554. [Leipzig, S. Hirzel, 1854]
  [248]-259 p. 24cm.
  Caption title.
  Detached from his Denkwürdigkeiten, Kap. VIII.
  1. Trials (Witchcraft)--Horn, Germany. 2. Trials (Witchcraft)--Germany. I. Title.

8

Hexenprocess zu Cösitz in Sachsen, vom J. 1657.

WITCHCRAFT
BF
1583
Z7
1657

Hexenprocess zu Cösitz in Sachsen, vom J. 1657. Aus den in der Registratur zu Cösitz noch befindlichen Original Acten.
  (In Stats-Anzeigen. Göttingen. 20cm. IV. Bd., Heft 15 (1784), p. 287-293)

  At head of title: 33.
  1. Winzer, Maria, d. 1657. 2. Trials (Witchcraft)--Saxony.

8

Ein Hexenprocess zu Schongau vom Jahre 1587.

WITCHCRAFT
BF
1583
Z7
1587a

Her,   , Rat.
  Ein Hexenprocess zu Schongau vom Jahre 1587. Aus den Originalacten geschichtlich dargestellt von Rath Her. München, Druck von G. Franz, 1849.
  19 p. 24cm.
  "Aus dem Oberbay. Archiv Bd. XI. Heft 1 besonders abgedruckt."
  1. Geiger, Lucia, fl. 1587. 2. Witchcraft--Bavaria. I. Title.

8

Hexenprocesse aus dem Hennebergschen.

WITCHCRAFT
BF
1583
Z7
1668

[Schlözer, August Ludwig] 1735-1809, ed.
  Hexen Processe aus dem Hennebergschen.
  (In Stats-Anzeigen. Göttingen. 22cm. 2. Bd., Heft 6 (1782), p. 161-168)

  At head of title: 14.
  1. Trials (Witchcraft)--Thuringia. 2. Motzen, Barbara, d. 1668. I. Title.

8
NIC

Die Hexenprocesse der beiden Städte Braunsberg.

WITCHCRAFT
BF
1583
L72

Lilienthal, J A von.
  Die Hexenprocesse der beiden Städte Braunsberg, nach den Criminalacten des Braunsberger Archivs. Königsberg, T. Theile, 1861.
  161 p. 23cm.

8
NIC   1. Witchcraft--Braunsberg, Ger. 2. Trials (Witchcraft)--Braunsberg, Ger.

CATALOGUE OF THE CORNELL WITCHCRAFT COLLECTION

Hexenprocesse im Gerichte Sankt Jürgen.

WITCHCRAFT
BF
1583
Z7
1550
 Krause,   Gymnasialdirector zu Rostock.
  Hexenprocesse im Gerichte S[ank]t Jürgen, Niederende, 1550 und 1551. Mitgetheilt vom Gymnasialdirector Krause zu Rostock. [n. p., 1867?]
  227-242 p. 20cm.
  Caption title.
  Detached copy.
  1. Trials (Witchcraft)--Sankt Jürgen, Ger. (Lower Saxony) I. Title.

8
NIC

Ein Hexenprozess.

Witchcraft
BF
1583
7
621
 Günther, Louis, 1859-
  Ein Hexenprozess; ein Kapitel aus der Geschichte des dunkelsten Aberglaubens. Giessen, A. Töpelmann, 1906.
  xii, 112 p. 22cm.
  1. Kepler, Katharina,1547-1622. 2. Witchcraft. 3. Trials (Witchcraft)--Germany. I. Title.

Eine Hexenprozess-Akte vom Jahre 1547.

Witchcraft
BF
1563
E92++
no.7
 Cassel, C
  Eine Hexenprozess-Akte vom Jahre 1547. Hannover, 1899.
  131-132 p. 32cm. (Hannoversche Geschichtsblätter, 2. Jahrg., No. 17)

Ein Hexenprozess aus dem Jahre 1676.

WITCHCRAFT
BF
1583
Z7
1676
 Trefftz, Johannes.
  Ein Hexenprozess aus dem Jahre 1676. (In Verein für Thüringische Geschichte und Altertumskunde. Zeitschrift. Jena. 23cm.) 29. Bd. Heft 1 (1912), p. [171]-180)
  At head of title: IV.
  1. Trials (Witchcraft)--Thuringia. 2. Hällwarth, Margarete--d. 1676. I. Title.

8
NIC

Ein Hexenprozess aus dem 17. Jahrhundert.

Witchcraft
BF
1583
Z7
1664
 Meyer, H
  Ein Hexenprozess aus dem 17. Jahrhundert. Aus den Acten dargestellt. Hannover, Schmorl & von Seefeld, 1867.
  19 p. 24cm.
  The trial of Margarethe Meineken at Rotenburg in 1664.
  1. Meineken, Margarethe. 2. Meineken, Catharine. 3. Trials (Witchcraft)--Rotenburg, Germany.

8
NIC

Ein Hexenprozess aus der Umgegend von Trier aus dem Jahre 1572.

WITCHCRAFT
BF
1583
Z7
1572
 Hennen, Gerhardus.
  Ein Hexenprozess aus der Umgegend von Trier aus dem Jahre 1572. Ein Beitrag zur Kulturgeschichte des Mosellandes von Dr. Hennen. St. Wendel, Druck von F. Maurer, 1887.
  24 p. 25cm.
  1. Trials (Witchcraft)--Germany. I. Title.

8

Ein Hexenprozess im Elsass vom Jahre 1616.

Witchcraft
BF
1583
Z7
1616
 Dennler, J.
  Ein Hexenprozess im Elsass vom Jahre 1616. Ein Beitrag zur Kulturgeschichte des Elsasses. Nach dem Rotbuch von Enzheim. Zabern, A. Fuchs, 1896.
  28 p. 21cm.
  1. Trials (Witchcraft)--Alsace. I. Title.

Ein Hexenprozess in Schleusingen aus dem Jahre 1663.

Witchcraft
BF
1583
Z7
1663
 Fuchs, Hugo.
  Ein Hexenprozess in Schleusingen aus dem Jahre 1663. Meiningen, Keyssner, 1889
  13 p. 25cm.
  1. Witchcraft. 2. Trials (Witchcraft)--Germany. I. Title.

Der Hexenprozess und seine Anwendung in Zürich.

WITCHCRAFT
BF
1584
S97
S41
 Schweizer, Paul, 1852-1932.
  Der Hexenprozess und seine Anwendung in Zürich. (In Zürcher Taschenbuch. Zürich. 22cm. n. F. 25. Jahrg. (1902), p. 1-63)
  1. Witchcraft--Switzerland. 2. Trials (Witchcraft)--Zürich. I. Title. II. Zürcher Taschenbuch.

8
NIC

Hexenprozesse. [Bamberg? 1617-1631]

MSS
Bd.
WITCHCRAFT
BF
H63++
 119 l. 34cm.
  Title from spine.
  Manuscript, on paper, in various 17th century hands.
  Contains 35 distinct documents concerning the witchcraft persecutions in Bamberg.
  Tipped inside front cover are two letters, dated 1832 and 1845, discussing the background of the documents.
  Bound in pl aid boards.
  1. Trials   (Witchcraft)--Bamberg.
  2. Witchcraft   --Bamberg.

Hexenprozesse.

BF
1566
K78
1966
 König, Bruno Emil, 1833-1902.
  Hexenprozesse; Ausgeburten des Menschenwahns im Spiegel der Hexenprozesse und der Autodafés. [1. Aufl. der Neuausgabe] Schwerte/Ruhr, H. Freistühler [1966]
  607 p. illus. 19cm.
  1. Witchcraft. 2. Superstition. I. Title.

Hexenprozesse.

WITCHCRAFT
BF
1569
S35
 Schnabel, Johannes.
  I. Hexenprozesse. II. Folgen des dreissigjährigen Krieges. Nach den besten Quellen bearbeitet. Brilon, M. Friedländer, 1864.
  16, 11 p. 19cm.
  Cover title.
  Each item has special t. p. and separate paging.
  1. Witchcraft--History--Addresses, essays, lectures. 2. Thirty Years' War--Destruction and pillage--Addresses, essays, lectures. I. His Folgen des dreissigjährigen Krieges. II. Title: Hexenprozesse.

8

Hexenprozesse aus dem Fränkischen.

Witchcraft
BF
1583
B39+
 Beck, Peter Paul.
  Hexenprozesse aus dem Fränkischen. [Stuttgart, 1883-1885]
  various pagings. 28cm.
  Five parts, extracted from Württembergische Vierteljahrshefte für Landesgeschichte, Jahrg. vi, vii (1883-1885).
  At head of title: Historischer Verein für das Württembergische Franken.
  1. Trials (Witchcraft)--Franconia. I. Title. II. Württembergische Vierjahrshefte für Landesgeschichte.

8

Hexenprozesse aus dem 17. Jahrhundert.

Witchcraft
BF
1583
W67
 Wilhelm, , Dr., of Diepholz, ed.
  Hexenprozesse aus dem 17. Jahrhundert. Mit höherer Genehmigung aus dem Archiv des Königlich Hannoverschen Amtsgerichts Diepholz mitgetheilt von dem Amtsrichter Dr. Wilhelm zu Diepholz. Hannover, Klindworth, 1862.
  91 p. 22cm.
  1. Trials (Witchcraft)--Diepholz, Germany. 2. Trials (Witchcraft)--Germany. I. Title.

8

Hexenprozesse aus dem Steinthal, 1607-1675. [Alsace, 1607-1675]

MSS
Bd.
WITCHCRAFT
BF
H64++
 294 l. 34cm.
  Title from spine.
  Manuscript, on paper, in various 17th century hands.
  Contains 87 trial documents in German or French, and other papers relating to witchcraft procedure in Alsace.
  Note by G. L. Burr inside cover discusses provenance of the collection.
  Bound in brown boards.
  1. Trials   (Witchcraft)--Alsace.
  2. Witchcraft   --Alsace.

Die Hexenprozesse: ein cultur-historischer Versuch nebst Dokumenten.

Witchcraft
BF
1583
H122
 Haas, Carl.
  Die Hexenprozesse: ein cultur-historischer Versuch nebst Dokumenten. Tübingen, Laupp & Siebeck, 1865.
  viii, 120 p. 18cm.
  1. Witchcraft. 2. Trials (Witchcraft)--Germany. I. Title.

Die Hexenprozesse im ehemaligen Fürstbisthum Basel.

WITCHCRAFT
BF
1584
S97
S334
 Schilliger, Josef, 1854-1920.
  Die Hexenprozesse im ehemaligen Fürstbisthum Basel. (In Vom Jura zum Schwarzwald. Aaran. 25cm. 8. Bd, 1. Heft (1891), p. 1-44)
  Obituary notice from Luzerner Tagblatt for November 8, 1920 (69. Jahrg., Nr. 264) in pocket.
  1. Trials (Witchcraft)--Basel. 2. Trials (Witchcraft)--Switzerland. 3. Schilliger, Josef, 1854-1920. I. Title. II. Vom Jura zum   Schwarzwald.

3
NIC

Die Hexenprozesse im Fürstentum Brixen.

Witchcraft
BF
1584
T9
A51
 Ammann, Hartmann.
  Die Hexenprozesse im Fürstentum Brixen. Innsbruck, Wagner, 1914.
  64 p. 23cm.
  "Sonderabdruck aus den 'Forschungen und Mitteilungen zur Geschichte Tirols und Vorarlbergs', XI. Jahrgang."
  1. Trials (Witchcraft)--Brixen. I. Title.

CATALOGUE OF THE CORNELL WITCHCRAFT COLLECTION

WITCHCRAFT
BF
1583
L87

Lory, Karl.
Hexenprozesse im Gebiete des ehemaligen Markgrafenlandes. [München, 1903]
[290]-304 p. 24cm.

Extract from Festgabe Karl Theodor von Heigel, 1903.

8
NIC

1. Witchcraft--Germany. 2. Trials (Witchcraft)--Germany.

Witchcraft
BF
1583
B17

Baldi, Alexander.
Die Hexenprozesse in Deutschland und ihr hervorragendster Bekämpfer; eine kulturhistorische Abhandlung. Würzburg, Stahel, 1874.
42 p. 24cm.

1. Trials (Witchcraft)--Germany. 2. Spee, Friedrich von, 1591-1635. I. Title.

WITCHCRAFT
BF
1584
H9
M32+

Marczali, Henrik, 1856-1940.
Hexenprozesse in Ungarn.

(In: Ungarische Rundschau für historische und soziale Wissenschaften. Leipzig. 26cm. Jahrg. 1, Heft 1, Jan. 1912. p.177-187)

8
NIC

1. Trials (Witchcraft)--Hungary. 2. Witchcraft--Hungary.

Witchcraft
BF
1584
S97
D48

Dettling, Alois.
Die Hexenprozesse im Kanton Schwyz. Schwyz, Buchdruckerei von C. Triner, 1907.
115 p. illus. 24cm.

1. Trials (Witchcraft)--Schwyz. I. Title.

DD
801
B322S37
v.56

Merzbacher, Friedrich.
Die Hexenprozesse in Franken. München, C.H. Beck, 1957.
ix, 186 p. maps. 25cm. (Schriftenreihe zur bayerischen Landesgeschichte, Bd.56)

1. Trials (Witchcraft)--Franconia. 2. Witchcraft--Franconia. I. Title.

WITCHCRAFT
BF
1584
A93
R55

Riegler, Ferdinand.
Hexenprozesse, mit besonderer Berücksichtigung des Landes Steiermark. Zur steiermärkischen Kultur. Graz, U. Moser, 1926.
viii, 119 p. 21cm.

"Zur Literatur": p. viii.

8
NIC

1. Trials (Witchcraft)--Styria. I. Title.

WITCHCRAFT
BF
1576
K32

Kempf, Oskar
Hexenprozesse in Amerika.
(In Die Kritik; Wochenschau des öffentlichen Lebens. Berlin, 1894-1902. 22cm. Nr. 16 (1895), p. 113-125)

Signed: Oskar Kempf.

8
NIC

1. Trials (Witchcraft)--New England. I. Title.

WITCHCRAFT
BF
1583
S85
1932

Spielmann, Karl Heinz.
Die Hexenprozesse in Kurhessen. Nach den Quellen dargestellt. 2. Aufl. Marburg, N. G. Elwert, 1932.
viii, 248 p. illus., facsims. (part fold.) 20cm.

1. Witchcraft--Hesse-Kassel. 2. Witchcraft--Germany. 3. Criminal procedure--Hesse-Kassel. I. Title.

8
NIC

Witchcraft
BF
1566
W65

Wigand, Paul, 1786-1866.
Die Hexenprozesse, und das Einschreiten des Kammergerichts gegen die dabei eingerissenen Misbräuche. [Leipzig, J. B. Hirschfeld, 1854]
[297]-339 p. 24cm.

Chapter X of the author's Denkwürdigkeiten für deutsche Staats- und Rechtswissenschaft, für rechtsalterthümer.
I. His Denkwürdigkeiten für deutsche Staats- und Rechtswissenschaft, für Rechtsalter thümer. II. Title.

WITCHCRAFT
BF
1583
H69

Höhn, W
Hexenprozesse in den hennebergischen Ämtern Schleusingen, Suhl und Ilmenau.
(In Hennebergischer Geschichtsverein. Schriften. Schleusingen. 22cm. Nr. 4. Jahrg. 1911 (1911), p. 24-137)

1. Trials (Witchcraft)--Henneberg, Germany. 2. Trials (Witchcraft)--Germany. I. Title. II. Hennebergischer Geschichtsver ein. Schriften.

8

WITCHCRAFT
DD
801
T4
T533
v.1-2

Hempel, Richard.
Hexenprozesse in Mühlhausen.
(In: Thüringer Monatshefte [under earlier title: Pflüger] Mühlhausen. 23cm. Jahrg.1 (1924) p. 164-169, 295-300; Jahrg. 2 (1925) p. 26-33, 116-122, 271-276, 343-348)

1. Witchcraft--Mühlhausen, Ger. (Thuringia) 2. Trials (Witchcraft)--Mühlhausen, Ger. (Thuringia)

8
NIC

WITCHCRAFT
BF
1566
S67

Snell, Otto.
Hexenprozesse und Geistesstörung. Psychiatrische Untersuchungen ... München, J. F. Lehmann, 1891.
130 p. 24cm.

I. Title.

8
NIC

DD
491
H34Q3
v.35

Hartmann, Wilhelm.
Die hexenprozesse in der stadt Hildesheim, von Wilhelm Hartmann. Hildesheim und Leipzig, A. Lax, 1927.
3 p. l., 107 p. 24½cm. (Added t.-p.: Quellen und darstellungen zur geschichte Niedersachsens ... bd. 35)

1. Witchcraft--Hildesheim. I. Title.

Library of Congress   DD491.H204.bd.35   28-30893
[2]

Witchcraft
BF
1584
T9
Z7
1644

Zingerle, Ignaz Vincenz, Edler von Summersberg, 1825-1892, ed.
Ein Beitrag zu den Hexenprozessen in Tirol im 17 Jahrhundert. Von Ignaz V. Zingerle. [Innsbruck, 1882]
[183]-189 p. 23cm.

Reprint from Zeitschrift des Ferdinandeum, 3. Folge, 26. Heft, 1882.

1. Pozza, Juliana de, fl. 1644. 2. Trials (Witchcraft)--Tyrol. I. Title: Die Hexenprozesse in Tirol im 17. Jahrhundert.

8

Witchcraft
BF
1584
A93
R22
1891

Rapp, Ludwig.
Die Hexenprozesse und ihre Gegner in Tirol. 2. verm. Aufl. Mit dem Bildnisse Tartarotti's. Brixen, A. Wegner, 1891.
iv, 170 p. pot. 22cm.

First published 1874 with title: Die Hexenprozesse und ihre Gegner aus Tirol.

1. Witchcraft--Austria. 2. Trials (Witchcraft)--Austria. 3. Tanner, Adam, 1572-1632. 4. Tartarotti, Girolamo, 1706-1761. 5. Sterzinger, Ferdinand, 1721-1779. I. Title.

8

WITCHCRAFT
BF
1583
H91

Humborg, Ludwig.
Die Hexenprozesse in der Stadt Münster. Ein Beitrag zur Kulturgeschichte Münsters. Münster (Westf.), Universitätsbuchhandlung F. Coppenrath, 1914.
135 p. 24cm. (Münstersche Beiträge zur Geschichtsforschung, n. F. XXXI)

1. Trials (Witchcraft)--Münster. 2. Witchcraft--Germany. 3. Münster--History. I. Title.

8
NIC

WITCHCRAFT
BF
1583
Z7
1628

Winkler, C
Die Hexenprozesse in Türkheim in den Jahren 1628-1630. Nach den Originalprotokolen der Stadt Türkheim. Gegeben von C. Winkler. Hiezu mehrere Ansichten der auf die Prozesse bezüglichen Lokalitäten und der Marterinstrumente. [Colmar, Buchdruckerei F. Waldmeyer, 1904]
45 p. illus. 23cm.

8

1. Trials (Witchcraft)--Türkheim. 2. Trials (Witchcraft)--Alsace. I. Title

---

PF
3025
G45
v.37
1968

Koch, Hugo.
... Hexenprozesse und reste des hexenglaubens in der Wetterau, von Hugo Koch. Giessen, 1935; Amsterdam, Swet & Zeitlinger, 1968.
40 p. 24½cm. (Giessener beiträge zur deutschen philologie ... XXXVII)

"Benutste darstellungen": p. 40.

1. Witchcraft--Wetterau. I. Title.

Univ. of Chicago   PF3025.G5 no. 37 Printed by L. C.   A C 85-2273

CATALOGUE OF THE CORNELL WITCHCRAFT COLLECTION

Der Hexenprozesz gegen den Fürstenbergischen Registrator Obervogteiverweser und Notar Mathias Tinctorius und Consorten zu Hüfingen.

Franck, Archivrath in Donaueschingen.
Der Hexenprozesz gegen den Fürstenbergischen Registrator Obervogteiverweser und Notar Mathias Tinctorius und Consorten zu Hüfingen. Ein Sittenbild aus den 1630er Jahren. Freiburg im Breisgau, F. X. Wangler, 1870.
42 p. 21cm.

1. Tinctorius, Mathias, d. 1632. I. Title.

Die Hexenrichter von Würzburg.

WITCHCRAFT
BF
1583
H11
1894

[Hacker, Franz Xavier] 1836-1894.
Die Hexenrichter von Würzburg. Historische Novelle von Franz von Seeburg [pseud.] 3. Aufl. Regensburg [etc.], F. Pustet, 1894.
iv, 297 p. 17cm.

1. Witchcraft--Fiction. 2. Witchcraft--Germany. 3. Spee, Friedrich von, 1591-1635--Fiction. I. Title.

Hexenspruch und Zauberbann.

Witchcraft
58
91

Frischbier, Hermann Karl, 1823-1891.
Hexenspruch und Zauberbann; ein Beitrag zur Geschichte des Aberglaubens in der Provinz Preussen. Berlin, T. C. F. Enslin, 1870.
x, 167 p. 19cm.

1. Incantations. 2. Magic. I. Title.

Das Hexenunwesen in Verden und sein Ende.

WITCHCRAFT
BF
1583
21

Mahnke, Dietrich, 1884-
Das Hexenunwesen in Verden und sein Ende. [Stade? 1923]
28 p. 23cm.

"Sonderdruck aus dem 'Stader Archiv' 1923, Neue Folge, Heft 13."

1. Witchcraft--Verden, Ger. 2. Trials (Witchcraft)--Verden, Ger.

Eine Hexenverbrennung in der Eifel.

Witchcraft
BF
1583
7
627a

Cremer, Tillmann.
Eine Hexenverbrennung in der Eifel; Kulturbild aus der Zeit des dreissigjährigen Krieges. Bonn, P. Hanstein, 1904.
342-346, 380-383 p. 23cm. (Rheinische Geschichtsblätter, 7. Jahrg., No. 11-12)

1. Trials (Witchcraft)--Germany. 2. Executions and executioners. I. Title.

Die Hexenverfolgung in Köln.

BF
1583
357

Siebel, Friedrich Wilhelm, 1932-
Die Hexenverfolgung in Köln. Bonn, 1959.
198 p. 21cm.

Diss.--Bonn.

1. Witchcraft--Cologne. I. Title.

Der Hexenwahn.

WITCHCRAFT
BF
1583
H36

Hauffen, Adolf, 1863-1930.
Der Hexenwahn. [Prag] 1897.
20 p. 22cm. (Sammlung gemeinnütziger Vorträge. No. 230)

Caption title.

1. Witchcraft--Germany. 2. Witchcraft--Austria. I. Title.

8

WITCHCRAFT
BF
1566
O38

Der Hexenwahn.

Ohle, Rudolf, 1857-
Der hexenwahn, von pfarrer lic. dr. R. Ohle ... 1.-5. tausend... Tübingen, J. C. B. Mohr (P. Siebeck) 1908.
47, [1] p. 20cm. (Religionsgeschichtliche volksbücher für die deutsche christliche gegenwart. IV. reihe, 8. hft. Hrsg. von ... F. M. Schiele ...)
"Literatur": p. 46-47.

1. Witchcraft--History. I. Title.

8
NIC   9-5135

Library of Congress   (Copyright 1909 Res. no. 2411)

Der Hexenwahn, ein Kulturbild aus Lauingens Vergangenheit.

WITCHCRAFT
BF
1583
R91

Rückert, Georg.
Der Hexenwahn, ein Kulturbild aus Lauingens Vergangenheit, von Gg. Rückert.
(In Alt-Lauingen; Organ des Altertumsvereins Lauingen. Lauingen a/D. 25cm. 2. Jahrg. (1907), p. [25]-27, 34-36, [41]-43, [49]-54, [57]-59, 69-71, [73]-77)

Caption title.

8
NIC

1. Witchcraft--Lauingen, Ger. I. Title.

Der Hexenwahn in neuester Beleuchtung.

WITCHCRAFT
BF
1566
O38
K78++

Königer, Albert Michael, 1874-
Der Hexenwahn in neuester Beleuchtung. Köln, 1909.
5 columns. 34cm.

In the Literarische Beilage der Kölnischen Volkszeitung for May 6, 1909.
In broadside box.

1. Ohle, Rudolf, 1857- . Der Hexenwahn. 2. Witchcraft--History. I. Title.

8
NIC

WITCHCRAFT
BF
1583
H618

Der Hexenwahn und die Hexenprozesse.
Barmen, H. Klein [1891]
58 p. 16cm. (Schriften für das evangelische Deutschland. Nr. 27)

1. Witchcraft--Germany. 2. Trials (Witchcraft)--Germany.

8

Hexenwahn und Hexenprozess, vornehmlich im 16. Jahrhundert.

WITCHCRAFT
BF
1571
P33

Paulus, Nicolaus, 1853-1930.
Hexenwahn und Hexenprozess, vornehmlich im 16. Jahrhundert. Von Nikolaus Paulus. Freiburg im Breisgau, Herder, 1910.
283 p. 20cm.

A collection and revision of 13 essays previously published in various journals.

1. Witchcraft--Hist. 2. Reformation. I. Title.

8

Hexenwahn und Hexenprozesse in der ehemaligen Reichsstadt und Landvogtei Hagenau.

WITCHCRAFT
BF
1582
K64

Kl616, J
Hexenwahn und Hexenprozesse in der ehemaligen Reichsstadt und Landvogtei Hagenau, von J. Kl616. Hagenau i. Els., F. Ruckstuhl, 1893.
viii, 177 p. 25cm.

1. Witchcraft--Haguenau, Alsace. 2. Trials (Witchcraft)--Haguenau, Alsace. I. Title.

8
NIC

Hexenwahn und Hexenprozesse in Deutschland.

WITCHCRAFT
BF
1583
K32

Kemper, Josef.
Hexenwahn und Hexenprozesse in Deutschland, von J. Kemper. Mit 13 Illustrationen. Regensburg, Verlagsanstalt vorm. G. J. Manz, 1908.
vi, 167, [1] p. illus. 20cm. (Geschichtliche Jugend- und Volksbibliothek, 16. Bd.)

Bibliography: p. [168]

1. Witchcraft--Germany. 2. Trials (Witchcraft)--Germany. 3. Torture--Germany. I. Title.

8
NIC

Hexenwahn und Hexenprozesse in Estland während der Schwedenherrschaft.

Witchcraft
BF
1584
E7
W77

Winkler, R
Über Hexenwahn und Hexenprozesse in Estland während der Schwedenherrschaft. Von Probst R. Winkler (Reval).
(In Baltische Monatschrift. Riga. 24cm. 67. Bd., Jahrg. 51, Heft 5 (1909), p. [321]-355)

1. Trials (Witchcraft)--Estonia. I. Title. II. Title: Hexenwahn und Hexenprozesse in Estland während der Schwedenherrschaft. III. Baltische Monatsschrift, Riga.

8

Hexenwahn und Protestantismus.

WITCHCRAFT
BF
1566
O38
P33++

Paulus, Nicolaus, 1853-1930.
Hexenwahn und Protestantismus. [Köln, 1909]
5 columns. 34cm.

Detached from the Kölnische Volkszeitung und Handels-Blatt, erste Beilage zur Sonntags-Ausgabe for February 14, 1909.
In broadside box.

1. Ohle, Rudolf, 1857- . Der Hexenwahn. 2. Witchcraft--History. I. Title.

8
NIC

Der Hexenwahn vor und nach der Glaubensspaltung in Deutschland.

Witchcraft
BF
1583
D55

Diefenbach, Johann.
Der Hexenwahn vor und nach der Glaubensspaltung in Deutschland. Mainz, F. Kirchheim, 1886.
viii, 360 p. 23cm.

1. Witchcraft--Germany. I. Title.

Das Hexenwesen im Elsass.

WITCHCRAFT
BF
1583
R44
S73

[Spach, Louis Adolphe]
Das Hexenwesen im Elsass. [n. p., ca. 1871]
6 p. 21cm.

Reprint from a review.

1. Reuss, Rodolphe Ernst, 1841-1924. La sorcellerie au seizième et au dix-septième siècle. 2. Witchcraft--Alsace. I. Title.

8
NIC

CATALOGUE OF THE CORNELL WITCHCRAFT COLLECTION

Das Hexenwesen im Gebiete Luzerns.

WITCHCRAFT
BF 1584 S97 S358
Schneller, Josef, 1801-1879.
  Das Hexenwesen im sechszehnten Jahrhundert. (Nach den Thurmbüchern Lucerns.) (In Der Geschichtsfreund. Einsiedeln. 23cm. 23. Bd. (1868), p. [351]-370)

  Title in table of contents: Das Hexenwesen im Gebiete Lucerns, am Ende des 16. Jahrhunderts.

  1. Witchcraft--Switzerland. 2. Trials (Witchcraft) --Lucerne. I. Title.

8 NIC

Das Hexenwesen im Kanton Bern.

WITCHCRAFT
BF 1584 S97 T78
Trechsel, Friedrich, 1805-1885.
  Das Hexenwesen im Kanton Bern. Aus archivalischen Quellen dargestellt. (In Berner Taschenbuch. Bern. 19cm. 19. Jahrg. (1870), p. 149-234)

  1. Witchcraft--Bern, Switzerland. 2. Witchcraft--Switzerland. I. Title.

8 NIC

Das Hexenwesen im Kanton Luzern nach den Prozessen von Luzern und Sursee, 1400-1675.

WITCHCRAFT
BF 1584 S97 S29
Schacher, Joseph.
  Das Hexenwesen im Kanton Luzern, nach den Prozessen von Luzern und Sursee 1400-1675. Luzern, Druck Räber, 1947.
  xvi, 112 p. 23cm.

  Diss.--Fribourg.

  1. Witchcraft--Luzern (Canton) 2. Trials (Witchcraft)--Switzerland. I. Title.

8 NIC

Das Hexenwesen im sechszehnten Jahrhundert.

WITCHCRAFT
BF 1584 S97 S358
Schneller, Josef, 1801-1879.
  Das Hexenwesen im sechszehnten Jahrhundert. (Nach den Thurmbüchern Lucerns.) (In Der Geschichtsfreund. Einsiedeln. 23cm. 23. Bd. (1868), p. [351]-370)

  Title in table of contents: Das Hexenwesen im Gebiete Lucerns, am Ende des 16. Jahrhunderts.

  1. Witchcraft--Switzerland. 2. Trials (Witchcraft) --Lucerne. I. Title.

8 NIC

Das Hexenwesen in Dänemark.

WITCHCRAFT
BF 1584 D4 P72
Plenkers, Wilhelm, d. 1889.
  Das Hexenwesen in Dänemark.
  (In: Stimmen aus Maria-Laach. Freiburg im Breisgau. 24cm. Jahrg. 1896. Heft 6, p.64-85; Heft 7, p. 175-191; Heft 9, p. 392-413; Heft 10, p. 494-515)

  1 Witchcraft--Denmark. 2. Trials (Witchcraft)--Denmark.

8 NIC

Das Hexenwesen in Ungarn.

WITCHCRAFT
BF 1584 H9 H61
  Das Hexenwesen in Ungarn.
  (In Das Ausland. Stuttgart. 32cm. (folded to 23cm) 52. Jahrg., Nr. 41 (1879), p. 815-818)

  In envelope.

  1. Witchcraft--Hungary. I. Das Ausland.

8 NIC

Hexenwesen und Zauberei in Pommern.

WITCHCRAFT
BF 1583 J25 1886
Jahn, Ulrich, 1861-1900.
  Hexenwesen und Zauberei in Pommern. Breslau, Im Commissionsverlag bei W. Koebner, 1886.
  196 p. 23cm.

  Originally published in Baltische Studien, Jahrg. 36. Also issued as a Separatabdruck thereof.

8 NIC

En Hexeproces fra Østerdalen i det 17de Aarhundrede.

WITCHCRAFT
BF 1584 S9 Z7 1670
Taranger, Absalon, 1858-1930.
  En Hexeproces fra Østerdalen i det 17de Aarhundrede. Ved A. Taranger.
  (In Vidar; Tidsskrift for Videnskab, Literatur og Politik. Christiania, 24cm. 7. Hefte (1887), p. [553]-560)

  1. Trials (Witchcraft)--Sweden. I. Title. II. Vidar; Tidsskrift for Videnskab, Literatur og Politik.

8 NIC

BF 1583 L65 1972
Leutenbauer, Siegfried.
  Hexerei- und Zaubereidelikt in der Literatur von 1450 bis 1550: mit Hinweisen auf d. Praxis im Herzogtum Bayern/ Siegfried Leutenbauer. -- Berlin: Schweitzer, 1972.
  xxv, 178 p.; 23cm. (Münchener Universitätsschriften. Juristische Fakultät. Abhandlungen zur rechtswissenschaftlichen Grundlagenforschung; Bd. 3)
  A revision of the author's thesis, Munich.
  Bibliography: p. xiv-xxv.
  1. Witchcraft--Bavaria--History. 2. Witchcraft--Germany--History. I. Title II. Series

NIC   JAN 16,'74   COxc   72-332940

Hexerey-Krieg.

WITCHCRAFT
BF 1565 S83 L88
[Loschert, Oswald] b.1704.
  Vorgängischer Versuch zu Erwürkung eines Vertrages zwischen den in dem bisherigen Hexerey-Kriege verwickelten Gelehrten. Wie auch zum nutzbaren Unterrichte, wie man von der Zauber- und Hexerey weder zu wenig, noch zu viel glauben soll. Unternommen von einem Verehrer der Gelehrten und Liebhaber der Christlichen Wahrheiten. [Bamberg] an dem Maynstrome [Göbhardt] 1767.
  86 p. 23 cm.

8 NIC
(Continued on next card)

Hexevaesen og hexelforfølgelser isaer i Denmark.

Witchcraft
BF 1584 D4 B21
Bang, Vilhelm.
  Hexevaesen og hexelforfølgelser isaer i Danmark. Kjøbenhavn, J. Frimodt, 1896.
  138 p. 22cm.

  1. Witchcraft. 2. Witchcraft--Denmark. I. Title.

Hexevaesen og troldskab i Norge.

WITCHCRAFT
BF 1584 N6 B14
[Baetzmann, Frederik] 1841-1913.
  Hexevaesen og troldskab i Norge. Meddelt til laesning for menigmand. Christiania, B. M. Bentzen, 1865.
  80 p. 16cm.

  1. Witchcraft--Norway. I. Title.

8

Heylsame Lehr-Stück, und Zauberey betreffende Anmerckungen.

MSS Bd.
WITCHCRAFT BF G12
Gaar, Georg, b. 1702.
  Heylsame Lehr-Stück, und Zauberey betreffende Anmerckungen in der christlichen, nach Hinrichtung Mariae Renatae einer Zauberin, gehaltenen Anred, einiger Massen zwar angereget, hernach aber ausführlicher erläutert ... An jetzo mit einem Zusatz vermehrt ... Wirtzburg, Marco Antonio Engman, 1750 [ca. 1900]
  38 p. 22cm.

  Carnap's manuscript copy.
  "Originaldruck in der Kgl. Universitätsbibliothek zu Würzburg,
(Continued on next card)

Heylsame Lehr-Stück, und Zauberey betreffende Anmerckungen.

MSS Bd.
WITCHCRAFT BF G12
Gaar, Georg, b. 1702. Heylsame Lehr-Stück ... 1750 [ca. 1900] (Card 2)
  44 S. in 4o."
  Numerals in margins indicate pagination of the original.
  In part a rebuttal of: Johann Christian Rinder. Eine Hexe nach ihrer gresslichen Gestalt und gerechter Strafe.
  Provoked in answer: Johann Christian Rinder. Kurtze doch nachdrückliche Abfertigung an den ... Herrn Georg Gaar.
(Continued on next card)

Heywood, Thomas, d. 1641.
  The late Lancashire witches.

PR 1259 W81 H62+
Heywood, Thomas, d. 1641.
  The poetry of witchcraft illustrated by copies of the plays on the Lancashire witches by Heywood and Shadwell. Reprinted under the direction of James O. Halliwell. Brixton Hill, Printed for priv. circ. only, 1853.
  238 p. 29cm.

  Eighty copies printed.
  Each play has also separate t.p.

(Continued on next card)

Heywood, Thomas, d. 1641.
  The late Lancashire witches.

PR 1259 W81 H62+
Heywood, Thomas, d. 1641. The poetry of witchcraft... 1853. (Card 2)

  Contents.--The Lancashire witches and Tegue o Divelly, the Irish priest, by Thomas Shadwell.--The late Lancashire witches, by Thomas Heywood and Richard Broome.

Witchcraft
PR 1259 W81 H62+
Heywood, Thomas, d. 1641.
  The poetry of witchcraft illustrated by copies of the plays on the Lancashire witches by Heywood and Shadwell. Reprinted under the direction of James O. Halliwell. Brixton Hill, Printed for priv. circ. only, 1853.
  238 p. 29cm.

  Eighty copies printed.
  Each play has also separate t.p.

(Continued on next card)

Witchcraft
PR 1259 W81 H62+
Heywood, Thomas, d. 1641. The poetry of witchcraft... 1853. (Card 2)

  Contents.--The Lancashire witches and Tegue o Divelly, the Irish priest, by Thomas Shadwell.--The late Lancashire witches, by Thomas Heywood and Richard Broome.
  I. Halliwell-Phillipps, James Orchard, 1-1889. II. Shadwell, Thomas, 1642?-1692. Lancashire witches and Tegue o Divelly. III. His The late Lancashire witches. IV. Broome, Richard, d. 1622? The late Lancashire witches. V. Title.

CATALOGUE OF THE CORNELL WITCHCRAFT COLLECTION

Hibbert-Ware, Samuel, 1782-1848.
A description of the Shetland Islands.

Witchcraft
BF
1581
Z7+
1644a

Trial of witches in Shetland, A. D. 1644. Intent upon pannel Marion Peebles alias Pardone, spouse to Swene in Hildiswick. [Edinburgh? 1822?]
10 p. 28cm.
Caption title.
Extract from Hibbert-Ware, Samuel, 1782-1848. A description of the Shetland Islands. Edinburgh, 1822. "... the original document was in the possession of a gentleman of Shetland, lately deceased."

(Continued on next card)

Hibernicus's letters.

Rare
PR
1365
H6
1734

[Arbuckle, James] 1700-1734? Hibernicus's letters: or, A philosophical miscellany. Containing (among many others) essays on the following useful and entertaining subjects, viz. Of happiness ... Of witches and apparitions ... Interspersed with several original poems and translations. Written by several eminent hands in Dublin. The 2d ed., with a compleat alphabetical index. London, Printed for J. Clark, 1734.
2 v. 21cm.

(Continued on next card)

Hibernicus's letters.

Rare
PR
1365
H6
1734

[Arbuckle, James] 1700-1734? Hibernicus's letters ... 1734. (Card 2)

"Chiefly the work of Arbuckle, though Francis Hutchison, Samuel Boyse, and the poet Parnell made a few contributions. This collection of papers, which first appeared in a Dublin journal, came to be known under the pen-name of the main contributor."--Cf. Halkett and Laing: Dictionary of anonymous and pseudonymous English literature, v. 3, p. 36.

I. Title.

Hicks, Elizabeth, 1707?-1716.

chcraft
3
++
23

The Whole trial and examination of Mrs. Mary Hicks and her daughter Elizabeth, but of nine years of age, who were condemn'd [sic] ... for witchcraft; and ... executed on Saturday the 28th of July, 1716 ... London, Printed by W. Matthews [1716. London, at the British Museum, 1923]
8 p. 18cm.

Photocopy (negative) 8 p. on 5 l. 20 x 32cm.
No. 23 in vol. lettered: Witchcraft tracts, chap-books and broadsides, 1579-1704; rotograph copies.

Hicks, Mary, d. 1716.

tchcraft
63
1++
.23

The Whole trial and examination of Mrs. Mary Hicks and her daughter Elizabeth, but of nine years of age, who were condemn'd [sic] ... for witchcraft; and ... executed on Saturday the 28th of July, 1716 ... London, Printed by W. Matthews [1716. London, at the British Museum, 1923]
8 p. 18cm.

Photocopy (negative) 8 p. on 5 l. 20x32cm.
No. 23 in vol. lettered: Witchcraft tracts, chap-books and broadsides, 1579-1704; rotograph copies.

Hieronymus à sancta Fide.

Witchcraft
BF
1565
T46
U584

[Gundling, Nicolaus Hieronymus] 1671-1729.
Gründliche Abfertigung der Unpartheyischen Gedancken eines ungenandten Auctoris, die er von der Lehre De crimine magiae, des hochberühmten Herrn D. Christiani Thomasii, neulichst heraus gegeben, gestellet von Hieronymo à sancta Fide. Franckfurth, 1703.
[48] p. 19cm.
Attribution by G. L. Burr.
1. Unpartheyische Gedancken über die Kurze Lehr-Sätze von dem Laster der Zauberey. 2. Witchcraft. I. Hieronymus à sancta Fide. II. Title.

8

WITCHCRAFT
BF
1565
H64
1631

Hildebrand, Wolffgang.
Goêtia, vel Theurgia, sive Praestigiarum magicarum descriptio, revelatio, resolutio, inquisitio, & executio. Das ist, Wahre vnd eigentliche Entdeckunge oder Erklärunge fürnemher Articul der Zauberey. Vnd was von Zauberern, Vnholden, Hexen, deren Händel, Art, Thun ... vnd ihrer Machination ... Etwan durch den wolgebornen Herrn Jacob Freyherrn von Liechtenberg &c. ... erfahren, durch den hochgelahrten Herrn

8
NIC

(Continued on next card)

WITCHCRAFT
BF
1565
H64
1631

Hildebrand, Wolffgang. Goêtia, vel Theurgia ... 1631. (Card 2)

Jacob Weckern M. D. etwas weitleufftiger beschrieben. Nun aber an jetzo mit allem Fleisse revidiret ... durch Wolfgangum Hildebrandum ... Leipzig, In Verlegung Joh. Francken S. Erben vnd Samuel Scheiben Buchh., 1631.
8 p. l., 342, [17] p. 18cm.
Title in red and black.

8

(Continued on next card)

WITCHCRAFT
BF
1565
H64
1631

Hildebrand, Wolffgang. Goêtia, vel Theurgia ... 1631. (Card 3)

1. Witchcraft. 2. Magic. 3. Devil--Legends. 4. Folk-lore--Germany. I. Liechtenberg, Jacob von, baron. Hexen-Büchlein. II. Wecker, Johann Jacob, 1528-1586. III. Title. IV. Title: Praestigiarum magicarum descriptio.

8

Hildebrand, Wolffgang.
Goetia, vel Theurgia.

WITCHCRAFT
BF
1603
H64
1704

Hildebrand, Wolffgang.
Wahre und eigentliche Entdeckung oder Erklärung der fürnemsten Artickul von der Zauberey und was von Zauberern, Vnholden, Hexen, derer Händel, Art, Thun, ... und vielen andern ihren Machinationen ... Durch den wohlgebohrnen Herrn Jacob Frey Herrn von Lichtenberg ... erfahren, und durch den hochgelahrten Herrn Jacob Weckern weitläufftiger beschrieben. Anitzo mit allem Fleiss übersehen und vermehret mit

8
NIC

(Continued on next card)

Hildebrand, Wolffgang.
Goetia, vel Theurgia.

WITCHCRAFT
BF
1603
H64
1704

Hildebrand, Wolffgang. Wahre und eigentliche Entdeckung oder Erklärung der fürnemsten Artickul von der Zauberey ...
[1704?] (Card 2)

vielen Artzeneyen ..., auch wie eine christliche Obrigkeit wider die Zauberer ... rechtlich verfahren soll, ... auch viele lustige und possierliche Historien von Erscheinungen allerhand Geister ... von neuen in Druck verfertiget durch Wolfgangum Hilde-

8
NIC

(Continued on next card)

Hildebrand, Wolffgang.
Goetia, vel Theurgia.

WITCHCRAFT
BF
1603
H64
1704

Hildebrand, Wolffgang. Wahre und eigentliche Entdeckung oder Erklärung der fürnemsten Artickul von der Zauberey ...
[1704?] (Card 3)

brandum. [Leipzig? 1704?]
11 p. l., 342, [18] p. front. 21cm.
Half title (follows Inhalt aller Capitel) agrees with original title: Goetia, vel Theurgia, sive Praestigiarum magicarum descriptio, and has imprint 1704.

8
NIC

(Continued on next card)

Hildebrand, Wolffgang.
Goetia, vel Theurgia.

WITCHCRAFT
BF
1603
H64
1704

Hildebrand, Wolffgang. Wahre und eigentliche Entdeckung oder Erklärung der fürnemsten Articul von der Zauberey. (Card 4)

Bound with his Neu-vermehrt, vortrefflich ... curieuses Kunst und Wunderbuch. Leipzig, 1704.
1. Witchcraft. 2. Magic. 3. Devil--Legends. 4. Folk-lore--Germany. I. His Goetia, vel Theurgia. II. Liechtenberg, Jacob von, baron. Hexen-Büchlein. III. Wecker, Johann Jacob, 1528-1586. IV. Title.

8
NIC

WITCHCRAFT
BF
1603
H64
1704

Hildebrand, Wolffgang.
Wahre und eigentliche Entdeckung oder Erklärung der fürnemsten Articul von der Zauberey und was von Zauberern, Vnholden, Hexen, derer Händel, Art, Thun, ... und vielen andern ihren Machinationen ... Durch den wohlgebohrnen Herrn Jacob Frey Herrn von Lichtenberg ... erfahren, und durch den hochgelahrten Herrn Jacob Weckern weitläufftiger beschrieben. Anitzo mit allem Fleiss übersehen und vermehret mit

8
NIC

(Continued on next card)

WITCHCRAFT
BF
1603
H64
1704

Hildebrand, Wolffgang. Wahre und eigentliche Entdeckung oder Erklärung der fürnemsten Artickul von der Zauberey ...
[1704?] (Card 2)

vielen Artzeneyen ..., auch wie eine christliche Obrigkeit wider die Zauberer ... rechtlich verfahren soll, ... auch viele lustige und possierliche Historien von Erscheinungen allerhand Geister ... von neuen in Druck verfertiget durch Wolfgangum Hilde-

8
NIC

(Continued on next card)

WITCHCRAFT
BF
1603
H64
1704

Hildebrand, Wolffgang. Wahre und eigentliche Entdeckung oder Erklärung der fürnemsten Artickul von der Zauberey ...
[1704?] (Card 3)

brandum. [Leipzig? 1704?]
11 p. l., 342, [18] p. front. 21cm.
Half title (follows Inhalt aller Capitel) agrees with original title: Goetia, vel Theurgia, sive Praestigiarum magicarum descriptio, and has imprint 1704.

8
NIC

(Continued on next card)

WITCHCRAFT
BF
1603
H64
1704

Hildebrand, Wolffgang. Wahre und eigentliche Entdeckung oder Erklärung der fürnemsten Articul von der Zauberey ... (Card 4)

Bound with his Neu-vermehrt, vortrefflich ... curieuses Kunst und Wunderbuch. Leipzig, 1704.
1. Witchcraft. 2. Magic. 3. Devil--Legends. 4. Folk-lore--Germany. I. His Goetia, vel Theurgia. II. Liechtenberg, Jacob von, baron. Hexen-Büchlein. III. Wecker, Johann Jacob, 1528-1586. IV. Title.

8
NIC

Hildebrand, Wolfgang.

see

Hildebrand, Wolffgang.

CATALOGUE OF THE CORNELL WITCHCRAFT COLLECTION

WITCHCRAFT
BT
770
H65

Hillinger, Johann Gottlieb, 1698-1732.
Herrn Johann Gottlieb Hillingers ... Zwey Predigten von der Ermunterung zu dem rechtschaffenen Kampffe gegen die bösen Geister, und von dem Glauben, der durch die Liebe thätig ist. Nebst einem Bedenken von der geistlichen Besitzung ... Jena, Bey J. R. Crökern, Druckts J. C. Cröker, 1733.
80 p. 19cm.
Title in red and black.
1. Faith—Sermons. 2. Devil. 3. Demoniac possession. I. Title.

8

Hincmarus, abp. of Reims, d. 882.

WITCHCRAFT
BF
1565
T83
1605

Trithemius, Johannes, 1462-1516.
Antipalus maleficiorvm Iohannis Tritemii Spanhemensis ... qvatvor libris comprehensvs. Mogvntiae, Apud Balthasarum Lippium, 1605.
275-861 p. 19cm.
According to a note by G. L. Burr inside front cover, this is detached from Paralipomena opusculorum Petri Blesensis, Joannes Trithemii, Hincmari, aliorumque, compiled and edited by Jean Buys.

8
NIC
(Continued on next card)

Hincmarus, abp. of Reims, d. 882.

WITCHCRAFT
BF
1565
T83
1605

Trithemius, Johannes, 1462-1516. Antipalvs maleficiorvm ... 1605. (Card 2)

Contents.—Antipalus maleficiorum.—Liber octo quaestionum, quas illi dissolvenda proposuit Maximilianus Caesar.—De laudibus ordinis Fratrum Carmelitarum.—Tractatus, De laudibus Sanctissimae Matris Annae.—Index Graecorum voluminum Ioannis Trithemii.—Hincmari Rhemensis ... Epistolae duae.—Hymni de solemnitate S. Wigberti.

8
NIC

Binding: 17th cent. blind stamped pig skin, with clasps.

(Continued on next card)

History of Science
QL
666
O6A11

Hippocrates.
Prognostica.
Cesalpino, Andrea, 1519-1603.
Daemonvm investigatio peripatetica. In qua explicatur locus Hippocratis Progn. Siquid diuinum in morbis habetur. Florentiae, Apud Iuntas, 1580.
24 l. 22cm.
Title vignette: Giunta's device; repeated at end in variant form.
Bound with Abati, Baldo Angelo. De admirabili viperae natvra ... Vrbini, 1589.

Witchcraft
Z
6880
Z9
D94

Hirsch, Emil, bookseller, Munich.
Du Prel, Karl Ludwig August Friedrich Maximilian Alfred, Freiherr, 1839-1899.
Bibliotheca occulta et philosophica; Sammlung Baron C. Du Prel, und kleine andere Beiträge (Inhaltsverzeichnis umstehend) Mit Vorwort von H. L. Held. München, E. Hirsch [193-]
104 p. 22cm.
Katalog 58.

Hirsul, die Hexe der Bielshöle.

WITCHCRAFT
PT
2435
M58
H6
1823

Moser, F W
Hirsul, die Hexe der Bielshöle. Merseburg, Sonntag, 1823.
188 p. 15cm.
Date changed by hand from 1843 to 1823.

8
NIC
I. Title.

Witchcraft
BF
1559
G25
Z63
no.5

Hirtenbrief des ... Herrn Anton Peters ... an die sämmtliche Geistlichkeit der Prager Erzdiöces im Jahre ... 1775.
Příchovský, Antonín Peter, Abp. of Prague, 1707-1793.
Hirtenbrief des hochwürdigsten und hochgebohrnen Fürsten und Herrn Herrn Anton Peters ... an die sämmtliche Geistlichkeit der Prager Erzdiöces im Jahre ... 1775. München [1775?]
31 p. 17cm.
"Nach dem Prager Original."
No. 5 in vol. lettered Gassneriana.
1. Exorcism. 2. Faith-cure. 3. Catholic Church—Pastoral letters and charges. I. Title.

8

WITCHCRAFT
BF
1517
F5
S96

Histoire abrégée de la possession des Ursulines de Loudun.
Surin, Jean Joseph, 1600-1665.
Histoire abrégée de la possession des Ursulines de Loudun, et des peines du père Surin; (ouvrage inédit faisant suite à ses oeuvres.) Paris, Chez l'éditeur, au Bureau de l'Association catholique du Sacré-Coeur, 1828.
365, [6] p. 18cm.
"D'après Sommervogel, publication partielle d'une copie d'un ms. de la fin du XVIIIe siècle, ayant pour titre: La vie

8
NIC
(Continued on next card)

WITCHCRAFT
BF
1517
F5
S96

Histoire abrégée de la possession des Ursulines de Loudun.
Surin, Jean Joseph, 1600-1665. Histoire abrégée de la possession des Ursulines de Loudun ... 1828. (Card 2)

du R. P. Surin, en laquelle il parle des maux qui lui sont arrivés ensuite de la possession des démons chassés par son ministère."— Note under Surin, Bibliothèque Nationale.
Surin's authorship has been questioned.
With this is bound his Triomphe de l'amour divin. Avignon, 1829.

8
NIC
(Continued on next card)

WITCHCRAFT
BF
1555
H678
1881

Histoire admirable de la maladie prodigieuse de Pierre Creusé, arrivée en la ville de Niort en 1628. Avec une introduction par L. Favre. Niort, Typ. de L. Favre, 1881.
iii, 84 p. 22cm.
Half title: Maladie prodigieuse de Pierre Creusé.
Includes reprint of the original t. p., whose title includes: "... auec vn plaidoyé de l'advocat du Roy de ladite

8
(Continued on next card)

WITCHCRAFT
BF
1555
H678
1881

Histoire admirable de la maladie prodigieuse de Pierre Creusé ... 1881. (Card 2)

ville sur le subjet de ladite maladie, & la sentence interuenue sur ledit plaidoyé: ensemble les certificats de medecins & chirurgiens dudit lieu. Niort, 1631."

1. Demoniac possession. 2. Creusé, Pierre, b. 1614. I. Favre, Léopold, 1817-1890, ed. II. Title: Maladie prodigieuse de Pierre Creusé.

8

WITCHCRAFT
BF
1517
F5
M62

Histoire admirable de la possession et conversion d'une penitente.
Michaelis, Sebastien, 1543?-1618.
Histoire admirable de la possession et conversion d'vne penitente, seduite par vn magicien, la faisant sorciere & princesse des sorciers au pays de Prouence, conduite à la S. Baume pour y estre exorcizee l'an M.DC.X. au mois de Nouembre, soubs l'authorité du R. P. F. Sebastien Michaelis ... Commis par luy aux exorcismes & recueil des actes le R. P. F. François Domptivs ... Ensemble la Pneumalogie, ou Discours du

8
(Continued on next card)

WITCHCRAFT
BF
1517
F5
M62

Histoire admirable de la possession et conversion d'une penitente.
Michaelis, Sebastien, 1543?-1618. Histoire admirable ... 1613. (Card 2)

susdit Pere Michaelis, reueu, corrigé, & augmenté par luy-mesme ... Paris, Chez Charles Chastellain, 1613.
16 p. l., 352, 124, 196, [30] p. 17cm.
"Actes recveillis ... par le reverend Pere Michaëlis" has separate paging.
"Discovrs des esprits" has special t. p. with imprint Paris, 1512, and separate paging.

8
(Continued on next card)

Witchcraft
BF
1555
H67
1886

Histoire admirable et veritable des choses advenues a l'endroict d'une religieuse professe.
La Possession de Jeanne Fery, religieuse professe du couvent des soeurs noires de la ville de Mons (1584) Paris, Aux bureaux du Progrès médical, 1886.
v, 109 p. 23cm. (Bibliothèque diabolique; Collection Bourneville)
Reprint of Histoire admirable et veritable des choses advenues a l'endroict d'une religieuse professe ..., pub. 1586.
Edited by D. B. Bourneville.
With facsimile of original t. p.

8
(Continued on next card)

WITCHCRAFT
BF
1555
H67
1589

Histoire admirable et veritable des choses advenues a l'endroict d'une religieuse professe. German.
Warhafft: vnd gründtlicher Bericht, sehr wunderlich: vnnd gleichsam vnerhörter Geschichten, so sich vnlangst zu Bergen [i.e., Mons] in Henogau, Ertzbisthumbs Cambrai, mit einer besessnen, vnd hernach widerledigten Closterfrawen verloffen. Auss frantzösischer Sprach, in Hochteutsch gebracht. [München, Gedruckt bey Adam Berg] 1589.
4 p. l., 47 numbered l. 19cm.
Illustrative title vignette.
With colophon.

8
(Continued on next card)

WITCHCRAFT
BF
1555
H67
1587

Histoire admirable et veritable des choses advenues a l'endroict d'une religieuse professe. German.
Warhafft: vnd gründtlicher Bericht, sehr wunderlich: 1589. (Card 2)

Translation of Histoire admirable et veritable des choses advenues a l'endroict d'une religieuse professe ... pub. 1586. Preface by Adam Berg.
1. Demoniac possession. 2. Fery, Jeanne, fl. 1584. I. Histoire admirable et veritable des choses advenues a l'endroict d'une religieuse professe. German. II. Berg, Adam, d. 1610.

8

Rare
BX
1735
L79
1818

Histoire critique de l'inquisition d'Espagne.
Llorente, Juan Antonio, 1756-1823.
Histoire critique de l'inquisition d'Espagne, depuis l'époque de son établissement par Ferdinand V, jusqu'au règne de Ferdinand VII; tirée des pièces originales des archives du Conseil de la Suprême et de celles des tribunaux subalternes du Saint-Office. Par D. Jean-Antoine Llorente ... Tr. de l'espagnol sur le manuscrit et sous les yeux de l'auteur, par Alexis Pellier. 2. éd. Paris, Treuttel et Würtz [etc.] 1818.
(Continued on next card)

Rare
BX
1735
L79
1818

Histoire critique de l'inquisition d'Espagne.
Llorente, Juan Antonio, 1756-1823. Histoire critique de l'inquisition d'Espagne ... 1818. (Card 2)

4 v. port., illus. (coat of arms) 21cm.

"Catalogue des manuscrits qui n'ont pas encore été publiés, et qui ont servi pour composer l'Histoire critique de l'inquisition d'Espagne": t.1, p. xxxj-xxxvj.
Translation of Historia critica de la inquisición de España.
(Continued on next card)

CATALOGUE OF THE CORNELL WITCHCRAFT COLLECTION

Histoire critique des pratiques superstitieuses.

Witchcraft
BF
1602
L45
1733
    Lebrun, Pierre, 1661-1729.
    Histoire critique des pratiques superstitieuses, qui ont séduit les peuples & embarrassé les savans. Avec la méthode & les principes pour discerner les effets naturels d'avec ceux qui ne le sont pas. 2d éd. augm. Amsterdam, J. F. Bernard, 1733-36.
    4 v. illus. 21cm.

    1. Superstition. 2. Magic. 3. Divining-rod. I. Title.

Histoire curieuse et pittoresque des sorciers ...

tchcraft
-12
1
49
    Giraldo, Mathias de, pseud.
    Histoire curieuse et pittoresque des sorciers, devins, magiciens, astrologues, voyants, revenants, ames en peine, vampires, spectres, fantomes apparitions, visions, gnomes, lutins, esprits malins, sorts jetés, exorcismes, etc. ... depuis l'antiquité jusqu'à nos jours, par le révérend père dominicain Mathias de Giraldo, ancien exorciste de l'Inquisition, rev. et augm. par M. Fornari, professeur de philosophie hermétique à Milan. Paris, Chez tous les libraires marchands de nouveautés [1849?]
    315 p. 4 fold. plates. 24cm.
    Half title: Histoire des sorciers.

Histoire de la diablerie chrétienne.

Witchcraft
BF
1565
B16
    Baissac, Jules, 1827-1898.
    Les grands jours de la sorcellerie. Paris, C. Klincksieck, 1890.
    v, 735 p. 25cm.

    Sequel to his Histoire de la diablerie chrétienne.

    1. Witchcraft--Hist. I. Title.

Histoire de la diablerie chrétienne.

itchcraft
F
549
16
    Baissac, Jules, 1827-1898.
    Histoire de la diablerie chrétienne. I. Le Diable; la personne du Diable, le personnel du Diable. Paris, M. Dreyfous [1882]
    ix, 611 p. 24cm.

    The second vol. of the series, published in 1890 under title: Les grands jours de la sorcellerie, does not have the general title Histoire de la diablerie chrétienne.
    1. Devil. I. Title: La diablerie chrétienne. II. Title.

Histoire de la fille maléficiée de Courson.

    Lange, , physician, of Lisieux.
CHCRAFT   Histoire de la fille maléficiée de Courson. Avec une dissertation physique sur ce maléfice. Par Monsieur Lange, Conseiller Médecin du Roy. Lisieux, Chez J. du Roncerey, 1717 [ca. 1900]
    34 p. 23cm.
    Carnap's manuscript copy.
    "Der Originaldruck von welchem diese Abschrift genommen wurde, befindet sich in der Bibliothè que Nationale zu Paris ... Eine Ab schrift fertigte der
    (Continued on next card)

Histoire de la fille maléficiée de Courson.

    Lange, , physician, of Lisieux.
    Histoire de la fille maléficiée ... 1717
TCHCRAFT [ca. 1900] (Card 2)

    daselbst angestellte Bibliothekar J. Herviant an; die vorliegende ist mit desselben wörtlich übereinstimmend."
    Numerals in the margins indicate pagination of the original work.
    "Notizen über diese Abhandlung" pp. 31-34.
    1. Diseases --Causes and theories of causation. 2. Witchcraft. 3. Morin, Madeleine. I. Title.

Histoire de la magie.

Witchcraft
BF
1589
C75
    [Constant, Alphonse Louis] 1810?-1875.
    Histoire de la magie, avec une exposition claire et precise de ses procédés, de ses rites et de ses mystères, par Éliphas Lévi [pseud.] ... Avec 18 planches représentant 90 figures. Paris, G. Baillière; Londres et New-York, H. Baillière; [etc., etc.] 1860.
    xvi, 560 p. front., plates. 22½ᶜᵐ.

    1. Magic. I. Title.

                          11-14511
Library of Congress   BF1589.C75

Histoire de la magie en France.

BF
1622
F7
G23
1965
    Garinet, Jules, 1797-1877.
    Histoire de la magie en France. Texte revu et présenté par Roland Villeneuve. Paris, Livre club du libraire, 1965.
    260 p. plates. 20 cm. 82 F.

                        (F 66-840)

    1. Magic—France. I. Villeneuve, Roland, 1922- ed. II. Title.

BF1622.F7G3   133.40944   66-72041

Library of Congress witchcraft [6]

Histoire de la magie en France depuis le commencement de la monarchie jusqu'a nos jours.

Witchcraft
BF
1622
F7
G23
    Garinet, Jules, 1797-1877.
    Histoire de la magie en France depuis le commencement de la monarchie jusqu'a nos jours. Paris, Foulon, 1818.
    liii, 363 p. front. 21cm.

    I. Title.

Histoire de la sorcellerie au comté de Bourgogne.

Witchcraft
BF
1582
D52
    Déy, Aristide, 1807-
    Histoire de la sorcellerie au comté de Bourgogne. Vesoul, Typographie de L. Suchaux, 1861.
    124 p. 22cm.

    1. Witchcraft--Burgundy, France--Hist. I. Title.

Histoire de M. Oufle.

Witchcraft
PQ
1957
B67
A64
1793
    Bordelon, Laurent, 1653-1730.
    Histoire de M. Oufle, par abbé Bordelon [retouchée et réduite par M. G.] et la Description du sabbat. Paris, Gay & Gide, 1793.
    360 p. 20cm.

    "...C'est ... un nouveau roman, mais ... nous sommes redevables néanmoins à l'abbé Bordelon...": p. 5-6.
    "Descripti on du sabbat" is not by Bordelon.

Histoire de Madeleine Bavent.

Witchcraft
BF
1582
Z7
1647
    Desmarets, oratorien.
    Histoire de Madeleine Bavent, religieuse du monastère de Saint-Louis de Louviers. Réimpression textuelle sur l'édition rarissime de 1652. Précédée d'une notice bio-bibliographique, et suivie de plusieurs pièces supplémentaires. Orné d'un front. et d' une vue de l'ancien couvent de Saint-Louis ... Rouen, J. Lemonnyer, 1878.
    xl, vii, 169 p. illus. 21cm.

    No. 141 of 177 copies printed.
    (Continued on next card)

Histoire de Madeleine Bavent.

Witchcraft
BF
1582
Z7
1647
    Desmarets, oratorien. Histoire de Madeleine Bavent ... 1878. (Card 2)

    Original t.p. reads: Historie de Magdelaine Bavent, religieuse du monastère de Saint Louis de Louviers, avec sa confession générale & testamentaire, où elle déclare les abominations, impietez, & sacrilèges qu'elle a pratiqué & veu pratiquer, tant ledit monastere, qu'au sabat, & les personnes qu'elle y a remarquées. Ensemble l'arrest
    (Continued on next card)

Histoire de Madeleine Bavent.

Witchcraft
BF
1582
Z7
1647
    Desmarets, oratorien. Histoire de Madeleine Bavent ... 1878. (Card 3)

    donné contre Mathurin Picard, Thomas Boullé & ladite Bavent, tous convaincus du crime de magie. Dedieé a Mme. la Dvchesse d'Orleans. Paris, J. Le Gentil, 1652.

    1. Bavent, Madeleine, ca.1608-1647. I. Title. II. Title: Historie de Magdelaine Bavent.

Histoire de Nicole de Vervins.

WITCHCRAFT
BX
2340
R72
    Roger, Joseph, abbé.
    Histoire de Nicole de Vervins d'après les historiens contemporains et témoins oculaires; ou, Le triomphe du saint sacrement sur le démon à Laon en 1566, par J. Roger ... Paris, H. Plon, 1863.
    495 p. fold. plate. 22cm.

8
NIC
    1. Nicole de Vervins. 2. Exorcism. I. Title. II. Title: Le triomphe du saint sacrement sur le démon à Laon en 1566.

Histoire de Satan.

WITCHCRAFT
BF
1505
L45
1882
    Lecanu, Auguste François, 1803-
    Histoire de Satan, sa chute, son culte, ses manifestations, ses oeuvres, la guerre qu'il fait à Dieu et aux hommes. Magie, possession... Paris, Féchoz et Letouzey [1882]
    506 p. 22cm.

8
NIC
    1. Devil. 2. Demonology. 3. Occult sciences. 4. Demoniac possession.

Histoire des diables de Loudun.

Witchcraft
BF
1517
F5
A892
1716
    [Aubin, Nicolas] b. ca. 1655.
    Cruels effets de la vengeance du Cardinal de Richelieu, ou Histoire des diables de Loudun, de la possession des religieuses ursulines, et de la condamnation et du suplice [sic] d'Urbain Grandier, curé de la même ville. Amsterdam, E. Roger, 1716.
    [10], 5-378 p. front. 17cm.
    Published also under titles: Histoire des diables de Loudun, ou, De la possession des religieuses ursulines ... Amsterdam, 1694; and Histoire d'Urbain Grandier, condamné comme magicien ... Amsterdam, 1735.

Histoire des diables de Loudun.

Witchcraft
BF
1517
F5
A893
1737
    [Aubin, Nicolas] b. ca. 1655.
    Histoire des diables de Loudun, ou De la possession des religieuses ursulines, et de la condamnation & du suplice d'Urbain Grandier, curé de la même ville. Cruels effets de la vengeance du Cardinal de Richelieu. Amsterdam, aux de'pens de la Compagnie, 1737.
    378 p. front. 17cm.
    "Published also under titles: Histoire d' Urbain Grandier, condamné comme magicien ... Amsterdam, 1735, and Cruels effets de la vengeance du Cardinal de Richelieu; ou, Histoire des diables de Loudun ... Amsterdam, 1716."--L.C.

CATALOGUE OF THE CORNELL WITCHCRAFT COLLECTION

Histoire des diables de Loudun.

WITCHCRAFT
BF
1517
F5
L22

La Menardaye, Jean Baptiste de.
Examen et discussion critique de l'histoire des diables de Loudun, de la possession des religieuses Ursulines, et de la condamnation d'Urbain Grandier. Paris, Chez Debure l'aîné, 1747.
xxix, 521 p. 17cm.

1. Demoniac possession. 2. Grandier, Urbain, 1590-1634. 3. Loudun, France. Ursuline convent. I. Title: Histoire des diables de Loudun. II. Title: Diables de Loudun.

8
NIC

L'histoire des imaginations extravagantes de M. Oufle.

Witchcraft
PQ
1957
B67
A64
1754

[Bordelon, Laurent] 1653-1730.
L'histoire des imaginations extravagantes de M. Oufle [pseud.] Servant de preservatif contre la lecture des livres qui traitent de la magie, du grimoire, des démoniaques, sorciers ... Avec un tresgrand nombre de nottes [sic] curieuses, qui rapportent fidellement [sic] les endroits des livres qui ont causé ces imaginations, & qui les combattent ... Paris, Duchesne, 1754.
5 v. in 2. illus. 17cm.
Imperfect: p. 3-24 of Part V are incorrectly bound between p. 4-25 of Part IV.
1. Occult sciences. 2. Apparitions. 3. Demonology. I. Title.

8

Histoire des moeurs.

WITCHCRAFT
BR
135
L14

Lacroix, Paul, 1806-1884.
Curiosités de l'histoire des croyances populaires au moyen âge, par P. L. Jacob [pseud.] Paris, A. Delahays, 1859.
323 p. 17cm.

Running title: Histoire des moeurs.
Includes bibliographies.
Contents.--Superstitions et croyances populaires.--Le juif-errant.--Les blasphé-

8
NIC   (Continued on next card)

Histoire des moeurs.

WITCHCRAFT
BR
135
L14

Lacroix, Paul, 1806-1884.
Curiosités de l'histoire des croyances populaires...1859.   (Card 2)

Contents--continued.
mateurs.--Les démons de la nuit.--Les sorciers et le sabbat.--Le boeuf gras.--Origines du mal de Naples.

1. Superstition. I. Title. II. Title: Histoire des moeurs.

Histoire des monstres depuis l'antiquité jusqu'à nos jours.

History of Science
QM
691
M37

Martin, Ernest.
Histoire des monstres depuis l'antiquité jusqu'à nos jours, par le docteur Ernest Martin ... Paris, C. Reinwald et cie, 1880.
vii, 415 p. 22cm.

"Bibliographie": p. [385]-407.

1. Monsters.   I. Title.

Histoire des oracles.

WITCHCRAFT
BF
1761
F68
1707

Fontenelle, Bernard Le Bovier de, 1657-1757.
Histoire des oracles. Nouvelle édition augmentée. Londres, Aux depens de Paul & Isaak Vaillant, 1707.
119, [1] p. front. 17cm.
Title in red and black.
Rifacimento of A. van Dale's De oraculis ethnicorum dissertationes duae, Amstelaedami, 1683.

I. Dale, Antonius van, 1638-1708. De oraculis ethnicorum. II. Title.

Histoire des sciences occultes depuis l'antiquité jusqu'à nos jours.

Witchcraft
BF
1410
D28
1883

Debay, Auguste, 1802-1890.
Histoire des sciences occultes depuis l'antiquité jusqu'à nos jours. 3. éd. ...
Paris, E. Dentu, 1883.
536 p. 18cm.

Histoire des sorciers.

Witchcraft
BF
1412
G51
1849

Giraldo, Mathias de, pseud.
Histoire curieuse et pittoresque des sorciers, devins, magiciens, astrologues, voyants, revenants, ames en peine, vampires, spectres, fantomes, apparitions, visions, gnomes, lutins, esprits malins, sorts jetés, exorcismes, etc. ... depuis l'antiquité jusqu'à nos jours, par le révérend père dominicain Mathias de Giraldo, ancien exorciste de l'Inquisition, rev. et augm. par M. Fornari, professeur de philosophie hermétique à Milan. Paris, Chez tous les libraires marchands de nouveautés [1849]
315 p. 4 fold. plates. 24cm.
Half title: Histoire des sorciers.

Histoire du diable.

WITCHCRAFT
PR
3404
H5
1745a

[Defoe, Daniel] 1660-1731.
Histoire du diable, traduite de l'anglois. Tome premier, contenant un détail des circonstances, où il s'est trouvé, depuis son bannissement du ciel ... Tome second, qui traite de la conduite qu'il a tenue jusqu'à-present ... Amsterdam, Aux dépens de la compagnie, 1729.
302 p. illus. 17cm.
Title in red and black.
Translation of The political history of the devil.

8   (Continued on next card)

Histoire du diable.

Witchcraft
BT
980
T94

Turmel, Joseph, 1859-
Histoire du diable. Paris, Rieder, 1931.
296 p. 19cm. (Christianisme. [38])

1. Devil. 2. Demonology. 3. Witchcraft. I. Title. II. Series.

8

Histoire du diable pendant la mission de Jésus-Christ en Palestine.

WITCHCRAFT
BT
980
M83

Morel, Auguste, 1820-1874.
Histoire du diable pendant la mission de Jésus-Christ en Palestine d'après les documents officiels, les travaux des publicistes et les monuments de l'art. Paris, E. Dentu, 1861.
193 p. 14cm.

8
NIC

1. Devil. 2. Jesus Christ. 3. Jesus Christ--Biblical teaching. 4. Devil--Temptation.

Histoire du merveilleux dans les temps modernes.

Witchcraft
BF
1412
F47
1860

Figuier, Louis, 1819-1894.
Histoire du merveilleux dans les temps modernes, par Louis Figuier ... Paris, L. Hachette et cie, 1860-61.
4 v. 18½cm.
Vols. 1-2, 2. édition.
CONTENTS.--t. 1. Introduction. Les diables de Loudun. Les convulsionnaires jansénistes.--t. 2. La baguette divinatoire. Les prophètes protestants.--t. 3. Le magnétisme animal.--t. 4. Les tables tournantes. Les médiums et les esprits.
1. Demonomania. 2. Divination. 3. Animal magnetism. 4. Spiritualism. I. Title.
[Full name: Guillaume Louis Figuier]

Library of Congress   BF1412.F4   11-20783 Revised

WITCHCRAFT
BF
1517
F5
H673
1875

Histoire espouventable et veritable arrivée en la ville de Soliers en Provence d'un homme qui s'estoit voué pour estre d'Esglise et qui n'ayant accomply son voeu, le diable lui a coupé les parties honteuses et couppé encore la gorge à une petite fille aagée de deux ans ou environs. Paris, Chez Nicolas Alexandre, 1619. [Lyon, Impr. L. Perrin, 1875]
15 p. 23cm.

8   1. Devil.   2. Vows.

Histoire et traité des sciences occultes.

Witchcraft
BF
1412
R43

Résie, Lambert Elisabeth d'Aubert, comte de.
Histoire et traité des sciences occultes; ou, Examen des croyances populaires sur les êtres surnaturels, la magie, la sorcellerie, la divination, etc., depuis le commencement du monde jusqu'à nos jours. Paris, Louis Vivès, 1857.
2 v. 23cm.

1. Occult sciences.   I. Title.

Histoire generale du monde, et de la nature.

WITCHCRAFT
BD
505
V14
1617

Valderrama, Pedro de
Histoire generale dv monde, et de la natvre. Ov Traictez theologiqves de la fabrique, composition, & conducite generale de l'vniuers. Divisez en trois livres. Le premier traictant de Dieu comme souuerain architecte du monde ... Le second de la conducte admirable du monde ... les intelligences celestes, la fabrique generale du ciel, les diuers degrez des anges ... Le troisies. des grades diuerses des de-

8   (Continued on next card)

Histoire generale du monde, et de la nature.

WITCHCRAFT
BD
505
V14
1617

Valderrama, Pedro de. Histoire generale dv monde ... 1617.   (Card 2)

mons, ... de leur science appellée magie ..., des diuerses partias di [sic] la magie & plusieurs autres illusions diaboliques. Le tout illustré d'vn grand nombre d'histoires & doctes exemples. Composé en espagnol par le R. P. P. Valderama, ... & traduit sur le manuscrit espagnol en nostre langue françoise, par le sieur de la Richardier. 2. éd. Paris, Chez Isaac Mesnier,

8   (Continued on next card)

Histoire generale du monde, et de la nature.

WITCHCRAFT
BD
505
V14
1617

Valderrama, Pedro de. Histoire generale dv monde ... 1617.   (Card 3)

1617-19 [v. 1.1619]
2 v. in 1. 18cm.

1. Cosmology. 2. God. 3. Angels. 4. Demonology. 5. Witchcraft. I. La Richardière, sieur de, tr. II. Title.

8

WITCHCRAFT
BF
1517
F5
H675
1880

Histoire horrible et espouuantable de ce q s'est fait & passé au foux-bourg S. Marcel, à mort d'vn miserable, qui a esté deuoré par plusieurs diables transformez en dogues, & ce pour auoir blasphemé le sainct nom de Dieu & battu sa mère. Imprimé nouuellement. [Arras, H. Schoutheer, 188-?]
11 p. 22cm.
Title vignette, tail-piece.
"L'original, imprimé vers 1640, appartient Monsieur Claudin ... à Paris. Réimprimé à Arr chez Schoutheer, par les soins de Margue et René Muffat de Menthon, bibliographes.
1. Demonology. 2. Exempla.

282

CATALOGUE OF THE CORNELL WITCHCRAFT COLLECTION

WITCHCRAFT
BF
1532
L24

Histoire mythique de Shatan.

Lancelin, Charles Marie Eugène, 1852-
Histoire mythique de Shatan. De la légende au dogme. Origine de l'idée démoniaque, ses transformations à travers les âges, d'après les textes et la tradition... Paris, H. Daragon, 1903-05.
2 v. in 1. illus. 20cm. (Bibliothèque des sciences maudites)

Vol. 2 has title: Le ternaire magique de Shatan; envoutement, incubat, vampirisme.
1. Devil. 2. Demonology. I. His
8   Le ternaire magique de Shatan.
NIC

WITCHCRAFT
BF
1517
F5
H676
1874
no.1

Histoire nouvelle merveilleuse et espouvantable d'un jeune homme d'Aix en Provence emporté par le diable et pendu à un amandier pour avoir impiement blasphémé le sainct nom de Dieu et mesprisé la saincte Messe; deux siens compagnons estant demeurez sans aucun mal... Iouxte la coppie imprimée à Lyon. Paris, Par Fleury Bourriquant [1614]. Lyon, Impr. L. Perrin, 1874]
13 p. 24cm.

(Continued on next card)

WITCHCRAFT
BF
1517
F5
H676
1874
no.1

Histoire nouvelle merveilleuse et espouvantable d'un jeune homme d'Aix en Provence ... [1874] (Card 2)

No. 1 in vol. lettered Histoire merveilleuse... 1614 [etc.]

1. Devil. 2. Exempla.

Witchcraft
BF
1412
F11

Histoire philosophique et politique de l'occulte: magie, sorcellerie, spiritisme.

Fabart, Félix.
Histoire philosophique et politique de l'occulte: magie, sorcellerie, spiritisme; avec une préface de Camille Flammarion. Paris, C. Marpon et E. Flammarion [1885?]
xx, 346 p. 19cm.

1. Occult sciences--Hist.

WITCHCRAFT

Histoire prodigieuse et espouvantable de plus de deux cens 50 sorciers et sorcières emmenez pour leur estre fait et parfait leur procez au Parlement de Tholoze: avec l'exécution exemplaire d'un grand nombre en divers lieux: ce qui a causé la cherté des bleds. Paris, Jouste la copie imprimée, 1649 [1901]
5 l. 19cm.

Carnap's manuscript copy.
"Originaldruck in der Bibliothèque Nationale zu Paris, 8 Seiten in 4°.
(Continued on next card)

WITCHCRAFT

Histoire prodigieuse et espouvantable de plus de deux cens 50 sorciers... 1649 [1901] (Card 2)

Copie angefertigt von der bei der Bibliothek angestellten Mr. Herviant -- Paris im Juni 1901. für 4,50 frcs."
Numerals in the margin indicate pagination of the original.

1. Witchcraft--Toulouse. 2. Witchcraft--France. 3. Devil.

WITCHCRAFT
BF
1517
F5
H676
1874
no.3

Histoire prodigieuse et punition de Dieu espouvantable naguères arrivée auprès de la ville d'Anduse au païs de Gevosdan d'un homme de la Religion pretendué qui vouloit travailler et faire travailler ses serviteurs le jour de la Feste Dieu dernierement passée. Paris, Chez Abraham Saugrain, 1618. [Lyon, Impr. L. Perrin, 1876]
10 p. 24cm.

No. 3 in vol. lettered Histoire merveilleuse... 1614 [etc.]
1. Church attendance (Canon law)
2. Visions.

Witchcraft
BF
1555
L57

Histoire veritable et memorable de ce qui c'est passé sous l'exorcisme.

Le Normant, Jean, sieur de Chiremont, ed.
Histoire veritable et memorable de ce qvi c'est passé sovs l'exorcisme de trois filles possedées és païs de Flandre, en la descouuerte & confession de Marie de Sains, soy disant Princesse de la magie, & Simone Dourlet, complice, & autres. Ov il est avssi traicte' de la police du sabbat, & secrets de la synagogue des magiciens & magiciennes. De l'antechrist, & de la fin du monde.

(Continued on next card)

Witchcraft
BF
1555
L57

Histoire veritable et memorable de ce qui c'est passé sous l'exorcisme.

Le Normant, Jean, sieur de Chiremont, ed.
Histoire veritable ... de trois filles possedées ... 1623. (Card 2)

Extraict des memoires de Nicolas de Momorenci, comte Destarre, & du F. Sebastien Michaëlis, & du François Donsieux. Paris, N. Bvon, 1623.
2 v. 17cm.

Vol. 2 has title: De la vocation des
(Continued on next card)

Witchcraft
BF
1555
L57

Histoire veritable et memorable de ce qui c'est passé sous l'exorcisme.

Le Normant, Jean, sieur de Chiremont, ed.
Histoire veritable ... de trois filles possedées... 1623. (Card 3)

magiciens et magiciennes par le ministre des demons...

1. Demoniac possession. I. Le Normant, Jean, sieur de Chiremont, ed. De la vocation des magiciens... II. Title.

WITCHCRAFT
BF
1517
F5
H678
1875

Histoire veritable et memorable de la grande cruauté et tyrannie faicte et exercée par un colonel signalé de l'armée de Gallas, lequel a tué, pillé et violé plusieurs paysans et paysannes. Qui a esté emporté et mangé visiblement par les diables et à la vue de beaucoup de personnes du pays d'Allemagne. Jouxte la copie imprimée à Aix en Allemagne. [n. p.] 1637. [Lyon, Imp. L. Perrin, 1875]
8 p. 22 cm.
(Continued on next card)

WITCHCRAFT
BF
1517
F5
H678
1875

Histoire veritable et memorable de la grande cruauté et tyrannie faicte ... par un colonel ... [1875] (Card 2)

1. Devil. 2. Exempla.

Witchcraft
BF
1520
W64P8
1579

Histoires, dispvtes et discovrs, des illusions et impostures des diables.

Wier, Johann, 1515-1588.
Histoires, dispvtes et discovrs, des illusions et impostures des diables, des magiciens infames, sorcieres & empoisonneurs: Des ensorcelez & demoniaques, & de la guerison d'iceux: Item de la punition que meritent les magiciens, les empoisonneurs, & les sorcieres. Le tout comprins en six livres... Devx dialogves de Thomas Erastvs ... touchant le pouuoir des sorcieres: & de la punition qu'elles meritent. Auec deux indices ... [Genève, Povr Iaqves Chovet, 1579.
(Continued on next card)

Witchcraft
BF
1520
W64P8
1579

Histoires, dispvtes et discovrs, des illusions et impostures des diables.

Wier, Johann, 1515-1588. Histoires, dispvtes et discovres des illusions et impostures des diables ... 1579. (Card 2)

[32], 875, [39] p. 18cm.

Translation of the author's De praestigiis daemonum.
"Devx dialogves de Thomas Erastvs" has special t. p.

Witchcraft
PQ
1914
R6
A72
1701

Les histoires tragiques de nostre temps, ou sont contenues les morts funestes & lamentables de plusieurs personnes ...

Rosset, François de, b. ca. 1570.
Les histoires tragiques de nostre temps, ou sont contenues les morts funestes & lamentables de plusieurs personnes, arrivées par leurs ambitions, amours dereglées, sortileges, vols, rapines, & par autres accidens divers & memorables, composées par François de Rosset. Derniere edition ... Lyon, Chez B. Vignieu, 1701.
4 p. l., 632 p. 18cm.

(Continued on next card)

Witchcraft
PQ
1914
R6
A72
1701

Les histoires tragiques de nostre temps, ou sont contenues les morts funestes & lamentables de plusieurs personnes ...

Rosset, François de, b. ca. 1570. Les histoires tragiques de nostre temps ... 1701. (Card 2)

First ed. published under title: Histoires mémorables et tragiques, Paris, 1619.
Imperfect: last page partly illegible.

1. Biography--17th century. 2. Biography--Collections. I. Title. II. His Histoires mémorables et tragiques.

WITCHCRAFT
BF
1582
H67
1874

Histoires véritables arrivées en la personne de deux bourgeois de la ville de Charleville qui ont esté estranglez et emportez par le diable dans la dite ville. Iouxte la copie imprimée à Charleville. [n. p.] 1637. [Lyon, Imprim. Louis Perrin, 1874]
13 p. 23cm.

1. Witchcraft--France. 2. Devil.
3. Witchcraft--Charleville, France.

Witchcraft
DL
45
M19+
1555

Historia de gentibus Septentrionalibus.
Magnus, Olaus, Abp. of Uppsala, 1490-1558.
Historia de gentibvs Septentrionalibvs, earvmqve diversis statibvs, conditionibvs, moribvs, ritibvs, svperstitionibvs, disciplinis, exercitiis, regimine, victu, bellis, structuris, instrumentis, ac mineris metallicis, & rebus mirabilibus, necnon vniuersis penè animalibus in Septentrione degentibus, eorumque natura ... Cum indice locupletissimo ... Romae [Impressvm apvd Ioannem Mariam De Viottis] 1555.
[82], 815 p. illus. 29cm.

(Continued on next card)

283

CATALOGUE OF THE CORNELL WITCHCRAFT COLLECTION

Witchcraft Historia de gentibus Septentrionalibus.
DL   Magnus, Olaus, Abp. of Uppsala, 1490-1558.
45   Historia de gentibvs Septentrionalibvs
M19+   ... 1555.   (Card 2)
1555
           On p. 815 large device of G. M. de Viottis.
           "De svperstitiosa cvltvra daemonvm popvlorvm Aquilonarium liber tertius": p. 96-128.

           1. Scandinavia--Hist. I. Title.

Witchcraft Historia de la hechicería y de las brujas.
BF   Bonilla García, Luis.
1566   Historia de la hechicería y de las brujas. Madrid.
B71   Biblioteca Nueva, 1962.
           301 p. illus. 23 cm.
           Includes bibliography.

           1. Witchcraft--Hist. I. Title.

BF1566.B6
Library of Congress

           Historia diaboli.
WITCHCRAFT
BF   Mayer, Johann Gottfried.
1520   Historia diaboli; seu, Commentatio de diaboli, malorumque spirituum exsistentia,
M46   statibus, iudiciis, consiliis, potestate.
1780   Editio altera. Tubingae, Sumtibus Ioh.
           Georgii Cottae, 1780.
           xvi, 712 p. 20cm.
8
NIC   1. Devil. 2. Demonology.

           Historia inquisitionis.
Rare   Limborch, Philippus van, 1633-1712.
BX   Historia inquisitionis. Cui subjungitur
1710   Liber sententiarum inquisitionis Tholosanae
L73++   ab anno Christi MCCCVII ad annum MCCCXXIII.
           Amstelodami, Apud Henricum Wetstenium, 1692.
           2 pts. in 1 v. plates. 33cm.

           Engraved title vignette.

           1. Inquisition--Hist. 2. Inquisition--
           Toulouse. I. Title.

           Historic Salem, Inc.
WITCHCRAFT
F   Proclamation concerning what is said to be
74   the oldest dwelling house in Salem Massachusetts: the Witch House, which is to be
S1   restored as it was in the year 1692
P96+   and to be retained as an everlasting monument to the courageous men who broke the
               shackles of theocratic authority and
               paved the way for that freedom of thought
               which has made this country great.
               [Salem? Mass., 1945?]
               2 l. illus. 30cm.
8   Probably issued by Historic Salem,
NIC   Inc.   (Continued on next card)

           A historical account of the belief in
Witchcraft   witchcraft in Scotland.
BF   Sharpe, Charles Kirkpatrick, 1781?-1851.
1581   A historical account of the belief
S53   in witchcraft in Scotland. London,
           Hamilton, Adams & Co.; Glasgow, Thomas D.
           Morison, 1884.
           268 p. 20cm.

           Originally published in 1819 as an
           introduction to Robert Law's "Memorialls".

           1. Witchcraft--Scotland. I. Title.

           An historical essay concerning witchcraft.
Witchcraft
BF   Hutchinson, Francis, bp. of Down and Connor,
1565   1660-1739.
H97   An historical essay concerning witchcraft.
1720   With observations upon matters of fact;
           tending to clear the texts of the sacred
           Scriptures, and confute the vulgar errors
           about that point. And also two sermons:
           one in proof of the Christian religion; the
           other concerning good and evil angels. By
           Francis Hutchinson ... 2d ed., with considerable additions. London, Printed for
           R. Knaplock [etc.] 1720.
           16 p. l.,   336 p. 20½cm.
           I. Title.

           An historical, physiological and theological treatise of spirits, apparitions,
           witchcrafts, and other magical practices.
Witchcraft
BF   Beaumont, John, d. 1731.
1445   An historical, physiological and theological treatise of spirits, apparitions,
B37   witchcrafts, and other magical practices ...
           With a refutation of Dr. Bekker's World
           bewitch'd; and other authors that have
           opposed the belief of them. By John Beaumont ... London, Printed for D. Browne [etc.]
           1705.
           8 p. l., 400 p. front. 20cm.

           Historie de Magdelaine Bavent.
Witchcraft
BF   Desmarets,   oratorien.
1582   Histoire de Madeleine Bavent, religieuse
Z7   du monastère de Saint-Louis de Louviers.
1647   Réimpression textuelle sur l'édition rarissime de 1652. Précédée d'une notice biobibliographique, et suivie de plusieurs pièces supplémentaires. Orné d'un front. et d'
           une vue de l'ancien couvent de Saint-Louis
           ... Rouen, J. Lemonnyer, 1878.
           xl, vii,169 p. illus. 21cm.

           No. 141 of   177 copies printed.
                           (Continued on next card)

           Historie de Magdelaine Bavent.
Witchcraft
BF   Desmarets,   oratorien. Histoire de
1582   Madeleine Bavent ... 1878. (Card 2)
Z7
1647   Original t.p. reads: Historie de Magdelaine
           Bavent, religieuse du monastère de Saint
           Louis de Louviers, avec sa confession
           générale & testamentaire, où elle déclare
           les abominations, impietez, & sacrilèges qu'
           elle a pratiqué & veu pratiquer, tan ledit
           monastere, qu'au sabat, & les personnes qu'
           ell y a remarquées. Ensemble l'arrest
                          (Continued on next card)

Witchcraft Historie de Magdelaine Bavent.
BF   Desmarets,   oratorien. Histoire
1582   de Madeleine Bavent... 1878. (Card 3)
Z7
1647   donné contre Mathurin Picard, Thomas Boullé
           & ladite Bavent, tous convaincus du crime de
           magie. Dediee a Mme. la Dvchesse d'Orleans.
           Paris, J. Le Gentil, 1652.

           1. Bavent, Madeleine, ca.1608-1647.
           I. Title. II. Title: Historie de Magdelaine
           Bavent.

           Historische en theologische Redeneringe,
              over het onlangs uitgegeve boek van ...
Witchcraft   Balthasar Bekker.
BF   Leydekker, Melchior, 1642-1721.
1410   Historische en theologische Redeneringe,
B42   over het onlangs uitgegeve Boek van ...
Z76   Balthasar Bekker, strekkende tot bevestinge
1692   der Waarheit en Authoriteit van de H.
           Schriftuur. Uit het Latijn overgebragt,
           engeschikt na het begrip van den Nederduitschen Leser. Waar achter gevoegd is
           een Brief van de Hr. D'Aillon, wegens sijn
           gevoelen van de Eenheit des Duyvels, geschreven uit   London, den 16 Decemb.

NIC   (Continued on next card)

           Historische en theologische Redeneringe,
              over het onlangs uitgegeve Boek van ...
Witchcraft   Balthasar Bekker.
BF   Leydekker, Melchior, 1642-1721. Historische
1410   en theologische Redeneringe ... (Card 2)
B42
Z76   1691. Utregt, By de Weduwe van W. Clerck,
1692   1692.
           64, 8 p. 20cm.

           Van der Linde 127.

NIC   (Continued on next card)

           Historische Relation, von denen ... der
              Zauberey halber beschreyten Kindern.
MSS   Haeberlin, Georg Heinrich, 1644-1727.
Bd.   Historische Relation, von denen in der
WITCHCRAFT hochfürstl. Würtemb. wolbenahmssten Amptsund Handel-Stadt Calw einige Zeit her der
BF   Zauberey halber beschreyten Kindern, und
H13   andern Personen. Sambt einer christlichen
           Predigt, wie solchen und dergleichen satanischen Anläufften christlich zu begegnen...
           In offentlicher Versammlung daselbsten gehalten, und in Truck gegeben von Georg
           Heinrich Hebe rlin ... Stuttgart,
           zu finden bey   Johann Gottfried Zubrodt,
                           (Continued on next card)

           Historische Relation, von denen ... der
              Zauberey halber beschreyten Kindern.
MSS   Haeberlin, Georg Heinrich, 1644-1727.
Bd.   Historische Relation ... 1685 [ca. 1900]
WITCHCRAFT   (Card 2)
BF
H13   daselbst gedruckt bey Melchior Gerhard
           Lorbern, 1685 [ca. 1900]
           36 p. 23cm.
           Carnap's manuscript copy.
           "Originaldruck in der Königlichen öff.
           Bibliothek zu Stuttgart 40 pag. S. in 4°.
           Numerals in   the margins indicate
           pagination of   the original.
                           (Continued on next card)

Witchcraft Historische und theologische Vorstellung
BF   des ebentheuerlichen Gespenstes ...
1429   Zobel, Enoch, 1653-1697.
G62   Historische und theologische Vorstellung
1704   des ebentheuerlichen Gespenstes, welches in
           einem Hause zu S. Annaberg, 2 Monat lang im
           neuligst 1691sten Jahr, viel Schrecken,
           Furcht und wunderseltsame Schauspiele angerichtet ... Leipzig, F. Lanckischens
           Erben, 1692.
           [32], 312, [22] p. illus. 18cm.

           Bound with Goldschmidt, P. Höllischer
           Morpheus.   Hamburg, 1704.
           I. Title.

           Historischer Bericht, den gantzen Verlauff mit dem Soldaten ... fürstellend.
WITCHCRAFT
BF   Scriver, Christian, 1629-1693.
1572   Das verlohrne und wiedergefundene
D4   Schäfflein, oder Historischer christlicher
S43   Bericht von einem jungen Menschen, der
           sich vom Satan mit ihm einen Bund zu machen
           und ihm in allerley gottlosen Wesen sechs
           Jahr zu dienen verleiten lassen, darauff
           durch des gerechten Gottes Urtheil in dessen leibliche Gewalt und Besitzung gerathen
           erschröcklich gequälet, endlich aber
           errettet und   befreyet worden ...

8
NIC   (Continued on next card)

           Historischer Bericht, den gantzen Verlauff
              mit dem Soldaten ... fürstellend.
WITCHCRAFT
BF   Scriver, Christian, 1629-1693. Das verlohrne und wiedergefundene Schäfflein ...
1572   1672.   (Card 2)
D4
S43   Magdeburg und Helmstadt, Johann und Friedrich Lüderwaldts Buchhändl., 1672.
           [116] p. 19cm.
           "Historischer Bericht, den gantzen Verlauff mit dem Soldaten, dessen in denen
           vorhergesätzten Predigten Meldung geschehen, fürstellend" has special t. p.

8
NIC   (Continued on next card)

284

CATALOGUE OF THE CORNELL WITCHCRAFT COLLECTION

Historischer Versuch von der Hexereÿ.

WITCHCRAFT

Hutchinson, Francis, bp. of Down and Connor, 1660-1739.
 Francisci Hutchinsons ... Historischer versuch von der hexereÿ, in einem gespräch zwischen einem geistlichen, einem schottländischen advocaten und englischen geschwornen; worinnen über würcklich geschehene dinge vernünfftige anmerckungen gemachet, die hieher gehörigen stellen aus der Heil. Schrifft richtig erkläret und die gemeinen irrthümer aufs bescheidenlichste widerleget werden. Nebst zwey vortrefflichen predigten, die erste zum beweiss der wahrheit christl. religion, die andere, von guten und bösen engeln; und einer vorrede des herrn geheimbden raths Thomasii. Aus
(Continued on next card)   32-6507

Historischer Versuch von der Hexereÿ.

WITCHCRAFT

Hutchinson, Francis, bp. of Down and Connor, 1660-1739.
 Francisci Hutchinsons ... Historischer versuch von der hexereÿ ... (Card 2)
 dem englischen ins teutsche übersetzet, auch mit kurtzen summarien und vollständigen registern versehen von Theodoro Arnold. Leipzig, J. C. Martini, 1726.
 [50], 332, [23] p. front. 22 cm.
 Head-pieces and initials.
 "Verzeichniss derer in diesem werck nur teutsch angeführten englischen autorum": p. [1]-[4] at end.
 With copies 1 and 2 are bound Saint André, F. de. Lesenswürdige Briefe ... uber die Materie von der Zauberey. Leipzig, 1727.   32-6507
 Library of Congress
 ——— Copy 2.   (Continued on next card)

Historisk efterretning om de i Ribe bye for hexerie forfulgte og braendte mennesker.

Witchcraft
BF
1584
D4
G87

Grönlund, David.
 Historisk efterretning om de i Ribe bye for hexerie forfulgte og braendte mennesker. Viborg, C.H. Mangor, 1780.
 250 p. 22cm.

 1. Witchcraft. 2. Trials (Witchcraft) --Denmark. I. Title.

Historisk efterretning om de i Ribe bye for hexerie forfulgte og braendte mennesker.

Grönlund, David, 1716-1784.
 Historisk efterretning om de i Ribe Bye for Hexerie forfulgte og braendte Mennesker. 2. udg. Genudg. ved Kirsten Agerbæk. Ølgod, Historisk samfund for Ribe Amt, Eksp.: S. Manøe Hansen, 1973.
 195 p. illus. 24 cm.
 Bibliography: p. 192-193.

 1. Witchcraft--Ribe, Denmark. I. Title

APP 01,'75   COCxc   74-314795

An history of apparitions.

[Bromhall, Thomas] ed. and tr.
 Treatise of specters; or, An history of apparitions, oracles ... with dreams, visions ... Collected out of sundry authours and delivered into English by T.B. Annexed, a learned treatise, confuting the opinions of Sadduces [sic] and epicures ... Written in French and now rendred [sic] into English. London, Printed by J. Streater, 1658.
 367 p. 28cm.
 With autograph: William Jones.
 1. Apparitions. I. Title. II. Title: An history of apparitions.

A history of crime in England.

Pike, Luke Owen, 1835-1915.
 A history of crime in England, illustrating the changes of the laws in the progress of civilisation; written from the public records and other contemporary evidence, by Luke Owen Pike ... London, Smith, Elder & co., 1873-76.
 2 v. fronts. (v. 1: facsim.) 22½cm.
 Contents--I. From the Roman invasion to the accession of Henry VII.--II. From the accession of Henry VII. to the present time.
 1. Crime and criminals--England. 2. Criminal law--England. I. Title.

The history of magic.

WITCHCRAFT
BF
1589
E59
1854

Ennemoser, Joseph, 1787-1854.
 The history of magic. Translated from the German by William Howitt. To which is added an appendix of the most remarkable and best authenticated stories of apparitions, dreams, second sight, somnambulism, predictions, divination, witchcraft, vampires, fairies, table-turning, and spirit-rapping. Selected by Mary Howitt. London, Henry G. Bohn, 1854.
 2 v. 19cm. (Bohn's scientific library)
 Translation of Geschichte der Magie.
 (Continued on next card)

The history of magic.

Witchcraft
BF
1589
S46+
1948

Seligmann, Kurt, 1900-
 The history of magic. [New York] Pantheon Books [c1948]
 504 p. 27cm.

 Also published the same year, by the same publisher, under title: The mirror of magic.

 1. Magic--Hist. I. Title. II. His The mirror of magic.

A history of magic and experimental science.

Witchcraft
Q
125
T49
1958

Thorndike, Lynn, 1882-
 A history of magic and experimental science. New York, Columbia University Press [1958-60, c1923-58]
 8 v. 23cm.

 Vols. 3-6 have series note on half-title: History of Science Society publications. New series IV.
 Contents.--v. 1-2. The first thirteen centuries of our era.--v. 3-4. Fourteenth

(Continued on next card)

A history of magic and experimental science.

Witchcraft
Q
125
T49
1958

Thorndike, Lynn, 1882-   A history of magic and experimental science. [1958-60, c1923-58]   (Card 2)

 Contents.--Continued.
 and fifteenth centuries.--v. 5-6. The sixteenth century. v. 7-8. The seventeenth century.

 I. Title.

The history of magic, including a clear and precise exposition of its procedure, its rites and its mysteries.

Witchcraft
BF
1589
C75
1949

Constant, Alphonse Louis, 1810-1875.
 The history of magic, including a clear and precise exposition of its procedure, its rites and its mysteries, by Eliphas Lévi (Alphonse Louis Constant) Tr., with a preface and notes, by Arthur Edward Waite. Los Angeles, Borden Pub. Co. [1949]
 384 p. illus. 22cm.
 Translation of Histoire de la magie.

An history of magic, witchcraft, and animal magnetism.

Witchcraft
BF
1589
C72

Colquhoun, John Campbell, 1785-1854.
 An history of magic, witchcraft, and animal magnetism. By J. C. Colquhoun ... London, Longman, Brown, Green, & Longmans; [etc., etc.] 1851.
 2 v. 19cm.

The history of magick by way of apology.

WITCHCRAFT
BF
1589
N29
1657

Naudé, Gabriel, 1600-1653.
 The history of magick by way of apology, for all the wise men who have unjustly been reputed magicians, from the creation, to the present age. Written in French, by G. Naudaeus ... Englished by J. Davies. London, Printed for John Streater, 1657.
 8 p. l., 306, [2] p. 18cm.
 Publisher's catalog p. [307]-[303].
 Translation of Apologie pour tous les grands personnages qui ont esté faussement soupçonnez de magie (1625).
 Wing N246.   (Continued on next card)

The history of Mother Shipton.

Witchcraft
BF
1815
S55
H43
1710

[Head, Richard] 1637?-1686?
 The history of Mother Shipton: containing an account of her strange and unnatural conception, her birth, life, actions and death: the correspondence she held with the devil, and the many strange and wonderful things perform'd by her. Together with all the predictions and prophecies that have been made by her, and since fulfilled, from the reign of King Henry the Seventh, to the third year of our Sovereign Lady Queen Anne ... London, Printed by and for W. Onley [ca. 1710]

(Continued on next card)

The history of Mother Shipton.

Witchcraft
BF
1815
S55
H43
1710

[Head, Richard] 1637?-1686?   The history of Mother Shipton ... [ca. 1710]   (Card 2)

 24 p. 21cm.

 Title vignette (woodcut)
 For authorship cf. Halkett & Laing. Dict. of anonymous and pseudonymous English lit., v. 3, p. 72.
 First published 1684 (or 1677) under title: The life and death of Mother Shipton.
 1. Shipton, Ursula. 2. Prophecies. I. Title. II. His The life and death of Mother Shipton.

The history of oracles.

WITCHCRAFT
BF
1761
F68
1753

Fontenelle, Bernard Le Bovier de, 1657-1757.
 The history of oracles, in two dissertations. Wherein are proved, I. That the oracles were not given out by daemons ... II. That the oracles did not cease at the coming of Jesus Christ ... Translated from the best edition of the original French. Glasgow, Printed by R. Urie, 1753.
 x, 144, [2] p. 17cm.
 Translation of Histoire des oracles, a rifacimento of A. van Dale's De oraculis ethnicorum dissertationes duae, Amstelaedami, 1683.

A history of penal methods.

HV
9644
I95

Ives, George Cecil, 1867-
 A history of penal methods; criminals, witches, lunatics, by George Ives, M.A. London, S. Paul & co. [1914]
 xi, 409 p. 23cm.

 "Index to authors [with titles of works]": p. 384-396.

A history of the delusion in Salem, in 1692.

Witchcraft
BF
1576
U68L4

Upham, Charles Wentworth, 1802-1875.
 Lectures on witchcraft, comprising a history of the delusion in Salem, in 1692. Boston, Carter, Hendee and Babcock, 1831.
 vii, 280 p. 16cm.

 I. Title. II. Title: A history of the delusion in Salem, in 1692.

CATALOGUE OF THE CORNELL WITCHCRAFT COLLECTION

The history of the Devil.

Witchcraft
PR
3404
H5
1780

[Defoe, Daniel] 1660-1731.
The history of the Devil, ancient and modern. In two parts. Part I. Containing a state of the Devil's circumstances, from his expulsion out of heaven to the creation; with remarks on the several mistakes concerning his fall. Part II. Containing his more private conduct down to the present times: his government, his appearance, his manner of working, and the tools he works with. In which is included a description of the Devil's dwelling. London, Printed for G. Hay, 1780.
viii, 340 p. 17cm.
(Continued on next card)

The history of the Devil.

Witchcraft
PR
3404
H5
1780

[Defoe, Daniel] 1660-1731. The history of the Devil ... 1780. (Card 2)

First ed. published in 1726 under title: The political history of the Devil.

I. Title: The history of the Devil.
II. His the political history of the devil.

The history of the devil and the idea of evil, from the earliest times to the present day.

Witchcraft
BF
1548
C32+

Carus, Paul, 1852-1919.
The history of the devil and the idea of evil, from the earliest times to the present day. Chicago, The Open Court Publishing Co.; [etc., etc.] 1900.
xvi, 496 p. illus. 28cm.

1. Devil. 2. Demonology. 3. Good and evil. I. Title.

The history of the devil, the horned God of the west.

Witchcraft
BT
980
T47

Thompson, Richard Lowe.
The history of the devil, the horned God of the west. London, Kegan Paul, Trench, Trubner & Co., Ltd., 1929.
xiv, 171 p. illus. 23cm.

The history of the devils of Loudun.

Witchcraft
BF
1517
F5
D46
1887

[Des Niau, ---]
The history of the devils of Loudun, the alleged possession of the Ursuline nuns, and the trial and execution of Urbain Grandier, told by an eye-witness. Translated from the original French, and edited by Edmund Goldsmid. Edinburgh, Priv. Print., 1887-88.
3 v. 18cm. (Collectanea Adamantaea, XXI.1)
Contains facsimile of original French t.p.: La véritable historie des diables de Loudun ... Poitiers, J. Thoreau, 1634.

The history of the Inquisition.

Rare
BX
1710
L73+
1731

Limborch, Philippus van, 1663-1712.
The history of the Inquisition. Translated into English by Samuel Chandler. To which is prefixed, a large introduction concerning the rise and progress of persecution and the real and pretended causes of it. London, Sold by J. Gray, 1731.
2 v. in 1. 26cm.

With autograph: John Kenrick.

1. Inquisition--Spain. I. Title.

A history of the Inquisition of Spain.

Witchcraft
BX
1735
L43
H3

Lea, Henry Charles, 1825-1909.
A history of the Inquisition of Spain. New York, London, The Macmillan Company, 1906-07.
4 v. 24cm.

I. Title.

The history of the inquisition of Spain.

BX
1735
L79
1827

Llorente, Juan Antonio, 1756-1823.
The history of the inquisition of Spain, from the time of its establishment to the reign of Ferdinand VII. Composed from the original documents of the Archives of the Supreme council, and from those of subordinate tribunals of the Holy office. Abridged and translated from the original works of D. Juan Antonio Llorente ... 2d. ed. London, Printed for G. B. Whittaker, 1827.
xx, 583, [1] p. 21½cm.
Translation of Historia critica.
1. Inquisition--Spain. I. Title.

A history of the Inquisition of the middle ages.

Witchcraft
BX
1711
L43
1888

Lea, Henry Charles, 1825-1909.
A history of the Inquisition of the middle ages. By Henry Charles Lea ... New York, Harper & brothers, 1888.
8 v. 23½cm.

The history of the life and adventures of Mr. Duncan Campbell.

Witchcraft
BF
1815
C2D31
1720

[Defoe, Daniel] 1660?-1731.
The history of the life and adventures of Mr. Duncan Campbell, a gentleman, who tho' deaf and dumb, writes down any stranger's name at first sight: with their future contingencies of fortune. Now living in Exeter-Court over-against the Savoy in the Strand ... 2d ed. cor. London, Printed for E. Curll, and sold by W. Mears [etc.] 1720.
xix, [4], 320 p. front.(port.) 4 pl. 19cm.

(Continued on next card)

The history of the life and adventures of Mr. Duncan Campbell.

Witchcraft
BF
1815
C2D31
1720

[Defoe, Daniel] 1660?-1731. The history of the life and adventures of Mr. Duncan Campbell, ... 1720. (Card 2)

Authorship disputed; probably by Defoe, though ascribed also to William Bond under whose name it appeared in 1728, with new title: The supernatural philosopher; or, The mysteries of magick ... unfolded by William Bond. cf. Dict. nat. biog.; Camb. hist. Eng. lit., v. 9; Dottin's "Daniel DeFoe et ses romans" (1924) p. 261.
Frontispiece wanting.

The history of the most remarkable tryals in Great Britain and Ireland, in capital cases ...

Rare
K
H675

The history of the most remarkable tryals in Great Britain and Ireland, in capital cases ... Both by the unusual methods of ordeal, combat, and attainder, and by the ecclesiastical, civil and common laws of these realms. Faithfully extracted from records, and from other authentick authorities, as well manuscript as printed. London, Printed for A. Bell [etc.] 1715.
5 p. l., 452, [4] p. 20cm.

1. Trials--Gt. Brit.--Hist.

A history of the ridiculous extravagancies of Monsieur Oufle.

Witchcraft
PQ
1957
B67
A64
1711

[Bordelon, Laurent] 1653-1730.
A history of the ridiculous extravagancies of Monsieur Oufle; occasion'd by his reading books treating of magick, the black-art, daemoniacks, conjurers, witches ... With notes containing a multitude of quotations out of those books, which have either caused such extravagant imaginations, or may serve to cure them. Written originally in French, by the Abbot B----; and now translated into English. London, Printed

8
(Continued on next card)

A history of the ridiculous extravagancies of Monsieur Oufle.

Witchcraft
PQ
1957
B67
A64
1711

[Bordelon, Laurent] 1653-1730. A history of the ridiculous extravagancies of Monsieur Oufle ... 1711. (Card 2)

for J. Morphew, 1711.
4 p. l., 303 [i.e., 319] p. 20cm.
Translation of Histoire des imaginations extravagantes de Monsieur Oufle.
Gathering G, between p. 96 and 97, incorrectly paged 81-96.
1. Occult sciences. 2. Apparitions.

8
(Continued on next card)

A history of the witches of Renfrewshire.

Witchcraft
BF
1581
H67

A history of the witches of Renfrewshire who were burned on the gallowgreen of Paisley. Published by the editor of the Paisley Repository. Paisley, Printed by J. Neilson for J. Millar, 1809.
iv, 200 p. 18cm.

At head of title: From authentic documents.

A history of the witches of Renfrewshire.

Witchcraft
BF
1581
H67
1877

A history of the witches of Renfrewshire. A new ed., with an introduction, embodying extracts, hitherto unpublished, from the records of the Presbytery of Paisley ... Paisley, A. Gardner, 1877.
2 p. l., [xi]-xxv (i. e. xxxv) p., 3 l., [5]-219, 6 p. front. 20½cm.
Introduction signed: J. D.
Includes reprint of original t.-p.: From authentic documents. A history of the witches of Renfrewshire, who were burned on the Gallowgreen of Paisley. Published by the editor of the Paisley repository ... Paisley, Printed by J. Neilson for J. Millar, 1809.
Comp. by J. Millar. Cf. p. [5]

1. Witchcraft--Scotland. I. Millar, John, comp.

Library of Congress   BF1581.A2 1809   11-14652

A history of the witches of Renfrewshire.

Witchcraft
BF
1581
M64
1877

[Millar, John] Bookseller.
A history of the witches of Renfrewshire. A new edition, with an introduction, embodying extracts, hitherto unpublished, from the records of the Presbytery of Paisley. Paisley [Scotland] Alex. Gardner, 1877.
xxv, 219, 6 p. front. 21cm.

Contains a reproduction of the original title-page with imprint: Paisley. Printed by J. Neilson, for John Millar, Bookseller, 1809.

1. Witchcraft--Renfrewshire, Scot. I. Title.

The history of witchcraft and demonology.

Witchcraft
BF
1566
S95H6

Summers, Montague, 1880-1948.
The history of witchcraft and demonology. London, Kegan Paul, Trench, Trubner & Co., Ltd., 1926.
xv, 353 p. illus. 24cm. (The history of civilization. Subject histories)

1. Witchcraft. 2. Demonology. I. Title.

CATALOGUE OF THE CORNELL WITCHCRAFT COLLECTION

A history of witchcraft in England from 1558 to 1718.

tchcraft
81
1
65

Notestein, Wallace, 1879-
A history of witchcraft in England from 1558 to 1718. New York, Russell & Russell, 1965.
xiv, 442 p. 23cm. (Prize essays of the American Historical Association)
"Awarded the Herbert Baxter Adams prize in European history for 1909."
1. Witchcraft--England. I. Title: Witchcraft in England from 1558 to 1718. II. Series: American Historical Association. Prize essays, 1909. III. Title.

History of witchcraft in Massachusetts.

WITCHCRAFT
BF 1576
M82
G641+

Goodell, Abner Cheney, 1831-1914.
[Reasons for concluding that the act of 1711, reversing the attainders of the persons convicted of witchcraft in Massachusetts in the year 1692, became a law. Being a reply to Supplementary notes, etc. by George H. Moore]
(In:. Massachusetts Historical Society. Proceedings. Boston. 26cm. Jan./Mar.1884. p.99-118)
With, in same issue: his Additional considerations on the history
(Continued on next card)

8
NIC

History of witchcraft in Massachusetts.

WITCHCRAFT
BF 1576
M82
G641+

Goodell, Abner Cheney, 1831-1914. [Reasons for concluding that the act of 1711... became a law] 1884. (Card 2)
of witchcraft in Massachusetts.
Running title: History of witchcraft in Massachusetts.
1. Witchcraft--Massachusetts. 2. Moore, George Henry, 1823-1892. Supplementary notes on witchcraft... I. His /History of witchcraft in Massachusetts. II. Title: History of witchcraft in Massachusetts. III. Title: Reasons for concluding that the act of 1711 became a law.

History of witchcraft in Massachusetts.

WITCHCRAFT
BF 1576
M82
G641+

Moore, George Henry, 1823-1892.
[Supplementary notes on witchcraft in Massachusetts]
(In: Massachusetts Historical Society. Proceedings. Boston. 26cm. Jan./Mar.1884. p.77-99)
With, in same issue; Goodell, Abner Cheney. Additional considerations on the history of witchcraft in Massachusetts.
Running title: History of witchcraft in Massachusetts.
Continues his Notes on the history
(Continued on next card)

8
NIC

History of witchcraft in Massachusetts.

WITCHCRAFT
BF 1576
M82
G641+

Moore, George Henry, 1823-1892. [Supplementary notes on witchcraft...] 1884. (Card 2)
of witchcraft in Massachusetts. Continued by his Final notes on witchcraft in Massachusetts.
1. Witchcraft--Massachusetts. 2. Goodell, Abner Cheney, 1831-1914. Further notes on the history of witchcraft... I. Title. II. His /History of witchcraft in Massachusetts. III. Title: History of witchcraft in Massachusetts.

History of witchcraft in Massachusetts.

ITCHCRAFT
F 576
821+
884

Moore, George Henry, 1823-1892.
Supplementary notes on witchcraft in Massachusetts; a critical examination of the alleged law of 1711 for reversing the attainders of the witches of 1692. Cambridge, J. Wilson, 1884.
25 p. facsim. 26cm.
Reprinted from the Proceedings of the Massachusetts Historical Society, Mar.1884.
Caption title: Witchcraft in Massachusetts.
(Running title of original article: History of witchcraft in Massachusetts)
(Continued on next card)

8
NIC

History of witchcraft in Massachusetts.

WITCHCRAFT
BF 1576
M821+
1884

Moore, George Henry, 1823-1892. Supplementary notes on witchcraft... 1884. (Card 2)
Continues his Notes on the history of witchcraft in Massachusetts. Continued by his Final notes on witchcraft in Massachusetts.
1. Witchcraft--Massachusetts. 2. Goodell, Abner Cheney, 1831-1914. Further notes on the history of witchcraft... I. Title. II. His Witchcraft in Massachusetts. III. Title: Witchcraft in Massachusetts. IV. His History of witchcraft in Massachusetts. V. Title: History of witchcraft in Massachusetts.

History of witches etc.

Witchcraft
BF 1566
M16

Macleod, Malcolm.
History of witches &c. The majesty of darkness discovered: in a series of tremendous tales ... of apparitions, witches, augers, magicians ... in confirmation of a future state, & the superintendency of a Divine Providence, by the agency of spirits & angels. With The prophecy of Pedan; or, The Caledonian apocalypse of the last century; sublimely adumbrating the awful events which now amaze and alarm all Europe. London, Printed by and for
(Continued on next card)

History of witches etc.

Witchcraft
BF 1566
M16

Macleod, Malcolm. History of witches &c... [1793] (Card 2)
I. Roach [1793]
97 p. front. 17cm.
Title vignette.
I. Title. II. Title: The majesty of darkness discovered. III. Title: The emphatical prophecy of Pedan.

Witchcraft
BF 1563
H67

The history of witches, ghosts, and highland seers: containing many wonderful well-attested relations of supernatural appearances, not published before in any similar collection. Designed for the conviction of the unbeliever, and the amusement of the curious. ... Berwick, Printed for R. Taylor [1800?]
xi, 263 p. front. 19cm.
1. Witchcraft. 2. Ghosts. 3. Apparitions.

Hobbes, Thomas, 1588-1679.
Elementa philosophica de cive.

Witchcraft
BF 1520
F17

Falck, Nathanael, 1663-1693.
Nathanaelis Falcken ... Dissertationes quatuor, De daemonologia recentiorum autorum falsa, Anno 1692. Wittebergae habitae, nunc verò praefixis literis Schomerianis ibidem recusae. [Wittebergae] Typis Martini Schultzii, 1694.
92 p. illus. initials. 20 x 16cm.
4°: A², B-M⁴, N².
Contents.--De falsa recentiorum auctorum daemonologia ... respondente Joh.
(Continued on next card)

8

Hobbes, Thomas, 1588-1679.
Elementa philosophica de cive.

Witchcraft
BF 1520
F17

Falck, Nathanael, 1663-1693. Nathanaelis Falcken ... Dissertationes quatuor ... 1694. (Card 2)
Contents--Continued.
Isaaco Trempenau.--Dissertatio II. Ortum daemonologiae falsae & progressum historicè declarans, respondente Johanne Furmann.--Dissertatio III. De daemonologia Hobbesii & Spinozae, respondente Jac. Friderico Mollero.--Dissertatio IV. De daemonolo-
(Continued on next card)

8

Hobbes, Thomas, 1588-1679.
Elementa philosophica de cive.

Witchcraft
BF 1520
F17

Falck, Nathanael, 1663-1693. Nathanaelis Falcken ... Dissertationes quatuor ... 1694. (Card 3)
gia Bekkeri & aliorum, respondente Georg. Abrahamo Wolf.
1. Demonology. 2. Hobbes, Thomas, 1588-1679. Elementa philosophica de cive. 3. Spinoza, Benedictus de, 1632-1677. Tractatus theologico-politicus. 4. Bekker, Balthasar, 1634-1698. De betoverde weereld. I. Title: De daemonologia recentiorum autorum falsa.

8

Hobbes, Thomas, 1588-1679.

WITCHCRAFT
BF 1581
A2
G551

Prior, Moody Erasmus, 1901-
Joseph Glanvill, witchcraft, and seventeenth-century science... Chicago, 1932.
167-193 p. 25cm.
"A part of a dissertation submitted to ...[the University of Chicago]...for the degree of Doctor of Philosophy."
Reprinted from Modern philology, v.30, no.2, 1932.
1. Glanvill, Joseph, 1636-1680. Saducismus triumphatus. 2. Hobbes, Thomas, 1588-1679. 3. Witchcraft.

8
NIC

WITCHCRAFT
BF 1565
R43

Ein hochgelehrter und gar vornehmer Juris Consultus.
Responsum juris, oder Rechtliches vnd ausführliches Bedencken von Zauberin, deren Thun, Wesen vnd Vermögen, auch was Gestalt dieselbe zubestraffen ... gestellet durch einen hochgelehrten vnd gar vornehmen JC^tum ... Franckfurt am Mayn, Erstmaln gedruckt vnd verlegt bey Johann-Friderich Weissen, 1637.
4 p. l., 126 [i.e., 162] p. 21cm.
Possibly by Philipp Hoffmann or Hofmann?
Running title: Rechtlich Bedencken von Zauberey.
(Continued on next card)

8
NIC

Hochnötige unterthanige wemütige Klage.

MSS
Bd.
WITCHCRAFT
BF
L82

Löher, Hermann, b. 1595.
Hochnötige unterthanige wemütige Klage der frommen Unschültigen; worin alle hohe und nidrige Oberkeit, sampt ihren Unterthanen klärlich, augenscheinlich zu sehen und zu lesen haben, wie die arme unschültige fromme Leute durch Fahm- und Ehrenrauber von den falschen Zauber-richtern angegriffen, durch die unchristliche Folter, und Pein-banck von ihnen gezwungen werden, erschreckliche, unthunliche Mord, und Todt, Sünden auff sich selbsten und
(Continued on next card)

Hochnötige unterthanige wemütige Klage.

MSS
Bd.
WITCHCRAFT
BF
L82

Löher, Hermann, b. 1595. Hochnötige unterthanige wemütige Klage ... 1676 [1896] (Card 2)
anderen mehr zu liegen, und sie ungerechtlich, falschlich zu besagen... durch Hermannum Löher. Amsterdam, Jacob de Jonge, 1676 [1896]
640 p. 10 plates, part folded. 19cm.
Carnap's manuscript copy.
"Originaldruck als einziges bekanntes Exemplar in der Bibliothek des Kgl.
(Continued on next card)

Hochnötige unterthanige wemütige Klage.

MSS
Bd.
WITCHCRAFT
BF
L82

Löher, Hermann, b. 1595. Hochnötige unterthanige wemütige Klage ... 1676 [1896] (Card 3)
Gymnasiums zu Münstereifel b/Bonn. 16 Bl. u. 608 pag. S. Von dort geliehen und abgeschrieben in der Zeit vom 12. Februar bis zum 9. März 1896."
Numerals in the margins indicate pagination of the original.
Imperfect: p. 84-86, 132-134, part of p. 354-355 are blank and
(Continued on next card)

287

CATALOGUE OF THE CORNELL WITCHCRAFT COLLECTION

Hochnötige unterthanige wemütige Klage.

MSS Bd. WITCHCRAFT BF L82
Löher, Hermann, b. 1595. Hochnötige unterthanige wemütige Klage ... 1676 [1896] (Card 4)

correspond to p. 45-48, 97-100 and 341-342 of the original, which the copyist states are missing.
Bibliography of literature referring to this work: p. 607-638.
Note by the copyist concerning the scarcity of the original   p. 639-640.
Plates are   photographic reproduc-
(Continued on next card)

Hochnötige unterthanige wemütige Klage.

MSS Bd. WITCHCRAFT BF L82
Löher, Hermann, b. 1595. Hochnötige unterthanige wemütige Klage ... 1676 [1896] (Card 5)

tions from the copper plates of the original, pasted on to extra leaves.
With note by G. L. Burr on inside front cover indicating provenance of the manuscript copy.

1. Trials (Witchcraft)--Germany.
2. Witchcraft --Germany. I. Title.

Hochstrassen, Jakob von, ca. 1460-1527.

see

Hoogstraten, Jacobus van, ca. 1460-1527.

Hochstraten, Jakob von, ca. 1460-1527.

see

Hoogstraten, Jacobus van, ca. 1460-1527.

Thesis 1911 338
Hodder, Mabel Elisabeth.
Peter Binsfeld and Cornelius Loos, an episode in the history of witchcraft. Ithaca, N. Y., 1911.
228 l. 29cm.

Thesis (Ph. D.)--Cornell University, 1911.

1. Binsfeld, Pierre, ca. 1540-1598. 2. Loos, Cornelius, 1546-1595.   3. Witchcraft.

Hoechstrassen, Jacobus, ca. 1460-1527.

see

Hoogstraten, Jacobus van, ca. 1460-1527.

WITCHCRAFT BF 1583 H69
Höhn, W
Hexenprozesse in den hennebergischen Ämtern Schleusingen, Suhl und Ilmenau. (In Hennebergischer Geschichtsverein. Schriften. Schleusingen. 22cm. Nr. 4. Jahrg. 1911 (1911), p. 24-137)

1. Trials (Witchcraft)--Henneberg, Germany. 2. Trials (Witchcraft)--Germany. I. Title. II. Hennebergischer Geschichtsver ein. Schriften.

Der höllische Intelligenz-Zettul.

Witchcraft BF 1555 B41
Beer, Johann Christoph, 1690-1760.
Der höllische Intelligenz-Zettul; das ist, Merckwürdige Betrachtungen über die dermahlige Verwirrung der gantzen Welt: verursachet durch vile tausend, von höllischen Geistern heimlich, und in der Still besessene Menschen. ... Augspurg, J. J. Mauracher [1753]
8 p. l., 472, [16] p. 18cm.

1. Demoniac possession. I. Title. II. Title: Merckwürdige Betrachtungen über di e dermahlige Verwirrung der gantzen We lt.

Der höllische Proteus.

Witchcraft BF 1445 F82 1695
Francisci, Erasmus, 1627-1694.
Der höllische Proteus, oder tausendkünstige Versteller, vermittelst Erzehlung der vielfältigen Bild-Verwechslungen erscheinender Gespenster, werffender und poltrender Geister ... wie auch andrer abentheurlicher Händel ... und von theils gelehrten, für den menschlichen Lebens-Geist irrig-angesehenen Betriegers, (nebst vorberichtlichem Grund-Beweis der Gewissheit, dass es würcklich Gespenster gebe)   ... Nürnberg, In Ver-
(Continued on next card)

Der höllische Proteus.

Witchcraft BF 1445 F82 1695
Francisci, Erasmus, 1627-1694. Der höllische Proteus ...   1695.   (Card 2)
legung Wolfgang Moritz Endters, 1695.
23 p. l., 1120, [46] p. front. 18cm.

First published 1690.

1. Ghosts. 2. Demonology. 3. Ghost stories. I. Title.

Die höllische Zauberin Circe, in ihren vermaledeyten Töchtern und verdammten Schwestern abgemahlet.

Witchcraft BL 820 C6 F12
Faber, Daniel.
Die höllische Zauberin Circe, in ihren vermaledeyten Töchtern und verdammten Schwestern abgemahlet. Auch alle Obrigkeiten und Richter der Welt zu ernstlicher Bestraffung derselben treuhertzig erinnert und angemahnet. Magdeburg, C. Seidel, 1699.
253 p. illus. 18cm.

1. Circe.   2. Witchcraft. I. Title.

Höllischer Morpheus.

Witchcraft BF 1429 G62 1704
Goldschmidt, Peter, d. 1713.
Höllischer Morpheus, welcher Kund wird durch die geschehene Erscheinungen derer Gespenster und Polter-Geister so bisshero zum Theil von keinen eintzigen Scribenten angeführet und bemercket worden sind ... Hamburg, G. Liebernickel, 1704.
[14], 409, [37] p. illus. 18cm.

With this are bound Glanvill, J. Saducismus triumphatus. Hamburg. 1701. Zobel, E. Historische und theologische Vorstellung des ebentheuer lichen Gespenstes. Leipzig. 1692; and. Declaratio apologetica. Leipz ig. 1695.

Witchcraft PT 1792 H69+
Hölscher, Otto.
Friedrich Spee von Langenfeld. Sein Leben und seine Schriften. Düsseldorf, Gedruckt von L. Boss [1871]
16 p. 27cm.

Accompanies "Programm" (zu den öffentlichen Prüfungen am 28., 29. und 30 August 1871)--Realschule erster Ordnung, Düsseldorf. Pages 13-16 give poems by Spee.

1. Spee, Fr iedrich von, 1591-1635. I. Title.

WITCHCRAFT BF 1569 H69
Hössli, Heinrich.
Hexenprocess -- und Glauben, Pfaffen und Teufel. Als Beitrag zur Cultur- und Sittengeschichte der Jahrhunderte. Leipzig, H. Barsdorf, 1892.
80 p. 22cm.

1. Witchcraft--History. 2. Superstition. I. Title.

NIC

WITCHCRAFT R 133 H71 1725
Hoffmann, Friedrich, 1660-1742.
Friderici Hoffmanni ... De diaboli potentia in corpora, dissertatio physico-medica curiosa. Emendatior jam edita. Halae Magdeburgicae, Typis Joh. Gruneri, 1725.
[39] p. 21cm.

First published 1703 under title: Disputatio inauguralis medico-philosophica De potentia diaboli in corpora.

1. Medici ne, Magic, mystic, and spagiric. 2.   Devil. I. His Disputatio inaugu ralis medico-philosophi-
(Over) ca De potent ia diaboli in corpora.

Hoffmann, Friedrich, 1660-1742.
De fato physico et medico ... disquisitio. German.

WITCHCRAFT R 133 H71 D2 1749
Hoffmann, Friedrich, 1660-1742.
D. Friedrich Hoffmanns ... Vernunfftmässige Abhandlung von dem heidnischen Fato, und der christlichen Providentz, in medicinisch- und physicalischen Dingen. Sorau, Bey G. Hebold, 1749.
116 p. 17cm.

Translation of De fato physico et medico ejusque rationali explicatione disquisitio. Halae Magdeb., 1724.

Added t. p.: D. Friedrich Hoffmanns ...

NIC   (Continued on next card)

Hoffmann, Friedrich, 1660-1742.
De fato physico et medico ... disquisitio. German.

WITCHCRAFT R 133 H71 D2 1749
Hoffmann, Friedrich, 1660-1742. ... Vernunfftmässige Abhandlung von dem heidnischen Fato ... 1749.   (Card 2)
Gründliche vernunfft- und schrifftmässige Betrachtung von der Würckung, Macht und Gewalt des Teuffels in der Lufft und menschlichen Körpern [translation of Disputatio inauguralis medico-philosophica De potentia diaboli in corpora. Halae, 1703]

1. Medicine, Magic, mystic, and spagiric 2. Fate and fatalism. 3. Medical delu-

NIC   (Continued on next card)

WITCHCRAFT R 133 H71
Hoffmann, Friedrich, 1660-1742, praeses.
Disputatio inauguralis medico-philosophica De potentia diaboli in corpora, quam ... praeside DN. Friderico Hoffmanno publico ... examini submittit Godofredus Büching. Halae, Typis Ioannis Gruneri [1703]
[39] p. 21cm.

Diss.--Halle (G. Büching, respondent)
NIC   I. Büching. Godofredus, respondent. II. Title.   III. Title: De potentia diaboli in corpora.

CATALOGUE OF THE CORNELL WITCHCRAFT COLLECTION

WITCHCRAFT
R
133
H71
1725

Hoffmann, Friedrich, 1660-1742.
   Disputatio inauguralis medico-philosophica De potentia diaboli in corpora.
Hoffmann, Friedrich, 1660-1742.
   Friderici Hoffmanni ... De diaboli potentia in corpora, dissertatio physico-medica curiosa. Emendatior jam edita. Halae Magdeburgicae, Typis Joh. Gruneri, 1725.
   [39] p. 21cm.
   First published 1703 under title: Disputatio inauguralis medico-philosophica De potentia diaboli in corpora.
   1. Medicine, Magic, mystic, and spagiric. 2. Devil. I. His Disputatio inauguralisca De potentia diaboli in corpora.

8

WITCHCRAFT
R
133
H71
1704

Hoffmann, Friedrich, 1660-1742.
   Disputatio inauguralis medico-philosophica De potentia diaboli in corpora. German.
[Hoffmann, Friedrich] 1660-1742.
   Philosophische Untersuchung von Gewalt und Wirckung des Teuffels in natürlichen Körpern. Franckfurt und Leipzig, 1704.
   29 p. 20cm.
   Translation of Disputatio inauguralis medico-philosophica De potentia diaboli in corpora. Halae, 1703.
   1. Medicine, Magic, mystic, and spagiric 2. Devil. I. His Disputatio inauguralis medico- philosophica De potentia diaboli in corpora. German. II. Title.

8
NIC

WITCHCRAFT
R
133
H71
D2
1749

Hoffmann, Friedrich, 1660-1742.
   Disputatio inauguralis medico-philosophica De potentia diaboli in corpora. German.
Hoffmann, Friedrich, 1660-1742.
   D. Friedrich Hoffmanns ... Vernunfftmässige Abhandlung von dem heidnischen Fato, und der christlichen Providentz, in medicinisch- und physicalischen Dingen. Sorau, Bey G. Hebold, 1749.
   116 p. 17cm.
   Translation of De fato physico et medico ejusque rationali explicatione disquisitio. Halae Magdeb., 1724.
   Added t. p.: D. Friedrich Hoffmanns ...
   (Continued on next card)

8
NIC

WITCHCRAFT
R
133
H71
D2
1749

Hoffmann, Friedrich, 1660-1742. ... Vernunfftmässige Abhandlung von dem heidnischen Fato ... 1749.   (Card 2)
   Gründliche vernunfft- und schrifftmässige Betrachtung von der Würckung, Macht und Gewalt des Teuffels in der Lufft und menschlichen Körpern [translation of Disputatio inauguralis medico-philosophica De potentia diaboli in corpora. Halae, 1703]
   1. Medicine, Magic, mystic, and spagiric 2. Fate and fatalism. 3. Medical delu-
   (Continued on next card)

8
NIC

WITCHCRAFT
R
133
H71
D2
1749

Hoffmann, Friedrich, 1660-1742.
   Gründliche vernunfft- und schrifftmässige Betrachtung von der Würckung ... des Teuffels.
Hoffmann, Friedrich, 1660-1742.
   D. Friedrich Hoffmanns ... Vernunfftmässige Abhandlung von dem heidnischen Fato, und der christlichen Providentz, in medicinisch- und physicalischen Dingen. Sorau, Bey G. Hebold, 1749.
   116 p. 17cm.
   Translation of De fato physico et medico ejusque rationali explicatione disquisitio. Halae Magdeb., 1724.
   Added t. p.: D. Friedrich Hoffmanns ...
   (Continued on next card)

8
NIC

WITCHCRAFT
R
133
H71
D2
1749

Hoffmann, Friedrich, 1660-1742.
   Gründliche vernunfft- und schrifftmässige Betrachtung von der Würckung ... des Teuffels.
Hoffmann, Friedrich, 1660-1742.   ... Vernunfftmässige Abhandlung von dem heidnischen Fato ... 1749.   (Card 2)
   Gründliche vernunfft- und schrifftmässige Betrachtung von der Würckung, Macht und Gewalt des Teuffels in der Lufft und menschlichen Körpern [translation of Disputatio inauguralis medico-philosophica De potentia diaboli in corpora. Halae, 1703]
   1. Medicine, Magic, mystic, and spagiric. 2. Fate and fatalism. 3. Medical delu-
   (Continued on next card)

8
NIC

WITCHCRAFT
R
133
H71
1704

[Hoffmann, Friedrich] 1660-1742.
   Philosophische Untersuchung von Gewalt und Wirckung des Teuffels in natürlichen Körpern. Franckfurt und Leipzig, 1704.
   29 p. 20cm.
   Translation of Disputatio inauguralis medico-philosophica De potentia diaboli in corpora. Halae, 1703.
   1. Medicine, Magic, mystic, and spagiric 2. Devil. I. His Disputatio inauguralis medico- philosophica De potentia diaboli in corpora. German. II. Title. III. Title: Gewalt und Wirckung des Teuffels.

8
NIC

WITCHCRAFT
R
133
H71
D2
1749

Hoffmann, Friedrich, 1660-1742. ... Vernunfftmässige Abhandlung von dem heidnischen Fato ... 1749.
   Added t. p.: D. Friedrich Hoffmanns ...
   (Continued on next card)

8
NIC

WITCHCRAFT
R
133
H71
D2
1749

Hoffmann, Friedrich, 1660-1742. ... Vernunfftmässige Abhandlung von dem heidnischen Fato ... 1749.   (Card 2)
   Gründliche vernunfft- und schrifftmässige Betrachtung von der Würckung, Macht und Gewalt des Teuffels in der Lufft und menschlichen Körpern [translation of Disputatio inauguralis medico-philosophica De potentia diaboli in corpora. Halae, 1703]
   1. Medicine, Magic, mystic, and spagiric 2. Fate and fatalism. 3. Medical delu-
   (Continued on next card)

8
NIC

WITCHCRAFT
R
133
H71
D2
1749

Hoffmann, Friedrich, 1660-1742.   ... Vernunfftmässige Abhandlung von dem heidnischen Fato ... 1749.   (Card 3)
   sions. 4. Devil. I. His De fato physico et medico ... disquisitio. German. II. His Gründliche vernunfft- und schrifftmässige Betrachtung von der Würckung ... des Teuffels. III. His Disputatio inauguralis medico-philosophica De potentia diaboli in corpora. German. IV. Title: Vernunfftmässige Abhandlung von dem heidnischen Fato. V. Title: Gründliche vernunfft- und schrifftmässige Betrachtung von der Würckung ...

8
NIC

RARE
HV
8593
D611
no.14

Hoffmann, Gottfried Daniel, 1719-1780, praeses.
   De continuatione torturae interruptae... praeside Godofredo Daniele Hoffmanno...disputabit Burcardus Fridericus Mauchart. Tubingae, Formis Erhardianis [1757]
   48 p. 21cm.
   Diss.--Tübingen (B. F. Mauchart, respondent)
   No. 14 in a vol. lettered: Dissertationes de tortura, 1697-1770.
   1. Torture. 2. Criminal procedure. I. Mauchart, Burcard Friedrich, respondent. II. Title.

8
NIC

WITCHCRAFT
BF
1565
R43

Hoffmann, Philipp, supposed author.
   Responsum juris, oder Rechtliches vnd auszführliches Bedencken von Zauberin, deren Thun, Wesen vnd Vermögen, auch was Gestalt dieselbe zubestraffen ... gestellet durch einen hochgelehrten vnd gar vornehmen JC^{tum} ... Franckfurt am Mayn, Erstmaln gedruckt vnd verlegt bey Johann-Friderich Weissen, 1637.
   4 p. l., 126 [i.e., 162] p. 21cm.
   Possibly by Philipp Hoffmann or Hofmann? Running title: Rechtlich Bedencken von Zauberey.
   (Continued on next card)

8
NIC

WITCHCRAFT
BF
1584
S97
H69

Hoffmann-Krayer, Eduard, 1864-1936.
   Luzerner Akten zum Hexen- und Zauberwesen.
   (In Schweizerisches Archiv für Volkskunde. Zürich. 25cm. 3. Jahrg. (1899), p. [22]-40, [81]-122, [191]-224, [291]-329)
   Includes illustrations.
   Also published as monograph, 1900.

8

WITCHCRAFT
BF
1584
S97
H69
1900

Hoffmann-Krayer, Eduard, 1864-1936.
   Luzerner Akten zum Hexen- und Zauberwesen. Zürich, Buchdruckerei E. Cotti's Witwe, 1900.
   144 p. 25cm.
   "Separat-Abdruck aus dem 'Schweiz. Archiv für Volkskunde.'"
   With this is bound his Ein Zauberprozess in Basel 1719. Zürich, 1898.
   1. Trials (Witchcraft)--Lucerne, Switzerland. 2. Trials (Witchcraft)-- Switzerland. I. Title.

8

WITCHCRAFT
BF
1584
S97
H69
1900

Hoffmann-Krayer, Eduard, 1864-1936.
   Ein Zauberprozess in Basel 1719.
   (In Schweizerisches Archiv für Volkskunde. Zürich. 25cm. 2. Jahrg., Heft 4 (1898), p. [283]-291)
   Bound with his Luzerner Akten zum Hexen- und Zauberwesen. Zürich, 1900.
   1. Charms. 2. Folk-lore--Switzerland. I. Title.

8

Witchcraft
BF
1565
D62
no.1

Hofmann, Johann.
   Apologia principum, in qua processus in causa sagarum continetur, et maleficorum argumenta refutantur ... a Johanne Hofmanno culmbacensi ... & authoris sumtibus in lucem edita. Erfurti, Typis Friderici Melchioris Dedekindi, 1636.
   [47] p. 20cm.
   No. 1 in vol. lettered Dissertationes de sagis. 1636-1714.
   1. Trials (Witchcraft). I. Title. II. Title: Processus in causa sagarum.

8

WITCHCRAFT
BF
1565
R43

Hofmann, Philipp, fl. 1593-1619, supposed author.
   Responsum juris, oder Rechtliches vnd auszführliches Bedencken von Zauberin, deren Thun, Wesen vnd Vermögen, auch was Gestalt dieselbe zubestraffen ... gestellet durch einen hochgelehrten vnd gar vornehmen JC^{tum} ... Franckfurt am Mayn, Erstmaln gedruckt vnd verlegt bey Johann-Friderich Weissen, 1637.
   4 p. l., 126 [i.e., 162] p. 21cm.
   Possibly by Philipp Hoffmann or Hofmann? Running title: Rechtlich Bedencken von Zauberey.
   (Continued on next card)

8
NIC

Hohenheim, Philipp Aureolus Theophrastus Bombast von, known as Paracelsus.

see

Paracelsus, 1493-1541.

CATALOGUE OF THE CORNELL WITCHCRAFT COLLECTION

R 133 A92
Hohman, Johann Georg.
Aurand, Ammon Monroe, 1895–
The "pow-wow" book; a treatise on the art of "healing by prayer" and "laying on of hands", etc., practiced by the Pennsylvania Germans and others; testimonials; remarkable recoveries; popular superstitions; etc., including an account of the famous "witch" murder trial, at York, Pa., by A. Monroe Aurand, jr. ... containing also the complete collection of remedies and cures in John George Hohman's "Pow-wows, or Long lost friend"; in popular use since 1820. Harrisburg, Pa., Priv. print. by The Aurand press, 1929.
x, 85, [1], 31, [1], xi, 13-64 p. incl. front., illus. 24cm. (Continued on next card)

R 133 A92
Hohman, Johann Georg.
Aurand, Ammon Monroe, 1895–   The "pow-wow" book ... 1929. (Card 2)
"An account of the 'witch' murder trial" ... and "John George Hohman's Pow-wows; or, Long lost friend" have special title-pages and pagination.
"Pow-wows; or Long lost friend" was published in 1819 under title: Der lange verborgene freund, oder: Getreuer und christlicher unterricht für jedermann.
"This edition of the 'Pow-wow' book is limited to one thousand copies; one hundred signed by the author. This is no. 309."
Bibliography: p. vi.
1. Medicine, Magic, mystic, and spagiric. 2. Superstition. 3. Folklore—Pennsylvania. 4. Witchcraft—Pennsylvania. 5. Blymyer, John H. 6. Rehmeyer, Nelson D., 1868-1928. I. Hohman, Johann Georg. II. Title. III. Title: "Witch" murder trial, York, Pa.
Library of Congress   R133.A8
—— Copy 2.   29-9468 Revised
Copyright A 7294   [d2]

BF 1581 H72M6
Hole, Christina.
A mirror of witchcraft.   London, Chatto & Windus, 1957.
260 p. illus. 23cm.
"Sources of extracts given": p. 9-16.
1. Witchcraft—England.   I. Title.

BF 1581 H72
Hole, Christina.
Witchcraft in England, by Christina Hole, illustrated by Mervyn Peake. London, B. T. Batsford ltd. [1945]
167, [1] p. front., illus., plates, ports. 22½ᶜᵐ.
"First published spring, 1945."
Bibliography: p. 161-165.
1. Witchcraft—England.   I. Title.
                                                45-4819
Library of Congress °   BF1581.H6
                  [3]   133.40942

BF 1581 H72 1947
Hole, Christina.
Witchcraft in England.   New York, C. Scribner's, 1947.
167 p. illus. 24cm.

WITCHCRAFT
BF 1583 H73
Hollenbach, Wilhelm.   Bilder aus Thüringen. I. Tragikomische Geisterbeschwörung auf dem Galgenberge bei Jena in der Christnacht des Jahres 1715. Nach den Originalquellen wahrheitsgetreu dargestellt ... Mit interessanten Bruchstücken der Streitschrift des Jenaischen Arztes Andreä und den Gutachten der theologischen und juristischen Fakultät zu Leipzig. Jena, F. Mauke (A. Schenk), 1885.
iv, 56 p.   21cm.
No more published?
8   (Continued on next card)

WITCHCRAFT
BF 1583 H73
Hollenbach, Wilhelm.   Bilder aus Thüringen. I. Tragikomische Geisterbeschwörung ... 1885.   (Card 2)
1. Witchcraft—Thuringia. 2. Witchcraft—Jena, Germany. 3. Devil. I. Title. II. Title: Tragikomische Geisterbeschwörung auf dem Galgenberg bei Jena ... 1715. III.   Andreä, Erdmann Friedrich.
8

Hollin, Maria, fl. 1594.
Witchcraft
BF 1583 Z7 1590
Weng, Johann Friedrich.
Die Hexen-Prozesse der ehemaligen Reichsstadt Nördlingen in den Jahren 1590-94. Aus den Kriminal-Akten des Nördlingischen Archives gezogen ... Nördlingen, C. H. Beck [1838]
60, 28 p.   22cm.
Aus der historisch-statistischen Zeitschrift: "Das Ries, wie es war und wie es ist" besonders abgedruckt.
1. Trials (Witchcraft)—Nördlingen. 2. Trials (Witchcraft)—Germany. 3. Hollin, Maria, fl. 1594.   I. Title.
8

WITCHCRAFT
BF 1584 D4 H742
[Holm, Viggo Valdemar] 1855-1899.
Fra Hexernes Tid. Kuriøse Historier af Woldemar [pseud.] Kjøbenhavn, P. G. Philipsen, 1887.
100, [4] p. 17cm.
Contents.—Hexerne.—Geworben.—Skielmen.—Dend brølendis Basune.—Margalitha.—Udi Linnehuuset.
1. Witchcraft—Denmark.   I. Title.
8

Witchcraft
BF 1584 D4 H74
[Holm, Viggo Valdemar] 1855-1899.
Kuriøse Historier fra Hexernes Tid af Woldemar [pseud.]   Kjøbenhavn, Gyldendalske Boghandel (F. Hegel & Søn) 1896.
151 p. 22cm.
Contents.—Halelu Jah, af I. Pedersson.—Menniskens Børn (af en gammel Krønike)—Hierichos Trummete, af Joannes Michaeli Søn.—Af Dirik Giglers Fortaellinger.
Each item has special t. p.; Halelu Jah also has imprint: Hafnia, 1589.
1. Witchcraft—Denmark.   I. Title.
8

Holman, Winnefred.
Witchcraft
Z 6490 H51+
Henkels, firm, auctioneers, Philadelphia.
The extraordinary collection of autograph letters belonging to the late Hon. Elliot Danforth ... To be sold ... Dec. 11, 1913, and ... Dec. 12, 1913 ... Stan. V. Henkels, auction commission merchant. Philadelphia, [M. H. Power, printer, 1913?]
135 p. facsims. 28cm.
Catalogue no. 1074, Part 3.
(Continued on next card)

Holman, Winnefred.
Witchcraft
Z 6490 H51+
Henkels, firm, auctioneers, Philadelphia.
The extraordinary collection of autograph letters...   [1913?]   (Card 2)
Contains facsimile of a letter signed by some of her neighbors, certifying that Winnefred Holman was not guilty of witchery.
1. Autographs—Collections. 2. Danforth, Elliot. 3. Holman, Winnefred.

Witchcraft
BF 1575 C23 H75
Holmes, Thomas James, 1874–
Cotton Mather and his writings on witchcraft. [Chicago, Univ. of Chicago Press, 1926]
29 p. 25cm.
"Reprinted for private distribution from Papers of the Bibliographical Society of America, vol. XVIII, Parts 1 and 2."
Bound with his The surreptitious printing of one of Cotton Mather's manuscripts.
1. Mather, Cotton, 1663-1728—Bibl. 2. Witchcraft—Bibl.   I. Title.

Witchcraft
BF 1575 C23 H75
Holmes, Thomas James, 1874–
The surreptitious printing of one of Cotton Mather's manuscripts, by Thomas J. Holmes ... Cambridge [Mass., Printed at the Harvard university press] 1925.
1 p. l., 12 p. 25cm.
"Reprinted from Bibliographical essays; a tribute to Wilberforce Eames."
With this is bound his Cotton Mather and his writings on witchcraft. [1926]
1. Calef, Robert, 1648-1719. More wonders of the invisible world. 2. Mather, Cotton, 1663-1728. 3. Witchcraft—New England.
Library of Congress   BF1575.C23H6
                                                41-38390
[2]   [159.96140974]   133.40974

The holocaust.
Witchcraft
BF 1775 B63
Blair, George.
The holocaust; or, The witch of Monzie, a poem illustrative of the cruelties of superstition. Lays of Palestine and other poems. To which is prefixed, Enchantment disenchanted; or, A treatise on superstition. ... London, J. F. Shaw, 1845.
xii, 277 p. 20cm.
1. Superstition.   I. Title. II. Title: The witch of Monzie.   III. Title: Lays of Palestine.   IV. Title: Enchantment disenchanted.

Witchcraft
BF 1410 B42 Z85 no.3
[Holy, Nikolaas Muys van] 1654–
Overweging van het hooftpoint in Do. Bekkers boek, genaamt De betoverde weereld, te weten, of de duyvel op een mensch werken kan. [Amsterdam, By P. Rotterdam, boekverkoper, 1692]
8 p. 19 x 16cm.
4°: A⁴.
Caption title.
Signed: Nicolaes Muys van Holy.
No. 3 in vol. lettered Stukken betrekkelijk Bekker.
8   (Continued on next card)

Witchcraft
BF 1410 B42 Z85 no.3
[Holy, Nikolaas Muys van] 1654–   Overweging van het hooftpoint in Do. Bekkers boek ... [1692]   (Card 2)
1. Bekker, Balthasar, 1634-1698. De betoverde weereld.   I. Title.

WITCHCRAFT
BF 1569 H76
Holzinger, J   B
Zur Naturgeschichte der Hexen. Vortrag gehalten vom Vereins-Präsidenten ... J. B. Holzinger, in der Jahres-Versammlung des Naturwissenschaftlichen Vereines für Steiermark am 16. December 1882. Graz, Verlag des Naturwissenschaftlichen Vereines für Steiermark, 1883.
40 p. 23cm.
"Separat-Abdruck aus den Mittheilungen des naturwissenschaftlichen Vereines für Steiermark Jahrgang 1882."
1. Witchcraft—History. 2. Science and civilization.   I. Title.
8

CATALOGUE OF THE CORNELL WITCHCRAFT COLLECTION

Witchcraft
BF
1517
G7
H76
   Homes, Nathaniel.
     Daemonologie and theologie. The first, the malady, demonstrating the diabolicall arts, and devillish hearts of men. The second, the remedy, demonstrating God, a rich supply of all good. London, Printed by T. Roycroft, and are to be sold by J. Martin and J. Ridley, 1650.
     208, 31 p. 15cm.

     The second part has special t.p.
     With bookplate of Sir William Grace, bart.
     I. Title.

WITCHCRAFT
BS
2675
H77
   Honert, Johan van den, 1693-1758, praeses.
     Dissertatio philologico-theologica, de velanda muliere propter angelos, ad locum I Cor. XI. vers 10. Lugduni Batavorum, 1738.
     14 p. 19cm.
     Diss.--Lund (G. Rekuc, respondent)

     1. Bible. N. T. 1 Corinthians XI, 10-- Criticism, interpretation, etc. I. Rekuc, Georgius, resp. II. Title: De velanda muliere propter angelos.

8
NIC

   Hoochstraten, Jacobus, ca. 1460-1527.
     see
   Hoogstraten, Jacobus van, ca. 1460-1527.

   Homma, Laurentius, d. 1681.

Witchcraft
BF
1410
B42
1691a
no.8
   Bekker, Balthasar, 1634-1698.
     Omstandig beright, van Balthasar Bekker, S. T. D. predikant tot Amsterdam, van sijne particuliere onderhandelinge met D. Laurentius Homma, sal. ged. in sijn leven mede predikant aldaar. Beneffens d'ontdekte lagen van Everhardus van der Hooght, en Jakob Lansman tegen denselven. Amsterdam, By D. vanden Dalen, boekverkooper, 1693.
     1 p. l., 22 p. title and end page vignettes, illus. initials. 20 x 16cm.
     4°: π1, A-C⁴ (-C4)

8   (Continued on next card)

Witchcraft
BF
1558
G86
1800
   Honorius III, Pope, d. 1227.
     Gremoire [sic] du Pape Honorius, avec un recueil des plus rares secrets. A Rome [i.e. Paris?] 1800.
     123 p. illus., 12 plates. 14cm.

     Text differs considerably from the Rome ed. of 1760.

     1. Incantations. 2. Magic. I. Honorius III, Pope, d. 1227. Spurious and doubtful works. II. Title: Grimoire du Pape Honorius.

8

Witchcraft
BS
1199
D4
H77
   Hood, Edwin Paxton, 1820-1885.
     Lectures on the Scriptural idea of the Devil. [187?]
     113-126 p. 23cm.

     Alternate pages blank.
     Evidently reprinted from a periodical.

     1. Devil--Biblical teaching. I. Title: The Scriptural idea of the Devil. II. Title.

   Homma, Laurentius, d. 1681.

Witchcraft
BF
1410
B42
1691a
no.8
   Bekker, Balthasar, 1634-1698. Omstandig beright ... 1693. (Card 2)

     Black letter.
     "Bedekte lagen van Everhard van der Hooght, predikant tot Nieuwendam, en Jakob Lansman, procureur en notaris tot Amsterdam: ontdekt aan Balthasar Bekker ...:" p. 17-22.
     Van der Linde 117.
     No. 8 in vol. lettered B. Bekker. Betoverde weereld.
     1. Hooght, Everard van der, d. 1716. 2. Lansman, Jakob. I. Homma, Laurentius, d. 1681. II. Title.

8

   Honorius III, Pope, d. 1227. Spurious and doubtful works.

Witchcraft
BF
1558
G86
1760a
     Grimoire du Pape Honorius, avec un recueil des plus rares secrets. A Rome, 1760. [Avignon, Offray ainé, ca. 1880]
     95 p. illus., 12 col. plates. 13cm.
     Title page is plate 2 (Pl. I in the numbering)
     Added title page preceeding text has title: Le grand grimoire, avec La grande clavicule de Salomon.
     1. Incantations. 2. Magic. I. Honorius III, Pope, d. 1227. Spurious and doubtful works. II. Title: Le grand grimoire.

8

Hooght, Everard Van Der

Witchcraft
BF
1410
B42
Z69
no.2
   [Hooght, Everard van der] d. 1716.
     Aanmerkingen van הגבר Φιλαληθής Haggébher Philaleethees, op de invoegselen van Do. Balthasar Bekker, voor zoo veel de zelve betreffen de stellingen, die reeds in sijne brieven tot noch toe zyn verhandelt, zynde een aanhangsel van den vyfden brief. Amsterdam, G. Borstius, 1691.
     124-134 p. 21cm.

     Signatures: 4°: A⁴, B².

NIC   (Continued on next card)

Witchcraft
BF
1410
B42
Z56
v.3
no.26
   Hooght, Everard van der, d. 1716.
     Antwoord van Everardus van der Hooght, aan den eerwaarden, godzaligen, hoog-geleerden heere, Do. Balthasar Bekker, S. Theologiae Doctor, yverig predikant tot Amsterdam. Amsterdam, By G. Borstius, boekverkoper, 1691.
     1 p. l., 8, [2] p. title vignette, illus. initial. 19 x 15cm.
     4°: π1, A⁴, [B]1.
     Black letter.
     Letter dated 29. Sept. 1691; postscript, 1 Oct. 1691.

     (Continued on next card)

Witchcraft
BF
1410
B42
Z69
no.13
   Hooght, Everard van der, d. 1716.
     Antwoord van Everardus van der Hooght, aan den eerwaarden, godzaligen, hoog-geleerden heere, Do. Balthasar Bekker, S. Theologiae Doctor, yverig predikant tot Amsterdam. Amsterdam, By G. Borstius, boekverkoper, 1691.
     1 p. l., 8, [2] p. title vignette, illus. initial. 21cm.
     4°: π1, A⁴, [B]1.
     Black letter.
     Letter dated 29 Sept. 1691; postscript, 1 Oct. 1691.

     (Continued on next card)

Witchcraft
BF
1410
B42
Z69
no.2
   [Hooght, Everard van der] d. 1716. Aanmerkingen van ... Haggébher Philaleethees ... 1691. (Card 2)

     Black letter.
     Van der Linde 102.
     No. 2 in a Collection of tracts against Balthasar Bekker and his Betoverde weereld.

     1. Bekker, Balthasar, 1634-1698. De betoverde weereld. 2. Jesus Christ --Temptation. 3. Bible. O.T. Job. I. Title.

NIC

Witchcraft
BF
1410
B42
Z56
v.3
no.26
   Hooght, Everard van der, d. 1716. Antwoord ... aan ... Do. Balthasar Bekker ... 1691. (Card 2)

     Van der Linde 106.
     No. 26 in vol. lettered Bekker III.

     I. Bekker, Balthasar, 1634-1698. Brief van den schrijver des boeks De betoverde weereld. I. Bekker, Balthasar, 1634-1698. II. Title.

Witchcraft
BF
1410
B42
Z69
no.13
   Hooght, Everard van der, d. 1716. Antwoord ... aan ... Do. Balthasar Bekker ... 1691. (Card 2)

     Van der Linde 106.
     No. 13 in a Collection of tracts against Balthasar Bekker and his Betoverde weereld.

CATALOGUE OF THE CORNELL WITCHCRAFT COLLECTION

Witchcraft
BF
1410
B42
Z56
v.3
no.25
[Hooght, Everard van der] d. 1716.
Derde briev van הגבר [Haggēbher]
ΦΙΛΑΛΗΘΗΣ [Philaleethees] geschreeven aan zynen vriend N. N. over het vervolg van de kerkelyke proceduuren tegen den persoon van Do. Balthasar Bekker; nevens de aan-merkingen over de gereformeerde confessie, ende over het gevoelen van de gesonde gereformeerde godsgeleerden, nopende het hooft-stuk van de natuure ende de werkingen der engelen. Amsterdam, By G. Borstius, boekverkoper, 1691.

8   (Continued on next card)

Witchcraft
BF
1410
B42
Z56
v.3
no.25
[Hooght, Everard van der] d. 1716. Derde briev ... aan zynen vriend N. N. ... 1691. (Card 2)

[39]-58 p. title vignette, illus. initial. 19 x 15cm.
4°: π1, A-B⁴, C1.
Black letter.
The friend N. N. is Jacobus Schuts?
Van der Linde 99.
No. 25 in vol lettered Bekker III.

                    (Continued on next card)

Witchcraft
BF
1410
B42
Z56
v.3
no.25
[Hooght, Everard van der] d. 1716. Derde briev ... aan zynen vriend N. N. ... 1691. (Card 3)

1. Bekker, Balthasar, 1634-1698. 2. Nederlandse Hervormde Kerk. 3. Spirits. I. Schuts, Jacobus. II. Title.

Witchcraft
BF
1410
B42
Z69
no.5
[Hooght, Everard van der] d. 1716.
Derde briev van הגבר [Haggēbher]
ΦΙΛΑΛΗΘΗΣ [Philaleethees] geschreeven aan zynen vriend N. N. over het vervolg van de kerkelyke proceduuren tegen den persoon van Do. Balthasar Bekker; nevens de aan-merkingen over de gereformeerde confessie, ende over het gevoelen van de gesonde gereformeerde godsgeleerden, nopende het hooft-stuk van de natuure ende de werkingen der engelen. Amsterdam, By G. Borstius, boekverkoper, 1691.

8   (Continued on next card)

Witchcraft
BF
1410
B42
Z69
no.5
[Hooght, Everard van der] d. 1716. Derde briev ... aan zynen vriend N. N. ... 1691. (Card 2)

[39]-58 p. title vignette, illus. initial. 21cm.
4°: π1, A-B⁴, C1.
Black letter.
The friend N. N. is Jacobus Schuts?
Van der Linde 99.
No. 5 in a Collection of tracts against Balthasar Bekker and his Betoverde weereld.

                    (Continued on next card)

Witchcraft
BF
1410
B42
Z69
no.5
[Hooght, Everard van der] d. 1716. Derde briev ... aan zynen vriend N. N. ... 1691. (Card 3)

1. Bekker, Balthasar, 1634-1698. 2. Nederlandse Hervormde Kerk. 3. Spirits. I. Schuts, Jacobus. II. Title.

Witchcraft
BF
1410
B42
Z69
no.3
[Hooght, Everard van der] d. 1716.
Eerste briev van הגבר Φιλαλήθης Haggēbher Philaleethees, geschreeven aan zynen vriend N. N. over den persoon en het boek van Do. Balthasar Bekker. In opzicht van de gudheyd, ende het gewichte zyner dwaling; nevens sijne onkunde in de godtgeleertheyd ende in de gronden van de Hebreeusche tale; demonstratiiv beweesen, uyt zyne verklaring van Gen. 18. ende Job 1. en 2. Amsterdam, G. Borstius, 1691.
20 p. 21cm.

NIC   (Continued on next card)

Witchcraft
BF
1410
B42
Z69
no.3
[Hooght, Everard van der] d. 1716. Eerste briev van ... Haggēbher Philaleethees... 1691. (Card 2)

Signatures: 4°: A-B⁴, C1.
Black letter.
N. N. is thought to be Jacobus Schuts.
Van der Linde 97.
No. 3 in a Collection of tracts against Balthasar Bekker and his Betoverde weereld.

NIC   (Continued on next card)

Witchcraft
BF
1410
B42
Z69
no.3
[Hooght, Everard van der] d. 1716. Eerste briev van ... Haggēbher Philaleethees ... 1691. (Card 3)

1. Bekker, Balthasar, 1634-1698. De betoverde weereld. I. Schuts, Jacobus. II. Title.

NIC

Witchcraft
BF
1410
B42
Z69
no.9
[Hooght, Everard van der] d. 1716.
Sesde briev van הגבר Φιλαλήθης Haggēbher Philaleethees, geschreeven aan zynen vriend N. N. vervattende: I. Een afwysing van vyfderley gewaande voorspraaken van D. Bekker. Ende II. een verhandeling van de De Daimonia, na hare beteekenisse voor, in, ende na de tyden Christi. Volgens het welke uyt het Hebreeusch Griekich en Syrisch klaar te sien is, dat De Daimonia zedert Christi tyden niet anders zyn, dan de Duyvelen. Amsterdam,

NIC   (Continued on next card)

Witchcraft
BF
1410
B42
Z69
no.9
[Hooght, Everard van der] d. 1716. Sesde briev van ... Haggēbher Philaleethees ... (Card 2)

G. Borstius, 1691.
135-176 p. 21cm.

Signatures: 4°: π1, A-E⁴, F1.
Black letter.
The friend N.N. may be Jacobus Schuts.
Van der Linde 103.
No. 9 in a Collection of tracts against Balthasar Bekker and his betoverde weereld.

NIC   (Continued on next card)

Witchcraft
BF
1410
B42
Z69
no.9
[Hooght, Everard van der] d. 1716. Sesde briev van ... Haggēbher Philaleethees... 1691. (Card 3)

1. Bekker, Balthasar, 1634-1698. 2. Leydekker, Melchior, 1642-1721. Historische en theologische redeneringe. 3. Schaak, Petrus, fl. 1691. 4. Daemonia (word) I. Schuts, Jacobus. II. Title.

NIC

Witchcraft
BF
1410
B42
Z69
no.12
Hooght, Everard van der, d. 1716.
Sesde briev van ... Haggēbher Philaleethees.
[Webbers, Zacharias]
In antwoort op het jonghste post scriptum van de VI. brief van Haggēbher Philaleethees tegens eene van de (soo hem dunkt) schadelyk helpers van Do. B. Bekker, raakende desselfs aanmerkingen over de predicatie van Do. Adrianus van Weesel, 's Sondags by sijn eerw. in de Wester Kerk den 25 Novemb. over Math. IV 5,6,7. Van de versoekinge onses saligmaker door den Duyvel, gedaan. Dienende dit tot krachtiger bewijs, dat deselve niet eygentlijk, maar by forme van een

NIC   (Continued on next card)

Witchcraft
BF
1410
B42
Z69
no.12
Hooght, Everard van der, d. 1716.
Sesde briev van ... Haggēbher Philaleethees.
[Webbers, Zacharias] In antwoort op het jonghste post scriptum ... (Card 2)

gesighte, en in den geest geschiet zy: door den zelven S. W. S. F. t'Amsterdam, by D. van den Dalen, 1692.
16 p. 21cm.

Signatures: 4°: A-B⁴.
Black letter.
No. 12 in a Collection of tracts against Balthasar Bekker and his Betoverde weereld.

NIC   (Continued on next card)

Witchcraft
BF
1410
B42
Z69
no.12
Hooght, Everard van der, d. 1716.
Sesde briev van ... Haggēbher Philaleethees.
[Webbers, Zacharias] In antwoort op het jonghste post scriptum ... 1692. (Card 3)

Attributed to Webbers by Aa, A. J. van der. Biographisch woordenboek der Nederlanden. Haarlem, 1852-78, and by Doorninck, J. I. van. Vermonde en naamlooze schrijvers ... Leiden, 1883-85.
Van der Linde 113.

NIC   (Continued on next card)

Witchcraft
BF
1410
B42
Z69
no.10
[Hooght, Everard van der] d. 1716.
Sevende briev van הגבר Φιλαλήθης geschreeven aan den E. Heer C. E. over den oorspronk, voortgang, ende het gebruyk der talen in het gemeen. Ende, in het byzondere, van de Duyvelen in het Oude Testament, onder de woorden scheedhijm, ende segnijrijm cap. 8. Item, een vertooning, dat de Heer Jesus ons de geheele Gods-geleertheyd in zijne dagen heest geleerd, na de waarheyd saake, ende nooit, tegen de waarheyd na de dwaling des volks. cap. Ende dat de beseetene ofte beduyvelde

NIC   (Continued on next card)

Witchcraft
BF
1410
B42
Z69
no.10
[Hooght, Everard van der] d. 1716. Sevende briev van ... (Card 2)

sijn geplaagt geworden van den Duyvel, als de naaste oorsaak van hare siektens, cap. Nevens een klaar vertoog, dat het niet de minste eygenschap en heeft, om zoo veele texten in Gods woord, alwaar de Satan, als een werker, benoemt word, alleen te willen betrekken op den Duyvel, voor soo veel hy geweest is de oorsaak van de eerste verleyding des menschen, cap. 11.

NIC   (Continued on next card)

Witchcraft
BF
1410
B42
Z69
no.10
[Hooght, Everard van der] d. 1716. Sevende briev van ... (Card 3)

Waar by koomen eenige invoegselen tegens sommige misduydingen, in het Post-script Met het vervolg der kerkelijke proceduur tegen D. B. Bekker. t'Amsterdam, By G. Borstius, 1692.
179-235 p. 21cm.

Signatures: 4°: π1, A-G⁴, H1.
Black letter.

NIC   (Continued on next card)

CATALOGUE OF THE CORNELL WITCHCRAFT COLLECTION

Witchcraft
BF
1410
B42
Z69
no.10

[Hooght, Everard van der] d. 1716. Sevende briev van ... 1692. (Card 4)

Van der Linde 104.
No. 10 in a collection of tracts against Balthasar Bekker and his Betoverde weereld.

1. Language and languages. 2. Devil. 3. Bekker, Balthasar, 1634-1698. I. Title.

NIC

Witchcraft
BF
1410
B42
Z69
no.6

[Hooght, Everard van der] d. 1716. Vierde briev van ... Haggébher Philaleethees ... (Card 2)

de authoriteyt van Gods woord, ende de eere des alderhoogsten. Amsterdam, G. Borstius, 1691.
59-96 p. 21cm.
Signatures: 4°: π1, A-C⁴, D².
Black letter.
Van der Linde 100.
No. 6 in a Collection of tracts
(Continued on next card)

NIC

Witchcraft
BF
1410
B42
Z69
v.2
no.23

Hooght, Everard van der, d. 1716. Zeedig ondersoek van het boek, ... [1692?] (Card 2)

antwoord op de brieven van B. Bekker. t'Amsterdam, By Dirk Boeteman [1692?]
4 p. l., 229, [1] p. [p. 231-232 blank] title and other vignettes, illus. initials.

(Continued on next card)

Witchcraft
BF
1410
B42
Z56
v.3
no.24

[Hooght, Everard van der] d. 1716. Tweede brief van הגבר [Haggébher] ΦΙΛΑΛΗΘΗΣ [philaleethees], geschreeven aan zynen vriend N. N. over de ordentelyke kerkelyke proceduuren, gehouden tegen den persoon ende het boek van Do. Balthasar Bekker, by zyn E. geintituleert De betoverde wereld. Met eenige ecclesiastique, theologische, philosophische ende philologische aanmerkingen over de zelve. Amsterdam, By G. Borstius, boekverkoper, 1691.
[19]-40 p. title vignette, illus. initial. 19 x 15cm.
8 (Continued on next card)

Witchcraft
BF
1410
B42
Z69
no.6

[Hooght, Everard van der] d. 1716. Vierde briev van ... Haggébher Philaleethees ... 1691. (Card 3)

against Balthasar Bekker and his Betoverde weereld.
N. N. is thought to be Jacobus Schuts.

1. God--Omnipotence. 2. Schaak, Petrus, fl. 1691. 3. Bekker, Balthasar, 1634-1698. De betoverde weereld. I. Title. II. Schuts, Jacobus.

NIC

Witchcraft
BF
1410
B42
Z56
v.2
no.23

Hooght, Everard van der, d. 1716. Zeedig ondersoek van ... de Betoverde weereld. (Card 3)

19 x 15cm. 4°, *⁴, A-2F⁴.
Black letter.
Autograph on back of t. p.: Ev. van der Hooght.
Van der Linde 114.
No. 23 in vol. lettered Bekker II.

(Continued on next card)

8

Witchcraft
BF
1410
B42
Z56
v.3
no.24

[Hooght, Everard van der] d. 1716. Tweede brief ... aan zynen vriend N. N. ... 1691. (Card 2)

4°: π1, A-B⁴, C².
Black letter.
The friend N. N. is Jacobus Schuts?
Van der Linde 98.
No. 24 in vol. lettered Bekker III.
1. Bekker, Balthasar, 1634-1698. 2. Bekker, Balthasar, 1634-1698. De betoverde weereld. 3. Nederlandse Hervormde Kerk. 4. Schuts, Jacobus. I. Title.

8

Witchcraft
BF
1410
B42
Z69
no.7

[Hooght, Everard van der] d. 1716. Vyfde briev van הגבר Φιλαληθης Haggébher Philaleethees, geschreeven aan zynen vriend N. N. over de versoekinge Christi in de woestyne, tot wederlegging van het 18 (ofte 20) capp. in het boek van D. Balthasar Bekker, genaamt de Betoverde wereld. Item, over de classicale proceduuren, &c. Amsterdam, G. Borstius, 1691.
99-123 p. 21cm.
Signatures: 4°: π1, A-C⁴, D¹.
Black letter. (Continued on next card)

NIC

Witchcraft
BF
1410
B42
Z56
v.2
no.23

Hooght, Everard van der, d. 1716. Zeedig ondersoek van ... de Betoverde weereld. (Card 4)

1. Bekker, Balthasar, 1634-1698. De betoverde weereld. 2. Bekker, Balthasar, 1634-1698. Twee brieven ... aan Everhardus vander Hooght. I. Title.

8

Witchcraft
BF
1410
B42
Z69
no.4

[Hooght, Everard van der] d. 1716. Tweede brief van הגבר [Haggébher] ΦΙΛΑΛΗΘΗΣ [philaleethees], geschreeven aan zynen vriend N. N. over de ordentelyke kerkelyke proceduuren, gehouden tegen den persoon ende het boek van Do. Balthasar Bekker, by zyn E. geintituleert De betoverde wereld. Met eenige ecclesiastique, theologische, philosophische ende philologische aanmerkingen over de zelve. Amsterdam, By G. Borstius, boekverkoper, 1691.
[19]-40 p. title vignette, illus. initial. 21cm.
8 (Continued on next card)

Witchcraft
BF
1410
B42
Z69
no.7

[Hooght, Everard van der] d. 1716. Vyfde briev van ... Haggébher Philaleethees ... 1691. (Card 2)

Van der Linde 101.
No. 7 in a Collection of tracts against Balthasar Bekker and his Betoverde weereld.
The friend N. N. is thought to be Jacobus Schuts.

NIC
(Continued on next card)

WITCHCRAFT
BF
1410
B42
Z69
no. 1

Hooght, Everard van der, d. 1716. Zeedig ondersoek van het boek, door den autheur, Balthasar Bekker, genaamt de Betoverde wereld. In het welke dat tweede boek, van vooren tot achteren, door alle de capittelen en paragraaphen, ordentelijk werd wederlegt. Door Everardus van der Hooght ... Welke achter dit werk gevoegt heeft; drie-der-ley registers; te weeten I. Van Bekkers valsche citatien. II. Een van de texten, ende III. Een van de verhandelde saaken, de welke of in dit boek, of, (Continued on next card)

8
NIC

Witchcraft
BF
1410
B42
Z69
no.4

[Hooght, Everard van der] d. 1716. Tweede brief ... aan zynen vriend N. N. ... 1691. (Card 2)

4°: π1, A-B⁴, C².
Black letter.
The friend N. N. is Jacobus Schuts?
Van der Linde 98.
No. 4 in a Collection of tracts against Balthasar Bekker and his Betoverde weereld.

8

Witchcraft
BF
1410
B42
Z69
no.7

[Hooght, Everard van der] d. 1716. Vyfde briev van ... Haggébher Philaleethees ... 1691. (Card 3)

1. Jesus Christ--Temptation. 2. Bekker, Balthasar, 1634-1698. De betoverde weereld. I. Schuts, Jacobus. II. Title.

NIC

WITCHCRAFT
BF
1410
B42
Z69
no. 1

Hooght, Everard van der, d. 1716. Zeedig ondersoek van het boek... (Card 2)

in de seven brieven, zijn verhandelt, met des autheurs antwoort op de brieven van B. Bekker. t' Amsterdam, By Dirk Boeteman [1692?]
4 p. l., 229, [1] p. [p. 231-232 blank] title and other vignettes, illus. initials. 21cm.
Signatures: 4°: *4, A-2E⁴, 2F³.
Black letter.
8 (Continued on next card)
NIC

Witchcraft
BF
1410
B42
Z69
no.6

[Hooght, Everard van der] d. 1716. Vierde briev van הגבר Φιλαληθης Haggébher Philaleethees, geschreeven aan zynen vriend N. N. over het weesen, denken, willen, vermoogen, ende de plaats der engelen in het gemeen, ende der quade geesten, in het byzonder. Item, van des menschen ziele, en harewerking, het zy afgesondert, ofte ook vereenigt met her lichaam; ende hoe verre de quade geesten op de selve konnen werken. Met een onder soek of D. Bekker wel kan seggen, dat syn E. zoekt te bewaren

NIC (Continued on next card)

Witchcraft
BF
1410
B42
Z56
v.2
no.23

Hooght, Everard van der, d. 1716. Zeedig ondersoek van het boek, door den autheur, Balthasar Bekker, genaamt de Betoverde weereld. In het welke dat tweede boek, van vooren tot achteren, door alle de capitelen en paragraaphen, ordentelijk werd wederlegt. Door Everardus van der Hooght ... Welke achter dit werk gevoegt heeft; drie-der-ley registers; te weeten I. Van Bekkers valsche citatien. II. Een van de texten, ende. III. Een van de verhandelde saaken, de welke of in dit boek, of, in de seven brieven, zijn verhandelt, met des autheurs (Continued on next card)

WITCHCRAFT
BF
1410
B42
Z69
no. 1

Hooght, Everard van der, d. 1716. Zeedig ondersoek van het boek... (Card 3)

With autograph: Ev. van der Hooght.
Van der Linde 114.
No. 1 in a Collection of tracts against Balthasar Bekker and his Betoverde weereld.

8

CATALOGUE OF THE CORNELL WITCHCRAFT COLLECTION

Hooght, Everard van der, d. 1716.

Witchcraft
BF 1410 B42 Z56 v.3 no.27

[Bekker, Balthasar] 1634-1698.
Brief van den schrijver des boeks De betoverde weereld genaamd, aan den eerwaardigen heere Everhard van der Hooght, yverigen leeraar van 's heeren gemeente tot Niewendam. Amsterdam, By G. Borstius, boekverkoper [1691]
11 p. [p. 12 is blank] title vignette, illus. initial.
4°: A⁴, [B²]
Van der Linde 105.
No. 27 in vol. lettered Bekker III.
8 (Continued on next card)

Hooght, Everard van der, d. 1716.

Witchcraft
BF 1410 B42 Z56 v.3 no.28

Bekker, Balthasar, 1634-1698.
Twee brieven van Balthasar Bekker predikant tot Amsterdam, aan Everhardus vander Hooght predikant tot Niewendam. D'eerste voor desen uitgegeven van den 25. September 1691, uit Amsterdam. D'andere nu daar by gevoegd, van den 3/13 Juny 1692, uit Franeker. Beide over het boek genaamd De betoverde weereld, en 't gene daar ontrent is voorgevallen. Met een kort beright over de voorrede van seker Opstel van aanmerkingen
8 (Continued on next card)

Hooght, Everard van der, d. 1716.

Witchcraft
BF 1410 B42 Z56 v.3 no.28

Bekker, Balthasar, 1634-1698. Twee brieven ... aan Everhardus vander Hooght ... 1692. (Card 2)
gemaakt door J. J. F. B. en tot Leewarden by Hero Nauta gedrukt. Franeker, By Leonardus Strik, boekverkoper, 1692.
2 p. l., 32 p. title vignette, illus. initials. 19 x 15cm.
4°: π², A-D⁴.
Back of t. p. autographed by Bekker.
8 (Continued on next card)

Hooght, Everard van der, d. 1716.

Witchcraft
BF 1410 B42 Z56 v.3 no.28

Bekker, Balthasar, 1634-1698. Twee brieven ... aan Everhardus vander Hooght ... 1692. (Card 3)
Variant of van der Linde 107: has p. 31-32.
No. 28 in vol. lettered Bekker III.
1. Bekker, Balthasar, 1634-1698. De betoverde weereld. 2. Opstel van enige aanmerkingen op het boek van B. Bekker. I. Hooght, Everard van der, d. 1716. II. Title.
8

Hooght, Everard van der, d. 1716.

Witchcraft
BF 1410 B42 Z56 v.3 no.29

Haak, Arent, ed.
Liefdelooze achterhoudinge van Do. Everhardus van der Hooght predikant tot Niewendam. Gebleeken in zijn schriftelyke onderhandelinge met Arent Haak. Amsterdam, By D. van den Dalen, boekverkooper, 1693.
32 p. title and end page vignettes, illus. initial. 20 x 15cm.
4°: A-D⁴.
Introduction by Haak: p. 3-9. The rest consists of letters exchanged by van der Hooght and Haak (in black letter),
8 (Continued on next card)

Hooght, Everard van der, d. 1716.

Witchcraft
BF 1410 B42 Z56 v.3 no.29

Haak, Arent, ed. Liefdelooze achterhoudinge van Do. Everhardus van der Hooght ... 1693. (Card 2)
on Balthasar Bekker's De betoverde weereld.
Van der Linde 118.
No. 29 in vol. lettered Bekker III.
1. Bekker, Balthasar, 1634-1698. De betoverde weereld. I. Hooght, Everard van der, d. 1716. II. Title.
8

Hooght, Everard van der, d. 1716.

Witchcraft
BF 1410 B42 1691a no.8

Bekker, Balthasar, 1634-1698.
Omstandig beright, van Balthasar Bekker, S. T. D. predikant tot Amsterdam, van sijne particuliere onderhandelinge met D. Laurentius Homma, sal. ged. in sijn leven mede predikant aldaar. Beneffens d'ontdekte lagen van Everhardus van der Hooght, en Jakob Lansman tegen denselven. Amsterdam, By D. vanden Dalen, boekverkooper, 1693.
1 p. l., 22 p. title and end page vignettes, illus. initials. 20 x 16cm.
4°: π 1, A- C⁴ (-C4)
8 (Continued on next card)

Hooght, Everard van der, d. 1716.

Witchcraft
BF 1410 B42 1691a no.8

Bekker, Balthasar, 1634-1698. Omstandig beright ... 1693. (Card 2)
Black letter.
"Bedekte lagen van Everhard van der Hooght, predikant tot Nieuwendam, en Jakob Lansman, procureur en notaris tot Amsterdam: ontdekt aan Balthasar Bekker ...:" p. 17-22.
Van der Linde 117.
No. 8 in vol. lettered B. Bekker. Betoverde weereld.
1. Hooght, Everard van der, d. 1716. 2. Lansman, Jakob. I. Homma, Laurentius, d. 1681. II. Title.
8

Hooght, Everard van der, d. 1716.

Witchcraft
BF 1410 B42 Z69 no.8

Een klaare uytlegginge, over de versoekinge des Heere Jesu Chriti in de woestyne. In antwoord op de vijfde brief van Philaleethees. t'Amsterdam, Voor den autheur gedrukt, en zijn volt te bekomen by P. Rotterdam [169-?]
24 p. 21cm.
Signatures: 4°, a², A-C⁴.
Black letter.
Van der Linde 110.
No. 8 in a Collection of tracts against Balthasar Bekker and his Betoverde weereld.
NIC (Continued on next card)

Hooght, Everard van der, d. 1716.

Witchcraft
BF 1410 B42 Z56 v.2 no.22

Noomtjins, Zalomon.
Spiegel voor den verwarden, en warzoekende Haggebher Philaleethees. Waar in, uit zyne 6 brieven, enz. getoond word, zyne onkunde, en verwarring, zoo in taal, als in zaaken. Ofte een briev van Zalomon Noomtjins, en Philaleethees. Geschreeven aan zynen vriend C.S.S. tot Buiksloot. Inhoudende (neevens andere zaaken) voornaamelijk, eenige aanmerkinges, over den perzoon, en de 6 brieven, enz. van Haggebher Philaleethees. Als meede over de briev, en perzoon van Everardus van der Hooght, en daar
8 (Continued on next card)

Hooght, Everard van der, d. 1716.

Witchcraft
BF 1410 B42 Z56 v.2 no.22

Noomtjins, Zalomon. Spiegel voor den verwarden, en warzoekende Haggebher Philaleethees. 1692. (Card 2)
by ook over zyne Aanmerkingen, over de ordre van een welgestelde predikatie. Mitsgaders d'ontdekking, der lasteringen van Brink. Amsterdam, By D. van den Dalen, boekverkooper, 1692.
33, [1] p. title and other vignettes. 19x15cm.
(Continued on next card)

Hooght, Everard van der, d. 1716.

Witchcraft
BF 1410 B42 Z56 v.2 no.22

Noomtjins, Zalomon. Spiegel voor den verwarden, en warzoekende Haggebher Philaleethees. 1692. (Card 3)
4°: A-D⁴, E1.
Black letter (except for introduction)
Attacks critics of Balthasar Bekker's De betoverde weereld.
G. L. Burr suggests Noomtjins may be a pseudonymn for Bekker.
Haggebher is a pseudonym of E. van der Hooght.
8 (Continued on next card)

Hooght, Everard van der, d. 1716.

Witchcraft
BF 1410 B42 Z56 v.2 no.22

Noomtjins, Zalomon. Spiegel voor den verwarden, en warzoekende Haggebher Philaleethees. 1692. (Card 4)
Van der Linde 111.
No. 22 in vol. lettered Bekker II.
1. Hooght, Everard van der, d. 1716. 2. Brink, Hendrik, 1645-1723. De godslasteringen van den amsterdamschen predikant Bekker. 3. Bekker, Balthasar, 1634-1698. De betoverde weereld. I. Title. II. Bekker, Balthasar, 1634-1698, supposed author.
8

Hooght, Everard van der, d. 1716.

Witchcraft
BF 1410 B42 Z69 no.14

[Seegen, Charinus van]
Oogmerck van Everardus van der Hoogt in sijn Brabbelen teegen het boek De Betoverde wereld genoemd. Sulx blijktuit de groote opheff, om D. Becker eens voor al, wel ter deegen, swart te maken ... t'Amsterdam, By D. van den Dalen, 1691.
16 p. 21cm.
Signatures: 4°: A-B⁴.
Black letter.
Signed: Charinus van Seegen.
Van der Linde 108.
No.14 in a Collection of tracts against Balthasar Bekker and his Betoverde weereld.

WITCHCRAFT
BF 1565 H77

Hoogstraten, Jacobus van, ca. 1460-1527.
Ad Reuerendissimū dñm dñm Philippū sancte ecclesie Coloniensis archiepm. Tractatus magistralis declarans q̄ grauiter peccēt q̄rentes auxiliū a maleficis copilat⁹ ab eximio sacre theologie professore & artiū magistro necnō heretice prauitatis inq̄sitore magistro Jacobo Hoechstrassen ordinis Predicatorū priore Ɔuentus Coloniensis. [Colonie, Impressum per Martinum de Werden 1510]
8 (Continued on next card)

WITCHCRAFT
BF 1565 H77

Hoogstraten, Jacobus van, ca. 1460-1527.
Ad Reuerendissimū dñm dñm Philippū sancte ecclesie Coloniensis archiepm ... [1510] (Card 2)
[16] p. illus. 18cm.
Woodcut illus. on p. [16].
Running title: Contra petentes remedia a maleficis.
1. Witchcraft. I. Title: Tractatus magistralis declarans quam graviter peccet querentes auxilium a maleficis. II. Title: Contra petentes remedia a maleficis. III. Title.
8

---

ar W 52854 no.2

Hopkin, Charles Edward, 1900–
... The share of Thomas Aquinas in the growth of the witchcraft delusion ... [by] Charles Edward Hopkin. Philadelphia, 1940.
viii, 27 p., 1 l., 29–127 p., 1 l., 129–188 p. 23ᵐ.
Thesis (PH. D.)—University of Pennsylvania, 1940.
CONTENTS.—Introduction.—pt. I. The demonology of Thomas Aquinas.—pt. II. Thomas Aquinas as mediator between earlier and later beliefs.—Conclusion.—Bibliography (p. 185–188)
No. 2 in vol. lettered: Pennsylvania dissertations
1. Thomas Aquinas, Saint, 1225?-1274. 2. Demonology. I. Title.

Library of Congress   B765.T54H6 1940   41—2305
Univ. of Pennsylvania   Libr.
— Copy 2.
Copyright A 140856   [41c2]   188

Witchcraft
BF 1565 H79

Hopkins, Matthew, d. 1647.
The discovery of witches: in answer to severall queries, lately delivered to the judges of assize for the county of Norfolk, and now published ... for the benefit of the whole kingdome ... London, Printed for R. Royston, 1647.
10 p. front. 20cm.
With book-plate of Herman Le Roy Edgar.
Binding by Rivière & Son. Full crushed maroon levant, gilt extra.
Wing H 2751.
1. Witchcraft—England. I. Title.

CATALOGUE OF THE CORNELL WITCHCRAFT COLLECTION

Witchcraft
BF
1563
T75

    Hopkins, Matthew, d. 1647.
        The discovery of witches: in answer to severall queries, lately delivered to the judges of assize for the county of Norfolk. And now published by Mathew Hopkins, witchfinder, for the benefit of the whole kingdome ... Reprinted verbatim from the original edition of 1647. Only 100 copies printed. Great Totham, Essex, Printed at C. Clark's private press, 1837.
        11 numbered leaves. port. 23cm.

8
        No. 1 in vo   1. lettered Tracts on witches.
        I. Title.

    Hopkins, Matthew, d. 1647.
        The discovery of witches.

Witchcraft
BF
1581
S95

    Summers, Montague, 1880-1948.
        The discovery of witches: a study of Master Matthew Hopkins commonly call'd witch finder generall, together with a reprint of The discovery of witches, from the rare original of 1647. London, Cayme Press, 1928.
        61 p. illus. 22cm. (Cayme Press pamphlet, no. 7)

    With facsimile of t.p. of original ed.

Witchcraft
BF
1565
G26

    Hopkins, Matthew, d. 1647.
    Gaule, John.
        Select cases of conscience touching witches and witchcrafts ... London, Printed by W. Wilson for R. Clutterbuck, 1646.
        208 p. 12cm.

    Contains a letter from Matthew Hopkins, called the witch-finder, announcing his intention of visiting Great Staughton (where Gaule was the preacher) "to search for evill disposed persons called witches."
    Has book-   plate of Edwd. Place, and his auto-   graph.

    Hopkins, Matthew, d. 1647.

Witchcraft
BF
1581
S95

    Summers, Montague, 1880-1948.
        The discovery of witches: a study of Matthew Hopkins commonly call'd witch finder generall, together with a reprint of The discovery of witches, from the rare original of 1647. London, Cayme Press, 1928.
        61 p. illus. 22cm. (Cayme Press pamphlet, no. 7)
    With facsimile of t.p. of original ed.

    Horn, Johann Benjamin, respondent.

Witchcraft
F
445
61
o.16

    Pistori, Gustav Friedrich, praeses.
        ... Dispvtatione secvnda existentiam spectrorvm, ex sagarum veneficarumque pactis cum daemone sancitis, declarabunt praeses M. Gvstavvs Fridericvs Pistori ... et respondens Ioannes Beniamin. Horn ... Vitembergae, Prelo Gerdesiano [1703]
        [16] p. 19cm. (bound in 21cm. vol.)
        No. 16 in vol. lettered Dissertationes de spectris. 1646-1753.
        1. Spirits. 2. Witchcraft. I.
    (Continued on next card)

Witchcraft
F
523
81

    Horst, Georg Conrad, 1767-1838?
        Dämonomagie, oder Geschichte des Glaubens an Zauberei und dämonische Wunder, mit besonderer Berücksichtigung des Hexenprocesses seit den Zeiten Innocentius des Achten. Nebst einer ausführlichen, nach Inquisitionsacten bearbeiteten Beschreibung des Hexenthurms zu Lindheim in der Wetterau ... Mit Kupfern. Frankfurt am Main, bei den Gebrüdern Wilmans, 1818.
        2 v. fold. plates. 20cm.
    I. Title. II. Title: Geschichte des Glaubens an Zau berei und dämonische Wunder.

    Horst, Georg Conrad, 1767-1838?
        Dämonomagie.

WITCHCRAFT
BF
1325
H81

    Horst, Georg Conrad, 1767-1838?
        Deuteroskopie, oder Merkwürdige psychische und physiologische Erscheinungen und Probleme aus dem Gebiete der Pneumatologie. Für Religionsphilosophen, Psychologen, und denkende Aerzte. Eine nöthige Beilage zur Dämonomagie, wie zur Zauber-Bibliothek. Frankfurt am Main, H. Wilmans, 1830.
        2 v. in 1. 21cm.
        1. Second sight. 2. Visions. I. His Dämonomagie. II. His Zauber-Bibliothek. III. Title.

8

WITCHCRAFT
BF
1325
H81

    Horst, Georg Conrad, 1767-1838?
        Deuteroskopie, oder Merkwürdige psychische und physiologische Erscheinungen und Probleme aus dem Gebiete der Pneumatologie. Für Religionsphilosophen, Psychologen, und denkende Aerzte. Eine nöthige Beilage zur Dämonomagie, wie zur Zauber-Bibliothek. Frankfurt am Main, H. Wilmans, 1830.
        2 v. in 1. 21cm.
        1. Second sight. 2. Visions. I. His Dämonomagie. II. His Zauber-Bibliothek. III. Title. IV. Title: Merkwürdige psych ische und physiologische Erscheinungen.

8

WITCHCRAFT
BF
1589
H81

    Horst, Georg Conrad, 1767-1838?
        Theurgie, oder Vom Bestreben der Menschen in der alten und neuen Zeit, zwischen sich und der Geisterwelt eine unmittelbare reale Verbindung zu bewirken. Mainz, Bei F. Kupferberg, 1820.
        91 p. 21cm.
        "Ankündigung. Zauber-Bibliothek," p. [83]-91, signed: Florian Kupferberg.
        Bound with his Von der alten und neuen Magie Ursprung. Mainz, 1820.
        1. Spiri ts. 2. Occult sciences --History. 3. His Zauber-Bibliothek. I. K upferberg, Florian. II. Title.

8
NIC

Witchcraft
BF
1405
H81

    Horst, Georg Conrad, 1767-1838?
        Zauber-Bibliothek; oder, Von Zauberei, Theurgie und Mantik, Zauberern, Hexen, und Hexenprocessen, Dämonen, Gespenstern, und Geistererscheinungen. Zur Beförderung einer rein-geschichtlichen, von Aberglauben und Unglauben freien Beurtheilung dieser Gegenstände. Mainz, F. Kupferberg, 1821-1826.
        6 v. 20cm.
        1. Witchcraft. I. Title. II. Title: Von Zauberei, Th eurgie und Mantik.

    Horst, Georg Conrad, 1767-1838?
        Zauber-Bibliothek.

WITCHCRAFT
BF
1325
H81

    Horst, Georg Conrad, 1767-1838?
        Deuteroskopie, oder Merkwürdige psychische und physiologische Erscheinungen und Probleme aus dem Gebiete der Pneumatologie. Für Religionsphilosophen, Psychologen, und denkende Aerzte. Eine nöthige Beilage zur Dämonomagie, wie zur Zauber-Bibliothek. Frankfurt am Main, H. Wilmans, 1830.
        2 v. in 1. 21cm.
        1. Second sight. 2. Visions. I. His Dämonomagie. II. His Zauber-Bibliothek. III. Title.

8

    Horst, Georg Conrad, 1767-1838?
        Zauber-Bibliothek.

WITCHCRAFT
BF
1589
H81

    Horst, Georg Conrad, 1767-1838?
        Theurgie, oder Vom Bestreben der Menschen in der alten und neuen Zeit, zwischen sich und der Geisterwelt eine unmittelbare reale Verbindung zu bewirken. Mainz, Bei F. Kupferberg, 1820.
        91 p. 21cm.
        "Ankündigung. Zauber-Bibliothek," p. [83]-91, signed: Florian Kupferberg.
        Bound with his Von der alten und neuen Magie Ursprung. Mainz, 1820.
        1. Spiri ts. 2. Occult sciences --History. 3. His Zauber-Bibliothek. I. K upferberg, Florian. II. Title.

8
NIC

WITCHCRAFT
BF
1589
H81

    Horst, Goerg Conrad, 1767-1838?
        Von der alten und neuen Magie Ursprung, Idee, Umfang, und Geschichte. Als Ankündigung der Zauber-Bibliothek und Verständigung mit dem Publikum über diess literarische Unternehmen. Mainz, Bei F. Kupferberg, 1820.
        83 p. 21cm.
        With this is bound his Theurgie. Mainz, 1820.
        1. Magic--History. 2. Occult sciences --History. 3. His Zauber-Bibliothek. I. Title.

8
NIC

    Hort an new schrecklich abentewr.

WITCHCRAFT
BF
1583
H82
1921

    En forskreckelig oc sand bescriffuelse om mange troldfolck; som ere forbrende for deris misgierninger skyld, fra det aar 1589... København [Bianco Lunos bogtrykkeri] 1921.
        [25] p. illus. 21cm. (Bianco Lunos bibliofiludgaver)
        Added t.-p.: Gammel dansk folkelitteratur.
        Flyveskrift første gang trykt i Köln paa Caspar Schumans af Eefurts bekostning og derefter i Kø benhavn af Laurentz

8
NIC   (Continued on next card)

    Hort an new schrecklich abentewr.

WITCHCRAFT
BF
1583
H82
1921

    En forskrechelig oc sand bescriffuelse om mange troldfolck... 1921. (Card 2)
    Benedicht, 1591.
        According to G. L. Burr, a translation of "Hort an new schrecklich abenthewr ... [Köln, 1589]."
        "Efter et gammelt flyveblad, der nu opbevares paa det Kongelige bibliotek i København ... paany ... udgivet ... efter ... modernise rede udkast."

8
NIC   (Continued on next card)

    Hort an new schrecklich abentewr.

WITCHCRAFT
BR
1583
H82
1921

    En forskreckelig oc sand bescriffeulse om mange troldfolck... 1921. (Card 3)
    "Stumme Peders graffschrift ... 1589": p. [14]
    "Oplysninger," af Emil Selmar p. [15]-[23] has special t. p.
    "Bogen er trykt i 500 ... ekspl. ... nr. 58."
        1. Witchcraft--Germany. 2. Witchcraft--Denmark. 3. Printing--History--Europe. I. Luno, Bianco, ed. II. Selmar, Emil. III. Hort an new schrecklich abentewr.

8
NIC

Witchcraft
F
7
H82

    Horton, Edward Augustus, 1843-
        The culmination of the Puritan theocracy, by Edward A. Horton. Boston, J.S. Lockwood, 1900.
        32 p. 24½cm.

    I. Title.

CATALOGUE OF THE CORNELL WITCHCRAFT COLLECTION

Hosman, Abraham, d. 1617.

see

Hossmann, Abraham, d. 1617.

Houghton, Richard Monckton Milnes, 1st. baron, 1809-1885, ed.
Witchcraft
Z
1009   Philobiblon Society, London.
P56   Miscellanies. London, Printed by C.
v.6,8   Whittingham and Wilkins, 1854-84.
          15 v. illus. 23cm.

    Edited for the most part by Richard Monckton Milnes, first lord Houghton.
    No more published; the society was disbanded in 1884.
    Partial contents.--v.5, 1858-59. 3. A discourse of witchcraft. As it was acted
                    (Continued on next card)

Howland, Arthur Charles, 1869-   ed.
Witchcraft
BF
1566   Lea, Henry Charles, 1825-1909, comp.
L43   Materials toward a history of witchcraft, collected by Henry Charles Lea ... arranged and edited by Arthur C. Howland .. with an introduction by George Lincoln Burr ... Philadelphia, University of Pennsylvania press, 1939.
          3 v. (xliv, 1548 p.) 24cm.

    1. Witchcraft. I. Howland, Arthur Charles, 1869-   ed II. Title
                                                         30-0021
    Library of Congress   BF1560.L4
    ———— Copy 2.
    Copyright A 128963

Hosmann, Abraham, d. 1617.

see

Hossmann, Abraham, d. 1617.

Houghton, Richard Monckton Milnes, 1st baron, 1809-1885, ed.
Witchcraft
Z
1009   Philobiblon Society, London.
P56   Miscellanies ... 1854-84.   (Card 2)

    in the family of Mr. Edward Fairfax ... 1621. By R. Monckton Milnes.--v.8, 1863-64. 5. L'enfer décrit par ceux qui l'ont vu. Essai philosophique et littéraire. Par Octave Delepierre. 9. The examination and confession of certain witches at Chelmsford, in the county of Essex. Communicated and prefaced by Hermann Beigel.
    I. Provenance-- Taunton, Lord (v.8); Sreys, (v.5). II. Autograph--
The Rev. Walter Milnes, Richard Monckton (v.5).

Howson, Robert.
WITCHCRAFT
BF
1555   The Second part of the Boy of Bilson: or, a true and particular relation of the impostor, Susanna Fowles ... who pretended her self possess'd with the Devil ... The whole being writ and attested by Robert Howson, clerk; Captain John Bonsey, and Mr. Nicholas Wade ... London, Printed by E. Whitlock, 1698.
          24 p. 20cm.

    1. Fowles, Susanna, fl. 1698. 2. Demoniac possession. I. Howson, Robert. II. Baddeley, Richard, fl. 1621. The
8   boy of Bilson.

WITCHCRAFT
QC
859   Hossmann, Abraham, d. 1617.
H82   De tonitru & tempestate, das ist: Nohtwendiger Bericht, von Donnern vnd Hagel-Wettern, wannen vnd woher sich dieselben verursachen, ob sie natürlich: Item, ob Teufel vnd Zäuberer auch Wetter machen können ... Neben Erzehlung etlicher seltzamen Fälle ... in Druck gegeben durch Abrahamum Hosmanum ... Leipzig, In Verlegung Henning Grossn des Ältern Buchhändl. [Typis Beerwaldin, durch Jacobum Popporeich] 1612.
          123, [1] p. 20cm.
8
NIC   (Continued on next card)

Hovhan Mandacuni, Patriarch of Armenia, d. ca. 490.

see

Hovhannes I Mandakuni, Patriarch of Armenia, d. ca. 490.

Witchcraft
BT
980   Hudson, William Henry, 1862-1918.
H88   The Satan of theology and how we came by him. Boston, American Unitarian Association [1891]
          42 p. 19cm.

    Author's autograph presentation copy to George Lincoln Burr.
    A lecture delivered in the First Unitarian Church, Ithaca, N. Y.

    1. Devil. I. Title.

WITCHCRAFT
QC
859   Hossmann, Abraham, d. 1617.   De tonitru
H82   & tempestate ... 1612.   (Card 2)
    Title in red and black, within ornamental border.
    With colophon.

    1. Meteorology--Early works to 1800. 2. Folk-lore, German. 3. Witchcraft. I. Title. II. Title: Von Donnern und Hagel-Wettern. III. Title: Nohtwendiger
8   Bericht, von Donnern und Hagel-
NIC   Wettern.

WITCHCRAFT
BV
4627   Hovhannes I Mandakuni, Patriarch of Armenia,
W8   d. ca. 490.
H84   Johannes Mantagunensis über Zauberei.
1851   [Tübingen, 1851]
          [85]-119 p. 21cm.
    At head of title: 3.
    Caption title.
    Article signed: Welte.
    Translation of a pastoral letter on witchcraft and fortune-telling.
    1. Witchcraft. 2. Fortune-telling.
    I. Welte, Benedict. II. Title.
8

Huger, Catherine, d. 1631.
Witchcraft
BF
1582   La sorcière de Munster [Catherine Huger;] sa torture à Wihr-au-Val et son exécution à Gunsbach, MDCXXXI. Colmar, E.
Z7   Barth, 1869.
1631   15 p. 23cm.

    Signed: J. D.

    1. Huger, Catherine, d. 1631. 2. Witchcraft. I. D., J. II. J. D.

Hott, Jane, d. 1645.
Witchcraft
BF
1563   The examination, confession, triall, and
T86   execution, of Joane Williford, Joan Cariden, and Jane Hott, who were executed at Feversham in Kent, for being witches, on Munday the 29 of September 1645... Taken by the major of Feversham and jurors for the said inquest. With the examination and confession of Elizabeth Harris, not yet executed. All attested under the hand of Robert Greenstreet, major of Feversham.   London, Printed for J. G., 1645.

                (Continued on next card)

Howitt, Mrs. Mary (Botham), 1799-1888, ed.
WITCHCRAFT
BF
1589   Ennemoser, Joseph, 1787-1854.
E59   The history of magic. Translated from
1854   the German by William Howitt. To which is added an appendix of the most remarkable and best authenticated stories of apparitions, dreams, second sight, somnambulism, predictions, divination, witchcraft, vampires, fairies, table-turning, and spirit-rapping. Selected by Mary Howitt. London, Henry G. Bohn, 1854.
          2 v. 19cm. (Bohn's scientific library)
    Translation   of Geschichte der Magie.
                (Continued on next card)

Hugo Farmers Versuch über die Dämonisch des Neuen Testamentes.
WITCHCRAFT
BF
1501   Farmer, Hugh, 1714-1787.
D12   Hugo Farmers Versuch über die Dämonisch
no.2   des Neuen Testamentes. Aus dem Englischen übersetzt von L. F. A. von Cölln. Nebst einer Vorrede D. Joh. Sal. Semlers. Bremen und Leipzig, Bey J. H. Cramer, 1776.
          38, 327 p. 17cm.
    Translation of An essay on the demoniacs of the New Testament.
    No. 2 in vol. lettered Dämonologische Schriften.
8   (Continued on next card)

Hott, Jane, d. 1645.
Witchcraft
BF
1563   The examination, confession, triall, and
T86   execution ... 1645.   (Card 2)

          6 p. 19cm.

    No. 5 in vol. lettered: Tracts of witches.

    1. Witchcraft. 2. Williford, Joane, d. 1645. 3. Cariden, Joan, d. 1645. 4. Hott, Jane, d. 1645. 5. Harris, Elizabeth, d. 1645.

Howitt, William, 1792-1879, tr.
WITCHCRAFT
BF
1589   Ennemoser, Joseph, 1787-1854.
E59   The history of magic. Translated from
1854   the German by William Howitt. To which is added an appendix of the most remarkable and best authenticated stories of apparitions, dreams, second sight, somnambulism, predictions, divination, witchcraft, vampires, fairies, table-turning, and spirit-rapping. Selected by Mary Howitt. London, Henry G. Bohn, 1854.
          2 v. 19cm. (Bohn's scientific library)
    Translation   of Geschichte der Magie.
                (Continued on next card)

Human, Armin, 1843-1923, ed.
Witchcraft
BF
1583   Saxe-Coburg. Laws, statutes, etc.
A2   Herzog Johann Casimirs "Gerichts-Ordnung die Hexerei betrf: Publiciret ahm 21.
S27+   February 1629." Aus dem Hildburghäuser
1898   Ratsarchiv mitgeteilt von Dr. A. Human.
          (In Verein für Sachsen-Meiningische Geschichte und Landeskunde, Meiningen. Schriften. Hildburghausen. 27cm. 29 (1898), p. 99-112)

8   (Continued on next card)

CATALOGUE OF THE CORNELL WITCHCRAFT COLLECTION

Witchcraft Human animals.
GR   Hamel, Frank.
325   Human animals. London, W. Rider, 1915.
H21   xii, 301 p. 23cm.

  1. Animal lore. 2. Occult sciences. I. Title.

TCHCRAFT
    Humborg, Ludwig.
       Die Hexenprozesse in der Stadt Münster.
    Ein Beitrag zur Kulturgeschichte Münsters.
    Münster (Westf.), Universitätsbuchhandlung
    F. Coppenrath, 1914.
       135 p. 24cm. (Münstersche Beiträge zur
    Geschichtsforschung, n. F. XXXI)

  1. Trials (Witchcraft)--Münster. 2. Witchcraft--Germany. 3. Münster--History. I. Title.

Witchcraft
BF   Hunger, Albert, 1545?-1604, praeses.
1520   De magia theses theologicae, ... per reuerendum & clarissimo viro M. Hectorem VVegman ... pro impetrando licentiae gradu, ad publicam disputationem propositae: praeside reuerendo & clarissimo viro Alberto Hvngero ... Ingolstadii, Ex officina VVeissenhorniana [1574]
H93   [23] p. 20cm.
        In MS at bottom of t. p.: Rdo dno M. Casparo Boos ddt   H. W.
                    (Continued on next card)

Witchcraft
BF   Hunger, Albert, 1545?-1604, praeses. De magia theses theologicae ... [1574] (Card 2)
1520
H93

  1. Demonology. 2. Magic. I. Wegman, Hector, respondent. I. Title.

Hutchinson, Francis, bp. of Down and Connor, 1660-1739.
    An historical essay concerning witchcraft. With observations upon matters of fact; tending to clear the texts of the sacred Scriptures, and confute the vulgar errors about that point. And also two sermons: one in proof of the Christian religion; the other concerning the good and evil angels. By Francis Hutchinson ... London, Printed for R. Knaplock, and D. Midwinter, 1718.
    xv, [4], 270 p. 19½cm.

  1. Witchcraft. 2. Angels. 3. Demonology.
                                11-9012

---

itchcraft
F   Hutchinson, Francis, bp. of Down and Connor, 1660-1739.
565   An historical essay concerning witchcraft. With observations upon matters of fact; tending to clear the texts of the sacred Scriptures, and confute the vulgar errors about that point. And also two sermons: one in proof of the Christian religion; the other concerning good and evil angels. By Francis Hutchinson ... 2d ed., with considerable additions. London, Printed for R. Knaplock [etc.] 1720.
97
720
        16 p. l., 336 p. 20½cm.
    I. Title.

            Hutchinson, Francis, bp. of Down and Connor, 1660-1739.
WITCHCRAFT   An historical essay concerning witchcraft.
BF   Hutchinson, Francis, bp. of Down and Connor, 1660-1739.
1555   Wilhelm Perry; oder: Der besessene Knabe.
H97   Ein Beitrag zu den Teufelsbesitzungen unsers
1799   Zeitalters. [Leipzig?] 1799.
              16 p. 19cm.
              Illustrative title vignette.
              "Ein Auszug aus Hutchinsons historischem Versuche über die Hexerey. Lpz. 1727": translation of Historical essay concerning witchcraft.
8
NIC   (Continued on next card)

            Hutchinson, Francis, bp. of Down and Connor, 1660-1739. An historical essay concerning witchcraft. German.
WITCHCRAFT Hutchinson, Francis, bp. of Down and Connor, 1660-1739.
BF   Francisci Hutchinsons ... Historischer versuch von der hexerey, in einem gespräch zwischen einem geistlichen, einem schottländischen advocaten und englischen geschworenen; worinnen über würcklich geschehene dinge vernünfftige anmerckungen gemachet, die hieher gehörigen stellen aus der Heil. Schrifft richtig erkläret und die gemeinen irrthümer aufs bescheidentlichste widerleget werden. Nebst zwey vortrefflichen predigten, die erste zum beweis der wahrheit christl. religion, die andere, von guten und bösen engeln; und einer vorrede des herrn geheimbden raths Thomasii. Aus
1565
H97
1726
                (Continued on next card)
8

            Hutchinson, Francis, bp. of Down and Connor, 1660-1739. An historical essay concerning witchcraft. German.
WITCHCRAFT Hutchinson, Francis, bp. of Down and Connor, 1660-1739.
BF   Francisci Hutchinsons ... Historischer versuch von der hexerey ... (Card 2)
1565
H97   dem englischen ins teutsche übersetzet, auch mit kurtzen summarien und vollständigen registern versehen von Theodoro Arnold. Leipzig, J. C. Martini, 1726.
1726
            [50], 332, [23] p. front. 22 cm.
            Head-pieces and initials.
            "Verzeichniss derer in diesem werck nur teutsch angeführten englischen autorum": p. [1]-[4] at end.
            With copies 1 and 2 are bound Saint André, F. de. Lesenswürdige Briefe ... über die Materie von der Zauberey. Leipzig, 1727.   32-6507
8   Library of Congress
                    (Continued on next card)
         Copy 2.

---

witchcraft   Hutchinson, Francis, Bp. of Down and Connor, 1660-1739.
BF   An historical essay concerning witchcraft.
1410   Boulton, Richard, fl. 1697-1724.
B76P8   The possibility and reality of magick, sorcery, and witchcraft, demonstrated. Or, A vindication of A compleat history of magick, sorcery, and witchcraft. In answer to Dr. Hutchinson's Historical essay ... In two parts ...   London, Printed for J. Roberts, 1722.
                xvi, [4], 184 p. 17cm.

            Hutchinson, Francis, bp. of Down and Connor, 1660-1739.
Witchcraft   An historical essay concerning witchcraft.
BF   Daillon, Jacques, ca. 1634-1726.
1505   Δαιμονολογία; or, A treatise of spirits. Wherein several places of Scripture are expounded, against the vulgar errors concerning witchcraft, apparitions, &c. To which is added, an appendix, containing some reflections on Mr. Boulton's answer to Dr. Hutchinson's Historical essay; entitled The possibility and reality of magick, sorcery and witchcraft demonstrated. London,
D13
                    Title transliterated:
                        Daimonología.
                (Continued on next card)

            Hutchinson, Francis, bp. of Down and Connor, 1660-1739. An historical essay concerning witchcraft.
Witchcraft Daillon, Jacques, ca. 1634-1726. Δαιμονολογία. (Card 2)
BF
1505   Printed for the author, 1723.
D13   182 p. 19cm.
               Ex libris Lord Hill.
               A Preface, consisting of eight pages, numbered iii-x, is inserted between the t.p. and p. v.
               With this is bound his The ax laid to the root of popery. [London? 1721?]

WITCHCRAFT Hutchinson, Francis, bp. of Down and Connor, 1660-1739.
BF   Francisci Hutchinsons ... Historischer versuch von der hexerey, in einem gespräch zwischen einem geistlichen, einem schottländischen advocaten und englischen geschworenen; worinnen über würcklich geschehene dinge vernünfftige anmerckungen gemachet, die hieher gehörigen stellen aus der Heil. Schrifft richtig erkläret und die gemeinen irrthümer aufs bescheidentlichste widerleget werden. Nebst zwey vortrefflichen predigten, die erste zum beweis der wahrheit christl. religion, die andere, von guten und bösen engeln; und einer vorrede des herrn geheimbden raths Thomasii. Aus
1565
H97
1726
2 copies
                (Continued on next card)
8   32-6507

WITCHCRAFT Hutchinson, Francis, bp. of Down and Connor, 1660-1739.
BF   Francisci Hutchinsons ... Historischer versuch von der hexerey ... (Card 2)
1565
H97   dem englischen ins teutsche übersetzet, auch mit kurtzen summarien und vollständigen registern versehen von Theodoro Arnold. Leipzig, J. C. Martini, 1726.
1726
            [50], 332, [23] p. front. 22 cm.
            Head-pieces and initials.
            "Verzeichniss derer in diesem werck nur teutsch angeführten englischen autorum": p. [1]-[4] at end.
            With copies 1 and 2 are bound Saint André, F. de. Lesenswürdige Briefe ... über die Materie von der Zauberey. Leipzig, 1727.   32-6507
8   Library of Congress
                    (Continued on next card)
         Copy 2.

WITCHCRAFT
BF   Hutchinson, Francis, bp. of Down and Connor, 1660-1739. Francisci Hutchinsons ... Historischer Versuch von der Hexerey ...
1565   (Card 3)
H97
1726

  1. Witchcraft. 2. Angels. 3. Demonology. I. Thomasius, Christian, 1655-1728. II. His An historical essay concerning witchcraft. German. III. Arnold, Theodor, 1683-1771, ed. and tr. IV. Title: Historischer Versuch von der Hexerey. V. Title.
8

            Hutchinson, Francis, bp. of Down and Connor, 1660-1739. Historischer Versuch von der Hexerey.
WITCHCRAFT Hutchinson, Francis, bp. of Down and Connor, 1660-1739.
BF   Wilhelm Perry; oder: Der besessene Knabe. Ein Beitrag zu den Teufelsbesitzungen unsers Zeitalters. [Leipzig?] 1799.
1555
H97   16 p. 19cm.
1799   Illustrative title vignette.
               "Ein Auszug aus Hutchinsons historischem Versuche über die Hexerey. Lpz. 1727": translation of Historical essay concerning witchcraft.
8
NIC   (Continued on next card)

            Hutchinson, Francis, bp of Down and Connor, 1660-1739. Historischer Versuch von der Hexerey.
WITCHCRAFT
BF   Saint André, François de.
1565   Mr. de St. André ... Lesenswürdige Briefe an einige seiner Freunde über die Materie von der Zauberey, den Ubelthaten, so dadurch angestifftet werden, und von den Zauberern und Hexen insbesondere; worinnen er die wunderbarsten Würckungen, die man gemeiniglich den Teuffeln zuschreibet, deutlich erkläret, und dabey zeiget, dass diese Geister offt
H97
1726
8
                (Continued on next card)

            Hutchinson, Francis, bp. of Down and Connor, 1660-1739. Historischer Versuch von der Hexerey.
WITCHCRAFT Saint André, François de.   Mr. de St. André ... Lesenswürdige Briefe ... 1727. (Card 2)
BF
1565
H97   nicht den geringsten Antheil daran haben ... Statt eines Suplements zum Hutchinson aus dem Frantzösischen ins Teutsche übersetzt ... von Theodoro Arnold. Leipzig, Bey J. C. Martini, 1727.
1726
               10 p. l., 204, [9] p. 22cm.
               Translation of Lettres ... à quelques-uns de ses amis, pub. 1725.
8
                (Continued on next card)

297

CATALOGUE OF THE CORNELL WITCHCRAFT COLLECTION

WITCHCRAFT
BF
1565
H97
1726
    Hutchinson, Francis, bp. of Down and Connor, 1660-1739.
        Historischer Versuch von der Hexerey. Saint André, François de. M^r. de S^t. André ... Lesenswürdige Briefe ... 1727. (Card 3)
    Title in red and black.
    Bound with Hutchinson, F. Historischer Versuch von der Hexerey. Leipzig, 1726.
    1. Witchcraft. 2. Magic. I. His Lettres ... à quelques-uns de ses amis. German. II. Hutchinson, Francis, bp. of Down and Connor, 1660-1739. Historischer Versuch von der Hexerey. III. Arnold, Theodor, 1683-1771, tr. IV. Title: Lesenswürdige Briefe ... über die Materie von der Zauberey.

8

WITCHCRAFT
BF
1555
H97
1799
    Hutchinson, Francis, bp. of Down and Connor, 1660-1739.
        Wilhelm Perry; oder: Der besessene Knabe. Ein Beitrag zu den Teufelsbesitzungen unsers Zeitalters. [Leipzig?] 1799.
    16 p. 19cm.
    Illustrative title vignette.
    "Ein Auszug aus Hutchinsons historischem Versuche über die Hexerey. Lpz. 1727": translation of Historical essay concerning witchcraft.

8
NIC
    (Continued on next card)

WITCHCRAFT
BF
1555
H97
1799
    Hutchinson, Francis, bp. of Down and Connor, 1660-1739. Wilhlem Perry ... 1799. (Card 2)
    1. Demoniac possession. 2. Perry, William. I. His Historischer Versuch von der Hexerey. II. His An historical essay concerning witchcraft. III. Title.

8
NIC

Witchcraft
BS
2545
D5
T97
no.8
    Hutchinson, Thomas, 1698-1769.
        Remarks upon a pamphlet intit'l'd, A review of the controversy about the meaning of demoniacs, &c. Wherein the sermon which asserteth the usual interpretation, &c., is vindicated from every exception of the reviewer. London, Printed for W. Innys and R. Manby, 1739.
    31 p. 21cm.
    No. 8 in   vol. lettered: Twells,
    (Continued on next card)

Witchcraft
BS
2545
D5
T97
no.8
    Hutchinson, Thomas, 1698-1769. Remarks upon a pamphlet intit'l'd, A review of the controversy ... 1739. (Card 2)
    Whiston, etc. Tracts on the demoniacs in the New Testament. London, 1738-1775.
    1. Sharpe, Gregory, 1713-1771. A review of the controversy about the meaning of demoniacks in the New Testament. 2. Hutchinson, Thomas, 1698-1769. The usual interpretation. I. Title.

Witchcraft
BS
2545
D5
T75
no.5
    Hutchinson, Thomas, 1698-1769.
        Remarks upon a pamphlet [by G. Sharpe] intitl'd, A review of the controversy about the meaning of demoniacs, &c. Wherein the sermon which asserteth the usual interpretation, &c. is vindicated from every exception of the reviewer. London, Printed for W. Innys and R. Manby, 1739.
    31 p. 20cm.
    No. 5 in vol. lettered: Tracts on demoniacks. 1737.

Witchcraft
BS
2545
D5
T75
no.4
    Hutchinson, Thomas, 1698-1769.
        The usual interpretation of ΔΑΙΜΟΝΕΣ and ΔΑΙΜΟΝΙΑ in the New Testament, asserted in a sermon preach'd before the University of Oxford at St. Mary's, on Sunday, March 5, 1737-8. Oxford, Printed at the Theatre for Mr. Clements, and sold by Mess. Innys and Manby, 1738.
    31 p. 20cm.
    No. 4 in vol. lettered: Tracts on demoniacks. 1737.
    I. Title.

Witchcraft
BS
2545
D5
T97
no.8
    Hutchinson, Thomas, 1698-1769.
    The usual interpretation.
        Remarks upon a pamphlet intit'l'd, A review of the controversy about the meaning of demoniacs, &c. Wherein the sermon which asserteth the usual interpretation, &c., is vindicated from every exception of the reviewer. London, Printed for W. Innys and R. Manby, 1739.
    31 p. 21cm.
    No. 8 in   vol. lettered: Twells,
    (Continued on next card)

Witchcraft
BS
2545
D5
T97
no.8
    Hutchinson, Thomas, 1698-1769. Remarks upon a pamphlet intit'l'd, A review of the controversy ... 1739. (Card 2)
    Whiston, etc. Tracts on the demoniacs in the New Testament. London, 1738-1775.
    1. Sharpe, Gregory, 1713-1771. A review of the controversy about the meaning of demoniacks in the New Testament. 2. Hutchinson, Thomas, 1698-1769. The usual interpretation. I. Title.

Witchcraft
BS
2545
D5
T75
no.3
    Hutchinson, Thomas, 1698-1769.
    The usual interpretation.
    [Sharpe, Gregory] 1713-1771.
        A review of the controversy about the meaning of demoniacks in the New-Testament. In which Mr. Hutchinson's sermon at Oxford ..., the Reply to the Further enquiry, Mr. Twell's Answer to the Further enquiry, and a tract, entitled, Some thoughts on the miracles of Jesus, by an impartial hand, are considered. By a lover of truth. ... London, Printed for J. Roberts, 1739.
    80 p. 20cm.
    No. 3 in vol. lettered: Tracts on demoniacks. 1737.

Witchcraft
F
7
H97
1870
    Hutchinson, Thomas, 1711-1780.
        The witchcraft delusion of 1692, by Gov. Thomas Hutchinson. From an unpublished manuscript (an early draft of his History of Massachusetts) in the Massachusetts archives. With notes by William Frederick Poole. Boston, Priv. print., 1870.
    43 p. 25cm.
    "Reprinted from the New-England historical and genealogical register for October, 1870."
    1. Witchcraft—New England. I. Poole, William Frederick, 1821-1894. II. Title.

Library of Congress   F7.H97   5-2279

Witchcraft
BF
1581
Z7+
1697d
    Hutchison, James.
        A sermon preached before the commissioners of justiciary appointed for triall of several persons suspected guilty of witchcraft: att Pasley the 13 Aprill 1697. [Glasgow, 1910] 390-399 p. 26cm.
    Running title: A sermon on witchcraft in 1697.
    Extract from The Scottish historical review, no. 28, July 1910. Contributed with a historical note, by Geo. Neilson.
    I. Neilson, George. II. Title. III. Title: A sermon on witchcraft.

BF
1517
F5H98
1952
    Huxley, Aldous Leonard, 1894–
        The devils of Loudun. [1st ed.] [New York] Harper [1952]
    340 p. illus., ports. 22cm.
    Bibliography: p. 329-330.

WITCHCRAFT
BF
1517
F5H98
1952
    Huxley, Aldous Leonard, 1894–
        The devils of Loudun. London, Chatto & Windus, 1952.
    376 p. illus., facsims. 21cm.
    I. Title.

Witchcraft
PQ
2309
H4
L111
    Huysmans, Joris Karl, 1848-1907.
    Là-bas.
    Bricaud, Joanny.
        J.-K. Huysmans et le satanisme, d'après des documents inédits. Paris, Bibliothèque Chacornac, 1913.
    77 p. 17cm.
    Inscribed by the author to "Monsieur J. Brien."
    1. Huysmans, Joris Karl, 1848-1907. Là-bas. 2. Devil. I. Title.

Witchcraft
BF
1549
B68
1897
    Huysmans, Joris Karl, 1848-1907.
    Bois, Jules, 1871–
        Le satanisme et la magie. Avec une étude de J.-K. Huysmans. Paris, Flammarion [1897]
    xxvii, 339 p. 19cm.
    With book-plate of Theodore Stanton.
    1. Satanism. 2. Magic. I. Huysmans, Joris Karl, 1848-1907. II. Title.

BF
1600
D36D6
1960
    Huysmans, Joris Karl, 1848-1907.
    Del Rio, Martin Antoine, 1551-1608.
        Le disquisizioni magiche: magia e stregoneria e i patti col diavolo, incubi e succubi, fatture e filtri d'amore e di morte, le statuette di cera, messe nere, le profezie, ecc. [Con uno studio sul "Satanismo" ai nostri giorni di J. K. Huysmans] Napoli, G. Rocco [1960?]
    124 p. 19cm.

WITCHCRAFT
BF
1584
D4
C551
    Hvorledes en hekseproces kommer i gang.
    Christensen, Christian Villads, 1864-1922.
        Hvorledes en hekseproces kommer i gang. En fortaelling fra Agernaes Birk.
    (In: Fra arkiv og museum, Kjøbenhavn. 23cm. v.1, no.2, 1900. p. [109]-134)

8
NIC
    1. Trials (Witchcraft)--Denmark. 2. Witchcraft--Denmark.

CATALOGUE OF THE CORNELL WITCHCRAFT COLLECTION

I

I. Iratiël Leetsosoneus

see

Hamer, Petrus, 1646-1716

Witchcraft BL 610 J27 1821

Iamblichus on the Mysteries of the Egyptians.
Jamblichus, of Chalcis.
[De mysteriis. English]
Iamblichus on the Mysteries of the Egyptians, Chaldeans, and Assyrians. Translated from the Greek by Thomas Taylor ... Chiswick, Printed by C. Whittinghams for the translator. 1821.

xxiv, 365 p. 22-1/2 cm.

"The epistle of Porphyry to the Egyptian Anebo": p. [1]-16.

Witchcraft BF 1508 B61 1699

Idée generale de la theologie payenne, servant de refutation au systeme de Mr. Bekker.
[Binet, Benjamin] 17th cent. Idée generale de la theologie payenne ... 1699. (Card 2)

Ex libris cabalisticis Kurt Seligmann.

1. Paganism. 2. Demonology. 3. Bekker, Balthasar, 1634-1698. De betoverde weereld. I. Title. II. His Traité historique des dieux et des demons du paganisme.

I. W.

Witchcraft X 479 42 11 o.14

Brief, aan een heer, waar in uyt de H. Schrift getoond werd, dat'er is een quade geest, die een redelijk schepsel is buyten de ziel des mensche. Met eenige aanmerkinge over het boek, De ware oorspronk, voort en ondergank des Satans. Door I. W. Amsterdam, By J. de Veer gedruckt, 1696.
64 p. title vignette, illus. initial.
20 x 15cm.
4°: A-H⁴.
Probably by Joannes van Wijk.

(Continued on next card)

Rare PQ 6437 T7A2 1575

Iardin de flores curiosas.
Torquemada, Antonio de, fl. 1553-1570.
Iardin de flores cvriosas, en qve se tratan algvnas materias de hvmanidad, philosophia, theologia, y geographia, con otros cosas curiosas, y apazibles ... Va hecho en seys tratados ... Anveres, En casa de Iuan Corderio, 1575.
[24], 538 p. 13cm.

Colophon: Antverpiae, Typis Gerardi Smits, 1575.

WITCHCRAFT RC 516 I19

Ideler, Karl Wilhelm, 1795-1860.
Ueber die Dämonomanie. Von Dr. Ideler, dirigirendem Arzte an der Irrenanstalt der Charité zu Berlin. [n. p., ca. 1840?]
[371]-408 p. 21cm.

Detached from Rust's Magazin, 48. Bd., 3. Heft.
At head of title: XII.

1. Demonomania. I. Title.

I. W.

itchcraft X 479 42 11 o.14

Brief, aan een heer, waar in uyt de H. Schrift getoond werd, dat'er is een quade geest ... 1696. (Card 2)

Supports Balthasar Bekker in the controversy over his De betoverde weereld.
No. 14 in vol. lettered B. Bekkers sterfbed en andere tractaten.
1. Devil. 2. Webbers, Zacharias. De waare oorspronk, voort- en onder-gank des Satans. 3. Bekker, Balthasar, 1634-1698. De betoverde weereld. I. Wijk, Joannes van. supposed author. II. I. W. III. W., I.

Witchcraft BF 1555 O29 1930

Ibberson, Dora, tr.
Oesterreich, Traugott Konstantin, 1880-1949.
Possession, demoniacal and other, among primitive races, in antiquity, the middle ages, and modern times, by T. K. Oesterreich ... New York, R. R. Smith, inc. 1930.
xi, 400 p. 24cm.

Lettered on cover: Demoniacal possession.
Printed in Great Britain.
"Authorized translation by D. Ibberson."
Translation of Die Besessenheit.

---

arW 37207

Ideler, Karl Wilhelm, 1795-1860.
Versuch einer Theorie des religiösen Wahnsinns; ein Beitrag zur Kritik der religiösen Wirren der Gegenwart. Halle, C. A. Schwetschke, 1848-1850.
2 v. 22cm.

1. Hallucinations and illusions. I. Title.

Iamblichos, of Chalcis

see

Jamblichus, of Chalcis

Witchcraft QP 251 M31

Idearum operatricium idea.
Marci a Kronland, Joannes Marcus, 1595-1667.
Idearvm operatricivm idea siue Hypotyposis et detectio illius occultae virtutis, quae semina faecundat, & ex ijsdem corpora organica producit ... [Pragae, Typis Seminarij Archiepiscopalis] 1635.
[176] l. illus. 21cm.

Signatures: 2 leaves unsigned, +, ++, +++, 1 leaf unsigned, A⁴, +, B-Z⁴, Aa-Tt⁴, Vu.
Engraved t. p.
I. Title.

WITCHCRAFT BF 1584 S7 I21

Idoate, Florencio, 1912-
Un documento de la Inquisición sobre brujería en Navarra. Pamplona, Editorial Aranzadi, 1972.
193 p. illus. (part fold.) 24cm.

1. Witchcraft--Navarre (Kingdom) 2. Inquisition. Spain. 3. Witchcraft--Spain. I. Title.

Iamblichus

see

Jamblichus, of Chalcis

Witchcraft BF 1508 B61 1699

Idée generale de la theologie payenne, servant de refutation au systeme de Mr. Bekker.
[Binet, Benjamin] 17th cent.
Idée generale de la theologie payenne, servant de refutation au systeme de Mr. Bekker. Touchant l'existence & l'operation des demons. Ou Traitté [sic] historique des dieux du paganisme. Par Mr. B***. Amsterdam, Chez J. du Fresne, 1699.
6 p. l., 227 p. 26cm.
12: *⁶, A-I¹², K⁶.
First published 1696 with title Traité historique des dieux et des demons du paganisme.

(Continued on next card)

WITCHCRAFT BF 1565 S43 1588

Ignotus Patronus Veritatis, pseud.
Examen epistolae et partis physiologiae de examine sagarum per aquam frigidam; à Gvilhelmo Adolpho Scribonio, medicinae et philosophiae doctore, diuersis temporibus in lucem editarum concinnatum à quodam Ignoto Patrono Veritatis. Epistola Scribonij, quae examinatur, in fine adiecta est. [Francofurti?] 1589.
78 p. 17cm.

"De examine et pvrgatione sagarvm per aqvam
(Continued on next card)

299

CATALOGUE OF THE CORNELL WITCHCRAFT COLLECTION

WITCHCRAFT
BF 1565 S43 1588
Ignotus Patronus Veritatis, pseud. Examen epistolae ... 1589. (Card 2)
frigidam epistola ... (with special t. p.): p. [51]-65.
Bound with Scribonius, Wilhelm Adolf. De sagarvm natvra. Marpurgi, 1588.

1. Scribonius, Wilhelm Adolf, 16th cent. De sagarum natura. 2. Witchcraft. I. Scribonius, Wilhelm Adolf, 16th cent. II. Title.

Witchcraft
BF 1565 S43 1588
Ignotus Patronus Veritatis, pseud.
Examen epistolae et partis physiologiae de examine sagarum per aquam frigidam. Scribonius, Wilhelm Adolf, 16th cent. Responsio ad examen Ignoti Patroni Veritatis de pvrgatione sagarum per aquam frigidam. Francofurti, Apud Joannem Wechelum, 1590.
[7], 56 p. 17cm.

Bound with his De sagarum natura. Marpurgi, 1588.

Witchcraft
BF 1565 S43 1588
Ignotus Patronus Veritatis, pseud.
Refvtatio responsionis Gvlielmi-Adolphi Scribonii, svperstitiosam sagarvm pvrgationem per aquam frigidam pertinacissimè defendentis; ab Ignoto Patrono Veritatis stylo Scriboniano conscripta ... Herbornae, 1591.
112 p. 17cm.

Bound with Scribonius, Wilhelm Adolf. De sagarvm natura. Marpurgi, 1588.
1. Scribonius, Wilhelm Adolph, 16th cent. Responsio ad examen Ignoti Patroni Veritatis de purgatione sagarum per aquam frigidam. I. Title.

Iiratiel Leetsosoneus

see

Hamer, Petrus, 1646-1716

BF 1566 K82
Het ijzige zaad van de duivel.
Koomen, Martin, 1939-
Het ijzige zaad van de duivel. Geschiedenis van heksen en demonen. Amsterdam, Wetenschappelijke Uitgeverij, 1973.
214 p. 20cm. (Unofficial history.)
Bibliography: p. 211-214.

NIC   COOdc   73-351717

WITCHCRAFT
BS 1325 L35
Illustrations and reflections on the story of Saul's consulting the witch of Endor.
Lathrop, Joseph, 1731-1820.
Illustrations and reflections on the story of Saul's consulting the witch of Endor. A discourse delivered at West-Springfield. Springfield, Mass., Henry Brewer, printer, 1806.
20 p. 21cm.

1. Endor, Witch of. (Biblical character) 2. Saul, king of Israel. 3. Bible. O.T. 1. Samuel XXVIII--Criticism, interpretation, etc. 4. Witchcraft in the Bible.

8 NIC

BF 411 T61
L'imagination: ses bienfaits et ses égarements.
Tissot, Claude Joseph, 1801-1876.
L'imagination: ses bienfaits et ses égarements surtout dans le domaine du merveilleux. Paris, Didier, 1868

1. Imagination. 2. Occult sciences. I. Title.

Witchcraft
BF 1555 W93
An impartial enquiry into the case of the Gospel demoniacks.
Worthington, William, 1703-1778.
An impartial enquiry into the case of the Gospel demoniacks. With an appendix, consisting of an essay on Scripture demonology. ... London, Printed for J. F. and C. Rivington, 1777.
349 p. 22cm.

"Books lately published": [1] p. at end.

1. Demonomania I. Title.

An Impartial Hand.

WITCHCRAFT
BF 1559 S69
Some thoughts on the miracles of Jesus; with an introduction to that of His casting out devils, which is particularly discuss'd. Occasioned by two late tracts, intitled, Enquiries into the meaning of demoniacks in the New Testament. By an Impartial Hand. London, Printed for John Clarke; and sold by J. Roberts, 1738.
69 p. 20cm.

8
1. Exorcism. 2. Demonology. 3. Enquiries into the meaning of demoniacks in the New Testament. I. An Impartial Hand.

Witchcraft
BF 1581 Z7 1712a
The impossibility of witchcraft, plainly proving, from Scripture and reason, that there never was a witch; and that it is both irrational and impious to believe there ever was. In which the depositions against Jane Wenham, lately try'd and condemn'd for a witch, at Hertford, are confuted and expos'd ... London, Printed and sold by J. Baker, 1712.
4 p. l., 31 p. 18½cm.

1. Witchcraft. 2. Wenham, Jane, d. 1730.

WITCHCRAFT
BF 1581 Z7 1712aa
The impossiblity of witchcraft, plainly proving, from Scripture and reason, that there never was a witch; and that it is both irrational and impious to believe there ever was. In which the depositions against Jane Wenham, lately try'd and condemn'd for a witch, at Hertford, are confuted and expos'd. 2d ed. London, Printed and sold by J. Baker, 1712.
4 p. l., 36 p. 18cm.
8   Imperfect copy: p. 17-24
NIC   (Continued on next card)

WITCHCRAFT
BF 1581 Z7 1712aa
The impossiblity of witchcraft... 1712. (Card 2)
erroneously numbered 25-32.
With this is bound The impossiblity of witchcraft further demonstrated. London, 1712.

1. Witchcraft--England. 2. Wenham, Jane, d. 1730. 3. Bragge, Francis, b. 1690. A full and impartial account of the discovery of sorcery and witchcraft.

8 NIC

The impossibility of witchcraft.

WITCHCRAFT
BF 1581 Z7 1712f
The Belief of witchcraft vindicated: proving, from Scripture, there have been witches; and, from reason, that there may be such still. In answer to a late pamphlet, intituled, The impossibility of witchcraft: plainly proving, from Scripture and reason that there never was a witch, &c. By G. R., A.M. London, Printed for J. Baker, 1712.
40 p. 19cm.
Sometimes attributed to F. Bragge.

(Continued on next card)

WITCHCRAFT
BF 1581 Z7 1712aa
The Impossibility of witchcraft further demonstrated, both from scripture and reason, wherein several texts of scripture relating to witches are prov'd to be falsly translated, with some cursory remarks on two trifling pamphlets in defence of the existence of witches. By the author of The impossibility of witchcraft, &c. London, Printed for J. Baker, 1712.
xv, 30, [2] p. 18cm.

8   (Continued on next card)

WITCHCRAFT
BF 1581 Z7 1712aa
The Impossibility of witchcraft further demonstrated ... 1712. (Card 2)
Bound with The impossibility of witchcraft. 2d ed. London, 1712.

1. Witchcraft. 2. Witchcraft in the Bible. 3. Bragge, Francis, b. 1690. Witchcraft farther display'd. I. The author of The impossibility of witchcraft.

8

Witchcraft
BF 1571 R63
The imposture of witchcraft.
Robbins, Rossell Hope, 1912-
The imposture of witchcraft. [London?] 1963.
545-562 p. 22cm.

"Read at the British Association for the Advancement of Science, Section H, Aberdeen, 3 September, 1963."
"Offprint from Folklore, Volume 74, Winter 1963."

1. Witchcraft. I. Title.

In antwoort op het jonghste post scriptum.

Witchcraft
BF 1410 B42 Z69 no.12
[Webbers, Zacharias]
In antwoort op het jonghste post scriptum van de VI. brief van Haggæoher Philaleethees tegens eene van de (soo hem dunkt) schaddyke helpers van Do. B. Bekker, raakende desselfs aanmerkinge over de predicatie van Do. Adrianus van Weesel, 's Sondags by sijn eerw. in de Wester Kerk den 25 Novemb. over Math. IV. 5,6,7. Van de versoekinge onses saligmakers door den Duyvel, gedaan. Dienende dit tot kraghtiger bewijs, dat deselve niet eygentlijk, maar by forme van een
NIC   (Continued on next card)

In antwoort op het jonghste post scriptum.

Witchcraft
BF 1410 B42 Z69 no.12
[Webbers, Zacharias] In antwoort op het jonghste post scriptum ... (Card 2)
gesighte, en in den geest geschiet zy: door den zelven S. W. S. F. t'Amsterdam, by D. van den Dalen, 1692.
16 p. 21cm.

Signatures: 4°: A-B⁴.
Black letter.
No. 12 in a Collection of tracts against Balthasar Bekker and his Betoverde weereld.
NIC   (Continued on next card)

CATALOGUE OF THE CORNELL WITCHCRAFT COLLECTION

In antwoort op het jonghste post scriptum.

Witchcraft
BF 1410
B42
Z69
no.12

[Webbers, Zacharias] In antwoort op het jonghste post scriptum ... 1692. (Card 3)

Attributed to Webbers by Aa, A. J. van der. Biographisch woordenboek der Nederlanden. Haarlem, 1852-78, and by Doorninck, J. I. van. Vermonde en naamlooze schrijvers ... Leiden, 1883-85.
Van der Linde 113.

NIC   (Continued on next card)

The inanity and mischief of vulgar superstitions.

Witchcraft
BF 1565
N33

Naylor, Martin Joseph.
The inanity [sic] and mischief of vulgar superstitions. Four sermons preached at All-Saint's church, Huntingdon, on the 25th day of March, in the years 1792, 1793, 1794, 1795. To which is added some account of the witches of Warboys ... Cambridge, Printed by B. Flower for J. Deighton & W. H. Lunn, 1795.
xi, 129 p. 21cm.

1. Superstition. 2. Witchcraft.
I. Title. II. Title: The witches of Warboys.

Inciarmatori, maghi e streghe di Benevento.

Witchcraft
BF 1584
I8
B64

Blasio, Abele de.
Inciarmatori, maghi e streghe di Benevento. Con prefazione di Enrico Morselli e proemio di G. Nicolucci. Napoli, L. Pierro, 1900.
249 p. illus. 20cm.

L'incredulité et mescreance du sortilege plainement convaincue.

WITCHCRAFT
BF 1602
L25
1622

L'Ancre, Pierre de, d. 1630.
L'incredvlité et mescreance dv sortilege plainement convaincve. Ov il est amplement et cvrievsement traicté, de la vérité ou illusion du sortilege, de la fascination, de l'attouchement, du scopelisme, de la diuination, de la ligature ou liaison magique, des apparitions: et d'vne infinité d'autres rares & nouueaux subjects. Paris, Chez Nicolas Bvon, 1622.
841, [10] p. port. 25cm.

I. Title.

L'incredulité sçavante, et la credulité ignorante.

Jacques d'Autun, Father, 1608 (ca.)-1678.
L'incredvlité sçavante, et la credvlité ignorante: au sujet des magiciens et des sorciers. Aueceque la response à vn liure intitulé Apologie pour tous les grands personnages, qui ont esté faussement soupçonnés de magie. Par le R.P. Iaqves d'Avtvn, predicateur Capucin. Lyon, Iean Certe, 1674.
[40], 1108, [24] p. 24cm.

Title vignette (woodcut)

Les incubes et les succubes...

Witchcraft

Delassus, Jules.
Les incubes et les succubes ... Paris, Société dv Mercvre de France [1897]
62 p. 19cm.

1. Demonology. I. Title.

Inderwick, F[rederick] A[ndrew]
Side-lights on the Stuarts; by F. A. Inderwick ... 2d ed. London, S. Low, Marston, Searle & Rivington, 1891.
4 p.l., 434 p., 1 l. 4 pl. (incl. col. front.) 7 port., 6 facsim. 22cm.

DA 375
I38
1891

1. Gt. Brit.--Hist.--Stuarts, 1603-1714. I. Title.

Index eorum, quae hoc in libro habentur.

WITCHCRAFT
PA 4220
L3
A4+
1516

Jamblichus, of Chalcis.
[De mysteriis. Latin]
Iamblichus De mysteriis Aegyptiorum, Chaldaeorum, Assyriorum. Proclus In Platonicum Alcibiadem de anima, atq[ue] demone. Proclus De sacrificio, & magia. Porphyrius De diuinis, atq[ue] daemonibus. Synesius Platonicus De somniis. Psellus De daemonibus. Expositio Prisciani, & Marsilii in Theophrastum De sensu, phantasia, & intellectu. Alcinoi Platonici philosophi, Liber de doctrina

8   (Continued on next card)

Index eorum, quae hoc in libro habentur.

WITCHCRAFT
PA 4220
L3
A4+
1516

Jamblichus, of Chalcis. [De mysteriis. Latin] [1516] (Card 2)

Platonis. Speusippi Platonis discipuli, Liber de Platonis definitionibus. Pythagorae philosophi Aurea uerba. Symbola Pythagorae philosophi. Xenocratis philosophi platonici, Liber de morte. Mercurii Trismegisti Pimander. Eiusdem Asclepius. Marsilii Ficini De triplici uita lib. II. Eiusdem Liber de uoluptate. Eiusdem

8   (Continued on next card)

Index eorum, quae hoc in libro habentur.

WITCHCRAFT
PA 4220
L3
A4+
1516

Jamblichus, of Chalcis. [De mysteriis. Latin] [1516] (Card 3)

De sole & lumine libri. II. Apologia eiusdem in librum suum de lumine. Eiusdem Libellus de magis. Quod necessaria sit securitas, & tranquillitas animi. Praeclarissimarum sententiarum huius operis breuis annotatio. [Venetiis, In aedibvs Aldi, et Andreae soceri, 1516]
177 [i.e., 175] numbered leaves.

8   29cm.   (Continued on next card)

Index eorum, quae hoc in libro habentur.

WITCHCRAFT
PA 4220
L3
A4+
1516

Jamblichus, of Chalcis. [De mysteriis] Latin. [1516] (Card 4)

At head of title: Index eorvm, qvae hoc in libro habentvr.
With colophon.
Provenance: Biblioteca SS. Me. Novelle.
Translations by M. Ficino.
1. Occult sciences. 2. Philosophy, Ancient--Collections. I. Proclus Diadochus. In Platonicum Alcibiadem. II. Proclus Diadochus. De sacrificio. III.

8   (Continued on next card)

Inductio sive directorium.

Witchcraft
BF 1583
A2
G74

Graminaeus, Theodor, b. ca. 1530.
Indvctio sive directorivm: das ist: Anleitung oder Vnderweisung, wie ein Richter in Criminal vnd peinlichen Sachen die Zauberer vnd Hexen belangendt, sich zuverhalten, vnd der Gebür damit zuverfahren haben soll, in zwey Theil getheilet, als wie von Amptsswegen, vnd sonst, so der Kläger Recht begert, zuverfahren ... Cölln, H. Falckenburg, 1594.
[8] 157 p. 15cm.

The infallible trve and assvred vvitch.

Witchcraft
BF 1565
C84
1624

Cotta, John, 1575?-1650?
The infallible trve and assvred vvitch; or, The second edition of The tryall of witch-craft. Shevving the right and trve methode of the discoverie; with a confvtation of erroneovs vvaies, carefvlly reviewed and more fully cleared and augmented. London, Printed by I. L. for R. Higginbotham, 1624.
155 p. 19cm.

STC 5837.
I. Title. II. His The tryall of witch-craft.

WITCHCRAFT
BF 1583
A2
I43

Informatio ivris, in causa poenali; vtrvm tres mvlieres maleficii, et veneficii, ceu reae, delatae capi, & torqueri potuerint, nécne? Qvad. Caroli V. imp. constitvtio criminalis aliqvot in locis declaratur. Rechtliches Bedencken, in Malefitzsachen; ob drey Weiber, der Zauberey halber angegeben, in gefängliche Verhafft angenommen, und peinlich befragt werden können, oder nicht? Darinnen Keyser Carols, dess Fünfften, hochlöblichister Gedächtnuss Peinliche, oder Halss-

8
NIC   (Continued on next card)

WITCHCRAFT
BF 1583
A2
I43

Informatio ivris, in causa poenali... (Card 2)

gerichtsordnunge in etlichen Articuln erkläret wirdt. Per H. A. B. V. I. D. Franckf[urt a. M.] Bey C. Egen[olffs] Erben, 1590.
68 l. 16cm.

1. Witchcraft--Germany. 2. Torture--Germany. I. B., H. A. II. H. A. B. III. Karl V, Emperor of Germany, 1500-1558. IV. Title: Recht liches Bedencken, in Malefitzsach en.

MSS Bd.
WITCHCRAFT
BF I53++

Ingolstadt. Universität. Juristische Fakultät.
Consilia der juridischen Facultät. Ingolstadt, 1618-1632.
17-123 p., [4] l., 124-249 p., [1] l. 33cm.

Title from spine.
Manuscript, on paper in various 17th century hands.
A collection of documents reporting the advice of the law faculty of the university in criminal cases,
(Continued on next card)

MSS Bd.
WITCHCRAFT
BF I53++

Ingolstadt. Universität. Juristische Fakultät. Consilia. 1618-1632. (Card 2)

five of which are witchcraft.
Bound in boards with gilded paper.

1. Advisory opinions--Ingolstadt. 2. Judicial opinions--Ingolstadt. 3. Trials (Witchcraft)--Ingolstadt. 4. Trials--Ingolstadt.

Witchcraft
BF 1578
B4
I54

Ingram, M V
An authenticated history of the famous Bell witch, the wonder of the 19th century, and unexplained phenomenon of the Christian era. The mysterious talking goblin that terrorized the west end of Robertson County, Tennessee, tormenting John Bell to his death. The story of Betsy Bell, her lover and the haunting sphinx. Clarksville, Tenn., 1894.
316 p. illus. 17cm.

Imprint covered by label: Setliff & Co., Nashville, Tenn.
(Over)

301

CATALOGUE OF THE CORNELL WITCHCRAFT COLLECTION

L'initiation à la sorcellerie et le sabbat.

Witchcraft
BF 1582 D34

Delcambre, Étienne.
Le concept de la sorcellerie dans le duché de Lorraine au XVIe et au XVIIe siècle ... Nancy, Société d'archéologie Lorraine, 1948.
v. 22cm. (Half-title: Recueil de documents sur l'histoire de Lorraine)
Contents.--fasc. 1. L'initiation à la sorcellerie et le sabbat.
1. Witchcraft--Lorraine--Hist. I. Title.

L'innocence opprimee.

MSS Bd. WITCHCRAFT BF L37

Laugeois, Antoine, d. 1674.
L'innocence opprimee; ou, Défense de Mathurin Picard, curé de Mesnil-Jourdain ... Par M. Laugeois, successeur immédiat dudit Picard - dans la cure de Mesnil-Jourdain. Ouvrage qui n'a jamais été imprimé et extrait sur l'original, par M. Chemin curé de Tourneville. [n. p. 17th cent.]
x, 102 p. title vignette. 18cm.
Manuscript, on paper.
Preface signed M. du Passeur (Gabriel), curé de Vironvay.
(Continued on next card)

L'innocence opprimee.

MSS Bd. WITCHCRAFT BF L37

Laugeois, Antoine, d. 1674. L'innocence opprimee...[17th cent.] (Card 2)
Notes by G. L. Burr inside front cover discuss history and provenance of the manuscript.
Bound in boards.
1. Demoniac possession. 2. Picard, Mathurin, d. 1647. 3. Bavent, Madeleine, b. 1607. 4. Louviers, France. St. Louis (Convent) 5. Witchcraft. I. Chemin, J B , 1725 -1781, ed. II. Title. III. Title: Défense de Mathurin Picard.

Innocencie appearing, through the dark mists of pretended guilt.

WITCHCRAFT BX 9339 P83 A17+ 1655

Pordage, John.
Innocencie appearing, through the dark mists of pretended guilt. Or, a full and true narration of the unjust and illegal proceedings of the commissioners of Berks, (for ejecting scandalous and insufficient ministers) against John Pordage of Bradfield in the same county. In which he is justly vindicated from the unjust and horrid aspersions of blasphemy, divelism or necromancie, scandal in his life ... London,
(Continued on next card)

8 NIC

Innocencie appearing, through the dark mists of pretended guilt.

WITCHCRAFT BX 9339 P83 A17+ 1655

Pordage, John. Innocencie appearing, through the dark mists of pretended guilt ... 1655. (Card 2)
Printed for Giles Calvert, 1655.
5 p. l., 114 p. port. 29cm.
1. Great Britain. Laws, statutes, etc. An ordinance for ejecting scandalous, ignorant and insufficient ministers and schoolmasters. 2. Visions. I. Title.

8 NIC

Der Innsbrucker Hexenprocess von 1485.

Witchcraft
BF 1584 A93 Z7 1485

Ammann, Hartmann.
Der Innsbrucker Hexenprocess von 1485. [Innsbruck, 1890]
1-87 p. 23cm.
Detached from Zeitschrift des Ferdinandeums für Tirol und Vorarlberg, 3. Folge, 34. Heft, 1890.
1. Trials (Witchcraft)--Tyrol. I. Title.

8

An inquiry into the extent of the witch persecutions in Germany.

Thesis Film 1894 48

Brown, Harriet Chedie (Connor), 1872-
An inquiry into the extent of the witch persecutions in Germany. Ithaca, N. Y., 1894.
151 l. 27cm.
Thesis (A. B.)--Cornell University, 1894.
Microfilm. Ithaca, N. Y., Photo Science, Cornell University, 1974. part of reel. 35mm.

14 NIC

I. Title.

An inquiry into the Scripture meaning of the word Satan.

Witchcraft
BF 1521 A82

[Ashdowne, William]
An inquiry into the Scripture meaning of the word Satan and its synonymous terms, the Devil, or the Adversary, and the Wicked-One. Wherein also the notions concerning devils or demons, are brought down to the standard of Scripture ... London, Printed for J. Wheble, 1772.
iii, 40, 77 p. 22cm.
With this is bound his An attempt to prove that the opinion concerning the Devil ... Canterbury, 1794.
With autographs of M.H.Black, Von Carnap, William Kite, William Ashdowne.
Interleaved, with ms. additions by author.

Inquisition. Rome.

Witchcraft
BX 1700 I59

Inquisition. Rome.
Instrvctio pro formandis processibus in causis strigum, sortilegiorum, & maleficiorum. [Romae, Ex typographia Reu. Cam. Apost., 1657]
[8] p. 22cm.
Caption title.
"Perhaps the only printed copy in existence of ... the official Instruction of the Roman Inquisition to the prosecution..." -- part of a long note by G. L. Burr inside front cover.
(Continued on next card)

8

Witchcraft

BX 1700 I59

Inquisition. Rome. Instrvctio pro formandis processibus in causis strigum ...

1. Trials (Witchcraft) I. Title.

8

L'inquisition en Dauphiné.

AS 162 B58 v.206

Marx, Jean, 1884-
L'inquisition en Dauphiné; étude sur le développement et la répression de l'hérésie et de la sorcellerie du XIVe siècle au début du règne de François Ier. Paris, H. Champion, 1914.
xxiii, 294 p. 25cm. (Bibliothèque de l'École des hautes études ... Sciences historiques et philologiques. 206. fasc.)
1. Inquisition. Dauphiné. 2. Waldenses. 3. Witchcraft--Dauphiné. I. Title.

The inquisition in the Spanish dependencies.

Witchcraft
BX 1735 L43 I5

Lea, Henry Charles, 1825-1909.
The inquisition in the Spanish dependencies: Sicily—Naples — Sardinia — Milan — the Canaries — Mexico — Peru—New Granada. By Henry Charles Lea ... New York, London, The Macmillan company, 1908.
1 p. l., vii-xvi, 564 p. 23½ cm.
1. Inquisition. I. Title.

8-1774

Library of Congress (Copyright 1907 A 196681)

Inquisition, Intoleranz, Exkommunication, Interdikt, Index, Zensur.

Z 2771 fasc.5 pt.5 no.2

Heinemann, Franz, 1870-
Inquisition, Intoleranz, Exkommunication, Interdikt, Index, Zensur. Sektenwesen, Hexenwahn und Hexenprozesse, Rechtsanschauungen. Bern, K. J. Wyss, 1908-09.
2 v. in 1. 22cm. (His Kulturgeschichte und Volkskunde (Folklore) der Schweiz, Heft 2)
Bibliographie der schweizerischen Landeskunde, Fasc. V5.

Inquisition und Hexenprocesse.

Witchcraft
BX 1711 D29

Deckert, Joseph.
Inquisition und Hexenprocesse. "Greuel der katholischen Kirche." Wien, "Sendboten des heil. Joseph" in Commission bei H. Kirsch 1896.
34 p. 21cm.
"Separat-Abdruck aus dem 'Sendboten des heil. Joseph."
1. Inquisition. 2. Trials (Witchcraft) I. Title.

Inquisition und Hexenverfolgung im Mittelalter.

WITCHCRAFT
BF 1566 H24 I5

Hansen, Joseph, 1862-1943.
Inquisition und Hexenverfolgung im Mittelalter. [München, 1898]
[385]-432 p. 23cm.
Detached from Historische Zeitschrift, 81. Bd., 3. Heft (1898)
1. Witchcraft--History. 2. Inquisition. I. Title.

8 NIC

CATALOGUE OF THE CORNELL WITCHCRAFT COLLECTION

Institoris, Henricus

Witchcraft
BF
1569
A2
I59
1582

Institoris, Henricus, d. 1508.
　Malleorum qvorvndam maleficarvm, tam vete-rvm quàm recentiorum authorum, tomi dvo. Quorum primus continet: I. Malleum male-ficarum Fr. Iacobi Sprenger, & Fr. Henri-ci Institoris: Inquisitorum. II. Fr. Ioannis Nider ... qui tractat de malefi-cis & eorum deceptionibus. Secvndvs verò tomus continet tractatus VII. ibi speci-atim nominatos ... Francofvrti [Svmp-tibvs Nicol　　　ai Bassaei] 1582.
　8 p. l.,　　　806, [35] p. 16cm.
　　　　　(Continued on next card)

Witchcraft
BF
1569
A2
I59
1582

Institoris, Henricus, d. 1508.
　Malleorum qvorvndam maleficarvm...1582.
　　　　　　　(Card 2)
　Vol. 2 of this ed. is not known to exist; however, vol. 2 of Bassaeus' edition of 1588 has title: Tomvs secvndvs malleorvm qvorvn-dam maleficarvm, and introduction dated 1582. This form of the title seems peculiar to these two volumes alone, out of the many editions of the Malleus maleficarum. We in-fer that the two belong together, vol. 1 of 1588 being a　　　"2d ed." of this issue.
　✓ I. His　　　Malleus maleficarum.
✓ II. Title.

Witchcraft
BF
1569
A2I59+
1487

[Institoris, Henricus] d. 1508.
　Malleus maleficarum ... [Speier, Peter Drach, before 15 Apr., 1487]
　[129] l. 28cm.
　Leaf [1a] blank.
　Leaf [1b]: Appologia auctoris in malleum maleficarum.
　Leaf [129b] (End): Sit laus deo. exter-miniū heresis. pax viuis. requies eterna defunctis. Amen.
　Signatures: a-p⁸, q⁹.
　　　　　(Continued on next card)

Witchcraft
BF
1569
A2I59+
1487

[Institoris, Henricus] d. 1508.　Malleus maleficarum ... [before 15 Apr., 1487]
　　　　　　　(Card 2)
　Capital spaces.
　By Henricus Institoris (Heinrich Krä-mer) and Jakob Sprenger.
　Hain. Repertorium (with Copinger's Sup-plement) *9238; Proctor, 526; Brit. Mus. Cat. (XV cent.) I, p. xxvi; Goff. Third census, I-163.
　With bookplate of J. B. Holzinger.
　　　　　(Continued on next card)

Witchcraft
BF
1569
A2I59+
1487

[Institoris, Henricus] d. 1508.　Malleus maleficarum ... [before 15 Apr., 1487]
　　　　　　　(Card 3)

　1. Witchcraft.　2. Demonology.　3. Crim-inal law.　4. Criminal procedure. ✓ I. Sprenger, Jakob, 1436 or 8-1495.　II. Title.

Witchcraft
BF
1569
A2I59+
1490

[Institoris, Henricus] d. 1508.
　Malleus maleficarum. [Speier, Peter Drach, about 1490-91]
　[102] l. 27cm.
　Leaf [1a] (Title): Malleus maleficarum.
　Leaf [1b]: Appologia auctoris in mal-leum maleficarum.
　Leaves [2a]-[3b]: Tenor bulle apostoli-ce aduersus heresim maleficarum cum appro-batione ɀ subscriptione doctorū alme vni-uersitatis Colonieñ. in sequentem tracta-tum.
　　　　　(Continued on next card)

Witchcraft
BF
1569
A2I59+
1490

[Institoris, Henricus] d. 1508.　Malleus maleficarum ... [about 1490-91]
　　　　　　　(Card 2)
　Leaf [102a] (End): Sit laus deo. exter-miniū heresis. pax viuis. requies eterna defunctis. amen.
　Signatures: a⁸, b-d⁶, ef⁸, g-h⁶, i⁸, k-r⁶; signatures ef being used together to mark a single gathering.
　Capital spaces.
　By Henricus Institoris (Heinrich Krämer)
　　　　　(Continued on next card)

Witchcraft
BF
1569
A2I59+
1490

[Institoris, Henricus] d. 1508.　Malleus maleficarum ... [about 1490-91]
　　　　　　　(Card 3)
　and Jakob Sprenger.
　Hain. Repertorium (with Copinger's Sup-plement) *9239; Proctor, 2383; Brit. Mus. Cat. (XV cent.) II, p. 498 (IB. 8615); Goff. Third census, I-164.

　1. Witchcraft.　2. Demonology.　3. Crim-inal law.　4. Criminal procedure. ✓ I. Sprenger, Jakob.　1436 or 8-1495.　II. Title.

Witchcraft
BF
1569
A2I59+
1494

[Institoris, Henricus] d. 1508.
　Malleus maleficarum.　Cologne, Johann Koelhoff, the Younger, 24 Nov. (in vigilia s. Katherine), 1494.
　[112] l. 27cm.
　Leaf [1a] (Title): Mallens maleficarnm.
　Leaf [1b]: Apologia autoris in malleū maleficarū.
　Leaves [1b]-[3a]: Tenor bulle apostoli-ce aduersus heresim maleficaɤ cū ɔpbatōe ɀ sb'scriptōe doctoɤ alme vniūsitatɜ Colon. ...
　　　　　(Continued on next card)

Witchcraft
BF
1569
A2I59+
1494

[Institoris, Henricus] d. 1508.　Malleus maleficarum ... 1494.　(Card 2)
　Leaf [112a] (Colophon): Liber Malleus maleficarū a suo editore nuncupatus Im-pressusq̕ per me Ioannem Koelhoff incolā Ciuitatis sancte Colonieñ. Anno salutɜ Mcccc.xciiij. in vigilia sanctɜ Katherine Regine ac Ʋginis martyrisq̕ finem accepit feliciter.
　Signatures: i-[iv], a-s⁶.　Leaves [5]-[112] numbered i-folio Cviij, with many
　　　　　(Continued on next card)

Witchcraft
BF
1569
A2I59+
1494

[Institoris, Henricus] d. 1508.　Malleus maleficarum ... 1494.　(Card 3)
　errors.
　Capital spaces, some with guide-letters. Capitals, paragraph-marks and initial-strokes supplied in red.
　By Henricus Institoris (Heinrich Krämer) and Jakob Sprenger.
　Hain. Repertorium (with Copinger's Sup-plement) 9244; Proctor, 1462; Brit. Mus. Cat. (XV cent.) I, p. 298 (IB. 5064); Goff.
　　　　　(Continued on next card)

Witchcraft
BF
1569
A2I59+
1494

[Institoris, Henricus] d. 1508.　Malleus maleficarum ... 1494.　(Card 4)
　Third census, I-167.
　Incomplete copy: lacks leaf xviij (c_{vi}). Ex libris cabalisticis Kurt Seligmann. Bound in brown morocco, by Sangorski and Sutcliffe.

　1. Witchcraft.　2. Demonology.　3. Crim-inal law.　4. Criminal procedure. ✓ I. Sprenger, Jakob, 1436 or 8-1495.　II. Title.

Witchcraft
BF
1569
A2I59
1519

[Institoris, Henricus] d. 1508.
　Malleus maleficarum maleficas et earum heresim vt phramea potentissima conterens. [Lugduni, Per Joannem Marion, 1519]
　[216] l. 15cm.
　Signatures: a-z⁸, A-D⁸.
　Printer's device on t. p.; variant form on verso of last leaf.
　Armorial book-plate of "Christophorus Baro à VVolcKhenstain, & Rodnegg, etc.", dated 1594. His arms are also stamped on
　　　　　(Continued on next card)

Witchcraft
BF
1569
A2I59
1519

[Institoris, Henricus] d. 1508.　Malleus maleficarum ... [1519]　(Card 2)
　the binding.
　By Henricus Institoris (Heinrich Krämer) and Jacob Sprenger.
　With this is bound Daneau, Lambert.　De veneficis ... Coloniae Agrippinae, 1575.

Witchcraft
BF
1569
A2I59
1519a

Institoris, Henricus, d. 1508.
　Malleus maleficarum.　Opus egregium: de varijs incantationum generibus origine: progressu: medela atque ordinaria damnatio-ne: compilatus ab eximijs Heinrico Instito-ris: et Jacobo Sprenger ordinis praedicato-rum, sacre pagine doctoribus et heretice pestis inquisitoribus: non tam vtilis quam necessarius ... [Nurenberge, Impressum in officina Frederici Peypus] 1519.
　clii, [10] l. 22cm.
　Title within　　ornamental border.

303

CATALOGUE OF THE CORNELL WITCHCRAFT COLLECTION

Witchcraft
BF 1569 A2I59 1520

[Institoris, Henricus] d. 1508.
Mallevs maleficarvm, maleficas, & earum haeresim, vt phramea potentissima conterens. [Coloniae, I. Gymnicus, 1520]
[268] l. 15cm.

Signatures: *8, a4, A-Z8, Aa-Ii8.
Colophon: Anno XX. Coloniae excvdebat Ioannes Gymnicvs.
By Henricus Institoris (Heinrich Krämer) and Jacob Sprenger.

WITCHCRAFT
BF 1569 A2 I59 1584

Institoris, Henricus, d. 1508.
Malleus maleficorvm...1584.   (Card 4)

Contents--continued.
Quaestio de strigibus seu maleficis. Eiusdem Apologia quadruplex de lamiis contra Io. Franciscum Ponzinibium.

WITCHCRAFT
BF 1569 A2 I59 1595

Institoris, Henricus, d. 1508.
Malleus maleficarvm, ex plvrimis avctoribvs coacervatvs, ac in dvos tomos distinctus. Quorum hic prior quos contineat, in altera pagella videbis. Accessit hvic editioni postremae, vt plusquam anteà plurimis mendis purgata sit quamplurimisque, in margine, additionibus illustrata & locupletata. Lvgdvni, Svmptibvs Petri Landry, 1595.

8
NIC
2 v. in 1.   18cm.

(Continued on next card)

Witchcraft
BF 1569 A2I59 1580

[Institoris, Henricus] d. 1508.
Mallevs maleficarvm in tres divisvs partes, in quibus concurrentia ad maleficia, maleficiorum effectus, remedia aduersus maleficia, et modum denique procedendi, ac puniendi maleficos abundè continetur, praecipuè autem omnibus inquisitoribus, et diuini verbi concionatoribus vtilis, ac necessarius. Auctore Jacobo Sprengero ... His nunc primum adiecimus, M. Bernhardi Basin opusculum de artibus magicis, ac magorum, maleficijs. Item. D. Vlrici Molitoris ...

(Continued on next card)

WITCHCRAFT
BF 1569 A2 I59 1588

Institoris, Henricus, d. 1508.
Malleus maleficarvm: De lamiis et strigibvs, et sagis, aliisqve magis & daemoniacis, eorumq3 arte, & potestate, & poena, tractatvs aliqvot tam veterum, quàm recentiorum auctorum: in tomos dvos distributi... Omnes de integro nvnc demvm in ordinem congestos, notis & explicationibus illustratos, atque ab innumeris ... mendis ... vindicatos [continet] ... Francofvrti [Sumpt   ibus N. Bassaei] 1588.
8
NIC   2v. 17cm.

(Continued on next card)

WITCHCRAFT
BF 1569 A2 I59 1595

Institoris, Henricus, d. 1508.
Malleus maleficarvm...1595.   (Card 2)

Title in red and black.
Vol. 2 has title: Mallei maleficarvm, ex multis auctoribus conflati ... tomvs alter.

Contents.---v. 1. Fr. Iacobi Sprengeri, & Fr. Henrici Institoris inquisitorũ haereticae prauitatis Malleum malsficarum. Fr. Ioannis Nideri ... Formicarium de maleficis.

(Continued on next card)

Witchcraft
BF 1569 A2I59 1580

[Institoris, Henricus] d. 1508. Mallevs maleficarvm ...   (Card 2)
de lamijs & Pythonicis mulieribus dialogum. Item. D. Ioannis de Gerson ... de probatione spirituum, libellum. Item. D. Thomae Murner ... libellum, de Pythonico contractu. Omnia summo studio illustrata, et multis mendis recens vindicata. Cum indice quaestionum & rerum ... Francofvrti ad Moenvm, apud Nicolaum Bassaeum, 1580.
[24], 737, [42] p. 16cm.

WITCHCRAFT
BF 1569 A2 I59 1588

Institoris, Henricus, d. 1508.
Malleus maleficarvm...1588.   (Card 2)

Printer's device on title-pages and at end of each vol.
Vol. 2 has title: Tomus secundus Malleorvm qvorvndam maleficarvm, tam vetervm, qvam recentivm avtorvm.
With autograph: Martinus Kimerlj.
Manuscript note on t. p.: Colleg. Societ. IESU Mindelh   emij, 1635.

(Continued on next card)

WITCHCRAFT
BF 1569 A2 I59 1595

Institoris, Henricus, d. 1508.
Malleus maleficarvm...1595.   (Card 3)

Contents--continued.
--v. 2. M. Bernhardi Basin Opusculum de artibus magicis. Vlrici Molitoris ... Dialogum de lamijs. Flagellum daemonum, seu Exorcismi efficacissimi ... per Fr. Hiero. Mengum. D. Ioannis de Gerson ... Libellus de probatione spirituum. M. Thomae Murner

(Continued on next card)

WITCHCRAFT
BF 1569 A2 I59 1584

Institoris, Henricus, d. 1508.
Malleus maleficorvm, ex plvrimis avthoribvs coaceruatus, ac in duos tomos distinctus ... Lvgdvni, Apud Ioannem Jacobi Iuntae F., 1584.
2 v. in 1. 18cm.

Title vignette: Giunta device.
Autograph on t. p.: Jr. Jo. Bap'ta Arrigonus ...

8
NIC
(Continued on next card)

WITCHCRAFT
BF 1569 A2 I59 1588

Institoris, Henricus, d. 1508.
Malleus maleficarvm...1588.   (Card 3)

Contemporary blind-stamped pigskin binding over wooden boards; metal clasps.
Contents.--v.1. Malleus maleficarum Iacobi Sprengeri, & Henrici Institoris. Ioannis Nideri Formicarius de maleficis, earumque praestigijs ac deceptionibus.--v.2. Bernhardi Basin Opusculum de artibus magicis, ac

(Continued on next card)

WITCHCRAFT
BF 1569 A2 I59 1595

Institoris, Henricus, d. 1508.
Malleus maleficarvm...1595.   (Card 4)

Contents--continued.
... Libellus de Pythonico contractu. Foelicis Malleoli [Hemmerli] ... Tractatus duo exorcismorum seu adiurationum. Item Tractatus eiusdem de credulitate demonibus adhibenda. Bartholomaei de Spina ... Quaestio de strigibus seu maleficis. Item eiusdem Apologia quadru   plex de lamijs contro Io. Francisc   um Ponzinibium.

WITCHCRAFT
BF 1569 A2 I59 1584

Institoris, Henricus, d. 1508.
Malleus maleficorvm...1584.   (Card 2)

Contents.--v.1. Iacobi Sprengeri & Henrici Institoris Malleus maleficarum. Ioannis Nider Formicarius, lib. V. De maleficis & eorum deceptionibus.--v.2. Bernhardi Basin De artibus magicis ac magorum maleficiis. Ulrici Molitoris De lamiis et Pythonicis mulieribus. Flagellum Daemonum per Hiero.

(Continued on next card)

WITCHCRAFT
BF 1569 A2 I59 1588

Institoris, Henricus, d. 1508.
Malleus maleficarvm...1588.   (Card 4)

Contents--continued.
magorum maleficijs. Vlrici Molitoris Dialogus de lamijs, & Pythonicis mulieribus. Flagellum daemonum ... per Ieron. Mengum. Ioannis de Gerson Libellus de probatione spirituum. Thomae Murner Libellus de Pythonico contractu. Foelicis Malleoli Tractatus duo

(Continued on next card)

WITCHCRAFT
BF 1569 A2 I59 1604

Institoris, Henricus, d. 1508.
Malleus maleficarvm ex variis avctoribvs concinnatus, & in tres tomos distinctus: qvorvm postremvs, qvi Fvstis daemonvm inscribitvr, nunc primum reliquis adiectus est. Postrema editio quamplurimis notis, explicationibus, & additionibus illustrata: atque ab innumeris ... mendis ... vindicata: Et vtilissimis, copiosissimisque indicibus locupletata ... Lvgdvni, Svmptibvs Petri Landry,   1604.
8
NIC   3v. in 2.   18cm.

(Continued on next card)

WITCHCRAFT
BF 1569 A2 I59 1584

Institoris, Henricus, d. 1508.
Malleus maleficorvm...1584.   (Card 3)

Contents--continued.
Mengum. Ioannis de Gerson Libellus de probatione spirituum. Thomae Murner, De Pythonico contractu. Anonymi cuiusdam [Felix Hemmerli] Tractatus duo exorcismorum seu adiurationum. Tractatus eiusdem de credulitate daemonibus adhibenda. Bartholomaei de Spina,

(Continued on next card)

WITCHCRAFT
BF 1569 A2 I59 1588

Institoris, Henricus, d. 1508.
Malleus maleficarvm...1588.   (Card 5)

Contents--continued.
contractu. Foelicis Malleoli Tractatus duo exorcismorum seu adiurationum. Tractatus eiusdem de credulitate daemonibus adhibenda. Bartholomaei de Spina Quaestio de strigibus seu maleficis. Eiusdem Apologia quadruplex de lamijs: contra Io. Franciscum Ponzinibium.

WITCHCRAFT
BF 1569 A2 I59 1604

Institoris, Henricus, d. 1508.
Malleus maleficarvm...1604.   (Card 2)

Title vignettes: device of P. Landry.
Vol. 2 has title: Mallei maleficarum, ex plvrimis avctoribvs coadunati ... tomvs secvndvs.
Vol. 3 has special t. p.: Fvstis daemonvm adivrationes formidabiles ... ad malignos spiritvs effvgandos de oppressis corporibus humanis ...   avctore Hieronymo Mengo.

(Continued on next card)

CATALOGUE OF THE CORNELL WITCHCRAFT COLLECTION

HCRAFT

    Institoris, Henricus, d. 1508.
      Malleus maleficarvm...1604.   (Card 3)

      With autograph: Joannes Peeters.
      With vol. 2-3 is bound Stampa, Pietro Antonio. Fuga Satanae. Lvgdvni, 1610.
      Contents.--v.1. Iacobi Sprengeri, & Henrici Institoris Malleus maleficarum. Ioannis Nideri Formicarius de maleficis, & earum praestigiis ac deceptionibus.--v.2. Bernhard Ba-

(Continued on next card)

WITCHCRAFT
BF
1569
A2
I59
1620

    Institoris, Henricus, d. 1508.
      Malleus maleficarvm...1620.   (Card 3)

      Stamp on t. p.: Couvent des Dominicains St. Romain, Toulouse.
      Contents.--v.1. Iacobi Sprengeri & Henrici Institoris Malleus maleficarum. Ioannis Nideri Formicarius de maleficis, & earum praestigiis ac deceptionibus.--v.2, pt.1. Bernhardi Basin Opusculum de artibus magicis

(Continued on next card)

WITCHCRAFT
BF
1569
A2
I59+
1669

    Institoris, Henricus, d. 1508.
      Malleus maleficarvm...   (Card 3)

    artis exorcisticae ...   Lvgdvni, Sumptibus Clavdii Bourgeat, 1669.
    4 v. in 2. 26cm.

      Engraved title vignettes.
      Vol. 2 issued in two parts, each with special t. p. and separate paging, and with

(Continued on next card)

HCRAFT

    Institoris, Henricus, d. 1508.
      Malleus maleficarvm...1604.   (Card 4)

      Contents--continued.
sin Opusculum de artibus magicis, ac magorum maleficijs. Vlrici Molitoris Dialogus de lamiis, & Pythonicis mulieribus. Flagellum daemonum, per Hieron. Mengum. Ioannis de Gerson Libellus de probatione spirituum. Thomae Murner Libellus de Pythonico contractu.

(Continued on next card)

WITCHCRAFT
BF
1569
A2
I59
1620

    Institoris, Henricus, d. 1508.
      Malleus maleficarvm...1620.   (Card 4)

      Contents--continued.
ac magorum maleficiis. Vlrici Molitoris Dialogus de lamiis, & Pythonicis mulieribus. Ioannis de Gerson Libellus de probatione spirituum. Thomae Murner Libellus de Pythonico contractu. Bartholomaei de Spina Quaestio de strigibus seu maleficis. Eiusdem Apolo-

(Continued on next card)

WITCHCRAFT
BF
1569
A2
I59+
1669

    Institoris, Henricus, d. 1508.
      Malleus maleficarvm...1669.   (Card 4)

    title: Mallei maleficarvm tractatvs aliqvot tam vetervm, qvam recentiorum in vnum corpus coaceruati ... tomi secvndi pars prior [-II].
      Vol. 3 has title: Daemonastix, sev adversvs daemones et maleficos, vniversi operis ad vsum praesertim exorcistarum concinnati tomus terti   us.

(Continued on next card)

HCRAFT

    Institoris, Henricus, d. 1508.
      Malleus maleficarvm...1604.   (Card 5)

      Contents--continued.
Foelicis Malleoli Tractatus duo exorcismorum seu adiurationum. Tractatus eiusdem de credulitate daemonibus adhibenda. Bartholomaei de Spina Quaestio de strigibus seu maleficis. Eiusdem Apologia quadruplex de lamiis contra Ponzinibium.--v.3. Fvstis daemonvm adivratio-

(Continued on next card)

WITCHCRAFT
BF
1569
A2
I59
1620

    Institoris, Henricus, d. 1508.
      Malleus maleficarvm...1620.   (Card 5)

      Contents--continued.
gia quadruplex contra Io. Franciscum Ponzinibium.--v.2, pt.2. Ioan. Laurentij Ananiae Libri 4. de natura daemonum. Bernardi Comensis Tractatus de strigibus. Ambrosij de Vignate Quaestio de lamiis, seu strigibus & earum delictis. Ioan. Gersonij Tractatus de

(Continued on next card)

WITCHCRAFT
BF
1569
A2
I59+
1669

    Institoris, Henricus, d. 1508.
      Malleus maleficarvm...1669.   (Card 5)

      T. p. of vol. 4 wanting.
      Contents.--v.1. Iacobi Sprengeri, & Henrici Institoris Malleus maleficarum. Ioannis Nideri Formicarius de maleficis, & earum praestigiis ac deceptionibus.--v.2, pt.1. Bernardi Basin Opusculum de artibus magicis ac magorum maleficiis. Vlrici Molitoris Dia-

(Continued on next card)

HCRAFT

    Institoris, Henricus, d. 1508.
      Malleus maleficarvm...1604.   (Card 6)

      Contents--continued.
nes formidabiles, et potentissimas ad malignos spiritvs effvgandos de oppressis corporibus humanis continens.

WITCHCRAFT
BF
1569
A2
I59
1620

    Institoris, Henricus, d. 1508.
      Malleus maleficarvm...1620.   (Card 6)

      Contents--continued.
erroribus circa artem magicam & articulis reprobatis. Ioan. Franc. Leonis Libellus de sortilegiis. Iacobi Simancae Titulus vnicus de lamiis. Alphonsi a Castro Zamorensis de impia sortilegarum, maleficarum & lamiarum haeresi, earúmque punitione, opusculum. Pauli Grilla   ndi Tractatus de sortilegiis, eorú   mque poenis.

WITCHCRAFT
BF
1569
A2
I59+
1669

    Institoris, Henricus, d. 1508.
      Malleus maleficarvm...1669.   (Card 6)

      Contents--continued.
logus de lamiis, & Pythonicis mulieribus. Ioannis de Gerson Libellus de probatione spirituum. Thomae Murner Libellus de Pythonico contractu. Bartholomaei de Spina Quaestio de strigibus seu maleficis. Eiusdem Apologia quadruplex de lamiis contra Ioan. Franciscum

(Continued on next card)

HCRAFT

    Institoris, Henricus, d. 1508.
      Malleus maleficarvm, maleficas et earvm haeresim framea conterens. Ex variis avctoribvs compilatus, & in tres tomos iustè distributus ... Lvgdvni, Sumptibus Clavdii Landry, 1620.
      2 v. 18cm.

      Title vignettes: device of C. Landry.
      Vol.2, pt.1-2 has title: Mallei malefica-

(Continued on next card)

WITCHCRAFT
BF
1569
A2
I59+
1669

    Institoris, Henricus, d. 1508.
      Malleus maleficarvm, maleficas et earvm haeresim frameâ conterens, ex variis avctoribvs compilatvs, & in quatuor tomos iustè distributus, qvorvm dvo priores vanas daemonvm versutias, praestigiosas eorum delusiones, superstitiosas strigimagarum caeremonias, horrendos etiam cum illis congressus; exactam denique tam pestiferae sectae disquisitionem, & punitionem com-

(Continued on next card)

WITCHCRAFT
BF
1569
A2
I59+
1669

    Institoris, Henricus, d. 1508.
      Malleus maleficarvm...1669.   (Card 7)

      Contents--continued.
Ponzinibium.--v.2, pt.2. Ioan. Laurentij Ananiae Libri 4. de natura daemonum. Bernardi Comensis Tractatus de strigibus. Ambrosij de Vignate Quaestio de lamiis seu strigibus & earum delictis. Ioan. Gersonij Tractatus de erroribus circa artem magicam & articulis

(Continued on next card)

HCRAFT

    Institoris, Henricus, d. 1508.
      Malleus maleficarvm...1620.   (Card 2)

    rvm tractavs aliqvot tam vetervm, quàm recentiorum in vnum corpus coaceruati ... tomi secvndi pars prior [-II].
      Colophon at end of each vol. reads: Ex Typographia Ioannis Royavlx ... 1620.
      Many irregularities in paging.
      A duplicate index for v.2, pt.2 is bound at end of v.   1.

(Continued on next card)

WITCHCRAFT
BF
1569
A2
I59+
1669

    Institoris, Henricus, d. 1508.
      Malleus maleficarvm...   (Card 2)

plectuntur. Tertius praxim exorcistarum ad daemonum, & strigimagarum maleficia de Christi fidelibus pellenda; quartus verò artem doctrinalem, benedictionalem, & exorcismalem continent ... Editio nouissima, infinitis penè mendis expurgata; cuique accessit Fuga daemonum & Complementum

(Continued on next card)

WITCHCRAFT
BF
1569
A2
I59+
1669

    Institoris, Henricus, d. 1508.
      Malleus maleficarvm...1669.   (Card 8)

      Contents--continued.
reprobatis. Ioan. Franc. Leonis Libellus de sortilegiis. Iacobi Simancae Titulus vnicus de lamiis. Alphonsi à Castro Zamorensis De impia sortilegarum, maleficarum & lamiarum haeresi, earúmque punitione, opusculum. Pauli Grillandi Tractatus de sortilegiis, eorúm-

(Continued on next card)

CATALOGUE OF THE CORNELL WITCHCRAFT COLLECTION

WITCHCRAFT
BF 1569 A2 I59+ 1669

Institoris, Henricus, d. 1508.
Malleus maleficarvm...1669. (Card 9)
Contents--continued.
que poenis.--v.3. Flagellum daemonum, autore Hieronymo Mengo. Fustis daemonum, eodem autore. Fuga Satanae, à Petro Antonio Stampa. Flagellum maleficorum autore Petro Mamoris. Tractatus de superstitiosis quibusdam casibus, compilatus per Henricum de Gorchen. --v.4. [Visconti, Zaccaria, Complementum artis exorcisticae.

Witchcraft
BF 1569 A2I59 1906

Institoris, Henricus, d. 1508.
Malleus maleficarum. Der Hexenhammer, verfasst von den beiden Inquisitoren Jakob Sprenger und Heinrich Institoris. Zum ersten Male ins Deutsche übertragen und eingeleitet von J. W. R. Schmidt. Berlin, H. Barsdorf, 1906.
3 v. 20cm.

Translation of Malleus maleficarum.

I. Institoris, Henricus, d. 1508. Malleus maleficarum--German. II. Schmidt, Richard, 1866-1939, tr. III. Title: Der Hexenhammer.

WITCHCRAFT
BF 1569 A2I59++ 1928

[Institoris, Henricus] d. 1508.
Malleus maleficarum, translated with an introduction, bibliography and notes by the Rev. Montague Summers. [London, J. Rodker, 1928.
xlv, 277, [1] p. front. (port.) 31cm.
By Henricus Institoris and Jacob Sprenger.
"This edition of Malleus maleficarum, comprising 1275 numbered copies, is here translated into English from the edition of 1489 for the first time ... This copy is out of series."
"A note upon the bibliography of the Malleus maleficarum": p. xli-xlii.
I. Sprenger, Jakob, 1436 or 8-1495. II. Summers, Montague, 1880-1948, ed. and tr. III. Title.

Witchcraft
BF 1569 A2I59 1948

[Institoris, Henricus] d. 1508.
Malleus maleficarum, translated with an introduction, bibliography and notes by the Rev. Montague Summers. London, Pushkin Press [1948]
xxi, 277 p. port. 23cm.
By Henricus Institoris (Heinrich Krämer) and Jacob Sprenger.
"A note upon the bibliography of the Malleus maleficarum": p. xvii-xviii.
I. Sprenger, Jakob, 1436 or 8-1495. II. Summers, Montague, 1880-1948, tr. III. Title.

WITCHCRAFT
BF 1569 A2 I59 1582

Institoris, Henricus, d. 1508.
Malleorum qvorvndam maleficarvm, tam vetervm quàm recentiorum authorum, tomi dvo. Quorum primus continet: I. Malleum maleficarum Fr. Iacobi Sprengeri, & Fr. Henrici Institoris: Inquisitorum. II. Fr. Ioannis Nider ... qui tractat de maleficis & eorum deceptionibus. Secvndvs verò tomus continet tractatus VII. ibi speciatim nominatos ... Francofvrti [Svmptibvs Nicolai Bassaei, 1582.
8 p. l., 806, [35] p. 16cm.
(Continued on next card)

8 NIC

WITCHCRAFT
BF 1569 A2 I59 1582

Institoris, Henricus, d. 1508.
Malleorum qvorvndam maleficarvm...1582. (Card 2)
Vol. 2 of this ed. is not known to exist; however, vol. 2 of Bassaeus' edition of 1588 has title: Tomvs secvndvs malleorvm qvorvndam maleficarvm, and introduction dated 1582. This form of the title seems peculiar to these two volumes alone, out of the many editions of the Malleus maleficarum. We infer that the two belong together, vol. 1 of 1588 being a "2d ed." of this issue.
I. His Malleus maleficarum. II. Title.

WITCHCRAFT
BF 1565 C36 1889

Institoris, Henricus, d. 1508.
Malleus maleficarum. German.
Catholic Church. Pope, 1484-1492 (Innocentius VIII) Summis desiderantes affectibus (9 Dec. 1484)
Die Hexenbulle, nebst Auszügen aus dem "Hexenhammer." Aus dem Lateinischen ins Deutsche übers. und mit erläuternden Anmerkungen versehen ... 2. Aufl., von Wilhelm Römer. Schaffhausen (Schweiz) 1889.
32 p. 21cm.
"Zum 400jährigen Jubiläum des 'Hexenhammers.'"
(Continued on next card)

8 NIC

WITCHCRAFT
BF 1565 C36 1889

Institoris, Henricus, d. 1508.
Malleus maleficarum. German.
Catholic Church. Pope, 1484-1492 (Innocentius VIII) Summis desiderantes affectibus (9 Dec. 1484)
Die Hexenbulle...1889. (Card 2)
Each page of the Hexenbulle has Latin text at the top, followed by German translation below.

1. Witchcraft. I. Institoris, Henricus, d. 1508. Malleus maleficarum. German. II. Römer, Wilhelm, ed. & tr. III. Title.

Witchcraft
BF 1569 A2I59 1906

Institoris, Henricus, d. 1508.
Malleus maleficarum. German.
Malleus maleficarum. Der Hexenhammer, verfasst von den beiden Inquisitoren Jakob Sprenger und Heinrich Institoris. Zum ersten Male ins Deutsche übertragen und eingeleitet von J. W. R. Schmidt. Berlin, H. Barsdorf, 1906.
3 v. 20cm.

Translation of Malleus maleficarum.

Witchcraft
BV 639 W7 C94+

Institoris, Henricus, d. 1508.
Malleus maleficarum.
Crohns, Hjalmar, 1862-1946.
Die Summa Theologica des Antonin von Florenz und die Schätzung des Weibes im Hexenhammer. [Helsingforsiae, ex Officina typographica Societatis litterariae fennicae, 1906]
1 p. l., 23 p. 28cm. ([Finska vetenskaps-societeten, Helsingfors] Acta Societatis scientiarum fennicae. t. xxxii, no. 4)

8

Witchcraft
BF 1569 A2 I594

Institoris, Henricus, d. 1508.
Malleus maleficarum.
Goff, Frederick Richmond, 1916-
The Library of Congress copy of the Malleus maleficarum, 1487. Copenhagen, Munksgaard, 1963.
[137]-141 p. facsim. 25cm.

"Separatum" from Libri; international library review and IFLA-Communications-FIAB, vol. 13, no. 2, 1963.

1. Institoris, Henricus, d. 1508. Malleus maleficarum. I. Title.

WITCHCRAFT
DD 741 W52 v.26 no.4

Institoris, Henricus, d. 1508.
Malleus maleficarum.
Hansen, Joseph, 1862-1943.
Der Hexenhammer, seine Bedeutung und die gefälschte Kölner Approbation vom Jahre 1487.
(In: Westdeutsche Zeitschrift für Geschichte und Kunst. Trier. 24cm. v.26 (1907) no.4. p. 372-404)

8 NIC

1. Institoris, Henricus, d.1508. Malleus maleficarum. I. Title.

WITCHCRAFT
DD 741 W52 v.27 no.2/3

Institoris, Henricus, d. 1508.
Malleus maleficarum.
Hansen, Joseph, 1862-1943.
Die Kontroverse über den Hexenhammer und seine Kölner Approbation vom Jahre 1487.
(In: Westdeutsche Zeitschrift für Geschichte und Kunst. Trier. 24cm. v.27 (1908) no.2/3. p.366-372)

8 NIC

1. Institoris, Henricus, d.1508. Malleus maleficarum. I. Title.

WITCHCRAFT
DD 741 W52 v.17 no.2

Institoris, Henricus, d. 1508.
Malleus maleficarum.
Hansen, Joseph, 1862-1943.
Der Malleus maleficarum, seine Druckausgaben und die gefälschte Kölner Approbation vom J. 1487.
(In: Westdeutsche Zeitschrift für Geschichte und Kunst. Trier. 24cm. v.17 (1898) no.2. p. 119-168)

8 NIC

1. Institoris, Henricus, d.1508. Malleus maleficarum. I. Title.

WITCHCRAFT
BF 1569 A2 I595

Institoris, Henricus, d. 1508.
Malleus maleficarum.
Hansen, Joseph, 1862-1943.
Der Malleus maleficarum, seine Druckausgaben und die gefälschte Kölner Approbation vom J. 1487. [Trier, 1898]
[119]-168 p. 23cm.
Caption title.
"Sonder-Abdruck aus Westdeutsche Zeitschrift für Geschichte und Kunst." [Bd. 17, Heft 2, 1898]

2 copies

1. Institoris, Henricus, d. 1508. Malleus maleficarum. I. Title.

8 NIC

WITCHCRAFT
BF 1583 A2 S744

Institoris, Henricus, d. 1508.
Malleus maleficarum.
A Jesuit philanthropist. Friedrich von Spee and the Würzburg witches.
(In The Church quarterly review. London. 23cm. v. 57, no. 114 (1904), p. 318-337)
Review of several books by Spee or about his times.
At head of title: Art. V.
1. Spee, Friedrich von, 1591-1635. Cautio criminalis. 2. Institoris, Henricus, d. 1508. Malleus maleficarum. 3. Witchcraft--Germany. I. Title.

8 NIC

BF 1569 Z69

Institoris, Henricus, d. ca. 1500.
Malleus maleficarum.
Zilboorg, Gregory, 1890-
... The medical man and the witch during the renaissance, by Gregory Zilboorg ... Baltimore, The Johns Hopkins press, 1935.
x, 215 p. front. (port.) illus., plates. 20½ᶜᵐ. (Publications of the Institute of the history of medicine, the Johns Hopkins university. ser., vol. II)
"The Hideyo Noguchi lectures."
CONTENTS.--The physiological and psychological aspects of the Malleus maleficarum (The witch's hammer)--Medicine and the witch in the sixteenth century.--Johann Weyer, the founder of modern psychiatry.
1. Witchcraft. 2. Psychology, Pathological. 3. Institoris, Henricus, d. ca. 1500. Malleus maleficarum. 4. Sprenger, Jakob, fl. 1494, joint author. Malleus maleficarum. 5. Wier, Johann, 1515-1588. 6. Renaissance. I. Title.

Library of Congress   HF1569.Z5
——— Copy 2.   35—12064
Copyright A 84565   [40n1]   [150:00140002] 133.40

Witchcraft
BF 1583 C94

Institoris, Henricus, d. 1508.
Crohns, Hjalmar, 1862-1946.
Zwei Förderer des Hexenwahns und ihre Ehrenrettung durch die ultramontane Wissenschaft. Stuttgart, Strecker & Schröder, 1905.
62 p. 20cm.

1. Institoris, Henricus, d. 1508. 2. Antoninus, Saint, abp. of Florence, 1389-1459. 3. Witchcraft. 4. Ultramontanism. I. Title.

CATALOGUE OF THE CORNELL WITCHCRAFT COLLECTION

WITCHCRAFT
BF
569
M2
I596

Institoris, Henricus, d. 1508.
   Müller, Karl Otto, 1884-
   Heinrich Institoris, der Verfasser des Hexenhammers, und seine Tätigkeit als Hexeninquisitor in Ravensburg im Herbst 1484.
   (In: Württembergische Vierteljahrshefte für Landesgeschichte. Stuttgart. 24cm. new ser. v.19, no.4. 1910. p. 397-417)

   1. Institoris, Henricus, d.1508. 2.Trials (Witchcraft) --Ravensburg, Ger.

8
NIC

WITCHCRAFT
4769
no.1

Instructio für die fürstliche Mecklenburgische Beampten und Stadt-Richtere, Mecklenburg. Laws, statutes, etc.
   Instructio für die fürstliche Mecklenburgische Beampten und Stadt-Richtere, wie wieder die dess Zauberlasters und Aberglaubischer-Dinge berüchtigte Personnen zu verfahren. Güstrow, Gedruckt durch Johann Spierling, 1681.
   [8] p. 21cm.
   No. 1 in a vol. of ordinances of Mecklenburg concerning witchcraft.
   1.Witchcraft--Laws and legislation--Mecklenburg. 2.Trials (Witchcraft)--Mecklenburg. I. Title.

8
NIC

Witchcraft
I700
I59

Instructio pro formandis processibus in causis strigum, sortilegiorum, & maleficiorum.
   Inquisition. Rome.
   Instrvctio pro formandis processibus in causis strigum, sortilegiorum, & maleficiorum. [Romae, Ex typographia Rev. Cam. Apost., 1657]
   [8] p. 22cm.
   Caption title.
   "Perhaps the only printed copy in existence of ... the official Instruction of the Roman Inquisition to the prosecution..." -- part of a long note by G. L. Burr inside front cover.
   (Continued on next card)

Witchcraft
I700
I59

Instructio pro formandis processibus in causis strigum, sortilegiorum, & maleficiorum.
   Inquisition. Rome. Instrvctio pro formandis processibus in causis strigum ...
   (Card 2)

   1. Trials (Witchcraft) I. Title.

Witchcraft

Instrumentu[m] cuiusdam sententie retractatis quicquid attentatum est p quoscunq, et qualitercunq +c. auctoritate cuiusdam asserte bulle Gregorii vndecimi contra doctrinam illuminati doctoris Raymundi lulli pii heremite. [Valencia, Impressum per Ioannem Iofredum, 1510]
   [31] p. 22cm.

   1. Lull, Ramón, d. 1315.

Witchcraft
17
I61

Interrogatoire de Maistre Vrbain Grandier, Prestre, Curé de S. Pierre du marché de Loudun, & Chanoyne de l'Eglise Saincte Croix dudit lieu. Avec les confrontations des Religieuses possedées contre le dit Grandier. Ensemble la liste & les noms des Iuges deputez par sa Majesté. A Paris, Chez Estienne Hebert, & Iacques Povllard, 1634.
   10 p. 16cm.
   1. Loudun, France. Ursuline Convent.
   2. Grandier, Urbain, 1590-1634.

WITCHCRAFT
BF
1582
G51
P96
v.1
no.8

Interrogatoires, recollement et confrontation du P. Girard, Jesuite.
   Cadière, Catherine, b. 1709.
   Interrogatoires, recollement et confrontation du P. Girard, Jesuite, et de la Demoiselle Cadière; avec des Observations. Ensemble la revocation de la variation de ladite Demoiselle Cadière, & la confrontation mutuelle avec le Père Nicolas, prieur des Carmes de Toulon. [s.l., 173-?]
   128 p. 17cm.

8
NIC

   No. 8 in vol. lettered: Procès de Girard. [v.1]
   (Continued on next card)

WITCHCRAFT
BT
960
V66

Intorno a' dimonii.
   Vieri, Francesco de, called Il Verino Secondo.
   Discorso dell' eccellentiss. filosofo M. Francesco de' Vieri cognominato il Secondo Verino. Intorno a' dimonii, volgarmente chiamati spiriti... Fiorenza, Appresso Bartolomeo Sermartelli, 1576.
   8 p. l., 108, [1] p. 17cm.

   1. Spirits. 2. Demonology. 3. Witchcraft. I. Title: Intorno a' dimonii.

8

Witchcraft
BF
1600
F62

Io. Ernesti Floerckii I. V. D. Commentatio de crimine conivrationis spirituum.
   Floercke, Johann Ernst von, 1695-1762.
   Io. Ernesti Floerckii I. V. D. Commentatio de crimine conivrationis spirituum eivs processv et poenis praemissis nonnvllis ad magiam svpernatvralem divinam daemoniacam et hvmanam nec non thevrgiam cabbalam et theologiam mysticam pertinentibvs ... Ienae, Apvd Io. Felic. Bielckivm, 1721.
   8 p. l., 522, [33] p. 21cm.
   Title in red and black.
   1. Magic. 2. Witchcraft. 3. Trials (Witchcraft) I. Title: De crimine conivrationis spirituum.

8

WITCHCRAFT
HQ
822
H33
1741

Io. Zachariae Hartmanni ... Commentatio iuridica De coniugibus incantatis.
   Hartmann, Johann Zacharias.
   Io. Zachariae Hartmanni ... Commentatio ivridica De conivgibvs incantatis eorvmqve separatione. Von bezauberten Ehe-Leuten, durch Nesselknüpfen, Schloss zuschnappen &c. und derselben Scheidung. Jenae, Ex officina Schilliana, 1741.
   40, 16 p. 22cm.
   Programma D. Ioh. Zach. Hartmanni ... Dispvtationi ivridicae has special t. p., and is paged separately.
   1. Marriage--Annulment. 2. Spells. I. Title: De conjugibus incantatis.

8

Witchcraft
BF
840
N66

Ioannis Lazari Gutierrii ... Opusculum de fascino.
   Gutierrez, Juan Lazaro, 17th cent.
   Ioannis Lazari Gvtierrii ... Opvscvlvm de fascino ... Lvgdvni, Sumpt. Philip. Borde, Lavr. Arnavd, & Cl. Rigavd, 1653.
   [8], 210, [15] p. 24cm.
   Engraved title vignette: publishers' device.
   Bound with Nicquet, Honorat. Physiognomia hvmana. Lvgdvni, 1648.

   1. Magic. 2. Witchcraft. I. Title: De fascino. II. Title. III. Title: Opusculum de fascino.

Witchcraft
BS
2545
D5
S47
1769

Ioannis Salomonis Semleri ... Commentatio de daemoniacis quorum in N. T. fit mentio.
   Semler, Johann Salomo, 1725-1791.
   Ioannis Salomonis Semleri ... Commentatio de daemoniacis qvorvm in N. T. fit mentio. Editio avctior. Halae Magdebvrgicae, Impensis I. C. Hendelii, 1769.
   62 p. 21cm.
   First published 1760 under title: De daemoniacis, quorum in Evangeliis fit mentio. (Title from Kayser)

WITCHCRAFT
BT
80
T83
1515

Ioannis Tritemii ... Liber octo questionū ad Maximilianum Cesarem.
   Trithemius, Johannes, 1462-1516.
   Ioannis Tritemii ... Liber octo questionū ad Maximilianum Cesarem. Cum priuilegio Cesaree maiestatis de nō imprimedo in regno ... [Oppenheym, Impressum impensis Iohānis Hasselbergen de Augia Constātiensis dyocesis, 1515]
   [78] p. 20cm.
   Title vignette with ports. of Maximilian and Trithemius.
   With colophon.

8
NIC
   (Continued on next card)

WITCHCRAFT
BF
1584
D4
Z7
1698a

Ipsen, Alfred, 1852-1922, ed.
   Arni Magnússon, 1663-1730.
   Kort og sandfærdig beretning om den vidtudraabte besættelse udi Thisted. Til alles efterretning af original-akter og troværdige dokumenter uddragen og sammenskreven af Arne Magnusson [sic]. Paany udgiven af Alfred Ipsen. Kjøbenhavn, J. Gjellerups Forlag, 1891.
   112 p. 18cm.
   Reprinted from ed. of 1699.
   1.Björn, Ole, b.1648. 2. Trials (Witchcraft) --Thisted, Denmark. I. Ipsen, Alfred, 1852-1922, ed. II. Title.

8
NIC

Witchcraft
BF
1565
T461
1729

Ipsen, Johann Paul, respondent.
   Thomasius, Christian, 1655-1728, praeses.
   Disputatio juris canonici De origine ac progressu processus inquisitorii contra sagas, quam ... praeside Dn. Christiano Thomasio ... subiicit die XXX. Aprilis A. M DCC XII ... Johannes Paulus Ipsen ... Halae Magdeburgicae, Apud J. C. Hendelium, 1729.
   68 [i.e. 76] p. 23cm.
   Pages 73-76 numbered 65-68.
   Diss.--Halle (J. P. Ipsen, respondent)

8
   (Continued on next card)

Witchcraft
BF
1581
S52
1913

Irish witchcraft and demonology.
   Seymour, St. John Drelincourt.
   Irish witchcraft and demonology. Baltimore, Norman, Remington & Co., 1913.
   vii, 255 p. 21cm.

   1. Witchcraft--Ireland. 2. Demonology. I. Title.

Witchcraft
BF
1040
I72
miniature

Irwin, Frank.
   The Blocksberg tryst. Franklin. N. H., Hillside Press, 1963.
   70 p. illus. 60 mm.
   "310 numbered copies ... Number 205."
   CONTENTS.--The Blocksberg tryst.--Peyote and pomades.--Magic under duress.--The Hexenhammer.--Dimensions beyond time.

   1. Psychical research. 2. Witchcraft. I. Title.

   BF1040.I7   63-3827
   Library of Congress   [1]

WITCHCRAFT
BF
1584
S9
I76

Isberg, Anders Ulrik Martin, 1867-1940.
   Häxboken; kulturhistoriska skildringar från det gamla Malmö, af A. U. Isberg. 1. delen. [Malmö, Bröderna Forssells boktryckeri, 1916]
   256 p. illus. 24cm.

   No more published?

   1. Witchcraft--Malmö, Sweden. I. Title.

8
NIC

CATALOGUE OF THE CORNELL WITCHCRAFT COLLECTION

WITCHCRAFT
BT 780 I85

Isolani, Isidoro, d. 1528.
 Libellus aduersus magos, diuinatores, maleficos, eosue qui ad religionē subeundam maleficis artib' quempiam cogi posse asseuerant. ₍Mediolani, Ex officina I. A. Scinzenzeler, 1506₎
 ₍56₎ p. 20cm.

8
NIC

 1. Conversion—Early works to 1800. 2. Occult sciences. I. Title.

Witchcraft
BF 1565 C12

Cäsar, Aquilin Julius.
 Ist die Nichtigkeit der Zauberey ganz erwiesen?
 Ist die Nichtigkeit der Zauberey ganz erwiesen? ₍München₎ 1789.
 56 p. 18cm.

 With this are bound his Abhandlung von Erscheinung der Geister. München, 1789, and his Meine Bedenken von den Besessenen der Welt vorgelegt. München, 1789.

 1. Witchcraft. I. Title.

HV 9644 I95

Ives, George Cecil, 1867-
 A history of penal methods; criminals, witches, lunatics, by George Ives, M.A. London, S. Paul & co. ₍1914₎
 xi, 409 p. 23cm.

 "Index to authors ₍with titles of works₎": p. 384-396.

 1. Prisons—Gt. Brit. 2. Crime and criminals—Gt. Brit. 3. Punishment. I. Title: Penal methods, A history of. II. Title.

CATALOGUE OF THE CORNELL WITCHCRAFT COLLECTION

J

J., M.

Witchcraft

The **Hartfordshire** wonder; or, Strange news from Ware. Being an exact and true relation of one Jane Stretton, the daughter of Thomas Stretton of Ware in the county of Herts, who hath been visited in a strange kind of manner by extraordinary and unusual fits, her abstaining from sustenance for the space of 9 months, being haunted by imps or devils in the form of several creatures here described, the parties adjudged of all by whom she was thus tormented and the occasion thereof ...

(Continued on next card) 17-20383

J., M.

Witchcraft

The **Hartfordshire** wonder ... (Card 2)
London: printed for J. Clark ... 1669. Reprinted with an introductory note by W. B. Gerish. Bishop's Stortford, 1908.
15 p. 22cm. (Hertfordshire folk lore. no. 8)
Preface signed: M. J.

1. Stretton, Jane, b. 1649. 2. Witchcraft—England. I. J., M. III. Gerish, William Blyth, ed.

17-20383

Library of Congress   GR142.H6A3 no. 5

J. D.

Witchcraft

La sorcière de Munster (Catherine Huger): sa torture à Wihr-au-Val et son exécution à Gunsbach, MDCXXXI. Colmar, E. Barth, 1869.
15 p. 23cm.

Signed: J. D.

1. Huger, Catherine, d. 1631. 2. Witchcraft. I. D., J. II. J. D.

J. D. V. B. T. K.

Witchcraft

Kort-bondige, en voor alle onpartydige, verstaanbare, en met de reeden overeenkomende verklaaringe; van de verleydinge onser eerste voor-ouderen, Adam ende Eva in het Paradys. Volgens de beschryving van Moses, in het boek der Scheppinge. Door J. D. V. B. T. K. Amsterdam, By J. Roman, boekverkoper, 1699.
22, (1) p. (p. 24 blank) title and end page vignettes, illus. initial. 20 x 15cm.
4°: A-C⁴.

(Continued on next card)

J. D. V. B. T. K.

Witchcraft

Kort-bondige, en voor alle onpartydige, verstaanbare ... verklaaringe ... 1699.
(Card 2)

Black letter.
No. 7 in vol. lettered B. Bekkers sterfbed en andere tractaten.

1. Fall of man. 2. Devil. I. J. D. V. B. T. K. II. K., J. D. V. B. T.

J. F. B.

Witchcraft
BD
428
B54

Bertram, Johann Friedrich, 1699-1741.
Ob die Thiere Teufel seyn? wird durch Veranlassung dess von einem Französischen Jesuiten P. Bonjeau unlängst ans Licht gestellten neuen Lehr-Begriffs von den Seelen der Thiere genannt: Amusements philosophiques sur le langage des bestes; oder: Philosophischer Zeit-Vertreib über die Thier-Sprache; in welchen sie zu Teufeln gemachet werden; nach Schrifft und Vernunfft untersuchet und beantwortet, von J.F. B. (Bremen) S. Pomarius (1740)
(15), 94 p. 16cm.

J. F. Z.

Witchcraft
BF
1565
S83
no.3

Drey Fragen zur Vertheidigung der Hexerey. I. Ob P. Angelus März die Rede des P. Don Ferdinand Sterzingers gründlich, und II. bescheiden widerleget habe? III. Und ob wohl diese akademische Rede dem heiligen Kreutze von Scheyrn in der That nachtheilig sey? Mit einem sichern Ja beantwortet, und dem P. Angelus März selbst dedicirt von J. F. Z. ... (München?) 1767.
28 p. 23cm.

8   (Continued on next card)

J. F. Z.

Witchcraft
BF
1565
S83
no.3

Drey Fragen zur Vertheidigung der Hexerey ... 1767.   (Card 2)

"In spite of the initials J. F. Z. (Johann Felix Zech) in the dedication, the work is probably by H. Braun. See Fieger, H. P. Don Ferdinand Sterzingers, 1907."—Note by G. L. Burr on his ms. catalog slip for this item.
No. 3 in vol. lettered Sterzinger über Hexerei, 1766-1767.

8   (Continued on next card)

J.-K. Huysmans et le satanisme, d'après des documents inédits.

Witchcraft
PQ
2309
H4
L111

Bricaud, Joanny.
J.-K. Huysmans et le satanisme, d'après des documents inédits. Paris, Bibliothèque Chacornac, 1913.
77 p. 17cm.

Inscribed by the author to "Monsieur J. Brien."

1. Huysmans, Joris Karl, 1848-1907. Là-bas. 2. Devil. I. Title.

J. N. A.

Witchcraft
BF
1565
S19

Samuel and the witch of Endor; or, The sin of witchcraft. (Battle Creek, Mich.) Seventh-Day Adventist Pub. Association, 18—)
32 p. 18cm.

Caption title.
Signed: J. N. A.

1. Witchcraft. I. Title: The sin of witchcraft. II. A., J. N. III. J. N. A.

J. P.

Witchcraft
BF
1410
B42
Z56
v.3
no.20

De Volmaakte kragt Godts verheerlykt. Nevens eenige aanmerkinge over de drie predikatien van Do. Petrus Schaak. Gedaan over Psal. 72: v. 18. Gen. 18: v. 1,2 ... en Gen. 32: v. 24, 25. In haar eigen gronden ondersogt, en met de waarheid vergeleken. En eenige andere aanmerkingen daar by gevoegd. Amsterdam, By D. vanden Dalen, boekverkooper, 1691.
47 p. (p. 48 blank) title and other vignettes illus. initial. 19 x 15cm.
4°: A-F⁴.

(Continued on next card)

J. P.

Witchcraft
BF
1410
B42
Z56
v.3
no.20

De Volmaakte kragt Godts verheerlykt. 1691.
(Card 2)

Black letter.
Preface signed: J: P. L: R.
Supports B. Bekker against Schaak's attacks on Bekker's De betoverde weereld.
Van der Linde 145.
No. 20 in vol. lettered Bekker III.

J. S.

Witchcraft
BX
9479
B42
B11
no.6

(Silvius, J)
Consideratien over het boek van de Heer Doctor Balthasar Bekker, genaamt De betoverde weereld, voorgestelt door J. S. Amsterdam, By G. Borstius, boekverkoper, 1691.
20 p. title vignette, illus. initials. 20 x 15cm.
4°: π1, A-B⁴, C1.
Black letter (except for introduction)
Ascribed to J. Silvius by Doorninck.
Variant of van der Linde 149:

8   (Continued on next card)

J. S.

Witchcraft
BX
9479
B42
B11
no.6

(Silvius, J) Consideratien over het boek van de Heer Doctor Balthasar Bekker ... 1691.   (Card 2)

only 20, instead of 22 p.
No. 6 in vol. lettered B. Bekkers sterfbed en andere tractaten.

1. Bekker, Balthasar, 1634-1698. De betoverde weereld. I. Title. II. J. S. III. S., J.

J. S. F.

Witchcraft
BF
1411
F73
1827

(Forsyth, J S)
Demonologia; or, Natural knowledge revealed; being an exposé of ancient and modern superstitions, credulity, fanaticism, enthusiasm, & imposture, as connected with the doctrine, caballa, and jargon, of amulets, apparitions, astrology, charms, demonology ... witchcraft, &c. ... By J. S. F. ... London, J. Bumpus, 1827.
1 p. l., (v)-xvi, 438 p. front. 19cm.
By J. S. Forsyth, cf. Halkett and Laing, Dict. anon. and pseud., new ed., 1926, v.2, p. 37.

CATALOGUE OF THE CORNELL WITCHCRAFT COLLECTION

Witchcraft
BV 30 G83
Jacobi Gretseri ... De festis Christianorum libri duo.
Gretser, Jacob, 1560-1625.
  Jacobi Gretseri ... De festis Christianorvm libri dvo. Adversvs Danaevm, Dresservm, Hospinianvm, aliosqve sectarios ... Ingolstadii, Excudebat Andreas Angermarivs, Sumptibvs Ioannis Hertsroy, 1612.
  16 p. l., 371, [25] p. 20cm.
  Gilt supra libros.
  With this is bound his Libri duo De benedictionibus, et tertius De maledictionibus. Ingolstadii, 1615.

8   (Continued on next card)

Witchcraft
PT 2430 M35 M3 1895
Jacobs, Joseph, 1854-1916, ed.
  Meinhold, Wilhelm, 1797-1851.
    The amber witch, a romance. Translated by Lady Duff Gordon. Edited, with an introd. by Joseph Jacobs, and illustrated by Philip Burne-Jones. London, D. Nutt, New York, Scribner, 1895.
    xxxviii, 221 p. illus. 20cm.
    Translation of his Maria Schweidler, die Bernsteinhexe.
  I. Title. II. Jacobs, Joseph, 1854-1916, ed. III. His   Maria Schweidler, die Bernsteinhexe--   English.

BF 1584 D4 J172
Jacobsen, Jørgen Carl, 1916-
  Christenze Kruckow. En adelig Troldkvinde fra Chr. IV's Tid. [Af] J. C. Jacobsen. København, Gad, 1972.
  8, 96 p. 25cm.

  1. Kruckow, Christence, d. 1621. 2. Trials (Witchcraft)--Denmark. I. Title.

3 NIC

BF 1584 D5 J17
Jacobsen, Jørgen Carl, 1916-
  Danske Domme i Trolddomssager i øverste Instans. Indledning og kommentar, af J. C. Jacobsen. [København] I kommission: G.E.C.Gad, 1966.
  20, 309 p. 24cm.
  Bibliography: p. xi-xx.

  1. Witchcraft--Denmark. I. Title.

BF 1584 D4 J171
Jacobsen, Jørgen Carl, 1916–
  Den sidste Hexebrænding i Danmark 1693. [Af] J. C. Jacobsen. København, Gad, 1971.
  xi, 110 p. 25 cm. kr27.60   D 71-26/27

3

  1. Witchcraft—Denmark. I. Title.
  BF1584.D4J3   77-853942
  ISBN 87-12-36475-4
  Library of Congress   71 [2]

MSS Bd. RARE B J17
Jacobus, of Jüterbogk, 1381-1465.
  De potestate daemonum, arte magica, superstitionibus ...
  Jacobus, of Jüterbogk, 1381-1465.
    [Treatises. s.l., 1762-65]
    10 pts. in 1 v. ([257] l.) 21cm.
    Copies of the original manuscripts, made 1762-65.
    Bound in boards with parchment back and corners.
    Contents.--Colloquium hominis ad animam suam.--De conflictu inter amorem dei & mundi.--De statibus mundi.--De VII statibus Ecclesiae in   Apocalypsi descriptis, & De authorita   te Ecclesiae ac eiusdem

8 NIC   (Continued on next card)

MSS Bd. RARE B J17
Jacobus, of Jüterbogk, 1381-1465.
  De potestate daemonum, arte magica, superstitionibus ...
  Jacobus, of Jüterbogk, 1381-1465.   [Treatises. 1762-65]   (Card 2)
  reformatione.--De statu securiori incedendi in hac vita.--De partitione reddituū inter religiosos.--De receptione & proventibus monialium & aliorum religiosorum deque propietate.--De contractibus & redemptionibus.--De indulgentiis anni jubilei.--De potestate daemonum, arte magica, superstitionibus & illusionibus   eorundem.

     (Continued on next card)

MSS Bd. RARE B J17
Jacobus, of Jüterbogk, 1381-1465.
  [Treatises. s.l., 1762-65]
  10 pts. in 1 v. ([257] l.) 21cm.
  Copies of the original manuscripts, made 1762-65.
  Bound in boards with parchment back and corners.
  Contents.--Colloquium hominis ad animam suam.--De conflictu inter amorem dei & mundi.--De statibus mundi.--De VII statibus Ecclesiae in   Apocalypsi descriptis, & De authorita   te Ecclesiae ac eiusdem

8 NIC   (Continued on next card)

MSS Bd. RARE B J17
Jacobus, of Jüterbogk, 1381-1465.   [Treatises. 1762-65]   (Card 2)
reformatione.--De statu securiori incedendi in hac vita.--De partitione reddituū inter religiosos.--De receptione & proventibus monialium & aliorum religiosorum deque propietate.--De contractibus & redemptionibus.--De indulgentiis anni jubilei.--De potestate daemonum, arte magica, superstitionibus & illusionibus   eorundem.

     (Continued on next card)

MSS Bd. RARE B J17
Jacobus, of Jüterbogk, 1381-1465.   [Treatises. 1762-65]   (Card 3)
  1. Theology--Collected works--Middle Ages. 2. Catholic Church--Collected works. 3. Monastic and religious life. 4. Demonology. 5. Devil. V. His/ De potestate daemonum, arte magica, superstitionibus... VI. Title: De potestate daemonum, arte magica, superstitionibus...

Jacobus, Hochstratus, ca. 1460-1527.
  see
Hoogstraten, Jacobus van, ca. 1460-1527.

BF 1602 J19
Jacques d'Autun, Father, 1608 (ca.)-1678.
  L'incredvlité sçavante, et la credvlité ignorante: au sujet des magiciens et des sorciers. Auecque la response à vn liure intitulé Apologie pour tous les grands personnages, qui ont esté faussement soupçonnés de magie. Par le P. Iaqves d'Avtvn, predicateur Capucin. Lyon, Iean Molin, 1671.
  [40], 1108, [24] p. 24cm.
  The leaf bearing p. 935-936 is mutilated, but between the last two leaves of the index

     (Continued on next card)

Witchcraft
BF 1602 J19
Jacques d'Autun, Father, 1608 (ca.)-1678.
  L'incredvlité sçavante ... 1671.   (Card 2)
  is inserted the same leaf of the edition of 1674, together with a fly-leaf.

Witchcraft
BF 1602 J19 1674
Jacques d'Autun, Father, 1608 (ca.)-1678.
  L'incredvlité sçavante, et la credvlité ignorante: au sujet des magiciens et des sorciers. Auecque la response à vn liure intitulé Apologie pour tous les grands personnages, qui ont esté faussement soupçonnés de magie. Par le R.P. Iaqves d'Avtvn, predicateur Capucin. Lyon, Iean Certe, 1674.
  [40], 1108, [24] p. 24cm.
  Title vignette (woodcut)
  I. Naudé, Gabriel, 1600-1653. Apologie pour tous les grands   personnages, qui ont esté faussement soupç   onnez de magie. II. Titl

---

Witchcraft
BF 1565 J19
Jacquier, Nicolas.
  Flagellvm haereticorvm fascinariorvm, avtor Nicolao Iaqverio. His accesservnt Lamberti Danaei de veneficis dialogi, Ioachimi Camerari in Plutarchi de oraculorum defectu epistola, Martini de Arles de superstitionibus tractatvs Ioannis Trithemii de reprobis atq; maleficis qvaestiones III, Thomae Erasti de strigibus liber. Francofvrti ad Moenvm [Impressvm apud N. Bassaeum] 1581.
  604 p. 17cm.

     (Continued on next card

Witchcraft
BF 1565 J19
Jacquier, Nicolas. Flagellvm haereticorvm fascinariorvm ... 1581.   (Card 2)
  1. Witchcraft. I. Daneau, Lambert, ca. 1530-1595. De veneficis. II. Camerarius, Joachim, 1500-1574. Prooemium in libellum Plutarchi de defectu oraculorum. III. Arles y Androsilla, Martín de. Tractatus de superstitionibus. IV. Trithemius, Johannes, 1462-1516. Tractatus de reprobis atque maleficis. V. Erastus, Thomas, 1524-1583. Dispvtatio de lamiis, sev strigibvs

     (Continued on next card)

Witchcraft
BF 1565 J19
Jacquier, Nicolas. Flagellvm haereticorvm fascinariorvm ... 1581.   (Card 3)
  VI. Myntzenbergius, Ioannes, ed. VII. Title. VIII. Title: De veneficis. IX. Title: Prooemium in libellum Plutarchi de defectu oraculorum. X. Title: Tractatus de superstitionibus. XI. Title: Tractatus de reprobis atque maleficis. XII. Title: Dispvtatio de lamiis, sev strigibv

---

Jäger,   Dr., Pfarrer in Pföring an der Donau.

  see

Jäger, Franz Anton, 1765-1835.

CATALOGUE OF THE CORNELL WITCHCRAFT COLLECTION

WITCHCRAFT

Jäger, Franz Anton, 1765-1835.
Geschichte des Hexenbrennens in Franken im siebzehnten Jahrhundert, aus Original-Prozess-Akten, von Dr. Jäger, Pfarrer in Pföring an der Donau. [Würzburg, 1834]
72 p. 23cm.

Caption title.
Detached from Historischer Verein von Unterfranken und Aschaffenburg. Archiv. 2. Bd.
1. Witchcraft--Franconia. I. Title.

WITCHCRAFT

Jahn, Ulrich, 1861-1900.
Hexenwesen und Zauberei in Pommern. Breslau, Im Commissionsverlag bei W. Koebner, 1886.
196 p. 23cm.

Originally published in Baltische Studien, Jahrg. 36. Also issued as a Separatabdruck thereof.
I. Title.

Jahn, Ulrich, 1861-1900.
Hexenwesen und Zauberei in Pommern. [Niederwalluf bei Wiesbaden] M. Sändig [1970]
196 p. 21cm.
Reprint of the 1886 ed.

1. Witchcraft--Pomerania. 2. Magic--Pomerania. I. Title

NOV 06, '73   00xc   72-548286

Witchcraft

Jamblichus of Chalcis.
[De mysteriis. Greek & Latin]
Ἰαμβλίχου Χαλκιδέως τῆς κοίλης Συρίας περὶ μυστηρίων λόγος. Iamblichi Chalcidensis ex Coele-Syria, de mysteriis liber. Praemittitur epistola Porphyrii ad Anebonem AEgyptium, eodem argumento. Thomas Gale Anglus graece nunc primum edidit, latine vertit, & notas adjecit. Oxonii, e theatro Sheldoniano, 1678.
20 p. l., 316, [6] p., 1 l. 32cm.
(Continued on next card)

Jamblichus of Chalcis. [De mysteriis. Greek & Latin] Ἰαμβλίχου Χαλκιδέως τῆς κοίλης Συρίας περὶ μυστηρίων λόγος. 1678. (Card 2)

Title vignette.
Greek and Latin in parallel columns.

1. Mysteries, Religious. I. Porphyrius. II. Gale, Thomas, 1635?-1702, ed. Title transliterated: Peri mysterion logos.

Witchcraft

Jamblichus, of Chalcis.
[De mysteriis. English]
Iamblichus on the Mysteries of the Egyptians, Chaldeans, and Assyrians. Translated from the Greek by Thomas Taylor ... Chiswick, Printed by C. Whittinghams for the translator. 1821.
xxiv, 365 p. 22-1/2 cm.

"The epistle of Porphyry to the Egyptian Anebo": p. [1]-16.
I. Porphyrius. II. Taylor, Thomas, 1758-1835, tr. III. Title.

WITCHCRAFT
PA 4220 L3 A4+ 1516

Jamblichus, of Chalcis.
[De mysteriis. Latin]
Iamblichus De mysteriis Aegyptiorum, Chaldaeorum, Assyriorum. Proclus In Platonicum Alcibiadem de anima, atq; daemone. Proclus De sacrificio, & magia. Porphyrius De diuinis, atq; daemonibus. Synesius Platonicus De somniis. Psellus De daemonibus. Expositio Prisciani, & Marsilii in Theophrastum De sensu, phantasia, & intellectu. Alcinoi Platonici philosophi, Liber de doctrina

8   (Continued on next card)

WITCHCRAFT
PA 4220 L3 A4+ 1516

Jamblichus, of Chalcis. [De mysteriis. Latin] [1516]   (Card 2)

Platonis. Speusippi Platonis discipuli, Liber de Platonis definitionibus. Pythagorae philosophi Aurea uerba. Symbola Pithagorae philosophi. Xenocratis philosophi platonici, Liber de morte. Mercurii Trismegisti Pimander. Eiusdem Asclepius. Marsilii Ficini De triplici uita lib. II. Eiusdem Liber de uoluptate. Eiusdem

8   (Continued on next card)

WITCHCRAFT
PA 4220 L3 A4+ 1516

Jamblichus, of Chalcis. [De mysteriis. Latin] [1516]   (Card 3)

De sole & lumine libri. II. Apologia eiusdem in librum suum de lumine. Eiusdem Libellus de magis. Quod necessaria sit securitas, & tranquillitas animi. Praeclarissimarum sententiarum huius operis breuis annotatio. [Venetiis, In aedibvs Aldi, et Andreae soceri, 1516]
177 [i.e., 175] numbered leaves.
8   29cm.   (Continued on next card)

WITCHCRAFT
PA 4220 L3 A4+ 1516

Jamblichus, of Chalcis. [De mysteriis] Latin. [1516]   (Card 4)

At head of title: Index eorvm, qvae hoc in libro habentvr.
With colophon.
Provenance: Bibliotec: SS. Me. Novelle.
Translations by M. Ficino.
1. Occult sciences. 2. Philosophy, Ancient--Collections. I. Proclus Diadochus. In Platonicum Alcibiadem. II. Proclus Diadochus. De sacrificio. III.
8   (Continued on next card)

WITCHCRAFT
PA 4220 L3 A4+ 1516

Jamblichus, of Chalcis. [De mysteriis. Latin] [1516]   (Card 5)

Porphyrius. De diuinis, atque daemonibus. IV. Synesius, Cyrenaeus, bp. of Ptolemais. De somniis. V. Psellus, Michael. De daemonibus. VI. Priscianus. Metaphrasis in Theophrasti De sensu. VII. Albinus. De doctrina Platonis liber. VIII. Speusippus, fl. 347-339 B. C. Liber de Platonis definitionibus. IX. Pythagoras. X.
8   Xenocrates, of Chalcedon, ca. 396-
         (Continued on next card)

WITCHCRAFT
PA 4220 L3 A4+ 1516

Jamblichus, of Chalcis. [De mysteriis. Latin] [1516]   (Card 6)

ca. 314 B. C. Spurious and doubtful works. De morte. XI. Hermes Trismegistus. Poemander. Latin. XII. Hermes Trismegistus. Asclepius. XIII. Ficino, Marsilio, 1433-1499. XIV. Title: Index eorum, quae hoc in libro habentur.

8

Witchcraft
PA 4220 L3 A4 1556

Jamblichus, of Chalcis.
[De mysteriis. Latin]
Iamblichvs De mysteriis Ægyptiorvm, nunc primùm ad uerbum de graeco expressus. Nicolao Scvtellio ... interprete. Adiecti de uita & secta Pythagorae flosculi, ab eodem Scutellio ex ipso Iamblicho collecti. Romæ, apvd Antonivm Bladum pontificis maximi excusorem, 1556.
[20], 148 p. 21cm.

"Ampliss. dominis s. r. e. cardinalibus ... Christophoro Madrutio ... & Othoni Trvccis ... Scipio Bongallus ... episcopus. s. p. d.": 2d-3d prelim. leaves.
"De uita & secta Pythagorae flosculi" not in this copy.
1. Religion--Philosophy. 2. Demonology. 3. Supernatural. 4. Mysticism. 5. Occult sciences. I. Scutelli, Niccolò, d. 1542, tr.
Library of Congress   [2]   CA 28-981 Unrev'd

Witchcraft
PA 4220 L3 A4 1577

Jamblichus, of Chalcis.
[De mysteriis. Latin]
Iamblichvs De mysteriis Ægyptiorvm, Chaldæorum, Assyriorum. Proclvs in Platonicum Alcibiadem de anima, atque dæmone. Porphyrvs De diuinis atq; dæmonib. Psellvs De dæmonibus. Mercvrii Trismegisti Pimander. Eiusdem Asclepius. Lvgdvni, apvd Ioan. Tornaesivm, 1577.
543, [1] p. 13cm.
Title vignette (printer's mark)
"Marsilivs Ficinvs ... se commendat": p. 3.
I. Proclus Diadochus. II. Porphyrius. III. Psellus, Michael. IV. Hermes Trismegistus. V. Ficino, Marsilio, 1433-1499, tr.   25-19681

Jamblichus, of Chalcis.
De mysteriis. Latin.

WITCHCRAFT
BF 1598 H55 A1 1532

Hermes Trismegistus.
[Poemander. Latin]
Mercvrii Trismegisti Pymander, De potestate et sapientia Dei. Eivsdem Asclepivs, De uoluntate Dei. Opuscula sanctissimis mysterijs, ac uerè coelestibus oraculis illustrissima. Iamblichvs De mysterijs Aegyptiorum, Chaldaeorum, & Assyriorū. Proclvs In Platonicum Alcibiadem, de anima & daemone. Idem De sacrificio & magia. Quae omnia solerti cura repurgata, ac suo tandem
8   (Continued on next card)

Jamblichus, of Chalcis.
De mysteriis. Latin.

WITCHCRAFT
BF 1598 H55 A1 1532

Hermes Trismegistus. [Poemander. Latin] 1532.   (Card 2)

candori restituta sunt. Basileae [Per Mich. Isingrinivm] 1532.
480, [3] p. 16cm.
With colophon.
The Asclepius translated by Apuleius Madaurensis; the rest by Marsilio Ficino.
I. Jamblichus, of Chalcis. De mysteriis. Latin. II. Proclus Diadochus. III. Apuleius Madaurensis, tr. IV. Ficino, Marsilio, 1433-1499, tr. V. His Asclepius.

WITCHCRAFT
DA 391 A13++

James I, king of Great Britain, 1566-1625.
The workes of the most high and mightie prince, Iames, by the grace of God, king of Great Britaine, France and Ireland, defender of the faith, &c. Pvblished by Iames, bishop of Winton, and dean of His Maiesties chappel royall. London, Printed by Robert Barker and Iohn Bill, printers to the Kings Most Excellent Maiestie. Anno 1616.
21 p. l., 569, [1] p. illus., port. 36cm.
8
NIC   (Continued on next card)

WITCHCRAFT
DA 391 A13++

James I, king of Great Britain, 1566-1625.
The workes of the most high and mightie prince... 1616.   (Card 2)
Added t. p., engraved.
First edition, first issue.
Contents.--A paraphrase vpon the Reuelation.--Daemonologie.--Basilicon-doron.--The trew law of free monarchies.--A counter-blast to tobacco.--A discourse of the powder treason.--An apologie for the oath of allegiance.--A praemonition
8
NIC   (Continued on next card)

CATALOGUE OF THE CORNELL WITCHCRAFT COLLECTION

WITCHCRAFT
DA
391
A13++

James I, king of Great Britain, 1566-1625.
The workes of the most high and mightie prince... 1616. (Card 3)

Contents--Continued.
to all Christian monarches, free princes and states.--A declaration against Vorstius.--A defence of the right of kings, against Cardinall Perron.--Fiue speaches.

8
NIC

FILM
470
reel
239

James I, king of Great Britain, 1566-1625.
Daemonologie, in forme of a dialogue, diuided in three bookes. Edinbvrgh Printed by Robert Walde-graue ... 1597 ...

"The preface to the reader" signed: Iames R.
University microfilms no. 12336 (case 40, carton 239)
Short-title catalogue no. 14364.

1. Demonology.

FILM
470
reel
239

James I, king of Great Britain, 1566-1625.
Daemonologie, in forme of a dialogue, diuided in three bookes. Edinbvrgh Printed by Robert Walde-graue ... 1597 ...

"The preface to the reader" signed: Iames R.
University microfilms no. 12336 (case 40, carton 239)
Short-title catalogue no. 14364 (variant).

1. Demonology.

Witchcraft
BF
1521
J28
1603

James I, King of Great Britain, 1566-1625.
Daemonologie, in forme of dialogve, diuided in three books ... London, Printed by Arnold Hatfield for Robert Wald-graue, 1603.
[8], 64 (i.e. 80) p. 18cm.

"The preface to the reader" signed: Iames R.
Errors in paging: 73 and 80 numbered 57 and 64.
With copy 2 of this is bound the author's An apologie for the oath of allegiance. London, 1609.

BF
1521
J28
1924

James I, king of Great Britain, 1566-1625.
King James, the First: Daemonologie (1597). Newes from Scotland, declaring the damnable life and death of Doctor Fian, a notable sorcerer who was burned at Edenbrough in Ianuary last (1591) London, J. Lane; New York, Dutton [1924]
xv, 81, 29 p. illus. 19cm. (The Bodley head quartos, no. 9)
With facsimiles of original title pages.
Newes from Scotland has been ascribed to James Carmichael, minister of
(Continued on next card)

BF
1521
J28
1924

James I, king of Great Britain, 1566-1625.
King James, the First: Daemonologie ... [1924] (Card 2)

Haddington. Cf. Sir James Melville, Memories, p. 195, and D. Webster, Collection of tracts on witchcraft, etc., 1820, p. 38.
1. Demonology. 2. Magic. 3. Witchcraft--Scotland. 4. Fian, John, d. 1591. I. Harrison, George Bagshawe, 1894- ed. II. Carmichael, James, d. 1628, supposed author. III. Title: Daemonologie. IV. Title: Newes from Scotland.

Witchcraft
BF
1581
K62
1912

Kittredge, George Lyman, 1860-1941.
English witchcraft and James the First, by George Lyman Kittredge; from Studies in the history of religions presented to Crawford Howell Toy, by pupils, colleagues and friends. New York The Macmillan company, 1912.
cover-title, 65 p. 23½cm.

With this is bound his King James I and The Devil is an ass.
Cover has initials of author (G.L.K.) and donor (J.M.H., i.e. J. M. Hart)

Witchcraft
BF
1563
W81++
no.9

James, Anthony, d. 1602.
The Most crvell and bloody mvrther committed by ... Annis Dell and her sonne George Dell, foure yeeres since, on ... Anthony Iames ... and now most miraculously reuealed by the sister of the said Anthony ... With the seuerall vvitchcrafts and most damnable practises of one Iohane Harrison and her daughter vpon seuerall persons ... who were all executed ... the 4 of August last past ... London, Printed for W. Firebrand
(Continued on next card)

Witchcraft
BF
1563
W81++
no.9

James, Anthony, d. 1602.
The Most crvell and bloody mvrther... 1606. [1923] (Card 2)

and J. Wright, 1606. [London, at the British Museum, 1923]
[24] p. 17cm.

Signatures: A-C⁴.
Photocopy (negative) 24 p. on 13 l. 20 x 32cm.
No. 9 in vol. lettered: Witchcraft tracts chapbooks and broadsides, 1579-1704; rotograph copies.

WITCHCRAFT
BF
1578
S55
A2
1894

James, Edward Wilson, d. 1906, ed.
Sherwood, Grace, defendant.
Grace Sherwood, the Virginia witch. Communicated by Edward W. James.

(In: William and Mary college quarterly historical magazine. Williamsburg, Va. 25cm. v.3, no.2, Oct. 1894, p. 96-101; v.3, no.3, Jan. 1895, p. 190-192)

Witchcraft Collection has only the first two of five articles. Cornell University Library has complete file of
(Continued on next card)

8
NIC

WITCHCRAFT
BF
1578
S55
A2
1894

James, Edward Wilson, d. 1906, ed.
Sherwood, Grace, defendant. Grace Sherwood, the Virginia witch. 1894-1895. (Card 2)

the periodical (F221 W71)
Contains court records of prosecutions of Grace Sherwood for witchcraft, in Princess Anne County, Virginia.
1. Witchcraft--Princess Anne Co., Virginia. 2. Trials (Witchcraft)--Princess Anne Co., Virginia. I. James, Edward Wilson, d.1906, ed. II. Title.

Rare
BX
890
A33
1651++

Jammy, Petrus, ed.
Albertus Magnus, Saint, Bp. of Ratisbon, 1193?-1280.

... Opera ... in lucem edita, studio & labore ... Petri Iammy. Lygdvni, Sumpt. Claudii Prost, Petri & Claudii Rigaud [etc] 1651.

21v. front. (v.1) 35cm.

Contents.--v.1. Logica.--v.2. Physica. De caelo & mundo. De generatione &
(Continued on next card)

Rare
BX
890
A33
1651++

Jammy, Petrus, ed.
Albertus Magnus, Saint, Bp. of Ratisbon, 1193?-1280. Opera ... 1651. (Card 2)

Contents:
Politicorum Aristotelis commentarii.--v.5. Parva natvralia.--v.6. De animalibvs.--v.7. Commentarii in Psalmos.--v.8. Commentarii in Threnos Ieremiae, in Baruch, in Danielem, in 12 proph. minores.--v.9. Commentarii in Matthaeum, in Marcum.--v.10. Commentarii in Lvcam.--v.11. Commentarii in Ioannem, in Apocalypsim.--v.12
(Continued on next card)

Rare
BX
890
A33
1651++

Jammy, Petrus, ed.
Albertus Magnus, Saint, Bp. of Ratisbon, 1193?-1280. Opera ... 1651. (Card 3)

Contents: (cont'd)
Sermones de tempore, de sanctis, de eucharista. Orationes super Evangelia dominicalia totius anni. de muliere forti liber.--v.13. Commentarij in D. Dionysium Compendij theologicae veritatis lib. VII. v.14-16. Commentarii in I.-IV. lib. Sententiarvm.--v.17-18. Svmma thologia.
(Continued on next card)

Rare
BX
890
A33
1651++

Jammy, Petrus, ed.
Albertus Magnus, Saint, Bp. of Ratisbon, 1193?-1280. Opera ... 1651. (Card 4)

Contents: (cont'd)
v.19. Svmma de creatvris.--v.20. Super missus. De laudibus Beatae Mariae. Biblia Mariana.--v.21. Philosophia pauperum.

I. Jammy, Petrus, ed.

HIST SCI
R
133
P74

Jancke, Johann Gottfried, b. 1762, respondent.
Pohl, Johann Ehrenfried, 1746-1800, praeses.
De medico exorcista...praeside Iohanne Ehrenfried Pohl...disputabit auctor ac respondens Iohannes Godofredus Iancke... Lipsiae, Ex officina Sommeria [1788]
26, xv p. 21cm.

Diss.--Leipzig (J. G. Jancke, respondent)
"Procancellarius D. Ernestus Gottlob Bose Panegyrin medicam...indicit. De phantasia laesa, gravium morborum matre.": xv p. at end.
(Continued on next card)

8
NIC

Witchcraft
BF
1565
S83
G19

Janser, B , supposed author.
[Ganser, Benno] 1728-1779?
Sendschreiben an einen gelehrten Freund betreffend die heutige Streitschriften von der Hexerey. Vom Donau-Strohm [1767?]
[12] p. 20cm.

Attribution by Holzmann and British Museum (the latter gives Christian name as Brenno), Fieger, in his P. Don Ferdinand Sterzinger, p. 136, gives the name as B. Janser: a misprint?
1. Sterzinger, Ferdinand, 1721-1786. 2. Witchcraft. I. Title. II. Janser, B , supposed author.

8

WITCHCRAFT
BF
1583
J37

Jaraczewsky, Adolph.
Zur Geschichte der Hexenprocesse in Erfurt und Umgegend; ein Beitrag zur Culturgeschichte des 17. Jahrhunderts ... von Dr. Jaraczewski. Erfurt, C. Villaret, 1876.
28 p. 22cm.

"Vortrag, gehalten im Verein für Geschicht und Alterthumskunde in Erfurt."

8
NIC

1. Trials (Witchcraft)--Erfurt. I. Title.

CATALOGUE OF THE CORNELL WITCHCRAFT COLLECTION

WITCHCRAFT
BF
1549
J41

Jaulmes, Alfred.
Essai sur le satanisme et la superstition au moyen age, précédé d'une introduction sur leurs origines. Étude historique. Montauban, Imprimerie typo-lithographique J. Granié, 1900.
110 p. 22cm.

Bibliography: p. ₍7₎-8.
Imprint stamped on t. p.: Paris, Librairie Fischbacher.
1. Satanism.   I. Title.

Witchcraft
BF
1581
Z7
1702

Jawson, Mary, fl. 1702.
A sad and lamentable account of one Mary Jawson ... who wickedly sold her self to the devil ... to be revenged on her aunt ... A dreadful story of a young maid in Devonshire, who, for renouncing her contract in marriage, had fearful judgements shewn on her. Also an account of a dreadful judgment on a rich man for the cruel usage of his servant ... To which is added three dreadful examples & judgments that hath befallen three notorious sinners. Glasgow, 1702.
(Continued on next card)

Witchcraft
BF
1581
Z7
1702

Jawson, Mary, fl. 1702.
A sad and lamentable account of one Mary Jawson ... 1702.   (Card 2)

12 p. 13cm.

Ex libris John A. Fairley.

1. Jawson, Mary, fl. 1702.

Witchcraft
BF
1565
A33
1723

Jeanne d'Arc, Saint, 1412-1431.
Alberti, Valentin, 1635-1697, praeses.
... Academische Abhandlung von den Hexen und dem Bündniss so sie mit dem Teuffel haben. Darinnen ... nebst Erörterung einiger andern curieusen Fragen, ob die bekannte Pucelle d'Orleans, ingleichen das rasende Weib, das den Attilam erschrecket, eine Hexe gewesen sei? Franckfurt und Leipzig, 1723.
₍56₎ p. front. 21cm.
Translation of his Dissertatio academica, De sagis, C. Stridtbeckh, respondent, Wittebergae, 1690.

(Continued on next card)

Witchcraft
BF
1565
D62
no.10

Jeanne d'Arc, Saint, 1412-1431.
Alberti, Valentin, 1635-1697, praeses.
Dissertatio academica, De sagis, sive foeminis, commercium cum malo spiritu habentibus, e christiana pnevmatologia desumpta, & sub praesidio ... Dn. D. Valentini Alberti ... publicae proposita ventilationi ... ab autore Christiano Stridtbekh ... Lipsiae, Typis Christoph. Fleischeri ₍1690₎
₍52₎ p. illus. 20cm.
No.10 in vol. lettered Dissertationes de sagis. 1636-1714.
(Continued on next card)

Witchcraft

Jeanne d'Arc, Saint, 1412-1431.
Thurston, Herbert, 1856-1939.
Was she a witch after all?
(In The month. London, 1922. 24cm. vol. 139, no. 691, p. ₍1₎-13)

1. Jeanne d'Arc, Saint, 1412-1431. I. Title.

WITCHCRAFT
BF
1517
F5
J43
1886

Jeanne des Anges, mère, 1602-1665.
Autobiographie.
Soeur Jeanne des Anges, supérieure des Ursulines de Loudun (XVIIe siècle) Autobiographie d'une hystérique possédée, d'après le manuscrit inédit de la bibliothèque de Tours. Annoté et publié par les docteurs Gabriel Legué et Gilles de la Tourette. Préface de M. le professeur Charcot. Paris, Aux Bureaux du Progrès, 1886.
xiv, 321 p. facsim. 24cm. (Bibliothèque diabolique ₍Collection Bourneville₎)
(Continued on next card)

8 NIC

WITCHCRAFT
BF
1517
F5
J43
1886

Jeanne des Anges, mère, 1602-1665.
Soeur Jeanne des Anges, supérieure des Ursulines de Loudun (XVIIe siècle) Autobiographie d'une hystérique possédée, d'après le manuscrit inédit de la bibliothèque de Tours. Annoté et publié par les docteurs Gabriel Legué et Gilles de la Tourette. Préface de M. le professeur Charcot. Paris, Aux Bureaux du Progrès, 1886.
xiv, 321 p. facsim. 24cm. (Bibliothèque diabolique ₍Collection Bourneville₎)
(Continued on next card)

8 NIC

WITCHCRAFT
BF
1517
F5
J43
1886

Jeanne des Anges, mère, 1602-1665. Soeur Jeanne des Anges...Autobiographie...1886
(Card 2)

1. Demoniac possession. 2. Loudun,France. Ursuline Convent. 3. Grandier, Urbain, 1590-1634. 4. Her Autobiographie. 5. Legué, Gabriel, d.1913, ed. 6. Gilles de la Tourette, Georges Albert Edouard Brutus, 1857- ed. 7. Title.

WITCHCRAFT
BF
1517
F5
S96

Jeanne des Anges, mère, 1602-1665.
Surin, Jean Joseph, 1600-1665.
Histoire abrégée de la possession des Ursulines de Loudun, et des peines du père Surin; (ouvrage inédit faisant suite à ses oeuvres.) Paris, Chez l'éditeur, au Bureau de l'Association catholique du Sacré-Coeur, 1828.
365, ₍6₎ p. 18cm.
"D'après Sommervogel, publication partielle d'une copie d'un ms. de la fin du XVIIIe siècle, ayant pour titre: La vie

(Continued on next card)

8 NIC

WITCHCRAFT
BF
1517
F5
S96

Jeanne des Anges, mère, 1602-1665.
Surin, Jean Joseph, 1600-1665. Histoire abrégée de la possession des Ursulines de Loudun ... 1828. (Card 2)
du R. P. Surin, en laquelle il parle des maux qui lui sont arrivés ensuite de la possession des démons chassés par son ministière." -- Note under Surin, Bibliothèque Nationale.
Surin's authorship has been questioned.
With this is bound his Triomphe de l'amour divin... Avignon, 1829.
(Continued on next card)

8 NIC

WITCHCRAFT
BF
1517
F5
S96

Jeanne des Anges, mère, 1602-1665.
Surin, Jean Joseph, 1600-1665.
Triomphe de l'amour divin sur les puissances de l'Enfer, en la possession de la Mère Prieure des Ursulines de Loudun, 1. partie; et Science expérimentale des choses de l'autre vie. Avec le moyen facile d'acquérir la paix du coeur. Ouvrages posthumes ... Avignon, Seguin aîné, 1829.
xj, 312 p. 18cm.
Parts 1 and 4 of Surin's posthumous works as published by Seguin.
(Continued on next card)

8 NIC

WITCHCRAFT
BF
1517
F5
S96

Jeanne des Anges, mère, 1602-1665.
Surin, Jean Joseph, 1600-1665. Triomphe de l'amour divin ... 1829. (Card 2)

Bound with his Histoire abrégée de la possession des Ursulines de Loudun. Paris, 1828.

1. Exorcism. 2. Jeanne des Anges, mère, 1602-1665. 3. Demonology. 4. Peace of mind. I. His Science expérimentale des choses de l'autre vie. II. Title.

8 NIC

Witchcraft
BF
1581
A2
W81
1866a
no.1

Jenkinson, Hellen, d. 1612.
The Witches of Northamptonshire. Agnes Browne. Ioane Vaughan. Arthur Bill. Hellen Ienkinson. Mary Barber. Witches. Who were all executed at Northampton the 22. of Iuly last. 1612. London, Printed by Tho: Purfoot, for Arthur Iohnson, 1612. ₍Northampton, England, Taylor & son, 1866₎
₍28₎ p. 22cm.
No. 1 in box lettered Witchcraft in Northamptonshire.
1. Witchcraft--Northamptonshire, England. I. Title: Witchcraft in Northamptonshire.

8

WITCHCRAFT
BF
1583
A2
S744

A Jesuit philanthropist. Friedrich von Spee and the Würzburg witches.
(In The Church quarterly review. London. 23cm. v. 57, no. 114 (1904), p. 318-337)
Review of several books by Spee or about his times.
At head of title: Art. V.
1. Spee, Friedrich von, 1591-1635. Cautio criminalis. 2. Institoris, Henricus, d. 1508. Malleus maleficarum. 3. Witchcraft--Germany. I. Title.

8 NIC

DQ
3
Q3
v.22

Jetzer, Johann, ca. 1483-ca. 1515.
Steck, Rudolf, 1842-1924, ed.
Die Akten des Jetzerprozesses nebst dem Defensorium. Basel, Verlag der Basler Buch- und Antiquariatshandlung vormals A. Geering, 1904.
xl, 679 p. illus. 23cm. (Quellen zur Schweizer Geschichte, 22. Bd.)
1. Jetzer, Johann, ca. 1483-ca. 1515. 2. Dominicans in Switzerland. 3. Bern--Church history--Sources. I. Title.

WITCHCRAFT
BX
3545
S9
S81

Jetzer, Johann, ca. 1483-ca. 1515.
Steck, Rudolf, 1842-1924.
Der Berner Jetzerprozess (1507-1509) in neuer Beleuchtung nebst Mitteilungen aus den noch ungedruckten Akten. Bern, Schmid & Francke, 1902.
87 p. illus. 24cm.
"Separat-Abdruck aus der 'Schweizerischen theolog. Zeitschrift' (Verlag von August Frick, Zürich II)."
Greatly expanded in his Die Akten des Jetzerprozesses nebst dem Defensorium. Basel, 1904.
(Continued on next card)

8 NIC

WITCHCRAFT
BX
3545
S9
S81

Jetzer, Johann, ca. 1483-ca. 1515.
Steck, Rudolf, 1842-1924. Der Berner Jetzerprozess ... 1902. (Card 2)

Stamped on cover: A. Francke, Verlags-Cto. vormals Schmid & Francke, Bern.

1. Jetzer, Johann, ca. 1483-ca. 1515. 2. Dominicans in Switzerland. 3. Bern--Church history--Sources. I. His Die Akten des Jetzerprozesses nebst dem Defensorium. II. Title.

8 NIC

CATALOGUE OF THE CORNELL WITCHCRAFT COLLECTION

Jiratiel Leetsosoneus

see

Hamer, Petrus, 1646-1716

WITCHCRAFT
BT 975 J61

Jirku, Anton, 1885-
Die Dämonen und ihre Abwehr im Alten Testament. Leipzig, A. Deichert, 1912.
viii, 99 p. 22cm.

"Literatur": p. [vii]-viii.

1. Demonology--Biblical teaching. I. Title.

8
NIC

Jo. Baptistae Viglioni ... Enchiridion.

WITCHCRAFT
BF 1068 V67 1734

Viglioni, Giovanni Battista.
Jo: Baptistae Viglioni ... Enchiridion quatuor tractatus complectens de somniis, cabalis, cacodaemonibus, et ludo in genere. Ad excellentiss. principem Julium Visconti Borromeum ... Nova editio. Neapoli, 1734.
xvi, 188, 51, 188-231 p. 23cm.
1. Sleep--Early works to 1800. 2. Dreams. 3. Cabala. 4. Demonology. 5. Games--Early works to 1800. I. Title: Enchiridion.

8

Witchcraft
BF 1815 J62 S28 1570

Joachim, Abbot of Fiore, 1132(ca.)-1202.
Spurious and doubtful works. Prophetiae. Scalichius, Paulus von Lika, count, 1534-1575.
Pavli principis de la Scala ... Primi tomi Miscellaneorvm, de rervm caussis & successibus atque secretiori methodo ibidem expressa, effigies ac exemplar, nimirum, vaticiniorum & imaginum Ioachimi Abbatis Florensis Calabriae, & Anselmi Episcopi Marsichani, super statu summorum Pontificum Rhomanae Ecclesiae, contra falsam, iniquam, vanam, confictam & seditiosam cuiusdam Pseudomagi, quae nuper nomine Theophrasti Paracelsi in lucem prodijt, pseudomagicam expositionem, vera, certa, & indubitata explanatio. (Continued on next card)

Witchcraft
BF 1815 J62 S78 1570

Joachim, Abbot of Fiore, 1132(ca.)-1202.
Spurious and doubtful works. Prophetiae. Scalichius, Paulus von Lika, count, 1534-1575.
... Primi tomi Miscellaneorvm ... effigies ...1570. (Card 2)

Coloniae Agrippinae, Ex Officina Typographica Theodori Graminaei, 1570.
[12], 152 p. illus. 21cm.

Title vignette.

Joannes XXII, pope, d. 1334.

WITCHCRAFT
BF 1582 Z7 1317

Albe, Edmond, 1861-
Autour de Jean XXII: Hugues Géraud, évêque de Cahors, l'affaire des poisons et des envoûtements en 1317. Cahors, J. Girma, 1904.
206 p. 25cm.
"Extrait du Bulletin de la Société des Études littéraires, Scientifiques et Artistiques du Lot, t. XXIX."
1. Géraud, Hugues, bp. of Cahors, fl. 1317. 2. Joannes XXII, pope, d. 1334. I. Title. II. Title: L'affaire des poisons.

Joannes Martacunes, Patriarch of Armenia, d. ca. 490.

see

Hovhannes I Mandakuni, Patriarch of Armenia, d. ca. 490.

WITCHCRAFT
DS 135 G4 B71

Joesten, Joseph, 1850-1909.
Zur Geschichte der Hexen und Juden in Bonn; eine kulturgeschichtliche Studie, von Dr. Joesten. Bonn, C. Georgi, 1900.
47 p. 24cm.

1. Jews in Bonn. 2. Witchcraft--Bonn. I. Title.

8
NIC

Johann VI, Count of Nassau-Dillenburg, 1535 or 6-1605 or 6.

Witchcraft
BF 1583 J65 Z6+

Götze, Ludwig.
Johanns VI., Grafen von Nassau-Dillenburg, Urteil über Hexenprocesse (1582) Mitgetheilt von Dr. L. Götze.
(In Verein für Nassauische Altertumskunde und Geschichtsforschung, Wiesbaden. Nassauische Annalen. Wiesbaden. 27cm. 13. Bd. (1874), p. [327]-329)
1. Johann VI, Count of Nassau-Dillenburg, 1535 or 6-1605 or 6. 2. Witchcraft--Nassau (Duc   hy) I. Verein für

8   (Continued on next card)

Johann VI, Count of Nassau-Dillenburg, 1535 or 6-1605 or 6.

Witchcraft
BF 1583 J65 Z6+

Götze, Ludwig.
Johanns VI., Grafen von Nassau-Dillenburg, Urteil über Hexenprocesse (1582) Mitgetheilt von Dr. L. Götze.
(In Verein für Nassauische Altertumskunde und Geschichtsforschung, Wiesbaden. Nassauische Annalen. Wiesbaden. 27cm. 13. Bd. (1874), p. [327]-329)
1. Johann VI, Count of Nassau-Dillenburg, 1535 or 6-1605 or 6. I. Verein für
--Nassau (Duc   hy)

8   (Continued on next card)

Johann VII von Schönenberg, abp. and elector of Treves.

WITCHCRAFT
BX 1935 N42

Neller, Georg Christoph, praeses.
...Conatus exegeticus in cap. Eam te 7 De rescriptis, quem una cum parergis, ex omni jure, nec non ex re monetaria, tum biblico-canonica, tum Trevirensi delibatis ...praeside...Georgio Christoph. Neller... publicae disputationi pro admissione ad tentamen graduandorum supposuit...Carolus Josephus Embden. Augustae Trevirorum, Typis Eschermannianis [1779]
48 p. front., plate. 22cm.

8   Burr's   note inside front cover:
NIC   (Continued on next card)

Johann VII von Schönenberg, abp. and elector of Treves.

WITCHCRAFT
BX 1935 N42

Neller, Georg Christoph, praeses. Conatus exegeticus in cap. Eam te 7 De rescriptis ...[1779]   (Card 2)

"This book is valuable in containing a... letter of the Elector, Johann VII of Treves asking the advice of the University theological faculty at Treves as to the trial of Dr. Dietrich Flade for witchcraft. (See pp. 32-35) It is to be noted that this student, writing under the eye of the eminent jurist   Neller in 1779, still believes in   witchcraft..."
(Continued on next card)

Johann Brenz und die Hexenfrage.

WITCHCRAFT
BR 350 B83 P33++

Paulus, Nicolaus, 1853-1930.
Johann Brenz und die Hexenfrage.
(In Wissenschaftliche Beilage zur Germania. Blätter für Literatur, Wissenschaft und Kunst. Berlin. 31cm. Jahrg. 1909, Nr. 26 (1909), p. [201]-204)
In double columns.
In broadside box.
1. Brenz, Johann, 1499-1570. 2. Witchcraft--Germany--History. I. Title.

8
NIC

Johann Casimir, Duke of Saxe-Coburg, 1564-1633.

Witchcraft
BF 1583 A2 S27+ 1898

Saxe-Coburg. Laws, statutes, etc.
Herzog Johann Casimirs "Gerichts-Ordnung die Hexerei betrf: Publiciret ahm 21. February 1629." Aus dem Hildburghäuser Ratsarchiv mitgeteilt von Dr. A. Human.
(In Verein für Sachsen-Meiningische Geschichte und Landeskunde, Meiningen. Schriften. Hildburghausen. 27cm. 29 (1898), p. 99-112)

8   (Continued on next card)

Johann Joseph Gassner, der berühmte Exorzist.

Witchcraft
BX 4705 G35406 Z74

Zimmermann, J   A
Johann Joseph Gassner, der berühmte Exorzist. Sein Leben und wundersames Wirken aus Anlass seiner hundertjährigen Todesfeier neuerdings erzählt und gewürdiget von J. A. Zimmermann. Kempten, J. Kösel'sche Buchhandlung, 1878.
viii, 122 p. 19cm.

1. Gassner, Johann Joseph, 1727-1779. 2. Exorcism. 3. Faith-cure.

8

Johann Michael Models, J. U. Lic. beantwortete Frage: Ob man die Ausfahrt der Hexen zulassen könne?

Witchcraft
BF 1565 S83 M69

Model, Johann Michael
Johann Michael Models, J. U. Lic. beantwortete Frage: Ob man die Ausfahrt der Hexen zulassen könne? Wider den heutigen Hexenstürmer P. Ferdinand Sterzinger. München, Bey J. A. Crätz, 1769.
36 p. 18cm.

1. Sterzinger, Ferdinand, 1721-1786. 2. Witchcraft. I. Title: Beantwortete Frage: Ob man die Ausfahrt der Hexen zulassen könne?   II. Title: Frage, Ob man die Ausfa   hrt der Hexen zulassen könne?

8

Johann Wagstaffs Gründlich ausgeführte Materie von der Hexerey.

WITCHCRAFT
BF 1565 W13 1711

Wagstaffe, John, 1633-1677.
Johann Wagstaffs Gründlich ausgeführte Materie von der Hexery, oder: Die Meynung derer jenigen welche da glauben, dass es Hexen gebe; deutlich widerlegt und mit vernünfftigen Anmerckungen über jedes Capitel erläutert. Aus dem Englischen übersetzt. Halle in Megdeburgischen, Im Rengerischen Buchladen, 1711.
16 p. l., 152 p. 16cm.

8   (Continued on next card)

Johann Wagstaffs Gründlich ausgeführte Materie von der Hexerey.

WITCHCRAFT
BF 1565 W13 1711

Wagstaffe, John, 1633-1677. Johann Wagstaffs Gründlich ausgeführte Materie von der Hexerey ... 1711.   (Card 2)

Translation of a revised version of The question of witchcraft debated.

1. Witchcraft. I. His The question of witchcraft debated. German. II. Title: Gründlich aus   geführte Materie von der Hexerey.

8

CATALOGUE OF THE CORNELL WITCHCRAFT COLLECTION

WITCHCRAFT
BX
2340
P33

Johann Wilhelm, Herzog von Jülich-Kleve-Berg, 1562-1609.
Pauls, Emil.
Der Exorcismus an Herzog Johann Wilhelm von Jülich in den Jahren 1604 und 1605.

(In: Historischer Verein für den Niederrhein. Annalen. Köln. 23cm. No.63 (1897) p. [27]-53)
With this, in the same issue, is: Keussen, Hermann. Zwei Hexenprozesse aus der Crefelder Gegend.
1. Exorcism. 2. Medicine, Magic, mystic and spagiric. 3. Johann Wilhelm, Herzog von Jülich-Kleve-Berg, 1562-1609.

8
NIC

Johannes Mantagunensis, Patriarch of Armenia, d. ca. 490.

see

Hovhannes I Mandakuni, Patriarch of Armenia, d. ca. 490.

WITCHCRAFT
BV
4627
W8
H84
1851

Johannes Mantagunensis über Zauberei.
Hovhannes I Mandakuni, Patriarch of Armenia, d. ca. 490.
Johannes Mantagunensis über Zauberei. [Tübingen, 1851].
[85]-119 p. 21cm.
At head of title: 3.
Caption title.
Article signed: Welte.
Translation of a pastoral letter on witchcraft and fortune-telling.
1. Witchcraft. 2. Fortune-telling.
I. Welte, Benedict. II. Title.

8

Johannes Polycarius.

Witchcraft
GT
6710
T76
1615

Tractatus tragicus De poenis omnium delictorum, quae adversus Deum aut homines admissa & mirabiliter vindicata sunt. Ex probatissimis omnium aetatum scriptoribus diligenter collectus ac libris duobus explicatus per Joannem Polycarium [pseud.?] [Islebiae?] Impensis Henningi Grosij, 1615.
4 p. l., 667, [32] p. 20cm.
With colophon.
First published 1597 under title:
(Continued on next card)

8

Johannes Polycarius.

Witchcraft
GT
6710
T76
1615

Tractatus tragicus De poenis omnium delictorum ... 1615. (Card 2)
Tragica, seu tristium historiarum de poenis criminalibus, and with dedication signed Henningus Grosius [sic]; no mention of J. Polycarius on t. p. or elsewhere.
This edition is the same printing as that of 1597, but with different t. p. and preliminary leaves.
Book I has caption title: Tragicorvm,
Continued on next card)

8

Johannes Polycarius.

Witchcraft
GT
6710
T76
1615

Tractatus tragicus De poenis omnium delictorum ... 1615. (Card 3)
seu sylvae tristivm, hoc est, Horribilium historiarum de poenis criminalibus.
Grässe, Bibliotheca magica, attributes this edition to Polycarpus, Johannes.
1. Punishment. 2. Crime and criminals --Biog. I. Grosse, Henning, 1553-1621, comp. II. Polycarius, Johannes. III. Polycarpus, Johannes. IV. Johannes Polycarius. V. Title: Tragicorum, seu sylvae tristium.

8

BX
4705
T83
S58

Johannes Trithemius; eine Monographie.
Silbernagl, Isidor, 1831-1904.
Johannes Trithemius; eine Monographie. Landshut, Krüll, 1868.
245 p. 22cm.

1. Trithemius, Johannes, 1462-1516. I. Title.

BX
1538
W95
Q3
v.23

Johannes Trithemius (1462-1516)
Arnold, Klaus.
Johannes Trithemius (1462-1516) Würzburg, Kommissionsverlag F. Schöningh, 1971.
xi, 319 p. ports. 23cm. (Quellen und Forschungen zur Geschichte des Bistums und Hochstifts Würzburg, Bd. 23)
Originally presented as the author's thesis, Würzburg.
Bibliography: p. 282-306.

1. Trithemius, Johannes, 1462-1516.

GR
530
J67

Johnson, Frank Roy, 1911-
Witches and demons in history and folklore, by F. Roy Johnson. Murfreesboro, N. C., Johnson Pub. Co. [1969]
262 p. illus. 22 cm.
Bibliographical references included in "Notes" (p. 237-252)

1. Witchcraft. I. Title.

GR530.J6   133.4   75-240086
Library of Congress   70 [2]   MARC

Witchcraft
PR
2610
A16
1905

Johnson, William Savage, ed.
Jonson, Ben, 1573?-1637.
The devil is an ass. Edited with introduction, notes, and glossary by William Savage Johnson. New York, Henry Holt and Co., 1905.
lxxix, 252 p. 24cm. (Yale studies in English, 29)

I. Johnson, William Savage, ed. II. Title.

PS
2142
W8

Johnston, Mary, 1870-1936.
The witch, by Mary Johnston. Boston and New York, Houghton Mifflin company, 1914.
v, [1] p., 1 l., 441, [1] p., 1 l. incl. col. front. 19½cm.

I. Title.

Witchcraft
BF
1555
J75

[Jollie, Thomas] 1629-1703.
The Surey demoniack; or, An account of Satans strange and dreadful actings, in and about the body of Richard Dugdale of Surey, near Whalley, in Lancashire; and how he was dispossest by Gods blessing on the fastings and prayers of divers ministers and people. The matter of fact attested by the oaths of several credible persons, before some of His Majesties justices of the peace in the said county. London, Printed for J. Robinson, 1697.
64 p. 20cm.

I. Title.

Witchcraft
BF
1555
J75T2

Jollie, Thomas, 1629-1703.
The Surey demoniack.
Taylor, Zachary, 1653-1705.
The Surey impostor: being an answer to a late pamphlet, entituled, The Surey demoniack. ... London, Printed for J. Jones, 1697.
75 p. front. 23cm.

1. Jollie, Thomas, 1629-1703. The Surey demoniack. 2. Demoniac possession. I. Title.

Witchcraft
BF
1555
J75V7

[Jollie, Thomas] 1629-1703.
A vindication of the Surey demoniack as no impostor: or, A reply to a certain pamphlet publish'd by Mr. Zach. Taylor, called The Surey impostor. With a further clearing and confirming of the truth as to Richard Dugdale's case and cure. By T. J., one of the ministers who attended upon that affair from first to last ... To which is annexed a brief narrative of the Surey demoniack, drawn up by the same author, for the satisfaction of such who have not
(Continued on next card)

Witchcraft
BF
1555
J75V7

[Jollie, Thomas] 1629-1703. A vindication of the Surey demoniack ... 1698. (Card 2)
seen the former narrative... London, Printed for N. Simmons, and sold by G. Conyers, 1698.
80 p. 21cm.

Wing J 889.

1. Dugdale, Richard. 2. Taylor, Zachary. The Surey imposter, being an answer to ... The Surey demoniack. I. Title.

RARE
HV
8593
J76

Jonctys, Daniel, 1600-1654.
De pyn-bank wedersproken, en bematigt, door Dan. Jonktys [sic] Rotterdam, By Ioannes Naeranus, 1651.
231, [12] p. 16cm.
Added t.p. engr.
"Gevoelen van Thomas Morus, dat dievery met de dood niet behoort gestraft te werden...uyt zijn boek...Utopia...": 12 p. at end.
1. Torture.

8
NIC

RARE
HV
8593
J76
1736

Jonctys, Daniel, 1600-1654.
De pyn-bank wedersproken, en bematigt, door Dan. Jonktys [sic]... Amsterdam, By Salomon Schouten, 1736.
268, [62] p. 16cm.
Added t.p. engr.
"Gevoelen van Thomas Morus, dat dievery met de dood niet behoort gestraft te werden...uyt zijn boek...Utopia": 14 p. after p. 268.
1. Torture. I. More, Sir Thomas, 1478-1535. Utopia. II. Title.

8
NIC

Jones, Henry, ed.

Witchcraft
BF
1575
M42
S8
1846

Mather, Cotton, 1663-1728.
Strange phenomena of New England: in the seventeenth century: including the "Salem witchcraft," "1692." From the writings of "the Rev. Cotton Mather, D. D." ... Collected and arranged for re-publication by Henry Jones ... New-York, Piercy and Reed, 1846.
iv, [5]-54 p. 24cm.

1. Witchcraft--New England. I. Jones, Henry, ed. II. Title.

11-8997

CATALOGUE OF THE CORNELL WITCHCRAFT COLLECTION

Witchcraft
BF
1445
L54
1605a

Jones, Zachary, tr.
Le Loyer, Pierre, sieur de La Brosse, 1550-1634.
A treatise of specters or straunge sights, visions and apparitions appearing sensibly vnto men. Wherein is delivered, the nature of spirites, angels, and divels: their power and properties: as also of witches, sorcerers, enchanters, and such like. With a table of the contents of the severall chapters annexed in the end of the booke. Newly done out of French into English. London, Printed by Val. S. for M. Lownes, 1605.
8 p. l., 145 numb. l., 1 l. 20cm.
(Continued on next card)

Witchcraft
BF
1445
L54
1605a

Jones, Zachary, tr.
Le Loyer, Pierre, sieur de La Brosse, 1550-1634.
A treatise of specters ... 1605 (Card 2)

Translated by Zachary Jones.
"A catalogue of the authours alledged in the Treatise of specters": prelim. leaves 5-8.
Translation of only the first book of IIII. ljvres des spectres.

Witchcraft
BF
1418
D9
J79
1955

Jong, Karel Hendrik Edward.
De zwarte magie. [2. herziene en verm. druk] 's-Gravenhage, H. P. Leopold [1955]
273 p. 24cm. (Parapsychologische bibliotheek, deel III)

1. Occult sciences. I. Title.

Witchcraft
PR
2610
A16
1905

Jonson, Ben, 1573?-1637.
The devil is an ass. Edited with introduction, notes, and glossary by William Savage Johnson. New York, Henry Holt and Co., 1905.
lxxix, 252 p. 24cm. (Yale studies in English, 29)

I. Johnson, William Savage, ed. II. Title.

Witchcraft
BF
1410
B42
Z56
v.2
no.24

Joosten, Lambert.
Bouman, Herman.
Brief van Lambert Joosten, met een antwoord op de selve, van Herman Bouman, waar in gehandelt word van de engelen en geesten, &c. En welk laatste een zedige verantwoordinge behelft, van de swaare gevolgen, of besluyten, die den autheur des briefs, uyt het gevoelen van H: B: tracht te maaken. Amsterdam, By A. van Damme, boekverkoper, 1696.
42 p. title vignette, illus. initial. 19 x 15cm.

(Continued on next card)

Witchcraft
BF
1410
B42
Z56
v.2
no.24

Joosten, Lambert.
Bouman, Herman. Brief van Lambert Joosten, met een antwoord op de selve ... 1696.
(Card 2)

4°: A-E⁴, F1.
Black letter (except for introduction)
Bouman divides Joosten's letter into sentences, and gives a refutation after each.
Van der Linde 80.
No. 24 in vol. lettered Bekker II.
1. Angels. 2. Spirits. I. Joosten, Lambert. II. Title.

8

Witchcraft
BF
1563
W81++
no.8

Jorden, Edward.
A briefe discovrse of a disease called the suffocation of the mother. Written vppon occasion which hath beene of late taken thereby, to suspect possession of an euill spirit, or some such like supernaturall power. Wherin is declared that diuers strange actions and passions of the body of man, which in the common opinion, are imputed to the Diuell, haue their true naturall causes, and do accompanie this disease. London, Printed by J. Windet, 1603. [London, at the British Museum, 1923]
(Continued on next card)

Witchcraft
BF
1563
W81++
no.8

Jorden, Edward. A briefe discovrse of a disease... 1603. [1923] (Card 2)

[58] p. 17cm.

Signatures: A-G⁴, H¹.
Photocopy (negative) 58 p. on 26 l. 20 x 32cm.
No. 8 in vol. lettered: Witchcraft tracts, chapbooks and broadsides, 1579-1704; rotograph copies.
1. Glover, Mary, fl. 1603.
2. Exorcism. I. Title.

MSS
Bd.
WITCHCRAFT
BF
B81

Jorden, Edward.
A briefe discourse of a disease called suffocation of the mother.
Bradwell, Stephan, fl. 1594-1636.
Marie Glovers late woefull case, together wth her joyfull deliverance written upon occasion of Dr. Jordens Discourse of the mother... With a defence of the truthe against D. J. his scandalous impugnations. [n.p.] 1603.
171 l. 20 x 29cm.
Photostatic copy of Sloan MSS 831 in the British Museum.
Second treatise, beginning on l. 42.
(Continued on next card)

MSS
Bd.
WITCHCRAFT
BF
B81

Jorden, Edward.
A briefe discourse of a disease called suffocation of the mother.
Bradwell, Stephan, fl. 1594-1636. Marie Glovers late woefull case...1603. (Card 2)

has caption title: A defence of the publique sentence of lawe, and of the iudgment, of certayne phisitions, t averred Marie Glouers case to be supernaturall: againste D. Jordens slie, but scandalous impugnations of bothe.
Bound in maroon buckram.
1. Glover, Mary, fl. 1603. 2. Demoniac possession. 3. Witchcraft--
(Continued on next card)

Witchcraft
BX
2340
B86
1725

Joseph de Jesus Maria, tr.
Brognolo, Candido.
Brognolo recopilado, e substanciado com addictamentos, de gravissimos authores. Methodo mais breve, muy suave, e utilissimo de exorcizar, expelindo Demonios, e desfazendo feytiços: segundo os dictames do Sagrado Evangelho ... Collegido, rezumido, e tradusido da lingua Latina, Italiana, e Hespanhola na Portugueza para clareza dos Exorcistas, e bem dos Exorcizados. Por Fr. Joseph de Jesus Maria Ullyssiponense ... Lisboa Oriental, Na Officina Ferreyriana, 1725.
(Continued on next card)

Witchcraft
BX
2340
B86
1725

Joseph de Jesus Maria, tr.
Brognolo, Candido. Brognolo recopilado ... 1725. (Card 2)

[24], 347 p. 15cm.

Translation of Manuale exorcistarum.

1. Exorcism. I. Brognolo, Candido. Manuale exorcistarum--Portuguese. II. Joseph de Jesus Maria, tr.

Witchcraft
BF
1559
G25

Joseph Gassners ... Antwort auf die Anmerkungen, welche in dem Münchnerischen Intelligenzblat ... gemacht worden.
Gassner, Johann Joseph, 1727-1779.
Joseph Gassners ... Antwort auf die Anmerkungen, welche in dem Münchnerischen Intelligenzblat vom 12. Nov. wider seine Gründe und Weise zu exorciren, wie auch von der deutschen Chronik, und andern Zeitungsschreibern gemacht worden. Augsburg, Bey J. Wolff, 1774.
48 p. 16cm. (bound in 19cm. vol.)
With this is bound Gründlicher Beweiss ... von einem Vertheidiger der Wahrheit ... Augsburg, 1775.

8 (Continued on next card)

WITCHCRAFT
BF
1581
A2
G551

Joseph Glanvill, witchcraft, and seventeenth-century science.
Prior, Moody Erasmus, 1901-
Joseph Glanvill, witchcraft, and seventeenth-century science... Chicago, 1932.
167-193 p. 25cm.

"A part of a dissertation submitted to ... [the University of Chicago] ... for the degree of Doctor of Philosophy."
Reprinted from Modern philology, v.30, no.2, 1932.
1. Glanvill, Joseph, 1636-1680. Saducismus triumphatus. 2. Hobbes, Thomas, 1588-16 79. 3. Witchcraft.

8
NIC

Witchcraft
Z
6876
J86

Jouin, Ernest.
Bibliographie occultiste et maçonnique. Répertoire d'ouvrages imprimés et manuscrits relatifs à la franc-maçonnerie, les sociétés secrètes, la magie, etc. publié d'après les fiches recueillies par A.-Peeters Baertsoen et avec des notes historiques et bibliographiques. Tome I. Jusqu'à l'année 1717. Paris, Revue internationale des sociétés secrètes, 1930.
653 p. 25cm.

At head of title: Mgr E. Jouin et V. Descreux.
No more published? (Over)

Rare
Z
6876
J86

Jouin, Ernest.
Bibliographie occultiste et maçonnique. Répertoire d'ouvrages imprimés et manuscrits relatifs à la franc-maçonnerie, les sociétés secrètes, la magie, etc. publié d'après les fiches recueillies par A.-Peeters Baertsoen et avec des notes historiques et bibliographiques. Tome I. Jusqu'à l'année 1717. Paris, Revue internationale des sociétés secrètes, 1930.
653 p. 25cm.

At head of title: Mgr E. Jouin et V. Descreux.
No more published?

Witchcraft
K
K383+

Judicium matris Kepleri.
Kepler, Katharina, 1547-1622, defendant.
Judicium matris Kepleri. [Francofurti a. M.? Heyder & Zimmer, 1870]
202 p. 27cm.

Offprint of Kepler, Johann, 1571-1630. ... opera omnia, ed. Ch. Frisch, 8. Bd., 1. Teil, p. [359]-562.

1. Trials (Witchcraft)--Germany. I. Title.

8

WITCHCRAFT
BF
1583
T15

Julii Tamiani Send-Schreiben an Hieronymum Pistellum.
Tamianus, Julius, pseud.
Julii Tamiani Send-Schreiben an Hieronymum Pistellum, worinne bey Veranlassung der unweit Jena unternommenen Satans-Beschwerung der Anfang und Fortgang der Magie wie nicht minder die Meynungen der Magorum untersuchet, auch von denen dabey gewöhnlichen Mitteln ... Bericht erstattet wird. Nebst einem Paquetgen an den verwegenen Authorem der sogenannten Gerichte Gottes und sinnreichen Überschrifft, so er Franco zu e

8
NIC (Continued on next card)

CATALOGUE OF THE CORNELL WITCHCRAFT COLLECTION

                Julii Tamiani Send-Schreiben an Hierony-
           mum Pistellum.

WITCHCRAFT
F
583
T5
    Tamianus, Julius, pseud. Julii Tamiani
  Send-Schreiben an Hieronymum Pistellum ...
                              (Card 2)

  halten hat. Zu Magiluna in Arabien [i.e.,
Jena?] 1716.
    52 p. 20cm.
    Illustrative title vignette.
    1. Witchcraft--Thuringia. 2. Witch-
craft--Jena, Germany. 3. Magic. I.
Pistellus, Hieronymus. II. Title:
Send-Schreiben an Hieronymum Pistel-
lum.

WITCHCRAFT
    Julliard, Isabelle
      Une possédée en 1862.   Paris, E. Dentu,
    1862.
      177 p. 18cm.

     I. Title.

          Junius, Franciscus, 1545-1602, tr.

WITCHCRAFT
F
520
66
581
    Bodin, Jean, 1530-1596.
      Io. Bodini Andegavensis De magovrvm dae-
monomania libri IV. Nvnc primvm e Gallico
in Latinum translati per Lotarivm Philopo-
nvm. Basileae, Per Thomam Guarinum, 1581.
    16 p. l., 488 p. 21cm.
    Translation of his De la démonomanie.

    I. Junius, Franciscus, 1545-1602, tr.

         Juridicus processus contra sagas et
            veneficos.
Witchcraft
BF
1565
L42
1710
    Laymann, Paul, 1574-1635, supposed author.
      Juridicus processus contra sagas et vene-
ficos: das ist: Ein rechtlicher Proceß gegen
die Unholden und zauberische Personen. In
welchen ordentlich docirt wird, und aus fürnehmen beyder Rechten Doctorn und berühmten
Scribenten vorgetragen wird ... Ist mit
guten [sic] Fleiß und gründlicher Probation
und Beweiß durch P. Paulum Laymann ... in
lateinischer Sprach beschrieben. Jetzt den
Gerichtshaltern   und guter Justici Be-

8   (Continued on next card)

         Juridicus processus contra sagas et
            veneficos.
Witchcraft
BF
1565
L42
1710
    Laymann, Paul, 1574-1635, supposed author.
      Juridicus processus contra sagas et vene-
    ficos ... 1710.   (Card 2)

    freunden zum besten verteutscht, auch mit
bewehrten Historien und andern Umständen
vermehrt, und in unterschiedliche Titul ordentlich abgetheilet ... Oettingen, Gedruckt bey Stephan Rolck; Augspurg, Zu finden bey Daniel Waldern, 1710.
      287 (i. e., 187), [3] p. fold.
t. p. 13cm.
8   (Continued on next card)

         Juridicus processus contra sagas et
            veneficos.
Witchcraft
BF
1565
L42
1710
    Laymann, Paul, 1574-1635, supposed author.
      Juridicus processus contra sagas et vene-
    ficos ... 1710.   (Card 3)

    Other editions have title: Processus
juridicus ...
    Ascribed also to Johann Jordanaeus and
to Hermann Goenhausen.

    I. His Processus juridicus contra
8 sagas et venefi   cos. II. Title.

Witchcraft
BF
1581
J98
    Juxon, Joseph.
      A sermon upon witchcraft. Occasion'd by
a late illegal attempt to discover witches by
swimming. Preach'd at Twyford, in the
county of Leicester, July 11, 1736. London,
Printed by H. Woodfall, and sold by J.
Roberts, 1736.
    32 p. 21cm.

    1. Witchcraft.   I. Title.

317

CATALOGUE OF THE CORNELL WITCHCRAFT COLLECTION

K

Witchcraft
BX 9479 B42 B11 no.8

K., A. W. S.
Het Woord Sitna verklaard, Gen. 26: 21. Met een vertoog, dat het woord Satan daar van afkomstig is. Waar by gevoegd word een verklaaring over 2 Sam. 24: 1, en 1 Chron. 21: 1. Door A. W. S. K. Amsterdam, By J. Roman, boekverkoper, 1699.
13 p. [p. 14 blank] title and end page vignettes. illus. initial. 20 x 15cm.
4°: A-B⁴(-B4)
Black letter.
No. 8 in vol. lettered B. Bekkers sterf-bed en andere tractaten.
(Continued on next card)

Witchcraft
BX 9479 B42 B11 no.7

K., J. D. V. B. T.
Kort-bondige, en voor alle onpartydige, verstaanbare en met de reeden overeenkomende verklaaringe; van de verleydinge onser eerste voor-ouderen, Adam ende Eva in het Paradys. Volgens de beschryving van Moses, in het boek der Scheppinge. Door J. D. V. B. T. K. Amsterdam, By J. Roman, boek-verkoper, 1699.
22, [1] p. [p. 24 blank] title and end page vignettes, illus. initial. 20 x 15cm.
4°: A-C⁴.
(Continued on next card)

Witchcraft
BX 9479 B42 B11 no.7

K., J. D. V. B. T.
Kort-bondige, en voor alle onpartydige, verstaanbare ... verklaaringe ... 1699.
(Card 2)
Black letter.
No. 7 in vol. lettered B. Bekkers sterf-bed en andere tractaten.

1. Fall of man. 2. Devil. I. J. D. V. B. T. K. II. K., J. D. V. B. T.

Witchcraft
BF 1410 B42 Z56 v.2 no.16

K. A. H.
Den verkeerden duyvel van den throon geschopt, en den rechten weder hervoort gebragt, verhandelende van engelen en duyvelen, hare macht ende werkinge, waar in besonderlyk getoont wort wat den duyvel is, schrift-matigh voorgestelt, waar in de swaarste stukken van die materie worden opgelost, noch noyt zoo voortgebracht. Door K. A. H. Amsterdam, By N. Holbeex, boekver-kooper, 1692.
2 p. l., 36 p. title and end page vignettes, illus. initials. 19 x 15cm.
(Continued on next card)

Witchcraft
BF 1410 B42 Z56 v.2 no.16

K. A. H.
Den verkeerden duyvel van den throon geschopt ... 1692. (Card 2)
4°: *², A-D⁴, E².
Black letter (except for introduction)
Modeled on Balthasar Bekker's De betoverde weereld, but not always supporting it.
Van der Linde 66.
No. 16 in vol. lettered Bekker II.
1. Demonology. 2. Angels. 3. Magic. 4. Witchcraft. 5. Bekker, Balthasar, 1634-1698. De betoverde weereld.
I. Title. II. K. A. H. III. H., K. A.

WITCHCRAFT
BF 1550 K12

Kaarsberg, Hans Sophus, 1854-1928.
Om satanismen, djaevlebesaettelse og hexevaesen, set fra et laegevidenskabeligt standpunkt. Kjøbenhavn, Gyldendal, 1896.
41 p. 25cm.

"Saertryk af 'Hospitalstidende.'"

1. Satanism. 2. Demoniac possession. 3. Witchcraft. I. Title.

8
NIC

WITCHCRAFT
BF 1584 S97 K12

Kämpfen, Peter Joseph.
Hexen & [i. e. und] Hexenprozesse im Wallis; nach bewährten Quellen bearb. und kritisch beleuchtet. Stans, C. von Matt, 1867.
76 p. 19cm.

1. Witchcraft--Valais (Canton) 2. Trials (Witchcraft)--Valais (Canton) I. Title.

8
NIC

Der Kaibenturm.
WITCHCRAFT
BF 1584 S97 S35

Schmidt von Kirchberg, Heinrich.
Der Kaibenturm. Eine Hexengeschichte. Nach Schweizer Prozess-Akten der dreissi-ger Jahre des achtzehnten Jahrhunderts. Dresden, H. R. Dohrn, 1903.
181 p. 20cm.

1. Witchcraft--Fiction. 2. Witch-craft--Switzerland. I. Title.

8
NIC

Kaisersberg, Johannes Geiler von, 1445-1510.
see
Geiler, Johannes, von Kaisersberg, 1445-1510.

Karakteristik des Unglaubens.
Witchcraft
BF 1555 E74

Eschenmayer, Carl Adolph von, 1770?-1852.
Karakteristik des Unglaubens, Halbglaubens und Vollglaubens, in Beziehung auf die neuern Geschichten besessener Personen. Nebst Beleuchtung der Kritik im Christenboten. Tübingen, Verlag der Buchhandlung Zu-Guttenberg, 1838.
110 p. 20cm.

1. Demoniac possession. I. Title.

WITCHCRAFT
BF 1581 K18

Karkeek, Paul Quick.
Devonshire witches, by Paul Q. Karkeek. (Read at Teignmouth, July, 1874) ... [London? 1874?]
30 p. 21cm.

"Reprinted from the Transactions of the Devonshire Association for the Advancement of Science, Literature, and Art. 1874."
With this are bound the author's Recent cases of supposed witchcraft in Devon-shire. [London? 1875?] and the au-
(Continued on next card)

8
NIC

WITCHCRAFT
BF 1581 K18

Karkeek, Paul Quick. Devonshire witches...
[1874?] (Card 2)
thor's A budget of witch stories. [London? 1882?]

1. Witchcraft--Devonshire, Eng. 2. Trials (Witchcraft)--Devonshire, Eng. I. Title.

WITCHCRAFT
BF 1581 K18

Karkeek, Paul Quick.
Recent cases of supposed witchcraft in Devonshire, by Paul Q. Karkeek. (Read at Torrington, July, 1875) ... [London? 1875?]
8 p. 21cm.

Caption title.
"Reprinted from the Transactions of the Devonshire Association for the Advancement of Science, Literature, and Art. 1875."
Bound with the author's Devonshire witches. [London? 1874?]
(Continued on next card)

8
NIC

WITCHCRAFT
BF 1581 K18

Karkeek, Paul Quick. Recent cases of sup-posed witchcraft in Devonshire... [1875?]
(Card 2)

1. Witchcraft--Devonshire, Eng. 2. Trials (Witchcraft)--Devonshire, Eng. I. Title.

Karl V, Emperor of Germany, 1500-1558.
WITCHCRAFT
BF 1583 A2 I43

Informatio ivris, in causa poenali; vtrvm tres mvlieres maleficii, et veneficii, cev reae, delatae capi, & torqueri potuerint, nécne? Qvad. Caroli V. imp. constitvtio criminalis aliqvot in locis declaratur. Rechtliches Bedencken, in Malefitzsachen; ob drey Weiber, der Zauberey halber ange-geben, in gefängliche Verhafft angenommen, und peinlich befragt werden können, oder nicht? Darinnen Keyser Carols, dess Fünfften, hochlöblichister Ge-dächtnuss Peinliche, oder Halss-
(Continued on next card)

8
NIC

318

CATALOGUE OF THE CORNELL WITCHCRAFT COLLECTION

Karl V, Emperor of Germany, 1500-1558.

WITCHCRAFT
BF
583
K3
 Informatio ivris, in causa poenali...
         (Card 2)

 gerichtsordnunge in etlichen Articuln erkläret wirdt. Per H. A. B. V. I. D. Franck[furt a. M.] Bey C. Egen[olffs] Erben, 1590.
 68 l. 16cm.
 1. Witchcraft--Germany. 2. Torture--Germany. I. B., H. A. II. H. A. B. III. Karl V, Emperor of Germany, 1500-1558. IV. Title: Recht liches Bedencken, in Malefitzsach en.

8

Karl XI. [i.e., der Elfte], Rabenius und der Hexenprozess.

Witchcraft
PT
9850
Z47
1846
 Zeipel, Carl von
  Karl XI. [i.e., der Elfte], Rabenius und der Hexenprozess. Historischer Roman von Carl von Zeipel. Aus dem Schwedischen übersetzt von G. Fink. Stuttgart, Franckh, 1846.
 2 v. in 1. 14cm. (Das belletristische Ausland, hrsg. Carl Spindler, 671.-679. Bd.)
 1. Rabenius, Nils, 1648-1717. 2. Witchcraft--Fiction. 3. Karl XI, King of Sweden, 1655-1697--Fiction. I. Title.

8

Karter, J.

WITCHCRAFT
BF
1558
K86
1750
 L'Art de commander les esprits célestes, aëriens, terrestres & infernaux. Suivi du Grand grimoire, de la magie noire et des forces infernales, du docteur J. Karter, La clavicule de Salomon, &c. Avec le vrai secret de faire parler les morts, pour découvrir tous les trésors cachés, &c. &c. [Paris?] 1421 [i. e., ca. 1750?]
 iv, 5-108 [i. e., 118], [2] p. illus. 16cm.
 Title in red and black.

      (Continued on next card)

Karter, J.

WITCHCRAFT
BF
1558
K86
1750
 L'Art de commander les esprits ... [1750?]
         (Card 2)

 Published also under other titles: Grimoire du Pape Honorius [best-known]; Le dragon rouge; and Le véritable dragon rouge.

 1. Incantations. 2. Magic. I. Karter, J. II. Title: Le grand grimoire. III. Title: Grimoire du Pape Honorius. IV. Title: Le dragon rouge. V. Title: Le véritable dragon rouge. VI. Title: La clav icule de Salomon.

Karter, J.

WITCHCRAFT
BF
1558
G86
1800a
 Le Véritable dragon rouge, ou l'Art de commander les esprits célestes, aériens, terrestres et infernaux, avec le secret de faire parler les morts; de gagner toutes les fois qu'on met aux loteries; de découvrir les trésors cachés; etc., etc.; suivi de La poule noire, cabale qui était restée inconnue jusqu'ici. [Lille, Imprimerie de Blocquel] 1521 [i.e., 18--]
 140 p. illus. 16cm.

8   (Continued on next card)

Karter, J.

WITCHCRAFT
BF
1558
K86
1800a
 Le Véritable dragon rouge ... [18--]
         (Card 2)

 Title in red and black.
 Chapter 1 signed: J. Karter, Venetiana.
 Published also under other titles: Grimoire du Pape Honorius [best-known]; Le dragon rouge; and L'art de commander les esprits.
 1. Incantations. 2. Magic. I. Karter, J. II. Title: Grimoire du Pape Honorius. III. Title: Le dragon rouge. IV. Title: L'art de com mander les esprits. V. Title: La poule noire.

Kartner, Gabriel, respondent.

Witchcraft
BF
1565
D62
no.15
 Hering, Johannes Ernst, praeses.
  Disputatio physica De hydromantia, qvoad sagas probandas per aqvam frigidam, qvam ... sub praesidio M. Johannis Ernesti Herings ... publicè ventilandam sistit respondens Gabriel Kartnerus reichenbergâ... [Wittebergae] In officina Finceliana exscribebat Michael Meyer [1667]
 [20] p. 18cm. (bound in 20cm. vol.)
 No. 15 in vol. lettered Dissertationes de sagis. 1636-1714.

8   (Continued on next card)

Katekismus von der Geisterlehre.

Witchcraft
BF
1603
S83
no.1
 [Sterzinger, Ferdinand] 1721-1786.
  ... Untersuchung ob es eine Festigkeit gebe dabey viele andere aberglaubische Irrthümer wiederleget werden nebst beygefügtem Katechismus von der Geisterlehre. München, W. Schwarzkopf, Buchhändler in Nürnberg, 1775.
 200 p. 17cm.
 At head of title: Francone dell' Amavero [pseud. of F. Sterzinger].
 No. 1 in vol. lettered Francone dell' Amavero (Ster zinger) Untersuchung [etc.]

8   (Continued on next card)

Katekismus von der Geisterlehre.

Witchcraft
BF
1603
S83
no.1
 [Sterzinger, Ferdinand] 1721-1786. ... Untersuchung ob es eine Festigkeit gebe ... 1775.   (Card 2)

 Attributed by British Museum and Kayser to A. U. Mayer.
 1. Magic. 2. Spells. I. His Katekismus von der Geisterlehre. II. Title. III. Mayer, Andreas Ulrich, 1732-1802, supposed author. IV. Title: Katekismus von der Geist erlehre.

8

Der katholische Weltmann.

WITCHCRAFT
BF
1565
W37
S347
 [Schmid, Franz Josef]
  Und der Satz: Teuflische Magie existirt, besteht noch. In einer Antwort des katholischen Weltmannes auf die von einem Herrn Landpfarrer herausgegebene Apologie der Professor Weberschen Hexenreformation. Augsburg, Bey J. N. Styx, 1791.
 xxiv, 350 p. 19cm.
 1. Bauer, Friedrich. Gedanken eines Landpfarrers über den Ungrund des Hexenglaubens. 2. We ber, Joseph, 1753-1831.

8   (Continued on next card)

Ein katholischer Weltmann.

WITCHCRAFT
BF
1565
W37
S34
 [Schmid, Franz Josef]
  Ueber die Hexenreformation des Herrn Professor Weber zu Dillingen ... Von einem katholischen Weltmanne. [Augsburg] 1787.
 86 p. 19cm.
 Attribution by Kayser and Deutsche Biographie (under Weber, Joseph).
 1. Weber, Joseph, 1753-1831. Ungrund des Hexen- und Gespenster-Glaubens. 2. Witchcraft. I. Ein katholischer Weltmann. II. Title.

8

WITCHCRAFT
BF
1583
K21
 Kausch, Friedrich.
  Hexenglaube und Hexenprozesse in unserer Heimat; ein Beitrag zur Geschichte der Provinz Sachsen und des Harzgebietes. Burg b. M., 1927.
 78 p. 19cm.

 1. Witchcraft--Saxony (Province) 2. Witchcraft--Harz Mountains. 3. Trials (Witchcraft)--Saxony (Province) 4. Trials (Witchcraft)--Harz Mountai ns. I. Title.

8
NIC

Witchcraft
BF
1565
K21
1771
 Kauz, Constantin Franz Florian Anton von, 1735-1797.
  Constantini Francisci de Cauz ... De cultibus magicis eorumque perpetuo ad ecclesiam et rempublicam habitu libri duo. ... Editio II. Aucta et emendata. Vindobonae, Literis Trattnerianis, 1771.
 18 p. l., 400, [6] p. 22cm.
 "ΕΠΙΜΕΤΡΟΝ. De ritu ignis natali Joannis Baptistae die accensi dissertatio," p. [377]-400, has special t. p. (First printed 1759)

8   (Continued on next card)

Witchcraft
BF
1565
K21
1771
 Kauz, Constantin Franz Florian Anton von, 1735-1797. ... De cultibus magicis ... 1771.   (Card 2)

 1. Witchcraft. 2. Catholic Church and occult sciences. 3. Trials (Witchcraft) 4. Fire in religion, folk-lore, etc. I. His Epimetron. II. His De ritu ignis. III. Title: De cultibus magicis. IV. Title: Epimetr on. De ritu ignis. V. Title.

8

Kauz, Constantin Franz Florian Anton von, 1735-1797.

Witchcraft
BF
1565
K21
1771
 De ritu ignis.
 Kauz, Constantin Franz Florian Anton von, 1735-1797.
  Constantini Francisci de Cauz ... De cultibus magicis eorumque perpetuo ad ecclesiam et rempublicam habitu libri duo. ... Editio II. Aucta et emendata. Vindobonae, Literis Trattnerianis, 1771.
 18 p. l., 400, [6] p. 22cm.
 "ΕΠΙΜΕΤΡΟΝ. De ritu ignis natali Joannis Baptistae die accensi dissertatio," p. [377]-400, has special t. p. (First printed 1759)

8   (Continued on next card)

Kauz, Constantin Franz Florian Anton von, 1735-1797.

Witchcraft
BF
1565
K21
1771
 Epimetron.
 Kauz, Constantin Franz Florian Anton von, 1735-1797.
  Constantini Francisci de Cauz ... De cultibus magicis eorumque perpetuo ad ecclesiam et rempublicam habitu libri duo. ... Editio II. Aucta et emendata. Vindobonae, Literis Trattnerianis, 1771.
 18 p. l., 400, [6] p. 22cm.
 "ΕΠΙΜΕΤΡΟΝ. De ritu ignis natali Joannis Baptistae die accensi dissertatio," p. [377]-400, has special t. p. (First printed 1759)

8   (Continued on next card)

Keisersperg, Johannes Geiler von, 1445-1510.

see

Geiler, Johannes, von Kaisersberg, 1445-1510.

WITCHCRAFT
PT
2376
K12
B7
 Keller, Karl, of Bunzlau.
  Bosheit und Wahnglaube; oder, Der Hexenprozess. Sittengemälde aus der Mitte des 17ten Jahrhunderts. Bunzlau, Appun, 1831.
 239 p. 19cm.

8
NIC I. Title.

CATALOGUE OF THE CORNELL WITCHCRAFT COLLECTION

WITCHCRAFT
BF 1555 K29
Keller, Ludwig, 1849-1915.
　　Die altevangelischen Gemeinden und der Hexenglaube.
　　(In [Geisteskultur;] Monatshefte der Comenius-Gesellschaft [für Geisteskultur und Volksbildung,] Berlin, 1892-1934. 25cm. 8. Bd., 1. und 2. Heft (1899), p. [30]-35)

　　Bibliographical footnotes.

　　1. Demoniac possession. 2. Waldenses. 3. Comenius, Johann Amos, 1592-1670. I. Title.
8 NIC

BT 975 K29
Kelly, Henry Ansgar.
　　The Devil, demonology, and witchcraft; the development of Christian beliefs in evil spirits. Garden City, N. Y., Doubleday, 1968.
　　vi, 187 p. 22 cm. (A Scott & Collins book) $4.95
　　Bibliographical footnotes.

　　1. Demonology. I. Title.

BT975.K42　　235'.4　　68-24838
Library of Congress　　[3]

Kelway, Thomas, fl. 1593, tr.

WITCHCRAFT
BF 51 S33
Schindler, Heinrich Bruno, 1797-1859.
　　Das magische Geistesleben. Ein Beitrag zur Psychologie. Breslau, W. G. Korn, 1857.
　　xvi, 356 p. 24cm.

　　1. Psychology, Religious. 2. Occult sciences--Psychology. I. Title.
8 NIC

WITCHCRAFT
BF 1583 K32
Kemper, Josef.
　　Hexenwahn und Hexenprozesse in Deutschland, von J. Kemper. Mit 13 Illustrationen. Regensburg, Verlagsanstalt vorm. G. J. Manz, 1908.
　　vi, 167, [1] p. illus. 20cm. (Geschichtliche Jugend- und Volksbibliothek, 16. Bd.)

　　Bibliography: p. [168]

　　1. Witchcraft--Germany. 2. Trials (Witchcraft)--Germany. 3. Torture--Germany. I. Title.
8 NIC

WITCHCRAFT
BF 1576 K32
Kempf, Oskar.
　　Hexenprozesse in Amerika.
　　(In Die Kritik; Wochenschau des öffentlichen Lebens. Berlin, 1894-1902. 22cm. Nr. 16 (1895), p. 113-125)

　　Signed: Oskar Kempf.

　　1. Trials (Witchcraft)--New England. I. Title.
8 NIC

Kepler, Johann, 1571-1630.
Witchcraft
QB 36 K38 K38
Keppler, Gustav, ed.
　　Familiengeschichte Keppler, bearb. und hrsg. von Oberpostinspektor Gustav Keppler, Stuttgart. 2. Bd. Görlitz, Verlag für Sippenforschung und Wappenkunde C. A. Starke, 1930.
　　864 p. port., plates. 15cm.
　　Added t. p.: Astronom Kepler und seine Zeit, mit Schilderung des Hexenprozesses gegen seine Mutter.
　　Band 1 apparently not published.
8
(Continued on next card)

Witchcraft
K K383+
Kepler, Katharina, 1547-1622, defendant.
　　Judicium matris Kepleri. [Francofurti a. M.?, Heyder & Zimmer, 1870]
　　202 p. 27cm.

　　Offprint of Kepler, Johann, 1571-1630. ... opera omnia, ed. Ch. Frisch, 8. Bd., 1. Teil, p. [359]-562.

　　1. Trials (Witchcraft)--Germany. I. Title.
8

Kepler, Katharina, 1547-1622.
Witchcraft
BF 1583 Z7 1621
Günther, Louis, 1859-
　　Ein Hexenprozess; ein Kapitel aus der Geschichte des dunkelsten Aberglaubens. Giessen, A. Töpelmann, 1906.
　　xii, 112 p. 22cm.

　　1. Kepler, Katharina, 1547-1622. 2. Witchcraft. 3. Trials (Witchcraft)--Germany. I. Title.

Kepler, Katharina, 1547-1622.
Witchcraft
QB 36 K38 K38
Keppler, Gustav, ed.
　　Familiengeschichte Keppler, bearb. und hrsg. von Oberpostinspektor Gustav Keppler, Stuttgart. 2. Bd. Görlitz, Verlag für Sippenforschung und Wappenkunde C. A. Starke, 1930.
　　864 p. port., plates. 15cm.
　　Added t. p.: Astronom Kepler und seine Zeit, mit Schilderung des Hexenprozesses gegen seine Mutter.
　　Band 1 apparently not published.
8
(Continued on next card)

Witchcraft
QB 36 K38 K38
Keppler, Gustav, ed. Familiengeschichte Keppler. 1930. (Card 2)

　　1. Kepler, Johann, 1571-1630. 2. Kepler, Katharina, 1547-1622. 3. Trials (Witchcraft)--Germany. I. Title. II. Title: Astronom Kepler und seine Zeit.
8

WITCHCRAFT
BF 1582 K39
Kerdaniel, Édouard Le Marant de, 1867-
　　Sorciers de Savoie [par] Édouard-L. de Kerdaniel. Annecy, Imprimerie Abry, 1900.
　　47 p. 19cm.

　　Bibliographical footnotes.

　　1. Witchcraft--Savoy. I. Title.
8 NIC

WITCHCRAFT
BF 1555 K39
Kerner, Justinus Andreas Christian, 1786-1862.
　　Geschichten Besessener neuerer Zeit; Beobachtungen aus dem Gebiete kakodämonisch-magnetischer Erscheinungen. Nebst Reflexionen von C. A. Eschenmayer über Besessenseyn und Zauber. Stuttgart, Druck von J. Wachendorf, 1834.
　　vi, 195 p. 19cm.

　　1. Demoniac possession. I. Eschenmayer, Carl Adolph von, 1770?-1852. Einige Reflexionen über Besitzung und Zauber. II. Title.
8 NIC

Witchcraft
Z 5761 K39
[Kernot, Henry] 1806-1874.
　　Bibliotheca diabolica; being a choice selection of the most valuable books relating to the Devil; his origin, greatness, and influence. Comprising the most important works on the devil, Satan, demons, hell, hell-torments, magic, witchcraft ... with some curious volumes on dreams and astrology. In two parts, pro and con, serious and humorous ... [New York] On sale by Scribner, Welford & Armstrong, 1874.
　　40 p. illus. 25cm.

　　1. Devil--Bibliography. I. Title.

Witchcraft
B 3998 K43
Kettner, Friedrich Ernst.
　　De duobus impostoribus, Benedicto Spinosa et Balthasare Bekkero. Lipsiae, Stanno Immanuelis Titii [1694]
　　[17] p. 20cm.

　　Diss.--Leipzig.

　　1. Spinoza, Benedictus de, 1632-1677. 2. Bekker, Balthasar, 1634-1698. I. Title.

Witchcraft
BF 1410 B42 Z56 v.3 no.8
Een Keuning-kaarsje voor den siender van Een vremt nagtgesigte, om te dienen tot opheldering van syn St. Niklaas-droom. Ezelenburg, Gedrukt in de Gulde Schoolplak [1692]
　　8 p. illus. initial. 20 x 15cm.
　　4°: A⁴.
　　Black letter.
　　Defending Molinaeus, and against Bekker.
　　Van der Linde 133.
　　No. 8 in vol. lettered Bekker III.
8
(Continued on next card)

Witchcraft
BF 1410 B42 Z56 v.3 no.8
Een Keuning-kaarsje voor den siender van Een vremt nagtgesigte ... [1692] (Card 2)

　　1. Beschryvinge van een vremd nagtgezigte. 2. Bekker, Balthasar, 1634-1698. 3. Molinaeus, Johannes, d. 1702.

Witchcraft
BF 1410 B42 Z69 no.26
Een Keuning-kaarsje voor den siender van Een vremt nagtgesigte, om te dienen tot opheldering van syn St. Niklaas-droom. Ezelenburg, Gedrukt in de Gulde Schoolplak [1692]
　　8 p. illus. initial. 21cm.
　　4°: A⁴.
　　Black letter.
　　Defending Molinaeus, and against Bekker.
　　Van der Linde 133.
　　No. 26 in a Collection of tracts against Balthasar Bekker and his Betoverde weereld.
8
(Continued on next card)

320

CATALOGUE OF THE CORNELL WITCHCRAFT COLLECTION

Witchcraft
BF
1410
B42
Z69
no.26

Een Keuning-kaarsje voor den siender van Een vremt nagtgesigte ... [1692] (Card 2)

1. Beschryvinge van een vremd nagt-gezigte. 2. Bekker, Balthasar, 1634-1698. 3. Molinaeus, Johannes, d. 1702.

WITCHCRAFT
BX
2340
P33

Keussen, Hermann, 1862–
Zwei Hexenprozesse aus der Crefelder Gegend.

(In: Historischer Verein für den Niederrhein. Annalen. Köln. 23cm. No.63 (1897) p. 111-119)

With, in the same issue: Pauls, Emil. Der Exorcismus an Herzog Johann Wilhelm von Jülich in den Jahren 1604 und 1605.

1. Trials (Witchcraft)—Krefeld, Ger. 2. Hagh, Catharina. 3. Blex, Sibilla. 4. Bleick, Anna. VI. Title.

8
NIC

WITCHCRAFT
BF
1563
K44

Keyser, Georg Adam, comp.
Uhuhu; oder Hexen-Gespenster-Schazgräber- und Erscheinungs-Geschichten. Erfurt, Bey G. A. Keyser, 1785-92.
7 v. in 3. Illus. 18cm.

Each vol. has lengthy introduction including bibliographical materials.

1. Witchcraft. 2. Ghost stories. 3. Occult sciences—Bibl. I. Title.

WITCHCRAFT
BF
1559
K5
K74a

Khueller, Sebastianus
Kurtze vnnd warhafftige Historia von einer Junckfrawen, welche mit etlich vnd dreissig bösen Geistern leibhafftig besessen, vnd in der Schloss Capeln zu Starnberg, im Ertz-hertzogthumb Österreich vnder der Enns, in beysein viler vom Adel, vnd ander ehrlichen leut, genedigklich daruon erlödiget worden. München, Getruckt bey Adam Berg [1574. Wien, 1885]
[14] p.   illus.   24cm.

(Continued on next card)

WITCHCRAFT
BF
1559
K5
K74a

Khueller, Sebastianus
Kurtze vnnd warhafftige Historia von einer Junckfrawen...[1885]   (Card 2)

Signed: Sebastianus Khüeller.
Facsimile reprint.

1. Exorcism. 2. Steiner, Veronica. 3. Title.

Kidder, Daniel Parish, 1815-1891, ed.

ar V
13956

Remarkable delusions; or, Illustrations of popular errors, revised by D. P. Kidder. New York, Carlton & Phillips, 1854.
213 p. 16cm.

I. Kidder, Daniel Parish, 1815-1891, ed.

Witchcraft
BF
1413
K47
G3

Kiesewetter, Karl, 1854-1895.
Die geheimwissenschaften. Von Karl Kiesewetter. Leipzig, W. Friedrich [1895]
iii-xxvii p., 1 l., 749, [1] p. illus., 2 port. 22cm.
Added t. p.: Geschichte des Occultismus.
Forms second part of the author's: Geschichte des neueren occultismus.
CONTENTS.—Die alchymie.—Die astrologie und das divinationswesen.—Das hexenwesen in seiner geschichte und seinen erscheinungen.—Die weisse magie. Die theurgie. Die nekromantie.—Vergleichung der spiritistischen phänomene mit den geheimwissenschaftlichen.

1. Occult sciences—Hist. I. His Geschichte des neueren Occultismus. II. His Geschichte des Occultismus. III. Title.

8   8-18781

Library of Congress, no.

Witchcraft
BF
1413
K47

Kiesewetter, Karl, 1854-1895.
Geschichte des neueren occultismus. Geheimwissenschaftliche systeme von Agrippa von Nettesheym bis zu Carl du Prel. Von Carl Kiesewetter ... Leipzig, W. Friedrich [1891]
xiv, 799, [2] p. illus. 22cm.
Half-title: Erster teil. Systeme und systematiker.
Pt. 2 issued under title: Die geheimwissenschaften.

1. Occult sciences—Hist. I. Title.

8   8-18764

Library of Congress, no.

Witchcraft
BF
1413
K47
G3

Kiesewetter, Karl, 1854-1895.
Geschichte des Occultismus.
Die geheimwissenschaften. Von Karl Kiesewetter. Leipzig, W. Friedrich [1895]
iii-xxvii p., 1 l., 749, [1] p. illus., 2 port. 22cm.
Added t. p.: Geschichte des Occultismus.
Forms second part of the author's: Geschichte des neueren occultismus.
CONTENTS.—Die alchymie.—Die astrologie und das divinationswesen.—Das hexenwesen in seiner geschichte und seinen erscheinungen.—Die weisse magie. Die theurgie. Die nekromantie.—Vergleichung der spiritistischen phänomene mit den geheimwissenschaftlichen.

1. Occult sciences—Hist. I. His Geschichte des neueren Occultismus. II. His Geschichte des Occultismus. III. Title.

8   8-18781

Library of Congress, no.

Witchcraft
BF
1413
K47
G3

Kiesewetter, Karl, 1854-1895.
Geschichte des Occultismus.
Die geheimwissenschaften. Von Karl Kiesewetter. Leipzig, W. Friedrich [1895]
iii-xxvii p., 1 l., 749, [1] p. illus., 2 port. 22cm.
Added t. p.: Geschichte des Occultismus.
Forms second part of the author's: Geschichte des neueren occultismus.
CONTENTS.—Die alchymie.—Die astrologie und das divinationswesen.—Das hexenwesen in seiner geschichte und seinen erscheinungen.—Die weisse magie. Die theurgie. Die nekromantie.—Vergleichung der spiritistischen phänomene mit den geheimwissenschaftlichen.

1. Occult sciences—Hist. I. His Geschichte des neueren Occultismus. II. His Geschichte des Occultismus. III. Title.

8   8-18781

Library of Congress, no.

BF
1566
K47

Kiessling, Edith.
Zauberei in den germanischen volksrechten, von dr. iur. Edith Kiessling ... Jena, G. Fischer, 1941.
79 p. pl. 23½cm. (Added t.-p.: Beiträge zur mittelalterlichen, neueren und allgemeinen geschichte, hrsg. von Friedrich Schneider. Bd. 17)
Issued also as inaugural dissertation, Frankfurt.
"Literaturverzeichnis": p. 76-79.
L. C. copy imperfect: plate wanting.

1. Witchcraft. 2. Law, Germanic. I. Title.

                                            43-47132
Library of Congress   BF1566.K47
                     [2]   133.40943

WITCHCRAFT
BF
1566
K49

Kimball, Mrs. Henrietta D.
Witchcraft illustrated. Witchcraft to be understood. Facts, theories and incidents. With a glance at old and new Salem and its historical resources. By Mrs. Henrietta D. Kimball. Boston, G. A. Kimball, 1892.
135 p. plates, ports. 20cm.

1. Witchcraft. 2. Salem, Mass.—Description. I. Title.

8
NIC   5-21280
Library of Congress

WITCHCRAFT
BF
1523
K78
K516

Kindleben, Christian Wilhelm, 1748-1785.
Der Teufeleien des achtzehnten Jahrhunderts letzter Akt, worinn des Emanuel Schwedenborgs demüthiges Danksagungsschreiben kürzlich beantwortet, der ganze bisher geführte Streit friedlich beygelegt, und in dem Büchlein über die Nonexistenz des Teufels manches zurückgenommen, ergänzt und berichtiget wird ... Leipzig, Bey C. F. Schneider, 1779.
63 p. 20cm.

8
NIC   (Continued on next card)

WITCHCRAFT
BF
1523
K78
K516

Kindleben, Christian Wilhelm, 1748-1785.
Der Teufeleien des achtzehnten Jahrhunderts letzter Akt...1779.   (Card 2)

1. Köster, Heinrich Martin Gottfried, 1734-1802. Emanuel Swedenborgs demüthiges Danksagungsschreiben. 2. Devil. I. His Ueber die Non-Existenz des Teufels. II. Title.

WITCHCRAFT
BF
1523
K78
K51

[Kindleben, Christian Wilhelm] 1748-1785.
Ueber die Non-Existenz des Teufels. Als eine Antwort auf die Demüthige Bitte um Belehrung an die grossen Männer, welche keinen Teufel glauben. Berlin, Bey G. A. Lange, 1776.
55 p.   17cm.
Attribution by Holzmann, Jocher, et al.

1. Köster, Heinrich Martin Gottfried, 1734-1802. Demüthige Bitte um Belehrung. 2. Devil. 2. Superstition. I. Title.

8

WITCHCRAFT
BF
1523
V19
no.3

[Kindleben, Christian Wilhelm] 1748-1785.
Ueber die Non-Existenz des Teufels. Als eine Antwort auf die Demüthige Bitte um Belehrung an die grossen Männer, welche keinen Teufel glauben. Berlin, Bey G. A. Lange, 1776.
55 p.   17cm.

Attribution by Holzmann, Jocher, et al.
No. 3 in vol. lettered Varia scripta demonolog.

8

WITCHCRAFT
BF
1501
D12
no.4

[Kindleben, Christian Wilhelm] 1748-1785.
Ueber die Non-Existenz des Teufels. Als eine Antwort auf die Demüthige Bitte um Belehrung an die grossen Männer, welche keinen Teufel glauben. Berlin, Bey G. A. Lange, 1776.
55 p.   17cm.
Attribution by Holzer, Jocher, et al.
No. 4 in vol. lettered Dämonologische Schriften.

8

Kindleben, Christian Wilhelm, 1748-1785.
Ueber die Non-Existenz des Teufels.

WITCHCRAFT
BF
1523
K78
K516

Kindleben, Christian Wilhelm, 1748-1785.
Der Teufeleien des achtzehnten Jahrhunderts letzter Akt, worinn des Emanuel Schwedenborgs demüthiges Danksagungsschreiben kürzlich beantwortet, der ganze bisher geführte Streit friedlich beygelegt, und in dem Büchlein über die Nonexistenz des Teufels manches zurückgenommen, ergänzt und berichtiget wird ... Leipzig, Bey C. F. Schneider, 1779.
63 p. 20cm.

8
NIC   (Continued on next card)

CATALOGUE OF THE CORNELL WITCHCRAFT COLLECTION

Kindleben, Christian Wilhelm, 1748-1785.
Ueber die Non-Existenz des Teufels.

WITCHCRAFT
BF 1523 K78 K513
[Köster, Heinrich Martin Gottfried] 1734-1802.
Emanuel Swedenborgs demüthiges Danksagungsschreiben an den grossen Mann, der die Nonexistenz des Teufels demonstrirt hat. Frankfurt und Leipzig, 1778.
46 p. 17cm.
Attribution by Holzmann.
1. Kindleben, Christian Wilhelm, 1748-1785. Ueber die Non-Existenz des Teufels. 2. Devil. I. Swedenborg, Emanuel, 1688-1772, supposed author. II. Title. III. Title: Demüthiges Danksagungsschre iben an den grossen Mann.
8

Kindlebn, Christian Wilhelm, 1748-1785.

see

Kindleben, Christian Wilhelm, 1748-1785.

The kingdom of darkness.

Witchcraft
BF 1565 C95
[Crouch, Nathaniel] 1632?-1725?
The kingdom of darkness: or, The history of daemons, specters, witches, apparitions, possessions, disturbances, and other wonderful and supernatural delusions, mischievous feats and malicious impostures of the Devil. ... By R. B. [pseud.] ... London, Printed for N. Crouch, 1688.
169, [9] p. illus. 15cm.

Publisher's catalogue: [9] p. at end.

WITCHCRAFT
DC 130 L97 K57
Kippenberg, Anton, 1874-1950.
Die Sage vom Herzog von Luxemburg und die historische Persönlichkeit ihres Trägers. Mit 2 Vollbildern und 11 Abbildungen im Text. Leipzig, W. Engelmann, 1901.
viii, 280 p. illus. 25cm.

Bibliography: p. [256]-280.

8 NIC
1. Luxembourg, François Henri de Montmorency, duc de, 1628-1695. I. Title.

Kirchberg, Marthe Margarethe, d. 1688, defendant.

Witchcraft
BF 1583 Z7 1688
Zwei Hexenprocesse aus dem Jahre 1688, geführt bei dem hochfürstlichen Amte in Ballenstedt. Quedlinburg, H. C. Huch, 1863.
104 p. 22cm.
Contents.--I. Acta inquisitionalia ... wider Marthen Margarethen Kirchbergs aus Reinstedt.--II. Acta inquisitionalia ... contra die Pfannenschmiedin Anna Teichmanns.
1. Trials (Witchcraft)--Saxony. I. Kirchberg, Marthe Margarethe, d. 1688, defendant. II. Teichmann, Anna, fl. 1688, defendant.

WITCHCRAFT
BT 980 K58
Kirchhof, Christian August Ludwig.
Christ. Aug. Lud. Kirchhoffs vollständige Beantwortung der Frage: Was läst sich nach Vernunft und Schrift vom Teufel glauben? Ein Beitrag zur Aufklärung besonders für Ungelehrte. Braunschweig, In Commission der Schröderschen Buchhandlung, 1789.
125 p. 17cm.

8 NIC
1. Devil--Biblical teaching. I. Title: Vollständige Beantwortung der Frage: Was läst sich nach Vernunft und Schrift vom Teufel glauben?

WITCHCRAFT
BF 1517 G3 K58
Kirchhoff, Theodor, 1853-1922.
Beziehungen des Dämonen- und Hexenwesens zur deutschen Irrenpflege, von Dr. Kirchhoff. (In Allgemeine Zeitschrift für Psychiatrie und ihre Grenzgebiete. Berlin, 1844-1949. 23cm. 44. Bd., 4. u. 5. Heft (1888), p. [329]-398)
Caption title.
Bibliographical footnotes.
1. Demonology. 2. Mental illness--Germany. 3. Mental illness (in religion, folk-lore, etc.) I. Title.

8 NIC

WITCHCRAFT
Z 6880 Z9C35 no.3
Kirchhoff & Wigand, Leipzig.
Culturgeschichte, Curiosa, Facetiae, ältere deutsche etc. Literatur, Vermischtes ... enthaltend auch die alten Sammlungen des ... Nationalökonomen Johann Georg Büsch über Hexen, Dämonologie, Alchemie und Geheime Wissenschaften im allgemeinen. New-York, G.E. Stechert [1885]
72 p. 23cm.

At head of title: Nr. 743.
No. 3 in vol. lettered:
(Continued on next card)

WITCHCRAFT
Z 6880 Z9C35 no.3
Kirchhoff & Wigand, Leipzig. Culturgeschichte, Curiosa, Facetiae, ältere deutsche etc. Literatur, Vermischtes ... [1885] (Card 2)

Catalogues of books on magic and witchcraft.

1. Bibliography--Rare books. 2. Occult sciences--Bibl.--Catalogs. 3. Witchcraft--Bibl.--Catalogs. I. Title.

Kirchmaier, Georg Caspar, 1635-1700.

see

Kirchmayer, Georg Caspar, 1635-1700.

Witchcraft
BF 1445 D61 no.10
Kirchmayer, Georg Caspar, 1635-1700, praeses.
Ad scriptores aliqvot Roman. veteres, De apparitionibus spectror. & spirituum, sub corpor. inprimis human. schemate, nec non visionibus naturae probabilibus, adversus atheos inprimis, dissertatio, sub moderamine ... Dn. Georgii Casparis Kirchmajeri, à Johanne Gottlieb Stoltzen ... ventilationi publicae exposita, die 27. Julii, anno 1692. Wittebergae, Typis Christiani Schrödteri [1692]
(Continued on next card)

8

Witchcraft
BF 1445 D61 no.10
Kirchmayer, Georg Caspar, 1635-1700, praeses. Ad scriptores ... De apparitionibus spectror. & spirituum ... [1692] (Card 2)

32, [2] p. 18cm. (bound in 21cm. vol.)
No. 10 in vol. lettered Dissertationes de spectris. 1646-1753.
1. Apparitions. I. Stoltze, Johann Gottlob, respondent. II. Title: De apparitionibus spectrorum et spirituum. III. Title: Ad scriptores aliqvot Roman. veteres, De apparitionibus spectror. & spirituum.

8

WITCHCRAFT
BF 1559 K62
Kittelman, Christian
Von dem Exorcismo; das ist, Von den Worten: Fahre aus du unreiner Geist, unnd gib Raum dem heiligen Geist, etc. Gründlich und bestendiger Bericht. [Vor, aus zu ersehen, das er melter, Exorcismus inn unsern Kirchen [billich] behalten werde, unnd das M. Wolffgang Amling keine erhebliche Ursachen gehabt, darumb er denselben zu Zerbst, und anderswo im Fürstenthumb Anhalt, abgeschafft. [Von] Christianus Kittelman ... [n. p.] 1591.
(Continued on next card)

8 NIC

WITCHCRAFT
BF 1559 K62
Kittelman, Christian
Von dem Exorcismo...1591. (Card 2)

Preface dated: Newemarckt, vor Halle, ... anno 1590.
Imperfect copy: t. p. mutilated. Missing words and letters supplied from The National union catalog, pre-1956 imprints.
"Consilium D. D. Martini Miri, amico cuidam priuatim cõmunicatum, super abrogatione Exorcismi": [18] manuscript pages bound at end.

(Continued on next card)

WITCHCRAFT
BF 1559 K62
Kittelman, Christian
Von dem Exorcismo...1591. (Card 3)

1. Exorcism. 2. Amling, Wolfgang, 1542-1606. I. Title.

Witchcraft
BF 1581 K62 1912
Kittredge, George Lyman, 1860-1941.
English witchcraft and James the First, by George Lyman Kittredge; from Studies in the history of religions presented to Crawford Howell Toy, by pupils, colleagues and friends. New York, The Macmillan company, 1912.
cover-title, 65 p. 23½cm.
With this is bound his King James I and The Devil is an ass.
Cover has initials of author (G.L.K.) and donor (J.M.H., i.e. J. M. Hart)
1. James I, king of Great Britain, 1566-1625. II. Title.

BF 1566 K62
Kittredge, George Lyman., 1860-1941.
Notes on witchcraft, by George Lyman Kittredge .. Worcester, Mass., The Davis press, 1907.
67 p. 26cm.
"Reprinted from the Proceedings of the American antiquarian society, vol. XVIII."

1. Witchcraft. I. Title.

15-3715

Library of Congress   BF1566.K5

Witchcraft
BF 1581 K62W8
Kittredge, George Lyman, 1860-1941.
Witchcraft in old and New England, by George Lyman Kittredge ... Cambridge, Mass., Harvard university press, 1929.
6 p. l., [3]-641 p. 24¼cm.
"Notes": p. [375]-598.
Presentation copy to Prof. Burr with author's autograph.

1. Witchcraft--England. 2. Witchcraft--New England. I. Title.

29-6482

Library of Congress   BF1581.K58
———— Copy 2.
Copyright A 5717   [5-2]

CATALOGUE OF THE CORNELL WITCHCRAFT COLLECTION

```
           Kittredge, George Lyman, 1860-1941.
BF             Witchcraft in Old and New England.  New York, Russell
1581        & Russell ₁1956₎
K62W8          641 p.  22 cm.
1956           Includes bibliography.


               1. Witchcraft—England. 2. Witchcraft—New England.

           BF1581.K58  1956         133.40942          58—12929 ‡
           Library of Congress         ₁59c7₎
```

```
              Klaare en beknopte verhandeling van de
              natuur en werkinge der menschelijke
Witchcraft    zielen, engelen en duivelen ...
BF           Blyenbergh, Willem van, 17th cent.
1410            Klaare en beknopte verhandeling van de
B42         natuur en werkinge der menschelijke zielen,
Z82         engelen en duivelen, vervat in gewisselde
no.3        brieven tusschen de heer Willem van Blyen-
            bergh en Willem Deurhoff.  Amsterdam, By
            J. ten Hoorn, boekverkooper, 1692.
               64 p.  title vignette, illus. initials.
            20 x 15cm.
               4°: A-H⁴.
               Discussion of questions raised in the
            contemporary        controversy over Bal-
                            (Continued on next card)
```

```
              Klaare en beknopte verhandeling van de
              natuur en werkinge der menschelijke
              zielen, engelen en duivelen ...
Witchcraft    Blyenbergh, Willem van, 17th cent.  Klaare
BF          en beknopte verhandeling van de natuur en
1410        werkinge der menschelijke zielen ... 1692.
B42                                      (Card 2)
Z82
no.3        thasar Bekker's De Betoverde weereld.
              Van der Linde 77.
              No. 3 in vol. lettered Over Bekkers
            Betoverde wereld.  1692.
              1. Soul.  2. Spirits.  3. Bekker, Bal-
            thasar.  De betoverde weereld.  I. Deurhoff,
            Willem, 1650-           1717.  II. Title.

8
```

```
Witchcraft
BF            Een klaare uytlegginge, over de versoekinge
1410        des Heere Jesu Christi in de woestyne.  In
B42         antwoord op de vijfde brief van Philalee-
Z69         thees.  t'Amsterdam, Voor den autheur ge-
no.8        drukt, en zijn volt te bekomen by P.
            Rotterdam ₁169-?₎
              24 p.  21cm.
              Signatures: 4°, a², A-C⁴.
              Black letter.
              Van der Linde 110.
              No. 8 in          a Collection of tracts
            against           Balthasar Bekker and his
            Betoverde          weereld.
NIC                       (Continued on next card)
```

```
Witchcraft
BF           Een klaare uytlegginge over de versoekinge
1410        des Heere Jesu Christi ...  ₁169-?₎
B42                                      (Card 2)
Z69
no.8           1. Jesus Christ—Temptation.  2. Bekker,
            Balthasar, 1634-1698.  De betoverde weereld.
            3. Hooght, Everard van der, d. 1716.  4.
            Nederlands Hervormde Kerk.



NIC
```

```
            Klein, Johann, 1659-1732.
              Juristische Untersuchung, was von der
Witchcraft    Hexen Bekäntniss zu halten.
BF          Thomasius, Christian, 1655-1728.
1565           Christ. Thomasii Kurtze Lehr-Sätze von
T46         dem Laster der Zauberey, mit dessen eige-
1717        nen Vertheidigung vermehret.  Worbey Johann
            Kleins ... Juristische Untersuchung, was von
            der Hexen Bekäntniss zu halten, dass solche
            aus schändlichem Beyschlaff mit dem Teuffel
            Kinder gezeuget.  Beydes aus dem Lateinischen
            ins Teutsche übersetzt.  Franckfurth und
            Leipzig, 1717.
              134 p.  18cm.     (Continued on next card)
8
```

```
             Klein, Johann, 1659-1732.
                Juristische Untersuchung, was von der
Witchcraft      Hexen Bekäntniss zu halten.
BF           Thomasius, Christian, 1655-1728.  Christ.
1565        Thomasii Kurtze Lehr-Sätze von dem Laster
T46         der Zauberey ... 1717.        (Card 2)
1717
              Title in red and black.
              Translation of Thomasius' Dissertatio de
            crimine magiae and of Klein's Meditatio aca-
            demica exhibens examen juridicum judicialis.
              Klein's Juristische Untersuchung, was von
            der Hexen Bekäntniss zu halten ..., p. ₁79₎-
            134, has special t. p.
8                       (Continued on next card)
```

```
             Klein, Johann, 1659-1732.
                Juristische Untersuchung, was von der
Witchcraft      Hexen Bekäntniss zu halten.
BF           Thomasius, Christian, 1655-1728.
1565           Christ. Thomasii Kurtze Lehr-Sätze von
T46         dem Laster der Zauberey, mit dessen eigenen
1717a       Vertheidigung vermehret.  Worbey Johann
            Kleins ... Juristische Untersuchung, was
            von der Hexen Bekäntniss zu halten, dass
            solche aus schändlichem Beyschlaf mit dem
            Teuffel Kinder gezeuget.  Beydes aus dem
            Lateinischen ins Teutsche übersetzt.
            Franckfurth und Leipzig, 1717.
              134 p.  front.  19cm.
8                       (Continued on next card)
```

```
             Klein, Johann, 1659-1732.
                Juristische Untersuchung, was von der
Witchcraft      Hexen Bekäntniss zu halten.
BF           Thomasius, Christian, 1655-1728.  Christ.
1565        Thomasii Kurtze Lehr-Sätze von dem Laster
T46         der Zauberey ... 1717.        (Card 2)
1717a
              Translation of his Dissertatio de crimi-
            ne magiae, J. Reiche, respondent; and of
            Meditatio academica, exhibens examen juri-
            dicum judicialis, by J. Klein (N. Putter,
            respondent.)
              Johann Kleins Juristische Untersuchung,
            p. ₁79₎-134, has     special t. p.
8                       (Continued on next card)
```

```
             Klein, Johann, 1659-1732.
                Juristische Untersuchung, was von der
Witchcraft      Hexen Bekäntniss zu halten.
BF           Thomasius, Christian, 1655-1728.  Christ.
1565        Thomasii Kurtze Lehr-Sätze von dem Laster
T46         der Zauberey ... 1717.        (Card 3)
1717a
              With this are bound Ludovici, Gottfried,
            1670-1724. ... Theologicum novae... Coburgi
            ₁1718₎ and Sturm, Johann Christoph, 1635-
            1703. ... Wahrhaffte und gründliche Vorstel-
            lung von der lügenhafften Stern-Wahrsagerey.
            Coburg, 1722.
              1. Witchcraft.  I. His Dissertatio
            de crimine mag     iae.— German.  II.
8                       (Continued on next card)
```

```
Witchcraft
BF            Klein, Johann, 1659-1732, praeses.
1565            Meditatio academica, exhibens examen
D62         juridicum judicialis lamiarum confessionis,
no.12       se ex nefando cum Satana coitu prolem sus-
            cepisse humanam, Was von der Hexen Bekänt-
            niss zu halten, dass sie aus schändlichen
            Beyschlaff mit dem Teuffel Kinder gezeuget?
            Qvam ... praeside Dn. Johanne Klein, ...
            submittit Nicolaus Putter, Strals. author.
            Rostochii, Typis Joh. Wepplingii ₁1698₎
              48 p.  20cm.
              No. 12 in         vol. lettered Dissertia-
            tiones de spec        tris. 1636-1714.
8
```

```
Witchcraft
BF            Klein, Johann, 1659-1732, praeses.
1572            Meditatio academica, exhibens examen
D4          jvridicvm jvdicialis lamiarvm confessionis,
K64         se ex nefando cvm Satana coitv prolem svs-
1731        cepisse hvmanam, Was von der Hexen Bekänt-
            niss zu halten, dass sie aus schändlichem
            Beyschlaff mit dem Teuffel Kinder gezeuget?
            Qvam ... praeside Dn. Johanne Klein, ...
            svbmittit Nicolavs Pvtter, Strals. Recvsa.
            ₁n. p.₎ 1731.
              48 p.  20cm.
              First publ        ished 1698.
8
```

```
Witchcraft
BF            Klein, Johann, 1659-1732, praeses.
1572            Meditatio academica exhibens examen
D4          ivridicvm ivdicialis lamiarvm confessionis
K64         se ex nefando cvm Satana coitv prolem svs-
1752        cepisse hvmanam.  Was von dem Bekenntniss
            der Hexen zu halten, dass sie aus schänd-
            lichen Beyschlaf mit dem Teufel Kinder ge-
            zeuget?  Praeside Domino Ioanne Klein ...
            svbmittit Nicolavs Pvtter ... Vitember-
            gae, Apvd Io. Christoph. Tzschiedrich, 1752.
              48 p.  21cm.
              First publ        ished 1698.
8                       (Continued on next card)
```

```
Witchcraft
BF            Klein, Johann, 1659-1732, praeses.  Medi-
1572        tatio academica exhibens examen ivridicvm
D4          ivdicialis lamiarvm confessionis ... 1752.
K64                                      (Card 2)
1752


              1. Witchcraft.  2. Devil.  I. Putter,
            Nicolaus, respondent.  II. Title: Examen
            juridicum judicialis lamiarum confessionis.
8           III. Title.
```

```
            Klein, Johann, 1659-1732.
              Meditatio academica exhibens examen
Witchcraft    juridicum judicialis—German.
BF          Thomasius, Christian, 1655-1728.
1565           Christ. Thomasii Kurtze Lehr-Sätze von
T46         dem Laster der Zauberey, mit dessen eige-
1717        nen Vertheidigung vermehret.  Worbey Johann
            Kleins ... Juristische Untersuchung, was von
            der Hexen Bekäntniss zu halten, dass solche
            aus schändlichem Beyschlaff mit dem Teuffel
            Kinder gezeuget.  Beydes aus dem Lateinischen
            ins Teutsche übersetzt.  Franckfurth und
            Leipzig, 1717.
              134 p.  18cm.     (Continued on next card)
8
```

```
            Klein, Johann, 1659-1732.
              Meditatio academica exhibens examen
Witchcraft    juridicum judicialis—German.
BF          Thomasius, Christian, 1655-1728.  Christ.
1565        Thomasii Kurtze Lehr-Sätze von dem Laster
T46         der Zauberey ... 1717.        (Card 2)
1717
              Title in red and black.
              Translation of Thomasius' Dissertatio de
            crimine magiae and of Klein's Meditatio aca-
            demica exhibens examen juridicum judicialis.
              Klein's Juristische Untersuchung, was von
            der Hexen Bekäntniss zu halten ..., p. ₁79₎-
            134, has special t. p.
8                       (Continued on next card)
```

```
            Klein, Johann, 1659-1732.
              Meditatio academica, exhibens examen
Witchcraft    juridicum judicialis—German.
BF          Thomasius, Christian, 1655-1728.
1565           Christ. Thomasii Kurtze Lehr-Sätze von
T46         dem Laster der Zauberey, mit dessen eigenen
1717a       Vertheidigung vermehret.  Worbey Johann
            Kleins ... Juristische Untersuchung, was von
            der Hexen Bekäntniss zu halten, dass
            solche aus schändlichem Beyschlaff mit dem
            Teuffel Kinder gezeuget.  Beydes aus dem
            Lateinischen ins Teutsche übersetzt.
            Franckfurth und Leipzig, 1717.
              134 p.  front.  19cm.
8                       (Continued on next card)
```

```
            Klein, Johann, 1659-1732.
              Meditatio academica, exhibens examen
Witchcraft    juridicum judicialis—German.
BF          Thomasius, Christian, 1655-1728.  Christ.
1565        Thomasii Kurtze Lehr-Sätze von dem Laster
T46         der Zauberey ... 1717.        (Card 2)
1717a
              Translation of his Dissertatio de crimi-
            ne magiae, J. Reiche, respondent; and of
            Meditatio academica, exhibens examen juri-
            dicum judicialis, by J. Klein (N. Putter,
            respondent.)
              Johann Kleins Juristische Untersuchung,
            p. ₁79₎-134, has     special t. p.
8                       (Continued on next card)
```

323

CATALOGUE OF THE CORNELL WITCHCRAFT COLLECTION

Witchcraft
BF
1565
T46
1717a

Klein, Johann, 1659-1732.
    Meditatio academica, exhibens examen juridicum judicialis--German.
    Thomasius, Christian, 1655-1728. Christ. Thomasii Kurtze Lehr-Sätze von dem Laster der Zauberey ... 1717. (Card 3)

    With this are bound Ludovici, Gottfried, 1670-1724. ... Theologicum novae... Coburgi [1718] and Sturm, Johann Christoph, 1635-1703. ... Wahrhaffte und gründliche Vorstellung von der lügenhafften Stern-Wahrsagerey. Coburg, 1722.

    1. Witchcraft. I. His Dissertatio de crimine mag   iae--German. II.

8   (Continued on next card)

Witchcraft
BF
1445
S595

Kleine Zweifeln über zwey Berichte von einer Hexen- oder Studenten-Geschichte.
    [Simon, Jordan] pater, 1719-1776.
    Nun, ja -- oder, Kleine Zweifeln über zwey Berichte von einer Hexen- oder Studenten-Geschichte die sich in dem Jahre 1768. den 10. 11. 12. und 13. Junius zu Ingolstadt in Bayern soll zugetragen haben. Gedruckt zu Unglauben, Mit der Akademicker Schriften [i. e., Leipzig, 1769]
    31 p. 21cm.
    Attribution by Holzmann; imprint from Kayser.

8   (Continued on next card)

Witchcraft
BF
1445
S595

Kleine Zweifeln über zwey Berichte von einer Hexen- oder Studenten-Geschichte.
    [Simon, Jordan] pater, 1719-1776. Nun, ja ... [1769] (Card 2)

    The "Berichte" are given, p. 3-11. Continued by Nicht doch -- oder, Auflösung der kleinen Zweifel über zwei Berichte. With this is bound his Nicht doch. [Leipzig? 1769]

    1. Ghosts. 2. Witchcraft--Ingolstadt, Bavaria. I. Title. II. Title: Kleine Zweifeln über zwey Berichte von einer Hexen- oder St   udenten-Geschichte.

Witchcraft
BF
1583
Z7
1629

Ein kleiner Beitrag zur Geschichte der Hexenprozesse.
    Englert, Anton, 1855-
    Ein kleiner Beitrag zur Geschichte der Hexenprozesse.
    (In Hessische Blätter für Volkskunde. Leipzig. 24cm. Bd. 5 (1906), p. [65]-71)

    1. Witchcraft--Dieburg, Germany. 2. Fleischbein, Hans, d. 1632. I. Title.

8

WITCHCRAFT
BF
1583
M945

Kleiner Beitrag zur Geschichte des Hexenwesens im XVI. Jahrhundert.
    Müller, Michael Franz Joseph.
    Kleiner Beitrag zur Geschichte des Hexenwesens im XVI. Jahrhundert, aus authentischen Akten ausgehoben. Trier, Bei J. J. Blattau, 1830.
    18 p. 19cm.

    With autograph: Geo. L. Burr.

8   1. Witchcraft--Hist. 2. Witchcraft--
NIC   Treves. 3. Trials (Witchcraft)--Treves.

WITCHCRAFT
BF
1582
K64

Klélé, J
    Hexenwahn und Hexenprozesse in der ehemaligen Reichsstadt und Landvogtei Hagenau, von J. Klélé. Hagenau i. Els., F. Ruckstuhl, 1893.
    viii, 177 p. 25cm.

    1. Witchcraft--Haguenau, Alsace. 2. Trials
8   (Witchcraft)--Haguenau, Alsace. I. Title.
NIC

Witchcraft
B
2605
Z7
K64

Klemperer,   Prediger zu Landsberg a. W.
    Christian Thomasius, ein Vorkämpfer der Volksaufklärung. Vortrag, gehalten vom Prediger Dr. Klemperer im Vereins-Verband für öffentliche Vorträge zu Landsberg a. W. am 15. Februar 1877. Landsberg a. W., Druck von F. Striewing, 1877.
    43 p. 21cm.

8   1. Thomasius, Christian, 1655-1728
    --Biog. I. Title.

HIST SCI
R
128
.7
A1
A33
no.22

Kletschke, David Gottfried, respondent.
    Alberti, Michael, 1682-1757, praeses.
    Dissertatio inauguralis medica De superstitione medica, quam...praeside Dn. D. Michaele Alberti...publicae ventilationi submittet David Godofred. Kletschke. Halae Magdeburgicae, Typis Ioanni [sic] Christiani Hendelii [1720]
    40 p. 20cm.

    Diss.--Halle (D. G. Kletschke, respondent)
    No.22 in a vol. of dissertations for which Alberti acted as praeses. (Vol. lettered: Dispv   tationvm medicarvm volu-
8   men LVI)
NIC   (Continued on next card)

History
of Science
R
133
A33

Kletschke, David Gottfried, respondent.
    Alberti, Michael, 1682-1757, praeses.
    Dissertatio inauguralis medica De superstitione medica, quam...praeside Dn. D. Michaele Alberti...publicae ventilationi submittet David Godofred. Kletschke. Halae Magdeburgicae, Typis Ioanni Christiani Hendelii [1720]
    40 p. 21cm.

    Diss.--Halle (D.G. Kletschke, respondent)

MSS
Bd.
WITCHCRAFT
BF
W792++

Klingler, Anton K., 1649-1713, plaintiff.
    Wirz, Bernhard, d. 1705, defendant.
    Processus wegen des vermeinten Gespengsts in dem Antistitio. [Zürich, 1705]
    402 p., [22] l. 34cm.

    Manuscript, on paper, in a German hand. According to G. L. Burr, probably the transcript of the court record.
    Bound in parchment.

    1. Trials (Witchcraft)--Zürich. 2. Trials (Malicious mi   schief)--Zürich. I. Klingler, Ant   on K., 1649-1713, plaintiff.   II. Title.

PD
25
P15
no.56

Klingner, Erich.
    ... Luther und der deutsche volksaberglaube. Von Erich Klingner. Berlin, Mayer & Müller, 1912.
    ix, 135, [1] p. 23½cm. (Palaestra. LVI)

    Chapters 1 and 2 appeared as the author's inaugural dissertation, Berlin.

    1. Luther, Martin, 1483-1546. 2. Folklore--Germany. I. Series. II. Title.

---

ar W
54764
no.5

Klingner, Erich, 1887-
    Luther und der deutsche Volksaberglaube. (Kapitel 1 und 2) [Göttingen, Dieterich'sche Univ.-Buchdr., 1912]
    75 p. 25cm.

    Inaug.-Diss.--Berlin.
    Chapters 1 and 2 of a larger work with the same title (Berlin, 1912)

Witchcraft
BF
1410
B42
Z56
v.3
no.10

Klinkende bel; of Uytroep om den verlorenen duyvel, door last van sijn liefhebbers. Rotterdam, Gedrukt by P. van Veen, boekdrukker, 1691.
    8 p. title vignette. 20 x 15cm.
    4°: A⁴.

    Poem supporting Balthasar Bekker against the Synode van Noordholland.
    "De duyvel roepende uyt sijn kerker, tot antwoord van den Uytroper:" p. 7-8. (Poem)
    Van der Lin   de 194.

8   (Continued on next card)

Witchcraft
BF
1410
B42
Z56
v.3
no.10

Klinkende bel; of Uytroep om den verlorenen duyvel ... 1691. (Card 2)

    No. 10 in vol. lettered Bekker III.

    1. Bekker, Balthasar, 1634-1698. 2. Nederlandse Hervormde Kerk. Synode van Noordholland, Edam, 1691. I. De duyvel roepende uyt sijn kerker. [poem]

Witchcraft
BF
1410
B42
Z892

Klinkende bel; of uytroep om den verloorenen duyvel.
    Vervolg van Verscheyde gedigten, &c. So voor als tegen het boek genaamt De betoverde werelt. [Amsterdam?] Gedrukt voor de liefhebbers, 1692.
    1 p. l., 54 p. title vignette, illus. initial. 20 x 16cm.
    4°: π1, A-F⁴, G3.

    Contains prose as well as poems.
    First poem has own t. p. with title: Verklaeringe van een turkse parabel ... door Mr. Gratianus   de Bly...

8   (Continued on next card)

Witchcraft
BF
1410
B42
Z892

Klinkende bel; of uytroep om den verloorenen duyvel.
    Vervolg van Verscheyde gedigten, &c. 1692. (Card 2)

    Klinkende bel; of uytroep om den verloorenen duyvel: P. 17-19. [Van der Linde 194]
    Variant of van der Linde 198: signatures differ (but not paging).

    1. Bekker, Balthasar, 1634-1698. De betoverde weer   eld. I. Verscheyde

    (Continued on next card)

Witchcraft
BF
1410
B42
Z892

Klinkende bel; of uytroep om den verloorenen duyvel.
    Vervolg van Verscheyde gedigten, &c. 1692. (Card 3)

    gedichten, so voor, als tegen het boek, genaamt: De betoverde weereld. II. Bly, Gratianus de. Verklaeringe van een turkse parabel. III. Klinkende bel; of uytroep om den verloorenen duyvel.

8

WITCHCRAFT
DL
271
R2
R19
1915-16

Klitgaard, Carl, 1868-
    Fra hexenes tid. I. Hexeprocesser fra Randers Amt. II. Hexene paa Mariageregnen
    (In: Randers Amts Historiske Samfund. Aarbog. Randers. 23cm. v.9 (1915) p. [97]-140; v.10 (1916) p. [86]-106)

    1 Witchcraft--Randers, Denmark. 2. Witchcraft--Denmark. 3. Trials (Witchcraft)--
8   Randers, Denm   ark. 4. Trials (Witch-
NIC   craft)--   Denmark. I. Title.

CATALOGUE OF THE CORNELL WITCHCRAFT COLLECTION

Kluge, Anna.

WITCHCRAFT
BF
1583
K
1652
   Könnecke, Max
     Zwei Hexenprozesse aus der Grafschaft
   Mansfeld.
     (In Mansfelder Blätter. Eisleben, 1887-
   1940? 23cm. 10. Jahrg. (1896), p. [32]-65)
     Caption title.
     "Inquisitionsakten wider die Pfarrwitwe
   Anna Kluge zu Ahlsdorf in Sachen beschuldigter Hexerei, 1652 und 1655": p. 34-51.
     "Inquisitionsakten wider Anna Traute
   Frohertzin und Marie Grösseln in Gerbstedt
   wegen beschul   digter Hexerei, 1689":
   p. 52-65.

NIC
     (Continued on next card)

Witchcraft

Knapp, Hermann, 1859-
   Alt-Regensburgs gerichtsverfassung, strafver-
fahren und strafrecht bis zur Carolina. Nach
urkundlichen quellen dargestellt von dr. Hermann
Knapp. Berlin, J. Guttentag, 1914.
   x, 275, [1] p. 23½cm.
   "Quellen und literatur": p. [1]-3.
   Bound with the author's Das alte Nürnberger
Kriminalrecht ... Berlin, 1896.

   1. Courts--Ratisbon. 2. Criminal procedure--
Ratisbon--Hist.   3. Criminal law--Ratisbon--
Hist.   I. Title.

Witchcraft

Knapp, Hermann, 1859-
   Das alte Nürnberger kriminalrecht. Nach rats-
urkunden erlautert [:] von dr. jur. Hermann
Knapp. Berlin, J. Guttentag, 1896.
   xviii, 307, [1] p. 23½cm.
   "Quellen": p. [xiii]-xiv; "Litteratur":
p. [xv]-xvi.
   With this is bound the author's Alt-Regens-
burgs Gerichtsverfassung, Strafverfahren und
Strafrecht bis zur Carolina ... Berlin, 1914.

   I. Title.

Knighton, William, d. 1900.
   Demoniacal possession in India.

Witchcraft
   Articles on mythology, etc. [v.p., 1871-1880]
   1 v. (various pagings) 25cm.

   Cover-title.
   Articles reprinted from Contemporary review
and Nineteenth century, with one from Once a
week.
   Contents.--On the philosophy of mythology,
by Max Müller.--Germanic mythology, by Karl
Blind.--The first sin, by François Lenormant.
--The myths of the   sea and the river of
     (Continued on next card)

Knighton, William, d. 1900.
   Demoniacal possession in India.

Witchcraft
   Articles on mythology, etc. 1871-1880.
     (Card 2)

   Contents--Continued.
death, by C. F. Keary.--Wind myths, by C. F.
Keary.--Forest and field myths, by W. R. S.
Ralston.--Cinderella, by W. R. S. Ralston.--
Demonology of the New Testament, by J. J. Owen.
--Demoniacal possession in India, by W.
Knighton.--Demonolatry, devil-dancing, and
demoniacal posse   ssion, by R. C. Caldwell.
--Witchcraft in   Devon.

WITCHCRAFT

Knortz, Karl, 1841-1918.
   Hexen, Teufel und Blocksbergspuk in Geschichte, Sage und Literatur. Annaberg,
Sachsen, Grasers Verlag (R. Liesche) [1913?]
   169 p. 19cm.

   Bibliographical footnotes.

   1. Witchcraft. 2. Demonology. 3. Supernatural in literature.   I. Title. II. Title:
Blocksbergsp   uk, Hexen, Teufel und.

Knott, Elizabeth, d. 1649.

Witchcraft
BF
1563
W81++
no.15
   The Divels delvsions; or, A faithfull relation of John Palmer and Elizabeth Knott,
two notorious vvitches lately condemned at
... St. Albans ... executed July 16. Also
their accusations of several vvitches in
... the county of Hartford. London,
Printed for R. Williams, 1649. [London,
at the British Museum, 1923]
   6 p. 16cm.

     (Continued on next card)

Knott, Elizabeth, d. 1649.

Witchcraft
BF
1563
W81++
no.15
   The Divels delvsions ... [1923] (Card 2)

   Photocopy (negative) 6 p. on 5 l. 20 x
32cm.
   No. 15 in vol. lettered: Witchcraft
tracts, chapbooks and broadsides, 1579-1704;
rotograph copies.

   1. Witchcraft--England. 2. Palmer, John,
d. 1649. 3. Knott, Elizabeth, d. 1649.

Witchcraft
GR
142
H6
A3
no.18
   Knott, Elizabeth, d. 1649.
     [Misodaimon, B.] pseud.
     The divel's delusions; or, A faithful relation of John
Palmer and Elizabeth Knott, two notorious vvitches,
lately condemned at the sessions of Oyer and Terminer
in St. Albans. Together with the confession of the aforesaid John Palmer and Elizabeth Knott, executed July 16.
Also their accusations of severall witches in Hitchen,
Norton, and other places in the county of Hartford. London, Printed for Richard Williams, stationer, at St. Albans, anno Dom, 1649. Reprinted with an introductory
by W. B. Gerish. Bishop's Stortford, 1914.
     13, [1] p. 21½cm. (Hertfordshire folk lore. no. 18)
     Signed: "B. Misodaimon."
     1. Witchcraft--England. 2. Palmer, John, d. 1649. 3. Knott,
Elizabeth, d. 1649. I. Gerish, William Blyth, ed. II. Title.

   Library of Congress   GR530.M55
                              16-25733

Witchcraft
BX
9479
B42
K74
   Knuttel, Willem Pieter Cornelis, 1854-1921.
     Balthasar Bekker de bestrijder van het
bijgeloof. 'S Gravenhage, M. Nijhoff,
1906.
     3 p. l., 368 p. port. 25cm.

     1. Bekker, Balthasar, 1634-1698--Biog.
I. Title.

Kober, Joachim Ernst, respondent.

WITCHCRAFT
K
B378
1717
   Bechmann, Johann Volkmar, 1624-1689, praeses.
     Discursus juridicus de crimine maleficii
vulgo Von Zauberey, sub praesidio Joh. Volk.
Bechmanns, submittit Joach. Ernst. Kober.
Nunc recusa. Jenae, 1717.
     30 p. 20cm.
     Originally published as dissertation, Jena,
1678 (Joachim Ernst Kober, respondent)

     1. Witchcraft. I. Kober, Joachim Ernst,
respondent.   II. Title. III. Title:
Von Zauberey.

NIC

PF
3025
G45
v.37
1968
   Koch, Hugo.
     ... Hexenprozesse und reste des hexenglaubens in der Wet-
terau, von Hugo Koch. Giessen, 1935; Amsterdam, Swets
& Zeitlinger, 1968.
     40 p. 24½ᶜᵐ. (Glessener beiträge zur deutschen philologie ... xxxvii)
     "Benutzte darstellungen": p. 40.

     1. Witchcraft--Wetterau. I. Title.
                             A C 35-2273
   Univ. of Chicago   PF3025.G5 no. 37 Printed by L. C.

Kochem, Martin von, pater, 1634?-1712.

  see

Martin von Cochem, pater, 1634?-1712.

WITCHCRAFT
BF
1583
Z7
1632d
   Köbbing, Georg, defendant.
     Merkwürdiger Hexen-Process gegen den Kauf-
mann G. Köbbing, an dem Stadtgerichte zu
Coesfeld im Jahre 1632 geführt. Vollständig aus den Original-Acten mitgetheilt und
mit einer Vorrede begleitet von Joseph Niesert. Coesfeld, Gedruckt bei Bernard
Wittneven, 1827.
     lii, 104 p. 19cm.

     1. Trials (Witchcraft)--Coesfeld, Germany.
8   I. Niesert,   Johann Heinrich Joseph,
NIC ed. II.   Title.

   Køge huskors.

DL
103
.5
D18+
no.61
   Brunsmand, Johan, 1637-1707.
     Køge huskors. Med indledning og noter
ved Anders Baeksted. København, E.
Munksgaard, 1953.
     320 p. illus. 22cm. (Danmarks
folkeminder, nr. 61)

     Includes reproduction of the title page
of the original edition published in 1674,
with title: Et forfaerdeligt huus-kaars.

     1. Witchcra   ft--Denmark. I.
Baeksted, And   ers. II. His Et
forfaerdeligt   huus-kaars. III. Title.

   Koelman, Jacobus, 1632-1695.
     Wederlegging van B. Bekkers Betoverde
Witchcraft   wereldt.
BF
1410
B42
Z56
v.2
no.14
   Dale, Antonius van, 1638-1708.
     Lasteringen van Jakob Koelman, in zijn
zoo genaamde wederlegging van B. Bekkers Betooverde wereld, zedelijk aangewesen in een
brief van Antony van Dale, med. doctor. Aan
zijnen vrind. Rotterdam, By I. van Ruynen,
boekverkooper, 1692.
     15, [1] p. title vignette, illus. initial.
19 x 15cm.
     4°: A-B⁴.

   Van der Lin   de 124.
   No. 14 in   vol. lettered Bekker II.
8   (Continued on next card)

Koelman, Jacobus, 1632-1695.

Witchcraft
BF
1410
B42
Z56
v.3
no.23
   Eenige originele brieven geschreven aan Do.
Balthasar Bekker, in zijn boek De betoverde werelt. Door Do. Jacobus Koelman.
En andere bekende, en onbekende persoonen.
Amsterdam, By D. van den Dalen, boekverkooper, 1692.
     1 p. l., 8 p. title and end page vig-
nettes. 19 x 15cm.
     4°: π1, *⁴.
     Four letters: one from Koelman, one
from Pieter   Hessels, and two signed
N. N. (but   not, apparently, by the
8   (Continued on next card)

Koelman, Jacobus, 1632-1695.

Witchcraft
BF
1410
B42
Z56
v.3
no.23
   Eenige originele brieven geschreven aan Do.
Balthasar Bekker ... 1692. (Card 2)

   same person.)
     Variant of van der Linde 123: lacks
second numbering (sign. A-C)
     No. 23 in vol. lettered Bekker III.
     1. Bekker, Balthasar, 1634-1698. De be-
toverde weereld. I. Koelman, Jacobus,
1632-1695.

8

CATALOGUE OF THE CORNELL WITCHCRAFT COLLECTION

WITCHCRAFT
BF 1566 K78
König, Bruno Emil, 1833-1902.
Ausgeburten des Menschenwahns im Spiegel der Hexenprozesse und der auto da fé's. Historische Schandsäulen des Aberglaubens. Eine Geschichte des After- und Aberglaubens bis auf die Gegenwart. Ein Volksbuch. Rudolstadt, A. Bock [1893].
811 p. plates (part fold.) 19cm.

Issued in 17 parts.

8 NIC
1. Witchcraft. 2. Superstition. I. Title.

WITCHCRAFT
BF 1566 K78 1966
König, Bruno Emil, 1833-1902.
Hexenprozesse; Ausgeburten des Menschenwahns im Spiegel der Hexenprozesse und der Autodafés. [1. Aufl. der Neuausgabe] Schwerte/Ruhr, H. Freistühler [1966]
607 p. illus. 19cm.

1. Witchcraft. 2. Superstition. I. Title.

WITCHCRAFT
BF 1566 O38 K78++
Königer, Albert Michael, 1874-
Der Hexenwahn in neuester Beleuchtung. Köln, 1909.
5 columns. 34cm.

In the Literarische Beilage der Kölnischen Volkszeitung for May 6, 1909. In broadside box.

8 NIC
1. Ohle, Rudolf, 1857- . Der Hexenwahn. 2. Witchcraft--History. I. Title.

WITCHCRAFT
BF 1583 Z7 1652
Könnecke, Max
Zwei Hexenprozesse aus der Grafschaft Mansfeld.
(In Mansfelder Blätter. Eisleben, 1887-1940? 23cm. 10. Jahrg. (1896), p. [32]-65)
Caption title.
"Inquisitionsakten wider die Pfarrwitwe Anna Kluge zu Ahlsdorf in Sachen, beschuldigter Hexerei, 1652 und 1655": p. 34-51.
"Inquisitionsakten wider Anna Traute Frohertzin und Marie Grösseln in Gerbstedt wegen beschuldigter Hexerei, 1689": p. 52-65.

8 NIC
(Continued on next card)

WITCHCRAFT
BF 1583 Z7 1652
Könnecke, Max
Zwei Hexenprozesse aus der Grafschaft Mansfeld... (Card 2)

1. Trials (Witchcraft)--Ahlsdorf, Ger. (Kreis Mansfeld) 2. Kluge, Anna. 3. Trials (Witchcraft)--Gerbstedt, Ger. 4. Frohertz, Anna Traute. 5. Grössel, Marie. I. Title.

WITCHCRAFT
BF 1569 K77
[Köppen, Karl Friedrich] 1808-1863.
Hexen und Hexenprocesse. Zur Geschichte des Aberglaubens und des inquisitorischen Processes. Leipzig, O. Wigand, 1855.
119 p. 15cm. (Reise-Lectüre. Bibliothèque des chemins de fer)

8

WITCHCRAFT
BF 1569 K77 1858
Köppen, Karl Friedrich, 1808-1863.
Hexen und Hexenprozesse. Zur Geschichte des Aberglaubens und des inquisitorischen Prozesses. Von K. F. Köppen. 2. Aufl. Leipzig, O. Wigand, 1858.
119 p. 14cm.

1. Witchcraft--History. 2. Trials (Witchcraft)--History. I. Title.

8

Körte, Friedrich Heinrich Wilhelm, 1776-1846, supposed author.
PT 1799 A1 W13
Wahrhafter Bericht vom Zauber-Sabbathe der St. Walpurgis-Nacht des dritten Reformations-Jubel-Jahres, enthaltend Satan's Reden an die auf dem Blocksberge versammelten Unholde Teutschlands, nebst vielen Parallel-Stellen von Dr. Martin Luther. Brockenhaus, 1817.
48 p. 18cm.
Possibly by F. H. W. Körte.
1. Political satire--Germany. 2. Luther, Martin-- Cartoons, satire, etc. I. Körte, Friedrich Heinrich Wilhelm, 1776-1846, supposed author.

8

WITCHCRAFT
BF 1523 K78 no.2
[Köster, Heinrich Martin Gottfried] 1734-1802.
Belehrung des Verfassers der Demüthigen Bitte an die grossen Männer welche keinen Teufel glauben. Mit Anmerkungen des Verfassers. [n. p.] 1776.
114 p. 17cm.
"Beurtheilung der demüthigen Bitte u.s.s. in der Lemgoer auserlesenen Bibliotheck 8. Band, S. 549": p. [5]-54. With commentary.
"Demüthigste Antwort eines geringen Land-

8
(Continued on next card)

WITCHCRAFT
BF 1523 K78 no.2
[Köster, Heinrich Martin Gottfried] 1734-1802.
Belehrung des Verfassers der Demüthigen Bitte ... 1776. (Card 2)

geistlichen ... Mit Anmerkungen," p. [57]-114, has special t. p. Text of the "Antwort" itself not included.
No. 2 in vol. lettered Ueber den Teufel.
1. Bonnet, Johann Carl. Demüthigste Antwort eines geringen Landgeistlichen. 2. Devil. 3. His Demüthige Bitte um Belehrung. I. Auserlesene Bibliothek der neuesten deutschen Literatur. Beurtheilung der demüthigen Bitte. II. Title.

8

WITCHCRAFT
BF 1523 V19 no.6
[Köster, Heinrich Martin Gottfried] 1734-1802.
Belehrung des Verfassers der Demüthigen Bitte an die grossen Männer welche keinen Teufel glauben. Mit Anmerkungen des Verfassers. [n. p.] 1776.
114 p. 17cm.

No. 6 in vol. lettered Varia scripta demonolog.

8

WITCHCRAFT
BF 1501 D12 no.3
[Köster, Heinrich Martin Gottfried] 1734-1802.
Demüthige Bitte um Belehrung an die grossen Männer welche keinen Teufel glauben. [Giessen, 1775]
56 p. 17cm.
First edition?
No. 3 in vol. lettered Dämonologische Schriften.

8

WITCHCRAFT
BF 1523 K78 no.1
[Köster, Heinrich Martin Gottfried] 1734-1802.
Demüthige Bitte um Belehrung an die grossen Männer, welche keinen Teufel glauben. 2. Aufl. In Deutschland, 1775.
54 p. 18cm.

Attribution by Holzmann, Jocher, et al.
No. 1 in vol. lettered Ueber den Teufel.

8

WITCHCRAFT
BF 1523 V19 no.2
[Köster, Heinrich Martin Gottfried] 1734-1802.
Demüthige Bitte um Belehrung an die grossen Männer, welche keinen Teufel glauben. 3. rechtmässige Aufl. In Deutschland, 1775.
56 p. 17cm.

Attribution by Holzmann, Jocher, et al.
No. 2 in vol. lettered Varia scripta demonolog.
1. Devil. 2. Devil--Biblical teaching. I. Title.

8

Köster, Heinrich Martin Gottfried, 1734-1802.
Demüthige Bitte um Belehrung.
WITCHCRAFT
BF 1523 V19 no.5
[Bonnet, Johann Carl]
Demüthigste Antwort eines geringen Landgeistlichen auf die Demüthige Bitte um Belehrung an die grossen Männer, welche keinen Teufel glauben. In Deutschland, 1776.
54 p. 17cm.
Attribution by Holzmann.
No. 5 in vol. lettered Varia scripta demonolog.
1. Köster, Heinrich Martin Gottfried, 1734-1802. Demüthige Bitte um Belehrung. 2. Devil. I. Ein geringer Landgeistlicher. II. Title.

8

Köster, Heinrich Martin Gottfried, 1734-1802.
Demüthige Bitte um Belehrung.
WITCHCRAFT
BF 1523 K78 K51
[Kindleben, Christian Wilhelm] 1748-1785.
Ueber die Non-Existenz des Teufels. Als eine Antwort auf die Demüthige Bitte um Belehrung an die grossen Männer, welche keinen Teufel glauben. Berlin, Bey G. A. Lange, 1776.
55 p. 17cm.
Attribution by Holzmann, Jocher, et al.
1. Köster, Heinrich Martin Gottfried, 1734-1802. Demüthige Bitte um Belehrung. 2. Devil. 2. Superstition. I. Title.

8

Köster, Heinrich Martin Gottfried, 1734-1802.
Demüthige Bitte um Belehrung.
WITCHCRAFT
BF 1523 K78 no.2
[Köster, Heinrich Martin Gottfried] 1734-1802.
Belehrung des Verfassers der Demüthigen Bitte an die grossen Männer welche keinen Teufel glauben. Mit Anmerkungen des Verfassers. [n. p.] 1776.
114 p. 18cm.
"Beurtheilung der demüthigen Bitte u.s.s. in der Lemgoer auserlesenen Bibliothek 8. Band, S. 549": p. [5]-54. With commentary.
"Demüthigste Antwort eines geringen Land-

8
(Continued on next card)

Köster, Heinrich Martin Gottfried, 1734-1802.
Demüthige Bitte um Belehrung.
WITCHCRAFT
BF 1523 K78 no.2
[Köster, Heinrich Martin Gottfried] 1734-1802. Belehrung des Verfassers der Demüthigen Bitte ... 1776. (Card 2)

geistlichen ... Mit Anmerkungen," p. [57]-114, has special t. p. Text of the "Antwort" itself not included.
No. 2 in vol. lettered Ueber den Teufel.
1. Bonnet, Johann Carl. Demüthigste Antwort eines geringen Landgeistlichen. 2. Devil. 3. His Demüthige Bitte um Belehrung. I. Auserlesene Bibliothek der neuesten deutschen Literatur. Beurtheilung der demüthigen Bitte. II. Title.

8

CATALOGUE OF THE CORNELL WITCHCRAFT COLLECTION

WITCHCRAFT
BF
1523
K78
no.4
    Köster, Heinrich Martin Gottfried, 1734-1802.
        Demüthige Bitte um Belehrung.
    [Köster, Heinrich Martin Gottfried] 1734-1802.
        Teufeleien des achtzehnten Jahrhunderts, von dem Verfasser der Demüthigen Bitte um Belehrung an die grossen Männer welche keinen Teufel glauben. 1. rechtmässige Aufl. Leipzig, Bey C. F. Schneidern, 1778.
        142 p. 18cm.
        No. 4 in vol. lettered Ueber den Teufel.
        1. His Demüthige Bitte um Belehrung.
8   2. Devil--Bi   bl. I. Title.

Witchcraft
BF
1550
K79
    Kohl, Carl.
        Satan og hans kultus. København, Nordiske forlag E. Bojesen, 1902.
        viii, 185, [1] p. 23cm.
        Autographed by the author.
        1. Devil. 2. Witchcraft. 3. Magic. I. Title.
8

Komenius, Amos, 1592-1670.
    see
Comenius, Johann Amos, 1592-1670.

WITCHCRAFT
BF
1523
K78
K513
    [Köster, Heinrich Martin Gottfried] 1734-1802.
        Emanuel Swedenborgs demüthiges Danksagungsschreiben an den grossen Mann, der die Nonexistenz des Teufels demonstrirt hat. Frankfurt und Leipzig, 1778.
        46 p. 17cm.
        Attribution by Holzmann.
        1. Kindleben, Christian Wilhelm, 1748-1785. Ueber die Non-Existenz des Teufels. 2. Devil. I. Swedenborg, Emanuel, 1688-1772, supposed author. II. Title. III. Title: Demüthiges Danksagungsschre iben an den grossen Mann.
8

WITCHCRAFT
JC
139
B66
K79
    Kohler, Josef, 1849-1919.
        Bodinus und die Hexenverfolgung. (In Archiv für Strafrecht und Strafprozess. Berlin, 1853-1933. 25cm. 66. Bd., 1. Heft (1918), p. 39-57)
        Caption title.
        Bibliographical footnotes.
        1. Bodin, Jean, 1530-1596. 2. Witchcraft.
8   I. Title.
NIC

Komenius, Johann Amos, 1592-1670.
    see
Comenius, Johann Amos, 1592-1670.

WITCHCRAFT
    Köster, Heinrich Martin Gottfried, 1734-1802.
BF
1523
K78
K516
        Emanuel Swedenborgs demüthiges Danksagungsschreiben.
    Kindleben, Christian Wilhelm, 1748-1785.
        Der Teufeleien des achtzehnten Jahrhunderts letzter Akt, worinn des Emanuel Schwedenborgs demüthiges Danksagungsschreiben kürzlich beantwortet, der ganze bisher geführte Streit friedlich beygeleget, und in dem Büchlein über die Nonexistenz des Teufels manches zurückgenommen, ergänzt und berichtiget wird ... Leipzig, Bey C. F. Schneider, 1779.
        63 p. 20cm.
8
NIC   (Continued on next card)

WITCHCRAFT
BM
645
A6
K79
    Kohut, Alexander, 1842-1894.
        Ueber die jüdische angelologie und daemonologie in ihrer abhängigkeit vom parsismus, von dr. Alexander Kohut. Leipzig, In commission bei F. A. Brockhaus, 1866.
        2 p. l., 105 p., 1 l. 22½cm. (Abhandlungen der Deutschen morgenländischen gesellschaft. iv. bd., no. 3)

        1. Angels (Judaism) 2. Demonology. 3. Jewish theology. 4. Zoroastrianism. I. Title.
        A C 34-3086
8   Title from Univ. of Chi- cago PJ5.D46 vol. 4
NIC Library of Congress [PJ5.D5 bd. 4, no. 3]
        [2]

Komenský, Jan Amos, 1592-1670.
    see
Comenius, Johann Amos, 1592-1670.

WITCHCRAFT
BF
1523
K78
no.4
    [Köster, Heinrich Martin Gottfried] 1734-1802.
        Teufeleien des achtzehnten Jahrhunderts, von dem Verfasser der Demüthigen Bitte um Belehrung an die grossen Männer welche keinen Teufel glauben. 1. rechtmässige Aufl. Leipzig, Bey C. F. Schneidern, 1778.
        142 p. 18cm.
        No. 4 in vol. lettered Ueber den Teufel.
        1. His Demüthige Bitte um Belehrung.
8   2. Devil--Bi   bl. I. Title.

WITCHCRAFT
BF
1559
K81
1893
    Koldewey, Friedrich, 1866-
        Der Exorcismus im Herzogtum Braunschweig seit den Tagen der Reformation; eine kirchenhistorische Studie. Wolfenbüttel, J. Zwissler, 1893.
        50 p. 24cm.
        Originally published as the author's dissertation, Jena.
        1. Exorci   sm. I. Title.
8
NIC

BF
1566
K82
    Koomen, Martin, 1939-
        Het ijzige zaad van de duivel. Geschiedenis van heksen en demonen. Amsterdam, Wetenschappelijke Uitgeverij, 1973.
        214 p. 20cm. (Unofficial history.)
        Bibliography: p. 211-214.

        1. Witchcraft. 2. Demonology. 3. Monsters. I. Title

NIC JUN 03,'74 COOm 73-351717

WITCHCRAFT
BF
1523
V19
no.7
    [Köster, Heinrich Martin Gottfried] 1734-1802.
        Teufeleien des achtzehnten Jahrhunderts, von dem Verfasser der Demüthigen Bitte um Belehrung an die grossen Männer welche keinen Teufel glauben. 1. rechtmässige Aufl. Leipzig, Bey C. F. Schneidern, 1778.
        142 p. 17cm.
        No. 7 in vol. lettered Varia scripta demonolog.
8

ar W
39971
    Koldewey, Friedrich, 1866-
        Der Exorcismus im Herzogtum Braunschweig seit den Tagen der Reformation. Wolfenbüttel, O. Wollermann, 1893.
        50 p. 22cm.

Witchcraft
BF
1410
K84
    Kornmann, Heinrich, fl. 1607.
        Henrici Kornmanni ... De miracvlis mortvorvm, opvs novvm et admirandum in decem partes distribvtum: in quo mirabilia Dei miracula & exempla mortuorum ex Veteri & Nouo Testamento, ex ecclesiasticis & prophanis historicis, summa opera & studio collecta habentur, quæstiones naturales, physicæ, medicæ, theologicæ & iuridicæ traduntur & artificiose pertractantur. Diu desideratum & expetitum, nunc vero primum in lucem editum. [Augustæ Vindelicorum?] typis I. Wolffii, sumptibus I. I. Porsii, 1610.
        [351] p. 15½cm.
        1. Miracles—Early works to 1800. 2. Death. 3. Witchcraft.
    I. Title: De miracvlis mortvorvm.
        10-33802 Revised
    Library of Congress BF1410.K8
        (Continued on next card)

WITCHCRAFT
BF
1523
K78
no.3
    [Köster, Heinrich Martin Gottfried] 1734-1802.
        Die Verbindung des Teufels mit den Gespenstern, nebst Anecdoten von Erscheinungen derselben. In Deutschland, 1777.
        118 p. 18cm.
        Attribution by Holzmann, Jocher, et al.
        No. 3 in vol. lettered Ueber den Teufel.
        1. Ghosts. 2. Apparitions. I. Title.
8

Witchcraft
BF
1565
S83
K81
    [Kollmann, Jacob Anton]
        Zweifel eines Baiers über die wirkende Zauberkunst und Hexerey. An dem Lechstrome [i.e., Augsburg] 1768.
        74, [1] p. 19cm.
        Attribution by British Museum and H. Fieger, P. Don Ferdinand Sterzinger, München, 1907.
        1. Sterzinger, Ferdinand, 1721-1786. Akademische Red von dem gemeinen Vorurtheile der ... Hex rey. 2. März Agnellus, 1726-1784. 3. Witchcraft. VII. Title.
8

Witchcraft
BF
1410
K84
    Kornmann, Heinrich, fl. 1607. ... De miracvlis mortvorvm ... 1610. (Card 2)
        Autograph on t. p. of copy 2: Sum ex libris M. Danielis Clasenij postridie Kalend. Octob. Anno M D CLI.
        With copy 2 of this is bound the author's Templvm natvrae historicvm. Darmstadii, 1611.

CATALOGUE OF THE CORNELL WITCHCRAFT COLLECTION

WITCHCRAFT
AC 31 K84 1694

Kornmann, Heinrich, fl. 1607.
  Henrici Kornmanni Opera curiosa in tractatus qvatuor distributa, qvorum I. Miracula vivorum; II. Miracula mortuorum ... III. Templum naturae historicum ... IV. Qvaestiones enucleatae de virginum statu ac jure ... Nunc in lucem edita. Francofurti ad Moenum, Ex officina Genschiana, 1694-96.
  6 v. in 2. 17cm.
  Vol. 3-6 have been bound in order: 5, 6, 4, 3.
2 copies of v. 5-6

8 NIC   (Continued on next card)

WITCHCRAFT
AC 31 K84 1694

Kornmann, Heinrich, fl. 1607.   Henrici Kornmanni Opera curiosa ... 1694-96. (Card 2)
  Each vol. also has special t. p.; vol. 5-6 also have special shared t. p.: Henrici Kornmanni tractatus duo ... qvorum prior Linea amoris ... posterior De annulo triplici ... with imprint 1696.
  Bound into copy 1 of vol. 5 is t. p. for Opera curiosa ... in 6 vols., with imprint 1696.
  1. Curiosities and wonders. I. Title: Opera curiosa. II. Title.

8 NIc

BF 1566 K84

Kors, Alan C., comp.
  Witchcraft in Europe, 1100-1700; a documentary history. Edited with an introd., by Alan C. Kors and Edward Peters. Philadelphia, University of Pennsylvania Press [1972]
  viii, 382 p. illus. 25 cm.
  Includes bibliographical references.

  1. Witchcraft--Europe--History--Sources. I. Peters, Edward M., joint comp. II. Title

NIC NOV 15, '73   COOxc   71-170267

UNDERGR
BF 1566 K84+

Kors, Alan C   comp.
  Witchcraft in Europe, 1100-1700; a documentary history. Edited with an introd., by Alan C. Kors and Edward Peters. Philadelphia, University of Pennsylvania Press [1972]
  viii, 382 p. illus. 26 cm. $17.50
  Includes bibliographical references.

  1. Witchcraft—Europe—History—Sources. I. Peters, Edward M., joint comp. II. Title.

4 NIC

Witchcraft
BF 1410 B42 1691b

Kort begrip van de twee boeken der Betooverde weereld ...
Bekker, Balthasar, 1634-1698.
  Kort begrip van de twee boeken der Betooverde weereld, in 't ligt gebragt door den heere Balthazar Bekker, S.T.D. en predikant te Amsterdam, zeer dienstig tot het recht verstaan (en teffens strekkende voor een bondig register) van dat vermaarde werk, opgesteld door een redenlievenden hater van bygeloof. Rotterdam, By I. van Ruynen, boekverkoper, 1691.
  2 p. l., 39 p. [p. 40 is blank] title

          (Continued on next card)

Witchcraft
BF 1410 B42 1691b

Kort begrip van de twee boeken der Betooverde weereld...
Bekker, Balthasar, 1634-1698. Kort begrip van de twee boeken der Betooverde weereld ... 1691. (Card 2)
  vignette, illus. initials. 20 x 16cm.
  4°: π², A-E⁴.
  Black letter.
  Preface signed: I. van Ruynen.
  Van der Linde 18.
  1. Demonology. 2. Angels. 3. Magic. 4. Witchcraft. I. His De betoverde weereld. II. Title. III. Ruynen, I. van. IV. Een redenlievende hater van bygeloof.

8

Witchcraft
BF 1410 B42 Z56 v.1 no.2

Kort beright van Balthasar Bekker S. T. D. predikant tot Amsterdam.
Bekker, Balthasar, 1634-1698.
  Kort beright van Balthasar Bekker S. T. D. predikant tot Amsterdam. Aangaande alle de schriften, welke over sijn boek De betoverde weereld enen tijd lang heen en weder verwisseld zijn. De tweede druk met enige stukken vermeerderd. Amsterdam, By D. vanden Dalen, boekverkoper [1692]
  80, 8 p. title vignette, illus. initials.
  19 x 16cm.
  4°: A-K⁴, A⁴.
  Black letter.

8   (Continued on next card)

Witchcraft
BF 1410 B42 Z56 v.1 no.2

Kort beright van Balthasar Bekker S. T. D. predikant tot Amsterdam.
Bekker, Balthasar, 1634-1698. Kort beright ... [1692] (Card 2)
  Dated Franeker den 21/31 Jul. 1692.
  Variant of van der Linde 76: t. p. includes statement De tweede druk...
  No. 2 in vol. lettered Bekker I.

  1. Bekker, Balthasar, 1634-1698. De betoverde weereld. I. Title.

8

Witchcraft
BX 9479 B42 B11 no.7

Kort-bondige, en voor alle onpartydige, verstaanbare, en met de reeden overeenkomende verklaaringe; van de verleydinge onser eerste voor-ouderen, Adam ende Eva in het Paradys. Volgens de beschryving van Moses, in het boek der Scheppinge. Door J. D. V. B. T. K. Amsterdam, By J. Roman, boekverkoper, 1699.
  22, [1] p. [p. 24 blank] title and end page vignettes, illus. initial. 20 x 15cm.
  4°: A-C⁴.

          (Continued on next card)

Witchcraft
BX 9479 B42 B11 no.7

Kort-bondige, en voor alle onpartydige, verstaanbare ... verklaaringe ... 1699. (Card 2)

  Black letter.
  No. 7 in vol. lettered B. Bekkers sterfbed en andere tractaten.

  1. Fall of man. 2. Devil. I. J. D. V. B. T. K. II. K., J. D. V. B. T.

Witchcraft
BF 1410 B42 Z56 v.1 no.5

Kort en waarachtig verhaal van 't gebeurde tsederd den 31. Mey 1691. tot den 21. Aug. 1692.
Bekker, Balthasar, 1634-1698.
  Kort en waarachtig verhaal van 't gebeurde tsederd den 31. Mey 1691. tot den 21. Aug. 1692. In den Kerkenraad en Classis van Amsterdam, en de Synode van Noord-Holland. In de sake van Balthasar Bekker, S.S. Th. Dr. en predikant tot Amsterdam; over sijn boek genaamd De betoverde weereld. Amsterdam, By D. van den Dalen, boekverkoper, 1692.
  2 p. l., 30 p. [p. 31-32 blank] title vignette, illus. initials.

          (Continued on next card)

Witchcraft
BF 1410 B42 Z56 v.1 no.5

Kort en waarachtig verhaal van 't gebeurde tsederd den 31. Mey 1691. tot den 21 Aug. 1692.
Bekker, Balthasar, 1634-1698. Kort en waarachtig verhaal ... 1692. (Card 2)
  19 x 16cm.
  4°: π², *-4*⁴
  Introductory letter autographed by Bekker.
  Van der Linde 47.
  No. 5 in vol. lettered Bekker I.

  1. Nederlandse Hervormde Kerk. 2. Bekker, Balthasar, 1634-1698. De betoverde weereld. I. Title.

8

WITCHCRAFT
BF 1584 D4 Z7 1698a

Kort og sandfaerdig beretning om den vidtudraabte besaettelse udi Thisted.
Árni Magnússon, 1663-1730.
  Kort og sandfaerdig beretning om den vidtudraabte besaettelse udi Thisted. Til alles efterretning af original-akter og trovaerdige dokumenter uddragen og sammenskreven (af Arne Magnussen [sic]) Paany udgiven af Alfred Ipsen. Kjøbenhavn, J. Gjellerups Forlag, 1891.
  112 p. 18cm.
  Reprinted from ed. of 1699.

  1. Björn, Ole, b.1648. 2. Trials (Witchcraft)--Thisted, Denmark. I. Ipsen, Alfred, 1852-1922, ed. II. Title.

8 NIC

Witchcraft
BF 1785 C73 1665

Kotter, Christoph, 17th cent.
[Comenius, Johann Amos] 1592-1670, comp.
  Lux e tenebris, novis radiis aucta. Hoc est: solemnissimae divinae revelationes, in usum seculi nostri factae ... Per immissas visiones, & angelica divinaqve alloqvia, facta I. Christophoro Kottero silesio, ab anno 1616, ad 1624. II. Christinae Poniatoviae bohemae, annis 1627, 1628, 1629, III. Nicolao Drabicio moravo, ab anno 1638, ad 1664 ... [Amstelodami] 1665.
  various pagings. illus., ports. 21cm.
  Added engr. t. p.

8   (Continued on next card)

Witchcraft
BF 1785 C73 1665

Kotter, Christoph, 17th cent.
[Comenius, Johann Amos] 1592-1670, comp.
  Lux e tenebris ... 1665. (Card 2)
  "Voluminis prophetici," first item, has special t. p. with imprint 1667.
  "Revelationes Christophoro Kottero" and "Revelationes Christinae Poniatoviae" each have special t. p. with imprint 1664.
  "Revelationes Nicolao Drabicio" has special t. p. without imprint.
  First published 1657 with title: Lux in tenebris.

8   (Continued on next card)

Krämer, Heinrich.

  see

Institoris, Henricus, d. 1508.

BF 1583 K89

Krämer, Wolfgang.
  Kurtrierische Hexenprozesse im 16. und 17. Jahrhundert, vornehmlich an der unteren Mosel; ein Beitrag zur Kulturgeschichte. München, 1959.
  118 p. illus. 21cm.

  1. Witchcraft--Treves (Electorate) I. Title.

WITCHCRAFT
BF 1559 K89

Krafft, Johann Melchior, 1673-1751.
  Ausführliche Historie vom Exorcismo, oder von dem Gebrauch bey der Kinder-Taufe dem unreinen Geist zu gebieten auszufahren und ihn zu beschwören, welche aus der Kirchen- und Gelehrten-Geschichte, aus vielen raren gedruckten und ungedruckten Schriften, vom andern Jahrhundert an bis auf gegenwärtige Zeiten ausgeführet, auch wie solcher sogleich bey der Reformation, und nachgehends an vielen Orten unserer Evangeli-

8 NIC   (Continued on next card)

328

CATALOGUE OF THE CORNELL WITCHCRAFT COLLECTION

WITCHCRAFT
BF
1559
K89

Krafft, Johann Melchior, 1673-1751.
Ausführliche Historie vom Exorcismo... (Card 2)
schen Kirchen abgeschaffet worden, gezeiget hat. Hamburg, C. W. Brandt, 1750.
1042 p. 18cm.

1. Exorcism. I. Title.

Witchcraft
BF
1520
K89

Krakevitz, Albert Joachim von, 1674-1734, praeses.
Facultatis theologicae ad hunc actum decanus Albertus Joach. de Krakevitz, ... suo & collegii theologici nomine ad disputationem inauguralem ... Dn. M. Fridemanni Andreae Zulichii, Jenens. De theologia daemonum ... invitat. Rostochii, Literis J. Wepplingi, Sereniss. Princ. & univ. typogr. [1715]
10 p. l., 68 p. 21cm.
The first section is a curriculum
(Continued on next card)

8

Witchcraft
BF
1520
K89

Krakevitz, Albert Joachim von, 1674-1734, praeses. ...De theologia daemonum ... [1715] (Card 2)
vitae.
The dissertation proper has special t. p.:
Auxiliante summo numine specimen inaugurale theologicum De theologia daemonum ...
Diss.--Rostock (F. A. Zulich, respondent)
1. Demonology. 2. Devil. I. Zulich, Fridemann Andreas, b. 1687, respondent.
II. His Specimen inaugurale theologicum De theologia daemonum. III. Title: De theologia daemonum.
(Over)

Krakevitz, Albert Joachim von, 1674-1734.
Specimen inaugurale theologicum De theologia daemonum.

Witchcraft
BF
1520
K89

Krakevitz, Albert Joachim von, 1674-1734, praeses.
Facultatis theologicae ad hunc actum decanus Albertus Joach. de Krakevitz, ... suo & collegii theologici nomine ad disputationem inauguralem ... Dn. M. Fridemanni Andreae Zulichii, Jenens. De theologia daemonum ... invitat. Rostochii, Literis J. Wepplingi, Sereniss. Princ. & univ. typogr. [1715]
10 p. l., 68 p. 21cm.
The first section is a curriculum
(Continued on next card)

8

Krakevitz, Albert Joachim von, 1674-1734.
Specimen inaugurale theologicum De theologia daemonum.

Witchcraft
BF
1520
K89

Krakevitz, Albert Joachim von, 1674-1734, praeses. ...De theologia daemonum ... [1715] (Card 2)
vitae.
The dissertation proper has special t. p.:
Auxiliante summo numine specimen inaugurale theologicum De theologia daemonum ...
Diss.--Rostock (F. A. Zulich, respondent)
1. Demonology. 2. Devil. I. Zulich, Fridemann Andreas, b. 1687, respondent.
II. His Specimen inaugurale theologici cum De theologia daemonum. III. Title: De theologia daemonum.

Kranz, Georg Christoph, respondent.

Witchcraft

Panecius, Nicolaus, praeses.
Dissertatio De generatione diaboli cum sagis, qvam ... sub praesidio M. Nicol. Panecii ... submittit autor respondens Georg. Christoph. Kranzius ... Wittebergae, Literis Johannis Wilckii [1693]
[16] p. 20cm.
No. 11 in vol. lettered Dissertationes de sagis. 1636-1714.
1. Witchcraft. 2. Devil. I. Kranz, Georg Christoph, respondent. II. Title: De generatione diaboli cum sagis.

WITCHCRAFT
BF
1583
Z7
1550

Krause, ____, Gymnasialdirector zu Rostock.
Hexenprocesse im Gerichte S[ank]t Jürgen, Niederende, 1550 und 1551. Mitgetheilt vom Gymnasialdirector Krause zu Rostock.
[n. p., 1867?]
227-242 p. 20cm.
Caption title.
Detached copy.

8
NIC

1. Trials (Witchcraft)--Sankt Jürgen, Ger. (Lower Saxony) I. Title.

Witchcraft
BF
1565
K91

Krause, Rudolph Wilhelm, 1642-1719, praeses.
Dissertatio medica inavgvralis De incantatis, qvam ... svb praesidio Rvdolffi VVilhelmi Cravsii ... subjicit Iohannes Ernestvs Rauschelbach ... Ienae, Literis Krebsianis [1701]
28 p. 20cm.
Diss.--Jena (J. E. Rauschelbach, respondent)
1. Witchcraft. 2. Personality, Disorders of. I. Rauschelbach, Johann Ernst, respondent. II. Title. III. Title: De incantatis.

8

WITCHCRAFT
BF
1556
K91

Krause, Rudolf Wilhelm, 1642-1719, praeses.
Dissertationem medicam inauguralem De incubo...praeside Dn. Rudolfo Wilhelmo Krauss ...publicae...disquisitioni submittit Daniel Christophorus Meineke... Jenae, Typis Viduae Samuelis Krebsii [1683]
[26] p. 20cm.
Diss.--Jena (D. C. Meineke, respondent)
1. Medicine, Magic, mystic and spagiric. 2. Medical delusions. I. Meineke, Daniel Christophorus, respondent. II. Title.

8
NIC

Witchcraft
GR
250
K91
S9+

Krauss, Friedrich Salomo, 1859-1938.
Südslavische Hexensagen. [Wien, 1884]
[13]-48 p. 29cm.
Caption title.
"Separatabdruck aus dem XIV. Bande [Neue Folge IV. Band] der 'Mittheilungen der Anthropologischen Gesellschaft in Wien'. 1884."
In double columns.
1. Folk-lore, Slavic. 2. Witchcraft --Yugoslavia. I. Title. II. Anthropologische Gesellschaft in Wien. Mitteilungen.

8

Krauss, Rudolf Wilhelm, 1642-1719.
see
Krause, Rudolf Wilhelm, 1642-1719.

WITCHCRAFT
BF
1555
K92

Kristeli, Placidus.
Scientia magica per triginta sex quaestiones deducta pro utilitate confessariorum, & animarum curatorum conscripta, atque per diversa quaesita pro notitia, & fraude daemonis cognoscenda explanata, cum supplemento benedictionum, & exorcismorum, tum maleficiatorum, tum daemoniacorum, tum etiam obsessorum, à Fr. P. Placido Kristelii. Viennae, J. J. Pentz, 1745.
1. Demoniac possession. 2. Exorcism. I. Title.

Kruckow, Christence, d. 1621.

WITCHCRAFT
BF
1584
D4
Z7
1621

Dom over Christence Kruchow for troldom, 1621.
(In: Nye danske magazin. Kjøbenhaven. 24cm. [ser.2] v.1, no.12, 1794, p.378-391)

8
NIC

1. Kruckow, Christence, d.1621. 2. Trials (Witchcraft)--Denmark.

Kruckow, Christence, d. 1621.

BF
1584
D4
J172

Jacobsen, Jørgen Carl, 1916-
Christence Kruckow. En adelig Troldkvinde fra Chr. IV's Tid. [Af] J. C. Jacobsen. København, Gad, 1972.
8, 96 p. 25cm.

1. Kruckow, Christence, d. 1621. 2. Trials (Witchcraft)--Denmark. I. Title.

3
NIC

WITCHCRAFT
BF
1583
K95

Kühnau, Richard, 1858-1930.
Hexen und Hexenzauber, nebst einem Anhang über Zauberer und Hexenmeister.
(In Schlesische Gesellschaft für Volkskunde, Breslau. Mitteilungen. Breslau, 1894/96-1938. 25cm. [Bd. 7] Heft 13 (1905), p. 82-98)
Caption title.

8
NIC

1. Witchcraft--Germany. I. Title.

Kulturbilder ur Finlands historia.

WITCHCRAFT
GR
200
H57

Hertzberg, Rafaël, 1845-1896.
Kulturbilder ur Finlands historia. Helsingfors, G. W. Edlund, 1885-88.
2 v. illus. 23cm.
Contents.--I. Skildringar och sägner från Finlands hednatid.--II. Hexprocesser på 1600 talet.
Incomplete: v. 2 lacking illus.
1. Folk-lore--Finland. 2. Witchcraft --Finland. I. Title.

8

Kulturgeschichtliche Bilder aus Mecklenburg.

Witchcraft
BF
1583
B57

Beyer, Conrad.
Kulturgeschichtliche Bilder aus Mecklenburg. Berlin, W. Süsserott, 1903.
131 p. 24cm. (Mecklenburgische Geschichte in Einzeldarstellungen. Heft 6)
Contents.--Zauberei und Hexenprozesse im evangelischen Mecklenburg.--Unter den Elenden und Ehrlosen.
1. Magic--Germany--Mecklenburg. 2. Trials (Witchcraft)--Mecklenburg, Ger. I. Title: Zauberei und Hexenprozesse im evangelischen Mecklenburg. II. Title.

DD
901
N9
K96
1970

Kunstmann, Hartmut Heinrich.
Zauberwahn und Hexenprozess in der Reichsstadt Nürnberg. [Von] Hartmut H[einrich] Kunstmann. (Nürnberg, Stadtarchiv; Korn u. Berg [in Komm.]) 1970.
xix, 214 p. with illus. 21cm. (Nürnberger Werkstücke zur Stadt- und Landesgeschichte, Bd. 1)
Originally presented as the author's thesis, Mainz.
(Continued on next card)

3

CATALOGUE OF THE CORNELL WITCHCRAFT COLLECTION

DD 901 N94 K96 1970
Kunstmann, Hartmut Heinrich. Zauberwahn und Hexenprozess in der Reichsstadt Nürnberg...1970. (Card 2)

1. Magic--Germany--Nuremberg. 2. Trials (Witchcraft)--Nuremberg. 3. Nuremberg--Social life and customs. I. Title. II. Series.

3

WITCHCRAFT BF 1583 A2 K96
Kuntz, Hans.
Newe [i. e. Neue] Zeitung, von einer erschrecklichen That, welche zu Dillingen, von einem Jhesuwider, vnd einer Hexen, geschehen ist, welche denn offentlich, durch strenge Marter, bekand haben, wie sie es getrieben, vnd was sie für grossen Schaden gethan. Auch in Sonderheit, von diesem grossen Gewitter, welches sie den 2. Augusti, dieses 1579. Jars, durch ire Zauberey gemacht haben. Dabeneben auch, von dem vngeschlach-

8 NIC (Continued on next card)

WITCHCRAFT BF 1583 A2 K96
Kuntz, Hans.
Newe [i. e. Neue] Zeitung, von einer erschrecklichen That... (Card 2)

ten Wetter, als Regen, vnd Kelte, welche dem Korn vnd Wein, zum grossen Schaden, vnd Nachtheil, geschehen ist. Auch ist die Hexe, welche 23. Jahr, mit dem bösen Feinde, dem leidigen Teuffel, gebuhlet, den 8. October, zu Dillingen, zum Fewr verurtheilet worden. Aber schrecklicher Weise, von dem

(Continued on next card)

WITCHCRAFT BF 1583 A2 K96
Kuntz, Hans.
Newe [i. e. Neue] Zeitung, von einer erschrecklichen That... (Card 3)

Teuffel aus dem Fewer, in den Lüfften weg geführet worden. Durch Hans Kuntzen beschrieben. Basel, Gedruckt durch Samuel Apiario [1579]
[8] p. 20cm.

1. Witchcraft--Dillingen, Ger. I. Title.

Witchcraft BF 1584 S97 K97+
Kuoni, Michael.
Die Hexengerichte im Prättigau. Kulturhistorische Skizze aus dem 17. Jahrhundert. (In Alpenrosen. Ein schweizerisches Sonntagsblatt. Bern. 27cm. 15. Jahrg. (1885), p. 366-367, 372-373)
Alpenrosen is a "Gratis-Beilage zum 'Intelligenzblatt der Stadt Bern'."
1. Witchcraft--Switzerland. I. Title. II. Alpenrosen. Ein schweizerisches Sonntagsblatt.

8

Kupferberg, Florian.
WITCHCRAFT BF 1589 H81
Horst, Georg Conrad, 1767-1838?
Theurgie, oder Vom Bestreben der Menschen in der alten und neuen Zeit, zwischen sich und der Geisterwelt eine unmittelbare reale Verbindung zu bewirken. Mainz, Bei F. Kupferberg, 1820.
91 p. 21cm.
"Ankündigung. Zauber-Bibliothek," p. [83]-91, signed: Florian Kupferberg.
Bound with his Von der alten und neuen Magie Ursprung. Mainz, 1820.

8 NIC
1. Spirits. 2. Occult sciences--History. 3. His Zauber-Bibliothek. I. Kupferberg, Florian. II. Title.

WITCHCRAFT BF 1555 K96
Kurella, Ernst Gottfried, 1725-1799.
Gedanken von Besessenen und Bezauberten. Halle im Magdeburgischen, C. H. Hemmerde, 1749.
64 p. 20cm.

8 NIC
1. Demoniac possession. I. Title.

Witchcraft BF 1584 D4 H74
Kuriøse Historier fra Hexernes Tid.
[Holm, Viggo Valdemar] 1855-1899.
Kuriøse Historier fra Hexernes Tid af Woldemar [pseud.] Kjøbenhavn, Gyldendalske Boghandel (F. Hegel & Søn) 1896.
151 p. 22cm.
Contents.--Halelu Jah, af I. Pedersson.--Menniskens Børn (af en gammel Krønike)--Hierichos Trummete, af Joannes Michaeli Søn.--Af Dirik Giglers Fortaellinger.
Each item has special t. p.; Halelu Jah also has imprint: Hafnia, 1589.
1. Witchcraft--Denmark. I. Title.

8

Kurtrierische Hexenprozesse im 16. und 17. Jahrhundert.
BF 1583 K89
Krämer, Wolfgang.
Kurtrierische Hexenprozesse im 16. und 17. Jahrhundert, vornehmlich an der unteren Mosel; ein Beitrag zur Kulturgeschichte. München, 1959.
118 p. illus. 21cm.

1. Witchcraft--Treves (Electorate) I. Title.

Witchcraft BF 1583 K96
Kurtz, Oswald Amand, 1889-
Beiträge zur Erklärung des volkstümlichen Hexenglaubens in Schlesien. Anlam, R. Poettke, 1916.
vi,150 p. 23cm.
Diss.--Greifswald.

1. Witchcraft--Silesia. I. Title.

BF 1583 K96
Kurtz, Oswald Amand, 1889-
Beiträge zur Erklärung des volkstümlichen Hexenglaubens in Schlesien. Anlam, R. Poettke, 1916.
vi,150 p. 23cm.
Diss.--Greifswald.

1. Witchcraft--Silesia.

Kurtze doch nachdrückliche Abfertigung an den ... Herrn Georg Gaar.
MSS Bd. WITCHCRAFT BF G12 R57
Rinder, Johann Christian.
Johann Christian Rinders ... Kurtze doch nachdrückliche Abfertigung an den würtzburgischen Pater Herrn Georg Gaar, Lojoliten, der ihn in einer öffentlichen und nun zum Druck gegebenen Canzelrede ... so gar mit Namen um der Wahrheit willen herum genommen, statt einer Franckfurter Messe dafür bey Gelegenheit derselben mit zu schuldig, übermacht. Jena, In der Cröckerischen Buchhandlung, 1750 [ca. 1900]
24 l. 23cm. (Continued on next card)

Kurtze doch nachdrückliche Abfertigung an den ... Herrn Georg Gaar.
MSS Bd. WITCHCRAFT BF G12 R57
Rinder, Johann Christian. ...Kurtze doch nachdrückliche Abfertigung ... 1750 [ca. 1900] (Card 2)
Carnap's manuscript copy.
"Originaldruck in der Kgl. Hof u. Staats-Bibliothek zu München. 46 S. in 4°."
Numerals in the margins indicate pagination of the original.
A defense of his Eine Hexe nach ihrer gresslichen Gestalt und gerechten Strafe.
1. Witchcraft--Germany. 2. Gaar, Georg, b. 1702. Heylsame Lehrstück, und Zauberey bet[...] reffende Anmerckungen.
(Continued on next card)

Kurtze Lehr-Sätze von dem Laster der Zauberey.
WITCHCRAFT BF 1565 R34
Reiche, Johann, ed.
Herrn D. Christian Thomasii ... Kurtze Lehr-Sätze von dem Laster der Zauberey, nach dem wahren Verstande des lateinischen Exemplars ins Deutsche übersetzet, und aus des berühmten Theologi D. Meyfarti, Naudaei, und anderer gelehrter Männer Schrifften erleutert ... nebst einigen Actis magicis heraus gegeben von Johann Reichen. Halle im Magdeburgischen, Im Rengerischen Buchladen, 1704.
2 v. in 1. 21cm.

8 NIC (Continued on next card)

Kurtze Lehr-Sätze von dem Laster der Zauberey.
WITCHCRAFT BF 1565 R34
Reiche, Johann, ed. Herrn D. Christian Thomasii ... Kurtze Lehr-Sätze ... 1704 (Card 2)

Vol. 1 has special t. p.: Fernerer Unfug der Zauberey. Halle im Magdeburgischen 1704.
Vol. 2 has special t. p.: Unterschiedliche Schrifften von Unfug des Hexen-Processes. Halle im Magdeburg, 1703.
Contents.--[1. Bd.] Gabriel Naudaei

8 NIC (Continued on next card)

Kurtze Lehr-Sätze von dem Laster der Zauberey.
WITCHCRAFT BF 1565 R34
Reiche, Johann, ed. Herrn D. Christian Thomasii ... Kurtze Lehr-Sätze ... 1704 (Card 3)
Contents.--Continued.
Schutz-Schrifft [tr. of Apologie pour tous les grands hommes]--Geschichte der Teuffel zu Lodun.--Trauer-Geschichte von der greulichen Zauberey Ludwig Goffredy [tr. of De l'horrible & épouvantable sorcellerie de Louis Goffredy, author F. de Rosset]--D. Christian Thomasii ... Kurtze Lehr-Sätze v[...]
8 NIC (Continued on next card)

Kurtze Lehr-Sätze vor dem Laster der Zauberey.
WITCHCRAFT BF 1565 R34
Reiche, Johann, ed. Herrn D. Christian Thomasii ... Kurtze Lehr-Sätze ... 1704 (Card 4)
Contents--Continued.
dem Laster der Zauberey [tr. of Dissertati[...] de crimine magiae, J. Reiche, respondent] [2. Bd.] Malleus judicum oder Gesetz-Hammer der unbarmhertzigen Hexen-Richter.--Cautio criminalis [von F. Spee]--D. Matthäus Meyfarths Christliche Erinnerung an Regenten.-- Viererley Sorten Hexen. Acta.
8 NIC (Continued on next card)

Kurtze Lehr-Sätze von dem Laster der Zaube[...]
Witchcraft BF 1555 A55 no.4
Thomasius, Christian, 1655-1728.
Kurtze Lehr-Sätze von dem Laster der Zaube[...] vormahls in einer Inaugural Disputation defen[...] dirt, nunmehro aber auff gut Befinden andrer Deutsche übersetzet von einem Liebhaber seine[r] Muttersprache. [n.p.] 1702.
[136] p. 14cm.
Translation of Dissertatio de crimine magi[ae]
No. 4 in vol. lettered Andreae. De angelor[...]

330

CATALOGUE OF THE CORNELL WITCHCRAFT COLLECTION

Kurtze Lehr-Sätze von dem Laster der Zauberey.

Witchcraft
BF
1565
T46
1712
    Thomasius, Christian, 1655-1728.
      Christ. Thomasii Kurtze Lehr-Sätze von dem Laster der Zauberey, aus dem Lateinischen ins Teutsche übersetzet, und mit des Autoris Vertheidigung vermehret. [n. p.] 1712.
      92 p. plate. 16cm.
      Title in red and black.
      Translation of Dissertatio de crimine magiae.
      Anhang, welcher aus des Autoris Erinne-

(Continued on next card)

Kurtze Lehr-Sätze von dem Laster der Zauberey.

Witchcraft
BF
1565
T46
1712
    Thomasius, Christian, 1655-1728. Christ. Thomasii Kurtze Lehr-Sätze von dem Laster der Zauberey ... 1712. (Card 2)

      rung wegen seiner künfftigen Winter-Lectionen, auff das 1702. und folgende Jahr genommen worden, und betrifft die Vertheidigung seiner selbst eigenen Lehr-Sätze von dem Laster der Zauberey, p. [85]-92, has special t. p.

8

Kurtze Lehr-Sätze von dem Laster der Zauberey.

Witchcraft
BF
1565
T46
1717
    Thomasius, Christian, 1655-1728.
      Christ. Thomasii Kurtze Lehr-Sätze von dem Laster der Zauberey, mit dessen eigenen Vertheidigung vermehret. Worbey Johann Kleins ... Juristische Untersuchung, was von der Hexen Bekäntniss zu halten, dass solche aus schändlichem Beyschlaff mit dem Teuffel Kinder gezeuget. Beydes aus dem Lateinischen ins Teutsche Übersetzt. Franckfurth und Leipzig, 1717.
      134 p. 18cm.

8   (Continued on next card)

Kurtze Lehr-Sätze von dem Laster der Zauberey.

Witchcraft
BF
1565
T46
1717
    Thomasius, Christian, 1655-1728. Christ. Thomasii Kurtze Lehr-Sätze von dem Laster der Zauberey ... 1717. (Card 2)

      Title in red and black.
      Translation of Thomasius' Dissertatio de crimine magiae and of Klein's Meditatio academica exhibens examen juridicum judicialis.
      Klein's Juristische Untersuchung, was von der Hexen Bekäntniss zu halten ..., p. [79]-134, has special t. p.

8   (Continued on next card)

Kurtze Lehr-Sätze von dem Laster der Zauberey.

Witchcraft
BF
1565
T46
1717a
    Thomasius, Christian, 1655-1728.
      Christ. Thomasii Kurtze Lehr-Sätze von dem Laster der Zauberey, mit dessen eigenen Vertheidigung vermehret. Worbey Johann Kleins ... Juristische Untersuchung, was von der Hexen Bekäntniss zu halten, dass solche aus schändlichem Beyschlaff mit dem Teuffel Kinder gezeuget. Beydes aus dem Lateinischen ins Teutsche übersetzt. Franckfurth und Leipzig, 1717.
      134 p. front. 19cm.

8   (Continued on next card)

Kurtze Lehr-Sätze von dem Laster der Zauberey.

Witchcraft
BF
1565
T46
1717a
    Thomasius, Christian, 1655-1728. Christ. Thomasii Kurtze Lehr-Sätze von dem Laster der Zauberey ... 1717. (Card 2)

      Translation of his Dissertatio de crimine magiae, J. Reiche, respondent; and of Meditatio academica, exhibens examen juridicum judicialis, by J. Klein (N. Putter, respondent).
      Johann Kleins Juristische Untersuchung, p. [79]-134, has special t. p.

8   (Continued on next card)

Kurtze Lehr-Sätze von dem Laster der Zauberey.

Witchcraft
BF
1565
T46
1717a
    Thomasius, Christian, 1655-1728. Christ. Thomasii Kurtze Lehr-Sätze von dem Laster der Zauberey ... 1717. (Card 3)

      With this are bound Ludovici, Gottfried, 1670-1724. ... Theologicum novae... Coburgi [1718] and Sturm, Johann Christoph, 1635-1703. ... Wahrhaffte und gründliche Vorstellung von der lügenhafften Stern-Wahrsagerey. Coburg, 1722.
      1. Witchcraft. I. His Dissertatio de crimine magiae.-- German. II.

8   (Continued on next card)

Kurtze vnnd warhafftige Historia von einer Junckfrawen.

WITCHCRAFT
BF
1559
K45
1574a
    Khueller, Sebastianus
      Kurtze vnnd warhafftige Historia von einer Junckfrawen, welche mit etlich vnd dreissig bösen Geistern leibhafftig besessen, vnd in der Schloss Capeln zu Starnberg, im Ertzhertzogthumb Osterreich vnder der Enns, in beysein viler vom Adel, vnd ander ehrlichen leut, genedigklich daruon erlödiget worden. München, Getruckt bey Adam Berg [1574].
Wien, [1885]
      [14] p. illus. 24cm.

8
NIC   (Continued on next card)

Kurtze vnnd warhafftige Historia von einer Junckfrawen.

WITCHCRAFT
BF
1559
K45
1574a
    Khueller, Sebastianus
      Kurtze vnnd warhafftige Historia von einer Junckfrawen... [1885] (Card 2)

      Signed: Sebastianus Khueller.
      Facsimile reprint.

      1. Exorcism. 2. Steiner, Veronica. I. Title.

WITCHCRAFT
BF
1552
K96
    Kurtze Untersuchung von Kobold, in so ferne gewisse phaenomena unter diesem Nahmen dem Teuffel zugeschrieben werden, aus Veranlassung einer besondern Begebenheit wobey überhaupt von denen sichtbaren Würckungen des Teuffels in und durch die natürlichen Cörper gehandelt. Auch hiernächst gezeiget wird wie der Herr autor seinen Lehr-Sätzen von dem Laster der Zauberey etliche hieher gehörige Schrifft-Stellen zur Ungebühr verdr ehet und überdis seine

8
NIC   (Continued on next card)

WITCHCRAFT
BF
1552
K96
    Kurtze Untersuchung von Kobold... (Card 2)

      gantze Meynung de pacto auf unbündige paralogismos gegründet. Von einen nach Engelland reisenden Passagier. Roterdam, 1719.
      108 p. front. 17cm.

      1. Demonology. 2. Witchcraft. 3. Thomasius, Christian, 1655-1728. Kurtze Lehr-Sätze von dem Laster der Zauberey. I. Ein nach Engelland reisender Passagier.

Kurtze Untersuchung von Kobold.

Witchcraft
BF
1565
F82
    Franck, Johannes Christophorus, fl. 1717.
      Gottfried Wahrliebs [pseud.] Deutliche vorstellung der nichtigkeit derer vermeynten hexereyen und des ungegründeten hexen-processes. Nebst einer Gründlichen beantwortung der unter dem nahmen eines nach Engelland reisenden passagiers unlängst heraus gekommenen Untersuchung vom kobold, darinnen die falschen auflagen / mit welchen derselbe so wohl den hrn. geheimbd. rath Thomasium als Johann Webstern ohne allen grund zu diffamiren gesucht. deutlich entdecket, wie auch die Thomasische. Lehr-sätze vom laster der

(Continued on next card)

Kurtze Untersuchung von Kobold.

Witchcraft
BF
1565
F82
    Franck, Johannes Christophorus, fl. 1717.
      Gottfried Wahrliebs [pseud.] Deutliche vorstellung der nichtigkeit derer vermeynten hexereyen ... [pref. 1720] (Card 2)

      zauberey wieder dessen ungegründete einwürffe zulänglich behauptet werden. Amsterdam, Nach erfindung der hexerey im dritten seculo, und nach einführung des hexen-processes im jahr 236 [pref. 1720]
      172, 78 p. front. 22cm.

(Continued on next card)

Kurtze Untersuchung von Kobold.

WITCHCRAFT
BF
1565
F82
    Franck, Johannes Christophorus, fl. 1717.
      Gottfried Wahrliebs [pseud.] Deutliche vorstellung der nichtigkeit derer vermeynten hexereyen...[pref. 1720] (Card 3)

      "Gründliche beantwortung der ... Untersuchung vom kobold" has separate paging and special t. p. with imprint: Amsterdam, 1720.

(Continued on next card)

Ein kurtzer Bericht, was von den abgötterischen Sägen und Beschweren zuhalten.

WITCHCRAFT
BF
1565
S767
    Spreter, Johann.
      Ein kurtzer Bericht, was von den abgötterischen Sägen vñ Beschweren, wie der etlich volbracht, vnnd das die ein Zauberey, auch Grewel vor Gott dem Herren seind. Durch den wirdigen vñ wolgelerten Herren Johañ. Spreter von Rotweil zůsamen gebracht ... [Basel, Getruckt durch Bartholomeum Westheymer, 1543]
      [12] p. 21cm.
      With colophon.

8
NIC   (Continued on next card)

Ein kurtzer Bericht, was von den abgötterischen Sägen und Beschweren zuhalten.

WITCHCRAFT
BF
1565
S767
    Spreter, Johann. Ein kurtzer Bericht ... [1543] (Card 2)

      Caption title: Von Sägen vnd Beschweren.
      Running title: Von abgötterischen Sägen vnd Beschweren.

      1. Witchcraft. 2. Magic. 3. Folk medicine. I. Title: Von abgötterischen Sägen und Beschweren.

8
NIC

Ein kurtzer doch gründlicher Bericht, wie vnd was gestalt, so woln bey dem rechtlichen Process ... zuuerfahren seye.

Witchcraft
BF
1565
L42
T3
1629
    Laymann, Paul, 1574-1635.
      Ein kurtzer doch gründlicher Bericht, wie vnd was gestalt, so woln bey dem rechtlichen Proceß als auch der Beicht mit den Hexen zuuerfahren seye. Auß deß ehrwurdigen hochgelehrten Herrn P. Pauli Läymanns ... Theologia morali gezogen, vñ den Richtern vñ Beichtvättern zu gutem absonderlich in den Truck gegeben. An jetzo aber männiglich zu gutem in die teutsche sprache vbersetzt. Durch Wolffgang Schilling ...

8   (Continued on next card)

Ein kurtzer doch gründlicher Bericht, wie vnd was gestalt, so woln bey dem rechtlichen Process ... zuuerfahren seye.

Witchcraft
BF
1565
L42
T3
1629
    Laymann, Paul, 1574-1635. Ein kurtzer doch gründlicher Bericht ... 1629. (Card 2)

      Wirtzburg, Gedruckt bey Stephan Fleischmann, 1629.
      129 p. 14cm.
      With colophon.
      According to G. L. Burr, the first part was printed in Aschaffenburg in 1629 under title: Aurea enucleatio atque disquisitio ... The second section, p. 60-129,

8   (Continued on next card)

CATALOGUE OF THE CORNELL WITCHCRAFT COLLECTION

```
              Ein kurtzer doch gründlicher Bericht, wie
              vnd was gestalt, so woln bey dem recht-
              lichen Process ... zuuerfahren seye.
Witchcraft
BF       Laymann, Paul, 1574-1635.  Ein kurtzer
1565        doch gründlicher Bericht ...  1629.
L42                                    (Card 3)
T3
1629     was published in 1629 by the same printer
         under title: Newer Tractat von der verführ-
         ten Kinder Zauberey, and is by Schilling.
            1. Trials (Witchcraft)  2. Confessors.
         I.  His  Theologia moralis. Selections.
         German.  II.  His  Aurea enucleatio. German.
         III. His  Neu   er Tractat von der ver-
  8      führten Kinder      Zauberey.  IV. Schil-
         ling, Wolfgang,     tr.  V. Title.


           Kurze Vertheidigung der thätigen Hex- und
              Zauberey.
Witchcraft
BF       März, Angelus, 1731-1784.
1565        P. Angelus März Kurze Vertheidigung der
S83      thätigen Hex- und Zauberey wider eine dem
M18      heiligen Kreuz zu Scheyrn nachtheilig- Aka-
1766     demische Rede, welche den 13. October 1766.
         von P. Don Ferdinand Sterzinger ... abgele-
         sen worden. 2. Aufl.   Jngolstadt, Gedruckt
         bey J. K. Gran ₍1766₎
           31 p.  21cm.
            1. Sterzinger, Ferdinand, 1721-1786. Aka-
         demische Rede     von dem gemeinen Vorur-
         theile der ...    Hexerey.  2. Witchcraft.
  8      I.  Title:  K    urze Vertheidigung der
         thätigen Hex-     und Zauberey.


             Kurzer Bericht von denen Geistern.
WITCHCRAFT
BF       Seidel, Abrahamus.
1445        ₍Pneumatologia₎ Πνευματολογία oder
S45      Kurtzer Bericht von denen Geistern, über der
         unlangst publicirten Frage ob natürliche
         gewisse Geister seyen, und einem Menschen
         gezieme solche an sich zu locken, und in de-
         ro Gemeinschafft zugerathen?... Erffurdt,
         In Verlegung Johann Birckners ₍Gedruckt in
         der Spangenbergischen Truckerey₎ 1648.
           ₍152₎ p.  illus.  14cm.
  8         One p. of        MS notes bound in at end.
NIC      Title in          red and black.
            1. Spiri      ts.  2. Witchcraft.  I.
         Title.


           Kurzgefasste Beschreibung des Lebens und
Witchcraft   der Thaten des Joseph Balsamo.
BF       ₍Barberi,     ₎
1598        Kurzgefasste Beschreibung des Lebens
C13      und der Thaten des Joseph Balsamo, oder
B23      sogenannten Grafen Kagliostro, gezogen aus
1791d    dem wider ihn zu Rom 1790; angestellten
         Prozesse: zur Beleuchtung der wahren
         Beschaffenheit der Freymaurersekte.  Aus
         dem Italiänischen ins Deutsche übersetzt.
         Augsburg, J. N. Styx, 1791.
           86, 40, 112, 23 p.  17cm.

                            (Continued on next card)


           Kurzgefasste Beschreibung des Lebens und
              der Thaten des Joseph Balsamo.
Witchcraft
BF       ₍Barberi,     ₎ Kurzgefasste Beschreibung
1598        des Lebens und der Thaten des Joseph
C13         Balsamo ... 1791.        (Card 2)
B23
1791d    Translation of Compendio della vita, e
         delle gesta di Giuseppe Balsamo.
            1. Cagliostro, Alessandro, conte di,
         assumed name of Giuseppe Balsamo, 1743-
         1795.  2. Freemasons.  I. His  Compendio
         della vita, e       delle gesta di Giuseppe
         Balsamo--Germ       an.  II. Title.
         III. Autograph-- Dumont, Paul.


ar W     Kutsche, Joseph.
36018       De incubo eiusque medela.   Berolini
         ₍1842₎
           32 p.  21cm.






            1. Spirits.   I. Title.
```

```
Witchcraft
BX       Kuyk, J     van.
9479        Disputatie over den duyvel, of dezelve
B42      is een geschaapen geest, buyten de zielen
B11      der menschen, dewelke afgevallen en boos ge-
no.16    worden is, ofte niet?  Voorgevallen tusschen
         J. van Kuyk, krankbesoeker, ter eenre, en
         H. Bouman, ter andere zyde ... op den 26 De-
         cember, 1694.  Door een liefhebber der waar-
         heyt, soo daar tegenwoordig was, opgestelt.
         Hier is noch by gevoegt een brief, aan ge-
         seyde J. van Kuyk ... den 27 January, 1693.

  8                        (Continued on next card)


Witchcraft
BX       Kuyk, J     van.  Disputatie over den
9479        duyvel ... 1695.          (Card 2)
B42
B11      aldaar bestelt; met redenen, waarom deselve
no.16    nu eerst door den druk gemeen gemaakt wort.
         Amsterdam, By E. Webber, boekverkooper, 1695.
           16 p.  title and end page vignettes.  20
         x 15cm.
           4°:  A-B⁴.
           Black letter (except introduction)
           Letter and          Na-reeden, p. 10-16,

  8                        (Continued on next card)


Witchcraft
BX       Kuyk, J     van.  Disputatie over den
9479        duyvel ... 1695.          (Card 3)
B42
B11      signed:  Z. W. ₍i. e., Zacharias Webbers₎
no.16    Van der Linde 79.
            No. 16 in vol. lettered B. Bekkers sterf-
         bed en andere tractaten.
            1. Devil.  I. Bouman, Herman.  II.
         Webbers, Zacharias.  III. Een liefhebber
         der waarheyt.  IV. Title.


  3


Witchcraft
BF       Kyteler, Alice, fl. 1324, defendant.
1581        A contemporary narrative of the proceedings against Dame
Z7       Alice Kyteler, prosecuted for sorcery in 1324, by Richard de
1324     Ledrede, bishop of Ossory.  Edited by Thomas Wright ...
         London, Printed for the Camden society, by J. B. Nichols and
         son, 1843.
           2 p. l., xlii p., 1 l., 61, ₍1₎ p.  21 x 17ᵐ.  ₍Camden society. Publications.
         no. XXIV₎
           Text in Latin.
           Printed from Harleian ms., no. 641.  cf. Introd.
            1. Witchcraft—Ireland.  I. Ledrede, Richard de, bp. of Ossory,
         d. 1360.  II. Wright, Thomas, 1810-1877, ed.  III. Title.
                                                             38-36518
           Library of Congress       DA20.C17  no. 24
           ———— Copy 2.    22½ x      17½ᵐ.
                                    ₍3₎


DA       Kyteler, Alice, fl. 1324, defendant.
20          A contemporary narrative of the proceed-
C17      ings against Dame Alice Kyteler, prosecuted
v. 24    for sorcery in 1324, by Richard de Ledrede,
         bishop of Ossory.  Edited by Thomas Wright
         ...  London, Printed for the Camden Society,
         by J. B. Nichols and son, 1843.
           2 p. l., xlii p., 1 l., 61, ₍1₎ p.  21 x
         17cm.  ₍Camden Society. Publications.  no.
         XXIV₎
           Text in Latin.
           Printed fr     om Harleian ms., no. 641.
```

L

L., M. J. J.

MSS Bd.
WITCHCRAFT
BF
E61

Der entlarvte Teuffel oder denkwürdige Geschichte von vielen warhaftig Besessenen, welche dieses Feindes Grausamkeit heftig erfahren, entlich aber durch den mächtigen Finger Gottes wieder erlediget worden. Zu mehrer Bekräftigung der von Doct. Beckern, in seiner verzauberten Welt, zweiffelhaft gemachten Kögischen Geschichte ... Zusammen getragen von M. J. J. L. Leipzig, Johann Melchior Liebe, 16   97 [ca. 1900]
(Continued on next card)

L., M. J. J.

MSS Bd.
WITCHCRAFT
BF
E61

Der entlarvte Teuffel ...   1697 [ca. 1900]
(Card 2)

77 p. 19cm.
Carnap's manuscript copy.
"Originaldruck in der Königl. öff. Bibliothek zu Dresden, 98 pag. Seiten in 8°."
"Diese Schrift bildet gewissermassen die Fortsetzung zu: "Das geängstigte Köge oder Eine warhaffte und denkwürdige Historie, von einer ent   setzlichen Versuchung, des leidigen   Satans zu Köge in
(Continued on next card)

L., M. J. J.

MSS Bd.
WITCHCRAFT
BF
E61

Der entlarvte Teuffel ...   1697 [ca. 1900]
(Card 3)

Seeland" wo in deutscher Sprache durch denselben Verfasser ... i. J. 1695 herausgegeben. Hieraus erklärt es sich, dass diese Schrift mit " die dritte Zugabe" anfängt, da "das geängstigte Köge mit der zweiten Zugabe abschliesst."
Marginal numerals and signatures indicate paginati   on ans signatures of the original.   (Continued on next card)

L., M. J. J.

MSS Bd.
WITCHCRAFT
BF
E61

Der entlarvte Teuffel ...   1697 [ca. 1900]
(Card 4)

Printed copy not in Van der Linde.

1. Demoniac possession. 2. Devil.
3. Bekker, Balthasar, 1634-1698. De betoverde weere   ld. I. Das geängstigte Köge.   II. M. J. J. L. III. L., M. J. J.

L--N. (pseud.)
see
Lorgion, Everardus Jan Diest, 1812-1876.

L. P.

Witchcraft
BX
9479
B42
B11
no.17

Brief van L. P. aan Herman Bouman; eerst in 't bysonder aan hem geschreeven, en nu door hem, met verlof van den autheur, gemeen gemaakt: behelsende sommige redenen waarom hy de soo genaamde Sleutel der geesten enz. van M. van Diepen, en J. Hubener niet, ofte niet zoodanig alse daar ligt, behoorde te beantwoorden; en teffens een volstrekte omkeering van de gronden van dat woest geschrift. Amsterdam, By   R. Blokland, boekverkoper, 1699.
(Continued on next card)

L. P.

Witchcraft
BX
9479
B42
B11
no.17

Brief van L. P. aan Herman Bouman ... 1699.
(Card 2)

2 p. l., 12 p. title and end page vignettes, illus. initials. 20 x 15cm.
4°: π², A⁴, B².
Written by a supporter of Balthasar Bekker, whom Diepen and Hubener attacked.
No. 17 in vol. lettered B. Bekkers sterfbed en andere tractaten.
1. Diepen,   Marcus van. De sleutel der geesten.   2. Bekker, Balthasar,
(Continued on next card)

L. R.

Witchcraft
BF
1410
B42
Z56
v.3
no.20

De Volmaakte kragt Godts verheerlykt. Nevens eenige aanmerkinge over de drie predikatien van Do. Petrus Schaak. Gedaan over Psal. 72: v.18. Gen. 18: v. 1,2,... en Gen. 32: v.24,25. In haar eigen gronden ondersogt, en met de waarheid vergeleken. En eenige andere aanmerkingen daar hy gevoegd. Amsterdam, By D. vanden Dalen, boekverkooper, 1691.
47 p. [p. 48 blank] title and other vignettes, illus. initial. 19 x 15cm.
4°: A-F⁴
Black letter.
(Continued on next card)

L. R.

Witchcraft
BF
1410
B42
Z56
v.3
no.20

De Volmaakte kragt Godts verheerlykt. 1691.
(Card 2)

Preface signed: J: P. L: R.
Supports B. Bekker against Schaak's attacks on Bekker's De betoverde weereld.
Van der Linde 145.
No.20 in vol. lettered Bekker III.

La Borie, François de, tr.

WITCHCRAFT
BT
960
M24
1616

Maldonado, Juan, 1534-1583.
Traicté des anges et demons, du R. P. Maldonat. Mis en françois, par maistre François de La Borie. Rouen, Chez Iacques Besongne, 1616.
242 l. 15cm.

Illustrated t.p.

1. Angels--Early works to 1800. 2. Demonology. I. La Borie, François de, tr. II. Title.

8
NIC

La Croix, Anthoine.

WITCHCRAFT
BF
1582
Z7
1700

Peyron, Paul Malo Théophile.
Procès pour faits de sorcellerie à la fin du XVIIe siècle. [Quimper? 190-?]
11 p. 23cm.

Signed: Peyron, chanoine.

8
NIC

1. Trials (Witchcraft)--Lesneven, France.
2. Maillé, Louis. 3. La Croix, Anthoine.

Lacroix, Paul, 1806-1884.

WITCHCRAFT
BR
135
L14

Curiosités de l'histoire des croyances populaires au moyen âge, par P. L. Jacob [pseud.] Paris, A. Delahays, 1859.
323 p. 17cm.

Running title: Histoire des moeurs.
Includes bibliographies.
Contents.--Superstitions et croyances populaires.--Le juif-errant.--Les blasphé-

8
NIC
(Continued on next card)

Lacroix, Paul, 1806-1884.

WITCHCRAFT
BR
135
L14

Curiosités de l'histoire des croyances populaires...1859.   (Card 2)

Contents--continued.
mateurs.--Les démons de la nuit.--Les sorciers et le sabbat.--Le boeuf gras.--Origines du mal de Naples.

1. Superstition. I. Title. II. Title: Histoire des   moeurs.

Lacroix, Paul, 1806-1884.

WITCHCRAFT
BF
1532
L14

Curiosités infernales, par P. L. Jacob [pseud.] Paris, Garnier frères, 1886.
ii, 396 p. 19cm.

Bibliographical footnotes.
Contents.--Les diables.--Les bons anges.--Le royaume des fées.--Nature troublée.--Monde des esprits.--Prodiges.--Empire des morts.--Présages.

8
NIC

1. Demonol   ogy. I. Title.

Ladame, Paul Louis, 1842-

DQ
441
S67M5
v.23

Les Mandragores ou diables familiers à Genève au 16e et au 17e siècle. (In Société d'histoire et d'archéologie de Genève. Mémoires et documents. v. 23, 1888/1894, pp. 237-281)

I. Title.

CATALOGUE OF THE CORNELL WITCHCRAFT COLLECTION

WITCHCRAFT
BF
1555
L15

Ladame, Paul Louis, 1842-1919.
Les possédés et les démoniaques à Genève au XVIIme siècle; étude historique de medecine mentale. [n. p., 189-?]
[156]-220 p. 21cm.

Caption title.
Signed: Paul Ladame.
Detached copy.

8
NIC

1. Demoniac possession. I. Title.

Ladame, Paul Louis, 1842-1919.

WITCHCRAFT
BF
1584
S97
Z7
1652

Chauderon, Michée, defendant.
Procès criminel de la dernière sorcière brulée à Genève le 6 avril 1652, publié d'après des documents inédits et originaux conservés aux Archives de Genève (N° 3465) par le d' Ladame. Paris, Aux Bureaux du Progrès médical, 1888.
xii, 52 p. 24cm. (Bibliothèque diabolique (Collection Bourneville))

8
NIC

Running title: Procès criminel de Michée Chauderon.
(Continued on next card)

WITCHCRAFT
BF
1584
B4
L15+

Laenen, Joseph, 1871-1940.
Heksenprocessen. Antwerpen, Algem. Katholieke Boekhandel "Veritas," 1914.
77 p. 26cm.

Bibliographical footnotes.

8
NIC

1. Trials (Witchcraft)--Belgium. 2. Witchcraft--Belgium. I. Title.

Längin, Georg, 1827-1897.
Religion und Hexenglaube.

Witchcraft
BF
1583
D55
Z3

Diefenbach, Johann.
Der Zauberglaube des sechzehnten Jahrhunderts nach den Katechismen Dr. Martin Luthers und des P. Canisius. Mit Berücksichtigung der Schriften Pfarrers Längin-Karlsruhe und des Professors Riezler-München. Mainz, F. Kirchheim, 1900.
xii, 209 p. 23cm.

1. Witchcraft--Germany. 2. Theology, Doctrinal--16th century. 3. Canisius, Petrus, Saint, 1521-1597. Catechismus.

8
(Continued on next card)

WITCHCRAFT
BF
1566
L153

Längin, Georg, 1827-1897.
Religion und Hexenprozess. Zur Würdigung des 400jährigen Jubiläums der Hexenbulle und des Hexenhammers sowie der neuesten katholischen Geschichtschreibung auf diesem Gebiete. Leipzig, O. Wigand, 1888.
xviii, 385 p. 24cm.

Autograph: Andrew Dickson White.

8
NIC

1. Witchcraft--Hist. 2. Trials (Witchcraft)--Hist. I. Title.

Laymann, Paul.
see
Laymann, Paul, 1574-1635.

WITCHCRAFT
BF
1582
L16

La Fons, Alexandre de, baron de Mélicocq.
Des sorciers aux XVme et XVIme siècles. [Abbeville, 1843]
[435]-448 p. 24cm.

Extract from Mémoires de la Société d'Abbeville, 1841-43.

8
NIC

1. Witchcraft--France. 2. Witchcraft--History. I. Title.

Witchcraft
BF
1711
B55
1730

Lambe, John, d. 1628.
A briefe description of the notoriovs life of Iohn Lambe, otherwise called Doctor Lambe, together with his ignominiovs death. Amsterdam, Printed 1628. [London, Barker, printer, 173-]

Facsimile reprint.

WITCHCRAFT
BF
1583
L22

Lamberg, G von
Criminal-Verfahren vorzüglich bei Hexenprozessen im ehemaligen Bissthum Bamberg während der Jahre 1624 bis 1630. Aus actenmässigen Urkunden gezogen von G. v. Lamberg. Nürnberg, Kiegel und Wiessner [1835]
39, 28 p. 19cm.

8
NIC

1. Trials (Witchcraft)--Bamberg (Diocese) I. Title.

WITCHCRAFT
BF
1517
F5
L22

La Menardaye, Jean Baptiste de.
Examen et discussion critique de l'histoire des diables de Loudun, de la possession des religieuses Ursulines, et de la condamnation d'Urbain Grandier. Paris, Chez Debure l'aîné, 1747.
xxix, 521 p. 17cm.

1. Demoniac possession. 2. Grandier, Urbain, 1590-1634. 3. Loudun, France. Ursuline convent. I. Title: Histoire des diables de Loudun. II. Title: Diables de Loudun.

8
NIC

Witchcraft
BF
1569
A2
V82
1490

Lamiarum sive striarum opuscula.
Visconti, Girolamo, fl. 1490-1512.
Lamiarum sive striarum opuscula. Milan, Leonardus Pachel, 13 Sept. 1490.
[24] l. 21cm.

Leaf [2a]: Magistri Hyeronimi Vicecomitis. Lamiarum siue striarum opusculum ad illustrissimum Mediolani ducem franciscum sfortiam Vicecomitem: Incipit feliciter.
Leaf [24b] (Colophon): Explicit Lamiarum tractatus magistri Iheronimi Vicecomitis predicatorum ordinis &c. Impressum
(Continued on next card)

Witchcraft
BF
1569
A2
V82
1490

Lamiarum sive striarum opuscula.
Visconti, Girolamo, fl. 1490-1512. Lamiarum sive striarum opuscula ... 1490.
(Card 2)

Mediolani per magistrum Leonerdum Pachel Anno Domini. M.cccc.xc. Die. xiii. Mensis Septēbris.
Signatures: a-c8.
Capital spaces, with guide-letters.
Edited by Aluisius de la Cruce.
Copinger. Supplement to Hain's Repertorium, 6200=3210; Proctor, 5986; Brit. Mus.
(Continued on next card)

Witchcraft
BF
1569
A2
V82
1490

Lamiarum sive striarum opuscula.
Visconti, Girolamo, fl. 1490-1512. Lamiarum sive striarum opuscula ... 1490.
(Card 3)

Cat. (XV cent.) VI, p. 778 (IA. 26646); Goff. Third census, V-272.

1. Witchcraft. I. Title. II. Title: Magistri Hyeronimi Vicecomitis. Lamiarum siue striarum opusculum.

Lancashire legends, traditions, &c.

DA
670
L2
H28

Harland, John, 1806-1868.
Lancashire legends, traditions, pageants, sports, etc., with an appendix containing a rare tract on the Lancashire witches, etc., by J. Harland and T. T. Wilkinson. London, G. Routledge, 1873.
xxxv, 283 p. illus. 20cm.

1. Lancashire, Eng.--Soc. life & customs. 2. Folk-lore--England--Lancashire. I. Wilkinson, T T joint author. II. Title.

WITCHCRAFT
BF
1532
L24

Lancelin, Charles Marie Eugène, 1852-
Histoire mythique de Shatan. De la légende au dogme. Origine de l'idée démoniaque, ses transformations à travers les âges, d'après les textes et la tradition... Paris, H. Daragon, 1903-05.
2 v. in 1. illus. 20cm. (Bibliothèque des sciences maudites)

Vol. 2 has title: Le ternaire magique de Shatan; envoutement, incubat, vampirisme.

8
NIC

1. Devil. 2. Demonology. I. His Le ternaire magique de Shatan. II. Title.

WITCHCRAFT
BF
1412
L24

Lancelin, Charles Marie Eugène, 1852-
La sorcellerie des campagnes. Paris, H. Durville [1912]
493 p. illus. 23cm.

8
NIC

1. Occult sciences--Hist. 2. Witchcraft--Hist. I. Title.

Lancelin, Charles Marie Eugène, 1852-
Le ternaire magique de Shatan.

WITCHCRAFT
BF
1532
L24

Lancelin, Charles Marie Eugène, 1852-
Histoire mythique de Shatan. De la légende au dogme. Origine de l'idée démoniaque, ses transformations à travers les âges, d'après les textes et la tradition... Paris, H. Daragon, 1903-05.
2 v. in 1. illus. 20cm. (Bibliothèque des sciences maudites)

Vol. 2 has title: Le ternaire magique de Shatan; envoutement, incubat, vampirisme.

8
NIC

1. Devil. 2. Demonology. I. His Le ternaire magique de Shatan.

WITCHCRAFT
BF
1602
L25
1622

L'Ancre, Pierre de, d. 1630.
L'incredvlité et mescreance dv sortilege plainement convaincve. Ov il est amplement et cvrievsement traicté, de la vérité ou illusion du sortilege, de la fascination, de l'attouchement, du scopelisme, de la diuination, de la ligature ou liaison magique, des apparitions: et d'vne infinité d'autres rares & nouueaux subjects. Paris, Chez Nicolas Bvon, 1622.
841, [10] p. port. 25cm.

I. Title.

CATALOGUE OF THE CORNELL WITCHCRAFT COLLECTION

BF 1522 L25 1612
L'Ancre, Pierre de, d. 1630.
Tableav de l'inconstance des mavvais anges et demons, ov il est amplement traicté des sorciers et de la sorcelerie ... Avec vn discours contenant la procedure faicte par les inquisiteurs d'Espagne et de Nauarre, à 53. magiciens, apostats, Juifs, et sorciers, en la ville de Logrogne en Castille, le 9. nouembre 1610 ... Paris, Chez Nicolas Bvon, 1612.
[36], 571, [24] p. 24cm.
(Continued on next card)

F 522 25 612
L'Ancre, Pierre de, d. 1630. Tableav de l'inconstance des mavvais anges et demons ... 1612. (Card 2)
In copy 1 signature Bbbb_iv (p. 567-568) is from a different impression, so that the closing paragraph of p. 567 is repeated on p. 568. Text ends on p. 570.
In copy 2 there are two signatures Cccc (p. 569-570) of different impressions. Page 569₁ begins: "tiere en trois lieux" and text ends on the same page; p. 570₁ is blank.
(Continued on next card)

F 522 25 612
L'Ancre, Pierre de, d. 1630. Tableav de l'inconstance des mavvais anges et demons ... 1612. (Card 3)
Page 569₂ begins: "Qvi me faict conclurre", and text ends on p. 570₂.

L'Ancre, Pierre de, d. 1630.
Tableav de l'inconstance des mavvais anges et demons, ou il est amplement traicté des sorciers et de la sorcellerie ... Avec vn discours contenant la procedure faicte par les inquisiteurs d'Espagne et de Nauarre, à 53. magiciens, apostats, Juifs, et sorciers, en la ville de Logrogne en Castille, le 9. nouembre 1610 ... Reueu, corrigé, & augmenté de plusieurs nouuelles obseruations, arrests, & autres choses notables. Paris, Nicolas Bvon, 1613.
[40], 590, [18] p. fold. pl. 24cm.
I. Title.

WITCHCRAFT BF 1583 L25
Landenberger, Johannes.
Stuttgarter Hexen-Geschichten. Kulturgeschichtliche Bilder aus vergangenen Tagen. Mit einer Einleitung. Lorch, K. Röhm [1904]
23 p. 17cm. (Deutsche Volks-Bibliothek, Nr.1)

8 NIC
1. Witchcraft--Stuttgart. I. Title.

Landsberg, Ernst, 1860-1927.
Zur biographie von Christian Thomasius, von prof. dr. Ernst Landsberg. Bonn, F. Cohen, 1894.
1 p. l., 36 p. 28½cm.
"Festschrift zur zweiten säcularfeier der Friedrichs-universität zu Halle."

1. Thomasius, Christian, 1655-1728. I. Title.
21-9110
Library of Congress   B2605.Z7L3

RARE HV 8593 D61 no.9
Lang, Johann Philibert.
Disputationem...inauguralem juridicam De quaestionibus seu torturis reorum...disquisitioni...subjiciet Joh. Philibertus Lang. Ob argumenti praestantiam denuo typis expressa. Basileae et Lipsiae, 1747.
80 p. 21cm.
Diss.--Basel, 1661.
No.9 in a vol. lettered: Dissertationes de tortura, 1667-1787.

8 NIC
1. Torture.   2. Criminal procedure.
I. Title.

MSS Bd. WITCHCRAFT RB L27
Lange,   , physician, of Lisieux.
Histoire de la fille maléficiée de Courson. Avec une dissertation physique sur ce maléfice. Par Monsieur Lange, Conseiller Médecin du Roy. Lisieux, Chez J. du Roncerey, 1717 [ca. 1900]
34 p. 23cm.
Carnap's manuscript copy.
"Der Originaldruck von welchem diese Abschrift genommen wurde, befindet sich in der Bibliothè que Nationale zu Paris ... Eine Ab schrift fertigte der
(Continued on next card)

MSS Bd. WITCHCRAFT RB L27
Lange,   , physician, of Lisieux.
Histoire de la fille maléficiée ... 1717 [ca. 1900]   (Card 2)
daselbst angestellte Bibliothekar J. Herviant an; die vorliegende ist mit desselben wörtlich übereinstimmend."
Numerals in the margins indicate pagination of the original work.
"Notizen über diese Abhandlung" pp. 31-34.
1. Diseases --Causes and theories of causation.   2. Witchcraft. 3. Morin, Madeleine. I. Title.

WITCHCRAFT BX 2340 L28+ 1910
Langlet, Louis.
Etude médicale d'une possession au XVIe siècle.
Une possession au XVIe siècle; étude médicale de la vie & de l'hystérie de Nicole Obry, dite Nicole de Vervins, 1566. Reims, Matot-Braine, 1910.
110 p. illus. 26cm.
Originally issued in the same year as thesis at the Faculté de médecine, Paris, with title: Etude médicale d'une possession au XVIe siècle...
1. Nicole   de Vervins. 2. Exorcism.
8 NIC
3. Hysteria.   I. His/Etude médicale d'une posses sion au XVIe siècle.

WITCHCRAFT BX 2340 L28+ 1910
Langlet, Louis.
Une possession au XVIe siècle; étude médicale de la vie & de l'hystérie de Nicole Obry, dite Nicole de Vervins, 1566. Reims, Matot-Braine, 1910.
110 p. illus. 26cm.
Originally issued in the same year as thesis at the Faculté de médecine, Paris, with title: Etude médicale d'une possession au XVIe siècle...
1. Nicole   de Vervins. 2. Exorcism.
8 NIC
3. Hysteria.   I. His/Etude médicale d'une posses sion au XVIe siècle.
II. Title.

WITCHCRAFT BF 1582 Z7 1605
Langlois, Ernest, 1857-1924.
Un évêque de Verdun, prince de Lorraine, ensorcelé, marié et condamné par le tribunal de l'inquisition. [Nancy, Impr. Berger-Levrault, 1895]
23 p. 20cm.
Concerning Erric, prince of Lorraine, bishop of Verdun.
Extract from Annales de l'est, Apr. 1895.

8 NIC
1. Erric, prince of Lorraine, bp. of Verdun, d.1623.   I. Title.

WITCHCRAFT BF 1003 U22+ v.24
Langner, Fritz.
Die Besessenheit (Dämonomanie)
(In: Die Übersinnliche Welt. Leipzig. 26cm. v.24 (1916) p. 118-130, 169-171, 212-215, 240-248)

8 NIC
1. Demoniac possession. 2. Demonomania
I. Title.

WITCHCRAFT BT 980 L28
Langton, Edward, 1886–
Satan, a portrait; a study of the character of Satan through all the ages, by Edward Langton ... London, Skeffington & son, ltd. [1946]
128 p. front., plates. 22cm.

1. Devil.   I. Title.
(Full name: Frederick Edward Palmer Langton)
46-4210
Library of Congress   BT980.L3
[r4]   235

Witchcraft BF 1410 B42 1691a no.8
Lansman, Jakob.
Bekker, Balthasar, 1634-1698.
Omstandig bericht, van Balthasar Bekker, S. T. D. predikant tot Amsterdam, van sijne particuliere onderhandelinge met D. Laurentius Homma, sal. ged. in sijn leven mede predikant ... Beneffens d'ontdekte lagen van Everhardus van der Hooght, en Jakob Lansman tegen denselven. Amsterdam, By D. vanden Dalen, boekverkooper, 1693.
1 p. l., 22 p. title and end page vignettes, illus. initials. 20 x 16cm.
4°: π 1, A- C⁴ (-C4)
8
(Continued on next card)

Witchcraft BF 1410 B42 1691a no.8
Lansman, Jakob.
Bekker, Balthasar, 1634-1698. Omstandig bericht ... 1693.   (Card 2)
Black letter.
"Bedekte lagen van Everhard van der Hooght, predikant tot Nieuwendam, en Jakob Lansman, procureur en notaris tot Amsterdam: ontdekt aan Balthasar Bekker ...:" p. 17-22.
Van der Linde 117.
No. 8 in vol. lettered B. Bekker. Betoverde weereld.
1. Hooght, Everard van der, d. 1716. 2. Lansman, Jako b.   I. Homma, Laurentius, d. 1681.   II. Title.
8

La Palud, Magdeleine de.
see
Palud, Magdeleine de la.

Witchcraft BS 2545 D5 L32
Lardner, Nathaniel, 1684-1768.
The case of the demoniacs mentioned in the New Testament: four discourses upon Mark V. 19. With an appendix for farther illustrating the subject. London, Printed for C. Henderson ... sold also by J. Buckland, 1758.
156 p. 21cm.

1. Demoniac possession. 2. Bible. N.T. Mark--Commen taries.   I. Title.

CATALOGUE OF THE CORNELL WITCHCRAFT COLLECTION

WITCHCRAFT
BF
1584
S97
L32
  Lardy, Charles Edouard, 1847-1923.
    Les procédures de sorcellerie à Neuchâtel.
Rapport présenté à la Conférence des avocats neuchâtelois le 11 avril 1866. Publié par décision de la conférence. Neuchâtel, J. Sandoz, 1866.
    45 p. facsim. 24cm.

8
NIC
  1. Trials (Witchcraft)--Neuchâtel.
  ✓ Title.

Witchcraft
BF
1575
M42
M5
1691
  Late memorable providences relating to witchcrafts and possessions.
  Mather, Cotton, 1663-1728.
    Late memorable providences relating to witchcrafts and possessions; clearly manifesting not only that there are witches, but that good men (as well as others) may possibly have their lives shortned by such evil instruments of Satan. 2d impression ... London, Printed for T. Parkhurst, 1691.
    144 p. 15cm.
  With autograph of R. Watts.
  Ex libris (supralibros) John Carter Brown.
  Holmes: C. M. #228B.

MSS
Bd.
WITCHCRAFT
BF
L37
  Laugeois, Antoine, d. 1674.
    L'innocence opprimee; ou, Défense de Mathurin Picard, curé de Mesnil-Jourdain ... Par M. Laugois, successeur immédiat dudit Picard - dans la cure de Mesnil-Jourdain. Ouvrage qui n'a jamais été imprimé et extrait sur l'original, par M. Chemin curé de Tourneville. [n.p.] 17th cent.
    x, 102 p. title vignette. 18cm.
  Manuscript, on paper.
  Preface signed M. du Passeur (Gabriel), curé de Vironvay.
    (Continued on next card)

WITCHCRAFT
BD
505
V14
1617
  La Richardière, sieur de, tr.
  Valderrama, Pedro de
    Histoire generale dv monde, et de la natvre. Ov Traictez theologiqves de la fabrique, composition, & conduicte generale de l'vniuers. Divisez en trois livres. Le premier traictant de Dieu comme souuerain architecte du monde ... Le second de la conduicte admirable du monde, les intelligences celestes, la fabrique generale du ciel, les diuers degrez des anges ... Le troisies. des grades diuerses des de-
8
    (Continued on next card)

WITCHCRAFT
BS
1325
L35
  Lathrop, Joseph, 1731-1820.
    Illustrations and reflections on the story of Saul's consulting the witch of Endor. A discourse delivered at West-Springfield. Springfield, Mass., Henry Brewer, printer, 1806.
    20 p. 21cm.

  ✓ 1. Endor, Witch of. (Biblical character) 2. Saul, king of Israel. 3. Bible. O.T. 1. Samuel XXVIII--Criticism, interpretation, etc. 4. Witchcraft in the Bible. I. Title.
8
NIC

MSS
Bd.
WITCHCRAFT
BF
L37
  Laugeois, Antoine, d. 1674. L'innocence opprimee... [17th cent.] (Card 2)
  Notes by G. L. Burr inside front cover discuss history and provenance of the manuscript.
  Bound in boards.
    1. Demoniac possession. ✓2. Picard, Mathurin, d. 1647. ✓3. Bavent, Madeleine, ca. 1608-1647. 4. Louviers, France. St. Louis (Convent) 5. Witchcraft. I. Chemin, J B , 1725-1781, ed. ✓II. Title.
✓III. Title: Défense de Mathurin Picard.

WITCHCRAFT
BD
505
V14
1617
  La Richardière, sieur de, tr.
  Valderrama, Pedro de. Histoire generale dv monde ... 1617. (Card 2)
mons, ... de leur science appellée magie ..., des diuerses parties di [sic] la magie, & plusieurs autres illusions diaboliques. Le tout illustré d'vn grand nombre d'histoires & doctes exemples. Composé en espagnol par le R. P. P. Valderama, ... & traduit sur le manuscrit espagnol en nostre langue françoise, par le sieur de la Richardier ... 2. éd. Paris, Chez Isaac Mesnier,
8
    (Continued on next card)

  Lauaterus, Lewes, 1527-1586.

    see

  Lavater, Ludwig, 1527-1586.

Laurent, Johannes Theodor, bp.

WITCHCRAFT
BF
1555
M69
  Möller, Karl.
    Eine Teufelaustreibung durch einen deutschen Bischof im 19. Jahrhundert. [Sonderabdruck aus der Rheinischen Correspondenz] Köln, C. Römcke, 1897.
    12 p. 23cm.
  Consists largely of extracts from his Leben und Briefe von Johannes Theodor Laurent, pub. 1887-89; the bishop's letters are quoted.
    1. Demoniac possession. 2. Exorcism. 3. Pfefferkorn, Maria Anna Katharina, fl. 1842. I. H is Leben und Briefe v Johannes Theodor Laurent. II. Laurent, Johannes Theodor, bp. III. Tit

---

WITCHCRAFT
BD
505
V14
1617
  La Richardière, sieur de, tr.
  Valderrama, Pedro de. Histoire generale dv monde ... 1617. (Card 3)
    1617-19 [v. 1.1619]
    2 v. in 1. 18cm.

  1. Cosmology. 2. God. 3. Angels. 4. Demonology. 5. Witchcraft. I. La Richardière, sieur de, tr. II. Title.
8

WITCHCRAFT
BF
1517
F5
C78
1634
  Laubardemont, Jean Martin de.
    Coppie d'v procez verbal faict le vingt & deuxiesme d'aoust mil six cens trente & quatre. Par Monsieur de Laubardemont conseller du roy en ses conseils d'estat & priué, sur le miracle fait dans la ville de Loudun. Poictiers, Par René Allain, 1634.
    9 p. 17cm.

  1. Loudun, France. Ursuline Convent. 2. Exorcism. I. Laubardemont, Jean Martin de.
8

Laurentius Heisterus ... programmate aus diabolic suppositis habitos ... rhachiticos fuisse...

WITCHCRAFT
BF
1552
H47
  Heister, Lorenz, 1683-1758, praeses.
    Lavrentivs Heistervs ... programmate avspicali qvo demonstrat infantes pro a diabolo svppositis habitos qvos vvlgo Wechselbälge appellarvnt rhachiticos fvisse ad clarissima medicinae candidati Io. Georgii de Broke ... dispvtationem inavgvralem invitat. Helmstadii, Literis Schnorrianis, 1725.
    [16] p. 21cm.

8
    (Continued on next card)

  La Rochelle, Jean François Née de, 1751-1838.

    see

  Née de la Rochelle, Jean François, 1751-1838.

Witchcraft
GR
830
W4
L36
  Laube, Theophilus.
    Dialogi und Gespräch von der Lycanthropia, oder der Menschen in Wölff-Verwandlung, darinnen vier gelehrte Personen, eine geistliche, eine rechts-gelehrte, eine arzney-verständige, und welt-weise von dieser Materi und andern merckwürdigen Sachen viel curieuses discuriren ... Auch durchgehends mit Kupffern aussgefertigt durch Theophilum Lauben. Franckfurt, Bey Arnold Heyl, 1686.
    6 p. l., 175 p. 9 plates. 13cm.
8
    (Continued on next card)

Der Lauterfresser.

Witchcraft
BF
1584
T9
Z59
  Zingerle, Ignaz Vincenz, Edler von Summersberg, 1825-1892, ed.
    Barbara Pachlerin, die Sarnthaler Hexe, und Mathias Perger, der Lauterfresser. Zwei Hexenprozesse, hrsg. von Dr. Ignaz Zingerle Innsbruck, Wagner, 1858.
    xii, 84 p. 19cm.
  Contents.--Barbara Pachlerin, die Sarnthaler Hexe.--Der Lauterfresser.--Anhang. Ein altes Loosbuch.
    Each item has special t. p.
8
    (Continued on next card)

Witchcraft
BF
1410
B42
Z56
v.2
no.14
  Lasteringen van Jakob Koelman, in zijn zoo genaamde wederlegging van B. Bekkers Betooverde wereld.
  Dale, Antonius van, 1638-1708.
    Lasteringen van Jakob Koelman, in zijn zoo genaamde wederlegging van B. Bekkers Betooverde wereld, zediglyk aangewesen in een brief van Antony van Dale, med. doctor. Aan zijnen vrind. Rotterdam, By I. van Ruynen, boekverkooper, 1692.
    15, [1] p. title vignette, illus. initial. 19 x 15cm.
    4°: A-B⁴.
  Van der Linde 124.
  No. 14 in vol. lettered Bekker II.
    (Continued on next card)

Witchcraft
GR
830
W4
L36
  Laube, Theophilus. Dialogi und Gespräch von der Lycanthrophia ... 1686. (Card 2)

    1. Werwolves. 2. Folk-lore--Germany.
✓ I. Title.

8

WITCHCRAFT
BF
1582
Z7
1631c
  La Vallée, Melchoir de.
  Lepage, Henri, 1814-1887.
    Melchoir de La Vallée et une gravure de Jacques Bellange. Nancy, René Wiener, 1882.
    56 p. illus., facsim. 23cm.

8
NIC
  1. La Vallée, Melchior de. 2. Trials (Witchcraft)--Nancy.

CATALOGUE OF THE CORNELL WITCHCRAFT COLLECTION

WITCHCRAFT
BF
1582
Z7
1477a
 Lavanchy, Joseph Marie, 1844-
  Sabbats ou synagogues sur les bords du lac d'Annecy. Procès inquisitorial à St.-Jorioz en 1477. 2.éd. Annecy Impr. Abry, 1896.
  64 p. 22cm.

8
NIC
  1. Trials (Witchcraft)--St. Jorioz, France. 2. Rose, Antoinette. 3. Title.

Witchcraft
BF
1559
G25
Z63
no.7
 Lavater, Johann Caspar, 1741-1801.
  Auszug der Frankfurter gelehrten Anzeigen Nro. 38 und 39 den 12. May 1775. Beytrag zur gelehrten Geschichte unserer Zeit. [Zürch, 1775]
  [8] p. 17cm.

  No. 7 in vol. lettered Gassneriana.

8
  1. Gassner, Johann Joseph, 1727-1779. I. Title. II. Title: Beytrag zur gelehrten Geschichte unserer Zeit.

WITCHCRAFT
BT
980
L39
 [Lavater, Johann Caspar] 1741-1801.
  Predigten über die Existenz des Teufels und seine Wirkungen, nach Anleitung der Versuchungsgeschichte Jesu. Von einem schweitzerischen Gottesgelehrten. Frankfurt und Leipzig, 1778.
  146 p. 18cm.

  Ex libris: Joan. Wilh. Dilichmann.
8
NIC
  1. Devil. 2. Devil--Biblical teaching. 3. Jesus Christ. 4. Jesus Christ--Temptation. I. Title.

WITCHCRAFT
BF
1557
L39
 Lavater, Johann Caspar, 1741-1801.
  Protokoll über den Spiritus Familiaris Gablidone. Mit Beylagen und einem Kupfer. Frankfurth und Leipzig, 1787.
  84 p. plate. 19cm.

8
NIC
  1. Spirits. 2. Demonology. 3. Talismans. I. Title. II. Title: Gablidone.

Lavater, Ludwig

WITCHCRAFT
BF
1445
L39
1575
 Lavater, Ludwig, 1527-1586.
  De spectris, lemvribvs et magnis atqve insolitis fragoribus, variísque praesagitionibus quae plerunque obitum hominum, magnas clades, mutationésque imperiorum praecedunt, liber vnvs. Lvdovico Lavatero Tigvrino avtore. Genevae, Apvd Evstathivm Vignon, 1575.
  8 p. l., 272 p. 18cm.
  First published Zürich, 1570.

8

WITCHCRAFT
BF
1445
L39
1659
 Lavater, Ludwig, 1527-1586. De spectris ... 1659. (Card 2)

  Added t. p., engraved.
  Error in paging: 244 numbered 144.
  Colophon: Lvgd. Batav., Ex Typogr. Joh. Z. Baron, 1659.

  1. Apparitions. 2. Ghosts. 3. Demonology. I. Title.

WITCHCRAFT Lavater, Ludwig, 1527-1586.
BF
1445
L39
1571
 Lavater, Ludwig, 1527-1586.
  Trois livres des apparitions des esprits, fantosmes, prodiges & accidens merueilleux qui precedent souuentesfois la mort de quelque personnage renommé, ou vn grand changement és choses de ce monde: traduits d'Alleman en François: conferez, reueus et augmentez sur le Latin. Plus trois questions proposees & resolues par M. Pierre Martyr excellent theologien, lesquelles conviennent à ceste matiere: traduites aussi de Latin en François. [Genève] De l'Imprimerie de François Perrin, pour Iean Durant, 1571.
  (Continued on next card)

hcraft
BF
1445
L39
1580
 Lavater, Ludwig, 1527-1586.
  De spectris, lemvribvs et magnis atqve insolitis fragoribus, variísque praesagitionibus, quae plerunque obitum hominum, magnas clades, mutationésque Imperiorum praecedunt, liber vnvs. Lvdovico Lavatero Tigvrino avtore. Genevae, Apvd Evstathivm Vignon, 1580.
  [16], 213 p. 17cm.

  Printer's device on t. p.
  Errors in paging: 77, 87, 124, 212 numbered 49, 78, 224, 112 respectively.

Lavater, Ludwig, 1527-1586.
De spectris, lemuribus magnis atque insolitis fragoribus. English.
WITCHCRAFT
BF
1445
L39
1596
 Lavater, Ludwig, 1527-1586.
  Of ghostes and spirites, walking by night, and of straunge noyses, crackes, and sundrie forewarnings, which commonly happen before the death of men: great slaughters, and alterations of kingdomes. One booke, written by Lewes Lauaterus of Tigurine. And translated into English by R. H. [i.e., Robert Harrison] London, Imprinted by Thomas Creede, 1596.
  10 p. l., 220 p. 18cm.
8
  (Continued on next card)

WITCHCRAFT Lavater, Ludwig, 1527-1586.
BF
1445
L39
1571
 De spectris--French.
 Lavater, Ludwig, 1527-1586. Trois livres des apparitions ... 1571. (Card 2)
  [16], 304, [11] p. 17cm.

  Translation of De spectris, lemuribus et magnis atque insolitis fragoribus.

  1. Apparitions. 2. Ghosts. 3. Demonology. I. Lavater, Ludwig, 1527-1586. De spectris, lemuribus et magnis atque insolitis fragoribus--French. II. Vermigli, Pietro Martire, 1500-1562.

WITCHCRAFT
BF
1445
L39
1659
 Lavater, Ludwig, 1527-1586.
  De spectris, lemuribus et magnis atque insolitis fragoribus, variisque praesagitionibus, quae plerunque obitum hominum, magnas clades, mvtationesque Imperiorum praecedunt. Liber vnvs. In tres partes distributus ... Authore Ludov. Lavatero Tigurino. Editio secunda priori multò emendatior. Lvgd. Batavorvm, Apud Henr. Verbiest, 1659.
  [18], 245 p. 13cm.
  (Continued on next card)

Lavater, Ludwig, 1527-1586.
De spectris, lemuribus magnis atque insolitis fragoribus. English.
WITCHCRAFT
BF
1445
L39
1596
 Lavater, Ludwig, 1527-1586. Of ghostes and spirites, walking by night ... 1596. (Card 2)

  Imperfect copy: p. 217-220 wanting.
  Translation of De spectris, lemuribus et magnis atque insolitis fragoribus.
  STC 15321.
  Armorial bookplate: Holland House.
  1. Apparitions. 2. Ghosts. 3. Demonology. I. His De spectris, lemuribus et magnis atque insolitis fragoribus. English. II. Harrison, Robert, d. 1585?, tr. III. Title.

FILM
470
reel
261
 Lavater, Ludwig, 1527-1586.
  Of ghostes and spirites walking by nyght, and of strange noyses, crackes, and sundry forewarnynges, whiche commonly happen before the death of menne, great slaughters, a alterations of kyngdomes ... written by Lewes Lauaterus ... And translated into Englyshe by R. H. [i.e. Robert Harrison] Printed at London by Henry Benneyman for Richard Watkyns. 1572.
  Colophon: Jmprinted at London, by Richard Watkins ... 1572.
  University microfilms no. 15866
  (Continued on next card)

CATALOGUE OF THE CORNELL WITCHCRAFT COLLECTION

FILM 470 reel 261 — Lavater, Ludwig, 1527-1586. Of ghostes and spirites walking by nyght ... 1572. (Card 2)

(case 44, carton 261)
Short-title catalogue no. 15320.

1. Apparitions. I. Harrison, Robert, d. 1585?, tr. II. Title.

WITCHCRAFT
BF 1445 L39 1596 — Lavater, Ludwig, 1527-1586.
Of ghostes and spirites, walking by night, and of straunge noyses, crackes, and sundrie forewarnings, which commonly happen before the death of men: great slaughters, and alterations of kyngdomes. One booke, written by Lewes Lauaterus of Tigurine. And translated into English by R. H. [i.e., Robert Harrison]. London, Imprinted by Thomas Creede, 1596.
10 p. l., 220 p. 18cm.

8 (Continued on next card)

WITCHCRAFT
BF 1445 L39 1596 — Lavater, Ludwig, 1527-1586. Of ghostes and spirites, walking by night ... 1596. (Card 2)

Imperfect copy: p. 217-220 wanting.
Translation of De spectris, lemuribus et magnis atque insolitis fragoribus.
STC 15321.
Armorial bookplate: Holland House.

1. Apparitions. 2. Ghosts. 3. Demonology. I. His De spectris, lemuribus et magnis atque insolitis fragoribus. English. II. Harrison, Robert, d. 1585?, tr. III. Title.

8

Film 470 reel 261 — Lavater, Ludwig, 1527-1586.
Of ghostes and spirites, walking by night, and of straunge noyses, crackes, and sundrie forewarnings, which commonly happen before the death of slaughters, and alterations of kingdomes ... written by Lewes Lauaterus ... And translated into English by R. H. [i.e. Robert Harrison], Imprinted at London by Thomas Creede, 1596.
University microfilms no. 15367 (case 44, carton 261)
Short-title catalogue no. 15321.
1. Apparitions. I. Harrison, Robert, d. 1585?, tr. II. Title.

BF 1445 L39 1929 — Lavater, Ludwig, 1527-1586.
... Of ghostes and spirites walking by nyght, 1572, edited with introduction and appendix by J. Dover Wilson ... and May Yardley ... Oxford, Printed for the Shakespeare association at the University press, 1929.
xxi, [15], 251, [1] p. 22½cm.
At head of title: Lewes Lavater.
With reproduction of original t.-p.: Of ghostes and spirites walking by nyght, and of strange noyses, crackes and sundry forewarnynges, which commonly happen
(Continued on next card)

BF 1445 L39 1929 — Lavater, Ludwig, 1527-1586. Of ghostes and spirites walking by nyght ... 1929. (Card 2)

before the death of menne, great slaughters, & alterations of kyngdomes. One booke, written by Lewes Lauaterus of Tigurine. And translated into Englyshe by R. H. [i.e. Robert Harrison]. Printed at London by Henry Benneyman for Richard Watkyns, 1572.
Contents.--The ghost-scenes in Hamlet in the light of Elizabethan spiritualism, by J. D. Wils on.--Of ghostes and
(Continued on next card)

BF 1445 L39 1929 — Lavater, Ludwig, 1527-1586. Of ghostes and spirites walking by nyght. 1572 ... 1929. (Card 3)

spirites walking by nyght.--The Catholic position in the ghost controversy of the sixteenth century, with special reference to Pierre Le Loyer's IIII livres des spectres (1586)

1. Apparitions. 2. Le Loyer, Pierre, sieur de La Brosse, 1550-1634. IIII livres des spectres. I. Harrison, Robert, d. 1585? tr. II. Wilson, John Dover, 1881- ed. III. Yardley, May, joint ed. IV. Shakespeare association, London. V. Title.

WITCHCRAFT
BF 1445 L39 1571 — Lavater, Ludwig, 1527-1586.
Trois livres des apparitions des esprits, fantosmes, prodiges & accidens merueilleux qui precedent souuentesfois la mort de quelque personnage renommé, ou vn grand changement és choses de ce monde: traduits d'Alleman en François: conferez, reueus et augmentez sur le Latin. Plus trois questions proposees & resolues par M. Pierre Martyr excellent theologien, lesquelles conviennent à ceste matiere: traduites aussi de Latin en François. [Genève] De l'Imprimerie de François Perrin, pour Iean Durant, 1571.
(Continued on next card)

WITCHCRAFT
BF 1445 L39 1571 — Lavater, Ludwig, 1527-1586. Trois livres des apparitions ... 1571. (Card 2)

[16], 304, [11] p. 17cm.
Translation of De spectris, lemuribus et magnis atque insolitis fragoribus.

1. Apparitions. 2. Ghosts. 3. Demonology. I. Lavater, Ludwig, 1527-1586. De spectris, lemuribus et magnis atque insolitis fragoribus-- French. II. Vermigli, Pietro Martire, 1500-1562. III. Title.

Lavaterus, Ludovicus, 1527-1586.

see

Lavater, Ludwig, 1527-1586.

Rare HV 6211 G28 1734 — La Ville, Jean Claude de, b. 1735.
Gayot de Pitaval, François, 1673-1743.
Causes célèbres et interessantes, avec les jugemens qui les ont décidées. La Haye, J. Neaulme, 1734-1751.
22 v. in 12. 17cm.

Imprint varies: v.1-2, Paris, J. de Nully.
Vol. 1-2 published under pseud. "M. ***, avocat au Parlement."

1. Crime and criminals. 2. Trials. I. La Ville, Jean Claude de, b. 1735. II. Title.

Rare DA 803 L41+ — Law, Robert, d. 1690?
Memorialls; or, The memorable things that fell out within this island of Brittain from 1638 to 1684. By the Rev. Mr. Robert Law. Ed. from the ms. by Charles Kirkpatrick Sharpe. Edinburgh, A. Constable and co., 1818.
cxiv, 277 p. front. 29cm.
Appendix: A true relation of an apparition ... which infected the house of Andrew Mackie ... 1695. By Mr. Alexander Telfair.
1. Scotland--Hist.--17th century. I. Title.

Witchcraft
BF 1581 L42 — The Lawes against witches, and conivration; and some brief notes and observations for the discovery of witches. Being very usefull for these times, wherein the Devil reignes and prevailes over the soules of poor creatures, in drawing them to that crying sin of witch-craft. Also, the confession of Mother Lakeland, who was arraigned and condemned for a witch, at Ipswich in Suffolke. ... London, Printed for R. W., 1645.
8 p. 19cm.

Lawrence, Henry, 1600-1664.
Militia spiritualis.

Witchcraft
BT 965 L42 — [Lawrence, Henry] 1600-1664.
Of our communion and warre with angels. Being certain meditations on that subject, bottom'd particularly (though not concluded within the compasse of that Scripture) on Ephes. 6.12. with the following verses to the 19. [Amsterdam] 1646.
189+ p. 21cm.

Epistle dedicatory signed Henry Lawrence.
Imperfect: index incomplete.
(Continued on next card)

Witchcraft
BT 965 L42 — Lawrence, Henry, 1600-1664. Militia spiritualis.
[Lawrence, Henry] 1600-1664. Of our communion and warre with angels ... 1646. (Card 2)

Wing L 665.
Reissued 1652 under title: Militia spiritualis; or, A treatise of angels.

I. Title. II. His Militia spiritualis.

Witchcraft
BT 965 L42 — [Lawrence, Henry] 1600-1664.
Of our communion and warre with angels. Being certain meditations on that subject, bottom'd particularly (though not concluded within the compasse of that Scripture) on Ephes. 6.12. with the following verses to the 19. [Amsterdam] 1646.
189+ p. 21cm.

Epistle dedicatory signed Henry Lawrence.
Imperfect: index incomplete.
(Continued on next card)

Witchcraft
BT 965 L42 — [Lawrence, Henry] 1600-1664. Of our communion and warre with angels ... 1646. (Card 2)

Wing L 665.
Reissued 1652 under title: Militia spiritualis; or, A treatise of angels.

I. Title. II. His Militia spiritualis.

The laws and customs of Scotland in matters criminal.

Rare K M15 L4+ — Mackenzie, Sir George, 1636-1691.
The laws and customs of Scotland in matters criminal. Wherein is to be seen how the civil law, and the laws and customs of other nations doth agree with, and supply ours. To this 2d ed. is now added ... a Treatise of mutilation and demembration and their punishments, by Sir Alexander Seton. Also a 2d ed. of the Observations upon the 18 Act. Parl. 23, K. James 6th, against dispositions made in defraud of creditors &c., corr. and ... enl. by the author
(Continued on next card)

CATALOGUE OF THE CORNELL WITCHCRAFT COLLECTION

The laws and customs of Scotland in matters criminal.

Mackenzie, Sir George, 1636-1691. The laws and customs of Scotland ... 1699. (Card 2)

... before his death. Edinburgh, Printed by the heirs and successors of A. Anderson for A. Symsonz, 1699.
291, 66, 62 p. 30cm.

Wing M 168.
With autographs: Charles Armstrong, and William Kirkpatrick.

(Continued on next card)

Lawson, Deodat.
Christ's fidelity the only shield against Satan's malignity. Asserted in a sermon deliver'd at Salem-village the 24th of March, 1692. Being lecture-day there, and a time of publick examination, of some suspected for witchcraft. By Deodat Lawson ... 2d ed. ... Printed at Boston in New-England, and Reprinted in London, by R. Tookey for the Author; and are to be sold by T. Parkhurst, at the Bible and Three Crowns in Cheapside; and J. Lawrence, at the Angel in the Poultry. 1704.
6 p. l., 120 p. 16cm.

(Continued on next card)

Library of Congress   25-13271
                          BF1575.L3 1704

Lawson, Deodat. Christ's fidelity the only shield against Satan's malignity. 1704. (Card 2)

Appendix (p. 93-120): "Brief account of the amazing things which occasioned that discourse to be delivered."

1. Witchcraft--Salem, Mass. I. Title.

Lawson, Deodat, fl. 1680-1698.
A true narrative of ... witchcraft at Salem.

Mather, Increase, 1639-1723.
A further account of the tryals of the New-England witches. With the observations of a person who was upon the place several days when the suspected witches were first taken into examination. To which is added, Cases of conscience concerning witchcrafts and evil spirits personating men. Written at the request of the ministers of New England. By Increase Mather, president of Harvard colledge ... London, Printed for J. Dunton, 1693.

(Continued on next card)
5-33455†

Lawson, Deodat, fl. 1680-1698.
A true narrative of ... witchcraft at Salem.

Mather, Increase, 1639-1723. A further account of the tryals of the New-England witches ... 1693. (Card 2)

1 p. l., 10 p., 1 l., [2], 39, [5] p. 20cm.
Title within double line border.
After year of imprint: Of whom may be had the third edition of Mr. Cotton Mather's first Account of the tryals of the New-England witches, Printed on the same size with this last account, that they may bind up together.
"Cases of conscience" has special t.-p. and separate paging.   (Continued on next card)

Lawson, Deodat, fl. 1680-1698.
A true narrative of ... witchcraft at Salem.

Mather, Increase, 1639-1723. A further account of the tryals of the New-England witches ... 1693. (Card 3)

"A true narrative of some remarkable passages relating to sundry persons afflicted by witchcraft at Salem village in New-England, which happened from the 19th of March to the 5th of April, 1692. Collected by Deodat Lawson": p.1-9.
"A further account of the tryals of the New-England witches, sent in a letter from thence, to a gentleman in London": p.9-10.
Wing M 1213.

Laymann, Paul 1574-1635.
Aurea enucleatio--German.

Witchcraft
BF   Laymann, Paul, 1574-1635.
1565   Ein kurtzer doch gründlicher Bericht,
L42   wie vnd was gestalt, so woln bey dem recht-
T3   lichen Proceß als auch der Beicht mit den
1629   Hexen zuuerfahren seye. Auß deß ehrwürdigen hochgelehrten Herrn P. Pauli Läymanns ... Theologia morali gezogen, vñ den Richtern vñ Beichtvättern zu gutem absonderlich in den Truck gegeben. An jetzo aber männiglich zu gutem in die teutsche Sprache vbersetzt. Durch Wolffgang Schilling ...
8   (Continued on next card)

Laymann, Paul, 1574-1635.
Aurea enucleatio--German.

Witchcraft
BF   Laymann, Paul, 1574-1635. Ein kurtzer
1565   doch gründlicher Bericht ... 1629.
L42   (Card 2)
T3
1629   Wirtzburg, Gedruckt bey Stephan Fleischmann, 1629.
129 p. 14cm.
With colophon.
According to G. L. Burr, the first part was printed in Aschaffenburg in 1629 under title: Aurea enucleatio atque disquisitio
8   ... The second section, p. 60-129,
                (Continued on next card)

Laymann, Paul, 1574-1635.
Aurea enucleatio--German.

Witchcraft
BF   Laymann, Paul, 1574-1635. Ein kurtzer
1565   doch gründlicher Bericht ... 1629.
L42   (Card 3)
T3
1629   was published in 1629 by the same printer under title: Newer Tractat von der verführten Kinder Zauberey, and is by Schilling.
1. Trials (Witchcraft) 2. Confessors.
I. His Theologia moralis. Selections.
German. II. His Aurea enucleatio. German.
III. His Neuer Tractat von der verführten Kinder Zauberey. IV. Schilling, Wolfgang, tr. V. Title.

Witchcraft
BF   Laymann, Paul, 1574-1635, supposed author.
1565   Juridicus processus contra sagas et veneficos: das ist: Ein rechtlicher Proceß gegen
L42   die Unholden und zauberische Personen. In
1710   welchen ordentlich docirt wird, und aus fürnehmen beyder Rechten Doctorn und berühmten Scribenten vorgetragen wird ... Ist mit guten [sic] Fleiß und gründlicher Probation und Beweiß durch P. Paulum Laymann ... in lateinischer Sprach beschrieben. Jetzt den Gerichtshaltern und guter Justici Be-
8   (Continued on next card)

Witchcraft
BF   Laymann, Paul, 1574-1635, supposed author.
1565   Juridicus processus contra sagas et veneficos ... 1710.   (Card 2)
L42
1710   freunden zum besten verteutscht, auch mit bewehrten Historien und andern Umbständen vermehrt, und in unterschiedliche Titul ordentlich abgetheilet ... Oettingen, Gedruckt bey Stephan Rolck; Augspurg, Zu finden bey Daniel Waldern, 1710.
287 (i. e., 187), [3] p. fold.
t. p. 13cm.
8   (Continued on next card)

Witchcraft
BF   Laymann, Paul, 1574-1635, supposed author.
1565   Juridicus processus contra sagas et veneficos ... 1710.   (Card 3)
L42
1710   Other editions have title: Processus juridicus ...
Ascribed also to Johann Jordanaeus and to Hermann Goehausen.

I. His Processus juridicus contra
8   sagas et veneficos. II. Title.

Laymann, Paul, 1574-1635.
Juridicus processus contra sagas et veneficos.

Witchcraft
BF   Laymann, Paul, 1574-1635, supposed author.
1565   Juridicus processus contra sagas et veneficos: das ist: Ein rechtlicher Proceß gegen
L42   die Unholden und zauberische Personen. In
1710   welchen ordentlich docirt wird, und aus fürnehmen beyder Rechten Doctorn und berühmten Scribenten vorgetragen wird ... Ist mit guten [sic] Fleiß und gründlicher Probation und Beweiß durch P. Paulum Laymann ... in lateinischer Sprach beschrieben. Jetzt den Gerichtshaltern und guter Justici Be-
8   (Continued on next card)

Laymann, Paul, 1574-1635.
Juridicus processus contra sagas et veneficos.

Witchcraft
BF   Laymann, Paul, 1574-1635, supposed author.
1565   Juridicus processus contra sagas et veneficos ... 1710.   (Card 2)
L42
1710   freunden zum besten verteutscht, auch mit bewehrten Historien und andern Umbständen vermehrt, und in unterschiedliche Titul ordentlich abgetheilet ... Oettingen, Gedruckt bey Stephan Rolck; Augspurg, Zu finden bey Daniel Waldern, 1710.
287 (i. e., 187), [3] p. fold.
t. p. 13cm.
8   (Continued on next card)

Laymann, Paul, 1574-1635.
Juridicus processus contra sagas et veneficos.

Witchcraft
BF   Laymann, Paul, 1574-1635, supposed author.
1565   Juridicus processus contra sagas et veneficos ... 1710.   (Card 3)
L42
1710   Other editions have title: Processus juridicus ...
Ascribed also to Johann Jordanaeus and to Hermann Goehausen.

I. His Processus juridicus contra
8   sagas et veneficos. II. Title.

Witchcraft
BF   Laymann, Paul, 1574-1635.
1565   Ein kurtzer doch gründlicher Bericht,
L42   wie vnd was gestalt, so woln bey dem rechtlichen Proceß als auch der Beicht mit den
T3   Hexen zuuerfahren seye. Auß deß ehrwürdigen hochgelehrten Herrn P. Pauli Läymanns
1629   ... Theologia morali gezogen, vñ den Richtern vñ Beichtvättern zu gutem absonderlich in den Truck gegeben. An jetzo aber männiglich zu gutem in die teutsche Sprache vbersetzt. Durch Wolffgang Schilling ...
8   (Continued on next card)

Witchcraft
BF   Laymann, Paul, 1574-1635. Ein kurtzer
1565   doch gründlicher Bericht ... 1629.
L42   (Card 2)
T3
1629   Wirtzburg, Gedruckt bey Stephan Fleischmann, 1629.
129 p. 14cm.
With colophon.
According to G. L. Burr, the first part was printed in Aschaffenburg in 1629 under title: Aurea enucleatio atque disquisitio
8   ... The second section, p. 60-129,
                (Continued on next card)

Witchcraft
BF   Laymann, Paul, 1574-1635. Ein kurtzer
1565   doch gründlicher Bericht ... 1629.
L42   (Card 3)
T3
1629   was published in 1629 by the same printer under title: Newer Tractat von der verführten Kinder Zauberey, and is by Schilling.
1. Trials (Witchcraft) 2. Confessors.
I. His Theologia moralis. Selections.
German. II. His Aurea enucleatio. German.
III. Schilling, Wolfgang. Newer Tractat von der verführten Kinder Zauberey. IV. Schilling, Wolfgang, tr. V. Title.
8

CATALOGUE OF THE CORNELL WITCHCRAFT COLLECTION

Witchcraft
BF   Laymann, Paul, 1574-1635, supposed author.
1565   Processvs ivridicvs contra sagas et vene-
L42   ficos: das ist, Ein rechtlicher Proceß gegen
1629 die Vnholden vnd zauberische Personen. In
      welchem ordentlich docirt vnd auß Fürneh-
      men beyder Rechten Doctoren vnd berümbten
      Scribenten vorgetragen wird ... Ist mit
      gutem Fleiß vnnd gründlicher Probation vnd
      Beweiß durch P. Pavlvm Laymann ... in la-
      teinischer Sprach beschrieben: jetzt den
      Gerichtshältern   vnd guter Iustici Be-
8   (Continued on next card)

Witchcraft
BF   Laymann, Paul, 1574-1635, supposed author.
1565   Processvs ivridicvs contra sagas et vene-
L42   ficos ...   1629.   (Card 2)
1629
      freundten zum besten verteutscht, auch mit
      bewährten Historien vnd andern Vmbständen
      vermehret vnd in vnderschiedlich Titeln
      ordentlich abgetheilt. Cölln, Gedruckt
      bey Peter Metternich, In Verlegung Cornelij
      ab Egmondt, Buchführrers, 1629.
          91 p. 19cm.
8   (Continued on next card)

Witchcraft
BF   Laymann, Paul, 1574-1635, supposed author.
1565   Processvs ivridicvs contra sagas et vene-
L42   ficos ...   1629.   (Card 3)
1629
         In Zeitschrift für katholische Theologie,
      Bd. 23 (1899), Bernhard Duhr questions Lay-
      mann's authorship of the work. He also
      notes that the putative Latin original is
      not known to have ever existed.
         G. L. Burr proposes Johann Jordanaeus as
      author (in his notes to the 1630 edition).
8   Others ascribe the work to Goehausen

Witchcraft
BF   [Laymann, Paul] 1574-1635, supposed author.
1565   Processus juridicus contra sagas & vene-
L42   ficos; das ist: Rechtlicher Proceß, wie man
1630 gegen Vnholdten vnd zauberische Personen ver-
      fahren soll. Mit erweglichen Exempeln vnd
      wunderbaren Geschichten, welche sich durch
      Hexerey zugetragen, außführlich erkläret.
      Vnàcum Decisionibus quaestionum ad hanc ma-
      teriam pertinentium. Herman. Goehavsen ...
      edidit et recensuit. Rintelij ad Visurgim,
      Typis exscripsit Petrus Lucius, 1630.
8   (Continued on next card)

Witchcraft
BF   [Laymann, Paul] 1574-1635, supposed author.
1565   Processus juridicus contra sagas & vene-
L42   ficos ...   1630.   (Card 2)
1630
         8 p. l., 447, 188 (i. e., 288) p. 16cm.
      Title in red and black.
         Decisiones aliquot quaestionum ad hanc
      materiam ... avctore Herman: Göehausen [sic]
      has special t. p. and is paged separately.
         Each Titulus followed by commentary in
      Latin.
8   (Continued on next card)

Witchcraft
BF   [Laymann, Paul] 1574-1635, supposed author.
1565   Processus juridicus contra sagas & vene-
L42   ficos ...   1630.   (Card 3)
1630
         Also ascribed to Johann Jordanaeus (see
      G. L. Burr's note facing t. p.) and Goe-
      hausen. (See Duhr, Bernhard, 1852-1635. Paul
      Laymann und die Hexenprozesse, in Zeit-
      schrift für katholische Theologie, Bd. 23
      (1899), p. 733-745, on authorship question)
         I. Goehausen, Herman, ed. II. Goe-
      hausen, Herman   n. Decisiones aliquot
8   quaestionum.

Witchcraft   Laymann, Paul, 1574-1635.
BF   Processus juridicus contra sagas et
1565   Duhr, Bernhard, 1852-1930.   veneficos.
L42   Paul Laymann und die Hexenprozesse.
D87   (In Zeitschrift für katholische Theolo-
          gie. Innsbruck. 23cm. 23. Bd., 4. Heft
          (1899), p. 733-745)

             1. Laymann, Paul, 1574-1635. Processus
          juridicus contra sagas et veneficos. 2.
          Trials (Witchcraft)--Germany. I. Title.
          II. Zeitschrift für katholische Theologie.
8

                 Laymann, Paul, 1574-1635.
                  [Theologia moralis. Selections.
Witchcraft   German]
BF   Laymann, Paul, 1574-1635.
1565   Ein kurtzer doch gründlicher Bericht,
L42   wie vnd was gestalt, so woln bey dem recht-
T3   lichen Proceß als auch der Beicht mit den
1629   Hexen zuuerfahren seye. Auß deß ehrwürdi-
          gen hochgelehrten Herrn P. Pauli Läymanns
          ... Theologia morali gezogen, vñ den Rich-
          tern vñ Beichtvättern zu gutem absonderlich
          in den Truck gegeben. An jetzo aber män-
          niglich zu gutem in die teutsche Sprache
          vbersetzt. Durch Wolffgang Schilling ...
8   (Continued on next card)

                 Laymann, Paul, 1574-1635.
                  [Theologia moralis. Selections.
Witchcraft   German]
BF   Laymann, Paul, 1574-1635. Ein kurtzer
1565   doch gründlicher Bericht ... 1629.
L42   (Card 2)
T3
1629   Wirtzburg, Gedruckt bey Stephan Fleisch-
          mann, 1629.
             129 p. 14cm.
             With colophon.
             According to G. L. Burr, the first part
          was printed in Aschaffenburg in 1629 under
          title: Aurea enucleatio atque disquisitio
          ... The second section, p. 60-129,
8   (Continued on next card)

                 Laymann, Paul, 1574-1635.
                  [Theologia moralis. Selections.
Witchcraft   German]
BF   Laymann, Paul, 1574-1635. Ein kurtzer
1565   doch gründlicher Bericht ... 1629.
L42   (Card 3)
T3
1629   was published in 1629 by the same printer
          under title: Newer Tractat von der verführ-
          ten Kinder Zauberey, and is by Schilling.
             1. Trials (Witchcraft) 2. Confessors.
          I. His   Theologia moralis. Selections.
          German. II. His   Aurea enucleatio. German.
          III. His   New   er Tractat von der ver-
          führten Kinder   Zauberey. IV. Schil-
8   ling, Wolfgang,   tr. V. Title.

                 Laymann, Paul, 1574-1635.
                  Tractatus de sagis et veneficis.
Witchcraft
BF   Diversi tractatvs: De potestate ecclesia-
1563   stica coercendi daemones circa energu-
D61   menos & maleficiatos, de potentia ac
          viribus daemonum. De modo procedendi ad-
          versvs crimina excepta; praecipuè contra
          sagas & maleficos ... Ex diversis jis-
          qve celeberrimis huius aeui scriptoribus
          ... disputantur. Coloniae Agrippinae,
          Sumptibus Constantini Munich bibliopolae,
          1629.
             8, 236,   166 p. 20cm.
8   (Continued on next card)

                 Laymann, Paul, 1574-1635.
                  Tractatus de sagis et veneficis.
Witchcraft
BF   Diversi tractatvs ... 1629.   (Card 2)
1563
D61   Contents.--Tractatvs de potestate eccle-
          siae coercendi daemones circa obsessos &
          maleficiatos, vnà cum praxi exorcistica, a
          R. della Torre.--Tractatvs theologicvs de
          processv adversvs crimina excepta, ac spe-
          ciatim aduersus crimen veneficij, aB A. Tan-
          ner.--Tractatvs alter theologicus de sagis
          et veneficis, a P. Laymanni.--Consilium de
          sagis, a M. A.   Peregrini.
8   (Continued on next card)

                 Laymann, Paul, 1574-1635.
                  Tractatus de sagis et veneficis.
Witchcraft
BF   Diversi tractatvs ... 1629.   (Card 3)
1563
D61   Title in red and black.
             In double columns except for t. p., ded-
          ication, and titles of first, second, and
          fourth works.
             1. Witchcraft. 2. Trials (Witchcraft)
          3. Exorcism. I. Torre, Raffaelle della.
          Tractatus de potestate ecclesiae coercendi
          daemones. II. Tanner, Adam, 1572-1632.
          Tractatus theologicus de processu adversus
8   (Continued on next card)

                 Laymann, Paul, 1574-1635.
ar W   Binz, Carl, 1832-1913.
53168   Miscellen. Pater P. Laymann, S. J., und
          die Hexenprocesse. Zur weiteren Ausklärung.
          [München, 190-]
             [290]-292 p. 22cm.

             "Sonderabzug aus der Historischen Zeit-
          schrift."

             1. Laymann, Paul, 1574-1635.

             Laymannus, Paulus.

                    see

             Laymann, Paul, 1574-1635.

                 Lays of Palestine.
Witchcraft
BF   Blair, George.
1775   The holocaust; or, The witch of Monzie, a
B63   poem illustrative of the cruelties of super-
          stition. Lays of Palestine and other poems.
          To which is prefixed, Enchantment disenchanted
          or, A treatise on superstition. ... London,
          J. F. Shaw, 1845.
             xii, 277 p. 20cm.

             1. Superstition. I. Title. II. Title: The
          witch of Monzie. III. Title: Lays of
          Palestine. IV.   Title: Enchantment dis-
          enchanted.

Witchcraft
BF   [Lea, Henry Charles] 1825-1909.
1555   The endemoniadas of Queretaro.   [Phila
L43   delphia, 1890]
             33-38 p. 25cm.

             Detached from the Journal of American
          folklore, v. 3, no. 8, 1890.

             1. Inquisition. Mexico. 2. Demoniac
          possession.   I. Title.

ar W   Lea, Henry Charles, 1825-1909.
39639   Geschichte der spanischen Inquisition;
          deutsch bearb. von P. Müllendorff. Leipzi
          Dyk, 1911-12.
             3 v. 25cm.

             Translation of History of the inquisiti
          of Spain.

             I. Lea, Henry Charles, 1825-1909.
          History of the   inquisition of Spain--
          German. II.   Title.

340

CATALOGUE OF THE CORNELL WITCHCRAFT COLLECTION

Witchcraft
BX 1735 L43 H3
Lea, Henry Charles, 1825-1909.
A history of the Inquisition of Spain. New York, London, The Macmillan Company, 1906-07.
4 v. 24cm.

I. Title.

Lea, Henry Charles, 1825-1909.
History of the inquisition of Spain--German.
Lea, Henry Charles, 1825-1909.
Geschichte der spanischen Inquisition; deutsch bearb. von P. Müllendorff. Leipzig, Dyk, 1911-12.
3 v. 25cm.

Translation of History of the inquisition of Spain.

I. Lea, Henry Charles, 1825-1909. History of the inquisition of Spain--German. II. Title.

---

tchcraft
Lea, Henry Charles, 1825-1909.
A history of the Inquisition of the middle ages. By Henry Charles Lea ... New York, Harper & brothers, 1888.
8 v. 23½cm.

1. Inquisition. I. Title.

---

tchcraft
Lea, Henry Charles, 1825-1909.
The inquisition in the Spanish dependencies; Sicily—Naples—Sardinia—Milan—the Canaries—Mexico—Peru—New Granada. By Henry Charles Lea ... New York, London, The Macmillan company, 1908.
1 p. l., vii-xvi, 564 p. 23½cm.

1. Inquisition. I. Title.

8-1774
Library of Congress (Copyright 1907 A 196681)

---

tchcraft
Lea, Henry Charles, 1825-1909, comp.
Materials toward a history of witchcraft, collected by Henry Charles Lea ... arranged and edited by Arthur C. Howland ... with an introduction by George Lincoln Burr ... Philadelphia, University of Pennsylvania press, 1939.
3 v. (xliv, 1548 p.) 24cm.

1. Witchcraft. I. Howland, Arthur Charles, 1869- ed II. Title.

Library of Congress BF1566.L4 39-5921
Copy 2.

Lea, Henry Charles, 1825-1909, comp.
Materials toward a history of witchcraft; arr. and edited by Arthur C. Howland. With an introd. by George Lincoln Burr. New York, T. Yoseloff [1957, c1939]
3 v. (xliv, 1548 p.) 22 cm.

1. Witchcraft--Hist. I. Title.

BF1566.L4 1957 133.409 57-59569
Library of Congress [2]

BF 1566 L43 1957
Lea, Henry Charles, 1825-1909, comp.
Materials toward a history of witchcraft. Arr. and edited by Arthur C. Howland; with an introd. by George Lincoln Burr. New York, T. Yoseloff [1957, c1939]
3 v. (xliv, 1548 p.) 22cm.

1. Witchcraft. I. Howland, Arthur Charles, 1869- ed. II. Title.

Witchcraft
HV 8497 L43 1866
Lea, Henry Charles, 1825-1909.
Superstition and force. Essays on the wager of law—the wager of battle—the ordeal—torture. By Henry C. Lea ... Philadelphia, H. C. Lea, 1866.
2 p. l., [13]-407 p. 20½cm.

1. Wager of law. 2. Wager of battle. 3. Ordeal. 4. Torture. I. Title.
15-6820

WITCHCRAFT
HV 8497 L43 1878
Lea, Henry Charles, 1825-1909.
Superstition and force. Essays on the wager of law—the wager of battle—the ordeal—torture. By Henry C. Lea ... 3d ed., rev. Philadelphia, H. C. Lea, 1878.
xii, [13]-552 p. 21cm.

1. Wager of law 2. Wager of battle. 3. Ordeal 4. Torture. I. Title.
Library of Congress 14-16066
Copy 2. HV8497.L4 1878
Copyright 1878: 8104

WITCHCRAFT
HV 8497 L43 1892
Lea, Henry Charles, 1825-1909.
Superstition and force. Essays on the wager of law—the wager of battle—the ordeal—torture. By Henry Charles Lea ... 4th ed., rev. Philadelphia, Lea brothers and co., 1892.
1 p. l., [vi]-xvi, [13]-627 p. 21cm.
"In a greatly condensed form the first three essays originally appeared in the North American review."—Pref.

1. Wager of law. 2. Wager of battle. 3. Ordeal. 4. Torture. I. Title.
Library of Congress HV8497.L4 12-36150
Copy 2.
Copyright 1892: 45625

Witchcraft
BX 1711 C26
Lea, Henry Charles, 1825-1909.
Cardew, Sir Alexander Gordon, 1861-
A short history of the inquisition, by Sir Alexander G. Cardew ... London, Watts & co. [1933]
viii, 115 p. 19cm.
"Mainly based on the exhaustive works of ... Dr. Henry Charles Lea—namely, Superstition and force, A history of the Inquisition in the middle ages, and A history of the inquisition in Spain."—Pref.
"First published April, 1933."

1. Inquisition--Hist. I. Lea, Henry Charles, 1825-1909. II. Title.
Library of Congress BX1711.C3 34-7592
[3] 272.2

RARE
B 485 L43
Leali, Josephus.
Paediae Scoticae, quibus subtilissima Scoti mens, Scotistis, & exteris, iuxta Aristotelis Principia, facili methodo, Scotice aperitur. Pars tertia, Libros de generatione, corruptione, meteoris, mundo, coelo, & magia, complectens. Auctore Iosepho Leali ... Venetiis, Apud Vitali, 1673.
150 p. 22cm.
Added t.p. engr.

1. Aristoteles. 2. Duns, Joannes, Scotus, 12 65?-1308? 3. Metaphysics. 4. Demonology. I. Title.

8 NIC

WITCHCRAFT
BX 4700 L6 S33 1877
Schick, J G
Leben des heiligen Alphons Maria von Liguori.
Leben des heiligen Alphons Maria von Liguori, Stifter des Redemptoristenordens, und des Pater Friedrich Spee, Priesters der Gesellschaft Jesu. 2. Aufl. Regensburg, G. J. Manz, 1877.
164 p. port. 19cm. (Leben ausgezeichneter Katholiken der drei letzten Jahrhunderte. 7. Bd. 2. Aufl.)
Leben des Pater Friedrich Spee, p. [129]-146, has special t. p.

8 NIC (Continued on next card)

WITCHCRAFT
BX 4700 L6 S33 1877
Schick, J G Leben des heiligen Alphons Maria von Liguori ... 1877. (Card 2)
Anhang, p. [147]-162, consists of selections from Spee's Trutz-Nachtigall.

1. Liguori, Alfonso Maria de', Saint, 1696-1787. 2. Spee, Friedrich von, 1591-1635. I. Spee, Friedrich von, 1591-1635. Trutz-Nachtigall. Selections. II. Title.

8 NIC

Witchcraft
BF 1598 C13 B23 1791c
[Barberi]
Leben und Thaten des Joseph Balsamo, sogenannten Grafen Cagliostro. Nebst einigen Nachrichten über die Beschaffenheit und den Zustand der Freymaurersekten. Aus den Alten des 1790 in Rom wider ihn geführten Prozesses gehoben, und aus dem in der päbstlichen Kammerdruckerey erschienen italienischen Originale übersetzt. Zürich, Orell, Gessner, Füssli, 1791.
xii, 171 p. 20cm.
Translation of Compendio della vita e delle gesta di Giuseppe Balsamo.

Witchcraft
BT 975 L44+
Le Blant, Edmond Frédéric, 1818-1897.
Les premiers chrétiens et le démon. Memoria del Socio Edmondo Le Blant, letta nella seduta del 22 gennaio 1888. [Roma, 1887]
161-168 p. 30cm.
Caption title.
Detached from Accademia nazionale dei Lincei, Rome. Classe di scienze morali storiche, critiche e filologiche. Memorie, ser. IV, v. 3.

1. Demonology. 2. Church history--Primitive and early church. I. Title. II. Title: Le démon.

8

WITCHCRAFT
BR 163 L44
Le Blant, Edmond Frédéric, 1818-1897.
Recherches sur l'accusation de magie dirigée contre les premiers chrétiens. Nogent-Le-Rotrou, A. Gouverneur, 1869.
36 p. 23cm.
Extract from Mémoires de la Société impériale des antiquaires de France, v.31.

1. Church history--Primitive and early church. 2. Magic. 3. Witchcraft. I. Title.

8 NIC

Witchcraft
BF 1602 L45 1702
[Lebrun, Pierre] 1661-1729.
Histoire critique des pratiques superstitieuses, qui ont seduit les peuples, & embarassé les sçavans. Avec la methode et les principes pour discerner les effets naturels d'avec ceux qui ne le sont pas. Par un Prêtre de l'Oratoire. A Rouen, a Paris, Chez Jean de Nully, 1702.
[52], 637, [39] p. illus. 17cm.

1. Superstition. 2. Magic. 3. Divining-rod. I. Title.

CATALOGUE OF THE CORNELL WITCHCRAFT COLLECTION

Witchcraft
BF 1602 L45 1733
   Lebrun, Pierre, 1661-1729.
     Histoire critique des pratiques superstitieuses, qui ont séduit les peuples & embarrassé les savans. Avec la méthode & les principes pour discerner les effets naturels d'avec ceux qui ne le sont pas. 2d éd. augm. Amsterdam, J. F. Bernard, 1733-36.
     4 v. illus. 21cm.

     1. Superstition. 2. Magic. 3. Divining-rod. I. Title.

WITCHCRAFT
BF 1505 L45 1882
   Lecanu, Auguste François, 1803-
     Histoire de Satan, sa chute, son culte, ses manifestations, ses oeuvres, la guerre qu'il fait à Dieu et aux hommes. Magie, possession... Paris, Féchoz et Letouzey [1882]
     506 p. 22cm.

8 NIC
     1. Devil. 2. Demonology. 3. Occult sciences. 4. Demoniac possession. I. Title.

WITCHCRAFT
DC 112 R38 L46 1869
   Leclerc, Laurent.
     Notice sur Nicolas Remy, procureur général de Lorraine; discours de réception à l'Académie de Stanislas, par L. Leclerc. Nancy, Sordoillet, imprimeurs de l'Académie de Stanislas, 1869.
     107 p. facsims., port. 23cm.

     "Extrait des Mémoires de l'Académie de Stanislas, 1868."

8 NIC
     1. Remi, Nicolas, 1530-1612. I. Title.

A lecture on the occult sciences.

Witchcraft
BF 1566 N54
   Newhall, James R[obinson]
     A lecture on the occult sciences: embracing some account of the New England witchcraft, with an attempt to exhibit the philosophy of spectre seeing, disease charming, &c. By James R. Newhall. [Published by request of auditors.] Salem, G.W. & E. Crafts, 1845.
     36 p. 22cm.

     Cover-title: An account of the great New England witchcraft ...

Lectures on the Scriptural idea of the Devil.

Witchcraft
BS 1199 D4 H77
   Hood, Edwin Paxton, 1820-1885.
     Lectures on the Scriptural idea of the Devil. [187?]
     113-126 p. 23cm.

     Alternate pages blank.
     Evidently reprinted from a periodical.

     1. Devil--Biblical teaching. I. Title: The Scriptural idea of the Devil.

Lectures on witchcraft, comprising a history of the delusion in Salem, in 1692.

Witchcraft
BF 1576 U68L4
   Upham, Charles Wentworth, 1802-1875.
     Lectures on witchcraft, comprising a history of the delusion in Salem, in 1692. Boston, Carter, Hendee and Babcock, 1831.
     vii, 280 p. 16cm.

     I. Title. II. Title: A history of the delusion in Salem, in 1692.

Witchcraft
BF 1581 Z7 1324
   Ledrede, Richard de, bp. of Ossory, d. 1360.
     Kyteler, Alice, fl. 1324, defendant.
     A contemporary narrative of the proceedings against Dame Alice Kyteler, prosecuted for sorcery in 1324, by Richard de Ledrede, bishop of Ossory. Edited by Thomas Wright ... London, Printed for the Camden society, by J. B. Nichols and son, 1843.
     2 p. l., xlii p., 1 l., 61, [1] p. 21x17cm.
     [Camden society. Publications. no. XXIV]
     Text in Latin.
     Printed from Harleian ms., no. 641. cf. Introd.

Lee, Frederick George, 1832-1902.
   Glimpses of the supernatural.

BF 1241 L47
   Lee, Frederick George, 1832-1902.
     The other world; or, Glimpses of the supernatural. Being facts, records, and traditions relating to dreams, omens, miraculous occurrences, apparitions, wraiths, warnings, second-sight, witchcraft, necromancy, etc. Ed. by the Rev. Frederick George Lee ... London, H. S. King and co., 1875.
     2 v. 18½cm.
     Published also under title: Glimpses of the supernatural.

     1. Supernatural. 2. Spiritualism. I. Lee, Frederick George, 1832-1902. Glimpses of the supernatural. II. Title.
     Library of Congress   BF1241.L48   10-32970

BF 1241 L47
   Lee, Frederick George, 1832-1902.
     The other world; or, Glimpses of the supernatural. Being facts, records, and traditions relating to dreams, omens, miraculous occurrences, apparitions, wraiths, warnings, second-sight, witchcraft, necromancy, etc. Ed. by the Rev. Frederick George Lee ... London, H. S. King and co., 1875.
     2 v. 18½cm.
     Published also under title: Glimpses of the supernatural.

     1. Supernatural. 2. Spiritualism. I. Lee, Frederick George, 1832-1902. Glimpses of the supernatural. II. Title.
     Library of Congress   BF1241.L48   10-32970

Lee, Prudence, d. 1652.

Witchcraft
BF 1581 Z7 1652a
   The Witch of Wapping; or, An exact and perfect relation of the life and devilish practises of Joan Peterson, who dwelt in Spruce Island, near Wapping; who was condemned for practising witch-craft, and sentenced to be hanged at Tyburn, on Munday the 11th [sic] of April, 1652... Together with the confession of Prudence Lee, who was burnt in Smithfield on Saturday the 10th. ... for the murthering her husband... London, Printed for Th. Spring, 1652.
     8 p. 20cm.
     (Continued on next card)

Lee, Prudence, d. 1652.

Witchcraft
BF 1581 Z7 1652a
   The Witch of Wapping ... 1652.   (Card 2)

     With this is bound A declaration in answer to several lying pamphlets concerning the witch of Wapping ... London, 1652.
     With book-plate of Francis Freeling.

     1. Peterson, Joan, d. 1652. 2. Lee, Prudence, d. 1652.

Leere van de geesten.

Witchcraft
BF 1445 G87
   Groenewegen, Hendrik.
     Pneumatica; ofte, Leere van de geesten, zijnde denkende en redelike wesens ... uytgegeven by gelegentheyd van 't boek De betooverde wereld, geschreven door Balthazar Bekker ... Enchuysen, H. van Straalen, 1692.
     88, 126, 56 p. 20cm.

     1. Ghosts. 2. Bekker, Balthasar, 1634-1698. De betooverde wereld. I. Title. II. Title: Leere van de geesten.

De leeringe der duyvelen.

Witchcraft
BT 980 O64 1691
   [Orchard, N   ] supposed author.
     De leeringe der duyvelen, beweezen te zyn de groote afval deezer laatste tyden. Of een proeve, strekkende om die onbehoorlyke kundigheden en bevattingen, welke de menschen van de demons en quaade geesten hebben, te verbéteren. In 't engelsch geschreeven door N. Orchard. En volgens de copy, gedrukt tot Londen in 't jaar 1676, vertaald door Wm. Sewel. t'Amsterdam, J. Broers, 1691.
     100 p. 21cm.

     (Continued on next card)

De leeringe der duyvelen.

Witchcraft
BT 980 O64 1691
   [Orchard, N   ] supposed author. De leeringe der duyvelen ... 1691. (Card 2)
     Translation of his The doctrine of devils ...
     Also attributed to Thomas Ady.

     1. Devil. 2. Demonology. I. Title. II. Orchard, N   supposed author. The doctrine of devils--Dutch. III. Ady, Thomas, supposed author.

Leetsosoneus, Iiratiel

     see

Hamer, Petrus, 1646-1716

Légendes des esprits et des démons qui circulent autour de nous ...

Witchcraft
BF 1552 C69
   Collin de Plancy, Jacques Albin Simon, 1794-1881.
     Légendes des esprits et des démons qui circulent autour de nous ... Paris, H. Plon [1864]
     395 p. col. front. 22cm.

     With this is bound his Légendes infernales. Paris [1862]

     1. Demonology. I. Title.

Witchcraft Légendes infernales.
BF 1552 C69
   Collin de Plancy, Jacques Albin Simon, 1794-1881.
     Légendes infernales. Relations et pactes des hôtes de l'enfer avec l'espèce humaine. Paris, H. Plon [1862]
     395 p. col. front. 22cm.

     Bound with his Légendes des esprits ... Paris [1864]

     I. Title

WITCHCRAFT
BF 1517 F5 L52 1874
   Legué, Gabriel, d. 1913.
     Documents pour servir à l'histoire des possédées de Loudun. Paris, A. Delahay 1874.
     90 p. 22cm.

     Issued also as diss.--Paris.

8 NIC
     1. Loudun, France. Ursuline Convent. 2. Demoniac possession. 3. Grandier, Ur 1590-1634. I. Title.

CATALOGUE OF THE CORNELL WITCHCRAFT COLLECTION

WITCHCRAFT
F
517
L521
884

Legué, Gabriel, d. 1913.
    Urbain Grandier et les possédées de Loudun. Nouv. éd. revue et augmentée. Paris, Charpentier, 1884.
    xii, 348 p. 19cm.

    1. Grandier, Urbain, 1590-1634. 2. Loudun, France. Ursuline Convent. 3. Demoniac possession. I. Title.

8
NIC

WITCHCRAFT
F
517
L5
43
886

Legué, Gabriel, d. 1913, ed.
    Jeanne des Anges, mère, 1602-1665.
    Soeur Jeanne des Anges, supérieure des Ursulines de Loudun (XVIIe siècle) Autobiographie d'une hystérique possédée, d'après le manuscrit inédit de la bibliothèque de Tours. Annoté et publié par les docteurs Gabriel Legué et Gilles de la Tourette. Préface de M. le professeur Charcot. Paris, Aux Bureaux du Progrès, 1886.
    xiv, 321 p. facsim. 24cm. (Bibliothèque diabolique [Collection Bourneville])

NIC

---

chcraft

Le Heurt, Matthieu, ed.
    Dupont, René.
    La philosophie des esprits, divisee en cinq livres, & generaux discours Chrestiens, specifiez en la page suiuante. Recueillie & mise en lumiere par F. M. Le Heurt ... 3. ed. Roven, R. Feron, 1628.
    [8], 257 [i.e. 267], [5] l. 17cm.

    1. Spirits. I. Le Heurt, Matthieu, ed. II. Title.

---

craft
F
038
18
52
898

Lehmann, Alfred Georg Ludvig, 1858-1921.
    Aberglaube und Zauberei von den ältesten Zeiten an bis in die Gegenwart. Deutsche autorisierte Ausgabe von Dr. Petersen ... Stuttgart, F. Enke, 1898.
    xii, 556 p. illus. 25cm.

Translation of Overtro og trolddom.

WITCHCRAFT

Lehmann, Alfred Georg Ludvig, 1858-1921.
    Aberglaube und Zauberei von den ältesten Zeiten an bis in die Gegenwart. Deutsche autorisierte Übersetzung von Dr. med. Petersen I. 2. umgearbeitete und erweiterte Auflage. Stuttgart, F. Enke, 1908.
    xii, 665 p. illus., facsims. 24cm.

Translation of Overtro og trolddom.

    I. His Overtro og trolddom--German. II. Petersen, Dominikus. III. Title.

Lehmann, Alfred Georg Ludvig, 1858-1921.
    Aberglaube und Zauberei von den ältesten Zeiten an bis in die Gegenwart. 3. deutsche Aufl., nach der 2. umgearb. dänischen Aufl., übersetzt und nach dem Tode des Verfassers bis in die Neuzeit ergänzt von Dr. Med. D. Petersen. Stuttgart, F. Enke, 1925.
    xvi, 752 p. illus., plates, facsims. 25cm.

WITCHCRAFT
BF
1038
D18
L52

Lehmann, Alfred Georg Ludvig, 1858-1921.
    Overtro og trolddom fra de aeldste tider til vore dage. Kjøbenhavn, J. Frimodt, 1893-[96]
    4 v. in 1. illus. 22cm.

T.p. for four vols. dated 1896.

    1. Magic. 2. Witchcraft. 3. Occult sciences. 4. Theosophy. 5. Spiritualism. 6. Superstition. 7. Dreams. 8. Hypnotism. 9. Occult sciences--Bibl. I. Title.

8
NIC

WITCHCRAFT
BF
1038
D18
L52
1908

Lehmann, Alfred Georg Ludvig, 1858-1921.
    Overtro og trolddom--German.
Lehmann, Alfred Georg Ludvig, 1858-1921.
    Aberglaube und Zauberei von den ältesten Zeiten an bis in die Gegenwart. Deutsche autorisierte Übersetzung von Dr. med. Petersen I. 2. umgearbeitete und erweiterte Auflage. Stuttgart, F. Enke, 1908.
    xii, 665 p. illus., facsims. 24cm.

Translation of Overtro og trolddom.

    I. His Overtro og trolddom--German. II. Petersen, Dominikus. III. Title.

WITCHCRAFT
BF
1584
S97
Z7
1782a

Lehmann, Heinrich Ludwig.
    Freundschaftliche und vertrauliche Briefe den so genannten sehr berüchtigten Hexenhandel zu Glarus betreffend. Zürich, Bey Johann Caspar Füessin, 1783.
    2 v. in 1. plate. 19cm.

No more published.

    1. Trials (Witchcraft)--Glarus (Canton) 2. Göldi, Anna. 3. Tschudi, Anna Maria. I. Title.

8
NIC

Witchcraft
BF
1548
A33

Die Lehre vom Teufel, allgemein fasslich dargestellt für liberale Protestanten aus dem Volk.
Albers, Johann Heinrich, 1840-
    Die Lehre vom Teufel, allgemein fasslich dargestellt für liberale Protestanten aus dem Volk. Eine Preisschrift. Strassburg, J. Schneider, 1878.
    58 p. 20cm.

    1. Devil. I. Title.

WITCHCRAFT
BT
980
L94

Die Lehren der Bibel und der ältesten christlichen Kirche über Satan und sein Reich.
Lützelberger, Ernst Carl Julius, 1802-1876.
    Die Lehren der Bibel und der ältesten christlichen Kirche über Satan und sein Reich. [Nürnberg, 1839]
    52-88 p. 21cm.

Extract from unidentified periodical.

8
NIC

    1. Devil. 2. Devil--Biblical teaching.

WITCHCRAFT
BF
1583
A2
L52

Leib, Johann, 1591-1666.
    Consilia, responsa ac deductiones juris variae, cumprimis vero processum contra sagas concernentia. Opus non tantum jurisconsultis et advocatis, sed & adsessoribus, iudicibus, aliiisque apprime utile ac necessarium. ...wie und welcher Gestalt der Process wider die Zauberer und Hexen anzustellen und hierinnen verantwortlich zuverfahren. Mit beygefügten underschiedlicher Universitäten über verschiedene schwere Fälle, Bedencken und Informationen...
    (Continued on next card)

8
NIC

WITCHCRAFT
BF
1583
A2
L52

Leib, Johann, 1591-1666. Consilia, responsa ac deductiones juris variae...1666.
    (Card 2)

Francofurti, Apud Hermannum à Sande, 1666.
    540 p. 21cm.

Text in Latin or German.

    1. Witchcraft--Germany. 2. Trials (Witchcraft)--Germany. 3. Torture--Germany. I. Title.

WITCHCRAFT
BF
1583
Z7
1749e

Leist, Friedrich, 1844-
    Aus Frankens Vorzeit.
    Maria Renata, die letzte Hexe Deutschlands.
    (In: His Aus Frankens Vorzeit. Würzburg, 1881. 18cm. p. 57-75)

    1. Sänger, Maria Renata von Mossau, ca. 1680-1749. 2. Trials (Witchcraft)--Germany. I. His Aus Frankens Vorzeit.

8
NIC

WITCHCRAFT
BF
1583
Z7
1749e

Leist, Friedrich, 1844-
    Maria Renata, die letzte Hexe Deutschlands.
    (In: His Aus Frankens Vorzeit. Würzburg, 1881. 18cm. p. 57-75)

    1. Sänger, Maria Renata von Mossau, ca. 1680-1749. 2. Trials (Witchcraft)--Germany. I. His Aus Frankens Vorzeit. II. Title.

8
NIC

WITCHCRAFT
BF
1555
L53

Leistle, David.
    Die Besessenheit mit besonderer Berücksichtigung der Lehre der hl. Väter. Dillingen, L. Keller's Witwe [1886]
    178 p. 23cm.

Programm--Dillingen.

    1. Demoniac possession. 2. Devil. 3. Demonology. I. Title.

8
NIC

WITCHCRAFT
BF
1413
L53

Leithäuser, Joachim G
    Das neue Buch vom Aberglauben; Geschichte und Gegenwart. Mit 117 Bildern auf Kunstdrucktafeln und 43 zeitgenössischen Darstellungen im Text. Berlin, Safari-Verlag [1964]
    412 p. illus. 25cm. (Die Welt des Wissens)

    1. Superstition. 2. Witchcraft--Hist. I. Title.

WITCHCRAFT
BF
1583
L53

Leitschuh, Friedrich, 1837-1898.
    Beiträge zur Geschichte des Hexenwesens in Franken. Bamberg, C. Hübischer, 1883.
    62, xviii, ii p. 22cm.

Note inside front cover by G.L. Burr: An extremely valuable contribution to the literature of the witch-persecution.

    1. Witchcraft--Franconia. 2. Trials (Witchcraft)--Franconia. I. Title.

8
NIC

CATALOGUE OF THE CORNELL WITCHCRAFT COLLECTION

Le Lorrain, Pierre, abbé de Vallemont.

see

Vallemont, Pierre Le Lorrain, abbé de, 1649-1721.

Witchcraft
BF 1445 L54

Le Loyer, Pierre, *sieur de La Brosse,* 1550-1634.
IIII. ljvres des spectres, ov apparitions et visions d'esprits, anges et démons se monstrans sensiblement aux hommes. Par Pierre Le Loyer ... Angers, G. Nepueu, 1586.
2 v. in 1. 22cm.
"Avctevrs allegvez ez Quatre liures des spectres": v. 1, prelim. leaves 3-5.

1. Apparitions. 2. Demonology. I. Title: Quatre livres des spectres.

Library of Congress BF1445.L4 11-20782

Le Loyer, Pierre, sieur de La Brosse, 1550-1634.
IIII. (Quatre) livres des spectres--English.
Le Loyer, Pierre, sieur de La Brosse, 1550-1634.

Witchcraft
BF 1445 L54 1605a

A treatise of specters or straunge sights, visions and apparitions appearing sensibly vnto men. Wherein is delivered, the nature of spirites, angels, and divels: their power and properties: as also of witches, sorcerers, enchanters, and such like. With a table of the contents of the severall chapters annexed in the end of the booke. Newly done out of French into English. London, Printed by Val. S. for M. Lownes, 1605.
8 p. l., 145 numb. l., 1 l. 20cm.
(Continued on next card)

WITCHCRAFT
BF 1445 L54 1608

Le Loyer, Pierre, sieur de La Brosse, 1550-1634.
Discovrs des spectres, ov visions et apparitions d'esprits, comme anges, demons, et ames, se monstrans visibles aux hommes, où sont rapportez les argvmens et raisons de cevx qui reuocquent en doute ce qui se dit sur ce subiect ... Le tovt en hvict livres ... 2. ed. reveve et avgmentee. Paris, Chez Nicolas Bvon, 1608.
12 p. l., 979, [43] p. 24cm.
(Continued on next card)

8

WITCHCRAFT
BF 1445 L54 1608

Le Loyer, Pierre, sieur de La Brosse, 1550-1634.
IIII. (Quatre) livres des spectres ou apparitions.
Le Loyer, Pierre, sieur de La Brosse, 1550-1634.
Discovrs des spectres, ov visions et apparitions d'esprits, comme anges, demons, et ames, se monstrans visibles aux hommes, où sont rapportez les argvmens et raisons de cevx qui reuocquent en doute ce qui se dit sur ce subiect ... Le tovt en hvict livres ... 2. ed. reveve et avgmentee. Paris, Chez Nicolas Bvon, 1608.
12 p. l., 979, [43] p. 24cm.
(Continued on next card)

8

Le Loyer, Pierre, sieur de La Brosse, 1550-1634.

Witchcraft
BF 1445 L54 1605a

A treatise of specters or straunge sights, ... 1605.
(Card 2)

Translated by Zachary Jones.
"A catalogue of the authours alledged in the Treatise of specters": prelim. leaves 5-8.
Translation of only the first book of IIII. ljvres des spectres.

WITCHCRAFT
BF 1445 L54 1604

Le Loyer, Pierre, sieur de La Brosse, 1550-1634. Discovrs des spectres ... 1608. (Card 2)

Title in red and black.
First published 1586 under title: IIII. Livres des spectres ou apparitions.

1. Apparitions. 2. Demonology. I. His IIII. (Quatre) livres des spectres ou apparitions. II. Title: Discours des spectres, ou visions.

8

WITCHCRAFT
BF 1445 L54 1604

Le Loyer, Pierre, sieur de La Brosse, 1550-1634. Discovrs des spectres ... 1608. (Card 2)

Title in red and black.
First published 1586 under title: IIII. Livres des spectres ou apparitions.

1. Apparitions. 2. Demonology. I. His IIII. (Quatre) livres des spectres ou apparitions. II. Title: Discours des spectres, ou visions.

8

Witchcraft
BF 1445 L54 1605a

Le Loyer, Pierre, sieur de La Brosse, 1550-1634.
A treatise of specters or straunge sights, ... 1605.
(Card 2)

Translated by Zachary Jones.
"A catalogue of the authours alledged in the Treatise of specters": prelim. leaves 5-8.
Translation of only the first book of IIII. ljvres des spectres.

I. Jones, Zachary, tr. II. Title. III. His IIII. (Quatre) livres des spectres--English.

WITCHCRAFT
BF 1445 L54 1605

Le Loyer, Pierre, sieur de La Brosse, 1550-1634.
Discovrs, et histoires des spectres, visions et apparitions des esprits, anges, demons, et ames, se monstrans visibles aux hommes. Divisez en hvict livres. Esqvels par les visions merveillevses, & prodigieuses apparitions avenuës en tous siecles, tirees & recueillies des plus celebres autheurs tant sacrez que prophanes, est manifestee la certitude des spectres & visions des esprits: &
(Continued on next card)

WITCHCRAFT
BF 1445 L54 1605

Le Loyer, Pierre, sieur de La Brosse, 1550-1634.
IIII. (Quatre) livres des spectres.
Le Loyer, Pierre, sieur de La Brosse, 1550-1634.
Discovrs, et histoires des spectres, visions et apparitions des esprits, anges, demons, et ames, se monstrans visibles aux hommes. Divisez en hvict livres. Esqvels par les visions merveillevses, & prodigieuses apparitions avenuës en tous siecles, tirees & recueillies des plus celebres autheurs tant sacrez que prophanes, est manifestee la certitude des spectres & visions des esprits: &
(Continued on next card)

WITCHCRAFT
BF 1445 L54 1605

Le Loyer, Pierre, sieur de la Brosse, 1550-1634. Discovrs, et histoires des spectres ... (Card 2)

sont baillees les causes des diverses sortes d'apparitions d'iceux, leurs effects, leurs differences, & les moyens pour recognoistre les bons & les mauuais, & chasser les demons. Avssi est traicté des extases et rauissemens: de l'essence, nature, et origine des ames, et de leur estat apres le deceds de leurs corps:
(Continued on next card)

WITCHCRAFT
BF 1445 L54 1605

Le Loyer, Pierre, sieur de La Brosse, 1550-1634. Discovrs, et histoires des spectres ... (Card 2)

sont baillees les causes des diverses sortes d'apparitions d'iceux, leurs effects, leurs differences, & les moyens pour recognoistre les bons & les mauuais, & chasser les demons. Avssi est traicté des extases et rauissemens: de l'essence, nature, et origine des ames, et de leur estat apres le deceds de leurs corps:
(Continued on next card)

WITCHCRAFT
BF 1566 L56

Lempens, Carl, 1839-
Geschichte der Hexen und Hexenprozesse.. St. Gallen (Schweiz), H. Fuhrimann, 1880.
80 p. 19cm.

8
NIC

1. Witchcraft--Hist. 2. Trials (Witchcraft)--Hist. I. Title.

Witchcraft
BF 1445 L54 1605

Le Loyer, Pierre, sieur de La Brosse, 1550-1634. Discovrs, et histoires des spectres ... (Card 3)

plus des magiciens et sorciers, de leur communication auec les malins esprits: ensemble des remedes pour se preseruer des illusions et impostures diaboliques. Paris, Chez Nicolas Bvon, 1605.
[26], 976, [39] p. 23cm.

2d ed. of IIII. ljvres des spectres.
I. His IIII. (Quatre) livres des spectres. II. Title.

Witchcraft
BF 1445 L54 1605

Le Loyer, Pierre, sieur de La Brosse, 1550-1634. Discovrs, et histoires des spectres ... (Card 3)

plus des magiciens et sorciers, de leur communication auec les malins esprits: ensemble des remedes pour se preseruer des illusions et impostures diaboliques. Paris, Chez Nicolas Bvon, 1605.
[26], 976, [39] p. 23cm.

2d ed. of IIII. ljvres des spectres.
I. His IIII. (Quatre) livres des spectres. II. Title.

Witchcraft
BF 1445 L56 1752

Lenglet Dufresnoy, Nicolas, 1674-1755.
Recueil de dissertations anciennes et nouvelles, sur les apparitions, les visions & les songes... Avignon, J. N. Leloup, 1751-52 [v.1, 1752]
2 v. 17cm.

"Liste des principaux auteurs qui ont traité des esprits, démons, apparitions, songes, magie & spectres": v.2, pt. 2, p. 223-287.

1. Apparitions. I. Title.

CATALOGUE OF THE CORNELL WITCHCRAFT COLLECTION

Witchcraft
BF 1445
L56
    Lenglet Dufresnoy, [Nicolas] 1674-1755.
    Traité historique et dogmatique sur les apparitions les visions & les révélations particuliéres. Avec des observations sur les Dissertations du r. p. Dom Calmet abbé de Sénones, sur les apparitions & les revenans Par M. l'abbé Lenglet Dufresnoy. Avignon & Paris Chez J. M. Leloup, 1751.
    2 v. pl. 18cm.   2-11834

    1. Apparitions. 2. Calmet, Augustin, 1672-1757. Dissertations sur les apparitions. I. Title.

Library of Congress, no.

Lenglet Dufresnoy, Nicolas, 1674-1755, ed.

Luther, Martin, 1483-1546.
    La conférence entre Luther et le diable au sujet de la messe; raconté par Luther lui-même. Trad. nouv. du latin par Isidore Liseux, avec les remarques et annotations des abbés de Cordemoy et Lenglet-Dufresnoy. Paris, 1875.
    viii, 91 p. 16cm.

    From Luther's tractate De missa privata atque sacerdotum unctione. Latin text parallel with French translation.

Le Normant, Jean, sieur de Chiremont, ed.
    De la vocation des magiciens.

Witchcraft
    Le Normant, Jean, sieur de Chiremont, ed.
    Histoire veritable et memorable de ce qvi c'est passé sovs l'exorcisme de trois filles possedées és païs de Flandre, en la descouuerte & confession de Marie de Sains, soy disant Princesse de la magie, & Simone Dourlet, complice, & autres. Ov il est avssi traicte' de la police du sabbat, & secrets de la synagogue des magiciens & magiciennes. De l'antechrist, & de la fin du monde.

    (Continued on next card)

Le Normant, Jean, sieur de Chiremont, ed.
    De la vocation des magiciens.

Witchcraft
BF 1555
L57
    Le Normant, Jean, sieur de Chiremont, ed.
    Histoire veritable ... de trois filles possedées ... 1623.   (Card 2)

    Extraict des memoires de Nicolas de Momorenci, comte Destarre, & du F. Sebastien Michaëlis, & du François Donsieux. Paris, N. Bvon, 1623.
    2 v. 17cm.

    Vol. 2 has title: De la vocation des
    (Continued on next card)

Le Normant, Jean, sieur de Chiremont, ed.
    De la vocation des magiciens.

Witchcraft
BF 1555
L57
    Le Normant, Jean, sieur de Chiremont, ed.
    Histoire veritable ... de trois filles possedées... 1623.   (Card 3)

    magiciens et magiciennes par le ministre des demons...

    1. Demoniac possession. I. Le Normant, Jean, sieur de Chiremont, ed. De la vocation des magiciens... II. Title.

Witchcraft
    Le Normant, Jean, sieur de Chiremont, ed.
    Histoire veritable et memorable de ce qvi c'est passé sovs l'exorcisme de trois filles possedées és païs de Flandre, en la descouuerte & confession de Marie de Sains, soy disant Princesse de la magie, & Simone Dourlet, complice, & autres. Ov il est avssi traicte' de la police du sabbat, & secrets de la synagogue des magiciens & magiciennes. De l'antechrist, & de la fin du monde.

    (Continued on next card)

Witchcraft
BF 1555
L57
    Le Normant, Jean, sieur de Chiremont, ed.
    Histoire veritable ... de trois filles possedées ... 1623.   (Card 2)

    Extraict des memoires de Nicolas de Momorenci, comte Destarre, & du F. Sebastien Michaëlis, & du François Donsieux. Paris, N. Bvon, 1623.
    2 v. 17cm.

    Vol. 2 has title: De la vocation des
    (Continued on next card)

Witchcraft
BF 1555
L57
    Le Normant, Jean, sieur de Chiremont, ed.
    Histoire veritable ... de trois filles possedées... 1623.   (Card 3)

    magiciens et magiciennes par le ministre des demons...

    1. Demoniac possession. I. Le Normant, Jean, sieur de Chiremont, ed. De la vocation des magiciens... II. Title.

Witchcraft
BF 1598
H55A4
1548
    Lenzoni, Carlo, d. 1551, ed.
    Hermes Trismegistus.
    [Poemander. Italian]
    Il Pimandro di Mercurio Trismegisto, tradotto da Tommaso Benci in lingua fiorentina. Firenze [L. Torrentino] 1548.
    [24], 119, [14] p. 18cm.

    Title vignette.
    Edited by Carlo Lenzoni.

    I. Benci, Tommaso, tr. II. Lenzoni, Carlo, d. 1551, ed.

Leo X, Pope, 1475-1521.

Witchcraft
BF 1775
W132
1849
    Der Wahre geistliche Schild, so vor 300 Jahren von dem heil. Papst Leo X. bestätigt worden, wider alle gefährliche böse Menschen sowohl als aller Hexerei und Teufelswerk entgegen gesetzt; darinnen sehr kräftiga Segen und Gebete ... Nebst einem Anhang heiliger Segen ... [n. p.] 1617. [Erie? 1849?]
    144, 35 p. illus. 12cm.
    Contents.--Andächtige Weise, dem Amt der heiligen Messe nützlich beizuwohnen.--Ein
    (Continued on next card)

Leo X, Pope, 1475-1521.

Witchcraft
BF 1775
W132
1849
    Der Wahre geistliche Schild ... [1849?]   (Card 2)

    Contents--Continued.
    schöner und wohlapprobirter heiliger Segen zu Wasser und Land wider alle seine Feinde.--Geistliche Schild-Wacht, darinnen der Mensch ihm für eine jegliche Stund ... einen besondern Patron aus den Heiligen Gottes erwähltet [sic].--Anhang. Heiliger Segen ... um in allen Gefahren, worein sowohl Men-
    (Continued on next card)

Leo X, Pope, 1475-1521.

Witchcraft
BF 1775
W132
1849
    Der Wahre geistliche Schild ... [1849?]   (Card 3)

    Contents--Continued.
    schen als Vieh oft gerathen, gesichert zu sein.
    Each item has special t. p.
    Geistliche Schild-Wacht has imprint 1840; the Anhang has imprint 1849 and is paged separately.

    1. Charms. 2. Prayers. I. Leo X, Pope, 1475-1521. II. Title: Heiliger Segen.

Leo XIII, Pope, 1810-1903.

WITCHCRAFT
BX 1374
R55
    Rieks, J
    Leo XIII. und der Satanskult, von J. Rieks. Berlin, H. Walther (F. Bechly) 1897.
    xx, 301 p. 19cm.

    Bibliographical footnotes.

8 NIC
    1. Leo XIII, Pope, 1810-1903. 2. Devil-worship. I. Title.

Leo XIII. und der Satanskult.

WITCHCRAFT
BX 1374
R55
    Rieks, J
    Leo XIII. und der Satanskult, von J. Rieks. Berlin, H. Walther (F. Bechly) 1897.
    xx, 301 p. 19cm.

    Bibliographical footnotes.

8 NIC
    1. Leo XIII, Pope, 1810-1903. 2. Devil-worship. I. Title.

Léonora Galigaï.

DC 123
.9
C6
M74
    Mongrédien, Georges, 1901-
    Léonora Galigaï. Un procès de sorcellerie sous Louis XIII. [Paris,] Hachette, 1968.
    234 p. 21 cm. (L'Envers de l'histoire) 16.50 F   (F***)
    Illustrated cover.
    Bibliography: p. [223]-232.

    1. Concini, Leonora (Dori) called Galigaï, d. 1617. 2. Trials (Witchcraft)--France. I. Title.

DC123.9.C62M6   68-134611

Library of Congress   [1]

WITCHCRAFT
BF 1582
Z7
1631c
    Lepage, Henri, 1814-1887.
    Melchior de La Vallée et une gravure de Jacques Bellange. Nancy, René Wiener, 1882.
    56 p. illus., facsim. 23cm.

8 NIC
    1. La Vallée, Melchior de. 2. Trials (Witchcraft)--Nancy. I. Title.

Lercheimer, Augustin, pseud.

see

Witekind, Hermann, 1522-1603.

WITCHCRAFT
BF 1517
F5
L61
    Leriche, Pierre Ambroise.
    Etudes sur les possessions en général et sur celle de Loudun en particulier. Précédées d'une lettre adressée à l'auteur par Ventura de Raulica. Paris, H. Plon, 1859.
    x, 258 p. 17cm.

8 NIC
    1. Demoniac possession. 2. Loudun, France. Ursuline Convent. 3. Grandier, Urbain, 1590-1634. I. Title.

CATALOGUE OF THE CORNELL WITCHCRAFT COLLECTION

Lesenswürdige Briefe ... über die Materie von der Zauberey.

WITCHCRAFT
BF
1565
H97
1726

Saint André, François de.
 Mʳ· de Sᵗ· André ... Lesenswürdige Briefe an einige seiner Freunde uber die Materie von der Zauberey, den Ubelthaten, so dadurch angestifftet werden, und von den Zauberern und Hexen insbesondere: worinnen es die wunderbarsten Würckungen, die man gemeiniglich den Teuffeln zuschreibet, deutlich erkläret, und dabey zeiget, dass diese Geister offt

8   (Continued on next card)

Lesenswürdige Briefe ... über die Materie von der Zauberey.

WITCHCRAFT
BF
1565
H97
1726

Saint André, François de. Mʳ· de Sᵗ· André ... Lesenswürdige Briefe ... 1727. (Card 2)

nicht den geringsten Antheil daran haben ... Statt eines Suplements zum Hutchinson aus dem Französischen ins Teutsche übersetzt ... von Theodoro Arnold. Leipzig, Bey J. C. Martini, 1727.
10 p. l., 204, [9] p. 22cm.
Translation of Lettres ... à quelques-uns de ses amis, pub. 1725.

8   (Continued on next card)

Lesenswürdige Briefe ... über die Materie von der Zauberey.

WITCHCRAFT
BF
1565
H97
1726

Saint André, François de. Mʳ· de Sᵗ· André ... Lesenswürdige Briefe ... 1727. (Card 3)

Title in red and black.
Bound with Hutchinson, F. Historischer Versuch von der Hexerey. Leipzig, 1726.
1. Witchcraft. 2. Magic. I. His Lettres ... à quelques-uns de ses amis. German. II. Hutchinson, Francis, bp. of Down and Connor, 1660-1739. Historischer Versuch von der Hexerey. III. Arnold, Theodor, 1683-1771, tr. IV. Title: Lesenswürdige Briefe ... über die Materie von der Zauberey.

8

Witchcraft
BF
1581
L63+

Lesley, Peter D
 Witchcraft in England: a study of the beliefs and of the predisposition to believe. [Middletown, Conn.?] 1967.
vi, 161 l. 29cm.

Thesis--Wesleyan University, Middletown, Conn.

1. Witchcraft--England. I. Title.

NIC

WITCHCRAFT
BF
1582
L63

Lespy, Jean Désiré, called Vastin, 1817-1897.
 Les sorcières dans le Béarn, 1393-1672. Pau, L. Ribaut, 1875.
72 p. 25cm.

Extract from Bulletin de la Société des sciences, lettres et arts de Pau, ser. 2, v.4.
1. Witchcraft--Béarn, France. 2. Trials (Witchcraft)--Béarn, France. I. Title.

8
NIC

Lessicomanzia.

Witchcraft
BF
1429
B57
1845

Bianco, Filippo.
 Lessicomanzia; ovvero, Dizionario degli esseri, dei personaggi, dei libri, dei fatti e delle cose, che riferisconsi alle apparizioni, alla divinazione, alla magia ec. Per servere di corredo alla storia degli scorsi secoli, con aggiunte interessanti in questa ed. Siena, Tipografia dell'Ancora, 1845.
xlix, 660 p. illus. 16cm.

1. Occult sciences--Dict. I. Title.

Witchcraft
BF
1531
S43
1830

Letters on demonology and witchcraft.
Scott, Sir Walter, bart., 1771-1832.
 Letters on demonology and witchcraft, addressed to J. G. Lockhart, esq., by Sir Walter Scott, bart. London, J. Murray, 1830.
ix, 402 p. front. 16 cm.

1. Demonology. 2. Witchcraft. I. Title.

Letters on natural magic.

WITCHCRAFT
BF
1042
B84
1842

Brewster, Sir David, 1781-1868.
 Letters on natural magic, addressed to Sir Walter Scott, bart ... 5th ed. London, J. Murray, 1842.
viii, 351 p. illus. diagrs. 16cm.
[Family library. Murray ed. v. 1]

1. Scientific recreations. I. Title. II. Title: Natural magic.

8
NIC

Lettre en forme de dissertation.

WITCHCRAFT
BF
1555
R47

Rhodes, de.
 Lettre en forme de dissertation de Mʳ. de Rhodes escuyer docteur en medecine, aggregé au college des medecins de Lyon. A monsievr Destaing comte de Lyon; au sujet de la prétenduë possession de Marie Volet de la paroisse de Pouliat en Bresse, dans laquelle il est traité des causes naturelles de ses accidens, & de sa guérison. Lyon, Chez Thomas Amaulry, 1691.
4 p. l., 75 p. 18cm.

8   Continued on next card)

Lettre en forme de dissertation.

WITCHCRAFT
BF
1555
R47

Rhodes, de. Lettre en forme de dissertation ... 1691. (Card 2)

Imperfect copy: p. 1-2 (second t. p.?) wanting.
With this is bound Sentimens d'Eudoxe et d'Aristée, sur le dialogue satirique de Mystagogue et de Neophile. 1691.

1. Demoniac possession. 2. Volet, Marie, fl. 1690. I. Title. II. Title: La prétenduë possession de Marie Volet.

8

Lettres ... à quelques-uns de ses amis.

WITCHCRAFT
BF
1565
S13

Saint André, François de.
 Lettres de Mʳ· de Sᵗ· André, conseiller-medecin ordinaire du roy; à quelques-uns de ses amis, au sujet de la magie, des maleficies et des sorciers ... Paris, R. M. Despilly, 1725.
4 p. l., 446, [2] p. 16½ᶜᵐ·
One of 4 Paris editions of this year; but listed first, in BN and Yves-Plessis.
Commentary in MS by G. L. Burr on flyleaf.
1. Witchcraft. 2. Magic. I. Title: Lettres ... à quelques-uns de ses amis.

8   11-15975

Library of Congress   BF1602.S2

Lettres de Mr. de St. André, ... à quelques-uns de ses amis.

WITCHCRAFT
BF
1565
S13

Saint André, François de.
 Lettres de Mʳ· de Sᵗ· André, conseiller-medecin ordinaire du roy; à quelques-uns de ses amis, au sujet de la magie, des maleficies et des sorciers ... Paris, R. M. Despilly, 1725.
4 p. l., 446, [2] p. 16½ᶜᵐ·
One of 4 Paris editions of this year; but listed first, in BN and Yves-Plessis.
Commentary in MS by G. L. Burr on flyleaf.
1. Witchcraft. 2. Magic. I. Title: Lettres ... à quelques-uns de ses amis.

8   11-15975

Library of Congress   BF1602.S2

Lettres philosophiques sur la magie.

Witchcraft
BF
1602
F44
1803

[Fiard, Jean Baptiste] 1736-1818.
 Lettres philosophiques sur la magie. Ed. corr. et augm. Paris, Grégoire, 1803.
130 p. 22cm.

First ed., Paris, 1791, had title: Lettres magiques, ou, Lettres sur le diable.
With this is bound his La France trompée par les magiciens ... Paris, 1803.

1. Magic. I. Title. II. Fiard, Jean Baptiste, 1736-1818. Lettres magique, ou, Lettres sur le diable.

Der letzte Hexenprocess.

WITCHCRAFT
BF
1584
897
Z7
1782

Osenbrüggen, Eduard, 1809-1879.
 Der letzte Hexenprocess. [Leipzig, 1867]
[513]-529 p. 24cm.

Extracted from Deutsches Museum, Nr. 17, Apr. 25, 1867.

1. Trials (Witchcraft)--Glarus (Canton) 2. Trials (Witchcraft)--Switzerland. 3. Göldi, Anna. 4. Tschudi, Anna Maria.

8
NIC

Die letzten Hexen Osnabrücks und ihr Richter.

WITCHCRAFT
BF
1583
L82

Lodtmann, Friedrich.
 Die letzten Hexen Osnabrücks und ihr Richter. Osnabrück, Im Selbstverlage des Vereins, 1875.
[97]-200 p. 23cm.

Detached from Mittheilungen des Historischen Vereins zu Osnabrück, v.10, 1875.

1. Witchcraft--Osnabrück. 2. Trials (Witchcraft)--Osnabrück.

8
NIC

WITCHCRAFT
BF
1555
L65

[Leu, Josef Burkard] 1808-1865.
 Die Teufels-Beschwörung in Stans; oder, Gutachten über die Broschüre: Ertheidigung der ehrw. Klosterfrau Maria Augusta Delphina im Frauenkloster zu Stans den 28. März 1848 durch P. Anizet Regli... Luzer X. Meyer, 1848.
15 p. 20cm.

1. Demoniac possession. 2. Devil. 3. Exorcism. 4. Delphina, Maria Augusta, fl.1848. 5. Regli, Anizet, fl. 1848. 6. Ertheidigung der ehrw. Klosterfrau Maria Augusta Delphina. 7. Title.

8
NIC

Witchcraft
GR
830
W4
L65

Leubuscher, Rudolph.
 Ueber die Wehrwölfe [sic] und Thierverwandlungen im Mittelalter. Ein Beitrag zur Geschichte der Psychologie. Berlin, G. Reimer, 1850.
65, [2] p. 24cm.

1. Werwolves. 2. Psychology, Pathological. I. Title.

8

BF
1583
L65
1972

Leutenbauer, Siegfried.
 Hexerei- und Zaubereidelikt in der Literatur von 1450 bis 1550: mit Hinweisen auf d. Praxis im Herzogtum Bayern/ Siegfried Leutenbauer. -- Berlin: Schweitzer, 1972.
xxv, 178 p.; 23cm. (Münchener Universitätsschriften. Juristische Fakultät. Abhandlungen zur rechtswissenschaftlichen Grundlagenforschung; Bd. 3)
A revision of the author's thesis, Munich.
Bibliography: p. xiv-xxv.
1. Witchcraft--Bavaria--History. 2. Witchcraft--Germany--History. I. Title II. Series

NIC   JAN 16, '74   COOxc   72-332

CATALOGUE OF THE CORNELL WITCHCRAFT COLLECTION

Witchcraft

Het Leven, de leer en lotgevallen van Balthazar Bekker beschouwd in twee redevoeringen. [Amsterdam] 1804.
3 pts. in 1. 23 x 14cm.

Detached from Vaderlandsche letteroefeningen. Mengelwerk, tot fraaije letteren, konsten en weetenschappen, betrekkelyk. Nos. 2-4, 1804, Amsterdam, p. [49]-66, [97]-112, [145]-158.

(Continued on next card)

Witchcraft

Het Leven, de leer en lotgevallen van Balthazar Bekker ... 1804. (Card 2)

With this is bound Arend, Johannes Pieter, 1796-1855. Verhandeling, over Balthasar Bekker. [Amsterdam] 1829.
I. Bekker, Balthasar, 1634-1698--Biog.
I. Vaderlandsche letteroefeningen. Mengelwerk. Nos. 2-4. 1804.

Lévi, Eliphas, pseud.

see

Constant, Alphonse Louis, 1810-1875.

Levin, David, 1924-
What happened in Salem? Documents pertaining to the 17th century witchcraft trials. Pref. by Theodore Morrison. [New York] Twayne Publishers, 1952.

Levin, David, 1924- ed.
What happened in Salem? Documents pertaining to the seventeenth-century witchcraft trials. Young Goodman Brown [by] Nathaniel Hawthorne [and] A mirror for witches [by] Esther Forbes. 2d ed. New York, Harcourt, Brace [1960]
238 p. 24cm. (Harbrace sourcebooks)
"The introduction and parts I and II ... were first published at Harvard in the sixth edition, 1950, of the Handbook for English A."
Includes bibliography.

1. Witchcraft--Salem, Mass. 2. Trials (Witchcraft)--Salem, Mass. I. Title.

WITCHCRAFT

Levin, Herman, 1862-
Forna tiders mörker och vidskepelse.

(In: Läsning för svenska folket. Stockholm. 20cm. 1909. p. 43-67, 92-115, 210-226)

1. Witchcraft--Sweden. 2. Witchcraft--Scandinavia. 3. Trials (Witchcraft)--Sweden. 4. Bure, Johan, 1568-1652. 5. Magnus, Olaus, abp. of Uppsala, 1490-1558. I. Läsning för svenska folket. II. Title.

Rare PQ 6437 T7A4 1618

Lewkenor, Sir Lewis, tr.
Torquemada, Antonio de, fl. 1553-1570. The Spanish Mandevile of myracles. Or The garden of curious flowers. Wherein are handled sundry points of humanity, philosophy, diuinity, and geography, beautified with many strange and pleasant histories: first written in Spanish by Anthonio de Torquemada, and translated out of that tongue into English. It is diuided into sixe treatises, composed in the manner of a dialogue ... London, Imprinted by Bernard Alsop, by the assigne of Richard Hawkins, 1618.
(Continued on next card)

Rare PQ 6437 T7A4 1618

Lewkenor, Sir Lewis, tr.
Torquemada, Antonio de, fl. 1553-1570. The Spanish Mandevile of myracles ... 1618. (Card 2)

[6], 325, [3] p. 20cm.

Translated by Lewis Lewkenor although the translation is usually attributed to Ferdinand Walker who published it.
Translation of Jardin de flores curiosas.
I. Lewkenor, Sir Lewis, tr. II. Walker, Ferdinand, fl. 1600, supposed tr. III. His Jardin de flores curiosas--English. IV. Title. V. Title: The garden of curious flowers.

Witchcraft BF 1410 B42 Z76 1692

Leydekker, Melchior, 1642-1721.
Historische en theologische Redeneringe, over het onlangs uitgegeve Boek van ... Balthasar Bekker, strekkende tot bevestinge der Waarheit en Authoriteit van de H. Schriftuur. Uit het Latijn overgebragt, engeschikt na het begrip van den Nederduitschen Leser. Waar achter gevoegt is een Brief van de Hr. D'Aillon, wegens sijn gevoelen van de Eenheit des Duyvels, geschreven uit London, den 16 Decemb.

NIC (Continued on next card)

Witchcraft BF 1410 B42 Z76 1692

Leydekker, Melchior, 1642-1721. Historische en theologische Redeneringe ... (Card 2)

1691. Utregt, By de Weduwe van W. Clerck, 1692.
64, 8 p. 20cm.

Van der Linde 127.

NIC (Continued on next card)

Witchcraft BF 1410 B42 Z76 1692

Leydekker, Melchior, 1642-1721. Historische en theologische Redeneringe ... 1692. (Card 3)

1. Bekker, Balthasar, 1634-1698. De betoverde Weereld. I. Daillon, Benjamin de. Brief ... over sijn gevoelen van de Eenheit des Duyvels. II. Title.

NIC

Witchcraft BF 1410 B42 Z69 no.27, 28

Leydekker, Melchior, 1642-1721.
Historische en theologische Redeneringe, over het onlangs uitgegeve Boek van ... Balthasar Bekker, strekkende tot bevestinge der Waarheit en Authoriteit van de H. Schriftuur. Uit het Latijn overgebragt, engeschikt na het begrip van den Nederduitschen Leser. Waar achter gevoegt is een Brief van de Hr. D'Aillon, wegens sijn gevoelen van de Eenheit des Duyvels, geschreven uit London, den 16 Decemb.

NIC (Continued on next card)

Witchcraft BF 1410 B42 Z69 no.27, 28

Leydekker, Melchior, 1642-1721. Historische en theologische Redeneringe ... (Card 2)

1691. Utregt, By de Weduwe van W. Clerck, 1692.
64, 8 p. 21cm.

Van der Linde 127, 75.
No. 28 has half-title only.
No. 27, 28 in a Collection of tracts against Balthasar Bekker and his Betoverde weereld.

NIC (Continued on next card)

Witchcraft BF 1410 B42 Z69 no.27,28

Leydekker, Melchior, 1642-1721. Historische en theologische Redeneringe ... 1692. (Card 3)

1. Bekker, Balthasar, 1634-1698. De betoverde Weereld. I. Daillon, Benjamin de. Brief ... over sijn gevoelen van de Eenheit des Duyvels.

NIC

Witchcraft BF 1410 B42 Z69 no.9

Leydekker, Melchior, 1642-1721. Historische en theologische redeneringe.
[Hooght, Everard van der] d. 1716. Sesde briev van הנבה Φιλαλήθης Haggebher Philaleethees, geschreeven aan zynen vriend N. N. vervattende: I. Een afwysing van vyfderley gewaande voorspraaken van D. Bekker. Ende II. een verhandeling van de De Daimonia, na hare beteekenisse voor, in, ende na de tyden Christi. Volgens het welke uyt het Hebreeusch Griekich en Syrisch klaar te sien is, dat De Daimonia zedert Christi tyden niet anders zyn, dan de Duyvelen. Amsterdam,

NIC (Continued on next card)

Witchcraft BF 1410 B42 Z69 no.9

Leydekker, Melchior, 1642-1721. Historische en theologische redeneringe.
[Hooght, Everard van der] d. 1716. Sesde briev van ... Haggebher Philaleethees ... (Card 2)

G. Borstius, 1691.
135-176 p. 21cm.

Signatures: 4°: Π1, A-E4, F1.
Black letter.
The friend N.N. may be Jacobus Schuts.
Van der Linde 103.
No. 9 in a Collection of tracts against Balthasar Bekker and his betoverde weereld.

NIC (Continued on next card)

Witchcraft BF 1410 B42 Z86 no.6

Leydekker, Melchior, 1642-1721. Historische en theologische redeneringe.
Missive van M. D. E. P. aan een vrind, over de zaak van Do. B: Bekker, en het boek van de Heer Professor M. Leydekker. Rotterdam, By J. Gysen, 1692.
8 p. 1. title vignette, illus. initial. 19 x 15cm.
4°: A-B.
Incomplete: second gathering wanting.
Van der Linde 129.
No. 6 in vol. lettered Tractaten voor en tegen B. Bekker.

(Continued on next card)

RARE HV 8593 D611 no.12

Leyser, Augustin, Reichsfreiherr von, 1683-1752, praeses.
De officio iudicis circa tormenta, praeside Augustino a Leyser...disputabit Georgius Guilielm..Büttnerus. Vitembergae, Typis Schlomachianis [1740]
28 p. 21cm.

Diss.--Wittenberg (G. W. Büttner, respondent)
No. 12 in a vol. lettered: Dissertationes de tortura, 1697-1770.
1. Torture. 2. Criminal procedure.
I. Büttner, Georg Wilhelm, respondent. II. Title.

NIC

CATALOGUE OF THE CORNELL WITCHCRAFT COLLECTION

WITCHCRAFT
K
L6795
1733
v.9

Leyser, Augustin, Reichsfreiherr von, 1683-1752.
　　Meditationes ad pandectas quibus praecipua juris capita ex antiquitate explicantur, cum juribus recentioribus conferuntur atque variis celebrium collegiorum responsis et rebus judicatis illustrantur. vol. IX. Editio secunda. Lipsiae et Guelpherbyti, Apud Joh. Christoph. Meisnerum, 1741.
　　962 p. 21cm.

8
NIC
"Specimen DCVIII. ad lib. XLVIII
(Continued on next card)

WITCHCRAFT
K
L6795
1733
v.9

Leyser, Augustin, Reichsfreiherr von, 1683-1752. Meditationes ad pandectas quibus praecipua juris capita...explicantur... vol. IX...1741. (Card 2)

tit. VIII De crimine magiae publice defensum a Frider. Christophoro Pfotenhauer... MDCCXXXVII.": p. 629-654. [Leyser probably acted as praeses]
　　1. Roman law   2.Civil law--Germany.
　　3. Criminal law--Germany. 4. Witchcraft--Germany. 5.　　　Trials (Witchcraft)--Germany. 2.　　Pfotenhauer, Friedrich Christoph.　　II. Title.

WITCHCRAFT
BF
1584
I8
D17

Leyva, Marianna de, known as Signora di Monza, 1575-1650.
　Dandolo, Tullio, conte, 1801-1870.
　　La signora di Monzi e le streghe del Tirolo, processi famosi del secolo decimosettimo per la prima volta cavati dalle filze originali. Milano, E. Besozzi, 1855.
　　259 p. port., facsims. 23cm.
　　1. Witchcraft--Tyrol. 2. Leyva, Marianna de, known as Signora di Monza, 1575-1650. 3. Manzoni, Alessandro, 1785-1873. I promessi sposi. I. Title.

8

WITCHCRAFT
BF
1555
L68
1963a

Lhermitte, Jacques Jean, 1877-
　　Diabolical possession, true and false. [This translation was made by P. J. Hepburne-Scott.] London, Burns & Oates [1963]
　　127 p. 20cm. (Faith and fact books, 57)

Translation of Vrais et faux possédés.
　　I. Title. II. His Vrais et faux possédés --English.

BF
1555
L68

Lhermitte, Jacques Jean, 1877-
　　Vrais et faux possédés. Paris, A. Fayard [1956]
　　170 p. 20 cm. (Bibliothèque Ecclesia, 19)

1. Demoniac possession.　I. Title.

BF1555.L55　　　　　　　56-36569 †
Library of Congress

WITCHCRAFT
BF
1555
L68
1963a

Lhermitte, Jacques Jean, 1877-
　Vrais et faux possédés--English.
　　Lhermitte, Jacques Jean, 1877-
　　Diabolical possession, true and false. [This translation was made by P. J. Hepburne-Scott.] London, Burns & Oates [1963]
　　127 p. 20cm. (Faith and fact books, 57)

Translation of Vrais et faux possédés.

WITCHCRAFT
BF
1524
P59

Libavius, Andreas, d. 1616.
　Pico della Mirandola, Giovanni Francesco, 1470-1533.
　　Strix; sive, De ludificatione daemonum dialogi tres. Nunc primum in Germania eruti ex bibliotheca M. Martini Weinrichii, cum ejusdem praefatione...itemque Epistola ad ...Andream Libavium de quaestione: Utrum in non maritatis & castis mola possit gigni? Et post mortem ejus editi studio & opera Caroli Weinrichii. Argentorati, Venundantur apud Paulum Ledertz, 1612.
　　160+ p. 18cm.

8
NIC
(Continued on next card)

WITCHCRAFT
BF
1524
P59

Libavius, Andreas, d. 1616.
　Pico della Mirandola, Giovanni Francesco, 1470-1533. Strix...1612. (Card 2)

Epistola to Libavius lacking.
　　With this is bound: Sennert, Daniel. De origine et natura animarum in brutis. 1638.
　　1.Magic. 2. Demonology. 3. Witchcraft. I. Weinrich, Martinus, 1548-1609. II. Weinrich, Carolus. III. Libavius, Andreas, d.1616. IV. Title.

Libbie, firm, auctioners, Boston.

Witchcraft
Z
6878
W8
G64

　Goodell, Abner Cheney, 1831-1914.
　　... Catalogue of the private library of the late Abner C. Goodell, Salem, Mass. ... Pt. II, P to Z and witchcraft collection, including Prince Society publications, Prynne's tracts, rare Quaker tracts ... valuable collection of books relating to witchcraft and demonology... Boston, C. F. Libbie, book and art auctioneers, 1918]
　　[93]-174 p. illus., facsims. 25cm.
　　At head of title: Auction sale: ... March 12th, 1918 ...
　　1. Witchcraft --Bibl.--Cat. I. Libbie, firm, actioners, Boston. II. Title.

WITCHCRAFT
BT
780
I85

Libellus aduersus magos, diuinatores, maleficos.
　Isolani, Isidoro, d. 1528.
　　Libellus aduersus magos, diuinatores, maleficos, eosque qui ad religionē subeundam maleficis artib' quempiam cogi posse asseuerant. [Mediolani, Ex officina I. A. Scinzenzeler, 1506]
　　[56] p. 20cm.

　　1. Conversion--Early works to 1800. 2. Occult sciences. I. Title.

8
NIC

Libellus benedictionum et exorcismorum.

Witchcraft
BX
2170
D6
C66
1737

　Martin von Cochem, pater, 1634?-1712.
　　Libellus infirmorum Germanico super additus. In quo breviter & practicè traditur quomodo administranda sint sacramenta infirmis deinde, quomodo piè assistendum sit moribundis ... Pro coronide additae sunt selectiores benedictiones et exorcismi ... authore R. P. Martino Cochemensi ordinis Capucinorum ... Editio novissima auctior & emendatior. Moguntiae & Francofurti, Sumptibus Joann is Mayeri per Joannem

8
(Continued on next card)

Libellus benedictionum et exorcismorum.

Witchcraft
BX
2170
D6
C66
1737

　Martin von Cochem, pater, 1634?-1712. Libellus infirmorum ... 1737. (Card 2)
　　Henricum Haeffner, 1737.
　　116, 488, [4] p. plate. 14cm.
　　Libellus benedictionum et exorcismorum has separate paging and special t. p. with imprint: Moguntiae & Francofurti, 1736.
　　1. Catholic Church--Prayer books and devotions. 2. Exorcism. I. Title. II. His Libellus benedictionum et exorcismorum. III. Title: Libellus benedictionum et exorcismorum.

8

Libellus consolatorius De spectris.

WITCHCRAFT
BF
1445
S327

　Scherertz, Sigismund, 1584-1639.
　　Libellus consolatorius De spectris, hoc est, apparitionibus & illusionibus daemonum. Pio studio conscriptus per Sigismundum Scherertzium ... Wittebergae, Typis Augusti Boreck, Sumptibus Pauli Helvvigij, 1621.
　　[158] p. 16cm.

　　1. Ghosts. 2. Spirits. 3. Demonology. I. Title.   II. Title: De spectris.

8
NIC

Libellus infirmorum Germanico super additus.

Witchcraft
BX
2170
D6
C66
1737

　Martin von Cochem, pater, 1634?-1712.
　　Libellus infirmorum Germanico super additus. In quo breviter & practicè traditur quomodo administranda sint sacramenta infirmis deinde, quomodo piè assistendum sit moribundis ... Pro coronide additae sunt selectiores benedictiones et exorcismi ... authore R. P. Martino Cochemensi ordinis Capucinorum ... Editio novissima auctior & emendatior. Moguntiae & Francofurti, Sumptibus Joann is Mayeri per Joannem

8
(Continued on next card)

Libellus infirmorum Germanico super additus.

Witchcraft
BX
2170
D6
C66
1737

　Martin von Cochem, pater, 1634?-1712. Libellus infirmorum ... 1737. (Card 2)
　　Henricum Haeffner, 1737.
　　116, 488, [4] p. plate. 14cm.
　　Libellus benedictionum et exorcismorum has separate paging and special t. p. with imprint: Moguntiae & Francofurti, 1736.
　　1. Catholic Church--Prayer books and devotions. 2. Exorcism. I. Title. II. His Libellus benedictionum et exorcismorum. III. Title: Libellus benedictionum et exorcismorum.

8

Liber apologeticus.

Witchcraft
BF
1520
W64
P8+
1582

　Wier, Johann, 1515-1588.
　　De praestigiis daemonum, & incantationibus ac ueneficiis libri sex, postrema editione sexta aucti & recogniti. Accessit Liber apologeticus, et Pseudomonarchia daemonum. Cum rerum ac uerborum copioso indice. Basileae, Ex Officina Oporiniana, 1583.
　　934 columns, [35] p. illus., port. 26cm.
　　Contents of De praestigiis daemonum are

8
(Continued on next card)

Liber apologeticus.

Witchcraft
BF
1520
W64
P8+
1582

　Wier, Johann, 1515-1588. De praestigiis daemonum ... 1583. (Card 2)
　　same as in 5th ed., 1577. Cf. Allgemeine deutsche Biographie, v. 42, p. 267.
　　Liber apologeticus, and Pseudomonarchia daemonum each with special t. p.
　　Colophon: Basileae, Ex Officina Oporiniana, per Balthasarvm Han, et Hieronymvm Gemvsaeum, Anno Salutis humanae M. D. LXXXIII mense Augusto.

8
(Continued on next card)

Liber apologeticus.

Witchcraft
BF
1520
W64
P8+
1582

　Wier, Johann, 1515-1588. De praestigiis daemonum ... 1583. (Card 3)
　　Bound with his De lamiis liber. Basileae, 1582.
　　Binding: blind stamped pigskin; front covered initialed B P I and dated 1588.
　　1. Demonology. 2. Witchcraft. 3. Magic. 4. Fasting. I. Title. II. His Liber apologeticus. III. His Pseudomonarchia daemonum. IV. Title: Liber apologeticus. V. Title: Pseudomonarchia dae monum.

8

CATALOGUE OF THE CORNELL WITCHCRAFT COLLECTION

Liber de ceremoniis magicis. English.

WITCHCRAFT
BF
410
A3
1655
    Henry Cornelius Agrippa's Fourth book of occult philosophy, and geomancy. Magical elements of Peter de Abano. Astronomical geomancy [by Gerardus Cremonensis]. The nature of spirits [by Georg Pictorius]: and Arbatel of magick. Translated into English by Robert Turner. Philomathées. London, 1655.
    9 p. l., [5]-266 [i.e., 286], [4] p. illus. 19cm.
    Neither Agrippa nor Abano wrote the works

(Continued on next card)

Liber de ceremoniis magicis. English.

WITCHCRAFT
BF
410
A3
1655
    Henry Cornelius Agrippa's Fourth book of occult philosophy, and geomancy ... 1655. (Card 2)
    here ascribed to them; the Heptameron, or Magical elements also was ascribed to Agrippa under the title: Les oeuvres magiques, with Abano as translator (!)
    Translation of a work variously titled Liber de ceremonijs magicis; and his De occulta philosophia, liber quartus.

(Continued on next card)

Liber de ceremoniis magicis. German.

    Heinrich Cornelius Agrippa's von Nettesheim Magische Werke : sammt den geheimnissvollen Schriften des Petrus von Abano, Pictorius von Villingen, Gerhard von Cremona, Abt Tritheim von Spanheim, dem Buche Arbatel, der sogenannten Heil. Geist-Kunst und verschiedenen anderen zum ersten Male vollständig in's Deutsche übersetzt : vollständig in fünf Theilen, mit einer Menge Abbildungen. -- 4. Aufl. -- Berlin : H. Barsdorf, 1921.
    5 v. in 3. : ill. ; 17 cm. -- (Geheime Wissenschaften ; 10-14)

(Continued on next card)

Liber de ceremoniis magicis. Italian. 1970?
    Le cerimonie magiche. Prima traduzione italiana dal testo latino preceduta da una introduzione. Roma, All'insegna della corona dei magi, [1970?]
    78 p. illus. 22cm.
    At head of title: Enrico Cornelio Agrippa.
    1. Occult sciences. I. Agrippa von Nettesheim, Heinrich Cornelius, 1486?-1535, supposed author. II. Title III. Title: De occulta philosophia liber quartus. Italian.

JAN 30, '74   COOxc

Liber octo questionum ad Maximilianum Cesarem.

WITCHCRAFT
    Trithemius, Johannes, 1462-1516.
    Ioannis Tritemii ... Liber octo questionū ad Maximilianum Cesarem. Cum priuilegio Cesaree maiestatis de nō imprimēdo in regno ... [Oppenheym, Impressum impensis Iohānis Hasselbergen de Augia Constātiensis dyocesis, 1515]
    [78] p. 20cm.
    Title vignette with ports. of Maximilian and Trithemius.
    With colophon.

(Continued on next card)

Witchcraft
    Librairie du Merveilleux, Paris.
    Catalogue périodique d'ouvrages anciens et modernes, neufs et d'occasion relatifs á l'étude des phénomènes et des sciences occultes, franc-maçonnerie & sociétés secretes. [no.] -15, -1911? Paris. nos. 24cm.
    No. 15 has title: Catalogue general de liquidation.
    No more published?
    1. Occult Sciences. 2. Secret Societies. I. Title.

The Library of Congress copy of the Malleus maleficarum, 1487.

Witchcraft
BF
1569
A2
I594
    Goff, Frederick Richmond, 1916-
    The Library of Congress copy of the Malleus maleficarum, 1487. Copenhagen, Munksgaard, 1963.
    [137]-141 p. facsim. 25cm.
    "Separatum" from Libri; international library review and IFLA-Communications-FIAB, vol. 13, no. 2, 1963.
    1. Institoris, Henricus, d. 1508. Malleus maleficarum. I. Title.

Libri duo De benedictionibus, et tertius De maledictionibus.

Witchcraft
BV
30
G83
    Gretser, Jacob, 1560-1625.
    Jacobi Gretseri ... Libri dvo De benedictionibvs, et tertivs De maledictionibvs ... Ingolstadii, Ex typographeo Ederiano, apud Elisabetham Angermariam, viduam, Impensis Ioannis Hertsroi, 1615.
    14 p. l., 288, [43] p. 20cm.
    Bound with his De festis Christianorum libri duo. Ingolstadii, 1612.
    1. Benediction. 2. Exorcism. 3. Blessing and cursing. I. Title: De benedictionibus. II. Title: De maledictionibus.

Die Licht- und Schattenseiten der Inquisition.

Witchcraft
BF
1566
F52
    Fischer, E
    Die Licht- und Schattenseiten der Inquisition; nebst einer Geschichte der Hexenprocesse und historischen Rückblicken auf die Geisselgesellschaften. Aus geschichtlichen Quellen geschöpft und parteilos. Wien, A. A. Benedikt [1881]
    310 p. 4 plates. 17cm.
    1. Inquisition. 2. Trials (Witchcraft) I. Title.

Lichtenberg, Jacob Freiherr von.

see

Liechtenberg, Jacob von, baron.

WITCHCRAFT
BF
1566
L71
    Lieberherr, Max von.
    Ueber Hexerei. Ein Vortrag gehalten am 21. Novbr. 1870 in der Aula der Universität zu Rostock. Rostock, Stiller, 1871.
    59 p. 14cm.

NIC   1. Witchcraft. I. Title.

Lieberwirth, Rolf, ed.

B
2605
Z7
T46
v.5
    Thomasius, Christian, 1655-1728.
    Über die Hexenprozesse. Überarb. und hrsg. von Rolf Lieberwirth. Weimar, Böhlau, 1967.
    232 p. 25cm. (Thomasiana, Heft 5)
    Contents.--Dissertatio de crimine magiae. Lateinische und deutsche Ausg.--Dissertatio de origine ac progressu processus inquisitorii sagas. Lateinische und deutsche Ausg.--Auszug aus: Christian Thomasens Erinnerung wegen seiner künfftigen Winterlektionen, so

(Continued on next card)

Lieberwirth, Rolf, ed.

B
2605
Z7
T46
v.5
    Thomasius, Christian, 1655-1728. Über die Hexenprozesse. 1967. (Card 2)
    nach Michaelis dieses 1702. Jahres ihren Anfang nehmen werden.--Verzeichnis der von Thomasius benutzten Literatur. (p. [225]-232)
    1. Trials (Witchcraft) I. Lieberwirth, Rolf, ed. II. Title.

Ein Liebhaber der Wahrheit.

Witchcraft
BF
1565
S83
M17
    [März, Agnellus] 1726-1784.
    Urtheil ohne Vorurtheil über die wirkend- und thätige Hexerey, abgefasset von einem Liebhaber der Wahrheit. [München] 1766.
    64 p. 20cm.
    1. Sterzinger, Ferdinand, 1721-1786. Akademische Rede von dem gemeinen Vorurtheile der ... Hexerey. 2. Witchcraft. I. Ein Liebhaber der Wahrheit. II. Title.

Ein Liebhaber der Wahrheit.

Witchcraft
BF
1565
S83
S835
    [März, Agnellus] 1726-1784.
    Vertheidigung wider die geschwulstige Vertheidigung der betrügenden Zauberkunst und traumenden Hexerey, verfasset von einem Liebhaber der Wahrheit. [München] 1767.
    [4] p.l., 104 p. 23cm.
    1. Sterzinger, Ferdinand, 1721-1786. Betrügende Zauberkunst und träumende Hexerey. I. Ein Liebhaber der Wahrheit. II. Title.

Ein Liebhaber der Wahrheit und Feind der Calumnien.

Witchcraft
BF
1565
T46
E358
    Das Wohl-meritirte und wohlverdiente Ehren=Kleid dem Anonymo und Autori des Gutachten von dem mit Herrn Doct. Thomasio erregten Streit über einige freye Meynungen in einem teutschen Programmate, und von Herrn D. Strykii Disputation de jure Sabbathi, zum Recompens vor die Mühe praesentiret von einem Liebhaber der Wahrheit und Feind der Calumnien. Freystatt, 1703.
    24 p. 18cm.

(Continued on next card)

Ein Liebhaber einer anständigen Freyheit.

MSS
Bd
Witchcraft
BF
G38
    Gespräche von verschiedenem Innhalte unter einer muntern Fastnachtcompagnie, verfasset von einem Liebhaber einer anständigen Freyheit. Gedruckt vor baares Geld, im Jahr, als noch im Märze Fasching war. [München? 1677]
    16 p. 22cm.
    Carnap's manuscript copy.
    Concerns the Sterzinger-März controversy.
    1. Sterzinger, Ferdinand, 1721-1786. 2. Superstition. I. Ein Liebhaber einer anständigen Freyheit.

Liebrecht, Felix, 1812-1890, ed.

ar W
9788
    Gervasius, of Tilbury.
    Otia imperialia. In einer Auswahl neu hrag. und mit Anmerkungen begleitet von Felix Liebrecht. Ein Beitrag zur deutschen Mythologie und Sagenforschung. Hannover, C. Rümpler, 1856.
    xxii, 274 p. 23cm.
    I. Liebrecht, Felix, 1812-1890, ed. II. Title.

CATALOGUE OF THE CORNELL WITCHCRAFT COLLECTION

WITCHCRAFT
BF
1565
H64
1631

Liechtenberg, Jacob von, baron.
   Hildebrand, Wolffgang.
     Goêtia, vel Theurgia, sive Praestigiarum magicarum descriptio, revelatio, resolutio, inquisitio, & executio. Das ist, Wahre vnd eigentliche Entdeckunge, Declaration oder Erklärunge fürnemher Articul der Zauberey. Vnd was von Zauberern, Vnholden, Hexen, deren Händel, Art, Thun ... vnd ihrer Machination ... Etwan durch den wolgebornen Herrn Jacob Freyherrn von Liechtenberg &c. ... erfahren, durch den hochgelahrten Herrn

8
NIC
           (Continued on next card)

WITCHCRAFT
BF
1565
H64
1631

Liechtenberg, Jacob von, baron.
   Hexenbüchlein.
   Hildebrand, Wolffgang. Goêtia, vel Theurgia ... 1631.   (Card 2)

Jacob Weckern M. D. etwas weitleufftiger beschrieben. Nun aber an jetzo mit allem Fleisse revidiret ... durch Wolfgangum Hildebrandum ... Leipzig, In Verlegung Joh. Francken S. Erben vnd Samuel Scheiben Buchh., 1631.
    8 p. l., 342, [17] p. 18cm.
    Title in red and black.

8
           (Continued on next card)

WITCHCRAFT
BF
1603
H64
1704

Liechtenberg, Jacob von, baron.
   Hexenbüchlein.
   Hildebrand, Wolffgang.
     Wahre und eigentliche Entdeckung oder Erklärung der fürnemsten Artickul von der Zauberey was von Zauberern, Vnholden, Hexen, derer Händel, Art, Thun, ... und vielen andern ihren Machinationen ... Durch den wohlgebohrnen Herrn Jacob Frey Herrn von Lichtenberg ... erfahren, und durch den hochgelahrten Herrn Jacob Weckern weitläufftiger beschrieben. Anitzo mit allem Fleiss übersehen und vermehret mit

8
NIC
           (Continued on next card)

WITCHCRAFT
BF
1603
H64
1704

Liechtenberg, Jacob von, baron.
   Hexenbüchlein.
   Hildebrand, Wolffgang. Wahre und eigentliche Entdeckung oder Erklärung der fürnemsten Artickul von der Zauberey ...
[1704?]   (Card 2)

vielen Artzeneyen ..., auch wie eine christliche Obrigkeit wider die Zauberer ... rechtlich verfahren soll, ... auch viele lustige und possierliche Historien von Erscheinungen allerhand Geister ... von neuen in Druck verfertiget durch Wolfgangum Hildebrandum.

8
NIC
           (Continued on next card)

WITCHCRAFT
BF
1603
H64
1704

Liechtenberg, Jacob von, baron.
   Hexenbüchlein.
   Hildebrand, Wolffgang. Wahre und eigentliche Entdeckung oder Erklärung der fürnemsten Artickul von der Zauberey ...
[1704?]   (Card 3)

brandum. [Leipzig? 1704?]
    11 p. l., 342, [18] p. front. 21cm.
    Half title (follows Inhalt aller Capitel) agrees with original title: Goetia, vel Theurgia, sive Praestigiarum magicarum descriptio, and has imprint 1704.

8
NIC
           (Continued on next card)

WITCHCRAFT
BF
1603
H64
1704

Liechtenberg, Jacob von, baron.
   Hexenbüchlein.
   Hildebrand, Wolffgang. Wahre und eigentliche Entdeckung oder Erklärung der fürnemsten Artickul von der Zauberey ...
[1704?]   (Card 4)

    Bound with his Neu-vermehrt, vortrefflich ... curieuses Kunst und Wunderbuch. Leipzig, 1704.
    1. Witchcraft. 2. Magic. 3. Devil--Legends. 4. Folk-lore--Germany. I. His Goetia, vel Theurgia. II. Liechtenberg, Jacob von, baron. Hexen-Büchlein. III. Wecker, Johann Jacob, 1528-1586. IV. Title.

8
NIC

Witchcraft
BF
1410
B42
Z56
v.3
no.29

Liefdelooze achterhoudinge.
   Haak, Arent, ed.
     Liefdelooze achterhoudinge van Do. Everhardus van der Hooght predikant tot Nieuwendam. Gebleeken in zijn schriftelyke onderhandelinge met Arent Haak. Amsterdam, By D. van den Dalen, boekverkooper, 1693.
    32 p. title and end page vignettes, illus. initial. 20 x 15cm.
    4°: A-D⁴.
    Introduction by Haak: p. 3-9. The rest consists of letters exchanged by van der Hooght and Haak (in black letter),

8
           (Continued on next card)

Witchcraft
BF
1410
B42
Z56
v.3
no.29

Liefdelooze achterhoudinge.
   Haak, Arent, ed. Liefdelooze achterhoudinge van Do. Everhardus van der Hooght ... 1693.   (Card 2)

on Balthasar Bekker's De betoverde weereld.
Van der Linde 118.
No. 29 in vol. lettered Bekker III.

    1. Bekker, Balthasar, 1634-1698. De betoverde weereld. I. Hooght, Everard van der, d. 1716. II. Title.

8

Witchcraft
BX
9479
B42
B11
no.13

Een liefhebber der waarheyt.
   Beknopte aanmerkingen over de korte opening van de plaatsen van 2 Pet. 2: 4 en Jud. v. 6. Voorgesteld aan R. A. predikant tot B. Als mede over de brief aan de selve. Waar in de bewysen over de gemelden plaatsen naarstiglyk ondersogt, en wederlegt werden. Door een liefhebber der waarheyt. Amsterdam, Gedrukt voor den autheur, 1697.
    4 p. l., 19 p. [p. 20 blank] title and other vignettes, illus. initials. 20 x 15cm.

8
           (Continued on next card)

Witchcraft
BX
9479
B42
B11
no.13

Een liefhebber der waarheyt.
   Beknopte aanmerkingen over de korte opening van de plaatsen van 2 Pet. 2: 4 en Jud. v. 6. 1697.   (Card 2)

    4°: A-C⁴, D².
    Black letter (except introduction)
    Supports Ruardus Andala in his controversy with Balthasar Bekker over Biblical spirits.
    No. 13 in vol. lettered B. Bekkers sterfbed en andere tractaten.
    1. Devil. 2. Bible. N. T. 2 Peter, II, 4--Criticism, interpretation, etc.

8
           (Continued on next card)

Witchcraft
BX
9479
B42
B11
no.16

Een liefhebber der waarheyt.
   Kuyk, J van.
     Disputatie over den duyvel, of dezelve is een geschaapen geest, buyten de zielen der menschen, dewelke afgevallen en boos geworden is, ofte niet? Voorgevallen tusschen J. van Kuyk, krankbesoeker, ter eenre, en H. Bouman, ter andere zyde ... op den 26 December, 1694. Door een liefhebber der waarheyt, soo daar tegenwoordig was, opgestelt. Hier is noch by gevoegt een brief, aan geseyde J. van Kuyk ... den 27 January, 1693.

8
           (Continued on next card)

Witchcraft
BX
9479
B42
B11
no.16

Een liefhebber der waarheyt.
   Kuyk, J van. Disputatie over den duyvel ... 1695.   (Card 2)

aldaar bestelt; met redenen, waarom deselve nu eerst door den druk gemeen gemaakt wort. Amsterdam, By E. Webber, boekverkooper, 1695.
    16 p. title and end page vignettes. 20 x 15cm.
    4°: A-B⁴.
    Black letter (except introduction)
    Letter and Na-reeden, p. 10-16,

8
           (Continued on next card)

Witchcraft
BX
9479
B42
B11
no.16

Een liefhebber der waarheyt.
   Kuyk, J van. Disputatie over den duyvel ... 1695.   (Card 3)

signed: Z. W. [i. e., Zacharias Webbers]
Van der Linde 79.
No. 16 in vol. lettered B. Bekkers sterfbed en andere tractaten.
    1. Devil. I. Bouman, Herman. II. Webbers, Zacharias. III. Een liefhebber der waarheyt. IV. Title.

8

Witchcraft
BF
1410
B42
Z56
v.2
no.8

Een liefhebber van vreede en waarheid.
   Copy van een brief geschreeve aan een heer, woonende tusschen Rotterdam en Dort. Raakende het gepasseerde in de saak van Dr. B. Bekker; door een liefhebber van vreede en waarheid. Dord, Gedrukt by G. Abramsz, 1692.
    18 p. [p. 19-20 blank] title vignette. 19 x 15cm.
    4°: A-B⁴, C².
    Signed: A. T.
    Van der Linde 48; 64.
    No. 8 in vol. lettered Bekker II.

8
           (Continued on next card)

WITCHCRAFT
DD
491
R4
A67
v.1

Liel, Anselm Franz Joseph.
   Merkwürdige Hexenprozesse...
   (In: Archiv für rheinische Geschichte. Coblenz. 23cm. v.1 (1833) p.47-80)

8
NIC
    1. Trials (Witchcraft)--Treves. 2. Witchcraft--Treves. I. Title.

WITCHCRAFT
DD
491
R4
A67
v.1

Liel, Anselm Franz Joseph.
   Die Verfolgung der Zauberer und Hexen in dem Kurfürstenthume Trier. Ein Beitrag zur vaterländischen Geschichte.
   (In: Archiv für rheinische Geschichte. Coblenz. 23cm. v.1 (1833) p.17-46)

8
NIC
    1. Witchcraft--Treves. 2. Trials (Witchcraft)--Treves. I. Title.

Witchcraft
BF
1563
T86

   The life and death of Lewis Gaufredy: a priest of the Church of the Accoules in Marseilles in France, (who ... committed many most abhominable sorceries, but chiefly vpō two very faire young gentle-women ... hee ... burnt aliue ... the last day of April, 1611. Together with the 53 articles of his confession ... Translated ... out of two French copies ... London, Printed by T. C. for R. Redmer, 1612.

           (Continued on next card)

Witchcraft
BF
1563
T86

   The life and death of Lewis Gaufredy ... 1612.   (Card 2)

    [34] p. 19cm.
    No. 11 in vol. lettered: Tracts of witches.

    1. Witchcraft. 2. Gaufridi, Louis, 1572-1611.

350

CATALOGUE OF THE CORNELL WITCHCRAFT COLLECTION

Witchcraft The life and death of Mother Shipton.
  [Head, Richard] 1637?-1686?
BF   The life and death of Mother Shipton.
1515   Being not only a true account of her strange
H5   birth, the most important passages of her life,
1687   but also all her prophesies ... until this
        present year 1667. Containing the most im-
        portant passages of state during the reigns
        of these kings and queens of England following:
        ... London, W. Harris, 1687.
          30 p. front. 23cm.

          1. Shipton, Ursula. 2. Prophecies. I.
        Title.

        The life of Henry Cornelius Agrippa von
          Nettesheim.
Witchcraft Morley, Henry, 1822-1894.
B   The life of Henry Cornelius Agrippa von
781   Nettesheim, doctor and knight, commonly known
A34   as a magician. London, Chapman and Hall,
M86   1856.
          2 v. 21cm.

          Title vignettes.
          At head of title: Cornelius Agrippa.

          1. Agrippa von Nettesheim, Heinrich
        Cornelius, 1486?-1535. I. Title.

        The life of the Count Cagliostro.
Witchcraft [Lucia] pseud.
          The life of the Count Cagliostro ... dedicat-
        ed to Madame la Comtesse de Cagliostro. 2d ed.
        London, Printed for the author, and sold by
        T. Hookham, 1787.
          viii, xxxii, 127 p. 22cm.

          Dedication signed: Lucia.

          Liguori, Alfonso Maria de', Saint,
            1696-1787.
WITCHCRAFT Schick, J   G
BX   Leben des heiligen Alphons Maria von
4700   Liguori, Stifter des Redemptoristenordens,
L6   und des Pater Friedrich Spee, Priesters
S33   der Gesellschaft Jesu, 2. Aufl. Regens-
1877   burg, G. J. Manz, 1877.
            164 p. port. 19cm. (Leben ausgezeich-
          neter Katholiken der drei letzten Jahrhun-
          derte. 7. Bd. 2. Aufl.)
            Leben des Pater Friedrich Spee, p. [129]-
          146, has special t. p.

                    (Continued on next card)

          Liguori, Alfonso Maria de', Saint,
            1696-1787.
WITCHCRAFT Schick, J   G   Leben des heili-
BX   gen Alphons Maria von Liguori ... 1877.
4700   (Card 2)
L6   Anhang, p. [147]-162, consists of selec-
S33   tions from Spee's Trutz-Nachtigall.
1877
            1. Liguori, Alfonso Maria de', Saint,
          1696-1787. 2. Spee, Friedrich von, 1591-
          1635. I. Spee, Friedrich von, 1591-1635.
          Trutz-Nachtigall. Selections. II. Title.

NIC

WITCHCRAFT Liisberg, Bering, 1854-1929.
BF   Vesten for sø og østen for hav; trolddom
1584   i København og i Edinburgh 1590, et bidrag
L4   til hekseprocessernes historie. Køben-
L72   havn, A. Christiansen, 1909.
            143 p. 20cm.

            1. Witchcraft--Copenhagen. 2. Witchcraft
          --Edinburgh. 3. Trials (Witchcraft)--
          Copenhagen.   4. Trials (Witchcraft)--
          Edinburgh.   I. Title.

NIC

WITCHCRAFT Lilienthal, J   A   von.
BF   Die Hexenprocesse der beiden Städte
1583   Braunsberg, nach den Criminalacten des
L72   Braunsberger Archivs. Königsberg, T.
          Theile, 1861.
            161 p. 23cm.

          8   1. Witchcraft--Braunsberg, Ger. 2.Trials
NIC   (Witchcraft) --Braunsberg, Ger.
              I. Title.

Rare   Limborch, Philippus van, 1633-1712.
BX   Historia inquisitionis. Cui subjungitur
1710   Liber sententiarum inquisitionis Tholosanae
L73++   ab anno Christi MCCCVII ad annum MCCCXXIII.
        Amstelodami, Apud Henricum Wetstenium, 1692.
          2 pts. in 1 v. plates. 33cm.

          Engraved title vignette.

          1. Inquisition--Hist. 2. Inquisition--
        Toulouse. I. Title.

Rare   Limborch, Philippus van, 1663-1712.
BX   The history of the Inquisition. Trans-
1710   lated into English by Samuel Chandler. To
L73+   which is prefixed, a large introduction con-
1731   cerning the rise and progress of persecu-
        tion and the real and pretended causes of it.
        London, Sold by J. Gray, 1731.
          2 v. in 1. 26cm.

          With autograph: John Kenrick.

          1. Inquisition--Spain. I. Title.

Witchcraft Linde, Antonius van der, 1833-1897.
Z   Balthasar Bekker. Bibliografie door Dr. A.
8086   van der Linde ... 's Gravenhage, M. Nijhoff,
.8   1869.
L74+   2 p. l., 57 p. 26cm.

          1. Bekker, Balthasar, 1634-1698--Bibl.
        I. Title.

          Lindemann, Ortia, fl. 1612.
Witchcraft Grote, Otto, Freiherr.
BF   Ortia Lindemann; oder, Der Zauberei-
1583   process zu Egeln 1612; mit Benutzung ge-
27   schichtlicher Quellen bearb. Osterwieck a.H.,
1612   A. W. Zickfeldt, 1877.
          62 p. 23cm.

          1. Witchcraft. 2. Trials (Witchcraft)
        --Germany. 3. Lindemann, Ortia, fl. 1612.
        I. Title.

WITCHCRAFT Linderholm, Emanuel, 1872-1937.
BF   De stora häxprocesserna i Sverige. Bi-
1584   drag till svensk kultur- och kyrkohistoria.
S9   1. delen: Inledning. Bohuslän. Uppsala,
L74   J. A. Lindblad [1918]
          xii, 272 p. 21cm.

          No more published.

        8   1. Trials (Witchcraft)--Sweden. 2.Witch-
NIC   craft--Sweden. I. Title.

WITCHCRAFT Lindinger, Johann Simon.
R   De Ebraeorum veterum arte medica, de dae-
135   mone, et daemoniacis. Servestae et Leu-
L74   coreae, Apud Sam. Godofr. Zimmermannum,
        1774.
          188 p. 20cm.

        8   1. Medicine, Ancient. 2. Demonology.
NIC   3. Demoniac possession. I. Title.

WITCHCRAFT Link, Johann Georg, respondent.
BT   Ohm, Gottfried, praeses.
960   De angelis malis ex lum. nat. demonstra-
038   bilibus, quam...disputatione publica...
        examini submittet praeses M. Godofredus
        Ohm respondente Joh. Georg. Linkio.
        Lipsiae, Literis Brandenburgerianis [1704]
          [28] p. 19cm.

        8   1. Devil. 2. Demonology. I. Link, Jo-
NIC   hann Georg, respondent.

Undergraduate
BF   Linton, Elizabeth (Lynn) 1822-1898,
1581   comp.
L76   Witch stories. New York, Barnes &
1861a   Noble Books [1972, i.e. 1973]
          iv, 428 p. 23 cm.
          Reprint of the 1861 ed. published by
        Champman and Hall, London.

          1. Witchcraft--Great Britain.
        I. Title

NIC APR 26,'74   COOxc   73-155608

Witchcraft
BF   Linton, Elizabeth (Lynn) 1822-1898, comp.
1581   Witch stories. A new ed. London,
L76   Chatto & Windus, 1883.
1883   320 p. 17cm.

          Contents.--Preface.--The witches of
        Scotland.--The witches of England.

          1. Witchcraft. I. Title.

          Lisbet Nypen; en hekseproces fra
            guldalen.
WITCHCRAFT Øverland, Ole Andreas, 1855-1911.
BF   Lisbet Nypen; en hekseproces fra gulda-
1584   len. Kristiania og København, A. Cammer-
N6   meyer [1896]
Z7   36 p. 19cm. (Historiske fortaellinger,
1670   nr.22)

          1. Nypen, Lisbet. 2. Witchcraft--Trond-
        8   heim. 3. Trials (Witchcraft)--
        NIC Trondheim. I. Title.

          Liseux, Isidore, 1835- , tr.
WITCHCRAFT Sinistrari, Luigi Maria, 1622-1701.
BF   De la démonialité et des animaux incubes
1556   et succubes ... par le R. P. Louis Marie
S61   Sinistrari d'Ameno ... Publié d'après le
1876   manuscrit original découvert à Londres en
        1872 et traduit du Latin par Isidore Li-
        seux. 2. éd. Paris, I. Liseux, 1876.
          xix, 267 p. 15cm.
          Title in red and black.
          Latin and French.
            Demonology. I. Liseux, Isidore,
        8   1835- , tr. II. His De daemoniali-
        NIC tate et incub is et succubis. III. His
            De daemoniali tate et incubis et succu-
            bis. French.   IV. Title.

CATALOGUE OF THE CORNELL WITCHCRAFT COLLECTION

Liseux, Isidore, 1835-   , tr.

Witchcraft
BF
1556
S61
1879

Sinistrari, Luigi Maria, 1622-1701.
Demoniality; or Incubi and succubi. A treatise wherein is shown that there are in existence on earth rational creatures besides man ... Published from the original Latin manuscript discovered in London in the year 1872, and translated into French by Isidore Liseux. Now first translated into English. With the Latin text. Paris, I. Liseux, 1879.
xvi, 251, [1] p. 17cm.

8   (Continued on next card)

Ein Lissaer Hexenprozess von 1740.

Pamphlet
B
124

Schottmüller, H
Ein Lissaer Hexenprozess von 1740. [Posen] 1902.
[65]-69 p. 23cm.

Detached from Historische Monatsblätter für die Provinz Posen, Jahrg. 3, Mai 1902, Nr. 5.

1. Witchcraft--Poland--Leszno. I. Title.

List of books on theosophy, archaeology, astrology, mesmerism ...

Witchcraft
Z
6880
Z9C35
no.6

Redway, George, London.
List of books on theosophy, archaeology, astrology, mesmerism, philology, spiritualism, freemasonry, alchemy, platonism, thought-reading, magic, the Rosicrucians, witchcraft, etc. by Fludd, Behmen, Paracelsus, Agrippa, Nostradamus, Van Helmont, & others. [London, 1885]
16 p. 23cm.

At head of title: No. 11, 1885.
No. 6 in vol. lettered: Catalogues of books on magic and witchcraft.

List of works in the New York public library relating to witchcraft.

Witchcraft
Z
6878
W8
N531+
1908

New York. Public library.
List of works in the New York public library relating to witchcraft in the United States. Comp. by George F. Black, of the Lenox staff. [New York, 1908]
18 p. 26cm.

Caption title.
"Reprinted from the Bulletin, November, 1908."
At end: 40 titles of works not in the library.

1. Witchcraft--U. S.--Bibl. I. Black, George Fraser, 1866- II. Title.

CA 9--2852 Unrev'd
Library of Congress   Z6878.W8N6

List of works relating to witchcraft in Europe.

Witchcraft
Z
6878
W8
N53+
1911

New York. Public library.
... List of works relating to witchcraft in Europe. New York, 1911.
31 p. 26½cm.

"Reprinted at the New York public library from the Bulletin, December, 1911."
Comp. by George F. Black.

The literature of occultism and archaeology.

Witchcraft
Z
6880
Z9C35
no.5

Redway, George, London.
The literature of occultism and archaeology. Being a Catalogue of books on sale relating to ancient worships, astrology, alchemy ...
[London, 1885]
48 p. 23cm.

At head of title: Part 1. December 1885.
No. 5 in vol. lettered: Catalogues of books on magic and witchcraft.

Witchcraft
Z
6879
W8
B96
1890

The literature of witchcraft.
Burr, George Lincoln, 1857-1938.
The literature of witchcraft. New York, Putnam, 1890.
37-66 p. 23cm.

Double paging.
"Reprinted from the Papers of the American Historical Association," vol. IV, p. 237-266.
Annotated by the author.

The literature of witchcraft in New England.

F
61
M427
v.6
no.14

Winsor, Justin, 1831-1897.
The literature of witchcraft in New England. By Justin Winsor. Worcester, Mass., Printed by C. Hamilton, 1896.
25 p. 25cm.

Reprinted, one hundred copies, from the Proceedings of the American Antiquarian Society, October, 1895.

The living librarie.

Rare
AC
14
C18+
1621

Camerarius, Philipp, 1537-1624.
The living librarie; or, Meditations and observations historical, natvral, moral, political, and poetical. Written in Latin by P. Camerarivs. And done into English by Iohn Molle, esquire. London, Printed by Adam Islip, 1621.

I. Molle, John, fl. 1621, tr. II. Molle, H., fl. 1625, tr. III. Baddeley, Richard, fl. 1621, ed. IV. Title.

Le livre d'Albert le Grand.

Witchcraft
BF
1582
Z7
1675

Hautefeuille,   lawyer.
Plaidoyez svr les magiciens et svr les sorciers, tenus en la cour de Liege, le 16. Decembre 1675. Ov on montre clairement qu'il n'y peut avoir de ces sortes de gens. Par les sieurs de Havte Fetille & Santevr advocats. Sur l'imprimé a Liege, Chez Iacqves Persois imprimeur, 1676.
120 p. 14cm.

"Le livre d'Albert le Grand, leqvel traite des merveilles du monde," p. [77]-

4   (Continued on next card)

Le livre d'Albert le Grand.

Witchcraft
BF
1582
Z7
1675

Hautefeuille,   lawyer. Plaidoyez svr les magiciens ... 1676. (Card 2)

120, has special t. p. with imprint: Lyon, Par Iean Hvgvetan, 1616. Text is taken from Les admirables secrets d'Albert le Grand.

1. Witchcraft. 2. Magic. 3. Sillieux, Sulpice, fl. 1675. I. Santeur, lawyer. II. Albertus Magnus, saint, bp. of Ratisbon, 1193?-1280. Spurious and doubtful works. Les admirables secrets d'Albert le Grand. III. Title: Plaidoyez sur les magiciens. IV. Title: Le livre d'Albert le Grand.

8

Livre des ruses, finesses et impostures des esprits malins.

MSS
Bd.
WITCHCRAFT
BF
D97

Du Triez, Robert.
Livre des ruses, finesses et impostures des esprits malins, oeuvre fort utile & delectable par un chacun a cause de la verité des choses estranges contenue en iceluy: Mis en lumiere par Robert du Triez. Cambray, Nicolas Lombart, 1563 [ca. 1900]
92 [i.e. 183], [14] p. illus. 19cm.
Signatures: A-Z⁴, AA-BB².
Carnap's manuscript copy.
"Die Seiten in dieser Abschrift
(Continued on next card)

Livre des ruses, finesses et impostures des esprits malins.

MSS
Bd.
WITCHCRAFT
BF
D97

Du Triez, Robert. Livre des ruses, finesses et impostures ... 1563 [ca. 1900]   (Card 2)

stimmen mit denjenigen der Originaldruckschrift überein."

1. Demonology. 2. Occult sciences. I. Title.

WITCHCRAFT
BF
1412
L78

Le Livre magique, histoire des événements et des personnages surnaturels; contenant des détails sur la démonologie, l'astrologie et la chiromancie...les spectres... les maléfices, les talismans... Ouvrage composé d'après les plus célèbres démonographes et cabalistes: Yles deux Albert, Eteilla, Cagliostro... Paris, Corbet ainé, 1835.
xx, 244 p. illus. 20cm.

8
NIC
1. Occult sciences--Hist. 2. Witchcraft--Hist.

Rare
BX
1735
L79
1818

Llorente, Juan Antonio, 1756-1823.
Histoire critique de l'inquisition d'Espagne, depuis l'époque de son établissement par Ferdinand V, jusqu'au règne de Ferdinand VII; tirée des pièces originales des archives du Conseil de la Suprême et de celles des tribunaux subalternes du Saint-Office. Par D. Jean-Antoine Llorente ... Tr. de l'espagnol sur le manuscrit et sous les yeux de l'auteur, par Alexis Pellier. 2. éd. Paris, Treuttel et Würtz [etc.] 1818.
(Continued on next card)

Rare
BX
1735
L79
1818

Llorente, Juan Antonio, 1756-1823. Histoire critique de l'inquisition d'Espagne ... 1818.   (Card 2)

4 v. port., illus. (coat of arms) 21cm.

"Catalogue des manuscrits qui n'ont pas encore été publiés, et qui ont servi pour composer l'Histoire critique de l'inquisition d'Espagne": t.1, p. xxxj-xxxvj.
Translation of Historia crítica de la inquisición de España.
(Continued on next card)

Rare
BX
1735
L79
1818

Llorente, Juan Antonio, 1756-1823. Histoire critique de l'inquisition d'Espagne...1818.   (card 3)

I. Pellier, Alexis, tr. II. His Historia crítica de la inquisición de España--French. III. Title.

Rare
BX
1735
L79
1818

Llorente, Juan Antonio, 1756-1823.
Historia crítica de la inquisición de España--French.
Llorente, Juan Antonio, 1756-1823.
Histoire critique de l'inquisition d'Espagne depuis l'époque de son établissement par Ferdinand V, jusqu'au règne de Ferdinand VII; tirée des pièces originales des archives du Conseil de la Suprême et de celles des tribunaux subalternes du Saint-Office. Par D. Jean-Antoine Llorente ... Tr. de l'espagnol sur le manuscrit et sous les yeux de l'auteur, par Alexis Pellier. 2. éd. Paris, Treuttel et Würtz [etc.] 1818.
(Continued on next card)

CATALOGUE OF THE CORNELL WITCHCRAFT COLLECTION

Llorente, Juan Antonio, 1756-1823.
   Historia crítica de la inquisición de España--French.
Llorente, Juan Antonio, 1756-1823. Histoire critique de l'inquisition d'Espagne ... 1818.   (Card 2)

   4 v. port., illus. (coat of arms) 21cm.

   "Catalogue des manuscrits qui n'ont pas encore été publiés, et qui ont servi pour composer l'Histoire critique de l'inquisition d'Espagne": t.1, p. xxxj-xxxvj.
   Translation of Historia crítica de la inquisición de España.
           (Continued on next card)

Llorente, Juan Antonio, 1756-1823.
   The history of the inquisition of Spain, from the time of its establishment to the reign of Ferdinand VII. Composed from the original documents of the Archives of the Supreme council, and from those of subordinate tribunals of the Holy office. Abridged and translated from the original works of D. Juan Antonio Llorente ... 2d. ed. London, Printed for G. B. Whittaker, 1827.
       xx, 583, [1] p. 21½cm.
       Translation of Historia crítica.
   1. Inquisition--Spain. I. Title.

Lloyd, Temperance, d. 1682.
   A true and impartial relation of the informations against three witches, viz.: Temperance Lloyd, Mary Trembles, and Susanna Edwards. Who were indicted, arraigned, and convicted, at the assizes holden for the county of Devon at the castle of Exon, Aug. 14, 1682. ... As also, their speeches, confessions, and behaviour, at the time and place of execution ... London, Printed by F. Collins, and are to be sold by T. Benskin and C. Yeo, 1682.
       40 p. 21cm.
               (Continued on next card)

Lloyd, Temperance, d. 1682.
   A true and impartial relation of the informations against three witches ... 1682.
                          (Card 2)

   With this is bound Stephens, Edward. A plain relation of the late action at sea ... London, 1690.

   1. Lloyd, Temperance, d. 1682. 2. Trembles, Mary, d. 1682. 3. Edwards, Susanna, d. 1682.

WITCHCRAFT

Lobau, Richard.
   Spaziergänge mit Planitz, dessen Ideen und Ansichten über Faust und Hexe. Tagenbuchnotizen. Wittenberg, A.Piehler [1924]
       vii, 96, 12 p. 19cm.
   Includes passages from Planitz' Die Hexe von Goslar, with commentary.
   1. Planitz, Ernst Alfons, Edler von der, 1857-   2. Witchcraft. 3. Goethe, Johann Wolfgang von,1749-1832. 4. Faust. 5. Planitz, Ernst Alfons, Edler von der, 1857- Die Hexe von Goslar. I. Planitz, Ernst Alfons, Edler von der, 1857- II. Planitz,Ernst Alfons, Edler von der, 1857- Die Hexe von Goslar.
   III. Title.

Locatellus, Petrus.
   Conjurationes potentissimae et efficaces...
Locatellus, Petrus.
   Exorcismi potentissimi, & efficaces, ad expellendas aëreas tempestates, a daemonibus per se, sive ad nutum cujusvis diabolici ministri excitatas... a ...Petro Locatello... Editio altera correctior. Labaci, Typis & impensis Joannis Bapt. Mayr, 1680.
       188 p. 14cm.
   Published earlier with title: Conjurationes potentissimae et efficaces ad expellendas aëreas tempestates...
               (Continued on next card)

Locatellus, Petrus.
   Conjurationes potentissimae et efficaces...
WITCHCRAFT
BX 2340
L81
1680
Locatellus, Petrus. Exorcismi potentissimi, & efficaces...1680.   (Card 2)

   With this is bound: Preces et coniurationes contra aëreas tempestates... Campidonae, 1667.

   1. Exorcism. I. Catholic Church. Liturgy and ritual. II. His Conjurationes potentissimae et efficaces... III. Title.
   IV. Title: Conjurationes potentissimae et eff   icaces...

WITCHCRAFT
BX 2340
L81
1680
Locatellus, Petrus.
   Exorcismi potentissimi, & efficaces, ad expellendas aëreas tempestates, a daemonibus per se, sive ad nutum cujusvis diabolici ministri excitatas... a ...Petro Locatello... Editio altera correctior.
   Labaci, Typis & impensis Joannis Bapt. Mayr, 1680.
       188 p. 14cm.
   Published earlier with title: Conjurationes potentiss imae et efficaces ad expellendas   aëreas tempestates...
               (Continued on next card)

8
NIC

WITCHCRAFT
BX 2340
L81
1680
Locatellus, Petrus. Exorcismi potentissimi, & efficaces...1680.   (Card 2)

   With this is bound: Preces et coniurationes contra aëreas tempestates... Campidonae, 1667.

   1. Exorcism. I. Catholic Church. Liturgy and ritual. II. His Conjurationes potentissimae et efficaces... III.Title.
   IV. Title: Conjurationes potentissimae et eff   icaces...

Locke, J. Courtenay, tr.

Witchcraft
BF 1412
G85+
1931
   Grillot de Givry, Émile Angelo, 1870-
   Witchcraft, magic & alchemy, by Grillot de Givry, translated by J. Courtenay Locke; with ten plates in colour and 366 illustrations in the text. London, G. G. Harrap [1931]
       394 p. illus. (part col.) 29cm.
   "A collection of the iconography of occultism."--Pref.
   Translation of Le musée des sorciers, mages et alchi mistes.
           (Continued on next card)

Witchcraft
BF 1531
S43
1830
Lockhart, John Gibson, 1794-1854.
   Scott, Sir Walter, bart., 1771-1832.
   Letters on demonology and witchcraft, addressed to J. G. Lockhart, esq., by Sir Walter Scott, bart. London, J. Murray, 1830.
       ix, 402 p. front. 16 cm.

   1. Demonology. 2. Witchcraft. I. Title.

Locupletissimus thesaurus continens varias & selectissimas benedictiones, conjurationes, exorcismos, absolutiones.
Witchcraft
BX 2340
C57
1733
   Cilia, Gelasius di.
   Locupletissimus thesaurus continens varias & selectissimas benedictiones, conjurationes, exorcismos, absolutiones ... ad utilitatem Christi fidelium, & commodiorem usum parochorum, omniúmque sacerdotum, tam saecularium, quàm religiosorum curam habentium, ex diversis ritualibus & probatissimis authoribus. Locupletior & correctior redditus a Gelasio di Cilia ... Ed. 4ª.
   Augustae Vindelicorum, Expensis F. A. Strötter, 1733.
               (Continued on next card)

Locupletissimus thesaurus continens varias & selectissimas benedictiones, conjurationes, exorcismos, absolutiones.
Witchcraft
BX 2340
C57
1733
   Cilia, Gelasius di. Locupletissimus thesaurus ... 1733.   (Card 2)

       774, [10] p. 17cm.

   1. Exorcism. 2. Benediction. 3. Prayers. I. Catholic Church. Liturgy and ritual. II. Title.

WITCHCRAFT
BF 1583
L82
Lodtmann, Friedrich.
   Die letzten Hexen Osnabrücks und ihr Richter. Osnabrück, Im Selbstverlage des Vereins, 1875.
       [97]-200 p. 23cm.
   Detached from Mittheilungen des Historischen Vereins zu Osnabrück, v.10, 1875.

   1. Witchcraft--Osnabrück. 2. Trials (Witchcraft)--Osnabrück. I. Title.

WITCHCRAFT
BT 965
L82
Löers, Johann Christian, 1675-1743.
   Dissertationes theologicae, quarum prima De angelorum corporibus, altera De homine ad gloriam Dei condito, tertia Qua hominem ad gloriam Dei conditum esse, ex facultate intelligendi probatur. Quibus accedit Jacobi Ode Dissertatio theologica De natura angelorum... Trajecti ad Rhenum, Apud Joannem Evelt, 1737.
       259 p. 21cm.
   1. Angels--Early works to 1800. 2. Man (Theology)--Early works to 1800. I. Ode, Jacobus, 1698-1751. Dissertatio theologica De natura angelorum.

MSS
Bd.
WITCHCRAFT
BF
L82
Löher, Hermann, b. 1595.
   Hochnötige unterthanige wemütige Klage der frommen Unschültigen; worin alle hohe und nidrige Oberkeit, sampt ihren Unterthanen klärlich, augenscheinlich zu sehen und zu lesen haben, wie die arme unschültige fromme Leute durch Fahm- und Ehrenrauber von den falschen Zauber-richtern angegriffen, durch die unchristliche Folter, und Pein-banck von ihnen gezwungen werden, erschreckliche, unthunliche Mord, und Todt, Sünden auff sich selbsten und
           (Continued on next card)

MSS
Bd.
WITCHCRAFT
BF
L82
Löher, Hermann, b. 1595. Hochnötige unterthanige wemütige Klage ... 1676 [1896]   (Card 2)

   anderen mehr zu liegen, und sie ungerechtlich, falschlich zu besagen... durch Hermannum Löher. Amsterdam, Jacob de Jonge, 1676 [1896]
       640 p. 10 plates, part folded. 19cm.
   Carnap's manuscript copy.
   "Originaldruck als einziges bekanntes Exemplar in der Bibliothek des Kgl.
           (Continued on next card)

MSS
Bd.
WITCHCRAFT
BF
L82
Löher, Hermann, b. 1595. Hochnötige unterthanige wemütige Klage ... 1676 [1896]   (Card 3)

   Gymnasiums zu Münstereifel b/Bonn. 16 Bl. u. 608 pag. S. Von dort geliehen und abgeschrieben in der Zeit vom 12. Februar bis zum 9. März 1896."
   Numerals in the margins indicate pagination of the original.
       Imperfect: p. 84-86, 132-134, part of p. 354-355 are blank and
           (Continued on next card)

CATALOGUE OF THE CORNELL WITCHCRAFT COLLECTION

MSS Bd.
WITCHCRAFT
BF
L82

Löher, Hermann, b. 1595. Hochnötige unter- thanige wemütige Klage ... 1676 [1896] (Card 4)

correspond to p. 45-48, 97-100 and 341-342 of the original, which the copyist states are missing.
Bibliography of literature referring to this work: p. 607-638.
Note by the copyist concerning the scarcity of the original p. 639-640.
Plates are photographic reproduc-
(Continued on next card)

MSS Bd.
WITCHCRAFT
BF
L82

Löher, Hermann, b. 1595. Hochnötige unter- thanige wemütige Klage ... 1676 [1896] (Card 5)

tions from the copper plates of the original, pasted on to extra leaves.
With note by G. L. Burr on inside front cover indicating provenance of the manu- script copy.

1. Trials (Witchcraft)--Germany.
2. Witchcraft --Germany. I. Title.

WITCHCRAFT
BF
1775
L82
1897

Löwenstimm, August.
Aberglaube und Strafrecht. Autorisierte Übersetzung aus dem Russischen. Mit einem Vorwort von J. Kohler. Berlin, J. Räde, 1897.
xv, 232 p. 19cm.

8
NIC

1. Superstition. I. Title.

Lohmännin, Anna Elisabeth.

see

Lohmannin, Anna Elisabeth.

Lohmannin, Anna Elisabeth.
WITCHCRAFT
BF
1555
M94
029
no.2

Das Bezauberte Bauermägdgen: oder Geschichte von dem anjetzo in Kemberg bey Wittenberg sich aufhaltenden Landmägdchen Johannen Elisabethen Lohmannin; aufgesetzt durch einen vom Vorurtheil Befreyeten, und mit Anmerkungen eines Rechtsgelahrten verse- hen. Breslau, Bey J. E. Meyer, 1760.
167 p. 18cm.
No. 2 in vol. lettered Oesfeld u. a. ...
"Eines Advocatens Ehrenrettung wider ...
Herrn Gottlieb Müllers Beschuldigung":
p. 51-162.

8
NIC
(Continued on next card)

Lohmannin, Anna Elisabeth.
WITCHCRAFT
BF
1555
M94
B66

[Bobbe, Johann Benjamin Gottlieb]
Vermischte Anmerkungen über Sr. Hoch- ehrwürden des Herrn Probstes und Superin- tendentens in Kemberg Herrn Gottlieb Müllers Gründlichen Nachricht und deren Anhang von einer begeisterten Weibesperson Annen Eli- sabeth Lohmännin, mitgetheilet von Antidä- moniacus. Bernburg, Bey C. G. Görner, 1760.
134 p. 18cm.
Attribution by Holzmann.

8
(Continued on next card)

Lohmannin, Anna Elisabeth.
WITCHCRAFT
BF
1555
M94
029
no.1

Oesfeld, Gotthelf Friedrich.
Gedanken von der Einwirkung guter und böser Geister in die Menschen. Nebst bey- gefügter Beurtheilung eines neuern Bey- spiels einer vermeynten leiblichen Besit- zung, herausgegeben von M. Gotthelf Fried- rich Oesfeld ... Wittenberg, J. J. Ahl- feldt, 1760.
110 p. 18cm.
No. 1 in vol. lettered Oesfeld u. a. ...
1. Spirits. 2. Demoniac possession. 3. Lohmannin, Anna Elisabeth. I. Title. II. Title: Einwirkung guter und böser Geister in die Menschen.

8
NIC

Lohmannin, Anna Elisabeth.
WITCHCRAFT
BF
1555
M94
029
no.4

Semler, Johann Salomo, 1725-1791.
D. Joh. Salomo Semlers ... Abfertigung der neuen Geister und alten Irtümer in der Lohmannischen Begeisterung zu Kemberg nebst theologischem Unterricht von dem Ungrunde der gemeinen Meinung von leiblichen Besit- zungen des Teufels und Bezauberungen der Christen. Halle, Bey J. J. Gebauer, 1760.
40, 328 p. 18cm.
Dedication and "Vorrede" comprise the first numbering.

8
NIC
(Continued on next card)

Lohmannin, Anna Elisabeth.
WITCHCRAFT
BF
1555
M94
029
no.4

Semler, Johann Salomo, 1725-1791. ...
Abfertigung der neuen Geister ... 1760. (Card 2)

"Anhang. Auszug aus des Chaufepiee [sic] Nouveau dictionnaire historique et critique, von dem Artikel Balthas. Bekker": p. 317- 328.
No. 4 in vol. lettered Oesfeld u. a. ...
1. Lohmannin, Anna Elisabeth. 2. Mül- ler, Gottlieb. Gründlicher Nachricht von einer begeisterten Weibesperson. 3. Devil. 4. Bekker, Balthasar, 1634-1698.

8
NIC
(Continued on next card)

Lohmannin, Anna Elisabeth.
WITCHCRAFT
BF
1555
M94
029
no.5

Semler, Johann Salomo, 1725-1791.
D. Joh. Salomo Semlers Anhang zu der Abfertigung der Lohmannischen Begeisterung, worin fernere historische Umstände gesamlet worden. Halle, Bey J. J. Gebauer, 1760.
112 p. 18cm.
Title of the original work reads: Ab- fertigung der neuen Geister und alten Irtü- mer der Lohmannischen Begeisterung. Halle, 1760.
No. 5 in vol. lettered Oesfeld u. a. ...

8 NIC
(Continued on next card)

WITCHCRAFT
DD
801
O6
L83

Lohmeyer, Heinrich Karl, 1832-1909.
Bearbeitung von Birkenfelder Kirchen- büchern. Teil I. Die geschichtlichen, kul- tur- und volkskundlichen Beziehungen.
Birkenfeld, F. Fillmann, 1909.
123 p. 22cm.

"Spuren des Hexenglaubens": p.27-41.

1. Birkenfeld (Landkreis) 2. Witchcraft --Birkenfeld (Landkreis) 3. Trials (Witchcraft) --Birkenfeld (Landkreis) I. Title.

8
NIC

F
5
C59

Longfellow's country.
Clarke, Helen Archibald, d. 1926.
Longfellow's country, by Helen Archibald Clarke ... New York, The Baker and Taylor company, 1909.
6 p. l., 252 p. front. (port.) 31 pl. 24cm.
Illus. end-papers.

Contents.--Along the coast of New England.-- Under the shadow of Blomidon.--Idyls from history --The New England tragedies.--The lore of Hiawatha.--In Cambridge.

Longin, César.

see

Longinus, Caesar.

WITCHCRAFT
BF
1405
L85
1611

Longinus, Caesar, ed.
Trinvm magicvm, siue Secretorvm magico- rvm opvs ... editum à Caesare Longino, phi- los. Offenbachii, Cura M. Georgij Beati, impensis Anthonij Hummij, Francof., 1611.
10 p. l., 635 p. 13cm.
Contents.--Marci Antonii Zimarae Tracta- tvs magicus.--Appendix De mirandis qvibvsdam natvrali magia factis operationibus. Ex lib 2. Mag. nat. Ioan. Bapt. Port.--Tractatvs De virtvtibvs herbarvm, lapidvm et animalium:

8
(Continued on next card)

WITCHCRAFT
BF
1405
L85
1611

Longinus, Caesar, ed. Trinvm magicvm ... 1611. (Card 2)

Contents.--Cont.
authore Alberto Magno.--Commentatio De mag- netica cvratione vvlnervm citra svperstiti- onem ... authore R. G. M. D.--Logia, siue Oracvla Zoroastri, ex Platonicorvm libris collecta.

Index in MS tipped in at end of text.

8

WITCHCRAFT
BF
1405
L85
1630

Longinus, Caesar, ed.
Trinvm magicvm, siue Secretorvm magico- rvm opvs ... Editum à Caesare Longino phi- los. Francofvrti, Sumptibus Conradi Eif- ridi, 1630.
12 p. l., 498 p. 13cm.
Contents.--Marci Antonii Zimarae Tracta- tvs magicus.--Appendix, De mirandis qvibvs- dam natvrali magia factis operationibus. E lib. 2. Mag. nat. Ioan. Bapt. Port.--Tracta- tvs De virtvtibvs qvarvndam herbarvm, lapi-

8
(Continued on next card)

WITCHCRAFT
BF
1405
L85
1630

Longinus, Caesar, ed. Trinvm magicvm ... 1630. (Card 2)

dum & animalium. A. M. A.--Commentatio De magnetica cvratione vvlnervm citra svpersti- tionem ... Authore R. G. M. D.--Logia, siu Oracvla Zoroastri ex Platonicorvm libris collecta.--Tractatvs De proprii cvivsqve na ti daemonis inqvisitione.

8

WITCHCRAFT
BF
1405
L85
1673

Longinus, Caesar, ed.
Trinum magicum, sive Secretorum magico rum opus ... Editum à Caesare Longino ph los. Francofurti, Sumptibus Jacobi Goth fredi Seyleri, 1673.
12 p. l., 498 p. 14cm.
Contents.--Marci Antonii Zimarae Tract tus magicus.--Appendix, De mirandis quibu dam naturali magia factis operationibus. Ex lib. 2. Mag. nat. Ioan. Bapt. Port.-- Tractatvs De virtutibus quarundam herbaru

8
(Continued on next card)

CATALOGUE OF THE CORNELL WITCHCRAFT COLLECTION

TCHCRAFT
-05
5
73

Longinus, Caesar, ed. Trinum magicum ...
1673. (Card 2)

lapidum & animalium. A. M. A.--Commentatio
De magnetica curatione vulnerum citra svperstitionem ... Authore R. G. M. D.--Logia,
sive Oracvla Zoroastri ex Platonicorum libris collecta.--Tractatus De proprii cujusqve nati daemonis inqvisitione.
Layout of text corresponds to that of
Frankfurt, 1630 ed. (C. Eifrid, printer)

(Continued on next card)

TCHCRAFT
-05
5
73

Longinus, Caesar, ed. Trinum magicum ...
1673. (Card 3)

1. Occult sciences. 2. Medicine, Medieval. 3. Demonology. 4. Incantations.
I. Zimara, Marco Antonio, 1460-1532. Antrum
magico-medicum. II. Albertus Magnus, bp. of
Ratisbon, 1193?-1280, supposed author. De
virtutibus quarundam herbarum, lapidum et
animalium. III. Porta, Giovanni Battista
della, 1535?-1615. Magiae naturalis libri

(Continued on next card)

HCRAFT

Longinus, Caesar, ed. Trinum magicum ...
1673. (Card 4)

viginti. IV. Title: De magnetica curatione vulnerum. V. Title: Oracula Zoroastri
ex Platonicorum libris collecta. VI. Title:
De proprii cujusque nati daemonis inqvisitione. VII. R. G., M. D. VIII. G., R., M. D.
IX. Title: Trinum magicum. X. Title:
Secretorum magicorum opus.

Loos, Cornelius, 1546-1595.
De vera et falsa magia. Trier, 1592;
HCRAFT 1886.
[4], [10]-171 l. 24cm.

Manuscript, on Japan vellum. Facsimile
copy made by George Lincoln Burr of a fragment of the original printer's copy of the
manuscript; title page supplied by Burr.
T. p. and index are loose, unnumbered.
The numbered leaves are tied in ten small
fascicles, forming only the first two
of the four books included in the

(Continued on next card)

Loos, Cornelius, 1546-1595.
[De vera et falsa magia. 1592; 1886] (Card 2)
CRAFT

index. There is a loose extra copy each
of l. 15, 20, 79.
In marbled case.
The original is in the Stadtbibliothek
Trier.
Partially printed in 1592.
With this is cased his Extracts from the
De vera et falsa magia. Köln, 1912.

Loos, Cornelius, 1546-1595.
[De vera et falsa magia. Köln? 1592?
RAFT ca. 1900]
[1], 96, [1], 89, [1] p.; 15 blank l.,
[1] p. 15cm.

Signatures: A-F⁸. (p. 1-96 only)
Carnap's manuscript copy of a printed
fragment, according to G. L. Burr, probably
as much as had been completed before
seizure by the Inquisition.
"Das Original befindet sich in der
Stadtbiblioth ek zu Köln ... 6 Bogen
(Continued on next card)

MSS
Bd.
WITCHCRAFT
BF
L86
1592b

Loos, Cornelius, 1546-1595. [De vera
et falsa magia. 1592? ca. 1900] (Card 2)

in Kl. 8°. Ein Titelblatt ist nicht vorhanden."
The second part, p. 1-89 consists of
bibliographical citations and excerpts
from articles concerning Loos and his work.

1. Demonology. 2. Witchcraft. 3. His
De vera et falsa magia. I. Title.

MSS
Bd.
WITCHCRAFT
BF
L86
1592b

Loos, Cornelius, 1546-1595.
De vera et falsa magia.
Loos, Cornelius, 1546-1595. [De vera et falsa magia. Köln? 1592?
ca. 1900]
[1], 96, [1], 89, [1] p.; 15 blank l.,
[1] p. 15cm.

Signatures: A-F⁸. (p. 1-96 only)
Carnap's manuscript copy of a printed
fragment, according to G. L. Burr, probably
as much as had been completed before
seizure by the Inquisition.
"Das Original befindet sich in der
Stadtbiblioth ek zu Köln ... 6 Bogen
(Continued on next card)

MSS
Bd.
WITCHCRAFT
BF
L86
1592b

Loos, Cornelius, 1546-1595.
De vera et falsa magia.
Loos, Cornelius, 1546-1595. [De vera
et falsa magia. 1592? ca. 1900] (Card 2)

in Kl. 8°. Ein Titelblatt ist nicht vorhanden."
The second part, p. 1-89 consists of
bibliographical citations and excerpts
from articles concerning Loos and his work.

1. Demonology. 2. Witchcraft. 3. His
De vera et falsa magia. I. Title.

MSS
Bd.
WITCHCRAFT
BF
L86
1592a

Loos, Cornelius, 1546-1595.
De vera et falsa magia.
Extracts from the De vera et falsa magia
of Cornelius Loos. (Made from the Ms. at
Trier and verified by the printed fragment
at Köln in July, 1912.) Köln, 1912.
4, 1-6, [1], 7-15, [1], 16-48 l. 20cm.

Manuscript, in small notebook of graph
paper, in the hand of G. L. Burr. P. 41-
48 are Notes on the printed fragment at
Cologne, by G. L. Burr.
Four loose typewritten leaves of
the Latin te xt are inserted inside
(Continued on next card)

MSS
Bd.
WITCHCRAFT
BF
L86
1592a

Loos, Cornelius, 1546-1595. Extracts from
the De vera et falsa magia ... 1912. (Card 2)
front cover.
In marbled case with his [De vera et
falsa magia. Trier, 1592; 1886]

1. Demonology. 2. Witchcraft. 3. His
De vera et falsa magia. I. Burr, George
Lincoln, 1857-1938.

MSS
Bd.
WITCHCRAFT
BF
L86
1592a

Loos, Cornelius, 1546-1595. Extracts from
the De vera et falsa magia ... 1912. (Card 2)
front cover.
In marbled case with his [De vera et
falsa magia. Trier, 1592; 1886]

1. Demonology. 2. Witchcraft. 3. His
De vera et falsa magia. I. Burr, George
Lincoln, 1857-1938.

Thesis
1911
338

Loos, Cornelius, 1546-1595.
Hodder, Mabel Elisabeth.
Peter Binsfeld and Cornelius Loos,
an episode in the history of witchcraft.
Ithaca, N. Y., 1911.
228 l. 29cm.

Thesis (Ph. D.)--Cornell University,
1911.

1. Binsfeld, Pierre, 1540-1598. 2. Loos,
Cornelius, 1546-1595. 3. Witchcraft.

Witchcraft
BF
1584
T9
Z59

Loosbuch.
Zingerle, Ignaz Vincenz, Edler von Summers-
berg, 1825-1892, ed.
Barbara Pachlerin, die Sarnthaler Hexe,
und Mathias Perger, der Lauterfresser. Zwei
Hexenprozesse, hrsg. von Dr. Ignaz Zingerle.
Innsbruck, Wagner, 1858.
xii, 84 p. 19cm.
Contents.--Barbara Pachlerin, die Sarn-
thaler Hexe.--Der Lauterfresser.--Anhang.
Ein altes Loosbuch.
8   Each item has special t. p.
(Continued on next card)

WITCHCRAFT
BF
1582
L86

Lorédan, Jean, 1853-
Un grand procès de sorcellerie au XVIIe
siècle: l'abbé Gaufridy et Madeleine de Demandolx (1600-1670) d'après des documents
inédits. Ouvrage orné de 9 gravures et de
2 fac-similés. Paris, Perrin, 1912.
xiv, 436 p. illus. 21cm.

1. Witchcraft--France. 2. Trials (Witchcraft)--France. 3. Gaufridi, Louis, 1572-
1611. 4. Demandolx, Madeleine de, 1593?-
8   1670. I. Title.
NIC

Witchcraft
BX
9479
B42
L872

Lorgion, Everardus Jan Diest, 1812-1876.
Balthasar Bekker in Amsterdam. Een
portret uit de zeventiende eeuw. Door
Dr. E. J. Diest Lorgion, schrijver van
Balthasar Bekker in Franker. Groningen,
H. R. Roelfsema, 1851.
2 v. title vignette (port.) 24 x 15cm.
8°: v. 1: π3, 1-19⁸, 20 1; v. 2: π²,
1-17⁸, 18⁴.
Title page on special paper, inserted.
Van der Linde 228.
1. Bekker, Balthasar, 1634-1698
--Biog. I. Title.

Witchcraft
BX
9479
B42
L87

[Lorgion, Everardus Jan Diest] 1812-1876.
Balthazar Bekker in Franeker. Een portret uit
de zeventiende eeuw. Groningen, H. R. Roelfsema,
1848.
4 p. l., 264 p. front. 23 x 14cm.
8°: π⁴, 1-16⁸, 17⁴.
Prefaced signed: L--N.
Van der Linde 227.

1. Bekker, Balthasar, 1634-1698--Biog.
I. Title.

CATALOGUE OF THE CORNELL WITCHCRAFT COLLECTION

Lorrain, Pierre Le, abbé de Vallemont.

see

Vallemont, Pierre Le Lorrain, abbé de, 1649-1721.

WITCHCRAFT
BF
1583
L87

Lory, Karl.
Hexenprozesse im Gebiete des ehemaligen Markgrafenlandes. [München, 1903]
[290]-304 p. 24cm.

Extract from Festgabe Karl Theodor von Heigel, 1903.

8
NIC
1. Witchcraft--Germany. 2. Trials (Witchcraft)--Germany. I. Title.

GR
540
L87+

Losch, Friedrich, comp.
Deutsche Segen, Heil- und Bannsprüche; nach gedruckten, schriftlichen und mündlichen Quellen zusammengestellt und hrsg. [Stuttgart, W. Kohlhammer, 1890]
157-259 p. 29cm.

Detached from Württembergische Vierteljahrshefte für Landesgeschichte, Jahrg. 13, Heft 3.

1. Incantations. 2. Exorcism. I. Title.

WITCHCRAFT
BF
1565
S83
L88

[Loschert, Oswald] b.1704.
Vorgängischer Versuch zu Erwürkung eines Vertrages zwischen den in dem bisherigen Hexerey-Kriege verwickelten Gelehrten. Wie auch zum nutzbaren Unterrichte, wie man von der Zauber- und Hexerey weder zu wenig, noch zu viel glauben soll. Unternommen von einem Verehrer der Gelehrten und Liebhaber der Christlichen Wahrheiten. [Bamberg] an dem Maynstrome [Göbhardt], 1767.
86 p. 23 cm.
(Continued on next card)

8
NIC

WITCHCRAFT
BF
1565
S83
L88

[Loschert, Oswald] b. 1704. Vorgängischer Versuch zu Erwürkung eines Vertrages zwischen den in dem bisherigen Hexerey-Kriege verwickelten Gelehrten...1767. (Card 2)

1. Witchcraft. 2. Sterzinger, Ferdinand, 1721-1786. Akademische Rede von dem gemeinen Vorurtheile der...Hexerey. I. Title. II. Title: Hexerey-Krieg.

WITCHCRAFT
BF
1412
L88

Louandre, Charles Léopold, 1812-1882.
La sorcellerie., Paris, L. Hachette, 1853.
146 p. 17cm.

8
NIC
1. Occult sciences. 2. Witchcraft. I. Title.

Witchcraft
BF
1517
F5
A89

Loudun, France. Ursuline convent.
[Aubin, Nicolas] b. ca. 1655.
The cheats and illusions of Romish priests and exorcists. Discovered in the history of the devils of Loudun: being an account of the pretended possession of the Ursuline nuns, and of the condemnation and punishment of Urban Grandier, a parson of the same town ... London, Printed for W. Turner and R. Bassett, 1703.
4 p. l., 331 p. 20cm.
Translation of Histoire des diables de Loudun Attributed also to M. Des Niau.
1. Loudun, France. Ursuline Convent. 2. Grandier, Urbain, 1590-1634. I. Des Niau, , supposed author. II. Title.

Witchcraft
BF
1517
F5
A892
1716

Loudun, France. Ursuline convent.
[Aubin, Nicolas] b. ca.1655.
Cruels effets de la vengeance du Cardinal de Richelieu, ou Histoire des diables de Loudun, de la possession des religieuses ursulines, et de la condamnation et du suplice [sic] d'Urbain Grandier, curé de la même ville. Amsterdam, E. Roger, 1716.
[10], 5-378 p. front. 17cm.
Published also under titles: Histoire des diables de Loudun, ou, De la possession des religieuses ursulines ... Amsterdam, 1694; and Histoire d'Urbain Grandier, condamné comme magicien... Amsterdam, 1735.

Witchcraft
BF
1517
F5
A893
1737

Loudun, France. Ursuline convent.
[Aubin, Nicolas] b. ca. 1655.
Histoire des diables de Loudun, ou De la possession des religieuses ursulines, et de la condamnation & du suplice d'Urbain Grandier, curé de la même ville. Cruels effets de la vengeance du Cardinal de Richelieu. Amsterdam, aux de'pens de la Compagnie, 1737.
378 p. front. 17cm.
"Published also under titles:
(Continued on next card)

Witchcraft
BF
1517
F5
A893
1737

Loudun, France. Ursuline convent.
[Aubin, Nicolas] b. ca. 1655. Histoire des diables de Loudun ... 1737. (Card 2)
Histoire d' Urbain Grandier, condamné comme magicien ... Amsterdam, 1735, and Cruels effets de la vengeance du Cardinal de Richelieu; ou, Histoire des diables de Loudun ... Amsterdam, 1716."--L.C.

1. Demoniac possession. 2. Grandier, Urbain, 1590-1634. 3. Loudun, France. Ursuline convent. I. Title: Les diables de Loudun.

Witchcraft
BF
1582
B54
1905

Loudun, France. Ursuline Convent.
Bertrand, Isidore.
Les possédées de Loudun, et Urbain Grandier. Étude historique. Paris, Bloud [1905?]
61 p. 18cm. (Science et religion: études pour le temps présent)

Includes bibliography (5 p.)
Bound with his La sorcellerie.

1. Demoniac possession. 2. Grandier, Urbain, 1590-1634. 3. Loudun, France. Ursuline Convent. I. Title.

Witchcraft
DC
801
L87
B64

Loudun, France. Ursuline Convent.
Bleau, Alphonse.
Précis d'histoire sur la ville et les possédées de Loudun. Poitiers, Typographie de H. Oudin, 1877.
246 p. 18cm.

1. Loudun, France--Hist. 2. Loudun, France. Ursuline Convent. 3. Grandier, Urbain, 1590-1634. 4. Demoniac possession. I. Title.

BF
1517
F5
C41

Loudun, France. Ursuline convent.
Certeau, Michel de.
La possession de Loudun, présentée par Michel de Certeau. [Paris, Julliard, 1970]
347 p. plates. 19 cm. (Collection Archives, 37) 9.00F F***
Includes bibliographical references.

4
1. Demoniac possession. 2. Loudun, France. Ursuline convent. 3. Grandier, Urbain, 1590-1634. I. Title.

BF1517.F5C47   76-575412
Library of Congress   71 [2]

WITCHCRAFT
BF
1517
F5
C78
1634

Loudun, France. Ursuline Convent.
Coppie d'v procez verbal faict le vingt & deuxiesme d'aoust mil six cens trente & quatre. Par Monsieur de Laubardement conseller du roy en ses conseils d'estat & priué, sur le miracle faict dans la ville de Loudun. Poictiers, Par René Allain, 1634.
9 p. 17cm.

8
1. Loudun, France. Ursuline Convent. 2. Exorcism. I. Laubardemont, Jean Martin de.

Witchcraft
BF
1517
F5
D46
1887

Loudun, France. Ursuline Convent.
[Des Niau, ---]
The history of the devils of Loudun, the alleged possession of the Ursuline nuns, and the trial and execution of Urbain Grandier, told by an eye-witness. Translated from the original French, and edited by Edmund Goldsmid. Edinburg, Priv. Print., 1887-88.
3 v. 18cm. (Collectanea Adamantaea, XXI.I)
Contains facsimile of original French t.p. La véritable historie des diables de Loudun ... Poitiers, J. Thoreau, 1634.

Witchcraft
BF
1517
F5
F81

Loudun, France. Ursuline convent.
France. Commission pour le jugement du procez criminel fait a l'encontre de Maistre Urbain Grandier & ses complices.
Extraict des registres de la Commission ordonnée par le Roy povr le ivgement ... Poictiers, Par I. Thoreav & la vefue d'A. Mesnier, 1634.
25 p. 16cm.

Witchcraft
BF
1517
F5I61

Loudun, France. Ursuline Convent.
Interrogatoire de Maistre Vrbain Grandier, Prestre, Curé de S. Pierre du marché de Loudun, & Chanoyne de l'Eglise Saincte Croix dudit lieu. Avec les confrontations des Religieuses possedées contre le dit Grandier. Ensemble la liste & les noms des Iuges deputez par sa Majesté. A Paris, Chez Estienne Hebert, & Iacqves Povllard, 1634.
10 p. 16cm.
1. Loudun, France. Ursuline Convent. 2. Grandier, Urbain, 1590-1634.

WITCHCRAFT
BF
1517
F5
M62
1613

Loudun, France. Ursuline convent.
Michaelis, Sebastien, 1543?-1618.
The admirable history of the possession and conversion of a penitent woman. Sedvced by a magician that made her to become a witch, and the princesse of sorcerers in the country of Prouince, who was brought to S. Baume to bee exorcised, in the yeere ... Wherevnto is annexed a pnevmology, or Discourse of spirits ... reuewed, corrected and enlarged ... Translated into English by W. B. London, Imprinted for Wil...
8   (Continued on next card)

CATALOGUE OF THE CORNELL WITCHCRAFT COLLECTION

Loudun, France. Ursuline convent.

WITCHCRAFT
BF
1517
F5
M62
1613

Michaelis, Sebastien, 1543?-1618. The admirable history of the possession ... of a penitent woman ... [1613]   (Card 2)

liam Aspley [1613]
24 p. l., 418, [10], 154, [34] p. 20cm.
Differs from another issue only in t. p. (lacks date; some spellings different)
Translation of Histoire admirable de la possession ... d'vne penitente, and of Discovrs des esprits.
"A discovrse of spirits" has special t. p. and separate paging.
(Continued on next card)

8

Loudun, France. Ursuline convent.

WITCHCRAFT
BF
1517
F5
M62
1613

Michaelis, Sebastien, 1543?-1618. The admirable history of the possession ... of a penitent woman ... [1613]   (Card 3)

STC 17854.
1. Palud, Magdeleine de la. 2. Gaufridi, Louis, 1572-1611. 3. Loudun, France. Ursuline convent. 4. Demoniac possession. 5. Exorcism. I. His Histoire admirable de la possession ... d'une penitente. English. II. His Discours des esprits. English. III. Title. IV. W. B., tr. V. B., W., tr.

Loudun, France. Ursuline convent.

WITCHCRAFT
BF
1517
F5
M62

Michaelis, Sebastien, 1543?-1618.
Histoire admirable de la possession et conversion d'vne penitente, seduite par vn magicien, la faisant sorciere & princesse des sorciers au pays de Prouence, conduite à la S. Baume pour y estre exorcizee l'an M.DC.X. au mois de Nouembre, soubs l'authorité du R. P. F. Sebastien Michaelis ... Commis par luy aux exorcismes & recueil des actes le R. P. F. François Domptivs ... Ensemble la Pneumalogie, ou Discours du
(Continued on next card)

Loudun, France. Ursuline convent.

WITCHCRAFT
BF
1517
F5
M62

Michaelis, Sebastien, 1543?-1618. Histoire admirable ... 1613.   (Card 2)

susdit Pere Michaelis, reueu, corrigé, & augmenté par luy-mesme ... Paris, Chez Charles Chastellain, 1613.
16 p. l., 352, 124, 196, [30] p. 17cm.
"Actes recveillis ... par le reverend Pere Michaëlis" has separate paging.
"Discovrs des esprits" has special t. p. with imprint Paris, 1512, and separate paging.
(Continued on next card)

Loudun, France. Ursuline Convent.

Witchcraft
17
R29

Recit veritable de ce qvi s'est passé à Lovdvn. Contre Maistre Vrbain Grandier, Prestre Curé de l'Eglise de S. Pierre de Loudun, attaint & convaincu du crime de Magie, malefice & possession, arriuée par son faict ès personne d'aucunes des Religieuses Vrseline de la ville de Loudun. A Paris, De l'Imprimerie de Pierre Targa, 1634.
15 p. 16cm.
1. Loudun, France. Ursuline Convent. 2. Grandier, Urbain, 1590-1634.

Loudun, France. Ursuline Convent.

WITCHCRAFT
17
8
35

Relation veritable de ce qvi s'est passé aux exorcismes des religieuses vrsulines possedees de Loudun, en la presence de Monsieur frere vnique du roy. Auec l'attestation des exorcistes. Paris, Chez Iean Martin, 1635.
46 p. 17cm.

"Iouxte la coppie imprimee à Poictiers."

1. Loudun, France. Ursuline Convent. 2. Exorcism. I. Gaston Jean Baptiste, duke of Orléans, 1608-1660.

Loudun, France. Ursuline convent.

WITCHCRAFT
BF
1517
F5
S26+

Sauzé, J.-Charles, 1815-
Essai médico-historique sur les possédés de Loudun. Paris, Impr. Rignoux, 1839.
59 p. 26cm.

Thèse--Paris.
"Questions sur diverses branches des sciences médicales": p. [51]-59.

1. Loudun, France. Ursuline convent. 2. Demoniac possession. 3. Psychical research. I. Title: Les possédés de Loudun.

8
NIC

Loudun, France. Ursuline convent.

WITCHCRAFT
BF
1517
F5
S96

Surin, Jean Joseph, 1600-1665.
Histoire abrégée de la possession des Ursulines de Loudun, et des peines du père Surin; (ouvrage inédit faisant suite à ses oeuvres.) Paris, Chez l'éditeur, au Bureau de l'Association catholique du Sacré-Coeur, 1828.
365, [6] p. 18cm.
"D'après Sommervogel, publication partielle d'une copie d'un ms. de la fin du XVIIIe siècle, ayant pour titre: La vie
(Continued on next card)

8
NIC

Loudun, France. Ursuline convent.

WITCHCRAFT
BF
1517
F5
S96

Surin, Jean Joseph, 1600-1665. Histoire abrégée de la possession des Ursulines de Loudun ... 1828.   (Card 2)

du R. P. Surin, en laquelle il parle des maux qui lui sont arrivés ensuite de la possession des démons chassés par son ministère." -- Note under Surin, Bibliothèque Nationale.
Surin's authorship has been questioned.
With this is bound his Triomphe de l'amour divin. Avignon, 1829.
(Continued on next card)

8
NIC

Loudun, France. Ursuline convent.

WITCHCRAFT
BF
1517
F5
T77
1634a

Tranquille de Saint-Rémi, capuchin.
Veritable relation des ivstes procedvres observees av faict de la possession des Vrsulines de Loudun. Et au procez d'Vrbain Grandier. Auec les theses generales touchant les diables exorcisez. Par le R. P. Tranquille, Capucin. La Fleche, Chez George Griveav, imprimeur ordinaire du roy, 1634.
80 p. 14cm.
Expanded version of the Poictiers text.
1. Loudun, France. Ursuline Convent. 2. Grandier, Urbain, 1590-1634. 3. Exorcism. I. Title.

WITCHCRAFT
BF
1582
L88

Louise, Théophile, b. 1822.
De la sorcellerie et de la justice criminelle à Valenciennes (XVIe et XVIIe siècles) Valenciennes, Typ. de E. Prignet, 1861.
iii, xix, 214 p. 6 plates. 22cm.

Pages 165-166 omitted in paging.

1. Witchcraft--France. 2. Trials (Witchcraft)--France. 3. Witchcraft. I. Title.

8
NIC

Witchcraft
GR
830
W4V73

Loups-garous et vampires.
Villeneuve, Roland, 1922-
Loups-garous et vampires. Paris, Genève, La Palatine [1963]
263 p. illus. 20cm.

1. Werwolves. 2. Vampires. I. Title.

Louviers, France. St. Louis (Convent)

WITCHCRAFT
BF
1555
E77
2 copies

Esprit du Bosroger, Capuchin.
La pieté affligee; ov, Discovrs historiqve & theologique de la possession des religieuses dittes de Saincte Elizabeth de Loüiers. Divisé en trois parties. Roven, Chez Iean le Bovlenger, 1652.
[30], 458, 67 p. front. 23cm.
Copy 1 imperfect: front. wanting.
Inserted at end of copy 1: 6 p. of ms.
1. Demoniac possession. 2. Bavent, Madeleine, b. 1607. 3. Louviers, France. St. Louis (Convent) 4. Witchcraft. I. Title.

Louviers, France. St. Louis (Convent)

WITCHCRAFT
BF
1555
R31

Recueil de pièces sur les possessions des religieuses de Louviers. Rouen [Imprimerie L. Deshays] 1879.
2 v. in 1. 25cm.

Title page and prefatory material bound following v. 1.
Contents.--[1] Histoire de Magdelaine Bavent, religieuse du monastere de Saint Loüis de Louviers (1652)--[2] I. Examen de la possession des religieuses de Louviers, par le Docteur Yvelin (1643)
(Continued on next card)

8
NIC

Louviers, France. St. Louis (Convent)

WITCHCRAFT
BF
1555
R31

Recueil de pièces sur les possessions des religieuses de Louviers...1879.   (Card 2)

Contents--continued.
II. Response à l'Examen de la possession des religieuses de Louviers (1643) III. Censure de l'Examen de la possession des religieuses de Louviers (1643) IV. Apologie pour l'autheur de l'Examen de la possession des religieuses de Louviers, attribuée au Docteur Yvelin (1643) V. Responce à l'Apologie de l'Examen du sieur Yvelin
(Continued on next card)

Louviers, France. St. Louis (Convent)

WITCHCRAFT
BF
1555
R31

Recueil de pièces sur les possessions des religieuses de Louviers...1879.   (Card 3)

Contents--continued.
(1644) VI. Recit veritable de ce qui s'est fait & passé à Louviers, touchant les religieuses possedées (1643) VII. Recit veritable de ce qui s'est fait & passé aux exorcismes de plusieurs religieuses de la ville de Louviers (1643) VIII. La deffense de la verité touchant la possession des religieuses de Louvier, par
(Continued on next card)

Louviers, France. St. Louis (Convent)

WITCHCRAFT
BF
1555
R31

Recueil de pièces sur les possessions des religieuses de Louviers...1879.   (Card 4)

Contents--continued.
Jean Le Breton (1643) IX. Attestation de messieurs les commissaires envoyez par sa Majesté pour prendre connoissance, avec monseigneur l'evesque d'Evreux, de l'estat des religieuses qui paroissent agitées au monastere de Saint Louys & Sainte Elizabeth de Louviers (1643?) X. Procés verbal de Monsieur le Peniten-
(Continued on next card)

Louviers, France. St. Louis (Convent)

WITCHCRAFT
BF
1555
R31

Recueil de pièces sur les possessions des religieuses de Louviers...1879.   (Card 5)

Contents--continued.
tier d'Evreux, de ce qui luy est arrivé dans la prison, interrogeant & consolant Magdelaine Bavent, magicienne, à une heureuse conversion & repentance, par Delangle (1643) XI. Lettre adressée à Monsieur D. L. V., medicin du Roy, & doyen de la Faculté de Paris, sur l'Apologie du sieur Yvelin, medicin, attribuée au doc-
(Continued on next card)

CATALOGUE OF THE CORNELL WITCHCRAFT COLLECTION

Louviers, France. St. Louis (Convent)
WITCHCRAFT
BF
1555
R31
    Recueil de pièces sur les possessions des religieuses de Louviers...1879. (Card 6)
    Contents--continued.
teur Maignart (1644) XII. Traicté des marques des possedez & la preuve de la veritable possession des religieuses de Louviers, par P. M., esc. d. en m. (attribué à Simon Pietre; 1644) XIII. Copie en forme de recueil de ce qui se fait de jour en jour dans le monastere des filles relligieuzes Saint Louis (1643) XIV. Pièces dé-
(Continued on next card)

Louviers, France. St. Louis (Convent)
WITCHCRAFT
BF
1555
R31
    Recueil de pièces sur les possessions des religieuses de Louviers...1879. (Card 7)
    Contents--continued.
tachées extraites du manuscrit H. F. n° 34 de la Bibliothèque Ste Geneviève, formant suite à la pièce précédente. XV. Notice sur la Mere Françoise, superieure des religieuses de la Place royale, au sujet de l'histoire des possedées de Louviers.
(Continued on next card)

A lover of truth.
Witchcraft
BS
2545
D5
T75
no.3
    [Sharpe, Gregory] 1713-1771.
    A review of the controversy about the meaning of demoniacks in the New-Testament. In which Mr. Hutchinson's sermon at Oxford [!], Mr. Twell's Reply to the Further enquiry, Mr. Twell's Answer to the Further enquiry, and a tract, entitled, Some thoughts on the miracles of Jesus, by an impartial hand, are considered. By a lover of truth. ... London, Printed for J. Roberts, 1739.
    80 p. 20cm.
    No. 3 in vol. lettered: Tracts on demoniacks. 1737.

Lowes, John, clerk, d. 1645.
WITCHCRAFT
BF
1581
Z7
1645
    Ewen, Cecil Henry L'Estrange, 1877-
    The trials of John Lowes, clerk. [London] 1937.
    7 p. 23cm.

    1. Lowes, John, clerk, d. 1645. 2. 2. Trials (Witchcraft)--Great Britain. I. Title.

8

Lowes, John, clerk, d. 1645.
Witchcraft
HV
6248
F78
    A Magazine of scandall; or, A heape of wickednesse of two infamous ministers, consorts, one named Thomas Fowkes of Earle Soham in Suffolk, convicted by law for killing a man, and the other named Iohn Lowes of Brandeston, who hath beene arraigned for witchcraft, and convicted by law for a common barretor. Together with the manner how my lord of Canterbury would put and keep them in the ministery, notwithstanding the many petitions and cer   tificates from their
(Continued on next card)

Lowes, John, clerk, d. 1645.
Witchcraft
HV
6248
F78
    A Magazine of scandall ... 1642. (Card 2)
    parishioners, and others... and against whom .. the county of Suffolke have [sic] petitioned to the Parliament ... because ... one of these scandalous ministers have [sic] abused the authority of the lords in Parliament ... London, Printed for R. H., 1642.
    [1]? p. 20cm.
    1. Fowkes, Thomas. 2. Lowes, John, clerk, d. 1645.

Lucanus, pseud.
WITCHCRAFT
AP
30
N4852
v.10
    Ein merkwürdiger Hexenprozess.
    (In: Neue gemeinnützige Blätter. Halberstadt. 16cm. v.10 (1800) p. [529]-540)
    Signed: Lucanus.
    Concerning the trial for witchcraft of a widow Siewerten, in 1577.

    1. Trials (Witchcraft)--Halberstadt. 2. Siewerten, defendant. I. Lucanus, pseud.

8
NIC

Lucerna inquisitorum haereticae.
Witchcraft
BT
1313
B52
    Bernardus Comensis.
    Lucerna inquisitorum haereticae pravitatis R. P. F. Bernardi Comensis... et eiusdem Tractatus de strigibus, cum annotationibus Francisci Pegnae... Additi sunt in hac impressione duo tractatus Joannis Gersoni... Roma, ex officina Bartholomaei Grassi, 1584.
    [4] l., 184, [28] p. 22cm.
    1. Heresies and heretics. I. Pegna, Francesco, ed. II. Gerson, Joannes, 1363-1429. III. Title.

WITCHCRAFT
DC
137
.15
L93
1786a
    [Luchet, Jean Pierre Louis de la Roche du Maine, marquis de] 1740-1792.
    Memoir authentique pour servir à l'histoire du comte de Cagliostro. Nouv. ed. Strasbourg, 1786.
    iv, 36 p. 22cm.

    1. Diamond necklace affair. 2. Cagliostro, Alessandro, conte di, assumed name of Giuseppe Balsamo, 1743-1795. I. Title.

8

Witchcraft
BF
1598
C13
L93
1787
    [Lucia] pseud.
    The life of the Count Cagliostro ... dedicated to Madame la Comtesse de Cagliostro. 2d ed. London, Printed for the author, and sold by T. Hookham, 1787.
    viii, xxxii, 127 p. 22cm.
    Dedication signed: Lucia.

    1. Cagliostro, Alessandro, conte di, assumed name of Giuseppe Balsamo, 1743-1795. I. Title.

Lucianus Samosatensis.
    Philopseudes.
Witchcraft
BF
1565
W13
    [Wagstaffe, John] 1633-1677.
    The question of witchcraft debated: or, A discourse against their opinion that affirm witches ... London, Printed for E. Willington, 1669.
    128 p. 14cm.
    Signatures: A-I[8].
    "... Lovers of lies. A dialogue made by the famous Lucian [translated by Sir Thomas More]: p. 83-128.

Lucianus Samosatensis.
    Philopseudes--English.
WITCHCRAFT
BF
1565
W13
1671
    Wagstaffe, John, 1633-1677.
    The question of witchcraft debated. Or a discourse against their opinion that affirm witches, considered and enlarged. The 2d ed. ... London, Printed for Edw. Millington, 1671.
    198 p. 15cm.

    "... Lovers of lies: a dialogue made by the famous Lucian [translated by Sir Thomas More]"
    I. Lucianus Samosatensis. Philopseudes. English. II. Title.

Witchcraft
B
2605
Z7
L94
    Luden, Heinrich, 1778?-1847.
    Christian Thomasius, nach seinen Schicksalen und Schriften dargestellt, von H. Luden. Mit einer Vorrede von Johann von Müller ... Berlin, Bei J. F. Unger, 1805.
    xvi, 311 p. 17cm.

    1. Thomasius, Christian, 1655-1728--Biog. I. Müller, Johannes von, 1752-1809. II. Title.

8

Witchcraft
BF
1565
T46
1717a
    Ludovici, Gottfried, 1670-1724. Theologicvm novae novi avtoris Francisci de Cordva anthropologiae et daemonologiae examen, nouitates vti alias, ab hoc in Schrifft- und Vernunfftmässigen Gedancken vom Schatzgraben und Beschwerung der Geister propositas ... Coburgi, Sumptu Pauli Güntheri Pfotenhaueri [1718]
    134 p. 19cm.
    Bound with Thomasius, Christian, 1655-1728. ... Kurtze Lehr-Sätze von dem
(Continued on next card)

8

Witchcraft
BF
1565
T46
1717a
    Ludovici, Gottfried, 1670-1724. Godofredo Ludovici ... Theologicvm novae ... anthropologiae ... examen ... [1718] (Card 2)
    Laster der Zauberey. Franckfurth, 1717.

    1. Franciscus de Cordua, pseud. Schrifft- und vernunfftmässige Gedancken vom Schatzgraben. 2. Demonology. I. Title: Theologicum novae ... anthropologiae ... examen. II. Title.

8

Ludwig, Gottfried, 1670-1724.
    see
Ludovici, Gottfried, 1670-1724.

Lueg, Severinus, ed.
WITCHCRAFT
BX
2045
B4
1849
    Catholic Church. Liturgy and ritual.
    Benedictional. Passau.
    Manuale benedictionum. Accedunt processiones variae publicis necessitatibus congruentes. Commodo animarum pastorum usui adaptavit Severinus Lueg... Editio secun[da] Passavii, Elsässer & Waldbauer, 1849.
    xix, 401 p. 17cm.
    "Additio. I. Benedictio a daemonio vexatorum. II. Exorcismus pro exorcizandis obsessis.": xix p. at beginning.
    1. Benediction. 2. Exorcism. I. Lueg, Severinus, ed. II. Title.

8
NIC

WITCHCRAFT
BT
980
L94
    Lützelberger, Ernst Carl Julius, 1802-187[?]
    Die Lehren der Bibel und der ältesten christlichen Kirche über Satan und sein Reich. [Nürnberg, 1839]
    52-88 p. 21cm.

    Extract from unidentified periodical.

    1. Devil. 2. Devil--Biblical teaching. I. Title.

8
NIC

CATALOGUE OF THE CORNELL WITCHCRAFT COLLECTION

Witchcraft
BF
1565
T19
M186+
   [Lugiato, Andrea]
     Osservazioni sopra l'opuscolo che ha per titolo Arte magica dileguata, di un prete dell' oratorio. Venezia, Presso Simone Occhi, 1750.
     3 p. l., 99 p. 27cm.
     Attributed to Lugiato by B. M. and Melzi; but Melzi also suggests one Lusato, veneziano.
     1. Maffei, Francesco Scipione, marchese, 1675-1755. Arte magica dileguata. 2. Magic. I. Lusato, veneziano, supposed author. II. Title.

8

Lugiato, Andrea.
     Osservazzioni sopra ... Arte magica dileguata.

Witchcraft
F
565
L9
L83
     Replica alla risposta intitolata Arte magica distrutta, di un dottore e sacerdote Veronese. Verona, Nella stamperìa Vescovile del seminario per Angelo Targa, 1751.
     68, [1] p. 24cm.
     Ascribed to P. Antonio Ballerini in a contempory hand on t. p. and in another hand on p. [69]
     "Melzi (II, p. 430) ascribes this to P. Andrea Lugiato, despite its praise of him;
     (Continued on next card)

Lugiato, Andrea.
     Osservazzioni sopra ... Arte magica dileguata.

Witchcraft
F
565
L9
L83
     Replica alla risposta intitolata Arte magica distrutta ... 1751. (Card 2)
     but Melzi knows nothing of the ascription to Ballerini."--Note of George Lincoln Burr on t. p.
     Bound with Fiorio, Antonio. Arte magica distrutta. Trento, 1750.
     1. Fiorio, Antonio. Arte magica distrutta. 2. Lugiato, Andrea. Osservazzioni sopra ... Arte magica dileguata.
     (Continued on next card)

Lugiato, Andrea, supposed author.

Witchcraft
F
565
L9
L83
     Replica alla risposta intitolata Arte magica distrutta, di un dottore e sacerdote Veronese. Verona, Nella stamperìa Vescovile del seminario per Angelo Targa, 1751.
     68, [1] p. 24cm.
     Ascribed to P. Antonio Ballerini in a contempory hand on t. p. and in another hand on p. [69]
     "Melzi (II, p. 430) ascribes this to P. Andrea Lugiato, despite its praise of him;
     (Continued on next card)

Lugiato, Andrea, supposed author.

Witchcraft
     Replica alla risposta intitolata Arte magica distrutta ... 1751. (Card 2)
     but Melzi knows nothing of the ascription to Ballerini."--Note of George Lincoln Burr on t. p.
     Bound with Fiorio, Antonio. Arte magica distrutta. Trento, 1750.
     1. Fiorio, Antonio. Arte magica distrutta. 2. Lugiato, Andrea. Osservazzioni sopra ... Arte magica dileguata.
     (Continued on next card)

Lugiato, Andrea, supposed author.

Witchcraft
F
504
L8
L56+
     Riflessioni sopra l'Arte magica annichilata. Venezia, Appresso Francesco Pitteri, 1755.
     130 p. 26cm.
     According to Melzi, may have been written by A. Lugiato.
     Ex libris F. G. Irwin.
     1. Maffei, Francesco Scipione, marchese, 1675-1755. Arte magica annichilata. 2. Magic. I. Lugiato, Andrea, supposed author.

WITCHCRAFT
BX
2340
L95
   Luis de la Concepción.
     Practica de conjurar, en que se contienen exorcismos, y conjuros contra los malos espiritus...y contra langosias y otros animales nocivos, y tempestades... Madrid, 1721.
     204 p. 16cm.

8
NIC
     1. Exorcism. I. Title.

Lujato, Andrea.

see

Lugiato, Andrea.

Lukins, George, fl. 1788.

Witchcraft
BF
1555
E13
   Easterbrook, Joseph.
     An appeal to the public respecting George Lukins (called the Yatton demoniac), containing an account of his affliction and deliverance, together with variety of circumstances which tend to exculpate him from the charge of imposture. Nottingham, Printed and sold by W. Gray [1788?]
     23 p. 20cm.
     1. Demoniac possession. 2. Lukins, George, fl. 1788. I. Title.

Lukins, George, fl. 1788.

WITCHCRAFT
BF
1555
E13
1788
   Easterbrook, Joseph.
     An appeal to the public respecting George Lukins, (called the Yatton demoniac,) containing an account of his affliction and deliverance; together with a variety of circumstances which tend to exculpate him from the charge of imposture ... Bristol, Printed for T. Mills [1788]
     31 p. 22cm.
     1. Demoniac possession. 2. Lukins, George, fl.1788. I.Title.

8

Lukins, George, fl. 1788.

WITCHCRAFT
BF
1555
N23
1788
   A Narrative of the extraordinary case, of Geo. Lukins, of Yatton, Somersetshire, who was possessed of evil spirits for near eighteen years, also an account of his remarkable deliverance ... extracted from the manuscripts of several persons who attended. To which is prefixed a letter from the Rev. W. R. W. With the Rev. Mr. Easterbrook's letter annex'd ... 2d ed. Bristol, Printed by Bulgin and Rosser, and sold by W. Bul-
     (Continued on next card)

Lukins, George, fl. 1788.

WITCHCRAFT
BF
1555
N23
1788
   A Narrative of the extraordinary case, of Geo. Lukins ... 1788. (Card 2)
     gin [etc] 1788.
     24 p. 21cm.
     1. Demoniac possession. 2. Exorcism. 3. Lukins, George, fl. 1788. I. W. R. W. II. W., R. W. III. Easterbrook, Joseph.

8

Lull, Ramón, d. 1315.

WITCHCRAFT
B
765
L84
I59
   Instrumentu[m], cuiusdam sentencie retractantis quicquid attentatum est p[er] quoscunq[ue], et qualitercunq[ue] +c. auctoritate cuiusda[m] asserte bulle Gregorii vndecimi contra doctrinam illuminati doctoris Raymundi lulii pii heremite. [Valencia, Impressum per Ioannem Iofredum, 1510]
     [31] p. 22cm.

8
NIC
     1. Lull, Ramón, d. 1315.

Witchcraft
BF
1587
D61
no.14
   Lunde, Nicolaus Johann, praeses.
     Theses de magis, volente Deo, publicè tuebimur Nicolaus Joh. Lunde praeses & Henricus Olai Butzow respondens ... Havniae, Ex Reg. Majest. & universit. typographéo [1709]
     8 p. 18cm. (bound in 21cm. vol.)
     No. 14 in vol. lettered Dissertationes de magia. 1623-1723.
     1. Witchcraft--Addresses, essays, lectures. I. Butzow, Henricus Olai, respondent. II. Title.

8

Lunge, Susann, fl. 1613.

Witchcraft
BF
1583
Z7+
1613
   Bacmeister, Dr., archivist.
     Zur Geschichte der Hexenprozesse. Concept Bedenkens über die zu Niedernhaal um Hexerei und Zauberei willen in verhaft liegende Susann, Michel Lunge's Weib, derem Aussage, und noch weiters angebene Personen. [Würtemberg, 1886]
     282-292 p. 30cm.
     Caption title.
     Detached from Württembergische Vierteljahrsheft für Landesgeschichte, IX, 1886.
     (Continued on next card)

Lunge, Susann, fl. 1613.

Witchcraft
BF
1583
Z7+
1613
   Bacmeister, Dr., archivist. Zur Geschichte der Hexenprozesse. (Card 2)
     In pamphlet binder with Bossert, Gustav. Fränkisches Gemeinderecht. [Würtemberg, 1886]
     1. Lunge, Susann, fl. 1613. 2. Witchcraft--Germany. I. Title.

Luno, Bianco, ed.

WITCHCRAFT
BF
1583
H82
1921
   En forskreckelig oc sand bescriffuelse om mange troldfolck; som ere forbrende for deris misgierninger skyld, fra det aar 1589... København [Bianco Lunos bogtrykkeri] 1921.
     [25] p. illus. 21cm. (Bianco Lunos bibliofiludgaver)
     Added t.-p.: Gammel dansk folkelitteratur.
     Flyveskrift første gang trykt i Köln paa Caspar Schumans af Eefurts bekostning og derefter i København af Laurentz
     (Continued on next card)

8
NIC

Luno, Bianco, ed.

WITCHCRAFT
BF
1583
H82
1921
   En forskrechelig oc sand bescriffuelse om mange troldfolck... 1921. (Card 2)
     Benedicht, 1591.
     According to G. L. Burr, a translation of "Hort an new schrecklich abenthewr ... [Köln, 1589?]
     "Efter et gammelt flyveblad, der nu opbevares paa det Kongelige bibliotek i København ... paany ... udgivet ... efter ... modernise[re]de udkast."
     (Continued on next card)

8
NIC

CATALOGUE OF THE CORNELL WITCHCRAFT COLLECTION

WITCHCRAFT
BR
1583
H82
1921

Luno, Bianco, ed.
    En forskreckelig oc sand bescriffeulse om
mange troldfolck... 1921.   (Card 3)

"Stumme Peders graffschrift ... 1589":
p. [14].
"Oplysninger," af Emil Selmar p. [15]-
[23] has special t. p.
"Bogen er trykt i 500 ... ekspl. ... nr.
58."
    1. Witchcraft--Germany. 2. Witchcraft--
Denmark. 3.   Printing--History--
Europe.   I. Luno, Bianco, ed.
II. Selmar,   Emil. III. Hort an new
schrecklich   abentewr.

8
NIC

Witchcraft
BF
1565
T19
M186+

Lusato, veneziano, supposed author.
    [Lugiato, Andrea]
    Osservazioni sopra l'opuscolo che ha per
titolo Arte magica dileguata, di un prete
dell' oratorio. Venezia, Presso Simone
Occhi, 1750.
    3 p. l., 99 p. 27cm.
    Attributed to Lugiato by B. M. and Mel-
zi; but Melzi also suggests one Lusato,
veneziano.
    1. Maffei, Francesco Scipione, marchese,
1675-1755. Arte   magica dileguata. 2. Magic. I. Lusato,   veneziano, supposed author. II. Ti   tle.

8

Witchcraft
BF
1583
D55
Z3

Luther, Martin, 1483-1546.
        Catechismus.
    Diefenbach, Johann.
    Der Zauberglaube des sechzehnten Jahr-
hunderts nach den Katechismen Dr. Martin
Luthers und des P. Canisius. Mit Berück-
sichtigung der Schriften Pfarrers Längin-
Karlsruhe und des Professors Riezler-Mün-
chen. Mainz, F. Kirchheim, 1900.
    xii, 209 p. 23cm.
    1. Witchcraft--Germany. 2. Theology,
Doctrinal--16th century. 3. Canisius,
Petrus, Saint,   1521-1597. Catechismus.

8   (Continued on next card)

BR
334
A2
C6
1875

Luther, Martin, 1483-1546.
    La conférence entre Luther et le diable
au sujet de la messe; raconté par Luther
lui-même. Trad. nouv. du latin par Isidore
Liseux, avec les remarques et annotations
des abbés de Cordemoy et Lenglet-Dufresnoy.
Paris, 1875.
    viii, 91 p. 16cm.

    From Luther's tractate De missa privata
atque sacerdotum unctione. Latin text
parallel with   French translation.
        (Continued on next card)

BR
334
A2
C6
1875

Luther, Martin, 1483-1546. La conférence
entre Luther et le diable...1875. (Card 2)

    I. Lenglet Dufresnoy, Nicolas, 1674-1755, ed.
II. Cordemoy, Géraud de, d. 1684, ed. III.
His De missa privata atque sacerdotum uncti-
one--French. IV. Title.

BR
334
A2
C6
1875

Luther, Martin, 1483-1546.
    De missa privata atque sacerdotum unctione
    --French.
    Luther, Martin, 1483-1546.
    La conférence entre Luther et le
diable au sujet de la messe; raconté par
Luther lui-même. Trad. nouv. du latin par
Isidore Liseux, avec les remarques et
annotations des abbés de Cordemoy et
Lenglet-Dufresnoy. Paris, 1875.
    viii, 91 p. 16cm.

    From Luther's tractate De missa privata
atque sacerdotum unctione. Latin text
parallel with   French translation.

Witchcraft
BT
965
L97
1531

Luther, Martin, 1483-1546.
    Eyn predig vonn den engeln. Do. Marti.
Luther. [Nürnberg, Jobst Gutknecht]
1531.
    [8] l. 21cm.
    Title within woodcut ornamental border.
    Signatures: A-B⁴ (last leaf blank)
    Benzing, J.: Lutherbibliographie, no.
2958.
    Bound by Sangorski and Sutcliffe.
    1. Angels--Early works to 1800. 2. Angels
--Sermons. I.   Title: Eine Predigt von
den Engeln. II. Binding--Sangorski &
Sutcliffe.   III. Title.

PD
25
P15
no.56

Luther, Martin, 1483-1546.
    Klingner, Erich.
    ... Luther und der deutsche volksaber-
glaube. Von Erich Klingner. Berlin,
Mayer & Müller, 1912.
    ix, 135, [1] p. 23½cm. (Palaestra. LVI)

    Chapters 1 and 2 appeared as the author's
inaugural dissertation, Berlin.

    1. Luther, Martin, 1483-1546. 2. Folk-
lore--Germany.   I. Series. II. Title.

WITCHCRAFT
BR
333
.5
W8
P33

Luther, Martin, 1483-1546--Theology.
    Paulus, Nicolaus, 1853-1930.
    Luther und die Hexen.
    (In Historisch-politische Blätter für
das katholische Deutschland. München.
23cm. 139. Bd., 8. Heft (1907), p. [557]-
575)

    At head of title: LV.

    1. Luther, Martin, 1483-1546--Theology.
    2. Witchcraft   --Germany--History. I.
8   Title.
NIC

PD
25
P15
no.56

Luther und der deutsche Volksaberglaube.
    Klingner, Erich.
    ... Luther und der deutsche volksaber-
glaube. Von Erich Klingner. Berlin,
Mayer & Müller, 1912.
    ix, 135, [1] p. 23½cm. (Palaestra. LVI)

    Chapters 1 and 2 appeared as the author's
inaugural dissertation, Berlin.

    1. Luther, Martin, 1483-1546. 2. Folk-
lore--Germany.   I. Series. II. Title.

WITCHCRAFT
BR
333
.5
W8
P33

Luther und die Hexen.
    Paulus, Nicolaus, 1853-1930.
    Luther und die Hexen.
    (In Historisch-politische Blätter für
das katholische Deutschland. München.
23cm. 139. Bd., 8. Heft (1907), p. [557]-
575)

    At head of title: LV.

    1. Luther, Martin, 1483-1546--Theology.
    2. Witchcraft   --Germany--History. I.
8   Title.
NIC

MSS
Bd.
WITCHCRAFT
BF
L97

Lutz, Reinhard.
    Warhafftige Zeitung. Von den gottlosen
Hexen, auch ketzerischen unnd Teufels
Weibern, die zu des heyligē römischeñ Reichsstatt Schletstat im Elsass, auff den zwey
und zwentzigsten Herbstmonats des verlauffenen siebentzigsten Jars, von wegen ihrer
schentlicher Teuffels Verpflichtung verbrent
worden, sampt einem kurtzen Extract und
Aussczug ettlicher Schrifften von Hexerey
zusamen gebra   cht durch Renhardum
Lutz ...   [n.p.] 1571 [ca. 1900]
        (Continued on next card)

MSS
Bd.
WITCHCRAFT
BF
L97

Lutz, Reinhard. Warhafftige Zeitung. Von
den gottlosen Hexen ... 1571 [ca. 1900]
        (Card 2)
    16 l. illus. 23cm.
    Signatures: A-D, E³.
    Carnap's manuscript copy.
    "Originaldruck in der Hof- u. Staats-
bibliothek zu München. 20 Bl. in 4°."
    Signatures and numerals in the margins
correspond to signatures and pagination of
the original.
    1. Witchcr   aft--Germany. 2. Demon-
    ology. 3.   Folk-lore of children.
    I. Title.

Lutz, Renhardus

    see

Lutz, Reinhard.

Witchcraft
BF
1785
C73
1665

Lux e tenebris, novis radiis aucta.
    [Comenius, Johann Amos] 1592-1670, comp.
    Lux e tenebris, novis radiis aucta. Hoc
est: solemnissimae divinae revelationes, in
usum seculi nostri factae ... Per immissas
visiones, & angelica divináqve alloqvia,
facta I. Christophoro Kottero silesio, ab
anno 1616, ad 1624. II. Christinae Poniatoviae bohemae, annis 1627, 1628, 1629,
III. Nicolao Drabicio moravo, ab anno 1638,
ad 1664 ... [Amstelodami] 1665.
    various pagings. illus., ports. 21cm.
    Added engr.   t. p.
8   (Continued on next card)

Witchcraft
BF
1785
C73
1665

Lux e tenebris, novis radiis aucta.
    [Comenius, Johann Amos] 1592-1670, comp.
Lux e tenebris ... 1665. (Card 2)

    "Voluminis prophetici," first item, has
special t. p. with imprint 1667.
    "Revelationes Christophoro Kottero" and
"Revelationes Christinae Poniatoviae" each
have special t. p. with imprint 1664.
    "Revelationes Nicolao Drabicio" has
special t. p. without imprint.
    First published 1657 with title: Lux
in tenebris.   (Continued on next card)

WITCHCRAFT
DC
130
L97
K57

Luxembourg, Francois Henri de Montmorency,
    duc de, 1628-1695.
    Kippenberg, Anton, 1874-1950.
    Die Sage vom Herzog von Luxemburg und die
historische Persönlichkeit ihres Trägers.
Mit 2 Vollbildern und 11 Abbildungen im
Text. Leipzig, W. Engelmann, 1901.
    viii, 280 p. illus. 25cm.

    Bibliography: p. [256]-280.

8
NIC

WITCHCRAFT
BF
1584
S97
H69
1900

Luzerner Akten zum Hexen- und Zauber-
    wesen.
    Hoffmann-Krayer, Eduard, 1864-1936.
    Luzerner Akten zum Hexen- und Zauberwe-
sen. Zürich, Buchdruckerei E. Gotti's
Witwe, 1900.
    144 p. 25cm.
    "Separat-Abdruck aus dem 'Schweiz. Ar-
chiv für Volkskunde.'"
    With this is bound his Ein Zauberproze
in Basel 1719. Zürich, 1898.
    1. Trials (Witchcraft)--Lucerne, Swit
erland. 2.   Trials (Witchcraft)--
8   Switzerland. I. Title.

360

CATALOGUE OF THE CORNELL WITCHCRAFT COLLECTION

Lysthenius, Georgius.
    An das Consistorium zu Leipzig: Drey un-
terschiedliche Schreiben als nemlich eine
Recusatio, Protestatio, Eefutatio [i.e.
Refutatio] M. Georgii Lysthenii wegen der
jtzigen newen Wittenberger Theologen ihme
und andern Superintendenten von oberwehntem Consistorio zugeschickten recht Zwinglischen und gut Caluinischen bedencken von
Abschaffung des Exorcismi bey der heiligen
Tauffe. Magdeburg, Bey Johan Francken,
1592.
    [37] p.   20cm.
           (Continued on next card)

WITCHCRAFT
BX
2340   Lysthenius, Georgius. An das Consistorium
L99   zu Leipzig...1592.   (Card 2)

    1. Exorcism. 2. Baptism--Early works to
1800. I. Title.

CATALOGUE OF THE CORNELL WITCHCRAFT COLLECTION

M

M., pseud.
Witchcraft
BF [Berns, Michael]
1410   Gründliche und völlige Wiederlegung der
B42   Bezauberten Welt Balthasar Beckers, D. Aus
Z57   der Heil. Schrifft gezogen. Wobey zugleich
1708 unzählige curioese Antiqvitaeten erläutert
und zum rechten Gebrauch angewendet werden;
und andere rare auch zu dieser Zeit höchstnöthige Materien. Nebst einem Anhange vom
Licht und Recht der Natur. Mit völligen Registern versehen. Von M. Hamburg, S. Heyl
und J. Liebezeit, 1708.

(Continued on next card)

M., pseud.
Witchcraft
BF [Berns, Michael] Gründliche und völlige
1410   Wiederlegung der Bezauberten Welt ...
B42   1708.   (Card 2)
Z57
1708   3 p. l., 958, [11] p. [p. [12] blank]
title and other vignettes, illus. initials.
21 x 17cm.
4°:)(3, A-I⁴, A-6D⁴, 6E3, 6F⁴, 6G².
Black letter.
According to J. G. T. Grässe, Bibliotheca
magica et pneu   matica, 1843, this work

8   (Continued on next card)

M., pseud.
Witchcraft
BF [Berns, Michael] Gründliche und völlige
1410   Wiederlegung der Bezauberten Welt ...
B42   1708.   (Card 3)
Z57
1708   first appeared in 1697 with title: Die
dreifache Welt als der Christen, Phantasten
und Bezauberten, in dreyen Büchern abgefasst.

1. Bekker, Balthasar, 1634-1698. De
betoverde weereld.   2. Christian life. 3.
Millennialism.   4. Spirits. I. Title.
II. M., pseud.   III. His Die dreifache Welt als   der Christen, Phantas-
8   ten und Bezaub   erten.

M., A. v.
WITCHCRAFT
BF   Neuester Hexenprozess aus dem aufgeklärten
1583   heutigen Jahrhundert; oder, So dumm liegt
A2   mein bayrisches Vaterland noch unter dem
N48   Joch der Mönche und des Aberglaubens.
Von A. v. M. [n.p.] 1786.
36 p. 16cm.

1. Superstition. 2. Witchcraft--Bavaria.
8   3. Trials (Witchcraft)--Bavaria. I. M.,
NIC   A.v.   II.   A. v. M.

M., T.
Witchcraft
BF   A relation of the diabolical practices of
1581   above twenty wizards and witches of the sher-
Z7   iffdom of Renfrew in the kingdom of Scotland,
1697 contain'd in their tryalls, examinations, and
confessions; and for which several of them have
been executed this present year, 1697. London, Printed for H. Newman [1697]
24 p. 21cm.

"To Sir T. M.", a letter signed: "T.P.":
p.3-4.
Wing R 823.

M. D. E. P.
Witchcraft
BF   Missive van M. D. E. P. aan een vrind, over
1410   de zaak van Do. B: Bekker, en het boek
B42   van de Heer Professor M. Leydekker. Rot-
Z86   terdam, By J. Gysen, 1692.
no.6   8 p. l. title vignette, illus. initial.
19 x 15cm. 4
4°: A-B⁴.
Incomplete: second gathering wanting.
Van der Linde 129.
No. 6 in vol. lettered Tractaten voor
en tegen B. Be   kker.

(Continued on next card)

Witchcraft
BF   M. F. S. B. jurium studiosi recentissimum
1445   monimentum De spectris ad ... dominvm
D61   Christophorum Schonbeck ... Lugduni
no.1 Batavorum, Typis Marsianis, 1646.
22, [2] p. 18cm. (bound in 21cm. vol.)

No. 1 in vol. lettered Dissertationes
de spectris. 1646-1753.

1. Apparitions.   I. B., F. S. II.
F. S. B.   III. Schonbeck, Christoph. IV.
8   Title: De sp   ectris.

M. G.
Witchcraft
PQ   Bordelon, Laurent, 1653-1730.
1957   Histoire de M. Oufle, par abbé Bordelon
B67   [retouchée et réduite par M. G.] et la
A64   Description du sabbat. Paris, Gay & Gide, 1793.
1793   360 p. 20cm.

"...C'est ... un nouveau roman, mais ...
nous sommes redevables néanmoins à l'abbé
Bordelon ...": p. 5-6.
"Description du sabbat" is not by Bordelon.

M. G.
Witchcraft
BX   Do. [i. e., doctor] B. Bekkers Sterf-bedde
9479   verdeedigt, tegens de zoo genaamde Nodi-
B42   ge aanmerkingen over het zelve: vervat
B11   in een brief aan den schryver; behelzende
no.3 een openbaar bewijs zijner onkunde in de
geschillen, en verdere ongegronde redeneeringen: tot wegschuiminge van zijn
alderhaatelijkste beschryving en veroordeeling van den overledene. Door M. G.
Amsterdam, By R. Blokland, boekverkooper,
1699.
1 p. l.,   16 p. title and end
8   (Continued on next card)

M. G.
Witchcraft
BX   Do. [i. e., doctor] B. Bekkers Sterf-bedde
9479   verdeedigt ... 1699.   (Card 2)
B42
B11   page vignettes, illus. initial. 20 x 16 cm.
no.3 4°: π1, A-B⁴.
Van der Linde 207.
No. 3 in vol. lettered B. Bekkers sterf-
bed en andere tractaten.
1. Bekker, Balthasar, 1634-1698. 2.
Bekker, Johannes Henricus, fl. 1698-1737.
Sterf-bedde van   ... Do. Balthazar Bekker.

(Continued on next card)

Witchcraft   M. J.
GR   The Hartfordshire wonder; or, Strange news from
142   Ware. Being an exact and true relation of one Jane
H6   Stretton, the daughter of Thomas Stretton of Ware in
A3   the county of Herts, who hath been visited in a strange
no.8 kind of manner by extraordinary and unusual fits, her
abstaining from sustenance for the space of 9 months,
being haunted by imps or devils in the form of several
creatures here described, the parties adjudged of all by
whom she was thus tormented and the occasion thereof ...

(Continued on next card)   17-20383

Witchcraft   M. J.
GR   The Hartfordshire wonder ... (Card 2)
142
H6   London: printed for J. Clark ... 1669. Reprinted with
A3   an introductory note by W. B. Gerish. Bishop's Stort-
no.8 ford. 1908.
15 p. 22ᶜᵐ. [Hertfordshire folk lore. no. 8]
Preface signed: M. J.

1. Stretton, Jane, b. 1649. 2. Witchcraft--England. I. J., M. II.
M J.   III. Gerish, William Blyth, ed.
17-20383
Library of Congress   GR142.H6A3 no. 5

M. J. J. L.
MSS   Der entlarvte Teuffel oder denkwürdige
Bd.   Geschichte von vielen warhaftig Beses-
WITCHCRAFT senen, welche dieses Feindes Grausamkeit
BF   heftig erfahren, entlich aber durch den
E61   mächtigen Finger Gottes wieder erledigt
worden. Zu mehrer Bekräftigung der von
Doct. Beckern, in seiner verzauberten
Welt, zweiffelhaft gemachten Kögischen
Geschichte ... Zusammen getragen von
M. J. J. L. Leipzig, Johann Melchior
Liebe, 16   97 [ca. 1900]

(Continued on next card)

M. J. J. L.
MSS   Der entlarvte Teuffel ... 1697 [ca. 1900]
Bd.   (Card 2)
WITCHCRAFT
BF   77 p. 19cm.
E61   Carnap's manuscript copy.
"Originaldruck in der Königl. öff.
Bibliothek zu Dresden, 98 pag. Seiten in 8°.
"Diese Schrift bildet gewissermassen die
Fortsetzung zu: "Das geängstigte Köge oder
Eine warhaffte und denkwürdige Historie,
von einer, ent   setzlichen Versuchung
des leidigen   Satans zu Köge in
(Continued on next card)

M. J. J. L.
MSS   Der entlarvte Teuffel ... 1697 [ca. 1900]
Bd.   (Card 3)
WITCHCRAFT
BF   Seeland" wo in deutscher Sprache durch
E61   denselben Verfasser ... i. J. 1695 herausgegeben. Hieraus erklärt es sich, dass
diese Schrift mit " die dritte Zugabe"
anfängt, da "das geängstigte Köge mit der
zweiten Zugabe abschliesst."
Marginal numerals and signatures indicate paginati   on ans signatures of
the original.   (Continued on next card)

362

CATALOGUE OF THE CORNELL WITCHCRAFT COLLECTION

M. J. J. L.
Der entlarvte Teuffel ... 1697 [ca. 1900]
(Card 4)

Printed copy not in Van der Linde.

1. Demoniac possession. 2. Devil. 3. Bekker, Balthasar, 1634-1698. De betoverde weereld. I. Das geängstigte Köge. II. M. J. J. L. III. L., M. J. J.

BF 1581 M14 1970
Macfarlane, Alan.
Witchcraft in Tudor and Stuart England; a regional and comparative study. New York, Harper & Row [1970]
xxi, 334 p. illus., facsims., maps. 24 cm. (J. & J. Harper editions) $8.50
"A torchbook library edition."
A modified version of the author's thesis, Oxford, 1967, published under the title: Witchcraft prosecutions in Essex, 1560-1680.
Bibliography: p. [313]-324.

1. Witchcraft—England. I. Title.
BF1581.M26 1970b 301.2 72-119635
Library of Congress 70 [4] MARC

Mackenzie, Sir George, 1636-1691.
The laws and customs of Scotland in matters criminal. Wherein is to be seen how the civil law, and the laws and customs of other nations doth agree with, and supply ours. To this 2d ed. is now added ... a Treatise of mutilation and demembration and their punishments, by Sir Alexander Seton. Also a 2d ed. of the Observations upon the 18 Act. Parl. 23, K. James 6th, against dispositions made in defraud of creditors &c., corr. and ... enl. by the author,
(Continued on next card)

Mackenzie, Sir George, 1636-1691. The laws and customs of Scotland ... 1699. (Card 2)

... before his death. Edinburgh, Printed by the heirs and successors of A. Anderson for A. Symsonz, 1699.
291, 66, 62 p. 30cm.

Wing M 168.
With autographs: Charles Armstrong, and William Kirkpatrick.

(Continued on next card)

Mackenzie, Sir George, 1636-1691. The laws and customs of Scotland ... 1699. (Card 3)

1. Criminal law--Scotland. 2. Criminal procedure--Scotland. 3. Bankruptcy--Scotland. I. Pittmedden, Sir Alexander Seton, Lord, 1639?-1719. A treatise of mutilation and demembration. II. His Observations upon the XVIII Act of Parl. XXIII. K. James VI, against dispositions made in defraud of creditors. III. Title.

Rare K M15 L4+
Mackenzie, Sir George, 1636-1691.
Observations upon the XVIII Act of Parl. XXIII, K. James VI, against dispositions made in defraud of creditors.
Mackenzie, Sir George, 1636-1691.
The laws and customs of Scotland in matters criminal. Wherein is to be seen how the civil law, and the laws and customs of other nations doth agree with, and supply ours. To this 2d ed. is now added ... a Treatise of mutilation and demembration and their punishments, by Sir Alexander Seton. Also a 2d ed. of the Observations upon the 18 Act. Parl. 23, K. James 6th, against dispositions made in defraud of creditors &c., corr. and ... enl. by the author,
(Continued on next card)

NIC

Rare K M15 L4+
Mackenzie, Sir George, 1636-1691.
Observations upon the XVIII Act of Parl. XXIII, K. James VI, against dispositions made in defraud of creditors.
Mackenzie, Sir George, 1636-1691. The laws and customs of Scotland ... (Card 2)

... before his death. Edinburgh, Printed by the heirs and successors of A. Anderson for A. Symsonz, 1699.
291, 66, 62 p. 30cm.

Wing M 168.
With autographs: Charles Armstrong, and William Kirkpatrick.

NIC (Continued on next card)

Witchcraft K M15 P7 1673
[Mackenzie, Sir George] 1636-1691.
Pleadings, in some remarkable cases, before the supreme courts of Scotland, since the year, 1661. To which the decisions are subjoyn'd ... Edinburgh, Printed by George Swintoun, James Glen, and Thomas Brown, 1673.
4 p. l., 232, [4] p. 19½cm.
Signatures: *⁴, q², A-Z⁴, Aa-Ff⁴.
Head-pieces; manuscript notes.
"In three of those pleadings, (viz. 2. 3. 7.) I have mingled with my own arguments, the arguments of such as pleaded with me. In the rest, I have used only my own."—The author's reflections.
With book-plate of George Lockhart of Carnwath.
I. Title.
29-39
Library of Congress [2]

Witchcraft BF 1566 M16
Macleod, Malcolm.
History of witches &c. The majesty of darkness discovered: in a series of tremendous tales ... of apparitions, witches, augers, magicians ... in confirmation of a future state, & the superintendency of a Divine Providence, by the agency of spirits & angels. With The prophecy of Pedan; or, The Caledonian apocalypse of the last century; sublimely adumbrating the awful events which now amaze and alarm all Europe. London, Printed by and for
(Continued on next card)

Witchcraft BF 1566 M16
Macleod, Malcolm. History of witches &c... [1793] (Card 2)
I. Roach [1793]
97 p. front. 17cm.

Title vignette.
I. Title. II. Title: The majesty of darkness discovered. III. Title: The emphatical prophecy of Pedan.

Witchcraft BF 1566 M16 1817
Macleod, Malcolm.
Macleod's History of witches, &c. &c. &c. The majesty of darkness discovered in a series of tremendous tales ... of apparitions, witches, augurs, magicians, dreams, visions and revelations, in confirmation of a future state and the superintendency of a Divine Providence, by the agency of spirits and angels. New York, 1817.
68 p. 18cm.

WITCHCRAFT BF 1523 R44
Das mächtige, doch umschränckte Reich des Teufels.
Reuter, Simon Henrich.
(Sulṭān al-Ẓulmah) سلطان الظلمة
das ist, Das mächtige, doch umschränckte Reich des Teufels; oder, Gründlicher und wahrhaftiger Bericht, was von der List, Macht und Wirckung des Satans und der bösen Geister zu halten sey, und was die Menschen durch derselben Kraft und Gemeinschaft wissen, thun und verrichten können ... Alles treulich aus Gottes Wort und vieler

8 NIC (Continued on next card)

WITCHCRAFT BF 1523 R44
Das mächtige, doch umschränckte Reich des Teufels.
Reuter, Simon Henrich.
(Sulṭān al-Ẓulmah)... (Card 2)
Gelehrten Bücher zusammen getragen, untersuchet und zur Warnung der glaubigen Kinder Gottes vorgestellet; auch mit einem nützlichen Register versehen. Lemgo, H. W. Meyer, 1716.
1293 p. 20cm.

(Continued on next card)

März, Agnellus, 1726-1784.
Augustinian father in Munich. Not to be confused with März, Angelus, 1731-1784, Benedictine father in Schreyer.

Witchcraft BF 1565 S83 M17
[März, Agnellus] 1726-1784.
Urtheil ohne Vorurtheil über die wirkend- und thätige Hexerey, abgefasset von einem Liebhaber der Wahrheit. [München] 1766.
64 p. 20cm.

1. Sterzinger, Ferdinand, 1721-1786. Akademische Rede von dem gemeinen Vorurtheile der ... Hexerey. 2. Witchcraft. I. Ein Liebhaber der Wahrheit. II. Title.

Witchcraft BF 1565 S83 S83
März, Agnellus, 1726-1784.
Urtheil ohne Vorurtheil über die wirkend- und thätige Hexerey.
Sterzinger, Ferdinand, 1721-1786.
Betrügende Zauberkunst und träumende Hexerey, oder Vertheidigung der akademischen Rede, von dem gemeinen Vorurtheile der wirkenden und thätigen Hexerey, wider das Urtheil ohne Vorurtheil &c. ... München, In der akademischen Buchhandlung, 1767.
4 p. l., 96, [2] p. 21cm.
1. His Akademische Rede von dem gemeinen Vorurtheile der . Hexerey. 2. Witchcraft. 3. März, Agnellus, 1726-1784. Urtheil ohne Vorurtheil über die wirkend- und thätige Hexerey. I. Title.

8

Witchcraft BF 1565 S83 M177
März, Agnellus, 1726-1784.
Urtheil ohne Vorurtheil über die wirkend- und thätige Hexerey.
[Sterzinger, Ferdinand] 1721-1786.
Gedanken über die Werke des Liebhabers der Wahrheit von der Hexerey. München, Bey J. A. Crätz, 1767.
27, [1] p. 21cm.
Attributed to Sterzinger by Holzmann and British Museum.

1. März, Agnellus, 1726-1784. Urtheil ohne Vorurtheil über die wirkend- und thätige Hexerey. 2. His Akademische Rede von dem gemeinen Vorurtheile der ... Hexerey. I. Title.

8

Witchcraft BF 1565 S83 S835
[März, Agnellus] 1726-1784.
Vertheidigung wider die geschwulstige Vertheidigung der betrügenden Zauberkunst und traumenden Hexerey, verfasset von einem Liebhaber der Wahrheit. [München] 1767.
[4] p.l., 104 p. 23cm.

1. Sterzinger, Ferdinand, 1721-1786. Betrügende Zauberkunst und träumende Hexerey. I. Ein Liebhaber der Wahrheit. II. Title.

8

CATALOGUE OF THE CORNELL WITCHCRAFT COLLECTION

März, Agnellus, 1726-1784.
   Vertheidigung wider die geschwulstige
Witchcraft   Vertheidigung der betrügenden Zauberkunst.
BF   [Mayer, Andreas Ulrich] 1732-1802.
1565   Sendschreiben an den Hochw. H. P. Agnel-
S83   lus März, ... Über seine Vertheidigung wider
S836   die schwulstige Vertheidigung der betrügen-
         den Zauberey und Hexerey, von F. N. Blocks-
         berger, Beneficiaten zu T. [pseud.]   Strau-
         bingen, 1767.
            5 pieces in 3 v.   23cm.
            Vol. 2 has caption title: Weitere Fort-
         setzung. Des F. N. Blockbergers [sic] zwey-
         tes Sendschreiben an H. P. Agnell &c. &c.
8   (Continued on next card)

März, Agnellus, 1726-1784.
   Vertheidigung wider die geschwulstige
Witchcraft   Vertheidigung der betrügenden Zauberkunst.
BF   [Mayer, Andreas Ulrich] 1732-1802. Send-
1565   schreiben an den Hochw. H. P. Agnellus
S83   März ... 1767.   (Card 2)
S836
         This vol. contains the 2. and 4. Sendschrei-
         ben, consecutively paged.
            Vol. 3 has caption title: Des F. N.
         Blockbergers [sic] fünftes Sendschreiben
         an H. P. Agnell, &c. &c. The vol. contains
         the 5. and 6. Sendschreiben, consecutively
         paged.
8   (Continued on next card)

März, Agnellus, 1726-1784.

Witchcraft
BF   [Durych, Fortunat] 1730-1802.
1565   Eutychii Beniamin Transalbini Dissertatio
D96   tio philologica De vocibus hhartymmim et
         belahatehem Exod. VII. 2.   [Vindobonae?]
         1767.
            20 p. 21cm.
            "Opusculi inscripti: Gedanken über die
         Werke des Liebhabers der Wahrheit von der
         Hexerey."
            1. Witchcraft in the Bible. 2. Bible.
         O.T.--Criticism, Textual. 3. Hartumim
8   (Continued on next card)

März, Agnellus, 1726-1784.

Witchcraft
BF   [Kollmann, Jacob Anton]
1565   Zweifel eines Baiers über die wirkende
S83   Zauberkunst und Hexerey.   An dem Lechstrome
K81   [i.e., Augsburg] 1768.
            74, [1] p. 19cm.
            Attribution by British Museum and H.
         Fieger, P. Don Ferdinand Sterzinger, Mün-
         chen, 1907.
            1. Sterzinger, Ferdinand, 1721-1786.
         Akademische Rede von dem gemeinen Vorurthei-
         le der ... Hexerey. 2. März, Agnellus,
         1726-1784. 3.   Witchcraft. II. Title.
8

März, Agnellus, 1726-1784.

Witchcraft
BF   Sonnenfels, Aloysius von
1565   Sendschreiben des hochedelgebohrnen Herrn
S69   Aloysius von Sonnenfels ... an den hochge-
         lehrten P. don Ferdinand Sterzinger, ...
         über zwey hebräische Wörter chartumim und
         belahatehem: nachmals zur nothwendigen Be-
         lehrung des sogenannten Liebhabers der Wahr-
         heit, und seines lateinischen Eutychii Ben-
         jamin Transalbini in ihrem Zauber- und Hexe-
         rey Streite zum Drucke befördert, von einem
         Verehrer des Sterzingerischen Namens.
8   (Continued on next card)

März, Agnellus, 1726-1784.

Witchcraft
BF   Sonnenfels, Aloysius von   Sendschreiben
1565   ... 1768.   (Card 2)
S69
         Wien, Gedruckt mit schulzischen Schriften,
         1768.
            30, [1] p. 21cm.
            1. Witchcraft in the Bible. 2. Bible.
         O.T.--Criticism, Textual. 3. Hartumim
         (The word) 4. Belahatehem (The word) 5.
         Durych, Fortunat, 1730-1802. Eutychii Ben-
         iamin Transalb   ini Dissertatio philo-
         logica... 6.   März, Agnellus, 1726-
         1784.
8

März, Angelus, 1731-1784.

         Benedictine father in Schreyer.
         Not to be confused with März,
         Agnellus, 1726-1784, Augustinian
         father in Munich.

März, Angelus, 1731-1784.
   Kurze Vertheidigung der thätigen Hex-
Witchcraft und Zauberey.
BF   P. Angelus März Kurze Vertheidigung der
1565   thätigen Hex- und Zauberey wider eine dem
S83   heiligen Kreuz zu Scheyrn nachtheilige- Aka-
M18   demische Rede, welche den 13. October 1766.
1766   von P. Don Ferdinand Sterzinger ... abgele-
         sen worden. 2. Aufl. Jngolstadt, Gedruckt
         bey J. K. Gran [1766]
            31 p. 21cm.
            1. Sterzinger, Ferdinand, 1721-1786. Aka-
         demische Rede   von dem gemeinen Vorur-
         theile der ...   Hexerey. 2. Witchcraft.
         I. Title: K   urze Vertheidigung der
         thätigen Hex-   und Zauberey. II. Title.
8

März, Angelus, 1731-1784.
   Kurze Vertheidigung der thätigen Hex-
Witchcraft und Zauberey.
BF   Anpreisung der allergnädigsten Landesverordnung Ihrer
1584   kaiserl. königl. apostolischen Majestät, wie es mit dem hexen-
A93   processe zu halten sey, nebst einer vorrede, in welcher die
A61   Kurze vertheidigung der hex- und zauberey, die herr pater
         Angelus März der Akademischen rede des herrn p. don Ferdi-
         nand Sterzingers über das vorurtheil der hexerey entgegen-
         gesetzet, beantwortet wird von einem gottesgelehrten. München,
         Akademische buchhandlung, 1767.
            4 p. l., 282, [2] p. 23cm.
                                                  42-40824
8   (Continued on next card)
                           [2]

März, Angelus, 1731-1784.
   Kurze Vertheidigung der thätigen Hex-
Witchcraft und Zauberey.
BF   Anpreisung der allergnädigsten Landesverordnung Ihrer
1584   kaiserl. königl. apostolischen Majestät ... 1767. (Card 2)
A93
A61   Variously ascribed to Jordan Simon and Andreas Ulrich Mayer.
            "Sr. kaiserlich-königlich-apostolischen Maje-
         stät allergnädigsten Landesordnung, wie es mit
         dem Hexenprocesse zu halten sey, mit kurzen An-
         preisungen für den gemeinen Mann erkläret," p.
         [1]-282, has special t.-p.
            1. Witchcraft—Austria. 2. März, Angelus, 1731-1784. Kurze Verthei-
         digung der thätigen Hex- und Zauberey. 3. Sterzinger, Ferdinand, 1721-
         1786. Akademische Rede von dem gemeinen Vorurtheile der ... Hexerey.
         I. Simon, Jordan, pater, 1719-1776, supposed ed. II. Mayer, Andreas Ul-
         rich, 1732-1802, supposed ed. III. Austria. Laws, statutes, etc. IV.
         Ein Gottesgelehrter.
                                                  42-40824
         Library of Congress   BF1584.A8A5
8   [2]

März, Angelus, 1731-1784.
   Kurze Vertheidigung der thätigen Hex-
Witchcraft und Zauberey.
BF   Drey Fragen zur Vertheidigung der Hexerey
1565   I. Ob P. Angelus März die Rede des P.
S83   Don Ferdinand Sterzingers gründlich, und
no.3   II. bescheiden widerleget habe? III.
         Und ob wohl diese akademische Rede dem
         heiligen Kreutze von Scheyrn in der That
         nachtheilig sey? Mit einem sichern Ja
         beantwortet, und dem P. Angelus März
         selbst dedicirt von J. F. Z. ...
         [München?] 1767.
            28 p. 23cm.
8   (Continued on next card)

März, Angelus, 1731-1784.
   Kurze Vertheidigung der thätigen Hex-
Witchcraft und Zauberey.
BF   Drey Fragen zur Vertheidigung der Hexerey
1565   ... 1767.   (Card 2)
S83
no.3   "In spite of the initials J. F. Z. (Jo-
         hann Felix Zech) in the dedication, the work
         is probably by H. Braun. See Fieger, H.
         P. Don Ferdinand Sterzinger, 1907."--Note
         by G. L. Burr on his ms. catalog slip for
         this item.
            No. 3 in vol. lettered Sterzinger über
         Hexerei, 1766-1767.
8   (Continued on next card)

März, Angelus, 1731-1784.
   Kurze Vertheidigung der thätigen Hex-
Witchcraft und Zauberey.
BF   März, Angelus, 1731-1784.
1565   P. Angeli März Verantwortung Über die
S83   vom (Titl) P. Don Ferdinand Sterzinger bey
M185   dem hochfürstlich-hochlöblich-geistlichen
         Rath zu Freysing freywillig wider ihn ge-
         stellten Fragen. Jngolstadt, Gedruckt
         bey J. K. Gran, 1767.
            42 p. 19cm.
            A copy of the questions may be found in:
         Fieger, Hans, 1857-   . P. Don Ferdinand
         Sterzinger, Mün   chen, 1907, p. 135.
8   (Continued on next card)

März, Angelus, 1731-1784.
   Kurze Vertheidigung der thätigen Hex-
Witchcraft und Zauberey.
BF   [Mayer, Andreas Ulrich] 1732-1802.
1565   Glückwünschungsschreiben an den Hochw.
S83   P. Angelus März, über seine Vertheidigung
M186   der Hex- und Zauberey, von F. N. Blocks-
         berger, Beneficiaten zu T. [pseud.]
         Straubingen, 1767.
            [16] p. 22cm.
            1. März, Agnellus, 1731-1784. ...
         Kurze Vertheidigung der thätigen Hex- und
         Zauberey. 2.   Sterzinger, Ferdinand,
         1721-1786. I.   Title.
8

März, Angelus, 1731-1784.
   Kurze Vertheidigung der thätigen Hex-
Witchcraft und Zauberey.
BF   [Mayer, Andreas Ulrich] 1732-1802.
1565   Nichtige, ungegründete, eitle, kahle und
S83   lächerliche Verantwortung des H. P. Angelus
no.4   März, Benedictiner zu Scheyrn, über die vom
         P. Don Ferdinand Sterzinger bey dem hoch-
         fürstlichen hochlöblichen geistlichen Rath
         in Freysing gestellten Fragen. Vom Mol-
         daustrom, 1767.
            57 p. 20cm. (bound in 23cm. vol.)
            Ascribed by Graesse, J. G. T., Biblio-
         theca magica et pneumatica and by Zapf.
8   (Continued on next card)

März, Angelus, 1731-1784.
   Kurze Vertheidigung der thätigen Hex-
Witchcraft und Zauberey.
BF   [Mayer, Andreas Ulrich] 1732-1802. Nich-
1565   tige, ungegründete, eitle ... Verantwortung
S83   des H. P. Angelus März ... 1767.
no.4   (Card 2)

            G. W., Zauberbibliothek, to F. N. Blocks-
         berger, which is A. U. Mayer's pseudonym.
         British Museum suggests F. Sterzinger
         as author.
            No. 4 in vol. lettered Sterzinger über
         Hexerei, 1766-1767.
8   (Continued on next card)

Witchcraft
BF   März, Angelus, 1731-1784.
1565   P. Angeli März Verantwortung über die
S83   vom (Titl) P. Don Ferdinand Sterzinger bey
M185   dem hochfürstlich-hochlöblich-geistlichen
         Rath zu Freysing freywillig wider ihn ge-
         stellten Fragen. Jngolstadt, Gedruckt
         bey J. K. Gran, 1767.
            42 p. 19cm.
            A copy of the questions may be found in:
         Fieger, Hans, 1857-   . P. Don Ferdinand
         Sterzinger, Mün   chen, 1907, p. 135.
8   (Continued on next card)

Witchcraft
BF   März, Angelus, 1731-1784. P. Angeli März
1565   Verantwortung ... 1767.   (Card 2)
S83
M185
            1. His   Kurze Vertheidigung der
         thätigen Hex- und Zauberey. 2. Sterzinger,
         Ferdinand, 1721-1786. I. Title: Verant-
         wortung über die vom ... P. Don Ferdinand
         Sterzinger ... gestellten Fragen. II. Title.
8

CATALOGUE OF THE CORNELL WITCHCRAFT COLLECTION

Matcke, Heinrich Andreas, respondent.

WITCHCRAFT
BT
960
.53
    Richter, David, of Güstrow, praeses.
        Qvadriga dispp. [i.e. disputationum, magico-thevrgicarum de conciliatione spirityvm, oder: Von der Kunst sich mit Geistern bekant zu machen, qvam svb praesidio Davidis Richteri habvervnt Henr. Andr. Matcke et Georg. Erhard. Hambergervs. Jena, J. B. Heller, 1716.
        86 p. 20cm.

(Continued on next card)

---

chcraft
    [Maffei, Francesco Scipione, marchese] 1675-1755.
        Arte magica annichilata. Libri tre. Con un' appendice. Verona, A. Andreoni, 1754.
        5 p. l., 328, [6] p. 25cm.
        Author's name appears in the dedication.
        The fifth preliminary leaf bound in back of vol.
        Work inspired by the controversy about G. Tartarotti's Del congresso notturno delle lammie.
        1. Magic. 2. Witchcraft. 3. Tartarotti, Girolamo, 1706-1761. Del congresso notturno delle lammie. I. Title.
    ——— Copy 2.

Maffei, Francesco Scipione, marchese, 1675-1755.
    Arte magica annichilata.

Witchcraft
BF
1604
.M8
.R56+
    Riflessioni sopra l'Arte magica annichilata. Venezia, Appresso Francesco Pitteri, 1755.
        130 p. 26cm.

    According to Melzi, may have been written by A. Lugiato.
    Ex libris F. G. Irwin.
    1. Maffei, Francesco Scipione, marchese, 1675-1755. Arte magica annichilata. 2. Magic. I. Lugiato, Andrea, supposed author.

Witchcraft
BF
1565
T19
M183+
    Maffei, Francesco Scipione, marchese, 1675-1755.
        Arte magica dileguata: lettera del Signor Marchese Maffei al Padre Innocente Ansaldi ... Verona, Per Agostino Carattoni, 1749.
        51 p. 26cm.
        With this are bound his Tre lettere. Verona, 1748; and Benvenuti, Giuseppe, 1728-ca. 1770. De daemoniacis dissertatio. Lucae, 1775.

(Continued on next card)

Witchcraft
    Maffei, Francesco Scipione, marchese, 1675-1755. Arte magica dileguata.
    1749.   (Card 2)

    1. Tartarotti, Girolamo, 1706-1761. Del congresso notturno delle lamie. 2. Magic. 3. Witchcraft. I. Title.

Maffei, Francesco Scipione, marchese, 1675-1755.
    Arte magica dileguata.

Witchcraft
BF
1565
T19
M183
    Fiorio, Antonio.
        Arte magica distrutta. Risposta di Don Antonio Fiorio Veronese. Trento, Per G. A. Brunati, 1750.
        47 p. 24cm.
        "As is pointed out on p. 4 of the Replica bound in these same covers, this imprint 'In Trento per G. A. Brunati' is stamped in by hand. Melzi, ii, p. 418, ascribes the pamphlet to Maffei himself." --Note of George Lincoln Burr on t. p.

(Continued on next card)

Maffei, Francesco Scipione, marchese, 1675-1755.
    Arte magica dileguata.

Witchcraft
BF
1565
T19
M183
    Fiorio, Antonio.   Arte magica distrutta.
    1750.   (Card 2)

    With this is bound Replica alla risposta intitolata Arte magica distrutta. Verona, 1751.
    1. Maffei, Francesco Scipione, marchese, 1675-1755. Arte magica dileguata. 2. Magic. I. Maffei, Francesco Scipione, marchese, 1675-1755, supposed author. II. Title.

Maffei, Francesco Scipione, marchese, 1675-1755.
    Arte magica dileguata.

Witchcraft
BF
1565
T19
M186+
    [Lugiato, Andrea]
        Osservazioni sopra l'opuscolo che ha per titolo Arte magica dileguata, di un prete dell' oratorio. Venezia, Presso Simone Occhi, 1750.
        3 p. l., 99 p. 27cm.
        Attributed to Lugiato by B. M. and Melzi; but Melzi also suggests one Lusato, veneziano.
        1. Maffei, Francesco Scipione, marchese, 1675-1755. Arte magica dileguata. 2. Magic. I. Lusato, veneziano, supposed author. II. Title.

Maffei, Francesco Scipione, marchese, 1675-1755.
    Arte magica dileguata.

Witchcraft
BF
1565
T192+
    Tartarotti, Girolamo, 1706-1761.
        Apologia del Congresso notturno delle lammie, o sia risposta di Girolamo Tartarotti all' Arte magica dileguata del Sig. March. Scipione Maffei, ed all' opposizione del Sig. Assessore Bartolommeo Melchiori. S'aggiunge una lettera del Sig. Clemente Baroni di Cavalcabò. Venezia, Presso Simone Occhi, 1751.
        4 p. l., 268 p. 26cm.
        1. His   Del congresso notturn-

(Continued on next card)

Witchcraft
BF
1412
C16
1759
    Maffei, Francesco Scipione, marchese, 1675-1755.
    Calmet, Augustin, 1672-1757.
        Traité sur les apparitions des esprits, et sur les vampires, ou les revenans de Hongrie, de Moravie, &c. Nouv. éd., rev., corr., & augm. Senones, Chez Joseph Pariset, 1759.
        2 v. 17cm.
        Later ed. of Dissertations sur les apparitions.
        "Lettre de M. le Marquis Maffei sur la magie": v. 2, p. 325-393.

Maffei, Francesco Scipione, marchese, 1675-1755, supposed author.

Witchcraft
BF
1565
T19
M183
    Fiorio, Antonio.
        Arte magica distrutta. Risposta di Don Antonio Fiorio Veronese. Trento, Per G. A. Brunati, 1750.
        47 p. 24cm.
        "As is pointed out on p. 4 of the Replica bound in these same covers, this imprint 'In Trento per G. A. Brunati' is stamped in by hand. Melzi, ii, p. 418, ascribes the pamphlet to Maffei himself." --Note of George Lincoln Burr on t. p.

(Continued on next card)

Maffei, Francesco Scipione, marchese, 1675-1755, supposed author.

Witchcraft
BF
1565
T19
M183
    Fiorio, Antonio.   Arte magica distrutta.
    1750.   (Card 2)

    With this is bound Replica alla risposta intitolata Arte magica distrutta. Verona, 1751.
    1. Maffei, Francesco Scipione, marchese, 1675-1755. Arte magica dileguata. 2. Magic. I. Maffei, Francesco Scipione, marchese, 1675-1755, supposed author. II. Title.

Witchcraft
BF
1604
P92
    Maffei, Francesco Scipione, marchese, 1675-1755.
    Preati, Bartolommeo.
        L'arte magica dimostrata. Dissertazione di Bartolammeo Preati, Vicentino, contra l'opinione del Signor Marchese Maffei. Venezia, Stamperia Remondini, 1751.
        95 p. 21cm.

    1. Magic. 2. Maffei, Francesco Scipione, marchese, 1675-1755. I. Title.

Mafteah Shelomo. French.

WITCHCRAFT
BF
1558
G86
1750
    L'Art de commander les esprits célestes, aériens, terrestres & infernaux. Suivi du Grand grimoire, de la magie noire et des forces infernales, du docteur J. Karter, La clavicule de Salomon, &c. Avec le vrai secret de faire parler les morts, pour découvrir tous les trésors caches, &c. &c. [Paris?] 1421 [i.e. ca.1750?]
        iv, 5-108 (i.e.118), [2] p. illus. 16cm.
        Title in red and black.
        Published also under other titles: Grimoire du Pape Honorius; Le dragon rouge; and Le véritable dragon rouge.

Witchcraft
HV
6248
F78
    A Magazine of scandall; or, A heape of wickednesse of two infamous ministers, consorts, one named Thomas Fowkes of Earle Soham in Suffolk, convicted by law for killing a man, and the other named Iohn Lowes of Brandeston, who hath beene arraigned for witchcraft, and convicted by law for a common barretor. Together with the manner how my lord of Canterbury would put and keep them in the ministery, notwithstanding the many petitions and cer tificates from their

(Continued on next card)

Witchcraft
HV
6248
F78
    A Magazine of scandall ... 1642.   (Card 2)

    parishioners, and others... and against whom .. the county of Suffolke have [sic] petitioned to the Parliament ... because ... one of these scandalous ministers have [sic] abused the authority of the lords in Parliament ... London, Printed for R. H., 1642.
        [12] p. 20cm.
        1. Fowkes, Thomas. 2. Lowes, John, clerk, d. 1645.

Witchcraft
Z
6878
W8
M19
    Maggs Bros., London.
        Witchcraft and magic; a catalogue of books relating to witchcraft, magic, necromancy, ghosts and apparitions, dreams, astrology, occult, prophecies, and strange happenings. London, 1969.
        38 p. illus. 23cm. (Its catalogue 921)
    2copies
    1. Witchcraft--Bibl.--Catalogs. 2. Magic-- Bibl.--Catalogs. I. Title.

I maghi.

GR
535
F41
    Feslikenian, Franca.
        I maghi. Storie vere di magie, riti e sortilegi. Milano, G. De Vecchi, 1970.
        195 p. plates. 20½ cm. L2500   It 71-Feb

    1. Witchcraft—Italy. I. Title.

GR535.F4   73-594798

Library of Congress   71 [2]

CATALOGUE OF THE CORNELL WITCHCRAFT COLLECTION

Witchcraft
BF
1565
A34

Magia; das ist, Christlicher Bericht von der Zauberey vnd Hexerey ins gemein. Albrecht, Bernhard.
Magia; das ist, Christlicher Bericht von der Zauberey vnd Hexerey ins gemein, vnd dero zwölfferley Sorten vnd Arten insonderheit ... Aus heiliger göttlicher Schrifft vnd andern bewährten Historien gestellet. Leipzig, G. Grosse, gedruckt durch J. A. Mintzeln, 1628.
314 p. 20cm.

1. Witchcraft. 2. Magic. I. Title.

WITCHCRAFT
BF
1595
N39

La magia nel secolo decimonono.
Negroni, Bernardino.
La magia nel secolo decimonono; racconti puramente storici. Bologna, Società tip. dei compositori, 1872.
2 v. in 1. 15cm.

8
NIC

1. Magic--Hist. 2. Occult sciences--Hist.

WITCHCRAFT
BF
1627
B82

A magia no mundo; catálogo da exposição.
Brazil. Biblioteca Nacional. Divisão de Publicações e Divulgação.
A magia no mundo; catálogo da exposição. [Rio de Janeiro] 1971.
79 p. illus. 23cm.

NIC 9

1. Magic--Exhibitions--Catalogs. I. Title.

Witchcraft
BF
1520
C57
1607

Magiæ omnifariæ.
Cigogna, Strozzi.
Magiæ omnifariæ, vel potius, Vniversæ natvræ theatrvm: in qvo a primis rervm principiis arcessita disputatione, vniuersa spiritvvm & incantationvm natura, &c. explicatur. Auctore d. Strozzio Cigogna ... ex italico latinitati donatum opera & studio Caspari Ens ... Coloniæ, sumptibus C. Butgenij, 1607.
4 p. l., 568 p. 16cm.

1. Demonology. 2. Exorcism. I. Ens, Gaspar, 1570-1636?, tr. II. Title.
11-9698

Rare
Z
6878
P8
P94

Magic--Bibliography.
Price, Harry, 1881-1948, compiler.
Short-title catalogue of works on psychical research, spiritualism, magic, psychology, legerdemain and other methods of deception, charlatanism, witchcraft, and technical works for the scientific investigation of alleged abnormal phenomena, from circa 1450 A. D. to 1929 A. D.
(In National Laboratory of Psychical Research, London. Proceedings. London. 25cm. v. 1 (1929) pt. 2, p. 67-422)

(over)

Witchcraft
Z
6880
Z9
C35
no.2

Magic--Bibliography--Catalogs.
Heberle, J M
Culturgeschichte und Curiositäten in Druckschriften, fliegenden Blättern, Bildern, Autographen und Monumenten. Aus den Sammlungen von Heinrich Lempertz... Zu beigesetzten Preisen vorräthig auf dem Bücher- und Kunstlager von J. M. Heberle (H. Lempertz' Söhne) in Cöln. Abth. E: Physiognomik, Phrenologie, Mimik, natürliche Magie, Kunststücke, Alchymie, etc. ... Abth. F: Zauberei und Hexerei, Faust, Cagliostro, Teufelswesen und
(Continued on next card)

Witchcraft
Z
6880
Z9
C35
no.2

Magic--Bibliography--Catalogs.
Heberle, J M
Culturgeschichte und Curiositäten... (Card 2)
Beschwörungen, Besessensein, etc. ... Cöln, Steven's Druckerei [1874?]
64 p. 23cm.

At head of title: Nro. 74.
No. 2 in vol. lettered: Catalogues of books on magic and witchcraft.
1. Occult sciences--Bibl.--Catalogs. 2. Witchcraft--Bibl.--Catalogs. 3. Magic--Bibl.--Catalogs.

Witchcraft
Z
6880
Z9C35
no.1

Magic--Bibliography--Catalogs.
Rosenthal, Ludwig, Munich.
Bibliotheca magica et pneumatica. Geheime Wissenschaften, Magie, gute und böse Geister, Gespenster, Volksaberglauben; Hexen und Hexenprocesse ... Ellwangen, L. Weil, [188-?]
148 p. 23cm.

"Katalog 45."
No. 1 in vol. lettered: Catalogues of books on magic and witchcraft.

Witchcraft
Z
6880
Z9
T35

Magic--Bibliography--Catalogs.
Teubner, Franz, bookseller, Bonn.
Bibliotheca magica et pneumatica. [Abth. I[-III, VI] Antiquaritäts-Katalog No. 49[-Nr. 51, 54. Bonn, 189-]
v. in . 22cm.
Abth. II and III in 1 vol.
At head of title, vol. I: Franz Teubner's Antiquariat (vorm. Antiquariat der Firma Paul Neubner in Köln)
1. Occult sciences--Bibl.--Catalogs. 2. Magic--Bibl.--Catalogs. I. Title.

8

Witchcraft
BF
1503
C69+
1863

Magic--Dictionaries.
Collin de Plancy, Jacques Albin Simon, 1794-1881.
Dictionnaire infernal. Répertoire universel des etres, des personnages, des livres, des faits et des choses qui tiennent aux esprits, aux démons, aux sorciers ... et généralement a toutes les fausses croyances merveilleuses, surprenantes, mystérieuses et surnaturelles. 6. éd., augm. et illustrée ... par M. L. Breton.   Paris, H. Plon, 1863.
723 p. illus., ports. 27cm.
1. Occult sciences--Dictionaries. 2. Magic--Dictionaries. I. Title.

Witchcraft
BF
1566
M71

Magic and witchcraft.
[Moir, George] 1800-1870.
Magic and witchcraft ... London, Chapman and Hall, 1852.
vi p, 1 l., 104 p. 17cm.

1. Magic. 2. Witchcraft. I. Title.
22-4737

Witchcraft
BF
1591
D25
1898

Magic, divination, and demonology among the Hebrews and their neighbours.
Davies, Thomas Witton, 1851-1923.
Magic, divination, and demonology among the Hebrews and their neighbours, including an examination of biblical references and of the biblical terms. London, J. Clarke [pref. 1898]
xvi,130 p. 20cm.

"This treatise was presented to the University of Leipzig [for the degree of doctor of philosophy] July 1897."--Pref.
Without thesis statement on t.p.
I. Title.

Witchcraft
BF
1639
H32+

Magic in the reign of Queen Elizabeth.
Hart, William Henry, d. 1888.
Observations on some documents relating to magic in the reign of Queen Elizabeth. Communicated to the Society of Antiquaries by W. H. Hart, esq. F.S.A. London, Printed by J. B. Nichols, 1867.
9 p. 30cm.

1. Alchemy. 2. Witchcraft--England. I. Society of Antiquaries of London. II. Title: Magic in the reign of Queen Elizabeth.

8

Witchcraft
BF
1589
B76
1960

Magic: its rites and history.
Bouisson, Maurice.
Magic: its rites and history. Translated from the French by G. Almayrac. London, Rider [1960]
319 p. illus. 24 cm.
Includes bibliography.
Translation of La magie; ses grands rites, son histoire.

1. Magic--Hist. I. Title. II. His La magie; ses grands rites, son histoire--English.
BF1589.B653   133.409   60-51858 ‡
Library of Congress   [2]

Witchcraft
BF
1593
R99
1879

The magic of the Middle Ages.
Rydberg, Viktor, 1828-1895.
The magic of the Middle Ages. Translated from the Swedish by August Hjalmar Edgren. New York, Holt, 1879.
231 p. 20cm.

Translation of his Medeltidens magi.

1. Magic. I. Title. II. Rydberg, Viktor, 1828-1895. Medeltidens magi--English.

WITCHCRAFT
GR
780
H59
1886

Magic plants.
Heucher, Johann Heinrich, 1677-1747.
Magic plants; being a translation of a curious tract entitled De vegetalibus magicis, written by M. J. H. Heucher. (1700.) Edited by Edmund Goldsmid. Edinburgh [Printed by E. & G. Goldsmid] 1886.
39 p. 23cm. (Bibliotheca curiosa)
Title in red and black.
"This edition is limited to 275 small-paper copies ..."
Translation of Ex historia naturali
(Continued on next card)

WITCHCRAFT
GR
780
H59
1886

Magic plants.
Heucher, Johann Heinrich, 1677-1747.
Magic plants ... 1886.   (Card 2)
de vegetalibus magicis generatim, by Heucher and J. Fabricius.
"I have given, as an Appendix, a translation from the Official records of the Royal Court of Guernsey, of the trials of three women for witchcraft in 1617. This translation is taken from Mr. J. L. Pitt's Witchcraft and Devil-Lore in the Channel Islands."--ed.

8
(Continued on next card)

WITCHCRAFT
BF
1589
B81
1852

Magic, witchcraft, animal magnetism, hypnotism, and electro-biology.
Braid, James, 1795?-1860.
Magic, witchcraft, animal magnetism, hypnotism, and electro-biology ... 3d. ed., greatly enl., embracing observations on J. C. Colquhon's "History of magic" ... London, J. Churchill, 1852.
122 p. 19cm.

1. Magic. 2. Witchcraft. 3. Animal magnetism. 4. Colquhon, John Campbell, 1785-1854. An history of magic. I. Title.

8
NIC

CATALOGUE OF THE CORNELL WITCHCRAFT COLLECTION

WITCHCRAFT
BF
1520
M19
    Magica, seu Mirabilium historiarum de spectris et apparitionibvs spiritvvm: item, De magicis & diabolicis incantationibus: De miraculis, oraculis, vaticinijs, diuinationibus, praedictionibus, visionibus, reuelationibus, & alijs eiusmodi multis ac varijs praestigijs, ludibrijs, & imposturis malorum daemonum libri II. Ex probatis, et fide dignis historiarum scriptoribus diligenter collecti. Islebiae, Cura, typis & sumptibus Henningi Grosij, 1597.

(Continued on next card)

CHCRAFT
20
    Magica, seu Mirabilium de spectris et apparitionibvs spiritvvm ... libri II ... 1597. (Card 2)

[16], 478, [28] p. 21cm.

Title within ornamental border; title vignette.
"Epistola dedicatoria" signed by the editor: Henningus Grosius.
Published in 1656 under title: Magica de spectris et apparitionibus spirituum, de vaticiniis, divinationibus, &c.
I. Magica de spectris et apparitionibus spirituum de vaticiniis, divinationibus.

WITCHCRAFT
BF
1520
M19
1656
    Magica de spectris et apparitionibus spiritū, de vaticiniis, divinationibus, &c. Lugd.Batavorvm, apud Franciscum Hackium, 1656.
12 p.l., 636, [33] p. 14cm.
Engraved t.-p.
First edition published under title: Magica; seu Mirabilium historiarum de spectris et apparitionibus spirituum ... libri II. Islebiae, typis et sumpt. Henningi Grosij, 1597.
"Epistola dedicatcria" signed by the editor: Henningus Grosius.
"Catalogus auctorum, e quibus historiae atque exempla ista congesta sunt": 11th -12th prelim. leaves.
I. Grosse, Henning, 1553-1621, ed.

---

chcraft
BF
1520
M19
    Magica de spectris et apparitionibus spirituum, de vaticiniis, divinationibus.
Magica, seu Mirabilium historiarum de spectris et apparitionibvs spiritvvm: item, De magicis & diabolicis incantationibus: De miraculis, oraculis, vaticinijs, diuinationibus, praedictionibus, visionibus, reuelationibus, & alijs eiusmodi multis ac varijs praestigijs, ludibrijs, & imposturis malorum daemonum libri II. Ex probatis, et fide dignis historiarum scriptoribus diligenter collecti. Islebiae, Cura, typis & sumptibus Henningi Grosij, 1597.

(Continued on next card)

---

chcraft
BF
1520
M19
    Magica de spectris et apparitionibus spirituum, de vaticiniis, divinationibus.
Magica, seu Mirabilium de spectris et apparitionibvs spiritvvm ... libri II ... 1597. (Card 2)

[16], 478, [28] p. 21cm.

Title within ornamental border; title vignette.
"Epistola dedicatoria" signed by the editor: Henningus Grosius.
Published in 1656 under title: Magica de spectris et apparitionibus spirituum, de vaticiniis, divinationibus, &c.

---

itchcraft
BF
879
2C75
896
    The magical ritual of the sanctum regnum interpreted by the tarot trumps.
[Constant, Alphonse Louis] 1810?-1875.
The magical ritual of the sanctum regnum interpreted by the tarot trumps. Translated from the mss. of Éliphaz Lévi [pseud.] and edited by W. Wynn Westcott. London, G. Redway, 1896.
x, 108 p. 8 col. plates. 19cm.

1. Magic. 2. Tarot. I. Westcott, William Wynn, 1848-1925, ed. and tr. II. Title.

WITCHCRAFT
R
133
C173
    Magici morbi historia attentius pensitata.
Camerarius, Elias, 1672-1734, praeses.
Magici morbi historia attentius pensitata. Hanc...praeside Elia Camerario...examini publico submittit Christianus Neufferus... Tubingae, Typis Georgii Friderici Pelickii [1724]
31 p. 20cm.

Diss.--Tübingen (C. Neuffer, respondent)
1. Medicine, Magic, mystic and spagiric. 2. Demonology. I. Neuffer, Christian, respondent.

8
NIC

Witchcraft
BF
1589
M45
1864
    La magie et l'astrologie dans l'antiquité et au moyen âge.
Maury, Louis Ferdinand Alfred, 1817-1892.
La magie et l'astrologie dans l'antiquité et au moyen âge; ou, Étude sur les superstitions païennes qui se sont perpétuées jusqu'à nos jours. 3. éd.revue et corrigée. Paris, Didier, 1864.
484 p. 18cm.

8
NIC

1. Magic. 2. Astrology. 3. Occult sciences. I. Title.

Witchcraft
BF
1434
F8
C37
    La magie et la sorcellerie en France.
Cauzons, Thomas de, pseud.
La magie et la sorcellerie en France ... par Th. de Cauzons ... Paris, Dorbon-aîné [1910-11?]
4 v. 20½cm.

Contents.--I. Origine de la sorcellerie. Ce qu'on racontait des sorcières. Opinions diverses à leur sujet.--II. Poursuite et châtiment de la magie jusqu'à la réforme protestante. Le procès des Templiers. Mission et procès de Jeanne d'Arc.--III. La sorcellerie de la réforme à la révolution. Les couvents possédés. La franc-maçonnerie. Le magnétisme animal.--
(Continued on next card)

Witchcraft
BF
1434
F8
C37
    La magie et la sorcellerie en France.
Cauzons, Thomas de, pseud. La magie et la sorcellerie en France ... [1910-11?] (Card 2)

Contents (cont'd)
IV. La magie contemporaine. Les transformations du magnétisme. Psychoses et névroses. Les esprits des vivants. Les esprits des morts. Le diable de nos jours. Le merveilleux populaire.

Witchcraft
BF
1612
P73
    La magie; les lois occultes.
Plytoff, G
La magie; les lois occultes, la théosophie, l'initiation, le magnétisme, le spiritisme, la sorcellerie, le sabbat, l'alchimie, la kabbale, l'astrologie. Paris, Librairie J.-B. Baillière et Fils, 1892.
viii, 312 p. illus. 20cm. (Bibliothèque scientifique contemporaine)

Witchcraft
BF
1412
C13
1858
    Magie magnétique.
Cahagnet, Louis Alphonse, 1809-1885.
Magie magnétique; ou, Traité historique et pratique de fascinations, miroirs cabalistiques, apports, suspensions, pactes, talismans ... 2. éd., corr. et augm. Paris, G. Baillière, 1858.
516 p. 18cm.
First published 1854.

1. Occult sciences--Hist. I. Title. II. Title: Traité historique et pratique des fascinations.

8

Witchcraft
BF
1603
H46
1750
    La magie naturelle.
Grimoire; ou La magie naturelle. La Haye, Aux dépens de la Compagnie [ca. 1750]
600 p. illus. 14cm.

"Traduction altérée d'un bizarre ouvrage allemand intitulé Heldenschutz"--Graesse, Trésor de livres rares et précieux.

1. Magic. 2. Receipts--Early works to 1800. 3. Handbooks, vade-mecums, etc. 4. Medicine--Formulae receipts, prescriptions, etc. I. Heldenschutz. French. II. Title: La magie naturelle.

8

Witchcraft
BF
1589
D19
    Magie und Geheimwissenschaft in ihrer Bedeutung für Kultur und Kulturgeschichte.
Danzel, Theodor Wilhelm, 1886-
Magie und Geheimwissenschaft in ihrer Bedeutung für Kultur und Kulturgeschichte. Stuttgart, Strecker und Schröder, 1924.
xv, 213 p. front. 22cm.

1. Magic. I. Title.

Witchcraft
BF
1587
D61
no.11
    Magiologia.
Büttner, Daniel, 1642-1696, praeses.
Magiologia seu Disputatio de magia licita et illicita qvam ... praeside Dn. Daniele Büttnero ... disquisitioni submittit Albertus zum Felde ... Hamburgi, Literis Conradi Neumanni [1693]
26, [6] p. 18cm. (bound in 21cm. vol.)
No. 11 in vol. lettered Dissertationes de magia. 1623-1723.

1. Magic--Addresses, essays, lectures. I. Felde, Albert zum, 1672-1720, respondent. II. Title. III. Title: De magia licita et illicita.

8

WITCHCRAFT
BF
1563
T86
    Das magische Geistesleben.
Ferrier, Auger, 1513-1588.
A learned astronomicall discovrse of the ivdjement of nativities; divided into three bookes ... by Oger Ferrier. Translated by Thomas Kelway. London, Printed by R. Cotes, and are to be sold by L. Chapman, 1642.
111 p. tables. 19cm.
Translation of Des jugements astronomiques sur les nativiez.
No. 10 in vol. lettered Tracts of witches.
I. His Des jugements astronomiques sur les nativitez. II. Kelway, Thomas, fl. 1593, tr. III. Title.

Witchcraft
BF
1555
H18
    Magister Ole Bjørn og de besatte i Thisted.
Hallager, Frederik, 1816-1876.
Magister Ole Bjørn og de besatte i Thisted. København, Dansk Sundhedstidendes Forlag, 1901.
188 p. 21cm.

1. Bjørn, Ole, b. 1648. 2. Demonology. 3. Exorcism. I. Title.

Witchcraft
BF
1569
A2
V82
1490
    Magistri Hyeronimi Vicecomitis. Lamiarum siue striarum opusculum.
Visconti, Girolamo, fl. 1490-1512.
Lamiarum sive striarum opuscula. Milan, Leonardus Pachel, 13 Sept. 1490.
[24] l. 21cm.

Leaf [2a]: Magistri Hyeronimi Vicecomitis. Lamiarum siue striarum opusculum ad illustrissimum Mediolani ducem franciscum sfortiam Vicecomitem: Incipit feliciter.
Leaf [24b] (Colophon): Explicit Lamiarum tractatus magistri Iheronimi Vicecomitis predicatorum ordinis &c. Impressum
(Continued on next card)

CATALOGUE OF THE CORNELL WITCHCRAFT COLLECTION

Witchcraft
BF
1569
A2
V82
1490

Magistri Hyeronimi Vicecomitis. Lamiarum siue striarum opusculum.
Visconti, Girolamo, fl. 1490-1512. Lamiarum sive striarum opuscula ... 1490. (Card 2)

Mediolani per magistrum Leonerdum Pachel Anno Domini. M.cccc.xc. Die. xiii. Mensis Septembris.
Signatures: a-c⁸.
Capital spaces, with guide-letters.
Edited by Aluisius de la Cruce.
Copinger. Supplement to Hain's Repertorium. 6200=3210; Proctor, 5986; Brit. Mus.
(Continued on next card)

Witchcraft
BF
1569
A2
V82
1490

Magistri Hyeronimi Vicecomitis. Lamiarum siue striarum opusculum.
Visconti, Girolamo, fl. 1490-1512. Lamiarum sive striarum opuscula ... 1490. (Card 3)

Cat. (XV cent.) VI, p. 778 (IA. 26646); Goff. Third census, V-272.

1. Witchcraft. I. Title. II. Title: Magistri Hyeronimi Vicecomitis. Lamiarum siue striarum opusculum.

Rare
BR
520
M42++

Magnalia Christi Americana.
Mather, Cotton, 1663-1728.
Magnalia Christi Americana; or, The ecclesiastical history of New-England, from its first planting in the year 1620, unto the year of Our Lord, 1698. London, Printed for T. Parkhurst, 1702.
7 pt. in 1 v. double map. 39cm.
Paging irregular: book 6, p. 24, 29, 86, incorrectly numbered 32, 37, 98 respectively; paging of book 4 begins with p. 125.
List of books printed for Parkhurst (2 p.) inserted at front; another
(Continued on next card)

Rare
BR
520
M42++

Magnalia Christi Americana.
Mather, Cotton, 1663-1728. Magnalia Christi Americana. London, 1702. (Card 2)

list of 2 p. at end.

Contents.--I. Antiquities.--II. Ecclesiarum clypei.--III. Polybivs.--IV. Sal gentium.--V. Acts and monuments.--VI. Thaumaturgus.--VII. Ecclesiarum praelia.

I. Title.

WITCHCRAFT
BF
1555
P61

Le magnétism, le somnambulisme et le spiritualisme dans l'histoire.
Piérart, Z J
Le magnétisme, le somnambulisme et le spiritualisme dans l'histoire. Affaire curieuse des possédées de Louviers...
Paris, Au Bureau du Journal du magnétisme, 1858.
39 p. 23cm.

Extract from Journal du magnétisme.
1. Demoniac possession. 2. Louviers, France. St. Louis (Convent) 3. Bavent, Madeleine, ca. 1608-1647. 4. Picard, Mathurin, d. 1647. 5. Boullé, Thomas.

8
NIC

WITCHCRAFT
BF
1132
P14

Le magnétisme, le spiritisme et la possession.
Pailloux, Xavier.
Le magnétisme, le spiritisme et la possession. Entretiens sur les esprits entre un théologien, un avocat, un philosophe et un médecin. Paris, J. Lecoffre, 1863.
xv, 460 p. 19cm.

1. Animal magnetism. 2. Demoniac possession. 3. Spirits. 4. Occult sciences. I. Title.

8
NIC

Witchcraft
DL
45
M19+
1555

Magnus, Olaus, Abp. of Uppsala, 1490-1558.
Historia de gentibvs Septentrionalibvs, earvmqve diversis statibvs, conditionibvs, moribvs, ritibvs, svperstitionibus, disciplinis, exercitiis, regimine, victu, bellis, structuris, instrumentis, ac mineris metallicis, & rebus mirabilibus, necnon vniuersis penè animalibus in Septentrione degentibus, eorumque natura ... Cum indice locupletissimo ... Romae [Impressvm apvd Ioannem Mariam De Viottis] 1555.
[82], 815 p. illus. 29cm.
(Continued on next card)

Witchcraft
DL
45
M19+
1555

Magnus, Olaus, Abp. of Uppsala, 1490-1558.
Historia de gentibvs Septentrionalibvs ... 1555. (Card 2)

On p. 815 large device of G. M. de Viottis.
"De svperstitiosa cvltvra daemonvm popvlorvm Aquilonarium liber tertius": p. 96-128.

1. Scandinavia--Hist. I. Title.

DL
45
M19+
1555a

Magnus, Olaus, Abp. of Uppsala, 1490-1558.
Historia de gentibus septentrionalibus: earumque diversis statibus, conditionibus, moribus, ritibus, superstitionibus, disciplinis, exercitiis, regimine, victu, bellis, structuris, instrumentis ac mineris metallicis & rebus mirabilibus ... Farnborough, Gregg, 1971.

[86], 815 p. illus. 28 cm. Index. £25.20   B 72-06924
Reprint of the 1555 ed.

9

1. Scandinavia. I. Title.

DL45.M17 1555a   72-184180
ISBN 0-576-78858-X
Library of Congress   72 [4]

WITCHCRAFT
BF
1584
S9
L66

Magnus, Olaus, abp. of Uppsala, 1490-1558.
Levin, Herman, 1862-
Forna tiders mörker och vidskepelse.

(In: Läsning för svenska folket. Stockholm. 20cm. 1909. p. 43-67, 92-115, 210-226)

1. Witchcraft--Sweden. 2. Witchcraft--Scandinavia. 3. Trials (Witchcraft)--Sweden. 4. Bure, Johan, 1568-1652. 5. Magnus, Olaus, abp. of Uppsala, 1490-1558. I. Läsning för svenska folket. II. Title.

8
NIC

Magnussen, Arne, 1663-1730.
see
Árni Magnússon, 1663-1730.

Magnússon, Arni, 1663-1730.
See
Árni Magnússon, 1663-1730.

BF
1584
H9
S37

Magyarországi boszorkányperek, 1529-1768.
Schram, Ferenc.
Magyarországi boszorkányperek, 1529-1768. Budapest, Akademiai Kiado, 1970.
2 v. 25 cm.
Bibliography: v. 2, p. 735-736.

NIC   FEB 21,'75   COOdc   74-203280

WITCHCRAFT
BF
1583
M21

Mahnke, Dietrich, 1884-
Das Hexenunwesen in Verden und sein Ende. [Stade? 1923]
28 p. 23cm.

"Sonderdruck aus dem 'Stader Archiv' 1923, Neue Folge, Heft 13."

1. Witchcraft--Verden, Ger. 2. Trials (Witchcraft)--Verden, Ger. I. Title.

8
NIC

Witchcraft
BF
1413
M21
1620

Maier, Michael, 1568?-1622.
Compendium Miraculorum, das ist: Kurtze, jedoch klare Beschreibung vnterschiedtlicher Wunderwercken vnd Geschichten: Insonderheit der Gänse, so in den Oradischen Insuln auff Bäumen wachsen: Dessgleichen von Vrsprung vnd Geburt etlicher sehr frembden Vegetabilien, Menschen vnd Thier: wie auch dem Vogel Phoenix, Wehrwölffen, Geniis, Waldtgöttern, Lamiis, Hexen, vnd anderer Gedächtnusswürdiger Sachen Erörterung. Von H. Michael Mayern ... Lateinisch beschrieben, vnd an jetzo ins
(Continued on next card)

Witchcraft
BF
1413
M21
1620

Maier, Michael, 1568?-1622. Compendium miraculorum ... (Card 2)

Teutsche vbersetzt, durch M. Georgivm Beatvm ... Franckfurt, Getruckt in Verlegung Lucae Jennis, 1620.
[16], 142 p. 17cm.

1. Occult sciences. 2. Marvelous, The. 3. Miracles--Early works to 1800. I. Title.

WITCHCRAFT
BF
1582
Z7
1700

Maillé, Louis.
Peyron, Paul Malo Théophile.
Procès pour faits de sorcellerie à la fin du XVIIe siècle. [Quimper? 190-?]
11 p. 23cm.

Signed: Peyron, chanoine.

1. Trials (Witchcraft)--Lesneven, France. 2. Maillé, Louis. 3. La Croix, Anthoine.

8
NIC

Witchcraft
BF
1566
M16

The majesty of darkness discovered.
Macleod, Malcolm.
History of witches &c. The majesty of darkness discovered: in a series of tremendous tales ... of apparitions, witches, augers, magicians ... in confirmation of a future state, & the superintendency of a Divine Providence, by the agency of spirits & angels. With The prophecy of Pedan; or, The Caledonian apocalypse of the last century; sublimely adumbrating the awful events which now amaze and alarm all Europe. London, Printed by and for
(Continued on next card)

368

CATALOGUE OF THE CORNELL WITCHCRAFT COLLECTION

The majesty of darkness discovered.

Witchcraft
Macleod, Malcolm. History of witches &c...
[1793] (Card 2)

I. Roach [1793]
97 p. front. 17cm.

Title vignette.
I. Title. II. Title: The majesty of darkness discovered. III. Title: The emphatical prophecy of Pedan.

Major, Ralph Hermon, 1884–
Faiths that healed, by Ralph H. Major ... New York, London, D. Appleton-Century company, incorporated, 1940.

x p., 1 l., 290 p. incl. plates. front., plates, ports. 21½ᶜᵐ.

1. Medicine, Magic, mystic, and spagiric. 2. Faith-cure. 3. Witchcraft. I. Title.

Library of Congress   RZ405.M3   40-5965

Maladie prodigieuse de Pierre Creusé.

WITCHCRAFT
555
678
881
Histoire admirable de la maladie prodigieuse de Pierre Creusé, arrivée en la ville de Niort en 1628. Avec une introduction par L. Favre. Niort, Typ. de L. Favre, 1881.
iii, 84 p. 22cm.
Half title: Maladie prodigieuse de Pierre Creusé.
Includes reprint of the original t. p., whose title includes: "... auec vn plaidoyé de l'ad uocat du Roy de ladite

(Continued on next card)

Maladie prodigieuse de Pierre Creusé.

WITCHCRAFT
555
678
881
Histoire admirable de la maladie prodigieuse de Pierre Creusé ... 1881.
(Card 2)

ville sur le subjet de ladite maladie, & la sentence interuenue sur ledit plaidoyé: ensemble les certificats de medecins & chirurgiens dudit lieu. Niort, 1631."

1. Demoniac possession. 2. Creusé, Pierre, b. 1614. I. Favre, Léopold, 1817-1890, ed. II. Title: Maladie prodigieuse de Pierre Creusé.

Les maladies épidémiques de l'esprit.

Witchcraft
Regnard, Paul, 1850–1927.
Les maladies épidémiques de l'esprit; sorcellerie, magnétisme, morphinisme, délire des grandeurs, par le dr Paul Regnard ... Ouvrage illustré de cent vingt gravures. Paris, E. Plon, Nourrit et cⁱᵉ, 1887.

iii–xii, 429 p., 1 l. incl. illus., pl., facsim. 27cm.
Contents.—Les sorcières.—Les miracles de Saint-Médard.—Sommeil et somnambulisme.—Deux poisons à la mode: la morphine et l'éther.—Le délire des grandeurs.
1. Psychology, Pathological. 2. Demoniac possession. 3. Hysteria. I. Title. II. Title: Sorcellerie, magnétism.
Library of Congress, no.

Malavesse, Catherine (David) fl. 1439.

Aubenas, Roger.
La sorcière et l'inquisiteur; épisode de l'Inquisition en Provence, 1439. Aix-en-Provence, La Pensée universitaire, 1956.
x, 81 p. facsims. 25 cm. (Archives de Provence, 1)
Bibliography: p. 79–80.

1. Malavesse, Catherine (David) fl. 1439. 2. Inquisition. Provence. I. Title. (Series)

BF1582.Z7 1439   57-36238
Library of Congress   [3]

MSS
Bd.
WITCHCRAFT
BT
M24
Maldonado, Juan, 1534–1583. Eruditissimi domini Joannis Maldonati...Disputatio De daemonum distinctione et de praestigiis hoc est de potestate, actione et fallacia eorundem. Paris, 1572.
[30] l. 23cm.
Manuscript, on paper.
The second part of a treatise which was never printed in the original Latin. A French translation of the entire work was published in   1605, 1616, 1617, 1619
with title: Traicté des anges et
(Continued on next card)

MSS
Bd.
WITCHCRAFT
BT
M24
Maldonado, Juan, 1534–1583. Eruditissimi domini Joannis Maldonati...Disputatio De daemonum distinctione...1572. (Card 2)

demons.
Signed: Sebastianus Hamelius.
Notes inside front cover of vol. discuss history and provenance of the manuscript. Originally the vol. was in the Lamoignon library, then passed to library of Prof. E. Dowden.
With this   ms. are bound three printed works: Nicaise, Claude. De
(Continued on next card)

MSS
Bd.
WITCHCRAFT
BT
M24
Maldonado, Juan, 1534–1583. Eruditissimi domini Joannis Maldonati...Disputatio De daemonum distinctione...1572. (Card 3)

nummo pantheo Hadriani imperatoris. Lugduni, 1690. Patin, Charles. Commentarius Caroli Patini in tres inscriptiones Graecas. Patavii, 1685. Rigord, Jean Pierre. Dissertation historique sur une medaille d'Herodes Antipas. Paris, 1689.
1. Demonology. 2. Devil. I. His Traicté des anges et demons. II. Title: Disputatio   De daemonum distinctione. III. Title: De daemonum distinctione.

WITCHCRAFT
BT
960
M24
1616
Maldonado, Juan, 1534–1583.
Traicté des anges et demons, du R. P. Maldonat. Mis en françois, par maistre François de La Borie. Rouen, Chez Iacques Besongne, 1616.
242 l. 15cm.

Illustrated t.p.

1. Angels—Early works to 1800. 2. Demonology. I. La Borie, François de, tr. II. Title.

MSS
Bd.
WITCHCRAFT
BT
M24
Maldonado, Juan, 1534–1583. Eruditissimi domini Joannis Maldonati...Disputatio De daemonum distinctione et de praestigiis hoc est de potestate, actione et fallacia eorundem. Paris, 1572.
[30] l. 23cm.
Manuscript, on paper.
The second part of a treatise which was never printed in the original Latin. A French translation of the entire work was published in   1605, 1616, 1617, 1619
with title: Traicté des anges et
(Continued on next card)

MSS
Bd.
WITCHCRAFT
BT
M24
Maldonado, Juan, 1534–1583. Eruditissimi domini Joannis Maldonati...Disputatio De daemonum distinctione...1572. (Card 2)

demons.
Signed: Sebastianus Hamelius.
Notes inside front cover of vol. discuss history and provenance of the manuscript. Originally the vol. was in the Lamoignon library, then passed to library of Prof. E. Dowden.
With this   ms. are bound three printed works: Nicaise, Claude. De
(Continued on next card)

MSS
Bd.
WITCHCRAFT
BT
M24
Maldonado, Juan, 1534–1583. Traicté des anges et demons.
Maldonado, Juan, 1534–1583. Eruditissimi domini Joannis Maldonati...Disputatio De daemonum distinctione...1572. (Card 3)

nummo pantheo Hadriani imperatoris. Lugduni, 1690. Patin, Charles. Commentarius Caroli Patini in tres inscriptiones Graecas. Patavii, 1685. Rigord, Jean Pierre. Dissertation historique sur une medaille d'Herodes Antipas. Paris, 1689.
1. Demonology. 2. Devil. I. His Traicté des anges et demons. II. Title: Disputatio   De daemonum distinctione. III. Title: De daemonum distinctione.

Maléfices et sortilèges.

Witchcraft
BF
1582
D59
Diricq, Édouard.
Maléfices et sortilèges: procès criminels de l'ancien évêché de Bâle pour faits de sorcellerie (1549–1670) Lausanne, Payot, 1910.
240 p. 18cm.

1. Witchcraft—Basel (Diocese)—History. I. Title.

WITCHCRAFT
DD
901
F9
M25
Malkmus, Georg Joseph.
Fuldaer Anekdotenbüchlein. Fulda, Druck der Fuldaer Aktienbuchdr., 1875.
viii, 151 p. 17cm.

"Eine Teufelsaustreibung.": p. 93–95.
"Noch eine Teufelsaustreibung.": p.95–97.
"Ein Hexenrichter.": p.101–151. An account, based on documents, of Balthasar Nuss and the witch trials in Fulda.
1. Fulda (craft)—Ful da, Ger. Ger. 2. Trials (Witch-3. Nuss, Balthasar. 4. Demoniac possession. I. Title.

Malleorum quorundam maleficarum.

WITCHCRAFT
BF
1569
A2
I59
1582
Institoris, Henricus, d. 1508.
Malleorum qvorvndam maleficarvm, tam vetervm quàm recentiorum authorum, tomi dvo. Quorum primus continet: I. Malleum maleficarum Fr. Iacobi Sprenger, & Fr. Henrici Institoris: Inquisitorum. II. Fr. Ioannis Nider ... qui tractat de maleficis & eorum deceptionibus. Secvndvs verò tomus continet tractatus VII. ibi speciatim nominatos ... Francofvrti [Svmptibvs Nicol   ai Bassaei, 1582.
8 p. l.,   806, [35] p. 16cm.
(Continued on next card)

Malleorum quorundam maleficarum.

WITCHCRAFT
BF
1569
A2
I59
1582
Institoris, Henricus, d. 1508.
Malleorum qvorvndam maleficarvm...1582.
(Card 2)
Vol. 2 of this ed. is not known to exist; however, vol. 2 of Bassaeus' edition of 1588 has title: Tomvs secvndvs malleorvm qvorvndam maleficarvm, and introduction dated 1582. This form of the title seems peculiar to these two volumes alone, out of the many editions of the Malleus maleficarum. We infer that the two belong together, vol. 1 of 1588 being a   "2d ed." of this issue.
I. His   Malleus maleficarum.
II. Title.

PQ
2625
A437
T8
Mallet-Joris, Françoise, 1930–
Trois âges de la nuit, histoires de sorcellerie [par] Françoise Mallet-Joris. Paris, B. Grasset, 1968.
377 p. 21cm.

1. Chantraine, Anne de—Fiction. 2. Ranfaing, Elisabeth de, 1592–1649—Fiction. 3. Harvilliers, Jeanne—Fiction. I. Title.

CATALOGUE OF THE CORNELL WITCHCRAFT COLLECTION

Witchcraft
BS
2545
D5A33

Malleus demonum.
Albertinus, Alexander.
Mallevs demonvm. Siue quatuor experimentatissimi exorcismi, ex Euangelijs collecti ... Veronae, Typis Bartholomaei Merli, 1620.
347 p. 17cm.

Imprint of colophon: Veronae, Typis Bartholomaei Meruli, 1621.

WITCHCRAFT
BF
1565
R34

8
NIC

Malleus judicum.
Reiche, Johann, ed. Herrn D. Christian Thomasii ... Kurtze Lehr-Sätze von dem Laster der Zauberey, nach dem wahren Verstande des lateinischen Exemplars ins Deutsche übersetzet, und aus des berühmten Theologi D. Meyfarti, Naudaei, und anderer gelehrter Männer Schrifften erleutert ... nebst einigen Actis magicis heraus gegeben von Johann Reichen. Halle im Magdeburgischen, Im Rengerischen Buchladen, 1704.
2 v. in 1. 21cm.
(Continued on next card)

WITCHCRAFT
BF
1565
R34

8
NIC

Malleus judicum.
Reiche, Johann, ed. Herrn D. Christian Thomasii ... Kurtze Lehr-Sätze ... 1704. (Card 2)

Vol. 1 has special t. p.: Fernerer Unfug der Zauberey. Halle im Magdeburgischen, 1704.
Vol. 2 has special t. p.: Unterschiedliche Schrifften von Unfug des Hexen-Processes. Halle im Magdeburg., 1703.
Contents.--[1. Bd.] Gabriel Naudaei
(Continued on next card)

WITCHCRAFT
BF
1565
R34

8
NIC

Malleus judicum.
Reiche, Johann, ed. Herrn D. Christian Thomasii ... Kurtze Lehr-Sätze ... 1704. (Card 3)

Contents.--Continued.
Schutz-Schrifft [tr. of Apologie pour tous les grands hommes]--Geschichte der Teuffel zu Lodün--Trauer-Geschichte von der greulichen Zauberey Ludwig Goffredy [tr. of De l'horrible & épouvantable sorcellerie de Louis Goffredy, author F. de Rosset]--D. Christian Thomasii ... Kurtze Lehr-Sätze von
(Continued on next card)

WITCHCRAFT
BF
1565
R34

8
NIC

Malleus judicum.
Reiche, Johann, ed. Herrn D. Christian Thomasii ... Kurtze Lehr-Sätze ... 1704. (Card 4)

Contents--Continued.
dem Laster der Zauberey [tr. of Dissertatio de crimine magiae, J. Reiche, respondent] [2. Bd.] Malleus judicum oder Gesetz-Hammer der unbarmhertzigen Hexen-Richter.-- Cautio criminalis [von F. Spee]--D. Johann Matthäus Meyfarths Christliche Erinnerung an Regenten.-- Viererley Sorten Hexen-Acta.
(Continued on next card)

Witchcraft
BF
1569
A2I59+
1487

Malleus maleficarum.
[Institoris, Henricus] d. 1508.
Malleus maleficarum. [Speier, Peter Drach, before 15 Apr., 1487]
[129] l. 28cm.

Leaf [1a] blank.
Leaf [1b]: Appologia auctoris in malleum maleficarum.
Leaf [129b] (End): Sit laus deo. exterminiū heresis. pax viuis. requies eterna defunctis. Amen.
Signatures: a-p8, q9.
(Continued on next card)

Witchcraft
BF
1569
A2I59+
1487

Malleus Maleficarum.
[Institoris, Henricus] d. 1508. Malleus maleficarum ... [before 15 Apr., 1487] (Card 2)

Capital spaces.
By Henricus Institoris (Heinrich Krämer) and Jakob Sprenger.
Hain. Repertorium (with Copinger's Supplement) *9238; Proctor, 526; Brit. Mus. Cat. (XV cent.) I, p. xxvi; Goff. Third census, I-163.
With bookplate of J. B. Holzinger.
(Continued on next card)

Witchcraft
BF
1569
A2I59+
1490

Malleus maleficarum.
[Institoris, Henricus] d. 1508.
Malleus maleficarum. [Speier, Peter Drach, about 1490-91]
[102] l. 27cm.

Leaf [1a] (Title): Malleus maleficarum.
Leaf [1b]: Appologia auctoris in malleum maleficarum.
Leaves [2a]-[3b]: Tenor bulle apostolice aduersus heresim maleficarum cum approbatione z subscriptione doctorū alme vniuersitatis Colonieñ. in sequentem tractatum.
(Continued on next card)

Witchcraft
BF
1569
A2I59+
1490

Malleus maleficarum.
[Institoris, Henricus] d. 1508. Malleus maleficarum ... [about 1490-91] (Card 2)

Leaf [102a] (End): Sit laus deo. exterminiū heresis. pax viuis. requies eterna defunctis. amen.
Signatures: a8, b-d6, ef8, g-h6, i8, k-p6; signatures ef being used together to mark a single gathering.
Capital spaces.
By Henricus Institoris (Heinrich Krämer)
(Continued on next card)

Witchcraft
BF
1569
A2I59+
1490

Malleus maleficarum.
[Institoris, Henricus] d. 1508. Malleus maleficarum ... [about 1490-91] (Card 3)

and Jakob Sprenger.
Hain. Repertorium (with Copinger's Supplement) *9239; Proctor, 2383; Brit. Mus. Cat. (XV cent.) II, p. 498 (IB. 8615); Goff. Third census, I-164.

1. Witchcraft. 2. Demonology. 3. Criminal law. 4. Criminal procedure. I. Sprenger, Jakob. 1436 or 8-1495. II. Title.

Witchcraft
BF
1569
A2I59+
1494

Malleus maleficarum.
[Institoris, Henricus] d. 1508.
Malleus maleficarum. Cologne, Johann Koelhoff, the Younger, 24 Nov. (in vigilia s. Katherine), 1494.
[112] l. 27cm.

Leaf [1a] (Title): Mallens maleficarnm.
Leaf [1b]: Apologia autoris in malleū maleficarū.
Leaves [1b]-[3a]: Tenor bulle apostolice aduersus heresim maleficaɤ cū ppbatōe z sb'scriptōe doctoɤ alme vniūsitatj Colon. ...
(Continued on next card)

Witchcraft
BF
1569
A2I59+
1494

Malleus maleficarum.
[Institoris, Henricus] d. 1508. Malleus maleficarum ... 1494. (Card 2)

Leaf [112a] (Colophon): Liber Malleus maleficarū a suo editore nuncupatus Impressusq̷ per me Ioannem Koelhoff incolā Ciuitatis sancte Colonieñ. Anno salutj Mcccc.xciiij. in vigilia sanctj Katherine Regine ac ɤginis martyrisq̷ finem accepit feliciter.
Signatures: i-[iv]; a-s6. Leaves [5]-[112] numbered i-folio Cviiij, with many
(Continued on next card)

Witchcraft
BF
1569
A2I59+
1494

Malleus maleficarum.
[Institoris, Henricus] d. 1508. Malleus maleficarum ... 1494. (Card 3)

errors.
Capital spaces, some with guide-letters.
Capitals, paragraph-marks and initial-strokes supplied in red.
By Henricus Institoris (Heinrich Krämer) and Jakob Sprenger.
Hain. Repertorium (with Copinger's Supplement) 9244; Proctor, 1462; Brit. Mus. Cat. (XV cent.) I, p. 298 (IB. 5064); Goff.
(Continued on next card)

Witchcraft
BF
1569
A2I59+
1494

Malleus maleficarum.
[Institoris, Henricus] d. 1508. Malleus maleficarum ... 1494. (Card 4)

Third census, I-167.
Incomplete copy: lacks leaf xviij (c_{vi}).
Ex libris cabalisticis Kurt Seligmann.
Bound in brown morocco, by Sangorski and Sutcliffe.

1. Witchcraft. 2. Demonology. 3. Criminal law. 4. Criminal procedure. I. Sprenger, Jakob, 1436 or 8-1495. II. Title.

WITCHCRAFT
BF
1569
A2I59++
1928

Malleus maleficarum.
[Institoris, Henricus] d. 1508.
Malleus maleficarum, translated with an introduction, bibliography and notes by the Rev. Montague Summers. [London] J. Rodker, 1928.
xlv, 277, [1] p. front. (port.) 31cm.
By Henricus Institoris and Jacob Sprenger.
"This edition of Malleus maleficarum, comprising 1275 numbered copies, is here translated into English from the edition of 1606 for the first time ... This copy is out of series."
"A note upon the bibliography of the Malleus maleficarum": p. xli-xlii.

Witchcraft
BF
1569
A2I59
1948

Malleus maleficarum.
[Institoris, Henricus] d. 1508.
Malleus maleficarum, translated with an introduction, bibliography and notes by the Rev. Montague Summers. London, Pushkin Press [1948]
xxi, 277 p. port. 23cm.

By Henricus Institoris (Heinrich Krämer) and Jacob Sprenger.
"A note upon the bibliography of the Malleus maleficarum": p. xvii-xviii.

WITCHCRAFT
DD
741
W52
v.17
no.2

8
NIC

Der Malleus maleficarum, seine Druckausgaben und die gefälschte Kölner Approbatio vom J. 1487.
Hansen, Joseph, 1862-1943.
Der Malleus maleficarum, seine Druckausgaben und die gefälschte Kölner Approbation vom J. 1487.

(In: Westdeutsche Zeitschrift für Geschichte und Kunst. Trier. 24cm. v.17 (1898) no.2. p. 119-168)

1. Institoris, Henricus, d.1508. Malleus maleficarum. I. Title.

WITCHCRAFT
BF
1569
A2
I595

2 copies

8
NIC

Der Malleus maleficarum, seine Druckausgaben und die gefälschte Kölner Approbation vom J. 1487.
Hansen, Joseph, 1862-1943.
Der Malleus maleficarum, seine Druckausgaben und die gefälschte Kölner Approbation vom J. 1487. [Trier, 1898]
[119]-168 p. 23cm.
Caption title.
"Sonder-Abdruck aus Westdeutsche Zeitschrift für Geschichte und Kunst." [Bd. 17, Heft 2, 1898]

1. Institoris, Henricus, d. 1508. Malleus maleficarum. I. Title.

CATALOGUE OF THE CORNELL WITCHCRAFT COLLECTION

WITCHCRAFT
BF
1584
S9
M25

Malmquist, H
  Om hexprocessen i Dalarne, 1757-1763; jemte öfversigt af föregående hexprocesser. Lund, F. Berling, 1877.
  45 p. 24cm.
  Diss.--Lund.

8
NIC

  1. Witchcraft--Dalecarlia, Sweden. 2. Trials (Witchcraft)--Dalecarlia, Sweden. I. Title.

DQ
441
S67M5
v.23

Les Mandragores ou diables familiers à Genève.
Ladame, Paul Louis, 1842-
  Les Mandragores ou diables familiers à Genève au 16e et au 17e siècle.
  (In Société d'histoire et d'archéologie de Genève. Mémoires et documents. v. 23, 1888/1894, pp. 237-281)

WITCHCRAFT
BF
1569
M28

Manser, Gallus, 1866-1950.
  Thomas von Aquin und der Hexenwahn.
  (In: Divus Thomas; Jahrbuch für Philosophie und spekulative Theologie. Wien. 23cm. ser.2, v.9 (1922) p.17-49, [81]-110)

8
NIC

  1. Witchcraft. 2. Witchcraft--Hist. 3. Demonology. 4. Thomas Aquinas, Saint, 1225?-1274. I. Title.

Mammoli, Domenico.
  Processo alla strega Matteuccia di Francesco, 20 marzo 1428. Todi, 1969.
  57 p. illus. 24cm. (Res Tudertinae. 8)

8

  1. Di Francesco, Matteuccia, fl. 1420. I. Title.

Witchcraft
HV
6025
B78

Les manières admirables povr de'covrir tovtes sortes de crimes et sortilèges.
Bouvet, prévost général des armées du roy en Italie.
  Les manières admirables povr de'covrir tovtes sortes de crimes et sortilèges. Avec l'instrvction solide povr bien ivger vn procez criminel. Ensemble l'espèce des crimes, & la punition d'iceux, suiuant les loix, ordonnances, canons, & arrests ... Paris, I. de la Caille, 1659.
  342 p. 17cm.

  1. Crime and criminals. I. Title.

Mantagunensis, Johannes, Patriarch of Armenia, d. ca. 490.

see

Hovhannes I Mandakuni, Patriarch of Armenia, d. ca. 490.

WITCHCRAFT
BF
1569
A2
.621

Mamoris, Petrus.
  Flagellum maleficorum authore M. Petro Mamoris. Cum indicibus. [Lugduni] 1621.
  82 p. 18cm.
  First published in Lyons about 1490. Later included in v.3 of 1669 ed. of Institoris' Malleus maleficarum.
  "Tractatus de superstitiosis quibusdam casibus, compilatus...per...Henricum de Gorchen.": p. 71-82.
  1. Witchcraft. 2. Demonology. 3. Superstition. 4. Heinrich von Gorkum, 1386 (ca.)-1431. I. Title.

WITCHCRAFT
BF
1775
M28

Mannhardt, Wilhelm, 1831-1880.
  Die praktischen Folgen des Aberglaubens, mit besonderer Berücksichtigung der Provinz Preussen. Berlin, C. Habel, 1878.
  88 p. 21cm. (Deutsche Zeit- und Streit-Fragen, Jahrg. 7, Heft 97/98)

8
NIC

  1. Superstition. 2. Witchcraft--Prussia. 3. Trials (Witchcraft)--Prussia. I. Title.

WITCHCRAFT
BX
2045
B4
1849

Manuale benedictionum.
Catholic Church. Liturgy and ritual. Benedictional. Passau.
  Manuale benedictionum. Accedunt processiones variae publicis necessitatibus congruentes. Commodo animarum pastorum usui adaptavit Severinus Lueg.... Editio secunda. Passavii, Elsässer & Waldbauer, 1849.
  xix, 401 p. 17cm.
  "Additio. I. Benedictio a daemonio vexatorum. II. Exorcismus pro exorcizandis obsessis.": xix p. at beginning.

8
NIC

  1. Benediction. 2. Exorcism. I. Lueg, Severinus, ed. II.Title.

Man muss auch dem Teufel nicht zu viel aufbürden. Bey Gelegenheit der Brochüre: Sollte der Teufel wirklich ein Unding seyn? etc. Beherziget von einem Freunde der Wahrheit ... Bremen, J. H. Cramer, 1776.
  xxxii, 426 p. 16cm.

  Attributed by various sources to C. H. Runge; cf. Holzmann, Michael. Deutsches Anonymenlexikon (Weimar, 1902-28)

(Continued on next card)

---

ar W
37208

Mannhardt, Wilhelm, 1831-1880.
  Die praktischen Folgen des Aberglaubens mit besonderer Berücksichtigung der Provinz Preussen. Berlin, C. Habel, 1878.
  88 p. 22cm.

WITCHCRAFT
BX
2045
B4
1671

Manuale benedictionum et rituum.
Catholic Church. Liturgy and ritual. Benedictional.
  Manuale benedictionum et rituum, qui saepius extra ecclesias exorcendi occurrunt, ex rituali Romano, Constantiensi, aliisque collectum. [Einsiedeln] Typis Monasterij Einsidlensis, per Nicolaum Wagenmann & Iosephum Reymann, 1671.
  114 p. 13cm.
  Includes rites for exorcism.
  With this is bound: Manuale exorcismorum et benedictionum...1671.

8
NIC

  1. Benediction. 2. Exorcism. I. Title.

Man muss auch dem Teufel nicht zu viel aufbürden...1776. (Card 2)

  1. Devil. 2. Demonology. I. Runge, Conrad Heinrich, supposed author. II. Ein Freund der Wahrheit. III. Sollte der Teufel wirklich ein Unding seyn?

WITCHCRAFT
BF
1413
M28
Z3
1897

Mannhardt, Wilhelm, 1831-1880.
  Zauberglaube und Geheimwissen im Spiegel der Jahrhunderte. Mit 44 teils farbigen Abbildungen. 3. Aufl. Leipzig, H. Barsdorf, 1897.
  284 p. illus. 21cm.
  "Die 'Truten-Zeitung'": p. 243-246. [Reprint of ed. of 1627]

8
NIC

  1. Occult sciences. I. Truten-Zeitung. II. Title.

BF
1614
P37

Manuale della magia e della stregoneria.
Pegaso, Osvaldo.
  Manuale della magia e della stregoneria. Milano, G. De Vecchi, 1967.
  438 p. 20½cm. L 8800

(It 67-8184)

  1. Magic. 2. Witchcraft. I. Title.

BF1614.P4   79-366201

Library of Congress   69 [18]

Mandakuni, Hovhannes I, Patriarch of Armenia, d. ca. 490.

see

Hovhannes I Mandakuni, Patriarch of Armenia, d. ca. 490.

WITCHCRAFT
R
133
M28

Manninen, Ilmari, 1894-1935.
  Die dämonistischen Krankheiten im finnischen Volksaberglauben; vergleichende volksmedizinische Untersuchung. Akademische Abhandlung. Loviisa, Loviisan Sanomain Osakeyhtion Kirjapaino, 1922.
  253 p. 22cm.
  Bibliography: p. 228-251.

8
NIC

  1. Medicine, Magic, mystic and spagiric. 2. Folk medicine--Finland. 3. Demonology. I. Title.

Witchcraft
BF
1414
M29
1864

  Manuale di spiriti folletti ossia Le apparizioni, le visioni spaventose, le streghe, la magia, i terremoti ed i fenomeni più ragguardevoli della natura, ecc. ecc. scritto da una Società di letterati italiani. Opera dilettevole ed istruttiva. 2a ed. Milano, A spese dell'editore, 1864.
  288 p. front. 16cm.

  1. Occult sciences.

CATALOGUE OF THE CORNELL WITCHCRAFT COLLECTION

Manuale exorcismorum.

WITCHCRAFT
BX
2340
E97
1709

Eynatten, Maximilian van, d. 1631.
Manuale exorcismorum, continens instructiones, et exorcismos ad ejiciendos è corporibus obsessis spiritus malignos, & ad quaevis maleficia depellenda, & ad quascumque infestationes daemonum reprimendas ... Antverpiae, Apud H. & C. Verdussen, 1709.
6 p. l., 291, [1] p. 17cm.

1. Exorcism. I. Title.

8

WITCHCRAFT
BX
2045
B4
1671

Manuale exorcismorum et benedictionum selectorum pro exorcistarum, parochorum, et aliorum quorumvis curatorum commodiori usu collectorum. [Einsiedeln] Typis Einsidlensibus, per Nicolaum Wagenmann & Josephum Reymann, 1671.
171 p. 13cm.

Bound with: Catholic Church. Liturgy and ritual. Benedictional. Constance. Manuale benedictionum et rituum. 1671.

8
NIC

1. Exorcism. 2. Catholic Church. Liturgy and ritual.

Witchcraft
BF
1555
B86
1714

Manuale exorcistarum, ac parochorum.
Brognolo, Candido.
Manuale exorcistarum, ac parochorum: hoc est Tractatus de curatione ac protectione divina; in quo reprobatis erroribus, verus, certus, securus, catholicus, apostolicus, & evangelicus eiiciendi daemones ab hominibus, & à rebus ad homines spectantibus: curandi infirmos: ab inimicis se tuendi: Deumque in cunctis necessitatibus propitium habendi modus traditur ... Venetiis, Apud Nicolaum Pezzana, 1714.
[22], 352, [24] p. 24cm.

(Continued on next card)

Witchcraft
BF
1555
B86
1714

Manuale exorcistarum, ac parochorum.
Brognolo, Candido. Manuale exorcistarum ... 1714. (Card 2)

Bound with the author's Alexicacon. Venetiis, 1714.

1. Exorcism. I. Title.

Witchcraft
BX
1710
A32
1642

Manuale qualificatorum sanctiss. Inquisitionis.
Alberghini, Giovanni, 1574-1644.
Manvale qvalificatorvm sanctiss. Inqvisitionis, in qvo omnia, qvae ad illvd tribvnal, ac haeresum censuram pertinent, breui methodo adducuntur ... Cum duplici indice ... Panormi, Apud Decium Cyrillum, 1642.
[24], 405, [3] p. 18cm.

Added t. p., engraved.

1. Inquisition. 2. Witchcraft. I. Title.

Witchcraft
BX
2048
B5
F92

Manuale selectissimarum benedictionum, conjurationum, exorcismorum, absolutionum, rituum.
Friz, Joannes Chrysostomus.
Manuale selectissimarum benedictionum, conjurationum, exorcismorum, absolutionum, rituum. Ad commodiorem usum parochorum, omniumque sacerdotum tam saecularium, quàm religiosorum. Ex diversis ritualibus et probatissimis auctoribus collectum, & novissime auctum per P.F. Joannem Chrysostomum Friz, Ord. Min. S. P. Francisci Reformat. Provinciae Tyrolensis. [Campidonae] Per Andream Stadler, 1737.
(Continued on next card)

8

Witchcraft
BX
2048
B5
F92

Manuale selectissimarum benedictionum, conjurationum, exorcismorum, absolutionum, rituum.
Friz, Joannes Chrysostomus. Manuale selectissimarum benedictionum ... 1737. (Card 2)

9 p. l., 657 p. 17cm.

1. Benediction. 2. Exorcism. I. Title.

8

Witchcraft
Z
6876
C13

Manuel bibliographique des sciences psychiques ou occultes.
Caillet, Albert Louis, 1869-
... Manuel bibliographique des sciences psychiques ou occultes ... Paris, L. Dorbon, 1912.
3 v. fold. tab. 25½ cm.

Covers dated 1913.
"Réunion de plusieurs bibliographies partielles et de catalogues, célèbres mais peu communs, fondus en un seul corps aussi homogène que possible."—Préf.
11,648 entries.

1. Occult sciences—Bibl. I. Title.

Z6876.C25   13—10632

Library of Congress   [53c1]

Witchcraft
BF
1582
Z7
1566

Le manvel de l'admirable victoire dv corps de Dieu svr l'esprit maling Beelzebub obtenue à Laon, 1566.
Boulaese, Jehan
Le manvel de l'admirable victoire dv corps de Dieu svr l'esprit maling Beelzebub obtenue à Laon, 1566 ... Liège, H. Houius, 1598.
392 p. 14cm.

Four pages of dedication bound between p. 24-25.
Colophon has date: M.D.IVC.

1. Witchcraft—France. I. Title.

RC
438
S98

The manufacture of madness.
Szasz, Thomas Stephen, 1920-
The manufacture of madness; a comparative study of the Inquisition and the mental health movement [by] Thomas S. Szasz. [1st ed.] New York, Harper & Row [1970]
xxvii, 383 p. 22cm.

About a third of the text deals with witchcraft.

1. Mental illness—History. I. Title.

WITCHCRAFT
BF
1584
I8
D17

Manzoni, Alessandro, 1785-1873.
I promessi sposi.
Dandolo, Tullio, conte, 1801-1870.
La signora di Monzi e le streghe del Tirolo, processi famosi del secolo decimosettimo per la prima volta cavati dalle filze originali. Milano, E. Besozzi, 1855.
259 p. port., facsims. 23cm.

1. Witchcraft—Tyrol. 2. Leyva, Marianna de, known as Signora di Monza, 1575-1650. 3. Manzoni, Alessandro, 1785-1873. I promessi sposi. I. Title.

8

Witchcraft
BF
1581
M29

Maple, Eric
The dark world of witches. London, R. Hale [1962]
192 p. illus. 23cm.

1. Witchcraft—Gt. Brit. I. Title.

WITCHCRAFT
BF
1582
Z7+
1642

Marais, Isaac.
Parfouru, Paul, 1846-1905.
Un procès de sorcellerie au Parlement de Bretagne. La condamnation de l'abbé Poussinière, 1642-1643. Rennes, Impr. A. Le Roy, 1893.
11 p. 26cm.

"Extrait de la revue L'Hermine."

8
NIC

1. Trials (Witchcraft)—Rennes. 2. Poussinière, Mathurin Trullier, known as l'abbé 3. Marais, Isaac. 4. France. Parlement (Rennes)

Witchcraft
BF
1583
Z7
1546

Ein Marburger Hexenprocess vom Jahre 1546.
Reichel, Rudolf.
Ein Marburger Hexenprocess vom Jahre 1546. Von Prof. Rudolf Reichel.
(In Historischer Verein für Steiermark, Graz. Mittheilungen. Graz. 23cm. 27. Heft (1879), p. [122]-135)

8

1. Trials (Witchcraft)—Germany. 2. Witchcraft—Germany. I. Title.

Witchcraft
BL
490
C35

Les marchands de miracles: histoire de la superstition humaine.
Caston, Alfred de
Les marchands de miracles: histoire de la superstition humaine, par Alfred de Caston. Paris, E. Dentu, 1864.
338 p. 20cm.

1. Superstition. 2. Occult sciences. I. Title.

8

Witchcraft
QP
251
M31

Marci a Kronland, Joannes Marcus, 1595-1667.
Idearvm operatricivm idea siue Hypotyposis et detectio illius occultae virtutis, quae semina faecundat, & ex ijsdem corpora organica producit ... [Pragae, Typis Seminarij Archiepiscopalis] 1635.
[176] l. illus. 21cm.

Signatures: 2 leaves unsigned, +, ++, +++, 1 leaf unsigned, A⁴, +, B-Z⁴, Aa-Tt⁴, Vu. Engraved t. p.

I. Title.

WITCHCRAFT
BF
1584
H9
M32+

Marczali, Henrik, 1856-1940.
Hexenprozesse in Ungarn.
(In: Ungarische Rundschau für historische und soziale Wissenschaften. Leipzig. 26c Jahrg. 1, Heft 1, Jan. 1912. p.177-187)

8
NIC

1. Trials (Witchcraft)—Hungary. 2. Witchcraft—Hungary. I. Title.

Maria Renata, nun, d. 1749.

see

Sänger, Maria Renata von Mossau, ca. 1680-1749.

CATALOGUE OF THE CORNELL WITCHCRAFT COLLECTION

Maria Renata, die letzte Hexe Deutschlands.

TCHCRAFT
    Leist, Friedrich, 1844-
      Maria Renata, die letzte Hexe Deutschlands.
33
49e
      (In: His Aus Frankens Vorzeit. Würzburg, 1881. 18cm. p. 57-75)

    1. Sänger, Maria Renata von Mossau, ca. 1680-1749. 2. Trials (Witchcraft)--Germany. I. His Aus Frankens Vorzeit.

Marie Glovers late woefull case.

HCRAFT
    Bradwell, Stephan, fl. 1594-1636.
      Marie Glovers late woefull case, together with her joyfull deliverance written upon occasion of Dr. Jordens Discourse of the mother... With a defence of the truthe against D. J. his scandalous impugnations. [n.p.] 1603.
      171 l. 20 x 29cm.
      Photostatic copy of Sloan MSS 831 in the British Museum.
      Second treatise, beginning on l. 42.
      (Continued on next card)

Marie Glovers late woefull case.

CHCRAFT
    Bradwell, Stephan, fl. 1594-1636. Marie Glovers late woefull case...1603. (Card 2)

has caption title: A defence of the publique sentence of lawe, and of the iudgment, of certayne phisitions, that averred Marie Glouers case to be supernaturall: againste D. Jordens slie, but scandalous impugnations of bothe.
    Bound in maroon buckram.
    1. Glover, Mary, fl. 1603. 2. Demoniac possession. 3. Witchcraft--
    (Continued on next card)

Mariken van Nimmegen.
    A marvelous history of Mary of Nimmegen, who for more than seven year lived and had ado with the devil. Translated from the Middle Dutch by Harry Morgan Ayres. With an introd. by Adriaan J. Barnouw. The Hague, M. Nijhoff, 1924.
    xxv, 78 p. 17cm. (The Dutch library. v. 3)
    "The English and the Dutch
    (Continued on next card)

Mariken van Nimmegen. A marvelous history of Mary of Nimmegen ... 1924. (Card 2)

versions are undated, but from the type and the printing devices used both are assigned to 1518-19. Hence a question has arisen as to the priority of the two versions. Some scholars regard the English version as an adaptation of the Dutch play, and others claim that both are based on a now lost Dutch prose original." Introd. of 1932 facsimile ed.
    I. Ayres, Harry Morgan, tr. II. Barnouw, Adriaan Jacob, 1877- III. Title.

Das Marile.
    Pastor, Karl.
445
3709
      Culturhistorische Bilder aus den Zeiten des Wahns. Bd. 1. Das Marile. Eine Geschichte aus der Zeit des Hexenwahns. Hamburg, Seelig & Ohmann, 1883.
883
      vi, 184 p. 21cm.
      No more published?
      I. Title. II. Title: Marile.

Marius, Simon, 1570-1624.

    see

Mayr, Simon, 1570-1624.

WITCHCRAFT
BF
1538
R9
M34
    Mark, abbot of the Simonov Monastery of Moscow.
      (Zlye dukhi i ikh vliianie na liudeĭ) Злые духи и ихъ вліяніе на людей. / Игумена Марка, Духовника Московскаго Ставропигіальнаго Симонова монастыря. С.-Петербургъ, Типо-лит. и переплетная Ю. А. Мансфельдъ, 1899.
      180 p. 25cm.
      1. Demonology. 2. Devil. I. Title.

Markophrates, pseud., trans.

Witchcraft
RX
1735
B39
    La Bruja; the witch; or, A picture of the court of Rome; found among the manuscripts of a respectable theologian, a great friend of that court. Translated from the Spanish by Markophrates [pseud.] London, J. Hatchard, 1840.
    188 p. 19cm.
    Added t. p. engr.
    1. Rome--Hist. 2. Inquisition. I. Title: The court of Rome.

Marquart, Antonius, respondent.

WITCHCRAFT
R
133
M62
    Michaelis, Johann, 1606-1667, praeses.
      Morbos ab incantatione et veneficiis oriundos...sub clypeo...Johannis Michaelis... publice examinandos proponit...Anton Marquart... [Lipsiae] Typis Haeredum Timothei Hönii, 1650.
      [56] p. 19cm.
      Diss.--Leipzig (A. Marquart, respondent)
      1. Medicine, Magic, mystic and spagiric.
8
NIC
      2. Devil. I. Marquart, Antonius, respondent.

Witchcraft
BF
1581
A2
W81
1866a
no.4
    [Marshall, F]
      A brief history of witchcraft, with especial reference to the witches of Northamptonshire. Collected in great part from original sources. Northampton, J. Taylor, 1866.
      18 p. illus. 22cm.
      No.4 in box lettered Witchcraft in Northamptonshire.
      1. Witchcraft--History. 2. Witchcraft--Northamptonshire, England. I. Title.
8

Witchcraft
BF
1581
A2
W81
1866b
    [Marshall, F]
      A brief history of witchcraft, with especial reference to the witches of Northamptonshire. Collected in great part from original sources. Northampton, J. Taylor, 1866.
      18 p. illus. 22cm.
      Differs from another issue only in advertisements following text.
8

HV
6535
E5
M36
    Marshburn, Joseph H   1890-
      Murder & witchcraft in England, 1550-1640, as recounted in pamphlets, ballads, broadsides, & plays, by Joseph H. Marshburn. [1st ed.] Norman, University of Oklahoma Press [1972, c1971]
      xxvii, 287 p. illus. 22 cm. $7.95
      Includes bibliographical references.

5
    1. Murder--England--History. 2. Witchcraft--England--History. I. Title.
    HV6535.E5M37   364.15′23′0942   78-160497
    ISBN 0-8061-0003-6   MARC
    Library of Congress   72 [4]

Witchcraft
BF
1524
M37
    Marsicani, Bernardo Maria
      Meditazioni filosofiche, teologico-morali sulla demonologia ... Napoli, Presso Domenico Pianese, 1788.
      148 p. 19cm.

    1. Demonology. I. Title.

Marsicani, Bernardo Maria.

Witchcraft
BF
1520
C27
    Caristinio, Dominico.
      ... Exercitatio per saturam, sive Diatriba theologico-critica daemonologiae elementa complectens, cui accedunt Meditationes philosophicae theologico morales super eodem subjecto, auctore Bernardo Maria Marsicani ... Neapoli, Typis Dominici Pianese, 1788.
      11 p. l., 207 p. 21cm.
      Marsicani's work not included; but dedication includes letter by and to him.
8
      1. Demonology. I. Marsicani, Bernardo Maria. II. Title. III. Title: Diatriba theologico-critica daemonologiae...

Witchcraft
K
M375
T7
    Marsiliis, Hippolytus de, 1451-1529.
      Tractatus De questionibus, in quo materie maleficiorum pertractant. , cū tabula p modū numeri et alfabeti nouissime recognit. [Lugduni, Impensis J. de Giuncta ac sociocū, 1524.
      [55], cxliiii [i.e. 288], p. 18cm.
      Printed 2 columns to a page.
      Engraved t.p.
      Commentary on Digesta, lib. XLVIII. tit. 18 (De quaestionibus)
8
NIC

WITCHCRAFT
K
M375
T7
1537
    Marsiliis, Hippolytus de, 1451-1529.
      Hippolyti de Marsiliis ... Tractatus de q̄stionibus nuperrime recognitus: in quo materie maleficiorū admodum diffuse subtiliterq̣ pertractant̄: cū tabula ... per modū numeri et alphabeti diligentissime distributa. Lugd[uni] Ueneunt apud Jacobum Giuncti, 1537.
      [27], cxliiij l. 18cm.
      Title within woodcut ornamental border; title vignette: author's portrait.
      Colophon (l. cxliiija): Hippolyti de Mar-
      (Continued on next card)

WITCHCRAFT
K
M375
T7
1537
    Marsiliis, Hippolytus de, 1451-1529. ...
      Tractatus de q̄stionibus ... 1537. (Card 2)

    silijs ... Lectura super titu. ff. de questionib⁹ explicit Lugduni impressa p Benedictū Bōnyn impensis ... D. Jacobi .q. Frācisci de Giuncta Florenti. ac sociorū. Anno domini .M. CCCCXXXVI. Die vero xxiij. mensis Nouembris.
    Giunta's device on l. cxliiijb.
    Commentary on Digesta, lib. XLVIII. tit. 18.
    (Continued on next card)

373

CATALOGUE OF THE CORNELL WITCHCRAFT COLLECTION

WITCHCRAFT
K
M375
T7
1537
 Marsiliis, Hippolytus de, 1451-1529. ...
Tractatus de q̄stionibus ... 1537.
(Card 3)
 From its dedication to Cardinal Grimani, the treatise bears, in some editions, the title Grimana.
 With this is bound the author's Singularia. Lugduni, 1546.
 1. Roman law. 2. Corpus juris civilis. Digesta. Lib. XLVIII, tit. 18. I. Title: Tractatus De quaestionibus. II. Title: Grimana.

Martacunes, Joannes, Patriarch of Armenia, d. ca. 490.

see

Hovhannes I Mandakuni, Patriarch of Armenia, d. ca. 490.

Witchcraft
BX
2170
D6
C66
1737
 Martin von Cochem, pater, 1634?-1712.
 Libellus benedictionum et exorcismorum.

 Martin von Cochem, pater, 1634?-1712.
 Libellus infirmorum Germanico super additus. In quo breviter & practicè traditur quomodo administranda sint sacramenta infirmis deinde, quomodo piè assistendum sit moribundis ... Pro coronide additae sunt selectiores benedictiones et exorcismi ... authore R. P. Martino Cochemensi ordinis Capucinorum ... Editio novissima auctior & emendatior. Moguntiae & Francofurti, Sumptibus Joann is Mayeri per Joannem
8
(Continued on next card)

Witchcraft
BX
2170
D6
C66
1737
 Martin von Cochem, pater, 1634?-1712. Libellus infirmorum ... 1737. (Card 2)
 Henricum Haeffner, 1737.
 116, 488, [4] p. plate. 14cm.
 Libellus benedictionum et exorcismorum has separate paging and special t. p. with imprint: Moguntiae & Francofurti, 1736.
 1. Catholic Church--Prayer books and devotions. 2. Exorcism. I. Title. II.
8 His Libellus benedictionum et exorcismorum. III. Title: Libellus benedictionum et exorcismorum.

Witchcraft
BX
2170
D6
C66
1737
 Martin von Cochem, pater, 1634?-1712.
 Libellus infirmorum Germanico super additus. In quo breviter & practicè traditur quomodo administranda sint sacramenta infirmis deinde, quomodo piè assistendum sit moribundis ... Pro coronide additae sunt selectiores benedictiones et exorcismi ... authore R. P. Martino Cochemensi ordinis Capucinorum ... Editio novissima auctior & emendatior. Moguntiae & Francofurti, Sumptibus Joann is Mayeri per Joannem
8
(Continued on next card)

Witchcraft
BX
2170
D6
C66
1737
 Martin von Cochem, pater, 1634?-1712. Libellus infirmorum ... 1737. (Card 2)
 Henricum Haeffner, 1737.
 116, 488, [4] p. plate. 14cm.
 Libellus benedictionum et exorcismorum has separate paging and special t. p. with imprint: Moguntiae & Francofurti, 1736.
 1. Catholic Church--Prayer books and devotions. 2. Exorcism. I. Title. II.
8 His Libellus benedictionum et exorcismorum. III. Title: Libellus benedictionum et exorcismorum.

History of Science
QM
691
M37
 Martin, Ernest.
 Histoire des monstres depuis l'antiquité jusqu'à nos jours, par le docteur Ernest Martin ... Paris, C. Reinwald et cie, 1880.
 vii, 415 p. 22cm.
 "Bibliographie": p. [385]-407.
 1. Monsters. I. Title.

WITCHCRAFT
BF
1575
M38
1692a
 Martin, Susanna, d.1692, defendant.
 The tryal of Susanna Martin, at the Court of Oyer and Terminer, held by adjournment at Salem, June 30, 1692... [Pasadena, Castle Press, 1932]
 xiii p. 23cm.
 "From 'The wonders of the invisible world' by the Rev. Cotton Mather, Boston, 1693."
 On cover: Susanna Martin, a martyr to superstition, was executed with others on July 19, 1692. This account of her
8
NIC trial is reprinted by permission
(Continued on next card)

WITCHCRAFT
BF
1575
M38
1692a
 Martin, Susanna, d.1692, defendant. The tryal of Susanna Martin...1932] (Card 2)
 from a rare copy in the Henry E. Huntington Library as a tribute from one of the eighth generation...
 Presentation copy from John Martin Vincent "to George L. Burr, master of the history of witchcraft."
 1.Trials (Witchcraft)--Salem,Mass. I.Mather,Cotton, 1663-1728. The wonders of the invis ible world. II.Title.

Witchcraft
BF
1587
D61
no.1
 Martini, Jacob, metaphysician, praeses.
 ΔΙΑΣΚΕΨΙΣ [i.e., diaskepsis] philosophica, De magicis actionibus earumque probationibus, ... praeside Jacobo Martini, ... respondente Henrico Nicolai. Ed. 2. [Wittebergae] Typis Christiani Tham, 1623.
 [24] p. 21cm.
 No. 1 in vol. lettered Dissertationes de magia. 1623-1723.
 1. Magic--Addresses, essays, lectures. 2. Witchcraft--Addresses, essays, lectures. I. Nicolai, Heinrich, 1605-1665, respondent. II. Title: Diaskepsis phi-
8 losophica, De magicis actionibus. (Over)

RARE
HV
8593
D61
no.16
 Martini, Werner Theodor, praeses.
 Disputatio juridica De quaestionibus et torturis, quam...sub praesidio...Werneri Theodori Martini ..publico examini subjicit autor Johannes Valerianus Fischer...
 [Wittebergae] Typis Matthaei Henckelii,1668.
 [28] p. 21cm.
 Diss.--Wittenberg (J. V. Fischer, respondent)
 No. 16 in a vol. lettered: Dissertationes de trotura, 1667-1787.
8 1.Torture. I. Fischer, Johann Valerian, respon dent. II. Title.
NIC

Martinus, Jacobus

see

Martini, Jacob, metaphysician

PT
5443
M33
1924
 A marvelous history of Mary of Nimmegen.
 Mariken van Nimmegen.
 A marvelous history of Mary of Nimmegen, who for more than seven year lived and had ado with the devil. Translated from the Middle Dutch by Harry Morgan Ayres. With an introd. by Adriaan J. Barnouw. The Hague, M. Nijhoff, 1924.
 xxv, 78 p. 17cm. (The Dutch library. v. 3)
 "The Engli sh and the Dutch
(Continued on next card)

PT
5443
M33
1924
 A marvelous history of Mary of Nimmegen.
 Mariken van Nimmegen. A marvelous history of Mary of Nimmegen ... 1924.
(Card 2)
 versions are undated, but from the type and the printing devices used both are assigned to 1518-19. Hence a question has arisen as to the priority of the two versions. Some scholars regard the English version as an adaptation of the Dutch play, and others claim that both are based on a now lost Dutch prose original." Introd. of 1932 facsimil e ed.
 I. Ayres, Harry Morgan, tr.

BF
1563
M39
 Marwick, Max, comp.
 Witchcraft and sorcery; selected readings, edited by Max Marwick. [Harmondsworth, Eng., Baltimore, Md.] Penguin Books [1970]
 416 p. 18 cm. (Penguin modern sociology readings) $1.95 (U. S.)
 Includes bibliographies.

 1. Witchcraft--Collections. I. Title.

4 BF1563.M3 1970 133.4'08 70-18967
 ISBN 0-14-080155-8 MARC
 Library of Congress 70 [2]

AS
162
B58
v.206
 Marx, Jean, 1884-
 L'inquisition en Dauphiné; étude sur le développement et la répression de l'hérésie et de la sorcellerie du XIVe siècle au début du règne de François Ier. Paris, H. Champion, 1914.
 xxiii, 294 p. 25cm. (Bibliothèque de l'école des hautes études ... Sciences historiques et philologiques. 206. fasc.)
 1. Inquisition. Dauphiné. 2. Waldenses. 3. Witchcraft --Dauphiné. I. Title.

Witchcraft
BF
1555
M39+
 Marx, Karl Friedrich Heinrich, 1796-1877.
 Ueber die Verdienste der Aerzte um das Verschwinden der dämonischen Krankheiten. Göttingen, Dieterich, 1859.
 66 p. 28cm.
 "Aus dem achten Band der Abhandlungen der Königlichen Gesellschaft der Wissenschaften zu Göttingen."
 1. Demoniac possession. 2. Medicine
8 --Practice. 3. Witchcraft. I. Title.

Witchcraft
PT
2430
M35
M3
1844
 Mary Schweidler, the amber witch.
 Meinhold, Wilhelm, 1797-1851.
 Mary Schweidler, the amber witch. The most interesting trial for witchcraft ever known. Printed from an imperfect manuscript by her father, Abraham Schweidler, the past[or] of Coserow, in the island of Usedom. Translated from the German by Lady Duff Gordon. London, J. Murray, 1844.
 xi, 171 p. 19cm.
 Translation of his Maria Schweidler die Bernstei nhexe.

CATALOGUE OF THE CORNELL WITCHCRAFT COLLECTION

Mary Schweidler, the amber witch.

WITCHCRAFT
T
430
S5
1894

Meinhold, Wilhelm, 1797-1851.
Sidonia, the sorceress, the supposed destroyer of the whole reigning ducal house of Pomerania, translated by Lady Wilde; Mary Schweidler, the amber witch... London, Reeves and Turner, 1894.
2 v. 20cm.

Translation of Sidonia von Bork, die Klosterhexe, and Maria Schweidler, die Bernsteinhexe.

(Continued on next card)

Mary Schweidler, the amber witch.

Witchcraft

Meinhold, Wilhelm, 1797-1851. Sidonia, the sorceress... 1894. (Card 2)

"Mary Schweidler" translated by Lady Duff Gordon.
1. Witchcraft--Pomerania. I. Meinhold, Wilhelm, 1797-1851. Sidonia von Bork, die Klosterhexe--English. II. Meinhold, Wilhelm, 1797-1851. Maria Schweidler, die Bernsteinhexe--English. III. Wilde, Jane Francesca (Elgee) lady, 1826-1896, tr. IV. Duff-Gordon, Lucie (Austin) lady, 1821-1869, tr. V. Title: Sidonia, the sorceress. VI. Title: Mary Schweidler, the amber witch.

WITCHCRAFT
BF
1584
M393

Maschek von Maasburg, Friedrich, 1838-1918.
Zur Entstehungsgeschichte der Theresianischen Halsgerichtsordnung, mit besonderer Rücksicht auf das im Artikel 58 derselben behandelte crimen magiae vel sortilegii. Wien, Manz, 1880.
vi, 60 p. 24cm.

8
NIC

1. Witchcraft--Laws and legislation--Austria. 2. Trials (Witchcraft)--Austria. I. Title.

WITCHCRAFT

Masecovius, Thomas.
Warhaffte und umbständliche Beschreibung der wunderbahren Geschichte, so sich mit einer angefochtenen Jungfer in dem 1683ten und folgenden Jahren zu Königsberg in Preussen... Nebst einer Vorrede D. Bernhard von Sanden...gerichtet wider die Bezauberte Welt D. Balthasar Beckers. Königsb., In Verlegung Heinrich Boye, Druckts Johann Zacharias Etoile, 1695.
363 p. 17cm.

1. Witchcraft. 2. Witchcraft--Germany I. Bekker, Balthasar, 1634-1698. De betoverde weereld. II. Sanden, Bernhard von. III. Title.

NIC

Witchcraft

[Masini, Eliseo] brother, 17th cent.
Sacro arsenale overo Prattica dell'Officio della Santa Inqvisitione. Genova, Appresso Givseppe Pavoni, 1621.
[4], 319, [40] p. 21cm.

Title vignette, engraved.

1. Inquisition. I. Title. II. Title: Prattica dell'Officio della Santa Inquisitione.
Secular name: Cesare Masini

BX
1710
M39
1639

[Masini, Eliseo] brother, 17th cent.
Sacro arsenale, overo Prattica dell'Officio della S. Inqvisitione. Ampliata. Roma, Appresso gl'Heredi del Corbelletti, 1639.
[8], 384, [46] p. 21cm.

Title vignette, engraved.
Colophon dated 1640. Corbelleti's device above colophon.

[Secular name: Cesare Masini]

Witchcraft
BX
1710
M39
1665

[Masini, Eliseo] brother, 17th cent.
Sacro arsenale ouero Prattica dell'Officio della Santa Inqvisitione. Di nuouo corretto, & ampliato. Bologna, Ad instanza del Baglioni, 1665.
432, [62], 32 p. 17cm.

Title vignette.
"Aggionte al Sacro arsenale della Santa Inqvisitione": 32 p. at end.

[Secular name: Cesare Masini]

Witchcraft
BX
1710
M39
1679

[Masini, Eliseo] brother, 17th cent.
Sacro arsenale, ouero Prattica dell'Officio della Santa Inqvisitione. Di nuouo corretto, & ampliato ... Bologna, Per Gioseffo Longhi, 1679.
[14], 528 p. 17cm.

Edited by Natale Doriguzzi.

I. Doriguzzi, Natale, ed. II. Title.

[Secular name: Cesare Masini]

Witchcraft
BX
1710
M39
1705

[Masini, Eliseo] brother, 17th cent.
[Sacro arsenale; overo, Prattica dell'Officio della S. Inquisitione con l'inserzione d'alcune regole fatte dal p. inquisitore Tomaso Menghini ... e di diverse annotationi del dott. Gio. Pasqualone ... Et in questa 2da impressione corretta in alcune cose la parte X. degl'avvertimenti. Roma, Nella Stamp. della Rev. Cam. Apost., 1705]
[6], 426, [46] p. 24cm.

(Continued on next card)

[Secular name: Cesare Masini]

Witchcraft
BX
1710
M39
1705

[Masini, Eliseo] brother, 17th cent. [Sacro arsenale ... 1705] (Card 2)

Edited by Luigi and Francesco Conti.
Ms. annotations on margins.
Imperfect copy: title page wanting. Title from the catalogue of Bibliothèque Nationale.

Witchcraft
BX
1710
M39
1730

[Masini, Eliseo] brother, 17th cent.
Sacro arsenale, ovvero Pratica dell'Uffizio della Santa Inquisizione; coll'inserzione di alcune regole fatte dal p. inquisitore Tommaso Menghini ... e di diverse annotazioni del dottore Gio: Pasqualone ... In questa 4. impressione aggiuntavi la Settima Denunzia fatta dal suddetto padre per li sponte comparenti, impressa in Ferrara 1687. e corretta in alcune cose la parte decima degli avvertimenti ... Roma, Nella Stamperia di
(Continued on next card)
Secular name: Cesare Masini

Witchcraft
BX
1710
M39
1730

[Masini, Eliseo] brother, 17th cent. Sacro arsenale ... (Card 2)
S. Michele a Ripa, 1730.
[6], 506, [54] p. 23cm.

Edited by Luigi and Francesco Conti.

1. Inquisition. I. Menghini, Tommaso, 17th cent. II. Pasqualone, Giovanni. III. Conti, Luigi. IV. Conti, Francesco. V. Title. VI. Title: Pratica dell'Uffizio della Santa Inquisizione.

WITCHCRAFT
BS
2745
.3
M39

Masius, Hector Gottfried, 1653-1709.
Hectoris Gothofr. Masii ... Disputatio theologica De doctrina daemoniorum ex I. Timoth. IV. v. 1 & seq. In abstinentiâ ab esu carnis potissimum monstratâ. Qvam respondente M. Severino Winthero, publicae disquisitioni exposuit ad 3. April. 1699. Wittebergae, Sumptibus A. Haeberi, 1709.
39 p. 20cm.

1. Bible. N.T. 1 Timothy IV--Criticism, interpretation, etc. 2. Heresy. I. Wintherus, Severinus, respondent. II. Title: De doctrina daemoniorum. III. Title: Disputatio theologica De doctrina daemoniorum.

WITCHCRAFT
BF
1565
M39

Mason, James, M.A.
The anotomie [sic] of sorcerie. Wherein the wicked impietie of charmers, inchanters, and such is discovered and confuted. London, Printed by John Legatt and are to be sold by Simon Waterson, 1612.
103 p. 19cm.

1. Witchcraft. 2. Occult sciences. I. Title. II. Title: The anatomie of sorcerie.

NIC

Massé, Pierre.
Abus des divins.

Witchcraft
BF
1410
M41

Massé, Pierre. De l'impostvre et tromperie des diables, devins, enchantevrs, sorciers, novevrs d'esguillettes, cheuilleurs, necromanciens, chiromanciens, & autres qui par telle inuocation diabolique, ars magiques & superstitions abusent le peuple. Par Pierre Massé du Mans, aduocat. Paris, Chez Iean Poupy, 1579.
various pagings. 17cm.
Printer's device on t. p.
(Continued on next card)

Massé, Pierre.
Abus des divins.

Witchcraft
BF
1410
M41

Massé, Pierre. De l'impostvre et tromperie des diables ... 1579. (Card 2)

Title on spine: Massé. Abus des divins.
Text proceeded by Petit fragment catechistic d'vne plvs ample catechese de la magie ... de M. René Benoist Angeuin ...; and followed by Benoist's Traicté enseignant en bref les cavses des malefices, sortileges et enchanteries... with special t. p. Declamation contre l'errevr execrable des

(Continued on next card)

Massé, Pierre.
Abus des divins.

Witchcraft
BF
1410
M41

Massé, Pierre. De l'impostvre et tromperie des diables ... 1579. (Card 3)

maleficiers ... par F. Pierre Nodé minime, has special t. p. with imprint Paris, Chez Iean du Carroy imprimeur, 1578, and is paged separately.
Trois sermons de S. Avgvstin ... traduits en françois par M. René Benoist, has special t. p. with imprint Paris, Chez Iean Poupy, 1579, and unnumbered pages.

(Continued on next card)

Witchcraft
BF
1410
M41

Massé, Pierre.
De l'impostvre et tromperie des diables, devins, enchantevrs, sorciers, novevrs d'esguillettes, cheuilleurs, necromanciens, chiromanciens, & autres qui par telle inuocation diabolique, ars magiques & superstitions abusent le peuple. Par Pierre Massé du Mans, aduocat. Paris, Chez Iean Poupy, 1579.
various pagings. 17cm.
Printer's device on t. p.
(Continued on next card)

375

CATALOGUE OF THE CORNELL WITCHCRAFT COLLECTION

Witchcraft
BF 1410 M41
Massé, Pierre. De l'impostvre et tromperie des diables ... 1579. (Card 2)

Title on spine: Massé. Abus des divins. Text preceeded by Petit fragment catechistic d'vne plvs ample catechese de la magie ... de M. René Benoist Angeuin ...; and followed by Benoist's Traicté enseignant en bref les cavses des malefices, sortileges et enchanteries... with special t. p. Declamation contre l'errevr execrable des

8   (Continued on next card)

Witchcraft
BF 1410 M41
Massé, Pierre. De l'impostvre et tromperie des diables ... 1579. (Card 3)

maleficiers ... par F. Pierre Nodé minime, has special t. p. with imprint Paris, Chez Iean du Carroy imprimeur, 1578, and is paged separately.
Trois sermons de S. Avgvstin ... traduits en françois par M. René Benoist, has special t. p. with imprint Paris, Chez Iean Poupy, 1579, and unnum bered pages.

8   (Continued on next card)

Witchcraft
BF 1410 M41
Massé, Pierre. De l'impostvre et tromperie des diables ... 1579. (Card 4)

1. Occult sciences. 2. Witchcraft. I. Benoist, René, 1521-1608. Petit fragment catechistic. II. Benoist, René, 1521-1608. Traicté enseignant en bref les causes des malefices. III. Nodé, Pierre. Declamation contre l'erreur execrable des maleficiers. IV. Augustinus, Aurelius, Saint, Bp. of Hippo. Trois sermons. V. Title: De l'imposture et tromperie des diables.

8   (Over)

WITCHCRAFT
RA 1195 M41
Masson, Albert. La sorcellerie et la science des poisons au XVIIe siècle. Paris, Hachette, 1904. 342 p. 19cm.

1. Poisons. 2. Toxicology--Hist. 3. Witchcraft. 4. Medicine--15th-18th centuries.

8 NIC   V. Title.

Witchcraft
BF 1556 M42
Masters, R E L
Eros and evil; the sexual psychopathology of witchcraft. New York, Julian Press, 1962. xviii, 322 p. 24cm.

Bibliography: p. [309]-313.

1. Witchcraft. 2. Sexual perversion. 3. Demonology.   I. Title.

Witchcraft
BF 1566 L43
Lea, Henry Charles, 1825-1909, comp. Materials toward a history of witchcraft, collected by Henry Charles Lea ... arranged and edited by Arthur C. Howland ... with an introduction by George Lincoln Burr ... Philadelphia, University of Pennsylvania press, 1939.
3 v. (xliv, 1548 p.) 24cm.

Witchcraft
BF 1566 L43 1957
Lea, Henry Charles, 1825-1909, comp. Materials toward a history of witchcraft; arr. and edited by Arthur C. Howland. With an introd. by George Lincoln Burr. New York, T. Yoseloff [1957, °1939]
3 v. (xliv, 1548 p.) 22 cm.

1. Witchcraft--Hist.   x. Title.

BF1566.L4 1957   133.409   57-59569
Library of Congress   [2]

Mather, Cotton

Witchcraft
BF 1575 M42 M5
Mather, Cotton, 1663-1728.
A discourse on witchcraft.
Mather, Cotton, 1663-1728.
Memorable providences, relating to witchcrafts and possessions. A faithful account of many wonderful and surprising things, that have befallen several bewitched and possessed persons in New-England. Particularly, a narrative of the marvellous trouble and reléef experienced by a pious family in Boston, very lately and sadly molested with evil spirits. Whereunto is added, a discourse delivered unto a congregation in Boston, on the occasion of that illustrious providence. As also, a dis-

(Continued on next card)   2-25219

Witchcraft
BF 1575 M42 M5
Mather, Cotton, 1663-1728.
A discourse on witchcraft.
Mather, Cotton, 1663-1728. Memorable providences ... (Card 2)
course delivered unto the same congregation; on the occasion of an horrible self-murder committed in the town. With an appendix, in vindication of a chapter in a late book of remarkable providences, from the calumnies of a Quaker at Pen-silvania. Written by Cotton Mather ... and recommended by the ministers of Boston and Charleston. Boston, Printed by R. P., 1689.
5 p. l., 75, 21, 40, [1], 14 p. 14cm.
The first of the two discourses is "On the power and malice of the devils," the second is "A discourse on witchcraft." The appendix is a reply to George Keith's "Churches in New-England brought to the test," etc.
With book-plate of James Brindley, no. 665.
Library of Congress, no.

Witchcraft
BF 1575 M42 M5 1691
Mather, Cotton, 1663-1728. Late memorable providences relating to witchcrafts and possessions; clearly manifesting not only that there are witches, but that good men (as well as others) may possibly have their lives shortned by such evil instruments of Satan. 2d impression... London, Printed for T. Parkhurst, 1691.
144 p. 15cm.

With autograph of R. Watts.
Ex libris (supralibros) John Carter Brown
Holmes: C. M. #228B.
I. Title.

Rare
BR 520 M42++
Mather, Cotton, 1663-1728. Magnalia Christi Americana; or, The ecclesiastical history of New-England, from its first planting in the year 1620, unto the year of Our Lord, 1698. London, Printed for T. Parkhurst, 1702.
7 pt. in 1 v. double map. 39cm.
Paging irregular: book 6, p. 24, 29, 86, incorrectly numbered 32, 37, 98 respectively; paging of book 4 begins with p. 125.
List of books printed for Parkhurst (2 p.) inserted at front; another
(Continued on next card)

Rare
BR 520 M42++
Mather, Cotton, 1663-1728. Magnalia Christi Americana. London, 1702. (Card 2)
list of 2 p. at end.

Contents.--I. Antiquities.--II. Ecclesiarum clypei.--III. Polybivs.--IV. Sal gentium.--V. Acts and monuments.--VI. Thaumaturgus.--VII. Ecclesiarum praelia.

I. Title.

Witchcraft
BF 1445 B35 1840
Mather, Cotton, 1663-1728. Magnalia Christi americana.
Baxter, Richard, 1615-1691. The certainty of the world of spirits fully evinced. To which is added, The wonders of the invisible world, by Cotton Mather. The former taken from the edition published by Mr. Baxter 1691, the latter from the Ecclesiastical history of New England, published 1702. With a preface by the editor. London, H. Howell, 1840.
245 p. 11cm.
The second part is not The wonders of the invisible world but only passages from Mather Magnalia; or, Ecclesiastical history of New England.

376

CATALOGUE OF THE CORNELL WITCHCRAFT COLLECTION

Witchcraft
F
575
42
5

Mather, Cotton, 1663-1728.
Memorable providences, relating to witchcrafts and possessions. A faithful account of many wonderful and surprising things, that have befallen several bewitched and possessed persons in New-England. Particularly, a narrative of the marvellous trouble and releef experienced by a pious family in Boston, very lately and sadly molested with evil spirits. Whereunto is added, a discourse delivered unto a congregation in Boston, on the occasion of that illustrious providence. As also, a dis-

(Continued on next card)   2-25219

Witchcraft
F
575
42
5

Mather, Cotton, 1663-1728. Memorable providences ... (Card 2)
course delivered unto the same congregation; on the occasion of an horrible self-murder committed in the town. With an appendix, in vindication of a chapter in a late book of remarkable providences, from the calumnies of a Quaker at Pen-silvania. Written by Cotton Mather ... and recommended by the ministers of Boston and Charleston. Boston, Printed by R. P., 1689.
5 p. l., 75, 21, 40, [1], 14 p. 14ᶜᵐ.
The first of the two discourses is "On the power and malice of the devils," the second is "A discourse on witchcraft." The appendix is a reply to George Keith's "Churches in New-England brought to the test," etc.
With book-plate of James Brindley, no. 665.
Library of Congress, no.   (Over)

Witchcraft
F
575
42
5

Mather, Cotton, 1663-1728. On the power and malice of the devils.
Mather, Cotton, 1663-1728.
Memorable providences, relating to witchcrafts and possessions. A faithful account of many wonderful and surprising things, that have befallen several bewitched and possessed persons in New-England. Particularly, a narrative of the marvellous trouble and releef experienced by a pious family in Boston, very lately and sadly molested with evil spirits. Whereunto is added, a discourse delivered unto a congregation in Boston, on the occasion of that illustrious providence. As also, a dis-

(Continued on next card)   2-25219

Witchcraft
BF
1575
M42
M5

Mather, Cotton, 1663-1728. On the power and malice of the devils.
Mather, Cotton, 1663-1728. Memorable providences ... (Card 2)
course delivered unto the same congregation; on the occasion of an horrible self-murder committed in the town. With an appendix, in vindication of a chapter in a late book of remarkable providences, from the calumnies of a Quaker at Pen-silvania. Written by Cotton Mather ... and recommended by the ministers of Boston and Charleston. Boston, Printed by R. P., 1689.
5 p. l., 75, 21, 40, [1], 14 p. 14ᶜᵐ.
The first of the two discourses is "On the power and malice of the devils," the second is "A discourse on witchcraft." The appendix is a reply to George Keith's "Churches in New-England brought to the test," etc.
With book-plate of James Brindley, no. 665.
Library of Congress, no.

Witchcraft
F
575
76
.2-3

Mather, Cotton, 1663-1728. Pietas in patriam. The life of Sir W. Phips
Calef, Robert, 1648-1719.
More wonders of the invisible world: or, The wonders of the invisible world, display'd in five parts. Part I. An account of the sufferings of Margaret Rule, written by the Reverend Mr. C. M. P. II. Several letters to the author, &c. And his reply relating to witchcraft. P. III. The differences between the inhabitants of Salem village, and Mr. Parris their minister, in New-England. P. IV. Letters of a gentleman uninterested, endeavouring to prove the received opinions about witchcraft to be orthodox. With short essays to their answers. P. v. A short historical accout [!] of matters of fact in that affair. To

(Continued on next card)
[r31e2]   2-13714 rev.

Mather, Cotton, 1663-1728. Pietas in patriam. The life of Sir W. Phips.
Calef, Robert, 1648-1719. More wonders of the invisible ... (Card 2)
which is added, a postscript relating to a book intitled, The life of Sir William Phips. Collected by Robert Calef, merchant, of Boston in New-England ... London, Printed for N. Hillar and J. Collyer, 1700.
Reprint. (In Drake, S. G. The witchcraft delusion in New England ... Roxbury, Mass., 1866. 21½ᶜᵐ. v. 2, p. 1-212; v. 3, p. 3-167)
Woodward's historical series. no. VI-VII.
Prefatory: by the editor: p. [v]-x. Pedigree of Calef: 1 fold. leaf. Memoir of Robert Calef: p. [xi]-xxix.
The text, here annotated, is that of the 1st edition, 1700. "It is given as exactly like the original as a much better type can be made to imitate an old type of 166 years ago."--Pref. by the editor. p. vi.

(Continued on next card)
[r31e2]   2-13714 rev.

Witchcraft
BF
1575
C14
1823

Mather, Cotton, 1663-1728. Pietas in patriam. The life of Sir W. Phips.
Calef, Robert, 1648-1719. More wonders of the invisible world ... 1700. (Card 3)
Appendix: I. Examination of Giles Cory.--II. Giles Corey and Goodwyfe Corey. A ballad of 1692.--III. Testimony of William Beale, of Marblehead, against Mr. Philip English of Salem, given Aug. 2d. 1692.--IV. [Examination of the Indian woman belonging to Mr. Parris's family].--V. The examination of Mary Clark of Haverhill.--VI. An account of the life and character of the Rev. Samuel Parris, of Salem village, and of his connection with the witchcraft delusion of 1692. By Samuel P. Fowler.

Witchcraft
BF
1575
C14
1823

Mather, Cotton, 1663-1728. Pietas in patriam. The life of Sir W. Phips
Calef, Robert, 1648-1719.
More wonders of the invisible world, or The wonders of the invisible world displayed. In five parts. Part I.--An account of the sufferings of Margaret Rule, written by the Rev. Cotton Mather. Part II.--Several letters to the author, &c. and his reply relating to witchcraft. Part III.--The differences between the inhabitants of Salem village, and Mr. Parris, their minister, in New-England. Part IV.--Letters of a gentleman uninterested, endeavouring to prove the received opinions about witch-

(Continued on next card)

Witchcraft
BF
1575
C14
1823

Mather, Cotton, 1663-1728. Pietas in patriam. The life of Sir W. Phips.
Calef, Robert, 1648-1719. More wonders of the invisible world ... 1823. (Card 2)
craft to be orthodox. With short essays to their answers. Part V.--A short historical account of matters of fact in that affair. To which is added a postscript [!] relating to a book entitled "The life of Sir Wm. Phips". Collected by Robert Calef, Merchant, of Boston, in New-England. Printed in London, 1700. Salem, Re-printed by J.D. & T.C. Cushing, jr. for Cushing and Appleton, 1823.
312 p. 18½ᶜᵐ.

(Continued on next card)

Witchcraft
BF
1575
C14
1823

Mather, Cotton, 1663-1728. Pietas in patriam. The life of Sir W. Phips.
Calef, Robert, 1648-1719. More wonders of the invisible world ... 1823. (Card 3)
Appended: Giles Cory [a report of his examination, taken from the witchcraft records] p. 310-312.
"The second Salem edition appears to have been copied from the first [Salem edition] that of 1796. In some instances slight departures are made from the copy ... such departures are also departures from the original [London edition of 1700]." -- S. G. Drake, pref. to ed. of 1866.

Mather, Cotton, 1663-1728. Pietas in patriam. The life of Sir W. Phips.
Witchcraft
BF
1575
C14
1828

Calef, Robert, 1648-1719.
Wonders of the invisible world, or, Salem witchcraft. In five parts. Boston, T. Bedlington [1828]
333 p. front. 14ᶜᵐ.

A reply to Cotton Mather's "Wonders of the invisible world."
First ed. published in 1700 under title: More wonders of the invisible world displayed.

(Continued on next card)

Mather, Cotton, 1663-1728. Pietas in patriam. The life of Sir W. Phips.
Witchcraft
BF
1575
C14
1828

Calef, Robert, 1648-1719. Wonders of the invisible world ... [1828] (Card 2)

Contents.--Part 1. An account of the sufferings of Margaret Rule, by Cotton Mather.--Part 2. Several letters from the author to Mr. Mather and others, relating to witchcraft.--Part 3. Account of the differences in Salem village between the villagers and their minister, Mr. Parris.--Part 4. Letters of a gentleman uninter-

(Continued on next card)

Mather, Cotton, 1663-1728. Pietas in patriam. The life of Sir W. Phips.
Witchcraft
BF
1575
C14
1828

Calef, Robert, 1648-1719. Wonders of the invisible world ... [1828] (Card 3)

ested, endeavouring to prove the received opinions about witchcraft to be orthodox.--Part 5. An impartial account of the most memorable matters of fact touching the supposed witchcraft in New-England.--Postscript, relating to Cotton Mather's life of Sir William Phips.--Giles Cory: a report of his examination, taken from the witchcraft files.

Witchcraft
BF
1575
M42
S8
1846

Mather, Cotton, 1663-1728.
Strange phenomena of New England: in the seventeenth century: including the "Salem witchcraft," "1692." From the writings of "the Rev. Cotton Mather, D. D." ... Collected and arranged for re-publication by Henry Jones ... New-York, Piercy and Reed, 1846.
iv, [5]-54 p. 24ᶜᵐ.

1. Witchcraft--New England. I. Jones, Henry, ed. II. Title.
11-8997
Library of Congress

WITCHCRAFT
BF
1575
M42
1862

Mather, Cotton, 1663-1728.
The wonders of the invisible world. Being an account of the tryals of several witches lately executed in New-England. To which is added A farther account of the tryals of the New-England witches. By Increase Mather. London, J. R. Smith, 1862.
xvi, 291 p. port. 18ᶜᵐ. (Library of old authors)
The wonders of the invisible world; A further account of the tryals of the New-England witches ... to which is added

(Continued on next card)
8

WITCHCRAFT
BF
1575
M42
1862

Mather, Cotton, 1663-1728. The wonders of the invisible world ... 1862. (Card 2)

Cases of conscience concerning witchcrafts; and Cases of conscience concerning evil spirits personating men, each have special facsimile t. p.
The two latter works by Increase Mather.

1. Witchcraft--New England. 2. Trials (Witchcraft)--New England. 3. Devil. I. Mather, Increase, 1639-1723. A further account of th e tryals of the New-England witches. II. Mather, Increase, 1639-1723. Cases of conscience. III. Title
8

Witchcraft
BF
1575
D76
v.1

Mather, Cotton, 1663-1728.
The wonders of the invisible world: being an account of the tryals of several vvitches, lately excuted [!] in New-England: and of several remarkable curiosities therein occurring. Together with, I. Observations upon the nature, the number, and the operations of the devils. II. A short narrative of a late outrage committed by a knot of witches in Swede-land, very much resembling, and so far explaining, that under which New-England

(Continued on next card)   2-13724

Witchcraft
BF
1575
D76
v.1

Mather, Cotton, 1663-1728. The wonders of the invisible world ... 1866. (Card 2)
has laboured. III. Some councels directing a due improvement of the terrible things lately done by the unusual and amazing range of evil-spirits in New-England. IV. A brief discourse upon those temptations which are the more ordinary devices of Satan. By Cotton Mather. Published by the special command of his excellency the govenour [!] of the province of the Massachusetts-Bay in

(Continued on next card)   2-13724

CATALOGUE OF THE CORNELL WITCHCRAFT COLLECTION

Witchcraft
BF
1575
D76
v.1

Mather, Cotton, 1663-1728. The wonders of the invisible world ... 1866. (Card 3)

New-England. Printed first, at Bostun [!] in New-England; and reprinted at London, for John Dunton, 1693.
(*Reprint. In* Drake, S. G. The witchcraft delusion in New England ... Roxbury, Mass., 1866. 21½ᶜᵐ. v. 1.
1 p. l., p. [1]–247)
Woodward's historical series. no. v.
The editor has followed the 1st London ed. "presuming that to be the most accurate, as the copy from which it was printed was doubtless furnished by the author." (Preface, p. vii)
1. Witchcraft—New England. 2. Trials (Witchcraft)—New England. I. Title.   2-13724

Library of Congress, no.

BF
1575
D76
v.1

Mather, Cotton, 1663-1728.
The wonders of the invisible world: being an account of the tryals of several vvitches, lately excuted [!] in New-England: and of several remarkable curiosities therein occurring. Together with, I. Observations upon the nature, the number, and the operations of the devils. II. A short narrative of a late outrage committed by a knot of witches in Swede-land, very much resembling, and so far explaining, that under which New-England

(Continued on next card)   2-13724

BF
1575
D76
v.1

Mather, Cotton, 1663-1728. The wonders of the invisible world ... 1866. (Card 2)

has laboured. III. Some councels directing a due improvement of the terrible things lately done by the unusual and amazing range of evil-spirits in New-England. IV. A brief discourse upon those temptations which are the more ordinary devices of Satan. By Cotton Mather. Published by the special command of his excellency the govenour [!] of the province of the Massachusetts-Bay in

(Continued on next card)   2-13724

BF
1575
D76
v.1

Mather, Cotton, 1663-1728. The wonders of the invisible world ... 1866. (Card 3)

New-England. Printed first, at Bostun [!] in New-England; and reprinted at London, for John Dunton, 1693.
(*Reprint. In* Drake, S. G. The witchcraft delusion in New England ... Roxbury, Mass., 1866. 21½ cm. v. 1.
1 p. l., p. [1]–247)
Woodward's historical series. no. v.
The editor has followed the 1st London ed. "presuming that to be the most accurate, as the copy from which it was printed was doubtless furnished by the author." (Preface, p. vii)
Subject entries: Witchcraft—New England. I. Title.   2-13724

Library of Congress, no.

Witchcraft
BF
1575
D76

Mather, Cotton, 1663-1728. The wonders of the invisible world.
Drake, Samuel Gardner, 1798-1875, comp.
The witchcraft delusion in New England; its rise, progress, and termination, as exhibited by Dr. Cotton Mather, in The wonders of the invisible world; and by Mr. Robert Calef, in his More wonders of the invisible world. With a preface, introduction, and notes, by Samuel G. Drake ... Roxbury, Mass., Printed for W. E. Woodward, 1866.
3 v. 21½x17cm. (Half-title: Woodward's historical series, no. V-VII)

(Continued on next card)

Witchcraft
BF
1575
D76

Mather, Cotton, 1663-1728. The wonders of the invisible world.
Drake, Samuel Gardner, 1798-1875, comp. The witchcraft delusion in New England...(Card 2) 1866.
No. 89 of an "edition in this size" of 280 copies.
Includes reprints of original title-pages.
Contents.—v.1. The wonders of the invisible world ... By Cotton Mather.—v.2-3. More wonders of the invisible world ... Collected by Robert Calef.

Mather, Cotton, 1663-1728.
WITCHCRAFT   The wonders of the invisible world.
BF   Martin, Susanna, d.1692, defendant.
1575   The tryal of Susanna Martin, at the
M38   Court of Oyer and Terminer, held by ad-
1692a   journment at Salem, June 30, 1692...
                [Pasadena, Castle Press, 1932]
                xiii p. 23cm.
                "From 'The wonders of the invisible world' by the Rev. Cotton Mather, Boston, 1693."
8   On cover: Susanna Martin, a martyr to superstition, was executed with others on
NIC   July 19,1692.   This account of her
                trial is   reprinted by permission
                          (Continued on next card)

Mather, Cotton, 1663-1728.
WITCHCRAFT   The wonders of the invisible world.
BF   Martin, Susanna, d.1692, defendant. The
1575   tryal of Susanna Martin...[1932] (Card 2)
M38
1692a   from a rare copy in the Henry E. Huntington Library as a tribute from one of the eighth generation...
                Presentation copy from John Martin Vincent "to George L. Burr, master of the history of witchcraft."
                  1.Trials (Witchcraft)—Salem,Mass. I.Mather,Cotton,   1663-1728. The wonders
                of the invis   ible world. II.Title.

Mather, Cotton, 1663-1728.
Witchcraft   The wonders of the invisible world.
BF   Calef, Robert, 1648-1719.
1575   More wonders of the invisible world: or, The wonders of the
D76   invisible world, display'd in five parts. Part I. An account of
v.2-3   the sufferings of Margaret Rule, written by the Reverend Mr.
                C. M. P. II. Several letters to the author, &c. And his reply relating to witchcraft. P. III. The differences between the inhabitants of Salem village, and Mr. Parris their minister, in New-England. P. IV. Letters of a gentleman uninterested, endeavouring to prove the received opinions about witchcraft to be orthodox. With short essays to their answers. P. v. A short historical accout [!] of matters of fact in that affair. To
                         (Continued on next card)   2-13714 rev.
                    [r31e2]

Mather, Cotton, 1663-1728.
Witchcraft   The wonders of the invisible world.
BF   Calef, Robert, 1648-1719.   More wonders of the invisible
1575   world ... (Card 2)
D76   which is added, a postscript relating to a book intiled, The
v.2-3   life of Sir William Phips. Collected by Robert Calef, merchant, of Boston in New-England ... London, Printed for N. Hillar and J. Collyer, 1700.
                Reprint. (In Drake, S. G. The witchcraft delusion in New England ... Roxbury, Mass., 1866. 21½ᶜᵐ. v. 2, p. 1-212; v. 3, p. 3-167)
                Woodward's historical series, no. VI-VII.
                Prefatory; by the editor: p. [v]-x. Pedigree of Calef: 1 fold. leaf.
                Memoir of Robert Calef: p. [xi]-xxix.
                The text, here annotated. is that of the 1st edition, 1700. "It is given as exactly like the original as a much better type can be made to imitate an old type of 166 years ago."—Pref. by the editor. p. vi.
                         (Continued on next card)   2-13714 rev.
                    [r31e2]

Mather, Cotton, 1663-1728.
Witchcraft   The wonders of the invisible world.
BF   Calef,Robert, 1648-1719. More wonders of the
1575   invisible world ... 1700. (Card 3)
D76   Appendix: I. Examination of Giles Cory.—
v.2-3   II. Giles Corey and Goodwyfe Corey. A ballad of 1692.—III. Testimony of William Beale, of Marblehead, against Mr. Philip English of Salem, given Aug. 2d. 1692.—IV. [Examination of the Indian woman belonging to Mr. Parris's family]—V. The examination of Mary Clark of Haverhill.—VI. An account of the life and character of the Rev. Samuel Parris, of Salem village, and of his connection with   the witchcraft delusion of 1692. By Samuel   P. Fowler.

Mather, Cotton, 1663-1728.
Witchcraft   The wonders of the invisible world.
BF   Calef, Robert, 1648-1719.
1575   More wonders of the invisible world, or The
C14   wonders of the invisible world displayed. In
1823   five parts. Part I.—An account of the sufferings of Margaret Rule, written by the Rev. Cotton Mather. Part II.—Several letters to the author, &c. and his reply relating to witchcraft. Part III.—The differences between the inhabitants of Salem village, and Mr. Parris, their minister, in New-England. Part IV.—Letters of a gentleman uninterested, endeavouring to prove the received opinions about witchcraft to be
                         (Continued on next card)

Witchcraft
BF
1575
C14
1823

Mather, Cotton, 1663-1728. The wonders of the invisible world.
Calef, Robert, 1648-1719. More wonders of the invisible world ... 1826. (Card 2)

orthodox. With short essays to their answers. Part V.—A short historical account of matters of fact in that affair. To which is added a postscript [!] relating to a book entitled "The life of Sir Wm. Phips". Collected by Robert Calef. Merchant, of Boston, in New-England. Printed in London, 1700. Salem, Re-printed by J.D. & T.C. Cushing, jr. for Cushing and Appleton, 1823.
312 p. 18½cm.   (Continued on next card)

Witchcraft
BF
1575
C14
1823

Mather, Cotton, 1663-1728. The wonders of the invisible world.
Calef, Robert, 1648-1719. More wonders of the invisible world ... 1823. (Card 3)

Appended: Giles Cory [a report of his examination, taken from the witchcraft records]: p. 310-312.
"The second Salem edition appears to have been copied from the first [Salem edition] that of 1796. In some instances slight departures are made from the copy ... such departures are also departures from the original [London edition of 1700.]"—S. G.   Drake, pref. to ed. of 1866.

Witchcraft
BF
1575
C14
1865

Mather, Cotton, 1663-1728.
The wonders of the invisible world.
Calef, Robert, 1648-1719.
Salem witchcraft: comprising More wonders of the invisible world, collected by Robert Calef; and Wonders of the invisible world, by Cotton Mather; together with notes and explanations by Samuel P. Fowler. Boston, William Veazie, 1865.
450 p. 22cm.

Witchcraft
BF
1575
C14
1828

Mather, Cotton, 1663-1728.
The wonders of the invisible world.
Calef, Robert, 1648-1719.
Wonders of the invisible world, or, Salem witchcraft. In five parts. Boston, T. Bedlington [1828]
333 p. front. 14cm.

A reply to Cotton Mather's "Wonders of the invisible world."
First ed. published in 1700 under title: More wonders of the invisible world displayed.

(Continued on next card)

Witchcraft
BF
1575
C14
1828

Mather, Cotton, 1663-1728.
The wonders of the invisible world.
Calef, Robert, 1648-1719. Wonders of the invisible world ... [1828] (Card 2)

Contents.—Part 1. An account of the sufferings of Margaret Rule, by Cotton Mather.—Part 2. Several letters from the author to Mr. Mather and others, relating to witchcraft.—Part 3. Account of the differences in Salem village between the villagers and their minister, Mr. Parris.—Part 4. Letter   s of a gentleman uninter-

(Continued on next card)

Witchcraft
BF
1575
C14
1828

Mather, Cotton, 1663-1728.
The wonders of the invisible world.
Calef, Robert, 1648-1719. Wonders of the invisible world ... [1828] (Card 3)

ested, endeavouring to prove the received opinions about witchcraft to be orthodox.—Part 5. An impartial account of the most memorable matters of fact touching the supposed witchcraft in New-England.—Postscript, relating to Cotton Mather's life of Sir William Phips.—Giles Cory: a report of his examinati   on, taken from the witchcraft files.

378

CATALOGUE OF THE CORNELL WITCHCRAFT COLLECTION

Mather, Cotton, 1663-1728.

WITCHCRAFT
BF
1576
P82
U673

Goddard, Delano Alexander, 1831-1882.
The Mathers weighed in the balances by Delano A. Goddard and found not wanting. Boston: Office of the Daily Advertiser; London: Office of H. Stevens, 1870.
32 p. 16cm.
Copy 1 is autograph presentation copy to A. D. White.
1. Upham, Charles Wentworth, 1802-1875. Salem witchcraft and Cotton Mather. 2. Mather, Increase, 1639-1723. 3. Mather, Cotton, 1663- 1728. I. Title.

Mather, Cotton, 1663-1728.

Witchcraft
BF
1576
P82

Poole, William Frederick, 1821-1894.
Cotton Mather and Salem witchcraft. By William Frederick Poole. ⟨Reprinted from the North American review for April, 1869.⟩ Boston [University press] 1869.
63 p. 24cm.
"One hundred copies printed."

1. Witchcraft—Salem, Mass. 2. Mather, Cotton, 1663-1728. I. Title.
3. Upham, Charles Wentworth, 1802-1875.
Salem witchcraft; with an account of Salem village.
Library of Congress   BF1576.P83

Mather, Cotton, 1663-1728.

WITCHCRAFT
BF
1576
P82
U67+

Upham, Charles Wentworth, 1802-1875.
Salem witchcraft and Cotton Mather. A reply [to W. F. Poole's Cotton Mather and Salem witchcraft] Morrisania, N. Y., 1869.
91 p. 19cm.
In double columns.
Reprint from the Historical Magazine.
1. Poole, William Frederick, 1821-1894. Cotton Mather and Salem witchcraft. 2. Mather, Cotton, 1663-1728. 3. Witchcraft—Salem, Mass. I. Title.

Mather, Cotton, 1663-1728.

Witchcraft
BF
1576
P82
U676

[Haven, Samuel Foster] 1806-1881.
[The Mathers and the witchcraft delusions. Boston, 1874]
14 p. 25cm.

Title on cover in ms.
"From the Proceedings of the meeting of the American Antiquarian Society in Boston, April 29, 1874. Report of the librarian."

1. Witchcraft—New England. 2. Mather, Cotton, 1663- 1728. I. Title.

Mather, Cotton, 1663-1728.

Witchcraft
BF
1576
P82
U676

[Poole, William Frederick] 1821-1894.
Cotton Mather & witchcraft; two notices of Mr. Upham, his reply. Boston, T. R. Marvin & son; [etc., etc.] 1870.
30 p. 17cm.

1. Witchcraft—Salem, Mass. 2. Mather, Cotton, 1663-1728. 3. Upham, Charles Wentworth, 1802-1875. I. Title.

11—9001

Library of Congress   BF1576.P8

Mather, Cotton, 1663-1728—Bibliography.

Witchcraft
BF
1575
C23
H75

Holmes, Thomas James, 1874–
Cotton Mather and his writings on witchcraft. [Chicago, Univ. of Chicago Press, 1926]
29 p. 25cm.

"Reprinted for private distribution from Papers of the Bibliographical Society of America, vol. XVIII, Parts 1 and 2."
Bound with his The surreptitious printing of one of Cotton Mather's manuscripts.
1. Mather, Cotton, 1663-1728—Bibl. 2. Witchcraft —Bibl. I. Title.

Mather, Cotton, 1663-1728.

Witchcraft
BF
1575
C23
H75

Holmes, Thomas James, 1874–
The surreptitious printing of one of Cotton Mather's manuscripts, by Thomas J. Holmes ... Cambridge [Mass., Printed at the Harvard university press] 1925.
1 p. l., 12 p. 25cm.

"Reprinted from Bibliographical essays; a tribute to Wilberforce Eames."

With this is bound his Cotton Mather and his writings on witchcraft. [1926]
1. Calef, Robert, 1648-1719. More wonders of the invisible world. 2. Mather, Cotton, 1663-1728. 3. Witchcraft—New England. I. Title.

Library of Congress   BF1575.C23H6
41-38390

Mather, Increase

Mather, Increase, 1639-1723.
Cases of conscience concerning evil spirits personating men, witchcrafts, infallible proofs of guilt in such as are accused of that crime. All considered according to the Scriptures, history, experience, and the judgment of many learned men... Boston, Printed and sold by B. Harris, 1693.
67 p. 15cm.

With autographs of John Dodge, 1692, Ebenezer Parker, John Temple, and Rebekah Temple.
(Continued on next card)

Mather, Increase, 1639-1723. Cases of conscience concerning evil spirits personating men ... 1693. (Card 2)

With book-plate of Matt. B. Jones. Seventeenth century binding. Original calf in full brown crushed levant solander case by Rivière & Son.
One of 2 known copies with inscription dated 1692 (December 13)
Holmes: I. M. #22; Wing M 1193.

1. Witchcraft. I. Title.

Mather, Increase, 1639-1723.
Cases of conscience.

WITCHCRAFT
BF
1575
M42
1862

Mather, Cotton, 1663-1728.
The wonders of the invisible world. Being an account of the tryals of several witches lately executed in New-England. To which is added A farther account of the tryals of the New-England witches. By Increase Mather. London, J. R. Smith, 1862.
xvi, 291 p. port. 18cm. (Library of old authors)
The wonders of the invisible world; A further account of the tryals of the New-England witches ... to which is added
(Continued on next card)

Mather, Increase, 1639-1723.
Cases of conscience.

WITCHCRAFT
BF
1575
M42
1862

Mather, Cotton, 1663-1728. The wonders of the invisible world ... 1862. (Card 2)

Cases of conscience concerning witchcrafts; and Cases of conscience concerning evil spirits personating men, each have special facsimile t. p.
The two latter works by Increase Mather.

1. Witchcraft—New England. 2. Trials (Witchcraft)—New England. 3. Devil. I. Mather, Increase, 1639-1723. A further account of the tryals of the New-England witches. II. Mather, Increase, 1639-1723. Cases of conscience. III. Title.

Mather, Increase, 1639-1723.

Witchcraft
BF
1575
M427

Cases of conscience concerning witchcrafts
Mather, Increase, 1639-1723.
A further account of the tryals of the New-England witches. With the observations of a person who was upon the place several days when the suspected witches were first taken into examination. To which is added, Cases of conscience concerning witchcrafts and evil spirits personating men. Written at the request of the ministers of New England. By Increase Mather, president of Harvard colledge ... London, Printed for J. Dunton, 1693.
(Continued on next card)

Mather, Increase, 1639-1723.

Witchcraft
BF
1575
M427

Cases of conscience concerning witchcrafts
Mather, Increase, 1639-1723. A further account of the tryals of the New-England witches ... 1693. (Card 2)
1 p. l., 10 p., 1 l., [2], 39, [5] p. 20cm.
Title within double line border.
After year of imprint: Of whom may be had the third edition of Mr. Cotton Mather's first Account of the tryals of the New-England witches, Printed on the same size with this last account, that they may bind up together.
"Cases of conscience" has special t.-p. and separate paging.   (Continued on next card)

CATALOGUE OF THE CORNELL WITCHCRAFT COLLECTION

Witchcraft
BF 1575
M427

Mather, Increase, 1639-1723.
Mather, Increase, 1639-1723. A further account of the tryals of the New-England witches ... 1693. (Card 3)
"A true narrative of some remarkable passages relating to sundry persons afflicted by witchcraft at Salem village in New-England, which happened from the 19th. of March to the 5th. of April, 1692. Collected by Deodat Lawson": p.1-9.
"A further account of the tryals of the New-England witches, sent in a letter from thence, to a gentleman in London": p. 9-10.
Wing M 1213.

Witchcraft
BF 1575
M427

Mather, Increase, 1639-1723.
A further account of the tryals of the New-England witches. With the observations of a person who was upon the place several days when the suspected witches were first taken into examination. To which is added, Cases of conscience concerning witchcrafts and evil spirits personating men. Written at the request of the ministers of New England. By Increase Mather, president of Harvard colledge ... London, Printed for J. Dunton, 1693.
(Continued on next card)
5-33455†

Witchcraft
BF 1575
M427

Mather, Increase, 1639-1723. A further account of the tryals of the New-England witches... 1693. (Card 2)
1 p. l., 10 p., 1 l., [2], 39, [5] p. 20cm.
Title within double line border.
After year of imprint: Of whom may be had the third edition of Mr. Cotton Mather's first Account of the tryals of the New-England witches. Printed on the same size with this last account, that they may bind up together.
"Cases of conscience" has special t.-p. and separate paging.
(Continued on next card)

Witchcraft
BF 1575
M427

Mather, Increase, 1639-1723. A further account of the tryals of the New-England witches ... 1693. (Card 3)
"A true narrative of some remarkable passages relating to sundry persons afflicted by witchcraft at Salem village in New-England, which happened from the 19th. of March to the 5th. of April, 1692. Collected by Deodat Lawson": p.1-9.
"A further account of the tryals of the New-England witches, sent in a letter from thence, to a gentleman in London": p. 9-10.
Wing M 1213.
I. Title. II. Lawson, Deodat, fl. 1680-1698. A true narrative of ... witchcraft at Salem. III. Mather, Increase, 1639-1723. Cases of conscience concerning witchcrafts.

WITCHCRAFT
BF 1575
M42 1862

Mather, Increase, 1639-1723.
A further account of the tryals of the New-England witches.
Mather, Cotton, 1663-1728.
The wonders of the invisible world. Being an account of the tryals of several witches lately executed in New-England. To which is added A farther account of the tryals of the New-England witches. By Increase Mather. London, J. R. Smith, 1862.
xvi, 291 p. port. 18cm. (Library of old authors)
The wonders of the invisible world; A further account of the tryals of the New-England witch es ... to which is added
(Continued on next card)

WITCHCRAFT
BF 1575
M42 1862

Mather, Increase, 1639-1723.
A further account of the tryals of the New-England witches.
Mather, Cotton, 1663-1728. The wonders of the invisible world ... 1862.
(Card 2)
Cases of conscience concerning witchcrafts; and Cases of conscience concerning evil spirits personating men, each have special facsimile t. p.
The two latter works by Increase Mather.
1. Witchcraft--New England. 2. Trials (Witchcraft)--New England. 3. Devil. I. Mather, Increase, 1639-1723. A further account of the tryals of the New-England witches. II. Mather, Increase, 1639-1723. Cases of conscience. III. Title.

Witchcraft
F 7
M42 1856

Mather, Increase, 1639-1723.
Remarkable providences illustrative of the earlier days of American colonisation. By Increase Mather. With introductory preface, by George Offor. London, J. R. Smith, 1856.
xix, [16], 262 p. front. (port.) 16½ᶜᵐ. (Half-title: Library of old authors)
1. New England--Hist.--Colonial period. I. Offor, George, 1787-1864, ed. II. Title.
18-11699
Library of Congress   F7.M436

WITCHCRAFT
BF 1576
P82
U673

Mather, Increase, 1639-1723.
Goddard, Delano Alexander, 1831-1882.
The Mathers weighed in the balances by Delano A. Goddard and found not wanting. Boston: Office of the Daily Advertiser; London: Office of H. Stevens, 1870.
2 copies
32 p. 16cm.
Copy 1 is autograph presentation copy to A. D. White.
1. Upham, Charles Wentworth, 1802-1875. Salem witchcraft and Cotton Mather. 2. Mather, Increase, 1639-1723. 3. Mather, Cotton, 1663- 1728. I. Title.
8 NIC

Witchcraft
BF 1576
H38

The Mathers and the witchcraft delusions.
[Haven, Samuel Foster] 1806-1881.
[The Mathers and the witchcraft delusions. Boston, 1874]
14 p. 25cm.
Title on cover in ms.
"From the Proceedings of the meeting of the American Antiquarian Society in Boston, April 29, 1874. Report of the librarian."
1. Witchcraft-- New England. 2. Mather, Cotton, 1663- 1728. I. Title.

WITCHCRAFT
BF 1576
P82
U673

The Mathers weighed in the balances.
Goddard, Delano Alexander, 1831-1882.
The Mathers weighed in the balances by Delano A. Goddard and found not wanting. Boston: Office of the Daily Advertiser; London: Office of H. Stevens, 1870.
2 copies
32 p. 16cm.
Copy 1 is autograph presentation copy to A. D. White.
1. Upham, Charles Wentworth, 1802-1875. Salem witchcraft and Cotton Mather. 2. Mather, Increase, 1639-1723. 3. Mather, Cotton, 1663- 1728. I. Title.
8 NIC

Witchcraft
BF 1548
M43

Matson, William A.
The Adversary, his person, power, and purpose; a study in satanology, by William A. Matson, D. D. New York, W. B. Ketcham [c1891]
xi, [13]-238 p. 19½ᶜᵐ.
1. Devil. 2. Demonomania. I. Title.
11—9194
Library of Congress   BF1548.M4
Copyright 1891: 37377   [a32b1]

Witchcraft
BF 1548
M43 1891

Matson, William A.
The Adversary, his person, power, and purpose; a study in satanology. [2d ed.] New York, W. B. Ketcham [c1891]
xi, 238 p. 20cm.
1. Devil. 2. Demonomania. I. Title.

RARE
HV 8593
D611
no.14

Mauchart, Burcard Friedrich, respondent.
Hoffmann, Gottfried Daniel, 1719-1780, praeses.
De continuatione torturae interruptae... praeside Godofredo Daniele Hoffmanno...disputabit Burcardus Fridericus Mauchart. Tubingae, Formis Erhardianis [1757]
48 p. 21cm.
Diss.--Tübingen (B. F. Mauchart, respondent)
No. 14 in a vol. lettered: Dissertationes de tortura, 1597-1770.
1. Torture. 2. Criminal procedure. I. Mauchart, Burcard Friedrich, respondent. II. Title.
8 NIC

WITCHCRAFT
BF 1584
N6
M44

Mauland, Torkell, 1848-1923.
Trolldom. Kristiania, J. W. Cappelen, 1911.
156 p. 22cm.
1. Witchcraft--Norway. 2. Trials (Witchcraft)--Norway. I. Title.
8 NIC

Witchcraft
BF 1565
M45

Mauritius, Erich, 1631-1692, praeses.
Dissertatio inauguralis, De denuntiatione sagarum, iisque quae ad eam recte intelligendam faciunt. Qvam ... praeside Erico Mauritio ... submittit Christophorus Daurer, Hamburg. Tubingae, Excudit Gregorius Kerner, 1664.
96 p. 20cm.
Diss.--Tübingen (C. Daurer, respondent)
1. Witchcraft. 2. Trials (Witchcraft) I. Daurer, Christophorus, respondent. II. Title: De denuntiatione sagarum. III. Title.
8

WITCHCRAFT
K
M452

Mauritius, Erich, 1631-1692.
Dissertatio inauguralis De denuntiatione sagarum.
Mauritius, Erich, 1631-1692.
Dissertationes et opuscula de selectis jurispublici, feudalis & privati vati argumentis conscripta, & seorsim antehac diversis locis edita, jam...in unum volumen collecta. Accessit praefatio Dn. Joannis Nicolai Hertii... Francofurti ad Moenum Sumptibus Christophori Olfen, 1692.
1256 p. 21cm.
"De denuntiatione sagarum dissertatio": p.1035-1138. Followed by an append containing Mauritius' opinion
(Continued on next card)
8 NIC

WITCHCRAFT
K
M452

Mauritius, Erich, 1631-1692. Dissertatio inauguralis De denuntiatione sagarum.
Mauritius, Erich, 1631-1692. Dissertationes et opuscula...1692. (Card 2)
in a witchcraft case. The dissertation was originally published at Tübingen in 1664 with title: Dissertatio inauguralis De denuntiatione sagarum. (Respondent: C. Daurer)
1. Law--Addresses, essays, lectures. 2. Witchcraft. 3. Trials (Witchcraft) I. Hi Dissertatio inauguralis De denuntiatione sagarum. II. Daurer, Christophorus, respondent. III.Title: De denuntiatione sagarum. IV. Hertius, Johann Nikol aus, 1651-1710, ed.

WITCHCRAFT
K
M452

Mauritius, Erich, 1631-1692.
Dissertationes et opuscula de selectis jurispublici, feudalis & privati vati argumentis conscripta, & seorsim antehac diversis locis edita, jam...in unum volumen collecta. Accessit praefatio Dn. Joannis Nicolai Hertii... Francofurti ad Moenum Sumptibus Christophori Olfen, 1692.
1256 p. 21cm.
"De denuntiatione sagarum dissertatio": p.1035-1138. Followed by an append containing Mauritius' opinion
(Continued on next card)
8 NIC

CATALOGUE OF THE CORNELL WITCHCRAFT COLLECTION

WITCHCRAFT
1452
Mauritius, Erich, 1631-1692. Dissertationes et opuscula...1692. (Card 2)

in a witchcraft case. The dissertation was originally published at Tübingen in 1664 with title: Dissertatio inauguralis De denuntiatione sagarum. (Respondent: C. Daurer)
  1. Law—Addresses, essays, lectures. 2. Witchcraft. 3. Trials (Witchcraft) I. His Dissertatio inauguralis De denuntiatione sagarum. II. Daurer, Christophorus, respondent. III. Title: De denuntiatione sagarum. IV. Hertius, Johann Nikolaus, 1651-1710, ed.

WITCHCRAFT
BF
1589
M45
1864

Maury, Louis Ferdinand Alfred, 1817-1892.
  La magie et l'astrologie dans l'antiquité et au moyen âge; ou, Étude sur les superstitions païennes qui se sont perpétuées jusqu'à nos jours. 3. éd. revue et corrigée. Paris, Didier, 1864.
  484 p. 18cm.

8
NIC

  1. Magic. 2. Astrology. 3. Occult sciences. I. Title.

Maury, Louis Ferdinand Alfred, 1817-1892.

WITCHCRAFT
BF
1582
T91+

Tuetey, Alexandre, 1842-1918.
  La sorcellerie dans le pays de Montbéliard au XVII siècle. D'après des documents inédits ... Avec une préface par Mr Alfred Maury ... Dôle (Jura), A. Vernier-Arcelin, 1886.
  x, 94 p. 26cm.

  1. Witchcraft—France. 2. Witchcraft—Montbéliard, France. I. Maury, Louis Ferdinand Alfred, 1817-1892. II. Title.

NIC

Le mauvais oeil, tradition dalmate.
Brisset, Joseph Mathurin, 1792-1856.
  Le mauvais oeil, tradition dalmate, suivi d'une nouvelle française. Paris, U. Canel, 1833.
  303 p. 22cm.

Maximilian I, Emperor of Germany, 1459-1519.

WITCHCRAFT
BF
1565
S83
1605

Trithemius, Johannes, 1462-1516.
  Antipalus maleficiorvm Iohannis Tritemii Spanhemensis ... qvatvor libris comprehensvs. Mogvntiae, Apud Balthasarum Lippium, 1605.
  275-861 p. 19cm.
  According to a note by G. L. Burr inside front cover, this is detached from Paralipomena opusculorum Petri Blesensis, Joannes Trithemii, Hincmari, aliorumque, compiled and edited by Jean Buys.
  (Continued on next card)

NIC

Maximilian I, Emperor of Germany, 1459-1519.

WITCHCRAFT
BF
1565
S83
1605

Trithemius, Johannes, 1462-1516. Antipalvs maleficiorvm ... 1605. (Card 2)

Contents.—Antipalus maleficiorum.—Liber octo quaestionum, quas illi dissolvenda proposuit Maximilianus Caesar.—De laudibus ordinis Fratrum Carmelitarum.—Tractatus, De laudibus Sanctissimae Matris Annae.—Index Graecorum voluminum Ioannis Trithemii.—Hincmari Rhemensis ... Epistolae duae.—Hymni de solemnitate S. Wigberti.
  Binding: 17th cent. blind stamped pig skin, with clasps.
  (Continued on next card)

NIC

Maximilian I, Emperor of Germany, 1459-1519.

WITCHCRAFT
BT
80
T83
1515

Trithemius, Johannes, 1462-1516.
  Ioannis Tritemii ... Liber octo questionū ad Maximilianum Cesarem. Cum priuilegio Cesaree maiestatis de nō imprimēdo in regno ... [Oppenheym, Impressum impensis Iohānis Hasselbergen de Augia Constātiensis dyocesis, 1515]
  [78] p. 20cm.
  Title vignette with ports. of Maximilian and Trithemius.
  With colophon.

8
NIC

(Continued on next card)

Witchcraft
BF
1565
S83
M186

[Mayer, Andreas Ulrich] 1732-1802.
  Glückwünschungsschreiben an den Hochw. P. Angelus März, über seine Vertheidigung der Hex- und Zauberey, von F. N. Blocksberger, Beneficiaten zu T. [pseud.] Straubingen, 1767.
  [16] p. 22cm.

  1. März, Angelus, 1731-1784. ... Kurze Vertheidigung der thätigen Hex- und Zauberey. 2. Sterzinger, Ferdinand, 1721-1786. I. Title.

8

Witchcraft
BF
1565
S83
no.4

[Mayer, Andreas Ulrich] 1732-1802.
  Nichtige, ungegründete, eitle, kahle und lächerliche Verantwortung des H. P. Angelus März, Benedictiner zu Scheyrn, über die vom P. Don Ferdinand Sterzinger bey dem hochfürstlichen hochlöblichen geistlichen Rath in Freysing gestellten Fragen. Vom Moldaustrom, 1767.
  57 p. 20cm. (bound in 23cm. vol.)
  Ascribed by Graesse, J. G. T., Bibliotheca magica et pneumatica and by Zapf,
  (Continued on next card)

8

Witchcraft
BF
1565
S83
no.4

[Mayer, Andreas Ulrich] 1732-1802. Nichtige, ungegründete, eitle ... Verantwortung des H. P. Angelus März ... 1767. (Card 2)

  G. W., Zauberbibliothek, to F. N. Blocksberger, which is A. U. Mayer's pseudonym.
  British Museum suggests F. Sterzinger as author.
  No. 4 in vol. lettered Sterzinger über Hexerei, 1766-1767.

8
(Continued on next card)

Witchcraft
BF
1565
S83
no.4

[Mayer, Andreas Ulrich] 1732-1802. Nichtige, ungegründete, eitle ... Verantwortung des H. P. Angelus März ... 1767. (Card 3)

  1. März, Angelus, 1731-1784. Kurze Vertheidigung der thätigen Hex- und Zauberey. 2. Sterzinger, Ferdinand, 1721-1786. I. Sterzinger, Ferdinand, 1721-1786, supposed author. II. Title: Nichtige, ungegründete, eitle ... Verantwortung des H. P. Angelus März.

8

Witchcraft
BF
1565
S83
S836

[Mayer, Andreas Ulrich] 1732-1802.
  Sendschreiben an den Hochw. H. P. Agnellus März, ... Über seine Vertheidigung wider die schwulstige Vertheidigung der betrügenden Zauberey und Hexerey, von F. N. Blocksberger, Beneficiaten zu T. [pseud.] Straubingen, 1767.
  5 pieces in 3 v. 23cm.
  Vol. 2 has caption title: Weitere Fortsetzung. Des F. N. Blockbergers [sic] zweytes Sendschreiben an H. P. Agnell &c. &c.
  (Continued on next card)

8

Witchcraft
BF
1565
S83
S836

[Mayer, Andreas Ulrich] 1732-1802. Sendschreiben an den Hochw. H. P. Agnellus März ... 1767. (Card 2)

  This vol. contains the 2. and 4. Sendschreiben, consecutively paged.
  Vol. 3 has caption title: Des F. N. Blockbergers [sic] fünftes Sendschreiben an H. P. Agnell, &c. &c. The vol. contains the 5. and 6. Sendschreiben, consecutively paged.
  (Continued on next card)

8

Witchcraft
BF
1565
S83
S836

[Mayer, Andreas Ulrich] 1732-1802. Sendschreiben an den Hochw. H. P. Agnellus März ... 1767. (Card 3)

  1. März, Agnellus, 1726-1784. Vertheidigung wider die geschwulstige Vertheidigung der betrügenden Zauberkunst. 2. Sterzinger, Ferdinand, 1721-1786. Betrügende Zauberkunst und träumende Hexerey. I. Title.

8

Mayer, Andreas Ulrich, 1732-1802, supposed ed.

Witchcraft
BF
1584
A93
A61

Anpreisung der allergnädigsten Landesverordnung Ihrer kaiserl. königl. apostolischen Majestät, wie es mit dem hexenprocesse zu halten sey, nebst einer vorrede, in welcher die Kurze vertheidigung der hex- und zauberey, die herr pater Angelus März der Akademischen rede des herrn p. don Ferdinand Sterzingers über das vorurtheil der hexerey entgegengesetzet, beantwortet wird von einem gottesgelehrten. München, Akademische buchhandlung, 1767.
  4 p. l., 282, [2] p. 23cm.
  (Continued on next card)

8
42-40824

Mayer, Andreas Ulrich, 1732-1802, supposed ed.

Witchcraft
BF
1584
A93
A61

Anpreisung der allergnädigsten Landesverordnung Ihrer kaiserl. königl. apostolischen Majestät ... 1767. (Card 2)

  Variously ascribed to Jordan Simon and Andreas Ulrich Mayer.
  "Sr. kaiserlich-königlich-apostolischen Majestät allergnädigsten Landesordnung, wie es mit dem Hexenprocesse zu halten sey, mit kurzen Anpreisungen für den gemeinen Mann erkläret," p. [1]- has special t.-p.
  1. Witchcraft—Austria. 2. März, Angelus, 1731-1784. Kurze Vertheidigung der thätigen Hex- und Zauberey. 3. Sterzinger, Ferdinand, 1721-1786. Akademische Rede von dem gemeinen Vorurtheile der ... Hexerey. I. Simon, Jordan, pater, 1719-1776, supposed ed. II. Mayer, Andreas Ulrich, 1732-1802, supposed ed. III. Austria. Laws, statutes, etc. IV. Ein Gottesgelehrter.

Library of Congress   BF1584.A8A5

8   42-40824   [2]

Mayer, Andreas Ulrich, 1732-1802, supposed author.

Witchcraft
BF
1603
S83
no.1

[Sterzinger, Ferdinand] 1721-1786.
  ... Untersuchung ob es eine Festigkeit gebe dabey viele andere aberglaubische Irrthümer widerleget werden nebst beygefügtem Katechismus von der Geisterlehre. München, W. Schwarzkopf, Buchhändler in Nürnberg, 1775.
  200 p. 17cm.
  At head of title: Francone dell' Amavero [pseud. of F. Sterzinger]
  No. 1 in vol. lettered Francone dell' Amavero (Sterzinger) Untersuchung [etc.]
  (Continued on next card)

8

Mayer, Andreas Ulrich, 1732-1802, supposed author.

Witchcraft
BF
1603
S83
no.1

[Sterzinger, Ferdinand] 1721-1786. ... Untersuchung ob es eine Festigkeit gebe ... 1775. (Card 2)

  Attributed by British Museum and Kayser to A. U. Mayer.
  1. Magic. 2. Spells. I. His Katekismus von der Geisterlehre. II. Title. III. Mayer, Andreas Ulrich, 1732-1802, supposed author. IV. Title: Katekismus von der Geisterlehre.

8

CATALOGUE OF THE CORNELL WITCHCRAFT COLLECTION

Witchcraft
BF
1410
C97

Mayer, Johann Friedrich, 1650-1712--
Fiction.
Curieuses Gespräche im Reiche derer Todten, zwischen zweyen hochberühmten Männern, Johann Friedrich Mayern, ... und Johann Wilhelm Petersen ... Darinnen nechst dieser beyder hochberühmten Männer Lebens-Particularitäten, von vielen curieusen und zu unserer Zeit strittig gewordenen Glaubens-Lehren, pro & contra gestritten wird. [Leipzig] 1732.
2 v. in 1. (128 p.) 2 plates, vignettes 21 x 17cm.

8 (Continued on next card)

Witchcraft
BF
1410
C97

Mayer, Johann Friedrich, 1650-1712--
Fiction.
Curieuses Gespräche im Reiche derer Todten, zwischen ...Johann Friedrich Mayern, ... und Johann Wilhelm Petersen ...   1732.
(Card 2)

4°: A3, B-H⁴, J3, K-Q⁴.
Black letter.
Vol. 2 has title: Gespräche im Reiche derer Todten ...
Bound with Curieuse Gespräche im Reiche derer Todten, zwischen ... Balthasar Beckern ... und ... Christian Scrivern ... 1731-[1734] (Continued on next card)

WITCHCRAFT
BF
1520
M46
1780

Mayer, Johann Gottfried.
Historia diaboli; seu, Commentatio de diaboli, malorumque spirituum exsistentia, statibus, iudiciis, consiliis, potestate. Editio altera. Tubingae, Sumtibus Ioh. Georgii Cottae, 1780.
xvi, 712 p. 20cm.

8
NIC 1. Devil. 2. Demonology. I. Title.

BF
1566
M46

Mayer, Phillip
Witches; inaugural lecture delivered at Rhodes University. Grahamstown, Rhodes University, 1954.
19 p. 22cm.

1. Witchcraft--Addresses, essays, lectures.
I. Title.

Mayer, Simon, 1570-1624.

see

Mayr, Simon, 1570-1624.

Mayerne, Louis Turquet de, d. 1618.

WITCHCRAFT
B
781
A33
I3
1582

Agrippa von Nettesheim, Heinrich Cornelius, 1486?-1535.
Declamation svr l'incertitvde, vanité, et abvs des sciences, traduite en françois du latin de Henry Corneille Agr. ...
[Paris] Par Iean Dvrand, 1582.
8 p. l., 551 p. 17cm.
First edition in French, of De incertitudine et vanitate omnium scientiarum et artium liber.
"Trad. par Louis de Mayerne Turquet. C'est la seule traduction qui n'a pas

8 (Continued on next card)

Mayerne, Louis Turquet de, d. 1618.

WITCHCRAFT
B
781
A33
I3
1582

Agrippa von Nettesheim, Heinrich Cornelius, 1486?-1535. Declamation svr l'incertitvde ... des sciences ... 1582. (Card 2)

été mutilée": in 17th century hand on flyleaf.
Gold stamped citron morocco binding with date 1695 on front and back covers.

1. Learning and scholarship. 2. Scholasticism. 3. Science--Early works to 1800. I. His De incertitudine et vanitate omnium scientiarum et artium liber, French. II. Mayerne, Louis Turquet, d. 1618. III. Title.

Mayr, Simon, 1570-1624.

WITCHCRAFT
BF
1555
S35

Schnabel, Joannes.
Warhafftige vnd erschröckliche Geschicht, welche sich newlicher Zeit zugetragen hat, mit einem jungen Handtwercks vnd Schmidtsgesellen, Hansen Schmidt genandt, ... der ... von einer gantzen Legion Teüffeln hefftig besessen vnd hernacher ... durch sonderbare Schickung Gottes Allmächtigen vnd zugethane verordtnete Mittel ... errettet ... worden ist ... Durch M. Ioannem Schnabeln ... vnd M. Simonem Marium ... Wirtzburg, Gedruckt

8
NIC (Continued on next card)

Mayr, Simon, 1570-1624.

WITCHCRAFT
BF
1555
S35

Schnabel, Joannes. Warhafftige vnd erschröckliche Geschicht ... [1589] (Card 2)

durch Henrich von Ach [1589]
[32] p. 20cm.
1. Demoniac possession. 2. Exorcism. 3. Schmidt, Hans, fl. 1589. I. Mayr, Simon, 1570-1624. II. Title.

8
NIC

Mazolini, Silvestro, 1456-1527.

see

Mazzolini, Silvestro, da Prierio, 1456-1523.

WITCHCRAFT
BF
1565
M47
1575

Mazzolini, Silvestro, da Prierio, 1456-1523.
Reverendi Patris F. Silvestri Prieriatis ... De strigimagarvm, daemonumque mirandis, libri tres ... Romae, In aedibus Po[puli] Ro[mani] 1575.
12 p. l., 262 p. 23cm.
With colophon.
With this is bound Spina, Bartolommeo. ... Quaestio de strigibus. Romae, 1576.

8
NIC 1. Witchcraft. 2. Demonology. I. Title. II. De strigimagarum... mirandis. Title.

WITCHCRAFT
K
M4769
no.4

Mecklenburg. Laws, statutes, etc.
Fürstl. Mecklenburg Anderweite Instruction und Verordnung, wie von denen Beampten E. E. Ritterschafft Gerichts-Verwaltern Bürgermeistern Richtern und Käthen und ins gemein andern Gerichts-vorwesern wieder die dess Zauberlasters und abergl[a]übischen Dinge berüchtigte Pehsonen und deren Complices zuverfahren sey. Güstrow, Gedruckt durch Johann Spierling, 1683.
[12] p. 21 cm.
No.4 in a vol. of ordinances of Mecklenburg concerning witchcraft.
(Continued on next card)

8
NIC

WITCHCRAFT
K
M4769
no.4

Mecklenburg. Laws, statutes, etc. Fürstl. Mecklenburg Anderweite Instruction und Verordnung...1683. (Card 2)

1. Witchcraft--Laws and legislation--Mecklenburg. 2. Trials (Witchcraft)--Mecklenburg. I. Title.

8
NIC

WITCHCRAFT
K
M4769
no.3

Mecklenburg. Laws, statutes, etc.
Fürstl. Mecklenb. Erweiterte Verordnung welcher massen es mit der befragunge der Zaubereyhalber eingezogenen Personen sonderlich mittelst adhibirter Tortur, wegen Ihrer complicum, zuhalten. Güstrow, Gedruckt durch Johann Spierling, 1683.
[7] p. 21cm.
No.3 in a vol. of ordinances of Mecklenburg concerning witchcraft.
1. Witchcraft--Laws and legislation--Mecklenburg. 2.Trials (Witchcraft)--Mecklenburg. I. Title.

8
NIC

WITCHCRAFT
K
M4769
no.2

Mecklenburg. Laws, statutes, etc.
Fürstl. Mecklenb. Verordnung wie nach diesem die der Zauberey halber gefänglich ein gezogene Personen bewahret werden sollen. Güstrow, Gedruckt durch Johann Spierling, 1682.
[6] p. 21cm.
No. 2 in a vol. of ordinances of Mecklenburg concerning witchcraft.
1. Witchcraft--Laws and legislation--Mecklenburg. 2. Trials (Witchcraft)--Mecklenburg. I. Title.

8
NIC

WITCHCRAFT
K
M4769
no.1

Mecklenburg. Laws, statutes, etc.
Instructio für die fürstliche Mecklenburgische Beampten und Stadt-Richtere, wie wieder die dess Zauberlasters und Aberglaubischer-Dinge berüchtigte Personen zu verfahren. Güstrow, Gedruckt durch Johann Spierling, 1681.
[8] p. 21cm.
No. 1 in a vol. of ordinances of Mecklenburg concerning witchcraft.
1.Witchcraft--Laws and legislation--Mecklenburg. 2.Trials (Witchcraft)--Mecklenburg. I. Title.

8
NIC

Witchcraft
BF
1410
B42
Z56
v.3
no.31

Eine Medaille, auf den weltberühmten Teufels-Banner, D. Balthasar Bekker, von A. 1692.
(In Wöchentliche historische Münz-Belustigung. Bremen? 21cm. 44. Stück (1736), p. 345-352)
4°: 2X⁴.
Both sides of coin are depicted.
No. 31 in vol. lettered Bekker III.

1. Bekker, Balthasar, 1634-1698.

8

Medelsky, Adolphus.

WITCHCRAFT
BX
2340
M66

Ministerium exorcisticum, quo exorcista possessos, obsessos, & maleficiatos a daemonijs...liberare potest. Cum annexis thesibus theologicis ad mentem...Joannis Duns-Scoti ex tribus libris sententiarum quas...publice defendendas susceperunt praeside M. R. P. Adolpho Medelsky... Franciscus Solanus Monschmidt &...Gelasius Stoephel .. Oppaviae, Typis Joannis W. Schindler [1738].
99 p. 17cm.
Apparently a cooperative undertaking of the Franciscan Father in Moravia.

8
NIC (Continued on next card)

382

CATALOGUE OF THE CORNELL WITCHCRAFT COLLECTION

Medeltidens magi.

Witchcraft
BF
1593
R99
1865

Rydberg, Victor, 1828-1895.
  Medeltidens magi. Stockholm, L. J.
Hiertas, 1865.
  140 p. 22cm.

"Förut utgifven i 'Svensk månadsskrift för fri forskning och allmän bildning af C. S. Warburg.'"

1. Magic. I. Title.

8

WITCHCRAFT
BF
1565
M48

Meder, David.
  Acht Hexenpredigten, darinnen von des Teuffels Mordtkindern, der Hexen, Unholden, Zauberischen, Drachenleuten, Milchdieben... gethan durch Davidem Mederum... Leipzig, Gedruckt bey Valentins am Ende Erben, in Versetzung Bartholomei Voigts, 1615.
  119 l. 20cm.

8
NIC

1. Witchcraft. 2. Devil. I. Title.

Les médiateurs et les moyens de la magie.

Witchcraft
BF
1032
G69

Gougenot des Mousseaux, Henri Roger, 1805-1876.
  Les médiateurs et les moyens de la magie, les hallucinations et les savants, le fantôme humain et le principe vital; par le chevalier Gougenot des Mousseaux ... Paris, H. Plon, 1863.
  2 p. l., xv, 447 p. 22½ cm.

1. Psychical research. I. Title.

                                          10-29937†
Library of Congress   BF1032.G6

The medical man and the witch during the renaissance.

BF
1569
Z69

Zilboorg, Gregory, 1890–
  ... The medical man and the witch during the renaissance, by Gregory Zilboorg ... Baltimore, The Johns Hopkins press, 1935.
  x, 215 p. front. (port.) illus., plates. 20½ᶜᵐ. (Publications of the Institute of the history of medicine, the Johns Hopkins university. 3d ser., v. 11)
  "The Hideyo Noguchi lectures."
  CONTENTS.—The physiological and psychological aspects of the Malleus maleficarum (The witch's hammer)—Medicine and the witch in the sixteenth century.—Johann Weyer, the founder of modern psychiatry.
  1. Witchcraft. 2. Psychology, Pathological. 3. Institoris, Henricus, d. ca. 1500. Malleus maleficarum. 4. Sprenger, Jakob, fl. 1494, joint author. Malleus maleficarum. 5. Wier, Johann, 1515-1588. 6. Renaissance. I. Title.

Library of Congress   BF1569.Z5   35—12064
                       Copy 2.
Copyright A 84565   [40n1] [150;00140002] 133.40002

Medien, Hexen und Geisterseher.

Witchcraft
BF
413
B91

Buchner, Eberhard, 1877- ed.
  Medien, Hexen und Geisterseher; kulturhistorisch interessante Dokumente aus alten deutschen Zeitungen und Zeitschriften (16. bis 18. Jahrhundert) München, A. Langen, 1926.
  359 p. 20cm.

1. Occult sciences--Germany. I. Title.

Meditatio academica exhibens examen ivridicvm ivdicialis lamiarvm confessionis.

Witchcraft
BF
4
64
752

Klein, Johann, 1659-1732, praeses.
  Meditatio academica exhibens examen ivridicvm ivdicialis lamiarvm confessionis se ex nefando cvm Satana coitv prolem svscepisse hvmanam. Was von dem Bekenntniss der Hexen zu halten, dass sie aus schändlichem Beyschlaf mit dem Teuffel Kinder gezeuget? Praeside Domino Ioanne Klein ... svbmittit Nicolavs Pvtter ... Vitembergae, Apvd Io. Christoph. Tzschiedrich, 1752.
  48 p. 21cm.
  First published 1698.
                (Continued on next card)

Meditationes ad pandectas quibus praecipua juris capita ex antiquitate explicantur.

WITCHCRAFT
K
L6795
1733
v.9

Leyser, Augustin, Reichsfreiherr von, 1683-1752.
  Meditationes ad pandectas quibus praecipua juris capita ex antiquitate explicantur, cum juribus recentioribus conferuntur atque variis celebrium collegiorum responsis et rebus judicatis illustrantur. vol. IX. Editio secunda. Lipsiae et Guelpherbyti, Apud Joh. Christoph. Meisnerum, 1741.
  962 p. 21cm.
                          DCVIII. ad lib. XLVIII.
  "Specimen   (Continued on next card)

8
NIC

Meditationes ad pandectas quibus praecipua juris capita ex antiquitate explicantur.

WITCHCRAFT
K
L6795
1733
v.9

Leyser, Augustin, Reichsfreiherr von, 1683-1752. Meditationes ad pandectas quibus praecipua juris capita...explicantur... vol. IX...1741.   (Card 2)

tit. VIII De crimine magiae publice defensum a Frider. Christophoro Pfotenhauer... MDCCXXXVII.": p. 629-654. [Leyser probably acted as praeses]
  1. Roman law   2. Civil law--Germany.
  3. Criminal law--Germany. 4. Witchcraft--Germany. 5.   Trials (Witchcraft)--
Germany. I.   Pfotenhauer, Friedrich
Christoph.   II. Title.

Meditazioni filosofiche, teologico-morali sulla demonologia.

Witchcraft
BF
1524
M37

Marsicani, Bernardo Maria.
  Meditazioni filosofiche, teologico-morali sulla demonologia ... Napoli, Presso Domenico Pianese, 1788.
  148 p. 19cm.

1. Demonology. I. Title.

WITCHCRAFT
BF
1555
M94
029
no.6

Meier, Georg Friedrich, 1718-1777.
  Georg Friedrich Meiers ... Philosophische Gedancken von den Würkungen des Teufels auf dem Erdboden. Halle, C. H. Hemmerde, 1760.
  168 p. 18cm.

No. 6 in vol. lettered Oesfeld u. a. ...

1. Müller, Gottlieb. Gründlicher Nachricht von einer begeisterten Weibesperson. 2.   Devil. I. Title:
Philosophische Gedanken von den
Würkungen des Teufels. II. Title.

8
NIC

Witchcraft
BF
1445
W41

Meier, Georg Friedrich, 1718-1777, supposed author.
  [Wegner, Georg Wilhelm]
  Gedancken von Gespenstern. Halle, C. H. Hemmerde, 1747.
  47 p. 18cm.
  Attributed to Wegner by Holzmann in v. 6 and 7 (correction of v. 2, which attributes the work to G. F. Meier)
  Second printing, 1749, spells title: Gedanken von Gespenstern.
  With this is bound Sucro, Johann Georg. Widerlegung der Gedancken von Gespenstern. Halle, 1748.

WITCHCRAFT
BF
1523
M51

Meigerius, Samuel.
  De panurgia lamiarum, sagarum, strigum ac veneficarum, totiusque cohortis magicae cacodaemonia libri tres... Hamborch, [Gedrücket durch Hans Binder], 1587.
  [438] p. 21cm.

Text in Low German.

8
NIC

1. Demonology. 2. Witchcraft. 3. Magic.
I. Title.

WITCHCRAFT
BF
1565
M498

Meinders, Hermann Adolph.
  Unvorgreifliche Gedancken und Monita, wie ohne blinden Eyfer und Übereilung mit denen Hexen-Processen und der Inquisition wegen der Zauberey, an Seiten des Richters so wol als des Königl. Preussischen Defensoris in denen Königl. Preussischen und Cuhrfürstlichen [sic] Brandenburgischen Landen ohnmassgeblich zu verfahren. Auf Königlichen Special-Befehl laut Edicti vom 13 Decembris 1714 zusammen getragen
                     (Continued on next card)

8
NIC

WITCHCRAFT
BF
1565
M498

Meinders, Hermann Adolph. Unvorgreifliche Gedancken und Monita...1716.   (Card 2)

und aufgesetzet von...Hermann Adolph Meinders. Lemgo, Druckts und verlegts Henrich Wilhelm Meyer, 1716.
  152 p. 22cm.

Collection of extracts from various sources concerning witchcraft, magic and trials for witchcraft.
  The most   extensive extract is
                     (Continued on next card)

WITCHCRAFT
BF
1565
M498

Meinders, Hermann Adolph. Unvorgreifliche Gedancken und Monita...1716.   (Card 3)

that from Pierre Bayle's Réponse aux questions d'un provincial. (in the original French, p. 12-93)

1. Witchcraft. 2. Trials(Witchcraft)
3. Magic. I. Bayle, Pierre, 1647-1706.
Réponse aux questions d'un provincial.
II. Title: Unvorgreifliche Gedancken und
Monita, wie   ...mit denen Hexen-Processen...zu   verfahren.

Meine Bedenken von den Besessenen der Welt vorgelegt.

Witchcraft
BF
1565
C12

Cäsar, Aquilin Julius.
  Meine Bedenken von den Besessenen der Welt vorgelegt. [München] 1789.
  56 p. 18cm.

Bound with his Ist die Nichtigkeit der Zauberey ganz erwiesen? München, 1789.

1. Demonology. I. Title.

Meineke, Daniel Christophorus, respondent.

WITCHCRAFT
BF
1556
K91

Krause, Rudolf Wilhelm, 1642-1719, praeses.
  Dissertationem medicam inauguralem De incubo...praeside Dn. Rudolfo Wilhelmo Krauss ...publicae...disquisitioni submittit Daniel Christophorus Meineke... Jenae, Typis Viduae Samuelis Krebsii [1683]
  [26] p. 20cm.

Diss.--Jena (D. C. Meineke, respondent)

8
NIC

WITCHCRAFT
BF
1583
Z7
1664

Meineken, Catharine.
Meyer, H
  Ein Hexenprozess aus dem 17. Jahrhundert. Aus den Acten dargestellt. Hannover, Schmorl & von Seefeld, 1867.
  19 p. 24cm.

The trial of Margarethe Meineken at Rotenburg in 1664.

1. Meineken, Margarethe. 2. Meineken, Catharine. 3. Trials (Witchcraft)--Rotenburg, Germany.

8
NIC

383

CATALOGUE OF THE CORNELL WITCHCRAFT COLLECTION

WITCHCRAFT
BF
1583
Z7
1664

Meineken, Margarethe.
    Meyer, H
       Ein Hexenprozess aus dem 17. Jahrhundert. Aus den Acten dargestellt. Hannover, Schmorl & von Seefeld, 1867.
       19 p. 24cm.

       The trial of Margarethe Meineken at Rotenburg in 1664.

       1. Meineken, Margarethe. 2. Meineken, Catharine. 3. Trials (Witchcraft)--Rotenburg, Germany.

8
NIC

WITCHCRAFT
BF
1517
G3
M51

Meiners, Christoph, 1747-1810.
    Geschichte einer merkwürdigen Teufels-Besitzung in Franken zwischen den Jahren 1740 und 1750. [Hannover, 1788]
    39 p. 20cm.

Detached from Göttingisches historisches Magazin, v.2, 1788.

    1. Demoniac possession. 2. Witchcraft--Franconia. 3. Sánger, Maria Renata von Mossau, ca.1680- 1749. I. Title.

WITCHCRAFT
D
1
G59
v.2

Meiners, Christoph, 1747-1810.
    Geschichte einer merkwürdigen Teufels-Besitzung in Franken zwischen den Jahren 1740-und 1750.

    (In: Göttingisches historisches Magazin. Hannover. 21cm. v.2 (1788) p.1-39)

    1. Demoniac possession. 2. Witchcraft--Franconia. 3. Sánger, Maria Renata von Mossau, ca. 1680-1749.

8
NIC

Witchcraft
PT
2430
M35
M3
1861

[Meinhold, Wilhelm] 1797-1851.
    The amber witch. The most romantic and extraordinary case of witchcraft extant. London, W. Tinsley, 1861.
    168 p. 17cm.

Translation of his Maria Schweidler, die Bernsteinhexe.
"The extraordinary romance upon which W. Vincent Wallace has founded his ... opera, 'The amber witch,' "--cover.
    I. Title. II. His Maria Schweidler, die Bernsteinhexe--English. III. Wallace, William Vincent, 1813-1865.

Witchcraft
PT
2430
M35
M3
1895

Meinhold, Wilhelm, 1797-1851.
    The amber witch, a romance. Translated by Lady Duff Gordon. Edited, with an introd. by Joseph Jacobs, and illustrated by Philip Burne-Jones. London, D. Nutt, New York, Scribner, 1895.
    xxxviii, 221 p. illus. 20cm.

Translation of his Maria Schweidler, die Bernsteinhexe.
    I. Title. II. Jacobs, Joseph, 1854-1916, ed. III. His Maria Schweidler, die Bernsteinhexe-- English.

Witchcraft
ML
50
W19
A4

Meinhold, Wilhelm, 1797-1851.
    Die Bernstein Hexe.
Wallace, William Vincent, 1812-1865.
    [The amber witch. Libretto. English]
    The amber witch: a romantic opera in four acts. The words by Henry F. Chorley, the music by W. Vincent Wallace. First represented at Her Majesty's Theatre, on Thursday, Feb. 28, 1861. London, Cramer, Beale & Chappell [1861?]
    48 p. 18cm.
    Based on the novel Maria Schweidler, die Bernstein Hexe, by Wilhelm Meinhold.
NIC   (Continued on next card)

Witchcraft
PT
2430
M35
M3
1846

Meinhold, Wilhelm, 1797-1851.
    Maria Schweidler, die Bernsteinhexe. Novelle, in der Sprache des siebenzehnten Jahrhunderts. 2. verb. Aufl. Leipzig, J. J. Weber, 1846.
    xxxvi, 285 p. 17cm. (His Gesammelte Schriften, Bd. 1)

PT
2430
M35
M3
1920

Meinhold, Wilhelm, 1797-1851.
    Maria Schweidler, die Bernsteinhexe; der interessanteste aller bisher bekannten Hexenprozesse, nach einer defekten Handschrift ihres Vaters, des Pfarrers Abraham Schweidler, in Coserow auf Usedom hrsg. Leipzig, Insel-Verlag [1920?]
    283 p. 19cm. (Bibliotek der Romane, 57)

Witchcraft
PT
2430
M35
M3
1861

Meinhold, Wilhelm, 1797-1851.
Maria Schweidler, die Bernsteinhexe--English.
    [Meinhold, Wilhelm] 1797-1851.
    The amber witch. The most romantic and extraordinary case of witchcraft extant. London, W. Tinsley, 1861.
    168 p. 17cm.

Translation of his Maria Schweidler, die Bernsteinhexe.
"The extraordinary romance upon which W. Vincent Wallace has founded his ... opera, 'The amber witch,' "--cover.
    I. Title. II. His Maria Schweidler, die Bernsteinhexe--English. III. Wallace, William Vincent, 1813-1865.

Witchcraft
PT
2430
M35
M3
1895

Meinhold, Wilhelm, 1797-1851.
Maria Schweidler, die Bernsteinhexe--English.
    Meinhold, Wilhelm, 1797-1851.
    The amber witch, a romance. Translated by Lady Duff Gordon. Edited, with an introd. by Joseph Jacobs, and illustrated by Philip Burne-Jones. London, D. Nutt, New York, Scribner, 1895.
    xxxviii, 221 p. illus. 20cm.

Translation of his Maria Schweidler, die Bernsteinhexe.
    I. Title. II. Jacobs, Joseph, 1854-1916, ed. III. His Maria Schweidler, die Bernsteinhexe-- English.

Witchcraft
PT
2430
M35
M3
1844

Meinhold, Wilhelm, 1797-1851.
Maria Schweidler, die Bernsteinhexe-- English.
    Meinhold, Wilhelm, 1797-1851.
    Mary Schweidler, the amber witch. The most interesting trial for witchcraft ever known. Printed from an imperfect manuscript by her father, Abraham Schweidler, the pastor of Coserow, in the island of Usedom. Translated from the German by Lady Duff Gordon. London, J. Murray, 1844.
    xi,171 p. 19cm.
    Translation of his Maria Schweidler, die Bernsteinhexe.

WITCHCRAFT
PT
2430
M35
S5
1894

Meinhold, Wilhelm, 1797-1851.
Maria Schweidler, die Bernsteinhexe-- English.
    Meinhold, Wilhelm, 1797-1851.
    Sidonia, the sorceress, the supposed destroyer of the whole reigning ducal house of Pomerania, translated by Lady Wilde; Mary Schweidler, the amber witch... London, Reeves and Turner, 1894.
    2 v. 20cm.

Translation of Sidonia von Bork, die Klosterhexe, and Maria Schweidler, die Bernsteinhexe.

    (Continued on next card)

Witchcraft
PT
2430
M35
S5
1894

Meinhold, Wilhelm 1797-1851.
Maria Schweidler, die Bernsteinhexe-- English.
    Meinhold, Wilhelm, 1797-1851. Sidonia, the sorceress... 1894. (Card 2)

"Mary Schweidler" translated by Lady Duff Gordon.

    1. Witchcraft--Pomerania. I. Meinhold, Wilhelm, 1797-1851. Sidonia von Bork, die Klosterhexe--English. II. Meinhold, Wilhelm, 1797-1851. Maria Schweidler, die Bernsteinhexe--English. III. Wilde, Jane Francesca (Elgee) lady, 1826-1896, tr. IV. Duff-Gordon, Lucie (Austin) lady, 1821-1869, tr. V. Title: Sidonia, the sorceress. VI. Title: Mary Schweidler, the amber witch.

PT
2430
M35M37
1948

Meinhold, Wilhelm, 1797-1851.
    Maria Schweidler.
Rysan, Josef, 1914-
    Wilhelm Meinhold's Bernsteinhexe: a study in witchcraft and cultural history. Chicago, 1948.
    iii l.,182 p. 23cm.

Thesis--Univ. of Chicago.
"Selected bibliography": p. 178-182.

---

ar W
1291

Meinhold, Wilhelm, 1797-1851.
    Mary Schweidler, the amber witch. The most interesting trial for witchcraft ever known. Printed from an imperfect manuscript by her father, Abraham Schweidler, the pastor of Coserow, in the island of Usedom. Translated from the German, by Lady Duff Gordon. New York, J. Winchester [184-?]
    60 p. 23cm.

With this is bound his Sidonia the sorceress. New York, 1860.

Witchcraft
PT
2430
M35
M3
1844

Meinhold, Wilhelm, 1797-1851.
    Mary Schweidler, the amber witch. The most interesting trial for witchcraft ever known. Printed from an imperfect manuscript by her father, Abraham Schweidler, the pastor of Coserow, in the island of Usedom. Translated from the German by Lady Duff Gordon. London, J. Murray, 1844.
    xi,171 p. 19cm.
    Translation of his Maria Schweidler, die Bernsteinhexe.
    I. His Maria Schweidler, die Bernsteinhexe--English. II. Title (Over)

PT
2430
M35M3
1845

Meinhold, Wilhelm, 1797-1851.
    Mary Schweidler, the amber witch; the most interesting trial for witchcraft ever known ... edited by W. Meinhold. Translated from the German by Lady Duff Gordon. New York, Wiley and Putnam, 1845.
    xi,180 p. 19cm.
    Translation of Maria Schweidler.

With this is bound La Motte-Fouqué, Friedrich Heinrich Karl, Freiherr de. Undine and Sintram and his companions. New York, 1845.

---

ar W
1291

Meinhold, Wilhelm, 1797-1851.
    Sidonia the sorceress, the supposed destroyer of the whole reigning Ducal house of Pomerania. New York, Harper, 1860.
    xiii,230 p. 23cm.

Bound with his Mary Schweidler, the amber witch, New York [184-]

    1. Witchcraft--Pomerania.

CATALOGUE OF THE CORNELL WITCHCRAFT COLLECTION

Witchcraft
PT 2430 M35S5+ 1893
Meinhold, Wilhelm, 1797-1851.
Sidonia the sorceress, translated by Francesca Speranza Lady Wilde. ₁Hammersmith, Eng., Kelmscott Press, 1893₃
xiv, 455 p. 30cm.

Translation of Sidonia von Bork, die Klosterhexe.
I. Wilde, Jane Francesca (Elgee) lady, 1826-1896, tr. II. His Sidonia von Bork, die Klosterhexe--English. III. Title.

WITCHCRAFT
PT 2430 M35 S5 1894
Meinhold, Wilhelm, 1797-1851.
Sidonia, the sorceress, the supposed destroyer of the whole reigning ducal house of Pomerania, translated by Lady Wilde; Mary Schweidler, the amber witch... London, Reeves and Turner, 1894.
2 v. 20cm.

Translation of Sidonia von Bork, die Klosterhexe, and Maria Schweidler, die Bernsteinhexe.
(Continued on next card)

Witchcraft
PT 2430 M35 S5 1894
Meinhold, Wilhelm, 1797-1851. Sidonia, the sorceress... 1894. (Card 2)

"Mary Schweidler" translated by Lady Duff Gordon.
1. Witchcraft--Pomerania. I. Meinhold, Wilhelm, 1797-1851. Sidonia von Bork, die Klosterhexe--English. II. Meinhold, Wilhelm, 1797-1851. Maria Schweidler, die Bernsteinhexe--English. III. Wilde, Jane Francesca (Elgee) lady, 1826-1896, tr. IV. Duff-Gordon, Lucie (Austin) lady, 1821-1869, tr. V. Title: Sidonia, the sorceress. VI. Title: Mary Schweidler, the amber witch.

Witchcraft
PT 2430 M35 S5 1847
Meinhold, Wilhelm, 1797-1851.
Sidonia von Bork, die Klosterhexe, angebliche Vertilgerin des gesammten herzoglich-pommerschen Regentenhauses ... Leipzig, J. J. Weber, 1847-48 ₁v. 1, 1848₃
3 v. fronts. 17cm. (His Gesammelte Schriften, Bd. 5-7)

I. Title.

Witchcraft
PT 2430 M35S5+ 1893
Meinhold, Wilhelm, 1797-1851.
Sidonia von Bork, die Klosterhexe--English.
Meinhold, Wilhelm, 1797-1851.
Sidonia the sorceress, translated by Francesca Speranza Lady Wilde. ₁Hammersmith, Eng., Kelmscott Press, 1893₃
xiv, 455 p. 30cm.

Translation of Sidonia von Bork, die Klosterhexe.

WITCHCRAFT
PT 2430 M35 S5 1894
Meinhold, Wilhelm, 1797-1851.
Sidonia von Bork, die Klosterhexe--English.
Meinhold, Wilhelm, 1797-1851.
Sidonia, the sorceress, the supposed destroyer of the whole reigning ducal house of Pomerania, translated by Lady Wilde; Mary Schweidler, the amber witch... London, Reeves and Turner, 1894.
2 v. 20cm.

Translation of Sidonia von Bork, die Klosterhexe, and Maria Schweidler, die Bernsteinhexe.
(Continued on next card)

Meinhold, Wilhelm, 1797-1851.
Sidonia von Bork, die Klosterhexe--English.
Witchcraft
PT 2430 M35 S5 1894
Meinhold, Wilhelm, 1797-1851. Sidonia, the sorceress... 1894. (Card 2)

"Mary Schweidler" translated by Lady Duff Gordon.
1. Witchcraft--Pomerania. I. Meinhold, Wilhelm, 1797-1851. Sidonia von Bork, die Klosterhexe--English. II. Meinhold, Wilhelm, 1797-1851. Maria Schweidler, die Bernsteinhexe--English. III. Wilde, Jane Francesca (Elgee) lady, 1826-1896, tr. IV. Duff-Gordon, Lucie (Austin) lady, 1821-1869, tr. V. Title: Sidonia, the sorceress. VI. Title: Mary Schweidler, the amber witch.

WITCHCRAFT
BT 980 M51
Meisner, Johann, praeses.
De apparitionibus daemonum exercitationem antipontificam praeside...Johanne Meisnero ...publico...examini...sistet M. Carolus Ortlob. ₁Wittebergae₃ Excudebatur literis Röhnerianis ₁1654₃
₁78₃ p. 20cm.

Diss.--Wittenberg (K. Ortlob, respondent)
1. Devil. 2. Demonology. 3. Apparitions.
8 NIC I. Ortlob, Karl, respondent. II. Title.

Meisner, Johann, praeses.
De apparitionibus daemonum.
WITCHCRAFT
BT 980 M51 1753
Meisner, Johann, praeses.
Tractatus anti pontificius De apparitionibus daemonibus ₁i.e. daemonum₃ Von Erscheinungen der Teufel. Francofurt. et Lipsiae, 1753.
94 p. 21cm.

Originally published as diss. at Wittenberg (K. Ortlob, respondent) in 1654, with title: De apparitionibus daemonum ...
1. Devil. 2. Demonology. 3. Apparitions.
8 NIC I. His ₁De apparitionibus daemonum. II. Ortlob, Karl, respondent.

WITCHCRAFT
BT 980 M51 1753
Meisner, Johann, praeses.
Tractatus anti pontificius De apparitionibus daemonibus ₁i.e. daemonum₃ Von Erscheinungen der Teufel. Francofurt. et Lipsiae, 1753.
94 p. 21cm.

Originally published as diss. at Wittenberg (K. Ortlob, respondent) in 1654, with title: De apparitionibus daemonum ...
1. Devil. 2. Demonology. 3. Apparitions.
8 NIC I. His ₁De apparitionibus daemonum. II. Ortlob, Karl, respondent. III. Title.

WITCHCRAFT
BF 1566 M51
Mejer, Ludwig.
Die Periode der Hexenprocesse. Hannover, Schmorl & von Seefeld, 1882.
100 p. 22cm.

2 copies

8 NIC 1. Witchcraft--Hist. 2. Trials (Witchcraft)--Hist. I. Title.

Melampronoea.
Witchcraft
BF 1521 H19
Hallywell, Henry, b. ca. 1630.
Melampronoea: or, A discourse of the polity and kingdom of darkness. Together with a solution of the chiefest objections brought against the being of witches ... London, Printed for Walter Kettilby, 1681.
₁16₃, 118 p. 15cm.

Melanchthon, Philipp, 1497-1560.
WITCHCRAFT
BX 2340 V94
Vom Exorcismo. Das dieser ohne Verletzung des Gewissens bey der Tauffe wol mag gebraucht vnd behalten werden: etliche Tractetlein. I. Iusti Menij. II. Lutheri Vorrede vber das Tauffbüchlein. III. Die gewöhnliche Gebet bey der Tauffe im Stifft vnd der Thumkirchen zu Cölln an der Sprew. IIII. Aus dem Appendice D. Vrbani Regij. V. Zwo Episteln Tilemanni Heshusij. VI. Eine Epistel Philippi Melanchton is. VII. D. Iacobi Co-
8 (Continued on next card)

Melanchthon, Philipp, 1497-1560.
WITCHCRAFT
BX 2340 V94
Vom Exorcismo ... 1591. (Card 2)
leri Büchlein. Alles zu guter Nachrichtung den einfeltigen Leyen zum besten zusammen bracht. ₁Franckfurt an der Oder, In Verlegung Johan vnd Friderich Hartmans, 1591.
₁269₃ p. 17cm.
Title in red and black.
With colophon: Gedruckt zu Franckfurt an der Oder, durch Nicolaum Voltzen, 1591.
8 (Continued on next card)

Melanchthon, Philipp, 1497-1560.
WITCHCRAFT
BX 2340 V94
Vom Exorcismo ... 1591. (Card 3)

Vom Exorcismo, oder Von dem Beschweren der Kinder bey der Tauffe. Drey Sendbriefe deren zwene D. Tilemannvs Heshvsivs: den dritten Herr Philippvs Melanchton geschrieben ... Verdeutscht durch Heinrich Rätel, has special t. p. with date 1590.
Vom Exorcismo bey der Tauffe ... durch Jacobum Colerum D. has special t. p., no date.
8 (Continued on next card)

WITCHCRAFT
BF 1565 M51
Melander, Otto, 1571-1640.
Resolutio praecipuarum quaestionum criminalis adversus sagas processus, cum refutatione nova tam juridica quam philosophica purgationis sagarum per aquam frigidam, adversus Guilielmum Adolphum Scribonium...Autore Otthone Melandro... Adjecta est .. Rodolphi Goclenii...Oratio...de natura sagarum in purgatione et examinatione per frigidam aquis innatantium. Lichae, Apud Nicolaum Erbenium, 1597.
8 NIC 131 p. 17cm. (Continued on next card)

WITCHCRAFT
BF 1565 M51
Melander, Otto, 1571-1640. Resolutio praecipuarum quaestionum criminalis adversus sagas processus... 1597. (Card 2)

1. Witchcraft. 2. Trials (Witchcraft) 3. Scribonius, Wilhelm Adolf, 16th cent. De sagarum natura. 4. Scribonius, Wilhelm Adolf, 16th cent. De examine et purgatione sagarum. 5. Goclenius, Rudolph, 1547-1628. II. Title.

Melchior de La Vallée et une gravure de Jacques Bellange.
WITCHCRAFT
BF 1582 Z7 1631c
Lepage, Henri, 1814-1887.
Melchior de La Vallée et une gravure de Jacques Bellange. Nancy, René Wiener, 1882.
56 p. illus., facsim. 23cm.

8 NIC I. La Vallée, Melchior de. 2. Trials (Witchcraft)--Nancy.

CATALOGUE OF THE CORNELL WITCHCRAFT COLLECTION

      Melchiori, Bartolommeo.

Witchcraft
BF   Tartarotti, Girolamo, 1706-1761.
1565   Apologia del Congresso notturno delle
T192+ lammie, o sia risposta di Girolamo Tarta-
      rotti all' Arte magica dileguata del Sig.
      March. Scipione Maffei, ed all' opposizione
      del Sig. Assessore Bartolommeo Melchiori.
      S'aggiunge una lettera del Sig. Clemente
      Baroni di Cavalcabò. Venezia, Presso
      Simone Occhi, 1751.
        4 p. l., 268 p. 26cm.
8   1. His   Del congresso nottur-
          (Continued on next card)

WITCHCRAFT
BF   Mell, Anton, 1865-1940.
1584   Zur Geschichte des Hexenwesens; ein Bei-
S8   trag aus steirischen Quellen. [Berlin?
M52   1891.
      [317]-335 p. 25cm.
      Extracted from Zeitschrift für deutsche
      Kulturgeschichte, 1891.

8   1. Witchcraft--Styria. 2. Trials (Witch-
NIC craft)--Styria.   I. Title.

      Melybog.

WITCHCRAFT
BF   Schrader, Ludwig Wilhelm.
1583   Die Sage von den Hexen des Brockens und
S37   deren Entstehen in vorchristlicher Zeit
      durch die Verehrung des Melybogs und der
      Frau Holle. Historisch bearbeitet ...
      Quedlinburg und Leipzig, G. Basse, 1839.
      48 p. 19cm.
      Sent to L. Freytag and published through
      him.
      1. Walpurgisnacht. 2. Witchcraft--
      Thuringia. 3. Folk-lore--Thuringia.
8   4. Melybog. 5. Frau Holle. I.
NIC Title.

      Ein Membrum des Collegii Curiosorum in
      Teutschland.
Witchcraft
BF   Unpartheyische Gedancken über die Kurtze
1565 Lehr-Sätze von dem Laster der Zauberey,
T46   welche der berühmte JCtus und Professor
U58   zu Halle, Herr D. Christianus Thomasius,
      damahls in einer Inaugural-Disputation
      defendiret, jetzo aber schon zum andern-
      mahl in teutsche Sprache übersetzet wor-
      den, nebst Anhang betreffende die Verthei-
      digung dieser Lehr-Sätze, kurtz gefasset
      und zum Druck befördert von einem Membro
      des Collegii Curiosorum in Teutsch-
8   (Continued on next card)

      Ein Membrum des Collegii Curiosorum in
      Teutschland.
Witchcraft
BF   Unpartheyische Gedancken über die Kurtze
1565 Lehr-Sätze von dem Laster der Zauberey ...
T46   1703.   (Card 2)
U58
      land. [n. p.] 1703.
      46 p. plate. 17cm.

      1. Thomasius, Christian, 1655-1728.
      Kurtze Lehr-Sätze von dem Laster der Zau-
      berey. 2. Witchcraft. I. Ein Membrum
      des Collegii Cu   riosorum in Teutschland.
8

WITCHCRAFT
BF   Memminger, Anton.
1583 Das verhexte Kloster. Nach den Akten dar-
Z7   gestellt. Würzburg, Memminger, 1904.
1749c   iv, 273 p. 19cm.

8   Sänger, Maria Renata von Mossau,
NIC ca. 1680-1749. Title.

WITCHCRAFT
BF   Memminger, Anton.
1583 Das verhexte Kloster. Nach den Akten dar-
Z7   gestellt. 2. verb. Aufl Würzburg,
1749d Memminger, 1908.
      181 p. 21cm. (Fränkische Bibliothek,
      Bd. 2)

8   Sänger, Maria Renata von Mossau, ca.
NIC 1680-1749. 2. Trials (Witchcraft)--Germany
      Title.

      Mémoir authentique pour servir à l'his-
      toire du comte de Cagliostro.
WITCHCRAFT
DC   [Luchet, Jean Pierre Louis de la Roche du
137   Maine, marquis de] 1740-1792.
.15   Memoir authentique pour servir à l'his-
L93   toire du comte de Cagliostro. Nouv. ed.
1786a Strasbourg, 1786.
      iv, 36 p. 22cm.

      1. Diamond necklace affair. 2. Cag-
      liostro, Alessandro, conte di, assumed name
      of Giuseppe Balsamo, 1743-1795. I.
8   Title.

      Memoir du P. et de la Cadier.
Witchcraft
BF   [Girard, Jean Baptiste] 1680-1733, defendant.
1582 Memoir [sic] du P. et de la Cadier [sic]
G51   [Aix, etc., De l'imprimerie de la veuve
M48++ de Joseph Senez, etc., 1731]
      various pagings. 32cm.
      Cover title.
      Contents.--Mémoire instructif, pour Mes-
      sire François Cadiere.--Observations sur le
      memoire manuscrit distribué par le P. Girard.
      --Memoire du Pere Girard.--Memoire instruc-
      tif, pour le Pere Nicolas de S. Joseph.--
8   (Continued on next card)

      Memoir du P. et de la Cadier.
Witchcraft
BF   [Girard, Jean Baptiste] 1680-1733, defendant
1582 Memoir du P. et de la Cadier. [1731]
G51   (Card 2)
M48++
      Contents--Continued.
      Reflexions sur la recrimination en pretendu
      complot imputé au Pere Estienne Thomas Ca-
      diere.--Observations sur les reponses per-
      sonnelles du P. Girard.--Second mémoire pour
      le Pere Girard.--Reponse a l'ecrit, qui a
      pour titre: Memoire des faits qui se
8   (Continued on next card)

      Memoir du P. et de la Cadier.
Witchcraft
BF   [Girard, Jean Baptiste] 1680-1733, defendant.
1582 Memoir du P. et de la Cadier. [1731]
G51   (Card 3)
M48++
      Contents--Continued.
      sont passez sour les yeux de M. l'Evêque de
      Toulon.--A nosseigneurs de Parlement [par
      Estienne-Thomas Cadiere]--A nosseigneurs de
      Parlement [par Catherine Cadiere]--A nos-
      seigneurs de Parlement [par Catherine Ca-
      diere]
8   (Continued on next card)

      Mémoire instructif, pour Demoiselle
      Catherine Cadière.
WITCHCRAFT
BF   Cadière, Catherine, b. 1709, appellant.
1582 Mémoire instructif, pour Demoiselle
G51   Catherine Cadière de ... Toulon, appelante
P96   comme d'abus de la procédure faite par
v.2   l'official en l'evêché de la même ville, à
no.3 la requête du promoteur & par appel simple
      de la procédure faite contr'elle par MM.
      les Commissaires du Parlement, du décret
      d'ajournement personnel contr'elle laxe, &
      à minima du décret d'assigné par eux rendu,
8   demanderesse en Lettres Royaux inci-
NIC dentes de   restitution, du 19 mai
        (Continued on next card)

      Mémoire instructif, pour Demoiselle
      Catherine Cadière.
WITCHCRAFT
BF   Cadière, Catherine, b. 1709, appellant.
1582 Mémoire instructif ...   (Card 2)
G51
P96   1731, & au principal querellante en enchante-
v.2   ment, rapt, inceste spirituel, avortement
no.3 & subornation de témoins. Contre le Père
      Jean Baptiste Girard, Jesuite ... intimé en
      appel à minima & querellé, & ... Mr. le
      P.G. du Roy, intimé aux autres appels: &
      tous deux défendeurs aux Lettres Royaux.
8   [s.l., 173-?]   17cm.
NIC 172 p.
       (Continued on next card)

      Mémoire instructif, pour Demoiselle
      Catherine Cadière.
WITCHCRAFT
BF   Cadière, Catherine, b. 1709, appellant.
1582 Mémoire instructif ... [173-?] (Card 3)
G51
P96   No. 3 in vol. lettered: Procès de Girard.
v.2   [v.2]
no.3

8   1. Girard, Jean Baptiste, 1680-1733,
NIC appellee.

      Mémoire instructif pour le père Jean-
      Baptiste Girard.
Witchcraft
BF   Girard, Jean Baptiste, 1680-1733.
1582 Mémoire instructif pour le père Jean-
G51M5 Baptiste Girard, jesuite ... contre Marie-
1731 Catherine Cadière; et encore M. le procur-
      eur général du roy, querellant. La Haye,
      H. Scheurleer, sur la copie imprimée à Paris,
      chez Gissey & Bordelet, 1731.
      284 p. 20cm.

      "Recueil des lettres du Père Girard et de
      la demoiselle Cadière, dont les ori-
        (Continued on next card)

      Mémoire instructif pour le père Jean-
Witchcraft Baptiste Girard.
BF   Girard, Jean Baptiste, 1680-1733. Mémoire
1582 instructif pour le père Jean-Baptiste
G51M5 Girard ... 1731.   (Card 2)
1731
      originaux ont été produits au procès": p.
      [141]-284.

      1. Cadière, Marie Catherine, fl. 1730.
      I. Cadière, Marie Catherine, fl. 1730. II.
      Title.

      Mémoire instructif, pour Messire François
WITCHCRAFT Cadière, prêtre de la ville de Toulon.
BF   Cadière, François, fl. 1730, appellant.
1582 Mémoire instructif, pour Messire François
G51   Cadière, prêtre de la ville de Toulon, ap-
P96   pellant du decret d'assigné contre lui ren-
v.2   du le 23. fév. dernier, & de ce qui s'en
no.1 est ensuivi, & demandeur en requête d'ad-
      hérance à l'appel comme d'abus relevé par
      la Demoiselle Cadière, sa soeur, & la pro-
      cedure faite à la requête du promoteur en
      l'evêché de Toulon. Contre M. le procu-
      reur général du Roy, intimé & défen-
8   deur.   [s.l., 1731]
NIC 131 p.   17cm.
       (Continued on next card)

      Mémoire instructif, pour Messire François
WITCHCRAFT Cadière, prêtre de la ville de Toulon.
BF   Cadière, François, fl. 1730, appellant.
1582 Mémoire instructif ... [1731?] (Card 2)
G51
P96   Signed: François Cadière. Bourgarel,
v.2   avocat. Simon, procureur.
no.1 No. 1 in vol. lettered: Procès de Girard.
      [v.2]

8   1. Girard, Jean Baptiste, 1680-1733. 2.
NIC Cadière,   Marie Catherine, fl. 173
      I. Title.

CATALOGUE OF THE CORNELL WITCHCRAFT COLLECTION

WITCHCRAFT
BF
1582
G51
M53

    Memoirs of Miss Mary-Catherine Cadiere, and Father Girard, Jesuit, containing an exact account of that extraordinary affairs interspers'd with letters and other original papers relating thereto, and which have hitherto been unknown to the publick. In an epistle from a person of quality at Paris to his correspondent in London. London, Printed for J. Isted, 1731.
    32 p. 20cm.
    1.Cadiere, Catherine, b.1709. 2. Girard, Jean Baptiste, 1680-1733. I. A Person of quality at Paris.

8
NIC

Rare
DA
803
L41+

    Memorialls.

Law, Robert, d. 1690?
    Memorialls; or, The memorable things that fell out within this island of Brittain from 1638 to 1684. By the Rev. Mr. Robert Law. Ed. from the ms. by Charles Kirkpatrick Sharpe. Edinburgh, A. Constable and co., 1818.
    cxiv, 277 p. front. 29cm.
    Appendix: A true relation of an apparition ... which infected the house of Andrew Mackie ... 1695. By Mr. Alexander Telfair.
    1. Scotland--Hist.--17th century. I. Title.

Witchcraft
BF
1565
M53

Mencken, Lüder, praeses.
    Commentationem ad titulum codicis De mathematicis maleficis et ceteris similibus praeside Lüdero Menckenio ... excutiendam publice proponet auctor et respondens Jacob. Benedictus Wincklerus ... Lipsiae, Literis I. Titii [1725].
    72 p. 20cm.
    1. Witchcraft. 2. Trials (Witchcraft) I. Winckler, Jacob Benedict, respondent. II. Title: De mathematicis maleficis et ceteris similibus. III. Title.

8

Menghi, Girolamo

WITCHCRAFT
F
524
54
582

Menghi, Girolamo, d. 1610.
    Compendio dell' arte essorcistica, et possibilita delle mirabili, et stvpende operationi delli demoni, et dei malefici. Con li rimedij opportuni alle infirmità maleficiali. Del R. P. F. Girolamo Menghi da Viadana ... Bologna, Nella stamperia di Giouanni Rossi, 1582.
    10 p. l., 614, [58] p. 15cm.
    Title in red and black.
    First published 1580.
    1. Demonology. 2. Witchcraft. 3. Exorcism. I. Title.

Witchcraft
BX
2340
M54
1587

Menghi, Girolamo, d. 1610.
    Flagellvm daemonvm exorcismos terribiles, potentissimos, et efficaces, remediaque probatissima, ac doctrinam singularem in malignos spiritus expellendos, facturasque et maleficia fuganda de obsessis corporibus complectens. Cum suis benedictionibus, & omnibus requisitis ad eorum expulsionem. Accessit postremò Pars secunda, quae Fustis daemonum inscribitur. Venetiis, Ad Signum Charitatis, 1587.
    [12], 172, [16], 160 p. 21cm.
    (Continued on next card)

Witchcraft
BX
2340
M54
1587

Menghi, Girolamo, d. 1610. Flagellvm daemonvm ... 1587. (Card 2)
    Title vignette.
    The Fustis daemonum has separate paging and special t. p.: Fvstis daemonvm, adivrationes formidabiles, potentissimas, et efficaces in malignos spiritvs fvgandos de oppressis corporibus humanis ... Venetiis, Ad Signum Charitatis, 1587.

WITCHCRAFT
F
40
4
89

Menghi, Girolamo, d. 1610.
    Flagellvm daemonvm. Exorcismos terribiles, potentissimos, et efficaces ... complectens ... Accessit postremò pars secunda, quae Fustis daemonum inscribitur. Quibus noui exorcismi, & alia nonnulla, quae prius desiderabantur, superaddita fuerunt. Auctore R. P. F. Hieronymo Mengo Vitellianensis ... Bononiae, Apud Ioannem Rossium, 1589.
    8 p. l., 247, [16], 350, 102, [2] p. 15cm.
    Title in red and black.
    (Continued on next card)

WITCHCRAFT
BX
2340
M54
1589

Menghi, Girolamo, d. 1610. Flagellvm daemonvm ... 1589. (Card 2)
    "Fvstis daemonvm" has special t. p. and separate paging.
    "Remedia efficacissima in malignos spiritvs expellendos," with caption title, is appended to "Fvstis daemonvm" and has separate paging.
    1. Exorcism. 2. Demonology. I. His Fustis daemonum. II. His Remedia efficacissima in malignos spiritus expellendos. III. Title: Flagellum daemonum. IV. Title: Remedia efficacissima. V. Title: Fustis daemonum.

8

WITCHCRAFT
BX
2340
M54
1608

Menghi, Girolamo, d. 1610.
    Flagellvm daemonvm, exorcismos terribiles, potentissimos, et efficaces ... complectens ... Accessit postremò pars secunda, quae Fustis daemonum inscribitur. Quibus noui exorcismi, & alia nonnulla, quae prius desiderabantur, superaddita fuerunt: avctore R. P. F. Hieronymo Mengo Vitellianensi ... Lvgdvni, Apud Franciscvm Arnovllet, 1608.
    8 p. l., 241 [i.e., 214], [2], [8], 208 p. 17cm.

8   (Continued on next card)

WITCHCRAFT
BX
2340
M54
1608

Menghi, Girolamo, d. 1610. Flagellvm daemonvm ... 1608. (Card 2)
    Title in red and black.
    "Fvstis daemonvm" has special t. p. and separate paging.
    Ex libris Aemilius Picard Avenionensis.

8

WITCHCRAFT
BX
2340
M54
1644

Menghi, Girolamo, d. 1610.
    Flagellvm daemonvm, exorcismos terribiles, potentissimos, et efficaces ... complectens ... Accessit postremò pars secunda, quae Fustis daemonum inscribitur. Quibus noui exorcismi, & alia nonnulla, quae prius desiderabantur, superaddita fuerunt. Auctore R. P. F. Hieronymo Mengo Vitellianensi ... Venetiis, Apud Io. Victorium Sauionum, 1644.
    244, [3], 222, [10] p. 17cm.
    "Fvstis daemonvm" has special t. p. and separate paging.

8

Witchcraft
BX
2340
M54
1683

Menghi, Girolamo, d. 1610.
    Flagellvm daemonvm, exorcismos terribiles, potentissimos, & efficaces, remediaque probatissima, ac doctrinam singularem in malignos spiritus expellendos, facturasque et maleficia fuganda de obsessis corporibus complectens, cum suis benedictionibus, et omnibus requisitis ad eorum expulsionem. Accessit postremò pars secunda, quae Fustis daemonum inscribitur. Quibus noui exorcismi, et alia nonnulla, quae priùs desiderabantur, superaddita fuerunt. Venetiis, Apud Paulum Balleonium, 1683.
    (Continued on next card)

Witchcraft
BX
2340
M54
1683

Menghi, Girolamo, d. 1610. Flagellvm daemonvm ... 1683. (Card 2)
    244, [3], 222, [10] p. 18cm.
    Title vignette.
    The Fustis daemonum has separate paging and special t. p.: Fvstis daemonvm, adivrationes formidabiles, potentissimas, & efficaces in malignos spiritus fugandos de oppressis corporibus humanis ... complectens ... Venetiis, Apud Paulum Balleonium, 1683.

Witchcraft
BX
2340
M54
1697

Menghi, Girolamo, d. 1610.
    Flagellvm daemonvm, exorcismos terribiles, potentissimos, & efficaces, remediaque probatissima, ac doctrinam singularem in malignos spiritus expellendos, facturasque et maleficia fuganda de obsessis corporibus complectens, cum suis benedictionibus, et omnibus requisitis ad eorum expulsionem. Accessit postremò pars secunda, quae Fustis daemonum inscribitur. Quibus noui exorcismi, et alia nonnulla, quae priùs desiderabantur, superaddita fuerunt. Venetiis, Apud Paulum Balleonium, 1697.
    (Continued on next card)

witchcraft
BX
2340
M54
1697

Menghi, Girolamo, d. 1610. Flagellvm daemonvm ... 1697. (Card 2)
    244, [3], 222, [10] p. 18cm.
    Title vignette.
    The Fustis daemonum has separate paging and special t. p.: Fvstis daemonvm, adivrationes formidabiles, potentissimas, & efficaces in malignos spiritus fugandos de oppressis corporibus humanis ... Venetiis, Apud Paulum Balleonem, 1697.

CATALOGUE OF THE CORNELL WITCHCRAFT COLLECTION

WITCHCRAFT
BX 2340 M54 1727
Menghi, Girolamo, d. 1610.
 Flagellum daemonum. Exorcismos terribiles, potentissimos, & efficaces ... complectens ... Accessit postremo pars secunda, quae Fustis daemonum inscribitur. Quibus novi exorcismi, & alia nonnulla, quae prius desiderabantur, super addita fuerunt. Auctore R. P. F. Hieronymo Mengo, Vitellianensi ... [Mediolani] 1727.
 7 p. l., 309, [3], [16], 308, [1] p. 18cm.
 "Fustis daemonum" has special t. p. and separate paging.
8 (Continued on next card)

WITCHCRAFT
BX 2340 M54 1727
Menghi, Girolamo, d. 1610. Flagellum daemonum ... 1727. (Card 2)

 1. Exorcism. 2. Demonology. I. His Fustis daemonum. II. Title. III. Title: Fustis daemonum.
8

Witchcraft
BF 1559 T41 1626
Menghi, Girolamo, d. 1610.
 Flagellum daemonum.
 Thesavrvs exorcismorvm atqve conivrationvm terribilivm, potentissimorum, efficacissimorum cum practica probatissima: qvibvs spiritvs maligni, daemones maleficiaque omnia de corporibus humanis obsessis, tanquam flagellis, fustibusque fugantur, expelluntur, doctrinis refertissimus atq. uberrimus: ad maximam exorcistarum commoditatem nunc vltimo plenariè in lucem editus & recusus: cuius authores, vt & singuli tractatus sequente pagellâ consignati, inueniuntur. Cum indice capitum, rerum & verborum ... Coloniae, sumptibus haeredum Lazari Zetzneri, 1626. (Continued on next card)

Witchcraft
BF 1559 T41 1626
Menghi, Girolamo, d. 1610.
 Flagellum daemonum.
 Thesavrvs exorcismorvm atqve conivrationvm terribilivm ... 1626. (Card 2)
 12 p. l., 1232, [39] p. 18cm.
 Previously published at Cologne in 1608.
 Contents.—F. Valerii Polydori ... Practica exorcistarum ad daemones & maleficia de Christi fidelibus pellendum, pars prima ... [et] secunda.—R. p. f. Hieronymi Mengi ... Flagellum daemonum.—Eivsdem Fvstis daemonvm.—F. Zachariae Vicecomitis ... Complementum artis exorcisticae. —Petri Antonii Stampae ... Fuga Satanae.—R. d. Maximiliani ab Eynatten ... Manuale exorcismorum.

WITCHCRAFT
BX 2340 M54 1589
Menghi, Girolamo, d. 1610.
 Fustis daemonum.
 Flagellvm daemonvm. Exorcismos terribiles, potentissimos, et efficaces ... complectens ... Accessit postremò pars secunda, quae Fustis daemonum inscribitur. Quibus novi exorcismi, & alia nonnulla, quae prius desiderabantur, superaddita fuerunt. Auctore R. P. F. Hieronymo Mengo Vitellianensis ... Bononiae, Apud Ioannem Rossium, 1589.
 8 p. l., 247, [16], 350, 102, [2] p. 15cm.
 Title in red and black.
8   (Continued on next card)

WITCHCRAFT
BX 2340 M54 1589
Menghi, Girolamo, d. 1610.
 Fustis daemonum.
 Flagellvm daemonvm ... 1589. (Card 2)
 "Fvstis daemonvm" has special t. p. and separate paging.
 "Remedia efficacissima in malignos spiritvs expellendos," with caption title, is appended to "Fvstis daemonvm" and has separate paging.
 1. Exorcism. 2. Demonology. I. His Fustis daemonum. II. His Remedia efficacissima in malignos spiritus expellendos. III. Tit le: Flagellum daemonum. IV. Title: Remedia efficacissima.
8

WITCHCRAFT
BX 2340 M54 1727
Menghi, Girolamo, d. 1610.
 Fustis daemonum.
 Flagellum daemonum. Exorcismos terribiles, potentissimos, & efficaces ... complectens ... Accessit postremo pars secunda, quae Fustis daemonum inscribitur. Quibus novi exorcismi, & alia nonnulla, quae prius desiderabantur, super addita fuerunt. Auctore R. P. F. Hieronymo Mengo, Vitellianensi ... [Mediolani] 1727.
 7 p. l., 309, [3], [16], 308, [1] p. 18cm.
 "Fustis daemonum" has special t. p. and separate paging.
8 (Continued on next card)

WITCHCRAFT
BX 2340 M54 1589
Menghi, Girolamo, d. 1610.
 Remedia efficacissima in malignos spiritus expellendos.
 Flagellvm daemonvm. Exorcismos terribiles, potentissimos, et efficaces ... complectens ... Accessit postremò pars secunda, quae Fustis daemonum inscribitur. Quibus novi exorcismi, & alia nonnulla, quae prius desiderabantur, superaddita fuerunt. Auctore R. P. F. Hieronymo Mengo Vitellianensis ... Bononiae, Apud Ioannem Rossium, 1589.
 8 p. l., 247, [16], 350, 102, [2] p. 15cm.
 Title in red and black.
8   (Continued on next card)

WITCHCRAFT
BX 2340 M54 1589
Menghi, Girolamo, d. 1610.
 Remedia efficacissima in malignos spiritus expellendos.
 Flagellvm daemonvm ... 1589. (Card 2)
 "Fvstis daemonvm" has special t. p. and separate paging.
 "Remedia efficacissima in malignos spiritvs expellendos," with caption title, is appended to "Fvstis daemonvm" and has separate paging.
 1. Exorcism. 2. Demonology. I. His Fustis daemonum. II. His Remedia efficacissima in malignos spiritus expellendos. III. Tit le: Flagellum daemonum. IV. Title: Remedia efficacissima.
8

Witchcraft
BX 1710 M39 1730
Menghini, Tommaso, 17th cent.
 [Masini, Eliseo] brother, 17th cent.
 Sacro arsenale, ovvero Pratica dell'Uffizio della Santa Inquisizione; coll'inserzione di alcune regole fatte dal p. inquisitore Tommaso Menghini ... e di diverse annotazioni del dottore Gio: Pasqualone ... In questa 4. impressione aggiuntavi la Settima Denunzia fatta dal suddetto padre per li sponte comparenti, impressa in Ferrara 1687. e corretta in alcune cose la parte decima degli avvertimenti ... Roma, Nella Stamperia di
 (Continued on next card)
 [Secular name: Cesare Masini]

Witchcraft
BX 1710 M39 1730
Menghini, Tommaso, 17th cent.
 [Masini, Eliseo] brother, 17th cent. Sacro arsenale ... (Card 2)
 S. Michele a Ripa, 1730.
 [6], 506, [54] p. 23cm.
 Edited by Luigi and Francesco Conti.
 1. Inquisition. I. Menghini, Tommaso, 17th cent. II. Pasqualone, Giovanni. III. Conti, Luigi. IV. Conti, Francesco. V. Title. VI. Title: Pratica dell'Uffizio della Santa Inquisi zione.

Mengi, Hieronymus, d. 1610.
 see
Menghi, Girolamo, d. 1610.

Mengo, Hieronymus, d. 1610.
 see
Menghi, Girolamo, d. 1610.

Mengus, Hieronymus, d. 1610.
 see
Menghi, Girolamo, d. 1610.

WITCHCRAFT
BX 2340 V94
Menius, Justus, 1499-1558.
 Vom Exorcismo.
 Vom Exorcismo. Das dieser ohne Verletzung des Gewissens bey der Tauffe wol mag gebraucht vnd behalten werden: etliche Tractetlein. I. Iusti Menij. II. Lutheri Vorrede vber das Tauffbüchlein. III. Die gewöhnliche Gebet bey der Tauffe im Stifft vnd der Thumkirchen zu Cölln an der Sprew. IIII. Aus dem Appendice D. Vrbani Regij. V. Zwc Episteln Tilemanni Heshusij. VI. Eine Epistel Philippi Melanchton is. VII. D. Iacobi Co-
8   (Continued on next card)

WITCHCRAFT
BX 2340 V94
Menius, Justus, 1499-1558.
 Vom Exorcismo.
 Vom Exorcismo ... 1591. (Card 2)
 leri Büchlein. Alles zu guter Nachrichtung den einfeltigen Leyen zum besten zusammen bracht. [Franckfurt an der Oder, In Verlegung Johan vnd Friderich Hartmans, 1591.
 [269] p. 17cm.
 Title in red and black.
 With colophon: Gedruckt zu Franckfurt an der Oder, durch Nicolaum Voltzen, 1591.
8   (Continued on next card)

WITCHCRAFT
BX 2340 V94
Menius, Justus, 1499-1558.
 Vom Exorcismo.
 Vom Exorcismo ... 1591. (Card 3)
 Vom Exorcismo, oder Von dem Beschweren der Kinder bey der Tauffe. Drey Sendbriefe deren zwene D. Tilemannvs Heshvsivs: den dritten Herr Philippvs Melanchton geschrieben ... Verdeutscht durch Heinrich Rätel, has special t. p. with date 1590.
 Vom Exorcismo bey der Tauffe ... durch Jacobum Colerum D. has special t. p., no date.
8   (Continued on next card)

WITCHCRAFT
BT 980 M54
[Menke, Karl F]
 Beitrag zur Dämonologie; oder, Widerlegung der exegetischen Aufsätze des Herrn Professor's Grimm. Von einem Geistlichen. Frankfurt und Leipzig, 1793.
 174 p. 17cm.
 With autograph: W. Wirbel?

8   1. Devil. 2. Demonology. 3. Grimm,
NIC   Heinrich Adolph, 1754-1813. 4. Title.

CATALOGUE OF THE CORNELL WITCHCRAFT COLLECTION

```
                    Mentzel, Andreas.
                        Gespräche, Fabeln und Erzählungen
Witchcraft      für niedre Schulen.
BF
1565                Om Hexemestere, Troldqvinder, Spøgelser,
M54             Gjengangere, Spaamaend, Forvarsler og Sand-
1800            sigere. En Bog for Almuen ... Oversat af
                het Tydske ved M. Hallager. Kjøbenhavn,
                Malling, 1800.
                    2 p. l., 39 p. 21cm.
                    Translation of part of his Gespräche,
                Fabeln und Erzählungen für niedre Schulen.
                    1. Witchcraft. 2. Occult sciences.
                I. His Gespräche, Fabeln und Erzählungen
                für niedre Schulen. Danish. III. Hal-
8               lager, Morton, 1740-1803, tr. II.
                Title.
```

```
Witchcraft      Mentzel, Andreas.
BF                  Om Hexemestere, Troldqvinder, Spøgelser,
1565            Gjengangere, Spaamaend, Forvarsler og Sand-
M54             sigere. En Bog for Almuen ... Oversat af
1800            het Tydske ved M. Hallager. Kjøbenhavn,
                Malling, 1800.
                    2 p. l., 39 p. 21cm.
                    Translation of part of his Gespräche,
                Fabeln und Erzählungen für niedre Schulen.
                    1. Witchcraft. 2. Occult sciences.
                I. His Gespräche, Fabeln und Erzählungen
8               für niedre Schulen. Danish. III. Hal-
                lager, Morton, 1740-1803, tr. II.
                Title.
```

```
                Mercklin, Georg Abraham, 1644-1700.
                    Sylloge physico-medicinalium casuum ...
WITCHCRAFT      Mercklin, Georg Abraham, 1644-1700.
R                   Tractatus physico-medicus de incantamen-
133             tis, sexaginta casus, maxime prae caeteris
M55             memorabiles, complectens; cum subnexis eo-
1715            rundem judiciis & curationibus cui mantis-
                sae loco accesserunt... Norimbergae, Im-
                pensis Joh Friderici Rudigeri, 1715.
                    254 p. plate. 21cm.
                    Reprint, with change of title, of his
                Sylloge physico-medicinalium casuum...
8                   1. Medicine, Magic, mystic and spa-
NIC             giric. I. His Sylloge physico-
                medicinalium casuum...
```

```
WITCHCRAFT      Mercklin, Georg Abraham, 1644-1700.
R                   Tractatus physico-medicus de incantamen-
133             tis, sexaginta casus, maxime prae caeteris
M55             memorabiles, complectens; cum subnexis eo-
1715            rundem judiciis & curationibus cui mantis-
                sae loco accesserunt... Norimbergae, Im-
                pensis Joh Friderici Rudigeri, 1715.
                    254 p. plate. 21cm.
                    Reprint, with change of title, of his
                Sylloge physico-medicinalium casuum...
8                   1. Medicine, Magic, mystic and spa-
NIC             giric. I. His Sylloge physico-
                medicinalium casuum... II. Title.
```

```
                Merckwürdige Betrachtungen über die der-
                    mahlige Verwirrung der gantzen Welt.
Witchcraft      Beer, Johann Christoph, 1690-1760.
                    Der höllische Intelligenz-Zettul; das
                ist, Merckwürdige Betrachtungen über die
                dermahlige Verwirrung der gantzen Welt:
                verursachet durch vile tausend, von hölli-
                schen Geistern heimlich, und in der Still
                besessene Menschen. ... Augspurg, J. J.
                Mauracher [1753]
                    8 p. l., 472, [16] p. 18cm.
                    1. Demoniac possession. I. Title.
                II. Title: Merckwürdige Betrach-
                tungen über die dermahlige Verwirrung
                der gantzen Welt.
```

```
                Mercurii Trismegisti Pymander, De potes-
                    tate et sapientia Dei.
WITCHCRAFT      Hermes Trismegistus.
BF                  [Poemander. Latin]
1598                Mercvrii Trismegisti Pymander, De potes-
H55             tate et sapientia Dei. Eivsdem Asclepivs,
A1              De uoluntate Dei. Opuscula sanctissimis
1532            mysterijs, ac uerè coelestibus oraculis il-
                lustrissima. Iamblichvs De mysterijs Aegyp-
                tiorum, Chaldaeorum, & Assyriorū. Proclvs
                In Platonicum Alcibiadem, de anima & daemo-
                ne. Idem De sacrificio & magia. Quae omnia
                solerti cura repurgata, ac suo tandem
                    (Continued on next card)
```

```
                Mercurii Trismegisti Pymander, De potes-
                    tate et sapientia Dei.
WITCHCRAFT      Hermes Trismegistus.
BF                  [Poemander. Latin] (Card 2)
1598                1532.
H55
A1                  candori restituta sunt. Basileae [Per
1532            Mich. Isingrinivm] 1532.
                    480, [3] p. 16cm.
                    With colophon.
                    The Asclepius translated by Apuleius
                Madaurensis; the rest by Marsilio Ficino.
                    I. Jamblichus, of Chalcis. De myste-
                riis. Latin. II. Proclus Diadochus.
                III. Apuleius Madaurensis, tr. IV.
                Ficino, Marsilio, 1433-1499, tr. V.
8               His Asclepius.
```

```
                Merkwürdige Hexenprozesse.
WITCHCRAFT      Liel, Anselm Franz Joseph.
DD                  Merkwürdige Hexenprozesse...
491
R4                  (In: Archiv für rheinische Geschichte.
A67             Coblenz. 23cm. v.1 (1833) p.47-80)
v.1

8                   1. Trials (Witchcraft)--Treves. 2. Witch-
NIC             craft--Treves.
```

```
                Merkwürdige psychische und physiologische
                    Erscheinungen.
WITCHCRAFT      Horst, Georg Conrad, 1767-1838?
BF                  Deuteroskopie, oder Merkwürdige psychi-
1325            sche und physiologische Erscheinungen und
H81             Probleme aus dem Gebiete der Pneumatologie.
                Für Religionsphilosophen, Psychologen, und
                denkende Aerzte. Eine nöthige Beilage zur
                Dämonomagie, wie zur Zauber-Bibliothek.
                Frankfurt am Main, H. Wilmans, 1830.
                    2 v. in 1. 21cm.
                    1. Second sight. 2. Visions. I. His
                Dämonomagie. II. His Zauber-Biblio-
8               thek. III. Title.
```

```
                Merkwürdiger Hexen-Process gegen den
                    Kaufmann G. Köbbing, an dem Stadtgerichte
WITCHCRAFT          zu Coesfeld im Jahre 1632 geführt.
BF              Köbbing, Georg, defendant.
1583                Merkwürdiger Hexen-Process gegen den Kauf-
Z7              mann G. Köbbing, an dem Stadtgerichte zu
1632d           Coesfeld im Jahre 1632 geführt. Vollstän-
                dig aus den Original-Acten mitgetheilt und
                mit einer Vorrede begleitet von Joseph Nie-
                sert. Coesfeld, Gedruckt bei Bernard
                Wittneven, 1827.
                    lii, 104 p. 19cm.

                    1. Trials (Witchcraft)--Coesfeld, Germany.
8               I. Niesert, Johann Heinrich Joseph,
NIC             ed. II. Title.
```

```
WITCHCRAFT      Ein merkwürdiger Hexenprozess.
AP
30                  (In: Neue gemeinnützige Blätter. Halber-
N4852           stadt. 16cm. v.10 (1800) p. [529]-540)
v.10
                    Signed: Lucanus.
                    Concerning the trial for witchcraft of
                a widow Siewerten, in 1577.

                    1. Trials (Witchcraft)--Halberstadt.
8               2. Siewerten, defendant. 3. Lucanus,
NIC             pseud.
```

```
Witchcraft      Merritt, Bertha (Sutermeister)
BF                  Witchcraft material gathered by Mrs.
1563            Merritt in preparation for her thesis.
M57+            Contains many notes and accounts of trials,
v.1-3           particularly in Alsace. Collected ca. 1926.
                    3 cases. 28cm.

                    1. Witchcraft. 2. Witchcraft--Alsace.
```

```
Thesis          Merritt, Bertha Sutermeister.
1926                Witchcraft trials in the Ban de la Roche,
M 572           Basse Alsace, 1607-1674 ... by Bertha Suter-
                meister Merritt.
                    [Ithaca, N.Y.] 1926.

                    Thesis (A.M.)--Cornell University, 1926.
                    Bibliography: p. 51-52.


                I. Title.
```

```
                Le merveilleux au XVe siècle.
WITCHCRAFT      Saint-Olive, Pierre.
BF                  Étude sur le merveilleux au XVe siècle.
1582            Un miracle à St.-Genis-d'Aoste. Une af-
S14             faire de sorcellerie aux Avenières. Bel-
                ley, Impr. L. Chaduc, 1912.
                    15 p. illus. 23cm.
                    "Extrait de la revue 'Le Bugey' Octobre
                1911. Tiré à 80 exemplaires. N°. 0014."
                    1. Witchcraft--France. 2. Witchcraft
                --Avenières, France. I. Title: Le mer-
8               veilleux au XVe siècle. II. Title: Un
NIC             miracle à St.-Genis-d'Aoste.
```

```
                Merz, Agnellus, 1726-1784.

                    see

                März, Agnellus, 1726-1784.
```

```
DD              Merzbacher, Friedrich.
801                 Die Hexenprozesse in Franken. München,
B322837         C.H. Beck, 1957.
v.56                ix,186 p. maps. 25cm. (Schriftenreihe
                zur bayerischen Landesgeschichte, Bd.56)


                    1. Trials (Witchcraft)--Franconia. 2.
                Witchcraft--Franconia. I. Title.
```

```
DD              Merzbacher, Friedrich.
801                 Die Hexenprozesse in Franken. (Mit 3 Ktn.) 2., erw.
B322            Aufl. München, Beck (1970).
S37                 xii, 257 p. maps. 24 cm. DM35.00       GDB 70-A48-102
v.56                Bibliography: p. 201-217.
1970


3                   1. Trials (Witchcraft)—Franconia.   I. Title.

                                                                74-565786
                ISBN 3-406-01982-X
                Library of Congress        71 [2]
```

```
WITCHCRAFT      Mesmer, Franz Anton, 1734-1815.
BF              Sierke, Eugen, 1845-
1408                Schwärmer und Schwindler zu Ende des
S57             achtzehnten Jahrhunderts. Leipzig, S.
                Hirzel, 1874.
                    vi, 462 p. 21cm.
                    1. Occult sciences--Biography. 2.
                Superstition. 3. Swedenborg, Emanuel,
                1688-1772. 4. Mesmer, Franz Anton, 1734-
                1815. 5. Gassner, Johann Joseph, 1727-
                1779. 6. Schrepfer, Johann Georg, 1730?-
8               1774. 7. Cagliostro, Alessandro,
NIC             conte de, assumed name of Giuseppe
                Balsamo, 1743-1795. I. Title.
```

CATALOGUE OF THE CORNELL WITCHCRAFT COLLECTION

Ein Messfremder.

WITCHCRAFT
BF
1523
H49
[Hempel, Christian Gottlob] 1748-
Von den bösen Geistern und der Zauberey: Ein Sendschreiben an den Herrn M. Haubold, Vesperprediger bei der Universitätskirche zu Leipzig, auf Veranlassung einer von demselben am letztverwichenen Michaelsfeste 1782 gehaltenen Nachmittagspredigt, von einem damals unter seinen Zuhörern gewesenen Messfremden. Sorau, 1783.
96 p. 19cm.
Attribution by Holzmann.
8 1. Demonology. 2. Witchcraft. I. Haubold,   , preacher. II. Ein Messfremder. III. Title.

Messmer, Franz Anton, 1734-1815.
see
Mesmer, Franz Anton, 1734-1815.

WITCHCRAFT
BF
1583
Z7
1664
Meyer, H
Ein Hexenprozess aus dem 17. Jahrhundert. Aus den Acten dargestellt. Hannover, Schmorl & von Seefeld, 1867.
19 p. 24cm.
The trial of Margarethe Meineken at Rotenburg in 1664.
1. Meineken, Margarethe. 2. Meineken, Catharine. 3. Trials (Witchcraft)--Rotenburg, Germany. I. Title.
8
NIC

Meyer, Heino, respondent.
Witchcraft
BF
1587
D61
no.7
Schütze, Bartholomaeus, praeses.
Disputatio physica De magia, quam ... exhibent praeses M. Bartholomaeus Schütze, ... & respondens Heino Meyer ... Rostochii, Typis Johannis Kilii [1669]
[24] p. 18cm. (bound in 21cm. vol.)
No. 7 in vol. lettered Dissertationes de magia. 1623-1723.
1. Magic--Addresses, essays, lectures. I. Meyer, Heino, respondent. II. Title: De magia.
8

WITCHCRAFT
GR
90
M61
Meyer, Karl Remigius, 1842-
Der Aberglaube des Mittelalters und der nächstfolgenden Jahrhunderte. Von Carl Meyer. Basel, F. Schneider, 1884.
viii, 382 p. 23cm.
1. Superstition. I. Title.
8

GR
90
M61
1971
Meyer, Karl Remigius, 1842-
Der Aberglaube des Mittelalters und der nächstfolgenden Jahrhunderte. Hildesheim, G. Olms, 1971.
viii, 382 p. 22cm. (Volkskundliche Quellen, 2)
Reprint of the ed. published in Basel by F. Schneider in 1884.
Includes bibliographical references.
1. Occult sciences--History. I. Title. II. Series.

WITCHCRAFT
BF
1555
M61+
Meyer, Ludwig.
Die Beziehungen der Geisteskranken zu den Besessenen und Hexen.
(In: Westermann's illustrirte deutsche Monatshefte. Wiesbaden. 26cm. No.57, June 1861. p. 258-264)
8
NIC
1. Demoniac possession. 2. Witchcraft. I. Title.

RARE
HV
8593
D61
no.23
Meyer, Philipp Carl, fl. 1787.
Observationes casibus quibusdam practicis de jurejurando, ceu remedio probandi in civilibus, et tortura, ceu remedio veritatem eruendi in criminalibus, caute nec sine summa necessitate decernendis, illustratae a Philippo Carolo Meyer. Oehringae, Typis J. L. Hollii, 1787.
80 p. 21cm.
No.23 in a vol. lettered: Dissertationes de tortura, 1667-1787.
1. Oaths--Holy Roman Empire. 2. Torture--Holy Roman Empire. 3. Criminal law--Holy Roman Empire. I. Title.
8
NIC

WITCHCRAFT
BX
1158
M61
Meyer, Raphael Ludwig, 1869-1925.
Gerbertsagnet; studie over middelalderlige djaevlekontrakthistorier. København, Det Nordiske Forlag, 1902.
170 p. 25cm.
8
NIC
1. Sylvester II, Pope, d. 1003. 2. Devil. 3. Demonology. 4. Title.

WITCHCRAFT
BF
1565
M61
Meyfart, Johann Matthäus, 1590-1642.
Christliche Erinnerung an gewaltige Regenten und gewissenhaffte Praedicanten wie das abscheiuliche Laster der Hexerey mit Ernst aussurotten... Schleusingen, Gedruckt durch Peter Schmiden, 1636.
272 p. 20cm.
8
NIC
1. Witchcraft. 2. Trials (Witchcraft) I. Title.

WITCHCRAFT
BF
1565
R34
Meyfart, Johann Matthäus, 1590-1642.
Christliche Erinnerung an Regenten.
Reiche, Johann, ed.
Herrn D. Christian Thomasii ... Kurtze Lehr-Sätze von dem Laster der Zauberey, nach dem wahren Verstande des lateinischen Exemplars ins Deutsche übersetzet, und aus des berühmten Theologi D. Meyfarti, Naudaei, und anderer gelehrter Männer Schrifften erleutert ... nebst einigen Actis magicis herausgegeben von Johann Reichen. Halle im Magdeburgischen, Im Rengerischen Buchladen, 1704.
2 v. in 1. 21cm.
8
NIC
(Continued on next card)

WITCHCRAFT
BF
1565
R34
Meyfart, Johann Matthäus, 1590-1642.
Christliche Erinnerung an Regenten.
Reiche, Johann, ed. Herrn D. Christian Thomasii ... Kurtze Lehr-Sätze ... 1704.
(Card 2)
Vol. 1 has special t. p.: Fernerer Unfug der Zauberey. Halle im Magdeburgischen, 1704.
Vol. 2 has special t. p.: Unterschiedliche Schrifften von Unfug des Hexen-Processes. Halle im Magdeburg., 1703.
Contents.--[1. Bd.] Gabriel Naudaei
8
NIC
(Continued on next card)

WITCHCRAFT
BF
1565
R34
Meyfart, Johann Matthäus, 1590-1642.
Christliche Erinnerung an Regenten.
Reiche, Johann, ed. Herrn D. Christian Thomasii ... Kurtze Lehr-Sätze ... 1704.
(Card 3)
Contents.--Continued.
Schutz-Schrifft [tr. of Apologie pour tous les grands hommes]--Geschichte der Teuffel zu Lodün.--Trauer-Geschichte von der greulichen Zauberey Ludwig Goffredy [tr. of De l'horrible & épouvantable sorcellerie de Louis Goffredy, author F. de Rosset]--D. Christian Thomasii ... Kurtze Lehr-Sätze von
8
NIC
(Continued on next card)

WITCHCRAFT
BF
1565
R34
Meyfart, Johann Matthäus, 1590-1642.
Christliche Erinnerung an Regenten.
Reiche, Johann, ed. Herrn D. Christian Thomasii ... Kurtze Lehr-Sätze ... 1704.
(Card 4)
Contents--Continued.
dem Laster der Zauberey [tr. of Dissertatio de crimine magiae, J. Reiche, respondent] [2. Bd.] Malleus judicum oder Gesetz-Hammer der unbarmhertziger Hexen-Richter.--Cautio criminalis [von F. Spee].--D. Johann Matthäus Meyfarths Christliche Erinnerung an Regenten.-- Viererley Sorten Hexen-Acta. (Continued on next card)
8
NIC

Witchcraft
BF
1623
A4
M61
Meyssonnier, Lazare, 1602-1672.
La philosophie des anges, contenant l'art de se rendre les bons esprits familiers. Avec l'histoire de S. Raphael, oeuvre nécessaire à tous ceux qui aspirent à la vie angelique. Par L. Meyssonnier. Lyon, Chez Pierre Compagnon, 1648.
8 p. l., 337, [3] p. 18cm.
1. Magic. 2. Angels. 3. Raphael, archangel. I. Title.
8

Michael, C., pseud.
See
Wolf, Marianne (Conrad) 1837-1886.

Michael, Gregorius.
Witchcraft
BF
1591
G13
1676
Gaffarel, Jacques, 1601-1681.
Curiositez inouyes, Hoc est: Curiositates inauditae de figvris Persarum talismannicis, horoscopo patriarcharum et characteribus coelestibus ... Latinè, cum Notis quibusdam ac figuris editae, operâ M. Gregorii Michaelis .. Hamburgi, Apud Gothofredum Schultzen, prostant & Amsterodami, Apud Jansonio-Waesbergios, 1676
2 v. in 1. plates (part fold.) 16cm.
Added t. p., engraved.
Vol. 2 has special t. p. only: M. Gregorii Michaelis Notae in Jacobi Gaffarelli Curiositates. (Continued on next card)

Michael, Gregorius.
Witchcraft
BF
1591
G13
1676
Gaffarel, Jacques, 1601-1681. Curiositez inouyes ... 1676. (Card 2)
Copy 1 imperfect: dedication ([48] p.), indexes of vol. 1 ([48] p. at end) and the who[le] vol. 2 (M. Gregorii Michaelis ... Notae in Jacobi Gaffarelli Curiositates) wanting.
Translation of Curiositez inouyes.
With copy 1 of this are bound Thavmatvrgi physici prodromvs (Coloniae, 1649); Ens, Gaspar Thavmatvrgvs mathematicvs (Coloniae, 1651); Marci a Kronland, Joannes Marcus. De longitudi[ne] (Pragae, 1650); Marci a Kronland, Joannes Marc[us] De natvra iridos (Pragae, 1650); Marci a Kronland, Joannes Marcus. De cavss[is] natvralibvs plvviae pvrpvreae Brvxellensis (Pragae, 1647).

CATALOGUE OF THE CORNELL WITCHCRAFT COLLECTION

WITCHCRAFT
R
-33
M62

    Michaelis, Johann, 1606-1667, praeses.
      Morbos ab incantatione et veneficiis oriundos...sub clypeo...Johannis Michaelis... publice examinandos proponit...Anton Marquart... [Lipsiae] Typis Haeredum Timothei Hönii, 1650.
      [56] p. 19cm.
      Diss.--Leipzig (A. Marquart, respondent)
      1. Medicine, Magic, mystic and spagiric. 2. Devil. I. Marquart, Antonius, respondent. II. Title.

WITCHCRAFT
BF
1517
F5
M62
1613a

    Michaelis, Sebastien, 1543?-1618.
      The admirable historie of the possession and conversion of a penitent woman. Sedvced by a magician that made her to become a witch, and the princes of sorcerers in the country of Prouince, who was brought to S. Baume to be exorcised, in the yeere 1610 ... Wherevnto is annexed a pnevmology, or Discourse of spirits ... reuiewed, corrected, and enlarged ... Translated into English by W. B. London, Imprinted for Wil-
      (Continued on next card)

WITCHCRAFT
BF
1517
F5
M62
1613a

    Michaelis, Sebastien, 1543?-1618. The admirable historie of the possession ... of a penitent woman ... 1613. (Card 2)
    liam Aspley, 1613.
      24 p. l., 418, [10], 154, [34] p. 20cm.
      Differs from another issue only in t. p. (has date; some spellings changed).
      Translation of Histoire admirable de la possession ... d'vne penitente, and of Discovrs des esprits.
      "A discovrse of spirits" has special t. p. and separate paging.
      STC 17854a.

WITCHCRAFT
BF
1517
F5
M62
1613

    Michaelis, Sebastien, 1543?-1618.
      The admirable history of the possession and conversion of a penitent woman. Sedvced by a magician that made her to become a witch, and the princesse of sorcerers in the country of Prouince, who was brought to S. Baume to bee exorcised, in the yeere 1610 ... Wherevnto is annexed a pnevmology, or Discourse of spirits ... reuewed, corrected, and enlarged ... Translated into English by W. B. London, Imprinted for Wil-
      (Continued on next card)

WITCHCRAFT
BF
1517
F5
M62
1613

    Michaelis, Sebastien, 1543?-1618. The admirable history of the possession ... of a penitent woman ... [1613] (Card 2)
    liam Aspley [1613]
      24 p. l., 418, [10], 154, [34] p. 20cm.
      Differs from another issue only in t. p. (lacks date; some spellings different)
      Translation of Histoire admirable de la possession ... d'vne penitente, and of Discovrs des esprits.
      "A discovrse of spirits" has special t. p. and separate paging.
      (Continued on next card)

WITCHCRAFT
BF
1517
F5
M62
1613

    Michaelis, Sebastien, 1543?-1618. The admirable history of the possession ... of a penitent woman ... [1613] (Card 3)
      STC 17854.
      1. Palud, Magdeleine de la. 2. Gaufridi, Louis, 1572-1611. 3. Loudun, France. Ursuline convent. 4. Demoniac possession. 5. Exorcism. I. His Histoire admirable de la possession ... d'une penitente. English. II. His Discours des esprits. English. III. Title. IV. W. B., tr. V. B., W., tr.

Film
470
reel
681

    Michaelis, Sebastien, 1543?-1618.
      The admirable history of the possession and conversion of a penitent woman. Seduced by a magician that made her to become a witch, and the princesse of sorcerers in the country of Prouince, who was brought to S. Baume to bee exorcised, in the yeere 1610. in the moneth of Nouember, by the authority of ... Sebastian Michaëlis, who appointed ... Frier Francis Domptius ... for the exorcisme and recollection of the acts. All faithfully set downe,
      (Continued on next card)

Film
470
reel
681

    Michaelis, Sebastien, 1543?-1618. The admirable history of the possession and conversion of a penitent woman ... (Card 2)
    and fully verified. Wherevnto is annexed a pnevmology, or discourse of spirits made by the said Father Michaëlis, and by him renewed, corr., and enl.: together with an explanatory apology of the many difficulties touching this history and the annotations. Translated into English by W. B. London, W. Aspley [1613]
      (Continued on next card)

Film
470
reel
681

    Michaelis, Sebastien, 1543?-1618. The admirable history of the possession and conversion of a penitent woman ... (Card 3)
      "A discourse of spirits" has special t.p. University microfilms no. 17885 (carton 681)
      Short-title catalogue no. 17854.

      1. Witchcraft. 2. Devil.
      MiU F56-843

WITCHCRAFT
BF
1517
F5
M62

    Michaelis, Sebastien, 1543?-1618.
      Discours des esprits.
    Michaelis, Sebastien, 1543?-1618.
      Histoire admirable de la possession et conversion d'vne penitente, seduite par vn magicien, la faisant sorciere & princesse des sorciers au pays de Prouence, conduite à la S. Baume pour y estre exorcizee l'an M.DC.X. au mois de Nouembre, soubs l'authorité du R. P. F. Sebastien Michaelis ... Commis par luy aux exorcismes & recueil des actes le R. P. F. François Domptivs ... Ensemble la Pneumalogie, ou Discours du
      (Continued on next card)

WITCHCRAFT
BF
1517
F5
M62

    Michaelis, Sebastien, 1543?-1618.
      Discours des esprits.
    Michaelis, Sebastien, 1543?-1618. Histoire admirable ... 1613. (Card 2)
      susdit Pere Michaëlis, reueu, corrigé, & augmenté par luy-mesme ... Paris, Chez Charles Chastellain, 1613.
      16 p. l., 352, 124, 196, [30] p. 17cm.
      "Actes recveillis ... par le reverend Pere Michaëlis" has separate paging.
      "Discovrs des esprits" has special t. p. with imprint Paris, 1512, and separate paging.
      (Continued on next card)

WITCHCRAFT
BF
1517
F5
M62
1613

    Michaelis, Sebastien, 1543?-1618.
      Discours des esprits. English.
    Michaelis, Sebastien, 1543?-1618.
      The admirable history of the possession and conversion of a penitent woman. Sedvced by a magician that made her to become a witch, and the princesse of sorcerers in the country of Prouince, who was brought to S. Baume to bee exorcised, in the yeere 1610 ... Wherevnto is annexed a pnevmology, or Discourse of spirits ... reuewed, corrected, and enlarged ... Translated into English by W. B. London, Imprinted for Wil-
      (Continued on next card)

WITCHCRAFT
BF
1517
F5
M62
1613

    Michaelis, Sebastien, 1543?-1618.
      Discours des esprits. English.
    Michaelis, Sebastien, 1543?-1618. The admirable history of the possession ... of a penitent woman ... [1613] (Card 2)
    liam Aspley [1613]
      24 p. l., 418, [10], 154, [34] p. 20cm.
      Differs from another issue only in t. p. (lacks date; some spellings different)
      Translation of Histoire admirable de la possession ... d'vne penitente, and of Discovrs des esprits.
      "A discovrse of spirits" has special t. p. and separate paging.
      (Continued on next card)

WITCHCRAFT
BF
1517
F5
M62
1613

    Michaelis, Sebastien, 1543?-1618.
      Discours des esprits. English.
    Michaelis, Sebastien, 1543?-1618. The admirable history of the possession ... of a penitent woman ... [1613] (Card 3)
      STC 17854.
      1. Palud, Magdeleine de la. 2. Gaufridi, Louis, 1572-1611. 3. Loudun, France. Ursuline convent. 4. Demoniac possession. 5. Exorcism. I. His Histoire admirable de la possession ... d'une penitente. English. II. His Discours des esprits. English. III. Title. IV. W. B., tr. V. B., W., tr.

WITCHCRAFT
BF
1517
F5
M62

    Michaelis, Sebastien, 1543?-1618.
      Histoire admirable de la possession et conversion d'vne penitente, seduite par vn magicien, la faisant sorciere & princesse des sorciers au pays de Prouence, conduite à la S. Baume pour y estre exorcizee l'an M.DC.X. au mois de Nouembre, soubs l'authorité du R. P. F. Sebastien Michaelis ... Commis par luy aux exorcismes & recueil des actes le R. P. F. François Domptivs ... Ensemble la Pneumalogie, ou Discours du
      (Continued on next card)

WITCHCRAFT
BF
1517
F5
M62

    Michaelis, Sebastien, 1543?-1618. Histoire admirable ... 1613. (Card 2)
      susdit Pere Michaëlis, reueu, corrigé, & augmenté par luy-mesme ... Paris, Chez Charles Chastellain, 1613.
      16 p. l., 352, 124, 196, [30] p. 17cm.
      "Actes recveillis ... par le reverend Pere Michaëlis" has separate paging.
      "Discovrs des esprits" has special t. p. with imprint Paris, 1512, and separate paging.
      (Continued on next card)

WITCHCRAFT
BF
1517
F5
M62

    Michaelis, Sebastien, 1543?-1618. Histoire admirable ... 1613. (Card 3)
      1. Palud, Magdeleine de la. 2. Gaufridi, Louis, 1572-1611. 3. Loudun, France. Ursuline convent. 4. Demoniac possession. 5. Exorcism. I. Title.

WITCHCRAFT
BF
1517
F5
M62
1613

    Michaelis, Sebastien, 1543?-1618.
      Histoire admirable de la possession ... d'une penitente. English.
    Michaelis, Sebastien, 1543?-1618.
      The admirable history of the possession and conversion of a penitent woman. Sedvced by a magician that made her to become a witch, and the princesse of sorcerers in the country of Prouince, who was brought to S. Baume to bee exorcised, in the yeere 1610 ... Wherevnto is annexed a pnevmology, or Discourse of spirits ... reuewed, corrected, and enlarged ... Translated into English by W. B. London, Imprinted for Wil-
      (Continued on next card)

CATALOGUE OF THE CORNELL WITCHCRAFT COLLECTION

WITCHCRAFT
BF
1517
F5
M62
1613

8

Michaelis, Sebastien, 1543?-1618.
　Histoire admirable de la possession
... d'une penitente. English.
　Michaelis, Sebastien, 1543?-1618. The admirable history of the possession ... of a penitent woman ... [1613]　(Card 2)
　　liam Aspley [1613]
　　24 p. l., 418, [10], 154, [34] p. 20cm.
　　Differs from another issue only in t. p.
(lacks date; some spellings different)
　　Translation of Histoire admirable de la possession ... d'vne penitente, and of Discovrs des esp　　rits.
　"A discov　　rse of spirits" has special t. p.　　and separate paging.
　　　　(Continued on next card)

Witchcraft
BF
1569
M62
1958

Michelet, Jules, 1798-1874.
　Satanism and witchcraft, a study in medieval superstition. Translated by A. R. Allinson. London, Arco Publications [1958]
　xx, 332 p. 21cm.

　Translation of La sorcière.

　1. Witchcraft. 2. Demonomania. 3. Civilization, Medieval. I. Allinson, Alfred Richard, tr. II. Michelet, Jules, 1798-1874. La sorcière.--English. III. Title.

BF
1582
M62
1966

Michelet, Jules, 1798-1874.
　La Sorcière. Chronologie et préface par Paul Viallaneix ... Paris, Garnier-Flammarion, 1966.
　318 p. 18cm. (Garnier-Flammarion. Texte intégral, 83) 3.95 F.

　Cover illustrated in color.
　Includes bibliographies.

　1. Witchcraft--Hist. 2. Demonomania.
3. Civilization, Medieval. I. Title.

WITCHCRAFT
BF
1517
F5
M62
1613

8

Michaelis, Sebastien, 1543?-1618.
　Histoire admirable de la possession
... d'une penitente. English.
　Michaelis, Sebastien, 1543?-1618. The admirable history of the possession ... of a penitent woman ... [1613]　(Card 3)
　STC 17854.
　1. Palud, Magdeleine de la. 2. Gaufridi, Louis, 1572-1611. 3. Loudun, France. Ursuline convent. 4. Demoniac possession. 5. Exorcism. I. His Histoire admirable de la possession ... d'une penitente. English. II. His Discours des esprits. English.　　III. Title. IV. W. B., tr. V. B.,　　W., tr.

Undergraduate Library
BF
1569
M62
1969

Michelet, Jules, 1798-1874.
　Satanism and witchcraft; a study in medieval superstition. Translated by A. R. Allinson. [9th paperbound ed.] New York, Citadel Press [1969]
　xx, 332 p. 21cm. (Citadel, C-89)
　Translation of La sorcière.

　1. Witchcraft. 2. Demonomania. 3. Civilization, Medieval. I. His La sorcière--English. II. Allinson, Alfred Richard, tr. III. Title.

Witchcraft
BF
1569
M62
1958

Michelet, Jules, 1798-1874.
　La sorcière. 1958.
　Satanism and witchcraft, a study in medieval superstition. Translated by A. R. Allinson. London, Arco Publications [1958]
　xx, 332 p. 21cm.

　Translation of La sorcière.

　1. Witchcraft. 2. Demonomania. 3. Civilization, Medieval. I. Allinson, Alfred Richard, tr. II. Michelet, Jules, 1798-1874. La sorcière.--English. III. Title.

WITCHCRAFT
BF
1582
Z7
1582c

8
NIC

Michaelis, Sébastien, 1543?-1618.
　[Pneumatologie] ou, Discours des esprits en tant qu'il est de besoing, pour entendre & resoudre la matière difficile des sorciers comprinse en la sentence contre eux dōnée en Avignon l'an de grace, 1582. Paris, G. Bichon, 1587]
　122 l. 18cm.

　T.p. lacking.
　1. Witchcraft--Avignon. 2. Trials (Witchcraft)--　　Avignon. 3. Devil. 4. Witchcraft.　　I. Title.

Witchcraft
BF
1569
M62
1862

Michelet, Jules, 1798-1874.
　La sorcière. Paris, E. Dentu, 1862.
　xxiv, 460 p. 18cm. (Collection Hetzel)

Witchcraft
BF
1445
D61
no.6

8

Michelmann, Christian, respondent.
　Drechssler, Johann Gabriel, d. 1677, praeses.
　De spectris, disputationem II. Inclut. facultat. philosoph. Lipsiensis consensu P. P. praeses M. Johannes Gabriel Drechssler ... et respondens Christianus Michelmann ... Lipsiae, Literis Johannis Erici Hahnii [1669]
　[12] p. 21cm.
　No. 6 in vol. lettered Dissertationes de spectris. 1646-1753.
　1. Rechenberg, Adam, 1642-1721, praeses. De spectris. 2. Apparitions. 3. Devil. I. Michelmann,　　Christian, respondent. II. Title.

WITCHCRAFT
BF
1508
P97
1688

8
NIC

Michaelou tou Psellou Peri energeias daimōnon dialogos.
　Psellus, Michael.
　[Michaelou tou Psellou Peri energeias daimōnon dialogos] Μιχαηλου του Ψελλου Περι ενεργειας δαιμόνων διάλογος. Michaelis Pselli De operatione daemonum dialogus. Gilbertus Gaulminus Molinensis primus Graece edidit & notis illustravit. E museo Dan. Hasenmülleri ... Kiloni, Sumtibus Joh. Sebastiani Richelii, 1688.
　6 p. l., 166 p. 15cm.

　(Continued on next card)

Witchcraft
BF
1569
M62
1867

Michelet, Jules, 1798-1874.
　La sorcière. Nouv. éd. Paris, Librairie Internationale, 1867.
　420 p. 19cm.

Witchcraft
BF
1439
M624+

Midelfort, H　　Christian Erik.
　Recent witch hunting research; or, Where do we go from here? [New York, 1968]
　373-420 p. 24cm.

　Extract from Bibliographical Society of America. Papers. v. 62 (1968)
　Bibliography: p. 385-420.
　Photocopy. 373-420 p. on 24 l. 24 x 3 cm.

　1. Witch　　craft. 2. Witchcraft
Bibl. I.　　Title.

WITCHCRAFT
BF
1508
P97
1688

8
NIC

Michaelou tou Psellou Peri energeias daimōnon dialogos.
　Psellus, Michael. [Michaelou tou Psellou Peri energeias daimōnon dialogos] 1688.
　　　　(Card 2)
　Latin and Greek on facing pages, with notes by Gaulmin at bottom of page.
　Latin translation by Petrus Morellus, "illius qui & Nicetae Thesaurum orthodoxae fidei de Graeco Latinum fecit."
　1. Demonology. I. Gaulmin, Gilbert, 1585-1665, ed. II. Morellus, Petrus, Turonensis,　　tr. III. Hasenmüller,
　　(Continued on next card)

Witchcraft
BF
1569
M62
1903

Michelet, Jules, 1798-1874.
　La sorcière. Etude par Gabriel Séailles. Paris, Calmann-Lévy [1903]
　xxxiv, 448 p. 18cm. (Oeuvres complètes de Michelet. Histoire sociale)

　1. Witchcraft. 2. Demonomania. 3. Civilization, Medieval. I. Séailles, Gabriel. II. Title.

BF
1583
M62

4

Midelfort, H　　Christian Erik.
　Witch hunting in southwestern Germany, 1562-1684; the social and intellectual foundations [by] H. C. Erik Midelfort. Stanford, Calif., Stanford University Press, 1972.
　viii, 306 p. illus. 24 cm. $11.50
　Bibliography: p. [261]-300.

　1. Witchcraft—Germany. 2. Trials (Witchcraft)—Germany. I. Title.

　BF1583.M5　　914.3'4'033　　75-1[?]891
　ISBN 0-8047-0805-3　　　　ARC
　Library of Congress　　72 [4]

WITCHCRAFT
BF
1582
Z7
1623

8

Michel, d. 1623.
　Discovrs admirable d'vn magicien de la ville de Moulins, qui auoit vn demon dans vne phiole, condemné d'estre bruslé tout vif par arrest de la Cour de Parlement. Paris, Chez Antoine Vitray, 1623.
　15 p. 16cm.

　1. Witchcraft--Moulins, France. I. France. Parlement (Moulin)

BF
1582
M62

v. 1 only

Michelet, Jules, 1798-1874.
　La sorcière. Édition originale, publiée avec notes et variantes par Lucien Refort. Paris, Didier, 1952-
　v. 19cm.

　At head of title: Société des textes français modernes.

　1. Witchcraft. I. Title.

BF
1501
S78

Milichius, Ludwig, d. 1575.
　Stambaugh, Ria, comp.
　Teufelbücher in Auswahl. Hrag. von Ria Stambaugh. Berlin, De Gruyter, 1970-
　v. 21cm. (Ausgaben deutscher Literatur des XV. bis XVIII. Jahrhunderts)

　Contents.--Bd. 1. Zauberteufel, Schrapteufe von L. Milichius.--Bd. 2. Kleiderteufel, von J. Strauss. Tanzteufel, von F. Daul. Hurenteuf von A. Hoppenrod. Hausteufel, von A. Schubart. Zehn Teufel, von N. Schmidt.

CATALOGUE OF THE CORNELL WITCHCRAFT COLLECTION

Witchcraft
F
1581
.64
M77

[Millar, John] Bookseller.
A history of the witches of Renfrewshire. A new edition, with an introduction, embodying extracts, hitherto unpublished, from the records of the Presbytery of Paisley. Paisley [Scotland] Alex. Gardner, 1877.
xxv, 219, 6 p. front. 21cm.
Contains a reproduction of the original title-page with imprint: Paisley: Printed by J. Neilson, for John Millar, Bookseller, 1809.
1. Witchcraft--Renfrewshire, Scot. I. Title.

Millar, John, comp.

Witchcraft
F
1581
.67
M77

A history of the witches of Renfrewshire. A new ed., with an introduction, embodying extracts, hitherto unpublished, from the records of the Presbytery of Paisley ... Paisley, A. Gardner, 1877.
2 p. l., (xii)-xxv (i.e. xxxv) p., 3 l., [5]-219, 6 p. front. 20½ᶜᵐ.
Introduction signed: J. D.
Includes reprint of original t.-p.: From authentic documents. A history of the witches of Renfrewshire, who were burned on the Gallowgreen of Paisley. Published by the editor of the Paisley repository ... Paisley, Printed by J. Neilson for J. Millar, 1809.
Comp. by J. Millar. Cf. p. [5]
1. Witchcraft--Scotland. I. Millar, John, comp.
Library of Congress   BF1581.A2 1809
                                    11-14652

Millies, Henricus Christianus, fl. 1801, respondent.

Witchcraft
BF
1775
.E16

Eberhard, Johann August, 1739-1809, praeses.
Dissertatio philosophica de superstitione, quam praeside ... Ioanne Augusto Eberhard ... A. D. 16 April 1801 publice defendet auctor Henricus Christianus Millies. Halis Saxonum, Typis Schimmelpfennigianis [1801]
51 p. 21cm.
Imperfect: t. p. badly worn.
Diss.--Halle (H. C. Millies, respondent)
2. Superstition. 2. Occult sciences. I. Millies, Henricus Christianus, fl. 1801, respondent. II. Title.

WITCHCRAFT
F
1584
.S7+
.M623

Millunzi, Gaetano.
Un processo di stregoneria nel 1623 in Sicilia, pubblicato e illustrato dal Can. Gaetano Millunzi e da Salvatore Salomone-Marino.
(In: Archivio storico siciliano. Palermo. 28cm. nuov. ser., anno 25, fasc. 3-4, 1901, p. [253]-379)
1. Trials (Witchcraft)--Sicily. 2. Adamo, Orazio di. 3. Cabala. 4. Occult sciences. I. Salomone-Marino, Salvatore, 1847-1916.

Minder, Robert.
Der Hexenglaube bei den Jatrochemikern des 17. Jahrhunderts. Zürich, Juris-Verlag, 1963.
26 p. illus. 23cm. (Zürcher medizingeschichtliche Abhandlungen, neue Reihe, Nr. 12)
Issued also as thesis, Zürich.
1. Medicine--15th-18th cent. 2. Witchcraft. I. Title.

Minerva met Mercurius. Aan de betoverde schrift-geleerden.
De Geharpoende muys. Of staatkundige consideratien, over zeekere arabische vertaalinge, uyt een turkx leeraar Hamets Sidach Effendi. Raakende het gewoel, over Do. Balthasar Bekkers Betoverde weereld. Beneffens Minerva, en Mercurius; aan de betoverde schriftgeleerden. [Amsterdam?] 1691.
12 p., title vignette. 19 x 15cm.
4°: A⁴, B²
Published also in Verscheyde gedichten, so voor, als tegen het boek, genaamt: De betoverde weereld.
No. 12 in vol. lettered Bekker II.

WITCHCRAFT
BX
2340
.M66

Ministerium exorcisticum, quo exorcista possessos, obsessos, & maleficiatos a daemonijs...liberare potest. Cum annexis thesibus theologicis ad mentem...Joannis Duns-Scoti ex tribus libris sententiarum, quas...publice defenderunt susceperunt praeside M. R. P. Adolpho Medelsky... Franciscus Solanus Monschmidt &...Gelasius Stoephel .. Oppaviae, Typis Joannis W. Schindler [1738]
99 p. 17cm.
Apparently a cooperative undertaking of the Franciscan Fathers in Moravia.
(Continued on next card)

8
NIC

WITCHCRAFT
BX
2340
.M66

Ministerium exorcisticum...[1738] (Card 2)
1. Exorcism. I. Medelsky, Adolphus. II. Monschmidt, Franciscus Solanus. III. Stoephel, Gelasius. IV. Duns, Joannes, Scotus, 1265?-1308?

Un miracle à St.-Genis-d'Aoste.

WITCHCRAFT
BF
1582
.S14

Saint-Olive, Pierre.
Étude sur le merveilleux au XVᵉ siècle. Un miracle à St.-Genis-d'Aoste. Une affaire de sorcellerie aux Avenières. Belley, Impr. L. Chaduc, 1912.
15 p. illus. 23cm.
"Extrait de la revue 'Le Bugey' Octobre 1911. Tiré à 80 exemplaires. Nᵒ. 0014."
1. Witchcraft--France. 2. Witchcraft--Avenières, France. I. Title: Le merveilleux au XVᵉ siècle. II. Title: Un miracle à St.-Genis-d'Aoste.

8
NIC

A mirror for witches.

PS
3511
.O64M6

Forbes, Esther.
A mirror for witches in which is reflected the life, machinations, and death of famous Doll Bilby, who, with a more than feminine perversity, preferred a demon to a mortal lover. Here is also told how and why a righteous and most awfull judgement befell her, destroying both corporeal body and immortal soul. By Esther Forbes, with woodcuts by Robert Gibbings. Boston and New York, Houghton Mifflin company, 1928.
4 p. l., 3-213, [1] p. front., illus., plates. 23½ᶜᵐ.

1. Witchcraft--Salem, Mass. I. Title.
Library of Congress   PZ3.F7418M1   28--12074
Copy 2.
Copyright A 1074255   [28e3]

The mirror of magic.

witchcraft
BF
1589
.S46+

Seligmann, Kurt, 1900-
The mirror of magic. 250 illus. [New York] Pantheon Books [1948]
504 p. illus., ports. 27 cm.
"Bibliographic résumé": p. 489-496.
1. Magic--Hist. I. Title.

A mirror of witchcraft.

BF
1581
.H72M6

Hole, Christina.
A mirror of witchcraft. London, Chatto & Windus, 1957.
260 p. illus. 23cm.
"Sources of extracts given": p. 9-16.
1. Witchcraft--England. I. Title.

Witchcraft
BF
1565
.D62
no.8

Mirus, Adam Erdmann, 1656-1727, praeses.
De conventu sagarum ad sua sabbata, qvae vocant, dissertationem, ... praeside M. Adamo Erdmann Miro ... exhibebit respondens Johannes Niessner ... Wittenbergae, Typis Matthaei Henckelii [1682]
[16] p. 20cm.
No. 8 in vol. lettered Dissertationes de sagis. 1636-1714.
1. Witchcraft. 2. Devil. I. Niessner, Johann, respondent. II. Title.

Mirville, Jacques Eudes, marquis de, 1802-73.
De l'esprit-saint ...

WITCHCRAFT
BF
1002
.M67
1854

Mirville, Jacques Eudes, marquis de, 1802-1873.
Pneumatologie. Des esprits et de leurs manifestations fluidiques. Mémoire adressé à l'Académie. 2. éd.... Paris, H. Vrayet de Surcy [etc.] 1854-68.
6 v. 24cm.
Vol. 1 only is of 2d ed.
Vols 2-5 have title: Pneumatologie. Des esprits et de leurs manifestations diverses. Vol. 6 has title: Des esprits. De l'esprit-saint et du miracle...
(Continued on next card)

8
NIC

Mirville, Jacques Eudes, marquis de, 1802-73.
De l'esprit-saint ...

WITCHCRAFT
BF
1002
.M67
1854

Mirville, Jacques Eudes, marquis de, 1802-1873. Pneumatologie...1854-68. (Card 2)
Vols. 2-5 also have special title: Manifestations historiques...I-IV.
Vol. 6 has also special title: Manifestations thaumaturgiques. I.
1. Psychical research. I. His Des esprits et de leurs manifestations... II.His De l'esprit-saint... III. His Manifestations historiques... IV. His Manifestations thaumaturgiques. V. Title.

Mirville, Jacques Eudes, Marquis de, 1802-73.
Des esprits et de leurs manifestations..

WITCHCRAFT
BF
1002
.M67
1854

Mirville, Jacques Eudes, marquis de, 1802-1873.
Pneumatologie. Des esprits et de leurs manifestations fluidiques. Mémoire adressé à l'Académie. 2. éd.... Paris, H. Vrayet de Surcy [etc.] 1854-68.
6 v. 24cm.
Vol. 1 only is of 2d ed.
Vols 2-5 have title: Pneumatologie. Des esprits et de leurs manifestations diverses. Vol. 6 has title: Des esprits. De l'esprit-saint et du miracle...
(Continued on next card)

8
NIC

Mirville, Jacques Eudes, marquis de, 1802-73.
Des esprits et de leurs manifestations...

WITCHCRAFT
BF
1002
.M67
1854

Mirville, Jacques Eudes, marquis de, 1802-1873. Pneumatologie...1854-68. (Card 2)
Vols. 2-5 also have special title: Manifestations historiques...I-IV.
Vol. 6 has also special title: Manifestations thaumaturgiques. I.
1. Psychical research. I. His Des esprits et de leurs manifestations... II.His De l'esprit-saint... III. His Manifestations historiques... IV. His Manifestations thaumaturgiques. V. Title.

Mirville, Jacques Eudes, marquis de, 1802-73.
Manifestations historiques ...

WITCHCRAFT
BF
1002
.M67
1854

Mirville, Jacques Eudes, marquis de, 1802-1873.
Pneumatologie. Des esprits et de leurs manifestations fluidiques. Mémoire adressé à l'Académie. 2. éd.... Paris, H. Vrayet de Surcy [etc.] 1854-68.
6 v. 24cm.
Vol. 1 only is of 2d ed.
Vols 2-5 have title: Pneumatologie. Des esprits et de leurs manifestations diverses. Vol. 6 has title: Des esprits. De l'esprit-saint et du miracle...
(Continued on next card)

8
NIC

CATALOGUE OF THE CORNELL WITCHCRAFT COLLECTION

WITCHCRAFT
BF
1002
M67
1854
  Mirville, Jacques Eudes, marquis de, 1802-73
    Manifestations historiques.
    Mirville, Jacques Eudes, marquis de, 1802-
    1873. Pneumatologie...1854-68. (Card 2)

    Vols. 2-5 also have special title: Manifestations historiques...I-IV.
    Vol. 6 has also special title: Manifestations thaumaturgiques. I.
    1. Psychical research. I. His Des esprits et de leurs manifestations... II. His De l'esprit-saint... III. His Manifestations historiques... IV. His Manifestations thaumaturgiques. V. Title.

8
NIC

WITCHCRAFT
BF
1584
S7
B55+
  Miscellaneous notes on witchcraft and alcahuetería.
  Berzunza, Julio, 1896-
    Miscellaneous notes on witchcraft and alcahuetería. [Lancaster, Pa., Lancaster Press, 1928]
    141-150 p. 26cm.

    Title on cover: Notes on witchcraft and alcahuetería.
    Reprinted from the Romanic review, v.19, no.2, Apr.-June 1928.

8
NIC
  1. Witchcraft--Spain. I. His Notes on witchcraft and alcahuetería.

Witchcraft
BF
1410
B42
Z86
no.6
  Missive van M. D. E. P. aan een vrind, over de zaak van Do. B: Bekker ... 1692.
                                              (Card 2)

  1. Bekker, Balthasar, 1634-1698. De betoverde weereld. 2. Leydekker, Melchior, 1642-1721. Historische en theologische redeneringe. I. M. D. E. P. II. P., M. D. E.

WITCHCRAFT
BF
1002
M67
1854
  Mirville, Jacques Eudes, marquis de, 1802-73.
    Manifestations thaumaturgiques.
    Mirville, Jacques Eudes, marquis de, 1802-1873.
    Pneumatologie. Des esprits et de leurs manifestations fluidiques. Mémoire addressé à l'Académie. 2. éd.... Paris, H. Vrayet de Surcy [etc.] 1854-68.
    6 v. 24cm.

    Vol. 1 only is of 2d ed.
    Vols 2-5 have title: Pneumatologie. Des esprits et de leurs manifestations diverses.
    Vol. 6 has title: Des esprits. De l'esprit-saint et du miracle...
              (Continued on next card)

8
NIC

Witchcraft
GR
142
H6
A3
no.18
  [Misodaimon, B.] pseud.
    The divel's delusions; or, A faithful relation of John Palmer and Elizabeth Knott, two notorious witches, lately condemned at the sessions of Oyer and Terminer in St. Albans. Together with the confession of the aforesaid John Palmer and Elizabeth Knott, executed July 16. Also their accusations of severall witches in Hitchen, Norton, and other places in the county of Hartford. London, Printed for Richard Williams, stationer, at St. Albans, anno Dom, 1649. Reprinted with an introductory by W. B. Gerish. Bishop's Stortford, 1914.
    13, [1] p. 21¾cm. [Hertfordshire folk lore. no. 18]
    Signed: "B. Misodaimon."
    1. Witchcraft--England. 2. Palmer, John, d. 1649. 3. Knott, Elizabeth, d. 1649. I. Gerish, William Blyth, ed. II. Title.

Library of Congress   GR530.M55
                              16-25733

Missot, M. J., 1801-1876.

see

Tissot, Claude-Joseph, 1801-1876.

WITCHCRAFT
BF
1002
M67
1854
  Mirville, Jacques Eudes, marquis de, 1802-73.
    Manifestations thaumaturgiques.
    Mirville, Jacques Eudes, marquis de, 1802-73. Pneumatologie...1854-68. (Card 2)

    Vols. 2-5 also have special title: Manifestations historiques...I-IV.
    Vol. 6 has also special title: Manifestations thaumaturgiques. I.
    1. Psychical research. I. His Des esprits et de leurs manifestations... II. His De l'esprit-saint... III. His Manifestations historiques... IV. His Manifestations thaumaturgiques. V. Title.

Witchcraft
BF
1410
B42
Z56
v.3
no.6
  Missive, aen D. Balthazar Bekker, in 't korte ontdekkende de gronden van sijn misgrepen ...
    [Schuts, Jacobus]
    Missive, aen D. Balthazar Bekker, in 't korte ontdekkende de gronden van sijn misgrepen, begaen in sijn drie tractaten De betooverde weereld, over den prophete Daniel, en van de cometen. Waer in N. Orchard, in sijn Leeringe der duivelen der grooten afval der Christenen, ende den spotterigen Philopater in sijn leven, ook hare voldoeninge konnen krygen. Tot Nederlands waerschouwinge en onderricht der Joden. Gravenhage, By B. Beek, konst- en boekverkoper, 1692.

8   (Continued on next card)

Witchcraft
BF
1566
M68
1839
  Mitchell, John, 1786-1856.
    The philosophy of witchcraft. By J. Mitchell and Jn. Dickie. Paisley, Murray and Stewart [etc., etc.] 1839.
    viii, 424 p. illus. 17cm.

    1. Witchcraft. I. Dickie, John, joint author. II. Title.

WITCHCRAFT
BF
1002
M67
1854
  Mirville, Jacques Eudes, marquis de, 1802-1873.
    Pneumatologie. Des esprits et de leurs manifestations fluidiques. Mémoire addressé à l'Académie. 2. éd.... Paris, H. Vrayet de Surcy [etc.] 1854-68.
    6 v. 24cm.

    Vol. 1 only is of 2d ed.
    Vols 2-5 have title: Pneumatologie. Des esprits et de leurs manifestations diverses.
    Vol. 6 has title: Des esprits. De l'esprit-saint et du miracle...
              (Continued on next card)

8
NIC

Witchcraft
BF
1410
B42
Z56
v.3
no.6
  Missive, aen D. Balthazar Bekker, in 't korte ontdekkende de gronden van sijn misgrepen ...
    [Schuts, Jacobus] Missive, aen D. Balthazar Bekker ... 1692.   (Card 2)

    10 p. l., 69 p. [p. 70-72 blank] title and other vignettes, illus. initials. 20 x 15cm.
    4°: a-b⁴, c², A-I⁴.
    Black letter.
    Signed and dated at end: N. N. Den 22 November 1691.
    Neither Orchard nor Philopater is mentioned in the text.

8   (Continued on next card)

Witchcraft
BF
1566
M68
1839
  Mitchell, John, 1786-1856.
    The philosophy of witchcraft. By J. Mitchell and Jn. Dickie ... Paisley, Murray and Stewart; Glasgow, W. Hamilton and P. Salmon; Edinburgh, N. Bowack; Montrose, J. & D. Nichol, 1839.
    viii, 424 p. front. 17cm.

WITCHCRAFT
BF
1002
M67
1854
  Mirville, Jacques Eudes, marquis de, 1802-1873. Pneumatologie...1854-68. (Card 2)

    Vols. 2-5 also have special title: Manifestations historiques..I-IV.
    Vol. 6 has also special title: Manifestations thaumaturgiques. I.
    1. Psychical research. I. His Des esprits et de leurs manifestations... II. His De l'esprit-saint... III. His Manifestations historiques... IV. His Manifestations thaumaturgiques. V. Title.

Witchcraft
BF
1410
B42
Z56
v.3
no.6
  Missive, aen D. Balthazar Bekker, in 't korte ontdekkende de gronden van sijn misgrepen ...
    [Schuts, Jacobus] Missive, aen D. Balthazar Bekker ... 1692.   (Card 3)

    Van der Linde 147.
    No. 6 in vol. lettered Bekker III.
    1. Bekker, Balthasar, 1634-1698. De betoverde weereld. 2. Bekker, Balthasar, 1634-1698. Ondersoek van de betekeninge der kometen. 3. Bekker, Balthasar, 1634-1698. Uitlegginge van den prophet Daniel. I. Title.

WITCHCRAFT
BF
1583
P77
2 copies
  Mittheilungen über den Hexenprozess in Deutschland.
    Pollack, Heinrich, 1844-1911.
    Mittheilungen über den Hexenprozess in Deutschland, insbesonders über verschiedene westphälische Hexenprozessakten. Berlin, Wallmann, 1885.
    50 p. 23cm.

    Two copies. On label pasted over imprint of copy 2: Berlin, F. Siemenroth, 1886.

8
NIC
    1. Trials (Witchcraft)--Germany. 2. Trials (Witchcraft)--Westphalia.

Witchcraft
GR
830
W4
A18
  Misantropus Audax.
    Acxtelmeier, Stanislaus Reinhard.
    Misantropus Audax; das ist: Der alles anbellende Menschen-Hund. Wider die Fehler, Irrthumer, Missbräuche, und aberglaubische, Gottes-lästerliche, teuffelische Zauber-Wercke, und andere Laster, welche leider, heutiges Tages häuffig im Schwung gehen, durch untadelhafftigen Tadel denen Irrgehenden zu Gemüth geleget, und im Reisen zusammen getragen. Augspurg, L. Kop, 1710.
    [3], 289 p.   16cm.
    I. Title. II. Title: Der alles anbellende Menschen-Hund.

Witchcraft
BF
1410
B42
Z86
no.6
  Missive van M. D. E. P. aan een vrind, over de zaak van Do. B: Bekker, en het boek van de Heer Professor M. Leydekker. Rotterdam, By J. Gysen, 1692.
    8 p. l. title vignette, illus. initial. 19 x 15cm.
    4°: A-B⁴.
    Incomplete: second gathering wanting.
    Van der Linde 129.
    No. 6 in vol. lettered Tractaten voor en tegen B. Bekker.

               (Continued on next card)

Witchcraft
BF
1565
S83
M69
  Model, Johann Michael
    Johann Michael Models, J. U. Lic. beantwortete Frage: Ob man die Ausfahrt der Hexen zulassen könne? Wider den heutigen Hexenstürmer P. Ferdinand Sterzinger. München, Bey J. A. Crätz, 1769.
    36 p. 18cm.
    1. Sterzinger, Ferdinand, 1721-1786. 2. Witchcraft. I. Title: Beantwortete Frage: Ob man die Ausfahrt der Hexen zulassen könne? II. Title: Frage, Ob man die Ausfahrt der Hexen zulassen könne? III. Title.

8

CATALOGUE OF THE CORNELL WITCHCRAFT COLLECTION

WITCHCRAFT
BF 1583
Z7
1907

Ein moderner Hexenprozess in Posen.
Hellwig, Albert Ernst Karl Max, 1880- , ed.
Ein moderner Hexenprozess in Posen. Von Dr. Albert Hellwig.
(In Schlesische Gesellschaft für Volkskunde. Mitteilungen. Breslau. 25cm. Bd. XII (1910), p. 191-215)

1. Witchcraft--Germany. I. Title.

8

Witchcraft
BF 1575
H16

A modest enquiry into the nature of witchcraft
Hale, John, 1636-1700.
A modest enquiry into the nature of witchcraft, and how persons guilty of that crime may be convicted: and the means used for their discovery discussed, both negatively and affirmatively, according to Scripture and experience. By John Hale, pastor of the Church of Christ in Beverley, anno Domini 1697 ... Boston in N. E., Printed by B. Green and J. Allen, for B. Eliot, 1702.
176 p. 15ᶜᵐ.
"An epistle to the reader," p. 3-7, signed: John Higginson, pastor of the church of Salem.
Imperfect: t.p., 7 l. at beginning and 3 l. at end lacking; supplied in ms.

Library of Congress   BF1575.H16
——— Copy 2.   11-9204

WITCHCRAFT
BX 2340
V82
1643

Modus interrogandi daemonem ab exorcista.
Visconti, Zaccaria.
Complementvm artis exorcisticae: cui simile nunquam visum est: cvm litaniis, benedictionibvs, & doctrinis nouis, exorcismis efficacissimis, ac remediis copiosis in maleficiatis expertis. Nuper correctum, & in tres partes diuisum. Qvarvm prima dicitvr doctrinalis. Secunda benedictionalis. Tertia exorcismalis. Cui addita est Oratio supra febricitantes. Avthore Fr. Zacharia Vicecomite ... Cui nupperrimè in hac

8   (Continued on next card)

WITCHCRAFT
BX 2340
V82
1643

Modus interrogandi daemonem ab exorcista.
Visconti, Zaccaria. Complementvm artis exorcisticae ... 1643. (Card 2)
postrema editione veneta. Pro vberiori complemento, additus est tractatus de Modo interrogandi daemonem ab exorcista ... Avthore Carolo de Bavcio ... Venetiis, Apud Turrinum, 1643.
8 p. l., 359, 85 p. 17cm.
"Modvs interrogandi daemonem ab exorcista," by Carlo de Baucio, has special t. p.

(Continued on next card)

Moebius, Friedrich Tobias, respondent.

Witchcraft
BL 325
M5
T46

Thomasius, Jacob, 1622-1684, praeses.
De transformatione hominum in bruta, dissertationem philosophicam priorem, inclytae facultatis philosophicae permissu & authoritate sub praesidio ... Dn. M. Jacobi Thomasii ... ventilationi subjicit ... Fridericus Tobias Moebius ... [Lipsiae?] Typis Joh. Wittigau [1667]
[20] p. 19cm.
Diss.--Leipzig (F. T. Moebius, respondent)
1. Metamorphosis (in religion, folk-lore, etc.) 2. Magic. I. Moebius, Friedrich Tobias, respondent. II. Title.

Möglichkeiten der Kritik am Hexen- und Zauberwesen im ausgehenden Mittelalter.

Ziegeler, Wolfgang.
Möglichkeiten der Kritik am Hexen- und Zauberwesen im ausgehenden Mittelalter: zeitgenöss. Stimmen u. ihre soziale Zugehörigkeit / Wolfgang Ziegeler. Köln, Wien: Böhlau, 1973.
xi, 231 p. 21 cm. (Kollektive Einstellungen und sozialer Wandel im Mittelalter, Bd. 2)
Bibliography: p. [206]-229.

C00dc   73-361719

WITCHCRAFT
DD 491
H2
H67
1842

Möhlmann, J H D
Actenmässige Darstellung der Theilnahme der Kalenbergischen Landstände an den durch angeschuldigte Zauberei und Giftmischerei zwischen dem Landesherrn Erich dem Jungern und seiner Gemahlinn Sidonia veranlassten Missverständnissen.
(In: Historischer Verein für Niedersachsen. Zeitschrift [under earlier title, Vaterländisches Archiv] Hannover. 19cm. 1842. p. 303- 323)

8
NIC   (Continued on next card)

WITCHCRAFT
DD 491
H2
H67
1842

Möhlmann, J H D
Actenmässige Darstellung der Theilnahme der Kalenbergischen Landstände an den durch angeschuldigte Zauberei...
(Card 2)

1. Braunschweig-und-Lüneburg, Sidonia, Herzogin zu. 2. Braunschweig-und-Lüneburg, Erich II, Herzog zu.
8   I. Title.
NIC

WITCHCRAFT
BF 1555
M69

Möller, Karl.
Leben und Briefe von Johannes Theodor Laurent.
Möller, Karl.
Eine Teufelaustreibung durch einen deutschen Bischof im 19. Jahrhundert. [Sonderabdruck aus der Rheinischen Correspondenz] Köln, C. Römcke, 1897.
12 p. 23cm.
Consists largely of extracts from his Leben und Briefe von Johannes Theodor Laurent, pub. 1887-89; the bishop's letters are quoted.
1. Demoniac possession. 2. Exorcism. 3. Pfefferkorn, Maria Anna Katharina, fl. 1842. I. H   is Leben und Briefe von Johannes Theodor Laurent. II. Laurent, Johannes Theodor, bp. III. Title.

8

WITCHCRAFT
BF 1555
M69

Möller, Karl.
Eine Teufelaustreibung durch einen deutschen Bischof im 19. Jahrhundert. [Sonderabdruck aus der Rheinischen Correspondenz] Köln, C. Römcke, 1897.
12 p. 23cm.
Consists largely of extracts from his Leben und Briefe von Johannes Theodor Laurent, pub. 1887-89; the bishop's letters are quoted.
1. Demoniac possession. 2. Exorcism. 3. Pfefferkorn, Maria Anna Katharina, fl. 1842. I. H   is Leben und Briefe von Johannes Theodor Laurent. II. Laurent, Johannes Theodor, bp. III. Title.

8

WITCHCRAFT
BF 1584
H9
M69

Möstl, Franz.
Ein Szegediner Hexenprocess. Culturhistorische Studie. Graz, Leykam-Josefsthal, 1879.
33 p. 18cm.
Includes account of trial in Szeged in 1728.

1. Witchcraft--Hungary. 2. Trials (Witchcraft)--Hungary. 3. Trials (Witchcraft)--Szeged, Hungary. I. Title.

8
NIC

Moeurs et pratiques des démons.

Witchcraft
BT 975
G69
1865

Gougenot des Mousseaux, Henri Roger, 1805-1876.
Moeurs et pratiques des démons ou des esprits visiteurs du spiritisme ancien et moderne ... Nouv. éd. entièrement refondue et fort augmentée. Paris, H. Plon, 1865.
xl, 436 p. 24cm.

1. Demonology. I. Title.

8

WITCHCRAFT
BF 1582
S83

Les moines et les sorcières d'Ancy au XVIᵉ siècle.
Sternon, Pierre.
Les moines et les sorcières d'Ancy au XVIᵉ siècle. Nancy, Imprimerie nouvelle, 1886.
148 p. 19cm.

1. Witchcraft--Fiction. 2. Witchcraft--France. I. Title.

8
NIC

Witchcraft
BF 1566
M71

[Moir, George] 1800-1870.
Magic and witchcraft ... London, Chapman and Hall, 1852.
vi p., 1 l., 104 p. 17cm.

1. Magic. 2. Witchcraft. I. Title.

WITCHCRAFT
BF 1584
N4
M71

Molhuysen, Philip Christiaan, 1870-1944.
Bijdrage tot de geschiedenis der heksenprocessen, in Gelderland. [n.p., n.d.]
16 p. 24cm.
Extract from Nieuwe bijdragen voor vaderl. geschiedenis en oudheidkunde, v.1, p.43-68.
With this is bound: Weerwolven. n.d.

8
NIC   1. Trials (Witchcraft)--Gelderland. I. Title.

Witchcraft
BF 1410
B42
Z86
no.5

Molinaeus, Johannes, d. 1702.
De betoverde werelt van D. Balthazar Bekker handelende van den aert en 't vermogen, van 't bewind en bedrijf der goede en quade engelen, onderzogt en wederleydt: in twee predikaetien; d' eerste van 't gebruik en misbruyk der philosophie; de tweede van den aert en 't bedrijf der goede engelen. En laetstelik in een verhandelinge van de booze geesten, of van den Duyvel en zijne engelen. Rotterdam, By B. Bos, boekverkooper, 1692.
6 p. l., 104 p. title vignette, illus. initials. 19 x 15 cm.
(Continued on next card)

Witchcraft
BF 1410
B42
Z86
no.5

Molinaeus, Johannes, d. 1702. De betoverde werelt van D. Balthazar Bekker ... 1692.
(Card 2)
4°: *⁴, 2*², A-N⁴.
Black letter (except for introduction)
Variant of van der Linde 131: 2*², H-N⁴ wanting in van der Linde copy.
No.5 in vol. lettered Tractaten voor en tegen B. Bekker.
1. Bekker, Balthasar, 1634-1698. De betoverde weereld. 2. Bible. N.T. Colossians II, 8--Criticism, interpretation, etc. 3. Bible. N.T. Hebrews I, 14--Criticism, interpretation, etc. I. Title.

WITCHCRAFT
BF 1410
B42
Z69
no. 24

Molinaeus, Johannes, d. 1702.
De betoverde werelt van D. Balthazar Bekker handelende van den aert en 't vermogen, van 't bewind en bedrijf der goede en quade engelen, onderzogt en wederleydt: in twee predikaetien; d' eerste van 't gebruik en misbruyk der philosophie; de tweede van den aert en 't bedrijf der goede engelen. En laetstelik in een verhandelinge van de booze geesten, of van den Duyvel en zijne engelen. Rotterdam, By B. Bos, boekverkooper, 1692.

8
NIC   (Continued on next card)

CATALOGUE OF THE CORNELL WITCHCRAFT COLLECTION

Witchcraft
BF
1410
B42
Z69
no. 24

Molinaeus, Johannes, d. 1702. De betoverde werelt van D. Balthazar Bekker...1692.
(Card 2)

6 p. l., 104 p. title vignette, illus. initials. 21cm.
4°: *⁴, 2*², A-N⁴.
Black letter (except for introduction).
Variant of van der Linde 131: 2*², H-N⁴ wanting in van der Linde copy.
No. 24 in a Collection of tracts against Balthasar Bekker and his Betoverde weereld.
(Continued on next card)

8
NIC

Witchcraft
BF
1410
B42
Z56
v.3
no.4

[Molinaeus, Johannes] d. 1702.
Paraenesis; ofte ernstige aenspraek aen den siender van Een vremt nagtgesigt. Rotterdam, By B. Bos, 1692.
1 p. l., 10 p. title vignette, illus. initial. 20 x 16cm.
4°: π 1, A⁴, B1.
Black letter.
Signed: J:M.
Defense of the author's attack on Balthasar Bekker and De betoverde weereld.

(Continued on next card)

Witchcraft
BF
1410
B42
Z56
v.3
no.21

Molinaeus, Johannes, d. 1702.
Rabus, Petrus, 1660-1702.
Ernstige en zedige verantwoording van P. Rabus, tegen de lasteringen des remonstrantschen predigers J. Molinaeus. Rotterdam, By P. Boekenes, boekverkooper, 1692.
1 p. l., 24 p. title and end page vignettes, illus. initial. 20 x 16cm.
4°: π1, A-C⁴.
Black letter.
In defense of Balthasar Bekker.
Van der Linde 135.
No. 21 in vol. lettered Bekker III.
(Continued on next card)

3

WITCHCRAFT
BF
1410
B42
Z69
no. 24

Molinaeus, Johannes, d. 1702. De betoverde werelt van D. Balthazar Bekker...1692.
(Card 3)

1. Bekker, Balthasar, 1634-1698. De betoverde weereld. 2. Bible. N. T. Colossians II, 8--Criticism, interpretation, etc. 3. Bible. N. T. Hebrews I, 14-- Criticism, interpretation, etc. I. Title.

8
NIC

Witchcraft
BF
1410
B42
Z56
v.3
no.4

[Molinaeus, Johannes] d. 1702. Paraenesis ... 1692. (Card 2)

Van der Linde 134.
No. 4 in vol. lettered Bekker III.

1. Bekker, Balthasar, 1634-1698. 2. Beschryvinge van een vremd nagt-gezigte. I. Title.

Witchcraft
BF
1555
M72
1873

[Molinier, Jean Baptiste] 1835-
Le Diable révolutionnaire; ou, Histoire d'une possédée encore vivante. Traduite de l'espagnol, avec introd. et conclusion sur les oeuvres diaboliques en général et sur les oeuvres diaboliques modernes en particulier, suivie d'un résumé en forme d'épilogue, ou catéchisme de Satan sur les principaux devoirs et les principales vérités du christianisme ... Par le comte Reinilom de Sneruab [pseud.] Toulouse, L. Hébrail, Durand & Delpuech, 1873.
133 p. 17cm.
1. Demoniac possession. 2. Trasfi, Carmette. I. Title.

Witchcraft
BF
1410
B42
Z56
v.2
no.7

Molinaeus, Johannes, d. 1702.
De betoverde werelt van D. Balthazar Bekker.
Beschryvinge van een vremd nagt-gezigte, vertoont aan een toehoorder der predikatie, die door den remonstrantsche leeraer Ds. Johannes Molinaeus voor 't vermogen des duivels, en tegen den aucteur van 't boek De betoverde weereld, onlangs te Rotterdam gedaan is. Logoochoorion, Gedrukt by den drukker van Haar Majesteit Krisis [1692]
2 p. l., 12 p. title vignette, illus. initial. 19 x 15cm.

(Continued on next card)

Witchcraft
BF
1410
B42
Z56
v.3
no.8

Molinaeus, Johannes, d. 1702.
Een Keuning-kaarsje voor den siender van Een vremt nagtgesigtie, om te dienen tot ophelderinge van syn St. Niklaas-droom. Ezelenburg, Gedrukt in de Gulde Schoolplak [1692]
8 p. illus. initial. 20 x 15cm.
4°: A⁴.
Black letter.
Defending Molinaeus, and against Bekker.
Van der Linde 133.
No. 8 in vol. lettered Bekker III.

(Continued on next card)

8

Witchcraft
BF
1520
B66
M72+

Molinier, Victor, 1799-1887.
Aperçus historiques et critiques sur la vie et les travaux de Jean Bodin, sur sa Démonomanie des sorciers, et sur les procès pour sorcellerie au seizième et au dix-septième siècle. Montpellier, Impr. typographique de Gras, 1867.
35 p. 28cm.

"Extrait de la Revue judiciaire du Midi, Cahiers de janvier et de février 1867."
1. Bodin, Jean, 1530-1596. De démonomanie des sorciers. I. Title.

Witchcraft
BF
1410
B42
Z56
v.2
no.7

Molinaeus, Johannes, d. 1702.
De betoverde werelt van D. Balthazar Bekker.
Beschryvinge van een vremd nagt-gezigte ... [1692] (Card 2)

4°: π², A⁴, B².
Black letter.
Van der Linde 132.
No. 7 in vol. lettered Bekker II.
1. Molinaeus, Johannes, d. 1702. De betoverde werelt van D. Balthazar Bekker. 2. Bekker, Balthasar, 1634-1698. De betoverde weereld. I. Title: Een vremd nagt-gezigt.

3

Molitor, Ulrich

Witchcraft
BF
1569
A2M72
1489

Molitor, Ulrich, fl. 1470-1501.
De lamiis et phitonicis mulieribus.
[Strassburg, Johann Prüss, not before 10 Jan., 1489]
[28] l. illus. (woodcuts) 21cm.

Leaf [1a] (Title): De laniis ε phitonicis mulieribus.
Leaf [2a]: Tractat⁹ ad illustrissimū prīcipem dnm Sigismundum archiducem austrie. Stirie carinthie τc. de lanijs ε phitonicis mulieribus per Ulricum molitoris de constan-
(Continued on next card)

Witchcraft
BF
1569
A2M72
1489

Molitor, Ulrich, fl. 1470-1501. De lamiis et phitonicis mulieribus ... [not before 10 Jan., 1489] (Card 2)

tia. studij papiensis. decretorum doctorem τ curie constantien. causarum patronum. ad honore eiusdē pncipis ac sub sue celsitudinis emēdatōe scriptis.
Leaf [27b] (End): Ex constañ. anno dñi. m.cccc.lxxxix. die decima ianuarij. Tue celsitudinis humilis cōsiliarius τ seruulus vlricus molitoris de constātia decre-
Continued on next card

Witchcraft
BF
1569
A2M72
1489

Molitor, Ulrich, fl. 1470-1501. De lamiis et phitonicis mulieribus ... [not before 10 Jan., 1489] (Card 3)

toꝛ doctor.
Leaf [28] blank; wanting in this copy.
Signatures: a-b⁸, c-d⁶.
Capital space on leaf [2a].
Six woodcuts (and a repeat) measuring about 120x75 mm., designed for the book, with a larger one (135x92 mm.) of a procession for exorcism from "De miseria cu-
(Continued on next card)

CATALOGUE OF THE CORNELL WITCHCRAFT COLLECTION

[Column 1, Card 1]

BF
569
2M72
489

Molitor, Ulrich, fl. 1470-1501. De lamiis et phitonicis mulieribus ... ₍not before 10 Jan., 1489₎ (Card 4)

ratorum (on leaf ₍1b₎)."
   Hain. Repertorium, *11535; Schramm. Bilderschmuck d. Frühdr., v.20, p. 27; Proctor, 562; Brit. Mus. Cat. (XV cent) I, p. 126 (IA. 1723; dated:₍about 1488-93₎); Goff. Third census, M-794.

   1. Witchcraft. 2. Demonology. I. Title.

[Column 1, Card 2]

aft
69
M72
93

Molitor, Ulrich, fl. 1470-1501.
   De lamiis et phitonicis mulieribus. German. ₍Strassburg, Johann Prüss, about 1493₎
   ₍30₎ l. 7 woodcuts. 19cm.

   Leaf ₍1a₎ (Title): Von den unholdē oder hexen.
   Leaf ₍2a₎: Tractatus von denn bosen wiber die man nennet die hexen &c. durch doctor vlrichen molitoris zu latin. vnd ouch czu tutsch gemacht. vnd dem durchluchtigistē Ertzhertzog Sigmund von osterrich als dem
          (Continued on next card)

[Column 1, Card 3]

aft
69
M72
93

Molitor, Ulrich, fl. 1470-1501. De lamiis et phitonicis mulieribus. German ... ₍about 1493₎

loblichen eren fursten zu corrigirē czu gesant.
   Leaf ₍29b₎: Datū zu costentz anno dn̄i. m.cccc.lxxxix. &c. Diner erhochsten furstlichen gnaden. demutiger raut vnd diener vlricus molitoris von costentz in den rechtenn doctor &c.
   Leaf ₍30₎ blank.
          (Continued on next card)

[Column 1, Card 4]

69
M72
93

Molitor, Ulrich, fl. 1470-1501. De lamiis et phitonicis mulieribus. German ... ₍about 1493₎ (Card 3)

   Signatures: A-F⁴, G⁶.
   Hain. Repertorium, 11539; Polain (B), 2767; Schramm, XX, p. 27; Goff. Third census, M-806.
   With manuscript marginal notes.

   1. Witchcraft. I. Title. II. Title: Von den Unholden oder Hexen.

[Column 1, Card 5]

Molitor, Ulrich, fl. 1470-1501.
   De lamiis et phitonicis mulieribus. ₍Paris, Georg Mittelhus?, about 1500₎
   ₍32₎ l. 14cm.

   Leaf ₍1a₎ (Title): Tractatus utilis et necessarius per viā dyalogi ymmo trilogi. De Phitonicis mulieribus. Unacum quodā paruo tractatulo doctissimi et acutissimi in sacra pagina doctoris Johān̄is de gersono cancellarii parisiensis De probatione spirituum.
   Leaf ₍1a-b₎: Tabula et capitula presentis
      (Continued on next card)

[Column 1, Card 6]

Molitor, Ulrich, fl. 1470-1501. De lamiis et phitonicis mulieribus ... ₍about 1500₎ (Card 2)

tractatus.
   Leaf ₍2₎: Epistola ... ad illustrissimū principē dominū Sigismundū archiducē Austrie Stirie Carinthie etc. ...
   The dialogue begins at the bottom of leaf ₍2b₎ and ends on leaf ₍27a₎
   "Johān̄is de gersonno ... tractatulus ... de probatione spirituum ...": leaf ₍27b₎
          (Continued on next card)

[Column 2, Card 1]

Witchcraft
BF
1569
A2M72
1500

Molitor, Ulrich, fl. 1470-1501. De lamiis et phitonicis mulieribus ... ₍about 1500₎ (Card 3)

   ₍32b₎
   Leaf ₍32b₎ (Colophon): Explicit tractatus de laniis ₍sic₎ et phitonicis mulieribus vna cū tractatu de probatio͂e sp̄uum venerabilis mgr̄i iohān̄is de gersono cācellarij parisiēsis.
   Signatures: a-d⁸.
   Copinger. Supplementum, 4341; Polain
          (Continued on next card)

[Column 2, Card 2]

Witchcraft
BF
1569
A2M72
1500

Molitor, Ulrich, fl. 1470-1501. De lamiis et phitonicis mulieribus ... ₍about 1500₎ (Card 4)

(B), 2763; Goff. Third census, M-805.

   1. Witchcraft. 2. Demonology. 3. Visions. I. Gerson, Joannes, 1363-1429. De probatione spirituum. II. Title. III. Title: De probatione spirituum.

[Column 2, Card 3]

WITCHCRAFT
BF
1569
A2
M72
1545

Molitor, Ulrich, fl. 1470-1501.
   De lamiis et phitonicis mulieribus.
   Hexen Meysterey. Dess hochgebornen Fürsten, Hertzog Sigmunds von Osterreich mit D. Vlrich Molitoris vnd Herr Cunrad Schatz, weilandt Burgermeister zů Costentz, ein schön Gesprech von den Onholden, ob die selben bösen Weyber, Hagel, Reiffen, vnd ander Ongefell, den Menschen zůschaden, machen können. Auch sunst ihrem gantzen Hexen Handel, waher der kumpt, vnd was dauon zůhalten sey, vnd zům   letsten, das sie auss R.
8
          (Continued on next card)

[Column 2, Card 4]

WITCHCRAFT
BF
1569
A2
M72
1545

Molitor, Ulrich, fl. 1470-1501. Hexen Meysterey ... 1545. (Card 2)

Rechten abzůthun seyen. &c. Weitleuffiger mit mer Exempeln der Alten, dann vor nie kains aussgangen. Nottwendig vnnd nutz aller Obergkeyt zůwissen. ₍Cölln?₎ 1545.
   ₍32₎ l. illus. 20cm.
   8 woodcuts (several repeated)
   For place, see Grässe, Trésor (describes 1544 ed.)
   Translati   on of De lamiis et phitonicis muli   eribus.
8   (Continued on next card)

[Column 2, Card 5]

WITCHCRAFT
BF
1569
A2
M72
1561

Molitor, Ulrich, fl. 1470-1501.
   De laniis ₍sic₎ et phitonicis mulieribus.
   Tractatvs De lamiis et pythonicis, autore Vlrico Molitore Constantiensi, ad Sigismundum Archiducem Austriae, anno 1489. Parisiis, Apud Aegidium Corrozet, 1561.
   40 numbered l. 17cm.
   First published under title: De laniis ₍sic₎ et phitonicis mulieribus.
   Imperfect copy: l. 38-40 damaged, some text of l. 40 wanting.
   1. Witchcraft. 2. Demonology. 3. Visions. I. His De laniis ₍sic₎
8 et phitonicis   mulieribus. II. Title.

[Column 2, Card 6]

Witchcraft
BF
1565
D17
1576

Molitor, Ulrich, fl. 1470-1501.
   De lamiis et phitonicis mulieribus--German.
   Daneau, Lambert, ca. 1530-1595.
   Von den Zauberern, Hexen, vnd Vnholden, drei christliche verscheidene ₍sic₎, vnnd zu diesen vnsern vngefärlichen Zeiten notwendige Bericht ... Durch die hoch vnd wohlgelehrte Herren, Lambertvm Danaeuvm, Iacobvm Vallick, vnnd Vlricvm Molitoris. ... Cölln, Gedruckt durch Johannem Gymnicum, 1576.
   2 v. in 1. 16cm.
   "Der ander Tractat von Zauberern, Hexen, vnd Vnholden,   durch J. Vallick, p.
          (Continued on next card)

[Column 3, Card 1]

Witchcraft
BF
1565
D17
1576

Molitor, Ulrich, fl. 1470-1501.
   De lamiis et phitonicis mulieribus--German.
   Daneau, Lambert, ca. 1530-1595. Von den Zauberern, Hexen, vnd Vnholden... 1576 (Card 2)

157-222 of v. 1, has special t. p.
   Translation of De veneficis, quos olim sortilegos ... vocant, by L. Daneau; of an unidentified work by J. Vallick; and of De lamiis et phitonicis mulieribus, by U. Molitor.
   1. Witchcraft. 2. Demonology. I. His De veneficis, quos olim sortilegos ... vo-
8   (Continued on next card)

[Column 3, Card 2]

Witchcraft
BF
1569
A2M72
1926

Molitor, Ulrich, fl. 1470-1501.
   Des sorcières et des devineresses par Ulric Molitor reproduit en fac-simile d'après l'édition latine de Cologne 1489 et traduit pour la première fois en français. Paris, E. Nourry, 1926.
   vii p., facsim. (₍56₎ p. illus.), 84 p. 25cm. (Bibliothèque magique des XVe et XVIe siècles, 1)

   Original t. p.: De lamiis et phitonicis mulieribus. (p. ₍1₎)
   "Tirage limité a 500 exemplaires sur vélin/a la cuve. N° 100.
   I. Title.   II. Title: De lamiis et phitonicis mulieribus.

[Column 3, Card 3]

WITCHCRAFT
BF
1569
A2
M72
1545

Molitor, Ulrich, fl. 1470-1501.
   Hexen Meysterey. Dess hochgebornen Fürsten, Hertzog Sigmunds von Osterreich mit D. Vlrich Molitoris vnd Herr Cunrad Schatz, weilandt Burgermeister zů Costentz, ein schön Gesprech von den Onholden, ob die selben bösen Weyber, Hagel, Reiffen, vnd ander Ongefell, den Menschen zůschaden, machen können. Auch sunst ihrem gantzen Hexen Handel, waher der kumpt, vnd was dauon zůhalten sey, vnd zům   letsten, das sie auss R.
8
          (Continued on next card)

[Column 3, Card 4]

WITCHCRAFT
BF
1569
A2
M72
1545

Molitor, Ulrich, fl. 1470-1501. Hexen Meysterey ... 1545. (Card 2)

Rechten abzůthun seyen. &c. Weitleuffiger mit mer Exempeln der Alten, dann vor nie kains aussgangen. Nottwendig vnnd nutz aller Obergkeyt zůwissen. ₍Cölln?₎ 1545.
   ₍32₎ l. illus. 20cm.
   8 woodcuts (several repeated)
   For place, see Grässe, Trésor (describes 1544 ed.)
   Translati   on of De lamiis et phitonicis muli   eribus.
8   (Continued on next card)

[Column 3, Card 5]

WITCHCRAFT
BF
1569
A2
M72
1545

Molitor, Ulrich, fl. 1470-1501. Hexen Meysterey ... 1545. (Card 3)

   1. Witchcraft. 2. Demonology. I. His De lamiis et phitonicis mulieribus. German. II. Title.

[Column 3, Card 6]

WITCHCRAFT
BF
1569
A2
M72
1561

Molitor, Ulrich, fl. 1470-1501.
   Tractatvs De lamiis et pythonicis, autore Vlrico Molitore Constantiensi, ad Sigismundum Archiducem Austriae, anno 1489. Parisiis, Apud Aegidium Corrozet, 1561.
   40 numbered l. 17cm.
   First published under title: De laniis ₍sic₎ et phitonicis mulieribus.
   Imperfect copy: l. 38-40 damaged, some text of l. 40 wanting.
   1. Witchcraft. 2. Demonology. 3. Visions. I. His De laniis ₍sic₎
8   et phitonicis   mulieribus. II. Title.
   III. Title: De lamiis et pythonicis.

CATALOGUE OF THE CORNELL WITCHCRAFT COLLECTION

Molitor, Ulrich, fl. 1470-1501.
Von Hexen unnd Unholden.

Witchcraft
BF   Daneau, Lambert, ca. 1530-1595.
1565   Von den Zauberern, Hexen, vnd Vnholden,
D17   drei christliche verscheidene [sic], vnnd
1576   zu diesen vnsern vngefärlichen Zeiten not-
         wendige Bericht ... Durch die hoch vnd
         wohlgelehrte Herren, Lambertvm Danaevm,
         Iacobvm Vallick, vnnd Vlricvm Molitoris.
         ... Cölln, Gedruckt durch Johannem Gym-
         nicum, 1576.
             2 v. in 1. 16cm.
             "Der ander Tractat von Zauberern, Hexen,
         vnd Vnholden,   durch J. Vallick, p.
8   (Continued on next card)

Molitor, Ulrich, fl. 1470-1501.
Von Hexen unnd Unholden.

Witchcraft
BF   Daneau, Lambert, ca. 1530-1595. Von den
1565   Zauberern, Hexen, vnd Vnholden... (Card 2)
D17
1576   157-222 of v. 1, has special t. p.
             Translation of De veneficis, quos olim
         sortilegos ... vocant, by L. Daneau; of an
         unidentified work by J. Vallick; and of
         De lamiis et phitonicis mulieribus, by
         U. Molitor.
             1. Witchcraft. 2. Demonology. I. His
         De veneficis, quos olim sortigelos ... vo-
8   (Continued on next card)

Rare   Molle, H., fl. 1625, tr.
AC   Camerarius, Philipp, 1537-1624.
14   The living librarie; or, Meditations and
C18+   observations historical, natvral, moral,
1621   political, and poetical. Written in Latin
         by P. Cameraivs. And done into English by
         Iohn Molle, esquire.   London, Printed
         by Adam Islip, 1621.
             I. Molle, John, fl. 1621, tr. II. Molle,
         H., fl. 1625, tr. III. Baddeley, Richard, fl.
         1621, ed. IV. Title.

Rare   Molle, John, fl. 1621, tr.
AC   Camerarius, Philipp, 1537-1624.
14   The living librarie; or, Meditations and
C18+   observations historical, natvral, moral,
1621   political, and poetical. Written in Latin
         by P. Cameraivs. And done into English by
         Iohn Molle, esquire.   London, Printed
         by Adam Islip, 1621.
             I. Molle, John, fl. 1621, tr. II. Molle,
         H., fl. 1625, tr. III. Baddeley, Richard, fl.
         1621, ed. IV. Title.

WITCHCRAFT
BT   Monceaux, François de.
960   Disquisitio de magia divinatrice & opera-
M73   trice... Auctore Francisco Moncaejo.
         Francofurti et Lipsiae, Sumtibus Joh. Chris-
         tiani Wohlfarti. 1683.
             184 p. 19cm.
             Date trimmed off by binder.
             Note by G.L. Burr: Is Moncaeus a pseud.
         of Joh. Praetorius? See Rosenthal, Cat. 83,
         no. 204.
             1. Supernatural. 2. Spirits. 3. Magic.
8   I. Praetorius,   Johannes, 1630-1680,
NIC   supposed au   thor. II. Title.

Le monde a l'empire et le monde demoniacle
fait par dialogues.
WITCHCRAFT
BF   Viret, Pierre, 1511-1571.
1547   Le monde a l'empire et le monde demoni-
V81   acle fait par dialogues. Revue et augu-
1561   mente ... Geneve, Par Guillaume de Lai-
         marie, 1561.
             8 p. l., 544 p. 15cm.
             Imperfect copy: t. p. and preliminary
         leaves, p. 391-394, and 543-544 wanting,
         and supplied in MS copy.
8   1. Demonology. I. Title.

Le monde enchanté.

Witchcraft
BF   Bekker, Balthasar, 1634-1698.
1410   Le monde enchanté; ou, Examen des communs
B42   sentimens touchant les esprits, leur nature,
1694   leur pouvoir, leur administration, & leurs
         opérations. Et touchant les éfets que les
         hommes sont capables de produire par leur com-
         munication & leur vertu, divisé en quatre
         parties, par Balthasar Bekker ... Tr. du hollan-
         dois. Amsterdam, P. Rotterdam, 1694.
             4 v. plates, port., title and other
         vignettes, illus. initials. 14cm.
             Translation of his De betoverde weereld.
             Dedication,   to M. Feyo Jean Winter,
         autographed by   Bekker.
                              (Continued on next card)

Le monde enchanté.

Witchcraft
BF   Bekker, Balthasar, 1634-1698. Le monde
1410   enchanté ... 1694.   (Card 2)
B42
1694   12°: vol. 1: *8, 2*-6*12, A-Q12, R4;
         vol. 2: *12, A-2F12; vol. 3: *12, 2*6,
         A-V12, X4; vol. 4: *12, 2*4, A-2G12, H7.
             Van der Linde 27.

             1. Demonology. 2. Angels. 3. Magic.
         4. Witchcraft. I. Title. II. His De
         betoverde weere   ld.

DC   Mongrédien, Georges, 1901-
123   Léonora Galigaï. Un procès de sorcellerie sous Louis
.9   XIII. [Paris], Hachette, 1968.
C6   234 p. 21 cm. (L'Envers de l'histoire) 16.50 F
M74   (F***)
             Illustrated cover.
             Bibliography: p. [223]-232.

             1. Concini, Leonora (Dori) called Galigaï, d. 1617. 2. Trials
         (Witchcraft)—France.   I. Title.

         DC123.9.C62M6   68-134611

         Library of Congress   [18]

WITCHCRAFT
BF   Monoyer, Jules Alfred, 1841-1887.
1584   Notices sur quelques points d'histoire
B4   et d'archéologie. III. La sorcellerie en
M75   Hainaut. Procès de 1568 à 1683. Mons,
         H. Manceaux, 1886.
             47 p. 23cm. (Essais d'histoire et d'ar-
         chéologie, t.5, fasc. 3)
             Half-title (also title on original cover):
         La sorcellerie en Hainaut, et plus spéci-
         alement aux environs du Roeulx...
             1.Witchcraft   --Hist. 2. Witchcraft--
         Hainaut. 3.   Trials (Witchcraft)--
8   Hainaut. I.   His La sorcellerie en
NIC   Hainaut.   II. Title.

WITCHCRAFT   La sorcellerie en Hainaut.
BF   Monoyer, Jules Alfred, 1841-1887.
1584   Notices sur quelques points d'histoire
B4   et d'archéologie. III. La sorcellerie en
M75   Hainaut. Procès de 1568 à 1683. Mons,
         H. Manceaux, 1886.
             47 p. 23cm. (Essais d'histoire et d'ar-
         chéologie, t.5, fasc. 3)
             Half-title (also title on original cover):
         La sorcellerie en Hainaut, et plus spéci-
         alement aux environs du Roeulx...
             1.Witchcraft   --Hist. 2. Witchcraft--
         Hainaut. 3.   Trials (Witchcraft)--
8   Hainaut. I.   His La sorcellerie en
NIC   Hainaut.

Monschmidt, Franciscus Solanus.
WITCHCRAFT
BX   Ministerium exorcisticum, quo exorcista
2340   possessos, obsessos, & maleficiatos a
M66   daemonijs...liberare potest. Cum annexis
         thesibus theologicis ad mentem...Joannis
         Duns-Scoti ex tribus libris sententiarum,
         quas...publice defendendas susceperunt
         praeside M. R. P. Adolpho Medelsky...
         Franciscus Solanus Monschmidt & ..Gela-
         sius Stoephel .. Oppaviae, Typis Joan-
         nis W. Schindler [1738]
             99 p. 17cm.
             Apparently   a cooperative under-
8   taking of   the Franciscan Fathers
NIC   in Moravia.   (Continued on next card)

WITCHCRAFT
BT   Monteacuto, Henricus a.
980   Daemonis mimica, in magiae progressu,
M77   tum in sectis errorum quorum author est...
         Parisiis, Apud Claudium Rigaud, 1612.
             410 p. 15cm.

             1. Devil. 2. Oracles. 3. Magic. 4.
8   NIC   Occult sciences.   V. Title.

Witchcraft
BF   [Montvalon, André Barrigue de] 1678-1779.
1582   Motifs des juges du parlement de Provence
G51   qui ont été d'avis de condamner le p. Jean
P9++   Baptiste Girard, envoyez à M. le Chancel-
         lier, le 31. decembre 1731. Ensemble la
         lettre de ce magistrat à Mr. le Président
         de Maliverney; la réponse de ce juge, &
         celle des autres messieurs qui ont été de
         son opinion. 3. éd. avec des notes cri-
         tiques tirées de la Procedure & des lettres
         écrites d'Aix, servant de motifs aux juges
         de l'opinion   contraire. On a cité
         ces lettres   sur la premiere éd.
                                  (Continued on next card)

Witchcraft
BF   [Montvalon, André Barrigue de] 1678-1779.
1582   Motifs des juges ...   (Card 2)
G51
P9++   qui en a été faite à Aix. [Aix?] 1733.
             67 p. 36cm.

             Bound with Girard, J. B. Procedure
         ... Aix, 1733.

             1. Girard, Jean Baptiste, 1680-1733.
             I. Title.

Moon, Anne (Hooper), fl. 1674.
WITCHCRAFT
BF   A Strange and wonderful relation from Shad-
1473   well; or, The Devil visible. Being a mos[t]
S52   true and faithful account how the Devil [in]
S89   human shape, on the 3d. of this instant
         July, made his appearance to one Mrs. M[oon?]
         there, ... with a bag of money in one
         hand, and a knife in the other, tempting
         her to murther one of her children. As
         also how she refused ... London, Print-
         ed for W. Smith, 1674.
             6 p. 19cm.
             1. Devil.   2. Shadwell, Stepney,
8   England. 3.   Moon, Anne (Hooper), fl.
         1674.

WITCHCRAFT
Z   Moore, George Henry, 1823-1892.
6878   Bibliographical notes on witchcraft in
W8   Massachusetts. Worcester, Printed for
M82   the author, 1888.
1888   31 p. 25cm.

             Read before the American Antiquarian
         Society, Apr. 25, 1888.
             Originally appeared in the Proceedings
         of the American Antiquarian Society, new
         ser., v.5, pt. 2, Apr.1888, p. 245-273,
8   with title: Notes on the bibliog-
NIC   phy of witch   craft in Massachusetts.
                                (Continued on next car[d])

WITCHCRAFT
Z   Moore, George Henry, 1823-1892. Biblio-
6878   graphical notes on witchcraft...1888.
W8
M82   (Card 2)
1888
             1. Witchcraft--Massachusetts--Bibl.
         I. His Notes on the bibliography of wit[ch]-
         craft in Massachusetts. II. Title.

CATALOGUE OF THE CORNELL WITCHCRAFT COLLECTION

Moore, George Henry, 1823-1892.
Final notes on witchcraft in Massachusetts: a summary vindication of the laws and liberties concerning attainders with corruption of blood, escheats, forfeitures for crime, and pardon of offenders, in reply to "Reasons," etc., of Hon. Abner C. Goodell, jr. ... By George H. Moore ... New York, Printed for the author, 1885.

120 p. 25½ cm.

"Pamphlets hitherto issued in this discussion": p. [2] Copy 1 is Autographed presentation copy from the author.
1. Witchcraft—Massachusetts. 2. Goodell, Abner Cheney, 1831-1914. Reasons for concluding that the act of 1711 ... became a law. I. Title. 11-13449

Library of Congress   BF1579.M8

Moore, George Henry, 1823-1892.
History of witchcraft in Massachusetts.
Moore, George Henry, 1823-1892.
[Supplementary notes on witchcraft in Massachusetts]

(In: Massachusetts Historical Society. Proceedings. Boston. 26 cm. Jan./Mar. 1884. p. 77-99)

With, in same issue: Goodell, Abner Cheney. Additional considerations on the history of witchcraft in Massachusetts.
Running title: History of witchcraft in Massachusetts.
Continues his Notes on the history
(Continued on next card)

Moore, George Henry, 1823-1892.
History of witchcraft in Massachusetts.
Moore, George Henry, 1823-1892. [Supplementary notes on witchcraft...] 1884.
(Card 2)
of witchcraft in Massachusetts. Continued by his Final notes on witchcraft in Massachusetts.
1. Witchcraft—Massachusetts. 2. Goodell, Abner Cheney, 1831-1914. Further notes on the history of witchcraft... I. Title. II. His History of witchcraft in Massachusetts. III. Title: History of witchcraft in Massachusetts.

Moore, George Henry, 1823-1892.
History of witchcraft in Massachusetts.
Moore, George Henry, 1823-1892.
Supplementary notes on witchcraft in Massachusetts; a critical examination of the alleged law of 1711 for reversing the attainders of the witches of 1692. Cambridge, J. Wilson, 1884.
25 p. facsim. 26 cm.

Reprinted from the Proceedings of the Massachusetts Historical Society, Mar. 1884.
Caption title: Witchcraft in Massachusetts.
(Running title of original article: History of witchcraft in Massachusetts)
(Continued on next card)

Moore, George Henry, 1823-1892.
History of witchcraft in Massachusetts.
Moore, George Henry, 1823-1892. Supplementary notes on witchcraft...1884.
(Card 2)
Continues his Notes on the history of witchcraft in Massachusetts. Continued by his Final notes on witchcraft in Massachusetts.
1. Witchcraft—Massachusetts. 2. Goodell, Abner Cheney, 1831-1914. Further notes on the history of witchcraft... I. Title. II. His Witchcraft in Massachusetts. III. Title: Witchcraft in Massachusetts. IV. His History of witchcraft in Massachusetts. V. Title: History of witchcraft in Massachusetts.

ITCHCRAFT
Moore, George Henry, 1823-1892.
Notes on the bibliography of witchcraft in Massachusetts.

(In: American Antiquarian Society. Proceedings. Worcester. 25 cm. new ser., v. 5, pt. 2, Apr. 1888. p. 245-273)

1. Witchcraft—Massachusetts—Bibl. I. Title.

WITCHCRAFT
Z 6878 W8 M82 1888
Moore, George Henry, 1823-1892.
Notes on the bibliography of witchcraft in Massachusetts.
Moore, George Henry, 1823-1892.
Bibliographical notes on witchcraft in Massachusetts. Worcester, Printed for the author, 1888.
31 p. 25 cm.

Read before the American Antiquarian Society, Apr. 25, 1888.
Originally appeared in the Proceedings of the American Antiquarian Society, new ser., v. 5, pt. 2, Apr. 1888, p. 245-273, with title: Notes on the bibliography of witchcraft in Massachusetts.
(Continued on next card)

Witchcraft
BF 1576 M82+
Moore, George Henry, 1823-1892.
Notes on the history of witchcraft in Massachusetts; with illustrative documents. From Proceedings at the annual meeting of the American antiquarian society, October 21, 1882. By George H. Moore. Worcester, Mass., Printed by C. Hamilton, 1883.
32 p. 26 cm.

Followed by the author's "Supplementary notes on witchcraft in Massachusetts" (Cambridge, 1884) reprinted from the Proceedings of the American antiquarian society, March 13, 1884; and by "Final notes on witchcraft in Massachusetts" (New York, 1885)
Autographed presentation copy from the author.
1. Witchcraft—Massachusetts. I. American Antiquarian Society, Worcester, Mass. II. Title.
Library of Congress   BF1576.M6   20-23088

WITCHCRAFT
BF 1576 M82 G64+
Moore, George Henry, 1823-1892.
Notes on the history of witchcraft in Massachusetts.
Goodell, Abner Cheney, 1831-1914.
[Further notes on the history of witchcraft in Massachusetts]

(In: Massachusetts Historical Society. Proceedings. Boston. 26 cm. June 1883. p. 280-326)

Running title: Witch-trials in Massachusetts.
Reply to George Henry Moore's Notes on the history of witchcraft in Massachusetts.
(Continued on next card)

WITCHCRAFT
BF 1576 M82 G641+
Moore, George Henry, 1823-1892.
[Supplementary notes on witchcraft in Massachusetts]

(In: Massachusetts Historical Society. Proceedings. Boston. 26 cm. Jan./Mar. 1884. p. 77-99)

With, in same issue: Goodell, Abner Cheney. Additional considerations on the history of witchcraft in Massachusetts.
Running title: History of witchcraft in Massachusetts.
Continues his Notes on the history
(Continued on next card)

WITCHCRAFT
BF 1576 M82 G641+
Moore, George Henry, 1823-1892. [Supplementary notes on witchcraft...] 1884.
(Card 2)
of witchcraft in Massachusetts. Continued by his Final notes on witchcraft in Massachusetts.
1. Witchcraft—Massachusetts. 2. Goodell, Abner Cheney, 1831-1914. Further notes on the history of witchcraft... I. Title. II. His History of witchcraft in Massachusetts. III. Title: History of witchcraft in Massachusetts.

WITCHCRAFT
BF 1576 M821+ 1884
Moore, George Henry, 1823-1892.
Supplementary notes on witchcraft in Massachusetts; a critical examination of the alleged law of 1711 for reversing the attainders of the witches of 1692. Cambridge, J. Wilson, 1884.
25 p. facsim. 26 cm.

Reprinted from the Proceedings of the Massachusetts Historical Society, Mar. 1884.
Caption title: Witchcraft in Massachusetts.
(Running title of original article: History of witchcraft in Massachusetts)
(Continued on next card)

WITCHCRAFT
BF 1576 M821+ 1884
Moore, George Henry, 1823-1892. Supplementary notes on witchcraft...1884.
(Card 2)
Continues his Notes on the history of witchcraft in Massachusetts. Continued by his Final notes on witchcraft in Massachusetts.
1. Witchcraft—Massachusetts. 2. Goodell, Abner Cheney, 1831-1914. Further notes on the history of witchcraft... I. Title. II. His Witchcraft in Massachusetts. III. Title: Witchcraft in Massachusetts. IV. His History of witchcraft in Massachusetts. V. Title: History of witchcraft in Massachusetts.

WITCHCRAFT
BF 1576 M82 G641+
Goodell, Abner Cheney, 1831-1914.
Reasons for concluding that the act of 1711, reversing the attainders of the persons convicted of witchcraft in Massachusetts in the year 1692, became a law. Being a reply to Supplementary notes, etc. by George H. Moore.

(In: Massachusetts Historical Society. Proceedings. Boston. 26 cm. Jan./Mar. 1884. p. 99-118)

With, in same issue: his Additional considerations on the history
(Continued on next card)

WITCHCRAFT
BF 1576 M82 G641+
Goodell, Abner Cheney, 1831-1914. [Reasons for concluding that the act of 1711... became a law] 1884.
(Card 2)
of witchcraft in Massachusetts.
Running title: History of witchcraft in Massachusetts.
1. Witchcraft—Massachusetts. 2. Moore, George Henry, 1823-1892. Supplementary notes on witchcraft... I. His History of witchcraft in Massachusetts. II. Title: History of witchcraft in Massachusetts. III. Title: Reasons for concluding that the act of 1711 became a law.

WITCHCRAFT
BF 1576 M821+ 1884
Moore, George Henry, 1823-1892.
Witchcraft in Massachusetts.
Moore, George Henry, 1823-1892.
Supplementary notes on witchcraft in Massachusetts; a critical examination of the alleged law of 1711 for reversing the attainders of the witches of 1692. Cambridge, J. Wilson, 1884.
2 copies
25 p. facsim. 26 cm.

Reprinted from the Proceedings of the Massachusetts Historical Society, Mar. 1884.
Caption title: Witchcraft in Massachusetts.
(Running title of original article: History of witchcraft in Massachusetts)
(Continued on next card)

WITCHCRAFT
BF 1576 M821 G64+ 1884
Goodell, Abner Cheney, 1831-1914.
Reasons for concluding that the act of 1711, reversing the attainders of the persons convicted of witchcraft in Massachusetts in the year 1692, became a law. Being a reply to Supplementary notes, etc. by George H. Moore. Cambridge, J. Wilson, 1884.
2 copies
21 p. 26 cm.

Originally appeared in the Proceedings of the Massachusetts Historical Society, Jan./Mar. 1884
(Continued on next card)

CATALOGUE OF THE CORNELL WITCHCRAFT COLLECTION

Moore, George Henry, 1823-1892.

WITCHCRAFT
BF
1576
M821
G64+
1884

Goodell, Abner Cheney, 1831-1914. Reasons for concluding that the act of 1711... became a law...1884. (Card 2)
Caption title: Witchcraft in Massachusetts. (Running title of original article: History of witchcraft in Massachusetts)
1. Witchcraft--Massachusetts. 2. Moore, George Henry, 1823-1892. Supplementary notes on witchcraft... I. His Witchcraft in Massachusetts. II. Title: Witchcraft in Massachusetts. III. His History of witchcraft in Massachusetts. IV. Title: History of witchcraft in Massachusetts. V. Title.

Moray, B   de.

WITCHCRAFT
BF
1555
P96
1883

Procès verbal fait povr délivrer vne fille possédée par le malin esprit à Lovviers. Publié d'après le manuscrit original et inédit de la Bibliothèque Nationale par Armand Benet ... précédé d'une introduction par B. de Moray. Paris, Aux bureaux du Progrès médical, 1883.
cxiv, 98 p. 22cm. (Bibliothèque diabolique)

8
NIC

1. Fontaine, Françoise, fl. 1591. 2. Demoniac possession. I. Moray, B   de. II. Bénet, Armand Eugène, 1858-

Morbos ab incantatione et veneficiis oriundos.

WITCHCRAFT
R
133
M62

Michaelis, Johann, 1606-1667, praeses. Morbos ab incantatione et veneficiis oriundos...sub clypeo...Johannis Michaelis... publice examinandos proponit...Anton Marquart... ₍Lipsiae₎ Typis Haeredum Timothei Hönii, 1650.
₍56₎ p. 19cm.
Diss.--Leipzig (A. Marquart, respondent)

8
NIC

1. Medicine, Magic, mystic and spagiric. 2. Devil. I. Marquart, Antonius, respondent.

Morduck, Sarah, fl. 1702.

WITCHCRAFT
K
H363
1754

Hathaway, Richard, fl. 1702, defendant.
The trial of Richard Hathaway, at Surrey assizes ... upon an information for being a cheat and impostor, and endeavouring to take away the life of Sarah Morduck, on a false accusation of witchcraft; in which is discovered the malicious designs of the said impostor, with an account of his pretended inchantments and witchcraft ... London, Printed for R. Griffiths, 1754.
92 p. 17cm.

8

(Continued on next card)

More, Sir Thomas, 1478-1535.
Utopia.

RARE
HV
8593
J76
1736

Jonctys, Daniel, 1600-1654.
De pyn-bank wedersproken, en bematigt, door Dan. Jonktys ₍sic₎... Amsterdam, By Salomon Schouten, 1736.
268, ₍62₎ p. 16cm.
Added t.p. engr.
"Gevoelen van Thomas Morus, dat dievery met de dood niet behoort gestraft te werden...uyt zijn boek...Utopia": 14 p. after p. 268.

8
NIC

1. Torture.   I. More, Sir Thomas, 1478-1535. ₍Utopia₎ II. Title.

More wonders of the invisible world.

Witchcraft
BF
1575
D76
v.2-3

Calef, Robert, 1648-1719.
More wonders of the invisible world: or, The wonders of the invisible world, display'd in five parts. Part I. An account of the sufferings of Margaret Rule, written by the Reverend Mr. C. M. P. II. Several letters to the author, &c. And his reply relating to witchcraft. P. III. The differences between the inhabitants of Salem village, and Mr. Parris their minister, in New-England. P. IV. Letters of a gentleman uninterested, endeavouring to prove the received opinions about witchcraft to be orthodox. With short essays to their answers. P. V. A short historical accout ₍!₎ of matters of fact in that affair. To
(Continued on next card) 2-18714 rev.
₍r31e2₎

More wonders of the invisible world.

Witchcraft
BF
1575
D76
v.2-3

Calef, Robert, 1648-1719.   More wonders of the invisible world ... (Card 2)
which is added, a postscript relating to a book intitled, The life of Sir William Phips. Collected by Robert Calef, merchant, of Boston in New-England ... London, Printed for N. Hillar and J. Collyer, 1700.
Reprint. (In Drake, S. G. The witchcraft delusion in New England ... Roxbury, Mass., 1866. 21½cm. v. 2, p. 1-212; v. 3, p. 3-167) Woodward's historical series. no. VI-VII.
Prefatory: by the editor: p. ₍v₎-x. Pedigree of Calef: 1 fold. leaf. Memoir of Robert Calef: p. ₍xi₎-xxix.
The text, here annotated, is that of the 1st edition, 1700. "It is given as exactly like the original as a much better type can be made to imitate an old type of 166 years ago."--Pref. by the editor. p. vi.
(Continued on next card)
2-18714 rev.
₍r31e2₎

More wonders of the invisible world.

Witchcraft
BF
1575
D76
v.2-3

Calef, Robert, 1648-1719. More wonders of the invisible world ... 1700.   (Card 3)
Appendix: I. Examination of Giles Cory.-- II. Giles Corey and Goodwyfe Corey. A ballad of 1692.--III. Testimony of William Beale, of Marblehead, against Mr. Philip English of Salem, given Aug. 2d. 1692.--IV. ₍Examination of the Indian woman belonging to Mr. Parris's family₎-- V. The examination of Mary Clark of Haverhill.-- VI. An account of the life and character of the Rev. Samuel Parris, of Salem village, and of his connection with the witchcraft delusion of 1692. By Samuel P.   Fowler.

More wonders of the invisible world, or The wonders of the invisible world displayed.

Witchcraft
BF
1575
C14
1823

Calef, Robert, 1648-1719.
More wonders of the invisible world, or The wonders of the invisible world displayed. In five parts. Part I.--An account of the sufferings of Margaret Rule, written by the Rev. Cotton Mather. Part II.--Several letters to the author, &c. and his reply relating to witchcraft. Part III.--The differences between the inhabitants of Salem village, and Mr. Parris, their minister, in New-England. Part IV.--Letters of a gentleman uninterested, endeavouring to prove the received opinions about witchcraft to be
(Continued on next card)

More wonders of the invisible world, or The wonders of the invisible world displayed.

Witchcraft
BF
1575
C14
1823

Calef, Robert, 1648-1719. More wonders of the invisible world ... 1823.   (Card 2)
orthodox. With short essays to their answers. Part V.--A short historical account of matters of fact in that affair. To which is added a postcript ₍!₎ relating to a book entitled "The life of Sir Wm. Phips". Collected by Robert Calef. Merchant, of Boston, in New-England. Printed in London, 1700. Salem, Re-printed by J.D. & T.C. Cushing, jr. for Cushing and Appleton, 1823.
312 p. 18½cm.

(Continued on next card)

More wonders of the invisible world, or The wonders of the invisible world displayed.

Witchcraft
BF
1575
C14
1823

Calef, Robert, 1648-1719. More wonders of the invisible world ... 1823.   (Card 3)
Appended: Giles Corey ₍a report of his examination, taken from the witchcraft records₎: p. 310-312.
"The second Salem edition appears to have been copied from the first ₍Salem edition₎ that of 1796. In some instances slight departures are made from the copy ... such departures are also departures from the original ₍London edition of 1700₎"--S. G. Drake, pref. to ed. of 1866.

Moreau, Pierre, Tourangeau.

see

Morellus, Petrus, Turonensis.

Moreau Tourangeau, Pierre.

see

Morellus, Petrus, Turonensis.

Morel, Auguste, 1820-1874.

WITCHCRAFT
BT
980
M83

Histoire du diable pendant la mission de Jésus-Christ en Palestine d'après les documents officiels, les travaux des publicistes et les monuments de l'art.   Paris, E. Dentu, 1861.
193 p. 14cm.

8
NIC

1. Devil.   2. Jesus Christ.   3. Jesus Christ--Temptation.   4. Devil --Biblical teaching.   I. Title.

Morel, Frédéric, 1558-1630.

WITCHCRAFT
BF
1508
P97
1615

Psellus, Michael.
₍Michaelou tou Psellou Peri energeias daimōnōn dialogos₎ Μιχαήλου του Ψέλλου Περὶ ἐνέργειας δαιμόνων διάλογος. Michaelis Pselli De operatione daemonum dialogus. Gilbertus Gavlminvs Molinensis primus Graecè edidit & notis illustrauit. Lvtetiae Parisiorvm, Sumptibus Hieronymi Drovart, 1615.
8 p. l., 153, ₍7₎ p. 17cm.
Latin and   Greek on facing pages.

8
NIC

(Continued on next card)

Morel, Frédéric, 1558-1630.

WITCHCRAFT
BF
1508
P97
1615

Psellus, Michael. ₍Michaelou tou Psellou Peri energeias daimōnōn dialogos₎   1615. (Card 2)

Latin translation by Petrus Morellus, "illius qui & Nicetae Thesaurum orthodoxe fidei de Graeco Latinum fecit."
Frédéric Morel also given credit in introduction for editing.
"Notae ad Michaelis Pselli dialogum," p. ₍103₎-153,   has special t. p.
I. Morel,   Frédéric, 1558-1630.

8
NIC

Morel, Petrus.

see

Morellus, Petrus, Turonensis.

Morellus, Petrus, Turonensis, tr.

WITCHCRAFT
BF
1508
P97
1688

Psellus, Michael.
₍Michaelou tou Psellou Peri energeias daimōnōn dialogos₎ Μιχαήλου του Ψέλλου Περὶ ἐνέργειας δαιμόνων διάλογος. Michaelis Pselli De operatione daemonum dialogus. Gilbertus Gaulminus Molinensis primus Graecè edidit & notis illustravit. E museo Dan. Hasenmülleri ... Kiloni, Sumtibus Joh. Sebastiani Richelii, 1688.
6 p. l., 166 p. 15cm.

8
NIC

(Continued on next card)

400

CATALOGUE OF THE CORNELL WITCHCRAFT COLLECTION

Morellus, Petrus, Turonensis, tr.
WITCHCRAFT   Psellus, Michael. [Michaelou tou Psellou
508   Peri energeias daimonon dialogos]   1688.
97   (Card 2)
88
Latin and Greek on facing pages, with
notes by Gaulmin at bottom of page.
Latin translation by Petrus Morellus,
"illius qui & Nicetae Thesaurum orthodoxae
fidei de Graeco Latinum fecit."
 1. Demonology. I. Gaulmin, Gilbert,
1585-1665, ed.   II. Morellus, Petrus,
C   Turonensis,   tr.   III. Hasenmüller,
               (Continued on next card)

Moreton, Andrew, pseud.

·see

Defoe, Daniel, 1660?-1731.

Morin, Madeleine.
     Lange,   , physician, of Lisieux.
        Histoire de la fille maléficiée de
CRAFT Courson. Avec une dissertation physique
     sur ce maléfice. Par Monsieur Lange, Con-
     seiller Médecin du Roy.   Lisieux, Chez
     J. du Roncerey, 1717 [ca. 1900]
        34 p. 23cm.
        Carnap's manuscript copy.
        "Der Originaldruck von welchem diese Ab-
     schrift genommen wurde, befindet sich in
     der Bibliothè- que Nationale zu Paris
     ... Eine Ab- schrift fertigte der
               (Continued on next card)

Morin, Madeleine.
     Lange,   , physician, of Lisieux.
        Histoire de la fille maléficiée ... 1717
HCRAFT [ca. 1900]   (Card 2)
     daselbst angestellte Bibliothekar J. Her-
     viant an; die vorliegende ist mit desselben
     wörtlich übereinstimmend."
        Numerals in the margins indicate pagina-
     tion of the original work.
        "Notizen über diese Abhandlung" pp. 31-34.
        1. Diseases   --Causes and theories of
     causation.   2. Witchcraft. 3. Morin,
     Madeleine.   I. Title.

---

tchcraft
     Morley, Henry, 1822-1894.
        The life of Henry Cornelius Agrippa von
1   Nettesheim, doctor and knight, commonly known
4   as a magician. London, Chapman and Hall,
5   1856.
        2 v. 21cm.
        Title vignettes.
        At head of title: Cornelius Agrippa.

        1. Agrippa von Nettesheim, Heinrich
     Cornelius,   1486?-1535. I. Title.

La mort et le diable.
craft Gener, Pompeyo, 1846-1920.
        La mort et le diable; histoire et philo-
+   sophie des deux négations suprêmes. Précé-
2   dé d'une lettre a l'auteur de E. Littré.
30   Paris, C. Reinwald, 1880.
        xl, 780 p. 24cm.
        At head of title: Contribution a l'étude
     de l'évolution des idées.
        1. Death. 2. Devil. 3. Good and evil.
     I. Title.

WITCHCRAFT Moser, F   W
PT   Hirsul, die Hexe der Bielshöle. Merse-
2435   burg, Sonntag, 1823.
M58   188 p. 15cm.
H6
1823   Date changed by hand from 1843 to 1823.

8
NIC   I. Title.

Moser, Johann Jacob, 1701-1785.
        Altes und Neues aus dem Reich Gottes.
MSS Hartmann, Andreas.
Bd.   Warhafftige und mit vielen glaubwürdigen
WITCHCRAFT Zeugen bewährte Relation was sich zu
BF   Döffingen, hoch-fürstl. württembergischer
H33 Herrschafft, und Böblinger Amts, mit zwey
     besessenen Weibs-Personen im Monat Decembr.
     1714. mercklich zugetragen hat ... Ans
     Licht gebracht von M. Andreas Hartmann ...
     [n.p.] 1716 [ca. 1900]
        14 l. 18cm.
        Carnap's manuscript copy.
        "Wörtliche   Abschrift aus: Altes
     und Neues aus   dem Reich Gottes und
               (Continued on next card)

Moser, Johann Jacob, 1701-1785.
        Altes und Neues aus dem Reich Gottes.
MSS Hartmann, Andreas. Warhafftige und mit
Bd. vielen glaubwürdigen Zeugen bewährte
WITCHCRAFT Relation ... 1716 [ca. 1900] (Card 2)
BF
H33 der übrigen guten und bösen Geister, etc.
     [hrsg. von J. J. Moser] 9ter Theil. Franck-
     furt u. Leipzig, 1734. 8°. S. 10-28."
        "NB. Diese Besessenheitsgeschichte steht
     auch wörtlich in: Guden, Friedrich,
     Schreckliche Geschichte Teuflischer Besitz-
     ung, in 3 merkw. Historien, etc. Budissin,
     1717. 8°. S.   159-188."
        1. Demoniac   possession. 2. Exorcism.
               (Continued on next card)

Witchcraft
BF   A Most certain, strange, and true discovery
1563   of a vvitch. Being taken by some of the
W81++   Parliament forces, as she was standing on
no.12   a small planck-board and sayling on it
        over the river of Newbury. Together with
        the strange and true manner of her death,
        with the propheticall words and speeches
        she vsed at the same time. [London?]
        Printed by J. Hammond, 1643. [London, at
        the British Museum, 1923]
        7 p. 16cm.
        Photocopy   (negative) 7 p. on 4 l.
     20 x 32cm.
               (Continued on next card)

Witchcraft
BF   A Most certain, strange, and true discovery
1563   of a witch. 1643 [1923] (Card 2)
W81++
no.12   No. 12 in vol. lettered: Witchcraft tracts,
     chapbooks and broadsides, 1579-1704; roto-
     graph copies.

        1. Witchcraft--England.

Witchcraft
BF   The Most crvell and bloody mvrther committed
1563   by ... Annis Dell and her sonne George
W81++   Dell, foure yeeres since, on ... Anthony
no.9   Iames ... and now most miraculously
        reuealed by the sister of the said
        Anthony ... With the seuerall vvitch-
        crafts and most damnable practises of one
        Iohane Harrison and her daughter vpon
        seuerall persons ... who were all
        executed ... the 4 of August last past ...
        London, Pr   inted for W. Firebrand
               (Continued on next card)

Witchcraft
BF   The Most crvell and bloody mvrther... 1606.
1563   [1923]   (Card 2)
W81++
no.9   and J. Wright, 1606. [London, at the British
     Museum, 1923]
        [24] p. 17cm.
        Signatures: A-C⁴.
        Photocopy (negative) 24 p. on 13 l. 20x32cm.
        No. 9 in vol. lettered: Witchcraft tracts
     chapbooks and broadsides, 1579-1704; rotograph
     copies.
        3. Dell, Mrs. Annis, d. 1606. 4. Dell, George,
     d. 1606. 5.   James, Anthony, d. 1602.

The most cruell and bloody murther,
Witchcraft committed by ... Annis Dell.
GR   A Hertfordshire miracle. The most cruell and bloody
142 murther, committed by an inkeeper's wife, called Annis
H6   Dell, and her sonne George Dell, four yeeres since, on the
A3   bodie of a childe called Anthony James in Bishop's Hat-
no.17 field in the countie of Hartford, and now most miracu-
     lously revealed by the sister of the said Anthony, who
     at the time of the murther had her tongue cut out, and
     four yeares remaynes dumme, and speechless, and now
     perfectly speaketh, revealing the murther, having no
               (Continued on next card)
                                            16-25741

The most cruell and bloody murther,
Witchcraft committed by ... Annis Dell.
GR   A Hertfordshire miracle ... (Card 2)
142 tongue to be seen. Who were executed at Hartford the
H6   4 of August last past 1606. Reprinted, with an intro-
A3   ductory by W. B. Gerish. Bishop's Stortford, 1913.
no.17   27 p. 22cm (Hertfordshire folk lore. no.
     The original pamphlet is in 2 parts and is entitled: The most cruell and
     bloody murther committed by ... Annis Dell ... With the severall witch-
     crafts and most damnable practises of one Johane Harrison and her
     daughter ... London, Printed for W. Ferebrand and J. Wright, 1606.
     1. Crime and criminals—England—Hertfordshire. 2. Dell, Mrs. Annis,
     d. 1606. 3. Dell, George, d. 1606. I. Gerish, William Blyth, ed. II. Title:
     The most cruell and bloody murther ...
                                            16-25741
     Library of Congress   GR142.H6A3 no. 13

The most cruell and bloody murther committed
         by ... Annis Dell.
Witchcraft
GR   The severall practices of Johane Harrison
142 and her daughter, condemned and executed
H6   at Hartford for witchcraft, the 4th
A3   August last, 1606. Reprinted from the
no.2 only known copy, with an introduction
     by W. B. Gerish. [Bishop's Stortford?]
     1909.
        15 p. 22cm. [Hertfordshire folk lore.
     no. 2]
        The original pamphlet is in 2 parts and is
     entitled: The mo   st cruell and
               (Continued on next card)

The most cruell and bloody murther committed
         by ... Annis Dell.
Witchcraft
GR   The severall practices of Johane Harrison
142   ... 1909. (Card 2)
H6
A3   bloody murther committed by ... Annis Dell
no.2 ... With the several witchcrafts and most
     damnable practises of one Johane Harrison
     and her daughter ... London, Printed for
     W. Ferebrand and J. Wright, 1606.

Witchcraft Motifs des juges du parlement de Provence.
BF   [Montvalon, André Barrigue de, 1678-1779.
1582   Motifs des juges du parlement de Provence
G51 qui ont été d'avis de condamner le p. Jean
P9++ Baptiste Girard, envoyez à M. le Chancel-
     lier, le 31. decembre 1731. Ensemble la
     lettre de ce magistrat à Mr. le Président
     de Maliverney; la réponse de ce juge, &
     celle des autres messieurs qui ont été de
     son opinion. 3. éd. avec des notes cri-
     tiques tirées de la Procedure & des lettres
     écrites d'Aix, servant de motifs aux juges
     de l'opinion   contraire. On a cité
     ces lettres   sur la premiere éd.
               (Continued on next card)

CATALOGUE OF THE CORNELL WITCHCRAFT COLLECTION

Witchcraft Motifs des juges du parlement de Provence.
BF   [Montvalon, André Barrigue de] 1678-1779.
1582   Motifs des juges ...   (Card 2)
G51
P9++   qui en a été faite à Aix. [Aix?], 1733.
        67 p. 36cm.

        Bound with Girard, J. B. Procedure
        ... Aix, 1733.

        1. Girard, Jean Baptiste, 1680-1733.
        I. Title.

Motzen, Barbara, d. 1668.
WITCHCRAFT
BF   [Schlözer, August Ludwig] 1735-1809, ed.
1583   Hexen Processe aus dem Hennebergschen.
Z7   (In Stats-Anzeigen. Göttingen. 22cm.
1668   2. Bd., Heft 6 (1782), p. 161-168)

        At head of title: 14.

        1. Trials (Witchcraft)--Thuringia.
        2. Motzen, Barbara, d. 1668. I. Title.
8
NIC

WITCHCRAFT
BF   Mouan, J L G
1582   Documents inédits sur un procès de magie
Z7   en Provence. (1318) Paris, Impr. impéri-
1318   ale, 1869.
        [169]-182 p. 25cm.

        Extract from the Mémoires lus à la Sor-
        bonne dans les séances extraordinaires du
        Comité impérial des travaux historiques et
        des sociétés savantes tenues les 14, 15, 16
        et 17 avril 1868. Histoire, philologie et
        sciences morales.
8   1. Trials (Witchcraft)--Aix, France.
NIC   2. Robert de Mauvoisin, abp. of Aix.
        I. Title.

The mowing-devil.
WITCHCRAFT
GR   Strange newes, out of Hartford-shire, and
525   Kent. 1. An account of a mowing-devil
M93   ... 2. A true narrative of a young maid
1679a   who was possest with several devils or
        evil spirits ... London, Printed for
        R. G., 1679 [n. p., 18--?]
        8 p. 14cm.
        Facsimile reprint.
        Item 1. first issued separately, 1678,
        under title: The mowing-devil: or, Strange
        news out of Hartford-shire.
8   1. Spirits. 2. Devil. 3. De-
        moniac possession. I. Title: The
        mowing-devil.

Mozolin, Silvestro, 1456-1527.

see

Mazzolini, Silvestro, da Prierio, 1456-1523.

Mr. de St. André ... Lesenswürdige
Briefe an einige seiner Freunde über
die Materie von der Zaubereÿ.
WITCHCRAFT
BF   Saint André, François de.
1565   Mr. de St. André ... Lesenswürdige Briefe
H97   an einige seiner Freunde uber die Materie
1726   von der Zaubereÿ, den Ubelthaten, so dadurch
        angestifftet werden, und von den Zauberern
        und Hexen insbesondere; worinnen er die wun-
        derbarsten Würckungen, die man gemeiniglich
        den Teuffeln zuschreibet, deutlich erkläret,
        und dabey zeiget, dass diese Geister offt
8
        (Continued on next card)

Mr. de St. André ... Lesenswürdige
Briefe an einige seiner Freunde über
WITCHCRAFT die Materie von der Zaubereÿ.
BF   Saint André, François de. Mr. de St. An-
1565   dré ... Lesenswürdige Briefe ... 1727.
H97   (Card 2)
1726
        nicht den geringsten Antheil daran haben ...
        Statt eines Suplements zum Hutchinson aus
        dem Frantzösischen ins Teutsche übersetzt
        ... von Theodoro Arnold. Leipzig, Bey
        J. C. Martini, 1727.
        10 p. l., 204, [9] p. 22cm.
        Translation of Lettres ... à quel-
8   ques-uns de ses amis, pub. 1725.
        (Continued on next card)

Mr. de St. André ... Lesenswürdige
Briefe an einige seiner Freunde über
WITCHCRAFT die Materie von der Zaubereÿ.
BF   Saint André, François de. Mr. de St. An-
1565   dré ... Lesenswürdige Briefe ... 1727.
H97   (Card 3)
1726
        Title in red and black.
        Bound with Hutchinson, F. Historischer
        Versuch von der Hexereÿ. Leipzig, 1726.
        1. Witchcraft. 2. Magic. I. His
        Lettres ... à quelques-uns de ses amis.
        German. II. Hutchinson, Francis, bp. of
        Down and Connor, 1660-1739. Historischer
        Versuch von der Hexereÿ. III. Arnold,
        Theodor, 1683-1771, tr. IV. Title: Le-
8   senswürdige Briefe ... Über die
        Materie von der Zaubereÿ.

Witchcraft
BF   Mudge, Zachariah Atwell, 1813-1888.
1576   Witch Hill: a history of Salem witchcraft.
M94   Including illustrative sketches of persons and
        places. By Rev. Z. A. Mudge ... Three illus-
        trations. New York, Carlton & Lanahan; San
        Francisco, E. Thomas; etc., etc., 1870.
        322 p. incl. front., 2 pl. 18cm.

        1. Witchcraft--Salem, Mass. I. Title.

WITCHCRAFT
BF   Mühe, Ernst.
1775   Der Aberglaube. Eine biblische Beleuch-
M945   ung der finstern Gebiete der Sympathie,
1886   Zauberei, Geisterbeschwörung &c. 2. verm.
        und verb. Aufl. Leipzig, G. Böhme, 1886.
        48 p. 21cm.

8
NIC   1. Superstition. I. Title.

WITCHCRAFT
BF   Müller, Curt.
1583   Hexenaberglaube und Hexenprozesse in
M94   Deutschland. Leipzig, P. Reclam Jun.
        [1893]
        172 p. 15cm. (Universal-Bibliothek,
        3166-3167)

8   1. Witchcraft--Germany. 2. Trials (Witch-
NIC   craft)--Germany. I. Title.

WITCHCRAFT
BF   Müller, Friedrich.
1584   Beiträge zur Geschichte des Hexenglaubens
T77   und des Hexenprocesses in Siebenbürgen.
M94   Braunschweig, C. A. Schwetschke, 1854.
        77 p. 22cm.

8   1. Witchcraft--Transylvania. 2. Trials
NIC   (Witchcraft)--Transylvania. I. Title.

Müller, Gottlieb.
        Gründlicher Nachricht von einer
WITCHCRAFT begeisterten Weibesperson.
BF   Das Bezauberte Bauermägdgen: oder Geschichte
1555   von dem anjetzo in Kemberg bey Wittenberg
M94   sich aufhaltenden Landmägdgen Johannen
029   Elisabethen Lohmännin; aufgesetzt durch
no.2   einen vom Vorurtheil Befreyeten, und mit
        Anmerkungen eines Rechtsgelahrten verse-
        hen. Breslau, Bey J. E. Meyer, 1760.
        167 p. 18cm.
        No. 2 in vol. lettered Oesfeld u. a. ...
        "Eines Advocatens Ehrenrettung wider ...
        Herrn Gottlieb Müllers Beschuldigung":
8   p. 51-162.
NIC   (Continued on next card)

Müller, Gottlieb.
        Gründlicher Nachricht von einer be-
WITCHCRAFT geisterten Weibesperson.
BF   [Bobbe, Johann Benjamin Gottlieb]
1555   Vermischte Anmerkungen über Sr. Hoch-
M94   ehrwürden des Herrn Probstes und Superin-
B66   tendentens in Kemberg Herrn Gottlieb Müllers
        Gründlichen Nachricht und deren Anhang von
        einer begeisterten Weibesperson Annen El-
        isabeth Lohmännin, mitgetheilet von Antidä-
        moniacus. Bernburg, Bey C. G. Cörner,
        1760.
        134 p. 18cm.
        Attribution by Holzmann.
8
                            (Continued on next card)

Müller, Gottlieb.
        Gründlicher Nachricht von einer be-
WITCHCRAFT geisterten Weibesperson.
BF   Meier, Georg Friedrich, 1718-1777.
1555   Georg Friedrich Meiers ... Philosophische
M94   Gedanken von den Würkungen des Teufels auf
029   dem Erdboden. Halle, C. H. Hemmerde, 1760.
no.6   168 p. 18cm.

        No. 6 in vol. lettered Oesfeld u. a. ...

        1. Müller, Gottlieb. Gründlicher
        Nachricht von einer begeisterten Weibes-
        person. 2.   Devil. I. Title:
        Philosophische Gedanken von den
8 NIC   Würkungen des Teufels.

Müller, Gottlieb.
        Gründlicher Nachricht von einer be-
WITCHCRAFT geisterten Weibesperson.
BF   Semler, Johann Salomo, 1725-1791.
1555   D. Joh. Salomo Semlers ... Abfertigung
M94   der neuen Geister und alten Irtümer in der
029   Lohmannischen Begeisterung zu Kemberg nebst
no.4   theologischem Unterricht von dem Ungrunde
        der gemeinen Meinung von leiblichen Besit-
        zungen der Teufels und Bezauberungen der
        Christen. Halle, Bey J. J. Gebauer, 1760.
        40, 328 p. 18cm.
        Dedication and "Vorrede" comprise the
        first numbering.
8
NIC   (Continued on next card)

Müller, Gottlieb.
        Gründlicher Nachricht von einer be-
WITCHCRAFT geisterten Weibesperson.
BF   Semler, Johann Salomo, 1725-1791. ...
1555   Abfertigung der neuen Geister ... 1760.
M94   (Card 2)
029
no.4   "Anhang. Auszug aus des Chaufepiée [sic]
        Nouveau dictionnaire historique et critique
        von dem Artikel Balthas. Bekker": p. 317-
        328.
        No. 4 in vol. lettered Oesfeld u. a. ...
        1. Lohmännin, Anna Elisabeth. 2. Mül-
        ler, Gottlieb. Gründlicher Nachricht von
        einer begeisterten Weibesperson. 3. Devil
        4. Bekker,   Balthasar, 1634-1698.
8
NIC   Continued on next card

Müller, Gottlieb.
        Gründlicher Nachricht von einer be-
WITCHCRAFT geisterten Weibesperson.
BF   Semler, Johann Salomo, 1725-1791.
1555   D. Joh. Salomo Semlers Anhang zu der
M94   Abfertigung der Lohmannischen Begeisterung,
029   worin fernere historische Umstände gesamlet
no.5   worden. Halle, Bey J. J. Gebauer, 1760.
        112 p. 18cm.
        Title of the original work reads: Ab-
        fertigung der neuen Geister und alten Irtü-
        mer der Lohmannischen Begeisterung. Halle
        1760.
        No. 5 in vol. lettered Oesfeld u. a. ...
8 NIC   (Continued on next card)

CATALOGUE OF THE CORNELL WITCHCRAFT COLLECTION

WITCHCRAFT
R
30
4
M94

Müller, Jacobus Friedrich, praeses.
Disputationem De λυκανθρωπία [lykanthrōpia], seu transmutatione hominum in lupos...examini sistunt publice praeses M. Jacobus Friedrich Müller et respondens Johan. Christoph. Pezelius... Lipsiae, Typis Viduae Joh. Wittigau [1673]
[20] p. 19cm.

Diss.--Leipzig (J. C. Pezelius, respondent

1. Werwolves. I. Pezelius, Johann Christoph, respondent. II. Title.

Witchcraft
BF
1445
D61
no.7

Müller, Jacobus Friedrich, respondent.
Drechssler, Johann Gabriel, d. 1677, praeses.
De spectris, & in specie eorum depulsione, disputationem III. Inclut. facultatis philosoph. Lipsiensis indultu, sub praesidio ... M. Johannis Gabrielis Drechsslers, ... publice defendet respondens Jacobus Friedrich Müller... Lipsiae, Excudebat Samuel Spörel [1670]
[20] p. illus. 21cm.

No. 7 in vol. lettered Dissertationes de spectris. 1646-1753.

(Continued on next card)

WITCHCRAFT
BS
2545
D5
S473

Müller, Joannes Stephanus.
De daemoniacis Semlerianis in duabus dissertationibus theologicis commentatur D. Ioannes Steph. Müllerus. Francofurti et Lipsiae, Apud Theodor. Vilhelm. Ern. Güthium, 1763.
95, 102 p. 23cm.

Each dissertation has separate t.p. (reprints of original title pages) No.1: Notionem δαιμονίου sive δαίμονος olim et inprimis Christi tempore non hoc (Continued on next card)

WITCHCRAFT
BS
2545
D5
S473

Müller, Joannes Stephanus. De daemoniacis Semlerianis...1763. (Card 2)

involuisse vi anima mortui daemon esse crederetur...demonstrat et...praeside...Ioanne Stephano Müllero...defendet Ioann. Burckhard. Caspari. Ienae [1761] No.2: Notio illa animam mortui esse et dici in evangeliis daemonem opinioni debetur...praeside ...Ioanne Stephano Müllero...defendere conatur Georg. Christ. Wagenbronner. Ienae [1762]

(Continued on next card)

WITCHCRAFT
BS
2545
D5
S473

Müller, Joannes Stephanus. De daemoniacis Semlerianis...1763. (Card 3)

I. Semler, Johann Salomo. 1725-1791. De daemoniacis, quorum in Evangeliis fit mentio. 2. Demoniac possession. II. Müller, Joannes Stephanus, praeses. / Notionem δαιμονίου [daimoniou]...anima mortui daemon esse crederetur... III. Müller, Joannes Stephanus, praeses. / Notio illa animam mortui esse et dici in evangeliis daemonem... IV. Caspari, Joannes Burckhardus, respondent. V. Wagenbronner, Georgius Christianus, respondent. VI. Title.

Müller, Joannes Stephanus, praeses.
Notio illa animam mortui esse et dici in evangeliis daemonem.
Müller, Joannes Stephanus.
De daemoniacis Semlerianis in duabus dissertationibus theologicis commentatur D. Ioannes Steph. Müllerus. Francofurti et Lipsiae, Apud Theodor. Vilhelm. Ern. Güthium, 1763.
95, 102 p. 23cm.

Each dissertation has separate t.p. (reprints of original title pages) No.1: Notionem δαιμονίου sive δαίμονος olim et inprimis Christi tempore non hoc (Continued on next card)

WITCHCRAFT
BS
2545
D5
S473

Müller, Joannes Stephanus, praeses.
Notio illa animam mortui esse et dici in evangeliis daemonem.
Müller, Joannes Stephanus. De daemoniacis Semlerianis...1763. (Card 2)

involuisse vi anima mortui daemon esse crederetur...demonstrat et...praeside...Ioanne Stephano Müllero...defendet Ioann. Burckhard. Caspari. Ienae [1761] No.2: Notio illa animam mortui esse et dici in evangeliis daemonem opinioni debetur...praeside ...Ioanne Stephano Müllero...defendere conatur Georg. Christ. Wagenbronner. Ienae [1762]

(Continued on next card)

WITCHCRAFT
BS
2545
D5
S473

Müller, Joannes Stephanus, praeses.
Notionem [daimoniou]...anima mortui daemon esse crederetur.
Müller, Joannes Stephanus. De daemoniacis Semlerianis...1763. (Card 2)

involuisse vi anima mortui daemon esse crederetur...demonstrat et...praeside...Ioanne Stephano Müllero...defendet Ioann. Burckhard. Caspari. Ienae [1761] No.2: Notio illa animam mortui esse et dici in evangeliis daemonem opinioni debetur...praeside ...Ioanne Stephano Müllero...defendere conatur Georg. Christ. Wagenbronner. Ienae [1762]

(Continued on next card)

WITCHCRAFT
BF
1413
M94

Müller, Johann Valentin, 1756-1813.
Entwurf einer gerichtlichen Arzneiwissenschaft.
Müller, Johann Valentin, 1756-1813.
Von Zauberey, Teufelsbesitzungen und Wunderkuren. [Frankfurt, 1796]
359-542 p. 21cm.

Extract from his Entwurf einer gerichtlichen Arzneiwissenschaft, v.2. (Comprises chapter 4)

1. Occult sciences. 2. Witchcraft. 3. Demoniac possession. 4. Medicine, Magic, mystic and spagiric. I. His / Entwurf einer gerichtlichen Arzneiwissenschaft.

WITCHCRAFT
BF
1413
M94

Müller, Johann Valentin, 1756-1813.
Von Zauberey, Teufelsbesitzungen und Wunderkuren. [Frankfurt, 1796]
359-542 p. 21cm.

Extract from his Entwurf einer gerichtlichen Arzneiwissenschaft, v.2. (Comprises chapter 4)

1. Occult sciences. 2. Witchcraft. 3. Demoniac possession. 4. Medicine, Magic, mystic and spagiric. I. His / Entwurf einer gerichtlichen Arzneiwissenschaft. II. Title.

Witchcraft
BF
1583
A2
M94

Müller, Johannes, praeses.
De conventu sagarum in monte Bruckterorum, nocte ante Calendas Maji, disputatio, quam ... praeside ... Dno. M. Johanne Müllern ... exponit Adamus Nicolaus Bersmannus ... Wittebergae, Ex typotheteo Hakiano [1675]
[16] p. 19cm.

1. Witchcraft--Brocken, Germany. 2. Walpurgisnacht. I. Bersmann, Adam Nicolaus, respondent. II. Title.

Witchcraft
BF
1565
D62
no.4

Müller, Johannes, praeses.
De conventu sagarum in monte Bruckterorum, nocte ante Calendas Maji, disputatio, quam ... praeside ... Dno. M. Johanes Müllern ... exponit Adamus Nicolaus Bersmannus ... Wittebergae, Ex typotheteo Hakiano [1675]
[16] p. 20cm.

Interleaved.
No. 4 in vol. lettered Dissertationes de sagis. 1636-1714.

Witchcraft
BF
1565
D62
no.6

Müller, Johannes, praeses.
Disputatio physica De magis tempestates cientibus, qvam ... sub praesidio ... Dn. M. Johannis Mülleri ... publicè pro virili defendet Gottlob Freygang ... Wittenbergae, Literis Matthaei Henckelii [1676]
[16] p. 20cm.

No. 6 in vol. lettered Dissertationes de sagis. 1636-1714.

1. Witchcraft. 2. Weather-lore. I. Freygang, Gottlob, respondent. II. Title: De magis tempestates cientibus. III. Disputatio physica De magis tempestates cientibus.

Müller, Johannes, of Stargard, respondent.

WITCHCRAFT
BF
1556
P47

Petermann, Andreas, 1649-1703, praeses.
Disputatio medica De ephialte seu incubo, quam...sub praesidio...Andr. Petermanni... publicè subjicit Johannes Müller ... Lipsiae, Typis Christophori Fleischeri [1688]
[40] p. 20cm.

Diss.--Leipzig (J. Müller, respondent)

1. Medicine, Magic, mystic and spagiric. 2. Demonology. 3. Diseases--Causes and theories of causation. I. Müller, Johannes, of Stargard, respondent.

Müller, Johannes von, 1752-1809.

Witchcraft
B
2605
Z7
L94

Luden, Heinrich, 1778?-1847.
Christian Thomasius, nach seinen Schicksalen und Schriften dargestellt, von H. Luden. Mit einer Vorrede von Johann von Müller ... Berlin, Bei J. F. Unger, 1805.
xvi, 311 p. 17cm.

1. Thomasius, Christian, 1655-1728--Biog. I. Müller, Johannes von, 1752-1809.

WITCHCRAFT
BF
1569
A2
I596

Müller, Karl Otto, 1884-
Heinrich Institoris, der Verfasser des Hexenhammers, und seine Tätigkeit als Hexeninquisitor in Ravensburg im Herbst 1484.
(In: Württembergische Vierteljahrshefte für Landesgeschichte. Stuttgart. 24cm. new ser. v.19, no.4. 1910. p. 397-417)

I. Institoris, Henricus, d.1508. 2.Trials (Witchcraft) --Ravensburg, Ger. I. Title.

Müller, Maria (Rhinow)

WITCHCRAFT
BF
1583
Z7
1667

Riedel, Adolph Friedrich Johann, 1809-1872.
Ein Hexenprocess, verhandelt bei dem Amtsgerichte zu Neustadt an der Dosse, im Jahre 1667; nach den Akten vom Geheimen Archivrathe Prof. Dr. Riedel. [Berlin, 18--]
[106]-119 p. 25cm.

Caption title.
Detached from Märkische Forschungen.

1. Trials (Witchcraft)--Neustadt, Ger. (Brandenburg) 2. Müller, Maria (Rhinow) I. Title.

403

CATALOGUE OF THE CORNELL WITCHCRAFT COLLECTION

WITCHCRAFT
BF 1583
M945

Müller, Michael Franz Joseph.
  Kleiner Beitrag zur Geschichte des Hexenwesens im XVI. Jahrhundert, aus authentischen Akten ausgehoben. Trier, Bei J. J. Blattau, 1830.
  18 p. 19cm.

  With autograph: Geo. L. Burr.

8
NIC
  1. Witchcraft--Hist. 2. Witchcraft--Treves. 3. Trials (Witchcraft)--Treves.
  I. Title.

---

ar V
13984

Müller, Michael Franz Joseph.
  Ueber das Geschichtliche der Folter und derselben Gebrauch und Missbrauch bei dem peinlichen Verfahren in dem Kurfürstenthum Trier im XVI, XVII und XVIII Jahrhundert, einige Worte. Trier, Blattau, 1831.
  17 p. 19cm.

  1. Torture.   I. Title.

Muis van Holy, Nikolaas, 1654-

see

Holy, Nikolaas Muys van, 1654-

Mulierum lavatio.

WITCHCRAFT
BF 1558
P79

Anten, Conradus ab.
  (Gynaikolousis) Γυναικόλουσις; seu, Mvliervm lavatio, qvam pvrgationem per aqvam frigidam vocant. Item vulgaris de potentia lamiarum opinio, quod vtraq; Deo, natvrae omni iuri et probatae consvetvdini sit contraria. Candida breuis & dilucida oratio. Autore Conrado ab Anten. Lvbecae, In officina typographica Assweri Crögeri, 1590.
  [102] p.   17cm.
  A small   portion of the text is

8
NIC
  (Continued on next card)

Mulierum lavatio.

WITCHCRAFT
BF 1558
P79

Anten, Conradus ab. (Gynaikolousis)
  Γυναικόλουσις...1590. (Card 2)

  in German.
  Bound with: Pomponazzi, Pietro, 1462-1524. De naturalium effectuum causis. Basileae, 1556.

  1. Witchcraft. 2. Trials (Witchcraft)
  I. Title. II. Title: Mulierum lavatio.

Mundane, sub-mundane and super-mundane spiritism.

Witchcraft
BF 1251
B86
A7

Britten, William, supposed author.
  Art magic; or, Mundane, sub-mundane and super-mundane spiritism. A treatise in three parts and twenty-three sections: descriptive of art magic, spiritism, the different orders of spirits in the universe known to be related to, or in communication with man; together with directions for invoking, controlling, and discharging spirits, and the uses and abuses, dangers and possibilities of magical art ... New York, The author, 1876.
  2 p. l., 467 p. front., illus. (incl. ports.) plates. 22½ᶜᵐ
  Copyrighted by William Britten.
  Ed. by Emma Hardinge Britten.
  1. Spiritualism. 2. Magic. ɪ. Britten, Mrs. Emma (Hardinge) ed.
  II. Title.
  Library of Congress   BF1251.B83   10-34083

Munich, Constantinus.

Witchcraft
BF 1563
D61

  Diversi tractatvs: De potestate ecclesiastica coercendi daemones circa energumenos & maleficiatos, de potentia ac viribus daemonum. De modo procedendi adversvs crimina excepta; praecipuè contra sagas & maleficos ... Ex diversis jisqve celeberrimis huius aeui scriptoribus ... disputantur. Coloniae Agrippinae, Sumptibus Constantini Munich bibliopolae, 1629.
  8, 236,   166 p. 20cm.

8
  (Continued on next card)

Munich, Constantinus.

Witchcraft
BF 1563
D61

  Diversi tractatvs ... 1629. (Card 2)

  Contents.--Tractatvs de potestate ecclesiae coercendi daemones circa obsessos & maleficiatos, vnà cum praxi exorcistica, a R. della Torre.--Tractatvs theologicvs de processv adversvs crimina excepta, ac speciatim aduersus crimen veneficij, ab A. Tanner.--Tractatvs alter theologicus de sagis et veneficis, a P. Laymanni.--Consilium de sagis, a M. A. Peregrini.

8
  (Continued on next card)

Munich, Constantinus.

Witchcraft
BF 1563
D61

  Diversi tractatvs ... 1629. (Card 3)

  Title in red and black.
  In double columns except for t. p., dedication, and titles of first, second, and fourth works.
  1. Witchcraft. 2. Trials (Witchcraft)
  3. Exorcism. I. Torre, Raffaelle della. Tractatus de potestate ecclesiae coercendi daemones. II. Tanner, Adam, 1572-1632. Tractatus theologicus de processu adversus

8
  (Continued on next card)

Murder and witchcraft in England, 1550-1640.

HV 6535
B5
M36

Marshburn, Joseph H   1890-
  Murder & witchcraft in England, 1550-1640, as recounted in pamphlets, ballads, broadsides, & plays, by Joseph H. Marshburn. [1st ed.] Norman, University of Oklahoma Press [1972, c1971]
  xxvii, 287 p. illus. 22 cm. $7.95
  Includes bibliographical references.

5
  1. Murder—England—History. 2. Witchcraft—England—History.
  I. Title.
  HV6535.E5M37   364.15'23'0942   78-160497
  ISBN 0-8061-0983-6   MARC
  Library of Congress   72 [4]

Witchcraft
BF 1569
A2
M97
1499

Murner, Thomas, 1475-1537.
  De pythonico contractu. [N. p., n. pr.], after 2 Oct., 1499]
  [12] l. 22cm.

  Leaf [1a] (Title): Tractatus perutilis de phitonico contractu fratris Thome murner liberaliū artium magistri ordinis minorum Ad instantiam Generosi domini Iohannis Wörnher de Mörsperg compilatus.
  Leaf [12a]: Ex vniuersitate Friburgeñ. Sole in .xvij. gradu libre gradiente. M.cccc.-xcix.
  (Continued on next card)

Witchcraft
BF 1569
A2
M97
1499

Murner, Thomas, 1475-1537. De pythonico contractu ... after 2 Oct., 1499. (Card 2)

  Signatures: a-b⁶.
  Ornamental capital I on leaf [2a].
  Hain. Repertorium (with Copinger's Supplement) *11647; Proctor, 3212; Brit. Mus. Cat. (XV cent.) III, 692 (IA. 14018); Goff. Third census, M-877.
  Brit. Mus. Catalog. gives as place and printer: Kirchheim in Elsass, Printer of
  (Continued on next card)

Witchcraft
BF 1569
A2
M97
1499

Murner, Thomas, 1475-1537. De pythonico contractu ... after 2 Oct., 1499. (Card 3)

  Sankt Brandons Leben or Strassburg, Matthias Hupfuff.
  49 blank sheets bound in at end.

  1. Witchcraft.   I. Title.

Witchcraft
BF 1566
M98
1917

Murray, Margaret Alice.
  The god of the witches. [Manchester, 1917]
  49-65 p. 24cm.

  Caption-title.
  "Reprinted from the Journal of the Manchester Egyptian and Oriental Society, 1916-1917."

Witchcraft
BF 1566
M98
1933

Murray, Margaret Alice.
  The god of the witches, by Margaret Alice Murray ... London. S. Low, Marston & co., ltd. [1933]
  ix, 214 p. plates, facsims. 23ᶜᵐ.
  "References": p. 201-208.
  Review copy from the American historical review to George Lincoln Burr.

  1. Witchcraft. 2. Demonology. 3. Magic. 4. Cultus.   I. Title.
  Library of Congress   BF1566.M8   34-41836

BF 1566
M98
1952

Murray, Margaret Alice.
  The god of the witches. New York, Oxford University Press, 1952.
  212 p. illus. 23cm.

  Bibliography: p. 198-207.

  1. Witchcraft. 2. Demonology. 3. Magic. 4. Cultus.   I. Title.

WITCHCRAFT
BF 1566
M98W8

Murray, Margaret Alice.
  The witch-cult in western Europe; a study in anthropology, by Margaret Alice Murray. Oxford, Clarendon press, 1921.
  303, [1] p. 23cm.
  Bibliography: p. [281]-285.
  Bibliographical foot-notes.
  "The mass of existing material on the subject is so great that I have not attempted to make a survey of the whole of European witchcraft, but have confined myself to an intensive study of the cult in Great Britain."--Pref.
  Same. An   other copy.
  I. Title.

BF 1581
M98
1962

Murray, Margaret Alice.
  The witch-cult in Western Europe. Oxford, Clarendon Press [1962]
  303 p. 20 cm. (Oxford paperbacks, no 53)

  1. Witchcraft—Gt. Brit.   I. Title.
  BF1581.M8 1962   133.4'0942   68-296
  Library of Congress   [2]

CATALOGUE OF THE CORNELL WITCHCRAFT COLLECTION

Muschamp children.

Witchcraft
F
563
81++
o.16
　　Wonderfull news from the north; or, A true relation of the sad and grievovs torments inflicted upon ... three children of Mr. George Muschamp ... by witch-craft; and how miraculously it pleased God to strengthen them and to deliver them; as also the prosecution of the sayd witches ... April 1650. Novemb. 25, 1650, Imprimatur John Downame.　London, Printed by T. H., and are to be sold by R. Harper, 1650. ₍London, at the British Museum, 1923₎
　　28 p.　16cm.

(Continued on next card)

Muschamp children.

Witchcraft
F
563
81++
o.16
　　Wonderfull news from the north ... 1650 ₍1923₎　(Card 2)

　　Photocopy (negative) 28 p. on 17 l.　20 x 32cm.
　　No. 16 in vol. lettered: Witchcraft tracts, chapbooks and broadsides, 1579-1704; rotograph copies.

　　1. Muschamp children.　2. Witchcraft--England.

Le musée des sorciers, mages et alchimistes.

Witchcraft
F
412
85+
　　Grillot de Givry, Émile Angelo, 1870-
　　Le musée des sorciers, mages et alchimistes, par Grillot de Givry.　Paris, Librairies de France, 1929.
　　4 p. l., 450 p. ccl. front., illus., col. plates, diagrs. 28cm.

　　"Recueil iconographique de l'occultisme."
　　--Préf.

　　1. Occult　　sciences.　I. Title.

---

ft

9
5
　　Musick, John Roy, 1849-1901.
　　The witch of Salem; or, Credulity run mad, by John R. Musick ... illustrations by F. A. Carter.　New York ₍etc.₎ Funk & Wagnalls company, 1893.
　　viii, 392p.　front., illus., plates, ports.　19ᶜᵐ.　(On cover: Columbian historical novels ₍v.7₎)

　　"Designed to cover twenty years in the history of the United States ... from 1680 to 1700, including all the principal features of this period."

　　1. Witchcraft--New England--Fiction. 2. U. S.--Hist.--Colonial period--Fiction. I. Title.

Library of Congress　　　Z3.F973Wi

7-33323†

WITCHCRAFT
T
80
99
　　Muthreich, Martin.
　　Theologischer Bericht von dem sehr schrecklichen Zornsturm des Teuffels, welchen er zu diese letzten Zeiten auch durch seine Getreue die Zauberer Hexen und der gleichen Unholden spüren lesset... Franckfurt an der Oder, Bey Johann Eichorns S. Wittib., 1649.
　　99 p. 19cm.

3
NIC
　　1. Devil. 2.　　Witchcraft. 3. Storms (in religion,　　folk-lore, etc.) I. Title.

Muys van Holy, Nicolaes, 1654-

see

Holy, Nikolaas Muys van, 1654-

Myntzenbergius, Ioannes, ed.

WITCHCRAFT
BF
1565
J19
　　Jacquier, Nicolas.
　　Flagellvm haereticorvm fascinariorvm, avtore Nicolao Iaqverio. His accesservnt Lamberti Danaei de veneficis dialogi, Ioachimi Camerarii in Plutarchi de oraculorum defectu epistola, Martini de Arles de superstitionibus tractatvs, Ioannis Trithemii de reprobis atq; maleficis qvaestiones III, Thomae Erasti de strigibus liber.　Studio Ioan. Myntzenbergii edita.　Francofvrti ad Moenvm ₍Impressvm apud N. Bassaeum₎ 1581.

8
NIC
　　604 p.　17　　cm.

(Continued on next card)

Les mystères de la science.

Witchcraft
BF
1412
F47
M9+
　　Figuier, Louis, 1819-1894.
　　Les mystères de la science, par Louis Figuier ... Paris, Librairie illustrée ₍1887₎
　　2 v. plates. 28½cm.
　　Contents.--₍I₎ Autrefois. Introduction. Les diables de Loudun. Les convulsionnaires jansénistes. Les prophètes protestants. La baguette divinatoire.--₍II₎ Aujourd'hui. Les prodiges de Cagliostro. Le magnétisme animal. Les magnétiseurs mystiques. La fille électrique. Les escargots sympathiques. Les esprits frappeurs. Les tables tournantes et les médiums. Les spirites.　　L'hypnotisme.

Mysteries.

Witchcraft
BF
1411
E46
2 copies
　　Elliott, Charles Wyllys, 1817-1883.
　　Mysteries; or, Glimpses of the supernatural, containing accounts of the Salem witchcraft, the Cock-lane ghost, the Rochester rappings, the Stratford mysteries, oracles, astrology, dreams, demons, ghosts, spectres, &c. ... New York, Harper & Brothers, 1852.
　　273 p. illus. (plan) 20cm.

I. Title.

The mysteries of all nations.

WITCHCRAFT
BF
1411
G76
　　Grant, James.
　　The mysteries of all nations: rise and progress of superstition, laws against and trials of witches, ancient and modern delusions, together with strange customs, fables, and tales ... Leith, Scot., Reid ₍1880₎
　　xxviii, 640 p. 23cm.

　　Title on spine: Superstitions, demonology, witchcraft and popular delusions.

　　1. Superstitions. I. Title.

Witchcraft
BF
1681
R62
　　The mysteries of astrology, and the wonders of magic.
　　Roback, C　　W
　　The mysteries of astrology, and the wonders of magic: including a history of the rise and progress of astrology, and the various branches of necromancy; together with valuable directions and suggestions relative to the casting of nativities, and predictions by geomancy, chiromancy, physiognomy, &c.; also, highly interesting narratives, anecdotes, &c., illustrative of the marvels of witchcraft, spiritual phenomena, and the results of supernatural influence.　Boston. Author, 1854.
　　ccxxxviii p.　24cm.

Witchcraft
BF
1612
C75
M9
　　The mysteries of magic.
　　₍Constant, Alphonse Louis₎ 1810?-1875.
　　The mysteries of magic: a digest of the writings of Éliphas Lévi ₍pseud.₎　With biographical and critical essay, by Arthur Edward Waite ... London, G. Redway, 1886.
　　xliii, 349 p. 22½ᶜᵐ.

1. Magic.　I. Waite, Arthur Edward, 1857-1942.　II. Title.

11--14358

Mysterium de daemonibus sive geniis atque intelligentiis philosophicum revelatum.

Witchcraft
BF
1520
F92
　　Frobes, Johann Nikolaus, 1701-1756.
　　Mysterivm de daemonibvs sive geniis atqve intelligentiis philosophicvm strictim et fideliter revelatvm.　Helmstadii, Ex Officina Schnorriana, 1748.
　　lxxv p. 22cm.

1. Demonology. 2. Spirits. 3. Angels.
I. Title: Mysterium de daemonibus sive geniis atque intelligentiis philosophicum revelatum.

The mystery of witch-craft.

Witchcraft
BF
1581
A2
C77
　　Cooper, Thomas, fl. 1598-1626.
　　The mystery of witch-craft, discovering the truth, nature, occasions, growth and power therof; together with the detection and punishment of the same. As also, the seuerall stratagems of Sathan ... London, N. Okes, 1617.
　　₍368₎ p. 14cm.

　　Later ed., 1622, has title: Sathan transformed into an　　angell of light.
　　1. Witch-　　craft. I. Title.

La mystique divine distinguée des contrefaçons diaboliques et des analogies humaines.

Witchcraft
BV
5091
C7
R48
1895
　　Ribet, Jérôme, 1837-1909.
　　La mystique divine distinguée des contrefaçons diaboliques et des analogies humaines. Nouv. éd. Paris, Ch. Poussielgue, 1895-1903.
　　4 v. 21cm.

　　Contents.--Part 1. Les phénomènes mystiques. v.1. La contemplation.--v.2. Les phénomènes distincts de la contemplation.--Part 2. Les causes des phénomènes mystiques. v.3. Les contrefaçons diaboliques.--v.4. Les analogies humaines.

Witchcraft
BV
5081
G59
1861
　　La mystique divine, naturelle et diabolique.
　　Görres, Johann Joseph von, 1776-1848.
　　La mystique divine, naturelle et diabolique; ouvrage traduit de l'allemand par M. Charles Sainte-Foi. 2. éd. Paris, Mᵐᵉ Vᵉ Poussielgue-Rusand, 1861-62.
　　5 v. 18cm.

　　Translation of Die christliche Mystik.

　　1. Mysticism. 2. Occult sciences. 3. Demonomania.　I. Görres, Johann Joseph von, 1776-1848. Die christliche Mystik--French. II. Sainte-Foi, Charles, 1806-1861, tr. III. Title.

CATALOGUE OF THE CORNELL WITCHCRAFT COLLECTION

N

Witchcraft
BX 9479 B42 B11 no.19
N., N.
Brief, aan een predikant, noopens den tegenwoordigen staat des geschils, over den duivel. Amsterdam, By J. de Veer gedrukt, 1696.
28 p. title vignette, illus. initial. 20 x 15cm.
4°: A-C⁴, D².
Signed: N. N. [not Jacobus Schuts]
On the controversy over Balthasar Bekker's De betoverde weereld.
No. 19 in vol. lettered B. Bekkers sterfbed en andere tractaten.

8 (Continued on next card)

Witchcraft
BX 9479 B42 B11 no.19
N. N.
Brief, aan een predikant, noopens den tegenwoordigen staat des geschils, over den duivel. Amsterdam, By J. de Veer gedrukt, 1696.
28 p. title vignette, illus. initial. 20 x 15cm.
4°: A-C⁴, D².
Signed: N. N. [not Jacobus Schuts]
On the controversy over Balthasar Bekker's De betoverde weereld.
No. 19 in vol. lettered B. Bekkers sterfbed en andere tractaten.

8 (Continued on next card)

Witchcraft
BF 1584 S9 B11
Några ord om trolldomswäsendet i Swerige på 1600-talet.
Bååth, Albert Ulrik, 1853-1912.
Några ord om trolldomswäsendet i Swerige på 1600-talet. [Stockholm, 1887]
[195]-205 p. 21cm.

Caption title.
Detached from Läsning för folket, 1887.

1. Witchcraft--Sweden. 2. Witchcraft--Dalecarlia, Sweden. I. Title. II. Läsning för svenska folket.

8

Witchcraft
BF 1410 B42 1691a no.5
Naakt verhaal van alle de kerkelike handelingen, voorgevallen in den Kerkenraad en de Classis van Amsterdam ...
Bekker, Balthasar, 1634-1698.
Naakt verhaal van alle de kerkelike handelingen, voorgevallen in den Kerkenraad en de Classis van Amsterdam, alsmede in de Synoden van Noord-Holland, tsedert den 31. May 1691. tot den 21. Aug. 1692. na vervolg des tijds uit de eigene acten en bygevoegde stukken der voornoemde kerklike vergaderingen tsaamgesteld, en met aantekeningen van den auteur over verscheidene omstandigheden breder verklaard. Amsterdam, By D. vanden Dalen, boekverkooper, 1692.

(Continued on next card)

Witchcraft
BF 1410 B42 1691a no.5
Naakt verhaal van alle de kerkelike handelingen, voorgevallen in den Kerkenraad en de Classis van Amsterdam ...
Bekker, Balthasar, 1634-1698. Naakt verhaal van alle de kerkelike handelingen ... 1692. (Card 2)
6 p. l., 80, 40, 78 p. [p. 79-80 blank] title vignette, illus. initials. 20 x 16cm.
4°: *⁴, 2*², A-C⁴, D², E-K⁴, L², 2A-2E⁴, 3A-3K⁴.
Black letter.
Introduction autographed by Bekker.
Variant of van der Linde 50:

(Continued on next card)

8

Witchcraft
BF 1410 B42 1691a no.5
Naakt verhaal van alle de kerkelike handelingen, voorgevallen in den Kerkenraad en de Classis van Amsterdam ...
Bekker, Balthasar, 1634-1698. Naakt verhaal van alle de kerkelike handelingen ... (Card 3)
Nader beright, p. 73-78, added.
No. 5 in vol. lettered B. Bekker. Betoverde weereld.
I. Nederlandse Hervormde Kerk. Classes. Amsterdam. II. Nederlandse Hervormde Kerk. Synode van Noordholland, Edam, 1691. III. Title.

8

Witchcraft
BF 1410 B42 Z86 no.1
Naakte uitbeeldinge van alle de vier boeken der Betoverde weereld.
Bekker, Balthasar, 1634-1698.
Naakte uitbeeldinge van alle de vier boeken der Betoverde weereld, uitgegeven door Baltasar Bekker, S. S. Th. Dr. predikant tot Amsterdam. Vertonende het oogmerk van den schryver, de schikkinge van 't werk en sijn eigentlyk gevoelen daar in voorgesteld en voorgestaan; tot wechneeminge van vooroordeelen, en een kort begryp des ganschen werx. Ingesteld door den selfden auteur. Amsterdam, By D. van den Dalen, boekverkoper, 1693.

(Continued on next card)

Witchcraft
BF 1410 B42 Z86 no.1
Naakte uitbeeldinge van alle de vier boeken der Betoverde weereld.
Bekker, Balthasar, 1634-1698. Naakte uitbeeldinge van alle de vier boeken der Betoverde weereld ... 1693. (Card 2)
2 p. l., 32 p. title and end page vignettes, illus. initials. 19 x 15cm.
4°: *², a-d⁴.
Black letter.
Introduction autographed by Bekker.
Van der Linde 21.
No. 1 in vol. lettered Tractaten voor en tegen B. Bekker.

(Continued on next card)

MSS Bd. WITCHCRAFT BF N12
Nachricht von einer Weibes-Person, so sich dem bösen Feinde mit Leib und Seel ergeben, auch wieder erlöset worden. Augspurg, 1671 [ca. 1900]
4 l. 23cm.

Carnap's manuscript copy.
"Originaldruck in der Kgl. Universitäts-Bibliothek zu Leipzig. 2 B. in 4°."
Numerals in the margins indicate pagination of the original.
1. Devil. 2. Witchcraft. 3. Schillerin, Regina.

Witchcraft
BF 1566 D13
Nachtfrauen und Galsterweiber.
Dahl, Jürgen.
Nachtfrauen und Galsterweiber; eine Naturgeschichte der Hexe. [Ebenhausen bei München] Langewiesche-Brandt [1960]
95 p. illus. 19cm.

WITCHCRAFT
BF 1566 S47
Die Nachtseite der Natur, Zauberwerk und Hexenwesen.
Sepp, Johann Nepomuk, 1816-1908.
Orient und Occident. Hundert Kapitel über die Nachtseite der Natur, Zauberwerk und Hexenwesen in alter und neuer Zeit. Berlin, A. Schwetschke, 1903.
312 p. 23cm.

1. Witchcraft. 2. Magic. 2. Folklore, Germanic. 4. Folk-lore--Classification. I. Title. II. Title: Die Nachtseite der Natur, Zauberwerk und Hexenwesen.

8 NIC

BF 1582 N25
Najean, Henry.
Le Diable et les sorcières chez les Vosgiens. 88 Saint-Dié, impr. Loos, 11, rue de Robache, 1970.
187 p. plates. 22cm.
Bibliography: p. [183]-[184]

1. Witchcraft--Vosges Mountains. 2. Demonology. I. Title

NIC   MAR 21, '74   COOxc   73-30902

WITCHCRAFT
BF 1555 N19
Nanz, Carl Friedrich.
Die Besessenen im Neuen Testamente. Ein exegetischer Versuch mit Rücksicht auf Dr. Strauss Leben Jesu. Reutlingen, J. C. Marcken, 1840.
ii, 42 p. 21cm.

1. Strauss, David Friedrich, 1808-1874. Das Leben Jesu. 2. Demoniac possession. 3. Bible. N.T.--Criticism, interpretation, etc. 4. Jesus Christ. I. Title.

8 NIC

Witchcraft
BF 1581 Z7 1762
A narrative of some extraordinary things that happened to Mr. Richard Giles's children at the Lamb...
Durbin, Henry.
A narrative of some extraordinary things that happened to Mr. Richard Giles's children at the Lamb, without Lawford's-Gate, Bristol, supposed to be the effect of witchcraft. By the late Mr Henry Durbin ... To which is added, a letter from the Rev. Mr. Bedford ... to the Bishop of Glocester, relative to one Thomas Perks, of Mangotsfield, who had dealings with familiar spirits. Bristol, Printed and sold by R. Edwards, 1800.
60 p. 21cm.

Witchcraft
BF 1581 Z7 1711
A narrative of some strange events that took place in Island Magee and neighbourhood, in 1711; in consequence of which several persons were tried and convicted at Carrickfergus, for witchcraft. By an eye witness Belfast, Printed by J. Smyth, 1822.
57 p. 19cm.

Appendix (p. [47]-57): Dr. Wm. Tisdall's account of the trial of eight reputed witches at Carrickfergus, March 31st, 1711. (Copied from the Hibernian magazine, for Jan. 1775, p. 52.) (Over)

CATALOGUE OF THE CORNELL WITCHCRAFT COLLECTION

WITCHCRAFT
BF
1555
N23
1788

A Narrative of the extraordinary case, of Geo. Lukins, of Yatton, Somersetshire, who was possessed of evil spirits for near eighteen years, also an account of his remarkable deliverance ... extracted from the manuscripts of several persons who attended. To which is prefixed a letter from the Rev. W. R. W. With the Rev. Mr. Easterbrook's letter annex'd ... 2d ed. Bristol, Printed by Bulgin and Rosser, and sold by W. Bulgin

(Continued on next card)

8

WITCHCRAFT
BF
1555
N23
1788

A Narrative of the extraordinary case, of Geo. Lukins ... 1788. (Card 2)

gin [etc] 1788.
24 p. 21cm.

1. Demoniac possession. 2. Exorcism. 3. Lukins, George, fl. 1788. I. W. R. W. II. W., R. W. III. Easterbrook, Joseph.

8

Witchcraft
BF
1581
Z7
1775

A Narrative of the sufferings and relief of a young girl [Christian Shaw] strangely molested by evil spirits and their instruments in the West; collected from authentic testimonies, with a preface and postscript. Containing reflections on what is most material or curious, either in the history or trial of the seven witches who were condemned and burnt in the Gallow-Green of Paisley ... Paisley, Printed and sold by A. Weir, 1775. 120 p. 17cm.

1. Shaw, Christian, fl. 1697. 2. Demoniac possession. 3. Witchcraft.

Narratives of sorcery and magic.
Wright, Thomas, 1810-1877.
Narratives of sorcery and magic, from the most authentic sources. By Thomas Wright ... New York, Redfield, 1852.
1 p. l., [5]-420 p. 19½ᶜᵐ.

First published in London, 1851.

1. Magic. 2. Witchcraft. I. Title.
                                           11—14498
Library of Congress   BF1589.W8 1852
                       [41d1]

Narratives of the witchcraft cases, 1648-1706.
Burr, George Lincoln, 1857-1938, ed.
Narratives of the witchcraft cases, 1648-1706, ed. by George Lincoln Burr ... with three facsimiles. New York, C. Scribner's sons, 1914.
xviii, 467 p. 3 facsim. 23cm. (Original narratives of early American history)

Inscribed to President A. D. White by the author.

(Continued on next card)

Narratives of the witchcraft cases, 1648-1706.
Burr, George Lincoln, 1857-1938, ed.
Narratives of the witchcraft cases ... 1914. (Card 2)

Contents.--From "An essay for the recording of illustrious providences" ... by Increase Mather, 1684.--The New York cases of Hall and Harrison, 1665, 1670.--"Lithobolia, or The stone-throwing devil", by Richard Chamberlain, 1698.--The Pennsylvania cases of Mattson, Hendrickson, and Guard, 1684, 1701.--"Memorable providences, relating to witchcrafts

(Continued on next card)

Narratives of the witchcraft cases, 1648-1706.
Witchcraft
BF
1573
A2
B96

Burr, George Lincoln, 1857-1938.
Narratives of the witchcraft cases ... 1914. (Card 3)

Contents--Continued.
and possessions", by Cotton Mather, 1689.--"A brief and true narrative of witchcraft at Salem village", by Deodat Lawson, 1692.--Letter of Thomas Brattle, F.R.S., 1692.--Letters of Governor Phips to the home government, 1692, 1693.--From "The wonders of the invisible world" by Cotton Mather, 1693.--"A brand pluck' out of the burning", by Cotton Mather, 1693.--

(Continued on next card)

Narratives of the witchcraft cases, 1648-1706.
Witchcraft
BF
1573
A2
B96

Burr, George Lincoln, 1857-1938, ed.
Narratives of the witchcraft cases... 1914. (Card 4)

Contents--Continued.
From "More wonders of the invisible world", by Robert Calef.--From "A modest inquiry into the nature of witchcraft", by John Hale, 1702.--The Virginia case of Grace Sherwood, 1706.

1. Witchcraft. 2. Witchcraft--New England. I. Title.

Nathanaelis Falcken ... Dissertationes quatuor, De daemonologia recentiorum autorum falsa.
Witchcraft
BF
1520
F17

Falck, Nathanael, 1663-1693.
Nathanaelis Falcken ... Dissertationes quatuor, De daemonologia recentiorum autorum falsa, Anno 1692. Wittebergae habitae, nunc verò praefixis literis Schomerianis ibidem recusae. [Wittebergae] Typis Martini Schultzii, 1694.
92 p. illus. initials. 20 x 16cm.
4°: A², B-M⁴, N².

Contents.--De falsa recentiorum auctorum daemonologia ... respondente Joh.

(Continued on next card)

8

Nathanaelis Falcken ... Dissertationes quatuor, De daemonologia recentiorum autorum falsa.
Witchcraft
BF
1520
F17

Falck, Nathanael, 1663-1693. Nathanaelis Falcken ... Dissertationes quatuor ... 1694. (Card 2)

Contents--Continued.
Isaaco Trempenau.--Dissertatio II. Ortum daemonologiae falsae & progressum historicè declarans, respondente Johanne Furmann.--Dissertatio III. De daemonologia Hobbesii & Spinozae, respondente Jac. Friderico Mollero.--Dissertatio IV. De daemonolo-

(Continued on next card)

8

Nathanaelis Falcken ... Dissertationes quatuor, De daemonologia recentiorum autorum falsa.
Witchcraft
BF
1520
F17

Falck, Nathanael, 1663-1693. Nathanaelis Falcken ... Dissertationes quatuor ... 1694. (Card 3)

gia Bekkeri & aliorum, respondente Georg. Abrahamo Wolf.

1. Demonology. 2. Hobbes, Thomas, 1588-1679. Elementa philosophica de cive. 3. Spinoza, Benedictus de, 1632-1677. Tractatus theologico-politicus. 4. Bekker, Balthasar, 1634-1698. De betoverde weereld. I. Title: De daemonologia recentiorum autorum falsa.

8

Natural magic.
WITCHCRAFT
BF
1042
B84
1842

Brewster, Sir David, 1781-1868.
Letters on natural magic, addressed to Sir Walter Scott, bart ... 5th ed. London, J. Murray, 1842.
viii, 351 p. illus., diagrs. 16cm.
[Family library. Murray ed. v. 1]

1. Scientific recreations. I. Title. II. Title: Natural magic.

8
NIC

The nature and circumstances of the demoniacks in the Gospels.
Witchcraft
BT
355
F23
1768

Barker, Thomas, 1722-1809.
The nature and circumstances of the demoniacks in the Gospels, stated and methodized, and considered in the several particulars. ... London, Printed for B. White, 1783.
vi, 56 p. 22cm.

Bound with c.1 of Farmer, Hugh. An inquiry into the nature and design of Christ's temptation in the wilderness. London [1768?]

1. Demoniac possession. 2. Bible. N.T.--Commentaries. I. Title.

Naturforschung und Hexenglaube.
WITCHCRAFT
BF
1566
Z94

Zuccalmaglio, Anton Wilhelm Florentin von, 1803-1869.
Naturforschung und Hexenglaube. Von Wilhelm von Waldbrühl [pseud.] Berlin, C. G. Lüderitz [1867].
39 p. 21cm. (Sammlung gemeinverständlicher wissenschaftlicher Vorträge, 2. Ser., Heft 46)

Note by G. L. Burr on p. [5]: "A very careless booklet. It has led many astray by its misstatements of fact -- me for instance."

8

Naturgeschichte des Teufels.
Witchcraft
BT
980
G73
1889

Graf, Arturo.
Naturgeschichte des Teufels. Einzige vom Verfasser autorisierte deutsche Ausg. Aus dem Italienischen von R. Teuscher. Jena, H. Costenoble [1889]
xviii, 448 p. 18cm.

1. Devil. I. Graf, Arturo. Il diavolo--German. II. Title.

Naudaeus, Gabriel, 1600-1653.

see

Naudé, Gabriel, 1600-1653.

WITCHCRAFT
BF
1589
N29
1712

Naudé, Gabriel, 1600-1653.
Apologie pour les grands hommes soupçonnez de magie. Dernière éd. où l'on a ajouté quelques remarques. Amsterdam, Chez Jean Frédéric Bernard, 1712.
470 p. front. 16cm.

First published in 1625 with title: Apologie pour tous les grands personnages qui ont esté faussement soupçonnez de magie.

Ex libris: Guillaume Doubigny.
I. Title.

8
NIC

Lavoisier
BF
1589
N29
1712

Naudé, Gabriel, 1600-1653.
Apologie pour les grands hommes soupçonnez de magie. Dernière éd. où l'on a ajouté quelques remarques. Amsterdam, Chez Jean Frédéric Bernard, 1712.
470 p. front. 16cm.

First published in 1625 with title: Apologie pour tous les grands personnages qui ont esté faussement soupçonnez de magie.

CATALOGUE OF THE CORNELL WITCHCRAFT COLLECTION

WITCHCRAFT
BF 1589
N29
1669
   Naudé, Gabriel, 1600-1653.
     Apologie pour tous les grands hommes, qui ont esté accusez de magie. Par Mr Navdé. Paris, Chez François Eschart, 1669.
     12 p. l., 502 p. 15cm.
     First published 1625 under title: Apologie pour tous les grands personnages qui ont esté faussement soupçonnez de magie.
     Half title: Apologie des grands hommes accusez de magie.
     Imperfect copy: p. 493-502 (end of Table des matieres) badly mutilated.
     I. Title.   II. Title: Apologie des grands hommes accusez de magie.
8 NIC

WITCHCRAFT
BF 1565
R34
   Naudé, Gabriel, 1600-1653.
     Apologie pour tous les grands hommes. German.
     Reiche, Johann, ed.
     Herrn D. Christian Thomasii ... Kurtze Lehr-Sätze von dem Laster der Zauberey, nach dem wahren Verstande des lateinischen Exemplars ins Deutsche übersetzet, und aus den berühmten Theologi D. Meyfarti, Naudaei, und anderer gelehrter Männer Schrifften erleutert ... nebst einigen Actis magicis herausgegeben von Johann Reichen. Halle im Magdeburgischen, Im Rengerischen Buchladen, 1704.
     2 v. in 1. 21cm.
8 NIC   (Continued on next card)

WITCHCRAFT
BF 1565
R34
   Naudé, Gabriel, 1600-1653. Apologie pour tous les grands hommes. German.
     Reiche, Johann, ed. Herrn D. Christian Thomasii ... Kurtze Lehr-Sätze ... 1704. (Card 2)
     Vol. 1 has special t. p.: Fernerer Unfug der Zauberey. Halle im Magdeburgischen, 1704.
     Vol. 2 has special t. p.: Unterschiedliche Schrifften von Unfug des Hexen-Processes. Halle im Magdeburg., 1703.
     Contents.--[1. Bd.] Gabriel Naudaei
8 NIC   (Continued on next card)

WITCHCRAFT
BF 1565
R34
   Naudé, Gabriel, 1600-1653. Apologie pour tous les grands hommes. German.
     Reiche, Johann, ed. Herrn D. Christian Thomasii ... Kurtze Lehr-Sätze ... 1704. (Card 3)
     Contents.--Continued.
     Schutz-Schrifft [tr. of Apologie pour tous les grands hommes]--Geschichte der Teuffel zu Loüin.--Trauer-Geschichte von der greulichen Zauberey Ludwig Goffredy [tr. of De l'horrible & épouvantable sorcellerie de Louis Goffredy, author F. de Rosset]--D. Christian Thomasii ... Kurtze Lehr-Sätze von
8 NIC   (Continued on next card)

WITCHCRAFT
BF 1565
R34
   Naudé, Gabriel, 1600-1653. Apologie pour tous les grands hommes. German.
     Reiche, Johann, ed. Herrn D. Christian Thomasii ... Kurtze Lehr-Sätze ... 1704. (Card 4)
     Contents--Continued.
     dem Laster der Zauberey [tr. of Dissertatio de crimine magiae, J. Reiche, respondent]--[2. Bd.] Malleus judicium oder Gesetz-Hammer der unbarmhertzigen Hexen-Richter.--Cautio criminalis [von F. Spee]--D. Johann Matthäus Meyfarths Christliche Erinnerung an Regenten.-- Viererley Sorten Hexen-Acta.
8 NIC   (Continued on next card)

WITCHCRAFT
BF 1589
N29
   Naudé, Gabriel, 1600-1653.
     Apologie povr tovs les grands personnages qui ont esté faussement soupçonnes de magie. Par G. Navdé paris. Paris, Chez François Targa, 1625.
     12 p. l., 615 [i.e., 649], [23] p. 17cm.
     Page 641-649 incorrectly numbered 607-615.
     First edition.
     1. Magic--History. 2. Learning and scholarship--History. I. Title: Apologie pour tous les grands personnages qui ont esté faussement soupçonnez de magie.
8

BF 1597
N29
1972
   Naudé, Gabriel, 1600-1653.
     Apologie pour tous les grands personnages qui ont esté faussement soupçonnez de magie, par G. Naudé. Farnborough, Gregg, 1972.
     [24], 638 [i. e. 672] p. 18 cm. index. £10.80   B 72-22086
     Reprint of the Paris, 1625 ed.

     1. Magic. I. Title.
4 NIC
BF1597.N3 1972   72-364008
ISBN 0-576-12183-9
Library of Congress   72

Witchcraft
BF 1602
J19
1674
   Naudé, Gabriel, 1600-1653. Apologie pour tous les grands personnages.
     Jacques d'Autun, Father, 1608 (ca.)-1678.
     L'incredvlité sçavante, et la credvlité ignorante: au sujet des magiciens et des sorciers. Auecque la response à vn liure intitulé Apologie pour tous les grands personnages, qui ont esté faussement soupçonnés de magie. Par le R.P. Iaqves d'Avtvn, predicateur Capucin. Lyon, Iean Certe, 1674.
     [40], 1108, [24] p. 24cm.
     Title vignette (woodcut)

WITCHCRAFT
BF 1589
N29
1657
   Naudé, Gabriel, 1600-1653.
     Apologie pour tous les grands personnages qui ont esté faussement soupçonnez de magie. English.
     The history of magick by way of apology, for all the wise men who have unjustly been reputed magicians, from the creation, to the present age. Written in French, by G. Naudaeus ... Englished by J. Davies. London, Printed for John Streater, 1657.
     8 p. l., 306, [2] p. 18cm.
     Publisher's catalog p. [307]-[308]
     Translation of Apologie pour tous les grands personnages qui ont esté faussement soupçonnez de magie (1625).
     Wing N246.
8   (Continued on next card)

WITCHCRAFT
BF 1589
N29
1657
   Naudé, Gabriel, 1600-1653.
     The history of magick by way of apology, for all the wise men who have unjustly been reputed magicians, from the creation, to the present age. Written in French, by G. Naudaeus ... Englished by J. Davies. London, Printed for John Streater, 1657.
     8 p. l., 306, [2] p. 18cm.
     Publisher's catalog p. [307]-[308]
     Translation of Apologie pour tous les grands personnages qui ont esté faussement soupçonnez de magie (1625).
     Wing N246.
8   (Continued on next card)

WITCHCRAFT
BF 1589
N29
1657
   Naudé, Gabriel, 1600-1653. The history of magick ... 1657. (Card 2)

     1. Magic--History. 2. Learning and scholarship--History. I. His Apologie pour tous les grands personnages qui ont esté faussement soupçonnez de magie. English. II. Davies, John, 1625-1693, tr. III. Title.
8

Witchcraft
BF 1598
A27
O2
1727
   Naudé, Gabriel, 1600-1653.
     Agrippa von Nettesheim, Heinrich Cornelius, 1486?-1535.
     La philosophie occulte. Divisée en trois livres, et traduite du Latin. La Haye, R. Chr. Alberts, 1727.
     2 v. in 1. illus. 19cm.
     Title vignettes, engraved.
     "Apologie pour Agrippa, par Mr. G. Naudé": v. 1, p. [3]-[21] (From his Apologie pour les grands hommes soupçonnez de magie)
     Translation of De occulta philosophia.

WITCHCRAFT
BT 980
N32
   Navarro, Gaspar.
     Tribunal de superstición ladina, explorador del saber, astucia, y poder del demonio en que se condena lo que suele correr por bueno en hechizos, agueros, ensalmos, vanos saludadores, maleficios, cõjuros, arte notoria, cavalista y paulina, y semejantes acciones vulgares. Dirigido a Jesus Nazareno. Huesca, Por Pedro Bluson, 1631.
     122 l. 21cm.

     1. Devil.   2. Demonology. 3. Occult sciences. I. Title.
8 NIC

Witchcraft
BF 1565
N33
   Naylor, Martin Joseph.
     The inanity [sic] and mischief of vulgar superstitions. Four sermons preached at All-Saint's church, Huntingdon, on the 25th day of March, in the years 1792, 1793, 1794, 1795. To which is added some account of the witches of Warboys ... Cambridge, Printed by B. Flower for J. Deighton & W. H. Lunn, 1795.
     xi, 129 p. 21cm.

     1. Superstition. 2. Witchcraft. I. Title. II. Title: The witches of Warboys.

Witchcraft
PS 2459
N28
R15
   Neal, John, 1793-1876.
     Rachel Dyer: a North American story. By John Neal. Portland [Me.] Shirley and Hyde, 1828.
     xx, [21]-276 p. 19cm.

     1. Witchcraft--New England--Fiction. I. Title.

Library of Congress   PZ3.N252R   7-33170†

Witchcraft
K F688
   Necyomantia ivrisperiti.
     Forcadel, Étienne, 1534-1579.
     Necyomantia ivrisperiti. Mira magiae descriptio, per quam euocati iurisconsulti, innumeros iuris ciuilis locos disertissimè declarant. Stephano Forcatvlo blyterensi ivriscos. avtore. Lvgdvni, Apvd Seb. Gryphivm, 1544.
     142 p. 19cm.

     1. Roman law--Interpretation and criticism. 2. Magic. I. Title.
8

   Nederlandsch Hervormde Kerk.

     see

   Nederlandse Hervormde Kerk.

Witchcraft
BF 1410
B42
Z56
v.3
no.13
   Nederlandse Hervormde Kerk.
     Brieven van eenige kerkenraden buyten de Provintie van Holland, namentlijk van 't Eerw. Classis van Walcheren, van de Eerwaardige Kerkenraden van Middelburg, Utrecht, Leeuwaarden, Groningen, aen de Eerwaardige Kerkenraad van Rotterdam, tot antwoord op haren Circulaire brief, rakende de sake van Dr. B. Bekker. Rotterdam, By R. van Doesburg, boekverkooper, 1692.
     16 p. title vignette, illus. initials. 19 x 15cm.

8   (Continued on next card)

CATALOGUE OF THE CORNELL WITCHCRAFT COLLECTION

chcraft
Nederlandse Hervormde Kerk. Brieven van eenige kerkenraden ... 1692. (Card 2)

4°: A-B⁴.
Van der Linde 36.
No. 13 in vol. lettered Bekker III.
1. Bekker, Balthasar, 1634-1698. De betoverde weereld. 2. Nederlandse Hervormde Kerk. Kerkenraden. Rotterdam. Circulaire brief ... wegens de saake van Dr. Balthasar Bekker. I. Nederlandse Hervormde Kerk. Kerkenraden. Rotterdam. II. Title.

Witchcraft
BX 9477 U92
Nederlandse Hervormde Kerk. Classes. Utrecht. Briev ... aan de Eerwaerde Classis van Amsterdam. 1692. (Card 2)

6 p. [p. 7-8 blank] title vignette, illus. initial. 22 x 17cm.
4°: A⁴.
Dated: 18 Martii ... 1692.
Van der Linde 34.

1. Bekker, Balthasar, 1634-1698. I. Nederlandse Hervormde Kerk. Classes. Amsterdam. II. Title.

Witchcraft
BF 1410 B42 Z56 v.3 no.13
Nederlandse Hervormde Kerk. Brieven van eenige kerkenraden ... 1692. (Card 2)

4°: A-B⁴.
Van der Linde 36.
No. 13 in vol. lettered Bekker III.
1. Bekker, Balthasar, 1634-1698. De betoverde weereld. 2. Nederlandse Hervormde Kerk. Kerkenraden. Rotterdam. Circulaire brief ... wegens de saake van Dr. Balthasar Bekker. I. Nederlandse Hervormde Kerk. Kerkenraden. Rotterdam. II. Title.

8

---

chcraft
Nederlandse Hervormde Kerk. Classes. Amsterdam. Vermeerderde articulen voor te stellen aen Do. B: Bekker. [Amsterdam, 1691]
[4] p. 19 x 16cm.
4°: π².
Caption title.
Text given also in its Autentyke copye van de articulen die ... den 23 Aug. 1691 opgestelt zyn. Van der Linde 30.
No. 1 in vol. lettered Stukken betrekkelijk Bekker.

(Continued on next card)

Witchcraft
BF 1410 B42 Z56 v.3 no.16
Nederlandse Hervormde Kerk. Kerkenraden. Rotterdam.
Circulaire brief van de Eerwaarde Kerkenraad van Rotterdam, geschreven aan de respective kerken-raden van Zuyd ende Noord Holland; misgaders aan de voornaamste steden van de verdere geunieerde provincien, wegens de saake van D Balthasar Bekker, en syn boek De betooverde weereld. [Rotterdam? 1692]
[4] p. 20 x 15cm.
4°: π².
Caption title.

(Continued on next card)

Witchcraft
BF 1410 B42 Z56 v.3 no.14
Nederlandse Hervormde Kerk. Kerkenraden. Utrecht.
Briev van de Eerwaarde Kerkenraad van Utrecht, aan de Eerw. Kerkenraad van Amsterdam, daar toe tendeerende dat de autheur van het boek, De betoverde wereld genaamt, niet wederom tot de bedieninge van het predikampt in de Gereformeerde Kerke mach werden toegelaten. [Amsterdam, 1692?]
4 p. 20 x 15cm.
4°: A².

(Continued on next card)

8

---

chcraft
Nederlandse Hervormde Kerk. Classes. Amsterdam. Vermeerderde articulen voor te stellen aen Do. B: Bekker. [1691] (Card 2)

I. Bekker, Balthasar, 1634-1698. II. Title. III. Nederlandse Hervormde Kerk. Classes. Amsterdam. Consistorie. Autentyke copye de articulen die ... den 23 Aug. 1691. opgestelt zyn.

Witchcraft
BF 1410 B42 Z56 v.3 no.16
Nederlandse Hervormde Kerk. Kerkenraden. Rotterdam. Circulaire brief ... [1692] (Card 2)
Van der Linde 33.
No. 16 in vol. lettered Bekker III.

1. Bekker, Balthasar, 1634-1698. De betoverde weereld. I. Nederlandse Hervormde Kerk. Kerkenraden. II. Title.

Witchcraft
BF 1410 B42 Z56 v.3 no.14
Nederlandse Hervormde Kerk. Kerkenraden. Utrecht. Briev ... aan de Eerw. Kerkenraad van Amsterdam ... [1692?] (Card 2)
Caption title.
"Gedrukt na de copie van Johannes Dale."
Variant of van der Linde 43, which is the printing by Johannes Dalé.
No. 14 in vol. lettered Bekker III.
1. Bekker, Balthasar, 1634-1698. I. Nederlandse Hervormde Kerk. Kerkenraden. Amsterdam. II. Title.

8

---

craft
Nederlandse Hervormde Kerk. Classes. Amsterdam. Consistorie.
Autentyke copye van de articulen die van het Eerwaarde Consistorie van Amsterdam. den 23 Aug. 1691. opgestelt zyn om voor te houden aen Do. B. Bekker en de aenbieding die Do. B. Bekker daar op gedaen heeft den 30 Augusti 1691. Amsterdam, Gedrukt by G. Borstius, boekverkooper [1691]
[8] p. title vignette. 19 x 15cm.
4°: A⁴.
Aenbieding van Do. B. Bekker: p. [7]-[8]

(Continued on next card)

Witchcraft
BF 1410 B42 Z56 v.1 no.1
Nederlandse Hervormde Kerk. Kerkenraden. Rotterdam. Circulaire brief ... wegens de saake van Dr. Balthasar Bekker.
Bekker, Balthasar, 1634-1698.
Nodige bedenkingen op de niewe beweegingen, onlangs verwekt door den circulairen brief en andere middelen, tegen den auteur van 't boek De betoverde weereld, door Balthasar Bekker, predikant tot Amsterdam. Amsterdam, Gedruckt by D. vanden Dalen, boekverkooper [1692?]
1 p. l., 62, [1] p. [p. 64 blank] title vignette, illus. initial. 19 x 16cm.
4°: π 1, A-H⁴.
Preface autographed by Bekker.

(Continued on next card)

Witchcraft
BF 1410 B42 1691a no.3
Nederlandse Hervormde Kerk. Synode van Noordholland, Edam, 1691.
Acten ofte handelingen van de Noord-Hollandsche Synodus, gehouden binnen Edam en Alcmaar, anno 1691. en 1692. Rakende Dr. Balthazar Bekker, en sijn boek De betoverde wereld, met alle de documenten daar toe behoorende, waar onder ook eenige, die in het synodale acten-boek niet en staan uyt-gedrukt; met een voor-reden, strekkende tot weder-legging van Dr. Bekkers Remonstrantie en verdere exceptien tegen de competentie van de Synodus. Enchuysen, Gedrukt by J. D. Kuyper, 1692. (Continued on next card)

8

---

craft
Nederlandse Hervormde Kerk. Classes. Amsterdam. Consistorie. Autentyke copye van de articulen van ... den 23 Aug.1691. ... [1691] (Card 2)

Van der Linde 30.
No. 1 in vol. lettered Bekker II.

1. Nederlandse Hervormde Kerk--Doctrinal and controversial works. I. Bekker, Balthasar, 1634-1698. II. Title.

Witchcraft
BF 1410 B42 Z56 v.1 no.1
Nederlandse Hervormde Kerk. Kerkenraden. Rotterdam. Circulaire brief ... wegens de saake van Dr. Balthasar Bekker.
Bekker, Balthasar, 1634-1698. Nodige bedenkingen op de niewe beweegingen ... [1692?] (Card 2)
Dated at end: den 9. July 1692.
Van der Linde 42.
No. 1 in vol. lettered Bekker I.
1. Nederlandse Hervormde Kerk. Kerkenraden. Rotterdam. Circulaire brief ... wegens de saake van Dr. Balthasar Bekker. 2. Nederlandse Hervormde Kerk--Doctrinal and controversial works. 3. Bekker, Balthasar, 1634-1698. De betoverde weereld. I. Title.

Witchcraft
BF 1410 B42 1691a no.3
Nederlandse Hervormde Kerk. Synode van Noordholland, Edam, 1691. Acten ofte handelingen van de Noord-Hollandsche Synodus, gehouden binnen Edam en Alcmaar ... 1692. (Card 2)

30 p. l., 102 p. title and end page vignettes., illus. initials. 20 x 16cm.
4°: *-7*⁴, 8*², A-N⁴(-N4)
Remonstrantie, by Bekker: p. 73-83.
Van der Linde 51.
No. 3 in vol. lettered B. Bekker. Betoverde weereld.

(Continued on next card)

8

---

chcraft
Nederlandse Hervormde Kerk. Classes. Utrecht.
Briev van de Eerwaerde Classis van Utreht, aan de Eerwaerde Classis van Amsterdam. Daer toe dienende, dat Dr. Bekker autheur van dat fameuse boek, De betoverde werelt genaemt, niet wederom tot de bedieninge van het predikampt in de Gereformeerde Kerck toegelaten werde. Gedruckt na de copy tot Utrecht. Amsterdam, By A. D. Oossaan, boekverkooper, 1692.

(Continued on next card)

Witchcraft
BF 1410 B42 Z56 v.3 no.13
Nederlandse Hervormde Kerk. Kerkenraden. Rotterdam. Circulaire brief ... wegens de saake van Dr. Balthasar Bekker.
Nederlandse Hervormde Kerk.
Brieven van eenige kerkenraden buyten de Provintie van Holland, namentlijk van 't Eerw. Classis van Walcheren, van de Eerwaardige Kerkenraden van Middelburg, Utrecht, Leeuwaarden, Groningen, aen de Eerwardige Kerkenraad van Rotterdam, tot antwoord op haren Circulaire brief, rakende de sake van Dr. B. Bekker. Rotterdam, By R. van Doesburg, boekverkooper, 1692.
16 p. title vignette, illus. initials. 19 x 15cm.

(Continued on next card)

8

Witchcraft
BF 1410 B42 1691a no.3
Nederlandse Hervormde Kerk. Synode van Noordholland, Edam, 1691. Acten ofte handelingen van de Noord-Hollandsche Synodus, gehouden binnen Edam en Alcmaar ... 1692. (Card 3)

1. Bekker, Balthasar, 1634-1698. De betoverde weereld. I. Bekker, Balthasar, 1634-1698. Remonstrantie in de Eerw. Synode van Noord-Holland ... op den 5. Aug. 1692. II. Title. III. Nederlandse Hervormde Kerk. Synode van Noordholland, Alcmaar, 1692.

8

409

CATALOGUE OF THE CORNELL WITCHCRAFT COLLECTION

```
WITCHCRAFT
BF        Nederlandse Hervormde Kerk.  Synode van
1410         Noordholland, Edam, 1691.
B42         Acten ofte handelingen van de Noord-Hol-
Z69      landsche Synodus, gehouden binnen Edam en
no. 33   Alcmaar, anno 1691. en 1692.  Rakende Dr.
         Balthazar Bekker, en sijn boek De betoverde
         wereld, met alle de documenten daar toe be-
         hoorende, waar onder ook eenige, die in het
         synodale acten-boek niet en staan uyt-gedrukt;
         met een voor-reden, strekkende tot weder-leg-
         ging van Dr. Bekkers Remonstrantie en verdere
         exceptien tege        n de competentie van de
8                             (Continued on next card)
NIC
```

```
WITCHCRAFT
BF        Nederlandse Hervormde Kerk.  Synode van
1410         Noordholland, Edam, 1691.  Acten ofte
B42         handelingen van de Noord-Hollandsche
Z69         Synodus, gehouden binnen Edam en Alcmaar.
no. 33                                 (Card 2)
         Synodus.  Enchuysen, Gedrukt by J. D.
         Kuyper, 1692.
            30 p. l., 102 p.  title and end page
         vignettes., illus. initials,  21cm.
         4°: *-7⁴, 8*², A-N⁴ (-N⁴)
8           Remonstrant          ie, by Bekker: p. 73-83.
NIC                         (Continued on next card)
```

```
WITCHCRAFT
BF        Nederlandse Hervormde Kerk.  Synode van
1410         Noordholland, Edam, 1691.  Acten ofte
B42         handelingen van de Noord-Hollandsche
Z69         Synodus, gehouden binnen Edam en Alcmaar...
no. 33      1692.                       (Card 3)
         Van der Linde 51.
         No. 33 in a Collection of tracts against
         Balthasar Bekker and his Betoverde weereld.
         With autograph: Petrus Jacobi.
8                           (Continued on next card)
NIC
```

```
WITCHCRAFT
BF        Nederlandse Hervormde Kerk.  Synode van
1410         Noordholland, Edam, 1691.  Acten ofte
B42         handelingen van de Noord-Hollandsche
Z69         Synodus, gehouden binnen Edam en Alcmaar...
no. 33      1692.                       (Card 4)
            1. Bekker, Balthasar, 1634-1698. De
         betoverde weereld.  I. Bekker, Balthasar,
         1634-1698. Remonstrantie in de Eerw. Synode
         van Noord-Holland ... op den 5. Aug. 1692.
         II. Title.  III. Nederlandse Hervormde
8        Kerk.  Synode      van Noordholland,
NIC      Alcmaar, 1692.
```

```
Witchcraft
BF        Nederlandse Hervormde Kerk.  Synode van
1410         Noordholland, Edam, 1691.
B42         Acten ofte handelingen van de Noord-Hol-
Z86      landsche Synodus, gehouden binnen Edam en
no.8     Alcmaar, anno 1691. en 1692. Rakende Dr.
         Balthazar Bekker, en sijn boek De betoverde
         wereld, met alle de documenten daar toe be-
         hoorende, waar onder ook eenige, die in het
         synodale acten-boek niet en staan uyt-gedrukt;
         met een voor-reden, strekkende tot weder-leg-
         ging van Dr. Bekkers Remonstrantie en verdere
         exceptien tege        n de competentie van de
         Synodus.  En          chuysen, Gedrukt by J. D.
8                              (Continued on next card)
```

```
Witchcraft
BF        Nederlandse Hervormde Kerk.  Synode van
1410         Noordholland, Edam, 1691. Acten ofte
B42         handelingen van de Noord-Hollandsche Sy-
Z86         nodus, gehouden binnen Edam en Alcmaar ...
no.8        1692.                       (Card 2)
         Kuyper, 1692.
            30 p. l., 102 p.  title and end page
         vignettes.  illus. initials.  19 x 15cm.
         4°: *-7*⁴, 8*², A-N⁴(-N⁴)
            Remonstrantie, by Bekker: p. 73-83.
         Van der Linde 51.
            No. 8 in           vol. lettered Tractaten
8        voor en teg          en B. Bekker.
```

```
              Nederlandse Hervormde Kerk. Synode van
              Noordholland, Edam, 1691.  Acten ofte
Witchcraft    handelingen van de Noord-Hollandsche
BF            Synodus, gehouden binnen Edam en Alcmaar.
1410         Bekker, Balthasar, 1634-1698.
B42             Aanmerkinge op de handelingen der twee
1691a        laatste noordhollandsche synoden, in de sake
no.4         van B. Bekker, ten opsighte van sijn boek
             genaamd De betoverde weereld; nu versch t'
             Enkhuisen gedrukt. En de verschoninge der-
             selve gemaakt in de voorrede daar voor,
             mitsgaders het reqvest der gedeputeerden van
             't voorleden jaar daar achter by gevoegd.
             [Amsterdam? 1692]
                16 p. 20 x 16cm.
                4°: A-B⁴.
8               Caption ti     tle.
                               (Continued on next card)
```

```
              Nederlandse Hervormde Kerk.  Synode van
              Noordholland, Edam, 1691.  Acten ofte
Witchcraft    handelingen van de Noord-Hollandsche
BF            Synodus, gehouden binnen Edam en Alcmaar.
1410         Bekker, Balthasar, 1634-1698.  Aanmerkinge
B42          op de handelingen der twee laatste noord-
1691a        hollandsche synoden ...  [1692]  (Card 2)
no.4
             In autograph on p. 16: a. 13. Octob.
         1692. Bekker.
             Van der Linde 52.
             No. 4 in vol. lettered B. Bekker. Beto-
         verde weereld.
             1. Nederlandse Hervormde Kerk.  Synode
         van Noordholland, Edam, 1691. Acten ofte
         handelingen van    de Noord-Hollandsche
         Synodus, gehou     den binnen Edam en Alc-
8        maar.  I. Tit     le.
```

```
              Née de la Rochelle, Jean François, 1751-
              1838, ed.
WITCHCRAFT       Courtilz, Gatien de, sieur de Sandras,
BF            1644?-1772.
1547             Les fredaines du diable; ou, Recueil de
C86           morceaux épars, pour servir à l'histoire
1797          du diable et de ses suppôts; tirés d'auteurs
              dignes de foi, par feu M. Sandras, avocat
              en Parlement; mis en nouveau style et pub-
              liés par J. Fr. N. D. L. R. [i.e., Jean
              François Née de la Rochelle]  Paris, Chez
              Merlin, 1797.
                 216 p.  17     cm.
8
NIC                         (Continued on next card)
```

```
              Née de la Rochelle, Jean François, 1751-
              1838, ed.
WITCHCRAFT       Courtilz, Gatien de, sieur de Sandras,
BF            1644?-1772. Les fredaines du diable ...
1547          1797.                       (Card 2)
C86
1797          Ascription by BM, Biographie universelle;
              and BN for entry under Née de la Rochelle
              as editor.
                 Author entry in BN: Sandras,
              advocat au Parlement.
                 1. Devil. 2. Devil--Bibliography.
8             I. Sandras,           advocat au Parlement,
NIC           supposed aut         her.  II. Née de la Ro-
              chelle, Jean         François, 1751-1838, ed.
              III. Title.
```

```
WITCHCRAFT
BF        Negroni, Bernardino.
1595         La magia nel secolo decimonono; racconti
N39       puramente storici.  Bologna, Società tip.
          dei compositori, 1872.
            2 v. in 1.  15cm.


8
NIC       √ 1. Magic--Hist. 2. Occult sciences--Hist.
            I. Title.
```

```
              Nehring, Johann Christoph, d. 1682,
              respondent.
Witchcraft
BF        Struve, Georg Adam, 1619-1692, praeses.
1565         Disputatio juridica De indiciis cui an-
D62       nectitur quaestio de proba per aquam frigi-
no.16     dam sagarum.  Von der Wasser-Prob der Hexen
          ... sub praesidio Dn. Georgii Adami Struven
          ... publicè proposita à Joh. Christoph.
          Nehringio ...  Jenae, Typis Pauli Ehrichii,
          1714.
             52 p.  20cm.
             No. 16 in vol. lettered Dissertationes
8         de sagis. 1636-1714.
                        (Continued on next card)
```

```
              Neilson, George.
Witchcraft
BF        Hutchison, James.
1581         A sermon preached before the commissioners
Z7+       of justiciary appointed for triall of several
1697d     persons suspected guilty of witchcraft: att
          Pasley the 13 Aprill 1697. [Glasgow, 1910]
             390-399 p.  26cm.

             Running title: A sermon on witchcraft in
          1697.
             Extract from The Scottish historical re-
          view, no. 28, July 1910.
             Contributed         with a historical note,
          by Geo.               Neilson.
             I. Neilson,        George.  II. Title.  III.
          Title: A sermo'       n on witchcraft.
```

```
WITCHCRAFT
BX        Neller, Georg Christoph, praeses.
1935         ...Conatus exegeticus in cap. Eam te 7
N42       De rescriptis, quem una cum parergis, ex
          omni jure, nec non ex re monetaria, tum
          biblico-canonica, tum Trevirensi delibatis
          ...praeside...Georgio Christoph. Neller...
          publicae disputationi pro admissione ad
          tentamen graduandorum supposuit...Carolus
          Josephus Embden.  Augustae Trevirorum,
          Typis Eschermannianis [1779]
             48 p.  front., plate.  22cm.

8            Burr's               note inside front cover.
NIC                         (Continued on next card)
```

```
WITCHCRAFT
BX        Neller, Georg Christoph, praeses. Conatus
1935         exegeticus in cap. Eam te 7 De rescriptis
N42       ...[1779]                   (Card 2)

          "This book is valuable in containing a...
          letter of the Elector, Johann VII of
          Treves asking the advice of the University
          theological faculty at Treves as to the
          trial of Dr. Dietrich Flade for witchcraft.
          (See pp. 32-35) It is to be noted that this
          student, writing under the eye of the emi-
          nent jurist          Neller in 1779, still
          believes in          witchcraft..."
                            (Continued on next card)
```

```
WITCHCRAFT
BX        Neller, Georg Christoph, praeses. Conatus
1935         exegeticus in cap. Eam te 7 De rescriptis
N42       ...[1779]                   (Card 3)

          √ 1. Catholic Church.  Codex iuris canonic
          2. Canon law--Sources. √3. Flade, Dietrich
          1534-1589. 4. Witchcraft. √I. Embden, Ca-
          rolus Josephus, respondent. √II. Johann VI
          von Schönenberg, abp. and elector of Treve
          III. Title.
```

```
Witchcraft
BF        Nemec, Jaroslav, 1910-
1565         Witchcraft and medicine (1484-1793)
N43+      [Washington] National Institutes of
          Health, 1974.
2 Copies    10 p.  illus. 26cm.  (NIH publication
          74-636)

            "Published in conjunction with an exhi-
          bit at the National Library of Medicine,
          March 25-July 19, 1974."

8           1. Witch          craft--Hist.  2.
NIC       Medicine.           I. Title.  II. United
          States.              National Library of
          Medicine.
```

```
          Das neue Buch vom Aberglauben.
BF        Leithäuser, Joachim G
1413         Das neue Buch vom Aberglauben; Geschichte
L53       und Gegenwart.  Mit 117 Bildern auf Kunst-
          drucktafeln und 43 zeitgenössischen Darstel-
          lungen im Text.  Berlin, Safari-Verlag
          [1964]
             412 p.  illus. 25cm.  (Die Welt des
          Wissens)

            1. Superstition. 2. Witchcraft--Hist.
          I. Title.
```

CATALOGUE OF THE CORNELL WITCHCRAFT COLLECTION

Witchcraft
PT
1792
D87

Neue Daten und Briefe zum Leben des P. Friedrich Spe.

Duhr, Bernhard, 1852-1930.
 Neue Daten und Briefe zum Leben des P. Friedrich Spe.
 (In Görres-Gesellschaft zur Pflege der Wissenschaft im katholischen Deutschland, Bonn. Historisches Jahrbuch. München. 24cm. 21. Bd., 2. u. 3. Heft (1900), p. [328]-352)
 1. Spee, Friedrich von, 1591-1635. 2. Witchcraft--Germany. I. Title. II. Görres-Gesellschaft zur Pflege der Wissenschaft im katholischen Deutschland, Bonn. Historisches Jahrbuch.

WITCHCRAFT
316++
582

Neue Ordnung des Durchläuchtigsten Fürsten ... Wilhelm Friederich, Marggrafens zu Brandenburg.

Brandenburg-Ansbach (Principality) Laws, statutes, etc.
 Neue Ordnung des Durchläuchtigsten Fürsten und Herrn, Herrn Wilhelm Friederich, Marggrafens zu Brandenburg ... Wie es in Criminal- und peinl. Sachen mit denen gütlichen und peinlichen Verhören, und inquisiterialischen Untersuchungen ... und sonsten mit denen Verurtheilten in dem Brandenburg-Onelzbachischen Fürstenthum und Landen des Burggrafthums Nürnberg unterhalb Gebürgs
 (Continued on next card)

WITCHCRAFT
316++
582

Neue Ordnung des Durchläuchtigsten Fürsten ... Wilhelm Friederich, Marggrafens zu Brandenburg.

Brandenburg-Ansbach (Principality) Laws, statutes, etc. Neue Ordnung ... 1720. (Card 2)

gehalten werden solle. Onelzbach, Gedruckt bey J. V. Lüders, 1720.
 34 p. 31cm.
 Bound with Brandenburg (Electorate) Laws, statutes, etc. Peinliche Halsgerichts Ordnung. Ansbach? 1582.

(Continued on next card)

WITCHCRAFT
BF
1583
A2
N48

Neuester Hexenprozess aus dem aufgeklärten heutigen Jahrhundert; oder, So dumm liegt mein bayrisches Vaterland noch unter dem Joch der Mönche und des Aberglaubens. Von A. v. M. [n.p.] 1786.
 36 p. 16cm.

 1. Superstition. 2. Witchcraft--Bavaria. 3. Trials (Witchcraft)--Bavaria. I. M., A. v. II. M., A. v.

Neuffer, Christian, respondent.

WITCHCRAFT
R
133
C173

Camerarius, Elias, 1672-1734, praeses.
 Magici morbi historia attentius pensitata Hanc...praeside Elia Camerario...examini publico submittit Christianus Neufferus... Tubingae, Typis Georgii Friderici Pelickii [1724]
 31 p. 20cm.

 Diss.--Tübingen (C. Neuffer, respondent)
 1. Medicine, Magic, mystic and spagiric. 2. Demonology. I. Neuffer, Christian, respondent.

Neun ausserlesen und wolgegründete Hexen Predigt.

Samson, Hermann.
 Neun ausserlesen und wolgegründete Hexen Predigt, darinnen der Terminus Magiae oder Zauberey nach den logicalischen Terminis ... erkläret und ausgeführet worden, und in der Thumb Kirchen zu Riga öffentlich gehalten durch M. Hermannum Sansonium ... Riga in Eiefland, durch und in Verlegung Gerhard Schröders, 1626 [ca. 1900]
 166 p. 24cm.
 Carnap's manuscript copy.
 "Originaldruck in der Universi-
 (Continued on next card)

Neun ausserlesen und wolgegründete Hexen Predigt.

MSS
Bd.
WITCHCRAFT
BF
S19

Samson, Hermann. Neun ausserlesen und wolgegründete Hexen Predigt ... 1626 [ca. 1900] (Card 2)

täts-Bibliothek zu Breslau. 42. Bl. in 4°."
 Title page in red and black.
 Numerals and signatures in the margins indicate pagination and signatures of the original.
 On the inside front cover the copyist has appended a note on the rarity of the printed work and given bibliographical
 (Continued on next card)

Neun ausserlesen und wolgegründete Hexen Predigt.

MSS
Bd.
WITCHCRAFT
BF
S19

Samson, Hermann. Neun ausserlesen und wolgegründete Hexen Predigt ... 1626 [ca. 1900] (Card 3)

references.
 Signed Geo. L. Burr.

 1. Witchcraft--Sermons. I. Title.

Névroses et possessions diaboliques.

WITCHCRAFT
BF
1555
H48
1898

Hélot, Charles.
 Névroses et possessions diaboliques. 2. éd. Paris, Bloud et Barral, 1898.
 556 p. 22cm.
 Contents.--1. ptie. Quelques faits à juger.--2. ptie. Le jugement de la science.--3. ptie. Jugement de l'Eglise.
 1. Demoniac possession. 2. Hysteria. 3. Somnambulism. 4. Hypnotism. 5. Exorcism. I. Title.

Witchcraft
BF
1565
E95

Neuwaldt, Hermann.
 Exegesis pvrgationis sive Examinis sagarum super aquam frigidam proiectarum: in qua refutata opinione Guilhelmi Adolphi Scribonij, de huius purgationis & aliarum similium origine, natura, & veritate agitur: omnibus ad rerum gubernacula sedentibus maximè necessaria ... Helmstadii, Excudebat Iacobus Lucius, 1584.
 [120] p. 17cm.
 Bound with Ewich, Johann, 1525-1588.
 (Continued on next card)

Witchcraft
BF
1565
E95

Neuwaldt, Hermann. Exegesis pvrgationis ... 1584. (Card 2)

De sagarum ... natura. Bremae, 1584.

 1. Scribonius, Wilhelm Adolf, 16th cent. De sagarum natura. 2. Witchcraft. I. Title: Exegesis purgationis.

Neuwaldt, Hermann.

WITCHCRAFT
BF
1565
S43
1588

Scribonius, Wilhelm Adolf, 16th cent.
 De sagarvm natura et potestate, deque his recte cognoscendis et pvniendis physiologia Gulielmi Adolphi Scribonii Marpurgensis. Vbi de pvrgatione earvm per aquam frigidam. Contra Joannem Evvichium ... & Her. Neuvvaldum ... doctores medicos & professores ... Marpurgi, typis Pauli Egenolphi, 1588.
 [8], 132 l. 17cm.

 In copy 2, contents in MS on l. [8]
 Title on spine of copy 1: Scribonius. Witchcraft pamphlets.
 (Continued on next card)

Neuwaldt, Hermann.

WITCHCRAFT
BF
1565
S43
1588

Scribonius, Wilhelm Adolf, 16th cent. De sagarvm natura ... 1588. (Card 2)

With copy 1 are bound Ignotus Patronus Veritatis, pseud. Examen epistolae et partis physiologiae de examine sagarum ([Francofurti] 1589); Scribonius, W. A. Responsio ad examen Ignoti Patroni Veritatis (Francofurdi, 1590); and Ignotus Patronus Veritatis, pseud. Refvtatio responsionis Gvlielmi-Adolphi Scribonii (Herbornae, 1591).
 1. Witchcraft. 2. Ewich, Johann, 1525-1588. 3. Neuwaldt, Hermann. I. Title: De sagarum natura.

Neuwaldus, Hermannus.

see

Neuwaldt, Hermann.

Witchcraft
BF
1576
N52
1892

Nevins, Winfield S.
 Witchcraft in Salem village in 1692, together with some account of other witchcraft prosecutions in New England and elsewhere; by Winfield S. Nevins ... Salem, Mass., North shore publishing company; Boston, Lee and Shepard, 1892.
 272 p. front., illus. (incl. facsim.) plates. 18½cm.

 1. Witchcraft--Salem, Mass. 2. Witchcraft--New England.

 Library of Congress   BF1576.N5   11-8999
 Copyright 1892: 22002

Witchcraft
BF
1576
N52
1916

Nevins, Winfield S.
 Witchcraft in Salem village in 1692; together with a review of the opinions of modern writers and psychologists in regard to outbreak of the evil in America. By Winfield S. Nevins. 5th ed., with new preface of striking interest. Salem, Mass., The Salem press company, 1916.
 2 p. l., lix, [2], 7-273 p. front., illus. (incl. facsim.) plates, ports. 18cm.

 1. Witchcraft--Salem, Mass. 2. Witchcraft--New England. I. Title.   17-18161
 Library of Congress   BF1576

The New-England tragedies in prose.

Witchcraft
BF
1576
A42

Allen, Rowland Hussey.
 The New-England tragedies in prose ... I. The coming of the Quakers. II. The witchcraft delusion. Boston, Nichols and Noyes, 1869.
 156 p. 19cm.

New England's place in the history of witchcraft.

Witchcraft
BF
1576
B96

Burr, George Lincoln, 1857-1938.
 ... New England's place in the history of witchcraft, by George Lincoln Burr ... Worcester, Mass., The Society, 1911.
 35 p. 25cm.

 At head of title: American antiquarian society.
 "Reprinted from the Proceedings of the American antiquarian society for October, 1911."

CATALOGUE OF THE CORNELL WITCHCRAFT COLLECTION

Witchcraft
BF
1576
P63

The new Puritan.
Pike, James Shepherd, 1811-1882.
    The new Puritan: New England two hundred years ago; some account of the life of Robert Pike, the Puritan who defended the Quakers, resisted clerical domination, and opposed the witchcraft prosecution ... New York, Harper & Brothers, 1879.
    237 p. 19cm.

    1. Pike, Robert, 1616-1706. I. Title.

Witchcraft
BF
1584
N4
Z7
1602a

New, unerhörte, erschröckliche, warhafftige Wundergeschicht, so sich in der Statt Edam in Holland den 24. Tag Hornung diss lauffenden 1602. Jahrs zugetragen ... Erstlich in flandrischer Sprache getruckt zu Brüssel ... Mit sampt einem Baderbornensischem Sendschreiben. Item: Dess ehrwürdigen hochgelehrten Herr Friderich Forner ... Sendtschreiben von erschröcklichem Vntergang sechs ketzerischen Personen ... in Francken bey Bamberg ...

8   (Continued on next card)

Witchcraft
BF
1584
N4
Z7
1602a

New, unerhörte, erschröckliche, warhafftige Wundergeschicht ... 1602. (Card 2)

jm Jahr 1601. Auss dem Latein ins Teutsch gebracht. Ingolstadt, Getruckt in der Ederischen Truckerey durch Andream Angermayer, 1602.
    17 p. 21cm.
    1. Witchcraft--Netherlands. 2. Witchcraft--Germany. I. Forner, Friedrich, Bp. of Hebron, d. 1630.

8

Witchcraft
Z
6878
W8
N531+
1908

New York. Public library.
    List of works in the New York public library relating to witchcraft in the United States. Comp. by George F. Black, of the Lenox staff. [New York, 1908]
    18 p. 26cm.
    Caption title.
    "Reprinted from the Bulletin, November, 1908."
    At end: 40 titles of works not in the library.

    1. Witchcraft--U. S.--Bibl. I. Black, George Fraser, 1866- II. Title.
        CA 9--2852 Unrev'd
    Library of Congress   Z6878.W8N6

Witchcraft
Z
6878
W8
N53+
1911

New York. Public library.
    ... List of works relating to witchcraft in Europe. New York, 1911.
    31 p. 26½cm.
    "Reprinted at the New York public library from the Bulletin, December, 1911."
    Comp. by George F. Black.

    1. Witchcraft--Bibl. I. Black, George Fraser, 1866- II. Title.
        12-9?
    Library of Congress   Z6878.W8N5

BF
1566
W81

Newall, Venetia, ed.
    The Witch figure; folklore essays by a group of scholars in England honouring the 75th birthday of Katharine M. Briggs. Edited by Venetia Newall. London, Boston, Routledge & Kegan Paul [1973]
    xiii, 239 p. illus. 23 cm.
    Includes bibliographical references.
    CONTENTS.--Michaelis-Jena, R. Katharine M. Briggs.--Blacker, C. Animal witchcraft in Japan.--Davidson, H. R. E. Hostile magic in the Icelandic sagas.--Dean-Smith, M. The ominous wood.--Grinsell, L. V. Witchcraft at some prehistoric sites.--Hole, C. Some instances of image-magic in Great Britain.--New all, V. The Jew as a witch figure.--Parrinder, G. The witch as vict im.--Ross, A. The
NIC   COOdc See next card

BF
1566
W81

Newall, Venetia, ed.
    The Witch figure; ... [1973] (Card 2) divine hag of the pagan Celts.--Simpson, J. Olaf Tryggvason versus the powers of darkness.--White, B. Cain's kin.--Widdowson, J. The witch as a frightening and threatening figure.--Publications by Katharine M. Briggs (p. 221)

NIC   COOdc   73-83077

MSS
Bd.
WITCHCRAFT
BF
C96

Newe Zeitung und ware Geschicht, dieses 76. Jars geschehen im Breissgaw.
Cudius, Hans.
    Newe Zeitung und ware Geschicht, dieses 76. Jars geschehen im Breissgaw, wie man da in etlichen Stätten und Flecken, in die 55. Unhulden gefangen und verbrent hat, auch wie sie schröckliche ding bekent haben ... Gestellt und gemacht durch Hans Cudium. [n.p.] 1576 [ca. 1900]
    4 l. 19cm.
    Carnap's manuscript copy.
    "Originaldr uck in der Stadtbibliothek zu Zür ich, 8 Seiten in 8°."
        (Continued on next card)

MSS
Bd.
WITCHCRAFT
BF
C96

Newe Zeitung und ware Geschicht, dieses 76. Jars geschehen im Breissgaw.
Cudius, Hans. Newe Zeitung ... 1576 [ca. 1900] (Card 2)
    Notations in the margins indicate foliation of the original.
    In verse.

    1. Witchcraft--Germany. I. Title.

MSS
Bd.
WITCHCRAFT
BF
N54

Newe Zeitung von den Hexen, oder Unhulden, so man verbrend hat, von dem 7. Februarj an, biss auff den 25. Junij, dieses 1580 Jar. Auch wirt darbey angezeigt, an was Ort und Enden, auch was sie bekent haben. In ein Liede verfasst. [n.p.] 1580 [ca. 1900]
    6 l. 19cm.
    Carnap's manuscript copy.
    "Originaldruck in der Stadtbibliothek zu Zürich, 7 Sei ten in 8°."
        (Continued on next card)

MSS
Bd.
WITCHCRAFT
BF
N54

Newe Zeitung von den Hexen, oder Unhulden ... 1580 [ca. 1900] (Card 2)
    In verse.
    Annotations in the margin indicate foliation of the original.

    1. Witchcraft--Germany.

WITCHCRAFT
BF
1583
A2
K96

Newe Zeitung, von einer erschrecklichen That.
Kuntz, Hans.
    Newe [i. e. Neue] Zeitung, von einer erschrecklichen That, welche zu Dillingen, von einem Jhesuwider, vnd einer Hexen, geschehen ist, welche denn offentlich, durch strenge Marter, bekand haben, wie sie es getrieben, vnd was sie für grossen Schaden gethan. Auch in Sonderheit, von diesem grossen Gewitter, welches sie den 2. Augusti, dieses 1579. Jars, durch ire Zauberey gemacht haben. Dabeneben au ch, von dem vngeschlach-

8
NIC   (Continued on next card)

WITCHCRAFT
BF
1583
A2
K96

Newe Zeitung, von einer erschrecklichen That.
Kuntz, Hans.
    Newe [i. e. Neue] Zeitung, von einer erschrecklichen That... (Card 2)

ten Wetter, als Regen, vnd Kelte, welche dem Korn vnd Wein, zum grossen Schaden, vnd Nachtheil, geschehen ist. Auch ist die Hexe, welche 23. Jahr, mit dem bösen Feinde, dem leidigen Teuffel, gebuhlet, den 8. October, zu Dillingen, zum Fewr verurtheilet worden. Aber schreck licher Weise, von dem

        (Continued on next card)

WITCHCRAFT
BF
1583
A2
K96

Newe Zeitung, von einer erschrecklichen That.
Kuntz, Hans.
    Newe [i. e. Neue] Zeitung, von einer erschrecklichen That... (Card 3)

Teuffel aus dem Fewer, in den Lüfften weg geführet worden. Durch Hans Kuntzen beschrieben. Basel, Gedruckt durch Samuel Apiario [1579]
    [8] p. 20cm.

    1. Witcher aft--Dillingen, Ger. I. Title.

WITCHCRAFT
BF
1572
C5
S33
1630

Newer Tractat von der verführten Kinder Zauberey.
[Schilling, Wolfgang]
    Newer Tractat von der verführten Kinder Zauberey. In welchem mit reifflichem Discurs ... vorgehalten wirdt, auss was Vrsachen viel vnerwachsene vnd vnmündige Kinder ... zu der verdampten Geister vnd Zauberer Gesellschafft vnd vnerhörter Weiss verführt werden ... auss lateinischer in die teutsche Sprach vbersetzt vnd in Truck gegeben ... durch VV. S. à V. C. & C. A. Aschaffenburg, Getruckt durch Quirin

8
NIC   (Continued on next card)

WITCHCRAFT
BF
1572
C5
S33
1630

Newer Tractat von der verführten Kinder Zauberey.
[Schilling, Wolfgang] Newer Tractat von der verführten Kinder Zauberey ... 1630. (Card 2)

Botzer, 1630.
    44 p. 21cm.
    Revised and augmented version of the "Appendix oder Nachtrab" (p. 60-129) published in his compilation on witchcraft from P. Laymann's Theologia moralis. (Laymann, P. Ein kurtzer doch gründlicher

8
NIC   (Continued on next card)

WITCHCRAFT
BF
1572
C5
S33
1630

Newer Tractat von der verführten Kinder Zauberey.
[Schilling, Wolfgang] Newer Tractat von der verführten Kinder Zauberey ... 1630. (Card 3)

Bericht wie ... mit den Hexen zuverfahren seye. Aschaffenburg, 1629.)

    1. Witchcraft. 2. Children--Management. I. Title. II. W. S. à V. C. & C. A. III. S., W., à V. C. & C. A.

8
NIC

BF
1521
J28
1924

Newes from Scotland.
James I, king of Great Britain, 1566-1625.
    King James, the First: Dæmonologie (1597). Newes from Scotland, declaring the damnable life and death of Doctor Fian, a notable sorcerer who was burned at Edenbrough in Ianuary last (1591) London, J. Lane; New York, Dutton [1924]
    xv, 81, 29 p. illus. 19cm. (The Bodley head quartos, no. 9)

    With facsimiles of original title pages.

        (Continued on next card)

CATALOGUE OF THE CORNELL WITCHCRAFT COLLECTION

Newes from Scotland.

James I, king of Great Britain, 1566-1625.
21   King James, the First: Daemonologie ...
8   [1924]   (Card 2)
24

Newes from Scotland has been ascribed to James Carmichael, minister of Haddington. cf. Sir James Melville, Memories, p. 195, and D. Webster, Collection of tracts on witchcraft, etc., 1820, p. 38.

Newhall, James R[obinson]
A lecture on the occult sciences: embracing some account of the New England witchcraft, with an attempt to exhibit the philosophy of spectre seeing, disease charming, &c. By James R. Newhall. ⟨Published by request of auditors.⟩ Salem, G. W. & E. Crafts, 1845.
36 p. 22cm.
Cover-title: An account of the great New England witchcraft ...

1. Occult sciences. 2. Witchcraft--Salem, Mass. I. Title.

Library of Congress   6-21183

---

tchcraft
45   [Newton, Thomas, bp. of Bristol] 1704-1782.
97   A dissertation on the demoniacs in the Gospels. London, Printed for J. and F. Rivington, 1775.
.1   63 p. 21cm.

No. 1 in vol. lettered: Twells, Whiston, etc. Tracts on the demoniacs in the New Testament. London, 1738-1775.

1. Demoniac possession. 2. Bible. N.T.--Commentaries. I. Title.

---

tchcraft
Nicholson, Isaac.
31   A sermon against witchcraft, preached in the parish church of Great Paxton, in the county of Huntingdon, July 17. 1808. With a brief account of the circumstances, which led to two atrocious attacks on the person of Ann Izzard, as a reputed witch. By the Reverend Isaac Nicholson ... London, Printed for J. Mawman, 1808.
1 p. l., ix, 35, [1] p. 22cm.

1. Witchcraft. I. Title.

11-15843

Library of Congress   BF1581.Z7 1808

Nicht doch --.

itchcraft
F   [Simon, Jordan] pater, 1719-1776.
445   Nicht doch -- oder, Auflösung der kleinen Zweifel über zwey Berichte von einer Hexen- oder Studenten-Geschichte die sich in dem Jahre 1768. den 10. 11. 12. und 13. Junius zu Ingolstadt in Bayern soll zugetragen haben. Aus einem dritten Berichte des Herrn Directors gezogen. Gedruckt zu Berichtshausen, Mit klaren Schriften [i.e., Leipzig] 1769?
27 p. 21cm.
(Continued on next card)

Nicht doch --.

itchcraft
F   [Simon, Jordan] pater, 1719-1776. Nicht doch -- ... [1769?]   (Card 2)
445
595

Attribution by Holzmann.
Continuation of his Nun, ja --. [Leipzig, 1769], with which this is bound.

1. Ghosts. 2. Witchcraft--Ingolstadt, Bavaria. I. His Nun, ja --. II. Title. III. Title: Auflösung der kleinen Zweifel über zwey Berichte von einer Hexen- oder Studenten-Geschichte.

Nichtige, ungegründete, eitle ... Verantwortung des H. P. Angelus März.

Witchcraft
BF   [Mayer, Andreas Ulrich] 1732-1802.
1565   Nichtige, ungegründete, eitle, kahle und lächerliche Verantwortung des H. P. Angelus
S83   März, Benedictiner zu Scheyrn, über die vom
no.4   P. Don Ferdinand Sterzinger bey dem hochfürstlichen hochlöblichen geistlichen Rath in Freysing gestellten Fragen. Vom Moldaustrom, 1767.
57 p. 20cm. (bound in 23cm. vol.)
Ascribed by Graesse, J. G. T., Bibliotheca magica et pneumatica and by Zapf,
8   (Continued on next card)

Nichtige, ungegründete, eitle ... Verantwortung des H. P. Angelus März.

Witchcraft
BF   [Mayer, Andreas Ulrich] 1732-1802. Nichtige, ungegründete, eitle ... Verantwortung
1565
S83   des H. P. Angelus März ... 1767.
no.4   (Card 2)

G. W., Zauberbibliothek, to F. N. Blocksberger, which is A. U. Mayer's pseudonym. British Museum suggests F. Sterzinger as author.
No. 4 in vol. lettered Sterzinger über Hexerei, 1766-1767.
8   (Continued on next card)

Die Nichtigkeit der Zauberey.

WITCHCRAFT
BF   Weber, Joseph, 1753-1831.
1565   Die Nichtigkeit der Zauberey, eine Vorlesung in den ökonomischen Lehrstunden.
W37   Salzburg, Im Verlage der hochfürstl. Wai-
1787   senhausbuchhandl., 1787.
32 p. 21cm.
Abbreviated version of his Ungrund des Hexen- und Gespenster-Glaubens.

1. Witchcraft. 2. Superstition. I. Title. II. His Ungrund des Hexen- und Gespenster-Glaubens.

Witchcraft
B   Nicoladoni, Alexander.
2605   Christian Thomasius. Ein Beitrag zur
Z7   Geschichte der Aufklärung. Dresden,
N63   Hönsch & Tiesler [1888]
vi, 140 p. port. 22cm.

1. Thomasius, Christian, 1655-1728--Biog. I. Title.

Nicolai, Ernst Anton, 1722-1802, praeses.
Dissertatio inauguralis medica De nyctalopia.

HIST SCI
RE   Gruner, Christian Gottfried, 1744-1815.
93   Decanus D. Christ. Godofredus Gruner...
N63   Dissertationem...Christiani Gottlob Rothe...
G89   indicit de daemoniacis a Christo Sospitatore percuratis breviter commentatus. Ienae, Litteris Fickelscherrii [1774]
16 p. 20cm.
Introductory to a diss. for which Nicolai acted as praeses, Rothe as respondent: Dissertatio inauguralis medica De nyctalopia ac hemeralopia visu simplici et duplici
1. Demoniac possession. 2. Rothe, Christian Gottlob, b.1750. 3. Nicolai, Ernst Anton,1722-1802,praeses. Dissertatio inauguralis medica De nyctalopia...

Witchcraft
BF   Nicolai, Heinrich, 1605-1665.
1600   De magicis actionibus tractatus singularis philosophico-theologicus & historicus,
N63   existentiam, definitionem, qvalitatem, cognitionem, probationem, averrionem, & remedia magicarum actionum discutens ... Exercitationibus quibusdam in Gymnasio Gedanensi percursus. Dantisci, E typographejo viduae G. Rhetii, 1649.
[8], 252 p. 19cm.

1. Magic. I. Title.

Nicolai, Heinrich, 1605-1665. respondent.

Witchcraft
BF   Martini, Jacob, metaphysician, praeses.
1587   ΔΙΑΣΚΕΨΙΣ [i.e., diaskepsis] philo-
D61   sophica, De magicis actionibus earumque pro-
no.1   bationibus, ... praeside Jacobo Martini, ... respondente Henrico Nicolai. Ed. 2. [Wittebergae] Typis Christiani Tham, 1623.
[24] p. 21cm.
No. 1 in vol. lettered Dissertationes de magia. 1623-1723.
1. Magic--Addresses, essays, lectures. 2. Witchcraft-- Addresses, essays, lectures. I. Nicolai, Heinrich, 1605-1665, respondent. I. Title: Diaskepsis philosophica, De magicis actionibus.

WITCHCRAFT   Nicolas de Saint Joseph, fl. 1730.
BF   Recueil des premières requestes de la
1582   Demoiselle Cadière, du Père Estienne
G51   Thomas Cadière, Jacobin, et du Père
P96   Nicolas, prieur des Carmes de Toulon.
v.3   [s.l., 173-?]
1 v. (various pagings) 17cm.
Binder's title: Procès de Girard. [v.3]

1. Girard, Jean Baptiste, 1680-1733. I. Cadière, Catherine, b. 1709. II. Cadière, Estienne Thomas, fl. 1730. III. Nicolas de Saint Joseph, fl. 1730.

8
NIC

Witchcraft
HV   Nicolas, Augustin, 1622-1695.
8593   An quaestione per tormenta criminum ve-
N63   ritas elucescat, dissertatio moralis et ju-
1697   ridica, quâ ordo & series instrumenti capitalis judicii, praesertim in causis sortilegii serio discutitur, & ad saniorem divinarum legum & juris antiqui usum revocatur ... Auctore Augustino Nicolao ... Argentorati, Sumptibus Joh. Friderici Spoor, 1697.
289, 80, [5] p. 17cm.
(Continued on next card)

Witchcraft
HV   Nicolas, Augustin, 1622-1695. An quaestione per tormenta criminum veritas elucescat, dissertatio ... 1697. (Card 2)
8593
N63
1697

"Instructio pro formandis processibus in causis strygum, sortilegorum & maleficorum": p. 271-289.
"Paradoxon de tortura in Christiana republica non exercenda ... à Jacobo Schallero"; 80 p. at end.

I. Schaller, Jacob, 1604-1676. Paradoxon de tortura in Christiana republica non exercenda. II. Title.

Witchcraft
HV   Nicolas, Augustin, 1622-1695.
8593   Si la torture est un moyen seur a verifier les crimes
N63   secrets; dissertation morale et juridique, par laquelle il
1681   est amplement traicté des abus qui se commettent par tout en l'instruction des procés criminels, & particulierement en la recherche du sortilege ... Par Mre. Augustin Nicolas ... A Amsterdam, Chez A. Wolfgang, 1681.
224, [8] p. 16cm.

1. Torture. 2. Witchcraft. I. Title.

13-26318

Library of Congress   HV8593.N5

Nicolas Remy et son oeuvre démonologique.

WITCHCRAFT
BF   Dintzer, Lucien.
1520   Nicolas Remy et son oeuvre démonologique.
R38   Lyon, L'imprimerie de Lyon, 1936.
D58   148 p. 25cm.
Thèse--Lyons.
At head of title: Université de Lyon, Faculté des lettres.
Bibliography: p. [135]-143.
1. Remi, Nicolas, 1530-1612. Daemonolatreiae libri tres. 2. Demonology. 3. Witchcraft. I. Title.

8
NIC

CATALOGUE OF THE CORNELL WITCHCRAFT COLLECTION

Nicole de Vervins.
WITCHCRAFT
BX   Langlet, Louis.
2340   Une possession au XVIe siècle; étude mé-
L28+ dicale de la vie & de l'hystérie de Nicole
1910 Obry, dite Nicole de Vervins, 1566.
      Reims, Matot-Braine, 1910.
      110 p. illus. 26cm.
      Originally issued in the same year as
      thesis at the Faculté de médecine, Paris,
      with title: Etude médicale d'une posses-
      sion au XVIe siècle...
          1. Nicole de Vervins. 2.Exorcism.
8   3. Hysteria. I. His Etude médicale
NIC   d'une possession au XVIe siècle.

Nicole de Vervins.
WITCHCRAFT
BX   Roger, Joseph, abbé.
2340   Histoire de Nicole de Vervins d'après les
R72   historiens contemporains et témoins oculai-
      res; ou, Le triomphe du saint sacrement sur
      le démon à Laon en 1566, par J. Roger ...
      Paris, H. Plon, 1863.
      495 p. fold. plate. 22cm.
          1. Nicole de Vervins. 2. Exorcism. I.
8   Title. II. Title: Le triomphe du saint sacre-
NIC   ment sur le   démon à Laon en 1566.

Witchcraft
BF   Nicuesa, Hilarius.
1559   Excorcismarivm, in duos libros dispositum:
N66   qvorvm annvale altervm, altervm sanctvarivm
      dicimvs conivrationvm. Qvibvs pro totivs
      anni feriis ... ex sacra scriptura & sanctis
      patribus apposita materia ... exorcistae
      non deest. Venice, Iunta, 1639.
      414 p. 23cm.
          1. Exorcism. I. Title.

Witchcraft
PA   Nider, Johannes, d. 1438.
8555   De visionibus ac revelationibus opus ra-
N59F7 rissimum Historiis Germaniae refertissimum,
1692 Anno 1517. Argentinae editum. Auspiciis...
      Rudolphi Augusti, Brunsvicens. ac Luneburg.
      Ducis, luci & integritati restitutum, re-
      censente Hermanno von der Hardt ... Hel-
      mestadii, Impensis Pauli Zeisingii, Typis
      Salomonis Schnorrii, 1692.
      [30], 669 p. front. 17cm.
          A reprint, under a new title, of Nider's
              (Continued on next card)

Witchcraft
PA   Nider, Johannes, d. 1438. De visionibus
8555 ... 1692.   (Card 2)
N59F7
1692 Formicarius.
      "Liber quintus: De maleficis & eorum de-
      ceptionibus": p. 514-669.
      Ex libris Kurt Seligmann.
          1. Conduct of life. 2. Christian life.
      3. Witchcraft. 4. Demonology. I. Hardt,
      Hermann von der, 1660-1746, ed. II. Nider,
      Johannes, d. 1438. Formicarius. III.
      Title. IV. Title: Formicarius.

Witchcraft Nider, Johannes, d. 1438.
PA   Formicarius
8555   Nider, Johannes, d. 1438.
N59F7   De visionibus ac revelationibus opus ra-
1692 rissimum Historiis Germaniae refertissimum,
      Anno 1517. Argentinae editum. Auspiciis...
      Rudolphi Augusti, Brunsvicens. ac Luneburg.
      Ducis, luci & integritati restitutum, re-
      censente Hermanno von der Hardt ... Hel-
      mestadii, Impensis Pauli Zeisingii, Typis
      Salomonis Schnorrii, 1692.
      [30], 669 p. front. 17cm.
          A reprint, under a new title, of Nider's
              (Continued on next card)

Witchcraft Nider, Johannes, d. 1438.
PA   Formicarius
8555   Nider, Johannes, d. 1438. De visionibus
N59F7   ... 1692.   (Card 2)
1692 Formicarius.
      "Liber quintus: De maleficis & eorum de-
      ceptionibus": p. 514-669.
      Ex libris Kurt Seligmann.
          1. Conduct of life. 2. Christian life.
      3. Witchcraft. 4. Demonology. I. Hardt,
      Hermann von der, 1660-1746, ed. II. Nider,
      Johannes, d. 1438. Formicarius. III.
      Title. IV. Title: Formicarius.

WITCHCRAFT
BF   Niehues, Bernhard, 1831-1909.
1583   Zur Geschichte des Hexenglaubens und der
N66   Hexenprozesse, vornehmlich im ehemaligen
      Fürstbisthum Münster. Münster, Coppenrath,
      1875.
      vi, 151 p. 23cm.
          1. Witchcraft--Münster (Diocese) 2.
8   Trials (Witchcraft)--Münster (Diocese)
NIC   I. Title.

WITCHCRAFT
BF   Niermeyer, Antonie.
1517   Verhandeling over het booze wezen in het
N4   bijgeloof onzer natie. Eene bijdrage tot
N67   de kennis onzer voorvaderlijke mythologie.
      Rotterdam, A. Wijnands, 1840.
      xiv, 115 p. 24cm.
          1. Devil. 2. Demonology. 3. Folk-lore--
8   Netherlands. I. Title.
NIC

Niesert, Johann Heinrich Joseph, ed.
WITCHCRAFT
BF   Köbbing, Georg, defendant.
1583   Merkwürdiger Hexen-Process gegen den Kauf-
Z7   mann G. Köbbing, an dem Stadtgerichte zu
1632d Coesfeld im Jahre 1632 geführt. Vollstän-
      dig aus den Original-Acten mitgetheilt und
      mit einer Vorrede begleitet von Joseph Nie-
      sert. Coesfeld, Gedruckt bei Bernard
      Wittneven, 1827.
      lii, 104 p. 19cm.
          1. Trials (Witchcraft)--Coesfeld, Germany.
8   I. Niesert, Johann Heinrich Joseph,
NIC   ed. II. Title.

Niessner, Johann, respondent.
Witchcraft
BF   Mirus, Adam Erdmann, 1656-1727, praeses.
1565   De conventu sagarum ad sua sabbata,
D62   qvae vocant, dissertationem, ... praeside
no.8 M. Adamo Erdmann Miro ... exhibebit res-
      pondens Johannes Niessner ... Witten-
      bergae, Typis Matthaei Henckelii [1682]
      [16] p. 20cm.
      No. 8 in vol. lettered Dissertationes
      de sagis. 1636-1714.
          1. Witchcraft. 2. Devil. I. Niess-
      ner, Johann, respondent. II. Title.

Nigal, Nicolle, d. 1582.
Witchcraft
BF   Badel, Émile, 1867-
1582   D'une sorcière qu'aultrefois on brusla
Z7   dans Sainct-Nicholas. Le tout habillé d'
1582 ymaiges [sic] par J. Jacquot. Nancy,
      Berger-Levrault, 1891.
      227 p. illus. 22cm.
          1. Nigal, Nicolle, d. 1582. 2. Witch-
      craft--France. I. Title.

Nigrinus, Georg, 1530-1601, tr.
Witchcraft
BF   Godelmann, Johann Georg, 1559-1611.
1565   Von Zäuberern Hexen vnd Vnholden, war-
G58   hafftiger vnd wolgegründter Bericht Herrn
1592 Georgii Gödelmanni ..., wie dieselben
      zuerkennen vnd zu straffen. Allen Beampten
      zu vnsern Zeitten von wegen vieler vngleich-
      er vnd streittigen Meynung sehr nützlich
      vnnd nothwendig zuwissen ... verteutschet
      ... durch Georgium Nigrinum ... Franck-
      fort am Mayn, Gedruckt durch Nicolaum Bas-
8   saeum, 1592.
              (Continued on next card)

Nigrinus, Georg, 1530-1601, tr.
Witchcraft
BF   Godelmann, Johann Georg, 1559-1611. Von
1565   Zäuberern Hexen vnd Vnholden ... 1592.
G58   (Card 2)
1592
      8 p. l., 483 p. illus. 20cm.
      Translation of Tractatus de magis, vene-
      ficis et lamiis.
          1. Witchcraft. 2. Demonology. 3.
      Trials (Witchcraft) I. His Tractatus de ma-
      gis, veneficis et lamiis. German.
      II. Title: Von Zäuberern, Hexen
8   und Unholden.

WITCHCRAFT
BF   Nippold, Friedrich Wilhelm Franz, 1838-
1566   Die gegenwärtige Wiederbelebung des Hexen-
N71   glaubens. Mit einem literarisch-kritischen
      Anhang über die Quellen und Bearbeitungen
      der Hexenprozesse. Berlin, C.G. Lüderitz,
      1875.
      95 p. 23cm. (Deutsche Zeit- und Streit-
      Fragen, Jahrg. 4, Heft 57/58)
          1. Witchcraft. 2. Witchcraft--Hist.
8   I. Title.
NIC

Nissenbaum, Stephen, joint author.
UNDERGR
BF   Boyer, Paul S
1576   Salem possessed; the social origins of
B79   witchcraft [by] Paul Boyer and Stephen Nissen-
      baum. Cambridge, Mass., Harvard University
      Press, 1974.
      xxi, 231 p. illus. 25 cm.

Nodé, Pierre.
      Declamation contre l'erreur execrable
      des maleficiers.
Witchcraft
BF   Massé, Pierre.
1410   De l'impostvre et tromperie des diables,
M41   devins, enchantevrs, sorciers, novevrs d'es-
      guillettes, cheuilleurs, necromanciens, chi-
      romanciens, & autres qui par telle inuoca-
      tion diabolique, ars magiques & superstit-
      ions abusent le peuple. Par Pierre Massé
      du Mans, aduocat. Paris, Chez Iean Poupy,
      1579.
      various pagings. 17cm.
8   Printer's device on t. p.
              (Continued on next card)

Nodé, Pierre.
      Declamation contre l'erreur execrable
Witchcraft des maleficiers.
BF   Massé, Pierre. De l'impostvre et tromperie
1410   des diables ... 1579.   (Card 2)
M41
      Title on spine: Massé. Abus des divins
      Text preceeded by Petit fragment cate-
      chistic d'vne plvs ample catechese de la
      magie ... de M. René Benoist Angeuin ...;
      and followed by Benoist's Traicté enseignan
      en bref les cavses des malefices, sortilege
      et enchanteries... with special t. p.
      Declamation contre l'errevr execrable de
8   (Continued on next card)

414

CATALOGUE OF THE CORNELL WITCHCRAFT COLLECTION

Nodé, Pierre.
Declamation contre l'erreur execrable des maleficiers.

Witchcraft
BF
1410
M41

Massé, Pierre. De l'imposture et tromperie des diables ... 1579. (Card 3)

maleficiers ... par F. Pierre Nodé minime, has special t. p. with imprint Paris, Chez Iean du Carroy imprimeur, 1578, and is paged separately.
Trois sermons de S. Avgvstin ... traduits en françois par M. René Benoist, has special t. p. with imprint Paris, Chez Iean Poupy, 1579, and unnum   bered pages.

8
(Continued on next card)

Nodige aanmerking over het Sterf-bedde van Balthasar Bekker.

Witchcraft
BX
9479
B42
B11
no.2

[Schuts, Jacobus]
Nodige aanmerking over het Sterf-bedde van Balthasar Bekker. Vertonende de openbare valsheyt van dat syn gevoelen, dat hy op syn dood-bedde segt hem voor paart en wagen verstrekt te hebben om hem te voeren na den hemel. Gravenhage, By P. van Tol, boekverkooper, 1698.
13 p. [p. 14 blank] title vignette, illus. initial. 20 x 16cm.
4°: A-B⁴(-B4)

8
(Continued on next card)

Nodige aanmerking over het Sterf-bedde van Balthasar Bekker.

Witchcraft
BX
9479
B42
B11
no.2

[Schuts, Jacobus] Nodige aanmerking over het Sterf-bedde van Balthasar Bekker. 1698. (Card 2)

Black letter.
Ascribed to Schuts by van der Linde.
Van der Linde 206.
No. 2 in vol. lettered B. Bekkers sterf-bed en andere tractaten.
1. Bekker, Balthasar, 1634-1698. 2. Bekker, Johannes Henricus, fl. 1698-1737. Sterf-bedde van ... Do. Balthazar Bekker. I. Title.

8

Witchcraft
BF
1410
B42
Z56
v.2
no.6

Nodige aanmerkinge omtrent eenige woorden gesprooken van D. Johannes Visscherus, in een catechisatie, over den 34 Sondag des Catechismus. Dog bysonderlijk over de 94 vrage, enz. voorgevallen op Sondag den 24 Augusty 1692. Door T. S. Amsterdam, By D. vanden Dalen, boekverkoper, 1692.
7 p. [p. 8 blank] title vignette. 19 x 15cm.
4°: A⁴.

8
(Continued on next card)

Witchcraft
BF
1410
B42
Z56
v.2
no.6

Nodige aanmerkinge omtrent eenige woorden gesprooken van D. Johannes Visscherus ... 1692. (Card 2)

Black letter.
Response to Visscher's attack on Balthasar Bekker.
No. 6 in vol. lettered Bekker II.
1. Visscher, Johannes, 161?-1694. 2. Bekker, Balthasar, 1634-1698. De betoverde weereld. I. T. S. II. S., T.

8

Nodige bedenkingen op de niewe beweegingen, onlangs verwekt door den circulairen brief en andere middelen ...

Witchcraft
BF
1410
B42
Z56
v.1
no.1

Bekker, Balthasar, 1634-1698.
Nodige bedenkingen op de niewe beweegingen, onlangs verwekt door den circulairen brief en andere middelen, tegen den auteur van 't boek De betoverde weereld, door Balthasar Bekker, predikant tot Amsterdam. Amsterdam, Gedruckt by D. vanden Dalen, boekverkoper [1692?]
1 p. l., 62, [1] p. [p. 64 blank] title vignette, illus. initial. 19 x 16cm.
4°: π1, A-H⁴.
Preface auto   graphed by Bekker.

(Continued on next card)

Nodige bedenkingen op de niewe beweegingen, onlangs verwekt door den circulairen brief en andere middelen ...

Witchcraft
BF
1410
B42
Z56
v.1
no.1

Bekker, Balthasar, 1634-1698. Nodige bedenkingen op de niewe beweegingen ... [1692?] (Card 2)

Dated at end: den 9. July 1692.
Van der Linde 42.
No. 1 in vol. lettered Bekker I.
1. Nederlandse Hervormde Kerk. Kerkenraden. Rotterdam. Circulaire brief wegens de saake van Dr. Balthasar Bekker. 2. Nederlandse Hervormde Kerk—Doctrinal and controversial works. 3. Bekker, Balthasar, 1634-1698. De betoverde weereld. I. Title.

8

WITCHCRAFT
QC
859
H82

Nohtwendiger Bericht, von Donnern und Hagel-Wettern.
Hossmann, Abraham, d. 1617.
De tonitru & tempestate, das ist: Nohtwendiger Bericht, von Donnern vnd Hagel-Wettern, wannen vnd woher sich dieselben verursachen, ob sie natürlich: Item, ob Teufel vnd Zäuberer auch Wetter machen können ... Neben Erzehlung etlicher seltzamen Fälle ... in Druck gegeben durch Abrahamum Hosmanum ... Leipzig, In Verlegung Henning Grossn des Ältern Buchhändl. [Typis Beerwaldin, durch Jacobum Popporeich] 1612.
123, [1] p. 20cm.

8
NIC
(Continued on next card)

WITCHCRAFT
QC
859
H82

Nohtwendiger Bericht, von Donnern und Hagel-Wettern.
Hossmann, Abraham, d. 1617. De tonitru & tempestate ... 1612. (Card 2)

Title in red and black, within ornamental border.
With colophon.
1. Meteorology—Early works to 1800. 2. Folk-lore, German. 3. Witchcraft. I. Title. II. Title: Von Donnern und Hagel-Wettern.

8
NIC

Witchcraft
BF
1410
B42
Z56
v.2
no.22

Noomtjins, Zalomon.
Spiegel voor den verwarden, en warzoekende Haggebher Philaleethees. Waar in, uit zyne 6 brieven, enz. getoond word, zyne onkunde, en verwarring, zoo in taal, als in zaaken. Ofte een briev van Zalomon Noomtjins, tot Amsteldam. Geschreeven aan zynen vriend C. S. S. tot Buiksloot. Inhoudende (neevens andere zaaken) voornaamelijk, eenige aanmerkingen, over den perzoon, en de 6 brieven, enz. van Haggebher Philaleethees. Als meede over de briev, en perzoon van Everardus van der Hooght, en daar by

(Continued on next card)

Witchcraft
BF
1410
B42
Z56
v.2
no.22

Noomtjins, Zalomon. Spiegel voor den verwarden, en warzoekende Haggebher Philaleethees. 1692. (Card 2)

ook over zyne Aanmerkingen, over de ordre van een welgestelde predikatie. Mitsgaders d'ontdekking, der lasteringen van Brink. Amsterdam, By D. van den Dalen, boekverkooper, 1692.
33, [1] p. title and other vignettes. 19 x 15cm.

(Continued on next card)

Witchcraft
BF
1410
B42
Z56
v.2
no.22

Noomtjins, Zalomon. Spiegel voor den verwarden, en warzoekende Haggebher Philaleethees. 1692. (Card 3)

4°: A-D⁴, E1.
Black letter (except for introduction)
Attacks critics of Balthasar Bekker's De betoverde weereld.
G. L. Burr suggests Noomtjins may be a pseudonymn for Bekker.
Haggebher is a pseudonym of E. van der Hooght.

(Continued on next card)

Witchcraft
BF
1410
B42
Z56
v.2
no.22

Noomtjins, Zalomon. Spiegel voor den verwarden, en warzoekende Haggebher Philaleethees. 1692. (Card 4)

Van der Linde 111.
No. 22 in vol. lettered Bekker II.
1. Hooght, Everard van der, d. 1716. 2. Brink, Hendrik, 1645-1723. De godslasteringen van den amsterdamschen predikant Bekker. 3. Bekker, Balthasar, 1634-1698. De betoverde weereld. I. Title. II. Bekker, Balthasar, 1634-1698, sup   posed author.

8

Witchcraft
BF
1410
B42
Z69
no.11

Noomtjins, Zalomon.
Spiegel voor den verwarden, en warzoekende Haggebher Philaleethees. Waar in, uit zyne 6 brieven, enz. getoond word, zyne onkunde, en verwarring, zoo in taal, als in zaaken. Ofte een briev van Zalomon Noomtjins, tot Amsteldam. Geschreeven aan zynen vriend C. S. S. tot Buiksloot. Inhoudende (neevens andere zaaken) voornaamelijk, eenige aanmerkingen, over den perzoon, en de 6 brieven, enz. van Haggebher Philaleethees. Als meede over de briev, en perzoon van Everardus van der Hooght, en daar by

(Continued on next card)

Witchcraft
BF
1410
B42
Z69
no.11

Noomtjins, Zalomon. Spiegel voor den verwarden, en warzoekende Haggebher Philaleethees. 1692. (Card 2)

by ook over zyne Aanmerkingen, over de ordre van een welgestelde predikatie. Mitsgaders d'ontdekking, der lasteringen van Brink. Amsterdam, By D. van den Dalen, boekverkooper, 1692.
33, [1] p. title and other vignettes. 21cm.

(Continued on next card)

Witchcraft
BF
1410
B42
Z69
no.11

Noomtjins, Zalomon. Spiegel voor den verwarden, en warzoekende Haggebher Philaleethees. 1692. (Card 3)

4°: A-D⁴, E1.
Black letter (except for introduction)
Attacks critics of Balthasar Bekker's De betoverde weereld.
G. L. Burr suggests Noomtjins may be a pseudonymn for Bekker.
Haggebher is pseudonym of E. van der Hooght.

(Continued on next card)

Witchcraft
BF
1410
B42
Z69
no.11

Noomtjins, Zalomon. Spiegel voor den verwarden, en warzoekende Haggebher Philaleethees. 1692. (Card 4)

Van der Linde 111.
No.11 in a Collection of tracts against Balthasar Bekker and his Betoverde weereld.

8

Nord-schwedische Hexerey.

WITCHCRAFT
BF
1584
S9
S61

Sincerus, Theophilus, pseud.
Nord-schwedische Hexerey, oder Simia Dei, Gottes Affe. Das ist: Ausführliche Beschreibung der schändlichen Verführungen des leidigen Satans, darinnen zu sehen Gottes erschröckliches Straff-Verhängen, wegen greulicher Sünden-Mengen. In einem Jammer-behertzigten Send-Schreiben am [sic] Tag gegeben, von Theophilo Sincero, an Christianum Piandrum. [Augsburg?] 1677.
[64] p. illus. 20cm.

8
NIC
(Continued on next card)

415

CATALOGUE OF THE CORNELL WITCHCRAFT COLLECTION

Nord-schwedische Hexerey.

WITCHCRAFT
BF
1584
S9
S61

Sincerus, Theophilus, pseud. Nord-schwedische Hexerey ... 1677. (Card 2)

"By Gottlieb Spitzel? See what Hauber says of the relation of this tract to his [i.e., Spitzel's] Die gebrochene Macht der Finsterniss. G. L. B."--Note in MS facing t. p.
Illustrative vignette on t. p.
1. Witchcraft--Sweden. 2. Witchcraft. I. Spitzel, Gottlieb, 1639-1691, supposed author. II. Title. III. Title: Simia Dei, Gottes Affe.

8
NIC

Normann, Martin, respondent.

Witchcraft
BF
1587
D61
no.13

Schack, Johann, praeses. Disputatio juridica ordinaria De probatione criminis magiae, qvam sub praesidio D. Johannis Schackii ... publice defendet Martinus von Normann ... Gryphiswaldiae, Typis Danielis Benjaminis Starckii [1706?] 26 p. 18cm. (bound in 21cm. vol.)
Pages 1-8 are bound between p. 72 & 73 of no. 12; rest of text follows no. 12.
No. 13 in vol. lettered Dissertationes de magia. 1623-1723.
1. Witchcraft--Addresses, essays, lectures. 2. Trials (Witchcraft) I. Normann, Martin, respondent. II. Title: De probatione criminis magiae.

8

Norske hexeformularer og magiske opskrifter.

AS
283
N86H6+
1901
no.1

Bang, Anton Christian, 1840-1913.
... Norske hexeformularer og magiske opskrifter ... Kristiania, I commission hos J. Dybwad, 1901-02.
xxxii, 761 p. 27½ᶜᵐ. (Videnskabs-selskabet i Christiania. Skrifter II. Historisk-filosofisk klasse, no. 1)
"Udgivet for Hans A. Benneches fond."
"Fremlagt i den Historisk-filosofisk klasse 19. jan. 1900."

I. Title.

3--24333

Library of Congress   AS283.057 1901 no.1
[a35b1]

The Northamptonshire witches.

Witchcraft
BF
1581
A2
W81
1866a
no.3

[Davis, Ralph] The Northamptonshire witches. Being a true and faithful account of the births, educations, lives, and conversations, of Elinor Shaw, and Mary Phillips, (the two notorious witches) that were executed at Northampton on Saturday, March the 17th, 1705, for bewitching a woman and two children to death. ... London, Printed for F. Thorn [1705] [Northampton, Taylor, 1866]
8 p. 22cm.

8
(Continued on next card)

The Northamptonshire witches.

Witchcraft
BF
1581
A2
W81
1866a
no.3

[Davis, Ralph] The Northamptonshire witches ... [1866] (Card 2)

No. 3 in box lettered Witchcraft in Northamptonshire.

1. Witchcraft--Northamptonshire, England. I. Title.

8

Witchcraft
F
67
N87
A2

Northend, William Dummer, 1823-1902.
Address before the Essex bar association, December 8, 1885. By William D. Northend ... Salem, Printed at the Salem press, 1885.
50 p. 22½ᶜᵐ
"From the Historical collections of the Essex Institute, vol. XXII."
"Members of the bar": p. [55]-59.

1. Law--Massachusetts--Hist. & crit. 2. Courts--Massachusetts. 3. Lawyers--Essex co., Mass. I. Title.

34--8901

Library of Congress   [2]

A noted case of witchcraft at North Moreton, Berks, in the early 17th century.

WITCHCRAFT
BF
1581
Z7
1605

Ewen, Cecil Henry L'Estrange, 1877-
A noted case of witchcraft at North Moreton, Berks, in the early 17th century. [London] 1936.
7 p. 23cm.

"Reprinted from the Berkshire archaeological journal, vol. 40, no.2."

1. Gunter, Anne, fl. 1605. 2. Witchcraft--Berkshire, England. I. Title.

8

Notes on the bibliography of witchcraft in Massachusetts.

WITCHCRAFT
Z
6878
W8
M82

Moore, George Henry, 1823-1892.
Notes on the bibliography of witchcraft in Massachusetts.

(In: American Antiquarian Society. Proceedings. Worcester. 25cm. new ser., v.5, pt.2, Apr. 1888. p. 245-273)

1. Witchcraft--Massachusetts--Bibl. I. Title.

8
NIC

Notes on the history of witchcraft in Massachusetts; with illustrative documents.

Witchcraft
BF
1576
M82+

Moore, George Henry, 1823-1892.
Notes on the history of witchcraft in Massachusetts; with illustrative documents. From Proceedings at the annual meeting of the American antiquarian society, October 21, 1882. By George H. Moore. Worcester, Mass., Printed by C. Hamilton, 1883.
32 p. 26ᶜᵐ.
Followed by the author's "Supplementary notes on witchcraft in Massachusetts" (Cambridge, 1884) reprinted from the Proceedings of the American antiquarian society, March 13, 1884; and by "Final notes on witchcraft in Massachusetts" (New York, 1885)
Autographed presentation copy from the author.
1. Witchcraft--Massachusetts. I. American Antiquarian Society, Worcester, Mass. II. Title.

24--23088

8
Library of Congress   BF1576.M6

Notes on witchcraft.

BF
1566
K62

Kittredge, George Lyman., 1860-1941.
Notes on witchcraft, by George Lyman Kittredge ... Worcester, Mass., The Davis press, 1907.
67 p. 26ᶜᵐ.

"Reprinted from the Proceedings of the American antiquarian society, vol. XVIII."

1. Witchcraft. I. Title.

15--3715

Library of Congress   BF1566.K5

Witchcraft
BF
1581
A2
N91

Notestein, Wallace, 1879-
A history of witchcraft in England from 1558 to 1718. Washington, American Historical Association, 1911.
xiv, 442 p. 20cm. (Prize essays of the American Historical Association, 1909)
"To this essay was awarded the Herbert Baxter Adam prize in European history for 1909."

3 copies

1. Witchcraft--England. I. American Historical Association. Prize essays, 1909.

Witchcraft
BF
1581
A2
N91
1965

Notestein, Wallace, 1879-
A history of witchcraft in England from 1558 to 1718. New York, Russell & Russell, 1965.
xiv, 442 p. 23cm. (Prize essays of the American Historical Association)

"Awarded the Herbert Baxter Adams prize in European history for 1909."
1. Witchcraft--England. I. Title: Witchcraft in England from 1558 to 1718. II. Series: American Historical Association. Prize essays, 1909. III. Title.

Notice sur Nicolas Remy.

WITCHCRAFT
DC
112
R38
L46
1869

Leclerc, Laurent.
Notice sur Nicolas Remy, procureur général de Lorraine; discours de réception à l'Académie de Stanislas, par L. Leclerc. Nancy, Sordoillet, imprimeurs de l'Académie de Stanislas, 1869.
107 p. facsims., port. 23cm.

"Extrait des Mémoires de l'Académie de Stanislas, 1868."

8
NIC

1. Remi, Nicolas, 1530-1612. I. Title.

Notices sur quelques points d'histoire et d'archéologie.

WITCHCRAFT
BF
1584
B4
M75

Monoyer, Jules Alfred, 1841-1887.
Notices sur quelques points d'histoire et d'archéologie. III. La sorcellerie en Hainaut. Procès de 1568 à 1683. Mons, H. Manceaux, 1886.
47 p. 23cm. (Essais d'histoire et d'archéologie, t.5, fasc. 3)
Half-title (also title on original cover): La sorcellerie en Hainaut, et plus spécialement aux environs du Roeulx...
1. Witchcraft--Hist. 2. Witchcraft--Hainaut. 3. Trials (Witchcraft)--Hainaut. 4. His La sorcellerie en Hainaut.

8
NIC

Notwendige Errinnerung. Vonn des Sathans letzten Zornsturm.

MSS
Bd.
WITCHCRAFT
BF
C39

Celichius, Andreas, d. 1599.
Notwendige Errinnerung. Vonn des Sathans letzten Zornsturm, und was es auff sich habe und bedeute, das nu zu dieser Zeit so viel Menschen an Leib und Seel vom Teuffel besessen werden durch Andream Celichium... Wittenberg, Zacharias Lehman, 1594 [ca. 1900]
59 p. 23cm.
Carnap's manuscript copy.
"Original druck in der Kgl.
(Continued on next card)

Notwendige Errinnerung. Vonn des Sathans letzten Zornsturm.

MSS
Bd.
WITCHCRAFT
BF
C39

Celichius, Andreas, d. 1599. Notwendige Errinnerung...1594 [ca. 1900] (Card 2)

Universit. Bibliothek zu Leipzig, 113 S. in 4°."
Title in red and black.
Numerals and signatures in the margins indicate pagination and signatures of the original.

1. Demoniac possession. 2. Exorcism. I. Title.

Witchcraft
Z
6880
Z9
N93

Nourry, Émile Dominique, 1870-1935.
Le bibliophile ès sciences psychiques. Catalogue de livres d'occasion sur les sciences occultes. Envente à la Librairie Ancienne et Moderne.
Paris.
nos. 24cm.

Subtitle varies.

Le nouveau Tarquin.

Witchcraft
BF
1582
G51R3
1731c

Girard, Jean Baptiste, 1680-1733, defendant.
Recueil général des pièces concernant le procez entre la Demoiselle Cadière de la ville de Toulon, et le père Girard, jesuite ... La Haye, Swart, 1731.
8 v. 17cm.

The trials were held before the Parlement of Aix.
A collection of items originally published separately; there is a general title
(Continued on next card)

416

CATALOGUE OF THE CORNELL WITCHCRAFT COLLECTION

Le nouveau Tarquin.

Witchcraft
BF
1582
G51R3
1731c

Girard, Jean Baptiste, 1680-1733, defendant.
Recueil général des pièces concernant le procez ... 1731. (Card 2)

page and a table of contents for each vol.
Bound with v.8 is Le nouveau Tarquin, usually attributed to Jean Jacques Bel.

I. Cadière, Catherine, b. 1709. II. France. Parlement (Aix) III. Title. IV. [Bel, Jean Jacques] 1693-1738. Le nouveau Tarquin. V. Title: Le nouveau Tarquin.

Novissimae consultationes cononicae.

Rare
BX
1939
.I4
P63++

Pignatelli, Giacomo, fl. 1668.
Novissimae consultationes canonicae, praecipue controversias, quae ad fidem, ejusque regulam spectant, in quibus errores atheorum, infidelium, schismaticorum, haereticorum, & aliorum Ecclesiae Catholicae hostium referuntur & refelluntur; praesertimque illas quae circa S. Inquisitionis Tribunal versantur ... complectentes. Opus prima vice praelo commissum ... Cum indice consultationum ... Cosmopoli, Apud Dominicum Puteanum, 1711.
2 v. in 1. 38cm.

WITCHCRAFT
BX
2340
N94
1675

Noydens, Benito Remigio, 1630-1685.
Practica de exorcistas y ministros de la iglesia, en que con mucha erudicion, y singular claridad, se trata de la instruccion de los exorcismos, para lançar, y auyentar los demonios, y curar espiritualmente todo genero de maleficio, y hechizos... Primera impression de Barcelona, añadida por su autor. Barcelona, Por Antonio Lacavalleria, 1675.
431 p. 14cm.

8
NIC
1. Exorcism. I. Title.

WITCHCRAFT
BX
2340
N96

Nucleus continens benedictiones rerum diversarum, item exorcismos ad varia maleficia depellenda, conjurationes item ad fugandas a daemonibus eorumque ministris excitatas aëreas tempestates... Constantiae, Ex typographia episcopali, apud Ioannem Geng., 1655.
196 p. 13cm.

8
NIC
Page 48 omitted in pagination.
1. Exorcism.

Nützlicher Unterricht wider den Teufel zu streiten.

Witchcraft
BF
1559
.G25
.N4
.775

Gassner, Johann Joseph, 1727-1779.
Weise fromm und gesund zu leben, auch ruhig und gottseelig zu sterben: oder, Nützlicher Unterricht wider den Teufel zu streiten: durch Beantwortung der Fragen: 1. Kann der Teufel dem Leibe der Menschen schaden? II. Welchen am mehresten? III. Wie ist zu helfen? 8. verb. Aufl. und vermehrt von Herrn Verfasser selbsten. Augsburg gedrucht, zu finden bey J. G. Bullman, 1775.
40 p. front. 17cm.

1. Exorcism. I. Title. II. Title: Nützlicher Unterricht wider den Teufel zu streiten.

Num daemon cum sagis generare possit.

Witchcraft
BF
1565
.W7

Wolf, Johann, praeses.
Disputationem physicam, evolventem qv. Num daemon cum sagis generare possit, ... sub praesidio Dn. M. Johannis Wolfii ... submittit Johann. Paulus Reineccius ... Wittenbergae, Typis Christiani Schrödteri [1676]
[16] p. 20cm.
No. 7 in vol. lettered Dissertationes de sagis. 1636-1714.
1. Witchcraft. 2. Devil. I. Reineck, Johann Paul, respondent. II. Title: Num daemon cum sagis generare possit.

Nun, ja --.

Witchcraft
BF
1445
S595

[Simon, Jordan] pater, 1719-1776.
Nun, ja -- oder, Kleine Zweifeln über zwey Berichte von einer Hexen- oder Studenten-Geschichte die sich in dem Jahre 1768. den 10. 11. 12. und 13. Junius zu Ingolstadt in Bayern soll zugetragen haben. Gedruckt zu Unglauben, Mit der Akademicker Schriften [i. e., Leipzig, 1769]
31 p. 21cm.
Attribution by Holzmann; imprint from Kayser.
(Continued on next card)

Nun, ja --.

Witchcraft
BF
1445
S595

[Simon, Jordan] pater, 1719-1776. Nun, ja ... [1769] (Card 2)

The "Berichte" are given, p. 3-11.
Continued by Nicht doch -- oder, Auflösung der kleinen Zweifel über zwei Berichte. With this is bound his Nicht doch. [Leipzig? 1769]
1. Ghosts. 2. Witchcraft--Ingolstadt, Bavaria. I. Title. II. Title: Kleine Zweifeln Über zwey Berichte von einer Hexen- oder Studenten-Geschichte.

Nuremberg.

MSS
Bd.
WITCHCRAFT
JS
N971++

Hals Gerichts Ordtnung. Ordnung des Hals-Gerichts zu Nürnberg. [17th cent.?]
99 l. 32 x 21cm.
Manuscript, on paper, in three different German hands. Only the first four leaves, dated 1526, are concerned with criminal procedure. The remaining leaves contain a listing and summary of trials which ended in sentences of execution from 1600-1692.
Notes inside front cover by G. L. Burr discuss origin of the manuscript and give bibliographical references.
(Continued on next card)

MSS
Bd.
WITCHCRAFT
JS
N971++

Nuremberg. Hals Gerichts Ordtnung.
[17th cent.?] (Card 2)
Bound in vellum with leather ties. The vellum is itself a manuscript: "... nearly complete (or quite complete) letter of Canton Zug, in Switzerland, to the city of Nuremberg relating to certain Swiss aggressions on the transalpine trade of that city. Its date is 1555 ... Its use suggests that the MS of the book may be the (or an) official original.
Accompanied by an incomplete
(Continued on next card)

MSS
Bd.
WITCHCRAFT
JS
N971++

Nuremberg. Hals Gerichts Ordtnung.
[17th cent.?] (Card 3)
transcript of the letter into a modern hand: 7 leaves, loose, in folder.
In sombre marbled case.
Ex libris: Gg. Wolfg. Carol. Lochner.

1. Criminal procedure--Nuremberg. 2. Criminal registers--Nuremberg. 3. Court records--Nuremberg. 4. Judgments, Criminal --Nuremberg. 5. Sentences (Criminal procedure)--Nuremberg.

Witchcraft
BF
1576
T17

Nurse, Mrs. Rebecca (Towne) 1621-1692.
Tapley, Charles Sutherland, 1899-
Rebecca Nurse, saint but witch victim. by Charles Sutherland Tapley. Boston, Mass., Marshall Jones company [1930]
xiii, 105 p. front. (port.) plates. 20cm.

1. Nurse, Mrs. Rebecca (Towne) 1621-1692. 2. Witchcraft--Salem, Mass. I. Title.

Library of Congress   BF1576.T23   30-33553
Copyright A 31490

Nuss, Balthasar.

WITCHCRAFT
DD
901
F9
M25

Malkmus, Georg Joseph.
Fuldaer Anekdotenbüchlein. Fulda, Druck der Fuldaer Aktienbuchdr., 1875.
viii, 151 p. 17cm.

"Eine Teufelsaustreibung.": p. 93-95.
"Noch eine Teufelsaustreibung.": p.95-97.
"Ein Hexenrichter.": p.101-151. An account, based on documents, of Balthasar Nuss and the witch trials in Fulda.
1. Fulda, Ger. 2. Trials (Witchcraft)--Fulda, Ger. 3. Nuss, Balthasar. 4. Demoniac possession. I. Title.

WITCHCRAFT
BF
1584
S28
N99

Nyerup, Rasmus, 1759-1829.
Udsigt over hexeprocesserne i Norden. Kjöbenhavn, Andreas Seidelin, 1823.
100 p. 18cm.

1. Witchcraft--Scandinavia. 2. Witchcraft--Iceland. 3. Trials (Witchcraft)--Scandinavia. 4. Trials (Witchcraft)--Iceland. I. Title.

WITCHCRAFT
BF
1565
N99

Nynauld, J de
De la lycanthropie, transformation, et extase des sorciers... Avec la refutation des argumens contraires que Bodin alleguë au 6. chap. de sa Demonomanie... Paris, Chez Iean Millot, 1615.
109 p. 16cm.

1. Witchcraft. 2. Demonomania. 3. Werwolves. 4. Bodin, Jean, 1530-1596. De la démonomanie des sorciers. I. Title.

Nypen, Lisbet

WITCHCRAFT
BF
1584
N6
Z7
1670

Øverland, Ole Andreas, 1855-1911.
Lisbet Nypen; en hekseproces fra guldalen. Kristiania og Kjøbenhavn, A. Cammermeyer [1896]
36 p. 19cm. (Historiske fortaellinger, nr.22)

1. Nypen, Lisbet. 2. Witchcraft--Trondheim. 3. Trials (Witchcraft)--Trondheim. I. Title.

WITCHCRAFT
BF
1566
N99

Nyström, Anton Kristen, 1842-1931.
Häxeriet och häxeriprocesserna. Stockholm, A. Bonnier [1896]
28 p. 22cm. (Studentföreningen Verdandis Småskrifter, 58)

1 Witchcraft--History. 2. Trials (Witchcraft)--History. I. Title.

O

Rare DA 448 P82++ 1679 no.2
Oates, Titus, 1649-1705.
The witch of Endor, or the witchcrafts of the Roman Jezebel: in which you have an account of the exorcisms and conjurations of the papists, as they be set forth in their agends, benedictionals, manuals, ... proposed and offered to the consideration of all sober Protestants. By Titus Otes. London, Printed for T. Parkhurst and T. Cockeril, 1679.
47 p. 31cm.
Wing O 62.
No. 2 in vol. lettered: Popish plot pamphlets, 1679.

Witchcraft BF 1565 O11 1736
[Oates, Titus] 1649-1705.
The witch of Endor: or, A plea for the divine administration by the agency of good and evil spirits. Written some years ago at the request of a lady; and now reprinted with a prefatory discourse, humbly addressed to the House of C-----s, who brought in their bill (Jan. 27) for repealing the statute of 1. Jac. cap. 12, concerning witchcraft. ... London, Printed and sold by J. Millan, 1736.
L, 102 p. 20cm.
I. Title.

Ob die Thiere Teufel seyn?
Witchcraft BD 428 B54
[Bertram, Johann Friedrich] 1699-1741.
Ob die Thiere Teufel seyn? wird durch Veranlassung dess von einem Französischen Jesuiten P. Bonjeau unlängst ans Licht gestellten neuen Lehr-Begriffs von den Seelen der Thiere genannt: Amusements philosophiques sur le langage des bestes; oder: Philosophischer Zeit-Vertreib über die Thier-Sprache; in welchen sie zu Teufeln gemachet werden; nach Schrifft und Vernunfft untersuchet und beantwortet, von J.F.B. [Bremen] S. Pomarius [1740]
[15], 94 p. 16cm.

WITCHCRAFT BF 1623 R7 O12
Obereit, Jacob Hermann, 1725-1798.
Gerade Schweizer-Erklärung von Centralismus, Exjesuiterey, Anecdoten, Aberglauben, Maulglauben und Unglauben, gegen einen neuen Rosenkreuz-Bruder in der Berliner Monatsschrift vom August 1785... Berlin, Bei August Mylius, 1786.
viii, 94 p. 17cm.
1. Rosicrucians. 2. Mysticism. 3. Superstition. 4. Jesuits--Controversial literature. Zimmermann, Johann Georg, Ritter von, 1728-1795.
8 NIC
I. Title. II. Title: Schweizer-Erklärung von Centralismus...

Observatio juris criminalis De applicatione tormentorum.
RARE HV 8593 G89
Grupen, Christian Ulrich, 1692-1767.
Observatio juris criminalis De applicatione tormentorum, insbesondere im Schnüren-Anfang, und in vollen Schnüren, mit einer dissertatione praeliminari von den tormentis Romanorum et Graecorum... Hannover, Bei Johann Christoph Richter, 1754.
xii, 442 (i.e. 244) p. 4 plates. 21cm.
With this is bound: Manipulus responsorum votorum ac de cendendi rationum... Ienae, 1726.
8 NIC
1. Torture. 2. Torture--Hist. I. Title.

Observationes casibus quibusdam practicis de jurejurando, ceu remedio probandi in civilibus.
RARE HV 8593 D61 no.23
Meyer, Philipp Carl, fl. 1787.
Observationes casibus quibusdam practicis de jurejurando, ceu remedio probandi in civilibus, et tortura, ceu remedio veritatem eruendi in criminalibus, caute nec sine summa necessitate decernendis, illustratae a Philippo Carolo Meyer. Oehringae, Typis J. L. Hollii, 1787.
80 p. 21cm.
No.23 in a vol. lettered: Dissertationes de tortura, 1667-1787.
8 NIC
1. Oaths--Holy Roman Empire. 2. Torture--Holy Roman Empire. 3. Criminal law--Holy Roman Empire. I. Title.

Observations suggested by the cattle plague.
Witchcraft BF 1775 C75
Constable, Henry Strickland, 1821-
Observations suggested by the cattle plague, about witchcraft, credulity, superstition, parliamentary reform, and other matters. By H. Strickland Constable ... London, Dalton & Lucy, 1866.
99 p. 21cm.

Observations sur le Mémoire manuscrit, attribué par le Père Girard, dans le cours de la plaidoirie de M. l'Avocat.
WITCHCRAFT BF 1582 G51 P96 v.1 no.7
[Cadière, Estienne Thomas] fl. 1730.
Observations sur le Mémoire manuscrit, attribué par le Père Girard, dans le cours de la plaidoirie de M. l'Avocat Général. [s.l., 173-?]
28 p. 17cm.
Signed: P. Etienne Thomas Cadière.
No. 7 in vol. lettered: Procès de Girard. [v.1]
8 NIC
1. Girard, Jean Baptiste, 1680-1733. I. Girard, Jean Baptiste, 1680-1733. II. Title.

The occult: a history.
BF 1429 W74
Wilson, Colin, 1931-
The occult : a history, by Colin Wilson. New York, Random House [c1971]
601 p. illus. 24cm.

1. Occult sciences. 2. Witchcraft. I. Title.

Occult sciences--Bibliography.
Witchcraft Z 6876 C13
Caillet, Albert Louis, 1869-
... Manuel bibliographique des sciences psychiques ou occultes ... Paris, L. Dorbon, 1912.
3 v. fold. tab. 25½cm.
Covers dated 1913.
"Réunion de plusieurs bibliographies partielles et de catalogues, célèbres mais peu communs, fondus en un seul corps aussi homogène que possible."--Pref.
11,648 entries.

1. Occult sciences--Bibl. I. Title.
Z6876.C25   13-10632
Library of Congress [53c1]

Occult sciences--Bibliography.
Witchcraft Z 6876 G73
Grässe, Johann Georg Theodor, 1814-1885.
Bibliotheca magica et pneumatica; oder, Wissenschaftlich geordnete bibliographie der wichtigsten in das gebiet des zauber-, wunder-, geister- und sonstigen aberglaubens vorzüglich älterer zeit einschlagenden werke. Mit angabe der aus diesen wissenschaften auf der Königl. Sächs. oeff. bibliothek zu Dresden befindlichen schriften. Ein beitrag zur sittengeschichtlichen literatur. Zusammengestellt und mit einem doppelten register versehen. Leipzig, W. Engelmann, 1843.
iv, 175 p. 22cm.
Copy 1 interleaved.
Manuscript notes, copy 1.
1. Occult sciences--Bibl. I. Title.

Occult sciences--Bibliography.
Witchcraft Z 6880 G94
Guaita, Stanislas de, 1860-1897.
Stanislas de Guaita et sa bibliothèque occulte. Paris, Dorbon, 1899.
1 p. l., vi p., 1 l., 299 p. front. (port.) plates, facsims. 24cm.
Preface by René Philipon.
A catalogue of 2,227 lots, offered for sale, with prices.
First issued in four parts, 1898-99, under title: Catalogue des livres et manuscrits relatifs aux sciences occultes.

1. Occult sciences--Bibl. I. Title.   3-22231
Library of Congress, no.   Z6880.G94

Occult sciences--Bibliography.
WITCHCRAFT BF 1563 K44
Keyser, Georg Adam, comp.
Uhuhu; oder Hexen-Gespenster-Schazgräber- und Erscheinungs-Geschichten. Erfurt, Bey G. A. Keyser, 1785-92.
7 v. in 3. illus. 18cm.
Each vol. has lengthy introduction including bibliographical materials.
8
1. Witchcraft. 2. Ghost stories. 3. Occult sciences--Bibl. I. Title.

Occult sciences--Bibliography.
QD 26 T41
Thesaurus incantatus: The enchanted treasure; or, The spagyric quest of Beroaldus Cosmopolita, in which is sophically and mystagorically declared the first matter of the stone. With a list of choice books on alchemy, magic, talismans, gems, mystics, neoplatonism, ancient worships, Rosicrucians, occult sciences, etc., etc. London, T. Marvell [1888?]
64 p. illus. 20cm.
1. Alchemy. 2. Occult sciences--Bibl. I. Title: The spagyric quest of Beroaldus Cosmopolita.

Occult sciences--Bibliography.
Witchcraft Z 6878 W8 Y98
Yve-Plessis, R[obert]
... Essai d'une bibliographie française méthodique & raisonnée de la sorcellerie et de la possession démoniaque; pour servir de suite et de complément à la Bibliotheca magica de Grässe, aux catalogues Sépher, Ouvaroff, D'Ourches et Guldenstubbe. S. de Guaita et aux divers travaux partiels publiés sur cette matière. Préface par Albert de Rochas. Paris, Bibliothèque Chacornac, 1900.
xiv, 254, [1] p. front., facsims., plates. 25cm.
"Il a été tiré de cet ouvrage : 10 exemplaires sur papier de Hollande et 500 exemplaires sur papier ordinaire, tous numérotés et paraphés. No. 13".
1,793 titles, classified.
1. Witchcraft--Bibl. 2. Occult sciences--Bibl. I. Grässe, Johann Georg Theodor, 1814-1885. Bibliotheca magica et pneumatica. II. Title.
Library of Congress, no.   Z6878.W8Y8.

CATALOGUE OF THE CORNELL WITCHCRAFT COLLECTION

Occult sciences--Bibliography--Catalogs.

Witchcraft
Z
6880
Z9A18
    Ackermann, Theodor, bookseller, Munich.
        Geheime Wissenschaften. 1-
1926-
    München.
        v. 21cm. (His Katalog 594-

        1. Occult sciences--Bibliography--Catalogs. I. Title.

Occult sciences--Bibliography--Catalogs.

Witchcraft
Z
6880
Z9
C35
no.2
    Heberle, J M
        Culturgeschichte und Curiositäten in Druckschriften, fliegenden Blättern, Bildern, Autographen und Monumenten. Aus den Sammlungen von Heinrich Lempertz... Zu beigesetzten Preisen vorräthig auf dem Bücher- und Kunstlager von J. M. Heberle (H. Lempertz' Söhne) in Cöln. Abth. E: Physiognomik, Phrenologie, Mimik, natürliche Magie, Kunststücke, Alchymie, etc. ... Abth. F: Zauberei und Hexerei, Faust, Cagliostro,
Teufelswesen und
        (Continued on next card)

Occult sciences--Bibliography--Catalogs.

Witchcraft
Z
6880
Z9R81
1903
    Rosenthal, J., firm, booksellers, Munich.
        Bibliotheca magica et pneumatica. Geheime Wissenschaften. Sciences occultes. Occult sciences. Folk-lore. München [1903]
        48, 680 p. 24cm. (Its Kataloge 31-35)

        Issued in parts.

        1. Occult sciences--Bibl.--Catalogs. 2. Folk-lore--Bibl.--Catalogs. 3. Curiosa--Bibl. I. Title.

Occult sciences--Bibliography--Catalogs.

Witchcraft
Z
6880
Z9A
181+
    Ackermann, Theodor, bookseller, Munich.
        Okkultismus und Verwandtes. Muenchen [1933?]
        10 p. 29 x 23cm. (Sonderliste, Nr. 58)

        1. Occult sciences--Bibl.--Catalogs. I. Title.

Occult sciences--Bibliography--Catalogs.

Z
6880
Z9
C35
no.2
    Heberle, J M
        Culturgeschichte und Curiositäten... [1874?] (Card 2)
    Beschwörungen, Besessensein, etc. ... Cöln, Steven's Druckerei [1874?]
        64 p. 23cm.

        At head of title: Nro. 74.
        No. 2 in vol. lettered: Catalogues of books on magic and witchcraft.
        1. Occult sciences--Bibl.--Catalogs. 2. Witchcraft--Bibl.--Catalogs. 3. Magic--Bibl.--Catalogs.

Occult sciences--Bibliography--Catalogs.

Witchcraft
Z
6880
Z9C35
no.1
    Rosenthal, Ludwig, Munich.
        Bibliotheca magica et pneumatica. Geheime Wissenschaften, Magie, gute und böse Geister, Gespenster, Volksaberglauben: Hexen und Hexenprocesse ... Ellwangen, L. Weil [188-?]
        148 p. 23cm.

        "Katalog 45."
        No. 1 in vol. lettered: Catalogues of books on magic and witchcraft.

Occult sciences--Bibliography--Catalogs.

Witchcraft
Z
6880
Z9
B66
    Bodin, Lucien, bookseller, Paris.
        Catalogue de livres d'occasion anciens et modernes relatifs aux sciences occultes et philosophiques. Paris.
        nos. 24cm.

        1. Occult sciences--Bibl.--Catalogs. 2. Witchcraft--Bibl.--Catalogs. I. Title.

WITCHCRAFT
Z
6880
Z9C35
no.3
    Occult sciences--Bibliography--Catalogs.
    Kirchhoff & Wigand, Leipzig.
        Culturgeschichte, Curiosa, Facetiae, ältere deutsche etc. Literatur, Vermischtes ... enthaltend auch die alten Sammlungen des ... Nationalökonomen Johann Georg Büsch über Hexen, Dämonologie, Alchemie und Geheime Wissenschaften im allgemeinen. New-York, G.E. Stechert [1885]
        72 p. 23cm.

    At head of title: Nr. 743.
    No. 3 in vol. lettered:
        (Continued on next card)

Occult sciences--Bibliography--Catalogs.

Witchcraft
Z
6880
Z9
S57
    Siegismund, Karl, bookseller, Berlin.
        Siegismund's vademecum der gesammten Litteratur über Occultismus. Alphabetische und systematische Zusammenstellung der litterarischen Erscheinungen in deutscher Sprache auf dem Gebiete der Mystik, Magie, des thierischen Magnetismus [u. s. w.] von 1800 bis Anfang 1888. Berlin, 1888.
        112 p. 22cm.
        1. Occult sciences--Bibl.--Catalogs. I. Title.

Occult sciences--Bibliography--Catalogs.

    Dorbon aîné, bookseller, Paris.
        Bibliotheca esoterica, catalogue annoté et illustré de 6707 ouvrages anciens et modernes, qui traitent des sciences occultes ... comme aussi des sociétés secrètes ... En vente à la Librairie Dorbon-aîné. Paris [1940]
        2 p. l., 656 p., 2 l. illus. (incl. music) plates, facsims. 25cm.

    1. Occult sciences—Bibl.—Catalogs. 2. Secret societies—Bibl.—Catalogs. I. Title.
    Library of Congress   Z6880.Z9D6   43-36450
    [3]   016.133

WITCHCRAFT
Z
6880
Z9C35
no.3
    Occult sciences--Bibliography--Catalogs.
    Kirchhoff & Wigand, Leipzig. Culturgeschichte, Curiosa, Facetiae, ältere deutsche etc. Literatur, Vermischtes ... [1885] (Card 2)

    Catalogues of books on magic and witchcraft.

        1. Bibliography--Rare books. 2. Occult sciences--Bibl.--Catalogs. 3. Witchcraft--Bibl.--Catalogs. I. Title.

Occult sciences--Bibliography--Catalogs.

Witchcraft
Z
6880
Z9
T35
    Teubner, Franz, bookseller, Bonn.
        Bibliotheca magica et pneumatica. [Abth.] I[-III, VI] Antiquaritäts-Katalog No. 49[-Nr. 51, 54. Bonn, 189-]
        v. in . 22cm.
        Abth. II and III in 1 vol.
        At head of title, vol. I: Franz Teubner's Antiquariat (vorm. Antiquariat der Firma Paul Neubner in Köln)
        1. Occult sciences--Bibl.--Catalogs. 2. Magic--Bibl.--Catalogs. I. Title.

Occult sciences--Bibliography--Catalogs.

Witchcraft
Z
6880
Z9
D685
    Dorbon, bookseller, Paris.
        Catalogue ... de livres et manuscrits relatifs aux sciences occultes ... Provenant de la bibliothèque de feu Stanislaus de Guaita ... En vente aux prix marqués à la Librairie Dorbon. Paris, 1898-1899.
        4 nos. 22cm. (Its Catalogue 180, 182, 184, 186)
        In envelope.
        1. Occult sciences--Bibl.--Catalogs. I. Guaita, Stanislaus de, 1860-1897.

Occult sciences--Bibliography--Catalogs.

Z
6880
Z9C35
no.6
    Redway, George, London.
        List of books on theosophy, archaeology, astrology, mesmerism, philology, spiritualism, freemasonry, alchemy, platonism, thought-reading, magic, the Rosicrucians, witchcraft, etc. by Fludd, Behmen, Paracelsus, Agrippa, Nostradamus, Van Helmont, & others. [London, 1885]
        16 p. 23cm.

        At head of title: No. 11, 1885.
        No. 6 in vol. lettered: Catalogues of books on magic and witchcraft.

Occult sciences--Dictionaries.

Witchcraft
BF
1429
B57
1845
    Bianco, Filippo.
        Lessicomanzia; ovvero, Dizionario degli esseri, dei personaggi, dei libri, dei fatti e delle cose, che riferisconsi alle apparizioni, alla divinazione, alla magia ec. Per servere di corredo alla storia degli scorsi secoli, con aggiunte interessanti in questa ed. Siena, Tipografia dell'Ancora, 1845.
        xlix,660 p. illus. 16cm.
        1. Occult sciences--Dict. I. Title.

Occult sciences--Bibliography--Catalogs.

    Du Prel, Karl Ludwig August Friedrich Maximilian Alfred, Freiherr, 1839-1899.
        Bibliotheca occulta et philosophica; Sammlung Baron C. Du Prel, und kleine andere Beiträge (Inhaltsverzeichnis umstehend) Mit Vorwort von H. L. Held. München, E. Hirsch [193-]
        104 p. 22cm.
        Katalog 58.

Occult sciences--Bibliography--Catalogs.

Witchcraft
Z
6880
Z9C35
    Redway, George, London.
        The literature of occultism and archaeology. Being a Catalogue of books on sale relating to ancient worships, astrology, alchemy ... [London, 1885]
        48 p. 23cm.

        At head of title: Part 1. December 1885.
        No. 5 in vol. lettered: Catalogues of books on magic and witchcraft.

Occult sciences--Dictionaries.

BF
1412
B74
    Bosc, Ernest, 1837-
        Petite encyclopédie synthétique des sciences occultes. Éd. de la curiosité. Nice, Bureau de la Curiosité, 1904.
        xiii, 285 p. 18cm.

        At head of title: Ernest Bosc de Vèze.

        1. Occult sciences--Dictionaries. I. Title.

CATALOGUE OF THE CORNELL WITCHCRAFT COLLECTION

Occult sciences--Dictionaries.

Witchcraft
BF 1503 C69+ 1863
Collin de Plancy, Jacques Albin Simon, 1794-1881.
Dictionnaire infernal. Répertoire universel des etres, des personnages, des livres, des faits et des choses qui tiennent aux esprits, aux démons, aux sorciers ... et généralement a toutes les fausses croyances merveilleuses, surprenantes, mystérieuses et surnaturelles. 6. éd., augm. et illustrée ... par M. L. Breton. Paris, H. Plon, 1863.
723 p. illus., ports. 27cm.
1. Occult sciences--Dictionaries. 2. Magic--Dictionaries. I. Title.

Occult sciences--Dictionaries.

BF 1025 S74+ 1920
Spence, Lewis, 1874- 1955.
An encyclopædia of occultism; a compendium of information on the occult sciences, occult personalities, psychic science, magic, demonology, spiritism and mysticism, by Lewis Spence. London, G. Routledge & sons, ltd., 1920.
3 p. l., ix-xii, [2], 451 p. illus., plates, ports. 25½ x 20¼ cm.
"Select bibliography": [2] p. after p. xii.

1. Occult sciences—Dictionaries. I. Title.

Library of Congress   BF1025.S7   20-7507
[4]

Occult sciences--Dictionaries--French.

BF 1503 B65 1971
Blocquel, Simon, 1780-1863.
Le triple vocabulaire infernal: manuel du démonomane; ou, Les ruses de l'enfer dévoilées, par Frinellan, démonographe. Paris, N. Bussière [1971?]
319 p. illus. 15 cm. 22.50F
"Réimpression photomécanique."
Frinellan, pseud. of Simon Blocquel.

1. Demonology—Dictionaries—French. 2. Occult sciences—Dictionaries—French. I. Title.

BF1503.B48 1971   74-875408
Library of Congress   71 [2]

BF 1411 O15
The Occult sciences; sketches of the traditions and superstitions of past times, and the marvels of the present day; by E. Smedley [and others] London, R. Griffin, 1855.
376 p. 19cm. (Encyclopaedia metropolitana [v. 31])

1. Occult sciences. I. Smedley, Edward, 1788-1836.

4

Witchcraft
BT 965 O23+ 1739
Ode, Jacobus, 1698-1751.
Commentarius de angelis. Trajecti ad Rhenum, Apud Matthaeum Visch, 1739.
[38], 1068, [46] p. 26cm.
Engraved title vignette.
Added t. p., engraved.

1. Angels--Early works to 1800. 2. Demonology. I. Title.

Ode, Jacobus, 1698-1751.
Dissertatio theologica De natura angelorum.

WITCHCRAFT
BT 965 L82
Löers, Johann Christian, 1675-1743.
Dissertationes theologicae, quarum prima De angelorum corporibus, altera De homine ad gloriam Dei condito, tertia Qua hominem ad gloriam Dei conditum esse, ex facultate intelligendi probatur. Quibus accedit Jacobi Ode Dissertatio theologica De natura angelorum. Trajecti ad Rhenum, Apud Joannem Evelt, 1737.
259 p. 21cm.
1. Angels--Early works to 1800. 2. Man (Theology)--Early works to 1800. I.Ode, Jacobus, 1698-1751. Dissertatio theologica De natura angelorum.

8 NIC

WITCHCRAFT
BF 1584 T9 O26
Odorici, Federico, 1807-1884.
Le streghe di Valtellina e la Santa Inquisizione. Milano, P. R. Carpano, 1862.
85-158 p. 19cm.
Part of unidentified work, but complete in itself.

1. Witchcraft--Tyrol. 2. Witchcraft--Valtellina. 3. Trials (Witchcraft)--Valtellina. 4. Inquisition. Valtellina. I. Title.

8 NIC

Örnhiälm, Claudius Arrhenius.
see
Örnhielm, Claudius Arrhenius, 1627-1695.

Witchcraft
BF 1587 D61 no.10
Örnhielm, Claudius Arrhenius, 1627-1675, praeses.
Dissertatio philosophica De magia qvam ... sub moderamine ... Dn. Claudii Arrhenii ... examinandam proponit ... Andreas Torselius ... Holmiae, Excudit Nicolaus Wankif [1679]
2 p. l., 41 p. 21cm.
Imperfect: p. 3-6 wanting.
No. 10 in vol. lettered Dissertationes de magia. 1623-1723.

8   (Continued on next card)

Witchcraft
BF 1587 D61 no.10
Örnhielm, Claudius Arrhenius, 1627-1675, praeses. Dissertatio philosophica De magia ... [1679]   (Card 2)

1. Magic--Addresses, essays, lectures. I. Torselius, Andreas, respondent. II. Title: De magia. III. Title.

8

Oernhjälm, Claudius Arrhenius.
see
Örnhielm, Claudius Arrhenius, 1627-1695.

WITCHCRAFT
BF 1583 O29 1862
[Oeser, Rudolf] 1807-1859.
Die Schreckensjahre von Lindheim. Ein Beitrag zur Sittengeschichte des siebzehnten Jahrhunderts. Für das Volk erzählt von O. Glaubrecht [pseud.] 4. Aufl. Frankfurt a. M. und Erlangen, Heyder & Zimmer, 1862.
vi, 93 p. front. 17cm.

1. Witchcraft--Fiction. 2. Witchcraft--Germany. I. Title.

8

Oeser, Rudolf Ludwig, 1807-1859.
see
Oeser, Rudolf, 1807-1859.

WITCHCRAFT
BF 1555 M94 O29 no.1
Oesfeld, Gotthelf Friedrich.
Gedanken von der Einwirkung guter und böser Geister in die Menschen. Nebst beygefügter Beurtheilung eines neuern Beyspiels einer vermeynten leiblichen Besitzung, herausgegeben von M. Gotthelf Friedrich Oesfeld ... Wittenberg, J. J. Ahlfeld, 1760.
110 p. 18cm.
No. 1 in vol. lettered Oesfeld u. a. ...
1. Spirits. 2. Demoniac possession. 3. Lohmann, Anna Elisabeth. I. Title. II. Title: Einwirkung guter und böser Geister in die Menschen.

8 NIC

WITCHCRAFT
BF 1555 O292 1921
Oesterreich, Traugott Konstantin, 1880-1949.
Die Besessenheit. Langensalza, Wendt & Klauwell, 1921.
vii, 403 p. 25cm.
Bibliographical notes: p. [387]-401.

8 NIC
1. Demoniac possession. I. Title.

Oesterreich, Traugott Konstantin, 1880-1949
Witchcraft   Die Besessenheit--English.
BF 1555 O292 1930
Oesterreich, Traugott Konstantin, 1880-1949.
Possession, demoniacal and other, among primitive races, in antiquity, the middle ages and modern times, by T. K. Oesterreich ... New York, R. R. Smith, inc., 1930.
xi, 400 p. 24cm.
Lettered on cover: Demoniacal possession.
Printed in Great Britain.
"Authorized translation by D. Ibberson."
Translation of Die Besessenheit.

Witchcraft
BF 1555 O292 1930
Oesterreich, Traugott Konstantin, 1880-1949.
Possession, demoniacal and other, among primitive races, in the middle ages, and modern times, by T. K. Oesterreich ... New York, R. R. Smith, inc., 1930.
xi, 400 p. 24cm.
Lettered on cover: Demoniacal possession.
Printed in Great Britain.
"Authorized translation by D. Ibberson."
Translation of Die Besessenheit.

1. Demoniac possession.   I. Ibberson, Dora, tr.   II. His Die Besessenheit--English.

Library of Congress   3F1555.O45   30-17623
[3]   133.4

WITCHCRAFT
BF 1602 O29 1788
Les Oeuvres magiques de Henri-Corneille Agrippa, par Pierre d'Aban, latin et français, avec des secrets occultes. Liege, 1547. [Liege? 1788?]
116, [4] p. illus. 12cm.
Caption title: Heptameron, ou Les éléments magiques de Pierre Aban, philosophe, disciple de Henri-Corneille Agrippa.
Has nothing to do with either Agrippa or Pietro d'Abano, who predeceased him by two centuries.
Has no Latin text; a few incantations are in Latin.

8

420

CATALOGUE OF THE CORNELL WITCHCRAFT COLLECTION

ITCHCRAFT
BF
602
C29
A830
    Les Oeuvres magiques de Henri-Corneille Agrippa, mises en français par Pierre d'Aban, avec des secrets occultes, notamment celui de la Reine des Mouches velues. Rome, 1744. [Lille, Impr. de Bloquel, ca. 1830]
    112 p. port., illus. (1 fold.) 14cm.
    Caption title: Heptameron, ou Les éléments magiques de Pierre d'Aban, philosophe, disciple de Henri Corneille Agrippa.
    Has nothing to do either with Agrip-
                (Continued on next card)

WITCHCRAFT
BF
602
C29
A830
    Les Oeuvres magiques de Henri-Corneille Agrippa ... [1830]   (Card 2)
    pa or with Pietro d'Abano, who predeceased him by 2 centuries.
    Copy 1 has list of similar items for sale, e.g., Le veritable dragon rouge, Enchiridion Leonis papae, Secrets merveilleux de la magie naturelle du Petit Albert ...
    1. Occult sciences. 2. Magic. 3. Charms.   (Continued on next card)

WITCHCRAFT
BF
602
C29
A830
    Les Oeuvres magiques de Henri-Corneille Agrippa ... [1830]   (Card 3)
    I. Agrippa von Nettesheim, Heinrich Cornelius, 1486?-1535, supposed author. Les oeuvres magiques. II. Abano, Pietro d', 1250-1315?, supposed author. Heptameron. III. Title: Heptameron, ou Les éléments magiques de Pierre d'Aban.

WITCHCRAFT
BF
1584
N6
27
1670
    Øverland, Ole Andreas, 1855-1911.
        Lisbet Nypen; en hekseproces fra guldalen. Kristiania og Kjøbenhavn, A. Cammermeyer [1896]
    36 p. 19cm. (Historiske fortaellinger, nr.22)

    1. Nypen, Lisbet. 2. Witchcraft--Trondheim. 3. Trials (Witchcraft)--Trondheim.   I. Title.
NIC

    Of credulity and incredulity; in things divine & spiritual.
chcraft
    Casaubon, Meric, 1599-1671.
        Of credulity and incredulity; in things divine & spiritval: wherein, (among other things) a true and faithful account is given of the Platonick philosophy, as it hath reference to Christianity: as also the business of witches and witchcraft, against a late writer, fully argued and disputed. By Merick Casaubon ... and one of the prebends of Christ-Church, Canturbury. London, Printed by T. N. for Samuel Lownds, 1670.
    2 p. l., 208 p. 17cm.
                (Continued on next card)

    Of credulity and incredulity; in things divine & spiritual.
chcraft
    Casaubon, Meric, 1599-1671. Of credulity and incredulity ... 1670.   (Card 2)

    A continuation of his Of credulity and incredulity; in things natural, civil and divine, first published 1688 without the third part on the divine.
    1. Credulity. 2. Christianity--Philosophy. 3. Plato. 4. Witchcraft. 5. Wagstaffe, John, 1633-1677. The question of witchcraft debated. I. His Of credulity and incredulity; in things natural, civil and divine. II. Title: Of credulity and incredulity; in things divine & spiritual.

    Of credulity and incredulity in things natural and civil.
Witchcraft
BF
773
C33
O3
1672
    Casaubon, Meric, 1599-1671.
        A treatise proving spirits, witches, and supernatural operations by pregnant instances and evidences. Together with other things worthy of note. London, Printed for B. Aylmer, 1672.
    316 p. 18cm.
    Caption title: Of credulity and incredulity in things natural and civil.
    First ed. puolished in 1668 under title: of credulity and incredulity;
                (Continued on next card)

    Of credulity and incredulity in things natural and civil.
Witchcraft
BF
773
C33
O3
1672
    Casaubon, Meric, 1599-1671. A treatise proving spirits, witches, and supernatural operations by pregnant instances and evidences ... 1672.   (Card 2)

    in things natural, civil and divine.
    "Reissue of first ed."--British Museum catalogue.
    Contains a preface "To the reader" dated 1688, which explains that the author was unable to write the third part mentioned in the title. The third part
                (Continued on next card)

    Of credulity and incredulity in things natural and civil.
Witchcraft
BF
773
C33
O3
1672
    Casaubon, Meric, 1599-1671. A treatise proving spirits, witches, and supernatural operations by pregnant instances and evidences ... 1672.   (Card 3)

    was published in 1670 under title: Of credulity and incredulity in things divine & spiritual ...
    1. Credulity. 2. Witchcraft. I. Title. II. His Of credulity and incredulity; in things natural, civil and divine. III. Title: Of credulity and incredulity in things natural and civil.

    Of ghostes and spirites, walking by night.
WITCHCRAFT
BF
1445
L39
1596
    Lavater, Ludwig, 1527-1586.
        Of ghostes and spirites, walking by night, and of straunge noyses, crackes, and sundrie forewarnings, which commonly happen before the death of men: great slaughters, and alterations of kingdomes. One booke, written by Lewes Lauaterus of Tigurine. And translated into English by R. H. [i.e., Robert Harrison], London, Imprinted by Thomas Creede, 1596.
    10 p. l., 220 p. 18cm.
8   (Continued on next card)

    Of ghostes and spirites, walking by night.
WITCHCRAFT
BF
1445
L39
1596
    Lavater, Ludwig, 1527-1586. Of ghostes and spirites, walking by night ... 1596.   (Card 2)

    Imperfect copy: p. 217-220 wanting.
    Translation of De spectris, lemuribus et magnis atque insolitis fragoribus.
    STC 15321.
    Armorial bookplate: Holland House.
    1. Apparitions. 2. Ghosts. 3. Demonology. I. His De spectris, lemuribus et magnis atque insolitis fragoribus. English. II. Harrison, Robert, d. 1585?, tr. III. Title.
8

    Of our communion and warre with angels.
Witchcraft
BT
965
L42
    [Lawrence, Henry] 1600-1664.
        Of our communion and warre with angels. Being certain meditations on that subject, bottom'd particularly (though not concluded within the compasse of that Scripture) on Ephes. 6.12. with the following verses to the 19. [Amsterdam] 1646.
    189+ p. 21cm.

    Epistle dedicatory signed Henry Lawrence.
    Imperfect: index incomplete.
                (Continued on next card)

    Of our communion and warre with angels.
Witchcraft
BT
965
L42
    [Lawrence, Henry] 1600-1664. Of our communion and warre with angels ... 1646. (Card 2)

    Wing L 665.
    Reissued 1652 under title: Militia spiritualis; or, A treatise of angels.

    Of superstition.
Witchcraft
BF
1775
H22
    [Hammond, Henry] 1605-1660.
        Of svperstition. ... Oxford, Printed by Henry Hall, Printer to the Universitie, 1645.
    25 p. 19cm.

    Wing H 566.

    1. Superstition. I. Title.

    Of the vanitie and uncertaintie of artes and sciences.
Witchcraft
B
781
A3313
1569
    Agrippa von Nettesheim, Heinrich Cornelius, 1486?-1535.
        Of the vanitie and vncertaintie of artes and sciences, Englished by Ja. San., gent. ... London, Imprinted by Henry Wykes, 1569.
    [8], 187 l. illus. 19cm.

    First edition.
    Translated by James Sandford.
    Title within ornamental border.
    Running title: Cornelius Agrippa of the vanities of sciences.
                (Continued on next card)

    Of the vanitie and uncertaintie of artes and sciences.
Witchcraft
B
781
A3313
1569
    Agrippa von Nettesheim, Heinrich Cornelius, 1486?-1535. Of the vanitie and vncertaintie of artes and sciences ... 1569.   (Card 2)

    Translation of De incertitudine et vanitate scientiarum atque artium declamatio invectiva.
    Imperfect copy: leaf 185 wanting.
    I. His De incertitudine et vanitate scientiarum. English. II. Sandford, James, fl. 1567, tr. III. Title.

F
7
M42
1856
    Offor, George, 1787-1864, ed.
    Mather, Increase, 1639-1723.
        Remarkable providences illustrative of the earlier days of American colonisation. By Increase Mather. With introductory preface, by George Offor. London, J. R. Smith, 1856.
    xix, [16], 262 p. front. (port.) 16½ᶜᵐ. (Half-title: Library of old authors)

    1. New England--Hist.--Colonial period. I. Offor, George, 1787-1864, ed. II. Title.

                          18-11699

    Library of Congress   F7.M436

WITCHCRAFT
BF
1583
O38+
    Ohle, Rudolf, 1857-
        Die Hexen in und um Prenzlau. Eine Untersuchung über Entstehung, Verlauf und Ausgang des Hexenwahnes.
    (In Uckermärkischer Museums- und Geschichts-Verein, Prenzlau. Mitteilungen. Prenzlau. 26cm. 4. Bd., 1. Heft (1908), p. [1]-86)

    1. Witchcraft--Prenzlau, Germany. 2. Witchcraft--Germany. I. Uckermärkischer Museums- und Geschichts-Verein, Prenzlau.   II. Title.
8
NIC

CATALOGUE OF THE CORNELL WITCHCRAFT COLLECTION

WITCHCRAFT
BF 1566 O38
8 NIC

Ohle, Rudolf, 1857–
    Der hexenwahn, von pfarrer lic. dr. R. Ohle ... 1.-5. tausend ... Tübingen, J. C. B. Mohr (P. Siebeck) 1908.
    47, (1) p. 20ᶜᵐ. (Religionsgeschichtliche volksbücher für die deutsche christliche gegenwart. iv. reihe, 8. hft. Hrsg. von ... F. M. Schiele ...)
    "Literatur": p. 46-47.

    1. Witchcraft--History. I. Title.

                            9-5135
Library of Congress   (Copyright 1909 Res. no. 2411)

Ohle, Rudolf, 1857–
Der Hexenwahn.

WITCHCRAFT
BF 1566 O38 K78++
8 NIC

Königer, Albert Michael, 1874–
    Der Hexenwahn in neuester Beleuchtung. Köln, 1909.
    5 columns. 34cm.

    In the Literarische Beilage der Kölnischen Volkszeitung for May 6, 1909.
    In broadside box.

    1. Ohle, Rudolf, 1857– . Der Hexenwahn. 2. Witchcraft--History. I. Title.

Ohle, Rudolf, 1857–
Der Hexenwahn.

WITCHCRAFT
BF 1566 O38 P33++
8 NIC

Paulus, Nicolaus, 1853-1930.
    Hexenwahn und Protestantismus. [Köln, 1909]
    5 columns. 34cm.

    Detached from the Kölnische Volkszeitung und Handels-Blatt, erste Beilage zur Sonntags-Ausgabe for February 14, 1909.
    In broadside box.

    1. Ohle, Rudolf, 1857– . Der Hexenwahn. 2. Witchcraft--History. I. Title.

WITCHCRAFT
BT 960 O38
8 NIC

Ohm, Gottfried, praeses.
    De angelis malis ex lum. nat. demonstrabilibus, quam...disputatione publica... examini submittet praeses M. Godofredus Ohm respondente Joh. Georg. Linkio. Lipsiae, Literis Brandenburgerianis [1704] [28] p. 19cm.

    1. Devil. 2. Demonology. I. Link, Johann Georg, respondent. II. Title.

Witchcraft
BF 1413 F86

Freimark, Hans, 1881–
    Okkultismus u. Sexualität. Beiträge zur Kulturgeschichte der Vergangenheit u. Gegenwart. Leipzig, Leipziger Verlag [1909]
    xvi, 433 p. 24cm.

    1. Occult sciences. 2. Sex. 3. Sexual perversion. 4. Psychical research. I. Title.

Witchcraft
Z 6880 Z9 A181+

Okkultismus und Verwandtes.
Ackermann, Theodor, bookseller, Munich.
    Okkultismus und Verwandtes. Muenchen [1937?]
    10 p. 29 x 23cm. (Sonderliste, Nr. 58)

    1. Occult sciences--Bibl.--Catalogs. I. Title.

Der Okkulttäter.

BF 1559 S29

Schäfer, Herbert.
    Der Okkulttäter (Hexenbanner, magischer Heiler, Erdentstrahler) Hamburg, Kriminalistik, Verlag für Kriminalistische Fachliteratur, 1959.
    xvi, 278 p. illus., maps. 24cm.

    1. Exorcism. 2. Witchcraft. 3. Medicine, Magic, mystic and spagiric. I. Title.

Witchcraft
BF 1583 A2S74 1632

Oldekop, Justus
    Cautelarum criminalium sylloge practica. Consiliarijs, maleficiorum judicibus, advocatis, inquisitoribus & actuarijs utilissima & pernecessaria ... Brunsvigae, Typis & sumptibus Gruberianis, 1633.
    [12], 363, [37] p. 17cm.

    Bound with [Spee, Friedrich von] Cautio criminalis. Editio secunda. Francofvrti, 1632.
    I. Title. 1. Witchcraft. 2. Witchcraft--Germany.

Olim.

Witchcraft
BF 1584 B4C22

Cannaert, Joseph Bernard, 1768-1848.
    Olim. Procès des sorcières en Belgique sous Philippe II et le gouvernement des archiducs. Tirés d'actes judiciaires et de documens inédits. Gand, C. Annoot-Braeckman, 1847.
    155 p. illus. 24cm.

Witchcraft
BF 1611 O49

Olliver, Charles Wolfran, 1895–
    An analysis of magic & witchcraft, a retrospective introduction to the study of modern metapsychics, by C. W. Olliver ... London, Rider & co. [1928]
    xi, 244 p. front., illus., plates, diagrs. 24ᶜᵐ.
    Bibliography: p. 235-244.

    1. Magic. 2. Witchcraft. 3. Phallicism. I. Title.

Library of Congress   BF1611.O5   29-24487 Revised
                       [r42d2]

Om heksetroen og om heksene i Thy og V. Hanherred.

WITCHCRAFT
DL 271 T44 H67 1919

Christensen, Severin, 1867–
    Om heksetroen og om heksene i Thy og V. Hanherred.
    (In: Historisk aarbog for Thisted Amt. København. 23cm. 1919. p. [3]-30)

    Continuation of an article in the 1917 issue.

    1. Witchcraft--Denmark. 2. Trials (Witchcraft)--Denmark.

Om Hexemestere, Troldqvinder, Spøgelser, Gjengangere, Spaamaend, Forvarsler og Sandsigere.

Witchcraft
BF 1565 M54 1800

Mentzel, Andreas.
    Om Hexemestere, Troldqvinder, Spøgelser, Gjengangere, Spaamaend, Forvarsler og Sandsigere. En Bog for Almuen ... Oversat af het Tydske ved M. Hallager. København, Malling, 1800.
    2 p. l., 39 p. 21cm.
    Translation of part of his Gespräche, Fabeln und Erzählungen für niedre Schulen.

    1. Witchcraft. 2. Occult sciences. I. His Gespräche, Fabeln und Erzählungen für niedre Schulen, Danish, tr. II. Hallager, Morton, 1740-1803, tr. III. Title.

Om hexprocessen i Dalarne, 1757-1763.

WITCHCRAFT
BF 1584 S9 M25

Malmquist, H
    Om hexprocessen i Dalarne, 1757-1763; jemte öfversigt af föregående hexprocesser. Lund, F. Berling, 1877.
    45 p. 24cm.
    Diss.--Lund.

    1. Witchcraft--Dalecarlia, Sweden. 2. Trials (Witchcraft)--Dalecarlia, Sweden.

Om satanismen, djaevlebesaettelse og hexevaesen.

WITCHCRAFT
BF 1550 K12

Kaarsberg, Hans Sophus, 1854-1928.
    Om satanismen, djaevlebesaettelse og hexevaesen, set fra et laegevidenskabeligt standpunkt. Kjøbenhavn, Gyldendal, 1896.
    41 p. 25cm.
    "Saertryk af 'Hospitalstidende.'"

    1. Satanism. 2. Demoniac possession. 3. Witchcraft. I. Title.

Om svartebøker.

WITCHCRAFT
BF 1558 T57

Tillier, S
    Om svartebøker. Av statsdyrlaege S. Tillier.
    (In Historielaget for Sogn, Bergen, Norway. Tidsskrift. Bergen. 23cm. No. 2 (1912), p. 47-92)
    Includes 2 fold. plates, 1 facsim.

    1. Magic. I. Title. II. Historielaget for Sogn, Bergen, Norway. Tidsskrift.

Om trolldomswäsendet i Dalarne under Karl XI:s regering.

Witchcraft
BF 1584 S9 B59

Billengren, Ehrenfried.
    Om trolldomswäsendet i Dalarne under Karl XI:s regering.
    (In Läsning för folket. Stockholm. 21cm. 7ᵉ Bandet, 2ª Häftet (1875), p. 97-139)
    Caption title.

    1. Witchcraft--Sweden. 2. Witchcraft--Dalecarlia, Sweden. I. Title. II. Läsning för svenska folket.

Omstandig beright, van Balthasar Bekker, S. T. D. predikant tot Amsterdam, van si particuliere onderhandelinge ...

Witchcraft
BF 1410 B42 1691a no.8

Bekker, Balthasar, 1634-1698.
    Omstandig beright, van Balthasar Bekker, S. T. D. predikant tot Amsterdam, van sijne particuliere onderhandelinge met D. Laurentius Homma, sal. ged. in sijn leven mede predikant aldaar. Beneffens d'ontdekte lagen van Everhardus van der Hooght, en Jakob Lansman tegen denselven. Amsterdam, By D. vanden Dalen, boekverkooper, 1693.
    1 p. l., 22 p. title and end page vignettes, illus. initials. 20 x 16cm.
    4º: π 1, A-   C⁴ (-C4)

(Continued on next card)

Omstandig beright, van Balthasar Bekker, S. T. D. predikant tot Amsterdam van si particuliere onderhandelinge ...

Witchcraft
BF 1410 B42 1691a no.8

Bekker, Balthasar, 1634-1698. Omstandig beright ... 1693. (Card 2)

    Black letter.
    "Bedekte lagen van Everhard van der Hoo predikant tot Nieuwendam, en Jakob Lansman procureur en notaris tot Amsterdam: ontde aan Balthasar Bekker ...:" p. 17-22.
    Van der Linde 117.
    No. 8 in vol. lettered B. Bekker. Beto verde weereld.

    1. Hooght, Everard van der, d. 1716. Lansman, Jako b. I. Homma, Laurentius, d. 1681. II. Title.

CATALOGUE OF THE CORNELL WITCHCRAFT COLLECTION

Witchcraft — Omstandig bewys, dat de daemones overgeset duyvelen ...
BF 1410 B42 Z56 v.3 no.5

Daillon, Benjamin de.
Omstandig bewys, dat de daemones overgeset duyvelen, geen quade geesten, maar zielen van menschen geweest zijn de welke op de wereld rechtvaardigh geleeft hadden, en dat de selve naar het gevoelen van d'oude heydenen, hare woonsteede in 't opperste en zuyverste deel van de lucht gehadt hebben, en ook middelaars tusschen de goden en menschen geweest zijn. Als ook datter maar eene duyvel of Satan is. Welk gevoelen met dat van d'Heer Predikant Bekker, in sijn boek De betoverde

8 (Continued on next card)

Witchcraft — Omstandig bewys, dat de daemones overgeset duyvelen ...
BF 1410 B42 Z56 v.3 no.5

Daillon, Benjamin de. Omstandig bewys, dat de daemones overgeset duyvelen ... 1692. (Card 2)

wereld genaamt vervat, over een stemt. Getrokken uyt de schriften van d'Heer Daillon frans predikant. Gravenhage, By M. Uytwerf, boekverkooper, 1692.
2 p. l., 43 p. [p. 44 blank] title vignette, illus. initial. 21 x 15cm.
4°: π², A-E⁴, E².

8 (Continued on next card)

Witchcraft — Omstandig bewys, dat de daemones overgeset duyvelen ...
BF 1410 B42 Z56 v.3 no.5

Daillon, Benjamin de. Omstandig bewys, dat de daemones overgeset duyvelen ... 1692. (Card 3)

Black letter.
Translation of selections from his Examen de l'opression des reformez en France ... avec l'explication de la doctrine des demons. Amsterdam, 1691.
Selections chosen to support Bekker's views in De betoverde weereld.
Van der Linde 74.

8 (Continued on next card)

Witchcraft — Omstandig bewys, dat de daemones overgeset duyvelen ...
BF 1410 B42 Z56 v.3 no.5

Daillon, Benjamin de. Omstandig bewys, dat de daemones overgeset duyvelen ... 1692. (Card 4)

No. 5 in vol. lettered Bekker III.

1. Devil. 2. Bekker, Balthasar, 1634-1698. De betoverde weereld. I. His Examen de l'opression des reformez en France ... Selections--Dutch. II. Title.

8

Witchcraft — Ondersoek en antwoord van Balthasar Bekker, S.S.Th.D. predikant tot Amsterdam, op 't request door de gedeputeerden ...
BF 1410 B42 591a p.7

Bekker, Balthasar, 1634-1698.
Ondersoek en antwoord van Balthasar Bekker, S.S.Th.D. predikant tot Amsterdam, op 't request door de gedeputeerden der Noordhollandsche Synode tot Edam, in den herfst des jaars 1691, ingegeven aan de Ed. Gr. Mog. Heeren Staten van Holland en West Friesland tegen sijn boek De betoverde weereld. Amsterdam, By D. vanden Dalen, boekverkooper, 1693.
2 p. l., 98 p. title vignette, illus. initials. 20 x 16cm.

8 (Continued on next card)

Witchcraft — Ondersoek en antwoord van Balthasar Bekker, S.S.Th.D predikant tot Amsterdam, op 't request door de gedeputeerden ...
BF 1410 B42 591a p.7

Bekker, Balthasar, 1634-1698. Ondersoek en antwoord ... 1693. (Card 2)

4°: *², A-M⁴, N1.
Black letter.
Prefatory letter autographed by Bekker.
Van der Linde 53.
No. 7 in vol. lettered B. Bekker. Betoverde weereld.
1. Nederlandsche Hervormde Kerk. Synode van Noordholland, Edam, 1691. 2. Bekker, Balthasar, 1634-1698. De betoverde weereld. I. Netherlands (United Provinces, 1581-1795) Staten General. II. Title.

8

Witchcraft
AG 27 O59 1764

Onomatologia cvriosa artificiosa et magica; oder, Ganz natürliches zauber-lexicon, welches das nöthigste, nützlichste und angenehmste in allen realen wissenschaften überhaupt und besonders in der naturlehre, mathematick, der haushaltungs- und natürlichen zauberkunst, und aller andern, vornemlich auch curieuser künste deutlich und vollständig nach alphabetischer ordnung beschreibet ... 2. vielvermehrte aufl. Nürnberg, Auf kosten der Raspischen handlung, 1764.
3 p. l., 1648 col. front., diagrs. (1 fold.) 21 cm.
In double columns.
Edited by Gotthart Hafner. cf. Meusel, J. G. Lexikon der vom jahr 1750 bis 1800 verstorbenen teutschen schriftsteller. v. 5, p. 36.
1. Encyclopedias and dictionaries, German. 2. Magic—Dictionaries. I. Hafner, Gotthart, 1707-1767, ed. II. Title: Zauber-lexicon.

8 Library of Congress   AG27.O8 1764   34-16288
                                                    [83]

Witchcraft
AG 27 O59 1784

Onomatologia cvriosa artificiosa et magica. Oder Natürliches Zauber-Lexicon, in welchem vieles Nützliche und Angenehme aus der Naturgeschichte, Naturlehre und natürlichen Magie nach alphabetischer Ordnung vorgetragen worden. 3. Aufl. Verbessert und mit vielen neuen Zusätzen vermehrt von Johann Christian Wiegleb. Nürnberg, Raspische Buchhandlung, 1784.
4 p. l., 1744 numb. columns. illus., fold. table. 22cm.

(Continued on next card)

WITCHCRAFT
AG 27 O59 1784

Onomatologia cvriosa artificiosa et magica ... 1784. (Card 2)

1. Encyclopedias and dictionaries, German. 2. Magic--Dictionaries. I. Wiegleb, Johann Christian, 1732-1800, ed. II. Title: Zauber-Lexicon.

8

Witchcraft — Ontdecking van tovery.
BF 1565 S42 1638

Scot, Reginald, 1538?-1599.
Ontdecking van tovery, beschreven int Engels door Reinald Scot, verduyscht by Th. en G. Basson. Beverwyck, Gedruckt by Frans Pels, 1638.
15 p. l., 351, [17] p. 15cm.
With engraved t. p., depicting a witch.
Abridgment and translation of Discoverie of witchcraft.
To this are appended: Historie van 't ghene gheschiet is in 't Graefschap van

8 (Continued on next card)

Witchcraft — Ontdecking van tovery.
BF 1565 S42 1638

Scot, Reginald, 1538?-1599. Ontdecking van tovery ... 1638. (Card 2)

Artoys ..., door J. DuClercq, with special t. p.; Extract uyt 't playdoye van M. L. Servin; Historie van de Maegt van Orleans ... Extract uyt J. P. van Bergamo; and various poems.
1. Witchcraft. 2. Magic. 3. Demonology. I. His Discoverie of witchcraft. Dutch. II. DuClercq, Jacques, seigneur

8 (Continued on next card)

Witchcraft — Oogmerck van Everardus van der Hoogt.
BF 1410 B42 Z69 no.14

[Seegen, Charinus van]
Oogmerck van Everardus van der Hooght in sijn Brabbelen teegen het boek De Betoverde wereld genoemd. Sulx blijkt uit de groote opheff, om D. Becker eens voor al, wel ter deegen, swart te maken ... t'Amsterdam, By D. van den Dalen, 1691.
16 p. 21cm.
Signatures: 4°: A-B⁴.
Black letter.

(Continued on next card)

Witchcraft — Oogmerck van Everardus van der Hoogt.
BF 1410 B42 Z69 no.14

[Seegen, Charinus van] Oogmerck van Everardus van der Hoogt ... 1691. (Card 2)

Signed: Charinus van Seegen.
Van der Linde 108.
No. 14 in a Collection of tracts against Balthasar Bekker and his Betoverde weereld.

WITCHCRAFT — Opera curiosa.
AC 31 K84 1694

Kornmann, Heinrich, fl. 1607.
Henrici Kornmanni Opera curiosa in tractatus qvatuor distributa, qvorum I. Miracula vivorum; II. Miracula mortuorum ... III. Templum naturae historicum ... IV. Qvaestiones enucleatae de virginum statu ac jure ... Nunc in lucem edita. Francofurti ad Moenum, Ex officina Genschiana, 1694-96.
6 v. in 2. 17cm.
Vol. 3-6 have been bound in order: 5, 6, 4, 3.

2 c. of v. 5-6

8 NIC (Continued on next card)

WITCHCRAFT — Opera curiosa.
AC 31 K84 1694

Kornmann, Heinrich, fl. 1607. Henrici Kornmanni Opera curiosa ... 1694-96. (Card 2)

Each vol. also has special t. p.; vol. 5-6 also have special shared t. p.: Henrici Kornmanni tractatus duo ... qvorum prior Linea amoris ... posterior De annulo triplici ... with imprint 1696.
Bound into copy 1 of vol. 5 is t. p. for Opera curiosa in 6 vols., with imprint 1696.
1. Curiosities and wonders. I. Title: Opera curiosa.

8 NIC

WITCHCRAFT — Opfer des Aberglaubens, Irrthums und Wahns.
PT 2583 W28 O6 1880

Wolf, Marianne (Conrad) 1837-1886.
Opfer des Aberglaubens, Irrthums und Wahns. Erzählungen und Erhüllungen aus uralter Zeit bis unsere Tage. Von C. Michael [pseud.] Leipzig, O. Spamer, 1880.
141 p. illus. 19cm. (Otto Spamer's Neue Volksbücher, no.6)

8 NIC   I. Title.

Witchcraft
BF 1565 O61

The opinion of witchcraft vindicated. In answer to a book intituled The question of witchcraft debated [by John Wagstaffe] Being a letter to a friend, by R. T. ... London, Printed by E. O. for F. Haley, 1670.
63 p. 15cm.

1. Witchcraft. 2. Wagstaffe, John, 1633-1677. The question of witchcraft debated. I. T., R.

WITCHCRAFT
BT 960 O61

Oporin, Joachim.
Der im Alten und Neuen Testament unterschiedene, auch ungleich eingesehene Dienst der guten Engel, nebst augenscheinlicher Rache des Messiae an dem Teufel. Das ist, Die erläuterte Lehre der Hebraeer und Christen von guten und bösen Engeln. Zamburg, Bey T. C. Felginers Wittwe gedruckt, 1735.
359p. 17cm.

8 NIC   1. Angels--Early works to 1800. 2. Devil. I. Title.

CATALOGUE OF THE CORNELL WITCHCRAFT COLLECTION

WITCHCRAFT
BF 1439
O62

8
NIC

En Oprigtig fortegnelse paa alle de hexer og troldfolk som have vaeret til siden Doctor Faust. Kiøbenhavn, T. Larsen Borups Efterieverste, 1771.
16 p. 18cm.

1. Witchcraft. 2. Occult sciences.

Witchcraft
BF 1410
B42
Z56
v.3
no.28

Opstel van enige aanmerkingen op het boek van B. Bekker.
Bekker, Balthasar, 1634-1698.
Twee brieven van Balthasar Bekker predikant tot Amsterdam, aan Everhardus vander Hooght predikant tot Niewendam. D'eerste voor desen uitgegeven van den 25. September 1691, uit Amsterdam. D'andere nu daar by gevoegd, van den 3/13 Juny 1692, uit Franeker. Beide over het boek genaamd De betoverde weereld, en 't gene daar ontrent is voorgevallen. Met een kort beright over de voorrede van seker Opstel van aanmerkingen

8   (Continued on next card)

Witchcraft
BF 1410
B42
Z56
v.3
no.28

Opstel van enige aanmerkingen op het boek van B. Bekker.
Bekker, Balthasar, 1634-1698. Twee brieven ... aan Everhardus vander Hooght ... 1692. (Card 2)
gemaakt door J. J. F. B. en tot Leewarden by Hero Nauta gedrukt. Franeker, By Leonardus Strik, boekverkoper, 1692.
2 p. l., 32 p. title vignette, illus. initials. 19 x 15cm.
4°: π², A-D⁴.
Back of t. p. autographed by Bekker.

8   (Continued on next card)

Witchcraft
BF 1410
B42
Z56
v.3
no.28

Opstel van enige aanmerkingen op het boek van B. Bekker.
Bekker, Balthasar, 1634-1698. Twee brieven ... aan Everhardus vander Hooght ... 1692. (Card 3)
Variant of van der Linde 107: has p. 31-32.
No. 28 in vol. lettered Bekker III.
1. Bekker, Balthasar, 1634-1698. De betoverde weereld. 2. Opstel van enige aanmerkingen op het boek van B. Bekker. I. Hooght, Everard van der, d. 1716. II. Title.

8

Witchcraft
BF 840
N66

Opusculum de fascino.
Gutiérrez, Juan Lazaro, 17th cent.
Ioannis Lazari Gvtierrii ... Opvscvlvm de fascino ... Lvgdvni, Sumpt. Philip. Borde, Lavr. Arnavd, & Cl. Rigavd, 1653.
[8], 210, [15] p. 24cm.

Engraved title vignette: publishers' device.
Bound with Nicquet, Honorat. Physiognomia hvmana. Lvgdvni, 1648.

1. Magic. 2. Witchcraft. I. Title: De fascino. II. Title. III. Title: Opusculum de fascino.

Witchcraft
BF 1520
P71

Opusculum de sagis maleficis.
Plantsch, Martinus, ca. 1460-1533.
Opusculum de sagis maleficis ... [Phorce, In Aedibus Thome Anshelmi impensisque Sigismundi Stir, 1507]
[49] l. 20cm.

Signatures: a-e⁸, f⁴, g⁵.
Edited by Heinrich Bebel.

1. Demonology. 2. Divination. 3. Magic. I. Bebel, Heinrich, 1472-ca. 1516, ed. II. Title: De sagis maleficis. III. Title.

MSS
Bd.
WITCHCRAFT
BF
V82

Opusculum ... in quo probatur lamias esse hereticas.
Visconti, Girolamo, fl. 1490-1512.
Opusculū magr̄i Hieronimi Vicecōm̄s ordis pd̄ica ͨt i q° pbat~ lamias eē heticas et nō laborare humore melancholico. [Milan? before Sept., 1490]
9 l. 19cm.
Manuscript, on vellum.
Title in red. 2 blue initials.
Marginal notes in hands differing from that of the text. According to G. L. Burr some of the notes are in the author's own hand.
(Continued on next card)

MSS
Bd.
WITCHCRAFT
BF
V82

Opusculum ... in quo probatur lamias esse hereticas.
Visconti, Girolamo, fl. 1490-1512. Opusculū ... i q° pbat~ lamias eē heticas ... [before Sept., 1490] (Card 2)
Text more complete than the printed version, which appears as the second part of his Lamiarum sive striarum opuscula. Milan, 1490.
Leaves sewn together but unbound. In case.
1. Witchcraft. I. His Lamiarum sive striarum opuscula. II. Title: Opusculum ... in quo probatur lamias esse hereti cas.

Witchcraft
BF 1761
C61

Oracula sibyllina.
Clasen, Daniel, 1623-1678.
De oraculis gentilium et in specie de vaticiniis sibyllinis libri tres, autore Daniele Clasen ... In fine adivncta svnt carmina sibyllina è versione Sebastiani Castalionis. Vt et Onuphrii Panvinii tractatvs de sibyllis. Helmstadii, apud H. Mullerum, 1673.
8 p. l., 824, [8], 104, [43] p. 20cm.

"Sibyllina oracula" has special t.-p. and separate paging.

WITCHCRAFT
BF 1405
L85
1673

Oracula Zoroastri ex Platonicorum libris collecta.
Longinus, Caesar, ed.
Trinum magicum, sive Secretorum magicorum opus ... Editum à Caesare Longino philos. Francofurti, Sumptibus Jacobi Gothofredi Seyleri, 1673.
12 p. l., 498 p. 14cm.
Contents.--Marci Antonii Zimarae Tractatus magicus.--Appendix, De mirandis quibusdam naturali magia factis operationibus. Ex lib. 2. Mag. nat. Ioan. Bapt. Port.-- Tractatvs De virtutibus quarundam herbarum,

8   (Continued on next card)

WITCHCRAFT
BF 1405
L85
1673

Oracula Zoroastri ex Platonicorum libris collecta.
Longinus, Caesar, ed. Trinum magicum ... 1673. (Card 2)
lapidum & animalium. A. M. A.--Commentatio De magnetica curatione vulnerum citra svperstitionem ... Authore R. G. M. D.--Logia, sive Oracvla Zoroastri ex Platonicorum libris collecta.--Tractatus De proprii cujusqve nati daemonis inqvisitione.
Layout of text corresponds to that of Frankfurt, 1630 ed. (C. Eifrid, printer)

8   (Continued on next card)

WITCHCRAFT
BX 2340
O63++

Oratio contra omnes tum maleficorum tum daemonum incursus. [s.l., ca.1550?]
4 items mounted on sheets. 41cm.

broadside box

Two variant copies of the prayer. At end of each: Fr. Bartholomeus Rocca de Palermo... vidit permittitque ut imprimatur. Mounted on sheet with each copy are illustrations of cross surrounded by ports. of various saints. One has German letter-press, the other Latin.
1. Exorcism. 2. Prayers.

Witchcraft
BT 980
O64

[Orchard, N], supposed author.
The doctrine of devils, proved to be the grand apostacy of these later times. An essay tending to rectifie those undue notions and apprehensions men have about daemons and evil spirits. London, Printed for the author, 1676.
205 p. 17cm.

Also attributed to Thomas Ady.
1. Devil. 2. Demonology. I. Title. II. Ady, Thomas, supposed author.

Witchcraft
BT 980
O64
1691

Orchard, N supposed author.
The doctrine of devils--Dutch.
[Orchard, N] supposed author.
De leeringe der duyvelen, beweezen te zyn de groote afval deezer laatste tyden. Of een proeve, strekkende om die onbehoorlyke kundigheden en bevattingen, welke de menschen van de demons en quaade geesten hebben, te verbéteren. In 't engelsch geschreeven door N. Orchard ... En volgens de copy, gedrukt tot Londen in 't jaar 1676, vertaald door Wm. Séwel. t'Amsterdam, J. Broers, 1691.
100 p. 21cm.
(Continued on next card)

Witchcraft
BT 980
O64
1691

Orchard, N supposed author.
The doctrine of devils--Dutch.
[Orchard, N], supposed author. De leeringe der duyvelen ... 1691. (Card 2)
Translation of his The doctrine of devils ...
Also attributed to Thomas Ady.

1. Devil. 2. Demonology. I. Title. II. Orchard, N supposed author. The doctrine of devils--Dutch. III. Ady, Thomas, supposed author.

Witchcraft
BF 1410
B42
Z82
no.2

Orchard, N , supposed author.
The doctrine of devils.
Hamer, Petrus, 1646-1716.
Voorlooper tot de volstrekte wederlegginge van het gene de heeren, Orchard, Daillon en Bekker hebben aen het licht gebragt; aengaende de werken, en macht der geesten: en met name der duivelen. Door Petrus Hamer, dienaer Jesus Christi in Numansdorp. Uitgegeven na kerken-ordre. Met belofte refutatoir van zekeren Brief aen een regent van Amsteldam. Dato 18 Maij 1692. Dordrecht, By C. Wilgaarts, boekverkooper, 1692.
4 p. l., 40 p. title vignette, illus.

8   (Continued on next card)

Witchcraft
BF 1410
B42
Z82
no.2

Orchard, N , supposed author.
The doctrine of devils.
Hamer, Petrus, 1646-1716. Voorlooper tot de volstrekte wederlegginge van... Orchard, Daillon en Bekker ... 1692. (Card 2)
initials. 20 x 15cm.
4°: *⁴, A-E⁴.
Van der Linde 95.
No. 2 in vol. lettered Over Bekkers Betoverde wereld. 1692.
1. Orchard, N , supposed author. The doctrine of devils. 2. Daillon, Benjamin de. Examen de l'opression

8   (Continued on next card)

Witchcraft
BT 980
O64
1691

[Orchard, N], supposed author.
De leeringe der duyvelen, beweezen te zyn de groote afval deezer laatste tyden. Of een proeve, strekkende om die onbehoorlyke kundigheden en bevattingen, welke de menschen van de demons en quaade geesten hebben, te verbéteren. In 't engelsch geschreeven door N. Orchard ... En volgens de copy, gedrukt tot Londen in 't jaar 1676, vertaald door Wm. Séwel. t'Amsterdam, J. Broers, 1691.
100 p. 21cm.
(Continued on next card)

424

CATALOGUE OF THE CORNELL WITCHCRAFT COLLECTION

Witchcraft
BF
1730
O64
1691

[Orchard, N   ] supposed author. De leeringe der duyvelen ... 1691. (Card 2)

Translation of his The doctrine of devils ...

Also attributed to Thomas Ady.

1. Devil. 2. Demonology. I. Title. II. Orchard, N   supposed author. The doctrine of devils--Dutch. III. Ady, Thomas, supposed author.

Ordo et methodus cognoscendi & curandi energumenos.

WITCHCRAFT
BF
1555
H49

Henckel, Elias Heinrich von, fl. 1654-1688.
Eliae Henrici Henckelii ... Ordo et methodus cognoscendi & curandi energumenos seu à Stygio cacodaemone obsessos. Antehac a nemine, quantum sunt, qui de obsessis scripserunt, tradita. Francofurti & Lipsiae, Sumptibus Nicolai Försteri, 1689.
7 p. l., 240, [16] p. 17cm.
Title in red and black.

1. Demoniac possession. 2. Medicine --15th-18th centuries. I. Title: Ordo et methodus cognoscendi & curandi energumenos.

WITCHCRAFT
BT
965
O66

Oregio, Agostino, cardinal, 1577-1635.
De angelis tractatus tertius, auctore Augustino Oregio. Romae, Ex typographia Vaticana, 1632.
216 p. 24cm.

Third in his series of theological tractates.
With this is bound his De opere sex dierum tractatus quartus. 1632.

1. Angels--Early works to 1800. I. Title.

NIC

L'Orgie satanique à travers les siècles.

Witchcraft

Brévannes, Roland.
L'orgie satanique à travers les siècles. Paris, C. Offenstadt, 1904.
268 p. illus. 19cm.

1. Demonology. I. Title.

Orient und Occident.

WITCHCRAFT

Sepp, Johann Nepomuk, 1816-1908.
Orient und Occident. Hundert Kapitel über die Nachtseite der Natur, Zauberwerk und Hexenwesen in alter und neuer Zeit. Berlin, A. Schwetschke, 1903.
312 p. 23cm.

1. Witchcraft. 2. Magic. 3. Folklore, Germanic. 4. Folk-lore--Classification. I. Title. II. Title: Die Nachtseite der Natur, Zauberwerk und Hexenwesen.

Origenes.
Contra Celsum.

Witchcraft

Thorndike, Lynn, 1882-
The attitude of Origen and Augustine toward magic. [Chicago, 1908]
[46]-66 p. 23cm.

Reprinted from The monist, v.18, Jan. 1908.

1. Origenes. Contra Celsum. 2. Augustinus Aurelius, Saint, bp. of Hippo. De civitate Dei. 3. Magic. I. Title.

Witchcraft
BF
1598
A27
O76

Orsier, Joseph.
... Henri Cornélis Agrippa, sa vie et son œuvre d'après sa correspondance (1486-1535) Paris, Chacornac, 1911.
142 p., 1 l. 25½cm.

CONTENTS.--1. ptie. La vie et l'œuvre d'Agrippa--2. ptie. Extraits, annotés et traduits pour la première fois du latin, de la correspondance d'Agrippa avec ses amis et les personnages de son temps.

1. Agrippa von Nettesheim, Heinrich Cornelius, 1486?-1535. I. Title.

Library of Congress   BF1598.A308   13-1681

Die Ortenau.

Witchcraft
BF
1583
R43

Rest, Josef, 1884-
Ettenheimer Hexenprozesse im 17. Jahrhundert.
(In Die Ortenau. Mitteilungen des historischen Vereins für Mittelbaden. Offenburg i. B. 25cm. 3. Heft (1912), p. [38]-56)
Includes transcripts of records.

1. Trials (Witchcraft)--Ettenheim, Germany. 2. Trials (Witchcraft)--Alsace. I. Title. II. Die Ortenau.

Ortia Lindemann.

Witchcraft
BF
1583
Z7
1612

Grote, Otto, Freiherr.
Ortia Lindemann; oder, Der Zaubereiprocess zu Egeln 1612; mit Benutzung geschichtlicher Quellen bearb. Osterwieck a.H., A. W. Zickfeldt, 1877.
62 p. 23cm.

1. Witchcraft. 2. Trials (Witchcraft) --Germany. 3. Lindemann, Ortia, fl. 1612. I. Title.

Ortlob, Karl, respondent.

WITCHCRAFT
BT
980
M51

Meisner, Johann, praeses.
De apparitionibus daemonum exercitationem antipontificam praeside...Johanne Meisnero ...publico...examini...sistet M. Carolus Ortlob. [Wittebergae] Excudebatur literis Köhnerianis [1654]
[78] p. 20cm.

Diss.--Wittenberg (K. Ortlob, respondent)

1. Devil. 2. Demonology. 3. Apparitions. I. Ortlob, Karl, respondent.

NIC

Ortlob, Karl, respondent.

WITCHCRAFT
BT
980
M51
1753

Meisner, Johann, praeses.
Tractatus anti pontificius De apparitionibus daemonibus [i.e. daemonum]. Von Erscheinungen der Teufel. Francofurt. et Lipsiae, 1753.
94 p. 21cm.

Originally published as diss. at Wittenberg (K. Ortlob, respondent) in 1654, with title: De apparitionibus daemonum ...

1. Devil. 2. Demonology. 3. Apparitions. I. His [De   ] apparitionibus daemonum. II. Ortlob, Karl, respondent.

NIC

Osa, Ardoino Ubbidente dell', pseud.

see

Simon, Jordan, pater, 1719-1776.

WITCHCRAFT
BF
1584
S97
Z7
1782

Osenbrüggen, Eduard, 1809-1879.
Der letzte Hexenprocess. [Leipzig, 1867]
[513]-529 p. 24cm.

Extracted from Deutsches Museum, Nr. 17, Apr. 25, 1867.

1. Trials (Witchcraft)--Glarus (Canton) 2. Trials (Witchcraft)--Switzerland. 3. Göldi, Anna. 4. Tschudi, Anna Maria. I. Title.

NIC

WITCHCRAFT
BF
1600
O82

Osiander, Johann Adam, 1622-1697.
Tractatus theologicus De magia, exhibens ejusdem etymologiam, synonymiam, homonymiam, existentiam & naturam, causas & effectus mirabiles... Tubingae, Sumptibus Christiani Mülleri, typis Viduae Johann-Henrici Reisii, 1687.
358 p. 20cm.

1. Magic. I. Title.

NIC

Osservazioni sopra l'opuscolo che ha per titolo Arte magica dileguata.

Witchcraft
BF
1565
T19
M186+

[Lugiato, Andrea]
Osservazioni sopra l'opuscolo che ha per titolo Arte magica dileguata, di un prete dell' oratorio. Venezia, Presso Simone Occhi, 1750.
3 p. l., 99 p. 27cm.

Attributed to Lugiato by B. M. and Melzi; but Melzi also suggests one Lusato, veneziano.

1. Maffei, Francesco Scipione, marchese, 1675-1755. Arte magica dileguata. 2. Magic. I. Lusato, veneziano, supposed author. II. Title.

WITCHCRAFT
BF
1525
O85
1602

Osuna, Francesco de, d. ca. 1540.
Flagellum diaboli; oder, Dess Teufels Gaissl. Darinn ...gehandlet wirt: Von der Macht und Gewalt dess bösen Feindts. Von den Effecten und Wirckungen der Zauberer, Unholdter uff Hexenmaister... Durch...Franciscum de Ossuna in spanischer Sprach aussgangen, und durch Egidium Albertinum...verteuscht. München, Getruckt bey Adam Berg, 1602.
78 (i.e.76) 1. 19cm.
1.Devil. 2.Demonology. 3.Witchcraft. I. Albertinus, Aegidius, 1560-1620, tr. II. Title.

NIC

The other world.

BF
1241
L47

Lee, Frederick George, 1832-1902.
The other world; or, Glimpses of the supernatural. Being facts, records, and traditions relating to dreams, omens, miraculous occurrences, apparitions, wraiths, warnings, second-sight, witchcraft, necromancy, etc. Ed. by the Rev. Frederick George Lee ... London, H. S. King and co., 1875.
2 v. 18½cm.

Published also under title: Glimpses of the supernatural.

1. Supernatural. 2. Spiritualism. I. Lee, Frederick George, 1832-1902. Glimpses of the supernatural. II. Title.

Library of Congress   BF1241.L48   10-32970

Othonis Casmanni Angelographia.

Witchcraft
BT
965
C33

Casmann, Otto, d. 1607.
Othonis Casmanni Angelographia; sive Commentationum disceptationumque physicarum prodromvs problematicvs, de angelis sev creatis spiritibvs a corporvm consortio abiunctis, ex Dei verbo, S. Patrvm monumentis, dd. scholasticis & physicis; cum veteribus, tum recentioribus, concinnatus, & in duas partes distinctus. Francofurti, In officina Palthenii typographi, 1605.
2 v. in 1.   15cm.

(Continued on next card)

CATALOGUE OF THE CORNELL WITCHCRAFT COLLECTION

Othonis Casmanni Angelographia.

Witchcraft
BT
965
C33
 Casmann, Otto, d. 1607. Othonis Casmanni Angelographia ... 1605. (Card 2)

 Consecutively paged: 8 p. l., 672 p.
 Vol. 2 has title: Othonis Casmanni Angelographiae, hoc est, descriptionis angelicae ... pars altera. Francofurti, Ex officina Zachariae Palthenii, 1605.

  1. Angels. 2. Demonology. 3. Devil.
 I. Title: Angelographia.

8

Otia imperialia.

ar W
9788
2 copies
 Gervasius, of Tilbury.
 Otia imperialia. In einer Auswahl neu hrsg. und mit Anmerkungen begleitet von Felix Liebrecht. Ein Beitrag zur deutschen Mythologie und Sagenforschung. Hannover, C. Rümpler, 1856.
 xxii, 274 p. 23cm.

 I. Liebrecht, Felix, 1812-1890, ed.
 II. Title.

Otte, Peter, fl. 1672.

WITCHCRAFT
BF
1572
D4
S43
 Scriver, Christian, 1629-1693.
 Das verlohrne und wiedergefundene Schäfflein, oder Historischer christlicher Bericht von einem jungen Menschen, der sich vom Satan mit ihm einen Bund zu machen und ihm in allerley gottlosen Wesen sechs Jahr zu dienen verleiten lassen, darauff durch des gerechten Gottes Urtheil in dessen leibliche Gewalt und Besitzung gerathen, erschröcklich gequälet, endlich aber ... errettet und befreyet worden ...

8
NIC
  (Continued on next card)

Otte, Peter, fl. 1672.

WITCHCRAFT
BF
1572
D4
S43
 Scriver, Christian, 1629-1693. Das verlohrne und wiedergefundene Schäfflein ... 1672. (Card 2)

 Magdeburg und Helmstadt, Johann und Friedrich Lüderwaldts Buchhändl., 1672.
 [116] p. 19cm.
 "Historischer Bericht, den gantzen Verlauff mit dem Soldaten, dessen in denen vorhergesätzten Predigten Meldung geschehen, fürstellend" has special t. p.

8
NIC
  (Continued on next card)

WITCHCRAFT
BF
1555
E74
O78
 Ottokar, Amadeus.
 Anti-Satan. Sendschreiben an Professor Eschenmayer betreffend dessen Entgegnung auf die Schrift: "Entdeckung eines Complots wider Religion und Christenthum etc." Nürnberg, Bauer und Raspe, 1838.
 24 p. 21cm.

 1. Devil. 2. Eschenmayer, Carl Adolph von, 1770?-1852. Karakteristik des Unglaubens...
 3. Eschenmayer, Carl Adolph von, 1770?-1852.
8
NIC I. Title.

Oufle, Monsieur, Histoire de.

Witchcraft
PQ
1957
B67
A64
1793
 Bordelon, Laurent, 1653-1730.
 Histoire de M. Oufle, par abbé Bordelon [retouchée et réduite par M. G.], et la Description du sabbat. Paris, Gay & Gide, 1793.
 360 p. 20cm.

 "...C'est ... un nouveau roman, mais ... nous sommes redevables néanmoins à l'abbé Bordelon ...": p. 5-6.
 "Description du sabbat" is not by Bordelon.

Oufle, Monsieur, A history of.

Witchcraft
PQ
1957
B67
A64
1711
 [Bordelon, Laurent] 1653-1730.
 A history of the ridiculous extravagancies of Monsieur Oufle; occasion'd by his reading books treating of magick, the black-art, daemoniacks, conjurers, witches ... With notes containing a multitude of quotations out of those books, which have either caused such extravagant imaginations, or may serve to cure them. Written originally in French, by the Abbot B----; and now translated into English. London, Printed

8 (Continued on next card)

Oufle, Monsieur, A history of.

Witchcraft
PQ
1957
B67
A64
1711
 [Bordelon, Laurent] 1653-1730. A history of the ridiculous extravagancies of Monsieur Oufle ... 1711. (Card 2)
 for J. Morphew, 1711.
 4 p. l., 303 [i.e., 319] p. 20cm.
 Translation of Histoire des imaginations extravagantes de Monsieur Oufle.
 Gathering G, between p. 96 and 97, incorrectly paged 81-96.
  1. Occult sciences. 2. Apparitions.

8 (Continued on next card)

Witchcraft
BF
1410
B42
Z56
v.2
no.18
 Overdenkinge op het boek Den Satan in zijn weesen, aard-bedryf, en guigelspel, &c. beschreven door Simon de Vries. Amsterdam, By D. van den Dalen, boekverkooper, 1691.
 15 p. [p. 16 blank] title vignette, illus. initial. 19 x 15cm.
 4°: A-B⁴.
 Black letter (except for introduction)
 Plea for tolerance in the controversy over Balthasar Bekker's De betoverde weereld.

8 (Continued on next card)

Witchcraft
BF
1410
B42
Z56
v.2
no.18
 Overdenkinge op het boek Den Satan in zijn weesen ... 1691. (Card 2)

 Van der Linde 154.
 No. 18 in vol. lettered Bekker II.

 1. Vries, Simon de, 1630- . De Satan in syn wesen, aart, bedryf en guychelspel. 2. Bekker, Balthasar, 1634-1698. De betoverde weereld.

Witchcraft
BF
1410
B42
Z69
no.19
 Overdenkinge op het boek Den Satan in zijn weesen, aard-bedryf, en guigelspel, &c. beschreven door Simon de Vries. Amsterdam, By D. van den Dalen, boekverkooper, 1691.
 15 p. [p. 16 blank] title vignette, illus. initial. 21cm.
 4°: A-B⁴.
 Black letter (except for introduction)
 Plea for tolerance in the controversy over Balthasar Bekker's De betoverde weereld.

8 (Continued on next card)

Witchcraft
BF
1410
B42
Z69
no.19
 Overdenkinge op het boek Den Satan in zijn weesen ... 1691. (Card 2)

 Van der Linde 154.
 No. 19 in a Collection of tracts against Balthasar Bekker and his Betoverde weereld.

Overtro og trolddom fra de aeldste tider til vore dage.

Witchcraft
BF
1038
D18
L52
 Lehmann, Alfred Georg Ludvig, 1858-1921.
 Overtro og trolddom fra de aeldste tider til vore dage. København, J. Frimodt, 1893-[96].
 4 v. in 1. illus. 22cm.

 T.p. for four vols. dated 1896.

 1. Magic. 2. Witchcraft. 3. Occult sciences. 4. Theosophy. 5. Spiritualism.
8 6. Superstition. 7. Dreams. 8. Hypnotism.
NIC 9. Occult sciences--Bibl. I.Title.

Overweging van het hooftpoint in Do. Bekkers boek, genaamt De betoverde weereld.

Witchcraft
BF
1410
B42
Z85
no.3
 [Holy, Nikolaas Muys van] 1654-
 Overweging van het hooftpoint in Do. Bekkers boek, genaamt De betoverde weereld, te weten, of de duyvel op een mensch werken kan. [Amsterdam, By P. Rotterdam, boekverkoper, 1692]
 8 p. 19 x 16cm.
 4°: A⁴.
 Caption title.
 Signed: Nicolaes Muys van Holy.
 No. 3 in vol. lettered Stukken betrekkelijk Bekker.

8 (Continued on next card)

Owen, John Jason, 1803-1869.
Demonology of the New Testament.

Witchcraft
BL
305
A79
 Articles on mythology, etc. [v.p.], 1871-1880.
 1 v. (various pagings) 25cm.

 Cover-title.
 Articles reprinted from Contemporary review and Nineteenth century, with one from Once a week.
 Contents.--On the philosophy of mythology, by Max Müller.--Germanic mythology, by Karl Blind.--The first sin, by François Lenormant.--The myths of the sea and the river of
  (Continued on next card)

Owen, John Jason, 1803-1869.
Demonology of the New Testament.

Witchcraft
BL
305
A79
 Articles on mythology, etc. 1871-1880.
  (Card 2)

 Contents--Continued.
death, by C. F. Keary.--Wind myths, by C. F. Keary.--Forest and field myths, by W. R. S. Ralston.--Cinderella, by W. R. S. Ralston.--Demonology of the New Testament, by J. J. Owen.--Demoniacal possession in India, by W. Knighton.--Demonolatry, devil-dancing, and demoniacal possession, by R. C. Caldwell.--Witchcraft in Devon.

CATALOGUE OF THE CORNELL WITCHCRAFT COLLECTION

P

P., C., bibliophile.
WITCHCRAFT
BT
980
D53
 Le Diable et ses métamorphoses; étude historique par le bibliophile C. P. Paris Sandoz et Thuillier, 1882.
 100 p. 19cm.

 1. Devil. 2. Devil in literature.
8 I. P., C., bibliophile. II. C. P., bibliophile.
NIC

P., J.
hcraft
 De Volmaakte kragt Godts verheerlykt. Nevens eenige aanmerkinge over de drie predikatien van Do. Petrus Schaak. Gedaan over Psal. 72: v. 18. Gen. 18: v. 1,2 ... en Gen. 32: v.24, 25. In haar eigen gronden ondersogt, en met de waarheid vergeleken. En eenige andere aanmerkingen daar by gevoegd. Amsterdam, By D. vanden Dalen, boekverkooper, 1691.
 47 p. [p. 48 blank] title and other vignettes illus. initial. 19 x 15cm.
 4°: A-F⁴.

(Continued on next card)

P., J.
hcraft
 De Volmaakte kragt Godts verheerlykt. 1691.
(Card 2)

 Black letter.
 Preface signed: J:P. L:R.
 Supports B. Bekker against Schaak's attacks on Bekker's De betoverde weereld.
 Van der Linde 145.
 No. 20 in vol. lettered Bekker III.

P., L.
itchcraft
X
479
42
11
o.17
 Brief van L. P. aan Herman Bouman; eerst in 't bysonder aan hem geschreeven, en nu door hem, met verlof van den autheur, gemeen gemaakt: behelsende sommige redenen waarom hy de soo genaamde Sleutel der geesten enz. van M. van Diepen, en J. Hubener niet, ofte niet zoodanig alse daar ligt, behoorde te beantwoorden; en teffens een volstrekte omkeering van de gronden van dat woest geschrift. Amsterdam, By R. Blokland, boekverkoper, 1699.

(Continued on next card)

P., L.
tchcraft
79
1
.17
 Brief van L. P. aan Herman Bouman ... 1699.
(Card 2)

 2 p. l., 12 p. title and end page vignettes, illus. initials. 20 x 15cm.
 4°: π², A⁴, B².

 Written by a supporter of Balthazar Bekker, whom Diepen and Hubener attacked.
 No. 17 in vol. lettered B. Bekkers sterfbed en andere tractaten.
 1. Diepen, Marcus van. De sleutel der geesten. 2. Bekker, Balthasar,

(Continued on next card)

P., M. D. E.
Witchcraft
BF
1410
B42
Z286
no.6
 Missive van M. D. E. P. aan een vrind, over de zaak van Do. B: Bekker, en het boek van de Heer Professor M. Leydekker. Rotterdam, By J. Gysen, 1692.
 8 p. l. title vignette, illus. initial.
 19 x 15cm.
 4°: A-B⁴.
 Incomplete: second gathering wanting.
 Van der Linde 129.
 No. 6 in vol. lettered Tractaten voor en tegen B. Bekker.

P., T.
Witchcraft
BF
1581
Z7
1697
 A relation of the diabolical practices of above twenty wizards and witches of the sheriffdom of Renfrew in the kingdom of Scotland, contain'd in their tryalls, examinations, and confessions; and for which several of them have been executed this present year, 1697. London, Printed for H. Newman [1697]
 24 p. 21cm.

 "To Sir T. M.", a letter signed: "T.P.": p.3-4.
 Wing R 823.

P. Angeli März Verantwortung über die vom ...
P. Don Ferdinand Sterzinger ... gestellten Fragen.
Witchcraft
BF
1565
S83
M185
 März, Angelus, 1731-1784.
 P. Angeli März Verantwortung über die vom (Titl) P. Don Ferdinand Sterzinger bey dem hochfürstlich-hochlöblich-geistlichen Rath zu Freysing freywillig wider ihn gestellten Fragen. Jngolstadt, Gedruckt bey J. K. Gran, 1767.
 42 p. 19cm.
 A copy of the questions may be found in: Fieger, Hans, 1857- . P. Don Ferdinand Sterzinger, München, 1907, p. 135.

P. Angelus März Kurze Vertheidigung der thätigen Hex- und Zauberey.
Witchcraft
BF
1565
S83
M18
1766
 März, Angelus, 1731-1784.
 P. Angelus März Kurze Vertheidigung der thätigen Hex- und Zauberey wider eine dem heiligen Kreuz zu Scheyrn nachtheilig- Akademische Rede, welche den 13. October 1766. von P. Don Ferdinand Sterzinger ... abgelesen worden. 2. Aufl. Jngolstadt, Gedruckt bey J. K. Gran [1766]
 31 p. 21cm.
 1. Sterzinger, Ferdinand, 1721-1786. Akademische Rede von dem gemeinen Vorurtheile der ... Hexerey. 2. Witchcraft.
8 I. Title: Kurze Vertheidigung der thätigen Hex- und Zauberev.

P. Don Ferdinand Sterzinger, Lector der Theatiner in München.
Witchcraft
BX
4705
S832
F45
1907
 Fieger, Hans, 1857-
 P. Don Ferdinand Sterzinger, Lector der Theatiner in München, Director der historischen Klasse der kurbayerischen Akademie der Wissenschaften, Bekämpfer des Aberglaubens und Hexenwahns und der Pfarrer Gassnerschen Wunderkuren. Ein Beitrag zur Geschichte der Aufklärung in Bayern unter Kurfürst Maximilian III. Joseph. München, R. Oldenbourg, 1907.
 xi, 275 p. 2 tables. 23cm.

8 (Continued on next card)

P. Don Ferdinand Sterzinger, Lector der Theatiner in München.
Witchcraft
BX
4705
S832
F45
1907
 Fieger, Hans, 1857- . P. Don Ferdinand Sterzinger ... 1907. (Card 2)
 Inaug.-diss.--München.
 Expansion of a Programmschrift: Pater Don Ferdinand Sterzingers Leben und Schriften, München, 1907.

 1. Sterzinger, Ferdinand, 1721-1786.
 2. Bavaria--Hist.--Maximilian III Joseph (1745-1777). I. Title.

Pachler, Barbara, d. 1540.
Witchcraft
BF
1584
T9
Z59
 Zingerle, Ignaz Vincenz, Edler von Summersberg, 1825-1892, ed.
 Barbara Pachlerin, die Sarnthaler Hexe, und Mathias Perger, der Lauterfresser. Zwei Hexenprozesse, hrsg. von Dr. Ignaz Zingerle. Innsbruck, Wagner, 1858.
 xii, 84 p. 19cm.
 Contents.--Barbara Pachlerin, die Sarnthaler Hexe.--Der Lauterfresser.--Anhang. Ein altes Loosbuch.
8 Each item has special t. p.

(Continued on next card)

Pachlerin, Barbara, d. 1540.

see

Pachler, Barbara, d. 1540.

Packet, Ysabeal, d. 1495.
WITCHCRAFT
BF
1582
Z7+
1495
 Tihon, Ferdinand, ed.
 Un procès de sorcellerie à Huy en 1495. [Liége] 1904.
 7 p. 26cm.
 "Extrait de Wallonia. Numéro de janvier 1904."
 Documents from Archives de l'état à Liége. Cour de justice de Huy. Reg. 4, fol. 81 v° et ss.
 1. Trials (Witchcraft)--Huy, France.
8 2. Packet, Ysabeal, d. 1495. I. Title.
NIC

Pacta und Gelübdnüss einer ... hohen Person.
Witchcraft
BF
1565
D62
no.9
 Pott, Johann Heinrich.
 Specimen juridicum, De nefando lamiarum cum diabolo coitu, von der Hexen schändlichen Beyschlaff mit dem bösen Feind, in quo abstrusissima haec materia dilucidē explicatur, quaestiones inde emergentes curatē resolvuntur, variisque non injucundis exemplis illustrantur, publicâ luce donatum â Johanne Henrico Pott ... Jenae, Prostat apud Tobiam Oehrlingium, 1689.
 72 p. 20cm.

8 (Continued on next card)

CATALOGUE OF THE CORNELL WITCHCRAFT COLLECTION

Pages d'histoire judiciaire.

WITCHCRAFT
BF
1569
T37
    Théaux, Marcel.
        Pages d'histoire judiciaire. Le crime de sorcellerie.
        (In La revue du palais. Paris. 25cm.
        1. année, no. 7 (1897), p. [103]-135)

        In envelope.

        1. Witchcraft--History. 2. Devil.
    3. Bavent, Madeleine, ca. 1608-1647. I. Title. II.   Title: Le crime de sorcellerie.

8
NIC

Paholaisen liittolaiset.

BF
1584
F5
H46
    Heikkinen, Antero
        Paholaisen liittolaiset. Noita- ja magiakäsityksiä ja -oikeudenkäyntejä Suomessa 1600-luvun jälkipuoliskolla (n. 1640-1712) Helsinki, 1969.
        394 p. map. 24cm. (Suomen Historiallinen Seura. Historiallisia tutkimuksia, 78)

        Summary in English.
        Yliopistollinen väitöskirja--Helsinki.
        Extra t.p., with thesis statement, inserted.

(Continued on next card)

WITCHCRAFT
BF
1132
P14
    Pailloux, Xavier.
        Le magnétisme, le spiritisme et la posession. Entretiens sur les esprits entre un théologien, un avocat, un philosophe et un médecin. Paris, J. Lecoffre, 1863.
        xv, 460 p. 19cm.

        1. Animal magnetism. 2. Demoniac possession. 3. Spirits. 4. Occult sciences.

8
NIC   I. Title.

BF
1572
S4
P14
    Paine, Lauran.
        Sex in witchcraft. New York, Taplinger Pub. Co. [1972]
        186 p. illus. 22 cm. $6.50
        Bibliography: p. [182]-183.

    1. Witchcraft and sex.   I. Title.

BF1572.S4P3 1972	133.4	72-76258
ISBN 0-8008-7151-0		MARC
4 Library of Congress	72 [4]	

Pale Hecate's team.

Witchcraft
BF
1581
B85
1962
    Briggs, Katharine Mary.
        Pale Hecate's team; an examination of the beliefs on witchcraft and magic among Shakespeare's contemporaries and his immediate successors. London, Routledge and K. Paul [1962]
        viii, 291 p. illus. 23 cm.

    1. Witchcraft--Gt. Brit. 2. Magic. 3. Folk-lore--Gt. Brit.
    I. Title.

BF1581.B7	133.40942	62-6110 ‡
Library of Congress	[2]	

Witchcraft
BF
1565
P16
1725
    Palingh, Abraham.
        't Afgerukt mom-aansight der tooverye: daar in het bedrogh der gewaande toverye, naakt ontdekt, en met gezonde redenen en exempelen dezer eeuwe aangewezen wort ... Den tweeden Druk ... Amsterdam, By Andries van Damme, 1725.
        [16], 429, [10] p. plates. 16cm.

        Title vignette, engraved.

        1. Witchcraft. 2. Magic.   I. Title.

Rare
BT
980
P16+
1484
    Palladinus, Jacobus, de Theramo, Bp. of Spoleto, 1349-1417.
        Consolatio peccatorum, seu Processus Belial. [Strassburg, Heinrich Knoblochtzer] 1484.
        [94] l. 30cm.

        Leaves [1], [93b] and [94] blank.
        Leaf [2a]: Reuerendi patris domini Iacobi de Theramo Compendium pbreue Consolatio peccatorum nun cupatū. Et apud nonnullos Belial vocitatū ad papā Vrbanum
(Continued on next card)

Rare
BT
980
P16+
1484
    Palladinus, Jacobus, de Theramo, Bp. of Spoleto, 1349-1417. Consolatio peccatorum ... 1484.   (Card 2)

        sextum conscriptum. Incipit feliciter.
        Leaf [93a] (Colophon): Explicit liber belial nucupat̄ al's peccatorum consolatio. Anno dn̄i Mº.ccccxxxiiij.
        Signatures: a-b⁸, c-d⁶, e-k⁸·⁶, l-n⁸.
        Capital spaces, mostly with guide-letters.
        Copinger.   Supplement to Hain's Repertorium,   5793; Proctor, 373;
(Continued on next card)

Rare
BT
980
P16+
1484
    Palladinus, Jacobus, de Theramo, Bp. of Spoleto, 1349-1417. Consolatio peccatorum ... 1484.   (Card 3)

        Brit. Mus. Cat. (SV cent.) I, p. 89 (IB. 1091; Javobus [Palladinus] de Theramo); Goff. Third census, J-70 (Jacobus de Theramo).

        1. Devil.   I. Title: Consolatio peccatorum.   II. Title: Processus Belial.

Palmer, John, d. 1649.

Witchcraft
BF
1563
W81++
no.15
    The Divels delvsions; or, A faithfull relation of John Palmer and Elizabeth Knott, two notorious vvitches lately condemned at ... St. Albans ... executed July 16. Also their accusations of several vvitches in ... the county of Hartford. London, Printed for R. Williams, 1649. [London, at the British Museum, 1923]
    6 p. 16cm.

(Continued on next card)

Palmer, John, d. 1649.

Witchcraft
BF
1563
W81++
no. 15
    The Divels delvsions ... [1923]   (Card 2)

        Photocopy (negative) 6 p. on 5 l. 20 x 32cm.
        No. 15 in vol. lettered: Witchcraft tracts, chapbooks and broadsides, 1579-1704; rotograph copies.

        1. Witchcraft--England. 2. Palmer, John, d. 1649. 3. Knott, Elizabeth, d. 1649.

Palmer, John, d. 1649.

Witchcraft
GR
142
H6
A3
no.18
    Misodaimon, B., *pseud.*
        The divel's delusions; or, A faithful relation of John Palmer and Elizabeth Knott, two notorious witches, lately condemned at the sessions of Oyer and Terminer in St. Albans. Together with the confession of the aforesaid John Palmer and Elizabeth Knott, executed July 16. Also their accusations of severall witches in Hitchen, Norton, and other places in the county of Hartford. London, Printed for Richard Williams, stationer, at St. Albans, anno Dom, 1649. Reprinted with an introductory by W. B. Gerish. Bishop's Stortford, 1914.
        13, [1] p. 21½ cm. [Hertfordshire folk lore. no. 18]
        Signed: "B. Misodaimon."

    1. Witchcraft--England.   2. Palmer, John, d. 1649. 3. Knott, Elizabeth, d. 1649.   I. Gerish, William Blyth, ed.   II. Title.

Library of Congress   GR530.M55   16-25733

BF
1566
P18
    Palou, Jean.
        De la sorcellerie, des sorciers & de leurs juges. Préf. de Robert Amadou. Sazeray, Indre, France, Presses des Mollets [1972]
        16, x, 132 p. illus. 24cm. (Fondation Jean Palou. Publications. Serie Recherches, 1)

        1. Witchcraft. 2. Witchcraft--France.   I. Title   II. Series

NIC   MAY 03,'74   COOxc

Palud, Magdeleine de la.

Witchcraft
BF
1582
A92
    [Augier, Adolphe Clovis]
        Les grandes victimes de l'hystérie: Louis Gaufridi, curé des Accoules, et Magdeleine de la Palud. Relation historique et rationnelle d'un procès de sorcellerie. Paris, L. Michaud [1907]
        313 p. 19cm.
        At head of title: Raoul Gineste [pseud. of A. C. Augier]

        1. Gaufridi, Louis, 1572-1611. 2. Palud, Magdeleine de la. 3. Witchcraft--Provence. I.   Title.

8

Palud, Magdeleine de la.

WITCHCRAFT
BF
1517
F5
M62
1613
    Michaelis, Sebastien, 1543?-1618.
        The admirable history of the possession and conversion of a penitent woman. Sedvced by a magician that made her to become a witch, and the princesse of sorcerers in the country of Prouince, who was brought to S. Baume to bee exorcised, in the yeere 16... Wherevnto is annexed a pnevmology, or Discourse of spirits ... reuewed, corrected and enlarged ... Translated into English by W. B. London, Imprinted for William
(Continued on next card)

Palud, Magdeleine de la.

WITCHCRAFT
BF
1517
F5
M62
1613
    Michaelis, Sebastien, 1543?-1618. The admirable history of the possession ... of a penitent woman ... [1613]   (Card 2)

        liam Aspley [1613]
        24 p. l., 418, [10], 154, [34] p. 20cm.
        Differs from another issue only in t. p. (lacks date; some spellings different)
        Translation of Histoire admirable de la possession ... d'vne penitente, and of Discovrs des esprits.
        "A discovrse of spirits" has special t. p.   and separate paging.
(Continued on next card)

Palud, Magdeleine de la.

WITCHCRAFT
BF
1517
F5
M62
1613
    Michaelis, Sebastien, 1543?-1618. The admirable history of the possession ... of a penitent woman ... [1613]   (Card 3)

        STC 17854.

        1. Palud, Magdeleine de la. 2. Gaufridi, Louis, 1572-1611. 3. Loudun, France, Ursuline convent. 4. Demoniac possession. 5. Exorcism. I. His Histoire admirable de la possession ... d'une penitente. English. II. His Discours des esprits. English.   III. Title. IV. W. B., tr. V. B., W., tr.

Palud, Magdeleine de la.

WITCHCRAFT
BF
1517
F5
M62
    Michaelis, Sebastien, 1543?-1618.
        Histoire admirable de la possession et conversion d'vne penitente, seduite par vn magicien, la faisant sorciere & princesse des sorciers au pays de Prouence, conduite à la S. Baume pour y estre exorcizee l'an M.DC.X. au mois de Nouembre, soubs l'authorité du R. P. F. Sebastien Michaelis ... Commis par luy aux exorcismes & recueil des actes le R. P. F. François Domptius ... Ensemble la Pneumalogie, ou Discours du
(Continued on next card)

CATALOGUE OF THE CORNELL WITCHCRAFT COLLECTION

Palud, Magdeleine de la.

WITCHCRAFT
BF
1517
F5
M62

Michaelis, Sebastien, 1543?-1618. Histoire admirable ... 1613. (Card 2)

susdit Pere Michaelis, reueu, corrigé, & augmenté par luy-mesme ... Paris, Chez Charles Chastellain, 1613.
16 p. l., 352, 124, 196, [30] p. 17cm.
"Actes recveillis ... par le reverend Pere Michaëlis" has separate paging.
"Discovrs des esprits" has special t. p. with imprint Paris, 1512, and separate paging.

8 (Continued on next card)

Pananti, Filippo, 1766-1837.

Witchcraft
BF
1566
Z29

Zangolini, Asclepiade.
Il diavolo e le streghe, ossia il pregiudizio popolare delle malie ragionamento del dottore Asclepiade Zangolini ... coll' aggiunta di alcuni racconti piacevoli del medesimo. Livorno, G. B. Rossi, 1864.
272 p. 13cm. (Biblioteca enciclopedica popolare)
Contents.--Il diavolo e le streghe.-- Racconti piacevoli.--Epigrammi editi ed inediti e novellet te inedite del dottore

(Continued on next card)

Pananti, Filippo, 1766-1837.

Witchcraft
BF
1566
Z29

Zangolini, Asclepiade. Il diavolo e le streghe ... 1864. (Card 2)

Filippo Pananti.
Racconti and Epigrammi each have special t. p.

1. Witchcraft. 2. Devil. I. His Racconti piacevoli. II. Pananti, Filippo, 1766-1837. III. Title.

8

Pandaemonium.

tchcraft

Bovet, Richard, b. ca. 1641.
Pandaemonium: or, The Devil's cloyster. Being a further blow to modern Sadduceism, proving the existence of witches and spirits. In a discourse deduced from the fall of the angels, the propagation of Satans kingdom before the flood ... With an account of the lives and transactions of several ... witches. Also a collection of several authentic relations of strange apparitions of daemons and specters, and fas cinations of witches ...

(Continued on next card)

Pandaemonium.

chcraft

Bovet, Richard, b. ca. 1641. Pandaemonium ... 1684. (Card 2)

London, Printed for J. Walthoe, 1684.
239 p. 16cm.

I. Title.

---

chcraft

Panecius, Nicolaus, praes.
Dissertatio De generatione diaboli cum sagis, qvam ... sub praesidio M. Nicol. Panecii ... submittit autor respondens Georg. Christoph. Kranzius ... Wittebergae, Literis Johannis Wilckii [1693]
[16] p. 20cm.
No. 11 in vol. lettered Dissertationes de sagis. 1636-1714.

1. Witchcraft. 2. Devil. I. Kranz, Georg Christoph, respondent. II. Title: De generatione diaboli cum sagis. III. Dissertatio De generatione diaboli cum sagis.

11

Panoplia armaturae Dei.

Witchcraft
BF
1520
F72
1626

Forner, Friedrich, Bp. of Hebron, d. 1630.
Panoplia armatvrae Dei, adversus omnem svperstitionvm, divinationvm, excantationvm, daemonolatriam, et vniversas magorvm, veneficorum, & sagarum, & ipsiusmet Sathanae insidias, praestigias & infestationes. Concionibvs ... instructa atq; inscripta a Friderico Fornero ... Ingolstadii, Typis Gregorii Haenlini, 1626.
20 p. l., 292 p. 20cm.
1. Demonology. 2. Witchcraft. I. Title: Panoplia armaturae Dei.

8

Pantopolion.

Witchcraft
BF
1623
A5P61

Pictorius, Georg.
Παντοπωλιον, continens omnivm ferme quadrupedum ... naturas, carmine elegiaco ... una cum ... de apibus ... methodo ... praeterea, de daemonum ... ortu ... Isagoge ... quibus accedit ... de speciebus magiae ceremonialis, quam Goëtiam vocant, epitome, et an sagae ... cremari debeant resolutio ... Basileae, Per Henricvm Petri, 1563.
123 p. 16cm.
With this is bound his De illorvm daemonvm.

I. Title.   Title transliterated: Pantopolion.

Witchcraft

Panvinio, Onofrio, 1529-1568.

Witchcraft
BF
1761
C61

Clasen, Daniel, 1623-1678.
De oraculis gentilium et in specie de vaticiniis sibyllinis libri tres, autore Daniele Clasen ... In fine adivncta svnt carmina sibyllina è versione Sebastiani Castalionis. Vt et Onuphrii Panvinii tractatvs de sibyllis. Helmstadii, apud H. Mullerum, 1673.
8 p. l., 824, [8], 104, [43] p. 20cm.
"Sibyllina oracula" has special t.-p. and separate paging.

Paracelsus, 1493-1541.

Witchcraft
BF
1815
J62
S28
1570

Scalichius, Paulus von Lika, count, 1534-1575.
Pavli principis de la Scala ... Primi tomi Miscellaneorvm, de rervm caussis & successibus atque secretiori methodo ibidem expressa, effigies ac exemplar, nimirum, vaticiniorum & imaginum Ioachimi Abbatis Florensis Calabriae, & Anselmi Episcopi Marsichani, super statu summorum Pontificum Rhomanae Ecclesiae, contra falsam, iniquam, vanam, confictam & seditiosam cuiusdam Pseudomagi, quae nuper nomine Theophrasti Paracelsi in lucem prodijt, pseudomagicam expositi onem, vera, certa, &

(Continued on next card)

Paracelsus, 1493-1541.

Witchcraft
BF
1815
J62
S28
1570

Scalichius, Paulus von Lika, count, 1534-1575. ... Primi tomi Miscellaneorvm ... effigies ... 1570. (Card 2)
indubitata explanatio. Coloniae Agrippinae, Ex Officina Typographica Theodori Graminaei, 1570.
[12], p. 152 p. illus. 21cm.

Title vignette.

Paradoxon de tortura in Christiana republica non exercenda.

RARE
HV
8593
S29
1742

Schaller, Jacob, 1604-1676.
Paradoxon de tortura in Christiana republica non exercenda... Lipsiae, Apud Io. Christianum Schroeterum, 1742.
48 p. 21cm.

8
NIC

1. Torture. I. Title.

Paraenesis; ofte ernstige aenspraek aen den siender van Een vremt nagtgesigt.

Witchcraft
BF
1410
B42
Z56
v.3
no.4

[Molinaeus, Johannes] d. 1702.
Paraenesis; ofte ernstige aenspraek aen den siender van Een vremt nagtgesigt. Rotterdam, By B. Bos, 1692.
1 p. l., 10 p. title vignette, illus. initial. 20 x 16cm.
4°: π 1, A⁴, B1.
Black letter.
Signed: J:M.
Defense of the author's attack on Balthasar Bekker and De betoverde weereld.

(Continued on next card)

Paraenesis; ofte ernstige aenspraek aen den siender van Een vremt nagtgesigt.

Witchcraft
BF
1410
B42
Z56
v.3
no.4

[Molinaeus, Johannes] d. 1702. Paraenesis ... 1692. (Card 2)

Van der Linde 134.
No. 4 in vol. lettered Bekker III.

1. Bekker, Balthasar, 1634-1698. 2. Beschryvinge van een vremd nagt-gezigte. I. Title.

Rare
BX
1710
P22+
1598

Paramo, Luis de, 1545-1619.
De origine et progressv officii Sanctae Inqvisitionis, eiúsque dignitate & vtilitate, de Romani Pontificis potestate & delegata inquisitorum: edicto Fidei, & ordine iudiciario Sancti Officij, quaestiones decem. Libri tres. Autore Ludouico á Paramo ... Matriti, Ex Typographia Regia, 1598.
[118], 887 p. 30cm.

Engraved title vignette.

(over)

WITCHCRAFT
BF
1582
Z7+
1642

Parfouru, Paul, 1846-1905.
Un procès de sorcellerie au Parlement de Bretagne. La condamnation de l'abbé Poussinière, 1642-1643. Rennes, Impr. A. Le Roy, 1893.
11 p. 26cm.
"Extrait de la revue L'Hermine."

1. Trials (Witchcraft)--Rennes. 2. Poussinière, Mathurin Trullier, known as l'abbé. 3. Marais, Isaac. 4. France. Parlement (Rennes) I. Title.

8
NIC

Witchcraft
BF
1577
M3
P23

Parke, Francis Neal
Witchcraft in Maryland, by Francis Neal Parke. [Baltimore?] 1937.
cover-title, 50 p. 25cm.

"A paper read in part before the Round table and the Maryland historical magazine of December, 1936."

With autograph: Joseph Foster.

1. Witchcraft--Maryland. I. Title.

Witchcraft
BF
1566
P26

Parrinder, Edward Geoffrey.
Witchcraft: European and African. London, Faber and Faber [1963]
215 p. 23 cm.

1. Witchcraft. 2. Witchcraft--Africa. I. Title.

BF1566.P3   133.9   63—4000 ‡

Library of Congress   [63r3]

429

CATALOGUE OF THE CORNELL WITCHCRAFT COLLECTION

Parris, Samuel, 1653-1720.

Witchcraft
BF   Calef, Robert, 1648-1719.
1575   More wonders of the invisible world: or, The wonders of the
D76   invisible world, display'd in five parts. Part I. An account of
v.2-3   the sufferings of Margaret Rule, written by the Reverend Mr.
       C. M. P. II. Several letters to the author, &c. And his reply
       relating to witchcraft. P. III. The differences between the in-
       habitants of Salem village, and Mr. Parris their minister, in
       New-England. P. IV. Letters of a gentleman uninterested,
       endeavouring to prove the received opinions about witchcraft
       to be orthodox. With short essays to their answers. P. V. A
       short historical account [!] of matters of fact in that affair. To
       (Continued on next card)
       [r31e2]   2-13714 rev.

Parris, Samuel, 1653-1720.

Witchcraft
BF   Calef, Robert, 1648-1719.   More wonders of the invisible
1575   world ... (Card 2)
D76   which is added, a postscript relating to a book intitled, The
v.2-3 life of Sir William Phips. Collected by Robert Calef, mer-
      chant, of Boston in New-England ... London, Printed for
      N. Hillar and J. Collyer, 1700.
        Reprint. (In Drake, S. G. The witchcraft delusion in New England
        ... Roxbury, Mass., 1866. 21½ᶜᵐ. v. 2, p. 1-212; v. 3, p. 3-167)
        Woodward's historical series. no. VI-VII.
        Prefatory: by the editor: p. [v]-x. Pedigree of Calef: 1 fold. leaf.
        Memoir of Robert Calef: p. [xi]-xxix.
        The text, here annotated. is that of the 1st edition, 1700. "It is given
        as exactly like the original as a much better type can be made to imi-
        tate an old type of 166 years ago."—Pref. by the editor. p. vi.
        (Continued on next card)
       [r31e2]   2-13714 rev.

Parris, Samuel, 1653-1720.

Witchcraft
BF   Calef, Robert, 1648-1719. More wonders of the
1575   invisible world ... 1700.   (Card 3)
D76   Appendix: I. Examination of Giles Cory.—
v.2-3 II. Giles Corey and Goodwyfe Corey. A ballad of
      1692.—III. Testimony of William Beale, of
      Marblehead, against Mr. Philip English of Salem,
      given Aug. 2d. 1692.—IV. [Examination of the
      Indian woman belonging to Mr. Parris's family]—
      V. The examination of Mary Clark of Haverhill.—
      VI. An account of the life and character of the
      Rev. Samuel Parris, of Salem village, and of his
      connection with the witchcraft delusion of 1692.
      By Samuel P.   Fowler.

Parris, Samuel, 1653-1720.

Witchcraft
BF   Calef, Robert, 1648-1719.
1575   More wonders of the invisible world, or The
C14   wonders of the invisible world displayed. In
1823 five parts. Part I.—An account of the suffer-
      ings of Margaret Rule, written by the Rev. Cott-
      on Mather. Part II.—Several letters to the
      author, &c. and his reply relating to witchcraft.
      Part III.—The differences between the inhabi-
      tants of Salem village, and Mr. Parris, their
      minister, in New-England. Part IV.—Letters of
      a gentleman uninterested, endeavouring to prove
      the received opinions about witchcraft to be
      (Continued on next card)

Parris, Samuel, 1653-1720.

Witchcraft
BF   Calef, Robert, 1648-1719. More wonders of the
1575   invisible world ... 1823.   (Card 2)
C14   orthodox. Part V.—A short historical account of matters
1823 of fact in that affair. To which is added a
      postscript (!) relating to a book entitled "The
      life of Sir Wm. Phips". Collected by Robert
      Calef. Merchant, of Boston, in New-England.
      Printed in London, 1700. Salem, Reprinted by
      J.D. & T.C. Cushing, jr. for Cushing and
      Appleton, 1823.
      312 p. 18½cm.

      (Continued on next card)

Parris, Samuel, 1653-1720.

Witchcraft
BF   Calef, Robert, 1648-1719. More wonders of the
1575   invisible world ... 1823. (Card 3)
C14
1823   Appended: Giles Cory [a report of his
      examination, taken from the witchcraft records]:
      p. 310-312.
      "The second Salem edition appears to have
      been copied from the first [Salem edition] that
      of 1796. In some instances slight departures are
      made from the copy ... such departures are also
      departures from the original [London edition of
      1700]"—S. G. Drake, pref. to ed. of 1866.

Parris, Samuel, 1653-1720.

Witchcraft
BF   Calef, Robert, 1648-1719.
1575   Wonders of the invisible world, or,
C14   Salem witchcraft. In five parts. Boston,
1828 T. Bedlington [1828]
      333 p. front. 14cm.

      A reply to Cotton Mather's "Wonders of
      the invisible world."
      First ed. published in 1700 under title:
      More wonders of the invisible world
      displayed.
        (Continued on next card)

Parris, Samuel, 1653-1720.

Witchcraft
BF   Calef, Robert, 1648-1719. Wonders of the
1575   invisible world ... [1828] (Card 2)
C14
1828   Contents.—Part 1. An account of the
      sufferings of Margaret Rule, by Cotton
      Mather.—Part 2. Several letters from the
      author to Mr. Mather and others, relating
      to witchcraft.—Part 3. Account of the
      differences in Salem village between the
      villagers and their minister, Mr. Parris.—
      Part 4. Letters of a gentleman uninter-
      (Continued on next card)

Parris, Samuel, 1653-1720.

Witchcraft
BF   Calef, Robert, 1648-1719. Wonders of the
1575   invisible world ... [1828] (Card 3)
C14
1828   ested, endeavouring to prove the received
      opinions about witchcraft to be orthodox.—
      Part 5. An impartial account of the most
      memorable matters of fact touching the
      supposed witchcraft in New-England.—Post-
      script, relating to Cotton Mather's life of
      Sir William Phips.—Giles Cory: a report of
      his examination, taken from the witch-
      craft files.

Parris, Samuel, 1653-1720.

Witchcraft
BF   Fowler, Samuel P[age] 1800-1888.
1575   An account of the life and character of the Rev. Sam-
D76   uel Parris, of Salem village, and of his connection with
v.3   the witchcraft delusion of 1692. By Samuel P. Fowler,
      esq. (In Drake, S. G. The witchcraft delusion in New
      England ... Roxbury, Mass., 1866. 21½ᶜᵐ. v. 3. p.
      198-222)
        Reprinted from Proceedings of the Essex Institute, v. 2, 1856-60, Salem,
      1862, p. 49-68.

        Subject entries: 1. Parris, Samuel, 1653-1720. 2. Witchcraft—New Eng-
      land. I. Title.
                                    2-13716
      Library of Congress, no.

Parris, Samuel, 1653-1720.

Witchcraft
F   Fowler, Samuel Page, 1800-1888.
74   An account of the life, character, &c.,
S1   of the Rev. Samuel Parris, of Salem village
P26 and of his connection with the witchcraft
      delusion of 1692. Read before the Essex
      Institute, Nov'r 14, 1856. Salem, W. Ives
      and G. W. Pease, printers, 1857.
      20 p. 24cm.

      Cover title.

      1. Parris, Samuel, 1653-1720. 2. Witch-
      craft—Salem,   Mass.

Witchcraft
PR   Parsons, Coleman Oscar.
5343   Witchcraft and demonology in Scott's
W8P26 fiction. With chapters on the super-
      natural in Scottish literature.
      Edinburgh and London, Oliver & Boyd, 1964.
      x, 363 p. 25cm.

      1. Scott, Sir Walter, bart., 1771-
      1832. 2. Witchcraft. 3. Demonology.
      I. Title.

Pasqualone, Giovanni.

Witchcraft
BX   [Masini, Eliseo] brother, 17th cent.
1710   Sacro arsenale, ovvero Pratica dell'Uffi-
M39 zio della Santa Inquisizione; coll'inserzio-
1730 ne di alcune regole fatte dal p. inquisitore
      Tommaso Menghini ... e di diverse annotazio-
      ni del dottore Gio: Pasqualone ... In questa
      4. impressione aggiuntavi la Settima Denun-
      zia fatta dal suddetto padre per li sponte
      comparenti, impressa in Ferrara 1687. E
      corretta in alcune cose la parte decima degli
      avvertimenti ...   Roma, Nella Stamperia di
      (Continued on next card)
      [Secular name: Cesare
        Masini]

Pasqualone, Giovanni.

Witchcraft
BX   [Masini, Eliseo] brother, 17th cent. Sacro
1710 arsenale ...   (Card 2)
M39
1730 S. Michele a Ripa, 1730.
      [6], 506, [54] p. 23cm.

      Edited by Luigi and Francesco Conti.

      1. Inquisition. I. Menghini, Tommaso,
      17th cent. II. Pasqualone, Giovanni. III.
      Conti, Luigi. IV. Conti, Francesco. V.
      Title. VI. Title: Pratica dell'Uffizio del-
      la Santa Inquisi-   zione.

Witchcraft
PT   Pastor, Karl.
2445   Culturhistorische Bilder aus den Zeiten
P3709 des Wahns. Bd. 1. Das Marile. Eine Ge-
1883 schichte aus der Zeit des Hexenwahns.
      Hamburg, Seelig & Ohmann, 1883.
      vi, 184 p. 21cm.

      No more published?

      I. Title. II. Title: Marile.

Pater Don Ferdinand Sterzingers Leben
   und Schriften.

Witchcraft
BX   Fieger, Hans, 1857-
4705   Pater Don Ferdinand Sterzingers Leben
S832 und Schriften. Ein Beitrag zur Geschichte
F45   der Aufklärungsepoche in Bayern. München,
      Druck von C. Gerber [1896]
      48 p. 2 tables (1 fold.) 24cm.
      Programmschrift—Königl. Ludwigs-Kreis-
      realschule, München.
      1. Sterzinger, Ferdinand, 1721-1786.
      2. Bavaria—Hist.—Maximilian III Joseph
      (1745-1777) I.   Title.
8

WITCHCRAFT
BF   Paterson, James, minister of the Associat
1566   Congregation, Midmar.
P29   A belief in witchcraft unsupported by
      scripture; an essay. Aberdeen, Printed
      by D. Chalmers, for A. Brown, 1815.
      vi, 134 p. 20cm.

8   1. Witchcraft. 2. Witchcraft in the
NIC Bible. I. Title.

Pathologia daemoniaca.

WITCHCRAFT
RC   Westphal, Johann Caspar.
340   D. Johannis-Caspari VVestphali, academi
W53 curiosi, Pathologia daemoniaca, id est Ob-
1707 servationes & meditationes physiologico-ma
      gico-medicae circa daemonomanias, similesq
      morbos convulsivos â fascino ortos, daemon
      bus olim Graecorum ethnicorum ac Judaeorum
      aëreis, hodiè verò obsessioni aliisque dia
      boli infernalis tentationibus & operation
      bus superstitiosè adscriptos ... Nunc ver
      philiatrorum   desiderio & adhortation
8   (Continued on next card)

CATALOGUE OF THE CORNELL WITCHCRAFT COLLECTION

Pathologia daemoniaca.

TCHCRAFT Westphal, Johann Caspar. ... Pathologia
           daemoniaca ... 1707. (Card 2)

bus revisae, & variis annotatis illustriores
redditae. Quibus accedunt Judicium physiologico-magico-medicum de viva jumentorum
contagio infectorum contumulatione, & Observationes atque experimenta chymico-physica
de prodigiis sangvinis, falsò hactenus proclamatis. Lipsiae, Apud haeredes F. Lanckisii, 1707.
  6 p. l., 148, [16] p. 22cm.
        (Continued on next card)

Pathologia daemoniaca.

TCHCRAFT Westphal, Johann Caspar. ... Pathologia
           daemoniaca ... 1707. (Card 3)

The first section, subtitled Historia
morbi & species facti, is German and Latin
in double columns.

1. Nervous system--Diseases. 2. Demonomania. 3. Epilepsy. 4. Hysteria. I.
Title: Pathologia daemoniaca.

Patronus nupturientium.

tchcraft   De injuriis, qvae haud raro novis nuptis,
I. Per sparsionem dissectorum culmorum
frugum Germ., durch das Herckerling-[sic]
Streuen; II. Per injustam interpellationem ulterioris proclamationis, durch
ungebührlichen Einspruch; III. Per ligationes magicas, durch das Nestel-Knüpf-
fen, inferri solent, qvas adjectis summariis & indice, per varias qvaestiones
practicas tractavit, examinavit, & praejudiciis hinc inde illustravit Patronus

        (Continued on next card)

Patronus nupturientium.

tchcraft   De injuriis, qvae haud raro novis nuptis
           ... inferri solent ... 1699. (Card 2)

Nupturientium. Qvedlinburg, Sumptibus
Gottlob Ernesti Strunzi, 1699.
123, [16] p. 21cm.

Title in red and black.

1. Marriage (Canon law) 2. Marriage
customs and ri   tes. 3. Charms. I.
Patronus nupt   urientium.

Paul Laymann und die Hexenprocesse.

tchcraft   Duhr, Bernhard, 1852-1930.
           Paul Laymann und die Hexenprozesse.
(In Zeitschrift für katholische Theologie. Innsbruck. 23cm. 23. Bd., 4. Heft
(1899), p. 733-745)

1. Laymann, Paul, 1574-1635. Processus
juridicus contra sagas et veneficos. 2.
Trials (Witchcraft)--Germany. I. Title.
II. Zeitschrift für katholische Theologie.

Pauli principis de la Scala ... Primi tomi
   miscellanea.

raft   Scalichius, Paulus von Lika, count, 1534-1575.
       Pavli principis de la Scala ... Primi tomi
Miscellaneorvm, de rervm caussis & successibus
atque secretiori methodo ibidem expressa, effigies ac exemplar, nimirum, vaticiniorum & imaginum Ioachimi Abbatis Florensis Calabriae, &
Anselmi Episcopi Marsichani, super statu summorum Pontificum Rhomanae Ecclesiae, contra falsam,
iniquam, vanam, confictam & seditiosam cuiusdam
Pseudomagi, quae nuper nomine Theophrasti Paracelsi in lucem prodijt, pseudomagicam expositionem, vera, certa, & indubitata explanatio.
        (Continued on next card)

Pauli principis de la Scala ... Primi tomi
Witchcraft miscellanea.
BF   Scalichius, Paulus von Lika, count, 1534-1575.
1815   ... Primi tomi Miscellaneorvm ... effigies ...
J62   1570. (Card 2)
S28
1570   Coloniae Agrippinae, Ex Officina Typographica
        Theodori Graminaei, 1570.
         [12], 152 p. illus. 21cm.

        Title vignette.

Die paulinische Angelologie und Dämonolo-
Witchcraft logie: ein biblisch-theologischer Versuch.
BS   Everling, Otto.
2655   Die paulinische Angelologie und Dämonolo-
A5   gie: ein biblisch-theologischer Versuch.
E93   Göttingen, Vandenhoeck und Ruprecht, 1888.
         126 p. 24cm.

        1. Bible. N. T. Epistles of Paul--
Theology. 2. Angels. 3. Demonology. I.
Title.

WITCHCRAFT
BX   Pauls, Emil.
2340   Der Exorcismus an Herzog Johann Wilhelm
P33   von Jülich in den Jahren 1604 und 1605.

        (In: Historischer Verein für den Nieder-
         rhein. Annalen. Köln. 23cm. No.63 (1897)
         p. [27]-53)

        With this, in the same issue, is: Keussen,
        Hermann. Zwei Hexenprozesse aus der Cre-
        felder Gegend.
8   1.Exorcism.   2.Medicine,Magic, mystic
NIC   and spagiric.   3. Johann Wilhelm, Her-
        zog von Jüli   ch-Kleve-Berg, 1562-1609.
         I. Title.

WITCHCRAFT
BF   Pauls, Emil.
1583   Zauberwesen und Hexenwahn am Niederrhein.
P33
        (In: Beiträge zur Geschichte des Nieder-
         rheins. Düsseldorf. 24cm. v.13 (1898)
         p. [134]-242)

8   1. Witchcraft--Germany. 2. Witchcraft--
NIC   History.   I. Title.

WITCHCRAFT
BF   Paulus, Nicolaus, 1853-1930.
1566   Bibel und protestantische Hexenverfolg-
P33   ung.
B5++   (In Wissenschaftliche Beilage zur Ger-
         mania. Blätter für Literatur, Wissenschaft
         und Kunst. Berlin. 31cm. Jahrg. 1907,
         Nr. 44 (1907), p. [345]-349)
        In columns.
        In broadside box.

        1. Witchcraft--History. 2. Witchcraft
8   in the Bible.   I. Title.
NIC

WITCHCRAFT
BF   Paulus, Nicolaus, 1853-1930.
1571   Hexenwahn und Hexenprozess, vornehmlich
P33   im 16. Jahrhundert. Von Nikolaus Paulus.
        Freiburg im Breisgau, Herder, 1910.
         283 p. 20cm.

        A collection and revision of 13 essays
        previously published in various journals.

        1. Witchcraft--Hist. 2. Reformation.
8   I. Title.

WITCHCRAFT
BF   Paulus, Nicolaus, 1853-1930.
1566   Hexenwahn und Protestantismus. [Köln,
038   1909]
P33++   5 columns. 34cm.

        Detached from the Kölnische Volkszeitung
        und Handels-Blatt, erste Beilage zur Sonn-
        tags-Ausgabe for February 14, 1909.
        In broadside box.

8   1. Ohle, Rudolf, 1857- .   Der Hexen-
NIC   wahn. 2. Wi   tchcraft--History. I.
        Title.

WITCHCRAFT
BR   Paulus, Nicolaus, 1853-1930.
350   Johann Brenz und die Hexenfrage.
B83   (In Wissenschaftliche Beilage zur Ger-
P33++   mania. Blätter für Literatur, Wissenschaft
         und Kunst. Berlin. 31cm. Jahrg. 1909,
         Nr. 26 (1909), p. [201]-204)
        In double columns.
        In broadside box.
        1. Brenz, Johann, 1499-1570. 2.
8   Witchcraft--Germany--History. I. Title.
NIC

WITCHCRAFT
BR   Paulus, Nicolaus, 1853-1930.
333   Luther und die Hexen.
.5   (In Historisch-politische Blätter für
W8   das katholische Deutschland. München.
P33   23cm. 139. Bd., 8. Heft (1907), p. [557]-
         575)

        At head of title: LV.

        1. Luther, Martin, 1483-1546--Theology.
8   2. Witchcraft   --Germany--History. I.
NIC   Title.

WITCHCRAFT
BF   Paulus, Nicolaus, 1853-1930.
1584   Rom und die Blütezeit der Hexenprozesse.
I8   (In Historisch-politische Blätter für
P33   das katholische Deutschland. München.
         22cm. 141. Bd., 1. Heft (1908), p. [241]-
         254)

        At head of title: XIX.

        1. Trials (Witchcraft)--Rome. I.
8   Title.
NIC

WITCHCRAFT
HV   Paulus, Nicolaus, 1853-1930.
8551   Der sächsische Kriminalist Carpzov und
P33++   seine 20 000 Todesurteile. [Köln, 1907]
         1 column. 58 cm. (folded to 34cm.)

        Detached from the Kölnische Volkszeitung
        und Handels-Blatt for February 18, 1907.
        In broadside box.

        1. Carpzov, Benedict, 1595-1666. 2.
8   Capital punishment--Germany. I. Title.
NIC

BF   Pazzini, Adalberto.
1555   Demoni, streghe e guaritori. [Milano] V. Bompiani, 1951.
P34   290 p. illus. 21 cm. (Avventure del pensiero, v. 80)
        "Opere consultate": p. [283]-[285]

        1. Demoniac possession. 2. Demonomania. 3. Witchcraft.
        I. Title.   A 52-10750

        Harvard Univ. Library
        for Library of Congress   [3]

CATALOGUE OF THE CORNELL WITCHCRAFT COLLECTION

Witchcraft
BF 1521
H17
    The pedigree of the devil.
Hall, Frederic Thomas.
    The pedigree of the devil. ... London, Trübner, 1883.
    xv, 256 p. illus. 22cm.

1. Devil. I. Title.

Witchcraft
BF 1581
Z7+
1644a
    Peebles, Marion, d. 1644.
    Trial of witches in Shetland, A. D. 1644. Intent upon pannel Marion Peebles alias Pardone, spouse to Swene in Hildiswick. [Edinburgh? 1822?]
    10 p. 28cm.
    Caption title.
    Extract from Hibbert-Ware, Samuel, 1782-1848. A description of the Shetland Islands. Edinburgh, 1822. "... the original document was in the possession of a gentleman of Shetland, lately deceased."

(Continued on next card)

BF 1581
P37
    Peel, Edgar.
    The trials of the Lancashire witches; a study of seventeenth-century witchcraft, by Edgar Peel and Pat Southern. Drawings by Pat Southern. New York, Taplinger Pub. Co. [1969]
    192 p. illus, facsim. geneal. table, map. 23 cm. 6.50
    Bibliography: p. 168-169.

1. Trials (Witchcraft)—Lancashire, Eng. I. Southern, Pat, joint author. II. Title.

343'.5   72-84973 MARC
Library of Congress   69 [3

Witchcraft
Z 6876
J86
    Peeters-Baertsoen, Adolphe, 1826-1875.
    Jouin, Ernest.
    Bibliographie occultiste et maçonnique. Répertoire d'ouvrages imprimés et manuscrits relatifs à la franc-maçonnerie, les sociétés secrètes, la magie, etc. publié d'après les fiches recueillies par A.-Peeters Baertsoen et avec des notes historiques et bibliographiques. Tome I. Jusqu'à l'année 1717. Paris, Revue internationale des sociétés secrètes, 1930.
    653 p. 25cm.
    At head of title: Mgr E. Jouin et V. Descreux.
    No more published?

BF 1614
P37
    Pegaso, Osvaldo.
    Manuale della magia e della stregoneria. Milano, G. De Vecchi, 1967.
    438 p. 20½ cm. L 3800
    (It 67-8184)

1. Magic. 2. Witchcraft. I. Title.

BF1614.P4   79-366201
Library of Congress   69 [18]

Witchcraft
BS 2545
D5
T75
no.6
    Pegge, Samuel, 1704-1796.
    An examination of the Enquiry into the meaning of demoniacs in the New Testament. In a letter to the author. Wherein it is shewn, that the word demon does not signify a departed soul, either in the classics or the Scriptures, and consequently, that the whole of the Enquiry is without foundation. London, Printed for F. Gyles, 1739.
    86 p. 20cm.
    No. 6 in vol. lettered: Tracts on demoniacks. 1737.

(Over)

Witchcraft
BT 1313
B52
    Pegna, Francesco, ed.
    Bernardus Comensis.
    Lucerna inquisitorum haereticae pravitatis R. P. F. Bernardi Comensis... et eiusdem Tractatus de strigibus, cum annotationibus Francisci Pegnae... Additi sunt in hac impressione duo tractatus Joannis Gersoni... Roma, ex officina Bartholomaei Grassi, 1584.
    [4] l., 184, [28] p. 22cm.

1. Heresies and heretics. I. Pegna, Francesco, ed. II. Gerson, Joannes, 1363-1429. III. Title.

Rare
K
A923++
    Peinliche Gerichtsordnung.
    Austria. Laws, statutes, etc.
    Constitutio criminalis Theresiana, oder Der Römisch-kaiserl. zu Hungarn und Böheim u. u. Königl. Apost. Majestät Mariä Theresiä, Erzherzogin zu Oesterreich, u. u., peinliche Gerichtsordnung. Wien, Gedruckt bey J. T. edlen von Trattnern, 1769.
    8 p.l., 282, lvi. p. incl. plates (part fold.) 35cm.
    Latin summary of paragraphs in margin.
    The plates (mostly printed on both

(Continued on next card)

Rare
K
A923++
    Peinliche Gerichtsordnung.
    Austria. Laws, statutes, etc. Constitutio criminalis Theresiana ... 1769. (Card 2)

sides) are illustrations of instruments of torture and their application.
    List of members of the commission entrusted with the elaboration of the code: p. lv-lvi.
    Note in manuscript on p. [2] of cover: Sehr selten, da die Exemplare unterdrückt wurden.

(Continued on next card)

Witchcraft
K
B816++
1582
    Peinliche Halssgerichts-Ordnung des durchleuchtigen hochgebornen Fürsten vnnd Herren, Herrn Georg Friedrichen.
    Brandenburg (Electorate) Laws, statutes, etc.
    Peinliche Halssgerichts-Ordnung, des Durchleuchtigen Hochgebornen Fürsten vnnd Herren, Herrn Georg Friderichen Marggrauen zu Brandenburg ... Welcher massen in J. F. G. Landen vnd Fürstenthumen in peinlichen Sachen einzuziehen, zufragen, zurichten, zustraffen, vnd zuuolfahren &c. Jtzo auff das Newe wider vbersehen, gemehrt vnd verbessert sampt einer Vor rede &c. [Ansbach?] Ge-

(Continued on next card)

Witchcraft
K
B816++
1582
    Peinliche Halssgerichts-Ordnung des durchleuchtigen hochgebornen Fürsten vnnd Herren, Herrn Georg Friedrichen.
    Brandenburg (Electorate) Laws, statutes, etc. Peinliche Halssgerichts-Ordnung ... 1582. (Card 2)

druckt zum Hoff durch Mattheum Pfeilschmidt, 1582.
    3 p. l., lxii numbered, 11 unnumbered l. 31cm.
    Interleaved, with ms. notes in contemporary hand; 7 l. appended at end.
    With colophon.
    Title in red and black, armorial device.

(Continued on next card)

Witchcraft
K
B816++
1582
    Peinliche Halssgerichts-Ordnung des durchleuchtigen hochgebornen Fürsten vnnd Herren, Herrn Georg Friedrichen.
    Brandenburg (Electorate) Laws, statutes, etc. Peinliche Halssgerichts-Ordnung ... 1582. (Card 3)

With this are bound Brandenburg-Ansbach (Principality) Laws, statutes, etc. Neue Ordnung ... Onolzbach, 1720; and Brandenburg-Ansbach (Principality) Laws, statutes, etc. Anhang zu der Anno 1720. ergangenen ... Gerichts-Ordnung. Onolzbach [1725]

1. Criminal procedure—Brandenburg (Electorate). I. Georg Friedrich, Margrave of Brandenburg, 1539-1603. II. Title.

Witchcraft
BF 1410
B42
Z56
v.3
no.19
    Pel, J
    De wonderdaden des Alderhoogsten, waar in aangewesen word, wat mogelyker en waarschijnelijker is, de verleidinge van den mensch door sig selfs, of door dat ding dat een afgevallen geest word genoemd; en dat den val van de denkende wesens onvereenigd met een lighaam, die engelen worden genoemt, niet alleen onbegrijpelijk maar ook onmogelijk is, ja dat hare scheppinge in 't werk der scheppinge, in den gehelen Bijbel niet te vinden is. ... Amsterdam, Gedrukt by W. de Coup, boekverkoper, 1693.

(Continued on next card)

Witchcraft
BF 1410
B42
Z56
v.3
no.19
    Pel, J   De wonderdaden des Alderhoogsten ... 1693.   (Card 2)

    4 p. l., [84], [8] p. title vignette, illus. initial. 19 x 15cm.
    4º: *⁴, A-L⁴, M².
    Incomplete: first gathering only.
    Van der Linde 137.
    No. 19 in vol. lettered Bekker III.

1. Devil. 2. Angels. I. Title.

Rare
BX 1735
L79
1818
    Pellier, Alexis, tr.
    Llorente, Juan Antonio, 1756-1823.
    Histoire critique de l'inquisition d'Espagne depuis l'époque de son établissement par Ferdinand V, jusqu'au règne de Ferdinand VII; tirée des pièces originales des archives du Conseil de la Suprême et de celles des tribunaux subalternes du Saint-Office. Par D. Jean-Antoine Llorente ... Tr. de l'espagnol sur le manuscrit et sous les yeux de l'auteur, par Alexis Pellier. 2. éd. Paris, Treuttel et Würtz [etc.], 1818.
    4 v. port., illus. (coat of arms) 21cm.

(Continued on next card)

Rare
BX 1735
L79
1818
    Pellier, Alexis, tr.
    Llorente, Juan Antonio, 1756-1823. Histoire critique de l'inquisition d'Espagne ... 1818.   (Card 2)

"Catalogue des manuscrits qui n'ont pas encore été publiés, et qui ont servi pour composer l'Histoire critique de l'inquisition d'Espagne": t.1, p. xxxj-xxxvj.
    Translation of Historia critica de la inquisición de España.

Rare
BX 1710
E97++
1578
    Peña, Francisco, 1540?-1612, ed.
    Eymerich, Nicolás, 1320-1399.
    Directorivm inqvisitorvm ... denvo ex collatione plvrivm exemplarium emendatum, et accessione multarum literarum Apostolicarum, officio Sanctae Inquisitionis deseruientium, locupletatum, cvm scholiis seu annotationibvs ... Francisci Pegnae Hispani, ... Accessit rerum & verborum ... index. ... Romae, In aedibvs Pop. Rom., 1578.
    3 pts. in 1 v. 34cm.

Title vignette.
Colophon of pt. 3 dated: 1579.

    Penal methods, A history of.

HV 9644
I95
    Ives, George Cecil, 1867-
    A history of penal methods; criminals, witches, lunatics, by George Ives, M.A. London, S. Paul & co., [1914]
    xi, 409 p. 23cm.

"Index to authors [with titles of works]" p. 384-396.

CATALOGUE OF THE CORNELL WITCHCRAFT COLLECTION

Pacta und Gelübdnüss einer ... hohen Person.
Pott, Johann Heinrich. Specimen juridicum ... 1689. (Card 2)

"Pacta und Gelübdnüss einer ... hohen Person, so dieselbe mit dem leydigen Satan soll haben getroffen," p. [69]-72, has special t. p.
No. 9 in vol. lettered Dissertationes de sagis. 1636-1714.
1. Witchcraft. 2. Devil. I. Title: De nefando lamiarum cum diabolo coitu. II. Title: Pacta und Gelübdnüss einer ... hohen Person.

Paediae Scoticae.
Leali, Josephus.
Paediae Scoticae, quibus subtilissima Scoti mens, Scotistis, & exteris, iuxta Aristotelis Principia, facili methodo, Scotice aperitur. Pars tertia, Libros de generatione, corruptione, meteoris, mundo, coelo, & magia, complectens. Auctore Iosepho Leali ... Venetiis, Apud Vitali, 1673.
150 p. 22cm.
Added t.p. engr.
1. Aristoteles. 2. Duns, Joannes, Scotus, 1265?-1308? 3. Metaphysics. 4. Demonology. I. Title.

Pagendarm, Johann Gerhard, respondent.
Pistori, Gustav Friedrich, praeses.
... Dispvtatione prima existentiam spectrorvm, praesertim ex sagarum veneficarumque pactis cum diabolo sancitis, benevolo facultatis philosophicae indultu demonstrabit praeses M. Gvstav. Frider. Pistori, ... et respondens Io. Gerhardvs Pagendarm ... Vitembergae, Praelo Christiani Gerdesii [ca. 1700]
[16] p. 18cm. (bound in 21cm. vol.)
No. 15 in vol. lettered Dissertationes de spectris. 1646-1753.
(Continued on next card)

Pépin, Étienne, fl. 1347.
Falgairolle, Edmond.
Un envoutement en Gévaudan en l'année 1347. Nîmes, Catélan, 1892.
117 p. 19cm.
Contains the complete proceedings of the trial of Etienne Pépin in Latin, and an abridged version in French.
1. Pépin, Étienne, fl. 1347. I. Title.

Peregrinus, Marcus Antonius, 1530-1616.
Consilium de sagis.
Diversi tractatvs: De potestate ecclesiastica coercendi daemones circa energumenos & maleficiatos, de potentia ac viribus daemonum. De modo procedendi adversvs crimina excepta; praecipuè contra sagas & maleficos ... Ex diversis jisqve celeberrimis huius aeui scriptoribus ... disputantur. Coloniae Agrippinae, Sumptibus Constantini Munich bibliopolae, 1629.
8, 236, 166 p. 20cm.
(Continued on next card)

Peregrinus, Marcus Antonius, 1530-1616.
Consilium de sagis.
Diversi tractatvs ... 1629. (Card 2)

Contents.--Tractatvs de potestate ecclesiae coercendi daemones circa obsessos & maleficiatos, vnà cum praxi exorcistica, a R. della Torre.--Tractatvs theologicvs de processv adversvs crimina excepta, ac speciatim adversus crimen veneficij, ab A. Tanner.--Tractatvs alter theologicus de sagis et veneficis, a P. Laymanni.--Consilium de sagis, a M. A. Peregrini.
(Continued on next card)

Peregrinus, Marcus Antonius, 1530-1616.
Consilium de sagis.
Witchcraft
BF 1563 D61
Diversi tractatvs ... 1629. (Card 3)

Title in red and black.
In double columns except for t. p., dedication, and titles of first, second, and fourth works.
1. Witchcraft. 2. Trials (Witchcraft) 3. Exorcism. I. Torre, Raffaele della. Tractatus de potestate ecclesiae coercendi daemones. II. Tanner, Adam, 1572-1632. Tractatus theologicus de processu adversus
(Continued on next card)

Witchcraft
BF 1600 P43 1591
Pereira, Benito, ca. 1535-1610.
Benedicti Pererii Valentini ... Adversvs fallaces et svperstitiosas artes, id est, De magia, de observatione somniorum, &, de diuinatione astrologica. Libri tres. Ingolstadii, Ex officina typographica Davidis Sartorii, 1591.
3 p. l., 139 p. 17cm.
Issued later under title: De magia, de observatione somniorum, et de divinatione astrologica.
Stamp on t.p.: Bibl. Buxheim.

Witchcraft
BF 1600 P43 1592
Pereira, Benito, ca. 1535-1610.
Benedicti Pererii Valentini ... Adversvs fallaces & superstitiosas artes, id est, De magia, de observatione somniorum, &, de diuinatione astrologica. Libri tres. Venetiis, Apud Ioan. Baptistam Ciottum, senensem, 1592.
3 p. l., 256, [8] p. 15cm.
First published 1591.
Later editions have title: De magia, de observatione somniorum, et de divinatione astrologica.
(Continued on next card)

Witchcraft
BF 1600 P43 1592
Pereira, Benito, ca. 1535-1610. Benedicti Pererii Valentini ... Adversus fallaces ... 1592. (Card 2)

Stamp of S. Michele in Bosco on cover.
1. Magic. 2. Dreams. 3. Astrology. I. Title: Adversus fallaces et superstitiosas artes. II. Title. III. his De magia, de observatione somniorum, et de divinatione astrologica.

WITCHCRAFT
BF 1600 P43 1603
Pereira, Benito, ca. 1535-1610.
Benedicti Pererii Valentini ... Adversvs fallaces et superstitiosas artes, id est, De magia, de observatione somniorum, & de diuinatione astrologica. Libri tres. Et à mendis quae anteà irrepserant accuratissimè repurgatus. Lvgdvni, Apvd Horativm Cardon, 1603.
5 p. l., 253, [8] p. 18cm.
Title in red and black.
1. Magic. 2. Dreams. 3. Astrology. I. Title: Adversus fallaces et superstitiosas artes.

Witchcraft
BF 1600 P43 1612
Pereira, Benito, ca. 1535-1610.
Benedicti Pererii ... De magia, de observatione somniorvm et de divinatione astrologica libri tres. Adversvs fallaces, et superstitiosas artes. Coloniae Agrippinae, Apud Ioannem Gymnicum, 1612.
324, [8] p. 13cm.
First published 1591 under title: ... Adversus fallaces et superstitiosas artes.
1. Magic. 2. Dreams. 3. Astrology. I. His ... Adversus fallaces et superstitiosas artes. II. Title: De magia, de observatione somniorum, et de divinatione astrologica.

Witchcraft
BF 1600 P43 1598
Pereira, Benito, 1535 (ca.)-1610.
De magia, de observatione somniorvm, et de divinatione astrologica, libri tres. Adversvs fallaces, et svperstitiosas artes. Avctore Benedicto Pererio Valentino ... Accesservnt indices dvo ... Coloniae Agrippinae, apud I. Gymnicum, 1598.
2 p. l., [1], 236, [8] p. 17cm.
First published 1591 under title: ... Adversus fallaces et superstitiosas artes.
11-15970 rev.
Library of Congress   BF1600.P4
——— Another issue.   BF1600.P42
[r38d2]

Witchcraft
BF 1600 P43 1612
Pereira, Benito, ca. 1535-1610.
Benedicti Pererii ... De magia, de observatione somniorvm et de divinatione astrologica libri tres. Adversvs fallaces, et superstitiosas artes. Coloniae Agrippinae, Apud Ioannem Gymnicum, 1612.
324, [8] p. 13cm.
First published 1591 under title: ... Adversus fallaces et superstitiosas artes.
1. Magic. 2. Dreams. 3. Astrology. I. His ... Adversus fallaces et superstitiosas artes. II. Title: De magia, de observatione somniorum, et de divinatione astrologica. III. Title.

Witchcraft
BF 1600 P43 1592
Pereira, Benito, ca. 1535-1610.
Benedicti Pererii Valentini ... Adversvs fallaces & superstitiosas artes, id est, De magia, de observatione somniorum, &, de diuinatione astrologica. Libri tres. Venetiis, Apud Ioan. Baptistam Ciottum, senensem, 1592.
3 p. l., 256, [8] p. 15cm.
First published 1591.
Later editions have title: De magia, de observatione somniorum, et de divinatione astrologica.
(Continued on next card)

Witchcraft
BF 1600 P43 1592
Pereira, Benito, ca. 1535-1610. Benedicti Pererii Valentini ... Adversus fallaces ... 1592. (Card 2)

Stamp of S. Michele in Bosco on cover.
1. Magic. 2. Dreams. 3. Astrology. I. Title: Adversus fallaces et superstitiosas artes.

Pererius, Benedictus, 1535 (ca.)-1610.
see
Pereira, Benito, 1535 (ca.)-1610.

Pererius Valentinus, Benedictus.
see
Pereira, Benito, 1535 (ca.)-1610.

433

CATALOGUE OF THE CORNELL WITCHCRAFT COLLECTION

WITCHCRAFT
R 133 P43+
Pereyra, Bernardo.
    Anacephaleosis medico-theologica, magica, juridica, moral, e politica na qual ... se mostra a infalivel certeza de haver qualidades maleficas ... e se descreve a cura assim em geral, como em particular, de que se devem valer nos achaques procedidos das dittas qualidades maleficas, e demoniacas, chamadas vulgarmente feitiços, obra necessaria para os medicos, e muito preciza para os exorcistas   Coimbra, Na officina de

8   (Continued on next card)

WITCHCRAFT
R 133 P43+
Pereyra, Bernardo. Anacephaleosis medico-theologica ... 1734. (Card 2)
    Francisco de Oliveyra, 1734.
      30 p. l., 432 p. 29cm.

    1. Medicine, Magic, mystic, and spagyric. 2. Magic. 3. Diseases--Causes and theories of causation. I. Title.

8

A perfect discovery of witches.

Witchcraft
BF 1565 A24 1661
[Ady, Thomas]
    [A perfect discovery of witches, shewing the divine cause of distractions of this kingdome, and also of the Christian world. London, 16--]
    [140] p. 20cm.

    Imperfect: lacks t.p. and all before p. 9, also p. 107-110; p. 9-18, 139-140 mutilated; page numbers and part of text lacking; t.p. in ms. supplied.
    First ed. published in 1656 under title: A candle in the dark.
    I. Title. II. His A candle in the dark.

Perger, Mathias, ca. 1580-1645?

Witchcraft
BF 1584 T9 Z59
Zingerle, Ignaz Vincenz, Edler von Summersberg, 1825-1892, ed.
    Barbara Pachlerin, die Sarnthaler Hexe, und Mathias Perger, der Lauterfresser. Zwei Hexenprozesse, hrsg. von Dr. Ignaz Zingerle. Innsbruck, Wagner, 1858.
    xii, 84 p. 19cm.
    Contents.--Barbara Pachlerin, die Sarnthaler Hexe.--Der Lauterfresser.--Anhang. Ein altes Loosbuch.
    Each item has special t. p.

8   (Continued on next card)

Peri energeias daimonon dialogos.

WITCHCRAFT
BF 1508 P97 1688
Psellus, Michael.
    [Michaelou tou Psellou Peri energeias daimonon dialogos] Μιχαήλου του Ψελλου Περὶ ἐνέργειας δαιμόνων διάλογος. Michaelis Pselli De operatione daemonum dialogus. Gilbertus Gaulminus Molinensis primus Graecè edidit & notis illustrauit. E museo Dan. Hasenmülleri ... Kiloni, Sumtibus Joh. Sebastiani Richelii, 1688.
    6 p. l., 166 p. 15cm.

8 NIC   (Continued on next card)

Peri energeias daimonon dialogos.

WITCHCRAFT
BF 1508 P97 1688
Psellus, Michael. [Michaelou tou Psellou] Peri energeias daimonon dialogos] 1688. (Card 2)

    Latin and Greek on facing pages, with notes by Gaulmin at bottom of page.
    Latin translation by Petrus Morellus, "illius qui & Nicetae Thesaurum orthodoxae fidei de Graeco Latinum fecit."
    1. Demonology. I. Gaulmin, Gilbert, 1585-1665, ed. II. Morellus, Petrus, Turonensis, tr. III. Hasenmüller,

8 NIC   (Continued on next card)

Die Periode der Hexenprocesse.

WITCHCRAFT
BF 1566 M51
Mejer, Ludwig.
    Die Periode der Hexenprocesse. Hannover, Schmorl & von Seefeld, 1882.
    100 p. 22cm.

2 copies

8 NIC   1. Witchcraft--Hist. 2. Trials (Witchcraft) --Hist.

WITCHCRAFT
BF 1565 P45 1608
Perkins, William, 1558-1602.
    A discovrse of the damned art of witchcraft; so farre forth as it is reuealed in the Scriptures, and manifest by true experience. Framed and delivered by M. William Perkins, in his ordinarie course of preaching, and now published by Tho. Pickering Batchelour of Diuinitie ... Wherevnto is adioyned a twofold table... [Cambridge, Eng.] Printed by Cantrel Legge, 1608.
    12 p. l., 257 p. 17cm.
    S.T.C. 19697.

8

FILM 470 reel 725
Perkins, William, 1558-1602.
    A discovrse of the damned art of witchcraft; so farre forth as it is reuealed in the Scriptures, and manifest by true experience. Framed and delivered by M. William Perkins, in his ordinarie course of preaching, and now published by Thomas Pickering. Wherevnto is adioyned a twofold table; one of the order and heades of the treatise; another of the texts of Scripture explaned, or vindicated from the corrupt inter pretation of the
    (Continued on next card)

FILM 470 reel 725
Perkins, William, 1558-1602. A discovrse of the damned art of witchcraft ... 1608. (Card 2)

adversarie. [Cambridge] Printed by C. Legge, 1608.
    University microfilms no. 21660 (carton 725)
    Short-title catalogue no. 19697.

1. Witchcraft.   MiU F57-527

FILM 470 reel 677
Perkins, William, 1558-1602.
    A discovrse of the damned art of witchcraft; so farre forth as it is reuealed in the Scriptures, and manifest by true experience. Framed and delivered by William Perkins in his ordinarie course of preaching and published by Thomas Pickering. [Cambridge, Eng.] Printed by C. Legge, 1609.
    From the author's Works? Cf. signatures and pagination.
    University microfilms no. 17770 (carton 677)
    (Continued on next card)

FILM 470 reel 677
Perkins, William, 1558-1602. A discovrse of the damned art of witchcraft ... 1609. (Card 2)

    Short-title catalogue no. 19649a [i.e. Bishop Checklist no. 19649.1]

    1. Witchcraft.   MiU F56-784

Witchcraft
BF 1565 P45 1610
Perkins, William, 1558-1602.
    A discovrse of the damned art of witchcraft, so farre forth as it is reuealed in the Scriptures, and manifest by true experience... Published by T. Pickering. Wherevnto is adioyned a twofold table; one of the order and heades of the treatise, another of the texts of Scripture explaned, or vindicated from the corrupt interpretation of the aduersarie. [Cambridge] Printed by C. Legge, printer to the Vniuersitie, 1610.
    16, [24], 256 p. 16cm.

    1. Witchcraft.

WITCHCRAFT
BF 1565 P45++ 1631
Perkins, William, 1558-1602.
    A discovrse of the damned art of witchcraft. So farre forth as it is revealed in the scriptvres, and manifested by true experience. Framed and delivered by Master William Perkins, in his ordinary course of preaching, and published by Thomas Pickering. London, Printed for Iames Boler, 1631.
    [10], 607-652 p. 33cm.

    Signatures: Llll-Oooo⁶.

    (Continued on next card)

WITCHCRAFT
BF 1565 P45++ 1631
Perkins, William, 1558-1602. A discovrse of the damned art of witchcraft ... 1631. (Card 2)
    Imperfect: last leaf mutilated.
    From the author's Works? Cf. signatures and pagination.
    With this is bound the author's A resolution to the countrey-man ... 1631.

    ✓ 1. Witchcraft. ✓ I. Pickering, Thomas, II. Title.

Perkins, William, 1558-1602.

BX 9339 P44 B11
Baarsel, Jan Jacobus van.
    William Perkins: eene bijdrage tot de kennis der religieuse ontwikkeling in Engeland, ten tijde van Koningin Elisabeth. 's-Gravenhage, H. P. de Swart [1912]
    321 p. illus. 25cm.

    1. Perkins, William, 1558-1602.

Perks, Thomas.

Witchcraft
BF 1581 Z7 1762
Durbin, Henry.
    A narrative of some extraordinary things that happened to Mr. Richard Giles's children the Lamb, without Lawford's-Gate, Bristol, supposed to be the effect of witchcraft. By the late Mr. Henry Durbin ... To which is added, letter from the Rev. Mr. Bedford ... to the Bishop of Glocester, relative to one Thomas P of Mangotsfield, who had dealings with famili spirits. Bristol, Printed and sold by R. Edwards, 1800.
    60 p. 21cm.

Witchcraft
BF 1576 P45
Perley, Martin Van Buren, 1835-
    A short history of the Salem village witchcraft trials illustrated by a verbatim report of the trial of Mrs. Elizabeth Howe; a memorial of her ... Map and half tone illustrations. [Souvenir ed.] Salem, Mass. M. V. B. Perley 1911.
    76 p. front., illus. (incl. map) 3 pl., ports., facsim. 19½ᶜᵐ $0.75

    1. Witchcraft--Salem, Mass. ✓ I. Title.

    Library of Congress   BF1576.P5   11-20600
    ——— Copy 2.
    Copyright A 295170

CATALOGUE OF THE CORNELL WITCHCRAFT COLLECTION

Witchcraft
Perley, Sidney, 1858-1928.
Where the Salem "witches" were hanged.
Salem, Mass., Essex Institute, 1921.
18 p. illus. 28cm.

"One hundred and fifty copies reprinted from the Historical collections of the Essex Institute, volume LVII."

1. Witchcraft--New England. I. Title.

Perneder, Andreas, d. 1543?
Von straff vnnd Peen aller vnnd yeder Malefitz handlungen ain kurtzer bericht, genommen vnd verfaszt ausz den gemainen Kayserlichen Rechten, mit Lateinischer Allegation derselben, auch daneben meldung der gebreüchlichen hierinn Hochteütschlands gewonhaiten: Nit anders zůachten dann ain Gerichtliche Practica aller Criminal oder peinlichen sachen ... Ingolstat, Gedruckt durch Alexander Weissenhorn, 1544.
[4], xxiiii l. 31cm.

Caption title A. Perneders halsgerichts ordnung. (over)

Perrault, François, 1572 or 77-1657.
L'Antidémon de Mascon--English.
Perrault, François, 1572 or 77-1657.
The Devill of Mascon; or, A true relation of the chiefe things which an vncleane spirit did, and said, at Mascon in Burgundy, in the house of Mr. Francis Perreand [sic] ... Published in French lately by himself; and now made English by one that hath a particular knowledge of the truth of this story [i.e. Peter Du Moulin. With a letter from the Hon. R. Boyle to the translator] Oxford, Printed by H. Hall, for R. Davis, 1658.
46 p. 15cm. (Continued on next card)

Perrault, François, 1572 or 77-1657.
L'Antidémon de Mascon--English.
Perrault, François, 1572 or 77-1657. The Devill of Mascon ... 1658. (Card 2)

Translation of his L'Antidémon de Mascon ...

1. Demonology. I. Title. II. Perrault, François, 1572 or 77-1657. L'Antidémon de Mascon--English.

Perrault, François, 1572 or 77-1657.
Demonologie ov Traitte des demons et sorciers: de leur puissance et impuissance: par Fr. Perreavd. Ensemble L'Antidemon de Mascon, ou Histoire veritable de ce qu'un demon a fait & dit, il y a quelques années, en la maison dudit Sr. Perreaud à Mascon ... Geneve, Chez Pierre Aubert, 1653.
2 pts. in 1 v. 15cm.

1. Demonology. I. Title. II. Title: L'Antidemon de Mascon.

Perrault, François, 1572 or 77-1657.
The Devill of Mascon; or, A true relation of the chiefe things which an vncleane spirit did, and said, at Mascon in Burgundy, in the house of Mr. Francis Perreand [sic] ... Published in French lately by himself; and now made English by one that hath a particular knowledge of the truth of this story [i.e. Peter Du Moulin. With a letter from the Hon. R. Boyle to the translator] Oxford, Printed by H. Hall, for R. Davis, 1658.
46 p. 15cm. (Continued on next card)

Witchcraft
BF
1555
P45
1658
Perrault, François, 1572 or 77-1657. The Devill of Mascon ... 1658. (Card 2)

Translation of his L'Antidémon de Mascon ...

1. Demonology. I. Title. II. Perrault, François, 1572 or 77-1657. L'Antidémon de Mascon--English.

Perry, William.
WITCHCRAFT
BF
1555
H97
1799
Hutchinson, Francis, bp. of Down and Connor, 1660-1739.
Wilhelm Perry; oder: Der besessene Knabe. Ein Beitrag zu den Teufelsbesitzungen unsers Zeitalters. [Leipzig?] 1799.
16 p. 19cm.
Illustrative title vignette.
"Ein Auszug aus Hutchinsons historischem Versuche über die Hexerey. Lpz. 1727": translation of Historical essay concerning witchcraft.

(Continued on next card)

A Person of quality at Paris.
WITCHCRAFT
BF
1582
G51
M53
Memoirs of Miss Mary-Catherine Cadiere, and Father Girard, Jesuit, containing an exact account of that extraordinary affairs interspers'd with letters and other original papers relating thereto, and which have hitherto been unknown to the publick. In an epistle from a person of quality at Paris to his correspondent in London. London, Printed for J. Isted, 1731.
32 p. 20cm.
1. Cadière, Catherine, b.1709. 2. Girard, Jean Baptiste, 1680-1733. I. A Person of quality at Paris.

The personality and history of Satan.
Witchcraft
BT
980
B88
Brown, Robert, of Barton-upon-Humber.
The personality and history of Satan. London, S. W. Partridge, 1887.
232 p. (p. [217]-232 advertisements) 19cm.

1. Devil. I. Title.

BF
1413
P45
Perty, Maximilian, 1804-1884.
Die sichtbare und die unsichtbare Welt, diesseits und jenseits. Leipzig, C. J. Winter, 1881.
320 p. 23cm.

1. Occult sciences. 2. Witchcraft. I. Title.

Thesis
1911
338
Peter Binsfeld and Cornelius Loos.
Hodder, Mabel Elisabeth.
Peter Binsfeld and Cornelius Loos, an episode in the history of witchcraft. Ithaca, N.Y., 1911.
228 l. 29cm.

Thesis (Ph.D.)--Cornell University, 1911.

WITCHCRAFT
BF
1556
P47
Petermann, Andreas, 1649-1703, praeses.
Disputatio medica De ephialte seu incubo, quam...sub praesidio...Andr. Petermanni... publico...examini subjicit Johannes Müller ... Lipsiae, Typis Christophori Fleischeri [1688]
[40] p. 20cm.

Diss.--Leipzig (J. Müller, respondent)

1. Medicine, Magic, mystic and spagiric. 2. Demonology. 3. Diseases--Causes and theories of causation. I. Müller, Johannes, of Stargard, respondent. II. Title.

BF
1566
K84
Peters, Edward M., joint comp.
Kors, Alan C., comp.
Witchcraft in Europe, 1100-1700; a documentary history. Edited with an introd., by Alan C. Kors and Edward Peters. Philadelphia, University of Pennsylvania Press [1972]
viii, 382 p. illus. 25 cm.
Includes bibliographical references.

1. Witchcraft--Europe--History--Sources. I. Peters, Edward M., joint comp. II. Title

NIC   NOV 15, '73   ⃝xc   71-170267

Petersen, Dominikus.
WITCHCRAFT
BF
1038
D18
L52
1908
Lehmann, Alfred Georg Ludvig, 1858-1921.
Aberglaube und Zauberei von den ältesten Zeiten an bis in die Gegenwart. Deutsche autorisierte Übersetzung von Dr. med. Petersen I. 2. umgearbeitete und erweiterte Auflage. Stuttgart, F. Enke, 1908.
xii, 665 p. illus., facsims. 24cm.

Translation of Overtro og trolddom.

I. His Overtro og trolddom--German. II. Petersen, Dominikus. III. Title.

Petersen, Friedrich Wilhelm--Fiction.
Witchcraft
BF
1410
C97
Curieuses Gespräche im Reiche derer Todten, zwischen zweyen hochberühmten Männern, Johann Friedrich Mayern, ... und Johann Wilhelm Petersen ... Darinnen nechst dieser beyder hochberühmten Männer Lebens-Particularitäten, von vielen curieusen und zu unserer Zeit strittig gewordenen Glaubens-Lehren, pro & contra gestritten wird. [Leipzig] 1732.
2 v. in 1. (128 p.) 2 plates, vignettes. 21 x 17cm.

(Continued on next card)

Petersen, Friedrich Wilhelm--Fiction.
Witchcraft
BF
1410
C97
Curieuses Gespräche im Reiche derer Todten, zwischen ... Johann Friedrich Mayern, ... und Johann Wilhelm Petersen ... 1732.
(Card 2)

4°: A3, B-H4, J3, K-Q4.
Black letter.
Vol. 2 has title: Gespräche im Reiche derer Todten ...
Bound with Curieuse Gespräche im Reiche derer Todten, zwischen ... Balthasar Beckern ... und ... Christian Scrivern ... 1731-[1734] (Continued on next card)

Peterson, Joan, d. 1652.
Witchcraft
BF
1581
Z7
1652a
A Declaration in answer to several lying pamphlets concerning the witch of Wapping. Being a more perfect relation of the arraignment, condemnation, and suffering of Jone Peterson, who was put to death on Munday the 12 of April, 1652. Shevving the bloudy plot and wicked conspiracy of one Abraham Vandenbemde, Thomas Crompton, Thomas Collet, and others. London, Printed in the year 1652.
11 p. 20cm.

(Continued on next card)

CATALOGUE OF THE CORNELL WITCHCRAFT COLLECTION

Peterson, Joan, d. 1652.
Witchcraft
BF   A Declaration in answer to several lying pam-
1581   phlets concerning the witch of Wapping...
Z7   1652.   (Card 2)
1652a
    Bound with The witch of Wapping. London,
    1652.
    With bookplate of Francis Freeling.

    1. Peterson, Joan, d. 1652.

Peterson, Joan, d. 1652.
Witchcraft
BF   The Tryall and examination of Mrs. Joan
1563   Peterson ... for her supposed witchcraft,
W81++   and poysoning of the lady Powel ...
no.17   together with her confession ... Also,
    the tryal, examination and confession of
    Giles Fenderlyn, who had made a convenant
    with the Devil for 14 years... London,
    Printed for G. Horton, 1652. [London,
    at the British Museum, 1923]
    8 p. 16cm.

                (Continued on next card)

Peterson, Joan, d. 1652.
Witchcraft
BF   The Tryall and examination of Mrs. Joan
1563   Peterson... [1923]   (Card 2)
W81++
no.17   Photocopy (negative) 8 p. on 7 l. 20 x
    32cm.
    No. 17 in vol. lettered: Witchcraft
    tracts, chapbooks and broadsides, 1579-
    1704; rotograph copies.

    1. Witchcraft--England. 2. Peterson, Joan,
    d, 1652. 3. Fenderlyn, Giles, d. 1652.

Peterson, Joan, d. 1652.
Witchcraft
BF   The Witch of Wapping; or, An exact and per-
1581   fect relation of the life and devilish
Z7   practises of Joan Peterson, who dwelt in
1652a   Spruce Island, near Wapping; who was con-
    demned for practising witch-craft, and sen-
    tenced to be hanged at Tyburn, on Munday the
    11th [sic] of April, 1652... Together with
    the confession of Prudence Lee, who was
    burnt in Smithfield on Saturday the 10th.
    ... for the murthering her husband...
    London, Print   ed for Th. Spring, 1652.
    8 p. 20cm.
                (Continued on next card)

Peterson, Joan, d. 1652.
Witchcraft
BF   The Witch of Wapping ... 1652.
1581   (Card 2)
Z7
1652a   With this is bound A declaration in answer
    to several lying pamphlets concerning the witch
    of Wapping ... London, 1652.
    With book-plate of Francis Freeling.

    1. Peterson, Joan, d. 1652. 2. Lee,
    Prudence, d. 1652.

    Petite encyclopédie synthétique des sciences
        occultes.
BF   Bosc, Ernest, 1837-
1412   Petite encyclopédie synthétique des sciences
B74   occultes. Éd. de la curiosité. Nice, Bureau
    de la Curiosité, 1904.
    xiii, 285 p. 18cm.

    At head of title: Ernest Bosc de Vèze.

    1. Occult sciences--Dictionaries. I. Title.

    Les petits sorciers du XVIIe siècle et
    la torture avant l'exécution.
Witchcraft
BF   [Gosselin, Louis Léon Théodore] 1857-1935.
1582   Les petits sorciers du XVIIe siècle et la
G67   torture avant l'exécution. [Paris? 19--]
    [80]-104 p. 25cm.

    Caption title.
    Detached from a periodical.

    1. Trials (Witchcraft)--France. 2.
    Torture--France. I. Title.
8

BF   Petrocchi, Massimo.
1559   Esorcismi e magia nell'Italia del Cin-
P49   quecento e del Seicento. Napoli, Libreria
    scientifica editrice, 1957.
    52 p. 20cm. (Collana di storia religiosa
    3)

    1. Exorcism. 2. Witchcraft--Italy.
    I. Title.

WITCHCRAFT
BF   Petto, Samuel, 1624?-1711.
1555   A faithful narrative of the wonderful
P51   and extraordinary fits which Mr. Tho. Spat-
1693   chet (late of Dunwich and Cookly) was un-
    der by witchcraft: or, a mysterious provi-
    dence in his even unparallel'd fits ...
    London, Printed for John Harris, 1693.
    2 p. l., 31, [1] p. 19cm.
    Also issued London, 1693, without printer
    or bookseller named.
    Wing P1897.
    1. Spatchet, Thomas, 1614- 2. Demoniac
    possession. 3. Convulsions. I. Title.
8

    Peucer, Caspar, 1525-1602.
        see
    Peucer, Kaspar, 1525-1602.

Witchcraft
BF   Peucer, Kaspar, 1525-1602.
1410   Commentarivs de praecipvis divinationvm
P51   generibvs, in quo a prophetiis diuina autori-
1553   tate traditis, et physicis praedictionibus,
    separantur diabolicae fraudes et superstitio-
    sae obseruationes, et explicantur fontes ac
    causae physicarum praedictionum, diabolicae
    et superstitiosae confutatae damnantur, ea
    serie, quam tabula indicis uice praefixa
    ostendit.   VVittebergae [Typis excudebat
    Iohannes Crato] 1553.
    [8], 335 l. fold. table. 17cm.

WITCHCRAFT
BF   Peucer, Kaspar, 1525-1602.
1410   Commentarivs de praecipvis divinationvm
P51   generibvs, in qvo a prophetijs autoritate
1560   diuina traditis & à physicis coniecturis,
    discernuntur artes et imposturae diabolicae,
    atq[ue] obseruationes natae ex superstitione et
    cum hac coniunctae. Et monstrantur fontes
    ac causae physicarum praedictionum. Diabo-
    licae uero superstitiosae confutatae damnan-
    tur ea serie, quam tabella indicis loco prae-
    fixa ostendit. Recens editus & auctus ac-
    cessione mult   iplici. Avtore Casparo
8   (Continued on next card)

WITCHCRAFT
BF   Peucer, Kaspar, 1525-1602. Commentarivs de
1410   praecipvis generibvs divinationvm ...
P51   1560.   (Card 2)
1560
    Pevcero. VVitebergae, Excvdebat Iohannes
    Crato, 1560.
    456 p. fold. table. 16cm.
    Table in back of vol.
    First published 1553 with title: Commen-
    tarivs de praecipvis divinationvm generibvs.
8

Witchcraft
BF   Peucer, Kaspar, 1525-1602.
1410   Commentarivs de praecipvis generibvs divi-
P51   nationvm, in qvo a prophetiis autoritate di-
1572   uina traditis, & à physicis coniecturis, dis-
    cernuntur artes & imposturae diabolicae, at-
    que obseruationes natae ex superstitione &
    cum hac coniunctae: et monstrantur fontes ac
    causae physicarum praedictionum: diabolicae
    vero ac superstitiosae confutatae damnantur
    ea serie, quam tabella praefixa ostendit.
    Recens editus, et auctus accessione multipli-
                    (Continued on next card)

Witchcraft
BF   Peucer, Kaspar, 1525-1602. Commentarivs de
1410   praecipvis generibvs divinationvm ...
P51   (Card 2)
1572
    ci, copiosoque rerum et uerborum indice ...
    VVitebergae, Excudebat Iohannes Lvfft, 1572.
    [7], 440, [30] l. fold. table. 18cm.

Witchcraft
BF   Peucer, Kaspar, 1525-1602.
1410   Commentarivs de praecipvis generibvs divi-
P51   nationvm, in qvo a prophetiis avtoritate diui-
1576   na traditis, & à physicis conjecturis, discer-
    nuntur artes & imposturae diabolicae, atque
    obseruationes natae ex superstitione & cum
    hac coniunctae: et monstrantur fontes ac cau-
    sae physicarum praedictionum: diabolicae verò
    ac superstitiosae confutatae damnantur ea se-
    rie, quam tabella praefixa ostendit. Recens
    editus & auctus accessione multiplici, copio-
    soque, rerum et verborum indice ... [VVite-
                    (Continued on next card)

Witchcraft
BF   Peucer, Kaspar, 1525-1602. Commentarivs de
1410   praecipvis generibvs divinationvm ...
P51   (Card 2)
1576
    bergae, Excudebat Iohan. Schvvertel [1576]
    [8], 452, [45] l. fold. table. 16cm.

WITCHCRAFT
BF   Peucer, Kaspar, 1525-1602.
1410   Commentarivs, de praecipvis divinationvm
P51   generibvs, in qvo a prophetiis, avthoritate
1593   diuina traditis, & à physicis coniecturis,
    discernuntur artes & imposturae diabolicae,
    atque obseruationes natae ex superstitione,
    & cum hac coniunctae: et monstrantur fontes
    ac causae physicarum praedictionum diabolic[ae]
    verò ac superstitiosae confutatae damnantur
    ea serie, quam tabella praefixa ostendit.
    Recognitus vltimò, & auctus, ab avthore ips[o]
    Casparo Pevcer   o D. Addita, singulis
8   (Continued on next card)

CATALOGUE OF THE CORNELL WITCHCRAFT COLLECTION

WITCHCRAFT
BF
1410
P51
1593

Peucer, Kaspar, 1525-1602. Commentarivs, de praecipvis divinationvm generibvs ... 1593. (Card 2)

voculis & sententiis Graecis, sua interpretatione. Francofvrti, Apud Andreae Wecheli heredes, Claudium Marnium, & Ioan. Aubrium, 1593.
16 p. l., 738, [51] p. 2 fold. tables. 18cm.
First published 1553.
1. Divination. 2. Prophecies. 3. Magic. 4. Witchcraft. I. Title.

Witchcraft
BF
1410
P51
1607

Peucer, Kaspar, 1525-1602.
Commentarivs de praecipvis divinationvm generibvs, in qvo a prophetiis, avthoritate diuina traditis, & à physicis coniecturis, discernuntur artes & imposturae diabolicae, atque obseruationes natae ex superstitione, & cum hac coniunctae: et monstrantur fontes ac causae physicarum praedictionum: diabolicae vero ac superstitiosae confutatae damnantur, ea serie, quam tabella praefixa ostendit. Recognitus vltimo, et auctus, ab avthore ipso Casparo Pevcero D. Addita, singulis
(Continued on next card)

Witchcraft
BF
1410
P51
1607

Peucer, Kaspar, 1525-1602. Commentarivs de praecipuis divinationvm generibvs ... (Card 2)

voculis et sententiis Graecis, sua interpretatione. Francofvrti, Typis Wechelianis apud Claudium Marnium & haeredes Ioan. Aubrii, 1607.
[32], 738, [51] p. diagr., fold. tables. 17cm.

WITCHCRAFT
BF
1410
P51
1584a

Peucer, Kaspar, 1525-1602. Commentarius de praecipuis generibus divinationum. French.
Peucer, Kaspar, 1525-1602.
Les devins, ov Commentaire des principales sortes de devinations: distingué en quinze liures, esquels les ruses & impostures de Satan sont descouuertes, solidement refutees, & separees d'auec les sainctes propheties & d'auec les predictions naturelles. Escrit en latin par M. Gaspar Pevcer, ... nouuellement tourné en françois par S. G. S. [i.e., Simon Goulart, Senlisien] ... Anvers, Par Hevdrik Connix, 1584.
8   (Continued on next card)

WITCHCRAFT
BF
1410
P51
1584a

Peucer, Kaspar, 1525-1602. Commentarius de praecipuis generibus divinationum. French.
Peucer, Kaspar, 1525-1602. Les devins, ov Commentaire des principales sortes de devinations ... 1584. (Card 2)

6 p. l., 653, [24] p. 24cm.
Translation of Commentarius de praecipuis generibus divinationum.
1. Divination. 2. Prophecies. 3. Magic. 4. Witchcraft. I. His Commentarius de praecipuis generibus divinationum. II. Goulart, Simon, 1543-1628, tr. III. Title.

Peucer, Kaspar, 1525-1602.
Les devins, ov Commentaire des principales sortes de devinations: distingué en quinze liures, esquels les ruses & impostures de Satan sont descouuertes, solidement refutees, & separees d'auec les sainctes propheties & d'auec les predictions naturelles. Escrit en latin par M. Gaspar Pevcer ... nouuellement tourné en françois par S. G. S. Auec les tables & indices necessaires pour le soulagement des lecteurs. Lyon, B. Honorati, 1584.
6 p. l., 653, [24] p. 24cm.
"... Tourné en françois par S. G. S." i. e. Simon Goulart, Senlisien.
Translation of Commentarius de praecipuis generibus divinationum.
Library of Congress   BF1410.P5   10-33806

WITCHCRAFT
BF
1410
P51
1584a

Peucer, Kaspar, 1525-1602.
Les devins, ov Commentaire des principales sortes de devinations: distingué en quinze liures, esquels les ruses & impostures de Satan sont descouuertes, solidement refutees, & separees d'auec les sainctes propheties & d'auec les predictions naturelles. Escrit en latin par M. Gaspar Pevcer, ... nouuellement tourné en françois par S. G. S. [i.e., Simon Goulart, Senlisien] ... Anvers, Par Hevdrik Connix, 1584.
8   (Continued on next card)

WITCHCRAFT
BF
1410
P51
1584a

Peucer, Kaspar, 1525-1602. Les devins, ov Commentaire des principales sortes de devinations ... 1584. (Card 2)

6 p. l., 653, [24] p. 24cm.
Translation of Commentarius de praecipuis generibus divinationum.
1. Divination. 2. Prophecies. 3. Magic. 4. Witchcraft. I. His Commentarius de praecipuis generibus divinationum. French. II. Goulart, Simon, 1543-1628, tr. III. Title.

WITCHCRAFT
BF
1582
Z7
1700

Peyron, Paul Malo Théophile.
Procés pour faits de sorcellerie à la fin du XVIIe siècle. [Quimper? 190-?]
11 p. 23cm.
Signed: Peyron, chanoine.

8
NIC   1. Trials (Witchcraft)--Lesneven, France. Maillé, Louis. La Croix, Anthoine. I. Title.

Pezelius, Johann Christoph, respondent.
WITCHCRAFT
GR
830
W4
M94

Müller, Jacobus Friedrich, praeses.
Disputationem De λυκανθρωπία [lykanthropia], seu transmutatione hominum in lupos...examini sistunt publice praeses M. Jacobus Friedrich Müller et respondens Johan. Christoph. Pezelius... Lipsiae, Typis Viduae Joh. Wittigau [1673]
[20] p. 19cm.
Diss.--Leipzig (J. C. Pezelius, respondent)

8
NIC   1. Werwolves. I. Pezelius, Johann Christoph, respondent.

WITCHCRAFT
BF
1569
P52+

Pfannenschmid, Heino, 1828-1906.
Erklärungsversuch einiger französischen, auf das Hexenwesen des Mittelalters bezüglichen Ausdrücke: Genot, Genocherie, Criage.

(In: La Revue nouvelle d'Alsace-Lorraine. Colmar. 26cm. v.4, no.1, June 1884. p. 36-47)

8
NIC   1. Witchcraft--Hist. 2. Witchcraft--France. I. Title.

Pfefferkorn, Maria Anna Katharina, fl. 1842.
WITCHCRAFT
BF
1555
M69

Möller, Karl.
Eine Teufelaustreibung durch einen deutschen Bischof im 19. Jahrhundert.
[Sonderabdruck aus der Rheinischen Correspondenz] Köln, C. Römcke, 1897.
12 p. 23cm.
Consists largely of extracts from his Leben und Briefe von Johannes Theodor Laurent, pub. 1887-89; the bishop's letters are quoted.
1. Demoniac possession. 2. Exorcism. 3. Pfefferkorn, Maria Anna Katharina, fl. 1842. I. H   is   Leben und Briefe von Johannes Theo   dor Laurent. II. Laurent, Johannes Theodor, bp. III. Title.

WITCHCRAFT
BF
1583
Z7
1592

Pflug, Walther.
Anna, eine Hexengeschichte. Dessau, M. Salzmann, 1929.
23 p. 23cm. (Aus der Vergangenheit unserer Heimat, Heft 4)
Subtitle on cover: eine Hexengeschichte aus Mosigkau.

8
NIC   1. Witchcraft--Dessau. 2. Trials (Witchcraft)--Dessau. I. Title.

Pfotenhauer, Friedrich Christoph.
WITCHCRAFT
K
L6795
1733
v.9

Leyser, Augustin, Reichsfreiherr von, 1683-1752.
Meditationes ad pandectas quibus praecipua juris capita ex antiquitate explicantur, cum juribus recentioribus conferuntur atque variis celebrium collegiorum responsis et rebus judicatis illustrantur. vol. IX. Editio secunda. Lipsiae et Guelpherbyti, Apud Joh. Christoph. Meisnerum, 1741.
962 p. 21cm.
8
NIC   "Specimen DCVIII. ad lib. XLVIII.
(Continued on next card)

Pfotenhauer, Friedrich Christoph.
WITCHCRAFT
K
L6795
1733
v.9

Leyser, Augustin, Reichsfreiherr von, 1683-1752. Meditationes ad pandectas quibus praecipua juris capita...explicantur... vol. IX...1741. (Card 2)

tit. VIII De crimine magiae publice defensum a Frider. Christophoro Pfotenhauer... MDCCXXXVII.": p. 629-654. [Leyser probably acted as praeses]
1. Roman law 2. Civil law--Germany. 3. Criminal law--Germany. 4. Witchcraft--Germany. 5.   Trials (Witchcraft)--Germany. I.   Pfotenhauer, Friedrich Christoph.   II. Title.

The phantom world; or, The philosophy of spirits, apparitions, etc.
Witchcraft
BF
1412
C16
1850

Calmet, Augustin, 1672-1757.
The phantom world; or, The philosophy of spirits, apparitions, etc. Edited with an introd. and notes by Henry Christmas. London, R. Bentley, 1850.
2 v. 20cm.
Translation of Dissertations sur les apparitions des anges, des démons & des esprits ... which was also published under title: Traité sur les   apparitions des esprits et sur les vamp   ires ...

Les phénomènes mystiques distingués de leurs contrefaçons humaines et diaboliques.
Witchcraft
BV
5090
F22

Farges, Albert, 1848-1926.
Les phénomènes mystiques distingués de leurs contrefaçons humaines et diaboliques. Traité de théologie mystique a l'usage des séminaires, du clergé et des gens du monde. Paris [1920]
640 p. 20cm.

1. Mysticism--Catholic church. I. Title.

Philalethes, pseud.
Witchcraft
BT
980
S97

[Swinton, John] 1703-1777.
A critical dissertation concerning the words ΔΑΙΜΩΝ and ΔΑΙΜΟΝΙΟΝ. Occasion'd by two late enquiries [by Arthur Ashley Sykes] into the meaning of demoniacs in the New Nestament. In a letter to a friend. By a Gentleman of Wadham College, Oxford. London, Printed for J. Crokatt; and sold by J. Roberts, 1738.
29 p. 20cm.
Also attributed to George Costard.
8   Letter sig   ned: Philalethes.
(Continued on next card)

437

CATALOGUE OF THE CORNELL WITCHCRAFT COLLECTION

Witchcraft
PS 991 A1 P54
Philip English's two cups. "1692."
New York, A. D. F. Randolph, 1869.
109 p. 19cm.

Dedication signed: M. B.

1. Witchcraft--Salem, Mass.--Fiction.
I. B., M.

Philips, Mary.
Witchcraft
BF 1563 W81++ no.20
Strange & terrible nevves from Cambridge, being a true relation of the Quakers bewitching of Mary Philips ...; likewise her speech to the scholars and countrey-men ... her oath before the judges and justices, and the names of the Quakers brought to tryal ... with the judgment of the court ... London, Printed for C. Brooks, 1659. [London, at the British Museum, 1923]
8 p. 16cm.
Photocopy (negative) 8 p. on 5 l. 20x32cm.
No.20 in vol. lettered: Witchcraft tracts, chapbooks and broadsides, 1579-1704; rotograph copies.

Phillips, Mary, d. 1705.
Witchcraft
BF 1581 A2 W81 1866a no.2
[Davis, Ralph]
An account of the tryals, examination and condemnation, of Elinor Shaw and Mary Phillip's (two notorious witches,) at Northampton assizes, on Wednesday the 7th of March 1705. ... London, Printed for F. Thorn [1705] [Northampton, Taylor, 1866]
8 p. 22cm.
No. 2 in box lettered Witchcraft in Northamptonshire.

1. Trials (Witchcraft)--Northamptonshire, England. I. Title.

8

Phillips, Mary, d. 1705.
Witchcraft
BF 1581 A2 W81 1866a no.3
[Davis, Ralph]
The Northamptonshire witches. Being a true and faithful account of the births, educations, lives, and conversations, of Elinor Shaw, and Mary Phillips, (the two notorious witches) that were executed at Northampton on Saturday, March the 17th, 1705, for bewitching a woman and two children to death. ... London, Printed for F. Thorn [1705] [Northampton, Taylor, 1866]
8 p. 22cm.
(Continued on next card)

Phillips, Mary, d. 1705.
Witchcraft
BF 1581 A2 W81 1866a no.3
[Davis, Ralph] The Northamptonshire witches ... [1866] (Card 2)

No. 3 in box lettered Witchcraft in Northamptonshire.

1. Witchcraft--Northamptonshire, England. I. Title.

8

Witchcraft
Z 1009 P56
Philobiblon Society, London.
Miscellanies. London, Printed by C. Whittingham and Wilkins, 1854-84.
15 v. illus. 23cm.
Edited for the most part by Richard Monckton Milnes, first lord Houghton.
No more published; the society was disbanded in 1884.
Partial contents.--v.5, 1858-59. 3. A discourse of witchcraft. As it was acted in the family of Mr. Edward Fairfax ... 1621.
(Continued on next card)

Witchcraft
Z 1009 P56
Philobiblon Society, London.
Miscellanies ... 1854-84. (Card 2)

in the family of Mr. Edward Fairfax ... 1621. By R. Monckton Milnes.--v.8, 1863-64. 5. L'enfer décrit par ceux qui l'ont vu. Essai philosophique et littéraire. Par Octave Delepierre. 9. The examination and confession of certain witches at Chelmsford, in the county of Essex. Communicated and prefaced by Hermann Beigel.
I. Provenance--Taunton, Lord (v.8); Sreys, The Rev. Walter (v.5). II. Autograph--Milnes, Richard M[onckton] (v.5). (Over)

Philoponus, Lotarius, pseud.

see

Junius, Franciscus, 1545-1602.

A philosophical essay on credulity and superstition.
Witchcraft
BF 1411 B63
Blakeman, Rufus.
A philosophical essay on credulity and superstition; and also on animal fascination, or charming. By Rufus Blakeman ... New York, D. Appleton & co.; New Haven, S. Babcock, 1849.
206 p. 18cm.
CONTENTS.--Mental origin of credulity and superstition, and its influence on ancient society.--Witchcraft.--Dreams.--Ghosts.--Ecstacy, trance, &c.--Empiricism and quackery.--Homœopathy.--Mesmerism.--Essay on animal fascination or charming.
1. Occult sciences. 2. Medical delusions. I. Title. II. Title: Animal fascination, or charming.

18-12143

La philosophie des anges...
Witchcraft
BF 1623 A4 M61
Meyssonnier, Lazare, 1602-1672.
La philosophie des anges, contenant l'art de se rendre les bons esprits familiers. Avec l'histoire de S. Raphael, oeuure necessaire à tous ceux qui aspirent à la vie angelique. Par L. Meyssonnier. Lyon, Chez Pierre Compagnon, 1648.
8 p. l., 337, [3] p. 18cm.

1. Magic. 2. Angels. 3. Raphael, archangel. I. Title.

8

Witchcraft
BT 960 D93 1628
La philosophie des esprits, divisee en cinq livres, & generaux discours Chrestiens.
Dupont, René.
La philosophie des esprits, divisee en cinq livres, & generaux discours Chrestiens, specifiez en la page suiuante. Recueillie & mise en lumiere par F. M. Le Heurt ... 3. ed. Rouen, R. Feron, 1628.
[8], 257 [i.e. 267], [5] l. 17cm.

1. Spirits. I. Le Heurt, Matthieu, ed. II. Title.

La philosophie occulte.
Witchcraft
BF 1598 A27 O2 1727
Agrippa von Nettesheim, Heinrich Cornelius, 1486?-1535.
La philosophie occulte. Divisée en trois livres, et traduite du Latin. La Haye, R. Chr. Alberts, 1727.
2 v. in 1. illus. 19cm.
Title vignettes, engraved.
"Apologie pour Agrippa, par Mr. G. Naudé": v. 1, p. [3]-[21] (From his Apologie pour les grands hommes soupçonnez de magie)
Translation of De occulta philosophia.

Philosophische Abhandlung von Gespenstern.
Witchcraft
BF 1445 W41 P5
Wegner, Georg Wilhelm.
Philosophische Abhandlung von Gespenstern, worinn zugleich eine kurtze Nachricht von dem Wustermarckischen Kobold gegeben wird. Berlin, Zu haben bey A. Haude u. C. Spener, 1747.
80 p. 17cm.

1. Ghosts. I. Title.

8

Philosophische Gedanken von den Würkungen des Teufels.
WITCHCRAFT
BF 1555 M94 O29 no.6
Meier, Georg Friedrich, 1718-1777.
Georg Friedrich Meiers ... Philosophische Gedanken von den Würkungen des Teufels auf dem Erdboden. Halle, C. H. Hemmerde, 1760.
168 p. 18cm.

No. 6 in vol. lettered Oesfeld u. a. ...

1. Müller, Gottlieb. Gründlicher Nachricht von einer begeisterten Weibesperson. 2. Devil. I. Title: Philosophisc he Gedanken von den Würkungen de s Teufels.

8 NIC

Philosophische Untersuchung von Gewalt und Wirckung des Teuffels.
WITCHCRAFT
R 133 H71 1704
[Hoffmann, Friedrich] 1660-1742.
Philosophische Untersuchung von Gewalt und Wirckung des Teuffels in natürlichen Körpern. Franckfurt und Leipzig, 1704.
29 p. 20cm.

Translation of Disputatio inauguralis medico-philosophica De potentia diaboli in corpora. Halae, 1703.

1. Medicine, Magic, mystic, and spagiric 2. Devil. I. His Disputatio inauguralis medico-philosophica De potentia diaboli in corpora. German. II. Title.

8 NIC

Philosophischer Zeit-Vertreib über die Thier-Sprache.
Witchcraft
BD 428 B54
Bertram, Johann Friedrich] 1699-1741.
Ob die Thiere Teufel seyn? wird durch Veranlassung dess von einem Französischen Jesuiten P. Bonjeau unlängst ans Licht gestellten neuen Lehr-Begriffs von den Seelen der Thiere genannt: Amusements philosophiques sur le langage des bestes; oder: Philosophischer Zeit-Vertreib über die Thier-Sprache; in welchen sie zu Teufeln gemachet werden; nach Schrifft und Vernunfft untersuchet und beantwortet, von J.F. B. [Bremen] S. Pomarius [1740]
[15], 94 p. 16cm.

The philosophy of mystery.
ar W 37205
Dendy, Walter Cooper, 1794-1871.
The philosophy of mystery. London, Longman, Orme, Brown, Green, & Longmans, 1841.
xii, 443 p. 23cm.

1. Psychical research. I. Title.

The philosophy of witchcraft.
Witchcraft
BF 1566 F35 1925
Ferguson, Ian.
The philosophy of witchcraft. New York D. Appleton, 1925.
218 p. 20cm.

1. Witchcraft. I. Title.

438

CATALOGUE OF THE CORNELL WITCHCRAFT COLLECTION

Witchcraft
BF
1566
M68

The philosophy of witchcraft.
Mitchell, John, 1786-1856.
The philosophy of witchcraft. By J. Mitchell and Jn. Dickie. Paisley, Murray and Stewart [etc., etc.] 1839.
viii, 424 p. illus. 17cm.

1. Witchcraft. I. Dickie, John, joint author. II. Title.

Phips, Sir William, 1651-1695.
Witchcraft
BF
1575
D76
v.2-3

Calef, Robert, 1648-1719.
More wonders of the invisible world ... display'd in five parts. Part I. An account of the sufferings of Margaret Rule, written by the Reverend Mr. C. M. P. II. Several letters to the author, &c. And his reply relating to witchcraft. P. III. The differences between the inhabitants of Salem village, and Mr. Parris their minister, in New-England. P. IV. Letters of a gentleman uninterested, endeavouring to prove the received opinions about witchcraft to be orthodox. With short essays to their answers. P. V. A short historical accout [!] of matters of fact in that affair. To
(Continued on next card)
[r31e2] 2-13714 rev.

Phips, Sir William, 1651-1695.
Calef, Robert, 1648-1719. More wonders of the invisible world ... (Card 2)
which is added, a postscript relating to a book intitled, The life of Sir William Phips. Collected by Robert Calef, merchant, of Boston in New-England ... London, Printed for N. Hillar and J. Collyer, 1700.
Reprint. (In Drake, S. G. The witchcraft delusion in New England ... Roxbury, Mass., 1866. 21½cm. v. 2, p. 1-212; v. 3, p. 3-167)
Woodward's historical series. no. VI-VII.
Prefatory: by the editor. p. [v]-x. Pedigree of Calef: 1 fold. leaf.
Memoir of Robert Calef: p. [xi]-xxix.
The text, here annotated, is that of the 1st edition, 1700. "It is given as exactly like the original as a much better type can be made to imitate an old type of 166 years ago."--Pref. by the editor, p. vi.
(Continued on next card)
[r31e2] 2-13714 rev.

Phips, Sir William, 1651-1695.
Calef, Robert, 1648-1719. More wonders of the invisible world ... 1700. (Card 3)
Appendix: I. Examination of Giles Cory.--II. Giles Corey and Goodwyfe Corey. A ballad of 1692 --III. Testimony of William Beale, of Marblehead, against Mr. Philip English of Salem, given Aug. 2d. 1692.--IV. [Examination of the Indian woman belonging to Mr. Parris's family]--V. The examination of Mary Clark of Haverhill.--VI. An account of the life and character of the Rev. Samuel Parris, of Salem village, and of his connection with the witchcraft delusion of 1692. By Samuel P. Fowler.

Phips, Sir William, 1651-1695.
Calef, Robert, 1648-1719.
More wonders of the invisible world, or The wonders of the invisible world displayed. In five parts. Part I.--An account of the sufferings of Margaret Rule, written by the Rev. Cotton Mather. Part II.--Several letters to the author, &c. and his reply relating to witchcraft. Part III.--The differences between the inhabitants of Salem village, and Mr. Parris, their minister, in New-England. Part IV.--Letters of a gentleman uninterested, endeavouring to prove the received opinions about
(Continued on next card)

Phips, Sir William, 1651-1695.
Calef, Robert, 1648-1719. More wonders of the invisible world ... 1823. (Card 2)
witchcraft to be orthodox. With short essays to their answers. Part V.--A short historical account of matters of fact in that affair. To which is added a postscript [!] relating to a book entitled "The life of Sir Wm. Phips". Collected by Robert Calef. Merchant, of Boston, in New-England. Printed in London, 1700. Salem, Re-printed by J.D. & T.C. Cushing, jr. for Cushing and Appleton, 1823.
(Continued on next card)

Phips, Sir William, 1651-1695.
Witchcraft
BF
1575
C14
1823

Calef, Robert, 1648-1719. More wonders of the invisible world ... 1823. (Card 3)
312 p. 18½cm.

Appended: Giles Cory [a report of his examination, taken from the witchcraft records]: p. 310-312.
"The second Salem edition appears to have been copied from the first [Salem edition], that of 1796. In some instances slight departures are made from the copy ... such departures are also departures from the original [London edition of 1700]." --S. G. Drake, pref. to ed. of 1866.

Phips, Sir William, 1651-1695.
Witchcraft
BF
1575
C14
1828

Calef, Robert, 1648-1719.
Wonders of the invisible world, or, Salem witchcraft. In five parts. Boston, T. Bedlington [1828]
333 p. front. 14cm.

A reply to Cotton Mather's "Wonders of the invisible world."
First ed. published in 1700 under title: More wonders of the invisible world displayed.

(Continued on next card)

Phips, Sir William, 1651-1695.
Witchcraft
BF
1575
C14
1828

Calef, Robert, 1648-1719. Wonders of the invisible world ... [1828] (Card 2)
Contents.--Part 1. An account of the sufferings of Margaret Rule, by Cotton Mather.--Part 2. Several letters from the author to Mr. Mather and others, relating to witchcraft.--Part 3. Account of the differences in Salem village between the villagers and their minister, Mr. Parris.-- Part 4. Letters of a gentleman uninter-

(Continued on next card)

Phips, Sir William, 1651-1695.
Witchcraft
BF
1575
C14
1828

Calef, Robert, 1648-1719. Wonders of the invisible world ... [1828] (Card 3)
ested, endeavouring to prove the received opinions about witchcraft to be orthodox.-- Part 5. An impartial account of the most memorable matters of fact touching the supposed witchcraft in New-England.--Postscript, relating to Cotton Mather's life of Sir William Phips.--Giles Cory: a report of his examination, taken from the witchcraft files.

Physica curiosa.
Witchcraft
BF
1410
S37
1697

Schott, Gaspar, 1608-1666.
Physica curiosa, sive Mirabilia naturae et artis libris XII. comprehensa, quibus pleraque, quae de angelis, daemonibus, hominibus, spectris, energumenis, monstris, portentis, animalibus, meteoris, &c. rara, arcana, curiosaque circumferuntur, ad veritatis trutinam expenduntur, variis ex historia ac philosophia petitis disquisitionibus excutiuntur, & innumeris exemplis illustrantur ... Editio tertia juxta exemplar secundae editionis auctioris. Herbipoli, Excudit Jobus Hertz,
(Continued on next card)

Physica curiosa.
Witchcraft
BF
1410
S37
1697

Schott, Gaspar, 1608-1666. Physica curiosa ... (Card 2)
Sumptibus Wolfgangi Mauritii Endteri, 1697.
[40], 1389, [21] p. plates (part fold.) 21cm.

Added t. p., engraved.
In two parts.

1. Demonology. 2. Deformities. 3. Monsters. 4. Zoology--Pre-Linnean works. I. Title.

Physikalische Abhandlung von der Gewalt des Teufels in die Körper.
WITCHCRAFT
BF
1547
R91
1753

Rübel, Johann Friedrich
Physikalische Abhandlung von der Gewalt des Teufels in die Körper ... mit vielen wichtigen Anmerkungen hrsg. von J. F. R. Nürnberg, In Commission in der Zimmermannischen Buchhandlung, 1753.
2 v. 23cm.

8
NIC

Contents.--[1] Die Fragen und Untersuchungen vorkommen: Ob der Teufel Wunderwerke thun Könne? Ob er die Leute holen, und durch die Luft fort, und in an-
(Continued on next card)

Physikalische Abhandlung von der Gewalt des Teufels in die Körper.
WITCHCRAFT
BF
1547
R91
1753

Rübel, Johann Friedrich
Physikalische Abhandlung des Teufels...1753. (Card 2)

Contents--continued.
dere Orte schleppen könne? Ob er allerhand Art von Ungeziefer in den Menschen hervorzubringen vermöge? Ob er den Menschen Krankheiten zuziehen könne? Was von Hexen, Zaubereyen, Gespenstern und Geistern zu halten? Von Beschwörung der Geister, etc.

(Continued on next card)

RARE
BX
1723
P58
1722

Piazza, Girolamo Bartolomeo.
A short and true account of the Inquisition and its proceeding, as it is practis'd in Italy, set forth in some particular cases. Whereunto is added, An extract out of an authentick book of legends of the Roman Church. London, W. Bowyer, 1722.
189 p. 21cm.

English and French; added t.p. in French.

1. Inquisition--Italy. I. Title.

Picard, Mathurin, d. 1647.
MSS
Bd.
WITCHCRAFT
BF
L37

Laugeois, Antoine, d. 1674.
L'innocence opprimee; ou, Défense de Mathurin Picard, curé de Mesnil-Jourdain ... Par M. Laugois, successeur immédiat dudit Picard - dans la cure de Mesnil-Jourdain. Ouvrage qui n'a jamais été imprimé et extrait sur l'original, par M. Chemin curé de Tourneville. [n. p. 17th cent.]
x, 102 p. title vignette. 18cm.
Manuscript, on paper.
Preface signed M. du Passeur (Gabriel), curé de Vironvay.
(Continued on next card)

Picard, Mathurin, d. 1647.
MSS
Bd.
WITCHCRAFT
BF
L37

Laugeois, Antoine, d. 1674. L'innocence opprimee...[17th cent.] (Card 2)

Notes by G. L. Burr inside front cover discuss history and provenance of the manuscript.
Bound in boards.
1. Demoniac possession. 2. Picard, Mathurin, d. 1647. 3. Bavent, Madeleine, b. 1607. 4. Louviers, France. St. Louis (Convent) 5. Witchcraft. I. Chemin, J B , 1725 -1781, ed. II. Title. III. Title: Défense de Mathurin Picard.

Picard, Mathurin, d. 1647.
WITCHCRAFT
BF
1555
P61

Piérart, Z J
Le magnétisme, le somnambulisme et le spiritualisme dans l'histoire. Affaire curieuse des possédées de Louviers. Paris, Au Bureau du Journal du magnétisme, 1858.
39 p. 23cm.

Extract from Journal du magnétisme.

1. Demoniac possession. 2. Louviers, France. St. Louis (Convent) 3. Bavent, Madeleine, ca. 1608-1647. 4. Picard, Mathurin, d. 1647. 5. Boullé, Thomas.

8
NIC

439

CATALOGUE OF THE CORNELL WITCHCRAFT COLLECTION

WITCHCRAFT
BF 1555 R31
8 NIC

Picard, Mathurin, d. 1647.
Recueil de pièces sur les possessions des religieuses de Louviers. Rouen [Imprimerie L. Deshays] 1879.
2 v. in 1. 25cm.

Title page and prefatory material bound following v. 1.
Contents.—[1] Histoire de Magdelaine Bavent, religieuse du monastere de Saint Loüis de Louviers (1652)—[2] I. Examen de la possession des religieuses de Louviers, par le Docteur Yvelin (1643)
(Continued on next card)

WITCHCRAFT
BF 1555 R31

Picard, Mathurin, d. 1647.
Recueil de pièces sur les possessions des religieuses de Louviers...1879. (Card 2)

Contents—continued.
II. Response à l'Examen de la possession des religieuses de Louviers (1643) III. Censure de l'Examen de la possession des religieuses de Louviers (1643) IV. Apologie pour l'autheur de l'Examen de la possession des religieuses de Louviers, attribuée au Docteur Yvelin (1643) V. Responce à l'Apologie de l'Examen du sieur Yvelin
(Continued on next card)

WITCHCRAFT
BF 1555 R31

Picard, Mathurin, d. 1647.
Recueil de pièces sur les possessions des religieuses de Louviers...1879. (Card 3)

Contents—continued.
(1644) VI. Recit veritable de ce qui s'est fait & passé à Louviers, touchant les religieuses possedées (1643) VII. Recit veritable de ce qui s'est fait & passé aux exorcismes de plusieurs religieuses de la ville de Louviers (1643) VIII. La deffense de la verité touchant la possession des religieuses de Louvier, par
(Continued on next card)

WITCHCRAFT
BF 1555 R31

Picard, Mathurin, d. 1647.
Recueil de pièces sur les possessions des religieuses de Louviers...1879. (Card 4)

Contents—continued.
Jean Le Breton (1643) IX. Attestation de messieurs les commissaires envoyez par sa Majesté pour prendre connoissance, avec monseigneur l'evesque d'Evreux, de l'estat des religieuses qui paroissent agitées au monastere de Saint Louys & Sainte Elizabeth de Louviers (1643?) X. Procés verbal de Monsieur le Peniten
(Continued on next card)

WITCHCRAFT
BF 1555 R31

Picard, Mathurin, d. 1647.
Recueil de pièces sur les possessions des religieuses de Louviers...1879. (Card 5)

Contents—continued.
tier d'Evreux, de ce qui luy est arrivé dans la prison, interrogeant & consolant Magdelaine Bavent, magicienne, à une heureuse conversion & repentance, par Delange (1643) XI. Lettre adressée à Monsieur D. L. V., medicin du Roy, & doyen de la Faculté de Paris, sur l'Apologie du sieur Yvelin, medicin, attribuée au docteur
(Continued on next card)

WITCHCRAFT
BF 1555 R31

Picard, Mathurin, d. 1647.
Recueil de pièces sur les possessions des religieuses de Louviers...1879. (Card 6)

Contents—continued.
teur Maignart (1644) XII. Traicté des marques des possedez & la preuve de la veritable possession des religieuses de Louviers, par P. M., esc. d. en m. (attribué à Simon Pietre; 1644) XIII. Copie en forme de recueil de ce qui se fait de jour en jour dans le monastere des filles relligieuses Saint Louis (1643) XIV. Pièces dé-
(Continued on next card)

WITCHCRAFT
BF 1555 R31

Picard, Mathurin, d. 1647.
Recueil de pièces sur les possessions des religieuses de Louviers...1879. (Card 7)

Contents—continued.
tachées extraites du manuscrit H. F. n° 34 de la Bibliothèque Ste Geneviève, formant suite à la pièce précédente. XV. Notice sur la Mere Françoise, superieure des religieuses de la Place royale, au sujet de l'histoire des possedées de Louviers.

(Continued on next card)

WITCHCRAFT
BF 1517 F5 P59
8 NIC

Pichard, Remy.
[Admirable vertu des saincts exorcismes sur les princes d'enfer possédants réellement vertueuse demoiselle Elisabeth de Ranfaing, avec ses justifications contre les ignorances et les calomnies de F. Claude Pithoys. Nancy, Par Sébastien Philippe, 1622]
674, 105 p. 14cm.

T.p. lacking. Handwritten t.p. substituted.
Bound in   after chapter 17 are
(Continued on next card)

WITCHCRAFT
BF 1517 F5 P59

Pichard, Remy. [Admirable vertu des saincts exorcismes...1622] (Card 2)

what appear to be the preface and table of contents of Stimuli virtutum adolescentiae Christianae, by Guglielmo Baldesano [considered by Bibliothèque nationale to be the pseudonym of Bernardino Rosignolo] The work itself is not in the vol.
The 105 pages at end consist of a reprint of Claude Pithois' La descouverture des faux possédez...la conférence
(Continued on next card)

WITCHCRAFT
BF 1517 F5 P59

Pichard, Remy. [Admirable vertu des saincts exorcismes...1622] (Card 3)

...touchant la prétendue possédée de Nancy [the work to which Pichard is replying] and chapter 18 of the Admirable vertu des saincts exorcismes.

1. Demoniac possession. 2. Exorcism. 3. Ranfaing, Elisabeth de, 1592-1649. I. Pithois, Claude, 1587-1676. La descouverture des faux possé   dez... II. Pithois, Claude, 1587-   1676. La descouverture des faux possé   dez... III. Title.

WITCHCRAFT
BF 1565 P45++ 1631

Pickering, Thomas.
Perkins, William, 1558-1602.
A discovrse of the damned art of witchcraft. So farre forth as it is revealed in the scriptvres, and manifested by true experience. Framed and delivered by Master William Perkins, in his ordinary course of preaching, and published by Thomas Pickering. London, Printed for Iames Boler, 1631.
[10], 607-652 p. 33cm.
Signatures: Llll-Oooo⁶.
Imperfect: last leaf mutilated.
From the author's Works? Cf. signatures and pagination.
With this is   bound the author's A resolvtion to the countrey-man ... 1631.

WITCHCRAFT
BF 1524 P59 1555

Pico della Mirandola, Giovanni Francesco, 1470-1533.
Dialogo intitolato La strega, overo De gli inganni de demoni dell' illustre Signor Giouan Francesco Pico conte de la Mirandola. Tradotto in lingva toscana per il Signor abate Turino Turini da Pescia ... In Pescia, 1555.
5 p. l., [17]-126 p., 1 l. 21½ᶜᵐ.
Title within ornamental border.
At end: Stampato in Pescia, appresso Lorenzo Torrentino, stampator ducale, MDLV.
Translation of Strix, sive De ludificatione daemonum dialogi tres.
With this is bound Cattani da Diacceto, F. Discorso ... sopra la superstizzione dell' arte magica. Fior   enza, 1567.   11-9699
(Continued on next card)

——— Copy 2.

WITCHCRAFT
BF 1524 P59 1555

Pico della Mirandola, Giovanni Francesco, 1470-1533. Dialogo intitolato La strega ... 1555. (Card 2)

1. Magic. 2. Demonology. 3. Witchcraft. I. His Strix, sive De ludificatione daemonum dialogi tres. Italian. II. Turini, Turino, tr. III. Title. IV. Title: La strega, overo De gli inganni de demoni.

WITCHCRAFT
BF 1524 P59 1864

Pico della Mirandola, Giovanni Francesco, 1470-1533.
La strega ovvero Degli inganni de' demoni. Dialogo di Giovan Franceso Pico della Mirandola, tradotto in lingva toscana da Turino Turini. Milano, D. Daelli, 1864.
xxiv, 135 p. 17cm. (Biblioteca rara, 40)
Translation of Strix, sive de ludificatione daemonum dialogi tres.
I. His Strix, sive de ludificatione daemonum dialogi tres. Italian. II. Turini, Turino, tr. III. Title.

WITCHCRAFT
BF 1524 P59
8 NIC

Pico della Mirandola, Giovanni Francesco, 1470-1533.
Strix, sive De ludificatione daemonum dialogi tres. Nunc primum in Germania eruti ex bibliotheca M. Martini Weinrichii, cum ejusdem praefatione...itemque Epistola ad ...Andream Libavium de quaestione: Utrum in non maritatis & castis mola possit gigni? Et post mortem ejus editi studio & opera Caroli Weinrichii. Argentorati, Venundantur apud Paulum Ledertz, 1612.
160+ p. 18cm.
(Continued on next card)

WITCHCRAFT
BF 1524 P59

Pico della Mirandola, Giovanni Francesco, 1470-1533. Strix...1612. (Card 2)

Epistola to Libavius lacking.
With this is bound: Sennert, Daniel. De origine et natura animarum in brutis. 1638.
1. Magic. 2. Demonology. 3. Witchcraft. I. Weinrich, Martinus, 1548-1609. II. Weinrich, Carolus. III. Libavius, Andreas, d.1616. IV. Title.

WITCHCRAFT
BF 1524 P59 1555

Pico della Mirandola, Giovanni Francesco, 1470-1533.
Dialogo intitolato La strega, overo De gli inganni de demoni dell' illustre Signor Giouan Francesco Pico conte de la Mirandola. Tradotto in lingva toscana per il Signor abate Turino Turini da Pescia ... In Pescia, 1555.
5 p. l., [17]-126 p., 1 l. 21½ᶜᵐ.
Title within ornamental border.
At end: Stampato in Pescia, appresso Lorenzo Torrentino, stampator ducale, MDLV.
Translation of Strix, sive De ludificatione daemonum dialogi tres.
With this is bound Cattani da Diacceto, F. Discorso ... sopra la superstizzione dell' arte magica. Fior   enza, 1567.   11-9699
(Continued on next card)

——— Copy 2.

WITCHCRAFT
BF 1524 P59 1864

Pico della Mirandola, Giovanni Francesco, 1470-1533.
La strega ovvero Degli inganni de' demoni. Dialogo di Giovan Franceso Pico della Mirandola, tradotto in lingua toscana da Turino Turini. Milano, D. Daelli, 1864.
xxiv, 135 p. 17cm. (Biblioteca rara, 40)
Translation of Strix, sive de ludificatione daemonum dialogi tres.

CATALOGUE OF THE CORNELL WITCHCRAFT COLLECTION

Witchcraft
BF
412
.B5
G58

A pictorial anthology of witchcraft, magic & alchemy.

Grillot de Givry, Émile Angelo, 1870-
A pictorial anthology of witchcraft, magic & alchemy. Translated by J. Courtenay Locke. New Hyde Park, N. Y., University Books [1958]
394 p. illus. 25cm.

Translation of Le musée des sorciers, mages et alchimistes.

Witchcraft
BF
1623
A5P61

Pictorius, Georg.
De illorvm daemonvm qvi svb lvnari collimitio uersantur ... Basileae, Per Henricvm Petri, 1563.
80 p. 16cm.

Bound with his Παντοπωλιον.

1. Magic. I. Title.

Witchcraft
BF
1623
A5P61

Pictorius, Georg.
Παντοπωλιον, continens omnivm ferme quadrupedum ... naturas, carmine elegiaco ... una cum ... de apibus ... methodo ... praeterea, de daemonum ... ortu ... Isagoge ... quibus accedit ... de speciebus magiae ceremonialis, quam Goëtiam vocant, epitome, et an sagae ... cremari debeant resolutio ... Basileae, Per Henricvm Petri, 1563.
123 p. 16cm.

With this is bound his De illorvm daemonvm.

I. Title.   Title transliterated: Pantopolion.

Witchcraft

Pictorius, Georg.
Heinrich Cornelius Agrippa's von Nettesheim Magische Werke : sammt den geheimnissvollen Schriften des Petrus von Abano, Pictorius von Villingen, Gerhard von Cremona, Abt Tritheim von Spanheim, dem Buche Arbatel, der sogenannten Heil. Geist-Kunst und verschiedenen anderen zum ersten Male vollständig in's Deutsche übersetzt : vollständig in fünf Theilen, mit einer Menge Abbildungen. -- 4. Aufl. -- Berlin : H. Barsdorf, 1921.
5 v. in 3. : ill. ; 17 cm. -- (Geheime Wissenschaften ; 10-14)

Pictorius, Georg.
WITCHCRAFT
BF
1410
L69
1655

Henry Cornelius Agrippa's Fourth book of occult philosophy, and geomancy. Magical elements of Peter de Abano. Astronomical geomancy [by Gerardus Cremonensis]. The nature of spirits [by Georg Pictorius]: and Arbatel of magick. Translated into English by Robert Turner. Philomathées. London, 1655.
9 p. l., [5]-266 [i.e., 286], [4] p. illus. 19cm.

8   Neither Agrippa nor Abano wrote the works
(Continued on next card)

Pictorius, Georg.
WITCHCRAFT
BF
1410
L69
1655

Henry Cornelius Agrippa's Fourth book of occult philosophy, and geomancy ...
1655.   (Card 2)

here ascribed to them; the Heptameron, or Magical elements also was ascribed to Agrippa under the title: Les oeuvres magiques, with Abano as translator (!)
Translation of a work variously titled Liber de ceremonijs magicis; and his De occulta philosophia, liber quartus.

8   (Continued on next card)

WITCHCRAFT
BF
1555
P61

Piérart, Z J
Le magnétisme, le somnambulisme et le spiritualisme dans l'histoire. Affaire curieuse des possédées de Louviers... Paris, Au Bureau du Journal du magnétisme, 1858.
39 p. 23cm.

Extract from Journal du magnétisme.
1. Demoniac possession. 2. Louviers, France. St. Louis (Convent) 3. Bavent, Madeleine, ca. 1608-1647. 4. Picard, Mathurin, d. 1647. 5. Boullé, Thomas. I. Title.

8
NIC

La pieté affligee.

WITCHCRAFT
BF
1555
E77

Esprit du Bosroger, Capuchin.
La pieté affligee; ov, Discovrs historiqve & theologique de la possession des religieuses dittes de Saincte Elizabeth de Louviers. Divisé en trois parties. Roven, Chez Iean le Bovlenger, 1652.
[30], 458, 8 p. front. 23cm.
Copy 1 imperfect: front. wanting.
Inserted at end of copy 1: 6 p. of ms.
1. Demoniac possession. 2. Bavent, Madeleine, b. 1607. 3. Louviers, France. St. Louis (Convent) 4. Witchcraft. I. Title.

WITCHCRAFT
BF
1584
P6
P62

Pietsch, Paul.
Die Doruchower Hexenverbrennung vom Jahre 1775.

(In: Historische Gesellschaft für die Provinz Posen. Zeitschrift. Posen. 24cm. v.14, no. 3/4, July/Dec. 1899. p. 336-339)

1. Witchcraft--Posen (Province) 2. Trials (Witchcraft) --Posen (Province)
I. Title.

8
NIC

Rare
BX
1939
H4
P63++

Pignatelli, Giacomo, fl. 1668.
Novissimae consultationes canonicae, praecipue controversias, quae ad fidem, ejusque regulam spectant, in quibus errores atheorum, infidelium, schismaticorum, haereticorum, & aliorum Ecclesiae Catholicae hostium referuntur & refelluntur; praesertimque illas quae circa S. Inquisitionis Tribunal versantur ... complectentes. Opus prima vice praelo commissum ... Cum indice consultationum ... Cosmopoli, Apud Dominicum Puteanum, 1711.
2 v. in 1. 38cm.
(over)

Witchcraft
BF
1576
P63

Pike, James Shepherd, 1811-1882.
The new Puritan: New England two hundred years ago; some account of the life of Robert Pike, the Puritan who defended the Quakers, resisted clerical domination, and opposed the witchcraft prosecution ... New York, Harper & Brothers, 1879.
237 p. 19cm.

1. Pike, Robert. 1616-1706. I. Title.

HV
6943
P63

Pike, Luke Owen, 1835-1915.
A history of crime in England, illustrating the changes of the laws in the progress of civilisation; written from the public records and other contemporary evidence, by Luke Owen Pike ... London, Smith, Elder & co., 1873-76.
2 v. fronts. (v. 1: facsim.) 22½cm.
Contents--I. From the Roman invasion to the accession of Henry VII.--II. From the accession of Henry VII. to the present time.
1. Crime and criminals--England.
2. Criminal law --England. I. Title.

Witchcraft
BF
1576
P63

Pike, James Shepherd, 1811-1882.
The new Puritan: New England two hundred years ago; some account of the life of Robert Pike, the Puritan who defended the Quakers, resisted clerical domination, and opposed the witchcraft prosecution ... New York, Harper & Brothers, 1879.
237 p. 19cm.

1. Pike, Robert, 1616-1706. I. Title.

Il Pimandro di Mercurio Trismegisto.

Witchcraft
BF
1598
H55A4
1548

Hermes Trismergistus.
[Poemander. Italian]

Il Pimandro di Mercurio Trismegisto, tradotto da Tommaso Benci in lingua fiorentina. Firenze [L. Torrentino] 1548.
[24], 119, [14] p. 18cm.

Title vignette.
Edited by Carlo Lenzoni.

WITCHCRAFT
BF
1559
P64

[Pinamonti, Giovanni Pietro] 1632-1703.
Exorcista rite' edoctus; seu, Accurata methodus omne maleficiorum genus probe ac prudenter curandi. Exposita a quodam religioso, & in lucem edita a quodam sacerdote ... Lucae, Typis Marescandoli, 1705.
154 p. 14cm.

"Formula exorcismi": p. 127-154.

8   1. Exorcism. 2. Witchcraft. 3. Demoniac
NIC possession.   I. Title.

WITCHCRAFT
BF
1559
P64
1737

Pinamonti, Giovanni Pietro, 1632-1703.
Exorcista rite' edoctus; seu, Accurata methodus omne maleficiorum genus probe ac prudenter curandi. Auctore R. P. Jo. Petro Pinamonti. Editio tertia. Venetiis, Ex Leonardo Pittono, 1737.
96 p. port. 16cm.

"Exorcismi": p. 88-91. (Abridged from the section, "Formula exorcismi" at the end of first ed., 1705)
1. Exorcism.   2. Witchcraft. 3. Demoniac possession.   I. Title.

8
NIC

WITCHCRAFT
BF
1410
P66
1635

Piperno, Pietro.
De magicis affectibus lib. VI. medice, stratagemmatice, divine, cum remediis electis, exorcismis, phisicis, ac curiosis, & De nuce Beneventana maga... [Neapoli, Typis Io. Dominici Montanati, 1635]
208, 24 p. 21cm.

The De nuce Beneventana maga has separate t.p. (title as: De nuce maga Beneventana) and pagination.
1. Occult sciences. 2. Demonology. 3. Medicine, Magic, mystic and spagiric. I. Title: De nuce maga Beneventana. II. His / De nuce maga Beneventana.

8
NIC

Piperno, Pietro.
De nuce maga Beneventana.

WITCHCRAFT
BF
1410
P66
1635

Piperno, Pietro.
De magicis affectibus lib. VI. medice, stratagemmatice, divine, cum remediis electis, exorcismis, phisicis, ac curiosis, & De nuce Beneventana maga... [Neapoli, Typis Io. Dominici Montanati, 1635]
208, 24 p. 21cm.

The De nuce Beneventana maga has separate t.p. (title as: De nuce maga Beneventana) and pagination.
1. Occult sciences. 2. Demonology. 3. Medicine, Magic, mystic and spagiric. I. Title: De nuce maga Beneventana. II. His / De nuce maga Beneventana.

8
NIC

CATALOGUE OF THE CORNELL WITCHCRAFT COLLECTION

Pistellus, Hieronymus.

WITCHCRAFT
BF
1583
T15

Tamianus, Julius, pseud.
Julii Tamiani Send-Schreiben an Hieronymum Pistellum, worinne bey Veranlassung der unweit Jena unternommenen Satans-Beschwerung der Anfang und Fortgang der Magie, wie nicht minder die Meynungen der Magorum untersuchet, auch von denen dabey gewöhnlichen Mitteln ... Bericht erstattet wird. Nebst einem Paquetgen an den verwegenen Authorem der sogenannten Gerichte Gottes und sinnreichen Überschrifft, so er Franco zu er-

8
NIC

(Continued on next card)

Pistellus, Hieronymus.

WITCHCRAFT
BF
1583
T15

Tamianus, Julius, pseud. Julii Tamiani Send-Schreiben an Hieronymum Pistellum ... (Card 2)

halten hat. Zu Magiluna in Arabien [i.e., Jena?] 1716.
52 p. 20cm.
Illustrative title vignette.
1. Witchcraft--Thuringia. 2. Witchcraft--Jena, Germany. 3. Magic. I. Pistellus, Hieronymus. II. Title: Send-Schreiben an Hieronymum Pistellum.

8
NIC

Witchcraft
BF
1445
D61
no.15

Pistori, Gustav Friedrich, praeses.
... Dispvtatione prima existentiam spectrorvm, praesertim ex sagarum veneficarumque pactis cum diabolo sancitis, benevolo facultatis philosophicae indultu demonstrabit praeses M. Gvstav. Frider. Pistori, ... et respondens Io. Gerhardvs Pagendarm ... Vitembergae, Praelo Christiani Gerdesii [ca. 1700]
[16] p. 18cm. (bound in 21cm. vol.)
No. 15 in vol. lettered Dissertationes de spectris. 1646-1753.

8

(Continued on next card)

Witchcraft
BF
1445
D61
no.15

Pistori, Gustav Friedrich, praeses. ... Dispvtatione prima existentiam spectrorvm ... demonstrabit ... Pistori ... [1700] (Card 2)

1. Demonology. 2. Witchcraft. I. Pagendarm, Johann Gerhard, respondent. II. Title: Disputatione prima existentiam spectrorum ...demonstrabit ... Pistori.

8

Witchcraft
BF
1445
D61
no.16

Pistori, Gustav Friedrich, praeses.
... Dispvtatione secvnda existentiam spectrorvm, ex sagarum veneficarumque pactis cum daemone sancitis, declarabunt praeses M. Gvstavvs Fridericvs Pistori ... et respondens Ioannes Beniamin. Horn ... Vitembergae, Prelo Gerdesiano [1703]
[16] p. 19cm. (bound in 21cm. vol.)
No. 16 in vol. lettered Dissertationes de spectris. 1646-1753.
1. Spirits. 2. Witchcraft. I.

8

(Continued on next card)

Witchcraft
BF
1445
D61
no.16

Pistori, Gustav Friedrich, praeses. ...
Dispvtatione secvnda existentiam spectrorvm ... declarabunt ... Pistori ... et ... Horn ... [1703] (Card 2)

Horn, Johann Benjamin, respondent. II. Title: Disputatione secunda existentiam spectrorum ... declarabunt ... Pistori ... et ... Horn.

WITCHCRAFT
BF
1520
P67

Pistorius, Johann, 1546-1608.
Dæmonomania Pistoriana. Magica et cabalistica morborum curandorum ratio, à Ioanne Pistorio Niddano ... ex lacunis judaicis ac gentilitiis hausta, pòst christianis proprinata. Cum antidoto prophylactico Iacobi Heilbronneri ... Lauingæ, typis Palatinis, 1601.
26 p. l., 1934 p. 16½ᵐ.

1. Dæmonomania. 2. Magic. I. Heilbronner, Jacob, 1548-1618. II. Title.

8
NIC

Library of Congress   BF1520.P5   11—0704

K
P674+

Pitcairn, Robert, comp., 1793-1835.
Criminal trials in Scotland, from A. D. 1488 to A. D. 1624, embracing the entire reigns of James IV. and V., Mary Queen of Scots, and James VI. Compiled from the original records and MSS., with historical notes and illustrations. Edinburgh, W. Tait, 1833.
3 v. in 4. 30cm.

Also published under title: Ancient criminal trials in Scotland.
(Continued on next card)

K
P674+

Pitcairn, Robert, comp., 1793-1835. Criminal trials in Scotland ... 1833. (Card 2)

Contents.--v.1, pt. 1. 1488-1568.--v.1, pt. 2. 1568-1592.--v.2 1596-1609.--v.3 1609-1624.

1. Trials--Scotland. I. Title.

WITCHCRAFT
BF
1517
F5
P59

Pithois, Claude, 1587-1676.
La descouverture des faux possédez ...
Pichard, Remy.
[Admirable vertu des saincts exorcismes sur les princes d'enfer possédants réellement vertueuse demoiselle Elisabeth de Ranfaing, avec ses justifications contre les ignorances et les calomnies de F.Claude Pithoys. Nancy, Par Sébastien Philippe, 1622]
674, 105 p. 14cm.

T.p. lacking. Handwritten t.p. substituted.
Bound in   after chapter 17 are
(Continued on next card)

8
NIC

WITCHCRAFT
BF
1517
F5
P59

Pithois, Claude, 1587-1676.
La descouverture des faux possédez ....
Pichard, Remy. [Admirable vertu des saincts exorcismes...1622]   (Card 2)

what appear to be the preface and table of contents of Stimuli virtutum adolescentiae Christianae, by Guglielmo Baldesano [considered by Bibliothèque nationale to be the pseudonym of Bernardino Rosignolo] The work itself is not in the vol.
The 105 pages at end consist of a reprint of Claude Pithois' La descouverture des faux possédez...la conférence
(Continued on next card)

WITCHCRAFT
BF
1517
F5
P59

Pithois, Claude, 1587-1676.
La descouverture des faux possédez ....
Pichard, Remy. [Admirable vertu des saincts exorcismes...1622]   (Card 3)

...touchant la prétendue possédée de Nancy [the work to which Pichard is replying] and chapter 18 of the Admirable vertu des saincts exorcismes.
1. Demoniac possession. 2. Exorcism. 3. Ranfaing, Elisabeth de, 1592-1649. 4. Pithois, Claude, 1587-1676. [La descouverture des faux possé dez... I. Pithois, Claude,1587-   1676. [La descouverture des faux pos   sedez... II. Title.

WITCHCRAFT
BF
1517
F5
P59

Pithois, Claude, 1587-1676.
La descouverture des faux possédez ...
Pichard, Remy.
[Admirable vertu des saincts exorcismes sur les princes d'enfer possédants réellement vertueuse demoiselle Elisabeth de Ranfaing, avec ses justifications contre les ignorances et les calomnies de F.Claude Pithoys. Nancy, Par Sébastien Philippe, 1622]
674, 105 p. 14cm.

T.p. lacking. Handwritten t.p. substituted.
Bound in   after chapter 17 are
(Continued on next card)

8
NIC

WITCHCRAFT
BF
1517
F5
P59

Pithois, Claude, 1587-1676.
La descouverture des faux possédez....
Pichard, Remy. [Admirable vertu des saincts exorcismes...1622]   (Card 2)

what appear to be the preface and table of contents of Stimuli virtutum adolescentiae Christianae, by Guglielmo Baldesano [considered by Bibliothèque nationale to be the pseudonym of Bernardino Rosignolo] The work itself is not in the vol.
The 105 pages at end consist of a reprint of Claude Pithois' La descouverture des faux possédez...la conférence
(Continued on next card)

WITCHCRAFT
BF
1517
F5
P59

Pithois, Claude, 1587-1676.
La descouverture des faux possédez....
Pichard, Remy. [Admirable vertu des saincts exorcismes...1622]   (Card 3)

...touchant la prétendue possédée de Nancy [the work to which Pichard is replying] and chapter 18 of the Admirable vertu des saincts exorcismes.
1. Demoniac possession. 2. Exorcism. 3. Ranfaing, Elisabeth de, 1592-1649. 4. Pithois, Claude, 1587-1676. [La descouverture des faux possé dez... I. Pithois, Claude,1587-   1676. [La descouverture des faux pos   sedez... II. Title.

BF
1713
P68
1972

Pithois, Claude, 1587-1676.
A seventeenth-century exposure of superstition: select texts of Claude Pithoys (1587-1676). Introd. and notes by P.J.S. Whitmore. The Hague, Nijhoff, 1972.
xliv, 263 p. 24cm. (International archives of the history of ideas, 49)

English, French or Latin.
Bibliography: p. [ix]-x, [248]-249.

1. Astrology. 2. Witchcraft. 3. Superstition. I. Whitmore, P J S II. Title. III. Series.

4
NIC

Pitt, John Linwood.

see

Pitts, John Linwood.

WITCHCRAFT
BT
125
P68

Pittis, Thomas, 1636-1687.
A discourse concerning the trial of spirits. Wherein inquiry is made into mens pretences to inspiration for publishing doctrines, in the name of God, beyond the rules of the Sacred Scriptures. In opposition to some principles and practices of papists and fanaticks; as they contradict the doctrines of the Church of England, defined in her Articles of religion, established by her ecclesiastical canons, and confirmed by acts of Parliament. By Thomas Pittis ... London, E. Vize, 1683.
4 p. l., 359 p. 18½ᵐ.
Wing P2313.
1. Inspiration. 2. Church of England--Doctrinal and controversial works. I. Title. II. Title: Trial of spirits.

8   Library of Congress   40-24455

BT125.P6   231.7

442

CATALOGUE OF THE CORNELL WITCHCRAFT COLLECTION

Rare K M15 L4+ NIC

Pittmedden, Sir Alexander Seton, Lord, 1639?-1719.
A treatise of mutilation and demembration
Mackenzie, Sir George, 1636-1691.
The laws and customs of Scotland in matters criminal. Wherein is to be seen how the civil law, and the laws and customs of other nations doth agree with, and supply ours. To this 2d ed. is now added ... a Treatise of mutilation and demembration and their punishments, by Sir Alexander Seton. Also a 2d ed. of the Observations upon the 18 Act. Parl. 23, K. James 6th, against dispositions made in defraud of creditors &c., corr. and ... enl. by the author,
(Continued on next card)

Rare K M15 L4+ NIC

Pittmedden, Sir Alexander Seton, Lord, 1639?-1719.
A treatise of mutilation and demembration ...
Mackenzie, Sir George, 1636-1691. The laws and customs of Scotland ... (Card 2)
... before his death. Edinburgh, Printed by the heirs and successors of A. Anderson for A. Symsonz, 1699.
291, 66, 62 p. 30cm.
Wing M 168.
With autographs: Charles Armstrong, and William Kirkpatrick.
(Continued on next card)

Witchcraft BF 1581 P69 C7

Pitts, John Linwood.
Confessions of witches under torture.
MDCXVII. Edinburgh, E. & G. Goldsmid, 1886.
15 p. 20cm. (In 25cm. envelope)
"This ... is taken from Mr. J. L. Pitt's [sic] Witchcraft and Devil-Lore in the Channel Islands." --Introduction, signed E. G.
"This edition is limited to 120 copies."

8
1. Witchcraft--Guernsey. I. His Witchcraft and devil lore in the Channel Islands. II. Title.

Witchcraft BF 1581 P69

Pitts, John Linwood.
Witchcraft and devil lore in the Channel Islands. Transcripts from the official records of the Guernsey Royal Court, with an English translation and historical introduction. By John Linwood Pitts ... Guernsey, Guille-Allès library and T. M. Bichard, printer to the states, 1886.
40 p. 22cm. (Guille-Allès Library series)
1. Trials (Witchcraft)--Channel Islands. 2. Channel Islands--Hist. I. Title.

WITCHCRAFT BR 480 .H59 .886

Pitts, John Linwood.
Witchcraft and devil-lore in the Channel Islands.
Heucher, Johann Heinrich, 1677-1747.
Magic plants; being a translation of a curious tract entitled De vegetalibus magicis, written by M. J. H. Heucher. (1700.) Edited by Edmund Goldsmid. Edinburgh [Printed by E. & G. Goldsmid] 1886.
39 p. 23cm. (Bibliotheca curiosa)
Title in red and black.
"This edition is limited to 275 small-paper copies ..."
Translation of Ex historia naturali
(Continued on next card)

WITCHCRAFT

Pitts, John Linwood.
Witchcraft and devil-lore in the Channel Islands.
Heucher, Johann Heinrich, 1677-1747.
Magic plants ... 1886. (Card 2)
de vegetalibus magicis generatim, by Heucher and J. Fabricius.
"I have given, as an Appendix, a translation from the Official records of the Royal Court of Guernsey, of the trials of three women for witchcraft in 1617. This translation is taken from Mr. J. L. Pitt's Witchcraft and Devil-Lore in the Channel Islands." --ed.
(Continued on next card)

Witchcraft BF 1581 P69 C7

Pitts, John Linwood.
Witchcraft and devil lore in the Channel Islands.
Pitts, John Linwood.
Confessions of witches under torture.
MDCXVII. Edinburgh, E. & G. Goldsmid, 1886.
15 p. 20cm. (In 25cm. envelope)
"This ... is taken from Mr. J. L. Pitt's [sic] Witchcraft and Devil-Lore in the Channel Islands." --Introduction, signed E. G.
"This edition is limited to 120 copies."

8 NIC
1. Witchcraft--Guernsey. I. His Witchcraft and devil lore in the Channel Islands. II. Title.

WITCHCRAFT BF 1559 P69

Pizzurini, Gervasio.
Enchiridion exorcisticum; compendiosissime continens diagnosim, prognosim, ac therapiam medicam et divinam affectionum magicarum. Lugduni, Apud Antonium Valançol, 1668.
133 p. 17cm.

8 NIC
1. Exorcism. 2. Medicine, Magic, mystic and spagiric. I. Title.

Witchcraft BF 1591 T49

The place of magic in the intellectual history of Europe.
Thorndike, Lynn, 1882-
The place of magic in the intellectual history of Europe. New York, Columbia Univ. Press, 1905.
110 p. 24cm. (Studies in history, economics and public law, edited by the Faculty of Political Science of Columbia University, v. 24, no. 1 [whole no. 62])

Witchcraft BF 1582 Z7 1675

Plaidoyez sur les magiciens.
Hautefeuille, lawyer.
Plaidoyez svr les magiciens et svr les sorciers, tenus en la cour de Liege, le 16. Decembre 1675. Ov on montre clairement qu'il n'y peut avoir de ces sortes de gens. Par les sieurs de Havte Feuille & Santevr advocats. Sur l'imprimé a Liege, Chez Iacqves Persois imprimeur, 1676.
120 p. 17cm.
"Le livre d'Albert le Grand, leqvel traite des merveilles du monde," p. [77]-

4
(Continued on next card)

Witchcraft BF 1582 Z7 1675

Plaidoyez sur les magiciens.
Hautefeuille, lawyer. Plaidoyez svr les magiciens ... 1676. (Card 2)
120, has special t. p. with imprint: Lyon, Par Iean Hvgvetan, 1616. Text is taken from Les admirables secrets d'Albert le Grand.
1. Witchcraft. 2. Magic. 3. Sillieux, Sulpice, fl. 1675. I. Santeur, lawyer. II. Albertus Magnus, saint, bp. of Ratisbon, 1193?-1280. Spurious and doubtful works. Les admirables secrets d'Albert le Grand. III. Title: Plaidoyez sur les magiciens. IV. Title: Le livre d'Albert le Grand.

8

Witchcraft BF 1565 P71+

Planch, Alexius M , praeses.
Dissertatio critico-scripturistica de magia diabolica, et magorum prodigiis Exod. 7. coram Pharaone patratis. Una cum conclusionibus ex utroque testamento desumptis, quas praeside D. Alexio M. Planch defendendas suscepere P. P. Chrysostomus M. Ennemoser, et Joan. Evang. M. Püchler ... [Oeniponti?] Litteris Wagnerianis [1767]
6 p. l., 66, [9] p. 28cm.

8
(Continued on next card)

Witchcraft BF 1565 P71+

Planch, Alexius M , praeses. Dissertatio critico-scripturistica de magia diabolica ... [1767] (Card 2)
Diss.--Innsbruck (C. M. Ennemoser and J. E. M. Püchler, respondents)
1. Witchcraft in the Bible. 2. Witchcraft. 3. Magic. I. Ennemoser, Chrysostomus M., respondent. II. Püchler, Johann Evangelica M., respondent. III. Title: De magia diabolica, et magorum prodigiis. IV. Title.

8

WITCHCRAFT BX 2340 P71

Planitius, Georgius.
Vom Exorcismo bey der heiligen Tauffe, und von der Christen Kinder Heiligkeit... [n.p.] 1591.
32 l. 20cm.

8 NIC
1. Exorcism. 2. Baptism--Early works to 1800. I. Title.

WITCHCRAFT PT 2631 L34 H61

Planitz, Ernst Alfons, Edler von der, 1857-
Die Hexe von Goslar.
Lobau, Richard.
Spaziergänge mit Planitz, dessen Ideen und Ansichten über Faust und Hexe. Tagenbuchnotizen. Wittenberg, A.Piehler [1924]
vii, 96, 12 p. 19cm.
Includes passages from Planitz' Die Hexe von Goslar, with commentary.
1. Planitz, Ernst Alfons, Edler von der, 1857- . 2. Witchcraft. 3. Goethe, Johann Wolfgang von, 1749-1832. 4. Faust. 4. Planitz, Ernst Alfons, Edler von der, 1857- . Die Hexe von Goslar. I. Planitz, Ernst Alfons, Edler von der, 1857- . Die Hexe von Goslar. II. Planitz, Ernst Alfons, Edler von der, 1857- . III. Title.

8 NIC

WITCHCRAFT PT 2631 L34 H61

Planitz, Ernst Alfons, Edler von der, 1857-
Die Hexe von Goslar.
Lobau, Richard.
Spaziergänge mit Planitz, dessen Ideen und Ansichten über Faust und Hexe. Tagenbuchnotizen. Wittenberg, A.Piehler [1924]
vii, 96, 12 p. 19cm.
Includes passages from Planitz' Die Hexe von Goslar, with commentary.
1. Planitz, Ernst Alfons, Edler von der, 1857- . 2. Witchcraft. 3. Goethe, Johann Wolfgang von, 1749-1832. 4. Faust. 4. Planitz, Ernst Alfons, Edler von der, 1857- . Die Hexe von Goslar. I. Planitz, Ernst Alfons, Edler von der, 1857- . Die Hexe von Goslar. II. Planitz, Ernst Alfons, Edler von der, 1857- . III. Title.

8 NIC

WITCHCRAFT PT 2631 L34 H61

Planitz, Ernst Alfons, Edler von der, 1857-
Lobau, Richard.
Spaziergänge mit Planitz, dessen Ideen und Ansichten über Faust und Hexe. Tagenbuchnotizen. Wittenberg, A.Piehler [1924]
vii, 96, 12 p. 19cm.
Includes passages from Planitz' Die Hexe von Goslar, with commentary.
1. Planitz, Ernst Alfons, Edler von der, 1857- . 2. Witchcraft. 3. Goethe, Johann Wolfgang von, 1749-1832. 4. Faust. 4. Planitz, Ernst Alfons, Edler von der, 1857- . Die Hexe von Goslar. I. Planitz, Ernst Alfons, Edler von der, 1857- . Die Hexe von Goslar. II. Planitz, Ernst Alfons, Edler von der, 1857- . III. Title.

8 NIC

CATALOGUE OF THE CORNELL WITCHCRAFT COLLECTION

Plants in witchcraft.

Witchcraft
BF
1623
P5
T44
    Thiselton-Dyer, Thomas Firminger, 1848-
       Plants in witchcraft.
      (In The popular science monthly. New York. 24cm. v. 34 (1889) p. 826-833)

   I. Title.

Witchcraft
BF
1520
P71
    Plantsch, Martinus, ca. 1460-1533.
      Opusculum de sagis maleficis ... [Phorce, In Aedibus Thome Anshelmi impensisque Sigismundi Stir, 1507]
    [49] l. 20cm.

    Signatures: a-e⁸, f⁴, g⁵.
    Edited by Heinrich Bebel.

   1. Demonology. 2. Divination. 3. Magic. I. Bebel, Heinrich, 1472-ca. 1516, ed. II. Title: De sagis maleficis. III. Title.

WITCHCRAFT
R
133
P72
    Plaz, Anton Wilhelm, 1708-1784.
      De magiae vanitate.
      Plaz, Anton Wilhelm, 1708-1784.
      Procancellarius D. Antonius Guilielmus Plaz Panegyrin medicam...indicit et de magiae vanitate iterum disserit. [Lipsiae, Ex officina Langenhemia, 1777]
    xvi p. 24cm.

    Introductory to a diss. for which Gehler acted as praeses Wildenhayn as respondent: De praeceptore medico.
    Bound with his: Procancellarius D. Antonius Guilielmus Plaz Panegyrin medicam...indicit et de magiae vanitate prolusione prima praefatur. 1777.
8 NIC
    (Continued on next card)

WITCHCRAFT
R
133
P72
    Plaz, Anton Wilhelm, 1708-1784.
      Procancellarius D. Antonius Guilielmus Plaz Panegyrin medicam...indicit et de magiae vanitate prolusione prima praefatur. [Lipsiae, Ex officina Langenhemia, 1777]
    xvi p. 24cm.

    Introductory to a diss. for which Gehler acted as praeses, Hendrich as respondent: De oleosis pinguibus rancidis.
    With this is bound his: Procancellarius D. Antonius Guilielmus Plaz Panegyrin medicam ...indicit et de magiae vanitate it erum disserit. 1777.
8 NIC
    (Continued on next card)

WITCHCRAFT
R
133
P72
    Plaz, Anton Wilhelm, 1708-1784. Procancellarius D. Antonius Guilielmus Plaz Panegyrin medicam...indicit et de magiae vanitate iterum disserit...[1777] (Card 2)

   1. Medical delusions. 2. Medicine, Magic, mystic and spagiric. 3. Wildenhayn, Joannes Guilielmus, b.1751. 4. His De magiae vanitate. 21. Title: De magiae vanitate.

WITCHCRAFT
R
133
P72
    Plaz, Anton Wilhelm, 1708-1784.
      Procancellarius D. Antonius Guilielmus Plaz Panegyrin medicam...indicit et de magiae vanitate prolusione prima praefatur. [Lipsiae, Ex officina Langenhemia, 1777] xvi p. 24cm.

    Introductory to a diss. for which Gehler acted as praeses, Hendrich as respondent: De oleosis pinguibus rancidis.
    With this is bound his: Procancellarius D. Antonius Guilielmus Plaz Panegyrin medicam ...indicit et de magiae vanitate it erum disserit. 1777.
8 NIC
    (Continued on next card)

WITCHCRAFT
R
133
P72
    Plaz, Anton Wilhelm, 1708-1784. Procancellarius D. Antonius Guilielmus Plaz Panegyrin medicam...indicit et de magiae vanitate iterum disserit...[1777] (Card 2)

   1. Medical delusions. 2. Medicine, Magic, mystic and spagiric. 3. Hendrich, Joannes Christianus Fridericus Aemilius, b.1748. 4. His De magiae vanitate. 21. Title: De magiae vanitate.

Pleadings; in some remarkable cases, before the supreme courts of Scotland.

Witchcraft
K
M15
P7
1673
    [Mackenzie, Sir George] 1636-1691.
      Pleadings, in some remarkable cases, before the supreme courts of Scotland, since the year, 1661. To which the decisions are subjoyn'd ... Edinburgh, Printed by George Swintoun, James Glen, and Thomas Brown, 1673.
    4 p. l., 232, [4] p. 19½ cm.

    Signatures: *⁴, q², A-Z⁴, Aa-Ff⁴.
    Head-pieces; manuscript notes.
    "In three of those pleadings, (viz. 2. 3. 7.) I have mingled with my own arguments, the arguments of such as pleaded with me. In the rest, I have used only my own."—The author's reflections.
    With book-plate of George Lockhart of Carnwath.

   I. Title.
    29—89
    Library of Congress   [2]

Witchcraft
BF
1565
P72
    A pleasant treatise of witches. Their imps, and meetings, persons bewitched, magicians, necromancers, incubus, and succubus's, familiar spirits, goblings, pharys, specters, phantasms, places haunted, and devillish impostures: with the difference between good and bad angels, and a true relation of a good genius. By a pen neer the Covent of Eluthery. London, Printed by H. B. for C. Wilkinson, and T. Archer and T. Burrell, 1673.
    126 p. 15cm.

    Wing P 2564.

WITCHCRAFT
BF
1584
D4
P72
    Plenkers, Wilhelm, d. 1889.
      Das Hexenwesen in Dänemark.

    (In: Stimmen aus Maria-Laach. Freiburg im Breisgau. 24cm. Jahrg. 1896. Heft 6, p.64-85; Heft 7, p. 175-191; Heft 9, p. 392-413; Heft 10, p. 494-515)

8 NIC
   1 Witchcraft—Denmark. 2. Trials (Witchcraft)—Denmark. I. Title.

Witchcraft
BF
1612
P73
    Plytoff, G
      La magie; les lois occulte, la théosophie, l'initiation, le magnétisme, le spiritisme, la sorcellerie, le sabbat, l'alchimie, la kabbale, l'astrologie. Paris, Librairie J.-B. Baillière et Fils, 1892.
    viii, 312 p. illus. 20cm. (Bibliothèque scientifique contemporaine)

   1. Magic. 2. Occult sciences. I. Title.

Pneumatica.

Witchcraft
BF
1445
G87
    Groenewegen, Hendrik.
      Pneumatica; ofte, Leere van de geesten, zijnde denkende en redelike wesens ... uytgegeven by gelegentheyd van 't boek De betooverde wereld, geschreven door Balthazar Bekker... Enchuysen, H. van Straalen, 1692.
    88, 126, 56 p. 20cm.

   1. Ghosts. 2. Bekker, Balthasar, 1634-1698. De betooverde wereld. I. Title. II. Title: Leere van de geesten.

Pneumatologia.

WITCHCRAFT
BF
1445
S45
    Seidel, Abrahamus.
      [Pneumatologia] Πνευματολογία oder Kurtzer Bericht von denen Geistern, über der unlangst publicirten Frage ob natürliche gewisse Geister seyen, und einem Menschen gezieme solche an sich zu locken, und in dero Gemeinschafft zugerathen?... Erffurdt, In Verlegung Johann Birckners [Gedruckt in der Spangenbergischen Truckerey] 1648.
    [152] p. illus. 14cm.

8 NIC
    One p. of MS notes bound in at end. Title in red and black.
   1. Spirits. 2. Witchcraft. I. Title.

Pneumatologie.

WITCHCRAFT
BF
1582
Z7
1582c
    Michaelis, Sébastien, 1543?-1618.
      [Pneumatologie; ou, Discours des esprits en tant qu'il est de besoing, pour entendr & resoudre la matière difficile des sorciers comprinse en la sentence contre eux dönee en Avignon l'an de grace, 1582. Paris, G. Bichon, 1587]
    122 l. 18cm.

    T.p. lacking.

8 NIC
   1. Witchcraft—Avignon. 2. Trials (Witchcraft)—Avignon. 3. Devil. 4. Witchcraft. I. Title.

Pneumatologie.

WITCHCRAFT
BF
1002
M67
1854
    Mirville, Jacques Eudes, marquis de, 1802-1873.
      Pneumatologie. Des esprits et de leurs manifestations fluidiques. Mémoire addressé à l'Académie. 2. éd.... Paris, H. Vrayet de Surcy [etc.] 1854-68.
    6 v. 24cm.

    Vol. 1 only is of 2d ed.
    Vols 2-5 have title: Pneumatologie. Des esprits et de leurs manifestations diverses. Vol. 6 has title: Des esprits, l'esprit-saint et du miracle..
8 NIC
    (Continued on next card)

Pneumatologie.

WITCHCRAFT
BF
1002
M67
1854
    Mirville, Jacques Eudes, marquis de, 1802-1873. Pneumatologie...1854-68. (Card 2)

    Vols. 2-5 also have special title: Manifestations historiques...I-IV.
    Vol. 6 has also special title: Manifestations thaumaturgiques. I.
   1. Psychical research. I. His Des esprits et de leurs manifestations... II. His De l'esprit-saint... III. His Manifestations historiques... IV. His Manifestations thaumaturgiques. V. Title.

The poetry of witchcraft.

Witchcraft
PR
1259
W81
H62+
    Heywood, Thomas, d. 1641.
      The poetry of witchcraft illustrated by copies of the plays on the Lancashire witches by Heywood and Shadwell. Reprinted under the direction of James O. Halliwell. Brixton Hill, Printed for priv. circ. only, 1853.
    238 p. 29cm.

    Eighty copies printed.
    Each play has also separate t.p.

    (Continued on next card)

CATALOGUE OF THE CORNELL WITCHCRAFT COLLECTION

Witchcraft
BF
1559
T2+

The poetry of witchcraft.
Heywood, Thomas, d. 1641. The poetry of witchcraft... 1853. (Card 2)

Contents.--The Lancashire witches and Tegue o Divelly, the Irish priest, by Thomas Shadwell.--The late Lancashire witches, by Thomas Heywood and Richard Broome.
I. Halliwell-Phillipps, James Orchard, 1820-1889. II. Shadwell, Thomas, 1642?-1692. The Lancashire witches and Tegue o Divelly. III. His The late Lancashire witches. IV. Broome, Richard, d. 1652? The late Lancashire witches V. Title.

HIST SCI
R
133
P74

Pohl, Johann Ehrenfried, 1746-1800, praeses.
De medico exorcista...praeside Iohanne Ehrenfried Pohl...disputabit auctor ac respondens Iohannes Godofredus Iancke... Lipsiae, Ex officina Sommeria [1788]
26, xv p. 21cm.
Diss.--Leipzig (J. G. Jancke, respondent)
"Procancellarius D. Ernestus Gottlob Bose panegyrin medicam...indicit. De phantasia laesa, gravium morborum matre.": xv p. at end.
(Continued on next card)

HIST SCI
R
133
P74

Pohl, Johann Ehrenfried, 1746-1800, praeses.
De medico exorcista...[1788] (Card 2)

1. Exorcism. 2. Medicine, Magic, mystic, and spagiric. 3. Hallucinations and illusions. 4. Mind and body--Early works to 1850. I. Jancke, Johann Gottfried, b.1762, respondent. II. Bose, Ernst Gottlob, 1723-1788. III. Title.

WITCHCRAFT
BF
1517
P75

Poitiers, Jean de.
Les diables de Loudun. Paris, Ghio, 1876
271 p. 17cm.

1. Demoniac possession. 2. Grandier, Urbain, 1590-1634. 3. Loudun, France. Ursuline convent. V. Title.

WITCHCRAFT
59
6

Polidoro, Valerio.
[Practica exorcistarum ... ad daemones et maleficia de Christifidelibus ejiciendum. Patavii, Apud Paulum Meietum, 1587]
2 v. in 1. 15cm.
Title page for vol. 1 lacking; title obtained from British Museum. Dept. of Printed Books. General catalogue of printed books. London, 1963. Running title: Expvlsio daemonvm.
Title for vol. 2: Dispersio daemonvm qvae
(Cont'd on next card)

WITCHCRAFT
59
6

Polidoro, Valerio. [Practica exorcistarum ...1587. (Card 2)

secvnda pars est practice exorcistarum. Additional exorcisms in ms. (16 p.) inserted.

1. Exorcism. I. Title. II. Title: Expvlsio daemonvm. III. Dispersio daemonvm.

Witchcraft
BF
1559
T41
1626

Polidoro, Valerio.
Practica exorcistarum.
Thesavrvs exorcismorvm atqve conivrationvm terribilivm, potentissimorum, efficacissimorum cum practica probatissima; qvibvs spiritvs maligni, daemones maleficiaque omnia de corporibus humanis obsessis, tanquam flagellis, fustibusque fugantur, expelluntur, doctrinis refertissimus atq. uberrimus: ad maximam exorcistarum commoditatem nunc vltimo plenarie in lucem editus & recusus; cuius authores, vt & singuli tractatus sequente pagella consignati, inueniuntur. Cum indice capitum, rerum & verborum ... Coloniae, sumptibus haeredum Lazari Zetzneri, 1626. (Continued on next card)

Witchcraft
BF
1559
T41
1626

Polidoro, Valerio.
Practica exorcistarum.
Thesavrvs exorcismorvm atqve conivrationvm terribilivm ... 1626. (Card 2)

12 p. l., 1232, [39] p. 18cm.
Previously published at Cologne in 1608.
Contents.--F. Valerii Polydori ... Practica exorcistarum ad daemones & maleficia de Christi fidelibus pellendum, pars prima ... [et] secunda.--R.p.f. Hieronymi Mengi ... Flagellum daemonum.--Eivsdem Fvstis daemonvm.--F. Zachariae Vicecomitis ... Complementum artis exorcisticae.-- Petri Antonii Stampae ... Fuga Satanae.-- R.d. Maximiliani ab Eynatten ... Manuale exorcismorum.

Witchcraft
PR
3404
H5
1739

The political history of the Devil.
[Defoe, Daniel] 1660-1731.
The political history of the Devil. Containing: his original; a state of his circumstances; his conduct [sic] publick and private; the various turns of his affairs from Adam down to this present time; the various methods he takes to converse with mankind; with the manner of his making witches, wizards, and conjurers, and how they sell their souls to him, &c. &c. The whole interspers'd with many of the Devil's
(Continued on next card)

Witchcraft
PR
3404
H5
1739

The political history of the Devil.
[Defoe, Daniel] 1660-1731. The political history of the Devil ... 1739. (Card 2)

adventures. To which is added, a description of the Devil's dwelling, vulgarly call'd hell. The 4th ed. London, Printed for J. Fisher, 1739.
351 p. 18cm.
I. Title.

Witchcraft
BF
1559
G25
Z63
no.3

Politische Frage, ob ein ... Landesfürst über die Gassnerischen Kuren ... gleichgültig seyn kann.
Was soll man an den Kuren des Herrn geistlichen Raths Gassner, die er bisher im Namen Jesu gemacht hat, noch untersuchen, so nicht schon längst hundertmal ist untersucht worden? Frankfurt und Berlin, 1775.
96 p. 17cm.
No. 3 in vol. lettered Gassneriana.
1. Gassner, Johann Joseph, 1727-1779. 2. Faith-cure. 3. Politische Frage, ob ein ... Landesfürst über die Gassnerischen Kuren ... gleichgültig seyn kann. 4. Sterzinger, Ferdinand, 1721-1786.

Witchcraft
BF
1521
H19

The polity and kingdom of darkness.
Hallywell, Henry, b. ca. 1630.
Melampronoea; or, A discourse of the polity and kingdom of darkness. Together with a solution of the chiefest objections brought against the being of witches ... London, Printed for Walter Kettilby, 1681.
[16], 118 p. 15cm.

WITCHCRAFT
BF
1583
P77

Pollack, Heinrich, 1844-1911.
Mittheilungen über den Hexenprozess in Deutschland, insbesondere über verschiedene westphälische Hexenprozessakten. Berlin, Wallmann, 1885.
50 p. 23cm.
Two copies. On label pasted over imprint of copy 2: Berlin, F. Siemenroth, 1886.
1. Trials (Witchcraft)--Germany. 2. Trials (Witchcraft)--Westphalia. I. Title.

Witchcraft
GT
6710
T76
1615

Polycarius, Johannes.
Tractatus tragicus De poenis omnium delictorum, quae adversus Deum aut homines admissa & mirabiliter vindicata sunt. Ex probatissimis omnium aetatum scriptoribus diligenter collectus ac libris duobus explicatus per Joannem Polycarium [pseud.?] [Islebiae?] Impensis Henningi Grosij, 1615.
4 p. l., 667, [32] p. 20cm.
With colophon.
First published 1597 under title:
(Continued on next card)

Witchcraft
GT
6710
T76
1615

Polycarius, Johannes.
Tractatus tragicus De poenis omnium delictorum ... 1615. (Card 2)

Tragica, seu tristium historiarum de poenis criminalibus, and with dedication signed Henningus Grosius [sic]; no mention of J. Polycarius on t. p. or elsewhere.
This edition is the same printing as that of 1597, but with different t. p. and preliminary leaves.
Book I has caption title: Tragicorvm,
Continued on next card)

Witchcraft
GT
6710
T76
1615

Polycarius, Johannes.
Tractatus tragicus De poenis omnium delictorum ... 1615. (Card 3)

seu sylvae tristivm, hoc est, Horribilium historiarum de poenis criminalibus.
Grässe, Bibliotheca magica, attributes this edition to Polycarpus, Johannes.
1. Punishment. 2. Crime and criminals --Biog. I. Grosse, Henning, 1553-1621, comp. II. Polycarius, Johannes. III. Polycarpus, Johannes. IV. Johannes Polycarius. V. Title: Tragicorum, seu sylvae tristium.

Witchcraft
GT
6710
T76
1615

Polycarpus, Johannes.
Tractatus tragicus De poenis omnium delictorum, quae adversus Deum aut homines admissa & mirabiliter vindicata sunt. Ex probatissimis omnium aetatum scriptoribus diligenter collectus ac libris duobus explicatus per Joannem Polycarium [pseud.?] [Islebiae?] Impensis Henningi Grosij, 1615.
4 p. l., 667, [32] p. 20cm.
With colophon.
First published 1597 under title:
(Continued on next card)

Witchcraft
GT
6710
T76
1615

Polycarpus, Johannes.
Tractatus tragicus De poenis omnium delictorum ... 1615. (Card 2)

Tragica, seu tristium historiarum de poenis criminalibus, and with dedication signed Henningus Grosius [sic]; no mention of J. Polycarius on t. p. or elsewhere.
This edition is the same printing as that of 1597, but with different t. p. and preliminary leaves.
Book I has caption title: Tragicorvm,
Continued on next card)

CATALOGUE OF THE CORNELL WITCHCRAFT COLLECTION

Polycarpus, Johannes.
Witchcraft
GT Tractatus tragicus De poenis omnium delic-
6710   torum ... 1615.   (Card 3)
T76
1615   seu sylvae tristivm, hoc est, Horribilium
        historiarum de poenis criminalibus.
        Grässe, Bibliotheca magica, attributes
        this edition to Polycarpus, Johannes.
        1. Punishment. 2. Crime and criminals
        --Biog. I. Grosse, Henning, 1553-1621,
        comp. II. Polycarius, Johannes. III.
8   Polycarpus, Johannes. IV. Johannes Poly-
        carius. V. Title: Tragicorum, seu sylvae
        tristivm.

WITCHCRAFT
BF   Pomponazzi, Pietro, 1462-1524.
1558   De naturalium effectuum causis, siue de
P79   incantationibus, opvs abstrvsioris philo-
        sophiae plenvm, & breuissimis historijs
        illustratum atq, ante annos xxxv composi-
        tum, nunc primum vero in lucem fideliter
        editum. Adiectis breuibus scholijs à Guliel-
        mo Grataroio. Basileae ₍per Henrichvm
        Petri, 1556₎
        349 p. 17cm.

8
NIC   (Cont'd on next card)

WITCHCRAFT
BF   Pomponazzi, Pietro, 1462-1524. De natura-
1558   lium effectuum causis...₍1556₎ (Card 2)
P79   Autograph on flyleaf: Gerardus Vossius,
        1577-1649.
        With this are bound: Landi, Bassiano. De
        incremento. Venetiis, 1556; Erastus,
        Thomas. Dispvtatio de avro potabili.
        Basileae, 1578; Anten, Conradus ab.
        (Gynaikolousis) sev mvlicrvm lavatio.
        Lvbecae,   1590.
        1. Demonolo-   gy. I. Grataroli, Gugli-
        elmo, 1516-   1568, ed. II. Title.

Poniatowska, Krystyna, 1610-1644.
Witchcraft
BF   ₍Comenius, Johann Amos₎ 1592-1670, comp.
1785   Lux e tenebris, novis radiis aucta. Hoc
C73   est: solemnissimae divinae revelationes, in
1665   usum seculi nostri factae ... Per immissas
        visiones, & angelica divindque alloqvia,
        facta I. Christophoro Kottero silesio, ab
        anno 1616, ad 1624. II. Christinae Poni-
        atoviae bohemae, annis 1627, 1628, 1629,
        III. Nicolao Drabicio moravo, ab anno 1638,
        ad 1664 ... ₍Amstelodami₎ 1665.
        various pagings. illus., ports. 21cm.
8   Added engr.   t. p.
                        (Continued on next card)

Poniatowska, Krystyna, 1610-1644.
Witchcraft
BF   ₍Comenius, Johann Amos₎ 1592-1670, comp.
1785   Lux e tenebris ... 1665.   (Card 2)
C73
1665   "Voluminis prophetici," first item, has
        special t. p. with imprint 1667.
        "Revelationes Christophoro Kottero" and
        "Revelationes Christinae Poniatoviae" each
        have special t. p. with imprint 1664.
        "Revelationes Nicolao Drabicio" has
        special t. p. without imprint.
        First published 1657 with title: Lux
8   in tenebris.
                        (Continued on next card)

Ponzinibius, Joannes Franciscus.
   De lamiis, et excellentia.
Witchcraft
BF   Grillando, Paolo.
1850   Tractatvs dvo: Vnus De sortilegiis D.
G85   Pavli Grillandi ... Alter De lamiis et ex-
1592   cellentia iuris vtriusque D. Ioannis Fran-
        cisci Ponzinibij Florentini ... Olim qvi-
        dem in lvcem editi; nunc verò recogniti, &
        ab innumeriis passim mendis vindicati; adiec-
        to indice locupletissimo. Francoforti ad
        Moenvm ₍Apvd Martinvm Lechlervm, Impensis
        Haeredvm Christiani Egenolphi₎ 1592.
        16 p. l., 29⁰ ₍2₎ p. 17cm.
8   With colop-   hon.
                        (Continued on next card)

Ponzinibius, Joannes Franciscus.
   De lamiis, et excellentia.
WITCHCRAFT
K   Ziletti, Giovanni Battista, fl. 1559, ed.
Z695   Volvmen praeclarissimvm ... omnivm trac-
1580   tatvvm criminalivm nvnc per D. Ioan. Bap-
        tistam Zilettum ab omnibus mendis expurga-
        tum ac omnino correctum ... Venetiis,
        Apud Io. Antonivm Bertanum, 1580.
        78 p. l., 473 numbered leaves. 21cm.
        Includes Tractatvs ... de lamijs ...
        Ioanni Francisci Ponzinibij, l. 89-99 v.;
        De sortilegiis tractatus Pauli Ghirlandi,
        l. 104 v.-138 v.
8   (Continued on next card)

Ponzinibius, Joannes Franciscus.
   De lamiis, et excellentia.
WITCHCRAFT
BF   Spina, Bartolommeo.
1565   Reverendi Patris F. Bartholomaei Spinei
M47   Pisani ... Qvaestio de strigibvs, vna cvm
1575   tractatv de praeeminentia Sacrae Theologiae,
        & quadruplici apologia de lamiis contra Pon-
        zinibium ... Romae, In aedibus Populi Ro-
        mani, 1576.
        4 p. l., 180 p. 23cm.
        Bound with Mazzolini, Silvestro, da Pri-
        erio. ... De strigmagarum... Romae, 1575.
        1. Witchcraft. 2. Theology, Doctrinal.
8   3. Ponzinib-   ius, Joannes Franciscus.
NIC   De lamiis,   et excellentia. I. Ti-
        tle: Quaes-   tio de strigibus.

Witchcraft
BF   Poole, William Frederick, 1821-1894.
1576   Cotton Mather and Salem witchcraft. By William
P82   Frederick Poole. ⟨Reprinted from the North American
        review for April, 1869.⟩ Boston ₍University press₎ 1869.
        63 p. 24ᶜᵐ.
        "One hundred copies printed."

        1. Witchcraft—Salem, Mass. 2. Mather, Cotton, 1663-1728. I. Title.
        3. Upham, Charles Wentworth, 1802-1875.
        Salem witchcraft;   with an account of
        Salem village.   15-15947
        Library of Congress   BF1576.P83

       Poole, William Frederick, 1821-1894.
           Cotton Mather and Salem witchcraft.
WITCHCRAFT
BF   Upham, Charles Wentworth, 1802-1875.
1576   Salem witchcraft and Cotton Mather. A
P82   reply ₍to W. F. Poole's Cotton Mather and
U67+   Salem witchcraft₎ Morrisania, N. Y.,
        1869.
        91 p. 19cm.
        In double columns.
        Reprint from the Historical Magazine.
        1. Poole, William Frederick, 1821-
        1894. Cotton Mather and Salem witchcraft.
        2. Mather, Cotton, 1663-1728. 3. Witch-
8   craft—Salem,   Mass. I. Title.

Witchcraft
BF   ₍Poole, William Frederick₎ 1821-1894.
1576   Cotton Mather & witchcraft; two notices of Mr. Upham,
P82   his reply. Boston, T. R. Marvin & son; ₍etc., etc.₎ 1870.
U676   30 p. 17cm.

        1. Witchcraft—Salem, Mass. 2. Mather, Cotton, 1663-1728. 3. Upham,
        Charles Wentworth, 1802-1875.   I. Title.
                                                        11—9001
        Library of Congress   BF1576.P8

       Poole, William Frederick, 1821-1894.
Witchcraft
F   The witchcraft delusion of 1692, by Gov. Thomas Hutch-
7   inson. From an unpublished manuscript (an early draft
H97   of his History of Massachusetts) in the Massachusetts
1870   archives. With notes by William Frederick Poole. Bos-
        ton, Priv. print., 1870.
        43 p. 25cm.
        "Reprinted from the New-England historical and genealogical register
        for October, 1870."

        1. Witchcraft—New England.   I. Poole, William Frederick, 1821-1894.
                                                        5—2279
        Library of Congress   F7.H97

       A popular history of witchcraft.
Witchcraft
BF   Summers, Montague, 1880-1948.
1566   A popular history of witchcraft, by Montague Summers.
S95   London, K. Paul, Trench, Trubner & co., ltd., 1937.
P8   xvi, 276 p. front., plates, facsims. 19ᵐᵐ.

        1. Witchcraft.   I. Title.
        ₍Full name: Alphonsus Joseph-Mary Augustus Montague Summers₎
                                                        37-22097
        Library of Congress   BF1566.S84
                                                        ₍8₎

Witchcraft
BF   Porath, Samuel, respondent.
1587   Bugges, Laurentius, praeses.
D61   Disputatio physica qva magiam doemonia-
no.6   cam ₍sic₎ ceu illicitam, & naturalem ceu
        licitam, in electorali ad albim academia
        explicabunt praeses M. Laurentius Bugges,
        ... respondens Samuel Porath ... Witte-
        bergae, Typis Johannis Haken, 1667.
        ₍12₎ p. 18cm. (bound in 21cm. vol.)
        No. 6 in vol. lettered Dissertationes de
        de magia. 1623-1723.
        1. Magic—   Addresses, essays, lec-
        tures. I. Po-   rath, Samuel, respondent.
8   II. Title: D   isputatio physica qua
        magiam ... ex   plicabunt...

WITCHCRAFT
BX   Pordage, John.
9339   Innocencie appearing, through the dark
P83   mists of pretended guilt. Or, a full and
A17+   true narration of the unjust and illegal
1655   proceedings of the commissioners of Berks,
        (for ejecting scandalous and insufficient
        ministers) against John Pordage of Bradfield
        in the same county. In which he is justly
        vindicated from the unjust and horrid as-
        persions of blasphemy, divelism or necroman-
        cie, scandal   in his life ... London,
8
NIC   (Continued on next card)

WITCHCRAFT
BX   Pordage, John. Innocencie appearing,
9339   through the dark mists of pretended guilt
P83   ... 1655.   (Card 2)
A17+
1655   Printed for Giles Calvert, 1655.
        5 p. l., 114 p. port. 29cm.

        1. Great Britain. Laws, statutes, etc.
        An ordinance for ejecting scandalous, ig-
        norant and insufficient ministers and school
        masters. 2. Visions. I. Title.

8
NIC

WITCHCRAFT
BF   Porée, Charles Gabriel.
1555   Le pour et contre de la possession des
P827   filles de la parroisse de Landes, diocese
        de Bayeux ₍par C. G. Porée et Dudouet,
        médicin₎ ... A Antioche, Chez les Héri-
        tiers de la bonne foy, 1738.
        275 p. 19cm.

8   1. Demoniac possession. I. Dudouet,
NIC   Dr. II. Title.

       Porphyrius.
           De divinis, atque daemonibus.
WITCHCRAFT
PA   Jamblichus, of Chalcis.
4220   ₍De mysteriis. Latin₎
L3
A4+   Iamblichus De mysteriis Aegyptiorum, Chal-
1516   daeorum, Assyriorum. Proclus In Platonicum
        Alcibiadem de anima, atq daemone. Proclus
        sacrificio, & magia. Porphyrius De divinis
        atq daemonibus. Synesius Platonicus De so-
        mniis. Psellus De daemonibus. Expositio
        Prisciani, & Marsilii in Theophrastum De sen-
        su, phantasia, & intellectu. Alcinoi Plat-
8   nici philoso   phi, Liber de doctrina
                    (Continued on next card)

446

CATALOGUE OF THE CORNELL WITCHCRAFT COLLECTION

WITCHCRAFT
PA
4220
L3
A4+
1516

Porphyrius.
De divinis, atque daemonibus.
Jamblichus, of Chalcis. [De mysteriis. Latin] [1516] (Card 2)
Platonis. Speusippi Platonis discipuli, Liber de Platonis definitionibus. Pythagorae philosophi Aurea uerba. Symbola Pythagorae philosophi. Xenocratis philosophi platonici, Liber de morte. Mercurii Trismegisti Pimander. Eiusdem Asclepius. Marsilii Ficini De triplici uita lib. II. Eiusdem Liber   de uoluptate. Eiusdem

8 (Continued on next card)

WITCHCRAFT
PA
4220
L3
A4+
1516

Porphyrius.
De divinis, atque daemonibus.
Jamblichus, of Chalcis. [De mysteriis. Latin] [1516] (Card 3)
De sole & lumine libri. II. Apologia eiusdem in librum suum de lumine. Eiusdem Libellus de magis. Quod necessaria sit securitas, & tranquillitas animi. Praeclarissimarum sententiarum huius operis breuis annotatio. [Venetiis, In aedibvs Aldi, et Andreae soceri, 1516]
177 [i.e., 175] numbered leaves.
29cm.

8 (Continued on next card)

WITCHCRAFT
PA
4220
L3
A4+
1516

Porphyrius.
De divinis, atque daemonibus.
Jamblichus, of Chalcis. [De mysteriis.] Latin] [1516] (Card 4)
At head of title: Index eorvm, qvae hoc in libro habentvr.
With colophon.
Provenance: Bibliotec: SS. Me. Novelle.
Translations by M. Ficino.
1. Occult sciences. 2. Philosophy, Ancient—Collections. I. Proclus Diadochus. In Platonicum Alcibiadem. II. Proclus Diadochus. De sacrificio. III.

8 (Continued on next card)

Witchcraft
A
220
++
578

Porphyrius.
Jamblicus, of Chalcis.
[De mysteriis. Greek & Latin]
Ἰαμβλίχου Χαλκιδέως τῆς κοίλης Συρίας περὶ μυστηρίων λόγος. Iamblichi Chalcidensis ex Coele-Syria, de mysteriis liber. Praemittitur epistola Porphyrii ad Anebonem AEgyptium, eodem argumento. Thomas Gale Anglus graece nunc primum edidit, latine vertit, & notas adjecit. Oxonii, e theatro Sheldoniano, 1678.
20 p.l., 316, [6] p., 1 l. 32cm.
(Continued on next card)

Witchcraft
A
220
++
578

Porphyrius.
Jamblicus, of Chalcis.
[De mysteriis. Greek & Latin] Ἰαμβλίχου Χαλκιδέως...περὶ μυστηρίων λόγος...1678. (Card 2)

Title vignette.
Greek and Latin in parallel columns.

Title transliterated:
Peri mystēriōn logos.

Witchcraft
L
10
27
1821

Porphyrius.
Jamblichus, of Chalcis.
[De mysteriis. English]
Iamblichus on the Mysteries of the Egyptians, Chaldeans, and Assyrians. Translated from the Greek by Thomas Taylor ... Chiswick, Printed by C. Whittinghams for the translator. 1821.
xxiv, 365 p. 22-1/2 cm.
"The epistle of Porphyry to the Egyptian Anebo": p. [1]-16.

Witchcraft
PA
4220
L3
A4
1577

Porphyrius.
Jamblichus, of Chalcis.
[De mysteriis. Latin]
Iamblichvs De mysteriis Ægyptiorvm, Chaldæorum, Assyriorum. Proclvs in Platonicum Alcibiadem de anima, atque dæmone. Idem De sacrificio & magia. Porphyrivs De diuinis atq; dæmonib. Psellvs De dæmonibus. Mercvrii Trismegisti Pimander. Eiusdem Asclepius. Lvgdvni, apvd Ioan. Tornaesivm, 1577.
543, [1] p. 13ᶜᵐ.
Title vignette (printer's mark)
"Marsilivs Ficinvs ... se commendat": p. 3.

[2] 25-19681

WITCHCRAFT
BF
1555
P83

Porri, Alessio.
Antidotario contro li demonii; nel qvale si tratta, come entrano ne' corpi humani, oue in quelli stiano, come da quelli si scacciano, & altre cose degne di sapersi ... In Venetia, Appresso R. Megietti, 1601.
291 p. 20cm.

8
NIC
1. Demoniac possession. 2. Exorcism.
I. Title.

WITCHCRAFT
BF
1405
L85
1673

Porta, Giovanni Battista della, 1535?-1615.
Magiae naturalis libri viginti.
Longinus, Caesar, ed.
Trinum magicum, sive Secretorum magicorum opus ... Editum à Caesare Longino philos. Francofurti, Sumptibus Jacobi Gothofredi Seyleri, 1673.
12 p. l., 498 p. 14cm.
Contents.—Marci Antonii Zimarae Tractatus magicus.—Appendix, De mirandis quibusdam naturali magia factis operationibus. Ex lib. 2. Mag. nat. Ioan. Bapt. Port.—Tractatvs De virtutibus quarundam herbarum,

8 (Continued on next card)

WITCHCRAFT
BF
1405
L85
1673

Porta, Giovanni Battista della, 1535?-1615.
Magiae naturalis libri viginti.
Longinus, Caesar, ed. Trinum magicum ... 1673. (Card 2)
lapidum & animalium. A. M. A.—Commentatio De magnetica curatione vulnerum citra svperstitionem ... Authore R. G. M. D.—Logia, sive Oracvla Zoroastri ex Platonicorum libris collecta.—Tractatus De proprii cujusqve nati daemonis inqvisitione.
Layout of text corresponds to that of Frankfurt, 1630 ed. (C. Eifrid, printer)

8 (Continued on next card)

Porta, Jean Baptiste, 1535?-1615.
see
Porta, Giovanni Battista della, 1535?-1615.

WITCHCRAFT
BF
1555
P84

Portal, Placido, 1793-1843.
Demonomania con commozione celebrale senza stravaso; osservazione fatta nel mese di novembre dell'anno 1833 nella R. Casa de' Matti in Palermo. Palermo, Dalla Tipografia del Giorn. letterario, 1834.
25, [4] p. port. 20cm.
"Autopsia cadaverica della demonomoniaca [sic] Rosa Cinexis ...": [4] p. at end.
Includes   bibliographical references.

8
NIC (Continued on next card)

WITCHCRAFT
BF
1555
P84

Portal, Placido, 1793-1843.
Demonomania con commozione celebrale senza stravaso...1834. (Card 2)

1. Demoniac possession. 2. Cinexis, Rosa. I. Title.

UNDERGR
BF
1576
B79

Porter family.
Boyer, Paul S
Salem possessed; the social origins of witchcraft [by] Paul Boyer and Stephen Nissenbaum. Cambridge, Mass., Harvard University Press, 1974.
xxi, 231 p. illus. 25 cm.

Witchcraft
BF
1410
B42
Z56
v.2
no.4

Portland, William Bentinck, 1st earl of, 1649-1709.
Walten, Ericus, 1663-1697.
Brief aan sijn Excellentie, de Heer Graaf van Portland, &c. &c. Rakende de persoon en het gevoelen van Dr. B. Bekker, en 't geen tegen hem, by eenige van sijn partyen, word verwagt, en uytgestrooyd, ten opsigte van sijn Koninglijke Majesteyt van Groot Britanjen. ... Door Ericus Walten ... Gedrukt voor den auteur. Gravenhage, By Meyndert Uytwerf, boekverkoper, 1692.
80 p. title vignette, illus. initial.
19 x 15cm.

4 (Continued on next card)

Witchcraft
BF
1410
B42
Z56
v.2
no.4

Portland, William Bentinck, 1st earl of, 1649-1709.
Walten, Ericus, 1663-1697. Brief aan sijn Excellentie, de Heer Graaf van Portland ... 1692. (Card 2)
4°: A-K⁴.
Van der Linde 174.
No. 4 in vol. lettered: Bekker II.

1. Bekker, Balthasar, 1634-1698. 2. Devil. I. Portland, William Bentinck, 1st earl of, 1649- 1709. II. William III, King of Great   Britain, 1649-1709.
III. Title.

8

Witchcraft
BF
1587
D61
no.2

Positionum decas de magia.
Sperling, Johann, 1603-1658, praeses.
Positionum decas de magia qvam ... sub ... M. Johannis Sperlings ... praesidio ... disqvisitioni publicè subjicit Henricus Solter ... aut. & respond. Wittebergae, Ex officinâ typographicâ Johannis Haken, 1648.
[32] p. 21cm.
No. 2 in vol. lettered Dissertationes de magia. 1623-1723.
1. Magic—Addresses, essays, lectures.
I. Solter, He   inrich, repsondent.
8 II. Title.

HIST SCI
BF
1445
P85

Posner, Caspar, praeses.
Diatribe physica De virunculis metallicis, quam...praeside...Casparo Posnero...publice ventilandam exhibet Michael Dachselt... Jenae, Literis Krebsianis, 1662.
[30] p. 20cm.

Diss.—Jena (M. Dachselt, respondent)

1. Apparitions. 2. Demonology. 3. Occult sciences. I. Dachselt, Michael, respondent.
8 II. Title.
NIC

447

CATALOGUE OF THE CORNELL WITCHCRAFT COLLECTION

Une possédée en 1862.

WITCHCRAFT
PQ 2311 J77 P6
Julliard, Isabelle
    Une possédée en 1862. Paris, E. Dentu, 1862.
    177 p. 18cm.

8 NIC
I. Title.

Les possédées de Loudun, et Urbain Grandier.

Witchcraft
BF 1582 B54 1905
Bertrand, Isidore
    Les possédées de Loudun, et Urbain Grandier. Étude historique. Paris, Bloud [1905?]
    61 p. 18cm. (Science et religion: études pour le temps présent)
    Includes bibliography (5 p.)
    Bound with his La sorcellerie.
    1. Demoniac possession. 2. Grandier, Urbain, 1590-1634. 3. Loudun, France. Ursuline Convent. I. Title.

Les possédées de Morzine.

WITCHCRAFT
BF 1555 T61
Tissot, Claude-Joseph, 1801-1876.
    Les possédées de Morzine, ou Le diable qui n'y voit goutte. Par M. J. Tissot. Paris, Didier, 1865.
    32 p. 24cm.
    "Extrait de la Revue moderne, du 1er mai 1865."
    1. Demoniac possession. 2. Morzine, France--History. I. Title. II. Title: Le diable qui n'y voit goutte.

8 NIC

Les possédés d'Illfurth.

BF 1555 G21
Gaquère, François, 1888-
    Les possédés d'Illfurth, de Natal et de Phat-Diem (1868-1906-1925) Genval, Éditions "Marie-Médiatrice" [1956]
    125 p. illus. 18cm.
    At head of title: P. Sutter [et] François Gaquère. Aux prises avec Satan.
    Although Sutter's name appears first (left top of the t.p.) the work is presumably chiefly (or only) by Gaquère. Cf. "Avant-propos" and cover.
    1. Demoniac possession. I. His Aux prises avec Satan. II. Sutter, P   III. Title. IV. Title: Aux prises avec Satan.

Les possédés de Loudun.

WITCHCRAFT
BF 1517 F5 S26+
Sauzé, J.-Charles, 1815-
    Essai médico-historique sur les possédés de Loudun. Paris, Impr. Rignoux, 1839.
    59 p. 26cm.
    Thèse--Paris.
    "Questions sur diverses branches des sciences médicales": p. [51]-59.
    1. Loudun, France. Ursuline convent. 2. Demoniac possession. 3. Psychical research. I. Title: Les possédés de Loudun.

8 NIC

Les possédés et les démoniaques à Genève au XVIIme siècle.

WITCHCRAFT
BF 1555 L15
Ladame, Paul Louis, 1842-1919.
    Les possédés et les démoniaques à Genève au XVIIme siècle; étude historique de medecine mentale. [n. p., 189-?]
    [156]-220 p. 21cm.
    Caption title.
    Signed: Paul Ladame.
    Detached copy.
    1. Demoniac possession. I. Title.

8 NIC

Une possession au XVIe siècle.

WITCHCRAFT
BX 2340 L28+ 1910
Langlet, Louis.
    Une possession au XVIe siècle; étude médicale de la vie & de l'hystérie de Nicole Obry, dite Nicole de Vervins, 1566. Reims, Matot-Braine, 1910.
    110 p. illus. 26cm.
    Originally issued in the same year as thesis at the Faculté de médecine, Paris, with title: Étude médicale d'une possession au XVIe siècle...
    1. Nicole de Vervins. 2. Exorcism 3. Hysteria. I. His Étude médicale d'une possession au XVIe siècle.

8 NIC

Witchcraft
BF 1555 H67 1886
La Possession de Jeanne Fery, religieuse professe du couvent des soeurs noires de la ville de Mons (1584) Paris, Aux bureaux du Progrès médical, 1886.
    v, 109 p. 23cm. (Bibliothèque diabolique; Collection Bourneville)
    Reprint of Histoire admirable et veritable des choses advenues a l'endroict d'une religieuse professe..., pub. 1586.
    Edited by D. B. Bourneville.
    With facsimile of original t. p.

8
(Continued on next card)

WITCHCRAFT
BF 1555 H67 1886
La Possession de Jeanne Fery ... 1886.
    (Card 2)
    1. Fery, Jeanne, fl. 1584. 2. Demoniac possession. I. Bourneville, Désiré Magloire, 1840-1909, ed. II. Histoire admirable et veritable des choses advenues a l'endroict d'une religieuse professe.

8

La possession de Loudun.

BF 1517 F5 C41
Certeau, Michel de.
    La possession de Loudun, présentée par Michel de Certeau. [Paris, Julliard, 1970]
    347 p. plates. 19 cm. (Collection Archives, 37) 9.00F F***
    Includes bibliographical references.

    1. Demoniac possession. 2. Loudun, France. Ursuline convent. 3. Grandier, Urbain, 1590-1634. I. Title.

4
BF1517.F5C47   76-575412
Library of Congress   71 [2]

Possession, demoniacal and other, among primitive races, in antiquity, the middle ages, and modern times.

Witchcraft
BF 1555 O29 1930
Oesterreich, Traugott Konstantin, 1880-1949.
    Possession, demoniacal and other, among primitive races, in antiquity, the middle ages, and modern times, by T. K. Oesterreich ... New York, R. R. Smith, inc., 1930.
    xi, 400 p. 24cm.
    Lettered on cover: Demoniacal possession.
    Printed in Great Britain.
    "Authorized translation by D. Ibberson."
    Translation of Die Besessenheit.

The possibility and reality of magick, sorcery, and witchcraft, demonstrated.

Witchcraft
BF 1410 B76P8
Boulton, Richard, fl. 1697-1724.
    The possibility and reality of magick, sorcery, and witchcraft, demonstrated. Or, A vindication of A compleat history of magick, sorcery, and witchcraft. In answer to Dr. Hutchinson's Historical essay ... In two parts ... London, Printed for J. Roberts, 1722.
    xvi, [4], 184 p. 17cm.

Witchcraft
BF 1565 D62 no.9
Pott, Johann Heinrich.
    Specimen juridicum, De nefando lamiarum cum diabolo coitu, von der Hexen schändlichen Beyschlaff mit dem bösen Feind, in quo abstrusissima haec materia dilucide explicatur, quaestiones inde emergentes curate resolvuntur, variisque non injucundis exemplis illustrantur, publicâ luce donatum à Johanne Henrico Pott ... Jenae, Prostat apud Tobiam Oehrlingium, 1689.
    72 p. 20cm.

8
(Continued on next card)

Witchcraft
BF 1565 D62 no.9
Pott, Johann Heinrich. Specimen juridicum ... 1689.   (Card 2)
    "Pacta und Gelübdnüss einer ... hohen Person, so dieselbe mit dem leydigen Satan soll haben getroffen," p. [69]-72, has special t. p.
    No. 9 in vol. lettered Dissertationes de sagis. 1636-1714.
    1. Witchcraft. 2. Devil. I. Title: De nefando lamiarum cum diabolo coitu. II. Title: Pacta und Gelübdnüss einer ... hohen Person. III. Title: Specimen juridicum, De nefando lamiarum cum diabolo coitu.

8

Witchcraft
BF 1581 P87
Potts, Thomas, fl. 1612-1618.
    Pott's Discovery of witches in the county of Lancaster, reprinted from the original ed. of 1613. With an introduction and notes, by James Crossley ... [Manchester] Printed for the Chetham society, 1745 [i.e. 1845]
    3 p. l., [iii]-lxxix, [190] p., 1 l., 51, 6 p. illus. 23x18cm. (Added t.-p.: Remains, historical & literary, connected with the palatine counties of Lancaster and Chester, pub. by the Chetham society. vol. VI)

(Continued on next card)

Witchcraft
BF 1581 P87
Potts, Thomas, fl. 1612-1618. Pott's Discovery of witches in the county of Lancaster.(Card 2)
    With reproduction of original t.-p.: The Wonderfvll Discoverie Of Witches In The Covntie Of Lancaster ... Together with the arraignement and triall of Iennet Preston, at the assizes holden at the Castle of Yorke ... London, 1613.
    "The arraignement and triall of Jennet Preston" has special t.-p. with imprint: London, 1612.
    Revised by Sir Edward Bromley.
    1. Witchcraft--Lancashire, Eng. 2. Preston, Jennet, d. 1612. I. Bromley, Sir Edward, fl. 1612. II. Crossley, James, 1800-188 ed. III. Title.

DA 35 T75 v.1
[Potts, Thomas] fl. 1612-1618.
    Trial of Jennet Preston, of Gisborne, in Craven, at the York Assizes, July, 1612; for practising devilish and wicked arts called witchcraft. Reprinted from the original edition printed at the end of "The wonderful discovery of witches in the Countie of Lancaster", 4 to. 1612. London, J. G. Bell, 1851.
    20 p. 19cm.
    "Only sixty copies printed."
    No. 9 in vol. lettered: Bell's rare tracts. Vol. I.
    1. Preston, Jennet, d. 1612. I. Title.

Witchcraft
BF 1581 P87T8 1929
[Potts, Thomas] fl. 1612-1618.
    The trial of the Lancaster witches A.D. MDCXII, edited with an introduction by G. B. Harrison. London, P. Davies, 1929.
    xlvi p., 1 l., 188 p. 1 illus. 21½cm.
    With reproduction of original t.-p.: The wonderfvll discoverie of witches in the covntie of Lancaster ... Together with the arraignement and triall of Iennet Preston, at the assizes holden at the Castle of Yorke ... By Thomas Potts ... London, 1613.
    "The arraignement and triall of Iennet Preston" has special t.-p. with
(Continued on next card)

CATALOGUE OF THE CORNELL WITCHCRAFT COLLECTION

Witchcraft
F
581
.87T8
1929

[Potts, Thomas] fl. 1612-1618. The trial of the Lancaster witches ... 1929. (Card 2)

imprint: London, 1612.
Revised by Sir Edward Bromley.

1. Witchcraft—Lancashire, Eng. 2. Preston, Jennet, d. 1612. I. Bromley, Sir Edward, fl. 1612. II. Harrison, George Bagshawe, 1894- ed. III. Title.

Witchcraft
F
581
.P87

Potts's Discovery of witches in the county of Lancaster.
Potts, Thomas, fl. 1612-1618.
Potts's Discovery of witches in the county of Lancaster, reprinted from the original ed. of 1613. With an introduction and notes, by James Crossley ... [Manchester] Printed for the Chetham society, 1745 [i.e. 1845]
3 p. l., [iii]-lxxix, [190] p., 1 l., 51, 6 p. illus. 23x18cm. (Added t.-p.: Remains, historical & literary, connected with the palatine counties of Lancaster and Chester, pub. by the Chetham society. vol. VI)

(Continued on next card)

Witchcraft
581
.P87

Potts's Discovery of witches in the county of Lancaster
Potts, Thomas, fl. 1612-1618. Potts's Discovery of witches in the county of Lancaster. (Card 2)

With reproduction of original t.-p.: The Wonderfvll Discoverie Of Witches In The Covntie Of Lancaster ... Together with the arraignement and triall of Iennet Preston, at the assizes holden at the Castle of Yorke ... London, 1613.
"The arraignement and triall of Iennet Preston" has special t.-p. with imprint: London, 1612.
Revised by Sir Edward Bromley.

WITCHCRAFT
BF
1558
.G86
1800a

La poule noire.
Le Véritable dragon rouge, ou l'Art de commander les esprits célestes, aériens, terrestres et infernaux, avec le secret de faire parler les morts; de gagner toutes les fois qu'on met aux loteries; de découvrir les trésors cachés; etc., etc.; suivi de La poule noire, cabale qui était restée inconnue jusqu'ici. [Lille, Imprimerie de Blocquel] 1521 [i.e., 18--]
140 p. illus. 16cm.

8   (Continued on next card)

WITCHCRAFT
BF
1558
.G86
1800a

La poule noire.
Le Véritable dragon rouge ... [18--]
(Card 2)
Title in red and black.
Chapter 1 signed: J. Karter, Venetiana.
Published also under other titles: Grimoire du Pape Honorius [best-known]; Le dragon rouge; and L'art de commander les esprits.

1. Incantations. 2. Magic. I. Karter, J. II. Title: Grimoire du Pape Honorius. III. Title: Le dragon rouge. IV. Title: L'art de commander les esprits. V. Title: La poule noire.

8

Witchcraft
BF
1412
.C16

Poupart, François.
Dissertation sur ce qu'on doit penser ...
Calmet, Augustin, 1672-1757.
Dissertations sur les apparitions des anges, des démons & des esprits, et sur les revenans et vampires de Hongrie, de Bohême, de Moravie & de Silesie. Paris, Chez de Bure l'aîné, 1746.
xxxvi, 500 p. 17cm.
Published also under title: Traité sur les apparitions des esprits ... Paris, 1751 [etc.]
"Dissertation sur ce qu'on doit penser
(Continued on next card)

Witchcraft
BF
1412
.C16

Poupart, François.
Dissertation sur ce qu'on doit penser ...
Calmet, Augustin, 1672-1757. Dissertations sur les apparitions des anges ... 1746. (Card 2)

de l'apparition des esprits, a l'occasion de l'avanture arrivée a Saint Maur. Paris, 1707: p. [467]-500, has special t. p., and is attributed to F. Poupart by the Bibliothèque Nationale.

1. Demonology. 2. Apparitions. I. Poupart, François. Dissertation sur ce qu'on doit penser... II. Title. III. Title: Dissertation sur ce qu'on doit penser de l'apparition des esprits.

8

WITCHCRAFT
BF
1555
.P827

Le pour et contre de la possession des filles de la parroisse de Landes.
Porée, Charles Gabriel.
Le pour et contre de la possession des filles de la parroisse de Landes, diocèse de Bayeux [par C.-G. Porée et Dudouet, médicin] ... A Antioche, Chez les Héritiers de la bonne foy, 1738.
275 p. 19cm.

8
NIC

1. Demoniac possession. I. Dudouet, Dr. III. Title.

WITCHCRAFT
BF
1582
.Z7+
1642

Pousinière, Mathurin Trullier, known as l'abbé.
Parfouru, Paul, 1846-1905.
Un procès de sorcellerie au Parlement de Bretagne. La condamnation de l'abbé Poussinière, 1642-1643. Rennes, Impr. A. Le Roy, 1893.
11 p. 26cm.
"Extrait de la revue L'Hermine."

1. Trials (Witchcraft)—Rennes. 2. Pousinière, Mathurin Trullier, known as l'abbé. 3. Marais, Isaac. 4. France. Parlement (Rennes)

8
NIC

R
133
.A92

The "pow-wow" book.
Aurand, Ammon Monroe, 1895-
The "pow-wow" book; a treatise on the art of "healing by prayer" and "laying on of hands", etc., practiced by the Pennsylvania-Germans and others; testimonials; remarkable recoveries; popular superstitions; etc., including an account of the famous "witch" murder trial, at York, Pa., by A. Monroe Aurand, jr. ... containing also the complete collection of remedies and cures in John George Hohman's "Pow-wows, or Long lost friend"; in popular use since 1820. Harrisburg, Pa., Priv. print. by The Aurand press, 1929.
x, 85, [1], 31, [1], xi, 13-64 p. incl. front., illus. 24cm.
(Continued on next card)

R
133
.A92

The "pow-wow" book.
Aurand, Ammon Monroe, 1895- The "pow-wow" book ... 1929. (Card 2)

"An account of the 'witch' murder trial" ... and "John George Hohman's Pow-wows; or, Long lost friend" have special title-pages and pagination.
"Pow-wows; or Long lost friend" was published in 1819 under title: Der lange verborgene Freund, oder: Getreuer und christlicher Unterricht für jedermann.
"This edition of the 'Pow-wow' book is limited to one thousand copies; one hundred signed by the author. This is no. 309."
Bibliography: p. vi.

1. Medicine, Magic, mystic, and spagiric. 2. Superstition. 3. Folk-lore—Pennsylvania. 4. Witchcraft—Pennsylvania. 5. Blymyer, John H. 6. Rehmeyer, Nelson D. 1868-1928. 7. Hohman, Johann Georg. II. Title. III. Title: "Witch" murder trial, York, Pa.

Library of Congress   R133.A8   29-9468 Revised
——— Copy 2.
Copyright A 7294   [29d2]

Witchcraft
BF
1584
.T9
.Z7
1644

Pozza, Juliana de, fl. 1644.
Zingerle, Ignaz Vincenz, Edler von Summersberg, 1825-1892, ed.
Ein Beitrag zu den Hexenprozessen in Tirol im 17. Jahrhundert. Von Ignaz V. Zingerle. [Innsbruck, 1882]
[183]-189 p. 23cm.
Reprint from Zeitschrift des Ferdinandeum, 3. Folge, 26. Heft, 1882.

1. Pozza, Juliana de, fl. 1644. 2. Trials (Witchcraft)—Tyrol. I. Title: Die Hexenprozesse in Tirol im 17. Jahrhundert.

8

WITCHCRAFT
BX
2340
.L95

Practica de conjurar, en que se contienen exorcismos.
Luis de la Concepción.
Practica de conjurar, en que se contienen exorcismos, y conjuros contra los malos espiritus...y contra langostas y otros animales nocivos, y tempestades... Madrid, 1721.
204 p. 16cm.

8
NIC

1. Exorcism. I. Title.

WITCHCRAFT
BX
2340
.N94
1675

Practica de exorcistas y ministros de la iglesia.
Noydens, Benito Remigio, 1630-1685.
Practica de exorcistas y ministros de la iglesia, en que con mucha erudicion, y singular claridad, se trata de la instruccion de los exorcismos, para lançar, y ayuentar los demonios, y curar espiritualmente todo genero de maleficio, y hechizos... Primera impression de Barcelona, añadida por su autor. Barcelona, Por Antonio Lacavalleria, 1675.
431 p. 14cm.

8
NIC

1. Exorcism. I. Title.

WITCHCRAFT
BX
2340
.R38
1678

Practica de exorcistas y ministros de la iglesia.
Remigio, Benito.
Practica de exorcistas y ministros de la iglesia. En qve con mvcha ervdicion ... se trata de la instruccion de los exorcismos, para lançar, y auy entar los demonios, y curar espiritualmente todo genero de maleficio, y hechizos. Por el P. Benito Remigio, noydens Antuerp ... 5. impression añadida ... Madrid, Por Andrés Garcia de la Iglesia, Acostade Francisco Serrano de Figùeroa, 1678.
7 p. l., 361 [i.e., 461] p. 15cm.

8   1. Exorcism. I. Title.

WITCHCRAFT
BF
1559
.P76

[Practica exorcistarum...ad daemones et maleficia de Christifidelibus ejiciendum]
Polidoro, Valerio.
[Practica exorcistarum ... ad daemones et maleficia de Christifidelibus ejiciendum. Patavii, Apud Paulum Meietum, 1587]
2 v. in 1. 15cm.
Title page for vol. 1 lacking; title obtained from British Museum. Dept. of Printed Books. General catalogue of printed books. London, 1963. Running title: Expvlsio daemonvm.

8
NIC

Title for vol. 2: Dispersio daemonvm qvae
(Cont'd on next card)

WITCHCRAFT
BF
1559
.P76

[Practica exorcistarum...ad daemones et maleficia de Christifidelibus ejiciendum]
Polidoro, Valerio. [Practica exorcistarum ...1587]
(Card 2)

secvnda pars est practice exorcistarum. Additional exorcisms in ms. (16 p.) inserted.

1. Exorcism. I. Title. II. Title: Expvlsio daemonvm. III. Dispersio daemonvm.

Rare
K
C287
.P8++
1658

Practica nova imperialis Saxonica rerum criminalium.
Carpzov, Benedict, 1595-1666.
Practicae novae imperialis Saxonicae rerum criminalium pars I.[-III.] ... Editio quarta correctior, cum indice rerum et verborum priore multum locupletiore. Francofurti et Wittebergae, Sumptibus Haeredum D. Tobiae Mevii, & Elerdi Schumacheri, Typis Balthasari Christophori VVustij, 1658.
3 v. 35cm.

For contents see Rare card.

(Continued on next card)

CATALOGUE OF THE CORNELL WITCHCRAFT COLLECTION

```
                    Praesidium angelicum.
WITCHCRAFT
BT        Scultetus, Marcus.
965         Praesidium angelicum. Ein nützlich Hand-
S43       büchlein. Von guten vnd bösen Engeln: vnd
          von derer beyder Wesen, Vhrsprung, Eigen-
          schafften, Ampt, Dienstbestallung vnnd Werk-
          ken gegen Gott vnd der christlichen Kirchen
          in allen Ständen ... Gestellet durch M.
          Marcvm Scvltetvm, Pfarrern zu Seehausen im
          Churfürstenthumb Sachsen. Wittenbergi,
          Gedruckt bey Georg Müller, in Verlegung
          Paul Heiwigs Buchf., 1616.
8           668 p.     vignettes. 17cm.
NIC                 (Continued on next card)
```

```
                    Praesidium angelicum.
WITCHCRAFT
BT        Scultetus, Marcus.  Praesidium angelicum
965         ...  1616.                (Card 2)
S43
            Title in red and black.
            Part 2 has title: Das ander Theil dieses
          Büchleins, Vnterricht von den bösen Engeln.

            1. Angels. 2. Demonology. I. Title.
          II. Title: Von guten und bösen Engeln.
8
NIC
```

```
              Praestigiarum magicarum descriptio.
WITCHCRAFT
BF        Hildebrand, Wolffgang.
1565        Goêtia, vel Theurgia, sive Praestigiarum
H64       magicarum descriptio, revelatio, resolutio,
1631      inquisitio, & executio. Das ist, Wahre vnd
          eigentliche Entdeckunge, Declaration oder
          Erklärunge fürnehmer Articul der Zauberey.
          Vnd was von Zauberern, Vnholden, Hexen,
          deren Händel, Art, Thun ... vnd ihrer Machi-
          nation ... Etwan durch den wolgebornen
          Herrn Jacob Freyherrn von Liechtenberg &c.
          ... erfahren, durch den hochgelahrten Herrn
8
NIC                 (Continued on next card)
```

```
              Praestigiarum magicarum descriptio.
WITCHCRAFT
BF        Hildebrand, Wolffgang.  Goêtia, vel Theur-
1565        gia ...  1631.              (Card 2)
H64
1631        Jacob Weckern M. D. etwas weitleufftiger
          beschrieben. Nun aber an jetzo mit allem
          Fleisse revidiret ... durch Wolfgangum Hil-
          debrandum ... Leipzig, In Verlegung Joh.
          Francken S. Erben vnd Samuel Scheiben Buchh.,
          1631.
            8 p. l., 342, [17] p. 18cm.
            Title in red   and black.
8
                    (Continued on next card)
```

```
WITCHCRAFT
BF        Praetorius, Antonius.
1565        Gründlicher Bericht von Zauberey vnd Zau-
P888      berern; deren Vrsprung, Vnterscheid, Vermögen
1629      vnd Handlungen; auch wie einer christlichen
          Obrigkeit, solchem schändlichen Laster zu
          begegnen, dasselbe auffzuheben, zu hindern
          vnd zu straffen gebühre vnd wol müglich seye.
          Auss göttlichem vnd kayserlichem Recht
          kurtzlich vnd ordentlich gestellt vnd zusam-
          men getragen. Männiglich, sonderlich aber
          den Hohen         vnd Nidern Obrigkeiten,
8         Richtern vnd              Gerichten, zu nohtwen-
NIC                 (Continued on next card)
```

```
WITCHCRAFT
BF        Praetorius, Antonius.
1565        Gründlicher Bericht von Zauberey vnd Zau-
P888      berern...                       (Card 2)
1629
            diger Nachrichtung sehr dienlich vnd nutz-
          lich zu lesen. Jetzo zum vierdtenmal in
          Truck gegeben, sampt einem vollkommenen
          Register. Franckfurt am Mayn, Getruckt
          durch J.-N. Stoltzenbergern; In Verlag J. C.
          Vnckels, 1629.
            174 p. 20    cm.

                    (Continued on next card)
```

```
WITCHCRAFT
BF        Praetorius, Antonius.
1565        Gründlicher Bericht von Zauberey vnd Zau-
P888      berern...1629.                  (Card 3)
1629
            Originally published under title: Von
          Zauberey und Zauberern, gründlicher Bericht.


            1. Witchcraft. I. His Von Zauberey und
          Zauberern, gründlicher Bericht. II. Title.
```

```
WITCHCRAFT
BF        Praetorius, Antonius.
1565        Von Zauberey vnd Zauberern, gründlicher
P888      Bericht; darinn der grawsamen Menschen
          thöriges, feindseliges, schändliches vor-
          nemmen, vnd wie christliche Oberkeit in
          rechter Amptspflege jhnen begegnen, jhr
          Werck straffen, auffheben, vnd hindern
          solle, vnd könne ... Hiezu ist gesetzet:
          Der Theologen zu Nürnberg gantz christlich
          Bedencken, vnd warhafftig Vrtheil von Zau-
          berey vnd He             xenwerck. Heydelberg,
8
NIC                 (Continued on next card)
```

```
WITCHCRAFT
BF        Praetorius, Antonius.
1565        Von Zauberey vnd Zauberern...   (Card 2)
P888
            Gedruckt durch J. Lancellot; In Verlegung
          A. Cambier, 1613.
            334 p. 20cm.



            I. Title.
```

```
              Praetorius, Antonius.
              Von Zauberey und Zauberern,
WITCHCRAFT    gründlicher Bericht.
BF        Praetorius, Antonius.
1565        Gründlicher Bericht von Zauberey vnd Zau-
P888      berern; deren Vrsprung, Vnterscheid, Vermögen
1629      vnd Handlungen; auch wie einer christlichen
          Obrigkeit, solchem schändlichen Laster zu
          begegnen, dasselbe auffzuheben, zu hindern
          vnd zu straffen gebühre vnd wol müglich seye.
          Auss göttlichem vnd kayserlichem Recht
          kurtzlich vnd ordentlich gestellt vnd zusam-
          men getragen. Männiglich, sonderlich aber
          den Hohen        vnd Nidern Obrigkeiten,
8
NIC       Richtern vnd            Gerichten, zu nohtwen-
                    (Continued on next card)
```

```
              Praetorius, Antonius.
              Von Zauberey und Zauberern,
WITCHCRAFT    gründlicher Bericht.
BF        Praetorius, Antonius.
1565        Gründlicher Bericht von Zauberey vnd Zau-
P888      berern...                       (Card 2)
1629
            diger Nachrichtung sehr dienlich vnd mutz-
          lich zu lesen. Jetzo zum vierdtenmal in
          Truck gegeben, sampt einem vollkommenen
          Register. Franckfurt am Mayn, Getruckt
          durch J.-N. Stoltzenbergern; In Verlag J. C.
          Vnckels, 1629.
            174 p. 20    cm.

                    (Continued on next card)
```

```
              Praetorius, Antonius.
              Von Zauberey und Zauberern,
WITCHCRAFT    gründlicher Bericht.
BF        Praetorius, Antonius.
1565        Gründlicher Bericht von Zauberey vnd Zau-
P888      berern...1629.                  (Card 3)
1629
            Originally published under title: Von
          Zauberey und Zauberern, gründlicher Bericht.


            1. Witchcraft. I. His Von Zauberey und
          Zauberern, gründlicher Bericht. II. Title.
```

```
WITCHCRAFT
BF        Praetorius, Johannes, 1630-1680.
1565        Blockes-Berges Verrichtung; oder, Ausführ-
P89       licher geographischer Bericht, von den hohen
          trefflich alt- und berühmten Blockes-Berge.
          Ingleichen von der Hexenfahrt, und Zauber-
          Sabbathe, so auff solchen Berge die Unholden
          aus gantz Teutschland, jährlich den 1. Maij
          in Sanct-Walpurgis Nachte anstellen sollen.
          Aus vielen autoribus abgefasset, und mit
          schönen Raritäten angeschmücket sampt zuge-
8         hörigen Figu           ren ... Leipzig,
NIC       J. Scheiben,             1668.
                    (Continued on next card)
```

```
WITCHCRAFT
BF        Praetorius, Johannes, 1630-1680.
1565        Blockes-Berges Verrichtung...1668.
P89                                       (Card 2)

            582 p. fold. front. 16cm.

            Copy 2 imperfect: pages trimmed too
          closely in binding.

            1. Witchcraft. I. Title. II. Title: Aus-
          führlicher                 geographischer Bericht,
          von den hohen             trefflich alt- und be-
          rühmten Block            es-Berge.
```

```
WITCHCRAFT    Praetorius, Johannes, 1630-1680,
                supposed author.
BT        Monceaux, François de.
960         Disquisitio de magia divinatrice & opera-
M73       trice... Auctore Francisco Moncaejo.
          Francofurti et Lipsiae, Sumtibus Joh. Chris-
          tiani Wohlfarti. 1683.
            184 p. 19cm.
            Date trimmed off by binder.
            Note by G.L. Burr: Is Moncaeus a pseud.
          of Joh. Praetorius? See Rosenthal, Cat. 83,
          no. 204.
            1. Supernatural. 2. Spirits. 3. Magic.
8         I. Praetorius,             Johannes, 1630-1680,
NIC       supposed au            thor. II. Title.
```

```
              Die praktischen Folgen des Aberglaubens.
WITCHCRAFT
BF        Mannhardt, Wilhelm, 1831-1880.
1775        Die praktischen Folgen des Aberglaubens,
M28       mit besonderer Berücksichtigung der Provinz
          Preussen. Berlin, C. Habel, 1878.
            88 p. 21cm. (Deutsche Zeit- und Streit-
          Fragen, Jahrg. 7, Heft 97/98)



            1. Superstition. 2. Witchcraft--Prussia.
8         3. Trials (Witchcraft)--Prussia.
NIC
```

```
              Pratica dell'Uffizio della Santa Inquisi-
Witchcraft      zione.
BX        [Masini, Eliseo] brother, 17th cent.
1710        Sacro arsenale, ovvero Pratica dell'Uf-
M39       fizio della Santa Inquisizione; coll'inserzio-
1730      ne di alcune regole fatte dal p. inquisitore
          Tommaso Menghini ... e di diverse annotazio-
          ni del dottore Gio. Pasqualone. In questa
          4. impressione aggiuntavi la Settima Denun-
          zia fatta dal suddetto padre per li sponte
          comparenti, impressa in Ferrara 1687. e cor-
          retta in alcune cose la parte decima degli
          avvertimenti ... Roma, Nella Stamperia di
                    (Continued on next card)
                    Secular name: Cesare
                        Masini]
```

```
              Pratica dell'Uffizio della Santa Inquisi-
Witchcraft      zione.
BX        [Masini, Eliseo] brother, 17th cent. Sacro
1710      arsenale ...                    (Card 2)
M39
1730      S. Michele a Ripa, 1730.
            [6], 506, [54] p. 23cm.

            Edited by Luigi and Francesco Conti.

            1. Inquisition. I. Menghini, Tommaso,
          17th cent. II. Pasqualone, Giovanni. III.
          Conti, Luigi. IV. Conti, Francesco. V.
          Title. VI. Title: Pratica dell'Uffizio del-
          la Santa Inquisi             zione.
```

CATALOGUE OF THE CORNELL WITCHCRAFT COLLECTION

```
Witchcraft
BF        Pratt, Sister Antoinette Marie, 1878-
1566          The attitude of the Catholic Church
P91        towards witchcraft and the allied practices
           of sorcery and magic.  Washington, D. C.
           [National Capital Press, Inc.] 1915.
               138 p.  23cm.

               Thesis (Ph. D.)--Catholic University
           of America.

               1. Witchcraft.  2. Magic.  3. Catholic
           Church--Hist.          I. Title.
```

```
ar W    Pratt, Sister Antoinette Marie, 1878-
48249      The attitude of the Catholic church towards witch-
no.4    craft and the allied practices of sorcery and magic, by
        Sister Antoinette Marie Pratt ...  Washington, D. C.
        [National capital press, inc.] 1915.
           138 p.  23cm.
           Thesis (PH. D.)--Catholic university of America, 1915.
           Vita.
           Bibliography: p. 125-132.

           1. Witchcraft.  2. Magic.  3. Catholic church—Hist.   I. Title.
                                                              15-21989
        Library of Congress        BF1566.P7
        Catholic Univ. of America  Libr.
```

```
Witchcraft
BX         Prattica dell'Officio della Santa Inquisi-
1710       tione.
M39        [Masini, Eliseo] brother, 17th cent.
1621           Sacro arsenale overo Prattica dell'Offi-
           cio della Santa Inqvisitione.  Genova,
           Appresso Givseppe Pavoni, 1621.
               [4], 319, [40] p.  21cm.

               Title vignette, engraved.

               1. Inquisition.  I. Title.  II. Title:
           Prattica dell'Officio della Santa Inquisi-
           tione.       Secular name: Cesare
                        Masini]
```

```
Witchcraft
BF        Preati, Bartolommeo.
1604         L'arte magica dimostrata.  Dissertazione
P92       di Bartolammeo Preati, Vicentino,
          contra l'opinione del Signor Marchese
          Maffei.  Venezia, Stamperia Remondini,
          1751.
              95 p.  21cm.

              1. Magic.  2. Maffei, Francesco
          Scipione, mar        chese, 1675-1755.  I.
8         Title.
```

```
WITCHCRAFT
BX        Preces et coniurationes contra aëreas tem-
2340         pestates, omnibus sacerdotibus utiles &
I81       necessariae...  [Campidonae] Typis Du-
1680      calis Monasterij Campidonensis, Per Ru-
          dolphum Dreherr, 1667.
              69 p.  14cm.

              Bound with: Locatellus, Petrus.  Exor-
          cismi potentissimi, & efficaces...  Labaci,
8         1680.
NIC           1. Prayers.  2. Benediction.  3.Exorcism.
```

```
          Précis d'histoire sur la ville et les
          possédées de Loudun.
itchcraft
C         Bleau, Alphonse.
01            Précis d'histoire sur la ville et les
87        possédées de Loudun.  Poitiers, Typographie
64        de H. Oudin, 1877.
              246 p.  18cm.

              1. Loudun, France--Hist.  2. Loudun,
          France.  Ursuline Convent.  3. Grandier,
          Urbain, 1590-1634.  4. Demoniac possession.
          I. Title.
```

```
                     Ein Predig von dem Teüffel.
Witchcraft
BF        Althamer, Andreas, ca. 1500-1539.
1550          Eyn [i. e., ein] Predig von dem Teüffel,
A46       das er alles Vnglück in der Welt anrichte.
          [Nuremberg, J. Gutknecht] 1532.
              [14] p.  21cm.

              1. Devil.  I. Title: Ein Predig von
          dem Teüffel.
8
```

```
Witchcraft  Eyn predig vonn den engeln.
BT        Luther, Martin, 1483-1546.
965           Eyn predig vonn den engeln.  Do. Marti.
L97       Luther.  [Nürnberg, Jobst Gutknecht]
1531      1531.
              [8] l.  21cm.

              Title within woodcut ornamental border.
              Signatures: A-B⁴ (last leaf blank)
              Benzing, J.: Lutherbibliographie, no.
          2958.
              Bound by Sangorski and Sutcliffe.

              1. Angels--Early works to 1800.  2. Angels
          --Sermons.  I.  Title: Eine Predigt von
          den Engeln.
```

```
Witchcraft  Eine Predigt von den Engeln.
BT        Luther, Martin, 1483-1546.
965           Eyn predig vonn den engeln.  Do. Marti.
L97       Luther.  [Nürnberg, Jobst Gutknecht]
1531      1531.
              [8] l.  21cm.

              Title within woodcut ornamental border.
              Signatures: A-B⁴ (last leaf blank)
              Benzing, J.: Lutherbibliographie, no.
          2958.
              Bound by Sangorski and Sutcliffe.

              1. Angels--Early works to 1800.  2. Angels
          --Sermons.  I.  Title: Eine Predigt von
          den Engeln.
```

```
             Predigten über die Existenz des Teufels
             und seine Wirkungen, nach Anleitung der
WITCHCRAFT   Versuchungsgeschichte Jesu.
BT        [Lavater, Johann Caspar] 1741-1801.
980           Predigten über die Existenz des Teufels
L39       und seine Wirkungen, nach Anleitung der
          Versuchungsgeschichte Jesu.  Von einem
          schweitzerischen Gottesgelehrten.  Frank-
          furt und Leipzig, 1778.
              146 p.  18cm.

              Ex libris: Joan. Wilh. Dilichmann.
              1. Devil.  2. Devil--Biblical teaching.
8         3. Jesus Christ.  4. Jesus Christ--Tempta-
NIC       tion.  I. Title.
```

```
Witchcraft
BF        Den predikant D. Balthasar Becker, seediglyk
1410         ondersogt so in zyn persoon als Schriften,
B42       ofhy die derst voorgeven, buyten hem alleen,
Z69       de gantsche werelt betovert te zyn, selfs
no.17,    hier af wel vry is, ende dat daar en boven
18        op hem niet soude werken, de geest van
          hovaardye en dwalinge voor ergernisse en van
          de kleine, en van de arme, en van de versla-
          gene van geest, en die beeven voor Godts
          woort.  By een missive den 19 January 1692,
          door H.v.G. van Amsterdam geschreven aan
          D.T.S. de Jonge tot Uytrecht.  Met zyn
                               (Continued on next card)
```

```
Witchcraft
BF        Den predikant D. Balthasar Becker ... (Card 2)
1410
B42           Andtwoord provisioneel tot nader berigt daar
Z69       op gevolgt, den 4. February desselven jaars.
no.17,    Uytregt, Gedrukt by W. Jansz, 1692.
18            32, 36 p.  21cm.

              Signatures: 4°: A-D⁴: A-D⁴, E².
              The Provisioneel Antwoord has special half-
          title and separate

                               (Continued on next card)
```

```
Witchcraft
BF        Den predikant D. Balthasar Becker ... 1692.
1410                                           (Card 3)
B42
Z69       paging.
no.17,    Van der Linde 63, 61.
18        "Extracten van ... De betoverde werelt,
          uytgetrokken en t'samengestelt door N. N.":
          p. 17-28 of the Provisioneel Antwoord; "Ex-
          tract van 'tgepasseerde des Synodi tot Edam,
          10. Aug. 1691. rakende D. Bekker ...": p. 28-
          29; "Articu       len voor te stellen aan
          Do. B.           Bekker" signed Leonardus
NIC                            (Continued on next card)
```

```
Witchcraft
BF        Den predikant D. Balthasar Becker ... 1692.
1410                                           (Card 4)
B42
Z69       Groenewegen: p. 29-31; "Eerste aanbieding van
No.17,    D. B. Bekker, op den 30. Aug. 1691": p. 31;
18        "Articulen tot satisfactie aan de Eerw.
          Classis van Amsterdam, van Do. Balthasar
          Bekker ... wegens ... de Betoverde wereld
          ...": p. 32-36.
              Nos. 17 & 18 in a Collection of tracts
          against            Balthasar Bekker and his
          Betoverde         weereld.
NIC                           (Continued on next card)
```

```
Witchcraft
BF        Den predikant D. Balthasar Becker ... 1692.
1410                                           (Card 5)
B42
Z69
no. 17,
18            1. Bekker, Balthasar, 1634-1698.  De be-
          toverde weerield.  I. Bekker, Balthasar, 1634-
          1698.  II. G., H. v.  III. H. v. G.  IV.
          S., D. T., Jr.  V. D. T. S. jr.  VI. Groene-
          wegen, Leonardus.

NIC
```

```
            Pregiudizi e superstizioni del popolo
            modenese.
Witchcraft
BF        Riccardi, Paolo, 1854-
1775          Pregiudizi e superstizioni del popolo
R48       modenese; contribuzione alla inchiesta
          intorno alle superstizioni e ai pregiudizi
          esistenti in Italia, ecc., ecc.  Modena,
          1890.
              84 p.  illus.  24cm.

              1. Superstition.  2. Folk-lore--Modena,
          Italy.  3. Witchcraft--Modena, Italy.
              I. Title.
```

```
                    Premb,        , supposed author.
Witchcraft
BF        Drey wichtige Fragen über das Hexen-System
1565          von einem gesunden, unverruckten Kopf
D77       disseits der Donau.  [n. p.] 1767.
              24 p.  21cm.
              H. Fieger, in P. Don Ferdinand Sterzin-
          ger, attributes this work to one "Premb,
          Weltpriester."
              1. Witchcraft.  2. Sterzinger, Fer-
          dinand, 1721-1786.  Akademische Rede von
          dem gemeinen Vorurtheile der ... Hexerey.
          I.  Premb,        , supposed author.
8         II. Ein gesu        nder, unverruckter
          Kopf disseits         der Donau.
```

```
            Le premier grand procès de sorcellerie
            aux Pays-Bas.
Witchcraft
BF        Duverger, Arthur.
1584          La vauderie dans les états de Philippe
B4        le Bon.  Arras, Imprimerie J. Moullé,
D98       1885.
              131 p.  19cm.
              At head of title: Le premier grand pro-
          cès de sorcellerie aux Pays-Bas.

              1. Witchcraft--Belgium.  I. Title.
          II. Title: Le premier grand procès de
8         sorcellerie aux      Pays-Bas.
```

CATALOGUE OF THE CORNELL WITCHCRAFT COLLECTION

Les premiers chrétiens et le démon.

Witchcraft
BT 975 L44+
Le Blant, Edmond Frédéric, 1818-1897.
Les premiers chrétiens et le démon. Memoria del Socio Edmondo Le Blant, letta nella seduta del 22 gennaio 1888. [Roma, 1887]
161-168 p. 30cm.
Caption title.
Detached from Accademia nazionale dei Lincei, Rome. Classe di scienze morali storiche, critiche e filologiche. Memorie, ser. IV, v. 3.

8
1. Demonology. 2. Church history--Primitive and early church. I. Title.

WITCHCRAFT
BF 1566 P93
Pressel, Wilhelm, writer on witchcraft.
Hexen und Hexenmeister; oder, Vollständige und getreue Schilderung und Beurtheilung des Hexenwesens. Stuttgart, C. Belser, 1860.
iv, 102 p. 19cm.

8
NIC
1. Witchcraft. I. Title. II. Title: Vollständige und getreue Schilderung und Beurtheilung des Hexenwesens.

Preston, Jennet, d. 1612.

Witchcraft
BF 1581 P87
Potts, Thomas, fl. 1612-1618.
Potts's Discovery of witches in the county of Lancaster, reprinted from the original ed. of 1613. With an introduction and notes, by James Crossley ... [Manchester] Printed for the Chetham society, 1745 [i.e. 1845]
3 p. l., [iii]-lxxix, [190] p., 1 l., 51, 6 p. illus. 23x18cm. (Added t.-p.: Remains, historical & literary, connected with the palatine counties of Lancaster and Chester, pub. by the Chetham society. vol. VI)

(Continued on next card)

Preston, Jennet, d. 1612.

Witchcraft
BF 1581 P87
Potts, Thomas, fl. 1612-1618. Potts's Discovery of witches in the county of Lancaster. (Card 2)
With reproduction of original t.-p.: The Wonderfvll Discoverie Of Witches In The Covntie Of Lancaster ... Together with the arraignement and triall of Iennet Preston, at the assizes holden at the Castle of Yorke ... London, 1613.
"The arraignment and triall of Iennet Preston" has special t.-p. with imprint: London, 1612.
Revised by Sir Edward Bromley.

Preston, Jennet, d. 1612.

DA 35 T75 v.1
[Potts, Thomas] fl. 1612-1618.
Trial of Jennet Preston, of Gisborne, in Craven, at the York Assizes, July, 1612; for practising devilish and wicked arts called witchcraft. Reprinted from the original edition; printed at the end of "The wonderful discovery of witches in the Countie of Lancaster", 4 to., 1612. London, J. G. Bell, 1851.
20 p. 19cm.
"Only sixty copies printed."
No. 9 in vol. lettered: Bell's rare tracts. Vol. I.
1. Preston, Jennet, d. 1612.

Preston, Jennet, d. 1612.

Witchcraft
BF 1581 P87T8 1929
[Potts, Thomas] fl. 1612-1618.
The trial of the Lancaster witches A.D. MDCXII, edited with an introduction by G. B. Harrison. London, P. Davies, 1929.
xlvi p., 1 l., 188 p. 1 illus. 21½cm.
With reproduction of original t.-p.: The wonderfvll discoverie of witches in the covntie of Lancaster ... Together with the arraignement and triall of Iennet Preston, at the assizes holden at the Castle of Yorke ... By Thomas Potts ... London, 1613.
"The arraignement and triall of Iennet Preston" has special t.-p. with imprint: London, 1612.
Revised by Sir Edward Bromley.

La prétendue possession de Marie Volet.

WITCHCRAFT
BF 1555 R47
Rhodes, de.
Lettre en forme de dissertation de M^r. de Rhodes escuyer docteur en medecine, aggregé au college des medecins de Lyon. A monsievr Destaing comte de Lyon; au sujet de la prétendue possession de Marie Volet de la parroisse de Pouliat en Bresse, dans laquelle il est traité des causes naturelles de ses accidens, & de sa guérison. Lyon, Chez Thomas Amaulry, 1691.
4 p. l., 75 p. 18cm.

8
(Continued on next card)

La prétendue possession de Marie Volet.

WITCHCRAFT
BF 1555 R47
Rhodes, de. Lettre en forme de dissertation ... 1691. (Card 2)
Imperfect copy: p. 1-2 (second t. p.?) wanting.
With this is bound Sentimens d'Eudoxe et d'Aristée, sur le dialogue satirique de Mystagogue et de Neophile. 1691.

8
1. Demoniac possession. 2. Volet, Marie, fl. 1690. I. Title. II. Title: La prétendue possession de Marie Volet.

Rare Z 6878 P8 P94
Price, Harry, 1881-1948, compiler.
Short-title catalogue of works on psychical research, spiritualism, magic, psychology, legerdemain and other methods of deception, charlatanism, witchcraft, and technical works for the scientific investigation of alleged abnormal phenomena, from circa 1450 A. D. to 1929 A. D.
(In National Laboratory of Psychical Research, London. Proceedings. London. 25cm. v. 1 (1929) pt. 2, p. 67-422)

(over)

Příchovický, Antonín Peter, Abp. of Prague, 1707-1793.

see

Příchovský, Antonín Peter, Abp. of Prague, 1707-1793.

Witchcraft
BF 1559 G25 Z63 no.5
Příchovský, Antonín Peter, Abp. of Prague, 1707-1793.
Hirtenbrief des hochwürdigsten und hochgebohrnen Fürsten und Herrn Herrn Anton Peters ... an die sämmtliche Geistlichkeit der Prager Erzdiöces im Jahre ... 1775. München [1775?]
31 p. 17cm.
"Nach dem Prager Original."
No. 5 in vol. lettered Gassneriana.
1. Exorcism. 2. Faith-cure. 3. Catholic Church--Pastoral letters and charges. I. Title.

8

Příchovský, Antonín Peter, Abp. of Prague, 1707-1793.

Witchcraft
BF 1559 G25 Z63 no.6
Eines redlichen Protestantens aufrichtige Erinnerung an den Verfasser des Exorcisten in seiner Blösse, den Prager Hirtenbrief betreffend. Frankfurt und Leipzig, 1776.
45 p. 17cm.
No. 6 in vol. lettered Gassneriana.
1. Gassner, Johann Joseph, 1727-1779.
2. Příchovský, Antonín Peter, Abp. of Prague, 1707-1793. Hirtenbrief ... 1775. 3. Der Exorcist in seiner Blösse. I. Ein redlicher Protestant.

8

Příchovský, Antonín Peter, Abp. of Prague, 1707-1793.

Witchcraft
BF 1559 G25 Z63 no.1
Hirtenbrief ... 1775.
Der Exorcist in seiner Blösse. [n. p.] 1776.
40 p. port. 17cm.
No. 1 in vol. lettered Gassneriana.

8
1. Gassner, Johann Joseph, 1727-1779.
2. Exorcism. 3. Příchovský, Antonín Peter, Abp. of Prague, 1707-1793. Hirtenbrief ... 1775.

Prierias, Sylvester, 1456-1527.

see

Mazzolini, Silvestro, da Prierio, 1456-1523.

Prierio, Silvester de, 1456-1527.

see

Mazzolini, Silvestro, da Prierio, 1456-1523.

WITCHCRAFT
GR 830 W4 P95
Prieur, Claude.
Dialogve de la lycanthropie, ov transformation d'hommes en lovps, vulgairement dits loups-garous, & si telle se peut faire; auquel en discourant est traicté de la maniere de se contregarder des enchantemens & sorcelleries, ensemble de plusieurs abus & superstitions, lesquelles se commettent en ce temps. Lovvain, I. Maes, 1596.
72 l. 15cm.

8
NIC
1. Werwolves. I. Title.

Primi tomi miscellanea.

Witchcraft
BF 1815 J62 S28 1570
Scalichius, Paulus von Lika, count, 1534-157
Pavli principis de la Scala ... Primi tomi Miscellaneorvm, de rervm caussis & successib atque secretiori methodo ibidem expressa, ef gies ac exemplar, nimirum, vaticiniorum & im num Ioachimi Abbatis Florensis Calabriae, & Anselmi Episcopi Marsichani, super statu sum um Pontificum Rhomanae Ecclesiae, contra fal iniquam, vanam, confictam & seditiosam cuius Pseudomagi, quae nuper nomine Theophrasti Pa celsi in lucem prodijt, pseudomagicam exposi nem, vera, certa, & indubitata explanatio.
(Continued on next car

Primi tomi miscellanea.

Witchcraft
BF 1815 J62 S28 1570
Scalichius, Paulus von Lika, count, 1534-157
... Primi tomi Miscellaneorvm ... effigie 1570. (Card 2)
Coloniae Agrippinae, Ex Officina Typographic Theodori Graminaei, 1570.
[12], 152 p. illus. 21cm.

Title vignette.

CATALOGUE OF THE CORNELL WITCHCRAFT COLLECTION

Prince, Raymond, ed.
  Bucke (R. M.) Memorial Society.
    Trance and possession states, edited by Raymond Prince. Proceedings [of the] second annual conference, R. M. Bucke Memorial Society, 4-6 March 1966, Montreal. [Montreal, R. M. Bucke Memorial Society, c1968]
    xii, 200 p. illus. 23cm.

  1. Demoniac possession--Addresses, essays, lectures. 2. Trance--Addresses, essays, lectures. I. Prince, Raymond, ed. II. Title.

WITCHCRAFT
BF
1581
A2
G551
  Prior, Moody Erasmus, 1901-
    Joseph Glanvill, witchcraft, and seventeenth-century science... Chicago, 1932.
    167-193 p. 25cm.
    "A part of a dissertation submitted to ...the University of Chicago...for the degree of Doctor of Philosophy."
    Reprinted from Modern philology, v.30, no.2, 1932.

8
NIC
  1. Glanvill, Joseph, 1636-1680. Saducismus triumphatus. 2. Hobbes, Thomas, 1588-1679. 3. Witchcraft. I. Title.

Priscianus.
  Metaphrasis in Theophrasti De sensu.
WITCHCRAFT
PA
4220
.3
.4+
.516
  Jamblichus, of Chalcis.
    [De mysteriis. Latin]
    Iamblichus De mysteriis Aegyptiorum, Chaldaeorum, Assyriorum. Proclus In Platonicum Alcibiadem de anima, atq, demone. Proclus De sacrificio, & magia. Porphyrius De diuinis, atq, daemonibus. Synesius Platonicus De somniis. Psellus De daemonibus. Expositio Prisciani, & Marsilii in Theophrastum De sensu, phantasia, & intellectu. Alcinoi Platonici philosophi, Liber de doctrina
    (Continued on next card)

Priscianus.
  Metaphrasis in Theophrasti De sensu.
WITCHCRAFT
  Jamblichus, of Chalcis. [De mysteriis. Latin] [1516]   (Card 2)

    Platonis. Speusippi Platonis discipuli, Liber de Platonis definitionibus. Pythagorae philosophi Aurea uerba. Symbola Pithagorae philosophi. Xenocratis philosophi platonici, Liber de morte. Mercurii Trismegisti Pimander. Euisdem Asclepius. Marsilii Ficini De triplici uita lib. II. Eiusdem Liber   de uoluptate. Eiusdem
    (Continued on next card)

Priscianus.
  Metaphrasis in Theophrasti De sensu.
WITCHCRAFT
  Jamblichus, of Chalcis. [De mysteriis. Latin] [1516]   (Card 3)

    De sole & lumine libri. II. Apologia eiusdem in librum suum de lumine. Eiusdem Libellus de magis. Quod necessaria sit securitas, & tranquillitas animi. Praeclarissimarum sententiarum huius operis breuis annotatio.
    [Venetiis, In aedibvs Aldi, et Andreae soceri, 1516]
    177 [i.e., 175] numbered leaves. 29cm.
    (Continued on next card)

Priscianus.
  Metaphrasis in Theophrasti De sensu.
WITCHCRAFT
  Jamblichus, of Chalcis. [De mysteriis.] Latin. [1516]   (Card 4)

    At head of title: Index eorvm, qvae hoc in libro habentvr.
    With colophon.
    Provenance: Biblioteo: SS. Me. Novelle.
    Translations by M. Ficino.
    1. Occult sciences. 2. Philosophy, Ancient--Collections. I. Proclus Diadochus. In Platonicum Alcibiadem. II. Proclus Diadochus. De sacrificio. III.
    (Continued on next card)

Problemata Iani Matthaei Durastantis.
Witchcraft
BF
1520
D94
  Durastante, Giano Matteo, 16th cent.
    Problemata Iani Matthaei Durastantis... I. Daemones an sint, & an morborum sint causae, pro theologorum, philosophorum, & medicorum sententiis. II. An uirium imbecillitati iuncta cacochymia per epicrasim curanda sit. III. Et, an rhabarbarum ob lienterian, dysenterian, & astrictionem sit comburendum. Venetijs, Ex officina Stellae, Iordani Ziletti, 1567.
    140 numb. l. 15cm.
8
    (Continued on next card)

Problemata Iani Matthaei Durastantis.
Witchcraft
BF
1520
D94
  Durastante, Giano Matteo, 16th cent. Problemata Iani Matthaei Durastantis ... 1567.   (Card 2)

    Printer's device on t. p. and verso of t. p.
    With this is bound his De aceti scillini ... compositione. Venetiis, 1567.

8
  1. Demonology. 2. Diseases--Causes and theories of causation. 3. Medicine--Early works to 1800. I. Title.

Procedure sur laquelle le pere Jean Baptiste Girard ... [est] été jugez.
Witchcraft
BF
1582
G51
P9++
  Girard, Jean Baptiste, 1680-1733, defendant.
    Procedure sur laquelle le pere Jean Baptiste Girard, jesuite, Catherine Cadiere, le pere Estienne Thomas Cadiere, dominicain, Mre. François Cadiere, prêtre, et le pere Nicolas de S. Joseph Carme Dechaussé, ont e'te' par arrêt du parlement de Provence du 10. octobre 1731 ... Aix, Chez J. David, 1733.
    422 p. 36cm.

    With this is bound Montvalon, A. B. de. Motifs des juges du parlement de Provence qui ont été
    (Continued on next card)

Procedure sur laquelle le pere Jean Baptiste Girard ... [est] été jugez.
Witchcraft
BF
1582
G51
P9++
  Girard, Jean Baptiste, 1680-1733, defendant.
    Procedure ... 1733.   (Card 2)

    d'avis de condamner le p. Jean Baptiste Girard ... [Aix?], 1733.

    I. France. Parlement (Aix) II. Cadière, Mary Catherine, fl. 1730. III. Cadière, Estienne Thomas, fl. 1730. IV. Cadière, François, fl. 1730. V. Dechaussé, Nicolas de S. Joseph Carme, fl. 1730. VI. Title: Procedure sur laquelle le pere Jean Baptiste Girard ... [est] été jugez.

Les procédures de sorcellerie à Neuchâtel.
WITCHCRAFT
BF
1584
S97
L32
  Lardy, Charles Edouard, 1847-1923.
    Les procédures de sorcellerie à Neuchâtel. Rapport présenté à la Conférence des avocats neuchâtelois le 11 avril 1866. Publié par décision de la conférence. Neuchâtel, J. Sandoz, 1866.
    45 p. facsim. 24cm.

8
NIC
  1. Trials (Witchcraft)--Neuchâtel. I. Title.

Procès criminel de la dernière sorcière brulée à Genève.
WITCHCRAFT
BF
1584
S97
Z7
1652
  Chauderon, Michée, defendant.
    Procès criminel de la dernière sorcière brulée à Genève le 6 avril 1652, publié d'après des documents inédits et originaux conservés aux Archives de Genève (N° 3465) par le d^r Ladame. Paris, Aux Bureaux du Progrès médical, 1888.
    xii, 52 p. 24cm. (Bibliothèque diabolique (Collection Bourneville))

8
NIC
    Running title: Procès criminel de Michée Chauderon.
    (Continued on next card)

Procès criminel de Michée Chauderon.
WITCHCRAFT
BF
1584
S97
Z7
1652
  Chauderon, Michée, defendant.
    Procès criminel de la dernière sorcière brulée à Genève le 6 avril 1652, publié d'après des documents inédits et originaux conservés aux Archives de Genève (N° 3465) par le d^r Ladame. Paris, Aux Bureaux du Progrès médical, 1888.
    xii, 52 p. 24cm. (Bibliothèque diabolique (Collection Bourneville))

8
NIC
    Running title: Procès criminel de Michée Chauderon.
    (Continued on next card)

Le procès de Guichard, Évêque de Troyes.
WITCHCRAFT
DC
92
R56+
  Rigault, Abel
    Le procès de Guichard, Évêque de Troyes (1308-1313) Paris, A. Picard, 1896.
    xii, 313 p. illus., facsim. 26cm. (Paris. Ecole des chartes. Société de l'Ecole des chartes. Mémoires et documents, 1)
    Bibliographical footnotes.
    1. Guichard, Bp. of Troyes, d. 1317. 2. France--History--Philip IV, 1285-1314. 3. Witchcraft--France. I. Title. II. Series.

8
NIC

Procès de Joseph Balsamo.
Witchcraft
BF
1598
C13
A2
1791
  Cagliostro, Alessandro, conte di, assumed name of Giuseppe Balsamo, 1743-1795, defendant.
    Procès de Joseph Balsamo, surnommé le comte Cagliostro. Commencé devant le Tribunal de la Ste. Inquisition en décembre 1790, & jugé définitivement par le pape le 7 avril 1791. Avec des éclaircissemens sur la vie de Cagliostro, & sur les différentes sectes de Francs-Maçons. Ouvrage traduit sur l'original publié à Rome ... Liège, J. J. Tutot, 1791.
    iv, 295 p. 17cm.
    Ex libris Arthur Flower-Ellis.

Un procès de sorcellerie à Huy en 1495.
WITCHCRAFT
BF
1582
Z7+
1495
  Tihon, Ferdinand, ed.
    Un procès de sorcellerie à Huy en 1495. [Liège] 1904.
    7 p. 26cm.
    "Extrait de Wallonia. Numéro de janvier 1904."
    Documents from Archives de l'état à Liège. Cour de justice de Huy. Reg. 4, fol. 81 v'et ss.
    1. Trials (Witchcraft)--Huy, France. 2. Packet, Ysabeal, d. 1495. I. Title.

8
NIC

Procès de sorcellerie au bailliage de Vesoul de 1606 à 1636.
Witchcraft
BF
1582
F51
  [Finot, Jules] 1842-1908?
    Procès de sorcellerie au bailliage de Vesoul de 1606 à 1636. [Vesoul, 1875]
    71 p. 23cm.
    Extract from Société d'agriculture, sciences et arts du département de la Haute-Saône, Vesoul. Bulletin. 3. sér., v. 3, 1875.
    1. Trials (Witchcraft)--Vesoul, France. I. Title.

Les procès de sorcellerie au XVII. siècle.
Witchcraft
BF
1571
D33
  Delacroix, Frédéric.
    Les procès de sorcellerie au XVII. siècle. Paris, Librairie de La Nouvelle Revue, 1894.
    328 p. 19cm.

    1. Trials (Witchcraft) I. Title.

453

CATALOGUE OF THE CORNELL WITCHCRAFT COLLECTION

Un procès de sorcellerie au Parlement de Bretagne.

WITCHCRAFT
BF
1582
Z7+
1642

Parfouru, Paul, 1846-1905.
  Un procès de sorcellerie au Parlement de Bretagne. La condamnation de l'abbé Poussinière, 1642-1643. Rennes, Impr. A. Le Roy, 1893.
  11 p. 26cm.
  "Extrait de la revue L'Hermine."

8
NIC

1. Trials (Witchcraft)--Rennes. 2. Poussinière, Mathurin Trullier, known as l'abbé. 3. Marais, Isaac. 4. France. Parlement (Rennes)

Les procès de sorcellerie dans l'ancienne France devant les juridictions séculières.

Witchcraft
BF
1582
F76

Foucault, Maurice.
  Les procès de sorcellerie dans l'ancienne France devant les juridictions séculières. Paris, Bonvalot-Jouve, 1907.
  362 p. 25cm.

  1. Trials (Witchcraft)--France. I. Title.

Les procès de sorcellerie et la suggestion hypnotique.

WITCHCRAFT
BF
1582
T45

Thomas, G
  Les procès de sorcellerie et la suggestion hypnotique. Discours prononcé par M. G. Thomas ... Nancy, Vagner, imprimeur, 1885.
  47 p. 23cm.
  At head of title: Cour d'appel de Nancy. Audience solennelle de rentrée du 16 octobre 1885.
  Half title: Rentrée de la Cour d'appel de Nancy.

8   (Continued on next card)

Les procès de sorcellerie et la suggestion hypnotique.

WITCHCRAFT
BF
1582
T45

Thomas, G   Les procès de sorcellerie et la suggestion hypnotique ... 1885.
                                        (Card 2)

  Includes part of the court's proceedings.
  1. Witchcraft--France--History. 2. Mental suggestion. I. France. Cour d'appel (Nancy) II. Title.

8

Procès de sorciers a Viry, bailliage de Ternier de 1534 à 1548.

Witchcraft
BF
1582
D98

Duval, César, comp.
  Procès de sorciers a Viry, bailliage de Ternier de 1534 à 1548. Documents inédits. Avec introduction par Eloy Duboin. [Genève, 1880]
  [299]-515 p. 23cm.

  From Institut national genevois. Bulletin, v. 24, 1880.
  1. Trials (Witchcraft)--Viry, France. I. Title.

Procès des sorcières en Belgique.

Witchcraft
BF
1584
B4C22

Cannaert, Joseph Bernard, 1768-1848.
  Olim. Procès des sorcières en Belgique sous Philippe II et le gouvernement des archiducs. Tirés d'actes judiciaires et de documens inédits. Gand, C. Annoot-Braeckman, 1847.
  155 p. illus. 24cm.

  1. Witchcraft--Belgium. I. Title. II. Title: Procès de sorcières en Belgique.

Procès pour faits de sorcellerie à la fin du XVIIe siècle.

WITCHCRAFT
BF
1582
Z7
1700

Peyron, Paul Malo Théophile.
  Procès pour faits de sorcellerie à la fin du XVIIe siècle. [Quimper? 190-?]
  11 p. 23cm.

  Signed: Peyron, chanoine.

8
NIC

1. Trials (Witchcraft)--Lesneven, France. 2. Maillé, Louis. 3. La Croix, Anthoine.

WITCHCRAFT
BF
1582
Z7
1619a

Procès verbal du crime détestable de trois sorcières surprinses es Faulx-Bourgs Sainct-Germain des Prez. Ensemble leur interrogatoire ... Paris, Chez Sylvestre Moreau, 1619. [Paris, Imprimerie Motteroz, 1876]
  10 p. 17cm.

  1. Trials (Witchcraft)--France. 2. Witchcraft--Paris.

8
NIC

Witchcraft
BF
1555
P96
1883

Procès verbal fait povr délivrer vne fille possédée par le malin esprit à Lovviers. Publié d'après le manuscrit original et inédit de la Bibliothèque Nationale par Armand Benet ... précédé d'une introduction par B. de Moray. Paris, Aux bureaux du Progrès médical, 1883.
  cxiv, 98 p. 22cm. (Bibliothèque diabolique)
  1. Fontaine, Françoise, fl. 1591. 2. Demoniac possession. I. Moray, B. de. II. Bénet, Armand Eugène, 1858-

---

Processo alla strega Matteuccia di Francesco.

DG
975
T65
R42
no.8

Mammoli, Domenico.
  Processo alla strega Matteuccia di Francesco, 20 marzo 1428. Todi, 1969.
  57 p. illus. 24cm. (Res Tudertinae. 8)

  1. Di Francesco, Matteuccia, fl. 1420. I. Title.

9

Processus Belial.

Rare
BT
980
P16+
1484

Palladinus, Jacobus, de Theramo, Bp. of Spoleto, 1349-1417.
  Consolatio peccatorum, seu Processus Belial. [Strassburg, Heinrich Knoblochtzer] 1484.
  [94] l. 30cm.

  Leaves [1], [93b] and [94] blank.
  Leaf [2a]: Reuerendi patris domini Iacobi de Theramo Compendium nbreue Consolatio peccatorum nuncupatū. Et apud nonnullos Belial vocitatū ad papā Vrbanum sextum con-
                                        (Continued on next card)

Processus Belial.

Rare
BT
980
P16+
1484

Palladinus, Jacobus, de Theramo, Bp. of Spoleto, 1349-1417. Consolatio peccatorum ... 1484.   (Card 2)

  scriptum. Incipit feliciter.
  Leaf [93a] (Colophon): Explicit liber belial nūcupat⁹ al's peccatorum consolatio. Anno dñi M°.ccccxxxiiij.
  Signatures: a-b⁸, c-d⁶, e-k⁸.⁶, l-n⁸.
  Capital spaces, mostly with guide-letters.
  Copinger. Supplement to Hain's Repertorium, 5793; Proctor, 373; Brit. Mus. Cat.
                                        (Continued on next card)

Processus Belial.

Rare
BT
980
P16+
1484

Palladinus, Jacobus, de Theramo, Bp. of Spoleto, 1349-1417. Consolatio peccatorum ... 1484.   (Card 3)

  (XV cent.) I, p. 89 (IB. 1091; Jacobus [Palladinus] de Theramo); Goff. Third census, J-70 (Jacobus de Theramo).

  1. Devil. I. Title: Consolatio peccatorum. II. Title: Processus Belial.

Processus in causa sagarum.

Witchcraft
BF
1565
D62
no.1

Hofmann, Johann.
  Apologia principum, in qua processus in causa sagarum continetur, et maleficorum argumenta refutantur ... a Johanne Hofmanno culmbacensi ... & authoris sumtibus in lucem edita. Erfurti, Typis Friderici Melchioris Dedekindi, 1636.
  [47] p. 20cm.
  No. 1 in vol. lettered Dissertationes de sagis. 1636-1714.
  1. Trials (Witchcraft). I. Title. II. Title: Processus in causa sagarum.

8

Processus wegen des vermeinten Gespengsts in dem Antistitio.

MSS
Bd.
WITCHCRAFT
BF
W792++

Wirz, Bernhard, d. 1705, defendant.
  Processus wegen des vermeinten Gespengsts in dem Antistitio. [Zürich, 1705]
  402 p., [22] l. 34cm.

  Manuscript, on paper, in a German hand. According to G. L. Burr, probably the transcript of the court record.
  Bound in parchment.
  1. Trials (Witchcraft)--Zürich. 2. Trials (Malicious mischief)--Zürich. I. Klingler, Ant   on K., 1649-1713, plaintiff.   II. Title.

Prock, Hans, d. 1610.

MSS
Bd.
WITCHCRAFT
BF
D77

Drey warhafftige grundtliche Zeitungen, die erste von ettlichen Hexen und Zauberin welche hin und wider in Ungern und Teutschland grossen Schaden angericht haben... Beschriben durch den hochgelerten Herrn Nicolaum Binder... Die ander von einem Burger und Thuchmacher der in grosser Unzucht ein zeitlang gelebt ... unnd wie er durch dess Teufels Eingebung 3. Kinder und sein Weib jämmer   licher weiss ermördet.. Die dritte   von Erscheinung zweyer
                                        (Continued on next card)

Prock, Hans, d. 1610.

MSS
Bd.
WITCHCRAFT
BF
D77

Drey warhafftige grundtliche Zeitungen ... 1610 [ca. 1900]   (Card 2)

  Engel... Beschriben durch den ehrwürdigen Herrn Joannem Röseler diser Zeit Pfarrern daselbsten. Erstlich Getruckt zu Tirnau in Ungern nachmals aber zu Freyburg, bey Georg Hofmann, 1610 [ca. 1900]
  [7] l. 24cm.

  T. p. add   ed by scribe: [Kerpffen
                                        (Continued on next card)

Prock, Hans, d. 1610.

MSS
Bd.
WITCHCRAFT
BF
D77

Drey warhafftige grundtliche Zeitungen ... 1610 [ca. 1900]   (Card 3)

  Drey warhafftige Zeitungen. Die erste von etlichen Hexen in Ungern, den 11. October 1609. Beschriben durch Nicolaus Binder. &c. 1610.
  Carnap's manuscript copy.
  "Originaldruck in der Stadtbibliothek zu Zürich. 4 Bl. in 4°."
  Numerals in   the margins indicate the paginati   on of the original.
                                        (Continued on next card

CATALOGUE OF THE CORNELL WITCHCRAFT COLLECTION

Prock, Hans, d. 1610.

MSS Bd.
WITCHCRAFT
BF
D77

Drey warhafftige grundtliche Zeitungen ... 1610 [ca. 1900] (Card 4)

In verse.

1. Witchcraft. 2. Apparitions. 3. Prock, Hans, d. 1610. I. Binder, Nicolaus. II. Röseler, Joannes.

WITCHCRAFT
F
74
S1
P96+

Proclamation concerning what is said to be the oldest dwelling house in Salem Massachusetts: the Witch House, which is to be restored as it was in the year 1692 and to be retained as an everlasting monument to the courageous men who broke the shackles of theocratic authority and paved the way for that freedom of thought which has made this country great. [Salem? Mass., 1945?]
2 l. illus 30cm.

8
NIC

Probably issued by Historic Salem, Inc. (Continued on next card)

WITCHCRAFT
F
74
S1
P96+

Proclamation concerning what is said to be the oldest dwelling house in Salem Massachusetts ... [1945?] (Card 2)

1. Salem, Mass.--History. 2. Witch House, Salem, Mass. I. Historic Salem, Inc.

8
NIC

Proclus Diadochus.
   De sacrificio.

WITCHCRAFT
PA
4220
L3
A4+
1516

Jamblichus, of Chalcis. [De mysteriis. Latin] [1516]

Iamblichus De mysteriis Aegyptiorum, Chaldaeorum, Assyriorum. Proclus In Platonicum Alcibiadem de anima, atq. demone. Proclus De sacrificio, & magia. Porphyrius De diuinis, atq. daemonibus. Synesius Platonicus De somniis. Psellus De daemonibus. Expositio Prisciani, & Marsilii in Theophrastum De sensu, phantasia, & intellectu. Alcinoi Platonici philoso   phi, Liber de doctrina

8

(Continued on next card)

Proclus Diadochus.
   De sacrificio.

WITCHCRAFT
PA
4220
L3
A4+
1516

Jamblichus, of Chalcis. [De mysteriis. Latin] [1516] (Card 2)

Platonis. Speusippi Platonis discipuli, Liber de Platonis definitionibus. Pythagorae philosophi Aurea uerba. Symbola Pithagorae philosophi. Xenocratis philosophi platonici, Liber de morte. Mercurii Trismegisti Pimander. Eiusdem Asclepius. Marsilii Ficini De triplici uita lib. II. Eiusdem Liber   de uoluptate. Eiusdem

8

(Continued on next card)

Proclus Diadochus.
   De sacrificio.

WITCHCRAFT
PA
4220
L3
A4+
1516

Jamblichus, of Chalcis. [De mysteriis. Latin] [1516] (Card 3)

De sole & lumine libri. II. Apologia eiusdem in librum suum de lumine. Eiusdem Libellus de magis. Quod necessaria sit securitas, & tranquillitas animi. Praeclarissimarum sententiarum huius operis breuis annotatio. [Venetiis, In aedibvs Aldi, et Andreae soceri, 1516]
177 [i.e., 175] numbered leaves.

8

29cm.   (Continued on next card)

Proclus Diadochus.
   De sacrificio.

WITCHCRAFT
PA
4220
L3
A4+
1516

Jamblichus, of Chalcis. [De mysteriis. Latin] [1516] (Card 4)

At head of title: Index eorvm, qvae hoc in libro habentvr.
With colophon.
Provenance: Bibliotec: SS. Me. Novelle.
Translations by M. Ficino.
1. Occult sciences. 2. Philosophy, Ancient--Collections. I. Proclus Diadochus. In Platonicum Alcibiadem. II. Proclus Diadoch   us. De sacrificio. III.

8

(Continued on next card)

Proclus Diadochus.
   In Platonicum Alcibiadem.

WITCHCRAFT
PA
4220
L3
A4+
1516

Jamblichus, of Chalcis. [De mysteriis. Latin]

Iamblichus De mysteriis Aegyptiorum, Chaldaeorum, Assyriorum. Proclus In Platonicum Alcibiadem de anima, atq. demone. Proclus De sacrificio, & magia. Porphyrius De diuinis, atq. daemonibus. Synesius Platonicus De somniis. Psellus De daemonibus. Expositio Prisciani, & Marsilii in Theophrastum De sensu, phantasia, & intellectu. Alcinoi Platonici philoso   phi, Liber de doctrina

8

(Continued on next card)

Proclus Diadochus.
   In Platonicum Alcibiadem.

WITCHCRAFT
PA
4220
L3
A4+
1516

Jamblichus, of Chalcis. [De mysteriis. Latin] [1516] (Card 2)

Platonis. Speusippi Platonis discipuli, Liber de Platonis definitionibus. Pythagorae philosophi Aurea uerba. Symbola Pithagorae philosophi. Xenocratis philosophi platonici, Liber de morte. Mercurii Trismegisti Pimander. Eiusdem Asclepius. Marsilii Ficini De triplici uita lib. II. Eiusdem Liber   de uoluptate. Eiusdem

8

(Continued on next card)

Proclus Diadochus.
   In Platonicum Alcibiadem.

WITCHCRAFT
PA
4220
L3
A4+
1516

Jamblichus, of Chalcis. [De mysteriis. Latin] [1516] (Card 3)

De sole & lumine libri. II. Apologia eiusdem in librum suum de lumine. Eiusdem Libellus de magis. Quod necessaria sit securitas, & tranquillitas animi. Praeclarissimarum sententiarum huius operis breuis annotatio. [Venetiis, In aedibvs Aldi, et Andreae soceri, 1516]
177 [i.e., 175] numbered leaves.

8

29cm.   (Continued on next card)

Proclus Diadochus.
   In Platonicum Alcibiadem.

WITCHCRAFT
PA
4220
L3
A4+
1516

Jamblichus, of Chalcis. [De mysteriis. Latin] [1516] (Card 4)

At head of title: Index eorvm, qvae hoc in libro habentvr.
With colophon.
Provenance: Bibliotec: SS. Me. Novelle.
Translations by M. Ficino.
1. Occult sciences. 2. Philosophy, Ancient--Collections. I. Proclus Diadochus. In Platonicum Alcibiadem. II. Proclus Diadoch   us. De sacrificio. III.

8

Proclus Diadochus.

WITCHCRAFT
BF
1598
H55
A1
1532

Hermes Trismegistus. [Poemander. Latin]

Mercvrii Trismegisti Pymander, De potestate et sapientia Dei. Eivsdem Asclepivs, De uoluntate Dei. Opuscula sanctissimis mysterijs, ac uerè coelestibus oraculis illustrissima. Iamblichvs De mysteriis Aegyptiorum, Chaldaeorum, & Assyriorū. Proclvs In Platonicum Alcibiadem, de anima & daemone. Idem De sacrificio & magia. Quae omnia solerti cura   repurgata, ac suo tandem

8

(Continued on next card)

Proclus Diadochus.

WITCHCRAFT
BF
1598
H55
A1
1532

Hermes Trismegistus. [Poemander. Latin] 1532. (Card 2)

candori restituta sunt. Basileae [Per Mich. Isingrinivm] 1532.
480, [3] p. 16cm.
With colophon.
The Asclepius translated by Apuleius Madaurensis; the rest by Marsilio Ficino.
I. Jamblichus, of Chalcis. De mysteriis. Latin.   II. Proclus Diadochus.   III. Apuleius Madaurensis, tr.   IV. Ficino, Marsilio, 1433-1499, tr.   V. His Asclepius.

8

Witchcraft
PA
4220
L3
A4
1577

Proclus Diadochus.
Jamblichus, of Chalcis.
[De mysteriis. Latin]

Iamblichvs De mysteriis Ægyptiorvm, Chaldæorum, Assyriorum. Proclvs in Platonicum Alcibiadem de anima, atque dæmone. Idem De sacrificio & magia. Porphyrivs De diuinis atq; dæmonib. Psellvs De dæmonibus. Mercvrii Trismegisti Pimander. Eiusdem Asclepius. Lvgdvni, apvd Ioan. Tornaesivm, 1577.
543, [1] p. 13cm.
Title vignette (printer's mark)
"Marsilvs Ficinvs ... se commendat": p. 3.

25-19681

Witchcraft
BF
1563
W81++
no.18

A Prodigious & tragicall history of the arraignment, tryall, confession, and condemnation of six witches at Maidstone in Kent, ... July ... 1652 ... Collected from the observations of E. G., Gent. (a learned person, present at their conviction and condemnation) and digested by H. F., Gent. To which is added a true relation of one Mrs. Atkins ... who was strangely carried away from her house in July last, and hath not been heard of since.   London, Printed for R. Harper, 1652. [London, at the British Museum, 1923]
8 p. 16cm.   (Continued on next card)

Witchcraft
BF
1563
W81++
no.18

A Prodigious & tragicall history of ... six witches at Maidstone ... 1652. (Card 2)

Photocopy (negative) 8 p. on 5 l. 20 x 32cm.
No. 18 in vol. lettered: Witchcraft tracts, chapbooks and broadsides, 1579-1704; rotograph copies.

1. Witchcraft--England. I. G., E. II. F., H.

Pröls, Georg, d. 1722.

Witchcraft
BF
1583
Z7
1722

Ausführliche Erzählung des Verhörs und der Hinrichtung des im Jahre 1722 der Hexerey beschuldigten Georg Pröls von Pfettrach in Baiern. Herausgezogen aus den Gerichts-Akten, und begleitet mit kritischen Anmerkungen zur Baierns Aufklärung. [n. p.] 1806.
271, [3] p. 18cm.
Vorrede signed: A**.
1. Trials (Witchcraft)--Bavaria. 2. Pröls, Georg, d. 1722. I. A**.

8

Den Professor J. van der Waeyen, ongelukkig en scandaleus verdeedigt van twee predikanten.

Witchcraft
BX
9479
B42
B11
no.18

Andala, Ruardus, 1665-1727.

Gansch desperaate en verlooren saake van D. Balthasar Bekker, getoont uit de nasnikken en genoegsaame bekentenisse van onmagt en verleegentheid van sijn voesterling ... Tot een volstrekt bewijs, dat D. Bekker deese schrijver aftedanken, en een beter, in de geestkunde bet geoefent, aan 't werk te stellen, of selve de hand aan de ploeg te slaan, of sijn sake ten besten te geven, genootsaakt is.   Franeker, Gedrukt by

(Continued on next card)

455

CATALOGUE OF THE CORNELL WITCHCRAFT COLLECTION

Witchcraft
BX
9479
B42
B11
no.18
    Den Professor J. van der Waeyen, ongelukkig en scandaleus verdeedigt van twee predikanten.
    Andala, Ruardus, 1665-1727. Gansch desperaate en verlooren saake.... 1698. (Card 2)
    H. Gyzelaar, ordinaris drukker der Eed. Mog. Heeren Staten, en der Academie van Friesland, 1698.
    35 p. [p. 36 blank] title and other vignettes, illus. initials. 20 x 15cm.
    4°: A-D⁴, E².
    Apparently refers to a work titled
    (Continued on next card)

Witchcraft
BX
9479
B42
B11
no.18
    Den Professor J. van der Waeyen, ongelukkig en scandaleus verdeedigt van twee predikanten.
    Andala, Ruardus, 1665-1727. Gansch desperaate en verlooren saake ... 1698. (Card 3)
    Den professor J. van der Waeyen, ongelukkig en scandaleus verdeedigt van twee predikanten, voormaals zijne discipulen, pub. 1697.
    No. 18 in vol. lettered B. Bekkers sterfbed en andere tractaten.
    1. van der Waeyen, J. ,ongelukkig en scandaleus verdeedigt van twee predikanten. 2. Bekker, Balthasar, 1634-1698. De betoverde weereld. 3. Devil. I. Title.

WITCHCRAFT
BV
810
G68
    Programma de baptismo diabolico.
    [Gottwald, Johannes Petrus]
    Programma de baptismo diabolico. [Coburgi, Typis I. N. Monachi, 1702]
    [8] p. 21cm.
    Introduction to an oral dissertation.
    1. Baptism--Early works to 1800. I. Title. II. Title: De baptismo diabolico.
8
NIC

Witchcraft
BF
1565
J19
    Prooemium in libellum Plutarchi de defectu oraculorum.
    Jacquier, Nicolas.
    Flagellvm haereticorvm fascinariorvm, avtore Nicolao Iaqverio. His accesservnt Lamberti Danaei de veneficis dialogi, Ioachimi Camerarii in Plutarchi de oraculorum defectu epistola, Martini de Arles de superstitionibus tractatvs, Ioannis Trithemii de reprobis atq; maleficis qvaestiones III, Thomae Erasti de strigibus liber. Studio Ioan. Myntzenbergii edita. Francofvrti ad Moenvm [Impressvm apud N. Bassaeum] 1581.
    604 p. 17cm.

Witchcraft
BF
1598
A27
P96
    Prost, Auguste, 1817-1896.
    Les sciences et les arts occultes au XVIe siècle. Corneille Agrippa, sa vie et ses oeuvres... Paris, Champion, 1881-82.
    2 v. 23cm.
    1. Agrippa von Nettesheim, Heinrich Cornelius, 1486?-1535. 2. Occult sciences. I. Title.

Witchcraft
BX
9476
N8
B42++
    Protest van Balthasar Bekker, S. S. T. D. en predikant tot Amsterdam, ter Synode van Noordholland.
    Bekker, Balthasar, 1634-1698.
    Protest van Balthasar Bekker, S. S. T. D. en predikant tot Amsterdam, ter Synode van Noordholland binnen Alkmaar ingeleverd, den 7 Aug. 1692. Alkmaar, 1692.
    broadside. illus. initial. 32 x 20cm.
    Van der Linde 46.
    With this is bound De betoverde weereld van den hooggeleerden heer, Dr. Balthasar Bekker... [poem. n. p., 169-]
    1. Nederlandse Hervormde Kerk. Synode van Noordholland, Alkmaar, 1692. 2. Nederlandse Hervormde Kerk. Classes. Amsterdam. I. Title.
8

WITCHCRAFT
BF
1557
L39
    Protokoll über den Spiritus familiaris Gablidone.
    Lavater, Johann Caspar, 1741-1801.
    Protokoll über den Spiritus Familiaris Gablidone. Mit Beylagen und einem Kupfer. Frankfurth und Leipzig, 1787.
    84 p. plate. 19cm.
8
NIC
    1. Spirits. 2. Demonology 3. Talismans. I. Title. II. Title: Gablidone.

MSS
Bd.
WITCHCRAFT
BF
P96+
    Protokolle von Hexenprocessen in Flamersheim. [Flamersheim? 1629-30]
    [54] l. 29cm.
    Manuscript, on paper, in a German hand. Leaves numbered as follows: 13-23, 25-29, 32-36, 39, 43, 51-61, 65-75, 82, 84. Followed by 7 unnumbered leaves, badly mutilated.
    Bound in green marbled boards.
    1. Trials (Witchcraft)--Germany. 2. Witchcraft--Flamersheim, Germany.

Witchcraft
B
781
B3
P96
    Province d'Anjou (periodical)
    IVe [i. e. Quatrième] centenaire Jean Bodin, 10 et 11 novembre 1929. [Angers, Société anonyme des Editions de l'Ouest, 1929]
    [359]-478 p. port. 25cm.
    Issued as 4. année, no. 20.
    1. Bodin, Jean, 1530-1596. I. Title.

    Przichowicky, Anton Peter von, Abp. of Prague, 1707-1793.
    see
    Příchovský, Antonín Peter, Abp. of Prague, 1707-1793.

    Przychowicki, Anton Peter, Abp. of Prague, 1707-1793.
    see
    Příchovský, Antonín Peter, Abp. of Prague, 1707-1793.

    Psellos, Constantinus, in religion Michael.
    see
    Psellus, Michael.

    Psellos, Michael.
    see
    Psellus, Michael.

WITCHCRAFT
PA
4220
L3
A4+
1516
    Psellus, Michael.
    De daemonibus.
    Jamblichus, of Chalcis. [De mysteriis. Latin]
    Iamblichus De mysteriis Aegyptiorum, Chaldaeorum, Assyriorum. Proclus In Platonicum Alcibiadem de anima, atq demone. Proclus De sacrificio, & magia. Porphyrius De diuinis, atq daemonibus. Synesius Platonicus De somniis. Psellus De daemonibus. Expositio Prisciani, & Marsilii in Theophrastum De sensu, phantasia, & intellectu. Alcinoi Platonici philosophi, Liber de doctrina
8
    (Continued on next card)

WITCHCRAFT
PA
4220
L3
A4+
1516
    Psellus, Michael.
    De daemonibus.
    Jamblichus, of Chalcis. [De mysteriis. Latin] [1516] (Card 2)
    Platonis. Speusippi Platonis discipuli, Liber de Platonis definitionibus. Pythagorae philosophi Aurea uerba. Symbola Pithagorae philosophi. Xenocratis philosophi platonici, Liber de morte. Mercurii Trismegisti Pimander. Eiusdem Asclepius. Marsilii Ficini De triplici uita lib. II. Eiusdem Liber de uoluptate. Eiusdem
8
    (Continued on next card)

WITCHCRAFT
PA
4220
L3
A4+
1516
    Psellus, Michael.
    De daemonibus.
    Jamblichus, of Chalcis. [De mysteriis. Latin] [1516] (Card 3)
    De sole & lumine libri. II. Apologia eiusdem in librum suum de lumine. Eiusdem Libellus de magis. Quod necessaria sit securitas & tranquillitas animi. Praeclarissimarum sententiarum huius operis breuis annotatio. [Venetiis, In aedibvs Aldi, et Andreae soceri, 1516]
    177 [i.e., 175] numbered leaves. 29cm.
8
    (Continued on next card)

WITCHCRAFT
PA
4220
L3
A4+
1516
    Psellus, Michael.
    De daemonibus.
    Jamblichus, of Chalcis. [De mysteriis. Latin. [1516] (Card 4)
    At head of title: Index eorvm, qvae hoc in libro habentvr.
    With colophon.
    Provenance: Bibliotec: SS. Me. Novelle. Translations by M. Ficino.
    1. Occult sciences. 2. Philosophy, Ancient--Collections. I. Proclus Diadochus. In Platonicum Alcibiadem. II. Proclus Diadochus. De sacrificio. III
8
    (Continued on next card)

WITCHCRAFT
BF
1508
P97
1838
    Psellus, Michael.
    Michael Psellus De operatione daemonum cum notis Gaulmini curante Jo. Fr. Boissenade. Accedunt inedita opuscula Pselli. Norimbergae, Apud F. N. Campe, 1838.
    xxvii, 348 p. 21cm.
    At head of title: Ψελλος.
    Greek text only: Peri energeias daimōnōn dialogos, with notes in Latin.
    1. Demonology. I. His Peri energeias daimonon dialogos. II. Gaulmin, Gilbert, 1585-1665, ed. III. Boissonade, Jean François, 1774-1857, ed. IV. Title.
8
NIC

CATALOGUE OF THE CORNELL WITCHCRAFT COLLECTION

WITCHCRAFT
BF
1508
P97
1615

Psellus, Michael.
⌈Michaelou tou Psellou Peri energeias daimōnon dialogos⌉ Μιχαήλου του Ψέλλου Περὶ ἐνέργειας δαιμόνων διάλογος. Michaelis Pselli De operatione daemonum dialogus. Gilbertvs Gavlminvs Molinensis primus Graecè edidit & notis illustravit. Lvtetiae Parisiorvm, Sumptibus Hieronymi Drovart, 1615.

8 p. l., 153, ⌈7⌉ p. 17cm.

8
NIC

Latin and Greek on facing pages.
(Continued on next card)

WITCHCRAFT
BF
1508
P97
1615

Psellus, Michael. ⌈Michaelou tou Psellou Peri energeias daimōnon dialogos⌉ 1615. (Card 2)

Latin translation by Petrus Morellus, "illius qui & Nicetae Thesaurum orthodoxe fidei de Graeco Latinum fecit."
Fédéric Morel also given credit in introduction for editing.
"Notae ad Michaelis Pselli dialogum," p. ⌈103⌉-153, has special t. p.

8
NIC

I. Morel, Fédéric, 1558-1630.

WITCHCRAFT
BF
1508
P97
1688

Psellus, Michael.
⌈Michaelou tou Psellou Peri energeias daimōnon dialogos⌉ Μιχαήλου του Ψέλλου Περὶ ἐνέργειας δαιμόνων διάλογος. Michaelis Pselli De operatione daemonum dialogus. Gilbertus Gaulminus Molinensis primus Graecè edidit & notis illustravit. E museo Dan. Hasenmülleri ... Kiloni, Sumtibus Joh. Sebastiani Richelii, 1688.

6 p. l., 166 p. 15cm.

8
NIC

(Continued on next card)

WITCHCRAFT
BF
1508
P97
1688

Psellus, Michael. ⌈Michaelou tou Psellou Peri energeias daimōnon dialogos⌉ 1688. (Card 2)

Latin and Greek on facing pages, with notes by Gaulmin at bottom of page.
Latin translation by Petrus Morellus, "illius qui & Nicetae Thesaurum orthodoxae fidei de Graeco Latinum fecit."

8
NIC

1. Demonology. I. Gaulmin, Gilbert, 1585-1665, ed. II. Morellus, Petrus, Turonensis, tr. III. Hasenmüller, (Continued on next card)

WITCHCRAFT
BF
1508
P97
1688

Psellus, Michael. ⌈Michaelou tou Psellou Peri energeias daimōnon dialogos⌉ 1688. (Card 3)

Daniel, 1651-1691. IV. His Peri energeias daimōnon dialogos. Latin. V. Title: Peri energeias daimōnon dialogos. VI. Title: De operatione daemonum dialogus.
VII. Title: Michaelou tou Psellou Peri energeias daimōnon dialogos.

8
NIC

Psellus, Michael.
Peri energeias daemōnōn dialogos.

WITCHCRAFT
BF
1508
P97
1838

Psellus, Michael.
Michael Psellus De operatione daemonum cum notis Gaulmini curante Jo. Fr. Boissenade. Accedunt inedita opuscula Pselli. Norimbergae, Apud F. N. Campe, 1838.
xxvii, 348 p. 21cm.
At head of title: Ψελλὸς.
Greek text only: Peri energeias daimōnōn dialogos, with notes in Latin.

1. Demonology. I. His Peri energeias daimōnōn dialogos. II. Gaulmin, Gilbert, 1585-1665, ed. III. Boissonade, Jean

8
NIC

François, 1774-1857, ed.

Psellus, Michael.
Peri energeias daimonon dialogos--Latin.

WITCHCRAFT
BF
1508
P97
1688

Psellus, Michael.
⌈Michaelou tou Psellou Peri energeias daimōnon dialogos⌉ Μιχαήλου του Ψέλλου Περὶ ἐνέργειας δαιμόνων διάλογος. Michaelis Pselli De operatione daemonum dialogus. Gilbertus Gaulminus Molinensis primus Graecè edidit & notis illustravit. E museo Dan. Hasenmülleri ... Kiloni, Sumtibus Joh. Sebastiani Richelii, 1688.

6 p. l., 166 p. 15cm.

8
NIC

(Continued on next card)

Psellus, Michael.
Peri energeias daimonon dialogos--Latin.

WITCHCRAFT
BF
1508
P97
1688

Psellus, Michael. ⌈Michaelou tou Psellou Peri energeias daimōnon dialogos⌉ 1688. (Card 2)

Latin and Greek on facing pages, with notes by Gaulmin at bottom of page.
Latin translation by Petrus Morellus, "illius qui & Nicetae Thesaurum orthodoxae fidei de Graeco Latinum fecit."

8
NIC

1. Demonology. I. Gaulmin, Gilbert, 1585-1665, ed. II. Morellus, Petrus, Turonensis, tr. III. Hasenmüller, (Continued on next card)

Witchcraft
PA
4220
L3
A4
1577

Jamblichus, of Chalcis.
⌈De mysteriis. Latin⌉
Iamblichvs De mysteriis Ægyptiorvm, Chaldæorvm, Assyriorum. Proclvs in Platonicum Alcibiadem de anima, atque dæmone. Idem De sacrificio & magia. Porphyrivs De diuinis atq; dæmonib. Psellvs De dæmonibus. Mercvrii Trismegisti Pimander. Eiusdem Asclepius. Lvgdvni, apvd Ioan. Tornaesivm, 1577.
543, ⌈1⌉ p. 13cm.
Title vignette (printer's mark)
"Marsilivs Ficinvs ... se commendat": p. 3.

25-19681

Psellus, Michael.

WITCHCRAFT
BF
1508
P97
S97

Swoboda, Karl Maria, 1889-
La démonologie de Michel Psellos (Démonologie Michala Psella) Brno, V komisi knihkupectví A. Piša, 1927.
60 p. 24cm. (Brno. Universita. Filosoficka faculta. Spisy. 22)

At head of title: K. Svoboda.
With summary in Czech.

1. Psellus. Michael. Peri energeias daimōnon dia logos. 2. Demonology. I. Title.

8
NIC

Pseudomonarchia daemonum.

Witchcraft
BF
1520
W64
P8+
1582

Wier, Johann, 1515-1588. De praestigiis daemonum, & incantationibus ac ueneficiis libri sex, postrema editione sexta aucti & recogniti. Accessit Liber apologeticus, et Pseudomonarchia daemonum. Cum rerum ac uerborum copioso indice. Basileae, Ex Officina Oporiniana, 1583.
934 columns, ⌈35⌉ p. illus., port. 26cm.
Contents of De praestigiis daemonum are

8
(Continued on next card)

Pseudomonarchia daemonum.

Witchcraft
BF
1520
W64
P8+
1582

Wier, Johann, 1515-1588. De praestigiis daemonum ... 1583. (Card 2)

same as in 5th ed., 1577. Cf. Allgemeine deutsche Biographie, v. 42, p. 267.
Liber apologeticus, and Pseudomonarchia daemonum each with special t. p.
Colophon: Basileae, Ex Officina Oporiniana, per Balthasarvm Han, et Hieronymvm Gemvsaeum, Anno Salutis humanae M. D. LXXXIII mense Augusto.

8
(Continued on next card)

Pseudomonarchia daemonum.

Witchcraft
BF
1520
W64
P8+
1582

Wier, Johann, 1515-1588. De praestigiis daemonum ... 1583. (Card 3)

Bound with his De lamiis liber. Basileae, 1582.
Binding: blind stamped pigskin; front covered initialed B P I and dated 1588.

1. Demonology. 2. Witchcraft. 3. Magic. 4. Fasting. I. Title. II. His Liber apologeticus. III. His Pseudomonarchia daemonum. IV. Title: Liber apologeticus. V. Title: Pseudomonarchia dae

8

monum.

The psychology of the Salem witchcraft excitement of 1692.

Witchcraft
BF
1576
B36

Beard, George Miller, 1839-1883.
The psychology of the Salem witchcraft excitement of 1692, and its practical application to our own time; by George M. Beard ... New York, G. P. Putnam's sons, 1882.
xx, 112 p. incl. front. 17½cm.
Largely a comparison of the witchcraft trials with those of Cadet Whittaker and Charles Guiteau.

1. Witchcraft — Salem, Mass. 2. Guiteau, Charles Julius, 1841-1882. 3. Insanity—Jurisprudence. I. Title.

Library of Congress   BF1576.B3   11-8994

Püchler, Johann Evangelica M., respondent.

Witchcraft
BF
1565
P71+

Planch, Alexius M   , praeses.
Dissertatio critico-scripturistica de magia diabolica, et magorum prodigiis Exod. 7. coram Pharaone patratis. Una cum conclusionibus ex utroque testamento desumptis, quas praeside P. Alexio M. Planch defendendas suscepere P. P. Chrysostomus M. Ennemoser, et Joan. Evang. M. Püchler ... ⌈Oeniponti?⌉ Litteris Wagnerianis ⌈1767⌉
6 p. l.,   66, ⌈9⌉ p. 28cm.

8
(Continued on next card)

Püchler, Johann Evangelica M., respondent.

Witchcraft
BF
1565
P71+

Planch, Alexius M, praeses. Dissertatio critico-scripturistica de magia diabolica ... ⌈1767⌉ (Card 2)

Diss.--Innsbruck (C. M. Ennemoser and J. E. M. Püchler, respondents)

1. Witchcraft in the Bible. 2. Witchcraft. 3. Magic. I. Ennemoser, Chrysostomus M., respondent. II. Püchler, Johann Evangelica M., respondent. III. Title: De magia diabolica, et magorum prodigiis.

8

The Puritan in England and New England.

BX
9321
B99
1896a

Byington, Ezra Hoyt, 1828-1901.
The Puritan in England and New England. By Ezra Hoyt Byington ... With an introduction by Alexander McKenzie ... London, S. Low, Marston & co., ltd., 1896.
xl, 406 p. 21½cm.
"List of authorities referred to": p. ⌈xxv⌉-xxix.

1. Puritans. 2. Witchcraft. 3. Pynchon, William, 1590?-1662. 4. Breck, Robert, 1713-1784. I. Title.

16-9631

Library of Congress

Witchcraft
BF
1576
P98

Putnam, Allen, 1802-1887.
Witchcraft of New England explained by modern spiritualism ... Boston, Colby and Rich, 1880.
482 p. 19cm.

1. Witchcraft--New England. I. Title.

CATALOGUE OF THE CORNELL WITCHCRAFT COLLECTION

Putnam family.

UNDERGR
BF
1576
B79
 Boyer, Paul S
  Salem possessed; the social origins of witchcraft [by] Paul Boyer and Stephen Nissenbaum. Cambridge, Mass., Harvard University Press, 1974.
  xxi, 231 p. illus. 25 cm.

Pynchon, William, 1590?-1662.

BX
9321
B99
1896a
 Byington, Ezra Hoyt, 1828-1901.
  The Puritan in England and New England. By Ezra Hoyt Byington ... With an introduction by Alexander McKenzie ... London, S. Low, Marston & co., ltd., 1896.
  xl, 406 p. 21½ᶜᵐ.
  "List of authorities referred to": p. [xxv]-xxix.
  1. Puritans. 2. Witchcraft. 3. Pynchon, William, 1590?-1662. 4. Breck, Robert, 1713-1784. I. Title.

16-9631

Library of Congress

Pythonissa Endorea.

WITCHCRAFT
BF
1565
W16
 Waldschmidt, Bernhard. Pythonissa Endorea ... 1660. (Card 2)
  16 p. l., 690, [26] p. port. 22cm.
  Added engr. t. p. facing portrait.
  "Ander Theil ... von den Gespensten ..." has special t. p.
  Title in red and black.
  1. Witchcraft. 2. Witchcraft in the Bible. 3. Ghosts. 4. Endor, Witch of (Biblical character) I. Title. II. Title: Ander Theil ... von den Gespensten.

8

Putter, Nicolaus, respondent.

Witchcraft
BF
1572
D4
K64
1752
 Klein, Johann, 1659-1732, praeses.
  Meditatio academica exhibens examen ivridicvm ivdicialis lamiarvm confessionis se ex nefando cvm Satana coitv prolem svscepisse hvmanam. Was von dem Bekenntniss der Hexen zu halten, dass sie aus schändlichem Beyschlaf mit dem Teufel Kinder gezeuget? Praeside Domino Ioanne Klein ... svbmittit Nicolavs Pvtter ... Vitembergae, Apvd Io. Christoph. Tzschiedrich, 1752.
  48 p. 21cm.
  First published 1698.

8 (Continued on next card)

Pythagoras.

WITCHCRAFT
PA
4220
L3
A4+
1516
 Jamblichus, of Chalcis.
  [De mysteriis. Latin]
  Iamblichus De mysteriis Aegyptiorum, Chaldaeorum, Assyriorum. Proclus In Platonicum Alcibiadem de anima, atq͏̄ demone. Proclus De sacrificio, & magia. Porphyrius De diuinis, atq͏̄ daemonibus. Synesius Platonicus De somniis. Psellus De daemonibus. Expositio Prisciani, & Marsilii in Theophrastum De sensu, phantasia, & intellectu. Alcinoi Platonici philoso phi, Liber de doctrina

8 (Continued on next card)

Putter, Nicolaus, respondent.

Witchcraft
BF
1565
T46
1717a
 Thomasius, Christian, 1655-1728.
  Christ. Thomasii Kurtze Lehr-Sätze von dem Laster der Zauberey, mit dessen eigenen Vertheidigung vermehret. Worbey Johann Kleins ... Juristische Untersuchung, was von der Hexen Bekäntniss zu halten, dass solche aus schändlichem Beyschlaff mit dem Teuffel Kinder gezeuget. Beydes aus dem Lateinischen ins Teutsche übersetzt. Franckfurth und Leipzig, 1717.
  134 p. front. 19cm.

8 (Continued on next card)

Pythagoras.

WITCHCRAFT
PA
4220
L3
A4+
1516
 Jamblichus, of Chalcis. [De mysteriis. Latin.] [1516.] (Card 2)
  Platonis. Speusippi Platonis discipuli, Liber de Platonis definitionibus. Pythagorae philosophi Aurea uerba. Symbola Pithagorae philosophi. Xenocratis philosophi platonici, Liber de morte. Mercurii Trismegisti Pimander. Eiusdem Asclepius. Marsilii Ficini De triplici uita lib. II. Eiusdem Liber de uoluptate. Eiusdem

8 (Continued on next card)

Putter, Nicolaus, respondent.

Witchcraft
BF
1565
T46
1717a
 Thomasius, Christian, 1655-1728. Christ. Thomasii Kurtze Lehr-Sätze von dem Laster der Zauberey ... 1717. (Card 2)
  Translation of his Dissertatio de crimine magiae, J. Reiche, respondent; and of Meditatio academica, exhibens examen juridicum judicialis, by J. Klein (N. Putter, respondent.)
  Johann Kleins Juristische Untersuchung, p. [79]-134, has special t. p.

8

Pythagoras.

WITCHCRAFT
PA
4220
L3
A4+
1516
 Jamblichus, of Chalcis. [De mysteriis. Latin] [1516] (Card 3)
  De sole & lumine libri. II. Apologia eiusdem in librum suum de lumine. Eiusdem Libellus de magis. Quod necessaria sit securitas, & tranquillitas animi. Praeclarissimarum sententiarum huius operis breuis annotatio. [Venetiis, In aedibvs Aldi, et Andreae soceri, 1516]
  177 [i.e., 175] numbered leaves.

8 29cm. (Continued on next card)

Putter, Nicolaus, respondent.

Witchcraft
BF
1565
T46
1717a
 Thomasius, Christian, 1655-1728. Christ. Thomasii Kurtze Lehr-Sätze von dem Laster der Zauberey ... 1717. (Card 3)
  With this are bound Ludovici, Gottfried, 1670-1724. ... Theologicum novae... Coburgi [1718] and Sturm, Johann Christoph, 1635-1703. ... Wahrhaffte und gründliche Vorstellung von der lügenhafften Stern-Wahrsagerey. Coburg, 1722.
  1. Witchcraft. I. His Dissertatio de crimine magiae—German. II.

8 (Continued on next card)

Pythagoras.

WITCHCRAFT
PA
4220
L3
A4+
1516
 Jamblichus, of Chalcis. [De mysteriis. Latin] [1516] (Card 4)
  At head of title: Index eorvm, qvae hoc in libro habentvr.
  With colophon.
  Provenance: Bibliotec: SS. Me. Novelle.
  Translations by M. Ficino.
  1. Occult sciences. 2. Philosophy, Ancient—Collections. I. Proclus Diadochus. In Platonicum Alcibiadem. II. Proclus Diadochus. De sacrificio. III.

8 (Continued on next card)

Witchcraft
BF
1520
B66
P99+
 [Puymaigre, Théodore Joseph Boudet, comte de] 1816-1901.
  Traité de la démonomanie contre les sorciers, par Jean Bodin. [Metz, ca. 1838]
  [169]-184, [236]-256, [307]-324 p. 26cm.
  Extracted from Revue de l'Austrasie, according to the Bibliothèque Nationale.
  1. Bodin, Jean, 1530-1596. De la démonomanie. 2. Witchcraft—France. 3. Witchcraft. I. Title.

8

Pythonissa Endorea.

WITCHCRAFT
BF
1565
W16
 Waldschmidt, Bernhard.
  Pythonissa Endorea, das ist: Acht vnd zwantzig Hexen- vnd Gespenstpredigten, genommen auss der Histori von der Zauberinn zu Endor ... Gehalten in der Kirchen zun Barfüssern in Franckfurt, vnd nunmehr mit nützlichen, auss vornehmer Theologorum vnd anderer berühmten Autorum Schrifften genommenen Anmerckungen vermehret ... Franckfurt, Johann-Wilhelm Ammon vnd Wilhelm Serlin, Gedruckt durch Hieronymum Polich, 1660.

8 (Continued on next card)

CATALOGUE OF THE CORNELL WITCHCRAFT COLLECTION

Q

Quadriga disputationum magico-theurgicarum de conciliatione spirituum.

WITCHCRAFT
BT
960
R53

Richter, David, of Güstrow, praeses.
Qvadriga dispp. [i.e. disputationum] magico-thevrgicarum de conciliatione spiritvvm, oder: Von der Kunst sich mit Geistern bekant zu machen, qvam svb praesidio Davidis Richteri habvervnt Henr. Andr. Mätcke et Georg. Erhard. Hambergervs. Jena, J. B. Heller, 1716.
86 p. 20cm.

8
NIC

(Continued on next card)

Quaestio de strigibus.

WITCHCRAFT
BF
1565
M47
1575

Spina, Bartolommeo.
Reverendi Patris F. Bartholomaei Spinei Pisani ... Qvaestio de strigibvs, vna cvm tractatv de praeeminentia Sacrae Theologiae, & quadruplici apologia de lamiis contra Ponzinibium ... Romae, In aedibus Populi Romani, 1576.
4 p. l., 180 p. 23cm.
Bound with Mazzolini, Silvestro, da Prierio. ... De strigmagarum... Romae, 1575.
1. Witchcraft. 2. Theology, Doctrinal. 3. Ponzinibius, Joannes Franciscus. De lamiis, et excellentia. I. Title: Quaestio de strigibus.

8
NIC

Quatorze histoires prodigieuses.

Witchcraft
AG
241
B66
1567

[Boaistuau, Pierre] d. 1566.
Qvatorze histoires prodigievses de novueau adioustées aux precedentes, recueillies par Claude de Tesserant Parisien. Paris, Chez Iean de Bordeaux [1567]
4 p. l., 278 [i.e. 557] p. illus. 12cm.
Tesserant's fourteen tales, p. 217-278, have caption title: Avtres histoires prodigievses ...
The illustrations are reduced copies of those in author's Histoires prodigievses,

(Continued on next card)

Quatorze histoires prodigieuses.

Witchcraft
AG
241
B66
1567

[Boaistuau, Pierre] d. 1566. Qvatorze histoires prodigievses ... [1567]
(Card 2)

published 1560 by V. Sertenas, Paris.
Introductory letter signed Lyon, 1567, by Claude de Tesserant.

1. Wonders. 2. Monsters. I. His Histoires prodigieuses. II. Tesserant, Claude de. III. Title: Quatorze histoires pro digieuses.

8

Quatre livres des spectres.

Witchcraft
BF
1445
L54

Le Loyer, Pierre, sieur de La Brosse, 1550-1634.
IIII. livres des spectres, ov apparitions et visions d'esprits, anges et démons se monstrans sensiblement aux hommes. Par Pierre Le Loyer ... Angers, G. Nepueu, 1586.
2 v. in l. 22cm.
"Avctevrs allegvez ez Quatre liures des spectres": v. 1, prelim. leaves 3-5.

1. Apparitions. 2. Demonology. I. Title: Quatre livres des spectres.

Library of Congress   BF1445.L4   11-20782

IVe [i. e. Quatrième] centenaire Jean Bodin.

Witchcraft
B
781
B3
P96

Province d'Anjou (periodical)
IVe [i. e. Quatrième] centenaire Jean Bodin, 10 et 11 novembre 1929. [Angers, Société anonyme des Editions de l'Ouest, 1929]
[359]-478 p. port. 25cm.

Issued as 4. année, no. 20.

1. Bodin, Jean, 1530-1596. I. Title.

Quellen und Untersuchungen zur Geschichte des Hexenwahns.

Witchcraft
BF
1569
H24

Hansen, Joseph, 1862-1943.
Quellen und Untersuchungen zur Geschichte des Hexenwahns und der Hexenverfolgung im Mittelalter. Mit einer Untersuchung der Geschichte des Wortes Hexe, von Johannes Franck. Bonn, C. Georgi, 1901.
xi, 703 p. illus. 24cm.

I. Franck, Johannes, 1854-   II. Title.

Quelques mots sur la sorcellerie dans les provinces de l'Ouest au XVIe et au XVIIe siècles.

Witchcraft
BF
1582
C31

Carré, Henri, 1850-
Quelques mots sur la sorcellerie dans les provinces de l'Ouest au XVIe et XVIIe siècles.
(In Société des antiquaires de l'Ouest. Bulletin. Poitiers. 24cm. sér. 3, t. 7 (1927) p. [631]-674)

The question of witchcraft debated.

Witchcraft
BF
1565
W13

[Wagstaffe, John] 1633-1677.
The question of witchcraft debated: or, A discourse against their opinion that affirm witches ... London, Printed for E. Millington, 1669.
128 p. 14cm.

Signatures: A-I⁸.
"... Lovers of lies. A dialogue made by the famous Lucian [translated by Sir Thomas More]: p. 83-128.

Questione de la Strie.

Witchcraft
BF
1569
A2S19

Samuel, Cassinensis.
Questione de le Strie. Questiones lamearuʒ fratris Samuelis de cassinis or. minorum ob. regularis. [Pavia? 1505]
[6] l. 21cm.

Signatures: a⁶.
Colophon (l. 6b): Editum a fratre Samuele de cassinis or. minoɹ ob. regularis die. 6. May anno. 1505.

Questiones lamearum.

Witchcraft
BF
1569
A2S19

Samuel, Cassinensis.
Questione de le Strie. Questiones lamearuʒ fratris Samuelis de cassinis or. minorum ob. regularis. [Pavia? 1505]
[6] l. 21cm.

Signatures: a⁶.
Colophon (l. 6b): Editum a fratre Samuele de cassinis or. minoɹ ob. regularis die. 6. May anno. 1505.

1. Witchcraft. I. Title. II. Title: Questiones lamearum.

The question of witchcraft debated.

WITCHCRAFT
BF
1565
W13
1671

Wagstaffe, John, 1633-1677.
The question of witchcraft debated. Or a discourse against their opinion that affirm witches, considered and enlarged. The 2d ed. ... London, Printed for Edw. Millington, 1671.
198 p. 15cm.

"... Lovers of lies: a dialogue made by the famous Lucian [translated by Sir Thomas More]."
I. Lucianus Samosatensis. Philopseudes. English. II. Title.

459

CATALOGUE OF THE CORNELL WITCHCRAFT COLLECTION

R

R., G., M. A.

WITCHCRAFT
BF
1581
Z7
1712f

The Belief of witchcraft vindicated: proving, from Scripture, there have been witches; and, from reason, that there may be such still. In answer to a late pamphlet, intituled, The impossibility of witchcraft: plainly proving, from Scripture and reason that there never was a witch, &c. By G. R., A.M. London, Printed for J. Baker, 1712.
40 p. 19cm.
Sometimes attributed to F. Bragge.

8   (Continued on next card)

Witchcraft
BF
1410
B42
Z56
v.3
no.20

R., L.

De Volmaakte kragt Godts verheerlykt. Nevens eenige aanmerkinge over de drie predikatien van Do. Petrus Schaak. Gedaan over Psal. 72: v. 18. Gen 18: v. 1,2... en Gen. 32: v. 24, 25. In haar eigen gronden ondersogt, en met de waarheid vergeleken. En eenige andere aanmerkingen daar by gevoegd. Amsterdam, By D. vanden Dalen, boekverkooper, 1691.
47 p. [p. 48 blank] title and other vignettes, illus. initial. 19 x 15cm.
4°: A-F4.
Black letter. (Continued on next card)

Witchcraft
BF
1410
B42
Z56
v.3
no.20

R., L.

De Volmaakte kragt Godts verheerlykt. 1691. (Card 2)
Preface signed: J: P. L: R.
Supports B. Bekker against Schaak's attacks on Bekker's De betoverde weereld.
Van der Linde 145.
No. 20 in vol. lettered Bekker III.

R. B.

WITCHCRAFT
BF
1501
C95

[Crouch, Nathaniel] 1632?-1725?
Wonderful prodigies of judgment and mercy: discovered in above three hundred memorable histories, containing I. Dreadful judgments upon atheists, perjured wretches, blasphemers ... II. The miserable ends of divers magicians, witches, conjurers, &c. with several strange apparitions. III. Remarkable presages of approaching death ... IV. The wicked lives, and woful deaths of wretched popes, apostates, and desperate

8   (Continued on next card)

R. B.

WITCHCRAFT
BF
1501
C95

[Crouch, Nathaniel] Wonderful prodigies of judgment and mercy ... 1682. (Card 2)
persecutors. V. Fearful judgments upon cruel tyrants, murderers, &c. ... VI. Admirable deliverances from imminent dangers ... VII. Divine goodness to penitents, with the dying thoughts of several famous men concerning a future state after this life. Imparti ally collected from antient

8   (Continued on next card)

R. B.

WITCHCRAFT
BF
1501
C95

[Crouch, Nathaniel] 1632?-1725? Wonderful prodigies of judgment and mercy ... 1682. (Card 3)
and modern authors ... By R. B. author of the History of the wars of England, and the Remarks of London, etc. London, Printed for Nath. Crouch, 1682.
2 p. l., 233, [3] p. illus. 15cm.
With added engr. t. p.
With armorial book plate: Hugh Cecil Earl of Lons   dale.

8   (Continued on next card)

R. B.

WITCHCRAFT
BF
1501
C95

[Crouch, Nathaniel] 1632?-1725? Wonderful prodigies of judgment and mercy ... 1682. (Card 4)

Wing C7361.

1. Devil--Collections. 2. Reward (Theology) 3. Marvelous, The. I. The author of the History of the wars of England. II. R. B. III. B., R. IV. Title.

8

R. G.

Witchcraft
BF
1546
G48

[Gilpin, Richard]
Daemonologia sacra: or, A treatise of Satans temptations ... By R. G. ... London, Printed by J. D. for R. Randel and P. Maplisden, 1677.
3 pts. in 1 v. 20cm.

1. Devil. I. Title. II. Title: Satans temptations. III. G., R. IV. R. G.

R. G., M. D.

WITCHCRAFT
BF
1405
L85
1673

Longinus, Caesar, ed.
Trinum magicum, sive Secretorum magicorum opus ... Editum à Caesare Longino philos. Francofurti, Sumptibus Jacobi Gothofredi Seyleri, 1673.
12 p. l., 498 p. 14cm.
Contents.--Marci Antonii Zimarae Tractatus magicus.--Appendix, De mirandis quibusdam naturali magia factis operationibus. Ex lib. 2. Mag. nat. Ioan. Bapt. Port.--Tractatvs De virtutibus quarundam herbarum,

8   (Continued on next card)

R. G., M. D.

WITCHCRAFT
BF
1405
L85
1673

Longinus, Caesar, ed. Trinum magicum ... 1673. (Card 2)
lapidum & animalium. A. M. A.--Commentatio De magnetica curatione vulnerum citra svperstitionem ... Authore R. G. M. D.--Logia, sive Oracvla Zoroastri ex Platonicorum libris collecta.--Tractatus De proprii cujusqve nati daemonis inqvisitione.
Layout of text corresponds to that of Frankfurt, 1630 ed. (C. Eifrid, printer)

8   (Continued on next card)

Raabin, Susanna, b. 1666.

MSS
Bd.
WITCHCRAFT
BF
F93

Fronmüller, Johann Christoph.
Die auss Gottes Zulass von dem abgesagten Gottes und Menschen-Feind, dem leidigen Teuffel eine geraume Zeit leiblich-besessene, und übel-geklagte, allein durch Gottes Gnade auf fleissiges Gebet vieler fromm Christen von der leiblichen Besitzung widerum befreÿdte ... Susanna Raabin. ...Theils auss den Actis, theils aber auss der Erfahrung selbsten zusamm getragen von Johann Christoff Fronmüller. 1696-[1703]
[1] l., 116 p. 18cm.
(Continued on next card)

Raabin, Susanna, b. 1666.

MSS
Bd.
WITCHCRAFT
BF
F93

Fronmüller, Johann Christoph. Die auss Gottes Zulass ... leiblich-besessene ... Susanna Raabin. 1696-[1703] (Card 2)
Manuscript, on paper, in a German hand.
Added leaf before t. p.: "Die Kÿrchendiener, welche auf Verordnung der hohen Obrigkeit die Susanna Raabin besuchten sind folgende ..."
Line frame on each page.
Bound in marbled boards.
1. Raabin, Susanna, b. 1666. 2. Demoniac possession. I. Title: Die auss Gottes Zulass... leiblich-besessene ... Susanna Raabin.

Witchcraft
BF
1520
R12

Rabener, Justus Gotthart, respondent.
Dissertatio philologica secunda de daemonibus, quam ... defendet M. Justus Gotthart Rabener ... Lipsiae, Literis Christiani Goezi [1707]
[40] p. 21cm.

First Dissertatio philologica de daemonibus published 1706.

8   1. Demonology. 2. De potentia, operationibus & cultus daemonum. I. Title. II. Title: De daemonibus.

Rabenius, Nils, 1648-1717.

Witchcraft
PT
9850
Z47
1846

Zeipel, Carl von
Karl XI. [i.e., der Elfte], Rabenius und der Hexenprozess. Historischer Roman von Carl von Zeipel. Aus dem Schwedischen übersetzt von G. Fink. Stuttgart, Franckh, 1846.
2 v. in 1. 14cm. (Das belletristische Ausland, hrsg. Carl Spindler, 671.-679. Bd.)
1. Rabenius, Nils, 1648-1717. 2. Witchcraft--Fiction. 3. Karl XI, King of Sweden, 1655-1697--Fiction. I. Title.

8

Witchcraft
BF
1410
B42
Z56
v.3
no.21

Rabus, Petrus, 1660-1702.
Ernstige en zedige verantwoording van P. Rabus, tegen de lasteringen des remonstrantsche prediger J. Molinaeus. Rotterdam, By P. Boekenes, boekverkooper, 1692.
1 p. l., 24 p. title and end page vignettes, illus. initial. 20x16cm.
4°: π1, A-C4.
Black letter.
In defense of Balthasar Bekker.
Van der Linde 135.
No. 21 in vol. lettered Bekker III.
(Continued on next card)

460

CATALOGUE OF THE CORNELL WITCHCRAFT COLLECTION

Witchcraft
Rabus, Petrus, 1660-1702. Ernstige en zedige verantwoording ... 1692. (Card 2)

1. Molinaeus, Johannes, d. 1702. 2. Bekker, Balthasar, 1634-1698. I. Title.

Witchcraft
BF
1566
R15
Raiponce, Léon.
Étude sur la sorcellerie. Dour, Typographie A. Vaubert, 1894.
105, [1] p. 19cm.

1. Witchcraft. 2. Witchcraft—France. I. Title.

Witchcraft
BF
1566
S968
Rannsakningarna om trolldomen i Bohuslän 1669-1672.
Svenungsson, Lars Manfred, 1889–
Rannsakningarna om trolldomen i Bohuslän 1669-1672. [Uddevalla, Sweden, Barneviks Tryckeri, 1970]
339 p. 23cm.

1. Witchcraft—Hist. I. Title.

NIC

Witchcraft
Rachel Dyer: a North American story.
Neal, John, 1793-1876.
Rachel Dyer: a North American story. By John Neal. Portland [Me.] Shirley and Hyde, 1828.
xx, [21]-276 p. 19cm.

1. Witchcraft—New England—Fiction. I. Title.

Library of Congress   PZ3.N252R   7-33170†

Rais, Gilles de Laval, seigneur de, 1404-1440.
Witchcraft
DC
102
.8
R2
V77
Vincent, Louis, 1876–
Gilles de Rais: the original Bluebeard, by A. L. Vincent & Clare Binns, introduction by M. Hamblin Smith ... London, A. M. Philpot, ltd., 1926.
2 p. l., 3-221, [1] p. illus., plates, 2 port. (incl. front.) 19½ cm.
"Genealogy of Gilles de Rais": p. 199-202.
"List of works consulted": p. 217-221.

1. Rais, Gilles de Laval, seigneur de, 1404-1440. I. Binns, Clare, joint author. II. Title.

Library of Congress   DC102.8.R2V6   27-18294 Revised
[r31c2]   8

Raphael, archangel.

Witchcraft
BF
1623
A4
M61
Meyssonnier, Lazare, 1602-1672.
La philosophie des anges, contenant l'art de se rendre les bons esprits familiers. Avec l'histoire de S. Raphael, oeuure necessaire à tous ceux qui aspirent à la vie angelique. Par L. Meyssonnier. Lyon, Chez Pierre Compagnon, 1648.
8 p. l., 337, [3] p. 18cm.

1. Magic. 2. Angels. 3. Raphael, archangel. I. Title.

8

Rätel, Heinrich, tr.
WITCHCRAFT
340
94
Vom Exorcismo. Das dieser ohne Verletzung des Gewissens bey der Tauffe wol mag gebraucht vnd behalten werden: etliche Tractetlein. I. Iusti Menij. II. Lutheri Vorrede vber das Tauffbüchlein. III. Die gewönliche Gebet bey der Tauffe im Stifft vnd der Thumkirchen zu Cölln an der Sprew. IIII. Aus dem Appendice D. Vrbani Regij. V. Zwo Episteln Tilemanni Heshusij. VI. Eine Epistel Philippi Melanchton is. VII. D. Iacobi Co—
(Continued on next card)

Ranfaing, Elisabeth de, 1592-1649.
WITCHCRAFT
BF
1517
F5
P59
Pichard, Remy.
[Admirable vertu des saincts exorcismes sur les princes d'enfer possédants réellement vertueuse demoiselle Elisabeth de Ranfaing, avec ses justifications contre les ignorances et les calomnies de F. Claude Pithoys. Nancy, Par Sébastien Philippe, 1622]
674, 105 p. 14cm.

T.p. lacking. Handwritten t.p. substituted.

8
NIC   Bound in   after chapter 17 are
(Continued on next card)

Witchcraft
BF
1584
A93
R22
Rapp, Ludwig.
Die Hexenprozesse und ihre Gegner aus Tirol. Ein Beitrag zur Kulturgeschichte. Innsbruck, Wagner'schen Universitäts-Buchhandlung, 1874.
iv, 180 p. 18cm.

8

Rätel, Heinrich, tr.
WITCHCRAFT
340
94
Vom Exorcismo ... 1591. (Card 2)
leri Büchlein. Alles zu guter Nachrichtung den einfeltigen Leyen zum besten zusammen bracht. [Franckfurt an der Oder. In Verlegung Johan vnd Friderich Hartmans, 1591.
[269] p. 17cm.
Title in red and black.
With colophon: Gedruckt zu Franckfurt an der Oder, durch Nicolaum Voltzen, 1591.
(Continued on next card)

Ranfaing, Elisabeth de, 1592-1649.
WITCHCRAFT
BF
1517
F5
P59
Pichard, Remy. [Admirable vertu des saincts exorcismes...1622] (Card 2)
what appear to be the preface and table of contents of Stimuli virtutum adolescentiae Christianae, by Guglielmo Baldesano [considered by Bibliothèque nationale to be the pseudonym of Bernardino Rosignolo] The work itself is not in the vol.
The 105 pages at end consist of a reprint of Claude Pithoys' La descouverture des faux pos   sédez...la conférence
(Continued on next card)

Witchcraft
BF
1584
A93
R22
1891
Rapp, Ludwig.
Die Hexenprozesse und ihre Gegner in Tirol. 2. verm. Aufl. Mit dem Bildnisse Tartarotti's. Brixen, A. Wegner, 1891.
iv, 170 p. pot. 22cm.
First published 1874 with title: Die Hexenprozesse und ihre Gegner aus Tirol.
1. Witchcraft—Austria. 2. Trials (Witchcraft)—Austria. 3. Tanner, Adam, 1572-1632. 4. Tartarotti, Girolamo, 1706-1761. 5. Ster   zinger, Ferdinand, 1721-
8   1786. I. Ti   tle.

Rätel, Heinrich, tr.
WITCHCRAFT
340
94
Vom Exorcismo ... 1591. (Card 3)
Vom Exorcismo, oder Von dem Beschweren der Kinder bey der Tauffe. Drey Sendbriefe deren zwene D. Tilemannvs Heshvsivs: den dritten Herr Philippvs Melanchton geschrieben ... Verdeutscht durch Heinrich Rätel, has special t. p. with date 1590.
Vom Exorcismo bey der Tauffe ... durch Jacobum Colerum D. has special t. p., no date.
(Continued on next card)

Ranfaing, Elisabeth de, 1592-1649.
WITCHCRAFT
BF
1517
F5
P59
Pichard, Remy. [Admirable vertu des saincts exorcismes...1622] (Card 3)
...touchant la prétendue possédée de Nancy [the work to which Pichard is replying] and chapter 18 of the Admirable vertu des saincts exorcismes.
1. Demoniac possession. 2. Exorcism. 3. Ranfaing, Elisabeth de, 1592-1649. 4. Pithois, Claude, 1587-1676. La descouverture des faux possé   dez... I. Pithois, Claude, 1587-   1676. La descouverture des faux pos   sédez... II. Title.

Ráth Végh, István, 1870-1959.
Az emberek butításának történetéböl—
Witchcraft   English.
BF
1418
H9
R23
1963
Ráth Végh, István, 1870-1959.
From the history of human folly. [Translated from the Hungarian by Zsuzsanna Horn. Budapest] Corvina [1963]
288, [1] p. 21cm.
Translation of his Az emberek butításának történetéböl.
"The translation has been revised by Elisabeth West."
(Continued on next card)

Ragionamento del padre Giorgio Gaar, della Compagnia di Gesu', fatto avanti al rogo di Maria Renata ...
Witchcraft
683
49a
Gaar, Georg, b. 1702.
Ragionamento del padre Giorgio Gaar, della Compagnia di Gesu', fatto avanti al rogo di Maria Renata, strega abbruciata in Erbipoli a' 21. di Giugno del corrente anno 1749. Tradotto del Tedesco nell' Italiano dal Dr. F. A. T. [Girolamo Tartarotti] Con alcune annotazioni critiche. Verona, Per D. Ramanzini [1749]
23 p. 24cm.
(Continued on next card)

Ranfaing, Elisabeth de, 1592-1649—
Fiction.
PQ
2625
A437
T8
Mallet-Joris, Françoise, 1930–
Trois âges de la nuit, histoires de sorcellerie [par] Françoise Mallet-Joris. Paris, B. Grasset, 1968.
377 p. 21cm.

1. Chantraine, Anne de—Fiction. 2. Ranfaing, Elisabeth de, 1592-1649—Fiction. 3. Harvilliers, Jeanne—Fiction. I. Title.

Witchcraft
BF
1418
H9
R23
1963
Ráth Végh, István, 1870-1959.
From the history of human folly. [Translated from the Hungarian by Zsuzsanna Horn. Budapest] Corvina [1963]
288, [1] p. 21cm.
Translation of his Az emberek butításának történetéböl.
"The translation has been revised by Elisabeth West."
(Continued on next card)

8

CATALOGUE OF THE CORNELL WITCHCRAFT COLLECTION

Witchcraft
BF 1418 H9 R23 1963
Ráth Végh, Istvan, 1870-1959. From the history of human folly. [1963] (Card 2)
1. Occult sciences—Hist. 2. Medicine, Magic, mystic, and spagiric. 3. Witchcraft—Hist. 4. Superstition. I. His Az emberek butításának történetéből—English. II. Title.

Witchcraft
BF 1583 R24
Rautert, Fr , ed.
Etwas Näheres über die Hexen-Prozesse der Vorzeit, aus authentischer Quelle von Fr. Rautert. Essen, Gedruckt bei G. D. Bädeker, 1827.
4 p. l., 79, [1] p. 22cm.
"Die Zeichnung für den Umschlag [ist] nach alten Holzschnitten aus dem 15ten und 16ten Jahrhundert."
Caption title: Hexen-Prozesse der Vorzeit.
8
1. Trials (Witchcraft)—Germany.
I. Title. II. Title: Hexen-Prozesse der Vorzeit.

Witchcraft
BF 1576 T17
Tapley, Charles Sutherland, 1899-
Rebecca Nurse, saint but witch victim, by Charles Sutherland Tapley. Boston, Mass., Marshall Jones company [1930]
xiii, 105 p. front. (port.) plates. 20cm.

1. Nurse, Mrs. Rebecca (Towne) 1621-1692. 2. Witchcraft—Salem, Mass. I. Title.

Library of Congress   BF1576.T23   30-33553
Copyright A 31490

The rational history of apparitions.
Witchcraft
BF 1052 B85 1853
Brierre de Boismont, Alexandre Jacques François, 1798-1881.
Hallucinations: or, The rational history of apparitions, visions, dreams, ecstasy, magnetism, and somnambulism. By A. Brierre de Boismont ... 1st American, from the 2d enl. and improved Paris ed. Philadelphia, Lindsay and Blakiston, 1853.
xx, [17]-553 p. 20cm.

A razor for a goat.
Witchcraft
BF 1566 R79
Rose, Elliot.
A razor for a goat; a discussion of certain problems in the history of witchcraft and diabolism. [Toronto] University of Toronto Press [1962]
257 p. 24 cm.
Includes bibliography.

1. Witchcraft. 2. Devil. I. Title.
BF1566.R6   133.4   62-3328 ‡
Library of Congress   [1]

Rebenstock, Heinrich Peter, tr.
Witchcraft
BF 1520 W64 P8++ 1586
Wier, Johann, 1515-1588.
De lamiis. Das ist: Von Teuffelsgespenst Zauberern vnd Gifftbereytern, kurtzer doch gründtlicher Bericht ... Sampt einem angehängten kleinen Tractätlein von dem falschen vnd erdichten Fasten ... in vnsere gemeine teutsche Sprache gebracht, durch Henricum Petrum Rebenstock ... Franckfort [sic] am Mayn, Gedruckt durch Nicolaum Basseum, 1586.
6 p. l., 90, [8] p. 34cm.
Title in red and black.
8
(Continued on next card)

Witchcraft
BF 1583 R23+
Raumer, Georg Wilhelm von, 1800-1856.
Actenmässige Nachrichten von Hexenprozessen und Zaubereien in der Mark Brandenburg vom sechzehnten bis ins achtzehnte Jahrhundert.
(In Märkische Forschungen (Verein für Geschichte der Mark Brandenburg) Berlin. 26cm. 1. Bd. (1841) p. [236]-265)
1. Witchcraft—Germany. 2. Trials (Witchcraft)—Germany. I. Märkische Forschungen (Verein für Geschichte der Mark Brandenburg) II. Title.

The real crime of witchcraft.
Witchcraft
BF 1566 R63
Robbins, Rossell Hope, 1912-
The real crime of witchcraft.
(In California monthly. Berkeley. 28cm. v. 76 (1966), p. 4-7)
Inscribed by the author to Cornell.
1. Inquisition. I. Title.

Rebenstock, Heinrich Peter, tr.
Witchcraft
BF 1520 W64 P8++ 1586
Wier, Johann, 1515-1588. De lamiis. Das ist: Von Teuffelsgespenst ... 1586.
(Card 2)
Originally published 1577 in Latin as an epitome of his De praestigiis daemonum. Cf. Allgemeine deutsche Biographie, v. 42, p. 267.
Bound with his De praestigiis daemonum. Von Teuffelsgespenst, Zauberern vnd Gifftbereytern. Franckfurt am Mayn,
8
(Continued on next card)

Raupach, Ernst, 1784-1852.
see
Raupach, Ernst Benjamin Salomon, 1784-1852.

Réalité de la magie et des apparitions.
WITCHCRAFT
BF 1503 C69 S61
[Simonnet, P. B.]
Réalité de la magie et des apparitions, ou Contrepoison du Dictionnaire infernal. Ouvrage dans lequel on prouve, par une multitude de faits et d'anecdotes authentiques ... l'existence des sorciers, la certitude des apparitions, la foi due aux miracles, la vérité des possessions, etc., ... précédé d'une Histoire très-précise de la magie ... Paris, P. Mongie aîné, 1819.
xxii, 152 p. 21cm.
Ascription by Barbier.
8 NIC
(Continued on next card)

Rebenstock, Heinrich Peter, tr.
Witchcraft
BF 1520 W64 P8++ 1586
Wier, Johann, 1515-1588. De lamiis. Das ist: Von Teuffelsgespenst ... 1586.
(Card 3)
1586.
Binding: blind stamped pigskin, with clasps (one wanting); front cover initialed A K A S H and dated 1589.
1. Demonology. 2. Witchcraft. 3. Magic. 4. Fasting. I. Title: Von Teuffelsgespenst, Zauberern und Gifftbe-
8
(Continued on next card)

Witchcraft
BL 65 C8 R24
Raupach, Ernst Benjamin Salomon, 1784-1852.
Der Aberglaube als weltgeschichtliche Macht. Vortrag im wissenschaftlichen Verein am 14. Februar 1852 von Dr. E. Raupach. Mit dem Bildnisse Raupach's aus früheren Jahren. Berlin [Druckerei von F. W. Gubitz] 1852.
27 p. port. 21cm.
1. Religion and culture. 2. Supernatural. I. Title.
8

Reasons for concluding that the act of
WITCHCRAFT 1711 became a law.
BF 1576 M82 G641+
Goodell, Abner Cheney, 1831-1914.
[Reasons for concluding that the act of 1711, reversing the attainders of the persons convicted of witchcraft in Massachusetts in the year 1692, became a law. Being a reply to Supplementary notes, etc. by George H. Moore]
(In:. Massachusetts Historical Society. Proceedings. Boston. 26cm. Jan./Mar. 1884. p.99-118)
With, in same issue: his Additional considerations on the history
8 NIC
(Continued on next card)

Recent cases of supposed witchcraft in Devonshire.
WITCHCRAFT
BF 1581]18
Karkeek, Paul Quick.
Recent cases of supposed witchcraft in Devonshire, by Paul Q. Karkeek. (Read at Torrington, July, 1875) ... [London? 1875]
8 p. 21cm.
Caption title.
"Reprinted from the Transactions of the Devonshire Association for the Advancement of Science, Literature, and Art. 1875."
Bound with the author's Devonshire witches. [London? 1874?]
8 NIC
(Continued on next card)

Witchcraft
BF 1565 K91
Rauschelbach, Johann Ernst, respondent.
Krause, Rudolph Wilhelm, 1642-1719, praeses.
Dissertatio medica inavgvralis De incantatis, qvam ... svb praesidio Rvdolffi VVilhelmi Cravsii ... subjicit Iohannes Ernestvs Rauschelbach ... Ienae, Literis Krebsianis [1701]
28 p. 20cm.
Diss.—Jena (J. E. Rauschelbach, respondent)
1. Witchcraft. 2. Personality, Disorders of. I. Rauschelbach, Johann Ernst, respondent. II. Title.
8

Reasons for concluding that the act of
WITCHCRAFT 1711 became a law.
BF 1576 M82 G641+
Goodell, Abner Cheney, 1831-1914. [Reasons for concluding that the act of 1711... became a law] 1884. (Card 2)
of witchcraft in Massachusetts.
Running title: History of witchcraft in Massachusetts.
1. Witchcraft—Massachusetts. 2. Moore, George Henry, 1823-1892. Supplementary notes on witchcraft... I. His History of witchcraft in Massachusetts. II. Title: History of witchcraft in Massachusetts. III. Title: Reasons for concluding that the act of 1711 became a law.

Recent witch hunting research.
Witchcraft
BF 1439 M62++
Midelfort, H Christian Erik
Recent witch hunting research; or, Where do we go from here? [New York, 1968]
373-420 p. 24cm.
Extract from Bibliographical Society of America. Papers. v. 62 (1968)
Bibliography: p. 385-420.
Photocopy. 373-420 p. on 24 l. 24 x cm.
1. Witchcraft. 2. Witchcraft—Bibl. I. Title.

462

CATALOGUE OF THE CORNELL WITCHCRAFT COLLECTION

Witchcraft
BF 1445
D61
no.5
   Rechenberg, Adam, 1642-1721, praeses.
   De spectris, incl. facult. philosoph. annuente, praeside Domino M. Adamo Rechenberg, ... publicè disputabit ... Johannes Gabriel Drechsler, ... A. & R. ... Lipsiae, Literis Johannis Erici Hahnii [1668] [20] p. 19cm. (bound in 21cm. vol.)

   No. 5 in vol. lettered Dissertationes de spectris. 1646-1753.

8
   1. Apparitions. I. Drechssler, Johann Gabriel, d. 1677, respondent. II. Title.

Witchcraft
BF 1445
D61
no.6
   Rechenberg, Adam, 1642-1721, praeses. De spectris.
   Drechssler, Johann Gabriel, d. 1677, praeses.
   De spectris, disputationem II. Inclut. facultat. philosoph. Lipsiensis consensu P. P. praeses M. Johannes Gabriel Drechssler ... et respondens Christianus Michelmann ... Lipsiae, Literis Johannis Erici Hahnii [1669] [12] p. 21cm.
   No. 6 in vol. lettered Dissertationes de spectris. 1646-1753.
   1. Rechenberg, Adam, 1642-1721, praeses. De spectris. 2. Apparitions. 3. Devil. I. Michelmann, Christian, respondent. II. Title.

WITCHCRAFT
BR 163
L44
   Recherches sur l'accusation de magie.
   Le Blant, Edmond Frédéric, 1818-1897.
   Recherches sur l'accusation de magie dirigée contre les premiers chrétiens. Nogent-Le-Rotrou, A. Gouverneur, 1869. 36 p. 23cm.

   Extract from Mémoires de la Société impériale des antiquaires de France, v.31.

8
NIC
   1. Church history--Primitive and early church. 2. Magic. 3. Witchcraft. I.Title.

Witchcraft
BF 1582
F26
   Recherches sur les procès de sorcellerie au XVIe siècle.
   Faure-Biguet, Albert.
   Recherches sur les procès de sorcellerie au XVIe siècle. Valence, Imprimerie de Chenevier, 1877. 45 p. 23cm.

   1. Trials (Witchcraft) I. Title.

WITCHCRAFT
BF 1555
M94
029
no.2
   Ein Rechtgelahrter.
   Das Bezauberte Bauermägdgen: oder Geschichte von dem anjetzo in Kemberg bey Wittenberg sich aufhaltenden Landmägdgen Johannen Elisabethen Lohmannin; aufgesetzt durch einen von Vorurtheil Befreyeten, und mit Anmerkungen eines Rechtsgelahrten versehen. Breslau, Bey J. E. Meyer, 1760. 167 p. 18cm.
   No. 2 in vol. lettered Oesfeld u. a. ...
   "Eines Advocatens Ehrenrettung wider ... Herrn Gottlieb Müllers Beschuldigung": p. 51-162.

8
NIC
(Continued on next card)

Witchcraft
BF 1565
R43
   Rechtlich Bedencken von Zauberey.
   Responsum juris, oder Rechtliches vnd auszführliches Bedencken von Zauberin, deren Thun, Wesen vnd Vermögen, auch was Gestalt dieselbe zubestraffen ... gestellet durch einen hochgelehrten vnd gar vornehmen JCtum ... Franckfurt am Mayn, Erstmaln gedruckt vnd verlegt bey Johann-Friderich Weissen, 1637. 4 p. l., 126 [i.e., 162] p. 21cm.
   Possibly by Philipp Hoffmann or Hofmann?
   Running title: Rechtlich Bedencken von Zauberey.

(Continued on next card)

WITCHCRAFT
BF 1583
A2
I43
   Rechtliches Bedencken, in Malefitzsachen.
   Informatio ivris, in causa poenali, vtrvm tres mvlieres maleficii, et veneficii, cev reae, delatae capi, & torqueri potuerint, nécne? Qvad. Caroli V. imp. constitvtio criminalis aliqvot in locis declaratur. Rechtliches Bedencken, in Malefitzsachen; ob drey Weiber, der Zauberey halber angegeben, in gefängliche Verhafft angenommen, und peinlich befragt werden können, oder nicht? Darinnen Keyser Carols, dess Fünfften, hochlöblichister Gedächtnuss Peinliche, oder Halss-

8
NIC
(Continued on next card)

WITCHCRAFT
BF 1583
A2
I43
   Rechtliches Bedencken, in Malefitzsachen.
   Informatio ivris, in causa poenali... (Card 2)
   gerichtsordnunge in etlichen Articuln erkläret wirdt. Per H. A. B. V. I. D. Franckfurt a. M., Bey C. Egenolffs Erben, 1590. 68 l. 16cm.
   1. Witchcraft--Germany. 2. Torture--Germany. I. B., H. A. II. H. A. B. III. Karl V, Emperor of Germany, 1500-1558. IV. Title: Rechtliches Bedencken, in Malefitzsachen.

Witchcraft
BF 1565
G61
   Rechtliches Bedencken, von Confiscation der Zauberer und Hexen-Güther.
   Goldast, Melchior, 1578-1635.
   Rechtliches Bedencken, von Confiscation der Zauberer und Hexen-Güther. Veber die Frage: Ob die Zauberer und Hexen, Leib und Guth mit und zugleich verwürcken, allso und dergestalt, dass sie nicht allein an Leib und Guth, können und sollen gestraffet werden? Sampt ein verliebtem kurtzem Bericht, von mancherley Arth der Zauberer und Hexen, und deren ungleiche Bestraffung ... Bremen, A. Wessels, 1661. 180 p. 21 cm.
   I. Title.

WITCHCRAFT
BF 1565
R43
   Rechtliches und auszführliches Bedencken von Zauberin.
   Responsum juris, oder Rechtliches vnd auszführliches Bedencken von Zauberin, deren Thun, Wesen vnd Vermögen, auch was Gestalt dieselbe zubestraffen ... gestellet durch einen hochgelehrten vnd gar vornehmen JCtum ... Franckfurt am Mayn, Erstmaln gedruckt vnd verlegt bey Johann-Friderich Weissen, 1637. 4 p. l., 126 [i.e., 162] p. 21cm.
   Possibly by Philipp Hoffmann or Hofmann?
   Running title: Rechtlich Bedencken von Zauberey.

8
NIC
(Continued on next card)

Witchcraft
BF 1517
F5R29
   Recit veritable de ce qvi s'est passé à Lovdvn. Contre Maistre Vrbain Grandier, Prestre Curé de l'Eglise de S. Pierre de Loudun, attaint & convaincu du crime de Magie, malefice & possession, arriuée par son faict és personne d'aucunes des Religieuses Vrseline de la ville de Loudun. A Paris, De l'Imprimerie de Pierre Targa, 1634. 15 p. 16cm.
   1. Loudun, France. Ursuline Convent. 2. Grandier, Urbain, 1590-1634.

Witchcraft
BF 1582
Z7
1637a
   Recit veritable de l'effet d'un malheureux sort magique nouvellement arrivé sur cinq habitans et deux damoiselles de la ville de Chasteaudun, et des effroyables actions qu'ils font journellement au grand estonnement du peuple. Avec tout ce qui s'est passé à ce sujet. Paris, Chez Claude Morlot, 1637. [Lyon, Imprim. L. Perrin, 1875] 11 p. 22cm.
   1. Witchcraft--Châteaudun, France. 2.

8
   Witchcraft--France.

Witchcraft
BF 1582
Z7
1630a
   Récit veritable des choses estranges et prodigieuses arrivées en l'execution de trois sorciers et magiciens deffaits en la ville de Lymoges le vingt quatriesme d'Avril mil six cens trente. Bourdeaux, Par J. du Coq [1630?] [Lyon, Imprim. Louis Perrin, 1875] 14 p. 23cm.
   "Jouxte la Coppie imprimée à Lymoges."
   1. Trials (Witchcraft)--France. 2.

8
   Trials (Witchcraft)--Limoges, France.

F 221
V824
C6
v.1
   Record of Grace Sherwood's trial for witchcraft.
   Sherwood, Grace, defendant.
   Record of Grace Sherwood's trial for witchcraft, in 1705, in Princess Anne County, Virginia. Presented by President Cushing, to the Virginia Historical and Philosophical Society on the 4th of February, 1833.
   (In Virginia Historical Society. Collections. Richmond, 1833. 24cm. v. 1, p. [69]-78)

   I. Title.

Witchcraft
BF 1575
R31
2 Copies
   Records of Salem witchcraft, copied from the original documents ... Roxbury, Mass., Priv. print. for W. E. Woodward, 1864. 2 v. 22 x 17cm. (Half title: Woodward's historical series. no. I-II)

   No. 104 of an edition of two hundred and fifteen copies. The second copy is not numbered.
   The 1st copy is defective, wanting pages 161-279 of Vol. 1. Pages from another work in the series are substituted.

Witchcraft
BF 1445
L56
1752
   Recueil de dissertations anciennes et nouvelles, sur les apparitions.
   Lenglet Dufresnoy, Nicolas, 1674-1755.
   Recueil de dissertations anciennes et nouvelles, sur les apparitions, les visions & les songes... Avignon, J. N. Leloup, 1751-52 [v.1, 1752] 2 v. 17cm.

   "Liste des principaux auteurs qui ont traité des esprits, démons, apparitions, songes, magie & spectres": v.2, pt. 2, p. 223-287.

   1. Apparitions. I. Title.

Witchcraft
BF 1602
S13
B68
   Recueil de lettres au sujet des malefices et du sortilege.
   Boissier, A.
   Recueil de lettres au sujet des malefices et du sortilege: servant de réponse aux Lettres du Sieur de Saint-André, medecin à Coutances, sur le même sujet. Avec la scavante remontrance du Parlement de Rouen faite au roy Louis XIV, au sujet du sortilege, du malefice, des sabats, & autres effets de la magie, pour la perfection du procez dont il est parlé dans ces Lettres. Paris, Brunet fils, 1731. xiii,387 p. 17cm.
   1. Saint-André, François de. 2. Witchcraft. 3. Sorcery. I. Title.

WITCHCRAFT
BF 1555
R31
   Recueil de pièces sur les possessions des religieuses de Louviers. Rouen, [Imprimerie L. Deshays] 1879. 2 v. in 1. 25cm.

   Title page and prefatory material bound following v. 1.
   Contents.--[1] Histoire de Magdelaine Bavent, religieuse du monastere de Saint Loüis de Louviers (1652)--[2] I. Examen de la possession des religieuses de Louviers, par le Docteur Yvelin (1643)

8
NIC
(Continued on next card)

463

CATALOGUE OF THE CORNELL WITCHCRAFT COLLECTION

WITCHCRAFT
BF 1555 R31
Recueil de pièces sur les possessions des religieuses de Louviers...1879. (Card 2)

Contents--continued.
II. Response à l'Examen de la possession des religieuses de Louviers (1643) III. Censure de l'Examen de la possession des religieuses de Louviers (1643) IV. Apologie pour l'autheur de l'Examen de la possession des religieuses de Louviers, attribuée au Docteur Yvelin (1643) V. Responce à l'Apologie de l'Examen du sieur Yvelin
(Continued on next card)

WITCHCRAFT
BF 1555 R31
Recueil de pièces sur les possessions des religieuses de Louviers...1879. (Card 3)

Contents--continued.
(1644) VI. Recit veritable de ce qui s'est fait & passé à Louviers, touchant les religieuses possedées (1643) VII. Recit veritable de ce qui s'est fait & passé aux exorcismes de plusieurs religieuses de la ville de Louviers (1643) VIII. La deffense de la verité touchant la possession des religieuses de Louvier, par
(Continued on next card)

WITCHCRAFT
BF 1555 R31
Recueil de pièces sur les possessions des religieuses de Louviers...1879. (Card 4)

Contents--continued.
Jean Le Breton (1643) IX. Attestation de messieurs les commissaires envoyez par sa Majesté pour prendre connoissance, avec monseigneur l'evesque d'Evreux, de l'estat des religieuses de plusieurs religieuses agitées au monastere de Saint Louys & Sainte Elizabeth de Louviers (1643?) X. Procés verbal de Monsieur le Peniten-
(Continued on next card)

WITCHCRAFT
BF 1555 R31
Recueil de pièces sur les possessions des religieuses de Louviers...1879. (Card 5)

Contents--continued.
tier d'Evreux, de ce qui luy est arrivé dans la prison, interrogeant & consolant Magdelaine Bavent, magicienne, à une heureuse conversion & repentance, par Delangle (1643) XI. Lettre adressée à Monsieur D. L. V., medicin du Roy, & doyen de la Faculté de Paris, sur l'Apologie du sieur Yvelin, medicin, attribuée au doc-
(Continued on next card)

WITCHCRAFT
BF 1555 R31
Recueil de pièces sur les possessions des religieuses de Louviers...1879. (Card 6)

Contents--continued.
teur Maignart (1644) XII. Traicté des marques des possedez & la preuve de la veritable possession des religieuses de Louviers, par P. M., esc. d. en m. (attribué à Simon Pietre; 1644) XIII. Copie en forme de recueil de ce qui se fait de jour en jour dans le monastere des filles relligieuzes Saint Louis (1643) XIV. Pièces dé-
(Continued on next card)

WITCHCRAFT
BF 1555 R31
Recueil de pièces sur les possessions des religieuses de Louviers...1879. (Card 7)

Contents--continued.
tachées extraites du manuscrit H. F. nº 34 de la Bibliotheque Ste Geneviève, formant suite à la pièce précédente. XV. Notice sur la Mere Françoise, superieure des religieuses de la Place royale, au sujet de l'histoire des possedées de Louviers.
(Continued on next card)

WITCHCRAFT
BF 1555 R31
Recueil de pièces sur les possessions des religieuses de Louviers...1879. (Card 8)

1. Demoniac possession. 2. Louviers, France. St. Louis (Convent) 3. Bavent, Madeleine, ca. 1608-1647. 4. Picard, Mathurin, d. 1647. 5. Boullé, Thomas.

Witchcraft
BF 1582 G51 P96 v.1 no.5
Girard, Jean Baptiste, 1680-1733.
Recueil des lettres du Père Girard & de la Demoiselle Cadière, dont les originaux ont été produits au procès. Réflexions générales sur ces lettres. [s.l., 173-?]
147 p. 17cm.

No. 5 in vol. lettered: Procès de Girard. [v.1]

8 NIC   I. Cadière, Catherine, b. 1709.

Witchcraft
BF 1582 G51R3 1731d
Girard, Jean Baptiste, 1680-1733, defendant.
[Recueil des pièces concernant le procez entre le père Girard, jesuite, et la Demoiselle Cadière. n.p., 1731?]
1 v. (various pagings) 17cm.

Cover-title: Procès de Girard. Tom. II.
Contents.--1. Mémoire instructif pour le p. Nicolas de Saint Joseph, Pazery.--2. Thorame, Cadière, M. C. Justi-
(Continued on next card)

Witchcraft
BF 1582 G51R3 1731d
Girard, Jean Baptiste, 1680-1733, defendant.
[Recueil des pièces concernant le procez ... n.p., 1731?] (Card 2)

Contents--Continued.
fication.--4. Premières actes et contrat protestatifs de la Demoiselle Cadière.--5. Mémoire des faits qui se sont passez sous les yeux de M. l'évêque de Toulon.--6. Cadière, M. C. Réponse à l'écrit de M. l'évêque de Toulon.--7. Cadière, François. Second
(Continued on next card)

Witchcraft
BF 1582 G51R3 1731d
Girard, Jean Baptiste, 1680-1733, defendant.
[Recueil des pièces concernant le procez ... n.p., 1731?] (Card 3)

Contents--Continued.
mémoire pour M. Cadière, prêtre.--8. Cadière, E. T. Réponse au second mémoire imprimé sous le nom du p. Girard, jesuite.

I. Cadière, Catherine, b. 1709.
II. Title.

WITCHCRAFT
BF 1582 G51 P96 v.3
Recueil des premières requestes de la Demoiselle Cadière, du Père Estienne Thomas Cadière, Jacobin, et du Père Nicolas, prieur des Carmes de Toulon. [s.l., 173-?]
1 v. (various pagings) 17cm.

Binder's title: Procès de Girard. [v.3]

8 NIC I. Girard, Jean Baptiste, 1680-1733. II. Cadière, Catherine, b. 1709. III. Estienne Thomas, fl. 1730. IV. Nicolas de Saint Joseph, fl. 1730.

Witchcraft
BF 1582 G51R3 1731c
Girard, Jean Baptiste, 1680-1733, defendant.
Recueil général des pièces concernant le procez entre la Demoiselle Cadière de la ville de Toulon, et le père Girard, jesuite ... La Haye, Swart, 1731.
8 v. 17cm.

The trials were held before the Parlement of Aix.
A collection of items originally published separately; there is a general title
(Continued on next card)

Witchcraft
BF 1582 G51R3 1731c
Girard, Jean Baptiste, 1680-1733, defendant.
Recueil général des pièces concernant le procez ... 1731. (Card 2)

page and a table of contents for each vol. Bound with v.8 is Le nouveau Tarquin, usually attributed to Jean Jacques Bel.

I. Cadière, Catherine, b. 1709.
II. France. Parlement (Aix) III. Title.
IV. [Bel, Jean Jacques], 1693-1738.
Le nouveau Tarquin. V. Title: Le nouveau Tarquin.

Witchcraft
BF 1582 G51R3 1731b
Girard, Jean Baptiste, 1680-1733, defendant.
Recueil général des pièces contenues au procez du Père Jean Baptiste Girard, Jesuite ... & de Demoiselle Catherine Cadière, querellante. Aix, J. David, 1731.
6 v. fronts. 17cm.

A collection of items originally published separately. There is a general title page and a table of contents for each vol. except vol. 6. Bound with v. 6 is Le nouveau
(Continued on next card)

Witchcraft
BF 1582 G51R3 1731b
Girard, Jean Baptiste, 1680-1733, defendant.
Recueil général des pièces contenues au procez ... 1731. (Card 2)

Tarquin, usually attributed to Jean Jacques Bel.

I. Cadière, Catherine, b. 1709.
II. Title.

Witchcraft
BF 1410 B42 1691b
Bekker, Balthasar, 1634-1698.
Kort begrip van de twee boeken der Betooverde weereld, in 't ligt gebragt door den heere Balthazar Bekker, S.T.D. en predikant te Amsterdam, zeer dienstig tot het recht verstaan (en teffens strekkende voor een bondig register) van dat vermaarde werk, opgesteld door een redenlievenden hater van bygeloof. Rotterdam, By I. van Ruynen, boekverkooper, 1691.
2 p. l., 39 p. [p. 40 is blank] title
(Continued on next card)

Een redenlievende hater van bygeloof.

Witchcraft
BF 1410 B42 1691b
Bekker, Balthasar, 1634-1698. Kort begrip van de twee boeken der Betooverde weereld ... 1691. (Card 2)

vignette, illus. initials. 20 x 16cm.
4°: π², A-E⁴.
Black letter.
Preface signed: I. van Ruynen.
Van der Linde 18.
1. Demonology. 2. Angels. 3. Magic. 4. Witchcraft. I. His De betoverde weereld. II. Title. III. Ruynen, I. van. IV. Een redenlievende hater van bygeloof.

8

464

CATALOGUE OF THE CORNELL WITCHCRAFT COLLECTION

Ein redlicher Protestant.

Witchcraft
BF
1559
G25
Z63
no.6

Eines redlichen Protestantens aufrichtige Erinnerung an den Verfasser des Exorcisten in seiner Blösse, den Prager Hirtenbrief betreffend. Frankfurt und Leipzig, 1776.
45 p. 17cm.
No. 6 in vol. lettered Gassneriana.
1. Gassner, Johann Joseph, 1727-1779. 2. Příchovský, Antonín Peter, Abp. of Prague, 1707-1793. Hirtenbrief ... 1775. 3. Der Exorcist in seiner Blösse. I. Ein redlicher Protestant.

Redway, George, London.
Z
6880
Z9C35
no.6

List of books on theosophy, archaeology, astrology, mesmerism, philology, spiritualism, freemasonry, alchemy, platonism, thought-reading, magic, the Rosicrucians, witchcraft, etc. by Fludd, Behmen, Paracelsus, Agrippa, Nostradamus, Van Helmont, & others. [London, 1885]
16 p. 23cm.
At head of title: No. 11, 1885.
No. 6 in vol. lettered: Catalogues of books on magic and witchcraft.
1. Occult sciences--Bibl.--Cat. 2. Witchcraft--Bibl.--Cat. I. Title.

Redway, George, London.
The literature of occultism and archaeology. Being a Catalogue of books on sale relating to ancient worships, astrology, alchemy ... [London, 1885]
48 p. 23cm.
At head of title: Part 1. December 1885.
No. 5 in vol. lettered: Catalogues of books on magic and witchcraft.
1. Occult sciences--Bibl.--Cat. I. Title.

Reflexions sur la récrimination en prétendu complot, imputé au Père Estienne Thomas Cadière.

WITCHCRAFT
BF
.582
.51
.96
v.1
no.6

Cadière, Estienne Thomas, fl. 1730.
Reflexions sur la récrimination en prétendu complot, imputé au Père Estienne Thomas Cadière ... par le P. Jean Baptiste Girard ... [s.l., 173-?]
144 p. 17cm.
No. 6 in vol. lettered: Procès de Girard. [v.1]
1. Girard, Jean Baptiste, 1680-1733. I. Title.

Refutatio responsionis Gulielmi-Adolphi Scribonii, superstitiosam sagarum purgationem per aquam frigidam.

Ignotus Patronus Veritatis, pseud.
Refvtatio responsionis Gvlielmi-Adolphi Scribonii, svperstitiosam sagarvm pvrgationem per aqvam frigidam pertinacissimè defendentis: ab Ignoto Patrono Veritatis stylo Scriboniano conscripta ... Herbornae, 1591.
112 p. 17cm.
Bound with Scribonius, Wilhelm Adolf. De sagarvm natura. Marpurgi, 1588.

Witchcraft
BF
1559
B61
1618a

Birette, Sanson.
Refvtation de l'errevr dv vvlgaire tovchant les responces des diables exorcizez ... Constances, I. le Carrel imprimeur, 1618.
143 numb. l. 15cm.
"Explication dv canon episcopi, 26. quest. 5.": verso l. 126-verso l. 139.
Imperfect: l. 11 mutilated; part of text missing.
1. Exorcism. 2. Demoniac possession. I. Title.

Regli, Anizet, fl. 1848.

MSS
Bd.
WITCHCRAFT
BF
E69

Erledigung der ehrw. Klosterfrau Maria Augusta Delphina, im Frauenkloster zu Stanz, den 28. März 1848 durch P. Anizet Regli, Guardian zu Stanz. [n.p.] Nach einem Original-Manuskripte getreu abgedruckt, 1848 [ca. 1900]
9 l. 19cm.
Carnap's manuscript copy.
"Originaldruck i. d. Stadtbibliothek zu Zürich. 13 S. in 8°."
Numerals in the margins indicate pagination of the original.
(Continued on next card)

Regli, Anizet, fl. 1848.

WITCHCRAFT
BF
1555
L65

[Leu, Josef Burkard] 1808-1865.
Die Teufels-Beschwörung in Stans; oder, Gutachten über die Broschüre: Erledigung der ehrw. Klosterfrau Maria Augusta Delphina im Frauenkloster zu Stans den 28. März 1848 durch P. Anizet Regli... Luzern, X. Meyer, 1848.
15 p. 20cm.
1. Demoniac possession. 2. Devil. 3. Exorcism. 4. Delphina, Maria Augusta, fl. 1848. 5. Regli, Anizet, fl. 1848. 6. Erledigung der ehrw. Klosterfrau Maria Augusta Delphina. I. Title.

8 NIC

Witchcraft
BF
173
R33+

Regnard, Paul, 1850-1927.
Les maladies épidémiques de l'esprit; sorcellerie, magnétisme, morphinisme, délire des grandeurs, par le dr Paul Regnard ... Ouvrage illustré de cent vingt gravures. Paris, E. Plon, Nourrit et cie, 1887.
iii-xii, 429 p., 1 l. incl. illus., pl., facsim. 27cm.
Contents.--Les sorcières.--Les miracles de Saint-Médard.--Sommeil et somnambulisme.--Deux poisons à la mode: la morphine et l'éther.--Le délire des grandeurs.
1. Psychology, Pathological. 2. Demoniac possession. 3. Hysteria. I. Title.
II. Title: Sorcellerie, magnétism.
Library of Congress, no.

BF
173
R33

Regnard, Paul, 1850-1927.
Les maladies épidémiques de l'esprit; sorcellerie, magnétisme, morphinisme, délire des grandeurs, par le dr Paul Regnard ... Ouvrage illustré de cent vingt gravures. Paris, E. Plon, Nourrit et cie, 1887.
iii-xii, 429 p., 1 l. incl. illus., pl., facsim. 25 cm.
Contents.--Les sorcières.--Les miracles de Saint-Médard.--Sommeil et somnambulisme.--Deux poisons à la mode: la morphine et l'éther.--Le délire des grandeurs.
1. Psychology, Pathological. 2. Demoniac possession. 3. Hysteria. I. Title.
II. Title: Sorcellerie, magnétism.
Library of Congress, no.

Witchcraft
BF
1569
R33

Regnard, Paul, 1850-1927.
Les sorcières. Conférence du 18 Mars 1882, faite à la Sorbonne. Paris, Gauthier-Villars, 1882.
41 p. 22cm.
At head of title: Association scientifique de France.
"Extrait des Bulletins hebdomadaires nos 106, 107."
1. Witchcraft--Addresses, essays, lectures. I. Title.

8

Regnard, Paul-Marie-Léon.

see

Regnard, Paul, 1850-1927.

Regnault, Jules, 1873-

see

Regnault, Jules Emile Joseph, 1873-

Witchcraft
BF
1572
M4
R33+

Regnault, Jules Emile Joseph, 1873-
La sorcellerie, ses rapports avec les sciences biologiques, par le docteur Jules Regnault ... Paris, G. Baillière, 1897.
350 p. 26cm.
1. Witchcraft. 2. Medicine, Magic, mystic, and spagiric. 3. Mental suggestion. I. Title.

8

Witchcraft
BF
1563
W81++
no.1

A Rehearsall both straung and true, of hainous and horrible actes committed by Elizabeth Stile, alias Rockingham, Mother Dutten, Mother Deuell, Mother Margaret, fower notorious witches, apprehended at Winsore in the countie of Barks, and at Abbington arraigned, condemned, and executed, on the 26 1 daye of Februarie laste, anno. 1579. London, Imprinted for E. White [1579?] London, at the British Museum, 1923]
Photocopy (negative) 19 p. on 10 l.
1. Stile, Elizabeth.

R
133
A92

Rehmeyer, Nelson D., 1868-1928.
Aurand, Ammon Monroe, 1895-
The "pow-wow" book: a treatise on the art of "healing by prayer" and "laying on of hands", etc., practiced by the Pennsylvania-Germans and others; testimonials; remarkable recoveries; popular superstitions; etc., including an account of the famous "witch" murder trial, at York, Pa. by A. Monroe Aurand, jr. ... containing also the complete collection of remedies and cures in John George Hohman's "Pow-wows, or Long lost friend"; in popular use since 1820. Harrisburg, Pa., Priv. print. by The Aurand press, 1929.
x, 85, [1] 31, [1], xi, 13-64 p. incl. front., illus. 24cm.
(Continued on next card)

R
133
A92

Rehmeyer, Nelson D., 1868-1928.
Aurand, Ammon Monroe, 1895-   The "pow-wow" book ... 1929. (Card 2)
"An account of the 'witch' murder trial" ... and "John George Hohman's Pow-wows; or, Long lost friend" have special title-pages and pagination.
"Pow-wows; or Long lost friend" was published in 1819 under title: Der lange verborgene freund, oder: Getreuer und christlicher unterricht für jedermann."
"This edition of the 'Pow-wow' book is limited to one thousand copies; one hundred signed by the author. This is no. 309."
Bibliography: p. vi.
1. Medicine, Magic, mystic, and spagiric. 2. Superstition. 3. Folklore--Pennsylvania. 4. Witchcraft--Pennsylvania. 5. Blymyer, John H. 6. Rehmeyer, Nelson D., 1868-1928. I. Hohman, Johann Georg. II. Title. III. Title: "Witch" murder trial, York, Pa.
Library of Congress   R133.A8   29-9468 Revised
——— Copy 2.
Copyright A 7294   [d2]

Witchcraft
BF
1578
B66

Rehmeyer, Nelson D., 1868-1928.
Blymyer, John H   defendant.
An account of the "witch" murder trial, York, Pa., January 7-9, 1929. Commonwealth of Pennsylvania vs. John Blymyer, et al. By A. Monroe Aurand, jr. ... Harrisburg, Pa., Priv. print. by the Aurand press, 1929.
31 p. 23cm.
1. Rehmeyer, Nelson D., 1868-1928. 2. Witchcraft--Pennsylvania. I. Aurand, Ammon Monroe, 1895-   II. Title: "Witch" murder trial, York, Pa., January 7-9, 1929. III. Title.
Library of Congress   29-23242
——— Copy 2.
Copyright A 4228   [2]

465

CATALOGUE OF THE CORNELL WITCHCRAFT COLLECTION

Reich, Johann.
  see
Reiche, Johann.

Witchcraft
BF 1547 R34

Reichard, Elias Caspar, 1714-1791.
Vermischte Beyträge zur Beförderung einer nähern Einsicht in das gesamte Geisterreich. Zur Verminderung und Tilgung des Unglaubens und Aberglaubens. Als eine Fortsetzung von D. David Eberhard Haubers Magischen Bibliothek herausgegeben. Helmstedt, Johann Heinrich Kühnlin, 1781-88.
2 v. 19cm.

Vol. 1 in 4 parts, each with special t.p.
I. Hauber, Eberhard David, 1695-1765. Biblioteca, acta et scripta magica. II. Ti tle.

WITCHCRAFT
BF 1565 R34

Reiche, Johann.
  Fernerer Unfug der Zauberey.
Reiche, Johann, ed.
Herrn D. Christian Thomasii ... Kurtze Lehr-Sätze von dem Laster der Zauberey, nach dem wahren Verstande des lateinischen Exemplars ins Deutsche übersetzet, und aus des berühmten Theologi D. Meyfarti, Naudaei, und anderer gelehrter Männer Schrifften erleutert ... nebst einigen Actis magicis herausgegeben von Johann Reichen. Halle im Magdeburgischen, Im Rengerischen Buchladen, 1704.
8   2 v. in 1.   21cm.
NIC   (Continued on next card)

WITCHCRAFT
BF 1565 R34

Reiche, Johann.
  Fernerer Unfug der Zauberey.
Reiche, Johann, ed. Herrn D. Christian Thomasii ... Kurtze Lehr-Sätze ... 1704.
(Card 2)

Vol. 1 has special t. p.: Fernerer Unfug der Zauberey. Halle im Magdeburgischen, 1704.
Vol. 2 has special t. p.: Unterschiedliche Schrifften von Unfug des Hexen-Processes. Halle im Magdeburg., 1703.
Contents.--[1. Bd.] Gabriel Naudaei
8
NIC   (Continued on next card)

WITCHCRAFT
BF 1565 R34

Reiche, Johann.
  Fernerer Unfug der Zauberey.
Reiche, Johann, ed. Herrn D. Christian Thomasii ... Kurtze Lehr-Sätze ... 1704.
(Card 3)

Contents.--Continued.

Schutz-Schrifft [tr. of Apologie pour tous les grands hommes]--Geschichte der Teuffel zu Loudun.--Trauer-Geschichte von der greulichen Zauberey Ludwig Goffredy [tr. of De l'horrible & épouvantable sorcellerie de Louis Goffredy, author F. de Rosset]--D. Christian Thomasii ... Kurtze Lehr-Sätze von
8
NIC   (Continued on next card)

WITCHCRAFT
BF 1565 R34

Reiche, Johann.
  Fernerer Unfug der Zauberey.
Reiche, Johann, ed. Herrn D. Christian Thomasii ... Kurtze Lehr-Sätze ... 1704.
(Card 4)

Contents--Continued.

dem Laster der Zauberey [tr. of Dissertatio de crimine magiae, J. Reiche, respondent] [2. Bd.] Malleus judicum oder Gesetz-Hammer der unbarmhertzigen Hexen-Richter.-- Cautio criminalis [von F. Spee]--D. Johann Matthäus Meyfarths Christliche Erinnerung an Regenten.-- Viererley Sorten Hexen-Acta.
8
NIC   (Continued on next card)

WITCHCRAFT
BF 1565 R34

Reiche, Johann, ed. Herrn D. Christian Thomasii ... Kurtze Lehr-Sätze von dem Laster der Zauberey, nach dem wahren Verstande des lateinischen Exemplars ins Deutsche übersetzet, und aus des berühmten Theologi D. Meyfarti, Naudaei, und anderer gelehrter Männer Schrifften erleutert ... nebst einigen Actis magicis herausgegeben von Johann Reichen. Halle im Magdeburgischen, Im Rengerischen Buchladen, 1704.
8   2 v. in 1.   21cm.
NIC   (Continued on next card)

WITCHCRAFT
BF 1565 R34

Reiche, Johann, ed. Herrn D. Christian Thomasii ... Kurtze Lehr-Sätze ... 1704.
(Card 2)

Vol. 1 has special t. p.: Fernerer Unfug der Zauberey. Halle im Magdeburgischen, 1704.
Vol. 2 has special t. p.: Unterschiedliche Schrifften von Unfug des Hexen-Processes. Halle im Magdeburg., 1703.
Contents.--[1. Bd.] Gabriel Naudaei
8
NIC   (Continued on next card)

WITCHCRAFT
BF 1565 R34

Reiche, Johann, ed. Herrn D. Christian Thomasii ... Kurtze Lehr-Sätze ... 1704.
(Card 3)

Contents.--Continued.

Schutz-Schrifft [tr. of Apologie pour tous les grands hommes]--Geschichte der Teuffel zu Loudun.--Trauer-Geschichte von der greulichen Zauberey Ludwig Goffredy [tr. of De l'horrible & épouvantable sorcellerie de Louis Goffredy, author F. de Rosset]--D. Christian Thomasii ... Kurtze Lehr-Sätze von
8
NIC   (Continued on next card)

WITCHCRAFT
BF 1565 R34

Reiche, Johann, ed. Herrn D. Christian Thomasii ... Kurtze Lehr-Sätze ... 1704.
(Card 4)

Contents--Continued.

dem Laster der Zauberey [tr. of Dissertatio de crimine magiae, J. Reiche, respondent] [2. Bd.] Malleus judicum oder Gesetz-Hammer der unbarmhertzigen Hexen-Richter.-- Cautio criminalis [von F. Spee]--D. Johann Matthäus Meyfarths Christliche Erinnerung an Regenten.-- Viererley Sorten Hexen-Acta.
8
NIC   (Continued on next card)

WITCHCRAFT
BF 1565 R34

Reiche, Johann, ed. Herrn D. Christian Thomasii ... Kurtze Lehr-Sätze ... 1704.
(Card 5)

1. Witchcraft. 2. Trials (Witchcraft)--Germany. I. His Fernerer Unfug der Zauberey. II. His Unterschiedliche Schrifften von Unfug des Hexen-Processes. III. Naudé, Gabriel, 1600-1659. Apologie pour tous les grands hommes. German. IV. Rosset, François de, b. ca. 1570. De l'horrible et épouvantable sorcellerie de Louis Goffredy. German. V. Thomasius,
8
NIC   (Continued on next card)

WITCHCRAFT
BF 1565 R34

Reiche, Johann, ed. Herrn D. Christian Thomasii ... Kurtze Lehr-Sätze ... 1704.
(Card 6)

Christian, 1655-1728. Dissertatio de crimine magiae. German. VI. Malleus judicum. VII. Spee, Friedrich von, 1591-1635. Cautio criminalis. VIII. Meyfart, Johann Matthäus, 1590-1642. Christliche Erinnerung an Regenten. IX. Title. X. Title: Fernerer Unfug der Zauberey. XI. Title: Unterschiedliche Schrifften von Unfug des Hexen-Processes.
8
NIC

Witchcraft
BF 1565 T46 1717a

Reiche, Johann, respondent.
Thomasius, Christian, 1655-1728.
Christ. Thomasii Kurtze Lehr-Sätze von dem Laster der Zauberey, mit dessen eigenen Vertheidigung vermehret. Worbey Johann Kleins ... Juristische Untersuchung, was von der Hexen Bekäntniss zu halten, dass solche aus schändlichem Beyschlaff mit dem Teuffel Kinder gezeuget. Beydes aus dem Lateinischen ins Teutsche übersetzt. Franckfurth und Leipzig, 1717.
8   134 p. fro nt. 19cm.
                (Continued on next card)

Witchcraft
BF 1565 T46 1717a

Reiche, Johann, respondent.
Thomasius, Christian, 1655-1728. Christ. Thomasii Kurtze Lehr-Sätze von dem Laster der Zauberey ... 1717. (Card 2)

Translation of his Dissertatio de crimine magiae, J. Reiche, respondent; and of Meditatio academica, exhibens examen juridicum judicialis, by J. Klein (N. Putter, respondent.)
Johann Kleins Juristische Untersuchung, p. [79]-134, has special t. p.
8
                (Continued on next card)

CATALOGUE OF THE CORNELL WITCHCRAFT COLLECTION

Reiche, Johann, respondent.

Witchcraft
BF
1565
T46
1717a

Thomasius, Christian, 1655-1728. Christ. Thomasii Kurtze Lehr-Sätze von dem Laster der Zauberey ... 1717.   (Card 3)

With this are bound Ludovici, Gottfried, 1670-1724. ... Theologicum novae... Coburgi [1718] and Sturm, Johann Christoph, 1635-1703. ... Wahrhaffte und gründliche Vorstellung von der lügenhafften Stern-Wahrsagerey. Coburg, 1722.
1. Witchcraft. I. His Dissertatio de crimine mag   iae.-- German. II.
(Continued on next card)

Reiche, Johann, respondent.

Witchcraft
BF
1565
T46

Thomasius, Christian, 1655-1728, praeses. Theses inavgvrales, De crimine magiae, qvas ... praeside D. Christiano Thomasio ... svbmittit M. Iohannes Reiche ... Halae Magdebvrgicae, Literis Christoph. Salfeldii [1701]
40 p. 21cm.
Diss.---Halle (J. Reiche, respondent)
Also known as Dissertatio de crimine magiae.
1. Witchcraft. I. Reiche, Johann, respondent. II. His Dissertatio de crimine magiae. III. Title: De crimine magiae.

Witchcraft
F
583
R7
546

Reichel, Rudolf.
Ein Marburger Hexenprocess vom Jahre 1546. Von Prof. Rudolf Reichel.
(In Historischer Verein für Steiermark, Graz. Mittheilungen. Graz. 23cm. 27. Heft (1879), p. [122]-135)

1. Trials (Witchcraft)--Germany. 2. Witchcraft--Germany. I. Title.

Witchcraft
C
340
R5
761

Reichle, Franciscus Antonius.
Der triumphierliche Namen Jesus, das ist: Allgemeines, unfehlbahres, und kräftiges Hilfs-Mittel, durch welches ein jeglicher catholischer Christ ... sich, und die seinige von allem Unheil bewahren, ... ja gar den leydigen Teufel selbsten ... verjagen, und überwinden kan. Zum Nutzen des christlichen gemeinen Volcks in teutscher Sprach verfasset ...; das jenige aber, so die Priester und Exorcisten   alleinig betrifft ...
(Continued on next card)

Witchcraft
C
340
R5
761

Reichle, Franciscus Antonius. Der triumphierliche Namen Jesus ... 1761.   (Card 2)

wird in lateinischer Sprach beygesetzt. Vermehrter in Druck gegeben von Franc. Ant. Reichle ... Costantz, Bey Antoni Labhart, Buchdr., 1761.
143 p. 13cm.
Appendix, p. 60-143, in Latin.
1. Exorcism. 2. Witchcraft. I. Catholic Church. Liturgy and ritual. II. Title.

Reineccius, Johann Paulus.

see

Reineck, Johann Paul.

Reineck, Johann Paul, respondent.

Witchcraft
BF
1565
D62
no.7

Wolf, Johann, praeses.
Disputationem physicam, evolventem qv. Num daemon cum sagis generare possit, ... sub praesidio Dn. M. Johannis Wolfii ... submittit Johann. Paulus Reineccius ... Wittenbergae, Typis Christiani Schrödteri [1676]
[16] p. 20cm.
No. 7 in vol. lettered Dissertationes de sagis. 1636-1714.
1. Witchcraft. 2. Devil. I. Reineck, Johann Paul, respondent. II. Title: Num daemon cum sagis generare possit.

Witchcraft
BF
1565
R37

[Reinking, Dietrich] 1590-1664.
Responsum juris, in ardua et gravi quadam causa, concernente processvm qvendam, contra sagam, nvlliter institutum, & inde exortam diffamationem. Ubi quaestiones quaedam, de nocturnis sagarum conventiculis, ... confessionibus, assertionibus & denuntiationibus, exactè examinantur, & requisita totius processus criminalis proponuntur ... Impertitum Gissae ... in anno 1621. Marpvrgi Cattorvm, Typis & sumptibus
(Continued on next card)

Witchcraft
BF
1565
R37

[Reinking, Dietrich] 1590-1664. Responsum juris ... 1630.   (Card 2)

bus Nicolai Hampelii, 1630.
10 p. l., 138 p. 20cm.
"This copy of the original impression lacks the first four leaves of the 'summaria' as well as a corner of the dedication leaf ..."--Note by G. L. Burr on front inside cover.

Witchcraft
HD
1239
G2
R37
1662

Reinking, Dietrich, 1590-1664.
Responsum juris, in ardua et gravi quadam causa, concernente processvm qvendam, contra sagam, nvlliter institutum, & inde exortam diffamationem. Ubi quaestiones quaedam, de nocturnis sagarum conventiculis, ... confessionibus, assertionibus & denuntiationibus, exactè examinantur, & requisita totius processus criminalis proponuntur ... auctore Theodoro Reinkingk ... Gissae Hassorvm.   Sumptibus Hermanni Vel-
(Continued on next card)

Witchcraft
HD
1239
G2
R37
1662

Reinking, Dietrich, 1590-1664. Responsum juris ... 1662.   (Card 2)

stenii, 1662.
9 p. l., 138 p. 19cm.
Detached from his Tractatus synopticus De retractu consanguinitatis.
In slipcase with his Tractatus synopticus, Gissae Hassorum, 1662.
1. Trials (Witchcraft) 2. Witchcraft. I. Title: Responsum juris, in ... causa, concernente processum ... contra sagam.

Witchcraft
HD
1239
G2
R37
1662

Reinking, Dietrich, 1590-1664.
Theodori Reinkingk ... Tractatus synopticus De retractu consangvinitatis ... in certas quaestiones collectus. Editio secunda priori correctior. Huic accessit ejusdem auctoris Responsum juris accuratè elaboratum de processu contra sagas et maleficos &c. Hactenus suppresso nomine editum.   Gissae Hassorvm, Sumptibus Hermanni Velstenii, 1662.
16 p. l., 420, [58] p. 14cm.
Added engraved t. p.
(Continued on next card)

Witchcraft
HD
1239
G2
R37
1662

Reinking, Dietrich, 1590-1664. Theodori Reinkingk ... Tractatus synopticus De retractu consangvinitatis ... 1662.   (Card 2)

Incomplete: Responsum juris ... wanting.
With this in slipcase is his Responsum juris ..., Gissae Hassorvm, 1662, detached from another copy of Tractatus synopticus.
1. Pre-emption--Germany. 2. Pre-emption (Roman law) I. Title: De retractu consanguinitatis.
(Over)

Reinkingk, Theodor, 1590-1664.

see

Reinking, Dietrich, 1590-1664.

WITCHCRAFT
AZ
999
H51

Eine Reise durch das Reich des Aberglaubens.
Henne am Rhyn, Otto, 1828-1914.
Eine Reise durch das Reich des Aberglaubens. Leipzig, M. Spohr [1893]
iv, 175 p. 22cm.

Rekuc, Georgius, resp.

WITCHCRAFT
BS
2675
H77

Honert, Johan van den, 1693-1758, praeses.
Dissertatio philologico-theologica, de velanda muliere propter angelos, ad locum I Cor. XI. vers 10. Lugduni Batavorum, 1738.
14 p. 19cm.
Diss.--Lund (G. Rekuc, respondent)

1. Bible. N. T. 1 Corinthians XI, 10-- Criticism, interpretation, etc. I. Rekuc, Georgius,   resp. II. Title: De velanda muliere propter angelos.

WITCHCRAFT
BF
1584
S7
R38

Relacion de las causas mas notables que siguio el tribunal de la inquisicion, contra los que se decian brujos, hechiceros, mágicos, nigrománticos, y aliados con el demonio; entre las que se refieren la del famoso mágico Torralba, Falso Nuncio de Portugal, Monja de Córdoba fingida santa, y otras de mucha nombradia sumamente curiosas. Sevilla, Imprenta de El Porvenir, 1839.
224 p. 14
1. Trials (Witchcraft)--Spain.
2. Inquisition. Spain.

Witchcraft
BF
1555
B35

Relation de l'état de quelques personnes pretenduës possédées.
Bayle, François.
Relation de l'état de quelques personnes pretenduës possédées. Faite d'autorité du Parlement de Toulouse, par Me. François Bayle & Me. Henri Grangeron ... Toulouse, Chez la veuve Pouchac & Bely, 1682.
118 p. 14cm.

467

CATALOGUE OF THE CORNELL WITCHCRAFT COLLECTION

Witchcraft
BF
1581
A2
W81
1866a
no.6

Relation of a memorable piece of witch-
craft, at Welton, near Daventry, in
Northamptonshire.
Clark, G
Relation of a memorable piece of witch-
craft, at Welton, near Daventry, in North-
amptonshire. ... Contained in a letter of
Mr. G. Clark to Mr. M. T. Northampton,
Taylor, 1867.
8 p. 22cm.
Letter dated 1658.
"Reprinted from Glanvil's Sadducismus
triumphatus. London, 1681."

8   No. 6 in box lettered Witchcraft in
Northamptonshire.
1. Ghosts. I. Title.

Witchcraft
GR
142
H6
A3
no.15

A relation of Mary Hall of Gadsden, reputed
to be possessed of two devils, 1664.
Drage, William, 1637?-1669.
A relation of Mary Hall of Gadsden, reputed
to be possessed of two devils, 1664, from
"A small treatise of sicknesses and diseases
from witchcraft," appended to "Physical experi-
ments," by William Drage, London. Printed for
Miller at the Star next the George in Little
Britain [1668] With an introductory by W. B.
Gerish. Bishop's Stortford, 1912.
28 p. 22cm. [Hertfordshire folk lore. no.15]

Witchcraft
BF
1581
Z7
1697

A relation of the diabolical practices of
above twenty wizards and witches of the sheriffdom of Renfrew in the kingdom of Scotland,
contain'd in their tryalls, examinations, and
confessions; and for which several of them have
been executed this present year, 1697. London, Printed for H. Newman [1697]
24 p. 21cm.
"To Sir T. M.", a letter signed: "T.P.":
p.3-4.   I. P., T. II. T. P.
Wing R 823.   III. M., T. IV. T. M.

Witchcraft
BF
1517
F5C75
1863

Relation sur une épidémie d'hystérodémono-
pathie en 1861.
Constans, Augustin.
Relation sur une épidémie d'hystérodémono-
pathie en 1861. 2. éd. Paris, A. Delahaye,
1863.
viii, 130 p. 24cm.

WITCHCRAFT
BF
1582
Z7
1649a

Relation véritable contenant ce qui s'est
passé aux exorcismes d'une fille appellée
Elisabeth Allier.
Farconnet, François.
Relation véritable contenant ce qui s'est
passé aux exorcismes d'une fille appellée
Elisabeth Allier, natife de la coste S. André en Dauphiné, possédée depuis vingt ans
par deux démons nommez Orgueuil et Bonifarce
et l'heureuse délivrance d'icelle fille après six exorcismes faits au couvent des F.
F. Prescheurs de Grenoble. Avec quelques
raisons pour obliger à croire la possession
& la délivrance. Jouxte la coppie [sic]
imprimée à Grenoble. Paris, P. Sevestre,
1649 [repr. Lyon, 1875]
29 p. 23 cm.
Title: Allier, Elisabeth, fl. 1649. I.

WITCHCRAFT
BF
1517
F5
R38
1635

Relation veritable de ce qvi s'est passé
aux exorcismes des religieuses vrsulines
possedees de Loudun, en la presence de
Monsieur frere vnique du roy. Auec l'attestation des exorcistes. Paris, Chez
Iean Martin, 1635.
46 p. 17cm.
"Iouxte la coppie imprimee à Poictiers."

8   1. Loudun, France. Ursuline Convent. 2.   Exorcism. I. Gaston
Jean Baptiste,   duke of Orléans, 1608-
1660.

WITCHCRAFT
BF
1552
R38

Der Relegirte Kobold. [Halle? 1704?]
44 p. front. 17cm.

8
NIC   1. Fairies.

BR
377
T45

Religion and the decline of magic.
Thomas, Keith Vivian.
Religion and the decline of magic [by] Keith Thomas.
New York, Scribner [1971]
xviii, 716 p. 25 cm. $17.50
Includes bibliographical references.

4   1. England—Religion. 2. Occult sciences—England.
3. Witchcraft—England. I. Title.
BR377.T48 1971b   133   74-141707
ISBN 0-684-10602-7   MARC
Library of Congress   71 [7]

WITCHCRAFT
BF
1566
S93

Religion und Aberglaube.
Stubenvoll, F   B
Religion und Aberglaube. Leipzig,
F. Jansa, 1897.
95 p. 20cm.

1. Witchcraft—History. 2. Superstition. I. Title.

8
NIC

---

ar V
13956

Remarkable delusions; or, Illustrations of
popular errors, revised by D. P. Kidder.
New York, Carlton & Phillips, 1854.
213 p. 16cm.

I. Kidder, Daniel Parish, 1815-1891, ed.

F
7
M42
1856

Remarkable providences illustrative of the
earlier days of American colonisation.
Mather, Increase, 1639-1723.
Remarkable providences illustrative of the earlier days
of American colonisation. By Increase Mather. With
introductory preface, by George Offor. London, J. R.
Smith, 1856.
xix, [16], 262 p. front. (port.) 16½ᶜᵐ. (Half-title: Library of old
authors)

1. New England—Hist.—Colonial period. I. Offor, George, 1787-1864,
ed. II. Title.
18-11699
Library of Congress   F7.M436

Witchcraft
BS
2545
D5
T97
no.8

Remarks upon a pamphlet intit'l'd, A
review of the controversy about the
meaning of demoniacs.
Hutchinson, Thomas, 1698-1769.
Remarks upon a pamphlet intit'l'd, A
review of the controversy about the
meaning of demoniacs, &c. Wherein the sermon which
asserteth the usual interpretation, &c., is
vindicated from every exception of the
reviewer. London, Printed for W. Innys
and R. Manby, 1739.
31 p. 21cm.

No. 8 in   vol. lettered: Twells,
(Continued on next card)

Witchcraft
BS
2545
D5
T97
no.8

Remarks upon a pamphlet intit'l'd, A
review of the controversy about the
meaning of demoniacs.
Hutchinson, Thomas, 1698-1769. Remarks
upon a pamphlet intit'l'd, A review of the
controversy ... 1739.   (Card 2)

Whiston, etc. Tracts on the demoniacs in
the New Testament. London, 1738-1775.

1. Sharpe, Gregory, 1713-1771. A review
of the controversy about the meaning of
demoniacks in the New Testament. 2.
Hutchinson, Thomas, 1698-1769. The
usual interpretation. I. Title.

WITCHCRAFT
BX
2340
M54
1589

Remedia efficacissima.
Menghi, Girolamo, d. 1610.
Flagellvm daemonvm. Exorcismos terribiles, potentissimos, et efficaces ... complectens ... Accessit postremò pars secunda,
quae Fustis daemonum inscribitur. Quibus noui exorcismi, & alia nonnulla, quae prius desiderabantur, superaddita fuerunt. Auctore
R. P. F. Hieronymo Mengo Vitellianensi ...
Bononiae, Apud Ioannem Rossium, 1589.
8 p. l., 247, [16], 350, 102, [2] p.
15cm.
8   Title in   red and black.
(Continued on next card)

WITCHCRAFT
BX
2340
M54
1589

Remedia efficacissima.
Menghi, Girolamo, d. 1610. Flagellvm daemonvm ... 1589.   (Card 2)
"Fvstis daemonvm" has special t. p. and
separate paging.
"Remedia efficacissima in malignos spiritvs expellendos," with caption title, is
appended to "Fvstis daemonvm" and has separate paging.
1. Exorcism. 2. Demonology. I. His
Fustis daemonum.   II. His Remedia efficacissima in malignos spiritus expellendos. III. Title: Flagellum daemonum.
IV. Title: Remedia efficacissima.

CATALOGUE OF THE CORNELL WITCHCRAFT COLLECTION

Remi, Nicolas

Remi, Nicolas, 1530-1612.
　Nicolai Remigii ... Daemonolatreiae libri tres. Ex iudicijs capitalibus nongentorum plus minus hominum, qui sortilegij crimen intra annos quindecim in Lotharingia capite luerunt ... Lvgdvni, In Officina Vincentii, 1595.
　[24], 394 p. 25cm.

　Title vignette: printer's device.

　1. Demonology. 2. Witchcraft--Lorraine. I. Title.

Remi, Nicolas, 1530-1612.
　Nicolai Remigii ... Daemonolatreiae libri tres. Ex iudicijs capitalibus nongentorum plus minus hominum, qui sortilegij crimen intra annos quindecim in Lotharingia capite luerunt ... Lvgdvni, In Officina Vincentii, 1595.
　[24], 394 p. 25cm.

　Title vignette: printer's device.
　Bound with Vairo, Leonardo. De fascino libri tres. Parisiis, 1583.

Remi, Nicolas, 1530-1612.
　Daemonolatreiae libri tres. Nicolai Remigii ... ex indiciis capitalibus DCCCC. plus minus hominum, qui sortilegii crimen intra annos XV. in Lotharingia capite luerunt. Miris ac iucundis narrationibus, variarum naturalium quaestionum ac mysteriorum daemonicorum discussionibus, valde suaues & grati, adque satis mouendos in primis apti. Francofvrti, in officina Palthenii, 1596.
　12 p. l., 407 p. 14½cm.

(Continued on next card)

Remi, Nicolas, 1530-1612. Daemonolatreiae
　... 1596. (Card 2)

　First edition, Lugduni, 1595.

　1. Demonology. 2. Witchcraft--Lorraine. I. Title.

Remi, Nicolas, 1530-1612.
　Daemonolatreiae libri tres.
Bodin, Jean, 1530-1596.
　Daemonomania; oder, Auszführliche Erzehlung des wütenden Teuffels in seinen damahligen rasenden Hexen und Hexenmeistern dero Bezauberungen, Beschwerungen, Vergifftungen, Gauckel- und Possen-Wercke... Welches der andere Theil Nicolai Remigii Daemonolatria. Wobey gleichfalls angehänget: Vielerhand warhaftige und erschreckliche Geschichte besessener Leute...nebst noch einigen betrieglichen ... und von Menschen
(Continued on next card)

Witchcraft
BF
1520
B66
1698

Remi, Nicolas, 1530-1612.
　Daemonolatreiae libri tres.
Bodin, Jean, 1530-1596. Daemonomania. 1698. (Card 2)

　practicirten kurtzweiligen Begenheiten. Hamburg, Gedruckt bey T. von Wiering, 1698.
　2 v. in 1. plates. 18cm.

　"Wiederlegung nebst der Schrifft des Hn. Weyer": v. 1, p. [400]-465.
　Translation of De la démonomanie.

Witchcraft
BF
1520
R38
1693

Remi, Nicolas, 1530-1612.
　Nicolai Remigii Daemonolatria, oder: Beschreibung von Zauberern und Zauberinnen. Mit wunderl. Erzehlungen, vielen natürlichen Fragen und teuflis. Geheimnissen vermischet. 1. Theil. Der ander Theil hält in sich: Wunder-seltzame Historien von des Teuffels Hinterlist, Betrug, Falschheit und Verführungen, an, bey und umb den Menschen ... Mit einem Anhange. Von falschen, erdichteten ... gespen stischen Begebenheiten.
(Continued on next card)

8

Witchcraft
BF
1520
R38
1693

Remi, Nicolas, 1530-1612. Daemonolatria, oder: Beschreibung von Zauberern und Zauberinnen. 1693. (Card 2)

　Hamburg, Gedruckt bey T. von Wiering, 1693.
　5 p. l., 288, 544, 96 p. 8 plates. 18cm.
　Part 2 has title: Der bösen Geister und Gespensten wunder-seltzame Historien ...
　Part 3 has title: Der Gespensten Gauckel-Wercks dritter Theil ...
(Continued on next card)

8

Witchcraft
BF
1520
R38
1693

Remi, Nicolas, 1530-1612. Daemonolatria, oder: Beschreibung von Zauberern und Zauberinnen. 1693. (Card 3)

　Translation of his Daemonolatreiae libri tres.

　1. Demonology. 2. Witchcraft--Lorraine. I. Title: Daemonolatria, oder: Beschreibung von Zauberern und Zauberinnen. II. His Daemonolatreiae libri tres --German.

8

Witchcraft
BF
1520
R38
1693

Remi, Nicolas, 1530-1612.
　Nicolai Remigii Daemonolatria, oder: Beschreibung von Zauberern und Zauberinnen. Mit wunderl. Erzehlungen, vielen natürlichen Fragen und teuflis. Geheimnissen vermischet. 1. Theil. Der ander Theil hält in sich: Wunder-seltzame Historien von des Teuffels Hinterlist, Betrug, Falschheit und Verführungen, an, bey und umb den Menschen ... Mit einem Anhange. Von falschen, erdichteten ... gespen stischen Begebenheiten.
(Continued on next card)

8

Witchcraft
BF
1520
R38
1693

Remi, Nicolas, 1530-1612. Daemonolatria, oder: Beschreibung von Zauberern und Zauberinnen. 1693. (Card 2)

　Hamburg, Gedruckt bey T. von Wiering, 1693.
　5 p. l., 288, 544, 96 p. 8 plates. 18cm.
　Part 2 has title: Der bösen Geister und Gespensten wunder-seltzame Historien ...
　Part 3 has title: Der Gespensten Gauckel-Wercks dritter Theil ...
(Continued on next card)

8

Witchcraft
BF
1520
R38
1693

Remi, Nicolas, 1530-1612. Daemonolatria, oder: Beschreibung von Zauberern und Zauberinnen. 1693. (Card 3)

　Translation of his Daemonolatreiae libri tres.

　1. Demonology. 2. Witchcraft--Lorraine. I. Title: Daemonolatria, oder: Beschreibung von Zauberern und Zauberinnen. II. His Daemonolatreiae libri tres --German.

8

BF
1520
R38+
1930

Remi, Nicolas, 1530-1612.
　Demonolatry. In 3 books; translated by E. A. Ashwin, edited with introd. and notes by Montague Summers. Drawn from the capital trials of 900 persons, more or less, who within the last fifteen years have in Lorraine paid the penalty of death for the crime of witchcraft. London, J. Rodker, 1930.
　xliii, 188 p. 27cm.

　French original first published, Lyon, 1595.

WITCHCRAFT
BF
1520
R38
D58

Remi, Nicolas, 1530-1612.
Dintzer, Lucien.
　Nicolas Remy et son oeuvre démonologique. Lyon, L'imprimerie de Lyon, 1936.
　148 p. 25cm.

　Thèse--Lyons.
　At head of title: Université de Lyon, Faculté des lettres.
　Bibliography: p. [135]-143.
　1. Remi, Nicolas, 1530-1612. Daemonolatreiae libri tres. 2. Demonology. 3. Witchcraft. I. Title.

8
NIC

WITCHCRAFT
DC
112
R38
L46
1869

Remi, Nicolas, 1530-1612.
Leclerc, Laurent.
　Notice sur Nicolas Remy, procureur général de Lorraine; discours de réception à l'Académie de Stanislas, par L. Leclerc. Nancy, Sordoillet, imprimeurs de l'Académie de Stanislas, 1869.
　107 p. facsims., port. 23cm.

　"Extrait des Mémoires de l'Académie de Stanislas, 1868."

8
NIC
　1. Remi, Nicolas, 1530-1612. I. Title.

CATALOGUE OF THE CORNELL WITCHCRAFT COLLECTION

WITCHCRAFT
BX 2340
R38
1678
Remigio, Benito.
  Practica de exorcistas y ministros de la iglesia. En qve con mvcha ervdicion ... se trata de la instrucion de los exorcismos, para lançar, y auy entar los demonios, y curar espiritualmente todo genero de maleficio, y hechizos. Por el P. Benito Remigio, noydens Antuerp ... 5. impression añadida ... Madrid, Por Andres Garcia de la Iglesia, Acostade Francisco Serrano de Figueroa, 1678.
  7 p. l., 361 [i.e., 461] p. 15cm.

8   1. Exorci   sm. I. Title.

Remigius, Nicolaus, 1530-1612.
  see
Remi, Nicolas, 1530-1612.

Remonstrance sur les jeux de sort.
Witchcraft
BF 1565
D17
1579
Daneau, Lambert, ca. 1530-1595?
  Devx traitez novveavx, tres-vtiles povr ce temps. Le premier tovchant les sorciers, auquel ce qui se dispute auiourd'huy sur cete matiere, est bien amplement resolu & augmenté de deux proces extraicts des greffes pour l'esclaircissement & confirmation de cet argument. Le second contient vne breue Remonstrance sur les ieux de cartes & de dez. Reu. & augm. par l'auteur M. Lambert Daneau. [Geneve?] Par Jaqves Bavmet, 1579.
  160 p. 15cm.
  "Dialogve des sorciers ov eriges" is transla- of most of his De   veneficis, qvos olim sortilegos ...   vocant.
8   (Continued on next card)
Library of Congress

Remonstrantie in de Eerw. Synode van Noord-Holland...
Witchcraft
BF 1410
B42
Z56
v.3
no.9
[Bekker, Balthasar] 1634-1698.
  Remonstrantie in de Eerw. Synode van Noord-Holland, jegenwoordig vergaderd tot Alkmaar, ingediend by ofte van wegen Balthasar Bekker, S.S.Th.Dr. ende predikant tot Amsterdam, op den 5. Aug. 1692. [Alkmaar? 1692]
  8 p. illus. initial. 20 x 15cm.
  4°: A⁴.
  Caption title.
  Signed: Bal   thasar Bekker.

                    (Continued on next card)

Remonstrantie in de Eerw. Synode van Noord-Holland...
Witchcraft
BF 1410
B42
Z56
v.3
no.9
[Bekker, Balthasar] 1634-1698. Remonstrantie in de Eerw. Synode van Noord-Holland ... [1692]   (Card 2)
  Describes Bekker's relations with the Classis of Amsterdam.
  Van der Linde 45.
  No. 9 in vol. lettered Bekker III.
  1. Nederlandse Hervormde Kerk. Classes. Amsterdam. I. Nederlandse Hervormde Kerk. Synode, Alkmaar, 1692. II. Title.

8

Remy, Nicolas, 1530-1612.
  see
Remi, Nicolas, 1530-1612.

WITCHCRAFT
BF 1773
R39
Renazzi, Filippo Maria, 1742-1808.
  De sortilegio et magia. Venetiis, Excudebant fratres Coletii, 1792.
  44 p. 23cm.

8
NIC   1. Divination. 2. Witchcraft. I. Title.

Repetitio dispvtationis de lamiis sev strigibvs.
Witchcraft
BF 1565
E65
Erastus, Thomas, 1524-1583.
  Repetitio dispvtationis de lamiis sev strigibvs: in qua plenè, solidè, & perspicuè, de arte earum, potestate, itemque poena disceptatur ... Basileae, Apud Petrum Pernam [1578]
  7 p. l., 127 p. 16cm.

  1. Witchcraft. I. Title.

8

Witchcraft
BF 1565
T19
M183
Replica alla risposta intitolata Arte magica distrutta, di un dottore e sacerdote Veronese. Verona, Nella stamperia Vescovile del seminario per Angelo Targa, 1751.
  68, [1] p. 24cm.
  Ascribed to P. Antonio Ballerini in a contempory hand on t. p. and in another hand on p. [69]
  "Melzi (II, p. 430) ascribes this to P. Andrea Lugiato, despite its praise of him;
8   (Continued on next card)

Witchcraft
BF 1565
T19
M183
Replica alla risposta intitolata Arte magica distrutta ... 1751. (Card 2)
  but Melzi knows nothing of the ascription to Ballerini."--Note of George Lincoln Burr on t. p.
  Bound with Fiorio, Antonio. Arte magica distrutta. Trento, 1750.
  1. Fiorio, Antonio. Arte magica distrutta. 2. Lugiato, Andrea. Osservazzioni sopra ... Arte magica dileguata.
8   (Continued on next card)

Witchcraft
BF 1565
T19
M183
Replica alla risposta intitolata Arte magica distrutta ... 1751. (Card 3)
  3. Magic. I. Ballerini, Antonio, supposed author. II. Lugiato, Andrea, supposed author.

8

The replie of Iohn Darrell, to the answer of Iohn Deacon, and Iohn Walker.
WITCHCRAFT
BF 1555
D22
Darrell, John, fl. 1562-1602.
  The replie of Iohn Darrell, to the answer of Iohn Deacon, and Iohn Walker, concerning the doctrine of the possession and dispossession of demoniakes. [London?] 1602.
  50, [8] p. 18cm.

  1. Deacon, John, preacher. A summarie answere. 2. Walker, John, preacher. 3. His A true   narration of the strange and grevous   vexation by the Devil. I. Title.

Witchcraft
BF 1761
F682
Baltus, Jean François, 1667-1743.
  Réponse à l'histoire des oracles, de Mr. de Fontenelle. Dans laquelle on réfute le systême de Mr. Van-Dale, sur les auteurs des oracles du paganisme, sur la cause & le temps de leur silence; & où l'on établit le sentiment des Pères de l'Eglise sur le même sujet. Strasbourg, J. R. Doulssecker, 1707.
  [42], 374, [13] p. front. 18cm.

  1. Fontenelle, Bernard Le Bovier de, 1657-1757. Histoire des oracles. 2. Oracles. 3. Dale, Anto   nius van, 1638-1708. De oraculis   ethnicorum.

Réponse à la seconde partie du Second Mémoire du Père Girard.
WITCHCRAFT
BF 1582
G51
P96
v.1
no.3
Cadière, Catherine, b. 1709, complainant.
  Réponse à la seconde partie du Second Mémoire du Père Girard. [s.l., 173-?]
  106 p. 17cm.
  No. 3 in vol. lettered: Procès de Girard. [v.1]

8
NIC   I. Girard, Jean Baptiste, 1680-1733, respondent. II. Title

Réponse au Second Mémoire instructif du Père Girard.
WITCHCRAFT
BF 1582
G51
P96
v.1
no.1
Cadière, Catherine, b. 1709, complainant.
  Réponse au Second Mémoire instructif du Père Girard, Jesuite, pour Demoiselle Catherine Cadière, de ... Toulon, querellante en crimes d'enchantement, d'inceste spirituel, d'avortement, & de subornation de témoins. Contre ledit Père Girard, querellé. [s.l., 173-?]
  104 p. 17cm.
  Signed: Catherine Cadière. Chaudron,
8 avocat.   Aubin, procurateur.
NIC De Ville   neuve d'Ansous, raporteur
                    (Continued on next card)

Réponse au Second Mémoire instructif du Père Girard.
WITCHCRAFT
BF 1582
G51
P96
v.1
no.1
Cadière, Catherine, b. 1709, complainant.
  Réponse au Second Mémoire ... du Père Girard. [173-?]   (Card 2)
  [sic]
  No. 1 in vol. lettered: Procès de Girard. [v.1]

8
NIC   1. Girard, Jean Baptiste, 1680-1733, respondent.   II. Title

Reprobacion de las svpersticiones y hechizerias.
Witchcraft
BF 1565
C57
R4
1551
Ciruelo, Pedro, 1470 (ca.)-1560.
  Reprobacion de las svpersticiones y hechizerias. Libro muy vtil, y necessario a todos los buenos christianos. ... Medina del Campo, Fue impresso en casa de Guillermo de millis, 1551.
  62 [i.e., 124] p. 20cm.

  Title vignette (printer's device)
  Imperfect: t. p. somewhat mutilated.

8

Witchcraft
BF 1410
B42
Z85
no.4
Request aan de Eerwaarde Kerkenraad van Amsterdam, overgelevert den 20 Maart. 1692. Ten eynde de suspensie van Do. Balthasar Bekker mochte werden gecontinueert. Amsterdam, By G. Borstius, boekverkooper [1692]
  11 p. [p. 12 blank] title vignette, illus. initial. 19 x 16cm.
  4°: A⁴, [B²]
  Van der Linde 39.
  No. 4 in vol. lettered Stukken betrekkelijk Bekker.

8   (Continued on next card)

470

CATALOGUE OF THE CORNELL WITCHCRAFT COLLECTION

Witchcraft
BF
410
.A2
.85
no.4
    Request aan de Eerwaarde Kerkenraad van Amsterdam ... [1692]   (Card 2)

    1. Bekker, Balthasar, 1634-1698.
I. Nederlandse Hervormde Kerk. Classes. Amsterdam.

Witchcraft
BF
1412
R43
    Résie, Lambert Elisabeth d'Aubert, comte de.
    Histoire et traité des sciences occultes; ou, Examen des croyances populaires sur les êtres surnaturels, la magie, la sorcellerie, la divination, etc., depuis le commencement du monde jusqu'à nos jours.   Paris, Louis Vivès, 1857.
    2 v. 23cm.

    1. Occult sciences.   I. Title.

WITCHCRAFT
BF
1565
M51

    Resolutio praecipuarum quaestionum criminalis adversus sagas processus.
    Melander, Otto, 1571-1640.
    Resolutio praecipuarum quaestionum criminalis adversus sagas processus, cum refutatione nova tam juridica quam philosophica purgationis sagarum per aquam frigidam, adversus Guilielmum Adolphum Scribonium... Autore Otthone Melandro... Adjecta est .. Rodolphi Goclenii...Oratio..de natura sagarum in purgatione et examinatione per frigidam aquis innatantium.   Lichae, Apud Nicolaum Erbenium, 1597.
8   131 p.   17cm.
NIC   (Continued on next card)

Witchcraft
BF
1565
G12
    Responsa ad annotationes criticas D. F. A. T. in sermonem de Maria Renata.
    Gaar, Georg, b. 1702.
    Responsa ad annotationes criticas D. F. A. T. [i.e. Girolamo Tartarotti] in sermonem de Maria Renata, saga supplicio addicta die 21. Junii Anno 1749. Herbipoli habitum, Veronae typis evulgatas, in lucem edita ab authore ejusdem sermonis P. Georgio Gaar, S.J. ... Wirceburgi, Typis M. A. Engman [1750?]
    55 p. 20cm.
8   (Continued on next card)

Witchcraft
BF
1565
G12
    Responsa ad annotationes criticas D. F. A. T. in sermonem de Maria Renata.
    Gaar, Georg, b. 1702.   Responsa ad annotationes criticas D. F. A. T. in sermonem de Maria Renata ... [1750]   (Card 2)

    His Ragionamento del padre Giorgio Gaar, p. [37]-55, has special t. p., facsimile of the Verona edition. This text includes Tartarotti's commentary.
    1. Tartarotti, Girolamo, 1706-1761. 2. His Ragionamento. 3. Witchcraft. 4. Sänger, Maria Renata von Mossau, ca. 1680-1749. I. His Ragionamento. II. Title.

Witchcraft
BF
1565
S43
1588
    Responsio ad examen Ignoti Patroni Veritatis.
    Scribonius, Wilhelm Adolf, 16th cent.
    Responsio ad examen Ignoti Patroni Veritatis de pvrgatione sagarum per aquam frigidam. Francofurdi, Apud Joannem Wechelum, 1590.
    [7], 56 p. 17cm.

    Bound with Scribonius, Wilhelm Adolf. De sagarvm natura. Marpurgi, 1588.
    1. Ignotus Patronus Veritatis, pseud. Examen epistolae et partis physiologiae de examine sagarum per aquam frigidam. 2. Witchcraft. I. Title.

Witchcraft
HD
1239
G2
R37
1662
    Responsum juris ... concernente processum ... contra sagam.
    Reinking, Dietrich, 1590-1664.
    Responsum juris, in ardua et gravi quadam causa, concernente processvm qvendam, contra sagam, nvlliter institutum, & inde exortam diffamationem. Ubi quaestiones quaedam, de nocturnis sagarum conventiculis, ... confessionibus, assertionibus & denuntiationibus, exactè examinantur, & requisita totius processus criminalis proponuntur ... auctore Theodoro Reinkingk ... Gissae Hassorvm, Sumptibus Hermanni Velstenii, 1662.
8   (Continued on next card)

Witchcraft
HD
1239
G2
R37
1662
    Responsum juris ... concernente processum ... contra sagam.
    Reinking, Dietrich, 1590-1664.   Responsum juris ... 1662.   (Card 2)
    9 p. l., 138 p. 19cm.
    Detached from his Tractatus synopticus De retractu consanguinitatis.
    In slipcase with his Tractatus synopticus. Gissae Hassorum, 1662.
    1. Trials (Witchcraft) 2. Witchcraft.
I. Title: Responsum juris, in ... causa, concernente processum ... contra sagam.

Witchcraft
BF
1583
A2
D23
    Responsum juris, in causa poenali maleficarum Winsiensium.
    Dassell, Artwig von.
    Hardevvici à Dassell j.c. Responsvm juris, in causa poenali maleficarum VVinsiensium. Pro defensione innoxiarvm, et condemnatione nocentum; ne quisquam ante judicium injuste innocenterq condemnetur; ad requisitionem quorundam Dominorum & amicorum, juris justitiaeq; amantium, conscriptum ... Hamburgi, Theodosius VVolderus, 1597.
    [96] p. 17cm.
    Title in red and black.
8   1. Trials (Witchcraft)--Germany.
I. Title: Responsum juris, in causa poenali maleficarum Winsiensium.

WITCHCRAFT
BF
1565
R43
    Responsum juris, oder Rechtliches vnd auszführliches Bedencken von Zauberin, deren Thun, Wesen vnd Vermögen, auch was Gestalt dieselbe zubestraffen ... gestellet durch einen hochgelehrten vnd gar vornehmen JC[tum] ... Franckfurt am Mayn, Erstmaln gedruckt vnd verlegt bey Johann-Friderich Weissen, 1637.
    4 p. l., 126 [i.e., 162] p. 21cm.
    Possibly by Philipp Hoffmann or Hofmann? Running title: Rechtlich Bedencken von Zauberey.
8
NIC   (Continued on next card)

WITCHCRAFT
BF
1565
R43
    Responsum juris, oder Rechtliches vnd auszführliches Bedencken von Zauberin ... 1637.   (Card 2)

    1. Witchcraft. 2. Trials (Witchcraft)
I. Hoffmann, Philipp, supposed author.
II. Hofmann, Philipp, fl. 1593-1619, supposed author. III. Ein hochgelehrter und gar vornehmer Juris Consultus. IV. Title: Rechtliches und auszführliches Bedencken von Zauberin.
V. Title: Rechtlich Bedencken von Zauberey.

Witchcraft
BF
1583
R43
    Rest, Josef, 1884-
    Ettenheimer Hexenprozesse im 17. Jahrhundert.
    (In Die Ortenau. Mitteilungen des historischen Vereins für Mittelbaden. Offenburg i. B. 25cm. 3. Heft (1912), p. [38]-56)
    Includes transcripts of records.
    1. Trials (Witchcraft)--Ettenheim, Germany. 2. Trials (Witchcraft)--Alsace. I. Title. II. Die Ortenau.

Witchcraft
BX
1070
A95
    Rettung der Catholischen Ehr und Wahrheit.
    Avertanus à S. Elia, Carmelite Prior at Ravensburg.
    Rettung der Catholischen Ehr vnd Wahrheit, auff etlich vnd zwantzig Fragen, vnder andern, ob von Silvestro II. biss auff Gregorium den VII. alle Päbst Zauberer gewesen? Wider die Lutherische Prædicanten daselbsten ... Ravenspurg, J. J. Wehrlin, 1669.
    iiij l., 120 p. 16cm.

    I. Title.

Rare
B
785
P5++
1572
    Reuchlin, Johann, 1455-1522.
    De arte cabalistica.
    Pico della Mirandola, Giovanni, 1463-1494.
    Opera omnia ... Item, tomo II. Ioannis Francisci Pici Principis ... opera quae extant omnia ... Accesservnt etiam indices dvo locvpletissimi ... Basileae, Ex Officina Henricpetrina [1572-73]
    2 v. 32cm.

    Device of Henricpetri on t. p. and on verso of last leaf.
    Includes also Johann Reuchlin's De arte cabalistica. ([20], 3001-3164 p. at end of v.1)
    (Continued on next card)

Rare
B
785
P5++
1572
    Reuchlin, Johann, 1455-1522.
    De arte cabalistica.
    Pico della Mirandola, Giovanni, 1463-1494.
    Opera omnia ... [1572-73]   (Card 2)

    Manuscript note on t. p.: Bibliothecae Limburgensis, 1719; and stamp: Bischöfliche Seminar-Bibliothek zu Limburg.
    16th century pigskin binding, blind-stamped, over wooden boards; clasps (one missing).

    I. Reuchlin, Johann, 1455-1522. De arte cabalistica.

WITCHCRAFT
BF
1583
R44
    Reuss, Rodolphe Ernst, 1841-1924.
    La sorcellerie au seizième et au dix-septième siècle, particulièrement en Alsace. D'après des documents en partie inédits. Paris, J. Cherbuliez, 1871.
    202 p. 24cm.

    1. Witchcraft--Alsace. 2. Witchcraft.
8   I. Title.
NIC

WITCHCRAFT
BF
1583
R44
S73
    Reuss, Rodophe Ernst, 1841-1924.
    La sorcellerie au seizième et au dix-septième siècle.
    [Spach, Louis Adolphe]
    Das Hexenwesen im Elsass. [n. p., ca. 1871]
    6 p. 21cm.

    Reprint from a review.

    1. Reuss, Rodolphe Ernst, 1841-1924. La sorcellerie au seizième et au dix-septième siècle. 2. Witchcraft--Alsace.
8   I. Title.
NIC

WITCHCRAFT
BF
1523
R44
    Reuter, Simon Henrich.
    (Sulṭān al-Ẓulmah)
    سلطان الظلمة
    das ist, Das mächtige, doch umschränckte Reich des Teufels; oder, Gründlicher und wahrhaftiger Bericht, was von der List, Macht und Wirckung des Satans und der bösen Geister zu halten sey, und was die Menschen durch derselben Kraft und Gemeinschaft wissen, thun und verrichten können ... Alles treulich aus Gottes Wort und vieler
8
NIC   (Continued on next card)

471

CATALOGUE OF THE CORNELL WITCHCRAFT COLLECTION

WITCHCRAFT
BF 1523
R44

Reuter, Simon Henrich.
(Sulṭān al-Ẓulmah)... (Card 2)

Gelehrten Bücher zusammen getragen, untersuchet und zur Warnung der glaubigen Kinder Gottes vorgestellet; auch mit einem nützlichen Register versehen. Lemgo, H. W. Meyer, 1716.
1293 p. 20cm.

(Continued on next card)

WITCHCRAFT
BF 1523
R44

Reuter, Simon Henrich.
(Sulṭān al-Ẓulmah)...1716. (Card 3)

1. Demonology. 2. Devil. I. Title. II. Title: Das mächtige, doch umschränckte Reich des Teufels. III. Title: Gründlicher und wahrhaftiger Bericht, was von der List, Macht und Wirckung des Satans ... zu halten sey.

Reverendi P. Petri Thyraei ... De variis tam spirituum, quam vivorum hominum prodigiosis apparitionibus ... libri tres.

WITCHCRAFT
BF 1445
T54
D2

Thyraeus, Pierre, 1546-1601.
Reverendi P. Petri Thyraei ... De variis tam spirityvm, qvam vivorvm hominvm prodigiosis apparitionibus, & nocturnis infestationibus libri tres. Quorum contenta pagina versa demonstrabit ... Coloniae Agrippinae, Ex officina Mater. Cholini, sumptibus Gosuini Cholini, 1594.
8 p. l., 159 p. 21cm.

8

1. Apparitions. 2. Ghosts. I. Title: De variis tam spirituum, quam vivorum hominum ... apparitionibus ... libri tres.

Reverendi Patris F. Bartholomaei Spinei Pisani ... Quaestio de strigibus.

WITCHCRAFT
BF 1565
M47
1575

Spina, Bartolommeo.
Reverendi Patris F. Bartholomaei Spinei Pisani ... Qvaestio de strigibvs, vna cvm tractatv de praeeminentia Sacrae Theologiae, & quadruplici apologia de lamiis contra Ponzinibium ... Romae, In aedibus Populi Romani, 1576.
4 p. l., 180 p. 23cm.
Bound with Mazzolini, Silvestro, da Prierio. ... De strigmagarum... Romae, 1576.

8
NIC

1. Witchcraft. 2. Theology, Doctrinal. 3. Ponzinibius, Joannes Franciscus. De lamiis, et excellentia. I. Title: Quaestio de strigibus.

Reverendi Patris F. Silvestri Prieriatis ... De strigimagarum, daemonumque mirandis.

WITCHCRAFT
BF 1565
M47
1575

Mazzolini, Silvestro, da Prierio, 1456-1523.
Reverendi Patris F. Silvestri Prieriatis ... De strigimagarvm, daemonumque mirandis, libri tres ... Romae, In aedibus Populi Romani, 1575.
12 p. l., 262 p. 23cm.
With colophon.
With this is bound Spina, Bartolommeo. ... Quaestio de strigibus. Romae, 1576.

8
NIC

1. Witch craft. 2. Demonology. I. Title: De strigimagarum... mirandis.

Reverendi patris Petri Thyraei ... De apparitionibus spirituum.

WITCHCRAFT
BF 1445
T54
D2
1600

Thyraeus, Pierre, 1546-1601.
Reverendi patris Petri Thyraei ... De apparitionibus spirituum tractatus duo: quorum prior agit de apparitionibvs omnis generis spirityvm, Dei, angelorvm, daemonvm, et animarum humanarum libro vno ... Posterior continet divinarvm sev Dei in Veteri Testamento apparitionum & locutionum tam externarum, quam internarum libros quatuor nunc primum editos. Coloniae Agrippinae, Ex officina Mater. Cholini, sumptibus Gosuini Cholini. 1600.

8

(Continued on next card)

Reverendi patris Petri Thyraei ... De apparitionibus spirituum.

WITCHCRAFT
BF 1445
T54
D2
1600

Thyraeus, Pierre, 1546-1601. ... De apparitionibvs spirituum tractatus duo ... 1600. (Card 2)

8 p. l., 486 p. 21cm.
Revised and expanded version of his De variis tam spirituum, quam vivorum hominum prodigiosis apparitionibus ... libri tres.
Binding: contemporary blind stamped pigskin, with clasps.
With this is bound his De prodigiosis. Wircebvrgi [1591?]

8

1. Apparitions. 2. Ghosts. I. His De variis tam spirituum, quam vivorum hominum ... a pparitionibus ... libri tres. II. Title: De apparitionibus spirituum tra ctatus duo.

A review of the controversy about the meaning of demoniacks in the New-Testament.

Witchcraft
BS 2545
D5
T75
no.3

[Sharpe, Gregory] 1713-1771.
A review of the controversy about the meaning of demoniacks in the New-Testament. In which Mr. Hutchinson's sermon at Oxford ..., the Reply to the Further enquiry, Mr. Twell's Answer to the Further enquiry, and a tract, entitled, Some thoughts on the miracles of Jesus, by an impartial hand, are considered. By a lover of truth. ... London, Printed for J. Roberts, 1739.
80 p. 20cm.
No. 3 in vol. lettered: Tracts on demoniacks. 1737.

Witchcraft
BF 1548
R45
1871

Réville, Albert, 1826-1906.
The devil his origin, greatness and decadence. London, Williams and Norgate, 1871.
xvi, 72 p. 18cm.

"Translator's prefatory notes", p. [v]-x, signed H. A. [i. e. Henry Attwell]

1. Devil. I. Réville, Albert, 1826-1906. Histoire du diable, ses origines, sa grandeur et sa décadence—English. II. Attwell, Henry, 1834- tr. III. Title.

Réville, Albert, 1826-1906. Histoire du diable ... —English.

WITCHCRAFT
BF 1548
R45
1871

Réville, Albert, 1826-1906.
The devil his origin, greatness and decadence. London, Williams and Norgate, 1871.
xvi, 72 p. 18cm.

"Translator's prefatory notes", p. [v]-x, signed H. A. [i. e. Henry Attwell]

1. Devil. I. Réville, Albert, 1826-1906. Histoire du diable, ses origines, sa grandeur et sa décadence—English. II. Attwell, Henry, 1834- tr. III. Title.

WITCHCRAFT
BF 1583
R46

Rhamm, A.
Hexenglaube und Hexenprocesse, vornämlich in den braunschweigischen Landen, von A. Rhamm. Wolfenbüttel, J. Zwissler, 1882.
104 p. 20cm.

Bibliographical footnotes.

8
NIC

1. Witchcraft—Brunswick (Duchy) 2. Trials (Witchcraft)—Brunswick (Duchy) I. Title.

Rhegius, Urbanus, 1489-1541.
Wie man fürsichtlich und ohne Ärgerniss reden soll.

WITCHCRAFT
BX 2340
V94

Vom Exorcismo ... Das dieser ohne Verletzung des Gewissens bey der Tauffe wol mag gebraucht vnd behalten werden: etliche Tractetlein. I. Iusti Menij. II. Lutheri Vorrede vber das Tauffbüchlein. III. Die gewöhnliche Gebet bey der Tauffe im Stifft vnd der Thumkirchen zu Cölln an der Sprew. IIII. Aus dem Appendice D. Vrbani Regij. V. Zwo Episteln Tilemanni Heshusij. VI. Eine Epistel Philippi Melanchton is. VII. D. Iacobi Co-

8

(Continued on next card)

Rhegius, Urbanus, 1489-1541.
Wie man fürsichtlich und ohne Ärgerniss reden soll.

WITCHCRAFT
BX 2340
V94

Vom Exorcismo ... 1591. (Card 2)

leri Büchlein. Alles zu guter Nachrichtung den einfeltigen Leyen zum besten zusammen bracht. [Franckfurt an der Oder, In Verlegung Johan vnd Friderich Hartmans, 1591.
[269] p. 17cm.
Title in red and black.
With colophon: Gedruckt zu Franckfurt an der Oder, durch Nicolaum Voltzen, 1591.

8

(Continued on next card)

Rhegius, Urbanus, 1489-1541.
Wie man fürsichtlich und ohne Ärgerniss reden soll.

WITCHCRAFT
BX 2340
V94

Vom Exorcismo ... 1591. (Card 3)

Vom Exorcismo, oder Von dem Beschweren der Kinder bey der Tauffe. Drey Sendbriefe deren zwene D. Tilemannvs Heshvsivs: den dritten Herr Philippvs Melanchton geschrieben ... Verdeutscht durch Heinrich Rätel, has special t. p. with date 1590.
Vom Exorcismo bey der Tauffe ... durch Jacobum Colerum D. has special t. p., no date.

8

(Continued on next card)

WITCHCRAFT
BF 1555
R47

Rhodes, de.
Lettre en forme de dissertation de M^r. de Rhodes escuyer docteur en mededine, aggregé au college des medecins de Lyon. A monsievr Destaing comte de Lyon; au sujet de la prétenduë possession de Marie Volet de la parroisse de Pouliat en Bresse, dans laquelle il est traité des causes naturelles de ses accidens, & de sa guérison. Lyon, Chez Thomas Amaulry, 1691.
4 p. l., 75 p. 18cm.

8

(Continued on next card)

WITCHCRAFT
BF 1555
R47

Rhodes, de. Lettre en forme de dissertation ... 1691. (Card 2)

Imperfect copy: p. 1-2 (second t. p.?) wanting.
With this is bound Sentimens d'Eudoxe et d'Aristée, sur le dialogue satirique de Mystagogue et de Neophile. 1691.

8

1. Demoniac possession. 2. Volet, Marie, fl. 1690. I. Title. II. Title: La prétenduë possession de Marie Volet. III. Destaing, count of Lyons.

Witchcraft
BV 5091
C7
R48
1895

Ribet, Jérôme, 1837-1909.
La mystique divine distinguée des contrefaçons diaboliques et des analogies humaines. Nouv. éd. Paris, Ch. Poussielgue, 1895-1903.
4 v. 21cm.

Contents.—Part 1. Les phénomènes mystiques. v.1. La contemplation.—v.2. Les phénomènes distincts de la contemplation.—Part 2. Les causes des phénomènes mystiques. v.3. Les contrefaçons diaboliques.—v.4. Les analogies humaines.
I. Title.

BF 1775
R48

Riccardi, Paolo, 1854-
Pregiudizi e superstizioni del popolo modenese; contribuzione alla inchiesta intorno alle superstizioni e ai pregiudizi esistenti in Italia, ecc., ecc. Modena, 1890.
84 p. illus. 24cm.

1. Superstition. 2. Folk-lore—Modena, Italy. 3. Witchcraft—Modena, Italy. I. Title.

CATALOGUE OF THE CORNELL WITCHCRAFT COLLECTION

hcraft
    Richel, Arthur.
        Zwei Hexenprozesse aus dem 16. Jahrhundert.
        (In Beiträge zur Kulturgeschichte. Weimar. 25cm. 2. Heft (1898), p. 1-17)

    1. Witchcraft--Germany. I. Title.

WITCHCRAFT
BF 1565 T75
    Rick, Jacobus, fl. 1580.
        Discursus de proba ut loquuntur aquae frigidae.
        Tractatus duo singulares de examine sagarum super aquam frigidam projectarum (Von der Wasser-Prob der Hexen) in quibus hujus purgationis origo, natura & veritas curiose inquiritur, variaeque quaestiones ê theologorum, JCtorum, medicorum & philosophorum scriptis petitae doctissime & jucunde resolvuntur. Francofurti, T. H. Grentz, 1686.
        155 p. 20cm.

8 NIC   (Continued on next card)

WITCHCRAFT
BX 1374 R55
    Rieks, J
        Leo XIII. und der Satanskult, von J. Rieks. Berlin, H. Walther (F. Bechly) 1897.
        xx, 301 p. 19cm.

    Bibliographical footnotes.

    1. Leo XIII, Pope, 1810-1903. 2. Devil-worship. I. Title.

8 NIC

CRAFT
    Richer, Paul Marie Louis Pierre, 1849-1933.
        Études cliniques sur la grande hystérie ou hystéro-épilepsie. 2. éd. rev. et considérablement augmentées. Paris, A. Delahaye et E. Lecrosnier, 1885.
        xv, 975 p. illus. 25cm.

    Imprint covered by label: Paris, O. Doin.
    1. Hysteria. 2. Hypnotism. I. Title. II. Title: La grande hystérie.

WITCHCRAFT
BF 1565 T75
    Rick, Jacobus, fl. 1580.
        Discursus de proba ut loquuntur aquae frigidae.
        Tractatus duo singulares de examine sagarum ... 1686. (Card 2)

    Scribonius' Epistola de purgatione sagarum previously published under title: De examine et purgatione sagarum per aquam frigidam epistola.
    Contents.--Jacobi Rickii Discursus de proba ut loquuntur aquae frigidae in examinatione maleficarum adhibenda.--Guilielmi Adolphi Scri   bonii Epistola de
        (Continued on next card)

Witchcraft
BF 1583 R56
    Riezler, Sigmund, Ritter von, 1843-1927.
        Geschichte der Hexenprozesse in Bayern. Im Lichte der allgemeinen Entwickelung dargestellt von Sigmund Riezler. Stuttgart, Verlag der J. G. Cotta'schen Buchhandlung Nachf., 1896.
        x, 340 p. 23cm.
    Includes excerpts from Johann Hartliebs Buch aller verbotenen Kunst.
    I. Hartlieb, Johann, fl. 1450. Buch aller verbotenen Kunst. II. Title.

---

craft
    Richer, Paul Marie Louis Pierre, 1849-1933, joint author.
    Charcot, Jean Martin, 1825-1893.
        Les démoniaques dans l'art, par J. M. Charcot et Paul Richer. Paris, A. Delahaye et E. Lecrosnier, 1887.
        116 p. 67 illus. 30cm.

WITCHCRAFT
BF 1565 T75
    Rick, Jacobus, fl. 1580.
        Discursus de proba ut loquuntur aquae frigidae.
        Tractatus duo singulares de examine sagarum ... 1686. (Card 3)

    purgatione sagarum super aquam frigidam projectarum.--Hermanni Neuvvalds Exegesis purgationis sive examinis sagarum super aquam frigidam projectarum in qua refutatur Cyrinio Guilielmi Adolphi Sbribonij [sic]
        (Continued on next card)

BF 1583 R56 1968
    Riezler, Sigmund, *Ritter von*, 1843-1927.
        Geschichte der Hexenprozesse in Bayern. Im Lichte der allgemeinen Entwickelung dargestellt. Neudruck der Ausg. Stuttgart 1896. Mit Nachwort, Register und Karte von Friedrich Merzbacher. Aalen, Scientia-Verlag, 1968.
        x, 404 p. map. 23 cm. 50.00   GDB 68-A35-356
    Includes excerpts from Johann Hartliebs Buch aller verbotenen Kunst.
    Bibliographical footnotes.

    1. Trials (Witchcraft)—Bavaria—History. I. Title: Die Hexenprozesse in Bayern.
        70-374271

Library of Congress   69 [1]

HCRAFT
    Richter, David, of Güstrow, praeses.
        Qvadriga dispp. [i.e. disputationum], magico-thevrgicarum de conciliatione spiritvvm, oder: Von der Kunst sich mit Geistern bekant zu machen, qvam svb praesidio Davidis Richteri habvervnt Henr. Andr. Mätcke et Georg. Erhard. Hambergervs. Jena, J. B. Heller, 1716.
        86 p. 20cm.

    (Continued on next card)

WITCHCRAFT
BF 1583 Z7 1667
    Riedel, Adolph Friedrich Johann, 1809-1872.
        Ein Hexenprocess, verhandelt bei dem Amtsgerichte zu Neustadt an der Dosse, im Jahre 1667; nach den Akten vom Geheimen Archivrathe Prof. Dr. Riedel. [Berlin, 18--]
        [106]-119 p. 25cm.

    Caption title.
    Detached from Märkische Forschungen.

8 NIC   1. Trials (Witchcraft)--Neustadt, Ger. (Brandenburg) 2. Müller, Maria (Rhinow) I. Title.

Witchcraft
BF 1583 D55 Z3
    Riezler, Sigmund, Ritter von, 1843-1927.
    Geschichte der Hexenprozesse in Bayern.
    Diefenbach, Johann.
        Der Zauberglaube des sechzehnten Jahrhunderts nach den Katechismen Dr. Martin Luthers und des P. Canisius. Mit Berücksichtigung der Schriften Pfarrers Längin-Karlsruhe und des Professors Riezler-München. Mainz, F. Kirchheim, 1900.
        xii, 209 p. 23cm.
    1. Witchcraft--Germany. 2. Theology, Doctrinal--16th century. 3. Canisius, Petrus, Saint, 1521-1597. Catechismus.

8   (Continued on next card)

CHCRAFT
    Richter, David, of Güstrow, praeses. Qvadriga dispp. [i.e. disputationum, magico-thevrgicarum...1716. (Card 2)

    1. Spirits. I. Mätcke, Heinrich Andreas, resp. II. Hamberger, Georg Erhard, 1697-1755, resp. III. Title. IV. Title: Von der Kunst sich mit Geistern bekant zu machen.

Witchcraft
BF 1600 R55
    Riegger, Paul Joseph, Ritter von, 1705-1775.
        Dissertatio de magia ... Vindobonae, Typis Ioan. Thomae nob. de Trattnern, 1773.
        104 p. 20cm.

    Title vignette: J. T. Trattner's device.

    1. Magic. I. Title.

Witchcraft
BF 1563 E92++ no. 3.
    Riezler, Sigmund, Ritter von, 1843-1927.
    Geschichte der Hexenprozesse in Bayern.
        Zur Geschichte des Hexenwahns. München, C. Wolf, 1897.
        316-317 p. 32cm. (Deutscher Merkur, 28. Jahrg., No. 40)
    A review of Riezler, S. Geschichte der Hexenprozesse in Bayern. Stuttgart, Cottas Nachfolger, 1896. [BF 1583 R56 1968]

    1. Witchcraft. 2. Trials (Witchcraft) 3. Riezler, Sigmund, Ritter von, 1843-1927. Geschichte der Hexenprozesse in Bayern.

---

hcraft
    Richtige Auslegung der Unterredung Sauls mit der Zauberin und mit einem Gespenste zu Endor.
    Bieler, Benjamin, 1693-1772.
        ... Richtige Auslegung der Unterredung Sauls mit der Zauberin und mit einem Gespenste zu Endor. 1. B. Sam. XXVIII. Auf Veranlassung eines gelehrten Mannes zur Vertheydigung seiner in der fortgesetzten Sammlung 1748 ans Licht gestellten schriftmässigen Betrachtung herausgegeben. Leipzig und Wittenberg, J. F. Schlomach, 1752.
        126 p. 18cm.

    (Continued on next card)

WITCHCRAFT
BF 1584 A93 R55
    Riegler, Ferdinand
        Hexenprozesse, mit besonderer Berücksichtigung des Landes Steiermark. Zur steiermärkischen Kultur. Graz, U. Moser, 1926.
        viii, 119 p. 21cm.

    "Zur Literatur": p. viii.

8 NIC   1. Trials (Witchcraft)--Styria. I. Title.

Witchcraft
BF 1604 M18 R56+
    Riflessioni sopra l'Arte magica annichilata. Venezia, Appresso Francesco Pitteri, 1755.
        130 p. 26cm.

    According to Melzi, may have been written by A. Lugiato.
    Ex libris F. G. Irwin.
    1. Maffei, Francesco Scipione, marchese, 1675-1755. Arte magica annichilata. 2. Magic. I. Lugiato, Andrea, supposed author.

8

473

CATALOGUE OF THE CORNELL WITCHCRAFT COLLECTION

WITCHCRAFT
DC
92
R56+

Rigault, Abel
Le procès de Guichard, Évêque de Troyes (1308-1313) Paris, A. Picard, 1896.
xii, 313 p. illus., facsim. 26cm.
(Paris. École des chartes. Société de l'École des chartes. Mémoires et documents, 1)

Bibliographical footnotes.
1. Guichard, Bp. of Troyes, d. 1317.
2. France-- History--Philip IV, 1285-1314. 3. Witchcraft--France.
I. Title. II. Series.

8
NIC

WITCHCRAFT
BF
1583
A2
R567

Rimphoff, Hinrich, 1599-1655.
Drachen-König; das ist: Warhafftige, deutliche, christliche, vnd hochnothwendige Beschreybunge, dess grawsamen, hochvermaledeyten Hexen, vnd Zauber Teuffels, welcher durch Gottes sonderbahre direction, Schikunge vnd Gnade, an diesem Ort bald fürm Jahr, durch ein neunjähriges Mägdelein, wieder aller Menschen Gedancken manifestirt, vnd gantz wunderbarlich aus Liecht gebracht. Zu Salvir, vnd Rettunge vieler christlicher, vnschuldiger, frommer
(Continued on next card)

8
NIC

WITCHCRAFT
BF
1583
A2
R567

Rimphoff, Hinrich, 1599-1655.
Drachen-König... (Card 2)

Hertzen dieses Orts, auch zur Warnunge aller Hexen Patronen, Adhaerenten, Vorfechteren vnd leichtfertigen Calumnianten. Sampt einem Appendice wider Johan Seiferten von Ulm ... Auss hoher Noth öffentlich in den Druck gegeben, durch Heinricum Rimphof. Rinteln, Druckts P. Lucius, 1647.
566 p. 16 cm.

(Continued on next card)

WITCHCRAFT
BF
1583
A2
R567

Rimphoff, Hinrich, 1599-1655.
Drachen-König...1647. (Card 3)

1. Witchcraft--Verden, Ger. 2. Seifert, Johan. I. Title.

WITCHCRAFT
BF
1583
A2
R57

Rinder, Johann Christian.
Eine Hexe nach ihrer greslichen Gestalt und gerechten Strafe, stellete auf das erschollene und sich weit ausbreitende Gerücht eines zu Apolda vermeintlich vorgegangenen Zauberwerks in nachmittäglicher Sonntags-Predigt den 17. Nov. 1748, aus einem besonders dazu erwehlten Text, 2 B. Mos. XXII, v. 18, Die Zauberinnen solt du nicht leben lassen, vor, und gabs nebst wahrhaftigem Bericht der ganzen Sache zum Druck. Jena, Im Verlag der Marggrafischen
(Continued on next card)

8
NIC

WITCHCRAFT
BF
1583
A2
R57

Rinder, Johann Christian.
Eine Hexe nach ihrer greslichen Gestalt und gerechten Strafe... (Card 2)

Buchhandlung [175-?]
44 p. 22cm.

1. Witchcraft--Apolda, Ger. 2. Witchcraft--Sermons. I. Title.

MSS
Bd.
WITCHCRAFT
BF
G12

Rinder, Johann Christian.
Eine Hexe nach ihrer gresslichen Gestalt und gerechten Strafe.
Gaar, Georg, b. 1702. Heylsame Lehr-Stück ... 1750 [ca. 1900]
44 S. in 4°."
Numerals in margins indicate pagination of the original.
In part a rebuttal of: Johann Christian Rinder. Eine Hexe nach ihrer gresslichen Gestalt und gerechter Strafe.
Provoked in answer: Johann Christian Rinder. Kurtze doch nachdrückliche Abfertigung an den ... Herrn Georg Gaar.
(Continued on next card)

MSS
Bd.
WITCHCRAFT
BF
G12
R57

Rinder, Johann Christian.
Eine Hexe nach ihrer gresslichen Gestalt und gerechten Strafe.
Johann Christian Rinders ... Kurtze doch nachdrückliche Abfertigung an den würtzburgischen Pater Herrn Georg Gaar, Lojoliten, der ihn in einer öffentlichen und nun zum Druck gegebenen Canzelrede ... so gar mit Namen um der Wahrheit willen herum genommen, statt einer Franckfurter Messe dafür bey Gelegenheit derselben wie schuldig, übermacht. Jena, In der Cröckerischen Buchhandlung, 1750 [ca. 1900]
24 l. 23cm. (Continued on next card)

MSS
Bd.
WITCHCRAFT
BF
G12
R57

Rinder, Johann Christian. ...Kurtze doch nachdrückliche Abfertigung ... 1750 [ca. 1900] (Card 2)

Carnap's manuscript copy.
"Originaldruck in der Kgl. Hof u. Staats-Bibliothek zu München. 46 S. in 4°."
Numerals in the margins indicate pagination of the original.
A defense of his Eine Hexe nach ihrer gresslichen Gestalt und gerechter Strafe.
1. Witchcraft--Germany. 2. Gaar, Georg, b. 1702. Heylsame Lehrstück, und Zauberey betreffende Anmerckungen.
(Continued on next card)

MSS
Bd.
WITCHCRAFT
BF
G12
R57

Rinder, Johann Christian.
Johann Christian Rinders ... Kurtze doch nachdrückliche Abfertigung an den würtzburgischen Pater Herrn Georg Gaar, Lojoliten, der ihn in einer öffentlichen und nun zum Druck gegebenen Canzelrede ... so gar mit Namen um der Wahrheit willen herum genommen, statt einer Franckfurter Messe dafür bey Gelegenheit derselben wie schuldig, übermacht. Jena, In der Cröckerischen Buchhandlung, 1750 [ca. 1900]
24 l. 23cm. (Continued on next card)

MSS
Bd.
WITCHCRAFT
BF
G12
R57

Rinder, Johann Christian. ...Kurtze doch nachdrückliche Abfertigung ... 1750 [ca. 1900] (Card 2)

Carnap's manuscript copy.
"Originaldruck in der Kgl. Hof u. Staats-Bibliothek zu München. 46 S. in 4°."
A defense of his Eine Hexe nach ihrer gresslichen Gestalt und gerechter Strafe.
1. Witchcraft--Germany. 2. Gaar, Georg, b. 1702. Heylsame Lehrstück, und Zauberey betreffende Anmerckungen.
(Continued on next card)

MSS
Bd.
WITCHCRAFT
BF
G12

Rinder, Johann Christian.
Eine Hexe nach ihrer gresslichen Gestalt und gerechten Strafe.
Gaar, Georg, b. 1702. Heylsame Lehr-Stück ... 1750 [ca. 1900] (Card 2)
44 S. in 4°."
Numerals in margins indicate pagination of the original.
In part a rebuttal of: Johann Christian Rinder. Eine Hexe nach ihrer gresslichen Gestalt und gerechter Strafe.
Provoked in answer: Johann Christian Rinder. Kurtze doch nachdrückliche Abfertigung an den ... Herrn Georg Gaar.
(Continued on next card)

MSS
Bd.
WITCHCRAFT
BF
G12
R57

Rinder, Johann Christian. ... Kurtze doch nachdrückliche Abfertigung ... 1750 [ca. 1900] (Card 3)

3. His / Eine Hexe nach ihrer gresslichen Gestalt und gerechten Strafe. I. Title: Kurtze doch nachdrückliche Abfertigung an den ... Herrn Georg Gaar.

MSS
Bd.
WITCHCRAFT
BF
G12

Rinder, Johann Christian.
...nachdrückliche Abfertigung ... an den ... Herrn Georg Gaar.
Gaar, Georg, b. 1702.
Heylsame Lehr-Stück, und Zauberey betreffende Anmerckungen in der christlichen, nach Hinrichtung Mariae Renatae einer Zauberin, gehaltenen Anred, einiger Massen zwar angeregt, hernach aber ausführlicher erläutert ... An jetzo mit einem Zusatz vermehrt ... Wirtzburg, Marco Antonio Engman, 1750 [ca. 1900]
38 p. 22cm.
Carnap's manuscript copy.
"Originaldruck in der Kgl. Universitätsbibliothek zu Würzburg,
(Continued on next card)

MSS
Bd.
WITCHCRAFT
BF
G12

Rinder, Johann Christian.
...nachdrückliche Abfertigung an den ... Herrn Georg Gaar.
Gaar, Georg, b. 1702. Heylsame Lehr-Stück ... 1750 [ca. 1900] (Card 2)
44 S. in 4°."
Numerals in margins indicate pagination of the original.
In part a rebuttal of: Johann Christian Rinder. Eine Hexe nach ihrer gresslichen Gestalt und gerechter Strafe.
Provoked in answer: Johann Christian Rinder. Kurtze doch nachdrückliche Abfertigung an den ... Herrn Georg Gaar.
(Continued on next card)

Witchcraft
BF
1547
F65
1741

Rinneberg, Johannes Andreas, respondent.
Förtsch, Michael, 1654-1724.
Commentatio de pactis hominvm cvm diabolo circa abditos in terra thesavros effodiendos et acqvirendos, ad casvm illvm tragicvm, qvi anno MDCCXV. in vigiliis festi Nativitatis Christi in agro Ienensi institvta. Von denen Bündnissen der Menschen mit dem Teufel bey dem Schatz-Graben. Editio novissima. Lipsiae, Apvd Christian. Schroetervm, 1741.
61, [2] p. 22cm.

A new edition of a dissertation at Jena,
(Continued on next card)

Witchcraft
BF
1547
F65
1741

Rinneberg, Johannes Andreas, respondent.
Förtsch, Michael, 1654-1724. Commentatio de pactis hominvm cvm diabolo ... 1741. (Card 2)

with Michael Förtsch as praeses and Johannes Andreas Rinneberg as respondent, published Jena, 1716.

1. Devil. 2. Treasure-trove. I. Rinneberg, Johannes Andreas, respondent. II. Title: De pactis hominum cum diabolo circa abditos in terra thesauros effodiendos. III. Title: Bündnisse der Menschen mit dem Teufel bey dem Schatz-Graben.

Witchcraft
BX
2340
C26

Ritualis Romani documenta de exorcizandis obsessis a daemonio comentariis.
Cardi, Paolo Maria, frater.
Ritualis Romani documenta de exorcizandis obsessis a daemonio comentariis ex SS. patribus, & Ecclesiasticis Scriptoribus potissimum depromptis, illustrata per Fr. Paulum Mariam Cardi ... Venetiis, Apud Josephum Corona, 1733.
8 p. l., 504 p. 18cm.

1. Exorcism. 2. Demonology. I. Catholic Church. Liturgy and ritual. II. Title.

8

CATALOGUE OF THE CORNELL WITCHCRAFT COLLECTION

hcraft
    Roback, C W
        The mysteries of astrology, and the wonders of magic: including a history of the rise and progress of astrology, and the various branches of necromancy; together with valuable directions and suggestions relative to the casting of nativities, and predictions by geomancy, chiromancy, physiognomy, &c.; also, highly interesting narratives, anecdotes, &c., illustrative of the marvels of witchcraft, spiritual phenomena, and the results of supernatural influence. Boston, Author, 1854.
        ccxxxviii p.   24cm.
        I. Title.

tchcraft
    Robbins, Rossell Hope, 1912–
        The encyclopedia of witchcraft and demonology. New York, Crown Publishers [1959]
        571 p. illus. 26 cm.
        Includes bibliography.

    1. Witchcraft—Dictionaries—English. 2. Demonology—Dictionaries—English. I. Title.

BF1503.R6   133.403   59-9155 ‡
Library of Congress   [80]

hcraft
    Robbins, Rossell Hope, 1912–
        The heresy of witchcraft. [Durham, N. C., 1966]
        [532]-543 p. 23cm.

        "Reprinted from The South Atlantic quarterly, vol. LXV, no. 4, Autumn 1966."
        Inscribed by the author.

        1. Witchcraft. 2. Heresy. I. The South Atlantic quarterly, vol. 65, no. 4, Autumn 1966. II. Title.

hcraft
    Robbins, Rossell Hope, 1912–
571   The imposture of witchcraft. [London?]
53   1963]
        545-562 p. 22cm.

        "Read at the British Association for the Advancement of Science, Section H, Aberdeen, 3 September, 1963."
        "Offprint from Folklore, Volume 74, Winter 1963."

        1. Witchcraft. I. Title.

tchcraft
    Robbins, Rossell Hope, 1912–
56   The real crime of witchcraft.
3   (In California monthly. Berkeley. 28cm. v. 76 (1966), p. 4-7)

        Inscribed by the author to Cornell.

        1. Inquisition. I. Title.

    Robert Calef, "Merchant, of Boston, in New England."

hcraft
    Harris, William Samuel, 1861–
        Robert Calef, "Merchant, of Boston, in New England."
        (In Granite monthly. Manchester, N. H. 26cm. v. 39 (1907) p. [157]-163)

        1. Calef, Robert, 1648-1719. I. Title.

    Robert de Mauvoisin, abp. of Aix.

WITCHCRAFT
BF   Mouan, J L G
1582   Documents inédits sur un procès de magie en Provence. (1318) Paris, Impr. impériale, 1869.
Z7
1318   [169]-182 p. 25cm.

        Extract from the Mémoires lus à la Sorbonne dans les séances extraordinaires du Comité impérial des travaux historiques et des sociétés savantes tenues les 14, 15, 16 et 17 avril 1868. Histoire, philologie et sciences morales.
8   1. Trials (Witchcraft)—Aix,France.
NIC   2. Robert de Mauvoisin, abp. of Aix.

Witchcraft
BF   Roberts, Alexander.
1581   A treatise of witchcraft: wherein sundry propositions are laid downe, plainely discouering the wickednesse of that damnable art ... With a true narration of the witchcrafts which Mary Smith ... did practise: of her contract vocally made between the Deuill and her, ... by whose meanes she hurt sundry persons whom she enuied ... London, Printed by N. O. for S. Man, 1616.
A2
R64
        80 p. 18cm.
        1. Witchcraft—England. I. Title.

    Rochelle, Jean François Née de la, 1751-1838.

        see

    Née de la Rochelle, Jean François, 1751-1838.

    Rodriguez de Gutierrez, Maria Garcia de, b. 1564.

        see

    Garcia de Rodriguez de Gutierrez, Maria, b. 1564.

    Römer, Wilhelm, ed. and tr.

WITCHCRAFT
BF   Catholic Church. Pope, 1484-1492 (Innocentius VIII) Summis desiderantes affectibus (9 Dec. 1484)
1565
C36
1889   Die Hexenbulle, nebst Auszügen aus dem "Hexenhammer." Aus dem Lateinischen ins Deutsche übers. und mit erläuternden Anmerkungen versehen ... 2. Aufl., von Wilhelm Römer. Schaffhausen (Schweiz) 1889.
        32 p. 21cm.

8   "Zum 400jährigen Jubiläum des
NIC   'Hexenhammers.'"
        (Continued on next card)

    Römer, Wilhelm, ed. and tr.

WITCHCRAFT
BF   Catholic Church. Pope, 1484-1492 (Innocentius VIII) Summis desiderantes affectibus (9 Dec. 1484)
1565
C36
1889   Die Hexenbulle...1889. (Card 2)

        Each page of the Hexenbulle has Latin text at the top, followed by German translation below.

        1. Witchcraft. I. Institoris, Henricus, d. 1508. Malleus maleficarum. German. II. Römer, Wilhelm, ed. & tr. III. Title.

    Das römische Inquisitionsverfahren in Deutschland bis zu den Hexenprozessen.

BR   Flade, Paul, 1860-1921.
141   Das römische inquisitionsverfahren in Deutschland bis zu den hexenprozessen, dargestellt von lic. theol. Paul Flade ... Leipzig, Dieterich, 1902.
S93
v.9
pt.1   4 p. l., [v]-x, 122 p. 22cm. (Added t.-p.: Studien zur geschichte der theologie und der kirche. 9. bd., hft. 1)

        1. Inquisition   I. Title.

WITCHCRAFT
BF   Röschen, Friedrich August
1566   Die Zauberei und ihre Bekämpfung.
R71   Gütersloh, C. Bertelsmann, 1886.
        110 p. 21cm.

8
NIC   1. Witchcraft. I. Title.

    Röseler, Joannes.

MSS   Drey warhafftige grundtliche Zeitungen,
Bd.   die erste von ettlichen Hexen und Zauberin welche hin und wider in Ungern und
WITCHCRAFT
BF   Teutschland grossen Schaden angericht
D77   haben... Beschriben durch den hochgelerten Herrn Nicolaum Binder... Die ander von einem Burger und Thuchmacher der in grosser Unzucht ein zeitlang gelebt ... unnd wie er durch dess Teufels Eingebung 3. Kinder und sein Weib jämmerlicher weiss ermördet... Die dritte von Erscheinung zweyer
        (Continued on next card)

    Röseler, Joannes.

MSS   Drey warhafftige grundtliche Zeitungen ...
Bd.   1610 [ca. 1900]   (Card 2)
WITCHCRAFT
BF   Engel... Beschriben durch den ehrwürdigen Herrn Joannem Röseler diser Zeit Pfarrern daselbsten. Erstlich Getruckt zu Tirnau in Ungern nachmals aber zu Freyburg, bey Georg Hofmann, 1610 [ca. 1900]
D77
        [7] l. 24cm.

        T. p. added by scribe: [Kerpffen]
        (Continued on next card)

    Röseler, Joannes.

MSS   Drey warhafftige grundtliche Zeitungen ...
Bd.   1610 [ca. 1900]   (Card 3)
WITCHCRAFT
BF   Drey warhafftige Zeitungen. Die erste von etlichen Hexen in Ungern, den 11. October 1609. Beschruben durch Nicolaus Binder. &c. 1610.
D77
        Carnap's manuscript copy.
        "Originaldruck in der Stadtbibliothek zu Zürich. 4 Bl. in 4°."
        Numerals in the margins indicate the paginati on of the original.
        (Continued on next card)

    Röseler, Joannes.

MSS   Drey warhafftige grundtliche Zeitungen ...
Bd.   1610 [ca. 1900]   (Card 4)
WITCHCRAFT
BF   In verse.
D77

        1. Witchcraft. 2. Apparitions. 3. Prock, Hans, d. 1610. I. Binder, Nicolaus. II. Röseler, Joannes

CATALOGUE OF THE CORNELL WITCHCRAFT COLLECTION

WITCHCRAFT
BX 2340
R72

Roger, Joseph, abbé.
    Histoire de Nicole de Vervins d'après les historiens contemporains et témoins oculaires; ou, Le triomphe du saint sacrement sur le démon à Laon en 1566, par J. Roger ... Paris, H. Plon, 1863.
    495 p. fold. plate. 22cm.

    1. Nicole de Vervins. 2. Exorcism. I. Title. II. Title: Le triomphe du saint sacrement sur le démon à Laon en 1566.

8
NIC

Rogers, Lydia.

Witchcraft
BF 1563
W81++
no.19

The Snare of the Devill discovered; or, A true and perfect relation of ... Lydia, the wife of John Rogers, ... how, she wanting money, the Devil appeared to her ... and brought her money ... Also her examination ... and her confession ... London, Printed for E. Thomas, 1658. [London, at the British Museum, 1923]
    [12] p. 16cm.
    Photocopy (negative) 12 p. on 8 l. 20 x 32cm.
    No. 19 in vol. lettered: Witchcraft tracts, chap- books and broadsides, 1579-1704; rotograph copies.

Witchcraft
BF 1556
R73

Rohr, Philipp, praeses.
    Dissertatio historico-philosophica De masticatione mortuorum, quam ... sistent praeses M. Philippus Rohr ... & respondens Benjamin Frizschius ... Lipsiae, Typis Michaelis Vogtii [1679]
    [24] p. 21cm.

    1. Vampires. 2. Devil. I. Fritzsch, Benjamin, respondent. II. Title: De masticatione mort uorum. III. Title.

8

    Rom und die Blütezeit der Hexenprozesse.

WITCHCRAFT
BF 1584
I8
P33

Paulus, Nicolaus, 1853-1930.
    Rom und die Blütezeit der Hexenprozesse. (In Historisch-politische Blätter für das katholische Deutschland. München. 22cm. 141. Bd., 1. Heft (1908), p. [241]-254)

    At head of title: XIX.

    1. Trials (Witchcraft)--Rome. I. Title.

8
NIC

Witchcraft
BF 1565
D62
no.13

Romanus, Carl Friedrich.
    Schediasma polemicum expendens quaestionem an dentur spectra magi et sagae. Una cum recensione historica plurimarum hac de re opinionum. Auctore Carolo Friderico Romano. Lipsiae, Apud Thomam. Fritsch, 1703.
    70 p. 20cm.

    No. 13 in vol. lettered Dissertationes de spectris. 1636-1714.

8

Witchcraft
BF 1445
D61
no.17

Romanus, Carl Friedrich.
    Schediasma polemicum expendens qvaestionem an dentur spectra magi et sagae; vulgo Ob wahrhafft Gespenster, Zauberer und Hexen seyn? Una cum recensione historica plurimarum hac de re opinionum auctore Carolo Friderico Romano. Lipsiae, Literis & sumpt. Andreae Martini Schedii, 1717.
    73 p. 21cm.
    First published 1703?
    No. 17 in vol. lettered Dissertationes de spectris. 1646-1753.

8
    (Continued on next card)

Witchcraft
BF 1445
D61
no.17

Romanus, Carl Friedrich. Schediasma polemicum ... 1717. (Card 2)

    1. Demonology. 2. Witchcraft. 3. Bekker, Balthasar, 1634-1698. De betoverde weereld. I. Title. II. Title: An dentur spectra magi et sagae.

8

WITCHCRAFT
BF 1584
N4
R78

Rooses, Max, writer on witchcraft.
    De heksenprocessen; eene volksvoordracht. [n. p., 187-?]
    [60]-87 p. 21cm.

    Caption title.
    Signed: Max. Rooses.
    Detached copy.

    1. Trials (Witchcraft)--Netherlands. I. Title.

8
NIC

    The roots of witchcraft.

BF 1566
H31

Harrison, Michael.
    The roots of witchcraft. [London] Muller [1973]
    278 p. illus. 24 cm.
    Bibliography: p. 265-269.

NIC   COOdc   74-152852

    Rose, Antoinette.

WITCHCRAFT
BF 1582
Z7
1477a

Lavanchy, Joseph Marie, 1844-
    Sabbats ou synagogues sur les bords du lac d'Annecy. Procès inquisitorial à St.-Jorioz en 1477. 2.éd. Annecy Impr. Abry, 1896.
    64 p. 22cm.

8
NIC

    1. Trials (Witchcraft)--St. Jorioz, France. 2. Rose, Antoinette. I. Title.

Witchcraft
BF 1566
R79

Rose, Elliot.
    A razor for a goat; a discussion of certain problems in the history of witchcraft and diabolism. [Toronto] University of Toronto Press [1962]
    257 p. 24cm.

    Includes bibliography.

    1. Witchcraft. 2. Devil. I. Title.

BF 1581
R81
1972

Rosen, Barbara, comp.
    Witchcraft. New York, Taplinger [1972, c1969]
    xii, 407 p. illus. 23 cm. (The Stratford-upon-Avon library 6)
    $9.95
    Bibliography: p. [385]-391.

4
    1. Witchcraft—England. I. Title.
    BF1581.R6 1972   133.4'0942   74-179662
    ISBN 0-8008-8372-1   MARC
    Library of Congress   72 [4]

Witchcraft
Z 6880
Z9R81
1903

Rosenthal, J., firm, booksellers, Munich.
    Bibliotheca magica et pneumatica. Geheime Wissenschaften. Sciences occultes. Occult sciences. Folk-lore. München [1903]
    48, 680 p. 24cm. (Its Kataloge 31-35)

    Issued in parts.

    1. Occult sciences--Bibl.--Catalogs. 2. Folk-lore--Bibl.--Catalogs. 3. Curiosa--Bibl. I. Title.

Witchcraft
Z 6880
Z9
C35
no.1

Rosenthal, Ludwig, Munich.
    Bibliotheca magica et pneumatica. Geheime Wissenschaften, Magie, gute und böse Geister, Gespenster, Volksaberglauben; Hexen und Hexenprocesse ... Ellwangen, L. Weil [188-?]
    148 p. 23cm.

    "Katalog 45."
    No. 1 in vol. lettered: Catalogues of books on magic and witchcraft.
    1. Occult sciences--Bibliography--Catalogs. 2. Witchcraft--Bibliography--Catalogs. 3. Magic--Bibliography--Catalogs. I. Title.

Witchcraft
BF 1550
R82

Roskoff, Gustav, 1814-1889.
    Geschichte des Teufels.
    Leipzig, F. A. Brockhaus, 1869.
    2 v. 23cm.

    1. Devil. 2. Witchcraft. I. Title.

    Ross Williamson, Hugh, 1901-

Witchcraft
BF 1565
S42+
1965

Scot, Reginald, 1538?-1599.
    The discoverie of witchcraft. Introduced by Hugh Ross Williamson. Carbondale, Southern Illinois University Press [1965, ¹1964]
    400 p. illus. 26 cm. ([Centaur classics])

    1. Witchcraft. 2. Magic. 3. Demonology. I. Title.
    II. Ross Williamson, Hugh, 1901-
    BF1565.S4 1965   133.4   64-18551
    Library of Congress

Witchcraft
PQ 1914
R6 A72
1701

Rosset, François de, b. ca. 1570.
    De l'horrible & épouvantable sorcellerie de Louis Goffredy, prêtre beneficié de Marseille.
    (In his Les histoires tragiques de nostre temps. Dernière éd. Lyon, 1701. 18cm. p. 27-56)

    1. Gaufridi, Louis, 1572-1611. I. Title.

    Rosset, François de, b. ca. 1570.
    De l'horrible et épouvantable sorcellerie de Louis Goffredy. German.

WITCHCRAFT
BF 1565
R34

Reiche, Johann, ed.
    Herrn D. Christian Thomasii ... Kurtze Lehr-Sätze von dem Laster der Zauberey, nach dem wahren Verstande des lateinischen Exemplars ins Deutsche übersetzet, und aus des berühmten Theologi D. Meyfarti, Naudaei, und anderer gelehrter Männer Schrifften erleutert ... nebst einigen Actis magicis heraus gegeben von Johann Reichen. Halle im Magdeburgischen, Im Rengerischen Buchladen, 1704.
    2 v. in 1. 21cm.

8
NIC
    (Continued on next card)

476

CATALOGUE OF THE CORNELL WITCHCRAFT COLLECTION

WITCHCRAFT
BF
1565
R34

Rosset, François de, b. ca. 1570.
De l'horrible et épouvantable sorcellerie de Louis Goffredy. German.
Reiche, Johann, ed. Herrn D. Christian Thomasii ... Kurtze Lehr-Sätze ... 1704.
(Card 2)

Vol. 1 has special t. p.: Fernerer Unfug der Zauberey. Halle im Magdeburgischen, 1704.
Vol. 2 has special t. p.: Unterschiedliche Schrifften von Unfug des Hexen-Processes. Halle im Magdeburg., 1703.
Contents.--[1. Bd.] Gabriel Naudaei

(Continued on next card)

NIC

WITCHCRAFT
BF
1565
R34

Rosset, François de, b. ca. 1570.
De l'horrible et épouvantable sorcellerie de Louis Goffredy. German.
Reiche, Johann, ed. Herrn D. Christian Thomasii ... Kurtze Lehr-Sätze ... 1704.
(Card 3)

Contents.--Continued.
Schutz-Schrifft [tr. of Apologie pour tous les grands hommes]--Geschichte der Teuffel zu Lodün.--Trauer-Geschichte von der greulichen Zauberey Ludwig Goffredy [tr. of De l'horrible & épouvantable sorcellerie de Louis Goffredy, author F. de Rosset]--D. Christian Thomasii ... Kurtze Lehr-Sätze von

(Continued on next card)

NIC

WITCHCRAFT
BF
1565
R34

Rosset, François de, b. ca. 1570.
De l'horrible et épouvantable sorcellerie de Louis Goffredy. German.
Reiche, Johann, ed. Herrn D. Christian Thomasii ... Kurtze Lehr-Sätze ... 1704.
(Card 4)

Contents--Continued.
dem Laster der Zauberey [tr. of Dissertatio de crimine magiae, J. Reiche, respondent] [2. Bd.] Malleus judicum oder Gesetz-Hammer der unbarmhertzigen Hexen-Richter.--Cautio criminalis [von F. Spee]--D. Johann Matthäus Meyfarths Christliche Erinnerung an Regenten.-- Viererley Sorten Hexen-Acta.

(Continued on next card)

NIC

Rosset, François de, b. ca. 1570.
Histoires mémorables et tragiques.

Witchcraft
PQ
1914
R6
A72
1701

Rosset, François de, b. ca. 1570.
Les histoires tragiques de nostre temps, ou sont contenues les morts funestes & lamentables de plusieurs personnes, arrivées par leurs ambitions, amours dereglées, sortileges, vols, rapines, & par autres accidens divers & memorables, composées par François de Rosset. Derniere edition ...
Lyon, Chez B. Vignieu, 1701.
4 p. l., 632 p. 18cm.

(Continued on next card)

Witchcraft
PQ
1914
R6
A72
1701

Rosset, François de, b. ca. 1570. Les histoires tragiques de nostre temps ... 1701.
(Card 2)

First ed. published under title: Histoires mémorables et tragiques, Paris, 1619.
Imperfect: last page partly illegible.

1. Biography--17th century. 2. Biography--Collections. I. Title. II. His Histoires mémorables et tragiques.

8
NIC

Witchcraft
PQ
1914
R6
A72
1701

Rosset, François de, b. ca. 1570.
Les histoires tragiques de nostre temps, ou sont contenues les morts funestes & lamentables de plusieurs personnes, arrivées par leurs ambitions, amours dereglées, sortileges, vols, rapines, & par autres accidens divers & memorables, composées par François de Rosset. Derniere edition ...
Lyon, Chez B. Vignieu, 1701.
4 p. l., 632 p. 18cm.

(Continued on next card)

Witchcraft
PQ
1914
R6
A72
1701

Rosset, François de, b. ca. 1570. Les histoires tragiques de nostre temps ... 1701.
(Card 2)

First ed. published under title: Histoires mémorables et tragiques, Paris, 1619.
Imperfect: last page partly illegible.

1. Biography--17th century. 2. Biography--Collections. I. Title. II. His Histoires mémorables et tragiques.

8
NIC

WITCHCRAFT
RC
438
R84

Rothe, A von
Geschichte der Psychiatrie in Polen, von A. v. Rothe. Leipzig, F. Deuticke, 1896.
99 p. 23cm.

Bibliographical footnotes.

1. Psychiatry--Poland--History. 2. Demonology. I. Title.

8
NIC

HIST SCI
RE
93
N63
G89

Rothe, Christian Gottlob, b. 1750.
Gruner, Christian Gottfried, 1744-1815.
Decanus D. Christ. Godofredus Gruner... Dissertationem...Christiani Gottlob Rothe... indicit de daemoniacis a Christo Sospitatore percuratis breviter commentatus. Ienae, Litteris Fickelscherrii [1774]
16 p. 20cm.

Introductory to a diss. for which Nicolai acted as praeses, Rothe as respondent: Dissertatio inauguralis medica De nyctalopia ac hemeralopia visu simplici et duplici.
1. Demoniac possession. 2. Rothe, Christian Gottlob, b.1750. 3. Nicolai, Ernst Anton, 1722-1802, praeses. Dissertatio inauguralis medica De nyctalopia...

Witchcraft
BF
1581
D248

Rowan tree and red thread.
Davidson, Thomas Douglas, 1911- comp.
Rowan tree and red thread. A Scottish witchcraft miscellany of tales, legends, and ballads; together with a description of the witches' rites and ceremonies. Edinburgh, Oliver and Boyd, 1949.
x, 286 p. front. 23cm.

Bibliography: p. 271-275.
With autograph: Joseph Foster.

Rudinger, J. C.

WITCHCRAFT
BF
1557
C64
1708

Clodius, Johann, 1645-1733, praeses.
De spiritibus familiaribus vulgo sic dictis, praeside Johanne Clodio, disseret Jo. Christophorus Rudingerus. Vitembergae, C. Schroedter, 1708.
[32] p. 20cm.

Originally issued as dissertation, Wittenberg, 1693 (J. C. Rudinger, respondent)
1. Demonology. I. Rudinger, J.C. II. Title.

8
NIC

WITCHCRAFT
BF
1583
R898

Rübel, Carl, 1848-1916.
Hexenaberglaube, Hexenprozesse und Zauberwahn in Dortmund, von Karl Rübel.
(In Beiträge zur Geschichte Dortmunds und der Grafschaft Mark. Dortmund. 23cm. v. 22 (1913), p. [96]-117)

Caption title.
Bibliographical footnotes.

8
NIC

1. Witchcraft--Dortmund. I. Title.

WITCHCRAFT
BF
1547
R91
1753

Rübel, Johann Friedrich
Physikalische Abhandlung von der Gewalt des Teufels in die Körper ... mit vielen wichtigen Anmerkungen hrsg. von J. F. R. Nürnberg, In Commission in der Zimmermannischen Buchhandlung, 1753.
2 v. 23cm.

Contents.--[1] Die Fragen und Untersuchungen vorkommen: Ob der Teufel Wunderwerke thun Könne? Ob er die Leute holen, und durch die Luft fort, und in an-
(Continued on next card)

8
NIC

WITCHCRAFT
BF
1547
R91
1753

Rübel, Johann Friedrich
Physikalische Abhandlung von der Gewalt des Teufels...1753. (Card 2)

Contents--continued.
dere Orte schleppen könne? Ob er allerhand Art von Ungeziefer in der Luft hervorzubringen vermöge? Ob er den Menschen Krankheiten zuziehen könne? Was von Hexen, Zaubereyen, Gespenstern und Geistern zu halten? Von Beschwörung der Geister, etc.

(Continued on next card)

WITCHCRAFT
BF
1547
R91
1753

Rübel, Johann Friedrich
Physikalische Abhandlung von der Gewalt des Teufels...1753. (Card 3)

1. Devil. 2. Demonology. I. Title.

WITCHCRAFT
BF
1583
R91

Rückert, Georg.
Der Hexenwahn, ein Kulturbild aus Lauingens Vergangenheit, von Gg. Rückert.
(In Alt-Lauingen; Organ des Altertumsvereins Lauingen. Lauingen a/D. 25cm. 2. Jahrg. (1907), p. [25]-27, 34-36, [41]-43, [49]-54, [57]-59, 69-71, [73]-77)

Caption title.

8
NIC

1. Witchcraft--Lauingen, Ger. I. Title.

WITCHCRAFT
BF
1565
R91

Rüdinger, Johannes
De magia illicita, decas concionum; zehen müthliche Predigten von der Zauber- vnd Hexenwerck aus Anleitung heiliger Schrifft vnd bewehrter Autorum rationibus nach dem bekanten Schul-Vers Quis? Quid? Ubi? vnd folgends andern Vmbstenden gehalten. Darinnen auff die von dieser Materia fürnembsten Fragen geantwortet, etliche darüber vngleiche Meynung erzehlet vnd dieselben kürtzlich wiederleget werden, durch

(Continued on next card)

8
NIC

WITCHCRAFT
BF
1565
R91

Rüdinger, Johannes
De magia illicita... (Card 2)

Johannem Rüdinger. Jehna, In Verlegung J. Reiffenberger, 1630.
406 p. 20cm.

1. Witchcraft--Sermons. I. Title. II. Title: Zehen müthliche Predigten von der Zauber- und Hexenwerck. III. Title: Von der Zauber- und Hexenwerck.

CATALOGUE OF THE CORNELL WITCHCRAFT COLLECTION

WITCHCRAFT
BF
1528
D9
T58

Rütz, Franz Georg Christoph.
Daemonologische fragmenten of byvoegsels tot de Oudheid- en geneeskundige verhandeling van den heer professor Theod. Gerhard Timmermann, over de daemonische menschen, waarvan in de geschiedverhaalen der Evangelien gewaagd wordt. Opgesteld en in 't licht gegeeven door F. G. C. Rütz ... Haarlem, By Plaat en Loosjes, 1789-90.
2 v. in 1. 22cm.
Vol. 2 has imprint: 'sGravenhage, by J. C. Lee uwestyn, 1790.
(Continued on next card)

8
NIC

WITCHCRAFT
BF
1528
D9
T58

Rütz, Franz Georg Christoph. Daemonologische fragmenten ... 1789-90. (Card 2)

1. Demonology. 2. Timmermann, Theodor Gerhard, 1727-1792. Diatribe antiquario-medica de daemoniacis Evangeliorum. 3. Demoniac possession. I. Title.

8
NIC

Witchcraft
BT
835
H46

Ruland, Martin, 1532-1602.
[Heilbronner, Philipp] 1546-1616, ed.
De Inferno sev cacodaemonum, damnatorumque domicilio: Tractatus ex Dei verbo, S. Patribvs atqve historijs permultis congestus, in quo nimirum Inferni locus, forma, poenae, earumque varietates ... demonstratur. Nunc recens ex bibliotheca ... Martini Rulandi depromtus, ac... in lucem editus. Cvi adivncta est figvra sive delineatio Inferni ex contextu libri concinnata. [n. p.] 1594.
[8], 130, [5] p. 17cm.
"Figura sive delineatio Inferni" not in this copy.

Witchcraft
CB
3
Z481

Ruland, Wilhelm, 1869-1927.
Steirische Hexenprozesse. Ein Beitrag zur Kulturgeschichte des 17. Jahrhunderts. (In Beiträge zur Kulturgeschichte. Weimar. 25cm. 2. Heft (1898), p. [45]-71)

1. Witchcraft--Germany. I. Title.

Witchcraft
BF
1575
D76
v.2-3

Rule, Margaret.
Calef, Robert, 1648-1719.
More wonders of the invisible world: or, The wonders of the invisible world, display'd in five parts. Part I. An account of the sufferings of Margaret Rule, written by the Reverend Mr. C. M. P. II. Several letters to the author, &c. And his reply relating to witchcraft. P. IV. The differences between the inhabitants of Salem village, and Mr. Parris their minister, in New-England. P. IV. Letters of a gentleman uninterested, endeavouring to prove the received opinions about witchcraft to be orthodox. With short essays to their answers. P. V. A short historical accout [!] of matters of fact in that affair. To
(Continued on next card)
[r31e2]
2-13714 rev.

Witchcraft
BF
1575
D76
v.2-3

Rule, Margaret.
Calef, Robert, 1648-1719. More wonders of the invisible world ... (Card 2)
which is added, a postscript relating to a book intitled, The life of Sir William Phips. Collected by Robert Calef, merchant, of Boston in New-England ... London, Printed for N. Hillar and J. Collyer, 1700.
Reprint. (In Drake, S. G. The witchcraft delusion in New England ... Roxbury, Mass., 1866. 21¼cm. v. 2, p. 1-212; v. 3, p. 3-167)
Woodward's historical series. no. VI-VII.
Prefatory; by the editor: p. [v]-x. Pedigree of Calef: 1 fold. leaf.
Memoir of Robert Calef: p. [xi]-xxix.
The text, here annotated, is that of the 1st edition, 1700. "It is given as exactly like the original as a much better type can be made to imitate an old type of 166 years ago."--Pref. by the editor, p. vi.
(Continued on next card)
[r31e2]
2-13714 rev.

Witchcraft
BF
1575
D76
v.2-3

Rule, Margaret.
Calef, Robert, 1648-1719. More wonders of the invisible world ... 1700. (Card 3)
Appendix: I. Examination of Giles Cory.--II. Giles Corey and Goodwyfe Corey. A ballad of 1692.--III. Testimony of William Beale, of Marblehead, against Mr. Philip English of Salem, given Aug. 2d. 1692.--IV. [Examination of the Indian woman belonging to Mr. Parris's family]--V. The examination of Mary Clark of Haverhill.--VI. An account of the life and character of the Rev. Samuel Parris, of Salem village, and of his connection with the witchcraft delusion of 1692. By Samuel P. Fowler.

Witchcraft
BF
1575
C14
1823

Rule, Margaret.
Calef, Robert, 1648-1719.
More wonders of the invisible world, or The wonders of the invisible world displayed. In five parts. Part I.--An account of the sufferings of Margaret Rule, written by the Rev. Cotton Mather. Part II.--Several letters to the author, &c. and his reply relating to witchcraft. Part III.--The differences between the inhabitants of Salem village, and Mr. Parris, their minister, in New-England. Part IV.--Letters of a gentleman uninterested, endeavouring to prove the received opinions about witchcraft to be
(Continued on next card)

Witchcraft
BF
1575
C14
1823

Rule, Margaret.
Calef, Robert, 1648-1719. More wonders of the invisible world ... 1823. (Card 2)
orthodox. With short essays to their answers. Part V.--A short historical account of matters of fact in that affair. To which is added a postscript [!] relating to a book entitled "The life of Sir Wm. Phips". Collected by Robert Calef. Merchant, of Boston, in New-England. Printed in London, 1700. Salem, Re-printed by J. D. & T. C. Cushing, jr. for Cushing and Appleton, 1823.
312 p. 18½cm. (Continued on next card)

Witchcraft
BF
1575
C14
1823

Rule, Margaret.
Calef, Robert, 1648-1719. More wonders of the invisible world ... 1823. (Card 3)
Appended: Giles Cory [a report of his examination, taken from the witchcraft records]: p. 310-312.
"The second Salem edition appears to have been copied from the first [Salem edition] that of 1796. In some instances slight departures are made from the copy ... such departures are also departures from the original [London edition of 1700]."--S.G.Drake, pref. to ed. of 1866.

Witchcraft
BF
1575
C14
1828

Rule, Margaret.
Calef, Robert, 1648-1719.
Wonders of the invisible world, or, Salem witchcraft. In five parts. Boston, T. Bedlington [1828]
333 p. front. 14cm.

A reply to Cotton Mather's "Wonders of the invisible world."
First ed. published in 1700 under title: More wonders of the invisible world displayed.
(Continued on next card)

Witchcraft
BF
1575
C14
1828

Rule, Margaret.
Calef, Robert, 1648-1719. Wonders of the invisible world ... [1828] (Card 2)
Contents.--Part 1. An account of the sufferings of Margaret Rule, by Cotton Mather.--Part 2. Several letters from the author to Mr. Mather and others, relating to witchcraft.--Part 3. Account of the differences in Salem village between the villagers and their minister, Mr. Parris.--Part 4. Letters of a gentleman uninter-
(Continued on next card)

Witchcraft
BF
1575
C14
1828

Rule, Margaret.
Calef, Robert, 1648-1719. Wonders of the invisible world ... [1828] (Card 3)
ested, endeavouring to prove the received opinions about witchcraft to be orthodox.--Part 5. An impartial account of the most memorable matters of fact touching the supposed witchcraft in New-England.--Postscript, relating to Cotton Mather's life of Sir William Phips.--Giles Cory: a report of his examination, taken from the witchcraft files.

P
9
F5
t.14,no.4

Runeberg, Arne.
Witches, demons and fertility magic; analysis of their significance and mutual relations in West-European folk religion. [With an appendix: Psychoanalytic interpretation of European bronze age religion.] Helsingfors, 1947.
xii, 273 p. 24cm. (Societas Scientiarum Fennica. Commentationes humanarum litterarum, XIV, 4)
"Authorities quoted": p. [252]-256.
Thesis--Helsingfors.
1. Witchcraft-- Europe. 2. Demonology.
3. Phallicism. 4. Magic--Europe.
I. Title.

WITCHCRAFT
BT
980
M26

Runge, Conrad Heinrich, supposed author.
Man muss auch dem Teufel nicht zu viel aufbürden. Bey Gelegenheit der Brochüre: Sollte der Teufel wirklich ein Unding seyn? etc. Beherziget von einem Freunde der Wahrheit ... Bremen, J. H. Cramer, 1776.
xxxii, 426 p. 16cm.

Attributed by various sources to C. H. Runge; cf. Holzmann, Michael. Deutsches Anonymenlexikon (Weimar, 1902-28)

8
NIC
(Continued on next card)

Witchcraft
BX
2340
R94++

Runge, Heinrich, 1817-1886, ed.
Adjurationen, Exorcismen und Benedictionen, vorzüglich zum Gebrauch bei Gottesgerichten. Ein Rheinauer Codex des eilften Jahrhunderts. Zürich, In Commission bei Meyer und Zeller, 1859.
[179]-203 p. facsim. 31cm. (Mittheilungen der antiquarischen Gesellschaft (der Gesellschaft für vaterländische Alterthümer) in Zürich. Bd. XII. Heft 5)
Imprint covered by bookseller's label.

8
(Continued on next card)

Witchcraft
BX
2340
R94++

Runge, Heinrich, 1817-1886, ed. Adjurationen ... 1859. (Card 2)

1. Exorcism. 2. Benediction. I. Rheinau, Switzerland. (Benedictine abbey) II. Title.

8

Witchcraft
BF
1569
R96

Russell, Jeffrey Burton.
Witchcraft in the Middle Ages. Ithaca, Cornell University Press [c1972]
ix, 394 p. 23cm.

1. Witchcraft--Hist. I. Title.

CATALOGUE OF THE CORNELL WITCHCRAFT COLLECTION

BF 569 .96
Russell, Jeffrey Burton.
    Witchcraft in the Middle Ages. Ithaca, Cornell University Press [1972]
    ix, 394 p. 23cm.

    1. Witchcraft--History. I. Title.

Ruynen, I. van.
Witchcraft
BF 1410 B42 1691b
    Bekker, Balthasar, 1634-1698.
    Kort begrip van de twee boeken der Betooverde weereld, in 't ligt gebragt door den heere Balthazar Bekker, S. T. D. en predikant te Amsterdam, zeer dienstig tot het recht verstaan (en taffens strekkende voor een bondig register) van dat vermaarde werk, opgesteld door een redenlievenden hater van bygeloof. Rotterdam, By I. van Ruynen, boekverkooper, 1691.
    2 p. l., 39 p. [p. 40 is blank] title

(Continued on next card)

Witchcraft
BF 1593 R99 1865
Rydberg, Victor, 1828-1895.
    Medeltidens magi. Stockholm, L. J. Hiertas, 1865.
    140 p. 22cm.

    "Förut utgifven i 'Svensk månadsskrift för fri forskning och allmän bildning af C. S. Warburg.'"

    1. Magic. I. Title.

8

Rutberg, Hulda, 1884-
    Häxprocesser i norska Finnmarken, 1620-1692. Stockholm, P. A. Norstedt, 1918.
    109 p. 24cm. (Bidrag till kännedom om svenska landsmålen ock svenskt folkliv. XVI.4)

    1. Witchcraft--Finmark, Norway. I. Title.

Ruynen, I. van.
Witchcraft
BF 1410 B42 1691b
    Bekker, Balthasar, 1634-1698. Kort begrip van de twee boeken der Betooverde weereld ... 1691. (Card 2)

    vignette, illus. initials. 20 x 16cm.
    $4°: \pi^2, A-E^4$.
    Black letter.
    Preface signed: I. van Ruynen.
    Van der Linde 18.
    1. Demonology. 2. Angels. 3. Magic. 4. Witchcraft. I. His De betoverde weereld. II. Title. III. Ruynen, I. van. IV. Een redenlievende hater van bygeloof.

8

Witchcraft
BF 1593 R99 1879
Rydberg, Viktor, 1828-1895.
    The magic of the Middle Ages. Translated from the Swedish by August Hjalmar Edgren. New York, Holt, 1879.
    231 p. 20cm.

    Translation of his Medeltidens magi.

    1. Magic. I. Title. II. Rydberg, Viktor, 1828-1895. Medeltidens magi--English.

Rydberg, Viktor, 1828-1895.
    Medeltidens magi--English.
Witchcraft
BF 1593 R99 1879
Rydberg, Viktor, 1828-1895.
    The magic of the Middle Ages. Translated from the Swedish by August Hjalmar Edgren. New York, Holt, 1879.
    231 p. 20cm.

    Translation of his Medeltidens magi.

    1. Magic. I. Title. II. Rydberg, Viktor, 1828-1895. Medeltidens magi--English.

WITCHCRAFT
Rutta, Carl.
    De angelorum existentia, natura, negotiis et in hominum vitae conditionem vel laetam vel tristem influxu. Auctore Carolo Rutta. Wirceburgi, C. G. Becker, 1823.
    46 p. 21cm.

    Inauguralis dissertatio--Würzburg.

    1. Angels. I. Title.

IC

Witchcraft
BF 1593 R99 1879
Rydberg, Viktor, 1828-1895.
    The magic of the Middle Ages. Translated from the Swedish by August Hjalmar Edgren. New York, Holt, 1879.
    231 p. 20cm.

    Translation of his Medeltidens magi.

    1. Magic. I. Title. II. Rydberg, Viktor, 1828-1895. Medeltidens magi--English.

PT 2430 M35M37
Rysan, Josef, 1914-
    Wilhelm Meinhold's Bernsteinhexe: a study in witchcraft and cultural history. Chicago, 1948.
    iii l.,182 p. 23cm.

    Thesis--Univ. of Chicago.
    "Selected bibiliography": p. 178-182.

CATALOGUE OF THE CORNELL WITCHCRAFT COLLECTION

S

S., D. T., jr.
Witchcraft
BF 1410 B42 Z69 no.17, 18

Den predikant D. Balthasar Becker, seediglyk ondersogt so in zyn persoon als Schriften, of hy die derst voorgeven, buyten hem alleen, de gantsche werelt betovert te zyn, selfs hier af wel vry is, ende dat daar en boven op hem niet soude werken, de geest van hovaardye en dwalinge tot ergernisse en van de kleine, en van de arme, en van de verslagene van geest, en die beeven voor Godts woort. By een missive den 19 January 1692, door H.v.G. van Amsterdam geschreven aan

NIC (Continued on next card)

S., D. T., jr.
Witchcraft
BF 1410 B42 Z69 no.17, 18

Den predikant D. Balthasar Becker ... (Card 2)
D. T. S. de Jonge tot Uytrecht. Met zyn Andtwoord provisioneel tot nader berigt daar op gevolgt, den 4. February desselven jaars. Uytregt, Gedrukt by W. Jansz, 1692.
32, 36 p. 21cm.
Signatures: 4°: A-D4. 4°: A-D4, E2.
The Provisioneel Antwoord has special half-title and separate

NIC (Continued on next card)

S., D. T., jr.
Witchcraft
BF 1410 B42 Z69 no.17, 18

Den predikant D. Balthasar Becker ... 1692. (Card 3)
paging.
Van der Linde 63, 61.
"Extractum van ... De betoverde werelt, uytgetrokken en t'samengestelt door N. N.": p. 17-28 of the Provisioneel Antwoord; "Extract van 'tgepasseerde des Synodi tot Edam, 10. Aug. 1691. rakende D. Bekker ...": p. 28-29; "Articulen voor te stellen aan Do. B. Bekker" signed Leonardus

NIC (Continued on next card)

S., D. T., jr.
Witchcraft
BF 1410 B42 Z69 No.17, 18

Den predikant D. Balthasar Becker ... 1692. (Card 4)
Groenewegen: p. 29-31; "Eerste aanbieding van D. B. Bekker, op den 30. Aug. 1691": p. 31; "Articulen tot satisfactie aan de Eerw. Classis van Amsterdam, van Do. Balthasar Bekker ... wegens ... de Betoverde wereld ...": p. 32-36.
Nos. 17 & 18 in a Collection of tracts against Balthasar Bekker and his Betoverde weereld.

NIC (Continued on next card)

S., J.
Witchcraft
BX 9479 B42 B11 no.6

[Silvius, J] Consideratien over het boek van de Heer Doctor Balthasar Bekker, genaamt De betoverde weereld, voorgestelt door J. S. Amsterdam, By G. Borstius, boekverkoper, 1691.
20 p. title vignette, illus. initials.
20 x 15cm.
4°: π1, A-B⁴, C1.
Black letter (except for introduction)
Ascribed to J. Silvius by Doorninck.
Variant of van der Linde 149:

(Continued on next card)

S., J.
Witchcraft
BX 9479 B42 B11 no.6

[Silvius, J] Consideratien over het boek van de Heer Doctor Balthasar Bekker ... 1691. (Card 2)
only 20, instead of 22 p.
No. 6 in vol. lettered B. Bekkers sterfbed en andere tractaten.
1. Bekker, Balthasar, 1634-1698. De betoverde weereld. I. Title. II. J. S. III. S., J.

S., T.
Witchcraft
BF 1410 B42 Z56 v.2 no.6

Nodige aanmerkinge omtrent eenige woorden gesprooken van D. Johannes Visscherus, in een catechisatie, over den 34 Sondag des Catechismus. Dog bysonderlijk over de 94 vrage, enz. voorgevallen op Sondag den 24 Augusty 1692. Door T. S. Amsterdam, By D. vanden Dalen, boekverkoper, 1692.
7 p. [p. 8 blank] title vignette. 19 x 15cm.
4°: A⁴.

3 (Continued on next card)

S., T.
Witchcraft
BF 1410 B42 Z56 v.2 no.6

Nodige aanmerkinge omtrent eenige woorden gesprooken van D. Johannes Visscherus ... 1692. (Card 2)
Black letter.
Response to Visscher's attack on Balthasar Bekker.
No. 6 in vol. lettered Bekker II.
1. Visscher, Johannes, 1617?-1694. 2. Bekker, Balthasar, 1634-1698. De betoverde weereld. I. T. S. II. S., T.

8

S., W., à V. C. & C. A.
WITCHCRAFT
BF 1572 C5 S33 1630

[Schilling, Wolfgang] Newer Tractat von der verführten Kinder Zauberey. In welchem mit reifflichem Discurs ... vorgehalten wirdt, auss was Vrsachen viel vnerwachsene vnd vnmündige Kinder ... zu der verdampten Geister vnd Zauberer Gesellschafft gebracht vnd vnerhörter Weiss verführt werden ... auss lateinischer in die teutsche Sprach vbersetzt vnd in Truck gegeben ... durch VV. S. à V. C. & C. A. Aschaffenburg, Getruckt durch Quirin

8 NIC (Continued on next card)

S., W., à V. C. & C. A.
WITCHCRAFT
BF 1572 C5 S33 1630

[Schilling, Wolfgang] Newer Tractat von der verführten Kinder Zauberey ... 1630. (Card 2)
Botzer, 1630.
44 p. 21cm.
Revised and augmented version of the "Appendix oder Nachtrab" (p. 60-129) published in his compilation on witchcraft from P. Laymann's Theologia moralis. (Laymann, P. Ein kurtzer doch gründlicher

8 NIC (Continued on next card)

S., W., à V. C. & C. A.
WITCHCRAFT
BF 1572 C5 S33 1630

[Schilling, Wolfgang] Newer Tractat von der verführten Kinder Zauberey ... 1630. (Card 3)
Bericht wie ... mit den Hexen zuverfahren seye. Aschaffenburg, 1629.)
1. Witchcraft. 2. Children--Management. I. Title. II. W. S. à V. C. & C. A. III. S., W., à V. C. & C. A.

8 NIC

S. F.
Witchcraft
BF 1152 D61+

Divination, witchcraft, and mesmerism. [New York, 1852]
198-213 p. 26cm.
Signed: S. F.
Detached from the International monthly magazine of literature, science, and art. v. 5.
1. Divination. 2. Witchcraft. 3. Mesmerism. I. F., S. II. S. F.

S. H.
Witchcraft
BF 1581 H32D6

[Harsnett, Samuel] archbishop of York, 1561-1631.
[A discovery of the fraudulent practises of John Darrell, bacheler of artes, in his proceedings concerning the pretended possession and dispossession of William Somers at Nottingham; of Thomas Darling, the boy of Burton at Caldwell; and of Katherine Wright at Mansfield, and Whittington; and of his dealings with one Mary Couper at Nottingham, detecting in some sort the deceitful trade in these latter day es of casting out deuils.
(Continued on next card)

S. H.
Witchcraft
BF 1581 H32D6

[Harsnett, Samuel] archbishop of York, 1561-1631. [A discovery of the fraudulent practises of John Darrell ... [1599] (Card 2)
London, 1599]
[328] p. 18cm.
Epistle to the reader signed: S. H.
Imperfect: t.-p. mounted, part of it missing; title taken from Halkett & Laing; pages cropped; numbers missing from 324-[328]
1. Darrell, John, fl. 1562-1602. I Title. II. S. H. III. H., S.

Le Sabbat des sorciers.
Witchcraft
BF 1566 B77

Bourneville, [Désiré Magloire] 1840-
Le Sabbat des sorciers, par Bournevill et E. Teinturier. Paris, Aux Bureaux Progrès médical; Delahaye et Lecrosnier, 1882.
38 p. illus. 22cm. (Bibliothèque diabolique)
1. Witchcraft. I. Teinturier, E. II. Title.

CATALOGUE OF THE CORNELL WITCHCRAFT COLLECTION

Sabbat, juges et sorciers.
Vartier, Jean.
Sabbat, juges et sorciers, quatre siècles de superstitions dans la France de l'Est. ₍Paris,₎ Hachette, 1968.
288 p. 21 cm. 20.00   F***
"Notes, eclaircissements et sources": p. ₍267₎-286.

1. Witchcraft—France. I. Title.

BF1582.V26   76-397594
Library of Congress   69 ₍4₎

Sabbats ou synagogues sur les bords du lac d'Annecy.
WITCHCRAFT
BF **Lavanchy, Joseph Marie,** 1844-
1582   Sabbats ou synagogues sur les bords du
Z7   lac d'Annecy. Procès inquisitorial à St.-
1477a Jorioz en 1477. 2. éd. Annecy Impr. Abry, 1896.
       64 p. 22cm.

1. Trials (Witchcraft)--St. Jorioz, France.
2. Rose, Antoinette. I. Title.

8
NIC

Sacro arsenale.
₍Masini, Eliseo₎ brother, 17th cent.
   Sacro arsenale overo Prattica dell'Officio della Santa Inqvisitione. Genova, Appresso Givseppe Pavoni, 1621.
   ₍4₎, 319, ₍40₎ p. 21cm.
Title vignette, engraved.

1. Inquisition. I. Title. II. Title: Prattica dell'Officio della Santa Inquisitione.
                    ₍Secular name: Cesare Masini₎

Sacro arsenale.
₍Masini, Eliseo₎ brother, 17th cent.
   Sacro arsenale, ouero Prattica dell'Officio della Santa Inqvisitione. Di nuouo corretto, & ampliato ... Bologna, Per Gioseffo Longhi, 1679.
   ₍14₎, 528 p. 17cm.
Edited by Natale Doriguzzi.

I. Doriguzzi, Natale, ed. II. Title.
                    ₍Secular name: Cesare Masini₎

Sacro arsenale.
₍Masini, Eliseo₎ brother, 17th cent.
   Sacro arsenale, ovvero Pratica dell'Uffizio della Santa Inquisizione; coll'inserzione di alcune regole fatte dal p. inquisitore Tommaso Menghini ... e di diverse annotazioni del dottore Gio: Pasqualone ... In questa 4. impressione aggiuntavi la Settima Denunzia fatta dal suddetto padre per li sponte comparenti, impressa in Ferrara 1687. e corretta in alcune cose la parte decima degli avvertimenti ... Roma, Nella Stamperia di
                    (Continued on next card)
                    ₍Secular name: Cesare Masini₎

Sacro arsenale.
Witchcraft
BX   ₍Masini, Eliseo₎ brother, 17th cent. Sacro
1710   arsenale ...   (Card 2)
M39
1730   S. Michele a Ripa, 1730.
       ₍6₎, 506, ₍54₎ p. 23cm.
Edited by Luigi and Francesco Conti.

1. Inquisition. I. Menghini, Tommaso, 17th cent. II. Pasqualone, Giovanni. III. Conti, Luigi. IV. Conti, Francesco. V. Title. VI. Title: Pratica dell'Uffizio della Santa Inquisizione.

Witchcraft
BF   A sad and lamentable account of one Mary
1581   Jawson ... who wickedly sold her self to
Z7   the devil ... to be revenged on her aunt
1702 ... A dreadful story of a young maid in
      Devonshire, who, for renouncing her contract in marriage, had fearful judgements shewn on her. Also an account of a dreadful judgment on a rich man for the cruel usage of his servant ... To which is added three dreadful examples & judgments that hath befallen three notorious sinners. Glasgow, 1702.
                    (Continued on next card)

Witchcraft
BF   A sad and lamentable account of one Mary
1581   Jawson ... 1702.   (Card 2)
Z7
1702 12 p. 13cm.
Ex libris John A. Fairley.

1. Jawson, Mary, fl. 1702.

Witchcraft
BF   Sadducismus debellatus; or, A true narra-
1581 tive of the sorceries and witchcrafts
Z7   exercis'd by the Devil and his instru-
1697a ments upon Mrs. Christian Shaw, daughter of Mr. John Shaw, of Bargarran in the County of Renfrew in the west of Scotland, from Aug. 1696 to Apr. 1697. Containing the journal of her sufferings ... Together with reflexions upon witchcraft in general, and the learned arguments of the lawyers, on both sides, at the
8   (Continued on next card)

Witchcraft
BF   Sadducismus debellatus ... 1698. (Card 2)
1581
Z7   trial of seven of those witches, who
1697a were condemned: and some passages which
      happened at their execution. London, Printed for H. Newman and A. Bell, 1698.
      4 p. l., 60 p. 22cm.

1. Shaw, Christian, fl. 1697. 2. Witchcraft--Scotland.

8

Der sächsische Kriminalist Carpzov und seine 20 000 Todesurteile.
WITCHCRAFT
HV   **Paulus, Nicolaus,** 1853-1930.
8551   Der sächsische Kriminalist Carpzov und
P33++ seine 20 000 Todesurteile. ₍Köln, 1907₎
      1 column. 58 cm. (folded to 34cm.)
Detached from the Kölnische Volkszeitung und Handels-Blatt for February 18, 1907.
In broadside box.

1. Carpzov, Benedict, 1595-1666. 2. Capital punishment--Germany. I. Title.

8
NIC

Ein sächsischer Hexenprozess aus dem 17. Jahrhundert.
Witchcraft
BF   Anna Renata Singer v. Mossau, die letzte
1583 deutsche Hexe. Ein Geschichtsbild, dar-
Z7   gestellt zur Erinnerung an den nunmehr
1749b hundertjährigen Niedergang eines langen und grauenvollen Irrwahns und an die Befreiung von der Schmach wälscher Inquisition in Deutschland. Nebst einem Abriss der Geschichte der Hexenprozesse im Allgemeinen und beiliegenden Actenstücken sowie einem sächsischen Hexenprocesse aus dem siebzehnten Jahrhun-
                    (Continued on next card)

Ein sächsischer Hexenprozess aus dem 17. Jahrhundert.
Witchcraft
BF   Anna Renata Singer v. Mossau ... 1849.
1583   (Card 2)
Z7
1749b   dert. ₍Leipzig, Bei F. Serig₎ 1849.
      142 p. 22cm.
"Kurzer Abriss der Geschichte des Hexentums" and the four Beilagen each have special t. p.
Includes Rede am Scheiterhaufen, von G. Gaar, and Ein sächsischer Hexenprozess, von G. A. Siebdrat.

8   (Continued on next card)

Sänger, Maria Renata Von Mossau

Sänger, Maria Renata von Mossau, ca. 1680-1749.
Witchcraft
BF   Anna Renata Singer v. Mossau, die letzte
1583   deutsche Hexe. Ein Geschichtsbild, dar-
Z7   gestellt zur Erinnerung an den nunmehr
1749b   hundertjährigen Niedergang eines langen
und grauenvollen Irrwahns und an die
Befreiung von der Schmach wälscher Inquisition in Deutschland. Nebst einem
Abriss der Geschichte der Hexenprocesse
im Allgemeinen und beiliegenden Actenstücken sowie einem sächsischen Hexenprocesse aus   dem siebzehnten Jahrhun-
8   (Continued on next card)

Sänger, Maria Renata von Mossau, ca. 1680-1749.
Witchcraft
BF   Anna Renata Singer v. Mossau ... 1849.
1583   (Card 2)
Z7
1749b   dert. [Leipzig, Bei F. Serig] 1849.
142 p. 22cm.
"Kurzer Abriss der Geschichte des Hexen-
tums" and the four Beilagen each have spe-
cial t. p.
Includes Rede am Scheiterhaufen, von G.
Gaar, and Ein sächsischer Hexenprozess, von
G. A. Siebdrat.
8

Witchcraft Sänger, Maria Renata von Mossau, ca. 1680-1749.
BF   Gaar, Georg, b. 1702.
1583   Christliche Anred nächst dem Scheiter-
Z7   Hauffen, worauf der Leichnam Mariae
1749   Renatae, einer durchs Schwerdt hingerichteten Zauberin, den 21. junii anno 1749 ausser
der Stadt Wirtzburg verbrennet worden, an
ein zahlreich-versammletes Volck gethan,
und hernach aus gnädigstem Befehl einer
Hohen Obrigkeit in offentlichen Druck gegeben. [Würzburg] M. A. Engmann [1749?]
[12] p. 21cm.

8

Sänger, Maria Renata von Mossau, ca. 1680-1749.
Witchcraft
BF   Gaar, Georg, b. 1702.
1583   Ragionamento del padre Giorgio Gaar,
Z7   della Compagnia di Gesu', fatto avanti al
1749a   rogo di Maria Renata, strega abbruciata
in Erbipoli a' 21. di Giugno del corrente
anno 1749. Tradotto del Tedesco nell'
Italiano dal Dr. F. A. T. [Girolamo Tar-
tarotti] Con alcune annotazioni critiche.
Verona, Per D. Ramanzini [1749]
23 p. 24cm.

Sänger, Maria Renata von Mossau, ca. 1680-1749.
Witchcraft
BF   Gaar, Georg, b. 1702.
1565   Responsa ad annotationes criticas D.
G12   F. A. T. [i.e. Girolamo Tartarotti] in
sermonem de Maria Renata, saga supplicio
addicta die 21. Junii Anno 1749. Herbipoli habitum, Veronae typis evulgatas, in
lucem edita ab authore ejusdem sermonis
P. Georgio Gaar, S.J. ... Wirceburgi,
Typis M. A. Engman [1750?]
55 p. 20cm.

8   (Continued on next card)

Sänger, Maria Renata von Mossau, ca. 1680-1749.
Witchcraft
BF   Gaar, Georg, b. 1702. Responsa ad anno-
1565   tationes criticas D. F. A. T. in sermonem
G12   de Maria Renata ...   [1750]   (Card 2)
His Ragionamento del padre Giorgio Gaar,
p. [37]-55, has special t. p., facsimile of
the Verona edition. This text includes
Tartarotti's commentary.
1. Tartarotti, Girolamo, 1706-1761. 2.
His Ragionamento. 3. Witchcraft. 4.
Sänger, Maria Renata von Mossau, ca. 1680-
8   1749. I. His Ragionamento. II.
Title.

Sänger, Maria Renata von Mossau, ca. 1680-1749.
Witchcraft
BV   Gätschenberger, Stephan.
4935   Zwei Klostergeschichten des vorigen Jahr-
G66   hunderts. Zum erstenmale nach den Inquisi-
G12   tions-Akten bearbeitet ... Leipzig, C. F.
Fleischer, 1858.
124 p. 18cm.
Contents.--1. Graf James Gordon oder Pater Marianus.--2. Die letzte Hexe in Deutsch
land.
1. Gordon, James, 1704-1734. 2. Conversion. 3. Sänger, Maria Renata von Mossau,
8   ca. 1680-1749. 4. Witchcraft. 5.
Martyrs. I.   Title.

Sänger, Maria Renata von Mossau, ca. 1680-1749.
WITCHCRAFT
BF   Leist, Friedrich, 1844-
1583   Maria Renata, die letzte Hexe Deutsch-
Z7   lands.
1749e
(In: His Aus Frankens Vorzeit. Würzburg,
1881. 18cm. p. 57-75)

1. Sänger, Maria Renata von Mossau, ca.
8   1680-1749. 2. Trials (Witchcraft)--Germany.
NIC   I. His Aus Frankens Vorzeit.

Sänger, Maria Renata von Mossau, ca.1680-1749.
WITCHCRAFT
D   Meiners, Christoph, 1747-1810.
1   Geschichte einer merkwürdigen Teufels-
G59   Besitzung in Franken zwischen den Jahren
v.2   1740-und 1750.

(In: Göttingisches historisches Magazin.
Hannover. 21cm. v.2 (1788) p.1-39)

1. Demoniac possession. 2. Witchcraft--
8   Franconia. 3. Sänger, Maria Renata von
NIC   Mossau, ca.   1680-1749.

Sänger, Maria Renata von Mossau, ca.1680-1749.
WITCHCRAFT
BF   Meiners, Christoph, 1747-1810.
1517   Geschichte einer merkwürdigen Teufels-
G3   Besitzung in Franken zwischen den Jahren
M51   1740 und 1750. [Hannover, 1788]
39 p. 20cm.

Detached from Göttingisches historisches
Magazin, v.2, 1788.

1. Demoniac possession. 2. Witchcraft--
Franconia. 3. Sänger, Maria Renata von Mossau, ca.1680-   1749.

Sänger, Maria Renata von Mossau, ca. 1680-1749.
WITCHCRAFT
BF   Memminger, Anton.
1583   Das verhexte Kloster. Nach den Akten dar-
Z7   gestellt. Würzburg, Memminger, 1904.
1749c   iv, 273 p. 19cm.

8
NIC

Sänger, Maria Renata von Mossau, ca. 1680-1749.
WITCHCRAFT
BF   Memminger, Anton.
1583   Das verhexte Kloster. Nach den Akten dar-
Z7   gestellt. 2. verb. Aufl Würzburg,
1749d   Memminger, 1908.
181 p. 21cm. (Fränkische Bibliothek,
Bd.2)

1. Sänger, Maria Renata von Mossau, ca.
8   1680-1749. 2. Trials (Witchcraft)--Germany.
NIC   I. Title.

Sänger, Maria Renata von Mossau, ca.1680-1749.
WITCHCRAFT
D   Wahrhafte und umständliche Nachricht von
1   dem Zufalle, so das jungfräuliche Kloster
G59   Unterzell nächst Würzburg des Praemon-
v.2   stratenser-Ordens betreffen.

(In: Göttingisches historisches Magazin.
Hannover. 21cm. v.2 (1788) p.594-631)

8   1. Demoniac possession. 2. Sänger, Maria
NIC   Renata von Mossau, ca. 1680-1749.

Die Sage vom Herzog von Luxemburg und die
historische Persönlichkeit ihres Trägers.
WITCHCRAFT
DC   Kippenberg, Anton, 1874-1950.
130   Die Sage vom Herzog von Luxemburg und die
L97   historische Persönlichkeit ihres Trägers.
K57   Mit 2 Vollbildern und 11 Abbildungen im
Text. Leipzig, W. Engelmann, 1901.
viii, 280 p. illus. 25cm.

Bibliography: p. [256]-280.

8   1. Luxembourg, François Henri de Mont-
NIC   morency, duc   de, 1628-1695. I.
Title.

Die Sage von den Hexen des Brockens.
WITCHCRAFT
BF   Schrader, Ludwig Wilhelm.
1583   Die Sage von den Hexen des Brockens und
S37   deren Entstehen in vorchristlicher Zeit
durch die Verehrung des Melybogs und der
Frau Holle. Historisch bearbeitet ...
Quedlinburg und Leipzig, G. Basse, 1839.
48 p. 19cm.
Sent to L. Freytag and published through
him.
1. Walpurgisnacht. 2. Witchcraft--
Thuringia. 3. Folk-lore--Thuringia.
8   4. Melybog.   5. Frau Holle. I.
NIC   Title.

CATALOGUE OF THE CORNELL WITCHCRAFT COLLECTION

CHCRAFT
    Saint André, François de.
      Mr. de St. André ... Lesenswürdige Briefe an einige seiner Freunde uber die Materie von der Zauberey, den Ubelthaten, so dadurch angestifftet werden, und von den Zauberern und Hexen insbesondere; worinnen er die wunderbarsten Würckungen, die man gemeiniglich den Teuffeln zuschreibet, deutlich erkläret, und dabey zeiget, dass diese Geister offt nicht den geringsten Antheil daran haben ... Statt eines Suplements zum Hutchinson aus dem Frantzösischen ins Teutsche übersetzt ... von Theodoro Arnold.
           (Continued on next card)

HCRAFT
    Saint André, François de. Mr. de St. André ... Lesenswürdige Briefe ... 1727. (Card 2)
      Leipzig, Bey J. C. Martini, 1727.
        10 p. l., 204, [9] p. 22cm.
      Translation of Lettres ... à quelques-uns de ses amis, pub. 1725.

          (Continued on next card)

ITCHCRAFT
565
97
726
    Saint André, François de. Mr. de St. André ... Lesenswürdige Briefe ... 1727. (Card 3)
      Title in red and black.
      Bound with Hutchinson, F. Historischer Versuch von der Hexerey. Leipzig, 1726.
      1. Witchcraft. 2. Magic. I. His Lettres ... à quelques-uns de ses amis. German. II. Hutchinson, Francis, bp. of Down and Connor, 1660-1739. Historischer Versuch von der Hexerey. III. Arnold, Theodor, 1683-1771, tr. IV. Title: Lesenswürdige Briefe ... über die Materie von der Zauberey. V. Title.

TCHCRAFT
    Saint André, François de.
      Lettres de Mr. de St. André, conseiller-medecin ordinaire du roy; à quelques-uns de ses amis, au sujet de la magie, des maleficres et des sorciers ... Paris, R. M. Despilly, 1725.
        4 p. l., 446, [2] p. 16½ cm.
      One of 4 Paris editions of this year; but listed first, in BN and Yves-Plessis.
      Commentary in MS by G. L. Burr on flyleaf.
      1. Witchcraft. 2. Magic. I. Title: Lettres ... à quelques-uns de ses amis. II. Title.

    Library of Congress   BF1602.S2
                        11-15975

    Saint André, François de.
      Lettres ... à quelques-uns de ses amis. German.

ITCHCRAFT
565
97
726
    Saint André, François de.
      Mr. de St. André ... Lesenswürdige Briefe an einige seiner Freunde uber die Materie von der Zauberey, den Ubelthaten, so dadurch angestifftet werden, und von den Zauberern und Hexen insbesondere; worinnen er die wunderbarsten Würckungen, die man gemeiniglich den Teuffeln zuschreibet, deutlich erkläret, und dabey zeiget, dass diese Geister offt

          (Continued on next card)

    Saint André, François de.
      Lettres ... à quelques-uns de ses amis. German.

TCHCRAFT
65
7
26
    Saint André, François de. Mr. de St. André ... Lesenswürdige Briefe ... 1727. (Card 2)
      nicht den geringsten Antheil daran haben ... Statt eines Suplements zum Hutchinson aus dem Französischen ins Teutsche übersetzt ... von Theodoro Arnold. Leipzig, Bey J. C. Martini, 1727.
        10 p. l., 204, [9] p. 22cm.
      Translation of Lettres ... à quelques-uns de ses amis, pub. 1725.
          (Continued on next card)

    Saint André, François de.
WITCHCRAFT   Lettres ... à quelques-uns de ses amis. German.
BF   Saint André, François de. Mr. de St. André ... Lesenswürdige Briefe ... 1727. (Card 3)
1565
H97   Title in red and black.
1726   Bound with Hutchinson, F. Historischer Versuch von der Hexerey. Leipzig, 1726.
      1. Witchcraft. 2. Magic. I. His Lettres ... à quelques-uns de ses amis. German. II. Hutchinson, Francis, bp. of Down and Connor, 1660-1739. Historischer Versuch von der Hexerey. III. Arnold, Theodor, 1683-1771, tr. IV. Title: Lesenswürdige Briefe ... über die
8   Materie von der Zauberey.

Witchcraft   Saint-André, François de.
      Lettres au sujet de la magie.
BF   Boissier, A.
1602   Recueil de lettres au sujet des malefices et du sortilege: servant de réponse aux
S13   Lettres du Sieur de Saint-André, medecin à
B68   Coutances, sur le même sujet. Avec la scavante remontrance du Parlement de Rouen faite au roy Louis XIV, au sujet du sortilege, du malefice, des sabats, & autres effets de la magie, pour la perfection du procez dont il est parlé dans ces Lettres. Paris, Brunet fils, 1731.
      xiii, 387 p. 17cm.
      1. Saint-André, François de. Lettres au sujet de la magie. 2. Witchcraft. 3. Sorcery. I. Title.

Witchcraft   St. Anthony's dance and witchcraft in colonial Connecticut.
BF   Vessie, Percy R., d. 1953.
1576   Hereditary chorea: St. Anthony's dance and witchcraft in colonial Connecticut.
V58+   [n. p., 1939]
      [7] p. illus. 28cm.

      "Reprinted from Journal of the Connecticut State Medical Society, vol. 3, no. 11, November, 1939."

      1. Witchcraft--Connecticut. 2. Chorea. I. Title. II. St. Anthony's dance and witchcraft in colonial Connecticut.

WITCHCRAFT
BF   Saint-Olive, Pierre.
1582   Étude sur le merveilleux au XVe siècle.
S14   Un miracle à St.-Genis-d'Aoste. Une affaire de sorcellerie aux Avenières. Belley, Impr. L. Chaduc, 1912.
      15 p. illus. 23cm.
      "Extrait de la revue 'Le Bugey' Octobre 1911. Tiré à 80 exemplaires. N°. 0014."
      1. Witchcraft--France. 2. Witchcraft--Avenières, France. I. Title: Le merveilleux au XVe siècle. II. Title: Un miracle à St.-Genis-d'Aoste. III. Title.
8
NIC

Witchcraft   Sainte-Foi, Charles, 1806-1861, tr.
BV   Görres, Johann Joseph von, 1776-1848.
5081   La mystique divine, naturelle et diabolique; ouvrage traduit de l'allemand par M.
G59   Charles Sainte-Foi. 2. éd. Paris, Mme
1861   Ve Poussielgue-Rusand, 1861-62.
      5 v. 18cm.
      Translation of Die christliche Mystik.
      1. Mysticism. 2. Occult sciences. 3. Demonomania. I. Görres, Johann Joseph von, 1776-1848. Die christliche Mystik--French. II. Sainte-Foi, Charles, 1806-1861, tr. III. Title.

WITCHCRAFT
Z   Salem, Mass. Public Library.
6878   [Witchcraft; special reading lists.]
W8
S16+   (In: Bulletin of the Salem Public Library. Salem, Mass. 26cm. v.1, no.3, July 1891, p.23-24; v.1, no.10, Feb. 1892, p.80)

8
NIC   1. Witchcraft--Bibl.

Witchcraft
PS   The Salem belle; a tale of 1692. Boston, Tappan & Dennet, 1842.
991   238 p. 17cm.
A1
S16

    Salem possessed.
UNDERGR
BF   Boyer, Paul S
1576   Salem possessed; the social origins of witchcraft [by] Paul Boyer and Stephen Nissenbaum. Cambridge, Mass., Harvard University Press, 1974.
B79
      xxi, 231 p. illus. 25 cm.

    The Salem village parsonage, 1681-1784.
Witchcraft
BF   Trask, Richard B
1576   The Devil amongst us; a history of the Salem village parsonage, 1681-1784.
T77   Danvers, Mass., Danvers Historical Society, 1971.
      12 p. illus. 23cm.

    1. Witchcraft--Salem, Mass. I. Title. II. Title: The Salem village parsonage, 1681- 1784.

Witchcraft   The Salem witch trials.
BF   Gemmill, William Nelson, 1860-
1576   The Salem witch trials, a chapter of New England history, by William Nelson Gemmill. Chicago, A. C. McClurg & co., 1924.
G32
      2 p l, iii p 1 l, 240 p. front. 19½ cm.

      1. Witchcraft--Salem, Mass. I. Title.
    Library of Congress   BF1576.G4
           Copy 2   25—471
    Copyright A 814302   [s25c3]

    Salem witchcraft and Cotton Mather. A reply.
WITCHCRAFT
BF   Upham, Charles Wentworth, 1802-1875.
1576   Salem witchcraft and Cotton Mather. A reply [to W. F. Poole's Cotton Mather and Salem witchcraft] Morrisania, N. Y., 1869.
P82
U67+
      91 p. 19cm.
      In double columns.
      Reprint from the Historical Magazine.
      1. Poole, William Frederick, 1821-1894. Cotton Mather and Salem witchcraft. 2. Mather, Cotton, 1663-1728. 3. Witchcraft--Salem, Mass. I. Title.
8

    Salem witchcraft and Cotton Mather. A reply.
BF   Upham, Charles Wentworth, 1802-1875.
1576   Salem witchcraft and Cotton Mather. A reply. Morrisania, N. Y., 1869.
U68S2+
      91 p. 29cm.

      A reply to an article that appeared in the North American review, April, 1869, concerning the author's Salem witchcraft.

      1. Witchcraft--Salem, Mass. 2. Mather, Cotton, 1663-1728. 1728. I. Title.

CATALOGUE OF THE CORNELL WITCHCRAFT COLLECTION

Witchcraft
BF
1575
C14
1865
    Salem witchcraft: comprising More wonders of the invisible world.
    Calef, Robert, 1648-1719.
        Salem witchcraft: comprising More wonders of the invisible world, collected by Robert Calef; and Wonders of the invisible world, by Cotton Mather; together with notes and explanations by Samuel P. Fowler. Boston, William Veazie, 1865.
        450 p. 22cm.

BF
1576
U67
    Salem witchcraft in outline.
    Upham, Mrs. Caroline E
        Salem witchcraft in outline. Salem, Mass., Salem Press, 1891.
        xiii,161 p. illus. 18cm.

    1. Witchcraft--Salem, Mass.
    I. Title.

Witchcraft
BF
1576
U68
1959
    Salem witchcraft; with an account of Salem village and a history of opinions on witchcraft.
    Upham, Charles Wentworth, 1802-1875.
        Salem witchcraft; with an account of Salem village and a history of opinions on witchcraft and kindred subjects. New York, F. Ungar Pub. Co. [1959]
        2 v. illus., ports., fold. map. 21 cm. (American classics)

    1. Witchcraft—Salem, Mass. 2. Salem, Mass.—Hist. I. Title.

BF1576.U56 1959   974.45   59—10887
Library of Congress   [60f5]

Witchcraft
AZ
999
S16
    Salgues, Jacques Barthélemy, 1760 (ca.)-1830.
        Des erreurs et des préjugés répandus dans la société ... Paris, Chez F. Buisson, 1810-15.
        3 v. 20cm.

    Vol. 2: "2. éd., revue et augmentée", with title: Des erreurs et des préjugés répandus dans les diverses classes de la société. Paris, Lepetit, 1815.
    Imprint of vol. 1 is partly covered by a bookplate.

(Over)

ar W
37210
    Salgues, Jacques Barthélemy, 1760 (ca.)-1830.
        Des erreurs et des préjugés répandus dans les dix-huitième et dix-neuvième siècles. Paris, J. G. Dentu, 1828.
        2 v. 22cm.

    1. Superstition. I. Title.

WITCHCRAFT
BF
1566
S16
    Salillas, Rafael.
        La fascinación en España. Estudio hecho con la información promovida por la Sección de Ciencias morales y políticas del Ateneo de Madrid. Madrid, Imprenta á cargo de E. Arias, 1905.
        107 p. 24cm.

    Subtitle on cover: Brujas--brujerías--amuletos.

8
NIC
    1. Witchcraft--Spain. 2. Amulets. I. Title.

WITCHCRAFT
BF
1584
I8
Z7+
1623
    Salomone-Marino, Salvatore, 1847-1916.
        Un processo di stregoneria nel 1623 in Sicilia, pubblicato e illustrato dal Can. Gaetano Millunzi e da Salvatore Salomone-Marino.
        (In: Archivio storico siciliano. Palermo. 28cm. nuov. ser., anno 25, fasc. 3-4, 1901, p. [253]-379)

    1. Trials (Witchcraft)--Sicily. 2. Adamo, Orazio di. 3. Cabala. 4. Occult sciences. I. Salomone-Marino, Salvatore, 1847-1916.

8
NIC

WITCHCRAFT
BF
1533
S18
    [Sambuga, Joseph Anton Franz Martin] 1752-1815.
        Der Teufel, ein Neujahrsgeschenk! Oder Prüfung des Glaubens an höllische Geister, nach der Lehre des hochwürdigen Herrn Peter Hartmann, Predigers zu Altenöting. [München] 1810.
        114 p. 21cm.
    Ascription by Holzmann and Kayser.

    1. Devil. 2. Hartmann, Peter, preacher.
    I. Title.

8

Witchcraft
BF
1559
G25
Z87
    Samlungen von Briefen und Aufsätzen über die Gassnerischen und Schröpferischen Geisterbeschwörungen.
    Semler, Johann Salomo, 1725-1791, ed.
        Samlungen von Briefen und Aufsätzen über die Gassnerischen und Schröpferischen Geisterbeschwörungen, mit eigenen vielen Anmerkungen hrsg. von Johann Salomo Semler ... Halle im Magdeburgischen, C. H. Hemmerde, 1776.
        2 v. in 1. 20cm.
    1. Gassner, Johann Joseph, 1727-1779. 2. Schrepfer, Johann Georg, 1730?-1774. 3. Exorcism. 4. Faith-cure.

8

Witchcraft
BF
1445
S18
    Sammlung vieler auserlesener und seltener Geschichte, und merkwürdiger Begebenheiten, welche sich mit erscheinenden Gespenstern, werfenden und rumorenden Poltergeistern, Vorboten des Todes-Fälle, Hexengespenstern, Zauberern, Zauberinnen, Schatzgräbern, u. d. g. ... Nebst gründlichem Beweis, dass es würklich Gespenster gebe. Nürnberg, W. M. Endterische Consorten und Engelbrechts seel. Wittib, 1753.

8
(Continued on next card)

Witchcraft
BF
1445
S18
    Sammlung vieler auserlesener und seltener Geschichte ... 1753.   (Card 2)
        24 p. l., 1120, [46] p. 19cm.

    1. Ghosts. 2. Ghost stories. 3. Folk-lore, German.

8

WITCHCRAFT
BF
1405
G28
    Sammlung von Natur- und Medicin- ... Geschichten.
        Geschichte der Natur u. Kunst von 1717-1726. Ausschnitte. [Bresslau, etc. 1718-1728]
        1 v. (various pagings) illus. 21cm.
    Cover title.
    Extracts from Sammlung von Natur- und Medicin- wie auch hierzu gehörigen Kunst- und Literatur-Geschichten, and Supplementum I-III. Curieuser und nutzbarer Anmerckungen von Natur- und Kunst-Geschichten.
    Paged (635) and with Register in MS.

8
NIC
    1. Occult sciences. 2. Curiosities and wonders. I. Sammlung von Natur- und Medicin- ... Geschichten.

MSS
Bd.
WITCHCRAFT
BF
S19
    Samson, Hermann.
        Neun ausserlesen und wolgegründete Hexen Predigt, darinnen der Terminus Magiae oder Zauberey nach den logicalischen Terminis ... erkläret und aussgeführet worden, und in der Thumb Kirchen zu Riga öffentlich gehalten durch M. Hermannum Sansonium ... Riga in Eieffland, durch und in Verlegung Gerhard Schröders, 1626 [ca. 1900]
        166 p. 24cm.
    Carnap's manuscript copy.
    "Originaldruck in der Universi-
(Continued on next card)

MSS
Bd.
WITCHCRAFT
BF
S19
    Samson, Hermann. Neun ausserlesen und wolgegründete Hexen Predigt ... 1626 [ca. 1900]   (Card 2)
    täts-Bibliothek zu Breslau. 42. Bl. in 4°."
    Title page in red and black.
    Numerals and signatures in the margins indicate pagination and signatures of the original.
    On the inside front cover the copyist has appended a note to the rarity of the printed work and given bibliographical
(Continued on next card)

MSS
Bd.
WITCHCRAFT
BF
S19
    Samson, Hermann. Neun ausserlesen und wolgegründete Hexen Predigt ... 1626 [ca. 1900]   (Card 3)
    references.
    Signed Geo. L. Burr.

    1. Witchcraft--Sermons. I. Title.

    Samsonius, Hermannus.

    see

    Samson, Hermann.

Witchcraft
BF
1569
A2S19
    Samuel, Cassinensis.
        Questione de le Strie. Questiones lamearum fratris Samuelis de cassinis or. minorum ob. regularis. [Pavia? 1505]
        [6] l. 21cm.

    Signatures: a6.
    Colophon (l. 6b): Editum a fratre Samuele de cassinis or. mino# ob. regularis die. 6. May anno. 1505.

    1. Witchcraft.   I. Title. II. Title: Questiones lamearum.

Witchcraft
BF
1565
S19
    Samuel and the witch of Endor; or, The sin of witchcraft. [Battle Creek, Mich.] Seventh-Day Adventist Pub. Association, 18--]
        32 p. 18cm.

    Caption title.
    Signed: J. N. A.

    1. Witchcraft.   I. Title: The sin of witchcraft. II. A., J. N. III. J. N. A.

CATALOGUE OF THE CORNELL WITCHCRAFT COLLECTION

Sanden, Bernhard von.

WITCHCRAFT
Masecovius, Thomas.
  Warhaffte und umbständliche Beschreibung der wunderbahren Geschichte, so sich mit einer angefochtenen Jungfer in dem 1683ten und folgenden Jahren zu Königsberg in Preussen... Nebst einer Vorrede D. Bernhard von Sanden...gerichtet wider die Bezauberte Welt D. Balthasar Beckers. Königsb., In Verlegung Heinrich Boye, Druckts Johann Zacharias Etoile, 1695.
    363 p. 17cm.
  1.Witchcraft. 2.Witchcraft--Germany 3.Bekker, Balthasar,1634-1698. ‹De betoverde weereld. I. Sanden, Bernhard von.

Sandford, James, fl. 1567, tr.
  Agrippa von Nettesheim, Heinrich Cornelius, 1486?-1535.
    Of the vanitie and vncertaintie of artes and sciences, Englished by Ja. San., gent. ... London, Imprinted by Henry Wykes, 1569.
    [8], 187 l. illus. 19cm.
  First edition.
  Translated by James Sandford.
  Title within ornamental border.
  Running title: Cornelius Agrippa of the vanities of sciences.
            (Continued on next card)

Sandford, James, fl. 1567, tr.
  Agrippa von Nettesheim, Heinrich Cornelius, 1486?-1535. Of the vanitie and vncertaintie of artes and sciences ... 1569. (Card 2)
  Translation of De incertitudine et vanitate scientiarum atque artium declamatio invectiva.
  Imperfect copy: leaf 185 wanting.
  I. His De incertitudine et vanitate scientiarum. English. II. Sandford, James, fl. 1567, tr. III. Title.

Sandras, , advocat au Parlement, supposed author.
WITCHCRAFT
  Courtilz, Gatien de, sieur de Sandras, 1644?-1722.
    Les fredaines du diable; ou, Recueil de morceaux épars, pour servir à l'histoire du diable et de ses suppôts; tirés d'auteurs dignes de foi, par feu M. Sandras, avocat en Parlement; mis en nouveau style et publiés par J. Fr. N. D. L. R. [i.e., Jean François Née de la Rochelle] Paris, Chez Merlin, 1797.
    216 p. 17 cm.
            (Continued on next card)

Sandras, , advocat au Parlement, supposed author.
WITCHCRAFT
  Courtilz, Gatien de, sieur de Sandras, 1644?-1722. Les fredaines du diable ... 1797. (Card 2)
  Ascription by BM, Biographie universelle; and BN for entry under Née de la Rochelle as editor.
  Author entry in BN: Sandras, , advocat au Parlement.
  1. Devil. 2. Devil--Bibliography. I. Sandras, , advocat au Parlement, supposed author. II. Née de la Rochelle, Jean François, 1751-1838, ed. III. Title.

Sandras de Courtilz, Gatien de, 1644?-1712.
  see
Courtilz, Gatien de, sieur de Sandras, 1644?-1712.

Witchcraft
DA 890 T77 S22
  Sands, J of Ormiston, Scotland.
    Sketches of Tranent in the olden time. Edinburgh, Printed for the author by J. Hogg, 1881.
    102 p. illus. 19cm.
  1. Tranent, Scotland. 2. Witchcraft--Scotland. I. Title.

WITCHCRAFT
BX 2340 S22 1761
  Sannig, Bernhard.
    Collectio, sive Apparatus absolutionum, benedictionum, conjurationum, exorcismorum, rituum, & ceremoniarum ecclesiasticarum, ac administrationis sacramentorum ... Coordinatum A. R. P. Bernardo Sannig. Venetiis, Apud J. B. Recurti, 1761.
    xii, 466 p. 15cm.
  1.Exorcism. 2. Benediction. I. Catholic Church. Liturgy and ritual. II. Title.

Santeur, lawyer.
Witchcraft
BF 1582 Z7 1675
  Hautefeuille, lawyer.
    Plaidoyez svr les magiciens et svr les sorciers, tenus en la cour de Liege, le 16. Decembre 1675. Ov on montre clairement qu'il n'y peut avoir de ces sortes de gens. Par les sieurs de Havte Feüille & Santevr advocats. Sur l'imprimé a Liege, Chez Iacqves Persois imprimeur, 1676.
    120 p. 14cm.
  "Le livre d'Albert le Grand, leqvel traite des merveilles du monde," p. [77]-
            (Continued on next card)

Santeur, lawyer.
Witchcraft
BF 1582 Z7 1675
  Hautefeuille, lawyer. Plaidoyez svr les magiciens ... 1676. (Card 2)
  120, has special t. p. with imprint: Lyon, Par Iean Hvgvetan, 1616. Text is taken from Les admirables secrets d'Albert le Grand.
  1. Witchcraft. 2. Magic. 3. Sillieux, Sulpice, fl. 1675. I. Santeur, lawyer. II. Albertus Magnus, saint, bp. of Ratisbon, 1193?-1280. Spurious and doubtful works. Les admirables secrets d'Albert le Grand. III. Title: Plaidoyez sur les magiciens. IV. Title: Le livre d'Albert le Grand.

Witchcraft
PQ 2422 S7 1904
  Sardou, Victorien, 1831-1908.
    La sorcière. Drame en cinq actes. [2. éd.] Paris, Calmann-Lévy [1904]
    242 p. 19cm.
  1. Witchcraft--Fiction. I. Title.

PQ 2422 S7 1904a
  Sardou, Victorien, 1831-1908.
    La sorcière; drame en cinq actes. [4. éd.] Paris, C. Lévy [1904]
    242 p. 18cm.

BF 1566 S24
  Sarpento, Lewis.
    Ze reden bij nacht ; de mysterieuze gruwelhistorie van de bokkerijders [door] Ben Lindekens. Amsterdam, Wetenschappelijke Uitgeverij, 1974.
    269 p. 20 cm. (Unofficial history)
    Bibliography: p. 262-269.
  1. Witchcraft. 2. Goats (in religion, folklore, etc.) I. Title
NIC AUG 26,'75   CoOexc   75-552134

RARE
HV 8593 B66 1726
  Sassen, Meint Johann, respondent.
    Bode, Heinrich von, 1652-1720, praeses.
    Tractatio juridica De usu & abusu torturae...quam...MDCXCVII habuit Heinricus de Boden [sic] Editio novissima. Halae Magdeb., sumtu Hendeliano, 1726.
    38 p. 21cm.
    Diss.--Halle (M. J. Sassen, respondent) 1697.
  1. Torture. I. Sassen, Meint Johann, respondent. II. Title.

RARE
HV 8593 D612 no.8
  Sassen, Meint Johann, respondent.
    Bode, Heinrich von, 1652-1720.
    Tractatio juridica De usu & abusu torturae...quam...habuit Heinricus de Boden. Editio novissima. Halae Magdeb., Sumtu Hendeliano, 1735.
    40 p. 22cm.
    Originally issued as diss., 1697, with M. J. Sassen as respondent.
    No.8 in a vol. lettered: Dissertation[e]s de tortura, 1721-92.
  1.Torture. I. Sassen, Meint Johann, respondent. II. Title.

WITCHCRAFT
BT 980 L28
  Satan, a portrait.
  Langton, Edward, 1886-
    Satan, a portrait; a study of the character of Satan through all the ages, by Edward Langton ... London, Skeffington & son, ltd. [1946]
    128 p. front., plates. 22cm.
  1. Devil. I. Title.
    [Full name: Frederick Edward Palmer Langton]
                                46-4210
  Library of Congress   BT980.L3
                      [1]   235

Witchcraft
BF 1528 D9 V98 1692
  De Satan, in sijn weesen, aert, bedryf, en guychel-spel...
  Vries, Simon de, b. 1630.
    De Satan, in sijn weesen, aert, bedryf, en guychel-spel, vertoond in een historische verhandelingh van duyvelen, gesighten, spoocken, voorseggingen, voorteeckenen, droomen, toveryen, betoveringen, beseetenheyd, en wat noch voorts deese stof aenhangigh is. Nevens afweeringh van 't geen daer tegens ingebraght werd met meenighvuldige verwringingen der H. Schrift, en tegenspraeck der geduerige ondervindingh.
            (Continued on next card)

Witchcraft
BF 1528 D9 V98 1692
  De Satan, in sijn weesen, aert, bedryf, en guychel-spel ...
    Vries, Simon de, b. 1630. De Satan ... 1692. (Card 2)
  Door S. de Vries. Utrecht, By A. Schouten, Boeckverkoper, 1692.
    20 p. l., 571, [57] p. title and other vignettes, illus. initials. 17 x 11cm.
    8°: *-2*8, 3*4, A-2Q8, 2R4.
  First published 1691.
  In part a refutation of Balthasar Bekker
            (Continued on next card)

CATALOGUE OF THE CORNELL WITCHCRAFT COLLECTION

De Satan, in sijn weesen, aert, bedryf, en guychel-spel.

Witchcraft
BF 1528 D9 V98 1692

Vries, Simon de, b. 1630. De Satan ... 1692. (Card 3)
ker's De betoverde weereld.
Van der Linde 153.

1. Devil. 2. Demonology. 3. Bekker, Balthasar, 1634-1698. De betoverde weereld. II. Title.

8

The Satan of theology and how we came by him.

Witchcraft
BT 980 H88

Hudson, William Henry, 1862-1918.
The Satan of theology and how we came by him. Boston, American Unitarian Association [1891]
42 p. 19cm.

Author's autograph presentation copy to George Lincoln Burr.
A lecture delivered in the First Unitarian Church, Ithaca, N. Y.

1. Devil. I. Title.

Satan og hans kultus.

Witchcraft
BF 1550 K79

Kohl, Carl.
Satan og hans kultus. København, Nordiske forlag E. Bojesen, 1902.
viii, 185, [1] p. 23cm.

Autographed by the author.

1. Devil. 2. Witchcraft. 3. Magic. I. Title.

8

Satan, satanism, and witchcraft.

BT 981 D32

DeHaan, Richard W
Satan, satanism, and witchcraft, by Richard W. Dehaan with Herbert Vander Lught. Grand Rapids, Mich., Zondervan Pub. House [1972]
125 p. 18 cm. (Zondervan books) $0.95
Bibliography: p. 123-125.

4

1. Devil. 2. Christianity and occult sciences. I. Vander Lught, Herbert, joint author. II. Title.

BT981.D44   235'.47   72-81786
                                        MARC
Library of Congress   72 [4]

Satanism and witchcraft.

Witchcraft
BF 1569 M62 1958

Michelet, Jules, 1798-1874.
Satanism and witchcraft, a study in medieval superstition. Translated by A. R. Allinson. London, Arco Publications [1958]
xx, 332 p. 21cm.

Translation of La sorcière.

1. Witchcraft. 2. Demonomania. 3. Civilization, Medieval. I. Allinson, Alfred Richard, tr. II. Michelet, Jules, 1798-1874. La sorcière.--English. III. Title.

Le satanisme et la magie.

Witchcraft
BF 1549 B68 1897

Bois, Jules, 1871-
Le satanisme et la magie. Avec une étude de J.-K. Huysmans. Paris, Flammarion [1897]
xxvii, 339 p. 19cm.

With book-plate of Theodore Stanton.

1. Satanism. 2. Magic. I. Huysmans, Joris Karl, 1848-1907. II. Title.

Satan's devices.

Witchcraft
PR 3404 H5 1817

[Defoe, Daniel] 1660-1731.
Satan's devices; or, The political history of the Devil, ancient and modern. In two parts. Part I. His original; a state of his circumstances; his conduct, public and private; the various turns of his affairs, from Adam down to this present time. Part II. The various methods he takes to converse with mankind; with the manner of his making witches, wizards, and conjurers; and how they sell their souls to him. The whole inter-
(Continued on next card)

Satan's devices.

Witchcraft
PR 3404 H5 1817

[Defoe, Daniel] 1660-1731. Satan's devices ... 1817. (Card 2)

spersed with many of the Devil's adventures. To which is added, a description of the Devil's dwelling, vulgarly called hell. A new ed., with engravings. London, T. Kelly, sold by W. Davies, 1817.
431 p. front. 21cm.

Added t.p. engr., with title The
(Continued on next card)

Satan's devices.

Witchcraft
PR 3404 H5 1817

[Defoe, Daniel] 1660-1731. Satan's devices ... 1817. (Card 3)

history of the Devil, ancient and modern, and imprint: Exeter, Davies & Eldridge, 1815.
First ed. published 1726 under title: The political history of the Devil.

1. Devil. I. Title. II. Defoe, Daniel, 1660-1731. The political history of the Devil.

Satans invisible world discovered.

Witchcraft
BF 1410 S61 1871

Sinclair, George, d. 1696.
Satans invisible world discovered. Reprinted from the original edition published in Edinburgh in 1685. Accompanied with a bibliographical notice and supplement, &c. Edinburgh, Thomas George Stevenson, 1871.
liii, 264, ciii p. 20cm.

Satans temptations.

Witchcraft
BF 1546 G48

[Gilpin, Richard]
Daemonologia sacra: or, A treatise of Satans temptations ... By R. G. ... London, Printed by J. D. for R. Randel and P. Maplisden, 1677.
3 pts. in 1 v. 20cm.

1. Devil. I. Title. II. Title: Satans temptations. III. G., R. IV. R. G.

Sathan transformed into an angell of light, expressing his dangerous impostures vnder glorious shewes.

Witchcraft
BF 1581 A2 C77 1622

Cooper, Thomas, fl. 1598-1626.
Sathan transformed into an angell of light, expressing his dangerous impostures vnder glorious shewes. Emplified specially in the doctrine of witch-craft, and such sleights of Satan as are incident thereunto. Very necessary to discerne the speci-plague (sic) raging in these dayes, and so to hide our selues from the snare thereof. London, B. Alsop, 1622.
368 p. 15cm.
Originally published in 1617 under title: The mystery of witch-craft.

Les satyres.

WITCHCRAFT
BL 820 S3 A89

Aubignac, François Hédelin, abbé d', 1604-1676.
Des satyres brvtes, monstres et demons. De levr natvre et adoration. Contre l'opinion de ceux qui ont estimé les satyres estre vne espece d'hommes distincts & separez des Adamicques ... Par F. Hedelin, aduocat en Parlement ... Paris, Chez Nicolas Bvon, 1627.
12 p. l., 236 p. 17cm.

8

Witchcraft
BT 965 S25

[Saunders, Richard] d. 1692.
Ἀγγελογραφία sive Πνεύματα λειτυργικά, Πνευματολογία: or, A discourse of angels: their nature and office, or ministry ... Also something touching devils and apparitions and impulses. With ... doctrine of angels ... London, Printed for T. Parkhurst, 1701.
314, [2] p. 21cm.
Preface signed: Geo. Hamond.
Publisher's advertisement: p. [315-316]

Title transliterated:
Angelographia sive Pneumata leiturgika ...
(Over)

WITCHCRAFT
BF 1569 S26

Sauter, Johann G
Zur Hexenbulle 1484. Die Hexerei, mit besonderer Berücksichtigung Oberschwabens. Eine culturhistorische Studie. Ulm, J. Ebner, 1884.
82 p. 21cm.

1. Witchcraft--History. 2. Witchcraft--Swabia. 3. Catholic Church. Pope, 1484-1492 (Innocenti VIII) Summis desiderantes affectibus (9 Dec. 1484) I. Title.

8
NIC

WITCHCRAFT
BF 1517 F5 S26+

Sauzé, J.-Charles, 1815-
Essai médico-historique sur les possédés de Loudun. Paris, Impr. Rignoux, 1839.
59 p. 26cm.

Thèse--Paris.
"Questions sur diverses branches des sciences médicales": p. [51]-59.

8
NIC

1. Loudun, France. Ursuline convent. 2. Demoniac possession. 3. Psychical research. I. Title: Les possédés de Loudun. II. Title.

Sawyer, Elizabeth, d. 1621.

Witchcraft
BF 1563 W81++ no.11

Goodcole, Henry.
The wonderfull discouerie of Elizabeth Sawyer, a witch, late of Edmonton, her convuiction and condemnation and death. Together with the relation of the Diuels accesse to her and their conference together. London, Printed for W. Butler, 1621. [London, at the British Museum, 1923]
[32] p. 16cm.
Signatures: A-D⁴.
Photocopy (negative) 31 p. on 15 l. 20 x 32cm.

Witchcraft
BF 1583 A2 S27+ 1898

Saxe-Coburg. Laws, statutes, etc.
Herzog Johann Casimirs "Gerichts-Ordnung die Hexerei betrf: Publiciret ahm 21. February 1629." Aus dem Hildburghäuser Ratsarchiv mitgeteilt von Dr. A. Human.
(In Verein für Sachsen-Meiningische Geschichte und Landeskunde, Meiningen. Schriften. Hildburghausen. 27cm. 29 (1898), p. 99-112)

8   (Continued on next card)

CATALOGUE OF THE CORNELL WITCHCRAFT COLLECTION

Witchcraft
Saxe-Coburg. Laws, statutes, etc. Herzog Johann Casimirs "Gerichts-Ordnung die Hexerei betrf ..." 1898.   (Card 2)

1. Witchcraft--Saxony. I. Johann Casimir, Duke of Saxe-Coburg, 1564-1633. II. Human, Armin, 1843-1923, ed. III. Verein für Saxen-Meiningische Geschichte und Landeskunde, Meiningen. Schriften. IV. Title: Herzog Johann Casimirs "Gerichts-Ordnung die Hexerei betreffend."

Scala, Paolo della, marquis of Verona, 1534-1575.

see

Scalichius, Paulus von Lika, count, 1534-1575.

Scala, Paulus de la, prince, 1534-1575.

see

Scalichius, Paulus von Lika, count, 1534-1575.

Scalich, Paul, 1534-1575.

see

Scalichius, Paulus von Lika, count, 1534-1575.

Scalichius, Paulus von Lika, count, 1534-1575.
Pavli principis de la Scala ... Primi tomi Miscellaneorvm, de rervm caussis & successibus atque secretiori methodo ibidem expressa, effigies ac exemplar, nimirum, vaticiniorum & imaginum Ioachimi Abbatis Florensis Calabriae, & Anselmi Episcopi Marsichani, super statu summorum Pontificum Rhomanae Ecclesiae, contra falsam, iniquam, vanam, confictam & seditiosam cuiusdam Pseudomagi, quae nuper nomine Theophrasti Paracelsi in lucem prodijt, pseudomagicam expositionem, vera, certa, & indubitata
(Continued on next card)

Scalichius, Paulus von Lika, count, 1534-1575. ... Primi tomi Miscellaneorvm ... effigies ... 1570.   (Card 2)
explanatio. Coloniae Agrippinae, Ex Officina Typographica Theodori Graminaei, 1570.
[12], 152 p. illus. 21cm.

Title vignette.
1. Joachim, Abbot of Fiore, 1132 (ca.)-1202. Spurious and doubtful works. Prophetiae de papis.
2. Anselmo, Saint, bp. of Marsico, d. 1210.
3. Paracelsus, 1493-1541. I. Title: Primi tomi Miscellaneorum.

Scaliger, Paulus, 1534-1575.

see

Scalichius, Paulus von Lika, count, 1534-1575.

Schaak, Petrus, fl. 1691.
Witchcraft
BF
1410
B42
Z69
no.9
[Hooght, Everard van der] d. 1716. Sesde briev van הגבר Φιλαλήθης Haggēbher Philaleethees, geschreeven aan zynen vriend N. N. vervattende: I. Een afwysing van vyfderley gewaande voorspraaken van D. Bekker. Ende II. een verhandeling van de De Daimonia, na hare beteekenisse voor, in, ende na de tyden Christi. Volgens het welke uyt het Hebreeusch Griekich en Syrisch klaar te sien is, dat De Daimonia zedert Christi tyden niet anders zyn, dan de Duyvelen. Amsterdam,
NIC   (Continued on next card)

Schaak, Petrus, fl. 1691.
Witchcraft
BF
1410
B42
Z69
no.9
[Hooght, Everard van der] d. 1716. Sesde briev van ... Haggēbher Philaleethees ...   (Card 2)

G. Borstius, 1691.
135-176 p. 21cm.
Signatures: 4°: Π1, A-E4, F1.
Black letter.
The friend N.N. may be Jacobus Schuts.
Van der Linde 103.
No. 9 in a Collection of tracts
against Balthasar Bekker and his
betoverde weereld.
NIC   (Continued on next card)

Schaak, Petrus, fl. 1691.
Witchcraft
BF
1410
B42
Z69
no.6
[Hooght, Everard van der] d. 1716. Vierde briev van הגבר Φιλαλήθης Haggēbher Philaleethees, geschreeven aan zynen vriend N. N. over het weesen, denken, willen, vermoogen, ende de plaats der engelen in het gemeen, ende der quade geesten, in het byzonder. Item, van des menschen ziele, en harewerking, het zy afgesondert, ofte ook vereenigt met het lichaam; ende hoe verre de quade geesten op de selve konnen werken. Met een onder soek van D. Bekker wel kan
seggen, dat syn E. zoekt te bewaren
NIC   (Continued on next card)

Schaak, Petrus, fl. 1691.
Witchcraft
BF
1410
B42
Z69
no.6
[Hooght, Everard van der] d. 1716. Vierde briev van ... Haggēbher Philaleethees ...   (Card 2)

de authoriteyt van Gods woord, ende de eere des alderhoogsten. Amsterdam, G. Borstius, 1691.
59-96 p. 21cm.
Signatures: 4°: Π1, A-C4, D2.
Black letter.
Van der Linde 100.
No. 6 in a Collection of tracts
NIC   (Continued on next card)

Schaak, Petrus, fl. 1691.
Witchcraft
BF
1410
B42
Z69
no.6
[Hooght, Everard van der] d. 1716. Vierde briev van ... Haggēbher Philaleethees ... 1691.   (Card 3)

against Balthasar Bekker and his Betoverde weereld.
N. N. is thought to be Jacobus Schuts.

1. God--Omnipotence. 2. Schaak, Petrus, fl. 1691. 3. Bekker, Balthasar, 1634-1698. De betoverde weereld.
I. Title. II. Schuts, Jacobus.
NIC

Schaak, Petrus, fl. 1691.
Witchcraft
BF
1410
B42
Z56
v.3
no.20
De Volmaakte kragt Godts verheerlykt. Nevens eenige aanmerkinge over de drie predikatien van Do. Petrus Schaak. Gedaan over Psal. 72: v. 18. Gen. 18: v. 1,2 ... en Gen. 32: v. 24, 25. In haar eigen grondon ondersogt, en met de waarheid vergeleken. En eenige andere aanmerkingen daar by gevoegd. Amsterdam, By D. vanden Dalen, boekverkooper, 1691.
47 p. [p. 48 blank] title and other vignettes, illus. initial. 19 x 15cm.
4°: A-F4.
Black letter.
(Continued on next card)

Schaak, Petrus, fl. 1691.
Witchcraft
BF
1410
B42
Z56
v.3
no.20
De Volmaakte kragt Godts verheerlykt. 1691   (Card 2)
Preface signed: J: P: L: R.
Supports B. Bekker against Schaak's attacks on Bekker's De betoverde weereld.
Van der Linde 145.
No. 20 in vol. lettered Bekker III.

Schaak, Petrus, fl. 1691.
Witchcraft
BF
1410
B42
Z56
v.3
no.3
Zeedige overweeging op de praedikatie van d'Hr. Petrus Schaak, gedaan in d'Oude Kerk op den 30 September 1691. Amsterdam, By A. Hendriksz [1691]
7 p. [p. 8 blank] title vignette, illus. initial. 20 x 16cm.
4°: A4.
Schaak's sermon was against De betoverde weereld, by Baltnasar Bekker.
Van der Linde 143.
No. 3 in vol. lettered Bekker III.
(Continued on next card)

WITCHCRAFT
BF
1584
S97
S29
Schacher, Joseph.
Das Hexenwesen im Kanton Luzern, nach den Prozessen von Luzern und Sursee 1400-1675. Luzern, Druck Räber, 1947.
xvi, 112 p. 23cm.

Diss.--Fribourg.

1. Witchcraft--Luzern (Canton) 2. Trials (Witchcraft)--Switzerland. I. Title.
8
NIC

Witchcraft
BF
1587
D61
no.13
Schack, Johann, praeses.
Disputatio juridica ordinaria De probatione criminis magiae, qvam sub praesidio D. Johannis Schackii ... publice defendet Martinus von Normann ... Gryphiswaldiae, Typis Danielis Benjaminis Starckii [1706?]
26 p. 18cm. (bound in 21cm. vol.)
Pages 1-8 are bound between p. 72 & 73 of no. 12; rest of text follows no. 12.
No. 13 in vol. lettered Dissertationes de magia. 1623-1723.
1. Witchcraft--Addresses, essays, lectures. 2. Trials (Witchcraft).
I. Normann, Martin, respondent. II.
Title: De pro batione criminis magiae.
III. Title.

BF
1559
S29
Schäfer, Herbert.
Der Okkulttäter (Hexenbanner, magischer Heiler, Erdentstrahler) Hamburg, Kriminalistik, Verlag für Kriminalistische Fachliteratur, 1959.
xvi, 278 p. illus., maps. 24cm.

1. Exorcism. 2. Witchcraft. 3. Medicine, Magic, mystic and spagiric. I. Title.

CATALOGUE OF THE CORNELL WITCHCRAFT COLLECTION

Schäfler, Anna, 1590-1654.

MSS
Bd.
WITCHCRAFT
BF
W275
Z88

Warhaffter sumarisch-ausssführlicher Bericht und Erzehlung. Was die in dess heyligen Röm- Reichsstatt Augspurg etlich Wochen lang in Verhafft gelegne zwo Hexen, benandtlich Barbara Frölin von Rieden unnd Anna Schäflerin von Eringen, wegen ihrer Hexereyen gut- und peinlich bekent ... und wie endtlich dise beede Unholden ihrem Verdienst nach, auff Sambstag den 18. Aprill diss 1654 Jahrs hingericht worden. Augspurg, Durch Andream Aperger, 1654 [ca. 1900]
(Continued on next card)

Schäfler, Anna, 1590-1654.

MSS
Bd.
WITCHCRAFT
BF
W275
Z88

Warhaffter sumarisch-ausssführlicher Bericht und Erzehlung ... 1654 [ca. 1900] (Card 2)

8 l. 24cm.
Carnap's manuscript copy.
"Originaldruck in der Gustav Freytag Biblioth. jetzt in der Stadtbibliothek zu Frankfurt a/M. 6 Blatt in 4°. Sig. Aij-B."
Numerals in the margins indicate pagination of the original.
1. Witchcraft --Augsburg. 2. Demoniac possession. 3. Frölin, Barbara, 1637-1654. 4. Schäfler, Anna, 1590-1654.

Schalich, Paul, 1534-1575.

see

Scalichius, Paulus von Lika, count, 1534-1575.

RARE
HV
8593
S29
1742

Schaller, Jacob, 1604-1676.
Paradoxon de tortura in Christiana republica non exercenda... Lipsiae, Apud Io. Christianum Schroeterum, 1742.
48 p. 21cm.

8
NIC

1. Torture. I. Title.

Witchcraft
HV
8593
N63
1697

Schaller, Jacob, 1604-1676. Paradoxon de tortura in Christiana.
Nicolas, Augustin, 1622-1695.
An quaestione per tormenta criminum veritas elucescat, dissertatio moralis et juridica, quâ ordo & series instrumenti capitalis judicii, praesertim in causis sortilegii serio discutitur, & ad saniorem divinarum legum & juris antiqui usum revocatur ... Auctore Augustino Nicolao ... Argentorati, Sumptibus Joh. Friderici Spoor, 1697.
289, 80, [5] p. 17cm.
(Continued on next card)

Witchcraft
HV
8593
N63
1697

Schaller, Jacob, 1604-1676. Paradoxon de tortura in Christiana.
Nicolas, Augustin, 1622-1695. An quaestione per tormenta criminum veritas elucescat, dissertatio ... 1697. (Card 2)

"Instructio pro formandis processibus in causis strygum, sortilegorum & maleficorum": p. 271-289.
"Paradoxon de tortura in Christiana republica non exercenda ... â Jacobo Schallero": 80 p. at end.
I. Schaller, Jacob, 1604-1676. Paradoxon de tortura in Christiana republica non exercenda. II. Title.

Witchcraft
BF
1775
W41

Schau-Platz vieler ungereimten Meynungen und Erzehlungen.
[Wegener, F G Wilhelm]
Schau-Platz vieler ungereimten Meynungen und Erzehlungen: worauf die unter dem Titul der Magiae Naturalis so hoch gepriesene Wissenschafften und Künste, ... ingleichen die mancherley Arten der Wahrsagerey, und viel andere fabelhaffte, abergläubische und ungegründete Dinge mehr, vorgestellet, geprüfet und entdecket werden ... von Tharsandern. Berlin und Leipzig, Bey Ambrosius Haude, 1735-42.
3 v. 17cm.
Planned originally as monthly issues to be bound together into two volumes.
Ex libris: v. Arnswaldt.

Witchcraft
BF
1410
B42
Z55

Schediasma critico-litterarivm de controversiis praecipvis Balthasari Bekkero...
Beckker, Wilhelm Heinrich.
Schediasma critico-litterarivm de controversiis praecipvis Balthasari Bekkero, theologo batavo qvondam motis, ob librvm cvi titvlvm fecit: Die bezauberte Welt. Adiecta in fine avctorvm farragine, qvi vel Bekkeri scriptvm refvtarvnt, vel asseclarvm more illvd defendervnt. Regiomonti ac Lipsiae, Impensis J. P. Hasii, 1721.
47 p. [p. 48 blank], title (port.), caption and end page vignettes. 19 x 16cm.
(Continued on next card)

Witchcraft
BF
1410
B42
Z55

Schediasma critico-litterarivm de controversiis praecipvis Balthasari Bekkero...
Beckker, Wilhelm Heinrich. Schediasma critico-litterarivm de controversiis praecipvis Balthasari Bekkero ... 1721. (Card 2)

4°: A-F⁴.
At head of title: M. Gvilielmi Henrici Beckker, Regiom. Prvssi.
Van der Linde 215.

1. Bekker, Balthasar, 1634-1698. De betoverde weereld. I. Title.

Witchcraft
BF
1445
D61
no.17

Schediasma polemicum expendens qvaestionem an dentur spectra magi et sagae.
Romanus, Carl Friedrich.
Schediasma polemicum expendens qvaestionem an dentur spectra magi et sagae; vulgo Ob wahrhafft Gespenster, Zauberer und Hexen seyn? Una cum recensione historica plurimarum hac de re opinionum auctore Carolo Friderico Romano. Lipsiae, Literis & sumpt. Andreae Martini Schedii, 1717.
73 p. 21cm.
First published 1703?
No. 17 in vol. lettered Dissertationes de spectris. 1646-1753.
(Continued on next card)

Witchcraft
BF
1555
D18

Scheid- und- Absag-Brieff einem ungenanten Priester ... gegeben.
Dannhauer, Johann Conrad, 1603-1666.
Scheid- vnd- Absag-Brieff einem vngenanten Priester auss Cöllen auff sein Antworts-Schreiben an einen seiner ... Freunde über das zu Strassburg (also titulirte) vom Teuffel besessene adeliche Jungfräwlin gegeben ... Strassburg, J. Städel, 1667.
396 p. 17cm.

The priest's letter is given in Latin and German.

1. Demoniac possession. I. Title.

WITCHCRAFT
BF
1572
M4
S32

Schelhammer, Günther Christoph, 1649-1716, praeses.
Disputatio inauguralis medica De morbis magicis quam ... sub praesidio ... Gunthero Christophori Schelhammeri ... submittet Christoph. Martinus Burchardus ... Kiloni, Literis B. Reutheri [1704].
40, [1] p. 20cm.

1. Witchcraft. 2. Diseases--Causes and theories of causation. I. Burchard, Christoph Martin, 1680-1742, respondent. II. Title: De morbis magicis. III. Title.

WITCHCRAFT
BF
1569
S32

Scheltema, Jacobus, 1767-1835.
Geschiedenis der heksenprocessen, eene bijdrage tot den roem des vaderlands. Door Mr. Jacobus Scheltema ... Haarlem, V. Loosjés, 1828.
2 p. l., xvi, 312, 101, [5] p. 23cm.
Engr. t-p., with portrait of J. Wier.
"Aanteekeningen en ophelderingen" has special t. p. and separate paging.

1. Witchcraft--History. 2. Trials (Witchcraft)--History. I. Title.
8
NIC
11-9021
Library of Congress BF1569.S3

WITCHCRAFT
BF
1555
S32

Scherer, Georg, 1539-1605.
Christliche Erinnerung, bey der Historien von jüngst beschehener Erledigung einer Junckfrawen, die mit zwölfftausent sechs hundert zwey vnd fünfftzig Teufel besessen gewesen. Geprediget zů Wien in Oesterreich Anno 1583 ... Jngolstatt, Getruckt durch David Sartorivm, 1584.
4 p. l., 63 p. 21cm.
Title in red and black.

1. Demoniac possession. 2. Exorcism. 3. Schultter bäwrin, Anna, fl. 1583. I. Title.

WITCHCRAFT
BF
1445
S327

Scherertz, Sigismund, 1584-1639.
Libellus consolatorius De spectris, hoc est, apparitionibus & illusionibus daemonum. Pio studio conscriptus per Sigismundum Scherertzium ... Wittebergae, Typis Augusti Boreck, Sumptibus Pauli Helvvigij, 1621.
[158] p. 16cm.

1. Ghosts. 2. Spirits. 3. Demonology. I. Title. II. Title: De spectris.

Scherertzius, Sigismundus, 1584-1639.

see

Scherertz, Sigismund, 1584-1639.

Witchcraft
BF
1520
S32

Scherzer, Johann Adam, praeses.
Daemonologia sive Duae disputationes theologicae de malis angelis ... praeside ... Dno. Joh. Adamo Scherzero ... nunc vero conjunctim editae â M. Christiano Trautmanno ... Lipsiae, Literis Spörelianis, 1672.
[64] p. 19cm. (bound in 21cm. vol.)
With this are bound Schwartz, Johann Conrad, 1677-1747. Dissertatio theologica De usu et praestantia daemonum. Altdorfii (Continued on next card)

Witchcraft
BF
1520
S32

Scherzer, Johann Adam, praeses. Daemonologia ... 1672. (Card 2)

Noric. [1715], and Breithaupt, Christian, 1689-1749, praeses. Commentatio secunda De existentia daemonum. Helmstadii [1722].
In vol. lettered Dissertationes de daemonibus. 1672-1722.

1. Demonology. 2. Angels. I. Trautmann, Christian, respondent. II. Title. III. Title: De malis angelis.

488

CATALOGUE OF THE CORNELL WITCHCRAFT COLLECTION

TCHCRAFT
    Schick, J   G
00   Leben des heiligen Alphons Maria von
    Liguori, Stifter des Redemptoristenordens,
3   und des Pater Friedrich Spee, Priesters
    der Gesellschaft Jesu. 2. Aufl. Regens-
77   burg, G. J. Manz, 1877.
       164 p. port. 19cm. (Leben ausgezeich-
    neter Katholiken der drei letzten Jahrhun-
    derte. 7. Bd. 2. Aufl.)
       Leben des Pater Friedrich Spee, p. [129]-
    146, has special t. p.

              (Continued on next card)

WITCHCRAFT
BX   Schick, J   G   Leben des heili-
4700   gen Alphons Maria von Liguori ... 1877.
L6   (Card 2)
S33   Anhang, p. [147]-162, consists of selec-
1877   tions from Spee's Trutz-Nachtigall.

       1. Liguori, Alfonso Maria de', Saint,
    1696-1787. 2. Spee, Friedrich von, 1591-
    1635. I. Spee, Friedrich von, 1591-1635.
    Trutz-Nachtigall. Selections. II. Title.

NIC

    Schickhart, Philipp.
       Zwo christliche Predigten, aber [sic]
CHCRAFT der Buss unnd Bekehrung, eines Jüngs,
    welcher sich, laut nachgesetzter Vorred,
    dem bösen Geist, auff siben Jar lang, mit
    Leib un Seel ergeben gehabt. Gehalten zu
    Göppingen, durch M. Philippum Schickardum ...
    Tübingen, Getruckt bey Johan Conrad Geyss-
    lern, 1631 [ca. 1900]
       [6], 48 p. title vignette. 19cm.
       Signatures: A-   G⁴, F.
       Carnap's man   uscript copy.
              (Continued on next card)

CHCRAFT Schickhart, Philipp. Zwo christliche
       Predigten ... 1631 [ca. 1900] (Card 2)

    "Original i. d. Kgl. Bibl. z. Stuttgart.
    Titelbl. 3 Bl. Vorrede u. 48 pag. S. Text.
    Sig. Aii-Giij."
    Bibliography: 1 leaf at end.
    "N. B. Die Seiten dieser Abschrift stimen
    mit denjenigen des Originals überein."
       1. Repentance--Sermons. 2. Conversion--
    Sermons. 3.   Devil. I. Title.

---

hcraft Schiess, Emil, 1894-
       Das Gerichtswesen und die Hexenprozesse in
    Appenzell. Trogen, Buchdr. O. Kübler, 1919.
       208 p. 20cm.

       Inaug.--Diss.--Bern.
       Anhang. Hexengeständnisse: p. [159]-204.

       1. Witchcraft--Switzerland. 2. Criminal
    procedure--Appenzell, Switzerland. I. Title.

    Schillerin, Regina.

       Nachricht von einer Weibes-Person, so
    sich dem bösen Feinde mit Leib und Seel
HCRAFT ergeben, auch wieder erlöset worden.
    Augspurg, 1671 [ca. 1900]
       4 l. 23cm.

       Carnap's manuscript copy.
    "Originaldruck in der Kgl. Universitäts-
    Bibliothek zu Leipzig. 2 B. in 4°."
    Numerals in the margins indicate pagina-
    tion of the original.
       1. Devil.   2. Witchcraft.
    3. Schillerin,   Regina.

WITCHCRAFT
BF   Schilliger, Josef, 1854-1920.
1584   Die Hexenprozesse im ehemaligen Fürst-
S97   bisthum Basel.
S334   (In Vom Jura zum Schwarzwald. Aaran.
    25cm. 8. Bd, 1. Heft (1891), p. 1-44)
      Obituary notice from Luzerner Tagblatt
    for November 8, 1920 (69. Jahrg., Nr. 264)
    in pocket.
      1. Trials (Witchcraft)--Basel. 2.
    Trials (Witchcraft)--Switzerland. 3.
    Schilliger, Josef, 1854-1920. I. Title. II
3   Vom Jura zum   Schwarzwald.
NIC

    Schilliger, Josef, 1854-1920.
WITCHCRAFT
BF   Schilliger, Josef, 1854-1920.
1584   Die Hexenprozesse im ehemaligen Fürst-
S97   bisthum Basel.
S334   (In Vom Jura zum Schwarzwald. Aaran.
    25cm. 8. Bd, 1. Heft (1891), p. 1-44)
      Obituary notice from Luzerner Tagblatt
    for November 8, 1920 (69. Jahrg., Nr. 264)
    in pocket.
      1. Trials (Witchcraft)--Basel. 2.
    Trials (Witchcraft)--Switzerland. 3.
    Schilliger, Josef, 1854-1920. I. Title. II.
3   Vom Jura zum   Schwarzwald.
NIC

WITCHCRAFT
BF   Schilling, A
1583   Drei Hexenverbrennungen zu Ulm. [Stutt-
S33+ gart, 1883]
       137-141 p. 28cm.

       Detached from Sitzungsberichte (?) of
    the Württembergischer Altertumsverein.

       1. Trials (Witchcraft)--Ulm, Germany.
    2. Witchcraft--Germany. I. Title.

8
NIC

WITCHCRAFT
BF   [Schilling, Wolfgang]
1572   Newer Tractat von der verführten Kinder
C5   Zauberey. In welchem mit reifflichem Dis-
S33   curs ... vorgehalten wirdt, auss was Vrsa-
1630 chen viel vnerwachsene vnd vnmündige Kinder
    ... zu der verdampten Geister vnd Zauberer
    Gesellschafft gebracht vnd vnerhörter Weiss
    verführt werden ... auss lateinischer in
    die teutsche Sprach vbersetzt vnd in Truck
    gegeben ... durch W. S. à V. C. & C. A.
8   Aschaffenburg,   Getruckt durch Quirin
NIC   (Continued on next card)

WITCHCRAFT
BF   [Schilling, Wolfgang] Newer Tractat von
1572   der verführten Kinder Zauberey ... 1630.
C5   (Card 2)
S33
1630 Botzer, 1630.
       44 p. 21cm.
       Revised and augmented version of the
    "Appendix oder Nachtrab" (p. 60-129) pub-
    lished in his compilation on witchcraft
    from P. Laymann's Theologia moralis. (Lay-
    mann, P. Ein   kurtzer doch gründlicher
8
NIC   (Continued on next card)

WITCHCRAFT
BF   [Schilling, Wolfgang] Newer Tractat von
1572   der verführten Kinder Zauberey ... 1630.
C5   (Card 3)
S33
1630 Bericht wie ... mit den Hexen zuverfahren
    seye. Aschaffenburg, 1629.)

       1. Witchcraft. 2. Children--Manage-
    ment. I. Title. II. W. S. à V. C. &
    C. A. III. S., W., à V. C. & C. A.

8
NIC

    Schilling, Wolfgang.
      Newer Tractat von der verführten
Witchcraft Kinder Zauberey.
BF   Laymann, Paul, 1574-1635. Ein kurtzer
1565   doch gründlicher Bericht,
L42   wie vnd was gestalt, so woln bey dem recht-
T3   lichen Proceß als auch der Beicht mit den
1629 Hexen zuuerfahren seye. Auß deß ehrwürdi-
    gen hochgelehrten Herrn P. Pauli Läymanns
    ... Theologia morali gezogen, vñ den Rich-
    tern vñ Beichtvättern zu gutem absonderlich
    in den Truck gegeben. An jetzo aber män-
    niglich zu gutem in die teutsche Sprache
    vbersetzt. Durch   Wolffgang Schilling ...
8   (Continued on next card)

    Schilling, Wolfgang.
      Newer Tractat von der verführten
Witchcraft Kinder Zauberey.
BF   Laymann, Paul, 1574-1635. Ein kurtzer
1565   doch gründlicher Bericht ... 1629.
L42   (Card 2)
T3
1629 Wirtzburg, Gedruckt bey Stephan Fleisch-
    mann, 1629.
       129 p. 14cm.
       With colophon.
       According to G. L. Burr, the first part
    was printed in Aschaffenburg in 1629 under
    title: Aurea enucleatio atque disquisitio
    ... The secon   d section, p. 60-129,
8   (Continued on next card)

    Schilling, Wolfgang.
      Newer Tractat von der verführten
Witchcraft Kinder Zauberey.
BF   Laymann, Paul, 1574-1635. Ein kurtzer
1565   doch gründlicher Bericht ... 1629.
L42   (Card 3)
T3
1629 was published in 1629 by the same printer
    under title: Newer Tractat von der verführ-
    ten Kinder Zauberey.
       1. Trials (Witchcraft) 2. Confessors.
    I. His   Theologia moralis. Selections.
    German. II. His Aurea enucleatio. German.
    III. His New   er Tractat von der ver-
    führten Kinder   Zauberey. IV. Schil-
8   ling, Wolfgang,   tr. V. Title.

    Schilling, Wolfgang, tr.

Witchcraft
BF   Laymann, Paul, 1574-1635.
1565   Ein kurtzer doch gründlicher Bericht,
L42   wie vnd was gestalt, so woln bey dem recht-
T3   lichen Proceß als auch der Beicht mit den
1629 Hexen zuuerfahren seye. Auß deß ehrwürdi-
    gen hochgelehrten Herrn P. Pauli Läymanns
    ... Theologia morali gezogen, vñ den Rich-
    tern vñ Beichtvättern zu gutem absonderlich
    in den Truck gegeben. An jetzo aber män-
    niglich zu gutem in die teutsche Sprache
    vbersetzt. Durch   Wolffgang Schilling ...
8   (Continued on next card)

    Schilling, Wolfgang, tr.

Witchcraft
BF   Laymann, Paul, 1574-1635. Ein kurtzer
1565   doch gründlicher Bericht ... 1629.
L42   (Card 2)
T3
1629 Wirtzburg, Gedruckt bey Stephan Fleisch-
    mann, 1629.
       129 p. 14cm.
       With colophon.
       According to G. L. Burr, the first part
    was printed in Aschaffenburg in 1629 under
    title: Aurea enucleatio atque disquisitio
    ... The secon   d section, p. 60-129,
8   (Continued on next card)

    Schilling, Wolfgang, tr.

Witchcraft
BF   Laymann, Paul, 1574-1635. Ein kurtzer
1565   doch gründlicher Bericht ... 1629.
L42   (Card 3)
T3
1629 was published in 1629 by the same printer
    under title: Newer Tractat von der verführ-
    ten Kinder Zauberey, and is by Schilling.
       1. Trials (Witchcraft) 2. Confessors.
    I. His   Theologia moralis. Selections.
    German. II. His Aurea enucleatio. German.
    III. His Neu   er Tractat von der ver-
    führten Kinder   Zauberey. IV. Schil-
8   ling, Wolfgang,   tr. V. Title.

CATALOGUE OF THE CORNELL WITCHCRAFT COLLECTION

BF 1532 S33 — Schindelholz, Georges. Grimoires et secrets. Porrentruy, Éditions Jurassiennes, 1970. 199 p. illus. 23 cm. 18.00F
Bibliography: p. 97-101.
1. Demonology. 2. Witchcraft—Jura Mountain region. 3. Magic. I. Title.
BF1532.S35   76-550819
Library of Congress   71 [2]

WITCHCRAFT
BF 1425 S33 — Schindler, Heinrich Bruno, 1797-1859. Der Aberglaube des Mittelalters. Ein Beitrag zur Culturgeschichte. Breslau, W. G. Korn, 1858. xxiv, 359 p. 23cm.
Bibliography: p. [xi]-xxii.
I. Title.

WITCHCRAFT
BF 1583 Z7 1668 — [Schlözer, August Ludwig] 1735-1809, ed. Hexen Processe aus dem Hennebergschen. (In Stats-Anzeigen. Göttingen. 22cm. 2. Bd., Heft 6 (1782), p. 161-168)
At head of title: 14.
1. Trials (Witchcraft)—Thuringia. 2. Motzen, Barbara, d. 1668. I. Title.

Witchcraft
BF 1445 D61 no.11 — Schlosser, Philipp Casimir, praeses. Disputatio inauguralis philosophica De spectris. Quam ... praeside ... M. Philippo Casimiro Schlossero ... pro lauru magisteriali rite & legitime impetranda, publice defendendam conscripsit, ac omnibus sobrie & candide philosophantibus subjicit A. & R. Johannes Philippus Hechler ... Gissae Hassorvm, Typis Christoph. Hermanni Kargeri [1693] 46 p. 21cm.
(Continued on next card)

Witchcraft
BF 1445 D61 no.11 — Schlosser, Philipp Casimis, praeses. Disputatio inauguralis philosophica De spectris ... [1693]   (Card 2)
Diss.--Giessen (J. P. Hechler, respondent)
No. 11 in vol. lettered Dissertationes de spectris. 1646-1753.
1. Apparitions. 2. Demonology. I. Hechler, Johann Philipp, respondent. II. Title: De spectris. III. Disputatio inauguralis De spectris.

Witchcraft
BS 1325 B59 — Schmersahl, Elias Friedrich, 1719-1775. Natürliche Erklärung der Geschichte Sauls mit der Betrügerin zu Endor. Bieler, Benjamin, 1693-1772. ... Richtige Auslegung der Unterredung Sauls mit der Zauberin und mit einem Gespenste zu Endor. 1. B. Sam. XXVIII. Auf Veranlassung seiner in der fortgesetzten Vertheydigung eines gelehrten Mannes zur Sammlung 1748 ans Licht gestellten schriftmässigen Betrachtung herausgegeben. Leipzig und Wittenberg, J. F. Schlomach, 1752. 126 p. 18cm.
(Continued on next card)

WITCHCRAFT
BF 1565 W37 S34 — [Schmid, Franz Josef] Ueber die Hexenreformation des Herrn Professor Weber zu Dillingen ... Von einem katholischen Weltmanne. [Augsburg] 1787. 86 p. 19cm.
Attribution by Kayser and Deutsche Biographie (under Weber, Joseph).
1. Weber, Joseph, 1753-1831. Ungrund des Hexen- und Gespenster-Glaubens. 2. Witchcraft. I. Ein katholischer Weltmann. II. Title.

WITCHCRAFT
BF 1565 W37 S347 — [Schmid, Franz Josef] Und der Satz: Teuflische Magie existirt, bestehet noch. In einer Antwort des katholischen Weltmannes auf die von einem Herrn Landpfarrer herausgegebene Apologie der Professor Weberschen Hexenreformation. Augsburg, Bey J. N. Styx, 1791. xxiv, 350 p. 19cm.
1. Bauer, Friedrich. Gedanken eines Landpfarrers über den Ungrund des Hexenglaubens. 2. Weber, Joseph, 1753-1831.
(Continued on next card)

WITCHCRAFT
BF 1565 W37 S347 — [Schmid, Franz Josef] Und der Satz: Teuflische Magie existirt, bestehet noch ... 1791.   (Card 2)
Ungrund des Hexen- und Gespenster-Glaubens. 3. Witchcraft. 4. Magic. I. Title. II. Title: Teuflische Magie existiert. III. Der katholische Weltmann. 5. Gedanken eines Landpfarrers über den Ungrund des Hexenglaubens.

Schmid, Johannes Andreas, 1652-1726.
see
Schmidt, Johann Andreas, 1652-1726.

Schmidius, Johannes Andreas.
see
Schmidt, Johann Andreas, 1652-1726.

Schmidt, Hans, fl. 1589.
WITCHCRAFT
BF 1555 S35 — Schnabel, Joannes. Warhafftige vnd erschröckliche Geschicht, welche sich newlicher Zeit zugetragen hat, mit einem jungen Handtwercks vnd Schmidtsgesellen, Hansen Schmidt genandt, ... der ... von einer gantzen Legion Teüffeln hefftig besessen vnd hernacher ... durch sondere Schickung Gottes Allmächtigen vnd zugethane verordnete Mittel ... errettet ... worden ist ... Durch M. Ioannem Schnabeln ... vnd M. Simonem Marium ... Wirtzburg, Gedruckt
(Continued on next card)

Schmidt, Hans, fl. 1589.
WITCHCRAFT
BF 1555 S35 — Schnabel, Joannes. Warhafftige vnd erschröckliche Geschicht ... [1589]   (Card 2)
durch Henrich von Ach [1589]
[32] p. 20cm.
1. Demoniac possession. 2. Exorcism. 3. Schmidt, Hans, fl. 1589. I. Mayr, Simon, 1570-1624. II. Title.

Witchcraft
BF 1583 A2S74 1703 — [Spee, Friedrich von] 1591-1635. ... Cautio criminalis; seu, De processibus contra sagas liber. Das ist: Peinliche Warschauung von Anstell- und Führung des Processes gegen die angegebene Zauberer, Hexen und Unholden ... ins Teutsch treulich übersetzt ... [Halle im Magdeburg, 1703] [49]-356 p. 21cm.
Imperfect: p. 89-218 wanting.
Translated by Hermann Schmidt.
(Continued on next card)

Witchcraft
BF 1583 A2S74 1703 — [Spee, Friedrich von] 1591-1635. Cautio criminalis ... [1703]   (Card 2)
From Unterschiedliche Schrifften von Unfug des Hexen-Processes, by Johann Reiche.
1. Witchcraft. 2. Witchcraft--Germany. I. Title. II. Title: De processus contra sagas liber. III. Schmidt, Hermann, tr.

Schmidt, Nicolaus, of Lübeck, respondent.
Witchcraft
BF 1587 D61 no.3 — Werger, Johann, praeses. De magia daemoniaca disquisitio physica, quam ... praeside M. Johanne Werger Lubec. ... exponit ... Nicolaus Schmidt Lubec. ... Wittebergae, Literis Oelschlegelianis [1657] [16] p. 21cm.
No. 3 in vol. lettered Dissertationes de magia. 1623-1723.
1. Occult sciences--Addresses, essays, lectures. I. Schmidt, Nicolaus, of Lübeck, respondent. II. Title.

Witchcraft
BF 1569 A2I59 1906 — Institoris, Henricus, d. 1508. Malleus maleficarum. Der Hexenhammer, verfasst von den beiden Inquisitoren Jakob Sprenger und Heinrich Institoris. Zum ersten Male ins Deutsche übertragen und eingeleitet von J. W. R. Schmidt. Berlin, H. Barsdorf, 1906. 3 v. 20cm.
Translation of Malleus maleficarum.

WITCHCRAFT
BF 1583 S35 — Schmidt, W. Anhaltische Hexenprozesse. (In Unser Anhaltland. Dessau. 32cm. (folded to 24cm.) 2. Jahrg., Nr. 1-2 (1902), p. [1]-5, [13]-17)
Subtitle: I. In Stadt und Amt Dessau. In envelope.
1. Trials (Witchcraft)--Saxony. 2. Trials (Witchcraft)--Dessau. I. Title.

CATALOGUE OF THE CORNELL WITCHCRAFT COLLECTION

WITCHCRAFT
BF 1584
S97
S35

Schmidt von Kirchberg, Heinrich.
Der Kaibenturm. Eine Hexengeschichte. Nach Schweizer Prozess-Akten der dreissiger Jahre des achtzehnten Jahrhunderts. Dresden, H. R. Dohrn, 1903.
181 p. 20cm.

1. Witchcraft--Fiction. 2. Witchcraft--Switzerland. I. Title.

NIC

Schmuckher, Aidano, joint author.
Delfino, Giuseppe.
Stregoneria, magia, credenze e superstizioni a Genova e in Liguria. Firenze, L. S. Olschki, 1973.
iv, 87 p. illus., plates. 21 cm. (Biblioteca di "Lares," v. 39)
L2200
At head of title: Giuseppe Delfino, Aidano Schmuckher.
Bibliography: p. 81-84.
It 73-Aug

1. Occult sciences--Genoa. 2. Occult sciences--Liguria. I. Schmuckher, Aidano, joint author. II. Title.

BF1434.I 8D44
Library of Congress   73 [2]
73-339982

WITCHCRAFT
[98]
3

Schmutzer, Joannes Gottfried.
De Michaele Scoto veneficii iniuste damnato disserit ... Iacobo Henrico Bornio ... qvvm is senator Lipsiensis in solemni Senatvs lectione ... nasceretvr hanc dignitatem gratvlatvrvs Ioannes Gottfried. Schmvtzervs. Lipsiae, Ex officina Langenhemiana [1739]
xvi p. 22cm.

1. Scott, Michael, 1175?-1234? 2. Witchcraft. 3. Born, Jakob Heinrich, 1717-1775. I. Title.

WITCHCRAFT
F
555
35

Schnabel, Joannes.
Warhafftige vnd erschröckliche Geschicht, welche sich newlicher Zeit zugetragen hat, mit einem jungen Handtwercks vnd Schmidtsgesellen, Hansen Schmidt genandt, ... der ... von einer gantzen Legion Teüffeln hefftig besessen vnd hernacher ... durch sondere Schickung Gottes Allmächtigen vnd zugethane verordtnete Mittel ... errettet ... worden ist ... Durch M. Ioannem Schnabeln ... vnd M. Simonem Marium ... Wirtzburg, Gedruckt
(Continued on next card)

WITCHCRAFT
F
555
35

Schnabel, Joannes. Warhafftige vnd erschröckliche Geschicht ... [1589]
(Card 2)
durch Henrich von Ach [1589]
[32] p. 20cm.

1. Demoniac possession. 2. Exorcism. 3. Schmidt, Hans, fl. 1589. I. Mayr, Simon, 1570-1624. II. Title.

Schnabel, Johannes.
Folgen des dreissigjährigen Krieges.

WITCHCRAFT
[569]
[35]

Schnabel, Johannes.
I. Hexenprozesse. II. Folgen des dreissigjährigen Krieges. Nach den besten Quellen bearbeitet. Brilon, M. Friedländer, 1864.
16, 11 p. 19cm.
Cover title.
Each item has special t. p. and separate paging.

1. Witchcraft--History--Addresses, essays, lectures. 2. Thirty Years' War--Destruction and pillage--Addresses, essays, lectures. I. His Folgen des dreissigjährigen Krieges. II. Title: Hexenprozesse.

WITCHCRAFT
BF 1569
S35

Schnabel, Johannes.
I. Hexenprozesse. II. Folgen des dreissigjährigen Krieges. Nach den besten Quellen bearbeitet. Brilon, M. Friedländer, 1864.
16, 11 p. 19cm.
Cover title.
Each item has special t. p. and separate paging.

1. Witchcraft--History--Addresses, essays, lectures. 2. Thirty Years' War--Destruction and pillage--Addresses, essays, lectures. I. His Folgen des dreissigjährigen Krieges. II. Title: Hexenprozesse.

8

WITCHCRAFT
BF 1583
S358

Schnell, Eugen.
Zur Geschichte der Criminal-Justiz und besonders der Hexenprozesse in Hohenzollern. Von Eugen Schnell, Fürstl. Hohenz. Archivar in Sigmaringen. [n. p., 1873]
[69]-99 p. 22cm.

Caption title.
Detached from a journal.

1. Witchcraft--Swabia. 2. Criminal procedure--Hohenzollern. I. Title.

8
NIC

WITCHCRAFT
BF 1584
S97
S358

Schneller, Josef, 1801-1879.
Das Hexenwesen im sechszehnten Jahrhundert. (Nach den Thurmbüchern Lucerns.)
(In Der Geschichtsfreund. Einsiedeln. 23cm. 23. Bd. (1868), p. [351]-370)

Title in table of contents: Das Hexenwesen im Gebiete Lucerns, am Ende des 16. Jahrhunderts.

1. Witchcraft--Switzerland. 2. Trials (Witchcraft)--Lucerne. I. Title. II. Title: Das Hexenwesen im Gebiete Luzerns.

8
NIC

WITCHCRAFT
BF 1569
S36

Scholtz, J A
Ueber den Glauben an Zauberei in den letztverflossenen vier Jahrhunderten. Vorgetragen in der schlesischen vaterländischen Gesellschaft ... Breslau, Gedruckt bei W. G. Korn, 1830.
134 p. 19cm.

1. Witchcraft--History. 2. Superstition. I. Title.

8
NIC

Schonbeck, Christoph.

Witchcraft
BF 1445
D61
no.1

M. F. S. B. jurium studiosi recentissimum monimentum De spectris ad ... dominvm Christophorum Schonbeck ... Lugduni Batavorum, Typis Marsianis, 1646.
22, [2] p. 18cm. (bound in 21cm. vol.)

No. 1 in vol. lettered Dissertationes de spectris. 1646-1753.

1. Apparitions. I. B., F. S. II. F. S. B. III. Schonbeck, Christoph. IV. Title: De sp ectris.

8

Witchcraft
BF 1410
S37
1667

Schott, Gaspar, 1608-1666.
Physica curiosa, sive Mirabilia naturae et artis libris XII. comprehensa, quibus pleraque, quae de angelis, daemonibus, hominibus, spectris, energumenis, monstris, portentis, animalibus, meteoris, &c. rara, arcana, curiosaque circumferuntur, ad veritatis trutinam expenduntur, variis ex historia ac philosophia petitis disquisitionibus excutiuntur, & innumeris exemplis illustrantur ... Editio altera auctior. Herbipoli, Sumptibus Johannis Andreae Endteri & Wolfgangi Jun. Haeredum,
(Continued on next card)

Witchcraft
BF 1410
S37
1667

Schott, Gaspar, 1608-1666. Physica curiosa
(Card 2)
Excudebat Jobus Hertz, 1667.
[56], 1389, [15] p. plates (part double) 21cm.
Added t. p., engraved.
In two parts.

1. Demonology. 2. Deformities. 3. Monsters. 4. Zoology--Pre-Linnean works. I. Title.

Witchcraft
BF 1410
S37
1697

Schott, Gaspar, 1608-1666.
Physica curiosa, sive Mirabilia naturae et artis libris XII. comprehensa, quibus pleraque, quae de angelis, daemonibus, hominibus, spectris, energumenis, monstris, portentis, animalibus, meteoris, &c. rara, arcana, curiosaque circumferuntur, ad veritatis trutinam expenduntur, variis ex historia ac philosophia petitis disquisitionibus excutiuntur, & innumeris exemplis illustrantur ... Editio tertia juxta exemplar secundae editionis auctioris. Herbipoli, Excudit Jobus Hertz,
(Continued on next card)

Witchcraft
BF 1410
S37
1697

Schott, Gaspar, 1608-1666. Physica curiosa
(Card 2)
Sumptibus Wolfgangi Mauritii Endteri, 1697.
[40], 1389, [21] p. plates (part fold.) 21cm.
Added t. p., engraved.
In two parts.

1. Demonology. 2. Deformities. 3. Monsters. 4. Zoology--Pre-Linnean works. I. Title.

Pamphlet
B
124

Schottmüller, H
Ein Lissaer Hexenprozess von 1740. [Posen] 1902.
[65]-69 p. 23cm.

Detached from Historische Monatsblätter für die Provinz Posen, Jahrg. 3, Mai 1902, Nr. 5.

1. Witchcraft--Poland--Leszno. I. Title.

WITCHCRAFT
BF 1583
S37

Schrader, Ludwig Wilhelm.
Die Sage von den Hexen des Brockens und deren Entstehen in vorchristlicher Zeit durch die Verehrung des Melybogs und der Frau Holle. Historisch bearbeitet ... Quedlinburg und Leipzig, G. Basse, 1839.
48 p. 19cm.
Sent to L. Freytag and published through him.

1. Walpurgisnacht. 2. Witchcraft--Thuringia. 3. Folk-lore--Thuringia. 4. Melybog. 5. Frau Holle. I. Title.

8
NIC

BF 1584
H9
S37

Schram, Ferenc.
Magyarországi boszorkányperek, 1529-1768. Budapest, Akadémiai Kiadó, 1970.
2 v. 25 cm.
Bibliography: v. 2, p. 735-736.

1. Trials (Witchcraft)--Hungary. I. Title

NIC   FEB 21,'75   200xc   74-203280

CATALOGUE OF THE CORNELL WITCHCRAFT COLLECTION

Die Schreckensjahre von Lindheim.

WITCHCRAFT
BF
1583
O29
1862

[Oeser, Rudolf] 1807-1859.
  Die Schreckensjahre von Lindheim. Ein Beitrag zur Sittengeschichte des siebzehnten Jahrhunderts. Für das Volk erzählt von O. Glaubrecht [pseud.] 4. Aufl. Frankfurt a. M. und Erlangen, Heyder & Zimmer, 1862.
  vi, 93 p. front. 17cm.

  1. Witchcraft--Fiction. 2. Witchcraft --Germany. I. Title.

8

Schreckliche Geschichte teuflischer Besitzung.

Witchcraft
BF
1555
G92

Guden, Friedrich,   ed.
  Schreckliche Geschichte teuflischer Besitzung; in 3 merckwürdigen Historien.
  [56], 188 p. 16cm.

Schrepfer, Johann Georg, 1730?-1774.

Witchcraft
BF
1432
E73

Erzstein, pseud., ed.
  Ertappter Briefwechsel von der Zauberey, Schröpfers Künsten, Nativitätstellen, Sympathie, Gespenstern u.d.g., gesammelt von einem Juristen, Mediciner, Philosophen und Theologen, und hrsg. von Erzstein. Leipzig, C. G. Huscher, 1777.
  282 p. 18cm.

Witchcraft
BF
1559
G25
Z87

Schrepfer, Johann Georg, 1730?-1774.
Semler, Johann Salomo, 1725-1791, ed.
  Samlungen von Briefen und Aufsätzen über die Gassnerischen und Schröpferischen Geisterbeschwörungen, mit eigenen vielen Anmerkungen hrsg. von Johann Salomo Semler ... Halle im Magdeburgischen, C. H. Hemmerde, 1776.
  2 v. in 1. 20cm.
  1. Gassner, Johann Joseph, 1727-1779. 2. Schrepfer, Johann Georg, 1730?-1774. 3. Exorcism. 4.   Faith-cure.

8

WITCHCRAFT
BF
1408
S57

Schrepfer, Johann Georg, 1730?-1774.
Sierke, Eugen, 1845-
  Schwärmer und Schwindler zu Ende des achtzehnten Jahrhunderts. Leipzig, S. Hirzel, 1874.
  vi, 462 p. 21cm.
  1. Occult sciences--Biography. 2. Superstition. 3. Swedenborg, Emanuel, 1688-1772. 4. Mesmer, Franz Anton, 1734-1815. 5. Gassner, Johann Joseph, 1727-1779. 6. Schrepfer, Johann Georg, 1730?-1774. 7. Cagliostro, Alessandro, conte de, as sumed name of Giuseppe Balsamo, 1743   -1795. I. Title.

8
NIC

Schrifft- und vernunfftmässige Gedanken vom Schatz-graben und Beschwerung der Geister.

Witchcraft
BF
1523
F81

Franciscus de Cordua, pseud.
  ... Schrifft- und vernunfftmässige Gedancken vom Schatz-graben und Beschwerung der Geister, aus dem Lateinischen ins Teutsche übersetzet. Hamburg, Bey Zacharias Schotken, 1716.
  141 p. 17cm.
  According to the "Vorrede," the author is French; however, the work exists only in German.
  1. Demonology. 2. Occult sciences. I. Title.

8

MSS
Bd.
WITCHCRAFT
BV
S38

Ein Schröckliche Antwort eines bösen Geists auss einer besessenen Person, als er beschworen, unnd ein verdampter Lugengeist gescholten worden ist, &c. Lieds weiss an Tag geben, zur Warnung und Straff aller unbussfertigen. [n.p.] 1596 [ca. 1900]
  4 l. title vignette. 19cm.
  Carnap's manuscript copy.
  "Originaldruck in der Königlichen Bibliothek zu Berlin, 4 Bl. in 16°."
  "Wahrscheinlich von Daniel Suderman.
  (Continued on next card)

MSS
Bd.
WITCHCRAFT
BV
S38

Ein Schröckliche Antwort eines bösen Geists ... 1596 [ca. 1900]   (Card 2)
  Diese Notiz steht mit Tinte geschrieben auf dem Titelblatte des Exemplars der Königl. Bibliothek zu Berlin."
  Numerals in the margins indicate pagination of the original.
  In verse.
  1. Admonition. I. Sudermann, Daniel, supposed author.

Schröpfer, Johann Georg, 1730?-1774.

see

Schrepfer, Johann Georg, 1730?-1774.

Witchcraft
BF
1565
D62
no.3

Schröter, Ernst Friedrich, 1621-1676, praeses.
  Dissertatio juridica De lamiis earumqve processu criminali, quam ... sub praesidio ... Dn. Ernesti Friderici Schröter ... publicae eruditorum censurae subjicit, Michael Paris Walburger ... Jenae, Literis Joh. Jacobi Bauhoferi, 1690.
  149, [3] p. 20cm.
  No. 3 in vol. lettered Dissertationes de sagis. 1636-1714.
  1. Witchcraft. 2. Trials (Witchcraft. I. Walburger, Michael Paris, respondent. I. Title: De lamiis.
(Over)

Witchcraft
BF
1520
S38

Schubart, Christoph, praeses.
  Dissertatio De potentia diaboli in sensu, quam ... sub praesidio M. Joh. Christophori Schubarti, die 23. April hor. 8. placidae eruditorum ventilationi in acroaterio philosophorum submittet respondens Paulus Nicolaus Einert ... Erfordiae, Literis Limprechtianis [1707]
  [14] p. 20cm.
  1. Devil. I. Einert, Paul Nicolaus, respo ndent. II. Title: De potentia diaboli in sensus. III. Title.

8

Schubert, Gotthilf Heinrich von, 1780-1860.
  Ansichten von der Nachtseite der Natur.

WITCHCRAFT
BF
1133
S38
1854

Schubert, Gotthilf Heinrich von, 1780-1860.
  Die Zaubereisünden in ihrer alten und neuen Form betrachtet ... Neuer unveränderter Abdruck. Erlangen, J. J. Palm und E. Enke, 1854.
  vii, 42 p. 22cm.
  Retraction of certain of his ideas as voiced in his Ansichten von der Nachtseite der Natur and related works.
  1. Mesmerism. 2. Subconsciousness. 3. Occult sciences. 4. His Ansichten von der Nachtseite der Natur. I. Title.

8

WITCHCRAFT
BF
1133
S38
1854

Schubert, Gotthilf Heinrich von, 1780-1860.
  Die Zaubereisünden in ihrer alten und neuen Form betrachtet ... Neuer unveränderter Abdruck. Erlangen, J. J. Palm und E. Enke, 1854.
  vii, 42 p. 22cm.
  Retraction of certain of his ideas as voiced in his Ansichten von der Nachtseite der Natur and related works.
  1. Mesmerism. 2. Subconsciousness. 3. Occult sciences. 4. His Ansichten von der Nachtseite der Natur. I. Title.

8
NIC

Witchcraft
BF
1583
Z7
1705

Schütz, W
  Ein Hexenprocess vom Jahre 1705, mitgetheilt von Herrn Amtscommissär W. Schütz in Weimar. [Jena, 1853]
  178-183 p. 23cm.
  In "Miscellen," detached from the Zeitschrift of the Verein für thüringische Geschichte und Altertumskunde, Jena, 1. Bd., 2. Heft, and bound in vol. lettered Miscellen über Hexerei.
  With this is bound Auen, Karl, Segen und Zauberformeln. [Jena, 1853]
  (Continued on next card)

8

Witchcraft
BF
1583
Z7
1705

Schütz, W   Ein Hexenprocess vom Jahre 1705 ... [1853]   (Card 2)

  1. Trials (Witchcraft)--Germany. 2. Hausberg, Anna Martha, 1663-1705. I. Title.

8

Witchcraft
BF
1587
D61
no.7

Schütze, Bartholomaeus, praeses.
  Disputatio physica De magia, quam ... exhibent praeses M. Bartholomaeus Schütze ... & respondens Heino Meyer ... Rostochii, Typis Johannis Kilii [1669]
  [24] p. 18cm. (bound in 21cm. vol.)
  No. 7 in vol. lettered Dissertationes de magia. 1623-1723.
  1. Magic--Addresses, essays, lectures. I. Meyer, Heino, respondent. II. Title: De magia. III.   Title.

8

WITCHCRAFT
BF
1775
S38
1757

Schütze, Heinrich Carl, 1700-1781.
  Vernunft- und schriftmässige Abhandlung von Aberglauben. Nebst einem Anhange von Astral-Geist. Wernigerode, J. G. Struck, 1757.
  9 p. l., 496, [16] p. front. 17cm.
  1. Superstition. 2. Occult sciences. I. Title. II. Title: Astral-Geist.

8
NIC

Schuller, Martin, respondent.

WITCHCRAFT
BF
1555
F11

Faber, Johann Gottlieb, 1717-1779, praeses.
  Disqvisitio academica An adaemonismvs cv fide et pietate Christiana conciliari possit? Qvam praeside ... Ioanne Gottlieb Faber ... svbmittit avctor defendens Martinvs Schvllervs ... Tvbingae, Literis Cottae et Revsii [1763]
  42 p. 21cm.
  Running title: De inflvxv adaemonismi in pietatem Christianam.
  1. Demoniac possession. I. Schuller, Martin, respondent. II. Title: An adaemonismus cum fide e pietate Christiana conciliari poss

8
NIC

492

CATALOGUE OF THE CORNELL WITCHCRAFT COLLECTION

Der Schulmeister zu Glücksfeld, pseud.

    Das Dorfconvent, welches allerley Gespräche von Hexen, Gespenstern, Schätzgräbern, und Naturerscheinungen enthält. Hrsg. vom Schulmeister zu Glücksfeld. Ganz neu gedruckt. [n. p., 1750?]
64 p. illus. 16cm.

    1. Folk-lore, German. I. Der Schulmeister zu Glücksfeld, pseud.

WITCHCRAFT
BF 1565 S38

Schultheis, Heinrich von. Eine ausführliche Instrvction ... 1634. (Card 3)

    1. Witchcraft. 2. Trials (Witchcraft) 3. Tanner, Adam, 1572-1632. Tractatus theologicus de processu adversus crimina excepta. I. Title.

8
NIC

Witchcraft
BF 1587 D61 no.9

Schultze, Georg, fl. 1671-1682, praeses.
    Decas qvaestionum ex magiae illicitae materia ... ventilationi propositarum â praeside M. Georg Schultzen ... respondente filio Christiano Schultzen, Halâ-Saxone ... [Lipsiae?] Typis viduae Joh. Wittigau [1677] [16] p. 21cm.
    No. 9 in vol. lettered Dissertationes de magia. 1623-1723.
    1. Magic--Addresses, essays, lectures. I. Schultze, Christian, respondent. II. Title: Decas quaestionum ex magiae illici tae materia.

8

WITCHCRAFT
BF 1555 S32

Schultterbäwrin, Anna, fl. 1583.

Scherer, Georg, 1539-1605.
    Christliche Erinnerung, bey der Historien von jüngst beschehener Erledigung einer Junckfrawen, die mit zwölfftausent sechs hundert zwey vnd fünfftzig Teufel besessen gewesen. Geprediget zů Wien in Oesterreich Anno 1583 ... Jngolstatt, Getruckt durch David Sartorivm, 1584.
    4 p. l., 63 p. 21cm.
    Title in red and black.
    1. Demoniac possession. 2. Exorcism. 3. Schultter bäwrin, Anna, fl. 1583. I. Title.

8
NIC

WITCHCRAFT
BF 1583 Z7 1669

Schulze, Barbara Elisabeth, fl. 1669, defendant.
    Barbara Elisabeth Schulzin. Ein Arnstädter Hexenprozess vom Jahre 1669. Nach den Originalprozessakten herausgegeben von Reinhold Stade. Arnstadt, Fürstl. Buchdruckerei von E. Protscher, 1904.
    75 p. 22cm.
    1. Trials (Witchcraft)--Germany. 2. Trials (Witchcraft)--Arnstadt, Germany. I. Stade, Reinhold, 1848- , ed. II. Title. III. Title: Ein Arnstädter Hexenprozess vom Ja hre 1669.

8
NIC

WITCHCRAFT
[65] [8]

Schultheis, Heinrich von.
    Eine ausführliche Instrvction, wie in Inqvisition Sachen des grewlichen Lasters der Zauberey gegen die Zaubere der göttlichen Majestät vnd der Christenheit Feinde ohn Gefahr der Vnschüldigen zu procediren ... In Form eines freundlichen Gesprächs gestelt ... Cölln, Bey Hinrich Berchem, Sumptibus authoris [gedruckt bey Gissbert Clemens] 1634.
    xiii, [7], 503 p. port.

    (Continued on next card)

Witchcraft
BF 1587 D61 no.9

Schultze, Christian, respondent.

Schultze, Georg, fl. 1671-1682, praeses.
    Decas qvaestionum ex magiae illicitae materia ... ventilationi propositarum â praeside M. Georg Schultzen ... respondente filio Christiano Schultzen, Halâ-Saxone ... [Lipsiae?] Typis viduae Joh. Wittigau [1677] [16] p. 21cm.
    No. 9 in vol. lettered Dissertationes de magia. 1623-1723.
    1. Magic--Addresses, essays, lectures. I. Schultze, Christian, respondent. II. Title: Decas quaestionum ex magiae illici tae materia.

8

Schulzin, Barbara Elisabeth, fl. 1669.

see

Schulze, Barbara Elisabeth, fl. 1669.

WITCHCRAFT
[65] [8]

Schultheis, Heinrich von. Eine ausführliche Instrvction ... 1634. (Card 2)

    Refutation of A. Tanner, p. 367-436, in Latin.
    "This book is, to my thinking, the most gruesome chapter in all the gruesome literature of witch-persecution; and there is good ground for suspecting it of being the only copy now surviving ..."--part of MS note by G. L. Burr tipped into back of vol.

    (Continued on next card)

Schuts, Jacobus

Witchcraft
F 410 42 69 no.16

[Schuts, Jacobus]
    De betoverde Bekker, ofte een overtuygent bewijs dat het boek vande Heer Bekker, genaemt de Betoverde weerelt, doorsaeyt is met de onredelijkste redenering, notoirste Onwaarheeden en andere schadelijcke gevolgen; waer door de waare reeden verlogent, de waarheyt vervalst, en de deught ontsenuwt wert. De Saduceen seggen datter geen Opstanding en is, noch Engel, noch Geest, maer de Fariseen gelooven het beyde Act VIII: vers 23. In 's Gravenhage,
    (Continued on next card)

IC

Witchcraft
BF 1410 B42 Z69 no.16

[Schuts, Jacobus] De betoverde Bekker ... 1691. (Card 3)

    No. 16 in a Collection of tracts against Balthasar Bekker and his Betoverde weereld. Van der Linde 146.

    1. Bekker, Balthasar, 1634-1698. De betoverde weereld. I. Title.

NIC

Witchcraft
BF 1410 B42 Z56 v.3 no.6

[Schuts, Jacobus] Missive, aen D. Balthazar Bekker ... 1692. (Card 2)

    10 p. l., 59 p. [p. 70-72 blank] title and other vignettes, illus. initials. 20 x 15cm.
    4°: a-b⁴, c², A-I⁴.
    Black letter.
    Signed and dated at end: N. N. Den 22 November 1691.
    Neither Orchard nor Philopater is mentioned in the text.

    (Continued on next card)

Witchcraft
[10] [59] [o.16]

[Schuts, Jacobus] De betoverde Bekker ... (Card 2)

    By B. Beek, 1691.
    [4] p. 21cm.
    Signatures: 4°: A3.
    Consists of the printer's letter to the reader only; followed by text of his Seedige aanmerkinge over ... De Godstlasteringe van ... Dr. Bekker, of which the t.p. and first 8 p. form no. 20 in this vol.

    (Continued on next card)

IC

Witchcraft
BF 1410 B42 Z56 v.3 no.6

    [Schuts, Jacobus]
    Missive, aen D. Balthazar Bekker, in 't korte ontdekkende de gronden van sijn misgrepen, begaen in sijn drie tractaten De betoverde weereld, over den prophete Daniel, en van de cometen. Waer in N. Orchard, in sijn Leeringe der duivelen den grooten afval der Christenen, ende den spotterigen Philopater in sijn leven, ook hare voldoeninge konnen krygen. Tot Nederlands waerschouwinge en onderricht der Joden. Gravenhage, By B. Beek, konst- en boekverkoper, 1692.

    (Continued on next card)

Witchcraft
BF 1410 B42 Z56 v.3 no.6

[Schuts, Jacobus] Missive, aen D. Balthazar Bekker ... 1692. (Card 3)

    Van der Linde 147.
    No. 6 in vol. lettered Bekker III.
    1. Bekker, Balthasar, 1634-1698. De betoverde weereld. 2. Bekker, Balthasar, 1634-1698. Ondersoek van de betekeninge der kometen. 3. Bekker, Balthasar, 1634-1698. Uitlegginge van den prophet Daniel. 4. Title.

8

CATALOGUE OF THE CORNELL WITCHCRAFT COLLECTION

Witchcraft
BF
1410
B42
Z69
no.29
  [Schuts, Jacobus]
    Missive, aen D. Balthazar Bekker, in 't korte ontdekkende de gronden van sijn misgrepen, begaen in sijn drie tractaten De betooverde weereld, over de prophete Daniel, en van de cometen. Waer in N. Orchard, in sijn Leeringe der duivelen den grooten afval der Christenen, ende den spotterigen Philopater in sijn leven, ook hare voldoeninge konnen krygen. Tot Nederlands waerschouwinge en onderricht der Joden. Gravenhage, By B. Beek, konst- en boekverkooper, 1692.
    (Continued on next card)

WITCHCRAFT
BF
1410
B42
Z69
no.29
  [Schuts, Jacobus] Missive, aen D. Balthazar Bekker...1692. (Card 2)
    10 p. l., 69 p. [p. 70-72 blank], title and other vignettes, illus. initials. 21cm.
    4°: a-b⁴, c², A-H⁴, I³.
    Black letter.
    Signed and dated at end: N. N. Den 22 November 1691.
    Neither Orchard nor Philopater is mentioned in the text.
8
NIC   (Continued on next card)

WITCHCRAFT
BF
1410
B42
Z69
no.29
  [Schuts, Jacobus] Missive, aen D. Balthazar Bekker...1692. (Card 3)
    Van der Linde 147.
    No. 29 in a Collection of tracts against Balthasar Bekker and his Betoverde weereld.

    1. Bekker, Balthasar, 1634-1698. De betoverde weereld. 2. Bekker, Balthasar, 1634-1698. Ondersoek van de betekeninge der kometen. 3. Bekker, Balthasar, 1634-1698. Uitlegginge va... n den prophet Daniel. I. Title.
8
NIC

Witchcraft
BX
9479
B42
B11
no.2
  [Schuts, Jacobus]
    Nodige aanmerking over het Sterf-bedde van Balthasar Bekker. Vertonende de openbare valsheyt van dat syn gevoelen, dat hy op syn dood-bedde segt hem voor paart en wagen verstrekt te hebben om hem te voeren na den hemel. Gravenhage, By P. van Tol, boekverkooper, 1698.
    13 p. [p. 14 blank], title vignette, illus. initial. 20 x 16cm.
    4°: A-B⁴(-B4)
    (Continued on next card)

Witchcraft
BX
9479
B42
B11
no.2
  [Schuts, Jacobus] Nodige aanmerking over het Sterf-bedde van Balthasar Bekker. 1698. (Card 2)
    Black letter.
    Ascribed to Schuts by van der Linde.
    Van der Linde 206.
    No. 2 in vol. lettered B. Bekkers sterf-bed en andere tractaten.
    1. Bekker, Balthasar, 1634-1698. 2. Bekker, Johannes Henricus, fl. 1698-1737. Sterf-bedde van ... Do. Balthazar Bekker. I. Title.
5

  Schuts, Jacobus.
    Nodige aanmerking over het Sterf-bedde van Balthasar Bekker.
Witchcraft
BX
9479
B42
B11
no.3
    Do. [i. e., doctor] B. Bekkers Sterf-bedde verdedigt, tegens de zoo genaamde Nodige aanmerkingen over het zelve: vervat in een brief aan den schryver; behelzende een openbaar bewijs zijner onkunde in de geschillen, en verdere ongegronde redeneeringen: tot wegschuiminge van zijn alderhaatelijkste beschryving en veroordeeling van den overledene. Door M. G. Amsterdam, By R. Blokland, boekverkooper, 1699.
    1 p. l., 16 p. title and end
8   (Continued on next card)

  Schuts, Jacobus.
    Nodige aanmerking over het Sterf-bedde van Balthasar Bekker.
Witchcraft
BX
9479
B42
B11
no.3
    Do. [i. e., doctor] B. Bekkers Sterf-bedde verdedigt ... 1699. (Card 2)
    page vignettes, illus. initial. 20 x 16 cm.
    4°: π1, A-B⁴.
    Van der Linde 207.
    No. 3 in vol. lettered B. Bekkers sterf-bed en andere tractaten.
    1. Bekker, Balthasar, 1634-1698. 2. Bekker, Johannes Henricus, fl. 1698-1737. Sterf-bedde van ... Do. Balthazar Bekker.
    (Continued on next card)
8

Witchcraft
BF
1410
B42
Z56
v.2
no.19
  [Schuts, Jacobus]
    Seedige aanmerkinge over de voorreden, genaamt: De godtslasteringe van den amsterdamsche predikant Dr. Bekker, ter waarschouwinge van alle vroome in den lande wederleyt, in de voorreden voor de toetsteen der waarheyt, ende der meyninge, door Henrikus Brink, &c. Door N. N. Amsterdam, By D. van den Dalen, boekverkooper, 1691.
    8, 88 p. title vignette, illus. initial. 19 x 15cm.
    (Continued on next card)
8

Witchcraft
BF
1410
B42
Z56
v.2
no.19
  [Schuts, Jacobus] Seedige aanmerkinge over de voorreden ... 1691. (Card 2)
    4°: A⁴, A-L⁴.
    Black letter.
    Signed on back of t. p.: J: C:
    Incomplete: all after first gathering wanting.
    Van der Linde 84.
    No. 19 in vol. lettered Bekker II.
    1. Brink, Hendrik, 1645-1723.
    (Continued on next card)

Witchcraft
BF
1410
B42
Z56
v.2
no.19
  [Schuts, Jacobus] Seedige aanmerkinge over de voorreden ... 1691. (Card 3)
    De godtslasteringen van den amsterdamschen predikant Bekker. 2. Bekker, Balthasar, 1634-1698. I. Title.

Witchcraft
BF
1410
B42
Z69
no.20
  [Schuts, Jacobus]
    Seedige aanmerkinge over de voorreden, genaamt: De godtslasteringe van den amsterdamsche predikant Dr. Bekker, ter waarschouwinge van alle vroome in den lande wederleyt, in de voorreden voor de toetsteen der waarheyt, ende der meyninge, door Henrikus Brink, &c. Door N. N. Amsterdam, By D. van den Dalen, boekverkooper, 1691.
    8, 88 p. title vignette, illus. initial. 21cm.
    (Continued on next card)
8

Witchcraft
BF
1410
B42
Z69
no.20
  [Schuts, Jacobus] Seedige aanmerkinge over de voorreden ... 1691. (Card 2)
    Signatures: 4°: A⁴, A-L⁴.
    Black letter.
    Signed on back of t.p.: J:C:
    Van der Linde 84.
    No. 20 in a Collection of tracts against Balthasar Bekker and his Betoverde weereld. The 88 p. of the 2d numbering are bound after no. 16.
NIC

Witchcraft
BF
1410
B42
Z69
no.30
  [Schuts, Jacobus]
    Tweede missive aen d'Heer Balthasar Bekker, over sijn Betoverde weereld, Daniel, en den 2den druk van de Cometen. Waar in benessens Orchards, en Philopaters genoegdoeninge, Daillions wederlegginge ook aangeroert word; en getoont, dat het woord Daimones met alle vereischte wettelijkheid vertaalt word Duivelen. Ende in het stuk van de Prophetien, en de Cometen word de saak eenigermate betrekkelijk gemaakt, op de Schriften van D. Koelman en D. Brink. Met den korten inhoud van de eerste
    (Continued on next card)

Witchcraft
BF
1410
B42
Z69
no.30
  [Schuts, Jacobus] Tweede missive aen d'Heer Balthasar Bekker ... 1692. (Card 2)
    Missive. D'Opdragt toont, dat Ericus Walten, in sijn Brief aan een Regent van Amsteldam, ydelijk voorgeest, dat het voor den Staat dezer Landen gevaarlijk is, de zaak van Dr. Bekker verder, in synoden, of andersins, te laten verhandelen, of Decideren. 's Gravenhage, By B. Beek en M. Uitwerf, 1692.
    [24] 72 p. 21cm.
    (Continued on next card)

Witchcraft
BF
1410
B42
Z69
no.30
  [Schuts, Jacobus] Tweede missive aen d'Heer Balthasar Bekker ... 1692. (Card 3)
    Signatures: 4°: †-3†⁴. A-I⁴, (Leaf I² is mis-signed as H²)
    Van der Linde 148.

    1. Bekker, Balthasar, 1634-1698. De betoverde weereld. I. Title.

  Schuts, Jacobus.
Witchcraft
BF
1410
B42
Z56
v.3
no.15
    Aanmerkingen van eenige rechtzinnige broederen over de Articulen van satisfactie, waar op men met D. B. Bekker een verdrag gemaakt heeft. Leyden, By F. Haring, boekverkooper, 1692.
    22, [l] p. [p. 24 blank] title vignette. 20 x 15cm.
    4°: A-C⁴.
    Consists of two letters, a short one signed N. N. [i. e., Jacobus Schuts], and one of 18 p. signed B. C.
8   (Continued on next card)

  Schuts, Jacobus.
Witchcraft
BF
1410
B42
Z56
v.3
no.15
    Aanmerkingen van eenige rechtzinnige broederen ... 1692. (Card 2)
    Van der Linde 38.
    No. 15 in vol. lettered Bekker III.
    1. Bekker, Balthasar, 1634-1698. Articulen tot satisfactie aan de Eerw. Classis van Amsterdam. I. Schuts, Jacobus. II. B. C. III. C., B.

  Schuts, Jacobus.
Witchcraft
BX
9479
B42
B11
no.10
  [Bouman, Herman]
    Aanleydinge, om klaar te konnen uytvinden wanneer men in de H. Schriftuur van duyvel, Satan, boose geest, &c. in ons Nederduyts leest, hoe het selve te verstaan zy. Waar na volgt, een korte verklaring over Matth. 8: 28-31. ... Ook zijn hier bygevoegt vier brieven, waar in over en weder gehandeld word van de versoekinge des Saligmakers Jesu Christi, van den hemel, de engelen, &c. 2. verm. druk. Amsterdam, By R. Blokland, boekverkooper, 1700.
    (Continued on next card)

494

CATALOGUE OF THE CORNELL WITCHCRAFT COLLECTION

Schuts, Jacobus.
tchcraft
[Bouman, Herman] Aanleydinge ... 1700.
(Card 2)
79
1
.10
2 p. l., 78 [i. e., 80] p. title vignette, illus. initials. 20 x 15cm.
4°: *², A-K⁴.
Black letter (except introduction and letters)
Introduction signed: H. Bouman.
Two letters are signed: N. N. [i. e., Jacobus Schuts]

(Continued on next card)

Schuts, Jacobus.
chcraft
[Bouman, Herman] Aanleydinge ... 1700.
(Card 3)
79
.10
Van der Linde 81.
No. 10 in vol. lettered B. Bekkers sterfbed en andere tractaten.

1. Devil. 2. Spirits. 3. Bible. N. T. Matthew VIII, 28-31--Criticism, interpretation, etc. I. Schuts, Jacobus. II. Title.

Schuts, Jacobus.
chcraft
Bouman, Herman, ed.
Disputatio van verscheyde saaken, raakende de wonderwerken, en of een schepsel die doen kan: item van de engelen, duyvelen, &c. Voorgevallen in de Menniste Kerk, het Lam genaamd, terwijl het oeffening was, den 7 Augustus, en den 29 Mey te vooren, deses jaars 1695. Door verscheyde broeders van deselve societeyt, die tegenwoordig waren, opgesteld, en nagesien van H: Bouman, die ook een kleyne voor-reden voor, en weynig aanmerkingen achter heeft bygevoegd.
(Continued on next card)

Schuts, Jacobus.
chcraft
Bouman, Herman, ed. Disputatio van verscheyde saaken ... 1695. (Card 2)
9
15
Amsterdam, By J. Snets en P. Dibbits, boekdrukkers, 1695.
23 p. [p. 24 blank] title vignette, illus. initials. 20 x 15cm.
4°: A-C⁴.
Black letter (except introduction and letters at end)
Letters of Bouman and N. N. [i. e.,

(Continued on next card)

Schuts, Jacobus.
chcraft
Bouman, Herman, ed. Disputatio van verscheyde saaken ... 1695. (Card 3)
9
15
Jacobus Schuts]: p. 22-23.
Van der Linde 78.
No. 15 in vol. lettered B. Bekkers sterfbed en andere tractaten.

1. Miracles--Early works to 1800. 2. Spirits. I. Schuts, Jacobus. II. Title.

Schuts, Jacobus.
chcraft
[Hooght, Everard van der] d. 1716.
Derde briev van הגבר [Haggēbher] ΦΙΛΑΛΗΘΗΣ [Philaleethees] geschreeven aan zynen vriend N. N. over het vervolg van de kerkelyke proceduuren tegen den persoon van Do. Balthasar Bekker; nevens de aanmerkingen over de gereformeerde confessie, ende over het gevoelen van de gesonde gereformeerde godsgeleerden, nopende het hooft-stuk van de natuure ende de werkingen der engelen. Amsterdam, By G. Borstius, boekverkoper, 1691.
(Continued on next card)

Schuts, Jacobus.
Witchcraft
BF
1410
B42
Z56
v.3
no.25
[Hooght, Everard van der] d. 1716. Derde briev ... aan zynen vriend N. N. ... 1691.
(Card 2)
[39]-58 p. title vignette, illus. initial. 19 x 15cm.
4°: π1, A-B⁴, C1.
Black letter.
The friend N. N. is Jacobus Schuts?
Van der Linde 99.
No. 25 in vol. lettered Bekker III.

(Continued on next card)

Schuts, Jacobus.
Witchcraft
BF
1410
B42
Z69
no.3
[Hooght, Everard van der] d. 1716.
Eerste briev van הגבר Φιλαλήθης Haggēbher Philaleethees, geschreeven aan zynen vriend N. N. over den persoon en het boek van Do. Balthasar Bekker. In opzicht van de gudheyd, ende het gewichte zyner dwaling; nevens sijne onkunde in de godtgeleertheyd ende in de gronden van de Hebreeusche tale; demonstratiiv beweesen, uyt zyne verklaring van Gen. 18. ende Job 1. en 2. Amsterdam, G. Borstius, 1691.
20 p. 21cm.
NIC
(Continued on next card)

Schuts, Jacobus.
Witchcraft
BF
1410
B42
Z69
no.3
[Hooght, Everard van der] d. 1716. Eerste briev van ... Haggēbher Philaleethees ... 1691. (Card 2)
Signatures: 4°: A-B⁴, C1.
Black letter.
N. N. is thought to be Jacobus Schuts.
Van der Linde 97.
No. 3 in a Collection of tracts against Balthasar Bekker and his Betoverde weereld.
NIC
(Continued on next card)

Schuts, Jacobus.
Witchcraft
BF
1410
B42
Z69
no.9
[Hooght, Everard van der] d. 1716.
Sesde briev van הגבר Φιλαλήθης Haggēbher Philaleethees, geschreeven aan zynen vriend N. N. vervattende: I. Een afwysing van vyfderley gewaande voorspraaken van D. Bekker. Ende II. een verhandeling van de De Daimonia na hare beteekenisse voor, in, ende na de tyden Christi. Volgens het welke uyt het Hebreeusch Griekich en Syrisch klaar te sien is, dat De Daimonia zedert Christi tyden niet anders zyn, dan de Duyvelen. Amsterdam,
NIC
(Continued on next card)

Schuts, Jacobus.
Witchcraft
BF
1410
B42
Z69
no.9
[Hooght, Everard van der] d. 1716. Sesde briev van ... Haggēbher Philaleethees ...
(Card 2)
G. Borstius, 1691.
135-176 p. 21cm.
Signatures: 4°: π1, A-E⁴, F1.
Black letter.
The friend N.N. may be Jacobus Schuts.
Van der Linde 103.
No. 9 in a Collection of tracts against Balthasar Bekker and his Betoverde weereld.
NIC
(Continued on next card)

Schuts, Jacobus.
Witchcraft
BF
1410
B42
Z56
v.3
no.24
[Hooght, Everard van der] d. 1716.
Tweede brief van הגבר [Haggēbher] ΦΙΛΑΛΗΘΗΣ [Philaleethees], geschreeven aan zynen vriend N. N. over de ordentelyke kerkelyke proceduuren, gehouden tegen den persoon ende het boek van Do. Balthasar Bekker, by zyn E. geintituleert De betoverde weereld. Met eenige ecclesiastique, theologische, philosophische ende philologische aanmerkingen over de zelve. Amsterdam, By G. Borstius, boekverkoper, 1691.
[19]-40 p. title vignette, illus. initial. 19 x 15cm.
8
(Continued on next card)

Schuts, Jacobus.
Witchcraft
BF
1410
B42
Z56
v.3
no.24
[Hooght, Everard van der] d. 1716. Tweede brief ... aan zynen vriend N. N. ... 1691.
(Card 2)
4°: π1, A-B⁴, C².
Black letter.
The friend N. N. is Jacobus Schuts?
Van der Linde 98.
No. 24 in vol. lettered Bekker III.
1. Bekker, Balthasar, 1634-1698. 2. Bekker, Balthasar, 1634-1698. De betoverde weereld. 3. Nederlandse Hervormde Kerk. I. Schuts, Jacobus. II. Title.

Schuts, Jacobus.
Witchcraft
BF
1410
B42
Z69
no.6
[Hooght, Everard van der] d. 1716.
Vierde briev van הגבר Φιλαλήθης Haggēbher Philaleethees, geschreeven aan zynen vriend N. N. over het weesen, denken, willen, vermoogen, ende de plaats der engelen in het gemeen, ende der quade geesten, in het byzonder. Item, van des menschen ziele, en harewerking, het zy afgesondert, ofte ook vereenigt met her lichaam; ende hoe verre de quade geesten op de selve konnen werken. Met een onder soek van D. Bekker wel kan seggen, dat syn E. zoekt te bewaren
NIC
(Continued on next card)

Schuts, Jacobus.
Witchcraft
BF
1410
B42
Z69
no.6
[Hooght, Everard van der] d. 1716. Vierde briev van ... Haggēbher Philaleethees ...
(Card 2)
de authoriteyt van Gods woord, ende de eere des alderhoogsten. Amsterdam, G. Borstius, 1691.
59-96 p. 21cm.
Signatures: 4°: π1, A-C⁴, D².
Black letter.
Van der Linde 100.
No. 6 in a Collection of tracts
NIC
(Continued on next card)

Schuts, Jacobus.
Witchcraft
BF
1410
B42
Z69
no.6
[Hooght, Everard van der] d. 1716. Vierde briev van ... Haggēbher Philaleethees ...
1691. (Card 3)
against Balthasar Bekker and his Betoverde weereld.
N. N. is thought to be Jacobus Schuts.

1. God--Omnipotence. 2. Schaak, Petrus, fl. 1691. 3. Bekker, Balthasar, 1634-1698. De betoverde weereld.
NIC I. Title. II. Schuts, Jacobus.

Schuts, Jacobus.
Witchcraft
BF
1410
B42
Z69
no.7
[Hooght, Everard van der] d. 1716.
Vyfde briev van הגבר Φιλαλήθης Haggēbher Philaleethees, geschreeven aan zynen vriend N. N. over de versoekinge Christi in de woestyne, tot vederlegging van het 18 (ofte 20) capp. in het boek van D. Balthasar Bekker, genaamt de Betoverde weereld. Item, over de classicale proceduuren, &c. Amsterdam, G. Borstius, 1691.
99-123 p. 21cm.
Signatures: 4°: π1, A-C⁴, D1.
Black letter.
NIC
(Continued on next card)

Schuts, Jacobus.
Witchcraft
BF
1410
B42
Z69
no.7
[Hooght, Everard van der] d. 1716. Vyfde briev van ... Haggēbher Philaleethees ...
1691. (Card 2)
Van der Linde 101.
No. 7 in a Collection of tracts against Balthasar Bekker and his Betoverde weereld.
The friend N. N. is thought to be Jacobus Schuts.

NIC
(Continued on next card)

495

CATALOGUE OF THE CORNELL WITCHCRAFT COLLECTION

Schuts, Jacobus.

Witchcraft
BF
1528
D9
W37
1729
[Webbers, Zacharias]
De waare oorspronk, voort- en onder-gank des Satans: behelzende, een buitengewoone, edog klare verhandeling, van de voornaamste plaatsen der Heilige Schrift, welke zyn spreekende van den Duivel. Dienende voor een inleiding tot de Bybelsche Godgeleerdheid, en het waare Christendom. Door Joan Adolphsz. 4. druk. Van nieuws oversien. Amsterdam, By Jacob Graal, boekverkooper, 1729.

8

(Continued on next card)

Schuts, Jacobus.

Witchcraft
BF
1528
D9
W37
1729
[Webbers, Zacharias] De waare oorspronk, voort- en onder-gank des Satans ... 1729.
(Card 2)

7 p. l., 418, 3 p. 17cm.
8°: *^{8} (-*1), A-2C^8, 2D3.
Black letter; title in red and black.
"De uitgever tot den leezer" signed:
N. N. (i. e., Jacobus Schuts)
First edition 1695.

8

(Continued on next card)

WITCHCRAFT
BF
1408
S57
Schwärmer und Schwindler zu Ende des achtzehnten Jahrhunderts.
Sierke, Eugen, 1845-
Schwärmer und Schwindler zu Ende des achtzehnten Jahrhunderts. Leipzig, S. Hirzel, 1874.
vi, 462 p. 21cm.

1. Occult sciences--Biography. 2. Superstition. 3. Swedenborg, Emanuel, 1688-1772. 4. Mesmer, Franz Anton, 1734-1815. 5. Gassner, Johann Joseph, 1727-1779. 6. Schrepfer, Johann Georg, 1730?-1774. 7. Cagliostro, Alessandro, conte de, as sumed name of Giuseppe Balsamo, 1743-1795. I. Title.

8
NIC

Witchcraft
BX
9479
B42
S39
Schwager, Johann Moritz.
Beytrag zur Geschichte der Intoleranz; oder Leben, Meynungen und Schicksale des ehemaligen Doct. der Theologie und reformierten Predigers in Amsterdam Balthasar Bekkers, meist nach kirchlichen Urkunden. ... Mit einer Vorrede Hrn. Doct. Joh. Salomo Semlers unter dessen Aufsicht nächstens herauskommenden verbesserten Auflage der bezauberten Welt. Leipzig, In der Weygandschen Buchhandlung, 1780.
10, LXXXXII, 190 p. 18 x 11cm.

8

(Continued on next card)

Witchcraft
BX
9479
B42
S39
Schwager, Johann Moritz. Beytrag zur Geschichte der Intoleranz ... 1780. (Card 2)

8°: a-g^8, A-M^8.

Van der Linde 217.

1. Bekker, Balthasar, 1634-1698--Biog. 2. Bekker, Balthasar, 1634-1698. De betoverde weereld. I. Semler, Johann Salomo, 1725-1791. II. Title.

8

Witchcraft
BF
1583
A2
S39
Schwager, Johann Moritz.
Versuch einer Geschichte der Hexenprozesse. Von Johann Moriz Schwager. 1. Bd. Berlin, J. F. Unger, 1784.
344 p. port. 23cm.

Includes transcripts of mss.
No more published.

1. Trials (Witchcraft)--Germany. 2. Witchcraft--Germany. I. Title.

8

Schwager, Johann Moritz, tr.

Witchcraft
BF
1410
B42
1781
Bekker, Balthasar, 1634-1698.
D. [i. e., Doktor] Balthasar Bekkers reformierten Predigers in Amsterdam bezauberte Welt. Neu übersetzt von Johann Moritz Schwager, Pastor zu Jöllenbeck; durchgesehen und vermehrt von D. Johann Salomo Semmler. Leipzig, In der Weygandschen Buchhandlung, 1781.
3 v. title vignette (port.), fold. plate. 20cm.
8°: vol. 1: a^8, b2, A-2F^8; vol. 2:

8

(Continued on next card)

Schwager, Johann Moritz, tr.

Witchcraft
BF
1410
B42
1781
Bekker, Balthasar, 1634-1698. D. Balthasar Bekkers ... bezauberte Welt. 1781.
(Card 2)

^{8} (- 8), A-2F^8, G^4; vol. 3: *^{8} (-*1, *8), A-2Y6.
Translation of his De betoverde weereld.

1. Demonology. 2. Angels. 3. Magic. 4. Witchcraft. I. Title. II. Title:

(Continued on next card)

MSS
Bd.
WITCHCRAFT
BF
S39
Schwann, Johan.
Zwo gründliche und warhafftige newe Zeitung, die Erste von den Hexen und Unholden Mann und Weibs Personen, so man in der churfürstlichen Statt zu Aschenburg unnd auch auff dem Land mit dem Fewer gestrafft unnd verbrandt hat ... Die ander Zeitung. Von dem erschröcklichen Jammer, so sich im Westerreich im Städtlein Sarwerth, begeben hatt und sehen lassen ... Gestelt durch Magister Joh   an Schwann ... Giesen, Bey Caspar   Kemla, 1612 [ca. 1900]
(Continued on next card)

MSS
Bd.
WITCHCRAFT
BF
S39
Schwann, Johan. Zwo gründliche und warhafftige newe Zeitung ... 1612 [ca. 1900]
(Card 2)

6 l. title vignette. 23cm.
Carnap's manuscript copy.
"Originaldruck in der Gust. Freytag Bibliothek; jetzt in der Stadtbibliothek zu Frankfurt a/M. 4 Bl. in 4°. Sig. Aij-Aiij."
Numerals and signatures in the margins indicate pagi   nation and signatures of the origi   nal.

(Continued on next card)

MSS
Bd.
WITCHCRAFT
BF
S39
Schwann, Johan. Zwo gründliche und warhafftige newe Zeitung ... 1612 [ca. 1900]
(Card 3)

In verse.

1. Witchcraft--Germany. 2. Apparitions. 3. Prophecies. I. Title: Von den Hexen und Unholden Mann und Weibs Personen ... zu Aschenburg. II. Title: Von dem erschröcklichen Jammer ... im Westerreich.

WITCHCRAFT
BF
1583
S39
Schwartz, Friedrich Leberecht Wilhelm, 1821-1899.
Zwei Hexengeschichten aus Waltershausen in Thüringen nebst einem mythologischen Excurs über Hexen- und ähnlichen Versammlungen. Von Direktor W. Schwartz. [Berlin, 1888]
395-419 p. 22cm.
Extract from Zeitschrift für Völkerpsychologie, v. 18.

1. Witchcraft--Thuringia. 2. Walpurgisnacht. I. Title.

8
NIC

Witchcraft
BF
1520
S32
Schwartz, Johann Conrad, 1677-1747.
Dissertatio theologica De vsv et praestantia daemonvm ad demonstrandam natvram Dei, qvam ... tvebitvr Io. Conradvs Schwartz ... Altdorfii Noric., Literis Iodoci Gvilielmi Kohlesii [1715]
26 p. 21cm.
Bound with Scherzer, Johann Adam, praeses. Daemonologia. Lipsiae, 1672.
In vol. lettered Dissertationes de daemonibus. 1672-1722.

1. God. 2. Demonology. I. Title: De usu et praestantia daemonum. II. Title.

8

WITCHCRAFT
BF
1593
U57
Die schwarze Magie: ihre Meister und ihre Opfer.
Unger, Franz, 1871-
Die schwarze Magie: ihre Meister und ihre Opfer. Coethen, R. Schumann [1904]
80 p. 20cm. (Collection rätselhafte Naturen Bd. VII)
Contents.--Präludium: Das Problem des übernatürlichen Geschlechtsverkehrs.--Geschlechtsverkehr zwischen Menschen, Teufeln und Dämonen.--Urbain Grandier und die Besessenen von Loudun.--Werke des Teufels in alter Zeit.

1. Magic. 2. Devil. 3. Grandier, Urbain, 1590-1634. I. Title.

8

WITCHCRAFT
BF
1584
S97
S41
Schweizer, Paul, 1852-1932.
Der Hexenprozess und seine Anwendung in Zürich.
(In Zürcher Taschenbuch. Zürich. 22cm. n. F. 25. Jahrg. (1902), p. 1-63)

1. Witchcraft--Switzerland. 2. Trials (Witchcraft)--Zürich. I. Title. II. Zürcher Taschenbuch.

8
NIC

WITCHCRAFT
BF
1623
R7
O12
Schweizer-Erklärung von Centralismus...
Obereit, Jacob Hermann, 1725-1798.
Gerade Schweizer-Erklärung von Centralismus, [Exjesuiterey, Anecdotenjagd, Aberglauben, Maulglauben und Unglauben, gegen einen neuen Rosenkreuz-Bruder in der Berliner Monatsschrift vom August 1785. Berlin, Bei August Mylius, 1786.
viii, 94 p. 17cm.

1. Rosicrucians. 2. Mysticism. 3. Superstition. 4. Jesuits--Controversial literature. I. Zimmermann, Johann Georg, Ritter von, 1728-1795. II. Title. III. Title: Schweizer Erklärung von Centralismus...

8
NIC

WITCHCRAFT
PQ
4416
C237
Schwickerath, Robert.
Attitude of the Jesuits in the trials for witchcraft.
(In The American Catholic quarterly review. Philadelphia. 25cm. v. 27, no. 107 (1902), p. 475-516)

1. Jesuits--Controversial literature. 2. Witchcraft--History. I. Title.

8
NIC

WITCHCRAFT
BF
1566
S41
Schwickerath, Robert.
Dr. White on witchcraft.
(In The Messenger. New York, N. Y. 25cm. v. 43, no. 6 (1905), p. 593-605)

With MS annotations by A. D. White.

1. White, Andrew Dickson, 1832-1918. Seven great statesmen in the warfare of humanity with unreason. 2. Witchcraft. I. Title.

8
NIC

CATALOGUE OF THE CORNELL WITCHCRAFT COLLECTION

Science and justice; the Massachusetts witchcraft trials.
Fox, Sanford J
  Science and justice; the Massachusetts witchcraft trials ₍by₎ Sanford J. Fox. Baltimore, Johns Hopkins Press ₍1968₎
    xix, 121 p. illus. 24 cm. $6.95
  Bibliographical footnotes.

  1. Witchcraft—Massachusetts. 2. Medical jurisprudence—Massachusetts. I. Title.

  KFM2478.8.W5F6   340'.6'09744   68-18771
  Library of Congress   ₍7₎

La science des esprits.
Witchcraft
BF
1412   ₍Constant, Alphonse Louis₎ 1810-1875.
C75   La science des esprits; révélation du dogme secret des kabbalistes esprit occulte des évangiles, appréciation des doctrines et des phénomènes spirites, par Eliphas Lévi ₍pseud.₎ Paris, Germer Baillière, 1865.
          507 p. 23cm. (His Philosophie occulte. 2. série)

  1. Occult sciences. 2. Spiritualism. I. Title.

Les sciences et les arts occultes au XVIe siècle.
Witchcraft
BF
1598   Prost, Auguste, 1817-1896.
A27   Les sciences et les arts occultes au XVIe siècle. Corneille Agrippa, sa vie et ses oeuvres... Paris, Champion, 1881-82.
P96   2 v. 23cm.

  1. Agrippa von Nettesheim, Heinrich Cornelius, 1486?-1535. 2. Occult sciences. I. Title.

Scientia magica.
WITCHCRAFT
BF
1555   Kristeli, Placidus.
K92   Scientia magica per triginta sex quaestiones deducta pro utilitate confessariorum, & animarum curatorum conscripta, atque per diversa quaesita pro notitia, & fraude daemonis cognoscenda explanata, cum supplemento benedictionum, & exorcismorum, tum maleficiatorum, tum daemoniacorum, tum etiam obsessorum, à Fr. P. Placido Kristelii. Viennae, J. J. Pentz, 1745.

  1. Demonia c possession. 2. Exorcism. I. Title.

Scot, Reginald

Scot, Reginald, 1538?-1599.
  The discouerie of witchcraft, wherein the lewde dealing of witches and witchmongers is notablie detected ... Hereunto is added a treatise vpon the nature and substance of spirits and diuels, &c: ... ₍London, Imprinted by William Brome₎ 1584.
  ₍28₎, 560, ₍16₎ p. 20cm.

  1. Witchcraft. 2. Magic. 3. Demonology. I. Title: The discovery of witchcraft.

Witchcraft
BF
1565   Scot, Reginald, 1538?-1599.
S42+   The discoverie of witchcraft. Introduced by Hugh Ross Williamson. Carbondale, Southern Illinois University Press ₍1965, ᶜ1964₎
1965   400 p. illus. 26 cm. (₍Centaur classics₎)

  1. Witchcraft. 2. Magic. 3. Demonology. I. Title.
  II. Ross Williamson, Hugh, 1901-
  BF1565.S4 1965   133.4   64-18551

Scot, Reginald, 1538?-1599.
Witchcraft   Discoverie of witchcraft--Dutch.
BF
1565   Scot, Reginald, 1538?-1599. Ontdecking
S42   van tovery ... 1638.   (Card 2)
1638
        Artoys ..., door J. DuClercq, with special t. p.; Extract uyt 't playdoye van M. L. Servin; Historie van de Maegt van Orleans ... Extract uyt J. P. van Bergamo; and various poems.

  1. Witchcraft. 2. Magic. 3. Demonology. I. His Discoverie of witchcraft. Dutch. II. DuClercq, Jacques, seigneur
8   (Continued on next card)

Scot, Reginald, 1538?-1599.
  The discouerie of witchcraft, wherein the lewde dealing of witches and witchmongers is notablie detected ... Hereunto is added a treatise vpon the nature and substance of spirits and diuels, &c: ... ₍London, Imprinted by William Brome₎ 1584.
  ₍28₎, 352, ₍4₎, 353-560, ₍16₎ p. illus. 20cm.

BF
1565   Scot, Reginald, 1538?-1599.
S42+   The discoverie of witchcraft. Introduced by Hugh Ross Williamson. Carbondale, Southern Illinois University Press ₍1965, c1964₎
1965   400 p. illus. 26cm. (₍Centaur classics₎)

  1. Witchcraft. 2. Magic. 3. Demonology. I. Title. II. Ross Williamson, Hugh, 1901-

---

Witchcraft
BF
1565   Scot, Reginald, 1538?-1599.
S42+   The discovery of witchcraft: proving, that
1665   the compacts and contracts of witches with devils and all infernal spirits or familiars, are but erroneous novelties and imaginary conceptions ... Wherein likewise the un-christian practices and inhumane dealings of searchers and witch-tryers upon aged, melancholly, and superstitious people, in extorting confessions by terrors and tortures ... are notably detected And the knavery of juglers, conjurers, charmers, soothsayers, figure-casters, dreamers, alchymists and philte rers; with many other
                              (Continued on next card)

Scot, Reginald, 1538?-1599.
  The discoverie of witchcraft. by Reginald Scot: with an introduction by the Rev. Montague Summers. ₍London₎ J. Rodker, 1930.
  xxxvii, 282, ₍1₎ p. illus. 30cm.
  "This edition ... is limited to 1275 copies ... This copy is no. 462."
  "The spelling ... is that of the edition of 1584."
  "A bibliographical note upon Scot's 'Discouerie': p. xxxiii-xxxvii.

  1. Witchcraft. 2. Magic. 3. Demonology. I. Summers, Montague, 1880-1948. II. Title: The discovery of witchcraft.
                              31-20328
  Library of Congress   BF1565.S4 1930

Scot, Reginald, 1538?-1599.
Witchcraft   Discoverie of witchcraft--Dutch.
BF
1565   Scot, Reginald, 1538?-1599.
S42   Ontdecking van tovery, beschreven int Engels door Reinald Scot, verduyscht by Th. en G. Basson. Beverwyck, Gedruckt by Frans Pels, 1638.
1638   15 p. l., 351, ₍17₎ p. 15cm.
        With engraved t. p., depicting a witch.
        Abridgment and translation of Discoverie of witchcraft.
        To this are appended: Historie van 't ghene gheschiet   is in 't Graefschap van
8   (Continued on next card)

Witchcraft
BF
1565   Scot, Reginald, 1538?-1599. The discovery of
S42+   witchcraft ... 1665.   (Card 2)
1665
        things ... fully opened and deciphered ... In sixteen books. Whereunto is added An excellent discourse of the nature and substance of devils and spirits, in two books ... London, Printed for A. Clark, 1665.
        ₍18₎, 292, ₍12₎, 72 p. illus. 29cm.

        "A discourse concerning the nature and substance of devils and spirits" has special t.p. and separate   paging.

497

CATALOGUE OF THE CORNELL WITCHCRAFT COLLECTION

Witchcraft
BF Scot, Reginald, 1538?-1599.
1565   Ontdecking van tovery, beschreven int
S42 Engels door Reinald Scot, verduyscht by
1638 Th. en G. Basson. Beverwyck, Gedruckt by
     Frans Pels, 1638.
       15 p. l., 351, [17] p. 15cm.
       With engraved t. p., depicting a witch.
       Abridgment and translation of Discoverie
     of witchcraft.
       To this are appended: Historie van 't
     ghene gheschiet is in 't Graefschap van
8   (Continued on next card)

Witchcraft
BF Scot, Reginald, 1538?-1599.   Ontdecking
1565   van tovery ... 1638.   (Card 2)
S42
1638 Artoys ..., door J. DuClercq, with special
     t. p.; Extract uyt 't playdoye van M. L.
     Servin; Historie van de Maegt van Orleans
     ... Extract uyt J. P. van Bergamo; and
     various poems.
       1. Witchcraft. 2. Magic. 3. Demono-
     logy. I. His Discoverie of witchcraft.
     Dutch. II. DuClercq, Jacques, seigneur
8   (Continued on next card)

Witchcraft
BF Scot, Reginald, 1538?-1599.   Ontdecking
1565   van tovery ... 1638.   (Card 3)
S42
1638
     de Beauvoir en Ternois, b. 1420. III.
     Servin, Louis, ca. 1555-1626. IV. Fore-
     sti, Jacopo Filippo, da Bergamo, 1434-1520.
     V. Basson, Govert, tr. VI. Basson, Tho-
     mas, 1555-1613, tr. VII. Title.

8

            Scott, Michael, 1175?-1234?
Witchcraft
Q   Brown, James Wood.
143   An enquiry into the life and legend
S42 of Michael Scot.   Edinburgh, David
B87 Douglas, 1897.
       xvi, 281 p. front. 23cm.

       1. Scott, Michael, 1175?-1234? I.
     Title.

             Scott, Michael, 1175?-1234?
WITCHCRAFT
BF   Schmutzer, Joannes Gottfried.
1598   De Michaele Scoto veneficii iniuste
S53 damnato disserit ... Iacobo Henrico Bor-
S35 nio ... qvvm is senator Lipsiensis in so-
     lemni Senatvs lectione ... nasceretvr hanc
     dignitatem gratvlatvrvs Ioannes Gottfried.
     Schmvtzervs. Lipsiae, Ex officina Langen-
     hemiana [1739]
       xvi p. 22cm.
8   1. Scott, Michael, 1175?-1234? 2.
NIC Witchcraft. 3. Born, Jakob Heinrich,
     1717-1775. I. Title.

Witchcraft
BT   Scott, Russell, Unitarian.
980   An analytical investigation of the
S42 scriptural claims of the devil: To
     which is added, an explanation of the
     terms Sheol, Hades, and Gehenna, as
     employed by the scripture writers: In
     a series of lectures delivered at
     Portsmouth. London, Sold by Rowland
     Hunter [etc., etc.] 1822.
       xxiv, 646 p. 22cm.

       1. Devil.   I. Title.

Witchcraft
BF   Scott, Walter, Pres. of Airedale College.
1531   The existence of evil spirits proved; and
S432 their agency, particularly in relation to the
     human race, explained and illustrated.
     London, Jackson and Walford, 1853.
       xx, 368 p. 20cm. (The Congregational lecture,
     ninth series)
       "New and uniform edition."

       1. Demonology. 2. Devil. I. Title.

Scott, Sir Walter

Witchcraft
BF   Scott, Sir Walter, bart., 1771-1832.
1531   Letters on demonology and witchcraft,
S43 addressed to J. G. Lockhart, esq., by Sir
1830 Walter Scott, bart. London, J. Murray,
     1830.
       ix, 402 p. front. 16 cm.

       1. Demonology. 2. Witchcraft. I. Title.
       II. Lockhart, John Gibson, 1794-1854.

Witchcraft
BF   Scott, Sir Walter, bart., 1771-1832.
1531   Letters on demonology and witchcraft,
S43 addressed to J. G. Lockhart, esq. 2d ed.
1831 London, J. Murray, 1831.
       ix, 396 p. front. 15cm.

Witchcraft
BF   Scott, Sir Walter, bart., 1771-1832.
1531   Letters on demonology and witchcraft.
S43 With an introduction by Henry Morley.
1884 London, New York, George Routledge and
     Sons, 1884.
       320 p. 20cm. (Morley's universal
     library)

       I. Morley, Henry, 1822-1894, ed.

Witchcraft
BF   Scott, Sir Walter, bart., 1771-1832.
1531   Letters on demonology and witchcraft.
S43 Addressed to J. G. Lockhart, esq. New-
1830a York, Printed by J. & J. Harper, 1830.
       338 p. 16cm. (Harper's family library,
     no. 11)
       At head of title: Harper's stereotype
     edition.

Witchcraft
BF   Scott, Sir Walter, bart., 1771-1832.
1531   Letters on demonology and witchcraft addressed
S43 to J. G. Lockhart, Esq. New York, Printed by
1832 J. & J. Harper; sold by Collins &Hannay, 1832.
       338 p. front. 16cm. (On cover: Harper's
     family library. No. XI)

Witchcraft
BF   Scott, Sir Walter, bart., 1771-1832.
1531   Letters on demonology and witchcraft.
S43 With an introduction by Henry Morley.
1887 3d ed.   London, George Routledge and
     Sons, 1887.
       320 p. 20cm. (Morley's universal
     library)

       I. Morley, Henry, 1822-1894, ed.

CATALOGUE OF THE CORNELL WITCHCRAFT COLLECTION

Scott, Sir Walter, bart., 1771-1832.
 Letters on demonology and witchcraft, with an introduction by Henry Morley. 4th ed. London, G. Routledge, 1898.
 320 p. 19cm. (Morley's Universal library, [12])

 Scott, Sir Walter, bart., 1771-1832.
WITCHCRAFT Brewster, Sir David, 1781-1868.
BF   Letters on natural magic, addressed to
1042   Sir Walter Scott, bart... 5th ed. Lon-
B84   don, J. Murray, 1842.
1842   viii, 351 p. illus., diagrs. 16cm.
       [Family library. Murray ed. v. 1]

       1. Scientific recreations. I. Title.
       II. Title: Natural magic.

 Scott, Sir Walter, bart., 1771-1832, ed.
 Somers, John Somers, baron, 1651-1716.
    A collection of scarce and valuable tracts ... [on] the history and constitution of these kingdoms ... 2d ed., rev., augm., and arr. by Walter Scott. London, Printed for T. Cadell and W. Davies, 1809-1815.
    13 v. 30cm.

    Ex libris Henry Thomas Buckle.

    1. Gt. Brit.--History--Modern period, 1485---Sources. 2. Pamphlets--Bibliography. I. Scott, Sir Walter, bart., 1771-1832, ed. II. Title.

 Scott, Sir Walter, bart., 1771-1832.
Witchcraft Parsons, Coleman Oscar.
PR   Witchcraft and demonology in Scott's
5343   fiction. With chapters on the super-
W8P26 natural in Scottish literature.
       Edinburgh and London, Oliver & Boyd, 1964.
       x, 363 p. 25cm.

       1. Scott, Sir Walter, bart., 1771-1832. 2. Witchcraft. 3. Demonology.

Scottish witchcraft trials.
 Black, George Fraser, 1866- ed.
   Some unpublished Scottish witchcraft trials; transcribed and annotated by Dr. George F. Black. New York, The New York public library, 1941.
   50 p. 25cm.
   "The following Scottish witchcraft trials were copied in 1894-1895 from a manuscript abridgment of the Books of adjournal in the library of the Society of antiquaries of Scotland. This abridgment ... contains records ... of the Court of Justiciary from 5th February, 1584, to 8th July, 1723."—p. 3.
   "Reprinted from the Bulletin of the New York public library of April-May-August-September 1941."
   1. Witchcraft—Scotland. I. Title: Scottish witchcraft trials.

   A 42-700
 New York. Public library
   for Library of Congress

Scottish witchcraft trials.
 Brodie-Innes, John William, 1848-
    Scottish witchcraft trials. By J. W. Brodie-Innes, master of the rolls to the Sette of odd volumes ... London, Imprinted at the Chiswick press, 1891.
    66 p., 1 l. 14x11½cm. (Half-title: Privately printed opuscula. Issued to members of the Sette of odd volumes. no. xxv)
    "This edition is limited to 245 copies, and is imprinted for private circulation only."
    "Read before the Sette at a meeting held at Limmer's hotel, on Friday, 7th November, 1890."
    Lists of club's publications and members: p. [51]-66.

        Scribonius, Wilhelm Adolf, 16th cent.
WITCHCRAFT De examine et purgatione sagarum.
BF   Melander, Otto, 1571-1640.
1565   Resolutio praecipuarum quaestionum cri-
M51   minalis adversus sagas processus, cum re-
        futatione nova tam juridica quam philoso-
        phica purgationis sagarum per aquam frigi-
        dam, adversus Guilielmum Adolphum Scribo-
        nium...Autore Otthone Melandro... Adjecta
        est .. Rodolphi Goclenii...Oratio...de na-
        tura sagarum in purgatione et examinatione
        per frigidam aquis innatantium. Lichae,
8   Apud Nicolaum Erbenium, 1597.
NIC   131 p.   17cm.
                              (Continued on next card)

WITCHCRAFT Scribonius, Wilhelm Adolf, 16th cent.
BF   De sagarvm natura et potestate, deque his
1565   recte cognoscendis et pvniendis physiologia
S43   Gulielmi Adolphi Scribonii Marpurgensis. Vbi
1588   de pvrgatione earvm per aquam frigidam. Con-
       tra Joannem Evvichium ... & Her. Neuvvaldum
       ... doctores medicos & professores ...
       Marpurgi, typis Pauli Egenolphi, 1588.
       [8], 132 l. 17cm.

       In copy 2, contents in MS on 1 [8b]
       Title on spine of copy 1:
8   Scribonius   Witchcraft pamphlets.
                              (Continued on next card)

WITCHCRAFT Scribonius, Wilhelm Adolf, 16th cent. De
BF   sagarvm natura ... 1588.   (Card 2)
1565
S43   With copy 1 are bound Ignotus Patronus
1588   Veritatis, pseud. Examen epistolae et partis
       physiologiae de examine sagarum ([Francofurti]
       1589); Scribonius, W. A. Responsio ad examen
       Ignoti Patroni Veritatis (Francofurti, 1590);
       and Ignotus Patronus Veritatis, pseud. Refvta-
       tio responsionis Gvlielmi-Adolphi Scribonii
       (Herbornae, 1591).
          1. Witchcraft   2. Ewich, Johann, 1525-
       1588. 3. Neuwaldt, Hermann. I. Title:
8   De sagarum natura. II. Title.

       Scribonius, Wilhelm Adolf, 16th cent.
WITCHCRAFT De sagarum natura.
BF   Ignotus Patronus Veritatis, pseud.
1565   Examen epistolae et partis physiologiae de
S43   examine sagarum per aquam frigidam; à Gvilhel-
1588   mo Adolpho Scribonio, medicinae et philosophiae
        doctore, diuersis temporibus in lucem editarum
        concinnata à quodam Ignoto Patrono Veritatis.
        Epistola Scribonij, quae examinatur, in fine
        adiecta est. [Francofurti?] 1589.
        78 p. 17cm.

        "De examine et pvrgatione sagarvm per aqvam
                              (Continued on next card)

       Scribonius, Wilhelm Adolf, 16th cent.
       De sagarum natura.
WITCHCRAFT Ignotus Patronus Veritatis, pseud. Examen
BF   epistolae ... 1589.   (Card 2)
1565
S43   frigidam epistola ... (with special t. p.):
1588   p. [51]-65.
       Bound with Scribonius, Wilhelm Adolf. De
       sagarvm natvra. Marpurgi, 1588.

       1. Scribonius, Wilhelm Adolf, 16th cent.
       De sagarum natura. 2. Witchcraft. I. Scri-
       bonius, Wilhelm Adolf, 16th cent. II. Title.

       Scribonius, Wilhelm Adolf, 16th cent.
WITCHCRAFT De sagarum natura.
BF   Melander, Otto, 1571-1640.
1565   Resolutio praecipuarum quaestionum cri-
M51   minalis adversus sagas processus, cum re-
        futatione nova tam juridica quam philoso-
        phica purgationis sagarum per aquam frigi-
        dam, adversus Guilielmum Adolphum Scribo-
        nium...Autore Otthone Melandro... Adjecta
        est .. Rodolphi Goclenii...Oratio...de na-
        tura sagarum in purgatione et examinatione
        per frigidam aquis innatantium. Lichae,
8   Apud Nicolaum Erbenium, 1597.
NIC   131 p.   17cm.
                              (Continued on next card)

       Scribonius, Wilhelm Adolf, 16th cent.
Witchcraft De sagarum natura.
BF   Neuwaldt, Hermann.
1565   Exegesis pvrgationis sive Examinis sa-
E95   garum super aquam frigidam proiectarum: in
        qua refutata opinione Guilhelmi Adolphi
        Scribonij, de huius purgationis & aliarum
        similium origine, natura, & veritate agi-
        tur: omnibus ad rerum gubernacula sedenti-
        bus maximè necessaria ... Helmstadii,
        Excudebat Iacobus Lucius, 1584.
        [120] p. 17cm.
        Bound with Ewich, Johann, 1525-1588.
8   (Continued on next card)

       Scribonius, Wilhelm Adolf, 16th cent.
Witchcraft De sagarum natura.
BF   Neuwaldt, Hermann. Exegesis pvrgationis
1565   ... 1584.   (Card 2)
E95
       De sagarum ... natura. Bremae, 1584.

       1. Scribonius, Wilhelm Adolf, 16th cent.
       De sagarum natura. 2. Witchcraft. I. Ti-
       tle: Exegesis purgationis.

8

       Scribonius, Wilhelm Adolf, 16th cent.
WITCHCRAFT Epistola de purgatione sagarum.
BF   Tractatus duo singulares de examine
1565   sagarum super aquam frigidam projectarum
T75   (Von der Wasser-Prob der Hexen) in quibus
        hujus purgationis origo, natura & veritas
        curiose inquiritur, variaeque quaestiones
        è theologorum, JCtorum, medicorum & philo-
        sophorum scriptis petitae doctissime &
        jucundè resolvuntur. Francofurti, T. H.
        Grentz, 1686.
        155 p. 20cm.
8
NIC   (Continued on next card)

       Scribonius, Wilhelm Adolf, 16th cent.
WITCHCRAFT Epistola de purgatione sagarum.
BF   Tractatus duo singulares de examine
1565   sagarum ... 1686.   (Card 2)
T75
          Scribonius' Epistola de purgatione sagarum
        previously published under title: De examine
        et purgatione sagarum per aquam frigidam
        epistola.
          Contents.--Jacobi Rickii Discurus de
        proba ut loquuntur aquae frigidae in exami-
        natione maleficarum adhibenda.--Guilielmi
        Adolphi Scri   bonii Epistola de
                              (Continued on next card)

       Scribonius, Wilhelm Adolf, 16th cent.
       Epistola de purgatione sagarum.
WITCHCRAFT Tractatus duo singulares de examine
BF   sagarum ... 1686.   (Card 3)
1565
T75
       purgatione sagarum super aquam frigidam
       projectarum.--Hermanni Neuvvalds Exegesis
       purgationis sive examinis sagarum super
       aquam frigidam projectarum in qua refutatur
       Cyrinio Guilielmi Adolphi Sbribonij [sic]

                              (Continued on next card)

Witchcraft Scribonius, Wilhelm Adolf, 16th cent.
BF   Responsio ad examen Ignoti Patroni Verita-
1565   tis de pvrgatione sagarum per aquam frigidam.
S43   Francofurdi, Apud Joannem Wechelum, 1590.
1588   [7], 56 p. 17cm.

        Bound with Scribonius, Wilhelm Adolf. De
        sagarvm natura. Marpurgi, 1588.

        1. Ignotus Patronus Veritatis, pseud. Exa-
        men epistolae et partis physiologiae de exami-
        ne sagarum per aquam frigidam. 2. Witchcraft.
        I. Title.

499

CATALOGUE OF THE CORNELL WITCHCRAFT COLLECTION

WITCHCRAFT
BF 1565 S43 R4

Scribonius, Wilhlem Adolf, 16th cent.
Responsio ad Examen Ignoti Patroni Veritatis de pvrgatione sagarum per aquam frigidam; auctore Gulielmo Adolpho Scribonio Marpurgensi. Francofurdi, Apud Joannem Wechelum, 1590.
3 p. l., 56 p. 15cm.

8 NIC

Witchcraft
BF 1565 S43 1588

Scribonius, Wilhelm Adolph, 16th cent.
Responsio ad examen Ignoti Patroni Veritatis de purgatione sagarum per aquam frigidam. Ignotus Patronus Veritatis, pseud.
Refvtatio responsionis Gvlielmi-Adolphi Scribonii, svperstitiosam sagarum pvrgationem per aquam frigidam pertinacissimè defendentis: ab Ignoto Patrono Veritatis stylo Scriboniano conscripta ... Herbornae, 1591.
112 p. 17cm.

Bound with Scribonius, Wilhelm Adolf. De sagarvm natvra. Marpurgi, 1588.

WITCHCRAFT
BF 1565 S43 1588

Scribonius, Wilhelm Adolf, 16th cent.
Ignotus Patronus Veritatis, pseud.
Examen epistolae et partis physiologicae de examine sagarum per aquam frigidam; à Gvilhelmo Adolpho Scribonio, medicinae et philosophiae doctore, diuersis temporibus in lucem editarum concinnatum à quodam Ignoto Patrono Veritatis. Epistola Scribonij, quae examinatur, in fine adiecta est. [Francofurti?] 1589.
78 p. 17cm.

"De examine et pvrgatione sagarvm per aqvam
(Continued on next card)

WITCHCRAFT
BF 1565 S43 1588

Scribonius, Wilhelm Adolf, 16th cent.
Ignotus Patronus Veritatis, pseud. Examen epistolae ... 1589. (Card 2)
frigidam epistola ... (with special t. p.): p. [51]-65.
Bound with Scribonius, Wilhelm Adolf. De sagarvm natvra. Marpurgi, 1588.

1. Scribonius, Wilhelm Adolf, 16th cent. De sagarum natura. 2. Witchcraft. I. Scribonius, Wilhelm Adolf, 16th cent.

Witchcraft
BS 1199 D4 H77

The Scriptural idea of the Devil.
Hood, Edwin Paxton, 1820-1885.
Lectures on the Scriptural idea of the Devil. [1877]
113-126 p. 23cm.

Alternate pages blank.
Evidently reprinted from a periodical.

1. Devil--Biblical teaching. I. Title: The Scriptural idea of the Devil.

Witchcraft
BT 975 Y73

The Scripture doctrine of devils.
Young, Joseph.
Demonology: or, The Scripture doctrine of devils. Edinburgh, T. Grant, 1856.
xviii, 460 p. 18cm.

1. Devil. I. Title: The Scripture doctrine of devils. II. Title: Demonology.

WITCHCRAFT
BF 1572 D4 S43

Scriver, Christian, 1629-1693.
Das verlohrne und wiedergefundene Schäfflein, oder Historischer christlicher Bericht von einem jungen Menschen, der sich vom Satan mit ihm einen Bund zu machen und ihm in allerley gottlosen Wesen sechs Jahr zu dienen verleiten lassen, darauff durch des gerechten Gottes Urtheil in dessen leibliche Gewalt und Besitzung gerathen, erschröcklich gequälet, endlich aber ... errettet und befreyet worden ...

8 NIC
(Continued on next card)

WITCHCRAFT
BF 1572 D4 S43

Scriver, Christian, 1629-1693. Das verlohrne und wiedergefundene Schäfflein ... 1672. (Card 2)
Magdeburg und Helmstadt, Johann und Friedrich Lüderwaldts Buchhändl., 1672.
[116] p. 19cm.

"Historischer Bericht, den gantzen Verlauff mit dem Soldaten, dessen in denen vorhergesätzten Predigten Meldung geschehen, fürstellend" has special t. p.

8 NIC
(Continued on next card)

WITCHCRAFT
BF 1572 D4 S43

Scriver, Christian, 1629-1693. Das verlohrne und wiedergefundene Schäfflein ... 1672. (Card 3)

1. Witchcraft. 2. Devil. 3. Demoniac possession. 4. Otte, Peter, fl. 1672. I. Title. II. Title: Historischer Bericht, den gantzen Verlauff mit dem Soldaten ... fürstellend.

8 NIC

Witchcraft
BF 1410 C97

Scriver, Christian, 1629-1693--Fiction.
Curieuse Gespräche im Reiche derer Todten, zwischen dem bekandten Auctore der bezauberten Welt, und ehemahligen Prediger in Holland Balthasar Beckern, der bey nahe wenig vom Teufel geglaubet; und zwischen dem in gantz Teutschland berühmten Theologo Christian Scrivern, der einen Menschen zurecht gebracht, so einen Pact mit dem Teufel gemacht; ... Leipzig und Braunschweig, 1731-[1734]
4 v. in 1. (208 p.) 4 plates, vignettes. 21 x 17cm.
(Continued on next card)

Witchcraft
BF 1410 C97

Scriver, Christian, 1629-1693--Fiction.
Curieuse Gespräche im Reiche derer Todten, zwischen .. Balthasar Beckern .. und .. Christian Scrivern ... 1731-[1734] (Card 2)

4°: A-P⁴, P3, Q-2C⁴.
Black letter.
Sometimes ascribed to David Fassmann.
Title of v. 2: Zweyte Unterredung oder Gespräche im Reiche derer Todten ...; of v. 3:
(Continued on next card)

Witchcraft
BF 1410 C97

Scriver, Christian, 1629-1693--Fiction.
Curieuse Gespräche im Reiche derer Todten, zwischen .. Balthasar Beckern .. und .. Christian Scrivern ... 1731-[1734] (Card 3)

Besonderes curieuses [sic] Gespräche im Reiche derer Todten ...; of v. 4: Curieuses Gespräche in dem Reiche derer Todten ...
With this is bound curieuses Gespräche im Reiche der Todten, zwischen .. Johann Friedrich Mayern .. und Johann Wilhelm Petersen ... [Leipzig] 1732.
(Continued on next card)

8

History of Science
BF 1471 D47

Scrutinium medicum De morbis a spectrorum apparitione oriundis.
Detharding, Georg Christoph, 1671-1747, praeses.
Scrutinium medicum De morbis a spectrorum apparitione oriundis, Von Gespenstern, wie weit solche durch ihre Erscheinung Kranckheiten verursachen, ed qvod ... praeside ... Georgio Dethardingio ... pro gradu doctorali summisque in arte medica honoribus insignibus ac privilegiis rite obtinendis, ... ad diem 27. Octobr. An. 1729. publico examini offert Georgius Erhard von Gehren...
(Continued on next card)

History of Science
BF 1471 D47

Scrutinium medicum De morbis a spectrorum apparitione oriundis.
Detharding, Georg Christoph, 1671-1747, praeses. Scrutinium medicum ... [1729] (Card 2)
Rostochii, Typis Io. Iacob. Adleri [1729]
38 p. 20cm.

Diss.--Rostock (G. E. von Gehren, respondent)

1. Apparitions. 2. Ghosts. 3. Medicine--15th-18th centuries. I. Gehren, Georg Erhard von, respondent. II. Title: De morbis a spectrorum apparitione oriundis. III. Title.

WITCHCRAFT
BF 1543 S43

Scultetus, Abraham, 1566-1624.
Der weisse Teuffel, so sich in menschlicher Verlarvung zu denen Einfältigen sichtbarlich gesellet, zu versuchen, ob er ihre Seelen durch allerhand Blendungen gewinnen möge? Wie er solches versuchet, indem er eine Bauer-Magd ... mit vielerley Schmeicheln und Drohungen aufgefodert hat, aber noch biss dato mit Schanden abziehen müssen ... Leipzig, Bey A. Martini, 1732.
70 p. 18cm.

8 NIC
1. Devil. 2. Exempla. I. Title.

WITCHCRAFT
BT 965 S43

Scultetus, Marcus.
Praesidium angelicum. Ein nützlich Hausbüchlein. Von guten vnd bösen Engeln: vn von derer beyder Wesen, Vhrsprung, Eigenschafften, Ampt, Dienstbestallung vnnd Werken gegen Gott vnd der christlichen Kirchen in allen Ständen ... Gestellet durch M. Marcvm Scvltetvm, Pfarrern zu Seehausen im Churfürstenthumb Sachsen. Wittenbergi, Gedruckt bey Georg Müller, in Verlegung Paul Helwigs Buchf., 1616.
668 p. vignettes. 17cm.
(Continued on next card)

8 NIC

WITCHCRAFT
BT 965 S43

Scultetus, Marcus. Praesidium angelicum ... 1616. (Card 2)

Title in red and black.
Part 2 has title: Das ander Theil dieses Büchleins, Vnterricht von den bösen Engeln.

1. Angels. 2. Demonology. I. Title. II. Title: Von guten und bösen Engeln.

8 NIC

Witchcraft
PA 4220 L3A4 1556

Scutelli, Niccolò, d. 1542, tr.
Jamblichus, of Chalcis.
[De mysteriis. Latin]
Iamblichvs De mysteriis AEgyptiorvm, nunc primum ad uerbum de graeco expressus. Nicol Scvtellio ... interprete. Adiecti de uita & secta Pythagorae flosculi, ab eodem Scutellio ex ipso Iamblicho collecti. Romae, apvd Antonivm Bladum pontificis maximi excusorem, 1556.
[20], 148 p. 21cm.

"Ampliss. dominis s. r. e. cardinalibus . Christophoro Madrutio ... & Othoni Truccis . Scipio Bongallus ... episcopus, s. p. d." 2d-3d prelim. leaves.
"De uita & secta Pythagorae flosculi" not this copy.

CATALOGUE OF THE CORNELL WITCHCRAFT COLLECTION

Séailles, Gabriel.

Witchcraft
BF
1569
M62
1903

    Michelet, Jules, 1798-1874.
        La sorcière. Etude par Gabriel Séailles. Paris, Calmann-Levy [1903]
        xxxiv, 448 p. 18cm. (Oeuvres complètes de Michelet. Histoire sociale)

        1. Witchcraft. 2. Demonomania. 3. Civilization, Medieval. I. Séailles, Gabriel. II. Title.

Séances and statutes.

Pamphlet
GR
1

    Ewen, Cecil Henry L'Estrange, 1877–
        Séances and statutes. Devon, C. L. Ewen, 1948.
        17 p. 22cm.

        1. Witchcraft. I. Title.

---

tchcraft
GR
162
B8
S44

    Sébillot, Paul, 1846-1918.
        Traditions et superstitions de la Haute-Bretagne. Paris, Maisonneuve, 1882.
        2 v. 17cm. (Les Littératures populaires de toutes les nations. 9-10)

        1. Folk-lore—Brittany. 2. Breton literature. I. Title. II. Series.

The second examination of mother Agnes Waterhouse.

Witchcraft
BF
1581
B42
1864

    Beigel, Hermann, 1830-1879, ed.
        The examination and confession of certain witches at Chelmsford in the county of Essex ... [London, Philobiblon Society, pref. 1864]
        49 p. 23cm.

        A reprint of two pamphlets in the library of Lambeth Palace, respectively entitled: The examination and confession of certaine wytches at Chensforde ... 1556 [i.e. 1566] ..." and

(Continued on next card)

The second examination of mother Agnes Waterhouse.

Witchcraft
BF
1581
B42
1864

    Beigel, Hermann, 1830-1879, ed. The examination and confession of certain witches ... [1864] (Card 2)

    The second examination of mother Agnes Waterhouse ... 1566 ....
    Offprint from Miscellanies of the Philobiblon Society, v. 8, 1863-63.

        1. Witchcraft—England. 2. Waterhouse, Agnes. I. Title. II. Title: The second examination of mother Agnes Waterhouse.

WITCHCRAFT
BF
1555
S44

    The Second part of the Boy of Bilson: or, a true and particular relation of the impostor, Susanna Fowles ... who pretended her self possess'd with the Devil ... The whole being writ and attested by Robert Howson, clerk; Captain John Bonsey, and Mr. Nicholas Wade ... London, Printed by E. Whitlock, 1698.
        24 p. 20cm.

        1. Fowles, Susanna, fl. 1698. 2. Demoniac possession. I. Howson, Robert. II. Baddeley, Richard, fl. 1621. The boy of Bilson.

8

Witchcraft
BF
1547
V81
1583

    The second part of The demoniacke vvorlde.
        [Viret, Pierre] 1511-1571.
        The second part of The demoniacke vvorlde, or, Worlde possessed with diuels, conteining three dialogues: 1. Of familiar diuels. 2. Of lunaticke diuels. 3. Of the coniuring of diuels. Translated out of French into English by T. S. [i.e. Thomas Stocker] London, Imprinted for I. Perin, and are to be sold in Paules church-yard at the signe of the Angell, 1583.
        1 v. (unpaged) 15cm.
        Bound with his The worlde possessed with deuils. London, 1583.

Witchcraft

    Secret societies—Bibliography —Catalogs.

Z
6880
Z9
D69

    Dorbon aîné, bookseller, Paris.
        Bibliotheca esoterica, catalogue annoté et illustré de 6707 ouvrages anciens et modernes, qui traitent des sciences occultes ... comme aussi des sociétés secrètes ... En vente à la Librairie Dorbon-aîné. Paris [1940]
        2 p. l., 656 p., 2 l. illus. (incl. music) plates, facsims. 25cm.

        1. Occult sciences—Bibl.—Catalogs. 2. Secret societies—Bibl.—Catalogs. I. Title.
    Library of Congress   Z6880.Z9D6   43-36450
        [3]   016.133

Der Secretarius.

WITCHCRAFT
BF
1555
S93

    [Stübel, Andreas] 1653-1725.
        Der mit allerhand Staats-Friedens-Kriegs-Hof-Literatur- wie auch Privat-Affairen beschäfftige Secretarius ... Freyburg [1709-21]
        various pagings. illus. (part fold.) 17cm.
        Attribution by Holzmann.
        Incomplete: detached sections dealing with supposed cases of demoniac possession. In form of "Expeditionen;" running

8
NIC

(Continued on next card)

Der Secretarius.

WITCHCRAFT
BF
1555
S93

    [Stübel, Andreas] 1653-1725. Der mit allerhand Staats-Friedens-Kriegs-Hof-Literatur- ... Affairen beschäfftige Secretarius ... [1709-21] (Card 2)

    title reads: Des beschäfftige Secretarii erste [zweite, dritte, u. s. w.] Expedition.
    Includes excerpts from Expedition 1, 5, 8, 10, 12, 18, 20, 24, 27, 28, 37-39, 42, 44, 45.
    Pages consecutively numbered in MS, and Register in MS bound in at end.

8
NIC

Secretorum magicorum opus.

WITCHCRAFT
BF
1405
L85
1673

    Longinus, Caesar, ed.
        Trinum magicum, sive Secretorum magicorum opus ... Editum à Caesare Longino philos. Francofurti, Sumptibus Jacobi Gothofredi Seyleri, 1673.
        12 p. l., 498 p. 14cm.
        Contents.—Marci Antonii Zimarae Tractatus magicus.—Appendix, De mirandis quibusdam naturali magia factis operationibus. Ex lib. 2. Mag. nat. Ioan. Bapt. Port.—Tractatvs De virtutibus quarundam herbarum,

8

(Continued on next card)

Secretorum magicorum opus.

WITCHCRAFT
BF
1405
L85
1673

    Longinus, Caesar, ed. Trinum magicum ... 1673. (Card 2)

    lapidum & animalium. A. M. A.—Commentatio De magnetica curatione vulnerum citra svperstitionem ... Authore R. G. M. D.—Logia, sive Oracvla Zoroastri ex Platonicorum libris collecta.—Tractatus De proprii cujusqve nati daemonis inqvisitione.
    Layout of text corresponds to that of Frankfurt, 1630 ed. (C. Eifrid, printer)

8

(Continued on next card)

Secrets merveilleux de la magie naturelle & cabalistique.

Witchcraft
BF
1602
A33
1743

    Albertus Parvus, Lucius, pseud.
        Secrets merveilleux de la magie naturelle & cabalistique du Petit Albert, traduits exactement sur l'original latin, intitulé Alberti Parvi Lucii Libellus de mirabilibus naturae arcanis. Enrichi de figures mistérieuses, & de la manière de les faire. Nouvelle edition corrigée & augmentée. Lion, Chez les Héritiers de Beringos Fratres, 1743.
        [12], 252 p. illus., plates (part fold.) 15cm.

(Continued on next card)

Secrets merveilleux de la magie naturelle et cabalistique.

Witchcraft
BF
1602
A33
1800

    Albertus Parvus, Lucius, pseud.
        Secrets merveilleux de la magie naturelle et cabalistique du Petit Albert. Traduits sur l'original latin intitulé: Alberti parvi Luci Libellus de mirabilibus naturae arcanis. Nouv. éd. Nouvelle-Orléans, Martin, frère [1800?]
        222 p. illus. 13cm.

        1. Magic. 2. Charms. 3. Medicine, Magic, mystic, and spagiric. I. His Libellus de mirabilibus naturae arcanis—Fren ch. II. Title.

8

The secrets of the invisible world laid open.

Witchcraft
BF
1445
D31
1770

    [Defoe, Daniel] 1660-1731.
        The secrets of the invisible world laid open; or, A general history of apparitions, sacred and prophane, whether angelical, diabolical, or departed souls. Shewing I. Their various returns to this world; with sure rules to know if they are good or evil. II. An enquiry into the scriptural doctrine of spirits. III. The different species of apparitions, with their real existence. IV. The nature of seeing ghosts, before

(Continued on next card)

The secrets of the invisible world laid open.

Witchcraft
BF
1445
D31
1770

    [Defoe, Daniel] 1660-1731. The secrets of the invisible world laid open. 1770. (Card 2)

    and after death. V. The effects of fancy, vapours, dreams, hyppo, and the difference between real or imaginary appearances. VI. A collection of the most authentic relations of apparitions, particularly that surprising one attested by the learned Dr. Scott. Likewise Mrs. Veal's appearance to

(Continued on next card)

The secrets of the invisible world laid open.

Witchcraft
BF
1445
D31
1770

    [Defoe, Daniel] 1660-1731. The secrets of the invisible world laid open. 1770. (Card 3)

    Mrs. Bargrave, Sir George Villers to the duke of Buckingham, &c. &c. Also the notions of the heathens concerning apparitions. Being the most entertaining, and, in quantity, the cheapest book of the kind. London, Printed for the Author and sold by D. Steel, 1770.

(Continued on next card)

The secrets of the invisible world laid open.

Witchcraft
BF
1445
D31
1770

    [Defoe, Daniel] 1660-1731. The secrets of the invisible world laid open. 1770. (Card 4)

    4, v, 252 p. 17cm.

    The first ed. was published anonymously, in 1727, under title: An essay on the history and reality of apparitions.

        1. Apparitions. I. Title. II. Defoe, Daniel, 1660-1731. An essay on the history and reality of apparitions.

CATALOGUE OF THE CORNELL WITCHCRAFT COLLECTION

BF 1584 S8 S45
Seebacher-Mesaritsch, Alfred, 1925–
Hexen-Report. Bericht über eine Massentragödie in d. Steiermark, 1425–1746. [Illustr.] Graz, Leykam (1972).
272 p. illus. 21cm.
Bibliography: p. 271.

1. Trials (Witchcraft)—Styria. I. Title.

NIC   JAN 23,'7?   xc   73-321799

Seeburg, Franz von, pseud.
see
Hacker, Franz Xavier, 1836–1894.

Witchcraft
BF 1410 B42 Z56 v.2 no.19
Seedige aanmerkinge over de voorreden, genaamt: De godtslasteringe van den amsterdamsche predikant Dr. Bekker ...
[Schuts, Jacobus]
Seedige aanmerkinge over de voorreden, genaamt: De godtslasteringe van den amsterdamsche predikant Dr. Bekker, ter waarschouwinge van alle vroome in den lande wederleyt, in de voorreden voor de toetsteen der waarheyt, ende der meyninge, door Henrikus Brink, &c. Door N. N. Amsterdam, By D. van den Dalen, boekverkooper, 1691.
8, 88 p. title vignette, illus. initial.
19 x 15cm.

(Continued on next card)

8

Witchcraft
BF 1410 B42 Z56 v.2 no.19
Seedige aanmerkinge over de voorreden, genaamt: De godtslasteringe van den amsterdamsche predikant Dr. Bekker ...
[Schuts, Jacobus] Seedige aanmerkinge over de voorreden ... 1691. (Card 2)
4°: A⁴, A-L⁴.
Black letter.
Signed on back of t. p.: J: C:
Incomplete: all after first gathering wanting.
Van der Linde 84.
No. 19 in vol. lettered Bekker II.
1. Brink, Hendrik, 1645-1723.

(Continued on next card)

Witchcraft
BF 1410 B42 Z69 no.14
[Seegen, Charinus van]
Oogmerck van Everardus van der Hoogt in sijn Brabbelen teegen het boek De Betoverde wereld genoemd. Sulx blijktuit de groote opheff, om D. Becker eens voor al, wel ter deegen, swart te maken ... t'Amsterdam, By D. van den Dalen, 1691.
16 p. 21cm.
Signatures: 4°: A-B⁴.
Black letter.
Signed: Charinus van Seegen.

(Continued on next card)

Witchcraft
BF 1410 B42 Z69 no.14
[Seegen, Charinus van] Oogmerck van Everardus van der Hoogt ... 1691. (Card 2)
Van der Linde 108.
No. 14 in a Collection of tracts against Balthasar Bekker and his Betoverde weereld.

1. Bekker, Balthasar, 1634-1698. De betoverde weereld. 2. Hooght, Everard van der, d. 1716. I. Title.

WITCHCRAFT
BF 1583 S45
Seemann, Otto, 1825-1901.
Über einige Hexenprozesse im Stift Essen.
(In Historischer Verein für Stadt und Stift Essen. Beiträge zur Geschichte von Stadt und Stift Essen. Essen. 20cm. 10. Heft (1886), p. [111]-131)

1. Trials (Witchcraft)—Essen, Germany.
2. Trials (Witchcraft)—Germany. I. Title.

8
NIC

Witchcraft
BF 1584 C3S45
Séguin, Robert Lionel.
La sorcellerie au Canada francais du xvii⁰ au xix⁰ siècles. Montréal, Librairie Ducharme, 1961.
191 p. illus. 23cm.

1. Witchcraft—Canada. I. Title.

WITCHCRAFT
BF 1555 T35
Seiberin, Johanna, fl. 1782.
Der Teufel zu Seefeld, noch 1783. Aus "Anmerkungen über den Teufel zu Seefeld in Tirol. [."] Verfasst von einem geistlichen Ganser der ExKlarisserinnen. Auf Unkosten der St. Monica Brüderschaft zu Seefeld. 1783, 8, 80 Seiten.
(In Stats-Anzeigen. Göttingen. 20 cm. 6. Bd., Heft 23 (1784), p. 274-294)
At head of title: 30.

WITCHCRAFT
BF 1445 S45
Seidel, Abrahamus.
[Pneumatologia] Πνευματολογία oder Kurtzer Bericht von denen Geistern, über der unlangst publicirten Frage ob natürliche gewisse Geister seyen, und einem Menschen gezieme solche an sich zu locken, und in dero Gemeinschafft zugerathen?... Erffurdt, In Verlegung Johann Birckners [Gedruckt in der Spangenbergischen Truckerey] 1648.
[152] p. illus. 14cm.
One p. of MS notes bound in at end. Title in red and black.

8
NIC
1. Spirits. 2. Witchcraft. I. Title. II. Title: Kurzer Bericht von denen Geistern.

Seifert, Johan.

WITCHCRAFT
BF 1583 A2 R567
Rimphoff, Hinrich, 1599-1655.
Drachen-König; das ist: Warhafftige, deutliche, christliche, vnd hochnothwendige Beschreybunge, dess grawsamen, vnd hochvermaledeyten Hexen, vnd Zauber Teuffels, welcher durch Gottes sonderbahre direction, Schikunge vnd Gnade, an diesem Ort bald fürm Jahr, durch ein neunjähriges Mägdelein, wieder aller Menschen Gedancken manifestirt, vnd gantz wunderbarlich aus Liecht gebracht. Zu Salvir, vnd Rettunge vieler christlicher, vnschuldiger, frommer
(Continued on next card)

8
NIC

Seifert, Johan.

WITCHCRAFT
BF 1583 A2 R567
Rimphoff, Hinrich, 1599-1655.
Drachen-König... (Card 2)
Hertzen dieses Orts, auch zur Warnunge aller Hexen Patronen, Adhaerenten, Vorfechteren vnd leichtfertigen Calumnianten. Sampt einem Appendice wider Johan Seiferten vom Ulm ... Auss hoher Noth öffentlich in den Druck gegeben, durch Heinricum Rimphof. Rintelen, Druckts P. Lucius, 1647.
566 p. 16 cm.

(Continued on next card)

Witchcraft
BF 1565 G26
Select cases of conscience touching witches and witchcrafts.
Gaule, John.
Select cases of conscience touching witches and witchcrafts ... London, Printed by W. Wilson for R. Clutterbuck, 1646.
208 p. 12cm.

Contains a letter from Matthew Wopkins, called the witch-finder, announcing his intention of visiting Great Staughton (where Gaule was the preacher) "to search for evill disposed persons called witches."
Has bookplate of Edwd. Place, and his autograph.

Witchcraft
BF 1589 S46+ 1948
Seligmann, Kurt, 1900–
The history of magic. [New York] Pantheon Books [c1948]
504 p. 27cm.

Also published the same year, by the same publisher, under title: The mirror of magic.

1. Magic—Hist. I. Title. II. His The mirror of magic.

Witchcraft
BF 1589 S46+
Seligmann, Kurt, 1900–
The mirror of magic. 250 illus. [New York] Pantheon Books [1948]
504 p. illus., ports. 27 cm.

"Bibliographic résumé": p. 489-496.

1. Magic—Hist. I. Title.

BF 1589 S46+
Seligmann, Kurt, 1900–
The mirror of magic. 250 illus. [New York] Pantheon Books [1948]
504 p. illus., ports. 27 cm.

"Bibliographic résumé": p. 489-496.

Seligmann, Kurt, 1900–
The mirror of magic.

Witchcraft
BF 1589 S46+ 1948
Seligmann, Kurt, 1900–
The history of magic. [New York] Pantheon Books [c1948]
504 p. 27cm.

Also published the same year, by the same publisher, under title: The mirror of magic.

1. Magic—Hist. I. Title. II. His The mirror of magic.

Selmar, Emil.

WITCHCRAFT
BF 1583 H82 1921
En forskreckelig oc sand bescriffuelse om mange troldfolck; som ere forbrende for deris misgierninger skyld, fra det aar 1589... København [Bianco Lunos bogtrykkeri] 1921.
[25] p. illus. 21cm. (Bianco Lunos bibliofiludgaver)
Added t.-p.: Gammel dansk folkelitteratur Flyveskrift første gang trykt i Køln paa Caspar Schumans af Eefurts bekostning og derefter i København af Laurentz
(Continued on next card)

8
NIC

CATALOGUE OF THE CORNELL WITCHCRAFT COLLECTION

Selmar, Emil.
WITCHCRAFT
F
583
S2
921

En forskreckelig oc sand bescriffuelse om mange troldfolck... 1921. (Card 2)
Benedicht, 1591.
According to G. L. Burr, a translation of "Hort an new schrecklich abenthewr ... [Köln, 1589?]
"Efter et gammelt flyveblad, der nu opbevares paa det Kongelige bibliotek i København ... paany ... udgivet ... efter ... modernise rede udkast."
(Continued on next card)

NIC

Selmar, Emil.
WITCHCRAFT
F
583
S2
921

En forskreckelig oc sand bescriffuelse om mange troldfolck... 1921. (Card 3)
"Stumme Peders graffschrift ... 1589": p. [14].
"Oplysninger," af Emil Selmar p. [15]-[23], has special t. p.
"Bogen er trykt i 500 ... ekspl. ... nr. 58."
1. Witchcraft--Germany. 2. Witchcraft--Denmark. 3. Printing--History--Europe. I. Lung, Bianco, ed. II. Selmar, Emil. III. Hort an new schrecklich abentewr.

NIC

WITCHCRAFT
BF
1555
M94
029
no.4

Semler, Johann Salomo, 1725-1791.
D. Joh. Salomo Semlers ... Abfertigung der neuen Geister und alten Irtümer in der Lohmannischen Begeisterung zu Kemberg nebst theologischem Unterricht von dem Ungrunde der gemeinen Meinung von leiblichen Besitzungen des Teufels und Bezauberungen der Christen. Halle, Bey J. J. Gebauer, 1760.
40, 328 p. 18cm.
Dedication and "Vorrede" comprise the first numbering.
(Continued on next card)

NIC

WITCHCRAFT
BF
1555
M94
029
no.4

Semler, Johann Salomo, 1725-1791. ...
Abfertigung der neuen Geister ... 1760. (Card 2)
"Anhang. Auszug aus des Chaufepiee [sic] Nouveau dictionnaire historique et critique, von dem Artikel Balthas. Bekker": p. 317-328.
No. 4 in vol. lettered Oesfeld u. a. ...
1. Lohmannin, Anna Elisabeth. 2. Müller, Gottlieb. Gründlicher Nachricht von einer begeisterten Weibesperson. 3. Devil. 4. Bekker, Balthasar, 1634-1698.
(Continued on next card)

NIC

WITCHCRAFT
F
555
94
29
.4

Semler, Johann Salomo, 1725-1791. ...
Abfertigung der neuen Geister ... 1760. (Card 3)
5. Demoniac possession.
I. Chauffepié, Jacques Georges de, 1702-1786. Nouveau dictionnaire historique et critique. II. Title: Abfertigung der neuen Geister und alten Irtümer. VIII. Title.

Semler, Johann Salomo, 1725-1791.
Abfertigung der neuen Geister und alten Irtümer.
WITCHCRAFT
555
94
29
.5

Semler, Johann Salomo, 1725-1791.
D. Joh. Salomo Semlers Anhang zu der Abfertigung der Lohmannischen Begeisterung, worin fernere historische Umstände gesamlet worden. Halle, Bey J. J. Gebauer, 1760.
112 p. 18cm.
Title of the original work reads: Abfertigung der neuen Geister und alten Irtümer der Lohmannischen Begeisterung. Halle, 1760.
No. 5 in vol. lettered Oesfeld u. a. ...
(Continued on next card)

NIC

WITCHCRAFT
BF
1555
M94
029
no.5

Semler, Johann Salomo, 1725-1791.
D. Joh. Salomo Semlers Anhang zu der Abfertigung der Lohmannischen Begeisterung, worin fernere historische Umstände gesamlet worden. Halle, Bey J. J. Gebauer, 1760.
112 p. 18cm.
Title of the original work reads: Abfertigung der neuen Geister und alten Irtümer der Lohmannischen Begeisterung. Halle, 1760.
No. 5 in vol. lettered Oesfeld u. a. ...
(Continued on next card)

8   NIC

WITCHCRAFT
BF
1555
M94
029
no.5

Semler, Johann Salomo, 1725-1791. ...
Anhang zu der Abfertigung der Lohmannischen Begeisterung ... 1760. (Card 2)

1. Müller, Gottlieb. 2. Lohmannin, Anna Elisabeth. 3. Demoniac possession.
I. His Abfertigung der neuen Geister und alten Irtümer. II. Title: Anhang zu der Abfertigung der Lohmannischen Begeisterung. III. Title.

8   NIC

WITCHCRAFT
BS
2545
D5
S47
1769

Semler, Johann Salomo, 1725-1791.
Ioannis Salomonis Semleri ... Commentatio de daemoniacis qvorvm in N. T. fit mentio. Editio avctior. Halae Magdebvrgicae, Impensis I. C. Hendelii, 1769.
62 p. 21cm.
First published 1760 under title: De daemoniacis, quorum in Evangeliis fit mentio. (Title from Kayser)
1. Demoniac possession. 2. Bible. N. T.--Commentaries. I. His De daemoniacis, quorum in Evangeliis fit mentio. II. Title: De daemoniacis quorum in N. T. fit mentio. (Over)

8

Semler, Johann Salomo, 1725-1791.
De daemoniacis, quorum in Evangeliis fit mentio.
WITCHCRAFT
BS
2545
D5
S47
1769

Semler, Johann Salomo, 1725-1791.
Ioannis Salomonis Semleri ... Commentatio de daemoniacis qvorvm in N. T. fit mentio. Editio avctior. Halae Magdebvrgicae, Impensis I. C. Hendelii, 1769.
62 p. 21cm.
First published 1760 under title: De daemoniacis, quorum in Evangeliis fit mentio. (Title from Kayser)
1. Demoniac possession. 2. Bible. N. T.--Commentaries. I. His De daemoniacis, quorum in Evangeliis fit mentio. II. Title: De daemoniacis quorum in N. T. fit mentio.

8

Semler, Johann Salomo, 1725-1791.
De daemoniacis, quorum in Evangeliis fit mentio.
WITCHCRAFT
BS
2545
D5
S472

Semler, Johann Salomo, 1725-1791.
D. Joh. Salomo Semlers ... Umständliche Untersuchung der dämonischen Leute oder sogenannten Besessenen, nebst Beantwortung einiger Angriffe. Halle, Bey J. I. Gebauer, 1762.
24 p. l., 272 p. 18cm.
Contents.--Auszug und Erleuterung der Dissertation: De daemoniacis, qvorum in Evangeliis fit mentio.--Auszug und Beantwortung der jenaischen Disputation.--Antwort
(Continued on next card)

8

Semler, Johann Salomo, 1725-1791.
De daemoniacis, quorum in Evangeliis fit mentio.
WITCHCRAFT
BS
2545
D5
S472

Semler, Johann Salomo, 1725-1791. ...Umständliche Untersuchung der dämonischen Leute ... 1762. (Card 2)
auf die unbillige Recension in den Auszügen aus Dispvtationibvs.
1. Demoniac possession. 2. His De daemoniacis, quorum in Evangeliis fit mentio. 3. Bible. N. T.--Commentaries. I. Title: Umständliche Untersuchung der dämonischen Leute oder sogenannten Besessenen.

8

Witchcraft
BF
1559
G25
Z87

Semler, Johann Salomo, 1725-1791, ed.
Samlungen von Briefen und Aufsätzen über die Gassnerischen und Schröpferischen Geisterbeschwörungen, mit eigenen vielen Anmerkungen hrsg. von Johann Salomo Semler. Halle im Magdeburgischen, C. H. Hemmerde, 1776.
2 v. in 1. 20cm.
1. Gassner, Johann Joseph, 1727-1779. 2. Schrepfer, Johann Georg, 1730?-1774. 3. Exorcism. 4. Faith-cure. I. Title.

8

Witchcraft
BS
2545
D5
S472

Semler, Johann Salomo, 1725-1791.
D. Joh. Salomo Semlers ... Umständliche Untersuchung der dämonischen Leute oder sogenannten Besessenen, nebst Beantwortung einiger Angriffe. Halle, Bey J. I. Gebauer, 1762.
24 p. l., 272 p. 18cm.
Contents.--Auszug und Erleuterung der Dissertation: De daemoniacis, qvorum in Evangeliis fit mentio.--Auszug und Beantwortung der jenaischen Disputation.--Antwort
(Continued on next card)

WITCHCRAFT
BS
2545
D5
S472

Semler, Johann Salomo, 1725-1791. ...Umständliche Untersuchung der dämonischen Leute ... 1762. (Card 2)
auf die unbillige Recension in den Auszügen aus Dispvtationibvs.
1. Demoniac possession. 2. His De daemoniacis, quorum in Evangeliis fit mentio. 3. Bible. N. T.--Commentaries. I. Title: Umständliche Untersuchung der dämonischen Leute oder sogenannten Besessenen.

8

Witchcraft
BF
1410
B42
1781

Semler, Johann Salomo, 1725-1791, ed.
Bekker, Balthasar, 1634-1698.
D. [i.e., Doktor] Balthasar Bekkers reformierten Predigers in Amsterdam bezauberte Welt. Neu übersetzt von Johann Moritz Schwager, Pastor zu Jöllenbeck; durchgesehen und vermehrt von D. Johann Salomo Semler. Leipzig, In der Weygandschen Buchhandlung, 1781.
3 v. title vignette (port.), fold. plate. 20cm.
8⁰: vol. 1: a⁸, b2¹ A-2F⁸; vol. 2: ⁸(- 8), A-2F⁸, G⁴; vol. 3: *⁸ (-*1, *8), A-2Y6.
Translation of De betoverde weereld.

WITCHCRAFT
BF
1501
D12
no.2

Semler, Johann Salomo, 1725-1791.
Farmer, Hugh, 1714-1787.
Hugo Farmers Versuch über die Dämonischen des Neuen Testamentes. Aus dem Englischen übersetzt von L. F. A. von Cölln. Nebst einer Vorrede D. Joh. Sal. Semlers. Bremen und Leipzig, Bey J. H. Cramer, 1776.
38, 327 p. 17cm.
Translation of An essay on the demoniacs of the New Testament.
No. 2 in vol. lettered Dämonologische Schriften.

8   (Continued on next card)

WITCHCRAFT
BF
1501
D12
no.1

Semler, Johann Salomo, 1725-1791.
[Hesse, Otto Justus Basilius] d. 1793.
Versuch einer biblischen Dämonologie, oder Untersuchung der Lehre der heil. Schrift vom Teufel und seiner Macht. Mit einer Vorrede und einem Anhang von D. Johann Salomo Semler. Halle im Magdeburgischen, C. H. Hemmerde, 1776.
28 p. l., 359 p. 17cm.
No. 1 in vol. lettered Dämonologische Schriften.
1. Devil. 2. Demonomania. 3. Bible--Criticism, interpretation, etc. I. Semler, Johann Salomo, 1725-1791. II. Title.

8

503

CATALOGUE OF THE CORNELL WITCHCRAFT COLLECTION

Semler, Johann Salomo, 1725-1791.

Witchcraft
BX 9479 B42 S39
Schwager, Johann Moritz.
Beytrag zur Geschichte der Intoleranz; oder Leben, Meynungen und Schicksale des ehemaligen Doct. der Theologie und reformierten Predigers in Amsterdam Balthasar Bekkers, meist nach kirchlichen Urkunden. ... Mit einer Vorrede Hrn. Doct. Joh. Salomo Semlers von einer unter dessen Aufsicht nächstens herauskommenden verbesserten Auflage der bezauberten Welt. Leipzig, In der Weygandschen Buchhandlung, 1780.
10, LXXXXII. 190 p. 18 x 11cm.

8 (Continued on next card)

Semler, Johann Salomo, 1725-1791.

Witchcraft
BX 9479 B42 S39
Schwager, Johann Moritz. Beytrag zur Geschichte der Intoleranz ... 1780. (Card 2)

8°: a-g⁸, A-M⁸.

Van der Linde 217.

1. Bekker, Balthasar, 1634-1698--Biog. 2. Bekker, Balthasar, 1634-1698. De betoverde weereld. I. Semler, Johann Salomo, 1725-1791. II. Title.

8

Semler, Johann Salomo, 1725-1791.

WITCHCRAFT
BS 2545 D5 S473
Müller, Joannes Stephanus.
De daemoniacis Semlerianis in duabus dissertationibus theologicis commentatur D. Ioannes Steph. Müllerus. Francofurti et Lipsiae, Apud Theodor. Vilhelm. Ern. Güthium, 1763.
95, 102 p. 23cm.

Each dissertation has separate t.p. (reprints of original title pages) No.1: Notionem δαιμονίου sive δαίμονος olim et inprimis Christi tempore non hoc
8 NIC (Continued on next card)

Semler, Johann Salomo, 1725-1791.

WITCHCRAFT
BS 2545 D5 S473
Müller, Joannes Stephanus. De daemoniacis Semlerianis...1763. (Card 2)

involuisse vi anima mortui daemon esse crederetur...demonstrat et...praeside...Ioanne Stephano Müllero...defendet Ioann. Burckhard. Caspari. Ienae [1761] No.2: Notio illa animam mortui esse et dici in evangeliis daemonem opinioni debetur...praeside ...Ioanne Stephano Müllero...defendere conatur Georg. Christ. Wagenbronner. Ienae [1762]
8 (Continued on next card)

Send-Schreiben an Hieronymum Pistellum.

WITCHCRAFT
BF 1583 T15
Tamianus, Julius, pseud.
Julii Tamiani Send-Schreiben an Hieronymum Pistellum, worinne bey Veranlassung der unweit Jena unternommenen Satans-Beschwerung der Anfang und Fortgang der Magie, wie nicht minder die Meynungen der Magorum untersuchet, auch von denen dabey gewöhnlichen Mitteln ... Bericht erstattet wird. Nebst einem Paquetgen an den verwegenen Authorem der sogenannten Gerichte Gottes und sinnreichen Uberschrifft, so er Franco zu er-
8 NIC (Continued on next card)

Send-Schreiben an Hieronymum Pistellum.

WITCHCRAFT
BF 1583 T15
Tamianus, Julius, pseud. Julii Tamiani Send-Schreiben an Hieronymum Pistellum ... (Card 2)

halten hat. Zu Magiluna in Arabien [i.e., Jena?] 1716.
52 p. 20cm.
Illustrative title vignette.
1. Witchcraft--Thuringia. 2. Witchcraft--Jena, Germany. 3. Magic. I. Pistellus, Hieronymus. II. Title: Send-Schreiben an Hieronymum Pistellum.

8 NIC

Sendschreiben an den Hochw. H. P. Agnellus März.

Witchcraft
BF 1565 S83 S836
[Mayer, Andreas Ulrich] 1732-1802.
Sendschreiben an den Hochw. H. P. Agnellus März, ... Über seine Vertheidigung wider die schwulstige Vertheidigung der betrügenden Zauberey und Hexerey, von F. N. Blocksberger, Beneficiaten zu T. [pseud] Straubingen, 1767.
5 pieces in 3 v. 23cm.
Vol. 2 has caption title: Weitere Fortsetzung. Des F. N. Blockbergers [sic] zweytes Sendschreiben an H. P. Agnell &c. &c.

8 (Continued on next card)

Sendschreiben an den Hochw. H. P. Agnellus März.

Witchcraft
BF 1565 S83 S836
[Mayer, Andreas Ulrich] 1732-1802. Sendschreiben an den Hochw. H. P. Agnellus März ... 1767. (Card 2)

This vol. contains the 2. and 4. Sendschreiben, consecutively paged.
Vol. 3 has caption title: Des F. N. Blockbergers [sic] fünftes Sendschreiben an H. P. Agnell, &c. &c. The vol. contains the 5. and 6. Sendschreiben, consecutively paged.

8 (Continued on next card)

Sendschreiben an einen gelehrten Freund betreffend die heutige Streitschriften von der Hexerey.

Witchcraft
BF 1565 S83 G19
[Ganser, Benno] 1728-1779?
Sendschreiben an einen gelehrten Freund betreffend die heutige Streitschriften von der Hexerey. Vom Donau-Strohm [1767?]
[12] p. 20cm.
Attribution by Holzmann and British Museum (the latter gives Christian name as Brenno), Fieger, in his P. Don Ferdinand Sterzinger, p. 136, gives the name as B. Janser: a misprint?
1. Sterzinger, Ferdinand, 1721-1786. 2. Witchcraft. I. Title. II. Janser, B , supposed author.

8

Sendschreiben des ... Aloysius von Sonnenfels ... an ... P. don Ferdinand Sterzinger, ... über zwey hebräische Wörter.

Witchcraft
BF 1565 S69
Sonnenfels, Aloysius von
Sendschreiben des hochedelgebohrnen Herrn Aloysius von Sonnenfels ... an den hochgelehrten P. don Ferdinand Sterzinger, ... über zwey hebräische Wörter chartumim und belahatehem: nachmals zur nothwendigen Belehrung des sogenannten Liebhabers der Wahrheit, und seines lateinischen Eutychii Benjamin Transalbini in ihrem Zauber- und Hexerey Streite zum Drucke befördert, von einem Verehrer des Ste rzingerischen Namens.
8 (Continued on next card)

Sendschreiben des ... Aloysius von Sonnenfels ... an ... P. don Ferdinand Sterzinger, ... über zwey hebräische Wörter.

Witchcraft
BF 1565 S69
Sonnenfels, Aloysius von Sendschreiben ... 1768. (Card 2)

Wjen, Gedruckt mit schulzischen Schriften, 1768.
30, [1] p. 21cm.
1. Witchcraft in the Bible. 2. Bible. O.T.--Criticism, Textual. 3. Ḥartumim (The word) 4. Belahatehem (The word) 5. Durych, Fortunat, 1730-1802. Eutychii Beniamin Transalb ini Dissertatio philologica... 6. März, Agnellus, 1726-1784.

8

WITCHCRAFT
BF 1566 S47
Sepp, Johann Nepomuk, 1816-1908.
Orient und Occident. Hundert Kapitel über die Nachtseite der Natur, Zauberwerk und Hexenwesen in alter und neuer Zeit. Berlin, A. Schwetschke, 1903.
312 p. 23cm.

1. Witchcraft. 2. Magic. 2. Folklore, Germanic. 4. Folk-lore--Classification. I. Title. II. Title: Die Nachtseite d er Natur, Zauberwerk und Hexenwesen.

8 NIC

WITCHCRAFT
BT 97 A2 S48
Serces, Jaques, 1695-1762.
Traité sur les miracles. Dans lequel on prouve que le diable n'en sauroit faire pour confirmer l'erreur ... et où l'on examine le système opposé, tel que l'a établi le Dr. Samuel Clarke, dans le chap. XIX. du II. vol. de son Traité sur la religion naturelle & chrétienne ... Amsterdam, Chez P. Humbert, 1729.
21 p. l., 371 p. 16cm.

8 Serces takes issue with Samuel
NIC (Continued on next card)

WITCHCRAFT
BT 97 A2 S48
Serces, Jaques, 1695-1762. Traité sur les miracles ... 1729. (Card 2)

Clarke's A discourse concerning the being and attributes of God, translated by P. Ricotier as De l'existence et des attributs de Dieu, Amsterdam, 1717. [See RARE B 1365 D32 F8 1717]
1. Miracles--Early works to 1800. 2. Clarke, Samuel, 1675-1729. A discourse concerning the being and attributes of God. 3. Magic. I. Title.

8 NIC

WITCHCRAFT
BF 1547 S48
Serclier, Jude, b. ca. 1568.
L'antidemon historial, où les sacrileges, larcins, ruses, & fraudes du Prince des tenebres, pour vsurper la Diuinité, sont amplement traictez, tant par le tesmoignage des S. Escritures, peres & docteurs de l'Eglise, qu'aussi par le rapport des historiens sacrez & profanes ... Lyon, Chez Pierre Rigavd, 1609.
10 p. l., 552, [15] p. 16cm.
Imperfect: last p. wanting.
1. Devil. 2. Gods. 3. Witchcraft. I. Title.

8 NIC

Witchcraft
BF 1566 S48
Sergeant, Philip Walsingham, 1872-
Witches and warlocks, by Philip W. Sergeant; with introduction by Arthur Machen; with 17 illustrations. London, Hutchinson & co., ltd. [1936].
290 p. front., plates, ports. 22ᶜᵐ.

1. Witchcraft. 2. Witchcraft--England. I. Title. II. Title: Warlocks.
36-35589
Library of Congress   BF1566.S4
Copyright A ad int. 22047   [159.9614] 133.4

A sermon against witchcraft.

Witchcraft
BF 1581 Z7 1808
Nicholson, Isaac.
A sermon against witchcraft, preached in the parish church of Great Paxton, in the county of Huntingdon, July 17. 1808. With a brief account of the circumstances, which led to two atrocious attacks on the person of Ann Izzard, as a reputed witch. By the Reverend Isaac Nicholson ... London, Printed for J. Mawman, 1808.
1 p. l., ix, 35, [1] p. 22ᶜᵐ.

1. Witchcraft. I. Title.
11-15843
Library of Congress   BF1581.Z7 1808

A sermon on witchcraft.

Witchcraft
BF 1581 Z7+ 1697d
Hutchison, James.
A sermon preached before the commissioners of justiciary appointed for triall of several persons suspected guilty of witchcraft: att Pasley the 13 Aprill 1697. [Glasgow, 1910].
390-399 p. 26cm.

Running title: A sermon on witchcraft in 1697.
Extract from The Scottish historical review, no. 28, July 1910.
Contributed with a historical note, by Geo. Neilson.
8 NIC 1. Neilson, George II. Title. III. Title: A sermon on witchcraft.

CATALOGUE OF THE CORNELL WITCHCRAFT COLLECTION

Witchcraft
Hutchison, James.
A sermon preached before the commissioners of justiciary appointed for triall of several persons suspected guilty of witchcraft: att Pasley the 13 Aprill 1697. [Glasgow, 1910]
390-399 p. 26cm.

Running title: A sermon on witchcraft in 1697.
Extract from The Scottish historical review, no. 28, July 1910. Contributed with a historical note, by Geo. Neilson.
I. Neilson, George. II. Title. III. Title: A sermon on witchcraft.

Witchcraft
Juxon, Joseph.
A sermon upon witchcraft. Occasion'd by a late illegal attempt to discover witches by swimming. Preach'd at Twyford, in the county of Leicester, July 11, 1736. London, Printed by H. Woodfall, and sold by J. Roberts, 1736.
32 p. 21cm.

1. Witchcraft.

Witchcraft
Guaita, Stanislas de, 1860-1897.
... Le serpent de la Genèse ... par Stanislas de Guaita. Paris, Librairie du merveilleux, 1891-
v. front, plates, ports. 23cm. (His Essais de sciences maudites II)
Books 1 and 2 only.
Vol. 2 has imprint: Bibliothèque Chacornac, 1897. Date on cover: 1902.
Vol. 1 has subtitle: Le temple de Satan.
Vol. 2 has subtitle: La clef de la magie noire.
Ex libris, vol. 2: Arthur Edward Waite.
1. Demonology. I. Title. II. His Essais de sciences maudites. III. Title: Le temple de Satan. IV. Title: La clef de la magie noire.
Library of Congress   BF1405.G8 vol.2

Witchcraft
Scot, Reginald, 1538?-1599.
Ontdecking van tovery, beschreven int Engels door Reinald Scot, verduyscht by Th. en G. Basson. Beverwyck, Gedruckt by Frans Pels, 1638.
15 p. l., 351, [17] p. 15cm.
With engraved t. p., depicting a witch.
Abridgment and translation of Discoverie of witchcraft.
To this are appended: Historie van 't ghene gheschiet is in 't Graefschap van
(Continued on next card)

Witchcraft
Scot, Reginald, 1538?-1599. Ontdecking van tovery ... 1638. (Card 2)
Artoys ..., door J. DuClercq, with special t. p.; Extract uyt 't playdoye van M. L. Servin; Historie van de Maegt van Orleans ... Extract uyt J. P. van Bergamo; and various poems.
1. Witchcraft. 2. Magic. 3. Demonology. I. His Discoverie of witchcraft. Dutch. II. DuClercq, Jacques, seigneur
(Continued on next card)

Witchcraft
[Hooght, Everard van der] d. 1716. Sesde briev van ... Haggébher Philaleethees, geschreeven aan zynen vriend N. N.
Haggébher Philaleethees, geschreeven aan zynen vriend N. N. vervattende: I. Een afwysing van vyfderley gewaande voorspraaken van D. Bekker. Ende II. een verhandeling van de De Daimonia, na hare beteekenisse voor, in, ende na de tyden Christi. Volgens het welke uyt het Hebreeusch Griekich en Syrisch klaar te sien is, dat De Daimonia zedert Christi tyden niet anders zyn, dan de Duyvelen. Amsterdam,
(Continued on next card)

Witchcraft
BF 1410 B42 Z69 no.9
[Hooght, Everard van der] d. 1716. Sesde briev van ... Haggébher Philaleethees ... (Card 2)
G. Borstius, 1691.
135-176 p. 21cm.
Signatures: 4°: ∏1, A-E⁴, F1.
Black letter.
The friend N.N. may be Jacobus Schuts.
Van der Linde 103.
No. 9 in a Collection of tracts against Balthasar Bekker and his betoverde weereld.
(Continued on next card)
NIC

BF 1581 S49 C5
Seth, Ronald.
Children against witches. New York, Taplinger Pub. Co. [1969]
190 p. illus. 23 cm. 4.95

1. Witchcraft—England. I. Title.
BF1581.S35 1969   133.4'0942   71-83224 MARC
Library of Congress   69 [2]

Witchcraft
BF 1581 S49
Seth, Ronald.
Stories of great witch trials. London, Barker [1967]
vii, 176 p. tables. 22½ cm. 21/-
(B 67-20430)
Bibliography: p. 169-171.

1. Trials (Witchcraft)—Gt. Brit. I. Title.
343'.3   67-105996
Library of Congress   [2]

BF 1566 S49
Seth, Ronald.
Witches and their craft. London, Odhams, 1967.
255 p. illus., 8 plates. 22 cm. 21/-
(B 67-11326)
Bibliography: p. 250-251.

1. Witchcraft. I. Title.
BF1566.S43   133.4   67-91518
Library of Congress   [3]

Witchcraft
BF 1410 B42 Z69 no.10
[Hooght, Everard van der] d. 1716.
Sevende briev van הגבר Φιλαλήθης geschreeven aan den E. Heer C. E. over den oorspronk, voortgang, ende het gebruyk der talen in het gemeen. Ende, in het byzonder, van de Duyvelen in het Oude Testament, onder de woorden scheedhijm, ende segnijrijm, cap. 8. Item, een vertooning, dat de Heere Jesus ons de geheele Gods-geleertheyd in zijne dagen heeft geleert, na de waarheyd der saake, ende nooit, tegen de waarheyd, na de dwaling des volks. cap. 9. Ende dat de beseetene ofte bedwyvelde
(Continued on next card)
NIC

Witchcraft
BF 1410 B42 Z69 no.10
[Hooght, Everard van der] d. 1716. Sevende briev van ... (Card 2)
sijn geplaagt geworden van den Duyvel, als de naaste oorsaak van hare siektens, cap. 10. Nevens een klaar vertoog, dat het niet de minste eygenschap en heeft, om zoo veele texten in Gods woord, alwaar de Satan, als een werker, benoemt word, alleen te willen betrekken op den Duyvel, voor zoo veel hy geweest is de oorsaak van de eerste verleyding des menschen, cap. 11.
(Continued on next card)
NIC

Witchcraft
BF 1410 B42 Z69 no.10
[Hooght, Everard van der] d. 1716. Sevende briev van ... (Card 3)
Waar by koomen eenige invoegselen tegens sommige misduydingen, in het Post-scriptum. Met het vervolg der kerkelijke proceduuren tegen D. B. Bekker. t'Amsterdam, By G. Borstius, 1692.
179-235 p. 21cm.
Signatures: 4°: ∏1, A-G⁴, H¹.
Black letter.
NIC   (Continued on next card)

Witchcraft
BF 1410 B42 Z69 no.10
[Hooght, Everard van der] d. 1716. Sevende briev van ... 1692. (Card 4)
Van der Linde 104.
No. 10 in a collection of tracts against Balthasar Bekker and his Betoverde weereld.

1. Language and languages. 2. Devil. 3. Bekker, Balthasar, 1634-1698. I. Title.
NIC

BF 1713 P68 1972
A seventeenth-century exposure of superstition.
Pithois, Claude, 1587-1676.
A seventeenth-century exposure of superstition: select texts of Claude Pithoys (1587-1676). Introd. and notes by P.J.S. Whitmore. The Hague, Nijhoff, 1972.
xliv, 263 p. 24cm. (International archives of the history of ideas, 49)

English, French or Latin.
Bibliography: p. [ix]-x, [248]-249.

1. Astrology. 2. Witchcraft. 3. Superstition. I. Whitmore, P J S II. Title. III. Series.
NIC

Witchcraft
GR 142 H6 A3 no.2
The severall practices of Johane Harrison and her daughter, condemned and executed at Hartford for witchcraft, the 4th August last, 1606. Reprinted from the only known copy, with an introduction by W. B. Gerish. [Bishop's Stortford?] 1909.
15 p. 22cm. (Hertfordshire folk lore. no. 2)
The original pamphlet is in 2 parts and is entitled: The most cruell and bloody murther committed by ... Annis Dell ... With the severall witchcrafts and most damnable practises of one Johane Harrison and her daughter ... London, Printed for W. Ferebrand and J. Wright, 1606.
1. Witchcraft—England. 2. Harrison, Johanna, d. 1606. 3. Harrison, Anne, d. 1606. I. Gerish, William Blyth, ed. II. Title: The most cruell and bloody murther committed by ... Annis Dell.
16-25735
Library of Congress   GR142.H6A3 no. 6

BF 1572 S4 P14
Sex in witchcraft.
Paine, Lauran.
Sex in witchcraft. New York, Taplinger Pub. Co. [1972]
186 p. illus. 22 cm. $8.50
Bibliography: p. [182]-183.

1. Witchcraft and sex. I. Title.
BF1572.S4P3 1972   133.4   72-76258 MARC
ISBN 0-8008-7151-0
Library of Congress   72 [4]

Witchcraft
BF 1581 S52 1913
Seymour, St. John Drelincourt.
Irish witchcraft and demonology. Baltimore, Norman, Remington & Co., 1913.
vii, 255 p. 21cm.

1. Witchcraft—Ireland. 2. Demonology. I. Title.

CATALOGUE OF THE CORNELL WITCHCRAFT COLLECTION

```
                    Shadwell, Thomas, 1642?-1692.
Witchcraft         The Lancashire witches and Tegue o
PR         Divelly.
1259       Heywood, Thomas, d. 1641.
W81            The poetry of witchcraft illustrated by
H62+       copies of the plays on the Lancashire witches
           by Heywood and Shadwell. Reprinted under the
           direction of James O. Halliwell.  Brixton
           Hill, Printed for priv. circ. only, 1853.
                238 p.  29cm.

                Eighty copies printed.
                Each play has also separate t.p.

                              (Continued on next card)
```

```
                    Shadwell, Thomas, 1642?-1692.
Witchcraft         The Lancashire witches and Tegue o
PR         Heywood, Thomas, d. 1641.   The poetry of
1259          witchcraft... 1853.    (Card 2)
W81
H62+         Contents.--The Lancashire witches and
           Tegue o Divelly, the Irish priest, by Thomas
           Shadwell.--The late Lancashire witches, by
           Thomas Heywood and Richard Broome.
             I. Halliwell-Phillipps, James Orchard, 1820
           -1889. II. Shadwell, Thomas, 1642?-1692. The
           Lancashire witches and Tegue o Divelly. III.
           His  The late Lancashire witches. IV. Broome
           Richard, d. 1622? The late Lancashire witches
           V. Title.
```

```
              The share of Thomas Aquinas in the growth of
                      the witchcraft delusion.
ar W     Hopkin, Charles Edward, 1900-
52854       ... The share of Thomas Aquinas in the witch-
no.2     craft delusion ... ₁by₁ Charles Edward Hopkin. Philadelphia.
         1940.
              viii, 27 p., 1 l., 29-127 p., 1 l., 129-188 p.  23cm.
              Thesis (PH. D.)—University of Pennsylvania, 1940.
              CONTENTS.—Introduction.—pt. I. The demonology of Thomas Aqui-
         nas.—pt. II. Thomas Aquinas as mediator between earlier and later be-
         liefs.—Conclusion.—Bibliography (p. 185-188)
              No. 2 in vol. lettered: Pennsylvania dissertations
              1. Thomas Aquinas, Saint, 1225?-1274.  2. Witchcraft.  3. Demonology.
              I. Title.
              Library of Congress        B765.T54H6 1940
                Univ. of Pennsylvania                Libr.
                    Copy 2.
              Copyright     A 146856    ₁41c2₁         189.4        41—2305
```

```
Witchcraft         Sharp, Granville, 1735-1813.
BF            The case of Saul, shewing that his disorder
1555       was a real spiritual possession, and proving
S53        (by the learned researches and labours of a
1807       strenuous promoter even of the contrary doc-
           trine( that actual possessions of spirits were
           generally acknowledged by the ancient writers
           among the heathens as well as among the Jews
           and Christians. ... To which is added a short
           tract, wherein the influence of demons are fur-
           ther illustrated by Remarks on 1. Timothy iv,
           1-3.  London,       Printed by W. Calvert for
           Vernor and          Hood, 1807.
                              (Continued on next card)
```

```
Witchcraft
BF         Sharp, Granville, 1735-1813. The case of Saul
1555          ... 1807.  (Card 2)
S53
1807           187, xv p.  19cm.

                The "Remarks on 1. Timothy ..." has separ-
           ate t.p.

                I. His  Remarks on 1. Timothy IV, 1-3.
           II. Title.
```

```
                    Sharp, Granville, 1735-1813.
Witchcraft         Remarks on 1. Timothy IV, 1-3.
BF         Sharp, Granville, 1735-1813.
1555          The case of Saul, shewing that his disorder
S53        was a real spiritual possession, and proving (by
1807       the learned researches and labours of a strenuous
           promoter even of the contrary doctrine (that
           actual possessions of spirits were generally
           acknowledged by the ancient writers among the
           heathens as well as among the Jews and
           Christians. ... To which is added a short tract,
           wherein the influence of demons are further
           illustrated by Remarks on 1. Timothy iv, 1-3.
           London, Printed by W. Calvert for Vernor and
           Hood, 1807.
           187, xv p.  19 cm.
           t.p. The "Remarks on 1. Timothy ..." has separate
```

```
Witchcraft
BF         Sharpe, Charles Kirkpatrick, 1781?-1851.
1581          A historical account of the belief
S53        in witchcraft in Scotland.  London,
           Hamilton, Adams & Co.; Glasgow, Thomas D.
           Morison, 1884.
                268 p.  20cm.

                Originally published in 1819 as an
           introduction to Robert Law's "Memorialls".

           1. Witchcraft--Scotland.   I. Title.
```

```
Witchcraft
BS         ₁Sharpe, Gregory₁ 1713-1771.
2545          A review of the controversy about the mean-
D5         ing of demoniacks in the New-Testament. In
T775       which Mr. Hutchinson's sermon at Oxford ...,
no.3       the Reply to the Further enquiry, Mr. Twell's
           Answer to the Further enquiry, and a tract, en-
           titled, Some thoughts on the miracles of Jesus,
           by an impartial hand, are considered.  By a
           lover of truth. ...  London, Printed for J.
           Roberts, 1739.
                80 p.  20cm.
                No. 3 in vol.        lettered: Tracts on de-
           moniacks. 1737.
                                                  (Over)
```

```
Witchcraft
BS         ₁Sharpe, Gregory₁ 1713-1771.
2545          A review of the controversy about the
D5         meaning of demoniacks in the New-Testament.
T97        In which Mr. Hutchinson's sermon at Oxford
no.7       ..., the Reply to the Further enquiry, Mr.
           Twell's Answer to the Further enquiry, and
           a tract, entitled, Some thoughts on the
           miracles of Jesus, by an impartial hand, are
           consider'd.  By a lover of truth ...  London,
           Printed for J. Roberts, 1739.
                80 p.  21cm.

                              (Continued on next card)
```

```
Witchcraft
BS         ₁Sharpe, Gregory₁ 1713-1771.  A review of
2545       the controversy about the meaning of
D5         demoniacks in the New-Testament ...
T97        1739.                (Card 2)
no.7
                No. 7 in vol. lettered: Twells, Whiston,
           etc. Tracts on the demoniacs in the New
           Testament.  London, 1738-1775.

           1. Demoniac possession.  2. Bible.
           N.T.--Commen       taries.  I. Title.
```

```
                    Sharpe, Gregory, 1713-1771.
                      A review of the controversy about the
Witchcraft         meaning of demoniacks in the New Testament.
BS         Hutchinson, Thomas, 1698-1769.
2545          Remarks upon a pamphlet intit'l'd, A
D5         review of the controversy about the meaning
T97        of demoniacs, &c.  Wherein the sermon which
no.8       asserteth the usual interpretation, &c., is
           vindicated from every exception of the
           reviewer.  London, Printed for W. Innys
           and R. Manby, 1739.
                31 p.  21cm.

                No. 8 in           vol. lettered: Twells,
                              (Continued on next card)
```

```
                    Sharpe, Gregory, 1713-1771.
                      A review of the controversy about the
Witchcraft         meaning of demoniacks in the New Testament
BS         Hutchinson, Thomas, 1698-1769.   Remarks
2545       upon a pamphlet intit'l'd, A review of the
D5         controversy ... 1739.   (Card 2)
T97
no.8       Whiston, etc. Tracts on the demoniacs in
           the New Testament.  London, 1738-1775.

                1. Sharpe, Gregory, 1713-1771. A review
           of the controversy about the meaning of
           demoniacks in the New Testament.  2.
           Hutchinson, Th    omas, 1698-1769. The
           usual interpr    etation. I. Title.
```

```
              Shaw, Christian, fl. 1697.
Witchcraft
BF         A Narrative of the sufferings and relief of a
1581       young girl ₁Christian Shaw₁ strangely mo-
Z7         lested by evil spirits and their instruments
1775       in the West; collected from authentic testi-
           monies, with a preface and postscript. Con-
           taining reflections on what is most material
           or curious, either in the history or trial
           of the seven witches who were condemned and
           burnt in the Gallow-Green of Paisley ...
           Paisley, Printed and sold by A. Weir, 1775.
                120 p.  17cm.

                1. Shaw, Chri     stian, fl. 1697. 2. Demoniac
           possession.         3. Witchcraft.
```

```
              Shaw, Christian, fl. 1697.
Witchcraft
BF         Sadducismus debellatus; or, A true narra-
1581       tive of the sorceries and witchcrafts
Z7         exercis'd by the Devil and his instru-
1697a      ments upon Mrs. Christian Shaw, daughter
           of Mr. John Shaw, of Bargarran in the
           County of Renfrew in the west of Scot-
           land, from Aug. 1696 to Apr. 1697. Con-
           taining the journal of her sufferings ...
           Together with reflexions upon witchcraft
           in general, and the learned arguments
           of the lawyers, on both sides, at the

        8                      (Continued on next card)
```

```
              Shaw, Christian, fl. 1697.
Witchcraft
BF         Sadducismus debellatus ...  1698.  (Card 2)
1581
Z7              trial of seven of those witches, who
1697a      were condemned: and some passages which
           happened at their execution ...  Lon-
           don, Printed for H. Newman and A. Bell,
           1698.
                4 p. l., 60 p.  22cm.

                1. Shaw, Christian, fl. 1697.  2.
           Witchcraft--Scotland.

        8
```

```
              Shaw, Elinor, d. 1705.
Witchcraft
BF         ₁Davis, Ralph₁
1581          An account of the tryals, examination
A2         and condemnation, of Elinor Shaw and Mary
W81        Phillip's (two notorious witches,) at North-
1866a      ampton assizes, on Wednesday the 7th of
no.2       March 1705. ...  London, Printed for F.
           Thorn ₁1705₁  ₁Northampton, Taylor, 1866₁
                8 p.  22cm.
                No. 2 in box lettered Witchcraft in
           Northamptonshire.
                1. Trials     (Witchcraft)--Northam
        8  tonshire, En      gland.  I. Title.
```

```
              Shaw, Elinor, d. 1705.
Witchcraft
BF         ₁Davis, Ralph₁
1581          The Northamptonshire witches. Being a
A2         true and faithful account of the births,
W81        educations, lives, and conversations, of
1866a      Elinor Shaw, and Mary Phillips, (the two
no.3       notorious witches) that were executed at
           Northampton on Saturday, March the 17th,
           1705, for bewitching a woman and two child-
           ren to death. ...  London, Printed for
           F. Thorn ₁1705₁  ₁Northampton, Taylor, 1866₁
                8 p.  22cm.

        8                      (Continued on next card)
```

```
              Shaw, Elinor, d. 1705.
Witchcraft
BF         ₁Davis, Ralph₁ The Northamptonshire
1581          witches ...  ₁1866₁     (Card 2)
A2
W81             No. 3 in box lettered Witchcraft in
1866a      Northamptonshire.
no.3
                1. Witchcraft--Northamptonshire, Eng-
           land.  I. Title.

        8
```

506

CATALOGUE OF THE CORNELL WITCHCRAFT COLLECTION

ITCHCRAFT
F
578
55
2
894
　　Sherwood, Grace, defendant.
　　　Grace Sherwood, the Virginia witch. Communicated by Edward W. James.
　　　(In: William and Mary college quarterly historical magazine. Williamsburg, Va. 25cm. v.3, no.2, Oct. 1894, p. 96-101; v.3, no.3, Jan. 1895, p. 190-192)

　　　Witchcraft Collection has only the first two of five articles. Cornell University Library has complete file of
(Continued on next card)

ITCHCRAFT
F
578
55
2
894
　　Sherwood, Grace, defendant. Grace Sherwood, the Virginia witch. 1894-1895. (Card 2)

the periodical (F221 W71)
　　Contains court records of prosecutions of Grace Sherwood for witchcraft, in Princess Anne County, Virginia.
　　1. Witchcraft--Princess Anne Co., Virginia. 2. Trials (Witchcraft)--Princess Anne Co., Virginia.　I. James, Edward Wilson, d.1906, ed. II. Title.

　　Sherwood, Grace, defendant.
　　　Record of Grace Sherwood's trial for witchcraft, in 1705, in Princess Anne County, Virginia. Presented by President Cushing, to the Virginia Historical and Philosophical Society on the 4th of February, 1833.
　　　(In Virginia Historical Society. Collections. Richmond, 1833. 24cm. v. 1, p. [69]-78)

I. Title.

WITCHCRAFT
BF
1578
S55
A2
1900
　　Sherwood, Grace, defendant.
　　　The story of Grace Sherwood. [n.p., ca. 1900?]
　　　12 p. 25cm.

　　Detached from unidentified periodical.
　　Contains court records of prosecutions of Grace Sherwood for witchcraft, in Princess Anne County, Virginia.
　　1. Witchcraft--Princess Anne Co., Virginia. 2. Trials (Witchcraft)--Princess Anne Co., Virginia.　I. Title.

tchcraft
BF
815
55
H43
710
　　Shipton, Ursula.
　　　[Head, Richard] 1637?-1686?
　　　The history of Mother Shipton: containing an account of her strange and unnatural conception, her birth, life, actions and death: the correspondence she held with the devil, and the many strange and wonderful things perform'd by her. Together with all the predictions and prophecies that have been made by her, and since fulfilled, from the reign of King Henry the Seventh, to the third year of our Sovereign Lady Queen Anne ... London, Printed by and for W. Onley [ca. 1710]
(Continued on next card)

craft
F
815
55
43
710
　　Shipton, Ursula.
　　　[Head, Richard] 1637?-1686? The history of Mother Shipton ... [ca. 1710] (Card 2)

24 p. 21cm.

Title vignette (woodcut)
For authorship cf. Halkett & Laing. Dict. of anonymous and pseudonymous English lit., v. 3, p. 72.
First published 1684 (or 1677) under title: The life and death of Mother Shipton.
1. Shipton, Ursula. 2. Prophecies. I. Title. II. His　The life and death of Mother Shipton.

Witchcraft
BF
1815
S55
H43
1687
　　Shipton, Ursula.
　　　[Head, Richard] 1637?-1686?
　　　The life and death of Mother Shipton. Being not only a true account of her strange birth, the most important passages of her life, but also all her prophesies ... until this present year 1667. Containing the most important passages of state during the reigns of these kings and queens of England following: ... London, W. Harris, 1687.
　　　30 p. front. 23cm.

　　1. Shipton, Ursula. 2. Prophecies. I. Title.

A short and true account of the Inquisition and its proceeding.

RARE
BX
1723
P58
1722
　　Piazza, Girolamo Bartolomeo.
　　　A short and true account of the Inquisition and its proceeding, as it is practis'd in Italy, set forth in some particular cases. Whereunto is added, An extract out of an authentick book of legends of the Roman Church. London, W. Bowyer, 1722.
　　　189 p. 21cm.

English and French; added t.p. in French.
　　1. Inquisition--Italy. I. Title.

Witchcraft
BX
1711
C26
　　A short history of the inquisition.
　　Cardew, Sir Alexander Gordon, 1861-
　　　A short history of the inquisition, by Sir Alexander G. Cardew ... London, Watts & co. [1933]
　　　viii, 115 p. 19cm.

"Mainly based on the exhaustive works of ... Dr. Henry Charles Lea—namely, Superstition and force, A history of the inquisition in the middle ages, and A history of the inquisition in Spain."—Pref.
"First published April, 1933."

1. Inquisition—Hist.　I. Lea, Henry Charles, 1825-1909.　II. Title.

Library of Congress　　BX1711.C3　　34-7592
　　　　　　　　　　　　　[3]　　　　272.2

Witchcraft
BF
1576
P45
　　Short history of the Salem village witchcraft trials.
　　Perley, Martin Van Buren, 1835-
　　　A short history of the Salem village witchcraft trials, illustrated by a verbatim report of the trial of Mrs. Elizabeth Howe; a memorial of her ... Map and half tone illustrations. [Souvenir ed.] Salem, Mass., M. V. B. Perley, 1911.
　　　76 p. front., illus. (incl. map) 3 pl., ports., facsim. 19½cm.　$0.75

1. Witchcraft—Salem, Mass.　I. Title.

Library of Congress　　BF1576.P5　　11-20600
─── ─── Copy 2.
Copyright A 295170

Witchcraft
GR
142
H6
A3
no.10
　　A short rehearsal of the sad condition of three of the children of John Baldwin of Sarret in the county of Hertford, and also the manner of their deliverance, 1717. The parents' evidence together with a summary of the testimonies of the children and friends and a brief introductory note by W. B. Gerish. Bishops' Stortford, 1915.
　　　19 p. 21¾cm. [Hertfordshire folk lore. no. 10]

1. Baldwin, Rebecca, 1688-1713.　2. Baldwin, Mary, b. 1690.　3. Essex, Mrs. Anne (Baldwin) b. 1686.　I. Gerish, William Blyth, ed.
　　　　　　　　　　　　　　　　　　　　　　　　　　　16-25743
Library of Congress　　GR142.H6A3 no. 17

Rare
Z
6878
P8
P94
　　Short-title catalogue of works on psychical research, spiritualism, magic, psychology ...
　　Price, Harry, 1881-1948, compiler.
　　　Short-title catalogue of works on psychical research, spiritualism, magic, psychology, legerdemain and other methods of deception, charlatanism, witchcraft, and technical works for the scientific investigation of alleged abnormal phenomena, from circa 1450 A. D. to 1929 A. D.
　　　(In National Laboratory of Psychical Research, London. Proceedings. London. 25cm. v. 1 (　　　1929) pt. 2, p. 67-422)
(over)

Witchcraft
BF
1563
W81++
no.4
　　A short treatise declaringe the detestable wickednesse of magicall sciences.
　　Coxe, Francis.
　　　A short treatise declaringe the detestable wickednesse of magicall sciences, as necromancie, coniurations of spirites, curiouse astrologie and such lyke ... [London, 1561. London, at the British Museum, 1923]
　　　[30] p. 14cm.
　　　Signatures: A⁸, B⁷.
　　　Photocopy (negative) 30 p. on 15 l. 20 x 32cm.
　　　No. 4 in vol. lettered: Witchcraft tracts, chapbooks and　　broadsides, 1579-1704; [p]hotograph copies.
　　I. Title.

Witchcraft
BF
1581
Z7
1664b
　　A short treatise touching sheriffs accompts.
　　Hale, Sir Matthew, 1609-1676.
　　　A short treatise touching sheriffs accompts. Written by the Honourable Sir Matthew Hale, kt. ... To which is added, A tryal of witches, at the assizes held at Bury St. Edmonds, for the county of Suffolk, on the 10th of March 1664, before the said Sir Matthew Hale, kt. London, Printed, and are to be sold by Will. Shrowsbery, 1683.
　　　4 p. l., 110 p., 2 l., 59 p. 19cm.
　　　Signatures: A⁴, B-H⁸ (last leaf blank) 2 leaves unsigned, B-D⁸, E⁶.
(Continued on next card)

Witchcraft
BF
1581
Z7
1664b
　　Hale, Sir Matthew, 1609-1676. A short treatise touching sheriffs accompts. 1683. (Card 2)

　　"A tryal of witches, at the assizes held at Bury St. Edmonds ... London, Printed for William Shrewsbery, 1682" (with special t.-p.): 2 l., 59 p. at end.
　　Wing H 260.

Witchcraft
HV
8593
N63
1681
　　Si la torture est un moyen seur a verifier les crimes secrets.
　　Nicolas, Augustin, 1622-1695.
　　　Si la torture est un moyen seur a verifier les crimes secrets; dissertation morale et juridique, par laquelle il est amplement traicté des abus qui se commettent par tout en l'instruction des procés criminels, & particulierement en la recherche du sortilege ... Par Mre. Augustin Nicolas ... A Amsterdam, Chez A. Wolfgang, 1681.
　　　224, [8] p. 16cm.

1. Torture. 2. Witchcraft.　I. Title.
　　　　　　　　　　　　　　　　　　　　　　　13-26318
Library of Congress　　HV8593.N5

WITCHCRAFT
BT
960
S56
1521
　　Sibylla, Bartholomaeus.
　　　Speculuȝ pegrinaȝ qōnuȝ eruditissimi viri Bartholomei Sybille Monopolitāi ... Tres decades cōplectēs: in ḡbus varie ǭones de aiab' rōnalib'ı ȝiūcro: τ separatȝ. Deqȝ angelis bōis τ malis multisqȝ alijs scitu dignissimis: τ ad ipsas rñsiones ponūtur. Ex ... theologoȝ: jurispōtificū: phōȝ ac astrologoȝū ... [Lugduni, Impressuȝ in edib' Iacobi Myt., 1521]
　　　ccxxviiȷ numb. l. 16cm.
8
(Continued on next card)

WITCHCRAFT
BT
960
S56
1521
　　Sibylla, Bartholomaeus. Speculuȝ pegrinaȝ qōnuȝ ... [1521]　　　(Card 2)

Title in red, in black ornamental woodcut border.

1. Future life. 2. Angels. 3. Demonology. 4. Man (Theology)　I. Title: Speculum peregrinarum questionum.
8

CATALOGUE OF THE CORNELL WITCHCRAFT COLLECTION

Sibylle, Bartholomaeus.

see

Sibylla, Bartholomaeus.

Sidonia, the sorceress.

Witchcraft
PT 2430 M35 S5 1894
Meinhold, Wilhelm, 1797-1851. Sidonia, the sorceress... 1894. (Card 2)

"Mary Schweidler" translated by Lady Duff Gordon.

1. Witchcraft--Pomerania. I. Meinhold, Wilhelm, 1797-1851. Sidonia von Bork, die Klosterhexe--English. II. Meinhold, Wilhelm, 1797-1851. Maria Schweidler, die Bernsteinhexe--English. III. Wilde, Jane Francesca (Elgee) lady, 1826-1896, tr. IV. Duff-Gordon, Lucie (Austin) lady, 1821-1869, tr. V. Title. Sidonia, the sorceress. VI. Title: Mary Schweidler, the amber witch.

Witchcraft
Z 6880 Z9 S57
Siegismund, Karl, bookseller, Berlin.
Siegismund's vademecum der gesammten Litteratur über Occultismus. Alphabetische und systematische Zusammenstellung der litterarischen Erscheinungen in deutscher Sprache auf dem Gebiete der Mystik, Magie, des thierischen Magnetismus [u. s. w.] von 1800 bis Anfang 1888. Berlin, 1888.

112 p. 22cm.

1. Occult sciences--Bibl.--Catalogs. I. Ti tle.

8

Die sichtbare und die unsichtbare Welt, diesseits und jenseits.

BF 1413 P45
Perty, Maximilian, 1804-1884.
Die sichtbare und die unsichtbare Welt, diesseits und jenseits. Leipzig, C. J. Winter, 1881.

320 p. 23cm.

1. Occult sciences. 2. Witchcraft.

Sidonia von Bork, die Klosterhexe.

Witchcraft
PT 2430 M35 S5 1847
Meinhold, Wilhelm, 1797-1851.
Sidonia von Bork, die Klosterhexe, angebliche Vertilgerin des gesammten herzoglich-pommerschen Regentenhauses ... Leipzig, J. J. Weber, 1847-48 [v. 1, 1848]

3 v. fronts. 17cm. (His Gesammelte Schriften, Bd. 5-7)

Siegismund's vademecum der gesammten Litteratur über Occultismus.

Witchcraft
Z 6880 Z9 S57
Siegismund, Karl, bookseller, Berlin.
Siegismund's vademecum der gesammten Litteratur über Occultismus. Alphabetische und systematische Zusammenstellung der litterarischen Erscheinungen in deutscher Sprache auf dem Gebiete der Mystik, Magie, des thierischen Magnetismus [u. s. w.] von 1800 bis Anfang 1888. Berlin, 1888.

112 p. 22cm.

1. Occult sciences--Bibl.--Catalogs. I. Ti tle.

8

Side-lights on the Stuarts.

DA 375 I38 1891
Inderwick, F[rederick] A[ndrew]
Side-lights on the Stuarts; by F. A. Inderwick ... 2d ed. London, S. Low, Marston, Searle & Rivington, 1891.

4 p.l., 434 p., 1 l. 4 pl. (incl. col. front.) 7 port., 6 facsim. 22cm.

1. Gt. Brit.--Hist.--Stuarts, 1603-1714. I. Title.

Den sidste hexebraending i Danmark 1693.

BF 1584 D4 J171
Jacobsen, Jørgen Carl, 1916-
Den sidste Hexebraending i Danmark 1693. [Af] J. C. Jacobsen. København, Gad, 1971.

xi, 110 p. 25cm.

WITCHCRAFT
BF 1408 S57
Sierke, Eugen, 1845-
Schwärmer und Schwindler zu Ende des achtzehnten Jahrhunderts. Leipzig, S. Hirzel, 1874.

vi, 462 p. 21cm.

1. Occult sciences--Biography. 2. Superstition. 3. Swedenborg, Emanuel, 1688-1772. 4. Mesmer, Franz Anton, 1734-1815. 5. Gassner, Johann Joseph, 1727-1779. 6. Schrepfer, Johann Georg, 1730?-1774. 7. Cagliostro, Alessandro, conte de, assumed name of Giuseppe Balsamo, 1743-1795. I. Title.

8 NIC

Sidonia, Herzogin zu Braunschweig-Lüneburg.

WITCHCRAFT
DD 491 H2 H67 1842
Havemann, Wilhelm, 1800-1869.
Sidonia, Herzogin zu Braunschweig-Lüneburg, geborene Herzogin von Sachsen.
(In: Historischer Verein für Niedersachsen Zeitschrift [under earlier title, Vaterländisches Archiv] Hannover. 19cm. 1842. p. 278-303)

1. Braunschweig-und-Lüneburg, Sidonia, Herzogin zu. 2. Braunschweig-und-Lüneburg, Erich II, Herzog zu.

8 NIC

Siebdrat, Gustav Albert.
Ein sächsischer Hexenprozess aus dem 17. Jahrhundert.

Witchcraft
BF 1583 Z7 1749b
Anna Renata Singer v. Mossau, die letzte deutsche Hexe. Ein Geschichtsbild, dargestellt zur Erinnerung an den nunmehr hundertjährigen Niedergang eines langen und grauenvollen Irrwahns und an die Befreiung von dem Schmach wälscher Inquisition in Deutschland. Nebst einem Abriss der Geschichte des Hexenprocesse im Allgemeinen und beiliegenden Actenstücken sowie einem sächsischen Hexenprocesse aus dem siebzehnten Jahrhun-

3 (Continued on next card)

Siewerten, defendant.

WITCHCRAFT
AP 30 N4852 v.10
Ein merkwürdiger Hexenprozess.
(In: Neue gemeinnützige Blätter. Halberstadt. 16cm. v.10 (1800) p. [529]-540)

Signed: Lucanus.
Concerning the trial for witchcraft of a widow Siewerten, in 1577.

1. Trials (Witchcraft)--Halberstadt. 2. Siewerten, defendant. I. Lucanus, pseud.

8 NIC

Siebdrat, Gustav Albert.
Ein sächsischer Hexenprozess aus dem 17. Jahrhundert.

Witchcraft
BF 1583 Z7 1749b
Anna Renata Singer v. Mossau ... 1849. (Card 2)

dert. [Leipzig, Bei F. Serig] 1849. 142 p. 22cm.

"Kurzer Abriss der Geschichte des Hexentums" and the four Beilagen each have special t. p.
Includes Rede am Scheiterhaufen, von G. Gaar, and Ein sächsischer Hexenprozess, von G. A. Siebdrat.

8 (Continued on next card)

Witchcraft
BF 1563 W81++ no.14
Signes and wonders from heaven. With a true relation of a monster borne in Ratcliffe Highway ... Also shewing how a cat kitned a monster in ... London... With divers other strange remarkable passages. London, Printed by I. H. [1645. London, at the British Museum, 1923]

5 p. 16cm.

Photocopy (negative) 5 p. on 4 l. 20 x 32cm.

(Continued on next card)

BF 1583 S57
Siebel, Friedrich Wilhelm, 1932-
Die Hexenverfolgung in Köln. Bonn, 1959.

198 p. 21cm.

Diss.--Bonn.

1. Witchcraft--Cologne. I. Title.

Witchcraft
BF 1563 W81++ no.14
Signes and wonders from heaven... [1923] (Card 2)

No. 14 in vol. lettered: Witchcraft tracts, chapbooks and broadsides, 1579-1704; rotograph copies.

1. Omens. 2. Witchcraft--England.

CATALOGUE OF THE CORNELL WITCHCRAFT COLLECTION

La signora di Monzi e le streghe del Tirolo.

WITCHCRAFT

34
7
Dandolo, Tullio, conte, 1801-1870.
La signora di Monzi e le streghe del Tirolo, processi famosi del secolo decimo-settimo per la prima volta cavati dalle filze originali. Milano, E. Besozzi, 1855.
259 p. port., facsims. 23cm.

1. Witchcraft--Tyrol. 2. Leyva, Marianna de, known as Signora di Monza, 1575-1650. 3. Manzoni, Alessandro, 1785-1873. I promessi sposi. I. Title.

Silbernagl, Isidor, 1831-1904.
Johannes Trithemius; eine Monographie. Landshut, Krüll, 1868.
245 p. 22cm.

1. Trithemius, Johannes, 1462-1516.
I. Title.

Sillieux, Sulpice, fl. 1675.

tchcraft

82
75
Hautefeuille, lawyer.
Plaidoyez svr les magiciens et svr les sorciers, tenus en la cour de Liege, le 16. Decembre 1675. Ov on montre clairement qu'il n'y peut avoir de ces sortes de gens. Par les sieurs de Havte Feville & Santevr advocats. Sur l'imprimé a Liege, Chez Iacqves Persois imprimeur, 1676.
120 p. 14cm.
"Le livre d'Albert le Grand, leqvel traite des merveilles du monde," p. [77]-

(Continued on next card)

Sillieux, Sulpice, fl. 1675.

tchcraft

82
75
Hautefeuille, lawyer. Plaidoyez svr les magiciens ... 1676. (Card 2)

120, has special t. p. with imprint: Lyon, Par Iean Hvgvetan, 1616. Text is taken from Les admirables secrets d'Albert le Grand.
1. Witchcraft. 2. Magic. 3. Sillieux, Sulpice, fl. 1675. I. Santeur, lawyer. II. Albertus Magnus, saint, bp. of Ratisbon, 1193?-1280. Spurious and doubtful works. Les admirables secrets d'Albert le Grand. III. Title: Plaidoyez sur les magiciens. IV. Title: Le livre d'Albert le Grand.

Silver, Richard, d. 1568.

see

Argentine, Richard, d. 1568.

Silvester de Prierio, 1456-1527.

see

Mazzolini, Silvestro, da Prierio, 1456-1523.

Witchcraft

BX
9479
B42
B11
no.6
[Silvius, J]
Consideratien over het boek van de Heer Doctor Balthasar Bekker, genaamt De betoverde weereld, voorgestelt door J. S. Amsterdam, By G. Borstius, boekverkoper, 1691.
20 p. title vignette, illus. initials. 20 x 15cm.
4°: π1, A-B⁴, C1.
Black letter (except for introduction)
Ascribed to J. Silvius by Doorninck.
Variant of van der Linde 149:

8

(Continued on next card)

Witchcraft

BX
9479
B42
B11
no.6
[Silvius, J] Consideratien over het boek van de Heer Doctor Balthasar Bekker ... 1691. (Card 2)

only 20, instead of 22 p.
No. 6 in vol. lettered B. Bekkers sterfbed en andere tractaten.

1. Bekker, Balthasar, 1634-1698. De betoverde weereld. I. Title. II. J. S. III. S., J.

Simia Dei, Gottes Affe.

WITCHCRAFT

BF
1584
S9
S61
Sincerus, Theophilus, pseud.
Nord-schwedische Hexerey, oder Simia Dei, Gottes Affe. Das ist: Ausführliche Beschreibung der schändlichen Verführungen des leidigen Satans, darinnen zu sehen Gottes erschröckliches Straff-Verhängen, wegen greulicher Sünden-Mengen. In einem Jammer-behertzigten Send-Schreiben am [sic] Tag gegeben, von Theophilo Sincero, an Christianum Piandrum. [Augsburg?] 1677.
[64] p. illus. 20cm.

8
NIC

(Continued on next card)

Simia Dei, Gottes Affe.

WITCHCRAFT

BF
1584
S9
S61
Sincerus, Theophilus, pseud. Nord-schwedische Hexerey ... 1677. (Card 2)

"By Gottlieb Spitzel? See what Hauber says of the relation of this tract to his [i.e., Spitzel's] Die gebrochene Macht der Finsterniss. G. L. B."--Note in MS facing t. p.
Illustrative vignette on t. p.
1. Witchcraft--Sweden. 2. Witchcraft.
I. Spitzel, Gottlieb, 1639-1691, supposed author. II. Title. III. Title: Simia Dei, Gottes Affe.

8
NIC

WITCHCRAFT

BF
1565
S59
[Simon, Jordan] pater, 1719-1776.
Das grosse Welt-betrügende Nichts; oder, Die heutige Hexerey und Zauberkunst in zweyen Büchern, von Ardoino Ubbidente dell'Osa [pseud.] entworfen ... Wirtzburg, J. J. Stahel, 1761.
4 p. l., 600 p. 17cm.
Second edition published under title: Die Nichtigkeit der Hexerey und Zauberkunst. (cf. Kayser)

8
NIC
Contents.-- 1. Th. Die Gründe und

(Continued on next card)

WITCHCRAFT

BF
1565
S59
[Simon, Jordan] pater, 1719-1776. Das grosse Welt-betrügende Nichts ... 1761. (Card 2)

Beweisthümer aus der Göttlichen Schrift ... dass die heutige Hexerey oder Zauberkunst ein leeres Nichts seye.--2. Th. Die Widerlegung der aus der Göttlichen Schrift gezogenen Beweis-Gründen, dass es Hexerey oder Zauberkunst gebe.
1. Witchcraft. 2. Witchcraft in the Bible. 3. Superstition. I. Title. II. Title: Die heutige Hexerey und Zauberkunst.

8
NIC

Witchcraft

BF
1445
S595
[Simon, Jordan] pater, 1719-1776.
Nicht doch --, oder, Auflösung der kleinen Zweifel über zwey Berichte von einer Hexen- oder Studenten-Geschichte die sich in dem Jahre 1768. den 10. 11. 12. und 13. Junius zu Ingolstadt in Bayern soll zugetragen haben. Aus einem dritten Berichte des Herrn Directors gezogen. Gedruckt zu Berichtshausen, Mit klaren Schriften [i.e., Leipzig? 1769?]
27 p. 21cm.

8

(Continued on next card)

Witchcraft

BF
1445
S595
[Simon, Jordan] pater, 1719-1776. Nicht doch -- ... [1769?] (Card 2)

Attribution by Holzmann.
Continuation of his Nun, ja --. [Leipzig, 1769], with which this is bound.

1. Ghosts. 2. Witchcraft--Ingolstadt, Bavaria. I. His Nun, ja --. II. Title. III. Title: Auflösung der kleinen Zweifel über zwey Berichte von einer Hexen- oder Studenten-Geschichte.

8

Simon, Jordan, pater, 1719-1776.
Nicht doch --.

Witchcraft

BF
1445
S595
[Simon, Jordan] pater, 1719-1776.
Nun, ja -- oder, Kleine Zweifeln über zwey Berichte von einer Hexen- oder Studenten-Geschichte die sich in dem Jahre 1768. den 10. 11. 12. und 13. Junius zu Ingolstadt in Bayern soll zugetragen haben. Gedruckt zu Unglauben, Mit der Akademicker Schriften [i. e., Leipzig, 1769]
31 p. 21cm.
Attribution by Holzmann; imprint from Kayser.

8

(Continued on next card)

Simon, Jordan, pater, 1719-1776.
Nicht doch --.

Witchcraft

BF
1445
S595
[Simon, Jordan] pater, 1719-1776. Nun, ja -- [1769] (Card 2)

The "Berichte" are given, p. 3-11.
Continued by Nicht doch -- oder, Auflösung der kleinen Zweifel über zwei Berichte. With this is bound his Nicht doch. [Leipzig? 1769?]
1. Ghosts. 2. Witchcraft--Ingolstadt, Bavaria. I. Title. II. Title: Kleine Zweifeln über zwey Berichte von einer Hexen- oder Studenten-Geschichte.

Witchcraft

BF
1445
S595
[Simon, Jordan] pater, 1719-1776.
Nun, ja -- oder, Kleine Zweifeln über zwey Berichte von einer Hexen- oder Studenten-Geschichte die sich in dem Jahre 1768. den 10. 11. 12. und 13. Junius zu Ingolstadt in Bayern soll zugetragen haben. Gedruckt zu Unglauben, Mit der Akademicker Schriften [i. e., Leipzig, 1769]
31 p. 21cm.
Attribution by Holzmann; imprint from Kayser.

8

(Continued on next card)

Witchcraft

BF
1445
S595
[Simon, Jordan] pater, 1719-1776. Nun, ja -- [1769] (Card 2)

The "Berichte" are given, p. 3-11.
Continued by Nicht doch -- oder, Auflösung der kleinen Zweifel über zwei Berichte. With this is bound his Nicht doch. [Leipzig? 1769?]
1. Ghosts. 2. Witchcraft--Ingolstadt, Bavaria. I. Title. II. Title: Kleine Zweifeln über zwey Berichte von einer Hexen- oder Studenten-Geschichte.
III. His Nicht doch --.

CATALOGUE OF THE CORNELL WITCHCRAFT COLLECTION

Simon, Jordan, pater, 1719-1776.
   Nun, ja --.

Witchcraft
BF   [Simon, Jordan] pater, 1719-1776.
1445   Nicht doch -- oder, Auflösung der kleinen
S595   Zweifel über zwey Berichte von einer Hexen-
        oder Studenten-Geschichte die sich in dem
        Jahre 1768. den 10. 11. 12. und 13. Junius
        zu Ingolstadt in Bayern soll zugetragen ha-
        ben. Aus einem dritten Berichte des Herrn
        Directors gezogen. Gedruckt zu Berichts-
        hausen, Mit klaren Schriften [i.e., Leip-
        zig? 1769?]
8   27 p. 21cm.
                   (Continued on next card)

Simon, Jordan, pater, 1719-1776.
   Nun, ja --.

Witchcraft
BF   [Simon, Jordan] pater, 1719-1776. Nicht
1445   doch -- ... [1769?]   (Card 2)
S595
        Attribution by Holzmann.
        Continuation of his Nun, ja --. [Leip-
        zig, 1769], with which this is bound.

        1. Ghosts. 2. Witchcraft--Ingolstadt,
        Bavaria. I. His Nun, ja --. II. Title.
        III. Title: Auflösung der kleinen Zweifel
8   über zwey Berichte von einer Hexen- oder
        Studenten-Ges   chichte.

Simon, Jordan, pater, 1719-1776, supposed ed.
Witchcraft
BF   Anpreisung der allergnädigsten Landesverordnung Ihrer
1584   kaiserl. königl. apostolischen Majestät, wie es mit dem hexen-
A93   processe zu halten sey, nebst einer vorrede, in welcher die
A61   Kurze vertheidigung der hex- und zauberey, die herr pater
        Angelus März der Akademischen rede des herrn p. don Ferdi-
        nand Sterzingers über das vorurtheil der hexerey entgegenge-
        setzet, beantwortet wird von einem gottesgelehrten. München,
        Akademische buchhandlung, 1767.
        4 p. l., 282, [2] p. 23ᵐ.
                  (Continued on next card)
8   [2]   42-40824

Simon, Jordan, pater, 1719-1776, supposed ed.
Witchcraft
BF   Anpreisung der allergnädigsten Landesverordnung Ihrer
1584   kaiserl. königl. apostolischen Majestät ... 1767. (Card 2)
A93
A61   Variously ascribed to Jordan Simon and Andreas Ulrich Mayer.
        "Sr. kaiserlich-königlich-apostolischen Ma-
        jestät allergnädigsten Landesordnung, wie es mit
        dem Hexenprocesse zu halten sey, mit kurzen An-
        preisungen für den gemeinen Mann erkläret," p.
        [129]-282, has special t.-p.
          1. Witchcraft--Austria. 2. März, Angelus, 1731-1784. Kurze Verthei-
        digung der thätigen Hex- und Zauberey. 3. Sterzinger, Ferdinand, 1721-
        1786. Akademische Rede von dem gemeinen Vorurtheile der ... Hexerey.
        I. Simon, Jordan, pater, 1719-1776, supposed ed. II. Mayer, Andreas Ul-
        rich, 1732-1802, supposed ed. III. Austria. Laws, statutes, etc. IV.
        Ein Gottesgelehrter.
8   Library of Congress   BF1584.A8A5
                                               42-40824
                               [2]

Simonnet, abbé.

      see

Simonnet, P. B.

WITCHCRAFT
BF   [Simonnet, P. B.]
1503   Réalité de la magie et des apparitions,
C69   ou Contrepoison du Dictionnaire infernal.
S61   Ouvrage dans lequel on prouve, par une mul-
        titude de faits et d'anecdotes authentiques
        ... l'existence des sorciers, la certitude
        des apparitions, la foi due aux miracles,
        la vérité des possessions, etc., pré-
        cédé d'une Histoire très-précise de la ma-
        gie ... Paris, P. Mongie aîné, 1819.
           xxii, 152 p. 21cm.
8   Ascription by Barbier.
NIC   (Continued on next card)

WITCHCRAFT
BF   [Simonnet, P. B.] Réalité de la magie ...
1503   1819.   (Card 2)
C69
S61
           1. Collin de Plancy, Jacques Albin Simon,
        1794-1881. Dictionnaire infernal. 2. Magic.
        3. Supernatural. I. Title. II. Title:
        Contrepoison du Dictionnaire infernal.

8
NIC

                The sin of witchcraft.
Witchcraft
BF   Samuel and the witch of Endor; or, The sin
1565   of witchcraft. [Battle Creek, Mich.,
S19   Seventh-Day Adventist Pub. Association, 18--]
           32 p. 18cm.

        Caption title.
        Signed: J. N. A.

           1. Witchcraft.   I. Title: The sin of
        witchcraft.   II. A., J. N. III.
        J. N. A.

WITCHCRAFT
BF   Sincerus, Theophilus, pseud.
1584   Nord-schwedische Hexerey, oder Simia
S9   Dei, Gottes Affe. Das ist: Ausführliche
S61   Beschreibung der schändlichen Verführungen
        des leidigen Satans, darinnen zu sehen
        Gottes erschröckliches Straff-Verhängen,
        wegen greulicher Sünden-Mengen. In einem
        Jammer-behertzigten Send-Schreiben am [sic]
        Tag gegeben, von Theophilo Sincero, an
        Christianum Piandrum. [Augsburg?] 1677.
           [64] p. illus. 20cm.
8
NIC   (Continued on next card)

WITCHCRAFT
BF   Sincerus, Theophilus, pseud. Nord-schwe-
1584   dische Hexerey ... 1677.   (Card 2)
S9
S61   "By Gottlieb Spitzel? See what Hauber
        says of the relation of this tract to his
        [i.e., Spitzel's] Die gebrochene Macht der
        Finsterniss. G. L. B."--Note in MS facing
        t. p.
        Illustrative vignette on t. p.
           1. Witchcraft--Sweden. 2. Witchcraft.
        I. Spitzel,   Gottlieb, 1639-1691, sup-
8   posed author.   II. Title. III. Title:
NIC   Simia Dei, Go   ttes Affe.

Witchcraft
BF   Sinclair, George, d. 1696.
1410   Satans invisible world discovered.
S61   Reprinted from the original edition
1871   published in Edinburgh in 1685.
        Accompanied with a bibliographical
        notice and supplement, &c. Edinburgh,
        Thomas George Stevenson, 1871.
           liii,264,ciii p. 20cm.

          ✓ I. Title.

BF   Sinclair, George. d. 1696.
1410   Satan's invisible world discovered. Gainesville, Fla.,
S61   Scholars' Facsimiles & Reprints, 1969.
1969   xxviii, xxx, 256 p. 23 cm. 12.50

        Reprint of the 1685 ed., with a new introd. by C. O. Parsons.

           1. Superstition. 2. Witchcraft. I. Title.

        BF1410.S5 1969   133.4   68-17017
        SBN 8201-1068-X   MARC
        Library of Congress   [2]

Sinclar, George, d. 1696.

      see

Sinclair, George, d. 1696.

Singer, Anna Renata von Mossau, ca.
   1680-1749.

      see

Sänger, Maria Renata von Mossau, ca. 1680-
   1749.

          Sinistrari, Luigi Maria, 1622-1701.
WITCHCRAFT   De daemonialitate et incubis et
BF   Sinistrari, Luigi Maria, 1622-1701. succubis.
1556   De la démonialité et des animaux incubes
S61   et succubes ... par le R. P. Louis Marie
1876   Sinistrari d'Ameno ... Publié d'après le
        manuscrit original découvert à Londres en
        1872 et traduit du Latin par Isidore
        Liseux. 2. éd. Paris, I. Liseux, 1876.
           xix, 267 p. 15cm.
        Title in red and black.
        Latin and French.
           1. Demonology. I. Liseux, Isidore,
8   1835-   , tr.   II. His De daemoniali-
NIC   tate et incub   is et succubis. III. His
        De daemoniali   tate et incubis et succu-
        bis. French.   IV. Title.

          Sinistrari, Luigi Maria, 1622-1701.
              De daemonialitate et incubis et succubis.
Witchcraft
BF   Sinistrari, Luigi Maria, 1622-1701.
1556   Demoniality; or Incubi and succubi. A
S61   treatise wherein is shown that there are in
1879   existence on earth rational creatures be-
        sides man ... Published from the original
        Latin manuscript discovered in London in
        the year 1872, and translated into French
        by Isidore Liseux. Now first translated
        into English. With the Latin text. Paris,
        I. Liseux, 1879.
           xvi, 251, [1] p. 17cm.

3   (Continued on next card)

          Sinistrari, Luigi Maria, 1622-1701.
              De daemonialitate et incubis et succubis
Witchcraft --English.
BF   Sinistrari, Luigi Maria, 1622-1701.
1556   Demoniality; or Incubi and succubi. A
S61   treatise wherein is shown that there are in
1879   existence on earth rational creatures be-
        sides man ... Published from the original
        Latin manuscript discovered in London in
        the year 1872, and translated into French
        by Isidore Liseux. Now first translated
        into English. With the Latin text. Paris,
        I. Liseux, 1879.
           xvi, 251, [1] p. 17cm.

3   (Continued on next card)

            Sinistrari, Luigi Maria, 1622-1701.
Witchcraft De daemonialitate et incubis et succubis--
BF   Sinistrari, Luigi Maria, 1622-1701. English.
1556   Demoniality. Translated into English
S61   from the Latin (with introd. and notes)
1927   by Montague Summers. London, Fortune
        Press [1927]
           xliii, 127 p. 23cm.

        No. 237 of 1200 copies.

           1. Demonology. I. Summers, Montague,
        1880-1948, tr.   II. Title. II. His
        De daemoniali   tate et incubis et
        succubis

510

CATALOGUE OF THE CORNELL WITCHCRAFT COLLECTION

WITCHCRAFT
BF
1556
S1
376

Sinistrari, Luigi Maria, 1622-1701.
De daemonialitate et incubis et succubis. French.
Sinistrari, Luigi Maria, 1622-1701.
De la démonialité et des animaux incubes et succubes ... par le R. P. Louis Marie Sinistrari d'Ameno ... Publié d'après le manuscrit original découvert à Londres en 1872 et traduit du Latin par Isidore Liseux. 2. éd. Paris, I. Liseux, 1876.
xix, 267 p. 15cm.
Title in red and black.
Latin and French.
1. Demonology. I. Liseux, Isidore, 1835- , tr. II. His De daemonialitate et incubis et succubis. III. His De daemonialitate et incubis et succubis. French. IV. Title.

Sinistrari, Luigi Maria, 1622-1701.
... De delictis, et poenis tractatus ... Venetiis, Apud Hieronymum Albriccium, 1700.
676 p. 34cm.

1. Criminal law (Roman law). 2. Canon law. I. Title.

WITCHCRAFT
BF
1556
S1
376

Sinistrari, Luigi Maria, 1622-1701.
De la démonialité et des animaux incubes et succubes ... par le R. P. Louis Marie Sinistrari d'Ameno ... Publié d'après le manuscrit original découvert à Londres en 1872 et traduit du Latin par Isidore Liseux. 2. éd. Paris, I. Liseux, 1876.
xix, 267 p. 15cm.
Title in red and black.
Latin and French.
1. Demonology. I. Liseux, Isidore, 1835- , tr. II. His De daemonialitate et incubis et succubis. III. His De daemonialitate et incubis et succubis. French. IV. Title.

Witchcraft
BF
1556
S1
79

Sinistrari, Luigi Maria, 1622-1701.
Demoniality; or Incubi and succubi. A treatise wherein is shown that there are in existence on earth rational creatures besides man ... Published from the original Latin manuscript discovered in London in the year 1872, and translated into French by Isidore Liseux. Now first translated into English. With the Latin text. Paris, I. Liseux, 1879.
xvi, 251, [1] p. 17cm.

(Continued on next card)

Witchcraft
BF
1556
S1
79

Sinistrari, Luigi Maria, 1622-1701. Demoniality ... 1879. (Card 2)

1. Demonology. I. Liseux, Isidore, 1835- , tr. II. Title. III. His De daemonialitate et incubis et succubis. IV. His De daemonialitate et incubis et succubis--English.

Witchcraft
BF
1556
S1
27

Sinistrari, Luigi Maria, 1622-1701.
Demoniality. Translated into English from the Latin (with introd. and notes) by Montague Summers. London, Fortune Press [1927]
xliii, 127 p. 23cm.

No. 237 of 1200 copies.

1. Demonology. I. Summers, Montague, 1880-1948, tr. II. Title. III. His De daemonialitate et incubis et succubis--English.

En skånsk hexprocess.
Witchcraft
BF
1584
S9
Z7
1706

Grünwall, F W
En skånsk hexprocess. Lund, E. Malmström, 1899.
18 p. 24cm.

"Särtryck ur Kulturhistoriska meddelanden."

Skalich, Paul, 1534-1575.
see
Scalichius, Paulus von Lika, count, 1534-1575.

Sketches of Tranent in the olden time.
Witchcraft
DA
890
T77
S22

Sands, J of Ormiston, Scotland.
Sketches of Tranent in the olden time. Edinburgh, Printed for the author by J. Hogg, 1881.
102 p. illus. 19cm.

Smedley, Edward, 1788-1836.
BF
1411
O15

The Occult sciences; sketches of the traditions and superstitions of past times, and the marvels of the present day; by E. Smedley [and others] London, R. Griffin, 1855.
376 p. 19cm. (Encyclopaedia metropolitana [v. 31])

1. Occult sciences. I. Smedley, Edward, 1788-1836.

Smeth, Joost de.
Witchcraft
BF
1410
B42
Z86
no.3

Bekker, Balthasar, 1634-1698. Brief van Baltasar [sic] Bekker, S. T. D. predikant tot Amsterdam, aan de Heeren Joost de Smeth, Willem Weyer, en Nikolaas vander Hagen, so tegenwoordig dienende als meermaals gediend hebbende ouderlingen der Gereformeerde Kerk aldaar. Tot antwoord op den brief van den Professor vander Waeyen aan deselven, gesteld voor sijn boek genaamd De betoverde weereld van B. B. ondersocht en wederleid. Hier achter is

(Continued on next card)

Smeth, Joost de.
Witchcraft
BF
1410
B42
Z86
no.3

Bekker, Balthasar, 1634-1698. Brief ... aan de Heeren Joost de Smeth, Willem Weyer, en Nikolaas vander Hagen ... 1693. (Card 2)

bygevoegd d'Opdraght-brief desselfden professors aan sijne Vorst. Doorl. den Prinsse van Nassaw Stadhouder &c. en d'Ed. Mog. Heeren Gedeputeerde Staten van Friesland, voor het selfde boek, met een antwoord op den selven. Amsterdam, By D. van den

(Continued on next card)

Smeth, Joost de.
Witchcraft
BF
1410
B42
Z86
no.3

Bekker, Balthasar, 1634-1698. Brief ... aan de Heeren Joost de Smeth, Willem Weyer, en Nikolaas vander Hagen ... 1693. (Card 3)

Dalen, boekverkoper, 1693.
16, 15*-16*, 17-24 p. title vignette, illus. initial. 19 x 15cm.
4°: A-B⁴, B*1, C⁴
Van der Linde 159.
No. 3 in vol. lettered Tractaten voor en tegen B. Bekker.

(Continued on next card)

WITCHCRAFT
BS
2545
D5
S64

Smit, Johannes.
De daemoniacis in historia Evangelica. Dissertatio exegetico-apologetica ... Romae, Sumptibus Pontificii Instituti Biblici, 1913.
xxii, 590 p. 25cm. (Rome (City) Pontificio Istituto Biblico. Scripta.)

1. Demoniac possession. 2. Bible. N.T.--Commentaries. 3. Bible--Psychology. I. Title. II. Series.

NIC

Smithe, Elleine.
Witchcraft
BF
1563
T75

Witchcraft at Maldon, Essex, in 1579. [Great Totham, Essex, Printed at C. Clark's private press, ca. 1840]
2 numbered leaves. 23cm.

Caption title.
Extract from A detection of damnable driftes ...
No. 2 in vol. lettered Tracts on witchcraft.

1. Smithe, Elleine. I. A detection of damnable driftes.

Witchcraft
BF
1563
W81++
no.19

The Snare of the Devill discovered; or, A true and perfect relation of ... Lydia, the wife of John Rogers, ... how, she wanting money, the Devil appeared to her ... and brought her money ... Also her examination ... and her confession ... London, Printed for E. Thomas, 1658. [London, at the British Museum, 1923]
[12] p. 16cm.
Photocopy (negative) 12 p. on 8 l. 20 x 32cm.
No. 19 in vol. lettered: Witchcraft tracts, chapbooks and broadsides, 1579-1704; rotograph copies.
1. Rogers, Lydia.

WITCHCRAFT
BF
1566
S67

Snell, Otto
Hexenprozesse und Geistesstörung. Psychiatrische Untersuchungen ... München, J. F. Lehmann, 1891.
130 p. 24cm.

I. Title.

NIC

BF
1566
S67

Snell, Otto
Hexenprozesse und Geistesstörung. Psychiatrische Untersuchungen. München, J.F. Lehmann, 1891.
130 p. 23cm.

1. Witchcraft. I. Title.

CATALOGUE OF THE CORNELL WITCHCRAFT COLLECTION

WITCHCRAFT
BF
1517
F5
J43
1886

Soeur Jeanne des Anges, supérieure des Ursulines de Loudun (XVIIe siècle) Autobiographie d'une hystérique possédée, Jeanne des Anges, mère, 1602-1665.
    Soeur Jeanne des Anges, supérieure des Ursulines de Loudun (XVIIe siècle) Autobiographie d'une hystérique possédée, d'après le manuscrit inédit de la bibliothèque de Tours. Annoté et publié par les docteurs Gabriel Legué et Gilles de la Tourette. Préface de M. le professeur Charcot. Paris, Aux Bureaux du Progrès, 1886.
    xiv, 321 p. facsim. 24cm. (Bibliothèque diabolique [Collection Bourneville,])

8
NIC   (Continued on next card)

WITCHCRAFT
BF
1523
M67
no.1

Die Sogenannten Werke des Teufels auf dem Erdboden. Horatius. Somnia, terrores magicos, miracvla, sagas, noctvrnos lemvres, portentaqve Thessala rides. Freyburg, 1751.
    312 p. front. 17cm.

    No. 1 on vol. lettered Miscellanien.

8
NIC   1. Devil. 2. Superstition. 3. Curiosities and wonders.

WITCHCRAFT
BF
1566
S68
B4

Soldan, Wilhelm Gottlieb, d. 1869.
    Ein Beitrag zur Geschichte der Hexenprocesse.
    (In Zeitschrift für deutsches Strafverfahren. Karlsruhe. 22cm. 3. Bd. (1843), p. [355]-378)
    At head of title: XXIII.
    1. Trials (Witchcraft)--Germany. I. His Geschichte der Hexenprocesse. II. Title.

8
NIC

Witchcraft
BF
1566
S68
1843

Soldan, Wilhelm Gottlieb, d. 1869.
    Geschichte der Hexenprocesse. Aus den Quellen dargestellt. Stuttgart, J. G. Cotta, 1843.
    xii, 512 p. 22cm.

    First ed.
    With autograph notes of A. D. White and Ernst Emil Hoffmann.

Witchcraft
BF
1566
S68
1880

Soldan, Wilhelm Gottlieb, d. 1869.
    Geschichte der Hexenprozesse. Neu bearbeitet von Dr. Heinrich Heppe. Stuttgart, J. G. Cotta, 1880.
    2 v. 22cm.

Witchcraft
BF
1566
S68
1912

Soldan, Wilhelm Gottlieb, d. 1869.
    Geschichte der Hexenprozesse. Neu bearbeitet und hrsg. von Max Bauer. München, G. Müller [1912]
    2 v. illus. 22cm.

    First ed. 1843; 2d ed., edited by Heinrich Heppe, published 1880. Cf. Allgemeine deutsche Biographie.

    1. Witchcraft. I. Heppe, Heinrich Ludwig Julius, 1820-1879, ed. II. Bauer, Max, 1861- ed. III. Title.

WITCHCRAFT
BF
1566
S68
B4

Soldan, Wilhelm Gottlieb, d. 1869.
    Ein Beitrag zur Geschichte der Hexenprocesse.
    (In Zeitschrift für deutsches Strafverfahren. Karlsruhe. 22cm. 3. Bd. (1843), p. [355]-378)
    At head of title: XXIII.
    1. Trials (Witchcraft)--Germany. I. His Geschichte der Hexenprocesse. II. Title.

8
NIC

WITCHCRAFT
BT
980
M26

Sollte der Teufel wirklich ein Unding seyn?
    Man muss auch dem Teufel nicht zu viel aufbürden. Bey Gelegenheit der Brochüre: Sollte der Teufel wirklich ein Unding seyn? etc. Beherziget von einem Freunde der Wahrheit ... Bremen, J. H. Cramer, 1776.
    xxxii, 426 p. 16cm.

    Attributed by various sources to C. H. Runge; cf. Holzmann, Michael. Deutsches Anonymenlexikon (Weimar, 1902-28)

8
NIC   (Continued on next card)

Witchcraft
BF
1587
D61
no.2

Solter, Heinrich, respondent.
    Sperling, Johann, 1603-1658, praeses.
    Positionum decas de magia qvam ... sub ... M. Johannis Sperlings ... praesidio ... disqvisitioni publicè subjicit Henricus Solter ... aut. & respond. ... Wittebergae, Ex officinâ typographicâ Johannis Haken, 1648.
    [32] p. 21cm.
    No. 2 in vol. lettered Dissertationes de magia. 1623-1723.
    1. Magic--Addresses, essays, lectures. I. Solter, Heinrich, respondent. II. Title.

8

Witchcraft
BF
1575
W69
1869

Some miscellany observations on our present debates respecting witchcrafts.
    [Willard, Samuel] 1640-1707.
    Some miscellany observations on our present debates respecting witchcrafts, in a dialogue between S. & B. By P. E. and J. A. [pseud.] Philadelphia, Printed by W. Bradford, for H. Usher. 1692. Boston, 1869.
    24 p. 23cm. ("Congregational quarterly" reprint, no. 1)

    No. 6 of an edition of 100 copies.

    1. Witchcraft. I. E., P. II. A., J. III. Title.

PA
19
S98
suppl.
v.20

Some notes on the demonology in the New Testament.
    Eitrem, Samson, 1872-
    Some notes on the demonology in the New Testament, by S. Eitrem. ed ed., rev. and enl. Osloae, In Aedibus Universitetsforlaget, 1966.
    78 p. 25cm. (Symbolae Osloenses Fasc. Supplet., 20)

    1. Demonology. 2. Bible. N.T.--Theology. I.Title.

Witchcraft
BF
1581
A2
G56

Some philosophical considerations touching the being of witches and witchcraft.
    [Glanvill, Joseph] 1636-1680.
    Some philosophical considerations touching the being of witches and witchcraft; written in a letter to Robert Hunt by J. G., a member of the Royal Society. London, Printed by E. C. for J. Collins, 1667.
    62 p. 21cm.
    Later incorporated into his Saducismus triumphatus.
    I. His Saducismus triumphatus. II. Title.

WITCHCRAFT
BF
1559
S69

Some thoughts on the miracles of Jesus; with an introduction to that of His casting out devils, which is particularly discuss'd. Occasioned by two late tracts, intitled, Enquiries into the meaning of demoniacks in the New Testament. By an Impartial Hand. London, Printed for John Clarke; and sold by J. Roberts, 1738.
    69 p. 20cm.
    1. Exorcism. 2. Demonology. 3. Enquiries into the meaning of demoniacks in the New Testament. I. An Impartial Hand.

8

Witchcraft
BS
2545
D5
T75
no.3

Some thoughts on the miracles of Jesus.
    [Sharpe, Gregory] 1713-1771.
    A review of the controversy about the meaning of demoniacks in the New-Testament. In which Mr. Hutchinson's sermon at Oxford ..., the Reply to the Further enquiry, Mr. Twell's Answer to the Further enquiry, and a tract, entitled, Some thoughts on the miracles of Jesus, by an impartial hand, are considered, by a lover of truth. ... London, Printed for J. Roberts, 1739.
    80 p. 20cm.
    No. 3 in vol. lettered: Tracts on demoniacks. 1737.

Witchcraft
BF
1581
B62
S6+
1941

Some unpublished Scottish witchcraft trials.
    Black, George Fraser, 1866- ed.
    Some unpublished Scottish witchcraft trials; transcribed and annotated by Dr. George F. Black. New York, The New York public library, 1941.
    50 p. 25cm.
    "The following Scottish witchcraft trials were copied in 1894-1895 from a manuscript abridgment of the Books of adjournal in the library of the Society of antiquaries of Scotland. This abridgment ... contains records ... of the Court of Justiciary from 8th February, 1584, to 8th July, 1723."--p. 3.
    "Reprinted from the Bulletin of the New York public library of April-May-August-September 1941."
    1. Witchcraft--Scotland.   I. Title: Scottish witchcraft trials.

New York. Public library
for Library of Congress   A 42-700

Rare
DA
300
S69+
1809

Somers, John Somers, baron, 1651-1716.
    A collection of scarce and valuable tracts ... [on] the history and constitution of these kingdoms ... 2d ed., rev., augm., and arr. by Walter Scott. London, Printed for T. Cadell and W. Davies, 1809-1815.
    13 v. 30cm.

    Ex libris Henry Thomas Buckle.

    1. Gt. Brit.--History--Modern period, 1485---Sources. 2. Pamphlets--Bibliography. I. Scott, Sir Walter, bart., 1771-1832, ed. II. Title.

Witchcraft
BF
1555
D22T6

Somers, William, fl. 1600.
    Darrell, John, fl. 1562-1602.
    A trve narration of the strange and grevous vexation by the Devil of 7. persons in Lancashire and VVilliam Somers of Nottingham. Wherein the doctrine of possession and dispossession of demoniakes ovt of the word of God is particularly applyed vnto Somers, and the rest of the persons controuerted, togeather with the use we are to make of these workes of God. [London?] 1600.
    24 [i.e. 23], 106 p. 19cm.

    1. Demoniac possession. 2. Somers, William, fl. 1600. II. Title.

Witchcraft
GR
730
A8
G87

Sonder- und wunderbare, doch wahre Geschichte, wie der Teufel +++ sich ... sehen liess.
    Gross, Wilibald.
    Sonder- und wunderbare, doch wahre Geschichte, wie der Teufel +++ sich einmal in der leiblichen Gestalt eines Esels auf dem Rathhause zu 3...r im W..b..g..schen sehen liess; zu Frommen und Besserung der izigen, höchst unglaubigen Welt, auch zum Beweiss des, in unsern Tagen so sehr geläugneten Daseyns eines Teufels +++, in Reimen, der bekannten Melodie: Ein Ritter, wie die Chronik sagt & c. &c. Im Manuscript aufgefunden und ans Licht gestellt

(Continued on next c)

CATALOGUE OF THE CORNELL WITCHCRAFT COLLECTION

Witchcraft
    Sonder- und wunderbare, doch wahre Geschichte, wie der Teufel +++ sich ... sehen liess.
    Gross, Wilibald. Sonder- und wunderbare, doch wahre Geschichte. Seefeld in Tyrol, 1786. (Card 2)

auch mit Anmerkungen vers. von Paul Weisshammer. [Seefeld in Tyrol] Gedrukt auf Kosten des Klosters, 1786.
    29 p. 18cm.

    I. Weisshammer, Paul, ed. II. Title.

Witchcraft
    Sonnenfels, Aloysius von
    Sendschreiben des hochedelgebohrnen Herrn Aloysius von Sonnenfels ... an den hochgelehrten P. don Ferdinand Sterzinger, ... Über zwey hebräische Wörter chartumim und belahatehem: nachmals zur nothwendigen Belehrung des sogenannten Liebhabers der Wahrheit, und seines lateinischen Eutychii Benjamin Transalbini in ihrem Zauber- und Hexerey Streite zum Drucke befördert, von einem Verehrer des Sterzingerischen Namens.
    (continued on next card)

Witchcraft
    Sonnenfels, Aloysius von   Sendschreiben ... 1768. (Card 2)
    Wien, Gedruckt mit schulzischen Schriften, 1768.
    30, [1] p. 21cm.
    1. Witchcraft in the Bible. 2. Bible. O.T.--Criticism, Textual. 3. Hartumim (The word) 4. Belahatehem (The word) 5. Durych, Fortunat, 1730-1802. Eutychii Beniamin Transalbini Dissertatio philologica. 6. März, Agnellus, 1726-1784. (Over)

La sorcellerie.

Witchcraft
    Bertrand, Isidore.
    La sorcellerie. 6. éd. Paris, Bloud [1905?]
    62 p. 18cm. (Science et religion: études pour le temps présent)

With this is bound his Les possédées de Loudun et Urbain Grandier. Paris [1905?]

    1. Witchcraft. I. Title.

La sorcellerie.

WITCHCRAFT
    Louandre, Charles Léopold, 1812-1882.
    La sorcellerie. Paris, L. Hachette, 1853.
    146 p. 17cm.

    1. Occult sciences. 2. Witchcraft.

WITCHCRAFT
    La Sorcellerie à Colmar et les environs. Instruction des procès: quarante-huit exécutions à Colmar, Ensisheim, Herrlisheim, Hattstadt, Wintzenheim, Soultzbach, Turckheim, Ammerschwihr, Sigolsheim, Ribeauvillé, Sainte-Marie-aux-Mines et Schlestadt. Colmar, E. Barth, 1869.
    11 p. 22cm.

    1. Trials (Witchcraft)--Alsace.

La sorcellerie à Toul aux XVIe & XVIIe siècles.

Witchcraft
BF 1582 D39
    Denis, Albert.
    La sorcellerie à Toul aux XVIe & XVIIe siècles. Étude historique. Toul, T. Lemaire, 1888.
    191 p. 19cm.

    1. Witchcraft--Toul, France. 2. Witchcraft--France. 3. Trials (Witchcraft)--France. I. Title.

La sorcellerie au Ban de Ramonchamp au XVIIe siècle.

WITCHCRAFT
BF 1582 T42
    Thiaucourt, Paul.
    La sorcellerie au Ban de Ramonchamp au XVIIe siècle. Remiremont, Imprim. H. Haut, 1906.
    54 p. 18cm.

    1. Witchcraft--Lorraine--History. I. Title.

La sorcellerie au Canada français du xviie au xixe siècles.

Witchcraft
BF 1584 C3S45
    Séguin, Robert Lionel.
    La sorcellerie au Canada français du XVIIe au XIXe siècles. Montréal, Librairie Ducharme, 1961.
    191 p. illus. 23 cm.

1. Witchcraft--Canada. I. Title.

BF1584.C3S4   64-27692 ‡
Library of Congress

La sorcellerie au seizième et au dix-septième siècle, particulièrement en Alsace.

WITCHCRAFT
BF 1583 R44
    Reuss, Rodolphe Ernst, 1841-1924.
    La sorcellerie au seizième et au dix-septième siècle, particulièrement en Alsace. D'après des documents en partie inédits. Paris, J. Cherbuliez, 1871.
    202 p. 24cm.

    1. Witchcraft--Alsace. 2. Witchcraft. I. Title.

La sorcellerie dans le pays de Montbéliard au XVII siècle.

WITCHCRAFT
BF 1582 T91+
    Tuetey, Alexandre, 1842-1918.
    La sorcellerie dans le pays de Montbéliard au XVII siècle. D'après des documents inédits ... Avec une préface par Mr Alfred Maury... Dôle (Jura), A. Vernier-Arcelin, 1886.
    x, 94 p. 26cm.

    1. Witchcraft--France. 2. Witchcraft--Montbéliard, France. I. Maury, Louis Ferdinand Alfred, 1817-1892. II. Title.

La sorcellerie des campagnes.

WITCHCRAFT
BF 1412 L24
    Lancelin, Charles Marie Eugène, 1852-
    La sorcellerie des campagnes. Paris, H. Durville [1912]
    493 p. illus. 23cm.

    1. Occult sciences--Hist. 2. Witchcraft--Hist. I. Title.

La sorcellerie en Béarn et dans le pays Basque.

Witchcraft
BF 1582 B28
    Barthety, Hilarion.
    La sorcellerie en Béarn et dans le pays Basque. Conférence publique à la mairie de Pau, suivie des pratiques de sorcellerie et superstitions populaires du Béarn. Pau, L. Ribaut, 1879.
    87 p. 25cm.

La sorcellerie en France.

BF 1622 F7 G232 1970
    Garinet, Jules, 1797-1877.
    La Sorcellerie en France, histoire de la magie jusqu'au XIXe siècle. Paris, F. Beauval [1970].
    254 p. illus., plates (part col.) 20 cm. 0.90F   F 72-7280
Includes bibliographical references.

1. Magic--France. 2. Demonology--History. I. Title.

NIC BF1622.F7G33 1970   72-357231
Library of Congress   72 [2]

La sorcellerie et la science des poisons au XVIIe siècle.

WITCHCRAFT
RA 1195 M41
    Masson, Albert.
    La sorcellerie et la science des poisons au XVIIe siècle. Paris, Hachette, 1904.
    342 p. 19cm.

    1. Poisons. 2. Toxicology--Hist. 3. Witchcraft. 4. Medicine--15th-18th centuries. I. Title.

Sorcellerie, magnétism.

Witchcraft
BF 173 R33+
    Regnard, Paul, 1850-1927.
    Les maladies épidémiques de l'esprit; sorcellerie, magnétisme, morphinisme, délire des grandeurs, par le d^r Paul Regnard ... Ouvrage illustré de cent vingt gravures. Paris, E. Plon, Nourrit et c^{ie}, 1887.
    iii-xii, 429 p., 1 l. incl. illus., pl., facsim. 27cm.
    Contents.--Les sorcières.--Les miracles de Saint-Médard.--Sommeil et somnambulisme.--Deux poisons à la mode: la morphine et l'éther.--Le délire des grandeurs.
    1. Psychology, Pathological. 2. Demoniac possession. 3. Hysteria. I. Title.
    II. Title: Sorcellerie, magnétism.
Library of Congress, no.

La sorcellerie, ses rapports avec les sciences biologiques.

Witchcraft
BF 1572 M4 R33+
    Regnault, Jules Émile Joseph, 1873-
    La sorcellerie, ses rapports avec les sciences biologiques, par le docteur Jules Regnault ... Paris, G. Baillière, 1897.
    350 p. 26cm.

    1. Witchcraft. 2. Medicine, Magic, mystic, and spagiric. 3. Mental suggestion. I. Title.

La sorcière.

WITCHCRAFT
BF 1569 M62 1863
    Michelet, Jules, 1798-1874.
    La sorcière: the witch of the middle ages. From the French of J. Michelet. By L. J. Trotter. London, Simpkin, Marshall and co., 1863.
    xii, 403 p. 20cm.

The only authorized English translation. "List of leading authorities": p. [402]-403.

CATALOGUE OF THE CORNELL WITCHCRAFT COLLECTION

La sorcière.

Witchcraft
BF
1569
M62
1903
 Michelet, Jules, 1798-1874.
  La sorcière. Etude par Gabriel Séailles.
Paris, Calmann-Levy [1903]
  xxxiv, 448 p. 18cm. (Oeuvres complètes
de Michelet. Histoire sociale)

  1. Witchcraft. 2. Demonomania. 3. Civilization, Medieval. I. Séailles, Gabriel.
II. Title.

La sorcière.

Witchcraft
PQ
2422
S7
1904
 Sardou, Victorien, 1831-1908.
  La sorcière. Drame en cinq actes. [2.
éd.] Paris, Calmann-Lévy [1904]
  242 p. 19cm.

8

Une sorcière au xviii⁰ siècle.

Witchcraft
BF
1582
L41
C88
 Coynart, Charles de, 1863-
  ... Une sorcière au XVIII⁰ siècle, Marie-Anne de La
Ville, 1680-1725, avec une préface de Pierre de Ségur.
Paris, Hachette et cⁱᵉ, 1902.
  2 p. l., iv, 286 p., 1 l. 19ᶜᵐ.

  1. La Ville, Marie Anne de, b. 1680. 2. Witchcraft--France. I. Title.

Library of Congress, no.

Witchcraft
BF
1582
Z7
1631
 La sorcière de Munster [Catherine Huger]: sa
torture à Wihr-au-Val et son exécution à
Gunsbach. MDCXXXI. Colmar, E. Barth, 1869.
  15 p. 23cm.

  Signed: J. D.

  1. Huger, Catherine, d. 1631. 2. Witchcraft.
I. D., J. II. J. D.

La sorcière et l'inquisiteur.

DC
611
P952
A67
v.1
 Aubenas, Roger.
  La sorcière et l'inquisiteur; épisode de l'Inquisition en
Provence, 1439. Aix-en-Provence, La Pensée universitaire,
1956.
  x, 81 p. facsims. 25 cm. (Archives de Provence, 1)
  Bibliography : p. 79–80.

  1. Malavesse, Catherine (David) fl. 1439. 2. Inquisition. Provence.
I. Title. (Series)
BF1582.Z7 1439   57-36238
Library of Congress   [3]

Les sorcières.

Witchcraft
BF
1569
R33
 Regnard, Paul, 1850-1927.
  Les sorcières. Conférence du 18 Mars
1882, faite à la Sorbonne. Paris, Gauthier-Villars, 1882.
  41 p. 22cm.
  At head of title: Association scientifique de France.
  "Extrait des Bulletins hebdomadaires nᵒˢ 106, 107."

8
  1. Witchcraft--Addresses, essays, lectures. I. Title.

Les sorcières dans le Béarn, 1393-1672.

WITCHCRAFT
BF
1582
L63
 Lespy, Jean Désiré, called Vastin, 1817-1897.
  Les sorcières dans le Béarn, 1393-1672.
Pau, L. Ribaut, 1875.
  72 p. 25cm.

  Extract from Bulletin de la Société des
sciences, lettres et arts de Pau, ser. 2,
v. 4.

8
NIC
  1. Witchcraft--Béarn, France. 2. Trials
(Witchcraft)-- Béarn, France. I.
Title.

Les sorcières de Bergheim.

Witchcraft
BF
1582
B22+
 Bapst, Edmond, 1858-
  Les sorcières de Bergheim; épisode de
l'histoire d'Alsace. Paris, A. Lahure,
1929.
  179 p. front. 30cm.

  1. Witchcraft--Germany--Bergheim. I. Title.

Les sorcières du Vivarais devant les
inquisiteurs de la foi.

Witchcraft
BF
1582
D14
 Dalmas, Jean Baptiste.
  Les sorcières du Vivarais devant les
inquisiteurs de la foi. Privas, Typographie et lithographie de Ph. Guiremand,
1865.
  251 p. port. 22cm.

  Bound in at end "Géologie et astronomie",
signed by Dalmas, 8 p.

  1. Witchcraft-- Vivarais, France. I.
Title. II. His Géologie et astronomie.
III. Géologie et astronomie.

Sorcières et loups-garous dans les Landes.

Witchcraft
BF
1582
F66
 [Foix, Vincent M.]
  Sorcières et loups-garous dans les
Landes. Auch, Imprimerie centrale, 1904.
  72 p. 25cm.

  Caption title: Folklore. Glossaire de
la sorcellerie landaise.

  1. Witchcraft--France--Dictionaries.
2. Werwolves--Dictionaries. I. Title.
II. Title: Glossaire de la sorcellerie landaise.
8

Les sorcières neuchateloises.

Witchcraft
BF
1566
C42
 Chabloz, Fritz.
  Les sorcières neuchateloises ... Neuchatel, Imprimerie de J. Attinger, 1868.
  512 p. 19cm.

  1. Witchcraft--Hist. I. Title.

Les sorciers de Lyon: episode judiciaire
du XVIII⁰ siècle.

Witchcraft
BF
1582
B38
 Beaune, Henri, 1833-1907.
  Les sorciers de Lyon: episode judiciaire du
XVIIIe siècle. [n.p., 18--]
  [65]-154 p. 22cm.

  Caption title.

Sorciers de Savoie.

WITCHCRAFT
BF
1582
K39
 Kerdaniel, Édouard Le Marant de, 1867-
  Sorciers de Savoie [par] Édouard-L. de
Kerdaniel. Annecy, Imprimerie Abry, 1900.
  47 p. 19cm.

  Bibliographical footnotes.

8
NIC
  1. Witchcraft--Savoy. I. Title.

Sotheby, firm, auctioneers, London.

Witchcraft
Z
6880
Z9
H37+
 Hauser, Lionel
  Catalogue of the very extensive and
important library of early books and
manuscripts relating to alchemy & the
occult & physical sciences, the property of
M. Lionel Hauser... and of four important
mediaeval manuscripts...which will be sold
by auction by Messrs. Sotheby and Co...the
16th of April, 1934... London, Printed by
J. Davy [1934]
  ii, 68 p. illus. 26cm.
  1. Alchemy--Bibl. 2. Occult sciences--Bibl. I. Sotheby, firm, auctioneers, London.

BF
1581
P37
 Peel, Edgar.
  The trials of the Lancashire witches; a study of seventeenth-century witchcraft, by Edgar Peel and Pat Southern. Drawings by Pat Southern. New York, Taplinger Pub. Co. [1969]
  192 p. illus., facsim., geneal. table, map. 23 cm. 6.50
  Bibliography: p. 168-169.

  1. Trials (Witchcraft)—Lancashire, Eng. I. Southern, Pat, joint author. II. Title.
  343'.5   72-84973
Library of Congress   69 [8]   MARC

WITCHCRAFT
BF
1583
R44
S73
 [Spach, Louis Adolphe]
  Das Hexenwesen im Elsass. [n. p., ca.
1871]
  6 p. 21cm.

  Reprint from a review.

8
NIC
  1. Reuss, Rodolphe Ernst, 1841-1924. Sorcellerie au seizième et au dix-septième siècle. 2. Witchcraft--Alsace.
I. Title.

Witchcraft
BF
1517
G7
S73
 Spalding, Thomas Alfred, 1850-
  Elizabethan demonology. An essay in
illustration of the belief in the existence
of devils, and the powers possessed by them,
as it was generally held during the period
of the Reformation, and the times immediately
succeeding; with special reference to
Shakspere and his works. London, Chatto and
Windus, 1880.
  xii, 151 p. 20cm.

  1. Demonology. 2. Shakespeare, William--Supernatural element.
I. Title.

BF
1517
G7
S73
1880a
 Spalding, Thomas Alfred, 1850-
  Elizabethan demonology; an essay in illustration of the
belief in the existence of devils, and the powers possessed
by them, as it was generally held during the period of the
Reformation, and the times immediately succeeding; with
special reference to Shakspere and his works. [Folcroft,
Pa.] Folcroft Press [1970]
  xii, 151 p. 22 cm.
  Reprint of the 1880 ed.
  Includes bibliographical references.

  1. Demonology. 2. Shakespeare, William—Supernatural element.
I. Title.
4
NIC
 BF1517.G7S7 1970   133.4'2'0942   72-19407
Library of Congress   72 [4]   MARC

514

CATALOGUE OF THE CORNELL WITCHCRAFT COLLECTION

The Spanish Mandevile of myracles.

Torquemada, Antonio de, fl. 1553-1570.
    The Spanish Mandevile of myracles. Or The garden of curious flowers. Wherein are handled sundry points of humanity, philosophy, diuinity, and geography, beautified with many strange and pleasant histories: first written in Spanish by Anthonio de Torquemada, and translated out of that tongue into English. It is diuided into sixe treatises, composed in the manner of a dialogue ... London, Imprinted by Bernard Alsop, by the assigne of Richard Hawkins, 1618.
            (Continued on next card)

37
44
18

The Spanish Mandevile of myracles.

Torquemada, Antonio de, fl. 1553-1570. The Spanish Mandevile of myracles ... 1618.
            (Card 2)

[6], 325, [3] p. 20cm.

    Translated by Lewis Lewkenor although the translation is usually attributed to Ferdinand Walker who published it.
    Translation of Jardin de flores curiosas.
    I. Lewkenor, Sir Lewis, tr. II. Walker, Ferdinand, fl. 1600, supposed tr. III. His Jardin de flores curiosas--English. IV. Title. V. Title: The garden of curious flowers.

37
44
18

Spatchet, Thomas, 1614-

WITCHCRAFT
BF
555
S51
693

Petto, Samuel, 1624?-1711.
    A faithful narrative of the wonderful and extraordinary fits which Mr. Tho. Spatchet (late of Dunwich and Cookly) was under by witchcraft: or, a mysterious providence in his even unparallel'd fits ... London, Printed for John Harris, 1693.
    2 p. l., 31, [1] p. 19cm.
    Also issued London, 1693, without printer or bookseller named.
    Wing P1897.
    1. Spatchet, Thomas, 1614- 2. Demoniac possession. 3. Convulsions. I. Title.

Spaziergänge mit Planitz, dessen Ideen und Ansichten über Faust und Hexe.

WITCHCRAFT
PT
2631
L34
H61

Lobau, Richard.
    Spaziergänge mit Planitz, dessen Ideen und Ansichten über Faust und Hexe. Tagebuchnotizen. Wittenberg, A.Piehler [1924]
    vii, 96, [2] p. 19cm.
    Includes passages from Planitz' Die Hexe von Goslar, with commentary.
    1.Planitz, Ernst Alfons, Edler von der, 1857- 2.Witchcraft. 3.Goethe, Johann Wolfgang von,1749-1832. 4.Faust. 4. Planitz, Ernst Alfons, Edler von der, 1857- Die Hexe von Goslar. I.Planitz, Ernst Alfons, Edler von der,1857- II. Planitz,Ernst Alfons,Edler von der, 1857- Die Hexe von Goslar. III. Title.

Spe, Friedrich, 1591-1635.

see

Spee, Friedrich von, 1591-1635.

Specimen juridicum, De nefando lamiarum cum diabolo coitu.

Witchcraft
BF
1565
D62
no.9

Pott, Johann Heinrich.
    Specimen juridicum, De nefando lamiarum cum diabolo coitu, von der Hexen schändlichen Beyschlaff mit dem bösen Feind, in quo abstrusissima haec materia dilucidè explicatur, quaestiones inde emergentes curatè resolvuntur, variisque non injucundis exemplis illustrantur, publicâ luce donatum à Johanne Henrico Pott ... Jenae, Prostat apud Tobiam Oehrlingium, 1689.
    72 p. 20cm.
            (Continued on next card)

8

Specimen juridicum, De nefando lamiarum cum diabolo coitu.

Witchcraft
BF
1565
D62
no.9

Pott, Johann Heinrich. Specimen juridicum ... 1689. (Card 2)

    "Pacta und Gelübdnüss einer ... hohen Person, so dieselbe mit dem leydigen Satan soll haben getroffen," p. [69]-72, has special t. p.
    No. 9 in vol. lettered Dissertationes de sagis. 1636-1714.
    1. Witchcraft. 2. Devil. I. Title: De nefando lamiarum cum diabolo coitu. II. Title: Pacta und Gelübdnüss einer ... hohen Person.

8

Spectrologia.

Witchcraft
BF
1445
D29

Decker, Johann Heinrich, 1665-1707.
    Spectrologia; h. e., Discursus ut plurimum philosophicus de spectris; brevibus & succinctis thesibus illorum existentiam, essentiam, qualitatem, &c, varias apparitionum formas, & fallacias exhibens. Hamburgi, Apud Gothofr. Liebernickel, Literis Brendekii, 1690.
    10 p. l., 197, [18] p. 14cm.
    Added engraved t. p.
    1. Apparitions. 2. Ghosts. I. Title.

8

Spectrum Endoreum, ex I. Sam. 28.

Witchcraft
BF
1445
D61
no.8

Gerhard, Johann Ernst, 1621-1668, praeses.
    Spectrum Endoreum, ex I. Sam. 28. Auspice numine summo, sub praesidio ... Johannis Eernesti Gerhardi ... Publicae eruditorum disquisitioni expositum, ab autore & respondente Benedicto Hahn ... ed. tertia auctior & ememdatior. Jenae, Literis Johannis Nisii, 1684.
    112 p. 21cm.
    No. 8 in vol. lettered Dissertationes de spectris. 1646-1753.

8   (Continued on next card)

Speculum peregrinarum questionum.

WITCHCRAFT
BT
960
S56
1521

Sibylla, Bartholomaeus.
    Speculuz pegrinaz q̃onuz eruditissimi viri Bartholomei Sybille Monopolitã: ... Tres decades cõplectes: in qbus varie qõnes de aiab' r̃onalib'i ?iũcro: z separatj. Deq̃ angelis b̃ois z malis multisq̃ alijs scitu dignissimis: z ad ipsas r̃nsiones ponũtur. Ex ... theologo&: jurispõtificũ: phõ ac astrologorũ ... [Lugduni, Impressuz in edib' Iacobi Myt., 1521]
    ccxxviij numb. l. 16cm.

8   (Continued on next card)

Speculum peregrinarum questionum.

WITCHCRAFT
BT
960
S56
1521

Sibylla, Bartholomaeus. Speculuz pegrinaz q̃onuz ... [1521] (Card 2)

    Title in red, in black ornamental woodcut border.

    1. Future life. 2. Angels. 3. Demonology. 4. Man (Theology) I. Title: Speculum peregrinarum questionum.

8

Spee, Friedrich Von

[Spee, Friedrich von] 1591-1635.
    Advis avx criminalistes svr les abvs qvi se glissent dans les proces de sorcelerie. Dediés aux magistrats d'Allemagne. Liure tres necessaire en ce temps icy, à tous iuges, conseillers, confesseurs ... inquisiteurs, predicateurs, aduocats, & mêmes aux medecins. Par le P. N. S. I. theologian romain. Imprimé en Latin pour la seconde fois à Francfort en l'annèe 1632. Et mis en françois par F. B. de Velledor [pseud.] M.A.D. Lyon,
            (Continued on next card)

Witchcraft
BF
1583
A2S74
1660

[Spee, Friedrich von] 1591-1635. Advis avx criminalistes ... (Card 2)

Aux dépens de l'autheur: Et se vend chez Claude Prost, 1660.
    [48], 336 p. 18cm.

    Translation of Cautio criminalis.
    I. His Cautio criminalis. French. II. Bouvot, Frédéric, tr. III. Title.

Witchcraft
BF
1583
A2S74
1631

[Spee, Friedrich von] 1591-1635.
    Cautio criminalis, seu De processibus contra sagas liber. Ad magistratus Germaniae hoc tempore necessarius, tum autem consiliariis, & confessariis Principum, inquisitoribus, judicibus, advocatis, confessariis reorum, concionatoribus, caeterisque lectu utilissimus. Avtore incerto theologo orthod. Rinthelii, Typis exscripsit Petrus Lucius, 1631.
    [8], 398, [2] p. 16cm.

CATALOGUE OF THE CORNELL WITCHCRAFT COLLECTION

Witchcraft
BF
1583
A2S74
1632

[Spee, Friedrich von] 1591–1635.
　　Cavtio criminalis, seu De processibvs contra sagas liber. Ad magistratvs Germaniae hoc tempore necessarius, tum autem consiliariis, et confessariis Principum, inquisitoribus, iudicibus, aduocatis, confessariis reorum, concionatoribus, caeterisque lectu vtilissimus. Avctore Incerto theologo Romano. Editio secunda. Francofvrti, Sumptibus Ioannis Gronaei, 1632.
　　[16], 459, [1] p. 17cm.

(Continued on next card)

Witchcraft
BF
1583
A2S74
1632

[Spee, Friedrich von] 1591–1635.　Cavtio criminalis ... 1632.　(Card 2)

With this is bound Oldekop, Justus. Cautelarum criminalium sylloge practica. Brunsvigae, 1633.

　1. Witchcraft. 2. Witchcraft--Germany. I. Title: Cautio criminalis.

Witchcraft
BF
1583
A2S74
1649

[Spee, Friedrich von] 1591–1635.
　　Cautio criminalis; sev, De processibus contra sagas liber. Das ist, Peinliche Warschauung von Anstell: vnd Führung dess Processes gegen die angegebene Zauberer, Hexen vnd Vnholden ... vnd männiglich zum besten ins Teutsch übersetzt ... durch H. S. S.　Franckfurt am Mayn, A. Hummen, 1649.
　　317 (i. e. 217) p. 20cm.

Witchcraft
BF
1583
A2S74
1695

[Spee, Friedrich von] 1591–1635.
　　Cautio criminalis, seu De processibus contra sagas liber, magistratibus Germaniae hoc tempore summè necessarius, praeprimis consiliariis et confessariis Principum, inquisitoribus, judicibus, advocatis, confessoribus reorum, concionatoribus, aliisque lectu utilissimus.　Solisbaci, Sumpt. Martini Endteri, 1695.
　　[22], 407, [1] p. 15cm.

　1. Witchcraft. 2. Witchcraft--Germany. I. Title.

Witchcraft
BF
1583
A2S74
1703

[Spee, Friedrich von] 1591–1635.
　　... Cautio criminalis; sev, De processibus contra sagas liber. Das ist: Peinliche Warschauung von Anstell - und Führung des Processes gegen die angegebene Zauberer, Hexen und Unholden ... ins Teutsch treulich übersetzt ... [Halle im Magdburg, 1703]
　　[49]-356 p. 21cm.

　Imperfect: p. 89-218 wanting.
　Translated by Hermann Schmidt.

(Continued on next card)

Witchcraft
BF
1583
A2S74
1703

[Spee, Friedrich von] 1591–1635.
　　Cautio criminalis ... [1703] (Card 2)

From Unterschiedliche Schrifften von Unfug des Hexen-Processes, by Johann Reiche.

　1. Witchcraft. 2. Witchcraft--Germany. I. Title. II. Title: De processus contra sagas liber. III. Schmidt, Hermann, tr.

BF
1583
A2S74
1939

Spee, Friedrich von, 1591–1635.
　　... Cautio criminalis; oder, Rechtliches bedenken wegen der hexenprozesse. Deutsche ausgabe von Joachim-Friedrich Ritter.　Weimar, H. Böhlaus nachf., 1939.
　　xlvii, 301 p. front. (port.) 23½ᶜᵐ. (Half-title: Forschungen zur geschichte des deutschen strafrechts, hrsg. von Eberhard Schmidt ... und Helmut v. Weber ... bd. 1)
　　Based upon the second edition, Frankfurt, 1632, with reproduction of title-pages.

　1. Witchcraft—Germany.　ɪ. Ritter, Joachim Friedrich, ed. and tr.
ɪɪ. Title: Cautio criminalis.

Library of Congress　　BF1583.A2S68　　41-22816
　　　　　　　　[2]　　　[159.96140943]　133.40943

WITCHCRAFT
BF
1565
R34

Spee, Friedrich von, 1591–1635.
　　Cautio criminalis.

Reiche, Johann, ed.
　　Herrn D. Christian Thomasii ... Kurtze Lehr-Sätze von dem Laster der Zauberey, nach dem wahren Verstande des lateinischen Exemplars ins Deutsche übersetzet, und aus des berühmten Theologi D. Meyfarti, Naudaei, und anderer gelehrter Männer Schrifften erleutert ... nebst einigen Actis magicis herausgegeben von Johann Reichen.　Halle im Magdeburgischen, Im Rengerischen Buchladen, 1704.
　　2 v. in 1.　21cm.

8
NIC

(Continued on next card)

WITCHCRAFT
BF
1565
R34

Spee, Friedrich von, 1591–1635.
　　Cautio criminalis.
Reiche, Johann, ed.　Herrn D. Christian Thomasii ... Kurtze Lehr-Sätze ... 1704.
　　　　　　　　　　　　(Card 2)

　Vol. 1 has special t. p.: Fernerer Unfug der Zauberey. Halle im Magdeburgischen, 1704.
　Vol. 2 has special t. p.: Unterschiedliche Schrifften von Unfug des Hexen-Processes. Halle im Magdeburg., 1703.
　Contents.--[1. Bd.] Gabriel Naudaei

8
NIC
(Continued on next card)

WITCHCRAFT
BF
1565
R34

Spee, Friedrich von, 1591–1635.
　　Cautio criminalis.
Reiche, Johann, ed.　Herrn D. Christian Thomasii ... Kurtze Lehr-Sätze ... 1704.
　　　　　　　　　　　　(Card 3)

Contents.--Continued.

Schutz-Schrifft [tr. of Apologie pour tous les grands hommes]--Geschichte der Teuffel zu Lodün,--Trauer-Geschichte von der greulichen Zauberey Ludwig Goffredy [tr. of De l'horrible & épouvantable sorcellerie de Louis Goffredy, author F. de Rosset]--D. Christian Thomasii ... Kurtze Lehr-Sätze von

8
NIC
(Continued on next card)

WITCHCRAFT
BF
1565
R34

Spee, Friedrich von, 1591–1635.
　　Cautio criminalis.
Reiche, Johann, ed.　Herrn D. Christian Thomasii ... Kurtze Lehr-Sätze ... 1704.
　　　　　　　　　　　　(Card 4)

Contents--Continued.

dem Laster der Zauberey [tr. of Dissertatio de crimine magiae, J. Reiche, respondent] [2. Bd.] Malleus judicum oder Gesetz-Hammer der unbarmhertzigen Hexen-Richter.--Cautio criminalis [von F. Spee]--D. Johann Matthäus Meyfarths Christliche Erinnerung an Regenten.--Viererley Sorten Hexen-Acta.--

8
NIC
(Continued on next card)

Witchcraft
BF
1583
A2S74
1660

Spee, Friedrich von, 1591–1635.
　　Cautio criminalis. French.
[Spee, Friedrich von] 1591–1635.
　　Advis avx criminalistes svr les abvs qvi se glissent dans les proces de sorcelerie. Dediés aux magistrats d'Allemagne. Liure tres necessaire en ce temps icy, à tous iuges, conseillers, confesseurs ... inquisiteurs, predicateurs, aduocats, & mêmes aux medecins. Par le P. N. S. I. theologian romain. Imprimé en Latin pour la seconde fois à Francfort en l'année 1632. Et mis en françois par F. B. de Velledor [pseud.] M.A.D.　Lyon,

(Continued on next card)

Witchcraft
BF
1583
A2S74
1660

Spee, Friedrich von, 1591–1635.
　　Cautio criminalis. French.
[Spee, Friedrich von] 1591–1635.　Advis avx criminalistes ...　(Card 2)

Aux dépens de l'autheur: Et se vend chez Claude Prost, 1660.
　　[48], 336 p. 18cm.

Translation of Cautio criminalis.

　I. His　Cautio criminalis. French.
　II. Bouvot, Frédéric, tr. III. Title.

WITCHCRAFT
PT
1792
C26

Spee, Friedrich von, 1591–1635.
　　Cautio criminalis.

Cardauns, Hermann, 1847-1925.
　　Friedrich Spee.　Frankfurt a. M., A. Foesser Nachf., 1884.
　　[103]-133 p. 23cm. (Frankfurter zeitgemässe Broschüren. N. F., Bd. 5, Heft 4)

　1. Spee, Friedrich von, 1591-1635. 2. Spee, Friedrich von, 1591-1635. Cautio criminalis. I. Series.

8
NIC

WITCHCRAFT
BF
1583
A2
S744

Spee, Friedrich von, 1591–1635.
　　Cautio criminalis.

A Jesuit philanthropist. Friedrich von Spee and the Würzburg witches. (In The Church quarterly review. London. 23cm. v. 57, no. 114 (1904), p. 318-337)
　　Review of several books by Spee or about his times.
　　At head of title: Art. V.
　1. Spee, Friedrich von, 1591-1635. Cautio criminalis. 2. Institoris, Henricus, d. 1508. Malleus maleficarum. 3. Witchcraft--Germany. I. Title.

8
NIC

PT
1792
Z97

Spee, Friedrich von, 1591–1635.
　　Cautio criminalis.

Zwetsloot, Hugo.
　　Friedrich Spee und die Hexenprozesse; die Stellung und Bedeutung der Cautio criminalis in der Geschichte der Hexenverfolgungen. Trier, Paulinus-Verlag, 1954.
　　345 p. illus., port. 24 cm.
　　Bibliography: p. 323-328.
　　"Ausgaben und Übersetzungen der Cautio criminalis": p. 329-331.

　1. Spee, Friedrich von, 1591-1635. Cautio criminalis. 2. Trials (Witchcraft)—Germany. I. Title.
　　　　　　　　　　　　　　　　　　　56-33376

WITCHCRAFT
BX
4700
L6
S33
1877

Spee, Friedrich von, 1591–1635.
　　Trutz-Nachtigall. Selections.

Schick, J　G
　　Leben des heiligen Alphohs Maria von Liguori, Stifter des Redemptoristenordens, und des Pater Friedrich Spee, Priesters der Gesellschaft Jesu,　2. Aufl. Regensburg, G. J. Manz, 1877.
　　164 p. port. 19cm. (Leben ausgezeichneter Katholiken der drei letzten Jahrhunderte. 7. Bd. 2. Aufl.)

　Leben des Pater Friedrich Spee, p. [129]-146, has special t. p.

8
NIC
(Continued on next card)

WITCHCRAFT
BX
4700
L6
S33
1877

Spee, Friedrich von, 1591–1635.
　　Trutz-Nachtigall. Selections.

Schick, J　G　Leben des heiligen Alphons Maria von Liguori ... 1877.　(Card 2)

　Anhang, p. [147]-162, consists of selections from Spee's Trutz-Nachtigall.

　1. Liguori, Alfonso Maria de', Saint, 1696-1787. 2. Spee, Friedrich von, 1591-1635. I. Spee, Friedrich von, 1591-1635. Trutz-Nachtigall. Selections. II. Title.

8
NIC

CATALOGUE OF THE CORNELL WITCHCRAFT COLLECTION

Spee, Friedrich von, 1591-1635.

Witchcraft
583
17
    Baldi, Alexander.
        Die Hexenprozesse in Deutschland und ihr hervorragendster Bekämpfer; eine kulturhistorische Abhandlung. Würzburg, Stahel, 1874.
        42 p. 24cm.

    1. Trials (Witchcraft)--Germany. 2. Spee, Friedrich von, 1591-1635. I. Title.

Spee, Friedrich von, 1591-1635.

ar W
25683
    Geilen, Heinz Peter, 1933-
        Die Auswirkungen der Cautio criminalis von Friedrich von Spee auf den Hexenprozess in Deutschland. [Köln, G. Wasmund, 1963]
        xviii, 92 p. 21cm.

    Inaug.-Diss.--Bonn.

Witchcraft
BF
1587
D61
no.2
    Sperling, Johann, 1603-1658, praeses.
        Positionum decas de magia qvam ... sub ... M. Johannis Sperlings ... praesidio ... disqvisitioni publicè subjicit Henricus Solter ... aut. & respond. ... Wittebergae, Ex officinā typographicā Johannis Haken, 1648.
        [32] p. 21cm.
    No. 2 in vol. lettered Dissertationes de magia. 1623-1723.
    1. Magic--Addresses, essays, lectures. I. Solter, Heinrich, repsondent. II. Title.

8

Spee, Friedrich von, 1591-1635.

Witchcraft
T
792
26
    Cardauns, Hermann, 1847-1925.
        Friedrich Spee. Frankfurt a. M., A. Foesser Nachf., 1884.
        [103]-133 p. 23cm. (Frankfurter zeitgemässe Broschüren. N. F., Bd. 5, Heft 4)

    1. Spee, Friedrich von, 1591-1635. 2. Spee, Friedrich von, 1591-1635. Cautio criminalis. I. Series.

NIC

Spee, Friedrich von, 1591-1635.

Witchcraft
PT
1792
H69+
    Hölscher, Otto.
        Friedrich Spee von Langenfeld. Sein Leben und seine Schriften. Düsseldorf, Gedruckt von L. Boss [1871]
        16 p. 27cm.
    Accompanies "Programm" (zu den öffentlichen Prüfungen am 28., 29. und 30 August 1871)--Realschule erster Ordnung, Düsseldorf.
    Pages 13-16 give poems by Spee.

8
    1. Spee, Friedrich von, 1591-1635. I. Title.

Speusippus, fl. 347-339 B. C.
    Liber de Platonis definitionibus.

WITCHCRAFT
PA
4220
L3
A4+
1516
    Jamblichus, of Chalcis. [De mysteriis. Latin]
        Iamblichus De mysteriis Aegyptiorum, Chaldaeorum, Assyriorum. Proclus In Platonicum Alcibiadem de anima, atq[ue] demone. Proclus De sacrificio, & magia. Porphyrius De diuinis, atq[ue] daemonibus. Synesius Platonicus De somniis. Psellus De daemonibus. Expositio Prisciani, & Marsilii in Theophrastum De sensu, phantasia, & intellectu. Alcinoi Platonici philosophi, Liber de doctrina

8
    (Continued on next card)

Spee, Friedrich von, 1591-1635.

Witchcraft
T
792
56
901
    Diel, Johannes Baptista, 1843-1875.
        Friedrich Spe. Von Johannes Diel. 2., umgearb. Aufl. von Barnhard Duhr. Freiburg i. B., Herder, 1901.
        viii, 147 p. port., facsim. 20cm. (Sammlung historischer Bildnisse. [IX])
    First published 1872 under title: Friedrich von Spee.
    Very extensively revised.
    1. Spee, Friedrich von, 1591-1635. I. Duhr, Bernhard, 1852-1930.

WITCHCRAFT
BX
4700
L6
S33
1877
    Schick, J G
        Leben des heiligen Alphons Maria von Liguori, Stifter des Redemptoristenordens, und des Pater Friedrich Spee, Priesters der Gesellschaft Jesu. 2. Aufl. Regensburg, G. J. Manz, 1877.
        164 p. port. 19cm. (Leben ausgezeichneter Katholiken der drei letzten Jahrhunderte. 7. Bd. 2. Aufl.)
    Leben des Pater Friedrich Spee, p. [129]-146, has special t. p.

8
NIC
    (Continued on next card)

Speusippus, fl. 347-339 B. C.
    Liber de Platonis definitionibus.

WITCHCRAFT
PA
4220
L3
A4+
1516
    Jamblichus, of Chalcis. [De mysteriis. Latin] [1516] (Card 2)

    Platonis. Speusippi Platonis discipuli, Liber de Platonis definitionibus. Pythagorae philosophi Aurea uerba. Symbola Pithagorae philosophi. Xenocratis philosophi platonici, Liber de morte. Mercurii Trismegisti Pimander. Eiusdem Asclepius. Marsilii Ficini De triplici uita lib. II. Eiusdem Liber de uoluptate. Eiusdem

8
    (Continued on next card)

Spee, Friedrich von, 1591-1635.

Witchcraft
T
792
56
    Diel, Johannes Baptista, 1843-1875.
        Friedrich Spe. Eine biographische und literarhistorische Skizze. Von J. B. M. Diel. Freiburg i. Br., Herder, 1872.
        119 p. port. 19cm. (Sammlung historischer Bildnisse. IX)
    Includes as "Beilage" selections from Spee's Trutznachtigall, in German and Latin.
    1. Spee, Friedrich von, 1591-1635. I. Spee, Friedrich von, 1591-1635. Trutz-Nachtigall. Selections. German and Latin.

NIC

WITCHCRAFT
BX
4700
L6
S33
1877
    Schick, J G   Leben des heiligen Alphons Maria von Liguori ... 1877. (Card 2)

    Anhang, p. [147]-162, consists of selections from Spee's Trutz-Nachtigall.

    1. Liguori, Alfonso Maria de', Saint, 1696-1787. 2. Spee, Friedrich von, 1591-1635. I. Spee, Friedrich von, 1591-1635. Trutz-Nachtigall. Selections. II. Title.

8
NIC

Speusippus, fl. 347-339 B. C.
    Liber de Platonis definitionibus.

WITCHCRAFT
PA
4220
L3
A4+
1516
    Jamblichus, of Chalcis. [De mysteriis. Latin] [1516] (Card 3)

    De sole & lumine libri. II. Apologia eiusdem in librum suum de lumine. Eiusdem Libellus de magis. Quod necessaria sit securitas, & tranquillitas animi. Praeclarissimarum sententiarum huius operis breuis annotatio. [Venetiis, In aedibvs Aldi, et Andreae soceri, 1516]
        177 [i.e., 175] numbered leaves.

8
    29cm.
    (Continued on next card)

Spee, Friedrich von, 1591-1635.

Witchcraft
T
792
087
    Duhr, Bernhard, 1852-1930.
        Neue Daten und Briefe zum Leben des P. Friedrich Spe.
    (In Görres-Gesellschaft zur Pflege der Wissenschaft im katholischen Deutschland, Bonn. Historisches Jahrbuch. München. 24cm. 21. Bd., 2. u. 3. Heft (1900), p. [328]-352)
    1. Spee, Friedrich von, 1591-1635. 2. Witchcraft--Germany. I. Title. II. Görres-Gesellschaft zur Pflege der Wissenschaft im katholischen Deutschland, Bonn. Historisches Jahrbuch.

BF
1025
S74+
1920
    Spence, Lewis, 1874-1955.
        An encyclopædia of occultism; a compendium of information on the occult sciences, occult personalities, psychic science, magic, demonology, spiritism and mysticism, by Lewis Spence. London, G. Routledge & sons, ltd., 1920.
        3 p. l., ix-xii, [2], 451 p. illus., plates, ports. 25½ x 20½ᶜᵐ.
    "Select bibliography": [2] p. after p. xii.

    1. Occult sciences—Dictionaries.   I. Title.

Library of Congress   BF1025.S7   20-7507
    [4]

Speusippus, fl. 347-339 B. C.
    Liber de Platonis definitionibus.

WITCHCRAFT
PA
4220
L3
A4+
1516
    Jamblichus, of Chalcis. [De mysteriis.] Latin. [1516] (Card 4)

    At head of title: Index eorvm, qvae hoc in libro habentvr.
    With colophon.
    Provenance: Bibliotec: SS. Me. Novelle.
    Translations by M. Ficino.
    1. Occult sciences. 2. Philosophy, Ancient--Collections. I. Proclus Diadochus. In Platonicum Alcibiadem. II. Proclus Diadochus. De sacrificio. III.

8
    (Continued on next card)

Spee, Friedrich von, 1591-1635.

    Ebner, Theodor.
        Friedrich von Spee und die Hexenprozesse seiner Zeit. Hamburg, Verlagsanstalt und Druckerei A.-G. (vormals J. F. Richter) 1898.
        47 p. 21cm. (Sammlung gemeinverständlicher wissenschaftlicher Vorträge, n.F., 13. Ser., Heft 291)

    1. Spee, Friedrich von, 1591-1635. 2. Witchcraft--Germany. I. Title.

BF
1025
S74+
1960
    Spence, Lewis, 1874-1955.
        An encyclopaedia of occultism; a compendium of information on the occult sciences, occult personalities, psychic science, magic, demonology, spiritism, mysticism and metaphysics. New Hyde Park, N. Y., University Books [c1960]
        xxiv, 440 p. plates, ports. 26cm.

Witchcraft
BF
1410
B42
Z56
v.2
no.22
    Spiegel voor den verwarden, en warzoekende Haggebher Philaleethees.
        Noomtjins, Zalomon.
        Spiegel voor den verwarden, en warzoekende Haggebher Philaleethees. Waar in, uit zyne 6 brieven, enz. getoond word, zyne onkunde, en verwarring, zoo in taal, als in zaaken. Ofte een brief van Zalomon Noomtjins, tot Amsterdam. Geschreeven aan zynen vriend C. S. S. tot Buiksloot. Inhoudende (neevens andere zaaken) voornaamelijk, eenige aanmerkingen, over den perzoon, en de 6 brieven, enz. van Haggebher Philaleethees. Als meede over de briev, en perzoon van Everardus van der Hooght, en daar

    (Continued on next card)

CATALOGUE OF THE CORNELL WITCHCRAFT COLLECTION

Witchcraft   Spiegel voor den verwarden, en warzoekende
BF   Noomtjins, Zalomon. Spiegel voor den verwarden,
1410   en warzoekende Haggebher Philaleethees. 1692.
B42   (Card 2)
Z56
v.2   by ook over zyne Aanmerkingen, over de ordre
no.22   van een welgestelde predikatie. Mitsgaders
         d'ontdekking, der lasteringen van Brink.
         Amsterdam, By D. van den Dalen, boekverkooper,
         1692.
         33, [1] p. title and other vignettes.
         19 x 15cm.

                     (Continued on next card)

Witchcraft   Spiegel voor den verwarden, en warzoekende
           Haggebher Philaleethees.
BF   Noomtjins, Zalomon. Spiegel voor den ver-
1410   warden, en warzoekende Haggebher Philalee-
B42   thees. 1692.   (Card 3)
Z56
v.2   4°: A-D⁴, E1.
no.22   Black letter (except for introduction)
         Attacks critics of Balthasar Bekker's De
         betoverde weereld.
         G. L. Burr suggests Noomtjins may be a
         pseudonym for Bekker.
         Haggebher is a pseudonym of E. van der
         Hooght.

                     (Continued on next card)

8

Witchcraft   Spiegel voor den verwarden, en warzoekende
           Haggebher Philaleethees.
BF   Noomtjins, Zalomon. Spiegel voor den ver-
1410   warden, en warzoekende Haggebher Philalee-
B42   thees. 1692.   (Card 4)
Z56
v.2   Van der Linde 111.
no.22   No. 22 in vol. lettered Bekker II.
         1. Hooght, Everard van der, d. 1716. 2.
         Brink, Hendrik, 1645-1723. De godslasteringen
         van den amsterdamschen predikant Bekker. 3.
         Bekker, Balthasar, 1634-1698. De betoverde
         weereld. I. Title. II. Bekker, Balthasar,
         1634-1698, sup   posed author.

8

Witchcraft   Spieghel der aenvechtinghe des Sathans eñ
           ware proeve des Gheloofs.
BT   [Amsweer, Doede van]
980   Spieghel der aenvechtinghe des Sathans eñ
A52   ware proeve des Gheloofs; daer in ons de streydt
         des bleesches teghen den Gheest die alle
         Christen in tyde van Cruyce ende teghenspoet
         in sich gevoelen levendich wort voor oogen
         ghestelt ... Door D.van A. Groeninghen, Ghe-
         druckt by H. S. Boeckdrucker, 1612.
         1 v. (unpaged) 15cm.

         1. Devil.   I.   Title.

WITCHCRAFT
BF   Spielmann, Karl Heinz.
1583   Die Hexenprozesse in Kurhessen. Nach
S85   den Quellen dargestellt. 2. Aufl. Mar-
1932   burg, N. G. Elwert, 1932.
         viii, 248 p. illus., facsims. (part
         fold.) 20cm.

         1. Witchcraft--Hesse-Kassel. 2.
         Witchcraft--Germany. 3. Criminal proce-
         dure--Hesse-   Kassel. I. Title.
8
NIC

           Spiess, Johannes Georg, respondent.
WITCHCRAFT
R   Ziegra, Christian Samuel, praeses.
133   Disputatio physica De magica morborum
Z66   curatione, qvam ... exponit praeses M.
         Christianus Samuel Ziegra ... respondente
         M. Johanne Georgio Spiess ... [Witte-
         bergae] Typis Matthaei Henckelii [1681]
         [24] p. 19cm.

         1. Medicine, Magic, mystic, and spa-
         giric. 2. Witchcraft. 3. Folk medicine.
         I. Spiess, Johannes Georg, respondent.
         II. Title: De magica morborum cu-
8   ratione.
NIC

WITCHCRAFT
BF   Spina, Bartolommeo.
1565   Reverendi Patris F. Bartholomaei Spinei
M47   Pisani ... Qvaestio de strigibvs, vna cvm
1575   tractatv de praeeminentia Sacrae Theologiae,
         & quadruplici apologia de lamiis contra Pon-
         zinibium ... Romae, In aedibus Populi Ro-
         mani, 1576.
         4 p. l., 180 p. 23cm.
         Bound with Mazzolini, Silvestro, da Pri-
         erio. ... De strigmagarum... Romae, 1575.
8   1. Witchcraft. 2. Theology, Doctrinal.
NIC   3. Ponzinib   ius, Joannes Franciscus.
         De lamiis,   et excellentia. I. Ti-
         tle: Quaes   tio de strigibus.
         II. Title.

WITCHCRAFT
BF   Spinaeus, Godofredus, praeses.
1559   Disputatio philosophica. Examinans
S85   quaestionem, Utrvm sonvs campanarvm ingru-
         entem tonitruum ac fulminum tempestatem,
         pruinas item, nec non spectra ac diabolum,
         depellere & abigere queat? Quam ... prae-
         side ... D. Godofredo Spinaeo ... Exerci-
         tationis ergo, publico subjicit examini,
         Joh. Iacobus Wagnerus ... Steinfvrti,
         Typis Cornelij Wellenberg, 1661.
         20 p. 19cm.

8   (Continued on next card)

WITCHCRAFT
BF   Spinaeus, Godofredus, praeses. Disputatio
1559   philosophica ... 1661.   (Card 2)
S85
         Diss.--Steinfurt (J. J. Wagner, respond-
         ent)

         1. Bells (in religion, folk-lore, etc.)
         2. Demonology. 3. Weather-lore. I.
         Wagner, Johann Jacob, respondent. II.
         Title: Utrum sonus campanarum ingruentem
         tonitruum ... tempestatem ... abigere
8   queat. III.   Title.

WITCHCRAFT
BF   Spinetti, Vittorio.
1584   Le streghe in Valtellina. Studio su
T9   vari documenti editi ed inediti dei sec.
S75   XV - XVI - XVII - XVIII. Sondrio, Stab.
         tip. E. Quadrio, 1903.
         131 p. 18cm.

         1. Witchcraft--Tyrol. 2. Witchcraft
         --Valtellina. I. Title.

8
NIC

           Spinoza, Benedictus de, 1632-1677.
            Tractatus theologico-politicus.
Witchcraft
BF   Falck, Nathanael, 1663-1693.
1520   Nathanaelis Falcken ... Dissertationes
F17   quatuor, De daemonologia recentiorum auto-
         rum falsa, Anno 1692. Wittebergae habitae,
         nunc verò praefixis literis Schomerianis
         ibidem recusae. [Wittebergae] Typis Mar-
         tini Schultzii, 1694.
         92 p. illus. initials. 20 x 16cm.
         4°: A², B-M⁴, N².
         Contents.--De falsa recentiorum aucto-
         rum daemonolog   ia ... respondente Joh.
8   (Continued on next card)

           Spinoza, Benedictus de, 1632-1677.
            Tractatus theologico-politicus.
Witchcraft
BF   Falck, Nathanael, 1663-1693. Nathanaelis
1520   Falcken ... Dissertationes quatuor ...
F17   1694.   (Card 2)

             Contents--Continued.
         Isaaco Trempenau.--Dissertatio II. Ortum
         daemonologiae falsae & progressum historicè
         declarans, respondente Johanne Furmann.--
         Dissertatio III. De daemonologia Hobbesii
         & Spinozae, respondente Jac. Friderico Mol-
         lero.--Dissert   atio IV. De daemonolo-
8   (Continued on next card)

           Spinoza, Benedictus de, 1632-1677.
            Tractatus theologico-politicus.
Witchcraft
BF   Falck, Nathanael, 1663-1693. Nathanaelis
1520   Falcken ... Dissertationes quatuor ...
F17   1694.   (Card 3)

         gia Bekkeri & aliorum, respondente Georg.
         Abrahamo Wolf.
         1. Demonology. 2. Hobbes, Thomas,
         1588-1679. Elementa philosophica de cive.
         3. Spinoza, Benedictus de, 1632-1677.
         Tractatus theologico-politicus. 4. Bek-
         ker, Balthasar,   1634-1698. De beto-
         verde weereld.   I. Title: De daemo-
8   nologia recen   tiorum autorum falsa.

Witchcraft   Spinoza, Benedictus de, 1632-1677.
B   Kettner, Friedrich Ernst.
3998   De duobus impostoribus, Benedicto Spinosa
K43   et Balthasare Bekkero. Lipsiae, Stannô
         Immanuelis Titii [1694]
         [17] p. 20cm.

         Diss.--Leipzig.

         1. Spinoza, Benedictus de, 1632-1677.
         2. Bekker, Balth   asar, 1634-1698.

           Spiritual and demonic magic from Ficino
            to Campanella.
BF   Walker, Daniel Pickering.
1593   Spiritual and demonic magic from Ficino
W17+   to Campanella. London, Warburg Institute,
         University of London, 1958.
         vi,244 p. illus. 27cm. (London.
         University. Warburg Institute. Studies,
         v. 22)

         1. Magic--Hist. I. Title. II. Series.

WITCHCRAFT
HV   Spitz, Erhard, fl. 1712-1716.
8609   De stigmatiis ... sine praeside dispv-
S76   tabit ... Erhardus Spitz Altdorfinus.
         [Altdorfii] Literis Kohlesii [ca. 1715?]
         50 p. 20cm.

         1. Punishment--History. 2. Cicatrice
         3. Birthmarks. 4. Witchcraft. I. Titl
8
NIC

WITCHCRAFT
BF   Spitzel, Gottlieb, 1639-1691.
1565   Die gebrochne Macht der Finsternüss,
S76   Zerstörte teuflische Bunds- und Buhl-Freu
         schafft mit den Menschen: das ist Gründ-
         licher Bericht, wie und welcher Gestalt d
         abscheuliche und verfluchte Zauber-Gemein
         schafft mit den bösen Geistern angehe; wi
         dieselbe zu- und fortgehe; ob und auf was
         Art und Weise sie widerum zergehe ... al
         Heyl- und Gnaden-begierigen und vom teufl
         Satan schänd   lich-berückten und ver
8   (Continued on next card
NIC

WITCHCRAFT
BF   Spitzel, Gottlieb, 1639-1691. Die ge-
1565   brochne Macht der Finsternüss ... 16
S76   (Card

         strickten Seelen zum nothwendigen Unterr
         und heylsamer Widerkehrung beschrieben .
         Augspurg, In Verlegung Gottlieb Göbels s
         Wittib, Gedruckt bey Jacob Koppmayer, 16
         24 p. l., 813, [18] p. 17cm.
         With added engr. t. p. for whole work
         and each of the   three Abtheilungen.
8   (Continued on next car
NIC

CATALOGUE OF THE CORNELL WITCHCRAFT COLLECTION

WITCHCRAFT
BF
1565
S76

Spitzel, Gottlieb, 1639-1691. Die gebrochne Macht der Finsternüss ... 1687.
(Card 3)

Title in red and black.
Cyprianvs magvs ... oder dess zu Christo
wunderbarlich bekehrten Ertz-Zauberers Cypriani von Antiochia hertzliche Buss und
Bekehrung: p. 778-813.
1. Witchcraft. 2. Devil. 3. Salva-
tion--Early works to 1800. I. Cyprianus,
of Antioch. Legend. II. Title.

8
NIC

WITCHCRAFT
BF
1584
S9
S61

Spitzel, Gottlieb, 1639-1691, supposed author.
Sincerus, Theophilus, pseud.
Nord-schwedische Hexerey, oder Simia
Dei, Gottes Affe. Das ist: Ausführliche
Beschreibung der schändlichen Verführungen
des leidigen Satans, darinnen zu sehen
Gottes erschröckliches Straff-Verhängen,
wegen greulicher Sünden-Mengen. In einem
Jammer-behertzigten Send-Schreiben am [sic]
Tag gegeben, von Theophilo Sincero, an
Christianum Piandrum. [Augsburg?] 1677.
[64] p. illus. 20cm.

8
NIC

(Continued on next card)

WITCHCRAFT
BF
1584
S9
S61

Spitzel, Gottlieb, 1639-1691, supposed author.
Sincerus, Theophilus, pseud. Nord-schwedische Hexerey ... 1677. (Card 2)

"By Gottlieb Spitzel? See what Hauber
says of the relation of this tract to his
[i.e., Spitzel's] Die gebrochene Macht der
Finsterniss. G. L. B."--Note in MS facing
t. p.
Illustrative vignette on t. p.
1. Witchcraft--Sweden. 2. Witchcraft.
I. Spitzel, Gottlieb, 1639-1691, supposed author. II. Title. III. Title:
Simia Dei, Gottes Affe.

NIC

WITCHCRAFT
BF
1566
S76

Spitzer, Johann.
Teufelsbündler. Zauber und Hexenglau-
ben und dessen kirchliche Ausbeutung zur
Schändung der Menschheit. Leipzig, O.
Wigand, 1871.
xx, 130 p. 20cm.
Includes list of folk spells.

1. Witchcraft--History. 2. Charms.
I. Title.

Sprenger, Jakob, 1436 or 8-1495, joint author.
Malleus maleficarum.

Zilboorg, Gregory, 1890-
... The medical man and the witch during the renaissance, by
Gregory Zilboorg ... Baltimore, The Johns Hopkins press,
1935.
x, 215 p. front. (port.) illus., plates. 20½ cm. (Publications of the
Institute of the history of medicine, the Johns Hopkins university. 3d
ser., vol. II)
"The Hideyo Noguchi lectures."
CONTENTS.—The physiological and psychological aspects of the Malleus maleficarum (The witch's hammer)—Medicine and the witch in the
sixteenth century—Johann Weyer, the founder of modern psychiatry.
1. Witchcraft. 2. Psychology, Pathological. 3. Institoris, Henricus,
d. ca. 1500. Malleus maleficarum. 4. Sprenger, Jakob, fl. 1494, joint
author. Malleus maleficarum. 5. Wier, Johann, 1515-1588. 6. Renaissance. I. Title.
Library of Congress   BF1569.Z5   35—12004
        Copy 2.
Copyright A 84565   [40n1]   [159.961140902]   133.40902

Sprenger, Jakob, 1436 or 8-1495.
[Institoris, Henricus] d. 1508.
Malleus maleficarum. [Speier, Peter
Drach, before 15 Apr., 1487]
[129] l. 28cm.

Leaf [1a] blank.
Leaf [1b]: Appologia auctoris in malleum maleficarum.
Leaf [129] (End): Sit laus deo. exter-
miniū heresis. pax viuis. requies eterna
defunctis. Amen.
Signatures: a-p⁸, q⁹.

(Continued on next card)

Witchcraft
BF
1569
A2I59+
1487

Sprenger, Jakob, 1436 or 8-1495.
[Institoris, Henricus] d. 1508. Malleus
maleficarum ... [before 15 Apr., 1487]
(Card 2)

Capital spaces.
By Henricus Institoris (Heinrich Krä-
mer) and Jakob Sprenger.
Hain. Repertorium (with Copinger's Sup-
plement) *9238; Proctor, 526; Brit. Mus.
Cat. (XV cent.) I, p. xxvi; Goff. Third
census, I-163.
With bookplate of J. B. Holzinger.

(Continued on next card)

Witchcraft
BF
1569
A2I59+
1490

Sprenger, Jakob, 1436 or 8-1495.
[Institoris, Henricus] d. 1508.
Malleus maleficarum. [Speier, Peter
Drach, about 1490-91]
[102] l. 27cm.

Leaf [1a] (Title): Malleus maleficarum.
Leaf [1b]: Appologia auctoris in malleum maleficarum.
Leaves [2a]-[3b]: Tenor bulle apostolice
aduersus heresim maleficarum cum appro-
batione z subscriptione doctorū alme vni-
uersitatis Colonien. in sequentem tracta-
tum.

(Continued on next card)

Witchcraft
BF
1569
A2I59+
1490

Sprenger, Jakob, 1436 or 8-1495.
[Institoris, Henricus] d. 1508. Malleus
maleficarum ... [about 1490-91]
(Card 2)

Leaf [102a] (End): Sit laus deo. exter-
miniū heresis. pax viuis. requies eterna
defunctis. amen.
Signatures: a⁸, b-d⁶, ef⁸, g-h⁶, i⁸,
k-r⁶; signatures ef being used together to
mark a single gathering.
Capital spaces.
By Henricus Institoris (Heinrich Krämer)

(Continued on next card)

Witchcraft
BF
1569
A2I59+
1490

Sprenger, Jakob, 1436 or 8-1495.
[Institoris, Henricus] d. 1508. Malleus
maleficarum ... [about 1490-91]
(Card 3)

and Jakob Sprenger.
Hain. Repertorium (with Copinger's Sup-
plement) *9239; Proctor, 2383; Brit. Mus.
Cat. (XV cent.) II, p. 498 (IB. 8615);
Goff. Third census, I-164.

1. Witchcraft. 2. Demonology. 3. Crim-
inal law. 4. Criminal procedure. I.
Sprenger, Jakob. 1436 or 8-1495. II.
Title.

Witchcraft
BF
1569
A2I59+
1494

Sprenger, Jakob, 1436 or 8-1495.
[Institoris, Henricus] d. 1508.
Malleus maleficarum. Cologne, Johann
Koelhoff, the Younger, 24 Nov. (in vigilia
s. Katherine), 1494.
[112] l. 27cm.

Leaf [1a] (Title): Mallens maleficarum.
Leaf [1b]: Apologia autoris in malleū
maleficarū.
Leaves [1b]-[3a]: Tenor bulle apostoli-
ce aduersus heresim maleficaȝ cū ppbatōe z
sbscriptōe doctoȝ alme vniūsitatȝ Colon.
...
(Continued on next card)

Witchcraft
BF
1569
A2I59+
1494

Sprenger, Jakob, 1436 or 8-1495.
[Institoris, Henricus] d. 1508. Malleus
maleficarum ... 1494. (Card 2)

Leaf [112a] (Colophon): Liber Malleus
maleficarū a suo editore nuncupatus Im-
pressusȝ per me Ioannem Koelhoff incolā
Ciuitatis sancte Colonien. Anno salutȝ
Mcccc.xciiij. in vigilia sanctȝ Katherine
Regine ac ẽginis martyrisȝȝ finem accepit
feliciter.
Signatures: i-[iv]; a-s⁶. Leaves [5]-
[112] numbered i-folio Cviij, with many

(Continued on next card)

Witchcraft
BF
1569
A2I59+
1494

Sprenger, Jakob, 1436 or 8-1495.
[Institoris, Henricus] d. 1508. Malleus
maleficarum ... 1494. (Card 3)

errors.
Capital spaces, some with guide-letters.
Capitals, paragraph-marks and initial-
strokes supplied in red.
By Henricus Institoris (Heinrich Krämer)
and Jakob Sprenger.
Hain. Repertorium (with Copinger's Sup-
plement) 9244; Proctor, 1462; Brit. Mus.
Cat. (XV cent.) I, p. 298 (IB. 5064); Goff.

(Continued on next card)

Witchcraft
BF
1569
A2I59+
1494

Sprenger, Jakob, 1436 or 8-1495.
[Institoris, Henricus] d. 1508. Malleus
maleficarum ... 1494. (Card 4)

Third census, I-167.
Incomplete copy: lacks leaf xviij (c_{vi}).
Ex libris cabalisticis Kurt Seligmann.
Bound in brown morocco, by Sangorski and
Sutcliffe.

1. Witchcraft. 2. Demonology. 3. Criminal law. 4. Criminal procedure. I.
Sprenger, Jakob, 1436 or 8-1495. II. Title.

WITCHCRAFT
BF
1569
A2I59++
1928

Sprenger, Jakob, 1436 or 8-1495.
[Institoris, Henricus] d. 1508.
Malleus maleficarum, translated with an
introduction, bibliography and notes by the
Rev. Montague Summers. [London] J. Rodker,
1928.
xlv, 277, [1] p. front. (port.) 31cm.
By Henricus Institoris and Jacob Sprenger.
"This edition of Malleus maleficarum, comprising 1275 numbered copies, is here translated into English from the edition of 1489
for the first time ... This copy is out of
series."
"A note upon the bibliography of the Malleus
maleficarum": p. xli-xlii.

Witchcraft
BF
1569
A2I59
1948

Sprenger, Jakob, 1436 or 8-1495.
[Institoris, Henricus] d. 1508.
Malleus maleficarum, translated with an
introduction, bibliography and notes by the
Rev. Montague Summers. London, Pushkin
Press [1948]
xxi, 277 p. port. 23cm.

By Henricus Institoris (Heinrich Krämer)
and Jacob Sprenger.
"A note upon the bibliography of the
Malleus maleficarum": p. xvii-xviii.

WITCHCRAFT
BF
1565
S767

Spreter, Johann.
Ein kurtzer Bericht, was von den abgötterischen Sägen vñ Beschweren zůhalten,
wie der etlich volbracht, vnnd das die ein
Zauberey, auch Greüwel vor Gott dem Herren
seind. Durch den wirdigen vñ wolgelerten
Herren Johañ. Spreter von Rotweil zůsamen
gebracht ... [Basel, Getruckt durch Bartholomeum Westheymer, 1543]
[12] p. 21cm.
With colophon.

8
NIC

(Continued on next card)

WITCHCRAFT
BF
1565
S767

Spreter, Johann. Ein kurtzer Bericht ...
[1543] (Card 2)

Caption title: Von Sägen vnd Beschweren.
Running title: Von abgötterischen Sägen
vnd Beschweren.

1. Witchcraft. 2. Magic. 3. Folk
medicine. I. Title: Von abgötterischen
Sägen und Beschweren. II. Title. III.
Title: Von Sägen und Beschweren.

8
NIC

519

CATALOGUE OF THE CORNELL WITCHCRAFT COLLECTION

Springinsgut, Daniel, respondent.

Witchcraft
BF 1555 D71 1743
    Dorsch, Johann Georg, 1597-1659, praeses.
    Dispvtatio theologica De horrenda et miserabili Satanae obsessione eivsdemqve ex obsessis expvlsione, von leibl. Besitzungen. Svb praesidio Dn. Io. Georg. Dorschei ...a. 1656 d. 23. Avg. pvblico ervditorvm examini svbmissa ab avtore et respondente Daniel Springinsgut ... Vitembergae, Ex officina Scheffleriana, 1743.
    48 p. 20cm.

8   (Continued on next card)

Springinsgut, Daniel, respondent.

Witchcraft
BF 1555 D71 1667
    Dorsch, Johann Georg, 1597-1659, praeses.
    Summi theologi D. Joh. Georgii Dorschei, dissertatio De horrenda & miserabili Satanae obsessione, ejusdemqve ex obsessis expulsione, multorum votis expetita, juventutis studiosae commodo iterum prodit. Rostochii, Typis Johannis Richelii, 1667.
    [24] p. 20cm.
    Presented August 23, 1656, with D. Springinsgut as respondent, and title: Disputatio theologica De horrenda et miserabili Satanae obsessione.

8   (Continued on next card)

Witchcraft
Z 1001 D28 1865
    Spurious reprints of early books.
    Deane, Charles, 1813-1889.
    ... Spurious reprints of early books. Boston [Cambridge, University press] 1865.
    19 p. 25cm. (Bibliographical tracts. no. 1)
    Signed at end "Delta."
    "From the Boston Daily advertiser of March 24, 1865. With additions and corrections. One hundred and thirty-one copies printed."
    "This reprint was not made by Mr. Deane."--Sabin.
    A review of "Salem witchcraft; comprising More wonders of the invisible world, collected by Robert Calef; and Wonders of the invisible world, by Cotton Mather. Together with notes and explanations by Samuel P. Fowler. Boston, W. Veazie, 1865" [reissue from the stereotyped plates of the Salem, 1861, edition]
    1. Fowler, Samuel Page, 1800-1888, ed. [Salem witchcraft ... Boston, 1865.]   I. Title.
    Library of Congress   Z1001.D28   2--13743

Stade, Reinhold, ed.

WITCHCRAFT
BF 1583 Z7 1669
    Schulze, Barbara Elisabeth, fl. 1669, defendant.
    Barbara Elisabeth Schulzin. Ein Arnstädter Hexenprozess vom Jahre 1669. Nach den Originalprozessakten herausgegeben von Reinhold Stade. Arnstadt, Fürstl. Buchdruckerei von E. Protscher, 1904.
    75 p. 22cm.
    1. Trials (Witchcraft)--Germany. 2. Trials (Witchcraft)--Arnstadt, Germany. I. Stade, Reinhold, 1848- , ed. II. Title. III. Title: Ein Arnstädter Hexenprozess vom Jahre 1669.

8 NIC

Stadebauer, Caroline.

Witchcraft
BF 1555 E74 C7
    Eschenmayer, Carl Adolph von, 1770?-1852.
    Conflict zwischen Himmel und Hölle, an dem Dämon eines besessenen Mädchens beobachtet von C. A. Eschenmayer in Kirchheim unter Teck. Nebst einem Wort an Dr. Strauss. Tübingen, Buchhandlung Zu-Guttenberg, 1837.
    xvi, 215 p. 17cm.

BF 1501 S78
    Stambaugh, Ria, comp.
    Teufelbücher in Auswahl. Hrsg. von Ria Stambaugh. Berlin, De Gruyter, 1970-
    ? v. 21cm. (Ausgaben deutscher Literatur des XV. bis XVIII. Jahrhunderts)
    Contents.--Bd. 1. Zauberteufel, Schrapteufel, von L. Milichius.--Bd. 2. Kleiderteufel, von J. Strauss. Tanzteufel, von F. Daul. Hurenteufel, von A. Hoppenrod. Hausteufel, von A. Schubart. Zehn Teufel, von N. Schmidt.--Bd. 3. Hoffartsteufel, von Joachim Westphal.
    1. Demonology--Collections. I. Milichius, Ludwig, d. 1575.   II. Title.

WITCHCRAFT
BF 1569 A2 I59 1604
    Stampa, Pietro Antonio.
    Fuga Satanae. Exorcismvs ex sacrarum litterarum fontibus, pioque sacros. Ecclesiae instituto exhaustus. Cum indice ad oram libri annexo. Lvgdvni, Svmptibvs Petri Landry, 1610.
    112 [i.e. 88], [5] p. 18cm.
    Many errors in paging.
    Bound with v. 2-3 of Institoris, Henricus. Malleus maleficarvm. Lvgdvni, 1604.

    1. Exorcism.   I. Title.

8 NIC

Witchcraft
BF 1559 T41 1626
    Stampa, Pietro Antonio.
    Fuga Satanae.
    Thesavrvs exorcismorvm atqve conivrationvm terribilivm, potentissimorum, efficacissimorum cum practica probatissima: qvibvs spiritvs maligni, daemones maleficiaque omnia de corporibus humanis obsessis, tanquam flagellis, fustibusque fugantur, expelluntur, doctrinis refertissimus atq; uberrimus: ad maximam exorcistarum commoditatem nunc vltimo plenariè in lucem editus & recusus: cuius authores, vt & singuli tractatus sequente pagellâ consignati, inueniuntur. Cum indice capitum, rerum & verborum ... Coloniae, sumptibus haeredum Lazari Zetzneri, 1626.
    (Continued on next card)

Witchcraft
BF 1559 T41 1626
    Stampa, Pietro Antonio.
    Fuga Satanae.
    Thesavrvs exorcismorvm atqve conivrationvm terribilivm ... 1626.   (Card 2)

    12 p. l., 1232, [39] p. 18cm.

    Previously published at Cologne in 1608.

    Contents.--F. Valerii Polydori ... Practica exorcistarum ad daemones & maleficia de Christi fidelibus pellendum, pars prima ... [et] secunda.--R. p. f. Hieronymi Mengi ... Flagellum daemonum.--Eivsdem Fvstis daemonvm.--F. Zachariae Vicecomitis ... Complementum artis exorcisticae.--Petri Antonii Stampae ... Fuga Satanae.--R. d. Maximiliani ab Eynatten ... Manuale exorcismorum.

Witchcraft
Z 6880 G94
    Stanislas de Guaita et sa bibliothèque occulte.
    Guaita, Stanislas de, 1860-1897.
    Stanislas de Guaita et sa bibliothèque occulte. Paris, Dorbon, 1899.
    1 p. l., vi p., 1 l., 299 p. front. (port.) plates, facsims. 24cm.
    Preface by René Philipon.
    A catalogue of 2,227 lots, offered for sale, with prices.
    First issued in four parts, 1898-99, under title: Catalogue des livres et manuscrits relatifs aux sciences occultes.

    1. Occult sciences--Bibl.   I. Title.   3--22281

    Library of Congress, no.   Z6880.G9

BF 1576 S79 1949
    Starkey, Marion Lena.
    The Devil in Massachusetts, a modern inquiry into the Salem witch trials. [1st ed.] New York, A.A. Knopf, 1949.
    xviii, 310, vii p. 22cm.

    "Selected bibliography": p. 301-310.

    1. Witchcraft--Salem, Mass.   I. Title.

BF 1576 S79 1961
    Starkey, Marion Lena.
    The devil in Massachusetts; a modern inquiry into the Salem witch trials. Garden City, N. Y., Doubleday [1961]
    310 p. 19cm. (Dolphin Books)

    1. Witchcraft--Salem, Mass.   I. Title.

Witchcraft
BF 1581 S79
    Stearne, John.
    A confirmation and discovery of witch-craft containing these severall particulars; that there are witches called bad witches, and witches untruely called good or white witches, and what manner of people they be, and how they may bee knowne, with many particulars thereunto tending. Together with the confessions of many of those executed since May 1645, in the severall counties hereafter mentioned. As also some objections answered. ... London, Printed by W. Wilson, 1648.
    61 p. 19cm.   (Continued on next card)

Witchcraft
BF 1581 S79
    Stearne, John. A confirmation and discovery of witch-craft containing these severall particulars ... 1648.   (Card 2)

    Binding by Douglas Cockerell, full brown niger, blind tooled, spine gilt, dated 1902.

    1. Witchcraft.   I. Title.

DQ 3 Q3 v.22
    Steck, Rudolf, 1842-1924, ed.
    Die Akten des Jetzerprozesses nebst dem Defensorium. Basel, Verlag der Basler Buch- und Antiquariatshandlung vormals A. Geering, 1904.
    xl, 679 p. illus. 23cm. (Quellen zur Schweizer Geschichte, 22. Bd.)

    1. Jetzer, Johann, ca. 1483-ca. 1515. 2. Dominicans in Switzerland. 3. Bern--Church history--Sources.   I. Title.

WITCHCRAFT
BX 3545 S9 S81
    Steck, Rudolf, 1842-1924.
    Die Akten des Jetzerprozesses nebst dem Defensorium.
    Steck, Rudolf, 1842-1924. Der Berner Jetzerprozess (1507-1509) in neuer Beleuchtung nebst Mitteilungen aus d[en] noch ungedruckten Akten. Bern, Schmid & Francke, 1902.
    87 p. illus. 24cm.
    "Separat-Abdruck aus der 'Schweizerisch[en] theolog. Zeitschrift' (Verlag von August Frick, Zürich II)."
    Greatly expanded in his Die Akten des Jetzerprozesses nebst dem Defensorium. Basel, 1904.   (Continued on next card)

8 NIC

WITCHCRAFT
BX 3545 S9 S81
    Steck, Rudolf, 1842-1924.
    Die Akten des Jetzerprozesses nebst dem Defensorium.
    Steck, Rudolf, 1842-1924. Der Berner Jetzerprozess ... 1902.   (Card 2)

    Stamped on cover: A. Francke, Verlags-Cto. vormals Schmid & Francke, Bern.

    1. Jetzer, Johann, ca. 1483-ca. 1515. 2. Dominicans in Switzerland. 3. Bern--Church history--Sources. I. His Die Akten des Jetzerprozesses nebst dem Defensorium.   II. Title.

8 NIC

WITCHCRAFT
BX 3545 S9 S81
    Steck, Rudolf, 1842-1924.
    Der Berner Jetzerprozess (1507-1509) in neuer Beleuchtung nebst Mitteilungen aus noch ungedruckten Akten. Bern, Schmid & Francke, 1902.
    87 p. illus. 24cm.
    "Separat-Abdruck aus der 'Schweizerisc[hen] theolog. Zeitschrift' (Verlag von August Frick, Zürich II)."
    Greatly expanded in his Die Akten des Jetzerprozesses nebst dem Defensorium. B[a]sel, 1904.   (Continued on next card)

8 NIC

CATALOGUE OF THE CORNELL WITCHCRAFT COLLECTION

WITCHCRAFT
BX
3545
S9
S81

 Steck, Rudolf, 1842-1924.   Der Berner Jetzerprozess ... 1902.   (Card 2)

 Stamped on cover: A. Francke, Verlags-Cto. vormals Schmid & Francke, Bern.

 1. Jetzer, Johann, ca. 1483-ca. 1515. 2. Dominicans in Switzerland. 3. Bern--Church history--Sources. I. His Die Akten des Jetzerprozesses nebst dem Defensorium. II. Title.

8
NIC

Witchcraft
F
410
B42
v.1
no.7

 Steenwinkel, Paulus, d. 1740.
 Bekker, Balthasar, 1634-1698.
 Brief van Balthasar Bekker S. T. D. en predikant tot Amsterdam. Aan twee waardige predikanten D. Joannes Aalstius tot Hoornaar, ende D. Paulus Steenwinkel tot Schelluinen, over derselver Zedige aanmerkingen op een deel des tweeden boex van sijn werk genaamd De betoverde weereld. Amsterdam, By D. vanden Dalen, boekverkoper, 1693.
 11 p. [p. 12 blank] title vignette, illus. initial. 19 x 16cm.

 (Continued on next card)

Witchcraft
F
410
B42
v.1
no.7

 Steenwinkel, Paulus, d. 1740.
 Bekker, Balthasar, 1634-1698. Brief van Balthasar Bekker ... aan ... Joannes Aalstius ... 1693.   (Card 2)

 4°: A⁴, B².
 Letter autographed by Bekker.
 Van der Linde 72.
 No. 7 in vol. lettered Bekker I.
 1. Aalst, Johannes, 1660-1712. Zedige aanmerkingen. I. Aalst, Johannes, 1660-1712. II. Steenwinkel, Paulus, d. 1740. III. Title.

Witchcraft
65
2
.5

 Stegmann, Christian, respondent.
 Wolf, Johann, praeses.
 De lacrymis sagarum. Disputationem physicam ... praeside Dn. M. Johanne Wolfio ... exponit Christianus Stegmann ... VVittebergae, Typis Christiani Schrödteri [1676]
 [16] 20cm.
 No. 5 in vol. lettered Dissertationes de sagis. 1636-1714.
 1. Witchcraft. 2. Crying. I. Stegmann, Christian, respondent. II. Title.

 Steiner, Veronica.

WITCHCRAFT
BF
1559
K45
1574a

 Khueller, Sebastianus
 Kurtze vnnd warhafftige Historia von einer Junckfrawen, welche mit etlich vnd dreissig bösen Geistern leibhafftig besessen, vnd in der Schloss Capeln zu Starnberg, im Ertzhertzogthumb Österreich vnder der Enns, in beysein viler vom Adel, vnd ander ehrlichen leut, genedigklich daruon erlödiget worden. München, Getruckt bey Adam Berg [1574.
Wien, 1885]
 [14] p.   illus. 24cm.

 (Continued on next card)

 Steiner, Veronica.

WITCHCRAFT
BF
1559
K45
1574a

 Khueller, Sebastianus
 Kurtze vnnd warhafftige Historia von einer Junckfrawen...[1885]   (Card 2)

 Signed: Sebastianus Khueller.
 Facsimile reprint.

 1. Exorcism. 2. Steiner, Veronica. I. Title.

 Steirische Hexenprozesse.

Witchcraft
CB
3
Z481

 Ruland, Wilhelm, 1869-1927.
 Steirische Hexenprozesse. Ein Beitrag zur Kulturgeschichte des 17. Jahrhunderts. (In Beiträge zur Kulturgeschichte. Weimar. 25cm. 2. Heft (1898), p. [45]-71)

 1. Witchcraft--Germany. I. Title.

 Stelligeri and other essays concerning America.

Witchcraft
PS
3158
W7S7

 Wendell, Barrett, 1855-1921.
 Stelligeri and other essays concerning America. New York, Charles Scribner's Sons, 1893.
 217 p. 18cm.
 Contents.--I. Stelligeri.--II. The four American centuries.--III. Some neglected characteristics of the New England Puritans.--IV. Were the Salem witches guiltless?--V. American literature.--VI. John Greenleaf Whittier.--VII. Mr. Lowell as a teacher.
 1. American literature--Addresses, essays, lectures. 2. United States--Hist.--Addresses, essays, lectures. I. Title.

8

 Die Stellung der Jesuiten in den deutschen Hexenprozessen.

Witchcraft
BF
1583
D87

 Duhr, Bernhard, 1852-1930.
 Die Stellungen der Jesuiten in den deutschen Hexenprozessen. Köln, J. P. Bachem, 1900.
 92 p. 25cm. (Görres-Gesellschaft zur Pflege der Wissenschaften im katholischen Deutschland, Bonn. Schriften, 1900, 1)

 Sterf-bedde, van den eerwaarden, godsaligen en seer geleerden, Do. Balthazar Bekker ...

Witchcraft
BX
9479
B42
B11
no.1

 Bekker, Johannes Henricus, fl. 1698-1737.
 Sterf-bedde, van den eerwaarden, godsaligen en seer geleerden, Do. Balthazar Bekker: in sijn leeven S. T. D. en predikant tot Amsterdam. Ofte een oprecht bericht hoe hy sich geduurende sijne siekte gedragen heeft; voornamentljik [sic] voorgestelt uit sijne redenen tegens verscheidene gebruikt: en sulks na een voor af-gaande kort ontwerp van sijn leeven, volgens sijn eigen handschrift, gevonden onder sijne nagelatene papieren. Te samen, tot stuitinge

 (Continued on next card)

 Sterf-bedde, van den eerwaarden, godsaligen en seer geleerden, Do. Balthazar Bekker ...

Witchcraft
BX
9479
B42
B11
no.1

 Bekker, Johannes Henricus, fl. 1698-1737.
 Sterf-bedde van ... Do. Balthazar Bekker ... [1698]   (Card 2)

 van valsche geruchten, uytgegeven door sijn soon Joannes Henricus Bekker ... Amsterdam, By D. vanden Dalen, boekverkooper [1698]
 3 p. l., 26 p. title vignette, illus. initials. 20 x 15cm.
 4°: *3, A-C⁴, D1.
 Black letter (except for introduction)

 (Continued on next card)

 Sterf-bedde, van den eerwaarden, godsaligen en seer geleerden, Do. Balthazar Bekker ...

Witchcraft
BX
9479
B42
B11
no.1

 Bekker, Johannes Henricus, fl. 1698-1737.
 Sterf-bedde van ... Do. Balthazar Bekker ... [1698]   (Card 3)

 No. 1 in vol. lettered B. Bekkers sterfbed en andere tractaten.

 1. Bekker, Balthasar, 1634-1698--Biog. I. Title.

WITCHCRAFT
BF
1582
S83

 Sternon, Pierre.
 Les moines et les sorcières d'Ancy au XVIᵉ siècle. Nancy, Imprimerie nouvelle, 1886.
 148 p. 19cm.

 1. Witchcraft--Fiction. 2. Witchcraft--France. I. Title.

8
NIC

 Sterzinger, Don Ferdinand, 1721-1786.

 see

 Sterzinger, Ferdinand, 1721-1786.

CATALOGUE OF THE CORNELL WITCHCRAFT COLLECTION

Sterzinger, Ferdinand

Witchcraft
BF 1565 S83 no.1

Sterzinger, Ferdinand, 1721-1786.
　　Akademische Rede von dem gemeinen Vorurtheil der wirkenden und thätigen Hexerey, welche an Sr. Churfürstl. Durchleucht in Baiern, &c. &c. &c. höchsterfreulichen Namensfeste abgelesen worden von P. Don Ferdinand Sterzinger ... Den 13. October 1766. München, Gedruckt bey M. M. Mayrin, Stadtbuchdruckerin [1766]
　　22 p. 20cm. (bound in 23cm. vol.)
　　No. 1 in vol. lettered Sterzinger über Hexerei, 1766-　　　1767.
　　　1. Witchcraft. I. Title.

8

Witchcraft
BF 1584 A93 A61

Sterzinger, Ferdinand, 1721-1786.
　　Akademische Rede von dem gemeinen Vorurtheile der ... Hexerey.
　　Anpreisung der allergnädigsten Landesverordnung Ihrer kaiserl. königl. apostolischen Majestät, wie es mit dem hexenprocesse zu halten sey, nebst einer vorrede, in welcher die Kurze vertheidigung der hex- und zauberey, die herr pater Angelus März der Akademischen rede des herrn p. don Ferdinand Sterzingers über das vorurtheil der hexerey entgegengesetzet, beantwortet wird von einem gottesgelehrten. München, Akademische buchhandlung, 1767.
　　4 p. l., 282, [2] p. 23cm.
(Continued on next card)
42-40824

8　[2]

Witchcraft
BF 1584 A93 A61

Sterzinger, Ferdinand, 1721-1786.
　　Akademische Rede von dem gemeinen Vorurtheile der ... Hexerey.
　　Anpreisung der allergnädigsten Landesverordnung Ihrer kaiserl. königl. apostolischen Majestät ... 1767. (Card 2)
　　Variously ascribed to Jordan Simon and Andreas Ulrich Mayer.
　　"Sr. kaiserlich-königlich-apostolischen Majestät allergnädigsten Landesordnung, wie es mit dem Hexenprocesse zu halten sey, mit kurzen Anpreisungen für den gemeinen Mann erkläret," p. [1]-132 has special t.-p.
　　1. Witchcraft--Austria. 2. März, Agnellus, 1731-1784. Kurze Vertheidigung der thätigen Hex- und Zauberey. 3. Sterzinger, Ferdinand, 1721-1786. Akademische Rede von dem gemeinen Vorurtheile der ... Hexerey. I. Simon, Jordan, pater, 1719-1776, supposed ed. II. Mayer, Andreas Ulrich, 1732-1802, supposed ed. III. Austria. Laws, statutes, etc. IV. Ein Gottesgelehrter.

Library of Congress　　BF1584.A8A5
42-40824
8　[2]

Witchcraft
BF 1565 S83 no.3

Sterzinger, Ferdinand, 1721-1786.
　　Akademische Rede von dem gemeinen Vorurtheile der Hexerey.
　　Drey Fragen zur Vertheidigung der Hexerey. I. Ob P. Angelus März die Rede des P. Don Ferdinand Sterzingers gründlich, und II. bescheiden widerleget habe? III. Und ob wohl diese akademische Rede dem heiligen Kreutze von Scheyrn in der That nachtheilig sey? Mit einem sichern Ja beantwortet, und dem P. Angelus März selbst dedicirt von J. F. Z. ... [München?] 1767.
　　28 p. 23cm.
(Continued on next card)

8

Witchcraft
BF 1565 S83 no.3

Sterzinger, Ferdinand, 1721-1786.
　　Akademische Rede von dem gemeinen Vorurtheile der Hexerey.
　　Drey Fragen zur Vertheidigung der Hexerey ... 1767. (Card 2)
　　"In spite of the initials J. F. Z. (Johann Felix Zech) in the dedication, the work is probably by H. Braun. See Fieger, H. P. Don Ferdinand Sterzinger, 1907."--Note by G. L. Burr on his ms. catalog slip for this item.
　　No. 3 in vol. lettered Sterzinger über Hexerei, 1766-1767.
(Continued on next card)

8

Witchcraft
BF 1565 D77

Sterzinger, Ferdinand, 1721-1786.
　　Akademische Rede von dem gemeinen Vorurtheile der ... Hexerey.
　　Drey wichtige Fragen über das Hexen-System von einem gesunden, unverruckten Kopf disseits der Donau. [n. p.] 1767.
　　24 p. 21cm.
　　H. Fieger, in P. Don Ferdinand Sterzinger, attributes this work to one "Premb, Weltpriester."
　　1. Witchcraft. 2. Sterzinger, Ferdinand, 1721-1786. Akademische Rede von dem gemeinen Vorurtheile der ... Hexerey.
I. Premb,　　, supposed author.
II. Ein gesunder, unverruckter Kopf disseits der Donau.

8

Witchcraft
BF 1565 S83 K81

Sterzinger, Ferdinand, 1721-1786.
　　Akademische Rede von dem gemeinen Vorurtheile der ... Hexerey.
　　[Kollmann, Jacob Anton]
　　Zweifel eines Baiers über die wirkende Zauberkunst und Hexerey. An dem Lechstrome [i.e., Augsburg] 1768.
　　74, [1] p. 19cm.
　　Attribution by British Museum and H. Fieger, P. Don Ferdinand Sterzinger, München, 1907.
　　1. Sterzinger, Ferdinand, 1721-1786. Akademische Rede von dem gemeinen Vorurtheile der ... Hexerey. 2. März, Agnellus, 1726-1784. 3. Witchcraft. II. Title.

8

Witchcraft
BF 1565 S83 M17

Sterzinger, Ferdinand, 1721-1786.
　　Akademische Rede von dem gemeinen Vorurtheile der ... Hexerey.
　　[März, Agnellus] 1726-1784.
　　Urtheil ohne Vorurtheil über die wirkend- und thätige Hexerey, abgefasset von einem Liebhaber der Wahrheit. [München] 1766.
　　64 p. 20cm.
　　1. Sterzinger, Ferdinand, 1721-1786. Akademische Rede von dem gemeinen Vorurtheile der ... Hexerey. 2. Witchcraft. I. Ein Liebhaber der Wahrheit. II. Title.

8

Witchcraft
BF 1565 S83 M18 1766

Sterzinger, Ferdinand, 1721-1786.
　　Akademische Rede von dem gemeinen Vorurtheile der ... Hexerey.
　　März, Angelus, 1731-1784.
　　P. Angelus März Kurze Vertheidigung der thätigen Hex- und Zauberey wider eine dem heiligen Kreuz zu Scheyrn nachtheilig-Akademische Rede, welche den 13. October 1766. von P. Don Ferdinand Sterzinger ... abgelesen worden. 2. Aufl. Jngolstadt, Gedruckt bey J. K. Gran [1766]
　　31 p. 21cm.
　　1. Sterzinger, Ferdinand, 1721-1786. Akademische Rede von dem gemeinen Vorurtheile der ... Hexerey. 2. Witchcraft. I. Title: Kurze Vertheidigung der thätigen Hex- und Zauberey.

8

Witchcraft
BF 1565 S83 S83

Sterzinger, Ferdinand, 1721-1786.
　　Betrügende Zauberkunst und träumende Hexerey, oder Vertheidigung der akademischen Rede, von dem gemeinen Vorurtheile der wirkenden und thätigen Hexerey, wider das Urtheil ohne Vorurtheil &c. ... München, In der akademischen Buchhandlung, 1767.
　　4 p. l., 96, [2] p. 21cm.
　　1. His Akademische Rede von dem gemeinen Vorurtheile der Hexerey. 2. Witchcraft. 3. März, Agnellus, 1726-1784. Urtheil ohne Vorurtheil über die wirkend- und thätige Hexere I. Title.

8

Witchcraft
BF 1565 S84

Sterzinger, Ferdinand, 1721-1786.
　　Akademische Rede von dem gemeinen Vorurtheile der ... Hexerey.
　　[Sterzinger, Joseph] 1746-1821.
　　Der Hexenprocess: ein Traum erzählt von einer unpartheyischen Feder im Jahre 1767. [München?] 1767.
　　18 p. 22cm.
　　Attribution and dates from Fieger, Hans. P. Don Ferdinand Sterzinger, München, 1907, p. 144-45. (Accepted also by Holzmann)
　　1. Sterzinger, Ferdinand, 1721-1786. Akademische Rede von dem gemeinen Vorurtheile der ... Hexerey. 2. Witchcraft. I. Eine unpartheyische Feder. II. Title.

8

Witchcraft
BF 1603 S83 G3

Sterzinger, Ferdinand, 1721-1786.
　　Die aufgedeckten Gassnerischen Wunderkuren.
　　Don Ferdinand Sterzingers Geister- und Zauberkatekismus. München, Bey J. N. Fritz, 1783.
　　72 p. 17cm.
　　Expansion of his Katekismus von der Geisterlehre, first published 1775 in his Untersuchung, ob es eine Festigkeit gebe, and again in his Die aufgedeckten Gassnerischen Wunderkuren, 1775.
　　1. Magic. 2. Witchcraft. 3. Spirits. I. Title: Geister- und Zauberkatekismus.

8

Witchcraft
BF 1410 S83 1785

Sterzinger, Ferdinand, 1721-1786.
　　Don Ferdinand Sterzingers Bemühung den Aberglaube zu stürzen. München, Bey J. Lentner, 1785.
　　6 p. l., 187 p. 21cm.
　　Table of contents bound by mistake between p. 186-187.
　　First published 1784, according to Kayser.
　　1. Occult sciences. 2. Superstition. I. Title: Bemühung den Aberglaube zu stürzen. II. Title.

8

Witchcraft
BF 1565 S83 S83

Sterzinger, Ferdinand, 1721-1786.
　　Betrügende Zauberkunst und träumende Hexerey oder Vertheidigung der Akademische Rede, von dem gemeinen Vorurtheile der wirkenden und thätigen Hexerey, wider das Urtheil ohne Vorurtheil &c. gestellet von P. Don Ferdinand Sterzinger ... München, In der akademischen Buchhandlung, 1767.
　　4 p. l., 96, [2] p. 21cm.

8

Witchcraft
BF 1565 S83 no.2

Sterzinger, Ferdinand, 1721-1786.
　　Betrügende Zauberkunst und träumende Hexerey, oder Vertheidigung der Akademische Rede, von dem gemeinen Vorurtheile der wirkenden und thätigen Hexerey, wider das Urtheil ohne Vorurtheil &c. gestellet von P. Don Ferdinand Sterzinger ... München, In der akademischen Buchhandlung, 1767.
　　4 p. l., 96, [2] p. 23cm.
　　Imperfect copy: t. p. damaged and all after p. 72 wanting.
　　No. 2 in vol. lettered Sterzinger über Hexerei, 1766-67.

8

CATALOGUE OF THE CORNELL WITCHCRAFT COLLECTION

Witchcraft
565
33
335

Sterzinger, Ferdinand, 1721-1786.
   Betrügende Zauberkunst und träumende Hexerey.
   [März, Agnellus] 1726-1784.
   Vertheidigung wider die geschwulstige Vertheidigung der betrügenden Zauberkunst und traumenden Hexerey, verfasset von einem Liebhaber der Wahrheit. [München] 1767.
   [4] p.l., 104 p. 23cm.

   1. Sterzinger, Ferdinand, 1721-1786. Betrügende Zauberkunst und träumende Hexerey. I. Ein Liebhaber der Wahrheit. II. Title.

Witchcraft
565
33
336

Sterzinger, Ferdinand, 1721-1786.
   Betrügende Zauberkunst und träumende Hexerey.
   [Mayer, Andreas Ulrich] 1732-1802. Sendschreiben an den Hochw. H. P. Agnellus März, ... über seine Vertheidigung wider die schwulstige Vertheidigung der betrügenden Zauberey und Hexerey, von F. N. Blocksberger, Beneficiaten zu T. [pseud.] Straubingen, 1767.
   5 pieces in 3 v. 23cm.
   Vol. 2 has caption title: Weitere Fortsetzung. Des F. N. Blockbergers [sic] zweytes Sendschreiben an H. P. Agnell &c. &c.

(Continued on next card)

Witchcraft
565
33
336

Sterzinger, Ferdinand, 1721-1786.
   Betrügende Zauberkunst und träumende Hexerey.
   [Mayer, Andreas Ulrich] 1732-1802. Sendschreiben an den Hochw. H. P. Agnellus März ... 1767. (Card 2)

   This vol. contains the 2. and 4. Sendschreiben, consecutively paged.
   Vol. 3 has caption title: Des F. N. Blockbergers [sic] fünftes Sendschreiben an H. P. Agnell, &c. &c. The vol. contains the 5. and 6. Sendschreiben, consecutively paged.

(Continued on next card)

Witchcraft
603
3
.3

[Sterzinger, Ferdinand] 1721-1786.
   Der in die katholische Schule geführte Fragensteller über den Katechismus von der Geisterlehre. [München?] 1775.
   29 p. 17cm.

   Ascribed to Sterzinger by British Museum.
   No. 3 in vol lettered Francone dell' Amavero (Sterzinger) Untersuchung [etc.]

   1. Frage, ob der Katechismus von der Geisterlehre e   in katholischer Katechismus sey? 2.   Magic. I. Title.

Witchcraft

[Sterzinger, Ferdinand] 1721-1786.
   Der in die katholische Schule geführte Fragensteller über den Katechismus von der Geisterlehre. [München?] 1775.
   29 p. 17cm.

   No. 4 in vol. lettered Gassneriana.

Witchcraft

Sterzinger, Ferdinand, 1721-1786.
   Der in die katholische Schule geführte Fragensteller.
   Der von seinem unglücklich gewählten Schüler abgefertigte Schulmeister. [n. p.] 1775.
   80 p. 17cm.

   No. 4 in vol. lettered Francone dell' Amavero (Sterzinger) Untersuchung [etc.]

   1. Sterzinger, Ferdinand, 1721-1786. Katekismus von der Geisterlehre. 2. Sterzinger, Ferdin   and, 1721-1786. Der in die kathol   ische Schule geführte Fragensteller.

Witchcraft
BF
1565
S83
M177

[Sterzinger, Ferdinand] 1721-1786.
   Gedanken über die Werke des Liebhabers der Wahrheit von der Hexerey. München, Bey J. A. Crätz, 1767.
   27, [1] p. 21cm.
   Attributed to Sterzinger by Holzmann and British Museum.

   1. März, Agnellus, 1726-1784. Urtheil ohne Vorurtheil über die wirkend- und thätige Hexerey. 2. His Akademische Rede von dem gemein   en Vorurtheile der ... Hexerey. I.   Title.

Witchcraft
BF
1603
S83
G3

Sterzinger, Ferdinand, 1721-1786.
   Don Ferdinand Sterzingers Geister- und Zauberkatekismus. München, Bey J. N. Fritz, 1783.
   72 p. 17cm.
   Expansion of his Katekismus von der Geisterlehre, first published 1775 in his Untersuchung, ob es eine Festigkeit gebe, and again in his Die aufgedeckten Gassnerischen Wunderkuren, 1775.
   1. Magic. 2. Witchcraft. 3. Spirits. I. Title: Geister- und Zauberkateki   smus. (ver)

Witchcraft
BF
1445
S83

Sterzinger, Ferdinand, 1721-1786.
   Die Gespenstererscheinungen, eine Phantasie oder Betrug, durch die Bibel, Vernunftlehre und Erfahrung bewiesen ... München, Bey J. Lentner, 1786.
   4 p. l., 123 p. 22cm.

   1. Ghosts. 2. Superstition. I. Title.

Witchcraft
BF
1603
S83
G3

Sterzinger, Ferdinand, 1721-1786.
   Katekismus von der Geisterlehre.
   Don Ferdinand Sterzingers Geister- und Zauberkatekismus. München, Bey J. N. Fritz, 1783.
   72 p. 17cm.
   Expansion of his Katekismus von der Geisterlehre, first published 1775 in his Untersuchung, ob es eine Festigkeit gebe, and again in his Die aufgedeckten Gassnerischen Wunderkuren, 1775.
   1. Magic. 2. Witchcraft. 3. Spirits. I. Title: Geister- und Zauberkateki   smus.

Witchcraft
BF
1603
S83
no.1

Sterzinger, Ferdinand, 1721-1786.
   Katekismus von der Geisterlehre.
   ... Untersuchung ob es eine Festigkeit gebe dabey viele andere aberglaubische Irrthümer wiederleget werden nebst beygefügtem Katechismus von der Geisterlehre. München, W. Schwarzkopf, Buchhändler in Nürnberg, 1775.
   200 p. 17cm.
   At head of title: Francone dell' Amavero [pseud. of F. Sterzinger]
   No. 1 in vol. lettered Francone dell' Amavero (Ster   zinger) Untersuchung [etc.]

(Continued on next card)

Witchcraft
BF
1603
S83
no.1

Sterzinger, Ferdinand, 1721-1786.
   Katekismus von der Geisterlehre.
   ... Untersuchung ob es eine Festigkeit gebe ... 1775. (Card 2)

   Attributed by British Museum and Kayser to A. U. Mayer.
   1. Magic. 2. Spells. I. His Katekismus von der Geisterlehre. II. Title. III. Mayer, Andreas Ulrich, 1732-1802, supposed author. IV. Title: Katekismus von der Geist   erlehre.

Witchcraft
BF
1603
S83
no.4

Sterzinger, Ferdinand, 1721-1786.
   Katekismus von der Geisterlehre.
   Der von seinem unglücklich gewählten Schüler abgefertigte Schulmeister. [n. p.] 1775.
   80 p. 17cm.

   No. 4 in vol. lettered Francone dell' Amavero (Sterzinger) Untersuchung [etc.]

   1. Sterzinger, Ferdinand, 1721-1786. Katekismus von der Geisterlehre. 2. Sterzinger, Ferdin   and, 1721-1786. Der in die kathol   ische Schule geführte Fragensteller.

Witchcraft
BF
1603
S83
no.2

Sterzinger, Ferdinand, 1721-1786.
   Katekismus von der Geisterlehre.
   Frage, ob der Katechismus von der Geisterlehre ein katholischer Katechismus sey? [Augsburg] 1775.
   45 p. 17cm.

   No. 2 in vol. lettered Francone dell' Amavero (Sterzinger) Untersuchung [etc.]

   1. Sterzinger, Ferdinand, 1721-1786. Katekismus von der Geisterlehre. 2. Miracles--Early works to 1800.

Witchcraft
BF
1603
S83
no.1

[Sterzinger, Ferdinand] 1721-1786.
   ... Untersuchung ob es eine Festigkeit gebe dabey viele andere aberglaubische Irrthümer wiederleget werden nebst beygefügtem Katechismus von der Geisterlehre. München, W. Schwarzkopf, Buchhändler in Nürnberg, 1775.
   200 p. 17cm.
   At head of title: Francone dell' Amavero [pseud. of F. Sterzinger]
   No. 1 in vol. lettered Francone dell' Amavero (Ster   zinger) Untersuchung [etc.]

(Continued on next card)

Witchcraft
BF
1603
S83
no.1

[Sterzinger, Ferdinand] 1721-1786. ... Untersuchung ob es eine Festigkeit gebe ... 1775. (Card 2)

   Attributed by British Museum and Kayser to A. U. Mayer.
   1. Magic. 2. Spells. I. His Katekismus von der Geisterlehre. II. Title. III. Mayer, Andreas Ulrich, 1732-1802, supposed author. IV. Title: Katekismus von der Geist   erlehre. V. Title: Francone dell' Amavero Untersuchung ob es eine Festigkeit gebe.

Witchcraft
BF
1603
S83
G3

Sterzinger, Ferdinand, 1721-1786.
   Untersuchung, ob es eine Festigkeit gebe.
   Don Ferdinand Sterzingers Geister- und Zauberkatekismus. München, Bey J. N. Fritz, 1783.
   72 p. 17cm.
   Expansion of his Katekismus von der Geisterlehre, first published 1775 in his Untersuchung, ob es eine Festigkeit gebe, and again in his Die aufgedeckten Gassnerischen Wunderkuren, 1775.
   1. Magic. 2. Witchcraft. 3. Spirits. I. Title: Geister- und Zauberkateki   smus.

Witchcraft
BF
1565
S83
no.4

Sterzinger, Ferdinand, 1721-1786, supposed author.
   [Mayer, Andreas Ulrich] 1732-1802.
   Nichtige, eitle, kahle und lächerliche Verantwortung des H. P. Angelus März, Benedictiner zu Scheyrn, über die vom P. Don Ferdinand Sterzinger bey dem hochfürstlichen hochlöblichen geistlichen Rath in Freysing gestellten Fragen. Vom Moldaustrom, 1767.
   57 p. 20cm. (bound in 23cm. vol.)
   Ascribed by Graesse, J. G. T., Bibliotheca magica et pneumatica and by Zapf,

(Continued on next card)

523

CATALOGUE OF THE CORNELL WITCHCRAFT COLLECTION

Sterzinger, Ferdinand, 1721-1786, supposed author.

Witchcraft
BF 1565 S83 no.4

[Mayer, Andreas Ulrich] 1732-1802. Nichtige, ungegründete, eitle ... Verantwortung des H. P. Angelus März ... 1767. (Card 2)

G. W., Zauberbibliothek, to F. N. Blocksberger, which is A. U. Mayer's pseudonym. British Museum suggests F. Sterzinger as author.
No. 4 in vol. lettered Sterzinger über Hexerei, 1766-1767.

8 (Continued on next card)

Sterzinger, Ferdinand, 1721-1786.

Witchcraft
BX 4705 S832 F45 1907

Fieger, Hans, 1857- . P. Don Ferdinand Sterzinger, Lector der Theatiner in München, Director der historischen Klasse der kurbayerischen Akademie der Wissenschaften, Bekämpfer des Aberglaubens und Hexenwahns und der Pfarrer Gassnerschen Wunderkuren. Ein Beitrag zur Geschichte der Aufklärung in Bayern unter Kurfürst Maximilian III. Joseph. München, R. Oldenbourg, 1907.
xi, 275 p. 2 tables. 23cm.

8 (Continued on next card)

Sterzinger, Ferdinand, 1721-1786.

Witchcraft
BX 4705 S832 F45 1907

Fieger, Hans, 1857- . P. Don Ferdinand Sterzinger ... 1907. (Card 2)
Inaug.-diss.--München.
Expansion of a Programmschrift: Pater Don Ferdinand Sterzingers Leben und Schriften, München, 1907.
1. Sterzinger, Ferdinand, 1721-1786. 2. Bavaria--Hist.--Maximilian III Joseph (1745-1777). I. Title.

8

Sterzinger, Ferdinand, 1721-1786.

Witchcraft
BF 1565 S83 G19

[Ganser, Benno] 1728-1779?
Sendschreiben an einen gelehrten Freund betreffend die heutige Streitschriften von der Hexerey. Vom Donau-Strohm [1767?]
[12] p. 20cm.
Attribution by Holzmann and British Museum (the latter gives Christian name as Brenno). Fieger, in his P. Don Ferdinand Sterzinger, p. 136, gives the name as B. Janser: a misprint?
1. Sterzinger, Ferdinand, 1721-1786. 2. Witchcraft. I. Title. II. Janser, B , supposed author.

8

Sterzinger, Ferdinand, 1721-1786.

Witchcraft
MSS Bd Witchcraft BF G38

Gespräche von verschiedenem Innhalte unter einer muntern Fastnachtcompagnie, verfasset von einem Liebhaber einer anständigen Freyheit. Gedruckt vor baares Geld, im Jahr, als noch im Märze Fasching war. [München? 1677]
16 p. 22cm.
Carnap's manuscript copy.
Concerns the Sterzinger-März controversy.
1. Sterzinger, Ferdinand, 1721-1786. 2. Superstition. I. Ein Liebhaber einer anständigen Freyheit.

8

Sterzinger, Ferdinand, 1721-1786.

WITCHCRAFT
BF 1565 S83 L88

[Loschert, Oswald] b.1704.
Vorgängischer Versuch zu Erwürkung eines Vertrages zwischen den in dem bisherigen Hexerey-Kriege verwickelten Gelehrten. Wie auch zum nutzbaren Unterrichte, wie man von der Zauber- und Hexerey weder zu wenig, noch zu viel glauben soll. Unternommen von einem Verehrer der Gelehrten und Liebhaber der Christlichen Wahrheiten. [Bamberg] an dem Maynstrome [Göbhardt] 1767.
86 p. 23 cm.

8 NIC (Continued on next card)

Sterzinger, Ferdinand, 1721-1786.

Witchcraft
BF 1565 S83 M185

März, Angelus, 1731-1784.
P. Angeli März Verantwortung über die vom (Titl) P. Don Ferdinand Sterzinger bey dem hochfürstlich-hochlöblich-geistlichen Rath zu Freysing freywillig wider ihn gestellten Fragen. Ingolstadt, Gedruckt bey J. K. Gran, 1767.
42 p. 19cm.
A copy of the questions may be found in: Fieger, Hans, 1857- . P. Don Ferdinand Sterzinger, München, 1907, p. 135.

8 (Continued on next card)

Sterzinger, Ferdinand, 1721-1786.

Witchcraft
BF 1565 S83 M186

[Mayer, Andreas Ulrich] 1732-1802.
Glückwünschungsschreiben an den Hochw. P. Angelus März, über seine Vertheidigung der Hex- und Zauberey, von F. N. Blocksberger, Beneficiaten zu T. [pseud.] Straubingen, 1767.
[16] p. 22cm.
1. März, Angelus, 1731-1784. ... Kurze Vertheidigung der thätigen Hex- und Zauberey. 2. Sterzinger, Ferdinand, 1721-1786. I. Title.

8

Sterzinger, Ferdinand, 1721-1786.

Witchcraft
BF 1565 S83 no.4

[Mayer, Andreas Ulrich] 1732-1802.
Nichtige, ungegründete, eitle, kahle und lächerliche Verantwortung des H. P. Angelus März, Benedictiner zu Scheyrn, über die vom P. Don Ferdinand Sterzinger bey dem hochfürstlichen hochlöblichen geistlichen Rath in Freysing gestellten Fragen. Vom Moldaustrom, 1767.
57 p. 20cm. (bound in 23cm. vol.)
Ascribed by Graesse, J. G. T., Bibliotheca magica et pneumatica and by Zapf,

8 (Continued on next card)

Sterzinger, Ferdinand, 1721-1786.

Witchcraft
BF 1565 S83 no.4

[Mayer, Andreas Ulrich] 1732-1802. Nichtige, ungegründete, eitle ... Verantwortung des H. P. Angelus März ... 1767. (Card 2)

G. W., Zauberbibliothek, to F. N. Blocksberger, which is A. U. Mayer's pseudonym. British Museum suggests F. Sterzinger as author.
No. 4 in vol. lettered Sterzinger über Hexerei, 1766-1767.

8 (Continued on next card)

Sterzinger, Ferdinand, 1721-1786.

Witchcraft
BF 1565 S83 M69

Model, Johann Michael
Johann Michael Models, J. U. Lic. beantwortete Frage: Ob man die Ausfahrt der Hexen zulassen könne? Wider den heutigen Hexenstürmer P. Ferdinand Sterzinger. München, Bey J. A. Crätz, 1769.
36 p. 18cm.
1. Sterzinger, Ferdinand, 1721-1786. 2. Witchcraft. I. Title: Beantwortete Frage: Ob man die Ausfahrt der Hexen zulassen könne? II. Title: Frage, Ob man die Ausfahrt der Hexen zulassen könne?

8

Sterzinger, Ferdinand, 1721-1786.

Witchcraft
BF 1584 A93 R22 1891

Rapp, Ludwig.
Die Hexenprozesse und ihre Gegner in Tirol. 2. verm. Aufl. Mit dem Bildnisse Tartarotti's. Brixen, A. Wegner, 1891.
iv, 170 p. port. 22cm.
First published 1874 with title: Die Hexenprozesse und ihre Gegner aus Tirol.
1. Witchcraft--Austria. 2. Trials (Witchcraft)--Austria. 3. Tanner, Adam, 1572-1632. 4. Tartarotti, Girolamo, 1706-1761. 5. Sterzinger, Ferdinand, 1721-1779. I. Title.

8

Sterzinger, Ferdinand, 1721-1786.

Witchcraft
BF 1559 G25 Z63 no.3

Was soll man an den Kuren des Herrn geistlichen Raths Gassner, die er bisher im Namen Jesu gemacht hat, noch untersuchen, so nicht schon längst hundertmal ist untersucht worden? Frankfurt und Berlin, 1775.
96 p. 17cm.
No. 3 in vol. lettered Gassneriana.
1. Gassner, Johann Joseph, 1727-1779. 2. Faith-cure. 3. Politische Frage, ob ein ... Landesfürst über die Gassnerischen Kuren ... gleichgültig seyn kann. 4. Sterzinger, Ferdinand, 1721-1786.

8

Sterzinger, Ferdinand, 1721-1786.

Witchcraft
BF 1565 S83 Z97

[Zapf, Georg Wilhelm] 1747-1810.
Zauberbibliothek. [München] 1776.
91 p. 19cm.
Based on annotated bibliography of the Gassner and Sterzinger controversies which first appeared in Allgemeine deutsche Bibliothek, Berlin, 1775-76. [BF 1565 S83 Z98] CUL holdings noted in ms. in text.
1. Sterzinger, Ferdinand, 1721-1786. 2. Gassner, Johann Joseph, 1727-1779. 3. Witchcraft-- Bibl. I. Title.

8

Sterzinger, Ferdinand, 1721-1786.

Witchcraft
BF 1565 S83 Z98

Zauberbibliothek. 1775-1776. [Berlin, 1775-76]
various pagings. 20cm.
Title from spine.
Consists of three sections detached from Allgemeine deutsche Bibliothek, titled: Zauberey; Teufeleyen; and Teufeleyen. Eine Fortsetzung der vorigen.
1. Sterzinger, Ferdinand, 1721-1786. 2. Gassner, Johann Joseph, 1727-1779. 3. Witchcraft--Bibl.

8

Sterzinger, Ferdinand, 1721-1786-- Biography.

Witchcraft
BX 4705 S832 F45

Fieger, Hans, 1857-
Pater Don Ferdinand Sterzingers Leben und Schriften. Ein Beitrag zur Geschichte der Aufklärungsepoche in Bayern. München, Druck von C. Gerber [1896]
48 p. 2 tables (1 fold.) 24cm.
Programmschrift--Königl. Ludwigs-Kreisrealschule, München.
1. Sterzinger, Ferdinand, 1721-1786. 2. Bavaria--Hist.--Maximilian III Joseph (1745-1777) I. Title.

8

Witchcraft
BF 1565 S83 S84

[Sterzinger, Joseph] 1746-1821.
Der Hexenprocess: ein Traum erzählt von einer unpartheyischen Feder im Jahre 1767. [München?] 1767.
18 p. 22cm.
Attribution and dates from Fieger, Hans. P. Don Ferdinand Sterzinger, München, 1907, p. 144-45. (Accepted also by Holzmann)
1. Sterzinger, Ferdinand, 1721-1786. Akademische Rede von dem gemeinen Vorurtheile der ... Hexerey. 2. Witchcraft. I. Eine unpartheyische Feder. II. Title.

8

Stever, Christianus, respondent.

WITCHCRAFT
RC 533 D47 1724

Detharding, Georg Christoph, 1671-1747, praeses.
Dissertatio medica inauguralis De obsessione eademque spuria, von Besessenen und vor besessen gehaltenen Menschen, qvam sub praesidio ... Georgii Dethardingii ... publice examinandam proponit Christ. Frider. Stever ... Rostochii, Recusa typis Io. Ioacob. Adleri [1724?]
[102] p. 19cm.
Diss.--Rostock (C. F. Stever, responder

8 NIC

CATALOGUE OF THE CORNELL WITCHCRAFT COLLECTION

Stiefel, Andreas, 1653-1725.

see

Stübel, Andreas, 1653-1725.

Witchcraft
CB
3
Z481

Stojentin, Max von.
Aktienmässige Nachrichten von Hexenprozessen und Zaubereien im ehemaligen Herzogtum Pommern.
(In Beiträge zur Kulturgeschichte. Weimar. 25cm. 2. Heft (1898), p. [18]-44)

1. Witchcraft--Germany. I. Title.

Witchcraft
BF
1581
S49

Seth, Ronald.
Stories of great witch trials. London, Barker [1967]
vii, 176 p. tables. 22½ cm. 21/-
Bibliography: p. 169-171.
(B 67-20430)

1. Trials (Witchcraft)--Gt. Brit.   I. Title.

343'.3   67-105996
Library of Congress   [2]

Stile, Elizabeth.
A Rehearsall both straung and true, of hainous and horrible actes committed by Elizabeth Stile, alias Rockingham, Mother Dutten, Mother Deuell, Mother Margaret, fower notorious witches, apprehended at Winsore in the countie of Barks, and at Abbington arraigned, condemned, and executed, on the 26¼ daye of Februarie laste, anno. 1579. London, Imprinted for E. White [1579?]
[London, at the British Museum, 1923]

Photocopy (negative) 19 p. on 10 l.

Stoltze, Johann Gottlieb.

see

Stoltze, Johann Gottlob.

WITCHCRAFT
BF
1578
S55
A2
1900

Sherwood, Grace, defendant.
The story of Grace Sherwood. [n.p., ca 1900?]
12 p. 25cm.

Detached from unidentified periodical. Contains court records of prosecutions of Grace Sherwood for witchcraft, in Princess Anne County, Virginia.

1. Witchcraft--Princess Anne Co., Virginia.
8   2. Trials (Witchcraft)--Princess Anne Co.,
NIC Virginia.   I. Title.

Stocker, Thomas, fl. 1569-1592, tr.
[Viret, Pierre] 1511-1571.
The second part of The demoniacke vvorlde, or, Worlde possessed with diuels, conteining three dialogues: 1. Of familiar diuels. 2. Of lunaticke diuels. 2. Of the coniuring of diuels. Translated out of French into English by T. S. [i.e. Thomas Stocker]   London, Imprinted for I. Perin, and are to be sold in Paules church-yard at the signe of the Angell, 1583.
1 v. (unpaged) 15cm.
Bound with   his The worlde possessed with deuils.   London, 1583.

Witchcraft
BF
1445
D61
no.10

Stoltze, Johann Gottlob, respondent.
Kirchmayer, Georg Caspar, 1635-1700, praeses.
Ad scriptores aliqvot Roman. veteres, De apparitionibus spectror. & spirituum, sub corpor. inprimis human. schemate, nec non visionibus naturae probabilibus, adversus atheos inprimis, dissertatio, sub moderamine ... Dn. Georgii Casparis Kirchmajeri, à Johanne Gottlieb Stoltzen ... ventilationi publicae exposita, die 27. Julii, anno 1692. Wittebergae, Typis Christiani Schrödteri
8   [1692]   (Continued on next card)

Witchcraft
BT
980
G73
1931

Graf, Arturo, 1848-1913.
The story of the devil, by Arturo Graf; translated from the Italian by Edward Noble Stone, with notes by the translator. New York, The Macmillan company, 1931.
xiv, 206 p. 22½cm.

Translation of Il diavolo.

Stöber, August, 1808-1884, ed.
Witchcraft
BX
890
G31
E5
1856

Geiler, Johannes, von Kaisersberg, 1445-1510.
Zur Geschichte des Volks-Aberglaubens im Anfange des XVI. Jahrhunderts. Aus Dr. Joh. Geilers von Kaisersberg Emeis. Mit einer Einleitung, Erläuterung und sonstigen literarischen Nachweisungen herausgegeben von August Stöber ... Basel, Schweighauser, 1856.
4 p. l., 92 p. 24cm.

Witchcraft
BF
1445
D61
no.10

Stoltze, Johann Gottlob, respondent.
Kirchmayer, Georg Caspar, 1635-1700, praeses. Ad scriptores ... De apparitionibus spectror. & spirituum ... [1692]
(Card 2)

32, [2] p. 18cm. (bound in 21cm. vol.) No. 10 in vol. lettered Dissertationes de spectris. 1646-1753.
1. Apparitions. I. Stoltze, Johann Gottlob, respondent. II. Title: De apparitionibus spectrorum et spirituum.

Thesis
1903
463

Stowell, Roy Sherman.
The English opponents of the witch persecution. Ithaca, N. Y., 1903.
[4], iv, 192 l. 28cm.

Thesis (A. M.)--Cornell University, June, 1903.

1. Witchcraft--England. I. Title.

Stoephel, Gelasius.
WITCHCRAFT
BX
2340
S66

Ministerium exorcisticum, quo exorcista possessos, obsessos, & maleficiatos a daemonijs...liberare potest. Cum annexis thesibus theologicis ad mentem...Joannis Duns-Scoti ex tribus libris sententiarum, quas...publice defendendas susceperunt praeside M. R. P. Adolpho Medelsky... Franciscus Solanus Monschmidt &...Gelasius Stoephel .. Oppaviae, Typis Joannis W. Schindler [1738]
99 p. 17cm.
Apparently   a cooperative undertaking of   the Franciscan Fathers in Moravia.
(Continued on next card)

Witchcraft
BT
980
G73
1931

Stone, Edward Noble, 1870-   tr.
Graf, Arturo, 1848-1913.
The story of the devil, by Arturo Graf; translated from the Italian by Edward Noble Stone, with notes by the translator. New York, The Macmillan company, 1931.
xiv, 206 p. 22½cm.

Translation of Il diavolo.

Witchcraft
BF
1563
T86

Strange and fearfull newes from Plaisto, in the parish of West-Ham, neere Bow, foure miles from London, in the house of one Paul Fox, a silke-weaver where is dayly to be seene throwing of stones, bric-bats, oystershels, bread, cutting his worke in peeces, breaking his windowes, stones of fifty wayt comming up the stayers, a sword flying about the roome, books going up and down the house ...   London, Printed by I. H. [1645]
(Continued on next card)

Stoiber, Ubaldus.
WITCHCRAFT
BX
2340
S87
1757

Armamentarium ecclesiasticum complectens arma spiritualia fortissima ad insultus diabolicos elidendos, & feliciter superandos ... Editio quarta ... Pedeponti, Sumptibus Joan. Gastl, 1757.
2 v. in 1. illus., diagrs, part folded. 18cm.
Contents.--Pars prima. Complectens materiam de energumenis liberandis.--Pars secunda. Materiam de maleficiis curandis, & domibus, aliis que locis à spectris, infestatis, ex purgandis, continens.
1. Exorcism. 2. Witchcraft. 3. Demonology.   I. Title.

De stora häxprocesserna i Sverige.
WITCHCRAFT
BF
1584
S9
L74

Linderholm, Emanuel, 1872-1937.
De stora häxprocesserna i Sverige. Bidrag till svensk kultur- och kyrkohistoria.
1. delen: Inledning. Bohuslän. Uppsala, J. A. Lindblad [1918]
xii, 272 p. 21cm.

No more published.

8   1. Trials (Witchcraft)--Sweden. 2. Witchcraft--Sweden.
NIC

Witchcraft
BF
1563
T86

Strange and fearfull newes from Plaisto ... [1645]   (Card 2)

8 p. 19cm.

No. 8 in vol. lettered: Tracts of witches

1. Witchcraft. 2. Fox, Paul.

525

CATALOGUE OF THE CORNELL WITCHCRAFT COLLECTION

Witchcraft
BF 1563
W81++
no.20

Strange & terrible nevves from Cambridge, being a true relation of the Quakers bewitching of Mary Philips ...; likewise her speech to the scholars and countrey-men ... her oath before the judges and justices, and the names of the Quakers brought to tryal ... with the judgment of the court ... London, Printed for C. Brooks, 1659. [London, at the British Museum, 1923]
8 p. 16cm.
Photocopy (negative) 8 p. on 5 l. 20x32cm.
(Continued on next card)

Witchcraft
BF 1563
W81++
no.20

Strange & terrible nevves from Cambridge ... 1659. [1923]   (Card 2)
No. 20 in vol. lettered: Witchcraft tracts, chapbooks and broadsides, 1579-1704; rotograph copies.

1. Witchcraft--England. 2. Philips, Mary.

WITCHCRAFT
BF 1555
S892

Strange and wonderful news from Wheelers Street in Spittle-Fields. Being a true and just account of a woman there living that hath lain for a long time under a great and heavy affliction of witch-craft, shewing also how the witch came in the shape of a great squirrill ... Also an account how her husband, going to a doctor to get help for her, saw the shape of a man and two women ... [London?] Printed for J. Clark [1683?]
8   8 p. 18cm.
(Continued on next card)

WITCHCRAFT
BF 1555
S892

Strange and wonderful news from Wheelers Street ... [London? 1683?] (Card 2)
Illustrative vignettes on t. p.
In MS on t. p.: 14. June. 1683.

1. Demoniac possession. 2. Witchcraft. 3. Wheelers Street, Stepney, England.
8

WITCHCRAFT
BF 1483
S89

Strange and wonderful news from Yowel [sic] in Surry; giving a true and just account of one Elizabeth Bvrgiss, who was most strangely bewitched and tortured ... As, also, how great stones ... were thrown at her ...; and after she came to her fathers house, the throwing of the pewter-dishes, candlesticks, and other clattering of houshold goods at her ... West-Smithfield, Printed for F. Clarke, seignior,   1681.
8   6 p. illus. 19cm.
(Continued on next card)

WITCHCRAFT
BF 1483
S89

Strange and wonderful news from Yowel [sic] in Surry ... 1681.   (Card 2)
Wing S5869b.
Illustrations are 5 woodcuts printed on verso of t. p.

1. Burgiss, Elizabeth, fl. 1681. 2. Ghosts--Ewell, Surrey, England. 3. Ghosts--England. 4. Witchcraft--England.
8

WITCHCRAFT
BF 1473
S52
S89

A Strange and wonderful relation from Shadwel; or, The Devil visible. Being a most true and faithful account how the Devil in human shape, on the 3d. of this instant July, made his appearance to one Mrs. Moon there, ... with a bag of money in one hand, and a knife in the other, tempting her to murther one of her children. As also how she refused ... London, Printed for W. Smith, 1674.
6 p. 19cm.
1. Devil.   2. Shadwell, Stepney, England. 3. Moon, Anne (Hooper), fl. 1674.
8

WITCHCRAFT
GR 525
M93
1679a

Strange newes, out of Hartford-shire, and Kent. 1. An account of a mowing-devil ... 2. A true narrative of a young maid who was possest with several devils or evil spirits ... London, Printed for R. G., 1679 [n. p., 18--?]
8 p. 21cm.
Facsimile reprint.
Item 1. first issued separately, 1678, under title: The mowing-devil: or, Strange news out of Hartford-shire.
8   1. Spirits. 2. Devil. 3. Demoniac possession. I. Title: The mowing-devil.

WITCHCRAFT
BF 1555
S89

Strange news from Arpington near Bexly in Kent: being a true narrative of a young maid who was possest with several devils or evil spirits, one of which ... was fetch out of her body, and appear'd in the room in the likeness of a large snake ... With an account also of other devils which yet remain in her ... London, Printed for R. G., 1679.
6 p. 18cm.
Not in Wing.
8

WITCHCRAFT
BF 1555
S89
1689

Strange news from Arpington near Bexly in Kent: being a true narrative of a young maid who was possest with several devils or evil spirits, one of which ... was fetch out of her body, and appear'd in the room in the likeness of a large snake ... With an account also of other devils which yet remain in her ... London, Printed for Benjamin Harris, 1689.
6 p. 19cm.
Imprint corrected in MS to 1679, which probably is   correct date.
8   Wing S5885.   (Continued on next card)

WITCHCRAFT
BF 1555
S89
1689

Strange news from Arpington ...   1689.
(Card 2)

1. Demoniac possession. 2. Arpington, Kent, England.
8

Strange phenomena of New England.

Witchcraft
BF 1575
M42
S8
1846

Mather, Cotton, 1663-1728.
Strange phenomena of New England: in the seventeenth century: including the "Salem witchcraft," "1692." From the writings of "the Rev. Cotton Mather, D. D." ... Collected and arranged for re-publication by Henry Jones ... New-York, Piercy and Reed, 1846.
iv, [5]-54 p. 24cm.

1. Witchcraft--New England. I. Jones, Henry, ed. II. Title.
11-8997

Rare
BR 304
A18
1631

Stratagematum Satanae.
Aconcio, Giacomo, 1492?-1566?
Stratagematvm Satanae, libri octo. Editio iterata & emendata. Oxonii, G. Webb, 1631.
426 p. 15cm.

"Iacobvs Acontivs Iohanni Wolfio": [26] p. at end.
Engr. t.p.
STC 93
1. Christianity--16th cent. 2. Creeds--Hist. & Crit. I. Wolf, Johann, 1522-1571. II. Title.

WITCHCRAFT
BF 1555
N19

Strauss, David Friedrich, 1808-1874.
Nanz, Carl Friedrich.
Die Besessenen im Neuen Testamente. Ein exegetischer Versuch mit Rücksicht auf Dr. Strauss Leben Jesu. Reutlingen, J. C. Marcken, 1840.
ii, 42 p. 21cm.

1. Strauss, David Friedrich, 1808-1874. Das Leben Jesu. 2. Demoniac possession. 3. Bible. N.T.--Criticism, interpretation, etc. 4.   Jesus Christ.
8
NIC

La strega, overo De gli inganni de demoni.

WITCHCRAFT
BF 1524
P59
1555

Pico della Mirandola, Giovanni Francesco, 1470-1533.
Dialogo intitolato La strega, overo De gli inganni de demoni dell' illustre Signor Giouan Francesco Pico conte de la Mirandola. Tradotto in lingva toscana per il Signor abate Turino Turini da Pescia ... In Pescia, 1555.
5 p. l., [17]-126 p., 1 l. 21½cm.
Title within ornamental border.
At end: Stampato in Pescia, appresso Lorenzo Torrentino, stampator ducale, MDLV.
Translation of Strix, sive De ludificatione daemonum dialogi tres.
With this is bound Cattani da Diacceto, F. Discorso ... sopra   la superstizzione dell' arte magica. Fiorenza, 1567.   11-9699
8   (Continued on next card)
Copy 2.

WITCHCRAFT
BF 1524
P59
1864

La strega ovvero Degli inganni de' demoni.
Pico della Mirandola, Giovanni Francesco, 1470-1533.
La strega ovvero Degli inganni de' demoni. Dialogo di Giovan Francesco Pico della Mirandola, tradotto in lingua toscana da Turino Turini. Milano, D. Daelli, 1864.
xxiv, 135 p. 17cm. (Biblioteca rara, 40)
Translation of Strix, sive de ludificatione daemonum dialogi tres.
8

Le streghe.

BF 1566
F15

Faggin, Giuseppe, 1906-
Le streghe. Milano, Longanesi [1959]
305 p. illus. 19cm. (I Marmi, v. 24)

Le streghe di Valtellina e la Santa Inquisizione.

WITCHCRAFT
BF 1584
T9
O26

Odorici, Federico, 1807-1884.
Le streghe di Valtellina e la Santa Inquisizione. Milano, P. R. Carpano, 1862.
85-158 p. 19cm.

Part of unidentified work, but complete in itself.

1. Witchcraft--Tyrol. 2. Witchcraft--Valtellina. 3. Trials (Witchcraft)--Valtellina. 4.   Inquisition. Valtelli. I. Title.
8
NIC

CATALOGUE OF THE CORNELL WITCHCRAFT COLLECTION

Le streghe e l'Inquisizione.

BF Ferraioni, Francesco
1584   Le streghe e l'Inquisizione; super-
I8   stizioni e realtà. Roma, Tipografia
F36   sallustiana, 1955.
     132, 6 p. illus. 21cm.

    1. Witchcraft—Italy. 2. Inquisition.
Italy. I. Title.

Le streghe in Valtellina.

WITCHCRAFT
BF   Spinetti, Vittorio.
1584   Le streghe in Valtellina. Studio su
T9   vari documenti editi ed inediti dei sec.
S75   XV - XVI - XVII - XVIII. Sondrio, Stab.
    tip. E. Quadrio, 1903.
     131 p. 18cm.

    1. Witchcraft—Tyrol. 2. Witchcraft
—Valtellina. I. Title.

8
NIC

Streghe, stregoni e stregonerie di
   Sicilia.

F
622   Ganci Battaglia, Giuseppe.
8   Streghe, stregoni e stregonerie di
19   Sicilia. Superstizione e magia, i
    misteri del mondo occulto, le avventure
    diaboliche del conte Cagliostro e della
    Vecchia dell'aceto. Palermo, D.
    Malato, [1972].
     218 p. plates. 21cm.
     Bibliography: p. 211-[219]

    1. Magic—Sicily. 2. Witchcraft—
Sicily. I. Title

NIC   FEB 28,'74   COOxc   73-321911

Stregoneria, magia, credenze e superstizioni
   a Genova e in Liguria.

GN
1   Delfino, Giuseppe.
L311   Stregoneria, magia, credenze e superstizioni a
B5   in Liguria. Firenze, L. S. Olschki, 1973.
v.39   iv, 87 p. illus., plates. 21 cm. (Biblioteca di "Lares," v. 39)

    L2200   It 73-Aug
    At head of title: Giuseppe Delfino, Aldano Schmuckher.
    Bibliography: p. 81-84.

9
NIC   1. Occult sciences—Genoa. 2. Occult sciences—Liguria.
    I. Schmuckher, Aldano, joint author. II. Title.

BF1434.I 8D44   73-339982

Library of Congress   73 [2]

Streitschrift vom dem Verbrechen der
   Zauber- und Hexerey.

Witchcraft
BF   Thomasius, Christian, 1655-1728.
1523   Christian Thomasii Gelehrte Streitschrift
E35   von dem Verbrechen der Zauber- und Hexerey.
    Aus dem Lateinischen übersetzt, und bey Ge-
    legenheit der Gassnerischen Wunderkuren zum
    Besten des Publikums herausgegeben. [Leip-
    zig?] 1775.
     95 p. 18cm.
     Bound with Einziger von Einzing, Johann
    Martin Maximilian, 1725-1798. Dämonologie.
    [Leipzig?] 1775.

8   Continued on next card)

Streitschrift von dem Verbrechen der
   Zauber- und Hexerey.

Witchcraft
BF   Thomasius, Christian, 1655-1728. Chris-
1523   tian Thomasii Gelehrte Streitschrift von
E35   dem Verbrechen der Zauber- und Hexerey ...
    1775.   (Card 2)

Translation of Dissertatio de crimine
magiae.
    1. Witchcraft. I. His Dissertatio
de crimine magiae. German. II. Title:
Streitschrift von dem Verbrechen der Zauber-
und Hexerey.

8

Witchcraft   Stretton, Jane, b. 1649.
GR   The Hartfordshire wonder; or, Strange news from
142   Ware. Being an exact and true relation of one Jane
H6   Stretton, the daughter of Thomas Stretton of Ware in
A3   the county of Herts, who hath been visited in a strange
no.8   kind of manner by extraordinary and unusual fits, her
    abstaining from sustenance for the space of 9 months,
    being haunted by imps or devils in the form of several
    creatures here described, the parties adjudged of all by
    whom she was thus tormented and the occasion thereof ...

    (Continued on next card)
    17-20383

Witchcraft   Stretton, Jane, b. 1649.
GR   The Hartfordshire wonder ... (Card 2)
142   London: printed for J. Clark ... 1669. Reprinted with
H6   an introductory note by W. B. Gerish. Bishop's Stort-
A3   ford, 1908.
no.8   15 p. 22cm. [Hertfordshire folk lore. no. 8]
    Preface signed: M. J.

    1. Stretton, Jane, b.1649. 2. Witchcraft—England. I. J., M. II.
M. J.   III. Gerish, William Blyth, ed.
    17-20383

Library of Congress   GR142.H6A3 no. 5

Witchcraft   Stridtbeckh, Christian, respondent.
BF   Alberti, Valentin, 1635-1697, praeses.
1565   ... Academische Abhandlung von den Hexen
A33   und dem Bündniss so sie mit dem Teuffel ha-
1723   ben. Darinnen ... nebst Erörterung einiger
    andern curieusen Fragen, ob die bekannte Pu-
    celle d'Orleans, ingleichen das rasende Weib,
    das den Attilam erschrecket, eine Hexe ge-
    wesen sei? Franckfurt und Leipzig, 1723.
     [56] p. front. 21cm.
    Translation of his Dissertatio academica,
De sagis, C. Stridtbeckh, respondent, Witte-
8   bergae, 1690.   (Continued on next card)

Witchcraft   Stridtbeckh, Christian, respondent.
BF   Alberti, Valentin, 1635-1697, praeses.
1565   Dissertatio academica, De sagis, sive
D62   foeminis, commercium cum malo spiritu haben-
no.10   tibus, e christiana pnevmatologia desumpta,
    & sub praesidio ... Dn. D. Valentini Al-
    berti ... publicae propositia ventilationi
    ... ab autore Christiano Stridtbeckh ...
    Lipsiae, Typis Christoph. Fleischeri
    [1690]
     [52] p. illus. 20cm.
    No.10 in vol. lettered Dissertationes
    de sagis.   1636-1714.
8   (Continued on next card)

   Strix; sive, De ludificatione daemonum
WITCHCRAFT   dialogi tres.
BF   Pico della Mirandola, Giovanni Francesco,
1524   1470-1533.
P59   Strix; sive, De ludificatione daemonum
    dialogi tres. Nunc primum in Germania eruti
    ex bibliotheca M. Martini Weinrichii, cum
    ejusdem praefatione...itemque Epistola ad
    ...Andream Libavium de quaestione: Utrum
    in non maritatis & castis mola possit gigni?
    Et post mortem ejus editi studio & opera
    Caroli Weinrichii. Argentorati, Venundan-
8   tur apud Paulum Ledertz, 1612.
NIC   160+ p.   18cm.
        (Continued on next card)

   Strix; sive, De ludificatione daemonum
WITCHCRAFT   dialogi tres.
BF   Pico della Mirandola, Giovanni Francesco,
1524   1470-1533. Strix...1612.   (Card 2)
P59

Epistola to Libavius lacking.
With this is bound: Sennert, Daniel. De
origine et natura animarum in brutis. 1638.

    1.Magic. 2. Demonology. 3. Witchcraft.
I. Weinrich, Martinus, 1548-1609. II. Weinrich, Carolus. III. Libavius, Andreas,
d.1616. IV. Title.

   Strutberger, Carel, tr.

MSS   Diszes Wonder, auch erschricklic Zaychen
Bd.   ist durch Zulassung Gottesz warhafftig
WITCHCRAFT   unnd thadlich gesehen in der Stat von
BF   Gent in Flandren, auff den XVIII. Augustii
D613   in Jaer, MDLXXXVI bey dem bossen Gayst
    unnd seinnesz Wercks, seer erschrocklich
    ist unnb zu leessen. Anntorff, By Paulus
    Brackfeldt, 1586 [ca. 1900]
     4 l. illus. 23cm.
     Carnap's manuscript copy.
    "Original   druck i. d. Gust. Frey-
tag Biblioth   ek, jetzt i. d. Stadt-
     (Continued on next card)

   Strutberger, Carel, tr.

MSS   Diszes Wonder, auch erschricklic Zaychen ...
Bd.   1586 [ca. 1900]   (Card 2)
WITCHCRAFT
BF   bibliothek zu Frankfurt a/M. 4 Bl. 4°."
D613   A letter received by D. H. V. W.
    At end: "Ghetranslateert durch M. Carel
    Strutberger."
    Numerals and signatures in the margins
    indicate pagination and signatures of the
    original.
    1. Apparitions. 2. Devil. I.
W., D. H. V.   II. Strutberger, Carel,
tr.

Witchcraft
BF   Struve, Georg Adam, 1619-1692, praeses.
1565   Disputatio juridica De indiciis cui an-
S92   nectitur quaestio de proba per aquam frigi-
    dam sagarum. Von der Wasser-Prob der Hexen
    ... sub praesidio Dn. Georgii Adami Struven
    ... publicè proposita à Iohanne Christo-
    phoro Nehringio ... [Jenae] Typis Johan-
    nis Jacobi Bauhoferi, 1666.
     [26] p. 20cm.

8   First edition.

Witchcraft
BF   Struve, Georg Adam, 1619-1692, praeses.
1565   Disputatio juridica De indiciis cui an-
D62   nectitur quaestio de proba per aquam frigi-
no.16   dam sagarum. Von der Wasser-Prob der Hexen
    ... sub praesidio Dn. Georgii Adami Struven
    ... publicè proposita à Joh. Christoph.
    Nehringio ... Jenae, Typis Pauli Ehrichii,
    1714.
     52 p. 20cm.
    No. 16 in vol. lettered Dissertationes
8   de sagis. 1636-1714.
     (Continued on next card)

Witchcraft
BF   Struve, Georg Adam, 1619-1692, praeses.
1565   Disputatio juridica De indiciis ...
D62   1714.   (Card 2)
no.16

    1. Trials (Witchcraft) 2. Witchcraft.
I. Nehring, Johann Christoph, d. 1682,
respondent. II. Title: De indiciis cui
annectitur quaestio de proba per aquam
frigidam sagarum. III. Title: Wasser-
Prob der Hexen. IV. Title.

8

Witchcraft
BF   Struve, Georg Adam, 1619-1692, praeses.
1565   Disputatio juridica De indiciis & proba
S92   per aquam frigidam sagarum. Wasser-Prob
1683   der Hexen. Sub praesidio Dn. Georgii Adami
    Struven ... publicè proposita à Johanne
    Christophoro Nehringio ... [Jenae?] Lite-
    ris Müllerianis, 1683.
     [54] p. 20cm.
    First published 1666 with title: Dis-
    putatio juridica De indiciis cui annectitur
    quaestio de proba per aquam frigidam saga-
8   rum.
    I. Title. II. Title: De indiciis et
proba per aquam frigidam sagarum.

CATALOGUE OF THE CORNELL WITCHCRAFT COLLECTION

Witchcraft
BF
1565
T46
E358

Stryk, Joannes Samuel, 1668-1715.
Disputatio de jure Sabbathi.
Das Wohl-meritirte und wohlverdiente Ehren=Kleid dem Anonymo und Autori des Gutachten von dem mit Herrn Doct. Thomasio erregten Streit über einige freye Meynungen in einem teutschen Programmate, und von Herrn D. Strykii Disputation de jure Sabbathi, zum Recompens vor die Mühe praesentiret von einem Liebhaber der Wahrheit und Feind der Calumnien. Freystatt, 1703.
24 p. 18cm.

8

WITCHCRAFT
BF
1555
S93

[Stübel, Andreas] 1653-1725. Der mit allerhand Staats-Friedens-Kriegs-Hof-Literatur- ... Affairen beschäfftige Secretarius ... [1709-21]   (Card 2)
title reads: Des beschäfftige Secretarii erste [zweite, dritte, u. s. w.] Expedition.
Includes excerpts from Expedition 1, 5, 8, 10, 12, 18, 20, 24, 27, 28, 37-39, 42, 44, 45.
Pages consecutively numbered in MS, and Register in MS bound in at end.
(Continued on next card)

8
NIC

Südslavische Hexensagen.

Witchcraft
GR
250
K91
S9+

Krauss, Friedrich Salomo, 1859-1938.
Südslavische Hexensagen. [Wien, 1884]
[13]-48 p. 29cm.
Caption title.
"Separatabdruck aus dem XIV. Bande [Neue Folge IV. Band] der 'Mittheilungen der Anthropologischen Gesellschaft in Wien'. 1884."
In double columns.
1. Folk-lore, Slavic. 2. Witchcraft--Yugoslavia.   I. Title. II. Anthropologische Gesellschaft in Wien. Mitteilungen.

8

Witchcraft
BF
1445
D61
no.14

Stryk, Joannes Samuel, 1668-1715, praeses.
Dispvtatio ivridica inavgvralis, De ivre spectrorvm, quam ... praeside Dn. Io. Samvele Strykio ... submittit Andreas Becker. Halae Magdebvrgicae, Literis Christiani Henckelii [1700]
43, [1] p. 18cm. (bound in 21cm. vol.)
Diss.--Halle (A. Becker, respondent.)
No. 14 in vol. lettered Dissertationes de spectris. 1646-1753.

8

WITCHCRAFT
BF
1555
S93

[Stübel, Andreas] 1653-1725. Der mit allerhand Staats-Friedens-Kriegs-Hof-Literatur- ... Affairen beschäfftige Secretarius ... [1709-21]   (Card 3)

1. Demoniac possession. 2. Curiosities and wonders. I. Title. II. Title: Der Secretarius.

8
NIC

WITCHCRAFT
BF
1566
S94

Sulle streghe: discorso istorico-critico.
Roma, Tip. Salviucci, 1875.
33 p. 21cm.

1. Witchcraft--History.

8
NIC

Witchcraft
BF
1445
S92
1738

Stryk, Joannes Samuel, 1668-1715, praeses.
Dispvtatio ivridica inavgvralis, De ivre spectrorvm qvam ... praeside Dn. Io. Samvele Strykio ... svbmittit Andreas Becker. Halae Magdebvrgicae, Literis Ioh. Christ. Grvnerti, 1738.
43, [1] p. 21cm.
Diss.--Halle (A. Becker, respondent)
German terms in black letter.
1. Ghosts. 2. Devil. 3. Witchcraft--Germany. I. Becker, Andreas, 1634-1698, respondent. II. Title: De iure spectrorum.

8

WITCHCRAFT
BF
1584
S97
S93

Stürler, Moritz von.
Urkunden über Hexenprozesse aus dem Staatsarchive in Bern. Mitgetheilt durch Herrn Staatsschreiber und Staatsarchivar Moritz von Stürler, korrespondierendes Mitglied der Basler historischen Gesellschaft. [Basel, 1854]
[284]-291 p. 23cm.
Extract from Beiträge zur vaterländischen Geschichte, Basel, v. 5, 1854.
1. Trials (Witchcraft)--Basel. 2. Trials (Witchcraft)--Switzerland. I. Title.

8

Sultān al-Zulmah.

WITCHCRAFT
BF
1523
R44

Reuter, Simon Henrich.
(Sultān al-Zulmah)
سلطان الظلمة
das ist, Das mächtige, doch umschränckte Reich des Teufels; oder, Gründlicher und wahrhaftiger Bericht, was von der List, Macht und Wirckung des Satans und der bösen Geister zu halten sey, und was die Menschen durch derselben Kraft und Gemeinschaft wissen, thun und verrichten können ... Alles treulich aus Gottes Wort und vieler

8
NIC

(Continued on next card)

WITCHCRAFT
BF
1566
S93

Stubenvoll, F   B
Religion und Aberglaube. Leipzig, F. Jansa, 1897.
95 p. 20cm.

1. Witchcraft--History. 2. Superstition. I. Title.

8
NIC

Stuttgarter Hexen-Geschichten.

WITCHCRAFT
BF
1583
L25

Landenberger, Johannes.
Stuttgarter Hexen-Geschichten. Kulturgeschichtliche Bilder aus vergangenen Tagen. Mit einer Einleitung. Lorch, K. Röhm [1904]
23 p. 17cm. (Deutsche Volks-Bibliothek, Nr.1)

1. Witchcraft--Stuttgart. I. Title.

8
NIC

WITCHCRAFT
BF
1523
R44

Reuter, Simon Henrich.
(Sultān al-Zulmah)...   (Card 2)
Gelehrten Bücher zusammen getragen, untersuchet und zur Warnung der glaubigen Kinder Gottes vorgestellet; auch mit einem nützlichen Register versehen. Lemgo, H. W. Meyer, 1716.
1293 p. 20cm.

Witchcraft
BF
1413
D94

Studien aus dem Gebiete der Geheimwissenschaften.
Du Prel, Karl Ludwig August Friedrich Maximilian Alfred, Freiherr, 1839-1899.
Studien aus dem Gebiete der Geheimwissenschaften. Erster Theil: Thatsachen und Probleme. Leipzig, W. Friedrich, 1890.
vii, 252 p. 22cm.
No more published?

1. Occult sciences.

Witchcraft
BF
1445
W41

[Sucro, Johann Georg]
Widerlegung der Gedancken von Gespenstern. Halle im Magdeburgischen, C. H. Hemmerde, 1748.
72 p. 18cm.
Attributed to Sucro by Holzmann.
Bound with Wegner, Georg Wilhelm. Gedancken von Gespenstern. Halle, 1747.
1. Wegner, Georg Wilhelm. Gedancken von Gespenstern. 2. Ghosts. 3. Hallucinations and illusions. I. Title.

8

Witchcraft
BV
639
W7
C94+

Die Summa Theologica des Antonin von Florenz und die Schätzung des Weibes i Hexenhammer.
Crohns, Hjalmar, 1862-1946.
Die Summa Theologica des Antonin von Florenz und die Schätzung des Weibes im Hexenhammer. [Helsingforsiae, ex Officina typographica Societatis litterariae fennicae, 1906]
1 p. l., 23 p. 28cm. ([Finska vetenskaps-societeten, Helsingfors] Acta Societatis scientiarum fennicae. t. xxxii, no. 4)

8

WITCHCRAFT
BF
1555
S93

[Stübel, Andreas] 1653-1725.
Der mit allerhand Staats-Friedens-Kriegs-Hof-Literatur- und Religions- wie auch Privat-Affairen beschäfftige Secretarius ... Freyburg [1709-21]
various pagings. illus. (part fold.) 17cm.
Attribution by Holzmann.
Incomplete: detached sections dealing with supposed cases of demoniac possession. In form of "Expeditionen;" running

8
NIC
(Continued on next card)

Sudermann, Daniel, supposed author.

MSS
Bd.
WITCHCRAFT
BV
S38

Ein Schröckliche Antwort eines bösen Geists auss einer besessenen Person, als er beschworen, unnd ein verdampter Lugengeist gescholten worden ist, &c. Lieds weiss an Tag geben, zur Wahrnung und Straff aller unbussfertigen. [n.p.] 1596 [ca. 1900]
4 l. title vignette. 19cm.
Carnap's manuscript copy.
"Originaldruck in der Königlichen Bibliothek zu Berlin 4 Bl. in 16°."
"Wahrscheinlich von Daniel Sudermañ.

Witchcraft
Z
1007
T46

Summarischer Nachrichten von auserlesenen mehrentheils alten in der Thomasischen Bibliotheque verhandenen Büchern.
Thomasius, Christian, 1655-1728, ed.
Summarischer Nachrichten von auserlesenen mehrentheils alten in der Thomasischen Bibliotheque verhandenen Büchern. 1.-[24.] Stück. Halle, J. F. Zeitler, 1715-18.
24 pt. in 1 v. fronts. (ports.) 18cm.

By various authors, edited by C. Thomasius

CATALOGUE OF THE CORNELL WITCHCRAFT COLLECTION

Summers, Montague

---

craft
    Summers, Montague, 1880-1948.
        The discovery of witches: a study of Master Matthew Hopkins commonly call'd with finder generall, together with a reprint of The discovery of witches, from the rare original of 1647. London, Cayme Press, 1928.
        61 p. illus. 22cm. (Cayme Press pamphlet, no. 7)

    With facsimile of t.p. of original ed.

    1. Hopkins, Matthew, d. 1647. I. Hopkins, Matthew, d. 1647. The discovery of witches. II. Title.

Witchcraft
BF 1566 S95 H6 1926
    Summers, Montague, 1880-1948.
        The history of witchcraft and demonology. New York, Knopf, 1926.
        xv, 353 p. plates. 24cm.

    With autograph: Geo. L. Burr.

Witchcraft
BF 1566 S95 P8
    Summers, Montague, 1880-1948.
        A popular history of witchcraft, by Montague Summers. London, K. Paul, Trench, Trubner & co., ltd., 1937.
        xvi, 278 p. front., plates, facsims. 19cm.

    1. Witchcraft. I. Title.
    [Full name: Alphonsus Joseph-Mary Augustus Montague Summers]

Library of Congress   BF1566.S84   37-22097
    [3]

Summers, Montague, 1880-1948.
    The geography of witchcraft. New York, A. A. Knopf, 1927.
    xi, 623 p. illus., facsim. 24cm. (The history of civilization. [Subject histories])

    "The present work may be regarded as a complementary volume to, or even a second volume of, my History of witchcraft and demonology."--Introd.

    I. His History of witchcraft and demonology. II. Title.

Witchcraft
BF 1566 S95 H6 1965
    Summers, Montague, 1880-1948.
        The history of witchcraft and demonology. London, Routledge & Kegan Paul Ltd. [1965, 1926]
        xv, 353 p. illus. 24cm. (The history of civilization)

    A reprint of the 1926 edition.

Witchcraft
GR 830 V3S95
    Summers, Montague, 1880-1948.
        The vampire, his kith and kin. London, Kegan Paul, Trench, Trubner & Co., Ltd., 1928.
        xv, 356 p. illus. 25cm.

    1. Vampires. I. Title.

Summers, Montague, 1880-1948.
    The geography of witchcraft. New York, A. A. Knopf, 1927.
    xi, 623 p. illus., facsim. 24cm. (The history of civilization. [Subject histories])

    "The present work may be regarded as a complementary volume to, or even a second volume of, my History of witchcraft and demonology."--Introd.

BF 1566 S95 H6 1965
Summers, Montague, 1880-1948.
    The history of witchcraft and demonology. London, Routledge & K. Paul [1965]
    xv, 353 p. facsims., plates. 25cm. (The History of civilization)

    Imprint covered by label: Barnes & Noble, New York.
    First published in 1926.

    1. Witchcraft --Hist. 2. Demonology. I. Title.

WITCHCRAFT
GR 830 V3 S95 1929
    Summers, Montague, 1880-1948.
        The vampire in Europe. London, K. Paul, Trench, Trubner & Co., 1929.
        xii, 330 p. plates, facsim. 25cm.

    1. Vampires. I. Title.

Undergraduate
    Summers, Montague, 1880-1948.
        The geography of witchcraft. Evanston [Ill.] University Books [1958]
        623 p. 22cm.

Undergraduate
BF 1566 S95 H6 1965
    Summers, Montague, 1880-1948.
        The history of witchcraft and demonology. London, Routledge & K. Paul [1965]
        xv, 353 p. facsims., plates. 25cm. (The History of civilization)

    First published in 1926.

    1. Witchcraft--Hist. 2. Demonology. I. Title.

GR 830 V3 S95 1968
    Summers, Montague, 1880-1948.
        The vampire in Europe. New Hyde Park, N. Y., University Books [1968]
        329 p. 24cm.

---

craft
    Summers, Montague, 1880-1948.
        The history of witchcraft and demonology. London, Kegan Paul, Trench, Trubner & Co., Ltd., 1926.
        xv, 353 p. illus. 24cm. (The history of civilization. Subject histories)

    1. Witchcraft. 2. Demonology. I. Title.

Witchcraft
BF 1566 S95 G3 1927
    Summers, Montague, 1880-1948.
        The history of witchcraft and demonology.
        Summers, Montague, 1880-1948.
        The geography of witchcraft. New York, A. A. Knopf, 1927.
        xi, 623 p. illus., facsim. 24cm. (The history of civilization. [Subject histories])

    "The present work may be regarded as a complementary volume to, or even a second volume of, my History of witchcraft and demonology."--Introd.

Witchcraft
GR 830 W4S95
    Summers, Montague, 1880-1948.
        The werewolf, by Montague Summers ... London, K. Paul, Trench, Trubner & co., ltd., 1933.
        xiv, 307 p. VIII pl. (incl. front.) 24½cm.
    Bibliography: p. 279-290.

    1. Werwolves. I. Title.
    [Full name: Alphonsus Joseph-Mary Augustus Montague Summers]

Library of Congress   GR830.W4S8   34-5257
    [3]   398.4

CATALOGUE OF THE CORNELL WITCHCRAFT COLLECTION

BF 1566 S95 [1945]
Summers, Montague, 1880-1948.
Witchcraft and black magic, by Montague Summers. With 24 illustrations. London, New York [etc.] Rider & co. ltd. [1945]
228 p. plates, facsims. 23½ᶜᵐ.

1. Witchcraft. 2. Magic.
[Full name: Alphonsus Joseph Marie Augustus Montague Summers]
A 46-5627
Harvard univ. Library for Library of Congress BF1566.S86
[4]†

Witchcraft
BF 1566 S95 1958
Summers, Montague, 1880-1948.
Witchcraft and black magic. London, Rider [1958]
228 p. illus. 24cm.

I. Title.

Summers, Montague, 1880-1948, ed.
Witchcraft
BF 1582 A2 B67 1929
Boguet, Henri, d. 1619.
An examen of witches, drawn from various trials of many of this sect in the district of Saint Oyan de Joux, commonly known as Saint Claude in the county of Burgundy, including the procedure necessary to a judge in trials for witchcraft. Tr. by E. Allen Ashwin, ed. by the Rev. Montague Summers. [London, J. Rodker, 1929.
liii, 328 p. 19cm.
8
"Edition limited to 1275 copies; this copy is number 290."

Summers, Montague, 1880-1948, ed. and tr.
WITCHCRAFT
BF 1569 A2I59++ 1928
[Institoris, Henricus, d. 1508.
Malleus maleficarum, translated with an introduction, bibliography and notes by the Rev. Montague Summers. [London, J. Rodker, 1928.
xlv, 277, [1] p. front.(port.) 31cm.
By Henricus Institoris and Jacob Sprenger.
"This edition of Malleus maleficarum, comprising 1275 numbered copies, is here translated into English from the edition of 1489 for the first time ... This copy is out of series."
"A note upon the bibliography of the Malleus maleficarum": p. xli-xlii.

Witchcraft
BF 1569 A2I59 1948
Summers, Montague, 1880-1948, tr.
[Institoris, Henricus, d. 1508.
Malleus maleficarum, translated with an introduction, bibliography and notes by the Rev. Montague Summers. London, Pushkin Press [1948]
xxi, 277 p. port. 23cm.
By Henricus Institoris (Heinrich Krämer) and Jacob Sprenger.
"A note upon the bibliography of the Malleus maleficarum": p. xvii-xviii.

Summers, Montague, 1880-1948, ed.
BF 1520 R38+ 1930
Remi, Nicolas, 1530-1612.
Demonolatry. In 3 books; translated by E. A. Ashwin, edited with introd. and notes by Montague Summers. Drawn from the capital trials of 900 persons, more or less, who within the last fifteen years have in Lorraine paid the penalty of death for the crime of witchcraft. London, J. Rodker, 1930.
xliii, 188 p. 27cm.
French original first published, Lyon, 1595.

Witchcraft
BF 1565 S42+ 1930
Scot, Reginald, 1538?-1599.
The discoverie of witchcraft, by Reginald Scot; with an introduction by the Rev. Montague Summers. [London] J. Rodker, 1930.
xxxvii, 282, [1] p. illus. 30cm.
"This edition ... is limited to 1275 copies ... This copy is no. 462."
"The spelling ... is that of the edition of 1584."
"A bibliographical note upon Scot's 'Discouerie'": p. xxxiii-xxxvii.

1. Witchcraft. 2. Magic. 3. Demonology. I. Summers, Montague, 1880-1948. II. Title: The discovery of witchcraft.
Library of Congress BF1565.S4 1930
31—20328

Summers, Montague, 1880-1948, tr.
Witchcraft
BF 1556 S61 1927
Sinistrari, Luigi Maria, 1622-1701.
Demoniality. Translated into English from the Latin (with introd. and notes) by Montague Summers. London, Fortune Press [1927]
xliii, 127 p. 23cm.

No. 237 of 1200 copies.

1. Demonology. I. Summers, Montague, 1880-1948, tr. II. Title. II. His De daemonialitate et incubis et succubis --English.

Summi theologi D. Joh. Georgii Dorschei, dissertatio De horrenda & miserabili Satanae obsessione.
Witchcraft
BF 1555 D71 1667
Dorsch, Johann Georg, 1597-1659, praeses.
Summi theologi D. Joh. Georgii Dorschei, dissertatio De horrenda & miserabili Satanae obsessione, ejusdemque ex obsessis expulsione, multorum votis expetita, juventutis studiosae commodo iterum prodit. Rostochii, Typis Johannis Richelii, 1667.
[24] p. 20cm.
Presented August 23, 1656, with D. Springinsgut as respondent, and title: Disputatio theologica De horrenda et miserabili Satanae obsessione.
8
(Continued on next card)

Summis desiderantes affectibus (9 Dec. 1484)
see
Catholic Church. Pope, 1484-1492 (Innocentius VIII) Summis desiderantes affectibus (9 Dec. 1484)

Superstition and force.
WITCHCRAFT
HV 8497 L43 1878
Lea, Henry Charles, 1825-1909.
Superstition and force. Essays on the wager of law—the wager of battle—the ordeal—torture. By Henry C. Lea ... 3d ed., rev. Philadelphia, H. C. Lea, 1878.
xii, [13]-552 p. 21ᶜᵐ.

1. Wager of law. 2. Wager of battle. 3. Ordeal. 4. Torture. I. Title.
14-16066
Library of Congress HV8497.L4 1878
——Copy 2.
Copyright 1878: 8104

The superstitions of witchcraft.
Witchcraft
BF 1566 W725
Williams, Howard, 1837-
The superstitions of witchcraft. London, Longmans, Green, Longman, Roberts & Green, 1865.
xi, 278 p. 21cm.

1. Witchcraft. I. Title.

La superstizione dell'arte magica.
WITCHCRAFT
BF 1524 P59 1555
Cattani da Diacceto, Francesco, bp. of Fiesole, d. 1595.
Discorso del reverendo M. Francesco de Cattani da Diacceto ... sopra la svperstizione dell'arte magica. Fiorenza, Appresso Valente Panizzi & Marco Peri C., 1567.
4 p. l., 36 numb. l. 23cm.
Bound with Pico della Mirandola, G. F. Dialogo intitolata La strega. Pescia, 1555.
1. Witchcraft. I. Title: La superstizzione dell'arte magica.
8

[Supplementary notes on witchcraft in Massachusetts]
WITCHCRAFT
BF 1576 M82 G641+
Moore, George Henry, 1823-1892.
[Supplementary notes on witchcraft in Massachusetts]
(In: Massachusetts Historical Society. Proceedings. Boston. 26cm. Jan./Mar. 1884. p.77-99)
With, in same issue: Goodell, Abner Cheney. Additional considerations on the history of witchcraft in Massachusetts.
Running title: History of witchcraft in Massachusetts.
8 Continues his Notes on the history
NIC (Continued on next card)

[Supplementary notes on witchcraft in Massachusetts]
WITCHCRAFT
BF 1576 M82 G641+
Moore, George Henry, 1823-1892. [Supplementary notes on witchcraft...] 1884.
(Card 2)
of witchcraft in Massachusetts. Continued by his Final notes on witchcraft in Massachusetts.
1. Witchcraft--Massachusetts. 2. Goodell, Abner Cheney, 1831-1914. Further notes on the history of witchcraft... I. Title. II. His History of witchcraft in Massachusetts. III. Title: History of witchcraft in Massachusetts.

Supplementary notes on witchcraft in Massachusetts.
WITCHCRAFT
BF 1576 M821+ 1884
Moore, George Henry, 1823-1892.
Supplementary notes on witchcraft in Massachusetts; a critical examination of the alleged law of 1711 for reversing the attainders of the witches of 1692. Cambridge, J. Wilson, 1884.
25 p. facsim. 26cm.
Reprinted from the Proceedings of the Massachusetts Historical Society, Mar. 1884.
Caption title: Witchcraft in Massachusetts
8 (Running title of original article: History of witchcraft in Massachusetts)
NIC (Continued on next card)

Supplementary notes on witchcraft in Massachusetts.
WITCHCRAFT
BF 1576 M821+ 1884
Moore, George Henry, 1823-1892. Supplementary notes on witchcraft...1884.
(Card 2)
Continues his Notes on the history of witchcraft in Massachusetts. Continued by his Final notes on witchcraft in Massachusetts.
1. Witchcraft--Massachusetts. 2. Goodell, Abner Cheney, 1831-1914. Further notes on the history of witchcraft... I. Title. II. His Witchcraft in Massachusetts. III. Title: Witchcraft in Massachusetts. IV. His History of witchcraft in Massachusetts. V. Title: History of witchcraft in Massachusetts.

Sur l'incertitude, aussi bien que la vanité des sciences et des arts.
WITCHCRAFT
B 781 A32 F8 1726
Agrippa von Nettesheim, Heinrich Cornelius, 1486?-1535.
Sur la noblesse, & excellence du sexe feminin, de sa preeminence sur l'autre sexe & du sacrement du mariage. Avec le traitté sur l'incertitude, aussi bien que la vanité des sciences & des arts ... traduit par M. de Guedeville. Leiden, Chez Theodore Haak, 1726.
3 v. front., port. 17cm.
Vols. 2-3 have title: Sur l'in-
8 (Continued on next card)
NIC

CATALOGUE OF THE CORNELL WITCHCRAFT COLLECTION

ITCHCRAFT
81
32
8
726

IC

Sur l'incertitude, aussi bien que la vanité des sciences et des arts.
Agrippa von Nettesheim, Heinrich Cornelius, 1486?-1535. Sur la noblesse, & excellence du sexe feminin ... 1726. (Card 2)

certitude, aussi bien que la vanité des sciences & des arts.
Translation of De nobilitate et praecellentia foeminei sexus, and De incertitudine et vanitate scientiarum et artium.
1. Woman. 2. Marriage. 3. Learning and scholarship. 4. Scholasticism. I.
(Continued on next card)

WITCHCRAFT
BF
1517
F5
S96

8
NIC

Surin, Jean Joseph, 1600-1665. Histoire abrégée de la possession des Ursulines de Loudun, et des peines du père Surin; (ouvrage inédit faisant suite à ses oeuvres.) Paris, Chez l'éditeur, au Bureau de l'Association catholique du Sacré-Coeur, 1828.
365, [6] p. 18cm.
"D'après Sommervogel, publication partielle d'une copie d'un ms. de la fin du XVIIIe siècle, ayant pour titre: La vie
(Continued on next card)

WITCHCRAFT
BF
1517
F5
S96

8
NIC

Surin, Jean Joseph, 1600-1665. Triomphe de l'amour divin ... 1829. (Card 2)

Bound with his Histoire abrégée de la possession des Ursulines de Loudun. Paris, 1828.

1. Exorcism. 2. Jeanne des Anges, mère, 1602-1665. 3. Demonology. 4. Peace of mind. I. His Science expérimentale des choses de l'autre vie. II. Title.

WITCHCRAFT
81
32
8
726

IC

Sur la noblesse, et excellence du sexe feminin.
Agrippa von Nettesheim, Heinrich Cornelius, 1486?-1535. Sur la noblesse, & excellence du sexe feminin, de sa preeminence sur l'autre sexe, & du sacrement du mariage. Avec le traitté sur l'incertitude, aussi bien que la vanité des sciences & des arts ... traduit par M. de Guedeville. Leiden, Chez Theodore Haak, 1726.
3 v. front., port. 17cm.
Vols. 2-3 have title: Sur l'in-
(Continued on next card)

WITCHCRAFT
BF
1517
F5
S96

8
NIC

Surin, Jean Joseph, 1600-1665. Histoire abrégée de la possession des Ursulines de Loudun ... 1828. (Card 2)

du R. P. Surin, en laquelle il parle des maux qui lui sont arrivés ensuite de la possession des démons chassés par son ministère." -- Note under Surin, Bibliothèque Nationale.
Surin's authorship has been questioned.
With this is bound his Triomphe de l'amour divin. Avignon, 1829.
(Continued on next card)

WITCHCRAFT
BF
1517
F5
S96

8
NIC

Surin, Jean Joseph, 1600-1665.
La vie du R. P. Surin.
Histoire abrégée de la possession des Ursulines de Loudun, et des peines du père Surin; (ouvrage inédit faisant suite à ses oeuvres.) Paris, Chez l'éditeur, au Bureau de l'Association catholique du Sacré-Coeur, 1828.
365, [6] p. 18cm.
"D'après Sommervogel, publication partielle d'une copie d'un ms. de la fin du XVIIIe siècle, ayant pour titre: La vie
(Continued on next card)

ITCHCRAFT
81
32
8
726

IC

Sur la noblesse, et excellence du sexe feminin.
Agrippa von Nettesheim, Heinrich Cornelius, 1486?-1535. Sur la noblesse, & excellence du sexe feminin ... 1726. (Card 2)

certitude, aussi bien que la vanité des sciences & des arts.
Translation of De nobilitate et praecellentia foeminei sexus, and De incertitudine et vanitate scientiarum et artium.
1. Woman. 2. Marriage. 3. Learning and scholarship. 4. Scholasticism. I.
(Continued on next card)

WITCHCRAFT
BF
1517
F5
S96

8
NIC

Surin, Jean Joseph, 1600-1665. Histoire abrégée de la possession des Ursulines de Loudun ... 1828. (Card 3)

1. Demonology. 2. Demoniac possession. 3. Jeanne des Anges, mère, 1602-1665. 4. Loudun, France. Ursuline convent. I. His La vie du R. P. Surin. II. Title.

WITCHCRAFT
BF
1517
F5
S96

8
NIC

Surin, Jean Joseph, 1600-1665.
La vie du R. P. Surin.
Histoire abrégée de la possession des Ursulines de Loudun ... 1828. (Card 2)

du R. P. Surin, en laquelle il parle des maux qui lui sont arrivés ensuite de la possession des démons chassés par son ministère." -- Note under Surin, Bibliothèque Nationale.
Surin's authorship has been questioned.
With this is bound his Triomphe de l'amour divin. Avignon, 1829.
(Continued on next card)

ITCHCRAFT
566
96

IC

Surbled, Georges, 1855-
Le diable et les sorciers. Arras, Impr. Sueur-Charruey, 1898.
23 p. 25cm.

"Extrait de la Science Catholique, XIIe année, Août 1898."

1. Witchcraft--History. I. Title.

WITCHCRAFT
BF
1517
F5
S96

8
NIC

Surin, Jean Joseph, 1600-1665.
Science expérimentale des choses de l'autre vie.
Triomphe de l'amour divin sur les puissances de l'Enfer, en la possession de la Mère Prieure des Ursulines de Loudun, 1. partie; et Science expérimentale des choses de l'autre vie. Avec le moyen facile d'acquérir la paix du coeur. Ouvrages posthumes ... Avignon, Seguin aîné, 1829.
xj, 312 p. 18cm.
Parts 1 and 4 of Surin's posthumous works as published by Seguin.
(Continued on next card)

Witchcraft
BF
1575
C23
H75

The surreptitious printing of one of Cotton Mather's manuscripts.
Holmes, Thomas James, 1874–
The surreptitious printing of one of Cotton Mather's manuscripts, by Thomas J. Holmes ... Cambridge [Mass., Printed at the Harvard university press] 1925.
1 p. l. 12 p. 25cm.
"Reprinted from Bibliographical essays; a tribute to Wilberforce Eames."
With this is bound his Cotton Mather and his writings on witchcraft. [1926]
1. Calef, Robert, 1648-1719. [More wonders of the invisible world. 2. Mather, Cotton, 1663-1728. 3. Witchcraft—New England. I. Title.
41-38390
Library of Congress   BF1575.C23H6

---

tchcraft
55
5

The Surey demoniack.
[Jollie, Thomas] 1629-1703.
The Surey demoniack; or, An account of Satans strange and dreadful actings, in and about the body of Richard Dugdale of Surey, near Whalley, in Lancashire, and how he was dispossest by Gods blessing on the fastings and prayers of divers ministers and people. The matter of fact attested by the oaths of several credible persons, before some of His Majesties justices of the peace in the said county. London, Printed for J. Robinson, 1697.
64 p. 20cm.
I. Title.

WITCHCRAFT
BF
1517
F5
S96

8
NIC

Surin, Jean Joseph, 1600-1665. Triomphe de l'amour divin ... 1829. (Card 2)

Bound with his Histoire abrégée de la possession des Ursulines de Loudun. Paris, 1828.

1. Exorcism. 2. Jeanne des Anges, mère, 1602-1665. 3. Demonology. 4. Peace of mind. I. His Science expérimentale des choses de l'autre vie. II. Title.

BF
1555
G21

Sutter, P.
Gaquère, François, 1888-
Les possédés d'Illfurth, de Natal et de Phat-Diem (1868-1906-1925) Genval, Éditions "Marie-Mediatrice" [1956]
125 p. illus. 18cm.
At head of title: P. Sutter [et] François Gaquère. Aux prises avec Satan.
Although Sutter's name appears first (left top of the t.p.) the work is presumably chiefly (or only) by Gaquère. Cf. "Avant-propos" and cover.
1. Demoniac possession. I. His Aux prises avec Satan. II. Sutter, P III. Title. IV. Title: Aux prises avec Satan.

---

tchcraft
55
5T2

The Surey imposter.
Taylor, Zachary, 1653-1705.
The Surey impostor: being an answer to a late pamphlet, entituled, The Surey demoniack. ... London, Printed for J. Jones, 1697.
75 p. front. 23cm.

1. Jollie, Thomas, 1629-1703. The Surey demoniack. 2. Demoniac possession. I. Title.

WITCHCRAFT
BF
1517
F5
S96

8
NIC

Surin, Jean Joseph, 1600-1665.
Triomphe de l'amour divin sur les puissances de l'Enfer, en la possession de la Mère Prieure des Ursulines de Loudun, 1. partie; et Science expérimentale des choses de l'autre vie. Avec le moyen facile d'acquérir la paix du coeur. Ouvrages posthumes ... Avignon, Seguin aîné, 1829.
xj, 312 p. 18cm.
Parts 1 and 4 of Surin's posthumous works as published by Seguin.
(Continued on next card)

RARE
K
S2545
1599

8
NIC

Suzaria, Guido de.
Tractatus II [i.e. duo] perutiles & quotidiani De indiciis, quaestionibus et tortura ... Guidonis de Suzaria & Pauli Grillandi de Castilione, una cum additionib. Ludovici Bolognini ... geordnet durch Ioannem Guörnerum de Vineca. Ursellis, Apud Nicolaum Henricum, sumptibus Cornelij Suterij, 1597.
291 p. 16cm.

Bound with: Saur, Abraham. Notarien Spiegel. Franckfort am Mayn, 1599.
(Continued on next card)

CATALOGUE OF THE CORNELL WITCHCRAFT COLLECTION

RARE K S2545 1599
Suzaria, Guido de. Tractatus II [i.e.duo] perutiles & quotidiani De indiciis... 1597. (Card 2)
1. Torture. 2. Criminal procedure. I. Grillando, Paolo. II. Bolognini, Ludovico, 1447 (ca.)-1508. III. Guornerus, Joannes, ed. IV. Title.

Witchcraft BF 1410 B42 Z56 v.3 no.22
Den swadder, die E. W. op Cartesianen en Coccejanen geworpen heeft ...
[Hamer, Petrus] 1646-1716. Den swadder, die E. W. op Cartesianen en Coccejanen geworpen heeft ... 1692. (Card 2)
4°: *², A-E⁴, F1.
Van der Linde 172.
No. 22 in vol. lettered Bekker III.

Witchcraft BS 2545 D5 T97 no.10
[Swinton, John] 1703-1777.
A critical dissertation concerning the words Δαι'μων and Δαιμο'νιον Occasion'd by two late enquiries into the meaning of demoniacks in the New Testament. In a letter to a friend. By a gentleman of Wadham College, Oxford. London, Printed for J. Crokatt, and sold by J. Roberts, 1738.
29 p. 21cm.
Also attributed to George Costard.
No. 10 in vol. lettered: Twells, Whiston, etc. Tracts on the demoniacs in the New Testament. London, 1738-1775.

DB 200 .5 S96
Svátek, Josef, 1835-
Culturhistorische Bilder aus Böhmen. Von Josef Svátek ... Wien, W. Braumüller, 1879.
vi p., 2 l., [3]-311 p. 23cm.
Contents.--Hexenprocesse in Böhmen.--Die Alchemie in Böhmen.--Adamiten und Deisten in Böhmen.--Ein griechischer Abenteurer in Prag.--Die Guillotine in Böhmen.--Bauern-Rebellionen in Böhmen.--Schiller in Böhmen.--Die Rudolfinische Kunstkammer in Prag.--Die Zigeuner in Böhmen.
I. Title.

Witchcraft BF 1563 W81++ no.7
Swan, John.
A trve and breife report of Mary Glovers vexation, and of her deliuerance by the meanes of fastinge and prayer. Performed by those whose names are sett downe in the next page. ... [London?] 1603. [London, at the British Museum, 1923]
[88] p. 14cm.
Signatures: A⁴, A-K⁴.
Photocopy (negative) 88 p. on 44 l. 20x32cm.
No. 7 in vol. lettered: Witchcraft tracts, chapbooks and broadsides, 1579-1704; rotograph copies.
1. Glover, Mary, fl. 1603.

WITCHCRAFT BF 1508 P97 S97
Svoboda, Karl Maria, 1889-
La démonologie de Michel Psellos (Démonologie Michala Psella) Brno, V komisi knihkupectví A. Piša, 1927.
60 p. 24cm. (Brno. Universita. Filosoficka faculta. Spisy. 22)
At head of title: K. Svoboda.
With summary in Czech.
1. Psellus, Michael. Peri energeias daimonon dia logos. 2. Demonology. I. Title.

8 NIC

Witchcraft BF 1566 S968
Svenungsson, Lars Manfred, 1889-
Rannsakningarna om trolldomen i Bohuslän 1669-1672. [Uddevalla, Sweden, Barneviks Tryckeri, 1970]
339 p. 23cm.
1. Witchcraft--Hist. I. Title.

NIC

WITCHCRAFT BF 1523 K78 K513
Swedenborg, Emanuel, 1688-1772, supposed author.
[Köster, Heinrich Martin Gottfried] 1734-1802.
Emanuel Swedenborgs demüthiges Danksagungsschreiben an den grossen Mann, der die Nonexistenz des Teufels demonstrirt hat. Frankfurt und Leipzig, 1778.
46 p. 14cm.
Attribution by Holzmann.
1. Kindleben, Christian Wilhelm, 1748-1785. Ueber die Non-Existenz des Teufels. 2. Devil. I. Swedenborg, Emanuel, 1688-1772, supposed author. II. Title. III. Title: Demüthiges Danksagungsschre iben an den grossen Mann.

8

Witchcraft BS 2545 D5 T97 no.2
[Sykes, Arthur Ashley] 1684?-1756.
An enquiry into the meaning of demoniacks in the New Testament. ... By T.P.A.P.O.A.B. I.T.C.O.S. 2d ed., corr. and amended. London, Printed for J. Roberts, 1737.
79 p. 21cm.
No. 2 in vol. lettered: Twells, Whiston, etc. Tracts on the demoniacs in the New Testament. London, 1738-1775.
1. Demoniac possession. 2. Bible. N.T.--Commentaries. I. Title.

PD 5001 S96 ser.1 v.13 no.6
Sverges sista häxprocess i Dalarne 1757-1763.
Fries, Ellen, 1855-1900.
... Sverges sista häxprocess i Dalarne 1757-1763, efter handlingarna i målet tecknad av Ellen Fries. Uppsala, Almqvist & Wicksells boktr.-aktiebolag. 1893.
73 p. 23½cm. ([Nyare] bidrag till kännedom om de svenska landsmålen ock svenskt folklif XIII. 6)
Forms 50. hft. of the whole series.
1. Witchcraft--Sweden. I. Title. 23--2440
Library of Congress PD5001.S9 50. hft., XIII. 6 [38b1]

WITCHCRAFT BF 1408 S57
Swedenborg, Emanuel, 1688-1772.
Sierke, Eugen, 1845-
Schwärmer und Schwindler zu Ende des achtzehnten Jahrhunderts. Leipzig, S. Hirzel, 1874.
vi, 462 p. 21cm.
1. Occult sciences--Biography. 2. Superstition. 3. Swedenborg, Emanuel, 1688-1772. 4. Mesmer, Franz Anton, 1734-1815. 5. Gassner, Johann Joseph, 1727-1779. 6. Schrepfer, Johann Georg, 1730?-1774. 7. Cagliostro, Alessandro, conte de, as sumed name of Giuseppe Balsamo, 1743-1795. I. Title.

8 NIC

Witchcraft BS 2545 D5 T75 no.1
[Sykes, Arthur Ashley] 1684?-1756.
An enquiry into the meaning of demoniacks in the New Testament. ... By T.P.A.P.O.A.B. I.T.C.O.S. The 2d ed. corr. and amended. London, Printed for J. Roberts, 1737.
79 p. 20cm.
No. 1 in vol. lettered: Tracts on demoniack 1737.

Svoboda, Karl, 1889-
see
Swoboda, Karl Maria, 1889-

Witchcraft BT 980 S97
[Swinton, John] 1703-1777.
A critical dissertation concerning the words ΔAIMΩN and ΔAIMONION. Occasion'd by two late enquiries [by Arthur Ashley Sykes] into the meaning of demoniacs in the New Nestament. In a letter to a friend. By a Gentleman of Wadham College, Oxford. London, Printed for J. Crokatt; and sold by J. Roberts, 1738.
29 p. 20cm.
Also attributed to George Costard.
Letter signed: Philalethes.
(Continued on next card)

8

Witchcraft BS 2545 D5 T759 no.1
[Sykes, Arthur Ashley] 1684?-1756.
An enquiry into the meaning of demoniack in the New Testament. ... By T.P.A.P.O.A.B I.T.C.O.S. The 2d ed. corr. and amended. London, Printed for J. Roberts, 1737.
79 p. 20cm.
No. 1 in vol. lettered: Tracks [sic] of demoniacks.

Witchcraft BF 1410 B42 Z56 v.3 no.22
Den swadder, die E. W. op Cartesianen en Coccejanen geworpen heeft ...
[Hamer, Petrus] 1646-1716.
Den swadder, die E. W. op Cartesianen en Coccejanen geworpen heeft, in sijn twee deelen van Aardige duivelarye zuiver af-gevaagt, met eer. het geschil dat Dr. Bekker ongegrond opwerpt, als of daimoon, &c. niet wel duivel overgezet wierd, kortelijk voldongen, en in staat van wijzen gebracht, door Iiratiel Leetsosoneus. Amsterdam, By G. Borstius, boekverkooper, 1692.
2 p. l., 42 p. title and other vignettes, illus. initia 1s. 20 x 15cm.
(Continued on next card)

Witchcraft BT 980 S97
[Swinton, John] 1703-1777. A critical dissertation ... 1738. (Card 2)
1. Demoniac possession. 2. Sykes, Arthur Ashley, 1684?-1756. An enquiry into the meaning of demoniacks in the New Testament. 3. Sykes, Arthur Ashley, 1684?-1756. A further enquiry into the meaning of demoniacks in the New Testament. I. Costard, George, 1710-1782, supposed author. II. Philalethes, pseud. III. Title: A critical dis sertation concerning the words DAIM ON and DAIMONION. (Over)

Witchcraft BS 2545 D5 C56
Sykes, Arthur Ashley, 1684?-1756.
An enquiry into the meaning of demoniack [Church, Thomas]
An essay towards vindicating the literal sense of the demoniacks in the New Testament. In answer to a late Enquiry into the meaning of them [by A.A. Sykes] ... London, Printed by J. Bettenhem, and sold by J. Roberts, 1737.
118 p. 19cm.
1. Demoniac possession. 2. Bible. N.T.--Commentaries. 3. Sykes, Arthur Ashley, 1684?-1756. [An en-quiry into the meaning of demoniacks in the New Testament. I. Title.

532

CATALOGUE OF THE CORNELL WITCHCRAFT COLLECTION

Sykes, Arthur Ashley, 1684?-1756.
    An enquiry into the meaning of demoniacks in the New Testament.
Pegge, Samuel, 1704-1796.
    An examination of the Enquiry into the meaning of demoniacs in the New Testament. In a letter to the author. Wherein it is shewn, that the word demon does not signify a departed soul, either in the classics or the Scriptures; and consequently, that the whole of the Enquiry is without foundation. London, Printed for F. Gyles, 1739.
    86 p. 20cm.

    No. 6 in vol. lettered: Tracts on demoniacks. 1737.

Sykes, Arthur Ashley, 1684?-1756.
    An enquiry into the meaning of demoniacks in the New Testament.
[Swinton, John] 1703-1777.
    A critical dissertation concerning the words ΔΑΙΜΩΝ and ΔΑΙΜΟΝΙΟΝ. Occasion'd by two late enquiries [by Arthur Ashley Sykes] into the meaning of demoniacs in the New Nestament. In a letter to a friend. By a Gentleman of Wadham College, Oxford. London, Printed for J. Crokatt; and sold by J. Roberts, 1738.
    29 p. 20cm.
    Also attributed to George Costard.
    Letter signed: Philalethes.
    (Continued on next card)

Sykes, Arthur Ashley, 1684?-1756.
    An enquiry into the meaning of demoniacks in the New Testament.
[Sykes, Arthur Ashley] 1684?-1756.
    A further enquiry into the meaning of demoniacks in the New Testament. Wherein the Enquiry is vindicated against the objections of ... Mr. Twells, and of the author of the Essay in answer to it [i.e. Thomas Church] ... London, Printed for J. Roberts, 1737.
    116 p. 21cm.

    No. 5 in vol. lettered: Twells, Whiston, etc. Tracts on the demoniacs in the New Testament. London, 1737-1775.

Sykes, Arthur Ashley, 1684?-1756.
    An enquiry into the meaning of demoniacks in the New Testament.
Twells, Leonard, d. 1742.
    An answer to the Enquiry into the meaning of demoniacks in the New Testament: shewing that the demons therein spoken of were fallen angels; and that the demoniacks were persons really possessed. In a letter to the author... London, Printed for R. Gosling, 1737.
    74 p. 21cm.

    No. 3 in vol. lettered: Twells, Whiston, etc. Tracts on the demoniacs in the New Testament. London, 1738-1775.

Sykes, Arthur Ashley, 1684?-1756.
    An enquiry into the meaning of daemoniacks in the New Testament.
Whiston, William, 1667-1752.
    An account of the daemoniacks, and of the power of casting out daemons, both in the New Testament, and in the four first centuries. Occasioned by a late pamphlet [by A. A. Sykes] intituled, An enquiry into the meaning of daemoniacks in the New Testament ... Added, an appendix, concerning the tythes and oblations paid by Christians ... London, Printed for J. Whiston, 1737.
    88 p. 21cm.

    (Continued on next card)

Sykes, Arthur Ashley, 1684?-1756.
    An enquiry into the meaning of daemoniacks in the New Testament.
Whiston, William, 1667-1752. An account of the daemoniacks, and of the power of casting out daemons ... 1737. (Card 2)

    No. 9 in vol. lettered: Twells, Whiston, etc. Tracts on the demoniacs in the New Testament. London, 1738-1775.

    1. Demoniac possession. 2. Bible. N.T.--Commentaries. 3. Tithes. I. Title.
Sykes, Arthur Ashley, 1684?-1756.
An enquiry into the meaning of daemoniacs in the New Testament.

Witchcraft
BS
2545
D5
T97
no.5

[Sykes, Arthur Ashley] 1684?-1756.
    A further enquiry into the meaning of demoniacks in the New Testament. Wherein the Enquiry is vindicated against the objections of ... Mr. Twells, and of the author of the Essay in answer to it [i.e. Thomas Church] ... London, Printed for J. Roberts, 1737.
    116 p. 21cm.

    No. 5 in vol. lettered: Twells, Whiston, etc. Tracts on the demoniacs in the New Testament. London, 1737-1775.
    (over)

Witchcraft
BS
2545
D5
T75
no.2

[Sykes, Arthur Ashley] 1684?-1756.
    A further enquiry into the meaning of demoniacks in the New Testament. Wherein the Enquiry is vindicated against the objections of ... Mr. Twells, and of the author of the Essay in answer to it [i.e. Thomas Church] ... London, Printed for J. Roberts, 1737.
    116 p. 20cm.

    No. 2 in vol. lettered: Tracts on demoniacks. 1737.

Witchcraft
BS
2545
D5
T759
no.2

[Sykes, Arthur Ashley] 1684?-1756.
    A further enquiry into the meaning of demoniacks in the New Testament. Wherein the Enquiry is vindicated against the objections of ... Mr. Twells, and of the author [i.e. T. Church] of the Essay in answer to it. ... London, Printed for J. Roberts, 1737.
    116 p. 20cm.

    No. 2 in vol. lettered: Tracts [sic] of demoniacks.

Witchcraft
BT
980
S97

Sykes, Arthur Ashley, 1684?-1756.
    A further enquiry into the meaning of demoniacks in the New Testament.
[Swinton, John] 1703-1777.
    A critical dissertation concerning the words ΔΑΙΜΩΝ and ΔΑΙΜΟΝΙΟΝ. Occasion'd by two late enquiries [by Arthur Ashley Sykes] into the meaning of demoniacs in the New Nestament. In a letter to a friend. By a Gentleman of Wadham College, Oxford. London, Printed for J. Crokatt; and sold by J. Roberts, 1738.
    29 p. 20cm.
    Also attributed to George Costard.
    Letter signed: Philalethes.
    (Continued on next card)

Witchcraft
BS
2545
D5
T97
no.6

Sykes, Arthur Ashley, 1684?-1756.
    A further enquiry into the meaning of demoniacks in the New Testament.
Twells, Leonard, d. 1742.
    An answer to the Further enquiry into the meaning of demoniacks in the New Testament. Wherein the arguments to prove that the demons of the New Testament were fallen angels are defended; and the objections against the scheme of the Enquiry are made good. In a second letter to the author. London, Printed for R. Gosling, 1738.
    92 p. 21cm.

    (Continued on next card)

Witchcraft
BS
2545
D5
T97
no.6

Sykes, Arthur Ashley, 1684?-1756.
    A further enquiry into the meaning of demoniacks in the New Testament.
Twells, Leonard, d. 1742. An answer to the Further enquiry into the meaning of demoniacks in the New Testament... 1738.
    (Card 2)

    No. 6 in vol. lettered: Twells, Whiston, etc. Tracts on the demoniacs in the New Testament. London, 1738-1775.

    1. Sykes, Arthur Ashley, 1684?-1756. A further enquiry into the meaning of demoniacks in the New Testament.

WITCHCRAFT
BX
1158
M61

Sylvester II, Pope, d. 1003.
    Meyer, Raphael Ludwig, 1869-1925.
        Gerbertsagnet; studie over middelalderlige djaevlekontrakthistorier. København, Det Nordiske Forlag, 1902.
        170 p. 25cm.

8
NIC

    1. Sylvester II, Pope, d. 1003. 2. Devil. 3. Demonology. I. Title.

Sylvester Prierias, 1456-1527.

    see

Mazzolini, Silvestro, da Prierio, 1456-1523.

Sylvius, Joannes Henricus, respondent.

WITCHCRAFT
BF
1445
T54
D2
1600

Thyraeus, Pierre, 1546-1601, praeses.
    De prodigiosis viuorum hominum apparitionibus. Dispvtatio theologica bipartita: et priori qvidem explicantvr illae, in quibus se viui sub propria forma, nunc vigilantibus, nunc dormientibus exhibent: posteriori verò, in quibus ijdem, sub brutorum animantium varijs formis conspiciuntur... Pro gradv responsvrvs est ... Ioannes Henricvs Sylvivs ... praeside P. Petro Thyraeo ... Wirceburgi, Ex officina typographica Henri-

8
    (Continued on next card)

Sylvius, Joannes Henricus, respondent.

WITCHCRAFT
BF
1445
T54
D2
1600

Thyraeus, Pierre, 1546-1601, praeses. De prodigiosis ... [1591?] (Card 2)
    ci Aquensis [1591?]
    [80] p. 21cm.
    Title in ornamental border.
    Binding: contemporary blind stamped pigskin, with clasps.
    Bound with his De apparitionibus spirituum tractatus duo. Coloniae Agrippinae, 1600.

    1. Apparitions. 2. Ghosts. I. Sylvius, Joannes Henricus, respondent. II. Title.

Sympathetic magic.

Witchcraft
BF
1531
F91

Friend, John Albert Newton, 1881-
    Demonology, sympathetic magic and witchcraft; a study of superstition as it persists in man and affects him in a scientific age. London, C. Griffin [1961]
    173 p. illus. 20 cm.
    Includes bibliography.

    1. Demonology. 2. Witchcraft. I. Title: Sympathetic magic.

    BF1531.F7   133.4   61-66183 ‡
    Library of Congress   [2]

Synesius, Cyrenaeus, bp. of Ptolemais.
    De somniis.

WITCHCRAFT
PA
4220
L3
A4+
1516

Jamblichus, of Chalcis.
    [De mysteriis. Latin]
    Iamblichus De mysteriis Aegyptiorum, Chaldaeorum, Assyriorum. Proclus In Platonicum Alcibiadem de anima, atq[ue] demone. Proclus De sacrificio, & magia. Porphyrius De diuinis, atq[ue] daemonibus. Synesius Platonicus De somniis. Psellus De daemonibus. Expositio Prisciani, & Marsilii in Theophrastum De sensu, phantasia, & intellectu. Alcinoi Platonici philosophi, Liber de doctrina

8
    (Continued on next card)

CATALOGUE OF THE CORNELL WITCHCRAFT COLLECTION

Synesius, Cyrenaeus, bp. of Ptolemais.
De somniis.

WITCHCRAFT
PA
4220　　Jamblichus, of Chalcis. [De mysteriis.
L3　　　　Latin.] [1516]　　　　(Card 2)
A4+
1516
　　Platonis. Speusippi Platonis discipuli,
Liber de Platonis definitionibus. Pythagorae philosophi Aurea uerba. Symbola Pithagorae philosophi. Xenocratis philosophi
platonici, Liber de morte. Mercurii Trismegisti Pimander. Eiusdem Asclepius. Marsilii Ficini De triplici uita lib. II.
8　　Eiusdem Liber　　de uoluptate. Eiusdem
　　　　　　(Continued on next card)

Synesius, Cyrenaeus, bp. of Ptolemais.
De somniis.

WITCHCRAFT
PA
4220　　Jamblichus, of Chalcis. [De mysteriis.
L3　　　　Latin] [1516]　　　　(Card 3)
A4+
1516
　　De sole & lumine libri. II. Apologia eiusdem in librum suum de lumine. Eiusdem Libellus de magis. Quod necessaria sit securitas,
& tranquillitas animi. Praeclarissimarum
sententiarum huius operis breuis annotatio.
[Venetiis, In aedibvs Aldi, et Andreae soceri, 1516]
8　　　　177 [i.e., 　　175] numbered leaves.
　　29cm.
　　　　　　(Continued on next card)

Synesius, Cyrenaeus, bp. of Ptolemais.
De somniis.

WITCHCRAFT
PA
4220　　Jamblichus, of Chalcis. [De mysteriis]
L3　　　　Latin. [1516]　　　　(Card 4)
A4+
1516
　　At head of title: Index eorvm, qvae hoc
in libro habentvr.
　　With colophon.
　　Provenance: Bibliotec: SS. Me. Novelle.
　　Translations by M. Ficino.
　　1. Occult sciences. 2. Philosophy,
Ancient--Collections. I. Proclus Diado-
chus. In Platonicum Alcibiadem. II. Pro-
8　　clus Diadoch　　us. De sacrificio. III.
　　　　　　(Continued on next card)

A system of magic.

Witchcraft
BF　　[Defoe, Daniel] 1660-1731.
1601　　A system of magic. In one volume.
D31　　Oxford, Printed by D. A. Talboys, for T.
1840　　Tegg, 1840.
　　xvii, 396 p. 18cm.

　　Reprint of the London ed. of 1728 with
a new t. p.

　　1. Magic. I. Title.

A system of magick.

Witchcraft
BF　　[Defoe, Daniel] 166 0-1731.
1601　　A system of magick; or, A history of the black art. Being
D31　　an historical account of mankind's most early dealing with
　　the devil; and how the acquaintance on both sides first began
　　... London, Printed: and sold by J. Roberts, MDCCXXVII.

　　6 p. l., 403 p. incl. front. 20ᶜᵐ.

　　First edition.

　　1. Magic.　　I. Title.

　　　　　　　　　　　　　　35—19190
Library of Congress　　　　BF1601.D3 1727
　　　　　　　　[42b1]　　[159.9614] 133.4

RC　　Szasz, Thomas Stephen, 1920-
438　　　The manufacture of madness; a compara-
S98　　tive study of the Inquisition and the mental
　　health movement [by] Thomas S. Szasz. [1st
　　ed.] New York, Harper & Row [1970]
　　xxvii, 383 p. 22cm.

　　About a third of the text deals with
witchcraft.
　　1. Mental illness--History. I. Title.

Ein Szegediner Hexenprocess.

WITCHCRAFT
BF　　Möstl, Franz.
1584　　Ein Szegediner Hexenprocess. Culturhis-
H9　　torische Studie. Graz, Leykam-Josefsthal,
M69　　1879.
　　33 p. 18cm.

　　Includes account of trial in Szeged in
1728.

　　1. Witchcraft--Hungary. 2. Trials (Witch-
　　craft)--Hungary. 3. Trials (Witchcraft)--
8　　Szeged, Hung　　ary.
NIC

534

CATALOGUE OF THE CORNELL WITCHCRAFT COLLECTION

T

T., A.

Witchcraft

Copy van een brief geschreeve aan een heer, woonende tusschen Rotterdam en Dort. Raakende het gepasseerde in de saak van Dr. B. Bekker; door een liefhebber van vreede en waarheid. Dord, Gedrukt by G. Abramsz, 1692.
18 p. [p. 19-20 blank] title vignette. 19 x 15cm.
4°: A-B⁴, C².
Signed: A. T.
Van der Lin de 48; 64.
No. 8 in vol. lettered Bekker II.
(Continued on next card)

T., R.

Witchcraft

The opinion of witchcraft vindicated. In answer to a book intituled The question of witchcraft debated [by John Wagstaffe] Being a letter to a friend, by R. T. ... London, Printed by E. O. for F. Haley, 1670.
63 p. 15cm.

1. Witchcraft. 2. Wagstaffe, John, 1633-1677. The question of witchcraft debated. I. T., R.

T. M.

Witchcraft

A relation of the diabolical practices of above twenty wizards and witches of the sheriffdom of Renfrew in the kingdom of Scotland, contain'd in their tryalls, examinations, and confessions; and for which several of them have been executed this present year, 1697. London, Printed for H. Newman [1697]
24 p. 21cm.

"To Sir T. M.", a letter signed: "T.P.": p.3-4.
Wing R 823.

T. P.

Witchcraft

A relation of the diabolical practices of above twenty wizards and witches of the sheriffdom of Renfrew in the kingdom of Scotland, contain'd in their tryalls, examinations, and confessions; and for which several of them have been executed this present year, 1697. London, Printed for H. Newman [1697]
24 p. 21cm.

"To Sir T. M.", a letter signed: "T.P.": p.3-4.
Wing R 823.

T. S.

Witchcraft

Nodige aanmerkinge omtrent eenige woorden gesprooken van D. Johannes Visscherus, in een catechisatie, over den 34 Sondag des Catechismus. Dog bysonderlijk over de 94 vrage, enz. voorgevallen op Sondag den 24 Augusty 1692. Door T. S. Amsterdam, By D. vanden Dalen, boekverkoper, 1692.
7 p. [p. 8 blank] title vignette. 19 x 15cm.
4°: A⁴.

(Continued on next card)

T. S.

Witchcraft
BF
1410
B42
Z56
v.2
no.6

Nodige aanmerkinge omtrent eenige woorden gesprooken van D. Johannes Visscherus ... 1692. (Card 2)

Black letter.
Response to Visscher's attack on Balthasar Bekker.
No. 6 in vol. lettered Bekker II.
1. Visscher, Johannes, 1617?-1694. 2. Bekker, Balthasar, 1634-1698. De betoverde weereld. I. T. S. II. S., T.

8

Witchcraft
BF
1522
L25
1613

Tableau de l'inconstance des mauvais anges et demons.
L'Ancre, Pierre de, d. 1630.
Tableav de l'inconstance des mavvais anges et demons, ov il est amplement traicté des sorciers et de la sorcellerie ... Avec vn discours contenant la procedure faicte par les inquisiteurs d'Espagne et de Nauarre, à 53. magiciens, apostats, Juifs, et sorciers, en la ville de Logrogne en Castille, le 9. nouembre 1610 ... Reueu, corrigé, & augmenté de plusieurs nouuelles obseruations, arrests, & autres choses notables. Paris, Nicolas Bvon, 1613.
[40], 590, [18] p. fold. pl. 24cm.

Witchcraft
BF
1411
D39

Tableau historique, analytique, et critique des sciences occultes.
Denis, Ferdinand, 1798-1890.
Tableau historique, analytique, et critique des sciences occultes, où l'on examine l'origine, le développement, l'influence et le caractère de la divination, de l'astrologie, des oracles ... Précédé d'une introduction et suivi d'une biographie, d'une bibliographie et d'un vocabulaire ... Paris, L'Encyclcpédie portative, 1830.
xii, 296 p. front. 13cm.
(Continued on next card)

Witchcraft
BF
1411
D39

Tableau historique, analytique, et critique des sciences occultes.
Denis, Ferdinand, 1798-1890. Tableau historique ... des sciences occultes ... 1830. (Card 2)

Half-title: Encyclopédie portative; ou, Résumé universel des sciences, des lettres et des arts, en une collection de tratiés séparés. Par une société de savans et de gens de lettres ...
Ex-libris Frédéric de Sevillia.

1. Occult sciences--Hist.

WITCHCRAFT
BS
2545
D5
T12

Taczak, Teodor, 1878-
Dämonische Besessenheit. Ein Kapitel aus der katholischen Lehre von der Herrschaft des Fursten der Sünde und des Todes. Von Theodor Taczak, Priester der Erzdiözese Gnesen-Posen. Münster i. W., Druck der Westfälischen Vereinsdruckerei [1903]
61, [4] p. 23cm.
Inaug.-diss.--Münster.
Contents.--Begriff und Tatsache der dämonischen Besessenheit.--Stellung der pro-

8
NIC
(Continued on next card)

WITCHCRAFT
BS
2545
D5
T12

Taczak, Teodor, 1878- . Dämonische Besessenheit ... [1903] (Card 2)

Contents--Continued.
testantischen Theologie zur Besessenheit. --Besessenheit und Besessenheitswahn.

1. Demoniac possession. 2. Devil. 3. Theology, Doctrinal. I. Title.

8
NIC

Taczak, Theodor, 1878-

see

Taczak, Teodor, 1878-

WITCHCRAFT
BL
25
R3805
v.7
no.3

Tambornino, Julius.
De antiquorum daemonismo. Giessen, A. Töpelmann, 1909.
112 p. 23cm. (Religionsgeschichtliche Versuche und Vorarbeiten, VII. Bd. 3. Heft)
"Kap. II und III sind auch gesondert als Dissertation von Münster 1909 unter dem Titel De antiquorum daemonismo capita duo erschienen."
1. Demoniac possession. 2. Occult sciences. 3. Classical literature (Selections: extracts, etc.) I. Title.

8
NIC

WITCHCRAFT
BF
1583
T15

Tamianus, Julius, pseud.
Julii Tamiani Send-Schreiben an Hieronymum Pistellum, worinne bey Veranlassung der unweit Jena unternommenen Satans-Beschwerung der Anfang und Fortgang der Magie, wie nicht minder die Meynungen der Magorum untersuchet, auch von denen dabey gewöhnlichen Mitteln ... Bericht erstattet wird. Nebst einem Paquetgen an den verwegenen Authorem der sogenannten Gerichte Gottes und sinnreichen Uberschrifft, so er Franco zu er-

8
NIC
(Continued on next card)

WITCHCRAFT
BF
1583
T15

Tamianus, Julius, pseud. Julii Tamiani Send-Schreiben an Hieronymum Pistellum ...
(Card 2)

halten hat. Zu Magiluna in Arabien [i.e., Jena?] 1716.
52 p. 20cm.
Illustrative title vignette.
1. Witchcraft--Thuringia. 2. Witchcraft--Jena, Germany. 3. Magic. I. Pistellus, Hieronymus. II. Title: Send-Schreiben an Hieronymum Pistellum. III. Title.

8
NIC

CATALOGUE OF THE CORNELL WITCHCRAFT COLLECTION

WITCHCRAFT
BF 1565 T16
8 NIC

Tandler, Tobias.
 Dissertatio de fascino & incantatione, sub auspicio praelectionum publ. habita, à Tobia Tandlero philos. & medicin. doctore, ac math. profess. 24. Octobris, anno 1606 ... VVitebergae, Sumptibus Clementis Bergeri, Excudebat Johann. Schmidt, 1606.
 8 p. l., 142 p. 16cm.
 Title in ornamental border.
 1. Witchcraft. 2. Evil eye. 3. Magic. I. Title: De fascino et incantatione. II. Title.

Witchcraft
BF 1563 D61
8

Tanner, Adam, 1572-1632.
 Tractatus theologicus de processu adversus crimina excepta.
 Diversi tractatvs: De potestate ecclesiastica coercendi daemones circa energumenos & maleficiatos, de potentia ac viribus daemonum. De modo procedendi adversvs crimina excepta; praecipuè contra sagas & maleficos ... Ex diversis jisqve celeberrimis huius aeui scriptoribus ... disputantur. Coloniae Agrippinae, Sumptibus Constantini Munich bibliopolae, 1629.
 8, 236, 166 p. 20cm.
 (Continued on next card)

Witchcraft
BF 1563 D61
8

Tanner, Adam, 1572-1632.
 Tractatus theologicus de processu adversus crimina excepta.
 Diversi tractatvs ... 1629. (Card 2)
 Contents.--Tractatvs de potestate ecclesiae coercendi daemones circa obsessos & maleficiatos, vnà cum praxi exorcistica, a R. della Torre.--Tractatvs theologicvs de processv adversvs crimina excepta, ac speciatim adversus crimen veneficij, a A. Tanner.--Tractatvs alter theologicus de sagis et veneficis, a P. Laymanni.--Consilium de sagis, a M. A. Peregrini.
 (Continued on next card)

Witchcraft
BF 1563 D61
8

Tanner, Adam, 1572-1632.
 Tractatus theologicus de processu adversus crimina excepta.
 Diversi tractatvs ... 1629. (Card 3)
 Title in red and black.
 In double columns except for t. p., dedication, and titles of first, second, and fourth works.
 1. Witchcraft. 2. Trials (Witchcraft) 3. Exorcism. I. Torre, Raffaelle della. Tractatus de potestate ecclesiae coercendi daemones. II. Tanner, Adam, 1572-1632. Tractatus theologicus de processu adversus
 (Continued on next card)

WITCHCRAFT
BF 1565 S38
8 NIC

Tanner, Adam, 1572-1632.
 Tractatus theologicus de processu adversus crimina excepta.
 Schultheis, Heinrich von.
 Eine aussführliche Instrvction, wie in Inqvisition Sachen des grewlichen Lasters der Zauberey gegen die Zaubere der göttlichen Majestät vnd der Christenheit Feinde ohn Gefahr der Vnschüldigen zu procediren ... In Form eines freundlichen Gesprächs gestelt ... Cölln, Bey Hinrich Berchem, Sumptibus authoris gedruckt bey Gissbert Clemens, 1634.
 xiii, [7], 503 p. port.
 (Continued on next card)

WITCHCRAFT
BF 1565 S38
8 NIC

Tanner, Adam, 1572-1632.
 Tractatus theologicus de processu adversus crimina excepta.
 Schultheis, Heinrich von. Eine aussführliche Instrvction ... 1634. (Card 2)
 Refutation of A. Tanner, p. 367-436, in Latin.
 "This book is, to my thinking, the most gruesome in all the gruesome literature of witch-persecution; and there is good ground for suspecting it of being the only copy now surviving ..."--part of MS note by G. L. Burr tipped into back of vol.
 (Continued on next card)

Witchcraft
BF 1584 A93 R22 1891
8

Tanner, Adam, 1572-1632.
 Rapp, Ludwig.
 Die Hexenprozesse und ihre Gegner in Tirol. 2. verm. Aufl. Mit dem Bildnisse Tartarotti's. Brixen, A. Wegner, 1891.
 iv, 170 p. pot. 22cm.
 First published 1874 with title: Die Hexenprozesse und ihre Gegner aus Tirol.
 1. Witchcraft--Austria. 2. Trials (Witchcraft)--Austria. 3. Tanner, Adam, 1572-1632. 4. Tartarotti, Girolamo, 1706-1761. 5. Sterzinger, Ferdinand, 1721-1779. I. Title.

Witchcraft
BF 1576 T17

Tapley, Charles Sutherland, 1899-
 Rebecca Nurse, saint but witch victim, by Charles Sutherland Tapley. Boston, Mass., Marshall Jones company [1930]
 xiii, 105 p. front. (port.) plates. 20cm.

 1. Nurse, Mrs. Rebecca (Towne) 1621-1692. 2. Witchcraft--Salem, Mass. I. Title.
 Library of Congress BF1576.T23 30-33553

WITCHCRAFT
BF 1584 S9 Z7 1670
8 NIC

Taranger, Absalon, 1858-1930.
 En Hexeproces fra Østerdalen i det 17de Aarhundrede. Ved A. Taranger.
 (In Vidar; Tidsskrift for Videnskab, Literatur og Politik. Christiania, 24cm. 7. Hefte (1887), p. [553]-560)
 1. Trials (Witchcraft)--Sweden. I. Title. II. Vidar; Tidsskrift for Videnskab, Literatur og Politik.

Witchcraft
BF 1565 T192+
8

Tartarotti, Girolamo, 1706-1761.
 Apologia del Congresso notturno delle lammie, o sia risposta di Girolamo Tartarotti all' Arte magica dileguata del Sig. March. Scipione Maffei, ed all' opposizione del Sig. Assessore Bartolommeo Melchiori. S'aggiunge una lettera del Sig. Clemente Baroni di Cavalcabò. Venezia, Presso Simone Occhi, 1751.
 4 p. l., 268 p. 26cm.
 1. His Del congresso notturno delle lammie.
 (Continued on next card)

Witchcraft
BF 1565 T192+
8

Tartarotti, Girolamo, 1706-1761. Apologia del Congresso notturno delle lammie ... 1751. (Card 2)
 ... no delle lammie. 2. Maffei, Francesco Scipione, marchese, 1675-1755. Arte magica dileguata. 3. Melchiori, Bartolommeo. I. Baroni Cavalcabò, Clemente, 1726-1796. Lettera ... ad un giornalista oltrammontano, sopra il Congresso notturno delle lammie. II. Title.

Witchcraft
BF 1565 T19
8

Tartarotti, Girolamo, 1706-1761.
 Del congresso notturno delle lammie, libri tre di Girolamo Tartarotti Roveretano. S'aggiungono due dissertazioni epistolari sopra l'arte magica... Rovereto, A spese di Giambatista Pasquali in Venezia, 1749.
 xxxii, 460 p. 24cm.
 Letter from Gianrinaldo Carli dated Padua, 1745, p. [317]-350, has special t. p.
 (Continued on next card)

Witchcraft
BF 1565 T19
8

Tartarotti, Girolamo, 1706-1761. Del congresso notturno delle lammie ... 1749. (Card 2)
 Letter of Tartarotti dated Rovereto, 1746, p. [351]-447, has special t. p.
 1. Witchcraft. 2. Magic. I. Carli, Giovanni Rinaldo, conte, 1720-1795. Lettera ... al signor Girolamo Tartarotti, intorno all' origine, e falsità della dottrina de' Maghi. II. Title.

Witchcraft
BF 1565 T19 B71
8

Tartarotti, Girolamo, 1706-1761. Del congresso notturno delle lammie.
 [Bonelli, Benedetto] 1704-1783.
 Animavversioni critiche sopra il Notturno congresso delle lammie, per modo di lettera indiritte ad un letterato. S'aggiunge il discorso del P. Gaar sulla strega d' Erbipoli, la Risposta dello stesso alle note, il Ragguaglio sulla strega di Salisburgo, e il Compendio storico della stregheria. Venezia, Presso Simone Occhi, 1751.
 6 p. l., 188 p. 25cm.
 (Continued on next card)

Witchcraft
BF 1565 T19 B71
8

Tartarotti, Girolamo, 1706-1761. Del congresso notturno delle lammie.
 [Bonelli, Benedetto] 1704-1783. Animavversioni critiche ... 1751. (Card 2)
 Attributed to Bonelli by Melzi.
 Each of the added items has special t. p. except the last, which has caption title.
 1. Tartarotti, Girolamo, 1706-1761. Del congresso notturno delle lammie. 2. Witchcraft. I. Title. II. Gaar, Georg, b. 1702. Ragionamento ... fatto avanti al rogo di Maria Renata.

Witchcraft
BF 1604 M18 1754
8

Tartarotti, Girolamo, 1706-1761. Del congresso notturno delle lammie.
 [Maffei, Francesco Scipione, marchese] 1675-1755.
 Arte magica annichilata. Libri tre. Con un' appendice. Verona, A. Andreoni, 1754.
 5 p. l., 328, [6] p. 25cm.
 Author's name appears in the dedication.
 The fifth preliminary leaf bound in back of vol.
 Work inspired by the controversy about G. Tartarotti's Del congresso notturno delle lammie.
 1. Magic. 2. Witchcraft. 3. Tartarotti, Girolamo, 1706-1761. Del congresso notturno delle lammie. I. Title.
 ——— Copy 2.

Witchcraft
BF 1565 T19 M18+
8

Tartarotti, Girolamo, 1706-1761. Del congresso notturno delle lamie.
 Maffei, Francesco Scipione, marchese, 1675-1755.
 Arte magica dileguata: lettera del Signor Marchese Maffei al Padre Innocente Ansaldi ... Verona, Per Agostino Carattoni, 1749.
 51 p. 26cm.
 With this are bound his Tre lettere. Verona, 1748; and Benvenuti, Giuseppe, 1728-ca. 1770. De daemoniacis dissertatio. Lucae, 1775.
 (Continued on next card)

Witchcraft
BF 1565 T192+
8

Tartarotti, Girolamo, 1706-1761.
 Apologia del Congresso notturno delle lammie, o sia risposta di Girolamo Tartarotti all' Arte magica dileguata del Sig. March. Scipione Maffei, ed all' opposizione del Sig. Assessore Bartolommeo Melchiori. S'aggiunge una lettera del Sig. Clemente Baroni di Cavalcabò. Venezia, Presso Simone Occhi, 1751.
 4 p. l., 268 p. 26cm.
 1. His Del congresso notturn-
 (Continued on next card)

CATALOGUE OF THE CORNELL WITCHCRAFT COLLECTION

Witchcraft
BF
1565
G12

Tartarotti, Girolamo, 1706-1761.
　　Ragionamento.
　　Gaar, Georg, b. 1702.
　　　　Responsa ad annotationes criticas D. F. A. T. [i.e. Girolamo Tartarotti] in sermonem de Maria Renata, saga supplicio addicta die 21. Junii Anno 1749. Herbipoli habitum, Veronae typis evulgatas, in lucem edita ab authore ejusdem sermonis P. Georgio Gaar, S.J. ... Wirceburgi, Typis M. A. Engman [1750?]
　　　　55 p. 20cm.

8　　　　　　　(Continued on next card)

Witchcraft
BF
1565
G12

Tartarotti, Girolamo, 1706-1761.
　　Ragionamento.
　　Gaar, Georg, b. 1702. Responsa ad annotationes criticas D. F. A. T. in sermonem de Maria Renata ... [1750] (Card 2)
　　　His Ragionamento del padre Giorgio Gaar, p. [37]-55, has special t. p., facsimile of the Verona edition. This text includes Tartarotti's commentary.
　　　1. Tartarotti, Girolamo, 1706-1761. 2. His Ragionamento. 3. Witchcraft. 4. Sänger, Maria Renata von Mossau, ca. 1680-1749. I. His Ragionamento. II. Title.

Witchcraft
BF
1583
Z7
1749a

Tartarotti, Girolamo, 1706-1761.
　　Gaar, Georg, b. 1702.
　　　Ragionamento del padre Giorgio Gaar, della Compagnia di Gesu', fatto avanti al rogo di Maria Renata, strega abbruciata in Erbipoli a' 21. di Giugno del corrente anno 1749. Tradotto del Tedesco nell' Italiano dal Dr. F. A. T. [Girolamo Tartarotti] Con alcune annotazioni critiche. Verona, Per D. Ramanzini [1749]
　　　23 p. 24cm.

(Continued on next card)

Witchcraft
BF
1565
G12

Tartarotti, Girolamo, 1706-1761.
　　Gaar, Georg, b. 1702. Responsa ad annotationes criticas D. F. A. T. [i.e. Girolamo Tartarotti] in sermonem de Maria Renata, saga supplicio addicta die 21. Junii Anno 1749. Herbipoli habitum, Veronae typis evulgatas, in lucem edita ab authore ejusdem sermonis P. Georgio Gaar, S.J. ... Wirceburgi, Typis M. A. Engman [1750?]
　　　55 p. 20cm.

8　　　　　　　(Continued on next card)

Witchcraft
BF
1565
G12

Tartarotti, Girolamo, 1706-1761.
　　Gaar, Georg, b. 1702. Responsa ad annotationes criticas D. F. A. T. in sermonem de Maria Renata ... [1750] (Card 2)
　　　His Ragionamento del padre Giorgio Gaar, p. [37]-55, has special t. p., facsimile of the Verona edition. This text includes Tartarotti's commentary.
　　　1. Tartarotti, Girolamo, 1706-1761. 2. His Ragionamento. 3. Witchcraft. 4. Sänger, Maria Renata von Mossau, ca. 1680-1749. I. His Ragionamento. II. Title.

Witchcraft
BF
1584
T93
1891

Tartarotti, Girolamo, 1706-1761.
　　Rapp, Ludwig.
　　　Die Hexenprozesse und ihre Gegner in Tirol. 2. verm. Aufl. Mit dem Bildnisse Tartarotti's. Brixen, A. Wegner, 1891.
　　　iv, 170 p. pot. 22cm.
　　　First published 1874 with title: Die Hexenprozesse und ihre Gegner aus Tirol.
　　　1. Witchcraft--Austria. 2. Trials (Witchcraft)--Austria. 3. Tanner, Adam, 1572-1632. 4. Tartarotti, Girolamo, 1706-1761. 5. Sterzinger, Ferdinand, 1721-1779. I. Title.

BF
1581
A2
W81+
1967

Taylor, John, 1831-1901, comp.
　　Witchcraft in Northamptonshire: facsimile reproduction of six rare and curious tracts dating from 1612 [collected by John Taylor]. [1st ed. reprinted]. Wilbarston (Northants.), Gerald Coe, Ltd., 1967.
　　[78] p. facsims. 26 cm. 15/-　　　　(B 68-00539)
　　Various pagings.
　　CONTENTS.--The witches of Northamptonshire.--An account of the tryals, examination and condemnation of Elinor Shaw and Mary Phillip.--A brief history of witchcraft.--Curious account of the remarkable case of the Duchess of Bedford.--Relation of a memorable piece of witchcraft at Welton.--The Northamptonshire witches.
　　1. Witchcraft--Northamptonshire, Eng.　I. Taylor, John, 1831-1901, comp.

BF1581.A2W5 1967　　133.4　　68-76836
Library of Congress　　[2]

Witchcraft
BF
1576
T24

Taylor, John Metcalf, 1845-1918.
　　The witchcraft delusion in colonial Connecticut 1647-1697. New York, The Grafton Press [c1908]
　　xv, 172 p. facsim. 20cm. (The Grafton historical series)

　　1. Witchcraft--Connecticut. I. Title.

Witchcraft
BL
610
J27
1821

Taylor, Thomas, 1758-1835, tr.
　　Jamblichus, of Chalcis.
　　　[De mysteriis. English]
　　　Iamblichus on the Mysteries of the Egyptians, Chaldeans, and Assyrians. Translated from the Greek by Thomas Taylor ... Chiswick, Printed by C. Whittinghams for the translator. 1821.
　　　xxiv, 365 p. 22-1/2 cm.
　　　"The epistle of Porphyry to the Egyptian Anebo": p. [1]-16.

Witchcraft
BF
1555
J75T2

Taylor, Zachary, 1653-1705.
　　The Surey impostor: being an answer to a late pamphlet, entituled, The Surey demoniack. ... London, Printed for J. Jones, 1697.
　　75 p. front. 23cm.

　　1. Jollie, Thomas, 1629-1703. The Surey demoniack. 2. Demoniac possession. I. Title.

Witchcraft
BF
1555
J75V7

Taylor, Zachary.
　　The Surey imposter, being an answer to ... The surey demoniack.
　　[Jollie, Thomas] 1629-1703.
　　A vindication of the Surey demoniack as no impostor: or, A reply to a certain pamphlet publish'd by Mr. Zach. Taylor, called The Surey impostor. With a further clearing and confirming of the truth as to Richard Dugdale's case and cure. By T. J., one of the ministers who attended upon that affair from first to last ... To which is annexed a brief narrative of the Surey demoniack, drawn up by the same author, for the satisfaction of such who have not
　　(Continued on next card)

Witchcraft
BF
1555
J75V7

Taylor, Zachary.
　　The Surey imposter, being an answer to ... The surey demoniack.
　　[Jollie, Thomas] 1629-1703. A vindication of the Surey demoniack ... 1698. (Card 2)
　　seen the former narrative... London, Printed for N. Simmons, and sold by G. Conyers, 1698.
　　80 p. 21cm.
　　Wing J 889.
　　1. Dugdale, Richard. 2. Taylor, Zachary. The Surey imposter, being an answer to ... The surey demoniack. I. Title.

GR
153
T25
1964

Teare, T Denys G
　　Folk-doctor's island, by T. D. G. Teare. [2d ed.] Douglass, Isle of Man, Times Press [1964]
　　222 p. illus. 19cm.

　　1. Folk-lore, Manx. 2. Witchcraft--Man, Isle of. I. Title.

Witchcraft
BF
1583
Z7
1688

Teichmann, Anna, fl. 1688, defendant.
　　Zwei Hexenprocesse aus dem Jahre 1688, geführt bei dem hochfürstlichen Amte in Ballenstedt. Quedlinburg, H. C. Huch, 1863.
　　104 p. 22cm.
　　Contents.--I. Acta inquisitionalia ... wider Marthen Margarethen Kirchbergs aus Reinstedt.--II. Acta inquisitionalia ... contra die Pfannenschmiedin Anna Teichmanns.
　　1. Trials (Witchcraft)--Saxony. I. Kirchberg, Marthe Margarethe, d. 1688, defendant. II. Teichmann, Anna, fl. 1688, defendant.

WITCHCRAFT
RC
547
T26

Teichmeyer, Hermann Friedrich, 1685-1746, praeses.
　　Dissertatio inavgvralis medica De incvbo qvam ... svb praesidio Herm. Frider. Teichmeyeri ... svbmittit Daniel Textoris ... Ienae, Litteris Wertherianis [1740]
　　26 [i.e., 28] p. 21cm.
　　Diss.--Jena (D. Textoris, respondent).
　　1. Sleep--Addresses, essays, lectures. 2. Folk-lore, German. I. Textoris, Daniel, respondent. II. Title: De incubo. III. Title.

8

Witchcraft
BF
1566
B77

Teinturier, E.
　　Bourneville, [Désiré Magloire] 1840-
　　　Le Sabbat des sorciers, par Bourneville et E. Teinturier. Paris, Aux Bureaux du Progrès médical; Delahaye et Lecrosnier, 1882.
　　　38 p. illus. 22cm. (Bibliothèque diabolique)

　　1. Witchcraft. I. Teinturier, E. II. Title.

Witchcraft
R
708
C18
T2

Temerarii circa magica judicii exemplum.
　　Camerarius, Elias, 1672-1734.
　　　Temerarii circa magica judicii exemplum. ... praeside Elia Camerario ... In dispvtatione inavgvrali pro summis in medicina honoribus obtendis ... publice defendet Johannes Dannenberger ... Tubingae, Literis Josephi Sigmundi [1729]
　　　18 p. 20cm.
　　　Diss.--Tübingen (J. Dannenberger, respondent).
　　　1. Medicine--Addresses, essays, lectures. 2. Magic. I. Dannenberger, Johannes, respondent. II. Title.

8

Witchcraft
BF
1505
G94

Le temple de Satan.
　　Guaita, Stanislas de, 1860-1897.
　　　... Le serpent de la Genèse ... par Stanislas de Guaita. Paris, Librairie du merveilleux, 1891-
　　　v. front., plates, ports. 23cm. (His Essais de sciences maudites II)
　　　Books 1 and 2 only.
　　　Vol. 2 has imprint: Bibliothèque Chacornac, 1897. Date on cover: 1902.
　　　Vol. 1 has subtitle: Le temple de Satan.
　　　Vol. 2 has subtitle: La clef de la magie noire.
　　　Ex libris, vol. 2: Arthur Edward Waite.
　　　1. Demonology. I. Title. II. His Essais de sciences maudites. III. Title: Le temple de Satan. IV. Title: La clef de la magie noire.
Library of Congress　　　BF1405.G8 vol.2

CATALOGUE OF THE CORNELL WITCHCRAFT COLLECTION

Witchcraft
BF
1565
D62
no.14
 Tentamen pnevmatologico physicvm De mancipiis diaboli sive sagis.
 Fischer, Daniel, 1695-1745.
  Tentamen pnevmatologico physicvm De mancipiis diaboli sive sagis. Avthore Daniele Fischero kesmarkiensi-hvngaro. Med. cvlt. Vitembergae, Ex officina Krevsigiana, 1716.
  24 p. 20cm.
  No. 14 in vol. lettered Dissertationes de sagis. 1636-1714.
  1. Witchcraft. I. Title: De mancipiis diaboli sive sagis. II. Title: De sagis.

8

Witchcraft
AG
241
B66
1567
 Tesserant, Claude de.
 [Boaistuau, Pierre] d. 1566.
  Qvatorze histoires prodigievses de novueau adioustées aux precedentes, recueillies par Claude de Tesserant Parisien. Paris, Chez Iean de Bordeaux [1567]
  4 p. l., 278 [i.e. 557] p. illus. 12cm.
  Tesserant's fourteen tales, p. 217-278, have caption title: Avtres histoires prodigievses ...
  The illustrations are reduced copies of those in author's Histoires prodigievses,
   (Continued on next card)

Witchcraft
AG
241
B66
1567
 Tesserant, Claude de.
 [Boaistuau, Pierre] d. 1566. Qvatorze histoires prodigievses ... [1567] (Card 2)
  published 1560 by V. Sertenas, Paris. Introductory letter signed Lyon, 1567, by Claude de Tesserant.
  1. Wonders. 2. Monsters. I. His Histoires prodigieuses. II. Tesserant, Claude de. III. Title: Quatorze histoires pro digieuses.

8

Witchcraft
Z
6880
Z9
T35
 Teubner, Franz, bookseller, Bonn.
  Bibliotheca magica et pneumatica. [Abth.] I[-III, VI] Antiquaritäts-Katalog No. 49[-Nr. 51, 54. Bonn, 189-]
  v. in . 22cm.
  Abth. II and III in 1 vol.
  At head of title, vol. I: Franz Teubner's Antiquariat (vorm. Antiquariat der Firma Paul Neubner in Köln)
  1. Occult sciences--Bibl.--Catalogs. 2. Magic--Bibl.--Catalogs. I. Title.

8

Witchcraft
BF
1505
D56
 Der Teufel als Sinnbild des Bösen im Kirchenglauben, in den Hexenprozessen und als Bundesgenosse der Freimaurer.
 Diestel, Ernst.
  Der Teufel als Sinnbild des Bösen im Kirchenglauben, in den Hexenprozessen und als Bundesgenosse der Freimaurer. Berlin, A. Unger, 1921.
  45 p. port. 22cm. (Comenius-Schriften zur Geistesgeschichte. Beihefte der Zeitschrift der Comenius-Gesellschaft "Geisteskultur und Volksbildung," 3. Heft)
  1. Devil. I. Title.

WITCHCRAFT
BF
1533
S18
 Der Teufel, ein Neujahrsgeschenk!
 [Sambuga, Joseph Anton Franz Martin] 1752-1815.
  Der Teufel, ein Neujahrsgeschenk! Oder Prüfung des Glaubens an höllische Geister, nach der Lehre des hochwürdigen Herrn Peter Hartmann, Predigers zu Altenöting. [München] 1810.
  114 p. 21cm.
  Ascription by Holzmann and Kayser.
  1. Devil. 2. Hartmann, Peter, preacher. I. Title.

8

Witchcraft
BT
980
H14
 Der Teufel im Lichte der Glaubensquellen.
 Hagen, Martin.
  Der Teufel im Lichte der Glaubensquellen. Freiburg im Breisgau, Herder, 1899.
  v, 69 p. 20cm.

  1. Devil--Bible teaching. I. Title.

Witchcraft
BF
1523
H51
 Der Teufel: sein Mythos und seine Geschichte im Christentum.
 Henning, Max.
  Der Teufel: sein Mythos und seine Geschichte im Christentum. Hamburg, P. Hartung [ca. 1910]
  123 p. 20cm.

  1. Devil. 2. Witchcraft. I. Title.

8

Witchcraft
N
8140
E33
 Der Teufel und seine Gesellen in der bildenen Kunst.
 Blomberg, Hugo, Freiherr von, 1820-1871.
  Der Teufel und seine Gesellen in der bildenen Kunst. Berlin, C. Duncker, 1867.
  133 p. 24cm. (Added t.p.: Studien zur Kunstgeschichte und Aesthetik. I.)

  1. Devil--Art. I. Title. II. Title: Studien zur Ku nstgeschichte und Aesthetik. I.

WITCHCRAFT
BF
1555
T35
 Der Teufel zu Seefeld, noch 1783. Aus "Anmerkungen über den Teufel zu Seefeld in Tirol. ["] Verfasst von einem geistlichen Ganser der ExKlarissennnen. Auf Unkosten der St. Monica Brüderschaft zu Seefeld. 1783, 8, 80 Seiten. (In Stats-Anzeigen. Göttingen. 20cm. 6. Bd., Heft 23 (1784), p. 274-294)
  At head of title: 30.
  1. Seiberin, Johanna, fl. 1782. 2. Demoniac possession.
  Title: Anmer kungen über den Teufel zu Seefeld in Tirol.

8

WITCHCRAFT
BF
1555
M69
 Eine Teufelaustreibung durch einen deutschen Bischof im 19. Jahrhundert.
 Möller, Karl.
  Eine Teufelaustreibung durch einen deutschen Bischof im 19. Jahrhundert. [Sonderabdruck aus der Rheinischen Correspondenz] Köln, C. Römcke, 1897.
  12 p. 23cm.
  Consists largely of extracts from his Leben und Briefe von Johannes Theodor Laurent, pub. 1887-89; the bishop's letters are quoted.
  1. Demoniac possession. 2. Exorcism. 3. Pfefferkorn, Maria Anna Katharina, fl. 1842. I. His Leben und Briefe von Johannes Theodor Laurent. II. Laurent, Johannes Theodor, bp. III. Title

8

Witchcraft
BF
1559
A92
 Eine Teufelaustreibung in Baiern.
 Aurelian, father, Capuchin.
  Eine Teufelaustreibung in Baiern. (In Kölnische Zeitung. Köln. 22cm. Nr. 375 (1892) p. [1])

  Later eds. published under title: Authentischer Bericht über die Teufelaustreibung...

  1. Exorcism. I. Title.

BX
2340
E71
 Teufelaustreibungen.
 Ernst, Cécile.
  Teufelaustreibungen; die Praxis der katholischen Kirche im 16. und 17. Jahrhundert. Bern, H. Huber [c1972]
  147 p. 23 cm. Sw***
  Bibliography: p. 135-141.

  1. Exorcism. I. Title.

| BX2340.E75 | 265'.9 | 73-188553 |
| ISBN 3-456-00282-3 | | |

3
NIC
 Library of Congress 72 [2]

BF
1501
S78
 Teufelbücher in Auswahl.
 Stambaugh, Ria, comp.
  Teufelbücher in Auswahl. Hrsg. von Ria Stambaugh. Berlin, De Gruyter, 1970-
  v. 21cm. (Ausgaben deutscher Literatur des XV. bis XVIII. Jahrhunderts)

  Contents.--Bd. 1. Zauberteufel, Schrapteufel, von L. Milichius.--Bd. 2. Kleiderteufel, von J. Strauss. Tanzteufel, von F. Daul. Hurenteufel, von A. Hoppenrod. Hausteufel, von A. Schubart. Zehn Teufel, von N. Schmidt.--Bd. 3. Hoffartsteufel, von Joa chim Westphal.

WITCHCRAFT
BF
1523
K78
no.4
 Teufeleien des achtzehnten Jahrhunderts.
 [Köster, Heinrich Martin Gottfried] 1734-1802.
  Teufeleien des achtzehnten Jahrhunderts, von dem Verfasser der Demüthigen Bitte um Belehrung an die grossen Männer welche keinen Teufel glauben. 1. rechtmässige Aufl. Leipzig, Bey C. F. Schneidern, 1778.
  142 p. 18cm.
  No. 4 in vol. lettered Ueber den Teufel.
  1. His Demüthige Bitte um Belehrung. 2. Devil--Bi bl. I. Title.

8

Witchcraft
BF
1565
S83
Z98
 Teufeleyen.
 Zauberbibliothek. 1775-1776. [Berlin, 1775-76]
  various pagings. 20cm.
  Title from spine.
  Consists of three sections detached from Allgemeine deutsche Bibliothek, titled: Zauberey; Teufeleyen; and Teufeleyen. Eine Fortsetzung der vorigen.
  1. Sterzinger, Ferdinand, 1721-1786. 2. Gassner, Johann Joseph, 1727-1779. 3. Witchcraft--Bibl.

8

WITCHCRAFT
BF
1555
L65
 Die Teufels-Beschwörung in Stans.
 [Leu, Josef Burkard] 1808-1865.
  Die Teufels-Beschwörung in Stans; oder, Gutachten über die Broschüre: Erledigung der ehrw. Klosterfrau Maria Augusta Delphina im Frauenkloster zu Stans den 28. März 1848 durch P. Anizet Regli... Luzern, X. Meyer, 1848.
  15 p. 20cm.
  1.Demoniac possession. 2. Devil. 3. Exorcism. 4.Delphina, Maria Augusta,fl.1848. 5.Regli,Anizet, fl. 1848. 6. Erledigung der ehrw. Klosterfrau Maria Augusta Delp hina. I. Title.

8
NIC

WITCHCRAFT
BF
1566
H51
 Der Teufels- und Hexenglaube.
 Henne am Rhyn, Otto, 1828-1914.
  Der Teufels- und Hexenglaube, seine Entwickelung, seine Herrschaft und sein Sturz. Leipzig, M. Spohr, 1892.
  vi, 159 p. 22cm.

  1. Witchcraft--Hist. 2. Demonology. I. Title.

8

CATALOGUE OF THE CORNELL WITCHCRAFT COLLECTION

Die Teufelsaustreibung im Wemdinger Kapuzinerkloster.

WITCHCRAFT
BT
1220
F67
W13
    Aurelian, father, Capuchin.
        Die Teufelsaustreibung im Wemdinger Kapuzinerkloster.
        (In Wahrmund, Ludwig. Ultramontan. München, 1908, p. [20]-30)
        First published 1892 under titles: Eine Teufelaustreibung in Baiern; and Authentischer Bericht über die Teufelaustreibung.
        1. Exorcism. I. His Authentischer Bericht über die Teufelaustreibung. II. Title.

8

WITCHCRAFT
BX
2340
T35
    Die Teufelsbeschwörungen, Geisterbannereien, Weihungen und Zaubereien der Kapuziner. Aus dem lateinischen Benedictionale übersetzt. [Bern?] ca. 1840[?]
        48 p. 17cm.
        Kayser's Bücher-Lexikon lists an edition of this item with much longer title, giving F. Ammann as translator and the imprint as: Bern, Jenni, Sohn, 1841.
        1. Exorcism. 2. Benediction. I. Ammann, Franz Sebastian, tr. II. Catholic Church. Liturgy and ritual. Benedictional.

8
NIC

Teufelsbündler.

WITCHCRAFT
BF
1566
S76
    Spitzer, Johann.
        Teufelsbündler. Zauber und Hexenglauben und dessen kirchliche Ausbeutung zur Schändung der Menschheit. Leipzig, O. Wigand, 1871.
        xx, 130 p. 20cm.
        Includes list of folk spells.
        1. Witchcraft--History. 2. Charms. I. Title.

8
NIC

Die Teufelscitation. Eine Anecdote ohne Zusaz -- nur mit Anmerkungen. [n.p.] Um drei Viertheil des jetzigen philosophischen Jahrhunderts gedruckt [i. e. 1775; ca. 1900]
    19 l. 19cm.
    Carnap's manuscript copy.
    "Druck in der Klg. Hof- u. Staatsbibliothek zu München. 32 S. in 8°."
    Numerals in the margins indicate pagination of the original.
    1. Superstition.

MSS
Bd.
WITCHCRAFT
BF
T35

Der Teufelskratz oder Hexenmal.

Witchcraft
BF
1439
B61
    Birlinger, Anton, 1834-1891.
        Der Teufelskratz oder Hexenmal.
        (In Im neuen Reich. Leipzig. 24cm. no. 32 (1879) p. 193-210)
        I. Title.

Eine Teufelsneurose im siebzehnten Jahrhundert.

BF
565
F79
924
    Freud, Sigmund, 1856-1939.
        Eine Teufelsneurose im siebzehnten Jahrhundert. Leipzig, Internationaler Psychoanalytischer Verlag, 1924.
        41 p. 23cm.
        Published first in Imago, Bd. 9, Heft 1.
        1. Witchcraft--17th cent. 2. Neuroses. I. Title.

Teuflische Magie existiert.

WITCHCRAFT
BF
1565
W37
S347
    [Schmid, Franz Josef]
        Und der Satz: Teuflische Magie existirt, besteht noch. In einer Antwort des katholischen Weltmannes auf die von einem Herrn Landpfarrer herausgegebene Apologie der Professor Weberschen Hexenreformation. Augsburg, Bey J. N. Styx, 1791.
        xxiv, 350 p. 19cm.
        1. Bauer, Friedrich. Gedanken eines Landpfarrers über den Ungrund des Hexenglaubens. 2. Weber, Joseph, 1753-1831.

8 (Continued on next card)

Textoris, Daniel, respondent.

WITCHCRAFT
RC
547
T26
    Teichmeyer, Hermann Friedrich, 1685-1746, praeses.
        Dissertatio inavgvralis medica De incvbo qvam ... svb praesidio Herm. Frider. Teichmeyeri ...svbmittit Daniel Textoris ... Ienae, Litteris Wertherianis [1740]
        26 [i.e., 28] p. 21cm.
        Diss.--Jena (D. Textoris, respondent)
        1. Sleep--Addresses, essays, lectures. 2. Folk-lore, German. I. Textoris, Daniel, respondent. II. Title: De incubo.

8

Witchcraft
BF
1411
T35
    Thacher, James, 1754-1844.
        An essay on demonology, ghosts, and apparitions, and popular superstitions. Also, an account of the witchcraft delusion at Salem in 1692 ... Boston, Carter and Hendee, 1831.
        234 p. 18cm.
        1. Demonology. 2. Apparitions. 3. Witchcraft--Superstition. Salem, Mass. 4. witchcraft delusion. I. Title. II. Title: The witchcraft delusion at Salem in 1692.

WITCHCRAFT
JN
3269
T36
    Thamm, Melchior, 1860-
        Femgericht und Hexenprozesse. Leipzig und Wien, Bibliographisches Institut [1903]
        179 p. 15cm. (Meyers Volksbücher. Nr. 1345-1347)
        1. Femic courts. 2. Witchcraft--Germany--History. I. Title.

8

Tharsander, pseud.
    see
Wegener, F   G   Wilhelm.

Theatrum chemicum britannicum.

HIST SCI
QD
25
A82
    Ashmole, Elias, 1617-1692, comp.
        Theatrum chemicum britannicum. Containing severall poeticall pieces of our famous English philosophers, who have written the hermetique mysteries in their owne ancient language. Faithfully collected into one volume, with annotations thereon, by Elias Ashmole, esq., qui est Mercuriophilus anglicus. The first part. London, Printed by J. Grismond for N. Brooke, 1652.
        8 p.l., 486 [8] p. illus. 19cm.

(Continued on next card)

Theatrum chemicum britannicum.

HIST SCI
QD
25
A82
    Ashmole, Elias, 1617-1692, comp. Theatrum chemicum britannicum ... London, 1652.
        (Card 2)
        No more published.
        Title vignette.
        Contains the Ordinall of alchemie by Thomas Norton, the Compound of alchemie by George Ripley, the Chanon's yeoman's tale by Chaucer, Sir Edward Kelley's Worke, Doctor John Dee's Testament, Secreta secretorum by John Lydgate, and other works.
        Wing A3987.
        1. Alchemy. I. Title.

Witchcraft
BF
1520
W64
P8++
1586
    Theatrvm [i. e., Theatrum] de veneficis.
        Das ist: Von Teuffelsgespenst, Zauberern vnd Gifftbereitern, Schwartzkünstlern, Hexen vnd Vnholden, vieler fürnemmen Historien vnd Exempel ... Sampt etlicher hingerichten zäuberischer Weiber gethaner Bekanntnuß, Examination, Prob, Vrgicht [sic] vnd Straff ... Allen Vögten, Schuldtheissen, Amptleuthen deß weltlichen Schwerdts, &c. sehr nützlich vnd dienstlich zu wissen, vnd keines wegs zu

8 (Continued on next card)

Witchcraft
BF
1520
W64
P8++
1586
    Theatrvm [i. e., Theatrum] de veneficis. 1586. (Card 2)
        verachten. Franckfurt am Mayn, Gedruckt durch Nicolaum Basseum, 1586.
        6 p. l., 396, [9] p. 34cm.
        Title in red and black.
        Preface signed: Nicolaus Bassaeus.
        Bound with Wier, Johann, 1515-1588. De praestigiis daemonum. Von Teuffelsgespenst, Zauberern, vnd Gifftbereytern.

8 (Continued on next card)

Witchcraft
BF
1520
W64
P8++
1586
    Theatrvm [i. e., Theatrum] de veneficis. 1586. (Card 3)
        Franckfurt am Mayn, 1586.
        Contents.--Warhafftige Zeittung von gottlosen Hexen, by R. Lutz.--Ein Gespräch von Zäuberern, welche man lateinisch Sortilegos oder Sortiarios nennet, by L. Daneus.--Von Zäuberern, Hexen, vnd Vnholden, by J. Vallick.--Von Hexen vnd Vnholden, by V. Molitoris, tr. by C. Lautenbach.--

8 (Continued on next card)

Witchcraft
BF
1520
W64
P8++
1586
    Theatrvm [i. e., Theatrum] de veneficis. 1586. (Card 4)
        Contents--Continued.
        Ein christlich vnd nothwendig Gespräch, von den bösen abtrünnigen Engeln, by A. Rheynmannus.--Von Gespensten, Vngehewren, Fällen, oder Poltern, vnd anderen wunderbaren Dingen, by L. Lavater.--Bedencken, was er von Exorcisterey halte, by L. Thurneysser.--Eine kurtze, trewe Warnung,

(Continued on next card)

Witchcraft
BF
1520
W64
P8++
1586
    Theatrvm [i. e., Theatrum] de veneficis. 1586. (Card 5)
        Contents--Continued.
        ... ob auch zu dieser vnser Zeit vnder vns Christen, Hexen, Zäuberer vnd Vnholden vorhanden, by A. Sawr.--Von deß Teuffels Nebelkappen, das ist: ein kurtzer Begriff, den gantzen Handel von der Zäuberey belangend, by P. Frisius.--Bericht von Erforschung, Prob vnd Erkäntniß der Zäuberinnen

8 (Continued on next card)

CATALOGUE OF THE CORNELL WITCHCRAFT COLLECTION

Witchcraft
BF
1520   Theatrvm [i. e., Theatrum] de veneficis.
W64   1586.   (Card 6)
P8++
1586   Contents--Continued.

        durchs kalte Wasser, by H. Neuwalt, tr. by
    H. Meybaum.--Ein christlich Bedencken vnnd
    Erjnnerung von Zauberey, by A. Lercheimer.
    --Wider die schwartzen Künst, by H. Bullin-
    ger.--Ware Entdeckung vnnd Erklärung aller
    fürnembster Artickel der Zauberey, by J.
    Freyherr von   Liechtenberger.--Von
8   (Continued on next card)

Witchcraft
BF
1520   Theatrvm [i. e., Theatrum] de veneficis.
W64   1586.   (Card 7)
P8++
1586   Contents--Continued.

        der Hexen, die man gemeiniglich Zauberin
    nennet, by J. Ewich.--Antwort auff etliche
    Fragen ... von ...Keyser Maximiliano, by
    J. Trithemius.--Consilia vnd Bedencken et-
    licher zu vnsern Zeiten rechtsgelehrten
    Juristen, von Hexen vnd Vnholden.

8
                             (Continued on next card)

Witchcraft
BF
1520   Theatrvm [i. e., Theatrum] de veneficis.
W64   1586.   (Card 8)
P8++
1586   Binding: blind stamped pigskin, with
    clasps (one wanting); front cover initialed
    A K A S H and dated 1589.
        1. Demonology. 2. Witchcraft. 3.
    Magic. I. Bassaeus, Nicolaus, d. 1599.
    II. Title: Von Teuffelsgespenst, Zau-
    berern und Gifftbereytern.

8

Witchcraft
BF
1603   Theatrvm diabolorum, das ist: Warhaffte
T37++   eigentliche vnd kurtze Beschreibung
1575   allerley grewlicher, schrecklicher vnd
            abschewlicher Laster ... Getruckt zu
            Franckfurt am Mayn, durch Peter
            Schmid [in Verlägung Sigismund
            Feyrabendt] 1575.
            568 l. 35cm.

        Foreword signed: Sigmund Feyrabend,
    Buchhandler.
        I. Feyer   abend, Sigmund, ca.
    1527-ca. 15   90.

Rare   Theatrum poenarum.
K   Döpler, Jacob, 17th cent.
            Theatrum poenarum, supplicorum et execu-
D65   tionum criminalium. Oder Schau-Platz, derer
1693   Leibes und Lebens-Straffen, welche nicht al-
        lein von alters bey allerhand Nationen und
        Völckern in Gebrauch gewesen, sondern auch
        noch heut zu Tage in allen vier Welt-Theilen
        üblich sind. Darinnen zugleich der gantze
        Inquisitions-Process, Captur, Examination,
        Confrontation, Tortur ... enthalten ... An-
        bei mit unterschiedlichen Protocollen, son-
        derlich bei den Zauber- und Hexen-Torturen...
                            (Continued on next card)

Rare   Theatrum poenarum.
K   Döpler, Jacob, 17th cent. Theatrum poena-
            rum ... 1693-97.   (Card 2)
D65
1693   Sondershausen, In Verlegung des Autoris,
        Druckts Ludwig Schönermarck, 1693-97.
            2 v. in 1. 21cm.

            Vol. 2 has special t. p.: Theatri poena-
        rum, suppliciorum et executionum criminalium,
        Oder Schau-Platzes derer Leibes- und Lebens-
        Strafen anderer Theil ... Leipzig, In Ver-
        legung Friedrich Lanckischen Erben, 1697.

            I. Title.

WITCHCRAFT
BF   Théaux, Marcel.
1569   Pages d'histoire judiciaire. Le crime
T37   de sorcellerie.
        (In La revue du palais. Paris. 25cm.
        1. année, no. 7 (1897), p. [103]-135)

            In envelope.

            1. Witchcraft--History. 2. Devil.
        3. Bavent, Madeleine, ca. 1608-1647. I.
8   Title. II. Title: Le crime de
NIC   sorcellerie.

                Theodor. Gerhard. Timmermann ... Diatribe
WITCHCRAFT   antiquario-medica De daemoniacis
BS   Evangeliorum.
2545   Timmermann, Theodor Gerhard, 1727-1792.
D5   Theodor. Gerhard. Timmermann ... Dia-
T58   tribe antiqvario-medica De daemoniacis
        Evangeliorvm. Rintelii, Apvd Ant. Henr.
        Boesendahl, 1786.
            90 p. 24cm.

            1. Demoniac possession. 2. Bible.
        N. T.--Commentaries. I. Title: De dae-
8   moniacis Evan   geliorum.
NIC

                Theodori Reinkingk ... Tractatus synop-
                  ticus De retractu consanguinitatis.
Witchcraft
HD   Reinking, Dietrich, 1590-1664.
1239   Theodori Reinkingk ... Tractatus synop-
G2   ticus De retractu consanguinitatis ... in
R37   certas quaestiones collectus. Editio secun-
1662   da priori correctior. Huic accessit ejusdem
        auctoris Responsum juris accuratè elaboratum
        de processu contra sagas et maleficos &c.
        Hactenus suppresso nomine editum. Gissae
        Hassorvm, Sumptibus Hermanni Velstenii, 1662.
            16 p. l., 420, [58] p. 14cm.
            Added engrav   ed t. p.
8
                           (Continued on next card)

                Theodori Reinkingk ... Tractatus synop-
                  ticus De retractu consanguinitatis.
Witchcraft
HD   Reinking, Dietrich, 1590-1664. Theodori
1239   Reinkingk ... Tractatus synopticus De re-
G2   tractu consangvinitatis ...   (Card 2)
R37
1662   Incomplete: Responsum juris ... wanting.
        With this in slipcase is his Responsum
        juris ..., Gissae Hassorvm, 1662, detached
        from another copy of Tractatus synopticus.
            1. Pre-emption--Germany. 2. Pre-emp-
        tion (Roman la   w) I. Title: De re-
8   tractu consan   guinitatis.

                A theological discourse of angels and their
                  ministries.
Witchcraft
BT   Camfield, Benjamin.
965   A theological discourse of angels and their
C18   ministries. Wherein their existence, nature,
        number, order and offices are modestly treated
        of: with the character of those for whose
        benefit especially they are commissioned and
        such practical inferences deduced as are most
        proper to the premises. Also an appendix
        containing some reflections upon Mr. Webster's
        Displaying supposed witchcraft. London,
        Printed by R. E.   for H. Brome, 1678.
            214 p.   19cm.
                          (Continued on next card)

                A theological discourse of angels and their
                  ministries.
Witchcraft
BT   Camfield, Benjamin. A theological discourse
965   of angels and their ministries ... 1678.
C18   (Card 2)

        "Appendix..." has separate t.p.
        Wing C 388.

            1. Angels. 2. Witchcraft. 3. Webster,
        John, 1610-1682. The displaying of supposed
        witchcraft. I. Title.

                Theologicum novae ... anthropologiae ...
                  examen.
Witchcraft
BF   Ludovici, Gottfried, 1670-1724.
1565   Godofredi Ludovici ... Theologicvm novae
T46   novi avtoris Francisci de Cordva anthropo-
1717a   logiae et daemonologiae examen, nouitates
        vti alias, ab hoc in Schrifft- und Vernunfft-
        mässigen Gedancken vom Schatzgraben und Be-
        schwerung der Geister propositas ... Cobur-
        gi, Sumptu Pauli Günthari Pfotenhaueri [1718]
            134 p. 19cm.

            Bound with Thomasius, Christian, 1655-
8   1728. ... Kurt   ze Lehr-Sätze von dem
                          (Continued on next card)

                Theologicum novae ... anthropologiae ...
                  examen.
Witchcraft
BF   Ludovici, Gottfried, 1670-1724. Godofredo
1565   Ludovici ... Theologicvm novae ... anthro-
T46   pologiae ... examen ... [1718] (Card 2)
1717a
        Laster der Zauberey. Franckfurth, 1717.

            1. Franciscus de Cordua, pseud.
        Schrifft- und vernunfftmässige Gedancken
        vom Schatzgraben. 2. Demonology. I.
        Title: Theologicum novae ... anthropolo-
8   giae ... examen.

                Theologischer Bericht von dem sehr
                  schrecklichen Zornsturm des Teuffels.
WITCHCRAFT
BT   Muthreich, Martin.
980   Theologischer Bericht von dem sehr schrec
M99   lichen Zornsturm des Teuffels, welchen er
        zu diese letzten Zeiten auch durch seine
        Getreue die Zauberer Hexen und die gleichen
        Unholden spüren lesset... Franckfurt an
        der Oder, Bey Johann Eichorns S. Wittib.,
        1649.
            99 p. 19cm.

            1.Devil. 2.   Witchcraft. 3. Storms
8   (in religion,   folk-lore, etc.)
NIC

                Theoria spectrorum philosophica.
Witchcraft
BF   Waller, Nicolai, praeses.
1445   Theoria spectrorum philosophica, quam
D61   ... praeside ... Dn. Nicolao Wallerio,
no.19   publico bonorum examini modeste offert ...
        Andreas Bäckerström ... Upsaliae, Excud.
        L. M. Höjer [1753]
            13, [1] p. 21cm.
            Imperfect copy: t. p. and other pages
        badly torn.
            No. 19 in vol. lettered Dissertationes
        de spectris. 1646-1753.
8   1. Appari   tions. 2. Demonology.
        I. Bäckerstr   öm, Andreas, respondent.
        II. Title.

                Theorica, e pratica per la vera in-
                  telligenza et cognitione intorno à
                  gli spiriti maligni ch' entrano ne'
Witchcraft   corpi humani.
BF   Bell'Haver, Giovanni Battista, fl. 1580-1623.
1555   Theorica, e pratica per la vera intelli-
B44   genza et cognitione intorno à gli spiriti
1616   maligni ch' entrano ne'corpi humani et an-
        co intorno all'arte essorcistica per discac-
        ciarli da essi ... Et vi si raccolgono poi
        alcuni più notabili casi scielti da graui
        autori con nuoui vtili documenti, et acute
        inuentioni fruttuosissime. Venetia, G. B.
        Combi, 1616.
            [32], 277 p. 16cm.

                Thesaurus ecclesiasticus ... de indul-
                  gentiis.
Witchcraft
BX   Fasciculus triplex exorcismorum, et bene-
2340   dictionum, in Romano-Catholica Ecclesia
F24   usitatarum, ex variis authoribus appro-
        batis collectus, & historiis, ac exem-
        plis subinde illustratus, cum adnexo
        Tractatu de indulgentiis, et jubilaeo,
        ac resolutionibus moralibus ... Tyr-
        naviae, Typis academicis, 1739.
            2 p. l., 148, 78, [7] p. 21cm.
            "Thesaurus ecclesiasticus ... de indul-
        gentiis ...,"   has special t. p. and
8   separate pagin   g.
                         (Continued on next card)

540

CATALOGUE OF THE CORNELL WITCHCRAFT COLLECTION

WITCHCRAFT
BF
1559
T41
    Thesaurus exorcismorum atque conjurationum terribilium, potentissimorum, efficacissimorum, cum practica probatissima: quibus spiritus maligni, daemones maleficiaq; omnia de corporibus humanis obsessis, tanquam flagellis fustibusque fugantur, expelluntur, doctrinis refertissimus atq; uberrimus: ad maximam exorcistarum commoditatem in lucem editus & recusus: cujus authores, ut & singuli tractatus, sequente Pagellâ consignati, inveniuntur.

8   (Continued on next card)

WITCHCRAFT
BF
1559
T41
    Thesaurus exorcismorum atque conjurationum terribilium ... 1608.   (Card 2)

    Coloniae, Impensis Lazari Zetzneri, 1608.
    8 p. l., 1272, [46] p. 17cm.
    Contents.--F. Valerii Polydori ... Practica exorcistarum ... pars prima ... [et] secunda.--F. Hieronymi Mengi ... Flagellum daemonum.--Ejusdem Fustis daemonum.--F. Zachariae Vicecomitis ... Complementum artis exorcisticae.-- Petri Antonii Stampae ... Fuga Satanae.

8

---

tchcraft
559
1
26
    Thesavrvs exorcismorvm atqve conivrationvm terribilivm, potentissimorvm, efficacissimorvm cum practica probatissima: qvibvs spiritvs maligni, daemones maleficiaqve omnia de corporibus humanis obsessis, tanquam flagellis, fustibusque fugantur, expelluntur, doctrinis refertissimus atqj uberrimus: ad maximam exorcistarum commoditatem nunc vltimo plenariè in lucem editus & recusus: cuius authores, vt & singuli tractatus sequente pagellâ consignati, inueniuntur. Cum indice capitum, rerum & verborum ... Coloniae, sumptibus haeredum
    (Continued on next card)

---

tchcraft
59
1
26
    Thesavrvs exorcismorvm atqve conivrationvm terribilivm ... 1626.   (Card 2)

    Lazari Zetzneri, 1626.
    12 p. l., 1232, [39] p. 18cm.
    Previously published at Cologne in 1608.

    Contents.--F. Valerii Polydori ... Practica exorcistarum ad daemones & maleficia de Christi fidelibus pellendum, pars prima ... [et] secunda.--R. p. f. Hieronymi Mengi ... Flagellum daemonum.--Eivsdem Fvstis daemonum.--
    (Continued on next card)

---

tchcraft
59
1
26
    Thesavrvs exorcismorvm atqve conivrationvm terribilivm ... 1626.   (Card 3)

    Contents:(cont'd.)
F. Zachariae Vicecomitis ... Complementum artis exorcisticae.--Petri Antonii Stampae ... Fuga Satanae.--R. d. Maximiliani ab Eynatten ... Manuale exorcismorum.

    1. Exorcism. 2. Demonomania. 3. Witchcraft. I. Polidoro, Valerio. Practica exorcistarum. II. Menghi, Girolamo, d. 1610. Flagellum daemonum. III. Visconti, Zaccaria. Complementum artis exorcisticae. IV. Stampa, Pietro Antonio. Fuga Satanae. V. Eynatten, Maximilian van, d. 1631. Manuale exorcismorum.

QD
26
41
    Thesaurus incantatus: The enchanted treasure; or, The spagyric quest of Beroaldus Cosmopolita, in which is sophically and mystagorically declared the first matter of the stone. With a list of choice books on alchemy, magic, talismans, gems, mystics, neoplatonism, ancient worships, Rosicrucians, occult sciences, etc., etc. London, T. Marvell [1888?]
    64 p. illus. 20cm.
    1. Alchemy. 2. Occult sciences--Bibl. I. Title: The spagyric quest of Beroaldus Cosmopolita.

Thesaurus sacer benedictionum veterum.

Witchcraft
BX
2340
F89
    Freyschmid, Joseph Caspar.
    Thesaurus sacer benedictionum veterum, ac novarum, ex sanctae ecclesiae ritibus, sanctorum virorum scriptis, probatis authoribus, & approbatissimo temporum usu collectus ... dicatus, dedicatus, consecratus a Josepho Casparo Freyschmid. Lincij, 1708.
    6 p. l., 725, [27] p. 14cm.
    Title in red and black.
    Benedictio numismatum crucis: Sancti Patris Benedicti   has special t. p.

8   (Continued on next card)

Thesaurus sacer benedictionum veterum.

Witchcraft
BX
2340
F89
    Freyschmid, Joseph Caspar. Thesaurus sacer benedictionum ... 1708. (Card 2)

    with imprint: Lincij, Typis Caspari Josephi Freyschmid, 1708, and is unpaged.

    1. Exorcism. 2. Benediction. I. Title. II. Title: Benedictio numismatum crucis.

8

Theses de magis, volente Deo.

Witchcraft
BF
1587
D61
no.14
    Lunde, Nicolaus Johann, praeses.
    Theses de magis, volente' Deo, publicè tuebimur Nicolaus Joh. Lunde praeses & Henricus Olai Butzow respondens ... Havniae, Ex Reg. Majest. & universit. typographeó [1709]
    8 p. 18cm. (bound in 21cm. vol.)
    No. 14 in vol. lettered Dissertationes de magia. 1623-1723.

    1. Witchcraft--Addresses, essays, lectures. I. Butzow, Henricus Olai, respondent. II. Title.

8

Theses inaugurales, De crimine magiae.

Witchcraft
BF
1565
T46
    Thomasius, Christian, 1655-1728, praeses.
    Theses inavgvrales, De crimine magiae, qvas ... praeside D. Christiano Thomasio ... svbmittit M. Iohannes Reiche ... Halae Magdebvrgicae, Literis Christoph. Salfeldii [1701]
    40 p. 21cm.
    Diss.--Halle (J. Reiche, respondent)
    Also known as Dissertatio de crimine magiae.
    1. Witchcraft. I. Reiche, Johann, respondent. II. His Dissertatio de crimine magiae. III. Title: De crimine magiae.

8

Theurgie.

WITCHCRAFT
BF
1589
H81
    Horst, Georg Conrad, 1767-1838?
    Theurgie, oder Vom Bestreben der Menschen in der alten und neuen Zeit, zwischen sich und der Geisterwelt eine unmittelbare reale Verbindung zu bewirken. Mainz, Bei F. Kupferberg, 1820.
    91 p. 21cm.
    "Ankündigung. Zauber-Bibliothek," p. [83]-91, signed: Florian Kupferberg.
    Bound with his Von der alten und neuen Magie Ursprung. Mainz, 1820.

8
NIC
    1. Spirits. 2. Occult sciences--History. 3. His Zauber-Bibliothek. I. Kupferberg, Florian. II. Title.

WITCHCRAFT
BF
1582
T42
    Thiaucourt, Paul.
    La sorcellerie au Ban de Ramonchamp au XVIIe siècle. Remiremont, Imprim. H. Haut, 1906.
    54 p. 18cm.

    1. Witchcraft--Lorraine--History. I. Title.

8

Witchcraft
BR
135
T43
    Thiers, Jean Baptiste, 1636-1703.
    Traité des superstitions selon l'Ecriture Sainte, les decrets des conciles, et les sentimens des saints peres, et des theologiens. Paris, Antoine Dezallier, 1679.
    [24], 454 p. 17cm.

    1. Superstition. I. Title.

Witchcraft
BF
1623
P5
T44
    Thiselton-Dyer, Thomas Firminger, 1848-
    Plants in witchcraft.
    (In The popular science monthly. New York. 24cm. v. 34 (1889) p. 826-833)

    I. Title.

Thomas Aquinas, Saint, 1225?-1274.

ar W
52854
no.2
    Hopkin, Charles Edward, 1900–
    ... The share of Thomas Aquinas in the growth of the witchcraft delusion ... [by] Charles Edward Hopkin. Philadelphia, 1940.
    viii, 27 p., 1 l., 29–127 p., 1 l., 129–188 p. 23^{cm}.
    Thesis (PH. D.)—University of Pennsylvania, 1940.
    CONTENTS.—Introduction.—pt. I. The demonology of Thomas Aquinas.—pt. II. Thomas Aquinas as mediator between earlier and later beliefs.—Conclusion.—Bibliography (p. 185–188)
    No. 2 in vol. lettered: Pennsylvania dissertations
    1. Thomas Aquinas, Saint, 1225?–1274. 2. Witchcraft. 3. Demonology. I. Title.
                                                          41—2305
    Library of Congress   BF1565.T34H6 1940
    Univ. of Pennsylvania Libr.
    ———— Copy 2.
    Copyright A 146856   [41c2]   189.4

Thomas Aquinas, Saint, 1225?-1274.

WITCHCRAFT
BF
1569
M28
    Manser, Gallus, 1866-1950.
    Thomas von Aquin und der Hexenwahn.
    (In: Divus Thomas; Jahrbuch für Philosophie und spekulative Theologie. Wien. 23cm. ser.2, v.9 (1922) p.17-49, [81]-110)

    1. Witchcraft. 2. Witchcraft--Hist. 3. Demonology. 4. Thomas Aquinas, Saint, 1225?-1274.

8
NIC

Thomas, Christian, 1655-1728.

    see

Thomasius, Christian, 1655-1728.

WITCHCRAFT
BF
1582
T45
    Thomas, G
    Les procès de sorcellerie et la suggestion hypnotique. Discours prononcé par M. G. Thomas ... Nancy. Vagner, imprimeur, 1885.
    47 p. 23cm.
    At head of title: Cour d'appel de Nancy. Audience solennelle de rentrée du 16 octobre 1885.
    Half title: Rentrée de la Cour d'appel de Nancy.

8   (Continued on next card)

CATALOGUE OF THE CORNELL WITCHCRAFT COLLECTION

WITCHCRAFT
BF
1582   Thomas, G   Les procès de sorcellerie
T45   et la suggestion hypnotique ... 1885.
                                                (Card 2)

   Includes part of the court's proceedings.
   1. Witchcraft--France--History. 2.
Mental suggestion. I. France. Cour d'appel (Nancy) II. Title.

8

BR
377   **Thomas, Keith Vivian.**
T45   Religion and the decline of magic ₍by₎ Keith Thomas.
       New York, Scribner ₍1971₎
         xviii, 716 p.   25 cm. $17.50
         Includes bibliographical references.

4   3. ₍₁₎ England--Religion. 2. Occult sciences--England.
           Witchcraft--Eng   land. I. Title.
        BR377.T48 1971b   133   74-141707
        ISBN 0-684-10662-7   MARC

        Library of Congress   71 ₍7₎

Thomas von Aquin und der Hexenwahn.

WITCHCRAFT
BF
1569   **Manser, Gallus,** 1866-1950.
M28   Thomas von Aquin und der Hexenwahn.

       (In: Divus Thomas; Jahrbuch für Philoso-
       phie und spekulative Theologie. Wien.
       23cm. ser.2, v.9 (1922) p.17-49, ₍81₎-110)

         1. Witchcraft. 2. Witchcraft--Hist.
8   3. Demonology. ✓. Thomas Aquinas, Saint.
NIC   1225?-1274.

Thomasius, Christian

              Thomasius, Christian, 1655-1728.
                Anhang zu denen Thomasischen gemischten
Witchcraft   Händeln.
B   Thomasius, Christian, 1655-1728.
2605   Vernünfftige und christliche aber nicht
V5   scheinheilige Thomasische Gedancken und
           Erinnerungen über allerhand gemischte phi-
           losophische und juristische Händel.   Halle
           im Magdeburg, In der Rengerischen Buchhand-
           lung, 1723-25.
             3 v. front. 18cm.
             Title of v. 1 in red and black.
             "Es folget ... jetzo der fünffte Theil
           der Juristischer Händel ₍1720-21₎, jedoch
8   (Continued on next card)

              Thomasius, Christian, 1655-1728.
                Anhang zu denen Thomasischen gemischten
Witchcraft   Händeln.
B   Thomasius, Christian, 1655-1728.   Vernünff-
2605   tige und christliche aber nicht scheinhei-
V5   lige Thomasische Gedancken ... 1723-25.
                                            (Card 2)

             mit einiger Änderung."--Vorrede, 1. Bd.
Witchcraft
B   ---Anhang zu denen Thomasischen gemischten
2605   Händeln.   Halle im Magdeburgischen, In der
V5   Rengerischen Buchhandlung, 1726.
suppl.   224 p. 18cm.
                          (Continued on next card)

              Thomasius, Christian, 1655-1728.
                Anhang zu denen Thomasischen
Witchcraft   gemischten Händeln.
B   Thomasius, Christian, 1655-1728.   Vernünff-
2605   tige und christliche aber nicht scheinhei-
V5   lige Thomasische Gedancken ... 1723-25.
suppl.   (Card 3)
             Bound with v. 2.

             1. Philosophers, German--Correspondence,
           reminiscences, etc. 2. Witchcraft. I.
           His Ernsthaffte aber doch muntere ... Ge-
           dancken ... Über ... juristische Händel.
8   II. His Anh   ang zu denen Thomasischen
           gemischten Hän   deln. III. Title.

           Thomasius, Christian, 1655-1728, praeses.
             De tortura ex foris Christianorum
                proscribenda.
RARE   Thomasius, Christian, 1655-1728, praeses.
HV   Disputatio inauguralis juridica De tortu-
8593   ra ex foris Christianorum proscribenda,
T46   quam...praeside Dn. Christiano Thomasio...
           discussioni submittit Martinus Bernhardi.
           Halae Magdeburgicae, Typis Christoph. An-
           dreae Zeitleri ₍1705₎
             38 p. 19cm.
8   Diss.--Halle (M. Bernhardi, respondent)
NIC   With this is bound the edition of 1759
           of the diss.   with title as: Tracta-
           tio juridica   De tortura ex foris
           Christianor   um proscribenda.
                                 (Continued on next card)

           Thomasius, Christian, 1655-1728, praeses.
             De tortura ex foris Christianorum
                proscribenda.
RARE   Thomasius, Christian, 1655-1728, praeses.
HV   Dissertatio juridica De tortura ex foris
8593   Christianorum proscribenda...quam praeside
T46   Christiano Thomasio...respondendo propugna-
1743   vit Martinus Bernhardi.   Halae Salicae,
           Ex officina Hendeliana, 1743.
             37 p. 20cm.
             Diss.--Halle, 1705 (M. Bernhardi, respon-
           dent)
             Originally published in 1705 with title:
           Disputatio   inauguralis juridica De
8   tortura ex   foris Christianorum pro-
NIC   scribenda.   (Continued on next card)

           Thomasius, Christian, 1655-1728.
             De tortura ex foris Christianorum
                proscribenda.
RARE   Thomasius, Christian, 1655-1728.
HV   Tractatio juridica De tortura ex foris
8593   Christianorum proscribenda.   Halae Magde-
T46   burgicae, Typis Io. Christ. Grunerti, 1759.
             38 p. 19cm.
             Originally issued in 1705 as diss. with
           M. Bernhardi as respondent, with title: Dis-
           putatio inauguralis juridica De tortura ex
           foris Christianorum proscribenda.
8   Bound with   the 1705 ed.
NIC
                             (Continued on next card)

RARE   Thomasius, Christian, 1655-1728, praeses.
HV   Disputatio inauguralis juridica De tortu-
8593   ra ex foris Christianorum proscribenda,
T46   quam...praeside Dn. Christiano Thomasio...
           discussioni submittit Martinus Bernhardi.
           Halae Magdeburgicae, Typis Christoph. An-
           dreae Zeitleri ₍1705₎
             38 p. 19cm.
8   Diss.--Halle (M. Bernhardi, respondent)
NIC   With this is bound the edition of 1759
           of the diss.   with title as: Tracta-
           tio juridica   De tortura ex foris
           Christianor   um proscribenda.
                                 (Continued on next card)

RARE   Thomasius, Christian, 1655-1728, praeses.
HV   Disputatio inauguralis juridica De tortura
8593   ... ₍1705₎   (Card 2)
T46

             1. Torture. I. Bernhardi, Martinus, re-
           spondent. II. His De tortura ex foris
           Christianorum proscribenda. III. Title.

           Thomasius, Christian, 1655-1728, praeses.
             De tortura ex foris Christianorum proscribenda.
RARE   Thomasius, Christian, 1655-1728, praeses.
HV   Dissertatio juridica De tortura ex foris
8593   Christianorum proscribenda...quam praeside
T46   Christiano Thomasio...respondendo propugna-
1743   vit Martinus Bernhardi.   Halae Salicae,
           Ex officina Hendeliana, 1743.
             37 p. 20cm.
             Diss.--Halle, 1705 (M. Bernhardi, respon-
           dent)
             Originally published in 1705 with title:
           Disputatio   inauguralis juridica De
8   tortura ex   foris Christianorum pro-
NIC   scribenda.   (Continued on next card)

           Thomasius, Christian, 1655-1728.
             De tortura ex foris Christianorum proscribenda.
RARE   Thomasius, Christian, 1655-1728.
HV   Tractatio juridica De tortura ex foris
8593   Christianorum proscribenda.   Halae Magde-
T46   burgicae, Typis Io. Christ. Grunerti, 1759.
             38 p. 19cm.
             Originally issued in 1705 as diss. with
           M. Bernhardi as respondent, with title: Dis-
           putatio inauguralis juridica De tortura ex
           foris Christianorum proscribenda.
8   Bound with   the 1705 ed.
NIC
                             (Continued on next card)

Witchcraft
BF   Thomasius, Christian, 1655-1728, praeses.
1565   Disputatio juris canonici De origine ac
T461   progressu processus inquisitorii contra sa-
           gas, quam ... praeside Dn. Christiano Tho-
           masio ... subjicit die XXX. Aprilis M.DCCXII
           ... Johannes Paulus Ipsen ... Halae
           Magdebvrgicae, Typis Johannis Christiani Zahnii
           ₍1712₎
             68 p. 17cm.
             Diss.--Halle (J. P. Ipsen, respondent)
8

Witchcraft
BF   Thomasius, Christian, 1655-1728, praeses.
1565   Disputatio juris canonici De origine ac
T461   progressu processus inquisitorii contra sa-
1729   gas, quam ... praeside Dn. Christiano Tho-
           masio ... subiicit die XXX. Aprilis A.
           M DCC XII ... Johannes Paulus Ipsen ...
           Halae Magdeburgicae, Apud J. C. Hendelium,
           1729.
             68 ₍i.e. 76₎ p. 23cm.
             Pages 73-76 numbered 65-68.
             Diss.--Halle   (J. P. Ipsen, respon-
8   dent)   (Continued on next card)

CATALOGUE OF THE CORNELL WITCHCRAFT COLLECTION

Witchcraft
F
565
461
1729

Thomasius, Christian, 1655-1728, praeses.
Disputatio juris canonici De origine ac progressu processus inquisitorii ... 1729.
(Card 2)

1. Trials (Witchcraft) 2. Witchcraft.
I. Ipsen, Johann Paul, respondent. II. Title: De origine ac progressu processus inquisitorii contra sagas. III. Title.

Witchcraft
F
565
R46

Thomasius, Christian, 1655-1728.
Dissertatio de crimine magiae.

Thomasius, Christian, 1655-1728, praeses.
Theses inavgvrales, De crimine magiae, qvas ... praeside D. Christiano Thomasio ... svbmittit M. Iohannes Reiche ... Halae Magdebvrgicae, Literis Christoph. Salfeldii [1701]
40 p. 21cm.
Diss.--Halle (J. Reiche, respondent)
Also known as Dissertatio de crimine magiae.
1. Witchcraft. I. Reiche, Johann, respondent. II. His Dissertatio de crimine magiae. III. Title: De crimine magiae.

Witchcraft
F
565
R34

Thomasius, Christian, 1655-1728.
Dissertatio de crimine magiae. German.

Reiche, Johann, ed.
Herrn D. Christian Thomasii ... Kurtze Lehr-Sätze von dem Laster der Zauberey, nach dem wahren Verstande des lateinischen Exemplars ins Deutsche übersetzet, und aus des berühmten Theologi D. Meyfarti, Naudaei, und anderer gelehrter Männer Schrifften erleutert ... nebst einigen Actis magicis herausgegeben von Johann Reichen. Halle im Magdeburgischen, Im Rengerischen Buchladen, 1704.
2 v. in 1. 21cm.
(Continued on next card)

Witchcraft
F
565
R34

Thomasius, Christian, 1655-1728.
Dissertatio de crimine magiae. German.

Reiche, Johann, ed. Herrn D. Christian Thomasii ... Kurtze Lehr-Sätze ... 1704.
(Card 2)

Vol. 1 has special t. p.: Fernerer Unfug der Zauberey. Halle im Magdeburgischen, 1704.
Vol. 2 has special t. p.: Unterschiedliche Schrifften von Unfug des Hexen-Processes. Halle im Magdeburg., 1703.
Contents.--[1. Bd.] Gabriel Naudaei
(Continued on next card)

Witchcraft
F
565
R34

Thomasius, Christian, 1655-1728.
Dissertatio de crimine magiae. German.

Reiche, Johann, ed. Herrn D. Christian Thomasii ... Kurtze Lehr-Sätze ... 1704.
(Card 3)

Contents.--Continued.

Schutz-Schrifft [tr. of Apologie pour tous les grands hommes]--Geschichte der Teuffel zu Lodün.--Trauer-Geschichte von der greulichen Zauberey Ludwig Goffredy [tr. of De l'horrible & épouvantable sorcellerie de Louis Goffredy, auther F. de Rosset]--D. Christian Thomasii ... Kurtze Lehr-Sätze von
(Continued on next card)

Witchcraft
F
565
R34

Thomasius, Christian, 1655-1728.
Dissertatio de crimine magiae. German

Reiche, Johann, ed. Herrn D. Christian Thomasii ... Kurtze Lehr-Sätze ... 1704.
(Card 4)

Contents--Continued.

dem Laster der Zauberey [tr. of Dissertatio de crimine magiae, J. Reiche, respondent] [2. Bd.] Malleus judicum oder Gesetz-Hammer der unbarmhertzigen Hexen-Richter.-- Cautio criminalis [von F. Spee]--D. Johann Matthäus Meyfarths Christliche Erinnerung an Regenten.-- Viererley Sorten Hexen-Acta.--
(Continued on next card)

Witchcraft
BF
1523
E35

Thomasius, Christian, 1655-1728.
Dissertatio de crimine magiae--German.

Thomasius, Christian, 1655-1728.
Christian Thomasii Gelehrte Streitschrift von dem Verbrechen der Zauber- und Hexerey. Aus dem Lateinischen übersetzet, und bey Gelegenheit der Gassnerischen Wunderkuren zum Besten des Publikums herausgegeben. [Leipzig?] 1775.
95 p. 18cm.
Bound with Einziger von Einzing, Johann Martin Maximilian, 1725-1798. Dämonologie. [Leipzig?] 1775.
(Continued on next card)

Witchcraft
BF
1523
E35

Thomasius, Christian, 1655-1728.
Dissertatio de crimine magiae--German.

Thomasius, Christian, 1655-1728. Christian Thomasii Gelehrte Streitschrift von dem Verbrechen der Zauber- und Hexerey ... 1775.
(Card 2)

Translation of Dissertatio de crimine magiae.
1. Witchcraft. I. His Dissertatio de crimine magiae. German. II. Title: Streitschrift von dem Verbrechen der Zauber- und Hexerey.

Witchcraft
BF
1555
A55
no.4

Thomasius, Christian, 1655-1728.
Dissertatio de crimine magiae--German.

Thomasius, Christian, 1655-1728.
Kurtze Lehr-Sätze von dem Laster der Zauberey, vormahls in einer Inaugural Disputation defendirt, nunmehre aber auff gut Befinden andrer ins Deutsche übersetzet von einem Liebhaber seiner Muttersprache. [n. p.] 1702.
[136] p. 14cm.
Translation of Dissertatio de crimine magiae.
No. 4 in vol. lettered Andreae. De angelorum...
(Continued on next card)

Witchcraft
BF
1565
T46
1712

Thomasius, Christian, 1655-1728.
Dissertatio de crimine magiae--German.

Thomasius, Christian, 1655-1728.
Christ. Thomasii Kurtze Lehr-Sätze von dem Laster der Zauberey, aus dem Lateinischen ins Teutsche übersetzet, und mit des Autoris Vertheidigung vermehret. [n. p.] 1712.
92 p. plate. 16cm.
Title in red and black.
Translation of Dissertatio de crimine magiae.
Anhang, welcher aus des Autoris Erinne-
(Continued on next card)

Witchcraft
BF
1565
T46
1712

Thomasius, Christian, 1655-1728.
Dissertatio de crimine magiae--German.

Thomasius, Christian, 1655-1728. Christ. Thomasii Kurtze Lehr-Sätze von dem Laster der Zauberey ... 1712. (Card 2)

rung wegen seiner künfftigen Winter-Lectionen, auff das 1702. und folgende Jahr genommen worden, und betrifft die Vertheidigung seiner selbst eigenen Lehr-Sätze von dem Laster der Zauberey, p. [85]-92, has special t. p.

Witchcraft
BF
1565
T46
1717

Thomasius, Christian, 1655-1728.
Dissertatio de crimine magiae--German.

Thomasius, Christian, 1655-1728.
Christ. Thomasii Kurtze Lehr-Sätze von dem Laster der Zauberey, mit dessen eigenen Vertheidigung vermehret. Worbey Johann Kleins ... Juristische Untersuchung, was von der Hexen Bekäntniss zu halten, dass solche aus schändlichem Beyschlaff mit dem Teuffel Kinder gezeuget. Beydes aus dem Lateinischen ins Teutsche übersetzt. Franckfurth und Leipzig, 1717.
134 p. 18cm. (Continued on next card)

Witchcraft
BF
1565
T46
1717

Thomasius, Christian, 1655-1728.
Dissertatio de crimine magiae--German.

Thomasius, Christian, 1655-1728. Christ. Thomasii Kurtze Lehr-Sätze von dem Laster der Zauberey ... 1717. (Card 2)

Title in red and black.
Translation of Thomasius' Dissertatio de crimine magiae and of Klein's Meditatio academica exhibens examen juridicum judicialis.
Klein's Juristische Untersuchung, was von der Hexen Bekäntniss zu halten ..., p. [79]-134, has special t. p.
(Continued on next card)

Witchcraft
BF
1565
T46
1717a

Thomasius, Christian, 1655-1728.
Dissertatio de crimine magiae--German.

Thomasius, Christian, 1655-1728.
Christ. Thomasii Kurtze Lehr-Sätze von dem Laster der Zauberey, mit dessen eigenen Vertheidigung vermehret. Worbey Johann Kleins ... Juristische Untersuchung, was von der Hexen Bekäntniss zu halten, dass solche aus schändlichem Beyschlaff mit dem Teuffel Kinder gezeuget. Beydes aus dem Lateinischen ins Teutsche übersetzt. Franckfurth und Leipzig, 1717.
134 p. front. 19cm.
(Continued on next card)

Witchcraft
BF
1565
T46
1717a

Thomasius, Christian, 1655-1728.
Dissertatio de crimine magiae--German.

Thomasius, Christian, 1655-1728. Christ. Thomasii Kurtze Lehr-Sätze von dem Laster der Zauberey ... 1717. (Card 2)

Translation of his Dissertatio de crimine magiae, J. Reiche, respondent; and of Meditatio academica, exhibens examen juridicum judicialis, by J. Klein (N. Putter, respondent.)
Johann Kleins Juristische Untersuchung, p. [79]-134, has special t. p.
(Continued on next card)

Witchcraft
BF
1565
T46
1717a

Thomasius, Christian, 1655-1728.
Dissertatio de crimine magiae--German.

Thomasius, Christian, 1655-1728. Christ. Thomasii Kurtze Lehr-Sätze von dem Laster der Zauberey ... 1717. (Card 3)

With this are bound Ludovici, Gottfried, 1670-1724. ... Theologicum novae... Coburgi [1718] and Sturm, Johann Christoph, 1635-1703. ... Wahrhaffte und gründliche Vorstellung von der lügenhafften Stern-Wahrsagerey. Coburg, 1722.
1. Witchcraft. I. His Dissertatio de crimine magiae.-- German. II.
(Continued on next card)

RARE
HV
8593
T46
1743

Thomasius, Christian, 1655-1728, praeses.
Dissertatio juridica De tortura ex foris Christianorum proscribenda...quam praeside Christiano Thomasio...respondendo propugnavit Martinus Bernhardi. Halae Salicae, Ex officina Hendeliana, 1743.
37 p. 20cm.
Diss.--Halle, 1705 (M. Bernhardi, respondent)
Originally published in 1705 with title: Disputatio inauguralis juridica De tortura ex foris Christianorum proscribenda.
(Continued on next card)

RARE
HV
8593
T46
1743

Thomasius, Christian, 1655-1728, praeses.
Dissertatio juridica De tortura...1743.
(Card 2)

1 Torture. I. Bernhardi, Martinus, respondent. II. His De tortura ex foris Christianorum proscribenda. III. His Disputatio inauguralis juridica De tortura ex foris Christianorum proscribenda. IV. Title.

543

CATALOGUE OF THE CORNELL WITCHCRAFT COLLECTION

Witchcraft
K Thomasius, Christian, 1655-1728.
T463   Ernsthaffte aber doch muntere und ver-
E7 nünfftige Thomasische Gedancken u. Errinne-
rungen über allerhand ausserlesene juris-
tische Händel.   Halle im Magdeburgischen,
In der Rengerischen Buchhandlung, 1720-21.
4 v. in 2. front. 22cm.
Title of v. 1 in red and black.
List of Thomasius' works in MS, from
S. Calvary & co., Berlin, tipped in before
8   t. p.
(Continued on next card)

Witchcraft
K Thomasius, Christian, 1655-1728. Ernst-
hafffte aber doch muntere und vernünfftige
T463 Thomasische Gedancken ... 1720-21.
E7 (Card 2)

Continued by his Vernünfftige und christ-
liche aber nicht scheinheilige Thomasische
Gedancken, 1723-25.
1. Law reports, digests, etc.--Germany.
I. His   Vernünfftige und christliche ...
Gedancken. II.   Title.

        Thomasius, Christian, 1655-1728.
        Ernsthaffte aber doch muntere ... Ge-
Witchcraft dancken ... über ... juristische Händel.
B Thomasius, Christian, 1655-1728.
2605 Vernünfftige und christliche aber nicht
V5 scheinheilige Thomasische Gedancken und
Erinnerungen über allerhand gemischte philosophische und juristische Händel. Halle
im Magdeburg, In der Rengerischen Buchhandlung, 1723-25.
3 v. front. 18cm.
Title of v. 1 in red and black.
"Es folget ... jetzo der fünffte Theil
der Juristischer Händel [1720-21], jedoch
8   (Continued on next card)

        Thomasius, Christian, 1655-1728.
        Ernsthaffte aber doch muntere ... Ge-
Witchcraft dancken ... über ... juristische Händel.
B Thomasius, Christian, 1655-1728. Vernünff-
2605 tige und christliche aber nicht scheinhei-
V5 lige Thomasische Gedancken ... 1723-25.
(Card 2)

mit einiger Änderung."--Vorrede, 1. Bd.
Witchcraft
B ---Anhang zu denen Thomasischen gemischten
2605 Händeln. Halle im Magdeburgischen, In der
V5 Rengerischen Buchhandlung, 1726.
suppl. 224 p. 18cm.
(Continued on next card)

        Thomasius, Christian, 1655-1728.
        Ernsthaffte aber doch muntere ... Ge-
Witchcraft dancken ... über ... juristische Händel.
B Thomasius, Christian, 1655-1728. Vernünff-
2605 tige und christliche aber nicht scheinhei-
V5 lige Thomasische Gedancken ... 1723-25.
suppl. (Card 3)

Bound with v. 2.

1. Philosophers, German--Correspondence,
reminiscences, etc. 2. Witchcraft. I.
His Ernsthaffte aber doch muntere ... Gedancken ... über ... juristische Händel.
8 II. His Anhang zu denen Thomasischer
gemischten Händeln. III. Title.

Witchcraft
BF Thomasius, Christian, 1655-1728.
1523   Christian Thomasii Gelehrte Streitschrift
E35 von dem Verbrechen der Zauber- und Hexerey.
Aus dem Lateinischen übersetzt, und bey Ge-
legenheit der Gassnerischen Wunderkuren zum
Besten des Publikums herausgegeben. [Leip-
zig?] 1775.
95 p. 18cm.
Bound with Einziger von Einzing, Johann
Martin Maximilian, 1725-1798. Dämonologie.
8 [Leipzig?] 1775.
Continued on next card)

Witchcraft
BF Thomasius, Christian, 1655-1728. Chris-
1523 tian Thomasii Gelehrte Streitschrift von
E35 dem Verbrechen der Zauber- und Hexerey ...
1775. (Card 2)
Translation of Dissertatio de crimine
magiae.
1. Witchcraft. I. His Dissertatio
de crimine magiae. German. II. Title:
Streitschrift von dem Verbrechen der Zauber-
und Hexerey. III. Title. 2. Gassner, Johann
8 Joseph, 1727- 1779.

Witchcraft
BF Thomasius, Christian, 1655-1728.
1555   Kurtze Lehr-Sätze von dem Laster der
A55 Zauberey, vormahls in einer Inaugural Dis-
no.4 putation defendirt, nunmehre aber auff
gut Befinden andrer ins Deutsche übersetzet
von einem Liebhaber seiner Muttersprache.
[n. p.] 1702.
[136] p. 14cm.
Translation of Dissertatio de crimine
magiae.
No. 4 in vol lettered Andreae. De
8 angelorum...
(Continued on next card)

Witchcraft
BF Thomasius, Christian, 1655-1728. Kurtze
1555 Lehr-Sätze von dem Laster der Zauberey ...
A55 1702. (Card 2)
no.4
1. Witchcraft. I. His Dissertatio
de crimine magiae--German. II. Title.

8

Witchcraft
BF Thomasius, Christian, 1655-1728.
1565   Christ. Thomasii Kurtze Lehr-Sätze von
T46 dem Laster der Zauberey, aus dem Lateini-
1712 schen ins Teutsche übersetzet, und mit des
Autoris Vertheidigung vermehret. [n. p.]
1712.
92 p. plate. 16cm.
Title in red and black.
Translation of Dissertatio de crimine
magiae.
Anhang, welcher aus des Autoris Erinne-
8 (Continued on next card)

Witchcraft
BF Thomasius, Christian, 1655-1728. Christ.
1565 Thomasii Kurtze Lehr-Sätze von dem Laster
T46 der Zauberey ... 1712. (Card 2)
1712

rung wegen seiner künfftigen Winter-Lectionen, auff das 1702. und folgende Jahr genommen worden, und betrifft die Vertheidigung seiner selbst eigenen Lehr-Sätze von
dem Laster der Zauberey, p. [85]-92, has
special t. p.
I. His Dissertatio de crimine magiae--
German. II. Title: Kurtze Lehr-Sätze von
8 dem Laster der   Zauberey.

Witchcraft
BF Thomasius, Christian, 1655-1728.
1565   Christ. Thomasii Kurtze Lehr-Sätze von
T46 dem Laster der Zauberey, mit dessen eige-
1717 nen Vertheidigung vermehret. Worbey Johann
Kleins ... Juristische Untersuchung, was von
der Hexen Bekäntniss zu halten, dass solche
aus schändlichem Beyschlaff mit dem Teuffel
Kinder gezeuget. Beydes aus dem Lateinischen
ins Teutsche übersetzt. Franckfurth und
Leipzig, 1717.
8 134 p. 18cm. (Continued on next card)

Witchcraft
BF Thomasius, Christian, 1655-1728. Christ.
1565 Thomasii Kurtze Lehr-Sätze von dem Laster
T46 der Zauberey ... 1717. (Card 2)
1717
Title in red and black.
Translation of Thomasius' Dissertatio de
crimine magiae and of Klein's Meditatio academica exhibens examen juridicum judicialis.
Klein's Juristische Untersuchung, was von
der Hexen Bekäntniss zu halten ..., p. [79]-
134, has special t. p.

8 (Continued on next card)

Witchcraft
BF Thomasius, Christian, 1655-1728. Christ.
1565 Thomasii Kurtze Lehr-Sätze von dem Laster
T46 der Zauberey ... 1717. (Card 3)
1717
1. Witchcraft. I. His Dissertatio de
crimine magiae.--German. II. Klein, Johann, 1659-1732. Juristische Untersuchung,
was von der Hexen Bekäntniss zu halten.
III. Klein, Johann, 1659-1732. Meditatio
academica exhibens examen juridicum judicialis.--German. IV. Title: Kurtze
8 Lehr-Sätze von dem Laster der Zauberey.

Witchcraft
BF Thomasius, Christian, 1655-1728.
1565   Christ. Thomasii Kurtze Lehr-Sätze von
T46 dem Laster der Zauberey, mit dessen eigenen
1717a Vertheidigung vermehret. Worbey Johann
Kleins ... Juristische Untersuchung, was
von der Hexen Bekäntniss zu halten, dass
solche aus schändlichem Beyschlaff mit dem
Teuffel Kinder gezeuget. Beydes aus dem
Lateinischen ins Teutsche übersetzt.
Franckfurth und Leipzig, 1717.
134 p. front. 19cm.
8 (Continued on next card)

Witchcraft
BF Thomasius, Christian, 1655-1728. Christ.
1565 Thomasii Kurtze Lehr-Sätze von dem Laster
T46 der Zauberey ... 1717. (Card 2)
1717a
Translation of his Dissertatio de crimine magiae, J. Reiche, respondent; and of
Meditatio academica, exhibens examen juridicum judicialis, by J. Klein (N. Putter,
respondent.)
Johann Kleins Juristische Untersuchung,
p. [79]-134, has special t. p.
8 (Continued on next card)

Witchcraft
BF Thomasius, Christian, 1655-1728. Christ.
1565 Thomasii Kurtze Lehr-Sätze von dem Laster
T46 der Zauberey ... 1717. (Card 3)
1717a
With this are bound Ludovici, Gottfried,
1670-1724. ... Theologicum novae... Coburgi
[1718] and Sturm, Johann Christoph, 1635-
1703. ... Wahrhaffte und gründliche Vorstellung von der lügenhafften Stern-Wahrsagerey.
Coburg, 1722.
1. Witchcraft. I. His Dissertatio
de crimine magiae.-- German. VII.
8 (Continued on next card)

Witchcraft
BF Thomasius, Christian, 1655-1728. Christ.
1565 Thomasii Kurtze Lehr-Sätze von dem Laster
T46 der Zauberey ... 1717. (Card 4)
1717a
Klein, Johann, 1659-1732. Meditatio acade-
mica, exhibens examen juridicum judicialis--
German. III. Klein, Johann, 1659-1732.
Juristische Untersuchung, was von der Hexen
Bekäntniss zu halten. IV. Reiche, Johann,
respondent. V.   Putter, Nicolaus, re-
spondent. VI.   Title: Kurtze Lehr-
Sätze von dem   Laster der Zauberey.
8 VII. Title.

CATALOGUE OF THE CORNELL WITCHCRAFT COLLECTION

Thomasius, Christian, 1655-1728.
   Kurtze Lehr-Sätze von dem Laster der Zauberey.
    Franck, Johannes Christophorus, fl. 1717.
      Gottfried Wahrliebs [pseud.] Deutliche vorstellung der nichtigkeit derer vermeynten hexereyen und des ungegründeten hexen-processes. Nebst einer Gründlichen beantwortung der unter dem nahmen eines nach Engelland reisenden passagiers unlängst heraus gekommenen Untersuchung vom kobold, darinnen die falschen auflagen / mit welchen derselbe so wohl den hrn. geheimbd. rath Thomasivm als Iohann Webstern ohne allen grund zu diffamiren gesucht. deutlich
              (Continued on next card)

Thomasius, Christian, 1655-1728.
   Kurtze Lehr-Sätze von dem Laster der Zauberey.
    Franck, Johannes Christophorus, fl. 1717.
      Gottfried Wahrliebs [pseud.] Deutliche vorstellung der nichtigkeit derer vermeynten hexereyen ... [pref. 1720]   (Card 2)

entdecket, wie auch die Thomasische Lehr-sätze vom laster der zauberey wieder dessen ungegründete einwürffe zulänglich behauptet werden. Amsterdam, Nach erfindung der hexerey in dritten seculo, und nach einführung des hexen-processes im jahr 236 [pref. 1720]
   172, 78 p.   front.   22cm.
           (Continued on next card)

Thomasius, Christian, 1655-1728.
   Kurtze Lehr-Sätze von dem Laster der Zauberey.
WITCHCRAFT
.565
.82
    Franck, Johannes Christophorus, fl. 1717.
      Gottfried Wahrliebs [pseud.] Deutliche vorstellung der nichtigkeit derer vermeynten hexereyen ... [pref. 1720]   (Card 3)

"Gründliche beantwortung der ... Untersuchung vom kobold" has separate paging and special t. p. with imprint: Amsterdam, 1720.

        ~~(Continued on next card)~~

Thomasius, Christian, 1655-1728.
   Kurtze Lehr-Sätze von dem Laster der Zauberey.
   Kurtze Untersuchung von Kobold, in so ferne gewisse phaenomena unter diesem Nahmen dem Teuffel zugeschrieben werden, auf Veranlassung einer besondern Begebenheit wobey überhaupt von denen sichtbaren Würckungen des Teuffels in und durch die natürlichen Cörper gehandelt. Auch hiernächst gezeiget wird wie der Herr autor derer Lehr-Sätze von dem Laster der Zauberey etliche hieher gehörige Schrifft-Stellen zur Ungebühr verdr   ehet und überdis seine
        (Continued on next card)

Thomasius, Christian, 1655-1728.
   Kurtze Lehr-Sätze von dem Laster der Zauberey.
   Kurtze Untersuchung von Kobold...   (Card 2)

gantze Meynung de pacto auf unbündige paralogismos gegründet. Von einem nach Engelland reisenden Passagier. Roterdam, 1719.
   108 p.   front.   17cm.

   1. Demonology. 2. Witchcraft. 3. Thomasius, Christian, 1655-1728. Kurtze Lehr-Sätze vom La   ster der Zauberey. I. Ein nach   Engelland reisender Passagier.

Thomasius, Christian, 1655-1728.
   Kurtze Lehr-Sätze von dem Laster der Zauberey.
   Unpartheyische Gedancken über die Kurtze Lehr-Sätze von dem Laster der Zauberey, welche der berühmte JCtus und Professor zu Halle, Herr D. Christianus Thomasius, damahls in einer Inaugural-Disputation defendiret, jetzo aber schon zum andernmahl in teutsche Sprache übersetzet worden, nebst Anhang betreffende die Vertheidigung dieser Lehr-Sätze, kurtz gefasset und zum Druck befördert von einem Membro des Collegii   Curiosorum in Teutsch-
        (Continued on next card)

Thomasius, Christian, 1655-1728.
Witchcraft
BF
1565
T46
U58
   Kurtze Lehr-Sätze von dem Laster der Zauberey.
   Unpartheyische Gedancken über die Kurtze Lehr-Sätze von dem Laster der Zauberey ... 1703.   (Card 2)

land.   [n. p.] 1703.
   46 p.   plate.   17cm.

   1. Thomasius, Christian, 1655-1728. Kurtze Lehr-Sätze von dem Laster der Zauberey. 2. Witchcraft. I. Ein Membrum des Collegii Cu   riosorum in Teutschland.

Witchcraft
Z
1007
T46
   Thomasius, Christian, 1655-1728, ed.
     Summarischer Nachrichten von auserlesenen mehrentheils alten in der Thomasischen Bibliotheque verhandenen [sic] Büchern. 1.-[24] Stück.   Halle, J. F. Zeitler, 1715-18.
   24 pt. in 1 v.   fronts. (ports.) 18cm.

   By various authors, edited by C. Thomasius.

   I. Title.   1. Books--Reviews.

Witchcraft
BF
1565
T46
   Thomasius, Christian, 1655-1728, praeses.
     Theses inavgvrales, De crimine magiae, qvas ... praeside D. Christiano Thomasio ... svbmittit M. Iohannes Reiche ... Halae Magdebvrgicae, Literis Christoph. Salfeldii [1701]
   40 p.   21cm.
   Diss.--Halle (J. Reiche, respondent)
   Also known as Dissertatio de crimine magiae.
   1. Witchcraft. I. Reiche, Johann, respondent. II. His Dissertatio de crimine magiae. III. Title: De crimine magiae.   (Over)

RARE
HV
8593
T46

   Thomasius, Christian, 1655-1728.
     Tractatio juridica De tortura ex foris Christianorum proscribenda. Halae Magdeburgicae, Typis Io. Christ. Grunerti, 1759.
   38 p.   19cm.

   Originally issued in 1705 as diss. with M. Bernhardi as respondent, with title: Disputatio inauguralis juridica De tortura ex foris Christianorum proscribenda.
   Bound with   the 1705 ed.
            (Continued on next card)

RARE
HV
8593
T46
   Thomasius, Christian, 1655-1728. Tractatio juridica De tortura...1759.   (Card 2)

   1. Torture. I. Bernhardi, Martinus, respondent. II. His De tortura ex foris Christianorum proscribenda. III. His Disputatio inauguralis juridica De tortura ex foris Christianorum proscribenda. IV. Title.

B
2605
Z7
T46
v.5
   Thomasius, Christian, 1655-1728.
     Über die Hexenprozesse. Überarb. und hrsg. von Rolf Lieberwirth. Weimar, Böhlau, 1967.
   232 p.   25cm.   (Thomasiana, Heft 5)
   Contents.--Dissertatio de crimine magiae. Lateinische und deutsche Ausg.--Dissertatio de origine ac progressu processus inquisitorii sagas. Lateinische und deutsche Ausg.--Auszug aus: Christian Thomasens Erinnerung wegen seiner künffti   gen Winterlektionen, so
         (Continued on next card)

B
2605
Z7
T46
v.5
   Thomasius, Christian, 1655-1728. Über die Hexenprozesse. 1967.   (Card 2)

nach Michaelis dieses 1702. Jahres ihren Anfang nehmen werden.--Verzeichnis der von Thomasius benutzten Literatur. (p. [225]-232)

   1. Trials (Witchcraft) I. Lieberwirth, Rolf, ed. II.   Title.

Witchcraft
B
2605
V5
   Thomasius, Christian, 1655-1728.
     Vernünfftige und christliche aber nicht scheinheilige Thomasische Gedancken und Erinnerungen über allerhand gemischte philosophische und juristische Händel. Halle im Magdeburg, In der Rengerischen Buchhandlung, 1723-25.
   3 v.   front.   18cm.
   Title of v. 1 in red and black.
   "Es folget ... jetzo der fünffte Theil der Juristischen Händel [1720-21], jedoch
        (Continued on next card)

Witchcraft
B
2605
V5
   Thomasius, Christian, 1655-1728. Vernünfftige und christliche aber nicht scheinheilige Thomasische Gedancken ... 1723-25.   (Card 2)

mit einiger Änderung."--Vorrede, 1. Bd.

Witchcraft
B
2605
V5
suppl.
   ---Anhang zu denen Thomasischen gemischten Händeln. Halle im Magdeburgischen, In der Rengerischen Buchhandlung, 1726.
   224 p.   18cm.

        (Continued on next card)

Witchcraft
B
2605
V5
suppl.
   Thomasius, Christian, 1655-1728. Vernünfftige und christliche aber nicht scheinheilige Thomasische Gedancken ... 1723-25.   (Card 3)

Bound with v. 2.

   1. Philosophers, German--Correspondence, reminiscences, etc. 2. Witchcraft. I. His Ernsthaffte aber doch muntere ... Gedancken ... über ... juristische Händel. II. His Anhang zu denen Thomasischen gemischten Händeln. III. Title. (Over)

Witchcraft
K
T463
E7
   Thomasius, Christian, 1655-1728. Vernünfftige und christliche ... Gedancken.
   Thomasius, Christian, 1655-1728.
     Ernsthaffte aber doch muntere und vernünfftige Thomasische Gedancken u. Errinnerungen über allerhand ausserlesene juristische Händel. Halle im Magdeburgischen, In der Rengerischen Buchhandlung, 1720-21.
   4 v. in 2.   front.   22cm.
   Title of v. 1 in red and black.
   List of Thomasius' works in MS, from S. Calvary & co., Berlin, tipped in before t. p.
        (Continued on next card)

Witchcraft
K
T463
E7
   Thomasius, Christian, 1655-1728. Vernünfftige und christliche ... Gedancken.
   Thomasius, Christian, 1655-1728. Ernsthaffte aber doch muntere und vernünfftige Thomasische Gedancken ... 1720-21.   (Card 2)

Continued by his Vernünfftige und christliche aber nicht scheinheilige Thomasische Gedancken, 1723-25.

   1. Law reports, digests, etc.--Germany. I. His   Vernünfftige und christliche ... Gedancken. II.   Title.

CATALOGUE OF THE CORNELL WITCHCRAFT COLLECTION

Thomasius, Christian, 1655-1728.
WITCHCRAFT
BF   Hutchinson, Francis, *bp. of Down and Connor*, 1660-1739.
1565   Francisci Hutchinsons ... Historischer versuch von der hexe-
H97   reÿ, in einem gespräch zwischen einem geistlichen, einem
1726 schottländischen advocaten und englischen geschwornen;
worinnen über würcklich geschehene dinge vernünfftige anmerckungen gemachet, die hieher gehörigen stellen aus der
Heil. Schrifft richtig erkläret und die gemeinen irrthümer
aufs bescheidentlichste widerleget werden. Nebst zwey vortrefflichen predigten, die erste zum beweiss der wahrheit
christl. religion, die andere, von guten und bösen engeln; und
einer vorrede des herrn geheimbden raths Thomasii. Aus
(Continued on next card)
8   32-6507

Thomasius, Christian, 1655-1728.
WITCHCRAFT
BF   Hutchinson, Francis, *bp. of Down and Connor*, 1660-1739.
1565   Francisci Hutchinsons ... Historischer versuch von der
H97   dem englischen ins teutsche übersetzet, auch mit kurtzen sum-
1726 marien und vollständigen registern versehen von Theodoro Arnold. Leipzig, J. C. Martini, 1726.
[50], 332, [23] p. front. 22 cm.
Head-pieces and initials.
"Verzeichniss derer in diesem werck nur teutsch angeführten englischen autorum": p. [1]-[4] at end.
With copies 1 and 2 are bound Saint André, F.
de. Lesenswürdige Briefe ... uber die Materie von
der Zauberey. Leipzig, 1727.   32-6507
Library of Congress
   —— Copy 2.   (Continued on next card)
8

Thomasius, Christian, 1655-1728.
Witchcraft
BF   Webster, John, 1610-1682.
1565   ... Untersuchung der vermeinten und so
W38   genannten Hexereÿen, worinn zwar zugegeben
1719 wird, daß es an mancherley Betrug und Aeffereyen nicht fehle ...: im Gegentheil aber
die Fabel, daß der Teuffel leibhafftig einen
Pact mit den Hexen mache ... durchaus geleugnet und umgestossen wird. Dabey auch
die Warheit, daß es allerdings Engel und
Geister, wie nicht weniger Erscheinungen
gebe, eröffnet ... Aus dem Englischen ins
8   Continued on next card)

Thomasius, Christian, 1655-1728.
Witchcraft
BF   Webster, John, 1610-1682. Untersuchung
1565 der vermeinten und so genannten Hexereÿen
W38   ... 1719.   (Card 2)
1719
Teutsche übersetzt, und nebst einer Vorrede
des Hrn. Geheimbden Raths Thomasii ...
Halle, im Magdeburgischen, In Verlegung der
Neuen Buchhandlung, 1719.
56, 611, [97] p. plate. 21cm.
1. Witchcraft. I. Thomasius, Christian,
1655-1728. II.   His The displaying of
supposed witch   craft. German. III.
Title.
8

Thomasius, Christian, 1655-1728.
Witchcraft
BF   Goldschmidt, Peter, d. 1713.
1565   Verworffener Hexen- und Zauberer-Advo-
G62   cat. Das ist: wolgegründete Vernichtung
des thörichten Vorhabens Hn. Christiani
Thomasii J. U. D. & Professoris Hallensis und
aller derer, welche durch ihre super-kluge Phantasie-Grillen dem teufflischen Hexen-Geschmeiss das Wort reden wollen ...
Hamburg, G. Liebernickel, 1705.
[13], 654, [19] p. illus. 18cm.
1. Thomasius, Christian, 1655-1728. I.
Title.

Thomasius, Christian, 1655-1728--Biography.
Witchcraft
B   Klemperer,   Prediger zu Landsberg a.
2605 W.
Z7   Christian Thomasius, ein Vorkämpfer
K64   der Volksaufklärung. Vortrag, gehalten vom
Prediger Dr. Klemperer im Vereins-Verband
für öffentliche Vorträge zu Landsberg a. W.
am 15. Februar 1877.   Landsberg a. W.,
Druck von F. Striewing, 1877.
43 p. 21cm.
1. Thomasius, Christian, 1655-1728
--Biog.
8

Thomasius, Christian, 1655-1728--Biography
Witchcraft
B   Luden, Heinrich, 1778?-1847.
2605   Christian Thomasius, nach seinen Schick-
Z7   salen und Schriften dargestellt, von H.
L94   Luden. Mit einer Vorrede von Johann von
Müller ... Berlin, Bei J. F. Unger, 1805.
xvi, 311 p. 17cm.

1. Thomasius, Christian, 1655-1728--
Biog. I. Müller, Johannes von, 1752-1809.
8

Thomasius, Christian, 1655-1728--
Witchcraft Biography.
B   Nicoladoni, Alexander.
2605   Christian Thomasius. Ein Beitrag zur
Z7   Geschichte der Aufklärung. Dresden,
N63   Hönsch & Tiesler [1888]
vi, 140 p. port. 22cm.

1. Thomasius, Christian, 1655-1728--
Biog.
8

Witchcraft
BL   Thomasius, Jacob, 1622-1684, praeses.
325   De transformatione hominum in bruta, dis-
M45   sertationem philosophicam priorem, inclytae
T46   facultatis philosophicae permissu & authoritate sub praesidio ... Dn. M. Jacobi Thomasii ... ventilationi subjicit ... Fridericus
Tobias Moebius ... [Lipsiae?] Typis Joh.
Wittigau [1667]
[20] p. 19cm.
Diss.--Leipzig (F. T. Moebius, respondent)
1. Metamorphosis (in religion, folk-lore,
etc.) 2. Magic. VI. Moebius, Fried-
8   rich Tobias,   respondent. VII. Title.

Witchcraft
BT   Thompson, Richard Lowe.
980   The history of the devil, the horned God of
T47   the west. London, Kegan Paul, Trench,
Trubner & Co., Ltd., 1929.
xiv, 171 p. illus. 23cm.

1. Devil. 2. Magic. 3. Witchcraft. I. Title.

Witchcraft
BF   Thorndike, Lynn, 1882-
1601   The attitude of Origen and Augustine toward
T49   magic. [Chicago, 1908]
[46]-66 p. 23cm.

Reprinted from The monist, v.18, Jan. 1908.

1. Origenes. Contra Celsum. 2. Augustinus
Aurelius, Saint, bp. of Hippo. De civitate Dei.
3. Magic. I. Title.

Q   Thorndike, Lynn, 1882-
125   A history of magic and experimental science ... by Lynn
T49   Thorndike ... New York, The Macmillan company, 1923-41.
1923 6 v. 23 cm.
Vols. III-VI have imprint: New York, Columbia university press.
Vols. III-VI have series note on half-title: History of science society
publications. New series IV.
Includes bibliographies.
CONTENTS.--v. 1-2. The first thirteen centuries of our era.--v. 3-4.
Fourteenth and fifteenth centuries.--v. 5-6. The sixteenth century.

1. Science--Hist. 2. Magic--Hist.

Q125.T52   509   23--2984
Library of Congress   [53r43p²]

Witchcraft
Q   Thorndike, Lynn, 1882-
125   A history of magic and experimental
T49   science. New York, Columbia University
1958 Press [1958-60, c1923-58]
8 v. 23cm.

Vols. 3-6 have series note on half-title:
History of Science Society publications.
New series IV.
Contents.--v. 1-2. The first thirteen
centuries of our era.--v. 3-4. Fourteenth
(Continued on next card)

Witchcraft
Q   Thorndike, Lynn, 1882-   A history of
125   magic and experimental science ...
T49   [1958-60, c1923-58]   (Card 2)
1958
Contents.--Continued.
and fifteenth centuries.--v. 5-6. The sixteenth century.--v. 7-8. The seventeenth
century.

   ✓ I. Title.
1. Science--History. 2. Magic--
History.

Witchcraft
BF   Thorndike, Lynn, 1882-
1591   The place of magic in the intellectual
T49   history of Europe.   New York, Columbia
Univ. Press, 1905.
110 p. 24cm. (Studies in history,
economics and public law, edited by the Faculty
of Political Science of Columbia University,
v. 24, no. 1 [whole no. 62])

   ✓ I. Title.

BF   Thót, László, d. 1935.
1566   Contra las brujas; procesos al demonio, la magia, y misas
T46   negras [por] Ladislao Thot. Buenos Aires, Ediciones La
Sirena [1969]
80 p. 20 cm.
                                        LACAP 69-8166
Bibliographical footnotes.

1. Witchcraft. ✓ I. Title.

BF1566.T47   133.4   74-427132
Library of Congress   69 [18]

Thoughts on dreaming.
WITCHCRAFT
BF   Branch, Thomas, fl. 1753.
1075   Thoughts on dreaming. Wherein the
B81   notion of the sensory, and the opinion
that it is shut up from the inspection
of the soul in sleep, and that spirits
supply us with all our dreams, are
examined by revelation and reason.
Occasioned by an essay on the phenomenon
of dreaming, in a book, entitled, An
enquiry into the nature of the human soul;
wherein the im   materiality of the
8   (Continued on next card
NIC

Thoughts on dreaming.
WITCHCRAFT
BF   Branch, Thomas, fl. 1753. Thoughts on
1075   dreaming...   (Card 2)
B81
soul is evinced from the principles of
reason and philosophy. By Tho. Branch.
London, Printed for R. Dodsley [etc.]
1738.
96 p. 21cm.
1. Dreams. 2. Soul. 3. Baxter, Andrew,
1686?-1750. An enquiry into the nature
of human soul.   I. Title.
8
NIC

CATALOGUE OF THE CORNELL WITCHCRAFT COLLECTION

Witchcraft　Three books of occult philosophy.
BF
1598　Agrippa von Nettesheim, Heinrich Cornelius,
A27　　1486?-1535.
O2　　　Three books of occult philosophy ...
1651　Translated out of the Latin into the English
tongue, by J. F[reake] London, Printed by
R. W. for Gregory Moule, and are to be sold
at the Sign of the three Bibles neer the
West-end of Pauls, 1651.
[26], 583, [12] p. port., illus., tables,
diagrs. 19cm.
Imprint of copy 3 varies slightly: London,
(Continued on next card)

itchcraft　Three books of occult philosophy.
BF
1598　Agrippa von Nettesheim, Heinrich Cornelius,
A27　　1486?-1535. Three books of occult phi-
O2　　　losophy ... 1651. (Card 2)
1651　Printed by R. W. for Gregory Moule, and are
to be sold neer the West-end of Pauls, 1651.
Copy 1 lacks portrait; copy 2 lacks "An
encomium on the three Books of Cornelius
Agrippa, by Eugenius Philalethes." (sig.a₂)
Portrait in copy 3 mounted.
Translation of De occulta philosophia
libri tres.
　I. His　　　　　De occulta philosophia
libri tres.　　　English. II. Freake,
J., tr. III.　　　Title.

WITCHCRAFT　Thresor d'histoires admirables et memorables
PN　　　de nostre temps.
6262　Goulart, Simon, 1543-1628.
G69　　Thresor d'histoires admirables et memo-
1610　rables de nostre temps. Recueilliies de
plusieurs autheurs, memoires, et auis de
diuers endroits. Mises en lvmiere par Simon Govlart Senlisien. [Genève?] Par
Pavl Marceav, 1610.
2 v. in 1. ([16], 1117, [35] p.) 18cm.

Title vignette.
First published Paris, 1600.

I. Title.

Witchcraft
DC　　Thurston, Herbert, 1856-1939.
104　　　Was she a witch after all?
.1　　　　(In The month. London, 1922. 24cm.
T54　　vol. 139, no. 691, p. [1]-13)

1. Jeanne d'Arc, Saint, 1412-1431. I. Title.

Thusius, Bloemardus, pseud.

see

Costerus, Florentius, fl. 1654-1703.

Thyraeus, Petrus, 1546-1601.

see

Thyraeus, Pierre, 1546-1601.

Thyraeus, Pierre

WITCHCRAFT
BF
1445　Thyraeus, Pierre, 1546-1601.
T54　　Daemoniaci, hoc est: De obsessis a spi-
1598a　ritibvs daemoniorvm hominibvs, liber vnvs.
In qvo daemonvm obsidentivm conditio: obsessorum hominum status ... et his similia,
discutiuntur et explicantur. Avthore Petro
Thyraeo ... Editio secvnda, correctior,
auctior, & exemplis facta illustrior.
Coloniae Agrippinae, Ex officini Mater.
Cholini, sumptib' Gosuini Cholini, 1598.
7 p. l., 3- 207 p. 22cm.
Bound with his Loca infesta. Coloniae Agrippin　　ae, 1598.
8
NIC

WITCHCRAFT
BF
1555　Thyraeus, Pierre, 1546-1601.
T54　　Daemoniaci, hoc est: De obsessis a spiri-
1603　tibvs daemoniorvm hominibvs, liber vnvs. In
qvo daemonvm obsidentivm conditio: obsessorum
hominum status ... et his similia, discutiuntur et explicantur, denuò omnia repurgata et
aucta. Avctore Petro Thyraeo ... Lvgdvni,
Apvd Ioannem Pillehotte, 1603.
324, [4] p. 17cm.

Title vignette (device of J. Pillehotte)
✓ I. Title. ✓ II. Title: De obsessis
a spiritibvs　　　daemoniorvm hominibvs,
liber vnvs.

hcraft
BF
1445　Thyraeus, Pierre, 1546-1601.
T54　　Daemoniaci, hoc est: De obsessis a spiri-
1599　tibvs daemoniorvm hominibvs, liber vnvs. In
qvo daemonvm obsidentivm conditio: obsessorum
hominum status ... et his similia, discutiuntur et explicantur, denuò omnia repurgata et
aucta. Avctore Petro Thyraeo ... Lvgdvni,
Apvd Ioannem Pillehotte, 1603.
324, [4] p. 17cm.

Title vignette (device of J. Pillehotte)
Bound with the author's Loca infesta.
Lvgdvni, 1599.

WITCHCRAFT
BF
1555　Thyraeus, Pierre, 1546-1601.
T54　　Daemoniaci cvm Locis infestis et Terri-
1604　cvlamentis noctvrnis. Id est, libri tres,
qvibvs spiritvvm homines obsidentium atque
infestantium genera, conditiones, &, quas
adferunt, molestiae, molestiarumq; causae
atque modi explicantur ... Coloniae Agrippinae, Ex officini Materni Cholini, Sumptibus Gosuini Cholini, 1604.
21 p. l., 3-210, 396 p. 21cm.
Loca infesta also published separately.
8
NIC

WITCHCRAFT
BF
1555　Thyraeus, Pierre, 1546-1601.
T54　　Daemoniaci cvm Locis infestis et terri-
1627　cvlamentis noctvrnis. Id est, libri tres,
qvibvs spiritvvm homines obsidentium atque
infestantium genera, conditiones, &, quas
adferunt, molestiae, molestiarumq; causae
atque modi explicantur ... Coloniae Agrippinae, Ex officina Choliniana, Sumptibus
Petri Cholini, 1627.
20 p. l., 164, 356 p. 21cm.
Loca infesta also published separately.
8
NIC　　　　(Continued on next card)

WITCHCRAFT
BF
1555　Thyraeus, Pierre, 1546-1601. Daemoniaci
T54　　cum Locis infestis et terricvlamentis noc-
1627　tvrnis ... 1627. (Card 2)

Daemoniaci first published 1694 under
title: De daemoniacis.
1. Demoniac possession. 2. Demonology.
3. Apparitions. 4. Ghosts. I. His De daemoniacis. II. His Loca infesta. III.
Title. IV. Title: Loca infesta.

8
NIC

WITCHCRAFT
BF
1445　Thyraeus, Pierre, 1546-1601.
T54　　Reverendi patris Petri Thyraei ... De
D2　　apparitionibvs spirituum tractatus duo:
1600　quorum prior agit de apparitionibvs omnis
generis spiritvvm, Dei, angelorvm, daemonvm,
et animarum humanarum libro vno ... Posterior continet divinarvm sev Dei in Veteri
Testamento apparitionum & locutionum tam
externarum, quam internarum libros quatuor
nunc primùm editos. Coloniae Agrippinae,
Ex officina Mater. Cholini, sumptibus Gosuini Cholini. 1600.
8　　　　　　(Continued on next card)

WITCHCRAFT
BF
1445　Thyraeus, Pierre, 1546-1601. ... De appari-
T54　　tionibvs spirituum tractatus duo ... 1600.
D2　　　　　　　　　　　　　　　　　(Card 2)
1600　8 p. l., 486 p. 21cm.
Revised and expanded version of his De variis tam spirituum, quam vivorum hominum prodigiosis apparitionibus ... libri tres.
Binding: contemporary blind stamped pigskin, with clasps.
With this is bound his De prodigiosis.
Wircebvrgi [1591?]
1. Apparitions. 2. Ghosts. I. His
De variis tam　　　spirituum, quam vivorum
hominum ... a　　pparitionibus ... libri
tres. II. T　　　itle: De apparitionibus
spirituum tra　　ctatus duo. III. Title.
8

WITCHCRAFT
BF
1445　Thyraeus, Pierre, 1546-1601.
T54　　Reverendi Patris Petri Thyraei ... De
1598a　apparitionibvs spirituum tractatus duo:
quorum prior agit de apparitionibvs omnis
generis spiritvvm, Dei, angelorvm, daemonvm, et animarum humanarum libro vno. Cum
duplici appendice de spirituum imaginibus &
cultu, deque Purgatorij veritate. Posterior continet Divinarvm sev Dei in Veteri
Testamento apparitionum & locutionum tam
externarum, quam internarum libros quatuor
8　　　　　　(Continued on next card)
NIC

547

CATALOGUE OF THE CORNELL WITCHCRAFT COLLECTION

WITCHCRAFT
BF 1445 T54 1598a

Thyraeus, Pierre, 1546-1601. ... De apparitionibvs spirituum tractatus duo ... (Card 2)
nunc primům editos. Coloniae Agrippinae, Officina Mater. Cholini, Sumptibus Gosuini Cholini, 1600.
8 p. l., 486 p. 22cm.
Revised and expanded version of his De variis tam spirituum, quam vivorum hominum prodigiosis apparitionibus ... libri tres.
Bound with his Loca infesta. Coloniae Agrippinae, 1598.

8 NIC

Witchcraft
BF 1555 T54

Thyraeus, Pierre, 1546-1601.
Reverendi p. Petri Thyraei ... De daemoniacis liber vnvs, in qvo daemonvm obsidentivm conditio; obsessorvm hominvm status; rationes item & modi, quibus ab obsessis daemones exiguntur, discutiuntur & explicantur. Cvm indice capitvm, et rervm ac sententiarum memorabilium. Coloniae Agrippinae, ex officina Mater. Cholini, sumptibus Gosuini Cholini, 1594.
5 p. l., 3-130 p. 21cm.
With this is bound his De variis tam spirituum, quam vivorum hominum prodigiosis apparitionibus ... libri tres. Coloniae Agrippinae, 1594.

WITCHCRAFT
BF 1555 T54 1627

Thyraeus, Pierre, 1546-1601.
De daemoniacis.
Thyraeus, Pierre, 1546-1601.
Daemoniaci cvm Locis infestis et terricvlamentis noctvrnis. Id est, libri tres, qvibvs spirituvm homines obsidentium atque infestantium genera, conditiones, &, quas adferunt, molestiae, molestiarumq; causae atque modi explicantur ... Coloniae Agrippinae, Ex officina Choliniana, Sumptibus Petri Cholini, 1627.
20 p. l., 164, 356 p. 21cm.
Loca infesta also published separately.
(Continued on next card)

8 NIC

WITCHCRAFT
BF 1555 T54 1627

Thyraeus, Pierre, 1546-1601.
De daemoniacis.
Thyraeus, Pierre, 1546-1601. Daemoniaci cum Locis infestis et terricvlamentis noctvrnis ... 1627. (Card 2)
Daemoniaci first published 1694 under title: De daemoniacis.
1. Demoniac possession. 2. Demonology. 3. Apparitions. 4. Ghosts. I. His De daemoniacis. II. His Loca infesta. III. Title. IV. Title: Loca infesta.

8 NIC

WITCHCRAFT
BF 1445 T54 D2 1600

Thyraeus, Pierre, 1546-1601, praeses.
De prodigiosis viuorum hominum apparitionibus. Dispvtatio theologica bipartita: et priori qvidem explicantvr illae, in quibus se viui sub propria forma, nunc vigilantibus, nunc dormientibus exhibent: posteriori vero, in quibus ijdem, sub brutorum animantium varijs formis conspiciuntur... Pro gradv responsvrvs est ... Ioannes Henricvs Sylvivs ... praeside P. Petro Thyraeo ... Wircebvrgi, Ex officina typographica Henri-
(Continued on next card)

8

WITCHCRAFT
BF 1445 T54 D2 1600

Thyraeus, Pierre, 1546-1601, praeses. De prodigiosis ... [1591?] (Card 2)
ci Aquensis [1591?]
[80] p. 21cm.
Title in ornamental border.
Binding: contemporary blind stamped pigskin, with clasps.
Bound with his De apparitionibus spirituum tractatus duo. Coloniae Agrippinae, 1600.
1. Apparitions. 2. Ghosts. I. Sylvius, Joannes Henricus, respondent. II. Title.

8

WITCHCRAFT
BF 1445 T54 D2

Thyraeus, Pierre, 1546-1601.
Reverendi P. Petri Thyraei ... De variis tam spirituvm, qvam vivorvm hominvm prodigiosis apparitionibus, & nocturnis infestationibus libri tres. Quorum contenta pagina versa demonstrabit ... Coloniae Agrippinae, Ex officina Mater. Cholini, sumptibus Gosuini Cholini, 1594.
8 p. l., 159 p. 21cm.

1. Apparitions. 2. Ghosts. I. Title: De variis tam spirituum, quam vivorum hominum ... apparitionibus ... libri tres. II. Title.

8

WITCHCRAFT
BF 1555 T54

Thyraeus, Pierre, 1546-1601.
Reverendi P. Petri Thyraei ... De variis tam spirituvm, qvam vivorvm hominvm prodigiosis apparitionibus, & nocturnis infestationibus libri tres. Quorum contenta pagina versa demonstrabit, et rervm ac sententiarum momorabilium. Coloniae Agrippinae, Ex officina Meter. Cholini, Sumptibus Gosuini Cholini, 1594.
8 p. l., 159 p. 21cm.
Bound with his De daemoniacis libri unus. Coloniae Agrippinae, 1594.

8 NIC

WITCHCRAFT
BF 1445 T54 D2 1600

Thyraeus, Pierre, 1546-1601.
De variis tam spirituum.
Thyraeus, Pierre, 1546-1601.
Reverendi patris Petri Thyraei ... De apparitionibvs spirituum tractatus duo: quorum prior agit de apparitionibvs omnis generis spirituvm, Dei, angelorvm, daemonvm, et animarum humanarum libro vno ... Posterior continet divinarvm sev Dei in Veteri Testamento apparitionum & locutionum tam externarvm, quam internarum libros quatuor nunc primům editos. Coloniae Agrippinae, Ex officina Mater. Cholini, sumptibus Gosuini Cholini. 1600.
(Continued on next card)

8

WITCHCRAFT
BF 1445 T54 D2 1600

Thyraeus, Pierre, 1546-1601.
De variis tam spirituum.
Thyraeus, Pierre, 1546-1601. ... De apparitionibvs spirituum tractatus duo ... 1600. (Card 2)
8 p. l., 486 p. 21cm.
Revised and expanded version of his De variis tam spirituum, quam vivorum hominum prodigiosis apparitionibus ... libri tres. Binding: contemporary blind stamped pigskin, with clasps.
With this is bound his De prodigiosis. Wircebvrgi [1591?].
1. Apparitions. 2. Ghosts. I. His De variis tam spirituum, quam vivorum hominum ... apparitionibus ... libri tres. II. Title: De apparitionibus spirituum tractatus duo.

8

Witchcraft
BF 1445 T54 1598

Thyraeus, Pierre, 1546-1601.
Loca infesta, hoc est: De infestis, ob molestantes daemoniorvm et defvnctorvm hominvm spirtvs, locis, liber vnvs. In qvo spirituvm infestantivm genera, conditiones, vires, discrimina, opera ... hisq; similia discutiuntur & explicantur. Avthore Petro Thyraeo ... Accessit eiusdem Libellus de terricvlamentis nocturnis, quae hominum mortem solent portendere. Coloniae Agrippinae, Ex officina Mater. Cholini, sumptib' Gosuini Cholini, 1598.
4 p. l., 352, [7] p. 20cm.

8

WITCHCRAFT
BF 1445 T54 1598a

Thyraeus, Pierre, 1546-1601.
Loca infesta, hoc est: De infestis, ob molestantes daemoniorvm et defvnctorvm hominvm spritvs, locis, liber vnvs. In qvo spirituvm infestantivm genera, conditiones, vires, discrimina, opera ... hisq; similia discutiuntur & explicantur. Avthore Petro Thyraeo ... Accessit eiusdem Libellus de terricvlamentis nocturnis, quae hominum mortem solent portendere. Coloniae Agrippinae, Ex officina Mater. Cholini, sumptib'
(Continued on next card)

8 NIC

WITCHCRAFT
BF 1445 T54 1598a

Thyraeus, Pierre, 1546-1601. Loca infesta ... 1598. (Card 2)
Gosuini Cholini, 1598.
8 p. l., 352 p. 22cm.
Differs from another copy in having the index bound in before p. 1.
With this are bound his Daemoniaci. Coloniae Agrippinae, 1598; and his De apparitionibus. Coloniae Agrippinae, 1600.
Binding: contemporary blind stamped pigskin, with clasps.

8 NIC

Witchcraft
BF 1445 T54 1599

Thyraeus, Pierre, 1546-1601.
Loca infesta, hoc est, De infestis, ob molestantes daemoniorvm et defunctorum hominum spiritus, locis, liber vnus. In qvo spirituvm infestantivm genera, conditiones, vires, discrimina, opera ... hisque similia discutiuntur et explicantur. Avthore Petro Thyraeo ... Accessit eiusdem Libellus de terricvlamentis nocturnis, quae hominum mortem solent portendere. Lvgdvni, Apvd Ioannem Pillehotte, 1599.
[24], 543 p. 18cm.
(Continued on next card)

Witchcraft
BF 1445 T54 1599

Thyraeus, Pierre, 1546-1601. Loca infesta ... 1599. (Card 2)
Title vignette (device of J. Pillehotte)
With this is bound the author's Daemoniaci. Lvgdvni, 1603.

1. Apparitions. 2. Ghosts. I. Title. II. Title: De infestis, ob molestantes daemoniorum et defunctorum hominum spiritus, locis.

WITCHCRAFT
BF 1555 T54 1627

Thyraeus, Pierre, 1546-1601.
Loca infesta.
Thyraeus, Pierre, 1546-1601. Daemoniaci cum Locis infestis et terricvlamentis noctvrnis ... 1627. (Card 2)
Daemoniaci first published 1694 under title: De daemoniacis.
1. Demoniac possession. 2. Demonology. 3. Apparitions. 4. Ghosts. I. His De daemoniacis. II. His Loca infesta. III. Title. IV. Title: Loca infesta.

8 NIC

WITCHCRAFT
BF 1555 T54 1627

Thyraeus, Pierre, 1546-1601.
Loca infesta.
Thyraeus, Pierre, 1546-1601. Daemoniaci cum Locis infestis et terricvlamentis noctvrnis ... 1627. (Card 2)
Daemoniaci first published 1694 under title: De daemoniacis.
1. Demoniac possession. 2. Demonology. 3. Apparitions. 4. Ghosts. I. His De daemoniacis. II. His Loca infesta. III. Title. IV. Title: Loca infesta.

8 NIC

Witchcraft
BF 1565 T56

Tiedemann, Dietrich, 1748-1803.
... Dispvtatio de qvaestione qvae fverit artivm magicarvm origo, qvomodo illae ab Asiae popvlis ad Graecos, atqve Romanos, et ab his ad ceteras gentes sint propagatae, qvibvsqve rationibvs addvcti fverint ii qvi ad nostra vsqve tempora easdem vel defenderent, vel oppvgnarent? ... Marbvrgi, In nova officina libraria academica, 1787.
158 p. 25cm.
With this is bound Ad Adonai, 3 leaves in MSS, in Latin in a German hand.
(Continued on next card)

8

CATALOGUE OF THE CORNELL WITCHCRAFT COLLECTION

Witchcraft
BF 1565 T56
Tiedemann, Dietrich, 1748-1803. ... Dispvtatio de qvaestione qvae fverit artivm magicarvm origo ... 1787. (Card 2)

1. Witchcraft. 2. Jamblichus, of Chalcis. I. Title: De quaestione quae fuerit artium magicarum origo. II. Title.

8

WITCHCRAFT
BF 1582 Z7+ 1495
Tihon, Ferdinand, ed.
Un procès de sorcellerie à Huy en 1495. [Liége] 1904.
7 p. 26cm.
"Extrait de Wallonia. Numéro de janvier 1904."
Documents from Archives de l'état à Liége. Cour de justice de Huy. Reg. 4, fol. 81 v'et ss.
1. Trials (Witchcraft)--Huy, France. 2. Packet, Ysabeal, d. 1495. I. Title.

8 NIC

Tilføjelser til efterretningerne om hexeforfølgelserne i Ribe.
WITCHCRAFT
BF 1584 D4 C552
Bang, Vilhelm.
Tilføjelser til efterretningerne om hexeforfølgelserne i Ribe.
(In: Samlinger til Jydsk historie of topografi. København. 22cm. ser.3, v.3, no.3. 1902. p.271-272)
With, in same issue: Christensen. Christian Villads. Besaettelsen i Thisted.
1. Witchcraft--Denmark. 2. Witchcraft--Ribe, Denmark.

8 NIC

Till Blåkulla.
BF 1584 S9 F15
Fahlgren, Karl.
Till Blåkulla. Trolldomsväsendet i Västerbotten 1675-1677. Umeå, Botnia, 1966.
115 p. 23 cm. 17.50 skr (unb. 9.50 skr).
(S 66-49)
Bibliographical references included in "Källor, litteratur och anmärkningar" (p. 100-115).

1. Witchcraft--Västerbotten, Sweden. I. Title.

67-81560
Library of Congress (2)

WITCHCRAFT
BJ 1408 T57
Tillich, Paul, 1886-1965.
Das Dämonische. Ein Beitrag zur Sinndeutung der Geschichte. Tübingen, J. C. B. Mohr (P. Siebeck), 1926.
44 p. 24cm. (Sammlung gemeinverständlicher Vorträge und Schriften aus dem Gebiet der Theologie und Religionsgeschichte, 119)
"... [ein] Aufsatz, der zwei Vorträge und einiges sonstige Material vereinigt ..."
1. Good and evil. 2. History--Philosophy. I. Title.

8 NIC

WITCHCRAFT
BF 1558 T57
Tillier, S
Om svartebøker. Av statsdyrlaege S. Tillier.
(In Historielaget for Sogn, Bergen, Norway. Tidsskrift. Bergen. 23cm. No. 2 (1912), p. 47-92)
Includes 2 fold. plates, 1 facsim.
1. Magic. I. Title. II. Historielaget for Sogn, Bergen, Norway. Tidsskrift.

8 NIC

WITCHCRAFT
BS 2545 D5 T58
Timmermann, Theodor Gerhard, 1727-1792.
Theodor. Gerhard. Timmermann ... Diatribe antiqvario-medica De daemoniacis Evangeliorvm. Rintelii, Apvd Ant. Henr. Boesendahl, 1786.
90 p. 24cm.

1. Demoniac possession. 2. Bible. N. T.--Commentaries. I. Title: De daemoniacis Evangeliorum. II. Title: Diatribe antiquario-medica De daemoniacis Evangeliorum. III. Title.

8 NIC

Timmermann, Theodor Gerhard, 1727-1792. Diatribe antiquario-medica de daemoniacis Evangeliorum.
WITCHCRAFT
BF 1528 D9 T58
Rütz, Franz Georg Christoph.
Daemonologische fragmenten of byvoegzels tot de Oudheid- en geneeskundige verhandeling van den heer professor Theod. Gerhard Timmerman, over de daemonische menschen, waarvan in de geschiedverhaalen der Evangelien gewaagd wordt. Opgesteld en in 't licht gegeeven door F. G. C. Rütz ... Haarlem, By Plaat en Loosjes, 1789-90.
2 v. in 1. 22cm.
Vol. 2 has imprint: 'sGravenhage, by J. C. Lee uwestyn, 1790.
(Continued on next card)

8 NIC

Tinctorius, Mathias, d. 1632.
Witchcraft
BF 1583 Z7 1632
Franck, Archivrath in Donaueschingen.
Der Hexenprozesz gegen den Fürstenbergischen Registrator Obervogteiverweser und Notar Mathias Tinctorius und Consorten zu Hüfingen. Ein Sittenbild aus den 1630er Jahren. Freiburg im Breisgau, F. X. Wangler, 1870.
42 p. 21cm.

1. Tinctorius, Mathias, d. 1632. I. Title.

Witchcraft
BF 1566 T58
Tindall, Gillian.
A handbook on witches. London, A. Barker [1965]
156 p. illus. 23cm.

1. Witchcraft. I. Title.

BF 1566 T58
Tindall, Gillian.
A handbook on witches. London, A. Barker [1965]
156 p. illus. 23cm.

1. Witchcraft. I. Title.

Tisdall, William, 1669-1735.
Witchcraft
BF 1581 Z7 1711
Account of the trial of eight reputed witches at Carrickfergus, March 31st, 1711
A narrative of some strange events that took place in Island Magee and neighbourhood, in 1711; in consequence of which several persons were tried and convicted at Carrickfergus, for witchcraft. By an eye witness. Belfast, Printed by J. Smyth, 1822.
57 p. 19cm.

Appendix (p. [47]-57); Dr. Wm. Tisdall's account of the trial of eight reputed witches at Carrickfergus, March 31st, 1711. (Copied from the Hibernian magazine, for Jan. 1775, p. 52.)

BF 411 T61
Tissot, Claude Joseph, 1801-1876.
L'imagination: ses bienfaits et ses égarements surtout dans le domaine du merveilleux. Paris, Didier, 1868

1. Imagination. 2. Occult sciences. I. Title.

WITCHCRAFT
BF 1555 T61
Tissot, Claude-Joseph, 1801-1876.
Les possédées de Morzine, ou Le diable qui n'y voit goutte. Par M. J. Tissot. Paris, Didier, 1865.
32 p. 24cm.

"Extrait de la Revue moderne, du 1er mai 1865."

1. Demoniac possession. 2. Morzine, France--History. I. Title. II. Title: Le diable qui n'y voit goutte.

8 NIC

Tissot, J , 1801-1876.
see
Tissot, Claude-Joseph, 1801-1876.

Tissot, Joseph, 1801-1876.
see
Tissot, Claude-Joseph, 1801-1876.

Een toehoorder, pseud.
Witchcraft
BF 1410 B42 1691a no.9
't Voorgevallene in de catechisatie, by Do. Adrianus van Wesel, op Sondagh den 28sten December. Ao. 1692. In de Oudezijds Kapel, opgesteld door een toehoorder. Amsterdam, By D. vanden Dalen, boekverkoper, 1693.
8 p. title vignette. 20 x 16cm.
4°: A⁴.
Black letter.
Van der Linde 177.
Argues for tolerance of views held by Balthasar Bekker and his followers.
(Continued on next card)

8

Een toehoorder, pseud.
Witchcraft
BF 1410 B42 1691a no.9
't Voorgevallene in de catechisatie, by Do. Adrianus van Wesel ... 1693. (Card 2)
No. 9 in vol. lettered B. Bekker. Betoverde weereld.

1. Nederlandse Hervormde Kerk--Doctrinal and controversial works. 2. Wesel, Adrianus van, d. 1710. 3. Bekker, Balthasar, 1634-1698. I. Een toehoorder, pseud.

8

549

CATALOGUE OF THE CORNELL WITCHCRAFT COLLECTION

BF 1503 T66 **Tondriau, Julien L**
Dictionnaire du diable et de la démonologie [par] J. Tondriau & R. Villeneuve. (Verviers, Gérard & Co., 1968).
333 p. illus., facsims., ports. 18 cm. (Marabout université, v. 154) bfr 80.—
(Be 68-3086)
Bibliography: p. [327]-330.

1. Demonology—Dictionaries—French. I. Villeneuve, Roland, 1922- joint author. II. Title.

BF1503.T6   133.4'2'03   78-365611
Library of Congress   69 [1¹]

Tonken, John, fl. 1686.
WITCHCRAFT
BF 1581 T858
A True account of a strange and wonderful relation of one John Tonken, of Pensans in Cornwall, said to be bewitched by some women; two of which on suspition are committed to prison. He vomiting up several pins, pieces of walnut-shels, an ear of rye, with a straw to it half a yard long ... London, Printed by George Croom, 1686.
6 p. 19cm.
Wing T2333.
1. Witchcraft—Cornwall. 2. Tonken, John, fl. 1686.
8

Rare PQ 6437 T7A2 1575
Torquemada, Antonio de, fl. 1553-1570.
Iardin de flores cvriosas, en qve se tratan algvnas materias de hvmanidad, philosophia, theologia, y geographia, con otros cosas curiosas, y apazibles ... Va hecho en seys tratados ... Anveres, En casa de Iuan Corderio, 1575.
[24], 538 p. 13cm.

Colophon: Antverpiae, Typis Gerardi Smits, 1575.
I. Iardin de flores curiosas.

Rare PQ 6437 T7A4 1618
Torquemada, Antonio de, fl. 1553-1570.
Jardin de flores curiosas—English.
Torquemada, Antonio de, fl. 1553-1570.
The Spanish Mandevile of myracles. Or The garden of curious flowers. Wherein are handled sundry points of humanity, philosophy, diuinity, and geography, beautified with many strange and pleasant histories: first written in Spanish by Anthonio de Torquemada, and translated out of that tongue into English. It is diuided into sixe treatises, composed in the manner of a dialogue ... London, Imprinted by Bernard Alsop, by the assigne of Richard Hawkins, 1618.
(Continued on next card)

Rare PQ 6437 T7A4 1618
Torquemada, Antonio de, fl. 1553-1570.
Jardin de flores curiosas—English.
Torquemada, Antonio de, fl. 1553-1570. The Spanish Mandevile of myracles ... 1618. (Card 2)
[6], 325, [3] p. 20cm.

Translated by Lewis Lewkenor although the translation is usually attributed to Ferdinand Walker who published it.
Translation of Jardin de flores curiosas.
I. Lewkenor, Sir Lewis, tr. II. Walker, Ferdinand, fl. 1600, supposed tr. III. His Jardin de flores curiosas—English. IV. Title. V. Title: The garden of curious flowers.

Rare PQ 6437 T7A4 1618
Torquemada, Antonio de, fl. 1553-1570.
The Spanish Mandevile of myracles. Or The garden of curious flowers. Wherein are handled sundry points of humanity, philosophy, diuinity, and geography, beautified with many strange and pleasant histories: first written in Spanish by Anthonio de Torquemada, and translated out of that tongue into English. It is diuided into sixe treatises, composed in the manner of a dialogue ... London, Imprinted by Bernard Alsop, by the assigne of Richard Hawkins, 1618.
(Continued on next card)

Rare PQ 6437 T7A4 1618
Torquemada, Antonio de, fl. 1553-1570. The Spanish Mandevile of myracles ... 1618. (Card 2)
[6], 325, [3] p. 20cm.

Translated by Lewis Lewkenor although the translation is usually attributed to Ferdinand Walker who published it.
Translation of Jardin de flores curiosas.
I. Lewkenor, Sir Lewis, tr. II. Walker, Ferdinand, fl. 1600, supposed tr. III. His Jardin de flores curiosas—English. IV. Title. V. Title: The garden of curious flowers.

Torre, Ludovicus de
see
Torre, Luis de, d. 1635

MSS Bd. WITCHCRAFT BF E736 Z55
Torre, Luis de, d. 1635, supposed author.
Erschröckliche doch warhaffte Geschicht, die sich in der spanischen Statt, Madrileschos genannt, mit einer verheuraten Weibss-person zugetragen, welche von einer gantzen Legion Teuffel siben Jar lang besessen gewest. Und durch Patrem Ludovicum de Torre ... widerumb erlediget worden. München, Durch Nicolaum Henricum, 1608 [ca. 1900]
11 l. illus. 24cm.
Carnap's manuscript copy.
(Continued on next card)

MSS Bd. WITCHCRAFT BF E736 Z55
Torre, Luis de, d. 1635, supposed author.
Erschröckliche doch warhaffte Geschicht, die sich in der spanischen Statt ... zugetragen ... 1608 [ca. 1900] (Card 2)

"Originaldruck in der Kgl. u. Staats-Bibliothek zu München. 8 Bl. in 4°. Sig. A²-B³."
Numerals in the margins indicate pagination of the original.
May have been written by De Torre himself.
1. Demoniac possession. 2. Exorcism. 3. Witchcraft—Spain. 4. Garcia de Rodriguez de Gutierrez, Maria, b. 1564. I. Torre, Luis de, d. 1635, supposed author.

Witchcraft BF 1563 D61
Torre, Raffaelle della.
Tractatus de potestate ecclesiae coercendi daemones.
Diversi tractatvs: De potestate ecclesiastica coercendi daemones circa energumenos & maleficiatos, de potentia ac viribus daemonum. De modo procedendi adversvs crimina excepta; praecipuè contra sagas & maleficos ... Ex diversis jisqve celeberrimis huius aevi scriptoribus ... disputantur. Coloniae Agrippinae, Sumptibus Constantini Munich bibliopolae, 1629.
8, 236, 166 p. 20cm.
(Continued on next card)

Witchcraft BF 1563 D61
Torre, Raffaelle della.
Tractatus de potestate ecclesiae coercendi daemones.
Diversi tractatvs ... 1629. (Card 2)
Contents.—Tractatvs de potestate ecclesiae coercendi daemones circa obsessos & maleficiatos, vnà cum praxi exorcistica, a R. della Torre.—Tractatvs theologicvs de processv adversvs crimina excepta, ac speciatim aduersus crimen veneficij, a A. Tanner.—Tractatvs alter theologicus de sagis et veneficis, a P. Laymanni.—Consilium de sagis, a M. A. Peregrini.
(Continued on next card)

Witchcraft BF 1563 D61
Torre, Raffaelle della.
Tractatus de potestate ecclesiae coercendi daemones.
Diversi tractatvs ... 1629. (Card 3)
Title in red and black.
In double columns except for t. p., dedication, and titles of first, second, and fourth works.
1. Witchcraft. 2. Trials (Witchcraft) 3. Exorcism. I. Torre, Raffaelle della. Tractatus de potestate ecclesiae coercendi daemones. II. Tanner, Adam, 1572-1632. Tractatus theologicus de processu adversus
8 (Continued on next card)

WITCHCRAFT BF 1565 T68 1623
Torreblanca Villalpando, Francisco.
Daemonologia sive De magia natvrali, daemoniaca, licita, & illicita, deq; aperta & occulta, interuentione & inuocatione daemonis libri quatuor ... Avctore Don Francisco Torreblanca Villalpando Cordvbensi ... Nunc cum summariis capitum, rerumq; indice iuris publici facti. Moguntiae, Impensis Ioh. Theowaldi Schönwetteri, 1623.
12 p. l., 632, [42], 76 p. 22cm.
8 (Continued on next card)

WITCHCRAFT BF 1565 T68 1623
Torreblanca Villalpando, Francisco. Daemonologia sive De magia ... 1623. (Card 2)
"Defensa en favor de los libros catolicos de la magia" separately paged.
Title in engraved illustrated border.
Provenance: Monast. S. Michaelis Archang. Bamberg.
Binding: contemporary blind stamped pigskin.
8 (Continued on next card)

WITCHCRAFT BF 1565 T68 1623
Torreblanca Villalpando, Francisco. Daemonologia sive De magia ... 1623. (Card 3)

1. Witchcraft. 2. Occult sciences. 3. Trials (Witchcraft) I. His Defensa en favor de los libros catolicos de la magia. II. Title. III. De magia naturali, daemoniaca, licita, & illicita.
8

WITCHCRAFT BF 1565 T68 1678
Torreblanca Villalpando, Francisco. Daemonologia sive De magia.
Torreblanca Villalpando, Francisco.
D. D. Francisci Torreblanca Cordubensis ... Epitome delictorum, sive De magia: in qva aperta vel occvlta invocatio daemonis intervenit. Editio novissima innvmeris mendis expvrgata, necnon indice rerum & verborum copiosissimo nunc primûm locupletata. Lugduni, Sumpt. Joannis Antonij Huguetan, & Soc., 1678.
4 p. l., 576, [107] p. 23cm.
Title in red and black.
First published 1618 under title Daemonologia sive De magia ...
8 (Continued on next card)

WITCHCRAFT BF 1565 T68 1623
Torreblanca Villalpando, Francisco.
Defensa en favor de los libros catolicos de la magia.
Torreblanca Villalpando, Francisco.
Daemonologia sive De magia natvrali, daemoniaca, licita, & illicita, deq; aperta & occulta, interuentione & inuocatione daemonis libri quatuor ... Avctore Don Francisco Torreblanca Villalpando Cordvbensi ... Nunc cum summariis capitum, rerumq; indice iuris publici facti. Moguntiae, Impensis Ioh. Theowaldi Schönwetteri, 1623.
12 p. l., 632, [42], 76 p. 22cm.
8 (Continued on next card)

CATALOGUE OF THE CORNELL WITCHCRAFT COLLECTION

Torreblanca Villalpando, Francisco.
Defensa en favor de los libros catolicos de la magia.

WITCHCRAFT
BF
1565
T68
1623

Torreblanca Villalpando, Francisco. Daemonologia sive De magia ... 1623.
(Card 2)

"Defensa en favor de los libros catolicos de la magia" separately paged.
Title in engraved illustrated border.
Provenance: Monast. S. Michaelis Archang. Bamberg.
Binding: contemporary blind stamped pigskin.

8   (Continued on next card)

WITCHCRAFT
BF
1565
T68
1678

Torreblanca Villalpando, Francisco.
D. D. Francisci Torreblanca Cordubensis ... Epitome delictorum, sive De magia: in qva aperta vel occvlta invocatio daemonis intervenit. Editio novissima innvmeris mendis expvrgata, necnon indice rerum & verborum copiosissimo nunc primùm locupletata. Lugduni, Sumpt. Joannis Antonij Huguetan, & Soc., 1678.
4 p. l., 576, [107] p. 23cm.
Title in red and black.
First published 1618 under title: Daemonologia sive De magia ...
(Continued on next card)

WITCHCRAFT
BF
1565
T68
1678

Torreblanca Villalpando, Francisco. ...
Epitome delictorum, sive De magia ... 1678. (Card 2)

1. Witchcraft. 2. Occult sciences.
3. Trials (Witchcraft) I. His Daemonologia sive De magia. II. Title: Epitome delictorum, sive De magia. III. Title: De magia. IV. Title.

Torselius, Andreas, respondent.

Witchcraft
BF
1587
D61
no.10

Örnhielm, Claudius Arrhenius, 1627-1675, praeses.
Dissertatio philosophica De magia qvam ... sub moderamine ... Dn. Claudii Arrhenii ... examinandam proponit ... Andreas Torselius ... Holmiae, Excudit Nicolaus Wankif [1679]
2 p. l., 41 p. 21cm.
Imperfect: p. 3-6 wanting.
No. 10 in vol. lettered Dissertationes de magia. 1623-1723.

8   (Continued on next card)

Witchcraft
BF
1552
B48

Tous les démons ne sont pas de l'autre monde.
Berbiguier de Terre-Neuve du Thym, Alexis Vincent Charles, 1765?-1851.
Les farfadets, ou Tous les démons ne sont pas de l'autre monde ... Paris Chez l'auteur [et] P. Gueffier, 1821.
3 v. plates. 21cm.

1. Fairies. 2. Spirits. 3. Demonology. 4. Superstition. I. Title.

566
73

Toussaint Raven, J   E 1934-
Heksenvervolging. [Door] J. E. Toussaint Raven. Bussum, Fibula-Van Dishoeck, 1972, [1973].
135 p. with illus. 21cm.
(Fibulareeks, 23)
Bibliography: p. 109-114.

1. Witchcraft. I. Title

Tractat' de hereticis et sortilegiis.

Witchcraft
BF
1565
G85
1536

Grillando, Paolo.
Paulus Grilládus. Tractat' de hereticis: z sortilegiis omnifariam coitu: eorumqʒ penis. Itē de questionibus: z tortura: ac de relaxatione carceratorum Domini Pauli Grillandi Castilionei: vltima hac impressione summa cura castigat': additis vbilibet sūmariis: prepositoqʒ perutili reptorio speciales sentētias aptissime continente. Veneūt Lugd., Apud Jacobū Giūcti, 1536.
16 p. l., cxxviii l. 17cm.

8   (Continued on next card)

Tractat' de hereticis et sortilegiis.

Witchcraft
BF
1565
G85
1536

Grillando, Paolo. ... Tractat' de hereticis ... 1536. (Card 2)

Title in red and black, with woodcut border.
Printed in double columns.

1. Witchcraft. 2. Heresy. 3. Torture. I. Title: De hereticis et sortilegiis.

Tractat von Bekanntnuss der Zauberer und Hexen.

Witchcraft
BF
1565
B61
1591a

Binsfeld, Pierre, ca. 1540-1598.
Tractat von Bekanntnuss der Zauberer vnd Hexen. Ob vnd wie viel denselben zu glauben. Anfänglich durch den hochwürdigen Herrn Petrum Binsfeldium ... in Latein beschrieben. Jetzt aber der Warheit zu stewr in vnser teutsche Sprach vertiert durch ... Bernhart Vogel ... München, Gedruckt bey Adam Berg, 1591.
4 p. l., 75 (i.e. 150), [6] p. 20cm.
Title in red and black.
With colophon.
(Continued on next card)

Tractat von Bekanntnuss der Zauberer und Hexen.

Witchcraft
BF
1565
B61
1591a

Binsfeld, Pierre, ca. 1540-1598. Tractat von Bekanntnuss der Zauberer vnd Hexen. 1591. (Card 2)

Translation of Tractatus de confessionibus maleficorum & sagarum.
Title vignette shows witches and devils.
1. Witchcraft. 2. Demonology. I. His Tractatus de confessionibus maleficorum & sagarum--German. II. Vogel, Bernhard, tr. III. Title: Tractat von Bekanntnuss der Zauberer und Hexen.

Tractatio juridica De tortura ex foris Christianorum proscribenda.

RARE
HV
8593
T46

Thomasius, Christian, 1655-1728.
Tractatio juridica De tortura ex foris Christianorum proscribenda. Halae Magdeburgicae, Typis Io. Christ. Grunerti, 1759.
38 p. 19cm.

Originally issued in 1705 as diss. with M. Bernhardi as respondent, with title: Disputatio inauguralis juridica De tortura ex foris Christianorum proscribenda.
Bound with the 1705 ed.

8
NIC   (Continued on next card)

Tractatio juridica De usu & abusu torturae.

RARE
HV
8593
B66
1726

Bode, Heinrich von, 1652-1720, praeses.
Tractatio juridica De usu & abusu torturae...quam...MDCXCVII habuit Heinricus de Boden [sic] Editio novissima. Halae Magdeb., sumtu Hendeliano, 1726.
38 p. 21cm.

Diss.--Halle (M. J. Sassen, respondent) 1697.
1. Torture. I. Sassen, Meint Johann, respondent. II. Title.

Tractatio juridica De usu & abusu torturae.

RARE
HV
8593
D612
no.8

Bode, Heinrich von, 1652-1720.
Tractatio juridica De usu & abusu torturae...quam...habuit Heinricus de Boden. Editio novissima. Halae Magdeb., Sumtu Hendeliano, 1735.
40 p. 22cm.

Originally issued as diss., 1697, with M. J. Sassen as respondent.
No.8 in a vol. lettered: Dissertation[e]s de tortura, 1721-92.

8   1.Torture.   I. Sassen, Meint Johann, respo-   ndent. II. Title.
NIC

Tractatus anti pontificius De apparitionibus daemonibus.

WITCHCRAFT
BT
980
M51
1753

Meisner, Johann, praeses.
Tractatus anti pontificius De apparitionibus daemonibus [i.e. daemonum, Von Erscheinungen der Teufel. Francofurt. et Lipsiae, 1753.
94 p. 21cm.

Originally published as diss. at Wittenberg (K. Ortlob, respondent) in 1654, with title: De apparitionibus daemonum ...

1. Devil. 2. Demonology. 3. Apparitions.
I. His [De apparitionibus daemonum.
II. Ortlob, Karl, respondent.

8
NIC

Tractatus contra demonum inuocatores.

Witchcraft
BF
1520
V85
1487

Vivetus, Johannes, fl. 1450.
Contra daemonum inuocatores. [Cologne, Ludwig von Renchen, about 1487]
[42] l. 20cm.

Leaf [1a] (Title): Tractatus contra demonū inuocatores
Leaf [1b]-[2b]: Tabula.
Leaf [3a]: Incipit tractatus ꝑtra demonū inuocatores ꝯpilatus per sacre theologie ꝑfessorē fratrem Johannē viueti. ordinis predicatoɼ inquisitorem apostolicū Carcassone.
(Continued on next card)

Tractatus contra demonum inuocatores.

Witchcraft
BF
1520
V85
1487

Vivetus, Johannes, fl. 1450. Contra daemonum invocatores ... [about 1487] (Card 2)

Leaf [41b] (End): Finit tractatus cōtra demonū inuocatores.
Leaf [42] blank; wanting in this copy.
Signatures: a-d⁸, e¹⁰.
Capital spaces. Capitals, paragraph-marks, initial-strokes and underlines supplied in red.
Copinger. Supplement to Hain's Repertorium, 6273*6274; Proctor, 1282; Brit. Mus.
Cat   (Continued on next card)

Tractatus contra demonum inuocatores.

Witchcraft
BF
1520
V85
1487

Vivetus, Johannes, fl. 1450. Contra daemonum invocatores ... [about 1487] (Card 3)

Cat (XV cent.) I, p. 269 (IA. 4514; author's name: Johannes, Vineti); Goff. Third census, V-310.
With a few manuscript marginal notes.

1. Demonology. 2. Magic. 3. Witchcraft.
I. Title. II. His Tractatus contra demonum inuocatores. III. Title: Tractatus contra demonum inuocatores.

Tractatus criminalis De veneficarum inquisitione.

WITCHCRAFT
BF
1565
H33
1639

Hartz, Konrad.
Tractatvs criminalis De veneficarum inquisitione Cunradi Hartz ... Editio secunda, priori longè auctiori & emendatiori. Rintelii ad Visvrgim, Typis exscripsit Petrus Lucius typog. acad., 1639.
394, [40] p. 15cm.
Published earlier as his Tractatus ... De reorum, inprimisque veneficarum, inquisitione juridice instituenda.
1. Trials (Witchcraft) 2. Witchcraft. I. His Tractatus ... De reorum, in primisque veneficarum, inquisitio   he ... II. Title.
De venefica   rum inquisitione.

XC   MAY 03,'74   COOxc   73-343289

CATALOGUE OF THE CORNELL WITCHCRAFT COLLECTION

Witchcraft
BF 1565
H33
1634

Tractatus criminalis theorico-practicus, De reorum, inprimisque veneficarum, inquisitione.

Hartz, Konrad.
Cunradi Hartz ... Tractatvs criminalis theorico-practicus, De reorum, inprimisque veneficarum, inquisitione juridice instituenda, in foro haud minus, quam scholis apprime utilis & jucundus. Nunc primùm in lucem editus ... cum notis ... anonymi cujusdam in Hassia LL. D. Marpvrgi, Typis & sumptibus Nicolai Hampelii, 1634.
189, [13] p. 20cm.
1. Trials (Witchcraft) 2. Witchcraft. I. Title: De reorum, inprimisque vene ficarum, inquisitione ...

8

Witchcraft
BF 1565
B61
1623

Tractatus de confessionibus maleficorum et sagarum.

Binsfeld, Pierre, ca. 1540-1598.
Tractatvs de confessionibvs maleficorvm et sagarvm. An & quanta fides ijs adhibenda sit? Auctore Petro Binsfeldio ... Accedit eiusdem auctoris Commentarius in tit. cod. lib. 9. de malefic. & mathematic. ... Item bvllae & extravagantes pontificum, &c. Editio quarta correctior & auctior. Coloniae Agrippinae, Sumptib. Petri Hennigij, 1623.
8 p. l., 638, [17] p. 16cm.

8
(Continued on next card)

Witchcraft
BF 1565
B61
1623

Tractatus de confessionibus maleficorum et sagarum.

Binsfeld, Pierre, ca. 1540-1598. Tractatvs de confessionibvs maleficorvm et sagarvm. 1623. (Card 2)

Commentarivs in titvlvm codicis lib. IX. de maleficis et mathematicis, p. 329-611, has special t. p.
Extravagantes et bvllae apostolicae diversorvm pontificum: p. 612-638.
"This was, I think, the last impression of Binsfeld's work. It is merely a reprint of the 4th ed. --that of 1596--the
8
(Continued on next card)

Witchcraft
BF 1565
B61
1623

Tractatus de confessionibus maleficorum et sagarum.

Binsfeld, Pierre, ca. 1540-1598. Tractatvs de confessionibvs maleficorvm et sagarvm. 1623. (Card 3)

last edited by himself. [Signed] G. L. B[urr]" in ms. inside front cover.

1. Witchcraft. 2. Demonology. I. Title: Tractatus de confessionibus maleficorum et sagarum. II. Title: De confessionibus maleficorum et sagarum. III. Title: Commentarius in titulum ... de maleficis et mathematicis.

8

Witchcraft
BF 1555
B86
1714

Tractatus de curatione ac protectione divina.

Brognolo, Candido.
Manuale exorcistarum, ac parochorum: hoc est Tractatus de curatione ac protectione divina; in quo reprobatis erroribus, verus, certus, securus, catholicus, apostolicus, & evangelicus eiiciendi daemones ab hominibus, & è rebus ad homines spectantibus: curandi infirmos: ab inimicis se tuendi: Deumque in cunctis necessitatibus propitium habendi modus traditur ... Venetiis, Apud Nicolaum Pezzana, 1714.
[22], 352, [24] p. 24cm.
(Continued on next card)

Witchcraft
BF 1555
B86
1714

Tractatus de curatione ac protectione divina.

Brognolo, Candido. Manuale exorcistarum ... 1714. (Card 2)
Bound with the author's Alexicacon. Venetiis, 1714.

1. Exorcism. I. Title.

Witchcraft
BF 1565
F93

Tractatus de fascinatione novus et singularis.

Frommann, Johann Christian, b. ca. 1640.
Tractatus de fascinatione novus et singularis, in quo fascinatio vulgaris profligatur, naturalis confirmatur, & magica examinatur ... Norimbergae, Sumtibus Wolfgangi Mauritii Endteri, & Johannis Andreae Endteri Haeredum, 1675.
[78], 1067, [45] p. 21cm.
Added t. p., engraved, dated: 1674.
Manuscript note on t. p.: Bibliotheca Scholar̄ Piar̄: 1783. Colleg. Loevenburgh.
(Continued on next card)

Witchcraft
BF 1565
F93

Tractatus de fascinatione novus et singularis.

Frommann, Johann Christian, b. ca. 1640.
Tractatus de fascinatione ... 1675. (Card 2)

Copy 2 has super exlibris: C[omes] W. G. V[on] N[ostitz]; autograph on t. p.: Jos. Bernhardt Graff von Herberstein; and 17th century vellum binding, with supra libros: I[oseph] B[ernhard] G[raf] V[on] H[erberstein], 1681.

1. Witchcraft. 2. Magic. 3. Superstition. I. Title.

Rare
K
F22T7
1619
++

Tractatus de haeresi.

Farinacci, Prospero, 1554-1618.
Tractatus de haeresi, qui est Opervm criminalivm pars VIII ... Prostat Francofvrti ad Moenum, Sumptibus Haeredum D. Zachariae Palthenij, 1619.

1. Heresy. 2. Canon law. I. Title.

Witchcraft
BF 1565
G85
1536

Tractatus de hereticis et sortilegiis.

Grillando, Paolo.
Paulus Grillādus. Tractat' de hereticis: z sortilegiis omnifariam coitu: eorumq; penis. Itē de questionibus: z tortura: ac de relaxatione carceratorum Domini Pauli Grillandi Castilionei: vltima hac impressione summa cura castigat': additis vbilibet sūmariis: prepositoq; perutili reptorio speciales sentētias aptissime continente. Veneūt Lugd., Apud Jacobū Giūcti, 1536.
16 p. l., cxxviii l. 17cm.

8
(Continued on next card)

Witchcraft
BF 1565
G85
1536

Tractatus de hereticis et sortilegiis.

Grillando, Paolo. ... Tractat' de hereticis ... 1536. (Card 2)

Title in red and black, with woodcut border.
Printed in double columns.

1. Witchcraft. 2. Heresy. 3. Torture. I. Title: De hereticis et sortilegiis.

8

WITCHCRAFT
BF 1569
A2
M72
1561

Tractatus De lamiis et pythonicis.

Molitor, Ulrich, fl. 1470-1501.
Tractatvs De lamiis et pythonicis, autore Vlrico Molitore Constantiensi, ad Sigismundum Archiducem Austriae, anno 1489. Parisiis, Apud Aegidium Gorrozet, 1561.
40 numbered l. 17cm.
First published under title: De laniis [sic] et phitonicis mulieribus.
Imperfect copy: l. 38-40 damaged, some text of l. 40 wanting.
1. Witchcraft. 2. Demonology. 3. Visions. I. His De laniis [sic] et phitonicis mulieribus. II. Title.

8

Witchcraft
BF 1565
G58
1601

Tractatus de magis, veneficis et lamiis.

Godelmann, Johann Georg, 1559-1611.
Tractatvs de magis, veneficis et lamiis, deqve his recte cognoscendis & puniendis ... publice in Academia Rostochiana olim praelectus, & in tres libros distributus, iam denuo recognitus, recensque allegationibus ab ipso contextu characterum diuersitate distinctis, editus à Ioanne Georgio Godelmanno ... Francoforti, Ex officina typographica Ioannis Saurii, Impensis Nicolai Bassaei, 1601.

8
(Continued on next card)

Witchcraft
BF 1565
G58
1601

Tractatus de magis, veneficis et lamiis.

Godelmann, Johann Georg, 1559-1601. Tractatvs de magis, veneficis et lamiis ... 1601. (Card 2)

3 v. in 1. 21cm.
Vols. 2 and 3 each have special t. p. Vol. 2 has title: De lamiis. Vol. 3 has title: Qvomodo contra magos, veneficas et lamias procedatur.

1. Witchcraft. 2. Demonology. 3. Trials (Witchcraft) I. Title: Tractatus de magis, vene ficis et lamiis.

8

Witchcraft
BX 1710
C27
T7

Tractatus de modo procedendi in causis S. Officii.

Carena, Cesare, fl. 1645.
Tractatvs de modo procedendi in cavsis S. Officii, Caesaris Carenae Cremonensis I. C. ... Auditoris, consultoris, & adu. fiscalis Sancti Officij, opus omnibus episcopis, inquisitoribus, & eorum ministris, ac etiam confessarijs perutile, & necessarium. Cremonae, Apud Marc'Ant. Belpıerum, 1636.
26 p. l., 385, [2] p. 20cm.
Later published as part 2 of his Trac-
8
(Continued on next card)

Witchcraft
BX 1710
C27
T7

Tractatus de modo procedendi in causis S. Officii.

Carena, Cesare, fl. 1645. Tractatvs de modo procedendi ... 1636. (Card 2)

tatvs de officio Sanctissimae Inqvisitonis.

1. Inquisition. 2. Heresy (Canon law) 3. Witchcraft. I. Title: Tractatus de modo procedendi in causis S. Officii. II. His Tractatus de officio Sanctissimae Inquisitionis.

8

WITCHCRAFT
K
M375
T7
1537

Tractatus De quaestionibus.

Marsiliis, Hippolytus de, 1451-1529.
Hippolyti de Marsiliis ... Tractatus de q̄stionibus nuperrime recognitus: in quo materie maleficiorū admodum diffuse subtiliterq; pertractant: cū tabula ... per modū numeri et alphabeti diligentissime distributa. Lugd[uni], Ueneunt apud Jacobum Giuncti, 1537.
[27], cxliiij l. 18cm.

Title within woodcut ornamental border; title vignette: author's portrait.
Colophon (l. cxliiija): Hippolyti de Mar-
(Continued on next card)

WITCHCRAFT
K
M375
T7
1537

Tractatus De quaestionibus.

Marsiliis, Hippolytus de, 1451-1529. ... Tractatus de q̄stionibus ... 1537. (Card 2)

silijs ... Lectura super titu. ff. de questionib9 explicit Lugduni impressa p Benedictū Bōnyn impensis ... D. Jacobi .q. Frācisci de Giuncta Florenti. ac sociorū. Anno domini .M.CCCCCXXXVI. Die vero xxiij. mensis Nouembris.
Giunta's device on l. cxliiijb.
Commentary on Digesta, lib. XLVIII, tit.

18.
(Continued on next card)

552

CATALOGUE OF THE CORNELL WITCHCRAFT COLLECTION

WITCHCRAFT Tractatus De quaestionibus.
K   Marsiliis, Hippolytus de, 1451-1529. ...
1375   Tractatus de q̄stionibus ... 1537.
.7   (Card 3)
.537
            From its dedication to Cardinal Grimani,
         the treatise bears, in some editions, the
         title Grimana.
            With this is bound the author's Singula-
         ria. Lugduni, 1546.

            1. Roman law. 2. Corpus juris civilis.
         Digesta. Lib. XLVIII, tit. 18. I. Title:
         Tractatus De quaestionibus. II. Title:
         Grimana.

             Tractatus de reprobis atque maleficis.
ITCHCRAFT
F   Jacquier, Nicolas.
565   Flagellvm haereticorvm fascinariorvm,
19   avtore Nicolao Iaqverio. His accesservnt
          Lamberti Danaei de veneficis dialogi, Ioa-
          chimi Camerarii in Plutarchi de oraculorum
          defectu epistola, Martini de Arles de super-
          stitionibus tractatvs, Ioannis Trithemii de
          reprobis atq; maleficis qvaestiones III,
          Thomae Erasti de strigibus liber. Studio
          Ioan. Myntzenbergij edita. Francofvrti ad
          Moenvm [Impressvm apud N. Bassaeum] 1581.
              604 p. 17   cm.
IC   (Continued on next card)

             Tractatus de superstitionibus.
Witchcraft
BR   Arles y Androsilla, Martín de.
135   Tractatvs de superstitionibus, contra
A72   maleficia sev sortilegia qvae hodie vigent
1559   in orbe terrarum: In lucem nuperrime edi-
          tus. Auctore D. Martino de Arles: in sacra
          theologia professore: ac canonico & archi-
          diacono Pamp. Romae, Apud Vincentium
          Luchinum, 1559.
              1 p. l., 71 numbered l. 15cm.
          Woodcut on t. p.
              Colophon: Romae apvd Vincentivm
          Lvcrinvm 1560.
                     (Continued on next card)

             Tractatus de superstitionibus.
ITCHCRAFT
          Jacquier, Nicolas.
565   Flagellvm haereticorvm fascinariorvm,
9   avtore Nicolao Iaqverio. His accesservnt
          Lamberti Danaei de veneficis dialogi, Ioa-
          chimi Camerarii in Plutarchi de oraculorum
          defectu epistola, Martini de Arles de super-
          stitionibus tractatvs, Ioannis Trithemii de
          reprobis atq; maleficis qvaestiones III,
          Thomae Erasti de strigibus liber. Studio
          Ioan. Myntzenbergij edita. Francofvrti ad
          Moenvm [Impressvm apud N. Bassaeum] 1581.
              604 p. 17   cm.
C   (Continued on next card)

           Tractatus duo perutiles et quotidiani De
                indiciis, quaestionibus et tortura.
ARE
          Suzaria, Guido de.
2545   Tractatus II [i.e. duo] perutiles & quoti-
599   diani De indiciis, quaestionibus et tortura
          ...Guidonis de Suzaria & Pauli Grillandi
          de Castilione, una cum additionib. Ludovici
          Bolognini...geordnet durch Ioannem Guörnerum
          de Vineca. Urselliis, Apud Nicolaum Henri-
          cum, sumptibus Cornelij Suterij, 1597.
              291 p. 16cm.
              Bound with: Saur, Abraham. Notarien Spie-
          gel. Franckfort am Mayn, 1599.
IC   (Continued on next card)

ITCHCRAFT
F   Tractatus duo singulares de examine
565   sagarum super aquam frigidam projectarum
75   (Von der Wasser-Prob der Hexen) in quibus
          hujus purgationis origo, natura & veritas
          curiose inquiritur, variaeque quaestiones
          è theologorum, JCtorum, medicorum & philo-
          sophorum scriptis petitae doctissime &
          jucundè resolvuntur. Francofurti, T. H.
          Grentz, 1686.
              155 p. 20cm.

IC   (Continued on next card)

WITCHCRAFT
BF   Tractatus duo singulares de examine
1565   sagarum ... 1686.   (Card 2)
T75
             Scribonius' Epistola de purgatione sagarum
          previously published under title: De examine
          et purgatione sagarum per aquam frigidam
          epistola.
             Contents.--Jacobi Rickii Discursus de
          proba ut loquuntur aquae frigidae in exami-
          natione maleficarum adhibenda.--Guilielmi
          Adolphi Scri   bonii Epistola de
                          (Continued on next card)

WITCHCRAFT
BF   Tractatus duo singulares de examine
1565   sagarum ... 1686.   (Card 3)
T75
          purgatione sagarum super aquam frigidam
          projectarum.--Hermanni Neuvvalds Exegesis
          purgationis sive examinis sagarum super
          aquam frigidam projectarum in qua refutatur
          Cyrinio Guilielmi Adolphi Sbribonij [sic]

                         (Continued on next card)

WITCHCRAFT
BF   Tractatus duo singulares de examine
1565   sagarum ... 1686.   (Card 4)
T75
             1. Witchcraft. I. Rick, Jacobus, fl.
          1580. Discursus de proba ut loquuntur
          aquae frigidae. II. Scribonius, Wilhelm
          Adolf, 16th cent. Epistola de purgatione
          sagarum. III. Scribonius, Wilhelm Adolf,
          16th cent. De examine et purgatione
          sagarum. IV.   Neuwaldt, Hermann.
                         (Continued on next card)

WITCHCRAFT
BF   Tractatus duo singulares de examine
1565   sagarum ... 1686.   (Card 5)
T75
          Exegesis purgationis. V. Title: Von der
          Wasser-Prob der Hexen. VI. Title: Discursus
          de proba ut loquuntur aquae frigidae. VII.
          Title: Epistola de purgatione sagarum.
          VIII. Title: Exegesis purgationis.

             Tractatus duo: Unus De sortilegiis.
Witchcraft
BF   Grillando, Paolo.
1850   Tractatvs dvo: Vnus De sortilegiis D.
G85   Pavli Grillandi ... Alter De lamiis et ex-
1592   cellentia iuris vtriusque D. Ioannis Fran-
          cisci Ponzinibij Florentini ... Olim qvi-
          dem in lvcem editi; nunc verò recogniti, &
          ab innumeris passim mendis vindicati: adiec-
          to indice locupletissimo. Francoforti ad
          Moenvm [Apvd Martinvm Lechlervm, Impensis
          Haeredvm Christiani Egenolphi] 1592.
              16 p. l.,   299, [1] p. 17cm.
              With colo   phon.
                       (Continued on next card)

           Tractatus magistralis declarans quam
             graviter peccent querentes auxilium a
WITCHCRAFT   maleficis.
BF   Hoogstraten, Jacobus van, ca. 1460-1527.
1565   Ad Reuerendissimū dn̄m dn̄m Philippū sanc-
H77   te ecclesie Coloniensis archiepm̄. Tractat⁹
          magistralis declarans q̄ grauiter peccēt
          q̄rentes auxiliū a maleficis cōpilat⁹ ab
          eximio sacre theologie professore & artiū
          magistro necnō heretice prauitatis inq̄si-
          tore magistro Jacobo Hoechstrassen ordinis
          Predicatorū priore ɋuentus Coloniensis.
          [Colonie, Impressum per Martinum de Werdena]
          1510]
8   (Continued on next card)

           Tractatus magistralis declarans quam
             graviter peccent querentes auxilium a
WITCHCRAFT   maleficis.
BF   Hoogstraten, Jacobus van, ca. 1460-1527.
1565   Ad Reuerendissimū dn̄m dn̄m Philippū sancte
H77   ecclesie Coloniensis archiepm̄ ... [1510]
                                         (Card 2)
              [16] p. illus. 18cm.
              Woodcut illus. on p. [16].
              Running title: Contra petentes remedia
          a maleficis.

              1. Witchcraft. I. Title: Tractatus
          magistralis declarans quam graviter peccent
          querentes au   xilium a maleficis. II.
8   Title: Cont   ra petentes remedia a
          maleficis.

           Tractatus physico-medicus de incantamen-
             tis, sexaginta casus.
WITCHCRAFT
R   Mercklin, Georg Abraham, 1644-1700.
133   Tractatus physico-medicus de incantamen-
M55   tis, sexaginta casus, maxime prae caeteris
1715   memorabiles, complectens; cum subnexis eo-
          rundem judiciis & curationibus cui mantis-
          sae loco accesserunt ... Norimbergae, Im-
          pensis Joh Friderici Rudigeri, 1715.
              254 p. plate. 21cm.

             Reprint, with change of title, of his
          Sylloge physico-medicinalium casuum...
             1. Medicine,   Magic, mystic and spa-
8   giric.   His [Sylloge physico-
NIC   medicinalium   casuum...

             Tractatus polyhistoricus magico-medicus
                 curiosus.
Witchcraft
BF   Gockel, Eberhard, 1636-1703.
1565   Tractatus polyhistoricus magico-medicus
G57   curiosus, oder Ein kurtzer, mit vielen ver-
          wunderlichen Historien untermengter Bericht
          von dem Beschreyen und Verzaubern, auch de-
          nen darauss entspringenden Kranckheiten und
          zauberischen Schäden ... Alles aus berühm-
          ter Alter und Neuer Medicorum Scriptis, auch
          auss eigner Erfahrung und 42jähriger Praxi
          zusammen getragen und hervor gegeben von
          Eberhardo Gockelio ... Franckfurt und
8   (Continued on next card)

             Tractatus polyhistoricus magico-medicus
                 curiosus.
Witchcraft
BF   Gockel, Eberhard, 1636-1703. Tractatus
1565   polyhistoricus ... 1699.   (Card 2)
G57
             Leipzig, Im Verlag Lorentz Kronigers, und
          Gottlieb Göbels sel. Erben Buchhändl. in
          Augspurg, 1699.
              4 p. l., 182 p. 17cm.
             "Mantissa oder ... Geheime Artzney. Mit-
          tel wider die zauberische Schäden und Kranck-
          heiten," p. [134]-182, has special t. p.
             1. Witchcraft. 2. Medicine, Magic, mys-
          tic, and spagi   ric. 3. Medicine--For-
8   mulae, receipt   s, prescriptions. I.
          Title.

           Tractatus posthumus Jani Jacobi Boissardi
             Vesvntini de divinatione et magicis
             praestigiis.
WITCHCRAFT
BF   Boissard, Jean Jacques, 1528-1602.
1750   Tractatus posthumus Jani Jacobi Bois-
B68++   sardi Vesvntini de divinatione et magicis
          praestigiis, quarum veritas ac vanitas
          solidè exponitur per descriptionem deorum
          fatidecorum qui olim responsa dederunt;
          eorundemque prophetarum, sacerdotum, phoe-
          badum, sibyllarum & divinorum, qui priscis
          temporibus celebres oraculis exstiterunt.
          Adjunctis ... effigiebus, ab ipso autore ...
          delineatis;   jam ... aeri incisis per
          Joh. Theodor   de Bry. Oppenheimii,
8   (Continued on next card)

           Tractatus posthumus Jani Jacobi Boissardi
             Vesvntini de divinatione et magicis
             praestigiis.
WITCHCRAFT
BF   Boissard, Jean Jacques, 1528-1602. Trac-
1750   tatus posthumus Jani Jacobi Boissardi
B68++   Vesvntini de divinatione et magicis
          praestigiis ...   (Card 2)

             typis H. Galleri [1616?]
              14 p. l., 358, [11] p. illus., ports.
          32cm.
              Engr. t.-p.
             Engraving on p. 151 (Nicostrata) is
          different in   the two copies.
8   (Continued on next card)

553

CATALOGUE OF THE CORNELL WITCHCRAFT COLLECTION

Tractatus synopticus De retractu consanguinitatis.

Witchcraft
HD
1239
G2
R37
1662

Reinking, Dietrich, 1590-1664.
Theodori Reinkingk ... Tractatus synopticus De retractu consangvinitatis ... in certas quaestiones collectus. Editio secunda priori correctior. Huic accessit ejusdem auctoris Responsum juris accuratè elaboratum de processu contra sagas et maleficos &c. Hactenus suppresso nomine editum. Gissae Hassorvm, Sumptibus Hermanni Velstenii, 1662.
16 p. l., 420, [58] p. 14cm.
Added engrav ed t. p.

8 (Continued on next card)

Tractatus synopticus De retractu consanguinitatis.

Witchcraft
HD
1239
G2
R37
1662

Reinking, Dietrich, 1590-1664. Theodori Reinkingk ... Tractatus synopticus De retractu consangvinitatis ... 1662. (Card 2)

Incomplete: Responsum juris ... wanting. With this in slipcase is his Responsum juris ..., Gissae Hassorvm, 1662, detached from another copy of Tractatus synopticus.
1. Pre-emption--Germany. 2. Pre-emption (Roman la w) I. Title: De retractu consan guinitatis.

8

Tractatus theologicus De magia.

WITCHCRAFT
BF
1600
O82

Osiander, Johann Adam, 1622-1697.
Tractatus theologicus De magia, exhibens ejusdem etymologiam, synonymiam, homonymiam, existentiam & naturam, causas & effectus mirabiles ... Tubingae, Sumptibus Christiani Mülleri, typis Viduae Johann-Henrici Reisii, 1687.
358 p. 20cm.

8
NIC   1. Magic. I. Title.

Witchcraft
GT
6710
T76
1615

Tractatus tragicus De poenis omnium delictorum, quae adversus Deum aut homines admissa & mirabiliter vindicata sunt. Ex probatissimis omnium aetatum scriptoribus diligenter collectus ac libris duobus explicatus per Joannem Polycarium [pseud.?] [Islebiae?] Impensis Henningi Grosij, 1615.
4 p. l., 667, [32] p. 20cm.
With colophon.
First published 1597 under title:
(Continued on next card)

8

Witchcraft
GT
6710
T76
1615

Tractatus tragicus De poenis omnium delictorum ... 1615. (Card 2)

Tragica, seu tristium historiarum de poenis criminalibus, and with dedication signed Henningus Grosius [sic]; no mention of J. Polycarius on t. p. or elsewhere.
This edition is the same printing as that of 1597, but with different t. p. and preliminary leaves.
Book I has caption title: Tragicorvm,
Continued on next card)

8

Witchcraft
GT
6710
T76
1615

Tractatus tragicus De poenis omnium delictorum ... 1615. (Card 3)

seu sylvae tristivm, hoc est, Horribilium historiarum de poenis criminalibus.
Grässe, Bibliotheca magica, attributes this edition to Polycarpus, Johannes.
1. Punishment. 2. Crime and criminals --Biog. I. Grosse, Henning, 1553-1621, comp. II. Polycarius, Johannes. III. Polycarpus, Johannes. IV. Johannes Polycarius. V. Title: Tragicorum, seu sylvae tristium.

8

Traditions et superstitions de la Haute-Bretagne.

Witchcraft
GR
162
B8
S44

Sébillot, Paul, 1846-1918.
Traditions et superstititons de la Haute-Bretagne. Paris, Maisonneuve, 1882.
2 v. 17cm. (Les Littératures populaires de toutes les nations. 9-10)

1. Folk-lore--Brittany. 2. Breton literature. I. Title. II. Series.

Witchcraft
GT
6710
T76

Tragica, seu tristium historiarum de poenis criminalibvs et exitv horribili eorum qui impietate, blasphemia, contemptu & abnegatione Dei, haeresi, magia, execratione, maledicentia ... & omnis generis illicita atq; execrabili vitę turpitudine vltionem diuinam prouocarunt, & mirabiliter perpessi sunt. Libri II ... Islebiae, Procurante & sumptum faciente Henningo Grosio, 1597.
8 p. l., 667. [32] p. 21cm.

8 (Continued on next card)

Witchcraft
GT
6710
T76

Tragica, seu tristium historiarum de poenis criminalibvs ... 1597. (Card 2)

With colophon.
Book I has caption title: Tragicorvm, seu sylvae tristivm, hoc est, Horribilium historiarum de poenis criminalibus.
1. Punishment. 2. Crime and criminals --Biog. I. Grosse, Henning, 1553-1621, comp. VII. Title: Tragicorum, seu sylvae tristium.

8

Witchcraft
GT
6710
T76
1615

Tractatus tragicus De poenis omnium delictorum, quae adversus Deum aut homines admissa & mirabiliter vindicata sunt. Ex probatissimis omnium aetatum scriptoribus diligenter collectus ac libris duobus explicatus per Joannem Polycarium [pseud.?] [Islebiae?] Impensis Henningi Grosij, 1615.
4 p. l., 667, [32] p. 20cm.
With colophon.
First published 1597 under title:
(Continued on next card)

8

Witchcraft
GT
6710
T76
1615

Tractatus tragicus De poenis omnium delictorum ... 1615. (Card 2)

Tragica, seu tristium historiarum de poenis criminalibus, and with dedication signed Henningus Grosius [sic]; no mention of J. Polycarius on t. p. or elsewhere.
This edition is the same printing as that of 1597, but with different t. p. and preliminary leaves.
Book I has caption title: Tragicorvm,
Continued on next card)

8

Witchcraft
GT
6710
T76
1615

Tractatus tragicus De poenis omnium delictorum ... 1615. (Card 3)

seu sylvae tristivm, hoc est, Horribilium historiarum de poenis criminalibus.
Grässe, Bibliotheca magica, attributes this edition to Polycarpus, Johannes.
1. Punishment. 2. Crime and criminals --Biog. I. Grosse, Henning, 1553-1621, comp. II. Polycarius, Johannes. IV. Johannes Polycarius. V. Title: Tragicorum, seu sylvae tristium.

8

Tragicorum, seu sylvae tristium.

Witchcraft
GT
6710
T76

Tragica, seu tristium historiarum de poenis criminalibvs et exitv horribili eorum qui impietate, blasphemia, contemptu & abnegatione Dei, haeresi, magia, execratione, maledicentia ... & omnis generis illicita atq; execrabili vitę turpitudine vltionem diuinam prouocarunt, & mirabiliter perpessi sunt. Libri II ... Islebiae, Procurante & sumptum faciente Henningo Grosio, 1597.
8 p. l., 667. [32] p. 21cm.

8 (Continued on next card)

Tragicorum, seu sylvae tristium.

Witchcraft
GT
6710
T76

Tragica, seu tristium historiarum de poenis criminalibvs ... 1597. (Card 2)

With colophon.
Book I has caption title: Tragicorvm, seu sylvae tristivm, hoc est, Horribilium historiarum de poenis criminalibus.
1. Punishment. 2. Crime and criminals --Biog. I. Grosse, Henning, 1553-1621, comp. II. Title: Tragicorum, seu sylvae tristium.

8

Tragikomische Geisterbeschwörung auf dem Galgenberg bei Jena ... 1715.

Witchcraft
BF
1583
H73

Hollenbach, Wilhelm.
Bilder aus Thüringen. I. Tragikomische Geisterbeschwörung auf dem Galgenberge bei Jena in der Christnacht des Jahres 1715. Nach den Originalquellen wahrheitsgetreu dargestellt ... Mit interessanten Bruchstücken der Streitschrift des Jenaischen Arztes Andreä und den Gutachten der theologischen und juristischen Fakultät zu Leipzig. Jena, F. Mauke (A. Schenk), 1885.
iv, 56 p. 21cm.
No more published?

Traicté des anges et demons.

WITCHCRAFT
BT
960
M24
1616

Maldonado, Juan, 1534-1583.
Traicté des anges et demons, du R. P. Maldonat. Mis en françois, par maistre François de La Borie. Rouen, Chez Iacques Besongne, 1616.
242 l. 15cm.

Illustrated t.p.

1. Angels--Early works to 1800. 2. Demonology. I. La Borie, François de, tr. II. Title.

8
NIC

Train, Joseph, 1779-1852, supposed author.

Witchcraft
BF
1581
W819

The Witch of Inverness and the fairies of Tomnahurich ... Inverness, J. Noble, 1891.
48 p. 19cm.

Attributed to Joseph Train.

1. Witchcraft--Scotland. 2. Folk-lore--Scotland. I. Train, Joseph, 1779-1852, supposed author.

Traité de la démonomanie contre les sorciers.

Witchcraft
BF
1520
B66
P99+

[Puymaigre, Théodore Joseph Boudet, comte de] 1816-1901.
Traité de la démonomanie contre les sorciers, par Jean Bodin. [Metz, ca. 1838]
[169]-184, [236]-256, [307]-324 p. 26cm.
Extracted from Revue de l'Austrasie, according to the Bibliothèque Nationale.
1. Bodin, Jean, 1530-1596. De la démonomanie. 2. Witchcraft--France. 3. Witchcraft. I. Title

8

CATALOGUE OF THE CORNELL WITCHCRAFT COLLECTION

Traité des superstitions selon l'Ecriture Sainte.

Thiers, Jean Baptiste, 1636-1703.
Traité des superstitions selon l'Ecriture Sainte, les decrets des conciles, et les sentimens des saints peres, et des theologiens. Paris, Antoine Dezallier, 1679.
[24], 454 p. 17cm.

1. Superstition. I. Title.

Traité historique et critique des principaux signes dont nous nous servons pour manifester nos pensées.

Witchcraft
B
51
83

Costadau, Alphonse.
Traité historique et critique des principaux signes dont nous nous servons pour manifester nos pensées ... Avec quantité de planches en taille-douce. Lyon, Chez la veuve de J. B. Guillimin & T. l'Abbé [etc.], 1717-20.
7 v. plates. 19cm.
Vols. 5-7 have title: Traité historique et critique des principaux signes qui servent a manifester les pensées, ou le com-
(Continued on next card)

Traité historique et critique des principaux signes dont nous nous servons pour manifester nos pensées.

Witchcraft
CB
51
83

Costadau, Alphonse. Traité historique et critique des principaux signes ... 1717-20. (Card 2)
merce des esprits. Seconde partie. Qui contient les signes superstitieux & diaboliques, pars lesquels certains hommes s'entendent avec les demons, & les demons avec certains hommes. Lyon, Chez les freres Bruyset, 1720.
Ex libris Congault.
(Continued on next card)

Traité historique et dogmatique sur les apparitions.

Witchcraft
BF
1445
L56

Lenglet Dufresnoy, [Nicolas] 1674-1755.
Traité historique et dogmatique sur les apparitions les visions & les révélations particuliéres. Avec des observations sur les Dissertations du r. p. Dom Calmet abbé de Sénones, sur les apparitions & les revenans Par M. l'abbé Lenglet Dufresnoy. Avignon & Paris Chez J. M. Leloup, 1751.
2 v. pl. 18cm.
2-11834

1. Apparitions. 2. Calmet, Augustin, 1672-1757. Dissertations sur les apparitions. I. Title.
Library of Congress, no.

Traité historique et pratique des fascinations.

Witchcraft

Gahagnet, Louis Alphonse, 1809-1885.
Magie magnétique; ou, Traité historique et pratique de fascinations, miroirs cabalistiques, apports, suspensions, pactes, talismans ... 2. éd., corr. et augm.
Paris, G. Baillière, 1858.
516 p. 18cm.
First published 1854.

1. Occult sciences--Hist. I. Title. II. Title: Traité historique et pratique des fascinations.

Traité sur la magie, le sortilege, les possessions, obsessions et malefices.

[Daugis, Antoine Louis]
Traité sur la magie, le sortilege, les possessions, obsessions et malefices, où l'on en démontre la verité & la réalité; avec une methode sûre & facile pour les discerner, & les reglemens contre les devins, sorciers, magiciens, &c. Ouvrage très-utile aux ecclesiastiques, aux medecins, & aux juges. Par m. D***.
Paris, P. Prault, 1732.
2 p. l., xxiv, [4], 304, 18 p. 17cm.

Traité sur les apparitions des esprits, et sur les vampires, ou les revenans de Hongrie, de Moravie, &c.

Witchcraft
BF
1412
C16
1759

Calmet, Augustin, 1672-1757.
Traité sur les apparitions des esprits, et sur les vampires, ou les revenans de Hongrie, de Moravie, &c. Nouv. éd., rev., corr., & augm. Senones, Chez Joseph Pariset, 1759.
2 v. 17cm.
Later ed. of Dissertations sur les apparitions.
"Lettre de M. le Marquis Maffei sur la magie": v. 2, p. 325-393.

Traité sur les miracles.

WITCHCRAFT
BT
97
A2
S48

Serces, Jaques, 1695-1762.
Traité sur les miracles. Dans lequel on prouve que le diable n'en sauroit faire pour confirmer l'erreur ... et où l'on examine le système opposé, tel que l'a établi le Dr. Samuel Clarke, dans le chap. XIX. du II. vol. de son Traité sur la religion naturelle & chrétienne ... Amsterdam, Chez P. Humbert, 1729.
21 p. l., 371 p. 16cm.

8
NIC
Serces takes issue with Samuel
(Continued on next card)

Traité sur les miracles.

WITCHCRAFT
BT
97
A2
S48

Serces, Jaques, 1695-1762. Traité sur les miracles ... 1729. (Card 2)
Clarke's A discourse concerning the being and attributes of God, translated by P. Ricotier as De l'existence et des attributs de Dieu, Amsterdam, 1717. [See RARE B 1365 D32 F8 1717]
1. Miracles--Early works to 1800. 2. Clarke, Samuel, 1675-1729. A discourse concerning the being and attributes of God. 3. Magic. I. Title.

8
NIC

Trall, Janet, d. 1623.

Witchcraft
BF
1581
T97
1676

Two witchcraft trials [of Janet Trall, of Perth, in 1623, and of Isabel Davidson of Aberdeenshire, in 1676.
(In North British advertiser & ladies' journal. Edinburgh. 25cm. v. 70 (1896) p.2.)
"Reprinted from the preface to the 'Presbytery book of Strathbogie.'"

Trance and possession states.

BF
1555
B92

Bucke (R. M.) Memorial Society.
Trance and possession states, edited by Raymond Prince. Proceedings [of the] second annual conference, R. M. Bucke Memorial Society, 4-6 March 1966, Montreal. [Montreal, R. M. Bucke Memorial Society, c1968]
xii, 200 p. illus. 23cm.

1. Demoniac possession--Addresses, essays, lectures. 2. Trance--Addresses, essays, lectures. I. Prince, Raymond, ed. II. Title.

Tranquille, capucin.
see
Tranquille de Saint-Rémi, capuchin.

Witchcraft
BF
1517
F5
T77
1634

[Tranquille de Saint-Rémi, capuchin]
Veritable relation des ivstes procedvres observees av faict de la possession des Vrsulines de Loudun. Et au procés d'Vrbain Grandier. Auec l'arrest donné contre ledit Grandier: ensemble les noms de messieurs les commissaires deputez par le roy. Poictiers, Par I. Thoreav, & la vefue d'An. Mesnier, imprimeurs ordinaires du roy, 1634.
39 p. 27cm.

1. Loudun, France. Ursuline Convent. 2. Grandier, Urbain, 1590-1634. I. Title.

WITCHCRAFT
BF
1517
F5
T77
1634a

Tranquille de Saint-Rémi, capuchin.
Veritable relation des ivstes procedvres observees av faict de la possession des Vrsulines de Loudun. Et au procez d'Vrbain Grandier. Auec les theses generales touchant les diables exorcisez. Par le R. P. Tranquille, Capucin. La Fleche, Chez George Griveav, imprimeur ordinaire du roy, 1634.
80 p. 14cm.
Expanded version of the Poictiers text.
1. Loudun, France. Ursuline Convent. 2. Grandier, Urbain, 1590-1634. 3. Exorcism. I. Title.

Transactiones diabolicae.

Witchcraft
BF
1520
W43

Weissenbach, Joseph Anton.
Transactiones diabolicae, ubi omnia malorum spirituum, quae nunc veniunt in contentionem, citra gratiam, clamorem, sine componuntur. In usus pherochorum scripsit Dr. Jos. Ant. Weissenbach, canonicus Duraquensis. Basileae, Typis E. Thurneysen, 1786.
160 p. 17cm.
With interesting bibliography, p. 148-160.
1. Demonology. 2. Witchcraft. I. Title.

8

Transcendental magic, its doctrine and ritual.

Witchcraft
BF
1612
C75
1938

[Constant, Alphonse Louis] 1810-1875.
Transcendental magic, its doctrine and ritual, by Eliphas Levi [pseud.], translated, annotated and introduced by Arthur Edward Waite. New and rev. ed. New York, E. P. Dutton & company, inc. [1938]
xxxiii p., 1 l., 521, [1] p. front. (port.) illus., plates. 22½cm.
Printed in Great Britain.
Translation of Dogme et rituel de la haute magie.
Imperfect: front. wanting.

Trasfi, Carmette.

Witchcraft
BF
1555
M72
1873

[Molinier, Jean Baptiste] 1835-
Le Diable révolutionnaire; ou, Histoire d'une possédée encore vivante. Traduite de l'espagnol, avec introd. et conclusion sur les oeuvres diaboliques en général et sur les oeuvres diaboliques modernes en particulier, suivie d'un résumé en forme d'épilogue, sur le catéchisme de Satan sur les principaux devoirs et les principales vérités du christianisme ... Par le comte Reinilom de Sneruab [pseud.] Toulouse, L. Hébrail, Durand & Delpuech, 1873.
133 p. 17cm.
1. Demoniac possession. 2. Trasfi, Carmette. I. Title.

Witchcraft
BF
1576
T77

Trask, Richard B
The Devil amongst us; a history of the Salem village parsonage, 1681-1784.
Danvers, Mass., Danvers Historical Society, 1971.
12 p. illus. 23cm.

1. Witchcraft--Salem, Mass. I. Title. II. Title: The Salem village parsonage, 1681-1784.

CATALOGUE OF THE CORNELL WITCHCRAFT COLLECTION

Trautmann, Christian, respondent.

Witchcraft
BF
1520　　Scherzer, Johann Adam, praeses.
S32　　　Daemonologia sive Duae disputationes
　　　theologicae de malis angelis ... praeside
　　　... Dno. Joh. Adamo Scherzero ... nunc
　　　vero conjunctim editae â M. Christiano
　　　Trautmanno ... Lipsiae, Literis Spöre-
　　　lianis, 1672.
　　　　[64] p. 19cm. (bound in 21cm. vol.)
　　　　With this are bound Schwartz, Johann
　　　Conrad, 1677-1747. Dissertatio theologica
　　　De usu et praestantia daemonum. Altdorfii
8
　　　　　　　(Continued on next card)

Trautmann, Christian, respondent.

Witchcraft
BF
1520　　Scherzer, Johann Adam, praeses. Daemono-
S32　　　logia ... 1672.　　(Card 2)

　　　　Noric. [1715], and Breithaupt, Christian,
　　　1689-1749, praeses. Commentatio secunda
　　　De existentia daemonum. Helmstadii [1722]
　　　　In vol. lettered Dissertationes de dae-
　　　monibus. 1672-1722.

8　　1. Demonology.　2. Angels.　I.
　　　Trautmann, Christian, respondent.
　　　II. Title.

Treasury of witchcraft.

Witchcraft
BF
1411　　Wedeck, Harry Ezekiel, 1894-
W38　　　Treasury of witchcraft. New York, Philosophical Li-
　　　brary [1961]
　　　　271 p. illus. 24 cm.
　　　　Includes bibliography.

　　　1. Occult sciences.　2. Witchcraft.　1. Title.

BF1411.W38　　　133.4　　　60-15049 ‡
Library of Congress　　[10]

A treatise concerning enthusiasme.

Rare
BF
575　　Casaubon, Meric, 1599-1671
E6 C33　　A treatise concerning enthusiasme, as
1656　　it is an effect of nature: but is mis-
2 copies　taken by many for either divine inspira-
　　　tion, or diabolicall possession. By Meric
　　　Casaubon, D.D. 2d ed.: rev., and enl. ...
　　　London, Printed by Roger Daniel, and are
　　　to be sold by Thomas Johnson, 1656.

　　　10 p. l., 297 p. 17cm.

　　　1. Enthusiasm.　I. Title.

Treatise of specters.

Witchcraft
BF
1445　　[Bromhall, Thomas]
B86+　　　Treatise of specters; or, An history
　　　of apparitions, oracles ... with dreams,
　　　visions ... Collected out of sundry au-
　　　thours and delivered into English by T.B.
　　　Annexed, a learned treatise, confuting the
　　　opinions of Sadduces [sic] and epicures
　　　... Written in French and now rendred
　　　[sic] into English. London, Printed by
　　　J. Streater, 1658.
　　　　367 p. 28cm.
　　　　With auto　　graph: William Jones.
　　　1. Appari　　tions.　I. Title.

A treatise of specters.

Witchcraft
BF
1445　　Le Loyer, Pierre, sieur de La Brosse, 1550-1634.
L54　　　A treatise of specters or straunge sights,
1605a　visions and apparitions appearing sensibly vnto
　　　men. Wherein is delivered, the nature of
　　　spirites, angels, and divels: their power and
　　　properties: as also of witches, sorcerers,
　　　enchanters, and such like. With a table of the
　　　contents the severall chapters annexed in the
　　　end of the booke. Newly done out of French into
　　　English. London, Printed by Val. S. for M.
　　　Lownes, 1605.
　　　　8 p. l., 145 numb. l., 1 l. 20cm.
　　　　　　　(Continued on next card)

A treatise of specters.

Witchcraft
BF
1445　　Le Loyer, Pierre, sieur de La Brosse, 1550-1634.
L54　　　A treatise of specters ... 1605.　(Card 2)
1605a
　　　　Translated by Zachary Jones.
　　　　"A catalogue of the authours alledged in the
　　　Treatise of specters": prelim. leaves 5-8.
　　　　Translation of only the first book of IIII.
　　　ljvres des spectres.

A treatise of spirits.

Witchcraft
BF
1505　　Daillon, Jacques, ca. 1634-1726.
D13　　　Δαιμονολογία; or, A treatise of
　　　spirits. Wherein several places of Scrip-
　　　ture are expounded, against the vulgar er-
　　　rors concerning witchcraft, apparitions, &c.
　　　To which is added, an appendix, containing
　　　some reflections on Mr. Boulton's answer to
　　　Dr. Hutchinson's Historical essay; entitled
　　　The possibility and reality of magick, sor-
　　　cery and witchcraft demonstrated. London,

　　　　Title transliterated:
　　　　Daimonología.
　　　(Continued on next card)

A treatise of spirits.

Witchcraft
BF
1505　　Daillon, Jacques, ca. 1634-1726. Δαιμονο-
D13　　　λογία. (Card 2)

　　　　Printed for the author, 1723.
　　　　182 p. 19cm.
　　　　Ex libris Lord Hill.
　　　　A Preface, consisting of eight pages,
　　　numbered iii-x, is inserted between the
　　　t.p. and p. v.
　　　　With this is bound his The ax laid to
　　　the root of popery. [London? 1721?]

A treatise of witchcraft.

Witchcraft
BF
1581　　Roberts, Alexander.
A2　　　A treatise of witchcraft: wherein sundry
R64　　propositions are laid downe, plainely discouer-
　　　ing the wickednesse of that damnable art ...
　　　With a true narration of the witchcrafts which
　　　Mary Smith ... did practise: of her contract
　　　vocally made between the Deuill and her, ...
　　　by whose meanes she hurt sundry persons whom
　　　she enuied ... London, Printed by N. O. for
　　　S. Man, 1616.
　　　　80 p. 18cm.

A treatise proving spirits, witches, and
supernatural operations by pregnant
instances and evidences.

Witchcraft
BF
773　　Casaubon, Meric, 1599-1671.
C33　　　A treatise proving spirits, witches, and
O3　　supernatural operations by pregnant instances
1672　and evidences. Together with other things
　　　worthy of note. London, Printed for B.
　　　Aylmer, 1672.
　　　　316 p. 18cm.

　　　　Caption title: Of credulity and incredu-
　　　lity in things natural and civil.
　　　　First ed. pub　　lished in 1668 under
　　　　　　　(Continued on next card)

A treatise proving spirits, witches, and
supernatural operations by pregnant
instances and evidences.

Witchcraft
BF
773　　Casaubon, Meric, 1599-1671.　A treatise
C33　　proving spirits, witches, and supernatural
O3　　operations by pregnant instances and
1672　evidences ... 1672.　(Card 2)

　　　title: Of credulity and incredulity; in
　　　things natural, civil and divine.
　　　　"Reissue of first ed."--British Museum
　　　catalogue.
　　　　Contains a preface "To the reader" dated
　　　1668, which　　explains that the author
　　　was unable to　　write the third part
　　　　　　　(Continued on next card)

A treatise proving spirits, witches, and
supernatural operations by pregnant
instances and evidences.

Witchcraft
BF
773　　Casaubon, Meric, 1599-1671.　A treatise
C33　　proving spirits, witches, and supernatural
O3　　operations by pregnant instances and
1672　evidences ... 1672.　(Card 3)

　　　mentioned in the title. The third part was
　　　published in 1670 under title: Of credulity
　　　and incredulity in things divine & spiritual
　　　...

　　　1. Credulity.　　I. Title.

WITCHCRAFT
BF
1584　　Trechsel, Friedrich, 1805-1885.
S97　　　Das Hexenwesen im Kanton Bern. Aus
T78　　archivalischen Quellen dargestellt.
　　　(In Berner Taschenbuch. Bern. 19cm.
　　　19. Jahrg. (1870), p. 149-234)

8　　1. Witchcraft--Bern, Switzerland.　2.
NIC　Witchcraft--Switzerland.　I. Title.

WITCHCRAFT
BF
1583　　Trefftz, Johannes.
Z7　　　Ein Hexenprozess aus dem Jahre 1676.
1676　　(In Verein für Thüringische Geschichte
2 copies　und Altertumskunde. Zeitschrift. Jena.
　　　23cm. 29. Bd. Heft 1 (1912), p. [171]-
　　　180)

　　　At head of title: IV.

8　　✓ 1. Trials (Witchcraft)--Thuringia.
NIC　 2. Hällwarth, Margarete, d. 1676.
　　 ✓I. Title.

Trembles, Mary, d. 1682.

Witchcraft
BF
1581　　A true and impartial relation of the infor-
T86　　mations against three witches, viz.: Tem-
　　　perance Lloyd, Mary Trembles, and Susanna
　　　Edwards. Who were indicted, arraigned, and
　　　convicted, at the assizes holden for the
　　　county of Devon at the castle of Exon, Aug.
　　　14, 1682. ... As also, their speeches, con-
　　　fessions, and behaviour, at the time and
　　　place of execution ... London, Printed by
　　　F. Collins, and are to be sold by T. Benskin
　　　and C. Yeo, 1682.
　　　　40 p. 21cm.
　　　　　　　(Continued on next card)

Trembles, Mary, d. 1682.

Witchcraft
BF
1581　　A true and impartial relation of the infor-
T86　　mations against three witches ... 1682.
　　　　　　　(Card 2)

　　　　With this is bound Stephens, Edward. A
　　　plain relation of the late action at sea ...
　　　London, 1690.

　　　1. Lloyd, Temperance, d. 1682.　2. Trembles,
　　　Mary, d. 1682.　3. Edwards, Susanna, d. 1682.

Trial of Jennet Preston.

DA
35　　[Potts, Thomas] fl. 1612-1618.
T75　　　Trial of Jennet Preston, of Gisborne, in
v.1　Craven, at the York Assizes, July, 1612; for
　　　practising devilish and wicked arts called
　　　witchcraft. Reprinted from the original edition;
　　　printed at the end of "The wonderful discovery
　　　of witches in the Countie of Lancaster", 4 to.,
　　　1612. London, J. G. Bell, 1851.
　　　　20 p. 19cm.
　　　　"Only sixty copies printed."
　　　　No. 9 in vol.　lettered: Bell's rare
　　　tracts. Vol. I.
　　　1. Preston,　　Jennet, d. 1612.

CATALOGUE OF THE CORNELL WITCHCRAFT COLLECTION

The trial of Richard Hathaway.

WITCHCRAFT

363
1754

Hathaway, Richard, fl. 1702, defendant.
The trial of Richard Hathaway, at Surrey assizes ... upon an information for being a cheat and impostor, and endeavouring to take away the life of Sarah Morduck, on a false accusation of witchcraft; in which is discovered the malicious designs of the said impostor, with an account of his pretended inchantments and witchcraft ... London, Printed for R. Griffiths, 1754.
92 p. 17cm.

(Continued on next card)

Trial of spirits.

CHCRAFT

Pittis, Thomas, 1636-1687.
A discourse concerning the trial of spirits. Wherein inquiry is made into mens pretences to inspiration for publishing doctrines, in the name of God, beyond the rules of the Sacred Scriptures. In opposition to some principles and practices of papists and fanaticks; as they contradict the doctrines of the Church of England, defined in her Articles of religion, established by her ecclesiastical canons, and confirmed by acts of Parliament. By Thomas Pittis ... London, E. Vize, 1683.
4 p. l., 359 p. 18½cm.
Wing P2313
1. Inspiration. 2. Church of England—Doctrinal and controversial works. I. Title. II. Title: Trial of spirits.
Library of Congress   BT125.P6   40-24455
231.74

The trial of the Lancaster witches A.D. MDCXII.

chcraft

8
9

[Potts, Thomas] fl. 1612-1618.
The trial of the Lancaster witches A.D. MDCXII, edited with an introduction by G. B. Harrison. London, P. Davies, 1929.
xlvi p., 1 l., 188 p. 1 illus. 21½cm.
With reproduction of original t.-p.: The wonderfvll discoverie of witches in the covntie of Lancaster ... Together with the arraignement and triall of Iennet Preston, at the assizes holden at the Castle of Yorke ... By Thomas Potts ... London, 1613.
"The arraignement and triall of Iennet Preston" has special t.-p. with imprint: London, 1612.
Revised by   Sir Edward Bromley.

Trial of witches at the Bury assizes.

tchcraft

81
64a

Hale, Sir Matthew, 1609-1676.
Trial of witches, at the Bury assizes, March 10, 1762 [i.e. 1664] before Sir Matthew Hale ... Rose Cullender and Amy Duny, ... were severally indicted for bewitching Elizabeth and Anne Durent ... and ... pleaded not guilty.
[n.p., 1762?]
57-64 p. 21cm.

Reprinted from the original ed. of 1682; evidently detached from a periodical

(Continued on next card)

Trial of witches at the Bury assizes.

tchcraft

581
64a

Hale, Sir Matthew, 1609-1676.
Trial of witches ... [1762?]   (Card 2)

(printed 1762?) but has no identification except paging and "Vol. III" at bottom of p. 57.
1. Cullender, Rose, fl. 1664. 2. Duny, Amy, fl. 1664. I. Title.

Trial of witches in Shetland, A. D. 1644.

81
4a

Intent upon pannel Marion Peebles alias Pardone, spouse to Swene in Hildiswick.
[Edinburgh? 1822?]
10 p. 28cm.
Caption title.
Extract from Hibbert-Ware, Samuel, 1782-1848. A description of the Shetland Islands. Edinburgh, 1822. "... the original document was in the possession of a gentleman of Shetland, lately deceased."

(Continued on next card)

Witchcraft
BF
1581
Z7+
1644a

Trial of witches in Shetland, A. D. 1644 ...
[1822]   (Card 2)

1. Trials (Witchcraft)—Scotland. 2. Peebles, Marion, d. 1644. I. Hibbert-Ware, Samuel, 1782-1848. A description of the Shetland Islands. 3. Guthramdaughter, Margaret, d. 1644.

8

Witchcraft
BF
1565
C84
1616

The triall of witch-craft.
Cotta, John, 1575?-1650?
The triall of witch-craft, shewing the trve and right methode of the discouery: with a confutation of erroneous wayes. London, Printed by George Pvrslowe for Samvel Rand, 1616.
[8], 128 p. 19cm.

1. Witchcraft. 2. Demonology. 3. Criminal procedure. I. Title.

The trials of John Lowes, clerk.

WITCHCRAFT
BF
1581
Z7
1645

Ewen, Cecil Henry L'Estrange, 1877-
The trials of John Lowes, clerk.
[London] 1937.
7 p. 23cm.

1. Lowes, John, clerk, d. 1645. 2. Trials (Witchcraft)—Great Britain. I. Title.

8

The trials of the Lancashire witches.

BF
1581
P37

Peel, Edgar.
The trials of the Lancashire witches; a study of seventeenth-century witchcraft, by Edgar Peel and Pat Southern. Drawings by Pat Southern. New York, Taplinger Pub. Co. [1969]
192 p. illus., facsim., geneal. table, map. 23 cm. 6.50
Bibliography: p. 168-169.

1. Trials (Witchcraft)—Lancashire, Eng.   I. Southern, Pat, joint author. II. Title.
343'.5   72-84973
Library of Congress   69   MARC

Tribunal de supersticion ladina.

WITCHCRAFT
BT
980
N32

Navarro, Gaspar.
Tribunal de supersticion ladina, explorador del saber, astucia, y poder del demonio en que se condena lo que suele correr por bueno en hechizos, agueros, ensalmos, vanos saludadores, maleficios, cōjuros, arte notoria, cavalista y paulina, y semejantes acciones vulgares. Dirigido a Jesus Nazareno. Huesca, Por Pedro Bluson, 1631.
122 l. 21cm.

8
NIC

1. Devil.   2. Demonology.   3. Occult sciences.   I. Title.

Tribunal magicum.

Witchcraft
BF
1600
C14
1658++

Caldera de Heredia, Gaspar.
Tribunal magicvm, quo omnia quae ad magiam spectant, accurate tranctantur & explanantur, seu Tribunalis medici [pars secunda] Lugduni Batavorum, apud Johannem Elsevirium, 1658.
194 p. 37cm.

I. Title.

Ein Trierer Hexenprocess.

Witchcraft
BF
1563
E92++
no.1

Evans, Edward Payson, 1831-1917.
Ein Trierer Hexenprocess. München, J. G. Cotta, 1892.
5-7 p. 32cm. (Beilage zur Allgemeinen Zeitung, Nr. 86)
No. 1 in vol. lettered Evans: Ein Trierer Hexenprocess, etc.

1. Witchcraft. 2. Trails (Witchcraft)—Germany.

Triez, Robert du.

see

Du Triez, Robert.

Witchcraft
BF
1555
G89

Triller, Daniel Wilhelm, 1695-1782.
Exercitatio medico-philologica De mirando lateris cordisque Christi vulnere.
Gruner, Christian Gottfried, 1744-1815.
Christiani Godofredi Grvner ... Commentatio de daemoniacis a Christo Sospitatore percvratis. Accedit Danielis Wilhelmi Trilleri ... Exercitatio medico-philologica De mirando lateris cordisqve Christi vvlnere atqve effvso inde largo sangvinis et aqvae proflvvio. Ienae, Litteris et impensis I. C. Stravssii, 1775.
6 p. l., 64, [3] p. 18cm.

8

1. Demoniac   possession. 2. Jesus
(Continued on next card)

Trinum magicum.

WITCHCRAFT
BF
1405
L85
1673

Longinus, Caesar, ed.
Trinum magicum, sive Secretorum magicorum opus ... Editum à Caesare Longino philos. Francofurti, Sumptibus Jacobi Gothofredi Seyleri, 1673.
12 p. l., 498 p. 14cm.
Contents.—Marci Antonii Zimarae Tractatus magicus.—Appendix, De mirandis quibusdam naturali magia factis operationibus. Ex lib. 2. Mag. nat. Ioan. Bapt. Port.—Tractatvs De virtutibus quarundam herbarum,

8   (Continued on next card)

Trinum magicum.

WITCHCRAFT
BF
1405
L85
1673

Longinus, Caesar, ed.   Trinum magicum ...
1673.   (Card 2)

lapidum & animalium. A. M. A.—Commentatio De magnetica curatione vulnerum citra svperstitionem ... Authore R. G. M. D.—Logia, sive Oracvla Zoroastri ex Platonicorum libris collecta.—Tractatus De proprii cujusqve nati daemonis inqvisitione.
Layout of text corresponds to that of Frankfurt, 1630 ed. (C. Eifrid, printer)

8   (Continued on next card)

Triomphe de l'amour divin sur les puissances de l'Enfer.

WITCHCRAFT
BF
1517
F5
S96

Surin, Jean Joseph, 1600-1665.
Triomphe de l'amour divin sur les puissances de l'Enfer, en la possession de la Mère Prieure des Ursulines de Loudun, 1. partie; et Science expérimentale des choses de l'autre vie. Avec le moyen facile d'acquérir la paix du coeur. Ouvrages posthumes ... Avignon, Seguin aîné, 1829.
xj, 312 p. 18cm.
Parts 1 and 4 of Surin's posthumous works as published   by Seguin.

8
NIC   (Continued on next card)

CATALOGUE OF THE CORNELL WITCHCRAFT COLLECTION

WITCHCRAFT
BF
1517
F5
S96
Triomphe de l'amour divin sur les puissances de l'Enfer.
Surin, Jean Joseph, 1600-1665. Triomphe de l'amour divin ... 1829. (Card 2)
Bound with his Histoire abrégée de la possession des Ursulines de Loudun. Paris, 1828.
1. Exorcism. 2. Jeanne des Anges, mère, 1602-1665. 3. Demonology. 4. Peace of mind. I. His Science expérimentale des choses de l'autre vie. II. Title.

8 NIC

WITCHCRAFT
BX
2340
R72
Le triomphe du saint sacrement sur le démon à Laon en 1566.
Roger, Joseph, abbé.
Histoire de Nicole de Vervins d'après les historiens contemporains et témoins oculaires; ou, Le triomphe du saint sacrement sur le démon à Laon en 1566, par J. Roger ... Paris, H. Plon, 1863.
495 p. fold. plate. 22cm.
1. Nicole de Vervins. 2. Exorcism. I. Title. II. Title: Le triomphe du saint sacrement sur le démon à Laon en 1566.

8 NIC

BF
1503
B65
1971
Le triple vocabulaire infernal.
Blocquel, Simon, 1780-1863.
Le triple vocabulaire infernal: manuel du démonomane; ou, Les ruses de l'enfer dévoilées, par Frinellan, démonographe. Paris, N. Bussière [1971]
319 p. illus. 15 cm. 22.50F
"Réimpression photomécanique."
Frinellan, pseud. of Simon Blocquel.
1. Demonology—Dictionaries—French. 2. Occult sciences—Dictionaries—French. I. Title.
BF1503.B48 1971   74-875408
Library of Congress 71 [2]

Tritemius, Johannes, 1462-1516.
see
Trithemius, Johannes, 1462-1516.

Tritheim, Johann, 1462-1516.
see
Trithemius, Johannes, 1462-1516.

Trithemius, Johannes

MSS
Bd.
WITCHCRAFT
BF
A32
1506
Trithemius, Johannes, 1462-1516.
Antipalus maleficiorum Johannis Trithemii ... [n.p. 16th cent.]
[182] l. 20cm.
Manuscript, on paper, in a Latin hand. Copy of an original in the library of the Elector Joachim.
T. p. and slight corrections to the text are in the hand of Henric Kuhnrath.
Note by G. L. Burr inside front cover states that th is manuscript contains much that was omitted from the (Continued on next card)

MSS
Bd.
WITCHCRAFT
BF
A32
1506
Trithemius, Johannes, 1462-1516. Antipalus malificiorum... [16th cent.] (Card 2)
printed version of 1605.
Bound with Albedach. Liber ... De sortilegiis. [n.p. 1506]
Bound in vellum.

WITCHCRAFT
BF
1565
T83
1605
Trithemius, Johannes, 1462-1516.
Antipalus maleficiorvm Iohannis Tritemii Spanhemensis ... qvatvor libris comprehensvs. Mogvntiae, Apud Balthasarum Lippium, 1605.
275-861 p. 19cm.
According to a note by G. L. Burr inside front cover, this is detached from Paralipomena opusculorum Petri Blesensis, Joannes Trithemii, Hincmari, aliorumque, compiled and edited by Jean Buys.
(Continued on next card)

8 NIC

WITCHCRAFT
BF
1565
T83
1605
Trithemius, Johannes, 1462-1516. Antipalvs maleficiorvm ... 1605. (Card 2)
Contents.—Antipalus maleficiorum.—Liber octo quaestionum, quas illi dissolvenda proposuit Maximilianus Caesar.—De laudibus ordinis Fratrum Carmelitarum.—Tractatus, De laudibus Sanctissimae Matris Annae.—Index Graecorum voluminum Ioannis Trithemii.—Hincmari Rhemensis ... Epistolae duae.—Hymni de solem nitate S. Wigberti.
Binding: 17th cent. blind stamped pig skin, wit h clasps.
(Continued on next card)

8 NIC

WITCHCRAFT
BF
1565
T83
1605
Trithemius, Johannes, 1462-1516. Antipalvs maleficiorvm ... 1605. (Card 3)
1. Witchcraft. I. His Liber octo quaestionum. II. His De laudibus ordinis Fratrum Carmelitarum. III. His De laudibus Sanctissimae Matris Annae. IV. Maximilian I, Emperor of Germany, 1459-1519. V. Hincmarus, abp. of Reims, d. 882. VI. Title: Antip alus maleficiorum.

8 NIC

WITCHCRAFT
BF
1565
T83
1605
Trithemius, Johannes, 1462-1516.
De laudibus ordinis Fratrum Carmelitarum.
Trithemius, Johannes, 1462-1516.
Antipalus maleficiorvm Iohannis Tritemii Spanhemensis ... qvatvor libris comprehensvs. Mogvntiae, Apud Balthasarum Lippium, 1605.
275-861 p. 19cm.
According to a note by G. L. Burr inside front cover, this is detached from Paralipomena opusculorum Petri Blesensis, Joannes Trithemii, Hincmari, aliorumque, compiled and edited by Jean Buys.
(Continued on next card)

8 NIC

WITCHCRAFT
BF
1565
T83
1605
Trithemius, Johannes, 1462-1516.
De laudibus ordinis Fratrum Carmelitarum.
Trithemius, Johannes, 1462-1516. Antipalvs maleficiorvm ... 1605. (Card 2)
Contents.—Antipalus maleficiorum.—Liber octo quaestionum, quas illi dissolvenda proposuit Maximilianus Caesar.—De laudibus ordinis Fratrum Carmelitarum.—Tractatus, De laudibus Sanctissimae Matris Annae.—Index Graecorum voluminum Ioannis Trithemii.—Hincmari Rhemensis ... Epistolae duae.—Hymni de solem nitate S. Wigberti.
Binding: 17th cent. blind stamped pig skin, wit h clasps.
(Continued on next card)

8 NIC

WITCHCRAFT
BF
1565
T83
1605
Trithemius, Johannes, 1462-1516.
De laudibus Sanctissimae Matris Annae.
Trithemius, Johannes, 1462-1516.
Antipalus maleficiorvm Iohannis Tritemii Spanhemensis ... qvatvor libris comprehensvs. Mogvntiae, Apud Balthasarum Lippium, 1605.
275-861 p. 19cm.
According to a note by G. L. Burr inside front cover, this is detached from Paralipomena opusculorum Petri Blesensis, Joannes Trithemii, Hincmari, aliorumque, compiled and edited by Jean Buys.
(Continued on next card)

8 NIC

WITCHCRAFT
BF
1565
T83
1605
Trithemius, Johannes, 1462-1516.
De laudibus Sanctissimae Matris Annae.
Trithemius, Johannes, 1462-1516. Antipalvs maleficiorvm ... 1605. (Card 2)
Contents.—Antipalus maleficiorum.—Liber octo quaestionum, quas illi dissolvenda proposuit Maximilianus Caesar.—De laudibus ordinis Fratrum Carmelitarum.—Tractatus, De laudibus Sanctissimae Matris Annae.—Index Graecorum voluminum Ioannis Trithemii.—Hincmari Rhemensis ... Epistolae duae.—Hymni de solem nitate S. Wigberti.
Binding: 17th cent. blind stamped pig skin, wit h clasps.
(Continued on next card)

8 NIC

CATALOGUE OF THE CORNELL WITCHCRAFT COLLECTION

Witchcraft
A
585
B586
536

Trithemius, Johannes, 1462-1516.
Epistolarum familiarium libri duo ad diuersos Germaniae principes, episcopos, ac eruditione praestantes uiros ... Haganoae, Ex Officina Petri Brubachij, 1536.
[16], 344 p. 20cm.

Title vignette.
Ex libris Frid. Zarncke.

I. Ex Libris--Zarncke, Friderich.
II. Title.

WITCHCRAFT
T
0
83
515

Trithemius, Johannes, 1462-1516.
Ioannis Tritemii ... Liber octo questionū ad Maximilianum Cesarem. Cum priuilegio Cesareae maiestatis de nō imprimēdo in regno ... [Oppenheym, Impressum impensis Iohānis Hasselbergen de Augia Constātiensis dyocesis, 1515]
[78] p. 20cm.
Title vignette with ports. of Maximilian and Trithemius.
With colophon.

NIC   (Continued on next card)

WITCHCRAFT
T
0
83
515

Trithemius, Johannes, 1462-1516. ... Liber octo questionu ad Maximilianum Cesarem ... [1515]   (Card 2)

1. Theology, Doctrinal--Addresses, essays, lectures. 2. Witchcraft. I. Maximilian I, Emperor of Germany, 1459-1519. II. Title: Liber octo questionum ad Maximilianum Cesarem. III. Title.

WITCHCRAFT
BF
1565
T83
1605

Trithemius, Johannes, 1462-1516.
Liber octo quaestionum.
Trithemius, Johannes, 1462-1516.
Antipalus maleficiorvm Iohannis Tritemii Spanhemensis ... qvatvor libris comprehensvs. Mogvntiae, Apud Balthasarum Lippium, 1605.
275-861 p. 19cm.
According to a note by G. L. Burr inside front cover, this is detached from Paralipomena opusculorum Petri Blesensis, Joannes Trithemii, Hincmari, aliorumque, compiled and edited by Jean Buys.

NIC   (Continued on next card)

WITCHCRAFT
65
3
05

Trithemius, Johannes, 1462-1516.
Liber octo quaestionum.
Trithemius, Johannes, 1462-1516. Antipalvs maleficiorvm ... 1605. (Card 2)

Contents.--Antipalus maleficiorum.--Liber octo quaestionum, quas illi dissolvenda proposuit Maximilianus Caesar.--De laudibus ordinis Fratrum Carmelitarum.--Tractatus, De laudibus Sanctissimae Matris Annae.--Index Graecorum volumium Ioannis Trithemii.--Hincmari Rhemensis ... Epistolae duae.--Hymni de solem nitate S. Wigberti.
Binding: 17th cent. blind stamped pig skin, wit h clasps.
(Continued on next card)

Trithemius, Johannes, 1462-1516.
Tractatus de reprobis atque maleficis.
Jacquier, Nicolas.
Flagellvm haereticorvm fascinariorvm, avtore Nicolao Iaqverio. His accesservnt Lamberti Danaei de veneficis dialogi, Ioachimi Camerarii in Plutarchi de oraculorum defectu epistola, Martini de Arles de superstitionibus tractatvs, Ioannis Trithemii de reprobis atq; maleficis qvaestiones III, Thomae Erasti de strigibus liber. Studio Ioan. Myntzenbergii edita.   Francofvrti ad Moenvm [Impressvm apud N. Bassaeum] 1581.
604 p. 17   cm.
(Continued on next card)

BF
1410
L69
1921

Trithemius, Johannes, 1462-1516.
Heinrich Cornelius Agrippa's von Nettesheim Magische Werke : sammt den geheimnissvollen Schriften des Petrus von Abano, Pictorius von Villingen, Gerhard von Cremona, Abt Tritheim von Spanheim, dem Buche Arbatel, der sogenannten Heil. Geist-Kunst und verschiedenen anderen zum ersten Male vollständig in's Deutsche übersetzt : vollständig in fünf Theilen, mit einer Menge Abbildungen.-- 4. Aufl. -- Berlin : H. Barsdorf, 1921.
5 v. in 3. : ill. ; 17cm. -- (Geheime Wissenschaften ; 10-14)

BX
1538
W95
Q3
v.23

Trithemius, Johannes, 1462-1516.
Arnold, Klaus.
Johannes Trithemius (1462-1516) Würzburg, Kommissionsverlag F. Schöningh, 1971.
xi, 319 p. ports. 23cm. (Quellen und Forschungen zur Geschichte des Bistums und Hochstifts Würzburg, Bd. 23)

Originally presented as the author's thesis, Würzburg.
Bibliography: p. 282-306.

1. Tritheminus, Johannes, 1462-1516.

BX
4705
T83
S58

Trithemius, Johannes, 1462-1516.
Silbernagl, Isidor, 1831-1904.
Johannes Trithemius; eine Monographie. Landshut, Krüll, 1868.
245 p. 22cm.

1. Trithemius, Johannes, 1462-1516.
I. Title.

Trittenhemius, Johann, 1462-1516.

see

Trithemius, Johannes, 1462-1516.

Witchcraft
BF
1410
B42
Z56
v.2
no.13

Den triumpheerenden duyvel spookende omtrent den Berg van Parnassus, en beginnende, na sijn gedaane triumph-spokery, te maalen, over seekere hem nog in de weg sijnde swarigheden; gelijk meede over seekere nu in 't ligt gekomene medailje, of penning, verbeeldende de duyvelisten en der selver doen; van welke medailje de beschrijvinge en uytlegginge hier agter gevoegd is.
[Middelburg, By G. Horthemels, boekverkoper, 1692]
24 p.   19 x 15cm.
(Continued on next card)

Witchcraft
BF
1410
B42
Z56
v.2
no.13

Den triumpheerenden duyvel spookende omtrent den Berg van Parnassus ... [1692] (Card 2)

4°: A-C⁴.
Satire defending Balthasar Bekker against the Reformed Church.
Van der Linde 185.
No. 13 in vol. lettered Bekker II.

1. Devil--Fiction. 2. Bekker, Balthasar, 1634-1698. 3. Nederlandse Hervormde Kerk.

Witchcraft
BX
2340
R35
1761

Der triumphierliche Namen Jesus.
Reichle, Franciscus Antonius.
Der triumphierliche Namen Jesus, das ist: Allgemeines, unfehlbahres, und kräftiges Hilfs-Mittel, durch welches ein jeglicher catholischer Christ ... sich, und die seinige von allem Unheil bewahren, ... ja gar den leydigen Teufel selbsten ... verjagen, und überwinden kan. Zum Nutzen des christlichen gemeinen Volcks in teutscher Sprach verfasset ...; das jenige aber, so die Priester und Exorcisten   alleinig betrifft ...

8   (Continued on next card)

Witchcraft
BX
2340
R35
1761

Der triumphierliche Namen Jesus.
Reichle, Franciscus Antonius. Der triumphierliche Namen Jesus ... 1761.
(Card 2)

wird in lateinischer Sprach beygesetzt. Vermehrter in Druck gegeben von Franc. Ant. Reichle ... Costantz, Bey Antoni Labhart, Buchdr., 1761.
143 p. 13cm.
Appendix, p. 60-143, in Latin.
1. Exorcis   m. 2. Witchcraft. I. Catholic Chur   ch. Liturgy and ritual. II. Title.

WITCHCRAFT
BX
2340
T83

Triumphus artis exorcisticae seu Compendiaria, et facillima ratio rite exorcizandi; benedictionis conficiendae super aegros, et aliarum cum suis exorcismis benedictionum; parochis utile, & exorcistis opusculum perutile. Lugani, Typis Agnelli, & soc., 1766.
xvi, 267 p. 18cm.

1. Exorcism. I. Title: Compendiaria, et facillima   ratio rite exorcizandi.

8
NIC

Witchcraft
BF
1775
G12

Tro och öfvertro i gångna tider.
Gadelius, Bror Edvard, 1862-
Tro och öfvertro i gångna tider, af Bror Gadelius.   Stockholm, H. Geber [1912-13]
2 v. illus. 23cm.

1. Superstition. 2. Occult sciences. 3. Folk-lore. I. Title.

8

PQ
2625
A437
T8

Trois âges de la nuit.
Mallet-Joris, Françoise, 1930-
Trois âges de la nuit, histoires de sorcellerie [par] Françoise Mallet-Joris.
Paris, B. Grasset, 1968.
377 p. 21cm.

1. Chantraine, Anne de--Fiction. 2. Ranfaing, Élisabeth de, 1592-1649--Fiction. 3. Harvilliers, Jeanne--Fiction. I. Title.

WITCHCRAFT
BF
1445
L39
1571

Trois livres des apparitions des esprits.
Lavater, Ludwig, 1527-1586.
Trois livres des apparitions des esprits, fantosmes, prodiges & accidens merueilleux qui precedent souuentesfois la mort de quelque personnage renommé, ou vn grand changement és choses de ce monde: traduits d'Alleman en François: conferez, reueus et augmentez sur le Latin. Plus trois questions proposees & resolues par M. Pierre Martyr excellent theologien, lesquelles conuiennent à ceste matiere: traduites aussi de Latin en François. [Genève] De l'Imprimerie de François Perrin, pour Iean Durant, 1571.
(Continued on next card)

559

CATALOGUE OF THE CORNELL WITCHCRAFT COLLECTION

Witchcraft
BF 1445 L39 1571
Lavater, Ludwig, 1527-1586. Trois livres des apparitions ... 1571. (Card 2)

[16], 304, [11] p. 17cm.

Translation of De spectris, lemuribus et magnis atque insolitis fragoribus.

WITCHCRAFT
BF 1584 N6 M44
Mauland, Torkell, 1848-1923.
Trolldom. Kristiania, J. W. Cappelen, 1911.
156 p. 22cm.

8
NIC
1. Witchcraft--Norway. 2. Trials (Witchcraft)--Norway.

WITCHCRAFT
BF 1584 S9 T84
Trolldom och folktro i Sverige på 1600- och 1700-talet. Ur häxprocessernas protokoll.

(In: Budkavlen. Vasa. 24cm. v.6 (1927) no.3, p. 76-84, no.4, p. 111-118)

8
NIC
1. Witchcraft--Sweden. 2. Trials (Witchcraft)--Sweden.

Trolldomsprocesserna i Sverige.
BF 1584 S9 A61
Ankarloo, Bengt, 1935-
Trolldomsprocesserna i Sverige. Stockholm, Nordiska bokhandeln (distr.), 1971.
355 p. illus. 24 cm. (Skrifter utg. av Institutet för rättshistorisk forskning. Serien 1: Rättshistoriskt bibliotek, bd. 17)   kr47.05
S 72-5/6
Thesis--Lund.
Summary in English.
Bibliography: p. 344-354.
1. Trials (Witchcraft)--Sweden. I. Title. II. Series: Institutet för rättshistorisk forskning. Stockholm. Skrifter. Serien 1: Rättshistoriskt bibliotek bd. 17.

3
Library of Congress   72 [2]   72-308069

Trotter, Lionel James, b. 1827, tr.
WITCHCRAFT
BF 1569 M62 1863
Michelet, Jules, 1798-1874.
La sorcière: the witch of the middle ages. From the French of J. Michelet. By L. J. Trotter. London, Simpkin, Marshall and co., 1863.
xii, 403 p. 20cm.

The only authorized English translation.
"List of leading authorities": p. [402]-403.

Truc, Gimel, d. 1609.
Witchcraft
BF 1582 Z7 1609a
Discours véritable d'un sorcier nommé Gimel Truc, natif de Léon en Bretaigne, surprins en ses charmes et sorcelleries au pays de Vivarois. Ensemble les receptes pour guarir le bestail que par sa subtil poison avait mis sur les champs. En l'année 1609. Paris, jouxte la coppie imprimée à Lyon, par H. Bottet, 1609 [1875]
13 p. 23cm.

WITCHCRAFT
BF 1581 T858
A True account of a strange and wonderful relation of one John Tonken, of Pensans in Cornwall, said to be bewitched by some women; two of which on suspition are committed to prison. He vomiting up several pins, pieces of walnut-shels, an ear of rye, with a straw to it half a yard long ... London, Printed by George Croom, 1686.
6 p. 19cm.
Wing T2333.
8   1. Witchcraft--Cornwall. 2. Tonken, John, fl. 1686.

Witchcraft
BF 1563 T86
A true and exact relation of the severall informations, examinations, and confessions of the late witches, arraigned and executed in the county of Essex. Who were arraigned and condemned at the late sessions, holden at Chelmesford before the Rt. Hon. Robert, earle of Warwicke, and severall of His Majesties justices of peace, the 29 of July, 1645... London, Printed by M. S. for H. Overton, 1645.
36 p. 19cm.
(Continued on next card)

Witchcraft
BF 1563 T86
A true and exact relation of the severall informations, examinations, and confessions of the late witches ... 1645. (Card 2)

Preface signed H. F.
No. 1 in vol. lettered: Tracts of witches.

1. Witchcraft.   I. F., H.   II. H.F.

A true and faithful relation of what passed for many yeers between Dr. John Dee ... and some spirits.
WITCHCRAFT
BF 1598 D31 A3++ 1659
Dee, John, 1527-1608.
A true & faithful relation of what passed for many yeers between Dr. John Dee ... and some spirits: tending (had it succeeded) to a general alteration of most states and kingdomes in the world. His private conferences with Rodolphe Emperor of Germany, Stephen K. of Poland, and divers other princes about it. The particulars of his cause, as it was agitated in the Emperors Court; by the Popes intervention: his banishment, and restoration in part. As also the letters of
(Continued on next card)

A true and faithful relation of what passed for many yeers between Dr. John Dee ... and some spirits.
WITCHCRAFT
BF 1598 D31 A3++ 1659
Dee, John, 1527-1608. A true and faithful relation...1659. (Card 2)
sundry great men and princes ... to the said D. Dee. Out of the original copy, written with Dr. Dees own hand: kept in the library of Sir Tho. Cotton ... With a preface confirming the reality ... of this relation ... by Meric. Casaubon. London, Printed by D. Maxwell, for T. Gartwait, 1659.
[78], 448, 45 p. front., 3 tables (1 fold.) 34 cm.
I. Title.

Witchcraft
BF 1581 T86
A true and impartial relation of the informations against three witches, viz.: Temperance Lloyd, Mary Trembles, and Susanna Edwards. Who were indicted, arraigned, and convicted, at the assizes holden for the county of Devon at the castle of Exon, Aug. 14, 1682. ... As also, their speeches, confessions, and behaviour, at the time and place of execution ... London, Printed by F. Collins, and are to be sold by T. Benskin and C. Yeo, 1682.
40 p. 21cm.
(Continued on next card)

Witchcraft
BF 1581 T86
A true and impartial relation of the informations against three witches ... 1682. (Card 2)

With this is bound Stephens, Edward. A plain relation of the late action at sea ... London, 1690.

1. Lloyd, Temperance, d. 1682. 2. Trembles, Mary, d. 1682. 3. Edwards, Susanna, d. 1682.

Witchcraft
BF 1563 W81++ no.3
A True and iust recorde of the information, examination and confession of all the witches taken at S. Oses in ... Essex; whereof some were executed, and other some entreated according to ... lawe. ... Written orderly as the cases were tryed by euidence, by W. W. [pseud.] London, Imprinted by T. Dawson, 1582. [London, at the British Museum, 1923]
[121] p. 14cm.
Signatures: A⁴, A-G⁸, χ¹.

(Continued on next card)
(Over)

Witchcraft
BF 1563 W81++ no.3
A true and iust recorde of ... witches ... at S. Oses ... 1582 [1923]   (Card 2)

"Dedicated to Justice Darcy; and ... evident that it was written by the judge himself."--Cf. Notestein, Wallace. A history of witchcraft in England from 1558 to 1718, p. 348.

Photocopy (negative) 121 p. on 53 l. 20 x 32cm.

No. 3 in vol. lettered: Witchcraft tracts, chapbooks and broadsides, 1579-1704; rotograph copies.

True narration of the strange and grevous vexation by the Devil of 7. persons.
Witchcraft
BF 1555 D22T8
Darrell, John, fl. 1562-1602.
A trve narration of the strange and grevous vexation by the Devil of 7. persons in Lancashire and VVilliam Somers of Nottingham. Wherein the doctrine of possession and dispossession of demoniakes ovt of the word of God is particularly applyed vnto Somers, and the rest of the persons controuerted, togeather with the use we are to make of these workes of God. [London?] 1600.
24 [i.e. 23], 106 p. 19cm.

Witchcraft
BF 1563 W81++ no.13
A True relation of the araignment of eighteene witches, that were tried, convicted, and condemned at ... St. Edmunds-bury... and so were executed the 27. day of August 1645. As also a list of the names of those that were executed, and their several confessions before their execution... London, Printed by I. H., 1645. [London, at the British Museum, 1923]
8 p. 16cm.

(Continued on next card)

Witchcraft
BF 1563 W81++ no.13
A True relation of the araignment of eighteene witches... [1923]   (Card 2)

Photocopy (negative) 8 p. on 5 l. 20 x 32cm.

No. 13 in vol. lettered: Witchcraft tracts, chapbooks and broadsides, 1579-1704; rotograph copies.

1. Witchcraft--England.

CATALOGUE OF THE CORNELL WITCHCRAFT COLLECTION

hcraft

A true relation of the araignment of thirty witches at Chensford in Essex, before Judge Coniers, fourteene whereof were hanged on Friday last, July 25, 1645 ... Setting forth the confessions of the principall of them. Also shewing how the divell had carnall copulation with Rebecca West, a young maid ... London, Printed by I. H. [1645]
6 p. 19cm.

No. 6 in vo   1. lettered: Tracts of witches.

---

itchcraft
775
51

Die trübe Quelle des Aberglaubens an dem Volksglauben und den Wundererscheinungen ... nachgewiesen.
Ammann, Franz Sebastian.
Die Trübe Quelle des Aberglaubens an dem Volksglauben und den Wundererscheinungen, namentlich an der Blutschwitzerin in Zug nachgewiesen. Zürich, Leuthy, 1850.
viii,152 p. 23cm.

1. Superstition. I. Title.

ITCHCRAFT
01
26
87

Trummer, Carl.
Vorträge über Tortur, Hexenverfolgungen, Vehmgerichte, und andere merkwürdige Erscheinungen in der Hamburgischen Rechtsgeschichte. Gehalten in der juristischen Section des geschichtlichen Vereins in Hamburg ... Mit vielen bisher ungedruckten Urkunden und Criminalfällen. Hamburg, J. A. Meissner, 1844-50.
3 v. in 1. 22cm.
Vol. 2 and   3 have title: Vorträge
(Continued on next card)

ITCHCRAFT
01
26
87

Trummer, Carl. Vorträge über Tortur, Hexenverfolgungen, Vehmgerichte ... 1844-50.   (Card 2)

Über merkwürdige Erscheinungen in der Hamburgischen Rechtsgeschichte.

1. Hamburg--History. 2. Law--Hamburg--History. 3. Hamburg--History--Sources. 4. Witchcraft--Hamburg. 5. Fehmic courts. 6. Torture--Germany. I. Title. II. Title: Vorträge über merkwürdigen Erscheinungen in der Hamburgischen Rechtsgeschichte.

---

chcraft

The tryal of Father John Baptist Girard.
Girard, Jean Baptiste, 1680-1733, defendant.
The tryal of Father John Baptist Girard on an accusation of quietism, sorcery, incest, abortion and subornation, before the great chamber of Parlement at Aix, at the instance of Miss Mary Catherine Cadiere ... London, Printed for J. Isted, 1732.
48 p. 23cm.
Bound in sprinkled calf gilt by W. Pratt.

1. Cadière,   Catherine, b. 1709. I. Title.

The tryal of Susanna Martin, at the Court of Oyer and Terminer.
Martin, Susanna, d.1692, defendant.
The tryal of Susanna Martin, at the Court of Oyer and Terminer, held by adjournment at Salem, June 30, 1692... [Pasadena, Castle Press, 1932]
xiii p. 23cm.
"From 'The wonders of the invisible world' by the Rev. Cotton Mather, Boston, 1693."
On cover: Susanna Martin, a martyr to superstition, was executed with others on July 19,1692.   This account of her trial is   reprinted by permission
(Continued on next card)

WITCHCRAFT
BF
1575
M38
1692a

The tryal of Susanna Martin, at the Court of Oyer and Terminer.
Martin, Susanna, d.1692, defendant. The tryal of Susanna Martin...[1932] (Card 2)

from a rare copy in the Henry E. Huntington Library as a tribute from one of the eighth generation...
Presentation copy from John Martin Vincent "to George L. Burr, master of the history of witchcraft."

1.Trials (Witchcraft)--Salem,Mass. I.Mather,Cotton, 1663-1728. The wonders of the invisible world. II.Title.

Witchcraft
BF
1581
Z7
1664b

A tryal of witches, at the assizes held at Bury St. Edmonds.
Hale, Sir Matthew, 1609-1676.
A short treatise touching sheriffs accompts. Written by the Honourable Sir Matthew Hale, kt. ... To which is added, A tryal of witches, at the assizes held at Bury St. Edmonds, for the county of Suffolk, on the 10th of March 1664, before the said Sir Matthew Hale, kt. London, Printed, and are to be sold by Will. Shrowsbery, 1683.
4 p. l., 110 p., 2 l., 59 p. 19cm.
Signatures: A⁴, B-H⁸ (last leaf blank)
2 leaves unsigned, B-B⁸, E⁶.
"A tryal of   witches, at the assizes held at Bury St. Edm   onds ... London, Printed for William Shre   wsbery, 1682" (with special t.-p.) : 2 l., 59 p. at end.

Witchcraft
BF
1563
T75

A tryal of witches, at the assizes held at Bury St. Edmonds.
Hale, Sir Matthew, 1609-1676.
A tryal of witches, at the assizes held at Bury St. Edmonds for the county of Suffolk; on the tenth day of March, 1664, before Sir Matthew Hale ... Reprinted verbatim from the original edition of 1682. With an appendix by C. Clark, esq., of Great Totham, Essex. London, J. R. Smith, 1838.
28 p. 23cm.
No. 3 in vol. lettered Tracts on witchcraft.

1. Trials (Witchcraft)--England.
2. Witchcraft--England. I. Title.

Witchcraft
BF
1563
W81++
no.17

The Tryall and examination of Mrs. Joan Peterson ... for her supposed witchcraft, and poysoning of the lady Powel ... together with her confession ... Also, the tryal, examination and confession of Giles Fenderlyn, who had made a convenant with the Devil for 14 years... London, Printed for G. Horton, 1652. [London, at the British Museum, 1923]
8 p. 16cm.

(Continued on next card)

Witchcraft
BF
1563
W81++
no.17

The Tryall and examination of Mrs. Joan Peterson... [1923]   (Card 2)

Photocopy (negative) 8 p. on 7 l. 20 x 32cm.
No. 17 in vol. lettered: Witchcraft tracts, chapbooks and broadsides, 1579-1704; rotograph copies.

1. Witchcraft--England. 2. Peterson, Joan, d.1652. 3. Fenderlyn, Giles, d. 1652.

Tschudi, Anna Maria.
WITCHCRAFT
BF
1584
S97
Z7
1782a

Lehmann, Heinrich Ludwig.
Freundschaftliche und vertrauliche Briefe den so genannten sehr berüchtigten Hexenhandel zu Glarus betreffend. Zürich, Bey Johann Caspar Füessin, 1783.
2 v. in 1. plate. 19cm.
No more published.

1. Trials (Witchcraft)--Glarus (Canton)
2. Göldi, Anna. 3. Tschudi, Anna Maria.

8 NIC

Tschudi, Anna Maria.
WITCHCRAFT
BF
1584
S97
Z7
1782

Osenbrüggen, Eduard, 1809-1879.
Der letzte Hexenprocess. [Leipzig, 1867]
[513]-529 p. 24cm.
Extracted from Deutsches Museum, Nr. 17, Apr. 25, 1867.

1. Trials (Witchcraft)--Glarus (Canton)
2. Trials (Witchcraft)--Switzerland.
3. Göldi,   Anna. 4. Tschudi, Anna Maria.

8 NIC

MSS
Bd.
WITCHCRAFT
BF
T91++

Tübingen. Universität. Theologische Fakultät.
Urtheil der Würtemb. theol. u. jurist. Facultät zu Tübingen über eine Hexenprozess, 1726. Tübingen, 1726.
[36] l. 33cm.
Manuscript, on paper.
Decision of the theological and law faculties of the university concerning the trial of Barbara Wackher for witchcraft.
On cover: University of Tubingen. Decision re   garding a witch. 1726.
(Continued on next card)

MSS
Bd.
WITCHCRAFT
BF
T91++

Tübingen. Universität. Theologische Fakultät. Urtheil ... über eine Hexenprozess...1726.   (Card 2)

Bound in marbled boards, half-leather.

1. Advisory opinions--Tübingen. 2. Judicial opinions--Tübingen. 3. Trials (Witchcraft)--Tübingen. I. Wackher, Barbara, b. 1680, defendant. II. Tübingen. Universität.   Juristische Facultät.

WITCHCRAFT
BF
1582
T91+

Tuetey, Alexandre, 1842-1918.
La sorcellerie dans le pays de Montbéliard au XVII siècle. D'après des documents inédits ... Avec une préface par Mr Alfred Maury ... Dôle (Jura), A. Vernier-Arcelin, 1886.
x, 94 p. 26cm.

1. Witchcraft--France. 2. Witchcraft--Montbéliard,   France. I. Maury, Louis Ferdin   and Alfred, 1817-1892. II. Title.

8 NIC

WITCHCRAFT
BF
1524
P59
1555

Turini, Turino, tr.
Pico della Mirandola, Giovanni Francesco, 1470-1533.
Dialogo intitolato La strega, overo De gli inganni de demoni dell' illustre Signor Giouan Francesco Pico conte de la Mirandola. Tradotto in lingva toscana per il Signor abate Turino Turini da Pescia ... In Pescia, 1555.
5 p. l., [17]-126 p., 1 l. 21½^cm.
Title within ornamental border.
At end: Stampato in Pescia, appresso Lorenzo Torrentino, stampator ducale, MDLV.
Translation of Strix, sive De ludificatione daemonum dialogi tres.
With this is bound Cattani da Diacceto, F. Discorso ... sopra   la superstizzione dell' arte magica. Fior   enza, 1567.   11-9699
Copy 2.   (Continued on next card)

8

WITCHCRAFT
BF
1524
P59
1864

Turini, Turino, tr.
Pico della Mirandola, Giovanni Francesco, 1470-1533.
La strega ovvero Degli inganni de' demoni. Dialogo di Giovan Francesco Pico della Mirandola, tradotto in lingua toscana da Turino Turini. Milano, D. Daelli, 1864.
xxiv, 135 p. 17cm. (Biblioteca rara, 40)
Translation of Strix, sive de ludificatione daemonum dialogi tres.

8

561

CATALOGUE OF THE CORNELL WITCHCRAFT COLLECTION

Witchcraft
BT
980
T94

Turmel, Joseph, 1859-
  Histoire du diable. Paris, Rieder, 1931.
  296 p. 19cm. (Christianisme. [38])

1. Devil. 2. Demonology. 3. Witchcraft. I. Title. II. Series.

8

WITCHCRAFT
BF
1410
L69
1655

Turner, Robert, fl. 1654-1655, tr.
  Henry Cornelius Agrippa's Fourth book of occult philosophy, and geomancy. Magical elements of Peter de Abano. Astronomical geomancy [by Gerardus Cremonensis]. The nature of spirits [by Georg Pictorius]: and Arbatel of magick. Translated into English by Robert Turner. Philomathées. London, 1655.
  9 p. l., [5]-266 [i.e., 286], [4] p. illus. 19cm.

8   Neither Agrippa nor Abano wrote the works

(Continued on next card)

WITCHCRAFT
BF
1410
L69
1655

Turner, Robert, fl. 1654-1655, tr.
  Henry Cornelius Agrippa's Fourth book of occult philosophy, and geomancy ... 1655. (Card 2)

here ascribed to them; the Heptameron, or Magical elements also was ascribed to Agrippa under the title: Les oeuvres magiques, with Abano as translator (!)
  Translation of a work variously titled Liber de ceremonijs magicis; and his De occulta philosophia, liber quartus.

8   (Continued on next card)

Rare
BL
230
T95++
1697

Turner, William, 1653-1701.
  A compleat history of the most remarkable providences, both of judgment and mercy, which have happened in this present age; extracted from the best writers ... to which is added whatever is curious in the works of nature and art ... being a work set on foot thirty years ago by the Reverend Mr. Pool ... London, John Dunton, 1697.
  1v. (various pagings) 35cm.

I. Title.

Twee brieven van Balthasar Bekker predikant tot Amsterdam, aan Everhardus vander Hooght predikant tot Niewendam.

Witchcraft
BF
1410
B42
Z56
v.3
no.28

Bekker, Balthasar, 1634-1698.
  Twee brieven van Balthasar Bekker predikant tot Amsterdam, aan Everhardus vander Hooght predikant tot Niewendam. D'eerste voor desen uitgegeven van den 25. September 1691, uit Amsterdam. D'andere nu daar by gevoegd, van den 3/13 Juny 1692, uit Franeker. Beide over het boek genaamd De betoverde weereld, en 't gene daar ontrent is voorgevallen. Met een kort beright over de voorrede van seker Opstel van aanmerkingen

8   (Continued on next card)

Twee brieven van Balthasar Bekker predikant tot Amsterdam, aan Everhardus vander Hooght predikant tot Niewendam.

Witchcraft
BF
1410
B42
Z56
v.3
no.28

Bekker, Balthasar, 1634-1698. Twee brieven ... aan Everhardus vander Hooght ... 1692. (Card 2)

gemaakt door J. J. F. B. en tot Leewarden by Hero Nauta gedrukt. Franeker, By Leonardus Strik, boekverkoper, 1692.
  2 p. l., 32 p. title vignette, illus. initials. 19 x 15cm.
  $4°: \pi^2, A-D^4$.
  Back of t. p. autographed by Bekker.

8   (Continued on next card)

Twee brieven van Balthasar Bekker predikant tot Amsterdam, aan Everhardus vander Hooght predikant tot Niewendam.

Witchcraft
BF
1410
B42
Z56
v.3
no.28

Bekker, Balthasar, 1634-1698. Twee brieven ... aan Everhardus vander Hooght ... 1692. (Card 3)

Variant of van der Linde 107: has p. 31-32.
  No. 28 in vol. lettered Bekker III.
  1. Bekker, Balthasar, 1634-1698. De betoverde weereld. 2. Opstel van enige aanmerkingen op het boek van B. Bekker. I. Hooght, Everard van der, d. 1716. II. Title.

8

Tweede brief van Haggébher philaleethees, geschreeven aan zynen vriend N. N. ...

Witchcraft
BF
1410
B42
Z56
v.3
no.24

[Hooght, Everard van der] d. 1716.
  Tweede brief van הגבר [Haggébher] ΦΙΛΑΛΗΘΗΣ [philaleethees], geschreeven aan zynen vriend N. N. over de ordentelyke kerkelyke proceduuren, gehouden tegen den persoon ende het boek van Do. Balthasar Bekker, by zyn E. geintitueleert De betoverde wereld. Met eenige ecclesiastique, theologische, dogmatische ende philologische aanmerkingen over de zelve. Amsterdam, By G. Borstius, boekverkoper, 1691.
  [19]-40 p. title vignette, illus. initial. 19 x 15cm.

8   (Continued on next card)

Tweede brief van Haggébher philaleethees, geschreeven aan zynen vriend N. N. ...

Witchcraft
BF
1410
B42
Z56
v.3
no.24

[Hooght, Everard van der] d. 1716. Tweede brief ... aan zynen vriend N. N. ... 1691. (Card 2)

$4°: \pi 1, A-B^4, C^2$.
  Black letter.
  The friend N. N. is Jacobus Schuts?
  Van der Linde 98.
  No. 24 in vol. lettered Bekker III.
  1. Bekker, Balthasar, 1634-1698. 2. Bekker, Balthasar, 1634-1698. De betoverde weereld. 3. Nederlandse Hervormde Kerk. I. Schuts, Jacobus. II. Title.

8

Tweede missive aen d'Heer Balthasar Bekker.

Witchcraft
BF
1410
B42
Z69
no.30

[Schuts, Jacobus]
  Tweede missive aen d'Heer Balthasar Bekker, over sijn Betooverde weereld, Daniel, en den 2den druk van de Cometen. Waar in benessens Orchards, en Philopaters genoegdoeninge, Daillions wederlegginge ook aangeroert word; en getoont, dat het woord Daimones met alle vereischte wettelijkheid vertaalt word Duivelen. Ende in het stuk van de Prophetien, en de Cometen word de saak eenigermate betrekkelijk gemaakt, op de Schriften van D. Koelman en D. Brink Met den korten inhoud van de eerste

(Continued on next card)

Tweede missive aen d'Heer Balthasar Bekker.

Witchcraft
BF
1410
B42
Z69
no.30

[Schuts, Jacobus] Tweede missive aen d'Heer Balthasar Bekker ... 1692. (Card 2)

Missive. D'Opdragt toont, dat Ericus Walten, in sijn Brief aan een Regent van Amsteldam, ydelijk voorgeest, dat het voor den Staat dezer Landen gevaarlijk is, de zaak van Dr. Bekker verder, in synoden, of andersins, te laten verhandelen, of Decideren. 's Gravenhage, By B. Beek en M. Uitwerf, 1692.
  [24], 72 p. 21cm.
  Signatures: $4°: †-3†^4, A-I^4$. (Leaf I^2 is mis-signed as H^2)
  Van der Linde 148.

Witchcraft
BS
2545
D5
T97
no.3

Twells, Leonard, d. 1742.
  An answer to the Enquiry into the meaning of demoniacks in the New Testament: shewing that the demons therein spoken of were fallen angels; and that the demoniacks were persons really possessed. In a letter to the author. ...
  London, Printed for R. Gosling, 1737.
  74 p. 21cm.

No. 3 in vol. lettered: Twells, Whiston, etc. Tracts on the demoniacs in the New Testament. London, 1738-1775.

1. Sykes, Arthur Ashley, 1684?-1756. An enquiry into the meaning of demoniacks in the New Testament. I. Title.

Witchcraft
BS
2545
D5
T97
no.5

Twells, Leonard, d. 1742.
  An answer to the Enquiry into the meaning of demoniacks in the New Testament.
  [Sykes, Arthur Ashley] 1684?-1756.
  A further enquiry into the meaning of demoniacks in the New Testament. Wherein the Enquiry is vindicated against the objections of ... Mr. Twells, and of the author of the Essay in answer to it [i.e. Thomas Church. ... London, Printed for J. Roberts, 1737.
  116 p. 21cm.

No. 5 in vol. lettered: Twells, Whiston, etc. Tracts on the demoniacs in the New Testament. London, 1737-1775.

Witchcraft
BS
2545
D5
T97
no.6

Twells, Leonard, d. 1742.
  An answer to the Further enquiry into the meaning of demoniacks in the New Testament. Wherein the arguments to prove that the demons of the New Testament were fallen angels are defended; and the objections against the scheme of the Enquiry are made good. In a second letter to the author.
  London, Printed for R. Gosling, 1738.
  92 p. 21cm.

(Continued on next card)

Witchcraft
BS
2545
D5
T97
no.6

Twells, Leonard, d. 1742. An answer to the Further enquiry into the meaning of demoniacks in the New Testament... 1738. (Card 2)

No. 6 in vol. lettered: Twells, Whiston, etc. Tracts on the demoniacs in the New Testament. London, 1738-1775.

1. Sykes, Arthur Ashley, 1684?-1756. A further enquiry into the meaning of demoniacks in the New Testament. I. Title.

Twells, Leonard, d. 1742. An answer to the Further enquiry into the meaning of demoniacks in the New Testament.

Witchcraft
BS
2545
D5
T75
no.3

[Sharpe, Gregory] 1713-1771.
  A review of the controversy about the meaning of demoniacks in the New-Testament. In which Mr. Hutchinson's sermon at Oxford ..., the Reply to the Further enquiry, Mr. Twell's Answer to the Further enquiry, and a tract, entitled, Some thoughts on the miracles of Jesus, by an impartial hand, are considered. By a lover of truth. ... London, Printed for J. Roberts, 1739.
  80 p. 20cm.
  No. 3 in vol. lettered: Tracts on demoniacks. 1737.

Witchcraft
BF
1581
T97
1676

Two witchcraft trials [of Janet Trall, of Perth, in 1623, and of Isabel Davidson, of Aberdeenshire, in 1676]
  (In North British advertiser & ladies' journal. Edinburgh. 25cm. v. 70 (1896) p. 2.)
  "Reprinted from the preface to the 'Presbytery book of Strathbogie.'"

1. Witchcraft--Scotland. 2. Trall, Janet d. 1623. 3. Davidson, Isabel, d. 1676.

FILM
470
reel
283

Twyne, Thomas, 1543-1613, supposed translator.
  Daneau, Lambert, ca. 1530-1595.
  A dialogue of witches in foretime named lot tellers, and novv commonly called sorcerers Written in Latin by Lambertus Danaeus. And translated into English. [London] Printed R. W[atkins], 1575.
  The translation is sometimes attributed to Thomas Twyne. cf. Short-title catalogue.
  Translation of De veneficis, quos olim sortilegos ... vocant.
  University microfilms no. 12047 (case 48, carton 283)
  Short-title catalogue no. 6226.

(Continued on next card)

CATALOGUE OF THE CORNELL WITCHCRAFT COLLECTION

Tyraeus, Pierre, 1546-1601.
   see
Thyraeus, Pierre, 1546-1601.

CATALOGUE OF THE CORNELL WITCHCRAFT COLLECTION

U

Ubbidente dell'Osa, Ardoino, pseud.

see

Simon, Jordan, pater, 1719-1776.

Udsigt over hexeprocesserne i Norden.

WITCHCRAFT
BF
1584
S28
N99

Nyerup, Rasmus, 1759-1829.
Udsigt over hexeprocesserne i Norden.
Kjöbenhavn, Andreas Seidelin, 1823.
100 p. 18cm.

1. Witchcraft--Scandinavia. 2. Witchcraft--Iceland. 3. Trials (Witchcraft)--Scandinavia. 4. Trials (Witchcraft)--Iceland.

8
NIC

WITCHCRAFT
BF
1555
U22

Ueber Besessenheitsfälle, deren Thatsächlichkeit und pastorale Behandlung. [Stuttgart, 1863]
[257]-336 p. 21cm.

Detached from Pastoral-theologische Blätter, 5. Stuttgart, 1863.

1. Demoniac possession.

8

WITCHCRAFT
BT
980
U22

Ueber das Besessenseyn, oder das Daseyn und den Einfluss des bösen Geisterreichs in der alten Zeit. Mit Berücksichtigung dämonischer Besitzungen der neuen Zeit. Heilbronn, C. Drechsler, 1833.
116 p. 20cm.

1. Devil--Biblical teaching. 2. Jesus Christ--Teachings. 3. Demoniac possession.

8

---

ar V
13984

Ueber das Geschichtliche der Folter und derselben Gebrauch und Missbrauch.

Müller, Michael Franz Joseph.
Ueber das Geschichtliche der Folter und derselben Gebrauch und Missbrauch bei dem peinlichen Verfahren in dem Kirfürstenthum Trier im XVI, XVII und XVIII Jahrhundert, einige Worte. Trier, Blattau, 1831.
17 p. 19cm.

1. Torture. I. Title.

WITCHCRAFT
BF
1569
S36

Ueber den Glauben an Zauberei in den letztverflossenen vier Jahrhunderten.

Scholtz, J A
Ueber den Glauben an Zauberei in den letztverflossenen vier Jahrhunderten. Vorgetragen in der schlesischen vaterländischen Gesellschaft ... Breslau, Gedruckt bei W. G. Korn, 1830.
134 p. 19cm.

1. Witchcraft--History. 2. Superstition. I. Title.

8
NIC

WITCHCRAFT
RC
516
I19

Ueber die Dämonomanie.

Ideler, Karl Wilhelm, 1795-1860.
Ueber die Dämonomanie. Von Dr. Ideler, dirigirendem Arzte an der Irrenanstalt der Charité zu Berlin. [n. p., ca. 1840?]
[371]-408 p. 21cm.

Detached from Rust's Magazin, 48. Bd., 3. Heft.
At head of title: XII.

1. Demonomania. I. Title.

Witchcraft
BF
1505
D61
1885

Ueber die Geschichte des Teufels. Vortrag.

Disselhoff, August.
Ueber die Geschichte des Teufels. Vortrag. 4. Aufl. Berlin N, Deutsche Evangelische Buch- und Tractat Gesellschaft, 1885.
32 p. 19cm.

1. Devil.

B
2605
Z7
T46
v.5

Über die Hexenprozesse.

Thomasius, Christian, 1655-1728.
Über die Hexenprozesse. Überarb. und hrsg. von Rolf Lieberwirth. Weimar, Böhlau, 1967.
232 p. 25cm. (Thomasiana, Heft 5)
Contents.--Dissertatio de crimine magiae. Lateinische und deutsche Ausg.--Dissertatio de origine ac progressu processus inquisitorii sagas. Lateinische und deutsche Ausg.--Auszug aus: Christian Thomasens Erinnerung wegen seiner künffti gen Winterlektionen, so
(Continued on next card)

B
2605
Z7
T46
v.5

Über die Hexenprozesse.

Thomasius, Christian, 1655-1728. Über die Hexenprozesse. 1967. (Card 2)

nach Michaelis dieses 1702. Jahres ihren Anfang nehmen werden.--Verzeichnis der von Thomasius benutzten Literatur. (p. [225]-232)

1. Trials (Witchcraft) I. Lieberwirth, Rolf, ed. II. Title.

WITCHCRAFT
BF
1565
W37
S34

Ueber die Hexenreformation des Herrn Professor Weber zu Dillingen.

[Schmid, Franz Josef]
Ueber die Hexenreformation des Herrn Professor Weber zu Dillingen ... Von einem katholischen Weltmanne. [Augsburg] 1787.
86 p. 19cm.

Attribution by Kayser and Deutsche Biographie (under Weber, Joseph).

1. Weber, Joseph, 1753-1831. Ungrund des Hexen- und Gespenster-Glaubens. 2. Witchcraft. I. Ein katholischer Weltmann. II. Title.

8

WITCHCRAFT
BM
645
A6
K79

Ueber die jüdische angelologie und daemonologie in ihrer abhängigkeit vom Parsismus.

Kohut, Alexander, 1842-1894.
Ueber die jüdische angelologie und daemonologie in ihrer abhängigkeit vom parsismus, von dr. Alexander Kohut. Leipzig, In commission bei F. A. Brockhaus, 1866.
2 p. l., 105 p., 1 l. 22½ᶜᵐ. (Abhandlungen der Deutschen morgenländischen gesellschaft. IV. bd., no. 3)

1. Angels (Judaism) 2. Demonology. 3. Jewish theology. 4. Zoroastrianism.

8
NIC

Title from Univ. of Chicago PJ5.D46 vol.4
Library of Congress [PJ5.D5 bd. 4, no. 3]

A C 34-3086

[2]

WITCHCRAFT
BF
1523
K78
K51

Ueber die Non-Existenz des Teufels.

[Kindleben, Christian Wilhelm] 1748-1785.
Ueber die Non-Existenz des Teufels. Als eine Antwort auf die Demüthige Bitte um Belehrung an die grossen Männer, welche keinen Teufel glauben. Berlin, Bey G. A. Lange, 1776.
55 p. 17cm.

Attribution by Holzmann, Jocher, et al.

1. Köster, Heinrich Martin Gottfried, 1734-1802. Demüthige Bitte um Belehrung. 2. Devil. 2. Superstition. I. Title.

8

Witchcraft
BF
1555
M39+

Ueber die Verdienste der Aerzte um das Verschwinden der dämonischen Krankheiten.

Marx, Karl Friedrich Heinrich, 1796-1877.
Ueber die Verdienste der Aerzte um das Verschwinden der dämonischen Krankheiten. Göttingen, Dieterich, 1859.
66 p. 28cm.

"Aus dem achten Band der Abhandlungen der Königlichen Gesellschaft der Wissenschaften zu Göttingen."

1. Demoniac possession. 2. Medicine--Practice. 3. Witchcraft. I. Title.

8

Witchcraft
GR
830
W4
L65

Ueber die Wehrwölfe [sic] und Thierverwandlungen im Mittelalter.

Leubuscher, Rudolph.
Ueber die Wehrwölfe [sic] und Thierverwandlungen im Mittelalter. Ein Beitrag zur Geschichte der Psychologie. Berlin, G. Reimer, 1850.
65, [2] p. 24cm.

1. Werwolves. 2. Psychology, Pathological. I. Title.

8

CATALOGUE OF THE CORNELL WITCHCRAFT COLLECTION

WITCHCRAFT
BF
.583
.7
.630
    Ueber einen Hexenprozess in München-Gladbach.
    Hesse, Werner.
      Ueber einen Hexenprozess in München-Gladbach.
    (In Rheinische Geschichtsblätter. Bonn. 23cm. 3. Jahrg., No. 8 (1897), p. [225]-232)

    1. Trials (Witchcraft)--Germany. 2. Trials (Witchcraft)--München-Gladbach, Germany. I. Title.

WITCHCRAFT
BF
1583
S45
    Über einige Hexenprozesse im Stift Essen.
    Seemann, Otto, 1825-1901.
      Über einige Hexenprozesse im Stift Essen.
    (In Historischer Verein für Stadt und Stift Essen. Beiträge zur Geschichte von Stadt und Stift Essen. Essen. 20cm. 10. Heft (1886), p. [111]-131)

    1. Trials (Witchcraft)--Essen, Germany. 2. Trials (Witchcraft)--Germany. I. Title.

NIC

Witchcraft
BF
1584
E7
W77
    Über Hexenwahn und Hexenprozesse in Estland während der Schwedenherrschaft.
    Winkler, R
      Über Hexenwahn und Hexenprozesse in Estland während der Schwedenherrschaft. Von Probst R. Winkler (Reval).
    (In Baltische Monatsschrift. Riga. 24cm. 67. Bd., Jahrg. 51, Heft 5 (1909), p. [321]-355)
    1. Trials (Witchcraft)--Estonia. I. Title. II. Title: Hexenwahn und Hexenprozesse in Estland während der Schwedenherrschaft. III. Baltische Monatsschrift, Riga.

8

WITCHCRAFT
BF
1566
L71
    Über Hexerei.
    Liebeherr, Max von.
      Ueber Hexerei. Ein Vortrag gehalten am 21. Novbr. 1870 in der Aula der Universität zu Rostock. Rostock, Stiller, 1871.
    59 p. 14cm.

8
NIC
    1. Witchcraft.

Witchcraft
BL
795
D2
G36+
    Über Wesen, Verwandtschaft und Ursprung der Dämonen und Genien.
    Gerhard, Eduard, 1795-1867.
      Über Wesen, Verwandtschaft und Ursprung der Dämonen und Genien. Gelesen in der königl. Akademie der Wissenschaften zu Berlin am 13. Mai 1852. Berlin, In Commission der Besserschen Buchhandlung (W. Hertz), 1852.
    [237]-266 p. 27cm.
    Repr. from Akademie der Wissenschaften, Berlin. Abhandlungen, v. 37 (1852) Philologische und hi   storische Abhandlungen.
    1. Spirit. I. Title.

Witchcraft
BF
1815
C2
D31
1742
    Der übernatürliche Philosoph.
    [Defoe, Daniel] 1660?-1731.
      Der Übernatürliche Philosoph, oder Die Geheimnisse der Magie, nach allen ihren Arten deutlich erkläret ... aus den bewährtesten Autoribus zusammen getragen und durch das Exempel und Leben des Herrn Duncan Campbells, des tauben und stummen Edelmanns, erörtert. Nebst D. Wallis Methode, taube und stumme lesen, schreiben und jede Sprache verstehen zu lernen, von W. Bond ... Aus dem Englischen

(Continued on next card)

Witchcraft
BF
1815
C2
D31
1742
    Der übernatürliche Philosoph.
    [Defoe, Daniel] 1660?-1731. Der Übernatürliche Philosoph ... 1742. (Card 2)

ins Deutsche übersetzt und mit einigen nöthigen und dienlichen Anmerkungen versehen ... Berlin, J. A. Rüdiger, 1742.
    [92], 432 p. front. (port.), 4 fold. plates. 17cm.
    First published 1720 anonymously with title: The history of the life and adventures of Mr. Duncan Campbell. Reissued 1728 with some additions as: The super-

(Continued on next card)

Witchcraft
BF
1815
C2
D31
1742
    Der übernatürliche Philosoph.
    [Defoe, Daniel] 1660?-1731. Der Übernatürliche Philosoph ... 1742. (Card 3)

natural philosopher, or, The mysteries of magick ... unfolded by William Bond, from which this is translated.
    Authorship disputed; probably by Daniel Defoe with the assistance of William Bond and possibly of Eliza Haywood.
    Imperfect: plate to p. [72] wanting.

BF
1429
B79
    Übersinnliche Erscheinungen bei Naturvölkern.
    Bozzano, Ernesto, 1862-1943.
      Übersinnliche Erscheinungen bei Naturvölkern. Mit einem Nachwort und einem Register von Gastone De Boni. Bern, A. Francke [1948]
    323 p. 18cm. (Sammlung DALP)

Bibliography: p. 299-301.

WITCHCRAFT
BF
1003
U22+
    Die Übersinnliche Welt. 1.-30. Jahrg., 1893-1922. Berlin [etc.]
    30 v. 26cm.

""Monatsschrift für wissenschaftliche Begründung des Okkultismus."
    Continued as a section, with its own numbering, in Psyche.

8
NIC
    1. Occult sciences--Period.

WITCHCRAFT
BF
1563
K44
    Uhuhu.
    Keyser, Georg Adam, comp.
      Uhuhu; oder Hexen-Gespenster-Schazgräber- und Erscheinungs-Geschichten. Erfurt, Bey G. A. Keyser, 1785-92.
    7 v. in 3. Illus. 18cm.

Each vol. has lengthy introduction including bibliographical materials.

    1. Witchcraft. 2. Ghost stories. 3. Occult sciences--Bibl. I. Title.

8

Witchcraft
BF
1410
B42
Z912
    Uiterste verleegentheid van Doctor Balt. Bekker.
    [Andala, Ruardus] 1665-1727.
      Uiterste verleegentheid van Doctor Balt. Bekker. Duidelijk aangeweesen door wederlegging van alle sijne aanmerkingen ende naleesingen gevoegt bi het slordige mengelmoes van sijn E. Voedsterlingen. Uitgegeeven door een discipel van de Heer J. vander Waeyen en voedsterling van de Academie van Friesland. Franeker, By H. Gyzelaar, ordinaris drukker der Eed. Mog. Heeren Staten, en der Academie van Friesland, 1696.
    4 p. l., 234, [6] p. title and

(Continued on next card)

Witchcraft
BF
1410
B42
Z912
    Uiterste verleegentheid van Doctor Balt. Bekker.
    [Andala, Ruardus] 1665-1727. Uiterste verleegentheid van Doctor Balt. Bekker. 1696. (Card 2)

other vignettes, illus. initials. 22 x 17cm.
    4°. *⁴, A-2G⁴.
    Van der Linde 166.
    Criticizes Bekker's critique of Waaijen's De betooverde weereld van D. Balthasar Bekker ondersogt en weederlegt.
    With this is bound Andala, Ruardus, 1665-1727. Balthazar Bekkers en

(Continued on next card)

R

Witchcraft
BF
1410
B42
Z912
    Uiterste verleegentheid van Doctor Balt. Bekker.
    [Andala, Ruardus] 1665-1727. Uiterste verleegentheid van Doctor Balt. Bekker. 1696. (Card 3)

insonderheyd sijner voedsterlingen onkunde... Franeker, 1696.
    1. Bekker, Balthasar, 1634-1698. De betooverde weereld. 2. Waaijen, Johannes van der, 1639-1701. De betooverde weereld van D. Balthasar Bekker ondersogt en weederlegt. I. Title.

WITCHCRAFT
BT
1220
F67
W13
    Ultramontan: eine Abwehr in vier Artikeln.
    Wahrmund, Ludwig, 1860-1932.
      Ultramontan: eine Abwehr in vier Artikeln. München, J. F. Lehmann, 1908.
    41 p. 22cm.
    Contents.--1. Herr P. Fonck S. J. als wissenschaftlicher Kritiker.--2. Die ultramontane Moral.--3. Die Teufelsaustreibung im Wemdinger Kloster.--4. Die "Religion" des Papstes Clemens VI.--Anhang. Einige berühmte Reliquienschätze.
    1. Fonck, Leopold, 1865-1930. Katholische Weltanschauung und freie Wissenschaft. 2. Ultramontanism. I. Title.

8

Witchcraft
BS
2545
D5
S472
    Umständliche Untersuchung der dämonischen Leute oder sogenannten Besessenen.
    Semler, Johann Salomo, 1725-1791.
      D. Joh. Salomo Semlers ... Umständliche Untersuchung der dämonischen Leute oder sogenannten Besessenen, nebst Beantwortung einiger Angriffe. Halle, Bey J. I. Gebauer, 1762.
    24 p. l., 272 p. 18cm.
    Contents.--Auszug und Erleuterung der Dissertation: De daemoniacis, qvorum in Evangeliis fit mentio.--Auszug und Beantwortung der jenaischen Disputation.--Antwort

(Continued on next card)

WITCHCRAFT
BS
2545
D5
S472
    Umständliche Untersuchung der dämonischen Leute oder sogenannten Besessenen.
    Semler, Johann Salomo, 1725-1791. ...Umständliche Untersuchung der dämonischen Leute ... 1762. (Card 2)

auf die unbillige Recension in den Auszügen aus Dispvtationibvs.
    1. Demoniac possession. 2. His De daemoniacis, quorum in Evangeliis fit mentio. 3. Bible. N. T.--Commentaries. I. Title: Umständliche Untersuchung der dämonischen Leute oder sogenannten Besessenen.

8

Witchcraft
BF
1555
F88
    Umständlicher Bericht, von dem Unlängst in Hamburg vom leidigen Satan besessenen Mägdlein.
    Frese, Jürgen, 1623-
      Umständlicher Bericht, von dem Unlängst in Hamburg vom leidigen Satan besessenen Mägdlein, wie auch Beantwortung einiger Fragen von der Universität Kiel, nebst des Autore Lebens-Lauf, worin gemeldet werden die Wunder von dem glühenden Rink und Kohlen, und noch beygefüget eine Trostschrift an einige betrübte Herzen. [Hamburg?] 1692.
    112 p. 17cm.

CATALOGUE OF THE CORNELL WITCHCRAFT COLLECTION

Und der Satz: Teuflische Magie existirt, besteht noch.

WITCHCRAFT
BF
1565
W37
S347

[Schmid, Franz Josef]
Und der Satz: Teuflische Magie existirt, besteht noch. In einer Antwort des katholischen Weltmannes auf die von einem Herrn Landpfarrer herausgegebene Apologie der Professor Weberschen Hexenreformation. Augsburg, Bey J. N. Styx, 1791.
xxiv, 350 p. 19cm.

1. Bauer, Friedrich. Gedanken eines Landpfarrers über den Ungrund des Hexenglaubens. 2. Weber, Joseph, 1753-1831.

8 (Continued on next card)

Die unfreie und die freie Kirche in ihren Beziehungen zur Sclaverei... und zum Dämonismus.

HT
913
B91

Buchmann, Jakob.
Die unfreie und die freie Kirche in ihren Beziehungen zur Sclaverei, zur Glaubens- und Gewissenstyrannei und zum Dämonismus. Breslau, A. Gosohorsky, 1873.
xvi, 331 p. 22cm.

1. Slavery and the church. 2. Demonology. I. Title.

WITCHCRAFT
BF
1593
U57

Unger, Franz, 1871-
Die schwarze Magie: ihre Meister und ihre Opfer. Coethen, R. Schumann [1904]
80 p. 20cm. (Collection rätselhafte Naturen Bd. VII)
Contents.--Präludium: Das Problem des übernatürlichen Geschlechtsverkehrs.--Geschlechtsverkehr zwischen Menschen, Teufeln und Dämonen.--Urbain Grandier und die Besessenen von Loudun.--Werke des Teufels in alter Zeit.

1. Magic. 2. Devil. 3. Grandier, Urbain, 1590-1634. I. Title.

8

Ungrund des Hexen- und Gespenster-Glaubens.

WITCHCRAFT
BF
1565
W37
1797

Weber, Joseph, 1753-1831.
Ungrund des Hexen- und Gespenster-Glaubens, in ökonomischen Lehrstunden dargestellt ... 2. verm. Aufl. Augsburg, C. F. Bürglen, 1797.
198 p. 19cm.
Preface dated: Dilingen am 29. Februars 1787.

1. Witchcraft. 2. Ghosts. 3. Superstition. I. Title.

8

U. S. National Library of Medicine.

Witchcraft
BF
1565
N43+

Nemec, Jaroslav, 1910-
Witchcraft and medicine (1484-1793) [Washington] National Institutes of Health, 1974.
10 p. illus. 26cm. (NIH publication 74-636)
"Published in conjunction with an exhibit at the National Library of Medicine, March 25-July 19, 1974."

NIC
1. Witchcraft--Hist. 2. Medicine. I. Title. II. United States. National Library of Medicine.

L'univers diabolique.

BF
1532
V73

Villeneuve, Roland, 1922-
L'univers diabolique. Paris, A. Michel [1972]
325, [8] p. plates. 22 cm. (Les Chemins de l'impossible) 24.00F F***
Bibliography: p. 323-[326]

4
1. Demonology. 2. Witchcraft. 3. Magic. I. Title.

BF1532.V54   72-326406
Library of Congress   72 [2]

Eine unpartheyische Feder.

Witchcraft
BF
1565
S83
S84

[Sterzinger, Joseph] 1746-1821.
Der Hexenprocess: ein Traum erzählt von einer unpartheyischen Feder im Jahre 1767. [München?] 1767.
18 p. 22cm.
Attribution and dates from Fieger, Hans. P. Don Ferdinand Sterzinger, München, 1907, p. 144-45. (Accepted also by Holzmann)

Witchcraft
BF
1565
T46
U58

Unpartheyische Gedancken über die Kurtze Lehr-Sätze von dem Laster der Zauberey, welche der berühmte JCtus und Professor zu Halle, Herr D. Christianus Thomasius, damahls in einer Inaugural-Disputation defendiret, jetzo aber schon zum andernmahl in teutsche Sprache übersetzet worden, nebst Anhang betreffende die Vertheidigung dieser Lehr-Sätze, kurtz gefasset und zum Druck befördert von einem Membro des Collegii Curiosorum in Teutsch-

8 (Continued on next card)

Witchcraft
BF
1565
T46
U58

Unpartheyische Gedancken über die Kurtze Lehr-Sätze von dem Laster der Zauberey ... 1703. (Card 2)

land. [n. p.] 1703.
46 p. plate. 17cm.

1. Thomasius, Christian, 1655-1728. Kurtze Lehr-Sätze von dem Laster der Zauberey. 2. Witchcraft. I. Ein Membrum des Collegii Curiosorum in Teutschland.

8

Unpartheyische Gedancken über die Kurze Lehr-Sätze von dem Laster der Zauberey.

Witchcraft
BF
1565
T46
U584

[Gundling, Nicolaus Hieronymus] 1671-1729.
Gründliche Abfertigung der Unpartheyischen Gedancken eines ungenandten Auctoris, die er von der Lehre De crimine magiae, des hochberühmten Herrn D. Christiani Thomasii, neulichst heraus gegeben, gestellet von Hieronymo à sancta Fide. Franckfurth, 1703.
[48] p. 19cm.
Attribution by G. L. Burr.

1. Unpartheyische Gedancken über die Kurze Lehr-Sätze von dem Laster der Zauberey. 2. Witchcraft. I. Hieronymus à sancta Fide. II. Title.

8

Witchcraft
BF
1559
G25
Z63
no.2

Unterricht für diejenigen, welche in ihren körperlichen Anliegenheiten, bey dem hochwürdigen Herrn Johann Joseph Gassner ... entweder Hülfe zu suchen gedenken, oder selbe schon gesucht, und gefunden haben. Als eine Fortsetzung des gründlichen Beweiss &c. von einem Vertheidiger der Wahrheit und aufrichtigem Menschenfreunde in öffentlichen Druck gegeben. Augsburg, Bey J. Wolff, 1775.
96 p. 17cm.

8 (Continued on next card)

Witchcraft
BF
1559
G25
Z63
no.2

Unterricht für diejenigen, welche ... Hülfe zu suchen gedenken ... 1775. (Card 2)

Attributed by British Museum to Gassner. No. 2 in vol. lettered Gassneriana.

1. Faith-cure. 2. Exorcism. I. Gassner, Johann Joseph, 1727-1779, supposed author. II. Gründlicher Beweiss ... von einem Vertheidiger der Wahrheit und aufrichtigem Menschenfreunde.

8

Unterschiedliche Schrifften von Unfug des Hexen-Processes.

WITCHCRAFT
BF
1565
R34

Reiche, Johann, ed.
Herrn D. Christian Thomasii ... Kurtze Lehr-Sätze von dem Laster der Zauberey, nach dem wahren Verstande des lateinischen Exemplars ins Deutsche übersetzet, und aus des berühmten Theologi D. Meyfarti, Naudaei, und anderer gelehrter Männer Schrifften erleutert ... nebst einigen Actis magicis herausgegeben von Johann Reichen. Halle im Magdeburgischen, Im Rengerischen Buchladen, 1704.
2 v. in 1. 21cm.

8
NIC (Continued on next card)

Unterschiedliche Schrifften von Unfug des Hexen-Processes.

WITCHCRAFT
BF
1565
R34

Reiche, Johann, ed. Herrn D. Christian Thomasii ... Kurtze Lehr-Sätze ... 1704. (Card 2)

Vol. 1 has special t. p.: Fernerer Unfug der Zauberey. Halle im Magdeburgischen, 1704.
Vol. 2 has special t. p.: Unterschiedliche Schrifften von Unfug des Hexen-Processes. Halle im Magdeburg., 1703.
Contents.--[1. Bd.] Gabriel Naudaei

8
NIC (Continued on next card)

Unterschiedliche Schrifften von Unfug des Hexen-Processes.

WITCHCRAFT
BF
1565
R34

Reiche, Johann, ed. Herrn D. Christian Thomasii ... Kurtze Lehr-Sätze ... 1704. (Card 3)

Contents.--Continued.

Schutz-Schrifft [tr. of Apologie pour tous les grands hommes]--Geschichte der Teuffel zu Lodün.--Trauer-Geschichte von der greulichen Zauberey Ludwig Goffredy [tr. of De l'horrible & épouvantable sorcellerie de Louis Goffredy, author F. de Rosset]--D. Christian Thomasii ... Kurtze Lehr-Sätze von

8
NIC (Continued on next card)

Unterschiedliche Schrifften von Unfug des Hexen-Processes.

WITCHCRAFT
BF
1565
R34

Reiche, Johann, ed. Herrn D. Christian Thomasii ... Kurtze Lehr-Sätze ... 1704. (Card 4)

Contents--Continued.

dem Laster der Zauberey [tr. of Dissertatio de crimine magiae, J. Reiche, respondent] [2. Bd.] Malleus judicum oder Gesetz-Hammer der unbarmhertzigen Hexen-Richter.--Cautio criminalis [von F. Spee].--D. Johann Matthäus Meyfarths Christliche Erinnerung an Regenten.-- Viererley Sorten Hexen-Acta.

8
NIC (Continued on next card)

WITCHCRAFT
BF
1523
U61

Untersuchung der Frage: ob der Satan Wunderwerke verrichten, ob er die Menschen hohlen [sic] und durch die Luft führen, auch ob derselbe einen Cörper in den andern verwandeln und ob er die Menschen besitzen könne oder nicht? Desgleichen was es mit denen Gespenstern, Hexen und der Erscheinung der Geister für eine Beschaffenheit habe &c &c. Frankfurt und Leipzig, 1770.
158 p. 20cm.

1. Devil. 2. Witchcraft. 3. Mental illness.

8

Untersuchung der vermeinten und so genannten Hexereÿen.

Witchcraft
BF
1565
W38
1719

Webster, John, 1610-1682.
... Untersuchung der vermeinten und so genannten Hexereÿen, worinn zwar zugegeben wird, daß es an mancherley Betrug und Aeffereyen nicht fehle ...: im Gegentheil aber die Fabel, daß der Teuffel leibhafftig einen Pact mit den Hexen mache ... durchaus geleugnet und umgestossen wird. Dabey auch die Warheit, daß es allerdings Engel und Geister, wie nicht weniger Erscheinungen gebe, eröffnet ... Aus dem Englischen ins

8 (Continued on next card)

566

CATALOGUE OF THE CORNELL WITCHCRAFT COLLECTION

Untersuchung der vermeinten und so genannten Hexereÿen.

Witchcraft
BF 1565
W38
1719

Webster, John, 1610-1682. Untersuchung der vermeinten und so genannten Hexereÿen ... 1719. (Card 2)

Teutsche übersetzt, und nebst einer Vorrede des Hrn. Geheimbden Raths Thomasii ... Halle, im Magdeburgischen, In Verlegung der Neuen Buchhandlung, 1719.
56, 611, [97] p. plate. 21cm.
1. Witchcraft. I. Thomasius, Christian, 1655-1728. II. His The displaying of supposed witchcraft. German. III. Title.

8

Untersuchung ob es eine Festigkeit gebe.

Witchcraft
BF 1603
S83
no.1

[Sterzinger, Ferdinand] 1721-1786.
... Untersuchung ob es eine Festigkeit gebe dabey viele andere aberglaubische Irrthümer wiederleget werden nebst beygefügtem Katechismus von der Geisterlehre. München, W. Schwarzkopf, Buchhändler in Nürnberg, 1775.
200 p. 17cm.
At head of title: Francone dell' Amavero [pseud. of F. Sterzinger]
No. 1 in vol. lettered Francone dell' Amavero (Sterzinger) Untersuchung [etc.]
(Continued on next card)

3

Untersuchung ob es eine Festigkeit gebe.

Witchcraft
BF 1603
S83
no.1

[Sterzinger, Ferdinand] 1721-1786. ... Untersuchung ob es eine Festigkeit gebe ... 1775. (Card 2)

Attributed by British Museum and Kayser to A. U. Mayer.
1. Magic. 2. Spells. I. His Katekismus von der Geisterlehre. II. Title. III. Mayer, Andreas Ulrich, 1732-1802, supposed author. IV. Title: Katekismus von der Geisterlehre.

3

ITCHCRAFT
F 523
19
o.1

Untersuchung und Beleuchtung der sogenannten biblischen Dämonologie, die mit Herrn D. Semlers Anhange herausgekommen ist. Danzig, Bey J. H. Flörke, 1778.
348 p. 17cm.
No. 1 in vol. lettered Varia scripta demonolog.
1. Devil--Biblical teaching. 2. Hesse, Otto Justus Basilius, d. 1793. Versuch einer biblischen Dämonologie. 3. Demonology.

Unvorgreifliche Gedancken und Monita, wie ... mit denen Hexen-Processen ... zu verfahren.

WITCHCRAFT
BF 1565
M498

Meinders, Hermann Adolph.
Unvorgreifliche Gedancken und Monita, wie ohne blinden Eyfer und Übereilung mit denen Hexen-Processen und der Inquisition wegen der Zauberey, an Seiten des Richters so wol als des königlichen Fiscalis und Defensoris in denen Königl. Preussischen und Cuhrfürstlichen [sic] Brandenburgischen Landen ohnmassgeblich zu verfahren. Auf königlichen Special-Befehl laut Edicti vom 13 Decembris 1714 zusammen getragen
(Continued on next card)

8
NIC

Unvorgreifliche Gedancken und Monita, wie ... mit denen Hexen-Processen ... zu verfahren.

WITCHCRAFT
BF 1565
M498

Meinders, Hermann Adolph. Unvorgreifliche Gedancken und Monita...1716. (Card 2)

und aufgesetzet von...Hermann Adolph Meinders. Lemgo, Druckts und verlegts Henrich Wilhelm Meyer, 1716
152 p. 22cm.
Collection of extracts from various sources concerning witchcraft, magic and trials for witchcraft.
The most extensive extract is
(Continued on next card)

Unvorgreifliche Gedancken und Monita, wie ... mit denen Hexen-Processen ... zu verfahren.

WITCHCRAFT
BF 1565
M498

Meinders, Hermann Adolph. Unvorgreifliche Gedancken und Monita...1716. (Card 3)

that from Pierre Bayle's Réponse aux questions d'un provincial. (in the original French, p. 12-93)
1. Witchcraft. 2. Trials (Witchcraft) 3. Magic. I. Bayle, Pierre, 1647-1706. Réponse aux questions d'un provincial. II. Title: Unvorgreifliche Gedancken und Monita, wie ...mit denen Hexen-Processen...zu verfahren.

BF 1576
U67

Upham, Mrs. Caroline E
Salem witchcraft in outline. Salem, Mass., Salem Press, 1891.
xiii, 161 p. illus. 18cm.

1. Witchcraft--Salem, Mass. I. Title.

Witchcraft
BF 1576
U68L4
4 copies

Upham, Charles Wentworth, 1802-1875.
Lectures on witchcraft, comprising a history of the delusion in Salem, in 1692. Boston, Carter, Hendee and Babcock, 1831.
vii, 280 p. 16cm.

I. Title. II. Title: A history of the delusion in Salem, in 1692.

Witchcraft
BF 1576
U68
2 copies

Upham, Charles Wentworth, 1802-1875.
Salem witchcraft; with an account of Salem Village, and a history of opinions on witchcraft and kindred subjects. Boston, Wiggin and Lunt, 1867.
2 v. illus., map. 21cm.

1. Witchcraft--Salem, Mass. 2. Salem, Mass.--Hist. I. Title.

BF 1576
U68
v.2

Upham, Charles Wentworth, 1802-1875.
Salem witchcraft; with an account of Salem Village, and a history of opinions on witchcraft and kindred subjects. Boston, Wiggin and Lunt, 1867.
2 v. illus., map. 21cm.

1. Witchcraft--Salem, Mass. 2. Salem, Mass.--Hist. I. Title.

Witchcraft
BF 1576
U68
1959

Upham, Charles Wentworth, 1802-1875.
Salem witchcraft; with an account of Salem village and a history of opinions on witchcraft and kindred subjects. New York, F. Ungar Pub. Co. [1959]
2 v. illus., ports. fold. map. 21 cm. (American classics)

1. Witchcraft—Salem, Mass. 2. Salem, Mass.--Hist. I. Title.

BF1576.U56 1959   974.45   59-10887
Library of Congress   [60f5]

Witchcraft
BF 1576
P82

Upham, Charles Wentworth, 1802-1875.
Salem witchcraft.
Poole, William Frederick, 1821-1894.
Cotton Mather and Salem witchcraft. By William Frederick Poole. [Reprinted from the North American review for April, 1869] Boston [University press] 1869.
63 p. 24cm.
"One hundred copies printed."

WITCHCRAFT
BF 1576
P82
U67+

Upham, Charles Wentworth, 1802-1875.
Salem witchcraft and Cotton Mather. A reply [to W. F. Poole's Cotton Mather and Salem witchcraft] Morrisania, N. Y., 1869.
91 p. 19cm.
In double columns.
Reprint from the Historical Magazine.
1. Poole, William Frederick, 1821-1894. Cotton Mather and Salem witchcraft. 2. Mather, Cotton, 1663-1728. 3. Witchcraft--Salem, Mass. I. Title.

8

WITCHCRAFT
BF 1576
P82
U673
2 copies

Upham, Charles Wentworth, 1802-1875.
Salem witchcraft and Cotton Mather.
Goddard, Delano Alexander, 1831-1882.
The Mathers weighed in the balances by Delano A. Goddard and found not wanting. Boston: Office of the Daily Advertiser; London: Office of H. Stevens, 1870.
32 p. 16cm.
Copy 1 is autograph presentation copy to A. D. White.
1. Upham, Charles Wentworth, 1802-1875. Salem witchcraft and Cotton Mather. 2. Mather, Increase, 1639-1723. 3. Mather, Cotton, 1663-1728. I. Title.

8
NIC

Witchcraft
BF 1576
P82
U676

Upham, Charles Wentworth, 1802-1875.
[Poole, William Frederick] 1821-1894.
Cotton Mather & witchcraft; two notices of Mr. Upham, his reply. Boston, T. R. Marvin & son; [etc., etc.] 1870.
30 p. 17cm.

1. Witchcraft—Salem, Mass. 2. Mather, Cotton, 1663-1728. 3. Upham, Charles Wentworth, 1802-1875. I. Title.

11—9001
Library of Congress   BF1576.P8

Witchcraft
BF 1576
N97
U67

Upham, William Phineas, 1836-1905.
Account of the Rebecca Nurse monument. Salem, Mass., Printed at the Salem Press, 1886.
41 p. 22cm.
With autograph: Joseph Foster.
"From the Historical collections of the Essex Institute, vol. XXIII."

1. Nurse, Rebecca (Towne) 1621-1692. I. Title: The Rebecca Nurse monument.

NIC

Urbain Grandier et les possédées de Loudun.

WITCHCRAFT
BF 1517
F5
L521
1884

Legué, Gabriel. d. 1913.
Urbain Grandier et les possédées de Loudun. Nouv. éd. revue et augmentée. Paris, Charpentier, 1884.
xii, 348 p. 19cm.

1. Grandier, Urbain, 1590-1634. 2. Loudun, France. Ursuline Convent. 3. Demoniac possession.

8
NIC

CATALOGUE OF THE CORNELL WITCHCRAFT COLLECTION

Urgicht und Verzaichnuss, so Walpurga Haussmännen ... bekandt hatt.

WITCHCRAFT
BF
1583
Z7
1587

Haussmännen, Walpurga, d. 1587, defendant.
Vrgicht vnd Verzaichnuss, so Walpurga Haussmännen zu Dillingen, inn ihrer peinlichen Marter bekandt hatt, was sy für Vbels vnd Jamers mit jhrer Hexerey, so sy biss in die 30. Jar getrüben, angericht vnd gestüfft hat, mit Hilff vnd Raht jhres Bülteüffels, so ihr darzu geholffen: welche Walburga Anno 1587. Jar, den 24. October, verbrandt vnd gericht ist worden, &c. [Dillingen?] 1588.
[20] p.   20cm.

8   (Continued on next card)

Urkunden über Hexenprozesse aus dem Staatsarchive in Bern.

WITCHCRAFT
BF
1584
S97
S93

Stürler, Moritz von.
Urkunden über Hexenprozesse aus dem Staatsarchive in Bern. Mitgetheilt durch Herrn Staatsschreiber und Staatsarchivar Moritz von Stürler, korrespondierendes Mitglied der Basler historischen Gesellschaft. [Basel, 1854]
[284]-291 p.   23cm.
Extract from Beiträge zur vaterländischen Geschichte, Basel, v. 5, 1854.
1. Trials (Witchcraft)--Basel. 2. Trials (Witchcraft)--Switzerland. I. Title.

8

Urtheil ohne Vorurtheil über die wirkend- und thätige Hexerey.

Witchcraft
BF
1565
S83
M17

[März, Agnellus] 1726-1784.
Urtheil ohne Vorurtheil über die wirkend- und thätige Hexerey, abgefasset von einem Liebhaber der Wahrheit. [München] 1766.
64 p.   20cm.

1. Sterzinger, Ferdinand, 1721-1786. Akademische Rede von dem gemeinen Vorurtheile der ... Hexerey. 2. Witchcraft.
I. Ein Liebhaber der Wahrheit. II. Title.

8

The usual interpretation of daimones and daimonia.

Witchcraft
BS
2545
D5
T75
no.4

Hutchinson, Thomas, 1698-1769.
The usual interpretation of ΔΑΙΜΟΝΕΣ and ΔΑΙΜΟΝΙΑ in the New Testament, asserted in a sermon preach'd before the University of Oxford at St. Mary's, on Sunday, March 5, 1737-8. Oxford, Printed at the Theatre for Mr. Clements, and sold by Mess. Innys and Manby, 1738.
31 p.   20cm.

No. 4 in vol. lettered: Tracts on demoniacks. 1737.

Utrum sonus campanarum ingruentem tonitruum ... tempestatem ... abigere queat.

WITCHCRAFT
BF
1559
S85

Spinaeus, Godofredus, praeses.
Disputatio philosophica. Examinans quaestionem, Utrvm sonvs campanarvm ingruentem tonitruum ac fulminum tempestatem, pruinas item, nec non spectra ac diabolum, depellere & abigere queat? Quam ... praeside ... D. Godofredo Spinaeo ... Exercitationis ergo, publico subjicit examini, Joh. Iacobus Wagnerus ... Steinfvrti, Typis Cornelij Wellenberg, 1661.
20 p.   19cm.

8   (Continued on next card)

Utrum sonus campanarum ingruentem tonitruum ... tempestatem ... abigere queat.

WITCHCRAFT
BF
1559
S85

Spinaeus, Godofredus, praeses. Disputatio philosophica ... 1661.   (Card 2)

Diss.--Steinfurt (J. J. Wagner, respondent)

1. Bells (in religion, folk-lore, etc.)
2. Demonology. 3. Weather-lore. I. Wagner, Johann Jacob, respondent. II. Title: Utrum sonus campanarum ingruentem tonitruum ... tempestatem ... abigere queat.

8

CATALOGUE OF THE CORNELL WITCHCRAFT COLLECTION

V

Vair, Léonard, Bp., ca. 1540-1603.

see

Vairo, Leonardo, Bp. ca. 1540-1603.

WITCHCRAFT
BF
1555
V14

8
NIC

Valcarenghi, Paolo.
De saxis, acubus, ferreis vitreisque frustis, non exiguae molis, variae superficiei & figurae, aliisque plurimis rebus, plerumque per vomitum, aliquando etiam per inferiores partes ejectis, tum & de miris animi & corporis morbosis affectionibus, quibus identidem per plures annos Cremonensis virgo quaedam obnoxia fuit, dissertatio epistolaris ... Cremonae, Apud P. Ricchini, 1746.
v-xx, 172 p. 23cm.
1. Demoniac possession. 2. Medicine-- 15th-18th centuries. I. Title.

Witchcraft
BF
1581
V17

Valiente, Doreen.
Where witchcraft lives. 1st ed. London, Aquarian Press, 1962.
xi, 7-112 p. 19 cm.

I. Title.

---

tchcraft

65
3

Vairo, Leonardo, Bp., ca. 1540-1603.
De fascino libri tres. In qvibvs omnes fascini species et cavsae optima methodo describuntur, & ex philosophorum ac theologorum sententiis scitè & eleganter explicantur: necnon contra praestigias, imposturas, illusionésque daemonum, cautiones & amuleta praescribuntur: ac denique nugae, quae de iisdem narrari solent, dilucidè confutantur. Accessit ad calcem index locupletissimus. Parisiis, Apud Nicolaum Chesneav, 1583.
[12], 275, [32] p. 23cm.
Title vignette : device of N. Chesneau.
With this is bound Remi, Nicolas. Daemonolatreiae libri tres. Lvgdvni, 1595.

Valderama, Pedro de.

see

Valderrama, Pedro de.

Witchcraft
BF
1558
V18+

Valle de Moura, Emanuel, fl. 1620.
De incantationibus sev ensalmis ...
Eborae, Typis Laurentij Crasbeeck, 1620.
[6], 11 l., 12-609, [1] p. 28cm.

Title vignette.

1. Magic. 2. Incantations. I. Title.

Witchcraft
BF
1565
V13
1589

Vairo, Leonardo, Bp., ca. 1540-1603.
De fascino libri tres. In quibus omnes fascini species, & causae optima methodo describuntur, & ex philosophorum ac theologorum sententijs eleganter explicantur: nec non contra praestigias, imposturas, allusionesque daemonum, cautiones & amuleta praescribuntur: ac denique nugae, quae de ijsdem narrari solent, dilucidè confutantur. Cum gemmino indice ... Venetiis, Apud Aldum, 1589.
[16], 375, [42] p. 17cm.
Aldine device on t. p.
I. Title.

WITCHCRAFT
BD
505
V14
1617

8

Valderrama, Pedro de
Histoire generale dv monde, et de la natvre. Ov Traictez theologiqves de la fabrique, composition, & conduicte generale de l'vniuers. Divisez en trois livres. Le premier traictant de Dieu comme souuerain architecte du monde ... Le second de la conduicte admirable du monde, les intelligences celestes, la fabrique generale du ciel, les diuers degrez des anges ... Le troisies. des grades diuerses des de-
(Continued on next card)

WITCHCRAFT
BF
1582
V18
1752a

8

Vallemont, Pierre Le Lorrain, abbé de, 1649-1721, supposed author.
[Valmont, de] Dissertation sur les maléfices et les sorciers selon les principes de la théologie et de la physique, ou l'on examine en particulier l'état de la fille de Tourcoing. Tourcoing, 1752. Lille, Leleu, 1862.
85 p. 16cm.
Title in red and black.
"Réimpression sur l'original à deux cents exemplaires."
Note in back of text claims Barbier attributed this item to the Abbé Vallemont.
(Continued on next card)

WITCHCRAFT
BF
1520
A53
1589

8

Vairo, Leonardo, bp., ca. 1540-1603.
De fascino libri tres, auctore Leonardo Vairo Beneventano ... Cum gemmino indice altero capitum, altero rerum memorabilium. Venetiis, Apud Aldum, 1589.
8 p. l., 375, [45] p. 17cm.

Bound with Anania, Giovanni Lorenzo d'. De natura daemonum. Venetiis, 1589.

WITCHCRAFT
BD
505
V14
1617

8

Valderrama, Pedro de. Histoire generale dv monde ... 1617. (Card 2)
mons ... de leur science appellée magie ..., des diuerses parties di [sic] la magie, & plusieurs autres illusions diaboliques. Le tout illustré d'vn grand nombre d'histoires & doctes exemples. Composé en espagnol par le R. P. P. Valderama, ... & traduit sur le manuscrit espagnol en nostre langue françoise, par le sieur de la Richardier ... 2. éd. Paris, Chez Isaac Mesnier,
(Continued on next card)

WITCHCRAFT
BF
1582
V18
1752a

Vallemont, Pierre Le Lorrain, abbé de, 1649-1721, supposed author.
[Valmont, de] Dissertation sur les maléfices et les sorciers ... 1862. (Card 2)
mont. However, the Abbé died 1721, and the introductory letter is dated 1751.

1. Witchcraft. I. Vallemont, Pierre Le Lorrain, abbé de, 1649-1721, supposed author. II. Title.

Vairus, Leonardus, Bp., ca. 1540-1603.

see

Vairo, Leonardo, Bp. ca. 1540-1603.

WITCHCRAFT
BD
505
V14
1617

8

Valderrama, Pedro de. Histoire generale dv monde ... 1617. (Card 3)
1617-19 [v. 1. 1619]
2 v. in 1. 18cm.

1. Cosmology. 2. God. 3. Angels. 4. Demonology. 5. Witchcraft. I. La Richardière, sieur de, tr. II. Title.

Witchcraft
BF
1565
D17
1576

8

Vallick, Jacob.
Ein Dialogus oder Gesprech von Zäuberey.
Daneau, Lambert, ca. 1530-1595.
Von den Zauberern, Hexen, vnd Vnholden, drei christliche verscheidene [sic], vnnd zu diesen vnsern vngefärlichen Zeiten notwendige Bericht ... Durch die hoch vnd wohlgelehrte Herren, Lambertvm Danaeuvm, Iacobvm Vallick, vnnd Vlricvm Molitoris. ... Cölln, Gedruckt durch Johannem Gymnicum, 1576.
2 v. in 1. 16cm.
"Der ander Tractat von Zauberern, Hexen, vnd Vnholden, durch J. Vallick, p.
(Continued on next card)

CATALOGUE OF THE CORNELL WITCHCRAFT COLLECTION

Vallick, Jacob.
　Ein Dialogus oder Gesprech von Zäuberey.

Witchcraft
BF　　Daneau, Lambert, ca. 1530-1595.　Von den
1565　　　Zauberern, Hexen, vnd Vnholden...　1576
D17　　　　　　　　　　　　　　　　(Card 2)
1576　　157-222 of v. 1, has special t. p.
　　Translation of De veneficis, quos olim
　sortilegos ... vocant, by L. Daneau; of an
　unidentified work by J. Vallick; and of
　De lamiis et phitonicis mulieribus, by
　U. Molitor.
　　1. Witchcraft. 2. Demonology. I. His
　De veneficis, quos olim sortigelos ... vo-
8
　　　　　(Continued on next card)

WITCHCRAFT
BF　　[Valmont,　　　de]
1582　　　Dissertation sur les maléfices et les
V18　　sorciers selon les principes de la théolo-
1752a　gie et de la physique, ou l'on examine en
　　particulier l'état de la fille de Tourcoing.
　　Tourcoing, 1752.　Lille, Leleu, 1862.
　　85 p. 16cm.
　　Title in red and black.
　　"Réimpression sur l'original à deux cents
　exemplaires."
　　Note in back of text claims Barbier at-
8　　tributed this　　item to the Abbé Valle-
　　　　　(Continued on next card)

WITCHCRAFT
BF　　[Valmont,　　　de]　Dissertation sur les
1582　　　maléfices et les sorciers ...　1862.
V18　　　　　　　　　　　　　　　　(Card 2)
1752a
　　mont. However, the Abbé died 1721, and the
　　introductory letter is dated 1751.

　　1. Witchcraft. I. Vallemont, Pierre
　Le Lorrain, abbé de, 1649-1721, supposed
　author. II. Title.

The vampire, his kith and kin.
Witchcraft
GR　　Summers, Montague, 1880-1948.
830　　　The vampire, his kith and kin.
V3S95　London, Kegan Paul, Trench, Trubner &
　　Co., Ltd., 1928.
　　xv, 356 p. illus. 25cm.

　　1. Vampires. I. Title.

The vampire in Europe.
WITCHCRAFT
GR　　Summers, Montague, 1880-1948.
830　　　The vampire in Europe.　London, K. Paul,
V3　　Trench, Trubner & Co., 1929.
S95　　xii, 330 p. plates, facsim. 25cm.
1929

　　1. Vampires. I. Title.

Vander Lught, Herbert, joint author.
BT　　DeHaan, Richard W
981　　　Satan, satanism, and witchcraft, by Richard W. Dehaan
D32　　with Herbert Vander Lught. Grand Rapids, Mich., Zonder-
　　van Pub. House [1972]
　　125 p. 18 cm. (Zondervan books) $0.95
　　Bibliography: p. 123-125.

4　　1. Devil. 2. Christianity and occult sciences. I. Vander Lught,
　Herbert, joint author. II. Title.
　BT981.D44　　　235'.47　　　72-81786
　　　　　　　　　　　　　　　MARC
　Library of Congress　　　72 [4]

Van Hoogstraten, Jacobus, ca. 1460-1527.
　see
　Hoogstraten, Jacobus van, ca. 1460-1527.

The vanity of arts and sciences.
Witchcraft
B　　Agrippa von Nettesheim, Heinrich Cornelius,
781　　1486?-1535.
A33I3　　The vanity of arts and sciences ...　Lon-
1694　　don, Printed by R. Everingham for R. Bentley,
　　and Dan. Brown, 1694.
　　[18], 368 p. 19cm.
　　Prefixed: The life of Henry Cornelius
　Agrippa; His epitaph; On the learned author
　... (verse, signed: S. S.)
　　Translation of De incertitudine et vanita-
　te scientiarum atque artium declamatio invec-
　tiva.

BF　　Vartier, Jean.
1582　　　Sabbat, juges et sorciers, quatre siècles de superstitions
V29　　dans la France de l'Est. [Paris,] Hachette, 1968.
　　288 p. 21 cm. 20.00　　　　　　　　　　　　F***
　　"Notes, eclaircissements et sources": p. [267]-286.

　　1. Witchcraft—France.　I. Title.
9
　BF1582.V26　　　　　　　　　76-397594
　Library of Congress　　69 [1!]

Vatter, Hanns, von Mellingen.
Witchcraft
BF　　Gründlicher vnnd warhaffter Bericht, was
1555　　sich mit dem Mann, der sich Hanns Vatter
G31　　von Mellingen, ausdem Landt zu Düringen
　　genennt, vnnd ein zeytlang im Teutschlandt
　　herumb gezogen, zur Buss geruffen, vnd
　　bey den Leuten fürgegeben, als ob er vom
　　Sathan gepunden vnnd geplagt würde, zu
　　Nürmberg zugetragen vnnd verloffen hat.
　　Nürmberg, Gedruckt bey Valentin Geyssler,
　　1562.
　　[20] p. 20cm.
8　　　　　(Continued on next card)

Vatter, Hanns, von Mellingen.
Witchcraft
BF　　Gründlicher vnnd warhaffter Bericht, was
1555　　sich mit ... Hanns Vatter ... zugetragen
G31　　hat ...　1562.　　　　　　(Card 2)
　　"Meniglich zu warhafftem Bericht verloff-
　ner Handlungen inn Druck gegeben durch mich
　Valtin Geyssler Buchdrucker zu Nürmberg."
　　Portrait of Vatter on t. p.

　　1. Vatter, Hanns, von Mellingen. 2.
8　Demoniac possession. I. Geyssler, Valentin.

La vauderie dans les états de Philippe
　le Bon.
Witchcraft
BF　　Duverger, Arthur.
1584　　　La vauderie dans les états de Philippe
B4　　le Bon.　Arras, Imprimerie J. Moullé,
D98　　1885.
　　131 p. 19cm.
　　At head of title: Le premier grand pro-
　cès de sorcellerie aux Pays-Bas.

　　1. Witchcraft—Belgium. I. Title.
8　II. Title: Le premier grand procès de
　sorcellerie aux　　Pays-Bas.

Vaughan, Joan, d. 1612.
Witchcraft
BF　　The Witches of Northamptonshire. Agnes
1581　　Browne. Ioane Vaughan. Arthur Bill.
A2　　Hellen Ienkinson. Mary Barber. Witches.
W81　　Who were all executed at Northampton the
1866a　22. of Iuly last. 1612.　London,
no.1　Printed by Thos Purfoot, for Arthur Iohn-
　　son, 1612. [Northampton, England, Tay-
　　lor & son, 1866]
　　[28] p. 22cm.
　　No. 1 in box lettered Witchcraft in
　Northamptonshire.
8　　1. Witchcraft—Northamptonshire,
　England.　I.　Title: Witchcraft in
　Northamptonshi　　re.

Vayra, Pietro, 1838-
BF　　Fabretti, Ariodante, 1816-1894.
1517　　　Il diavolo ad Issime. Il più
I8　　sensazionale processo del Seicento.
F22　　Torino, Piemonte in bancarella, 1970.
1970　　99 p. illus. 18cm.
　　At head of title: A Fabretti and P.
　Vayra.
　　Includes bibliographical references.

　　1. Demonology. I. Vayra, Pietro,
　1838-　II. Title

NIC　APR 25,'7.　　　　　　OxC　　72-33387

Vehmgerichte und Hexenprozesse in
　Deutschland.
WITCHCRAFT
JN　　Wächter, Oskar Eberhard Siegfried von,
3269　　1825-1902.
W12　　　Vehmgerichte und Hexenprozesse in
　　Deutschland, nach den Quellen dargestellt
　　von Oskar Wächter. Stuttgart, W. Spemann
　　[1882]
　　221 p. 19cm. (Collection Spemann)
　　(Deutsche Hand- und Hausbibliothek)

　　1. Femic courts. 2. Witchcraft—
8　Germany—Hist. I. Title.

Venefica.
Witchcraft
BF　　Gebhard, Johann.
1565　　　Canidia, hoc est, Venefica, fetura caco-
G29　　daemonis spurcissimi ex creaturis praepoten-
　　tiae divinae pulcerrimis nobilissimisq facta
　　spurcissimarum omnium spurcissima; non peni-
　　culo pigmentario, sed vivo vocis characte-
　　re ex lyrici Venusini Epodis V. & XVII adumbra-
　　ta, inq; theatro Gymnasii Vratislaviensium
　　Elisabetani publico ad contemplandum ... pro-
　　ponenda, curante Johanne Gebhardo ...　Wra-
　　tislaviae, Typ　　is Baumannianis, Per
8　　　　　(Continued on next card)

Venefica.
Witchcraft
BF　　Gebhard, Johann. Canidia ...　[1651]
1565　　　　　　　　　　　　　　　(Card 2)
G29
　　Gottfridum Gründerum [1651]
　　[8] p. 20cm.

　　1. Witchcraft. I. Title. II. Title:
8　Venefica.

Venitiana, Antonio, del Rabbina.
WITCHCRAFT
BF　　Le Dragon rouge, ou l'art de commander les
1558　　　esprits célestes, aériens, terrestres,
G86　　infernaux, avec le vrai secret de faire
1823　　parler les morts, de gagner toutes les
　　fois qu'on met aux loteries, de décou-
　　vrir les trésors cachés, etc., etc.
　　Imprimé sur un manuscrit de 1522.
　　Nismes, Chez Gaude, 1823.
　　108 p. illus. 15cm.
　　Published also under other titles: Gri-
　moire du Pape　　Honorius [best-known];
8　　　　　(Continued on next card)

CATALOGUE OF THE CORNELL WITCHCRAFT COLLECTION

Venitiana, Antonio, del Rabbina.

    Le Dragon rouge ... 1823.   (Card 2)

    Le véritable dragon rouge; and L'art de commander les esprits.
        Chapter 1 signed: Antonio Venitiana, del Rabbina.

Verantwortung über die vom ... P. Don Ferdinand Sterzinger ... gestellten Fragen.

Witchcraft
BF
1565
S83
M185

    März, Angelus, 1731-1784.
        P. Angeli März Verantwortung über die vom (Titl) P. Don Ferdinand Sterzinger bey dem hochfürstlich-hochlöblich-geistlichen Rath zu Freysing freywillig wider ihn gestellten Fragen. Jngolstadt, Gedruckt bey J. K. Gran, 1767.
        42 p. 19cm.
        A copy of the questions may be found in: Fieger, Hans, 1857- . P. Don Ferdinand Sterzinger, München, 1907, p. 135.

8   (Continued on next card)

Die Verbindung des Teufels mit den Gespenstern.

WITCHCRAFT
BF
1523
K78
no.3

    [Köster, Heinrich Martin Gottfried] 1734-1802.
        Die Verbindung des Teufels mit den Gespenstern, nebst Anecdoten von Erscheinungen derselben. In Deutschland, 1777.
        118 p. 18cm.

        Attribution by Holzmann, Jocher, et al.
        No. 3 in vol. lettered Ueber den Teufel.

        1. Ghosts. 2. Apparitions. I. Title.

Das Verbrechen der Zauberei (crimen magiae)

Witchcraft

    Byloff, Fritz, 1875-
        Das Verbrechen der Zauberei (crimen magiae) Ein Beitrag zur Geschichte der Strafrechtspflege in Steiermark. Graz, Leuschner & Lubensky, 1902.
        440 p. 24cm.

        1. Criminal law-- Styria. 2. Witchcraft--Styria. I. Title.

WITCHCRAFT
BF
1566
V47

Die Verbreitung des Glaubens an Hexerei.
    (In Globus. Braunschweig. 32cm. Bd. 26, no. 19 (1874), p. 298-301)

    Folded, in envelope.

    1. Witchcraft--Hist.

8

WITCHCRAFT
BF
1511
V48

    Verdun, Paul, 1861-
        Le diable dans la vie des saints. Paris, Delhomme et Briguet [1897]
        2 v. 18cm.

        Contents.--T. 1. Du Xe au XIVe siècle.
        --T. 2. Du XVe au XIXe siècle.

        1. Demonology. 2. Devil. 3. Exorcism. 4. Demoniac possession. 5. Saints--Biog. I. Title.

Die Verfolgung der Zauberer und Hexen in dem Kurfürstenthume Trier.

WITCHCRAFT
DD
491
R4
A67
v.1

    Liel, Anselm Franz Joseph.
        Die Verfolgung der Zauberer und Hexen in dem Kurfürstenthume Trier. Ein Beitrag zur vaterländischen Geschichte.
        (In: Archiv für rheinische Geschichte Coblenz. 23cm. v.1 (1833) p.17-46)

8
NIC

        1. Witchcraft--Treves. 2. Trials (Witchcraft)--Treves.

Verhandeling, over Balthasar Bekker.

Witchcraft
BX
9479
B42
A68

    Arend, Johannes Pieter, 1796-1855.
        Verhandeling, over Balthasar Bekker. Door J. P. Arend, Lector in de hoogduitsche en engelsche talen en letterkunde aan de doorluchtige school te Deventer.
        (In Vaderlandsche letteroefeningen. Mengelwerk, tot fraaije letteren, konsten en weetenschappen, betrekkelyk. Amsterdam. 23cm. no. 16 (1829), p. [713]-743)
        8°: 3A-3B^8, 3B^6.
        This issue   paged: [713]-756.

        (Continued on next card)

Verhandeling over het booze wezen in het bijgeloof onzer natie.

WITCHCRAFT
BF
1517
N4
N67

    Niermeyer, Antonie.
        Verhandeling over het booze wezen in het bijgeloof onzer natie. Eene bijdrage tot de kennis onzer voorvaderlijke mythologie. Rotterdam, A. Wijnands, 1840.
        xiv, 115 p. 24cm.

8
NIC

        1. Devil. 2. Demonology. 3. Folk-lore--Netherlands.

Das verhexte Kloster.

WITCHCRAFT
BF
1583
Z7
1749c

    Memminger, Anton.
        Das verhexte Kloster. Nach den Akten dargestellt. Würzburg, Memminger, 1904.
        iv, 273 p. 19cm.

8
NIC

Das verhexte Kloster.

WITCHCRAFT
BF
1583
Z7
1749d

    Memminger, Anton.
        Das verhexte Kloster. Nach den Akten dargestellt. 2. verb. Aufl Würzburg, Memminger, 1908.
        181 p. 21cm. (Fränkische Bibliothek, Bd.2)

        1. Sánger, Maria Renata von Mossau, ca. 1680-1749. 2. Trials (Witchcraft)--Germany. I. Title.

8
NIC

Verhörsprotokoll über einen der Hexerei Angeklagten.

WITCHCRAFT
BF
1583
Z7
1680

    Hessler, Matthes, defendant.
        Verhörsprotokoll über einen der Hexerei Angeklagten. Fröstedt, den 27. July 1680.
        (In Aus der Heimath. Blätter der Vereinigung für Gothaische Geschichte und Alterthumsforschung. Gotha. 25cm. 1. Jahrg., Nr. 3 (1897), p. 41-43)

        1. Trials (Witchcraft)--Germany. I. Title. II. Aus der Heimath.

8

Il Verino Secondo.

    see

Vieri, Francesco de, called Il Verino Secondo.

WITCHCRAFT
BF
1558
G86
1800a

Le Véritable dragon rouge, ou l'Art de commander les esprits célestes, aériens, terrestres et infernaux, avec le secret de faire parler les morts; de gagner toutes les fois qu'on met aux loteries; de découvrir les trésors cachés; etc., etc.; suivi de La poule noire, cabale qui était restée inconnue jusqu'ici.
    [Lille, Imprimerie de Blocquel] 1521 [i.e., 18--]
    140 p. illus. 16cm.

8   (Continued on next card)

WITCHCRAFT
BF
1558
G86
1800a

Le Véritable dragon rouge ... [18--]
        (Card 2)

    Title in red and black.
    Chapter 1 signed: J. Karter, Venetiana.
    Published also under other titles: Grimoire du Pape Honorius [best-known]; Le dragon rouge; and L'art de commander les esprits.

    1. Incantations. 2. Magic. I. Karter, J. II. Title: Grimoire du Pape Honorius. III. Title: Le dragon rouge. IV. Title: L'art de commander les esprits. V. Title: La poule noire.

8

Le véritable dragon rouge.

WITCHCRAFT
BF
1558
G86
1750

L'Art de commander les esprits célestes, aériens, terrestres & infernaux. Suivi du Grand grimoire, de la magie noire et des forces infernales, du docteur J. Karter, La clavicule de Salomon, &c. Avec le vrai secret de faire parler les morts, pour découvrir tous les trésors caches, &c. &c. [Paris?] 1421 [i.e., ca. 1750?]
    iv, 5-108 [i. e., 118], [2] p. illus. 16cm.
    Title in red and black.

8   (Continued on next card)

Le véritable dragon rouge.

WITCHCRAFT
BF
1558
G86
1750

L'Art de commander les esprits ... [1750?]
        (Card 2)

    Published also under other titles: Grimoire du Pape Honorius [best-known]; Le dragon rouge; and Le véritable dragon rouge.

    1. Incantations. 2. Magic. I. Karter, J. II. Title: Le grand grimoire. III. Title: Grimoire du Pape Honorius. IV. Title: Le dragon rouge. V. Title: Le véritable dragon rouge. VI. Title: La clavicule de Salomon.

8

Le véritable dragon rouge.

WITCHCRAFT
BF
1558
G86
1823

Le Dragon rouge, ou l'art de commander les esprits célestes, aériens, terrestres, infernaux, avec le vrai secret de faire parler les morts, de gagner toutes les fois qu'on met aux loteries, de découvrir les trésors cachés, etc.
    Imprimé sur un manuscrit de 1522.
    Nismes, Chez Gaude, 1823.
    108 p. illus. 15cm.
    Published also under other titles: Grimoire du Pape   Honorius [best-known];

3   (Continued on next card)

CATALOGUE OF THE CORNELL WITCHCRAFT COLLECTION

```
                Le véritable dragon rouge.
WITCHCRAFT
BF           Le Dragon rouge ... 1823.   (Card 2)
1558
G86          Le véritable dragon rouge; and L'art de
1823      commander les esprits.
               Chapter 1 signed: Antonio Venitiana,
          del Rabbina.

             1. Incantations. 2. Magic. I. Veni-
          tiana, Antonio, del Rabbina. II. Title:
          Grimoire du Pape Honorius. III. Title:
 8        Le véritable       dragon rouge. IV. Ti-
          tle: L'art       de commander les esprits.
```

```
              Le véritable dragon rouge--German.
WITCHCRAFT
BF            Der Wahrhaftige feurige Drache; oder, Herr-
1405        schaft über die himmlischen und hölli-
S41         schen Geister und über die Mächte der
no.6        Erde und Luft ... Nebst den geheimen
            Mitteln, sich die schwarze Henne mit der
            goldnen Eiern zu verschaffen ... Nach
            einem in Frankreich aufgefundenen Manu-
            script von 1522. Nebst einem Postscrip-
            tum aus dem grossen Buche von König Salo-
            mo, mit einigen köstlichen Recepten, ge-
            funden bei Peter Michel, dem letzten
 8
NIC                         (Continued on next card)
```

```
              Le véritable dragon rouge--German.
WITCHCRAFT
BF            Der Wahrhaftige feurige Drache ...  [ca.
1405          1880]                           (Card 2)
S41
no.6        Karthäuser zu Erfurt. [Berlin, E. Bar-
            tels, ca. 1880]
              125 p. illus. 17cm.
              Translation of Le véritable dragon rouge,
            which was published under a variety of ti-
            tles, the best-known being Grimoire du Pape
            Honorius.
              Erstes Buch, erstes Kapitel signed: Rab-
 8
NIC                         (Continued on next card)
```

```
              Le véritable dragon rouge--German.
WITCHCRAFT
BF            Der Wahrhaftige fuerige Drache ... [ca.
1405          1880]                          (Card 3)
S41
no.6         bi Anton Moses el Arradsch.
             No. 6 in vol. lettered Der schwarze Raabe.

            1. Incantations. 2. Magic. I. Anton
          Moses el Arradsch. II. Le véritable dragon
          rouge. German. III. Grimoire du Pape
          Honorius. German.

 8
NIC
```

```
              Veritable relation des iustes procedures
                observees au faict de la possession des
WITCHCRAFT       Ursulines de Loudun.
BF            Tranquille de Saint-Rémi, capuchin.
1517          Veritable relation des ivstes procedvres
F5          observees av faict de la possession des Vr-
T77         sulines de Loudun. Et au procez d'Vrbain
1634a       Grandier. Auec les theses generales touchant
            les diables exorcisez. Par le R. P. Tran-
            quille, Capucin. La Fleche, Chez George
            Griveav, imprimeur ordinaire du roy, 1634.
              80 p. 14cm.
              Expanded version of the Poictiers text.
              1. Loudun,        France. Ursuline Convent.
            2. Grandier,      Urbain, 1590-1634. 3.
            Exorcism. I.     Title.
```

```
Witchcraft
BF            Den verkeerden duyvel van den throon geschopt,
1410        en den rechten weder hervoort gebragt, ver-
B42         handeelde van engelen en duyvelen, hare
Z56         macht ende werkinge, waar in besonderlyk
v.2         getoont wort wat den duyvel is, schrift-
no.16       matigh voorgestelt, waar in de swaarste
            stukken van die materie worden opgelost,
            noch noyt zoo voortgestelt. Door K. A.
            H. Amsterdam, By N. Holbeex, boekver-
            kooper, 1692.
              2 p. 1., 36 p.  title and end page vi-
            gnettes, illus.     initials. 19 x 15cm.

                            (Continued on next card)
```

```
Witchcraft
BF            Den verkeerden duyvel van den throon geschopt
1410        ... 1692.                       (Card 2)
B42
Z56           4°: *², A-D⁴, E².
v.2
no.16         Black letter (except for introduction)
              Modeled on Balthasar Bekker's De betoverde
            weereld, but not always supporting it.
              Van der Linde 66.
              No. 16 in vol. lettered Bekker II.
              1. Demonology. 2. Angels. 3. Magic.
            4. Witchcraft.     5. Bekker, Balthasar,
            1634-1698.         De betoverde weereld.
            I. Title.          II. K. A. H. III.
 8          H., K. A.
```

```
              Verklaeringe van een turkse parabel: of
                Voorbeeld der mahumetaense kerktucht.
Witchcraft
BF            Bly, Gratianus de
1410          Verklaeringe van een turkse parabel: of
B42         Voorbeeld der mahumetaense kerktucht: in
Z56         rijm gesteld door Mr. Gratianus de Bly, vol-
v.3         gens de vertaelinge uit seker arabisch
no.2        schrijver. ... [Amsterdam?] By J. Rieu-
            wertsz, boekverkooper, 1691.
              54 p. end page vignette, illus. initial.
            19 x 15cm.
              4°: A-G⁴(-G4)
              A collection      of satirical verse and
            prose, other        authors included, in
 8
                            (Continued on next card)
```

```
              Verklaeringe van een turkse parabel: of
                Voorbeeld der mahumetaense kerktucht.
Witchcraft
BF            Bly, Gratianus de  Verklaeringe van een
1410        turkse parabel ... 1691.    (Card 2)
B42
Z56         defense of Balthasar Bekker.
v.3           Gratianus de Bly is possibly a pseudonym.
no.2          No. 2 in vol. lettered Bekker III.
              1. Bekker, Balthasar, 1634-1698. I.
            Title.
```

```
                Das verlohrne und wiedergefundene
                  Schäfflein.
WITCHCRAFT
BF            Scriver, Christian, 1629-1693.
1572          Das verlohrne und wiedergefundene
D4          Schäfflein, oder Historischer christlicher
S43         Bericht von einem jungen Menschen, der
            sich vom Satan mit ihm einen Bund zu machen
            und ihm in allerley gottlosen Wesen sechs
            Jahr zu dienen verleiten lassen, darauff
            durch des gerechten Gottes Urtheil in des-
            sen leibliche Gewalt und Besitzung gerathen,
            erschröcklich gequälet, endlich aber ...
            errettet und         befreyet worden ...
 8
NIC                         (Continued on next card)
```

```
              Das verlohrne und wiedergefundene
                Schäfflein.
WITCHCRAFT
BF            Scriver, Christian, 1629-1693.  Das ver-
1572        lohrne und wiedergefundene Schäfflein ...
D4          1672.                           (Card 2)
S43
            Magdeburg und Helmstedt, Johann und Fried-
            rich Lüderwaldts Buchhändl., 1672.
              [116] p. 19cm.
              "Historischer Bericht, den gantzen Ver-
            lauff mit dem Soldaten, dessen in denen
            vorhergesätzten Predigten Meldung gesche-
            hen, fürstellend" has special t. p.
 8
NIC                         (Continued on next card)
```

```
              Vermeerderde articulen voor te stellen
                aen Do. B: Bekker.
Witchcraft
BF            Nederlandse Hervormde Kerk.   Classes.
1410        Amsterdam.
B42           Vermeerderde articulen voor te stellen
Z85         aen Do. B: Bekker. [Amsterdam, 1691]
no.1          [4] p. 19 x 16cm.
              4°: π².
              Caption title.
              Text given also in its Autentyke copye
            van de articulen ... den 23 Aug. 1691
            opgestelt zyn. [Van der Linde 30]
              No. 1 in vol.     lettered Stukken betrek-
            kelijk Bekker.
 8                          (Continued on next card)
```

```
WITCHCRAFT Vermigli, Pietro Martire, 1500-1562.
BF           Lavater, Ludwig, 1527-1586.
1445         Trois livres des apparitions des esprits,
L39        fantosmes, prodiges & accidens merueilleux qui
1571       precedent souuentesfois la mort de quelque per-
           sonnage renommé, ou vn grand changement és
           choses de ce monde: traduits d'Alleman en Fran-
           çois: conferez, reueus et augmentez sur le La-
           tin. Plus trois questions proposees & resolues
           par M. Pierre Martyr excellent theologien, les-
           quelles conuiennent à ceste matiere: traduites
           aussi de Latin en François. [Genève] De
           l'Imprimerie de François Perrin, pour Iean Du-
           rant, 1571.
                            (Continued on next card)
```

```
WITCHCRAFT Vermigli, Pietro Martire, 1500-1562.
BF           Lavater, Ludwig, 1527-1586. Trois livres des
1445       apparitions ... 1571.         (Card 2)
L39
1571         [16], 304, [11] p. 17cm.

             Translation of De spectris, lemuribus et
           magnis atque insolitis fragoribus.

             1. Apparitions. 2. Ghosts. 3. Demonology.
           I. Lavater, Ludwig, 1527-1586. De spectris,
           lemuribus et magnis atque insolitis fragoribus--
           French. II. Vermigli, Pietro Martire, 1500-
           1562.
```

```
              Vermischte Anmerkungen über ... Gottlieb
                Müllers Gründlichen Nachricht.
WITCHCRAFT
BF           [Bobbe, Johann Benjamin Gottlieb]
1555          Vermischte Anmerkungen über Sr. Hoch-
M94        ehrwürden des Herrn Probstes und Superin-
B66        tendentens in Kemberg Herrn Gottlieb Müllers
           Gründlichen Nachricht und deren Anhang von
           einer begeisterten Weibesperson Annen Eli-
           sabeth Lohmännin, mitgetheilet von Antidä-
           moniacus. Bernburg, Bey C. G. Cörner,
           1760.
             134 p. 18cm.
             Attribution by Holzmann.
 8
                            (Continued on next card)
```

```
              Vermischte Beyträge zur Beförderung einer
                nähern Einsicht in das gesamte Geisterreich.
Witchcraft
BF           Reichard, Elias Caspar, 1714-1791.
1547          Vermischte Beyträge zur Beförderung einer
R34        nähern Einsicht in das gesamte Geisterreich.
           Zur Verminderung und Tilgung des Unglaubens
           und Aberglaubens. Als eine Fortsetzung von
           D. David Eberhard Haubers Magischen Biblio-
           thek herausgegeben. Helmstedt, Johann
           Heinrich Kühnlin, 1781-88.
             2 v. 19cm.

             Vol. 1 in 4 parts, each with special t.p.
```

```
              Vernünfftige und christliche aber nicht
                scheinheilige Thomasische Gedancken und
                Erinnerungen.
Witchcraft
B            Thomasius, Christian, 1655-1728.
2605          Vernünfftige und christliche aber nicht
V5         scheinheilige Thomasische Gedancken und
           Erinnerungen über allerhand gemischte phi-
           losophische und juristica Händel. Halle
           im Magdeburg, In der Rengerischen Buchhand-
           lung, 1723-25.
             3 v. front. 18cm.
             Title of v. 1 in red and black.
             "Es folgt ... jetzo der fünffte Theil
           der Juristischen    Händel [1720-21], jedoch
                            (Continued on next card)
```

```
              Vernünfftige und christliche aber nicht
                scheinheilige Thomasische Gedancken und
                Erinnerungen.
Witchcraft
B            Thomasius, Christian, 1655-1728. Vernünff-
2605       tige und christliche aber nicht scheinhei-
V5         lige Thomasische Gedancken ... 1723-25.
                                             (Card 2)

           mit einiger Änderung."--Vorrede, 1. Bd.
Witchcraft
B          ---Anhang zu denen Thomasischen gemischten
2605       Händeln. Halle im Magdeburgischen, In der
V5         Rengerischen Buchhandlung, 1726.
suppl.        224 p. 18cm.

                            (Continued on next card)
```

572

CATALOGUE OF THE CORNELL WITCHCRAFT COLLECTION

Witchcraft
B
2605
V5
suppl.
    Vernünfftige und christliche aber nicht scheinheilige Thomasische Gedancken und Erinnerungen.
    Thomasius, Christian, 1655-1728. Vernünfftige und christliche aber nicht scheinheilige Thomasische Gedancken ... 1723-25. (Card 3)

    Bound with v. 2.

    1. Philosophers, German--Correspondence, reminiscences, etc. 2. Witchcraft. I. His Ernsthaffte aber doch muntere ... Gedancken ... Über ... juristische Händel. II. His Anhang zu denen Thomasischen gemischten Händeln. III. Title.

WITCHCRAFT
R
133
H71
D2
1749
    Vernunfftmässige Abhandlung von dem heidnischen Fato.
    Hoffmann, Friedrich, 1660-1742.
    D. Friedrich Hoffmanns ... Vernunfftmässige Abhandlung von dem heidnischen Fato, und der christlichen Providentz, in medicinisch- und physicalischen Dingen. Sorau, Bey G. Hebold, 1749.
    116 p. 17cm.
    Translation of De fato physico et medico ejusque rationali explicatione disquisitio. Halae Magdeb., 1724.
    Added t. p.: D. Friedrich Hoffmanns ...

8
NIC
(Continued on next card)

WITCHCRAFT
R
133
H71
D2
1749
    Vernunfftmässige Abhandlung von dem heidnischen Fato.
    Hoffmann, Friedrich, 1660-1742. ... Vernunfftmässige Abhandlung von dem heidnischen Fato ... 1749. (Card 2)
    Gründliche vernunfft- und schrifftmässige Betrachtung von der Würckung, Macht und Gewalt des Teuffels in der Lufft und menschlichen Körpern [translation of Disputatio inauguralis medico-philosophica De potentia diaboli in corpora. Halae, 1703]
    1. Medicine, Magic, mystic, and spagiric 2. Fate and fatalism. 3. Medical delusions.

8
NIC
(Continued on next card)

WITCHCRAFT
BF
1775
S38
1757
    Vernunft- und schriftmässige Abhandlung von Aberglauben.
    Schütze, Heinrich Carl, 1700-1781.
    Vernunft- und schriftmässige Abhandlung von Aberglauben. Nebst einem Anhange von Astral-Geist. Wernigerode, J. G. Struck, 1757.
    9 p. l., 496, [16] p. front. 17cm.

    1. Superstition. 2. Occult sciences. I. Title. II. Title: Astral-Geist.

8
NIC

Witchcraft
BF
1410
B42
Z88
    Verrijn, Johannes, d. 1698.
    Aenmerckingen op De betoverde werelt van Dr. Balthazar Bekker, nopende de geesten, en hun vermogen, en byzonderlijck den staet, en magt des duyvels. Door J. Verryn. Amsterdam, By G. Slaats, boekverkoper, 1692.
    4 p. l., 136 p. title and end page vignettes, illus. initials. 22 x 17cm.
    4⁰: *⁴, A-R⁴.
    Black letter.
    Van der Linde 150.
(Continued on next card)

Witchcraft
BF
1410
B42
Z88
    Verrijn, Johannes, d. 1698. Aenmerckingen op De betoverde werelt van Dr. Balthazar Bekker ... 1692. (Card 2)

    1. Bekker, Balthasar, 1634-1698. De betoverde wereld. 2. Devil. 3. Spirits. I. Title.

Witchcraft
BF
1410
B42
Z69
no.15
    Verrijn, Johannes, d. 1698.
    Aenmerckingen op De betoverde werelt van Dr. Balthazar Bekker, nopende de geesten, en hun vermogen, en byzonderlijck den staet, en magt des duyvels. Door J. Verryn. Amsterdam, By G. Slaats, boekverkoper, 1692.
    4 p. l., 136 p. title and end page vignettes, illus. initials. 21cm.
    4⁰; *⁴, A-R⁴.
    Black letter.
    Van der Linde 150.
(Continued on next card)

Witchcraft
BF
1410
B42
Z69
no.15
    Verrijn, Johannes, d. 1698. Aenmerckingen op De betoverde werelt van Dr. Balthazar Bekker ... 1692. (Card 2)

    No. 15 in a Collection of tracts against Balthasar Bekker and his Betoverde weereld.

Witchcraft
BF
1410
B42
Z86
no.10
    Verrijn, Johannes, d. 1698.
    Aenmerckingen op De betoverde werelt van Dr. Balthazar Bekker, nopende de geesten, en hun vermogen, en byzonderlijck den staet, en magt des duyvels. Door J. Verryn. Amsterdam, By G. Slaats, boekverkoper, 1692.
    4 p. l., 136 p. title and end page vignettes, illus. initials. 19 x 15cm.
    4⁰: *⁴, A-R⁴.
    Black letter.
    Van der Linde 150.
    No. 10 in vol. lettered Tractaten voor en tegen B. Bekker.

8

    Verryn, J

        see

    Verrijn, Johannes, d. 1698.

Witchcraft
BF
1410
B42
Z89
    Verscheyde gedichten, so voor, als tegen het boek, genaamt: De betoverde weereld. [Amsterdam?] Gedrukt voor de liefhebbers, 1691.
    1 p. l., 12, 9-32 p. title vignettes, illus. initials. 20 x 15cm.
    4⁰: π1, A⁶, B-D⁴.
    First poem has own t. p. with title: Gestroojde zeegen-palmen, op het doorwrogte werk van de Heer Balthasar Bekker ... genaamd De betooverde weereld. [Van der Linde 188]
(Continued on next card)

Witchcraft
BF
1410
B42
Z89
    Verscheyde gedichten, so voor, als tegen het boek, genaamt: De betoverde weereld. 1691. (Card 2)
    Includes other works published separately: De betoverde predikant Dr. Balthasar Bekker [van der Linde 189]; Verta[e]ling uit seker arabisch schryver; De geharpoende muys.
    Van der Linde 197.
    1. Bekker, Balthasar, 1634-1698. De betoverde weereld. I. Gestroojde zeegen-
(Continued on next card)

8

Witchcraft
BF
1410
B42
Z89
    Verscheyde gedichten, so voor, als tegen het boek, genaamt: De betoverde weereld. 1691. (Card 3)
    palmen. II. De betoverde predikant Dr. Balthasar Bekker. III. Vertaeling uit seker arabisch schryver. IV. De geharpoende muys.

Witchcraft
BF
1410
B42
Z892
    Vervolg van Verscheyde gedigten, &c. voor als tegen het boek genaamt De betoverde werelt. [Amsterdam?] Gedrukt voor de liefhebbers, 1692.
    1 p. l., 54 p. title vignette, illus. initial. 20 x 16cm.
    4⁰: π 1, A-F⁴, G3.
    Contains prose as well as poems.
    First poem has own t. p. with title: Verklaeringe van een turkse parabel ... door Mr. Gratianus de Bly...

8
(Continued on next card)

Witchcraft
BF
1410
B42
Z892
    Vervolg van Verscheyde gedigten, &c. 1692. (Card 2)
    Klinkende bel; of uytroep om den verlooren duyvel: P. 17-19. [Van der Linde 194]
    Variant of van der Linde 198: signatures differ (but not paging).

    1. Bekker, Balthasar, 1634-1698. De betoverde wereld. I. Verscheyde
(Continued on next card)

WITCHCRAFT
BT
980
V83
    Verstooringe des Satans Ryck.
    Visscher, Volkard, 1639-1678.
    Verstooringe des Satans Ryck; voorgestelt in zwee Predikatien over 1. Cor. 10: vers 20. en Matt. 4, vers 1, &c. Onlanghs openttlyck geleert door de Eerwaerdige en Hoogh-Geleerden, nu Zal: Heer. En nu in 't Licht gegeven tot onderwijs van de eenduldigen en obertuygingh aller Lastertongen; door een Liefhebber van Godts Herck. t'Amsterdam, by J. van Someren, 1678.
    24 p. 20cm.

8
NIC
    1. Devil--Biblical teaching. 2. Bible. N. T.--Commentaries. 3. Jesus Christ--Temptation.

WITCHCRAFT
BF
1501
D12
no.1
    Versuch einer biblischen Dämonologie.
    [Hesse, Otto Justus Basilius] d. 1793.
    Versuch einer biblischen Dämonologie, oder Untersuchung der Lehre der heil. Schrift vom Teufel und seiner Macht. Mit einer Vorrede und einem Anhang von D. Johann Salomo Semler. Halle im Magdeburgischen, C. H. Hemmerde, 1776.
    28 p. l., 359 p. 17cm.
    No. 1 in vol. lettered Dämonologische Schriften.
    1. Devil. 2. Demonomania. 3. Bible--Criticism, interpretation, etc. I. Semler, Johann Salomo, 1725-1791. II. Title.

8

Witchcraft
BF
1583
A2
S39
    Versuch einer Geschichte der Hexenprozesse.
    Schwager, Johann Moritz.
    Versuch einer Geschichte der Hexenprozesse. Von Johann Moriz Schwager. 1. Bd. Berlin, J. F. Unger, 1784.
    344 p. port. 23cm.

    Includes transcripts of mss.
    No more published.

    1. Trials (Witchcraft)--Germany. 2. Witchcraft--Germany. I. Title.

8

CATALOGUE OF THE CORNELL WITCHCRAFT COLLECTION

Versuch einer Theorie des religiösen Wahnsinns.

arW 37207
Ideler, Karl Wilhelm, 1795-1860.
Versuch einer Theorie des religiösen Wahnsinns; ein Beitrag zur Kritik der religiösen Wirren der Gegenwart. Halle, C. A. Schwetschke, 1848-1850.
2 v. 22cm.

1. Hallucinations and illusions. I. Title.

Versuch über die Dämonischen des Neuen Testamentes.

WITCHCRAFT
BF 1501
D12
no.2

Farmer, Hugh, 1714-1787.
Hugo Farmers Versuch über die Dämonischen des Neuen Testamentes. Aus dem Englischen übersetzt von L. F. A. von Cölln. Nebst einer Vorrede D. Joh. Sal. Semlers. Bremen und Leipzig, Bey J. H. Cramer, 1776.
38, 327 p. 17cm.
Translation of An essay on the demoniacs of the New Testament.
No. 2 in vol. lettered Dämonologische Schriften.

8   (Continued on next card)

Witchcraft
BF 1410
B42
Z56
v.2
no.11

Vertaeling uit seker arabisch schryver. Hamets Sidach Effendi, voornaem turks leeraer, verhaelt in syne wederlegginge van 't gevoelen der Sadduceen, een parabel of gelykenisse, die, hoewel Mahometans, echter in dese tyden met vrucht onder de Christenen kan gelesen worden. [Amsterdam, By P. Rotterdam, 1692]
4 p. illus. initial. 19 x 15cm.
4°: A².
Caption title.
                    (Continued on next card)

Witchcraft
BF 1410
B42
Z56
v.2
no.11

Vertaeling uit seker arabisch schryver. [1691]
                    (Card 2)
"Redenering over de nuttigheid der fabelen": p. 3-4.
Parable itself published also in Verscheyde gedichten, so voor, als tegen het boek, genaamt: De betoverde weereld.
No. 11 in vol. lettered Bekker II.

1. Parables. 2. Bekker, Balthasar, 1634-1698. De betoverde weereld.

Witchcraft
BF 1410
B42
Z89

Vertaeling uit seker arabisch schryver.
Verscheyde gedichten, so voor, als tegen het boek, genaamt: De betoverde weereld. [Amsterdam?] Gedrukt voor de liefhebbers, 1691.
1 p. l., 12, 9-32 p. title vignettes, illus. initials. 20 x 15cm.
4°: π1, A⁶, B-D⁴.
First poem has own t. p. with title: Gestroojde zeegen-palmen, op het doorwrogte werk van de Heer Balthasar Bekker ... genaamd De betoverde weereld. [Van der Linde 188]

8   (Continued on next card)

Witchcraft
BF 1410
B42
Z89

Vertaeling uit seker arabisch schryver.
Verscheyde gedichten, so voor, als tegen het boek, genaamt: De betoverde weereld.
                    (Card 2)
1691.
Includes other works published separately: De betoverde predikant Dr. Balthasar Bekker [van der Linde 189]; Verta[e]ling uit seker arabisch schryver; De geharpoende muys. Van der Linde 197.
1. Bekker, Balthasar, 1634-1698. De betoverde weereld. I. Gestroojde zeegen-

8   (Continued on next card)

Witchcraft
BF 1410
B42
Z56
v.2
no.12

vertaeling uit seker arabisch schryver.
De Geharpoende muys. Of staatkundige consideratien, over zeekere arabische vertaalinge, uyt een turkx leeraar Hamets Sidach Effendi. Raakende het gewoel, over Do. Balthasar Bekkers Betoverde weereld. Beneffens Minerva en Mercurius; aan de betoverde schriftgeleerden. [Amsterdam?] 1691.
12 p. title vignette. 19 x 15cm.
4°: A⁴, B².
Published also in Verscheyde gedichten, so voor, als tegen het boek, genaamt: De betoverde weereld.
No.12 in vol. lettered Bekker II.

Ein Vertheidiger der Wahrheit und aufrichtiger Menschenfreund.

Witchcraft
BF 1559
G25

Gründlicher Beweiss, dass die Art, mit welcher der nun in ganz Deutschland berühmte hochw. Herr Pfarrer zu Klösterl Johann Joseph Gassner die Krankheiten zu heilen pflegt, den evangelischen Grundsätzen und den Gesinnungen der allerersten Kirche ganz gleichförmig sey. Von einem Vertheidiger der Wahrheit und aufrichtigem Menschenfreunde in öffentlichen Druck gegeben. Augsburg, Bey J. Wolff, 1775.
93 p. 19cm.

8   (Continued on next card)

Ein Vertheidiger der Wahrheit und aufrichtiger Menschenfreund.

Witchcraft
BF 1559
G25

Gründlicher Beweiss ... von einem Vertheidiger der Wahrheit ... 1775. (Card 2)

Bound with Gassner, Johann Joseph, 1727-1779. Antwort auf die Anmerkungen, welche in dem Münchnerischen Intelligenzblat ... gemacht worden. Augsburg, 1774.

1. Gassner, Johann Joseph, 1727-1779. 2. Exorcism. 3. Medicine, Magic, mystic, and spagiric. I. Ein Vertheidiger der Wahrheit und aufrichtiger Menschenfreund.

Vertheidigung wider die geschwulstige Vertheidigung der betrügenden Zauberkunst und traumenden Hexerey.

Witchcraft
BF 1565
S83
S835

März, Agnellus [1726-1784]
Vertheidigung wider die geschwulstige Vertheidigung der betrügenden Zauberkunst und traumenden Hexerey, verfasset von einem Liebhaber der Wahrheit. [München] 1767.
[4] p.l., 104 p. 23cm.

1. Sterzinger, Ferdinand, 1721-1786. Betrügende Zauberkunst und träumende Hexerey. I. Ein Liebhaber der Wahrheit. II. Title.

Witchcraft
BF 1410
B42
Z892

Vervolg van Verscheyde gedigten, &c. So voor als tegen het boek genaamt De betoverde werelt. [Amsterdam?] Gedrukt voor de liefhebbers, 1692.
1 p. l., 54 p. title vignette, illus. initial. 20 x 16cm.
4°: π1, A-F⁴, G3.
Contains prose as well as poems.
First poem has own t. p. with title: Verklaeringe van een turkse parabel ... door Mr. Gratianus de Bly...

                    (Continued on next card)

Witchcraft
BF 1410
B42
Z892

Vervolg van Verscheyde gedigten, &c. 1692.
                    (Card 2)
Klinkende bel; of uytroep om den verlorenen duyvel: P. 17-19. [Van der Linde 194]
Variant of van der Linde 198: signatures differ (but not paging).

1. Bekker, Balthasar, 1634-1698. De betoverde weereld. I. Verscheyde

                    (Continued on next card)

Witchcraft
BF 1410
B42
Z892

Vervolg van Verscheyde gedigten, &c. 1692.
                    (Card 3)
gedichten, so voor, als tegen het boek, genaamt: De betoverde weereld. II. Bly, Gratianus de. Verklaering van een turkse parabel. III. Klinkende bel; of uytroep om den verloorenen duyvel.

Die Verwaltung des Exorcistats nach Massgabe des römischen Benediktionale.

Witchcraft
BX 2340
B62
1893

Bischofberger, Theobald.
Die Verwaltung des Exorcistats nach Massgabe des römischen Benediktionale. 2. verm. und verb. Aufl. Neue Ausg. Stuttgart, J. Roth, 1893.
57 p. 18cm.

Verworffener Hexen- und Zauberer-Advocat.

Witchcraft
BF 1565
G62

Goldschmidt, Peter, d. 1713.
Verworffener Hexen- und Zauberer-Advocat. Das ist: wolgegründete Vernichtung des thörichten Vorhabens Hn. Christiani Thomasii J. U. D. & Professoris Hallensis und aller derer, welche durch ihre super-kluge Phantasie-Grillen dem teufflischen Hexen-Geschmeiss das Wort reden wollen ... Hamburg, G. Liebernickel, 1705.
[13], 654, [19] p. illus. 18cm.
1. Thomasius, Christian, 1655-1728. I. Title.

Witchcraft
BF 1576
V58+

Vessie, Percy R., d. 1953.
Hereditary chorea: St. Anthony's dance and witchcraft in colonial Connecticut. [n. p., 1939]
[7] p. illus. 28cm.

"Reprinted from Journal of the Connecticut State Medical Society, vol. 3, no. 11, November, 1939."

1. Witchcraft--Connecticut. 2. Chorea. I. Title. II. St. Anthony's dance and witchcraft in colonial Connecticut.

Vesten for sø og østen for hav; trolddom i København og i Edinburgh 1590, et bidrag til hekseprocessernes historie.

WITCHCRAFT
BF 1584
D4
L72

Liisberg, Bering, 1854-1929.
Vesten for sø og østen for hav; trolddom i København og i Edinburgh 1590, et bidrag til hekseprocessernes historie. København, A. Christiansen, 1909.
143 p. 20cm.

1. Witchcraft--Copenhagen. 2. Witchcraft--Edinburgh. 3. Trials (Witchcraft)--Copenhagen. 4. Trials (Witchcraft)--Edinburgh. I. Title.

8
NIC

Vicecomes, Zacharias.

see

Visconti, Zaccaria.

574

CATALOGUE OF THE CORNELL WITCHCRAFT COLLECTION

Vidas magicas e Inquisición.

Witchcraft
BF 1595
C29

Caro Baroja, Julio, 1914-
  Vidas magicas e Inquisición. Madrid, Taurus, 1967.
  2 v. 24cm.

1. Witchcraft--Spain. 2. Magic--Spain. I. Inquisition. Spain. II. Title.

Vie de Joseph Balsamo.

Witchcraft
BF 1598
C13
B23
1791

[Barberi]
  Vie de Joseph Balsamo, connu sous le nom de comte Cagliostro. Extraite de la procédure instruite contre lui à Rome en 1790. Traduite d'après l'original italien, imprimé à la Chambre apostolique. Enrichie de notes curieuses, et ornée de son portrait. 2. éd. Paris, Onfroy, 1791.
  xxvi, 239 p. front. (port.) 19cm.

Translation of Compendio della vita e delle gesta di Giuseppe Balsamo.
(Continued on next card)

Vie de Joseph Balsamo.

Witchcraft
BF 1598
C13
B23
1791

[Barberi]   Vie de Joseph Balsamo
  ... 1791.   (Card 2)

With this is bound Goupil, P. E. A. Essais historiques sur ... Marie Antoinette. Londres, 1789.

1. Cagliostro, Alessandro, conte di, assumed name of Giuseppe Balsamo, 1743-1795. I. Barberi. Compendio della vita e delle gesta di Giuseppe Balsamo--French. II. Title.

La vie exécrable de Guillemette Babin.

Witchcraft
513
4
26

Garçon, Maurice, 1899-
  ... La vie exécrable de Guillemette Babin, sorcière. Paris, H. Piazza [1926]
  viii, 151, [1] p., 2 l. plates. 21cm.
  "Exemplaire n° 220."

I. Title.
Library of Congress   PQ2613.A44V5 1926   26-17655
Copyright A--Foreign   31061
                        [2]

Vierde briev van Haggébher Philaleethees, geschreeven aan zynen vriend N. N.

Witchcraft
BF 1410
B42
Z69
no.6

[Hooght, Everard van der] d. 1716.
  Vierde briev van הגבר Φιλαληθης Haggébher Philaleethees, geschreeven aan zynen vriend N. N. over het weesen, denken, willen, vermoogen, ende de plaats der engelen in het gemeen, ende der quade geesten, in het byzonder. Item, van des menschen ziele, en harewerking, het zy afgesondert, ofte ook vereenigt met her lichaam; ende hoe verre de quade geesten op de selve konnen werken. Met een onder   soek of D. Bekker wel kan seggen, dat   syn E. zoekt te bewaren

NIC   (Continued on next card)

Vierde briev van Haggébher Philaleethees, geschreeven aan zynen vriend N. N.

Witchcraft
BF 1410
B42
Z69
no.6

[Hooght, Everard van der] d. 1716. Vierde briev van ... Haggébher Philaleethees ... (Card 2)

de authoriteyt van Gods woord, ende de eere des alderhoogsten. Amsterdam, G. Borstius, 1691.
  59-96 p. 21cm.
  Signatures: 4°: ¶1, A-C⁴, D².
  Black letter.
  Van der   Linde 100.
  No. 6 in   a Collection of tracts
NIC   (Continued on next card)

Vierde briev van Haggébher Philaleethees, geschreeven aan zynen vriend N. N.

Witchcraft
BF 1410
B42
Z69
no.6

[Hooght, Everard van der] d. 1716. Vierde briev van ... Haggébher Philaleethees ... 1691.   (Card 3)

against Balthasar Bekker and his Betoverde weereld.
  N. N. is thought to be Jacobus Schuts.

1. God--Omnipotence. 2. Schaak, Petrus, fl. 1691.   3. Bekker, Balthasar, 1634-1698.   De betoverde weereld.
NIC   I. Title.   II. Schuts, Jacobus.

WITCHCRAFT
BT 960
V66

Vieri, Francesco de, called Il Verino Secondo.
  Discorso dell' eccellentiss. filosofo M. Francesco de' Vieri cognominato il Secondo Verino. Intorno a' dimonii, volgarmente chiamati spiriti... Fiorenza, Appresso Bartolomeo Sermartelli, 1576.
  8 p. l., 108, [1] p. 17cm.

1. Spirits. 2. Demonology. 3. Witchcraft. I. Title: Intorno a' dimonii.
8   II. Title.

Viervoudige beantwoordinge van beswaarnissen, voorgesteld aan Balthasar Bekker...

Witchcraft
BF 1410
B42
V6

Bekker, Balthasar, 1634-1698.
  Viervoudige beantwoordinge van beswaarnissen, voorgesteld aan Balthasar Bekker, S. S. Th. Dr. predikant tot Amsterdam, over sijn boek, genaamd De betoverde weereld. ... Amsterdam, By D. van den Dalen, boekverkoper, 1692.
  3 p. l., 74, 95, [1] p. title vignette, illus. initials. 21 x 17cm.
  4°: *⁴, A-J⁴, K1, a-m⁴.

8   (Continued on next card)

Viervoudige beantwoordinge van beswaarnissen, voorgesteld aan Balthasar Bekker ...

Witchcraft
BF 1410
B42
V6

Bekker, Balthasar, 1634-1698. Viervoudige beantwoordinge van beswaarnissen ... 1692.
                                       (Card 2)

Black letter.
Preface autographed by Bekker.
Includes actions taken by the church.
Variant of van der Linde 49: four final gatherings wanting.
  1. Bekker, Balthasar, 1634-1698. De betoverde weereld. I. Nederlandse Hervormde Kerk. II.   Title.

8

Witchcraft
AG 241
V67

A View of human nature; or, Select histories; giving an account of persons who have been most eminently distinguish'd by their virtues or vices, their perfections or defects, either of body or mind; or who have been, in any respect, remarkable instances of divine Providence. The whole collected from the best authors in various languages, with the addition of several curious particulars never before publish'd ... London, Printed for S. Birt, 1750.
  312 p. 18cm.

1. Curiosa.

WITCHCRAFT
BF 1068
V67
1734

Viglioni, Giovanni Battista.
  Jo: Baptistae Viglioni ... Enchiridion quatuor tractatus complectens de somniis, cabalis, cacodaemonibus, et ludo in genere. Ad excellentiss. principem Julium Visconti Borromeum ... Nova editio. Neapoli, 1734.
  xvi, 188, 51, 188-231 p. 23cm.
  1. Sleep--Early works to 1800. 2. Dreams. 3. Cabala. 4. Demonology. 5. Games--Early works to 1800. I. Title: Enchiridion.   II. Title.
8

Witchcraft
GR 830
W4V73

Villeneuve, Roland, 1922-
  Loups-garous et vampires. Paris, Genève, La Palatine [1963]
  263 p. illus. 20cm.

1. Werwolves. 2. Vampires.   I. Title.

BF 1532
V73

Villeneuve, Roland, 1922-
  L'univers diabolique. Paris, A. Michel [1972]
  325, [8] p. plates. 22 cm. (Les Chemins de l'impossible)   24.00F
  Bibliography: p. 323-[326]

4
  1. Demonology. 2. Witchcraft. 3. Magic. I. Title.
  BF1532.V54   72-326406
  Library of Congress   72 [2]

Villeneuve, Roland, 1922-   ed.

BF 1622
F7
G23
1965

Garinet, Jules, 1797-1877.
  Histoire de la magie en France. Texte revu et présenté par Roland Villeneuve. Paris, Livre club du libraire, 1965.
  260 p. plates. 20 cm. 82 F.
                                              (F 66-840)

  1. Magic--France.   I. Villeneuve, Roland, 1922-   ed.
  II. Title.
  BF1622.F7G3   133.40944   66-72041
  Library of Congress witchcraft [5]

Villeneuve, Roland, 1922-   joint author.

BF 1503
T66

Tondriau, Julien L
  Dictionnaire du diable et de la démonologie [par] J. Tondriau & R. Villeneuve. (Verviers, Gérard & Co., 1968).
  333 p. illus., facsims., ports. 18 cm. (Marabout université, v. 154)   bfr 80.--
                                              (Be 68-3086)
  Bibliography: p. [327]-330.

  1. Demonology--Dictionaries--French.   I. Villeneuve, Roland, 1922-   joint author. II. Title.
  BF1503.T6   133.4'2'03   78-365611
  Library of Congress   69 [1]

Vilmar, August Friedrich Christian, 1800-1868.

Witchcraft
BF 1583
A2
W82
1888

Witekind, Hermann, 1522-1603.
  Augustin Lercheimer (Professor H. Witekind in Heidelberg) und seine Schrift wider den Hexenwahn. Lebensgeschichtliches und Abdruck der letzten vom Verfasser besorgten Ausgabe von 1597. Sprachlich bearbeitet durch Anton Birlinger. Hrsg. von Carl Binz. Strassburg, J. H. E. Heitz (Heitz und Mündel) 1888.
  xxxii, 188 p. 21cm.

(Continued on next card)

Vilmar, August Friedrich Christian, 1800-1868.

Witchcraft
BF 1583
A2
W82
1888

Witekind, Hermann, 1522-1603. Augustin Lercheimer ... und seine Schrift wider den Hexenwahn. 1888.   (Card 2)

Includes reprint of original t.p.: Christlich bedencken vnd Erinnerung von Zauberey.
Contents.--Mitteilungen über die Person und die Schriften des Professors H. Witekind.--Text.--Sprachliches, Wort- und Sachbestand, Textesunterschiede.--Vilmar über Witekind.
  Ex libris Fri   d. Zarncke.

CATALOGUE OF THE CORNELL WITCHCRAFT COLLECTION

Witchcraft
DC
102
.8
R2
V77

Vincent, Louis, 1876–
  Gilles de Rais: the original Bluebeard, by A. L. Vincent & Clare Binns, introduction by M. Hamblin Smith ... London, A. M. Philpot, ltd., 1926.
  2 p. l., 3–221, [1] p. illus., plates, 2 port. (incl. front.) 19½ᶜᵐ.
  "Genealogy of Gilles de Rais": p. 199–202.
  "List of works consulted": p. 217–221.

  1. Rais, Gilles de Laval, seigneur de, 1404–1440. I. Binns, Clare, joint author. II. Title.
                                                    27-18294 Revised
8 Library of Congress   DC102.8.R2V6
                    [r31c2]

Witchcraft
BT
980
G21
1929

Vinchon, Jean, 1884–   joint author.
  Garçon, Maurice.
    The devil; an historical, critical and medical study. London, V. Gollancz, 1929.
    288 p. 22cm.
    At head of title: Maurice Garçon & Jean Vinchon, translated by Stephen Haden Guest from the sixth French edition.

  1. Devil. 2. Demonomania. 3. Demonology. I. Vinchon, Jean, 1884– joint author. II. Garçon, Maurice. Le diable.--English. III. Title.

Witchcraft
BF
1410
B76P8

A vindication of A compleat history of magick, sorcery, and witchcraft.
  Boulton, Richard, fl. 1697–1724.
    The possibility and reality of magick, sorcery, and witchcraft, demonstrated. Or, A vindication of A compleat history of magick, sorcery, and witchcraft. In answer to Dr. Hutchinson's Historical essay ... In two parts ... London, Printed for J. Roberts, 1722.
    xvi, [4], 184 p. 17cm.

Witchcraft
BF
1555
J75V7

A vindication of the Surey demoniack as no imposter.
  [Jollie, Thomas] 1629–1703.
    A vindication of the Surey demoniack as no impostor: or, A reply to a certain pamphlet publish'd by Mr. Zach. Taylor, called The Surey impostor. With a further clearing and confirming of the truth as to Richard Dugdale's case and cure. By T. J., one of the ministers who attended upon that affair from first to last ... To which is annexed a brief narrative of the Surey demoniack, drawn up by the same author, for the satisfaction   of such who have not
                     (Continued on next card)

Witchcraft
BF
1555
J75V7

A vindication of the Surey demoniack as no imposter.
  [Jollie, Thomas] 1629–1703. A vindication of the Surey demoniack ... 1698. (Card 2)
    seen the former narrative... London, Printed for N. Simmons, and sold by G. Conyers, 1698.
    80 p. 21cm.
    Wing J 889.

  1. Dugdale, Richard. 2. Taylor, Zachary. The Surey imposter, being an answer to ... The   surey demoniack. I. Title.

WITCHCRAFT
BF
1547
V81
1561

Viret, Pierre, 1511–1571.
  Le monde a l'empire et le monde demoniacle fait par dialogues. Revue et augmente ... Geneve, Par Guillaume de Laimarie, 1561.
  8 p. l., 544 p.
  Imperfect copy: t. p. and preliminary leaves, p. 391–394, and 543–544 wanting, and supplied in MS copy.

  1. Demonology. I. Title.
8

Witchcraft
BF
1547
V81
1583

Viret, Pierre, 1511–1571.
  Le monde à l'empire--English.
  [Viret, Pierre] 1511–1571.
    The second part of The demoniacke vvorlde, or, Worlde possessed with diuels, conteining three dialogues: 1. Of familiar diuels. 2. Of lunaticke diuels. 2. Of the coniuring of diuels. Translated out of French into English by T. S. [i.e. Thomas Stocker] London, Imprinted for I. Perin, and are to be sold in Paules church-yard at the signe of the Angell, 1583.
    1 v. (unpaged) 15cm.
    Bound with   his The worlde possessed with deuils.   London, 1583.

Witchcraft
BF
1547
V81
1583

[Viret, Pierre] 1511–1571.
  The second part of The demoniacke vvorlde, or, Worlde possessed with diuels, conteining three dialogues: 1. Of familiar diuels. 2. Of lunaticke diuels. 2. Of the coniuring of diuels. Translated out of French into English by T. S. [i.e. Thomas Stocker] London, Imprinted for I. Perin, and are to be sold in Paules church-yard at the signe of the Angell, 1583.
    1 v. (unpaged) 15cm.
    Bound with   his The worlde possessed with deuils.   London, 1583.
                                            (over)

Witchcraft
BF
1547
V81
1583

[Viret, Pierre] 1511–1571.
  The worlde possessed with deuils, conteinyng three dialogues. 1. Of the deuill let loose. 2. Of blacke deuils. 3. Of white deuils. And of the commyng of Jesus Christe to judgement, a verie necessarie and comfortable discourse for these miserable and daungerous daies. London, Imprinted for I. Perin, and are to be sold in Paules churchyard at the signe of the Angell, 1583.
    1 v. (unpaged) 15cm.
                     (Continued on next card.)

Witchcraft
BF
1547
V81
1583

[Viret, Pierre] 1511–1571. The worlde possessed with deuils. 1583. (Card 2)
  A translation by Thomas Stocker of the second part of his Le monde à l'empire et le monde démoniacle fait par dialogues. Cf. Haag. La France protestante.
  With this is bound his The second part of The demoniacke vvorlde, or, Worlde possessed with diuels. London, 1583.

  1. Demonology. I. Title.

Witchcraft
BF
1547
V81
1583

Worlde possessed with diuels.
  [Viret, Pierre] 1511–1571.
    The second part of The demoniacke vvorlde, or, Worlde possessed with diuels, conteining three dialogues: 1. Of familiar diuels. 2. Of lunaticke diuels. 2. Of the coniuring of diuels. Translated out of French into English by T. S. [i.e. Thomas Stocker] London, Imprinted for I. Perin, and are to be sold in Paules church-yard at the signe of the Angell, 1583.
    1 v. (unpaged) 15cm.
    Bound with   his The worlde possessed with deuils.   London, 1583.

Witchcraft
BF
1569
A2
V82
1490

Visconti, Girolamo, fl. 1490–1512.
  Lamiarum sive striarum opuscula. Milan, Leonardus Pachel, 13 Sept. 1490.
  [24] l. 21cm.
  Leaf [2a]: Magistri Hyeronimi Vicecomitis. Lamiarum siue striarum opusculum ad illustrissimum Mediolani ducem franciscum sfortiam Vicecomitem: Incipit feliciter.
  Leaf [24b] (Colophon): Explicit Lamiarum tractatus magistri Iheronimi Vicecomitis predicatorum ordinis &c. Impressum
                     (Continued on next card)

Witchcraft
BF
1569
A2
V82
1490

Visconti, Girolamo, fl. 1490–1512. Lamiarum sive striarum opuscula ... 1490.
                                            (Card 2)
  Mediolani per magistrum Leonerdum Pachel Anno Domini. M.cccc.xc. Die. xiii. Mensis Septēbris.
  Signatures: a–c8.
  Capital spaces, with guide-letters.
  Edited by Aluisius de la Cruce.
  Copinger. Supplement to Hain's Repertorium, 6200=3210; Proctor, 5986; Brit. Mus.
                     (Continued on next card)

Witchcraft
BF
1569
A2
V82
1490

Visconti, Girolamo, fl. 1490–1512. Lamiarum sive striarum opuscula ... 1490.
                                            (Card 3)
  Cat. (XV cent.) VI, p. 778 (IA. 26646); Goff. Third census, V–272.

  1. Witchcraft. I. Title. II. Title: Magistri Hyeronimi Vicecomitis. Lamiarum siue striarum   opusculum.

MSS
Bd.
WITCHCRAFT
BF
V82

Visconti, Girolamo, fl. 1490–1512.
  Lamiarum sive striarum opuscula.
  Visconti, Girolamo, fl. 1490–1512.
    Opusculū magr̄i Hieronimi Vicecom̄s ordis pdicat̄ i q° pbat̄ lamias ēe hēticas et nō laborare humore melancholico. [Milan? before Sept., 1490]
    9 l. 19cm.
    Manuscript, on vellum.
    Title in red. 2 blue initials.
    Marginal notes in hands differing from that of the text. According to G. L. Burr some of the   notes are in the author's own hand.
                     (Continued on next card)

MSS
Bd.
WITCHCRAFT
BF
V82

Visconti, Girolamo, fl. 1490–1512.
  Lamiarum sive striarum opuscula.
  Visconti, Girolamo, fl. 1490–1512. Opusculū ... i q° pbat̄ lamias ēe hēticas...
    [before Sept., 1490]   (Card 2)
  Text more complete than the printed version, which appears as the second part of his Lamiarum sive striarum opuscula. Milan, 1490.
  Leaves sewn together but unbound. In case.
    1. Witchcraft. I. His Lamiarum sive striarum opus cula. II. Title: Opusculum ... in   quo probatur lamias esse hereti   cas.

MSS
Bd.
WITCHCRAFT
BF
V82

Visconti, Girolamo, fl. 1490–1512.
  Opusculū magr̄i Hieronimi Vicecom̄s ordis pdicat̄ i q° pbat̄ lamias ēe hēticas et nō laborare humore melancholico. [Milan? before Sept., 1490]
  9 l. 19cm.
  Manuscript, on vellum.
  Title in red. 2 blue initials.
  Marginal notes in hands differing from that of the text. According to G. L. Burr some of the   notes are in the author's own hand.
                     (Continued on next card)

MSS
Bd.
WITCHCRAFT
BF
V82

Visconti, Girolamo, fl. 1490–1512. Opusculū ... i q° pbat̄ lamias ēe hēticas...
  [before Sept., 1490]   (Card 2)
  Text more complete than the printed version, which appears as the second part of his Lamiarum sive striarum opuscula. Milan, 1490.
  Leaves sewn together but unbound. In case.
    1. Witchcraft. I. His Lamiarum sive striarum opus cula. II. Title: Opusculum ... in   quo probatur lamias esse hereti   cas.

CATALOGUE OF THE CORNELL WITCHCRAFT COLLECTION

WITCHCRAFT
BX
2340
V82
    Visconti, Zaccaria.
        Complementvm artis exorcisticae, cui simile nunquàm visum est: cum litanijs, benedictionibus, & doctrinis nouis, exorcismis efficacissimis, ac remedijs copiosis in maleficiatis expertis. In tres partes diuisum. Quarum prima dicitur doctrinalis. Secunda benedictionalis. Tertia exorcismalis. Cui addita est Oratio supra febricitantes. Avthore F. Zacharia Vicecomite ... Venetiis, Apud Franciscum Barilettum, 1600.
        3 p. l.,   716, [30] p. 15cm.
        First edition, apparently.

8

WITCHCRAFT
BX
2340
V82
1643
    Visconti, Zaccaria.
        Complementvm artis exorcisticae: cui simile nunquam visum est: cvm litaniis, benedictionibvs, & doctrinis nouis, exorcismis efficacissimis, ac remedijs copiosis in maleficiatis expertis. Nuper correctum, & in tres partes diuisum. Qvarvm prima dicitvr doctrinalis. Secunda benedictionalis. Tertia exorcismalis. Cui addita est Oratio supra febricitantes. Avthore Fr. Zacharia Vicecomite ... Cui nupperrimè in hac
                (Continued on next card)

8

WITCHCRAFT
BX
2340
V82
1643
    Visconti, Zaccaria.   Complementvm artis exorcisticae ... 1643.   (Card 2)
        postrema editione veneta. Pro vberiori complemento, additus est tractatus de Modo interrogandi daemonem ab exorcista ... Avthore Carolo de Bavcio ... Venetiis, Apud Turrinum, 1643.
        8 p. l., 359, 85 p. 17cm.
        "Modvs interrogandi daemonem ab exorcista," by Carlo de Baucio, has special t. p.
                (Continued on next card)

8

WITCHCRAFT
BX
2340
V82
1643
    Visconti, Zaccaria.   Complementvm artis exorcisticae ... 1643.   (Card 3)

        1. Exorcism. 2. Benediction. 3. Demonology. I. Title: Complementum artis exorcisticae. II. Baucio, Carlo de. Modus interrogandi daemonem ab exorcista. III. Title: Modus interrogandi daemonem ab exorcista.

8

    Visconti, Zaccaria.
tchcraft   Complementum artis exorcisticae. Thesavrvs exorcismorvm atqve conivrationvm terribilivm, potentissimorum, efficacissimorum cum practica probatissima: qvibvs spiritvs maligni, daemones maleficiaque omnia de corporibus humanis obsessis, tanquam flagellis, fustibusque fugantur, expelluntur, doctrinis refertissimus atqu; uberrimus: ad maximam exorcistarum commoditatem nunc vltimo plenariè in lucem editus & recusus: cuius authores, vt & singuli tractatus sequente pagellā consignati, inueniuntur. Cum indice capitum, rerum & verborum ...
                (Continued on next card)

    Visconti, Zaccaria.
CHCRAFT   Complementum artis exorcisticae. Thesavrvs exorcismorvm atqve conivrationvm terribilivm...1626.   (Card 2)
Coloniae, sumptibus haeredum Lazari Zetzneri, 1626.
    12 p. l., 1232, [39] p. 18cm.
    Previously published at Cologne in 1608.
    Contents.--F. Valerii Polydori...Practica exorcistarum ad daemones & maleficia de Christi fidelibus pellendum, pars prima...[et] secunda.--R.p.f. Hieronymi Mengi...Flagellum daemonum.--Eivsdem Fvstis daemonvm.--F. Zachariae Vicecomitis...Complementum artis exorcisticae.--Petri Antonii Stampae...Fuga Satanae.--R.d. Maximiliani ab Eynatten... Manuale exorcismorum.

WITCHCRAFT
BF
1517
F5
V83
1620a
    La Vision pvbliqve d'vn horrible & tres-espouuantable demon, sur l'Eglise Cathedralle de Quinpercorentin en Bretagne. Le premier iour de ce mois de feurier 1620. Lequel demon consomma vne pyramide par feu, & y suruint vn grand tonnerre & foudre du ciel.   Paris, Chez Abraham-Saugrin, 1620. [Arras, Imprimerie de Rousseau-Leroy, ca. 1865]
    8 p. 19cm. (bound in 23cm. vol.) (Portefeuille de l'ami des livres.)
                (Continued on next card)

8

WITCHCRAFT
BF
1517
F5
V83
1620a
    La Vision pvbliqve d'vn horrible & tres-espouuantable demon ... [Ca. 1865]
                (Card 2)

    Caption title reads: Le grand fev, tonnerre & foudre du ciel ..."
    "Iouxte la copie imprimee à Rennes."

    1. Demonology. 2. Quimper, France. Cathedrale. I. Title: Le grand feu, tonnerre & foudre du ciel.

8

    Visscher, Johannes, 1617?-1694.
Witchcraft
BF
1410
B42
Z56
v.2
no.6
    Nodige aanmerkinge omtrent eenige woorden gesprooken van D. Johannes Visscherus, in een catechisatie, over den 34 Sondag des Catechismus. Dog bysonderlijk over de 94 vrage, enz. voorgevallen op Sondag den 24 Augusty 1692. Door T. S. Amsterdam, By D. vanden Dalen, boekverkoper, 1692.
    7 p. [p. 8 blank] title vignette. 19 x 15cm.
    4°: A⁴.
                (Continued on next card)

8

    Visscher, Johannes, 1617?-1694.
Witchcraft
BF
1410
B42
Z56
v.2
no.6
    Nodige aanmerkinge omtrent eenige woorden gesprooken van D. Johannes Visscherus ... 1692.   (Card 2)

    Black letter.
    Response to Visscher's attack on Balthasar Bekker.
    No. 6 in vol. lettered Bekker II.
    1. Visscher, Johannes, 1617?-1694. 2. Bekker, Balthasar, 1634-1698. De betoverde weereld. I. T. S. II. S., T.

8

WITCHCRAFT
BT
980
V83
    Visscher, Volkard, 1639-1678.
        Verstooringe des Satans Ryck; voorgestelt in zwee Predikatien over 10. Cor. 10: vers 20. en Matt. 4, vers 1, &c. Onlanghs opentlijck geleert door de Eerwaerdige en Hoogh-Geleerden, nu Zal: Heer. En nu in 't Licht gegeben tot onderwijs van de eenduldigen en obertuygingh aller Lastertongen; door een Liefhebber van Godts Herck. t'Amsterdam, by J. van Someren, 1678.
    24 p.   20cm.
8
NIC
    1.Devil--   Biblical teaching. 2. Bible. N. T.   --Commentaries. 3. Jesus Christ   --Temptation. I. Title.

    Visscherus, Johannes, 1617?-1694.

    see

    Visscher, Johannes, 1617?-1694.

WITCHCRAFT
BF
1508
V83
    Visser, Johannes Theodoor de, 1857?-1932.
        De daemonologie van het Oude Testament ... Utrecht, A. F. Blanche, 1880.
    x, 177 p. 24cm.

    Diss.--Utrecht.

    1. Demonology. 2. Devil. 3. Bible. O.T.--Criticism, interpretation, etc. I. Title.

8

BF
1576
V85
    Vivan, Itala.
        Caccia alle streghe nell'America puritana. Milano, Rizzoli, 1972.
    751 p. illus. 20½ cm. (Nuova collana) L7500   It 72-June
    Includes bibliographical references.

9
NIC
    1. Witchcraft—New England.   I. Title.

    BF1576.V58   72-340534

    Library of Congress   72 [2]

Witchcraft
BF
1520
V85
1487
    Vivetus, Johannes, fl. 1450.
        Contra daemonum invocatores. [Cologne, Ludwig von Renchen, about 1487]
    [42] l. 20cm.

    Leaf [1a] (Title): Tractatus contra demonū inuocatores
    Leaf [1b]-[2b]: Tabula.
    Leaf [3a]: Incipit tractatus ɔtra demonū inuocatores ɔpilatus per sacre theologie pfessorē fratrem Johannē viueti. ordinis predicatoɣ inquisitorem apostolicū Carcassone.
                (Continued on next card)

Witchcraft
BF
1520
V85
1487
    Vivetus, Johannes, fl. 1450.   Contra daemonum invocatores ... [about 1487]   (Card 2)

    Leaf [41b] (End): Finit tractatus cōtra demonū inuocatores.
    Leaf [42] blank; wanting in this copy.
    Signatures: a-d⁸, e¹⁰.
    Capital spaces. Capitals, paragraph-marks, initial-strokes and underlines supplied in red.
    Copinger. Supplement to Hain's Repertorium, 6273=6274; Proctor, 1282; Brit. Mus.
                (Continued on next card)

Witchcraft
BF
1520
V85
1487
    Vivetus, Johannes, fl. 1450. Contra daemonum invocatores ... [about 1487]   (Card 3)

    Cat (XV cent.) I, p. 269 (IA. 4514; author's name: Johannes, Vineti); Goff. Third census, V-310.
    With a few manuscript marginal notes.

    1. Demonplogy. 2. Magic. 3. Witchcraft. I. Title. II. His Tractatus contra demonum inuocatores. III. Title: Tractatus contra demonum inuocatores.

    Vivetus, Johannes, fl. 1450.
Witchcraft   Tractatus contra demonum inuocatores.
BF
1520
V85
1487
    Vivetus, Johannes, fl. 1450.
        Contra daemonum invocatores. [Cologne, Ludwig von Renchen, about 1487]
    [42] l. 20cm.

    Leaf [1a] (Title): Tractatus contra demonū inuocatores
    Leaf [1b]-[2b]: Tabula.
    Leaf [3a]: Incipit tractatus ɔtra demonū inuocatores ɔpilatus per sacre theologie pfessorē fratrem Johannē viueti. ordinis predicatoɣ inquisitorem apostolicū Carcassone.
                (Continued on next card)

CATALOGUE OF THE CORNELL WITCHCRAFT COLLECTION

Vivetus, Johannes, fl. 1450.
Tractatus contra demonum inuocatores.

Witchcraft
BF 1520 V85 1487

Vivetus, Johannes, fl. 1450. Contra daemonum invocatores ... [about 1487] (Card 2)

Leaf [41b] (End): Finit tractatus cōtra demonũ inuocatores.
Leaf [42] blank; wanting in this copy.
Signatures: a-d⁸, e¹⁰.
Capital spaces. Capitals, paragraph-marks, initial-strokes and underlines supplied in red.
Copinger. Supplement to Hain's Repertorium, 6273=6274; Proctor, 1282; Brit. Mus.
(Continued on next card)

Vivetus, Johannes, fl. 1450.
Tractatus contra demonum inuocatores.

Witchcraft
BF 1520 V85 1487

Vivetus, Johannes, fl. 1450. Contra daemonum invocatores ... [about 1487] (Card 3)

Cat (XV cent.) I, p. 269 (IA. 4514; author's name: Johannes, Vineti); Goff. Third census, V-310.
With a few manuscript marginal notes.

1. Demonology. 2. Magic. 3. Witchcraft. I. Title. II. His Tractatus contra demonum inuocatores. III. Title: Tractatus contra demonum inuocatores.

Vogel, Bernhard, tr.

Witchcraft
BF 1565 B61 1591a

Binsfeld, Pierre, ca. 1540-1598. Tractat von Bekanntnuss der Zauberer vnd Hexen. Ob vnd wie viel denselben zu glauben. Anfänglich durch den hochwürdigen Herrn Petrum Binsfeldium ... in Latein beschrieben. Jetzt aber der Warheit zu stewr in vnser teutsche Sprach vertiert durch ... Bernhart Vogel ... München, Gedruckt bey Adam Berg, 1591.
4 p. l., 75 (i.e. 150), [6] p. 20cm.
Title in red and black.
With coloph on.
(Continued on next card)

8

Vogel, Bernhard, tr.

Witchcraft
BF 1565 B61 1591a

Binsfeld, Pierre, ca. 1540-1598. Tractat von Bekanntnuss der Zauberer vnd Hexen. 1591. (Card 2)

Translation of Tractatus de confessionibus maleficorum & sagarum.
Title vignette shows witches and devils.
1. Witchcraft. 2. Demonology. I. His Tractatus de confessionibus maleficorum & sagarum--German. II. Vogel, Bernhard, tr. III. Title: Tractat von Bekanntnuss der Zauberer und Hexen.

8

Witchcraft
BF 1565 D62 no.2

Voigt, Gottfried, 1644-1682, praeses. De conventu sagarum ad sua sabbata, qvae vocant ... praeside ... Dn. M. Gothofredo Voigt ... responsurus Philipp. David Fuhrmann ... Wittebergae, Typis Johannis Borckardi [1667]
[16] p. 20cm.
No. 2 in vol. lettered Dissertationes de sagis. 1636-1714.
1. Witchcraft. I. Fuhrmann, Philipp David, respondent. II. Title.

8

Witchcraft
QL 50 V89

Voigt, Gottfried, 1644-1682. Gothofrei Voigtii ... Deliciae physicae ΕΠΙΔΙΕΣΚΕΥΑΣΜΕΝΑΙ, de stillicidio sanguinis ex interemti hominis cadavere praesente occisore, lacrymis crocodili, catulis ursarum, amore ovis et lupi, piscibus fossilibus et volatilibus, conventu sagarum ad sua sabbata, infantibus supposititiis, cornu cervi, et stellis cadentibus accurata methodo conscr[ ]iptae. Rostochii, Im-
(Continued on next card)

8

Witchcraft
QL 50 V89

Voigt, Gottfried, 1644-1682. ...Deliciae physicae ... 1671. (Card 2)

primebat Johannes Kilius, 1671.
7 p. l., 369, [1] p. 17cm.
Title in red and black.

1. Natural history--Curiosa and miscellany. 2. Animal lore. 3. Witchcraft. I. Title: Deliciae physicae. II. Title.

8

Volet, Marie, fl. 1690.

WITCHCRAFT
BF 1555 R47

Rhodes, de. Lettre en forme de dissertation de Mr. de Rhodes escuyer docteur en medecine, aggregé au college des medecins de Lyon. A monsievr Destaing comte de Lyon; au sujet de la prétenduë possession de Marie Volet de la parroisse de Pouliat en Bresse, dans laquelle il est traité des causes naturelles de ses accidens, & de sa guérison. Lyon, Chez Thomas Amaulry, 1691.
4 p. l., 75 p. 18cm.
(Continued on next card)

8

Volet, Marie, fl. 1690.

WITCHCRAFT
BF 1555 R47

Rhodes, de. Lettre en forme de dissertation ... 1691. (Card 2)

Imperfect copy: p. 1-2 (second t. p.?) wanting.
With this is bound Sentimens d'Eudoxe et d'Aristée, sur le dialogue satirique de Mystagogue et de Neophile. 1691.

1. Demoniac possession. 2. Volet, Marie, fl. 1690. I. Title. II. Title: La prétenduë possession de Marie Volet.

8

WITCHCRAFT
BF 1583 V91

Volk, Franz. Hexen in der Landvogtei Ortenau und Reichsstadt Offenburg. Ein Beitrag zur Sittengeschichte von Franz Volk, Bürgermeister in Offenburg. Lahr, M. Schauenburg, 1882.
154 p. 22cm.

1. Witchcraft--Baden. 2. Witchcraft--Germany. I. Title.

8

Volkskundliches aus strafprozessen der österreichischen Alpenländer.

Witchcraft
BF 1584 A93 B991

Byloff, Fritz, 1875– Volkskundliches aus strafprozessen der österreichischen Alpenländer, mit besonderer berücksichtigung der zauberei- und hexenprozesse 1455 bis 1850; gesammelt, hrsg. und mit anmerkungen versehen von Fritz Byloff. Berlin und Leipzig, W. de Gruyter & co., 1929.
68 p. 24½ cm. (Added t.-p.: Quellen zur deutschen volkskunde ... 3. hft.)
"Literaturverzeichnis": p. [59]-60.

1. Folk-lore--Austria. 2. Witchcraft--Austria. 3. Trials--Austria. I. Title.

Library of Congress   36-6690

WITCHCRAFT
BF 1566 V92

Vollert, Anton, 1828-1897. Die Hexen und Hexenprocesse. Eine criminal-historische Skizze. Von Dr. A. Vollert, Herausgeber des "neuen Pitaval". [Leipzig? 1871]
[595]-603 p. 23cm.
Caption title.
Extract from a periodical.
Incomplete copy: part one only of 2.
1. Witchcraft. 2. Trials (Witchcraft) I. Title.

8

Vollmöller, Karl Gustav, 1848-1922, ed.

PN 674 H57

Hertz, Wilhelm, 1835-1902. Aus dichtung und sage; vorträge und aufsätze von Wilhelm Hertz. Hrsg. von Karl Vollmöller. Stuttgart und Berlin, J. G. Cotta nachfolger, 1907.
x, 219, [1] p. 18½ᵐ.
Reprinted from different periodicals.
CONTENTS.--Über den ritterlichen frauendienst.--Die Walküren.--Die Nibelungensage.--Altfranzösische volkslieder.--Beowulf, das älteste germanische epos.--Mythologie der schwäbischen volkssagen.--Die hexenprobe.--Mörikes "Feuerreiter".

1. Literature, Medieval--Hist. & crit. 2. Witchcraft. 3. Folk-songs--France. 4. Mörike, Eduard Friedrich, 1804-1875. Der feuerreiter. 5. Folk literature--Swabia. I. Vollmöller, Karl Gustav, 1848-1922, ed. II. Title.
32-10346
Library of Congress   PN674.H4   804

Vollständige Beantwortung der Frage: Was läst sich nach Vernunft und Schrift vom Teufel glauben?

WITCHCRAFT
BT 980 K58

Kirchhof, Christian August Ludwig. Christ. Aug. Lud. Kirchhoffs vollständige Beantwortung der Frage: Was läst sich nach Vernunft und Schrift vom Teufel glauben? Ein Beytrag zur Aufklärung besonders für Ungelehrte. Braunschweig, In Commission der Schröderschen Buchhandlung, 1789.
125 p. 17cm.

1. Devil--Biblical teaching. I. Title: Vollständige Beantwortung der Frage: Was läst sich nach Vernunft und Schrift vom Teufel glauben?

8 NIC

Vollständige und getreue Schilderung und Beurtheilung des Hexenwesens.

WITCHCRAFT
BF 1566 P93

Pressel, Wilhelm, writer on witchcraft. Hexen und Hexenmeister; oder, Vollständige und getreue Schilderung und Beurtheilung des Hexenwesens. Stuttgart, C. Belser, 1860.
iv, 102 p. 19cm.

1. Witchcraft. I. Title. II. Title: Vollständige und getreue Schilderung und Beurtheilung des Hexenwesens.

8 NIC

Witchcraft
BF 1410 B42 Z56 v.3 no.20

De Volmaakte kragt Godts verheerlykt. Nevens eenige aanmerkinge over de drie predikatien van Do. Petrus Schaak. Gedaan over Psal. 72: v. 18. Gen. 18: v. 1,2 ... en Gen. 32: v. 24, 25. In haar eigen gronden ondersogt, en met de waarheid vergeleken. En eenige andere aanmerkingen daar by gevoegd. Amsterdam, By D. vanden Dalen, boekverkooper, 1691.
47 p. [p. 48 blank] title and other vignettes, illus. initial. 19 x 15cm.
4°: A-F⁴.
Black letter.
Preface signed : J: P: L: R:
(Continued on next card)

Witchcraft
BF 1410 B42 Z56 v.3 no.20

De Volmaakte kragt Godts verheerlykt. 1691. (Card 2)

Supports B. Bekker against Schaak's attacks on Bekker's De betoverde weereld.
Van der Linde 145.
No. 20 in vol. lettered Bekker III.

1. Schaak, Petrus, fl. 1691. 2. Spirits. 3. Bekker, Balthasar, 1634-1698. De betoverde weereld. I. J. P. II. P., J. III. L. R. IV. R., L.

Volumen praeclarissimum ... omnium tractatuum criminalium.

WITCHCRAFT
K Z695 1580

Ziletti, Giovanni Battista, fl. 1559, ed. Volvmen praeclarissimvm ... omnivm tractatvvm criminalivm nvnc per D. Ioan. Baptistam Zilettum ab omnibus mendis expurgatum ac omnino correctum ... Venetiis, Apud Io. Antonium Bertanum, 1580.
78 p. l., 473 numbered leaves. 21cm.
Includes Tractatvs ... de lamijs ... Ioanni Francisci Ponzinibij, l. 89-99 v.; De sortilegiis tractatus Pauli Ghirlandi, l. 104 v.-138 v.
(Continued on next card)

8

578

CATALOGUE OF THE CORNELL WITCHCRAFT COLLECTION

WITCHCRAFT
BM
610
V94

Volz, Paul, 1871-
Das Dämonische in Jahwe ... Vortrag auf dem Alttestamentlertag in München. Tübingen, J. C. B. Mohr (P. Siebeck), 1924.
41 p. 24cm. (Sammlung gemeinverständlicher Vorträge und Schriften aus dem Gebiet der Theologie und Religionsgeschichte 110)
1. God (Judaism) 2. God--Attributes.
I. Title.

Vom aussgelasnen wütigen Teuffelsheer.
Bodin, Jean, 1530-1596.
Vom aussgelasnen wütigen Teuffelsheer. Übers. v. Johann Fischart. (Um ein neues Vorw. verm. Nachdr. d. Ausg. Strassburg 1591.) Vorw.: Hans Biedermann. Graz, Akadem. Druck- u. Verlagsanst., 1973.
vii p., 372 p. of facsims. 28 cm. S720.00 Au 73-17-273
Translation of De la démonomanie des sorciers.
Bibliography: p. vii.
1. Witchcraft. 2. Magic. 3. Demonology. I. Fischart, Johann, 1550 (ca.)-1590?, tr. II. Biedermann, Hans, fl. 1968- ed. III. Title. IV. His De la démonomanie des sorciers. German.   73-349006
ISBN 3-201-00821-4
Library of Congress   73 ₍₂₎

NIC

WITCHCRAFT
BX
2340
V94

Vom Exorcismo. Das dieser ohne Verletzung des Gewissens bey der Tauffe wol mag gebraucht vnd behalten werden: etliche Tractetlein. I. Iusti Menij. II. Lutheri Vorrede vber das Tauffbüchlein. III. Die gewöhnliche Gebet bey der Tauffe im Stifft vnd der Thumkirchen zu Cölln an der Sprew. IIII. Aus dem Appendice D. Vrbani Regij. V. Zwo Episteln Tilemanni Heshusij. VI. Eine Epistel Philippi Melanchton is. VII. D. Iacobi Co-
(Continued on next card)

WITCHCRAFT
BX
2340
V94

Vom Exorcismo ... 1591.   (Card 2)
leri Büchlein. Alles zu guter Nachrichtung den einfeltigen Leyen zum besten zusammen bracht. ₍Franckfurt an der Oder₎ In Verlegung Johan vnd Friderich Hartmans, 1591.
₍269₎ p. 17cm.
Title in red and black.
With colophon: Gedruckt zu Franckfurt an der Oder, durch Nicolaum Voltzen, 1591.
(Continued on next card)

WITCHCRAFT
BX
2340
V94

Vom Exorcismo ... 1591.   (Card 3)
Vom Exorcismo, oder Von dem Beschweren der Kinder bey der Tauffe. Drey Sendbriefe deren zwene D. Tilemannvs Heshvsivs: den dritten Herr Philippvs Melanchton geschrieben ... Verdeutscht durch Heinrich Rätel, has special t. p. with date 1590.
Vom Exorcismo bey der Tauffe ... durch Jacobum Colerum D. has special t. p., no date.
(Continued on next card)

WITCHCRAFT
BX
2340
V94

Vom Exorcismo ... 1591.   (Card 4)
1. Exorcism. 2. Baptism--Early works to 1800. I. Menius, Justus, 1499-1558. Vom Exorcismo. II. Rhegius, Urbanus, 1489-1541. Wie man fürsichtlich und ohne Ärgerniss reden soll. III. Heshusius, Tilemann, 1527-1588. IV. Melanchthon, Philipp, 1497-1560. V. Coler, Jacob, 1537-1612. Vom Exorcismo bey der Taufe. VI. Rätel, Heinrich, tr.

Vom Exorcismo bey der heiligen Tauffe.
WITCHCRAFT
BX
2340
P71

Planitius, Georgius.
Vom Exorcismo bey der heiligen Tauffe, und von der Christen Kinder Heiligkeit...
₍n.p.₎ 1591.
32 l. 20cm.

8
NIC

1. Exorcism. 2. Baptism--Early works to 1800.

Vom Geitz Teuffel.
Witchcraft
BV
4627
A8
B81

Brandmüller, Johann.
Vom Geitz Teuffel. Ein christliche und heilsame Predig, gethan zů Basel, unnd hernach auss Bitt eines christenlichen Bruders auch geschrieben. Durch Johansen Brandmüllern. Basel, P. Perna, 1579.
30 p. 17cm.

1. Avarice. 2. Devil. 3. Sermons, Swiss.
I. Title.

Vom Zaubereiunwesen anfangs des 14. Jahrhunderts.
Witchcraft
BF
1569
E86

Eubel, Conrad, 1842-1923.
Vom Zaubereiunwesen anfangs des 14. Jahrhunderts. (Mit urkundlichen Beilagen) München, Herder, 1897.
608-631 p. 24cm. (Historisches Jahrbuch der Görres-Gesellschaft, 18. Bd., 3. Heft)

1. Witchcraft.

Von abgötterischen Sägen und Beschweren.
WITCHCRAFT
BF
1565
S767

Spreter, Johann.
Ein kurtzer Bericht, was von den abgötterischen Sägen vñ Beschweren zůhalten, wie der etlich volbracht, vnnd das die ein Zauberey, auch Greüwel vor Gott dem Herren seind. Durch den wirdigen vñ wolgelerten Herren Johañ. Spreter von Rotweil zůsamen gebracht ... ₍Basel, Getruckt durch Bartholomeum Westheymer, 1543₎
₍12₎ p. 21cm.
With colophon.

8
NIC

Von abgötterischen Sägen und Beschweren.
WITCHCRAFT
BF
1565
S767

Spreter, Johann. Ein kurtzer Bericht ...
₍1543₎   (Card 2)
Caption title: Von Sägen vnd Beschweren.
Running title: Von abgötterischen Sägen vnd Beschweren.

1. Witchcraft. 2. Magic. 3. Folk medicine. I. Title: Von abgötterischen Sägen und Beschweren.

8
NIC

Von dem erschröcklichen Jammer ... im Westerreich.
MSS
Bd.
WITCHCRAFT
BF
S39

Schwann, Johan.
Zwo gründliche und warhafftige newe Zeitung, die Erste von den Hexen und Unholden Mann und Weibs Personen, so man in der churfürstlichen Statt zu Aschenburg unnd auch auff dem Land mit dem Fewer gestrafft unnd verbrandt hat ... Die ander Zeitung.
Von dem erschröcklichen Jammer, so sich im Westerreich im Städtlein Sarwerth, begeben hatt und sehen lassen ... Gestelt durch Magister Joh   an Schwann ... Giesen, Bey Caspar   Kemla, 1612 ₍ca. 1900₎
(Continued on next card)

Von dem erschröcklichen Jammer ... im Westerreich.
MSS
Bd.
WITCHCRAFT
BF
S39

Schwann, Johan. Zwo gründliche und warhafftige newe Zeitung ... 1612 ₍ca. 1900₎
    (Card 2)
6 l. title vignette. 23cm.
Carnap's manuscript copy.
"Originaldruck in der Gust. Freytag Bibliothek; jetzt in der Stadtbibliothek zu Frankfurt a/M. 4 Bl. in 4°. Sig. Aij-Aiij."
Numerals and signatures in the margins indicate pagi   nation and signatures of the origi   nal.
(Continued on next card)

Von dem erschröcklichen Jammer ... im Westerreich.
MSS
Bd.
WITCHCRAFT
BF
S39

Schwann, Johan. Zwo gründliche und warhafftige newe Zeitung ... 1612 ₍ca. 1900₎
    (Card 3)
In verse.

1. Witchcraft--Germany. 2. Apparitions. 3. Prophecies. I. Title: Von den Hexen und Unholden Mann und Weibs Personen ... zu Aschenburg. II. Title: Von dem erschröcklichen Jammer ... im Westerreich.

Von dem Exorcismo.
WITCHCRAFT
BF
1559
K62

Kittelman, Christian
Von dem Exorcismo; das ist, Von den Wor₍t₎en: Fahre aus du unreiner Geist, unnd gib Raum dem heiligen Geist, etc. Gründlich und bestendiger Bericht. ₍Vor₎aus zu ersehen, das er₍melter₎, Exorcismus inn unsern Kirchen ₍billich₎ behalten werde, unnd das M. Wolffgang Amling keine erhebliche Ursachen gehabt, darumb er denselben zu Zerbst, und anderswo im Fürstenthumb Anhalt, abgeschafft. ₍Von₎ Christianus   Kittelman ... ₍n. p.₎ 1591.
(Continued on next card)

8
NIC

Von dem Exorcismo.
WITCHCRAFT
BF
1559
K62

Kittelman, Christian
Von dem Exorcismo...1591.   (Card 2)
Preface dated: Newemarckt, vor Halle, ... anno 1590.
Imperfect copy: t. p. mutilated. Missing words and letters supplied from The National union catalog, pre-1956 imprints.
"Consilium D. D. Martini Miri, amico cuidam priuatim cõmunicatum, super abrogatione Exorcismi": ₍18₎ manuscript pages bound at end.
(Continued on next card)

Von den bösen Geistern und der Zauberey.
WITCHCRAFT
BF
1523
H49

₍Hempel, Christian Gottlob₎ 1748-
Von den bösen Geistern und der Zauberey: Ein Sendschreiben an den Herrn M. Haubold, Vesperprediger bei der Universitätskirche zu Leipzig, auf Veranlassung einer von demselben am letztverwichenen Michaelsfeste 1782 gehaltenen Nachmittagspredigt, von einem damals unter seinen Zuhörern gewesenen Messfremden. Sorau, 1783.
96 p. 19cm.
Attribution by Holzmann.
1. Demonolo   gy. 2. Witchcraft. I. Haubold,   , preacher. II. Ein Messfremder.   III. Title.

8

Von den Hexen.
Witchcraft
BF
1565
A33
1723

Alberti, Valentin, 1635-1697, praeses.
... Academische Abhandlung von den Hexen und dem Bündniss so sie mit dem Teuffel haben. Darinnen ... nebst Erörterung einiger andern curieusen Fragen, ob die bekannte Pucelle d'Orleans, ingleichen das rasende Weib, das den Attilam erschrecket, eine Hexe gewesen sei? Franckfurt und Leipzig, 1723.
₍56₎ p. front. 21cm.
Translation of his Dissertatio academica, De sagis, C. Stridtbeckh, respondent, Wittebergae, 1690.
(Continued on next card)

8

CATALOGUE OF THE CORNELL WITCHCRAFT COLLECTION

Von den Hexen und Unholden Mann und Weibs Personen ... zu Aschenburg.

MSS Bd.
WITCHCRAFT
BF
S39

Schwann, Johan.
Zwo gründliche und warhafftige newe Zeitung, die Erste von den Hexen und Unholden Mann und Weibs Personen, so man in der churfürstlichen Statt zu Aschenburg unnd auch auff dem Land mit dem Fewer gestrafft unnd verbrandt hat ... Die ander Zeitung. Von dem erschröcklichen Jammer, so sich im Westerreich im Städtlein Sarwerth, begeben hatt und sehen lassen ... Gestelt durch Magister Johan Schwann ... Giesen, Bey Caspar Kemla, 1612 ₍ca. 1900₎
(Continued on next card)

Von den Hexen und Unholden Mann und Weibs Personen ... zu Aschenburg.

MSS Bd.
WITCHCRAFT
BF
S39

Schwann, Johan. Zwo gründliche und warhafftige newe Zeitung ... 1612 ₍ca. 1900₎ (Card 2)

6 l. title vignette. 23cm.
Carnap's manuscript copy.
"Originaldruck in der Gust. Freytag Bibliothek; jetzt in der Stadtbibliothek zu Frankfurt a/M. 4 Bl. in 4°. Sig. Aij-Aiij."
Numerals and signatures in the margins indicate pagination and signatures of the original.
(Continued on next card)

Von den Hexen und Unholden Mann und Weibs Personen ... zu Aschenburg.

MSS Bd.
WITCHCRAFT
BF
S39

Schwann, Johan. Zwo gründliche und warhafftige newe Zeitung ... 1612 ₍ca. 1900₎ (Card 3)

In verse.

1. Witchcraft--Germany. 2. Apparitions. 3. Prophecies. I. Title: Von den Hexen und Unholden Mann und Weibs Personen ... zu Aschenburg. II. Title: Von dem erschröcklichen Jammer ... im Westerreich.

Von den Unholden oder Hexen.

Witchcraft
BF
1569
A2M72
1493

Molitor, Ulrich, fl. 1470-1501.
De lamiis et phitonicis mulieribus. German. ₍Strassburg, Johann Prüss, about 1493₎
₍30₎ l. 7 woodcuts. 19cm.

Leaf ₍1a₎ (Title): Von den unholdẽ oder hexen.
Leaf ₍2a₎: Tractatus von denn bosen wiber die man nennet die hexen &c. durch doctor vlrichen molitoris zu latin, vnd ouch czu tutsch gemacht. vnd dem durchleuchtigistẽ Ertzhertzog Sigmund von osterrich als dem
(Continued on next card)

Von den Unholden oder Hexen.

Witchcraft
BF
1569
A2M72
1493

Molitor, Ulrich, fl. 1470-1501. De lamiis et phitonicis mulieribus. German ... ₍about 1493₎ (Card 2)

loblichen eren fursten zu corrigirẽ czu gesant.
Leaf ₍29b₎: Datũ zu costentz anno dñi. m.cccc.lxxxix. &c. Diner erhochsten furstlichen gnaden. demutiger raut vnd diener vlricus molitoris von costentz in den rechtenn doctor &c.
Leaf ₍30₎ blank.
(Continued on next card)

Von den Unholden oder Hexen.

Witchcraft
BF
1569
A2M72
1493

Molitor, Ulrich, fl. 1470-1501. De lamiis et phitonicis mulieribus. German ... ₍about 1493₎ (Card 3)

Signatures: A-F⁴, G⁶.
Hain. Repertorium, 11539; Polain (B), 2767; Schramm, XX, p. 27; Goff. Third census, M-806.
With manuscript marginal notes.

1. Witchcraft. I. Title. II. Title: Von den Unholden oder Hexen.

Von den Zauberern, Hexen vnd Vnholden, drei christliche verscheidene, vnnd zu diesen vnsern vngefärlichen Zeiten notwendige Bericht.

Witchcraft
BF
1565
D17
1576

Daneau, Lambert, ca. 1530-1595.
Von den Zauberern, Hexen, vnd Vnholden, drei christliche verscheidene ₍sic₎, vnnd zu diesen vnsern vngefärlichen Zeiten notwendige Bericht ... Durch die hoch vnd wohlgelehrte Herren, Lambertvm Danaevvm, Iacobvm Vallick, vnnd Vlricvm Molitoris. ... Cölln, Gedruckt durch Johannem Gymnicum, 1576.
2 v. in 1. 16cm.
"Der ander Tractat von Zauberern, Hexen, vnd Vnholden, durch J. Vallick, p.
(Continued on next card)

Von den Zauberern, Hexen vnd Vnholden, drei christliche verscheidene, vnnd zu diesen vnsern vngefärlichen Zeiten notwendige Bericht.

Witchcraft
BF
1565
D17
1576

Daneau, Lambert, ca. 1530-1595. Von den Zauberern, Hexen, vnd Vnholden... 1576 (Card 2)

157-222 of v. 1, has special t. p. Translation of De veneficis, quos olim sortilegos ... vocant, by L. Daneau; of an unidentified work by J. Vallick; and of De lamiis et phitonicis mulieribus, by U. Molitor.

1. Witchcraft. 2. Demonology. I. His De veneficis, quos olim sortigelos ... vo-
(Continued on next card)

Von der alten und neuen Magie Ursprung.

WITCHCRAFT
BF
1589
H81

Horst, Goerg Conrad, 1767-1838?
Von der alten und neuen Magie Ursprung, Idee, Umfang, und Geschichte. Als Ankündigung der Zauber-Bibliothek und Verständigung mit dem Publikum über diess literarische Unternehmen. Mainz, Bei F. Kupferberg, 1820.
83 p. 21cm.
With this is bound his Theurgie. Mainz, 1820.

1. Magic--History. 2. Occult sciences--History. 3. His Zauber-Bibliothek. I. Title.

8 NIC

Von der Kunst sich mit Geistern bekant zu machen.

WITCHCRAFT
BT
960
R53

Richter, David, of Güstrow, praeses.
Qvadriga dispp. ₍i.e. disputationum₎ magico-thevrgicarum de conciliatione spirituum, oder: Von der Kunst sich mit Geistern bekant zu machen, qvam svb praesidio Davidis Richteri habvervnt Henr. Andr. Mätcke et Georg. Erhard. Hambergervs. Jena, J. B. Heller, 1716.
86 p. 20cm.

8 NIC

(Continued on next card)

Von der Zauber- und Hexenwerck.

WITCHCRAFT
BF
1565
R91

Rüdinger, Johannes
De magia illicita, decas concionum; zehen müthliche Predigten von der Zauber- vnd Hexenwerck aus Anleitung heiliger Schrifft vnd bewehrter Autorum rationibus nach dem bekanten Schul-Vers Quis? Quid? Ubi? vnd folgends andern Vmbstenden gehalten. Darinnen auff die von dieser Materia fürnembsten Fragen geantwortet, etliche darüber vngleiche Meynung erzehlet vnd dieselben kürtzlich wiederleget werden, durch

8 NIC

(Continued on next card)

Von der Zauber- und Hexenwerck.

WITCHCRAFT
BF
1565
R91

Rüdinger, Johannes
De magia illicita... (Card 2)

Johannem Rüdinger. Jehna, In Verlegung J. Reiffenberger, 1630.
406 p. 20cm.

1. Witchcraft--Sermons. I. Title. II. Title: Zehen müthliche Predigten von der Zauber- und Hexenwerck. III. Title: Von der Zauber- und Hexenwerck.

Von Donnern und Hagel-Wettern.

WITCHCRAFT
QC
859
H82

Hossmann, Abraham, d. 1617.
De tonitru & tempestate, das ist: Nohtwendiger Bericht, von Donnern vnd Hagel-Wettern, wannen vnd woher sich dieselbe verursachen, ob sie natürlich: Item, ob Teufel vnd Zäuberer auch Wetter machen können ... Neben Erzehlung etlicher seltzamen Fälle ... in Druck gegeben durch Abrahamum Hosmanum ... Leipzig, In Verlegung Henning Grossn des Ältern Buchhändl. ₍Typis Beerwaldin, durch Jacobum Popporeich₎ 1612.
123, ₍1₎ p. 20cm.

8 NIC

(Continued on next card)

Von Donnern und Hagel-Wettern.

WITCHCRAFT
QC
859
H82

Hossmann, Abraham, d. 1617. De tonitru & tempestate ... 1612. (Card 2)

Title in red and black, within ornamental border.
With colophon.

1. Meteorology--Early works to 1800. 2. Folk-lore, German. 3. Witchcraft. I. Title. II. Title: Von Donnern und Hagel-Wettern.

8 NIC

Von dreyen Hexen-Pfaffen.

MSS
Bd.
WITCHCRAFT
BF
Z98
Z65

Zwo Hexenzeitung, die erste, Von dreyen Hexen-Pfaffen, unnd einem Organisten zu Ellwang, wie dieselbe Christo abgesagt, unnd dem bösen Geist mit Leib und Seel sich ergeben, und die Zauberkunst von ime erlernet ... Die ander: Von einer Unholdin oder Hexen, wie sie mit ihren Gespilen alles zu verderben unterstanden, der Satan aber, ihnen Ursachen, warum sie solches sollen bleiben lassen angezeigt, auch nicht gestatten, oder geschehen lassen wöllen. Nürnberg,
(Continued on next card)

Von dreyen Hexen-Pfaffen.

MSS
Bd.
WITCHCRAFT
BF
Z98
Z65

Zwo Hexenzeitung, die erste, Von dreyen Hexen-Pfaffen ... 1615 ₍ca. 1900₎ (Card 2)

1615 ₍ca. 1900₎
4 l. title vignette. 19cm.
Carnap's manuscript copy.
"Original i. d. Kgl. öff. Bibl. z. Stuttgart 4 unpag. Bl. incl. Titelbl. ohne Signat."
1. Witchcraft. I. Title: Von dreyen Hexen-Pfaffen. II. Title: Von einer Unholdin oder Hexen.

Von einem Studenten, welchen der Teuffel ... in grewliche Sünden gestürzt.

MSS
Bd.
WITCHCRAFT
BF
W277
Z92

Warhafftige und erschreckliche newe Zeittunge von einer jungen Diernen, welche sich dem Teuffel auf sechs Jar lang ergeben ... Item, von einem Studenten, welchen der Teuffel gleichfals in grewliche Sünden gestürzt ... Item, von den ungestümen Wettern am den 12. Maij dieses 82. Jars in Baijern ... grossen Schaden, an Menschen und Wiese gethan haben. Dresdzen, Gimel Bergen, 1582 ₍ca. 1900₎
6 l. 19 cm.
(Continued on next card)

Von einem Studenten, welchen der Teuffel ... in grewliche Sünden gestürzt.

MSS
Bd.
WITCHCRAFT
BF
W277
Z92

Warhafftige und erschreckliche newe Zeittunge von einer jungen Diernen ... 1582 ₍ca. 1900₎ (Card 2)

Carnap's manuscript copy.
"Originaldruck in der Stadtbibliothek zu Zürich, 8 Seiten in 4°."
Signatures in the margins indicate signatures of the original.
1. Devil. 2. Nature (in religion, folk-lore, etc.) I. Title: Von einer jungen Diernen, welche sich dem
(Continued on next card)

CATALOGUE OF THE CORNELL WITCHCRAFT COLLECTION

Von einer jungen Diernen, welche sich dem Teuffel ... ergeben.

S
TCHCRAFT
77
2

Warhafftige und erschreckliche neue Zeittunge von einer jungen Diernen, welche sich dem Teuffel auf sechs Jar lang ergeben ... Item, von einem Studenten, welchen der Teuffel gleichfals in grewliche Sünden gestürzt ... Item, von grewlichen ungestümen Wettern so den 12. Maij dieses 82. Jars in Baijern ... grossen Schaden, an Menschen und Wiese gethan haben. Dreszden, Gimel Bergen, 1582 [ca. 1900]
6 l. 19   cm.
(Continued on next card)

Von einer jungen Diernen, welche sich dem Teuffel ... ergeben.

S
TCHCRAFT
77
2

Warhafftige und erschreckliche neue Zeittunge von einer jungen Diernen ... 1582 [ca. 1900] (Card 2)

Carnap's manuscript copy.
"Originaldruck in der Stadtbibliothek zu Zürich, 8 Seiten in 4°."
Signatures in the margins indicate signatures of the original.
1. Devil. 2. Nature (in religion, folklore, etc.) I. Title: Von einer jungen Diernen, welche sich dem (Continued on next card)

Von einer Unholdin oder Hexen.

S
TCHCRAFT

Zwo Hexenzeitung, die erste, Von dreyen Hexen-Pfaffen, unnd einem Organisten zu Ellwang, wie dieselbe Christo abgesagt, unnd dem bösen Geist mit Leib und Seel sich ergeben, und die Zauberkunst von ime erlernet ... Die ander: Von einer Unholdin oder Hexen, wie sie mit ihren Gespilen alles zu verderben unterstanden, der Satan aber, ihnen Ursachen, warum sie solches sollen bleiben lassen angezeigt, auch nicht gestatten, oder geschehen lassen wöllen. Nürnberg,
(Continued on next card)

Von einer Unholdin oder Hexen.

S
TCHCRAFT

Zwo Hexenzeitung, die erste, Von dreyen Hexen-Pfaffen ... 1615 [ca. 1900] (Card 2)

1615 [ca. 1900]
4 l. title vignette. 19cm.
Carnap's manuscript copy.
"Original i. d. Kgl. öff. Bibl. z. Stuttgart 4 unpag. Bl. incl. Titelbl. ohne Signat."
1. Witchcraft. I. Title: Von dreyen Hexen-Pfaffen. II. Title: Von einer Unholdin oder Hexen.

Von etlichen Hexen oder Unholden ... im Stifft Mäntz.

S
TCHCRAFT
77
3

Ein Warhafftige Zeitung von etlichē Hexen oder Unholden, welche man kürtzlich im Stifft Mäntz, zu Ascheburg, Dipperck, Ostum, Rönsshoffen, auch andern Orten, verbrendt, was Ubels sie gestifft, und bekandt haben. [Franckfurt, 1603; ca. 1900]
5 l. 19cm.
Carnap's manuscript copy.
"Originaldruck in der Königl. Bibliothek zu Berlin 4 Bl.   in 12°."
Numerals in the margins indicate (Continued on next card)

Von etlichen Hexen oder Unholden ... im Stifft Mäntz.

S
TCHCRAFT
77
3

Ein Warhafftige Zeitung von etlichē Hexen ... [1603; ca. 1900] (Card 2)

pagination of the original.
In verse.

1. Witchcraft--Germany. I. Title: Von etlichen Hexen oder Unholden ... im Stifft Mäntz.

Von grewlichen ungestümen Wettern.

MSS
Bd.
WITCHCRAFT
BF
W277
Z92

Warhafftige und erschreckliche neue Zeittunge von einer jungen Diernen, welche sich dem Teuffel auf sechs Jar lang ergeben ... Item, von einem Studenten, welchen der Teuffel gleichfals in grewliche Sünden gestürzt ... Item, von grewlichen ungestümen Wettern so den 12. Maij dieses 82. Jars in Baijern ... grossen Schaden, an Menschen und Wiese gethan haben. Dreszden, Gimel Bergen, 1582 [ca. 1900]
6 l. 19   cm.
(Continued on next card)

Von grewlichen ungestümen Wettern.

MSS
Bd.
WITCHCRAFT
BF
W277
Z92

Warhafftige und erschreckliche neue Zeittunge von einer jungen Diernen ... 1582 [ca. 1900] (Card 2)

Carnap's manuscript copy.
"Originaldruck in der Stadtbibliothek zu Zürich, 8 Seiten in 4°."
Signatures in the margins indicate signatures of the original.
1. Devil. 2. Nature (in religion, folklore, etc.) I. Title: Von einer jungen Diernen, welche sich dem (Continued on next card)

Von guten und bösen Engeln.

WITCHCRAFT
BT
965
S43

Scultetus, Marcus.
Praesidium angelicum. Ein nützlich Handbüchlein. Von guten vnd bösen Engeln: vnd von derer beyder Wesen, Vhrsprung, Eigenschafften, Ampt, Dienstbestallung vnnd Wercken gegen Gott vnd der christlichen Kirchen in allen Ständen ... Gestellet durch M. Marcvm Scvltetvm, Pfarrern zu Seehausen im Churfürstenthumb Sachsen. Wittenbergi, Gedruckt bey Georg Müller, in Verlegung Paul Heiwigs   Buchf., 1616.
668 p.   vignettes. 17cm.
(Continued on next card)

8
NIC

Von guten und bösen Engeln.

WITCHCRAFT
BT
965
S43

Scultetus, Marcus. Praesidium angelicum ... 1616.   (Card 2)

Title in red and black.
Part 2 has title: Das ander Theil dieses Büchleins, Vnterricht von den bösen Engeln.

1. Angels. 2. Demonology. I. Title. II. Title: Von guten und bösen Engeln.

8
NIC

Von Hexen und Wildem Gejäg.

BF
1566
H2

Haan, Jean.
Von Hexen und wildem Gejäg. Mit mittelalterlichen Holzschnitten und Kupferstichen sowie Zeichnungen von Félix Mersch, Gab Weis und Pit Weyer. Luxembourg, Edi-Centre, 1971.
159 p. illus. 24 cm. (Am Sagenborn des Luxemburger Volkes, Bd. 3)
Bibliography: p. 159.

1. Witchcraft. I. Title. II. Series.

BF1566.H3   70-594907

Library of Congress   [1] [2]

Von Hexen unnd Unholden.

Witchcraft
BF
1565
D17
1576

Daneau, Lambert, ca. 1530-1595.
Von den Zauberern, Hexen, vnd Vnholden, drei christliche verscheidene [sic], vnnd zu diesen vnsern vngefärlichen Zeiten notwendige Bericht ... Durch die hoch vnd wohlgelehrte Herren, Lambertvm Danaevm, Iacobvm Vallick, vnnd Vlricvm Molitoris. ... Cölln, Gedruckt durch Johannem Gymnicum, 1576.
2 v. in 1. 16cm.
"Der ander Tractat von Zauberern, Hexen, vnd Vnholden,   durch J. Vallick, p.
(Continued on next card)

8

Von Hexen unnd Unholden.

Witchcraft
BF
1565
D17
1576

Daneau, Lambert, ca. 1530-1595. Von den Zauberern, Hexen, vnd Vnholden... 1576 (Card 2)

157-222 of v. 1, has special t. p.
Translation of De veneficis, quos olim sortilegos ... vocant, by L. Daneau; of an unidentified work by J. Vallick; and of De lamiis et phitonicis mulieribus, by U. Molitor.
1. Witchcraft. 2. Demonology. I. His De veneficis, quos olim sortigelos ... vo-
(Continued on next card)

8

Von Hundert und vir und dreyssig Unholden.

MSS
Bd.
WITCHCRAFT
BF
W272

Warhaffte und glaubwirdige Zeytung. Von Hundert und vir und dreyssig Unholden, so umb ihrer Zauberey halben, diss verschinen LXXXij. Jars, zu Gefencknus gebracht ... zum Fewer verdambt unnd verbrennet worden ... wie dañ die Ort do sich solches alles verloffen, ordenlich hernach werden vermelt und angezeigt. Strassburg, Bey Nicolaus Wiriod, 1583 [ca. 1900]
4 l. 24cm.
Carnap's   manuscript copy.
(Continued on next card)

Von Hundert und vir und dreyssig Unholden.

MSS
Bd.
WITCHCRAFT
BF
W272

Warhaffte und glaubwirdige Zeytung. Von Hundert und vir und dreyssig Unholden ... 1583 [ca. 1900] (Card 2)

"Originaldruck in der Königl. Hof- u. Staats-Bibliothek zu München, 4 Bl. in 4°."
Numerals in the margins indicate pagination of the original.

1. Witchcraft--Germany. I. Title: Von Hundert und vir   und dreyssig Unholden.

Von Sägen und Beschweren.

WITCHCRAFT
BF
1565
S767

Spreter, Johann.
Ein kurtzer Bericht, was von den abgötterischen Sägen vñ Beschweren zůhalten, wie der etlich volbracht, vnnd das die ein Zauberey, auch Grewel vor Gott dem Herren seind. Durch den wirdigen vñ wolgelerten Herren Johañ. Spreter von Rotweil zůsamen gebracht ... [Basel, Getruckt durch Bartholomeum Westheymer, 1543]
[12] p. 21cm.
With colophon.
(Continued on next card)

8
NIC

Von Sägen und Beschweren.

WITCHCRAFT
BF
1565
S767

Spreter, Johann. Ein kurtzer Bericht ... [1543]   (Card 2)

Caption title: Von Sägen vnd Beschweren.
Running title: Von abgötterischen Sägen vnd Beschweren.

1. Witchcraft. 2. Magic. 3. Folk medicine. I. Title: Von abgötterischen Sägen und Beschweren.

8
NIC

Von straff vnnd Peen aller vnnd yeder Malefitz handlungen ain kurtzer bericht.

Rare
K
Perneder, Andreas, d. 1543?
P44
V9++
1544

Von straff vnnd Peen aller vnnd yeder Malefitz handlungen ain kurtzer bericht, genommen vnd verfaszt ausz den gemainen Kayserlichen Rechten, mit Lateinischer Allegation derselben, auch daneben meldung der gebreüchlichen hierinn Hochteütschlands gewonhaiten: Nit anders zůachten dann ain Gerichtliche Practica aller Criminal oder peinlichen sachen ... Ingolstat, Gedruckt durch Alexander Weissenhorn, 1544.
[4], xxiiii l. 31cm.
Caption title   A. Perneders halsgerichts ordnung.

CATALOGUE OF THE CORNELL WITCHCRAFT COLLECTION

Von Teuffelsgespenst, Zauberern und Gifftbereytern.

Witchcraft
BF 1520 W64 P8++ 1586

Theatrvm [i. e., Theatrum] de veneficis. Das ist: Von Teuffelsgespenst, Zauberern vnd Gifftbereitern, Schwartzkünstlern, Hexen vnd Vnholden, vieler fürnemmen Historien vnd Exempel ... Sampt etlicher hingerichten zäuberischer Weiber gethaner Bekanntnuß, Examination, Prob, Vrgicht [sic] vnd Straff ... Allen Vögten, Schuldtheissen, Amptleuthen deß weltlichen Schwerdts, &c. sehr nützlich vnd dienstlich zu wiss en, vnd keines wegs zu

8 (Continued on next card)

Von Teuffelsgespenst, Zauberern und Gifftbereytern.

Witchcraft
BF 1520 W64 P8++ 1586

Theatrvm [i. e., Theatrum] de veneficis. 1586. (Card 2)

verachten. Franckfurt am Mayn, Gedruckt durch Nicolaum Basseum, 1586.
6 p. l., 396, [9] p. 34cm.
Title in red and black.
Preface signed: Nicolaus Bassaeus.
Bound with Wier, Johann, 1515-1588. De praestigiis daemonum. Von Teuffelsgespenst, Zauberern, vnd Gifftbereytern.

8 (Continued on next card)

Von Teuffelsgespenst, Zauberern und Gifftbereytern.

Witchcraft
BF 1520 W64 P8++ 1586

Theatrvm [i. e., Theatrum] de veneficis. 1586. (Card 3)

Franckfurt am Mayn, 1586.
Contents.--Warhafftige Zeittung von gottlosen Hexen, by R. Lutz.--Ein Gespräch von Zäuberern, welche man lateinisch Sortilegos oder Sortiarios nennet, by L. Daneus.--Von Zäuberern, Hexen, vnd Vnholden, by J. Vallick.--Von Hexen vnd Vnholden, by V. Molitoris, tr. by C. Lautenbach.--

8 (Continued on next card)

Von Teuffelsgespenst, Zauberern und Gifftbereytern.

Witchcraft
BF 1520 W64 P8++ 1586

Theatrvm [i. e., Theatrum] de veneficis. 1586. (Card 4)

Contents--Continued.
Ein christlich vnd nothwendig Gespräch, von den bösen abtrünnigen Engeln, by A. Rheynmannus.--Von Gespensten, Vngehewren, Fällen, oder Poltern, vnd anderen wunderbaren Dingen, by L. Lavater.--Bedencken, was er von Exorcisterey halte, by L. Thurneysser.--Eine kurtze, trewe Warnung,

8 (Continued on next card)

Von Teuffelsgespenst, Zauberern und Gifftbereytern.

Witchcraft
BF 1520 W64 P8++ 1586

Theatrvm [i. e., Theatrum] de veneficis. 1586. (Card 5)

Contents--Continued.
... ob auch zu dieser vnser Zeit vnder vns Christen, Hexen, Zäuberer vnd Vnholden vorhanden, by A. Sawr.--Von deß Teuffels Nebelkappen, das ist: ein kurtzer Begriff, den gantzen Handel von der Zäuberey belangend, by P. Frisius.--Bericht von Erforschung, Prob vnd Erkän ntniß der Zäuberinnen

8 (Continued on next card)

Von Teuffelsgespenst, Zauberern und Gifftbereytern.

Witchcraft
BF 1520 W64 P8++ 1586

Theatrvm [i. e., Theatrum] de veneficis. 1586. (Card 6)

Contents--Continued.
durchs kalte Wasser, by H. Neuwalt, tr. by H. Meybaum.--Ein christlich Bedencken vnnd Erjnnerung von Zauberey, by A. Lercheimer.--Wider die schwartzen Künst, by H. Bullinger.--Ware Entdeckung vnd Erklärung aller fürnembster Articckel der Zauberey, by J. Freyherr von Liechtenberg.--Von

8 (Continued on next card)

Von Teuffelsgespenst, Zauberern und Gifftbereytern.

Witchcraft
BF 1520 W64 P8++ 1586

Theatrvm [i. e., Theatrum] de veneficis. 1586. (Card 7)

Contents--Continued.
der Hexen, die man gemeiniglich Zauberin nennet, by J. Ewich.--Antwort auff etliche Fragen ... von ... Keyser Maximiliano, by J. Trithemius.--Consilia vnd Bedencken etlicher zu vnsern Zeiten rechtsgelehrten Juristen, von Hexen vnd Vnholden.

8 (Continued on next card)

Von Teuffelsgespenst, Zauberern und Gifftbereytern.

Witchcraft
BF 1520 W64 P8++ 1586

Theatrvm [i. e., Theatrum] de veneficis. 1586. (Card 8)

Binding: blind stamped pigskin, with clasps (one wanting); front cover initialed A K A S H and dated 1589.
1. Demonology. 2. Witchcraft. 3. Magic. I. Bassaeus, Nicolaus, d. 1599. II. Title: Von Teuffelsgespenst, Zauberern und Gifftbereytern.

8

Von Teuffelsgespenst, Zauberern und Gifftbereytern.

Witchcraft
BF 1520 W64 P8++ 1586

Wier, Johann, 1515-1588. De lamiis. Das ist: Von Teuffelsgespenst, Zauberern vnd Gifftbereytern, kurtzer doch gründtlicher Bericht ... Sampt einem angehängten kleinen Tractätlein von dem falschen vnd erdichten Fasten ... in vnsere gemeine teutsche Sprache gebracht, durch Henricum Petrum Rebenstoek ... Franckfort [sic] am Mayn, Gedruckt durch Nicolaum Basseum, 1586.
6 p. l., 90, [8] p. 34cm.
Title in red and black.

8 (Continued on next card)

Von Teuffelsgespenst, Zauberern und Gifftbereytern.

Witchcraft
BF 1520 W64 P8++ 1586

Wier, Johann, 1515-1588. De lamiis. Das ist: Von Teuffelsgespenst ... 1586. (Card 2)

Originally published 1577 in Latin as an epitome of his De praestigiis daemonum. Cf. Allgemeine deutsche Biographie, v. 42, p. 267.
Bound with his De praestigiis daemonum. Von Teuffelsgespenst, Zauberern vnd Gifftbereytern. Franckfurt am Mayn,

8 (Continued on next card)

Von Teuffelsgespenst, Zauberern, und Gifftbereytern.

Witchcraft
BF 1520 W64 P8++ 1586

Wier, Johann, 1515-1588. De lamiis. Das ist: Von Teuffelsgespenst ... 1586. (Card 3)

1586.
Binding: blind stamped pigskin, with clasps (one wanting); front cover initialed A K A S H and dated 1589.
1. Demonology. 2. Witchcraft. 3. Magic. 4. Fasting. I. Title: Von Teuffelsgespenst, Zauberern und Gifftbe-

8

Von Teuffelsgespenst, Zauberern, und Gifftbereytern.

Witchcraft
BF 1520 W64 P8++ 1586

Wier, Johann, 1515-1588. De praestigiis daemonvm. Von Teuffelsgespenst, Zauberern vnd Gifftbereytern, Schwartzkünstlern, Hexen vnd Vnholden, darzu jrer Straff, auch von den Bezauberten, vnd wie jhnen zuhelffen sey, ordentlich vnd eigentlich mit sondern Fleiß in VI. Bücher getheilet: darinnen gründlich vnd eigentlich dargethan, was von solchen jeder zeit disputiert, vnd gehalten worden. Erstlich durch D. Johannem Weier in Latein

8 (Continued on next card)

Von Teuffelsgespenst, Zauberern, und Gifftbereytern.

Witchcraft
BF 1520 W64 P8++ 1586

Wier, Johann, 1515-1588. De praestigiis daemonvm. Von Teuffelsgespenst, Zauberern vnd Gifftbereytern ... 1586. (Card 2)

beschrieben, nachmals von Johanne Fuglino verteutscht, jetzund aber nach dem letzten lateinischen außgangenen Original auffs neuw vbersehen, vnnd mit vielen heilsamen nützlichen Stücken: auch sonderlich hochdienlichen newen Zusätzen, so im Lateinischen nicht gelesen, als im folgenden Blat

8 (Continued on next card)

Von Teuffelsgespenst, Zauberern, und Gifftbereytern.

Witchcraft
BF 1520 W64 P8++ 1586

Wier, Johann, 1515-1588. De praestigiiis daemonvm. Von Teuffelsgespenst, Zauberern vnd Gifftbereytern ... 1586. (Card 3)

zufinden, so der Bodinus mit gutem Grundt nicht widerlegen kan, durchauß gemehret vnd gebessert. Sampt zu Endt angehencktem newem vnd volkommenen Register. Franckfurt am Mayn, Getruckt durch Nicolaum Basseum, 1586.
12 p. l., 575, [20] p. illus. 34cm.

8 (Continued on next card)

Von Teuffelsgespenst, Zauberern, und Gifftbereytern.

Witchcraft
BF 1520 W64 P8++ 1586

Wier, Johann, 1515-1588. De praestigiis daemonvm. Von Teuffelsgespenst, Zauberern vnd Gifftbereytern ... 1586. (Card 4)

Title in red and black.
Includes translations of his Liber apologeticus and Pseudomonarchia daemonum.
With this are bound his De Lamiis. Das ist: Von Teuffelsgespenst ... Franckfort am Mayn, 1586; and Theatrum de veneficis. Franckfurt am Mayn, 1586.

8 (Continued on next card)

Von Teuffelsgespenst, Zauberern, und Gifftbereytern.

Witchcraft
BF 1520 W64 P8++ 1586

Wier, Johann, 1515-1588. De praestigiis daemonvm. Von Teuffelsgespenst, Zauberern vnd Gifftbereytern ... 1586. (Card 5)

Binding: blind stamped pigskin, with clasps (one wanting); front cover initialed A K A S H and dated 1589.
1. Demonology. 2. Witchcraft. 3. Magic. 4. Fasting. I. Title: Von Teuffelsgespenst, Zauberern und Gifftbereytern. II. His De praestigiis daemo-

8 (Continued on next card)

Von Zäuberern, Hexen und Unholden.

Witchcraft
BF 1565 G58 1592

Godelmann, Johann Georg, 1559-1611. Von Zäuberern Hexen vnd Vnholden, warhafftiger vnd wolgegründter Bericht Herrn Georgii Gödelmanni ..., wie dieselbigen zuerkennen vnd zu straffen, Allen Beampten zu vnsern Zeiten von wegen vieler vngleicher vnd streittigen Meynung sehr nützlich vnnd nothwendig zuwissen ... verteutscht ... durch Georgium Nigrinum ... Franckfort am Mayn, Gedruckt durch Nicolaum Bassaeum, 1592.

8 (Continued on next card)

Von Zäuberern, Hexen und Unholden.

Witchcraft
BF 1565 G58 1592

Godelmann, Johann Georg, 1559-1611. Von Zäuberern Hexen vnd Vnholden ... 1592. (Card 2)

8 p. l., 483 p. illus. 20cm.
Translation of Tractatus de magis, veneficis et lamiis.
1. Witchcraft. 2. Demonology. 3. Trials (Witchcraft) I. His Tractatus de magis, veneficis et lamiis-- German. II. Title: Von Zäuberern, Hexen und Unholden.

8

CATALOGUE OF THE CORNELL WITCHCRAFT COLLECTION

Witchcraft
BF
1405
H81

Von Zauberei, Theurgie und Mantik.
Horst, Georg Conrad, 1767-1838?
Zauber-Bibliothek; oder, Von Zauberei, Theurgie und Mantik, Zauberern, Hexen, und Hexenprocessen, Dämonen, Gespenstern, und Geistererscheinungen. Zur Beförderung einer rein-geschichtlichen, von Aberglauben und Unglauben freien Beurtheilung dieser Gegenstände. Mainz, F. Kupferberg, 1821-1826.
6 v. 20cm.

---

von Hohenheim, Philipp Aureolus Theophrastus Bombast, known as Paracelsus.

see

Paracelsus, 1493-1541.

WITCHCRAFT
BF
1565
S83
L88

8
NIC

Vorgängischer Versuch zu Erwürkung eines Vertrages.
[Loschert, Oswald,] b.1704.
Vorgängischer Versuch zu Erwürkung eines Vertrages zwischen den in dem bisherigen Hexerey-Kriege verwickelten Gelehrten. Wie auch zum nutzbaren Unterrichte, wie man von der Zauber- und Hexerey weder zu wenig, noch zu viel glauben soll. Unternommen von einem Verehrer der Gelehrten und Liebhaber der Christlichen Wahrheiten. [Bamberg,] an dem Maynstrome [Göbhardt,] 1767.
86 p. 23 cm.
(Continued on next card)

Witchcraft
BF
1584
S8
V94+

Von Zauberern, Hexen und Wolfsbannern. Actenstücke, Processe wider Zauberer und Hexen betreffend, 1602-1701. Origg. u. Copp. im Landesarchive u. zu Admont. (In Steiermärkische Geschichtsblätter. Graz. 26cm. 3. Jahrg., 3. u. 4.? Heft (1882), p. [129]-180, 201-216)
Probably edited by J. von Zahn.
1. Witchcraft--Styria. 2. Trials (Witchcraft)--Styria. I. Zahn, Josef von.
II. Steiermärkische Geschichtsblätter.

Von Przichowicky, Anton Peter, Abp. of Prague, 1707-1793.

see

Přichovský, Antonín Peter, Abp. of Prague, 1707-1793.

Witchcraft
BF
1528
D9
V981

8

Vorst, Conrad, 1569-1622.
Vries, Simon de, b. 1630.
Wercksaeme duyvelen in de weereld: of Vervolgh vande Satan in sijn weesen, aert, bedryf en guygchelspel: vertoond in een historische verhandelingh van duyvelsche gesighten, spoocken, droomen, voorteeckenen, voorseggingen, tovereyen, en wat voorts deese stof aenhangigh is. Nevens afweeringh van 't geen daer tegens ingebraght werd, met meenighvuldige verwringingen der H. Schrift. Door S. de Vries. Utrecht,
(Continued on next card)

WITCHCRAFT
K
B378
1717

8
NIC

Von Zauberey.
Bechmann, Johann Volkmar, 1624-1689, praeses.
Discursus juridicus de crimine maleficii, vulgo Von Zauberey, sub praesidio Joh. Volk. Bechmanns, submittit Joach. Ernst. Kober. Nunc recusa. Jenae, 1717.
30 p. 20cm.
Originally published as dissertation, Jena, 1678 (Joachim Ernst Kober, respondent)
1. Witchcraft. I. Kober, Joachim Ernst, respondent. II. Title. III. Title: Von Zauberey.

Witchcraft
BF
1410
B42
1691a
no.9

8

't Voorgevallene in de catechisatie, by Do. Adrianus van Wesel, op Sondagh den 28sten December. Ao. 1692. In de Oudezijds Kapel, opgesteld door een toehoorder. Amsterdam, By D. van den Dalen, boekverkoper, 1693.
8 p. title vignette. 20 x 16cm.
4°: A⁴.
Black letter.
Van der Linde 177.
Argues for tolerance of views held by Balthasar Bekker and his followers.
(Continued on next card)

Witchcraft
BF
1528
D9
V981

8

Vorst, Conrad, 1569-1622.
Vries, Simon de, b. 1630. Wercksaeme duyvelen in de weereld ... 1692. (Card 2)
By Anthoni Schouten, boeckverkoper, 1692.
34 p. l., 590, [50] p. title and other vignettes. 16cm.
8°: *-4*⁸, 5*1, A-2R⁸.
Title in red and black.
Imperfect: p. 271-272 wanting.
Running title: De Satan vertoond in
(Continued on next card)

WITCHCRAFT
BF
1413
M94

8
NIC

Von Zauberey, Teufelsbesitzungen und Wunderkuren.
Müller, Johann Valentin, 1756-1813.
Von Zauberey, Teufelsbesitzungen und Wunderkuren. [Frankfurt, 1796]
359-542 p. 21cm.
Extract from his Entwurf einer gerichtlichen Arzneiwissenschaft, v.2. (Comprises chapter 4)
1. Occult sciences. 2. Witchcraft. 3. Demoniac possession. 4. Medicine, Magic, mystic and spagiric. I. His / Entwurf einer gerichtlichen Arzneiwissenschaft.

Witchcraft
BF
1410
B42
1691a
no.9

8

't Voorgevallene in de catechisatie, by Do. Adrianus van Wesel ... 1693. (Card 2)
No. 9 in vol. lettered B. Bekker. Betoverde weereld.
1. Nederlandse Hervormde Kerk--Doctrinal and controversial works. 2. Wesel, Adrianus van, d. 1710. 3. Bekker, Balthasar, 1634-1698. I. Een toehoorder, pseud.

Witchcraft
BF
1528
D9
V981

8

Vorst, Conrad, 1569-1622.
Vries, Simon de, b. 1630. Wercksaeme duyvelen in de weereld ... 1692. (Card 3)
sijn weesen, aert, bedrijf, en guygchelspel.
Preface discusses the opinions of Conrad Vorst.
1. Devil. 2. Demonology. 3. Vorst, Conrad, 1569-1622. I. His De Satan in sijn weesen, aert, bedryf, en guychelspel. II. Title.

WITCHCRAFT
BF
1565
P888

8
NIC

Von Zauberey vnd Zauberern, gründlicher Bericht.
Praetorius, Antonius.
Von Zauberey vnd Zauberern, gründlicher Bericht; darinn der grawsamen Menschen thöriges, feindseliges, schändliches vornemmen, vnd wie christliche Oberkeit in rechter Amptspflege jhnen begegnen, jhr Werck straffen, auffheben, vnd hindern solle, vnd könne ... Hiezu ist gesetzet: Der Theologen zu Nürnberg gantz christlich Bedencken, vnd warhafftig Vrtheil von Zauberey vnd Hexenwerck. Heydelberg,
(Continued on next card)

Witchcraft
BF
1410
B42
Z82
no.2

8

Voorlooper tot de volstrekte wederlegginge van het gene de heeren, Orchard, Daillon en Bekker hebben aen het licht gebragt.
Hamer, Petrus, 1646-1716.
Voorlooper tot de volstrekte wederlegginge van het gene de heeren, Orchard, Daillon en Bekker hebben aen het licht gebragt; aengaende de werken, en macht der geesten: en met name der duivelen. Door Petrus Hamer, dienaer Jesus Christi in Numansdorp. Uitgegeven na kerken-ordre. Met belofte refutatoir van zekeren Brief aen een regent van Amsteldam. Dato 18 Maij 1692. Dordrecht, By C. Wilgaarts, boekverkooper, 1692.
4 p. l., 40 p. title vignette, illus.
(Continued on next card)

WITCHCRAFT
DD
901
H26
T87

8
NIC

Vorträge über merkwürdige Erscheinungen in der Hamburgischen Rechtsgeschichte.
Trummer, Carl.
Vorträge über Tortur, Hexenverfolgungen, Vehmgerichte, und andere merkwürdige Erscheinungen in der Hamburgischen Rechtsgeschichte. Gehalten in der juristischen Section des geschichtlichen Vereins in Hamburg ... Mit vielen bisher ungedruckten Urkunden und Criminalfällen. Hamburg, J. A. Meissner, 1844-50.
3 v. in 1. 22cm.
Vol. 2 and 3 have title: Vorträge
(Continued on next card)

WITCHCRAFT
BF
1565
P888

Von Zauberey vnd Zauberern, gründlicher Bericht.
Praetorius, Antonius.
Von Zauberey vnd Zauberern... (Card 2)
Gedruckt durch J. Lancellot; In Verlegung A. Cambier, 1613.
334 p. 20cm.

I. Title.

Witchcraft
BF
1410
B42
Z82
no.2

8

Voorlooper tot de volstrekte wederlegginge van het gene de heeren, Orchard, Daillon en Bekker hebben aen het licht gebragt.
Hamer, Petrus, 1646-1716. Voorlooper tot de volstrekte wederlegginge van... Orchard, Daillon en Bekker ... 1692. (Card 2)
initials. 20 x 15cm.
4°: *⁴, A-E⁴.
Van der Linde 95.
No. 2 in vol. lettered Over Bekkers Betoverde wereld. 1692.
1. Orchard, N , supposed author. The doctrine of devils. 2. Daillon, Benjamin de. Examen de l'opression
(Continued on next card)

WITCHCRAFT
DD
901
H26
T87

8
NIC

Vorträge über merkwürdige Erscheinungen in der Hamburgischen Rechtsgeschichte.
Trummer, Carl. Vorträge über Tortur, Hexenverfolgungen, Vehmgerichte ... 1844-50. (Card 2)
Über merkwürdige Erscheinungen in der Hamburgischen Rechtsgeschichte.
1. Hamburg--History. 2. Law--Hamburg --History. 3. Hamburg--History--Sources. 4. Witchcraft--Hamburg. 5. Fehmic courts. 6. Torture--Germany. I. Title. II. Title: Vorträge über merkwürdige Erscheinungen in der Hamburgischen Rechtsgeschichte.

CATALOGUE OF THE CORNELL WITCHCRAFT COLLECTION

WITCHCRAFT
DD
901
H26
T87

Vorträge über Tortur, Hexenverfolgungen, Vehmgerichte, und andere merkwürdige Erscheinungen.
Trummer, Carl.
Vorträge über Tortur, Hexenverfolgungen, Vehmgerichte, und andere merkwürdige Erscheinungen, in der Hamburgischen Rechtsgeschichte. Gehalten in der juristischen Section des geschichtlichen Vereins in Hamburg ... Mit vielen bisher ungedruckten Urkunden und Criminalfällen. Hamburg, J. A. Meissner, 1844-50.
3 v. in 1. 22cm.
Vol. 2 and 3 have title: Vorträge

8
NIC
(Continued on next card)

WITCHCRAFT
DD
901
H26
T87

Vorträge über Tortur, Hexenverfolgungen, Vehmgerichte, und andere merkwürdige Erscheinungen.
Trummer, Carl. Vorträge über Tortur, Hexenverfolgungen, Vehmgerichte ... 1844-50. (Card 2)
Über merkwürdige Erscheinungen in der Hamburgischen Rechtsgeschichte.

1. Hamburg—History. 2. Law—Hamburg—History. 3. Hamburg—History—Sources. 4. Witchcraft—Hamburg. 5. Fehmic courts. 6. Torture—Germany. I. Title. II. Title: Vorträge über merkwürdige Erscheinungen in der Hamburgischen Rechtsgeschichte.

8
NIC

Witchcraft
BF
1559
G25
Z92
1796

Das Vorurtheil, Glaub, und Unglaub, bey denen Gassnerischen Kuren, oder, Etwas für diejenigen, die keinen Teufel glauben. Nebst einem Verzeichniss von denen pro und contra herausgekommenen Schriften. [n. p.] 1796.
77 p. 18cm.
British Museum, whose edition has imprint Sulzbach, 1775, attributes work to Gassner.
1. Gassner, Johann Joseph, 1727-1779. 2. Exorcism. I. Gassner, Johann Joseph, 1727-1779, supposed author.

8

BF
1555
L68

Vrais et faux possédés.
Lhermitte, Jacques Jean, 1877–
Vrais et faux possédés. Paris, A. Fayard [1956]
170 p. 20 cm. (Bibliothèque Ecclesia, 19)

1. Demoniac possession. I. Title.

BF1555.L55   56-36569 ‡
Library of Congress

Witchcraft
BF
1410
B42
Z56
v.2
no.7

Een vremd nagt-gezigt.
Beschryvinge van een vremd nagt-gezigte, vertoont aan een toehoorder der predikatie, die door den remonstrantsche leeraer Ds. Johannes Molinaeus voor 't vermogen des duivels, en tegen den aucteur van 't boek De betooverde weereld, onlangs te Rotterdam gedaan is. Logoochoorion, Gedrukt by den drukker van Haar Majesteit Krisis [1692]
2 p. l., 12 p. title vignette, illus. initial. 19 x 15cm.

(Continued on next card)

Witchcraft
BF
1410
B42
Z56
v.2
no.7

Een vremd nagt-gezigt.
Beschryvinge van een vremd nagt-gezigte ... [1692] (Card 2)
4°: π², A⁴, B².
Black letter.
Van der Linde 132.
No. 7 in vol. lettered Bekker II.
1. Molinaeus, Johannes, d. 1702. De betooverde werelt van D. Balthazar Bekker. 2. Bekker, Balthasar, 1634-1698. De betoverde weereld. I. Title: Een vremd nagt-gezigt.

8

Witchcraft
BF
1528
D9
V98
1692

Vries, Simon de, b. 1630.
De Satan, in sijn weesen, aert, bedryf, en guychel-spel, vertoond in een historische verhandelingh van duyvelen, gesichten, spoocken, voorseggingen, voorteeckenen, droomen, toveryen, betoveringen, beseetenheyd, en wat noch voorts deese stof aenhangigh is. Nevens afweeringh van 't geen daer tegens ingebraght werd met meenighvuldige verwringingen der H. Schrift, en tegenspraeck der geduerige ondervindingh.

8
(Continued on next card)

Witchcraft
BF
1528
D9
V98
1692

Vries, Simon de, b. 1630.   De Satan ...
1692.   (Card 2)
Door S. de Vries. Utrecht, By A. Schouten, Boeckverkoper, 1692.
20 p. l., 571, [57] p. title and other vignettes, illus. initials. 17 x 11cm.
8°: *-2*⁸, 3*⁴, A-2Q⁸, 2R⁴.
First published 1691.
In part a refutation of Balthasar Bekker's De betoverde weereld.

8
(Continued on next card)

Witchcraft
BF
1528
D9
V98
1692

Vries, Simon de, b. 1630.   De Satan ...
1692.   (Card 3)
ker's De betoverde weereld.
Van der Linde 153.

1. Devil. 2. Demonology. 3. Bekker, Balthasar, 1634-1698. De betoverde weereld. II. Title.

8

Witchcraft
BF
1528
D9
V981

Vries, Simon de, b. 1630.
De Satan in sijn weesen, aert, bedryf, en guychelspel.
Vries, Simon de, b. 1630.
Wercksaeme duyvelen in de weereld: of Vervolgh vande Satan in sijn weesen, aert, bedryf en guygchelspel: vertoond in een historische verhandelingh van duyvelsche gesichten, spoocken, droomen, voorteeckenen, voorseggingen, tovereyen, en wat voorts deese stof aenhangigh is. Nevens afweeringh van 't geen daer tegens ingebraght werd, met meenighvuldige verwringingen der H. Schrift. Door S. de Vries. Utrecht,

8
(Continued on next card)

Witchcraft
BF
1528
D9
V981

Vries, Simon de, b. 1630.   Wercksaeme duyvelen in de weereld ... 1692.   (Card 2)
By Anthoni Schouten, boeckverkoper, 1692.
34 p. l., 590, [50] p. title and other vignettes. 16cm.
8°: *-4*⁸, 5*1, A-2R⁸.
Title in red and black.
Imperfect: p. 271-272 wanting.
Running title: De Satan vertoond in

8
(Continued on next card)

Witchcraft
BF
1528
D9
V981

Vries, Simon de, b. 1630.   Wercksaeme duyvelen in de weereld ... 1692.   (Card 3)
sijn weesen, aert, bedrijf, en guygchelspel.
Preface discusses the opinions of Conrad Vorst.

1. Devil. 2. Demonology. 3. Vorst, Conrad, 1569-1622. I. His De Satan in sijn weesen, aert, bedryf, en guygchelspel. II. Title.

8

Witchcraft
BF
1410
B42
Z56
v.2
no.18

Vries, Simon de, 1630–
De Satan in syn wesen, aart, bedryf en guychelspel.
Overdenkinge op het boek Den Satan in zijn weesen, aard-bedryf, en guigelspel, &c. beschreven door Simon de Vries. Amsterdam, By D. van den Dalen, boekverkooper, 1691.
15 p. [p. 16 blank] title vignette, illus. initial. 19 x 15cm.
4°: A-B⁴.
Black letter (except for introduction)
Plea for tolerance in the controversy over Balthasar Bekker's De betoverde weereld.

8
(Continued on next card)

Witchcraft
BF
1410
B42
Z56
v.2
no.18

Vries, Simon de, 1630–
De Satan in syn wesen, aart, bedryf en guychelspel.
Overdenkinge op het boek Den Satan in zijn weesen ... 1691.   (Card 2)
Van der Linde 154.
No. 18 in vol. lettered Bekker II.

1. Vries, Simon de, 1630- De Satan in syn wesen, aart, bedryf en guychelspel. 2. Bekker, Balthasar, 1634-1698. De betoverde weereld.

8

Witchcraft
BF
1528
D9
V981

Vries, Simon de, b. 1630.
Wercksaeme duyvelen in de weereld: of Vervolgh vande Satan in sijn weesen, aert, bedryf en guygchelspel: vertoond in een historische verhandelingh van duyvelsche gesichten, spoocken, droomen, voorteeckenen, voorseggingen, tovereyen, en wat voorts deese stof aenhangigh is. Nevens afweeringh van 't geen daer tegens ingebraght werd, met meenighvuldige verwringingen der H. Schrift. Door S. de Vries. Utrecht,

8
(Continued on next card)

Witchcraft
BF
1528
D9
V981

Vries, Simon de, b. 1630.   Wercksaeme duyvelen in de weereld ... 1692.   (Card 2)
By Anthoni Schouten, boeckverkoper, 1692.
34 p. l., 590, [50] p. title and other vignettes. 16cm.
8°: *-4*⁸, 5*1, A-2R⁸.
Title in red and black.
Imperfect: p. 271-272 wanting.
Running title: De Satan vertoond in

8
(Continued on next card)

Witchcraft
BF
1410
B42
Z69
no.7

Vyfde briev van ... Haggébher Philaleethees, geschreeven aan zynen vriend N. N.
[Hooght, Everard van der] d. 1716.
Vyfde briev van הגבר Φιλαλήθης Haggébher Philaleethees, geschreeven aan zynen vriend N. N. over de versoekinge Christi in de woestyne, tot wederlegging van het 18 (ofte 20) capp. in het boek van D. Balthasar Bekker, genaamt de Betoverde wereld. Item, over de classicale proceduuren, &c. Amsterdam, G. Borstius, 1691.
99-123 p. 21cm.
Signatures: 4°: π1, A-C⁴, D1.
Black letter.
NIC
(Continued on next card)

Vyfde briev van ... Haggébher Philalee-
    thees, geschreeven aan zynen vriend N. N.

[Hooght, Everard van der] d. 1716. Vyfde
    briev van ... Haggébher Philaleethes ...
    1691.   (Card 2)

    Van der Linde 101.
    No. 7 in a Collection of tracts against
Balthasar Bekker and his Betoverde weereld.
    The friend N. N. is thought to be Jacobus
Schuts.

        (Continued on next card)

CATALOGUE OF THE CORNELL WITCHCRAFT COLLECTION

W

W., D. H. V.

MSS Bd. WITCHCRAFT BF D613

Diszes Wonder, auch erschricklic Zaychen ist durch Zulassung Gottesz warhafftig unnd thadlich gesehen in der Stat von Gent in Flandren, auff den XVIII. Augustii in Jaer, MDLXXXVI bey dem bossen Gayst unnd seinnesz Wercks, seer erschrocklich ist unnb zu leessen. Anntorff, By Paulus Brackfeldt, 1586 [ca. 1900]
4 l. illus. 23cm.
Carnap's manuscript copy.
"Original druck i. d. Gust. Freytag Bibliothek, jetzt i. d. Stadt-
(Continued on next card)

W., D. H. V.

MSS Bd. WITCHCRAFT BF D613

Diszes Wonder, auch erschricklic Zaychen ... 1586 [ca. 1900] (Card 2)
bibliothek zu Frankfurt a/M. 4 Bl. 4°."
A letter received by D. H. V. W.
At end: "Ghetranslateert durch M. Carel Strutberger."
Numerals and signatures in the margins indicate pagination and signatures of the original.
1. Apparitions. 2. Devil. I. W., D. H. V. II. Strutberger, Carel, tr.

W., I.

Witchcraft BX 9479 B42 B11 no.14

Brief, aan een heer, waar in uyt de H. Schrift getoond werd, dat'er is een quade geest, die een redelijk schepsel is buyten de ziel des mensche. Met eenige aanmerkinge over het boek, De ware oorspronk, voort en ondergank des Satans. Door I. W. Amsterdam, By J. de Veer gedrukt, 1696.
64 p. title vignette, illus. initial. 20x15cm.
4°: A-H⁴.
Probably by Joannes van Wijk.
Supports Balthasar Bekker in the controversy over his De betoverde weereld.
No.14 in vol. lettered B. Bekkers sterfbed en andere tractaten.

W., R. W.

WITCHCRAFT BF 1555 N23 1788

A Narrative of the extraordinary case, of Geo. Lukins, of Yatton, Somersetshire, who was possessed of evil spirits for near eighteen years, also an account of his remarkable deliverance ... extracted from the manuscripts of several persons who attended. To which is prefixed a letter from the Rev. W. R. W. With the Rev. Mr. Easterbrook's letter annex'd ... 2d ed. Bristol, Printed by Bulgin and Rosser, and sold by W. Bulgin [etc.] 1788.
(Continued on next card)

8

W., R. W.

WITCHCRAFT BF 1555 N23 1788

A Narrative of the extraordinary case, of Geo. Lukins ... 1788. (Card 2)
gin [etc] 1788.
24 p. 21cm.
1. Demoniac possession. 2. Exorcism. 3. Lukins, George, fl. 1788. I. W. R. W. II. W., R. W. III. Easterbrook, Joseph.

8

W., W.

Witchcraft BF 1563 W81++ no.3

A True and iust recorde of the information, examination and confession of all the witches taken at S. Oses in ... Essex; whereof some were executed, and other some entreated according to ... lawe. ... Written orderly as the cases were tryed by euidence, by W. W. [pseud.] London, Imprinted by T. Dawson, 1582. [London, at the British Museum, 1923]
[121] p. 14cm.
Signatures: A⁴, A-G⁸, χ¹.
(Continued on next card)

W., W.

Witchcraft BF 1563 W81++ no.3

A true and iust recorde of ... witches ... at S. Oses ... 1582 [1923] (Card 2)
"Dedicated to Justice Darcy; and ... evident that it was written by the judge himself."--Cf. Notestein, Wallace. A history of witchcraft in England from 1558 to 1718, p. 348.
Photocopy (negative) 121 p. on 53 l. 20 x 32cm.
No. 3 in vol. lettered: Witchcraft tracts, chapbooks and broadsides, 1579-1704; rotograph copies.

W. B., tr.

WITCHCRAFT BF 1517 F5 M62 1613

Michaelis, Sebastien, 1543?-1618.
The admirable history of the possession and conversion of a penitent woman. Sedvced by a magician that made her to become a witch, and the princesse of sorcerers in the country of Prouince, who was brought to S. Baume to bee exorcised, in the yeere 1610 ... Wherevnto is annexed a pnevmology, or Discourse of spirits ... reuewed, corrected, and enlarged ... Translated into English by W. B. London, Imprinted for William Aspley [1613]
(Continued on next card)

8

W. B., tr.

WITCHCRAFT BF 1517 F5 M62 1613

Michaelis, Sebastien, 1543?-1618. The admirable history of the possession ... of a penitent woman ... [1613] (Card 2)
liam Aspley [1613]
24 p. l., 418, [10], 154, [34] p. 20cm.
Differs from another issue only in t. p. (lacks date; some spellings different)
Translation of Histoire admirable de la possession ... d'vne penitente, and of Discovrs des esprits.
"A discovrse of spirits" has special t. p. and separate paging.
(Continued on next card)

8

W. B., tr.

WITCHCRAFT BF 1517 F5 M62 1613

Michaelis, Sebastien, 1543?-1618. The admirable history of the possession ... of a penitent woman ... [1613] (Card 3)
STC 17854.
1. Palud, Magdeleine de la. 2. Gaufridi, Louis, 1572-1611. 3. Loudun, France. Ursuline convent. 4. Demoniac possession. 5. Exorcism. I. Histoire admirable de la possession ... d'une penitente. English. II. His Discours des esprits. English. III. Title. IV. W. B., tr. V. B., W., tr.

8

W. R. W.

WITCHCRAFT BF 1555 N23 1788

A Narrative of the extraordinary case, of Geo. Lukins, of Yatton, Somersetshire, who was possessed of evil spirits for near eighteen years, also an account of his remarkable deliverance ... extracted from the manuscripts of several persons who attended. To which is prefixed a letter from the Rev. W. R. W. With the Rev. Mr. Easterbrook's letter annex'd ... 2d ed. Bristol, Printed by Bulgin and Rosser, and sold by W. Bulgin
(Continued on next card)

8

W. R. W.

WITCHCRAFT BF 1555 N23 1788

A Narrative of the extraordinary case, of Geo. Lukins ... 1788. (Card 2)
gin [etc] 1788.
24 p. 21cm.
1. Demoniac possession. 2. Exorcism. 3. Lukins, George, fl. 1788. I. W. R. W. II. W., R. W. III. Easterbrook, Joseph.

8

W. S. à V. C. & C. A.

WITCHCRAFT BF 1572 C5 S33 1630

[Schilling, Wolfgang]
Newer Tractat von der verführten Kinder Zauberey. In welchem mit reifflichem Discurs ... vorgehalten wirdt, auss was Vrsachen viel vnerwachsene vnd vnmündige Kinder ... zu der verdampten Geister vnd Zauberer Gesellschafft gebracht vnd vnerhörter Weiss verführt werden ... auss lateinischer in die teutsche Sprach vbersetzt vnd in Truck gegeben ... durch VV. S. à V. C. & C. A. Aschaffenburg, Getruckt durch Quirin
(Continued on next card)

8 NIC

W. S. à V. C. & C. A.

WITCHCRAFT BF 1572 C5 S33 1630

[Schilling, Wolfgang] Newer Tractat von der verführten Kinder Zauberey ... 1630. (Card 2)
Botzer, 1630.
44 p. 21cm.
Revised and augmented version of the "Appendix oder Nachtrab" (p. 60-129) published in his compilation on witchcraft from P. Laymann's Theologia moralis. (Laymann, P. Ein kurtzer doch gründlicher
(Continued on next card)

8 NIC

W. S. à V. C. & C. A.

WITCHCRAFT BF 1572 C5 S33 1630

[Schilling, Wolfgang] Newer Tractat von der verführten Kinder Zauberey ... 1630. (Card 3)
Bericht wie ... mit den Hexen zuverfahren seye. Aschaffenburg, 1629.)
1. Witchcraft. 2. Children--Management. I. Title. II. W. S. à V. C. & C. A. III. S., W., à V. C. & C. A.

8 NIC

CATALOGUE OF THE CORNELL WITCHCRAFT COLLECTION

```
                W. W.
Witchcraft
BF          A True and iust recorde of the information,
1563          examination and confession of all the
W81++         witches taken at S. Oses in ... Essex;
no.3          whereof some were executed, and other
              some entreated according to ... lawe.
              ... Written orderly as the cases were
              tryed by euidence, by W. W. [pseud.]
              London, Imprinted by T. Dawson, 1582.
              [London, at the British Museum, 1923]
              [121] p. 14cm.
              Signatures: A⁴, A-G⁸, χ¹.

                                (Continued on next card)
```

```
                W. W.
Witchcraft
BF          A true and iust recorde of ... witches ...
1563          at S. Oses ... 1582 [1923]  (Card 2)
W81++
no.3          "Dedicated to Justice Darcy; and ... evi-
              dent that it was written by the judge himself."
              --Cf. Notestein, Wallace. A history of witch-
              craft in England from 1558 to 1718, p. 348.
              Photocopy (negative) 121 p. on 53 l.  20
              x 32cm.
              No. 3 in vol. lettered: Witchcraft tracts,
              chapbooks and broadsides, 1579-1704; roto-
              graph copies.
```

```
Witchcraft
BF          Waaijen, Johannes van der, 1639-1701.
1410          De betoverde weereld van D. Balthasar
B42         Bekker ondersogt en weederlegt door Johannes
Z91         vander Waeyen.  Franeker, By L. Strik en
              J. Horreus, boekverkoopers, 1693.
              1 p. l., VIII, 3-16, 651, [11] p. title
              vignette, illus. initials. 20 x 16cm.
              4°: π1, *⁴, *2-2*⁴, A-K⁴, L3, M-O⁴, P².
              Black letter.
              Van der Linde 156.
              1. Bekker,       Balthasar, 1634-1698.
              De betoverde    weereld. I. Title.
```

```
              Waaijen, Johannes van der, 1639-1701.
                De betoverde weereld van D. Balthasar
                Bekker ondersogt en weederlegt.
Witchcraft
BF          [Andala, Ruardus] 1665-1727.
1410          Uiterste verleegentheid van Doctor Balt.
B42         Bekker. Duidelijk aangeweesen door weder-
Z912        legginge van alle sijne aanmerkingen ende
              naleesingen gevoegt bi het slordige mengel-
              moes van sijn E. Voedsterlingen.  Uitgegeeven
              door een discipel van de Heer J. vander
              Waeyen en voedsterling van de Academie van
              Friesland.  Franeker, By H. Gyzelaar, ordi-
              naris drukker der Eed. Mog. Heeren Staten,
              en der Academie van Friesland, 1696.
              4 p. l., 234, [6] p. title and
                                (Continued on next card)
```

```
              Waaijen, Johannes van der, 1639-1701.
                De betoverde weereld van D. Balthasar
                Bekker ondersogt en weederlegt.
Witchcraft
BF          [Andala, Ruardus] 1665-1727.  Uiterste
1410          verleegentheid van Doctor Balt. Bekker.
B42           1696.                            (Card 2)
Z912
              other vignettes, illus. initials. 22 x 17cm.
              4°: *⁴, A-2G⁴.
              Van der Linde 166.
              Criticizes Bekker's critique of Waaijen's
              De betoverde weereld van D. Balthasar Bekker
              ondersogt en weederlegt.
                With this  is bound Andala, Ruardus,
                1665-1727.           Balthazar Bekkers en
                                (Continued on next card)
```

```
              Waaijen, Johannes van der, 1639-1701.
                De betoverde weereld van D. Balthasar
Witchcraft    Bekker ondersogt en weederlegt.
BF          [Andala, Ruardus] 1665-1727.  Uiterste
1410          verleegentheid van Doctor Balt. Bekker.
B42           1696.                            (Card 3)
Z912
              insonderheyd sijner voedsterlingen onkunde...
              Franeker, 1696.
              1. Bekker, Balthasar, 1634-1698. De
              betoverde weereld.  2. Waaijen, Johannes
              van der, 1639-1701. De betoverde weereld
              van D. Balthasar Bekker ondersogt en weeder-
              legt. I. Title.
```

```
              Waaijen, Johannes van der, 1639-1701.
                De betoverde weereld van D. Balthasar
Witchcraft    Bekker ondersogt en weederlegt.
BF            Bekker, Balthasar, 1634-1698.
1410            Brief van Baltasar [sic] Bekker, S. T. D.
B42           predikant tot Amsterdam, aan de Heeren
Z86           Joost de Smeth, Willem Weyer, en Nikolaas
no.3          vander Hagen, so tegenwoordig dienende als
              meermaals gediend hebbende ouderlingen der
              Gereformeerde Kerk aldaar. Tot antwoord
              op den brief van den Professor vander
              Waeyen aan deselven, gesteld voor sijn
              boek genaamd De betoverde weereld van B. B.
              ondersocht en wederleid.  Hier achter is
                                (Continued on next card)
     8
```

```
              Waaijen, Johannes van der, 1639-1701.
                De betoverde weereld van D. Balthasar
Witchcraft    Bekker ondersogt en weederlegt.
BF            Bekker, Balthasar, 1634-1698.  Brief ...
1410          aan de Heeren Joost de Smeth, Willem
B42           Weyer, en Nikolaas vander Hagen ...  1693.
Z86                                              (Card 2)
no.3
              bygevoegd d'Opdraght-brief desselfden pro-
              fessors aan sijne Vorst. Doorl. den Prinsse
              van Nassaw Stadhouder &c. en d'Ed. Mog.
              Heeren Gedeputeerde Staten van Friesland,
              voor het selfde boek, met een antwoord op
              den selven.  Amsterdam, By D. van den
                                (Continued on next card)
     8
```

```
              Waaijen, Johannes van der, 1639-1701.
                De betoverde weereld van D. Balthasar
Witchcraft    Bekker ondersogt en weederlegt.
BF            Bekker, Balthasar, 1634-1698.  Brief ...
1410          aan de Heeren Joost de Smeth, Willem
B42           Weyer, en Nikolaas vander Hagen ...  1693.
Z86                                              (Card 3)
no.3
              Dalen, boekverkoper, 1693.
              16, 15*-16*, 17-24 p.  title vignette,
              illus. initial. 19 x 15cm.
              4°: A-B⁴, B*1, C⁴.
              Van der Linde 159.
              No. 3 in vol. lettered Tractaten voor
              en tegen B. Be    kker.
                                (Continued on next card)
     8
```

```
              Waaijen, Johannes van der, 1639-1701.
Witchcraft
BF            Bekker, Balthasar, 1634-1698.
1410            Brief van Balthasar Bekker, S. Th. Dr.
B42           predikant tot Amsterdam. Aan den Heer
Z86           Joannes vander Waeyen, S. Theol. Dr. en
no.2          professor in de loffelike en vermaarde
              Universiteit tot Franeker. In antwoord
              op desselven brief, waarmede hy hem sijn
              boek tegen De betoverde weereld onlangs
              uitgegeven, heeft toegesonden. [Amster-
              dam? 1693]
                8 p. illus. initial. 19 x 15cm.
                                (Continued on next card)
     8
```

```
              Waaijen, Johannes van der, 1639-1701.
Witchcraft
BF            Bekker, Balthasar, 1634-1698.  Brief ...
1410          aan den Heer Joannes vander Waeyen ...
B42           [1693]                           (Card 2)
Z86
no.2          4°: A⁴.
              Caption title.
              Dated: Amsterdam den 8 Augusty 1693.
              Van der Linde 157.
              No. 2 in vol. lettered Tractaten voor
              en tegen B. Bekker.
              1. His  De betoverde weereld.  I.
              Waaijen, Joha    nnes van der, 1639-
              1701. II. T      itle.
     8
```

```
              De waare oorspronk, voort- en onder-gank des
                Satans.
Witchcraft
BF          [Webbers, Zacharias]
1528          De waare oorspronk, voort- en onder-gank des
D9            Satans: behelzende, een buitengewoone, edog
W37           klare verhandeling, van de voornaamste plaatsen
1729          der Heilige Schrift, welke zyn spreekende van
              den Duivel. Dienende voor een inleiding tot de
              Bybelsche Godgeleerdheid, en het waare
              Christendom. Door Joan Adolphsz. 4. druk.
              Van nieuws overzien. Amsterdam, By Jacob Graal,
              boekverkooper, 1729.
                                (Continued on next card)
```

```
              De waare oorspronk, voort- en onder-gank
                des Satans.
Witchcraft
BF          [Webbers, Zacharias]  De waare oorspronk,
1528          voort- en onder-gank des Satans ...  1729.
D9                                               (Card 2)
W37
1729          7 p. l., 418, 3 p. 17cm.
              8°: *⁸ (-*1), A-2C⁸, 2D3.
              Black letter; title in red and black.
              "De uitgever tot den leezer" signed:
              N. N. (i. e., Jacobus Schuts)
              First edition 1695.
     8                          (Continued on next card)
```

```
              Wackher, Barbara, b. 1680, defendant.
MSS
Bd.           Tübingen. Universität. Theologische Fakultät.
WITCHCRAFT      Urtheil der Würtemb. theol. u. jurist.
BF            Facultät zu Tübingen über eine Hexenprozess,
T91++         1726. Tübingen, 1726.
              [36] l. 33cm.
              Manuscript, on paper.
              Decision of the theological and law faculties
              of the university concerning the trial of
              Barbara Wackher for witchcraft.
              On cover: University of Tubingen. Decision
              regarding a witch. 1726.
              Bound in marbled boards, half-leather.
```

```
K           Wächter, Carl Georg von, 1797-1880.
              Beiträge zur deutschen Geschichte, insbesondere zur
W12         Geschichte des deutschen Strafrechts. [Von] Karl Georg
              von Wächter. Neudr. d. Ausg. Tübingen 1845. Aalen,
              Sciencia-Verl., 1970.
                 viii, 331 p. 22 cm.  DM50.00       GDB 70-A39-128
                 Includes bibliographical references.

3             1. Law—Germany—History and criticism.  2. Criminal law—
              Germany—History.  3. Fehmic courts.  4. Witchcraft—Germany.
              I. Title.

              ISBN 3-511-00425-X
                                                      75-583846
              Library of Congress              71 [2]
```

```
              Wächter, Oskar, 1825-1902.

                see

              Wächter, Oskar Eberhard Siegfried von,
                1825-1902.
```

```
WITCHCRAFT
JN            Wächter, Oskar Eberhard Siegfried von,
3269            1825-1902.
W12             Vehmgerichte und Hexenprozesse in
              Deutschland, nach den Quellen dargestellt
              von Oskar Wächter.  Stuttgart, W. Spemann
              [1882]
                221 p. 19cm. (Collection Spemann)
              (Deutsche Hand- und Hausbibliothek)

                1. Femic courts.  2. Witchcraft--
              Germany--Hist.  I. Title.
     8
```

```
              Waeyen, Johannes van der, 1639-1701.

                see

              Waaijen, Johannes van der, 1639-1701.
```

CATALOGUE OF THE CORNELL WITCHCRAFT COLLECTION

WITCHCRAFT
BS
2545
D5
S473

Wagenbronner, Georgius Christianus, respondent.
Müller, Joannes Stephanus.
De daemoniacis Semlerianis in duabus dissertationibus theologicis commentatur D. Ioannes Steph. Müllerus. Francofurti et Lipsiae, Apud Theodor. Vilhelm. Ern. Güthium, 1763.
95, 102 p. 23cm.

Each dissertation has separate t.p. (reprints of original title pages) No.1: Notionem δαιμονίου sive δαίμονος olim et inprimis Christi tempore non hoc
(Continued on next card)

8
NIC

WITCHCRAFT
BS
2545
D5
S473

Wagenbronner, Georgius Christianus, respondent.
Müller, Joannes Stephanus. De daemoniacis Semlerianis...1763. (Card 2)
involuisse vi anima mortui daemon esse crederetur...demonstrat et...praeside...Ioanne Stephano Müllero...defendet Ioann. Burckhard. Caspari. Ienae [1761]. No.2: Notio illa animam mortui esse et dici in evangeliis daemonem opinioni debetur...praeside...Ioanne Stephano Müllero...defendere conatur Georg. Christ. Wagenbronner. Ienae [1762].

Witchcraft
PT
1793
T4
W13+

Wagner, B. A
Christian Thomasius; ein Beitrag zur Würdigung seiner Verdienste um die deutsche Literatur. Berlin, W. Weber, 1872.
26 p. 27cm.

1. Thomasius, Christian, 1655-1728.
II. Title.

8

PT
1793
T4
W13+

Wagner, B. A
Christian Thomasius; ein Beitrag zur Würdigung seiner Verdienste um die deutsche Literatur. Berlin, W. Weber, 1872.
26 p. 27cm.

1. Thomasius, Christian, 1655-1728.
2. German literature--Early modern (to 1700)--Hist. & crit.

WITCHCRAFT
BF
1559
S85

Wagner, Johann Jacob, respondent.
Spinaeus, Godofredus, praeses.
Disputatio philosophica. Examinans quaestionem, Utrvm sonvs campanarvm ingruentem tonitruum ac fulminum tempestatem, pruinas item, nec non spectra ac diabolum, depellere & abigere queat? Quam ... praeside ... D. Godofredo Spinaeo ... Exercitationis ergo, publico subjicit examini, Joh. Iacobus Wagnerus ... Steinfvrti, Typis Cornelij Wellenberg, 1661.
20 p. 19cm.

8 (Continued on next card)

WITCHCRAFT
BF
1559
S85

Wagner, Johann Jacob, respondent.
Spinaeus, Godofredus, praeses. Disputatio philosophica ... 1661. (Card 2)
Diss.--Steinfurt (J. J. Wagner, respondent)

1. Bells (in religion, folk-lore, etc.)
2. Demonology. 3. Weather-lore. I. Wagner, Johann Jacob, respondent. II. Title: Utrum sonus campanarum ingruentem tonitruum ... tempestatem ... abigere queat.

8

Wagstaff, Johann, 1633-1677.

see

Wagstaffe, John, 1633-1677.

WITCHCRAFT
BF
1565
W13
1711

Wagstaffe, John, 1633-1677.
Johann Wagstaffs Gründlich ausgeführte Materie von der Hexerey, oder: Die Meynung derer jenigen so da glauben, dass es Hexen gebe; deutlich widerlegt und mit vernünfftigen Anmerckungen über jedes Capitel erläutert. Aus dem Englischen übersetzt. Halle in Megdeburgischen, Im Rengerischen Buchladen, 1711.
16 p. l., 152 p. 16cm.

8 (Continued on next card)

WITCHCRAFT
BF
1565
W13
1711

Wagstaffe, John, 1633-1677. Johann Wagstaffs Gründlich ausgeführte Materie von der Hexerey ... 1711. (Card 2)

Translation of a revised version of The question of witchcraft debated.

1. Witchcraft. I. His The question of witchcraft debated. German. II. Title: Gründlich aus geführte Materie von der Hexerey. III. Title.

8

Witchcraft
BF
1565
W13

[Wagstaffe, John] 1633-1677.
The question of witchcraft debated: or, A discourse against their opinion that affirm witches ... London, Printed for E. Millington, 1669.
128 p. 14cm.

Signatures: A-I⁸.
"... Lovers of lies. A dialogue made by the famous Lucian [translated by Sir Thomas More]: p. 83-128.

(Over)

WITCHCRAFT
BF
1565
W13
1671

Wagstaffe, John, 1633-1677.
The question of witchcraft debated. Or a discourse against their opinion that affirm witches, considered and enlarged. The 2d ed. ... London, Printed for Edw. Millington, 1671.
198 p. 15cm.

"... Lovers of lies: a dialogue made by the famous Lucian [translated by Sir Thomas More]."
I. Lucianus Samosatensis. Philopseudes. English. II. Title.

WITCHCRAFT
BF
1565
W13
1711

Wagstaffe, John, 1633-1677.
The question of witchcraft debated. German.
Johann Wagstaffs Gründlich ausgeführte Materie von der Hexerey, oder: Die Meynung derer jenigen so da glauben, dass es Hexen gebe; deutlich widerlegt und mit vernünfftigen Anmerckungen über jedes Capitel erläutert. Aus dem Englischen übersetzt. Halle in Megdeburgischen, Im Rengerischen Buchladen, 1711.
16 p. l., 152 p. 16cm.

8 (Continued on next card)

WITCHCRAFT
BF
1565
W13
1711

Wagstaffe, John, 1633-1677.
The question of witchcraft debated. German.
Wagstaffe, John, 1633-1677. Johann Wagstaffs Gründlich ausgeführte Materie von der Hexerey ... 1711. (Card 2)

Translation of a revised version of The question of witchcraft debated.

1. Witchcraft. I. His The question of witchcraft debated. German. II. Title: Gründlich aus geführte Materie von der Hexerey.

8

Witchcraft
BF
773
C33

Wagstaffe, John, 1633-1677.
The question of witchcraft debated.
Casaubon, Meric, 1599-1671.
Of credulity and incredulity; in things divine & spiritval: wherein, (among other things) a true and faithful account is given of the Platonick philosophy, as it hath reference to Christianity: as also the business of witches and witchcraft, against a late writer, fully argued and disputed. By Merick Casaubon ... and one of the prebends of Christ-Church, Canturbury. London, Printed by T. N. for Samuel Lownds, 1670.
2 p. l., 208 p. 17cm.

8 (Continued on next card)

Witchcraft
BF
773
C33

Wagstaffe, John, 1633-1677.
The question of witchcraft debated.
Casaubon, Meric, 1599-1671. Of credulity and incredulity ... 1670. (Card 2)

A continuation of his Of credulity and incredulity; in things natural, civil and divine, first published 1688 without the third part on the divine.
1. Credulity. 2. Christianity--Philosophy. 3. Plato. 4. Witchcraft. 5. Wagstaffe, John, 1633-1677. The question of witchcraft debated. I. His Of credulity and incredulity; in things natural, civil and divine. II. Title: Of credulity and incredulity; in things divine & spiritual.

8

Witchcraft
BF
1565
061

Wagstaffe, John, 1633-1677.
The question of witchcraft debated.
The opinion of witchcraft vindicated. In answer to a book intituled The question of witchcraft debated [by John Wagstaffe] Being a letter to a friend, by R. T. ... London, Printed by E. O. for F. Haley, 1670.
63 p. 15cm.

1. Witchcraft. 2. Wagstaffe, John, 1633-1677. The question of witchcraft debated. I. T., R.

Witchcraft
BF
1775
W132
1840

Der Wahre geistliche Schild, so vor 300 Jahren von dem heil. Papst Leo X. bestätigt worden, wider alle gefährliche böse Menschen sowohl, als aller Hexerei und Teufelswerk entgegengesetzt. Darinnen sehr kräftige Segen und Gebete ... Nebst einem Anhang heiliger Segen ... [n. p.] 1747. Erie, Bei J. Keim [1840?]
180 p. illus. 12cm.
Contents.--Andächtige Weis dem Amt der heiligen Mess nützlich beizuwohnen.--Ein
(Continued on next card)

Witchcraft
BF
1775
W132
1840

Der Wahre geistliche Schild ... [1840?] (Card 2)

Contents--Continued.
schöner und wohl approbirter heiliger Segen zu Wasser und Land wider alle seine Feinde.--Geistliche Schild-Wacht, darinnen einer alle Stund einen besonderen erwählen kann.--Anhang. Heiliger Segen ... um in allen Gefahren, worein sowohl Menschen als Vieh oft gerathen, gesichert zu sein.

8 (Continued on next card)

CATALOGUE OF THE CORNELL WITCHCRAFT COLLECTION

Witchcraft
BF
1775
W132
1840

Der Wahre geistliche Schild ... [1840?] (Card 3)

Each item has special t. p. Geistliche Schild-Wacht and Anhang have imprint 1840.
In case.

8

Witchcraft
BF
1775
W132
1849

Der Wahre geistliche Schild, so vor 300 Jahren von dem heil. Papst Leo X. bestätigt worden, wider alle gefährliche böse Menschen sowohl als aller Hexerei und Teufelswerk entgegen gesetzt; darinnen sehr kräftige Segen und Gebete ... Nebst einem Anhang heiliger Segen ... [n. p.] 1617. [Erie? 1849?]
144, 35 p. illus. 12cm.
Contents.--Andächtige Weise, dem Amt der heiligen Messe nützlich beizuwohnen.--Ein

8   (Continued on next card)

Witchcraft
BF
1775
W132
1849

Der Wahre geistliche Schild ... [1849?] (Card 2)

Contents--Continued.
schöner und wohlapprobirter heiliger Segen zu Wasser und Land wider alle seine Feinde. --Geistliche Schild-Wacht, darinnen der Mensch ihm für eine jegliche Stund ... einen besondern Patron aus den Heiligen Gottes erwählet [sic].--Anhang. Heiliger Segen ... um in allen Gefahren, worein sowohl Men-

8   (Continued on next card)

Witchcraft
BF
1775
W132
1849

Der Wahre geistliche Schild ... [1849?] (Card 3)

Contents--Continued.
schen als Vieh oft gerathen, gesichert zu sein.
Each item has special t. p.
Geistliche Schild-Wacht has imprint 1840; the Anhang has imprint 1849 and is paged separately.
1. Charms.   2. Prayers. I. Leo X, Pope, 1475-1521. II. Title: Heiliger Segen.

8

Witchcraft
BF
1775
W13
1800

Der Wahre geistliche Schild. 2. Th. Oder: Heiliger Segen aller heil. Apostel und Jünger Jesu Christi ..., um alle unheilbaren Krankheiten der Menschen zu vertreiben, und alle Anfälle des Satans abzuwenden. Sammt dem wunderthätigen Gertrauden-Büchlein, das ist: Der heil. Jungfrau und Abtissin Gertraud himmlische Anmuthungen und Gebete um zeitliche und ewige Güter. Salzburg, 1667. [n. p., 18--]
148 p. illus. 16cm.

8   (Continued on next card)

Witchcraft
BF
1775
W13
1800

Der Wahre geistliche Schild ... [18--] (Card 2)

Heiliger Segen aller heiligen Apostel ... has special t. p.
Der heiligen Jungfrauen und Abtissin Gertraud himmlische Anmuthungen und Gebeter has special t. p. and imprint Cöln, 1506.
1. Charms. 2. Prayers. I. Gertrude, Saint, surnamed the Great, 1256-1302? supposed author. II. Title: Heiliger Segen aller heiligen Apostel. III. Title: Der heiligen Jungfrauen ...Gertraud himmlische Anmuthungen.

8

WITCHCRAFT
BF
1603
H64
1704

Wahre und eigentliche Entdeckung oder Erklärung der fürnemsten Artickul von der Zauberey.
Hildebrand, Wolffgang.
Wahre und eigentliche Entdeckung oder Erklärung der fürnemsten Artickul von der Zauberey und was von Zauberern, Vnholden, Hexen, derer Händel, Art, Thun, ... und vielen andern ihren Machinationen ... Durch den wohlgebohrnen Herrn Jacob Frey Herrn von Lichtenberg ... erfahren, und durch den hochgelahrten Herrn Jacob Weckern weitläufftiger beschrieben. Anitzo mit allem Fleiss übersehen und vermehret mit

8   (Continued on next card)
NIC

WITCHCRAFT
BF
1603
H64
1704

Wahre und eigentliche Entdeckung oder Erklärung der fürnemsten Artickul von der Zauberey.
Hildebrand, Wolffgang. Wahre und eigentliche Entdeckung oder Erklärung der fürnemsten Artickul von der Zauberey ... [1704?] (Card 2)

vielen Artzeneyen ..., auch wie eine christliche Obrigkeit wider die Zauberer ... rechtlich verfahren soll, ... auch viele lustige und possierliche Historien von Erscheinungen allerhand Geister ... von neuen in Druck verfertiget durch Wolfgangum Hilde-

8   (Continued on next card)
NIC

WITCHCRAFT
BF
1603
H64
1704

Wahre und eigentliche Entdeckung oder Erklärung der fürnemsten Artickul von der Zauberey.
Hildebrand, Wolffgang. Wahre und eigentliche Entdeckung oder Erklärung der fürnemsten Artickul von der Zauberey ... [1704?] (Card 3)

brandum. [Leipzig? 1704?]
11 p. l., 342, [18] p. front. 21cm.
Half title (follows Inhalt aller Capitel) agrees with original title: Goetia, vel Theurgia, sive Praestigiarum magicarum descriptio, and has imprint 1704.

8   (Continued on next card)
NIC

WITCHCRAFT
BF
1603
H64
1704

Wahre und eigentliche Entdeckung oder Erklärung der fürnemsten Artickul von der Zauberey.
Hildebrand, Wolffgang. Wahre und eigentliche Entdeckung oder Erklärung der fürnemsten Artickul von der Zauberey ... [1704?] (Card 4)

Bound with his Neu-vermehrt, vortrefflich ... curieuses Kunst und Wunderbuch. Leipzig, 1704.
1. Witchcraft. 2. Magic. 3. Devil--Legends. 4. Folk-lore--Germany. I. His Goetia, vel Theurgia. II. Liechtenberg, Jacob von, baron. Hexen-Büchlein. III. Wecker, Johann Jacob, 1528-1586. IV. Title.

8
NIC

MSS
Bd.
WITCHCRAFT
BF
W13

Wahrhafte Nachricht von einer Beschwerung des Satans so in der letzt abgewichenen heiligen Christ-Nacht 1730 zwischen 11 und 12 Uhr von 5 Bürgern in der Stadt Lindau vorgenommen worden. [n.p.] 1731 [ca. 1900]
2 l. illus. 23cm.

Carnap's manuscript copy.
"Originaldruck i. d. Kgl. Univers. Bibliothek zu Halle a/S. ... 2 Bl. in 4°."
1. Devil.   2. Exorcism.

WITCHCRAFT
D
1
G59
v.2

Wahrhafte und umständliche Nachricht von dem Zufalle, so das jungfräuliche Kloster Unterzell nächst Würzburg des Praemonstratenser-Ordens betreffen.

(In: Göttingisches historisches Magazin. Hannover. 21cm. v.2 (1788) p.[594]-631)

8   1. Demoniac possession. 2. Sänger, Maria
NIC   Renata von Mossau, ca. 1680-1749.

WITCHCRAFT
PT
1799
A1
W13

Wahrhafter Bericht vom Zauber-Sabbathe der St. Walpurgis-Nacht des dritten Reformations-Jubel-Jahres, enthaltend Satan's Reden an die auf dem Blocksberge versammelten Unholde Teutschlands, nebst vielen Parallel-Stellen von Dr. Martin Luther. Brockenhaus, 1817.
48 p. 18cm.
Possibly by F. H. W. Körte.
1. Political satire--Germany. 2. Luther, Martin--Cartoons, satire, etc. I. Körte, Friedrich Heinrich Wilhelm, 1776-1846, supposed author.

8

WITCHCRAFT
BF
1405
S41
no.6

Der Wahrhaftige feurige Drache; oder, Herrschaft über die himmlischen und höllischen Geister und über die Mächte der Erde und Luft ... Nebst den geheimen Mitteln, sich die schwarze Henne mit den goldnen Eiern zu verschaffen ... Nach einem in Frankreich aufgefundenen Manuscript von 1522. Nebst einem Postscriptum aus dem grossen Buche von König Salomo, mit einigen köstlichen Recepten, gefunden bei Peter Michel, dem letzten

8   (Continued on next card)
NIC

WITCHCRAFT
BF
1405
S41
no.6

Der Wahrhaftige feurige Drache ... [ca. 1880] (Card 2)

Karthäuser zu Erfurt. [Berlin, E. Bartels, ca. 1880]
125 p. illus. 17cm.
Translation of Le véritable dragon rouge, which was published under a variety of titles, the best-known being Grimoire du Pape Honorius.
Erstes Buch, erstes Kapitel signed: Rab-

8   (Continued on next card)
NIC

WITCHCRAFT
BF
1405
S41
no.6

Der Wahrhaftige fuerige Drache ... [ca. 1880] (Card 3)

bi Anton Moses el Arradsch.
No. 6 in vol. lettered Der schwarze Raabe.
1. Incantations. 2. Magic. I. Anton Moses el Arradsch. II. Le véritable dragon rouge. German. III. Grimoire du Pape Honorius. German.

8
NIC

WITCHCRAFT
BF
1003
U22+
v.24

Die Wahrheit im Zauber- und Hexenwesen.
Berg, W
Die Wahrheit im Zauber- und Hexenwesen.

(In: Die Übersinnliche Welt. Leipzig. 26cm. v.24 (1916) p.[249]-271, 287-310, 331-337, 356-367)

8   1. Witchcraft. 2. Magic. 3. Occult
NIC   sciences.

Wahrlieb, Gottfried, pseud.

see

Franck, Johannes Christophorus, fl. 1717

589

CATALOGUE OF THE CORNELL WITCHCRAFT COLLECTION

WITCHCRAFT
BT 1220 F67 W13
Wahrmund, Ludwig, 1860-1932.
Ultramontan: eine Abwehr in vier Artikeln. München, J. F. Lehmann, 1908.
41 p. 22cm.
Contents.--1. Herr P. Fonck S. J. als wissenschaftlicher Kritiker.--2. Die ultramontane Moral.--3. Die Teufelsaustreibung im Wemdinger Kloster.--4. Die "Religion" des Papstes Clemens VI.--Anhang. Einige berühmte Reliquienschätze.
1. Fonck, Leopold, 1865-1930. Katholische Weltanschauung und freie Wissenschaft. 2. Ultramontanism. I. Title.
8

Witchcraft
BF 1589 C75 1949
Waite, Arthur Edward, 1857-1942, tr.
Constant, Alphonse Louis, 1810-1875.
The history of magic, including a clear and precise exposition of its procedure, its rites and its mysteries, by Éliphas Lévi (Alphonse Louis Constant) Tr., with a preface and notes, by Arthur Edward Waite. Los Angeles, Borden Pub. Co. [1949]
384 p. illus. 22cm.
Translation of Histoire de la magie.

Witchcraft
BF 1612 C75 M9
Waite, Arthur Edward, 1857-1942.
[Constant, Alphonse Louis] 1810?-1875.
The mysteries of magic: a digest of the writings of Éliphas Lévi [pseud.] With biographical and critical essay, by Arthur Edward Waite ... London, G. Redway, 1886.
xliii, 349 p. 22½ cm.

1. Magic. I. Waite, Arthur Edward, 1857-1942. II. Title.
11—14358

Walburger, Michael Paris, respondent.
Witchcraft
BF 1565 D62 no.3
Schröter, Ernst Friedrich, 1621-1676, praeses.
Dissertatio juridica De lamiis earumqve processu criminali, quam ... sub praesidio ... Dn. Ernesti Friderici Schröter ... publicae eruditorum censurae subjicit, Michael Paris Walburger ... Jenae, Literis Joh. Jacobi Bauhoferi, 1690.
149, [3] p. 20cm.
No. 3 in vol. lettered Dissertationes de sagis. 1636-1714.
1. Witchcraft. 2. Trials (Witchcraft) I. Walburger, Michael Paris, respondent. II. Title: De lamiis.
8

Wald, Georg am.
Gerichtlicher Process.
WITCHCRAFT
GT 6260 W15
Wald, Georg am.
Gerichts Teuffel, darin angezeigt vnd gehandelt wirt, wie vnnd in was massen der leidig Sathan bissweylen Vnordnung vnd Zerrüttung in Gerichten durch die Richter, Cleger, Beklagten, Aduocaten, Procuratoren, Zeugen vnd dergleichen Personen, so zu einem Gericht gehören, anrichten thut ...
Zu End ist auch angehenckt der Gerichtlich Process ... Durch Georgen am Wald, der Rechten Licentiaten ... S. Gallen,
(Continued on next card)
8

Wald, Georg am.
Gerichtlicher Process.
WITCHCRAFT
GT 6260 W15
Wald, Georg am. Gerichts Teuffel ... 1580. (Card 2)
Gedruckt bey Leonhart Straub, 1580.
[98] p. 20cm.
Title in red and black.
Gerichtlicher Process, wie er im gemeinen geschriben bäpstlichen vnnd keyserlichen Rechten gegründet ... has special t. p., and is in verse.
1. Germany--Social life and customs. 2. Procedure(Law)--Germany. 3. Trial practice--Germany. I. His Gerichtlicher Process. II. Title.
8

WITCHCRAFT
GT 6260 W15
Wald, Georg am.
Gerichts Teuffel, darin angezeigt vnd gehandelt wirt, wie vnnd in was massen der leidig Sathan bissweylen Vnordnung vnd Zerrüttung in Gerichten durch die Richter, Cleger, Beklagten, Aduocaten, Procuratoren, Zeugen vnd dergleichen Personen, so zu einem Gericht gehören, anrichten thut ...
Zu End ist auch angehenckt der Gerichtlich Process ... Durch Georgen am Wald, der Rechten Licentiaten ... S. Gallen,
(Continued on next card)
8

WITCHCRAFT
GT 6260 W15
Wald, Georg am. Gerichts Teuffel ... 1580. (Card 2)
Gedruckt bey Leonhart Straub, 1580.
[98] p. 20cm.
Title in red and black.
Gerichtlicher Process, wie er im gemeinen geschrioen bäpstlichen vnnd keyserlichen Rechten gegründet ... has special t. p., and is in verse.
1. Germany--Social life and customs. 2. Procedure(Law)--Germany. 3. Trial practice--Germany. I. His Gerichtliche r Process. II. Title.
8

Waldbrühl, Wilhelm von, pseud.
see
Zuccalmaglio, Anton Wilhelm Florentin von, 1803-1869.

Waldenses.
WITCHCRAFT
BF 1555 K29
Keller, Ludwig, 1849-1915.
Die altevangelischen Gemeinden und der Hexenglaube.
(In [Geisteskultur;] Monatshefte der Comenius-Gesellschaft [für Geisteskultur und Volksbildung,] Berlin, 1892-1934. 25cm. 8. Bd., 1. und 2. Heft (1899), p. [30]-35)
Bibliographical footnotes.
1. Demoniac possession. 2. Waldenses. 3. Comenius, Johann Amos, 1592-1670. I. Title.
8
NIC

Rare
HV 8593 W16
Waldkirch, Johann Rudolf von.
Der gerechte Folter-Banck; das ist, Eine rechtliche und gründliche Anweisung und Untersuchung ob, wie und wann eine christliche Obrigkeit die verdächtigen Maleficanten könne oder solle peinlich befragen.. Bern, Bey Daniel Tschiffeli, 1710.
95 p. 19cm.
"Von Zauberey": p. 74-77.
1. Torture. I. Title.
8
NIC

WITCHCRAFT
BF 1565 W16
Waldschmidt, Bernhard.
Pythonissa Endorea, das ist: Acht vnd zwantzig Hexen- vnd Gespenstpredigten, genommen auss der Histori von der Zauberinn zu Endor ... Gehalten in der Kirchen zun Barfüssern in Franckfurt, vnd nunmehr mit nützlichen, auss vornehmer Theologorum vnd anderer berühmten Autorum Schrifften genommenen Anmerckungen vermehret ... Franckfurt, Johann-Wilhelm Ammon vnd Wilhelm Serlin, Gedruckt durch Hieronymum Polich, 1660.
(Continued on next card)
8

WITCHCRAFT
BF 1565 W16
Waldschmidt, Bernhard. Pythonissa Endorea ... 1660. (Card 2)
16 p. l., 690, [26] p. port. 22cm.
Added engr. t. p. facing portrait.
"Ander Theil ... von den Gespensten ..." has special t. p.
Title in red and black.
1. Witchcraft. 2. Witchcraft in the Bible. 3. Ghosts. 4. Endor, Witch of (Biblical character) I. Title. II. Title: Ander Theil ... von den Gespensten. III. His Von den Gespensten.
8

Waldschmidt, Bernhard.
Von den Gespensten.
WITCHCRAFT
BF 1565 W16
Waldschmidt, Bernhard.
Pythonissa Endorea, das ist: Acht vnd zwantzig Hexen- vnd Gespenstpredigten, genommen auss der Histori von der Zauberinn zu Endor ... Gehalten in der Kirchen zun Barfüssern in Franckfurt, vnd nunmehr mit nützlichen, auss vornehmer Theologorum vnd anderer berühmten Autorum Schrifften genommenen Anmerckungen vermehret ... Franckfurt, Johann-Wilhelm Ammon vnd Wilhelm Serlin, Gedruckt durch Hieronymum Polich, 1660.
(Continued on next card)
8

Waldschmidt, Bernhard.
Von den Gespensten.
WITCHCRAFT
BF 1565 W16
Waldschmidt, Bernhard. Pythonissa Endorea ... 1660. (Card 2)
16 p. l., 690, [26] p. port. 22cm.
Added engr. t. p. facing portrait.
"Ander Theil ... von den Gespensten ..." has special t. p.
Title in red and black.
1. Witchcraft. 2. Witchcraft in the Bible. 3. Ghosts. 4. Endor, Witch of (Biblical character) I. Title. II. Title: Ander Theil ... von den Gespensten.
8

BF 1593 W17+
Walker, Daniel Pickering.
Spiritual and demonic magic from Ficino to Campanella. London, Warburg Institute, University of London, 1958.
vi, 244 p. illus. 27cm. (London. University. Warburg Institute. Studies, v. 22)

1. Magic--Hist. I. Title. II. Series.

Rare
PQ 6437 T7A4 1618
Walker, Ferdinand, fl. 1600, supposed tr.
Torquemada, Antonio de, fl. 1553-1570.
The Spanish Mandevile of myracles. Or The garden of curious flowers. Wherein are handled sundry points of humanity, philosophy, diuinity, and geography, beautified with many strange and pleasant histories: first written in Spanish by Anthonio de Torquemada, and translated out of that tongue into English. It is diuided into sixe treatises, composed in the manner of a dialogue ... London, Imprinted by Bernard Alsop, by the assigne of Richard Hawkins, 1618.
(Continued on next card)

Rare
PQ 6437 T7A4 1618
Walker, Ferdinand, fl. 1600, suppposed tr.
Torquemada, Antonio de, fl. 1553-1570. The Spanish Mandevile of myracles ... 1618. (Card 2)
[6], 325, [3] p. 20cm.
Translated by Lewis Lewkenor although the translation is usually attributed to Ferdinand Walker who published it.
Translation of Jardin de flores curiosas.
I. Lewkenor, Sir Lewis, tr. II. Walker, Ferdinand, fl. 1600, supposed tr. III. His Jardin de flores curiosas--English. IV. Title. V. Title: The garden of curious flowers.

CATALOGUE OF THE CORNELL WITCHCRAFT COLLECTION

Witchcraft
BF
1565
D27
Copies

Walker, John, preacher, joint author.
    Deacon, John, Preacher.
        Dialogicall discourses of spirits and divels, declaring their proper essence, natures, dispositions, and operations, and dispossessions: with other the appendantes ... By John Deacon [and] John Walker ... Londini, G. Bishop, 1601.
        356 p. 20cm.

    1. Witchcraft. I. Walker, John, Preacher, joint author. II. Title.

WITCHCRAFT
BF
1555
D22

Walker, John, preacher.
    Darrell, John, fl. 1562-1602.
        The replie of Iohn Darrell, to the answer of Iohn Deacon, and Iohn Walker, concerning the doctrine of the possession and dispossession of demoniakes. [London?] 1602.
        50, [8] p. 18cm.

    1. Deacon, John, preacher. A summarie answere. 2. Walker, John, preacher. His A true narration of the strange and grevous vexation by the Devil. I. Title.

Witchcraft
ML
50
W19
A4

Wallace, William Vincent, 1812-1865.
    [The amber witch. Libretto. English]
        The amber witch: a romantic opera in four acts. The words by Henry F. Chorley, the music by W. Vincent Wallace. First represented at Her Majesty's Theatre, on Thursday, Feb. 28, 1861. London, Cramer, Beale & Chappell [1861?]
        48 p. 18cm.

    Based on the novel Maria Schweidler, die Bernstein Hexe, by Wilhelm Meinhold.

NIC   (Continued on next card)

Witchcraft
ML
50
W19
A4

Wallace, William Vincent, 1812-1865. [The amber witch. Libretto. English] The amber witch. [1861?] (Card 2)

    1. Operas--Librettos. I. Chorley, Henry Fothergill, 1808-1872. [The amber witch. II. Meinhold, Wilhelm, 1797-1851. Die Bernstein Hexe. III. Title.

NIC

Witchcraft
PT
2430
M35
M3
1861

Wallace, William Vincent, 1813-1865.
    [Meinhold, Wilhelm] 1797-1851.
        The amber witch. The most romantic and extraordinary case of witchcraft extant. London, W. Tinsley, 1861.
        168 p. 17cm.

    Translation of his Maria Schweidler, die Bernsteinhexe.
    "The extraordinary romance upon which W. Vincent Wallace has founded his ... opera, 'The amber witch.'"--cover.
    I. Title. II. His Maria Schweidler, die Bernsteinhexe--English. III. Wallace, William Vincent, 1813-1865.

Witchcraft
BF
1445
D61
no.19

Waller, Nicolai, praeses.
    Theoria spectrorum philosophica, quam ... praeside ... Dn. Nicolao Wallerio, ... publico bonorum examini modeste offert ... Andreas Bäckerström ... Upsaliae, Excud. L. M. Höjer [1753]
    13, [1] p. 21cm.
    Imperfect copy: t. p. and other pages badly torn.
    No. 19 in vol. lettered Dissertationes de spectris. 1646-1753.

8   1. Apparitions. 2. Demonology. I. Bäckerström, Andreas, respondent. II. Title.

WITCHCRAFT
BF
1583
S37

Walpurgisnacht.
    Schrader, Ludwig Wilhelm.
        Die Sage von den Hexen des Brockens und deren Entstehen in vorchristlicher Zeit durch die Verehrung des Melybogs und der Frau Holle. Historisch bearbeitet ... Quedlinburg und Leipzig, G. Basse, 1839.
        48 p. 19cm.
    Sent to L. Freytag and published through him.
    1. Walpurgisnacht. 2. Witchcraft--Thuringia. 3. Folk-lore--Thuringia. 4. Melybog. 5. Frau Holle. I. Title.

8
NIC

WITCHCRAFT
BF
1583
S39

Walpurgisnacht.
    Schwartz, Friedrich Leberecht Wilhelm, 1821-1899.
        Zwei Hexengeschichten aus Waltershausen in Thüringen nebst einem mythologischen Excurs über Hexen- und ähnlichen Versammlungen. Von Direktor W. Schwartz. [Berlin, 1888]
        395-419 p. 22cm.
    Extract from Zeitschrift für Völkerpsychologie, v. 18.
    1. Witchcraft--Thuringia. 2. Walpurgisnacht. I. Title.

8
NIC

Witchcraft
BF
1563
W81++
no.5

Walsh, John.
    The Examination of John Walsh, before Master Thomas Williams ... upon certayne interrogatories touchyng wytchcrafte and sorcerye, in the presence of diuers gentlemen and others, the XX. of August, 1566. London, Imprinted by J. Awdely, 1566. [London, at the British Museum, 1923]
        [16] p. 14cm.
    Signature: A⁸.

    (Continued on next card)

Witchcraft
BF
1563
W81++
no.5

Walsh, John.
    The Examination of John Walsh... 1566. [1923]
        Photocopy (negative) 16 p. on 8 l. 20 x 32cm.
    No. 5 in vol. lettered: Witchcraft tracts, chapbooks and broadsides, 1579-1704; rotograph copies.

    1. Witchcraft--England. 2. Walsh, John.

Witchcraft
BF
1410
B42
Z92

[Walten, Ericus] 1663-1697.
    Aardige duyvelary, voorvallende in dese dagen. Begrepen in een brief van een heer te Amsterdam, geschreven aan een van sijn vrienden te Leeuwaerden, in Vriesland. [Amsterdam, 1691]
        45 p. [p. 46-48 blank] illus. initial. 19 x 16cm.
    4°: A-F⁴.
    Defense of B. Bekker and his book De betoverde weereld.
    Van der Linde 170.

    (Continued on next card)

Witchcraft
BF
1410
B42
Z92

[Walten, Ericus] 1663-1697. Aardige duyvelary, voorvallende in dese dagen. [1691] (Card 2)

    Stamped: Koninkl. bibliothek te 's Hage. 1698. Eenige extracten uyt Dr. Bekkers Betooverder weerelt, tweede deel. [n.p.] 1691.

    1. Bekker, Balthasar, 1634-1698. De betoverde weereld. I. Title.

Witchcraft
BF
1410
B42
Z56
v.3
no.7

Walten, Ericus, 1663-1697.
    Bekker door Bekker overtuygt. Uytgewerckt in een brief hem schriftelijk toegesonden in welke vertocnt wort dat Do. Bekker, en uyt Gods woort, en ook uyt sijn eygen grond regels en belydenis; van de valscheyt sijnes gevoelens, aengaende de goede en quade geesten, moetover tuygt sijn. Neffens. Een korte aenmerking over twee geschrifte in faveur van Do. Bekker in 't ligt gebracht, her [sic] eerste geschreven aan een heer tot Uytrecht, en het andere genaemt de Aerdige duyvelarye.

8   (Continued on next card)

Witchcraft
BF
1410
B42
Z56
v.3
no.7

Walten, Ericus, 1663-1697.
    Aardige duyvelary.
    Bekker door Bekker overtuygt. 1692.
        (Card 2)
    Gravenhage, By B. Beek, konst-en boekverkooper, 1692.
        5 p. l., 18 p. title and other vignettes, illus. initials. 20 x 16cm.
    4°: π1, *⁴, A-B⁴, C1.
    Black letter (second numbering only)
    Van der Linde 173.
    No. 7 in vol. lettered Bekker III.

8   (Continued on next card)

Witchcraft
BF
1410
B42
Z56
v.3
no.22

Walten, Ericus, 1663-1697.
    Aardige duyvelary.
    [Hamer, Petrus] 1646-1716.
        Den swadder, die E. W. op Cartesianen en Coccejanen geworpen heeft, in sijn twee deelen van Aardige duivelarye zuiver af-gevaagt, met een het geschil dat Dr. Bekker ongegrond opwerpt, als of daimoon, &c. niet wel duivel overgezet wierd, kortelijk voldongen, en in staat van wijzen gebracht, door Iiratiel Leetsosoneus. Amsterdam, By G. Borstius, boekverkooper, 1692.
        2 p. l., 42 p. title and other vignettes, illus. initials. 20 x 15 cm.
    4°: *2, A-E⁴, F1.
    Van der Linde 172.
    No. 22 in vol. lettered Bekker III.

Witchcraft
BF
1410
B42
Z82
no.1

[Walten, Ericus] 1663-1697.
    Brief aan een regent der Stad Amsterdam. Behelsende een regtsinnige uytlegginge, en redenmatige verklaringe, van de articulen die D. Balthasar Bekker op den 22 Januarij 1692 heeft overgeleverd aan de Classis van Amsterdam, wegens sijn uytgegeven boek, genaamd, De betoverde wereld; met eenige philosophische redeneringen, seer nut en dienstig, om verscheidene dingen in 't selve boek wel te verstaan; en een kort verhaal van den uytslag der kerkelijke proceduyren, daar

    (Continued on next card)

Witchcraft
BF
1410
B42
Z82
no.1

[Walten, Ericus] 1663-1697. Brief aan een regent der Stad Amsterdam. 1692.
        (Card 2)
    over gehouden. ... Gravenhage, By M. Uytwerf, boekverkooper, 1692.
        135 p. [p. 136 blank] title vignette. 19 x 15cm.
    4°: A-R⁴.
    Signed: Ericus Walten. 18. Mey 1692.
    Van der Linde 41.
    No. 1 in vol. lettered Over Bekkers Betoverde wereld. 1692.

    (Continued on next card)

Witchcraft
BF
1410
B42
Z82
no.1

[Walten, Ericus] 1663-1697. Brief aan een regent der Stad Amsterdam. 1692.
        (Card 3)

    1. Bekker, Balthasar, 1634-1698. De betoverde weereld. 2. Bekker, Balthasar, 1634-1698. Articulen tot satisfactie aan de Eerw. Classis van Amsterdam. I. Nederlandse Hervormde Kerk. Classes. Amsterdam. II. Nederlandse Hervormde Kerk. Synode van Noordholland, Alkmaar, 1692. III. Title.

591

CATALOGUE OF THE CORNELL WITCHCRAFT COLLECTION

Witchcraft
BF 1410 B42 Z56 v.3 no.17
[Walten, Ericus,] 1663-1697.
　　Brief aan een regent der Stad Amsterdam. Behelsende een regtsinnige uytlegginge, en redenmatige verklaringe, van de articulen die D. Balthasar Bekker op den 22 Januarij 1692 heeft overgeleverd aan de Classis van Amsterdam, wegens sijn uytgegeven boek, genaamd, De betoverde wereld; met eenige philosophische redeneringen, seer nut en dienstig, om verscheidene dingen in 't selve boek wel te verstaan; en een kort verhaal van de uytslag der kerke　　　　lijke proceduyren, daar

8　　　　　(Continued on next card)

Witchcraft
BF 1410 B42 Z56 v.3 no.17
[Walten, Ericus,] 1663-1697. Brief aan een regent der Stad Amsterdam. 1692. (Card 2)
over gehouden. ... Gravenhage, By M. Uytwerf, boekverkooper, 1692.
　135 p. [p. 136 blank] title vignette.
　19 x 15cm.
　4°: A-R⁴.
　Signed: Ericus Walten. 18. Mey 1692.
　Van der Lin　　de 41.
　No. 17 in　　　vol. lettered Bekker III.

Witchcraft
BF 1410 B42 Z82 no.2
Walten, Ericus, 1663-1697.
　　Brief aan een regent der Stad Amsterdam.
Hamer, Petrus, 1646-1716.
　　Voorlooper tot de volstrekte wederlegginge van het gene de heeren, Orchard, Daillon en Bekker hebben aen het licht gebragt; aengaende de werken, en macht der geesten: en met name der duivelen. Door Petrus Hamer, dienaer Jesus Christi in Numansdorp. Uitgegeven na kerken-ordre. Met belofte refutatoir van zekeren Brief aen een regent van Amsteldam. Dato 18 Maij 1692. Dordrecht, By C. Wilgaarts, boekverkooper, 1692.
　4 p. l., 40　　p. title vignette, illus.

8　　　　　(Continued on next card)

Witchcraft
BF 1410 B42 Z82 no.2
Walten, Ericus, 1663-1697.
　　Brief aan een regent der Stad Amsterdam.
Hamer, Petrus, 1646-1716. Voorlooper tot de volstrekte wederlegginge van... Orchard, Daillon en Bekker ... 1692. (Card 2)
initials. 20 x 15cm.
　4°: *⁴, A-E⁴.
　Van der Linde 95.
　No. 2 in vol. lettered Over Bekkers Betoverde wereld. 1692.
　1. Orchard, N　　, supposed author. The doctrine of　　devils. 2. Daillon, Benjamin de.　　Examen de l'opression
(Continued on next card)

Witchcraft
BF 1410 B42 Z56 v.2 no.4
Walten, Ericus, 1663-1697.
　　Brief aan sijn Excellentie, de Heer Graaf van Portland, &c. &c. Rakende de persoon en het gevoelen van Dr. B. Bekker, en 't geen tegen hem, by eenige van sijn partyen, word verwagt, en uytgestrooyd, ten opsigte van sijn Koninglijke Majesteyt van Groot Britanjen. ...Door Ericus Walten ... Gedrukt voor den auteur. Gravenhage, By Meyndert Uytwerf, boekverkoper, 1692.
　80 p. title vignette, illus. initial.
　19 x 15cm. (Continued on next card)

Witchcraft
BF 1410 B42 Z56 v.2 no.4
Walten, Ericus, 1663-1697. Brief aan sijn Excellentie, de Heer Graaf van Portland ... 1692. (Card 2)
　4°: A-K⁴.
　Van der Linde 174.
　No. 4 in vol. lettered: Bekker II.
　1. Bekker, Balthasar, 1634-1698. 2. Devil. I. Portland, William Bentinck, 1st earl of, 1649-　　1709. II. William III, King of Great　　Britain, 1649-1709.
　III. Title.

8

Witchcraft
BF 1410 B42 Z82 no.4
Walten, Ericus, 1663-1697.
　　Brief aan sijn Excellentie, de Heer Graaf van Portland, &c. &c. Rakende de persoon en het gevoelen van Dr. B. Bekker, en 't geen tegen hem, by eenige van sijn partyen, ten opsigte van sijn Koninglijke Majesteyt van Groot Britanjen. ...Door Ericus Walten ... Gedrukt voor den auteur. Gravenhage, By M. Uytwerf, boekverkoper, 1692.
　80 p. title vignette, illus. initial.
　20 x 15cm.
　　　(Continued on next card)

Witchcraft
BF 1410 B42 Z82 no.4
Walten, Ericus, 1663-1697. Brief aan sijn Excellentie, de Heer Graaf van Portland ... 1692. (Card 2)
　4°: A-K⁴.
　Van der Linde 174.
　No. 4 in vol. lettered Over Bekkers Betoverde wereld. 1692.

8

Walter, Ericus, 1663-1697.
　　see
Walten, Ericus, 1663-1697.

WITCHCRAFT
BF 1583 W23
Walter, Theobald.
　　Die Hexenplätze der Rufacher Hexenurkunden.
　　(In Jahrbuch für Geschichte, Sprache und Litteratur Elsass-Lothringens. Strassburg. 24cm. 12. Jahrg. (1896), p. [40]-43)

8　　1. Witchcraft--Alsace. I. Title.

Walton, Ericus, 1663-1697.
　　see
Walten, Ericus, 1663-1697.

WITCHCRAFT
BF 1555 H67 1589
Warhafft: vnd gründtlicher Bericht, sehr wunderlich: vnnd gleichsam vnerhörter Geschichten, so sich vnlangst zu Bergen [i.e., Mons] in Henogau, Ertzbisthumbs Cambrai, mit einer besessnen, vnd hernach widerloeseten Closterfrawen verloffen. Auss frantzösischer Sprach, in Hochteutsch gebracht. [München, Gedruckt bey Adam Berg] 1589.
　4 p. l., 47 numbered l. 19cm.
8　Illustrati　　ve title vignette.
　　With colo　　phon.
　　　(Continued on next card)

WITCHCRAFT
BF 1555 H67 1587
Warhafft: vnd gründtlicher Bericht, sehr wunderlich ... 1589. (Card 2)
Translation of Histoire admirable et veritable des choses advenues a l'endroict d'une religieuse professe ... pub. 1586. Preface by Adam Berg.
　1. Demoniac possession. 2. Fery, Jeanne, fl. 1584. I. Histoire admirable et veritable des choses advenues a l'endroict d'une　　religieuse professe.
8　German. II. Berg, Adam, d. 1610.

MSS Bd. WITCHCRAFT BF W272
Warhaffte und glaubwirdige Zeytung. Von Hundert und vir und dreyssig Unholden, so umb ihrer Zauberey halben, diss verschinen lXXXij. Jars, zu Gefencknus gebracht ... zum Fewer verdambt unnd verbrennet worden ... wie dañ die Ort do sich solches alles verloffen, ordenlich hernach werden vermelt und angezeigt. Strassburg, Bey Nicolaus Wiriod, 1583 [ca. 1900]
　4 l. 24cm.
　Carnap's　　manuscript copy.
　　　(Continued on next card)

MSS Bd. WITCHCRAFT BF W272
Warhaffte und glaubwirdige Zeytung. Von Hundert und vir und dreyssig Unholden ... 1583 [ca. 1900] (Card 2)
"Originaldruck in der Königl. Hof- u. Staats-Bibliothek zu München, 4 Bl. in 4°."
Numerals in the margins indicate pagination of the original.
　1. Witchcraft--Germany. I. Title: Von Hundert und vir　　und dreyssig Unholden.

WITCHCRAFT
BF 1583 A2 M39
Warhaffte und umbständliche Beschreibung der wunderbahren Geschichte, so sich mit einer angefochtenen Jungfer...
Masecovius, Thomas.
　　Warhaffte und umbständliche Beschreibung der wunderbahren Geschichte, so sich mit einer angefochtenen Jungfer in dem 1683ten und folgenden Jahren zu Königsberg in Preussen... Nebst einer Vorrede D. Bernhard von Sanden...gerichtet wider die Bezauberte Welt D. Balthasar Beckers. Königsb., In Verlegung Heinrich Boye, Druckts Johann Zacharias Etoile, 1695.
　363 p. 17cm.
8　1. Witchcraft. 2. Witchcraft--Germany—
NIC　Bekker, Balthasar, 1634-1698. [De　betoverde　weereld.] I. Sanden, Bernhard von.

MSS Bd. WITCHCRAFT BF W275 Z55
Warhaffter Bericht und denckwürdiger Verlauff, welcher Gestalten in dem 1664. Jahr den 3. Tag Jenners, durch die Barmhertzigkeit Gottes auff Anruffung dess H. Francisci Xaverii ... die wol-edle und tugendreiche Junckfraw Anna Elisabetha Susanna, nunmehr aber Maria Francisca de la Haye von den bösen Geistern, so sie besessen und verfolgt, in unser Frauen Kirchen ... wunderbarlich ist erlediget worden. St　　raubing, Bey Magdalena Haanin, 16　　65 [ca. 1900]
(Continued on next card)

MSS Bd. WITCHCRAFT BF W275 Z55
Warhaffter Bericht und denckwürdiger Verlauff ... 1665 [ca. 1900] (Card 2)
　97 p. 19cm.
Carnap's manuscript copy.
"Originaldruck in der Königlichen u. Staats-Bibliothek zu München, VIII + 83 S. S. in 8°."
Numerals in the margins indicate pagination of the original.
　1. Demoniac　　possession. 2. De la Haye, Maria　　Francisca.

592

CATALOGUE OF THE CORNELL WITCHCRAFT COLLECTION

MSS
Bd.
WITCHCRAFT
F
275
B8

Warhaffter sumarisch-aussführlicher Bericht und Erzehlung. Was die in dess heyligen Röm- Reichsstatt Augspurg etlich Wochen lang in Verhafft gelegne zwo Hexen, benandtlich Barbara Frölin von Rieden unnd Anna Schäflerin von Eringen, wegen ihrer Hexereyen gut- und peinlich bekent ... und wie endtlich dise beede Unholden ihrem Verdienst nach, auff Sambstag den 18. Aprill diss 1654 Jahrs hingericht worden. Augspurg, Durch Andream Aperger, 1654 [ca. 1900]
(Continued on next card)

MSS
Bd.
WITCHCRAFT
BF
W54

Warhafftige und ein erschröckliche newe Zeitung, des grossen Wasserguss.
Wetz, Ambrosius. Warhafftige und ein erschröckliche newe Zeitung, des grossen Wasserguss ... [1578? ca. 1900] (Card 2)

Annotations in the margins indicate foliation of the original.
In verse.

1. Witchcraft--Austria. I. Title.
II. Title: Des grossen Wasserguss.

MSS
Bd.
WITCHCRAFT
BF
H33

Warhafftige und mit vielen glaubwürdigen Zeugen bewährte Relation.
Hartmann, Andreas. Warhafftige und mit vielen glaubwürdigen Zeugen bewährte Relation was sich zu Döffingen, hoch-fürstl. württembergischer Herrschafft, und Böblinger Amts, mit zwey besessenen Weibs-Personen im Monat Decembr. 1714, mercklich zugetragen hat ... Ans Licht gebracht von M. Andreas Hartmann ... [n.p.] 1716 [ca. 1900]
14 l. 18cm.
Carnap's manuscript copy.
"Wörtliche Abschrift aus: Altes und Neues aus dem Reich Gottes und
(Continued on next card)

MSS
Bd.
WITCHCRAFT
F
275
B8

Warhaffter sumarisch-aussführlicher Bericht und Erzehlung ... 1654 [ca. 1900] (Card 2)
8 l. 24cm.
Carnap's manuscript copy.
"Originaldruck in der Gustav Freytag Biblioth. jetzt in der Stadtbibliothek zu Frankfurt a/M. 6 Blatt in 4°. Sig. Aij-B."
Numerals in the margins indicate pagination of the original.

1. Witchcraft--Augsburg. 2. Demoniac possession. 3. Frölin, Barbara, 1637-1654. 4. Schäfler, Anna, 1590-1654.

MSS
Bd.
WITCHCRAFT
BF
W277
Z92

Warhafftige und erschreckliche neue Zeittunge von einer jungen Diernen, welche sich dem Teuffel auf sechs Jar lang ergeben ... Item, von einem Studenten, welchen der Teuffel gleichfals in grewliche Sünden gestürzt ... Item, von grewlichen ungestümen Wettern so den 12. Maij dieses 82. Jars in Baijern ... grossen Schaden, an Menschen und Wiese gethan haben. Dresden, Gimel Bergen, 1582
6 l. 19 cm.
(Continued on next card)

MSS
Bd.
WITCHCRAFT
BF
H33

Warhafftige und mit vielen glaubwürdigen Zeugen bewährte Relation.
Hartmann, Andreas. Warhafftige und mit vielen glaubwürdigen Zeugen bewährte Relation ... 1716 [ca. 1900] (Card 2)

der übrigen guten und bösen Geister, etc. [hrsg. von J. J. Moser] 9ter Theil. Franckfurt u. Leipzig, 1734. 8°. S. 10-28."
"NB. Diese Besessenheitsgeschichte steht auch wörtlich in: Guden, Friedrich, Schreckliche Geschichte Teuflischer Besitzung, in 3 merkw. Historien, etc. Budissin, 1717. 8°. S. 159-188."

1. Demoniac possession. 2. Exorcism.
(Continued on next card)

MSS
Bd.
WITCHCRAFT
BF
W277
Z75

Warhafftige newe Zeyttung, so den 18. Martii, in diesem 75. Jar, zu Bramberg im Pintzkaw, ein Meilwegs von Mittersel im Bisthumb Saltzburg, mit einem Pfarrer und seiner Köchin zugetragen hat, unnd wie sie auch hernach umb ihre Missethat hingericht worden sind. Wien, Steffan Creutzer, 1575 [ca. 1900]
6 l. 19cm.
Carnap's manuscript copy.
"Originaldruck in der Stadtbibliothek zu Züri[ch, 14 S. in 8°."
(Continued on next card)

MSS
Bd.
WITCHCRAFT
BF
W277
Z92

Warhafftige und erschreckliche neue Zeittunge von einer jungen Diernen ... 1582 [ca. 1900] (Card 2)

Carnap's manuscript copy.
"Originaldruck in der Stadtbibliothek zu Zürich, 8 Seiten in 4°."
Signatures in the margins indicate signatures of the original.

1. Devil. 2. Nature (in religion, folk-lore, etc.) I. Title: Von einer jungen Diern[en, welche sich dem
(Continued on next card)

MSS
Bd.
WITCHCRAFT
BF
L97

Warhafftige Zeitung. Von den gottlosen Hexen.
Lutz, Reinhard. Warhafftige Zeitung. Von den gottlosen Hexen, auch ketzerischen unnd Teufels Weibern, die zu des heyligē römischen Reichssstatt Schletstat im Elsass, auff den zwey und zwentzigsten Herbstmonats des verlauffenen siebentzigsten Jars, von wegen ihrer schentlicher Teuffels Verpflichtung verbrent worden, sampt einem kurtzen Extract und Ausszug ettlicher Schrifften von Hexerey zusamen gebra[cht durch Renhardum Lutz ... [n.p.] 1571 [ca. 1900]
(Continued on next card)

MSS
Bd.
WITCHCRAFT
BF
W277
Z75

Warhafftige newe Zeyttung, so den 18. Martii ... mit einem Pfarrer und seiner Köchin zugetragen hat ... 1575 [ca. 1900] (Card 2)

Signatures in the margins indicate signatures of the original.

1. Witchcraft--Austria.

MSS
Bd.
WITCHCRAFT
BF
W277
Z92

Warhafftige und erschreckliche neue Zeittunge von einer jungen Diernen ... 1582 [ca. 1900] (Card 3)

Teuffel ... ergeben. II. Title: Von einem Studenten, welchen der Teuffel ... in grewliche Sünden gestürzt. III. Title: Von grewlichen ungestümen Wettern.

MSS
Bd.
WITCHCRAFT
BF
L97

Lutz, Reinhard. Warhafftige Zeitung. Von den gottlosen Hexen ... 1571 [ca. 1900] (Card 2)
16 l. illus. 23cm.
Signatures: A-D, E^3.
Carnap's manuscript copy.
"Originaldruck in der Hof- u. Staatsbibliothek zu München. 20 Bl. in 4°."
Signatures and numerals in the margins correspond to signatures and pagination of the original.

1. Witchcraft--Germany. 2. Demonology. 3. Folk-lore of children.
I. Title.

WITCHCRAFT
BF
1555
S35

8
NIC

Warhafftige und erschröckliche Geschicht, welche sich newlicher Zeit ... mit einem jungen Handtwercks.
Schnabel, Joannes.
Warhafftige vnd erschröckliche Geschicht welche sich newlicher Zeit zugetragen hat, mit einem jungen Handtwercks vnd Schmidtsgesellen, Hansen Schmidt genannt, ... der ... von einer gantzen Legion Teüffeln hefftig besessen vnd hernacher ... durch sondere Schickung Gottes Allmächtigen vnd zugethane verordtnete Mittel ... errettet ist ... Durch M. Ioannem Schnabeln ... vnd M. Simonem Marium ... Wirtzburg, Gedruckt
(Continued on next card)

MSS
Bd.
WITCHCRAFT
BF
W277
Z98

Ein Warhafftige Zeitung von etlichē Hexen oder Unholden, welche man kürtzlich im Stifft Mäntz, zu Ascheburg, Dipperck, Ostum, Rönsshoffen, auch andern Orten, verbrendt, was Ubels sie gestifft, und bekandt haben. [Franckfurt, 1603; ca. 1900]
5 l. 19cm.
Carnap's manuscript copy.
"Originaldruck in der Königl. Bibliothek zu Berlin 4 Bl. in 12°."
Numerals in the margins indicate
(Continued on next card)

Warhafftige Relation, was sich in Hamburg den 16 Martii Anno 1683 mit einem vom Sathan besessenen Mägdlein, Nahmens Catharina, dessen Vater Martin Grambeck, ein frommer Mann, zugetragen ... [n.p., 1683; ca. 1900]
1 l. 24cm.
Carnap's manuscript copy.
"Originaldruck in der Commerz-Bibliothek zu Hamburg - 1 Bl. in fol."

1. Demoniac possession.

WITCHCRAFT
BF
1555
S35

8
NIC

Warhafftige und erschröckliche Geschicht, welche sich newlicher Zeit ... mit einem jungen Handtwercks.
Schnabel, Joannes. Warhafftige vnd erschröckliche Geschicht ... [1589] (Card 2)

durch Henrich von Ach [1589]
[32] p. 20cm.

1. Demoniac possession. 2. Exorcism. 3. Schmidt, Hans, fl. 1589. I. Mayr, Simon, 1570-1624. II. Title.

MSS
Bd.
WITCHCRAFT
BF
W277
Z98

Ein Warhafftige Zeitung von etlichē Hexen ... [1603; ca. 1900] (Card 2)

pagination of the original.
In verse.

1. Witchcraft--Germany. I. Title: Von etlichen Hexen oder Unholden ... im Stifft Mäntz.

Warhafftige und ein erschröckliche newe Zeitung, des grossen Wasserguss.
Wetz, Ambrosius. Warhafftige und ein erschröckliche newe Zeitung, des grossen Wasserguss, so den 15. May diss lauffenden 78. Jahrs, zu Horb geschehen ... wie man hernach alda etlich Unholden verbrent hatt, wie sie schröcklich Ding bekendt haben ... durch Ambrosium Wetz ... [n.p., 1578? ca. 1900]
4 l. 19cm.
Carnap's manuscript copy.
"Originaldr[uck in der Stadtbibliothek zu Züri[ch, 8 Seiten in 8°."
(Continued on next card)

593

CATALOGUE OF THE CORNELL WITCHCRAFT COLLECTION

Warlocks.

Witchcraft
BF 1566 S48
 Sergeant, Philip Walsingham, 1872-
  Witches and warlocks, by Philip W. Sergeant; with introduction by Arthur Machen; with 17 illustrations. London, Hutchinson & co., ltd. [1936]
  290 p. front., plates, ports. 22cm.

Webber, Zacharias.
  see
Webbers, Zacharias.

Witchcraft
BF 1528 D9 W37 1729
 [Webbers, Zacharias] De waare oorspronk, voort- en onder-gank des Satans ... 1729. (Card 2)
  7 p. l., 418, 3 p. 17cm.
  8°: *⁸ (-*1), A-2C⁸, 2D3.
  Black letter; title in red and black.
  "De uitgever tot den leezer" signed: N. N. (i. e., Jacobus Schuts)
  First edition 1695.

8   (Continued on next card)

Was she a witch after all?

Witchcraft
DC 104 .1 T54
 Thurston, Herbert, 1856-1939.
  Was she a witch after all?
  (In The month. London, 1922. 24cm. vol. 139, no. 691, p. [1]-13)

  1. Jeanne d'Arc, Saint, 1412-1431. I. Title.

Witchcraft
BF 1410 B42 Z69 no.12
 [Webbers, Zacharias]
  In antwoort op het jonghste post scriptum van de VI. brief van Haggebher Philaleethees tegens eene van de (soo hem dunkt) schadelyke helpers van Do. B. Bekker, raakende desselfs aanmerkinge over de predicatie van Do. Adrianus van Weesel, 's Sondags by sijn eerw. in de Wester Kerk den 25 Novemb. over Math. IV. 5,6,7. Van de versoekinge onses saligmakers door den Duyvel, gedaan. Dienende dit tot kraghtiger bewijs dat deselve niet eygentlijk, maar by forme van een

NIC   (Continued on next card)

Witchcraft
BF 1528 D9 W37 1729
 [Webbers, Zacharias] De waare oorspronk, voort- en onder-gank des Satans ... 1729. (Card 3)
  1. Devil--Biblical teaching. 2. Jesus Christ--Temptation. 3. Bekker, Balthasar, 1634-1698. De betoverde wereld. I. Schuts, Jacobus. II. Title.

8

Witchcraft
BF 1559 G25 Z63 no.3
 Was soll man an den Kuren des Herrn geistlicher Raths Gassner, die er bisher im Namen Jesu gemacht hat, noch untersuchen, so nicht schon längst hundertmal ist untersucht worden? Frankfurt und Berlin, 1775.
  96 p. 17cm.
  No. 3 in vol. lettered Gassneriana.
  1. Gassner, Johann Joseph, 1727-1779. 2. Faith-cure. 3. Politische Frage, ob ein Landes fürst über die Gassnerischen Kuren ... gleichgültig seyn kann. 4. Sterzinger, Ferdinand, 1721-1786.

8

Wasser-Prob der Hexen.

Witchcraft
BF 1565 D62 no.16
 Struve, Georg Adam, 1619-1692, praeses.
  Disputatio juridica De indiciis cui annectitur quaestio de proba per aquam frigidam sagarum. Von der Wasser-Prob der Hexen ... sub praesidio Dn. Georgii Adami Struven ... publicè proposita à Joh. Christoph. Nehringio ... Jenae, Typis Pauli Ehrichii, 1714.
  52 p. 20cm.
  No. 16 in vol. lettered Dissertationes de sagis. 1636-1714.

8   (Continued on next card)

Witchcraft
BF 1410 B42 Z69 no.12
 [Webbers, Zacharias] In antwoort op het jonghste post scriptum ... (Card 2)
  gesighte, en in den geest geschiet zy: door den zelven S. W. S. F. t'Amsterdam, by D. van den Dalen, 1692.
  16 p. 21cm.
  Signatures: 4°: A-B⁴.
  Black letter.
  No. 12 in a Collection of tracts against Balthasar Bekker and his Betoverde weereld.

NIC   (Continued on next card)

Webbers, Zacharias.
 De waare oorspronk, voort- en onder-gank des Satans.

Witchcraft
BX 9479 B42 B11 no.14
 Brief, aan een heer, waar in uyt de H. Schrift getoond werd, dat'er is een quade geest, die een redelijk schepsel is buyten de ziel des mensche. Met eenige aanmerkinge over het boek, De ware oorspronk, voort en ondergank des Satans. Door I. W. Amsterdam, By J. de Veer gedruckt, 1696.
  64 p. title vignette, illus. initial. 20 x 15cm.
  4°: A-H⁴.
  Probably by Joannes van Wijk.

8   (Continued on next card)

Witchcraft
BF 1410 B42 Z69 no.12
 [Webbers, Zacharias] In antwoort op het jonghste post scriptum ... 1692. (Card 3)
  Attributed to Webbers by Aa, A. J. van der. Biographisch woordenboek der Nederlanden. Haarlem, 1852-78, and by Doorninck, J. I. van. Vermonde en naamlooze schrijvers ... Leiden, 1883-85.
  Van der Linde 113.

NIC   (Continued on next card)

Webbers, Zacharias.
 De waare oorspronk, voort- en onder-gank des Satans.

Witchcraft
BX 9479 B42 B11 no.14
 Brief, aan een heer, waar in uyt de H. Schrift getoond werd, dat'er is een quade geest ... 1696. (Card 2)
  Supports Balthasar Bekker in the controversy over his De betoverde weereld.
  No. 14 in vol. lettered B. Bekkers sterfbed en andere tractaten.

Waterhouse, Agnes.

Witchcraft
BF 1581 B42 1864
 Beigel, Hermann, 1830-1879, ed.
  The examination and confession of certain witches at Chelmsford in the county of Essex ... [London, Philobiblon Society, pref. 1864]
  49 p. 23cm.
  A reprint of two pamphlets in the library of Lambeth Palace, respectively entitled: The examination and confession of certaine wytches at Chensforde ... 1556 [i.e. 1566] ..." and

  (Continued on next card)

Witchcraft
BF 1410 B42 Z69 no.12
 [Webbers, Zacharias] In antwoort op het jonghste post scriptum ... 1692. (Card 4)
  1. Bekker, Balthasar, 1634-1698. De betoverde weereld. 2. Hooght, Everard van der, d. 1716. Sesde briev van ... Haggebher Philaleethees. I. Title.

NIC

Witchcraft
BX 9479 B42 B11 no.16
 Kuyk, J van.
  Disputatie over den duyvel, of dezelve is een geschaapen geest, buyten de zielen der menschen, dewelke afgevallen en boos geworden is, ofte niet? Voorgevallen tusschen J. van Kuyk, krankbesoeker, ter eenre, en H. Bouman, ter andere zyde ... op den 26 December, 1694. Door een liefhebber der waarheyt, soo daar tegenwoordig was, opgestelt. Hier is noch by gevoegt een brief, aan geseyde J. van Kuyk ... den 27 January, 1693.

8   (Continued on next card)

Waterhouse, Agnes.

Witchcraft
BF 1581 B42 1864
 Beigel, Hermann, 1830-1879, ed. The examination and confession of certain witches ... [1864] (Card 2)
  The second examination of mother Agnes Waterhouse ... 1566 ...
  Offprint from Miscellanies of the Philobiblon Society, v. 8, 1863-63.

  1. Witchcraft--England. 2. Waterhouse, Agnes. I. Title. II. Title: The second examination of mother Agnes Waterhouse.

Witchcraft
BF 1528 D9 W37 1729
 [Webbers, Zacharias]
  De waare oorspronk, voort- en onder-gank des Satans: behelzende, een buitengewoone, edog klare verhandeling, van de voornaamste plaatsen der Heilige Schrift, welke zyn spreekende van den Duivel. Dienende voor een inleiding tot de Bybelsche Godgeleerdheid, en het waare Christendom. Door Joan Adolphsz. 4. druk. Van nieuws overzien. Amsterdam, By Jacob Graal, boekverkooper, 1729.

  (Continued on next card)

Witchcraft
BX 9479 B42 B11 no.16
 Kuyk, J van. Disputatie over den duyvel ... 1695. (Card 2)
  aldaar bestelt; met redenen, waarom deselve nu eerst door den druk gemeen gemaakt wort. Amsterdam, By E. Webber, boekverkooper, 1695.
  16 p. title and end page vignettes. 20 x 15cm.
  4°: A-B⁴.
  Black letter (except introduction)
  Letter and Na-reeden, p. 10-16,

8   (Continued on next card)

594

CATALOGUE OF THE CORNELL WITCHCRAFT COLLECTION

```
              Webbers, Zacharias.
Witchcraft
BX       Kuyk, J    van. Disputatie over den
9479        duyvel ... 1695.       (Card 3)
342
811      signed: Z. W. ₍i. e., Zacharias Webbers₎
no.16       Van der Linde 79.
            No. 16 in vol. lettered B. Bekkers sterf-
         bed en andere tractaten.
            1. Devil.  I. Bouman, Herman.  II.
         Webbers, Zacharias.  III. Een liefhebber
         der waarheyt.  IV. Title.
```

```
                    Webberus, Zacharias.
                         see
                    Webbers, Zacharias.
```

Weber, Joseph

```
WITCHCRAFT
BF       Weber, Joseph, 1753-1831.
1565        Die Nichtigkeit der Zauberey, eine Vor-
W37      lesung in den ökonomischen Lehrstunden.
1787     Salzburg, Im Verlage der hochfürstl. Wai-
         senhausbuchhandl., 1787.
            32 p. 21cm.
            Abbreviated version of his Ungrund des
         Hexen- und Gespenster-Glaubens.
            1. Witchcraft. 2. Superstition.  I.
8        Title.  II. His  Ungrund des Hexen- und
         Gespenster-Gl   aubens.
```

```
WITCHCRAFT
BF       Weber, Joseph, 1753-1837.
1565        Ungrund des Hexen- und Gespenster-Glau-
W37      bens.  ₍Dilingen, B. Kälin, 1787₎
            108 p. 21cm.
            Added engr. t. p.
            Consists of two lectures; "Ungrund des
         Hexenglaubens. Zweite Vorlesung" has spe-
         cial t. p.

8
```

```
WITCHCRAFT
BF       Weber, Joseph, 1753-1831.
1565        Ungrund des Hexen- und Gespenster-Glaubens,
W37      bens, in ökonomischen Lehrstunden darge-
1797     stellt ... 2. verm. Aufl. Augsburg,
         C. F. Bürglen, 1797.
            198 p. 19cm.
            Preface dated: Dilingen am 29. Februars
         1787.
            1. Witchcraft. 2. Ghosts. 3. Super-
8        stition.  I.      Title.
```

```
              Weber, Joseph, 1753-1831.
                 Ungrund des Hexen- und Gespenster-
                    Glaubens.
WITCHCRAFT
BF       Weber, Joseph, 1753-1831.
1565        Die Nichtigkeit der Zauberey, eine Vor-
W37      lesung in den ökonomischen Lehrstunden.
1787     Salzburg, Im Verlage der hochfürstl. Wai-
         senhausbuchhandl., 1787.
            32 p. 21cm.
            Abbreviated version of his Ungrund des
         Hexen- und Gespenster-Glaubens.
            1. Witchcraft. 2. Superstition. I.
8        Title.  II. His  Ungrund des Hexen- und
         Gespenster-Gl   aubens.
```

```
              Weber, Joseph, 1753-1831.
                 Ungrund des Hexen- und Gespenster-
WITCHCRAFT       Glaubens.
BF       ₍Schmid, Franz Josef₎
1565        Ueber die Hexenreformation des Herrn
W37      Professor Weber zu Dillingen ... Von
S34      einem katholischen Weltmanne.  ₍Augsburg₎
         1787.
            86 p. 19cm.
            Attribution by Kayser and Deutsche Bio-
         graphie (under Weber, Joseph).
            1. Weber, Joseph, 1753-1831. Ungrund
         des Hexen- und Gespenster-Glaubens. 2.
         Witchcraft.      I. Ein katholischer
8        Weltmann.        II. Title.
```

```
              Weber, Joseph, 1753-1831.
                 Ungrund des Hexen- und Gespenster-
WITCHCRAFT       Glaubens.
BF       ₍Schmid, Franz Josef₎
1565        Und der Satz: Teuflische Magie existirt,
W37      bestecht noch. In einer Antwort des katho-
S347     lischen Weltmannes auf die von einem Herrn
         Landpfarrer herausgegebene Apologie der
         Professor Weberschen Hexenreformation.
         Augsburg, Bey J. N. Styx, 1791.
            xxiv, 350 p. 19cm.
            1. Bauer, Friedrich.  Gedanken eines
         Landpfarrers über den Ungrund des Hexenglau-
         bens. 2. We    ber, Joseph, 1753-1831.
8                          (Continued on next card)
```

```
Witchcraft
BF       ₍Webster, David₎
1581        A collection of rare and curious tracts on
W37      witchcraft and the second sight; with an
         original essay on witchcraft.    Edinburgh,
         Printed for D. Webster, 1820.
            iv,183 p. 20cm.

            1. Witchcraft--Scotland. 2. Second sight.
          I. Title.
```

```
Witchcraft
BF       Webster, John, 1610-1682.
1565        The displaying of supposed witchcraft.
W38+     Wherein is affirmed that there are many sorts of
         deceivers and impostors, and divers persons
         under a passive delusion of melancholy and fancy.
         But that there is a corporeal league made
         betwixt the devil and the witch, or that he
         sucks on the witches body ... or the like, is
         utterly denied and disproved. Wherein also is
         handled, the existence of angels and spirits,
         the truth of apparitions ... the force of charms,
         and philters; with other abstruse matters. By
         John Webster ...     London, Printed by J. M.,
         1677.
            7 p. l., 346,  ₍4₎ p.  30 cm.
                                           (over)
```

```
              Webster, John, 1610-1682.
                 The displaying of supposed witchcraft.
Witchcraft
BF       Webster, John, 1610-1682.
1565        ... Untersuchung der vermeinten und so
W38      genannten Hexereÿen, worinn zwar zugegeben
1719     wird, daß es an mancherley Betrug und Aef-
         fereyen nicht fehle ...: im Gegentheil aber
         die Fabel, daß der Teuffel leibhafftig einen
         Pact mit den Hexen mache ... durchaus ge-
         leugnet und umgestossen wird. Dabey auch
         die Warheit, daß es allerdings Engel und
         Geister, wie nicht weniger Erscheinungen
         gebe, eröffnet ... Aus dem Englischen ins
8                          ₍Continued on next card)
```

```
              Webster, John, 1610-1682.
                 The displaying of supposed witchcraft.
Witchcraft
BF       Webster, John, 1610-1682. Untersuchung
1565     der vermeinten und so genannten Hexereÿen
W38      ... 1719.                  (Card 2)
1719
            Teutsche übersetzt, und nebst einer Vorrede
         des Hrn. Geheimbden Raths Thomasii ...
         Halle, im Magdeburgischen, In Verlegung der
         Neuen Buchhandlung, 1719.
            56, 611, ₍97₎ p. plate. 21cm.
            1. Witchcraft.  I. Thomasius, Christian,
         1655-1728.  II.     His  The displaying of
         supposed witch     craft. German. III.
8        Title.
```

```
              Webster, John, 1610-1682.
                 The displaying of supposed witchcraft.
Witchcraft
BT       Camfield, Benjamin.
965         A theological discourse of angels and their
C18      ministries. Wherein their existence, nature,
         number, order and offices are modestly treated
         of: with the character of those for whose
         benefit especially they are commissioned and
         such practical inferences deduced as are most
         proper to the premises. Also an appendix
         containing some reflections upon Mr. Webster's
         Displaying supposed witchcraft.   London,
         Printed by R. E.    for H. Brome, 1678.
            214 p.          19cm.
                                  (Continued on next card)
```

```
              Webster, John, 1610-1682.
                 The displaying of supposed witchcraft.
Witchcraft
BT       Camfield, Benjamin.   A theological discourse
965         of angels and their ministries ... 1678.
C18                                       (Card 2)

            "Appendix..." has separate t.p.
         Wing C 388.

            1. Angels. 2. Witchcraft. 3. Webster,
         John, 1610-1682. The displaying of supposed
         witchcraft.  I. Title.
```

CATALOGUE OF THE CORNELL WITCHCRAFT COLLECTION

Webster, John, 1610-1682.
  The displaying of supposed witchcraft.

Witchcraft
BF   Franck, Johannes Christophorus, fl. 1717.
1565   Gottfried Wahrliebs [pseud.] Deutliche vor-
F82   stellung der nichtigkeit derer vermeynten
        hexereyen und des ungegründeten hexen-processes.
        Nebst einer gründlichen beantwortung der unter
        dem nahmen eines nach Engelland reisenden
        passagiers unlängst heraus gekommenen Unter-
        suchung vom kobold, darinnen die falschen
        auflagen / mit welchen derselbe so wohl den hrn.
        geheimbd. rath Thomasivm als Iohann Webstern
        ohne allen grund zu diffamiren gesucht. deutlich
                        (Continued on next card)

Webster, John, 1610-1682.
Witchcraft   The displaying of supposed witchcraft.
BF   Franck, Johannes Christophorus, fl. 1717.
1565   Gottfried Wahrliebs [pseud.] Deutliche
F82   vorstellung der nichtigkeit derer vermeynten
        hexereyen ... [pref. 1720]   (Card 2)

        entdecket, wie auch die Thomasische, Lehr-sätze
        vom laster der zauberey wieder dessen ungegründ-
        ete einwürffe zulänglich behauptet werden.
        Amsterdam, Nach erfindung der hexerey im dritten
        seculo, und nach einführung des hexen-processes
        im jahr 236 [pref. 1720]
          172, 78 p. front. 22cm.
                        (Continued on next card)

Webster, John, 1610-1682.
  The displaying of supposed witchcraft.
WITCHCRAFT
BF   Franck, Johannes Christophorus, fl. 1717.
1565   Gottfried Wahrliebs [pseud.] Deutliche
F82   vorstellung der nichtigkeit derer vermeyn-
        ten hexereyen...[pref. 1720]   (Card 3)

        "Gründliche beantwortung der ... Unter-
        suchung vom kobold" has separate paging and
        special t. p. with imprint: Amsterdam, 1720.

                        (Continued on next card)

Witchcraft
BF   Webster, John, 1610-1682.
1565   ... Untersuchung der vermeinten und so
W38   genannten Hexereÿen, worinn zwar zugegeben
1719   wird, daß es an mancherley Betrug und Aef-
        fereyen nicht fehle ...: im Gegentheil aber
        die Fabel, daß der Teuffel leibhafftig einen
        Pact mit den Hexen mache ... durchaus ge-
        leugnet und umgestossen wird. Dabey auch
        die Warheit, daß es allerdings Engel und
        Geister, wie nicht weniger Erscheinungen
        gebe, eröffnet ... Aus dem Englischen ins
8   Continued on next card)

Witchcraft
BF   Webster, John, 1610-1682. Untersuchung
1565   der vermeinten und so genannten Hexereÿen
W38   ... 1719.   (Card 2)
1719
        Teutsche übersetzt, und nebst einer Vorrede
        des Hrn. Geheimbden Raths Thomasii ...
        Halle, im Magdeburgischen, In Verlegung der
        Neuen Buchhandlung, 1719.
          56, 611, [97] p. plate. 21cm.
          1. Witchcraft. I. Thomasius, Christian,
        1655-1728. II. His The displaying of
8   supposed witch   craft. German. III.
        Title.

        Wechselbälge.
WITCHCRAFT
BF   Heister, Lorenz, 1683-1758, praeses.
1552   Lavrentivs Heistervs ... programmate
H47   avspicali qvo demonstrat infantes pro a
        diabolo svppositis habitos qvos vvlgo
        Wechselbälge appellarvnt rhachiticos fvisse
        ad clarissima medicinae candidati Io. Ge-
        orgii de Broke ... dispvtationem inavgvra-
        lem invitat. Helmstadii, Literis Schnor-
        rianis, 1725.
          [16] p. 21cm.
8
                       (Continued on next card)

Wecker, Hanss Jacob, 1528-1586.

  see

Wecker, Johann Jacob, 1528-1586.

Wecker, Jacob, 1528-1586.

  see

Wecker, Johann Jacob, 1528-1586.

Wecker, Johann Jacob, 1528-1586.
WITCHCRAFT
BF   Hildebrand, Wolffgang.
1565   Goêtia, vel Theurgia, sive Praestigiarum
H64   magicarum descriptio, revelatio, resolutio,
1631   inquisitio, & executio. Das ist, Wahre vnd
        eigentliche Entdeckunge, Declaration oder
        Erklärunge fürnehmer Articul der Zauberey.
        Vnd was von Zauberern, Vnholden, Hexen,
        deren Händel, Art, Thun ... vnd ihrer Machi-
        nation ... Etwan durch den wohlgebornen
        Herrn Jacob Freyherrn von Liechtenberg &c.
        ... erfahren, durch den hochgelahrten Herrn
8   (Continued on next card)
NIC

Wecker, Johann Jacob, 1528-1586.
WITCHCRAFT
BF   Hildebrand, Wolffgang. Goêtia, vel Theur-
1565   gia ... 1631.   (Card 2)
H64
1631   Jacob Weckern M. D. etwas weitleufftiger
        beschrieben. Nun aber an jetzo mit allem
        Fleisse revidiret ... durch Wolfgangum Hil-
        debrandum ... Leipzig, In Verlegung Joh.
        Francken S. Erben vnd Samuel Scheiben Buchh.,
        1631.
          8 p. l., 342, [17] p. 18cm.
          Title in red and black.
8   (Continued on next card)

Wecker, Johann Jacob, 1528-1586.
WITCHCRAFT
BF   Hildebrand, Wolffgang.
1603   Wahre und eigentliche Entdeckung oder
H64   Erklärung der fürnemsten Articul von der
1704   Zauberey und was von Zauberern, Vnholden,
        Hexen, derer Händel, Art, Thun, ... und
        vielen andern ihren Machinationen ...
        Durch den wohlgebohrnen Herrn Jacob Frey
        Herrn von Lichtenberg ... erfahren, und
        durch den hochgelahrten Herrn Jacob Weckern
        weitläufftiger beschrieben. Anitzo mit
        allem Fleiss übersehen und vermehret mit
8   (Continued on next card)
NIC

Wecker, Johann Jacob, 1528-1586.
WITCHCRAFT
BF   Hildebrand, Wolffgang. Wahre und eigent-
1603   liche Entdeckung oder Erklärung der für-
H64   nemsten Articul von der Zauberey ...
1704   [1704?]   (Card 2)

        vielen Artzeneyen ..., auch wie eine christ-
        liche Obrigkeit wider die Zauberer ...
        rechtlich verfahren soll, ... auch viele
        lustige und possierliche Historien von Er-
        scheinungen allerhand Geister ... von neuen
        in Druck verfertiget durch Wolfgangum Hilde-
8   (Continued on next card)
NIC

Wecker, Johann Jacob, 1528-1586.
WITCHCRAFT
BF   Hildebrand, Wolffgang. Wahre und eigent-
1603   liche Entdeckung oder Erklärung der für-
H64   nemsten Articul von der Zauberey ...
1704   [1704?]   (Card 3)

        brandum. [Leipzig? 1704?]
          11 p. l., 342, [18] p. front. 21cm.
          Half title (follows Inhalt aller Capitel)
        agrees with original title: Goetia, vel
        Theurgia, sive Praestigiarum magicarum des-
        criptio, and has imprint 1704.
8   (Continued on next card)
NIC

Wecker, Johann Jacob, 1528-1586.
WITCHCRAFT
BF   Hildebrand, Wolffgang. Wahre und eigent-
1603   liche Entdeckung oder Erklärung der für-
H64   nemsten Articul von der Zauberey ...
1704   [1704?]   (Card 4)

        Bound with his Neu-vermehrt, vortrefflich
        ... curieuses Kunst und Wunderbuch. Leip-
        zig, 1704.
          1. Witchcraft. 2. Magic. 3. Devil--
        Legends. 4. Folk-lore--Germany. I. His
        Goetia, vel Theurgia. II. Liechtenberg,
        Jacob von, ba   ron. Hexen-Büchlein.
8   III. Wecker,   Johann Jacob, 1528-1586.
NIC   IV. Title.

Witchcraft
BF   Wedeck, Harry Ezekiel, 1894–
1411   Treasury of witchcraft. New York, Philosophi Li-
W38   brary [c1961]
          271 p. illus. 24 cm.
          Includes bibliography.

          1. Occult sciences. 2. Witchcraft. I. Title.

          BF1411.W38   133.4   60-15949
          Library of Congress   [10]

BF   Wedeck, Harry Ezekiel, 1894–
1411   Treasury of witchcraft. New York, Philo-
W38   sophical Library [c1961]

          271 p. illus. 24 cm.

          Includes bibliography.

        Wedel, Ernst Heinrich, 1671-1709, respond-
        ent.
Witchcraft
BF   Wedel, Georg Wolfgang, 1645-1721, praeses.
1445   Dissertatio medica De spectris, praeside
D61   Georgio Wolffgango VVedelio ... proposita
no.13   ab Ernesto Henrico Wedelio ... Editio
        secunda. Jenae, Litteris Krebsianis,
        1698.
          39, [1] p. 19cm. (bound in 21cm. vol.)

          Diss.--Jena (E. H. Wedel, respondent)
          No. 13 in vol. lettered Dissertationes
8   de spectris. 1646-1753.

Witchcraft
RC   Wedel, Georg Wolfgang, 1645-1721, praeses.
547   Dissertatio medica De incvbo, ex epito-
W39   me praxeos clinicae Georgii Wolffgangi We-
        delii ... eodem praeside, pvblicae ... dis-
        qvisitioni svbiecta a Christophoro Lvdovi-
        co Göckelio ... Ienae, Litteris Krebsia-
        nis [1708]
          20 p. 21cm.

          Diss.--Jena (C. L. Göckelius, respondent
        √I. Göckelius. Christophorus Ludovicus,
8   respondent. √II. Title. √III. Title:
        incubo.

596

CATALOGUE OF THE CORNELL WITCHCRAFT COLLECTION

Wedel, Georg Wolfgang, 1645-1721, praeses.
Dissertatio medica De incubo, ex epitome praxeos clinicae Georgii Wolffgangi Wedelii ...eodem praeside publicae... disquisitioni subiecta a Christophoro Ludovico Göckelio... Ienae, Litteris Krebsianis, [1708].
20 p. 20cm.

Diss.--Jena (C. L. Göckelius, respondent)
1. Insomnia. 2. Sedatives. I. Göckelius, Christophorus Ludovicus, respondent.

Witchcraft
F
445
61
no.13

Wedel, Georg Wolfgang, 1645-1721, praeses.
Dissertatio medica De spectris, praeside Georgio Wolffgango Wedelio ... proposita ab Ernesto Henrico Wedelio ... Editio secunda. Jenae, Litteris Krebsianis, 1698.
39, [1] p. 19cm. (bound in 21cm. vol.)

Diss.--Jena (E. H. Wedel, respondent)
No. 13 in vol. lettered Dissertationes de spectris. 1646-1753.
I. Wedel, Ernst Heinrich, 1671-1709, respondent. II. Title. III. Title: De spectris.

WITCHCRAFT
BF
1584
N4
M71

8
NIC

Weerwolven. [n.p., n.d.]
[117]-119 p. 14cm. (in vol. 24cm.)
Extract from unidentified work.
Bound with: Molhuysen, Philip Christiaan. Bijdrage tot de geschiedenis der heksenprocessen in Gelderland. n.d.
1. Werwolves.

Witchcraft
F
589
B88

Wegelin, Johann Reinhard.
Bruckner, Wilhelm Hieronymus.
De magicis personis et artibvs disserit, et ea omnino dari ostendit. Von zauberischen Leuten und Künsten, das solche warhafftig anzutreffen und nicht in einer blossen Einbildung bestehen, occasione legis 6. c. de malef. & mathem. a nobilissimo jurium candidato Jo. Reinhardo Wegelino ... solemni lectione ... explicandae die IX. Maji M DCC XII ... [Jena?] 1723.
28 p. 20cm.

Witchcraft
775
41

[Wegener, F G Wilhelm]
Schau-Platz vieler ungereimten Meynungen und Erzehlungen: worauf die unter dem Titul der Magiae Naturalis so hoch gepriesene Wissenschafften und Künste, ... ingleichen die mancherley Arten der Wahrsagerey, und viel andere fabelhaffte, abergläubische und ungegründete Dinge mehr, vorgestellet, geprüfet und entdecket werden ... von Tharsandern. Berlin und Leipzig, Bey Ambrosius Haude, 1735-42.
3 v. 17cm.
(Continued on next card)

Witchcraft
75

[Wegener, F G Wilhelm] Schau-Platz vieler ungereimten Meynungen und Erzehlungen ... 1735-42. (Card 2)
Planned originally as monthly issues to be bound together into two volumes.
Ex libris: v. Arnswaldt.

1. Superstition. 2. Occult sciences. 3. Magic. 4. Folk-lore--Germany. I. Title.

Wegman, Hector, respondent.

Witchcraft
BF
1520
H93

Hunger, Albert, 1545?-1604, praeses.
De magia theses theologicae, ... per reuerendum & eruditum virum M. Hectorem VVegman ... pro impetrando licentiae gradu, ad publicam disputationem propositae: praeside reuerendo & clarissimo viro Alberto Hvngero ... Ingolstadii, Ex officina VVeissenhorniana [1574]
[23] p. 20cm.
In MS at bottom of t. p.: Rdo dno M. Casparo Boos ddt H. W.

8 (Continued on next card)

Witchcraft
BF
1445
W41

[Wegner, Georg Wilhelm]
Gedancken von Gespenstern. Halle, C. H. Hemmerde, 1747.
47 p. 18cm.
Attributed to Wegner by Holzmann in v. 6 and 7 (correction of v. 2, which attributes the work to G. F. Meier)
Second printing, 1749, spells title: Gedanken von Gespenstern.
With this is bound Sucro, Johann Georg. Widerlegung der Gedancken von Gespenstern. Halle, 1748.

8 (Continued on next card)

Witchcraft
BF
1445
W41

[Wegner, Georg Wilhelm] Gedancken von von Gespenstern. 1747 (Card 2)

1. Ghosts. I. Meier, Georg Friedrich, supposed author. II. Title. III. Title: Gedanken von Gespenstern.

8

Wegner, Georg Wilhelm.
Gedancken von Gespenstern.

Witchcraft
BF
1445
W41

[Sucro, Johann Georg]
Widerlegung der Gedancken von Gespenstern. Halle im Magdeburgischen, C. H. Hemmerde, 1748.
72 p. 18cm.
Attributed to Sucro by Holzmann.
Bound with Wegner, Georg Wilhelm. Gedancken von Gespenstern. Halle, 1747.
1. Wegner, Georg Wilhelm. Gedancken von Gespenstern. 2. Ghosts. 3. Hallucinations and illusions. I. Title.

8

Witchcraft
BF
1445
W41
P5

Wegner, Georg Wilhelm.
Philosophische Abhandlung von Gespenstern, worinn zugleich eine kurtze Nachricht von dem Wustermarckischen Kobold gegeben wird. Berlin, Zu haben bey A. Haude u. C. Spener, 1747.
80 p. 17cm.

1. Ghosts. I. Title. II. Title: Georg Wilhelm Wegners ... philosophische Abhandlung von Gespenstern.

8

Witchcraft
BF
1583
A2
B89
1727

Weidner, Johann Joachim, 1672-1732.
Christ-bescheidentliche Gegen-Erinnerungen, worinnen der teuffelischen Wirckungen halber, umständliche Nachricht geschehen, und zugleich Jacobi Brunnemanni Anmerckungen, mit guten Grunde und nach Gottes Wort geprüfet und hingeleget seyn ... Rostock, Kissner, 1730.
143, [11] p. 22cm.
Bound with Brunnemann, Jacob. Discours von betrüglichen Kennzeichen.Halle, 1727.
1. Witchcraft. 2. Trials (Witchcraft)-- Germany. I. Brunnemann, Jacob, d. 1735. II. Title.

Weidner, Johann Joachim, 1672-1732.

Witchcraft
BF
1583
A2
B89
1727

Brunnemann, Jacob, d. 1735.
Discours von betrüglichen Kennzeichen der Zauberey, worinnen viel abergläubische Meinungen freymüthig untersuchet und verworffen, wie auch Carpzovii, Berlichii, Crusii ... missliche und leichtgläubige Lehr-Sätze von der Zauberey erwogen, zugleich J. J. Weidnerii Gegensätze wider diesen Discours kurtz und bescheidentlich beantwortet werden ... Halle, J. E. Fritsch, 1727.
[32], 228, [16] p. 22cm.
(Continued on next card)

Weidner, Johann Joachim, 1672-1732.

Witchcraft
BF
1583
A2
B89
1727

Brunnemann, Jacob, d. 1735. Discours von betrüglichen Kennzeichen der Zauberey ... 1727. (Card 2)
With this is bound Weidner, J. J. Christbescheidentliche Gegen-Erinnerungen. Rostock, 1730.
1. Witchcraft. 2. Trials (Witchcraft)-- Germany. I. Weidner, Johann Joachim, 1672-1732.

Weier, Johann, 1515-1588.
see
Wier, Johann, 1515-1588.

Weinrich, Carolus.

WITCHCRAFT
BF
1524
P59

Pico della Mirandola, Giovanni Francesco, 1470-1533.
Strix; sive, De ludificatione daemonum dialogi tres. Nunc primum in Germania eruti ex bibliotheca M. Martini Weinrichii, cum ejusdem praefatione...itemque Epistola ad ...Andream Libavium de quaestione: Utrum in non maritatis & castis mola possit gigni? Et post mortem ejus editi studio & opera Caroli Weinrichii. Argentorati, Venundantur apud Paulum Ledertz, 1612.

8
NIC   160+ p.   18cm.
(Continued on next card)

Weinrich, Carolus.

WITCHCRAFT
BF
1524
P59

Pico della Mirandola, Giovanni Francesco, 1470-1533. Strix...1612. (Card 2)
Epistola to Libavius lacking.
With this is bound: Sennert, Daniel. De origine et natura animarum in brutis. 1638.
1. Magic. 2. Demonology. 3. Witchcraft. I. Weinrich, Martinus, 1548-1609. II. Weinrich, Carolus. III. Libavius, Andreas, d.1616. IV. Title.

Weinrich, Martinus, 1548-1609.

WITCHCRAFT
BF
1524
P59

Pico della Mirandola, Giovanni Francesco, 1470-1533.
Strix; sive, De ludificatione daemonum dialogi tres. Nunc primum in Germania eruti ex bibliotheca M. Martini Weinrichii, cum ejusdem praefatione...itemque Epistola ad ...Andream Libavium de quaestione: Utrum in non maritatis & castis mola possit gigni? Et post mortem ejus editi studio & opera Caroli Weinrichii. Argentorati, Venundantur apud Paulum Ledertz, 1612.

8
NIC   160+ p.   18cm.
(Continued on next card)

CATALOGUE OF THE CORNELL WITCHCRAFT COLLECTION

Weinrich, Martinus, 1548-1609.
WITCHCRAFT
BF Pico della Mirandola, Giovanni Francesco,
1524   1470-1533. Strix...1612.   (Card 2)
P59
    Epistola to Libavius lacking.
    With this is bound: Sennert, Daniel. De
origine et natura animarum in brutis. 1638.
        1. Magic. 2. Demonology. 3. Witchcraft.
    I. Weinrich, Martinus, 1548-1609. II. Weinrich, Carolus. III. Libavius, Andreas, d.1616. IV. Title.

        Weise fromm und gesund zu leben, auch ruhig
        und gottseelig zu sterben.
Witchcraft
BF   Gassner, Johann Joseph, 1727-1779.
1559   Weise fromm und gesund zu leben, auch ruhig
G25 und gottseelig zu sterben: oder, Nützlicher
W4   Unterricht wider den Teufel zu streiten: durch
1775 Beantwortung der Fragen: 1. Kann der Teufel
     dem Leibe der Menschen schaden? II. Welchen am
     mehresten? III. Wie ist zu helfen? 8. verb.
     Aufl. und vermehrt von Herrn Verfasser selbsten.
     Augsburg gedruckt, zu finden bey J. G. Bullman,
     1775.
        40 p. front.   17cm.
        1. Exorcism.   I. Title. II. Title:
    Nützlicher Unterricht wider den Teufel
    zu streiten.

Witchcraft
RA   Weiss, Georg Franz.
1201   Alexiterium; sive Opusculum continens remedia adversus venena et maleficia auctore
W43 Georgio Francisco Weiss, philosophiae & medicinae doctore urbis Marcoduranae physico
     ... Coloniae Agrippinae, Typis Petri Theodori Hilden, 1698.
        7 p. l., 172, [1] p. 16cm.
        Provenance: Bibl. Buxheim (Carthusian convent)
        1. Poisons.   2. Toxicology.   I.
8   Title.

        Der weisse Teuffel, so sich in menschlicher Verlarvung zu denen Einfältigen
WITCHCRAFT sichtbarlich gesellet.
BF   Scultetus, Abraham, 1566-1624.
1543   Der weisse Teuffel, so sich in menschlicher Verlarvung zu denen Einfältigen
S43 sichtbarlich gesellet, zu versuchen, ob er
     ihre Seelen durch allerhand Blendungen gewinnen möge? Wie er solches versuchet, indem er eine Bauer-Magd ... mit vielerley
     Schmeicheln und Drohungen aufgefodert hat,
     aber noch biss dato mit Schanden abziehen
     müssen ... Leipzig, Bey A. Martini, 1732.
        70 p. 18cm.
8   1. Devil.   2. Exempla. I. Title.
NIC

Witchcraft
BF   Weissenbach, Joseph Anton.
1520   Transactiones diabolicae, ubi omnia malorum spirituum, quae nunc veniunt in contentionem, citra gratiam, clamorem, odium
W43 componuntur. In usus parochorum scripsit Dr.
     Jos. Ant. Weissenbach, canonicus Duraquensis.
     Basileae, Typis E. Thurneysen, 1786.
        160 p. 17cm.
        With interesting bibliography, p. 148-160.
        1. Demonology. 2. Witchcraft. I.
8   Title. 3. Witchcraft--Bibliography.

        Weisshammer, Paul, ed.
Witchcraft
GR   Gross, Wilibald.
730   Sonder- und wunderbare, doch wahre Geschichte, wie der Teufel ††† sich einmal in
A8   der leiblichen Gestalt eines Esels auf dem
G87 Rathhause im W..r im W..b..g..schen sehen
     liess; zu Frommen und Besserung der izigen,
     höchst unglaubigen Welt, auch zum Beweiss
     des, in unsern Tagen so sehr geläugneten
     Daseyns eines Teufels †††, in Reimen, nach
     der bekannten Melodie: Ein Ritter, wie die
     Chronik sagt &   c. &c. Im Manuscript
     aufgefunden u   nd ans Licht gestellt,
                    (Continued on next card)

        Weisshammer, Paul, ed.
Witchcraft
GR   Gross, Wilibald. Sonder- und wunderbare,
730 doch wahre Geschichte. Seefeld in Tyrol,
A8   1786.   (Card 2)
G87
    auch mit Anmerkungen vers. von Paul Weisshammer. [Seefeld in Tyrol] Gedrukt auf
    Kosten des Klosters, 1786.
        29 p. 18cm.

        I. Weisshammer, Paul, ed. II. Title.

WITCHCRAFT   Welte, Benedict.
BV   Hovhannes I Mandakuni, Patriarch of Armenia,
4627 d. ca. 490.
W8   Johannes Mantagunensis über Zauberei.
H84 [Tübingen, 1851]
1851   [85]-119 p. 21cm.
        At head of title: 3.
        Caption title.
        Article signed: Welte.
        Translation of a pastoral letter on
    witchcraft and fortune-telling.
        1. Witchcraft. 2. Fortune-telling.
8   I. Welte, Benedict. II. Title.

Witchcraft
PS   Wendell, Barrett, 1855-1921.
3158   Stelligeri, and other essays concerning
W7S7 America. New York, Charles Scribner's Sons,
     1893.
        217 p. 18cm.
        Contents.--I. Stelligeri.--II. The four
    American centuries.--III. Some neglected
    characteristics of the New England Puritans.--
    IV. Were the Salem witches guiltless?--
    V. American literature.--VI. John Greenleaf
    Whittier.--VII. Mr. Lowell as a teacher.
        1. American literature--Addresses, essays,
    lectures. 2. United States--Hist.--Addresses,
    essays, lectures. I. Title. II. His Were the
    Salem witches guiltless?

Witchcraft
PS   Wendell, Barrett, 1855-1921.
3158   Stelligeri, and other essays concerning
W7S7 America.   New York, Scribner's, 1893.
        217 p. 18cm.
        Contents.--Stelligeri.--The four American
    centuries.--Some neglected characteristics
    of the New England Puritans.--Were the Salem
    witches guiltless?--American literature.--
    John Greenleaf Whittier.--Mr. Lowell as a
    teacher.

                    (over)

Witchcraft
BF   Wendell, Barrett, 1855-1921.
1576   Were the Salem witches guiltless? A
W46+ paper read before the Essex Institute,
     February 29, 1892. Salem, Mass., 1892.
        19 p. 26cm.
        Reprinted "from the Historical collections
    of the Essex Institute, vol. XXIX, 1892."

        1. Witchcraft--Salem, Mass. I. Title.

             Wendell, Barrett, 1855-1921.
Witchcraft   Were the Salem witches guiltless?
PS   Wendell, Barrett, 1855-1921.
3158   Stelligeri and other essays concerning
W7S7 America. New York, Charles Scribner's
     Sons, 1893.
        217 p. 18cm.
        Contents.--I. Stelligeri.--II. The four
    American centuries.--III. Some neglected
    characteristics of the New England Puritans.
    --IV. Were the Salem witches guiltless?--
    V. American literature.--VI. John Greenleaf Whittier.--VII. Mr. Lowell as a teacher.
        1. American literature--Addresses, essays,
    lectures. 2. United States--Hist.--
8   Addresses, essays, lectures. I.
    Title.

Witchcraft   Weisshammer, Paul, ed.
BF   Weng, Johann Friedrich.
1583   Die Hexen-Prozesse der ehemaligen Reichsstadt Nördlingen in den Jahren 1590-94. Aus
Z7   den Kriminal-Akten des Nördlingischen Archives gezogen ... Nördlingen, C. H. Beck
1590 [1838].
        60, 28 p. 22cm.
        Aus der historisch-statistischen Zeitschrift: "Das Ries, wie es war und wie es
    ist" besonders abgedruckt.
        1. Trials (Witchcraft)--Nördlingen.
        2. Trials (Witchcraft)--Germany. 3.
8   Hollin, Maria, fl. 1594. I. Title.

Witchcraft   Wenham, Jane, d. 1730.
BF   Bragge, Francis.
1581   A defense of the proceedings against Jane
Z7   Wenham, wherein the possibility and reality of
1712c witchcraft are demonstrated from Scripture, and
     the concurrent testimonies of all ages. In
     answer to two pamphlets, entituled, I. The
     impossibility of witchcraft, &c. II. A full
     confutation of witchcraft. By Francis Bragge ...
     London, Printed for E. Curll, 1712.
        2 p. l., 36 p. 18½cm.

             Wenham, Jane, d. 1730.
Witchcraft
BF   [Bragge, Francis]
1581   A full and impartial account of the discovery of sorcery and witchcraft, practis'd
Z7   by Jane Wenham of Walkerne in Hertfordshire,
1712 upon the bodies of Anne Thorn, Anne Street,
     &c. The proceedings against her from her
     being first apprehended, till she was committed to gaol by Sir Henry Chauncy. Also
     her tryal at the assizes at Hertford before
     Mr. Justice Powell, where she was found guilty
     of felony and witchcraft, and receiv'd sen-
                    (Continued on next card)

             Wenham, Jane, d. 1730.
Witchcraft
BF   [Bragge, Francis] A full and impartial
1581 account of the discovery of sorcery and
Z7   witchcraft ... 1712.   (Card 2)
1712
    tence of death for the same, March 4, 1711-12.
    London, Printed for E. Curll, 1712.
        2 p. l., 36 p. 19cm.

        1. Wenham, Jane, d. 1730. 2. Witchcraft--
    England. I. Title.

Witchcraft   Wenham, Jane, d. 1730.
BF   Bragge, Francis.
1581   The witch of Walkerne. Being, I. A full
Z7   and impartial account of the discovery of
1712d sorcery and witchcraft, practis'd by Jane
     Wenham of Walkerne in Hertfordshire ...
     II. Witchcraft farther display'd. Containing an account of the witchcraft practis'd
     by Jane Wenham, since her condemnation, etc.
     ... III. A defense of the proceedings
     against Jane Wenham ... In answer to two
     pamphlets, entituled, 1. The impossibility
     of witchcraft. 2. A full confutation of
                    (Continued on next card)

Witchcraft   Wenham, Jane, d 1730.
BF   Bragge, Francis. The witch of Walkerne ...
1581   (Card 2)
Z7
1712d witchcraft. IV. A general preface to the
     whole. 5th ed. London, Printed for E.
     Curll, 1712.
        3 pts. in 1 v. 20cm.

        Parts 2 and 3 have special title pages.

        1. Witchcraft--England. 2. Wenham, Jane,
    d. 1730. I. Title.

598

CATALOGUE OF THE CORNELL WITCHCRAFT COLLECTION

Wenham, Jane, d. 1730.
WITCHCRAFT
F
581
7
712b
  [Bragge, Francis]
    Witchcraft farther display'd. Containing I. An account of the witchcraft practis'd by Jane Wenham of Walkerne, in Hertfordshire, since her condemnation, upon the bodies of Anne Thorn and Anne Street. II. An answer to the most general objections against the being and power of witches: with some remarks upon the case of Jane Wenham in particular, and on Mr. Justice Powel's procedure therein. To which are added, the tryals of Florence
       (Continued on next card)

Wenham, Jane, d. 1730.
WITCHCRAFT
581
712b
  [Bragge, Francis] Witchcraft farther display'd ...   (Card 2)
    Newton, a famous Irish witch, at the assizes held at Cork, anno 1661; as also of two witches at assizes held at Bury St. Edmonds in Suffolk, anno 1664, before Sir Matthew Hale ... who were found guildty and executed. London, Printed for E. Curll, 1712.
       2 p. l., 39 p.   19cm.
       Introduction signed: F. B.
       Bound with A Full confutation of witchcraft.   London, 1712.
         (Continued on next card)

Wenham, Jane, d. 1730.
Witchcraft
81
12e
    The case of the Hertfordshire witchcraft consider'd. Being an examination of a book, entitl'd, A full and impartial account of the discovery of sorcery & witchcraft, practis'd by Jane Wenham of Walkern, upon the bodies of Anne Thorne, Anne Street, &c. London, Printed for J. Pemberton, 1712.
       3 p. l., vi, 86 p. 20 cm.
       With copy 1 is bound [Bragge, Francis] Witchcraft farther display'd. London, 1712.

Wenham, Jane, d. 1730.
hcraft
    A full confutation of witchcraft: more particularly of the depositions against Jane Wenham, lately condemned for a witch; at Hertford. In which the modern notions of witches are overthrown, and the ill consequences of such doctrines are exposed by arguments; proving that, witchcraft is priestcraft ... In a letter from a physician in Hertfordshire, to his friend in London. London, Printed for J. Baker, 1712.
       48 (i.e. 40) p. 18½cm.
       With this is bound [Bragge, Francis] Witchcraft farther display'd. London, 1712.

Wenham, Jane, d. 1730.
hcraft
  Gerish, William Blyth.
    A Hertfordshire witch: or, The story of Jane Wenham, the "wise woman" of Walkern, by W. B. Gerish. [Bishop's Stortford? 1906]
       cover-title, 13 p. 23ᶜᵐ. [Hertfordshire folk lore. no. 7]
       With facsimile of the t.-p. of the Rev. Francis Bragge's pamphlet: A full and impartial account of the discovery of sorcery and witchcraft, practis'd by Jane Wenham ... 3d ed. London, 1712.

       1. Wenham, Jane, d. 1730. 2. Witchcraft—England.
                                            17-20384

Wenham, Jane, d. 1730.
hcraft
    The impossibility of witchcraft, plainly proving, from Scripture and reason, that there never was a witch; and that it is both irrational and impious to believe there ever was. In which the depositions against Jane Wenham, lately try'd and condemn'd for a witch, at Hertford, are confuted and expos'd ... London, Printed and sold by J. Baker, 1712.
       4 p. l., 31 p. 18½cm.

Wenham, Jane, d. 1730.
WITCHCRAFT
BF
1581
Z7
1712aa
    The impossiblity of witchcraft, plainly proving, from Scripture and reason, that there never was a witch; and that it is both irrational and impious to believe there ever was. In which the depositions against Jane Wenham, lately try'd and condemn'd for a witch, at Hertford, are confuted and expos'd. 2d ed. London, Printed and sold by J. Baker, 1712.
       4 p. l.,   36 p. 18cm.
8   Imperfect   copy: p. 17-24
NIC   (Continued on next card)

Wenham, Jane, d. 1730.
WITCHCRAFT
BF
1581
Z7
1712aa
    The impossiblity of witchcraft... 1712. (Card 2)
       erroneously numbered 25-32.
       With this is bound The impossiblity of witchcraft further demonstrated. London, 1712.

       1. Witchcraft—England. 2. Wenham, Jane, d. 1730. 3. Bragge, Francis, b. 1690. A full and impartial account of the discovery of sorcery and witchcraft.
8
NIC

Witchcraft
GR
580
W48
  Wenzel, Gottfried Immanuel, 1754-1809.
    Geist-Wunder-Hexen- und Zaubergeschichten, vorzüglich neuester Zeit. Erzählt und erklärt von Gottfried Immanuel Wenzel ... Prag und Leipzig, In der von Schönfeldschen Buchhandlung, 1793.
       4 p. l., 160 p. 20cm.
       Illustrative vignette on t. p.

       1. Ghost stories. 2. Magic. 3. Superstition. I. Title.
8

Wercksaeme duyvelen in de weereld.
Witchcraft
BF
1528
D9
V981
  Vries, Simon de, b. 1630.
    Wercksaeme duyvelen in de weereld: of Vervolgh vande Satan in sijn weesen, aert, bedryf en guygchelspel: vertoond in een historische verhandelingh van duyvelsche gesighten, spoocken, droomen, voorteeckenen, voorseggingen, tovereyen, en wat voorts deese stof aenhangigh is. Nevens afweeringh van 't geen daer tegens ingebragt werd, met meenighvuldige verwringingen der H. Schrift. Door S. de Vries. Utrecht,
8   (Continued on next card)

Wercksaeme duyvelen in de weereld.
Witchcraft
BF
1528
D9
V981
  Vries, Simon de, b. 1630. Wercksaeme duyvelen in de weereld ... 1692. (Card 2)
    By Anthoni Schouten, boeckverkoper, 1692.
       34 p. l., 590, [50] p. title and other vignettes. 16cm.
       8°: *-4*⁸, 5*¹, A-2R⁸.
       Title in red and black.
       Imperfect: p. 271-272 wanting.
       Running title: De Satan vertoond in
8   (Continued on next card)

Wercksaeme duyvelen in de weereld.
Witchcraft
BF
1528
D9
V981
  Vries, Simon de, b. 1630. Wercksaeme duyvelen in de weereld ... 1692. (Card 3)
    sijn weesen, aert, bedrijf, en guygchelspel.
    Preface discusses the opinions of Conrad Vorst.

       1. Devil. 2. Demonology. 3. Vorst, Conrad, 1569-1622. I. His De Satan in sijn weesen, aert, bedryf, en guychelspel. II. Title.
8

Were the Salem witches guiltless?
Witchcraft
BF
1576
W46+
  Wendell, Barrett, 1855-1921.
    Were the Salem witches guiltless? A paper read before the Essex Institute, February 29, 1892. Salem, Mass., 1892.
       19 p. 26cm.

       Reprinted "from the Historical collections of the Essex Institute, vol. XXIX, 1892."

       1. Witchcraft—Salem, Mass. I. Title.

The werewolf.
Witchcraft
GR
830
W4S95
  Summers, Montague, 1880–
    The werewolf, by Montague Summers ... London, K. Paul, Trench, Trubner & co., ltd., 1933.
       xiv, 307 p. VIII pl. (incl. front.) 24½ᶜᵐ.
       Bibliography: p. 279-290.

       1. Werwolves. I. Title.
       [Full name: Alphonsus Joseph-Mary Augustus Montague Summers]

Library of Congress   GR830.W4S8   34-5257
                           [3]   398.4

Witchcraft
BF
1587
D61
no.3
  Werger, Johann, praeses.
    De magia daemoniaca disquisitio physica, quam ... praeside M. Johanne Werger Lubec. ... exponit ... Nicolaus Schmidt Lubec. ... Wittebergae, Literis Oelschlegelianis [1657]
       [16] p. 21cm.
       No. 3 in vol. lettered Dissertationes de magia. 1623-1723.

       1. Occult sciences—Addresses, essays, lectures. I. Schmidt, Nicolaus, of Lübeck, respondent. II. Title.
8

Der Werwolf.
ar W
6460
  Hertz, Wilhelm, 1835-1902.
    Der Werwolf; Beitrag zur Sagengeschichte. Stuttgart, A. Kröner, 1862.
       134 p. 22cm.

       Bound with Rochholz, E. L. Gauggöttinnen: Walburg, Verena und Gertrud. Leipzig, 1870.

       1. Werwolves. I. Title.

Wesel, Adrianus van, d. 1710.
Witchcraft
BF
1410
B42
1691a
no.9
    't Voorgevallene in de catechisatie, by Do. Adrianus van Wesel, op Sondagh den 28sten December. Ao. 1692. In de Oudezijds Kapel, opgesteld door een toehoorder. Amsterdam, By D. vanden Dalen, boeckverkoper, 1693.
       8 p. title vignette. 20 x 16cm.
       4°: A⁴.
       Black letter.
       Van der Linde 177.
       Argues for tolerance of views held by Balthasar Bekker and his followers.
8   (Continued on next card)

Wesel, Adrianus van, d. 1710.
Witchcraft
BF
1410
B42
1691a
no.9
    't Voorgevallene in de catechisatie, by Do. Adrianus van Wesel ... 1693. (Card 2)
       No. 9 in vol. lettered B. Bekker. Betoverde weereld.

       1. Nederlandse Hervormde Kerk—Doctrinal and controversial works. 2. Wesel, Adrianus van, d. 1710. 3. Bekker, Balthasar, 1634-1698. I. Een toehoorder, pseud.
8

599

CATALOGUE OF THE CORNELL WITCHCRAFT COLLECTION

Witchcraft
N 8217
D5
W51
    Wessely, Joseph Eduard, 1826-1895.
        Die Gestalten des Todes und des Teufels in der darstellenden Kunst. Von J. E. Wesseley. Mit 2 Radirungen des Verfassers und 21 Illustrationen in Holzschnitt. Leipzig, H. Vogel (früher R. Weigel) 1876.
        123 p. illus. (part col.) 23cm.
        Contents.--I. Iconographie des Todes.--II. Iconographie des Teufels.
        Each part has special t. p.
        1. Death--   Art. 2. Devil--Art.
8   I. Title.

Witchcraft
BF 1879
T2C75
1896
    Westcott, William Wynn, 1848-1925, ed. and tr.
    [Constant, Alphonse Louis] 1810?-1875.
        The magical ritual of the sanctum regnum interpreted by the tarot trumps. Translated from the mss. of Éliphaz Lévi [pseud.] and edited by W. Wynn Westcott. London, G. Redway, 1896.
        x, 108 p. 8 col. plates. 19cm.

        1. Magic. 2. Tarot. I. Westcott, William Wynn, 1848-1925, ed. and tr. II. Title.

WITCHCRAFT
RC 340
W53
1707
    Westphal, Johann Caspar.
        D. Johannis-Caspari VVestphali, academici curiosi, Pathologia daemoniaca, id est Observationes & meditationes physiologico-magico-medicae circa daemonomanias, similesque morbos convulsivos â fascino ortos, daemonibus olim Graecorum ethnicorum ac Judaeorum aëreis, hodiè verò obsessioni aliisque diaboli infernalis tentationibus & operationibus superstitiosè adscriptos ... Nunc verò philiatrorum   desiderio & adhortationi-
8   (Continued on next card)

WITCHCRAFT
RC 340
W53
1707
    Westphal, Johann Caspar. ... Pathologia daemoniaca ... 1707.   (Card 2)
    bus revisae, & variis annotatis illustriores redditae. Quibus accedunt Judicium physiologico-magico-medicum de viva jumentorum contagio infectorum contumulatione, & Observationes atque experimenta chymico-physica de prodigiis sanguinis, falsò hactenus proclamatis. Lipsiae, Apud haeredes F. Lanckisii, 1707.
    6 p. l.,   148, [16] p. 22cm.
8   (Continued on next card)

WITCHCRAFT
RC 340
W53
1707
    Westphal, Johann Caspar. ... Pathologia daemoniaca ... 1707.   (Card 3)
    The first section, subtitled Historia morbi & species facti, is German and Latin in double columns.

    1. Nervous system--Diseases. 2. Demonomania. 3. Epilepsy. 4. Hysteria. I. Title: Pathologia daemoniaca. II. Title

8

MSS
Bd.
WITCHCRAFT
BF
W54
    Wetz, Ambrosius.
        Warhafftige und ein erschröckliche newe Zeitung, des grossen Wasserguss, so den 15. May diss lauffenden 78. Jahrs, zu Horb geschehen ... wie man hernach alda etlich Unhulden verbrent hatt, wie sie schröcklich Ding bekendt haben ... durch Ambrosium Wetz ... [n.p., 1578? ca. 1900]
    4 l. 19cm.
    Carnap's manuscript copy.
    "Originaldruck in der Stadtbibliothek zu Züri   ch, 8 Seiten in 8°."
    (Continued on next card)

MSS
Bd.
WITCHCRAFT
BF
W54
    Wetz, Ambrosius. Warhafftige und ein erschröckliche newe Zeitung, des grossen Wasserguss ... [1578? ca. 1900] (Card 2)
    Annotations in the margins indicate foliation of the original.
    In verse.

    1. Witchcraft--Austria.   I. Title.
    II. Title: Des grossen Wasserguss.

    Weyer, Johann, 1515-1588.
    see
    Wier, Johann, 1515-1588.

    What happened in Salem?
BF 1575
L66
1960
    Levin, David, 1924- ed.
        What happened in Salem? Documents pertaining to the seventeenth-century witchcraft trials. Young Goodman Brown [by] Nathaniel Hawthorne [and] A mirror for witches [by] Esther Forbes. 2d ed. New York, Harcourt, Brace [1960]
    238 p. 24cm. (Harbrace sourcebooks)
    "The introduction and parts I and II ... were first published at Harvard in the sixth edition, 1950, of the Handbook for English A."
    Includes bibliography.

BF 1411
W55+
    Wheatley, Dennis, 1897-
        The devil and all his works. New York, American Heritage Press [1971]
    302 p. illus. (part. col.), maps, ports. 29cm.

    1. Occult sciences. 2. Psychical research. I. Title.

    Where the Salem "witches" were hanged.
Witchcraft
BF 1576
P451+
1921
    Perley, Sidney, 1858-1928.
        Where the Salem "witches" were hanged. Salem, Mass., Essex Institute, 1921.
    18 p. illus. 28cm.
    "One hundred and fifty copies reprinted from the Historical collections of the Essex Institute, volume LVII."

    1. Witchcraft--New England. I. Title.

    Where witchcraft lives.
Witchcraft
BF 1581
V17
    Valiente, Doreen.
        Where witchcraft lives. 1st ed. London, Aquarian Press, 1962.
    xi, 7-112 p. 19 cm.

Witchcraft
BS 2545
D5
T97
no.9
    Whiston, William, 1667-1752.
        An account of the daemoniacks, and of the power of casting out daemons, both in the New Testament, and in the four first centuries. Occasioned by a late pamphlet [by A. A. Sykes] intituled, An enquiry into the meaning of daemoniacks in the New Testament ... Added, an appendix, concerning the tythes and oblations paid by Christians ... London, Printed for J. Whiston, 1737.
    88 p. 21cm.

    (Continued on next card)

Witchcraft
BS 2545
D5
T97
no.9
    Whiston, William, 1667-1752. An account of the daemoniacks, and of the power of casting out daemons ... 1737. (Card 2)
    No. 9 in vol. lettered: Twells, Whiston, etc. Tracts on the demoniacs in the New Testament. London, 1738-1775.

    1. Demoniac possession. 2. Bible. N.T.--Commentaries. 3. Tithes. 4. Sykes, Arthur Ashley, 1684?-1756. An enquiry into the meaning of daemoniacks in the New Testament. I. Title.

Witchcraft
BS 2545
D5
T759
no.3
    Whiston, William, 1667-1752.
        An account of the daemoniacks, and of the power of casting out daemons, both in the New Testament, and in the four first centuries. Occasioned by a late pamphlet [by A. A. Sykes] intituled, An enquiry into the meaning of daemoniacks in the New Testament ... Added, an appendix, concerning the tythes and oblations paid by Christians ... London, Printed for J. Whiston, 1737.

    (Continued on next card)

Witchcraft
BS 2545
D5
T759
no.3
    Whiston, William, 1667-1752. An account of the daemoniacks ... 1737. (Card 2)
    88 p. 20cm.

    No. 3 in vol. lettered: Tracks [sic] of demoniacks.

WITCHCRAFT
BF 1566
S41
    White, Andrew Dickson, 1832-1918.
        Seven great statesmen in the warfare of humanity with unreason.
    Schwickerath, Robert.
        Dr. White on witchcraft.
        (In The Messenger. New York, N. Y. 25cm. v. 43, no. 6 (1905), p. 593-605)

    With MS annotations by A. D. White.

    1. White, Andrew Dickson, 1832-1918. Seven great statesmen in the warfare of humanity with unreason. 2. Witchcraft.
8   I. Title.
NIC

BF 1713
P68
1972
    Whitmore, P   J   S
    Pithois, Claude, 1587-1676.
        A seventeenth-century exposure of superstition: select texts of Claude Pithoys (1587-1676). Introd. and notes by P.J.S. Whitmore. The Hague, Nijhoff, 1972.
    xliv, 263 p. 24cm. (International archiv[es] of the history of ideas, 49)

    English, French or Latin.
    Bibliography: p. [ix]-x, [248]-249.

    1. Astrology.   2. Witchcraft. 3. Superstition.   I. Whitmore, P
4   J   S   II. Title. III.
NIC   Series.

CATALOGUE OF THE CORNELL WITCHCRAFT COLLECTION

```
chcraft      Who is the devil?
             Gostick, Jesse.
 8              Who is the devil? (Twentieth thousand)
             London, Printed for the Trade [1871]
 1              12 p. 19cm.


                1. Devil. I. Title.
```

```
Witchcraft
BF         Wickwar, John William.
1566          Witchcraft and the black art; a book dealing with the psy-
W63        chology and folklore of the witches, by J. W. Wickwar ...
           London, H. Jenkins limited [1925?]
              320 p. 19cm.
              "Second printing completing 6,500 copies."


              1. Witchcraft.    I. Title.
                                                            26—7666
           Library of Congress          BF1566.W6
                                        [827e2]
```

```
Witchcraft                Wiegleb, Johann Christian, 1732-1800, ed.
AG            Onomatologia cvriosa artificiosa et magica.
27         Oder Natürliches Zauber-Lexicon, in welchem
059        vieles Nützliche und Angenehme aus der
1784       Naturgeschichte, Naturlehre und natürlichen
           Magie nach alphabetischer Ordnung vorgetragen
           worden. 3. Aufl. Verbessert und mit vielen
           neuen Zusätzen vermehrt von Johann Christian
           Wiegleb. Nürnberg, Raspische Buchhandlung,
           1784.
              4 p. l., 1744 numb. columns. illus., fold.
           table. 22cm.
```

```
craft      The Whole trial and examination of Mrs. Mary
           Hicks and her daughter Elizabeth, but of nine
           years of age, who were condemo'd [sic] ...
           for witchcraft; and ... executed on Saturday
           the 28th of July, 1716 ... London, Printed
           by W. Matthews [1716. London, at the British
           Museum, 1923]
              8 p. 18cm.
              Photocopy (negative) 8 p. on 5 l. 20x32cm.
              No.23 in vol. lettered: Witchcraft tracts,
           chapbooks and broadsides, 1579-1704; rotograph
           copies.
              1. Witchcraft—England. 2. Hicks, Mary,
           d. 1716. 3. Hicks, Elizabeth, 1707?-1716.
```

```
Witchcraft              Widerlegung der Gedancken von Gespenstern.
BF         [Sucro, Johann Georg]
1445          Widerlegung der Gedancken von Gespen-
W41        stern. Halle im Magdeburgischen, C. H.
           Hemmerde, 1748.
              72 p. 18cm.
              Attributed to Sucro by Holzmann.
              Bound with Wegner, Georg Wilhelm. Ge-
           dancken von Gespenstern. Halle, 1747.
              1. Wegner, Georg Wilhelm. Gedancken
           von Gespenstern. 2. Ghosts. 3. Hallu-
           cinations and illusions. I. Title.
 8
```

Wier, Johann

```
raft       Wier, Johann, 1515-1588.
              Opera omnia. Quorum contenta versa pagi-
           na exhibet. Editio nova & hactenus deside-
           rata. Accedunt indices rerum & verborum co-
           piosissimi. Amstelodami, Apud Petrum Van-
           den Berge, 1660.
              [44], 1002 p. illus. 23cm.
```

```
Witchcraft
BF         Wier, Johann, 1515-1588. Cinq livres de
1520       l'imposture et tromperie des diables ...
W64        1569.                          (Card 2)
P8
1569          bert. Essai d'une bibliographie ... de la
           sorcellerie, p. 104, no. 832.
              A t. p. in G. L. Burr's hand indicates
           this edition of the work; however, a long
           note by Burr on facing page claims the edi-
           tion agrees with no. 833 in Yve-Plessis.
           But no. 833 consists of 6 books, not
           5.
 8                          (Continued on next card)
```

```
Witchcraft
BF         Wier, Johann, 1515-1588. De commentitiis
1520       ieivniis. Cum rerum ac uerborum copioso
W64        indice ... Basileae, Ex Officina Opo-
P8+        riniana, 1582.
1582          138 columns, [7] p. illus., port. 26cm.
              Title vignette: device of J. Oporinus.
              First published 1577, as an epitome of
           his De praestigiis daemonum. Cf. Allge-
           meine deutsche Biographie, v. 42, p. 267.
 8                          (Continued on next card)
```

```
craft      Wier, Johann, 1515-1588.
              Cinq livres de l'impostvre et tromperie
           des diables; des enchantements & sorcelleries.
           Pris du latin de Iean Vvier, par Iaques
           Gréuin. Paris, I. du Pays, 1567.
              1 v. in 2 (460 p.) 17cm.
              Translation of De praestigiis daemonum.
              Ex libris Prof. Deneux.
```

```
Witchcraft
BF         Wier, Johann, 1515-1588. Cinq livres de
1520       l'imposture et tromperie des diables ...
W64        1569.                          (Card 3)
P8
1569          Translation of his De praestigiis dae-
           monum.
              1. Demonology. 2. Witchcraft. 3. Ma-
           gic. 4. Fasting. I. Grévin, Jacques,
           1538?-1570, tr. II. His De praestigiis
           daemonum—French. III. Title. IV. Title:
           De l'imposture et tromperie des diables.
 8
```

```
Witchcraft
BF         Wier, Johann, 1515-1588. De lamiis liber
1520           ... 1582.                   (Card 2)
W64
P8+           With this is bound his De praestigiis
1582       daemonum. Basileae, 1583.
              Binding: blind stamped pigskin; front
           cover initialed B P I and dated 1588.
              1. Demonology. 2. Witchcraft. 3.
           Magic. 4. Fasting. I. His De prae-
           stigiis daemonum. II. Title: De lamiis.
           III. Title: De commentitiis ieiuniis.
 8
```

```
tchcraft   Wier, Johann, 1515-1588.
520           Cinq livres de l'imposture et tromperie
54         des diables: des enchantements et sorcel-
           leries. Pris du latin de Iean Uvier et
569        faits françois par Iaques Gréuin de Cler-
           mont en Beauuoisis, médicin à Paris.
           Paris, Iaques du Puys, 1569.
              468, [79] p. 16cm.
              Incomplete: t. p. and all before p. 1
           wanting.
              Title taken from Yve-Plessis, Ro-
                           (Continued on next card)
```

```
Witchcraft
BF         Wier, Johann, 1515-1588.
1520          De lamiis liber: item De commentitiis
W64P8      ieivniis. Cum rerum ac uerborum copioso
1577       indice ... Basileae, Ex Officina Opo-
           riniana, 1577.
              134 columns, [7] p. illus. 25cm.
              Title vignette: device of J. Oporinus.
              Published as an epitome of the author's
           De praestigiis daemonum.—Cf. Allgemeine
           deutsche Biographie, v. 42, p. 267.
```

```
Witchcraft
BF         Wier, Johann, 1515-1588.
1520          De lamiis. Das ist: Von Teuffelsgespenst,
W64        Zauberern vnd Gifftbereytern, kurtzer doch
P8++       gründtlicher Bericht ... Sampt einem ange-
1586       hängten kleinen Tractätlein von dem falschen
           vnd erdichten Fasten ... in vnsere gemeine
           teutsche Sprach gebracht, durch Henricum
           Petrum Rebenstoek [sic] am
           Mayn, Gedruckt durch Nicolaum Basseum, 1586.
              6 p. l., 90, [8] p. 34cm.
              Title in red and black.
 8                          (Continued on next card)
```

CATALOGUE OF THE CORNELL WITCHCRAFT COLLECTION

Witchcraft
BF 1520 W64 P8++ 1586
Wier, Johann, 1515-1588. De lamiis. Das ist: Von Teuffelsgespenst ... 1586. (Card 2)
Originally published 1577 in Latin as an epitome of his De praestigiis daemonum. Cf. Allgemeine deutsche Biographie, v. 42, p. 267.
Bound with his De praestigiis daemonum. Von Teuffelsgespenst, Zauberern vnd Gifftbereytern. Franckfurt am Mayn,
8
(Continued on next card)

WITCHCRAFT
BF 1520 B66 1616
Wier, Johann, 1515-1588.
De lamiis.
Bodin, Jean, 1530-1596.
Le fleav des demons et sorciers, par I. B. angevin. Reueu & corrigé de plusieurs fautes qui s'estoyent glissees és precedentes impressions ... Derniere ed. Nyort, Par Dauid du Terroir, 1616.
2 p. l., 38, 556, [21] p. 17cm.
Title in ornamental woodcut border.
First published under title: De la daemonomanie.
"Refvtation des opinions de Iean VVier": p. 476-556.
8
(Continued on next card)

Witchcraft
BF 1520 W64 P8+ 1582
Wier, Johann, 1515-1588. De praestigiis daemonum ... 1583. (Card 2)
same as in 5th ed., 1577. Cf. Allgemeine deutsche Biographie, v. 42, p. 267.
Liber apologeticus, and Pseudomonarchia daemonum each with special t. p.
Colophon: Basileae, Ex Officina Oporiniana, per Balthasarvm Han, et Hieronymvm Gemvsaeum, Anno Salutis humanae M. D. LXXXIII mense Augusto.
8
(Continued on next card)

Witchcraft
BF 1520 W64 P8++ 1586
Wier, Johann, 1515-1588. De lamiis. Das ist: Von Teuffelsgespenst ... 1586. (Card 3)
1586.
Binding: blind stamped pigskin, with clasps (one wanting); front cover initialed A K A S H and dated 1589.
1. Demonology. 2. Witchcraft. 3. Magic. 4. Fasting. I. Title: Von Teuffelsgespenst, Zauberern und Gifftbe-
8
(Continued on next card)

Witchcraft
BF 1520 W64 P8 1563
Wier, Johann, 1515-1588.
De praestigiis daemonvm, et incantationibus, ac ueneficijs, libri V ... Basileae, Per Ioannem Oporinum, 1563.
479 p. 18cm.
Contemporary binding: fragment of a German manuscript on vellum, partly covered with blind stamped pigskin.
1. Demonology. 2. Magic. 3. Witchcraft.
I. Title.
8

Witchcraft
BF 1520 W64 P8+ 1582
Wier, Johann, 1515-1588. De praestigiis daemonum ... 1583. (Card 3)
Bound with his De lamiis liber. Basileae, 1582.
Binding: blind stamped pigskin; front covered initialed B P I and dated 1588.
1. Demonology. 2. Witchcraft. 3. Magic. 4. Fasting. I. Title. II. His Liber apologeticus. III. His Pseudomonarchia daemonum. IV. Title: Liber apologeticus. V. Title: Pseudomonarchia dae-   monum.
8

Witchcraft
BF 1520 W64 P8++ 1586
Weir, Johann, 1515-1588. De lamiis. Das ist: Von Teuffelsgespenst ... 1586. (Card 4)
reytern. II. His De lamiis--German. III. Rebenstock, Heinrich Peter, tr.
8

Witchcraft
BF 1520 W64 P8 1564
Wier, Johann, 1515-1588.
De praestigiis daemonvm, et incantationibus ac ueneficijs, libri V. recogniti, & ualde aucti ... Accessit index amplissimus. Basileae, Per Ioannem Oporinum, 1564.
565, [58] p. 18cm.
Ex libris Benno Loewy.
I. Title.
8

Witchcraft
BF 1520 W64 P8++ 1586
Wier, Johann, 1515-1588.
De praestigiis daemonvm. Von Teuffelsgespenst, Zauberern vnd Gifftbereytern, Schwartzkünstlern, Hexen vnd Vnholden, darzu jrer Straff, auch von den Bezauberten, vnd wie jhnen zuhelffen sey, ordentlich vnd eigentlich mit sondern Fleiß in VI. Bücher getheilet: darinnen gründlich vnd eigentlich dargethan, was von solchen jeder zeit disputiert, vnd gehalten worden. Erstlich durch D. Johannem Weier in Latein
8
(Continued on next card)

Witchcraft
BF 1520 W64 P8++ 1586
Wier, Johann, 1515-1588.
De lamiis--German.
De lamiis. Das ist: Von Teuffelsgespenst, Zauberern vnd Gifftbereytern, kurtzer doch gründtlicher Bericht ... Sampt einem angehängten kleinen Tractätlein von dem falschen vnd erdichten Fasten ... in vnsere gemeine teutsche Sprach gebracht, durch Henricum Petrum Rebenstoek [sic] am Mayn, Gedruckt durch Nicolaum Basseum, 1586.
6 p. l., 90, [8] p. 34cm.
Title in red and black.
8
(Continued on next card)

Witchcraft
BF 1520 W64 P8 1568
Wier, Johann, 1515-1588.
De praestigiis daemonvm, et incantationibus ac ueneficijs libri sex, aucti & recogniti. Accessit rerum & uerborum copiosus index. (4. ed.) Basileae, Ex Officina Oporiniana, 1568.
697, [55] p. title vignette. 21cm.
Ex libris: Johannes Daniel Crugius; D. Biener; C. F. Illgen; Fletcher & Maude Battershall; Cabalisticis Kurt Seligmann.
Binding: blind stamped pigskin, with clasps, ca. 1590.
8

Witchcraft
BF 1520 W64 P8++ 1586
Wier, Johann, 1515-1588. De praestigiis daemonvm. Von Teuffelsgespenst, Zauberern vnd Gifftbereytern ... 1586. (Card 2)
beschrieben, nachmals von Johanne Fuglino verteutscht, jetzund aber nach dem letzten lateinischen außgangenen Original auffs neuw vbersehen, vnnd mit vielen heilsamen nützlichen Stücken: auch sonderlich hochdienlichen newen Zusätzen, so im Lateinischen nicht gelesen, als im folgenden Blat
8
(Continued on next card)

Witchcraft
BF 1520 W64 P8++ 1586
Wier, Johann, 1515-1588. De lamiis--German.
Wier, Johann, 1515-1588. De lamiis. Das ist: Von Teuffelsgespenst ... 1586. (Card 2)
Originally published 1577 in Latin as an epitome of his De praestigiis daemonum. Cf. Allgemeine deutsche Biographie, v. 42, p. 267.
Bound with his De praestigiis daemonum. Von Teuffelsgespenst, Zauberern vnd Gifftbereytern. Franckfurt am Mayn,
8
(Continued on next card)

WITCHCRAFT
BF 1520 W64 P8 1577a
Wier, Johann, 1515-1588.
Ioannis VVieri De praestigiis daemonum, & incantationibus ac ueneficiis libri sex, postrema editione quinta aucti & recogniti. Accessit Liber apologeticvs, et Psevdomonarchia daemonvm. Cum rerum ac uerborum copioso indice. Basileae, Ex officina Oporiniana, 1577.
934 numbered columns, [34] p. port. 25cm.
Liber apologeticus and Pseudomonarchia each has special t. p.
With colophon.
8

Witchcraft
BF 1520 W64 P8++ 1586
Wier, Johann, 1515-1588. De praestigiis daemonvm. Von Teuffelsgespenst, Zauberern vnd Gifftbereytern ... 1586. (Card 3)
zufinden, so der Bodinus mit gutem Grundt nicht widerlegen kan, durchauß gemehret vnd gebessert. Sampt zu Endt angehencktem newem vnd volkommenem Register. Franckfurt am Mayn, Getruckt durch Nicolaum Basseum, 1586.
12 p. l., 575, [20] p. illus. 34cm.
8
(Continued on next card)

Witchcraft
BF 1520 W64 P8++ 1586
Wier, Johann, 1515-1588. De lamiis. Das ist: Von Teuffelsgespenst ... 1586. (Card 3)
1586.
Binding: blind stamped pigskin, with clasps (one wanting); front cover initialed A K A S H and dated 1589.
1. Demonology. 2. Witchcraft. 3. Magic. 4. Fasting. I. Title: Von Teuffelsgespenst, Zauberern und Gifftbe-
8
(Continued on next card)

Witchcraft
BF 1520 W64 P8+ 1582
Wier, Johann, 1515-1588.
De praestigiis daemonum, & incantationibus ac ueneficiis libri sex, postrema editione sexta aucti & recogniti. Accessit Liber apologeticus, et Pseudomonarchia daemonum. Cum rerum ac uerborum copioso indice. Basileae, Ex Officina Oporiniana, 1583.
934 columns, [35] p. illus., port. 26cm.
Contents of De praestigiis daemonum are
8
(Continued on next card)

Witchcraft
BF 1520 W64 P8++ 1586
Wier, Johann, 1515-1588. De praestigiis daemonvm. Von Teuffelsgespenst, Zauberern vnd Gifftbereytern ... 1586. (Card 4)
Title in red and black.
Includes translations of his Liber apologeticus and Pseudomonarchia daemonum.
With this are bound his De Lamiis. Das ist: Von Teuffelsgespenst ... Franckfort am Mayn, 1586; and Theatrum de veneficis. Franckfurt am Mayn, 1586.
8
(Continued on next card)

CATALOGUE OF THE CORNELL WITCHCRAFT COLLECTION

Witchcraft
BF 1520 W64 P8++ 1586

Wier, Johann, 1515-1588. De praestigiis daemonvm. Von Teuffelsgespenst, Zauberern vnd Gifftbereytern ... 1586. (Card 5)

Binding: blind stamped pigskin, with clasps (one wanting); front cover initialed A K A S H and dated 1589.
1. Demonology. 2. Witchcraft. 3. Magic. 4. Fasting. I. Title: Von Teuffelsgespenst, Zauberern und Gifftbereytern. II. His De praestigiis daemo-

(Continued on next card)

8

Witchcraft
BF 1520 W64 P8++ 1586

Wier, Johann, 1515-1588. De praestigiis daemonvm. Von Teuffelsgespenst, Zauberern vnd Gifftbereytern ... 1586. (Card 6)

num.--German. III. His Liber apologeticus.--German. IV. His Pseudomonarchia daemonum.--German. V. Füglin, Johann, tr.

8

Wier, Johann, 1515-1588.
De praestigiis daemonum.

Witchcraft
BF 1520 W64 P8+ 1582

Wier, Johann, 1515-1588. De lamiis liber: item De commentitiis ieiuniis. Cum rerum ac uerborum copioso indice ... Basileae, Ex Officina Oporiniana, 1582.
138 columns, [7] p. illus., port. 26cm.
Title vignette: device of J. Oporinus.
First published 1577, as an epitome of his De praestigiis daemonum. Cf. Allgemeine deutsche Biographie, v. 42, p. 267.

8

(Continued on next card)

Wier, Johann, 1515-1588.
De praestigiis daemonum.

Witchcraft
BF 1520 W64 P8+ 1582

Wier, Johann, 1515-1588. De lamiis liber ... 1582. (Card 2)

With this is bound his De praestigiis daemonum. Basileae, 1583.
Binding: blind stamped pigskin; front cover initialed B P I and dated 1588.
1. Demonology. 2. Witchcraft. 3. Magic. 4. Fasting. I. His De praestigiis daemonum. II. Title: De lamiis. III. Title: De commentitiis ieiuniis.

8

Wier, Johann, 1515-1588.
De praestigiis daemonum--French.

Witchcraft
BF 1520 W64 P8 1569

Wier, Johann, 1515-1588.
Cinq livres de l'imposture et tromperie des des enchantements et sorcelleries. Pris du latin de Iean Uvier et faits françois par Iaques Gréuin de Clermont en Beauuoisis, médicin à Paris. Paris, Iaques du Puys, 1569.
468, [79] p. 16cm.
Incomplete: t. p. and all before p. 1 wanting.
Title taken from Yve-Plessis, Ro-

8

(Continued on next card)

Wier, Johann, 1515-1588.
De praestigiis daemonum--French.

Witchcraft
BF 1520 W64 P8 1569

Wier, Johann, 1515-1588. Cinq livres de l'imposture et tromperie des diables ... 1569. (Card 2)

bert. Essai d'une bibliographie ... de la sorcellerie, p. 104, no. 832.
A t. p. in G. L. Burr's hand indicates this edition of the work; however, a long note by Burr on facing page claims the edition agrees with no. 833 in Yve-Plessis. But no. 833 consists of 6 books, not 5.

8

(Continued on next card)

Wier, Johann, 1515-1588.
De praestigiis daemonum--French.

Witchcraft
BF 1520 W64 P8 1569

Wier, Johann, 1515-1588. Cinq livres de l'imposture et tromperie des diables ... 1569. (Card 3)

Translation of his De praestigiis daemonum.
1. Demonology. 2. Witchcraft. 3. Magic. 4. Fasting. I. Grévin, Jacques, 1538?-1570, tr. II. His De praestigiis daemonum--French. III. Title. IV. Title: De l'imposture et tromperie des diables.

8

Wier, Johann, 1515-1588.
De praestigiis daemonum--French.

Witchcraft
BF 1520 W64P8 1579

Wier, Johann, 1515-1588.
Histoires, dispvtes et discovrs, des illusions et impostures des diables, des magiciens infames, sorcieres & empoisonneurs: Des ensorcelez & demoniaques, & de la guerison d'iceux: Item de la punition que meritent les magiciens, les empoisonneurs, & les sorcieres. Le tout comprins en six livres ... Devx dialogves de Thomas Erastvs ... touchant le pouuoir des sorcieres: & de la punition qu'elles meritent. Auec deux indices ... [Genève] Povr Iaqves Chovet, 1579.

8

(Continued on next card)

Wier, Johann, 1515-1588.
De praestigiis daemonum--French.

Witchcraft
BF 1520 W64P8 1579

Wier, Johann, 1515-1588. Histoires, dispvtes et discovres, des illusions et impostures des diables ... 1579. (Card 2)

[32], 875, [39] p. 18cm.

Translation of the author's De praestigiis daemonum.
"Devx dialogves de Thomas Erastvs" has special t. p.

8

Wier, Johann, 1515-1588.
De praestigiis daemonum--German.

Witchcraft
BF 1520 W64 P8++ 1586

Wier, Johann, 1515-1588. De praestigiis daemonvm. Von Teuffelsgespenst, Zauberern vnd Gifftbereytern, Schwartzkünstlern, Hexen vnd Vnholden, darzu jrer Straff, auch von den Bezauberten, vnd wie jhnen zuhelffen sey, ordentlich vnd eigentlich mit sonderm Fleiß in VI. Bücher getheilet: darinnen gründlich vnd eigentlich dargethan, was von solchen jeder zeit disputiert, vnd gehalten worden. Erstlich durch D. Johannem Weier in Latein

8

(Continued on next card)

Wier, Johann, 1515-1588.
De praestigiis daemonum--German.

Witchcraft
BF 1520 W64 P8++ 1586

Wier, Johann, 1515-1588. De praestigiis daemonvm. Von Teuffelsgespenst, Zauberern vnd Gifftbereytern ... 1586. (Card 2)

beschrieben, nachmals von Johanne Fuglino verteutscht, jetzund aber nach dem letzten lateinischen auβgangenen Original auffs neuw vbersehen, vnnd mit vielen heilsamen nützlichen Stücken: auch sonderlich hochdienlichen newen Zusätzen, so im Lateinischen nicht gelesen, als im folgenden Blat

8

(Continued on next card)

Witchcraft
BF 1520 W64 P8++ 1586

Wier, Johann, 1515-1588. De praestigiis daemonvm. Von Teuffelsgespenst, Zauberern vnd Gifftbereytern ... 1586. (Card 3)

zufinden, so der Bodinus mit gutem Grundt nicht widerlegen kan, durchauß gemehret vnd gebessert. Sampt zu Endt angehencktem newem vnd volkommenen Register. Franckfurt am Mayn, Getruckt durch Nicolaum Basseum, 1586.
12 p. l., 575, [20] p. illus. 34cm.

8

(Continued on next card)

Wier, Johann, 1515-1588.
De praestigiis daemonum--German.

Witchcraft
BF 1520 W64 P8++ 1586

Wier, Johann, 1515-1588. De praestigiis daemonvm. Von Teuffelsgespenst, Zauberern vnd Gifftbereytern ... 1586. (Card 4)

Title in red and black.
Includes translations of his Liber apologeticus and Pseudomonarchia daemonum.
With this are bound his De Lamiis. Das ist: Von Teuffelsgespenst ... Franckfort am Mayn, 1586; and Theatrum de veneficis. Franckfurt am Mayn, 1586.

8

(Continued on next card)

Wier, Johann, 1515-1588.
De praestigiis daemonum--German.

Witchcraft
BF 1520 W64 P8++ 1586

Wier, Johann, 1515-1588. De praestigiis daemonvm. Von Teuffelsgespenst, Zauberern vnd Gifftbereytern ... 1586. (Card 5)

Binding: blind stamped pigskin, with clasps (one wanting); front cover initialed A K A S H and dated 1589.
1. Demonology. 2. Witchcraft. 3. Magic. 4. Fasting. I. Title: Von Teuffelsgespenst, Zauberern und Gifftbereytern. II. His De praestigiis daemo-

8

(Continued on next card)

Wier, Johann, 1515-1588.
De praestigiis daemonum.

Witchcraft
BF 1520 W64 P83

Eschbach, H
Dr. med. Johannes Wier, der Leibarzt des Herzogs Wilhelm III. von Cleve-Jülich-Berg. Ein Beitrag zur Geschichte der Hexenprozesse.
(In Düsseldorfer Jahrbuch. Beiträge zur Geschichte des Niederrheins. Düsseldorf. 23cm. 1. Band (1886), p. [57]-174)

Witchcraft
BF 1520 W64P8 1579

Wier, Johann, 1515-1588.
Histoires, dispvtes et discovrs, des illusions et impostures des diables, des magiciens infames, sorcieres & empoisonneurs: Des ensorcelez & demoniaques, & de la guerison d'iceux: Item de la punition que meritent les magiciens, les empoisonneurs, & les sorcieres. Le tout comprins en six livres ... Devx dialogves de Thomas Erastvs ... touchant le pouuoir des sorcieres: & de la punition qu'elles meritent. Auec deux indices ... [Genève] Povr Iaqves Chovet, 1579.

(Continued on next card)

Witchcraft
BF 1520 W64P8 1579

Wier, Johann, 1515-1588. Histoires, dispvtes et discovres, des illusions et impostures des diables ... 1579. (Card 2)

[32], 875, [39] p. 18cm.

Translation of the author's De praestigiis daemonum.
"Devx dialogves de Thomas Erastvs" has special t. p.
✓ I. His De praestigiis daemonum.--French.
✓ II. Erastus, Thomas, 1524-1583. ✓ III. Title.

Witchcraft
BF 1520 W64 P8 1885

Wier, Johann, 1515-1588.
Histoires, dispvtes et discovrs des illvsions et impostvres des diables, des magiciens infames, sorcieres et empoissonevrs ... Devx dialogves tovchant le povvoir des sorcieres et de la pvnition qv'elles meritent, par Thomas Erastvs. Avec devx indices. Paris, Aux bureaux du Progrès médical, A. Delahaye et Lecrosnier, 1885.
2 v. front. (port.) 22cm. (Bibliotheque diabolique)
Translation of his De praestigiis daemonum.

603

CATALOGUE OF THE CORNELL WITCHCRAFT COLLECTION

Witchcraft
BF
1520
W64
P8+
1582

Wier, Johann, 1515-1588.
Liber apologeticus.

Wier, Johann, 1515-1588.
De praestigiis daemonum, & incantationibus ac ueneficiis libri sex, postrema editione sexta aucti & recogniti. Accessit Liber apologeticus, et Pseudomonarchia daemonum. Cum rerum ac uerborum copioso indice. Basileae, Ex Officina Oporiniana, 1583.
934 columns, [35] p. illus., port. 26cm.
Contents of De praestigiis daemonum are
8 (Continued on next card)

Witchcraft
BF
1520
W64
P8+
1582

Wier, Johann, 1515-1588.
Liber apologeticus.

Wier, Johann, 1515-1588. De praestigiis daemonum ... 1583. (Card 2)
same as in 5th ed., 1577. Cf. Allgemeine deutsche Biographie, v. 42, p. 267.
Liber apologeticus, and Pseudomonarchia daemonum each with special t. p.
Colophon: Basileae, Ex Officina Oporiniana, per Balthasarvm Han, et Hieronymvm Gemvsaeum, Anno Salutis humanae M. D. LXXXIII mense Augusto.
8 (Continued on next card)

Witchcraft
BF
1520
W64
P8+
1582

Wier, Johann, 1515-1588.
Liber apologeticus.

Wier, Johann, 1515-1588. De praestigiis daemonum ... 1583. (Card 3)
Bound with his De lamiis liber. Basileae, 1582.
Binding: blind stamped pigskin; front covered initialed B P I and dated 1588.
1. Demonology. 2. Witchcraft. 3. Magic. 4. Fasting. I. Title. II. His Liber apologeticus. III. His Pseudomonarchia daemonum. IV. Title: Liber apologeticus. V. Title: Pseudomonarchia daemonum.
8

Witchcraft
BF
1520
W64
P8++
1586

Wier, Johann, 1515-1588.
Liber apologeticus--German.

Wier, Johann, 1515-1588.
De praestigiis daemonvm. Von Teuffelsgespenst, Zauberern vnd Gifftbereytern, Schwartzkünstlern, Hexen vnd Vnholden, darzu jrer Straff, auch von den Bezauberten, vnd wie jhnen zuhelffen sey, ordentlich vnd eigentlich mit sondern Fleiß in VI. Bücher getheilet: darinnen gründlich vnd eigentlich dargethan, was von solchen jeder zeit disputiert, vnd gehalten worden. Erstlich durch D. Johannem Weier in Latein
8 (Continued on next card)

Witchcraft
BF
1520
W64
P8++
1586

Wier, Johann, 1515-1588.
Liber apologeticus--German.

Wier, Johann, 1515-1588. De praestigiis daemonvm. Von Teuffelsgespenst, Zauberern vnd Gifftbereytern ... 1586. (Card 2)
beschrieben, nachmals von Johanne Fuglino verteutscht, jetzund aber nach dem letzten lateinischen außgangenen Original auffs neuw vbersehen, vnnd mit vielen heilsamen nützlichen Stücken: auch sonderlich hochdienlichen newen Zusätzen, so im Lateinischen nicht gelesen, als im folgenden Blat
8 (Continued on next card)

Witchcraft
BF
1520
W64
P8++
1586

Wier, Johann, 1515-1588.
Liber apologeticus--German.

Wier, Johann, 1515-1588. De praestigiis daemonvm. Von Teuffelsgespenst, Zauberern vnd Gifftbereytern ... 1586. (Card 3)
zufinden, so der Bodinus mit gutem Grundt nicht widerlegen kan, durchauß gemehret vnd gebessert. Sampt zu Endt angehencktem newem vnd volkommenen Register. Franckfurt am Mayn, Getruckt durch Nicolaum Basseum, 1586.
12 p. l., 575, [20] p. illus. 34cm.
8 (Continued on next card)

Witchcraft
BF
1520
W64
P8++
1586

Wier, Johann, 1515-1588.
Liber apologeticus--German.

Wier, Johann, 1515-1588. De praestigiis daemonvm. Von Teuffelsgespenst, Zauberern vnd Gifftbereytern ... 1586. (Card 4)
Title in red and black.
Includes translations of his Liber apologeticus and Pseudomonarchia daemonum.
With this are bound his De Lamiis. Das ist: Von Teuffelsgespenst ... Franckfort am Mayn, 1586; and Theatrum de veneficis. Franckfurt am Mayn, 1586.
8 (Continued on next card)

Witchcraft
BF
1520
W64
P8++
1586

Wier, Johann, 1515-1588.
Liber apologeticus--German.

Wier, Johann, 1515-1588. De praestigiis daemonvm. Von Teuffelsgespenst, Zauberern vnd Gifftbereytern ... 1586. (Card 5)
Binding: blind stamped pigskin, with clasps (one wanting); front cover initialed A K A S H and dated 1589.
1. Demonology. 2. Witchcraft. 3. Magic. 4. Fasting. I. Title: Von Teuffelsgespenst, Zauberern und Gifftbereytern. II. His De praestigiis daemo-
8 (Continued on next card)

Witchcraft
BF
1520
W64
P8+
1582

Wier, Johann, 1515-1588.
Pseudomonarchia daemonum.

Wier, Johann, 1515-1588.
De praestigiis daemonum, & incantationibus ac ueneficiis libri sex, postrema editione sexta aucti & recogniti. Accessit Liber apologeticus, et Pseudomonarchia daemonum. Cum rerum ac uerborum copioso indice. Basileae, Ex Officina Oporiniana, 1583.
934 columns, [35] p. illus., port. 26cm.
Contents of De praestigiis daemonum are
8 (Continued on next card)

Witchcraft
BF
1520
W64
P8+
1582

Wier, Johann, 1515-1588.
Pseudomonarchia daemonum.

Wier, Johann, 1515-1588. De praestigiis daemonum ... 1583. (Card 2)
same as in 5th ed., 1577. Cf. Allgemeine deutsche Biographie, v. 42, p. 267.
Liber apologeticus, and Pseudomonarchia daemonum each with special t. p.
Colophon: Basileae, Ex Officina Oporiniana, per Balthasarvm Han, et Hieronymvm Gemvsaeum, Anno Salutis humanae M. D. LXXXIII mense Augusto.
8 (Continued on next card)

Witchcraft
BF
1520
W64
P8+
1582

Wier, Johann, 1515-1588.
Pseudomonarchia daemonum.

Wier, Johann, 1515-1588. De praestigiis daemonum ... 1583. (Card 3)
Bound with his De lamiis liber. Basileae, 1582.
Binding: blind stamped pigskin; front covered initialed B P I and dated 1588.
1. Demonology. 2. Witchcraft. 3. Magic. 4. Fasting. I. Title. II. His Liber apologeticus. III. His Pseudomonarchia daemonum. IV. Title: Liber apologeticus. V. Title: Pseudomonarchia daemonum.
8

Witchcraft
BF
1520
W64
P8++
1586

Wier, Johann, 1515-1588.
Pseudomonarchia daemonum--German.

Wier, Johann, 1515-1588.
De praestigiis daemonvm. Von Teuffelsgespenst, Zauberern vnd Gifftbereytern, Schwartzkünstlern, Hexen vnd Vnholden, darzu jrer Straff, auch von den Bezauberten, vnd wie jhnen zuhelffen sey, ordentlich vnd eigentlich mit sondern Fleiß in VI. Bücher getheilet: darinnen gründlich vnd eigentlich dargethan, was von solchen jeder zeit disputiert, vnd gehalten worden. Erstlich durch D. Johannem Weier in Latein
8 (Continued on next card)

Witchcraft
BF
1520
W64
P8++
1586

Wier, Johann, 1515-1588.
Pseudomonarchia daemonum--German.

Wier, Johann, 1515-1588. De praestigiis daemonvm. Von Teuffelsgespenst, Zauberern vnd Gifftbereytern ... 1586. (Card 2)
beschrieben, nachmals von Johanne Fuglino verteutscht, jetzund aber nach dem letzten lateinischen außgangenen Original auffs neuw vbersehen, vnnd mit vielen heilsamen nützlichen Stücken: auch sonderlich hochdienlichen newen Zusätzen, so im Lateinischen nicht gelesen, als im folgenden Blat
8 (Continued on next card)

Witchcraft
BF
1520
W64
P8++
1586

Wier, Johann, 1515-1588.
Pseudomonarchia daemonum--German.

Wier, Johann, 1515-1588. De praestigiis daemonvm. Von Teuffelsgespenst, Zauberern vnd Gifftbereytern ... 1586. (Card 3)
zufinden, so der Bodinus mit gutem Grundt nicht widerlegen kan, durchauß gemehret vnd gebessert. Sampt zu Endt angehencktem newem vnd volkommenen Register. Franckfurt am Mayn, Getruckt durch Nicolaum Basseum, 1586.
12 p. l., 575, [20] p. illus. 34cm.
8 (Continued on next card)

Witchcraft
BF
1520
W64
P8++
1586

Wier, Johann, 1515-1588.
Pseudomonarchia daemonum--German.

Wier, Johann, 1515-1588. De praestigiis daemonvm. Von Teuffelsgespenst, Zauberern vnd Gifftbereytern ... 1586. (Card 4)
Title in red and black.
Includes translations of his Liber apologeticus and Pseudomonarchia daemonum.
With this are bound his De Lamiis. Das ist: Von Teuffelsgespenst ... Franckfort am Mayn, 1586; and Theatrum de veneficis. Franckfurt am Mayn, 1586.
8 (Continued on next card)

Witchcraft
BF
1520
W64
P8++
1586

Wier, Johann, 1515-1588.
Pseudomonarchia daemonum--German.

Wier, Johann, 1515-1588. De praestigiis daemonvm. Von Teuffelsgespenst, Zauberern vnd Gifftbereytern ... 1586. (Card 5)
Binding: blind stamped pigskin, with clasps (one wanting); front cover initialed A K A S H and dated 1589.
1. Demonology. 2. Witchcraft. 3. Magic. 4. Fasting. I. Title: Von Teuffelsgespenst, Zauberern und Gifftbereytern. II. His De praestigiis daemo-
8 (Continued on next card)

Witchcraft
BF
1520
B66
1698

Wier, Johann, 1515-1588.

Bodin, Jean, 1530-1596.
Daemonomania; oder, Ausführliche Erzehlung des wütenden Teuffels in seinen damahligen rasenden Hexen und Hexenmeistern dero Bezauberungen, Beschwerungen, Vergifftungen, Gauckel- und Possen-Wercke... Welches der andere Theil Nicolai Remigii Daemonolatria. Wobey gleichfalls angehänget: Vielerhand warhaftige und erschreckliche Geschichte besessener Leute...nebst noch einigen betrieglichen und von Menschen
(Continued on next card)

Witchcraft
BF
1520
B66
1698

Wier, Johann, 1515-1588.

Bodin, Jean, 1530-1596. Daemonomania. 1698. (Card 2)
practicirten kurtzweiligen Begenheiten. Hamburg, Gedruckt bey T. von Wiering, 1698.
2 v. in 1. plates. 18cm.
"Wiederlegung nebst der Schrifft des Hn. Weyer": v. 1, p. [400]-465.
Translation of De la démonomanie.

CATALOGUE OF THE CORNELL WITCHCRAFT COLLECTION

Wier, Johann, 1515-1588.

Witchcraft
R
512
W64
B61
1896

Binz, Carl, 1832-1913.
Doctor Johann Weyer: ein rheinischer Arzt, der erste Bekämpfer des Hexenwahns. Ein Beitrag zur Geschichte der Aufklärung und der Heilkunde. 2., umgearb. u. verm. Aufl. Mit dem Bildnisse Johann Weyers. Berlin, A. Hirschwald, 1896.
vii, 189 p. port. 24cm.

8

Wier, Johann, 1515-1588.

WITCHCRAFT
BF
1520
B66
1598

Bodin, Jean, 1530-1596. La demonomanie des sorciers ... 1598. (Card 2)

First published under title: De la demonomanie des sorciers.

1. Demonomania. 2. Witchcraft. 3. Magic. 4. Wier, Johann, 1515-1588. I. His De la démonomanie des sorciers. II. Title.

8

Wigand, Paul, 1786-1866.

Witchcraft
BF
1566
W65

Denkwürdigkeiten für deutsche Staats-wissenschaft.
Wigand, Paul, 1786-1866.
Die Hexenprozesse, und das Einschreiten des Kammergerichts gegen die dabei eingerissenen Misbräuche. [Leipzig, J. B. Hirschfeld, 1854]
[297]-339 p. 24cm.

Chapter X of the author's Denkwürdigkeiten für deutsche Staats- und Rechtswissenschaft, für rechtsalterthümer.

Wier, Johann, 1515-1588.

Witchcraft
R
512
W64
B612

Binz, Carl, 1832-1913.
Doctor Johann Weyer. (1515-1588) Eine Nachlese. [Düsseldorf, Gedruckt bei E. Voss] 1889.
36 p. facsim. 23cm.
"Sonderabdruck aus dem 24. Band der Zeitschrift des Bergischen Geschichtsvereins."
Includes further discussion of the question raised in his Wier oder Weyer? [Düsseldorf, 1887]

Wier, Johann, 1515-1588.

Witchcraft
BF
1563
E92++
no. 4-6

Die ersten Bekämpfer des Hexenwahns. München, C. Wolf, 1897.
[321]-323, [329]-331, 338-339 p. 32cm. (Deutscher Merkur, 28. Jahrg., No. 41-43)

A review of Binz. Doktor Johann Weyer, der erste Bekämpfer des Hexenwahns.

Witchcraft
BF
1555
W65

Wigand, Paul, 1786-1866.
Epidemie der vom Teufel Besessenen. 44. Criminal-Prozess gegen Besessene, und Untersuchung, ob sie wirklich vom Teufel besessen seinen, oder nicht. 1664 und 1666. [Leipzig, S. Hirzel, 1854]
[320]-339 p. 23cm.
Caption title.
Detached from Denkwürdigkeiten, Kap. XI.

1. Demoniac possession. 2. Witchcraft--Germany. I. Title. II. Title: Criminal-Prozess gegen Besessene ... 1664 und 1666.

Wier, Johann, 1515-1588.

Witchcraft
R
512
W64
B618

Binz, Carl, 1832-1913.
Wier oder Weyer? Nachträgliches über den ersten Bekämpfer des Hexenwahns in Deutschland. [Düsseldorf, 1877]
11 p. 23cm.
"Sonderabdruck aus: Beiträge zur Geschichte des Niederrheins, Band II."
In ms. on t. p.: Sent me by Dr. Binz himself, Nov. 1890. G. L. B[urr]

Wier, Johann, 1515-1588.

Witchcraft
BF
1520
W64
P83

Eschbach, H
Dr. med. Johannes Wier, der Leibarzt des Herzogs Wilhelm III. von Cleve-Jülich-Berg. Ein Beitrag zur Geschichte der Hexenprozesse. (In Düsseldorfer Jahrbuch. Beiträge zur Geschichte des Niederrheins. Düsseldorf. 23cm. 1. Band (1886), p. [57]-174)

Witchcraft
BF
1566
W65

Wigand, Paul, 1786-1866.
Die Hexenprozesse, und das Einschreiten des Kammergerichts gegen die dabei eingerissenen Misbräuche. [Leipzig, J. B. Hirschfeld, 1854]
[297]-339 p. 24cm.

Chapter X of the author's Denkwürdigkeiten für deutsche Staats- und Rechtswissenschaft, für rechtsalterthümer.

I. His Denkwürdigkeiten für deutsche Staats- und Rechtswissenschaft, für Rechtsalterthümer. II. Title.

Wier, Johann, 1515-1588.

Witchcraft
BF
1520
B66
1593

Bodin, Jean, 1530-1596.
De la demonomanie des sorciers. A Monseignevr M. Chrestofle de Thou ... Seigneur de Coeli ... Par I. Bodin Angevin. Lyon, Povr P. Frellon et A. Cloqvemin, 1593.
604 p. 17cm.

"Réfutation des opinions de Jean Wier": p. 522-604.

1. Wier, Johann, 1515-1588. II. Title.

Wier, Johann, 1515-1588.

BF
1569
Z69

Zilboorg, Gregory, 1890–
... The medical man and the witch during the renaissance, by Gregory Zilboorg ... Baltimore, The Johns Hopkins press, 1935.
x, 215 p. front. (port.) illus., plates. 20½ᶜᵐ. (Publications of the Institute of the history of medicine, the Johns Hopkins university. 3d ser., vol. II)
"The Hideyo Noguchi lectures."
Contents.—The physiological and psychological aspects of the Malleus maleficarum (The witch's hammer)—Medicine and the witch in the sixteenth century—Johann Weyer, the founder of modern psychiatry.
1. Witchcraft. 2. Psychology, Pathological. 3. Institoris, Henricus, d. ca. 1500. Malleus maleficarum. 4. Sprenger, Jakob, fl. 1494, joint author. Malleus maleficarum. 5. Wier, Johann, 1515-1588. 6. Renaissance. I. Title.

Library of Congress   BF1569.Z5   35—12004
— Copy 2.
Copyright A 84565   [40n1]   [150.00140002] 133.40002

Witchcraft
BF
1583
Z7
1554

Wigand, Paul, 1786-1866.
Zur Geschichte der Hexenprocesse. 1) Ein Hexenprocess vor dem Criminalgericht zu Horn im Fürstenthum Lippe. 1554. [Leipzig, S. Hirzel, 1854]
[248]-259 p. 24cm.
Caption title.
Detached from his Denkwürdigkeiten, Kap. VIII.

1. Trials (Witchcraft)--Horn, Germany.
2. Trials (Witchcraft)--Germany. I. Title. II. Title: Ein Hexenprocess vor dem Criminalgericht zu Horn im Fürstenthum Lippe.

WITCHCRAFT
BF
1520
B66
1592

Bodin, Jean, 1530-1596.
Demonomania de gli stregoni, cioè Fvrori, et malie de' demoni, col mezo de gl'hvomini: Diuisa in libri IIII. Di Gio. Bodino Francese, tradotta dal K.ʳ Hercole Cato ... Di nuouo purgata, & ricorretta. Venetia, Presso Aldo, 1592.
26 p. l., 419 p. 22cm.
"Confvtatione delle opinioni di Giovanni VVier": p. [360]-419.
Translation of De la démonomanie.

8

(Continued on next card)

Wier oder Weyer?

Witchcraft
R
512
W64
B618

Binz, Carl, 1832-1913.
Wier oder Weyer? Nachträgliches über den ersten Bekämpfer des Hexenwahns in Deutschland [Düsseldorf, 1877]
11 p. 23cm.
"Sonderabdruck aus: Beiträge zur Geschichte des Niederrheins, Band II."
In ms. on t. p.: Sent me by Dr. Binz himself, Nov. 1890. G. L. B[urr]

Wijk, Joannes van, supposed author.

Witchcraft
BX
9479
B42
B11
no.14

Brief, aan een heer, waar in uyt de H. Schrift getoond werd, dat'er is een quade geest, die een redelijk schepsel is buyten de ziel des mensche. Met eenige aanmerking over het boek, De ware oorspronk, voort en ondergank des Satans. Door I. W. Amsterdam, By J. de Veer gedruckt, 1696.
64 p. title vignette, illus. initial. 20 x 15cm.
4°: A-H⁴.
Probably by Joannes van Wijk.
Supports Balthasar Bekker in the controversy over his De beto verde weereld.
No.14 in vol. lettered B. Bekkers sterfbed en andere tractaten.

WITCHCRAFT
BF
1520
B66
1598

Bodin, Jean, 1530-1596.
La demonomanie des sorciers. Par I. Bodin angevin. Reueuë & corrigee d'vne infinité de fautes qui se sont passees és precedentes impressions. Auec vn indice des choses les plus remarquables contenuës en ce liure. Edition derniere. Paris, Chez Estienne Prevosteav, 1598.
604, [31] p. 15cm.
"Refvtation des opinions de Iean Wier": p. 523-604.

8

(Continued on next card)

Wierus, Joannes, 1515-1588.

see

Wier, Johann, 1515-1588.

Wilcken, Hermann, 1522-1603.

see

Witekind, Hermann, 1522-1603.

CATALOGUE OF THE CORNELL WITCHCRAFT COLLECTION

Witchcraft
PT 2430
M35S5+
1893
Wilde, Jane Francesca (Elgee) lady, 1826-1896, tr.
Meinhold, Wilhelm, 1797-1851.
Sidonia the sorceress, translated by Francesca Speranza Lady Wilde. [Hammersmith, Eng., Kelmscott Press, 1893]
xiv, 455 p. 30cm.

Translation of Sidonia von Bork, die Klosterhexe.

WITCHCRAFT
PT 2430
M35
S5
1894
Wilde, Jane Francesca (Elgee) lady, 1826-1896, tr.
Meinhold, Wilhelm, 1797-1851.
Sidonia, the sorceress, the supposed destroyer of the whole reigning ducal house of Pomerania, translated by Lady Wilde; Mary Schweidler, the amber witch... London, Reeves and Turner, 1894.
2 v. 20cm.

Translation of Sidonia von Bork, die Klosterhexe, and Maria Schweidler, die Bernsteinhexe.
(Continued on next card)

Witchcraft
PT 2430
M35
S5
1894
Wilde, Jane Francesca (Elgee) lady, 1826-1896, tr.
Meinhold, Wilhelm, 1797-1851. Sidonia, the sorceress... 1894. (Card 2)

"Mary Schweidler" translated by Lady Duff Gordon.

1. Witchcraft--Pomerania. I. Meinhold, Wilhelm, 1797-1851. Sidonia von Bork, die Klosterhexe--English. II. Meinhold, Wilhelm, 1797-1851. Maria Schweidler, die Bernsteinhexe--English. III. Wilde, Jane Francesca (Elgee) lady, 1826-1896, tr. IV. Duff-Gordon, Lucie (Austin) lady, 1821-1869, tr. V. Title: Sidonia, the sorceress. VI. Title: Mary Schweidler, the amber witch.

WITCHCRAFT
R
133
P72
Wildenhayn, Joannes Guilielmus, b. 1751.
Plaz, Anton Wilhelm, 1708-1784.
Procancellarius D. Antonius Guilielmus Plaz Panegyrin medicam...indicit et de magiae vanitate iterum disserit. [Lipsiae, Ex officina Langenhemia, 1777]
xvi p. 24cm.

Introductory to a diss. for which Gehler acted as praeses Wildenhayn as respondent: De praeceptore medico.

Bound with his: Procancellarius D. Antonius Guilielmus Plaz Panegyrin medicam...in dicit et de magiae vanitate prolusi one prima praefatur.1777.
8
NIC
(Continued on next card)

RARE
HV
8593
D611
no.2
Wildvogel, Christian, 1644-1728, praeses.
Dissertationem juridicam inauguralem De arbitrio judicis circa torturam, quam... sub praesidio Dn. Christiani Wildvogelii.. submittit Iohann Iacob Arnold. Jenae, Litteris Müllerianis [1710]
54 p. 21cm.

Diss.--Jena (J. J. Arnold, respondent)
No. 2 in a vol. lettered: Dissertationes de tortura, 1697-1770.
1. Torture. I. Arnold, Johann Jacob, respondent. II. Title.

WITCHCRAFT
K
B816++
1582
Wilhelm Friedrich, Margrave of Brandenburg-Ansbach, 1685-1723.
Brandenburg-Ansbach (Principality) Laws, statutes, etc.
Neue Ordnung des Durchläuchtigsten Fürsten und Herrn, Herrn Wilhelm Friederich, Marggrafens zu Brandenburg ... Wie es in Criminal- und peinl. Sachen mit denen gütlichen und peinlichen Verhören, und inquisitorialischen Untersuchungen ... und sonsten mit denen Verurtheilten in dem Brandenburg-Onolzbachischen Fürstenthum und Landen des Burggrafthums Nürnberg unterhalb Gebürgs
8
NIC
(Continued on next card)

WITCHCRAFT
K
B816++
1582
Wilhelm Friedrich, Margrave of Brandenburg-Ansbach, 1685-1723.
Brandenburg-Ansbach (Principality) Laws, statutes, etc. Neue Ordnung ... 1720. (Card 2)

gehalten werden solle. Onolzbach, Gedruckt bey J. V. Lüders, 1720.
34 p. 31cm.
Bound with Brandenburg (Electorate) Laws, statutes, etc. Peinliche Halsgerichts-Ordnung. Ansbach? 1582.
8
NIC
(Continued on next card)

Witchcraft
BF
1583
W67
Wilhelm, , Dr., of Diepholz, ed.
Hexenprozesse aus dem 17. Jahrhundert. Mit höherer Genehmigung aus dem Archiv des Königlich Hannoverschen Amtsgerichts Diepholz mitgetheilt von dem Amtsrichter Dr. Wilhelm zu Diepholz. Hannover, Klindworth, 1862.
91 p. 22cm.
1. Trials (Witchcraft)--Diepholz, Germany. 2. Trials (Witchcraft)--Germany. I. Title.

PT
2430
M35M37
Wilhelm Meinhold's Bernsteinhexe: a study in witchcraft and cultural history.
Rysan, Josef, 1914-
Wilhelm Meinhold's Bernsteinhexe: a study in witchcraft and cultural history. Chicago, 1948.
iii l.,182 p. 23cm.

Thesis--Univ. of Chicago.
"Selected bibliography": p. 178-182.

WITCHCRAFT
BF
1555
H97
1799
Wilhelm Perry.
Hutchinson, Francis, bp. of Down and Connor, 1660-1739.
Wilhelm Perry; oder: Der besessene Knabe. Ein Beitrag zu den Teufelsbesitzungen unsers Zeitalters. [Leipzig?] 1799.
16 p. 19cm.
Illustrative title vignette.
"Ein Auszug aus Hutchinsons historischem Versuche über die Hexerey. Lpz. 1727": translation of Historical essay concerning witchcraft.
8
NIC
(Continued on next card)

DA
670
L2
H28
Wilkinson, T. T., joint author.
Harland, John, 1806-1868.
Lancashire legends, traditions, pageants, sports, etc., with an appendix containing a rare tract on the Lancashire witches, etc. etc., by J. Harland and T. T. Wilkinson. London, G. Routledge, 1873.
xxxv. 283 p. illus. 20cm.

1. Lancashire, Eng.--Soc. life & custom. 2. Folk-lore--England--Lancashire. I. Wilkinson, T. T., joint author. II. Title.

Witchcraft
BF
1575
W69
1869
[Willard, Samuel] 1640-1707.
Some miscellany observations on our present debates respecting witchcrafts, in a dialogue between S. & B. By P. E. and J. A. [pseud.] Philadelphia, Printed by W. Bradford, for H. Usher. 1692. Boston, 1869.
24 p. 23cm. ("Congregational quarterly" reprint, no. 1)

No. 6 of an edition of 100 copies.

1. Witchcraft. I. E., P. II. A., J. III. Title.

Witchcraft
F
74
G88
G794
Willard, Samuel, 1640-1707.
Green, Samuel Abbott, 1830-1918.
Groton in the witchcraft times. By Samuel A. Green, M. D. Groton, Mass. [J. Wilson and son, Cambridge] 1883.
29 p. 24cm.
"A briefe account of a strange & unusuall providence of God befallen to Elizabeth Knap of Groton. p me Samll Willard": p. 7-21.
8
NIC

BX
9339
P44
B11
William Perkins: eene bijdrage tot de kennis der religieuse ontwikkeling in Engeland.
Baarsel, Jan Jacobus van.
William Perkins: eene bijdrage tot de kennis der religieuse ontwikkeling in Engeland, ten tijde van Koningin Elisabeth. 's-Gravenhage, H. P. de Swart [1912]
321 p. illus. 25cm.

1. Perkins, William, 1558-1602.

Witchcraft
BF
1566
W72
1941
Williams, Charles, 1886-1945.
Witchcraft, by Charles Williams. London, Faber and Faber limited [1941]
3 p. l., 9-316 p. 22½cm.

"First published in March Mcmxii."

1. Witchcraft. I. Title.
[Full name: Charles Walter Stansby Williams]

Witchcraft
BF
1566
W725
Williams, Howard, 1837-
The superstitions of witchcraft. London, Longmans, Green, Longman, Roberts & Green, 1865.
xi,278 p. 21cm.

1. Witchcraft. I. Title.

Witchcraft
BF
1563
T86
Williford, Joane, d. 1645.
The examination, confession, triall, and execution, of Joane Williford, Joan Cariden, and Jane Hott, who were executed at Feversham in Kent, for being witches, on Munday the 29 of September 1645... Taken by the major of Feversham and jurors for the said inquest. With the examination and confession of Elizabeth Harris, not yet executed. All attested under the hand of Robert Greenstreet, major of Feversham. London, Printed for J. G., 1645.
(Continued on next card)

Witchcraft
BF
1563
T86
Williford, Joane, d. 1645.
The examination, confession, triall, and execution ... 1645. (Card 2)

6 p. 19cm.

No. 5 in vol. lettered: Tracts of witches.

CATALOGUE OF THE CORNELL WITCHCRAFT COLLECTION

Willimot, Joanne, d. 1618.

Witchcraft
BF
1563
T75
The Wonderfvl discoverie of the witchcrafts of Margaret and Phillip[pa] Flower, daughters of Joan Flower neere Beuer Castle ... Together with the seuerall examinations and confessions of Anne Baker, Ioan Willimot, and Ellen Greene, witches in Leicestershire. London, Printed by G. Eld for I Barnes, 1619. [Greenwich, Reprinted by H. S. Richardson, ca. 1840]
26 p. title vignettes. 23cm.

8
(Continued on next card)

Willimot, Joanne, d. 1618.

Witchcraft
BF
1563
T75
The Wonderfvl discoverie of the witchcrafts of Margaret and Phillip[pa] Flower ... [1840] (Card 2)

The examinations of Anne Baker, Ioanne Willimot, and Ellen Greene has special t. p. No. 4 in vol. lettered Tracts on witchcraft.

8

BF
1429
W74
Wilson, Colin, 1931-
The occult: a history, by Colin Wilson. New York, Random House [c1971]
601 p. illus. 24cm.   4

1. Occult sciences. 2. Witchcraft. I. Title.

Winckler, Jacob Benedict, respondent.

Witchcraft
BF
1565
M53
Mencken, Lüder, praeses.
Commentationem ad titulum codicis De mathematicis maleficis et ceteris similibus praeside Lüdero Menckenio ... excutiendam publice proponet auctor et respondens Jacob. Benedictus Wincklerus ... Lipsiae, Literis I. Titii [1725]
72 p. 20cm.

1. Witchcraft. 2. Trials (Witchcraft) I. Winckler, Jacob Benedict, respondent. II. Title: De mathematicis maleficis et ceteris sim ilibus.

8

WITCHCRAFT
BF
1583
Z7
1628
Winkler, C
Die Hexenprozesse in Türkheim in den Jahren 1628-1630. Nach den Originalprotokolen der Stadt Türkheim. Gegeben von C. Winkler. Hiezu mehrere Ansichten der auf die Prozesse bezüglichen Lokalitäten und der Marterinstrumente. [Colmar, Buchdruckerei F. Waldmeyer, 1904]
45 p. illus. 23cm.

8
1. Trials (Witchcraft)--Türkheim. 2. Trials (Witchcraft)--Alsace. I. Title.

Witchcraft
BF
1584
E7
W77
Winkler, R
Über Hexenwahn und Hexenprozesse in Estland während der Schwedenherrschaft. Von Probst R. Winkler (Reval).
(In Baltische Monatsschrift. Riga. 24cm. 67. Bd., Jahrg. 51, Heft 5 (1909), p. [321]-355)
1. Trials (Witchcraft)--Estonia. I. Title. II. Title: Hexenwahn und Hexenprozesse in Estland während der Schwedenherrschaft. III. Baltische Monatsschrift, Riga.

8

F
61
M427
v.6
no.14
Winsor, Justin, 1831-1897.
The literature of witchcraft in New England. By Justin Winsor. Worcester, Mass., Printed by C. Hamilton, 1896.
25 p. 25cm.

Reprinted, one hundred copies, from the Proceedings of the American Antiquarian Society, October, 1895.

1. Witchcraft--New England--Bibliography. I. Title.

Witchcraft
BF
1548
W78
Winterbottom, Vera.
The devil in Lancashire. With drawings and cover design by Barbara Tomlinson. [Stockport, Heaton Mersey, Eng., Cloister Press, 1962]
87 p. illus. 23cm.

1. Devil. 2. Witchcraft--Lancashire, Eng. I. Title.

Wintherus, Severinus, respondent.

WITCHCRAFT
BS
2745
.3
M39
Masius, Hector Gottfried, 1653-1709.
Hectoris Gothofr. Masii ... Disputatio theologica De doctrina daemoniorum ex I. Timoth. IV. v. 1 & seq. In abstinentiâ ab esu carnis potissimum monstratâ. Qvam respondente M. Severino Winthero, publicae disquisitioni exposuit ad 3. April. 1699. Wittebergae, Sumptibus A. Haeberi, 1709.
39 p. 20cm.
1. Bible. N.T. 1 Timothy IV--Criticism, interpretation, etc. 2. Heresy. I. Wintherus, Severinus, respondent.
8   II. Title: De doctrina daemoniorum.

Witchcraft
BF
1530
W79
Winzer, Julius Friedrich.
De daemonologia in sacris Novi Testamenti libris proposita. Commentatio prima. Scripsit ... pro licentia svmmos in theologia honores capessendi ... sine praeside ... pvblice defendet Ivlivs Fridericvs Winzer ... Vitebergae, Literis C. H. Graessleri [1812]
57 p. 22cm.
Diss.--Wittenberg.
With this is bound his De daemonologia ... Commentatio secvnda. Vitebergae [1813]
1. Demonology. 2. Bible. N.T.--Theology. I. Title.

8

Witchcraft
BF
1530
W79
Winzer, Julius Friedrich.
De daemonologia in sacris Novi Testamenti libris proposita. Commentatio secvnda. Qva ad aviendam orationem aditialem ... recitandam hvmanissime invitat D. Ivlivs Fridericvs Winzer ... Vitebergae, Literis C. H. Graessleri [1813]
22 p. 22cm.
Bound with his De daemonologia ... Commentatio prima. Vitebergae [1812]
1. Demonology. 2. Bible--N.T.--Theology. I. Title.

8

Winzer, Maria, d. 1657.

Witchcraft
BF
1583
Z7
1657
Hexenprocess zu Cösitz in Sachsen, vom J. 1657. Aus den in der Registratur zu Cösitz noch befindlichen Original Acten.
(In Stats-Anzeigen. Göttingen. 20cm. IV. Bd., Heft 15 (1784), p. 287-293)

At head of title: 33.

MSS
Bd.
WITCHCRAFT
BF
W792++
Wirz, Bernhard, d. 1705, defendant.
Processus wegen des vermeinten Gespengsts in dem Antistitio. [Zürich, 1705]
402 p., [22] l. 34cm.

Manuscript, on paper, in a German hand. According to G. L. Burr, probably the transcript of the court record.
Bound in parchment.

1. Trials (Witchcraft)--Zürich. 2. Trials (Malicious mi schief)--Zürich. I. Klingler, Ant on K., 1649-1713, plaintiff. II. Title.

The wisdom of our ancestors.

Witchcraft
PR
4712
G14
W8
1830
Gaspey, Thomas, 1788-1871.
The witch-finder; or, The wisdom of our ancestors. London, H. Lea [183-?]

I. Title. II. Title: The wisdom of our ancestors.

The witch.

PS
2142
W8
Johnston, Mary, 1870-1936.
The witch, by Mary Johnston. Boston and New York, Houghton Mifflin company, 1914.
v, [1]p., 1 l., 441, [1] p., 1 l. incl. col. front. 19½cm.

I. Title.

The witch-cult in western Europe.

WITCHCRAFT
BF
1566
M98W8
Murray, Margaret Alice.
The witch-cult in western Europe; a study in anthropology, by Margaret Alice Murray. Oxford, Clarendon press, 1921.
303, [1] p. 23cm.
Bibliography: p. [281]-285.
Bibliographical foot-notes.
"The mass of existing material on the subject is so great that I have not attempted to make a survey of the whole of European witchcraft, but have confined myself to an intensive study of the cult in Great Bri tain."--Pref.
Same. An other copy.

BF
1566
W81
The Witch figure; folklore essays by a group of scholars in England honouring the 75th birthday of Katharine M. Briggs. Edited by Venetia Newall. London, Boston, Routledge & Kegan Paul [1973]
xiii, 239 p. illus. 23 cm.
Includes bibliographical references.
CONTENTS.--Michaelis-Jena, R. Katharine M. Briggs.--Blacker, C. Animal witchcraft in Japan.--Davidson, H. R. E. Hostile magic in the Icelandic sagas.--Dean-Smith, M. The ominous wood.--Grinsell, L. V. Witchcraft at some prehistoric sites.--Hole, C. Some instances of image-magic in Great Britain.--New all, V. The Jew as a witch figure. --Parrinder, G. The witch as vict im.--Ross, A. The
NIC SEP 17,'74 COOxc See next card

BF
1566
W81
The Witch figure; ... [1973] (Card 2)
divine hag of the pagan Celts.-- Simpson, J. Olaf Tryggvason versus the powers of darkness.--White, B. Cain's kin.--Widdowson, J. The witch as a frightening and threatening figure.-- Publications by Katharine M. Briggs (p 221)

1. Witchcraft--Addresses, essays, lectures. 2. Magic--Addresses, essays, lectures. 3. Briggs, Katharine Mary. I. Briggs, Katharine Mary. II. Newall, Venetia, ed.

NIC SEP 17,'74 COOxc 73-83077

CATALOGUE OF THE CORNELL WITCHCRAFT COLLECTION

Witchcraft
PR
4712
G14
W8
1830
The witch-finder.
Gaspey, Thomas, 1788-1871.
The witch-finder; or, The wisdom of our ancestors. London, H. Lea [183-?]

I. Title. II. Title: The wisdom of our ancestors.

Witchcraft
BF
1576
M94
Witch Hill.
Mudge, Zachariah Atwell, 1813-1888.
Witch Hill: a history of Salem witchcraft. Including illustrative sketches of persons and places. By Rev. Z. A. Mudge ... Three illustrations. New York, Carlton & Lanahan; San Francisco, E. Thomas; etc., etc., 1780.
322 p. incl. front., 2 pl. 18cm.

WITCHCRAFT
F
74
S1
P96+

8
NIC
Witch House, Salem, Mass.
Proclamation concerning what is said to be the oldest dwelling house in Salem Massachusetts: the Witch House, which is to be restored as it was in the year 1692 and to be retained as an everlasting monument to the courageous men who broke the shackles of theocratic authority and paved the way for that freedom of thought which has made this country great. [Salem? Mass., 1945?]
2 l. illus. 30cm.
Probably issued by Historic Salem, Inc. (Continued on next card)

Witchcraft
Z
987
B96
1902
A witch-hunter in the book-shops.
Burr, George Lincoln, 1857-1938.
A witch-hunter in the book-shops. [n.p., 1902]
[16] p. facsims. 25cm.

"Reprinted from The bibliographer, December 1902."

1. Book collecting. 2. Libraries, Private. 3. Witchcraft-- Bibl. I. Title.

Witchcraft
BF
1581
E94
W8
1929
Witch hunting and witch trials; the indictments for witchcraft from the records of 1373 assizes
Ewen, Cecil Henry L'Estrange, 1877- ed.
Witch hunting and witch trials; the indictments for witchcraft from the records of 1373 assizes held for the home circuit A.D. 1559-1736, collected and edited by C. L'Estrange Ewen, with an introduction. New York, L. MacVeagh, The Dial Press, 1929.
xiii, 345 p. front., plates, facsims., diagrs. 23cm.

"Appendix I. Essex gaol delivery
(Continued on next card)

Witchcraft
BF
1581
E94
W8
1929
Witch hunting and witch trials; the indictments for witchcraft from the records of 1373 assizes ...
Ewen, Cecil Henry L'Estrange, 1877- ed.
Witch hunting and witch trials... 1929. (Card 2)

roll, summer 1645": 1 folded leaf inserted.
"Volumes relating to witchcraft in England ... most useful for reference": p. ix-x.

1. Witchcraft. 2. Criminal law--Great Britain. 3. Criminal procedure--Great Britain. I. Great Britain. Courts of assize and nisi prius. II. Title.

BF
1583
M62
Witch hunting in southwestern Germany.
Midelfort, H Christian Erik.
Witch hunting in southwestern Germany, 1562-1684; the social and intellectual foundations [by] H. C. Erik Midelfort. Stanford, Calif., Stanford University Press, 1972.
viii, 306 p. illus. 24 cm. $11.50
Bibliography: p. [261]-300.

1. Witchcraft—Germany. 2. Trials (Witchcraft)—Germany. I. Title.

BF1583.M5   914.3'4'033   75-151891
ISBN 0-8047-0805-3   ♭ ABC
Library of Congress   72 [4]

R
133
A92
"Witch" murder trial, York, Pa.
Aurand, Ammon Monroe, 1895-
The "pow-wow" book; a treatise on the art of "healing by prayer" and "laying on of hands", etc., practiced by the Pennsylvania-Germans and others; testimonials; remarkable recoveries; popular superstitions; etc., including an account of the famous "witch" murder trial, at York, Pa., by A. Monroe Aurand, jr. ... containing also the complete collection of remedies and cures in John George Hohman's "Pow-wows, or Long lost friend"; in popular use since 1820. Harrisburg, Pa., Priv. print. by The Aurand press, 1929.
x, 85, [1], 31, [1], xi, 13-64 p. incl. front., illus. 24cm.
(Continued on next card)

R
133
A92
"Witch" murder trial, York, Pa.
Aurand, Ammon Monroe, 1895- The "pow-wow" book ... 1929. (Card 2)
"An account of the 'witch' murder trial" ... and "John George Hohman's Pow-wows; or, Long lost friend" have special title-pages and pagination.
"Pow-wows; or Long lost friend" was published in 1819 under title: Der lange verborgene freund, oder: Getreuer und christlicher unterricht für jedermann.
"This edition of the 'Pow-wow' book is limited to one thousand copies; one hundred signed by the author. This is no. 309."
Bibliography: p. vi.
1. Medicine, Magic, mystic, and spagiric. 2. Superstition. 3. Folklore—Pennsylvania. 4. Witchcraft—Pennsylvania. 5. Blymyer, John H. 6. Rehmeyer, Nelson D., 1868-1928. I. Hohman, Johann Georg. II. Title: "Witch" murder trial, York, Pa.

Library of Congress   R133.A8   29-9468 Revised
------ Copy 2.
Copyright A 7294   [d2]

Witchcraft
BF
1578
B66
"Witch" murder trial, York, Pa., January 7-9, 1929.
Blymyer, John H   defendant.
An account of the "witch" murder trial, York, Pa., January 7-9, 1929. Commonwealth of Pennsylvania vs. John Blymyer, et al. By A. Monroe Aurand, jr. ... Harrisburg, Pa., Priv. print. by the Aurand press, 1929.
31 p. 23½cm.

1. Rehmeyer, Nelson D., 1868-1928. 2. Witchcraft—Pennsylvania. I. Aurand, Ammon Monroe, 1895- II. Title: "Witch" murder trial, York, Pa., January 7-9, 1929. III. Title.

Library of Congress   29-23242
------ Copy 2.
Copyright A 4228   [2]

Witchcraft
BF
1565
O11
1736
The witch of Endor.
[Oates, Titus] 1649-1705.
The witch of Endor: or, A plea for the divine administration by the agency of good and evil spirits. Written some years ago at the request of a lady; and now reprinted with a prefatory discourse, humbly addressed to the House of C-----s, who brought in their bill (Jan. 27) for repealing the statute of 1. Jac. cap. 12, concerning witchcraft. ... London, Printed and sold by J. Millan, 1736.
L, 102 p. 20cm.

Witchcraft
BF
1581
W819
The Witch of Inverness and the fairies of Tomnahurich ... Inverness, J. Noble, 1891.
48 p. 19cm.

Attributed to Joseph Train.

1. Witchcraft--Scotland. 2. Folk-lore--Scotland. I. Train, Joseph, 1779-1852, supposed author.

Witchcraft
BF
1775
B63
The witch of Monzie.
Blair, George.
The holocaust; or, The witch of Monzie, a poem illustrative of the cruelties of superstition. Lays of Palestine and other poems. To which is prefixed, Enchantment disenchanted; or, A treatise on superstition. ... London, J. F. Shaw, 1845.
xii, 277 p. 20cm.

1. Superstition. I. Title. II. Title: The witch of Monzie. III. Title: Lays of Palestine. IV. Title: Enchantment disenchanted.

Witchcraft
PS
2459
M985
W8
The witch of Salem.
Musick, John Roy, 1849-1901.
The witch of Salem; or, Credulity run mad. By John R. Musick ... illustrations by F. A. Carter. New York [etc.] Funk & Wagnalls company, 1893.
viii, 392 p. front., illus., plates, ports. 19cm. (On cover: Columbian historical novels [v. 7])
"Designed to cover twenty years in the history of the United States ... from 1680 to 1700, including all the principal features of this period."

1. Witchcraft--New England--Fiction. 2. U. S.--Hist.--Colonial period--Fiction. I. Title.

Library of Congress   23.F973W7   7-33323†

Witchcraft
BF
1581
Z7
1712d
The witch of Walkerne.
Bragge, Francis.
The witch of Walkerne. Being, I. A full and impartial account of the discovery of sorcery and witchcraft, practis'd by Jane Wenham of Walkerne in Hertfordshire ... II. Witchcraft farther display'd. Containing an account of the witchcraft practis'd by Jane Wenham, since her condemnation, etc. ... III. A defense of the proceedings against Jane Wenham ... In answer to two pamphlets, entituled, 1. The impossibility of witchcraft. 2. A full confutation of
(Continued on next card)

Witchcraft
BF
1581
Z7
1712d
The witch of Walkerne.
Bragge, Francis. The witch of Walkerne ... (Card 2)

witchcraft. IV. A general preface to the whole. 5th ed. London, Printed for E. Curll, 1712.
3 pts. in 1 v. 20cm.

Parts 2 and 3 have special title pages.

1. Witchcraft--England. 2. Wenham, Jane, d. 1730. I. Title.

Witchcraft
BF
1581
Z7
1652a
The Witch of Wapping; or, An exact and perfect relation of the life and devilish practises of Joan Peterson, who dwelt in Spruce Island, near Wapping; who was condemned for practising witch-craft, and sentenced to be hanged at Tyburn, on Munday the 11th [sic] of April, 1652 ... Together with the confession of Prudence Lee, who was burnt in Smithfield on Saturday the 10th. ... for the murthering her husband ... London, Printed for Th. Spring, 1652.
8 p. 20cm.
(Continued on next card)

Witchcraft
BF
1581
Z7
1652a
The Witch of Wapping ... 1652. (Card 2)

With this is bound A declaration in answer to several lying pamphlets concerning the witch of Wapping ... London, 1652.
With book-plate of Francis Freeling.

✓1. Peterson, Joan, d. 1652. 2. Lee, Prudence, d. 1652.

CATALOGUE OF THE CORNELL WITCHCRAFT COLLECTION

The witch-persecutions.

Witchcraft
BF
1565
B96

Burr, George Lincoln, 1857-1938.
The witch-persecutions. Philadelphia, Dept. of History, Univ. of Pennsylvania, 1897.
cover-title, 36 p. 22cm. (Translations and reprints from the original sources of European history, v. III, no. 4, [1896])

With this is bound a revised ed. of the above, 1903.

1. Witchcraft-- Hist. I. Title.

Witchcraft Witch stories.
BF
1581
L76
1883

Linton, Elizabeth (Lynn) 1822-1898, comp.
Witch stories. A new ed. London, Chatto & Windus, 1883.
320 p. 17cm.

Contents.--Preface.--The witches of Scotland.--The witches of England.

1. Witchcraft. I. Title.

Witch-trials in Massachusetts.

WITCHCRAFT
BF
1576
M82
G641+

Goodell, Abner Cheney, 1831-1914.
[Additional considerations on the history of witchcraft in Massachusetts]

(In: Massachusetts Historical Society. Proceedings. Boston. 26cm. Jan./Mar.1884. p.65-71)
Running title: Witch-trials in Massachusetts.
With this, in same issue, are: Moore, George Henry. Supplementary notes on witchcraft in Massachusetts; and Goodell's Reasons for concluding that the act of 1711 became a law.

8
NIC

(Continued on next card)

Witch-trials in Massachusetts.

WITCHCRAFT
BF
1576
M82
G64+

Goodell, Abner Cheney, 1831-1914.
[Further notes on the history of witchcraft in Massachusetts]

(In: Massachusetts Historical Society. Proceedings. Boston. 26cm. June 1883. p. 280-326)
Running title: Witch-trials in Massachusetts.
Reply to George Henry Moore's Notes on the history of witchcraft in Massachusetts.

8
NIC

(Continued on next card)

Witch, warlock, and magician.

Witchcraft
BF
1581
A22

Adams, William Henry Davenport, 1828-1891.
Witch, warlock, and magician. Historical sketches of magic and witchcraft in England and Scotland, by W. H. Davenport Adams ... London, Chatto & Windus, 1889.
vi p., 1 l., 428 p. 23cm.

Witchcraft--Bibliography.

Witchcraft
Z
987
B96
1902

Burr, George Lincoln, 1857-1938.
A witch-hunter in the book-shops. [n.p., 1902]
[16] p. facsims. 25cm.

"Reprinted from The bibliographer, December 1902."

1. Book collecting. 2. Libraries, Private. 3. Witchcraft-- Bibl. I. Title.

Witchcraft--Bibliography.

Witchcraft
Z
6878
W8G54+

Glasgow. University. Hunterian Library.
An exhibition of books on witchcraft and demonology. January-March, 1966.
[Glasgow? 1966]
24 p. 26cm.

1. Witchcraft--Exhibitions.
2. Witchcraft--Bibl. I. Title.

Witchcraft--Bibliography.

Witchcraft
BF
1547
H36

Hauber, Eberhard David, 1695-1765.
Bibliotheca, acta et scripta magica. Gründliche Nachrichten und Urtheile von solchen Büchern und Handlungen, welche die Macht des Teufels in leiblichen Dingen betreffen ... Lemgo, Gedruckt bey J. H. Meyer, 1738-45.
36 pts. in 3 v. plates (part fold.) ports. 18cm.

Vol.[1]: 1. Stück. 2. und verbesserter Druck. 1739.
For detailed contents see J. G. T. Grässe:

(Continued on next card)

Witchcraft--Bibliography.

Witchcraft
BF
1547
H36

Hauber, Eberhard David, 1695-1765. Bibliotheca, acta et scripta magica ... 1738-45. (Card 2)

Bibliotheca magica, p. 118-130.

1. Devil. 2. Devil--Bibl. 3. Witchcraft. 4. Witchcraft--Bibl. 5. Occult sciences. I. Title.

Witchcraft--Bibliography.

Z
2771
B58
fasc.5
pt.5
no.2

Heinemann, Franz, 1870-
Inquisition, Intoleranz, Exkommunikation, Interdikt, Index, Zensur. Sektenwesen, Hexenwahn und Hexenprozesse, Rechtsanschauungen. Bern, K. J. Wyss, 1908-09.
2 v. in 1. 22cm. (His Kulturgeschichte und Volkskunde (Folklore) der Schweiz, Heft 2)

Bibliographie der schweizerischen Landeskunde, Fasc. V5.

Witchcraft--Bibliography.

Witchcraft
BF
1575
C23
H75

Holmes, Thomas James, 1874-
Cotton Mather and his writings on witchcraft. [Chicago, Univ. of Chicago Press, 1926]
29 p. 25cm.

"Reprinted for private distribution from Papers of the Bibliographical Society of America, vol. XVIII, Parts 1 and 2."
Bound with his The surreptitious printing of one of Cotton Mather's manuscripts.
1. Mather, Cotton, 1663-1728--Bibl.
2. Witchcraft --Bibl. I. Title.

Witchcraft--Bibliography.

Rare
Z
6878
P8
P94

Price, Harry, 1881-1948, compiler.
Short-title catalogue of works on psychical research, spiritualism, magic, psychology, legerdemain and other methods of deception, charlatanism, witchcraft, and technical works for the scientific investigation of alleged abnormal phenomena, from circa 1450 A. D. to 1929 A. D.

(In National Laboratory of Psychical Research, London. Proceedings. London. 25cm. v. 1 (1929) pt. 2, p. 67-422)

(over)

Witchcraft--Bibliography.

Witchcraft
BF
1520
W43

Weissenbach, Joseph Anton.
Transactiones diabolicae, ubi omnia malorum spirituum, quae nunc veniunt in contentionem, citra gratiam, clamorem, odium componuntur. In usus parochorum scripsit Dr. Jos. Ant. Weissenbach, canonicus Duraquensis. Basileae, Typis E. Thurneysen, 1786.
160 p. 17cm.
With interesting bibliography, p. 148-160.
1. Demonology. 2. Witchcraft. I. Title.

8

Witchcraft--Bibliography.

Witchcraft
Z
6878
W8
Y98

Yve-Plessis, R[obert]
...Essai d'une bibliographie française méthodique & raisonnée de la sorcellerie et de la possession démoniaque; pour servir de suite et de complément à la Bibliotheca magica de Graesse, aux catalogues Sépher, Ouvaroff, D'Ourches et Guldenstubbe, S. de Guaita et aux divers travaux partiels publiés sur cette matière. Préface par Albert de Rochas. Paris, Bibliothèque Chacornac, 1900.
xiv p., 1 l., 254, [1] p. front., facsims., plates. 25cm.
"Il a été tiré de cet ouvrage : 10 exemplaires sur papier de Hollande et 500 exemplaires sur papier ordinaire, tous numérotés et paraphés. No. 13."
1,793 titles, classified.
1. Witchcraft--Bibl. 2. Occult sciences--Bibl.
I. Grässe, Johann Georg Theodor, 1814-1885. Bibliotheca magica et pneumatica. II. Title.
Library of Congress, no. Z6878.W8Y8.

Witchcraft--Bibliography.

Witchcraft
BF
1565
S83
Z97

[Zapf, Georg Wilhelm] 1747-1810.
Zauberbibliothek. [München] 1776.
91 p. 19cm.

Based on annotated bibliography of the Gassner and Sterzinger controversies which first appeared in Allgemeine deutsche Bibliothek, Berlin, 1775-76. [BF 1565 S83 Z98] CUL holdings noted in ms. in text.
1. Sterzinger, Ferdinand, 1721-1786. 2. Gassner, Johann Joseph, 1727-1779. 3. Witchcraft-- Bibl. I. Title.

8

Witchcraft--Bibliography.

Witchcraft
BF
1565
S83
Z98

Zauberbibliothek. 1775-1776. [Berlin, 1775-76]
various pagings. 20cm.
Title from spine.
Consists of three sections detached from Allgemeine deutsche Bibliothek, titled: Zauberey; Teufeleyen; and Teufeleyen. Eine Fortsetzung der vorigen.
1. Sterzinger, Ferdinand, 1721-1786. 2. Gassner, Johann Joseph, 1727-1779. 3. Witchcraft--Bibl.

8

Witchcraft--Bibliography--Catalogs.

Witchcraft
Z
6880
Z9B66

Bodin, Lucien, bookseller, Paris.
Catalogue de livres d'occasion anciens et modernes relatifs aux sciences occultes et philosophiques.
Paris.
nos. 24cm.

1. Occult sciences--Bibl.--Catalogs.
2. Witchcraft-- Bibl.--Catalogs.
I. Title.

Witchcraft--Bibliography--Catalogs.

Witchcraft
Z
6878
W8
G64

Goodell, Abner Cheney, 1831-1914.
... Catalogue of the private library of the late Abner C. Goodell, Salem, Mass. ... Pt. II, P to Z and witchcraft collection, including Prince Society publications, Prynne's tracts, rare Quaker tracts ... valuable collection of books relating to witchcraft and demonology... Boston, C. F. Libbie, book and art auctioneers, 1918.
[93]-174 p. illus., facsims. 25cm.
At head of title: Auction sale: ... March 12th, 1918 ...
1. Witchcraft --Bibl.--Cat. I. Libbie, firm, auctioneers, Boston. II. Title.

CATALOGUE OF THE CORNELL WITCHCRAFT COLLECTION

```
Witchcraft--Bibliography--Catalogs.
Witchcraft
Z           Heberle, J       M
6880          Culturgeschichte und Curiositäten in
Z9          Druckschriften, fliegenden Blättern,
C35         Bildern, Autographen und Monumenten. Aus
no.2        den Sammlungen von Heinrich Lempertz...
            Zu beigesetzten Preisen vorräthig auf dem
            Bücher- und Kunstlager von J. M. Heberle
            (H. Lempertz' Söhne) in Cöln. Abth. E:
            Physiognomik, Phrenologie, Mimik, natürliche
            Magie, Kunststücke, Alchymie, etc. ... Abth.
            F: Zauberei           und Hexerei, Faust,
            Cagliostro,           Teufelswesen und
                        (Continued on next card)
```

```
Witchcraft--Bibliography--Catalogs.
Witchcraft
Z           Heberle, J       M
6880          Culturgeschichte und Curiositäten...
Z9          [1874?]                    (Card 2)
C35         Beschwörungen, Besessensein, etc. ...
no.2        Cöln, Steven's Druckerei [1874?]
            64 p. 23cm.
            At head of title: Nro. 74.
            No. 2 in vol. lettered: Catalogues of
            books on magic and witchcraft.
                1. Occult      sciences--Bibl.--
                Catalogs.   2. Witchcraft--Bibl.--
                Catalogs.   3. Magic--Bibl.--
                Catalogs.
```

```
                 Witchcraft--Bibliography--Catalogs.
WITCHCRAFT
Z           Kirchhoff & Wigand, Leipzig.
6880           Culturgeschichte, Curiosa, Facetiae,
Z9C35       ältere deutsche etc. Literatur, Vermischtes
no.3        ... enthaltend auch die alten Sammlungen des
            ... Nationalökonomen Johann Georg Büsch über
            Hexen, Dämonologie, Alchemie und Geheime
            Wissenschaften im allgemeinen. New-York,
            G.E. Stechert [1885]
               72 p. 23cm.
            At head of     title: Nr. 743.
            No. 3 in       vol. lettered:
                         (Continued on next card)
```

```
                 Witchcraft--Bibliography--Catalogs.
WITCHCRAFT
Z           Kirchhoff & Wigand, Leipzig.  Culturge-
6880        schichte, Curiosa, Facetiae, ältere
Z9C35       deutsche etc. Literatur, Vermischtes ...
no.3        [1885]                    (Card 2)
            Catalogues of books on magic and witchcraft.
                1. Bibliography--Rare books. 2. Occult
            sciences--Bibl.--Catalogs. 3. Witchcraft--
            Bibl.--Catalogs. I. Title.
```

```
Witchcraft        Witchcraft--Bibliography--Catalogs.
Z           Redway, George, London.
6880          List of books on theosophy, archaeology,
Z9C35       astrology, mesmerism, philology, spiritualism,
no.6        freemasonry, alchemy, platonism, thought-read-
            ing, magic, the Rosicrucians, witchcraft, etc.
            by Fludd, Behmen, Paracelsus, Agrippa, Nostra-
            damus, Van Helmont, & others.   [London, 1885]
               16 p. 23cm.
            At head of title: No. 11, 1885.
            No. 6 in vol. lettered: Catalogues of books
            on magic and witchcraft.
```

```
              Witchcraft--Bibliography--Catalogs.
Witchcraft
Z           Rosenthal, Ludwig, Munich.
              Bibliotheca magica et pneumatica. Geheime
            Wissenschaften, Magie, gute und böse Geister,
            Gespenster, Volksaberglauben; Hexen und Hexen-
            processe ... Ellwangen, L. Weil [188-?]
               148 p. 23cm.
            "Katalog 45."
            No. 1 in vol. lettered: Catalogues of books
            on magic and witchcraft.
```

```
          Witchcraft--Dictionaries--English.
BF          Robbins, Rossell Hope, 1912-
1503          The encyclopedia of witchcraft and demonology. New
R63+        York, Crown Publishers [1959]
               571 p. illus. 26 cm.
               Includes bibliography.

               1. Witchcraft—Dictionaries—English. 2. Demonology—Diction-
            aries—English. I. Title.

            BF1503.R6             133.403           59-9155 ‡
            Library of Congress   [30]
```

```
                  Witchcraft--Fiction.
Witchcraft
PT          Zeipel, Carl von
9850          Karl XI. [i.e., der Elfte], Rabenius und
Z47         der Hexenprozess. Historischer Roman von
1846        Carl von Zeipel. Aus dem Schwedischen über-
            setzt von G. Fink. Stuttgart, Franckh,
            1846.
               2 v. in 1. 14cm. (Das belletristische
            Ausland, hrsg. Carl Spindler, 671.-679. Bd.)
               1. Rabenius, Nils, 1648-1717. 2. Witch-
            craft--Fiction. 3. Karl XI, King of Sweden,
8           1655-1697--Fict    ion. I. Title.
```

```
            Witchcraft--New England--Bibliography.
F           Winsor, Justin, 1831-1897.
61            The literature of witchcraft in New England.
M427        By Justin Winsor. Worcester, Mass., Printed by
v.6         C. Hamilton, 1896.
no.14         25 p. 25cm.
            Reprinted, one hundred copies, from the
            Proceedings of the American Antiquarian
            Society, October, 1895.
```

```
               Witchcraft--Scotland--Bibliography.
Witchcraft
Z           Ferguson, John, 1837-1916.
6878          Bibliographical notes on the witchcraft
W8          literature of Scotland.
F35            (In The Edinburgh Bibliographical Society.
            [Publications] Session 1896-97. Edinburgh.
            25cm. v. 3 (1897) p. [37]-124)
```

```
Witchcraft        Witchcraft--U. S.--Bibliography.
Z           New York. Public library.
6878          List of works in the New York public library relating
W8          to witchcraft in the United States. Comp. by George F.
N531+       Black, of the Lenox staff. [New York, 1908]
1908           18 p. 26 cm.
               Caption title.
               "Reprinted from the Bulletin, November, 1908."
               At end: 40 titles of works not in the library.

               1. Witchcraft—U. S.—Bibl.   I. Black, George Fraser, 1866-
            II. Title.
                                              CA 9—2852 Unrev'd
            Library of Congress       Z6878.W8N6
```

```
                  Witchcraft.
BF          Hart, Roger.
1566          Witchcraft. London, Wayland Publishers [1971]
H32            128 p. illus., facsims., port. 24 cm. index. (The Wayland docu-
            mentary history series)                            B 71–14448
               Bibliography: p. 128.

               1. Witchcraft.   I. Title.
            BF1566.H37            133.4'094        73–599830
            ISBN 0-85340-150-0                       MARC
            Library of Congress    71 [2]
```

```
                  Witchcraft.
BF          Rosen, Barbara, comp.
1581          Witchcraft. New York, Taplinger [1972, c1969]
R81            xii, 407 p. illus. 23 cm. (The Stratford-upon-Avon library 6)
1972        $9.95
               Bibliography: p. [385]-391.

4              1. Witchcraft—England.   I. Title.
            BF1581.R6 1972         133.4'0942      74-179662
            ISBN 0-8008-8372-1                       MARC
            Library of Congress     72 [4]
```

```
                  Witchcraft.
BF          Williams, Charles, 1886-1945.
1566          Witchcraft, by Charles Williams. London,
W72         Faber and Faber limited [1941]
1941           3 p. l., 9-316 p. 22½cm.
               "First published in March Mcmxii."
```

```
               Witchcraft and black magic.
Witchcraft
BF          Summers, Montague, 1880-1948.
1566          Witchcraft and black magic. London,
S95         Rider [1958]
1958           228 p. illus. 24cm.
```

```
               Witchcraft and Christianity.
Witchcraft
BL          [Doughty, Henry Montagu]
490           Witchcraft and Christianity. [Edinburgh,
D73         1898]
               378-397 p. 24cm.
               Extract from Blackwood's Edinburgh
            magazine, vol. 163, March 1898.

               1. Superstition. I. Title.
```

```
            witchcraft and demonianism; a concise ac-
            count derived from sworn depositions and
Witchcraft  confessions obtained in the courts of
BF          Ewen, Cecil Henry L'Estrange, 1877-   England and Wales.
1581          Witchcraft and demonianism; a concise
E94         account derived from sworn depositions and
            confessions obtained in the courts of England
            and Wales, by C. L'Estrange Ewen ... with
            eight contemporary illustrations. London,
            Heath, Cranton, limited, 1933.
               495 p. front., plates, port., facsims.,
            fold. tab. 23cm.
               With autogr     aph: Geo. L. Burr.
               1. Witcher     aft. 2. Demonology.
```

```
            Witchcraft and demonology in Scott's
Witchcraft  fiction.
PR          Parsons, Coleman Oscar.
5343          Witchcraft and demonology in Scott's
W8P26       fiction. With chapters on the super-
            natural in Scottish literature.
            Edinburgh and London, Oliver & Boyd, 1964.
               x,363 p. 25cm.

               1. Scott, Sir Walter, bart., 1771-
            1832. 2. Witchcraft. 3. Demonology.
            I. Title.
```

CATALOGUE OF THE CORNELL WITCHCRAFT COLLECTION

Witchcraft and devil lore in the Channel Islands.

Witchcraft
BF
1581
P69

Pitts, John Linwood.
Witchcraft and devil lore in the Channel Islands. Transcripts from the official records of the Guernsey Royal Court, with an English translation and historical introduction. By John Linwood Pitts ... Guernsey, Guille-Allès library and T. M. Bichard, printer to the states, 1886.
40 p. 22cm. (Guille-Allès Library series)

8
1. Trials (Witchcraft)--Channel Islands. 2. Channel Islands--Hist. I. Title.

Witchcraft and magic; a catalogue of books relating to witchcraft ...

Witchcraft
Z
6878
W8
M19

Maggs Bros., London.
Witchcraft and magic; a catalogue of books relating to witchcraft, magic, necromancy, ghosts and apparitions, dreams, astrology, occult, prophecies, and strange happenings. London, 1969.
38 p. illus. 23cm. (Its catalogue 921)

8
NIC
1. Witchcraft--Bibl.--Catalogs. 2. Magic--Bibl.--Catalogs. I. Title.

Witchcraft and medicine (1484-1793)

Witchcraft
BF
1565
N43+

Nemec, Jaroslav, 1910-
Witchcraft and medicine (1484-1793) [Washington] National Institutes of Health, 1974.
10 p. illus. 26cm. (NIH publication 74-636)
"Published in conjunction with an exhibit at the National Library of Medicine, March 25-July 19, 1974."

8
NIC
1. Witchcraft--Hist. 2. Medicine. I. Title. II. United States. National Library of Medicine.

Witchcraft & second sight in the Highlands & islands of Scotland.

Witchcraft
BF
1581
C18

Campbell, John Gregerson, 1836-1891.
Witchcraft & second sight in the Highlands & islands of Scotland; tales and traditions collected entirely from oral sources. Glasgow, J. MacLehose, 1902.
xii, 314 p. 21 p.

1. Witchcraft. 2. Second sight. 3. Folk-lore--Scotland. I. Title.

Witchcraft and sorcery.

BF
1563
M39

Marwick, Max, comp.
Witchcraft and sorcery; selected readings, edited by Max Marwick. [Harmondsworth, Eng., Baltimore, Md.] Penguin Books [1970]
416 p. 18 cm. (Penguin modern sociology readings) $1.95 (U.S.)
Includes bibliographies.

1. Witchcraft--Collections. I. Title.

4
BF1563.M3 1970   133.4'08   70-18967
ISBN 0-14-080155-3   MARC
Library of Congress   70 [2]

Witchcraft and the black art.

Witchcraft
F
566
63

Wickwar, John William.
Witchcraft and the black art: a book dealing with the psychology and folklore of the witches, by J. W. Wickwar ... London, H. Jenkins limited [1925?]
320 p. 19cm.

"Second printing completing 6,500 copies."

Witchcraft and the evil eye in Guernsey.

DA
670
G9
G93
no.3

Dewar, Stephen.
Witchcraft and the evil eye in Guernsey. Guernsey, Toucan P., 1968.
12 p. illus. 19 cm. (Guernsey historical monographs, no. 3)
2/6
Bibliography: p. 12.   (B 68-14255)

1. Witchcraft--Guernsey. 2. Evil eye. I. Title.
DA670.G9G85 no. 3   133.4   72-354498
Library of Congress   69 [1₈]

Witchcraft
BF
1563
T75

Witchcraft at Maldon, Essex, in 1579.
[Great Totham, Essex, Printed at C. Clark's private press, ca. 1840]
2 numbered leaves. 23cm.

Caption title.
Extract from A detection of damnable driftes ...
No. 2 in vol. lettered Tracts on witchcraft.

8
1. Smithe, Elleine. I. A detection of damnable driftes.

Witchcraft at Salem.

BF
1576
H24

Hansen, Chadwick, 1926-
Witchcraft at Salem. New York, G. Braziller [1969]
xvii, 252 p. 22 cm. 6.95
Includes bibliographical references.

1. Witchcraft--Salem, Mass. I. Title.
BF1576.H26   133.4   69-15825
                              MARC
Library of Congress

Witchcraft cast out from the religious seed and Israel of God.

Witchcraft
BF
1565
F23

[Farnworth, Richard]
Witchcraft cast out from the religious seed and Israel of God. And the black art of nicromancery, inchantments, sorcerers, wizards ... Also some things to clear the truth from reproaches, lies and slanders ... occasioned by Daniel Bott... Written in Warwickshire, the ninth moneth, 1654. As a judgement upon witchcraft, and a deniall, testimony and declaration against witchcraft, from those that the world
(Continued on next card)

Witchcraft cast out from the religious seed and Israel of God.

Witchcraft
BF
1565
F23

[Farnworth, Richard] Witchcraft cast out from the religious seed and Israel of God. 1655.
(Card 2)

reproachfully calleth Quakers. London, Printed for G. Calvert, 1655.
20 p. 20cm.

With book-plate of Francis Freeling.

The witchcraft delusion at Salem in 1692.

Witchcraft
BF
1411
T35

Thacher, James, 1754-1844.
An essay on demonology, ghosts, and apparitions, and popular superstitions. Also, an account of the witchcraft delusion at Salem in 1692 ... Boston, Carter and Hendee, 1831.
234 p. 18cm.

The witchcraft delusion in colonial Connecticut 1647-1697.

Witchcraft
BF
1576
T24

Taylor, John Metcalf, 1845-1918.
The witchcraft delusion in colonial Connecticut 1647-1697. New York, The Grafton Press [c1908]
xv, 172 p. facsim. 20cm. (The Grafton historical series)

The witchcraft delusion in New England.

Witchcraft
BF
1575
D76

Drake, Samuel Gardner, 1798-1875, comp.
The witchcraft delusion in New England; its rise, progress, and termination, as exhibited by Dr. Cotton Mather, in The wonders of the invisible world; and by Mr. Robert Calef, in his More wonders of the invisible world. With a preface, introduction, and notes, by Samuel G. Drake ... Roxbury, Mass., Printed for W. E. Woodward, 1866.
3 v. 21½x17cm. (Half-title: Woodward's historical series, no. V-VII)
No. 89 of an "edition in this size" of 280 copies.
(Continued on next card)

The witchcraft delusion in New England.

Witchcraft
BF
1575
D76

Drake, Samuel Gardner, 1798-1875, comp. The witchcraft delusion in New England. 1866.
(Card 2)

Includes reprints of original title-pages.
Contents.--v.1. The wonders of the invisible world ... By Cotton Mather. v.2-3. More wonders of the invisible world ... Collected by Robert Calef.

The witchcraft delusion of 1692.

Witchcraft
F
7
H97
1870

Hutchinson, Thomas, 1711-1780.
The witchcraft delusion of 1692, by Gov. Thomas Hutchinson. From an unpublished manuscript (an early draft of his History of Massachusetts) in the Massachusetts archives. With notes by William Frederick Poole. Boston, Priv. print., 1870.
43 p. 25cm.
"Reprinted from the New-England historical and genealogical register for October, 1870."

1. Witchcraft--New England. I. Poole, William Frederick, 1821-1894. II. Title.
                                                                5-2279
Library of Congress   F7.H97

Witchcraft: European and African.

Witchcraft
BF
1566
P26

Parrinder, Edward Geoffrey.
Witchcraft: European and African. London, Faber and Faber [1963]
215 p. 23 cm.

1. Witchcraft. 2. Witchcraft--Africa. I. Title.
BF1566.P3   133.9   63—4000 ‡
Library of Congress   [63f3]

Witchcraft farther display'd.

WITCHCRAFT
BF
1581
Z7
1712b

[Bragge, Francis]
Witchcraft farther display'd. Containing I. An account of the witchcraft practis'd by Jane Wenham of Walkerne, in Hertfordshire, since her condemnation, upon the bodies of Anne Thorn and Anne Street. II. An answer to the most general objections against the being and power of witches: with some remarks upon the case of Jane Wenham in particular, and on Mr. Justice Powel's procedure therein. To which are added, the tryals of Florence
8   (Continued on next card)

CATALOGUE OF THE CORNELL WITCHCRAFT COLLECTION

Witchcraft farther display'd.

WITCHCRAFT
BF
1581
Z7
1712b

[Bragge, Francis] Witchcraft farther display'd ... (Card 2)
Newton, a famous Irish witch, at the assizes held at Cork, anno 1661; as also of two witches at assizes held at Bury St. Edmonds in Suffolk, anno 1664, before Sir Matthew Hale ... who were found guildty and executed. London, Printed for E. Curll, 1712.
2 p. l., 39 p. 19cm.
Introduction signed: F. B.
Bound with A Full confutation of witchcraft. London, 1712.
8 (Continued on next card)

Witchcraft illustrated.

WITCHCRAFT
BF
1566
K49

Kimball, Mrs. Henrietta D.
Witchcraft illustrated. Witchcraft to be understood. Facts, theories and incidents. With a glance at old and new Salem and its historical resources. By Mrs. Henrietta D. Kimball. Boston, G. A. Kimball, 1892.
135 p. plates, ports. 20cm.

1. Witchcraft. 2. Salem, Mass.--Description. I. Title.

8
NIC
Library of Congress   5-21280

Witchcraft in Devon.

Witchcraft
BL
305
A79

Articles on mythology, etc. [v.p., 1871-1880]
1 v. (various pagings) 25cm.
Cover-title.
Articles reprinted from Contemporary review and Nineteenth century, with one from Once a week.
Contents.--On the philosophy of mythology, by Max Müller.--Germanic mythology, by Karl Blind.--The first sin, by François Lenormant.--The myths of the sea and the river of
(Continued on next card)

Witchcraft in Devon.

Witchcraft
BL
305
A79

Articles on mythology, etc. 1871-1880.
(Card 2)
Contents--Continued.
death, by C. F. Keary.--Wind myths, by C. F. Keary.--Forest and field myths, by W. R. S. Ralston.--Cinderella, by W. R. S. Ralston.--Demonology of the New Testament, by J. J. Owen.--Demoniacal possession in India, by W. Knighton.--Demonolatry, devil-dancing, and demoniacal possession, by R. C. Caldwell.--Witchcraft in Devon.

Witchcraft in England.

BF
1581
H72

Hole, Christina
Witchcraft in England, by Christina Hole, illustrated by Mervyn Peake. London, B. T. Batsford ltd. [1945]
167, [1] p. front., illus., plates, ports. 22½cm.
"First published spring, 1945."
Bibliography: p. 161-165.

1. Witchcraft--England. I. Title.

45-4819
Library of Congress   BF1581.H6
[3]   133.40942

Witchcraft in England.

Witchcraft
BF
1581
L63+

Lesley, Peter D
Witchcraft in England: a study of the beliefs and of the predisposition to believe. [Middletown, Conn.?] 1967.
vi, 161 l. 29cm.
Thesis--Wesleyan University, Middletown, Conn.

1. Witchcraft--England. I. Title.

Witchcraft in England from 1558 to 1718

Witchcraft
BF
1581
A2
N91
1965

Notestein, Wallace, 1879-
A history of witchcraft in England from 1558 to 1718. New York, Russell & Russell, 1965.
xiv, 442 p. 23cm. (Prize essays of the American Historical Association)

"Awarded the Herbert Baxter Adams prize in European history for 1909."

1. Witchcraft--England. I. Title: Witchcraft in England from 1558 to 1718. II. Series: American Historical Association. Prize essays, 1909. III. Title.

Witchcraft in Europe, 1100-1700.

BF
1566
K84

Kors, Alan C, comp.
Witchcraft in Europe, 1100-1700; a documentary history. Edited with an introd., by Alan C. Kors and Edward Peters. Philadelphia, University of Pennsylvania Press [1972]
viii, 382 p. illus. 25 cm.
Includes bibliographical references.

1. Witchcraft--Europe--History--Sources. I. Peters, Edward M., joint comp. II. Title

NIC   NOV 15,'73   [?]xc   71-170267

Witchcraft in Ireland.

BF
1581
B99

Byrne, Patrick F
Witchcraft in Ireland, by Patrick F. Byrne. Cork, Mercier Press [1967]
75 p. 18cm. (A Mercier original paperback)

1. Witchcraft--Ireland. I. Title.

Witchcraft in Kenmore, 1730-57: extracts from the kirk session records of the parish.

Witchcraft
BF
1581
A2C55

Christie, John, comp.
Witchcraft in Kenmore, 1730-57: extracts from the kirk session records of the parish. Aberfeldy, D. Cameron, 1893.
19 p. 19cm.

1. Witchcraft--Kenmore (Scotland) I. Church of Scotland. Presbytery of Kenmore. II. Title.

Witchcraft in Maryland.

Witchcraft
BF
1577
M3
P23

Parke, Francis Neal.
Witchcraft in Maryland, by Francis Neal Parke. [Baltimore?] 1937.
cover-title, 50 p. 25cm.

"A paper read in part before the Round table and the Maryland historical society, and published in part in the Maryland historical magazine of December, 1936."
With autograph: Joseph Foster.

Witchcraft in Massachusetts.

WITCHCRAFT
BF
1576
M821
G64+
1884

Goodell, Abner Cheney, 1831-1914.
Reasons for concluding that the act of 1711, [reversing the attainders of the persons convicted of witchcraft in Massachusetts in the year 1692, became a law. Being a reply to Supplementary notes, etc. by George H. Moore. Cambridge, J. Wilson, 1884.
21 p. 26cm.
2 copies

Originally appeared in the Proceedings of the Massachusetts Historical Society, Jan./Mar. 1884.

8
NIC (Continued on next card)

Witchcraft in Massachusetts.

WITCHCRAFT
BF
1576
M821
G64+
1884

Goodell, Abner Cheney, 1831-1914. Reasons for concluding that the act of 1711... became a law...1884. (Card 2)

Caption title: Witchcraft in Massachusetts. (Running title of original article: History of witchcraft in Massachusetts)

1. Witchcraft--Massachusetts. 2. Moore, George Henry, 1823-1892. Supplementary notes on witchcraft... I. His Witchcraft in Massachusetts. II. Title: Witchcraft in Massachusetts. III. His History of witchcraft in Massachusetts. IV. Title: History of witchcraft in Massachusetts. V. Title.

Witchcraft in Massachusetts.

WITCHCRAFT
BF
1576
M821+
1884

Moore, George Henry, 1823-1892.
Supplementary notes on witchcraft in Massachusetts; a critical examination of the alleged law of 1711 for reversing the attainders of the witches of 1692. Cambridge, J. Wilson, 1884.
25 p. facsim. 26cm.
2 copies

Reprinted from the Proceedings of the Massachusetts Historical Society, Mar.1884.
Caption title: Witchcraft in Massachusetts. (Running title of original article: History of witchcraft in Massachusetts)

8
NIC   (Continued on next card)

Witchcraft in Massachusetts.

WITCHCRAFT
BF
1576
M821+
1884

Moore, George Henry, 1823-1892. Supplementary notes on witchcraft...1884. (Card 2)

Continues his Notes on the history of witchcraft in Massachusetts. Continued by his Final notes on witchcraft in Massachusetts.

1. Witchcraft--Massachusetts. 2. Goodell, Abner Cheney, 1831-1914. Further notes on the history of witchcraft... I. Title. II. His Witchcraft in Massachusetts. III. Title: Witchcraft in Massachusetts. IV. His History of witchcraft in Massachusetts. V. Title: History of witchcraft in Massachusetts.

Witchcraft
BF
1581
A2
W81
1866

Witchcraft in Northamptonshire.--1470-1850.
[Northampton, Taylor & son, 187-]
7 v. in 1. facsims. 23cm.
Title on spine.
Facsimile reproductions of tracts dating 1612, collected by John Taylor, and published in his series of "Rare and curious tracts illustrative of the history of Northamptonshire."
Contents.--Curious account of the remarkable case of the Duchess of Bedford.--

8
(Continued on next card)

Witchcraft
BF
1581
A2
W81
1866
1870.

Witchcraft in Northamptonshire.--1470-1850. (Card 2)

Contents. Continued.
The witches of Northamptonshire.--Relation of a memorable piece of witchcraft, at Welton.--An account of the tryals, examination and condemnation, of Elinor Shaw, and Mary Phillip's.--The Northamptonshire witches.--The Barby apparition.--A brief history of witchcraft.

8

BF
1581
A2
W81+
1967

Witchcraft in Northamptonshire: facsimile reproduction of six rare and curious tracts dating from 1612 [collected by John Taylor]. [1st ed. reprinted]. Wilbarston (Northants.), Gerald Coe, Ltd., 1967.
[78] p. facsims. 26 cm. 15/-
Various pagings.   (B 68-00539)
CONTENTS.--The witches of Northamptonshire.--An account of the tryals, examination and condemnation of Elinor Shaw and Mary Phillip.--A brief history of witchcraft.--Curious account of the remarkable case of the Duchess of Bedford.--Relation of a memorable piece of witchcraft at Welton.
1. Witchcraft--Northamptonshire, Eng.   I. Taylor, John, 1831-1901, comp.
BF1581.A2W5 1967   133.4   68-76836
Library of Congress   [2]

612

CATALOGUE OF THE CORNELL WITCHCRAFT COLLECTION

Witchcraft in Northamptonshire.

Witchcraft
BF
1581
A2
W81
1866a
no.1

The Witches of Northamptonshire. Agnes Browne. Ioane Vaughan. Arthur Bill. Hellen Ienkinson. Mary Barber. Witches. Who were all executed at Northampton the 22. of Iuly last. 1612. London, Printed by Thos Purfoot, for Arthur Iohnson, 1612. [Northampton, England, Taylor & son, 1866]
[28] p. 22cm.

No. 1 in box lettered Witchcraft in Northamptonshire.

1. Witchcraft—Northamptonshire, England. I. Title: Witchcraft in Northamptonshire.

Witchcraft in old and New England.

Witchcraft
BF
1581
K62W8

Kittredge, George Lyman, 1860–1941.
Witchcraft in old and New England, by George Lyman Kittredge ... Cambridge, Mass., Harvard university press, 1929.
6 p. l., [3]–641 p. 24½cm.
"Notes": p. [375]–598.
Presentation copy to Prof. Burr with author's autograph.

1. Witchcraft—England. 2. Witchcraft—New England. I. Title.

Library of Congress   BF1581.K58
———— Copy 2.   29-6482
Copyright A 5717   [5-2]

Witchcraft in Salem village.

Witchcraft
BF
1576
F54
1923

Fiske, John, 1842–1901.
Witchcraft in Salem village, by John Fiske ... Boston and New York, Houghton Mifflin company, 1923.
2 p. l., 60 p. illus. (incl. ports., facsims.) 19½cm.

"This account ... is reprinted from the author's 'New France and New England'."

Witchcraft in Salem village in 1692.

Witchcraft
BF
1576
N52
1916

Nevins, Winfield S.
Witchcraft in Salem village in 1692; together with a review of the opinions of modern writers and psychologists in regard to outbreak of the evil in America. By Winfield S. Nevins. 5th ed., with new preface of striking interest. Salem, Mass., The Salem press company, 1916.
2 p. l., lix, [2], 7–273 p. front., illus. (incl. facsim.) plates, ports. 18cm.

1. Witchcraft—Salem, Mass. 2. Witchcraft—New England. I. Title.
17-18161

Library of Congress   BF1576

Witchcraft in the Middle Ages.

Witchcraft
BF
1569
R96

Russell, Jeffrey Burton.
Witchcraft in the Middle Ages. Ithaca, Cornell University Press [c1972]
ix, 394 p. 23cm.

1. Witchcraft—Hist. I. Title.

Witchcraft in the Star chamber.

Witchcraft
BF
1581
E94
W81

Ewen, Cecil Henry L'Estrange, 1877–
Witchcraft in the Star chamber, by C. L'Estrange Ewen. [London] The author, 1938.
68 p. 23cm.

1. Witchcraft—England. 2. Great Britain. Court of Star chamber. I. Title.

Witchcraft in Tudor and Stuart England.

BF
1581
M14
1970

Macfarlane, Alan.
Witchcraft in Tudor and Stuart England; a regional and comparative study. New York, Harper & Row [1970]
xxi, 334 p. illus., facsims., maps. 24 cm. (J. & J. Harper editions) $8.50
"A torchbook library edition."
A modified version of the author's thesis, Oxford, 1967, published under the title: Witchcraft prosecutions in Essex, 1560–1680.
Bibliography: p. [313]–324.

1. Witchcraft—England. I. Title.

BF1581.M26 1970b   301.2   72-119635
Library of Congress   70 [4]   MARC

Witchcraft in Yorkshire.

BF
1581
C95

Crowther, Patricia.
Witchcraft in Yorkshire. [Clapham, Yorkshire], Dalesman, 1973.
72 p. illus., facsims., map. 21 cm.

1. Witchcraft—Yorkshire, Eng. I. Title

NIC   MAR 21, '74   (OOxc   73-168514

Witchcraft, magic & alchemy.

Witchcraft
BF
1412
G85+
1931

Grillot de Givry, Émile Angelo, 1870–
Witchcraft, magic & alchemy, by Grillot de Givry, translated by J. Courtenay Locke; with ten plates in colour and 366 illustrations in the text. London, G. G. Harrap [1931]
394 p. illus. (part col.) 29cm.
"A collection of the iconography of occultism."—Pref.
Translation of Le musée des sorciers, mages et alchimistes.
(Continued on next card)

WITCHCRAFT
BF
1563
W797++

[Witchcraft newspaper clippings, photographs, etc. v.p., 1857–1921]
broadside box. 44x31cm.

The newspaper clippings are chiefly from New York papers, including a group dated 1857 concerning practitioners of palmistry, astrology, etc.

NIC   1. Witchcraft.   2. Occult sciences.

Witchcraft of New England explained by modern spiritualism.

Witchcraft
BF
1576
P98

Putnam, Allen, 1802–1887.
Witchcraft of New England explained by modern spiritualism ... Boston, Colby and Rich, 1880.
482 p. 19cm.

1. Witchcraft—New England. I. Title.

Witchcraft trials in the Ban de la Roche.

Thesis
1926
M 572

Merritt, Bertha Sutermeister.
Witchcraft trials in the Ban de la Roche, Basse Alsace, 1607–1674 ... by Bertha Sutermeister Merritt.
[Ithaca, N.Y.] 1926.

Thesis (A.M.)—Cornell University, 1926.
Bibliography: p. 51–52.

I. Title.

Witches.

BF
1566
M46

Mayer, Phillip
Witches; inaugural lecture delivered at Rhodes University. Grahamstown, Rhodes University, 1954.
19 p. 22cm.

1. Witchcraft—Addresses, essays, lectures. I. Title.

Witches and demons in history and folklore.

GR
530
J67

Johnson, Frank Roy, 1911–
Witches and demons in history and folklore, by F. Roy Johnson. Murfreesboro, N. C., Johnson Pub. Co. [1969]
262 p. illus. 22 cm.
Bibliographical references included in "Notes" (p. 237–252)

1. Witchcraft. I. Title.

GR530.J6   133.4   75-240086
Library of Congress   70 [2]   MARC

Witches and sorcerers.

Witchcraft
BF
1566
D21

Daraul, Arkon.
Witches and sorcerers. London, F. Muller [1962]
270 p. illus. 23cm.

1. Witchcraft. I. Title.

Witches and their craft.

BF
1566
S49

Seth, Ronald.
Witches and their craft. London, Odhams, 1967.
255 p. illus., 8 plates. 22 cm. 21/-
Bibliography: p. 250–251.
(B 67-11326)

1. Witchcraft. I. Title.

BF1566.S43   133.4   67-91518
Library of Congress   [3]

Witches and warlocks.

Witchcraft
BF
1566
S48

Sergeant, Philip Walsingham, 1872–
Witches and warlocks, by Philip W. Sergeant; with introduction by Arthur Machen; with 17 illustrations. London, Hutchinson & co., ltd. [1936]
290 p. front., plates, ports. 22cm.

1. Witchcraft. 2. Witchcraft—England. I. Title. II. Title: Warlocks.
36-35589

Library of Congress   BF1566.S4
Copyright A ad int. 22047   [159.9614] 133.4

Witches, demons and fertility magic.

P
9
F5
t.14, no.4

Runeberg, Arne.
Witches, demons and fertility magic; analysis of their significance and mutual relations in West-European folk religion. [With an appendix: Psychoanalytic interpretation of European bronze age religion.] Helsingfors, 1947.
xii, 273 p. 24cm. (Societas Scientiarum Fennica. Commentationes humanarum litterarum, XIV, 4)
"Authorities quoted": p. [252]–256.
Thesis—Helsingfors.

613

CATALOGUE OF THE CORNELL WITCHCRAFT COLLECTION

Witches in Salem and elsewhere.

Witchcraft
BF 1576 C43
Chadwick, John White, 1840-1904.
Witches in Salem and elsewhere. [n. p., 1885?]
[63]-82 p. 24cm.

Caption title.

The witches of Hvntingdon.

Witchcraft
BF 1581 Z7 1646
[Davenport, John] ed.
The witches of Hvntingdon, their examinations and confessions; exactly taken by His Majesties justices of peace for that county. Whereby will appeare how craftily and dangerously the Devill tempeth and seizeth on poore soules ... London, Printed by W. Wilson for R. Clutterbuck, 1646.
15 p. 19cm.
With book-plate of Herman Le Roy Edgar.
Bound in full 19th century diced red roan, triple gilt fillets on covers, spine gilt extra.

Witchcraft
BF 1581 A2 W81 1866a no.1
The Witches of Northamptonshire. Agnes Browne. Ioane Vaughan. Arthur Bill. Hellen Ienkinson. Mary Barber. Witches. Who were all executed at Northampton the 22. of Iuly last. 1612. London, Printed by Tho: Purfoot, for Arthur Iohnson, 1612. [Northampton, England, Taylor & son, 1866]
[28] p. 22cm.
No. 1 in box lettered Witchcraft in Northamptonshire.

8
1. Witchcraft--Northamptonshire, England. I. Title: Witchcraft in Northamptonshire. (Over)

The witches of Warboys.

Witchcraft
BF 1565 N33
Naylor, Martin Joseph.
The inanity [sic] and mischief of vulgar superstitions. Four sermons preached at All-Saint's church, Huntingdon, on the 25th day of March, in the years 1792, 1793, 1794, 1795. To which is added some account of the witches of Warboys ... Cambridge, Printed by B. Flower for J. Deighton & W. H. Lunn, 1795.
xi, 129 p. 21cm.
1. Superstition. 2. Witchcraft. I. Title. II. Title: The witches of Warboys.

Witchcraft
BF 1583 A2 W82 1888
Witekind, Hermann, 1522-1603.
Augustin Lercheimer (Professor H. Witekind in Heidelberg) und seine Schrift wider den Hexenwahn. Lebensgeschichtliches und Abdruck der letzten vom Verfasser besorgten Ausgabe von 1597. Sprachlich bearbeitet durch Anton Birlinger. Hrsg. von Carl Binz. Strassburg, J. H. E. Heitz (Heitz und Mündel) 1888.
xxxii, 188 p. 21cm.

(Continued on next card)
(over)

Witchcraft
BF 1583 A2 W82 1888
Witekind, Hermann, 1522-1603. Augustin Lercheimer ... und seine Schrift wider den Hexenwahn. 1888. (Card 2)
Includes reprint of original t.p.: Christlich bedencken vnd Erinnerung von Zauberey.
Contents.--Mitteilungen über die Person und die Schriften des Professors H. Witekind.--Text.--Sprachliches, Wort- und Sachbestand, Textesunterschiede.--Vilmar über Witekind.
Ex libris Fri d. Zarncke.

Witchcraft
BF 1583 A2 W82 1593
Witekind, Hermann, 1522-1603.
Christlich Bedencken vnnd Erinnerung von Zauberey, woher, was, vnd wie vielfältig sie sey, wem sie schaden könne oder nicht, wie diesem Laster zu wehren, vnd die so damit behafft, zu bekehren, oder auch zu straffen seyn. Beschrieben durch Augustin Lercheimer [pseud.] von Steinfelden. Aut assentire his, aut meliora doce. Jetzund auffs new gemehret vnd gebessert. Basel, Getruckt durch Sebastia num Henricpetri [1593]

8 (Continued on next card)

Witchcraft
BF 1583 A2 W82 1593
Witekind, Hermann, 1522-1603. Christlich Bedencken vnnd Erinnerung von Zauberey ... [1593] (Card 2)
280, [3] p. 17cm.
With colophon and printer's device.
Woodcut of a witches' sabbath on t. p.
Commentary by G. L. Burr on front inside cover.
1. Witchcraft. 2. Trials (Witchcraft)--Germany. I. Title: Christlich Bedencken und Erinnerung von Zauberey.

Witekind, Hermann, 1522-1603.
Christlich Bedencken und Erinnerung von Zauberey

Witchcraft
BF 1583 A2 W82 1888
Witekind, Hermann, 1522-1603.
Augustin Lercheimer (Professor H. Witekind in Heidelberg) und seine Schrift wider den Hexenwahn. Lebensgeschichtliches und Abdruck der letzten vom Verfasser besorgten Ausgabe von 1597. Sprachlich bearbeitet durch Anton Birlinger. Hrsg. von Carl Binz. Strassburg, J. H. E. Heitz (Heitz und Mündel) 1888.
xxxii, 188 p. 21cm.

(Continued on next card)

Witekind, Hermann, 1522-1603.
Christlich Bedencken und Erinnerung von Zauberey

Witchcraft
BF 1583 A2 W82 1888
Witekind, Hermann, 1522-1603. Augustin Lercheimer ... und seine Schrift wider den Hexenwahn. 1888. (Card 2)
Includes reprint of original t.p.: Christlich bedencken vnd Erinnerung von Zauberey.
Contents.--Mitteilungen über die Person und die Schriften des Professors H. Witekind.--Text.--Sprachliches, Wort- und Sachbestand, Textesunterschiede.--Vilmar über Witekind.
Ex libris Fri d. Zarncke.

Witchcraft
BF 1555 B57
Witmer, Georg, joint author.
[Bewerlein, Sixtus]
Erschröckliche gantz warhafftige Geschicht, welche sich mit Apolonia, Hannsen Geißlbrechts Burgers zu Spalt inn dem Lystätter Bistumb, Hauβfrawen, so den 20. Octobris, Anno 82. von dem bösen Feind gar hart besessen, vnnd doch den 24. gedachts Monats widerumb durch Gottes gnädige Hilff, auβ solcher grossen Pein vnnd Marter entlediget worden, verlauffen hat. Allen gottlosen, zänckischen, vbelfluchenden Eheleuten, vnnd andern zu sonderer Warnung in Truck gegeben. Durch M. Sixtum Agricolam [pseud.] ...

8 (Continued on next card)

Witchcraft
BF 1555 B57
Witmer, Georg, joint author.
[Bewerlein, Sixtus] Erschröckliche gantz warhafftige Geschicht ... 1584. (Card 2)
... vnd dann D. Georgium Witmerum ... Ingolstatt, Getruckt durch Wolffgang Eder, 1584.
3 p. l., 49 p. 20cm.
Title in red and black.
1. Demoniac possession. 2. Exorcism. 3. Geisslbrecht, Anna, fl. 1584. I. Witmer, Georg, joint author. II. Title.

HIST SCI
BF 1555 W82 2 copies
Witt, Joannes Michael.
De obsessis falsis atque veris...disserit Joannes Michael Witt... Erfordiae, Prelo Heringiano [1739]
32 p. 21cm.

Diss.--Erfurt.

1. Demoniac possession. 2. Obsessive-compulsive neuroses. I. Title.

Witchcraft
BF 1583 W83
Wittig, Gregor Constantin.
Hexenaberglaube in Schlesien.
(In Psychische Studien. Leipzig. 23cm. 25. Jahrg., 9. Heft (1898), p. 443-450)

In envelope.

1. Witchcraft--Silesia. I. Title.

Witchcraft
BF 1565 T46 E358
Das Wohl-meritirte und wohlverdiente Ehren=Kleid dem Anonymo und Autori des Gutachten von dem mit Herrn Doct. Thomasio erregten Streit über einige freye Meynungen in einem teutschen Programmate, und von Herrn D. Strykii Disputation de jure Sabbathi, zum Recompens vor die Mühe praesentiret von einem Liebhaber der Wahrheit und Feind der Calumnien. Freystatt, 1703.
24 p. 18cm.

8 (Continued on next card)

Witchcraft
BF 1565 T46 E358
Das Wohl-meritirte und wohlverdiente Ehren=Kleid ... 1703. (Card 2)

1. Eines Anonymi Gutachten von dem mit Herrn D. Thomasio erregten Streit über einige freye Meynungen. 2. Gutachten von dem mit Herrn D. Thomasio erregten Streit. 3. Stryk, Joannes Samuel, 1668-1715. Disputatio de jure Sabbathi. I. Ein Liebhaber der Wahrheit und Feind der Calumnien.

CATALOGUE OF THE CORNELL WITCHCRAFT COLLECTION

Woldemar [pseud.]

see

Holm, Viggo Valdemar, 1855-1899.

Witchcraft
BF
1565
D62
no.5

Wolf, Johann, praeses.
De lacrymis sagarum. Disputationem physicam ... praeside Dn. M. Johanne Wolfio ... exponit Christianus Stegmann ... VVittebergae, Typis Christiani Schrödteri [1676]
[16] p. 20cm.
No. 5 in vol. lettered Dissertationes de sagis. 1636-1714.
1. Witchcraft. 2. Crying. I. Stegmann, Christian, respondent. II. Title.

8

Witchcraft
BF
1565
D62
no.7

Wolf, Johann, praeses.
Disputationem physicam, evolventem qv. Num daemon cum sagis generare possit, ... sub praesidio Dn. M. Johannis Wolfii ... submittit Johann.Paulus Reineccius ... Wittenbergae, Typis Christiani Schrödteri [1676]
[16] p. 20cm.
No. 7 in vol. lettered Dissertationes de sagis. 1636-1714.
1. Witchcraft. 2. Devil. I. Reineck, Johann Paul, respondent. II. Title.
Num daemon cum sagis generare possit. III. Title.

8

Rare
BR
304
A18
1631

Wolf, Johann, 1522-1571.
Aconcio, Giacomo, 1492?-1566?
Stratagematvm Satanae, libri octo. Editio iterata & emendata. Oxonii, G. Webb, 1631.
426 p. 15cm.
"Iacobvs Acontivs Iohanni Wolfio": [26] p. at end.
Engr. t.p.
STC 93
1. Christianity--16th cent. 2. Creeds-- Hist. & Crit. I. Wolf, Johann, 1522-1571. II. Title.

WITCHCRAFT
PT
2583
W28
06
1880

Wolf, Marianne (Conrad) 1837-1886.
Opfer des Aberglaubens, Irrthums und Wahns. Erzählungen und Enthüllungen aus uralter Zeit bis auf unsere Tage. Von C. Michael [pseud.] Leipzig, O. Spamer, 1880.
141 p. illus. 19cm. (Otto Spamer's Neue Volksbücher, no.6)

8
NIC

I. Title.

Woman-burning in England [letter]

Witchcraft
BF
1581
B96

Burr, George Lincoln, 1857-1938.
Woman-burning in England [letter] (In the Nation. New York. 17cm. v. 49 (1889) p. 169)
With, in envelope, his [Letter] to the editor of the Nation [about witch-burning in England] 1889.
1. Witchcraft--England. I. Title.

Witchcraft
BF
1410
B42
Z56
v.3
no.19

Pel, J
De wonderdaden des Alderhoogsten, waar in aangewesen word, wat mogelijker en waarschijnelijker is ...
De wonderdaden des Alderhoogsten, waar in aangewesen word, wat mogelijker en waarschijnelijker is, de verleidinge van den mensch door sig selfs, of door dat ding dat een afgevallen geest word genoemt; en dat den val van de denkende wesens onvereenigd met een lighaam, die engelen worden genoemt, niet alleen onbegrijpelijk maar ook onmogelijk is, ja dat hare scheppinge in 't werk der scheppinge, in den gehelen Bijbel niet te vinden is. ... Amsterdam, Gedrukt by W. de Coup, boekverkoper, 1693.
(Continued on next card)

Witchcraft
BF
1410
B42
Z56
v.3
no.19

Pel, J   De wonderdaden des Alderhoogsten ... 1693.   (Card 2)
4 p. l., [84], [8] p. title vignette, illus. initial. 19 x 15cm.
4°: *⁴, A-L⁴, M².
Incomplete: first gathering only.
Van der Linde 137.
No. 19 in vol. lettered Bekker III.
1. Devil. 2. Angels. I. Title.

8

Witchcraft
BF
1563
T75

The Wonderfvl discoverie of the witchcrafts of Margaret and Phillip [pa] Flower, daughters of Joan Flower neere Beuer Castle ... Together with the seuerall examinations and confessions of Anne Baker, Ioan Willimot, and Ellen Greene, witches in Leicestershire. London, Printed by G. Eld for I Barnes, 1619. [Greenwich, Reprinted by H. S. Richardson, ca. 1840]
26 p. title vignettes. 23cm.

8   (Continued on next card)

Witchcraft
BF
1563
T75

The Wonderfvl discoverie of the witchcrafts of Margaret and Phillip [pa] Flower ... [1840]   (Card 2)
The examinations of Anne Baker, Ioanne Willimot, and Ellen Greene has special t. p.
No. 4 in vol. lettered Tracts on witchcraft.
1. Flower, Margaret, d. 1618. 2. Flower, Philippa, d. 1618. 3. Baker, Anne, d. 1618. 4. Willimot, Joanne, d. 1618. 5. Greene, Ellen, d. 1618.

8

BF
1581
Z7
1618a

The Wonderfvl discoverie of the witchcrafts of Margaret and Phillip [i. e. Philippa] Flower ... together with the seuerall examinations and confessions of Anne Baker, Ioan Willimot and Ellen Greene, witches in Leicestershire. London. Printed by G. Eld for I. Barnes, 1619. Leicester, Vance Harvey Publishing, 1970.
26, 17 p. 1 illus. 22 cm. 18/-   B 70-27926
"Limited to fivehundred copies, of which the first fifty are numbered and bound in hard covers, printed and gold blocked."
Facsimile reprint of one of A collection of rare and curious tracts relating to witchcraft ... London, 1838.
1. Witchcraft—England. 2. Flower, Margaret, d. 1618. 3. Flower, Philippa, d. 1618.
BF1581.Z7 1618ba   133.4'0922   76-860173
ISBN 0-85544-000-7   MARC
Library of Congress   71 [2]

4

WITCHCRAFT
BF
1501
C95

Wonderful prodigies of judgment and mercy.
[Crouch, Nathaniel] 1632?-1725?
Wonderful prodigies of judgment and mercy: discovered in above three hundred memorable histories, containing I. Dreadful judgments upon atheists, perjured wretches, blasphemers ... II. The miserable ends of divers magicians, witches, conjurers, &c. with several strange apparitions. III. Remarkable presages of approaching death ... IV. The wicked lives, and woful deaths of wretched popes, apostates, and desperate

8   (Continued on next card)

WITCHCRAFT
BF
1501
C95

Wonderful prodigies of judgment and mercy.
[Crouch, Nathaniel] 1632?-1725? Wonderful prodigies of judgment and mercy ... 1682.   (Card 2)

persecutors. V. Fearful judgments upon cruel tyrants, murderers, &c. ... VI. Admirable deliverances from imminent dangers ... VII. Divine goodness to penitents, with the dying thoughts of several famous men concerning a future state after this life. Impartially collected from antient

8   (Continued on next card)

WITCHCRAFT
BF
1501
C95

Wonderful prodigies of judgment and mercy.
[Crouch, Nathaniel] 1632?-1725? Wonderful prodigies of judgment and mercy ... 1682.   (Card 3)

and modern authors ... By R. B. author of the History of the wars of England, and the Remarks of London, etc. London, Printed for Nath. Crouch, 1682.
2 p. l., 233, [3] p. illus. 15cm.
With added engr. t. p.
With armorial book plate: Hugh Cecil Earl of Lonsdale.

8   (Continued on next card)

WITCHCRAFT
BF
1501
C95

Wonderful prodigies of judgment and mercy.
[Crouch, Nathaniel] 1632?-1725? Wonderful prodigies of judgment and mercy ... 1682.   (Card 4)

Wing C7361.

1. Devil--Collections. 2. Reward (Theology) 3. Marvelous, The. I. The author of the History of the wars of England. II. R. B. III. B., R. IV. Title.

8

Witchcraft
BF
1563
W81++
no.11

The wonderfull discouerie of Elizabeth Sawyer.
Goodcole, Henry.
The wonderfull discouerie of Elizabeth Savvyer, a witch, late of Edmonton, her conuiction and condemnation and death. Together with the relation of the Diuels accesse to her and their conference together. London, Printed for VV. Butler, 1621. [London, at the British Museum, 1923]
[32] p. 16cm.
Signatures: A-D⁴.
Photocopy (negative) 31 p. on 15 l. 20 x 32cm.
1. Sawyer, Elizabeth, d. 1621.
I. Title.

Witchcraft
BF
1563
W81++
no.16

Wonderfull news from the north; or, A true relation of the sad and grievovs torments inflicted upon ... three children of Mr. George Muschamp ... by witch-craft; and how miraculously it pleased God to strengthen them and to deliver them; as also the prosecution of the sayd witches ... April 1650. Novemb. 25, 1650, Imprimatur John Downame. London, Printed by T. H., and are to be sold by R. Harper, 1650. [London, at the British Museum, 1923]
28 p. 16cm.

(Continued on next card)

Witchcraft
BF
1563
W81++
no.16

Wonderfull news from the north ... 1650 [1923]   (Card 2)

Photocopy (negative) 28 p. on 17 l. 20 x 32cm.
No. 16 in vol. lettered: Witchcraft tracts, chapbooks and broadsides, 1579-1704; rotograph copies.

1. Muschamp children. 2. Witchcraft-- England.

CATALOGUE OF THE CORNELL WITCHCRAFT COLLECTION

The wonders of the invisible world.

Witchcraft
BF   Mather, Cotton, 1663-1728.
1575   The wonders of the invisible world. Being an
M42   account of the tryals of several witches lately
1862 executed in New-England. To which is added
      A farther account of the tryals of the New-
    England witches. By Increase Mather. London,
    J. R. Smith, 1862.
      xvi, 291 p. port. 18cm. (Library of old
    authors)
      The wonders of the invisible world; A further
    account of the tryals of the New-England witches
    ... to which is added Cases of conscience
                     (Continued on next card)

The wonders of the invisible world.

Witchcraft
BF   Mather, Cotton, 1663-1728. The wonders of the
1575   invisible world ... 1862.   (Card 2)
M42
1862 concerning witchcrafts; and Cases of conscience
    concerning evil spirits personating men, each
    have special facsimile t. p.
      The two latter works by Increase Mather.

Witchcraft The wonders of the invisible world.
BF   Mather, Cotton, 1663-1728.
1575   The wonders of the invisible world: being an account
D76 of the tryals of several vvitches, lately excuted [!] in New-
v.1   England: and of several remarkable curiosities therein
    occurring. Together with, I. Observations upon the
    nature, the number, and the operations of the devils.
    II. A short narrative of a late outrage committed by a
    knot of witches in Swede-land, very much resembling,
    and so far explaining, that under which New-England
               (Continued on next card)
                                2-13724

Witchcraft The wonders of the invisible world.
BF   Mather, Cotton, 1663-1728. The wonders of the in-
1575   visible world ... 1866. (Card 2)
D76
v.1   has laboured. III. Some councels directing a due im-
    provement of the terrible things lately done by the un-
    usual and amazing range of evil-spirits in New-England.
    IV. A brief discourse upon those temptations which are
    the more ordinary devices of Satan. By Cotton Mather.
    Published by the special command of his excellency the
    govenour [!] of the province of the Massachusetts-Bay in
           (Continued on next card)
                                2-13724

Witchcraft The wonders of the invisible world.
BF   Mather, Cotton, 1663-1728. The wonders of the in-
1575   visible world ... 1866. (Card 3)
D76
v.1   New-England. Printed first. at Bostun [!] in New-Eng-
    land; and reprinted at London, for John Dunton, 1693.
    (*Reprint. In* Drake, S. G. The witchcraft delusion in
    New England ... Roxbury, Mass., 1866. 21½ᶜᵐ. v. 1.
    1 p. l., p. [1]-247)
    Woodward's historical series. no. v.
    The editor has followed the 1st London ed. "presuming that to be the
    most accurate, as the copy from which it was printed was doubtless furnished
    by the author." (Preface, p, vii)
      1. Witchcraft--New England. 2. Trials (Witch-
    craft)--New England.   I. Title.   2-13724

Library of Congress, no.

Wonders of the invisible world, or,
Salem witchcraft.

Witchcraft
BF   Calef, Robert, 1648-1719.
1575   Wonders of the invisible world, or,
C14   Salem witchcraft. In five parts. Boston,
1828 T. Bedlington [1828]
      333 p. front. 14cm.

    A reply to Cotton Mather's "Wonders of
    the invisible world."
      First ed. published in 1700 under title:
    More wonders of the invisible world
    displayed.
                 (Continued on next card)

Wonders of the invisible world, or,
Salem witchcraft.

Witchcraft
BF   Calef, Robert, 1648-1719. Wonders of the
1575   invisible world ... [1828]   (Card 2)
C14
1828 Contents.--Part 1. An account of the
    sufferings of Margaret Rule, by Cotton
    Mather.--Part 2. Several letters from the
    author to Mr. Mather and others, relating
    to witchcraft.--Part 3. Account of the
    differences in Salem village between the
    villagers and their minister, Mr. Parris.--
    Part 4. Letter   s of a gentleman uninter-
              (Continued on next card)

Wonders of the invisible world, or,
Salem witchcraft.

Witchcraft
BF   Calef, Robert, 1648-1719. Wonders of the
1575   invisible world ... [1828]   (Card 3)
C14
1828 ested, endeavouring to prove the received
    opinions about witchcraft to be orthodox.--
    Part 5. An impartial account of the most
    memorable matters of fact touching the
    supposed witchcraft in New-England.--Post-
    script, relating to Cotton Mather's life of
    Sir William Phips.--Giles Cory: a report of
    his examinati   on, taken from the witch-
    craft files.

Witchcraft
BF   Woodward, Thomas.
1555   Demoniacal possession, its nature and ces-
W89 sation. An essay. London, J. Masters, 1849.
    60 p. 22cm.

    1. Demoniac possession. I. Title.

Witchcraft
BX   Het Woord Sitna verklaard, Gen. 26: 21. Met
9479 een vertoog, dat het woord Satan daar van
B42 afkomstig is. Waar by gevoegd word een
B11 verklaaring over 2 Sam. 24: 1, en 1 Chron.
no.8 21: 1. Door A. W. S. K. Amsterdam, By
    J. Roman, boekverkoper, 1699.
      13 p. [p. 14 blank] title and end page
    vignettes, illus. initial. 20 x 15cm.
      4°: A-B⁴(-B4)
      Black letter.
      No. 8 in vol.   lettered B. Bekkers sterf-
    bed en andere   tractaten.
                 (Continued on next card)

Witchcraft
BX   Het Woord Sitna verklaard, Gen. 26:21.
9479   1699.   (Card 2)
B42
B11   1. Bible. O. T. Genesis XXVI, 21--
no.8 Criticism, interpretation, etc. 2. Devil.
    3. Bible. O. T. 2 Samuel XXIV, 1--Criti-
    cism, interpretation, etc. 4. Bible. O. T.
    1 Chronicles XXI, 1--Criticism, interpreta-
    tion, etc. I. A. W. S. K. II. K., A. W.
    S.

The world bewitch'd.

Witchcraft
BF   Bekker, Balthasar, 1634-1698.
1410   The world bewitch'd; or, An examination
B42 of the common opinions concerning spirits:
1695 their nature, power, administration, and
    operations. As also, the effects men are
    able to produce by their communication.
    Divided into IV parts. By Balthazar Bekker,
    D. D. and pastor at Amsterdam. Vol. I.
    Translated from a French copy, approved of
    and subscribed by the author's own hand.
    [London] Printed for R. Baldwin, 1695.
               (Continued on next card)

The world bewitch'd.

Witchcraft
BF   Bekker, Balthasar, 1634-1698. The world
1410   bewitch'd ... 1695.   (Card 2)
B42
1695   41 p. 1., 264 p. 17 x 10cm.
      12°: a⁶(-a1), b-d¹², B-M¹².
      No more published.
      Half title: The world bewitch'd, &c.
      Vol. I.
      Translation of vol. 1 of Le monde enchanté,
    Amsterdam, 1694, which is a translation of
    his De betoverde weereld, Amsterdam, 1691-93.
               (Continued on next card)

The world bewitch'd.

Witchcraft
BF   Bekker, Balthasar, 1634-1698. The world
1410   bewitch'd ... 1695.   (Card 3)
B42
1695   Reissued in 1700 under title: The world
    turn'd upside down.
      Autograph on t. p.: Ch. Whittuck.
      Wing B 1781.
      Variant of van der Linde 28: 12°, not 8°.
      1. Demonology. 2. Angels. 3. Magic.
    4. Witchcraft. I. Title. II. His De
    betoverde weereld--English. III. His Le
    monde enchanté   --English.

The world of the witches.

Witchcraft
BF   Caro Baroja, Julio.
1566   This world of the witches. Translated by
C29 O. N. V. Glendinning. [Chicago] University of
    Chicago Press [1964]
      xiv, 313 p. illus. 22cm. (The Nature of
    human society series)

    Translation of Las brujas y su mundo.
    Bibliographical references included in "Notes"
    (p. 259-306)

The world turn'd upside down.

Witchcraft
BF   [Bekker, Balthasar] 1634-1698.
1410   The world turn'd upside down: or, A plain
B42 detection of errors, in the common or vulgar
1700 belief, relating to spirits, spectres or
    ghosts, daemons, witches, &c. In a due and
    serious examination of their nature, power,
    administration, and operation. In what forms
    or shape incorporeal spirits appear to men,
    by what means, and of what elements they take
    to themselves, and form appearances of bodies,
    visible to mort   al eyes; why they
               (Continued on next card)

The world turn'd upside down.

Witchcraft
BF   [Bekker, Balthasar] 1634-1698. The world
1410   turn'd upside down ... 1700.   (Card 2)
B42
1700 appear, and what frights and force of imag-
    ination often delude us into the appre-
    hensions of supposed phantasms, through the
    intimidation of the mind, &c. Also what evil
    tongues have power to produce of hurt of man-
    kind, or irational [sic] creatures; and the
    effects men and   women are able to produce
    by their commun   ication with good or evil
               (Continued on next card)

The world turn'd upside down.

Witchcraft
BF   [Bekker, Balthasar] 1634-1698. The world
1410   turn'd upside down ... 1700.   (Card 3)
B42
1700 spirits, &c. Written at the request of a
    person of honour, by B. B., a Protestant min-
    ister for publick information. London,
    Printed for E. Harris, 1700.
      37 p. 1., 264 p. 16cm.
      12°: π1, b-d¹², B-M¹².
      With two old prints of devils inserted at
    front and back of book.

                 (Continued on next card)

CATALOGUE OF THE CORNELL WITCHCRAFT COLLECTION

The world turn'd upside down.

Witchcraft
BF
1410
B42
1700
[Bekker, Balthasar] 1634-1698. The world turn'd upside down ... 1700. (Card 4)
Title on spine: Bekker's World bewitch'd.
First published in 1695 with title: The world bewitch'd. This is same, with new t. p. and lacking the dedication.
Translation of Book 1 of his Le monde enchanté, which is a translation of De betoverde weereld.
Variant of van der Linde 28.

(Continued on next card)

The worlde possessed with deuils, conteinyng three dialogues.

Witchcraft
BF
1547
V81
1583
[Viret, Pierre] 1511-1571.
The worlde possessed with deuils, conteinyng three dialogues. 1. Of the deuill let loose. 2. Of blacke deuils. 3. Of white deuils. And of the commyng of Jesus Christe to judgement, a verie necessarie and comfortable discourse for these miserable and daungerous daies. London, Imprinted for I. Perin, and are to be sold in Paules churchyard at the signe of the Angell, 1583.
1 v. (unpaged) 15cm.

(Continued on next card.)

The worlde possessed with deuils.

Witchcraft
BF
1547
V81
1583
[Viret, Pierre] 1511-1571. The worlde possessed with deuils. 1583. (Card 2)
A translation by Thomas Stocker of the second part of his Le monde à l'empire et le monde démoniacle fait par dialogues. Cf. Haag. La France protestante.
With this is bound his The second part of The demoniacke vvorlde, or, Worlde possessed with diuels. London, 1583.

1. Demonology.   I. Title.

Witchcraft
BF
1555
W93
Worthington, William, 1703-1778.
An impartial enquiry into the case of the Gospel demoniacks. With an appendix, consisting of an essay on Scripture demonology. ... London, Printed for J. F. and C. Rivington, 1777.
349 p. 22cm.
"Books lately published": [1] p. at end.

1. Demonomania.   I. Title.

Witchcraft
BF
1581
A2
W81
1866a
no.5
Wright, Thomas, 1810-1877, ed.
Curious account of the remarkable case of the Duchess of Bedford, in the reign of Edward IV., who was charged with having by witchcraft fixed the love of the king on her daughter Queen Elizabeth. Furnished by the rolls of Parliament of 9th Edward IV. Northampton, J. Taylor, 1867.
8 p. 22cm.
"In the Proceedings against Dame Alice Kyteler, for the Camden Society."

(Continued on next card)

Witchcraft
BF
1581
A2
W81
1866a
no.5
Wright, Thomas, 1810-1877, ed. Curious account of the remarkable case of the Duchess of Bedford ... 1867. (Card 2)
No. 5 in box lettered Witchcraft in Northamptonshire.

1. Bedford, Jaquetta of Luxembourg, duchess of. 2. Edward IV, King of England, 1442-1483. I. Title.

8

Witchcraft
BF
1589
W95
1851
Wright, Thomas, 1810-1877.
Narratives of sorcery and magic, from the most authentic sources. London, R. Bentley, 1851.
2v. in 1. 20cm.

1. Magic. 2. Witchcraft.

Witchcraft
BF
1589
W95
1852
Wright, Thomas, 1810-1877.
Narratives of sorcery and magic, from the most authentic sources. By Thomas Wright ... New York, Redfield, 1852.
1 p. l., [5]-420 p. 19½ᶜᵐ.
First published in London, 1851.

1. Magic. 2. Witchcraft.   I. Title.

Library of Congress   BF1589.W8 1852
[41d1]   11—14498

WITCHCRAFT
BF
1565
G45
1842
Wright, Thomas, 1810-1877, ed.
Gifford, George, d. 1620.
A dialogue concerning witches & witchcrafts, by George Gifford. Reprinted from the edition of 1603. London, Printed for the Percy society [by T. Richards] 1842.
viii, v, [7]-119 p. 20cm.
With reproduction of the t.-p. of the London edition of 1603.
Edited by Thomas Wright.

1. Witchcraft. I. Wright, Thomas, 1810-1877, ed. II. Title.

Witchcraft
BF
1581
Z7
1324
Wright, Thomas, 1810-1877, ed.
Kyteler, Alice, fl. 1324, defendant.
A contemporary narrative of the proceedings against Dame Alice Kyteler, prosecuted for sorcery in 1324, by Richard de Ledrede, bishop of Ossory. Edited by Thomas Wright ... London, Printed for the Camden society, by J. B. Nichols and son, 1843.
2 p. l., xiii p., 1 l., 61, [1] p. 21x17cm.
[Camden society. Publications. no. XXIV]
Text in Latin.
Printed from Harleian ms. no. 641. cf. Introd.

Witchcraft
BF
1563
E92++
no. 2.
[Württemberger Hexenprocess] München, C. Wolf, 1897.
p. 222. 32cm. (Deutsche Merkur, 28. Jahrg., No. 28)

1. Witchcraft. 2. Trials (Witchcraft) --Germany.

MSS
Bd.
WITCHCRAFT
BF
W96
Ein Wunderbarlich erschrockenlich Handelunge, so sich auff den grün Dornstag dis Jars, ynn dem Stedlein Schiltach, mit einer Brunst durch den bösen Geyst gestifft, begeben hat, ym MDxxxiij. [n.p., 1553? ca. 1900]
4 l. 21cm.
Signatures: A⁴.
Carnap's manuscript copy.
"Original i. d. Kgl. Bibl. zu Berlin, ehemals im Heyse Bücherschatz."

1. Ghosts.   2. Devil.

MSS
Bd.
WITCHCRAFT
BV
W96
Eyn Wunderliches Gesicht und Geschicht von der hellen Pein, über die bösen Gottlosen Verächter des heyligen Evangelii zu eyner Warnung und Besserung, in disem XLIX. Jare offenbart. [n.p.] 1549 [ca. 1900]
6 l. illus. 23cm.
Carnap's manuscript copy.
"Originaldruck in der Gust. Freytag Bibliothek; jetzt in der Stadtbibliothek zu Frankfurt a/M. 8 Bl. in 4°. Sig. Aij-Biij."

(Continued on next card)

MSS
Bd.
WITCHCRAFT
BV
W96
Eyn Wunderliches Gesicht ... 1549 [ca. 1900] (Card 2)
Numerals and signatures in the margins indicate pagination of the original.

1. Exempla. 2. Admonition.

617

X

```
                    Xenocrates, of Chalcedon, ca. 396-ca.
                     314 B. C. Spurious and doubtful works.
WITCHCRAFT          De morte.
PA          Jamblichus, of Chalcis.
4220          [De mysteriis. Latin]
L3
A4+           Iamblichus De mysteriis Aegyptiorum, Chal-
1516        daeorum, Assyriorum. Proclus In Platonicum
            Alcibiadem de anima, atq̃ dęmone. Proclus De
            sacrificio, & magia. Porphyrius De diuinis,
            atq̃ daemonibus. Synesius Platonicus De som-
            niis. Psellus De daemonibus. Expositio
            Prisciani, & Marsilii in Theophrastum De sen-
            su, phantasia, & intellectu. Alcinoi Plato-
            nici philoso    phi, Liber de doctrina
8
                         (Continued on next card)
```

```
                    Xenocrates, of Chalcedon, ca. 396-ca.
                     314 B. C. Spurious and doubtful works.
WITCHCRAFT          De morte.
PA          Jamblichus, of Chalcis. [De mysteriis.
4220          Latin.]  [1516]              (Card 2)
L3
A4+           Platonis. Speusippi Platonis discipuli,
1516        Liber de Platonis definitionibus. Pythago-
            rae philosophi Aurea uerba. Symbola Pitha-
            gorae philosophi. Xenocratis philosophi
            platonici, Liber de morte. Mercurii Tris-
            megisti Pimander. Euisdem Asclepius. Mar-
            silii Ficini De triplici uita lib. II.
            Eiusdem Liber      de uoluptate. Eiusdem
8
                         (Continued on next card)
```

```
                    Xenocrates, of Chalcedon, ca. 396-
                     ca. 314 B. C., Spurious and doubtful
WITCHCRAFT          works. De morte.
PA          Jamblichus, of Chalcis. [De mysteriis.
4220          Latin]  [1516]              (Card 3)
L3
A4+           De sole & lumine libri. II. Apologia eius-
1516        dem in librum suum de lumine. Eiusdem Libel-
            lus de magis. Quod necessaria sit securitas,
            & tranquillitas animi. Praeclarissimarum
            sententiarum huius operis breuis annotatio.
            [Venetiis, In aedibvs Aldi, et Andreae soce-
            ri, 1516]
                177 [i.e.,    175] numbered leaves.
8           29cm.
                         (Continued on next card)
```

```
                    Xenocrates, of Chalcedon, ca. 396-ca.
                     314 B. C., Spurious and doubtful works.
WITCHCRAFT          De morte.
PA          Jamblichus, of Chalcis. [De mysteriis.]
4220          Latin.  [1516]              (Card 4)
L3
A4+           At head of title: Index eorvm, qvae hoc
1516        in libro habentvr.
              With colophon.
              Provenance: Bibliotec: SS. Me. Novelle.
            Translations by M. Ficino.
              1. Occult sciences. 2. Philosophy,
            Ancient--Collections. I. Proclus Diado-
            chus. In Platonicum Alcibiadem. II. Pro-
8           clus Diadoch    us. De sacrificio. III.
```

Y

WITCHCRAFT [Young, Arthur] 1693-1759.
A dissertation on the Gospel Daemoniacs, occasioned by the Bp. of St. David's answer to Mr. Woolston. [n.p., before 1760]
64 l. 23cm.
Manuscript, on paper, with gilt edges.
"...This dissertation ... was printed in 1760... It is not improbable that this is the author's autograph": G. L. Burr's note at beginning.
Bound in gilt-stamped black leather.
1. Demoniac possession. 2. Bible. N. T.--Commentaries. I. Title.

Witchcraft
Young, Arthur, 1693-1759.
A dissertation on the Gospel-daemoniacs. London, Printed for the Editor, and sold by G. Woodfall, 1760.
45 p. 20cm.

No. 4 in vol. lettered: Tracks [sic] of demoniacks.

Witchcraft
BT
975
Y73
Young, Joseph.
Demonology: or, The Scripture doctrine of devils. Edinburgh, T. Grant, 1856.
xviii, 460 p. 18cm.

1. Devil. I. Title: The Scripture doctrine of devils. II. Title: Demonology.

Yovhannes I Mandakuni, Patriarch of Armenia, d. ca. 490.

see

Hovhannes I Mandakuni, Patriarch of Armenia, d. ca. 490.

Witchcraft
Z
6878
W8
Y98
Yve-Plessis, R[obert]
...Essai d'une bibliographie française méthodique & raisonnée de la sorcellerie et de la possession démoniaque; pour servir de suite et de complément à la Bibliotheca magica de Græsse, aux catalogues Sépher, Ouvaroff, D'Ourches et Guldenstubbe, S. de Guaita et aux divers travaux partiels publiés sur cette matière. Préface par Albert de Rochas. Paris, Bibliothèque Chacornac, 1900.
xiv p., 1 l., 254, [1] p. front., facsims., plates. 25ᶜᵐ.
"Il a été tiré de cet ouvrage: 10 exemplaires sur papier de Hollande et 500 exemplaires sur papier ordinaire, tous numérotés et paraphés. No. 13".
1,793 titles, classified.
1. Witchcraft—Bibl. 2. Occult sciences—Bibl.
I. Grässe, Johann Georg Theodor, 1814-1885. Bibliotheca magica et pneumatica. II. Title.
Library of Congress, no. Z6878.W8Y8.

CATALOGUE OF THE CORNELL WITCHCRAFT COLLECTION

Z

Z., J. F.

Witchcraft
BF
1565
S83
no.3

Drey Fragen zur Vertheidigung der Hexerey. I. Ob P. Angelus März die Rede des P. Don Ferdinand Sterzingers gründlich, und II. bescheiden widerleget habe? III. Und ob wohl diese akademische Rede dem heiligen Kreutze von Scheyrn in der That nachtheilig sey? Mit einem sichern Ja beantwortet, und dem P. Angelus März selbst dedicirt von J. F. Z. ... [München?] 1767.
28 p. 23cm.

8   (Continued on next card)

Z., J. F.

Witchcraft
BF
1565
S83
no.3

Drey Fragen zur Vertheidigung der Hexerey ... 1767.   (Card 2)

"In spite of the initials J. F. Z. (Johann Felix Zech) in the dedication, the work is probably by H. Braun. See Fieger, H. P. Don Ferdinand Sterzinger, 1907."--Note by G. L. Burr on his ms. catalog slip for this item.
No. 3 in vol. lettered Sterzinger über Hexerei, 1766-1767.

8   (Continued on next card)

Zahn, Josef von.

Witchcraft
BF
1584
S8
V94+

Von Zauberern, Hexen und Wolfsbannern. Actenstücke, Processe wider Zauberer und Hexen betreffend, 1602-1701. Origg. u. Copp. im Landesarchive u. zu Admont. (In Steiermärkische Geschichtsblätter. Graz. 26cm. 3. Jahrg., 3. u. 4.? Heft (1882), p. [129]-180, 201-216)
Probably edited by J. von Zahn.
1. Witchcraft--Styria. 2. Trials (Witchcraft)--Styria. I. Zahn, Josef von. II. Steiermärkische Geschichtsblätter.

Witchcraft
BF
1566
Z29

Zangolini, Asclepiade.
Il diavolo e le streghe, ossia il pregiudizio popolare delle malie ragionamento del dottore Asclepiade Zangolini ... coll' aggiunta di alcuni racconti piacevoli del medesimo. Livorno, G. B. Rossi, 1864.
272 p. 13cm. (Biblioteca enciclopedica popolare)
Contents.--Il diavolo e le streghe.--Racconti piacevoli.--Epigrammi editi ed inediti e novellette inedite del dottore

8   (Continued on next card)

Witchcraft
BF
1566
Z29

Zangolini, Asclepiade. Il diavolo e le streghe ... 1864.   (Card 2)

Filippo Pananti.
Racconti and Epigrammi each have special t. p.

1. Witchcraft. 2. Devil. I. His Racconti piacevoli. II. Pananti, Filippo, 1766-1837. III. Title.

Zangolini, Asclepiade.
Racconti piacevoli.

Witchcraft
BF
1566
Z29

Zangolini, Asclepiade.
Il diavolo e le streghe, ossia il pregiudizio popolare delle malie ragionamento del dottore Asclepiade Zangolini ... coll' aggiunta di alcuni racconti piacevoli del medesimo. Livorno, G. B. Rossi, 1864.
272 p. 13cm. (Biblioteca enciclopedica popolare)
Contents.--Il diavolo e le streghe.--Racconti piacevoli.--Epigrammi editi ed inediti e novellette inedite del dottore

8   (Continued on next card)

Zangolini, Asclepiade.
Racconti piacevoli.

Witchcraft
BF
1566
Z29

Zangolini, Asclepiade. Il diavolo e le streghe ... 1864.   (Card 2)

Filippo Pananti.
Racconti and Epigrammi each have special t. p.

1. Witchcraft. 2. Devil. I. His Racconti piacevoli. II. Pananti, Filippo, 1766-1837. III. Title.

Witchcraft
BF
1565
S83
Z97

[Zapf, Georg Wilhelm] 1747-1810.
Zauberbibliothek. [München] 1776.
91 p. 19cm.
Based on annotated bibliography of the Gassner and Sterzinger controversies which first appeared in Allgemeine deutsche Bibliothek, Berlin, 1775-76. [BF 1565 S83 Z98] CUL holdings noted in ms. in text.
1. Sterzinger, Ferdinand, 1721-1786. 2. Gassner, Johann Joseph, 1727-1779. 3. Witchcraft-- Bibl. I. Title.

Zauber-Bibliothek.

Witchcraft
BF
1405
H81

Horst, Georg Conrad, 1767-1838?
Zauber-Bibliothek; oder, Von Zauberei, Theurgie und Mantik, Zauberern, Hexen, und Hexenprocessen, Dämonen, Gespenstern, und Geistererscheinungen. Zur Beförderung einer rein-geschichtlichen, von Aberglauben und Unglauben freien Beurtheilung dieser Gegenstände. Mainz, F. Kupferberg, 1821-1826.
6 v. 20cm.

1. Witchcraft. I. Title. II. Title: Von Zauberei, Theurgie und Mantik.

Zauber-lexicon.

Witchcraft
AG
27
O59
1764

Onomatologia cvriosa artificiosa et magica; oder, Ganz natürliches zauber-lexicon, welches das nöthigste, nützlichste und angenehmste in allen realen wissenschaften überhaupt und besonders in der naturlehre, mathematick, der haushaltungs- und natürlichen zauberkunst, und aller andern, vornemlich auch curieuser künste deutlich und vollständig nach alphabetischer ordnung beschriebet ... 2. vielvermehrte aufl. Nürnberg, Auf kosten der Raspischen handlung, 1764.
3 p. l., 1648 col. front., diagrs. (1 fold.) 21cm.

(Continued on next card)

Zauber-lexicon.

Witchcraft
AG
27
O59
1764

Onomatologia cvriosa artificiosa et magica. 1764.   (Card 2)

In double columns.
Edited by Gotthart Hafner. cf. Meusel, J.G. Lexikon der vom jahr 1750 bis 1800 verstorbenen teutschen schriftsteller. v. 5, p. 36.

Zauber-Lexicon.

Witchcraft
AG
27
O59
1784

Onomatologia cvriosa artificiosa et magica. Oder Natürliches Zauber-Lexicon, in welchem vieles Nützliche und Angenehme aus der Naturgeschichte, Naturlehre und natürlichen Magie nach alphabetischer Ordnung vorgetragen worden. 3. Aufl. Verbessert und mit vielen neuen Zusätzen vermehrt von Johann Christian Wiegleb. Nürnberg, Raspische Buchhandlung, 1784.
4 p. l., 1744 numb. columns. illus., fold. table. 22cm.

Das Zauber- und Hexenwesen, dann der Glauben an Vampyre in Mähren und Oesterr. Schlesien.

Witchcraft
BF
1583
E51+
1859

Elvert, Christian, Ritter d', 1803-1896.
Das Zauber- und Hexenwesen, dann der Glauben an Vampyre in Mähren und Oesterr. Schlesien. [Brunn, 1859]
319-[421] p. 26cm. (Schriften der Historisch-Statistischen Section der Mähr.-Schles. Gesellschaft zur Beförderung der Natur- und Landeskunde, Bd. 12)

1. Witchcraft. 2. Vampires. I. Title.

Witchcraft
BF
1565
S83
Z98

Zauberbibliothek. 1775-1776. [Berlin, 1775-76]
various pagings. 20cm.
Title from spine.
Consists of three sections detached from Allgemeine deutsche Bibliothek, titled: Zauberey; Teufeleyen; and Teufeleyen. Eine Fortsetzung der vorigen.
1. Sterzinger, Ferdinand, 1721-1786. 2. Gassner, Johann Joseph, 1727-1779. 3. Witchcraft--Bibl. I. Title: Zauberey. II. Title: Teufeleyen.

Zauberbibliothek.

Witchcraft
BF
1565
S83
Z97

[Zapf, Georg Wilhelm] 1747-1810.
Zauberbibliothek. [München] 1776.
91 p. 19cm.
Based on annotated bibliography of the Gassner and Sterzinger controversies which first appeared in Allgemeine deutsche Bibliothek, Berlin, 1775-76. [BF 1565 S83 Z98] CUL holdings noted in ms. in text.
1. Sterzinger, Ferdinand, 1721-1786. 2. Gassner, Johann Joseph, 1727-1779. 3. Witchcraft-- Bibl. I. Title.

CATALOGUE OF THE CORNELL WITCHCRAFT COLLECTION

Zauberei in den germanischen Volksrechten.

Kiessling, Edith.
 Zauberei in den germanischen volksrechten, von dr. iur. Edith Kiessling ... Jena, G. Fischer, 1941.
 79 p. pl. 23½ᶜᵐ. (Added t.-p.: Beiträge zur mittelalterlichen, neueren und allgemeinen geschichte, hrsg. von Friedrich Schneider. Bd. 17)
 Issued also as inaugural dissertation, Frankfurt.
 "Literaturverzeichnis": p. 76-79.
 L. C. copy imperfect: plate wanting.

 1. Witchcraft. 2. Law, Germanic. I. Title.

 43-47132
 Library of Congress   BF1566.K47
 [2]   133.40943

Zauberei und Aberglaube.

Witchcraft
BF
1595
F45

Fiedler, Hermann.
 Zauberei und Aberglaube. Eine kulturhistorische und kritische Beleuchtung dieser Erscheinungen. Bernburg, J. Bacmeister [1884]
 37 p. 21cm.

 1. Magic. 2. Superstition. I. Title.

Zauberei und Hexenprozess.

Witchcraft
BF
1411
D88

Dumcke, Julius, 1867-
 Zauberei und Hexenprozess. Berlin, A. Scherl [1921]
 323 p. 17cm.

 1. Occult Sciences. I. Title.

Zauberei und Hexenprozesse im evangelischen Mecklenburg.

Witchcraft
BF
1583
B57

Beyer, Conrad.
 Kulturgeschichtliche Bilder aus Mecklenburg. Berlin, W. Süsserott, 1903.
 131 p. 24cm. (Mecklenburgische Geschichte in Einzeldarstellungen. Heft 6)

 Contents.--Zauberei und Hexenprozesse im evangelischen Mecklenburg.--Unter den Elenden und Ehrlosen.

 1. Magic--Germany--Mecklenburg. 2. Trials (Witchcraft)--Mecklenburg, Ger. I. Title: Zauberei und Hexenprozesse im evangelischen Mecklenburg. II. Title.

Zauberei und Hexerei.

Witchcraft

Brauchitsch, C   von
 Zauberei und Hexerei.
 (In Die Grenzboten. Zeitschrift für Politik, Literatur und Kunst. Leipzig. 25cm. Jahrg. 36 (1877) p. [281]-294)

 1. Occult sciences. I. Title.

Die Zauberei und ihre Bekämpfung.

WITCHCRAFT
BF
1566
R71

Röschen, Friedrich August.
 Die Zauberei und ihre Bekämpfung. Gütersloh, C. Bertelsmann, 1886.
 110 p. 21cm.

 1. Witchcraft. I. Title.

 8
 NIC

Die Zaubereisünden in ihrer alten und neuen Form betrachtet.

WITCHCRAFT
BF
1133
S38
1854

Schubert, Gotthilf Heinrich von, 1780-1860.
 Die Zaubereisünden in ihrer alten und neuen Form betrachtet ... Neuer unveränderter Abdruck. Erlangen, J. J. Palm und E. Enke, 1854.
 vii, 42 p. 22cm.
 Retraction of certain of his ideas as voiced in his Ansichten von der Nachtseite der Natur and related works.

 1. Mesmerism. 2. Subconsciousness. 3. Occult sciences. 4. His Ansichten von der Nachtseite der Natur. I. Title.

 8
 NIC

Zauberey.

Witchcraft
BF
1565
S83
Z98

Zauberbibliothek. 1775-1776. [Berlin, 1775-76]
 various pagings. 20cm.
 Title from spine.
 Consists of three sections detached from Allgemeine deutsche Bibliothek, titled: Zauberey; Teufeleyen; and Teufeleyen. Eine Fortsetzung der vorigen.

 1. Sterzinger, Ferdinand, 1721-1786. 2. Gassner, Johann Joseph, 1727-1779. 3. Witchcraft--Bibl.

 8

Der Zauberglaube des sechzehnten Jahrhunderts nach den Katechismen Dr. Martin Luthers und des P. Canisius.

Witchcraft
BF
1583
D55
Z3

Diefenbach, Johann.
 Der Zauberglaube des sechzehnten Jahrhunderts nach den Katechismen Dr. Martin Luthers und des P. Canisius. Mit Berücksichtigung der Schriften Pfarrers Längin-Karlsruhe und des Professors Riezler-München. Mainz, F. Kirchheim, 1900.
 xii, 209 p. 23cm.

 1. Witchcraft--Germany. 2. Theology, Doctrinal--16th century. 3. Canisius, Petrus, Saint, 1521-1597. Catechismus.

 8   (Continued on next card)

Zauberglaube und Geheimwissen im Spiegel der Jahrhunderte.

WITCHCRAFT
BF
1413
M28
Z3
1897

Mannhardt, Wilhelm, 1831-1880.
 Zauberglaube und Geheimwissen im Spiegel der Jahrhunderte. Mit 44 teils farbigen Abbildungen. 3. Aufl. Leipzig, H. Barsdorf, 1897.
 284 p. illus. 21cm.

 "Die 'Truten-Zeitung'": p. 243-246. [Reprint of ed. of 1627]

 1. Occult sciences. I. Truten-Zeitung. II. Title.

 8
 NIC

Ein Zauberprozess in Basel 1719.

WITCHCRAFT
BF
1584
S97
H69
1900

Hoffmann-Krayer, Eduard, 1864-1936.
 Ein Zauberprozess in Basel 1719.
 (In Schweizerisches Archiv für Volkskunde. Zürich. 25cm. 2. Jahrg., Heft 4 (1898), p. [283]-291)

 Bound with his Luzerner Akten zum Hexen- und Zauberwesen. Zürich, 1900.

 1. Charms. 2. Folk-lore--Switzerland. I. Title.

 8

Zauberwahn, Inquisition und Hexenprozess im Mittelalter.

WITCHCRAFT
BF
1566
H24

Hansen, Joseph, 1862-1943.
 Zauberwahn, inquisition und hexenprozess im mittelalter und die entstehung der grossen hexenverfolgung. Von Joseph Hansen. München und Leipzig, R. Oldenbourg, 1900.
 xv, 538 p. 22ᶜᵐ. (Historische bibliothek. 12. bd.)   2-20753

 1. Witchcraft--History. 2. Inquisition. 3. Trials (Witchcraft)--History. I. Title. II. Series.

 8
 NIC

 Library of Congress, no.

Zauberwahn und Hexenprozess in der Reichsstadt Nürnberg.

DD
901
N94
K96
1970

Kunstmann, Hartmut Heinrich.
 Zauberwahn und Hexenprozess in der Reichsstadt Nürnberg. [Von] Hartmut H[einrich] Kunstmann. (Nürnberg, Stadtarchiv; Korn u. Berg [in Komm.]) 1970.
 xix, 214 p. with illus. 21cm. (Nürnberger Werkstücke zur Stadt- und Landesgeschichte, Bd. 1)
 Originally presented as the author's thesis, Mainz.

 3   (Continued on next card)

Zauberwesen und Hexenwahn am Niederrhein.

WITCHCRAFT
BF
1583
P33

Pauls, Emil.
 Zauberwesen und Hexenwahn am Niederrhein.
 (In: Beiträge zur Geschichte des Niederrheins. Düsseldorf. 24cm. v.13 (1898) p. [134]-242)

 1. Witchcraft--Germany. 2. Witchcraft--History.

 8
 NIC

Ze reden bij nacht; de mysterieuze gruwelhistorie van de bokkerijders.

BF
1566
S24

Sarpento, Lewis.
 Ze reden bij nacht; de mysterieuze gruwelhistorie van de bokkerijders [door] Ben Lindekens. Amsterdam, Wetenschappelijke Uitgeverij, 1974.
 269 p. 20cm. (Unofficial history)
 Bibliography: p. 262-269.

Zech, Johann Nepomuk Felix, supposed author.

Witchcraft
BF
1565
S83
no.3

Drey Fragen zur Vertheidigung der Hexerey. I. Ob P. Angelus März die Rede des P. Don Ferdinand Sterzingers gründlich, und II. bescheiden widerleget habe? III. Und ob wohl diese akademische Rede dem heiligen Kreutze von Scheyrn in der That nachtheilig sey? Mit einem sichern Ja beantwortet, und dem P. Angelus März selbst dedicirt von J. F. Z. ... [München?] 1767.
 28 p. 23cm.

 8   (Continued on next card)

Zech, Johann Nepomuk Felix, supposed author.

Witchcraft
BF
1565
S83
no.3

Drey Fragen zur Vertheidigung der Hexerey ... 1767.   (Card 2)

 "In spite of the initials J. F. Z. (Johann Felix Zech) in the dedication, the work is probably by H. Braun. See Fieger, H. P. Don Ferdinand Sterzinger, 1907."--Note by G. L. Burr on his ms. catalog slip for this item.
 No. 3 in vol. lettered Sterzinger Über Hexerei, 1766-1767.

 8   (Continued on next card)

Zeedig ondersoek van het boek, door den autheur, Balthasar Bekker ... 1716.

Witchcraft
BF
1410
B42
Z56
v.2
no.23

Hooght, Everard van der, d. 1716.
 Zeedig ondersoek van het boek, door den autheur, Balthasar Bekker, genaamt de Betoverde weereld. In het welke dat tweede boek, van vooren tot achteren, door alle de capittelen en paragraaphen, ordentelijk werd wederlegt. Door Everardus van der Hooght ... Welke achter dit werk gevoegt heeft; drie-der-ley registers; te weeten I. Van Bekkers valsche citatien. II. Een van de texten, ende. III. Een van de verhandelde saaken, de welke of in dit boek,
 (Continued on next card)

CATALOGUE OF THE CORNELL WITCHCRAFT COLLECTION

Witchcraft
BF
1410
B42
Z56
v.2
no.23

Hooght, Everard van der, d. 1716. Zeedig ondersoek van het boek, door den autheur, Balthasar Bekker ... [1692?] (Card 2)

of, in de seven brieven, zijn verhandelt, met des autheurs antwoort op de brieven van B. Bekker. t' Amsterdam, By Dirk Boeteman [1692?]

4 p. l., 229, [1] p. [p. 231-232 blank] title and other vignettes, illus. initials

(Continued on next card)

Witchcraft
BF
1410
B42
Z56
v.2
no.23

Hooght, Everard van der, d. 1716. Zeedig ondersoek van ... de Betoverde weereld. (Card 3)

19 x 15cm.
4°: *⁴, A-2F⁴.
Black letter.
Autograph on back of t. p.: Ev. van der Hooght.
Van der Linde 114.
No. 23 in vol. lettered Bekker II.

(Continued on next card)

8

Witchcraft
BF
1410
B42
Z56
v.3
no.3

Zeedige overweeging op de praedikatie van d'Hr. Petrus Schaak, gedaan in d'Oude Kerk op den 30 September 1691. Amsterdam, By A. Hendriksz [1691]

7 p. [p. 8 blank] title vignette, illus. initial. 20 x 16cm.
4°: A⁴.
Schaak's sermon was against De betoverde weereld, by Balthasar Bekker.
Van der Linde 143.
No. 3 in vol. lettered Bekker III.
1. God--Omnipotence. 2. Schaak, Petrus, fl. 1691. 3. Bekker, Balthasar, 1634-1698. De betoverde weereld.

Witchcraft
BF
1410
B42
Z56
v.2
no.10

Zeedige overweeging op de praedikatie van d'Hr. Petrus Schaak, gedaan in d'Oude Kerk op den 30 September 1691. Amsterdam, By A. Hendriksz [1691]

7 p. [p. 8 blank] title vignette, illus. initial. 20 x 16cm.
4°: A⁴.
Schaak's sermon was against De betoverde weereld, by Balthasar Bekker.
Van der Linde 143.
No. 10 in vol. lettered Bekker II.

8

Zehen mütliche Predigten von der Zauber- und Hexenwerck.

WITCHCRAFT
BF
1565
R91

Rüdinger, Johannes
De magia illicita, decas concionum; zehen mütliche Predigten von der Zauber- vnd Hexenwerck aus Anleitung heiliger Schrifft vnd bewehrter Autorum rationibus nach dem bekanten Schul-Vers Quis? Quid? Ubi? vnd folgends andern Vmbstenden gehalten. Darinnen auff die von dieser Materia fürnembsten Fragen geantwortet, etliche darüber vngleiche Meynung erzehlet vnd dieselben kürtzlich wiederleget werden, durch

8
NIC

(Continued on next card)

Zehen mütliche Predigten von der Zauber- und Hexenwerck.

WITCHCRAFT
BF
1565
R91

Rüdinger, Johannes
De magia illicita... (Card 2)

Johannem Rüdinger. Jehna, In Verlegung J. Reiffenberger, 1630.
406 p. 20cm.

1. Witchcraft--Sermons. I. Title. II. Title: Zehen mütliche Predigten von der Zauber- und Hexenwerck. III. Title: Von der Zauber- und Hexenwerck.

Witchcraft
BF
1565
Z44

Zehner, Joachim, 1566-1612.
Fünff Predigten von den Hexen, ihren Anfang, Mittel vnd End in sich haltend vnd erklärend. Aus heiliger göttlicher Schrifft vnd vornembsten alten Kirchenlehrern zusammen getragen vnd vor dessen gehalten in der Pfarrkirchen zu Schleusingen durch Ioachimum Zehner... Leipzig, In Verlegung Thomae Schürers Buchhändlers [Gedruckt durch Michael Lantzenbergers Erben] 1613.
3 p. l., 90, [2] p. 20cm.

8

(Continued on next card)

Witchcraft
BF
1565
Z44

Zehner, Joachim, 1566-1612. Fünff Predigten von den Hexen ... 1613. (Card 2)

Title in woodcut border.
With colophon.

1. Witchcraft. 2. Witchcraft in the Bible. I. Title.

8

Witchcraft
PT
9850
Z47
1846

Zeipel, Carl von
Karl XI. [i.e., der Elfte], Rabenius und der Hexenprozess. Historischer Roman von Carl von Zeipel. Aus dem Schwedischen übersetzt von G. Fink. Stuttgart, Franckh, 1846.
2 v. in 1. 14cm. (Das belletristische Ausland, hrsg. Carl Spindler, 671.-679. Bd.)
1. Rabenius, Nils, 1648-1717. 2. Witchcraft--Fiction. 3. Karl XI, King of Sweden, 1655-1697--Fiction. I. Title.

8

Zeltner, Gustav Georg, 1672-1738.

Witchcraft
BF
1555
B71

Bonnhöfer, Johann Friedrich.
... Erbauliche Abhandlung von dem erschröcklichen und Jammer-vollen Zustand der geist- und leiblichen Besitzung des Teuffels. In zweyen Betrachtungen aus Heil. Schrifft erwiesen und mit historischen Exempeln erleutert ... mit einer Vorrede Gustav Georg Zeltners, D. worinnen er seine Gedancken vom Binden des Satans, Offenb. 20, 2. eröffnet. Nürnberg, Bey J. W. Rönnagel, 1733.
26 p. l., 884, [36] p. port. 17cm.

8

(Continued on next card)

Witchcraft
BF
1583
Z56

Zenz, Emil
Dr. Dietrich Flade, ein Opfer des Hexenwahnes. Trier, J. Lintz, 1962.
41-69 p. 24cm.

Caption title.
"Kurtrierisches Jahrbuch. Jahrgang 2, 1962. Sonderabdruck."

1. Flade, Dietrich, 1534-1589. 2. Witchcraft--Germany. I. Title.

Zeugnisse zum Hexenwahn des 17. Jahrh.

Witchcraft
BF
1584
V9
A43

Allgäuer, Emil.
Zeugnisse zum Hexenwahn des 17. Jahrh. (Ein Beitrag zur Volkskunde Vorarlbergs) Salzburg, Gedruckt bei R. Kiesel, 1914.

Accompanies Programm--K.K. Staats-Gymnasium, Salzburg.

1. Witchcraft--Vorarlberg. I. Title

Witchcraft
BF
1569
Z66

Ziegeler, Wolfgang.
Möglichkeiten der Kritik am Hexen- und Zauberwesen im ausgehenden Mittelalter: zeitgenöss. Stimmen u. ihre soziale Zugehörigkeit / Wolfgang Ziegeler. Köln, Wien: Böhlau, 1973.
xi, 231 p. 21 cm. (Kollektive Einstellungen und sozialer Wandel im Mittelalter; Bd. 2)
Bibliography: p. [206]-229.

1. Witchcraft--History. 2. Magic--History. I. Title II. Series

NIC   JUN 27.'74   COOxc   73-361719

WITCHCRAFT
R
133
Z66

Ziegra, Christian Samuel, praeses.
Disputatio physica De magica morborum curatione, qvam ... exponit praeses M. Christianus Samuel Ziegra ... respondente M. Johanne Georgio Spiess ... [Wittebergae] Typis Matthaei Henckelii [1681]
[24] p. 19cm.

1. Medicine, Magic, mystic, and spagiric. 2. Witchcraft. 3. Folk medicine. I. Spiess, Johannes Georg, respondent. II. Title: De magica morborum curatione. III. Title.

8
NIC

Witchcraft
BF
1587
D61
no.5

Ziegra, Constantinus, praeses.
Disputatio physica exhibens I. Doctrinam de magia. II. Theoremata miscellanea ex parte tùm generali tùm speciali physicae. Qvam sub praesidio ... Dn. Constantini Ziegra ... ventilationi subjiciet M. Elias Conradi ... aut. & resp. Wittebergae, Typis Jobi Wilhelmi Fincelii, 1661.
[36] p. 21cm.
No. 5 in vol. lettered Dissertationes de magia. 1623- 1723.
1. Occult sciences--Addresses, essays, lectures. I. Conradi, Elias, respondent. II. Title.

8

Witchcraft
HQ
822
H33
1731

Hartmann, Johann Zacharias, praeses.
Dispvtatio inavgvralis ivridica De conivgibvs incantatis eorvmqve separatione, Germanice: Von bezauberten Ehe-Leuten und derselben Scheidung, qvam ... svb praesidio ... Io. Zachariae Hartmanni ... pvblico ervditorvm examini svbiicit avctor Ioannes Helvigivs Zielinski ... Ienae, Recvsa per I. B. Hellervm, 1731.
38, [2] p. 21cm.
Diss.--Jena   (J. H. Zielinski, respondent, 1727)

8

(Continued on next card)

BF
1569
Z69

Zilboorg, Gregory, 1890-
... The medical man and the witch during the renaissance, by Gregory Zilboorg ... Baltimore, The Johns Hopkins press, 1935.
x, 215 p. front. (port.) illus., plates. 20½ᶜᵐ. (Publications of the Institute of the history of medicine, the Johns Hopkins university. 3d ser., vol. II)
"The Hideyo Noguchi lectures."
CONTENTS.--The physiological and psychological aspects of the Malleus maleficarum (The witch's hammer)--Medicine and the witch in the sixteenth century.--Johann Weyer, the founder of modern psychiatry.

1. Witchcraft. 2. Psychology, Pathological. 3. Institoris, Henricus, d. ca. 1500. Malleus maleficarum. 4. Sprenger, Jakob, fl. 1494, joint author. Malleus maleficarum. 5. Wier, Johann, 1515-1588. 6. Renaissance.   I. Title.
                                                    35--12004
Library of Congress   BF1569.Z5
——— Copy 2.
Copyright   A 84565   [40n1]   [150.9614002]   133.40002

Rare
K
Z695
1563

Ziletti, Giovanni Battista, fl. 1559, ed.
Volvmen praeclarissimvm ... omnivm tractatvvm criminalivm nunc per d. Ioan. Baptistam Zilettum Venetum ab omnibus mendis expurgatum ac omnino correctum, & longè diligentius accuratius ac fœlicius quàm unquam antea, in lucem proditum. Nam praeter omnes tractatvs, qui sunt antea in hac materia editi, non hoc volumine quamplurimi alii tractatus ... continentur, qui cùm essent manu scripti. Svnt svmma cvra diligentia stvdio ac sumptu nunc nouiter è manibus doctissimorum ac praestantissimorum omnium aetatis nostre iurisperitorum ex-

(Continued on next card)   38-33484

CATALOGUE OF THE CORNELL WITCHCRAFT COLLECTION

Rare   Ziletti, Giovanni Battista, *fl.* 1559, *ed.*   Volvmen praecla-
K   rissimvm ... (Card 2)
Z695
.563   cerpti ... cvm eivsdem d. Ioan. Baptistæ Ziletti, omnium ma-
teriarum indice multò quàm antea pleniore. Venetiis [apud
Cominum de Tridino Montisferrati] M D LXIII.
   68 p. l., 416 numb. l. illus. 21ᶜᵐ.
   Title vignette.

   1. Roman law. 2. Criminal law (Roman law) I. Title.

                                  38-33484

Library of Congress   [8]

WITCHCRAFT
K   Ziletti, Giovanni Battista, fl. 1559, ed.
Z695   Volvmen praeclarissimvm ... omnivm trac-
1580   tatvvm criminalivm nvnc per D. Ioan. Baptistam Zilettum ab omnibus mendis expurgatum ac omnino correctum ... Venetiis,
Apud Io. Antonium Bertanum, 1580.
   78 p. l., 473 numbered leaves. 21cm.
   Includes Tractatvs ... de lamijs ...
Ioanni Francisci Ponzinibij, l. 89-99 v.;
De sortilegiis tractatus Pauli Ghirlandi,
l. 104 v.-138 v.
8   (Continued on next card)

WITCHCRAFT
K   Ziletti, Giovanni Battista, fl. 1559, ed.
Z695   Volvmen praeclarissivm...1580. (Card 2)
1580

   1. Roman law. 2. Criminal law (Roman
law) I. Grillando, Paolo. De sortilegiis.
II. Ponzinibius, Joannes Franciscus. De
lamiis. III. Title: Volumen praeclarissimum ... omnium tractatuum criminalium.
8

   Zimara, Marco Antonio, 1460-1532.
     Antrum magico-medicum.
WITCHCRAFT
BF   Longinus, Caesar, ed.
1405   Trinum magicum, sive Secretorum magico-
L85   rum opus ... Editum à Caesare Longino phi-
1673   los. Francofurti, Sumptibus Jacobi Gothofredi Seyleri, 1673.
   12 p. l., 498 p. 14cm.
   Contents.--Marci Antonii Zimarae Tractatus magicus.--Appendix, De mirandis quibusdam naturali magia factis operationibus.
Ex lib. 2. Mag. natur. Ioan. Bapt. Port.--
Tractatvs De virtutibus quarundam herbarum,
8   (Continued on next card)

   Zimara, Marco Antonio, 1460-1532.
     Antrum magico-medicum.
WITCHCRAFT
BF   Longinus, Caesar, ed. Trinum magicum ...
1405   1673. (Card 2)
L85
1673   lapidum & animalium. A. M. A.--Commentatio
De magnetica curatione vulnerum citra svperstitionem ... Authore R. G. M. D.--Logia,
sive Oracvla Zoroastri ex Platonicorum libris collecta.--Tractatus De proprii cujusqve nati daemonis inqvisitione.
   Layout of text corresponds to that of
Frankfurt, 1630 ed. (C. Eifrid, printer)
8   (Continued on next card)

Witchcraft
BX   Zimmermann, J   A
4705   Johann Joseph Gassner, der berühmte Exor-
G35406   zist. Sein Leben und wundersames Wirken aus
Z74   Anlass seiner hundertjährigen Todesfeier
neuerdings erzählt und gewürdiget von J. A.
Zimmermann. Kempten, J. Kösel'sche Buchhandlung, 1878.
   viii, 122 p. 19cm.

   1. Gassner, Johann Joseph, 1727-1779.
8   2. Exorcism. 3. Faith-cure. I. Title.

WITCHCRAFT   Zimmermann, Johann Georg, Ritter von,
BF   1728-1795.
1623   Obereit, Jacob Hermann, 1725-1798.
R7   Gerade Schweizer-Erklärung von Centralis-
012   mus, [Exjesuiterey, Anecdoten]agd, Aberglauben, Maulglauben und Unglauben, gegen einen
neuen Rosenkreuz-Bruder in der Berliner
Monatsschrift vom August 1785... Berlin,
Bei August Mylius, 1786.
   viii, 94 p. 17cm.

   1. Rosicrucians. 2. Mysticism. 3. Superstition. 4. Jesuits--Controversial literature. I. Zimmermann, Johann
   Georg, Ritt   er von, 1728-1795.
8   II. Title. III. Title: Schweizer-
N.C.   Erklärung von Centralismus...

Witchcraft
BF   Zingerle, Ignaz Vincenz, Edler von Summers-
1584   berg, 1825-1892, ed.
T9   Barbara Pachlerin, die Sarnthaler Hexe,
Z59   und Mathias Perger, der Lauterfresser. Zwei
Hexenprozesse, hrsg. von Dr. Ignaz Zingerle.
Innsbruck, Wagner, 1858.
   xii, 84 p. 19cm.
   Contents.--Barbara Pachlerin, die Sarn-
thaler Hexe.--Der Lauterfresser.--Anhang.
Ein altes Loosbuch.
8   Each item has special t. p.
   (Continued on next card)

Witchcraft
BF   Zingerle, Ignaz Vincenz, Edler von Summers-
1584   berg, 1825-1892, ed. Barbara Pachlerin,
T9   die Sarnthaler Hexe ... 1858. (Card 2)
Z59

   1. Pachler, Barbara, d. 1540. 2. Per-
ger, Mathias, ca. 1580-1645? 3. Witchcraft
--Tyrol. 4. Fortune-telling. I. Title:
Der Lauterfresser. II. Title: Loosbuch.
8   III. Title: Barbara Pachlerin, die Sarnthaler
Hexe. IV. Title: Ein altes Loosbuch.

Witchcraft
BF   Zingerle, Ignaz Vincenz, Edler von Summers-
1584   berg, 1825-1892, ed.
T9   Ein Beitrag zu den Hexenprozessen in
Z7   Tirol im 17 Jahrhundert. Von Ignaz V. Zin-
1644   gerle. [Innsbruck, 1882]
   [183]-189 p. 23cm.
   Reprint from Zeitschrift des Ferdinandeum, 3. Folge, 26. Heft, 1882.
   1. Pozza, Juliana de, fl. 1644. 2.
Trials (Witchcraft)--Tyrol. I. Title:
Die Hexenproze   sse in Tirol im 17.
8   Jahrhundert. II. Title.

   Zlye dukhi i ikh vliianie na liudei.
WITCHCRAFT
BF   Mark, abbot of the Simonov Monastery of
1538   Moscow.
R9   (Zlye dukhi i ikh vliianie na liudei) Злые
M34   духи и ихъ влiянiе на людей. / Игумена Марка,
Духовника Московскаго Ставропигiальнаго Симо-
нова монастыря. С.-Петербургъ, Типо-лит.
и переплетная Ю. А. Мансфельдъ, 1899.
   180 p. 25cm.

   1. Demonology. 2. Devil. I. Title.

Witchcraft
BF   Zobel, Enoch, 1653-1697.
1429   Declaratio apologetica, das ist: Schutz-
G62   schriftliche und fernere Erklärung, uber [sic]
1704   die St. Annabergische Gespensts-Historie,
wider Herrn Balthasar Bekkers ... heraus-gegebenes Buch, genannt Die bezauberte Welt,
abgefasset von M. Enoch Zobeln, Archi-Diac.
zu St Annaberg. Leipzig, Verlegt von den
Lanckischen Erben, 1695.
   7 p. l., 174, [1] p. [p. 176 blank]
front., vignettes. 17 x 10cm.

   (Continued on next card)

Witchcraft
BF   Zobel, Enoch, 1653-1697. Declaratio apo-
1429   logetica ... 1695. (Card 2)
G62
1704   8°: χ⁸(-)(8), A-L⁸.
   Black letter.
   At head of title: B. C. D.
   Autograph on p. [176]: Adolph Gerhard
Eduard Grovermann.
   Bound with Goldschmidt, P. Höllischer
Morpheus. Hamburg, 1704.
   1. Ghosts--Germany. 2. Bekker, Baltha-
   (Continued on next card)

Witchcraft
BF   Zobel, Enoch, 1653-1697. Declaratio apo-
1429   logetica ... 1695. (Card 3)
G62
1704   sar, 1634-1698. De betoverde weereld. 3.
His Historische und theologische Vorstel-
lung des ebentheuerlichen Gespenstes. I.
Title.

Witchcraft
BF   Zobel, Enoch, 1653-1697.
1483   Die ebenthürliche [sic] Beschreibung des
Z84   Gespenstes, welches in einem Hause zu St.
1692   Annaberg, im abgelegten 1691 Jahr 2 Month
lang, viel Schrecken, Furcht und wunderseltzame Schau-Spiele angerichtet. Beschrieben
von des Hauses Eigenthumbs-Herrn, M. Enoch
Zobeln, Arch. Diac. daselbst. Hamburg, Zu
bekommen bey T. von Wiering [1692]
   [24] p. 18cm.
   Reproduces p. [1]-48 of the author's
   (Continued on next card)

Witchcraft
BF   Zobel, Enoch, 1653-1697. Die ebenthürliche
1483   Beschreibung des Gespenstes ... [1692]
Z84
1692   (Card 2)

   Historische und theologische Vorstellung des
ebenteuerlichen Gespenstes ... Leipzig, 1692.

   1. Ghosts--Germany. I. Title. II.
His Historische und theologische Vorstellung des ebenteuerlichen Gespenstes.

Witchcraft
BF   Zobel, Enoch, 1653-1697.
1429   Historische und theologische Vorstellung
G62   des ebentheuerlichen Gespenstes, welches in
1704   einem Hause zu S. Annaberg, 2 Monat lang im
neuligst 1691sten Jahr, viel Schrecken,
Furcht und wunderseltsame Schauspiele angerichtet ... Leipzig, F. Lanckischens
Erben, 1692.
   [32], 312, [22] p. illus. 18cm.

   Bound with Goldschmidt, P. Höllischer
Morpheus. Ham   burg, 1704.
   I. Title.

   Zobel, Enoch, 1653-1697.
Witchcraft   Historische und theologische Vorstellung
BF   Zobel, Enoch, 1653-1697.
1483   Die ebenthürliche [sic] Beschreibung des
Z84   Gespenstes, welches in einem Hause zu St.
1692   Annaberg, im abgelegten 1691 Jahr 2 Monath
lang, viel Schrecken, Furcht und wunderseltzame Schau-Spiele angerichtet. Beschrieben
von des Hauses Eigenthumbs-Herrn, M. Enoch
Zobeln, Arch. Diac. daselbst. Hamburg, Zu
bekommen bey T. von Wiering [1692]
   [24] p. 18cm.
   Reproduces p. [1]-48 of the author's
   (Continued on next card)

CATALOGUE OF THE CORNELL WITCHCRAFT COLLECTION

Zobel, Enoch, 1653-1697.
Historische und theologische Vorstellung des ebenteuerlichen Gespenstes.

Witchcraft
BF
1483
Z84
1692

Zobel, Enoch, 1653-1697. Die ebenthürliche Beschreibung des Gespenstes ... [1692] (Card 2)

Historische und theologische Vorstellung des ebenteuerlichen Gespenstes ... Leipzig, 1692.

1. Ghosts--Germany. I. Title. II. His Historische und theologische Vorstellung des ebenteuerlichen Gespenstes.

8

Zobel, Enoch, 1653-1697.
Historische und theologische Vorstellung des ebenteuerlichen Gespenstes.

Witchcraft
BF
1429
G62
1704

Zobel, Enoch, 1653-1697. Declaratio apologetica, das ist: Schutz-schriftliche und fernere Erklärung, uber [sic] die St. Annabergische Gespensts-Historie, wider Herrn Balthasar Bekkers ... heraus-gegebenes Buch, genannt Die bezauberte Welt, abgefasset von M. Enoch Zobeln, Archi-Diac. zu St. Annaberg. Leipzig, Verlegt von den Lanckischen Erben, 1695.

7 p. l., 174, [1] p. [p. 176 blank] front., vignettes. 17 x 10cm.

(Continued on next card)

Zobel, Enoch, 1653-1697.
Historische und theologische Vorstellung des ebenteuerlichen Gespenstes.

Witchcraft
BF
1429
G62
1704

Zobel, Enoch, 1653-1697. Declaratio apologetica ... 1695. (Card 2)

8°: χ⁸ (-)(8), A-L⁸.
Black letter.
At head of title: B. C. D.
Autograph on p. [176]: Adolph Gerhard Eduard Grovermann.
Bound with Goldschmidt, P. Höllischer Morpheus. Hamburg, 1704.

1. Ghosts--Germany. 2. Bekker, Baltha-

(Continued on next card)

WITCHCRAFT
BF
1566
Z94

Zuccalmaglio, Anton Wilhelm Florentin von, 1803-1869.
Naturforschung und Hexenglaube. Von Wilhelm von Waldbrühl [pseud.] Berlin, C. G. Lüderitz, [1867]
39 p. 21cm. (Sammlung gemeinverständlicher wissenschaftlicher Vorträge, 2. Ser., Heft 46)
Note by G. L. Burr on p. [5]: "A very careless booklet. It has led many astray by its misstatements of fact -- me for instance."

8

I. Title.

AC
30
S18
no.46

Zuccalmaglio, Anton Wilhelm Florentin von, 1803-1869.
Naturforschung und Hexenglaube, von Wilhelm von Waldbrühl [pseud.] Berlin, C. G. Lüderitz, 1867.
38 p. 21cm. (Sammlung gemeinverständlicher wissenschaftlicher Vorträge, II. Ser., Heft 46)

1. Witchcraft.

Zulich, Fridemann Andreas, b. 1687, respondent.

Witchcraft
BF
1520
K89

Krakevitz, Albert Joachim von, 1674-1734, praeses.
Facultatis theologicae ad hunc actum decanus Albertus Joach. de Krakevitz, ... suo & collegii theologici nomine ad disputationem inauguralem ... Dn. M. Fridemanni Andreae Zulichii, Jenens. De theologia daemonum ... invitat. Rostochii, Litteris J. Wepplingi, Sereniss. Princ. & univ. typogr. [1715]
10 p. l., 68 p. 21cm.

8   The first se   ction is a curriculum
(Continued on next card)

Zulich, Fridemann Andreas, b. 1687, respondent.

Witchcraft
BF
1520
K89

Krakevitz, Albert Joachim von, 1674-1734, praeses. ...De theologia daemonum ... [1715] (Card 2)

vitae.
The dissertation proper has special t. p.: Auxiliante summo numine specimen inaugurale theologicum De theologia daemonum ...
Diss.--Rostock (F. A. Zulich, respondent.

1. Demonology. 2. Devil. I. Zulich, Fridemann Andreas, b. 1687, respondent. II. His Specimen inaugurale theologicum De theologia daemonum. III. Title: De theologia daemonum.

8

Zur Biographie von Christian Thomasius.

Witchcraft
B
2605
Z7
L26+

Landsberg, Ernst, 1860-1927.
Zur biographie von Christian Thomasius, von prof. dr. Ernst Landsberg. Bonn, F. Cohen, 1894.
1 p. l., 36 p. 28½ᶜᵐ.
"Festschrift zur zweiten säcularfeier der Friedrichs-universität zu Halle."

8

1. Thomasius, Christian, 1655-1728.

21-9110

Library of Congress   B2605.Z7L3

Zur Entstehungsgeschichte der Theresianischen Halsgerichtsordnung.

WITCHCRAFT
BF
1584
A93
M39

Maschek von Maasburg, Friedrich, 1838-1918.
Zur Entstehungsgeschichte der Theresianischen Halsgerichtsordnung, mit besonderer Rücksicht auf das im Artikel 58 derselben behandelte crimen magiae vel sortilegii. Wien, Manz, 1880.
vi, 60 p. 24cm.

8
NIC

1. Witchcraft--Laws and legislation--Austria. 2. Trials (Witchcraft)--Austria.

Zur Geschichte der Criminal-Justiz und besonders der Hexenprozesse in Hohenzollern.

WITCHCRAFT
BF
1583
S358

Schnell, Eugen.
Zur Geschichte der Criminal-Justiz und besonders der Hexenprozesse in Hohenzollern. Von Eugen Schnell, Fürstl. Hohenz. Archivar in Sigmaringen. [n. p., 1873]
[69]-99 p. 22cm.

Caption title.
Detached from a journal.

8
NIC

1. Witchcraft--Swabia. 2. Criminal procedure-- Hohenzollern. I. Title.

Zur Geschichte der Hexen und Juden in Bonn.

WITCHCRAFT
DS
135
G4
B71

Joesten, Joseph, 1850-1909.
Zur Geschichte der Hexen und Juden in Bonn; eine kulturgeschichtliche Studie, von Dr. Joesten. Bonn, C. Georgi, 1900.
47 p. 24cm.

8
NIC

1. Jews in Bonn. 2. Witchcraft--Bonn. I. Title.

Zur Geschichte der Hexenprocesse.

Witchcraft
BF
1583
Z7
1554

Wigand, Paul, 1786-1866.
Zur Geschichte der Hexenprocesse. 1) Ein Hexenprocess vor dem Criminalgericht zu Horn im Fürstenthum Lippe. 1554. [Leipzig, S. Hirzel, 1854]
[248]-259 p. 24cm.
Caption title.
Detached from his Denkwürdigkeiten, Kap. VIII

Zur Geschichte der Hexenprocesse in Erfurt und Umgegend.

WITCHCRAFT
BF
1583
J37

Jaraczewsky, Adolph.
Zur Geschichte der Hexenprocesse in Erfurt und Umgegend; ein Beitrag zur Culturgeschichte des 17. Jahrhunderts ... von Dr. Jaraczewski. Erfurt, C. Villaret, 1876.
28 p. 22cm.

"Vortrag, gehalten im Verein für Geschichte und Alterthumskunde in Erfurt."

8
NIC

1. Trials (Witchcraft)--Erfurt.
I. Title.

Zur Geschichte der Hexenprozesse.

Witchcraft
BF
1583
Z7+
1613

Bacmeister, Dr., archivist.
Zur Geschichte der Hexenprozesse. Concept Bedenkens über die zu Niedernhaal um Hexerei und Zauberei willen in verhaft liegende Susann, Michel Lunge's Weib, derem Aussage, und noch weiters angebene Personen. [Würtemberg, 1886]
282-292 p. 30cm.

Caption title.
Detached from Württembergische Vierteljahrsheft für Landesgeschichte, IX, 1886.

(Continued on next card)

Zur Geschichte der Hexenprozesse.

Witchcraft
BF
1583
Z7+
1613

Bacmeister, Dr., archivist. Zur Geschichte der Hexenprozesse. (Card 2)

In pamphlet binder with Bossert, Gustav. Frankisches Gemeinderecht. [Würtemberg, 1886]

1. Lunge, Susann, fl. 1613. 2. Witchcraft--Germany. I. Title.

Zur Geschichte des Glaubens an Zauberer, Hexen, und Vampyre in Mähren und Osterr. Schlesien.

Witchcraft
BF
1413
B62+
1859

Bischof, Ferdinand.
Zur Geschichte des Glaubens an Zauberer, Hexen, und Vampyre in Mähren und Oesterr. Schlesien. Von Ferdinand Bischof und Christian d'Elvert. Brünn, Buchdruckerei von R. Rohrer's Erben, 1859.
164 p. 26cm.

"Aus dem XII. Bande der Schriften der historisch-statistischen Sektion der k. k. mähr. schles. Gesellschaft zur Beförderung des Ackerbaues, der Natur- und Landeskunde besonders abgedruckt."

Zur Geschichte des Hexenglaubens und der Hexenprozesse.

WITCHCRAFT
BF
1583
N66

Niehues, Bernhard, 1831-1909.
Zur Geschichte des Hexenglaubens und der Hexenprozesse, vornehmlich im ehemaligen Fürstbisthum Münster. Münster, Coppenrath, 1875.
vi, 151 p. 23cm.

8
NIC

1. Witchcraft--Münster (Diocese) 2. Trials (Witchcraft)--Münster (Diocese)

Zur Geschichte des Hexenwahns.

Witchcraft
BF
1563
E92++
no.3

München, C. Wolf, 1897.
316-317 p. 32cm. (Deutscher Merkur, 28. Jahrg., No. 40)
A review of Riezler, S. Geschichte der Hexenprozesse in Bayern. Stuttgart, Cottas Nachfolger, 1896. [BF 1583 R56 1968]
No. 3 in vol. lettered Evans: Ein Trierer Hexenprocess, etc.

1. Witchcraft. 2. Trials (Witchcraft)
3. Riezler, Sigmund, Ritter von, 1843-1927. Geschichte der Hexenprozesse in Bayern.

624

CATALOGUE OF THE CORNELL WITCHCRAFT COLLECTION

Zur Geschichte des Hexenwesens.

WITCHCRAFT
34
2
Mell, Anton, 1865-1940.
Zur Geschichte des Hexenwesens; ein Beitrag aus steirischen Quellen. [Berlin? 1891]
[317]-335 p. 25cm.

Extracted from Zeitschrift für deutsche Kulturgeschichte, 1891.

1. Witchcraft--Styria. 2. Trials (Witchcraft)--Styria.

Witchcraft
3
4
Zur Geschichte des Hexenwesens in Mähren und Schlesien. [Brunn? 1865]
395-424 p. 26cm. (Schriften der historisch- statistischen Section der mährschlesischen Gesellschaft zur Beförderung des Ackerbaues, der Natur- u. Landeskunde, 4)

1. Witchcraft. 2. Trials (Witchcraft)--Germany. I. Elvert, Christian, Ritter d', 1803-1896, supposed author.

Zur Geschichte des Volks-Aberglaubens im Anfange des XVI. Jahrhunderts.

Witchcraft
40
41
56
Geiler, Johannes, von Kaisersberg, 1445-1510.
Zur Geschichte des Volks-Aberglaubens im Anfange des XVI. Jahrhunderts. Aus Dr. Joh. Geilers von Kaisersberg Emeis. Mit einer Einleitung, Erläuterung und sonstigen literarischen Nachweisungen herausgegeben von August Stöber ... Basel, Schweighauser, 1856.
4 p. l., 92 p. 24cm.

Zur Hexenbulle 1484.

WITCHCRAFT
569
6
Sauter, Johann G
Zur Hexenbulle 1484. Die Hexerei, mit besonderer Berücksichtigung Oberschwabens. Eine culturhistorische Studie. Ulm, J. Ebner, 1884.
82 p. 21cm.

1. Witchcraft--History. 2. Witchcraft--Swabia. 3. Catholic Church. Pope, 1484-1492(Innocentius VIII) Summis desiderantes affectibus (9 Dec. 1484) I. Title.

Zur Naturgeschichte der Hexen.

WITCHCRAFT
69
6
Holzinger, J B
Zur Naturgeschichte der Hexen. Vortrag gehalten vom Vereins-Präsidenten ... J. B. Holzinger, in der Jahres-Versammlung des Naturwissenschaftlichen Vereines für Steiermark am 16. December 1882. Graz, Verlag des Naturwissenschaftlichen Vereines für Steiermark, 1883.
40 p. 23cm.
"Separat-Abdruck aus den Mittheilungen des naturwissenschaftlichen Vereines für Steiermark Jahrgang 1882."

1. Witchcraft--History. 2. Science and civilization. I. Title.

De zwarte magie.

Witchcraft
48
Jong, Karel Hendrik Edward.
De zwarte magie. [2. herziene en verm. druk] 's-Gravenhage, H. P. Leopold [1955]
273 p. 24cm. (Parapsychologische bibliotheek, deel III)

1. Occult sciences. I. Title.

MSS
Bd.
WITCHCRAFT
BT
Z97
Zween erschreckliche Geschicht, gesangsweise.
Die erste, von einem Wirt im Allgergaw, Bastian Schönmundt genandt ... wie er sein ehelich Wieb [sic], so schwanger Leibs gewesen, dreyen Mördern verkaufft ... Die ander, eine erschreckliche und warhafftige neue Zeitung, wie sich im 1596. Jahres ... hat zugetragen, das ein schwanger Weib vom Teuffel besessen, iren Man sampt drey Kindern, auch sich selbs mit ihrer Leibesfrucht jemmerlich ermordt und umbgebracht hat.
(Continued on next card)

MSS
Bd.
WITCHCRAFT
BT
Z97
Zween erschreckliche Geschicht, gesangsweise ... [1596; ca. 1900] (Card 2)
[n.p., 1596; ca. 1900]
6 l. 19cm.
Carnap's manuscript copy.
"Druck in der Königl. Bibliothek zu Berlin; 4 Bl. in 16°."
In verse.
1. Providence and government of God. 2. Demoniac possession.

Zwei Förderer des Hexenwahns und ihre Ehrenrettung.

Witchcraft
BF
1583
C94
Crohns, Hjalmar, 1862-1946.
Zwei Förderer des Hexenwahns und ihre Ehrenrettung durch die ultramontane Wissenschaft. Stuttgart, Strecker & Schröder, 1905.
62 p. 20cm.

1. Institoris, Henricus, d. ca. 1500. 2. Antoninus, Saint, abp. of Florence, 1389-1459. 3. Witchcraft. 4. Ultramontanism. I. Title.

Zwei Hexengeschichten aus Waltershausen in Thüringen.

WITCHCRAFT
BF
1583
S39
Schwartz, Friedrich Leberecht Wilhelm, 1821-1899.
Zwei Hexengeschichten aus Waltershausen in Thüringen nebst einem mythologischen Excurs über Hexen- und ähnlichen Versammlungen. Von Direktor W. Schwartz. [Berlin, 1888]
395-419 p. 22cm.
Extract from Zeitschrift für Völkerpsychologie, v. 18.

1. Witchcraft--Thuringia. 2. Walpurgisnacht. I. Title.

Witchcraft
BF
1583
Z7
1688
Zwei Hexenprocesse aus dem Jahre 1688, geführt bei dem hochfürstlichen Amte in Ballenstedt. Quedlinburg, H. C. Huch, 1863.
104 p. 22cm.
Contents.--I. Acta inquisitionalia ... wider Marthen Margarethen Kirchbergs aus Reinstedt.--II. Acta inquisitionalia ... contra die Pfannenschmiedin Anna Teichmanns.
1. Trials (Witchcraft)--Saxony. I. Kirchberg, Marthe Margarethe, d. 1688, defendant. II. Teichmann, Anna, fl. 1688, defendant.

Witchcraft
BF
1584
B6
Z68
Zwei Hexenprozesse zu Braunau.
(In Verein für Geschichte der Deutschen in Böhmen. Mittheilungen. Prag. 23cm. 33. Jahrg., Nr. 3 (1895), p. 285-292)
An editorial, probably by G. Biermann.

1. Trials (Witchcraft)--Bohemia. I. Biermann, Gottlieb, 1824- , supposed author.

Zwei Hexenprozesse aus dem 16. Jahrhundert.

Witchcraft
CB
3
Z481
Richel, Arthur.
Zwei Hexenprozesse aus dem 16. Jahrhundert.
(In Beiträge zur Kulturgeschichte. Weimar. 25cm. 2. Heft (1898), p. 1-17)

1. Witchcraft--Germany. I. Title.

Zwei Hexenprozesse aus der Crefelder Gegend.

WITCHCRAFT
BX
2340
P33
Keussen, Hermann, 1862-
Zwei Hexenprozesse aus der Crefelder Gegend.
(In: Historischer Verein für den Niederrhein. Annalen. Köln. 23cm. No.63 (1897) p. 111-119)
With, in the same issue: Pauls, Emil. Der Exorcismus an Herzog Johann Wilhelm von Jülich in den Jahren 1604 und 1605.
1. Trials (Witchcraft)--Krefeld, Ger. 2. Hagh, Catharina. 3. Blex, Sibilla. 4. Bleick, Anna.

Zwei Hexenprozesse aus der Grafschaft Mansfeld.

WITCHCRAFT
BF
1583
Z7
1652
Könnecke, Max.
Zwei Hexenprozesse aus der Grafschaft Mansfeld.
(In Mansfelder Blätter. Eisleben, 1887-1940? 23cm. 10. Jahrg. (1896), p. [32]-65)
Caption title.
"Inquisitionsakten wider die Pfarrwitwe Anna Kluge zu Ahlsdorf in Sachen beschuldigter Hexerei, 1652 und 1655": p. 34-51.
"Inquisitionsakten wider Anna Traute Frohertzin und Marie Grösseln in Gerbstedt wegen beschuldigter Hexerei, 1689": p. 52-65.
(Continued on next card)

Zwei Klostergeschichten des vorigen Jahrhunderts.

Witchcraft
BV
4935
G66
G12
Gätschenberger, Stephan.
Zwei Klostergeschichten des vorigen Jahrhunderts. Zum erstenmale nach den Inquisitions-Akten bearbeitet ... Leipzig, C. F. Fleischer, 1858.
124 p. 18cm.
Contents.--1. Graf James Gordon oder Pater Marianus.--2. Die letzte Hexe in Deutschland.
1. Gordon, James, 1704-1734. 2. Conversion. 3. Sänger, Maria Renata von Mossau, ca. 1680-1749. 4. Witchcraft. 5. Martyrs. I. Title.

Zweifel eines Baiers über die wirkende Zauberkunst und Hexerey.

Witchcraft
BF
1565
S83
K81
[Kollmann, Jacob Anton]
Zweifel eines Baiers über die wirkende Zauberkunst und Hexerey. An dem Lechstrome [i.e., Augsburg] 1768.
74, [1] p. 19cm.
Attribution by British Museum and H. Fieger, P. Don Ferdinand Sterzinger, München, 1907.

1. Sterzinger, Ferdinand, 1721-1786. Akademische Rede von dem gemeinen Vorurtheile der ... Hexerey. 2. März, Agnellus, 1726-1784. 3. Witchcraft. II. Title.

PT
1792
Z97
Zwetsloot, Hugo.
Friedrich Spee und die Hexenprozesse; die Stellung und Bedeutung der Cautio criminalis in der Geschichte der Hexenverfolgungen. Trier, Paulinus-Verlag, 1954.
345 p. illus., port. 24 cm.
Bibliography: p. 323-328.
"Ausgaben und Übersetzungen der Cautio criminalis": p. 329-331.

1. Spee, Friedrich von, 1591-1635. Cautio criminalis. 2. Trials (Witchcraft)--Germany. I. Title.

56-33376

CATALOGUE OF THE CORNELL WITCHCRAFT COLLECTION

WITCHCRAFT
BT
770
H65

Zwey Predigten von der Ermunterung zu dem rechtschaffenen Kampffe gegen die bösen Geister.
 Hillinger, Johann Gottlieb, 1698-1732.
  Herrn Johann Gottlieb Hillingers ... Zwey Predigten von der Ermunterung zu dem rechtschaffenen Kampffe gegen die bösen Geister, und von dem Glauben, der durch die Liebe thätig ist. Nebst einem Bedenken von der geistlichen Besitzung ... Jena, Bey J. R. Crökern, Druckts J. C. Cröker, 1733.
  80 p. 19cm.
  Title in red and black.
8   1. Faith——Sermons. 2. Devil. 3. Demoniac possession.

MSS
Bd.
WITCHCRAFT
BT
S33

Zwo christliche Predigten aber der Buss unnd Bekehrung.
 Schickhart, Philipp.
  Zwo christliche Predigten, aber [sic] der Buss unnd Bekehrung, eines Jüngs, welcher sich, laut nachgesetzter Vorred, dem bösen Geist, auff siben Jar lang, mit Leib uñ Seel ergeben gehabt. Gehalten zu Göppingen, durch M. Philippum Schickardum ... Tübingen, Getruckt bey Johan Conrad Geysslern, 1631 [ca. 1900]
  [6], 48 p. title vignette. 19cm.
  Signatures: A- G⁴, F.
  Carnap's manuscript copy.
(Continued on next card)

MSS
Bd.
WITCHCRAFT
BT
S33

Zwo christliche Predigten aber der Buss unnd Bekehrung.
 Schickhart, Philipp. Zwo christliche Predigten ... 1631 [ca. 1900] (Card 2)
 "Original i. d. Kgl. Bibl. z. Stuttgart. Titelbl. 3 Bl. Vorrede u. 48 pag. S. Text. Sig. Aiij-Giij."
 Bibliography: 1 leaf at end.
 "N. B. Die Seiten dieser Abschrift stimen mit denjenigen des Originals überein."
 1. Repentance--Sermons. 2. Conversion--Sermons. 3. Devil. I. Title.

MSS
Bd.
WITCHCRAFT
BF
Z98
Z65

Zwo Hexenzeitung, die erste, Von dreyen Hexen-Pfaffen, unnd einem Organisten zu Ellwang, wie dieselbe Christo abgesagt, unnd dem bösen Geist mit Leib und Seel sich ergeben, und die Zauberkunst von ime erlernet ... Die ander: Von einer Unholdin oder Hexen, wie sie mit ihren Gespilen alles zu verderben unterstanden, der Satan aber, ihnen Ursachen, warum sie solches sollen bleiben lassen angezeigt, auch nicht gestatten, oder geschehen las sen wöllen. Nürnberg,
(Continued on next card)

MSS
Bd.
WITCHCRAFT
BF
Z98
Z65

Zwo Hexenzeitung, die erste, Von dreyen Hexen-Pfaffen ... 1615 [ca. 1900] (Card 2)
 1615 [ca. 1900]
 4 l. title vignette. 19cm.
 Carnap's manuscript copy.
 "Original i. d. Kgl. öff. Bibl. z. Stuttgart 4 unpag. Bl. incl. Titelbl. ohne Signat."
 1. Witchcraft. I. Title: Von dreyen Hexen-Pfaffen. II. Title: Von einer Unholdin oder Hexen.

MSS
Bd.
WITCHCRAFT
BF
Z98
Z97

Zwo warhafftige newe Zeittung. Die erste ist ein warhafftige Propheceyung, was sich diss tausent sechzehenhundert und 28. Jahr wird verlauffen und zutragen ... Die ander Zeittung ist auss dem Bistumb Würtzburg und Bamberg, auch sonst auss andern Herrschafften, wie man viel Hexen unnd Gabelreutersen verbrennen lest, und noch viel gefangen liegen ... Würtzburg, 1627 [ca. 1900]
 4 l. title vignette. 24cm.
 Carnap's manuscript copy.
(Continued on next card)

MSS
Bd.
WITCHCRAFT
BF
Z98
Z97

Zwo warhafftige newe Zeittung. Die erste ist ein warhafftige Propheceyung ... 1627 [ca. 1900] (Card 2)
 "Originaldruck i. d. Stadtbibliothek zu Frankfurt a/Main. 4 Bl. in 4°."
 In verse.

 1. Prophecies. 2. Deformities. 3. Witchcraft.

626

CATALOGUE OF THE CORNELL WITCHCRAFT COLLECTION

Manuscripts

Witchcraft

Aa, Jacob van der, 1792-1857.

am Bekker (Balthazar)

₍1844-1846, Amsterdam₎
2 ll.

Copy of the article on Bekker in his Nieuw biographisch, anthologisch en critisch woordenboek van Nederlandsche dichters, Amsterdam, W. de Grebber, 1844-1846, v. 1, p. 101.

Witchcraft

Anschütz, Anna, defendant.

AM Zeugenn Verhör, inn Beschuldigten unndt sehr Verdechtigenn Hexerij sachen, zwischen Michaellen Kreijenbergern, und Annen, Walten Anschützen des Köhlers Haussfrau allenn zue Mehliss, den 3. Augustj Anno 1615.

1615 Mehliss, Germany
48 ll.

Fragments of the trial for witchcraft, containing the accusations against the defendant and the examination of witnesses.

MSS Bd. WITCHCRAFT JS A92

Augsburg.

Kurzer Bericht Was alhier Malefiz-Recht gehalten wird, oder, Modius Procedendi in Malefiz Sachen wie auch eine richtige Verzeichnis aller und jeder Maleficanten, welche in der H: R: Statt Augsburg von anno 1353: bis zu disen unseren Zeiten ...
₍18th cent.?₎
₍6₎ l., 166 p. 20 x 16cm.
Manuscript, on paper, in five different hands. Hand-ruled frame on each page. The statement of court procedure, l. ₍1-6₎, and the list of court cases from
(Continued on next card)

MSS Bd. WITCHCRAFT JS A92

Augsburg. Kurzer Bericht Was alhier Malefiz-Recht gehalten wird. ₍18th cent.?₎ (Card 2)
1353 to 1747 are in one hand. Cases from 1747 to 1760 are recorded in four additional hands. Index, p. 147-163 again in the first hand. P. 139-146, 164-166 blank.
Bound in worn leather.
Ex libris: Xaverii Mösman.

1. Criminal procedure--Augsburg.
2. Criminal registers--Augsburg.
(Continued on next card)

MSS Bd. WITCHCRAFT JS A92

Augsburg. Kurzer Bericht Was alhier Malefiz-Recht gehalten wird. ₍18th cent.?₎ (Card 3)

3. Judgments, Criminal--Augsburg. 4. Sentences (Criminal procedure)--Augsburg.
5. Court records--Augsburg.

Witchcraft

B. Bekker betreffende is te vinden in

AM

₍n.d., n.p₎
2 ll.

List of works containing passages on Bekker.

Witchcraft

Baer, Joseph & co., Frankfurt am Main.

ALS to George Lincoln Burr

January 6, ₍1900₎ Frankfurt, Dear Sir/
We received with thanks
2 ll.

The letter is mis-dated 1899.
Acknowledging payment for documents of the witch trials of Sister Maria Renata Sänger and Hans Loder's wife.
With envelope.

Witchcraft

Baer, Joseph & co., Frankfurt am Main.

ALS to ₍Andrew Dickson White₎

November 8, 1899. Frankfurt. Euer Excellenz/ Beehren wir uns in/ Anlage den Brief des Eigen-
2 ll.

Concerns the purchase of documents of the witch trials of Sister Maria Renata Sänger and Hans Loder's wife.

Witchcraft

Baer, Joseph & co., Frankfurt am Main.

ALS to Andrew D. White

November 15, 1899. Frankfurt. Er. Excellenz/ Rechnung für Herrn Botschafter Andrew D. White, Berlin.
1 l.

A bill for the purchase of documents of the witch trials of Sister Maria Renata Sänger and Hans Loder's wife.
With envelope.

Witchcraft

Baer, Joseph & Co., Frankfurt am Main.

TLS to Sr. Excellenz Herrn A. D. White.

den 7. Februar 1900. Frankfurt.
Ew. Excellenz,/ Mr. Burr hat vor einiger Zeit bei uns angefragt, ob wir noch weitere/
1 l.

Concerns the purchase of Hexenprozesse. ₍Bamberg? 1617- 1631₎

Witchcraft
BX
890
G31
E5+
1517

Barack,

ALS to M. Spirgatis

30 Dez., 1895. Strassburg. Geilers Emeis, Strassburg 1517 ist textlich vollständlich, wie auch eine Ver-/
1 l.

Attached inside the front cover of Johannes Geiler von Kaisersberg. Die emeis, and concerns the apparent lacuna of leaves v and vi of this work.

Witchcraft

Basler Buch- und Antiquariatshandlung.

ALS to Herrn Professor G. L. Burr.

den 29/V/1907. Basel. Dear Sir!/
I have been much enjoyed to receive the signs/
1 l.

Signed Adolf Geering.
Concerns the purchase of Hexenprozesse aus dem Steinthal, 1607-1675. ₍Alsace, 1607-1675₎
With envelope.

Witchcraft

Basler Buch- und Antiquariatshandlung.

ALS to Herrn Dr. George Lincoln Burr.

den 27/VI/1907. Basel. Hochgeehrter Herr !/ Da Sie ja ganz gut deutsch verstehen, so/
1 l.

Signed Adolf Geering.
With envelope.
Concerns the purchase of Hexenprozesse aus dem Steinthal, 1607-1675. ₍Alsace 1607-1675₎

MSS Bd. WITCHCRAFT JS B35+

Bavaria. Instruction. Wie sich in denen Landten zu Bayen ₍sic₎ die Pfleger, Landtrichter, Pflegs Comisary, unnd Anwalten, auch Gerichtsschreiber, und andere Bediente in Malefizsachen in ain: und andern zu verhalten. Was sy wegen der Inquisition, Incarceration, in: und bey dem Examen Einhaltung der Erfahrungen: Vornembung der Inspection, Confrontation: Tortur: Erstattung der Berichten, bei dem Leben Abthundten, gegen denen begleitten: in Verfassung der Ur gichten: unnd bey
(Continued on next card)

MSS Bd. WITCHCRAFT JS B35+

Bavaria. Instruction. Wie sich in denen Landten zu Bayen ₍sic₎ ... in Malefizsachen ... zu verhalten ... ₍17th cent.₎ (Card 2)

Exequierung diser, und einer Urtls zu thunn: unnd zu observieren haben. ₍17th cent.₎
83, ₍4₎ l. 30 x 21cm.
Manuscript, on paper in a seventeenth century German hand. Index on last 4 leaves. Bound in boards with vellum spine. On spine: Instruction für Beamte.
1. Criminal procedure--Bavaria. 2. Criminal justice, Administration of--Bavaria.

627

CATALOGUE OF THE CORNELL WITCHCRAFT COLLECTION

MSS   Beauvois de Chauvincourt, sieur de.
Bd.   Discovrs de la lycantropie ou de la trans-
WITCHCRAFT mutation des hommes en loups: par le Sieur
GR   de Beauvoys de Chauvincourt; gentil-homme
B38   Angevin. Paris, chez Jacques Rezé, 1599
        [ca. 1900]
        [8], 31, [1] p. title vignette, illus.
     initial. 19cm.
        Signatures: A-E^4.
        Carnap's manuscript copy.
        "Original i.   d. Grossherz. H. Bib-
liothek zu   Darmstadt."
        (Continued on next card)

MSS   Beauvois de Chauvincourt, sieur de. Dis-
Bd.   covrs de la lycantropie ... 1599 [ca.
WITCHCRAFT 1900]   (Card 2)
GR
B38   "Die Seiten-zahlen dieser Abschrift
stimmen mit denjenigen der Originaldruck-
schrift überein."

    1. Werwolves. 2. Metamorphosis (in
religion, folk-   lore, etc.) I. Title.

Witchcraft
    Bekker, Balthasar, 1634-1698.

        am[copy] Aan Saalems vreede schrijver
doomienee Zaaloomon val til.

      February 7, 1678. Weesp, Netherlands.
      5 ll.

      Poem. The date and Bekker's name are
appended by the copyist. Acquired,
according to G.L. Burr, "with the bulk
of our Bekker books."

Witchcraft
    Bekker, Balthasar, 1634-1698.

      am[copy] Allinga Tegen de Luyterse-
Aan Den Autheur.

      January 1, 1679. Weesp, Netherlands.
      3 ll. With: his Lof Geedight op Den
Roem der kristenen...

      Poem on Lutheranism. The copyist has
appended Bekker's name and the date.

Witchcraft
    Bekker, Balthasar, 1634-1698.

      am[copy] Bijschriften door B: Bekker
voorkomende in de gedichten uit het
stamboek van ... Johanna Koerten.

      [n.d., n.p.]
      1 l.

Witchcraft
    Bekker, Balthasar, 1634-1698.

      am[copy] Brief aan zijn huisvrouw,
Frouk Fullenia.

      August, 1691 [n.p.]
      2 ll.

Witchcraft
    Bekker, Balthasar, 1634-1698.

      am[copy] Lof Gedight op het euwig
evangelium Gemaakt Door Joohannis Vlak
prediekant tee Zutven.

      [n.d., n.p.]
      2 ll.

      Poem. The copyist has appended Bekker's
name. Acquired, according to G.L. Burr,
"with the bulk of our Bekker books."

Witchcraft
    Bekker, Balthasar, 1634-1698.

      am[copy] Lof Geedight op Den Roem
der kristenen Geemaakt door Heeroo
Siebersmaa Prediekandt tot Amsterdam
aan den drukker.

      January 7, 1687 Amsterdam.
      2 ll.

      Poem in praise of the printer who
published Siebersmaa's "Den Roem der
kristenen."

Witchcraft
    Bekker, Balthasar, 1634-1698.

      am[copy] Lof geedight over het ver-
klaare van den eerste brief van Peetrus
door Doomiene Golsieus, prediekant tot
hindeloopen.

      [n.d., n.p.]
      1 l.

      Poem. Bekker's name is appended by the
copyist. Ac   quired, according to G.
L. Burr, "wi   th the bulk of our Bekker
books."

Witchcraft
    Bekker, Balthasar, 1634-1698.

      am[copy] Uittreksel uit het Kort
bericht van B. Bekker aangaande alle de
schriften, welke over zijn boek De betoverde
weereld enen tijd lang heen en weder verwisseld zijn.

      [n.d., n.p.]
      2 ll.

      Copied from his Kort berigt van B.
Bekker...   Aangaande alle de
      (Continued on next card)

Witchcraft
    Bekker, Balthasar, 1634-1698. Uittreksel
      uit het Kort bericht aangaande alle de
      schriften...[n.d.]   (Card 2)

      schriften, welke over syn boek de B.W.
enen tijd lang heen en weder verwisseld
zijn. Franeker, by Leonardus Strik,
1692.

MSS
Bd.   Bradwell, Stephan, fl. 1594-1636.
WITCHCRAFT Marie Glovers late woefull case, together
BF   wth her joyfull deliverance written upon
B81   occasion of Dr. Jordens Discourse of the
mother... With a defence of the truthe
against D. J. his scandalous impugnations.
    [n.p.] 1603.
    171 l. 20 x 29cm.
    Photostatic copy of Sloan MSS 831 in the
British Museum.
    Second trea   tise, beginning on l. 42,
      (Continued on next card)

MSS
Bd.   Bradwell, Stephan, fl. 1594-1636. Marie
WITCHCRAFT Glovers late woefull case...1603. (Card 2)
BF
B81   has caption title: A defence of the pub-
lique sentence of lawe, and of the iudgment,
of certayne phisitions, $\overset{t}{y}$ averred Marie
Glouers case to be supernaturall: againste
D. Jordens slie, but scandalous impugna-
tions of bothe.
    Bound in maroon buckram.
  1. Glover,   Mary, fl. 1603. 2.
Demoniac poss   ession. 3. Witchcraft--
      (Continued on next card)

MSS
Bd.   Bradwell, Stephan, fl. 1594-1636. Marie
WITCHCRAFT Glovers late woefull case...1603. (Card 3)
BF
B81
    England. 4. Jorden, Edward. A briefe
discourse of a disease called suffocation
of the mother. I. Title.

Witchcraft
    Braun, Marta, defendant, b. 1582.

      AM[copy] Gut und peinliche Aussage
Marta, Hans Georg Braunen zu Mergentheim,
Frau.

      1628. Neuhaus.
      6 l.

      At head of title: Abschrift eines
Hexen-Processes.

Witchcraft
    Brockhaus' konversations-lexikon.

      am[copy] Bekker/Balthasar/

      [n. p., n.d.]
      1 l.

      A copy of the article on Balthasar
Bekker in Brockhaus' Konversations-
lexikon, vol. 10, pp. 172-173, edition
and year not indicated.

Witchcraft
    Brussen, Agnes, d. 1679.

      ADS Processus Inquisitorius c. Agnes
Brussen, Michell Hoogen Wittibe zum Grands-
hagen in po Incantationis.

      22 May-14 June, 1679. Treptow, Germany.
      34 ll.

      Includes the testimony of Agnes' neighbors,
her own inquisition, letters of testimony
from clergy, an order for torture from the
Juristic Faculty   of the University of
      (Continued on next card)

Witchcraft
    Brussen, Agnes, d. 1679. ADS Processus
      Inquisitorius...1679.   (Card 2)

      Greifswald, her confession, and the sentence,
according to which she was to be burnt.

CATALOGUE OF THE CORNELL WITCHCRAFT COLLECTION

Witchcraft
    Büchler, Cathrina, defendant.

        AD Acta inquisitionalia Cathrinen Büchlers, die sogenannte alte Beckerin zu Gross Mühlingen betr. in po. Veneficii.

        1688-1689. Gross-Mühlingen, Germany.
        128 ll.

        Trial documents and the letters concerning the witchcraft case, sewn into one fascicle. The defendant was finally released for lack of evidence.
        With a description by Joseph Baer &
        (Continued on next card)

Witchcraft
    Büchler, Cathrina, defendant. AD Acta inquisitionalia ... 1688-1689. (Card 2)

        Co., the dealer from whom it was bought, invoice, and envelope.

Witchcraft
    Büder, Gela, defendant.

        AD[frag.] Gela Hermann Büder Wittwe zu Rodenbach Clägerin. Contra Die Gemeindte desselbsten und sonderlich Johannes Krüdelbach und Johann Hansen itzo Heimbergern beiden selbigen Orths beilecgte, Bezüchtigung Zauberey belangend.

        1650-1651. Rodenbach, Germany.
        29 ll.

        Documents from Gela Büder's trial, consisting of her accusers' statements and her answers thereto. With note by G. L. Burr.

Witchcraft
    Burr, George Lincoln, 1857-1938.

        A & TM Cards for unpublished witch-trials and documents belonging to witch-trials, or for other Mss relating to witchcraft

        [n.d.] [Ithaca, New York]

        Filed in card box shelved with witchcraft manuscripts.

Witchcraft
    Burr, George Lincoln, 1857-1938.

        TM [Catalog cards for Graf Carnap's manuscript copies of printed works]

        [n.d.] [Ithaca, New York]

        Filed in card box shelved with witchcraft manuscripts.

Witchcraft
    Burr, George Lincoln, 1857-1938.

        A & TM [Catalog slips for the witchcraft collection]

        [n.d.] [Ithaca, New York]

        Burr's own slips, many with bibliographical and historical annotations and references to related material.
        Filed in card box shelved with witchcraft manuscripts.

Witchcraft
    Burr, George Lincoln, 1857-1938.

        AM [List of unpublished witch-trials and documents belonging to witch-trials in the President White Library]

        [n.d.] [Ithaca, New York]

        Catalog slips listing the manuscripts, with a short bibliographical annotation for each.
        Filed in card box shelved with witchcraft manuscripts.

Witchcraft
    Burr, George Lincoln, 1857-1938.

        AM On the Loos MS.

        [October?, 1886] [Ithaca, New York?]
        15 ll.

        Speech delivered at a meeting of the History and Political Science Association October 6, 1886.

Witchcraft
    Burr, George Lincoln, 1857-1938.

        TM[copy] On the Loos MS.

        October?, 1886 [Ithaca, New York?]
        12 ll.

        Speech delivered at a meeting of the History and Political Science Association October 6, 1886.
        With a carbon copy, 13 ll.

ARCHIVES   14/17/22

    Burr, George Lincoln, 1857-1938.
    Papers, 1862-1938.

        AM The fate of Dietrich Flade.

        (In Box 38: Witchcraft material collected by Burr and Charles H. Lea.)

    Burr, George Lincoln, 1857-1938.
        LETTERS FROM

Baer, Joseph & co., Frankfurt am Main.
Basler Buch- und Antiquariatshandlung.
Ewen, Cecil Henry L'Estrange, 1877-
Godard, George S
Halle, J., firm, booksellers, Munich.
Nicholson, Jno. W
White, Andrew Dickson, 1832-1918.

Witchcraft
    Bussbacher, Margaretha, defendant, b. 1596.

        AM Aussag.

        1628. Zeyl, Germany.
        8 l.

        Contains the confrontation with the witnesses and the defendant's statement of her case.
        No. 2 in a fascicle of trial documents from Franken.
        Filed with Seebawer, K. AM Aussag. Zeyl, 1692.

Witchcraft
K
T463
E7
    Calvary, S., & co., Berlin.

        AM [List of works by Christian Thomasius]

        [n.d.] Berlin.
        2 ll.

        Pasted inside front cover of the first volume of Thomasius, Christian, 1655-1728. Ernsthaffte aber doch muntere und vernünfftige Thomasische Gedancken u. Erinnerungen über allerhand ausserlesene juristische Händel.

Witchcraft
    Carpenter, William H

        AM Extracts from the MS. of the witch trial of Dr. Dietrich Flade

        1833. Ithaca, New York.
        11 ll.

        Included is his article "Dietrich Flade" from the Library of Cornell University, vol. I., no. 5, Ithaca, 1833.

MSS
Bd.
WITCHCRAFT
BF
C39
    Celichius, Andreas, d. 1599.
    Notwendige Errinnerung. Vonn des Sathans letzten Zornsturm, und was es auff sich habe und bedeute, das nu zu dieser Zeit so viel Menschen an Leib und Seel vom Teuffel besessen werden durch Andream Celichium... Wittenberg, Zacharias Lehman, 1594 [ca. 1900]
        59 p. 23cm.
        Carnap's manuscript copy.
        "Original druck in der Kgl.
        (Continued on next card)

MSS
Bd.
WITCHCRAFT
BF
C39
    Celichius, Andreas, d. 1599. Notwendige Errinnerung...1594 [ca. 1900] (Card 2)

        Universit. Bibliothek zu Leipzig, 113 S. in 4°."
        Title in red and black.
        Numerals and signatures in the margins indicate pagination and signatures of the original.

        1. Demoniac possession. 2. Exorcism. I. Title.

MSS
Bd.
WITCHCRAFT
AG
C73
    [Compendium of folklore and popular beliefs of the seventeenth century. n.p. late 17th - early 18th cent.]
    [389] l. illus. 23cm.
        Manuscript, on paper, in an 18th century German hand.
        Text rubricated in red and green. Richly illustrated with colored drawings, charts, calendars and astrological tables.
        Bound in vellum.
        Ex libris: Kurt Seligmann.
        1. Folk-lore--Collections. 2. Occult sciences--Collections.

MSS
Bd.
WITCHCRAFT
BF
C96
    Cudius, Hans.
    Newe Zeitung und ware Geschicht, dieses 76. Jars geschehen im Breissgaw, wie man da in etlichen Stätten und Flecken, in die 55. Unhulden gefangen und verbrent hat, auch wie sie schröckliche ding bekent haben ... Gestellt und gemacht durch Hans Cudium.
    [n.p. 1576 [ca. 1900]
    4 l. 19cm.
        Carnap's manuscript copy.
        "Originaldruck in der Stadtbibliothek zu Zürich, 8 Seiten in 8°."
        (Continued on next card)

CATALOGUE OF THE CORNELL WITCHCRAFT COLLECTION

MSS
Bd.
WITCHCRAFT
BF
C96

Cudius, Hans. Newe Zeitung ... 1576
[ca. 1900] (Card 2)
Notations in the margins indicate foliation of the original.
In verse.

1. Witchcraft--Germany. I. Title.

MSS
Bd.
WITCHCRAFT
BF
D27

De vampiri vnico trattato. In cui si dimostra che l'apparizioni di spettri, larve, fantasme, e dette con altri termini, larve, lenture, mani, lari, genij, ó siano fale, monacchi, incubi non sono altro che imagini formate dall 'vmana fantasia alterate, e guasta. [n.p. after 1738]
112 p. 22cm.
Manuscript, on paper, in an Italian hand. Note on fly-leaf by a former owner states that the manuscript was never printed.
Bound in vellum.
1. Vampires.   2. Apparitions.

MSS
Bd.
WITCHCRAFT
BF
D61

Discours sur la mort et condemnation de Charles de Franchillon, Baron de Chenevières, exécuté en la place de Grève, par arrest de la Cour de Parlement de Paris pour crime de sortilege et de magie, du jeudy 14. may 1626. Paris, chez P. Mettayer, 1626 [1901]
6 l. 19cm.

Carnap's manuscript copy.
"Originaldruck in der Bibliothèque Nationale zu Paris (Imprimés Ln 27.
(Continued on next card)

MSS
Bd.
Rare
BX
D28

De compunctione et fuga demonum. 1488-89.
[72] l. (29 lines) 21.2 x 14.2cm.
Ms. written at Foligno, Italy; on paper. Signatures (with catch-words): a-e^{12}, f^{14} (last 2 ff. wanting, would have been blank) Later hand has partially obliterated the words "compunctione et fuga" in the title and written "fuga" above.
Inscription on f. 1^r (in margin): Die conceptionis beate/ virginis [8 Dec.] 1488 fulginii. Inscription on f. 72^v: finis. die viij. Januarij. mccccxxxviiij. Laus deo.
(Continued on next card)

Witchcraft

De la Monidemiere...
ALS to Armand Jean du Plessis, Cardinal, Duc de Richelieu
October 5, 1635. Loudun, France.
Vostre Eminence aura bien par les lettres que Monsieur
1 l., incl. address-leaf, with seals intact.
Describes the phenomenon in which
(Continued on next card)

MSS
Bd.
WITCHCRAFT
BF
D61

Discours sur la mort et condemnation de Charles de Franchillon ... 1626 [1901] (Card 2)
4768.) Copie davon genomen durch M^r. Herviant - Paris im Mai 1901, wonach die vorliegende gemacht. (pet. in 4° de 16 pp.)"
Numerals in margin indicate pagination of the original.

1. Witchcraft--France. 2. Franchillon, Charles de, d. 1626.

MSS
Bd.
Rare
BX
D28

De compunctione et fuga demonum. 1488-89.
(Card 2)
Bound in original wooden boards and stamped calf.
DeRicci, II, p. 1233.

Witchcraft

De la Monidemiere... ALS to Armand Jean du Plessis, Cardinal, Duc de Richelieu ... 1635. (Card 2)
the Mother Superior of the Ursuline convent, in a demoniac convulsion, found the name "Joseph" written upon her left arm. Details of the event appear in Des Niau. La véritable histoire des diables de Loudun, and many other sources.

MSS
Bd.
WITCHCRAFT
BX
D61
no.2

Dissertazione circa la streg^{h}eria con apendice della magia diabolica. [Milan? early 18th cent.]
26 l. 22 x 16cm.
Manuscript, in an eighteenth century Italian hand, on paper.
Bound in gray boards.
No. 2 in vol. of anonymous dissertations on theology and witchcraft.

1. Witchcraft.   2. Magic.

M
Bd.
Pictorius

De Incantatione et adiuratione, collique suspensione, Epistola incerti authoris
Late 17th century   18cm.
[10] ll.
Bound with: Pictorius -- De speciebus magiae; An sagae, vel mulieres quas expiatrices vulgatim nominamus; and De Illorum daemonum. Also, Geomantiae Astronomicae [By Gerardus Cremonensis]; De Magia
(Continued on next card)

Witchcraft

Der Nürnbergischen Theologen ainhellige Antwort, über etliche Puncten, die Unhulden betreffent.
AMS
1590 [Nuremberg?]
18 ll.
Signed by six clergymen of Nuremberg. Statement of procedures for dealing with witches and explanation of the scriptural basis for these procedures.
With a handwritten copy made in 1900.

MSS
Bd.
WITCHCRAFT
BF
D61
no.3

Dissertazione intorno a veri, e falsi miracoli. [n.p. early 18th cent.]
15 l. 22 x 16cm.
Manuscript, in an eighteenth century Italian hand, on paper.
Bound in gray boards.
No. 3 in a vol. of anonymous dissertations on theology and witchcraft.

1. Witchcraft. 2. Magic. 3. Miracles.

M
Bd.
Pictorius

De Incantatione et adiuratione ... (Card 2)
veterum [Arbatel de Magia]; Ars notoria; and Diversa divinationum genera.

Witchcraft

Discours Sur la mort et condemnation de Charles de Franchillon, Baron de Chenevières, exécuté en la place de Grève, par arrest de la Cour de Parlement de Paris pour crime de Sortilege et de Magie, du Jeudy. 14 May 1626. A. Paris chez P. Mettayer, Imprimeur et libraire ordinaire du Roy. M.DCXXVI.
AM[copy]
[n.d.] [Paris]
10 ll.
(Continued on next card)

MSS
Bd.
WITCHCRAFT
BF
D613

Diszes Wonder, auch erschricklic Zaychen ist durch Zulassung Gottesz warhafftig unnd thadlich gesehen in der Stat von Gent in Flandren, auff den XVIII. Augustii in Jaer, MDLXXXVI bey dem bossen Gayst unnd seinnesz Wercks, seer erschrocklich ist unnb zu leessen.   Anntorff, By Paulus Brackfeldt, 1586 [ca. 1900]
4 l. illus. 23cm.
Carnap's manuscript copy.
"Original druck i. d. Gust. Freytag Biblioth ek, jetzt i. d. Stadt-
(Continued on next card)

M
Bd.
Pictorius

De Magia veterum summum sapientiae studium [Arbatel de Magia]
[Late 17th century] 18cm.
[48] ll.
Bound with: Pictorius -- De Speciebus magiae; An Sagae, vel mulieres quas expiatrices vulgatim nominamus; and De Illorum daemonum. Also, Geomantiae Astronomicae [by Gerardus Cremonensis]; Ars notoria; De Incantatione et adiuratione; and Diversa divinationum genera.

Witchcraft

Discours Sur la mort et condemnation de Charles de Franchillon ... AM[copy]
(Card 2)
Copy, in small notebook on lined paper, of the original printed work in the Bibliothèque Nationale "Imprimés Le 27 4768".
Numerals in the margin indicate pagination of the original.
The hand on the cover is the same as in Carnap's manuscript copies of works in French.

MSS
Bd.
WITCHCRAFT
BF
D613

Diszes Wonder, auch erschricklic Zaychen ...
1586 [ca. 1900] (Card 2)
bibliothek zu Frankfurt a/M. 4 Bl. 4°."
A letter received by D. H. V. W.
At end: "Ghetranslateert durch M. Carel Strutberger."
Numerals and signatures in the margins indicate pagination and signatures of the original.
1. Apparitions. 2. Devil. I. W., D. H. V.   II. Strutberger, Carel, tr.

CATALOGUE OF THE CORNELL WITCHCRAFT COLLECTION

Witchcraft

Drencken, Catarina, defendant.

AD₍frag.₎ Criminal Proces ... Lasters der Zaubereiyen

June 28, 1613. Neuerburg, Luxemburg.
4 ll.

Preliminary statement by the prosecutor and testimony against Catarina Drencken by one witness.

MSS Bd. WITCHCRAFT BF D77

Drey warhafftige grundtliche Zeitungen, die erste von ettlichen Hexen und Zauber- in welche hin und wider in Ungern und Teutschland grossen Schaden angerichtet haben... Beschriben durch den hochgelerten Herrn Nicolaum Binder... Die ander von einem Burger und Thuchmacher der in grosser Unzucht ein zeitlang gelebt ... unnd wie er durch dess Teufels Eingebung 3. Kinder und sein Weib jämmer licher weiss ermördet... Die dritte von Erscheinung zweyer
(Continued on next card)

MSS Bd. WITCHCRAFT BF D77

Drey warhafftige grundtliche Zeitungen ... 1610 ₍ca. 1900₎ (Card 2)

Engel... Beschriben durch den ehrwürdigen Herrn Joannem Röseler diser Zeit Pfarrern daselbsten. Erstlich Getruckt zu Tirnau in Ungern nachmals aber zu Freyburg, bey Georg Hofmann, 1610 ₍ca. 1900₎
₍7₎ l. 24cm.

T. p. add ed by scribe: ₍Kerpffen₎
(Continued on next card)

MSS Bd. WITCHCRAFT BF D77

Drey warhafftige grundtliche Zeitungen ... 1610 ₍ca. 1900₎ (Card 3)

Drey warhafftige Zeitungen. Die erste von etlichen Hexen in Ungern, den 11. October 1609. Beschriben durch Nicolaus Binder. &c. 1610.
Carnap's manuscript copy.
"Originaldruck in der Stadtbibliothek zu Zürich. 4 Bl. in 4°."
Numerals in the margins indicate the paginati on of the original.
(Continued on next card)

MSS Bd. WITCHCRAFT BF D77

Drey warhafftige grundtliche Zeitungen ... 1610 ₍ca. 1900₎ (Card 4)

In verse.

1. Witchcraft. 2. Apparitions. 3. Prock, Hans, d. 1610. I. Binder, Nicolaus. II. Röseler, Joannes.

MSS Bd. WITCHCRAFT BF D97

Du Triez, Robert.
Livre des ruses, finesses et impostures des esprits malins, oeuvre fort utile & delectable par un chacun a cause de la verité des choses estranges contenue en iceluy: Mis en lumiere par Robert du Triez. Cambray, Nicolas Lombart, 1563 ₍ca. 1900₎
92 ₍i.e. 183₎, ₍14₎ p. illus. 19cm.
Signatures: A-Z⁴, AA-BB².
Carnap's m anuscript copy.
"Die Seit en dieser Abschrift
(Continued on next card)

MSS Bd. WITCHCRAFT BF D97

Du Triez, Robert. Livre des ruses, finesses et impostures ... 1563 ₍ca. 1900₎ (Card 2)

stimmen mit denjenigen der Originaldruckschrift überein."

1. Demonology. 2. Occult sciences. I. Title.

Witchcraft

Eismennin, Margretha.

AM Extrahirte Aussag.

₍n.d., n.p.₎
2 l.

Incomplete summary of her trial.
No. 4 in a fascicle of trial documents from Franken.
Filed with Seebawer, K. AM Aussag. Zeyl, 1629.

MSS Bd. WITCHCRAFT BF E46++

Engelhard, Elsa, defendant.
Inquisitions-acta contra Elsa und Margreta Engelhardin, Geschwister zu Cabartz und Klein Cabartz w.gn. verdächtiger Hexerei. ₍Reinhardsbrunn?₎ 1686₎-87.
94 l. 34cm.
Manuscript, on paper, in various 17th century hands.
2 extra leaves inserted between l. 91, 92 and 93, 94 form one sheet and are a fragment of anoth er court document having noth ing to do with the
(Continued on next card)

MSS Bd. WITCHCRAFT BF E46++

Engelhard, Elsa, defendant. Inquisitions-acta ... ₍1686₎-87. (Card 2)

trial.
Note by G. L. Burr inside front cover discusses the trial.
Bound in gray marbled boards with vellum spine. On spine: Trial for witchcraft of Elsa and Margaret Engelhardt. 1687.
1. Trials (Witchcraft)--Saxony. 2. Witchcraft--Saxony. I. Engelhard, Margreta, defendant.

MSS Bd. WITCHCRAFT BF E61

Der entlarvte Teuffel oder denkwürdige Geschichte von vielen warhaftig Besessenen, welche dieses Feindes Grausamkeit heftig erfahren, entlich aber durch den mächtigen Finger Gottes wieder erlediget worden. Zu mehrer Bekräftigung der von Doct. Beckern, in seiner verzauberten Welt, zweiffelhaft gemachten Kögischen Geschichte ... Zusammen getragen von M. J. J. L. Leipzig, Johann Melchior Liebe, 16 97 ₍ca. 1900₎
(Continued on next card)

MSS Bd. WITCHCRAFT BF E61

Der entlarvte Teuffel ... 1697 ₍ca. 1900₎ (Card 2)

77 p. 19cm.
Carnap's manuscript copy.
"Originaldruck in der Königl. öff. Bibliothek zu Dresden, 98 pag. Seiten in 8°."
"Diese Schrift bildet gewissermassen die Fortsetzung zu: "Das geängstigte Köge oder Eine warhaffte und denkwürdige Historie, von einer ent setzlichen Versuchung des leidigen Satans zu Köge in
(Continued on next card)

MSS Bd. WITCHCRAFT BF E61

Der entlarvte Teuffel ... 1697 ₍ca. 1900₎ (Card 3)

Seeland" wo in deutscher Sprache durch denselben Verfasser ... i. J. 1695 herausgegeben. Hieraus erklärt es sich, dass diese Schrift mit " die dritte Zugabe" anfängt, da "das geängstigte Köge mit der zweiten Zugabe abschliesst".
Marginal numerals and signatures indicate paginati on ans signatures of the original.
(Continued on next card)

MSS Bd. WITCHCRAFT BF E61

Der entlarvte Teuffel ... 1697 ₍ca. 1900₎ (Card 4)

Printed copy not in Van der Linde.

1. Demoniac possession. 2. Devil. 3. Bekker, Balthasar, 1634-1698. De betoverde weere ld. I. Das geängstigte Köge. II. M. J. J. L. III. L., M. J. J.

MSS Bd. WITCHCRAFT BF E69

Erledigung der ehrw. Klosterfrau Maria Augusta Delphina, im Frauenkloster zu Stanz, den 28. März 1848 durch P. Anizet Regli, Guardian zu Stanz. ₍n.p.₎ Nach einem Original-Manuskripte getreu abgedruckt, 1848 ₍ca. 1900₎
9 l. 19cm.
Carnap's manuscript copy.
"Originaldruck i. d. Stadtbibliothek zu Zürich. 13 S. in 8°."
Numerals i n the margins indicate pagination of the original.
(Continued on next card)

MSS Bd. WITCHCRAFT BF E69

Erledigung der ehrw. Klosterfrau Maria Augusta Delphina ... 1848 ₍ca. 1900₎ (Card 2)

1. Demoniac possession. 2. Delphina, Maria Augusta, fl. 1848. I. Regli, Anizet, fl. 1848.

MSS Bd. WITCHCRAFT BF E733

Erschreckliche newe Zeitung, welche sich begeben und zugetragen in diesem 1650. Jahr, in der Osternacht, im Schweitzer Gebirge, bey der Stadt Dillhofen auff einem Dorffe Dinndurff genandt, in welchem drey Hexen gewohnet ... Dilhofen, Matthias Hammer, 1650 ₍ca. 1900₎
₍6₎ p. 19cm.
Carnap's manuscript copy.
"Originaldruck in der Königl. Bibliothek zu Berlin, (Me usebach'sche Sa͠mlung), 4 Bl. in 16°."
(Continued on next card)

MSS Bd. WITCHCRAFT BF E733

Erschreckliche newe Zeitung ... 1650 ₍ca. 1900₎ (Card 2)

In verse.

1. Witchcraft--Switzerland.

CATALOGUE OF THE CORNELL WITCHCRAFT COLLECTION

MSS
Bd.
WITCHCRAFT
BF
E735
    Ein Erschröcklich Geschicht vom Tewfel und einer Unhulden, beschehen zu Schilta bey Rotweil in der Karwochen MDXXXIII. Jar. [n.p., 1533? ca. 1900]
    2 l. 19cm.

    Carnap's manuscript copy.
    "Originaldruck in der Stadtbibliothek zu Zürich. 1 Bl. Fol."
    At end: Steffan hamer, Briefmaler.
    1. Exempla.   2. Devil. I. Hamer, Steffan.

MSS
Bd.
WITCHCRAFT
BF
E736
Z55
    Erschröckliche doch warhaffte Geschicht, die sich in der spanischen Statt, Madrileschos genannt, mit einer verheuraten Weibss-person zugetragen, welche von einer gantzen Legion Teuffel siben Jar lang besessen gewest. Und durch Patrem Ludovicum de Torre ... widerumb erlediget worden. München, Durch Nicolaum Henricum, 1608 [ca. 1900]
    11 l. illus. 24cm.
    Carnap's manuscript copy.
    (Continued on next card)

MSS
Bd.
WITCHCRAFT
BF
E736
Z55
    Erschröckliche doch warhaffte Geschicht, die sich in der spanischen Statt ... zugetragen ... 1608 [ca. 1900] (Card 2)
    "Originaldruck in der Kgl. u. Staatsbibliothek zu München. 8 Bl. in 4°. Sig. A²–B³."
    Numerals in the margins indicate pagination of the original.
    May have been written by De Torre himself.
    1. Demoniac possession. 2. Exorcism. 3. Witchcraft--Spain. 4. Garcia de Rodriguez de Gutierrez, Maria, b. 1564. I. Torre, Luis de, d. 1635, supposed author.

MSS
Bd.
WITCHCRAFT
BF
E738
    Erweytterte Unholden Zeyttung. Kurtze Erzelung wie viel der Unholden hin und wider, sonderlich inn dem Obern Teutschland, gefängklich eingezogen: was für grossen Schaden sie den Menschen, vermög ihrer Urgicht, zugefüget, und wieviel ungefehrlich deren, inn disem 1590. Jar, biss auff den 21. Julij, von dem Leben zum Todt hingerichtet und verbrandt worden seyen. [Ulm, 1590? ca. 1900]
    6 l. illus., end vignette. 24cm.
    Carnap's manuscript copy.
    (Continued on next card)

MSS
Bd.
WITCHCRAFT
BF
E738
    Erweytterte Unholden Zeyttung. [1590? ca. 1900] (Card 2)
    "Originaldruck i. d. Kgl. Bibliothek zu Berlin, 6 Bl. in 4°. Sig. Aij--Bij."
    Numerals and signatures in the margins indicate pagination and signatures of the original.

    1. Witchcraft. 2. Trials (Witchcraft)--Germany.

Witchcraft
    Essex County, Mass. Sheriff.
    ADS Returne confirming the execution of Bridgett Bishop
    June 11, 1692. [Salem]
    1 l. (2 copies)
    Filed with: Massachusetts (Colony) Courts (Essex Co.) Order of execution of Bridgett Bishop.   Facsimile
    Letter signed by George Corwin, sheriff of Essex County. Photograph obtained from the New York Public Library.

Witchcraft
    Esty, Mary, of Topsfield, Mass., d. 1692.
    AM The humble petition of Mary Estey unto the honored Judges...
    [September?] 1692. [Salem, Mass.?]
    1 l.
    FACSIMILE
    Mary Esty was hanged for witchcraft on September 22, 1692. She here pleads for clemency for those to follow her.

Witchcraft
    Ewen, Cecil Henry L'Estrange, 1877-
    ALS to George L. Burr
    [Nov. 1929] London. Dear Sir, Your very kind letter was most welcome to/ one
    2 ll.
    With envelope.
    Taken from copy 2 of Ewen's Witch hunting and witch trials, 1929.

Witchcraft
    Ewen, Cecil Henry L'Estrange, 1877-
    ALS to George L. Burr
    Aug. 1, 1930. London. Dear Sir, I have to thank you for so kindly/ sending
    1 l.
    With envelope.
    Taken from copy 2 of Ewen's Witch hunting and witch trials, 1929.

Witchcraft
    Ewen, Cecil Henry L'Estrange, 1877-
    TLS to George L. Burr
    Oct. 13, 1933. London. My dear Sir, I have to thank you for your kind reply to my/ enquiry
    1 l.
    With envelope and circular mentioned in the letter.
    Taken from copy 2 of Ewen's Witch hunting and witch trials, 1929.

Witchcraft
    Ewen, Cecil Henry L'Estrange, 1877-
    TLS to George L. Burr
    Nov. 5, 1934. London. My dear Sir, I beg to thank you for the reprint of your review of Witchcraft
    2 ll.
    With envelope.
    Taken from copy 2 of Ewen's Witch hunting and witch trials, 1929.

Witchcraft
    Ewen, Cecil Henry L'Estrange, 1877-
    TLS to George L. Burr
    Dec. 6, 1934. London. My dear Sir, I have to acknowledge your kind reply of 17th inst., and I am/ very pleased
    1 l.
    With envelope.
    Taken from copy 2 of Ewen's Witch hunting and witch trials, 1929.

Witchcraft
    Ewen, Cecil Henry L'Estrange, 1877-
    TLS to George L. Burr
    May 28, 1935. London. My dear Sir, I have to thank you for your very kind thought in sending me
    1 l.
    With envelope.
    Taken from copy 2 of Ewen's Witch hunting and witch trials, 1929.

Witchcraft
    Extract Pfarr Protocoll, te Anno 1651. 9. Jan.
    ADS
    March 28, 1653. [Tenneberg? Germany]
    2 ll.

    Signed Martin Wandersleben.
    Statement by several witnesses that the wife of Gabriel Stolz could supposedly turn herself into a wolf.

Witchcraft
    F.
    ALS to ?
    August 23, 1634. Poitiers, France. Monsieur, Grandier est mort et fut
    1 l.

    Eye-witness description of the last hours and death of Urbain Grandier, priest of Loudun and victim of Cardinal Richelieu's demoniac possession hoax in the Ursuline convent at Loudun.

MSS
Bd.
WITCHCRAFT
BF
F24
    Fassiculus [sic] artis exorcisticae ex varijs authorib. collectus. Ad omnes infirmitates tam maleficiales quam demoniacas manifestandas, ac propulsandas vtilis, ac per necessarius. [n.p., 16th cent?]
    150 l. illus. 21cm.
    Manuscript, on paper, in a Latin hand. The illustrations and illustrated initials have been cut out of printed works and pasted in. Line borders on each page.
    Bound in brown boards.
    1. Exorcism.

Witchcraft
    Fiedler, Hanss, defendant.
    ADS Inquisition-Acta contra Hanss Fiedlern ... undt Margarethen dessen Eheweib zu Schönau wegen verdächtiger Hexerey
    1662-1663. Schleusingen, Germany.
    122 ll.

    Contains the preliminary statement of neighbors as well as the trial proper of Hanss Fiedler and his wife Margareth for witchcraft. A note is added to p. 1
    (Continued on next card)

Witchcraft
    Fiedler, Hanss, defendant. ADS Inquisition-Acta ... 1662-1663. (Card 2)

    stating that after Margareth's death under torture, Hanss was released.

CATALOGUE OF THE CORNELL WITCHCRAFT COLLECTION

MSS
Bd.
WITCHCRAFT
BF
F57++

Flade, Dietrich, 1534-1589, defendant.
[Minutes of the trial for witchcraft of Dr. Dietrich Flade of Trier, 1589. Trier, 1589]
127 l. 34cm.
Manuscript, on paper, in a 16th century German hand.
Title page supplied by G. L. Burr.
The first leaf is detached and badly mutilated. A transcription of it in a 19th century German hand has been added.
(Continued on next card)

MSS
Bd.
WITCHCRAFT
BF
F57++

Flade, Dietrich, 1534-1589, defendant.
[Minutes of the trial for witchcraft ... 1589]   (Card 2)
L. 2 is missing and supplied in transcript by G. L. Burr from the fragment at Trier.
L. 105-106 are blank, and represent a lacuna.
Bound in brown boards with leather spine.
On spine: Hexenprozesse 1589.
1. Trials (Witchcraft)--Trier.
2. Witchcraft --Trier.

Witchcraft

Flade, Dietrich, 1534-1589, defendant.
ams[copy] Transcript of the trial for witchcraft of Dr. Dietrich Flade of Trier, 1589.
1589. Trier.
67 ll.
With the mutilated first page restored from the autograph protocol of the notary, in the city library at Trier. Copy made by George L. Burr, 1885-1886.

Witchcraft

Fragenden contra Elss Misseler.
AM
[n.d., n.p.]
2 l.
A summary of the first 36 leaves of Protokolle von Hexenprocessen in Flamersheim. [Flamersheim? 1629-30]

MSS
Bd.
WITCHCRAFT
BF
F93

Fronmüller, Johann Christoph.
Die auss Gottes Zulass von dem abgesagten Gottes und Menschen-Feind, dem leidigen Teuffel eine geraume Zeit leiblich-besessene, und übel-geklagte, allein durch Gottes Gnade auf fleissiges Gebet vieler fromm Christen von der leiblichen Besitzung widerum befreyde ... Susanna Raabin. ...Theils auss den Actis, theils aber auss der Erfahrung selbsten zusamm getragen von Johann Christoff Fronmüller. 1696-[1703]
[1] l., 116 p. 18cm.
(Continued on next card)

MSS
Bd.
WITCHCRAFT
BF
F93

Fronmüller, Johann Christoph. Die auss Gottes Zulass ... leiblich-besessene ... Susanna Raabin...1696-[1703] (Card 2)
Manuscript, on paper, in a German hand.
Added leaf before t. p.: "Die Kyrchendiener, welche auf Verordnung der hohen Obrigkeit die Susanna Raabin besuchten sind folgende ..."
Line frame on each page.
Bound in marbled boards.
1. Raabin, Susanna, b. 1666. 2. Demoniac possession. I. Title: Die auss Gottes Zulass... leiblich-besessene ... Susanna Raabin.

Witchcraft

Furman, Gabriel, 1800-1854.
AM American legends, ghost stories and witchcrafts.
1825. Brooklyn, New York.
64 ll. of which 15 are blank.
Contents: 1. Daemon ships 2. Michael Burn 3. The Hermit of Shawagunk Mountain 4. Poem from U.S. Literary Gazette 5. The Witch of Champlain,[frag.]
Bought from the library of Hon. Henry C. Murphy March, 1884.

Witchcraft

Furman, Gabriel, 1800-1854.
AM [Notes on witchcraft in America]
[n.d.] [Brooklyn, New York?]
17 pieces.
A collection of notes, folklore and anecdotes concerning supposed witches in America. Bought from the library of Hon. Henry C. Murphy, March, 1884.

MSS
Bd.
WITCHCRAFT
BF
G12

Gaar, Georg, b. 1702.
Heylsame Lehr-Stück, und Zauberey betreffende Anmerckungen in der christlichen, nach Hinrichtung Mariae Renatae einer Zauberin, gehaltenen Anred, einiger Massen zwar angeregt, hernach aber ausführlicher erläutert ... An jetzo mit einem Zusatz vermehrt ... Wirtzburg, Marco Antonio Engman, 1750 [ca. 1900]
38 p. 22cm.
Carnap's manuscript copy.
"Originaldruck in der Kgl. Universitätsbibliothek zu Würzburg,
(Continued on next card)

MSS
Bd.
WITCHCRAFT
BF
G12

Gaar, Georg, b. 1702. Heylsame Lehr-Stück ... 1750 [ca. 1900] (Card 2)
44 S. in 4°."
Numerals in margins indicate pagination of the original.
In part a rebuttal of: Johann Christian Rinder. Eine Hexe nach ihrer gresslichen Gestalt und gerechter Strafe.
Provoked in answer: Johann Christian Rinder. Kurtze doch nachdrückliche Abfertigung an den ... Herrn Georg Gaar.
(Continued on next card)

MSS
Bd.
WITCHCRAFT
BF
G12

Gaar, Georg, b. 1702. Heylsame Lehr-Stück ... 1750 [ca. 1900] (Card 3)
1. Witchcraft--Germany. 2. Witchcraft--Sermons. 3. Rinder, Johann Christian. Eine Hexe nach ihrer gresslichen Gestalt und gerechten Strafe. I. Rinder, Johann Christian. Kurtze doch nachdrückliche Abfertigung an den ... Herrn Georg Gaar. II. Title.

Witchcraft

Gasserstedt, Hansswolff, defendant.
ADS [Litigation concerning the payment of court costs]
1654-1655. Tennenberg, Germany.
18 ll.
Documents concerning the defendant's payment of the court costs for his suit in behalf of his wife, Judith Rommelmann, who had been banished for witchcraft.

MSS
Bd.
WITCHCRAFT
BF
G27++

Gause, Anna, defendant.
Inquisitions Acten wider Anna Gausen, sel. Claus Zaumanns Witwe in puncto beschuldigter Zauberei. Wittenburg, 1689.
29 l. 33cm.
Manuscript, on paper, in the hands of the official notary, Joachim Ehler and other jurists.
T. p. supplied by a former owner.
At head of first leaf: "Protocollum gehalten Wittemburgk... In Inquisition Sachen wieder Anna Gausen,
(Continued on next card)

MSS
Bd.
WITCHCRAFT
BF
G27++

Gause, Anna, defendant. Inquisitions Acten...1689. (Card 2)
sehl. Claus Zaumans nachgelassene Witwen in pō. beschüldigter Zaubereÿ."
Slightly mutilated but mended.
Bound in black boards.
On spine: Hexenprocess-Akten 1689.
1. Trials (Witchcraft)--Wittenburg.
2. Witchcraft-- Wittenburg.

Witchcraft

Gause, Anna, defendant.
A & TM [Partial transcript and notes on the manuscript of her trial]
-1931. [n.p.]
10 l.
In the hands of Georg Sello and G. L. Burr.

MSS
Bd.
WITCHCRAFT
BF
G31

Geistliches Zeug-Hauss in sich haltend starckhe und geistliche Waysen, die teuflische Anfäll glücklich zu yberwinden.
[n.p. 17th cent.]
473 p. 17cm.
Manuscript, on paper, in a 17th century German hand.
Bound in vellum.
1. Demoniac possession. 2. Exorcism. 3. Witchcraft.

MSS
Bd.
WITCHCRAFT
BF
G38

Gespräche von verschiedenem Innhalte unter einer muntern Fastnachtcompagnie, verfasset von einem Liebhaber einer anständigen Freyheit. Gedruckt vor baares Geld, im Jahr, als noch im Märze Fasching war. [München? 1677]
16 p. 22cm.
Carnap's manuscript copy.
Concerns the Sterzinger-März controversy.
1. Sterzinger, Ferdinand, 1721-1786. 2. Superstition. I. Ein Liebhaber einer anständigen Freyheit.

MSS
Bd.
WITCHCRAFT
BF
H63+

Glaser,
ALS to Prof. Dr. Budfurt.
20 Nov. 1845. Bamberg. Verehrtester Freund!/ Unter den alten Papieren auf dem/
1 l.
Tipped in Hexenprozesse. [Bamberg? 1617-1631]

CATALOGUE OF THE CORNELL WITCHCRAFT COLLECTION

Witchcraft
    Godard, George S

        TM List of material on <u>witchcraft</u> in the Connecticut State Library.

        [February, 1914. Hartford]
        3 ll.

        Lists 31 titles. With the letter of transmittal by Godard.

Witchcraft
    Godard, George S

        TLS to George Lincoln Burr

        February 21, 1914. Hartford. As per your request and my promise in/ Charleston
        1 l.

        Filed with his List of material on <u>witchcraft</u> in the Connecticut State Library.

Witchcraft
    Good, William.

        ALS to The Honourable Committee.

        Sept. 13, 1710. Salem, Mass. The humble representation of Willm Good of the Damage Sustained by him in the year 1692...

        William Good's wife, Sarah, was executed as a witch July 19, 1692.
        Purchased from Goodspeed's catalogue #96, Jan., 1913, item 805.
        (Continued on next card)

Witchcraft
    Good, William. ALS to The Honourable Committee...1710. (Card 2)

        Included are two letters from G. F. Dow, secretary of the Essex Institute, 1913, concerning the document.

MSS   Grave, Gerhard, 1598-1675.
Bd.   Abgenötigte Rettung und Erklärung, zweyer
WITCHCRAFT zu Rinteln, jüngsthin, gedruckter Send-
HV   brieffe, so mit Arrest sind hieselbst be-
G77   fangen: in welchen wird gehandelt: Von der Wasser Prob oder vermeintem Hexenbaden ... Durch M. Gerhardum Graven ... Rinteln an der Weser, Gedruckt durch Petrum Lucium, 1640 [ca. 1900]
    157 p. 24cm.
    Carnap's manuscript copy.
    "Originaldruck in der Stadtbiblio-
    (Continued on next card)

MSS   Grave, Gerhard, 1598-1675. Abgenötigte
Bd.   Rettung ... 1640 [ca. 1900] (Card 2)
WITCHCRAFT
HV   thek zu Braunschweig im Samelbande 900.C.
G77   794. 157 Seiten in 4° u. 6 Bl. Register."
    Numerals in the margins indicate pagination of the original.

    1. Trials (Witchcraft) 2. Torture. 3. Water (in religion, folk-lore, etc.) I. Title.

Witchcraft
    Greiess, Eva, defendant, d. 1629.

        ADS Zwuschen ... Wilhelm von ... Neuerreburgh ... und Greiess Eva von Empweiller Zauberey halber Behaftin

        22 September, 1629. Neuerburg? Luxemburg.
        2 ll.

        Advice of the Luxemburg government ordering the torture and execution of Eva Greiess for witchcraft. Signed J. Lud[hug?] and Aut. Lan [ser?]
        (Continued on next card)

witchcraft
    Greiess, Eva, defendant, d. 1629. ADS Zwuschen ... Wilhelm von ... 1629.(Card 2)

        For G. L. Burr's notes on this trial, see Stein, Susanna, defendant, d. 1627. ADS Criminalische Handlung.

Witchcraft
    Gröling, Margaretha, defendant, b. 1587.

        AM Güet unnd peinliche Aussag.

        [1617] [n.p.]
        10 l.

        The defendant's statement under torture. No. 7 in a fascicle of trial documents from Franken.
        Filed with Seebawer, K. AM Aussag. Zeyl, 1629.

MSS   Haeberlin, Georg Heinrich, 1644-1727.
Bd.   Historische Relation, von denen in der
WITCHCRAFT hochfürstl. Würtemb. wohlbenahmssten Ampts-
BF   und Handel-Stadt Calw einige Zeit her der
H13   Zauberey halber beschreyten Kindern, und andern Personen. Sambt einer christlichen Predigt, wie solchen und dergleichen satanischen Anläufften christlich zu begegnen... In öffentlicher Versammlung daselbsten gehalten, und in Truck gegeben von Georg Heinrich Hebe   rlin ... Stuttgart, zu finden bey Johann Gottfried Zubrodt,
    (Continued on next card)

MSS   Haeberlin, Georg Heinrich, 1644-1727.
Bd.   Historische Relation ... 1685 [ca. 1900]
WITCHCRAFT   (Card 2)
BF
H13   daselbst gedruckt bey Melchior Gerhard Lorbern, 1685 [ca. 1900]
    36 p. 23cm.
    Carnap's manuscript copy.
    "Originaldruck in der Königlichen öff. Bibliothek zu Stuttgart 40 pag. S. in 4°."
    Numerals in the margins indicate pagination of the original.
    (Continued on next card)

MSS   Haeberlin, Georg Heinrich, 1644-1727.
Bd.   Historische Relation ... 1685 [ca. 1900]
WITCHCRAFT   (Card 3)
BF
H13

    1. Demoniac possession. 2. Witchcraft--Sermons. 3. Devil. I. Title: Historische Relation, von denen ... der Zauberey halber beschreyten Kindern.

Witchcraft
    Hall, Ralph, defendant.

        ad[copy] Bill of indictment. [Against Ralph Hall and his wife Mary for witchcraft]

        [October 2] 1665. New York.
        3 ll.

        One of two copies of the bill of indictment and procedures of the trial made by Judge Gabriel Furman. His appended comments differ from those accompanying the other copy. On the verso of the third
        (Continued on next card)

Witchcraft
    Hall, Ralph, defendant. ad[copy] Bill of indictment...1665. (Card 2)

    l. and continuing for two more ll. begins Furman's account of "The extraordinary case of Rachel Baker" as he copied it from the National Advocate of New York, March 17, [1816?]

Witchcraft
    Hall, Ralph, defendant.

        ad[copy] Trial for witchcraft.

        October 2, 1665. New York.
        4 ll. [2nd is blank]

        One of two copies of the bill of indictment and procedures of the trial against Ralph Hall and his wife Mary, made by Judge Gabriel Furman. This copy was written on an unused legal form for summons to jury duty in Brooklyn. Furman's
        (continued on next card)

Witchcraft
    Hall, Ralph, defendant. Trial for witchcraft.
        (card 2)

    appended comments differ from those accompanying the other copy.

Witchcraft
    Halle, J., firm, booksellers, Munich.

        TLS to George Lincoln Burr, Esq.

        6. November 1906. München.
    J can report:/ <u>Protokolle von Hexenprocessen zu Flamersheim im Rheinland aus d. J. 1629-/</u>
    2 l.
    With envelope.
    Concerns the purchase of Protokolle von Hexenprocessen in Flamersheim. [Flamersheim? 1629- 30]

Witchcraft
    Happe, Hans.

        TM[copy] Alchemical receptary in German.

        Nov. 8, 1933. [Washington, D. C.?]
        14 l.

        Partial transcription and bibliographic description of Happe, H. Alchamigia. [Nordt Haussen? 1572-73]
        Perhaps done by the Library of Congress.

CATALOGUE OF THE CORNELL WITCHCRAFT COLLECTION

Witchcraft
 Harrison, Katherine, of Wethersfield.
  td₍copy₎ Answer to witnesses
  ₍1669. Hartford, Connecticut₎
  7 ll.
  Mrs. Harrison's reply to her accusers at her trial for witchcraft. The original ms is part of the "Winthrop Papers" preserved by the Massachusetts Historical Society (vol. 14, p.8). Copy made by G. L. Burr from photographs. With envelope and note to Burr concerning the ms.

Witchcraft
 Hencke, Barbara, defendant.
  ADS Zwischen Steins Heinrichen ... und Henckis Barbaren daselbsten Beclagtin und Behaftin
  4 March, 1621. Luxemburg.
  2 ll.
  Judicial order for the torture of Barbara Hencke on the charge of witchcraft. Signed: M. Weser and W. Fünck.

MSS
Bd.
WITCHCRAFT
BF
H63++
 Hexenprozesse. ₍Bamberg? 1617-1631₎
 119 l. 34cm.
 Title from spine.
 Manuscript, on paper, in various 17th century hands.
 Contains 35 distinct documents concerning the witchcraft persecutions in Bamberg.
 Tipped inside front cover are two letters, dated 1832 and 1845, discussing the background of the documents.
 Bound in pl aid boards.
 1. Trials (Witchcraft)--Bamberg.
 2. Witchcraft --Bamberg.

MSS
d.
ITCHCRAFT
F
32
 Hartlieb, Johann, fl. 1450.
 Dr. Hartlieb's Buch aller verbotenen Kunst, Unglaubens und der Zauberei. ₍n.p. 1456; 1896₎
 153 p. 23cm.
 Carnap's manuscript copy.
 "Wörtlich genaue Abschrift der Handschrift ... in der Herzoglichen Bibliothek zu Wolfenbüttel."
 Numerals in the margins indicate foliation of the origin al.
    (Continued on next card)

Witchcraft
 Henot, Catharina, defendant, d. 1627.
  AD₍frag.₎ ₍Trial for witchcraft₎
  16 March, 1627. Cologne.
  3 ll. Facsimile
 Photostat copies of the evidence against the defendant in the hand of a notary, and her protestation of innocence in her own hand.
 With a letter from Dr. Joseph Hansen, discoverer of th e ms., to Lois Gibbons,
    (Continued on next card)

MSS
Bd.
WITCHCRAFT
BF
H64++
 Hexenprozesse aus dem Steinthal, 1607-1675. ₍Alsace, 1607-1675₎
 294 l. 34cm.
 Title from spine.
 Manuscript, on paper, in various 17th century hands.
 Contains 87 trial documents in German or French, and other papers relating to witchcraft procedure in Alsace.
 Note by G. L. Burr inside cover discusses provenance of the collection.
 Bound in brown boards.
 1. Trials (Witchcraft)--Alsace.
 2. Witchcraft --Alsace.

MSS
Bd.
WITCHCRAFT
BF
H32
 Hartlieb, Johann, fl. 1450. Buch aller verbotenen Kunst ... ₍1456; 1896₎ (Card 2)
 Between pages 134 and 135 are inserted 5 unnumbered leaves of "Erlauterungen".
 P. 135-153 are copies of short articles on the original work.
 1. Magic. 2. Witchcraft. 3. Devil.
 I. Title.

Witchcraft
 Henot, Catharina, defendant, d. 1627. AD ₍frag.₎ ₍Trial for witchcraft₎ (Card 2)
 to whom he sent the facsimile and who later gave it to Cornell; envelope and notes by G. L. Burr.

Witchcraft
 Hinteregger, Catharina, defendant.
  AD ₍Trial for witchcraft₎
  1686-1687 Cärnthen, Austria.
  50 ll.
  Documents from the trial of Catharina, her sons Thomerl, Einhardt and Christian, and Christian's wife Agnes.

MSS
Bd.
WITCHCRAFT
BF
H33
 Hartmann, Andreas.
 Warhafftige und mit vielen glaubwürdigen Zeugen bewährte Relation was sich zu Döffingen, hoch-fürstl. würtembergischer Herrschafft, und Böblinger Amts, mit zwey besessenen Weibs-Personen im Monat Decembr. 1714, merckllich zugetragen hat ... Ans Licht gebracht von M. Andreas Hartmann ... ₍n.p.₎ 1716 ₍ca. 1900₎
 14 l. 18cm.
 Carnap's manuscript copy.
 "Wörtliche Abschrift aus: Altes und Neues aus dem Reich Gottes und
    (Continued on next card)

MSS
Bd.
WITCHCRAFT
BF
H61+
 Hexen-Processe im Elsass. Vom Jahre 1615 bis 1635. ₍Hamburg₎ 1835 ₍ca. 1900₎
 5 l. 27cm.
 Carnap's typewritten copy of an article in Die Börsen-Halle, no. 1092-1093, Hamburg, 1835.
 1. Trials (W itchcraft)--Alsace.

MSS
Bd.
WITCHCRAFT
BF
H67
 Histoire prodigieuse et espouvantable de plus de deux cens 50 sorciers et sorcières emmenez pour leur estre fait et parfait leur procez au Parlement de Tholoze: avec l'exécution exemplaire d'un grand nombre en divers lieux: ce qui a causé la cherté des bleds. Paris, Jouste la copie imprimée, 1649 ₍1901₎
 5 l. 19cm.
 Carnap's manuscript copy.
 "Originaldr uck in der Bibliothèque Nationale zu Paris, 8 Seiten in 4°.
    (Continued on next card)

MSS
Bd.
WITCHCRAFT
BF
H33
 Hartmann, Andreas. Warhafftige und mit vielen glaubwürdigen Zeugen bewährte Relation ... 1716 ₍ca. 1900₎ (Card 2)
 der übrigen guten und bösen Geister, etc. ₍hrsg. von J. J. Moser₎ 9ter Theil. Franckfurt u. Leipzig, 1734. 8°. S. 10-28."
 "NB. Diese Besessenheitsgeschichte steht auch wörtlich in: Guden, Friedrich, Schreckliche Geschichte Teuflischer Besitzung, in 3 merkw. Historien, etc. Budissin, 1717. 8°. S. 159-188."
 1. Demoniac possession. 2. Exorcism.
    (Continued on next card)

Witchcraft
 ₍Hexenprozess. Luxemburg. 1621₎
  ADS₍frag.₎
  1621. ₍Luxemburg?₎
  4 ll.
  Testimony of other accused witches against the defendant who is not named, but who seems to have been condemned to be burned on March 12, 1621. G.L. Burr suggests she was very possibly Barbara Hencke, for which see Hencke, Barbara, defendant.
    (Continued on next card)

MSS
Bd.
WITCHCRAFT
BF
H67
 Histoire prodigieuse et espouvantable de plus de deux cens 50 sorciers ... 1649 ₍1901₎ (Card 2)
 Copie angefertigt von der bei der Bibliothek angestellten Mr. Herviant -- Paris im Juni 1901. für 4,50 frs."
 Numerals in the margin indicate pagination of the original.
 1. Witchcraft --Toulouse. 2. Witchcraft--France. 3. Devil.

MSS
Bd.
WITCHCRAFT
BF
H33
 Hartmann, Andreas. Warhafftige und mit vielen glaubwürdigen Zeugen bewährte Relation ... 1716 ₍ca. 1900₎ (Card 3)
 I. Guden, Friedrich, ed. Schreckliche Geschichte teuflischer Besitzung. II. Moser, Johann Jacob, 1701-1785. Altes und Neues aus dem Reich Gottes. III. Title.

Witchcraft
 ₍Hexenprozess₎ ADS₍frag.₎ ... 1621. (Card 2)
 ADS Zwischen Steins Heinrichen ...
 Signed: Joes Dietz.
 Third leaf torn.

Witchcraft
BF
1563
W81++
no. 10
 How to dishroud a witch
  early 17th century 16 cm.
  1 l. Facsimile
 No. 10 in vol. lettered: Witchcraft tracts, chapbooks and broadsides, 1579-1704; rotograph copies.
 Description of va rious tests to determine whether or not a person is a witch.

CATALOGUE OF THE CORNELL WITCHCRAFT COLLECTION

MSS
Bd.
WITCHCRAFT
BF
I53++

Ingolstadt. Universität. Juristische Fakultät.
Consilia der juridischen Facultät. Ingolstadt, 1618-1632.
17-123 p., [4] l., 124-249 p., [1] l. 33cm.
Title from spine.
Manuscript, on paper in various 17th century hands.
A collection of documents reporting the advice of the law faculty of the university in criminal cases,
(Continued on next card)

MSS
Bd.
WITCHCRAFT
BF
I53++

Ingolstadt. Universität. Juristische Fakultät. Consilia. 1618-1632.
(Card 2)
five of which are witchcraft.
Bound in boards with gilded paper.
1. Advisory opinions--Ingolstadt. 2. Judicial opinions--Ingolstadt. 3. Trials (Witchcraft)--Ingolstadt. 4. Trials--Ingolstadt.

Witchcraft
James I, king of Great Britain, 1566-1625.
tm[copy] Tolbooth speech as to witchcraft, as reported by the English envoy.
1591. Edinburgh.
4 ll.
Speech made at the inquest of Barbara Neparre for witchcraft. Copy made by Lucy Dreicker in 1929 from the State Papers, Scotland, v. 47, no. 61. With her handwritten copy of the same (9 ll.),
(Continued on next card)

Witchcraft
James I, king of Great Britain, 1566-1625.
Tolbooth speech as to witchcraft...1591.
(Card 2)
letter to G. L. Burr requesting payment, his note of approval, bank receipt for the draft, and a typewritten note by Burr concerning the speech.

Witchcraft
Keiner, Osanna, defendant, d. 1662.
ADS [Trial for witchcraft]
March-April, 1662. Suhl, Germany.
4 ll.
Two documents relating to her trial for witchcraft: one describing the great "tumult" which took place in her cell and was supposedly caused by supernatural events, and the other attributing her death under torture to strangulation by the devil.

Witchcraft
De Klinkende bel.
am[copy]
[n.d., n.p.]
3 ll.
Poem copied from "Vervolg van verscheyde gedigten, &c. so voor als tegen het boek genaamt de betoverde werelt" Voor de Liefhebbers, 1692.

Witchcraft
Knoulton, Thomas.
A(aman?) [Deposition against Rachel Clinton for practice of witchcraft]
1687? Salem, Massachusetts? 31 cm.
1 l. + typed transcription.
The original leaf has been mounted on later heavy paper.

Witchcraft
Kort-bondige, en voor alle onpartydige, verstaanbare, en met de reeden overeenkomende verklaaringe; van de verleydinge onser eeerste voor-ouderen, Adam ende Eva in het Paradys. Volgens de beschryving van Moses, in het boek der Scheppinge. [Review and critique]
AM
[n.d., n.p.]
4 ll.
(Continued on next card)

Witchcraft
Kort-bondige ... verklaaringe...[n.d.]
(Card 2)
MS review of the article by J.D.V.B.T.K., t'Amsterdam, by Johannes Roman, Boekverkooper, 1699.

Witchcraft
Krämer, Margaretha, defendant, d. 1662.
AD [Trial for witchcraft]
May-October, 1662 Suhl, Germany
55 ll.
Various documents relating to her trial for witchcraft, sewn together in one fascicle.
With note by G. L. Burr.

Witchcraft
Krist, N C
AMS[init.] Bekker's portret.
[1838?] [n.p.]
1 l.
A description of Balthasar Bekker based upon his portraits. The page is headed by the title: Nederlandsch Archief voor Kerkelyke Geschiedenis door N.C. Krist en H.J. Royaards Negende Deel, but the article does not appear in print in that issue (1838).

Witchcraft
Kühn, Sebastianus.
ADS [Receipt for 2 fl. 5 g. 3 d.]
April 12, 1665 Schleusingen, Germany
1 l.
Receipt to the court clerk Sebastian Bentzinger for the sum paid to Kühn and 4 clergymen from the estate of Irmel Wagnerin, executed for witchcraft on April 8, 1665.
With note by G. L. Burr.

Witchcraft
Künnen, Reygers, defendant.
AM Erste güetliche unn[d] peinliche Aussag.
[1616] Geroltzh[ausen?]
10 l.
The defendant's statement.
No. 6 in a fascicle of trial documents from Franken.
Filed with Seebawer, K. AM Aussag. Zeyl, 1629.

Witchcraft
[Lach?], Johanes.
a[aman.]ls to ? Weiss
17. Februar, 1808. [illegible] Hochzuverehrenten Hern./ in dem, Bitte ich Aller Gehorsamst
2 ll.
The author writes that he has found an "olympian water" and the conjuration for the spirit which governs it.

Witchcraft
Lamkers, Maria, defendant.
ad [Deposition for witchcraft]
[c. 1630?] Neuerburg, Luxemburg.
2 ll.
The deposition against Maria Lamkers was presented by the attorney for the city of Neuerburg.

MSS
Bd.
WITCHCRAFT
RB
L27

Lange, , physician, of Lisieux.
Histoire de la fille maléficiée de Courson. Avec une dissertation physique sur ce maléfice. Par Monsieur Lange, Conseiller Médecin du Roy. Lisieux, Chez J. du Roncerey, 1717 [ca. 1900]
34 p. 23cm.
Carnap's manuscript copy.
"Der Originaldruck von welchem diese Abschrift genommen wurde, befindet sich in der Bibliothèque Nationale zu Paris ... Eine Abschrift fertigte der
(Continued on next card)

MSS
Bd.
WITCHCRAFT
RB
L27

Lange, , physician, of Lisieux.
Histoire de la fille maléficiée ... 1717
[ca. 1900] (Card 2)
daselbst angestellte Bibliothekar J. Herviant an; die vorliegende ist mit desselben wörtlich übereinstimmend."
Numerals in the margins indicate pagination of the original work.
"Notizen über diese Abhandlung" pp. 31-34.
1. Diseases --Causes and theories of causation. 2. Witchcraft. 3. Morin, Madeleine. I. Title.

MSS
Bd.
WITCHCRAFT
BF
L37

Laugeois, Antoine, d. 1674.
L'innocence opprimee; ou, Défense de Mathurin Picard, curé de Mesnil-Jourdain ... Par M. Laugois, successeur immédiat dudit Picard - dans la cure de Mesnil-Jourdain. Ouvrage qui n'a jamais été imprimé et extrait sur l'original, par M. Chemin curé de Tourneville. [n. p. 17th cent.]
x, 102 p. title vignette. 18cm.
Manuscript, on paper.
Preface signed M. du Passeur (Gabriel), curé de Vironvay.
(Continued on next card)

636

CATALOGUE OF THE CORNELL WITCHCRAFT COLLECTION

MSS
d.
ITCHCRAFT
37

Laugeois, Antoine, d. 1674. L'innocence opprimee...₍17th cent.₎ (Card 2)

Notes by G. L. Burr inside front cover discuss history and provenance of the manuscript.
Bound in boards.
1. Demoniac possession. 2. Picard, Mathurin, d. 1647. 3. Bavent, Madeleine, b. 1607. 4. Louviers, France. St. Louis (Convent) 5. Witchcraft. I. Chemin, J B , 1725 -1781, ed. II. Title. III. Title: Défense de Mathurin Picard.

Witchcraft

₍List of works concerning Balthasar Bekker₎

AM₍frag.₎

₍n.d., n.p.₎
1 l.

List of 12 articles.

MSS
Bd.
WITCHCRAFT
BF
L82

Löher, Hermann, b. 1595. Hochnötige unterthanige wemütige Klage ... 1676 ₍1896₎ (Card 3)

Gymnasiums zu Münstereifel b/Bonn. 16 Bl. u. 608 pag. S. Von dort geliehen und abgeschrieben in der Zeit vom 12. Februar bis zum 9. März 1896."
Numerals in the margins indicate pagination of the original.
Imperfect: p. 84-86, 132-134, part of p. 354-355 are blank and
(Continued on next card)

Witchcraft

Lea, Henry Charles, 1825-1909, comp.

TM₍copy₎ ₍Clippings relating to witchcraft₎

₍n.d.₎ ₍Ithaca, New York₎
79 l.

Transcription of clippings collected by Lea, which he lent to the library for copying.

Witchcraft

Liveyra, Maria Antonia de, defendant.

am Sentença De Maria Antonia Natural da Freguezia de Valga, e moradora no lugar do Seixo Comarca da Villa da Feyra, Bisp.do do Porto, Que se lhe leo no Auto publico da Fee que se celebrou em a Cidade de Coimbra em 21 de Fevr. de 1673...

₍c.1710₎ ₍Lisbon₎
5 ll.

An account of the trial conducted
(Continued on next card)

MSS
Bd.
WITCHCRAFT
BF
L82

Löher, Hermann, b. 1595. Hochnötige unterthanige wemütige Klage ... 1676 ₍1896₎ (Card 4)

correspond to p. 45-48, 97-100 and 341-342 of the original, which the copyist states are missing.
Bibliography of literature referring to this work: p. 607-638.
Note by the copyist concerning the scarcity of the original p. 639-640.
Plates are photographic reproduc-
(Continued on next card)

Witchcraft

Leitschuh, Dr. Fr₍anz Friedrich₎

ALS to ₍Joseph Baer & Co.₎

November 1, 1899. Strassburg. Sehr geehrte Herren !/ Zu meinem Bedauern ist es mir nicht möglich,
2 ll.

Concerns his offer to sell this dealer the documents of the witch trial of Sister Maria Renata Sänger and Hans Loder's wife. For these trials see Loder, Mrs. Hans, defendant.
(Continued on next card)

Witchcraft

Liveyra, Maria Antonia de, defendant. am Sentença ... (Card 2)

by the Portuguese Inquisition. The accused was convicted of witchcraft after confessing to charges of effecting magical cures.

MSS
Bd.
WITCHCRAFT
BF
L82

Löher, Hermann, b. 1595. Hochnötige unterthanige wemütige Klage ... 1676 ₍1896₎ (Card 5)

tions from the copper plates of the original, pasted on to extra leaves.
With note by G. L. Burr on inside front cover indicating provenance of the manuscript copy.

1. Trials (Wi tchcraft)--Germany.
2. Witchcraft --Germany. I. Title.

Witchcraft

Leitschuh, Dr. Fr₍anz Friedrich₎ ALS. (Card 2)

ADS₍frag.₎ ₍Trial for witchcraft₎ and Sänger, Maria Renata von Mossau, ca. 1680-1749. ADS ₍Trial for witchcraft₎

Witchcraft

Loder, Mrs. Hans, defendant.

ADS₍frag.₎ ₍Trial for witchcraft₎

1584-85. Arnstein, Germany.
17 ll.

Nine different documents plus one duplicate, all addressed to the Prince-Bishop of Würzburg.
See also: Leitschuh, Dr. Fr₍anz Friedrich₎ ALS to ₍Joseph Baer & Co.₎

MSS
Bd.
WITCHCRAFT
BF
L86
1592a

Loos, Cornelius, 1546-1595.
₍De vera et falsa magia. Trier, 1592;
₍⁴₎, ₍10₎-171 l. 24cm.
Manuscript, on Japan vellum. Facsimile copy made by George Lincoln Burr of a fragment of the original printer's copy of the manuscript; title page supplied by Burr.
T. p. and index are loose, unnumbered.
The numbered leaves are tied in ten small fascicles, for ming only the first two of the four books included in the
(Continued on next card)

Witchcraft

Leonhardtz, Hupricht, d. 1621, defendant.

AM Verbal zwischen Steins Henrichen aus Oberweiss formal Clegern ahn einem, geg und wider Leonhardtz Huprichten von Oberweiss lasters Zauberey halb Inquirirten andern Theilss.

1621. Neuerburg, Luxemburg.
20 l.

The original, in the hand of the notary, Joh annes Dietz.

MSS
Bd.
WITCHCRAFT
BF
L82

Löher, Hermann, b. 1595.
Hochnötige unterthanige wemütige Klage der frommen Unschültigen; worin alle hohe und nidrige Oberkeit, sampt ihren Unterthanen klärlich, augenscheinlich zu sehen und zu lesen haben, wie die arme unschüldige fromme Leute durch Fahm- und Ehrenrauber von den falschen Zauber-richtern angegriffen, durch die unchristliche Folter, und Pein-banck von ihnen gezwungen werden, erschreckliche, unthunliche Mord, und Todt, Sünden auff sich selbsten und
(Continued on next card)

MSS
Bd.
WITCHCRAFT
BF
L86
1592a

Loos, Cornelius, 1546-1595. ₍De vera et falsa magia. 1592; 1886₎ (Card 2)
index. There is a loose extra copy each of l. 15, 20, 79.
In marbled case.
The original is in the Stadtbibliothek Trier.
Partially printed in 1592.
With this is cased his Extracts from the De vera et falsa magia. Köln, 1912.

Witchcraft

Lijst der werken van B. Bekker voor en tegen schriften, enz., enz., enz.

AM

₍n.p., n.d₎
6 ll.

List enumerates, besides Bekker's own works, some 170 titles.

MSS
Bd.
WITCHCRAFT
BF
L82

Löher, Hermann, b. 1595. Hochnötige unterthanige wemütige Klage ... 1676 ₍1896₎ (Card 2)

anderen mehr zu liegen, und sie ungerechtlich, falschlich zu besagen... durch Hermannum Löher. Amsterdam, Jacob de Jonge, 1676 ₍1896₎
640 p. 10 plates, part folded. 19cm.
Carnap's manuscript copy.
"Originaldruck als einziges bekanntes Exemplar in der Bibliothek des Kgl.
(Continued on next card)

MSS
Bd.
WITCHCRAFT
BF
L86
1592b

Loos, Cornelius, 1546-1595.
₍De vera et falsa magia. Köln? 1592?
ca. 1900₎
₍1₎, 96, ₍1₎, 89, ₍1₎ p.; 15 blank l., ₍1₎ p. 15cm.
Signatures: A-F⁸. (p. 1-96 only)
Carnap's manuscript copy of a printed fragment, according to G. L. Burr, probably as much as had been completed before seizure by the Inquisition.
"Das Original befindet sich in der Stadtbiblioth ek zu Köln ... 6 Bogen
(Continued on next card)

CATALOGUE OF THE CORNELL WITCHCRAFT COLLECTION

MSS Bd. WITCHCRAFT BF L86 1592b
Loos, Cornelius, 1546-1595. [De vera et falsa magia. 1592? ca. 1900] (Card 2)
in Kl. 8°. Ein Titelblatt ist nicht vorhanden."
The second part, p. 1-89 consists of bibliographical citations and excerpts from articles concerning Loos and his work.
1. Demonology. 2. Witchcraft. 3. His De vera et falsa magia. I. Title.

MSS Bd. WITCHCRAFT BF L86 1592a
Loos, Cornelius, 1546-1595. Extracts from the De vera et falsa magia of Cornelius Loos. (Made from the Ms. at Trier and verified by the printed fragment at Köln in July, 1912.) Köln, 1912. 4, 1-6, [1], 7-15, [1], 16-48 l. 20cm.
Manuscript, in small notebook of graph paper, in the hand of G. L. Burr. P. 41-48 are Notes on the printed fragment at Cologne, by G. L. Burr.
Four loose typewritten leaves of the Latin text are inserted inside
(Continued on next card)

MSS Bd. WITCHCRAFT BF L86 1592a
Loos, Cornelius, 1546-1595. Extracts from the De vera et falsa magia ... 1912. (Card 2) front cover.
In marbled case with his [De vera et falsa magia. Trier, 1592; 1886]
1. Demonology. 2. Witchcraft. 3. His De vera et falsa magia. I. Burr, George Lincoln, 1857-1938.

MSS Bd. WITCHCRAFT BF L97
Lutz, Reinhard.
Warhafftige Zeitung. Von den gottlosen Hexen, auch ketzerischen unnd Teufels Weibern, die zu des heyligē römischeñ Reichsstatt Schletstat im Elsass, auff den zwey und zwentzigsten Herbstmonats des verlauffenen siebentzigsten Jars, von wegen ihrer schentlicher Teuffels Verpflichtung verbrent worden, sampt einem kurtzen Extract und Aussszug ettlicher Schrifften von Hexerey zusammen gebracht durch Renhardum Lutz ... [n.p.] 1571 [ca. 1900]
(Continued on next card)

MSS Bd. WITCHCRAFT BF L97
Lutz, Reinhard. Warhafftige Zeitung. Von den gottlosen Hexen ... 1571 [ca. 1900] (Card 2)
16 l. illus. 23cm.
Signatures: A-D, E³.
Carnap's manuscript copy.
"Originaldruck in der Hof- u. Staatsbibliothek zu München. 20 Bl. in 4°."
Signatures and numerals in the margins correspond to signatures and pagination of the original.
1. Witchcraft--Germany. 2. Demonology. 3. Folk-lore of children. I. Title.

MSS Bd. WITCHCRAFT BT M24
Maldonado, Juan, 1534-1583. Eruditissimi domini Joannis Maldonati... Disputatio De daemonum distinctione et de praestigiis hoc est de potestate, actione et fallacia eorundem. Paris, 1572. [30] l. 23cm.
Manuscript, on paper.
The second part of a treatise which was never printed in the original Latin. A French translation of the entire work was published in 1605, 1616, 1617, 1619 with title: Traicté des anges et
(Continued on next card)

MSS Bd. WITCHCRAFT BT M24
Maldonado, Juan, 1534-1583. Eruditissimi domini Joannis Maldonati... Disputatio De daemonum distinctione... 1572. (Card 2) demons.
Signed: Sebastianus Hamelius.
Notes inside front cover of vol. discuss history and provenance of the manuscript. Originally the vol. was in the Lamoignon library, then passed to library of Prof. E. Dowden.
With this ms. are bound three printed works: Nicaise, Claude. De
(Continued on next card)

MSS Bd. WITCHCRAFT BT M24
Maldonado, Juan, 1534-1583. Eruditissimi domini Joannis Maldonati... Disputatio De daemonum distinctione... 1572. (Card 3)
nummo pantheo Hadriani imperatoris. Lugduni, 1690. Patin, Charles. Commentarius Caroli Patini in tres inscriptiones Graecas. Patavii, 1685. Rigord, Jean Pierre. Dissertation historique sur une medaille d'Herodes Antipas. Paris, 1689.
1. Demonology. 2. Devil. I. His Traicté des anges et demons. II. Title: Disputatio De daemonum distinctione. III. Title: De daemonum distinctione.

Witchcraft
Margareth, of Körperich, defendant.
ads Präparatorische Information durch ... Hans Jacob von Preisgin ... wegen criminalist Inditien über Margareth von Körperich
September 9, 1600. Neuerburg, Luxemburg. 2 ll.
Margaret's confession that she had been led to become a witch by her grandmother. Signed: Hrn. Johann.

Witchcraft
Martin, Margreta, defendant, d. 1620.
ADS Bericht. Wegen der verstorbnen Hexen der Märtins Greten
January 22, 1620. [Lowenberg, Germany] 2 ll.
Report on the torture of Margreta Martin and her ensuing "inexplicable" death.

Witchcraft
Martin, Margreta, defendant, d. 1620.
AD Peinliche Anclag ad Torturam
December 12, 1619. Lowenberg, Germany. 4 ll.
Deposition against Margreta Martin for witchcraft, culminating in a request for the application of torture.

Witchcraft
Massachusetts (Colony) Courts (Essex Co.)
ADS Order of execution of Bridgett Bishop
June, [1692] Salem.
1 l. (2 copies)   **Facsimile**
Letter from Judge William Stoughton to George Corwin, sheriff of Essex County, ordering the execution of Bridgett Bishop, who was convicted of witchcraft.
In the same photograph is the answering letter of Corwin, confirming that the execution was completed.

Rare BF 1563 M57+ v.1-3
Merritt, Bertha (Sutermeister)
Witchcraft material gathered by Mrs. Merritt in preparation for her thesis. Contains many notes and accounts of trials, particularly in Alsace. Collected ca. 1926. 3 cases. 28cm.
1. Witchcraft. 2. Witchcraft--Alsace.

Witchcraft
Miller, Johannes, Anglican minister.
AM[copy] [Answer to the seven questions posed by Joseph Dudley]
October, 1692 New York. **Facsimile**
2 ll. (2 copies, positive and negative)
Miller's own copy (made in 1717) of his original answers to the seven questions posed by Dudley on October 5, 1692, concerning the Church's definition of witchcraft and punishment thereof. Photostats from the New York Public Library.

WITCHCRAFT BF 1559 K62
Mirus, Martin, 1532-1593.
AM Consilium D. D. Martini Miri, amico cuidam priuatim cōmunicatum, super abrogatione Exorcismi.
[n.d., n.p.]
9 l.
Tipped in Kittelman, Christian. Von dem Exorcismo. [n.p.] 1591.

MSS Bd. WITCHCRAFT BF N12
Nachricht von einer Weibes-Person, so sich dem bösen Feinde mit Leib und Seel ergeben, auch wieder erlöset worden.
Augspurg, 1671 [ca. 1900]
4 l. 23cm.
Carnap's manuscript copy.
"Originaldruck in der Kgl. Universitäts-Bibliothek zu Leipzig. 2 B. in 4°."
Numerals in the margins indicate pagination of the original.
1. Devil. 2. Witchcraft. 3. Schillerin, Regina.

Witchcraft
National advocate.
am[copy] The extraordinary case of Rachel Baker.
March 17, [1816?] New York.
3 ll.
Filed with Hall, Ralph, defendant. Bill of Indictment.
Copy of a newspaper article made by Judge Gabriel Furman. The first l. is on the verso of the 3rd l. of the Bill of Indictment against Ralph Hall.

Witchcraft
Nederlandse hervormde kerk. Kerkelijk register der predikanten.
am[copy] Article on Balthasar Bekker.
[n.d., n.p.]
2 ll.
Copy of the article on Bekker in the Kerkelijk register der predikanten, p. 110.

CATALOGUE OF THE CORNELL WITCHCRAFT COLLECTION

Witchcraft
    9 [i.e., Negen] deelen voor en tegen B. Bekker.
    AM
    [n.d., n.p.]
    8 ll.
    List of pamphlets relating to the Bekker controversy. Titles and imprints are given with great fullness.

Witchcraft
    Novelles voor en tegen B. Bekker.
    AM
    [n.d., n.p.]
    4 ll.
    Enumerates some 117 titles (7 deelen) of pamphlets concerning Bekker.

Witchcraft
    Picken, Magdalen, defendant.
    ADS Criminal Proces ... zwischent ... Hern Cristoffeln de la Val ... und Picken Hansen Hausfrauen Magdalenen Lasters der Zaubereyen halber gedagtin und belagten
    1613. Neueurburg, Luxemburg.
    11 ll.
    Her first examination and testimony of seven other convicted witches who had accused her.

Witchcraft
    9 [i.e., Negen] deelen voor en tegen B. Bekker.
    AM [frag.]
    [n.d., n.p.]
    3 ll.
    Contains the end of the 6th, complete 7th and 8th, and beginning of the 9th parts.

MSS
Bd.
WITCHCRAFT
JS
N971++
    Nuremberg.
    Hals Gerichts Ordtnung. Ordnung des Hals-Gerichts zu Nürnberg. [17th cent.?]
    99 l. 32 x 21cm.
    Manuscript, on paper, in three different German hands. Only the first four leaves, dated 1526, are concerned with criminal procedure. The remaining leaves contain a listing and summary of trials which ended in sentences of execution from 1600-1692.
    Notes inside front cover by G. L. Burr discuss origin of the manuscript and give bibliog raphical references.
    (Continued on next card)

M
Bd.
Pictorius
    Pictorius, Georg.
    am An sagae mulieres quas expiatrices vulgatim nominanus, ignis mulcta sunt damnadae, resolutio.
    [Late 17th century] 18cm.
    [3] ll.
    Bound with: his De Speciebus magiae; and De Illorum daemonum. Also, Geomantiae Astronomicae [by Gerardus Cremonensis]; De Magia veterum [Arbatel de Magia]; Ars notoria; De incantatione et adiuratione; and Diversa divinationum genera.

Witchcraft
    New York (State) University, Binghamton. Center for Medieval and Early Renaissance Studies.
    Witchcraft and the occult in the Middle ages and early Renaissance.
    Binghamton, 1973
    [4] p.
    Printed program for the Center's Seventh Annual Confer ence, May 5-6, 1973.

MSS
Bd.
WITCHCRAFT
JS
N971++
    Nuremberg. Hals Gerichts Ordtnung.
    [17th cent.?] (Card 2)
    Bound in vellum with leather ties. The vellum is itself a manuscript: "... nearly complete (or quite complete) letter of Canton Zug, in Switzerland, to the city of Nuremberg relating to certain Swiss aggressions on the transalpine trade of that city. Its date is 1555 ... Its use suggests that the MS of the book may be the (or an) official origi nal."
    Accompanied by an incomplete
    (Continued on next card)

M
Bd.
Pictorius
    Pictorius, Georg.
    am De illorum daemonum qui sub lunari collimitio versantur, ortu, nominibus, officiis, illusionibus, potestate, vaticiniis, miraculis, et quibus mediis in fugam compellantur. [With the Colloquntur Castor et Pollux].
    [Late 17th century] 18cm.
    [44] ll.
    Descriptions of the Spirits, their power, and how they may be expelled.
    (Continued on next card)

MSS
Bd.
WITCHCRAFT
BF
N54
    Newe Zeitung von den Hexen, oder Unhulden, so mañ verbrend hat, von dem 7. Februarj an, biss auff den 25. Junij, dieses 1580 Jar. Auch wirt darbey angezeigt, an was Ort und Enden, auch was sie bekent haben. In ein Liede verfasst. [n.p.] 1580 [ca. 1900]
    6 l. 19cm.
    Carnap's manuscript copy.
    "Originaldruck in der Stadtbibliothek zu Zürich, 7 Sei ten in 8°."
    (Continued on next card)

MSS
Bd.
WITCHCRAFT
JS
N971++
    Nuremberg. Hals Gerichts Ordtnung.
    [17th cent.?] (Card 3)
    transcript of the letter into a modern hand: 7 leaves, loose, in folder.
    In sombre marbled case.
    Ex libris: Gg. Wolfg. Carol. Lochner.
    1. Criminal procedure--Nuremberg. 2. Criminal registers--Nuremberg. 3. Court records--Nuremberg. 4. Judgments, Criminal --Nuremberg. 5. Sentences (Criminal procedure)-- Nuremberg.

M
Bd.
Pictorius
    Pictorius, Georg. am De illorum daemonum ... (Card 2)
    Bound with: his De Speciebus magiae; and An sagae, vel mulieres quas expiatrices vulgatim nominamus. Also, Geomantiae Astronomicae [by Gerardus Cremonensis]; De Magia veterum [Arbatel de Magia]; Ars notoria; De Incantatione et adiuratione; and Diversa divinationum genera.

MSS
Bd.
WITCHCRAFT
BF
N54
    Newe Zeitung von den Hexen, oder Unhulden ... 1580 [ca. 1900] (Card 2)
    In verse.
    Annotations in the margin indicate foliation of the original.
    1. Witchcraft--Germany.

Witchcraft
    Onder het Monument von B. Bekker staat alz volgt.
    am
    [n.d., n.p.]
    1 l.
    Inscription on Bekker's monument and list of portraits of him.

M
Bd.
Pictorius
    Pictorius, Georg.
    am De speciebus magiae ceremonialis quam Goëtiam vocant, epitome per Georgium Pictorium Vigillanum, doctorem medicum, nuperrime conscripta.
    [Late 17th century] 18cm.
    [28] ll.
    Deals with various types of ceremonial magic.
    Bound with: his An Sagae, vel mulieres quas expiatrices vul gatim nominamus; and De
    (Continued on next card)

Witchcraft
    Nicholson, Jno. W
    ALS to Prof. Geo. L. Burr
    Sept. 28, 1908. Puncoteague, Va.
    My dear Sir:/ I received by mail/ from Scribner's Sons a discriptive
    2 ll.
    Informs Burr that he has a "facsimile copy" of the trial of Grace Sherwood.
    With envelope.

Witchcraft
    Pennsylvania gazette.
    am [copy] Trial for witchcraft.
    October 22, 1730 Philadelphia.
    4 ll.
    Copy made by Judge Gabriel Furman at Burlington, October 12, [n.y.], of an article in the issue of October 22, 1730. The last half of the 2nd l. is taken up by the copy of a poem called Majesty in misery, by King Charles 1st.

M
Bd.
Pictorius
    Pictorius, Georg. am De speciebus magiae ceremonialis ... (Card 2)
    Illorum daemonum. Also Geomantiae Astronomicae [by Gerardus Cremonensis]; De Magia veterum [Arbatel de Magia]; Ars notoria; De Incantatione et adiuratione; and Diversa divinationum genera.

CATALOGUE OF THE CORNELL WITCHCRAFT COLLECTION

Witchcraft
    Pollmann, Anna, defendant.

    AD₍frag.₎ Untersuchungs Protokoll gegen die Ehefrau dess Jürgen Pollmann, Anna geboren Nolte in Rinteln, wegen Zauberei.

    1660-1664. Rinteln, Germany.
    143 ll.

    With catalog and note by George L. Burr.

MSS Bd. WITCHCRAFT BF G12 R57
    Rinder, Johann Christian. ...Kurtze doch nachdrückliche Abfertigung ... 1750 ₍ca. 1900₎   (Card 2)

    Carnap's manuscript copy.
    "Originaldruck in der Kgl. Hof u. Staats-Bibliothek zu München. 46 S. in 4°."
    Numerals in the margins indicate pagination of the original.
    A defense of his Eine Hexe nach ihrer gresslichen Gestalt und gerechten Strafe.
    1. Witchcraft--Germany. 2. Gaar, Georg, b. 1702. Heyls ame Lehrstück, und Zauberey bet reffende Anmerckungen.
    (Continued on next card)

MSS Bd. WITCHCRAFT BF S19
    Samson, Hermann. Neun ausserlesen und wolgegründete Hexen Predigt ... 1626 ₍ca. 1900₎   (Card 2)

    täts-Bibliothek zu Breslau. 42. Bl. in 4°."
    Title page in red and black.
    Numerals and signatures in the margins indicate pagination and signatures of the original.
    On the inside front cover the copyist has appended a no   te on the rarity of the printed work   and given bibliographical
    (Continued on next card)

MSS Bd. WITCHCRAFT BF P96+
    Protokolle von Hexenprocessen in Flamersheim. ₍Flamersheim? 1629-30₎
    ₍54₎ l. 29cm.

    Manuscript, on paper, in a German hand.
    Leaves numbered as follows: 13-23, 25-29, 32-36, 39, 43, 51-61, 65-75, 82, 84.
    Followed by 7 unnumbered leaves, badly mutilated.
    Bound in green marbled boards.
    1. Trials (Wi   tchcraft)--Germany.
    2. Witchcraft --Flamersheim, Germany.

MSS Bd. WITCHCRAFT BF G12 R57
    Rinder, Johann Christian. ... Kurtze doch nachdrückliche Abfertigung ... 1750 ₍ca. 1900₎   (Card 3)

    3. His Eine Hexe nach ihrer gresslichen Gestalt und gerechten Strafe. I. Title: Kurtze doch nachdrückliche Abfertigung an den ... Herrn Georg Gaar.

MSS Bd. WITCHCRAFT BF S19
    Samson, Hermann. Neun ausserlesen und wolgegründete Hexen Predigt ... 1626 ₍ca. 1900₎   (Card 3)

    references.
    Signed Geo. L. Burr.

    1. Witchcraft--Sermons. I. Title.

Witchcraft
    Prütinger, Cunz, defendant.

    ADS ₍Order for examination by torture on the charge of witchcraft₎

    September 7, 1621. Bamberg, Germany.
    2 ll.

    Issued by the Chancellor and Council of the Prince-Bishop of Bamberg and Würzburg.

Witchcraft
    Rosenthal, Ludwig, Munich.

    AL to The President White Library

    May, 1900. Munich.

    Post card offering for sale Hexen Buechlein. Pencilled on the card is a note by G. L. Burr indicating that the book was not ordered.

MSS Bd. WITCHCRAFT BT S33
    Schickhart, Philipp.
    Zwo christliche Predigten, aber ₍sic₎ der Buss unnd Bekehrung, eines Jüngs, welcher sich, laut nachgesetzter Vorred, dem bösen Geist, auff siben Jar lang, mit Leib uñ Seel ergeben gehabt. Gehalten zu Göppingen, durch M. Philippum Schickardum ... Tübingen, Getruckt bey Johan Conrad Geysslern, 1631 ₍ca. 1900₎
    ₍6₎, 48 p. title vignette. 19cm.
    Signatures: A-   G⁴, F.
    Carnap's man   uscript copy.
    (Continued on next card)

Witchcraft
    Reinhard, Ursula, defendant.

    ADS Summarische Erkundigung -- wegen verdächtiger Zauberey wider Ursel Reinhardin ... itszo -- Judith Rommelmann Ernst Hansen Wittibe -- und Caspar Hessen Weib

    1649-1654. Tenneberg, Germany.
    208 ll.

    Documents from the trials of all 3 accused witches, of which the first 106 ll. are sewn together in one   fascicle and concern
    (Continued on next card)

Witchcraft
    Sänger, Maria Renata von Mossau, defendant, ca. 1680-1749.

    ADS ₍Trial for witchcraft₎

    1749. ₍n.p.₎
    35 ll.

    Contents: Ratione corporis delecti, a brief of the case against her; 3 lists of questions to be asked her; her examination and confession, signed in her hand at the bottom of the first page and at the   end; a document sentencing
    (Continued on next card)

MSS Bd. WITCHCRAFT BT S33
    Schickhart, Philipp. Zwo christliche Predigten ... 1631 ₍ca. 1900₎   (Card 2)

    "Original i. d. Kgl. Bibl. z. Stuttgart. Titelbl. 3 Bl. Vorrede u. 48 pag. S. Text. Sig. Aii-Giij."
    Bibliography: 1 leaf at end.
    "N. B. Die Seiten dieser Abschrift stimen mit denjenigen des Originals überein."
    1. Repentance--Sermons. 2. Conversion--Sermons. 3. Devil. I. Title.

Witchcraft
    Reinhard, Ursula, defendant. ADS Summarische Erkundigung ...   (Card 2)

    only Ursula Reinhard. Followed by 93 loose ll. relating also to her trial, 2 ll. relating to Judith Rommelmann, and 7 ll. from the trial of Caspar Hess' wife.
    With a note by G. L. Burr.

Witchcraft
    Sänger, Maria Renata von Mossau, defendant, ca. 1680-1749. ADS ₍Trial ...₎ (Card 2)

    cing her to trial by a secular court; two legal briefs discussing her penalty and torture; two short statements accusing her of further bewitching her companions; a brief summation of her career, trial and execution; two accounts of her secular trial and execution.
    With notes by George L. Burr.
    See also Wahrhaffte und umständige Nachricht ... AM. and White, Andrew Dickson, 1832-1918. TLS   to Proffessor George L. Burr, September   30, 1899.

Witchcraft
    Schlott,   defendant.

    AM Notamina ulteriora

    1750? ₍n.p.₎
    4 ll.

    Deposition for witchcraft against one Schlott, who was secretary for the convent of Unterzell, near Würzburg.

MSS Bd. WITCHCRAFT BF G12 R57
    Rinder, Johann Christian.
    Johann Christian Rinders ... Kurtze doch nachdrückliche Abfertigung an den würtzburgischen Pater Herrn Georg Gaar, Lojoliten, der ihn in einer öffentlichen und nun zum Druck gegebenen Canzelrede ... so gar mit Namen um der Wahrheit willen herum genommen, statt einer Franckfurter Messe dafür bey Gelegenheit derselben wie schuldig, übermacht. Jena, In der Cröckerischen Buchhandlung, 1750   ₍ca. 1900₎
    24 l. 23cm.
    (Continued on next card)

MSS Bd. WITCHCRAFT BF S19
    Samson, Hermann.
    Neun ausserlesen und wolgegründete Hexen Predigt, darinnen der Terminus Magiae oder Zauberey nach den logicalischen Terminis ... erkläret und aussgeführet worden, und in der Thumb Kirchen zu Riga öffentlich gehalten durch M. Hermannum Sansonium ... Riga in Eiffland, durch und in Verlegung Gerhard Schröders, 1626 ₍ca. 1900₎
    166 p. 24cm.
    Carnap's ma   nuscript copy.
    "Original   ruck in der Universi-
    (Continued on next card)

MSS Bd. WITCHCRAFT BF H63+
    Schneider, Dr.

    ALS to den Herrn Grafen und Appellations-Gerichts-Präsidenten von Bamberg.

    d. 19 Mai 1832. Fulda.

    Hochgeborner Herr Graf, hochwohlgeborner Herr Präsident !/ Balthasar Voss ist uns hier durch seine Hexenunsage und Grausamkeit tradition   ell noch/
    Tipped in   Hexenprozesse. ₍Bamberg 1617-1631₎

CATALOGUE OF THE CORNELL WITCHCRAFT COLLECTION

MSS
Bd.
WITCHCRAFT
BV
S38

Ein Schröckliche Antwort eines bösen Geists auss einer besessenen Person, als er beschworen, unnd ein verdampter Lugengeist gescholten worden ist, &c. Lieds weiss an Tag geben, zur Wahrnung und Straff aller unbussfertigen. [n.p.] 1596 [ca. 1900]
4 l. title vignette. 19cm.
Carnap's manuscript copy.
"Originaldruck in der Königlichen Bibliothek zu Berlin, 4 Bl. in 16°."
"Wahrscheinlich von Daniel Sudermañ.
(Continued on next card)

MSS
Bd.
WITCHCRAFT
BV
S38

Ein Schröckliche Antwort eines bösen Geists ... 1596 [ca. 1900] (Card 2)
Diese Notiz steht mit Tinte geschrieben auf dem Titelblatte des Exemplars der Königl. Bibliothek zu Berlin."
Numerals in the margins indicate pagination of the original.
In verse.
1. Admonition. I. Sudermann, Daniel, supposed author.

Witchcraft

Schuster, Barbara Schröchlin, defendant, b. 1590.
AM[frag.] Aussag.
[1630] Bamberg.
4 l.
An incomplete summary of her trial.
No. 3 in a fascicle of trial documents from Franken.
Filed with Seebawer, K. AM Aussag. Zeyl, 1629.

MSS
Bd.
WITCHCRAFT
PT
S39

Schuster, Michael.
Verkehrter bekehrter und wider bethörter Ophiletes auf die Traur-Bühne gestellet von Sibylla Schusterin. [Kurzer historischer Innhalt dess Traurspiels] Oettingen, Stephan Rolk, 1685 [ca. 1900]
7 l. 19cm.
Carnap's manuscript copy of an excerpt from Michael Schuster's preface Kurzer historischer Innhalt dess Traurspiels.
"Ausschnitt: Blatt, Sign. v-viij
(Continued on next card)

MSS
Bd.
WITCHCRAFT
PT
S39

Schuster, Michael. Verkehrter bekehrter ... Ophiletes ... [Kurzer historischer Innhalt ...] 1685 [ca. 1900] (Card 2)
der Vorrede, von Michael Schuster."
"Original i. d. Kgl. Bibl. z. Berlin. Bildniss, Titel, 2 unpag. Blätter Widmung, 9 unpag. Blätter Vorrede u. Einführung. 226 pag. Seiten Text. 12°."
I. Schuster, Sibylla (Neithart), 1639-1685. Verkehrter bekehrter und wider bethörter Ophiletes. II. Title.

MSS
Bd.
WITCHCRAFT
BF
S39

Schwann, Johan.
Zwo gründliche und warhafftige newe Zeitung, die Erste von den Hexen und Unholden Mann und Weibs Personen, so man in der churfürstlichen Statt zu Aschenburg unnd auch auff dem Land mit dem Fewer gestrafft unnd verbrandt hat ... Die ander Zeitung. Von dem erschröcklichen Jammer, so sich im Westerreich im Städtlein Sarwerth, begeben hatt und sehen lassen ... Gestelt durch Magister Johan Schwann ... Giesen, Bey Caspar Kemla, 1612 [ca. 1900]
(Continued on next card)

MSS
Bd.
WITCHCRAFT
BF
S39

Schwann, Johan. Zwo gründliche und warhafftige newe Zeitung ... 1612 [ca. 1900] (Card 2)
6 l. title vignette. 23cm.
Carnap's manuscript copy.
"Originaldruck in der Gust. Freytag Bibliothek; jetzt in der Stadtbibliothek zu Frankfurt a/M. 4 Bl. in 4°. Sig. Aij-Aiij."
Numerals and signatures in the margins indicate pagination and signatures of the original.
(Continued on next card)

MSS
Bd.
WITCHCRAFT
BF
S39

Schwann, Johan. Zwo gründliche und warhafftige newe Zeitung ... 1612 [ca. 1900] (Card 3)
In verse.
1. Witchcraft--Germany. 2. Apparitions. 3. Prophecies. I. Title: Von den Hexen und Unholden Mann und Weibs Personen ... zu Aschenburg. II. Title: Von dem erschröcklichen Jammer ... im Westerreich.

WITCHCRAFT
PQ
4416
C237

Schwickerath, Robert.
ALS to Mr. George Lincoln Burr
August 6, 1902. Woodstock, Md. Dear sir:/ I send you herewith the "American/ Catholic Quarterly Review," July 1902, containing/
1 l.
Tipped inside the issue sent by Schwickerath, containing his article "The Attitude of the Jesuits in the Trial for Witch-
(Continued on next card)

WITCHCRAFT
PQ
4416
C237

Schwickerath, Robert. ALS to Mr. George Lincoln Burr...1902. (Card 2)
craft," in which he comments on Burr's "The Fate of Dietrich Flade."

Witchcraft

Seebawer, Küngundtis, defendant, 1601-1629.
AM Aussag.
1629. Zeyl, Germany.
1 l.
Contains testimony of the witnesses and an account of the procedure of her trial and execution.
No. 1 in a fascicle of trial documents from Franken.
With 2 letters from the dealer from whom the manuscript was bought.

Witchcraft

Seublin, Agnes, defendant.
ADS[frag.] [Trial for witchcraft]
27 May-20 August, 1629. Leonberg, Germany.
12 l.
6 documents and a postscript scrap belonging to the trial of Agnes Seublin of Warmbrunn, near Stuttgart.

Witchcraft

Spingel, Sunna, defendant.
ADS Extract auss Gelen Sunnen von Feulssdorff volefuhrten criminalischen Process
16 March, 1621. Neuerburg, Luxemburg.
2 ll.
Testimony against Sunna Spingel extracted from the trial of Sunna Gelen, who was burned as a witch on July 23, 1619. Extract made and signed by Joes Dietz.

Witchcraft
BX
890
G31
E5+
1517

Spirgatis, M[ax Ludwig]
ALS to Geo[rge] L. Burr.
Dec. 27, 1895. Leipzig. Dear Sir,/ Your favour of Dec. 14 reached me
2 ll.
Attached inside the front cover of Johannes Geiler von Kaisersberg. Die emeis, and concerns the apparent lacuna of leaves v and vi of this work.

Witchcraft
BX
890
G31
E5+
1517

Spirgatis, M[ax Ludwig]
ALS to Geo[rge] L. Burr.
Jan. 2, 1896. Leipzig. Dear Sir, confirming my respects of
2 ll.
Attached inside the front cover of Johannes Geiler von Kaisersberg. Die emeis, and concerns the apparent lacuna of leaves v and vi of this work.

Witchcraft

Stein, Susanna, defendant, d. 1627.
ADS Criminalische Handlung zwischen gemeinen Herr zur Neuerburg ex officio Cleger gegen und wider Steins Dietherich Haussfrau Susanna
6 August-20 November, 1627. Neuerburg, Luxemburg.
4 ll., 31 ll., 1 l.
Includes the trial proper, signed by Joes Dietz, the indictment, and an advice of the Luxemburg government
(Continued on next card)

Witchcraft

Stein, Susanna, defendant, d. 1627. ADS Criminalische Handlung... (Card 2)
advising postponement of torture until further evidence is received, dated 24 August, 1627 and signed J. Zorn and C. Binsfelt.
With G. L. Burr's notes and the catalog from which it was bought.

Witchcraft

Stein, Susanna, defendant, d. 1627.
ads[copy] Criminalische Handlung zwischen gemeinen Herr zur Neuerburg ex officio Cleger gegen und wider Steins Dietherich Haussfrau Susanna
6 August-20 November, 1627. Neuerburg, Luxemburg.
18 ll.
Copy of the trial proper made by Pastor Dransfeld.
For G. L. Burr's notes on this
(Continued on next card)

CATALOGUE OF THE CORNELL WITCHCRAFT COLLECTION

Witchcraft
    Stein, Susanna, defendant, d. 1627. ads
    [copy] Criminalische Handlung... (Card 2)

    trial, see the original ms., her ADS
    Criminalische Handlung...

MSS
Bd.   Tübingen. Universität. Theologische Fakultät.
Witchcraft Urtheil der Würtemb. theol. u. jurist.
BF   Facultät zu Tübingen über eine Hexenprozess,
T91++ 1726. Tübingen, 1726.
    [36] l. 33cm.
    Manuscript, on paper.
    Decision of the theological and law faculties
of the university concerning the trial of
Barbara Wackher for witchcraft.
    On cover: University of Tubingen. Decision
regarding a witch. 1726.
        (Continued on next card)

Witchcraft
    Wahrhaffte und umständige Nachricht von
    dem Zufahl, so das jungfräuliche Closter
    Unter-Cell des heiligen canonischen
    Praemonstratenser Ordens im Jahr 1749
    betroffen hat.

AM
[n.d., n.p.]
23 ll.

    Sometimes attributed to Oswald Löschert.
    An account of Sister Maria Renata's
        (Continued on next card)

Witchcraft
    Stübler, Magdalena, defendant.

    ADS [Trial for witchcraft]

    1619-1620. Leonberg, Germany.
    32 ll.

    16 documents relating to the trial of
Magdalena Stübler of Menssen, at Leonberg,
near Stuttgart.

MSS
Bd.   Tübingen. Universität. Theologische Fakultät.
Witchcraft Urtheil ... über eine Hexenprozess ... 1726.
BF   (Card 2)
T91++

    Bound in marbled boards, half-leather.

    1. Advisory opinions--Tübingen. 2. Judicial
opinions--Tübingen. 3. Trials (Witchcraft)--
Tübingen. I. Wackher, Barbara, b. 1680,
defendant. II. Tübingen. Universität.
Juristische Facul tät.

Witchcraft
    Wahrhaffte und umständige Nachricht von dem
    Zufahl ... AM. (Card 2)

    career from the time she entered the cloister
through her trial and execution for witchcraft.
    For the printed version of the ms., without the post-script, see Horst, Georg Conrad.
Zauber-Bibliothek, Mainz, F. Kupferberg,
1821-1826, v. 3.
    For the trial documents themselves see
Sänger, Maria Renata von Mossau, defendant,
ca. 1680-1749. ADS [Trial for witchcraft]

Witchcraft
    Taylor, G A

    ALS to J. J. Adams

    May 23, 1926. Boston. My dear Prof.
Adams:- I am sending you today under/
separate cover a little "effusion"
    1 l.

Witchcraft
    Verfast Urtheil der sechs Zauberischen
    Persohnen[sic] als. Anna Schneiderin,
    Lud. Staudtin, Magdhalena Stüberich,
    Anna Stuberich ir Mud, Ottilia Dehinn
    und Clauss Winckelmann von Frankenweisheim.
AM
1616. [n.p.]
2 l.

    Sentence passed upon 6 people convicted
of witchcraft.
    No. 5 in a fascicle of trial
        (Continued on next card)

MSS
Bd.   Wahrhafte Nachricht von einer Beschwerung
WITCHCRAFT des Satans so in der letzt abgewichenen
BF   heiligen Christ-Nacht 1730 zwischen 11
W13   und 12 Uhr von 5 Bürgern in der Stadt
    Lindau vorgenommen worden. [n.p.]
    1731 [ca. 1900]
    2 l. illus. 23cm.

    Carnap's manuscript copy.
    "Originaldruck i. d. Kgl. Univers. Bibliothek zu Ha lle a/S. ... 2 Bl. in 4°."
    1. Devil. 2. Exorcism.

MSS
Bd.   Trithemius, Johannes, 1462-1516.
WITCHCRAFT Antipalus maleficiorum Johannis Trithemii ... [n.p. 16th cent.]
BF
A32   [182] l. 20cm.
1506 Manuscript, on paper, in a Latin hand.
    Copy of an original in the library of the
Elector Joachim.
    T. p. and slight corrections to the text
are in the hand of Henric Kuhnrath.
    Note by G. L. Burr inside front cover
states that th is manuscript contains
much that was omitted from the
        (Continued on next card)

Witchcraft
    Verfast Urtheil der sechs Zauberischen
    Persohnen...1616. (Card 2)

    documents from Franken.
    Filed with Seebawer, K. AM Aussag.
Zeyl, 1629.

MSS
Bd.   Warhaffte und glaubwirdige Zeytung. Von
WITCHCRAFT Hundert und vir und dreyssig Unholden,
BF   so umb ihrer Zauberey halben, diss verschinen LXXXij. Jars, zu Gefencknus
W272 gebracht ... zum Fewer verdambt unnd verbrennet worden ... wie dañ die Ort do sich
    solches alles verloffen, ordenlich hernach werden vermelt und angezeigt.
    Strassburg, Bey Nicolaus Wiriod, 1583
    [ca. 1900]
    4 l. 24cm.
    Carnap's manuscript copy.
        (Continued on next card)

MSS
Bd.   Trithemius, Johannes, 1462-1516. Antipalus
WITCHCRAFT malificiorum...[16th cent.] (Card 2)
BF
A32   printed version of 1605.
1506 Bound with Albedach. Liber ... De sortilegiis. [n.p. 1506]
    Bound in vellum.

MSS
Bd.   Visconti, Girolamo, fl. 1490-1512.
WITCHCRAFT Opusculũ magri Hieronimi Vicecõms ordis
BF   pdicat i q° pbat~ lamias ẽe heticas et nõ
V82   laborare humore melancholico. [Milan?
    before Sept., 1490]
    9 l. 19cm.
    Manuscript, on vellum.
    Title in red. 2 blue initials.
    Marginal notes in hands differing from
that of the text. According to G. L. Burr
some of the notes are in the author's
own hand.
        (Continued on next card)

MSS
Bd.   Warhaffte und glaubwirdige Zeytung. Von
WITCHCRAFT Hundert und vir und dreyssig Unholden ...
BF   1583 [ca. 1900] (Card 2)
W272

    "Originaldruck in der Königl. Hof- u.
Staats-Bibliothek zu München, 4 Bl. in 4°."
    Numerals in the margins indicate pagination of the original.

    1. Witchcraft--Germany. I. Title: Von
Hundert und vir und dreyssig Unholden.

Witchcraft
    Trithemius, Johannes, 1462-1516.

    am Citatio.

    [1616?] [n.p.]
    6 ll.

    A collection of conjurations attributed
to the Abbot of Spannheim, Joannes Trithemius.

MSS
Bd.   Visconti, Girolamo, fl. 1490-1512. Opus-
WITCHCRAFT culũ ... i q° pbat~ lamias ẽe heticas...
BF   [before Sept., 1490] (Card 2)
V82
    Text more complete than the printed
version, which appears as the second part
of his Lamiarum sive striarum opuscula.
Milan, 1490.
    Leaves sewn together but unbound. In case.
    1. Witchcraft. I. His Lamiarum sive
striarum opus cula. II. Title: Opusculum ... in quo probatur lamias
esse hereti cas.

MSS
Bd.   Warhaffter Bericht und denckwürdiger Verlauff, welcher Gestalten in dem 1664.
WITCHCRAFT Jahr den 3. Tag Jenners, durch die Barmhertzigkeit Gottes auff Anruffung dess
BF   H. Francisci Xaverii ... die wol-edle und
W275 tugendreiche Junckfraw Anna Elisabetha
Z55   Susanna, nunmehr aber Maria Francisca de
la Haye von den bösen Geistern, so sie
besessen und verfolgt, in unser Frauen
Kirchen ... wunderbarlich ist erlediget
worden. St raubing, Bey Magdalena
Haanin, 16 65 [ca. 1900]
        (Continued on next card)

CATALOGUE OF THE CORNELL WITCHCRAFT COLLECTION

MSS
Bd.
WITCHCRAFT
BF
W275
Z55

Warhaffter Bericht und denckwürdiger Verlauff ... 1665 [ca. 1900] (Card 2)

97 p. 19cm.
Carnap's manuscript copy.
"Originaldruck in der Königlichen u. Staats-Bibliothek zu München, VIII + 83 S. S. in 8°."
Numerals in the margins indicate pagination of the original.
1. Demoniac possession. 2. De la Haye, Maria Francisca.

MSS
Bd.
WITCHCRAFT
BF
W275
.88

Warhaffter sumarisch-aussführlicher Bericht und Erzehlung. Was die in dess heyligen Röm- Reichsstatt Augspurg etlich Wochen lang in Verhafft gelegne zwo Hexen, benandtlich Barbara Frölin von Rieden unnd Anna Schäflerin von Eringen, wegen ihrer Hexereyen gut- und peinlich bekent ... und wie endtlich dise beede Unholden ihrem Verdienst nach, auff Sambstag den 18. Aprill diss 1654 Jahrs hingericht worden. Augspurg, Durch Andream Aperger, 1654 [ca. 1900]
(Continued on next card)

MSS
Bd.
WITCHCRAFT
BF
W275
Z88

Warhaffter sumarisch-aussführlicher Bericht und Erzehlung ... 1654 [ca. 1900] (Card 2)

8 l. 24cm.
Carnap's manuscript copy.
"Originaldruck in der Gustav Freytag Biblioth. jetzt in der Stadtbibliothek zu Frankfurt a/M. 6 Blatt in 4°. Sig. Aij-B."
Numerals in the margins indicate pagination of the original.
1. Witchcraft --Augsburg. 2. Demoniac possession. 3. Frölin, Barbara, 1637-1654. 4. Schäfler, Anna, 1590-1654.

MSS
Bd.
WITCHCRAFT
BF
W277
Z75

Warhafftige newe Zeyttung, so den 18. Martii, in diesem 75. Jar, zu Bramberg im Pintzkaw, ein Meilwegs von Mittersel im Bisthumb Saltzburg, mit einem Pfarrer und seiner Köchin zugetragen hat, unnd wie sie auch hernach umb ihre Missethat hingericht worden sind. Wien, Steffan Creutzer, 1575 [ca. 1900]
6 l. 19cm.
Carnap's manuscript copy.
"Originaldr uck in der Stadtbibliothek zu Züri ch, 14 S. in 8°."
(Continued on next card)

MSS
Bd.
WITCHCRAFT
BF
W277
Z75

Warhafftige newe Zeyttung, so den 18. Martii ... mit einem Pfarrer und seiner Köchin zugetragen hat ... 1575 [ca. 1900] (Card 2)

Signatures in the margins indicate signatures of the original.

1. Witchcraft--Austria.

MSS
Bd.
WITCHCRAFT
BF
W277
Z87

Warhafftige Relation, was sich in Hamburg den 16 Martii Anno 1683 mit einem vom Sathan besessenen Mägdlein, Nahmens Catharina, dessen Vater Martin Grambeck, ein frommer Mann, zugetragen ... [n.p., 1683; ca. 1900]
1 l. 24cm.
Carnap's manuscript copy.
"Originaldruck in der Commerz-Bibliothek zu Hamburg - 1 Bl. in fol."
1. Demoniac possession.

MSS
Bd.
WITCHCRAFT
BF
W277
Z92

Warhafftige und erschreckliche newe Zeittunge von einer jungen Diernen, welche sich dem Teuffel auf sechs Jar lang ergeben ... Item, von einem Studenten, welchen der Teuffel gleichfals in grewliche Sünden gestürzt ... Item, von grewlichen ungestümen Wettern so den 12. Maij dieses 82. Jars in Baijern ... grossen Schaden, an Menschen und Wiese gethan haben. Dresdzen, Gimel Bergen, 1582 [ca. 1900]
6 l. 19 cm.
(Continued on next card)

MSS
Bd.
WITCHCRAFT
BF
W277
Z92

Warhafftige und erschreckliche newe Zeittunge von einer jungen Diernen ... 1582 [ca. 1900] (Card 2)

Carnap's manuscript copy.
"Originaldruck in der Stadtbibliothek zu Zürich, 8 Seiten in 4°."
Signatures in the margins indicate signatures of the original.
1. Devil. 2. Nature (in religion, folklore, etc.). I. Title: Von einer jungen Diern en, welche sich dem
(Continued on next card)

MSS
Bd.
WITCHCRAFT
BF
W277
Z92

Warhafftige und erschreckliche newe Zeittunge von einer jungen Diernen ... 1582 [ca. 1900] (Card 3)

Teuffel ... ergeben. II. Title: Von einem Studenten, welchen der Teuffel ... in grewliche Sünden gestürzt. III. Title: Von grewlichen ungestümen Wettern.

MSS
Bd.
WITCHCRAFT
BF
W277
Z98

Ein Warhafftige Zeitung von etlichē Hexen oder Unholden, welche man kürtzlich im Stifft Mäntz, zu Ascheburg, Dipperck, Ostum, Rönsshoffen, auch andern Orten, verbrendt haben, was Ubels sie gistifft, und bekandt haben. [Franckfurt, 1603; ca. 1900]
5 l. 19cm.
Carnap's manuscript copy.
"Originaldruck in der Königl. Bibliothek zu Berlin 4 Bl. in 12°."
Numerals in the margins indicate
(Continued on next card)

MSS
Bd.
WITCHCRAFT
BF
W277
Z98

Ein Warhafftige Zeitung von etlichē Hexen ... [1603; ca. 1900] (Card 2)

pagination of the original.
In verse.

1. Witchcraft--Germany. I. Title: Von etlichen Hexen oder Unholden ... im Stifft Mäntz.

Witchcraft

Weittlufft, Niclass, defendant.

AD Prothocollvm gehalten und gevüerth zue Schwäb. Gemünde über den incarcerirten Maleficanten Niclass Weittlufften Spittal Pfrüendner daselbsten und einen Bettelbueben, Zacherlen genadt, in Crimine Veneficii Anno: 1650

1650. Schwäbisch-Gmünd.
50 ll.

With two cat alogs and note by George Lincoln Burr.
(Continued on next card)

Witchcraft

Weittlufft, Niclass, defendant. AD Prothocollvm ... 1650. (Card 2)

Between ll. 45 and 46 is tipped in: Einnemen Handelohn und Wecglöszin Anno: 1645. AD.

Witchcraft

Wendel, Regina, b. 1714, defendant.

ADS [Verhör]

26 July-20 August, 1722. Oltingen, Germany. 13 ll.

Four documents from the hearing of 8 year old Regina Wendel, who was supposedly under the influence of the devil. Includes a statement of the original accusation, a report on a preliminary hearing, the examination of the defendant and witnesses, and a final decision by a "specialus" who acquitted her. 2 ll. torn.

MSS
Bd.
WITCHCRAFT
BF
W54

Wetz, Ambrosius.
Warhafftige und ein erschröckliche newe Zeitung, des grossen Wasserguss, so den 15. May diss lauffenden 78. Jahrs, zu Horb geschehen ... wie man hernach alda etlich Unholden verbrent hatt, wie sie schröcklich Ding bekendt haben ... durch Ambrosium Wetz ... [n.p., 1578? ca. 1900]
4 l. 19cm.
Carnap's manuscript copy.
"Originaldr uck in der Stadtbibliothek zu Züri ch, 8 Seiten in 8°."
(Continued on next card)

MSS
Bd.
WITCHCRAFT
BF
W54

Wetz, Ambrosius. Warhafftige und ein erschröckliche newe Zeitung, des grossen Wasserguss ... [1578? ca. 1900] (Card 2)

Annotations in the margins indicate foliation of the original.
In verse.

1. Witchcraft--Austria. I. Title. II. Title: Des grossen Wasserguss.

Witchcraft

Weyer, Lehna, defendant, d. 1628.

ADS Zwischen Anwaldh ... der Herrschaft Neurerburgh ex officio Klegern eins, gegen und wider Weyer Hansen Haussfrauen Lehna ... Lasters der Zauberey halber Behafftin anderen theils.

14 January, 1628. Neuerburg? Luxemburg. 2 ll.

Advice of the Luxemburg government for the torture and execution of Lehna Weyer for witch craft. Signed: P. Stro
(Continued on next card)

Witchcraft

Weyer, Lehna, defendant, d. 1628. ADS Zwischen Anwaldh... (Card 2)

and C. Binsfelt.
For G. L. Burr's notes concerning this trial, see Stein, Susanna, defendant, d. 1627. ADS Criminalische Handlung.

643

CATALOGUE OF THE CORNELL WITCHCRAFT COLLECTION

Witchcraft
 White, Andrew Dickson, 1832-1918.
  TLS to Proffessor [sic] George L. Burr
  September 30, 1899. Berlin. My dear friend:/ I have just received from Joseph Baer &
  Discusses the contents and purchase of the documents of the witchcraft trial of Sister Maria Renata Sänger of Unterzell. See also Sänger, Maria Renata von Mossau, defendant, ca. 1680-1749.

MSS Bd. WITCHCRAFT BV W96
 Eyn Wunderliches Gesicht und Geschicht von der hellen Pein, über die bösen Gottlosen Verächter des heyligen Evangelii zu eyner Warnung und Besserung, in disem XLIX. Jare offenbart. [n.p.] 1549 [ca. 1900]
 6 l. illus. 23cm.
 Carnap's manuscript copy.
 "Originaldruck in der Gust. Freytag Bibliothek; jetzt in der Stadtbibliothek zu Frankfurt a/M. 8 Bl. in 4°. Sig. Aij-Biij."
  (Continued on next card)

MSS Bd. WITCHCRAFT BF Z98 Z65
 Zwo Hexenzeitung, die erste, Von dreyen Hexen-Pfaffen ... 1615 [ca. 1900] (Card 2)
 1615 [ca. 1900]
 4 l. title vignette. 19cm.
 Carnap's manuscript copy.
 "Original i. d. Kgl. öff. Bibl. z. Stuttgart 4 unpag. Bl. incl. Titelbl. ohne Signat."
 1. Witchcraft. I. Title: Von dreyen Hexen-Pfaffen. II. Title: Von einer Unholdin oder Hexen.

Witchcraft
 White, Andrew Dickson, 1832-1918.
  TLS to Professor George L. Burr.
  February 10, 1900. Berlin. My dear friend:/ The enclosed letter will explain itself./
  1 l.
  With envelope.
  Concerns the purchase of Hexenprozesse. [Bamberg? 1617- 1631]

MSS Bd. WITCHCRAFT BV W96
 Eyn Wunderliches Gesicht ... 1549 [ca. 1900] (Card 2)
 Numerals and signatures in the margins indicate pagination of the original.

 1. Exempla. 2. Admonition.

MSS Bd. WITCHCRAFT BF Z98 Z97
 Zwo warhafftige newe Zeitung. Die erste ist ein warhafftige Propheceyung, was sich diss tausent sechzehenhundert und 28. Jahr wird verlauffen und zutragen ... Die ander Zeitung ist aus dem Bistumb Würtzburg und Bamberg, auch sonst aus andern Herrschafften, wie man viel Hexen unnd Gabelreutersen verbrennen lest, und noch viel gefangen liegen ... Würtzburg, 1627 [ca. 1900]
 4 l. title vignette. 24cm.
 Carnap's manuscript copy.
  (Continued on next card)

White, Andrew Dickson, 1832-1918.
 LETTERS FROM
 Baer, Joseph & co., Frankfurt am Main.

MSS Bd. WITCHCRAFT BS Y68
 [Young, Arthur] 1693-1759.
 A dissertation on the Gospel Daemoniacs, occasioned by the Bp. of St. David's answer to Mr. Woolston. [n.p.] before 1760.
 64 l. 23cm.
 Manuscript, on paper, with gilt edges.
 "...This dissertation ... was printed in 1760... It is not improbable that this is the author's autograph": G. L. Burr's note at beginning.
 Bound in gilt-stamped black leather.
 1. Demoniac possession. 2. Bible. N. T.--Commentaries. I. Title.

MSS Bd. WITCHCRAFT BF Z98 Z97
 Zwo warhafftige newe Zeitung. Die erste ist ein warhafftige Propheceyung ... 1627 [ca. 1900] (Card 2)
 "Originaldruck i. d. Stadtbibliothek zu Frankfurt a/Main. 4 Bl. in 4°."
 In verse.
 1. Prophecies. 2. Deformities. 3. Witchcraft.

Witchcraft
 Wick, Johann Jacob, 1522-1588.
  am[copy] [Wick Mss]
  [c. 1560-1588] Zurich.
  63 ll. in 5 small notebooks.
  Extracts made in 1888 by George L. Burr and Earl Barnes from the Wick Mss in the Zurich Zentralbibliothek. With annotations and descriptions by Burr. The Mss, 24 vols., are a chronicle of occult and mysterious events occurring in the years 1560-1587.

MSS Bd. WITCHCRAFT BT Z97
 Zween erschreckliche Geschicht, gesangsweise. Die erste, von einem Wirt im Allgergaw, Bastian Schönmundt genandt ... wie er sein ehelich Wieb [sic], so schwanger Leibs gewesen, dreyen Mördern verkaufft ... Die ander, eine erschreckliche und warhafftige newe Zeitung, wie sich im 1596. Jahres ... hat zugetragen, das ein schwanger Weib vom Teuffel besessen, iren Man sampt drey Kindern, auch sich selbs mit ihrer Leibesfrucht jemmerlich ermordt und umbgebracht hat.
  (Continued on next card)

MSS Bd. WITCHCRAFT BF W792++
 Wirz, Bernhard, d. 1705, defendant.
 Processus wegen des vermeinten Gespengsts in dem Antistitio. [Zürich, 1705]
 402 p., [22] l. 34cm.
 Manuscript, on paper, in a German hand. According to G. L. Burr, probably the transcript of the court record.
 Bound in parchment.
 1. Trials (Witchcraft)--Zürich. 2. Trials (Malicious mischief)--Zürich. I. Klingler, Anton K., 1649-1713, plaintiff. II. Title.

MSS Bd. WITCHCRAFT BT Z97
 Zween erschreckliche Geschicht, gesangsweise ... [1596; ca. 1900] (Card 2)
 [n.p., 1596; ca. 1900]
 6 l. 19cm.
 Carnap's manuscript copy.
 "Druck in der Königl. Bibliothek zu Berlin; 4 Bl. in 16°."
 In verse.
 1. Providence and government of God. 2. Demoniac possession.

MSS Bd. WITCHCRAFT BF W96
 Ein Wunderbarlich erschrockenlich Handelunge, so sich auff den grün Dornstag dis Jars, ynn dem Stedlein Schiltach, mit einer Brunst durch den bösen Geyst gestifft, begeben hat, ym MDxxxiij. [n.p., 1553? ca. 1900]
 4 l. 21cm.
 Signatures: A⁴.
 Carnap's manuscript copy.
 "Original i. d. Kgl. Bibl. zu Berlin, ehemals im Heyse Bücherschatz."
 1. Ghosts. 2. Devil.

MSS Bd. WITCHCRAFT BF Z98 Z65
 Zwo Hexenzeitung, die erste, Von dreyen Hexen-Pfaffen, unnd einem Organisten zu Ellwang, wie dieselbe Christo abgesagt, unnd dem bösen Geist mit Leib und Seel sich ergeben, und die Zauberkunst von ime erlernet ... Die ander: Von einer Unholdin oder Hexen, wie sie mit ihren Gespilen alles zu verderben unterstanden, der Satan aber, ihnen Ursachen, warum sie solches sollen bleiben lassen angezeigt, auch nicht gestatten, oder geschehen lassen wöllen. Nürnberg,
  (Continued on next card)

INDEX

INDEX

Agrippa von Nettesheim, Heinrich Cornelius, 401, 425, 456
Alchemy, 82, 249, 541, 634; history of, 6; *see also* Catalogues
Angels, 18, 95, 108, 217, 297, 338, 369, 390, 420, 423, 432, 479, 486, 488, 500
Animals, 66, 74, 118, 428, 485, 508, 511, 578
Apparitions, 22, 85, 90, 92, 101, 104, 117, 126–127, 154, 155, 158–159, 180, 184, 185, 190, 223–224, 238–239, 241, 242–243, 287, 322, 337–338, 344–345, 363, 385, 447, 462, 486, 490, 496, 539, 546–547, 591, 630, 631, 641
Astrology, 74, 433, 475
Austria, witchcraft in, 14, 19, 96, 264, 461, 593, 600, 643; Styria, 96, 386, 583; Tyrol, 16, 420, 578, 623; Vorarlberg, 16; *see also* Legislation *and* Trials

Babin, Guillemette, 223
Baker, Anne, 615
Baker, Rachel, 634, 638
Balsano, Giuseppe, *see* Cagliostro, Alessandro
Bateman, Mary (Harker), 201
Bavent, Madeleine, 165, 196, 336, 441, 462–463, 540, 636–637
Bedford, Jaquetta of Luxembourg, duchess of, 617
Bekker, Balthasar, 17, 22, 34, 39, 53, 57, 62, 63, 66, 67, 68, 71, 75–76, 88–89, 93, 123, 124, 128, 134, 135, 170, 181, 189, 194, 203, 228, 250, 256, 259–260, 290, 291, 292–293, 320–321, 323, 324, 325, 347, 351, 355, 375, 382, 394, 395–396, 408–410, 415, 426, 433, 451, 460–461, 470–471, 476, 493–494, 496, 502, 503, 509, 559, 573, 574, 578, 583, 584, 587, 591–592, 594, 622, 623, 626, 627, 628, 631, 636, 638–639; bibliography, 637, 639
Belgium, witchcraft in, 105, 187, 264, 398; *see also* Trials
Bell witch, 301
Bible, 22, 25, 64, 70, 82, 134, 138, 179, 187, 251, 257, 266, 291, 423, 430, 431, 432, 434, 443, 509, 513, 590, 619; New Testament, 14, 24, 35, 63, 114, 190, 198, 204, 228–229, 257; Old Testament, 186, 190, 616; Witch of Endor, 231, 336, 418, 484, 590
Bilby, Doll, 211
Bishop, Bridgett, 632, 638
Bleick, Anna, 321
Blex, Sibilla, 321
Bodenham, Anne, 85
Bodin, Jean, 327, 396, 417, 456–457, 458
Braun, Marta, 628
Braunschweig-und-Lüneburg, Sidonia, Herzogin zu, 384–385
Brussen, Agnes, 628
Büchler, Cathrina, 629
Büder, Gela, 629
Bussbacher, Margaretha, 629
Buts, Joan, 4

Cadière, Catherine, 97–100, 235, 236–237, 387, 463
Cagliostro, Alessandro, pseud., 35, 101, 358, 508
Campbell, Duncan, 157
Canada, witchcraft in, 502
Cariden, Joan, 4, 199
Catalogues: alchemy, 109, 262, 264, 465; magic, 109, 265, 365, 476, 538; occult sci-

ences, 4, 109, 182, 186, 264, 265, 322, 416, 465, 476, 508, 538; witchcraft, 265, 322, 365, 465, 476
Catholic church, 5, 110, 190, 200, 201, 204, 205, 213, 268, 319, 374, 431, 442, 451, 496, 518, 523, 525; papal bulls, 110, 307, 486; practice of exorcism, 195, 204, 353, 372, 418, 452, 467, 485; *see also* Inquisition
Charms, 13, 117, 171, 262, 289, 420–421, 519, 588–589
Circe, 202
Clinton, Rachel, 636
Concini, Leonara (Dori), called Galigaï, 398
Crime and criminals, 84, 86–87, 96, 226, 245, 270–271, 308, 441, 515–516, 554, 587
Criminal procedure, 107, 198, 199, 303–306, 325, 335, 363, 413, 417, 431, 435, 489, 491, 492, 518, 531–532, 590, 622–623, 627, 639, 640
Cullender, Rose, 258

Davidson, Isabel, 562
Demoniac possession, 12, 14, 16–17, 18, 24, 26–27, 35, 38, 40, 67, 68, 69, 73, 75, 76, 81, 85, 91, 94, 108, 111, 114, 117, 121, 137, 162, 171, 172, 179, 180, 182, 183, 190, 194, 195, 196, 197, 202, 204, 216, 217, 223, 229, 232, 248, 253, 257, 261–262, 265, 267, 268, 280, 282, 288, 298, 313, 315, 317, 318, 320, 329, 330, 334, 335, 336, 340–341, 342–343, 345, 346, 348, 351, 369, 373, 374, 384, 387–388, 390, 391, 395, 396, 403, 406, 407, 408, 413, 420, 428, 431, 436, 440, 441, 445, 446, 447, 448, 454, 462–463, 465, 472, 486, 488, 491, 492, 500, 501, 503, 506, 511, 526, 528, 531, 532, 533, 535, 537, 538, 546, 549, 562, 564, 569, 571, 589, 592, 593, 600, 605, 614, 616, 619, 625, 628, 629, 630, 631, 632, 633, 634, 635, 636–637, 642–643, 644
Demonology, 7, 11–12, 14–15, 17, 22, 24, 25, 26, 41–42, 52, 53, 54, 57–58, 65, 71–72, 74, 75, 77–78, 79–80, 81–82, 88, 92, 94, 96, 101, 104, 105, 106, 107, 108, 109, 111, 113, 114, 116, 117, 123, 124, 125–126, 128, 133, 134, 135–137, 138, 160, 184, 186–187, 188, 190, 196, 197, 198, 202, 203, 204, 205, 207, 212, 214, 217, 223, 227, 230, 240–241, 242, 245, 248–249, 253, 254, 259, 266, 268, 271, 282, 290, 294, 295, 297, 303–306, 310, 311–312, 313, 314, 318, 320, 322, 325, 327, 329, 331, 333, 334, 335, 337–338, 341, 342, 343, 344, 351, 352, 354–355, 358, 360, 369, 371, 372, 373, 375, 376, 380, 382, 383, 385, 387–388, 390, 396–397, 404, 406, 408, 414, 420, 422, 424–425, 429, 435, 440, 441, 442, 444, 446, 447, 457, 460, 469, 471–472, 476, 477, 478, 488, 490, 491, 496, 497–500, 505, 506, 507, 511, 512, 514, 518, 525, 531, 532, 539, 546, 549, 562, 569, 571, 572, 575, 576, 577, 579,
584, 591, 598, 601–604, 607, 619, 630, 631, 637, 638; collections, 520; dictionaries, 475, 550; history, 73, 205, 208, 223, 295, 476, 529; *see also* Spirits
Demonomania, 77–78, 91, 111, 117, 183, 190, 206, 207, 223, 242, 271, 298, 299, 335, 392, 417, 431, 432, 442, 447, 541, 600, 616
Devil, 5, 7, 11, 12, 15, 16, 25, 32, 39, 63, 66, 69, 75, 80, 81, 83, 84, 87, 88, 92, 94, 96, 107, 108, 111, 117, 123, 125–127, 128, 134, 156–158, 160, 168, 169, 170, 172, 173, 177, 184, 186, 189, 190, 194, 195, 196, 210, 216, 223, 224, 227–228, 229, 231, 232, 234, 244, 245, 251, 254–255, 257, 259–260, 262, 268, 271, 279, 280, 282, 283, 288, 289, 290, 291, 292–293, 296, 310, 316, 320, 321, 322, 323, 326, 327, 328, 329, 332, 333, 334, 335, 337, 338, 342, 343, 346, 358, 360, 369, 371, 373, 377–378, 380, 382, 383, 385, 388, 390, 392, 393, 398, 400, 405, 406, 408, 414, 422, 423, 424–425, 426, 428, 433, 448, 471–472, 473, 476, 477, 479, 484, 486, 489, 492, 498, 500, 503, 504, 511, 512, 526, 535, 540, 546, 559, 562, 564, 566, 567, 571, 573, 584, 589, 590, 593, 600, 607, 617, 620, 630, 631, 632, 634, 635, 638, 640, 641, 642, 643, 644; in art, 600; in biblical teaching, 577, 594, 607, 616, 619, 644; bibliography, 125, 202, 263, 327
Di Francesco, Matteuccia, 371
Drencken, Catarina, 631
Duny, Amy, 258

Edwards, Susanna, 560
Engelhard, Elsa and Margreta, 192, 631
Esty, Mary, 632
Europe, witchcraft in, 429, 478; *see also under individual countries*
Evil eye, 91, 168, 536
Executions, *see* Witches, executions of
Exorcism, 12, 25, 26–27, 64, 65, 68, 73, 82, 91–92, 106, 109–110, 111, 114, 120, 123, 133, 180–181, 182, 183, 184, 186, 188, 195, 196, 200, 201, 203, 204, 216, 217, 224, 229, 248, 252–253, 254, 259, 261–262, 316, 321, 322, 327, 328–329, 335, 346, 353, 356, 359, 361, 371, 374, 387–388, 391, 393, 395, 407, 414, 417, 424, 430, 436, 440, 441, 443, 445, 447, 451, 467, 468, 470, 476, 478, 487, 488, 491, 503, 512, 520, 525, 531, 539, 541, 549, 559, 566, 571, 577, 579, 589, 623, 629, 632, 633, 636, 638, 642

Farmer, Hugh, 205
Fiedler, Margarethe, 632
Flade, Dietrich, 95, 209, 410, 622, 629, 633, 641
Flower, Margaret and Philippa, 615
Foster, Ann, 218

Index

France, witchcraft in, 11, 26–27, 32, 79–80, 82, 97–98, 100, 107, 111, 125, 159, 164, 165, 172, 173, 196, 210, 214, 223, 236–237, 283, 320, 334, 336, 346, 350, 355, 357, 387, 392, 428, 437, 458, 461, 474, 483, 500, 514, 521, 541–542, 561, 570, 630, 635, 636–637; Alsace, 34, 164, 208, 274, 275, 324, 389, 471, 592, 607, 627, 638; Auxonne, 223; Avignon, 392; Basque provinces, 35; Burgundy, 169; Châteaudun, 462; Dauphiné, 374; Douay, 173; Labourd, 66; Léon, 173; Limoges, 462; Lorraine, 160, 335, 469, 541; Loudun, 26–27, 67, 74, 111, 123, 165, 207, 213, 246, 298, 307, 313, 334, 342–343, 345, 391, 445, 462, 468, 486, 531, 555, 566, 630, 632; Louviers, 165, 196, 336, 441, 462–463, 540, 636–637; Luxeuil, 38; Morzines, 121; Moulins, 172; Normandy, 238; Paris, 454; Provence, 235; Savoy, 320; Vivarais, 135; Vosges, 406
Franchillon, Charles de, 173, 630
Frohertz, Anna Traute, 326

Gardner, Gerald Brosseau, 85
Gassner, Johann Joseph, 190, 200, 252–253, 257, 337, 503, 575, 594, 620, 623
Gaufridi, Louis, 27, 211, 350, 355, 391, 476
Gause, Anna, 226, 633
Geiger, Lucia, 269
Géraud, Hugues, bishop of Cahors, 11
Germany, witchcraft in, 32, 66, 92, 93, 95, 127, 171, 182, 186, 188, 190, 191, 193, 196, 212, 214, 217, 221–222, 228, 257, 264, 268, 273, 277, 296, 301, 313, 320, 325, 329, 343, 347–348, 353–354, 356, 360, 392, 395, 401, 402, 412, 420, 421, 422, 431, 441, 462, 473, 474, 478, 496, 515–516, 525, 539, 587, 592, 593, 605, 617, 622, 629–630, 631, 632, 633, 636, 637, 638, 639, 640, 641, 642, 643; Augsburg, 593; Baden, 578; Bamberg, 275, 635, 640; Bavaria, 27, 32, 37, 269, 346, 411, 522; Bergheim, 34; Birkenfeld, 354; Bonn, 314; Braunsberg, 351; Braunschweig, 472; Brocken, 403; Cologne, 508; Dessau, 429; Dillingen, 330; Dortmund, 477; Erkelenz, 224; Flamersheim, 456; Franconia, 343, 384, 389; Fulda, 369; Halberstadt, 389; Hamburg, 561; Harz Mountains, 319; Hesse, 215, 518; Hildesheim, 263; Ingolstadt, 509; Jena, 290; Lauingen, 477; Marburg, 467; Münster, 297, 414, 514; Osnabrück, 353; Pomerania, 311, 384–385; Prussia, 371, 375; Rotenberg, 390; Saxony, 192, 319, 472, 486–487, 631; Silesia, 330, 614; Stuttgart, 335; Swabia, 486, 491; Thuringia, 268, 290, 491, 496, 535; Trier, 209, 328, 350, 404, 410, 633; Ulm, 489; Verden, 368; Westphalia, 314; Wetterau, 325; Wittenberg, 226, 633; *see also* Legislation *and* Trials
Ghosts, 101, 104, 119, 155, 196, 287, 327, 337–338, 344, 484, 488, 509, 523, 526, 528, 546–547, 571, 590, 595, 597, 599, 617, 623–624, 644; *see also* Apparitions
Girard, Jean Baptiste, 97–98, 100, 235–237, 387, 398, 463
Glanvill, Joseph, 453
Glover, Mary, 85, 532, 628
Göldi, Anna, 425
Good, Sarah, 634
Grandier, Urbain, 26–27, 74, 111, 165, 213, 246, 307, 313, 334, 342–343, 345, 445, 462, 555, 566, 632
Great Britain, witchcraft in, 5, 322, 351, 372, 404, 512; *see also* Ireland, Legislation *and* Trials
────── England, 4, 20, 40, 54, 85–86, 90, 94, 96, 108, 115, 137, 138, 166, 168, 180, 187, 196, 198, 199, 201, 218, 226, 258, 262, 263, 265, 290, 294–295, 301, 308, 322–323, 346, 351, 363, 365, 373, 401, 416, 438, 441, 455, 465, 475, 476, 504, 505, 508, 525, 526, 542, 560, 561, 562, 608, 615, 617; Berkshire, 198; Channel Islands, 272, 443, 537; Devonshire, 318, 560; Essex, 560, 561, 611; Hertfordshire, 86, 108, 218, 231, 270–271, 300, 394, 401, 505, 507; Lancashire, 261, 278, 432, 448–449, 607; Northamptonshire, 138, 218, 373, 612, 614
────── Scotland, 74, 87, 91, 105, 113, 138, 205, 286, 312, 351, 393, 408, 468, 481, 485, 506, 595, 608
Greene, Ellen, 615
Greiess, Eva, 634
Grössel, Marie, 326
Gunter, Anne, 198
Guthramdaughter, Margaret, 255

Hagh, Catharina, 321
Hall, Mary, 634
Hallucinations and illusions, 299, 528
Harris, Elizabeth, 199
Harrison, Johanna, 401, 505
Harrison, Katherine, 635
Hathaway, Richard, 263
Hausberg, Anna Martha, 492
Hencke, Barbara, 635
Henot, Catharina, 635
Heresies and heretics, 109, 204, 248, 441, 475
Hicks, Mary and Elizabeth, 601
Hinteregger, Catharina, 635
Hobbes, Thomas, 203, 453
Holman, Winnefred, 268
Hooght, Everard van der, 502
Hott, Jane, 4, 199
Huger, Catherine, 514
Hungary, witchcraft in, 278, 372, 395, 631; *see also* Trials

Iceland, witchcraft in, 417; *see also* Trials
Incantations, 24, 106, 114, 117, 183–184, 217, 248, 354–355, 356, 569, 571, 589, 630
Inquisition, 26, 93, 160, 201, 206, 208, 209, 260, 266, 299, 302, 341, 374, 375, 429, 441, 467, 475, 534, 637; history, 340–341, 351, 352–353, 420
Institoris, Henricus, 403
Ireland, witchcraft in, 96, 332, 406, 505
Italy, witchcraft in, 74, 81, 156, 206, 222, 234, 371, 393, 436, 472; *see also* Trials

James I, king of Great Britain, 322, 636
Jeanne d'Arc, Saint, 12, 111, 546

Keiner, Osanna, 636
Kepler, Katharina, 254, 320
Kirchberg, Marthe Margarethe, 625
Kluge, Anna, 326
Knott, Elizabeth, 180, 394
Krämer, Margaretha, 636
Kruckow, Christence, 310
Kyteler, Alice, 332

Lamb, John, 85, 90
Lamkers, Maria, 636
La Ville, Marie Anne de, 125
Laymann, Paul, 73, 186
Legislation concerning witchcraft, 198; Austria, 27–28, 375; England, 20, 174, 198; France, 214; Germany, 32, 321, 382, 445; Massachusetts, 244
Lindemann, Ortia, 251
Liveyra, Maria Antonia de, 637
Lloyd, Temperance, 560
Loder, Mrs. Hans, 637
Lohmannin, Anna Elisabeth, 76, 420, 503
Loudun, *see* France
Louviers, *see* France
Lowes, John, 198, 365
Lunge, Susann, 32
Luther, Martin, 431, 589, 628
Luxembourg, witchcraft in, 636; *see also* Trials

März, Agnellus, 187, 327, 513; *see also* Sterzinger, Ferdinand
März, Angelus, 19, 381; *see also* Sterzinger, Ferdinand
Magic, 4, 5, 8, 11, 12, 13, 24, 27, 36, 37, 41–42, 52, 53, 54, 57–58, 65, 68, 70, 73, 76, 77–78, 80, 82, 83, 86, 87, 88, 90, 91, 92–93, 94, 102, 104, 105, 107, 110, 111, 112, 117, 119, 121–122, 134, 137, 138, 143, 156, 159, 161–162, 171, 173, 180, 183–184, 186, 188, 190, 196, 203, 206, 207, 208, 210, 211, 216, 217, 222, 228, 229, 241, 244, 248, 249, 255, 257, 262, 264, 265, 266, 268, 272, 279, 297, 310, 311, 312, 316, 327, 329, 341–342, 343, 359, 365, 367, 374, 383, 390, 395, 398, 404, 413, 420–421, 422, 425, 428, 432, 433, 434, 436–437, 440, 441, 442, 444, 451, 466, 470, 473, 478, 483, 490, 492, 493, 497–498, 504, 510, 517, 519, 523, 530, 535, 536, 539–540, 546, 549, 566, 569, 571, 572, 575, 577, 589, 597, 599, 601–604, 607, 617, 630, 635, 369; bibliography, 452, 476, 538; dictionaries, 117, 423; history, 118, 121, 193, 206, 223, 251, 260, 295, 381, 407–408, 410, 475, 479, 502, 546, 590, 622
Malavesse, Catherine (David), 26
Margareth, of Körperich, 638
Martin, Margreta, 638
Martin, Susanna, 374
Maryland, witchcraft in, 429
Mather, Cotton, 38, 102–103, 184, 240, 264, 290, 446, 567
Mather, Increase, 240
Medicine, magic, mystic, and spagiric, 72, 80, 111, 172, 183, 184, 203, 223, 224, 240, 252–253, 268, 288, 289, 329, 351, 354–355, 369, 371, 376, 389, 391, 403, 431, 434, 435, 441, 443, 445, 461–462, 487; medical aspects of witchcraft, 72, 111, 172, 183, 184, 203, 322, 329, 335, 369, 374, 393, 410, 444, 465, 488, 537, 569, 596–597, 600, 622, 636; psychopathology of witchcraft, 473, 511, 534, 566, 601, 622
Meineken, Margarethe, 390
Metamorphosis, 39, 546, 628, 638
Miribilia (curiosities and wonders), 25, 223–224, 232, 245, 327, 328, 368, 512, 528, 550, 575
Misseler, Elss, 633
Molinaeus, Johannes, 320–321, 460–461
Monsters, 374, 491
Moore, George Henry, 243
Morduck, Sarah, 263
Morin, Madeleine, 335, 636
Motzen, Barbara, 490
Müller, Gottlieb, 76, 383, 503
Müller, Maria (Rhinow), 473
Mysticism, 118, 204, 242, 311, 418, 472

Neparre, Barbara, 363
Netherlands, witchcraft in, 412; *see also* Trials
New England, witchcraft in, 75, 95, 96, 102–103, 111, 115, 138, 184, 213, 248, 264, 295, 298, 322–323, 376, 377–378, 380, 408, 411, 416, 434–435, 441, 446, 457, 577, 607; bibliography, 398–399, 607; *see also* Trials
―――― Connecticut, 537, 574, 635
―――― Massachusetts, 213, 243, 244, 398–399; Salem, 39, 85, 94, 102–103, 111, 151, 191,

Index

209, 211, 213, 229, 260, 321, 339, 347, 377, 380, 402, 405, 411, 413, 434–435, 438, 446, 455, 462, 483, 520, 536, 539, 555, 567, 598, 632, 634, 636, 638
Nigal, Nicolle, 32
Nypen, Lisbet, 421

Occult sciences, 5–6, 8–11, 12, 13, 35, 37, 39, 65, 69, 74, 75, 80, 81–82, 85, 87, 94, 101, 105, 111, 117, 118, 121, 124, 125, 159, 160, 161, 186, 187, 188, 207, 214, 215, 222, 229, 232, 235, 242, 244, 249, 254, 259, 260, 263, 269, 270, 308, 310, 311, 316, 319, 321, 342, 343, 349, 354–355, 356, 368, 371, 372, 375–376, 381, 389, 393, 398, 403, 408, 413, 420–421, 424, 428, 435, 441, 444, 447, 456, 492, 522, 535, 542, 549, 550–551, 597, 599, 600, 607, 622, 631; bibliography, 4, 79, 102, 182, 186, 245, 253, 265, 266, 316, 322, 465, 476, 508, 538, 541, 619; collections, 119, 613, 629, 644; history, 6, 14, 109, 155, 164, 193, 202, 295, 321, 334, 352, 390, 410, 461–462, 471, 484, 565, 693; *see also* Catalogues
Oracles, 25, 115, 134–135, 211, 270, 398

Pachler, Barbara, 623
Packet, Ysabeal, 549
Palmer, John, 180, 394
Palud, Magdeleine de la, 27, 391
Parris, Samuel, 213
Peebles, Marion, 550
Pennsylvania, witchcraft in, 27, 76; *see also* Trials
Pépin, Etienne, 203
Peterson, Joan, 155, 561, 608
Phillips, Mary, 138, 526, 612
Picken, Magdalen, 639
Plants in witchcraft, 74, 272, 541
Poisons, 116, 214, 376, 465, 598; affair of the, 11
Poland, witchcraft in, 491
Pollman, Anna, 640
Portugal, witchcraft in, 637; *see also* Trials
Preston, Jennet, 448–449
Příchovský, Antonín Peter, 190, 200
Pröls, Georg, 27
Prophesies, 265, 401, 436–437, 496, 626, 641, 644

Rais, Gilles de Laval, seigneur de, 576
Reinhard, Ursula, 640

Sänger, Maria Renata von Mossau, 19, 221–222, 343, 384, 386, 589, 627, 637, 640, 642, 644
Satanism, *see* Demonology *and* Devil

Sawyer, Elizabeth, 243
Scandinavia, witchcraft in, 368, 417; Denmark, 32, 33, 34, 93, 113, 212, 250, 267, 290, 310, 324, 351, 421, 444; Finland, 126, 264, 271; Norway, 15, 32, 33, 380, 479; Sweden, 19, 71, 74, 203, 217, 250, 307, 347, 351, 371, 510, 560, 622; *see also* Trials
Schillerin, Regina, 406, 638
Schlott, 640
Schulze, Barbara Elisabeth, 493
Schuster, Barbara Schröchlin, 641
Schweidler, Maria, 384, 479
Scott, Michael, 92
Scott, Sir Walter, 430
Seebawer, Küngundtis, 641
Seublin, Agnes, 641
Sermons, 212, 221–222, 280, 298, 317, 424, 474, 477, 484, 489, 578, 617, 622, 633, 634, 640
Shakespeare, William, 90; supernatural elements in, 514
Shaw, Christian, 407, 481
Shaw, Elinor, 138, 612
Sherwood, Grace, 507, 639
Shipton, Ursula, 265
Siewerten, 389
Smith, Mary, 475
Sorcery, 93, 97–98, 100, 101, 111, 117, 171, 202, 216, 242, 249, 300, 310, 321, 334, 335, 339–340, 369, 450, 475
Spain, witchcraft in, 67, 107, 195, 299, 484; *see also* Trials
Spee, Friedrich von, 33, 105, 171, 186, 188, 228, 257, 288, 313, 489, 625
Spells, 11, 84, 523
Spingel, Sunna, 641
Spinoza, Benedictus de, 203, 320
Spirits, 75–76, 83, 84, 86, 96, 104, 108, 157, 182, 183–184, 186, 187, 217, 229, 230, 254–255, 292, 295, 322, 332, 337, 344, 396, 420, 428, 442, 468, 473, 488, 502, 523, 526, 573, 575, 578, 639; *see also* Ghosts
Stein, Susanna, 641–642
Sterzinger, Ferdinand, 19, 164, 184–185, 207, 213, 223, 233, 327, 356, 363, 364, 381, 394, 524, 620, 633
Stile, Elizabeth, 465
Stübler, Magdalena, 642
Supernatural, 342, 398, 462, 510
Superstition, 3, 15, 23, 27, 33, 37, 38, 65, 74, 91, 106, 109, 111, 115, 117, 121, 135, 161, 183, 188, 205, 207, 208, 212, 216, 217, 222, 223–224, 235, 247, 252, 254, 260, 267, 268, 288, 310, 313, 324, 341–342, 354, 371, 381, 392, 402, 408, 411, 418, 420, 442, 452, 461–462, 466, 468, 472, 484, 491, 492, 501, 508, 509, 510, 512, 522, 523, 528, 539, 541, 595, 597, 599, 606, 633; history, 107, 208, 217, 229, 254, 265, 321, 326, 333, 343, 368, 390, 490, 570